Diederich

## How to Use the Maps in *World History, 5th Edition*

Here are some basic map concepts that will help you to get the most out of the maps in this textbook.

- Always look at the scale, which allows you to determine the distance in miles or kilometers between locations on the map.
- Examine the legend carefully. It explains the colors and symbols used on the map.
- Note the locations of mountains, rivers, oceans, and other geographic features, and consider how these would affect such human activities as agriculture, commerce, travel, and warfare.
- Read the map caption thoroughly. It provides important information, sometimes not covered in the text itself, and poses a thought question to encourage you to think beyond the mere appearance of the map and make connections across chapters, regions, and concepts.
- Several "spot maps" appear in each chapter, to allow you to view in detail smaller areas that may not be apparent in larger maps. For example, a spot map in Chapter 12 lets you zoom in on Charlemagne's Empire.
- Many of the text's maps also carry a globe icon alongside the title, which indicates that the map appears in interactive form on the text's website:

http://history.wadsworth.com/duikerspielvogel05/

# A best-selling text that takes a comparative approach to the human experience

Balanced and engaging, **World History,** Fifth Edition, explores the common challenges and experiences that unify the human past, as well as global patterns over time. Respected scholars and teachers William J. Duiker and Jackson J. Spielvogel integrate thorough coverage of political, economic, social, religious, intellectual, cultural, and military history into a chronologically ordered synthesis to give students an appreciation and understanding of the distinctive character and development of individual cultures.

With this edition, Duiker and Spielvogel enhance the book's comparative exploration of the human experience. Their global approach to world history places an emphasis on analytical comparisons between and among cultures throughout history. This approach helps students link together events in a broad comparative and global framework, placing the history of each of the world's cultures in a more meaningful context.

The Fifth Edition is rich with new content, including greatly expanded coverage of Islam, as well as improved pedagogy to help students study more effectively and efficiently. For a complete list of chapter-by-chapter changes and additions, see the text Preface.

## *World History is available in four volume options—choose the one that's right for your course!*

**World History,**
Fifth Edition
(Chapters 1-29)
**0-495-05012-1**

**World History, Volume I: To 1800,**
Fifth Edition
(Chapters 1-17)
**0-495-05053-9**

**World History, Volume II: From 1500,**
Fifth Edition
(Chapters 13-29)
**0-495-05054-7**

**World History to 1500,**
Fifth Edition
(Chapters 1-12)
**0-495-05060-1**

PREVIEW

# Comparative

**Duiker and Spielvogel's World History is renowned for its comparative approach, and with this edition you'll find even more comparisons between and among cultures.**

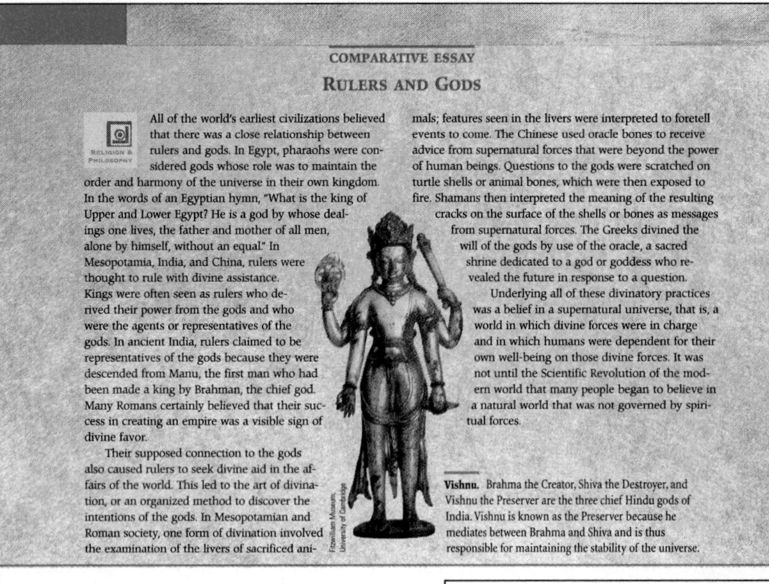

COMPARATIVE ESSAY

RULERS AND GODS

RELIGION & PHILOSOPHY

All of the world's earliest civilizations believed that there was a close relationship between rulers and gods. In Egypt, pharaohs were considered gods whose role was to maintain the order and harmony of the universe in their own kingdom. In the words of an Egyptian hymn, "What is the king of Upper and Lower Egypt? He is a god by whose dealings one lives, the father and mother of all men, alone by himself, without an equal." In Mesopotamia, India, and China, rulers were thought to rule with divine assistance. Kings were often seen as rulers who derived their power from the gods and who were the agents or representatives of the gods. In ancient India, rulers claimed to be representatives of the gods because they were descended from Manu, the first man who had been made a king by Brahman, the chief god. Many Romans certainly believed that their success in creating an empire was a visible sign of divine favor.

Their supposed connection to the gods also caused rulers to seek divine aid in the affairs of the world. This led to the art of divination, or an organized method to discover the intentions of the gods. In Mesopotamian and Roman society, one form of divination involved the examination of the livers of sacrificed animals; features seen in the livers were interpreted to foretell events to come. The Chinese used oracle bones to receive advice from supernatural forces that were beyond the power of human beings. Questions to the gods were scratched on turtle shells or animal bones, which were then exposed to fire. Shamans then interpreted the meaning of the resulting cracks on the surface of the shells or bones as messages from supernatural forces. The Greeks divined the will of the gods by use of the oracle, a sacred shrine dedicated to a god or goddess who revealed the future in response to a question.

Underlying all of these divinatory practices was a belief in a supernatural universe, that is, a world in which divine forces were in charge and in which humans were dependent for their own well-being on those divine forces. It was not until the Scientific Revolution of the modern world that many people began to believe in a natural world that was not governed by spiritual forces.

Fitzwilliam Museum, University of Cambridge

**Vishnu.** Brahma the Creator, Shiva the Destroyer, and Vishnu the Preserver are the three chief Hindu gods of India. Vishnu is known as the Preserver because he mediates between Brahma and Shiva and is thus responsible for maintaining the stability of the universe.

63 B.C.E., and by 6 C.E., Judaea (which embraced the lands of the old Jewish kingdom of Judah) had been made a province and placed under the direction of a Roman procurator. But unrest continued, augmented by divisions among the Jews themselves. The Sadducees fa-

The

Jesus

Jew w

milita

his fe

◀ A **new** *Comparative Essay* in every chapter empowers students to see similarities and differences between and among cultures. Keyed to the seven major themes of world history (as discussed on the next page of this Preview), these essays help students draw comparisons and contrasts across geographic, cultural, and chronological lines. Examples include "History and the Environment," "Trade and Civilization," "Rulers and Gods," and "The Migration of Peoples."

▶ Each chapter now includes one or more **new** *Comparative Illustrations* that show students cross-cultural comparisons of rituals, art, war, and other topics. Examples include "The Afterlife and Prized Possessions," "The Stele," "Popular Culture—East and West," and "War in the Rice Paddies." Each *Comparative Illustration* is specifically keyed to at least one of the book's seven overarching themes, thus helping students categorize these connections.

© Werner Forman/Art Resource, NY

© Réunion des Musées Nationaux/Art Resource, NY

© Borromeo/Art Resource, NY

ARTS & IDEAS

COMPARATIVE ILLUSTRATION

**The Stele.** A stele is a stone slab or pillar, usually decorated or inscribed, and placed upright. Stelae were often used to commemorate the accomplishments of a ruler or significant figure. Shown at the left is the tallest of the Axum stelae still standing, in present-day Ethiopia. The stone stelae in Axum in the fourth century B.C.E. marked the location of royal tombs with inscriptions commemorating the glories of the kings. An earlier famous stele, seen in the center, is that of Hammurabi (who ruled from 1792 to 1750 B.C.E.; see Chapter 1), which depicts Hammurabi standing in front of a seated god. Below the scene is an inscription of the Code of Hammurabi. A similar kind of stone pillar, shown at the right, was erected in India during the reign of Ashoka in the third century B.C.E. (see Chapter 2) to commemorate events in the life of the Buddha. Archaeologists have also found stelae in ancient China, Greece, and Mexico.

The most famous stone buildings in sub-Saharan Africa are those at Great Zimbabwe. Constructed without mortar, the outer wall and public buildings at Great Zimbabwe are an impressive monument to the architectural creativity of the peoples of the region.

Literature

was transmitted orally from generation to generation. In many West African societies, bards were highly esteemed and served as counselors to kings as well as protectors of local tradition. Bards were revered for their oratory and singing skills, phenomenal memory, and astute interpretation of history. As one African scholar wrote, the death of a bard was equivalent to the burning of a library.

Bards served several necessary functions in society. They were chroniclers of history, preservers of social cus- and proper conduct, and entertainers who possessed a

The book's comparisons reveal the importance and uniqueness of each individual civilization. Examples include early Chinese religion compared with that of Mesopotamia and Greece; comparisons of the building techniques of the Inca and Great Zimbabwe; and the School of Mind compared with Greek philosophy. A complete chapter-by-chapter list appears in the text Preface.

# Thematic

**This Fifth Edition is organized around new themes that are especially relevant in understanding the course of world history.**

The book's seven major themes, pertinent to all cultures from all time periods, make the narrative more cohesive while helping students make connections and comparisons across chapters. These themes are:

| Science & Technology | Politics & Government | Religion & Philosophy | Earth & Environment | Arts & Ideas | Family & Society | Interaction & Exchange |
|---|---|---|---|---|---|---|

Politics & Government

The authors refer to the themes throughout the book, as well as within every *Comparative Essay* and *Comparative Illustration,* where icons highlight the appropriate theme or themes.

© Art Institute of Chicago, Clarence Buckingham Collection

COMPARATIVE ILLUSTRATION

**Popular Culture: East and West**

By the eighteenth century, a popular culture distinct from the elite culture of the nobility was beginning to emerge in the urban worlds of both the East and the West. At the left is a scene from the "floating world," as the pleasure district in Edo, Japan, was called. Seen here are courtesans, storytellers, jesters, and various other entertainers. Below is a scene from the celebration of Carnival on the Piazza Sante Croce in Florence, Italy. Carnival was a period of festivities before Lent, mostly celebrated in Roman Catholic countries. Carnival became an occasion for indulgence in food, drink, games, and practical jokes.

© Scala/Art Resource, NY

tronomy, and languages and also led to experimentation with oil painting and Western ideas of perspective and the interplay of light and dark. Some painters depicted the "southern barbarians," with their strange ships and costumes, large noses, and plumed hats. Europeans desired Japanese lacquerware and metalwork, inlaid with ivory and mother-of-pearl, and especially the ceramics, which were now as highly prized as those of the Chinese.

Perhaps the most famous of all Japanese art of the Tokugawa era is the woodblock print. Genre painting, or representations of daily life, began in the sixteenth century and found its new mass-produced form in the eighteenth-century woodblock print. The now literate mercantile class was eager for illustrated texts of the amusing and bawdy tales that had circulated in oral tradition. At first, these prints were done in black and white,

THE EAST ASIAN WORLD 471

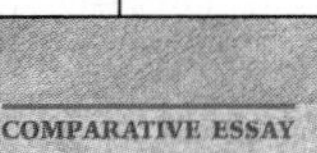

COMPARATIVE ESSAY

**THE USE OF METALS**

Around 6000 B.C.E., people in western Asia discovered how to use metals. They soon realized the advantage in using metal rather than stone to make both tools and weapons. Metal could be shaped more exactly, allowing artisans to make more refined tools and weapons with sharp edges and more precise shapes. Copper, silver, and gold, which were commonly found in their elemental form, were the first metals to be used. These were relatively soft and could be easily pounded into different shapes. But an important step was taken when people discovered that a rock that contained metal could be heated to liquefy the metal (a process called smelting). The liquid metal could then be poured into molds of clay or stone to make precisely shaped tools and weapons.

Copper was the first metal to be used in making tools. The first known copper smelting furnace, dated to 3800 B.C.E., was found in the Sinai. At about the same time, however, artisans in Southeast Asia discovered that tin could be added to copper to make bronze. By 3000 B.C.E., artisans in West Asia were also making bronze. Bronze has a lower melting point that makes it easier to cast, but it is also a harder metal than copper and corrodes less. By 1400 B.C.E., the Chinese were making bronze decorative objects as well as battle-axes and helmets. The widespread use of bronze has led historians to speak of the period from around 3000 to 1200 B.C.E. as the Bronze Age, although this is somewhat misleading in that many peoples continued to use stone tools and weapons even after bronze became available.

But there were limitations to the use of bronze. Tin was not as available as copper, which made bronze tools and weapons expensive. After 1200 B.C.E., bronze was increasingly replaced by iron, which was probably first used around 1500 B.C.E. in western Asia, where the Hittites made new weapons from it. Between 1500 and 600 B.C.E., iron-making spread across Europe, North Africa, and Asia. Bronze continued to be used, but mostly for jewelry and other domestic purposes. Iron was used to make tools and weapons with sharper edges. Because iron weapons were cheaper than bronze ones, larger numbers of warriors could be armed, and wars could be fought on a larger scale.

Iron was handled differently from bronze: it was heated until it could be beaten into a desired shape. Each hammering produced increased strength for the metal. This wrought iron, as it was called, was typical of iron manufacturing in the West until the late Middle Ages. In China, however, the use of heat-resistant clay in the walls of their blast furnaces raised temperatures to 1,537 degrees Celsius, enabling artisans already in the fourth century B.C.E. to liquefy iron so that it too could be cast in a mold. Europeans would not develop such blast furnaces until the fifteenth century C.E.

©British Museum

**Bronze Axhead.** This axhead was made around 2000 B.C.E. by pouring liquid metal into an ax-shaped mold of clay or stone. Artisans would then polish the surface of the ax to produce a sharp cutting edge.

# Visual

## The book's renowned—and now enhanced—map and photo program creates interest and offers increased clarity.

**Gateway to Slavery.** Of the twenty million slaves shipped from Africa to other parts of the world, a good number passed through this doorway (right) on Gorée (top), a small island in a bay just off the coast of Senegal, near Cape Verde. Beginning in the sixteenth century, European traders began to ship Africans from this region to the Americas to be used as slave labor on sugar plantations. Some victims were kept in a prison on the island, which was first occupied by the Portuguese and later by the Dutch, the British, and the French. It also served as an entrepôt and a ...

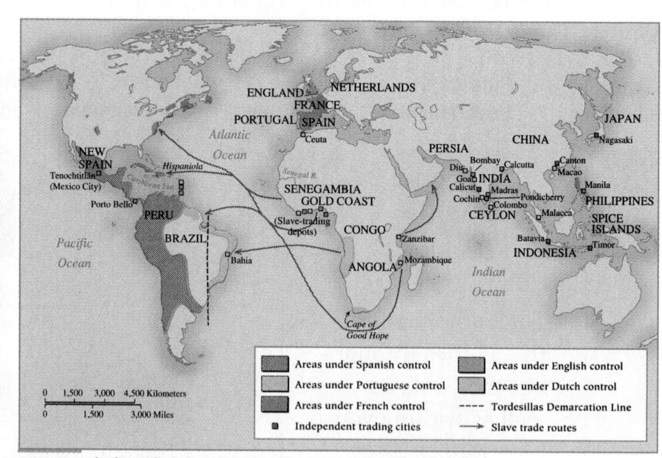


MAP 13.4 **The Slave Trade.** Beginning in the sixteenth century, the trade in African slaves to the New World became a major source of profit to European merchants. This map traces the routes taken by slave trading ships, as well as the territories and ports of call of European powers in the seventeenth century. What were the major destinations for the slave trade? **View an animated version of this map or related maps at** http://history.wadsworth.com/duikerspielvogel05/

▶ Bright maps feature a **new**, more contrasting palette, making them easier to read and understand. Continuing the book's comparative approach, some maps are paired with photos to underline comparisons and bring geography to life. For example Map 13.4, "The Slave Trade," is paired with photographs of the African slave port on Gorée. Expanded map captions encourage readers to think beyond the mere appearance of each map and to make connections across chapters, regions, and concepts. Many maps are also available in interactive form on the **Book Companion Website** (see Preview page 6).

▶ In all, the book contains over 150 four-color maps and 400 pieces of artwork throughout. More than 80 photographs are **new** to this edition.

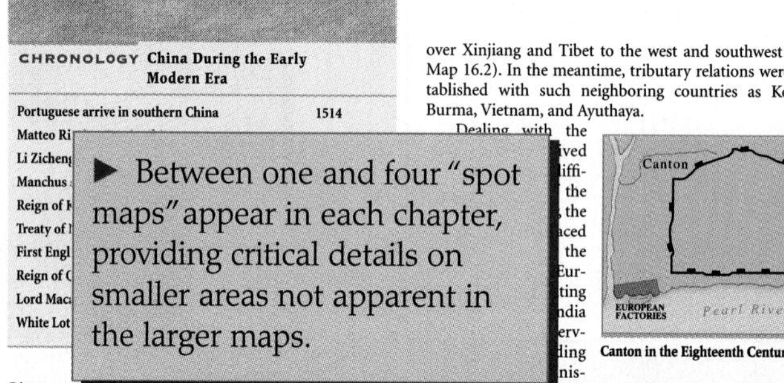

CHRONOLOGY **China During the Early Modern Era**

Portuguese arrive in southern China 1514

over Xinjiang and Tibet to the west and southwest (see Map 16.2). In the meantime, tributary relations were established with such neighboring countries as Korea, Burma, Vietnam, and Ayuthaya.



**Canton in the Eighteenth Century**

Qing court ... for regular trade between the two countries. Through such arrangements, the Manchus were able not only to pacify the northern frontier but also to extend their rule

... territories in Asia, the English established their first trading post at Canton in 1699. Over the next decades, trade with China, notably the export of tea and silk to England, increased rapidly. To limit

▶ Between one and four "spot maps" appear in each chapter, providing critical details on smaller areas not apparent in the larger maps.

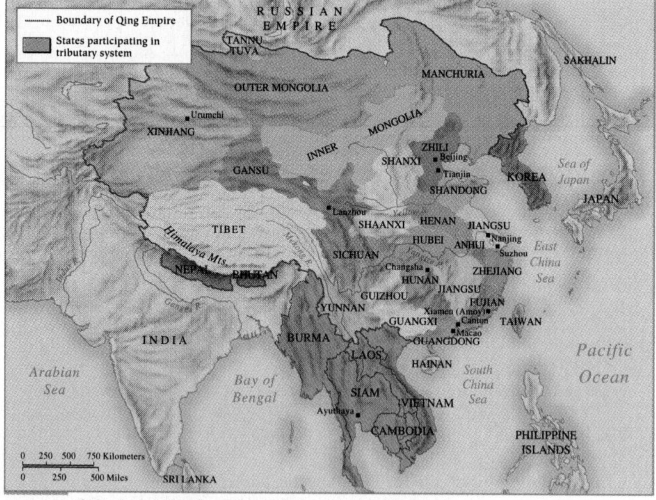


MAP 16.2 **The Qing Empire in the Eighteenth Century.** The boundaries of the Chinese Empire at the height of the Qing dynasty in the eighteenth century are shown on this map. What areas were linked in tributary status to the Chinese empire? **View an animated version of this map or related maps at** http://history.wadsworth.com/duikerspielvogel05/

THE EAST ASIAN WORLD 455

# Compelling

**Primary sources paint powerful pictures of the past, while newly revised *Timelines* put the course of history in perspective.**

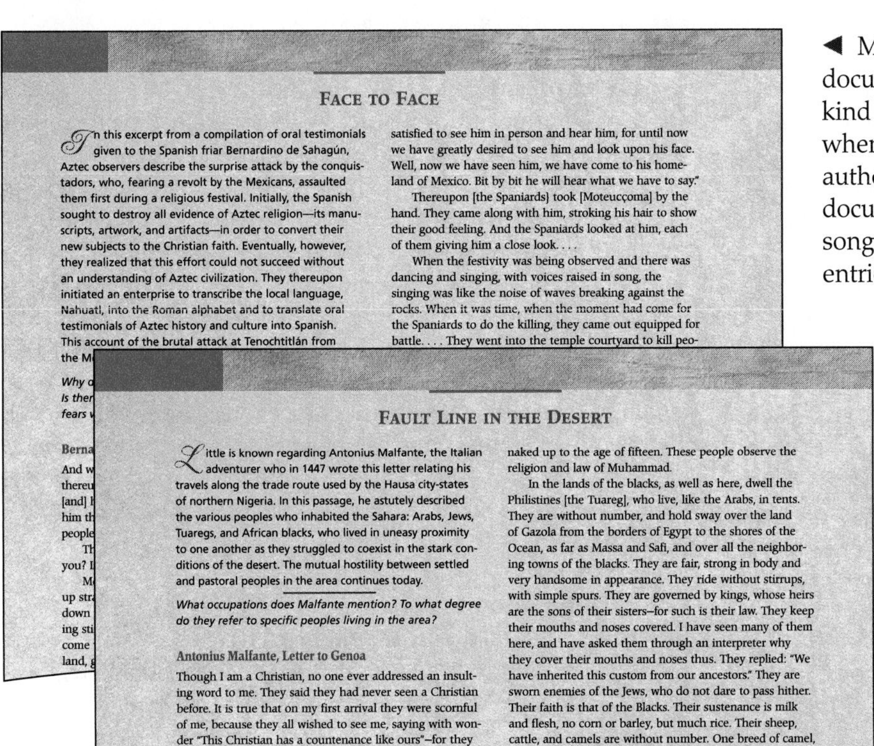

FACE TO FACE

In this excerpt from a compilation of oral testimonials given to the Spanish friar Bernardino de Sahagún, Aztec observers describe the surprise attack by the conquistadors, who, fearing a revolt by the Mexicans, assaulted them first during a religious festival. Initially, the Spanish sought to destroy all evidence of Aztec religion—its manuscripts, artwork, and artifacts—in order to convert their new subjects to the Christian faith. Eventually, however, they realized that this effort could not succeed without an understanding of Aztec civilization. They thereupon initiated an enterprise to transcribe the local language, Nahuatl, into the Roman alphabet and to translate oral testimonials of Aztec history and culture into Spanish. This account of the brutal attack at Tenochtitlán from the M

satisfied to see him in person and hear him, for until now we have greatly desired to see him and look upon his face. Well, now we have seen him, we have come to his homeland of Mexico. Bit by bit he will hear what we have to say."

Thereupon [the Spaniards] took [Moteucçoma] by the hand. They came along with him, stroking his hair to show their good feeling. And the Spaniards looked at him, each of them giving him a close look. . . .

When the festivity was being observed and there was dancing and singing, with voices raised in song, the singing was like the noise of waves breaking against the rocks. When it was time, when the moment had come for the Spaniards to do the killing, they came out equipped for battle. . . . They went into the temple courtyard to kill peo-

FAULT LINE IN THE DESERT

Little is known regarding Antonius Malfante, the Italian adventurer who in 1447 wrote this letter relating his travels along the trade route used by the Hausa city-states of northern Nigeria. In this passage, he astutely described the various peoples who inhabited the Sahara: Arabs, Jews, Tuaregs, and African blacks, who lived in uneasy proximity to one another as they struggled to coexist in the stark conditions of the desert. The mutual hostility between settled and pastoral peoples in the area continues today.

*What occupations does Malfante mention? To what degree do they refer to specific peoples living in the area?*

**Antonius Malfante, Letter to Genoa**

Though I am a Christian, no one ever addressed an insulting word to me. They said they had never seen a Christian before. It is true that on my first arrival they were scornful of me, because they all wished to see me, saying with wonder "This Christian has a countenance like ours"—for they believed that Christians had disguised faces. Their curosity was soon satisfied, and now I can go alone anywhere, with no one to say an evil word to me.

There are many Jews, who lead a good life here, for they are under the protection of the several rulers, each of whom defends his own clients. Thus they enjoy very secure social standing. Trade is in their hands, and many of them are to be trusted with the greatest confidence.

This locality is a mart of the country of the Moors [Berbers] to which merchants come to sell their goods: gold is carried hither, and bought by those who come up from the coast. . . .

It never rains here: if it did, the houses, being built of salt in the place of reeds, would be destroyed. It is scarcely ever cold here: in summer the heat is extreme, wherefore

naked up to the age of fifteen. These people observe the religion and law of Muhammad.

In the lands of the blacks, as well as here, dwell the Philistines [the Tuareg], who live, like the Arabs, in tents. They are without number, and hold sway over the land of Gazola from the borders of Egypt to the shores of the Ocean, as far as Massa and Safi, and over all the neighboring towns of the blacks. They are fair, strong in body and very handsome in appearance. They ride without stirrups, with simple spurs. They are governed by kings, whose heirs are the sons of their sisters—for such is their law. They keep their mouths and noses covered. I have seen many of them here, and have asked them through an interpreter why they cover their mouths and noses thus. They replied: "We have inherited this custom from our ancestors." They are sworn enemies of the Jews, who do not dare to pass hither. Their faith is that of the Blacks. Their sustenance is milk and flesh, no corn or barley, but much rice. Their sheep, cattle, and camels are without number. One breed of camel, white as snow, can cover in one day a distance which would take a horseman four days to travel. Great warriors, these people are continually at war amongst themselves.

The states which are under their rule border upon the land of the blacks . . . which have inhabitants of the faith of Muhammad. In all, the great majority are blacks, but there are a small number of whites [i.e. tawny Moors]. . . .

To the south of these are innumerable great cities and territories, the inhabitants of which are all blacks and idolators, continually at war with each other in defense of their law and faith of their idols. Some worship the sun, others the moon, the seven planets, fire, or water; others a mirror which reflects their faces, which they take to be the images of gods; others groves of trees, the seats of a spirit to whom they make sacrifice; others again, statues of wood and stone, with which, they say, they commune by incantations.

◀ More than 200 primary source documents give students access to the kind of material historians draw on when doing their research. The authors include a variety of documents such as letters, memoirs, song lyrics, official documents, diary entries, menus, poetry, plays, and more. Examples include "Face to Face," the Aztec point of view on the arrival of the conquistadors, and "Fault Line in the Desert," on Antonius Malfante's travels along the Hausa trade route. With this edition, the authors add **new** questions to each document, to guide students in thinking more critically, comparatively, and thematically. Also included with some primary sources are references to related documents available online.

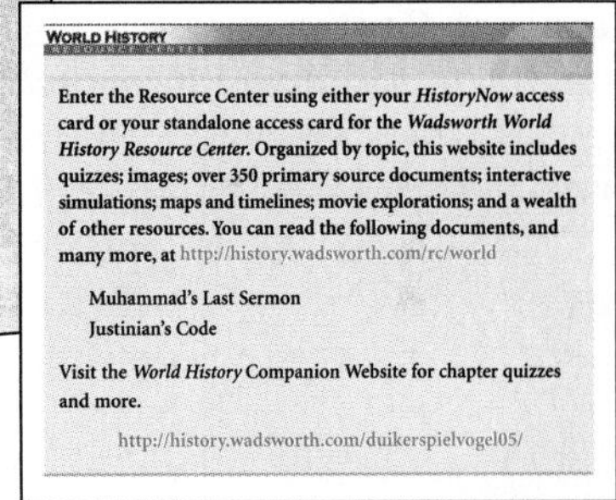

WORLD HISTORY RESOURCE CENTER

Enter the Resource Center using either your *HistoryNow* access card or your standalone access card for the *Wadsworth World History Resource Center*. Organized by topic, this website includes quizzes; images; over 350 primary source documents; interactive simulations; maps and timelines; movie explorations; and a wealth of other resources. You can read the following documents, and many more, at http://history.wadsworth.com/rc/world

Muhammad's Last Sermon
Justinian's Code

Visit the *World History* Companion Website for chapter quizzes and more.

http://history.wadsworth.com/duikerspielvogel05/

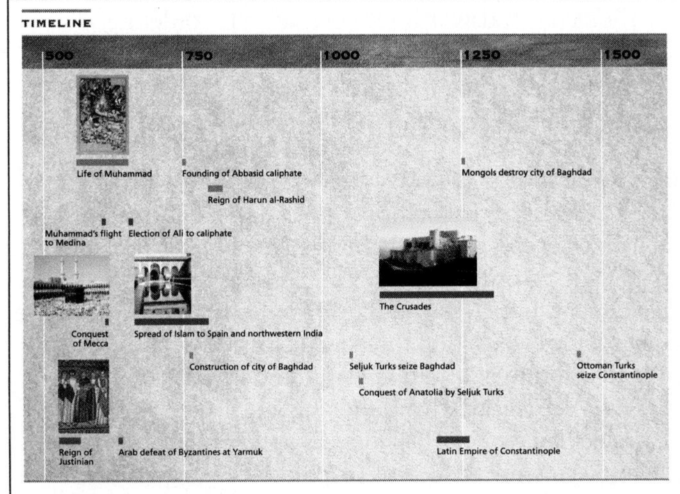


▲ Many primary source documents and end-of-chapter learning materials—including *Timelines*—are available online at the **Wadsworth World History Resource Center** and the **Book Companion Website.** (See the inside cover of this book and the next page of this Preview for details on this powerful resource.)

▲ A *Timeline* in every chapter features **new** thumbnail photos to bring events to life, chronologically lists the dates important to the understanding of a period, and places historical people and events in a comparative setting.

# Interactive

**World History** is enriched by a variety of teaching and learning resources that bring history to life through interactive exploration.

## History Now

**HistoryNow™: World History**

This web-based, intelligent study system saves time for students and instructors by providing a complete package of diagnostic quizzes, a personalized study plan, integrated multimedia elements, primary sources, learning modules, and an instructor grade book. With **HistoryNow** to accompany Duiker and Spielvogel's **World History, Fifth Edition,** students can focus their studies, increase their understanding of key concepts, and improve their performance in your course. This passcode-protected website includes direct access to the **Wadsworth World History Resource Center** with over 350 primary sources, as well as photographs, simulations, maps, and more. Visit **http://history.wadsworth.com** for a demo of **HistoryNow.** Contact your Thomson Wadsworth representative for ordering information.

**Wadsworth World History Resource Center**
**http://history.wadsworth.com/rc/world**

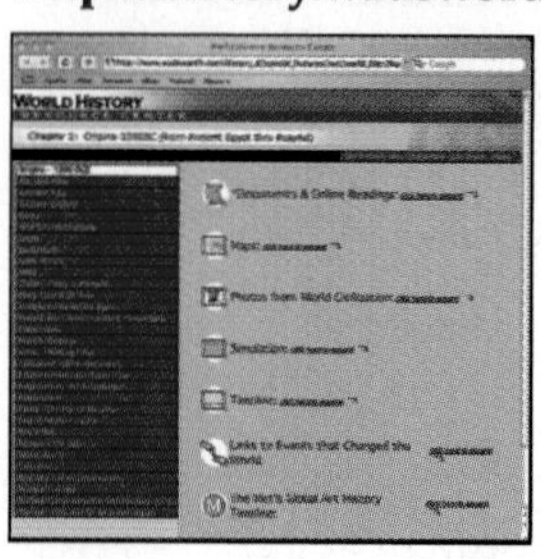

*Significantly expanded!* Now topically organized with a user-friendly timeline navigation bar, this resource center acts as a primary source e-reader with over 300 primary source documents and features numerous resources—such as timelines, photos, interactive maps, exercises, and more! Your students can gain access to the resource center with **HistoryNow.** If you wish for your students to have access only to the **Wadsworth World History Resource Center** you can package an access code with Duiker and Spielvogel's text; contact your Thomson Wadsworth representative for ordering information. Demo the resource center at **http://history.wadsworth.com.**

## HistoryUnbound

**Online Explorations in World History**

**History Unbound** provides access to a visually driven journey that takes you and your students through more than 30 unique explorations of world history. Each exploration consists of a module complete with interactive maps and timelines, hundreds of art images, over 450 primary and secondary source readings, as well as a glossary and questions. Allowing students to explore the past in a new way, **HistoryUnbound** comes with a book-specific *Correlation Guide* consisting of a brief description of each module, along with its list of readings, critical thinking section questions, and module-level questions. The access code can be packaged with any volume of the text; contact your Thomson representative for ordering information. Visit **http://history.wadsworth.com** for a demo of these modules.

**Book Companion Website**
**http://history.wadsworth.com/duiker05/**

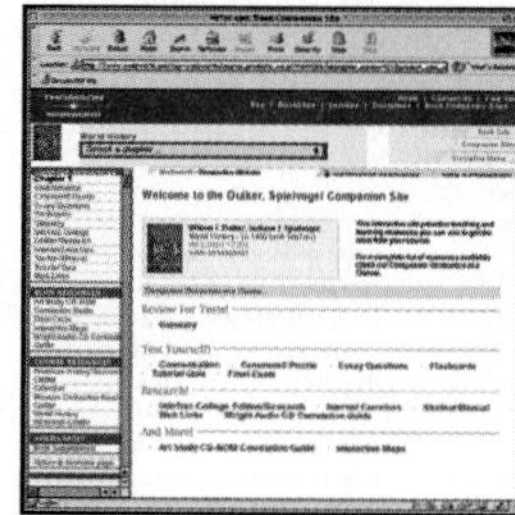

Both instructors and students will enjoy the chapter-by-chapter resources for Duiker and Spielvogel's **World History.** Text-specific content for students includes interactive maps and timelines, tutorial quizzes, glossary, hyperlinks, **InfoTrac® College Edition** exercises, Internet activities, and an annotated bibliography. Instructors also have access to the AP Instructor's Guide and updates, the Instructor's Manual, and Microsoft® PowerPoint® slides. Access code required; contact your Thomson Wadsworth representative for ordering information.

**WebTUTOR™ Advantage on Blackboard® and WebCT®**

**Blackboard: 0-495-09464-1 • WebCT: 0-495-09463-3**

With the text-specific, preformatted content and total flexibility of **WebTutor™ Advantage,** you can easily create and manage your own custom course website! The course management tool gives you the ability to provide virtual office hours, post syllabi, set up threaded discussions, track student progress with the quizzing material, and much more. For students, **WebTutor Advantage** offers real-time access to a full array of study tools, including chapter outlines, learning objectives, glossary flashcards (with audio), practice quizzes, and more. Instructors can access password-protected resources for lectures and class preparation.

Due to contractual reasons certain ancillaries are available only in higher education or U.S. domestic markets. Minimum purchases may apply to receive the ancillaries at no charge. For more information, please contact your local Thomson sales representative.

# Student support

**Student exploration is enhanced with these readers, workbooks, and multimedia explorations of history.**

## Readers & Primers

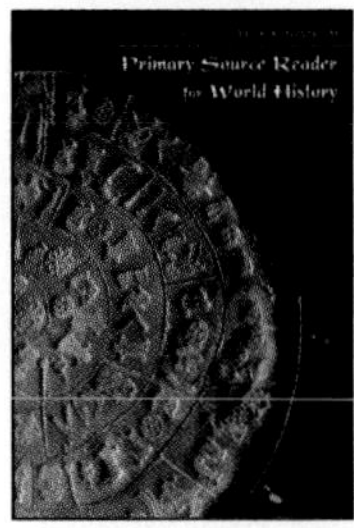

**Primary Source Reader for World History**
**Volume I/To 1500: 0-495-00609-2**
**Volume II/Since 1500: 0-495-00610-6**
*Edited by Elsa A. Nystrom.* Each volume includes primary source documents essential to world history. More than 50 percent of the primary source documents are non-Western, giving students a broad perspective on the history of the world.

**Sources in World History, Fourth Edition**
**Volume I: 0-495-09151-0**
**Volume II: 0-534-58690-2**
*Edited by Mark A. Kishlansky.* These volumes include diverse documents from world history. They provide a balance of constitutional documents, political theory, philosophy, imaginative literature, and social description.

**A Civilization Primer, Fifth Edition**
**0-15-506318-9**
*By Edward M. Anson.* This primer helps history students develop their knowledge of core social science concepts and terminology. Anson defines and clarifies the basics of history, culture, religion, government, economics, and geography.

***Scientific American:* Ancient Civilizations**
Bring your students into current activity in the field with *Scientific American* magazine. As an exclusive offer from Thomson, this magazine is available as a package item for your course; contact your representative for ordering information. *Not available separately.*

***Many of these items can be packaged with your text at considerable savings; contact your Thomson Wadsworth representative for ordering information.***

## Workbooks

**Document Exercise Workbook for World History, Third Edition**
**Volume I: 0-534-57177-8**
**Volume II: 0-534-57178-6**
*Prepared by Donna Van Raaphorst.* These workbooks provide exercises based on primary sources in history.

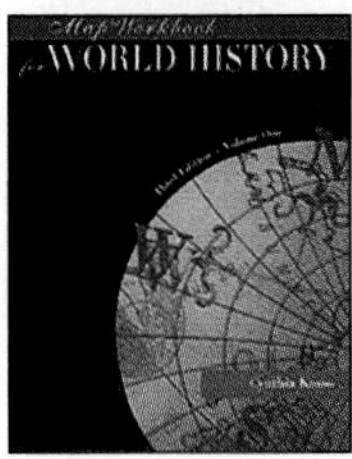


**Map Exercise Workbook, Third Edition**
**Volume I: 0-534-57179-4**
**Volume II: 0-534-57180-8**
*Prepared by Cynthia Kosso.* With approximately 30 map exercises, this workbook has students identify places while improving their geographic understanding of world history. Also includes critical thinking questions for each unit. Contact your local sales representative for package pricing.

**Magellan World History Atlas**
**0-534-56866-1**
This atlas contains 45 four-color historical maps in a practical 8″ x 10″ format. Package item only; contact your local sales representative for pricing. *Not available separately.*

## Multimedia

**Journey of Civilization: The World and Western Traditions CD-ROM**
**0-314-20620-5**
This CD-ROM takes the student on 18 interactive journeys through history. Enhanced with QuickTime™ movies, animations, sound clips, maps, and more, the journeys allow students to engage in history as active participants rather than as readers of past events.

**Migration in Modern World History 1500–2000 CD-ROM with User Guide**
**0-534-57439-4**
*Developed by Patrick Manning and the World History Center at Northeastern University.* This interactive media curriculum goes beyond the mere chronicling of migratory paths. Over 400 primary source documents in migration provide a springboard to explore a wide range of global issues in social, cultural, economic, and political history during the period 1500–2000.

Due to contractual reasons certain ancillaries are available only in higher education or U.S. domestic markets. Minimum purchases may apply to receive the ancillaries at no charge. For more information, please contact your local Thomson sales representative.

# Instructor support

**Everything you need for time-saving course preparation and lecture enrichment.**

## Course Preparation

**Resource Integration Guide**

The **Resource Integration Guide** makes it easy for you to find and integrate the text's topics with a rich array of multimedia resources and print materials. For each chapter of the text you'll find compelling applications and relevant supplemental material. With this easy-to-use tool, you can quickly compile a teaching and learning program that complements both the text's coverage and your own personal instructional style. The **Resource Integration Guide** is included with the **Instructor's Resource CD-ROM** and in the **Instructor's Manual.**

ExamView

**Multimedia Manager with Instructor's Resources: A Microsoft® PowerPoint® Tool**
**0-495-13017-6**

The most comprehensive instructor's resource you'll find! The CD-ROM includes the **Instructor's Manual, Resource Integration Guide, ExamView® Computerized Testing,** and Microsoft® PowerPoint® slides with lecture outlines and images that can be used as offered or customized. **ExamView** allows you to create, deliver, and customize tests and study guides (both print and online) in minutes with its easy-to-use assessment and tutorial system. It offers both a *Quick Test Wizard* and an *Online Test Wizard* that guide you step by step through the process of creating tests. Using the complete word-processing capabilities of **ExamView,** you can enter an unlimited number of new questions or edit existing questions.

**eBank Instructor's Manual and Test Bank**
**0-495-09446-3**

Filled with everything you need for your course, this resource includes lecture outlines reflecting the main chapter headings; class lecture/discussion topics; thought/discussion questions for the boxed documents; possible student projects; and examination questions (essays, identifications, and 50 multiple-choice questions, the latter with correct answers and text page references indicated). Also available on the **Multimedia Manager** and at the **Book Companion Website.**

**AP Instructor's Guide for World History**
**0-495-09442-0**

ISBN 0-495-12723-X
90000
9 780495 127239

## Presentation Tools

JoinIn™ on TurningPoint®

**JoinIn™ on TurningPoint®**
**0-495-09461-7**

**JoinIn™ on TurningPoint®** is the easiest way to turn your lecture hall into a personal, fully interactive experience for your students. **JoinIn** turns your ordinary PowerPoint® application into powerful audience response software allowing you to: take attendance, poll students on key issues to spark discussion, check student comprehension of difficult concepts, collect student demographics to better assess student needs, and even administer quizzes without collecting papers or grading. In addition, we provide interactive slide sets for many of our leading products that you can modify and merge with any existing PowerPoint® lecture slides for a seamless classroom presentation.

**Sights and Sounds of History VHS**
**0-314-09355-9**

Short, focused video clips, photos, artwork, animations, music, and dramatic readings are used to bring life to historical topics and events which are most difficult for students to appreciate from a textbook alone. For example, students will experience the grandeur of Versailles and the defeat felt by a German soldier at Stalingrad. The video segments average four minutes in length and make excellent lecture launchers.

**Transparency Acetates for World History**
**0-495-12868-6**

Each package contains more than 100 four-color map images from the text and other sources. Packages are three-hole punched and shrink-wrapped. Map commentary is provided by James Harrison of Siena College.

**Music CDs**
**2-CD Set: 0-534-60374-2**
**6-CD Set: 0-534-60375-0**

Available to instructors upon request, this CD-ROM set includes musical selections from Purcell through Ravi Shankar to enrich lectures. A correlation guide is available in the **Instructor's Resource CD-ROM** and the **Instructor's Manual and Test Bank.**

Due to contractual reasons certain ancillaries are available only in higher education or U.S. domestic markets. Minimum purchases may apply to receive the ancillaries at no charge. For more information, please contact your local Thomson sales representative.

THOMSON
WADSWORTH

**Publisher** *Clark Baxter*
**Senior Development Editor** *Sue Gleason*
**Assistant Editor** *Paul Massicotte*
**Editorial Assistant** *Lucinda Bingham*
**Technology Project Manager** *David Lionetti*
**Marketing Manager** *Lori Grebe Cooke*
**Marketing Assistant** *Teresa Jessen*
**Advertising Project Manager** *Tami Strang*
**Project Manager, Editorial Production** *Katy German*
**Art Director** *Maria Epes*
**Creative Director** *Rob Hugel*
**Print Buyer** *Rebecca Cross*
**Permissions Editor** *Sarah Harkrader*
**Production Service** *Dovetail Publishing Services*
**Text and Cover Designer** *Kathleen Cunningham*
**Photo Researcher** *Lili Weiner*
**Copy Editor** *Bruce Emmer*
**Illustrator** *Dovetail Publishing Services*
**Cover Image** *The Art Archive/Topkapi Museum Istanbul / Dagli Orti (A). Procession of the Trade Corporations during festival of 1720 in Constantinople; Turkish miniature from Vehbi's* Surname *or* Book of Festival, *c. 1720.*
**Cover Printer** *Phoenix Color Corp*
**Compositor** *Graphic World, Inc.*
**Printer** *The Courier Corporation/Kendallville*



Printed in the United States of America
1 2 3 4 5 6 7 09 08 07 06 05



Library of Congress Control Number: 2005932428
ISBN 0-495-05012-1

**Thomson Higher Education**
10 Davis Drive
Belmont, CA 94002-3098
USA

## ABOUT THE AUTHORS

**WILLIAM J. DUIKER** is liberal arts professor emeritus of East Asian studies at The Pennsylvania State University. A former U.S. diplomat with service in Taiwan, South Vietnam, and Washington, D.C., he received his doctorate in Far Eastern history from Georgetown University in 1968, where his dissertation dealt with the Chinese educator and reformer Cai Yuanpei. At Penn State, he has written widely on the history of Vietnam and modern China, including the widely acclaimed *The Communist Road to Power in Vietnam* (revised edition, Westview Press, 1996), which was selected for a Choice Outstanding Academic Book Award in 1982–1983 and 1996–1997. Other recent books are *China and Vietnam: The Roots of Conflict* (Berkeley, 1987), *Sacred War: Nationalism and Revolution in a Divided Vietnam* (McGraw-Hill, 1995), and *Ho Chi Minh* (Hyperion, 2000). While his research specialization is in the field of nationalism and Asian revolutions, his intellectual interests are considerably more diverse. He has traveled widely and has taught courses on the History of Communism and non-Western civilizations at Penn State, where he was awarded a Faculty Scholar Medal for Outstanding Achievement in the spring of 1996.

To Yvonne,
for adding sparkle to this book, and to my life
W.J.D.

**JACKSON J. SPIELVOGEL** is associate professor emeritus of history at The Pennsylvania State University. He received his Ph.D. from The Ohio State University, where he specialized in Reformation history under Harold J. Grimm. His articles and reviews have appeared in such journals as *Moreana, Journal of General Education, Catholic Historical Review, Archiv für Reformationsgeschichte,* and *American Historical Review.* He has also contributed chapters or articles to *The Social History of the Reformation, The Holy Roman Empire: A Dictionary Handbook, Simon Wiesenthal Center Annual of Holocaust Studies,* and *Utopian Studies.* His work has been supported by fellowships from the Fulbright Foundation and the Foundation for Reformation Research. At Penn State, he helped inaugurate the Western civilization course as well as a popular course on Nazi Germany. His book *Hitler and Nazi Germany* was published in 1987 (fifth edition, 2005). He is the author of *Western Civilization,* published in 1991 (sixth edition, 2006). Professor Spielvogel has won five major university-wide teaching awards. During the year 1988–1989, he held the Penn State Teaching Fellowship, the university's most prestigious teaching award. In 1996, he won the Dean Arthur Ray Warnock Award for Outstanding Faculty Member and in 2000 received the Schreyer Honors College Excellence in Teaching Award.

To Diane,
whose love and support made it all possible
J.J.S.

# Brief Contents

# Detailed Contents

# PART V
# TOWARD A GLOBAL CIVILIZATION? THE WORLD SINCE 1945 720

## 25 IN THE GRIP OF THE COLD WAR: THE BREAKDOWN OF THE YALTA SYSTEM 722



## 26 BRAVE NEW WORLD: COMMUNISM ON TRIAL 750



## 27 EUROPE AND THE WESTERN HEMISPHERE SINCE 1945 783

## 28 Challenges of Nation-Building in Africa and the Middle East 815



## 29 Toward the Pacific Century? 851

# MAPS

# Chronologies

# Documents



## Chapter 1

**THE CODE OF HAMMURABI 13**
Pritchard, James B., ed., *Ancient Near Eastern Texts Relating to the Old Testament,* 3rd Edition with Supplement. Copyright © 1950, 1955, 1969, renewed 1978 by Princeton University Press. Reprinted by permission of Princeton University Press.

**THE GREAT FLOOD 16**
From *The Epic of Gilgamesh* translated by N K Sandars (Penguin Classics 1960, Third Edition 1972). Copyright © N K Sandars, 1960, 1964, 1972. Reproduced by permission of Penguin Books Ltd.

**THE SIGNIFICANCE OF THE NILE RIVER AND THE PHAROAH 18**
Pritchard, James B., ed., *Ancient Near Eastern Texts Relating to the Old Testament,* 3rd Edition with Supplement. Copyright © 1950, 1955, 1969, renewed 1978 by Princeton University Press. Reprinted by permission of Princeton University Press. "Hymn to the Pharoah": Reprinted from The Literature Of The Ancient Egyptians, Adolf Ermann. Copyright © 1927 by E. P. Dutton.

**AKHENATON'S HYMN TO ATON 22**
Pritchard, James B., ed., *Ancient Near Eastern Texts Relating to the Old Testament,* 3rd Edition with Supplement. Copyright © 1950, 1955, 1969, renewed 1978 by Princeton University Press. Reprinted by permission of Princeton University Press.

**THE COVENANT AND THE LAW: THE BOOK OF EXODUS 27**
Reprinted from the Holy Bible, New International Version.

**THE HEBREW PROPHETS: MICAH, ISAIAH, AND AMOS 28**
Reprinted from the Holy Bible, New International Version.

**THE ASSYRIAN MILITARY MACHINE 30**
"King Sennacherib (704–681 B.C.E.) Describes a battle with the Elamites in 691": Reprinted with permission from Pan Macmillan, London, from *The Might That Was Assyria* by H. W. Saggs. Copyright © 1984 by Sidgwick & Jackson Limited. Pritchard, James B., ed., *Ancient Near Eastern Texts Relating to the Old Testament,* 3rd Edition with Supplement. Copyright © 1950, 1955, 1969, renewed 1978 by Princeton University Press. Reprinted by permission of Princeton University Press.

## Chapter 2

**THE ORIGINS OF KINGSHIP 44**
Excerpt from *Sources of Indian Tradition,* by William Theodore de Bary. Copyright © 1988 by Columbia University Press.

**THE DUTIES OF A KING 45**
Excerpt from *Sources of Indian Tradition,* by William Theodore de Bary. Copyright © 1988 by Columbia University Press. Reprinted with the permission of the publisher.

**SOCIAL CLASSES IN ANCIENT INDIA 46**
Excerpt from *Sources of Indian Tradition,* by William Theodore de Bary. Copyright © 1988 by Columbia University Press. Reprinted with the permission of the publisher.

**IN THE BEGINNING 50**
From *The Upanishads,* translated by Juan Mascaro. Viking Press, 1965.

**HOW TO ACHIEVE ENLIGHTENMENT 54**
From *The Teachings of the Compassionate Buddha,* E. A. Burtt, ed. Copyright 1955 by Mentor. Used by permission of the E. A. Burtt Estate.

**THE VOICES OF SILENCE 55**
"Sumangalamata" (A woman well set free! How free I am), translated from Pali by Uma Chakravarti and Kumkum Roy from *Women Writing in India: 600 B.C. to the Present,* Vol. I, ed. by Susie Tharu and K. Lalita, The Feminist Press at the City University of New York. Copyright © 1991 by Susie Tharu and K. Lalita. Reprinted by permission. "Venmanipputi" (What she said to her girlfriend), translated by A. K. Ramanujan from *The Interior Landscape* edited by A. K. Ramanujan, 1967. Reprinted by permission of Peter Owen Ltd, London.

**DRAUPADI'S HUMILIATION 58**
From *The Mahabharata,* William Buck, et al. (Eds.), University of California Press, 2000.

**RAMA AND SITA 59**
From *The Ramayana* by R. K. Narayan. Viking Books, 1972.

## Chapter 3

**A TREATISE ON THE YELLOW RIVER AND ITS CANALS 68**
Excerpt from *Records of the Grand Historian of China,* by Burton Watson, trans. Copyright © 1961 Columbia University Press. Reprinted with the permission of the publisher.

**LIFE IN THE FIELDS 70**
Reprinted from *Ancient China in Transition,* by Cho-yun Hsu, with the permission of the publishers, Stanford University Press, www.sup.org. Copyright © 1965 by the Board of Trustees of the Leland Stanford Junior University.

Continues on page 911

# Preface

For several million years after primates first appeared on the surface of the earth, human beings lived in small communities, seeking to survive by hunting, fishing, and foraging in a frequently hostile environment. Then suddenly, in the space of a few thousand years, there was an abrupt change of direction as human beings in a few widely scattered areas of the globe began to master the art of cultivating food crops. As food production increased, the population in those areas rose correspondingly, and people began to congregate in larger communities. Governments were formed to provide protection and other needed services to the local population. Cities appeared and became the focal point of cultural and religious development. Historians refer to this process as the beginnings of civilization.

For generations, historians in Europe and the United States pointed to the rise of such civilizations as marking the origins of the modern world. Courses on Western civilization conventionally began with a chapter or two on the emergence of advanced societies in Egypt and Mesopotamia and then proceeded to ancient Greece and the Roman Empire. From Greece and Rome, the road led directly to the rise of modern civilization in the West.

There is nothing inherently wrong with this approach. Important aspects of our world today can indeed be traced back to these early civilizations, and all human beings the world over owe a considerable debt to their achievements. But all too often this interpretation has been used to imply that the course of civilization has been linear in nature, leading directly from the emergence of agricultural societies in ancient Mesopotamia to the rise of advanced industrial societies in Europe and North America. Until recently, most courses on world history taught in the United States routinely focused almost exclusively on the rise of the West, with only a passing glance at other parts of the world, such as Africa, India, and East Asia. The contributions made by those societies to the culture and technology of our own time were often passed over in silence.

Two major reasons have been advanced to justify this approach. Some have argued that it is more important that young minds understand the roots of their own heritage than that of peoples elsewhere in the world. In many cases, however, the motivation for this Eurocentric approach has been the belief that since the time of Socrates and Aristotle Western civilization has been the sole driving force in the evolution of human society.

Such an interpretation, however, represents a serious distortion of the process. During most of the course of human history, the most advanced civilizations have been not in the West, but in East Asia or the Middle East. A relatively brief period of European dominance culminated with the era of imperialism in the late nineteenth century, when the political, military, and economic power of the advanced nations of the West spanned the globe. During recent generations, however, that dominance has gradually eroded, partly as the result of changes taking place within Western societies and partly because new centers of development are emerging elsewhere on the globe—notably in East Asia, where the growing economic strength of China and Japan and many of their neighbors has led to the now familiar prediction that the twenty-first century will be known as the Pacific Century.

World history, then, has been a complex process in which many branches of the human community have taken an active part, and the dominance of any one area of the world has been a temporary rather than a permanent phenomenon. It will be our purpose in this book to present a balanced picture of this story, with all respect for the richness and diversity of the tapestry of the human experience. Due attention must be paid to the rise of the West, of course, since that has been the most dominant aspect of world history in recent centuries. But the contributions made by other peoples must be given adequate consideration as well, not only in the period prior to 1500 when the major centers of civilization were located in Asia, but also in our own day, where a multipolar picture of development is clearly beginning to emerge.

Anyone who wishes to teach or write about world history must decide whether to present the topic as an integrated whole or as a collection of different cultures. The world that we live in today, of course, is in many respects an interdependent one in terms of economics as well as culture and communications, a reality that is often expressed by the phrase "global village." The convergence of peoples across the surface of the earth into an integrated world system began in early times and intensified after the rise of capitalism in the early modern era. In growing recognition of this trend, historians trained in global history, as well as instructors in the growing number of world history courses, have now begun to speak and write of a "global approach" that turns attention away from the study of individual civilizations and focuses instead on the "big picture" or, as the world historian Fernand Braudel termed it, interpreting world history as a river with no banks.

On the whole, this development is to be welcomed as a means of bringing the common elements of the evolution of human society to our attention. But there is a problem involved in this approach. For the vast majority of their time on earth, human beings have lived in partial or virtually total isolation from each other. Differences in climate, location, and geographical features have created human societies very different from each other in culture and historical experience. Only in relatively recent times (the commonly accepted date has long been the beginning of the age of European exploration at the end of the fifteenth century, but some would now push it back to the era of the Mongol empire or even further) have cultural interchanges begun to create a common "world system," in which events taking place in one part of the world are rapidly transmitted throughout the globe, often with momentous consequences. In recent generations, of course, the process of global interdependence has been proceeding even more rapidly. Nevertheless, even now the process is by no means complete, as ethnic and regional differences continue to exist and to shape the course of world history. The tenacity of these differences and sensitivities is reflected not only in the rise of internecine conflicts in such divergent areas as Africa, India, and Eastern Europe, but also in the emergence in recent years of such regional organizations as the Organization of African Unity, the Association for the Southeast Asian Nations, and the European Union.

The second problem is a practical one. College students today are all too often not well informed about the distinctive character of civilizations such as China and India and, without sufficient exposure to the historical evolution of such societies, will assume all too readily that the peoples in these countries have had historical experiences similar to ours and will respond to various stimuli in a similar fashion to those living in Western Europe or the United States. If it is a mistake to ignore those forces that link us together, it is equally a mistake to underestimate those factors that continue to divide us and to differentiate us into a world of diverse peoples.

Our response to this challenge has been to adopt a global approach to world history while at the same time attempting to do justice to the distinctive character and development of individual civilizations and regions of the world. The presentation of individual cultures will be especially important in Parts I and II, which cover a time when it is generally agreed that the process of global integration was not yet far advanced. Later chapters will begin to adopt a more comparative and thematic approach, in deference to the greater number of connections that have been established among the world's peoples since the fifteenth and sixteenth centuries. Part V will consist of a series of chapters that will center on individual regions of the world while at the same time focusing on common problems related to the Cold War and the rise of global problems such as overproduction and environmental pollution.

We have sought balance in another way as well. Many textbooks tend to simplify the content of history courses by emphasizing an intellectual or political perspective or, most recently, a social perspective, often at the expense of sufficient details in a chronological framework. This approach is confusing to students whose high school social studies programs have often neglected a systematic study of world history. We have attempted to write a well-balanced work in which political, economic, social, religious, intellectual, cultural, and military history have been integrated into a chronologically ordered synthesis.

To enliven the past and let readers see for themselves the materials that historians use to create their pictures of the past, we have included primary sources (boxed documents) in each chapter that are keyed to the discussion in the text. The documents include examples of the religious, artistic, intellectual, social, economic, and political aspects of life in different societies and reveal in a vivid fashion what civilization meant to the individual men and women who shaped it by their actions. We have added questions to help guide students in analyzing the documents, as well as references to related documents that are available online.

Each chapter has a lengthy introduction and conclusion to help maintain the continuity of the narrative and to provide a synthesis of important themes. Anecdotes in the chapter introductions convey more dramatically the major theme or themes of each chapter. Timelines, now with thumbnail images illustrating major events and figures, at the end of each chapter enable students to see the major developments of an era at a glance and within cross-cultural categories, while the more detailed chronologies reinforce the events discussed in the text. An annotated bibliography at the end of each chapter reviews the most recent literature on each period and also gives references to some of the older, "classic" works in each field.

Updated maps and extensive illustrations serve to deepen the reader's understanding of the text. Map captions are designed to enrich students' awareness of the importance of geography to history, and numerous spot maps enable students to see at a glance the region or subject being discussed in the text. Map captions also include a question to guide students' reading of the map, as well as references to online interactive versions of the maps. To facilitate understanding of cultural movements, illustrations of artistic works discussed in the text are placed near the discussions. Chapter outlines and focus and critical thinking questions have been combined in a new format at the beginning of each chapter to help students with an overview and guide them to the main subjects of each chapter. A glossary of important terms (now boldfaced in the text when they are introduced and defined) and a pronunciation guide are provided at the back of the book to maximize reader comprehension.

After reexamining the entire book and analyzing the comments and reviews of many colleagues who have found the book to be a useful instrument for introducing their students to world history, we have also made a number of other changes for the fifth edition. In the first place, we have reorganized the material by ending Part II at 1500, reversing the order of Chapters 13 and 14, and redoing Chapter 12, "The Making of Europe." The Renaissance is now covered in Chapter 12, and Chapter 14, "Europe Transformed: Reform and State Building," begins with the Reformation.

Second, we have sought to strengthen the global framework of the book, but not at the expense of reducing the attention assigned to individual regions of the world. New comparative essays have been added to each chapter. Keyed to the seven major themes of world history (see p. xxxi), these essays enable us to more concretely draw comparisons and contrasts across geographical, cultural, and chronological lines. Moreover, additional comparative material has been added to each chapter to help students be aware of similar developments globally. Among other things, this material includes new comparative sections as well as comparative illustrations in each chapter that are keyed to the seven major themes of world history. We hope that these techniques will assist instructors who wish to encourage their students to adopt a comparative approach to their understanding of the human experience.

Third, this new edition contains additional information on the role of women in world history. In conformity with our own convictions, as well as what we believe to be recent practice in the field, we have tried where possible to introduce such material at the appropriate point in the text, rather than to set aside separate sections devoted exclusively to women's issues.

Finally, a number of new illustrations, boxed documents, and maps have been added, and the bibliographies have been revised to take account of newly published material. The chronologies and maps have been fine-tuned as well, to help the reader locate in time and space the multitude of individuals and place names that appear in the book. To keep up with the ever-growing body of historical scholarship, new or revised material has been added throughout the book on many topics.

*Chapter 1* New material on Paleolithic painting; the Code of Hammurabi; urbanization in the first civilizations; gender issues in Mesopotamia; and mummification. New comparative illustration on early writing. New comparative essay, "From Hunter-Gatherers and Herders to Farmers."

*Chapter 2* New material on Hinduism and Buddhism, and ancient Indian achievements in mathematics. New comparative illustration on the Buddha and Jesus. New comparative essay, "Writing and Civilization."

*Chapter 3* New material on early Chinese religion compared with that in Mesopotamia and Greece; the evolution of autocratic rule in ancient China; and bronze-casting factories. New comparative illustration on the afterlife and prized possessions. New comparative essay, "The Use of Metals."

*Chapter 4* New material on Hellenistic urbanization; trade and cultural diffusion; Alexander's connections to the East; Greek science in the classical and Hellenistic periods; Minoan Crete; Troy; the effects of colonization; and the development of Athenian democracy, especially under Pericles. New comparative illustration on Hellenistic versus Eastern sculpture. New comparative essay, "*Demos* and Despots."

*Chapter 5* New material on trade between Rome and China; Magna Graeca; Marius; the Etruscans; Mount Vesuvius; slaves; and the crises of the third century and the end of the Western Empire. New comparative illustration on Roman and Chinese Roads. New comparative essay, "Rulers and Gods."

*Chapter 6* New material on the Maya; Caral and Chavín de Huantar; environmental problems in ancient South America; and the Anasazi. New comparative illustration of pyramids. New comparative essay, "History and the Environment."

*Chapter 7* New material on early Islam; early Muslim brotherhoods; and iconoclasm in Islam. New comparative illustration of medieval castles. New comparative essay, "Trade and Civilization."

*Chapter 8* New material on the Husuni Kubwa; comparison of building techniques of the Inka and Great Zimbabwe; the Khoi and the San; and African wood carving. New comparative illustration of the stele. New comparative essay, "The Migration of Peoples." New spot map of the Swahili coast.

*Chapter 9* New comparative illustration of rock architecture. New comparative essay, "Caste, Class, and Family."

*Chapter 10* New material on the Silk Road and the School of Mind compared with Greek philosophy. New comparative illustration of grand canals. New comparative essay, "The Spread of Technology."

*Chapter 11* New comparative illustration of urban life in medieval Japan and Europe. New comparative essay, "Feudal Orders Around the World."

*Chapter 12* New material on decentralization versus centralization of state power in the Middle Ages and Renaissance; long-distance trade with the East during the Renaissance; feudalism as a modern construct; combination of the Roman and Germanic worlds in the making of Europe; and the rise of Italian communes. New comparative illustration of new agriculture in the medieval world. New comparative essay, "The Role of Disease."

*Chapter 13* New material on the Middle Passage and an overall assessment of the Age of Exploration. New comparative illustration of Christianity in Asia. New comparative essay, "Marriage in the Early Modern World."

*Chapter 14* New material on the military revolution of the seventeenth century, connecting wars of religion with state building, and Jesuit missionary activities in Asia. New comparative illustrations on sun kings, west and east. New comparative essay, "Marriage in the Early Modern World."

*Chapter 15* New material on Safavid Iran. New comparative illustration of war commemorations. New comparative essay, "The Changing Face of War."

*Chapter 16* New comparative illustration on popular culture. New comparative essay, "Population Explosion."

*Chapter 17* New material on women thinkers during the Enlightenment. New comparative illustration on revolution and revolt in France and China. New comparative essay, "The Scientific Revolution."

*Chapter 18* New material on the origins of the Industrial Revolution in Britain and the spread of the Industrial Revolution on the Continent; nationalism; and a changed interpretation of the Battle of Königgrätz. New comparative illustration of textile factories. New comparative essay, "The Industrial Revolution."

*Chapter 19* New material on trade unions; reforms in Great Britain; Canada; westernizers, slavophiles, and anarchists in Russia; and social Darwinism. New comparative illustration of painting. New comparative essay, "The Rise of Nationalism."

*Chapter 20* New comparative illustration on cultural influences. New comparative essay, "Imperialism: The Balance Sheet."

*Chapter 21* New comparative illustration of female rulers. New comparative essay, "Imperialism and the Global Environment."

*Chapter 22* New material on the Russian Revolution; casualties of World War I; genocide of Armenians by Turks at end of World War I; and Dadaism. New comparative illustration of soldiers from around the world. New comparative essay, "A Revolution in the Arts."

*Chapter 23* New material on women's rights in India and early twentieth-century nation building in Iraq. New comparative illustration of communist leaders. New comparative essay, "Out of the Doll's House."

*Chapter 24* New material on Stalin and the Soviet Union; Mussolini and the Fascist movement in Italy; and Japanese motives for expansion. New comparative illustration of the bombing of civilians. New comparative essay, "Paths to Modernization."

*Chapter 25* New comparative illustration, "War in the Rice Paddies." New comparative essay, "One World, One Environment." New map of the Chinese civil war; new spot map of South Vietnam at war.

*Chapter 26* New comparative illustration of student rebellions. New comparative essay, "Family and Society in an Era of Change."

*Chapter 27* New sections on the European Union and "The West and Islam." New material on Yugoslavia; immigration laws in Europe; postmodernism; and science and technology. All nations updated to the present. New comparative illustration on international terrorism. New comparative essay, "From the Industrial to the Technological Revolution." New spot map of Central America.

*Chapter 28* New material on Muslim fundamentalism and the growth of Islam in the West, and society and culture in the Middle East. All nations updated to the present. New comparative illustration on traditional patterns in the countryside. New comparative essay, "Religion and Society." New spot map of present-day Iraq.

*Chapter 29* All nations updated to the present. New comparative illustration on the exchange of foods. New comparative essay, "Global Village or Clash of Civilizations?"

Because courses in world history at American and Canadian colleges and universities follow different chronological divisions, a one-volume comprehensive edition, a two-volume edition of this text, and a volume covering events to 1500 are being made available to fit the needs of instructors. Teaching and learning ancillaries include:

*Multimedia Manager for World History with Instructor's Resources: A Microsoft® Powerpoint® Tool* Includes the Instructor's Manual, Resource Integration Guide (grids that link each chapter of the text to instructional ideas and corresponding supplemental resources), ExamView® computerized testing, and Microsoft® PowerPoint® slides with lecture outlines and images that can be used as offered, or customized by importing personal lecture slides or other material. ExamView allows you to create, deliver, and customize tests and study guides (both print and online) in minutes with its easy-to-use assessment and tutorial system. It offers both a Quick Test Wizard and an Online Test Wizard that guide you step by step through the process of creating tests, while its "what you see is what you get" capability allows you to see the test you are creating on the screen exactly as it will print or display online. You can build tests of up to 250 questions using up to 12 question types. Using ExamView's complete word-processing capabilities, you can enter an unlimited number of new questions or edit existing questions.

*Instructor's Manual with Test Bank* Prepared by Eugene Larson, Los Angeles Pierce College. Includes chapter outlines reflecting the main headings; class lecture/discussion topics; thought/discussion questions for the boxed documents; possible student projects; and examination questions (essay, identification, and 50 multiple-choice questions, the latter with correct answers and text page references indicated). Also available on the Multimedia Manager.

*AP Instructor's Guide for World History* This instructor's guide is designed specifically for teachers of Advanced Placement World History courses. It includes a master AP Resource Integration Guide; correlations of the text and the test bank with the most recent released AP exam; sample syllabi; essays on "Making AP Accessible" and "Utilizing Library Resources"; "What to Do After the AP Exam"; learning objectives; lecture outlines; lesson plans keyed to the AP World History Standards; suggested class times; glossary items; lecture and discussion topics; group work suggestions and possible projects; and document-based questions (DBQs).

*Transparency Acetates for World History* Each package contains more than 100 four-color map images from the text and other sources. Packages are three-hole punched and shrinkwrapped. Map commentary is provided by James Harrison, Siena College.

*Sights and Sounds of History* Prepared by David Redles, Cuyahoga Community College. Short, focused VHS video clips, photos, artwork, animations, music, and dramatic readings are used to bring life to historical topics and events which are most difficult for students to appreciate from a textbook alone. For example, students will experience the grandeur of Versailles and the defeat felt by a German soldier at Stalingrad. The video segments average 4 minutes in length and make excellent lecture launchers.

*JoinIn™ on TurningPoint®—World History JoinIn™ on TurningPoint®* is the easiest way to turn your lecture hall into a personal, fully interactive experience for your students. JoinIn turns your ordinary PowerPoint® application into powerful audience response software, allowing you to take attendance, poll students on key issues to spark discussion, check student comprehension of difficult concepts, collect student demographics to better assess student needs, and even administer quizzes without collecting papers or grading. In addition, we provide interactive slide sets for many of our leading products that you can modify and merge with any existing PowerPoint lecture slides for a seamless classrooom presentation.

*Music CDs* Available to instructors upon request, these CDs include musical selctions from Henry Purcell through Ravi Shankar to enrich lectures. A correlation guide is available in the Resource Integration Guide in the Multimedia Manager and the Multimedia Manager.

*HistoryUnbound Web Tutor™ Advantage for World History (for Blackboard® and WebCT®)* This web-based teaching and learning tool is rich with study and mastery tools, communication tools, and course content. Use WebTutor™ to provide virtual office hours, post syllabi, set up threaded discussions, track student progress with quizzing material, and more. For students, Web Tutor offers real-time access to a full array of study tools, including flashcards (with audio), practice quizzes, online tutorials, and web links. Professors can customize the content by uploading images and other resources, adding web links, or creating their own practice materials. Web Tutor also provides rich communication tools including a course calendar, asynchronous discussion, "real-time" chat, and an integrated e-mail system. HistoryUnbound WebTutor Advantage gives you access to all HistoryUnbound online modules.

*HistoryNow* Available via access card, this web-based intelligent study system saves time for students and instructors by providing a complete package of diagnostic quizzes, a personalized study plan, integrated multimedia, over 450 primary source readings, and an instructor gradebook.

*HistoryUnbound: Online Explorations in World History* *HistoryUnbound*'s online modules bring the past to life through seamless integration of interactive maps and timelines, images, and primary-source readings. Available as a bundle item or as a standalone product, the *HistoryUnbound* access code is packaged with a text-specific Correlation Guide.

*Wadsworth History Resource Center* Wadworth History Resource Centers (http://history.wadsworth.com/rc/world) for American History, World History, and Western Civilization have significantly expanded! Now chronologically organized with a user-friendly timeline navigation bar, these centers act as a primary source e-reader with over 300 primary source documents and feature numerous resources, such as timelines, photos, interactive maps, exercises, and more. Your students obtain access to the appropriate resource center when you package an access code with any Thomson Wadsworth history textbook. Access codes are available free when packaged with most new books and at a nominal price when packaged with our Thomson Advantage Books. If need be, you can also order it by itself. All access codes last for one complete year. Demo the resource centers at htto://history.wadsworth.com, by clicking on your area (American, Western Civilization, World Civilization) on the left-hand navigation bar, and then contact your local representative for ordering details.

*Book Companion Web Site*

http://history.wadsworth.com/duikerspielvogel05/

Both instructors and students will enjoy the chapter-by-chapter resources for Duiker and Spielvogel's *World History*, with access to the Wadsworth World History Resource Center. Text-specific content for students includes interactive maps, interactive timelines, tutorial quizzes, glossary, hyperlinks, InfoTrac College Edition exercises, Internet activities, and an annotated bibliography. Instructors also have access to the Instructor's Manual and PowerPoint slides (access code required). From the History homepage, instructors and students can access many selections, such as primary source documents, interactive simulations, an Internet Guide for History, a career center, lessons on surfing the web, the World History Image Bank, and links to great history-related web sites.

*The Journey of Civilization* Prepared by David Redles, Cuyahoga Community College. This CD-ROM takes the student on 18 interactive journeys through history. Enhanced with QuickTime movies, animations, sound clips, maps, and more, the journeys allow students to engage in history as active participants rather than as readers of past events. Contact your local sales representative for bundle pricing.

*Migrations in Modern World History 1500–2000 CD-ROM with User Guide (Student Version)* An interactive multimedia curriculum on CD-ROM developed by Patrick Manning and the World History Center at Northeastern University. *Migration* goes beyond the mere chronicling of migratory paths. Over 400 primary source documents in *Migration* provide a springboard to explore a wide range of global issues in social, cultural, economic, and political history during the period 1500–2000.

*InfoTrac® College Edition with InfoMarks®* Now available, free four-month access to InfoTrac® College Edition's online database of more than 18 million reliable, full-length articles from 5,000 academic journals and periodicals (including *the New York Times, Science, Forbes,* and *USA Today*) includes access to InfoMarks—stable URLs that can be linked to articles, journals, and searches. InfoMarks allow you to use a simple "copy and paste" technique to create instant and continually updated online readers, content services, bibliographies, elecronic "reserve" readings, and current topic sites. And incorporating InfoTrac College Edition into your course is easy—references to this virtual library are built into many of our texts in margins, exercises, and so forth. In addition, ask about other InfoTrac College Edition resources available, including InfoMarks print and online readers with readings, activities, and exercises hand selected to work with the text. And to help students use the research they gather, their free four-month subscription to InfoTrac College Edition includes access to InfoWrite, a complete set of online critical thinking and paper writing tools. To take a quick tour of InfoTrac College Edition, visit http://www.infotrac-college.com/ and select the "User Demo." (Journals subject to change. Certain restrictions may apply. For additional information, please consult your local Thomson representative.)

*A Civilization Primer, 5th Edition* This proven supplement for the introductory Western civilization course, by Edward M. Anson, University of Arkansas, Little Rock, is designed to help history students develop their knowledge of core social science concepts and terminology. This brief text defines and clarifies the basics of history, culture, religion, government, economics, and geography.

*Document Exercise Workbook for World History, 3rd Edition* Prepared by Donna Van Raaphorst, Cuyahoga Community College, this two-volume workbook provides a collection of exercises based around primary source documents in history. Contact your local sales representative for bundle pricing.

*Magellan World History Atlas* Available to bundle with any history text. Contains 44 four-color historical maps, including The Conflict in Afghanistan, 2001, and States of the World, 2001. Contact your local sales representative for bundle pricing.

*Map Exercise Workbook, 3rd Edition* Prepared by Cynthia Kosso, Northern Arizona University, this two-volume workbook features approximately 30 map exercises. Designed to help students feel comfortable with maps by having them work with different kinds of maps to identify places and improve their geographic understanding of world history. Contact your local sales representative for bundle pricing.

*Scientific American—Ancient Civilizations* Bring your students into current activity in the field with *Scientific American* magazine. As an exclusive offer from Thomson, this magazine is available as a bundle item for your course. This issue includes coverage by region, including such topics as the Iceman, Death Cults of Prehistoric Malta, Keys to the Lost Indus Cities, Women and Men at Catalhuyuk, Rock Art in Southern Africa, Life and Death in Nabada, Tapestry of Power in a Mesopotamian City, Daily Life in Ancient Egypt, Great Zimbabwe, Precious Metal Objects of the Middle Sican, Life in the Provinces of the Aztec Empire, Reading the Bones of La Florida, and more.

*Sources of World History* This two-volume reader, edited by Mark Kishlansky, Harvard University, is a collection of primary source documents designed to supplement any world history text. Provides a balance of constitutional documents, political theory, philosophy, imaginative literature, and social description. Contact your local sales representative for bundle pricing.

*Primary Source Reader for World History* Edited by Elsa A. Nystrom, Kennesaw State University. A thoughtful collection of important primary source documents essential to world history, this two-volume reader is an affordable supplement for students and a valuable complement to any world history or world civilization class. More than 50 percent of the primary source documents are non-Western, giving students a broad perspective on the history of the world. The readings are divided by eras and organized according to principal themes, such as religion, law and government, and everyday life. Each group of readings has a section describing the signficance of subsequent readings and how those readings interrelate. Individual readings include a headnote and various study questions intended to guide student reading and understanding.

*A Custom Reader for Western Civilization* Written by leading educators and historians, this fully customizable reader of primary and secondary sources, appropriate for the text's European coverage, is enhanced with an online collection of visual sources, including maps, animations and interactive exercises. Each reading also comes with an introduction and a series of review questions. To learn more visit www.ThomsonCustom.com or call Thomson Custom Publishing at 1-800-355-9983.

# Acknowledgments

BOTH AUTHORS GRATEFULLY acknowledge that without the generosity of many others, this project could not have been completed.

William Duiker would like to thank Kumkum Chatterjee and On-cho Ng for their helpful comments about issues related to the history of India and premodern China. His longtime colleague Cyril Griffith, now deceased, was a cherished friend and a constant source of information about modern Africa. Art Goldschmidt has been of invaluable assistance in reading several chapters of the manuscript, as well as in unraveling many of the mysteries of Middle Eastern civilization. Finally, he remains profoundly grateful to his wife, Yvonne V. Duiker, Ph.D. She has not only given her usual measure of love and support when this appeared to be an insuperable task, but she has also contributed her own time and expertise to enrich the sections on art and literature, thereby adding life and sparkle to this, as well as the earlier editions of the book. To her, and to his daughters Laura and Claire, he will be forever thankful for bringing joy to his life.

Jackson Spielvogel would like to thank Art Goldschmidt, David Redles, and Christine Colin for their time and ideas. Daniel Haxall and Kathryn Spielvogel of The Pennsylvania State University provided valuable assistance with materials on postwar art, popular culture, and Postmodern art and thought. Above all, he thanks his family for their support. The gifts of love, laughter, and patience from his daughters, Jennifer and Kathryn, his sons, Eric and Christian, and daughters-in-law, Liz and Laurie, and his son-in-law, Daniel, were invaluable. Diane, his wife and best friend, provided him with editorial assistance, wise counsel, and the loving support that made a project of this magnitude possible.

Thanks to Wadsworth's comprehensive review process, many historians were asked to evaluate our manuscript. We are grateful to the following for the innumerable suggestions that have greatly improved our work. Members of this edition's Editorial Review Board (asterisked) deserve our particular thanks.

Najia Aarim
*SUNY College at Fredonia*

*Jacob Abadi
*U.S. Air Force Academy*

Henry Maurice Abramson
*Florida Atlantic University*

Wayne Ackerson
*Salisbury University*

Charles F. Ames, Jr.
*Salem State College*

Nancy Anderson
*Loyola University*

J. Lee Annis
*Montgomery College*

*Monty Armstrong
*Cerritos High School*

Gloria M. Aronson
*Normandale College*

Charlotte Beahan
*Murray State University*

Doris Bergen
*University of Vermont*

Martin Berger
*Youngstown State University*

Deborah Biffton
*University of Wisconsin—LaCrosse*

Charmarie Blaisdell
*Northeastern University*

Brian Bonhomme
*Youngstown State University*

Patricia J. Bradley
*Auburn University at Montgomery*

Dewey Browder
*Austin Peay State University*

Nancy Cade
*Pikeville College*

Antonio Calabria
*University of Texas at San Antonio*

Alice-Catherine Carls
*University of Tennessee—Martin*

Yuan Ling Chao
*Middle Tennessee State University*

Mark W. Chavalas
*University of Wisconsin*

Hugh Clark
*Ursinus College*

Joan Coffey
*Sam Houston State University*

*Eleanor A. Congdon
*Youngstown State University*

Edward R. Crowther
*Adams State College*

John Davis
*Radford University*

Ross Dunn
*San Diego State University*

Lane Earn
*University of Wisconsin—Oshkosh*

Roxanne Easley
*Central Washington University*

C. T. Evans
*Northern Virginia Community College*

Edward L. Farmer
*University of Minnesota*

William W. Farris
*University of Tennessee*

Ronald Fritze
*Lamar University*

Joe Fuhrmann
*Murray State University*

Robert Gerlich
*Loyola University*

Marc J. Gilbert
*North Georgia College*

William J. Gilmore-Lehne
*Richard Stockton College of New Jersey*

Richard M. Golden
*University of North Texas*

Candice Goucher
*Washington State University—Vancouver*

Joseph M. Gowaskie
*Rider College*

Jonathan Grant
*Florida State University*

Don Gustafson
*Augsburg College*

Deanna Haney
*Lansing Community College*

Jason Hardgrave
*University of Southern Indiana*

Jay Harmon
*Catholic High School*

Ed Haynes
*Winthrop College*

*Marilynn Jo Hitchens
*University of Colorado—Denver*

*Tamara L. Hunt
*University of Southern Indiana*

Linda Kerr
*University of Alberta at Edmonton*

David Koeller
*North Park University*

Zoltan Kramar
*Central Washington University*

Douglas Lea
*Kutztown University*

David Leinweber
*Emory University*

Thomas T. Lewis
*Mount Senario College*

Craig A. Lockard
*University of Wisconsin—Green Bay*

George Longenecker
*Norwich University*

*Norman D. Love
*El Paso Community College*

Robert Luczak
*Vincennes University*

Aran MacKinnon
*State University of West Georgia*

Patrick Manning
*Northeastern University*

Dolores Nason McBroome
*Humboldt State University*

John McDonald
*Northern Essex Community College*

Andrea McElderry
*University of Louisville*

Jeff McEwen
*Chattanooga State Technical Community College*

Margaret McKee
*Castilleja High School*

Nancy McKnight
*Stockton High School*

David L. McMullen
*University of North Carolina at Charlotte*

John A. Mears
*Southern Methodist University*

David A. Meier
*Dickinson State University*

Marc A. Meyer
*Berry College*

Stephen S. Michot
*Mississippi County Community College*

John Ashby Morton
*Benedict College*

William H. Mulligan
*Murray State University*

*Henry A. Myers
*James Madison University*

Marian P. Nelson
*University of Nebraska at Omaha*

Sandy Norman
*Florida Atlantic University*

Patrick M. O'Neill
*Broome Community College*

Roger Pauly
*University of Central Arkansas*

Norman G. Raiford
*Greenville Technical College*

Jane Rausch
*University of Massachusetts—Amherst*

Dianna K. Rhyan
*Columbus State Community College*

Merle Rife
*Indiana University of Pennsylvania*

Patrice C. Ross
*Columbus State Community College*

John Rossi
*LaSalle University*

Eric C. Rust
*Baylor University*

Maura M. Ryan
*Springbrook High School*

Jane Samson
*University of Alberta*

Keith Sandiford
*University of Manitoba*

Elizabeth Sarkinnen
*Mt. Hood Community College*

*Pamela Sayre
*Henry Ford College*

Bill Schell
*Murray State University*

Robert M. Seltzer
*Hunter College*

David Shriver
*Cuyahoga Community College*

Amos E. Simpson
*University of Southwestern Louisiana*

Wendy Singer
*Kenyon College*

Marvin Slind
*Washington State University*

Paul Smith
*Washington State University*

John Snetsinger
*California Polytechnic State University*

George Stow
*LaSalle University*

John C. Swanson
*Utica College of Syracuse*

Patrick Tabor
*Chemeketa Community College*

Tom Taylor
*Seattle University*

John G. Tuthill
*University of Guam*

Joanne Van Horn
*Fairmont State College*

Salli Vaegis
*Georgia Perimeter College*

Peter von Sivers
*University of Utah*

*Christopher J. Ward
*Clayton College and State University*

Pat Weber
*University of Texas—El Paso*

Douglas L. Wheeler
*University of New Hampshire*

David L. White
*Appalachian State University*

Elmira B. Wicker
*Southern University—Baton Rouge*

Glee Wilson
*Kent State University*

Harry Zee
*Cumberland County College*

The authors are truly grateful to the people who have helped us to produce this book. We especially want to thank Clark Baxter, whose faith in our ability to do this project was inspiring. Sue Gleason thoughtfully and cheerfully guided the overall development of the fifth edition, and Paul Massicotte orchestrated the preparation of outstanding teaching and learning ancillaries. Bruce Emmer was, as usual, an outstanding copyeditor. Lili Weiner provided valuable assistance in obtaining permissions for the illustrations. Jon Peck, of Dovetail Publishing Services, was as cooperative and cheerful as he was competent in matters of production management.

# A Note to Students About Language and the Dating of Time

One of the most difficult challenges in studying world history is coming to grips with the multitude of names, words, and phrases in unfamiliar languages. Unfortunately, this problem has no easy solution. We have tried to alleviate the difficulty, where possible, by providing an English-language translation of foreign words or phrases, a glossary, and a pronunciation guide. The issue is especially complicated in the case of Chinese, since two separate systems are commonly used to transliterate the spoken Chinese language into the Roman alphabet. The Wade-Giles system, invented in the nineteenth century, was the most frequently used until recent years, when the pinyin system was adopted by the People's Republic of China as its own official form of transliteration. We have opted to use the latter, since it appears to be gaining acceptance in the United States, but the initial use of a Chinese word is accompanied by its Wade-Giles equivalent in parentheses for the benefit of those who may encounter the term in their outside reading.

In our examination of world history, we need also to be aware of the dating of time. In recording the past, historians try to determine the exact time when events occurred. World War II in Europe, for example, began on September 1, 1939, when Adolf Hitler sent German troops into Poland, and ended on May 7, 1945, when Germany surrendered. By using dates, historians can place events in order and try to determine the development of patterns over periods of time.

If someone asked you when you were born, you would reply with a number, such as 1987. In the United States, we would all accept that number without question, because it is part of the dating system followed in the Western world (Europe and the Western Hemisphere). In this system, events are dated by counting backward or forward from the birth of Christ (assumed to be the year 1). An event that took place 400 years before the birth of Christ would most commonly be dated 400 B.C. (before Christ). Dates after the birth of Christ are labeled as A.D. These letters stand for the Latin words *anno domini*, which mean "in the year of the Lord" (or the year of the birth of Christ). Thus an event that took place 250 years after the birth of Christ is written A.D. 250, or in the year of the Lord 250. It can also be written as 250, just as you would not give your birth year as A.D. 1987, but simply 1987.

Some historians now prefer to use the abbreviations B.C.E. ("before the common era") and C.E. ("common era") instead of B.C. and A.D. This is especially true of world historians who prefer to use symbols that are not so Western or Christian oriented. The dates, of course, remain the same. Thus, 1950 B.C.E. and 1950 B.C. would be the same year, as would A.D. 40 and 40 C.E. In keeping with the current usage by many world historians, this book will use the terms B.C.E. and C.E.

Historians also make use of other terms to refer to time. A decade is 10 years; a century is 100 years; and a millennium is 1,000 years. The phrase fourth century B.C.E. refers to the fourth period of 100 years counting backward from 1, the assumed date of the birth of Christ. Since the first century B.C.E. would be the years 100 B.C.E. to 1 B.C.E., the fourth century B.C.E. would be the years 400 B.C.E. to 301 B.C.E. We could say, then, that an event in 350 B.C.E. took place in the fourth century B.C.E.

The phrase fourth century C.E. refers to the fourth period of 100 years after the birth of Christ. Since the first period of 100 years would be the years 1 to 100, the fourth period or fourth century would be the years 301 to 400. We could say, then, for example, that an event in 350 took place in the fourth century. Likewise, the first millennium B.C.E. refers to the years 1000 B.C.E. to 1 B.C.E.; the second millennium C.E. refers to the years 1001 to 2000.

The dating of events can also vary from people to people. Most people in the Western world use the Western calendar, also known as the Gregorian calendar after Pope Gregory XIII who refined it in 1582. The Hebrew calendar, on the other hand, uses a different system in which the year 1 is the equivalent of the Western year 3760 B.C.E., considered by Jews to be the date of the creation of the world. Thus, the Western year 2006 will be the year 5766 on the Jewish calendar. The Islamic calendar begins year 1 on the day Muhammad fled Mecca, which is the year 622 on the Western calendar.

# Themes for Understanding World History

As they pursue their craft, historians often organize their material on the basis of themes that enable them to ask and try to answer basic questions about the past. Such is our intention here. In preparing the fifth edition of this book, we have selected several major themes that we believe are especially important in understanding the course of world history. These themes transcend the boundaries of time and space and have relevance to all cultures since the beginning of the human experience.

In the chapters that follow, we will refer to these themes frequently as we advance from the prehistoric era to the present. Where appropriate, we shall make comparisons across cultural boundaries, or across different time periods. To facilitate this process, we have included a comparative essay in each chapter that focuses on a particular theme within the specific time period dealt with in that section of the book. For example, the comparative essays in Chapters 1 and 6 deal with the human impact on the natural environment during the premodern era, while those in Chapters 21 and 25 discuss the issue during the age of imperialism and in the contemporary world. Each comparative essay is identified with a particular theme, although it will be noted that many essays deal with several themes at the same time.

We have sought to illustrate these themes through the use of comparative illustrations in each chapter. These illustrations are comparative in nature and seek to encourage the reader to think about thematic issues in cross-cultural terms, while not losing sight of the unique characteristics of individual societies. Our seven themes, each divided into two subtopics, are listed below.

1. *Politics and Government* The study of politics seeks to answer certain basic questions that historians have about the structure of a society: How were people governed? What was the relationship between the ruler and the ruled? What people or groups of people (the political elites) held political power? What actions did people take to guarantee their security or change their form of government?

2. *Arts and Ideas* We cannot understand a society without looking at its culture, or the common ideas, beliefs, and patterns of behavior that are passed on from one generation to the next. Culture includes both high culture and popular culture. High culture consists of the writings of a society's thinkers and the works of its artists. A society's popular culture is the world of ideas and experiences of ordinary people. Today the media have embraced the term popular culture to describe the current trends and fashionable styles.

3. *Religion and Philosophy* Throughout history, people have sought to find a deeper meaning to human life. How have the world's great religions, such as Hinduism, Buddhism, Judaism, Christianity, and Islam, influenced people's lives? How have they spread to create new patterns of culture in other parts of the world?

4. *Family and Society* The most basic social unit in human society has always been the family. From a study of family and social patterns, we learn about the different social classes that make up a society and their relationships with one another. We also learn about the role of gender in individual societies. What different roles did men and women play in their societies? How and why were those roles different?

5. *Science and Technology* For thousands of years, people around the world have made scientific discoveries and technological innovations that have changed our world. From the creation of stone tools that made farming easier to advanced computers that guide our airplanes, science and technology have altered how humans have related to their world.

6. *Earth and the Environment* Throughout history, peoples and societies have been affected by the physical world in which they live. Climatic changes alone have been an important factor in human history. Through their economic activities, peoples and societies, in turn, have also made an impact on their world. Human activities have affected the physical environment and even endangered the very existence of entire societies and species.

7. *Interaction and Exchange* Many world historians believe that the exchange of ideas and innovations is the driving force behind the evolution of human societies. The introduction of agriculture, writing and printing, metal working, and navigational techniques, for example, spread gradually from one part of the world to other regions and eventually changed the face of the entire globe. The process of cultural and technological exchange took place in various ways, including trade, conquest, and the migration of peoples.

PART

# I

# The First Civilizations and the Rise of Empires (Prehistory to 500 C.E.)



**For hundreds of thousands** of years, human beings lived in small communities, seeking to survive by hunting, fishing, and foraging in an often hostile environment. Then, in the space of a few thousand years, there was an abrupt change of direction as human beings in a few widely scattered areas of the globe began to master the art of cultivating food crops. As food production increased, the population in such areas grew, and people began to congregate in larger communities. Cities appeared and became centers of cultural and religious development. Historians refer to these changes as the beginnings of civilization.

How and why did the first civilizations arise? What role did cross-cultural contacts play in their development? What was the nature of the relationship between these permanent settlements and nonagricultural peoples living elsewhere in the world? Finally, what brought about the demise of these early civilizations, and what legacy did they leave for their successors in the region? The first civilizations that emerged in Mesopotamia, Egypt, India, and China in the fourth and third millennia B.C.E. all shared a number of basic characteristics. Each developed in a river valley that was able to provide the agricultural resources needed to maintain a large population.

The appearance of these sedentary societies had a major impact on the social organizations, religious beliefs, and ways of life of the peoples living within their boundaries. With the increase in population and the development of centralized authority came the emergence of cities. Within the cities, new forms of livelihood appeared to satisfy the growing need for social services and consumer goods. Some people became artisans or merchants, while others became warriors, scholars, or priests. In some cases, the physical divisions within the first cities reflected the strict hierarchical character of the society as a whole, with a royal palace surrounded by an imposing wall and separate from the remainder of the urban population.

Although the emergence of the first civilizations led to the appearance of major cities, the vast majority of the population undoubtedly consisted of peasants or slaves working on the lands of the wealthy. In general, rural peoples were less affected by the change than their urban counterparts. Farmers continued to live in simple mud-and-thatch huts, and many still faced severe legal restrictions on their freedom of action and movement. Slavery was still commonly practiced in virtually all ancient societies.

Within these civilizations, the nature of social organization and relationships also began to change. As the concept of private property spread, people were less likely to live in large kinship groups, and the concept of the nuclear family became increasingly prevalent. Gender roles came to be differentiated, with men working in the fields or at various specialized occupations and women remaining in the home. Wives were less likely to be viewed as partners than as possessions under the control of their husbands.

These new civilizations were also the scene of significant religious and cultural developments. All of them gave birth to new religions as a means of explaining the functioning of the

forces of nature. The approval of gods was deemed crucial to a community's chances of success, and a professional class of priests emerged to govern relations with the divine world.

Writing was an important development in the evolution of these new civilizations. Eventually, all of them used writing as a primary means of communication and of creative expression.

From the beginnings of the first civilizations around 3000 B.C.E., there was an ongoing movement toward the creation of larger territorial states with more sophisticated systems of control. This process reached a high point in the first millennium B.C.E. Between 1000 and 500 B.C.E., the Assyrians and Persians amassed empires that encompassed large areas of the ancient Middle East. The conquests of Alexander the Great in the fourth century B.C.E. created an even larger, if short-lived, empire that soon divided into four kingdoms. Later, the western portion of these kingdoms as well as the Mediterranean world and much of western Europe fell subject to the mighty empire of the Romans. At the same time, much of India became part of the Mauryan Empire. Finally, in the last few centuries B.C.E, the Qin and Han dynasties of China created a unified Chinese empire.

At first, these new civilizations had relatively little contact with peoples in the surrounding regions. But there is growing evidence that a pattern of regional trade had begun to develop in the Middle East, and probably in southern and eastern Asia as well, at a very early date. As the population increased, the volume of trade undoubtedly rose with it, and the new civilizations began to move outward to acquire new lands and access needed resources. As they expanded, they began to encounter peoples along the periphery of their growing empires.

Not much evidence has survived to chronicle the nature of these first encounters, but it is likely that the results varied widely according to time and place. In some cases, the growing civilizations found it relatively easy to absorb isolated communities of agricultural or food-gathering peoples whom they encountered. Such was the case in southern China and in the southern part of the South Asian peninsula. But in other instances, notably among the nomadic or seminomadic peoples in central and northeastern Asia, the problem was more complicated and often resulted in bitter and extended conflict.

Contacts between these nomadic or seminomadic peoples and settled civilizations probably developed gradually over an extended period of time. Often the relationship, at least at the outset, was mutually beneficial, as each needed goods produced by the other. Nomadic peoples in Central Asia also served as an important conduit for goods and ideas between sedentary civilizations transporting goods over long distances as early as 3000 B.C.E. Overland trade throughout southwestern Asia was already well established by the third millennium B.C.E.

Eventually, the relationship between the settled peoples and the nomadic peoples became increasingly characterized by conflict. Where conflict occurred, the governments of the sedentary civilizations used a variety of techniques to resolve the problem, including negotiations, conquest, or alliance with other pastoral peoples to isolate their primary tormentors.

In the end, these early civilizations collapsed not only as a result of nomadic invasions but also because of their own weaknesses, which made them increasingly vulnerable to attacks along the frontier. Some of their problems were political, and others were related to climatic change or environmental problems.

The fall of the ancient empires did not mark the end of civilization, of course, but rather a transition to a new stage of increasing complexity in the evolution of human society. ◆

CHAPTER

# 1

# The First Civilizations: The Peoples of Western Asia and Egypt

© Nik Wheeler/CORBIS

*Ruins of the ancient Sumerian city of Uruk*

## CHAPTER OUTLINE AND FOCUS QUESTIONS

### The First Humans

- How did the Neolithic agricultural revolution occur, and how did it affect the lives of men and women?

### The Emergence of Civilization

- What are the characteristics of civilization, and what are some explanations for why early civilizations emerged?

### Civilization in Mesopotamia

- How are the chief characteristics of civilization evident in ancient Mesopotamia?

### Egyptian Civilization: "The Gift of the Nile"

- What was the role of geography and religion in the civilization of ancient Egypt?

### New Centers of Civilization

- How did Judaism and Zoroastrianism differ from the religions of Mesopotamia and Egypt?

### The Rise of New Empires

- What methods and institutions did the Assyrians and Persians use to amass and maintain their respective empires?

### CRITICAL THINKING

- In what ways were the civilizations of Mesopotamia and Egypt alike? In what ways were they different? What accounts for the similarities and differences?

IN 1849, A DARING YOUNG ENGLISHMAN made a hazardous journey into the deserts and swamps of southern Iraq. Braving high winds and temperatures that reached 120 degrees Fahrenheit, William Loftus led a small expedition southward along the banks of the Euphrates River in search of the roots of civilization. As he said, "From our childhood we have been led to regard this place as the cradle of the human race."

Guided by native Arabs into the southernmost reaches of Iraq, Loftus and his small band of explorers were soon overwhelmed by what they saw. He wrote, "I know of nothing more exciting or impressive than the first sight of one of these great piles, looming in solitary grandeur from the surrounding plains and marshes." One of these piles, known to the natives as the mound of Warka, contained the ruins of Uruk, one of the first cities in the world and part of the world's first civilization.

Southern Iraq, known to ancient peoples as Mesopotamia, was one of the areas in the world where civilization began. In the fertile valleys of large rivers—the Tigris and Euphrates in Mesopotamia, the Nile in Egypt, the Indus in India, and the Yellow River in China–intensive agriculture became capable of supporting large groups of people. In these regions, civilization was born. The first civilizations emerged in western Asia (now known as the Middle East) and Egypt, where people developed organized societies and created the ideas and institutions that we associate with civilization.

Before considering the early civilizations of western Asia and Egypt, however, we must briefly examine our prehistory and observe how human beings made the shift from hunting and gathering to agricultural communities and ultimately to cities and civilization. ◇

**CHRONOLOGY The First Humans**

| | |
|---|---|
| Australopithecines | flourished c. 2–4 million years ago |
| *Homo habilis* | flourished c. 1–4 million years ago |
| *Homo erectus* | flourished c. 100,000–1.8 million years ago |
| *Homo sapiens:* | |
| Neanderthals | flourished c. 100,000–30,000 B.C.E. |
| *Homo sapiens sapiens* | emerged c. 200,000 B.C.E. |

# The First Humans

Historians rely mostly on documents to create their pictures of the past, but no written records exist for the prehistory of humankind. In their absence, the story of early humanity depends on archaeological and, more recently, biological information, which anthropologists and archaeologists use to formulate theories about our early past.

Although science has given us more precise methods for examining prehistory, much of our understanding of early humans still relies on considerable conjecture. Given the rate of new discoveries, the following account of the current theory of early human life might well be changed in a few years. As the great British archaeologist Louis Leakey reminded us years ago, "Theories on prehistory and early man constantly change as new evidence comes to light."

The earliest humanlike creatures—known as **hominids**—lived in Africa some three to four million years ago. Called Australopithecines, or "southern apemen," by their discoverers, they flourished in eastern and southern Africa and were the first hominids to make simple stone tools. Australopithecines were also bipedal—that is, they walked upright on two legs, a trait that enabled them to move over long distances and make use of their arms and legs for different purposes.

In 1959, Louis and Mary Leakey discovered a new form of hominid in Africa that they labeled *Homo habilis* ("handy human"). The Leakeys believed that *Homo habilis* was the earliest toolmaking hominid, which had a brain almost 50 percent larger than that of the Australopithicenes. Their larger brains and the ability to walk upright allowed these hominids to become more sophisticated in the search for meat, seeds, and nuts for nourishment.

A new phase in early human development occurred around 1.8 million years ago with the emergence of *Homo erectus* ("upright human"). A more advanced human form, *Homo erectus* made use of larger and more varied tools and was the first hominid to leave Africa and move into Europe and Asia.

## The Emergence of *Homo sapiens*

Around 250,000 years ago, a third and crucial phase in human development began with the emergence of *Homo sapiens* ("wise human"). By 100,000 B.C.E., two groups of *Homo sapiens* had developed. One type was the Neanderthal, whose remains were first found in the Neander valley in Germany. Neanderthal remains have since been found in both Europe and the Middle East and have been dated to between 100,000 and 30,000 B.C.E. Neanderthals relied on a variety of stone tools and were the first early people to bury their dead. (Some scientists maintain that burial of the dead indicates a belief in an afterlife.) Neanderthals in Europe made clothes from the skins of animals that they had killed for food.

The first anatomically modern humans, known as *Homo sapiens sapiens* ("wise, wise human"), appeared in Africa between 200,000 and 150,000 years ago. Recent evidence indicates that they began to spread outside Africa around 100,000 years ago. Map 1.1 shows probable dates for different movements, although many of these dates are still controversial. By 30,000 B.C.E., *Homo sapiens sapiens* had replaced the Neanderthals, who had largely become extinct.

The movement of the first modern humans was rarely deliberate. Groups of people advanced beyond their old hunting grounds at a rate of only 2 to 3 miles per generation. This was enough, however, to populate the world in some tens of thousands of years. Some scholars have suggested that such advanced human creatures may have emerged independently in different parts of the world, rather than in Africa alone, but the latest genetic evidence strongly supports the out-of-Africa theory as the most likely explanation of human origin. In any case, by 10,000 B.C.E., members of the *Homo sapiens sapiens* species could be found throughout the world. By that time, it was the only human species left. All humans today, be they Europeans, Australian Aborigines, or Africans, belong to the same subspecies of human being.

## The Hunter-Gatherers of the Paleolithic Age

One of the basic distinguishing features of the human species is the ability to make tools. The earliest tools were

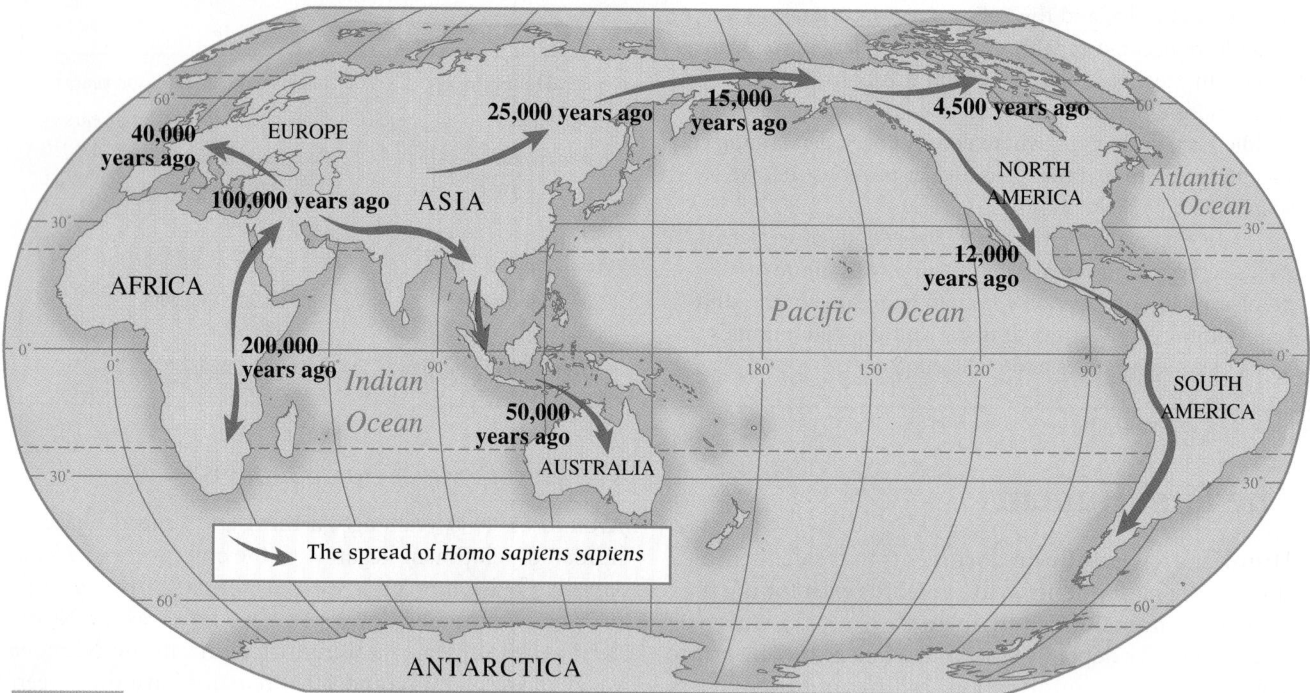


**MAP 1.1 The Spread of Homo *sapiens sapiens.*** *Homo sapiens sapiens* spread from Africa beginning about 100,000 years ago. Living and traveling in small groups, these anatomically modern humans were hunter-gatherers. ? Given that some diffusion of humans occurred during ice ages, how would such climate change affect humans and their movements, especially from Asia to Australia and Asia to North America?

**View an animated version of this map or related maps at** http://history.wadsworth .com/duikerspielvogel05/

made of stone, and so this early period of human history (c. 2,500,000–10,000 B.C.E.) has been designated the **Paleolithic Age** (*paleolithic* is Greek for "old stone").

For hundreds of thousands of years, humans relied on hunting and gathering for their daily food. Paleolithic peoples had a close relationship with the world around them, and over a period of time, they came to know which animals to hunt and which plants to eat. They did not know how to grow crops or raise animals, however. They gathered wild nuts, berries, fruits, and a variety of wild grains and green plants. Around the world, they captured and consumed various animals, including buffalo, horses, bison, wild goats, reindeer, and fish.

The hunting of animals and the gathering of wild plants no doubt led to certain patterns of living. Archaeologists and anthropologists have speculated that Paleolithic people lived in small bands of twenty to thirty individuals. They were nomadic (they moved from place to place) because they had no choice but to follow animal migrations and vegetation cycles. Hunting depended on careful observation of animal behavior patterns and required a group effort to have any real degree of success. Over the years, tools became more refined and more useful. The invention of the spear, and later the bow and arrow, made hunting considerably easier. Harpoons and fishhooks made of bone increased the catch of fish.

Both men and women were responsible for finding food—the chief work of Paleolithic people. Since women bore and raised the children, they generally stayed close to the camps, but they played an important role in acquiring food by gathering berries, nuts, and grains. Men hunted for wild animals, an activity that took them far from camp. Because both men and women played important roles in providing for the band's survival, scientists have argued that a rough equality existed between men and women. Indeed, some speculate that both men and women made the decisions that governed the activities of the Paleolithic band.

These groups of Paleolithic peoples, especially those who lived in cold climates, found shelter in caves. Over time, they created new types of shelter as well. Perhaps the most common was a simple structure of wood poles or sticks covered with animal hides. Where wood was scarce, Paleolithic hunter-gatherers might use the bones of mammoths for the framework and cover it with animal hides. The systematic use of fire, which archaeologists believe began around 500,000 years ago, made it possible for the caves and human-made structures to have a source of light and heat. Fire also enabled early humans to cook their food, making it taste better, last longer, and in the case of some plants, such as wild grains, easier to chew and digest.

The making of tools and the use of fire—two important technological innovations of Paleolithic peoples—remind us how crucial the ability to adapt was to human survival. Changing physical conditions during periodic ice ages posed a considerable threat to human existence.

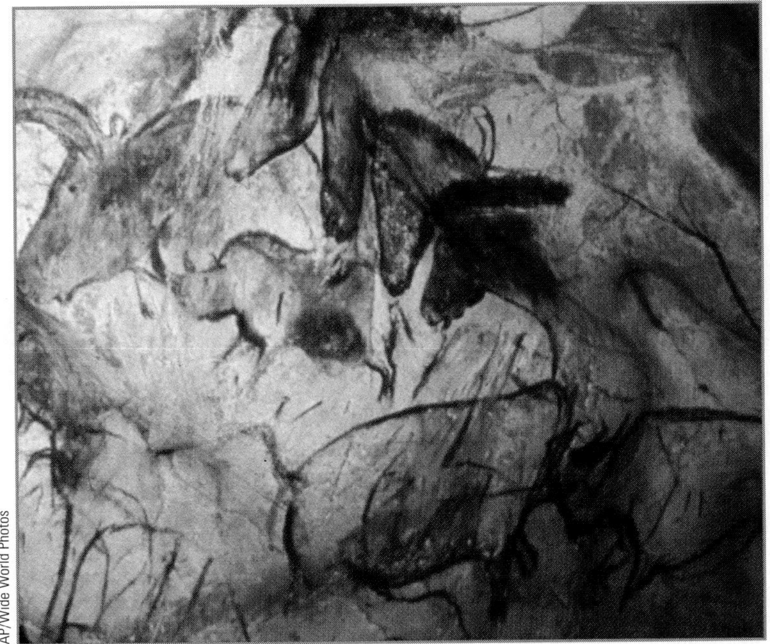

AP/Wide World Photos

**Paleolithic Cave Painting: The Chauvet Cave.** Cave paintings of large animals reveal the cultural creativity of Paleolithic peoples. This scene is part of a mural in a large underground chamber at Vallon-Pont-d' Arc, France, discovered in December 1994. It dates from around 30,000–28,000 B.C.E. and depicts aurochs (long-horned wild oxen), horses, and rhinoceroses. To make their paintings, Paleolithic artists used stone lamps in which they burned animal fat to illuminate the cave walls and combined powdered mineral ores with animal fat to create red, yellow, and black pigments. Some artists even made brushes out of animal hairs with which to apply the paints.

Paleolithic peoples used their technological innovations—such as the ability to make tools and use fire—to change their physical environment. By working together, they found a way to survive. And by passing on their common practices, skills, and material products to their children, they ensured that later generations, too, could survive in a harsh environment.

But Paleolithic peoples did more than just survive. The cave paintings of large animals found in southwestern France and northern Spain bear witness to the cultural activity of Paleolithic peoples. A cave discovered in southern France in 1994 (known as the Chauvet cave after the leader of the expedition that found it) contains more than three hundred paintings of lions, oxen, owls, panthers, and other animals. Most of these are animals that Paleolithic people did not hunt, which suggests to some scholars that the paintings were made for religious or even decorative purposes. The discoverers were overwhelmed by what they saw: "There was a moment of ecstasy. . . . They overflowed with joy and emotion in their turn. . . . These were moments of indescribable madness."[1]

## The Neolithic Revolution, c. 10,000–4000 B.C.E.

The end of the last ice age around 10,000 B.C.E. was followed by what is called the **Neolithic Revolution** because it ushered in the New Stone Age (*neolithic* is Greek for "new stone"). The name New Stone Age is misleading, however. Although Neolithic peoples made a new type of polished stone axes, this was not the most significant change they introduced.

**A Revolution in Agriculture** The biggest change was the shift from hunting animals and gathering plants for sustenance to producing food by systematic agriculture (see Map 1.2). The planting of grains and vegetables provided a regular supply of food, while the taming of animals, such as sheep, goats, cattle, and pigs, added a steady source of meat, milk, and fibers such as wool for clothing. Larger animals could also be used as beasts of burden. The growing of crops and the taming of food-producing animals created a new relationship between humans and nature. Historians like to speak of this as an agricultural revolution. Revolutionary change is dramatic and requires great effort, but the ability to acquire food on a regular basis gave humans greater control over their environment. It also enabled them to give up their nomadic ways of life and begin to live in settled communities.

The shift from hunting and gathering to food producing was not as sudden as was once believed, however. The **Mesolithic Age** ("Middle Stone Age," c. 10,000–7000 B.C.E.) saw a gradual transition from a food-gathering and hunting economy to a food-producing one and witnessed a gradual domestication of animals as well. Likewise, the movement toward the use of plants and their seeds as an important source of nourishment was also not sudden. Evidence seems to support the possibility that the Paleolithic hunters and gatherers had already grown crops to supplement their traditional sources of food. Moreover, throughout the Neolithic period, hunting and gathering as well as nomadic herding remained ways of life for many people around the world.

Systematic agriculture developed independently in different areas of the world between 8000 and 5000 B.C.E. Inhabitants of the Middle East began cultivating wheat and barley and domesticating pigs, cattle, goats, and sheep by 8000 B.C.E. From the Middle East, farming spread into the Balkans region of Europe by 6500 B.C.E. By 4000 B.C.E., it was well established in the south of

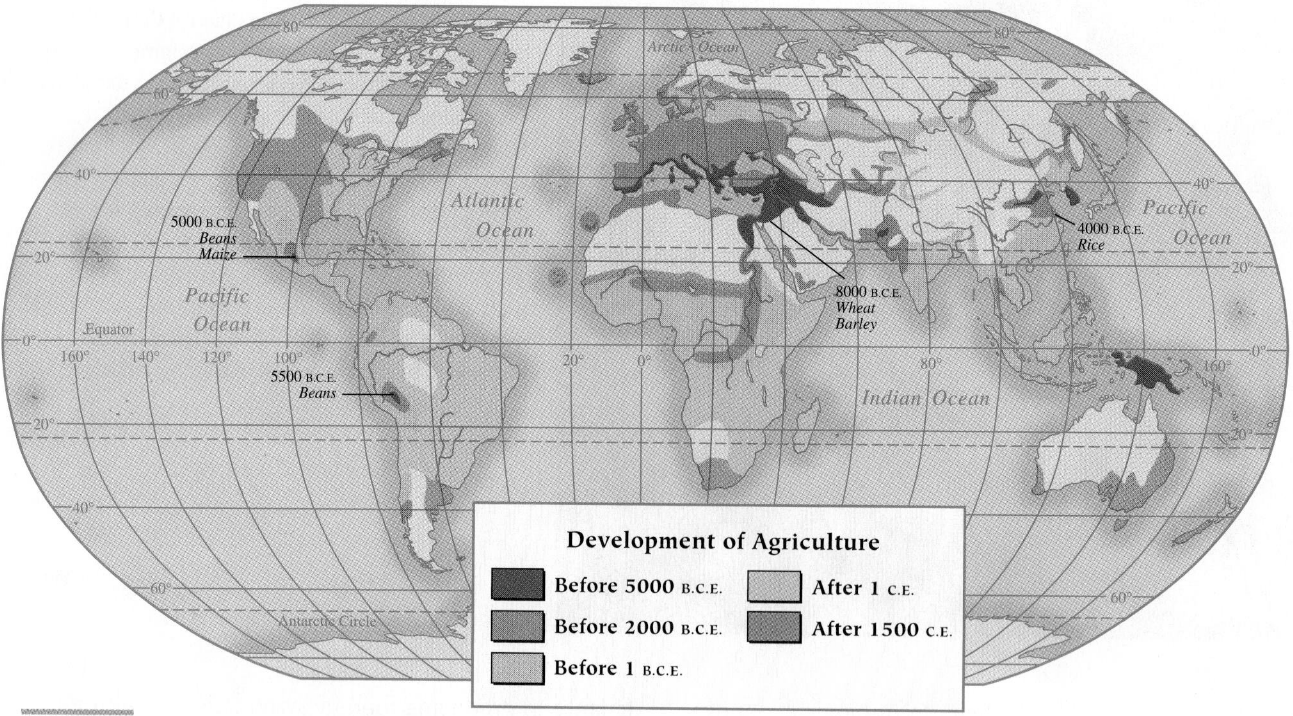


**MAP 1.2 The Development of Agriculture.** Agriculture first began between 8000 and 7000 B.C.E. in four different areas. It allowed the establishment of permanent settlements where crops could be grown and domesticated animals that produced meat and milk could be easily tended. ? What geographical and human factors might explain relationships between latitude and the beginning of agriculture?
**View an animated version of this map or related maps at** http://history.wadsworth.com/duikerspielvogel05/

France, central Europe, and the coastal regions of the Mediterranean. The cultivation of wheat and barley also spread from western Asia into the Nile valley of Egypt by 6000 B.C.E. and soon spread up the Nile to other areas of Africa, especially the Sudan and Ethiopia. In the woodlands and tropical forests of Central Africa, a separate agricultural system emerged based on the cultivation of tubers or root crops such as yams and tree crops such as bananas. The cultivation of wheat and barley also eventually moved eastward into the highlands of northwestern and central India, between 7000 and 5000 B.C.E. By 5000 B.C.E., rice was being cultivated in southeastern Asia, from where it spread into southern China. In northern China, the cultivation of millet and the domestication of pigs and dogs seem well established by 6000 B.C.E. In the Western Hemisphere, Mesoamericans (inhabitants of present-day Mexico and Central America) domesticated beans, squash, and maize (corn) as well as dogs and fowl between 7000 and 5000 B.C.E. (see the comparative essay "From Hunter-Gatherers and Herders to Farmers" on p. 7)

**Neolithic Farming Villages** The growing of crops on a regular basis gave rise to relatively permanent settlements, which historians refer to as Neolithic farming villages or towns. Although Neolithic villages appeared in Europe, India, Egypt, China, and Mesoamerica, the oldest and most extensive ones were located in the Middle East. Jericho, in Palestine near the Dead Sea, was in existence by 8000 B.C.E. and covered several acres by 7000 B.C.E. It had a wall several feet thick that enclosed houses made of sun-dried mudbricks. Çatal Hüyük, located in modern Turkey, was an even larger community. Its walls enclosed 32 acres, and its population probably reached six thousand inhabitants during its high point from 6700 to 5700 B.C.E. People lived in simple mudbrick houses that were built so close to one another that there were few streets. To get to their homes, people would walk along the rooftops and enter the house through a hole in the roof.

Archaeologists have discovered twelve cultivated products in Çatal Hüyük, including fruits, nuts, and three kinds of wheat. People grew their own food and stored it in storerooms in their homes. Domesticated animals, especially cattle, yielded meat, milk, and hides. Hunting scenes on the walls would indicate that the people of Çatal Hüyük hunted as well, but unlike earlier hunter-gatherers, they no longer relied on hunting to survive. Food surpluses also made it possible for people to do things other than farming. Some people became artisans and made weapons and jewelry that were traded with neighboring peoples, thus connecting the inhabitants of Çatal Hüyük to the wider world around them.

## COMPARATIVE ESSAY

# From Hunter-Gatherers and Herders to Farmers

About ten thousand years ago, human beings began to practice the cultivation of crops and the domestication of animals. The exact time and place that crops were first cultivated successfully is uncertain. The first farmers undoubtedly used simple techniques and still relied primarily on other forms of food production, such as hunting, foraging, and pastoralism, or herding. The real breakthrough came when farmers began to cultivate crops along the flood plains of river systems. The advantage was that crops grown in such areas were not as dependent upon rainfall and therefore produced a more reliable harvest. An additional benefit was that the sediment carried by the river waters deposited nutrients in the soil, thus enabling the farmer to cultivate a single plot of ground for many years without moving to a new location. Thus, the first truly sedentary (nonmigratory) societies were born.

The spread of river valley agriculture in various parts of Asia and Africa was the decisive factor in the rise of the first civilizations. The increase in food production in these regions led to a significant growth in population, while efforts to control the flow of water to maximize the irrigation of cultivated areas and to protect the local inhabitants from hostile forces outside the community provoked the first steps toward cooperative activities on a large scale. The need to oversee the entire process brought about the emergence of an elite that was eventually transformed into a government.

We shall investigate this process in the next several chapters as we explore the rise of civilizations in the Mediterranean, the Middle East, South Asia, China, and the Americas. We shall also raise a number of important questions: Why did human communities in some areas that had the capacity to support agriculture not take the leap to farming? Why did other groups that had managed to master the cultivation of crops not take the next step to create large and advanced societies? Finally, what happened to the existing communities of hunter-gatherers who were overrun or driven out as the agricultural revolution spread its way rapidly throughout the world?

Over the years, a number of possible reasons, some of them biological, others cultural or environmental in nature, have been advanced to explain such phenomena. According to Jared Diamond, in his highly acclaimed work *Guns, Germs, and Steel: The Fates of Human Societies,* the ultimate causes of such differences lie not within the character or cultural values of the resident population, but in the nature of the local climate and topography. These influence the degree to which local crops and animals can be put to human use and then be transmitted to adjoining regions. In Mesopotamia, for example, the widespread availability of edible crops, such as wheat and barley, helped promote the transition to agriculture in the region. At the same time, the lack of land barriers between Mesopotamia and its neighbors to the east and west facilitated the rapid spread of agricultural techniques and crops to climatically similar regions in the Indus River valley and Egypt.

---

Religious shrines housing figures of gods and goddesses have been found at Çatal Hüyük, as have a number of female statuettes. Molded with noticeably large breasts and buttocks, these "earth mothers" perhaps symbolically represented the fertility of both "our mother" earth and human mothers. Both the shrines and the statues point to the growing role of religion in the lives of these Neolithic peoples.

**Consequences of the Neolithic Revolution** The Neolithic agricultural revolution had far-reaching consequences. Once people settled in villages or towns, they built houses for protection and other structures for the storage of goods. As organized communities stored food and accumulated material goods, they began to engage in trade. In the Middle East, for example, the new communities exchanged such objects as shells, flint, and semiprecious stones. People also began to specialize in certain crafts, and a division of labor developed. Pottery was made from clay and baked in fire to make it hard. The pots were used for cooking and to store grains. Woven baskets were also used for storage. Stone tools became refined as flint blades were used to make sickles and hoes for use in the fields. In the course of the Neolithic Age, many of the food plants still in use today came to be cultivated. Moreover, vegetable fibers from such plants as flax and cotton were used to make thread that was woven into cloth.

The change to systematic agriculture in the Neolithic Age also had consequences for the relationship between men and women. Men assumed the primary responsibility for working in the fields and herding animals, jobs that kept them away from the home. Women remained behind, caring for the children and weaving cloth, making cheese from milk, and performing other household tasks that required considerable labor. In time, as work outside the home was increasingly perceived as more important

**Statues from Ain Ghazal.** These life-size statues made of plaster and bitumen dating from 6500 B.C.E. were discovered in 1984 in Ain Ghazal, an archaeological site near Amman, Jordan. They are among the oldest known statues of the human figure. Although they appear lifelike, their features are considered generic rather than portraits of individual faces. The purpose and meaning of these sculptures may never be known.

than work done in the home, men came to play the more dominant role in human society, a basic pattern that would persist until our own times.

Other patterns set in the Neolithic Age also proved to be enduring elements of human history. Fixed dwellings, domesticated animals, regular farming, a division of labor, men holding power—all of these are part of the human story. For all of our scientific and technological progress, human survival still depends on the growing and storing of food, an accomplishment of people in the Neolithic Age. The Neolithic Revolution was truly a turning point in human history.

Between 4000 and 3000 B.C.E., significant technical developments began to transform the Neolithic towns. The invention of writing enabled records to be kept, and the use of metals marked a new level of human control over the environment and its resources. Already before 4000 B.C.E., artisans had discovered that metal-bearing rocks could be heated to liquefy the metal, which could then be cast in molds to produce tools and weapons that were more useful than stone instruments. Although copper was the first metal to be used for producing tools, after 4000 B.C.E., metalworkers in western Asia discovered that a combination of copper and tin produced bronze, a much harder and more durable metal than copper. Its widespread use has led historians to call the period from around 3000 to 1200 B.C.E. the Bronze Age; thereafter, bronze was increasingly replaced by iron.

At first, Neolithic settlements were hardly more than villages. But as their inhabitants mastered the art of farming, more complex human societies gradually emerged. As wealth increased, these societies sought to protect it from being plundered by outsiders and so began to develop armies and to build walled cities. By the beginning of the Bronze Age, the concentration of larger numbers of people in river valleys was leading to a whole new pattern for human life.

## The Emergence of Civilization

As we have seen, early human beings formed small groups that developed a simple culture that enabled them to survive. As human societies grew and developed greater complexity, civilization came into being. A **civilization** is a complex culture in which large numbers of people share a variety of common elements. Historians have identified a number of basic characteristics of civilization, including the following:

1. *An urban focus.* Cities became the centers for political, economic, social, cultural, and religious development. The cities that emerged were much larger than the Neolithic towns that preceded them.
2. *New political and military structures.* An organized government bureaucracy arose to meet the administrative demands of the growing population, and armies were organized to gain land and power.
3. *A new social structure based on economic power.* While kings and an upper class of priests, political leaders, and warriors dominated, there also existed large groups of free common people (farmers, artisans, craftspeople) and, at the very bottom socially, a class of slaves.
4. *The development of more complexity in a material sense.* Abundant agricultural yields created opportunities for

economic specialization as a surplus of goods enabled some people to work in occupations other than farming. The demand of ruling elites for luxury items encouraged artisans and craftspeople to create new products. As urban populations exported finished goods in exchange for raw materials from neighboring populations, organized trade grew substantially.

5. *A distinct religious structure.* The gods were deemed crucial to the community's success, and professional priestly classes, as stewards of the gods' property, regulated relations with the gods.
6. *The development of writing.* Kings, priests, merchants, and artisans used writing to keep records.
7. *New and significant artistic and intellectual activity.* For example, monumental architectural structures, usually religious, occupied a prominent place in urban environments.

## Early Civilizations Around the World

The first civilizations that developed in Mesopotamia and Egypt will be examined in detail in this chapter. But civilizations also developed independently in other parts of the world. Between 3000 and 1500 B.C.E., the valleys of the Indus River in India supported a flourishing civilization that extended hundreds of miles from the Himalayas to the coast of the Arabian Sea (see Chapter 2). This Indus valley civilization carried on extensive trade with city-states in Mesopotamia.

Another river valley civilization emerged along the Yellow River in northern China about four thousand years ago (see Chapter 3). Under the Shang dynasty of kings, which ruled from 1750 to 1122 B.C.E., this civilization contained impressive cities with huge city walls, royal palaces, and large royal tombs. A system of irrigation enabled early Chinese civilization to maintain a prosperous farming society ruled by an aristocratic class whose major concern was war.

Scholars have believed for a long time that civilization emerged only in these four areas—the fertile river valleys of the Tigris and Euphrates, the Nile, the Indus, and the Yellow River. Recently, however, archaeologists have discovered two other early civilizations. One of these flourished in Central Asia (in what are now the republics of Turkmenistan and Uzbekistan) around four thousand years ago. People in this civilization built mudbrick buildings, raised sheep and goats, had bronze tools, used a system of irrigation to grow wheat and barley, and had a writing system.

**Central Asian Civilization**

Another early civilization was discovered in the Supe River valley of Peru. At the center of this civilization was the city of Caral, which flourished around 2600 B.C.E. It contained buildings for officials, apartment buildings, and grand residences, all built of stone. The inhabitants of Caral also developed a system of irrigation by diverting a river more than a mile upstream into their fields.

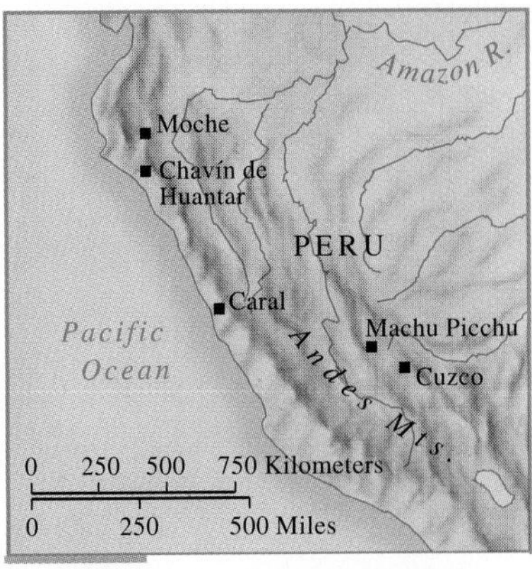


**Caral, Peru**

## Causes of Civilization

Why civilizations developed remains difficult to explain. Since civilizations developed independently in different parts of the world, can general causes be identified that would tell us why all of these civilizations emerged? A number of possible explanations of the beginning of civilization have been suggested. A theory of challenge and response maintains that challenges forced human beings to make efforts that resulted in the rise of civilization. Some scholars have adhered to a material explanation. Material forces, such as the accumulation of food surpluses, made possible the specialization of labor and development of large communities with bureaucratic organization. But some areas were not naturally conducive to agriculture. Abundant food could be produced only through a massive human effort to carefully manage the water, an effort that created the need for organization and bureaucratic control and led to civilized cities. Some historians have argued that nonmaterial forces, primarily religious, provided the sense of unity and purpose that made such organized activities possible. Finally, some scholars doubt that we are capable of ever discovering the actual causes of early civilization.

# Civilization in Mesopotamia

The Greeks spoke of the valley between the Tigris and Euphrates Rivers as Mesopotamia, the land "between the rivers." The region receives little rain, but the soil of the plain of southern Mesopotamia was enlarged and enriched over the years by layers of silt deposited by the two rivers. In late spring, the Tigris and Euphrates overflow their banks and deposit their fertile silt, but since this flooding depends on the melting of snows in the upland mountains where the rivers begin, it is irregular and sometimes catastrophic. In such circumstances, farming could be accomplished only with human intervention in the form of irrigation and drainage ditches. A complex system was required to control the flow of the rivers and

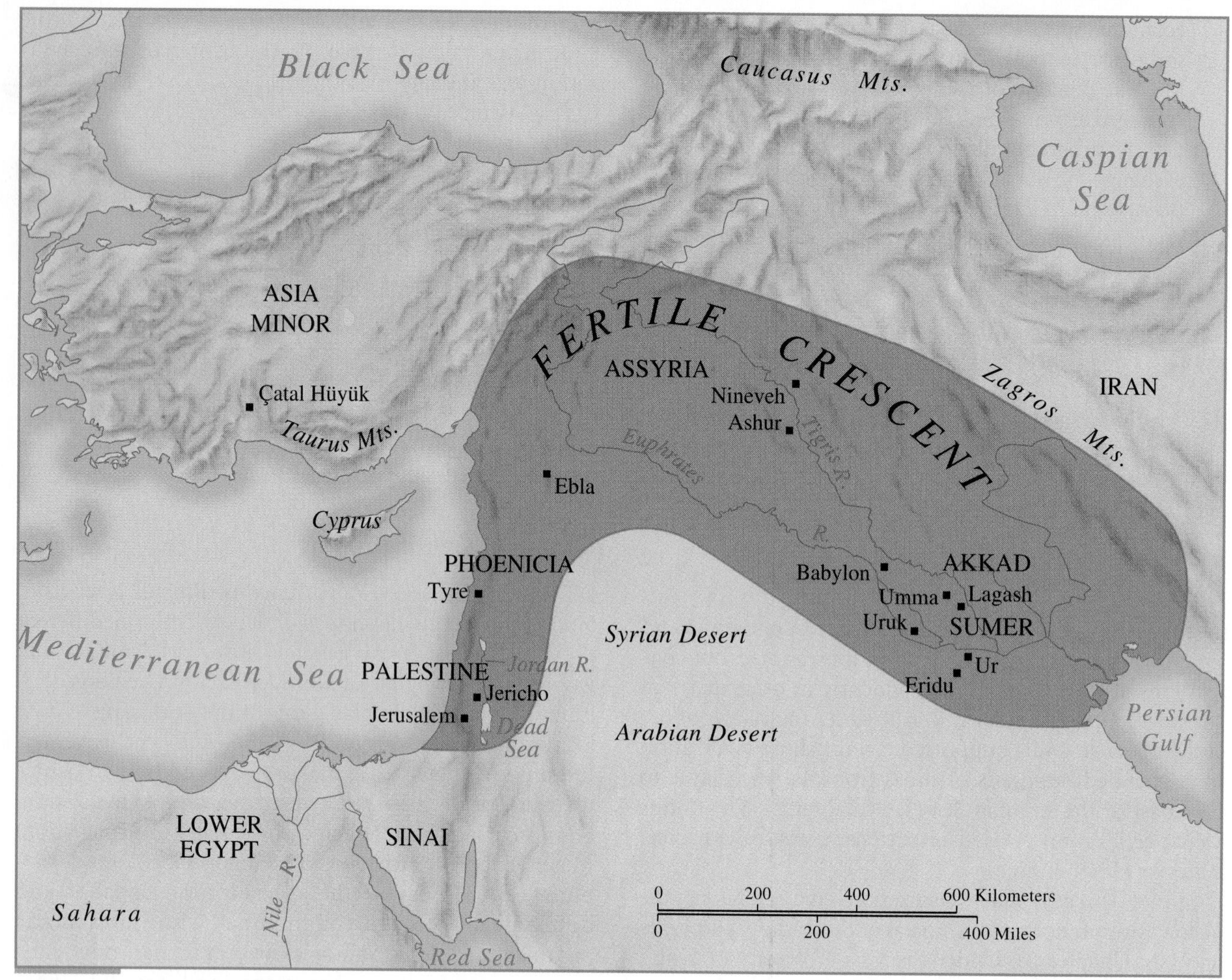


**MAP 1.3 The Ancient Near East.** The Fertile Crescent encompassed land with access to water. Employing flood management and irrigation systems, the peoples of the region established civilizations based on agriculture. These civilizations developed writing, law codes, and economic specialization. ? What geographical aspects of the Mesopotamian city-states made conflict between them likely? **View an animated version of this map or related maps at http://history.wadsworth.com/duikerspielvogel05/**

produce the crops. Large-scale irrigation made possible the expansion of agriculture in this region, and the abundant food provided the material base for the emergence of civilization in Mesopotamia.

## The City-States of Ancient Mesopotamia

The creators of the first Mesopotamian civilization were the Sumerians, a people whose origins remain unclear. By 3000 B.C.E., they had established a number of independent cities in southern Mesopotamia, including Eridu, Ur, Uruk, Umma, and Lagash (see Map 1.3). As the cities expanded, they came to exercise political and economic control over the surrounding countryside, forming city-states, which were the basic units of Sumerian civilization.

**Sumerian Cities** Sumerian cities were surrounded by walls. Uruk, for example, was encircled by a wall 6 miles long with defense towers located along it every 30 to 35 feet. City dwellings, built of sun-dried bricks, included both the small flats of peasants and the larger dwellings of the civic and priestly officials. Although Mesopotamia had little stone or wood for building purposes, it did have plenty of mud. Mudbricks, easily shaped by hand, were left to bake in the hot sun until they were hard enough to use for building. People in Mesopotamia were remarkably innovative with mudbricks, inventing the arch and the dome and constructing some of the largest brick buildings in the world. Mudbricks are still used in rural areas of the Middle East today.

The most prominent building in a Sumerian city was the temple, which was dedicated to the chief god or goddess of the city and often built atop a massive stepped tower called a **ziggurat.** The Sumerians believed that gods and goddesses owned the cities, and much wealth was used to build temples as well as elaborate houses for the priests and priestesses who served the deities. Priests and priestesses, who supervised the temples and their property, had great

© British Museum

**The "Royal Standard" of Ur.** This detail is from the "Royal Standard" of Ur, a box dating from around 2700 B.C.E. that was discovered in a stone tomb from the royal cemetery of the Sumerian city-state of Ur. The scenes on one side of the box depict the activities of the king and his military forces. Shown in the bottom panel are four Sumerian battle chariots. Each chariot held two men, one who held the reins and the other armed with a spear for combat. A special compartment in the chariot held a number of spears. The charging chariots are seen defeating the enemy. In the middle band, the Sumerian soldiers round up the captured enemies. In the top band, the captives are presented to the king, who has alighted from his chariot and is shown standing above all the others in the center of the panel.

power. In fact, historians believe that in the early stages of the city-states, priests and priestesses played an important role in ruling. The Sumerians believed that the gods ruled the cities, making the state a **theocracy** (government by a divine authority). Eventually, however, ruling power passed into the hands of worldly figures, known as kings.

**Kingship** Sumerians viewed kingship as divine in origin—kings, they believed, derived their power from the gods and were the agents of the gods. As one person said in a petition to his king: "You in your judgement, you are the son of Anu [god of the sky]; Your commands, like the word of a god, cannot be reversed, Your words, like rain pouring down from heaven, are without number."[2] Regardless of their origins, kings had power—they led armies and organized workers for the irrigation projects on which Mesopotamian farming depended. The army, the government bureaucracy, and the priests and priestesses all aided the kings in their rule. Befitting their power, Sumerian kings lived in large palaces with their wives and children.

**Economy and Society** The economy of the Sumerian city-states was primarily agricultural, but commerce and industry became important as well. The people of Mesopotamia produced woolen textiles, pottery, and metalwork. The Sumerians imported copper, tin, and timber in exchange for dried fish, wool, barley, wheat, and metal goods. Traders traveled by land to the eastern Mediterranean in the west and by sea to India in the east. The introduction of the wheel, which had been invented around 3000 B.C.E. by nomadic people living in the region north of the Black Sea, led to carts with wheels that made the transport of goods easier.

Sumerian city-states contained three major social groups: nobles, commoners, and slaves. Nobles included royal and priestly officials and their families. Commoners were the nobles' clients, who worked for the palace and temple estates, and other free citizens, who worked as farmers, merchants, fishers, and craftspeople. At least 90 percent of the population was engaged in farming. Slaves belonged to palace officials, who used them in building projects; to temple officials, who used mostly female slaves to weave cloth and grind grain; and to rich landowners, who used them for farming and domestic work.

## Empires in Ancient Mesopotamia

As the number of Sumerian city-states grew and the states expanded, new conflicts arose as city-state fought city-state for control of land and water. The fortunes of various city-states rose and fell over the centuries. The constant wars, with their burning and sacking of cities, left many Sumerians in deep despair, as is evident in the words of this Sumerian poem from the city of Ur: "Ur is destroyed, bitter is its lament. The country's blood now fills its holes like hot bronze in a mold. Bodies dissolve like fat in the sun. Our temple is destroyed, the gods have abandoned us, like migrating birds. Smoke lies on our city like a shroud."

**TABLE 1.1 Some Semitic Languages**

| | | |
|---|---|---|
| *Akkadian* | *Assyrian* | Hebrew |
| Arabic | *Babylonian* | *Phoenician* |
| Aramaic | *Canaanitic* | *Syriac* |

NOTE: Languages in italic type are no longer spoken.

**Stele of Hammurabi (Code of Hammurabi, King of Babylonia).** Although the Sumerians compiled earlier law codes, Hammurabi's code was the most famous in early Mesopotamian history. The upper section of the stele depicts Hammurabi standing in front of the seated sun god Shamash. The king raises his hand in deference to the god, who gives Hammurabi the power to rule and orders the king to record the law. The lower section of the stele contains the actual code.

**Sargon's Empire** Located in the flat land of Mesopotamia, the Sumerian city-states were also open to invasion. To the north of the Sumerian city-states were the Akkadians. We call them a Semitic people because of the type of language they spoke (see Table 1.1). Around 2340 B.C.E., Sargon, leader of the Akkadians, overran the Sumerian city-states and established an empire that included most of Mesopotamia as well as lands westward to the Mediterranean. Even in the first millennium B.C.E., Sargon was still remembered in chronicles as a king of Akkad who "had no rival or equal, spread his splendor over all the lands, and crossed the sea in the east. In his eleventh year, he conquered the western land to its furthest point, and brought it under his sole authority."[3] Attacks from neighboring hill peoples eventually caused the Akkadian empire to fall, and its end by 2100 B.C.E. brought a return to the system of warring city-states. It was not until 1792 B.C.E. that a new empire came to control much of Mesopotamia under Hammurabi, who ruled over the Amorites or Old Babylonians, a large group of Semitic-speaking seminomads.

**Hammurabi's Empire** Hammurabi (1792–1750 B.C.E.) employed a well-disciplined army of foot soldiers who carried axes, spears, and copper or bronze daggers. He learned to divide his opponents and subdue them one by one. Using such methods, he gained control of Sumer and Akkad, creating a new Mesopotamian kingdom. After his conquests, he called himself "the sun of Babylon, the king who has made the four quarters of the world subservient," and established a new capital at Babylon.

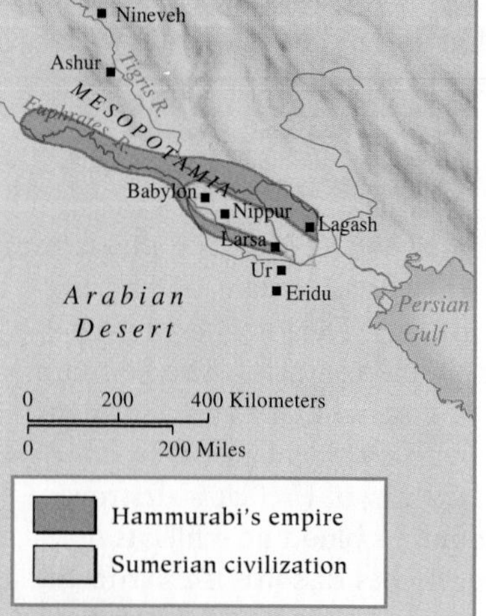


**Hammurabi's Empire**

Hammurabi, the man of war, was also a man of peace. A collection of his letters, found by archaeologists, reveals that he took a strong interest in state affairs. He built temples, defensive walls, and irrigation canals; encouraged trade; and brought about an economic revival. Indeed, Hammurabi saw himself as a shepherd to his people: "I am indeed the shepherd who brings peace, whose scepter is just. My benevolent shade was spread over my city. I held the people of the lands of Sumer and Akkad safely on my lap."[4] After his death, however, a series of weak kings were unable to keep Hammurabi's empire united, and it finally fell to new invaders.

**The Code of Hammurabi: Society in Mesopotamia** Hammurabi is best remembered for his law code, a collection of 282 laws. Although many scholars today view Hammurabi's collection less as a code of laws and more as the attempt of Hammurabi to portray himself as the source of justice to his people, the code still gives us a glimpse of the Mesopotamian society of his time (see the box on p. 13).

The Code of Hammurabi reveals a society with a system of strict justice. Penalties for criminal offenses were severe and varied according to the social class of the victim. A crime against a member of the upper class (a noble) by a member of the lower class (a commoner) was punished more severely than the same offense against a member of the lower class. Moreover, the principle of "an

## THE CODE OF HAMMURABI

Although there were earlier Mesopotamian law codes, Hammurabi's is the most complete. The law code emphasizes the principle of retribution ("an eye for an eye") and punishments that vary according to social status. Punishments could be severe. The following examples illustrate these concerns.

*What do these points of law from the Code of Hammurabi reveal to you about Mesopotamian society?*

25. If fire broke out in a free man's house and a free man, who went to extinguish it, cast his eye on the goods of the owner of the house and has appropriated the goods of the owner of the house, that free man shall be thrown into that fire.

129. If the wife of a free man has been caught while lying with another man, they shall bind them and throw them into the water. If the husband of the woman wishes to spare his wife, then the king in turn may spare his subject.

131. If a free man's wife was accused by her husband, but she was not caught while lying with another man, she shall make affirmation by god and return to her house.

196. If a free man has destroyed the eye of a member of the aristocracy, they shall destroy his eye.

198. If he has destroyed the eye of a commoner or broken the bone of a commoner, he shall pay one mina of silver.

199. If he has destroyed the eye of a free man's slave or broken the bone of a free man's slave, he shall pay one-half his value.

209. If a free man struck another free man's daughter and has caused her to have a miscarriage, he shall pay ten shekels of silver for her fetus.

210. If that woman has died, they shall put his daughter to death.

211. If by a blow he has caused a commoner's daughter to have a miscarriage, he shall pay five shekels of silver.

212. If that woman has died, he shall pay one-half mina of silver.

213. If he struck a free man's female slave and has caused her to have a miscarriage, he shall pay two shekels of silver.

214. If that female slave has died, he shall pay one-third mina of silver.

**HistoryNow**™ To read a full version of this document, enter the *HistoryNow* documents area using the access card that is available for *World History.*

eye for an eye, a tooth for a tooth" was fundamental to this system of justice. This meant that punishments should fit the crime: "If a freeman has destroyed the eye of a member of the aristocracy, they shall destroy his eye." Hammurabi's code also had an impact on legal ideas in southwestern Asia for hundreds of years, as the following verse from the Hebrew Bible (Leviticus 24:19–20) demonstrates: "If anyone injures his neighbor, whatever he has done must be done to him: fracture for fracture, eye for eye, tooth for tooth. As he has injured the other, so he is to be injured."

The largest category of laws in the Code of Hammurabi focused on marriage and the family. Parents arranged marriages for their children. After marriage, the parties involved signed a marriage contract; without it, no one was considered legally married. While the husband provided a bridal payment to the bride's parents, the woman's parents were responsible for a dowry to the new husband.

As in many patriarchal societies, women possessed far fewer privileges and rights in the married relationship than men. A woman's place was in the home, and failure to fulfill her expected duties was grounds for divorce. If she was not able to bear children, her husband could divorce her. Furthermore, a wife who was a "gadabout, . . . neglecting her house [and] humiliating her husband," could be drowned. We do know that in practice, not all women remained at home. Some worked in the fields and others in business, where they were especially prominent running taverns.

Women were guaranteed some rights, however. If a woman was divorced without good reason, she received the dowry back. A woman could seek divorce and get her dowry back if her husband was unable to show that she had done anything wrong. In theory, a wife was guaranteed the use of her husband's legal property in the event of his death. A mother could also decide which of her sons would receive an inheritance.

Sexual relations were strictly regulated as well. Husbands, but not wives, were permitted sexual activity outside marriage. A wife and her lover caught committing adultery were pitched into the river, although if the husband pardoned his wife, the king could pardon the guilty man. Incest was strictly forbidden. If a father had incestuous relations with his daughter, he would be banished. Incest between a son and his mother resulted in both being burned.

Fathers ruled their children as well as their wives. Obedience was duly expected: "If a son has struck his father, they shall cut off his hand." If a son committed a serious enough offense, his father could disinherit him, although fathers were not permitted to disinherit their sons arbitrarily.

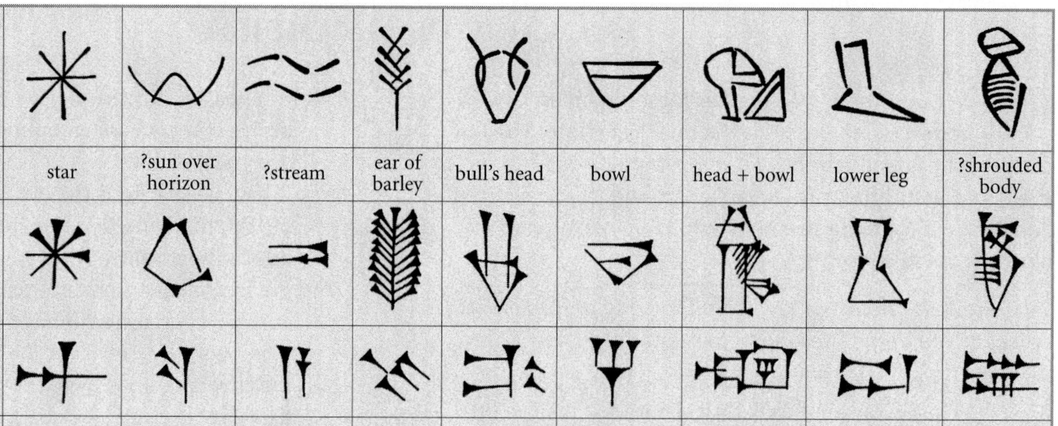

| Pictographic sign, c. 3100 B.C.E. | | | | | | | | | |
|---|---|---|---|---|---|---|---|---|---|
| Interpretation | star | ?sun over horizon | ?stream | ear of barley | bull's head | bowl | head + bowl | lower leg | ?shrouded body |
| Cuneiform sign, c. 2400 B.C.E. | | | | | | | | | |
| Cuneiform sign c. 700 B.C.E. (turned through 90°) | | | | | | | | | |
| Phonetic value* | dingir, an | $u_4$, ud | a | še | $gu_4$ | $nig_2$, ninda | $ku_2$ | du, gin, gub | $lu_2$ |
| Meaning | god, sky | day, sun | water, seed, son | barley | ox | food, bread | to eat | to walk, to stand | man |

*Some signs have more than one phonetic value and some sounds are represented by more than one sign; for example, $u_4$ means the fourth sign with the phonetic value *u*.

**The Development of Cuneiform Writing.** This chart shows the evolution of writing from pictographic signs around 3100 B.C.E. to cuneiform signs by about 700 B.C.E. Note that the sign for *star* came to mean "god" or "sky." Pictographic signs for *head* and *bowl* came eventually to mean "to eat" in their simplified cuneiform version.

## The Culture of Mesopotamia

A spiritual worldview was of fundamental importance to Mesopotamian culture. To the peoples of Mesopotamia, the gods were living realities who affected all aspects of life. It was crucial, therefore, that the correct hierarchies be observed. Leaders could prepare armies for war, but success really depended on a favorable relationship with the gods. This helps explain the importance of the priestly class and is the reason why even the kings took great care to dedicate offerings and monuments to the gods.

**The Importance of Religion** The physical environment had an obvious impact on the Mesopotamian view of the universe. Ferocious floods, heavy downpours, scorching winds, and oppressive humidity were all part of the Mesopotamian climate. These conditions and the resulting famines easily convinced Mesopotamians that this world was controlled by supernatural forces and that the days of human beings "are numbered; whatever he may do, he is but wind," as *The Epic of Gilgamesh* put it. In the presence of nature, Mesopotamians could easily feel helpless, as this poem relates:

> *The rampant flood which no man can oppose,*
> *Which shakes the heavens and causes earth to tremble,*
> *In an appalling blanket folds mother and child,*
> *Beats down the canebrake's full luxuriant greenery,*
> *And drowns the harvest in its time of ripeness.*[5]

The Mesopotamians discerned cosmic rhythms in the universe and accepted its order but perceived that it was not completely safe because of the presence of willful, powerful cosmic powers that they identified with gods and goddesses.

With its numerous gods and goddesses animating all aspects of the universe, Mesopotamian religion was a form of **polytheism**. The four most important deities were An, god of the sky and hence the most important force in the universe; Enlil, god of wind; Enki, god of the earth, rivers, wells, and canals as well as inventions and crafts; and Ninhursaga, a goddess associated with soil, mountains, and vegetation, who came to be worshiped as a mother goddess, a "mother of all children," who manifested her power by giving birth to kings and conferring the royal insignia on them.

Human relationships with the gods were based on subservience since, according to Sumerian myth, human beings were created to do the manual labor the gods were unwilling to do for themselves. Moreover, humans were insecure because they could never predict the gods' actions. But humans did attempt to relieve their anxiety by discovering the intentions of the gods through **divination.**

Divination took a variety of forms. A common form, at least for kings and priests who could afford it, involved killing animals, such as sheep or goats, and examining their livers or other organs. Supposedly, features seen in the organs of the sacrificed animals foretold events to come. Thus one handbook states that if the animal organ has shape *x*, the outcome of the military campaign will be *y*. The Mesopotamian arts of divination arose out of the desire to discover the purposes of the gods. If people could decipher the signs that foretold events, the events would be predictable and humans could act wisely.

**The Cultivation of Writing and Sciences** The realization of writing's great potential was another aspect of Mesopotamian culture. The oldest Mesopotamian texts date to

© Réunion des Musées Nationaux/Art Resource, NY

© British Museum

COMPARATIVE ILLUSTRATION

**Early Writing** Pictured at top left is the upper part of the cone of Uruinimgina, an example of early cuneiform script from an early Sumerian dynasty. The first Egyptian writing was also pictographic, as shown in the hieroglyphs from the Book of the Dead papyrus of the Lady Anhai during the New Kingdom (lower right). In Central America, the Mayan civilization had a well-developed writing system, also based on hieroglyphs, as seen in this text carved in 766 C.E. on the wall of Tikal's Temple of the Inscriptions (upper right). The deciphering of hieroglyphic scripts was a difficult task. The discovery in Egypt in 1799 of the Rosetta Stone (lower left), a granite block with texts in hieroglyphics (top row in illustration) and Greek (bottom row) enabled Jean-François Champollion, a French linguistic genius, to provide the foundation for deciphering Egyptian hieroglyphics. Mayan hieroglyphs were not deciphered until the second half of the twentieth century.

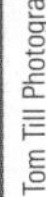

© Tom Till Photography

© Michael Holford

around 3000 B.C.E. and were written by the Sumerians, who used a **cuneiform** ("wedge-shaped") system of writing. Using a reed stylus, they made wedge-shaped impressions on clay tablets, which were then baked or dried in the sun. Once dried, these tablets were virtually indestructible, and the several hundred thousand that have been found so far have been a valuable source of information for modern scholars. Sumerian writing evolved from pictures of

## The Great Flood

The great epic poem of Mesopotamian literature, *The Epic of Gilgamesh*, includes an account by Utnapishtim (a Mesopotamian version of the later biblical Noah), who had built a ship and survived the flood unleashed by the gods to destroy humankind. In this selection, Utnapishtim recounts his story to Gilgamesh, telling how the god Ea advised him to build a boat and how he came to land the boat at the end of the flood.

*What does this selection from* The Epic of Gilgamesh *tell you about the relationship between the Mesopotamians and their gods? How might you explain the differences between this account and the biblical flood story in Genesis?*

### *The Epic of Gilgamesh*

In those days the world teemed, the people multiplied, the world bellowed like a wild bull, and the great god was aroused by the clamor. Enlil heard the clamor and he said to the gods in council, "The uproar of mankind is intolerable and sleep is no longer possible by reason of the babel." So the gods agreed to exterminate mankind. Enlil did this, but Ea [Sumerian Enki, god of the waters] because of his oath warned me in a dream, ". . . Tear down your house and build a boat, abandon possessions and look for life, despise worldly goods and save your soul alive. Tear down your house, I say, and build a boat. . . . then take up into the boat the seed of all living creatures. . . ." [Utnapishtim did as he was told, and then the destruction came.]

For six days and six nights the winds blew, torrent and tempest and flood overwhelmed the world, tempest and flood raged together like warring hosts. When the seventh day dawned the storm from the south subsided, the sea grew calm, the flood was stilled; I looked at the face of the world and there was silence, all mankind was turned to clay. The surface of the sea stretched as flat as a rooftop; I opened a hatch and the light fell on my face. Then I bowed low, I sat down and I wept, the tears streamed down my face, for on every side was the waste of water. I looked for land in vain, but fourteen leagues distant there appeared a mountain, and there the boat grounded; on the mountain of Nisir the boat held fast, she held fast and did not budge. . . . When the seventh day dawned I loosed a dove and let her go. She flew away, but finding no resting place she returned. Then I loosed a swallow, and she flew away but finding no resting place she returned. I loosed a raven, she saw that the waters had retreated, she ate, she flew around, she cawed, and she did not come back. Then I threw everything open to the four winds, I made a sacrifice and poured out a libation on the mountaintop.

**HistoryNow™** To read a full version of this document, enter the *HistoryNow* documents area using the access card that is available for *World History.*

concrete objects to simplified and stylized signs, leading eventually to a phonetic system that made possible the written expression of abstract ideas.

Mesopotamian peoples used writing primarily for record keeping, but cuneiform texts were also used in schools set up to teach the cuneiform system of writing. The primary goal of scribal education was to produce professionally trained scribes for careers in the temples and palaces, the military, and government service. Pupils were male and primarily from wealthy families.

Writing was important because it enabled a society to keep records and maintain knowledge of previous practices and events. Writing also made it possible for people to communicate ideas in new ways, which is especially evident in the most famous piece of Mesopotamian literature, *The Epic of Gilgamesh,* an epic poem that records the exploits of a legendary king of Uruk (see the box above). Gilgamesh, wise, strong, and perfect in body, part man and part god, befriends a hairy beast named Enkidu. Together they set off in pursuit of heroic deeds. When Enkidu dies, Gilgamesh experiences the pain of mortality and begins a search for the secret of immortality. But his efforts fail. Gilgamesh remains mortal. The desire for immortality, one of humankind's great searches, ends in complete frustration. "Everlasting life," as this Mesopotamian epic makes clear, is only for the gods.

Mesopotamians also made outstanding achievements in mathematics and astronomy. In math, the Sumerians devised a number system based on 60, using combinations of 6 and 10 for practical solutions. Geometry was used to measure fields and erect buildings. In astronomy, the Sumerians made use of units of 60 and charted the heavenly constellations. Their calendar was based on twelve lunar months and was brought into harmony with the solar year by adding an extra month from time to time.

# Egyptian Civilization: "The Gift of the Nile"

"The Egyptian Nile," wrote one Arab traveler, "surpasses all the rivers of the world in sweetness of taste, in length of course and usefulness. No other river in the world can show such a continuous series of towns and villages along its banks." The Nile River was crucial to the development of Egyptian civilization (see the box on p. 18). Egypt, like Mesopotamia, was a river valley civilization.

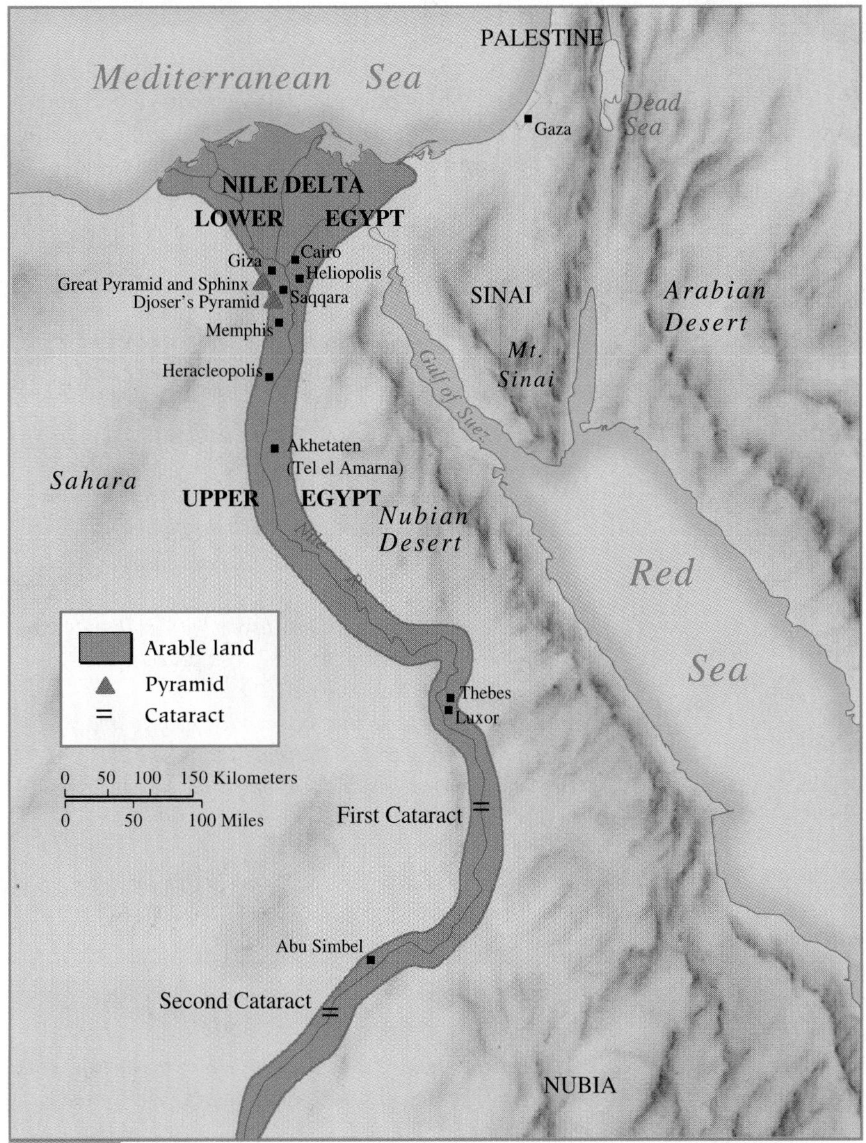


**MAP 1.4 Ancient Egypt.** Egyptian civilization centered on the life-giving water and flood silts of the Nile River, with most of the population living in Lower Egypt, where the river splits to form the Nile delta. Most of the pyramids, built during the Old Kingdon, are clustered south and west of Cairo. ? How did the lands to the east and west of the river make invasions of Egypt difficult? **View an animated version of this map or related maps at http://history.wadsworth.com/duikerspielvogel05/**

## The Impact of Geography

The Nile is a unique river, beginning in the heart of Africa and coursing northward for thousands of miles. It is the longest river in the world. The Nile was responsible for creating an area several miles wide on both banks of the river that was fertile and capable of producing abundant harvests. The "miracle" of the Nile was its annual flooding. The river rose in the summer from rains in Central Africa, crested in Egypt in September and October, and left a deposit of silt that enriched the soil. The Egyptians called this fertile land the "Black Land" because it was dark in color from the silt and crops grew on it so densely. Beyond these narrow strips of fertile fields lay the deserts (the "Red Land"). About 100 miles before it empties into the Mediterranean, the river splits into two major branches, forming the delta, a triangular-shaped territory called Lower Egypt to distinguish it from Upper Egypt, the land upstream to the south (see Map. 1.4). Egypt's important cities developed at the tip of the delta. Even today, most of Egypt's people are crowded along the banks of the Nile River.

Unlike Mesopotamia's rivers, the flooding of the Nile was gradual and usually predictable, and the river itself was seen as life-enhancing, not life-threatening. Although a system of organized irrigation was still necessary, the small villages along the Nile could create such systems without the massive state intervention that was required in Mesopotamia. Egyptian civilization consequently tended to remain more rural, with many small population centers congregated along a narrow band on both sides of the Nile.

The surpluses of food that Egyptian farmers grew in the fertile Nile valley made Egypt prosperous. But the Nile also served as a unifying factor in Egyptian history. In ancient times, the Nile was the fastest way to travel through the land, making both transportation and communication easier. Winds from the north pushed sailboats south, and the current of the Nile carried them north.

Unlike Mesopotamia, which was subject to constant invasion, Egypt had natural barriers that fostered isolation, protected it from invasion, and gave it a sense of security. These barriers included deserts to the west and east; cataracts (rapids) on the southern part of the Nile, which made defense relatively easy; and the Mediterranean Sea to the north. These barriers, however, did not prevent the development of trade. Indeed, there is evidence of very early trade between Egypt and Mesopotamia.

The regularity of the Nile floods and the relative isolation of the Egyptians created a sense of security and a feeling of changelessness. To the ancient Egyptians, when the Nile flooded each year, "the fields laugh, and people's faces light up." Unlike people in Mesopotamia, Egyptians faced life with a spirit of confidence in the stability of things. Ancient Egyptian civilization was characterized by a remarkable degree of continuity for thousands of years.

## The Significance of the Nile River and the Pharaoh

Two of the most important sources of life for the ancient Egyptians were the Nile River and the pharaoh. Egyptians perceived that the Nile River made possible the abundant food that was a major source of their well-being. This *Hymn to the Nile,* probably from the nineteenth and twentieth dynasties in the New Kingdom, expresses the gratitude Egyptians felt for the Nile.

*How do these two hymns underscore the importance of the Nile River and the institution of the pharaoh to Egyptian civilization?*

### Hymn to the Nile

*Hail to you, O Nile, that issues from the earth*
*and comes to keep Egypt alive! . . .*
*He that waters the meadows which Re created,*
*in order to keep every kid alive.*
*He that makes to drink the desert and the place*
*distant from water: that is his dew coming down*
*from heaven. . . .*
*The lord of fishes, he who makes the marsh-birds to*
*go upstream. . . .*
*He who makes barley and brings emmer into being,*
*that he may make the temples festive.*
*If he is sluggish, then nostrils are stopped up, and*
*everybody is poor. . . .*
*When he rises, then the land is in jubilation, then*
*every belly is in joy, every backbone takes on*
*laughter, and every tooth is exposed.*
*The bringer of good, rich in provisions, creator of all*
*good, lord of majesty, sweet of fragrance. . . .*
*He who makes every beloved tree to grow, without*
*lack of them.*

The Egyptian king, or pharaoh, was viewed as a god and the absolute ruler of Egypt. His significance and the gratitude of the Egyptian people for his existence are evident in this hymn from the reign of Sesotris III (c. 1880–1840 B.C.E.).

### Hymn to the Pharaoh

*He has come unto us that he may carry away Upper*
*Egypt; the double diadem [crown of Upper and*
*Lower Egypt] has rested on his head.*
*He has come unto us and has united the Two Lands;*
*he has mingled the reed with the bee [symbols*
*of Lower and Upper Egypt].*
*He has come unto us and has brought the Black*
*Land under his sway; he has apportioned to*
*himself the Red Land.*
*He has come unto us and has taken the Two Lands*
*under his protection; he has given peace to the*
*Two Riverbanks.*
*He has come unto us and has made Egypt to live;*
*he has banished its suffering.*
*He has come unto us and has made the people to*
*live; he has caused the throat of the subjects*
*to breathe. . . .*
*He has come unto us and has done battle for*
*his boundaries; he has delivered them that*
*were robbed.*

**HistoryNow™** To read a full version of *Hymn to the Nile*, enter the *HistoryNow* documents area using the access card that is available for *World History.*

## The Old and Middle Kingdoms

Modern historians have divided Egyptian history into three major periods, known as the Old Kingdom, the Middle Kingdom, and the New Kingdom. These were periods of long-term stability characterized by strong monarchical authority, competent bureaucracy, freedom from invasion, much construction of temples and pyramids, and considerable intellectual and cultural activity. But between the periods of stability were times of political chaos known as the Intermediate Periods, which were characterized by weak political structures and rivalry for leadership, invasions, a decline in building activity, and a restructuring of society.

**The Old Kingdom** According to the Egyptians' own tradition, their land consisted initially of numerous populated areas ruled by tribal chieftains. Around 3100 B.C.E., the first Egyptian royal dynasty, under a king called Menes, united Upper and Lower Egypt into a single kingdom. Henceforth, the king would be called "King of Upper and Lower Egypt," and the royal crown would be a double diadem, signifying the unification of all Egypt. Just as the Nile served to unite Upper and Lower Egypt physically, kingship served to unite the two areas politically.

The Old Kingdom encompassed the third through sixth dynasties of Egyptian kings, lasting from around 2686 to 2125 B.C.E. It was an age of prosperity and splendor, made visible in the construction of the greatest and largest pyramids in Egypt's history. The capital of the Old Kingdom was located at Memphis, south of the delta.

Kingship was a divine institution in ancient Egypt and formed part of a universal cosmic scheme (see the box above): "What is the king of Upper and Lower Egypt? He is a god by whose dealings one lives, the father and mother of all men, alone by himself, without an equal."[6] In obeying their king, subjects helped maintain the cosmic order. A breakdown in royal power could

**Pair Statue of King Menkaure and His Queen.** During the Old Kingdom, kings (eventually called pharaohs) were regarded as gods, divine instruments who maintained the fundamental order and harmony of the universe and wielded absolute power. Seated and standing statues of kings were commonly placed in Egyptian royal tombs. Seen here are the standing portraits of King Menkaure and his queen, Khamerernebty, from the fourth dynasty. By artistic convention, kings and their queens were shown in a rigid pose, reflecting their timeless nature. Husband and wife show no emotion but are seen looking out into space.

only mean that citizens were offending divinity and weakening the universal structure. Among the various titles of Egyptian kings, that of **pharaoh** (originally meaning "great house" or "palace") eventually came to be the most common.

Although they possessed absolute power, Egyptian kings were not supposed to rule arbitrarily but according to set principles. The chief principle was called *Ma'at*, a spiritual precept that conveyed the ideas of truth and justice and especially right order and harmony. To ancient Egyptians, this fundamental order and harmony had existed throughout the universe since the beginning of time. Pharaohs were the divine instruments who maintained it and were themselves subject to it.

Although theoretically absolute in their power, in practice Egyptian kings did not rule alone. Initially, members of the king's family performed administrative tasks, but by the fourth dynasty, a bureaucracy with regular procedures had developed. Especially important was the office of vizier, "steward of the whole land." Directly responsible to the king, the vizier was in charge of the bureaucracy. For administrative purposes, Egypt was divided into provinces, or *nomes* as they were later called by the Greeks—twenty-two in Upper Egypt and twenty in Lower Egypt. A governor, called by the Greeks a *nomarch*, was head of each nome and was responsible to the king and vizier. Nomarchs, however, tended to build up large holdings of land and power within their nomes, creating a potential rivalry with the pharaohs.

**The Middle Kingdom** Despite the theory of divine order, the Old Kingdom eventually collapsed, ushering in a period of chaos. Finally, a new royal dynasty managed to pacify all Egypt and inaugurated the Middle Kingdom, a period of stability lasting from around 2055 to 1650 B.C.E. Egyptians later portrayed the Middle Kingdom as a golden age, a clear indication of its stability. Several factors contributed to its vitality. The nome structure was reorganized. The boundaries of each nome were now settled precisely, and the obligations of the nomes to the state were clearly delineated. Nomarchs were confirmed as hereditary officeholders but with the understanding that their duties must be performed faithfully. These included the collection of taxes for the state and the recruitment of labor forces for royal projects, such as stone quarrying.

The Middle Kingdom was characterized by a new concern of the pharaohs for the people. In the Old Kingdom, the pharaoh had been viewed as an inaccessible god-king. Now he was portrayed as the shepherd of his people with the responsibility to build public works and provide for the public welfare. As one pharaoh expressed it: "He [a particular god] created me as one who should do that which he had done, and to carry out that which he commanded should be done. He appointed me herdsman of this land, for he knew who would keep it in order for him."[7]

## Society and Economy in Ancient Egypt

Egyptian society had a simple structure in the Old and Middle Kingdoms; basically, it was organized along hierarchical lines with the god-king at the top. The king was surrounded by an upper class of nobles and priests who participated in the elaborate rituals of life that surrounded the pharaoh. This ruling class ran the government and managed its own landed estates, which provided much of its wealth.

Below the upper classes were merchants and artisans. Merchants engaged in an active trade up and down the Nile as well as in town and village markets. Some merchants also engaged in international trade; they were sent by the king to Crete and Syria, where they obtained wood and other products. Expeditions traveled into Nubia for ivory and down the Red Sea to Punt for incense and spices. Eventually, trade links were established between ports in the Red Sea and countries as far away as the Indonesian archipelago. Egyptian artisans made an incredible variety of well-built and beautiful goods: stone dishes; painted boxes made of clay; wooden furniture; gold, silver, and copper tools and containers; paper and rope made of papyrus; and linen clothing.

By far the largest number of people in Egypt simply worked the land. In theory, the king owned all the land but granted portions of it to his subjects. Large sections were in the possession of nobles and the temple complexes. Most of the lower classes were serfs, or common people bound to the land, who cultivated the estates. They paid taxes in the form of crops to the king, nobles, and priests; lived in small villages or towns; and provided military service and forced labor for building projects.

## The Culture of Egypt

Egypt produced a culture that dazzled and awed its later conquerors. The Egyptians' technical achievements, especially visible in the construction of the pyramids, demonstrated a measure of skill unequaled in the world at that time. To the Egyptians, all of these achievements were part of a cosmic order suffused with the presence of the divine.

**Spiritual Life in Egyptian Society** The Egyptians had no word for religion because it was an inseparable element of the entire world order to which Egyptian society belonged. The Egyptians were polytheistic and had a remarkable number of gods associated with heavenly bodies and natural forces. Two groups, sun gods and land gods, came to have special prominence, hardly unusual in view of the importance to Egypt's well-being of the sun, the river, and the fertile land along its banks. The sun was the source of life and hence worthy of worship. The sun god took on different forms and names, depending on his specific role. He was worshiped as Atum in human form and also as Re, who had a human body but the head of a falcon. The pharaoh took the title of "Son of Re," since he was regarded as the earthly form of Re. Eventually, Re became associated with Amon, an air god of Thebes, as Amon-Re.

River and land deities included Osiris and Isis with their child Horus, who was related to the Nile and to the sun as well. Osiris became especially important as a symbol of resurrection or rebirth. A famous Egyptian myth told of the struggle between Osiris, who brought civilization to Egypt, and his evil brother Seth, who killed him, cut his body into fourteen parts, and tossed them into the Nile River. Osiris' faithful wife Isis found the pieces and, with help from other gods, restored Osiris to life. As a symbol of resurrection and as judge of the dead, Osiris took on an important role for the Egyptians. By identifying with Osiris, one could hope to gain new life just as Osiris had done. The dead, embalmed and mummified, were placed in tombs (in the case of kings, in pyramidal tombs), given the name of Osiris, and by a process of magical identification became Osiris. Like Osiris, they could then be reborn. The flood of the Nile and the new life it brought to Egypt were symbolized by Isis gathering all of Osiris' parts together and were celebrated each spring in the Festival of the New Land.

**The Pyramids** One of the great achievements of Egyptian civilization, the building of pyramids, occurred in the time of the Old Kingdom. Pyramids were built as part of a larger complex of buildings dedicated to the dead—in effect, a city of the dead. The area included a large pyramid for the king's burial, smaller pyramids for his family, and *mastabas*, rectangular structures with flat roofs, as tombs for the pharaoh's noble officials.

The tombs were well prepared for their residents, their rooms furnished and stocked with numerous supplies, including chairs, boats, chests, weapons, games, dishes, and a variety of foods. The Egyptians believed that human beings had two bodies, a physical one and a spiritual one they called the *ka*. If the physical body was properly preserved (by mummification) and the tomb was furnished with all the objects of regular life, the *ka* could return, surrounded by earthly comforts, and continue its life despite the death of the physical body.

To preserve the physical body after death, the Egyptians practiced mummification, a process of slowly drying a dead body to prevent it from decomposing. Special workshops, run by priests, performed this procedure, primarily for the wealthy families who could afford it. According to an ancient Greek historian who visited Egypt around 450 B.C.E., "The most refined method is as follows: first of all they draw out the brain through the nostrils with an iron hook. . . . Then they make an incision in the flank with a sharp Ethiopian stone through which they extract all the internal organs." The liver, lungs, stomach, and intestines were placed in four special jars that were put in the tomb with the mummy. The priests then covered the corpse with a natural salt that absorbed the body's water. Later, they filled the body with spices and wrapped it with layers of linen soaked in resin. At the end of the process, which took about seventy days, a lifelike mask was placed over the head and shoulders of the mummy, which was then sealed in a case and placed in its tomb.

Pyramids were tombs for the mummified bodies of the pharaohs. The largest and most magnificent of all the pyramids was built under King Khufu. Constructed at Giza around 2540 B.C.E., this famous Great Pyramid covers 13 acres, measures 756 feet at each side of its base, and stands 481 feet high (see the comparative illustration in Chapter 6, p. 165). Its four sides are almost precisely oriented to the four points of the compass. The interior included a grand gallery to the burial chamber, which was built of granite with a lidless sarcophagus for the pharaoh's body. The Great Pyramid still stands as a visible symbol of the power of Egyptian kings and the spiritual

**CHRONOLOGY The Egyptians**

| | |
|---|---|
| Early Dynastic Period (Dynasties 1–2) | c. 3100–2686 B.C.E. |
| Old Kingdom (Dynasties 3–6) | c. 2686–2125 B.C.E. |
| First Intermediate Period (Dynasties 7–10) | c. 2125–2055 B.C.E. |
| Middle Kingdom (Dynasties 11–12) | c. 2055–1650 B.C.E. |
| Second Intermediate Period (Dynasties 13–17) | c. 1650–1550 B.C.E. |
| New Kingdom (Dynasties 18–20) | c. 1550–1070 B.C.E. |
| Post-Empire (Dynasties 21–31) | c. 1070–30 B.C.E. |

conviction that underlay Egyptian society. No pyramid built later ever matched its size or splendor. The pyramid was not only the king's tomb; it was also an important symbol of royal power. It could be seen from miles away, a visible reminder of the glory and might of the ruler who was a living god on earth.

**Art and Writing** Commissioned by kings or nobles for use in temples and tombs, Egyptian art was largely functional. Wall paintings and statues of gods and kings in temples served a strictly spiritual purpose. They were an integral part of the performance of ritual, which was thought necessary to preserve the cosmic order and hence the well-being of Egypt. Likewise, the mural scenes and sculptured figures found in the tombs had a specific function: they were supposed to assist the journey of the deceased into the afterworld.

Egyptian art was also formulaic. Artists and sculptors were expected to observe a strict canon of proportions that determined both form and presentation. This canon gave Egyptian art a distinctive appearance for thousands of years. Especially characteristic was the convention of combining the profile, semiprofile, and frontal views of the human body in relief work and painting in order to represent each part of the body accurately. The result was an art that was highly stylized yet still allowed distinctive features to be displayed.

Writing emerged in Egypt during the first two dynasties. The Greeks later called Egyptian writing **hieroglyphics,** meaning "priest-carvings" or "sacred writings." Hieroglyphs were sacred characters used as picture signs that depicted objects and had a sacred value at the same time. Although hieroglyphs were later simplified into two scripts for writing purposes, they never developed into an alphabet. Egyptian hieroglyphs were initially carved in stone, but later the two simplified scripts were written on papyrus, a paper made from the reeds that grew along the Nile. Most of the ancient Egyptian literature that has come down to us was written on papyrus rolls and wooden tablets.

## Chaos and a New Order: The New Kingdom

The Middle Kingdom came to an end around 1650 B.C.E. with the invasion of Egypt by a people from western Asia known to the Egyptians as the Hyksos. The Hyksos used horse-drawn war chariots and overwhelmed the Egyptian soldiers, who fought from donkey carts. For almost a hundred years, the Hyksos ruled much of Egypt, but the conquered took much from their conquerors. From the Hyksos, the Egyptians learned to use bronze in making new farming tools and weapons. They also mastered the military skills of the Hyksos, especially the use of horse-drawn war chariots.

**The Egyptian Empire** Eventually, a new line of pharaohs—the eighteenth dynasty—made use of the new weapons to throw off Hyksos domination, reunite Egypt, establish the New Kingdom (c. 1550–1085 B.C.E.), and launch the Egyptians along a new militaristic path. During the period of the New Kingdom, Egypt created an empire and became the most powerful state in the Middle East.

Massive wealth aided the power of the New Kingdom pharaohs. The Egyptian rulers showed their wealth by building new temples. Queen Hatshepsut (c. 1503–1480 B.C.E.), in particular, one of the first women to become pharaoh in her own right, built a great temple at Deir el Bahri near Thebes. As pharaoh, Hatshepsut sent out military expeditions, encouraged mining, fostered agriculture, and sent a trading expedition up the Nile. Because pharaohs were almost always male, Hatshepsut's official statues show her clothed and bearded like a king. She was addressed as "His Majesty." Hatshepsut was succeeded by her nephew, Thutmosis III (c. 1480–1450 B.C.E.), who led seventeen military campaigns into Syria and Palestine and even reached the Euphrates River. Egyptian forces occupied Palestine and Syria and also moved westward into Libya.

**Akhenaten and Religious Change** The eighteenth dynasty was not without its troubles, however. Amenhotep IV (c. 1364–1347 B.C.E.) introduced the worship of Aten, god of the sun disk, as the chief god (see the box on p. 22) and pursued his worship with great enthusiasm. Changing his own name to Akhenaten ("It is well with Aten"), the pharaoh closed the temples of other gods and especially endeavored to lessen the power of Amon-Re and his priesthood at Thebes. Akhenaten strove to reduce their influence by replacing Thebes as the capital of Egypt with Akhetaten ("dedicated to Aten"), a new city located near modern Tel el Amarna, 200 miles north of Thebes.

Akhenaten's attempt at religious change failed. It was too much to ask Egyptians to give up their traditional ways and beliefs, especially since they saw the destruction of the old gods as subversive of the very cosmic order on which Egypt's survival and continuing prosperity depended. Moreover, the

## Akhenaten's Hymn to Aten

Amenhotep IV, more commonly known as Akhenaten, created a religious upheaval in Egypt by introducing the worship of Aten, god of the sun disk, as the sole god. Akhenaten's attitude to Aten is seen in this hymn. Some authorities have noted a similarity in spirit and wording to the 104th Psalm of the Old Testament.

*What does this hymn tell you about Akhenaten's religious beliefs?*

### Hymn to Aten

*Your rays suckle every meadow.*
*When you rise, they live, they grow for you.*
*You make the seasons in order to rear all that you have made,*
*The winter to cool them,*
*And the heat that they may taste you.*
*You have made the distant sky in order to rise therein,*
*In order to see all that you do make.*
*While you were alone,*
*Rising in your form as the living Aten,*
*Appearing, shining, withdrawing or approaching,*
*You made millions of forms of yourself alone.*
*Cities, towns, fields, road, and river–*
*Every eye beholds you over against them,*
*For you are the Aten of the day over the earth. . . .*
*The world came into being by your hand,*
*According as you have made them.*
*When you have risen they live,*
*When you set they die.*
*You are lifetime your own self,*
*For one lives only through you.*
*Eyes are fixed on beauty until you set.*
*All work is laid aside when you set in the west.*
*But when you rise again,*
*Everything is made to flourish for the king, . . .*
*Since you did found the earth*
*And raise them up for your son,*
*Who came forth from your body:*
*the King of Upper and Lower Egypt, . . .*
*Akn-en-Aten, . . . and the Chief Wife of the King . . .*
*Nefert-iti, living and youthful forever and ever.*

priests at Thebes were unalterably opposed to the changes, which had diminished their influence and power. At the same time, Akhenaten's preoccupation with religion caused him to ignore foreign affairs and led to the loss of both Syria and Palestine. Akhenaten's changes were soon undone after his death by those who influenced his successor, the boy-pharaoh Tutankhamun (1347–1338 B.C.E.). Tutankhamun returned the government to Thebes and restored the old gods. The Aten experiment had failed to take hold, and the eighteenth dynasty itself came to an end in 1333.

**Decline of the Egyptian Empire** The nineteenth dynasty managed to restore Egyptian power one more time. Under Rameses II (c. 1279–1213 B.C.E.), the Egyptians regained control of Palestine but were unable to reestablish the borders of their earlier empire. New invasions in the thirteenth century by the "Sea Peoples," as the Egyptians called them, destroyed Egyptian power in Palestine and drove the Egyptians back within their old frontiers. The days of Egyptian empire were ended, and the New Kingdom itself expired with the end of the twentieth dynasty in 1070. For the next thousand years, despite periodical revivals of strength, Egypt was dominated by Libyans, Nubians, Persians, and finally Macedonians, after the conquest of Alexander the Great (see Chapter 4). In the first century B.C.E., Egypt became a province in Rome's mighty empire. Egypt continued, however, to influence its conquerors through the richness of its heritage and the awesome magnificence of its physical remains.

## Daily Life in Ancient Egypt: Family and Marriage

Ancient Egyptians had a very positive attitude toward daily life on earth and followed the advice of the wisdom literature, which suggested that people marry young and establish a home and family. Monogamy was the general rule, although a husband was allowed to keep additional wives if his first wife was childless. Pharaohs, of course, were entitled to harems. The queen was acknowledged, however, as the Great Wife, with a status higher than that of the other wives. The husband was master in the house, but wives were very much respected and in charge of the household and education of the children. From a book of wise sayings (which the Egyptians called "instructions") came this advice:

> If you are a man of standing, you should found your household and love your wife at home as is fitting. Fill her belly; clothe her back. Ointment is the prescription for her body. Make her heart glad as long as you live. She is a profitable field for her lord. You should not contend with her at law, and keep her far from gaining control. . . . Let her heart be soothed through what may accrue to you; it means keeping her long in your house.[9]

Women's property and inheritance remained in their hands, even in marriage. Although most careers and public offices were closed to women, some did operate businesses. Peasant women worked long hours in the fields and at numerous domestic tasks. Upper-

**Nubians in Egypt.** During the New Kingdom, Egypt expanded to the north, into Palestine and Syria, and to the south, into the African kingdom of Nubia. Nubia had first emerged as an African kingdom around 2300 B.C.E. (see Chapter 8). Shown here in a fourteenth-century B.C.E. painting from an Egyptian official's tomb in Nubia are Nubians arriving in Egypt with bags and rings of gold. Nubia was a rich source of gold for the Egyptians.

class women could function as priestesses, and a few queens, such as Hatshepsut, even became pharaohs in their own right.

Little is known about marital arrangements and ceremonies, although it does appear that marriages were arranged by parents. The primary concerns were family and property, and the chief purpose of marriage was to produce children, especially sons. From the New Kingdom came this piece of wisdom: "Take to yourself a wife while you are [still] a youth, that she may produce a son for you."[10] Only sons could carry on the family name. Daughters were not slighted, however. Numerous tomb paintings show the close and affectionate relationship parents had with both sons and daughters. Although marriages were arranged, some of the surviving love poems from ancient Egypt suggest that some marriages included an element of romance. Here is the lament of a lovesick boy for his "sister" (lovers referred to each other as "brother" and "sister"):

*Seven days to yesterday I have not seen the sister,*
*and a sickness has invaded me;*
*My body has become heavy,*
*And I am forgetful of my own self.*
*If the chief physicians come to me,*
*My heart is not content with their remedies. . . .*
*What will revive me is to say to me: "Here she is!"*
*Her name is what will lift me up. . . .*
*My health is her coming in from outside:*
*When I see her, then I am well.*[11]

Marriages could and did end in divorce, which was allowed, apparently with compensation for the wife. Adultery, however, was strictly prohibited, with stiff punishments—especially for women, who could have their noses cut off or be burned at the stake.

## New Centers of Civilization

Our story of civilization so far has been dominated by Mesopotamia and Egypt. But significant developments were also taking place on the fringes of these civilizations. Farming had spread into the Balkan peninsula of Europe by 6500 B.C.E., and by 4000 B.C.E., it was well established in southern France, central Europe, and the coastal regions of the Mediterranean. Although migrating farmers from the Anatolian peninsula may have brought some farming techniques into Europe, some historians believe that the Neolithic peoples of Europe domesticated animals and began to farm largely on their own.

One outstanding feature of late Neolithic Europe was the building of megalithic structures. ***Megalith*** is Greek for "large stone." Radiocarbon dating, a technique that allows scientists to determine the ages of objects, shows that the first megalithic structures were built around 4000 B.C.E., more than a thousand years before the great pyramids were built in Egypt. Between 3200 and 1500 B.C.E., standing stones that were placed in circles or lined up in rows were erected throughout the British Isles and northwestern France. Other megalithic constructions have been found as far north as Scandinavia

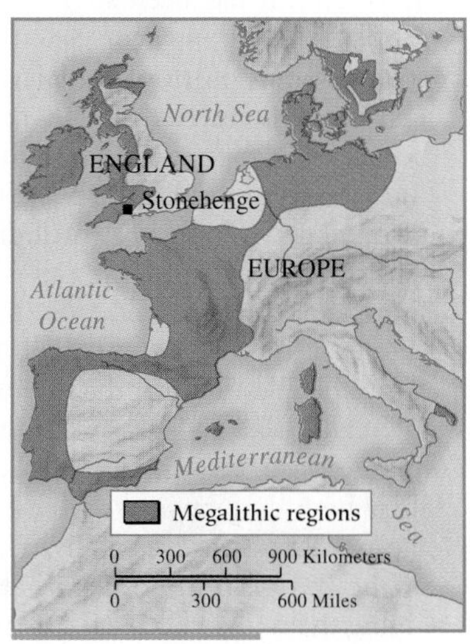


**Stonehenge and Other Megalithic Regions in Europe**

**Stonehenge.** By far the most famous megalithic construction, Stonehenge in England consists of a series of concentric rings of standing stones. Its construction sometime between 2100 and 1900 B.C.E. was no small accomplishment. The eighty bluestones used at Stonehenge weighed 4 tons each and were transported to the site from 135 miles away. Like other megalithic structures, Stonehenge indicates a remarkable awareness of astronomy on the part of its builders, as well as an elaborate coordination of workers.

and as far south as the islands of Corsica, Sardinia, and Malta. Archaeologists have demonstrated that the stone circles were used as observatories to detect not only such simple astronomical phenomena as midwinter and midsummer sunrises but also such sophisticated phenomena as the major and minor standstills of the moon.

## The Impact of the Indo-Europeans

In large part, both the details of construction and the purpose of the megalithic structures of Europe remain a mystery. Also puzzling is the role of the Indo-European peoples. The term *Indo-European* refers to people who used a language derived from a single parent tongue. *Indo-European* languages include Greek, Latin, Persian, Sanskrit, and the Germanic and Slavic languages (see Table 1.2). It has been suggested that the original Indo-European–speaking peoples were based somewhere in the steppe region north of the Black Sea or in southwestern Asia, in modern Iran or Afghanistan. Although there had been earlier migrations, around 2000 B.C.E. the original Indo-European–speaking peoples began major nomadic movements into Europe (including present-day Italy and Greece), India, and western Asia. One group of Indo-Europeans who moved into Asia Minor and Anatolia (modern Turkey) around 1750 B.C.E. coalesced with the native peoples to form the Hittite kingdom, with its capital at Hattusha (Bogazköy in modern Turkey).

Between 1600 and 1200 B.C.E., the Hittites created their own empire in western Asia and even threatened the power of the Egyptians. The Hittites were the first of the Indo-European peoples to make use of iron, enabling them to construct weapons that were stronger and cheaper to make because of the widespread availability of iron ore. But around 1200 B.C.E., new waves of invading Indo-European peoples destroyed the Hittite empire. The destruction of the Hittite kingdom and the weakening of Egypt around 1200 B.C.E. temporarily left no dominant powers in western Asia, allowing a patchwork of petty kingdoms and city-states to emerge, especially in the area of Syria and Palestine. The Phoenicians were one of these peoples.

## The Phoenicians

A Semitic-speaking people, the Phoenicians lived in the area of Palestine along the Mediterranean coast on a narrow band of land 120 miles long. Their newfound political independence after the demise of Hittite and Egyptian power helped the Phoenicians expand the trade that was already the foundation of their prosperity. The chief cities of Phoenicia—Byblos, Tyre, and Sidon—were ports on the eastern Mediterranean, but they also served as distribution centers for the lands to the east in Mesopotamia. The Phoenicians themselves produced a number of goods for foreign markets, including purple dye, glass, wine, and lumber from the famous cedars of Lebanon. In addition, the Phoenicians improved their ships and became great international sea traders. They charted new routes, not only in the Mediterranean but also in the Atlantic Ocean, where they reached Britain and sailed south along the west coast of Africa. The Phoenicians established a number of colonies in the western Mediterranean, including settlements in southern Spain, Sicily, and Sardinia. Carthage, the Phoenicians' most famous colony, was located on the north coast of Africa.

Culturally, the Phoenicians are best known as transmitters. Instead of using pictographs or signs to represent whole words and syllables as the Mesopotamians and Egyptians did, the Phoenicians simplified their writing by

**TABLE 1.2 Some Indo-European Languages**

| Subfamily | Languages |
|---|---|
| Indo-Iranian | *Sanskrit,* Persian |
| Balto-Slavic | Russian, Serbo-Croatian, Czech, Polish, Lithuanian |
| Hellenic | Greek |
| Italic | *Latin,* Romance languages (French, Italian, Spanish, Portuguese, Romanian) |
| Celtic | Irish, Gaelic |
| Germanic | Swedish, Danish, Norwegian, German, Dutch, English |

NOTE: Languages in italic type are no longer spoken.

using twenty-two different signs to represent the sounds of their speech. These twenty-two characters or letters could be used to spell out all the words in the Phoenician language. Although the Phoenicians were not the only people to invent an alphabet, theirs would have special significance because it was eventually passed on to the Greeks. From the Greek alphabet was derived the Roman alphabet that we still use today (Table 1.3 shows the derivation of the letters A to F). The Phoenicians achieved much while independent, but they ultimately fell subject to the Assyrians and Persians.

## The Hebrews: The "Children of Israel"

To the south of the Phoenicians lived another group of Semitic-speaking people known as the Hebrews. Although they were a minor factor in the politics of the region, their **monotheism**—belief in but one God—known as Judaism, later influenced both Christianity and Islam and flourished as a world religion in its own right. The Hebrews had a tradition concerning their origins and history that was eventually written down as part of the Hebrew Bible, known to Christians as the Old Testament. Describing them as a nomadic people, the Hebrews' own tradition states that they were descendants of the patriarch Abraham, who had migrated from Mesopotamia to the land of Palestine, where the Hebrews became identified as the "Children of Israel." Moreover, according to tradition, a drought in Palestine caused many Hebrews to migrate to Egypt, where they lived peacefully until they were enslaved by pharaohs who used them as laborers on building projects. The Hebrews remained in bondage until Moses led his people out of Egypt in the well-known "exodus," which some historians have argued would have occurred in the first half of the thirteenth century B.C.E. According to the biblical account, the Hebrews then wandered for many years in the desert until they entered Palestine. Organized into twelve tribes, the Hebrews became embroiled in conflict with the Philistines, a people who had settled in the coastal area of Palestine but were beginning to move into the inland areas.

Many scholars today doubt that the early books of the Hebrew Bible reflect the true history of the early Israelites. They argue that the early books of the Bible, written centuries after the events described, preserve only what the Israelites came to believe about themselves and that recent archaeological evidence often contradicts the details of the biblical account. Some of these scholars have even argued that the Israelites were not nomadic invaders but indigenous peoples in the Palestinian hill country. What is generally agreed, however, is that between 1200 and 1000 B.C.E., the Israelites emerged as a distinct group of people, possibly organized into tribes or a league of tribes, who established a united kingdom known as Israel.

**The United Kingdom of Israel** The first king of the Israelites was Saul (c. 1020–1000 B.C.E.), who initially achieved some success in the ongoing struggle with the Philistines. But after his death in a disastrous battle with this enemy, a brief period of anarchy ensued, until one of Saul's lieutenants, David (c. 1000–970 B.C.E.), reunited the Israelites, defeated the Philistines, and established control

**TABLE 1.3 The Phoenician, Greek, and Roman Alphabets**

| PHOENICIAN | | | GREEK | | | ROMAN | |
|---|---|---|---|---|---|---|---|
| *Phoenician* | *Phoenician Name* | *Modern Symbol* | *Early Greek* | *Classical Greek* | *Greek Name* | *Early Latin* | *Classical Latin* |
| 𐤀 | 'aleph | ' | Α | Α | alpha | A | A |
| 𐤁 | beth | b | Β | Β | beta | | B |
| 𐤂 | gimel | g | Γ | Γ | gamma | | C |
| 𐤃 | daleth | d | Δ | Δ | delta | D | D |
| 𐤄 | he | h | Ε | Ε | epsilon | E | E |
| 𐤅 | waw | w | Ϝ | | digamma | F | F |

SOURCE: Andrew Robinson, *The Story of Writing* (London, 1995), p. 170.

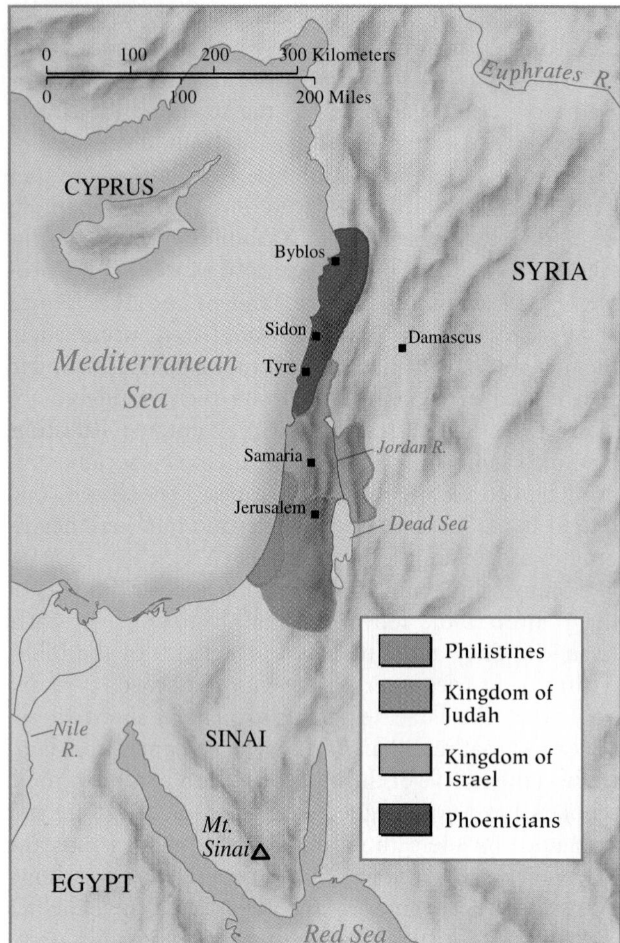


**MAP 1.5 Palestine in the First Millennium B.C.E.** United under Saul, David, and Solomon, greater Israel split into two states—Israel and Judah—after the death of Solomon. With power divided, the Israelites could not resist invasions that dispersed many Jews from Palestine. Some, such as the "ten lost tribes," never returned. Others were sent to Babylon but were later allowed to return under the rule of the Persians. Why was Israel more vulnerable to the Assyrian Empire than Judah was? **View an animated version of this map or related maps at** http://history.wadsworth.com/duikerspielvogel05/

over all of Palestine. Among David's conquests was the city of Jerusalem, which he made into the capital of a united kingdom. David centralized Israel's organization and accelerated the integration of the Israelites into a settled community based on farming and urban life.

David's son Solomon (c. 970–930 B.C.E.) did even more to strengthen royal power. He expanded the political and military establishments and was especially active in extending the trading activities of the Israelites. Solomon is known for his building projects, of which the most famous was the Temple in the city of Jerusalem. The Israelites viewed the Temple as the symbolic center of their religion and hence of the kingdom of Israel itself. The Temple now housed the Ark of the Covenant, the holy chest containing the sacred relics of the Hebrew religion and, symbolically, the throne of the invisible God of Israel. Under Solomon,

### CHRONOLOGY The Israelites

| | |
|---|---|
| **Israelites** | |
| **Saul (first king)** | **c. 1020–1000 B.C.E.** |
| **King David** | **c. 1000–970 B.C.E.** |
| **King Solomon** | **c. 970–930 B.C.E.** |
| **Northern kingdom of Israel destroyed by Assyria** | **722 or 721 B.C.E.** |
| **Fall of southern kingdom of Judah to Chaldeans; destruction of Jerusalem** | **586 B.C.E.** |
| **Return of exiles to Jerusalem** | **538 B.C.E.** |

ancient Israel was at the height of its power, but his efforts to extend royal power throughout his kingdom led to dissatisfaction among some of his subjects.

**The Divided Kingdom** After Solomon's death, tensions between the northern and southern tribes within Israel led to the establishment of two separate kingdoms—a kingdom of Israel, composed of the ten northern tribes, with its capital eventually at Samaria, and a southern kingdom of Judah, consisting of two tribes, with its capital at Jerusalem (see Map 1.5). In 722 or 721 B.C.E., the Assyrians destroyed Samaria, overran the kingdom of Israel, and deported many Hebrews to other parts of the Assyrian Empire. These dispersed Hebrews (the "ten lost tribes") merged with neighboring peoples and gradually lost their identity.

The southern kingdom of Judah was also forced to pay tribute to Assyria but managed to retain its independence as Assyrian power declined. However, a new enemy appeared on the horizon. The Chaldeans defeated Assyria, conquered the kingdom of Judah, and completely destroyed Jerusalem in 586 B.C.E. Many upper-class people from Judah were deported to Babylonia; the memory of their exile is still evoked in the stirring words of Psalm 137:

*By the rivers of Babylon, we sat and wept when we remembered Zion. . . .*
*How can we sing the songs of the Lord while in a foreign land?*
*If I forget you, O Jerusalem, may my right hand forget its skill.*
*May my tongue cling to the roof of my mouth if I do not remember you,*
*If I do not consider Jerusalem my highest joy.*[12]

But the Babylonian captivity of the people of Judah did not last. A new set of conquerors, the Persians, destroyed the Chaldean kingdom and allowed the people of Judah to return to Jerusalem and rebuild their city and Temple. The revived kingdom of Judah remained under Persian control until the conquests of Alexander the Great in the fourth century B.C.E. The people of Judah survived, even-

## The Covenant and the Law: The Book of Exodus

According to the biblical account, it was during the exodus from Egypt that the Israelites made their covenant with Yahweh. They agreed to obey their God and follow his law. In return, Yahweh promised to take special care of his chosen people. This selection from Exodus describes the making of the covenant and God's commandments to the Hebrews.

*What was the nature of the covenant between Yahweh and the Hebrews? What was its moral significance for the Hebrew people? How might you explain its differences from Hammurabi's Code?*

### Exodus 19:1–8

In the third month after the Israelites left Egypt—on the very day—they came to the Desert of Sinai. After they set out from Rephidim, they entered the desert of Sinai, and Israel camped there in the desert in front of the mountain. Then Moses went up to God, and the Lord called to him from the mountain, and said, "This is what you are to say to the house of Jacob and what you are to tell the people of Israel: 'You yourselves have seen what I did to Egypt, and how I carried you on eagles' wings and brought you to myself. Now if you obey me fully and keep my covenant, then out of all nations you will be my treasured possession. Although the whole earth is mine, you will be for me a kingdom of priests and a holy nation.' These are the words you are to speak to the Israelites." So Moses went back and summoned the elders of the people and set before them all the words the Lord had commanded him to speak. The people all responded together, "We will do everything the Lord has said." So Moses brought their answer back to the Lord.

### Exodus 20:1–3, 7–17

And God spoke all these words, "I am the Lord your God, who brought you out of Egypt, out of the land of slavery. You shall have no other gods before me. . . . You shall not misuse the name of the Lord your God, for the Lord will not hold anyone guiltless who misuses his name. Remember the Sabbath day by keeping it holy. Six days you shall labor and do all your work, but the seventh day is a Sabbath to the Lord your God. On it you shall not do any work, neither you, nor your son or daughter, nor your manservant or maidservant, nor your animals, nor the alien within your gates. For in six days the Lord made the heavens and the earth, the sea, and all that is in them, but he rested on the seventh day. Therefore the Lord blessed the Sabbath day and made it holy. Honor your father and your mother, so that you may live long in the land the Lord your God is giving you. You shall not murder. You shall not commit adultery. You shall not steal. You shall not give false testimony against your neighbor. You shall not covet your neighbor's house. You shall not covet your neighbor's wife, or his manservant or maidservant, his ox or donkey, or anything that belongs to your neighbor."

**HistoryNow™** To read a full version of this document, enter the *HistoryNow* documents area using the access card that is available for *World History.*

**The King of Israel Pays Tribute to the King of Assyria.** By the end of the ninth century B.C.E., the kingdom of Israel had been forced to pay tribute to the Assyrian Empire. The Assyrians overran the kingdom in 722 B.C.E. and destroyed the capital city of Samaria. In this scene from a black obelisk, Jehu, king of Israel, is shown paying tribute to the king of Assyria.

tually becoming known as the Jews and giving their name to Judaism, the religion of Yahweh, the Jewish God.

**The Spiritual Dimensions of Israel** According to the Jewish conception, there is but one God, called Yahweh, who is the creator of the world and everything in it. The Jewish God ruled the world; he was subject to nothing. This omnipotent creator, however, was not removed from the life he had created but was a just and good God who expected goodness from his people. If they did not obey his will, they would be punished. But he was primarily a God of mercy and love: "The Lord is gracious and compassionate, slow to anger and rich in love. The Lord is good to all; he has compassion on all he has made."[13] Each individual could have a personal relationship with this being.

Three aspects of the Jewish religious tradition had special significance: the covenant, the law, and the prophets. The Israelites believed that during the exodus from Egypt, when Moses had supposedly led his people out of bondage and into the Promised Land, God made a covenant or contract with the tribes of Israel, who believed that Yahweh had spoken to them through Moses (see the box above). The

## Three Hebrew Prophets: Micah, Isaiah, and Amos

The Hebrew prophets warned the Israelites that they must obey God's commandments or face being punished for breaking their covenant with God. These selections from the prophets Micah, Isaiah, and Amos make clear that God's punishment would fall on the Israelites for their sins. Even the Assyrians, as Isaiah indicated, would be used as God's instrument to punish them.

*What did the Hebrew prophets focus on as the transgressions of the Hebrew people? What do these selections tell you about the nature of the Hebrews as a "chosen" people?*

### Micah 6:9–16

Listen! The Lord is calling to the city–and to fear your name is wisdom–"Heed the rod and the One who appointed it. Am I still to forget, O wicked house, your ill-gotten treasures . . . ? Shall I acquit a man with dishonest scales, with a bag of false weights? Her rich men are violent; her people are liars and their tongues speak deceitfully. Therefore, I have begun to destroy you, to ruin you because of your sins. You will eat but not be satisfied; your stomach will still be empty. You will store up but save nothing, because what you save I will give to the sword. You will plant but not harvest; you will press olives but not use the oil on yourselves, you will crush grapes but not drink the wine. . . . Therefore I will give you over to ruin and your people to derision; you will bear the scorn of the nations."

### Isaiah 10:1–6

Woe to those who make unjust laws, to those who issue oppressive decrees, to deprive the poor of their rights and withhold justice from the oppressed of my people, making widows their prey and robbing the fatherless. What will you do on the day of reckoning, when disaster comes from afar? To whom will you run for help? Where will you leave your riches? Nothing will remain but to cringe among the captives or fall among the slain. Yet for all this, his anger is not turned away, his hand is still upraised. "Woe to the Assyrian, the rod of my anger, in whose hand is the club of my wrath! I send him against a godless nation, I dispatch him against a people who anger me, to seize loot and snatch plunder, and to trample them down like mud in the streets."

### Amos 3:1–2

Hear this word the Lord has spoken against you, O people of Israel–against the whole family I brought up out of Egypt: "You only have I chosen of all the families of the earth; therefore I will punish you for all your sins."

**History Now™** To read full versions of these documents, enter the *HistoryNow* documents area using the access card that is available for *World History.*

Israelites promised to obey Yahweh and follow his law. In return, Yahweh promised to take special care of his chosen people, "a peculiar treasure unto me above all people."

This covenant between Yahweh and his chosen people could be fulfilled, however, only by obedience to the law of God. Most important were the ethical concerns that stood at the center of the law. Sometimes these took the form of specific standards of moral behavior: "You shall not murder. You shall not commit adultery. You shall not steal."[14] True freedom consisted of following God's moral standards voluntarily. If people chose to ignore the good, suffering and evil would follow.

The Israelites believed that certain religious teachers, called prophets, were sent by God to serve as his voice to his people (see the box above). The golden age of prophecy began in the mid-eighth century B.C.E. and continued during the time when the people of Israel and Judah were threatened by Assyrian and Chaldean conquerors. The "men of God" went through the land warning the Israelites that they had failed to keep God's commandments and would be punished for breaking the covenant: "I will punish you for all your iniquities."

Out of the words of the prophets came new concepts that enriched the Jewish tradition. The prophets embraced a concern for all humanity. All nations would someday come to the God of Israel: "All the earth shall worship thee." This vision encompassed the elimination of war and the establishment of peace for all the nations of the world. In the words of the prophet Isaiah: "He will judge between the nations and will settle disputes for many people. They will beat their swords into plowshares and their spears into pruning hooks. Nation will not take up sword against nation, nor will they train for war anymore."[15]

Although the prophets developed a sense of universalism, the demands of the Jewish religion (the need to obey God) eventually encouraged a separation between the Jews and their non-Jewish neighbors. Unlike most other peoples of the Middle East, Jews could not simply be amalgamated into a community by accepting the gods of their conquerors and their neighbors. To remain faithful to the demands of their God, they might even have to refuse loyalty to political leaders.

# The Rise of New Empires

A small and independent Jewish state could exist only as long as no larger state dominated western Asia. New empires soon arose, however, and conquered vast stretches of the ancient world.

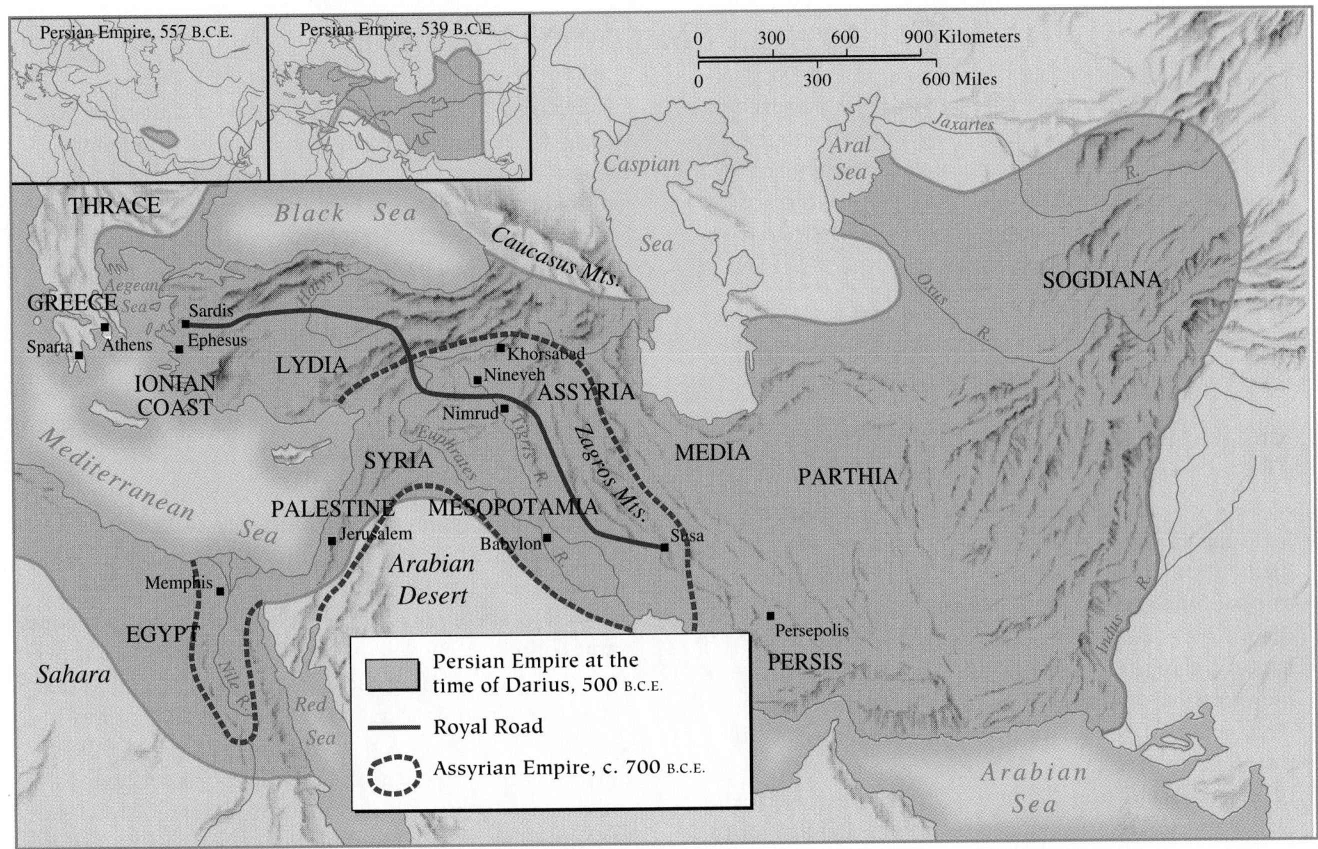


**MAP 1.6 The Assyrian and Persian Empires.** Cyrus the Great united the Persians and led them in a successful conquest of much of the Near East, including most of the lands of the Assyrian Empire. By the time of Darius, the Persian Empire was the largest the world had yet seen. How did Persian policies attempt to overcome the difficulties of governing far-flung provinces? **View an animated version of this map or related maps at** http://history.wadsworth.com/duikerspielvogel05/

## The Assyrian Empire

The first of these empires was formed in Assyria, located on the upper Tigris River, an area that brought it into both cultural and political contact with southern Mesopotamia. The Assyrians were a Semitic-speaking people who exploited the use of iron weapons, first developed by the Hittites, to establish an empire that by 700 B.C.E. included Mesopotamia, parts of the Iranian Plateau, sections of Asia Minor, Syria, Palestine, and Egypt down to Thebes (see Map 1.6). Ashurbanipal (669–626 B.C.E.) was one of the strongest Assyrian rulers, but during his reign it was already becoming apparent that the Assyrian Empire was greatly overextended. Moreover, subject peoples, such as the Babylonians, greatly resented Assyrian rule and rebelled against it. Soon after Ashurbanipal's reign, the Assyrian Empire began to disintegrate rapidly. The capital city of Nineveh fell to a coalition of Chaldeans and Medes in 612 B.C.E., and in 605 B.C.E., the rest of the empire was finally divided between the two powers.

At its height, the Assyrian Empire was ruled by kings whose power was considered absolute. Under their leadership, the empire came to be well organized. Local officials were directly responsible to the king. The Assyrians also developed an efficient system of communication to administer their empire more effectively. A network of staging posts was established throughout the empire that used relays of horses (mules or donkeys in mountainous terrain) to carry messages. The system was so effective that a provincial governor anywhere in the empire (except Egypt) could send a question and receive an answer from the king in his palace within a week.

The Assyrians' ability to conquer and maintain an empire was due to a combination of factors. Over many years of practice, the Assyrians developed effective military leaders and fighters. They were able to enlist and deploy troops numbering in the hundreds of thousands, although most campaigns were not on such a large scale. Size alone was not decisive, however. The Assyrian army was well organized and disciplined. It included a standing army of infantrymen as its core, accompanied by cavalry and horse-drawn war chariots that were used as mobile platforms for shooting arrows. The Assyrian army was also capable of waging guerrilla warfare in the mountains and set battles on open ground as well as laying siege to cities.

Another factor in the effectiveness of the Assyrian military machine was its use of terror as an instrument of

## The Assyrian Military Machine

The Assyrians achieved a reputation for possessing a mighty military machine. They were able to use a variety of military tactics and were successful whether they were waging guerrilla warfare, fighting set battles, or laying siege to cities. In these three selections, Assyrian kings boast of their military conquests.

*As seen in their own descriptions, what did Assyrian kings believe was important for military success? Do you think their accounts may be exaggerated? Why?*

### King Sennacherib (704–681 B.C.E.) Describes a Battle with the Elamites in 691

At the command of the god Ashur, the great Lord, I rushed upon the enemy like the approach of a hurricane. . . . I put them to rout and turned them back. I transfixed the troops of the enemy with javelins and arrows. . . . I cut their throats like sheep. . . . My prancing steeds, trained to harness, plunged into their welling blood as into a river; the wheels of my battle chariot were bespattered with blood and filth. I filled the plain with the corpses of their warriors like herbage. . . . As to the sheikhs of the Chaldeans, panic from my onslaught overwhelmed them like a demon. They abandoned their tents and fled for their lives, crushing the corpses of their troops as they went. . . . In their terror they passed scalding urine and voided their excrement into their chariots.

### King Sennacherib Describes His Siege of Jerusalem in 701

As to Hezekiah, the Jew, he did not submit to my yoke. I laid siege to 46 of his strong cities, walled forts, and the countless small villages in their vicinity, and conquered them by means of well-stamped earth-ramps, and battering-rams brought thus near to the walls combined with the attack by foot soldiers, using mines, breeches, as well as sapper work. I drove out of them 200,150 people, young and old, male and female, horses, mules, donkeys, camels, big and small cattle beyond counting, and considered them booty. Himself I made a prisoner in Jerusalem, his royal residence, like a bird in a cage. I surrounded him with earthwork in order to molest those who were leaving his city's gate.

### King Ashurbanipal (669–626 B.C.E.) Describes His Treatment of Conquered Babylon

I tore out the tongues of those whose slanderous mouths had uttered blasphemies against my god Ashur and had plotted against me, his god-fearing prince; I defeated them completely. The others, I smashed alive with the very same statues of protective deities with which they had smashed my own grandfather Sennacherib—now finally as a belated burial sacrifice for his soul. I fed their corpses, cut into small pieces, to dogs, pigs, . . . vultures, the birds of the sky, and also to the fish of the ocean. After I had performed this and thus made quiet again the hearts of the great gods, my lords, I removed the corpses of those whom the pestilence had felled, whose leftovers after the dogs and pigs had fed on them were obstructing the streets, filling the places of Babylon, and of those who had lost their lives through the terrible famine.

History Now™ To read full versions of these documents, or related documents, enter the *HistoryNow* documents area using the access card that is available for *World History.*

warfare (see the box above). As a matter of regular policy, the Assyrians laid waste the land in which they were fighting, smashing dams, looting and destroying towns, setting crops on fire, and cutting down trees, particularly fruit trees. The Assyrians were especially known for committing atrocities on their captives. King Ashurnasirpal recorded this account of his treatment of prisoners:

> 3000 of their combat troops I felled with weapons. . . . Many of the captives taken from them I burned in a fire. Many I took alive; from some of these I cut off their hands to the wrist, from others I cut off their noses, ears and fingers; I put out the eyes of many of the soldiers. . . . I burned their young men and women to death.[16]

After conquering another city, the same king wrote: "I fixed up a pile of corpses in front of the city's gate. I flayed the nobles, as many as had rebelled, and spread their skins out on the piles. . . . I flayed many within my land and spread their skins out on the walls."[17] It should be noted that this policy of extreme cruelty to prisoners was not used against all enemies but was primarily reserved for those who were already part of the empire and then rebelled against Assyrian rule.

**Assyrian Society** Assyrian deportation policies created a polyglot society in which ethnic differences were not very important. What gave identity to the Assyrians themselves was their language, although even that was akin to the language of their southern neighbors in Babylonia, who also spoke a Semitic language. Religion was also a cohesive force. Assyria was literally "the land of Ashur," a reference to its chief god. The king, as the human representative of the god Ashur, provided a final unifying focus.

Agriculture formed the principal basis of Assyrian life. Assyria was a land of farming villages with relatively few significant cities, especially in comparison to southern Mesopotamia. Unlike the river valleys, where farming required the minute organization of large numbers of people to control irrigation, Assyrian farms received sufficient moisture from regular rainfall.

**King Ashurbanipal's Lion Hunt.** This relief, sculpted on alabaster as a decoration for the northern palace in Nineveh, depicts King Ashurbanipal engaged in a lion hunt. Lion hunts were not done in the wild but under controlled circumstances. The king and his retainers faced lions released from cages in an arena. The purpose of the scene was to glorify the king as a conqueror of the king of beasts. Relief sculpture, one of the best-known forms of Assyrian art, reached its high point under Ashurbanipal at about the time that the Assyrian empire began to disintegrate.

Trade was second to agriculture in economic importance. For internal trade, metals—such as gold, silver, copper, and bronze—were used as a medium of exchange. Various agricultural products also served as a form of payment or exchange. Because of their geographical location, the Assyrians served as intermediaries and participated in an international trade in which they imported timber, wine, and precious metals and stones while exporting textiles produced in palaces, temples, and private workshops.

**Assyrian Culture** The culture of the Assyrian Empire was essentially a hybrid. The Assyrians assimilated much of Mesopotamian civilization and saw themselves as guardians of Sumerian and Babylonian culture. Assyrian kings also tried to maintain old traditions when they rebuilt damaged temples by constructing the new buildings on the original foundations, not in new locations.

Among the best-known objects of Assyrian art are the relief sculptures found in the royal palaces in three of the Assyrian capital cities, Nimrud, Nineveh, and Khorsabad. These reliefs, which were begun in the ninth century and reached their high point in the reign of Ashurbanipal in the seventh century, depicted two different kinds of subject matter: ritual or ceremonial scenes revolving around the person of the king and scenes of hunting and war. The latter show realistic action scenes of the king and his warriors engaged in battle or hunting animals, especially lions. These pictures depict a strongly masculine world where discipline, brute force, and toughness are the enduring values—indeed, the very values of the Assyrian military monarchy.

## The Persian Empire

After the collapse of the Assyrian Empire, the Chaldeans, under their king Nebuchadnezzar II (605–562 B.C.E.), made Babylonia the leading state in western Asia. Nebuchadnezzar rebuilt Babylon as the center of his empire, giving it a reputation as one of the great cities of the ancient world. But the splendor of Chaldean Babylonia proved to be short-lived when Babylon fell to the Persians in 539 B.C.E.

The Persians were an Indo-European–speaking people who lived in southwestern Iran. Primarily nomadic, the Persians were organized into tribes until the Achaemenid dynasty managed to unify the Persians. One of its members, Cyrus (559–530 B.C.E.), created a powerful Persian state that rearranged the political map of western Asia.

**Cyrus the Great** In 550 B.C.E., Cyrus extended Persian control over the Medes, making Media the first Persian **satrapy,** or province. Three years later, Cyrus defeated the prosperous Lydian kingdom in western Asia Minor, and Lydia became another Persian satrapy. Cyrus' forces then went on to conquer the Greek city-states that had been established on the Ionian coast. Cyrus then turned eastward, subduing the eastern part of the Iranian Plateau, Sogdia, and even western India. His eastern frontiers secured, Cyrus entered Mesopotamia in 539 and captured Babylon (see Map 1.6). His treatment of Babylonia showed remarkable restraint and wisdom. Babylonia was made into a Persian province under a Persian **satrap,** or governor, but many government officials were kept in their positions. Cyrus took the title "King of All, Great King, Mighty King, King of Babylon, King of the Land of Sumer and Akkad, King of the Four Rims [of the earth], the Son of Cambyses the Great King, King of Anshan"[18] and insisted that he stood in the ancient, unbroken line of Babylonian kings. By appealing to the vanity of the Babylonians, he won their loyalty. Cyrus also issued an edict permitting the Jews, who had been brought to Babylon in the sixth century B.C.E., to return to Jerusalem with their sacred objects and to rebuild their Temple as well.

To his contemporaries, Cyrus deserved to be called Cyrus the Great. The Greek historian Herodotus recounted that the Persians viewed him as a "father," a ruler who was "gentle, and procured them all manner of goods."[19] Cyrus must have been an unusual ruler for his time, a man who demonstrated considerable wisdom and compassion in the conquest and organization of his empire. He won approval by using not only Persians but also native peoples as government officials in their own states. Unlike the Assyrian rulers of an earlier empire, he had a reputation for mercy. Medes, Babylonians, and Jews all accepted him as their legitimate ruler. Indeed, the Jews regarded him as the anointed one of God: "I am the Lord who says of Cyrus, 'He is my shepherd and will accomplish all that I please'; he will say of Jerusalem, 'Let it be rebuilt'; and of the Temple, 'Let its foundations be laid.' This is what the Lord says to his anointed, to Cyrus, whose right hand I take hold of to subdue nations before him."[20] Cyrus had a genuine respect for ancient civilizations—in building his palaces, he made use of Assyrian, Babylonian, Egyptian, and Lydian practices.

**Expanding the Empire** Cyrus's successors extended the territory of the Persian Empire. His son Cambyses (530–522 B.C.E.) undertook a successful invasion of Egypt. Darius (521–486 B.C.E.) added a new Persian province in western India that extended to the Indus River and moved into Europe proper, conquering Thrace and making the Macedonian king a vassal. A revolt of the Ionian Greek cities in 499 B.C.E. resulted in temporary freedom for these communities in western Asia Minor. Aid from the Greek mainland, most notably from Athens, encouraged the Ionians to invade Lydia and burn Sardis, center of the Lydian satrapy. This event led to Darius' involvement with the mainland Greeks. After reestablishing control of the Ionian Greek cities, Darius undertook an invasion of the Greek mainland, which culminated in the famous Athenian victory in the Battle of Marathon, in 490 B.C.E. (see Chapter 4).

**Governing the Empire** By the reign of Darius, the Persians had created the largest empire the world had yet seen. It not only included all the old centers of power in Egypt and western Asia but also extended into Thrace and Asia Minor in the west and into India in the east. For administrative purposes, the empire had been divided into approximately twenty satrapies. Each province was ruled by a satrap, literally a "protector of the kingdom." Satraps collected tributes, were responsible for justice and security, raised military levies for the royal army, and normally commanded the military forces within their satrapies. In terms of real power, the satraps were miniature kings who created courts imitative of the Great King's.

An efficient system of communication was crucial to sustaining the Persian Empire. Well-maintained roads facilitated the rapid transit of military and government personnel. One in particular, the so-called Royal Road, stretched from Sardis, the center of Lydia in Asia Minor, to Susa, the chief capital of the Persian Empire. Like the Assyrians, the Persians established staging posts equipped with fresh horses for the king's messengers.

**CHRONOLOGY Early Empires**

| | |
|---|---|
| **The Assyrians** | |
| Height of power | 700 B.C.E. |
| Ashurbanipal | 669–626 B.C.E. |
| Fall of Nineveh | 612 B.C.E. |
| Assyrian Empire destroyed | 605 B.C.E. |
| **The Persians** | |
| Unification under Achaemenid dynasty | 600s B.C.E. |
| Persian control over Medes | 550 B.C.E. |
| Conquests of Cyrus the Great | 559–530 B.C.E. |
| Cambyses and conquest of Egypt | 530–522 B.C.E. |
| Reign of Darius | 521–486 B.C.E. |

**The Great King** In this vast administrative system, the Persian king occupied an exalted position. Although not considered a god in the manner of an Egyptian pharaoh, he was nevertheless the elect one or regent of the Persian god Ahuramazda (see the next section, "Persian Religion"). All subjects were the king's servants, and he was the source of all justice, possessing the power of life and death over everyone. Persian kings were largely secluded and not easily accessible. They resided in a series of splendid palaces. Darius in particular was a palace builder on a grand scale. His description of the construction of a palace in the chief Persian capital of Susa demonstrated what a truly international empire Persia was:

> This is the . . . palace which at Susa I built. From afar its ornamentation was brought. . . . The cedar timber was brought from a mountain named Lebanon; the Assyrians brought it to Babylon, and from Babylon the Carians and Ionians brought it to Susa. Teakwood was brought from Gandara and from Carmania. The gold which was used here was brought from Sardis and from Bactria. The stone—lapis lazuli and carnelian—was brought from Sogdiana. . . . The silver and copper were brought from Egypt. The ornamentation with which the wall was adorned was brought from Ionia. The ivory was brought from Ethiopia, from India, and from Arachosia. The stone pillars were brought from . . . Elam. The artisans who dressed the stone were Ionians and Sardians. The goldsmiths who wrought the gold were Medes and Egyptians. . . . Those who worked the baked brick [with figures] were Babylonians. The men who adorned the wall were Medes and Egyptians. At Susa here a splendid work was ordered; very splendid did it turn out.[21]

But Darius was unhappy with Susa. He did not really consider it his homeland, and it was oppressively hot in the summer months. He built another residence at Persepolis, a new capital located to the east of the old one and at a higher elevation.

The policies of Darius also tended to widen the gap between the king and his subjects. As the Great King himself said of all his subjects: "What was said to them by me, night and day it was done."[22] Over a period of time, the Great Kings in their greed came to hoard immense quantities of gold and silver in the various treasuries located in the capital cities. Both their hoarding of wealth and their later overtaxation of their subjects are considered crucial factors in the ultimate weakening of the Persian Empire.

In its heyday, however, the empire stood supreme, and much of its power depended on the military. By the time of Darius, the Persian monarchs had created a standing army of professional soldiers. This army was truly international in character, composed of contingents from the various peoples who made up the empire. At its core was a cavalry force of ten thousand and an elite infantry force of ten thousand Medes and Persians known as the Immortals because they were never allowed to fall below ten thousand in number. When one was killed, he was immediately replaced.

**Persian Religion** Of all the Persians' cultural contributions, the most original was their religion, **Zoroastrianism.** According to Persian tradition, Zoroaster was born in 660 B.C.E. After a period of wandering and solitude, he experienced revelations that caused him to be revered as a prophet of the "true religion." His teachings were eventually written down in the third century B.C.E. in the *Zend Avesta,* the sacred book of Zoroastrianism.

Like the Hebrews', Zoroaster's spiritual message was monotheistic. To Zoroaster, Ahuramazda was the only god, and the religion he preached was the only perfect one. Ahuramazda (the "Wise Lord") was the supreme deity who brought all things into being. According to Zoroaster, Ahuramazda also possessed qualities that all humans should aspire to, such as good thought, right, and piety. Although Ahuramazda was supreme, he was not unopposed. At the beginning of the world, the good spirit of Ahuramazda was opposed by the evil spirit, later identified as Ahriman.

Humans also played a role in this cosmic struggle between good and evil. Ahuramazda, the creator, gave all humans free will and the power to choose between right and wrong. The good person chooses the right way of Ahuramazda. Zoroaster taught that there would be an end to the struggle between good and evil. Ahuramazda would eventually triumph, and at the last judgment at the end of the world, the final separation of good and evil would occur. Individuals, too, would be judged. Each soul faced a final evaluation of its actions. If a person had performed good deeds, he or she would achieve paradise; if evil deeds, the soul would be thrown into an abyss of torment.

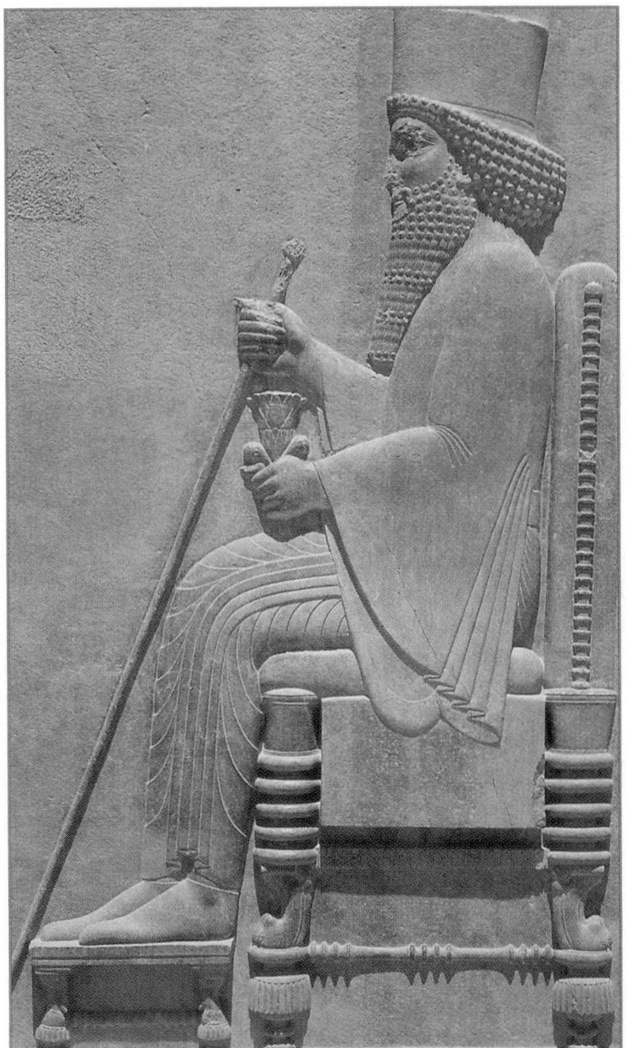



**Darius, the Great King.** Darius ruled the Persian Empire from 521 to 486 B.C.E. He is shown here on his throne in Persepolis, a new capital city that he built. In his right hand, Darius holds the royal staff. In his left hand, he grasps a lotus blossom with two buds, a symbol of royalty.

## CONCLUSION

**THE PEOPLES OF MESOPOTAMIA AND EGYPT,** like the peoples of India and China, built the first civilizations. Blessed with an abundant environment in their fertile river valleys, they built technologically advanced societies, developed cities, and struggled with the problems of organized states. They developed writing to keep records and created literature. They constructed monumental architecture to please their gods, symbolize their power, and preserve their culture for all time. They developed new political, military, social, and religious structures to deal with the basic problems of human existence and organization. These first literate civilizations left detailed records that allow us to view how they grappled with three of the fundamental problems that humans have pondered: the nature of human relationships, the nature of the universe, and the role of divine forces in that cosmos. Although other peoples would provide different answers from those of the Mesopotamians and Egyptians, they posed the questions, gave answers, and wrote them down. Human memory begins with the creation of civilizations.

By the middle of the second millennium B.C.E., much of the creative impulse of the Mesopotamian and Egyptian civilizations was beginning to wane. Around 1200 B.C.E., the decline of the Hittites and Egyptians had created a power vacuum that allowed a number of small states to emerge and flourish temporarily. All of them were eventually overshadowed by the rise of the great empires of the Assyrians and Persians. The Assyrian Empire was the first to unite almost all of the ancient Middle East. Even larger, however, was the empire of the Great Kings of Persia. Although it owed much to the administrative organization created by the Assyrians, the Persian Empire had its own peculiar strengths. Persian rule was tolerant as well as efficient. Conquered peoples were allowed to keep their own religions, customs, and methods of doing business. The many years of peace that the Persian Empire brought to the Middle East facilitated trade and the general well-being of its peoples. It is no wonder that many peoples expressed their gratitude for being subjects of the Great Kings of Persia. Among these peoples were the Jews, who created no empire but nevertheless left an important spiritual legacy. The evolution of monotheism created in Judaism one of the world's greatest religions; moreover, Judaism influenced the development of both Christianity and Islam.

The Persians also extended their empire to the Indus River, which brought them into contact with another river valley civilization that had developed independently of the civilizations in the Middle East and Egypt. It is to South Asia that we now turn.

## CHAPTER NOTES

1. J. M. Chauvet et al., *Dawn of Art: The Chauvet Cave* (New York, 1996), pp. 49–50.
2. Quoted in A. Kuhrt, *The Ancient Near East, c. 3000–330 B.C.* (London, 1995), vol. 1, p. 68.
3. Quoted in M. Van de Mieroop, *A History of the Ancient Near East, ca. 3000–323 B.C.* (Oxford, 2004), p. 69.
4. Quoted in ibid., p. 106
5. Quoted in T. Jacobsen, "Mesopotamia," in H. Frankfort et al., *Before Philosophy* (Baltimore, 1949), p. 139.
6. Quoted in M. Covensky, *The Ancient Near Eastern Tradition* (New York, 1966), p. 51.
7. Quoted in B. G. Trigger et al., *Ancient Egypt: A Social History* (Cambridge, 1983), p. 74.
8. Quoted in R-M. Hagen and R. Hagen, *Egypt: People, Gods, Pharaohs* (Cologne, 2002), p. 148.
9. J. B. Pritchard, *Ancient Near Eastern Texts,* 3d ed. (Princeton, N.J., 1969), p. 413.
10. Ibid., p. 420.
11. Quoted in J. A. Wilson, *The Culture of Ancient Egypt* (Chicago, 1956), p. 264.
12. Psalms 137:1, 4–6.
13. Psalms 145:8–9.
14. Exodus 20:13–15.
15. Isaiah 2:4.
16. Quoted in H. W. F. Saggs, *The Might That Was Assyria* (London, 1984), p. 261.
17. Ibid., p. 262.
18. Quoted in J. M. Cook, *The Persian Empire* (New York, 1983), p. 32.
19. Herodotus, *The Persian Wars,* trans. G. Rawlinson (New York, 1942), p. 257.
20. Isaiah, 44:28, 45:1.
21. Quoted in A. T. Olmstead, *History of the Persian Empire* (Chicago, 1948), p. 168.
22. Quoted in Cook, *The Persian Empire,* p. 76.

## SUGGESTED READING

To examine some of the issues raised in the comparative essay for Chapter 1, see **J. Diamond, *Guns, Germs, and Steel: The Fates of Human Societies*** (New York, 1997). The following works are of considerable value in examining the prehistory of humankind: **R. Leakey, *The Making of Mankind*** (London, 1981); **R. J. Wenke, *Patterns in Prehistory: Humankind's First Three Million Years,*** 4th ed. (New York, 1999); **P. Mellars and C. Stringer, *The Human Revolution*** (Edinburgh, 1989); and **D. O. Henry, *From Foraging to Agriculture*** (Philadelphia, 1989). For a study of the role of women in early human society, see **E. Barber, *Women's Work: The First 20,000 Years*** (New York, 1994).

An excellent reference tool on the ancient Near East can be found in **P. Bienkowski and A. Milward, eds., *Dictionary of the Ancient Near East*** (Philadelphia, 2000). A very competent general survey of the ancient Near East is **M. Van de Mieroop, *A History of the Ancient Near East, ca. 3000–323 B.C.*** (Oxford, 2004). Also valuable is **A. B. Knapp, *The History and Culture of Ancient Western Asia and Egypt*** (Chicago, 1987). For a detailed survey, see **A. Kuhrt, *The Ancient Near East, c. 3000–330 B.C.,*** 2 vols. (London, 1996). **H. W. F. Saggs, *Babylonians*** (Norman, Okla., 1995), provides an overview of the people of ancient Mesopotamia. On the economic and social history of the ancient Near East, see **D. C. Snell, *Life in the Ancient Near East*** (New Haven, Conn., 1997). The fundamental collection of translated documents from the ancient Near East is **J. B. Pritchard, *Ancient Near Eastern Texts,*** 3d ed. (Princeton, N.J., 1969).

General works on ancient Mesopotamia include **J. N. Postgate, *Early Mesopotamia: Society and Economy at the Dawn of History*** (London, 1992), and **S. Lloyd, *The Archaeology of Mesopotamia,*** rev. ed. (London, 1984). A beautifully illustrated survey can be found in **M. Roaf, *Cultural Atlas of Mesopotamia and the Ancient Near East*** (New York, 1996). The world of the Sumerians has been well described

## TIMELINE

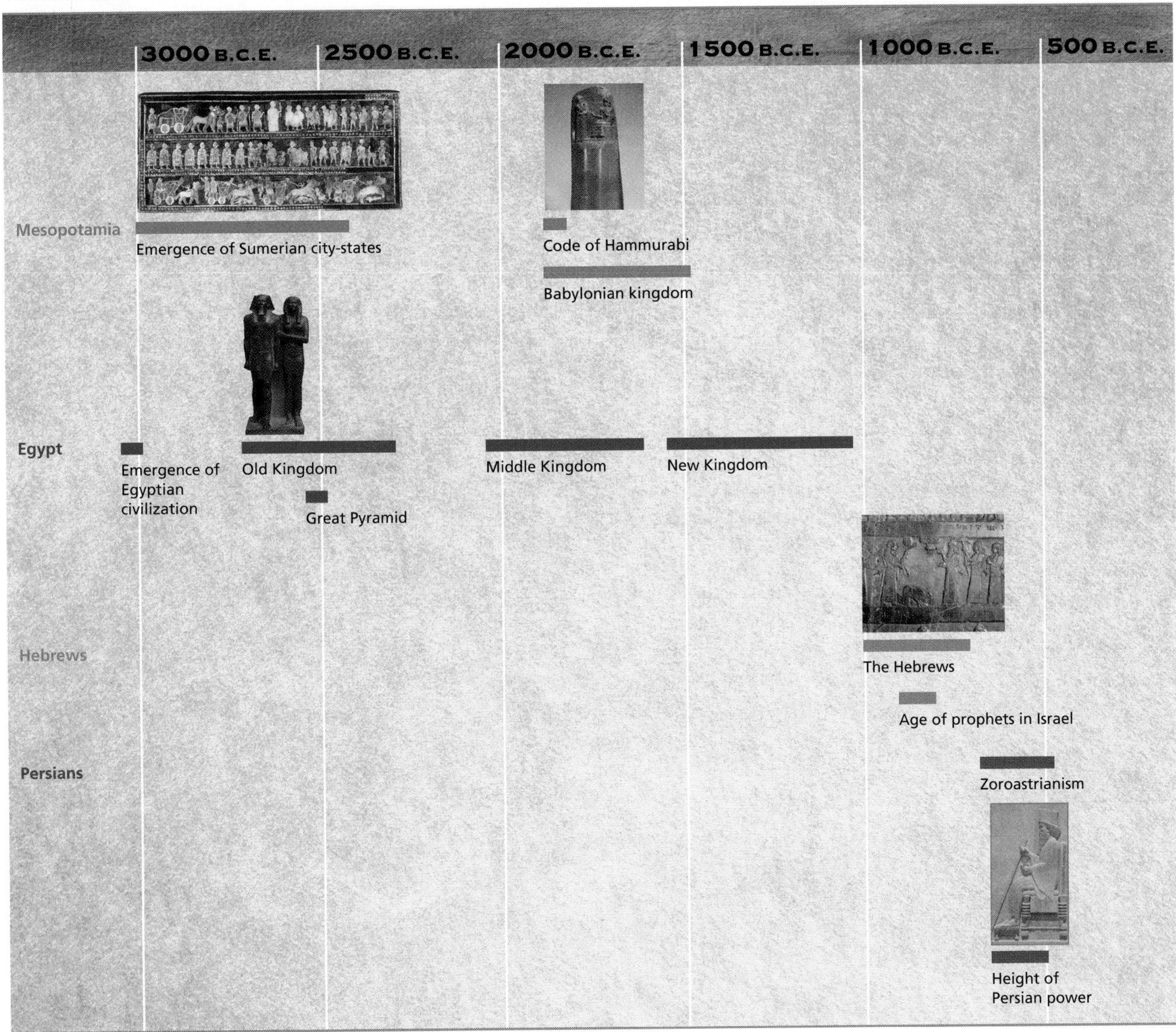


in **S. N. Kramer, *The Sumerians*** (Chicago, 1963) and ***History Begins at Sumer*** (New York, 1959). See also the summary of the historical and archaeological evidence by **H. Crawford, *Sumer and the Sumerians*** (Cambridge, 1991). For a reference work on daily life, see **S. Bertman, *Handbook to Life in Ancient Mesopotamia*** (New York, 2003).

For a good introduction to ancient Egypt, see the beautifully illustrated works by **M. Hayes, *The Egyptians*** (New York, 1997); **J. Baines and J. Málek, *The Cultural Atlas of the World: Ancient Egypt*** (Alexandria, Va., 1991); and **D. P. Silverman,** ed., ***Ancient Egypt*** (New York, 1997). Other general surveys include **N. Grant, *The Egyptians*** (New York, 1996); **I. Shaw,** ed., ***The Oxford History of Ancient Egypt*** (New York, 2000); and **N. Grimal, *A History of Ancient Egypt,*** trans. I. Shaw (Oxford, 1992). Egyptian religion is covered in **S. Quirke, *Ancient Egyptian Religion*** (London, 1992). On culture in general, see **J. A. Wilson, *The Culture of Ancient Egypt*** (Chicago, 1956). Daily life in ancient Egypt can be examined in **E. Strouhal, *Life of the Ancient Egyptians*** (Norman, Okla., 1992). An important study on women is **G. Robins, *Women in Ancient Egypt*** (Cambridge, Mass., 1993).

On the Sea Peoples, see the standard work by **N. Sanders, *The Sea Peoples: Warriors of the Ancient Mediterranean*** (London, 1978). Surveys on the Hittites can be found in **O. R. Gurney, *The Hittites,*** rev. ed (Harmondsworth, England, 1990), and **T. Bryce, *The Kingdom of the Hittites*** (Oxford, 1998).

For a good account of Phoenician domestic history and overseas expansion, see **D. Harden, *The Phoenicians*,** rev. ed. (Harmondsworth, England, 1980). See also **M. E. Aubet, *The Phoenicians and the West: Politics, Colonies and Trade*** (Cambridge, 1993), and **G. Markoe, *Phoenicians*** (London, 2000). There is an enormous literature on ancient Israel. Two good studies on the archaeological aspects are **A. Mazar, *Archaeology of the Land of the Bible*** (New York, 1992), and **A. Ben-Tor,** ed., ***The***

*Archaeology of Ancient Israel* (New Haven, Conn., 1992). For historical narratives, see especially **J. Bright, *A History of Israel,*** 3d ed. (Philadelphia, 1981), a fundamental study; the survey by **M. Grant, *The History of Ancient Israel*** (New York, 1984); and **H. Shanks, *Ancient Israel: A Short History from Abraham to the Roman Destruction of the Temple*** (Englewood Cliffs, N.J., 1988). For general studies on the religion of the Hebrews, see **R. Albertz, *A History of Israelite Religion in the Old Testament Period*** (Louisville, Ky., 1994), and **W. J. Doorly, *The Religion of Israel*** (New York, 1997). On the origins of the Israelites, see **W. G. Dever, *Who Were the Early Israelites and Where Did They Come From?*** (Grand Rapids, Mich., 2003).

A detailed account of Assyrian political, economic, social, military, and cultural history is **H. W. F. Saggs, *The Might That Was Assyria*** (London, 1984). The Chaldean empire can be examined in **Saggs's *Babylonians*** (Norman, Okla., 1995).

The classic work on the Persian Empire is **A. T. Olmstead, *History of the Persian Empire*** (Chicago, 1948), but a more recent work by **J. M. Cook, *The Persian Empire*** (New York, 1983), provides new material and fresh interpretations. Also of value is **J. Curtis, *Ancient Persia*** (Cambridge, Mass., 1990). On the history of Zoroastrianism, see **S. A. Nigosian, *The Zoroastrian Faith: Tradition and Modern Research*** (New York, 1993).

## History Now™

**Enter *HistoryNow* using the access card that is available with this text. *HistoryNow* will assist you in understanding the content in this chapter with lesson plans generated for your needs, as well as provide you with a connection to the *Wadsworth World History Resource Center* (see description below for details).**

### World History Resource Center

**Enter the Resource Center using either your *HistoryNow* access card or your standalone access card for the *Wadsworth World History Resource Center.* Organized by topic, this website includes quizzes; images; over 350 primary source documents; interactive simulations; maps and timelines; movie explorations; and a wealth of other resources. You can read the following documents, and many more, at http://history.wadsworth.com/rc/world**

*Enuma Elish*

Herodotus, History, book 2, chapters 124–127

Visit the *World History* Companion Website for chapter quizzes and more.

http://history.wadsworth.com/duikerspielvogel05/

CHAPTER

# 2

# ANCIENT INDIA

Krishna and Arjuna preparing for battle



## CHAPTER OUTLINE AND FOCUS QUESTIONS

### The Emergence of Civilization in India: Harappan Society

- What were the chief features of Harappan civilization, and in what ways was it similar to the civilizations that arose in Egypt and Mesopotamia?

### The Arrival of the Aryans

- What effects did the class system and the family have on Indian civilization?

### Escaping the Wheel of Life: The Religious World of Ancient India

- What are the main tenets of Hinduism and Buddhism, and how did each religion influence Indian civilization?

### The Rule of the Fishes: India After the Mauryas

- Why was India unable to maintain a unified empire in the first millennium B.C.E., and how was the Mauryan Empire temporarily able to overcome the tendencies toward disunity?

### The Exuberant World of Indian Culture

- In what ways did the culture of ancient India resemble and differ from the cultural experience of ancient Mesopotamia and Egypt?

### CRITICAL THINKING

- What are some of the key factors that explain why India became one of the first regions to create an advanced technological society in the ancient world? To what degree does it merit comparison with Mesopotamia and Egypt as the site of the first civilizations?

**ARJUNA WAS DESPONDENT** as he prepared for battle. In the opposing army were many of his friends and colleagues, some of whom he had known since childhood. In despair, he turned for advice to Krishna, his chariot driver, who, unknown to Arjuna, was in actuality an incarnation of the Indian deity Vishnu. "Do not despair of your duty," Krishna advised his friend.

*To be born is certain death,*
*to the dead, birth is certain.*
*It is not right that you should sorrow*
*for what cannot be avoided. . . .*
*If you do not fight this just battle*
*you will fail in your own law*
*and in your honor,*
*and you will incur sin.*

Krishna's advice to Arjuna is contained in the Bhagavad Gita, one of India's most sacred classical writings, and reflects one of the key tenets in Indian philosophy—the belief in reincarnation, or rebirth of the soul. It also points up the importance of doing one's duty without regard for the consequences. Arjuna was a warrior, and according to Aryan tribal tradition, he was obliged to follow the code of his class. "There is more joy in doing one's own duty badly," advised Krishna, "than in doing another man's duty well."

In advising Arjuna to fulfill his obligation as a warrior, the author of the Bhagavad Gita, writing around the second century B.C.E. about a battle that took place almost a thousand years earlier, was by implication urging all readers to adhere to their own responsibility as members of one of India's major classes. Henceforth, this hierarchical vision of a society divided into groups, each with clearly distinct roles, would become a defining characteristic of Indian history.

The Bhagavad Gita is part of a larger work that deals with the early history of the Aryan peoples who entered India from beyond the mountains north of the Khyber Pass between 1500 and 1000 B.C.E. When the Aryans arrived, India had already had a thriving civilization for almost two thousand years. The Indus valley civilization, although not as well known today as the civilizations of Mesopotamia and Egypt, was just as old; and its political, social, and cultural achievements were also impressive. That civilization, known to historians by the names of its two major cities, Harappa and Mohenjo-Daro, emerged in the late fourth millennium B.C.E., flourished for over one thousand years, and then came to an abrupt end about 1500 B.C.E. It was soon replaced by a new society dominated by the Aryan peoples. The new civilization that emerged represented a rich mixture of the two cultures–Harappan and Aryan–and evolved over the next three thousand years into what we know today as India. ◇

# The Emergence of Civilization in India: Harappan Society

Although today this beautiful mosaic of peoples and cultures has been broken up into a number of separate independent states, the region still possesses a coherent history that despite its internal diversity is recognizably Indian.

## A Land of Diversity

India was and still is a land of diversity. This diversity is evident in its languages and cultures as well as in its physical characteristics. India possesses an incredible array of languages. It has a deserved reputation, along with the Middle East, as a cradle of religion. Two of the world's major religions, Hinduism and Buddhism, originated in India; and a number of others, including Sikhism and Islam (the latter of which entered the South Asian subcontinent in the ninth or tenth century C.E.), continue to flourish there.

In its size and diversity, India seems more like a continent than a single country. That diversity begins with the geographical environment. The Indian subcontinent, shaped like a spade hanging from the southern ridge of Asia, is composed of a number of core regions. In the far north are the Himalayan and Karakoram mountain ranges, home to the highest mountains in the world. Directly to the south of the Himalayas and the Karakoram range is the rich valley of the Ganges, India's "holy river" and one of the core regions of Indian culture. To the west is the Indus River valley. Today the latter is a relatively arid plateau that forms the backbone of the modern state of Pakistan, but in ancient times it enjoyed a more balanced climate and served as the cradle of Indian civilization.

South of India's two major river valleys lies the Deccan, a region of hills and an upland plateau that extends from the Ganges valley to the southern tip of the Indian subcontinent. The interior of the plateau is relatively hilly and dry, but the eastern and western coasts are occupied by lush plains, which are historically among the most densely populated regions of India. Off the southeastern coast is the island known today as Sri Lanka. Although Sri Lanka is now a separate country quite distinct politically and culturally from India, the island's history is intimately linked with that of its larger neighbor.

In this vast region live a rich mixture of peoples: Dravidians, probably descended from the Indus River culture that flourished at the dawn of Indian civilization, over four thousand years ago; Aryans, descended from the pastoral peoples who flooded southward from Central Asia in the second millennium B.C.E.; and hill peoples, who may have lived in the region prior to the rise of organized societies and thus may have been the earliest inhabitants of all.

## Harappan Civilization: A Fascinating Enigma

In the 1920s, archaeologists discovered the existence of agricultural settlements dating back well over six thousand years in the lower reaches of the Indus River valley in modern Pakistan. Those small mudbrick villages eventually gave rise to the sophisticated human communities that historians call Harappan civilization. Although today the area is relatively arid, during the third and fourth millennia B.C.E., it evidently received much more abundant rainfall, and the valleys of the Indus River and its tributaries supported a thriving civilization that may have covered a total area of over 600,000 square miles, from the Himalayas to the coast of the Indian Ocean. More than seventy sites have been unearthed since the area was first discovered in the 1850s, but the main sites are at the two major cities, Harappa, in the Punjab, and Mohenjo-Daro, nearly 400 miles to the south near the mouth of the Indus River (see Map 2.1).

The origin of the Harappans is still debated, but some scholars have suggested on the basis of ethnographic and linguistic analysis that the language and physical characteristics of the Harappans were similar to those of the Dravidian peoples who live in the Deccan Plateau today. If that is so, Harappa is not simply a dead civilization,

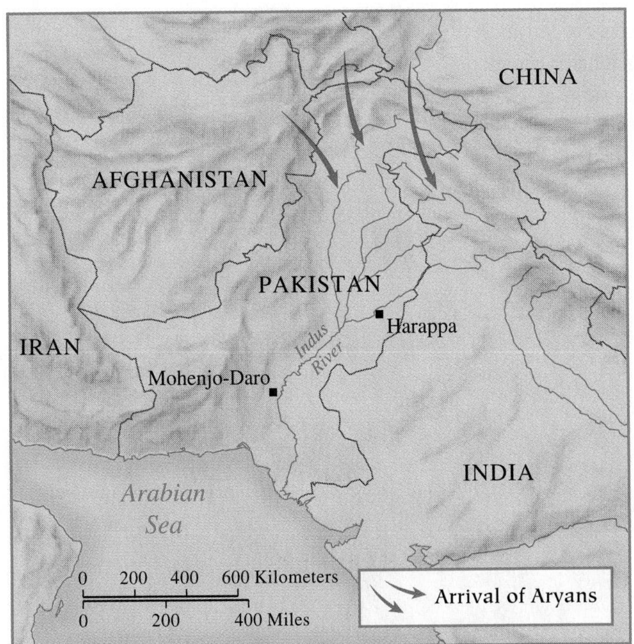


**MAP 2.1 Ancient Harappan Civilization.** This map shows the location of the first civilization that arose in the Indus River valley, which today is located in the contemporary state of Pakistan. ? What were the names of the two largest urban centers that have so far been excavated? **View an animated version of this map or related maps at** http://history.wadsworth.com/duikerspielvogel05/

whose culture and peoples have disappeared into the sands of history, but a part of the living culture of the Indian subcontinent.

**Political and Social Structures** In several respects, Harappan civilization closely resembled the cultures of Mesopotamia and the Nile valley. Like them, it probably began in tiny farming villages scattered throughout the river valley, some dating back to as early as 6500 or 7000 B.C.E. These villages thrived and grew until by the middle of the third millennium B.C.E. they could support a privileged ruling elite living in walled cities of considerable magnitude and affluence. The center of power was the city of Harappa, which was surrounded by a brick wall over 40 feet thick at its base and more than 3½ miles in circumference. The city was laid out on an essentially rectangular grid, with some streets as wide as 30 feet. Most buildings were constructed of kiln-dried mudbricks and were square in shape, reflecting the grid pattern. At its height, the city may have had as many as 80,000 inhabitants, as large as some of the most populous urban centers in Sumerian civilization.

Both Harappa and Mohenjo-Daro were divided into large walled neighborhoods, with narrow lanes separating the rows of houses. Houses varied in size, with some as high as three stories, but all followed the same general plan based on a square courtyard surrounded by rooms. Bathrooms featured an advanced drainage system, which carried wastewater out to drains located under the streets and thence to sewage pits beyond the city walls. But the cities also had the equivalent of the modern slum. At Harappa, tiny dwellings for workers have been found near metal furnaces and the open areas used for pounding grain.

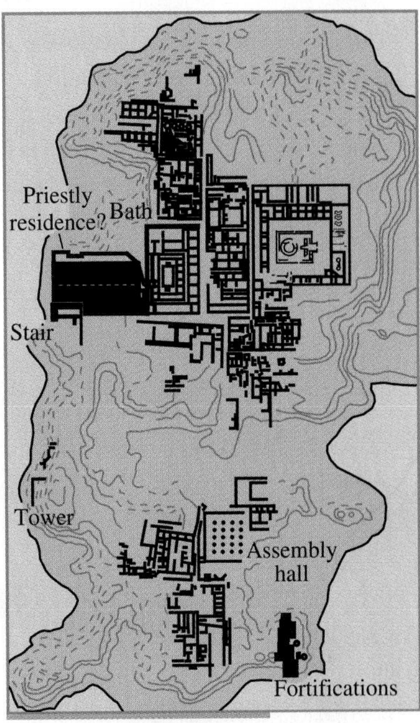


**The City of Mohenjo-Daro**

Unfortunately, Harappan writing has not yet been deciphered, so historians know relatively little about the organization of the Harappan state (see the comparative essay, "Writing and Civilization," on p. 41). However, recent archaeological evidence suggests that unlike its contemporaries in Egypt and Sumer, Harappa was not a centralized monarchy with a theocratic base but a collection of over fifteen hundred towns and cities loosely connected by ties of trade and alliance and ruled by a coalition of landlords and rich merchants. There were no royal precincts or imposing burial monuments, and there are few surviving stone or terra-cotta images that might represent kings, priests, or military commanders. It is possible that religion had advanced beyond the stage of spirit worship to belief in a single god or goddess of fertility. Presumably, priests at court prayed to this deity to maintain the fertility of the soil and guarantee the annual harvest.

As in Mesopotamia and Egypt, the Harappan economy was based primarily on agriculture. Wheat, barley, rice, and peas were apparently the primary crops. The presence of cotton seeds at various sites suggests that the Harappan peoples may have been the first to master the cultivation of this useful crop and possibly introduced it, along with rice, to other societies in the region. But Harappa also developed an extensive trading network that extended to Sumer and other civilizations to the west. Textiles and foodstuffs were apparently imported from Sumer in exchange for metals such as copper, lumber, precious stones, and various types of luxury goods. Much of this trade was conducted by ship via the Persian Gulf, although some undoubtedly went by land.

**Harappan Culture** Archaeological remains indicate that the Indus valley peoples possessed a culture as sophisticated in some ways as that of the Sumerians to the west. Although Harappan architecture was purely functional and shows little artistic sensitivity, the aesthetic quality of some of the pottery and sculpture is superb. Harappan painted pottery, wheel-turned and kiln-fired, rivals equivalent work produced elsewhere. Sculpture, however, was the

**The City of the Dead.** Mohenjo-Daro (below) was one of the two major cities of the ancient Indus River civilization. In addition to rows on rows of residential housing, it had a ceremonial center, with a royal palace and a sacred bath that was probably used by the priests as a means of achieving ritual purity. The bath is reminiscent of water tanks in modern Hindu temples, such as the Minakshi Temple in Madurai (on the right), where the faithful wash their feet prior to religious devotion. Water was an integral part of Hindu temple complexes, as symbolically it represented Vishnu's cosmic ocean and Shiva's reception of the holy Ganges on his head. Psychologically, water was a vital necessity in India's arid climate.

Courtesy of William J. Duiker

© Borromeo/Art Resource NY

© Royal Smeets Offset, Weert

**The Dancing Girl.** Relatively little has survived reflecting the creative talents of the Harappan peoples. This 5-inch bronze figure of a young dancer in repose is one of the few surviving metal sculptures from Mohenjo-Daro. The detail and grace of her stance reflect the skill of the artist who molded her four thousand years ago.

## COMPARATIVE ESSAY

# WRITING AND CIVILIZATION

In the year 3250 B.C.E., King Scorpion of Egypt issued an edict announcing a major victory for his army over rival forces in the region. Inscribed in limestone on a cliff face in the Nile River valley, that edict is perhaps the oldest surviving historical document in the world today.

According to prehistorians, human beings began to create the first spoken language about 50,000 years ago. As human beings spread from Africa to other continents, that first system gradually fragmented into innumerable separate languages. By the time the agricultural revolution began about 10,000 years ago, there were perhaps nearly twenty distinct language families in existence around the world.

During the later stages of the agricultural revolution, the first writing systems also began to be created in various regions around the world. The first successful efforts were apparently achieved in Mesopotamia and Egypt, but knowledge of writing soon spread to peoples along the shores of the Mediterranean and in the Indus River valley in South Asia. Wholly independent systems were also invented in China and Mesoamerica. Writing was used for a variety of purposes. King Scorpion's edict suggests that one reason was to enable a ruler to communicate with his subjects on matters of official concern. In other cases, the purpose was to enable human beings to communicate with supernatural forces. In China and Egypt, for example, priests used writing to communicate with the gods. In Mesopotamia and in the Indus River valley, merchants used writing to record commercial and other legal transactions. Finally, writing was also used to present ideas in new ways, giving rise to such early Mesopotamian literature as *The Epic of Gilgamesh*.

How did such early written languages evolve into the complex systems in use today? In almost all cases, the first systems consisted of pictographs, pictorial images of various concrete objects such as trees, water, cattle, body parts, and the heavenly bodies. Eventually such signs became more stylized to facilitate transcription–much as we often use a cursive script instead of block printing today. Finally, and most important for their future development, these pictorial images began to take on specific phonetic meaning so that they could represent sounds in the written language. Most sophisticated written systems eventually evolved to a phonetic script, based on an alphabet of symbols to represent all sounds in the spoken language, but others went only part way by adding phonetic signs to the individual character to suggest pronunciation while keeping part of the original pictograph to indicate meaning. Most of the latter systems, such as hieroglyphics in Egypt and cuneiform in Mesopotamia, eventually became extinct, but the ancient Chinese writing system survives today, although in changed form.

---

Harappans' highest artistic achievement. Some artifacts possess a wonderful vitality of expression. Fired clay seals show a deft touch in carving animals such as elephants, tigers, rhinoceros, and antelope, and figures made of copper or terra-cotta show a lively sensitivity and a sense of grace and movement that is almost modern.

Writing was another achievement of Harappan society and dates back at least to the beginning of the third millennium B.C.E. (see the comparative essay "Writing and Civilization" above). Unfortunately, the only surviving examples of Harappan writing are the pictographic symbols inscribed on the clay seals. The script contained more than four hundred characters, but most are too stylized to be identified by their shape, and scholars have thus far been unable to decipher them. There are no apparent links with Mesopotamian scripts, although, like the latter, the primary purpose may have been to carry on commercial transactions. Until the script is deciphered, much about the Harappan civilization must remain, as one historian termed it, a fascinating enigma.

**Harappan Seals.** The Harappan peoples, like their contemporaries in Mesopotamia, developed a writing system to record their spoken language. Unfortunately, it has not yet been deciphered. Most extant examples of Harappan writing are found on fired clay seals depicting human figures and animals. These seals have been found in houses and were probably used to identify the owners of goods for sale. Other seals may have been used as amulets or have had other religious significance. Several depict religious figures or ritualistic scenes of sacrifice.

### A Lost Civilization?

Until recently, the area north of the Indus River was presumed to be isolated from the emerging river valley civilizations to the south. But archaeologists have now discovered the remnants of a lost culture there that dates back at least to the late third millennium B.C.E. Bronze Age mudbrick settlements surrounded by irrigated fields have been found along a series of oases that stretch several hundred miles from the Caspian Sea into modern-day Afghanistan. There are also clear indications of the domestication of sheep and goats and of widespread trade with other societies in the region, along with tantalizing hints—in the form of an engraved stone seal found at one site—that the inhabitants of the region were in the process of developing their own form of writing. Although the founders of this mysterious civilization remain unknown, it is now clear that the rudiments of civilization in ancient times were not limited to the great river valleys located on the edges of the African and Asian continents.

## The Arrival of the Aryans

One of the great mysteries of Harappan civilization is how it came to an end. Archaeologists working at Mohenjo-Daro have discovered signs of first a gradual decay and then a sudden destruction of the city and its inhabitants around 1500 B.C.E. Many of the surviving skeletons have been found in postures of running or hiding, reminiscent of the ruins of the Roman city of Pompeii, destroyed by the eruption of Mount Vesuvius in 79 C.E.

These tantalizing signs of flight before a sudden catastrophe once led scholars to surmise that the city of Mohenjo-Daro (the name was applied by archaeologists and means "city of the dead") and perhaps the remnants of Harappan civilization were destroyed by the Aryans, nomads from the north, who arrived in the subcontinent around the middle of the second millennium B.C.E. Although the Aryans were perhaps not as sophisticated culturally as the Harappans, like many nomadic peoples they excelled at the art of war. As in Mesopotamia and the Nile valley, most contacts between pastoral and agricultural peoples proved unstable and often ended in armed conflict. Nevertheless, it is doubtful that the Aryan peoples were directly responsible for the final destruction of Mohenjo-Daro. More likely, Harappan civilization had already fallen on hard times, perhaps as a result of climatic change in the Indus valley. Archaeologists have found clear signs of social decay, including evidence of trash in the streets, neglect of public services, and overcrowding in urban neighborhoods. Mohenjo-Daro itself may have been destroyed by an epidemic or by natural phenomena such as floods, an earthquake, or a shift in the course of the Indus River. If that was the case, the Aryans arrived in the area after the greatness of Harappan civilization had already passed.

### The Early Aryans

Historians know relatively little about the origins and culture of the Aryans before they entered India, although they were part of the extensive group of Indo-European–speaking peoples who inhabited vast areas in what is now Siberia and the steppes of Central Asia. Whereas other Indo-European–speaking peoples moved westward and eventually settled in Europe, the Aryans moved south across the Hindu Kush into the plains of northern India. Between 1500 and 1000 B.C.E., they gradually advanced eastward from the Indus valley, across the fertile plain of the Ganges, and later southward into the Deccan Plateau until they had eventually extended their political mastery over the entire subcontinent and its Dravidian inhabitants, although the indigenous culture survived to remain a prominent element in the evolution of traditional Indian civilization.

After they settled in India, the Aryans gradually adapted to the geographical realities of their new homeland and abandoned the pastoral life for agricultural pursuits. They were assisted by the introduction of iron, which probably came from the Middle East, where it had first been introduced by the Hittites (see Chapter 1) about 1500 B.C.E. The invention of the iron plow, along with the development of irrigation, allowed the Aryans and their indigenous subjects to clear the dense jungle growth along the Ganges River and transform the Ganges valley into one of the richest agricultural regions in all of South Asia. The Aryans also developed their first writing system, based on the Aramaic script in the Middle East, and were thus able to transcribe the legends that previously had been passed down from generation to generation by memory (see Map 2.2). Most of what is known about the early Aryans is based on oral traditions passed on in the Rig Veda, an ancient work that was written down after the Aryans arrived in India (it is one of several Vedas, or collections of sacred instructions and rituals).

As in other Indo-European societies, each of the various Aryan tribes was led by a chieftain, called a ***raja,*** who was assisted by a council of elders composed of other leading members of the tribe; like them, he was normally a member of the warrior class, called the ***kshatriya.*** The chief derived his power from his ability to protect his tribe from rival groups, an ability that was crucial in the warring kingdoms and shifting alliances that were typical of early Aryan society. Though the rajas claimed to be representatives of the gods, they were not viewed as gods themselves (see the box on p. 44).

As Aryan society grew in size and complexity, the chieftains began to be transformed into kings, usually called ***maharajas*** ("great *rajas*"). Nevertheless, the tradition that the ruler did not possess absolute authority remained strong. Like all human beings, the ruler was required to follow the ***dharma,*** a set of laws that set behavioral standards for all individuals and classes in Indian society.

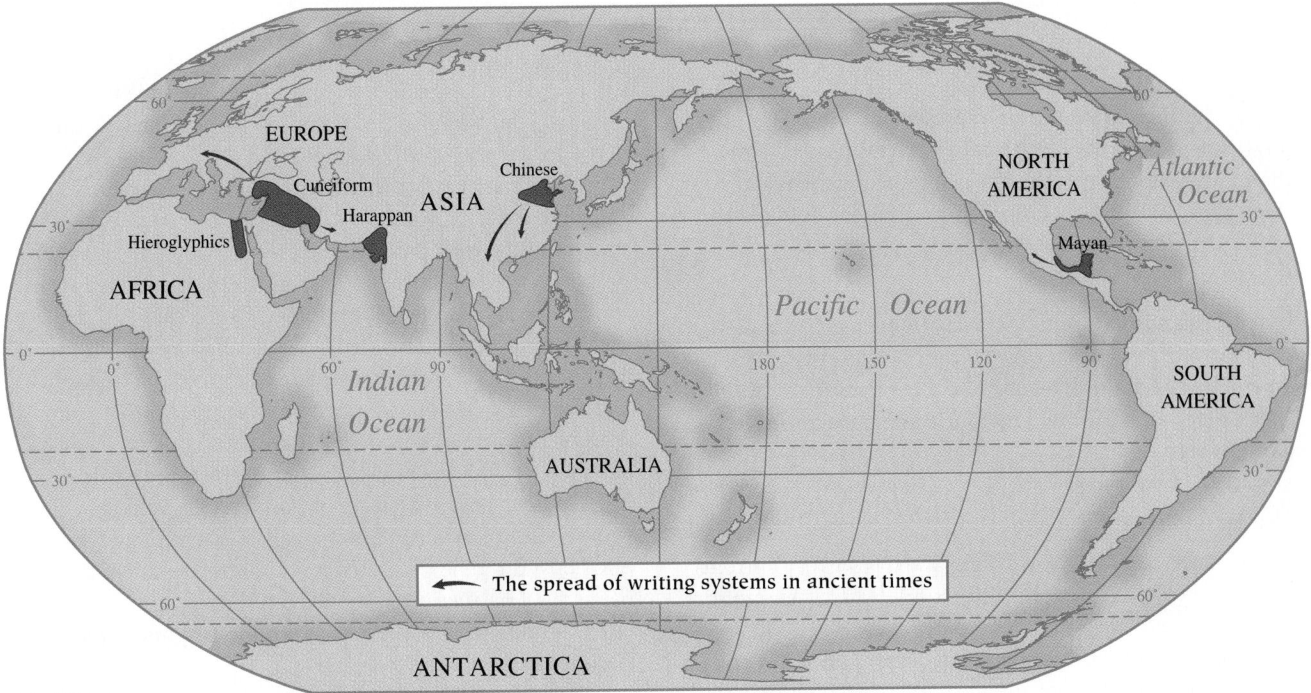


**MAP 2.2 Writing Systems in the Ancient World.** One of the chief characteristics of the first civilizations was the development of a system of written communication. In what ways were these first writing systems similar, and how were they different? **View an animated version of this map or related maps at** http://history.wadsworth.com/duikerspielvogel05/

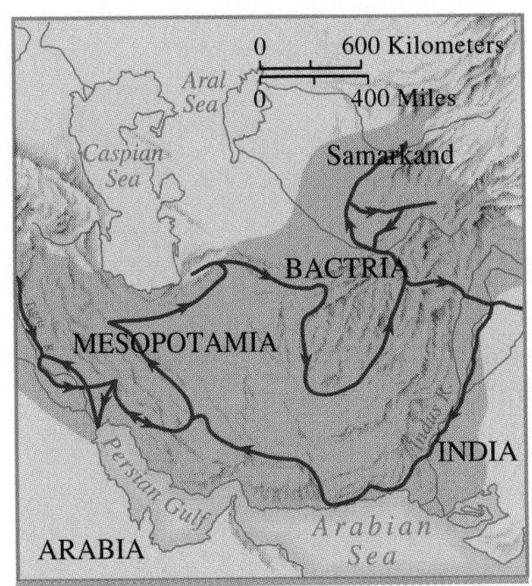


**Alexander the Great's Movements in Asia**

**The Impact of the Greeks** While competing groups squabbled for precedence in India, powerful new empires were rising to the west. First came the Persian Empire of Cyrus and Darius. Then came the Greeks. After two centuries of sporadic rivalry and warfare, the Greeks achieved a brief period of regional dominance in the late fourth century B.C.E. with the rise of Macedonia under Alexander the Great. Alexander had heard of the riches of India, and in 330 B.C.E., after conquering Persia, he launched an invasion of the east (see Chapter 4). In 326, his armies arrived in the plains of northwestern India and the Indus River valley. They departed almost as suddenly as they had come, leaving in their wake Greek administrators and a veneer of cultural influence that would affect the area for generations to come.

## The Mauryan Empire

The Alexandrian conquest was only a brief interlude in the history of the Indian subcontinent, but it played a formative role, for on the heels of Alexander's departure came the rise of the first dynasty to control much of the region. The founder of the new state, who took the royal title Chandragupta Maurya (324–301 B.C.E.), drove out the Greek administrators who had remained after the departure of Alexander and solidified his control over the northern Indian plain. He established the capital of his new Mauryan Empire at Pataliputra (modern Patna) in the Ganges valley (see the map on p. 56). Little is known of his origins, although some sources say he had originally fought on the side of the invading Greek forces but then angered Alexander with his outspoken advice.

Little, too, is known of Chandragupta Maurya's empire. Most accounts of his reign rely on a lost work written by Megasthenes, a Greek ambassador to the Mauryan court, in about 302 B.C.E. Chandragupta Maurya was apparently advised by a brilliant court official named Kautilya, whose name has been attached to a treatise on politics called the *Arthasastra* (see the box on p. 45). The work actually dates from a later time, but it may well reflect Kautilya's ideas.

Although the author of the *Arthasastra* follows Aryan tradition in stating that the happiness of the king lies in the happiness of his subjects, the treatise also asserts that when the sacred law of the *dharma* and practical politics collide, the latter must take precedence: "Whenever there is disagreement between history and sacred law or between evidence and sacred law, then the matter should be settled in accordance with sacred law. But whenever sacred law is in conflict with rational law, then reason

## The Origins of Kingship

Both India and China had a concept of a golden age in the remote past that provided a model for later governments and peoples to emulate. This passage from the famous Indian epic the Mahabharata describes a three-stage process in the evolution of government in human society. Yudhishthira and Bhishma are two of the main characters in the story.

*What is the author's purpose here? How does this vision compare with the views then current on the reasons for the emergence of political leadership? How does it compare with Chinese theories regarding the Mandate of Heaven (see Chapter 3)?*

### The Mahabharata

Yudhisthira said: "This word 'king' [raja] is so very current in this world, O Bharata; how has it originated? Tell me that O grandfather."

Bhishma said: "Currently, O best among men, do you listen to everything in its entirety–how kingship originated first during the golden age [krtayuga]. Neither kingship nor king was there in the beginning, neither scepter [danda] nor the bearer of a scepter. All people protected one another by means of righteous conduct, O Bharata, men eventually fell into a state of spiritual lassitude. Then delusion overcame them. Men were thus overpowered by infatuation, O leader of men, on account of the delusion of understanding; their sense of righteous conduct was lost. When understanding was lost, all men, O best of the Bharatas, overpowered by infatuation, became victims of greed. Then they sought to acquire what should not be acquired. Thereby, indeed, O lord, another vice, namely, desire overcame them. Attachment then attacked them, who had become victims of desire. Attached to objects of sense, they did not discriminate between what should be said and what should not be said, between the edible and inedible and between right and wrong. When this world of men had been submerged in dissipation, all spiritual knowledge [brahman] perished; and when spiritual knowledge perished, O king, righteous conduct also perished."

When spiritual knowledge and righteous conduct perished, the gods were overcome with fear, and fearfully sought refuge with Brahma, the creator. Going to the great lord, the ancestor of the worlds, all the gods, afflicted with sorrow, misery, and fear, with folded hands said: "O Lord, the eternal spiritual knowledge, which had existed in the world of men, has perished because of greed, infatuation, and the like, therefore we have become fearful. Through the loss of spiritual knowledge, righteous conduct also has perished, O God. Therefore, O Lord of the three worlds, mortals have reached a state of indifference. Verily, we showered rain on earth, but mortals showered rain [i.e., oblations] up to heaven. As a result of the cessation of ritual activity on their part, we faced a serious peril. O grandfather, decide what is most beneficial to use under these circumstances."

Then, the self-born lord said to all those gods: "I will consider what is most beneficial; let your fear depart, O leaders of the gods."

Thereupon he composed a work consisting of a hundred thousand chapters out of his own mind, wherein righteous conduct [dharma], as well as material gain [artha] and enjoyment of sensual pleasures [kama] were described. This group, known as the threefold classification of human objectives, was expounded by the self-born lord; so, too, a fourth objective, spiritual emancipation [moksha], which aims at a different goal, and which constitutes a separate group by itself.

Then the gods approached Vishnu, the lord of creatures, and said: "Indicate to us that one person among mortals who alone is worthy of the highest eminence." Then the blessed lord god Narayana reflected, and brought forth an illustrious mind-born son, called Virajas [who, in this version of the origins of the Indian state, became the first king].

shall be held authoritative."[1] The *Arthasastra* also emphasizes ends rather than means, achieved results rather than the methods employed. For this reason, it has often been compared to Machiavelli's famous political treatise of the Italian Renaissance, *The Prince,* written more than a thousand years later (see Chapter 14).

As described in the *Arthasastra,* Chandragupta Maurya's government was highly centralized and even despotic: "It is power and power alone which, only when exercised by the king with impartiality, and in proportion to guilt, over his son or his enemy, maintains both this world and the next."[2] The king possessed a large army and a secret police responsible to his orders (according to the Greek ambassador Megasthenes, Chandragupta Maurya was chronically fearful of assassination, a not unrealistic concern for someone who had allegedly come to power by violence). Reportedly, all food was tasted in his presence, and he made a practice of never sleeping twice in the same bed in his sumptuous palace. To guard against corruption, a board of censors was empowered to investigate cases of possible malfeasance and incompetence within the bureaucracy.

The ruler's authority beyond the confines of the capital may often have been limited, however. The empire

## The Duties of a King

Kautilya, India's earliest known political philosopher, was an adviser to the Mauryan rulers. The *Arthasastra,* though written down at a later date, very likely reflects his ideas. This passage sets forth some of the necessary characteristics of a king, including efficiency, diligence, energy, compassion, and concern for the security and welfare of the state. In emphasizing the importance of results rather than motives, Kautilya resembles the Italian Renaissance thinker Machiavelli. But in focusing on winning popular support as the means of becoming an effective ruler, the author echoes the view of the Chinese philosopher Mencius, who declared that the best way to win the empire is to win the people (see Chapter 3).

*To whom was the author of this document directing his advice? How do the ideas expressed here compare with political thinkers during the time of Confucius in China and of Socrates and Plato in Classical Greece?*

### The *Arthasastra*

Only if a king is himself energetically active do his officers follow him energetically. If he is sluggish, they too remain sluggish. And, besides, they eat up his works. He is thereby easily overpowered by his enemies. Therefore, he should ever dedicate himself energetically to activity. . . .

A king should attend to all urgent business; he should not put it off. For what has been thus put off becomes either difficult or altogether impossible to accomplish.

The vow of the king is energetic activity; his sacrifice is constituted of the discharge of his own administrative duties; his sacrificial fee [to the officiating priests] is his impartiality of attitude toward all; his sacrificial consecration is his anointment as king.

In the happiness of the subjects lies the happiness of the king; in their welfare, his own welfare. The welfare of the king does not lie in the fulfillment of what is dear to him; whatever is dear to the subjects constitutes his welfare.

Therefore, ever energetic, a king should act up to the precepts of the science of material gain. Energetic activity is the source of material gain; its opposite, of downfall.

In the absence of energetic activity, the loss of what has already been obtained and of what still remains to be obtained is certain. The fruit of one's works is achieved through energetic activity–one obtains abundance of material prosperity.

was divided into provinces that were ruled by governors. At first, most of these governors were appointed by and reported to the ruler, but later the position became hereditary. The provinces themselves were divided into districts, each under a chief magistrate appointed by the governor. At the base of the government pyramid was the village, where the vast majority of the Indian people lived. The village was governed by a council of elders; membership in the council was normally hereditary and was shared by the wealthiest families in the village.

## Caste and Class: Social Structures in Ancient India

When the Aryans arrived in India, they already possessed a social system based on a ruling warrior class and other groupings characteristic of a pastoral society. In India, they encountered peoples living in an agricultural society and assigned them a lower position in the community. The result was a set of social institutions and class divisions that have persisted with only minor changes down to the present day.

**The Class System** At the base of the social system that emerged from the clash of cultures was the concept of the superiority of the invading peoples over their conquered subjects. In a sense, it became an issue of color, because the Aryan invaders, a primarily light-skinned people, were contemptuous of their subjects, who were dark. Light skin came to imply high status, whereas dark skin suggested the opposite.

The concept of color, however, was only the physical manifestation of a division that took place in Indian society on the basis of economic functions. Indian classes (called ***varna,*** literally, "color," and commonly but mistakenly known as "castes" in English) did not simply reflect an informal division of labor. Instead, at least in theory they were a set of rigid social classifications that determined not only one's occupation but also one's status in society and one's hope for ultimate salvation (see "Escaping the Wheel of Life" later in this chapter). There were five major *varna* in Indian society in ancient times (see the box on p. 46). At the top were two classes, collectively viewed as the aristocracy, which represented the ruling elites in Aryan society prior to their arrival in India: the priests and the warriors.

The priestly class, known as the ***brahmins,*** was usually considered to be at the top of the social scale. Descended from seers who had advised the ruler on religious matters in Aryan tribal society (*brahmin* meant "one possessed of ***Brahman,***" a term for the supreme god in the Hindu religion), they were eventually transformed

## Social Classes in Ancient India

*The Law of Manu* is a set of behavioral norms allegedly prescribed by India's mythical founding ruler, Manu. The treatise was probably written in the first or second century B.C.E. The following excerpt describes the various social classes in India and their prescribed duties. Many scholars doubt that the social system in India was ever as rigid as it was portrayed here, and some suggest that upper-class Indians may have used the idea of *varna* to enhance their own status in society.

*How might the class system in ancient India, as described here, be compared with social class divisions in other societies in Asia? Why do you think the class system as described here developed in India? What is the difference between the class system* (varna) *and the* jati?

### The Law of Manu

For the sake of the preservation of this entire creation, the Exceedingly Resplendent One [the Creator of the Universe] assigned separate duties to the classes which had sprung from his mouth, arms, thighs, and feet.

Teaching, studying, performing sacrificial rites, so too making others perform sacrificial rites, and giving away and receiving gifts—these he assigned to the [*brahmins*].

Protection of the people, giving away of wealth, performance of sacrificial rites, study, and nonattachment to sensual pleasures—these are, in short, the duties of a *kshatriya*.

Tending of cattle, giving away of wealth, performance of sacrificial rites, study, trade and commerce, usury, and agriculture—these are the occupations of a *vaisya*.

The Lord has prescribed only one occupation [*karma*] for a *sudra*, namely, service without malice of even these other three classes.

Of created beings, those which are animate are the best; of the animate, those which subsist by means of their intellect; of the intelligent, men are the best; and of men, the [brahmins] are traditionally declared to be the best.

The code of conduct—prescribed by scriptures and ordained by sacred tradition—constitutes the highest *dharma;* hence a twice-born person, conscious of his own Self [seeking spiritual salvation], should be always scrupulous in respect of it.

**HistoryNow™** To read a full version of *The Law of Manu*, enter the *HistoryNow* documents area using the access card that is available for *World History*.

into an official class after their religious role declined in importance. Megasthenes described this class as follows:

> From the time of their conception in the womb they are under the care and guardianship of learned men who go to the mother and . . . give her prudent hints and counsels, and the women who listen to them most willingly are thought to be the most fortunate in their offspring. After their birth the children are in the care of one person after another, and as they advance in years their masters are men of superior accomplishments. The philosophers reside in a grove in front of the city within a moderate-sized enclosure. They live in a simple style and lie on pallets of straw and [deer] skins. They abstain from animal food and sexual pleasures, and occupy their time in listening to serious discourse and in imparting knowledge to willing ears.[3]

The second class was the *kshatriya*, the warriors. Although often listed below the *brahmins* in social status, many *kshatriyas* were probably descended from the ruling warrior class in Aryan society prior to the conquest of India and thus may have originally ranked socially above the *brahmins*, although they were ranked lower in religious terms. Like the *brahmins*, the *kshatriyas* were originally identified with a single occupation—fighting—but as the character of Aryan society changed, they often switched to other forms of employment. At the same time, new conquering families from other classes were sometimes tacitly accepted into the ranks of the warriors.

The third-ranked class in Indian society was the ***vaisya*** (literally, "commoner"). The *vaisyas* were usually viewed in economic terms as the merchant class. Some historians have speculated that the *vaisyas* were originally guardians of the tribal herds but that after settling in India, many moved into commercial pursuits. Megasthenes noted that members of this class "alone are permitted to hunt and keep cattle and to sell beasts of burden or to let them out on hire. In return for clearing the land of wild beasts and birds which infest sown fields, they receive an allowance of corn from the king. They lead a wandering life and dwell in tents."[4] Although this class was ranked below the first two in social status, it shared with them the privilege of being considered **"twice-born,"** a term referring to a ceremony at puberty whereby young males were initiated into adulthood and introduced into Indian society. After the ceremony, male members of the top three classes were allowed to wear the "sacred thread" for the remainder of their lives.

Below the three "twice-born" classes were the ***sudras,*** who represented the great bulk of the Indian population. The *sudras* were not considered fully Aryan, and the term probably originally referred to the indigenous population. Most *sudras* were peasants or artisans or worked at other forms of manual labor. They had only limited rights in society. In recent years, DNA samples have revealed that most upper-class South Indians share more genetic characteristics with Europeans than their lower-class counterparts do, thus tending to confirm the hypothesis that the Aryans established their political and social dominance over the indigenous population.

At the lowest level of Indian society, and in fact not even considered a legitimate part of the class system itself, were the untouchables (also known as outcastes, or **pariahs**). The untouchables probably originated as a slave class consisting of prisoners of war, criminals, ethnic minorities, and other groups considered outside Indian society. Even after slavery was outlawed, the untouchables were given menial and degrading tasks that other Indians would not accept, such as collecting trash, handling dead bodies, or serving as butchers or tanners (handling dead meat). According to the estimate of one historian, they may have accounted for a little more than 5 percent of the total population of India in antiquity.

The life of the untouchables was extremely demeaning. They were not considered human, and their very presence was considered polluting to members of the other *varna.* No Indian would touch or eat food handled or prepared by an untouchable. Untouchables lived in special ghettos and were required to tap two sticks together to announce their presence when they traveled outside their quarters so that others could avoid them.

Technically, these class divisions were absolute. Individuals supposedly were born, lived, and died in the same class. In practice, upward or downward mobility probably took place, and there was undoubtedly some flexibility in economic functions. But throughout most of Indian history, class taboos remained strict. Members were generally not permitted to marry outside their class (although in practice, men were occasionally allowed to marry below their class but not above it). At first, attitudes toward the handling of food were relatively loose, but eventually that taboo grew stronger, and social mores dictated that sharing meals and marrying outside one's class were unacceptable.

**The *Jati*** The people of ancient India did not belong to a particular class as individuals but as part of a larger kin group commonly referred to as the ***jati*** (in Portuguese, *casta,* which evolved into the English term *caste*), a system of extended families that originated in ancient India and still exists in somewhat changed form today. Although the origins of the *jati* system are unknown (there are no indications of strict class distinctions in Harappan society), the *jati* eventually became identified with a specific kinship group living in a specific area and carrying out a specific function in society. Each *jati* was identified with a particular *varna,* and each had its own separate economic function.

*Jatis* were thus the basic social organization into which traditional Indian society was divided. Each *jati* was itself composed of hundreds or thousands of individual nuclear families and was governed by its own council of elders. Membership in this ruling council was usually hereditary and was based on the wealth or social status of particular families within the community.

**CHRONOLOGY** **Ancient India**

| | |
|---|---|
| Harappan civilization | c. 2600–1900 B.C.E. |
| Arrival of the Aryans | c. 1500 B.C.E. |
| Life of Gautama Buddha | c. 560–480 B.C.E. |
| Invasion of India by Alexander the Great | 326 B.C.E. |
| Mauryan dynasty founded | 324 B.C.E. |
| Reign of Chandragupta Maurya | 324–301 B.C.E. |
| Reign of Ashoka | 269–232 B.C.E. |
| Collapse of Mauryan dynasty | 183 B.C.E. |
| Rise of Kushan kingdom | c. first century C.E. |

In theory, each *jati* was assigned a particular form of economic activity. Obviously, though, not all families in a given *jati* could take part in the same vocation, and as time went on, members of a single *jati* commonly engaged in several different lines of work. Sometimes an entire *jati* would have to move its location in order to continue a particular form of activity. In other cases, a *jati* would adopt an entirely new occupation in order to remain in a certain area. Such changes in habitat or occupation introduced the possibility of movement up or down the social scale. In this way, an entire *jati* could sometimes engage in upward mobility, even though it was not normally possible for individuals, who were tied to their class identity for life.

The class system in ancient India may sound highly constricting, but there were persuasive social and economic reasons why it survived for so many centuries. In the first place, it provided an identity for individuals in a highly hierarchical society. Although an individual might rank lower on the social scale than members of other classes, it was always possible to find others ranked even lower. Class was also a means for new groups, such as mountain tribal people, to achieve a recognizable place in the broader community. Perhaps equally important, the *jati* was a primitive form of welfare system. Each was obliged to provide for any of its members who were poor or destitute. It also provided an element of stability in a society that all too often was in a state of political turmoil.

## Daily Life in Ancient India

Beyond these rigid social stratifications was the Indian family. Not only was life centered around the family, but the family, not the individual, was the most basic unit in society.

**The Family** The ideal social unit was an extended family, with three generations living under the same roof. It was essentially patriarchal, except along the Malabar coast, near the southwestern tip of the subcontinent, where a matriarchal form of social organization prevailed down to modern times. In the rest of India, the oldest male traditionally possessed legal authority over the entire family unit.

The family was linked together in a religious sense by a series of commemorative rites to ancestral members. This ritual consisted of family ceremonies to honor the departed and to link the living and the dead. The male family head was responsible for leading the ritual. At his death, his eldest son had the duty of conducting the funeral rites.

The importance of the father and the son in family ritual underlined the importance of males in Indian society. Male superiority was expressed in a variety of ways. Women could not serve as priests (although some were accepted as seers), nor were they normally permitted to study the Vedas. In general, males had a monopoly on education, since the primary goal of learning to read was to carry on family rituals. In high-class families, young men, after having been initiated into the sacred thread, began Vedic studies with a ***guru*** (teacher). Some then went on to higher studies in one of the major cities. The goal of such an education might be either professional or religious. Such young men were not supposed to marry until after twelve years of study.

**Marriage** In general, only males could inherit property, except in a few cases where there were no sons. According to law, a woman was always considered a minor. Divorce was prohibited, although it sometimes took place. According to the *Arthasastra*, a wife who had been deserted by her husband could seek a divorce. Polygamy was fairly rare and apparently occurred mainly among the higher classes, but husbands were permitted to take a second wife if the first was barren. Producing children was an important aspect of marriage, both because children provided security for their parents in old age and because they were a physical proof of male potency. Child marriage was common for young girls, whether because of the desire for children or because daughters represented an economic liability to their parents. But perhaps the most graphic symbol of women's subjection to men was the ritual of ***sati*** (often written *suttee*), which required the wife to throw herself on her dead husband's funeral pyre. The Greek visitor Megasthenes reported "that he had heard from some persons of wives burning themselves along with their deceased husbands and doing so gladly; and that those women who refused to burn themselves were held in disgrace."[5] All in all, it was undoubtedly a difficult existence. According to the *Law of Manu*, an early treatise on social organization and behavior in ancient India, probably written in the first or second century B.C.E., women were subordinated to men—first to their father, then to their husband, and finally to their sons:

*She should do nothing independently*
*even in her own house.*
*In childhood subject to her father,*
*in youth to her husband,*
*and when her husband is dead to her sons,*
*she should never enjoy independence. . . .*

*She should always be cheerful,*
*and skillful in her domestic duties,*
*with her household vessels well cleansed,*
*and her hand tight on the purse strings. . . .*

*Though he be uncouth and prone to pleasure,*
*though he have no good points at all,*
*the virtuous wife should ever*
*worship her lord as a god.*[6]

**The Role of Women** At the root of female subordination to the male was the practical fact that as in most agricultural societies, men did most of the work in the fields. Females were viewed as having little utility outside the home and indeed were considered an economic burden, since parents were obliged to provide a dowry to acquire a husband for a daughter. Female children also appeared to offer little advantage in maintaining the family unit, since they joined the families of their husbands after the wedding ceremony.

Despite all of these indications of female subjection to the male, there are numerous signs that in some ways women often played an influential role in Indian society, and the Hindu code of behavior stressed that they should be treated with respect. Indians appeared to be fascinated by female sexuality, and tradition held that women often used their sexual powers to achieve domination over men. The author of the Mahabharata, a vast epic of early Indian society, complained that "the fire has never too many logs, the ocean never too many rivers, death never too many living souls, and fair-eyed woman never too many men." Despite the legal and social constraints, women often played an important role within the family unit, and many were admired and honored for their talents. It is probably significant that paintings and sculpture from ancient and medieval India frequently show women in a role equal to that of men, and the tradition of the henpecked husband is as prevalent in India as in many Western societies.

## The Economy

The Aryan conquest did not drastically change the economic character of Indian society. Not only did most Aryans take up farming, but it is likely that agriculture expanded rapidly under Aryan rule with the invention of the iron plow and the spread of northern Indian culture into the Deccan Plateau. One consequence of this process was to shift the focus of Indian culture from the Indus valley farther eastward to the Ganges River valley, which even today is one of the most densely populated regions on earth. The flatter areas in the Deccan Plateau and in the coastal plains were also turned into cropland.

**Indian Farmers** For most Indian farmers, life was harsh. Among the most fortunate were those who owned their own land, although they were required to pay taxes to the state. Many others were sharecroppers or landless laborers. They were subject to the vicissitudes of the market and often paid exorbitant rents to their landlord. Concentration of land in large holdings was limited by the tradition of dividing property among all the sons, but large estates worked by hired laborers or rented out to sharecroppers were not uncommon, particularly in areas where local *rajas* derived much of their wealth from their property.

Another problem for Indian farmers was the unpredictability of the climate. India is in the monsoon zone. The monsoon is a seasonal wind pattern in southern Asia that blows from the southwest during the summer months and from the northeast during the winter. The southwest monsoon is commonly marked by heavy rains. When the rains were late, thousands starved, particularly in the drier areas, which were especially dependent on rainfall. Strong governments attempted to deal with such problems by building state-operated granaries and maintaining the irrigation works, but strong governments were rare, and famine was probably all too common. The staple crops in the north were wheat, barley, and millet, with wet rice common in the fertile river valleys. In the south, grain and vegetables were supplemented by various tropical products, cotton, and spices such as pepper, ginger, cinnamon, and saffron.

**Trade and Manufacturing** By no means were all Indians farmers. As time passed, India became one of the most advanced trading and manufacturing civilizations in the ancient world. After the rise of the Mauryas, India's role in regional trade began to expand, and the subcontinent became a major transit point in a vast commercial network that extended from the rim of the Pacific to the Middle East and the Mediterranean Sea. This regional trade went both by sea and by camel caravan. Maritime trade across the Indian Ocean may have begun as early as the fifth century B.C.E. It extended eastward as far as Southeast Asia and China and southward as far as the straits between Africa and the island of Madagascar. Westward to Egypt, on ships carrrying up to 1,000 tons in cargo, went spices, teakwood, perfumes, jewels, textiles, precious stones and ivory, and wild animals. In return, India received gold, tin, lead, and wine. The subcontinent had become a major crossroads of trade in the ancient world.

India's expanding role as a manufacturing and commercial hub was undoubtedly a spur to the growth of the state. Under Chandragupta Maurya, the central government became actively involved in commercial and manufacturing activities. It owned mines and land and undoubtedly earned massive profits from its role in regional commerce. Separate government departments were established for trade, agriculture, mining, and the manufacture of weapons, and the movement of private goods was vigorously taxed. Nevertheless, a significant private sector also flourished; it was dominated by great caste guilds, which monopolized key sectors of the economy. A money economy probably came into operation during the second century B.C.E., when copper and gold coins were introduced from the Middle East. This in turn led to the development of banking. But village trade continued to be conducted by means of cowry shells (highly polished shells used as a medium of exchange throughout much of Africa and Asia) or barter throughout the ancient period.

## Escaping the Wheel of Life: The Religious World of Ancient India

Like Indian politics and society, Indian religion is a blend of Aryan and Dravidian culture. The intermingling of those two civilizations gave rise to an extraordinarily complex set of religious beliefs and practices, filled with diversity and contrast. Out of this cultural mix came two of the world's great religions, Buddhism and **Hinduism,** and several smaller ones, including Jainism and Sikhism.

### Hinduism

Evidence about the earliest religious beliefs of the Aryan peoples comes primarily from sacred texts such as the Vedas, a set of four collections of hymns and religious

Courtesy of William J. Duiker

**Dancing Shiva.** The Hindu deity Shiva is often presented in the form of a bronze statue, performing a cosmic dance in which he simultaneously creates and destroys the universe. While his upper right hand creates the cosmos, his upper left hand reduces it in flames, and the lower two hands offer eternal blessing. Shiva's dancing statues present to his followers the visual message of his power and compassion.

## In The Beginning

As Indians began to speculate about the nature of the cosmic order, they came to believe in the existence of a single monistic force in the universe, a form of ultimate reality called *Brahman*. Today the early form of Hinduism is sometimes called Brahmanism. In the Upanishads, the concept began to emerge as an important element of Indian religious belief. It was the duty of the individual self—called the *Atman*—to achieve an understanding of this ultimate reality so that after death the self would merge in spiritual form with *Brahman*. Sometimes *Brahman* was described in more concrete terms as a creator god—eventually known as Vishnu—but more often in terms of a shadowy ultimate reality. In the following passage from the Upanishads, the author speculates on the nature of ultimate reality.

*How does this concept of the origins of the universe compare with versions proposed in other early civilizations? How does it compare with metaphysical explanations in Buddhism?*

### The Upanishads

In the beginning . . . , this world was just being, one only, without a second. Some people, no doubt, say: "In the beginning . . . , this world was just nonbeing, one only, without a second; from that nonbeing, being was produced." But how indeed . . . could it be so? How could being be produced from nonbeing? . . .

In the beginning this world was being alone, one only, without a second. Being thought to itself: "May I be many, may I procreate." It produced fire. That fire thought to itself: "May I be many, may I procreate." It produced water. Therefore, whenever a person grieves or perspires, then it is from fire [heat] alone that water is produced. That water thought to itself: "May I be many, may I procreate." It produced food; it is from water alone that food for eating is produced. . . . That divinity [Being] thought to itself: "Well, having entered into these three divinities [fire, water, and food] by means of this living self, let me develop names and forms.

HistoryNow™ To read more of the Upanishads, enter the *HistoryNow* documents area using the access card that is available for *World History*.

ceremonies transmitted by memory through the centuries by Aryan priests. Many of these religious ideas were probably common to all of the Indo-European peoples before their separation into different groups at least four thousand years ago. Early Aryan beliefs were based on the common concept of a pantheon of gods and goddesses representing great forces of nature similar to the immortals of Greek mythology. The Aryan ancestor of the Greek father-god Zeus, for example, may have been the deity known in early Aryan tradition as Dyaus (see Chapter 4).

The parent god Dyaus was a somewhat distant figure, however, who was eventually overshadowed by other, more functional gods possessing more familiar human traits. For a while, the primary Aryan god was the great warrior god Indra. Indra summoned the Aryan tribal peoples to war and was represented in nature by thunder. Later, Indra declined in importance and was replaced by Varuna, lord of justice. Other gods and goddesses represented various forces of nature or the needs of human beings, such as fire, fertility, and wealth (see the box above).

The concept of sacrifice was a key element in Aryan religious belief in Vedic times. As in many other ancient cultures, the practice may have begun as human sacrifice, but later animals were used as substitutes. The priestly class, the *brahmins*, played a key role in these ceremonies.

Another element of Indian religious belief in ancient times was the ideal of *asceticism*. Although there is no reference to such practices in the Vedas, by the sixth century B.C.E., self-discipline or subjecting oneself to painful stimuli had begun to replace sacrifice as a means of placating or communicating with the gods. Apparently, the original motive for asceticism was to achieve magical powers, but later, in the Upanishads (a set of commentaries on the Vedas compiled in the sixth century B.C.E.), it was seen as a means of spiritual meditation that would enable the practitioner to reach beyond material reality to a world of truth and bliss beyond earthly joy and sorrow: "Those who practice penance and faith in the forest, the tranquil ones, the knowers of truth, living the life of wandering mendicancy—they depart, freed from passion, through the door of the sun, to where dwells, verily . . . the imperishable Soul."[7] It is possible that another motive was to permit those with strong religious convictions to communicate directly with metaphysical reality without having to rely on the priestly class at court.

Asceticism, of course, has been practiced in other religions, including Christianity and Islam, but it seems particularly identified with Hinduism, the religion that emerged from early Indian religious tradition. Eventually, asceticism evolved into the modern practice of body training that we know as *yoga* (union), which is accepted today as a meaningful element of Hindu religious practice.

**Reincarnation** Another new concept also probably began to appear around the time the Upanishads were written—the idea of **reincarnation.** This is the idea that the individual soul is reborn in a different form after death and progresses through several existences on the wheel of life until it reaches its final destination in a union with the Great World Soul, *Brahman.* Because life is harsh, this final release is the objective of all living souls. From this concept comes the term *Brahmanism,* referring to the early form of Aryan religious tradition.

A key element in this process is the idea of ***karma***—that one's rebirth in a next life is determined by one's *karma* (actions) in this life. Hinduism, as it emerged from Brahmanism, placed all living species on a vast scale of existence, including the four classes and the untouchables in human society. The current status of an individual soul, then, is not simply a cosmic accident but the inevitable result of actions that that soul has committed in a past existence.

At the top of the scale are the *brahmins,* who by definition are closest to ultimate release from the law of reincarnation. The *brahmins* are followed in descending order by the other classes in human society and the world of the beasts. Within the animal kingdom, an especially high position is reserved for the cow, which even today is revered by Hindus as a sacred beast. Some have speculated that the unique role played by the cow in Hinduism derives from the value of cattle in Aryan pastoral society. But others have pointed out that cattle were a source of both money and food and suggest that the cow's sacred position may have descended from the concept of the sacred bull in Harappan culture.

The concept of *karma* is governed by the *dharma,* or the law. A law regulating human behavior, the *dharma* imposes different requirements on different individuals depending on their status in society. Those high on the social scale, such as *brahmins* and *kshatriyas,* are held to a stricter form of behavior than *sudras* are. The *brahmin,* for example, is expected to abstain from eating meat, because that would entail the killing of another living being, thus interrupting its *karma.*

How the concept of reincarnation originated is not known, although it was apparently not unusual for early peoples to believe that the individual soul would be reborn in a different form in a later life. In any case, in India the concept may have had practical causes as well as consequences. In the first place, it tended to provide religious sanction for the rigid class divisions that had begun to emerge in Indian society after the Aryan conquest, and it provided moral and political justification for the privileges of those on the higher end of the scale.

At the same time, the concept of reincarnation provided certain compensations for those lower on the ladder of life. For example, it gave hope to the poor that if they behaved properly in this life, they might improve their condition in the next. It also provided a means for unassimilated groups such as ethnic minorities to find a place in Indian society while at the same time permitting them to maintain their distinctive way of life.

The ultimate goal of achieving "good" *karma,* as we have seen, was to escape the cycle of existence. To the sophisticated, the nature of that release was a spiritual union of the individual soul with the Great World Soul, *Brahman,* described in the Upanishads as a form of dreamless sleep, free from earthly desires. Such a concept, however, was undoubtedly too ethereal for the average Indian, who needed a more concrete form of heavenly salvation, a place of beauty and bliss after a life of disease and privation.

**Hindu Gods and Goddesses** It was probably for this reason that the Hindu religion—in some ways so otherworldly and ascetic—came to be peopled with a multitude of very human gods and goddesses. It has been estimated that the Hindu pantheon contains more than 33,000 deities. Only a small number are primary ones, however, notably the so-called trinity of gods: Brahman the Creator, Vishnu the Preserver, and Shiva (originally the Vedic god Rudra) the Destroyer. Although Brahman (sometimes in his concrete form called Brahma) is considered to be the highest god, Vishnu and Shiva take precedence in the devotional exercises of many Hindus, who can be roughly divided into Vishnuites and Shaivites. In addition to the trinity of gods, all of whom have wives with readily identifiable roles and personalities, there are countless minor deities, each again with his or her own specific function, such as bringing good fortune, arranging a good marriage, or guaranteeing a son in childbirth.

The rich variety and earthy character of many Hindu deities is somewhat misleading, however, for Hindus regard the multitude of gods as simply different manifestations of one ultimate reality. The various deities also provide a useful means for ordinary Indians to personify their religious feelings. Even though some individuals among the early Aryans attempted to communicate with the gods through animal sacrifice or asceticism, most Indians undoubtedly sought to satisfy their own individual religious needs through devotion, which they expressed through ritual ceremonies and offerings at a Hindu temple. Such offerings were not only a way to seek salvation but also a means of satisfying all the aspirations of daily life.

Over the centuries, then, Hinduism changed radically from its origins in Aryan tribal society and became a religion of the vast majority of the Indian people. Concern with a transcendental union between the individual soul and the Great World Soul contrasted with practical desires for material wealth and happiness; ascetic self-denial contrasted with an earthy emphasis on the pleasures and values of sexual union between marriage partners. All of these became aspects of Hinduism, the religion of 70 percent of the Indian people.

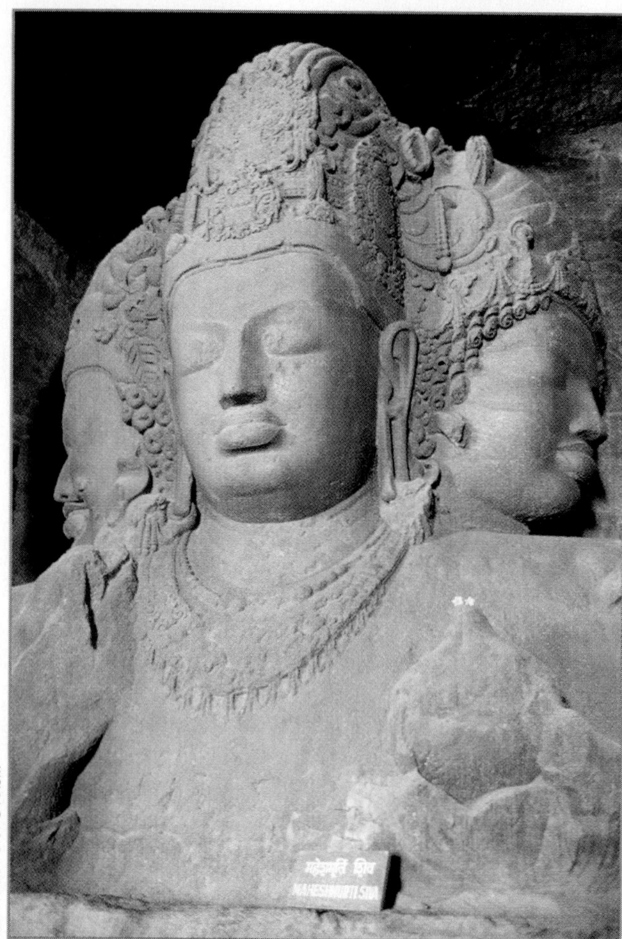


ACSAA slide # 3101 © AAUM

**The Three Faces of Shiva.** In the first centuries of the first millennium C.E., Hindus began to adopt Buddhist rock art. One of the most outstanding examples is at the Elephanta Caves, near the modern city of Mumbai (Bombay). Dominating the cave is this 18-foot-high triple-headed statue of Shiva, representing the Hindu deity in all his various aspects. The central figure presents him in total serenity, enveloped in absolute knowledge. The angry profile on the left portrays him as the destroyer, struggling against time, death, and other negative forces. The right-hand profile shows his loving and feminine side in the guise of his beautiful wife Parvati.

## Buddhism: The Middle Path

In the sixth century B.C.E., a new doctrine appeared in northern India that would eventually begin to rival Hinduism's growing popularity throughout the subcontinent. This new doctrine was called Buddhism.

**The Life of Siddhartha Gautama** The historical founder of **Buddhism,** Siddhartha Gautama, was a native of a small principality in the foothills of the Himalaya Mountains in what is today southern Nepal. He was born in the mid-sixth century B.C.E., the son of a ruling *kshatriya* family. According to tradition, the young Siddhartha was raised in affluent surroundings and trained, like many other members of his class, in the martial arts. On reaching maturity, he married and began to raise a family. However, at the age of twenty-nine he suddenly discovered the pain of illness, the sorrow of death, and the degradation caused by old age in the lives of ordinary people and exclaimed: "Would that sickness, age, and death might be forever bound!" From that time on, he decided to dedicate his life to determining the cause and seeking the cure for human suffering.

To find the answers to these questions, Siddhartha abandoned his home and family and traveled widely. At first he tried to follow the model of the ascetics, but he eventually decided that self-mortification did not lead to a greater understanding of life and abandoned the practice. Then one day after a lengthy period of meditation under a tree, he finally achieved enlightenment as to the meaning of life and spent the remainder of his life preaching it. His conclusions, as embodied in his teachings, became the philosophy (or as some would have it, the religion) of Buddhism. According to legend, the Devil (the Indian term is *Mara*) attempted desperately to tempt him with political power and the company of beautiful girls. But Siddhartha Gautama resisted:

> *Pleasure is brief as a flash of lightning*
> *Or like an autumn shower, only for a moment. . . .*
> *Why should I then covet the pleasures you speak of?*
> *I see your bodies are full of all impurity:*
> *Birth and death, sickness and age are yours.*
> *I seek the highest prize, hard to attain by men–*
> *The true and constant wisdom of the wise.*[8]

How much the modern doctrine of Buddhism resembles the original teachings of Siddhartha Gautama is open to debate, since much time has elapsed since his death and original texts relating his ideas are lacking. Nor is it certain that Siddhartha even intended to found a new religion or doctrine. In some respects, his ideas could be viewed as a reformist form of Hinduism, designed to transfer responsibility from the priests to the individual, much as Martin Luther saw Protestantism as a reformation of Christianity. Siddhartha accepted much of the belief system of Hinduism, if not all of its practices. For example, he accepted the concept of reincarnation and the role of *karma* as a means of influencing the movement of individual souls up and down in the scale of life. He followed Hinduism in praising nonviolence and borrowed the idea of living a life of simplicity and chastity from the ascetics. Moreover, his vision of metaphysical reality—commonly known as **Nirvana**—is closer to the Hindu concept of *Brahman* than it is to the Christian concept of heavenly salvation. Nirvana, which involves an extinction of selfhood and a final reunion with the Great World Soul, is sometimes likened to a dreamless sleep or to a kind of "blowing out" (as of a candle). Buddhists occasionally remark that someone who asks for a description does not understand the concept.

At the same time, the new doctrine differed from existing Hindu practices in a number of key ways. In the first place, Siddhartha denied the existence of an individ-

© Freer Gallery of Art, Smithsonian Institution, Washington, DC

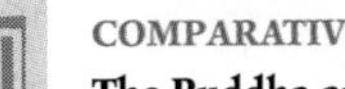

RELIGION & PHILOSOPHY

COMPARATIVE ILLUSTRATION

**The Buddha and Jesus** As Buddhism evolved, transforming Gautama Buddha from mortal to god, Buddhist art changed as well. The representation of the Buddha in statuary and in relief panels began to illustrate the story of his life. In the frieze shown on the left, the infant Siddhartha Gautama is seen emerging from the hip of his mother, Queen Maya. Although dressed in draperies that reflect Greek influences from Alexander's brief incursion into northwest India, her sensuous stance and the touching of the tree evoke the traditional female earth spirit. On the right is a fifth-century mosaic depicting Jesus as the Good Shepherd. Notice that the heads of both the Buddha and Jesus are surrounded by a halo. The halo—or circle of light—is an ancient symbol of divinity. In ancient Hindu, Greek, and Roman art, the heads of gods were shown to emit a sunlike divine radiance. Early kings adopted crowns of gold and precious gems to symbolize their own divine authority.

© Scala/Art Resource, NY

ual soul. To him, the Hindu concept of *Atman*—the individual soul—meant that the soul was subject to rebirth and thus did not achieve a complete liberation from the cares of this world. In fact, Siddhartha denied the ultimate reality of the material world in its entirety and taught that it was an illusion that had to be transcended. Siddhartha's idea of achieving Nirvana was based on his conviction that the pain, poverty, and sorrow that afflict human beings are caused essentially by their attachment to the things of this world. Once worldly cares are abandoned, pain and sorrow can be overcome. With this knowledge comes ***bodhi,*** or wisdom (source of the term *Buddhism* and the familiar name for Gautama the Wise: Gautama Buddha).

Achieving this understanding is a key step on the road to Nirvana, which, as in Hinduism, is a form of release from the wheel of life. According to tradition, Siddhartha transmitted this message in a sermon to his disciples in a deer park at Sarnath, not far from the modern city of Varanasi (also known as Benares). Like so many messages, it is deceptively simple and is enclosed in four noble truths: life is suffering, suffering is caused by desire, the way to end suffering is to end desire, and the way to end desire is to avoid the extremes of a life of vulgar materialism and a life of self-torture and to follow the **Middle Path.** This Middle Path, which is also known as the Eightfold Way, calls for right knowledge, right purpose, right speech, right conduct, right occupation, right effort, right awareness, and right meditation (see the box on p. 54).

Buddhism also differed from Hinduism in its relative egalitarianism. Although Siddhartha accepted the idea of reincarnation (and hence the idea that human beings differ as a result of *karma* accumulated in a previous existence), he rejected the Hindu division of humanity into rigidly defined classes based on previous reincarnations and taught that all human beings could aspire to Nirvana as a result of their behavior in this life—a message that likely helped Buddhism win support among people at the lower end of the social scale.

In addition, Buddhism was much simpler than Hinduism. Siddhartha rejected the panoply of gods that had become identified with Hinduism and forbade his followers to worship his person or his image after his death. In fact, many Buddhists view Buddhism as a philosophy rather than a religion.

# How to Achieve Enlightenment

One of the most famous passages in Buddhist literature is the sermon at Sarnath, which Siddhartha Gautama delivered to his followers in a deer park outside the holy city of Varanasi (Benares), in the Ganges River valley. Here he set forth the key ideas that would define Buddhist beliefs for centuries to come.

*How did Siddhartha Gautama reach the conclusion that the "Four Noble Truths" was the proper course in living a moral life? How do his ideas compare with the biblical Ten Commandments or with the moral teachings of Confucius?*

## The Sermon at Benares

Thus have I heard: at one time the Lord dwelt at Benares at Isipatana in the Deer Park. There the Lord addressed the five monks:–

"These two extremes, monks, are not to be practiced by one who has gone forth from the world. What are the two? That conjoined with the passions and luxury, low, vulgar, common, ignoble, and useless; and that conjoined with self-torture, painful, ignoble, and useless. Avoiding these two extremes the Tathagata has gained the enlightenment of the Middle Path, which produces insight and knowledge and tends to calm, to higher knowledge, enlightenment, Nirvana.

"And what, monks, is the Middle Path, of which the Tathagata has gained enlightenment, which produces insight and knowledge, and tends to calm, to higher knowledge, enlightenment, Nirvana? This is the noble Eightfold Way: namely, right view, right intention, right speech, right action, right livelihood, right effort, right mindfulness, right concentration. This, monks, is the Middle Path, of which the Tathagata has gained enlightenment, which produces insight and knowledge, and tends to calm, to higher knowledge, enlightenment, Nirvana.

1. Now this, monks, is the noble truth of pain: birth is painful, old age is painful, sickness is painful, death is painful, sorrow, lamentation, dejection, and despair are painful. Contact with unpleasant things is painful, not getting what one wishes is painful. In short the five groups of graspings are painful.
2. Now this, monks, is the noble truth of the cause of pain: the craving, which tends to rebirth, combined with pleasure and lust, finding pleasure here and there; namely, the craving for passion, the craving for existence, the craving for nonexistence.
3. Now this, monks, is the noble truth of the cessation of pain, the cessation without a remainder of craving, the abandonment, forsaking, release, nonattachment.
4. Now this, monks, is the noble truth of the way that leads to the cessation of pain: this is the noble Eightfold Way; namely, right view, right intention, right speech, right action, right livelihood, right effort, right mindfulness, right concentration.

"And when, monks, in these four noble truths my due knowledge and insight with its three sections and twelve divisions was well purified, then, monks, . . . I had attained the highest complete enlightenment. This I recognized. Knowledge arose in me, insight arose that the release of my mind is unshakable; this is my last existence; now there is no rebirth."

**HistoryNow™** To read more writings of Siddhartha Gautama, enter the *HistoryNow* documents area using the access card that is available for *World History.*

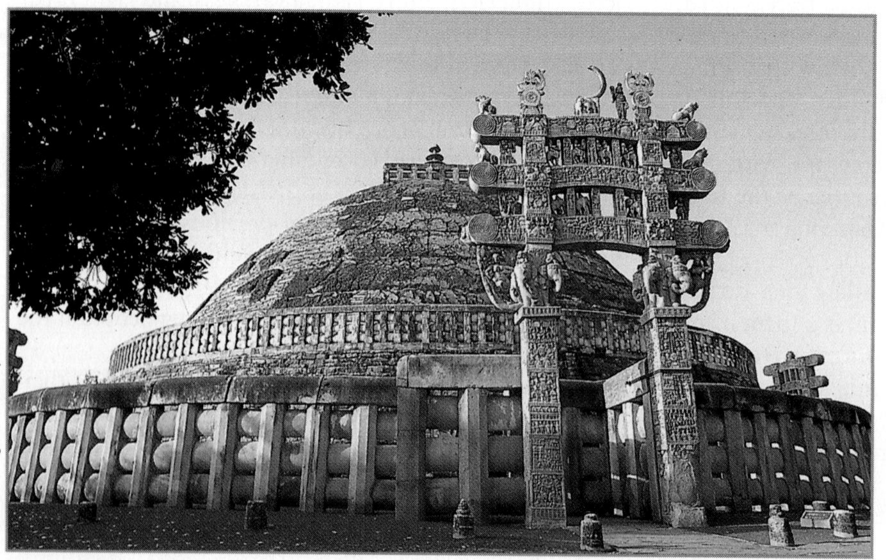



**Sanchi Gate and Stupa.** First constructed during the reign of Emperor Ashoka in the third century B.C.E., the stupa at Sanchi was enlarged over time, eventually becoming the greatest Buddhist monument in the entire Indian subcontinent. Originally intended to house a relic of the Buddha, the stupa became a holy place for devotion and a familiar form of Buddhist architecture. Sanchi's four elaborately carved stone gates, each over 40 feet high, tell the stories of the Buddha set in joyful scenes of everyday life. Christian churches would later portray events in the life of Jesus to instruct the faithful.

## THE VOICES OF SILENCE

Most of what is known about the lives of women in ancient India comes from the Vedas or other texts written by men. Classical Sanskrit was the exclusive property of upper-class males for use in religious and court functions. There are a few examples of women's writings that date from this period. In the first poem quoted here, a Buddhist nun living in the sixth century B.C.E. reflects on her sense of spiritual salvation and physical release from the drudgery of daily life. The other two poems were produced several hundred years later in southern India by anonymous female authors at a time when strict Hindu traditions had not yet been established in the area. Poetry and song were an essential part of daily life, as women sang while working in the fields, drawing water at the well, or reflecting on the hardships of their daily lives. The second poem quoted here breathes the sensuous joy of sex, while the third expresses the simultaneous grief and pride of a mother as she sends her only son off to war.

*What are the various points of view that are being expressed in these short poems? Can you think of any equivalents from other ancient civilizations at this time?*

### "A Woman Well Set Free!"

*A woman well set free! How free I am,*
*How wonderfully free, from kitchen drudgery.*
*Free from the harsh grip of hunger,*
*And from empty cooking pots,*
*Free too of that unscrupulous man,*
*The weaver of sunshades.*
*Calm now, and serene I am,*
*All lust and hatred purged.*
*To the shade of the spreading trees I go*
*And contemplate my happiness.*

Translated by Uma Chakravarti
and Kumkum Roy

### "What She Said to Her Girlfriend"

*What she said to her girlfriend:*
*On beaches washed by seas*
*older than the earth,*
*in the groves filled with bird-cries,*
*on the banks shaded by a* punnai
*clustered with flowers,*
*when we made love*
*my eyes saw him*
*and my ears heard him;*

*my arms grow beautiful*
*in the coupling*
*and grow lean*
*as they come away.*
*What shall I make of this?*

Translated by A. K. Ramanujan

### "Her Purpose Is Frightening, Her Spirit Cruel"

*Her purpose is frightening, her spirit cruel.*
*That she comes from an ancient house is fitting, surely.*
*In the battle the day before yesterday,*
*her father attacked an elephant and died there on the field.*
*In the battle yesterday,*
*her husband faced a row of troops and fell.*
*And today,*
*she hears the battle drum,*
*and, eager beyond reason, gives him a spear in his hand,*
*wraps a white garment around him,*
*smears his dry tuft with oil,*
*and, having nothing but her one son,*
*"Go!" she says, sending him to battle.*

Translated by George L. Hart III

After Siddhartha Gautama's death in 480 B.C.E., dedicated disciples carried his message the length and breadth of India. Buddhist monasteries were established throughout the subcontinent, and temples and **stupas** (stone towers housing relics of the Buddha) sprang up throughout the countryside.

Women were permitted to join the monastic order but only in an inferior position. As Siddhartha had explained, women are "soon angered," "full of passion," and "stupid": "That is the reason . . . why women have no place in public assemblies . . . and do not earn their living by any profession." Still, the position of women tended to be better in Buddhist societies than it was elsewhere in ancient India (see the box above).

**Jainism** During the next centuries, Buddhism began to compete actively with Hindu beliefs, as well as with another new faith known as **Jainism.** Jainism was founded by Mahavira, a contemporary of Siddhartha Gautama. Resembling Buddhism in its rejection of the reality of the material world, Jainism was more extreme in practice. Where Siddhartha Gautama called for the "middle way" between passion and luxury and pain and self-torture, Mahavira preached a doctrine of extreme simplicity to his followers, who kept no possessions and relied on begging for a living. Some even rejected clothing and wandered through the world naked. Perhaps because of its insistence on a life of poverty, Jainism failed to attract enough adherents to become a major doctrine and never

Courtesy of the British Library, Oriental and India Office Collection

**Female Earth Spirit.** This 2,200-year-old earth spirit, sculpted on a sandstone gatepost from the Buddhist stupa at Bharhut, illustrates how earlier Indian representations of the fertility goddess were incorporated into Buddhist art. Women were revered as powerful fertility symbols, represented first on Harappan seals, later on Buddhist shrines, and later still on Hindu temples. Voluptuous and idealized, these earth spirits could allegedly cause a tree to blossom if they merely touched a branch with their arm or wrapped a leg around its trunk.

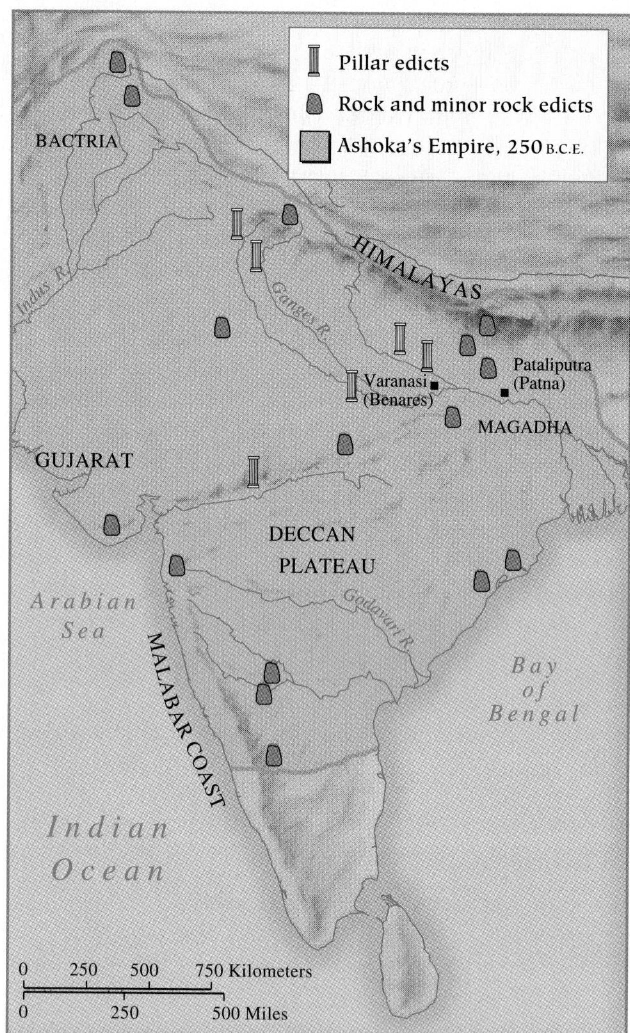


**MAP 2.3 The Empire of Ashoka.** Ashoka, the greatest of Indian monarchs, reigned over the Mauryan dynasty in the third century B.C.E. This map shows the extent of his empire, with the location of the pillar edicts that were erected along major trade routes. ? What were the purposes of these pillars?

**View an animated version of this map or related maps at http:// history.wadsworth.com/duikerspielvogel05/**

received official support. According to tradition, however, Chandragupta Maurya accepted Mahavira's doctrine after abdicating the throne and fasted to death in a Jain monastery.

**Ashoka, a Buddhist Monarch** Buddhism received an important boost when Ashoka, the grandson of Chandragupta Maurya, converted to Buddhism in the third century B.C.E. Ashoka (269–232 B.C.E.) is widely considered the greatest ruler in the history of India. By his own admission, as noted in rock edicts placed around his kingdom, Ashoka began his reign conquering, pillaging, and killing, but after his conversion to Buddhism, he began to regret his bloodthirsty past and attempted to rule benevolently.

Ashoka directed that banyan trees and shelters be placed along the road to provide shade and rest for weary travelers. He sent Buddhist missionaries throughout India and ordered the erection of stone pillars with official edicts and Buddhist inscriptions to instruct people in the proper way (see Map 2.3 and the illustration on p. 236). According to tradition, his son converted the island of Sri Lanka to Buddhism, and the peoples there accepted a tributary relationship with the Mauryan Empire.

## The Rule of the Fishes: India After the Mauryas

After Ashoka's death in 232 B.C.E., the Mauryan Empire began to decline. In 183 B.C.E., the last Mauryan ruler was overthrown by one of his military commanders, and

India slipped back into disunity. A number of new kingdoms, some of them perhaps influenced by the memory of the Alexandrian conquests, arose along the fringes of the subcontinent in Bactria, known today as Afghanistan. In the first century C.E., Indo-European–speaking peoples fleeing from the nomadic Xiongnu warriors in Central Asia seized power in the area and proclaimed the new Kushan kingdom (see Chapter 9). For the next two centuries, the Kushanas extended their political sway over northern India as far as the central Ganges valley, while other kingdoms scuffled for predominance elsewhere on the subcontinent. India would not see unity again for another five hundred years.

Several reasons for India's failure to maintain a unified empire have been proposed. Some historians suggest that a decline in regional trade during the first millennium C.E. may have contributed to the growth of small land-based kingdoms, which drew their primary income from agriculture. The tenacity of the Aryan tradition, with its emphasis on tribal rivalries, may also have contributed. Although the Mauryan rulers tried to impose a more centralized organization, clan loyalties once again came to the fore after the collapse of the Mauryan dynasty. Furthermore, the behavior of the ruling class was characterized by what Indians call the "rule of the fishes," which glorified warfare as the natural activity of the king and the aristocracy. The *Arthasastra,* which set forth a model of a centralized Indian state, assumed that war was the "sport of kings." Still, this was not an uneventful period in the history of India, as Indo-Aryan ideas continued to spread toward the south and both Hinduism and Buddhism evolved in new directions.

## The Exuberant World of Indian Culture

Few cultures in the world are as rich and varied as that of India. Most societies excel in some forms of artistic and literary achievement and not in others, but India has produced great works in almost all fields of cultural endeavor—art and sculpture, science, architecture, literature, and music.

### Literature

The earliest known Indian literature consists of the four Vedas, which were passed down orally from generation to generation until they were finally written down after the Aryan conquest of India. The Rig Veda dates from the second millennium B.C.E. and consists of over a thousand hymns that were used at religious ceremonies. The other three Vedas were written considerably later and contain instructions for performing ritual sacrifices and other ceremonies. The Brahmanas and the Upanishads served as commentaries on the Vedas.

The language of the Vedas was **Sanskrit,** one of the Indo-European family of languages. After the Aryan conquest of India, Sanskrit gradually declined as a spoken language and was replaced in northern India by a simpler tongue known as **Prakrit.** Nevertheless, Sanskrit continued to be used as the language of the bureaucracy and literary expression for many centuries after that and, like Latin in medieval Europe, served as a common language of communication between various regions of India. In the south, a variety of Dravidian languages continued to be spoken.

As early as the fifth century B.C.E., Indian grammarians had already codified Sanskrit in order to preserve the authenticity of the Vedas for the spiritual edification of future generations. A famous grammar written by the scholar Panini in the fourth century B.C.E. set forth four thousand grammatical rules prescribing the correct usage of the spoken and written language. This achievement is particularly impressive in that Europe did not have a science of linguistics until the nineteenth century, when it was developed partly as a result of the discovery of the works of Panini and later Indian linguists.

After the development of a writing system sometime in the first millennium B.C.E., India's holy literature was probably inscribed on palm leaves stitched together into a book somewhat similar to the bamboo strips used during the same period in China. Also written for the first time were India's great historical epics, the Mahabharata and the Ramayana. Both of these epics may have originally been recited at religious ceremonies, but they are essentially historical writings that recount the martial exploits of great Aryan rulers and warriors.

The Mahabharata, consisting of more than 90,000 stanzas, was probably written about 100 B.C.E. and describes in great detail a war between cousins for control of the kingdom about 1000 B.C.E. Interwoven in the narrative are many fantastic legends of the Hindu gods. Above all, the Mahabharata is a tale of moral confrontations and an elucidation of the ethical precepts of the *dharma* (see the box on p. 58). The most famous section of the book is the so-called Bhagavad Gita, a sermon by the legendary Indian figure Krishna on the eve of a major battle. In this sermon, mentioned at the beginning of this chapter, Krishna sets forth one of the key ethical maxims of Indian society: in taking action, one must be indifferent to success or failure and consider only the moral rightness of the act itself.

The Ramayana, written at about the same time, is much shorter than the Mahabharata. It is an account of a semilegendary ruler named Rama who, as the result of a palace intrigue, is banished from the kingdom and forced to live as a hermit in the forest. Later, he fights the demon-king of Sri Lanka, who has kidnapped his beloved wife, Sita. Like the Mahabharata, the Ramayana is strongly imbued with religious and moral significance. Rama himself is portrayed as the ideal Aryan hero, a perfect ruler and an ideal son, while Sita projects the supreme duty of

## Draupadi's Humiliation

In the Mahabharata, the great Indian epic, Draupadi, wife of the five Pandava brothers, is humiliated by both her husbands and their enemies. One of her husbands insults her by betting and losing her in a dice game to their rival cousins, who in turn demand that Draupadi be summoned immediately to be disrobed in public. Furious, she arrives with her hair unbraided, a sign that she is undergoing her monthly cycle. During such periods women were segregated from men to safeguard the latter from menstrual pollution.

Humiliated, Draupadi implores Lord Krishna for assistance in reinstating her honor. As one of the cousins attempts to unravel her sari, all are amazed at the never-ending folds of her garment. Although the disrobing is foiled, Draupadi's humiliation is complete. She vows revenge, refusing to rebraid her hair until it is bathed in the blood of the cousin. The famous scene has remained a favorite and occurs at a pivotal climax of the epic.

*What is the purpose of the author in reciting this tale of Draupadi's humiliation? Can you think of any other examples of a woman seeking revenge from her tormenters in the classical literature?*

### The Mahabharata

Then how was it that a woman like me, wife to the Parthas, friend to you, Lord Krishna, sister of Dhristadyumna, came to be dragged into the hall? Subjected to the law of women, stained with blood, shuddering in my sole piece of clothing, I was grievously dragged into the assembly of the Kurus. In the midst of the kings, inside the hall, overrun by my menses, they watched me, the Dhartarastras [the sons of Dhrtarashtra], and burst out laughing, the foul-minded! . . . Am I not . . . [Draupadi], by Law the daughter-in-law of Bhisma and Dhrtarashtra? And I was forcibly reduced to a slave!

female chastity and wifely loyalty to her husband. The Ramayana is a story of the triumph of good over evil, duty over self-indulgence, and generosity over selfishness. It combines filial and erotic love, conflicts of human passion, character analysis, and poetic descriptions of nature (see the box on p. 59).

The Ramayana also has all the ingredients of an enthralling adventure: giants, wondrous flying chariots, invincible arrows and swords, and magic potions and mantras. One of the real heroes of the story is the monkey-king Hanuman, who flies from India to Sri Lanka to set the great battle in motion. It is no wonder that for millennia the Ramayana has remained a favorite among Indians of all age groups, including a hugely popular TV version produced in recent years.

## Architecture and Sculpture

After literature, the greatest achievements of early Indian civilization were in architecture and sculpture. Some of the earliest examples of Indian architecture stem from the time of Emperor Ashoka, when Buddhism became the religion of the state. Until the time of the Mauryas, Aryan buildings had been constructed of wood. With the rise of the empire, stone began to be used as artisans arrived in India seeking employment after the destruction of the Persian Empire by Alexander. Many of these stone carvers accepted the patronage of Emperor Ashoka, who used them to spread Buddhist ideas throughout the subcontinent.

There were three main types of religious structure: the pillar, the stupa, and the rock chamber. During Ashoka's reign, many stone columns were erected alongside roads to commemorate the events in the Buddha's life and mark pilgrim routes to holy places. Weighing up to 50 tons each and rising as high as 32 feet, these polished sandstone pillars were topped with a carved capital, usually depicting lions uttering the Buddha's message. Ten remain standing today.

A stupa was originally meant to house a relic of the Buddha, such as a lock of his hair or a branch of the famous Bodhi tree (the tree beneath which Siddhartha Gautama had first achieved enlightenment) and was constructed in the form of a burial mound (the pyramids in Egypt also derived from burial mounds). Eventually, the stupa became a place for devotion and the most familiar form of Buddhist architecture. It rose to considerable heights and was surmounted with a spire, possibly representing the stages of existence en route to Nirvana. According to legend, Ashoka ordered the construction of 84,000 stupas throughout India to promote the Buddha's message. A few survive today, including the famous stupa at Sanchi, begun under Ashoka and completed two centuries later.

The final form of early Indian architecture is the rock chamber carved out of a cliff on the side of a mountain. Ashoka began the construction of these chambers to provide rooms to house monks or wandering ascetics and to serve as halls for religious ceremonies. The chambers were rectangular in form, with pillars, an altar, and a vault, reminiscent of Roman basilicas in the West. The three most famous chambers of this period are at Bhaja, Karli, and Ajanta; this last one contains twenty-nine rooms.

All three forms of architecture were embellished with decorations. Consisting of detailed reliefs and freestanding statues of deities, other human figures, and animals, these decorations are permeated with a sense of nature and the

## Rama and Sita

Over the ages, the conclusion of the Indian epic, the Ramayana, has been the focus of considerable debate. After a long period of captivity at the hands of the demon Ravana, Sita is finally liberated by her husband, King Rama. Although the two enjoy a joyful reunion, the people of Rama's kingdom continue to voice suspicions that she has been defiled by her captor, and he is forced to banish her to a forest, where she gives birth to twin sons. The account reflects the tradition, expressed in the *Arthasastra,* that a king must place the needs of his subjects over his personal desires. Here we read of Rama's anguished decision as he consults with his brother, Lakshmana.

By accepting banishment, Sita bows to the authority of her husband and the established moral order. Subservient and long-suffering, she has been lauded as the ideal heroine and feminine role model, imitated by generations of Indian women. At the close of the Ramayana, Rama decides to take Sita back "before all my people." She continues to feel humiliated, however, and begs Mother Earth to open up and swallow her.

*How does this story reflect some of the basic values of traditional Indian civilization? Why do you think it was necessary to have an unhappy ending to the story, unlike the ending to Homer's epic* The Odyssey?

### The Ramayana

"A king must be blameless."

"Such words pierce my heart," said Lakshmana. "Fire himself proved her innocent. She is fired gold, poured into golden fire!"

Rama said, "Lakshmana, consider what is a king. Kings cannot afford blame. Ill fame is evil to kings; they above all men must be beyond reproach. . . . See into what a chasm of sorrow a King may fall. . . . "

Lakshmana said, "Gradually everything seems to change again, and even an Emperor must pay his way through life."

Rama faced his brother. "It must be! It's all the same, can't you see? Where there is growth there is decay; where there is prosperity there is ruin; and where there is birth there is death."

Lakshmana sighed hopelessly. "Well, what will you do?"

"Sita expects to go to the forests tomorrow. Let Sumantra the Charioteer drive you both there, and when you arrive by the river Ganga abandon her."

"She will die. Your child will die!"

"No," said Rama. "I command you! Not a word to anyone."

Lakshmana said, "Surely a king is remote and lonely, and very far from reason. We cannot speak to you. . . . "

Rama said, "Each person can be told what he will understand of the nature of the world, and no more than that–for the rest, take my word. . . . "

Sita was forever beautiful. Wearing her ornaments she turned slowly around and looked at every person there. "Rama, let me prove my innocence, here before everyone."

"I give my permission," said Rama.

Then Sita stepped a little away from him and said, "Mother Earth, if I have been faithful to Rama take me home, hide me!"

Earth rolled and moved beneath our feet. With a great rumbling noise the ground broke apart near Sita and a deep chasm opened, lighted from below with bright lights like lightning flashes, from the castles of the Naga serpent kings. . . .

On that throne sat Mother Earth. Earth was not old, she was fair to look on, she was not sad but smiling. She wore flowers and a girdle of seas. Earth supports all life, but she feels no burden in all that. She is patient. She was patient then, under the Sun and Moon and through the rainfalls of countless years. She was patient with seasons and with kings and farmers; she endured all things and bore no line of care from it.

But this was the end of her long patience with Rama. Earth looked at her husband Janaka and smiled. Then she stretched out her arms and took her only child Sita on her lap. She folded her beautiful arms around her daughter and laid Sita's head softly against her shoulder as a mother would. Earth stroked her hair with her fair hands, and Sita closed her eyes like a little girl.

The throne sank back underground and they all were gone; the Nagas dove beneath the ground and the crevice closed gently over them, forever.

vitality of life. Many reflect an amalgamation of popular and sacred themes, of Buddhist, Vedic, and pre-Aryan religious motifs, such as male and female earth spirits. Until the second century C.E., Siddhartha Gautama was represented only through symbols, such as the wheel of life, the Bodhi tree, and the footprint, perhaps because artists deemed it improper to portray him in human form, since he had escaped his corporeal confines into enlightenment. After the spread of Mahayana Buddhism in the second century, when the Buddha was no longer portrayed as a teacher but rather as a god, his image began to appear in stone as an object for divine worship.

By this time, India had established its own unique religious art. The art is permeated by sensuousness and exuberance and is often overtly sexual. These scenes are meant to express otherworldly delights, not the pleasures

© ephotocorp.com

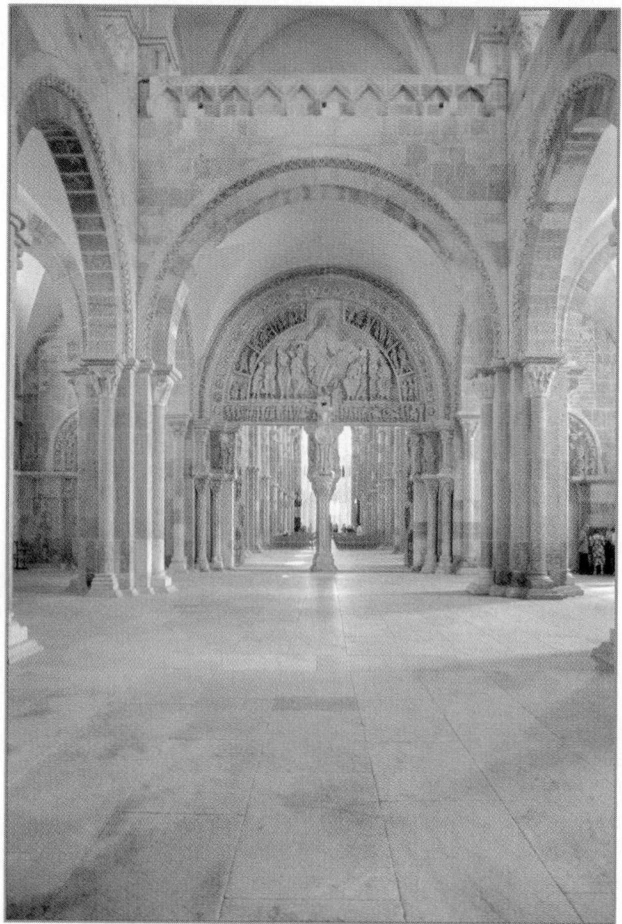

© Vanni/Art Resource, NY

**Carved Chapels.** Carved out of solid rock cliffs during the Mauryan dynasty, these rock chambers served as meditation halls for traveling Buddhist monks. Initially, they resembled freestanding shrines of wood and thatch from the Vedic period but evolved into magnificent chapels carved deep into the mountainside such as this one at Karli (left). Working downward from the top, the stone cutters removed tons of rock while sculptors embellished and polished the interior decor. Notice the rounded vault and multicolumned sides reminiscent of Roman basilicas in the West. This style would reemerge in medieval chapels such as the one shown here in southern France (right).

**Symbols of the Buddha.** Pre–Christian Era Buddhist sculptures referred to the Buddha only through visual symbols representing his life on the path to enlightenment. In this relief, from the second-century B.C.E. stupa at Bharhut, we see four devotees paying homage to the Buddha, who is portrayed as a giant wheel, dispensing his "Wheel of the Law."

Courtesy of William J. Duiker

of this world. The sensuous paradise that adorned the religious art of ancient India represented salvation and fulfillment for the ordinary Indian.

## Science

Our knowledge of Indian science is limited by the paucity of written sources, but it is evident that ancient Indians had amassed an impressive amount of scientific knowledge in a number of areas. Especially notable was their work in mathematics, where they devised the numerical system that we know as Arabic numbers and use today, and in astronomy, where they charted the movements of the heavenly bodies and recognized the spherical nature of the earth at an early date. Their ideas of physics were similar to those of the Greeks; matter was divided into the five elements of earth, air, fire, water, and ether. Many of their technological achievements are impressive, notably the quality of their textiles and the massive stone pillars erected during the reign of Ashoka. As noted, the pillars weighed up to 50 tons each and were transported many miles to their final destination.

## TIMELINE

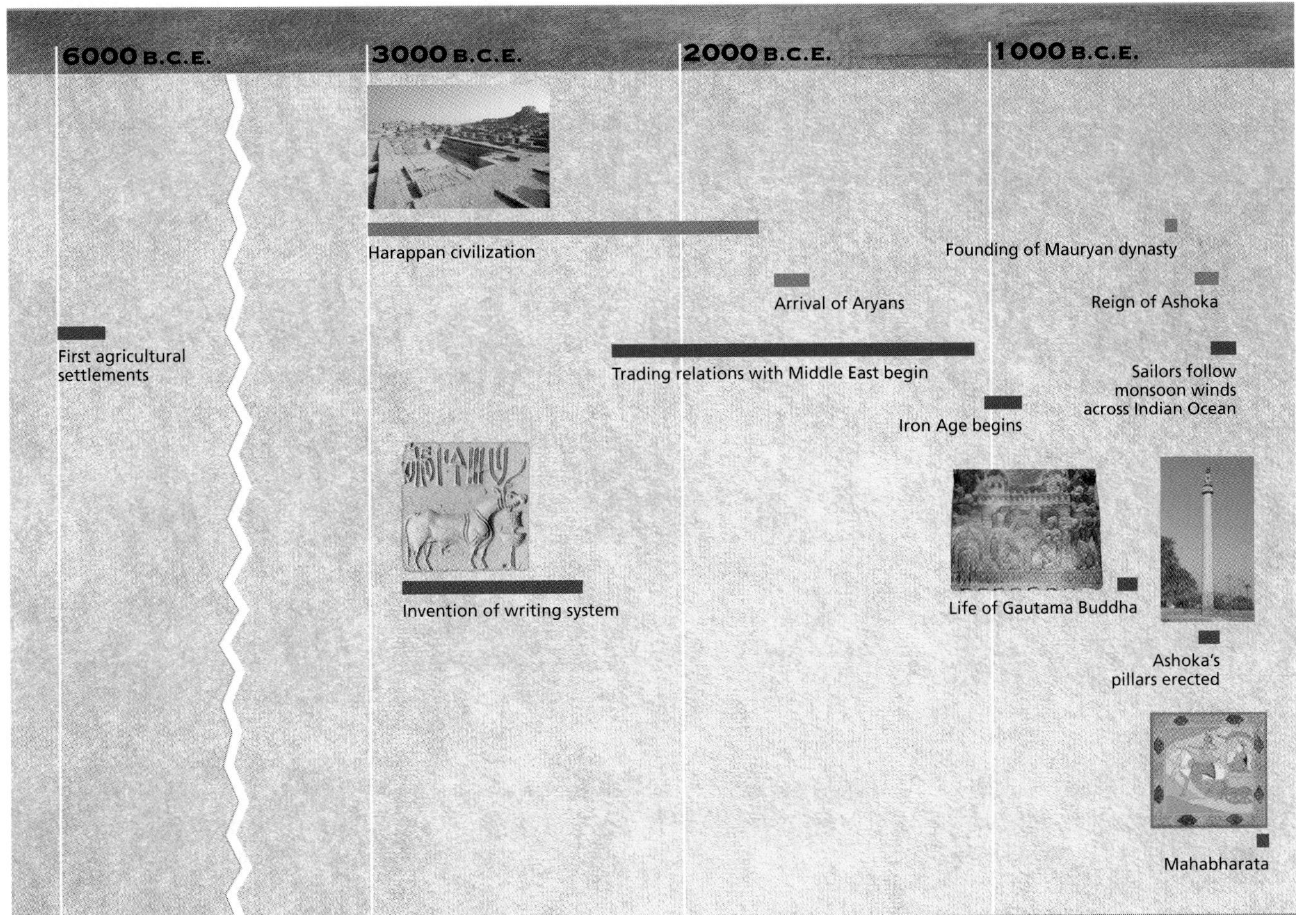


## CONCLUSION

While the peoples of North Africa and the Middle East were actively building the first civilizations, a similar process was getting under way in the Indus River valley. Much has been learned about the nature of the Indus valley civilization in recent years, but without written records there are inherent limits to our understanding. How did the Harappan people deal with the fundamental human problems mentioned at the close of Chapter 1? The answers remain tantalizingly elusive.

As often happened elsewhere, however, the collapse of Harappan civilization did not lead to the total disappearance of its culture. The new society that eventually emerged throughout the subcontinent after the coming of the Aryans was an amalgam of two highly distinctive cultures, Aryan and Dravidian, each of which made a significant contribution to the politics, the social institutions, and the creative impulse of ancient Indian civilization.

With the rise of the Mauryan dynasty in the fourth century B.C.E., the distinctive features of a great civilization begin to be clearly visible. It was extensive in its scope, embracing the entire Indian subcontinent and eventually, in the form of Buddhism and Hinduism, spreading to China and Southeast Asia. But the underlying ethnic, linguistic, and cultural diversity of the Indian people posed a constant challenge to the unity of the state. After the collapse of the Mauryas, the subcontinent would not come under a single authority again for several hundred years.

In the meantime, another great experiment was taking place far to the northeast, across the Himalaya Mountains. Like many other civilizations of antiquity, the first Chinese state was concentrated on a major river system. And like them, too, its political and cultural achievements eventually spread far beyond their original habitat. In the next chapter, we turn to the civilization of ancient China.

## CHAPTER NOTES

1. Quoted in R. Lannoy, *The Speaking Tree: A Study of Indian Culture and Society* (London, 1971), p. 318.
2. The quotation is from ibid., p. 319. Note also that the *Law of Manu* says that "punishment alone governs all created beings. . . . The whole world is kept in order by punishment, for a guiltless man is hard to find."
3. Strabo's *Geography,* bk. 15, quoted in M. Edwardes, *A History of India: From the Earliest Times to the Present Day* (London, 1961), p. 55.
4. Ibid., p. 54.
5. Ibid., p. 57.
6. From the *Law of Manu,* quoted in A. L. Basham, *The Wonder That Was India* (London, 1961), pp. 180–181.
7. Mundaka Upanishad 1:2, quoted in W. T. de Bary et al., eds., *Sources of Indian Tradition* (New York, 1966), pp. 28–29.
8. Quoted in A. K. Coomaraswamy, *Buddha and the Gospel of Buddhism* (New York, 1964), p. 34.

## SUGGESTED READING

Several standard histories of India provide a good overview of the ancient period. One of the most readable and reliable is **S. Wolpert, *New History of India,*** 3d ed. (New York, 1989).

By far the most informative and readable narrative on the cultural history of India in premodern times is still **A. L. Basham, *The Wonder That Was India*** (London, 1961), which, although somewhat out of date, contains informative sections on prehistory, economy, language, art and literature, society, and everyday life. **R. Thapar, *Early India: From the Origins to AD 1300*** (London, 2002), provides a recent view by an Indian historian.

Because of the relative paucity of archaeological exploration in South Asia, evidence for the Harappan period is not as voluminous as for areas such as Mesopotamia and the Nile valley. Some of the best work has been written by scholars who actually worked at the sites. For a recent account, see **J. M. Kenoyer, *Ancient Cities of the Indus Valley Civilization*** (Karachi, 1998). A somewhat more extensive study is **B. Allchin** and **R. Allchin, *The Birth of Indian Civilization, India and Pakistan Before 500 B.C.*** (New York, 1968). For a detailed and well-illustrated analysis, see **G. L. Possehl,** ed., ***The Harappan Civilization: A Contemporary Perspective*** (Amherst, N.Y., 1983). Commercial relations between Harappa and its neighbors are treated in **S. Ratnagar, *Encounters: The Westerly Trade of the Harappan Civilization*** (Oxford, 1981).

There are a number of good books on the introduction of Buddhism into Indian society. Buddha's ideals are presented in **P. Williams** (with **A. Tribe**), ***Buddhist Thought: A Complete Introduction to the Indian Tradition*** (London, 2000). Also see **H. Nakamura** and **M. B. Dasgupta, *Indian Buddhism: A Survey with Bibliographical Notes*** (New Delhi, 1987). **H. Akira, *A History of Indian Buddhism: From Sakyamuni to Early Mahayana*** (Honolulu, 1990), provides a detailed analysis of early activities by Siddhartha Gautama and his followers. The intimate relationship between Buddhism and commerce is discussed in **Liu Hsin-ju, *Ancient India and Ancient China: Trades and Religious Exchanges*** (Oxford, 1988).

There are a number of excellent surveys of Indian art, including the comprehensive **S. L. Huntington, *The Art of Ancient India: Buddhist, Hindu, Jain*** (New York, 1985), and the concise ***Indian Art,*** rev. ed. (London, 1997) by **R. Craven.** See also **V. Dehejia's *Devi: The Great Goddess*** (Washington, D.C., 1999) and ***Indian Art*** (London, 1997).

Many editions of Sanskrit literature are available in English translation. Many are available in the multivolume ***Harvard Oriental Series.*** For a shorter annotated anthology of selections from the Indian classics, consult **S. N. Hay,** ed., ***Sources of Indian Tradition,*** 2 vols. (New York, 1988), or **J. B. Alphonso-Karkala, *An Anthology of Indian Literature,*** 2d rev. ed. (New Delhi, 1987), put out by the Indian Council for Cultural Relations.

The Mahabharata and Ramayana have been rewritten for 2,500 years. Fortunately, the vibrant versions, retold by **William Buck** and condensed to 400 pages each, reproduce the spirit of the originals and enthrall today's imagination. See **W. Buck, *Mahabharata*** (Berkeley,

Calif., 1973) and ***Ramayana*** (Berkeley, Calif., 1976). On the role played by women writers in ancient India, see **S. Tharu** and **K. Lalita,** eds., ***Women Writing in India: 600 B.C. to the Present,*** vol. 1 (New York, 1991).

For additional information on the invention of the first writing systems, see **J. T. Hooker,** (ed.), ***Reading the Past: Ancient Writing from Cuneiform to the Alphabet*** (London, 1990), and A. Hurley, ***The Alphabet: The History, Evolution, and Design of the Letters We Use Today*** (New York, 1995).

**History Now™**

**Enter *HistoryNow* using the access card that is available with this text. *HistoryNow* will assist you in understanding the content in this chapter with lesson plans generated for your needs, as well as provide you with a connection to the *Wadsworth World History Resource Center* (see description at right for details).**

**WORLD HISTORY**
RESOURCE CENTER

**Enter the Resource Center using either your *HistoryNow* access card or your standalone access card for the *Wadsworth World History Resource Center.* Organized by topic, this website includes quizzes; images; over 350 primary source documents; interactive simulations; maps and timelines; movie explorations; and a wealth of other resources. You can read the following documents, and many more, at http://history.wadsworth.com/rc/world**

*The Law of Manu*
The Rig Veda

Visit the World History Companion Web Site for chapter quizzes and more.

**http://history.wadsworth.com/duikerspielvogel05/**

CHAPTER

# 3

# CHINA IN ANTIQUITY

Confucius and his disciples

© Topham/The Image Works

## CHAPTER OUTLINE AND FOCUS QUESTIONS

### The Dawn of Chinese Civilization

- How did geography influence the civilization that arose in China?

### The Zhou Dynasty

- What were the major tenets of Confucianism, Legalism, and Daoism, and what role did each play in early Chinese history?

### The Rise of the Chinese Empire: the Qin and the Han

- What role did nomadic peoples play in early Chinese history? How did that role compare with conditions in other parts of Asia?

### Daily Life in Ancient China

- What were the key aspects of social and economic life in early China?

### Chinese Culture

- What were the chief characteristics of the Chinese writing system? How and why had it been developed?

### CRITICAL THINKING

- The civilization of ancient China resembles those of its contemporaries in Mesopotamia and Egypt in several respects, but the contrasts were equally significant. What were some of these differences, and how might geography and the environment have been factors in determining them?

THE MASTER SAID: "If the government seeks to rule by decree, and to maintain order by the use of punishment, the people will seek to evade punishment and have no sense of shame. But if government leads by virtue and governs through the rules of propriety, the people will feel shame and seek to correct their mistakes."

That statement is from the *Analects,* a collection of remarks by the Chinese philosopher Confucius that were gathered together by his disciples and published after his death in the fifth century B.C.E. Confucius lived at a time when Chinese society was in a state of increasing disarray. The political principles that had governed society since the founding of the Zhou dynasty six centuries earlier were widely ignored, and squabbling principalities scuffled for primacy as the power of the Zhou court steadily declined. The common people groaned under the weight of an oppressive manorial system that left them at the mercy of their aristocratic lords.

In the midst of this turmoil, Confucius traveled the length of the kingdom observing events and seeking employment as a political counselor. In the process, he attracted a number of disciples, to whom he expounded a set of ideas that in later years served as the guiding principles for the Chinese empire. Some of his ideas are strikingly modern in their thrust. Among them is the revolutionary proposition that government depends on the will of the people.

On the other hand, the principles that Confucius sought to instill into his society had, in his view, all been previously established many centuries in the past—during an alleged "Golden Age" at the dawn of Chinese history. In that sense, Confucius was a profoundly conservative thinker, seeking to preserve elements in Chinese history that had been neglected by his contemporaries. The dichotomy between tradition and change was thus a key component in Confucian philosophy that would be reflected in many ways over the course of the next 2,500 years of Chinese history.

The civilization that produced Confucius had originated more than fifteen hundred years earlier along the two great river systems of East Asia, the Yellow and the Yangtze. This vibrant new civilization, which we know today as ancient China, expanded gradually over its neighboring areas. By the third century B.C.E., it had emerged as a great empire, as well as the dominant cultural and political force in the entire region.

Like Sumer, Harappa, and Egypt, the civilization of ancient China began as a collection of autonomous villages cultivating food crops along a major river system. Improvements in agricultural techniques led to a food surplus and the growth of an urban civilization characterized by more complex political and social institutions, as well as new forms of artistic and intellectual creativity.

Like its counterparts elsewhere, ancient China faced the challenge posed by the appearance of pastoral peoples on its borders. Unlike Harappa, Sumer, and Egypt, however, ancient China was able to surmount that challenge, and many of its institutions and cultural values survived intact down to the beginning of the twentieth century. For that reason, Chinese civilization is sometimes described as the oldest continuous civilization on earth. ◇

# The Dawn of Chinese Civilization

According to Chinese legend, Chinese society was founded by a series of rulers who brought the first rudiments of civilization to the region nearly five thousand years ago. The first was Fu Xi (Fu Hsi), the ox-tamer, who "knotted cords for hunting and fishing," domesticated animals, and introduced the beginnings of family life. The second was Shen Nong (Shen Nung), the divine farmer, who "bent wood for plows and hewed wood for plowshares." He taught the people the techniques of agriculture. Last came Huang Di (Huang Ti), the Yellow Emperor, who "strung a piece of wood for the bow, and whittled little sticks of wood for the arrows." Legend credits Huang Di with creating the Chinese system of writing, as well as with inventing the bow and arrow.[1] Modern historians, of course, do not accept the literal accuracy of such legends but view them instead as part of the process whereby early peoples attempt to make sense of the world and their role in it. Nevertheless, such re-creations of a mythical past often contain an element of truth. Although there is no clear evidence that the "three sovereigns" actually existed, their achievements do symbolize some of the defining characteristics of Chinese civilization: the interaction between nomadic and agricultural peoples, the importance of the family as the basic unit of Chinese life, and the development of a unique system of writing.

## The Land and People of China

Human communities have existed in China for several hundred thousand years. Sometime around the eighth millennium B.C.E., the early peoples living along the riverbanks of northern China began to master the cultivation of crops. A number of these early agricultural settlements were in the neighborhood of the Yellow River, where they gave birth to two Neolithic societies known to archaeologists as the **Yangshao** and the **Longshan** cultures (sometimes identified in terms of their pottery as the painted and black pottery cultures, respectively). Similar communities have been found in the Yangtze valley in central China and along the coast to the south. The southern settlements were based on the cultivation of rice rather than dry crops such as millet, barley, and wheat, but they were as old as those in the north. Thus agriculture, and perhaps other elements of early civilization, may have developed spontaneously in several areas of China rather than radiating outward from one central region.

At first, these simple Neolithic communities were hardly more than villages, but as the inhabitants mastered the rudiments of agriculture, they gradually gave rise to more sophisticated and complex societies. In a pattern that we have already seen elsewhere, civilization gradually spread from these nuclear settlements in the valleys of the Yellow and Yangtze Rivers to other lowland areas of eastern and central China. The two great river valleys, then, can be considered the core regions in the development of Chinese civilization.

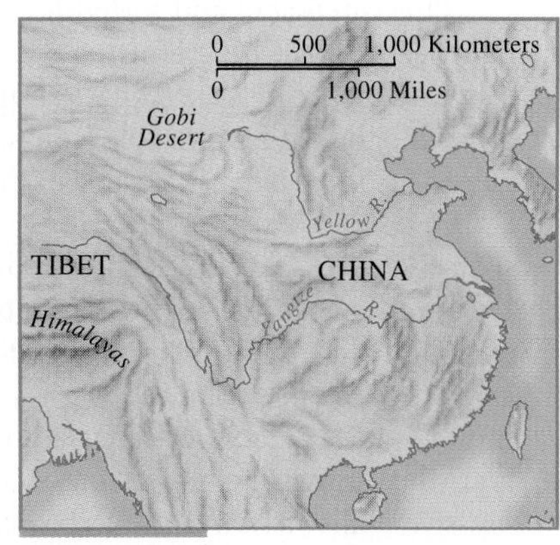

Neolithic China

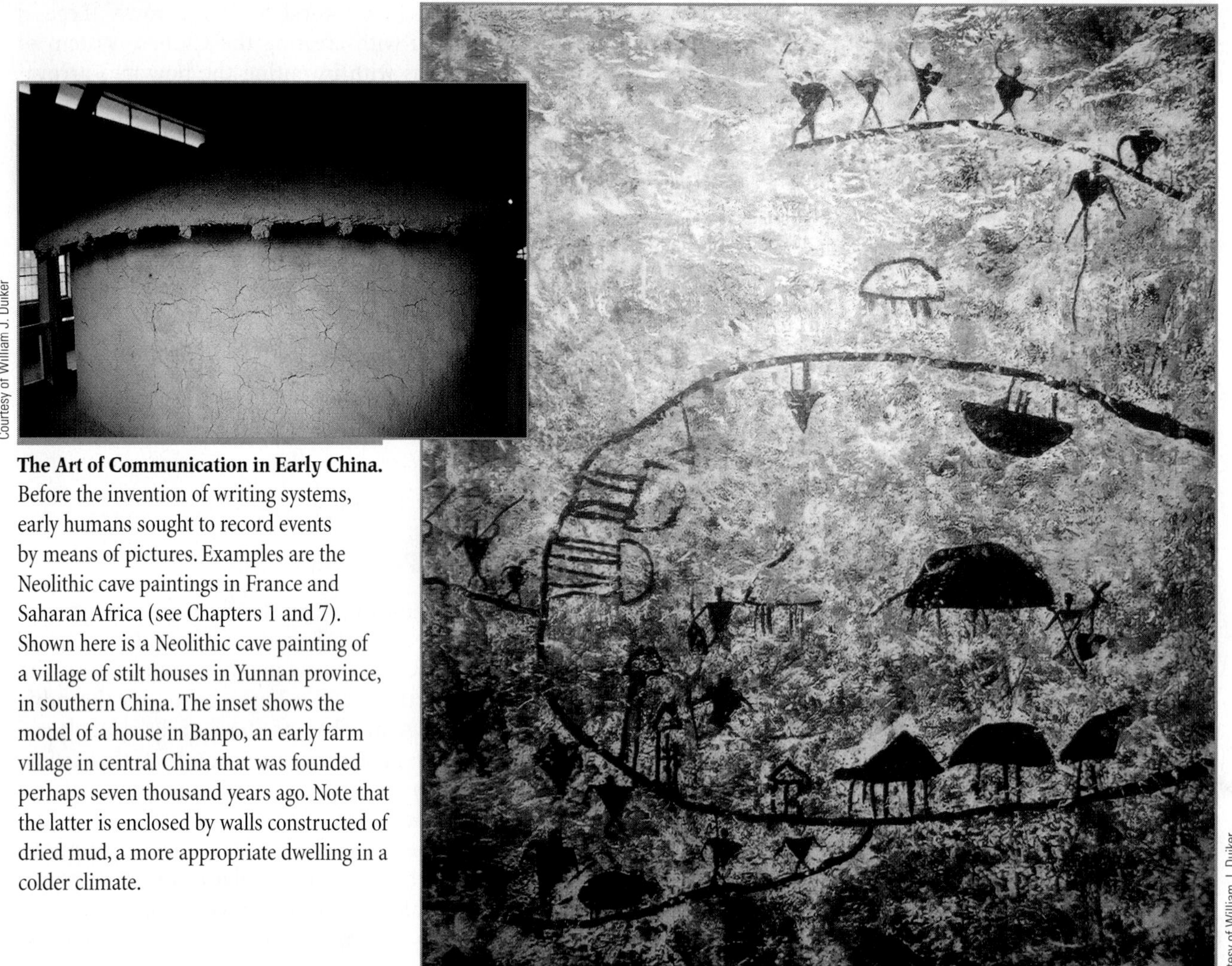

Courtesy of William J. Duiker

Courtesy of William J. Duiker

**The Art of Communication in Early China.** Before the invention of writing systems, early humans sought to record events by means of pictures. Examples are the Neolithic cave paintings in France and Saharan Africa (see Chapters 1 and 7). Shown here is a Neolithic cave painting of a village of stilt houses in Yunnan province, in southern China. The inset shows the model of a house in Banpo, an early farm village in central China that was founded perhaps seven thousand years ago. Note that the latter is enclosed by walls constructed of dried mud, a more appropriate dwelling in a colder climate.

Although these densely cultivated valleys eventually became two of the great food-producing areas of the ancient world, China is more than a land of fertile fields. In fact, only 12 percent of the total land area is arable, compared with 23 percent in the United States. Much of the remainder consists of mountains and deserts that ring the country on its northern and western frontiers.

This often arid and forbidding landscape is a dominant feature of Chinese life and has played a significant role in Chinese history. The geographical barriers served to isolate the Chinese people from advanced agrarian societies in other parts of Asia. The frontier regions in the Gobi Desert, Central Asia, and the Tibetan plateau were sparsely inhabited by peoples of Mongolian, Indo-European, or Turkish extraction. Most were pastoral societies, and like the other river valley civilizations, their contacts with the Chinese were often characterized by mutual distrust and conflict. Although less numerous than the Chinese, many of these peoples possessed impressive skills in war and were sometimes aggressive in seeking wealth or territory in the settled regions south of the Gobi Desert. Over the next two thousand years, the northern frontier became one of the great fault lines of conflict in Asia as Chinese armies attempted to protect precious farmlands from marauding peoples from beyond the frontier. When China was unified and blessed with capable rulers, it could usually keep the nomadic intruders at bay and even bring them under a loose form of Chinese administration. But in times of internal weakness, China was vulnerable to attack from the north, and on several occasions, nomadic peoples succeeded in overthrowing native Chinese rulers and setting up their own dynastic regimes.

From other directions, China normally had little to fear. To the east lay the China Sea, a lair for pirates and the source of powerful typhoons that occasionally ravaged the Chinese coast but otherwise rarely a source of concern. South of the Yangtze River was a hilly region inhabited by a mixture of peoples of varied language and ethnic stock who lived by farming, fishing, or food gathering. They were gradually absorbed in the inexorable expansion of Chinese civilization.

## The Shang Dynasty

Historians of China have traditionally dated the beginning of Chinese civilization to the founding of the Xia (Hsia) dynasty more than four thousand years ago. Although the precise date for the rise of the Xia is in dispute, recent archaeological evidence confirms its existence. Legend maintains that the founder was a ruler named Yu, who is also credited with introducing irrigation and draining the floodwaters that periodically threatened to inundate the northern China plain (see the box on p. 68). The Xia dynasty was replaced by a second dynasty, the Shang, around the sixteenth century B.C.E. The late Shang capital at Anyang, just north of the Yellow River in north-central China, has been excavated by archaeologists. Among the finds were thousands of so called oracle bones, ox and chicken bones or turtle shells that were used by Shang rulers for divination and to communicate with the gods. The inscriptions on these oracle bones are the earliest known form of Chinese writing and provide much of our information about the beginnings of civilization in China. They describe a culture gradually emerging from the Neolithic to the early Bronze Age.

0 200 400 600 Kilometers
0 200 400 Miles
Anyang
Luoyang
Yellow R.
Yellow Sea
Huai R.
Yangtze R.
Major regions of the late Shang state

**Shang China**

**Political Organization** China under the Shang dynasty was a predominantly agricultural society ruled by an aristocratic class whose major occupation was war. One ancient chronicler complained that "the big affairs of state consist of sacrifice and soldiery."[2] Combat was carried on by means of two-horse chariots. The appearance of chariots in China in the mid-second millennium B.C.E. coincides roughly with similar developments elsewhere, leading some historians to suggest that the Shang ruling class may originally have invaded China from elsewhere in Asia. But items found in Shang burial mounds are similar to Longshan pottery, implying that the Shang ruling elites were linear descendants of the indigenous Neolithic peoples in the area. If that was the case, the Shang may have acquired their knowledge of horse-drawn chariots through contact with the peoples of neighboring regions.

Some recent support for that assumption has come from evidence unearthed in the sandy wastes of Xinjiang, China's far-northwestern province. There archaeologists have discovered corpses dating back as early as the second millennium B.C.E. with physical characteristics that are clearly European. They are also clothed in textiles similar to those worn at the time in Europe, suggesting that they may have been members of an Indo-European migration from areas much farther to the west. If that is the case, they were probably familiar with advances in chariot making that occurred a few hundred years earlier in southern Russia and Kazakstan. By about 2000 B.C.E., spoked wheels were being deposited at grave sites in the Ukraine and also in the Gobi Desert, just north of the great

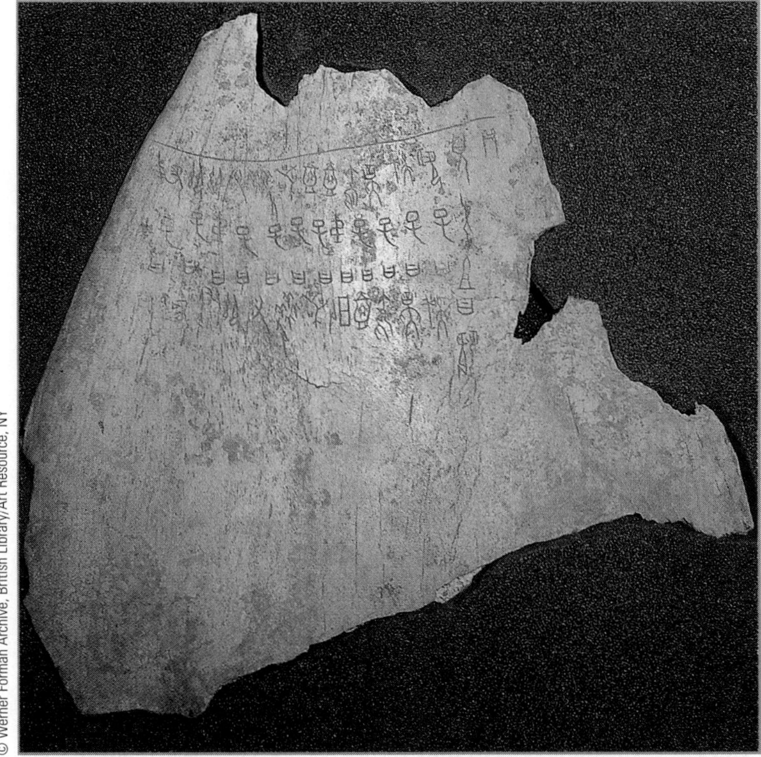



**Shell and Bone Writing.** The earliest known form of true writing in China dates back to the Shang dynasty and was inscribed on shells or animal bones. Questions for the gods were scratched on bones, which cracked after being exposed to fire. The cracks were then interpreted by sorcerers. The questions often expressed practical concerns: Will it rain? Will the king be victorious in battle? Will he recover from his illness? Originally composed of pictographs and ideographs four thousand years ago, Chinese writing has evolved into an elaborate set of symbols that combine meaning and pronunciation in a single character.

## A Treatise on the Yellow River and Its Canals

Sima Qian (Szu-ma Ch'ien) was a famous historian of the Han dynasty who lived during the second and first centuries B.C.E. In his most famous work, titled *Historical Records,* he describes the public works projects undertaken during the Xia dynasty to convert the dangerous waters of the Yellow River to human use. Although the identification of irrigation with Yu may be apocryphal, irrigation works were under way in central China at least as early as the sixth century B.C.E., and China later became one of the foremost hydraulic societies in the ancient world.

*For ancient China, controlling the flow of water on the country's major river systems was essential to survival. To what degree was this true of the other major civilizations we have encountered in Part I of this book, and how did they deal with the problem?*

### Sima Qian, *Historical Records*

The documents on the Hsia dynasty tell us that Emperor Yu spent thirteen years controlling and bringing an end to the floods, and during that period, though he passed by the very gate of his own house, he did not take the time to enter. On land he traveled in a cart and on water in a boat; he rode a sledge to cross the mud and wore cleated shoes in climbing the mountains. In this way he marked out the nine provinces, led the rivers along the bases of the mountains, decided what tribute was appropriate for each region in accordance with the quality of its soil, opened up the nine roads, built embankments around the nine marshes, and made a survey of the nine mountains.

Of all the rivers, the Yellow River caused the greatest damage to China by overflowing its banks and inundating the land, and therefore he turned all his attention to controlling it. Thus he led the Yellow River in a course from Chi-shih past Lung-men and south to the northern side of Mount Hua; from there eastward along the foot of Ti-chu Mountain, past the Meng Ford and the confluence of the Lo River to Ta-p'ei. At this point Emperor Yu decided that, since the river was descending from high ground and the flow of the water was rapid and fierce, it would be difficult to guide it over level ground without danger of frequent disastrous breakthroughs. He therefore divided the flow into two channels, leading it along the higher ground to the north, past the Chiang River and so to Ta-lu. There he spread it out to form the Nine Rivers, brought it together again to make the Backward-Flowing River [i.e., tidal river], and thence led it into the Gulf of Pohai. When he had thus opened up the rivers of the nine provinces and fixed the outlets of the nine marshes, peace and order were brought to the lands of the Hsia, and his achievements continued to benefit the Three Dynasties which followed.

**History Now™** To read other works by Sima Qian, enter the *HistoryNow* documents area using the access card that is available for *World History.*

bend of the Yellow River. It is thus likely that the new technology became available to the founders of the Shang dynasty and may have aided their rise to power in northern China.

The Shang king ruled with the assistance of a central bureaucracy in the capital city. His realm was divided into a number of territories governed by aristocratic chieftains, but the king appointed these chieftains and could apparently depose them at will. He was also responsible for the defense of the realm and controlled large armies that often fought on the fringes of the kingdom. The transcendent importance of the ruler was graphically displayed in the ritual sacrifices undertaken at his death, when hundreds of his retainers were buried with him in the royal tomb.

As the inscriptions on the oracle bones make clear, the Chinese ruling elite believed in the existence of supernatural forces and thought that they could communicate with those forces to obtain divine intervention on matters of this world. In fact, the purpose of the oracle bones was to communicate with the gods. This evidence also suggests that the king was already being viewed as an intermediary between heaven and earth. In fact, an early Chinese character for king (王) consists of three horizontal lines connected by a single vertical line; the middle horizontal line represents the king's place between human society and the divine forces in nature.

The early Chinese also had a clear sense of life in the hereafter. Though some of the human sacrifices discovered in the royal tombs were presumably intended to propitiate the gods, others were meant to accompany the king or members of his family on the journey to the next world. From this conviction would come the concept of the **veneration of ancestors** (mistakenly known in the West as "ancestor worship") and the practice, which continues to the present day in many Chinese communities, of burning replicas of physical objects to accompany the departed on their journey to the next world.

**Social Structures** In the Neolithic period, the farm village was apparently the basic social unit of China, at least in the core region of the Yellow River valley. Villages were

© ChinaStock

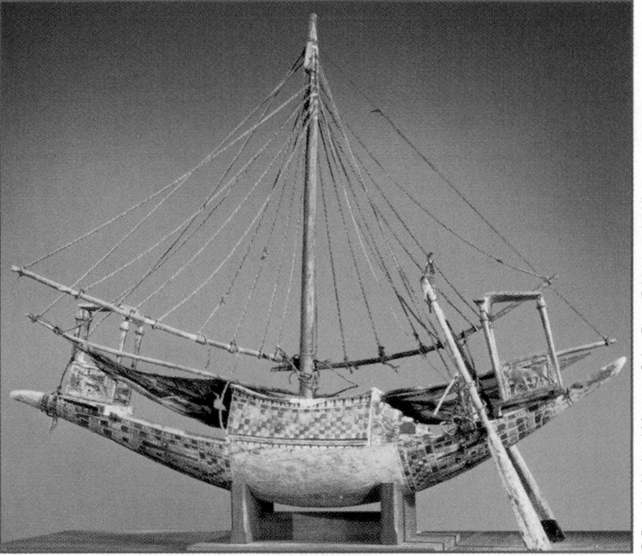
© Egyptian National Museum, Cairo, Egypt/Bridgeman Art Library

Religion & Philosophy

COMPARATIVE ILLUSTRATION

**The Afterlife and Prized Possessions.** Like the pharaohs in Egypt, Chinese rulers filled their tombs with prized possessions from daily life. It was believed that if the tombs were furnished and stocked with supplies, including chairs, boats, chests, weapons, games, and dishes, the spiritual body could continue its life despite the death of the physical body. At left, we see the remains of a chariot and horses in a burial pit in Hebei province in China that dates from the early Zhou dynasty. At right, we see a small model boat from the tomb of Tutankhamun in the Valley of the Kings in Egypt.

organized by clans rather than by nuclear family units, and all residents probably took the common clan name of the entire village. In some cases, a village may have included more than one clan. At Banpo (Pan P'o), an archaeological site near modern Xian that dates back at least eight thousand years, the houses in the village are separated by a ditch, which some scholars think may have served as a divider between two clans. The individual dwellings at Banpo housed nuclear families, but a larger building in the village was apparently used as a clan meeting hall. The tribal origins of Chinese society may help explain the continued importance of the joint family in traditional China, as well as the relatively small number of family names in Chinese society. Even today there are only about four hundred commonly used family names in a society of more than one billion people, and the colloquial name for the common people in China today is "the old hundred names."

By Shang times, the classes were becoming increasingly differentiated. It is likely that some poorer peasants did not own their farms but were obliged to work the land of the chieftain and other elite families in the village (see the box on p. 70). The aristocrats not only made war and served as officials (indeed, the first Chinese character for *official* originally meant "warrior"), but they were also the primary landowners. In addition to the aristocratic elite and the peasants, there were a small number of merchants and artisans, as well as slaves, probably consisting primarily of criminals or prisoners taken in battle.

The Shang are perhaps best known for their mastery of the art of bronze casting. Utensils, weapons, and ritual objects made of bronze (see the comparative essay "The Use of Metals" on p. 71) have been found in royal tombs in urban centers throughout the area known to be under Shang influence. It is also clear that the Shang had achieved a fairly sophisticated writing system that would

## Life in the Fields

The following passage is from *The Book of Songs*, a classic written during the early Zhou dynasty. This excerpt describes the calendar of peasant life on an estate in ancient China and indicates the various types of service that peasants provided for their lord.

*Who is the presumed author of this document? Are there suggestions here that men and women had different job responsibilities on the estate? How does this compare with the situation in other ancient civilizations?*

### The Book of Songs

*In the seventh month the Fire Star passes the meridian;*
*In the ninth month clothes are given out.*
*In the days of [our] first month, the wind blows cold;*
*In the days of [our] second, the air is cold.*
*Without coats, without garments of hair,*
*How could we get to the end of the year?*
*In the days of [our] third month we take our plows in hand;*
*In the days of [our] fourth we make our way to the fields.*
*Along with wives and children,*
*We eat in those south-lying acres.*
*The surveyor of the fields comes and is glad.*

*In the seventh month the Fire Star passes the meridian;*
*In the ninth month clothes are given out.*
*With the spring days the warmth begins,*
*And the oriole utters its song.*
*The young women take their deep baskets*
*And go along the small paths,*
*Looking for the tender [leaves of the] mulberry trees*
*As the spring days lengthen out,*
*They gather in crowds the white southern wood.*
*The girl's heart is wounded with sadness,*
*For she will soon be going with one of the young lords*
. . . .
*In the eighth month spinning is begun;*
*We make dark fabrics and yellow,*
*"With our red dye so bright,*
*We make robes for our young lords."*

*In the ninth month we prepare the stockyard,*
*And in the tenth we bring in the harvest.*
*The millets, the early and the late,*
*Together with paddy and hemp, beans and wheat.*
. . .
*Now we go up to work in the manor.*
*"In the day you gather the thatch-reeds;*
*In the evening twist them into rope;*
*Go quickly on to the roofs;*
*Soon you are to sow the grain."*

*In the days of [our] second month we cut the ice with tingling blows;*
*In the days of [our] third month [it is] stored in the icehouse.*
*In the days of [our] fourth month, very early,*
*A lamb with scallions is offered in sacrifice.*
*In the ninth month are shrewd frosts;*
*In the tenth month the stockyard is cleared.*
*With twin pitchers we hold the feast,*
*Killed for it is a young lamb.*
*Up we go into the lord's hall,*
*Raise the cup of buffalo horn;*
*"Long life for our lord; may he live forever and ever!"*

eventually spread throughout East Asia and evolve into the written language that is still used in China today.

# The Zhou Dynasty

In the eleventh century B.C.E., the Shang dynasty was overthrown by an aggressive young state located somewhat to the west of Anyang, the Shang capital, and near the great bend of the Yellow River as it begins to flow directly eastward to the sea. The new dynasty, which called itself the Zhou (Chou), survived for about eight hundred years and was thus the longest-lived dynasty in the history of China. According to tradition, the last of the Shang rulers was a tyrant who oppressed the people (Chinese sources assert that he was a degenerate who built "ponds of wine" and ordered the composing of lustful music that "ruined the morale of the nation"),[3] leading the ruler of the principality of Zhou to revolt and establish a new dynasty.

The Zhou located their capital in their home territory, near the present-day city of Xian. Later they established a second capital city at modern Luoyang, farther to the east, to administer new territories captured from the Shang. This established a pattern of eastern and western capitals that would endure off and on in China for nearly two thousand years.

## Political Structures

The Zhou dynasty (1045–221 B.C.E.) adopted the political system of its predecessors, with some changes. The Shang practice of dividing the kingdom into a number of territories governed by officials appointed by the king was continued under the Zhou. At the apex of the government

## COMPARATIVE ESSAY

# THE USE OF METALS

Around 6000 B.C.E., people in western Asia discovered how to use metals. They soon realized the advantage in using metal rather than stone to make both tools and weapons. Metal could be shaped more exactly, allowing artisans to make more refined tools and weapons with sharp edges and more precise shapes. Copper, silver, and gold, which were commonly found in their elemental form, were the first metals to be used. These were relatively soft and could be easily pounded into different shapes. But an important step was taken when people discovered that a rock that contained metal could be heated to liquefy the metal (a process called smelting). The liquid metal could then be poured into molds of clay or stone to make precisely shaped tools and weapons.

Copper was the first metal to be used in making tools. The first known copper smelting furnace, dated to 3800 B.C.E., was found in the Sinai. At about the same time, however, artisans in Southeast Asia discovered that tin could be added to copper to make bronze. By 3000 B.C.E., artisans in West Asia were also making bronze. Bronze has a lower melting point that makes it easier to cast, but it is also a harder metal than copper and corrodes less. By 1400 B.C.E., the Chinese were making bronze decorative objects as well as battle-axes and helmets. The widespread use of bronze has led historians to speak of the period from around 3000 to 1200 B.C.E. as the Bronze Age, although this is somewhat misleading in that many peoples continued to use stone tools and weapons even after bronze became available.

But there were limitations to the use of bronze. Tin was not as available as copper, which made bronze tools and weapons expensive. After 1200 B.C.E., bronze was increasingly replaced by iron, which was probably first used around 1500 B.C.E. in western Asia, where the Hittites made new weapons from it. Between 1500 and 600 B.C.E., ironmaking spread across Europe, North Africa, and Asia. Bronze continued to be used, but mostly for jewelry and other domestic purposes. Iron was used to make tools and weapons with sharper edges. Because iron weapons were cheaper than bronze ones, larger numbers of warriors could be armed, and wars could be fought on a larger scale.

Iron was handled differently from bronze: it was heated until it could be beaten into a desired shape. Each hammering produced increased strength for the metal. This wrought iron, as it was called, was typical of iron manufacturing in the West until the late Middle Ages. In China, however, the use of heat-resistant clay in the walls of their blast furnaces raised temperatures to 1,537 degrees Celsius, enabling artisans already in the fourth century B.C.E. to liquefy iron so that it too could be cast in a mold. Europeans would not develop such blast furnaces until the fifteenth century C.E.

©British Museum

**Bronze Axhead.** This axhead was made around 2000 B.C.E. by pouring liquid metal into an ax-shaped mold of clay or stone. Artisans would then polish the surface of the ax to produce a sharp cutting edge.

hierarchy was the Zhou king, who was served by a bureaucracy of growing size and complexity. It now included several ministries responsible for rites, education, law, and public works. Beyond the capital, the Zhou kingdom was divided into a number of principalities, governed by members of the hereditary aristocracy, who were appointed by the king and were at least theoretically subordinated to his authority.

**The Mandate of Heaven** But the Zhou kings also introduced some innovations. According to the *Rites of Zhou*, one of the oldest surviving documents on statecraft, the Zhou dynasty ruled China because it possessed the **"mandate of Heaven."** According to this concept, Heaven (viewed as an impersonal law of nature rather than as an anthropomorphic deity) maintained order in the universe through the Zhou king, who thus ruled as a representative of Heaven but not as a divine being. The king, who was selected to rule because of his talent and virtue, was then responsible for governing the people with compassion and efficiency. It was his duty to appease the gods in order to protect the people from natural calamities or bad harvests. But if the king failed to rule effectively, he could, theoretically at least, be overthrown and replaced by a new ruler. As noted earlier, this idea was used to justify the Zhou conquest of the Shang. Eventually, the concept of the heavenly mandate would become a cardinal principle of Chinese statecraft.[4] Each founder of a new dynasty would routinely assert that he had earned the mandate of Heaven, and who could disprove it except by overthrowing the king? As a pragmatic Chinese proverb put it, "He who wins is the king; he who loses is the rebel."

In asserting that the ruler had a direct connection with the divine forces presiding over the universe, Chinese tradition reflected a belief that was prevalent in all ancient civilizations. But whereas in some societies, notably in Mesopotamia and Greece (see Chapter 4), the gods were seen as capricious and not subject to human understanding, in China, Heaven was viewed as an essentially benevolent force devoted to universal harmony and order that could be influenced by positive human action. Was this attitude a consequence of the fact that the Chinese environment, though subject to some of the same climatic vicissitudes that plagued other parts of the world, was somewhat more predictable and beneficial than in climatically harsh regions like the Middle East?

By the sixth century B.C.E., the Zhou dynasty began to decline. As the power of the central government disintegrated, bitter internal rivalries arose among the various principalities, where the governing officials had succeeded in making their positions hereditary at the expense of the king. As the power of these officials grew, they began to regulate the local economy and seek reliable sources of revenue for their expanding armies, such as a uniform tax system and government monopolies on key commodities such as salt and iron.

## Economy and Society

During the Zhou dynasty, the essential characteristics of Chinese economic and social institutions began to take shape. The Zhou continued the pattern of land ownership that had existed under the Shang: the peasants worked on lands owned by their lord but also had land of their own that they cultivated for their own use. The practice was called the **well field system,** since the Chinese character for well (井) resembles a simplified picture of the division of the farmland into nine separate segments. Each peasant family tilled an outer plot for its own use and then joined with other families to work the inner one for the hereditary lord (see the box on p. 70). How widely this system was used is unclear, but it represented an ideal described by Confucian scholars of a later day. As the following poem indicates, life for the average farmer was a difficult one. The "big rat" is probably a reference to the high taxes imposed on the peasants by the government or lord.

*Big rat, big rat*
*Do not eat my millet!*
*Three years I have served you,*
*But you will not care for me.*
*I am going to leave you*
*And go to that happy land;*
*Happy land, happy land,*
*Where I will find my place.*[5]

Trade and manufacturing were carried out by merchants and artisans, who lived in walled towns under the direct control of the local lord. Merchants did not operate independently but were considered the property of the local lord and on occasion could even be bought and sold like chattels. A class of slaves performed a variety of menial tasks and perhaps worked on local irrigation projects. Most of them were probably prisoners of war captured during conflicts with the neighboring principalities. Scholars do not know how extensive slavery was in ancient times, but slaves probably did not constitute a large portion of the total population.

The period of the later Zhou, from the sixth to the third century B.C.E., was an era of significant economic growth and technological innovation, especially in agriculture. During that time, large-scale water control projects were undertaken to regulate the flow of rivers and distribute water evenly to the fields, as well as to construct canals to facilitate the transport of goods from one region to another (see the box on p. 68). Perhaps the most impressive technological achievement of the period was the construction of the massive water control project on the Min River, a tributary of the Yangtze. This system of canals and spillways, which was put into operation by the state of Qin a few years prior to the end of the Zhou dynasty, diverted excess water from the river into the local irrigation network and watered an area populated by as many as five million people. The system is still in use today, over two thousand years later.

Food production was also stimulated by a number of advances in farm technology. By the mid-sixth century B.C.E., the introduction of iron had led to the development of iron plowshares, which permitted deep plowing for the first time. Other innovations dating from the later Zhou were the use of natural fertilizer, the collar harness, and the technique of leaving land fallow to preserve or replenish nutrients in the soil (see the box on p. 73). By the late Zhou dynasty, the cultivation of wet rice had become one of the prime sources of food in China. Although rice was difficult and time-consuming to produce, it replaced other grain crops in areas with a warm climate because of its good taste, relative ease of preparation, and high nutritional value.

The advances in agriculture, which enabled the population of China to rise as high as twenty million people during the late Zhou era, were also undoubtedly a major factor in the growth of commerce and manufacturing. During the late Zhou, economic wealth began to replace noble birth as the prime source of power and influence. Utensils made of iron became more common, and trade developed in a variety of useful commodities, including cloth, salt, and various manufactured goods.

One of the most important items of trade in ancient China was silk. There is evidence of silkworm raising as early as the Neolithic period. Remains of silk material have been found on Shang bronzes, and a large number of fragments have been recovered in tombs dating from the mid-Zhou era. Silk cloth was used not only for clothing and quilts but also to wrap the bodies of the dead prior to burial. Fragments have been found throughout Central Asia and as far away as Athens, suggesting that the famous

## Environmental Concerns in Ancient China

Even in antiquity, China possessed a large population that often stretched the limits of the productive potential of the land. In the following excerpt, the late Zhou philosopher Mencius appeals to his sovereign to adopt policies that will conserve precious resources and foster the well-being of his subjects. Clearly, Mencius was concerned that environmental needs were being neglected. Unfortunately, his advice has not always been followed, and environmental degradation remains a problem in China today. The destruction of the forests, for example, has deprived China of much of its wood resources, and the present government has launched an extensive program to plant trees.

*Are these recommendations realistic in terms of what a monarch in ancient China might hope to achieve? Or might farmers resist some of these proposals as likely to harm their own interests?*

### The *Book of Mencius*

If you do not interfere with the busy season in the fields, then there will be more grain than the people can eat; if you do not allow nets with too fine a mesh to be used in large ponds, then there will be more fish and turtles than they can eat; if hatchets and axes are permitted in the forests on the hills only in the proper seasons, then there will be more timber than they can use. When the people have more grain, more fish and turtles than they can eat, and more timber than they can use, then in the support of their parents when alive and in the mourning of them when dead, they will be able to have no regrets over anything left undone. This is the first step along the Kingly way.

If the mulberry is planted in every homestead of five mu of land, then those who are fifty can wear silk; if chickens, pigs, and dogs do not miss their breeding season, then those who are seventy can eat meat; if each lot of a hundred mu is not deprived of labor during the busy seasons, then families with several mouths to feed will not go hungry. Exercise due care over the education provided by the village schools, and discipline the people by teaching them the duties proper to sons and younger brothers, and those whose heads have turned gray will not be carrying loads on the roads. When those who are seventy wear silk and eat meat and the masses are neither cold nor hungry, it is impossible for their prince not to be a true King.

Now when food meant for human beings is so plentiful as to be thrown to dogs and pigs, you fail to realize that it is time for garnering, and when men drop dead from starvation by the wayside, you fail to realize that it is time for distribution. When people die, you simply say, "It is none of my doing. It is the fault of the harvest." In what way is that different from killing a man by running him through, while saying all the time, "It is none of my doing. It is the fault of the weapon." Stop putting the blame on the harvest and the people of the whole Empire will come to you.

**HistoryNow™** To read other selections by Mencius, enter the *HistoryNow* documents area using the access card that is available for *World History*.

Silk Road stretching from central China westward to the Middle East and the Mediterranean Sea was in operation as early as the fifth century B.C.E. (see Map 3.2 on p. 83; see also Chapter 10).

With the development of trade and manufacturing, China began to move toward a money economy. The first form of money, as in much of the rest of the world, may have been seashells (the Chinese character for goods or property contains the ideographic symbol for "shell": 貝), but by the Zhou dynasty, pieces of iron shaped like a knife or round coins with a hole in the middle so they could be carried in strings of a thousand were being used. Most ordinary Chinese, however, simply used a system of barter. Taxes, rents, and even the salaries of government officials were normally paid in grain.

## The Hundred Schools of Ancient Philosophy

In China, as in other great river valley societies, the birth of civilization was accompanied by the emergence of an organized effort to comprehend the nature of the cosmos and the role of human beings within it. Speculation over such questions began in the very early stages of civilization and culminated at the end of the Zhou era in the "hundred schools" of ancient philosophy, a wide-ranging debate over the nature of human beings, society, and the universe.

**Early Beliefs** The first hint of religious belief in ancient China comes from relics found in royal tombs of Neolithic times. By then, the Chinese had already developed a religious sense beyond the primitive belief in the existence of spirits in nature. The Shang had begun to believe in the existence of one transcendent god, known as Shang Di, who presided over all the forces of nature. As time went on, the Chinese concept of religion evolved from a vaguely anthropomorphic god to a somewhat more impersonal symbol of universal order known as Heaven (*Tian*, or *T'ien*). There was also much speculation among Chinese intellectuals about the nature of the cosmic order. One of the earliest ideas was that the universe was divided into two primary forces of good and evil, light and dark, male and female, called the *yang* and the *yin*, represented symbolically by the sun (*yang*) and the moon (*yin*). According to this theory, life was a dynamic process of interaction between the forces of *yang* and *yin*. Early Chinese could attempt only to understand the process and perhaps to have some minimal effect on its operation. They could not hope to reverse it. It is sometimes asserted that this belief has contributed to the heavy element of fatalism in Chinese popular wisdom. The Chinese have traditionally believed that bad times will be followed by good times, and vice versa.

The belief that there was some mysterious "law of nature" that could be interpreted by human beings led to various attempts to predict the future, such as the Shang oracle bones and other methods of divination. Philosophers invented ways to interpret the will of nature, while shamans, playing a role similar to the *brahmins* in India, were employed at court to assist the emperor in his policy deliberations until at least the fifth century C.E. One of the most famous manuals used for this purpose was the *Yi Jing* (*I Ching*), known in English as the *Book of Changes*.

**Confucianism** Such efforts to divine the mysterious purposes of Heaven notwithstanding, Chinese thinking about metaphysical reality also contained a strain of pragmatism, which is readily apparent in the ideas of the great philosopher Confucius. Confucius (the name is the Latin form of his honorific title, Kung Fuci, or K'ung Fu-tzu, meaning Master Kung) was born in the state of Lu (in the modern province of Shandong) in 551 B.C.E. After reaching maturity, he apparently hoped to find employment as a political adviser in one of the principalities into which China was divided at that time, but he had little success in finding a patron. Nevertheless, he made an indelible mark on history as an independent (and somewhat disgruntled) political and social philosopher.

In conversations with his disciples contained in the *Analects*, Confucius often adopted a detached and almost skeptical view of Heaven. "You are unable to serve man," he commented on one occasion, "how then can you hope to serve the spirits? While you do not know life, how can you know about death?" In many instances, he appeared to advise his followers to revere the deities and the ancestral spirits but to keep them at a distance. Confucius believed it was useless to speculate too much about metaphysical questions. Better by far to assume that there was a rational order to the universe and then concentrate one's attention on ordering the affairs of this world.[6]

Confucius' interest in philosophy, then, was essentially political and ethical. The universe was constructed in such a way that if human beings could act harmoniously in accordance with its purposes, their own affairs would prosper. Much of his concern was with human behavior. The key to proper behavior was to behave in accordance with the ***Dao*** (Way). Confucius assumed that all human beings had their own *Dao*, depending on their individual role in life, and it was their duty to follow it. Even the ruler had his own *Dao*, and he ignored it at his peril, for to do so could mean the loss of the mandate of Heaven. The idea of the *Dao* is reminiscent of the concept of *dharma* in ancient India and played a similar role in governing the affairs of society.

Two elements in the Confucian interpretation of the *Dao* are particularly worthy of mention. The first is the concept of duty. It was the responsibility of all individuals to subordinate their own interests and aspirations to the broader need of the family and the community. Confucius assumed that if each individual worked hard to fulfill his or her assigned destiny, the affairs of society as a whole would prosper as well. In this respect, it was important for the ruler to set a good example. If he followed his "kingly way," the beneficial effects would radiate throughout society (see the box on p. 75).

The second key element is the idea of humanity, sometimes translated as "human-heartedness." This concept involves a sense of compassion and empathy for others. It is similar in some ways to Christian concepts, but with a subtle twist. Where Christian teachings call on human beings to "behave toward others as you would have them behave toward you," the Confucian maxim is put in a different way: "Do not do unto others what you would not wish done to yourself." To many Chinese, this attitude symbolizes an element of tolerance in the Chinese character that has not always been practiced in other societies.[7]

Confucius may have considered himself a failure because he never attained the position he wanted, but many of his contemporaries found his ideas appealing, and in the generations after his death, his message spread widely throughout China. Confucius was an outspoken critic of his times and lamented the disappearance of what he regarded as the Golden Age of the early Zhou.

In fact, however, Confucius was not just another disgruntled Chinese conservative mourning the passing of the good old days; rather, he was a revolutionary thinker, many of whose key ideas looked forward rather than backward. Perhaps his most striking political idea was that the government should be open to all men of superior quality, not limited to those of noble birth. As one of his disciples reports in the *Analects*: "The Master said, by nature, men are nearly alike; by practice, they get to be wide apart."[8] Confucius undoubtedly had himself in mind as one of those "superior" men, but the rapacity of the hereditary lords must have added strength to his convictions.

The concept of rule by merit was, of course, not an unfamiliar idea in the China of his day; the *Rites of Zhou* had clearly stated that the king himself deserved to rule because of his talent and virtue, rather than as the result of noble birth. In practice, however, aristocratic privilege must often have opened the doors to political influence, and many of Confucius' contemporaries must have regarded his appeal for government by talent as both exciting and dangerous. Confucius did not explicitly question the right of the hereditary aristocracy to play a leading role in the political process, nor did his ideas have much effect in his lifetime. Still, they introduced a new concept that was later implemented in the form of a bureaucracy selected through a civil service examination (see "Confucianism and the State" later in this chapter).

## THE WAY OF THE GREAT LEARNING

Few texts exist today that were written by Confucius himself. Most were written or edited by his disciples. The following text, titled *The Great Learning,* was probably written two centuries after Confucius' death, but it illustrates his view that good government begins with the cultivation of individual morality and proper human relationships at the basic level. This conviction that to bring peace to the world, you must cultivate your own person continued to win general approval down to modern times. There are interesting similarities between such ideas and the views expressed in the Indian treatise *Arthasastra,* discussed in Chapter 2.

*Compare these views, which reflect one of the most basic elements in Confucian thought—that proper moral behavior must begin at the level of the individual if it is to succeed within the framework of the larger community—with moral teachings expressed in other ancient civilizations. Would the Indian political adviser Kautilya, for example, agree with such views?*

### The Great Learning

The Way of the Great Learning consists in clearly exemplifying illustrious virtue, in loving the people, and in resting in the highest good.

Only when one knows where one is to rest can one have a fixed purpose. Only with a fixed purpose can one achieve calmness of mind. Only with calmness of mind can one attain serene repose. Only in serene repose can one carry on careful deliberation. Only through careful deliberation can one have achievement. Things have their roots and branches; affairs have their beginning and end. He who knows what comes first and what comes last comes himself near the Way.

The ancients who wished clearly to exemplify illustrious virtue throughout the world would first set up good government in their states. Wishing to govern well their states, they would first regulate their families. Wishing to regulate their families, they would first cultivate their persons. Wishing to cultivate their persons, they would first rectify their minds. Wishing to rectify their minds, they would first seek sincerity in their thoughts. Wishing for sincerity in their thoughts, they would first extend their knowledge. The extension of knowledge lay in the investigation of things. For only when things are investigated is knowledge extended; only when knowledge is extended are thoughts sincere; only when thoughts are sincere are minds rectified; only when minds are rectified are our persons cultivated; only when our persons are cultivated are our families regulated; only when families are regulated are states well governed; and only when states are well governed is there peace in the world.

From the emperor down to the common people, all, without exception, must consider cultivation of the individual character as the root. If the root is in disorder, it is impossible for the branches to be in order. To treat the important as unimportant and to treat the unimportant as important–this should never be. This is called knowing the root; this is called the perfection of knowledge.

Confucius' ideas, passed on to later generations through the *Analects* as well as through writings attributed to him, had a strong impact on Chinese political thinkers of the late Zhou period, a time when the existing system was in disarray and open to serious question. But as with most great thinkers, Confucius' ideas were sufficiently ambiguous to be interpreted in contradictory ways. Some, like the philosopher Mencius (370–290 B.C.E.), stressed the humanistic side of Confucian ideas, arguing that human beings were by nature good and hence could be taught their civic responsibilities by example. He also stressed that the ruler had a duty to govern with compassion:

> It was because Chieh and Chou lost the people that they lost the empire, and it was because they lost the hearts of the people that they lost the people. Here is the way to win the empire: win the people and you win the empire. Here is the way to win the people: win their hearts and you win the people. Here is the way to win their hearts: give them and share with them what they like, and do not do to them what they do not like. The people turn to a human ruler as water flows downward or beasts take to wilderness.[9]

Here is a prescription for political behavior that could win wide support in our own day. Other thinkers, however, rejected Mencius' rosy view of human nature and argued for a different approach.

**Legalism** One school of thought that became quite popular during the "hundred schools" era in ancient China was the philosophy of Legalism. Taking issue with the view of Mencius and other disciples of Confucius that human nature was essentially good, the Legalists argued that human beings were by nature evil and would follow the correct path only if coerced by harsh laws and stiff punishments. These thinkers were referred to as the School of Law because they rejected the Confucian view that government by "superior men" could solve society's problems and argued instead for a system of impersonal laws.

The Legalists also disagreed with the Confucian belief that the universe has a moral core. They therefore believed that only firm action by the state could bring about social order. Fear of harsh punishment, more than the promise of material reward, could best motivate the common people to serve the interests of the ruler. Because

© Topham/The Image Works

**Confucius and Lao Tzu.** It is not likely that the two ancient Chinese philosophers ever met, for little is known about the life of Lao Tzu, but according to tradition the two allegedly held a face-to-face meeting. The discussion must have interesting, for their points of view about the nature of reality were diametrically opposed. The Chinese have managed to preserve both traditions throughout history, however, perhaps a reflection of the dualities represented in the Chinese approach to life. A similar duality existed among Platonists and Aristotelians in ancient Greece (see Chapter 4).

human nature was essentially corrupt, officials could not be trusted to carry out their duties in a fair and even-handed manner, and only a strong ruler could create an orderly society. All human actions should be subordinated to the effort to create a strong and prosperous state subject to his will.

**Daoism** One of the most popular alternatives to **Confucianism** was the philosophy of **Daoism** (frequently spelled Taoism). According to Chinese tradition, the Daoist school was founded by a contemporary of Confucius popularly known as Lao Tzu (Lao Zi), or the Old Master. Many modern scholars, however, are skeptical that Lao Tzu actually existed.

Obtaining a clear understanding of the original concepts of Daoism is difficult because its primary document, a short treatise known as the *Dao De Jing* (sometimes translated as *The Way of the Tao*), is an enigmatic book whose interpretation has baffled scholars for centuries. The opening line, for example, explains less what the *Dao* is than what it is not: "The Tao [Way] that can be told of is not the eternal Tao. The name that can be named is not the eternal name."[10]

Nevertheless, the basic concepts of Daoism are not especially difficult to understand. Like Confucianism, Daoism does not anguish over the underlying meaning of the cosmos. Rather, it attempts to set forth proper forms of behavior for human beings here on earth. In most other respects, however, Daoism presents a view of life and its ultimate meaning that is almost diametrically opposed to that of Confucianism. Where Confucian doctrine asserts that it is the duty of human beings to work hard to improve life here on earth, Daoists contend that the true way to interpret the will of Heaven is not action but inaction *(wu wei)*. The best way to act in harmony with the universal order is to act spontaneously and let nature take its course (see the box on p. 77).

Such a message could be very appealing to people who were uncomfortable with the somewhat rigid flavor of the Confucian work ethic and preferred a more individualistic approach. This image would eventually find graphic expression in Chinese landscape painting, which in its classical form would depict naturalistic scenes of mountains, water, and clouds and underscore the fragility and smallness of individual human beings.

Daoism achieved considerable popularity in the waning years of the Zhou dynasty. It was especially popular among intellectuals, who may have found it appealing as an escapist antidote in a world characterized by growing disorder.

**Popular Beliefs** Daoism also played a second role as a loose framework for popular spiritualistic and animistic beliefs among the common people. Popular Daoism was less a philosophy than a religion; it comprised a variety of rituals and forms of behavior that were regarded as a means of achieving heavenly salvation or even a state of immortality on earth. Daoist sorcerers practiced various types of mind- or body-training exercises in the hope of achieving power, sexual prowess, and long life. It was primarily this form of Daoism that survived into a later age.

The philosophical forms of Confucianism and Daoism did not provide much meaning to the mass of the population, for whom philosophical debate over the ultimate meaning of life was not as important as the daily struggle for survival. Even among the elites, interest in the occult and in astrology was high, and magicoreligious ideas coexisted with the interest in natural science and humanistic philosophy throughout the ancient period.

For most Chinese, Heaven was not a vague, impersonal law of nature, as it was for many Confucian and Daoist intellectuals, but a terrain peopled with innumerable gods and spirits of nature, both good and evil, who existed in trees, mountains, and streams as well as in heavenly bodies. As human beings mastered the techniques of farming, they called on divine intervention to guarantee a good harvest. Other gods were responsible for the safety of fishers, transportation workers, or prospective mothers.

## The Daoist Answer to Confucianism

The *Dao De Jing* (*The Way of the Tao*) is the great classic of philosophical Daoism (Taoism). Traditionally attributed to the legendary Chinese philosopher Lao Tzu (Old Master), it was probably written sometime during the era of Confucius. This opening passage illustrates two of the key ideas that characterize Daoist belief: it is impossible to define the nature of the universe, and "inaction" (not Confucian "action") is the key to ordering the affairs of human beings.

*What is Lao Tzu, the presumed author of this document, trying to express about the basic nature of the universe? Is there a moral order that can be comprehended by human thought? What would Lao Tzu have to say about Confucian moral teachings?*

### The Way of the Tao

*The Tao that can be told of is not the eternal Tao;*
*The name that can be named is not the eternal name.*
*The Nameless is the origin of Heaven and Earth;*
*The Named is the mother of all things.*

*Therefore let there always be nonbeing, so we may see their subtlety.*
*And let there always be being, so we may see their outcome.*
*The two are the same,*
*But after they are produced, they have different names.*
*They both may be called deep and profound.*
*Deeper and more profound,*
*The door of all subtleties!*
*When the people of the world all know beauty as beauty,*
*There arises the recognition of ugliness.*
*When they all know the good as good,*
*There arises the recognition of evil.*
*Therefore:*
*Being and nonbeing produce each other;*
*Difficult and easy complete each other;*
*Long and short contrast each other;*
*High and low distinguish each other;*
*Sound and voice harmonize each other;*
*Front and behind accompany each other.*

*Therefore the sage manages affairs without action*
*And spreads doctrines without words.*
*All things arise, and he does not turn away from them.*
*He produces them but does not take possession of them.*
*He acts but does not rely on his own ability.*
*He accomplishes his task but does not claim credit for it.*
*It is precisely because he does not claim credit that his accomplishment remains with him.*

**History Now**™ To read more selections from the *Dao De Jing*, enter the *HistoryNow* documents area using the access card that is available for *World History*.

Another aspect of popular religion was the belief that the spirits of deceased human beings lived in the atmosphere for a time before ascending to heaven or descending to hell. During that period, surviving family members had to care for the spirits through proper ritual, or they would become evil spirits and haunt the survivors.

Thus in ancient China, human beings were offered a variety of interpretations of the nature of the universe. Confucianism satisfied the need for a rational doctrine of nation building and social organization at a time when the existing political and social structure was beginning to disintegrate. Philosophical Daoism provided a more sensitive approach to the vicissitudes of fate and nature, and a framework for a set of diverse animistic beliefs at the popular level. But neither could satisfy the deeper emotional needs that sometimes inspire the human spirit. Neither could effectively provide solace in a time of sorrow or the hope of a better life in the hereafter. Something else would be needed to fill the gap.

# The Rise of the Chinese Empire: The Qin and the Han

During the last two centuries of the Zhou dynasty (the fourth and third centuries B.C.E.), the authority of the king became increasingly nominal, and several of the small principalities into which the Zhou kingdom had been divided began to evolve into powerful states that presented a potential challenge to the Zhou ruler himself. Chief among these were Qu (Ch'u) in the central Yangtze valley, Wu in the Yangtze delta, and Yue (Yueh) along the southeastern coast. At first, their mutual rivalries were in check, but by the late fifth century B.C.E., competition intensified into civil war, giving birth to the so-called Period of the Warring States (see the box on p. 79). Powerful principalities vied with each other for preeminence and largely ignored the now purely titular authority of the Zhou court (see Map 3.1). New forms of warfare also

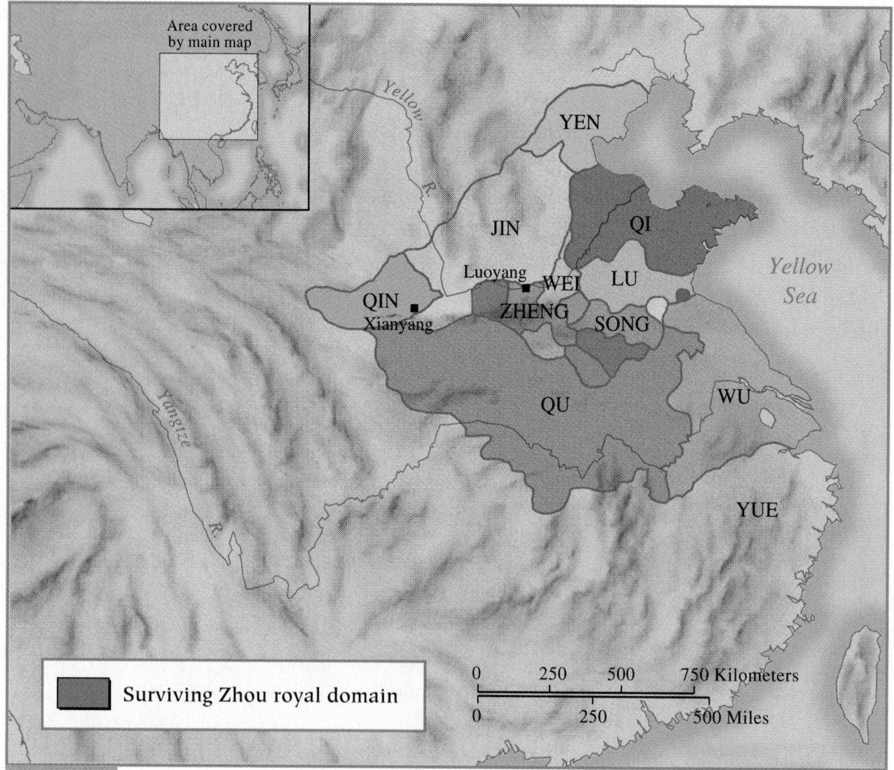


**MAP 3.1 China During the Period of the Warring States.** From the fifth to the third centuries B.C.E, China was locked in a time of civil strife known as the Period of the Warring States. This map shows the Zhou dynasty capital at Luoyang, along with the major states that were squabbling for precedence in the region. The state of Qin would eventually suppress its rivals and form the first unified Chinese empire, with its capital at Xianyang (near modern Xian). ? Where is Qin located on the map? **View an animated version of this map or related maps at** http://history.wadsworth.com/duikerspielvogel05/

emerged with the invention of iron weapons and the introduction of the foot soldier. Cavalry, too, made its first appearance, armed with the powerful crossbow.

Eventually, the relatively young state of Qin, located in the original homeland of the Zhou, became a key player in these conflicts. Benefiting from a strong defensive position in the mountains to the west of the great bend of the Yellow River, as well as from their control of the rich Sichuan plains, the Qin gradually subdued their main rivals through conquest or diplomatic maneuvering. In 221 B.C.E.., the Qin ruler declared the establishment of a new dynasty, the first truly unified government in Chinese history.

## The Qin Dynasty (221–206 B.C.E.)

One of the primary reasons for the triumph of the Qin was probably the character of the Qin ruler, known to history as Qin Shi Huangdi (Ch'in Shih Huang Ti), or the First Emperor of Qin. A man of forceful personality and immense ambition, Qin Shi Huangdi had ascended to the throne of Qin in 246 B.C.E. at the age of thirteen. Described by the famous Han dynasty historian Sima Qian as having "the chest of a bird of prey, the voice of a jackal, and the heart of a tiger," the new king of Qin found the Legalist views of his adviser Li Su (Li Ssu) only too appealing. In 221 B.C.E. Qin Shi Huangdi defeated the last of his rivals and founded a new dynasty with himself as emperor.

**Political Structures** The Qin dynasty transformed Chinese politics. Philosophical doctrines that had proliferated during the late Zhou period were prohibited, and Legalism was adopted as the official ideology. Those who opposed the policies of the new regime were punished and sometimes executed, while books presenting ideas contrary to the official orthodoxy were publicly put to the torch, perhaps the first example of book burning in history (see the box on p. 80).

Legalistic theory gave birth to a number of fundamental administrative and political developments, some of which would survive the Qin and serve as a model for future dynasties. In the first place, unlike the Zhou, the Qin was a highly centralized state. The central bureaucracy was divided into three primary ministries: a civil authority, a military authority, and a censorate, whose inspectors surveyed the efficiency of officials throughout the system. This would later become standard administrative procedure for future Chinese dynasties.

Below the central government were two levels of administration: provinces and counties. Unlike the Zhou system, officials at these levels did not inherit their positions but were appointed by the court and were subject to dismissal at the emperor's whim. Apparently, some form of merit system was used, although there is no evidence that selection was based on performance in an examination. The civil servants may have been chosen on the recommendation of other government officials. A penal

**The Qin Empire, 221–206 B.C.E.**

## The Art of War

With the possible exception of the nineteenth-century German military strategist Karl von Clausewitz, there is probably no more famous or respected writer on the art of war than the ancient Chinese thinker Sun Tzu. Yet surprisingly little is known about him. Recently discovered evidence suggests that he lived sometime in the fifth century B.C.E., during the chronic conflict of the Period of Warring States, and that he was an early member of an illustrious family of military strategists who advised Zhou rulers for more than two hundred years. But despite the mystery surrounding his life, there is no doubt of his influence on later generations of military planners. Among his most avid followers in our century have been the revolutionary leaders Mao Zedong and Ho Chi Minh, as well as the Japanese military strategists who planned the attacks on Port Arthur and Pearl Harbor.

The following brief excerpt from his classic *The Art of War* provides a glimmer into the nature of his advice, still so timely today.

*Why are the ideas of Sun Tzu about the art of war still so popular among military strategists after 2,500 years? How might he advise U.S. and other statesmen to deal with the problem of international terrorism today?*

### Selections from Sun Tzu

Sun Tzu said:

"In general, the method for employing the military is this: . . . Attaining one hundred victories in one hundred battles is not the pinnacle of excellence. Subjugating the enemy's army without fighting is the true pinnacle of excellence. . . .

"Thus the highest realization of warfare is to attack the enemy's plans; next is to attack their alliances; next to attack their army; and the lowest is to attack their fortified cities.

"This tactic of attacking fortified cities is adopted only when unavoidable. Preparing large movable protective shields, armored assault wagons, and other equipment and devices will require three months. Building earthworks will require another three months to complete. If the general cannot overcome his impatience but instead launches an assault wherein his men swarm over the walls like ants, he will kill one-third of his officers and troops, and the city will still not be taken. This is the disaster that results from attacking [fortified cities].

"Thus one who excels at employing the military subjugates other people's armies without engaging in battle, captures other people's fortified cities without attacking them, and destroys others people's states without prolonged fighting. He must fight under Heaven with the paramount aim of 'preservation.' . . .

"In general, the strategy of employing the military is this: If your strength is ten times theirs, surround them; if five, then attack them; if double, then divide your forces. If you are equal in strength to the enemy, you can engage him. If fewer, you can circumvent him. If outmatched, you can avoid him. . . .

"Thus there are five factors from which victory can be known:

*"One who knows when he can fight, and when he cannot fight, will be victorious.*
*"One who recognizes how to employ large and small numbers will be victorious.*
*"One whose upper and lower ranks have the same desires will be victorious.*
*"One who, fully prepared, awaits the unprepared will be victorious.*
*"One whose general is capable and not interfered with by the ruler will be victorious.*

"These five are the Way (Tao) to know victory. . . .

"Thus it is said that one who knows the enemy and knows himself will not be endangered in a hundred engagements. One who does not know the enemy but knows himself will sometimes be victorious, sometimes meet with defeat. One who knows neither the enemy nor himself will invariably be defeated in every engagement."

**History Now**™ To read more of *The Art of War,* enter the *HistoryNow* documents area using the access card that is available for *World History.*

code provided for harsh punishments for all wrongdoers. Officials were watched by the censors, who reported directly to the throne. Those guilty of malfeasance in office were executed.

**Society and the Economy** Qin Shi Huangdi, who had a passion for centralization, unified the system of weights and measures, standardized the monetary system and the written forms of Chinese characters, and ordered the construction of a system of roads extending throughout the empire. He also attempted to eliminate the remaining powers of the landed aristocrats and divided their estates among the peasants, who were now taxed directly by the state. He thus eliminated potential rivals and secured tax revenues for the central government. Members of the aristocratic clans were required to live in the capital city at Xianyang (Hsien-yang), just north of modern Xian, so that the court could monitor their activities. Such a

## Memorandum on the Burning of Books

Li Su, the author of the following passage, was a chief minister of the First Emperor of Qin. An exponent of Legalism, Li Su hoped to eliminate all rival theories on government. His recommendation to the emperor on the subject was recorded by the Han dynasty historian Sima Qian. The emperor approved the proposal and ordered all books contrary to the spirit of Legalist ideology to be destroyed on pain of death. Fortunately, some texts were preserved by being hidden or even memorized by their owners and were thus available to later generations. For centuries afterward, the First Emperor of Qin and his minister were singled out for criticism because of their intolerance and their effort to control the very minds of their subjects. Totalitarianism, it seems, is not exclusively a modern concept.

*Why does the Legalist thinker Li Su feel that his proposal to destroy dangerous ideas is justified? Are there examples of similar thinking in our own time? Are there occasions when it might be permissible to outlaw unpopular ideas?*

### Sima Qian, *Historical Records*

In earlier times the empire disintegrated and fell into disorder, and no one was capable of unifying it. Thereupon the various feudal lords rose to power. In their discourses they all praised the past in order to disparage the present and embellished empty words to confuse the truth. Everyone cherished his own favorite school of learning and criticized what had been instituted by the authorities. But at present Your Majesty possesses a unified empire, has regulated the distinctions of black and white, and has firmly established for yourself a position of sole supremacy. And yet these independent schools, joining with each other, criticize the codes of laws and instructions. Hearing of the promulgation of a decree, they criticize it, each from the standpoint of his own school. At home they disapprove of it in their hearts; going out they criticize it in the thoroughfare. They seek a reputation by discrediting their sovereign; they appear superior by expressing contrary views, and they lead the lowly multitude in the spreading of slander. If such license is not prohibited, the sovereign power will decline above and partisan factions will form below. It would be well to prohibit this.

Your servant suggests that all books in the imperial archives, save the memoirs of Ch'in, be burned. All persons in the empire, except members of the Academy of Learned Scholars, in possession of the *Book of Odes,* the *Book of History,* and discourses of the hundred philosophers should take them to the local governors and have them indiscriminately burned. Those who dare to talk to each other about the *Book of Odes* and the *Book of History* should be executed and their bodies exposed in the marketplace. Anyone referring to the past to criticize the present should, together with all members of his family, be put to death. Officials who fail to report cases that have come under their attention are equally guilty. After thirty days from the time of issuing the decree, those who have not destroyed their books are to be branded and sent to build the Great Wall. Books not to be destroyed will be those on medicine and pharmacy, divination by the tortoise and milfoil, and agriculture and arboriculture. People wishing to pursue learning should take the officials as their teachers.

system may not have been advantageous to the peasants in all respects, however, since the central government could now collect taxes more effectively and mobilize the peasants for military service and for various public works projects.

The Qin dynasty was equally unsympathetic to the merchants, whom it viewed as parasites. Private commercial activities were severely restricted and heavily taxed, and many vital forms of commerce and manufacturing, including mining, wine making, and the distribution of salt, were placed under a government monopoly.

Qin Shi Huangdi was equally aggressive in foreign affairs. His armies continued the gradual advance to the south that had taken place during the final years of the Zhou dynasty, extending the border of China to the edge of the Red River in modern Vietnam. To supply the Qin armies operating in the area, a canal was dug that provided direct inland navigation from the Yangtze River in central China to what is now the modern city of Guangzhou (Canton) in the south.

**Beyond the Frontier: The Nomadic Peoples and the Great Wall** The main area of concern for the Qin emperor, however, was in the north, where a nomadic people, known to the Chinese as the Xiongnu (Hsiung-nu) and possibly related to the Huns (see Chapter 5), had become increasingly active in the area of the Gobi Desert. The area north of the Yellow River had been sparsely inhabited since prehistoric times. During the Qin period, the climate of northern China was somewhat milder and moister than it is today, and parts of the region were heavily forested. The local population probably lived by hunting and fishing, practicing limited forms of agriculture, or herding animals such as cattle or sheep.

As the climate gradually became drier, people were forced to rely increasingly on animal husbandry as a means of livelihood. Their response was to master the art of riding on horseback and to adopt the nomadic life. Organized loosely into communities consisting of a number of kinship groups, they ranged far and wide in search of pasture for their herds of cattle, goats, or sheep. As they moved seasonally from one pasture to another, they often traveled several hundred miles carrying their goods and their circular felt tents, called *yurts.*

But the new way of life presented its own challenges. Increased food production led to a growing population, which in times of drought outstripped the available resources. Rival groups then competed for the best pastures. After they mastered the art of fighting on horseback sometime during the middle of the first millennium B.C.E., territorial warfare became commonplace throughout the entire frontier region from the Pacific Ocean to Central Asia.

By the end of the Zhou dynasty in the third century B.C.E., the nomadic Xiongnu posed a serious threat to the security of China's northern frontier, and a number of Chinese principalities in the area began to build walls and fortifications to keep them out. But warriors on horseback possessed significant advantages over the infantry of the Chinese.

Qin Shi Huangdi's answer to the problem was to strengthen the walls to keep the marauders out. In Sima Qian's words:

> [The] First Emperor of the Ch'in dispatched Meng T'ien to lead a force of a hundred thousand men north to attack the barbarians. He seized control of all the lands south of the Yellow River and established border defenses along the river, constructing forty-four walled district cities overlooking the river and manning them with convict laborers transported to the border for garrison duty. Thus he utilized the natural mountain barriers to establish the border defenses, scooping out the valleys and constructing ramparts and building installations at other points where they were needed. The whole line of defenses stretched over ten thousand *li* [a *li* is one-third of a mile] from Lin-t'ao to Liao-tung and even extended across the Yellow River and through Yang-shan and Pei-chia.[11]

Today, of course, we know Qin Shi Huangdi's project as the Great Wall, which extends nearly 4,000 miles from the sandy wastes of Central Asia to the sea. It is constructed of massive granite blocks, and its top is wide enough to serve as a roadway for horse-drawn chariots. Although the wall that appears in most photographs today was built 1,500 years after the Qin, during the Ming dynasty, some of the walls built by the Qin remain standing. Their construction was a massive project that required the efforts of thousands of laborers, many of whom met their deaths there and, according to legend, are now buried within the wall.

**The Fall of the Qin** The Legalist system put in place by the First Emperor of Qin was designed to achieve maximum efficiency as well as total security for the state. It did neither. Qin Shi Huangdi was apparently aware of the dangers of factions within the imperial family and established a class of **eunuchs** (males whose testicles have been removed) who served as personal attendants for himself and female members of the royal family. The original idea may have been to restrict the influence of male courtiers, and the eunuch system later became a standard feature of the Chinese imperial system. But as confidential advisers to the royal family, eunuchs were in a position of influence. The rivalry between the "inner" imperial court and the "outer" court of bureaucratic officials led to tensions that persisted until the end of the imperial system.

By ruthlessly gathering control over the empire into his own hands, Qin Shi Huangdi had hoped to establish a rule that, in the words of Sima Qian, "would be enjoyed by his sons for ten thousand generations." In fact, his centralizing zeal alienated many key groups. Landed aristocrats and Confucian intellectuals, as well as the common people, groaned under the censorship of thought and speech, harsh taxes, and forced labor projects. "He killed men," recounted the historian, "as though he thought he could never finish, he punished men as though he were afraid he would never get around to them all, and the whole world revolted against him."[12] Shortly after the emperor died in 210 B.C.E., the dynasty quickly descended into factional rivalry, and four years later it was overthrown.

The disappearance of the Qin brought an end to an experiment in absolute rule that later Chinese historians would view as a betrayal of humanistic Confucian principles. But in another sense, the Qin system was a response—though somewhat extreme—to the problems of administering a large and increasingly complex society. Although later rulers would denounce Legalism and enthrone Confucianism as the new state orthodoxy, in practice they would make use of a number of the key tenets of Legalism to administer the empire and control the behavior of their subjects.

## The Glorious Han Dynasty (202 B.C.E.–221 C.E.)

The fall of the Qin was followed by a brief period of civil strife as aspiring successors competed for hegemony. Out of this strife emerged one of the greatest and most durable dynasties in Chinese history—the Han. The Han dynasty would later become so closely identified with the advance of Chinese civilization that even today the Chinese sometimes refer to themselves as "people of Han" and to their language as the "language of Han."

The founder of the Han dynasty was Liu Bang (Liu Pang), a commoner of peasant origin who would be known historically by his title of Han Gaozu (Han Kao Tsu, or Exalted Emperor of Han). Under his strong rule and that of his successors, the new dynasty quickly moved to consolidate its control over the empire and promote the welfare of its subjects. Efficient and benevolent, at least by the standards of the time, Gaozu maintained the centralized political institutions of the Qin but abandoned their harsh Legalistic approach to law enforcement. Han rulers also reversed the effort by the First Emperor of Qin to enforce a single ideology and discovered in Confucian principles a useful foundation for the creation of a new state philosophy. Under the Han,

Confucianism began to take on the character of an official ideology.

**Confucianism and the State** The integration of Confucian doctrine with Legalist practice, creating a system generally known as **State Confucianism,** did not take long to accomplish. Although the founding Han ruler declared his intention to discard the harsh methods adopted by the Qin, he and his successors found it convenient to retain many of the institutions introduced by the First Emperor of Qin. For example, they borrowed the tripartite division of the central government into civilian and military authorities and a censorate. The government was headed by a "grand council" including representatives from all three segments of government. The Han also retained the system of local government, dividing the empire into provinces and districts.

Finally, and perhaps most important, the Han continued the Qin system of selecting government officials on the basis of merit rather than birth. Shortly after founding the new dynasty, Emperor Gaozu decreed that local officials would be asked to recommend promising candidates for public service. Thirty years later, in 165 B.C.E., the first known **civil service examination** was administered to candidates for positions in the bureaucracy. Shortly after that, an academy was established to train candidates. Nevertheless, the first candidates were almost all from aristocratic or other wealthy families, and the Han bureaucracy itself was still dominated by the traditional hereditary elite. Still, the principle of selecting officials on the basis of talent had been established and would eventually become standard practice.

Under the Han dynasty, the population increased rapidly—by some estimates rising from about twenty million to over sixty million at the height of the dynasty—creating a growing need for a large and efficient bureaucracy to maintain the state in proper working order. Unfortunately, the Han were unable to resolve all of the problems left over from the past. Factionalism at court remained a serious problem and undermined the efficiency of the central government. Equally important, despite their efforts, the Han rulers were never able to restrain the great aristocratic families, who continued to play a dominant role in political and economic affairs. The failure to curb the power of the wealthy clans eventually became a major factor in the collapse of the dynasty.

Why did Chinese rulers under the Qin and the Han dynasties decide to adopt an autocratic system of government headed by a hereditary monarch, rather than a more decentralized system such as we shall encounter in later chapters? Some scholars have speculated that the need to establish and regulate a vast public irrigation network, as had been created in China under the Zhou dynasty, led naturally to the emergence of a form of **Oriental despotism** that would henceforth be applied in all such **hydraulic societies.** Recent evidence, however, disputes this view, suggesting that the emergence of strong central government followed, rather than preceded, the establishment of a large irrigation system. The preference for autocratic rule is probably better explained by the desire to limit the emergence of powerful regional landed interests and maintain control over a vast empire.

**Society and Economy in the Han Empire** Han rulers also retained some of the economic and social policies of their predecessors. In particular, they saw that a free peasantry paying taxes directly to the state would both limit the wealth and power of the great noble families and increase the state's revenues. The Han had difficulty preventing the recurrence of the economic inequities that had characterized the last years of the Zhou, however. The land taxes were relatively light, but the peasants also faced a number of other exactions, including military service and forced labor of up to one month annually. Although the use of iron tools brought new lands under the plow and food production increased steadily, the trebling of the population under the Han eventually reduced the average size of the individual farm plot to about one acre per capita, barely enough for survival. As time went on, many poor peasants were forced to sell their land and become tenant farmers, paying rents ranging up to half of the annual harvest. Thus land once again came to be concentrated in the hands of the powerful landed clans, which often owned thousands of acres worked by tenants and mustered their own military forces to bully free farmers into becoming tenants.

Although such economic problems contributed to the eventual downfall of the dynasty, in general the Han era was one of unparalleled productivity and prosperity. The period was marked by a major expansion of trade, both domestic and foreign. This was not necessarily due to official encouragement. In fact, the Han were as suspicious of private merchants as their predecessors had been and levied stiff taxes on trade in an effort to limit commercial activities. Merchants were also subject to severe social constraints. They were disqualified from seeking office, restricted in their place of residence, and viewed in general as parasites providing little true value to Chinese society.

The state itself directed much trade and manufacturing; it manufactured weapons, for example, and operated shipyards, granaries, and mines. The government also moved cautiously into foreign trade, mostly with neighboring areas in Central and Southeast Asia, although trade relations were established with countries as far away as India and the Mediterranean, where active contacts were maintained with the Roman Empire (see Map 3.2). Some of this long-distance trade was carried by sea through southern ports like Guangzhou, but more was transported by overland caravans on the Silk Road (see Chapter 10) and other routes that led westward into Central Asia. Some of the trade was organized in the form of tribute missions, with neighboring countries providing local specialties like tropical products and precious stones in return for Chinese silks, glazed pottery (an early form

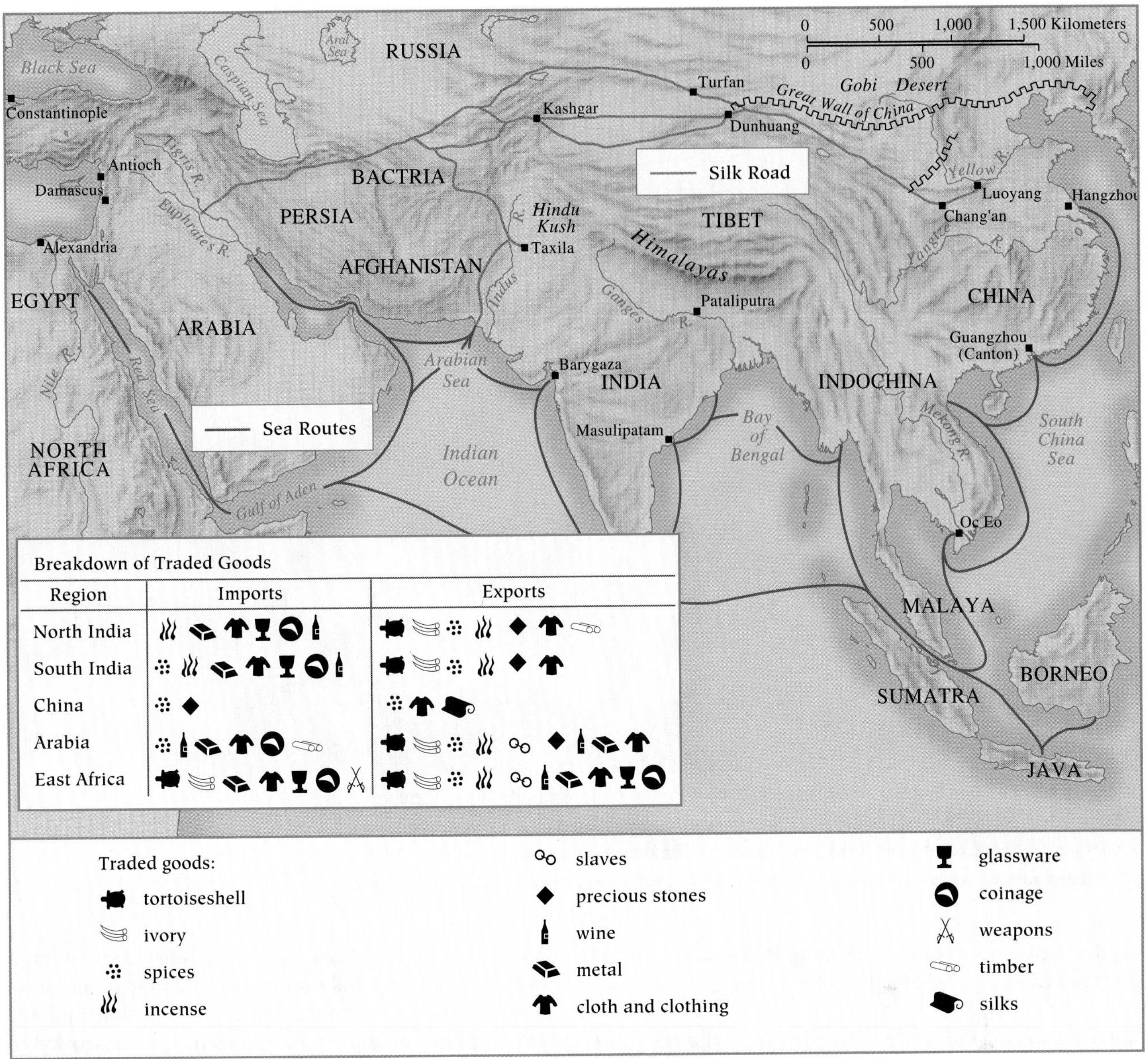


**MAP 3.2 Trade Routes of the Ancient World.** This map shows the various land and maritime routes that extended from China toward other civilizations that were located to the south and west of the Han empire. The various goods that were exchanged are identified at the bottom of the map. **?** What were the major goods exported by China? **View an animated version of this map or related maps at** http://history.wadsworth.com/duikerspielvogel05/

of porcelain), and various manufactured products. China often gave more than it received to ensure that neighboring monarchs would accept China's benevolent protection and not harbor its enemies.

New technology contributed to the economic prosperity of the Han era. Significant progress was achieved in such areas as textile manufacturing, water mills, and iron casting; skill at ironworking led to the production of steel a few centuries later. Paper was invented under the Han, and the development of the rudder and fore-and-aft rigging permitted ships to sail into the wind for the first time. Thus equipped, Chinese merchant ships carrying heavy cargoes could sail throughout the islands of Southeast Asia and into the Indian Ocean.

**Expansion Abroad** Finally, the Han emperors continued the process of territorial expansion and consolidation that had begun under the Zhou and the Qin. Han rulers, notably Han Wudi (Han Wu Ti, or Martial Emperor of Han), successfully completed the assimilation into the empire of the regions south of the Yangtze River, including the Red River delta in what is today northern Vietnam. Han armies also marched westward as far as the Caspian Sea, pacifying nomadic tribal peoples and extending China's boundary far into Central Asia (see Map 3.3). The Han continued to have problems with the Xiongnu beyond the Great Wall to the north. Nomadic raids on Chinese territory continued intermittently to the end of the dynasty, once reaching almost to the gates of the

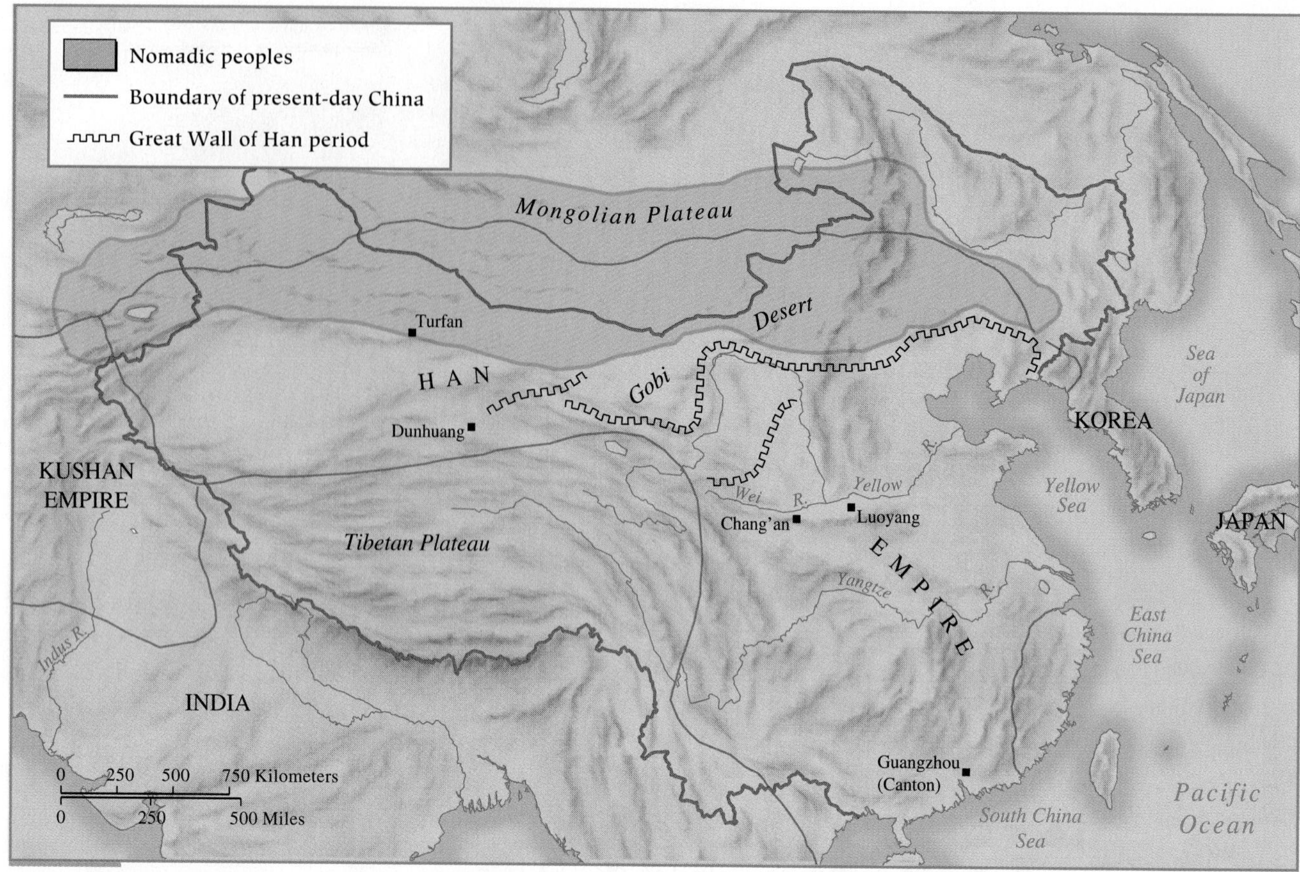


**MAP 3.3 The Han Empire.** This map shows the territory under control of the Han empire at its greatest extent during the first century B.C.E. Note the expansion of Han rule to the west, as Chinese armies penetrated across the Silk Road into Central Asia. ? Where is the Great Wall on the map?

**View an animated version of this map or related maps at** http://history.wadsworth.com/duikerspielvogel05/

capital city, now located at Chang'an (Ch'ang An, or Eternal Peace), on the site of modern Xian.

**The Decline and Fall of the Han** In 9 C.E., the reformist official Wang Mang, who was troubled by the plight of the peasants, seized power from the Han court and declared the foundation of the Xin (New) dynasty. The empire had been crumbling for decades. As frivolous or depraved rulers amused themselves with the pleasures of court life, the power and influence of the central government began to wane, and the great noble families filled the vacuum, amassing vast landed estates and transforming free farmers into tenants. Wang Mang tried to confiscate the great estates, restore the ancient well field system, and abolish slavery. In so doing, however, he alienated powerful interests, who conspired to overthrow him. In 23 C.E., beset by administrative chaos and a collapse of the frontier defenses, Wang Mang was killed in a coup d'état.

For a time, strong leadership revived some of the glory of the early Han. The court did attempt to reduce land taxes and carry out land resettlement programs. The growing popularity of nutritious crops like rice, wheat, and soybeans, along with the introduction of new crops such as alfalfa and grapes, helped boost food production. But the monopoly of land and power by the great landed families continued. Weak rulers were isolated within their imperial chambers and dominated by eunuchs and other powerful figures at court. Official corruption and the concentration of land in the hands of the wealthy led to widespread peasant unrest. The population of the empire, which had been estimated at about sixty million in China's first census in the year 2 C.E., had shrunk to less than one-third that number two hundred years later. In the early third century C.E., the dynasty was finally brought to an end when power was seized by Cao Cao (Ts'ao Ts'ao), a general known to later generations as one of the main characters in the famous Chinese epic *The Romance of the Three Kingdoms.* But Cao Cao was unable to consolidate his power, and China entered a period of almost constant anarchy and internal division, compounded by invasions by northern tribal peoples. The next great dynasty did not arise until the beginning of the seventh century, four hundred years later.

## Daily Life in Ancient China

Few social institutions have been as closely identified with China as the family. As in most agricultural civilizations, the family served as the basic economic and social unit in

**CHRONOLOGY Ancient China**

| | |
|---|---|
| Xia (Hsia) dynasty | ?–c. 1570 B.C.E |
| Shang dynasty | c. 1570–c. 1045 B.C.E |
| Zhou (Chou) dynasty | c. 1045–221 B.C.E |
| Life of Confucius | 551–479 B.C.E |
| Period of the Warring States | 403–221 B.C.E |
| Life of Mencius | 370–290 B.C.E |
| Qin (Ch'in) dynasty | 221–206 B.C.E |
| Life of the First Emperor of Qin | 259–210 B.C.E |
| Formation of Han dynasty | 202 B.C.E |
| Wang Mang interregnum | 9–23 C.E. |
| Collapse of Han dynasty | 221 C.E. |

society. In traditional China, however, it took on an almost sacred quality as a microcosm of the entire social order.

## The Role of the Family

In Neolithic times, the farm village, organized around the clan, was the basic social unit in China, at least in the core region of the Yellow River valley. Even then, however, the smaller family unit was becoming more important, at least among the nobility, who attached considerable significance to the ritual veneration of their immediate ancestors.

During the Zhou dynasty, the family took on increasing importance, in part because of the need for cooperation in agriculture. The cultivation of rice, which had become the primary crop along the Yangtze River and in the provinces to the south, is highly labor-intensive. The seedlings must be planted in several inches of water in a nursery bed and then transferred individually to the paddy beds, which must be irrigated constantly. During the harvest, the stalks must be cut and the kernels carefully separated from the stalks and husks. As a result, children—and the labor they supplied—were considered essential to the survival of the family, not only during their youthful years but also later, when sons were expected to provide for their parents. Loyalty to family members came to be considered even more important than loyalty to the broader community or the state. Confucius commented that it is the mark of a civilized society that a son should protect his father even if the latter has committed a crime against the community.

At the crux of the concept of family was the idea of **filial piety,** which called on all members of the family to subordinate their personal needs and desires to the patriarchal head of the family. More broadly, it created a hierarchical system in which every family member had his or her place. All Chinese learned the **five relationships** that were the key to a proper social order. The son was subordinate to the father, the wife to her husband, the younger brother to the older brother, and all were subject to their king. The final relationship was the proper one between

Courtesy of William J. Duiker

**Flooded Rice Fields.** Rice, which was first cultivated in China seven or eight thousand years ago, is a labor-intensive crop that requires many workers to plant the seedlings and organize the distribution of water. Initially, the fields are flooded to facilitate the rooting of the rice seedlings and to add nutrients to the soil. Fish breeding in the flooded fields help keep mosquitoes and other insects in check. As the plants mature, the fields are drained, and the plants complete their four-month growing cycle in dry soil. Shown here is an example of terracing on a hillside to preserve water for the nourishment of young seedlings. Compare this with the photo of terracing on page 274.

friend and friend. Only if all members of the family and the community as a whole behaved in a properly filial manner would society function effectively.

A stable family system based on obedient and hard-working members can serve as a bulwark for an efficient government, but putting loyalty to the family and the clan over loyalty to the state can also present a threat to a centralizing monarch. For that reason, the Qin dynasty attempted to destroy the clan system in China and assert the primacy of the state. Legalists even imposed heavy taxes on any family with more than two adult sons in order to break down the family concept. The Qin reportedly also originated the practice of organizing several family units into larger groups of five and ten families that would exercise mutual control and surveillance. Later dynasties continued the practice under the name of the ***Bao-jia*** (*Pao-chia*) ***system.***

But the efforts of the Qin to eradicate or at least reduce the importance of the family system ran against tradition and the dynamics of the Chinese economy, and under the Han, the family revived and increased in importance. With official encouragement, the family system began to take on the character that it would possess until our own day. The family was not only the basic economic unit; it was also the basic social unit for education, religious observances, and training in ethical principles.

## Lifestyles

We know much more about the lifestyle of the elites than that of the common people in ancient China. The first houses were probably constructed of wooden planks, but later Chinese mastered the art of building in tile and brick. By the first millennium B.C.E., most public buildings and the houses of the wealthy were probably constructed in this manner. By Han times, most Chinese probably lived in simple houses of mud, wooden planks, or brick with thatch or occasionally tile roofs. But in some areas, especially the loess (pronounced "less," a type of soil common in North China) regions of northern China, cave dwelling remained common down to modern times. The most famous cave dweller of modern times was Mao Zedong, who lived in a cave in Yan'an during his long struggle against Chiang Kai-shek.

Chinese houses usually had little furniture; most people squatted or sat with their legs spread out on the packed mud floor. Chairs were apparently not introduced until the sixth or seventh century C.E. Clothing was simple, consisting of cotton trousers and shirts in the summer and wool or burlap in the winter.

The staple foods were millet in the north and rice in the south. Other common foods were wheat, barley, soybeans, mustard greens, and bamboo shoots. In early times, such foods were often consumed in the form of porridge, but by the Zhou dynasty, stir-frying in a wok was becoming common. When possible, the Chinese family would vary its diet of grain foods with vegetables, fruit (including pears, peaches, apricots, and plums), and fish or meat; but for most, such additions to the daily plate of rice, millet, or soybeans were a rare luxury.

Alcohol in the form of ale was drunk at least by the higher classes and by the early Zhou era had already begun to inspire official concern. According to the *Book of History,* "King Wen admonished . . . the young nobles . . . that they should not ordinarily use spirits; and throughout all the states he required that they should be drunk only on occasion of sacrifices, and that then virtue should preside so that there might be no drunkenness."[13]

Courtesy of William J. Duiker

**Heartland of Ancient China.** The Yellow River valley and its neighboring regions have always been viewed as the heartland of ancient Chinese civilization. Rich clay soils, known as geologists as loess and carried southward by the winds from the vast Gobi Desert, created a thick blanket of rich loam in which to plant the grain crops that sustained the Chinese people. In the photograph here, even the walls of the village are constructed of this rich yellow earth. The hills in the background are pockmarked with cave dwellings (see inset) that have housed the local inhabitants since prehistoric times.

### Cities

Most Chinese, then as now, lived in the countryside. But as time went on, cities began to play a larger role in Chinese society. The first towns were little more than forts for the local aristocracy; they were small in size and limited in population. By the Zhou era, however, larger towns, usually located on the major trade routes, began to combine administrative and economic functions, serving as regional markets or manufacturing centers. Such cities were usually surrounded by a wall and a moat, and a raised platform might be built within the walls to provide a place for ritual ceremonies and housing for the ruler's family.

By the Han, the major city in China was Chang'an, the imperial capital. The city covered a total area of nearly 16 square miles and was enclosed by a 12-foot earthen wall surrounded by a moat. Twelve gates provided entry into the city, and eight major avenues ran east-west or north-south. Each avenue was nearly 150 feet wide; a center strip in each avenue was reserved for the emperor, whose palace and gardens occupied nearly half the southern and central part of the city.

### The Humble Estate: Women in Ancient China

Female subservience was a key element in the social system of ancient China. As in many traditional societies, the male was considered of transcendent importance because of his role as food procurer or, in the case of farming communities, food producer. In ancient China, men worked in the fields and women raised children and served in the home. The Chinese written language graphically demonstrates how ancient Chinese society regarded the sexes. The character for man (男) combines the symbols for strength and a rice field, whereas the character for woman (女) represents a person in a posture of deference and respect. The character for peace (安) is a woman under a roof. A wife is symbolized by a woman with a broom.

Confucian thought, while not denigrating the importance of women as mothers and homemakers, accepted the dual roles of men and women in Chinese society. Men governed society. They carried on family ritual through the veneration of ancestors. They were the warriors, scholars, and ministers. Their dominant role was firmly enshrined in the legal system. Men were permitted to have more than one wife and to divorce a spouse who did not produce a male child. Women were denied the right to own property, and there was no dowry system in ancient China that would have provided the wife with a degree of financial security from her husband and his family. As the third-century C.E. woman poet Fu Xuan lamented:

*How sad it is to be a woman*
*Nothing on earth is held so cheap.*
*No one is glad when a girl is born.*
*By her the family sets no store.*
*No one cries when she leaves her home*
*Sudden as clouds when the rain stops.*[14]

Not surprisingly, women were taught to accept their secondary role in life. Ban Zhao, a prominent female historian of the Han dynasty whose own career was an exception to the rule, described that role as follows:

> To be humble, yielding, respectful and reverential; to put herself after others—these qualities are those exemplifying woman's low and humble estate. To retire late and rise early; not to shirk exertion from dawn to dark—this is called being diligent. To behave properly and decorously in serving her husband; to be serene and self-possessed, shunning jests and laughter—this is called being worthy of continuing the husband's lineage. If a woman possess the above-mentioned three qualities, then her reputation shall be excellent.[15]

Some women did become a force in politics, especially at court, where wives of the ruler or other female members of the royal family were often influential in palace intrigues. Such activities were frowned on, however, as the following passage from the *Book of Songs* attests:

*A clever man builds a city,*
*A clever woman lays one low;*
*With all her qualifications, that clever woman*
*Is but an ill-omened bird.*
*A woman with a long tongue*
*Is a flight of steps leading to calamity;*
*For disorder does not come from heaven,*
*But is brought about by women.*
*Among those who cannot be trained or taught*
*Are women and eunuchs.*[16]

## Chinese Culture

Modern knowledge about artistic achievements in ancient civilizations is limited because often little has survived the ravages of time. Fortunately, many ancient civilizations, such as Egypt and Mesopotamia, were located in relatively arid areas where many artifacts were preserved, even over thousands of years. In more humid regions, such as China and South Asia, the cultural residue left by the civilizations of antiquity has been adversely affected by climate.

As a result, relatively little remains of the cultural achievements of the prehistoric Chinese aside from Neolithic pottery and the relics found at the site of the Shang dynasty capital at Anyang. In recent years, a rich trove from the time of the Qin Empire has been unearthed near the tomb of Qin Shi Huangdi near Xian in central China and at Han tombs nearby. But little remains of the literature of ancient China and almost none of the painting, architecture, and music.

### Metalwork and Sculpture

Discoveries at archaeological sites indicate that ancient China was a society rich in cultural achievement. The pottery found at Neolithic sites such as Longshan and

**A Shang Wine Vessel.** Used initially as food containers in royal ceremonial rites during the Shang dynasty, Chinese bronzes were the product of an advanced technology unmatched by any contemporary civilization. This wine vessel displays a deep green patina as well as a monster motif, complete with large globular eyes, nostrils, and fangs, typical of many Shang bronzes. Known as the *taotie,* this fanciful beast is normally presented in silhouette as two dragons face to face so that each side forms half of the mask. Although the *taotie* presumably served as a guardian force against evil spirits, scholars are still not aware of its exact significance for early Chinese peoples.

Yangshao exhibits a freshness and vitality of form and design, and the ornaments, such as rings and beads, show a strong aesthetic sense.

**Bronze Casting** The pace of Chinese cultural development began to quicken during the Shang dynasty, which ruled in northern China from the sixteenth to the eleventh century B.C.E. At that time, objects cast in bronze began to appear. Various bronze vessels were produced for use in preparing and serving food and drink in the ancestral rites. Later vessels were used for decoration or for dining at court.

The method of casting used was one reason for the extraordinary quality of Shang bronze work. Bronze workers in most ancient civilizations used the lost-wax method, for which a model was first made in wax. After a clay mold had been formed around it, the model was heated so that the wax would melt away, and the empty space was filled with molten metal. In China, clay molds composed of several sections were tightly fitted together prior to the introduction of the liquid bronze. This technique, which had evolved from ceramic techniques used during the Neolithic period, enabled the artisans to apply the design directly to the mold and thus contributed to the clarity of line and rich surface decoration of the Shang bronzes.

Bronze casting became a large-scale business, and more than ten thousand vessels of an incredible variety of form and design survive today. Factories were located not only in the Yellow River valley but also in Sichuan Province, in southern China. The art of bronze working continued into the Zhou and the Han dynasties, but the quality and originality declined. The Shang bronzes remain the pinnacle of creative art in ancient China.

One reason for the decline of bronze casting in China was the rise in popularity of iron. Ironmaking developed in China around the ninth or eighth century B.C.E., much later than in the Middle East, where it had been mastered almost a millennium earlier. Once familiar with the process, however, the Chinese quickly moved to the forefront. Ironworkers in Europe and the Middle East, lacking the technology to achieve the high temperatures necessary to melt iron ore for casting, were forced to work with wrought iron, a cumbersome and expensive process. By the fourth century B.C.E., the Chinese had invented the technique of the blast furnace, powered by a person operating a bellows. They were therefore able to manufacture cast-iron ritual vessels and agricultural tools centuries before an equivalent technology appeared in the West.

Another reason for the deterioration of the bronze-casting tradition was the development of cheaper materials such as lacquerware and ceramics. Lacquer, made from resins obtained from the juices of sumac trees native to the region, had been produced since Neolithic times, and by the Han era it had become a popular method of applying a hard coating to objects made of wood or fabric. Pottery, too, had existed since early times, but technological advances during the Han led to the production of a high-quality form of pottery covered with a brown or gray-green glaze, the latter known popularly as celadon. During the Han, both lacquerware and pottery replaced bronze in popularity and value.

**The First Emperor's Tomb** In 1974, in a remarkable discovery, farmers digging a well about 35 miles east of Xian unearthed a number of terra-cotta figures in an underground pit about one mile east of the burial mound of the First Emperor of Qin. Chinese archaeologists sent to work at the site discovered a vast terra-cotta army that they believed was a re-creation of Qin Shi Huangdi's imperial guard, which was to accompany the emperor on his journey to the next world.

One of the astounding features of the terra-cotta army is its size. The army is enclosed in four pits that were

Courtesy of William J. Duiker

**Han Dynasty Horse.** This terra-cotta horse head is a striking example of Han artistry. Although the Chinese had domesticated the smaller Mongolian pony as early as 2000 B.C.E., it would be toward the end of the first millennium B.C.E., as a result of military expeditions into Central Asia, that the Chinese acquired horses. Admired for their power and grace, horses made of terra-cotta or bronze were often placed in Qin and Han tombs. This magnificent head suggests the divine power that the Chinese of this time attributed to horses.

originally encased in a wooden framework, which has since disintegrated. More than a thousand figures have been unearthed in the first pit, along with horses, wooden chariots, and seven thousand bronze weapons. Archaeologists estimate that there are more than six thousand figures in that pit alone.

Equally impressive is the quality of the work. Slightly larger than life-size, the figures were molded of finely textured clay and then fired and painted. The detail on the uniforms is realistic and sophisticated, but the most striking feature is the individuality of the facial features of the soldiers. Apparently, ten different head shapes were used and were then modeled further by hand to reflect the variety of ethnic groups and personality types in the army.

The discovery of the terra-cotta army also shows that the Chinese had come a long way from the human sacrifices that had taken place at the death of Shang sovereigns more than a thousand years earlier. But the project must have been ruinously expensive and is additional evidence of the burden the Qin ruler imposed on his subjects. One historian has estimated that one-third of the national income in Qin and Han times may have been spent on preparations for the ruler's afterlife. The emperor's mausoleum has not yet been unearthed, but it is enclosed in a mound nearly 250 feet high and is surrounded by a rectangular wall nearly 4 miles around. According to the Han historian Sima Qian, the ceiling is a replica of the heavens, while the floor contains a relief model of the entire Qin kingdom, with rivers flowing in mercury. According to tradition, traps were set within the mausoleum to prevent intruders, and the workers applying the final touches were buried alive in the tomb with its secrets.

Qin Shi Huangdi's ambitious effort to provide for his immortality became a pattern for his successors during the Han dynasty, although apparently on a somewhat more modest scale. In 1990, Chinese workers discovered a similar underground army for a Han emperor of the second century B.C.E. Like the imperial guard of the First Qin Emperor, the underground soldiers were buried in parallel pits and possessed their own weapons and individual facial features. But they were smaller—only one-third the height of the average human adult—and were armed with wooden weapons and dressed in silk clothing, now decayed. A burial pit nearby indicates that as many as ten thousand workers, probably slaves or prisoners, died in the process of building the emperor's mausoleum, which took an estimated ten years to construct.

## Language and Literature

Precisely when writing developed in China cannot be determined, but certainly by Shang times, as the oracle bones demonstrate, the Chinese had developed a simple but functional script. Like many other languages of antiquity, it was primarily ideographic and pictographic in form. Symbols, usually called "characters," were created to represent an idea or to form a picture of the object to be represented. For example, the Chinese characters for mountain (山), the sun (日), and the moon (月) were meant to represent the objects themselves. Other characters, such as "big" (大) (a man with his arms outstretched), represent an idea. The word "east" (東) symbolizes the sun coming up behind the trees.

Each character, of course, would be given a sound by the speaker when pronounced. In other cultures, this process led to the abandonment of the system of ideographs and the adoption of a written language based on phonetic symbols. The Chinese language, however, has never entirely abandoned its original ideographical format, although the phonetic element has developed into a significant part of the individual character. In that sense, the Chinese written language is virtually unique in the world today.

**Pictographs in Ancient Cultures.** Virtually all written language evolved from pictographs—representations of physical objects that were eventually stylized and tied to sounds in the spoken language. This chart shows pictographs that originated independently in three ancient cultures and the stylized modern characters into which the Chinese oracle pictographs evolved.

| | | | | | |
|---|---|---|---|---|---|
| Mesopotamian Cuneiform | | | | | |
| Egyptian Hieroglyphics | | | | | |
| Oracle Bone Script | | | | | |
| Modern Chinese | 日 sun | 山 hill | 水 water | 男 man | 女 woman |

One reason the language retained its ideographic quality may have been the aesthetics of the written characters. By the time of the Han dynasty, if not earlier, the written language came to be seen as an art form as well as a means of communication, and calligraphy became one of the most prized forms of painting in China.

Even more important, if the written language had developed in the direction of a phonetic alphabet, it could no longer have served as the written system for all the peoples of an expanding civilization. Although the vast majority spoke a tongue derived from a parent Sinitic language (a system distinguished by its variations in pitch, a characteristic that gives Chinese its lilting quality even today), the languages spoken in various regions of the country differed from each other in pronunciation and to a lesser degree in vocabulary and syntax; for the most part, they were (and are today) mutually unintelligible.

The Chinese answer to this problem was to give all the spoken languages the same writing system. Although any character might be pronounced differently in different regions of China, that character would be written the same way (after the standardization undertaken under the Qin) no matter where it was written. This system of written characters could be read by educated Chinese from one end of the country to the other. It became the language of the bureaucracy and the vehicle for the transmission of Chinese culture to all Chinese from the Great Wall to the southern border and even beyond. The written language, however, was not identical with the spoken. Written Chinese evolved a totally separate vocabulary and grammatical structure from the spoken tongues. As a result, those who used it required special training.

The earliest extant form of Chinese literature dates from the Zhou dynasty. It was written on silk or strips of bamboo and consisted primarily of historical records such as the *Rites*

Courtesy of William J. Duiker

China Photos/Getty Images

**Qin Shi Huangdi's Tomb.** The First Emperor of Qin ordered the construction of an elaborate mausoleum, an underground palace complex protected by an army of terra-cotta soldiers and horses to accompany him on his journey to the afterlife. This massive formation of six thousand life-size armed soldiers, discovered accidentally by farmers in 1974, reflects Qin Shi Huangdi's grandeur and power.

## Love Spurned in Ancient China

*The Book of Songs* is an anthology of about three hundred poems written during the early Zhou dynasty. According to tradition, they were selected by Confucius from a much larger collection. In later years, many were given political interpretations. The poem reprinted here, however, expresses a very human cry of love spurned.

*It has been said that traditional Chinese thought lacked a sense of tragedy similar to the great dramatic tragedies composed in ancient Greece. Does this passage qualify as tragedy? If not, why not?*

### *The Book of Songs:* The Odes

*You seemed a guileless youth enough,*
*Offering for silk your woven stuff;*
*But silk was not required by you;*
*I was the silk you had in view.*
*With you I crossed the ford, and while*
*We wandered on for many a mile*
*I said, "I do not wish delay,*
*But friends must fix our wedding-day. . . .*
*Oh, do not let my words give pain,*
*But with the autumn come again."*

*And then I used to watch and wait*
*To see you passing through the gate;*
*And sometimes, when I watched in vain,*
*My tears would flow like falling rain;*
*But when I saw my darling boy,*
*I laughed and cried aloud for joy.*
*The fortune-tellers, you declared,*
*Had all pronounced us duly paired;*
*"Then bring a carriage," I replied,*
*"And I'll away to be your bride."*

*The mulberry tree upon the ground,*
*Now sheds its yellow leaves around.*
*Three years have slipped away from me*
*Since first I shared your poverty;*
*And now again, alas the day!*
*Back through the ford I take my way.*

*My heart is still unchanged, but you*
*Have uttered words now proved untrue;*
*And you have left me to deplore*
*A love that can be mine no more.*

*For three long years I was your wife,*
*And led in truth a toilsome life;*
*Early to rise and late to bed,*
*Each day alike passed o'er my head.*
*I honestly fulfilled my part,*
*And you—well, you have broke my heart.*
*The truth my brothers will not know,*
*So all the more their gibes will flow.*
*I grieve in silence and repine*
*That such a wretched fate is mine.*

*Ah, hand in hand to face old age!—*
*Instead, I turn a bitter page.*
*O for the riverbanks of yore;*
*O for the much-loved marshy shore;*
*The hours of girlhood, with my hair*
*Ungathered, as we lingered there.*
*The words we spoke, that seemed so true,*
*I little thought that I should rue;*
*I little thought the vows we swore*
*Would some day bind us two no more.*

*of Zhou*, philosophical treatises such as the *Analects* and *The Way of the Tao*, and poetry, as recorded in *The Book of Songs* and the *Song of the South* (see the box above). In later years, when Confucian principles had been elevated to a state ideology, the key works identified with the Confucian school were integrated into a set of so-called Confucian Classics. These works became required reading for generations of Chinese schoolchildren and introduced them to the forms of behavior that would be required of them as adults.

Under the Han dynasty, although poetry and philosophical essays continued to be popular, historical writing became the primary form of literary creativity. Historians such as Sima Qian and Ban Gu (the dynasty's official historian and the older brother of the female historian Ban Zhao) wrote works that became models for later dynastic histories. These historical works combined political and social history with biographies of key figures. Like so much literary work in China, their primary purpose was moral and political—to explain the underlying reasons for the rise and fall of individual human beings and dynasties.

### Music

From early times in China, music was viewed not just as an aesthetic pleasure but also as a means of achieving political order and refining the human character. In fact, music may have originated as an accompaniment to sacred rituals at the royal court. According to the *Historical Records*, a history written during the Han dynasty: "When our sage-kings of the past instituted rites and music, their objective was far from making people indulge in the . . . amusements of singing and dancing. . . . Music is produced to purify the heart, and rites introduced to rectify the behavior."[17] Eventually, however, music began to be appreciated for its own sake as well as to accompany singing and dancing.

© Bradley D. Appleby

**Music in the Confucian Era.** According to Confucius, "If a man lack benevolence, what has he to do with music?" The purpose of music, to followers of the Master, was to instill in the listener a proper respect for ethical conduct. Foremost among the instruments in the Confucian era were bronze bells. Some weighed over two tons and, in combination as shown here, covered a range of several octaves. Bronze bells have not been found in any other contemporary civilization and are considered one of the great cultural achievements of ancient China. The largest known bell dating from the Roman Empire, for example, is only 6 centimeters high.

A wide variety of musical instruments were used, including flutes, various stringed instruments, bells and chimes, drums, and gourds. Bells cast in bronze were first used as musical instruments in the Shang period; they were hung in rows and struck with a wooden mallet. The finest were produced during the mid-Zhou era and are considered among the best examples of early bronze work in China.

By the late Zhou era, bells had begun to give way as the instrument of choice to strings and wind instruments, and the purpose of music shifted from ceremony to entertainment. This led conservative critics to rail against the onset of an age of debauchery.

Ancient historians stressed the relationship between music and court life, but it is highly probable that music, singing, and dancing were equally popular among the common people. The *Book of History,* purporting to describe conditions in the late third millennium B.C.E., suggests that ballads emanating from the popular culture were welcomed at court. Nevertheless, court music and popular music differed in several respects. Among other things, popular music was more likely to be motivated by the desire for pleasure than for the purpose of law and order and moral uplift. Those differences continued to be reflected in the evolution of music in China down to modern times.

## CONCLUSION

**OF THE GREAT CLASSICAL CIVILIZATIONS** discussed in Part I of this book, China was the last to come into full flower. By the time the Shang began to emerge as an organized state, the societies in Mesopotamia and the Nile valley had already reached an advanced level of civilization. Unfortunately, not enough is known about the early stages of these civilizations to allow us to determine why some developed earlier than others, but one likely reason for China's late arrival was that it was virtually isolated from other emerging centers of culture elsewhere in the world and thus was compelled to develop essentially on its own. Only at the end of the first millennium B.C.E. did the Han dynasty come into regular contact with other civilizations in South Asia, the Middle East, and the Mediterranean.

Once embarked on its own path toward the creation of a complex society, however, China achieved results that were in all respects the equal of its counterparts elsewhere. During the glory years of the Han dynasty, China extended the boundaries of its empire far into the sands of Central Asia and southward along the coast of the South China Sea into what is now Vietnam. The doctrine of State Confucianism provided an effective ideology for the state, and Chinese culture appeared unrivaled. In many respects, its scientific and technological achievements were unsurpassed.

One reason for China's striking success was undoubtedly that unlike its contemporary civilizations, it long was able to fend off the danger from nomadic peoples (along the northern frontier). By the end of the second century B.C.E., however, the Xiongnu were looming ominously, and tribal warriors began to nip at the borders of the empire. While the dynasty was strong, the problem was manageable, but when internal difficulties began to corrode the unity of the state, China became increasingly vulnerable to the threat from the north and entered its own time of troubles.

During the glory years of the Han, another great civilization was beginning to take form on the northern shores of the Mediterranean Sea. Unlike China and the other ancient societies discussed thus far, this new civilization in Europe was based as much on trade as on agriculture. Yet the political and cultural achievements of ancient Greece were the equal of any of the great human experiments that had preceded it and soon began to exert a significant impact on the rest of the ancient world.

## TIMELINE

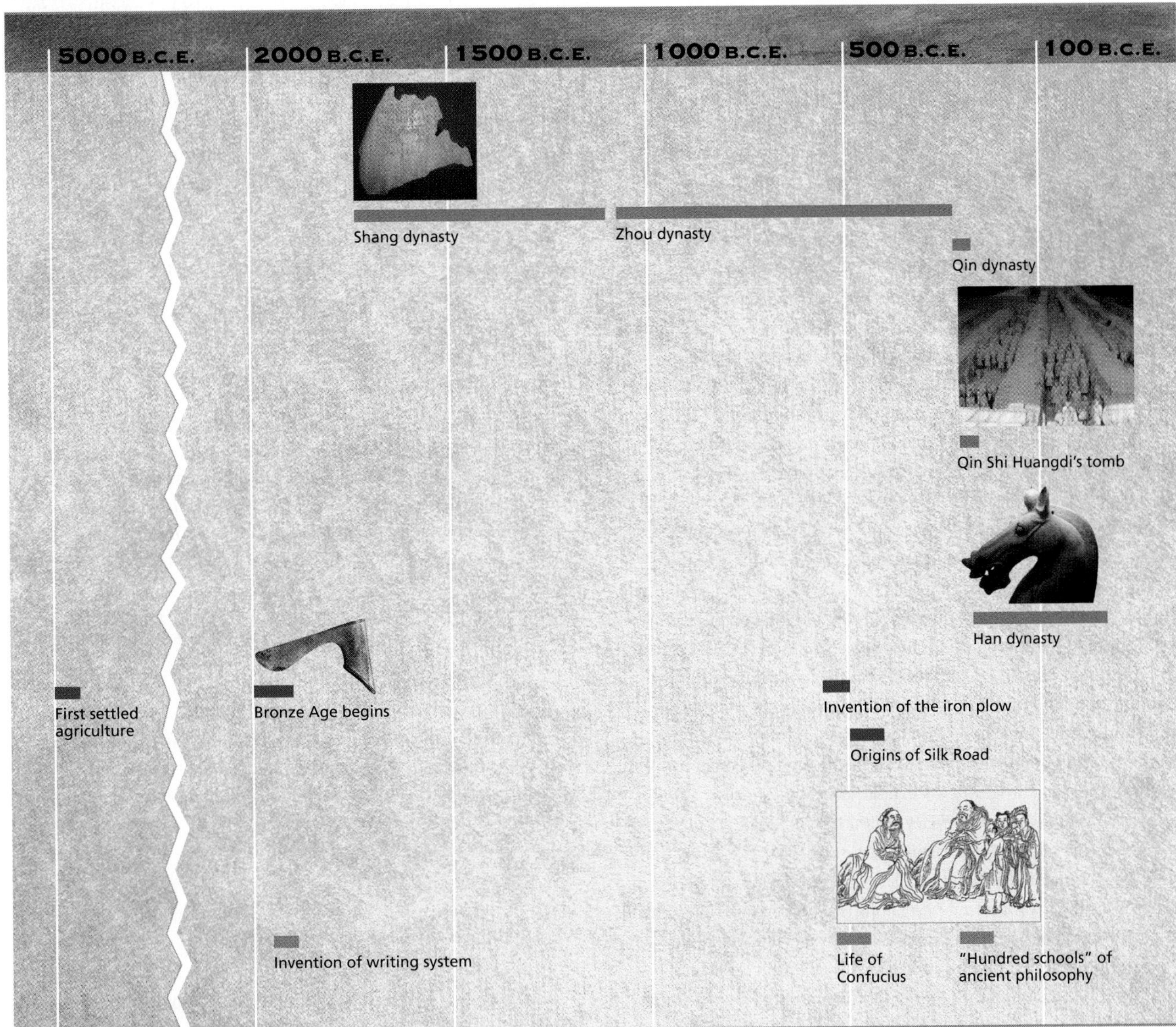


## CHAPTER NOTES

1. *Book of Changes*, quoted in Chang Chi-yun, *Chinese History of Fifty Centuries*, vol. 1, *Ancient Times* (Taipei, 1962), pp. 15, 31, and 65.
2. Ibid., p. 381.
3. Quoted in E. N. Anderson, *The Food of China* (New Haven, Conn., 1988), p. 21.
4. According to Chinese tradition, the *Rites of Zhou* was written by the duke of Zhou himself near the time of the founding of the Zhou dynasty. However, modern historians believe that it was written much later, perhaps as late as the fourth century B.C.E.
5. From *The Book of Songs*, quoted in S. de Grazia, ed., *Masters of Chinese Political Thought: From the Beginnings to the Han Dynasty* (New York, 1973), pp. 40–41.

6. *Confucian Analects* (Lun Yu), ed. J. Legge (Taipei, 1963), 11:11 and 6:20.
7. Ibid., 15:23.
8. Ibid., 17:2.
9. *Book of Mencius* (Meng Zi), 4A:9, quoted in W. T. de Bary et al., eds., *Sources of Chinese Tradition* (New York, 1960), p. 107.
10. Quoted in de Bary, *Sources of Chinese Tradition,* p. 53.
11. B. Watson, *Records of the Grand Historian of China* (New York, 1961), vol. 2, pp. 155, 160.
12. Ibid., pp. 32, 53.
13. C. Waltham, *Shu Ching: Book of History* (Chicago, 1971), p. 154.
14. A. Waley, ed., *Chinese Poems* (London, 1983), p. xx.
15. Quoted in L. E. Eastman, *Family, Fields, and Ancestors: Constancy and Change in China's Social and Economic History, 1550–1949* (New York, 1988), p. 19.
16. Quoted in H. A. Giles, *A History of Chinese Literature* (New York, 1923), p. 19.
17. Chang Chi-yun, *Chinese History of Fifty Centuries,* vol. 1, p. 183.

## SUGGESTED READING

Several general histories of China provide a useful overview of the period of antiquity. Perhaps the best known is the classic ***East Asia: Tradition and Transformation*** (Boston, 1973), by **J. K. Fairbank, E. O. Reischauer,** and **A. M. Craig.** For an authoritative overview of the ancient period, see **M. Loewe** and **E. L. Shaughnessy, *The Cambridge History of Ancient China from the Origins of Civilization to 221 B.C.*** (Cambridge, 1999). Political and social maps of China can be found in **A. Herrmann, *A Historical Atlas of China*** (Chicago, 1966).

The period of the Neolithic era and the Shang dynasty has received increasing attention in recent years. For an impressively documented and annotated overview, see **Kwang-chih Chang, *Shang Civilization*** (New Haven, Conn., 1980) and ***Studies in Shang Archaeology*** (New Haven, Conn., 1982). **D. Keightley, *The Origins of Chinese Civilization*** (Berkeley, Calif., 1983), presents a number of interesting articles on selected aspects of the period.

The Zhou and Qin dynasties have also received considerable attention. The former is exhaustively analyzed in **Cho-yun Hsu** and **J. M. Linduff, *Western Zhou Civilization*** (New Haven, Conn., 1988), and **Li Xueqin, *Eastern Zhou and Qin Civilizations*** (New Haven, Conn., 1985). The latter is a translation of an original work by a mainland Chinese scholar and is especially interesting for its treatment of the development of the silk industry and the money economy in ancient China. On bronze casting, see **E. L. Shaughnessy, *Sources of Eastern Zhou History*** (Berkeley, Calif., 1991).

There are a number of useful books on the Han dynasty. **Zhongshu Wang, *Han Civilization*** (New Haven, Conn., 1982), presents evidence from the mainland on excavations from **Han** tombs and the old imperial capital of Chang'an. Also see the lavishly illustrated ***Han Civilization of China*** (Oxford, 1982) by **M. P. Serstevens.** For a firsthand view, see **B. Watson, *Records of the Grand Historian of China*** (New York, 1961), a translation of key passages from Sima Qian's history of the period.

The philosophy of ancient China has attracted considerable attention from Western scholars. For excerpts from all the major works of the "hundred schools," consult **W. T. de Bary** and **I. Bloom,** eds., ***Sources of Chinese Tradition,*** vol 1 (New York, 1999). On Confucius, see **B. W. Van Norden,** ed., ***Confucius and the Analects: New Essays*** (Oxford, 2002). Also see **F. Mote, *Intellectual Foundations of China,*** 2d ed. (New York, 1989).

For works on general culture and science, consult the illustrated work by **R. Temple, *The Genius of China: 3000 Years of Science, Discovery, and Invention*** (New York, 1986), and **J. Needham, *Science in Traditional China: A Comparative Perspective*** (Boston, 1981). See also **E. N. Anderson, *The Food of China*** (New Haven, Conn., 1988). Environmental issues are explored in **M. Elvin, *The Retreat of the Elephants: An Environmental History of China*** (New Haven, Conn., 2004).

For an introduction to classical Chinese literature, consult the three standard anthologies: **Liu Wu-Chi, *An Introduction to Chinese Literature*** (New York, 1961); **V. H. Mair,** ed., ***The Columbia Anthology of Traditional Chinese Literature*** (New York, 1994); and **S. Owen,** ed., ***An Anthology of Chinese Literature: Beginnings to 1911*** (New York, 1996). For a comprehensive introduction to Chinese art, consult **M. Sullivan, *The Arts of China,*** 4th ed. (Berkeley, Calif., 1999), with good illustrations in color. Also see **M. Tregear, *Chinese Art,*** rev. ed. (London, 1997), and ***Art Treasures in China*** (New York, 1994). Also of interest is **P. B. Ebrey, *The Cambridge Illustrated History of China*** (Cambridge, 1999). For recent finds, consult **J. Rowson, *Mysteries of Ancient China: New Discoveries from the Early Dynasties*** (New York, 1996).On music, see **J. F. So,** ed., ***Music in the Age of Confucius*** (Washington, D.C., 2000).



*I Ching*

Confucius, *Analects*

CHAPTER

# 4

# THE CIVILIZATION OF THE GREEKS

## CHAPTER OUTLINE AND FOCUS QUESTIONS

### Early Greece

- Why was Homer used as the basis for Greek education?

### The Greek City-States (c. 750–c. 500 B.C.E.)

- What was the *polis,* or city-state, and how did the city-states of Athens and Sparta differ?

### The High Point of Greek Civilization: Classical Greece

- What did the Greeks mean by democracy, and in what ways was the Athenian political system a democracy?

### The Rise of Macedonia and the Conquests of Alexander

- How was Alexander the Great able to amass his empire, and what was his legacy?

### The World of the Hellenistic Kingdoms

- How did the political, economic, and social institutions of the Hellenistic world differ from those of classical Greece?

### CRITICAL THINKING

- In what ways did the schools of philosophy and major religions of the Hellenistic period differ from those of the classical period, and what do those differences suggest about society in the two periods?

akg-images/John Hios

*A statue of Pericles in Athens*

DURING THE ERA OF CIVIL WAR in China known as the Period of the Warring States, a civil war also erupted on the northern shores of the Mediterranean Sea. In 431 B.C.E., two very different Greek city-states—Athens and Sparta—fought for domination of the Greek world. The people of Athens felt secure behind their walls and in the first winter of the war held a public funeral to honor those who had died in battle. On the day of the ceremony, the citizens of Athens joined in a procession, with the relatives of the dead wailing for their loved ones. As was the custom in Athens, one leading citizen was asked to address the crowd, and on this day it was Pericles who spoke to the people. He talked about the greatness of Athens and reminded the Athenians of the strength of their political system: "Our constitution," he said, "is called a democracy because power is in the hands not of a minority but of the whole people. When it is a question of settling private disputes, everyone is equal before the law. . . . Just as our political life is free and open, so is our day-to-day life in our relations with each other. . . . Here each individual is interested not only in his own affairs but in the affairs of the state as well."

In this famous funeral oration, Pericles gave voice to the ideals of democracy and the importance of the individual, ideals that were quite different from those of some other ancient societies, in which the individual was subordinated to a larger order based on obedience to an exalted emperor. The Greeks asked some basic questions about human life: What is the nature of the universe? What is the purpose of human existence? What is our relationship to divine forces? What constitutes a community? What constitutes a state? What is true education? What are the true sources of law? What is truth itself, and how do we realize it? Not only did the Greeks answer these questions, but they also created a system of logical, analytical thought to examine them. Their answers and their system of rational thought laid the intellectual foundation for Western civilization's understanding of the human condition.

The remarkable story of ancient Greek civilization begins with the arrival of the Greeks around 1900 B.C.E. By the eighth century B.C.E., the characteristic institution of ancient Greek life, the *polis,* or city-state, had emerged. Greek civilization flourished and reached its height in the classical era of the fifth century B.C.E., but the inability of the Greek city-states to end their fratricidal warfare eventually left them vulnerable to the Macedonian king Philip II and helped bring an end to the era of independent Greek city-states.

Although the city-states were never the same after their defeat by the Macedonian monarch, this defeat did not bring an end to the influence of the Greeks. Philip's son Alexander led the Macedonians and Greeks on a spectacular conquest of the Persian Empire and opened the door to the spread of Greek culture throughout the Middle East. ◇

# Early Greece

Geography played an important role in Greek history. Compared to Mesopotamia and Egypt, Greece occupied a small area, a mountainous peninsula that encompassed only 45,000 square miles of territory, about the size of the state of Louisiana. The mountains and the sea were especially significant. Much of Greece consists of small plains and river valleys surrounded by mountain ranges 8,000 to 10,000 feet high. The mountains isolated Greeks from one another, causing Greek communities to follow their own separate paths and develop their own way of life. Over a period of time, these communities became so fiercely attached to their independence that they were willing to fight one another to gain advantage. No doubt the small size of these independent Greek communities fostered participation in political affairs and unique cultural expressions, but the rivalry among them also led to the internecine warfare that ultimately devastated Greek society.

The sea also influenced Greek society. Greece had a long seacoast, dotted by bays and inlets that provided numerous harbors. The Greeks also inhabited a number of islands to the west, south, and particularly the east of the Greek mainland. It is no accident that the Greeks became seafarers who sailed out into the Aegean and Mediterranean Seas to make contact with the outside world and later to establish colonies that would spread Greek civilization throughout the Mediterranean.

Greek topography helped determine the major territories into which Greece was ultimately divided (see Map 4.1). South of the Gulf of Corinth was the Peloponnesus, virtually an island attached by a tiny isthmus to the mainland. Consisting mostly of hills, mountains, and small valleys, the Peloponnesus was the location of Sparta, as well as the site of Olympia, where athletic games were held. Northeast of the Peloponnesus was the Attic peninsula (or Attica), the home of Athens, hemmed in by mountains to the north and west and surrounded by the sea to the south and east. Northwest of Attica was Boeotia in central Greece, with its chief city of Thebes. To the north of Boeotia was Thessaly, which contained the largest plains and became a great producer of grain and horses. To the north of Thessaly lay Macedonia, which was not of much importance in Greek history until 338 B.C.E., when the Macedonian king Philip II conquered the Greeks.

## Minoan Crete

The earliest civilization in the Aegean region emerged on the large island of Crete, southeast of the Greek mainland. A Bronze Age civilization that used metals, especially bronze, in making weapons had been established there by 2800 B.C.E. This civilization was discovered at the turn of the twentieth century by the English archaeologist Arthur Evans, who named it "Minoan" after Minos, a legendary king of Crete. In language and religion, the Minoans were not Greek, although they did have some influence on the peoples of the Greek mainland.

Evans's excavations on Crete unearthed an enormous palace complex at Knossus, near modern Heracleion. The remains revealed a rich and prosperous culture with Knossus as the apparent center of a far-ranging "sea empire," probably largely commercial in nature. We know from the archaeological remains that the people of Minoan Crete were accustomed to sea travel and had made contact with the more advanced civilization of Egypt. Egyptian products have been found in Crete and Cretan products in Egypt. Minoan Cretans also had contacts with and exerted influence on the Greek-speaking inhabitants of the Greek mainland.

The Minoan civilization reached its height between 2000 and 1450 B.C.E. The palace at Knossus, the royal seat of the kings, was an elaborate structure that included numerous private living rooms for the royal family and workshops for making decorated vases, ivory figurines, and jewelry. Even bathrooms, with elaborate drains, like those found at Mohenjo-Daro in India, formed part of the complex. The rooms were decorated with brightly colored frescoes showing sporting events and nature scenes. Storerooms in the palace held enormous jars of oil, wine, and grain, paid as taxes in kind to the king.

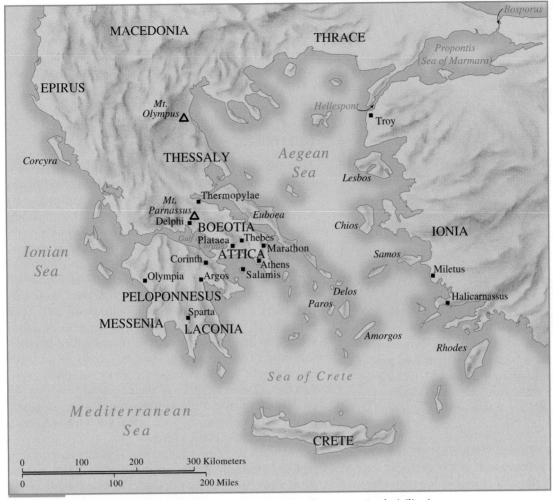

**MAP 4.1 Ancient Greece (c. 750–338 B.C.E.).** Between 750 and 500 B.C.E., Greek civilization witnessed the emergence of the city-state as the central institution in Greek life and the Greeks' colonization of the Mediterranean and Black Seas. Classical Greece lasted from about 500 to 338 B.C.E. and encompassed the high points of Greek civilization in arts, science, philosophy, and politics, as well as the Persian Wars and the Peloponnesian War. How does the geography of Greece help explain the rise and development of the Greek city-state? **View an animated version of this map or related maps at http://history.wadsworth.com/duikerspielvogel05/**

The centers of Minoan civilization on Crete suffered a sudden and catastrophic collapse around 1450 B.C.E. Some historians believe that a tsunami triggered by a powerful volcanic eruption on the island of Thera was responsible for the devastation. That explosion, however, had taken place almost two hundred years earlier, and most historians today maintain that the destruction was the result of invasion and pillage of a weakened Cretan society by mainland Greeks known as the Mycenaeans.

## The First Greek State: Mycenae

The term *Mycenaean* is derived from Mycenae, a remarkable fortified site excavated by the amateur German archaeologist Heinrich Schliemann starting in 1870. Mycenae was one center in a Mycenaean Greek civilization that flourished between 1600 and 1100 B.C.E. The Mycenaean Greeks were part of the Indo-European family of peoples (see Chapter 1) who spread from their original location into southern and western Europe, India, and Persia. One group entered the territory of Greece from the north around 1900 B.C.E. and eventually managed to gain control of the Greek mainland and develop a civilization.

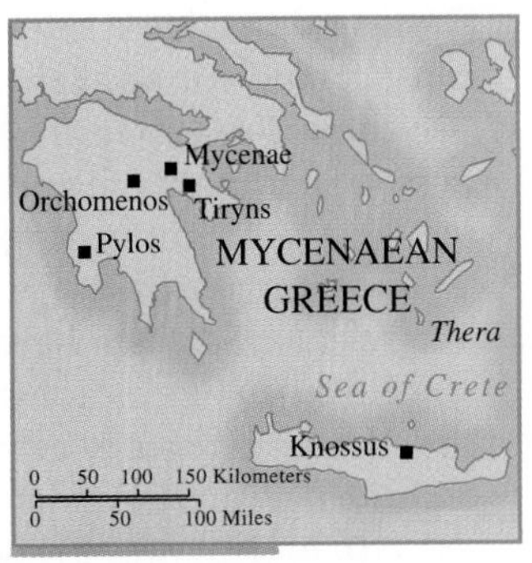


**Minoan Crete and Mycenaean Greece**

Mycenaean civilization, which reached its high point between 1400 and 1200 B.C.E., consisted of a number of powerful monarchies based in fortified palace complexes, which were built on hills and surrounded by gigantic stone walls, such as those

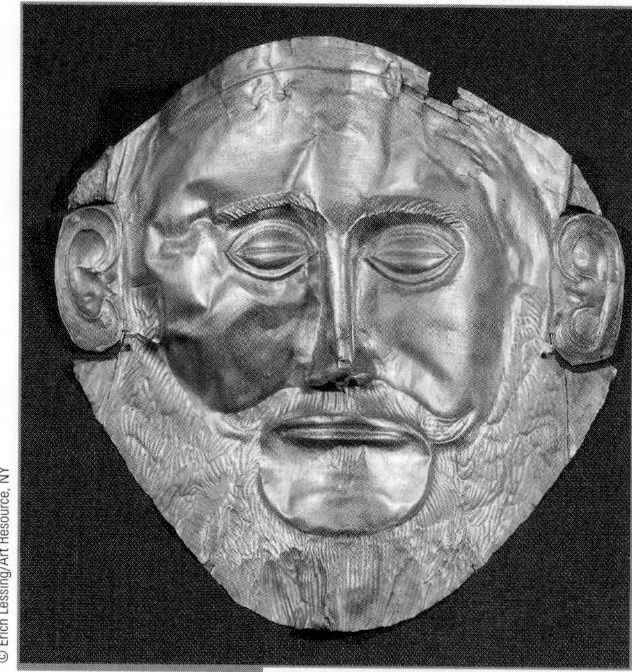

© Erich Lessing/Art Resource, NY

**A Mycenaean Death Mask.** This death mask of thin gold was one of several found by Heinrich Schliemann in his excavation of Grave Circle A at Mycenae. These masks are similar to the gold mummy mask used in Egyptian royal tombs. Schliemann claimed—incorrectly—that he had found the mask of Agamemnon, king of Mycenae in Homer's *Iliad.*

found at Mycenae, Tiryns, Pylos, Thebes, and Orchomenos. These various centers of power probably formed a loose confederacy of independent states, with Mycenae the strongest.

The Mycenaeans were above all a warrior people who prided themselves on their heroic deeds in battle. Archaeological evidence indicates that the Mycenaean monarchies also developed an extensive commercial network. Mycenaean pottery has been found throughout the Mediterranean basin, in Syria and Egypt to the east and Sicily and southern Italy to the west. But some scholars also believe that the Mycenaeans, led by Mycenae itself, spread outward militarily, conquering Crete and making it part of the Mycenaean world. The most famous of all their supposed military adventures has come down to us in the epic poetry of Homer (discussed later in this chapter). Did the Mycenaean Greeks, led by Agamemnon, king of Mycenae, sack the city of Troy on the northwestern coast of Asia Minor around 1250 B.C.E.? Scholars have been debating this question since Schliemann's excavations began. Many believe in the Homeric legend, even if the details have become shrouded in mystery. Many historians today believe that the city of Troy was a vassal of the Hittite Empire and guarded the southern entrance to the Hellespont (today known as the Dardanelles). If so, the Greeks may have had an economic motive for seizing Troy and opening a trade route to the Black Sea.

By the late thirteenth century, Mycenaean Greece was showing signs of serious trouble. Mycenae itself was burned around 1190 B.C.E., and other Mycenaean centers show a similar pattern of destruction as new waves of Greek-speaking invaders moved into Greece from the north. By 1100 B.C.E, the Mycenaean culture was coming to an end, and the Greek world was entering a new period of considerable insecurity.

## The Greeks in a Dark Age (c. 1100–c. 750 B.C.E.)

After the collapse of Mycenaean civilization, Greece entered a difficult era of declining population and falling food production; not until 850 B.C.E. did farming—and Greece itself—revive. Because of both the difficult conditions and the fact that we have few records to help us reconstruct what happened in this period, historians refer to it as the Dark Age.

During the Dark Age, large numbers of Greeks left the mainland and migrated across the Aegean Sea to various islands and especially to the southwestern shore of Asia Minor, a strip of territory that came to be called Ionia. Two other major groups of Greeks settled in established parts of Greece. The Aeolian Greeks of northern and central Greece colonized the large island of Lesbos and the adjacent territory of the mainland. The Dorians established themselves in southwestern Greece, especially in the Peloponnesus, as well as on some of the south Aegean islands, including Crete.

As trade and economic activity began to recover, iron replaced bronze in the construction of weapons, making them affordable for more people. At some point in the eighth century B.C.E., the Greeks adopted the Phoenician alphabet to give themselves a new system of writing. And near the very end of the Dark Age appeared the work of Homer, who has come to be viewed as one of the great poets of all time.

**Homer and Homeric Greece** The *Iliad* and the *Odyssey,* the first great epic poems of early Greece, were based on stories that had been passed down from generation to generation. It is generally assumed that Homer made use of these oral traditions to compose the *Iliad,* his epic poem of the Trojan War. The war was caused when Paris, a prince of Troy, kidnapped Helen, wife of the king of the Greek state of Sparta, outraging all the Greeks. Under the leadership of the Spartan king's brother, Agamemnon of Mycenae, the Greeks attacked Troy. After ten years of combat, the Greeks finally sacked the city. The *Iliad* is not so much the story of the war itself, however, as it is the tale of the Greek hero Achilles and how the "wrath of Achilles" led to disaster.

The *Odyssey,* Homer's other masterpiece, is an epic romance that recounts the journeys of one of the Greek heroes, Odysseus, from the fall of Troy until his eventual return to his wife, Penelope, after twenty years. But there is a larger vision here as well: the testing of the heroic stature of Odysseus until, by both cunning and patience, he prevails. In the course of this testing, the underlying moral message is "that virtue is a better policy than vice."[1]

## HOMER'S IDEAL OF EXCELLENCE

The *Iliad* and the *Odyssey,* which the Greeks believed were both written by Homer, were used as basic texts for the education of Greeks for hundreds of years during antiquity. This passage from the *Iliad,* describing the encounter between Hector, prince of Troy, and his wife Andromache, illustrates the Greek ideal of gaining honor through combat. At the end of the passage, Homer also reveals what became the Greek attitude toward women: they are supposed to spin and weave and take care of their households and children.

*What important ideals for Greek men and women are revealed in this passage from the* Iliad? *How do the women's ideals compare with those for ancient Indian and Chinese women?*

### Homer, *Iliad*

Hector looked at his son and smiled, but said nothing. Andromache, bursting into tears, went up to him and put her hand in his. "Hector," she said, "you are possessed. This bravery of yours will be your end. You do not think of your little boy or your unhappy wife, whom you will make a widow soon. Some day the Achaeans [Greeks] are bound to kill you in a massed attack. And when I lose you I might as well be dead. . . . I have no father, no mother, now. . . . I had seven brothers too at home. In one day all of them went down to Hades' House. The great Achilles of the swift feet killed them all. . . .

"So you, Hector, are father and mother and brother to me, as well as my beloved husband. Have pity on me now; stay here on the tower; and do not make your boy an orphan and your wife a widow. . . ."

"All that, my dear," said the great Hector of the glittering helmet, "is surely my concern. But if I hid myself like a coward and refused to fight, I could never face the Trojans and the Trojan ladies in their trailing gowns. Besides, it would go against the grain, for I have trained myself always, like a good soldier, to take my place in the front line and win glory for my father and myself. . . . "

As he finished, glorious Hector held out his arms to take his boy. But the child shrank back with a cry to the bosom of his girdled nurse, alarmed by his father's appearance. He was frightened by the bronze of the helmet and the horsehair plume that he saw nodding grimly down at him. His father and his lady mother had to laugh. But noble Hector quickly took his helmet off and put the dazzling thing on the ground. Then he kissed his son, dandled him in his arms, and prayed to Zeus and the other gods: "Zeus, and you other gods, grant that this boy of mine may be, like me, preeminent in Troy; as strong and brave as I; a mighty king of Ilium. May people say, when he comes back from battle, 'Here is a better man than his father.' Let him bring home the bloodstained armor of the enemy he has killed, and make his mother happy."

Hector handed the boy to his wife, who took him to her fragrant breast. She was smiling through her tears, and when her husband saw this he was moved. He stroked her with his hand and said, "My dear, I beg you not to be too much distressed. No one is going to send me down to Hades before my proper time. But Fate is a thing that no man born of woman, coward or hero, can escape. Go home now, and attend to your own work, the loom and the spindle, and see that the maidservants get on with theirs. War is men's business; and this war is the business of every man in Ilium, myself above all."

**HistoryNow™** To read Book 1 of the *Iliad,* enter the *HistoryNow* documents area using the access card that is available for *World History.*

Although the *Iliad* and the *Odyssey* supposedly deal with the heroes of the Mycenaean age of the thirteenth century B.C.E., many scholars believe that they really describe the social conditions of the Dark Age. According to the Homeric view, Greece was a society based on agriculture in which a landed warrior-aristocracy controlled much wealth and exercised considerable power. Homer's world reflects the values of aristocratic heroes.

**Homer's Enduring Importance** This, of course, explains the importance of Homer to later generations of Greeks. Homer did not so much record history as make it. The Greeks regarded the *Iliad* and the *Odyssey* as authentic history. They gave the Greeks an ideal past, somewhat like the concept of the Golden Age in ancient China, with a legendary age of heroes and came to be used as standard texts for the education of generations of Greek males. As one Athenian stated, "My father was anxious to see me develop into a good man . . . and as a means to this end he compelled me to memorize all of Homer."[2] The values Homer inculcated were essentially the aristocratic values of courage and honor (see the box above). It was important to strive for the excellence befitting a hero, which the Greeks called *arete.* In the warrior-aristocratic world of Homer, *arete* is won in struggle or contest. Through his willingness to fight, the hero protects his family and friends, preserves his own honor and his family's, and earns his reputation. In the Homeric world, aristocratic women, too, were expected to pursue excellence. Penelope, for example, the wife of Odysseus, the hero of the *Odyssey,* remains faithful to her husband and displays great courage and intelligence in preserving their household during her

**The Slaying of Hector.** This scene from a late-fifth-century B.C.E. Athenian vase depicts the final battle between Achilles and the Trojan hero Hector. Achilles is shown lunging forward with his spear to deliver the final, deadly blow to the Trojan prince, a scene taken from Homer's *Iliad.* The *Iliad,* together with the *Odyssey,* Homer's other masterpiece, was important to later Greeks as a means of teaching the aristocratic values of courage and honor.



husband's long absence. Upon his return, Odysseus praises her for her excellence: "Madame, there is not a man in the wide world who could find fault with you. For your fame has reached heaven itself, like that of some perfect king, ruling a populous and mighty state with the fear of god in his heart, and upholding the right."[3]

To later generations of Greeks, these heroic values formed the core of aristocratic virtue, a fact that explains the tremendous popularity of Homer as an educational tool. Homer gave to the Greeks a single universally accepted model of heroism, honor, and nobility. But in time, as a new world of city-states emerged in Greece, new values of cooperation and community also transformed what the Greeks learned from Homer.

# The Greek City-States (c. 750–c. 500 B.C.E.)

During the Dark Age, Greek villages gradually expanded and evolved into independent city-states. By the eighth century B.C.E., the city-state, or what the Greeks called a ***polis*** (plural, *poleis*), had emerged as a unique and fundamental institution in Greek society.

## The *Polis*

In the most basic sense, a *polis* could be defined as a small but autonomous political unit in which all major political, social, and religious activities were carried out at one central location. The *polis* consisted of a city, town, or village and its surrounding countryside. The city, town, or village was the focus, a central point where the citizens of the *polis* could assemble for political, social, and religious activities. In some *poleis,* this central meeting point was a hill, like the Acropolis at Athens, which could serve as a place of refuge during an attack and later in some sites came to be the religious center on which temples and public monuments were erected. Below the acropolis would be an *agora,* an open place that served both as a market and as a place where citizens could assemble.

*Poleis* varied greatly in size, from a few square miles to a few hundred square miles. They also varied in population. Athens had a population of about 250,000 by the fifth century B.C.E. But most *poleis* were much smaller, consisting of only a few hundred to several thousand people.

Although our word *politics* is derived from the Greek term *polis,* the *polis* itself was much more than a political institution. It was a community of citizens in which all political, economic, social, cultural, and religious activities were focused. As a community, the *polis* consisted of citizens with political rights (adult males), citizens with no political rights (women and children), and noncitizens (slaves and resident aliens). All citizens of a *polis* possessed fundamental rights, but these rights were coupled with responsibilities. The Greek philosopher Aristotle argued that the citizen did not just belong to himself: "We must rather regard every citizen as belonging to the state." However, the loyalty that citizens had to their city-states also had a negative side. City-states distrusted one an-

© Scala/Art Resource, NY

**The Hoplite Forces.** The Greek hoplites were infantrymen equipped with large round shields and long thrusting spears. In battle, they advanced in tight phalanx formation and were dangerous opponents as long as this formation remained unbroken. This vase painting of the seventh century B.C.E. shows two groups of hoplite warriors engaged in battle. The piper on the left is leading another line of soldiers preparing to enter the fray.

other, and the division of Greece into fiercely patriotic independent units helped bring about its ruin.

**A New Military System: The Hoplites** The development of the *polis* was paralleled by the emergence of a new military system. Greek fighting had previously been dominated by aristocratic cavalrymen, who reveled in individual duels with enemy soldiers. But by the end of the eighth century B.C.E., a new military order came into being that was based on **hoplites,** heavily armed infantrymen who wore bronze or leather helmets, breastplates, and greaves (shin guards). Each carried a round shield, a short sword, and a thrusting spear about 9 feet long. Hoplites advanced into battle as a unit, forming a **phalanx** (a rectangular formation) in tight order, usually eight ranks deep. As long as the hoplites kept their order, were not outflanked, and did not break, they either secured victory or, at the very least, suffered no harm. The phalanx was easily routed, however, if it broke its order. Thus the safety of the phalanx depended above all on the solidarity and discipline of its members. As one seventh-century B.C.E. poet noted, a good hoplite was "a short man firmly placed upon his legs, with a courageous heart, not to be uprooted from the spot where he plants his legs."[4]

The hoplite force had political as well as military repercussions. The aristocratic cavalry was now outdated. Since each hoplite provided his own armor, men of property, both aristocrats and small farmers, made up the new phalanx. Those who could become hoplites and fight for the state could also challenge aristocratic control.

## Colonization and the Growth of Trade

Between 750 and 550 B.C.E., large numbers of Greeks left their homeland to settle in distant lands. The growing gulf between rich and poor, overpopulation, and the development of trade were all factors that spurred the establishment of colonies. Invariably, each colony saw itself as an independent *polis* whose links to the mother *polis* (the *metropolis*) were not political but based on sharing common social, economic, and especially religious practices.

In the western Mediterranean, new Greek settlements were established along the coastline of southern Italy, southern France, eastern Spain, and northern Africa west of Egypt. To the north, the Greeks set up colonies in Thrace, where they sought good agricultural lands to grow grains. Greeks also settled along the shores of the Black Sea and secured the approaches to it with cities on the Hellespont and Bosporus, most notably Byzantium, site of the later Constantinople (Istanbul). In establishing these settlements, the Greeks spread their culture throughout the Mediterranean basin. Moreover, colonization helped the Greeks foster a greater sense of Greek identity. Before the eighth century, Greek communities were mostly isolated from one another, leaving many neighboring states on unfriendly terms. Once Greeks from different communities went abroad and found peoples with different languages and customs, they became more aware of their own linguistic and cultural similarities.

Colonization also led to increased trade and industry. The Greeks on the mainland sent their pottery, wine, and olive oil to these areas; in return, they received grains and metals from the west and fish, timber, wheat, metals, and slaves from the Black Sea region. In many *poleis,* the expansion of trade and industry created a new group of rich men who desired political privileges commensurate with their wealth but found such privileges impossible to gain because of the power of the ruling aristocrats.

## Tyranny in the Greek *Polis*

The aspirations of the new industrial and commercial groups laid the groundwork for the rise of **tyrants** in the seventh and sixth centuries B.C.E. They were not necessarily oppressive or wicked, as the modern English word *tyrant* connotes. Greek tyrants were rulers who came to power in an unconstitutional way; a tyrant was not subject to the law. Many tyrants were actually aristocrats who opposed the control of the ruling aristocratic faction in their cities. The support for the tyrants, however, came from the new rich who made their money in trade and industry, as well as from poor peasants who were becoming increasingly indebted to landholding aristocrats. Both groups were opposed to the domination of political power by aristocratic **oligarchies** (an oligarchy is rule by a few).

Once in power, the tyrants built new marketplaces, temples, and walls that not only glorified the city but also enhanced their own popularity. Tyrants also favored the interests of merchants and traders. Despite these achievements, however, **tyranny** was largely extinguished by the end of the sixth century B.C.E. Greeks believed in the rule of law, and tyranny made a mockery of that ideal.

Although tyranny did not last, it played a significant role in the evolution of Greek history by ending the rule of narrow aristocratic oligarchies. Once the tyrants were eliminated, the door was opened to the participation of new and more people in governing the affairs of the community. Although this trend culminated in the development of democracy in some communities, in other states expanded oligarchies of one kind or another managed to remain in power. Greek states exhibited considerable variety in their governmental structures; this can perhaps best be seen by examining the two most famous and most powerful Greek city-states, Sparta and Athens.

## Sparta

Located in the southwestern Peloponnesus, Sparta, like other Greek states, faced the need for more land. Instead of sending its people out to found new colonies, the Spartans conquered the neighboring Laconians and later, beginning around 730 B.C.E., undertook the conquest of neighboring Messenia despite its larger size and population. Messenia possessed a large, fertile plain ideal for growing grain. After its conquest in the seventh century B.C.E., the Messenians, like the Laconians earlier, were reduced to serfdom (they were known as ***helots,*** a name derived from a Greek word for "capture") and made to work for the Spartans. To ensure control over their conquered Laconian and Messenian helots, the Spartans made a conscious decision to create a military state.

**The New Sparta** Between 800 and 600 B.C.E., the Spartans instituted a series of reforms that are associated with the name of the lawgiver Lycurgus (see the box on p. 103). Although historians are not sure that Lycurgus ever existed, there is no doubt about the result of the reforms that were made: the lives of Spartans were now rigidly organized and tightly controlled (to this day, the word *spartan* means "highly self-disciplined"). Boys were taken from their mothers at the age of seven and put under control of the state. They lived in military-style barracks, where they were subjected to harsh discipline to make them tough and given an education that stressed military training and obedience to authority. At twenty, Spartan males were enrolled in the army for regular military service. Although allowed to marry, they continued to live in the barracks and ate all their meals in public dining halls with their fellow soldiers. Meals were simple; the famous Spartan black broth consisted of a piece of pork boiled in blood, salt, and vinegar, causing a visitor who ate in a public mess to remark that he now understood why Spartans were not afraid to die. At thirty, Spartan males were recognized as mature and allowed to vote in the assembly and live at home, but they remained in military service until the age of sixty.

While their husbands remained in military barracks until age thirty, Spartan women lived at home. Because of this separation, Spartan women had greater freedom of movement and greater power in the household than was common for women elsewhere in Greece. Spartan women were encouraged to exercise and remain fit to bear and raise healthy children. Like the men, Spartan women engaged in athletic exercises in the nude. Many Spartan women upheld the strict Spartan values, expecting their husbands and sons to be brave in war. The story is told that as a Spartan mother was burying her son, an old woman came up to her and said, "You poor woman, what a misfortune." "No," replied the mother, "because I bore him so that he might die for Sparta, and that is what has happened, as I wished."[5]

## The Lycurgan Reforms

To maintain their control over the conquered Messenians, the Spartans instituted the reforms that created their military state. In this account of the lawgiver Lycurgus, the Greek historian Plutarch discusses the effect of these reforms on the treatment and education of boys.

*What does this passage from Plutarch's account of Lycurgus reveal about the nature of the Spartan state? Why would this whole program have been distasteful to the Athenians?*

### Plutarch, *Lycurgus*

Lycurgus was of another mind; he would not have masters bought out of the market for his young Spartans, . . . nor was it lawful, indeed, for the father himself to breed up the children after his own fancy; but as soon as they were seven years old they were to be enrolled in certain companies and classes, where they all lived under the same order and discipline, doing their exercises and taking their play together. Of these, he who showed the most conduct and courage was made captain; they had their eyes always upon him, obeyed his orders, and underwent patiently whatsoever punishment he inflicted; so that the whole course of their education was one continued exercise of a ready and perfect obedience. The old men, too, were spectators of their performances, and often raised quarrels and disputes among them, to have a good opportunity of finding out their different characters, and of seeing which would be valiant, which a coward, when they should come to more dangerous encounters. Reading and writing they gave them, just enough to serve their turn; their chief care was to make them good subjects, and to teach them to endure pain and conquer in battle. To this end, as they grew in years, their discipline was proportionately increased; their heads were close-clipped, they were accustomed to go barefoot, and for the most part to play naked.

After they were twelve years old, they were no longer allowed to wear any undergarments; they had one coat to serve them a year; their bodies were hard and dry, with but little acquaintance of baths and unguents; these human indulgences they were allowed only on some few particular days in the year. They lodged together in little bands upon beds made of the rushes which grew by the banks of the river Eurotas, which they were to break off with their hands with a knife; if it were winter, they mingled some thistledown with their rushes, which it was thought had the property of giving warmth. By the time they were come to this age there was not any of the more hopeful boys who had not a lover to bear him company. The old men, too, had an eye upon them, coming often to the grounds to hear and see them contend either in wit or strength with one another, and this as seriously . . . as if they were their fathers, their tutors, or their magistrates; so that there scarcely was any time or place without someone present to put them in mind of their duty, and punish them if they had neglected it.

[Spartan boys were also encouraged to steal their food.] They stole, too, all other meat they could lay their hands on, looking out and watching all opportunities, when people were asleep or more careless than usual. If they were caught, they were not only punished with whipping, but hunger, too, being reduced to their ordinary allowance, which was but very slender, and so contrived on purpose, that they might set about to help themselves, and be forced to exercise their energy and address. This was the principal design of their hard fare.

**HistoryNow™** To read more of Plutarch's *Life of Lycurgus*, enter the *HistoryNow* documents area using the access card that is available for *World History.*

**The Spartan State** The so-called Lycurgan reforms also reorganized the Spartan government, creating an oligarchy. Two kings were primarily responsible for military affairs and served as the leaders of the Spartan army on its campaigns. The two kings shared power with a body called the *gerousia*, a council of elders. It consisted of twenty-eight citizens over the age of sixty, who were elected for life, and the two kings. The primary task of the *gerousia* was to prepare proposals that would be presented to the *apella*, an assembly of all male citizens. The assembly did not debate but only voted on the proposals put before it by the *gerousia;* rarely did the assembly reject these proposals. The assembly also elected the *gerousia* and another body known as the *ephors*, a group of five men who were responsible for supervising the education of youth and the conduct of all citizens.

To make their new military state secure, the Spartans deliberately turned their backs on the outside world. Foreigners, who might bring in new ideas, were discouraged from visiting Sparta. Nor were Spartans, except for military reasons, allowed to travel abroad, where they might pick up new ideas dangerous to the stability of the state. Likewise, Spartan citizens were discouraged from studying philosophy, literature, or the arts—subjects that might encourage new thoughts. The art of war was the Spartan ideal, and all other arts were frowned on.

In the sixth century, Sparta used its military might and the fear it inspired to gain greater control of the Peloponnesus by organizing an alliance of almost all the Peloponnesian states. Sparta's strength enabled it to dominate this Peloponnesian League and determine its policies. By 500 B.C.E., the Spartans had organized a powerful

## COMPARATIVE ESSAY

# *DEMOS* AND DESPOTS

The origins of modern government lie in the agricultural revolution, when sedentary peoples began to seek organized protection from threats and dangers arising from within and outside the community. Influential figures, known to sociologists as "big men," emerged as community leaders in farm villages or pastoral communities to provide protection and to perform other services of importance to the local population. As these societies grew in size and complexity, such informal authority figures began to assume greater power and influence and to surround themselves with relatives and retainers serving as a ruling elite. By the time of the emergence of ancient civilizations, the former "big men" had begun to assume divine or semidivine powers to ensure their hereditary status and bolster their authority over their subjects. Examples appeared in Egypt with the reign of kings around 3100 B.C.E., in Mesopotamia a few hundred years later, and in China by the end of the second millennium B.C.E.

The power of these rulers over their subject peoples was not necessarily absolute. In many cases (see Chapter 2) government was decentralized rather than focused on one single authority. In China under the Zhou dynasty, the concept that the ruler governed by divine mandate (the Mandate of Heaven) became widely accepted. With this concept came the belief that if the ruler did not govern effectively, he could be overthrown and replaced by a new ruler. This view culminated with the ideas of the Zhou dynasty philosopher Confucius, and his disciple Mencius, who declared that "the people are first in importance, the nation is next, while the ruler is of the least importance, since it is the people who make him the Son of Heaven."

But it was in the region of the Mediterranean Sea that the most effective statement against the power of the ruler was proclaimed. In the sixth century B.C.E., political thinkers in Greece—notably in the city-state of Athens—began to reject the idea of the *despot* (from the Greek word for "master"), which they identified with the rulers of the Persian Empire, in favor of government based on the will of the people (in Greek, *demos*). Such views represent the first glimmerings of the modern concept of *democracy.* The Greek experiment was brief, however, as despotic forces soon brought an end to Athenian democracy. On the nearby Italian peninsula to the west, an early Roman Republic was eventually replaced by a monarchy based on the divine power of the emperor. But the vision of democracy did not entirely vanish and was revived with even greater force in Europe and North America at the end of the eighteenth century.

military state that maintained order and stability in the Peloponnesus. Raised from early childhood to believe that total loyalty to the Spartan state was the basic reason for existence, the Spartans viewed their strength as justification for their militaristic ideals and regimented society.

## Athens

By 700 B.C.E., Athens had established a unified *polis* on the peninsula of Attica. Although early Athens had been ruled by a monarchy, by the seventh century B.C.E. it had fallen under the control of its aristocrats. They possessed the best land and controlled political and religious life by means of a council of nobles, assisted by a board of nine officials called archons. Although there was an assembly of full citizens, it possessed few powers.

Near the end of the seventh century B.C.E., Athens faced political turmoil because of serious economic problems. Increasing numbers of Athenian farmers found themselves sold into slavery when they were unable to repay loans they had obtained from their aristocratic neighbors, pledging themselves as collateral. Repeatedly, there were cries to cancel the debts and give land to the poor.

**The Reforms of Solon** The ruling Athenian aristocrats responded to this crisis by choosing Solon, a reform-minded aristocrat, as sole archon in 594 B.C.E. and giving him full power to make changes. Solon canceled all land debts, outlawed new loans based on humans as collateral, and freed people who had fallen into slavery for debts. He refused, however, to carry out land redistribution and hence failed to deal with the basic cause of the economic crisis. This failure, however, was overshadowed by the commercial and industrial prosperity that Athens began to experience in the following decades.

Like his economic reforms, Solon's political measures were also a compromise. Though by no means eliminating the power of the aristocracy, they opened the door to the participation of new people, especially the nonaristocratic wealthy, in the government. But Solon's reforms, though popular, did not truly solve Athens's problems. Aristocratic factions continued to vie for power, and the poorer peasants resented Solon's failure to institute land redistribution. Internal strife finally led to the very institution Solon had hoped to avoid—tyranny. Pisistratus, an aristocrat, seized power in 560 B.C.E. Pursuing a foreign policy that aided Athenian trade, Pisistratus remained popular with the mercantile and industrial classes. But the Athenians rebelled against his son and ended the tyranny in 510 B.C.E. Although the aristocrats attempted to reestablish an aristocratic oligarchy, Cleisthenes, another aristocratic reformer, opposed this plan and, with the backing of the Athenian people, gained the upper hand in 508 B.C.E.

**The Reforms of Cleisthenes** Cleisthenes created a new Council of Five Hundred, chosen by lot by the ten tribes in which all citizens had been enrolled. The Council of Five Hundred was responsible for the administration of both foreign and financial affairs and prepared the business that would be handled by the assembly. This assembly of all male citizens had final authority in the passing of laws after free and open debate; thus Cleisthenes' reforms had reinforced the central role of the assembly of citizens in the Athenian political system.

The reforms of Cleisthenes created the foundations for Athenian democracy (see the comparative essay "*Demos* and Despots" on p. 104). More changes would come in the fifth century, when the Athenians themselves would begin to use the word *democracy* to describe their system (from the Greek words *demos*, "people," and *kratia*, "power"). By 500 B.C.E., Athens was more united than it had been and was on the verge of playing a more important role in Greek affairs.

# The High Point Of Greek Civilization: Classical Greece

Classical Greece is the name given to the period of Greek history from around 500 B.C.E. to the conquest of Greece by the Macedonian king Philip II in 338 B.C.E. Many of the cultural contributions of the Greeks occurred during this period. The age began with a mighty confrontation between the Greek states and the mammoth Persian Empire.

## The Challenge of Persia

As the Greeks spread throughout the Mediterranean, they came into contact with the Persian Empire to the east (see Chapter 1). The Ionian Greek cities in western Asia Minor had already fallen subject to the Persian Empire by the mid-sixth century B.C.E. An unsuccessful revolt by the Ionian cities in 499 B.C.E.—assisted by the Athenian navy—led the Persian ruler Darius to seek revenge by attacking the mainland Greeks. In 490 B.C.E., the Persians landed an army on the plain of Marathon, only 26 miles from Athens. The Athenians and their allies were clearly outnumbered, but led by Miltiades, one of the Athenian leaders who insisted on attacking, the Greek hoplites charged across the plain of Marathon and crushed the Persian forces.

Xerxes, the new Persian monarch after the death of Darius in 486 B.C.E., vowed revenge and planned to invade. In preparation for the attack, some of the Greek states formed a defensive league under Spartan leadership, while the Athenians pursued a new military policy by developing a navy. By the time of the Persian invasion

The Art Archive/Acropolis Museum Athens/Dagli Orti

Courtesy of William M. Murray

**The Greek Trireme.** The trireme became the standard warship of ancient Greece. Highly maneuverable, fast, and outfitted with metal prows, Greek triremes were especially effective at ramming enemy ships. The strenuous work of the oarsmen aboard a trireme is shown in the relief dating from the fourth century B.C.E. The photo shows the *Olympias*, a trireme reconstructed by the Greek navy.

in 480 B.C.E., the Athenians had produced a fleet of about two hundred vessels.

Xerxes led a massive invasion force into Greece: close to 150,000 troops, almost seven hundred naval ships, and hundreds of supply ships to keep the large army fed. The Greeks tried to delay the Persians at the pass of Thermopylae, along the main road into central Greece. A Greek force numbering close to nine thousand, under the leadership of the Spartan king, Leonidas, and his contingent of three hundred Spartans, held off the Persian army for two days. The Spartan troops were especially brave. When told that Persian arrows would darken the sky in battle, one Spartan warrior supposedly responded, "That is good news. We will fight in the shade!" Unfortunately for the Greeks, a traitor told the Persians how to use a mountain path to outflank the Greek force. The Spartans fought to the last man.

The Athenians, now threatened by the onslaught of the Persian forces, abandoned their city. While the Persians sacked and burned Athens, the Greek fleet remained offshore near the island of Salamis and challenged the Persian navy to fight. Although the Greeks were outnumbered, they managed to outmaneuver the Persian fleet and utterly defeated it. A few months later, early in 479 B.C.E., the Greeks formed the largest Greek army seen up to that time and decisively defeated the Persian army at Plataea, northwest of Attica. The Greeks had won the war and were now free to pursue their own destiny.

## The Growth of an Athenian Empire in the Age of Pericles

After the defeat of the Persians, Athens took over the leadership of the Greek world by forming a defensive alliance against the Persians called the Delian League in the winter of 478–477 B.C.E. Its main headquarters was on the island of Delos, but its chief officials, including the treasurers and commanders of the fleet, were Athenian. Under the leadership of the Athenians, the Delian League pursued the attack against the Persian Empire. Virtually all of the Greek states in the Aegean were liberated from Persian control. Arguing that the Persian threat was now over, some members of the Delian League wished to withdraw. But the Athenians forced them to remain in the league and to pay tribute. In 454 B.C.E the Athenians moved the treasury of the league from Delos to Athens. By controlling the Delian League, Athens had created an empire.

At home, Athenians favored the new imperial policy, especially after 461 B.C.E., when a political faction, led by a young aristocrat named Pericles, triumphed. Under Pericles, who remained a dominant figure in Athenian politics for more than three decades, Athens embarked on a policy of expanding democracy at home and its new empire abroad. This period of Athenian and Greek history, which historians have subsequently labeled the Age of Pericles, witnessed the height of Athenian power and the culmination of its brilliance as a civilization.

**CHRONOLOGY The Persian Wars**

| | |
|---|---|
| Rebellion of Greek cities in Asia Minor | 499–494 B.C.E. |
| Battle of Marathon | 490 B.C.E. |
| Xerxes invades Greece | 480–479 B.C.E. |
| Battles of Thermopylae and Salamis | 480 B.C.E. |
| Battle of Plataea | 479 B.C.E. |

In the Age of Pericles, the Athenians became deeply attached to their democratic system. The sovereignty of the people was embodied in the assembly, which consisted of all male citizens over eighteen years of age. In the 440s, that was probably a group of about 43,000. Not all attended, however, and the number present at the meetings, which were held every ten days on a hillside east of the Acropolis, seldom reached 6,000. The assembly passed all laws and made final decisions on war and foreign policy.

Routine administration of public affairs was handled by a large body of city magistrates, usually chosen by lot without regard to class and usually serving only one-year terms. This meant that many male citizens held public office at some time in their lives. A board of ten officials known as generals (*strategoi*) were elected by public vote to guide affairs of state, although their power depended on the respect they had attained. Generals were usually wealthy aristocrats, even though the people were free to select otherwise. The generals could be reelected, enabling individual leaders to play an important political role. Pericles' frequent reelection (fifteen times) as one of the ten generals made him one of the leading politicians between 461 and 429 B.C.E.

Pericles expanded the Athenians' involvement in democracy, which is what by now the Athenians had come to call their form of government (see the box on p. 107). Power was in the hands of the people; male citizens voted in the assemblies and served as jurors in the courts. Lower-class citizens were now eligible for public offices formerly closed to them. Pericles also introduced state pay for office-holders, including the widely held jury duty. This meant that even poor citizens could hold public office and afford to participate in public affairs. Nevertheless, although the Athenians developed a system of government that was unique in its time in which citizens had equal rights and the people were the government, aristocrats continued to hold the most important offices, and many people, including women, slaves, and foreigners residing in Athens, were not given the same political rights.

Under Pericles, Athens became the leading center of Greek culture. The Persians had destroyed much of the city during the Persian Wars, but Pericles used the treasury money of the Delian League to set in motion a massive rebuilding program. New temples and statues soon made the greatness of Athens more visible. Art, architecture, and philosophy flourished, and Pericles broadly boasted that Athens had become the "school of Greece."

## Athenian Democracy: The Funeral Oration of Pericles

In his *History of the Peloponnesian War,* the Greek historian Thucydides presented his reconstruction of the eulogy given by Pericles in the winter of 431–430 B.C.E. to honor the Athenians killed in the first campaigns of the Great Peloponnesian War. It is a magnificent, idealized description of Athenian democracy at its height.

*In the eyes of Pericles, what are the ideals of Athenian democracy? In what ways does Pericles exaggerate his claims? Why would the Athenian passion for debate described by Pericles have been distasteful to the Spartans? On the other hand, how does eagerness for discussion perfectly suit democracy?*

### Thucydides, *History of the Peloponnesian War*

Our constitution is called a democracy because power is in the hands not of a minority but of the whole people. When it is a question of settling private disputes, everyone is equal before the law; when it is a question of putting one person before another in positions of public responsibility, what counts is not membership of a particular class, but the actual ability which the man possesses. No one, so long as he has it in him to be of service to the state, is kept in political obscurity because of poverty. And, just as our political life is free and open, so is our day-to-day life in our relations with each other. We do not get into a state with our next-door neighbor if he enjoys himself in his own way, nor do we give him the kind of black looks which, though they do no real harm, still do hurt people's feelings. We are free and tolerant in our private lives; but in public affairs we keep to the law. This is because it commands our deep respect.

We give our obedience to those whom we put in positions of authority, and we obey the laws themselves, especially those which are for the protection of the oppressed, and those unwritten laws which it is an acknowledged shame to break. . . . Here each individual is interested not only in his own affairs but in the affairs of the state as well: even those who are mostly occupied with their own business are extremely well-informed on general politics–this is a peculiarity of ours: we do not say that a man who takes no interest in politics is a man who minds his own business; we say that he has no business here at all. We Athenians, in our own persons, take our decisions on policy or submit them to proper discussions: for we do not think that there is an incompatibility between words and deeds; the worst thing is to rush into action before the consequences have been properly debated. . . . Taking everything together then, I declare that our city is an education to Greece, and I declare that in my opinion each single one of our citizens, in all the manifold aspects of life, is able to show himself the rightful lord and owner of his own person, and do this, moreover, with exceptional grace and exceptional versatility. And to show that this is no empty boasting for the present occasion, but real tangible fact, you have only to consider the power which our city possesses and which has been won by those very qualities which I have mentioned.

**HistoryNow**™ To read more of Thucydides' *History,* enter the *HistoryNow* documents area using the access card that is available for *World History.*

But the achievements of Athens alarmed the other Greek states, especially Sparta, and soon all Greece was confronting a new war.

## The Great Peloponnesian War and the Decline of the Greek States

During the forty years after the defeat of the Persians, the Greek world came to be divided into two major camps: Sparta and its supporters and the Athenian maritime empire. Sparta and its allies feared the growing Athenian empire. Then, too, Athens and Sparta had created two very different kinds of societies, and neither state was able to tolerate the other's system. A series of disputes finally led to the outbreak of war in 431 B.C.E.

At the beginning of the war, both sides believed they had winning strategies. The Athenians planned to remain behind the protective walls of Athens while the overseas empire and the navy would keep them supplied. Pericles knew that the Spartans and their allies could beat the Athenians in open battles, which was the chief aim of the Spartan strategy. The Spartans and their allies invaded Attica and ravaged the fields and orchards, hoping that the Athenians would send out their army to fight beyond the walls. But Pericles was convinced that Athens was secure behind its walls and stayed put.

In the second year of the war, however, plague devastated the crowded city of Athens and wiped out possibly one-third of the population. Pericles himself died the following year (429 B.C.E.), a severe loss to Athens. Despite the losses from the plague, the Athenians fought on in a struggle that dragged on for another twenty-seven years. A final crushing blow came in 405 B.C.E., when the Athenian fleet was destroyed at Aegospotami on the Hellespont. Athens was besieged and surrendered in 404. Its walls were torn down, the navy was disbanded, and the Athenian empire was no more. The great war was finally over.

The Great Peloponnesian War weakened the major Greek states and destroyed any possibility of cooperation among the Greek states. The next seventy years of

Greek history are a sorry tale of efforts by Sparta, Athens, and Thebes, a new Greek power, to dominate Greek affairs. In continuing their petty wars, the Greek states remained oblivious to the growing power of Macedonia to their north.

## The Culture of Classical Greece

Classical Greece saw a period of remarkable intellectual and cultural growth throughout the Greek world, and Periclean Athens was the most important center of classical Greek culture.

**The Writing of History** History as we know it, as the systematic analysis of past events, was introduced to the Western world by the Greeks. Herodotus (c. 484–c. 425 B.C.E.) wrote *History of the Persian Wars,* a work commonly regarded as the first real history in Western civilization. The central theme of Herodotus' work is the conflict between the Greeks and the Persians, which he viewed as a struggle between freedom and despotism. Herodotus traveled extensively and questioned many people to obtain his information. He was a master storyteller and sometimes included considerable fanciful material, but he was also capable of exhibiting a critical attitude toward the materials he used.

Thucydides (c. 460–c. 400 B.C.E.) was a better historian by far; indeed, he is considered the greatest historian of the ancient world. Thucydides was an Athenian and a participant in the Peloponnesian War. He had been elected a general, but a defeat in battle led the fickle Athenian assembly to send him into exile, which gave him the opportunity to write his *History of the Peloponnesian War.*

Unlike Herodotus, Thucydides was not concerned with underlying divine forces or gods as explanatory causal factors in history. He saw war and politics in purely rational terms, as the activities of human beings. He examined the causes of the Peloponnesian War in a clear, methodical, objective fashion, placing much emphasis on accuracy and the precision of his facts. As he stated:

> With regard to my factual reporting of the events of the war I have made it a principle not to write down the first story that came my way, and not even to be guided by my own general impressions; either I was present myself at the events which I have described or else I heard of them from eyewitnesses whose reports I have checked with as much thoroughness as possible.[6]

Thucydides also provided remarkable insight into the human condition. He believed that political situations recur in similar fashion and that the study of history is therefore of great value in understanding the present.

**Greek Drama** Drama as we know it in Western culture was originated by the Greeks. Plays were presented in outdoor theaters as part of religious festivals. The form of Greek plays remained rather stable. Three male actors who wore masks acted all the parts. A chorus, also male, spoke lines that explained what was going on. Action was very limited because the emphasis was on the story and its meaning.

The first Greek dramas were tragedies, plays based on the suffering of a hero and usually ending in disaster. Aeschylus (525–456 B.C.E.) is the first tragedian whose plays are known to us. As was customary in Greek tragedy, his plots are simple, and the entire drama focuses on a single tragic event and its meaning. Greek tragedies were sometimes presented in a trilogy (a set of three plays) built around a common theme. The only complete trilogy we possess, called the *Oresteia,* was composed by Aeschylus. The theme of this trilogy is derived from Homer. Agamemnon, the king of Mycenae, returns a hero from the defeat of Troy. His wife, Clytemnestra, avenges the sacrificial death of her daughter Iphigenia by murdering Agamemnon, who had been responsible for Iphigenia's death. In the second play of the trilogy, Agamemnon's son Orestes avenges his father by killing his mother. Orestes is then pursued by the avenging Furies, who torment him for killing his mother. Evil acts breed evil acts, and suffering is one's lot, suggests Aeschylus. But Orestes is put on trial and acquitted by Athena, the patron goddess of Athens. Personal vendetta has been eliminated, and law has prevailed.

Another great Athenian playwright was Sophocles (c. 496–406 B.C.E.), whose most famous play was *Oedipus the King.* In this play, the oracle of Apollo foretells that a man (Oedipus) will kill his own father and marry his mother. Despite all attempts at prevention, the tragic events occur. Although it appears that Oedipus suffered the fate determined by the gods, Oedipus also accepts that he himself as a free man must bear responsibility for his actions: "It was Apollo, friends, Apollo, that brought this bitter bitterness, my sorrows to completion. But the hand that struck me was none but my own."[7]

The third outstanding Athenian tragedian, Euripides (c. 485–406 B.C.E.), moved beyond his predecessors by creating more realistic characters. His plots also became more complex, with a greater interest in real-life situations. Euripides was controversial; he questioned traditional moral and religious values. For example, he was critical of the traditional view that war was glorious. He portrayed war as brutal and barbaric.

Greek tragedies dealt with universal themes still relevant to our day. They probed such problems as the nature of good and evil, the rights of the individual, the nature of divine forces, and the nature of human beings. Over and over, the tragic lesson was repeated: humans were free and yet could operate only within limitations imposed by the gods. To strive to do the best may not always gain a person success in human terms but is nevertheless worthy of the endeavor. Greek pride in human accomplishment and independence is real. As the chorus chants in Sophocles' *Antigone:* "Is there anything more wonderful on earth, our marvelous planet, than the miracle of man?"[8]

## Athenian Comedy: Sex as an Antiwar Instrument

Greek comedy became a regular feature of the dramatic presentations at the festival of Dionysus in Athens beginning in 488–487 B.C.E. Aristophanes used his comedies to present political messages, especially to express his antiwar sentiments. The plot of *Lysistrata* centers on a sex strike by wives in order to get their husbands to end the Peloponnesian War. In this scene from the play, Lysistrata (whose name means "she who dissolves the armies") has the women swear a special oath. The oath involves a bowl of wine offered as a libation to the gods.

*How does this selection from Aristophanes illustrate the political use of comedy?*

### Aristophanes, *Lysistrata*

LYSISTRATA: LAMPITO: all of you women: come, touch the bowl, and repeat after me: I WILL HAVE NOTHING TO DO WITH MY HUSBAND OR MY LOVER
KALONIKE: I will have nothing to do with my husband or my lover
LYSISTRATA: THOUGH HE COME TO ME IN PITIABLE CONDITION
KALONIKE: Though he come to me in pitiable condition (Oh, Lysistrata! This is killing me!)
LYSISTRATA: I WILL STAY IN MY HOUSE UNTOUCHABLE
KALONIKE: I will stay in my house untouchable
LYSISTRATA: IN MY THINNEST SAFFRON SILK
KALONIKE: In my thinnest saffron silk
LYSISTRATA: AND MAKE HIM LONG FOR ME.
KALONIKE: And make him long for me.
LYSISTRATA: I WILL NOT GIVE MYSELF
KALONIKE: I will not give myself
LYSISTRATA: AND IF HE CONSTRAINS ME
KALONIKE: And if he constrains me
LYSISTRATA: I WILL BE AS COLD AS ICE AND NEVER MOVE
KALONIKE: I will be as cold as ice and never move
LYSISTRATA: I WILL NOT LIFT MY SLIPPERS TOWARD THE CEILING
KALONIKE: I will not lift my slippers toward the ceiling
LYSISTRATA: OR CROUCH ON ALL FOURS LIKE THE LIONESS IN THE CARVING
KALONIKE: Or crouch on all fours like the lioness in the carving
LYSISTRATA: AND IF I KEEP THIS OATH LET ME DRINK FROM THIS BOWL
KALONIKE: And if I keep this oath let me drink from this bowl
LYSISTRATA: IF NOT, LET MY OWN BOWL BE FILLED WITH WATER.
KALONIKE: If not, let my own bowl be filled with water.
LYSISTRATA: You have all sworn?
MYRRHINE: We have

Greek comedy developed later than tragedy. The plays of Aristophanes (c. 450–c. 385 B.C.E.), who used both grotesque masks and obscene jokes to entertain the Athenian audience, are examples of Old Comedy. But comedy in Athens was also more clearly political than tragedy. It was used to attack or savagely satirize both politicians and intellectuals. Of special importance to Aristophanes was his opposition to the Peloponnesian War. *Lysistrata*, performed in 411 B.C.E., when Athens was in serious danger of losing the war, had a comic but effective message against the war (see the box above).

**The Arts: The Classical Ideal** The artistic standards established by the Greeks of the classical period have largely dominated the arts of the Western world. Greek art was concerned with expressing eternally true ideals. Its subject matter was basically the human being, expressed harmoniously as an object of great beauty. The classic style, based on the ideals of reason, moderation, symmetry, balance, and harmony in all things, was meant to civilize the emotions.

In architecture, the most important form was the temple dedicated to a god or goddess. At the center of Greek temples were walled rooms that housed the statues of deities and treasuries in which gifts to the gods and goddesses were safeguarded. These central rooms were surrounded by a screen of columns that made Greek temples open structures rather than closed ones. The columns were originally made of wood but were changed to marble in the fifth century B.C.E.

Some of the finest examples of Greek classical architecture were built in fifth-century Athens. The most famous building, regarded as the greatest example of the classical Greek temple, was the Parthenon, built between 447 and 432 B.C.E. Consecrated to Athena, the patron goddess of Athens, the Parthenon was also dedicated to the glory of the city-state and its inhabitants. The Parthenon typifies the principles of classical architecture: calmness, clarity, and the avoidance of superfluous detail.

Greek sculpture also developed a classical style that differed significantly from the artificial stiffness of the figures of an earlier period, which had been influenced by Egyptian sculpture. Statues of the male nude, the favorite subject of Greek sculptors, now exhibited more relaxed attitudes; their faces were self-assured, their bodies flexible and smooth-muscled. Although the figures possessed natural features that made them lifelike, Greek sculptors

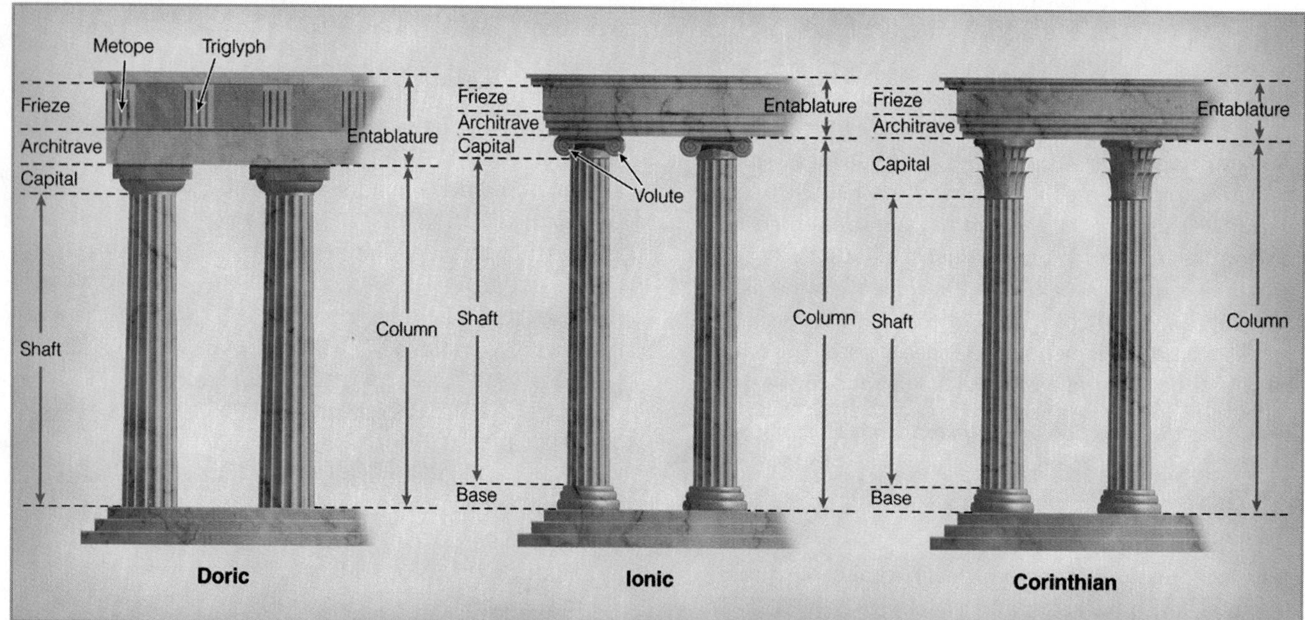


© Art Resource, NY

**Doric, Ionic, and Corinthian Orders.** The Greeks used different shapes and sizes in the columns of their temples. The Doric order, evolved first in the Dorian Peloponnesus, consisted of thick, fluted columns with simple capitals (the decorated tops of the columns). The Greeks considered the Doric order grave, dignified, and masculine. The Ionic style was first developed in western Asia Minor and consisted of slender columns with spiral-shaped capitals. The Greeks characterized the Ionic order as slender, elegant, and feminine in principle. Corinthian columns, with their more detailed capitals modeled after acanthus leaves, came later, near the end of the fifth century B.C.E.

© Michael Holford, London

**The Parthenon.** The arts in classical Greece were designed to express the eternal ideals of reason, moderation, symmetry, balance, and harmony. In architecture, the most important form was the temple, and the classical example of this kind of architecture is the Parthenon, built between 447 and 432 B.C.E. Located on the Acropolis, the Parthenon was dedicated to Athena, the patron goddess of Athens, but it also served as a shining example of the power and wealth of the Athenian empire.

sought to achieve not realism but a standard of ideal beauty. Polyclitus, a fifth-century sculptor, authored a treatise (now lost) on a canon of proportions that he illustrated in a work known as the *Doryphoros.* His theory maintained that the use of ideal proportions, based on mathematical ratios found in nature, could produce an ideal human form, beautiful in its perfected and refined features. This search for ideal beauty was the dominant feature of the classical standard in sculpture.

**The Greek Love Of Wisdom** *Philosophy* is a Greek word that originally meant "love of wisdom." Early Greek philosophers were concerned with the development of critical or rational thought about the nature of the universe and the place of divine forces and souls in it.

Much of early Greek philosophy focused on the attempt to explain the universe on the basis of unifying principles. Thales of Miletus, an Ionian Greek who lived around 600 B.C.E., postulated the unity of the universe. All things were linked by water as the basic substance. Another Ionian Greek, Pythagoras (c. 580–c. 490 B.C.E.), taught that the essence of the universe could be found in music and number. These early Greek philosophers may have eliminated the role of the gods as they were portrayed in Greek myths, but they did not eliminate divinity itself from the world, tending instead to identify it with the underlying, unchanging forces that govern the universe.

Many Greeks, however, were simply not interested in such speculations. The **Sophists** were a group of philosophical teachers in the fifth century B.C.E. who rejected such speculation as foolish. Like their near contemporary Confucius in China (see Chapter 3), they argued that understanding the universe was beyond the reach of

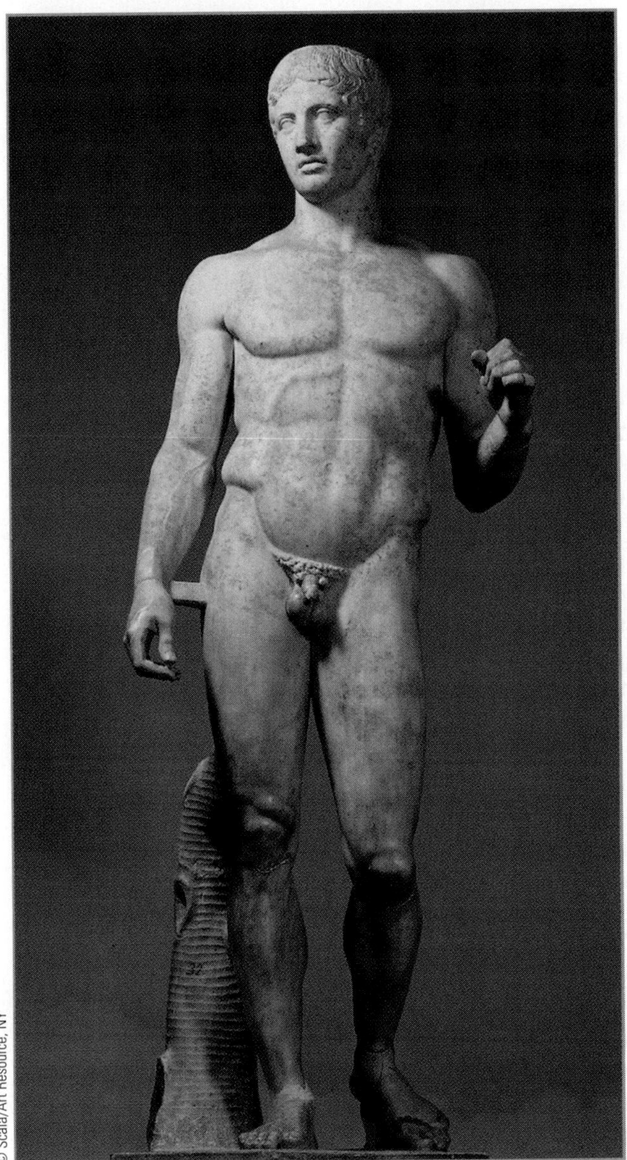


**Doryphoros.** This statue, known as the *Doryphoros,* or spear-carrier, is by the fifth-century B.C.E. sculptor Polyclitus, who believed it illustrated the ideal proportions of the human figure. Classical Greek sculpture moved away from the stiffness of earlier figures but retained the young male nude as the favorite subject matter. The statues became more lifelike, with relaxed poses and flexible, smooth-muscled bodies. The aim of sculpture, however, was not simply realism but rather the expression of ideal beauty.

the human mind. It was more important for individuals to improve themselves, so the only worthwhile object of study was human behavior. The Sophists were wandering scholars who sold their services as professional teachers to the young men of Greece, especially those of Athens. The Sophists stressed the importance of **rhetoric** (the art of persuasive oratory) in winning debates and swaying an audience, a skill that was especially valuable in democratic Athens. Unlike Confucius, however, the Sophists tended to be skeptics who questioned the traditional values of their societies. To the Sophists, there was no absolute right or wrong. True wisdom consisted of being able to perceive and pursue one's own good. Because of these ideas, many people viewed the Sophists as harmful to society and especially dangerous to the values of young people.

In classical Greece, Athens became the foremost intellectual and artistic center. Its reputation is perhaps strongest of all in philosophy. After all, Socrates, Plato, and Aristotle raised basic questions that have been debated for two thousand years; these are still largely the same philosophical questions we wrestle with today.

Socrates (469–399 B.C.E.) left no writings, but we know about him from his pupils. Socrates was a stonemason whose true love was philosophy. He taught a number of pupils, although not for pay, because he believed that the goal of education was to improve the individual. His approach, still known as the **Socratic method,** employs a question-and-answer technique to lead pupils to see things for themselves using their own reason. Socrates believed that all knowledge is within each person; only critical examination was needed to call it forth. This was the real task of philosophy, since "the unexamined life is not worth living."

Socrates questioned authority, and this soon led him into trouble. Athens had had a tradition of free thought and inquiry, but defeat in the Peloponnesian War had created an environment intolerant of open debate and soulsearching. Socrates was accused and convicted of corrupting the youth of Athens by his teaching. An Athenian jury sentenced him to death.

One of Socrates' disciples was Plato (c. 429–347 B.C.E.), considered by many the greatest philosopher of Western civilization. Unlike his master Socrates, who wrote nothing, Plato wrote a great deal. He was fascinated with the question of reality: How do we know what is real? According to Plato, a higher world of eternal, unchanging Ideas or Forms has always existed. To know these Forms is to know truth. These ideal Forms constitute reality and can only be apprehended by a trained mind—which, of course, is the goal of philosophy. The objects that we perceive with our senses are simply reflections of the ideal Forms. They are shadows; reality is in the Forms themselves.

Plato's ideas of government were set out in his dialogue titled *The Republic.* Based on his experience in Athens, Plato had come to distrust the workings of democracy. It was obvious to him that individuals could not attain an ethical life unless they lived in a just and rational state. Plato's search for the just state led him to construct an ideal state in *The Republic,* in which the population was divided into three basic groups. At the top was an upper class, a ruling elite, the philosopher-kings: "Unless . . . political power and philosophy meet together . . . , there can be no rest from troubles . . . for states, nor yet, as I believe, for all mankind."[9] The second group were those who showed courage; they would be the warriors who protected the society. All the rest made up the masses, essentially people driven not by wisdom or courage but by desire. They would be the producers of society—the artisans, tradespeople, and farmers. Contrary to common Greek custom, Plato also believed that men and women should have the same education and equal access to all positions.

Plato established a school at Athens known as the Academy. One of his pupils, who studied there for twenty years, was Aristotle (384–322 B.C.E.), who later became a tutor to Alexander the Great. Aristotle did not accept Plato's theory of ideal Forms. Instead he believed that by examining individual objects, we can perceive their form and arrive at universal principles, but that these principles do not exist as a separate higher world of reality beyond material things but are a part of things themselves. Aristotle's interests, then, lay in analyzing and classifying things based on thorough research and investigation. His interests were wide-ranging, and he wrote treatises on an enormous number of subjects: ethics, logic, politics, poetry, astronomy, geology, biology, and physics.

Like Plato, Aristotle wished for an effective form of government that would rationally direct human affairs. Unlike Plato, he did not seek an ideal state based on the embodiment of an ideal Form of justice but tried to find the best form of government by a rational examination of existing governments. For his *Politics,* Aristotle examined the constitutions of 158 states and arrived at general categories for organizing governments. He identified three good forms of government: monarchy, aristocracy, and constitutional government. But based on his examination, he warned that monarchy can easily turn into tyranny, aristocracy into oligarchy, and constitutional government into radical democracy or anarchy. He favored constitutional government as the best form for most people.

Aristotle's philosophical and political ideas played an enormous role in the development of Western thought during the Middle Ages (see Chapter 12). So did his ideas on women. Aristotle maintained that women were biologically inferior to men: "A woman is, as it were, an infertile male. She is female in fact on account of a kind of inadequacy." Therefore, according to Aristotle, women must be subordinated to men, not only in the community but also in marriage: "The association between husband and wife is clearly an aristocracy. The man rules by virtue of merit, and in the sphere that is his by right; but he hands over to his wife such matters as are suitable for her."[10]

## Greek Religion

As was the case throughout the ancient world, religion played an important role in Greek society and was intricately connected to every aspect of daily life; it was both social and practical. Public festivals, which originated from religious practices, served specific functions: boys were prepared to be warriors, girls to be mothers. Because religion was related to every aspect of life, citizens had to have a proper attitude toward the gods. Religion was a civic cult necessary for the well-being of the state. Temples dedicated to a god or goddess were the major buildings in Greek cities.

The poetry of Homer gave an account of the gods that provided Greek religion with a definite structure. Over a period of time, all Greeks came to accept a common religion. There were twelve chief gods who supposedly lived on Mount Olympus, the highest mountain in Greece. Among the twelve were Zeus, the chief deity and father of the gods; Athena, goddess of wisdom and crafts; Apollo, god of the sun and poetry; Aphrodite, goddess of love; and Poseidon, brother of Zeus and god of the seas and earthquakes. Although the twelve Olympian gods were common to all Greeks, each *polis* usually singled out one of the twelve Olympians as a guardian deity for the community. Athena was the patron goddess of Athens, for example.

Greek religion did not have a body of doctrine, nor did it focus on morality. It gave little or no hope of life after death for most people. Because the Greeks wanted the gods to look favorably on their activities, ritual assumed enormous proportions in Greek religion. Prayers were often combined with gifts to the gods based on the principle "I give so that you, the gods, will give in return." Yet the Greeks were well aware of the capricious nature of the gods, who were assigned recognizably human qualities and often engaged in fickle or even vengeful behavior toward other deities or human beings.

Festivals also developed as a way to honor the gods and goddesses. Some of these (the Panhellenic celebrations) came to have international significance and were held at special locations, such as those dedicated to the worship of Zeus at Olympia or to Apollo at Delphi. Numerous events were held in honor of the gods at the great festivals, including athletic competitions to which all Greeks were invited. The first such games were held at the Olympic festival in 776 B.C.E. and were then held every four years thereafter to honor Zeus. Initially, the Olympic contests consisted of footraces and wrestling, but later boxing, javelin throwing, and various other contests were added.

As another practical side of Greek religion, Greeks wanted to know the will of the gods. To do so, they made use of the oracle, a sacred shrine dedicated to a god or goddess who revealed the future. The most famous was the oracle of Apollo at Delphi, located on the side of Mount Parnassus, overlooking the Gulf of Corinth. At Delphi, a priestess listened to questions while in a state of ecstasy that was believed to be induced by Apollo. Her responses were interpreted by the priests and given in verse form to the person asking questions. Representatives of states and individuals traveled to Delphi to consult the oracle of Apollo. States might inquire whether they should undertake a military expedition; individuals might raise such questions as "Heracleidas asks whether he will have offspring from the wife he has now." Responses were often enigmatic and at times even politically motivated. Croesus, the king of Lydia in Asia Minor who was known for his incredible wealth, sent messengers to the oracle at Delphi, asking whether he should go to war with the Persians. The oracle replied that if Croesus attacked the Persians, he would destroy a mighty empire. Overjoyed to hear these words, Croesus made war on the Persians but was crushed. A mighty empire was indeed destroyed—his own.

## Daily Life in Classical Athens

The *polis* was above all a male community: only adult male citizens took part in public life. In Athens, this meant the exclusion of women, slaves, and foreign residents, or roughly 85 percent of the total population in Attica. There were probably 150,000 citizens in Athens, of whom about 43,000 were adult males who exercised political power. Resident foreigners, who numbered about 35,000, received the protection of the laws but were also subject to some of the responsibilities of citizens, namely, military service and the funding of festivals. The remaining social group, the slaves, numbered around 100,000. Most slaves in Athens worked in the home as cooks and maids or toiled in the fields. Some were owned by the state and work on public construction projects.

**Women in the Loom Room.** In Athens, women were citizens and could participate in religious cults and festivals, but they had no rights and were barred from political activity. Women were thought to belong in the house, caring for the children and the needs of the household. A principal activity of Greek women was the making of clothes. This vase shows two women working on a warp-weighted loom.

**Economy and Lifestyle** The Athenian economy was largely based on agriculture and trade. Athenians grew grains, vegetables, and fruit for local consumption. Grapes and olives were cultivated for wine and olive oil, which were used locally and also exported. The Athenians raised sheep and goats for wool and dairy products. Because of the size of the population in Attica and the lack of abundant fertile land, Athens had to import 50 to 80 percent of its grain, a staple in the Athenian diet. Trade was thus very important to the Athenian economy. Perhaps that is one reason why the Greeks were among the first to mint silver coins, a practice that caused environmental problems by releasing toxic lead into the atmosphere.

The Athenian lifestyle was basically simple. Athenian houses were furnished with necessities bought from artisans, such as beds, couches, tables, chests, pottery, stools, baskets, and cooking utensils. Wives and slaves made clothes and blankets at home. The Athenian diet was rather plain and relied on such basic foods as barley, wheat, millet, lentils, grapes, figs, olives, almonds, bread made at home, vegetables, eggs, fish, cheese, and chicken. Olive oil was widely used, not only for eating but also for burning in lamps and rubbing on the body after washing and exercise. Although country houses kept animals, they were used for reasons other than their flesh: oxen for plowing, sheep for wool, and goats for milk and cheese.

**Family and Relationships** The family was a central institution in ancient Athens. It was composed of husband, wife, and children (a nuclear family), although other dependent relatives and slaves were regarded as part of the family economic unit. The family's primary social function was to produce new citizens. Strict laws of the fifth century had stipulated that a citizen must be the offspring of a legally acknowledged marriage between two Athenian citizens whose parents were also citizens.

Adult female citizens could participate in most religious cults and festivals but were otherwise excluded from public life. They could not own property beyond personal items and always had a male guardian. An Athenian woman was expected to be a good wife. Her foremost obligation was to bear children, especially male children who would preserve the family line. A wife was also to take care of her family and her house, either doing the household work herself or supervising the slaves who did the actual work (see the box on p. 114).

Women were kept under strict control. Because they were married at fourteen or fifteen, they were taught about their responsibilities early. Although many managed to learn to read and play musical instruments, they were not given any formal education. And women were expected to remain at home out of sight unless attending funerals or festivals. If they left the house, they were to be accompanied. A woman working alone in public was either poverty-stricken or not a citizen.

Male homosexuality was also a prominent feature of Athenian life. The Greek homosexual ideal was a relationship between a mature man and a young male. It is most likely that this was an aristocratic ideal and not one practiced by the common people. While the relationship was

## HOUSEHOLD MANAGEMENT AND THE ROLE OF THE ATHENIAN WIFE

In fifth-century Athens, a woman's place was in the home. She had two major responsibilities: the bearing and raising of children and the management of the household. In his dialogue on estate management, Xenophon relates the advice of an Attican gentleman on how to train a wife.

*What does the selection from Xenophon tell you about the role of women in the Athenian household? How do these requirements compare with those applied in ancient India and ancient China?*

### Xenophon, *Oeconomicus*

[Ischomachus addresses his new wife.] For it seems to me, dear, that the gods with great discernment have coupled together male and female, as they are called, chiefly in order that they may form a perfect partnership in mutual service. For, in the first place, that the various species of living creatures may not fail, they are joined in wedlock for the production of children. Secondly, offspring to support them in old age is provided by this union, to human beings, at any rate. Thirdly, human beings live not in the open air, like beasts, but obviously need shelter. Nevertheless, those who mean to win stores to fill the covered place, have need of someone to work at the open-air occupations; since plowing, sowing, planting, and grazing are all such open-air employments; and these supply the needful food. . . . For he made the man's body and mind more capable of enduring cold and heat, and journeys and campaigns; and therefore imposed on him the outdoor tasks. To the woman, since he has made her body less capable of such endurance, I take it that God has assigned the indoor tasks. And knowing that he had created in the woman and had imposed on her the nourishment of the infants, he meted out to her a larger portion of affection for newborn babes than to the man. . . . Now since we know, dear, what duties have been assigned to each of us by God, we must endeavor, each of us, to do the duties allotted to us as well as possible. . . .

Your duty will be to remain indoors and send out those servants whose work is outside, and superintend those who are to work indoors, and to receive the incomings, and distribute so much of them as must be spent, and watch over so much as is to be kept in store, and take care that the sum laid by for a year be not spent in a month. And when wool is brought to you, you must see that cloaks are made for those that want them. You must see too that the dry corn is in good condition for making food. One of the duties that fall to you, however, will perhaps seem rather thankless: you will have to see that any servant who is ill is cared for.

**History Now™** TTo read other works by Xenophon, enter the *HistoryNow* documents area using the access card that is available for *World History.*

frequently physical, the Greeks also viewed it as educational. The older male (the "lover") won the love of his "beloved" through his value as a teacher and the devotion he demonstrated in training his charge. In a sense, this love relationship was seen as a way of initiating young males into the male world of political and military dominance. The Greeks did not feel that the coexistence of homosexual and heterosexual predilections created any special problems for individuals or their society.

# The Rise of Macedonia and the Conquests of Alexander

While the Greek city-states were continuing to fight each other, to their north a new and ultimately powerful kingdom was emerging in its own right. Its people, the Macedonians, were viewed as barbarians by their southern neighbors, the Greeks. The Macedonians were mostly rural folk, organized in tribes, not city-states, and not until the end of the fifth century B.C.E. did Macedonia emerge as an important kingdom. But when Philip II (359–336 B.C.E.) came to the throne, he built an efficient army and turned Macedonia into the strongest power of the Greek world—one that was soon drawn into the conflicts among the Greeks.

The Athenians at last took notice of the new contender. Fear of Philip led them to ally with a number of other Greek states and confront the Macedonians at the Battle of Chaeronea, near Thebes, in 338 B.C.E. The Macedonian army crushed the Greeks, and Philip was now free to consolidate his control over the Greek peninsula. The Greek states were joined together in an alliance that we call the Corinthian League because they met at Corinth. All members took an oath of loyalty: "I swear by Zeus, Earth, Sun, Poseidon, Athena, Ares, and all the gods and goddesses. I will abide by the peace, and I will not break the agreements with Philip the Macedonian, nor will I take up arms with hostile intent against any one of those who abide by the oaths either by land or by sea."[11] Philip insisted that the Greek states end their bitter rivalries and cooperate with him in a war against Persia. Before Philip could undertake his invasion of Asia, however, he was assassinated, leaving the task to his son Alexander.

## Alexander the Great

Alexander was only twenty when he became king of Macedonia. He was in many ways prepared to rule by his

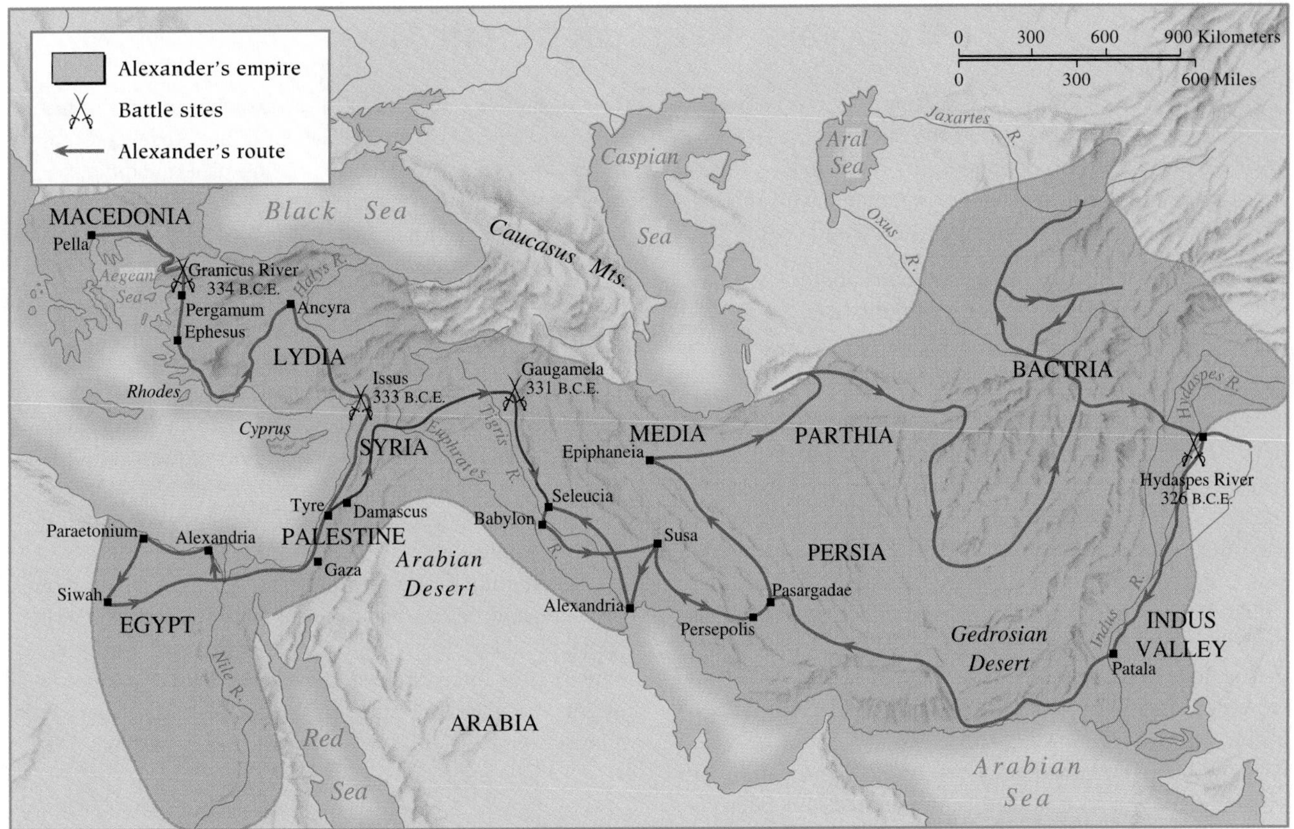


**MAP 4.2 The Conquests of Alexander the Great.** In just twelve years, Alexander the Great conquered vast territories. Dominating lands from west of the Nile to east of the Indus, he brought the Persian Empire, Egypt, and much of the Middle East under his control and laid the foundations for the Hellenistic world. ? Approximately how far did he and his troops travel during those twelve years?

**View an animated version of this map or related maps at** http://history.wadsworth.com/duikerspielvogel05/

father, who had taken Alexander along on military campaigns and had given him control of the cavalry at the important battle of Chaeronea. After his father's assassination, Alexander moved quickly to assert his authority, securing the Macedonian frontiers and smothering a rebellion in Greece. He then turned to his father's dream, the invasion of the Persian Empire.

**Alexander's Conquests** There is no doubt that Alexander was taking a chance in attacking the Persian Empire, which was still a strong state. In the spring of 334 B.C.E., Alexander entered Asia Minor with an army of 37,000 men. About half were Macedonians, the rest Greeks and other allies. The cavalry, which would play an important role as a striking force, numbered about 5,000.

Alexander's first confrontation with the Persians, at a battle at the Granicus River in 334 B.C.E., almost cost him his life but resulted in a major victory. By the following spring, the entire western half of Asia Minor was in Alexander's hands (see Map 4.2). Meanwhile, the Persian king, Darius III, mobilized his forces to stop Alexander's army. Although the Persian troops outnumbered Alexander's, the Battle of Issus was fought on a narrow field that canceled the advantage of superior numbers and resulted in another Macedonian success. After his victory at Issus in 333 B.C.E., Alexander turned south, and by the winter of 332, Syria, Palestine, and Egypt were under his domination. He took the traditional title of pharaoh of Egypt and founded the first of a series of cities named after him (Alexandria) as the Greek administrative capital of Egypt. It became (and remains today) one of Egypt's and the Mediterranean world's most important cities.

In 331 B.C.E., Alexander renewed his offensive, moved into the territory of the ancient Mesopotamian kingdoms, and fought a decisive battle with the Persians at Gaugamela, northwest of Babylon. After his victory, Alexander entered Babylon and then proceeded to the Persian capitals at Susa and Persepolis, where he acquired the Persian treasuries and took possession of vast quantities of gold and silver. By 330, Alexander was again on the march, pursuing Darius. After Darius was killed by one of his own men, Alexander took the title and office of Great King of the Persians.

But Alexander was not content to rest with the spoils of the Persian Empire. Over the next three years, he moved east and northeast, as far as modern Pakistan. By the summer of 327 B.C.E., he had entered India, which at that time was divided into a number of warring states. In 326 B.C.E., Alexander and his armies arrived in the plains of northwestern India. At the Battle of

## Alexander Meets an Indian King

In his campaigns in India, Alexander fought a number of difficult battles. At the Battle of the Hydaspes River, he faced a strong opponent in the Indian king Porus. After defeating Porus, Alexander treated him with respect, according to Arrian, Alexander's ancient biographer.

*What do we learn from Arrian's account about Alexander's military skills and Indian methods of fighting?*

### Arrian, *The Campaigns of Alexander*

Throughout the action Porus had proved himself a man indeed, not only as a commander but as a soldier of the truest courage. When he saw his cavalry cut to pieces, most of his infantry dead, and his elephants killed or roaming riderless and bewildered about the field, his behaviour was very different from that of the Persian King Darius: unlike Darius, he did not lead the scramble to save his own skin, but so long as a single unit of his men held together, fought bravely on. It was only when he was himself wounded that he turned the elephant on which he rode and began to withdraw. . . . Alexander, anxious to save the life of this great soldier, sent. . . [to him] an Indian named Meroes, a man he had been told had long been Porus's friend. Porus listened to Meroes's message, stopped his elephant, and dismounted; he was much distressed by thirst, so when he had revived himself by drinking, he told Meroes to conduct him with all speed to Alexander.

Alexander, informed of his approach, rode out to meet him. . . . When they met, he reined in his horse, and looked at his adversary with admiration: he was a magnificent figure of a man, over seven feet high and of great personal beauty; his bearing had lost none of its pride; his air was of one brave man meeting another, of a king in the presence of a king, with whom he had fought honourably for his kingdom.

Alexander was the first to speak. "What," he said, "do you wish that I should do with you?" "Treat me as a king ought," Porus is said to have replied. "For my part," said Alexander, pleased by his answer, "your request shall be granted. But is there not something you would wish for yourself? Ask it." "Everything," said Porus, "is contained in this one request."

The dignity of these words gave Alexander even more pleasure, and he restored to Porus his sovereignty over his subjects, adding to his realm other territory of even greater extent. Thus he did indeed use a brave man as a king ought, and from that time forward found him in every way a loyal friend.

the Hydaspes River, Alexander won a brutally fought battle (see the box above). When Alexander made clear his determination to march east to conquer more of India, his soldiers, weary of campaigning year after year, mutinied and refused to go on. Reluctantly, Alexander turned back, leading his men across the arid lands of southern Persia. Conditions in the desert were appalling; the blazing sun and lack of water led to thousands of deaths before Alexander and his remaining troops reached Babylon. Alexander planned still more campaigns, but in June 323 B.C.E., weakened from wounds, fever, and probably excessive alcohol consumption, he died at the age of thirty-two.

**The Legacy of Alexander** Alexander is one of the most puzzling great figures in history. Historians relying on the same sources give vastly different pictures of him. Some portray him as an idealistic visionary and others as a ruthless Machiavellian. How did Alexander the Great view himself? We know that he sought to imitate Achilles, the warrior-hero of Homer's *Iliad.* Alexander kept a copy of the *Iliad*—and a dagger—under his pillow. He also claimed to be descended from Heracles, the Greek hero who came to be worshiped as a god.

**Bust of Alexander the Great.** This bust of Alexander the Great is a Roman copy of the head of a statue, possibly by Lysippus. Alexander was partial to Lysippus' portraits, believing that the sculptor was the only one who had the ability to portray Alexander's true essence. Alexander claimed to be descended from Heracles, a Greek hero worshiped as a god, and as pharaoh of Egypt, he gained recognition as a living deity. It is reported that on the base of one of his statues, now lost, in which Alexander was shown gazing at Zeus were the words "I place the earth under my sway; you, O Zeus, keep Olympus."

| CHRONOLOGY The Rise of Macedonia and the Conquests of Alexander | |
|---|---|
| Reign of Philip II | 359–336 B.C.E. |
| Battle of Chaeronea; Philip II conquers Greece | 338 B.C.E. |
| Reign of Alexander the Great | 336–323 B.C.E. |
| Alexander invades Asia; Battle of Granicus River | 334 B.C.E. |
| Battle of Issus | 333 B.C.E. |
| Battle of Gaugamela | 331 B.C.E. |
| Fall of Persepolis, the Persian capital | 330 B.C.E. |
| Alexander enters India | 327 B.C.E. |
| Battle of Hydaspes River | 326 B.C.E. |
| Death of Alexander | 323 B.C.E. |

Regardless of his ideals, motives, or views about himself, one fact stands out: Alexander truly created a new age, the Hellenistic era. The word *Hellenistic* is derived from a Greek word meaning "to imitate Greeks." It is an appropriate way, then, to describe an age that saw the extension of the Greek language and ideas to the non-Greek world of the Middle East. Alexander's destruction of the Persian monarchy created opportunities for Greek engineers, intellectuals, merchants, soldiers, and administrators. Those who followed Alexander and his successors participated in a new political unity based on the principle of monarchy. His successors used force to establish military monarchies that dominated the Hellenistic world after his death. Autocratic power became a regular feature of those Hellenistic monarchies and was part of Alexander's political legacy to the Hellenistic world. His vision of empire no doubt inspired the Romans, who were, of course, the real heirs of Alexander's legacy.

But Alexander also left a cultural legacy. As a result of his conquests, Greek language, art, architecture, and literature spread throughout the Middle East. The urban centers of the Hellenistic age, many founded by Alexander and his successors, became springboards for the diffusion of Greek culture. While the Greeks spread their culture in the east, they were also inevitably influenced by eastern ways. Thus Alexander's legacy created one of the basic characteristics of the Hellenistic world: the clash and fusion of different cultures.

# The World of the Hellenistic Kingdoms

The united empire that Alexander created by his conquests disintegrated after his death. All too soon, Macedonian military leaders were engaged in a struggle for power, and by 301 B.C.E., any hope of unity was dead.

## Hellenistic Monarchies

Eventually, four Hellenistic kingdoms emerged as the successors to Alexander (see Map 4.3). In Macedonia, the struggle for power led to the extermination of Alexander the Great's dynasty. Not until 276 B.C.E. did Antigonus Gonatus, the grandson of one of Alexander's generals, succeed in establishing the Antigonid dynasty as rulers of Macedonia and Greece. Another Hellenistic kingdom emerged in Egypt, where a Macedonian general named Ptolemy established himself as king in 305 B.C.E., creating the Ptolemaic dynasty of pharaohs. A third Hellenistic kingdom came into being in 230 B.C.E. when Attalus I declared himself king of Pergamum in Asia Minor and established the Attalid dynasty.

**The Seleucid Kingdom and India** By far the largest of the Hellenistic kingdoms was founded by the general Seleucus, who established the Seleucid dynasty of Syria, which controlled much of the old Persian Empire from Turkey in the west to India in the east. The Seleucids, however, found it increasingly difficult to maintain control of the eastern territories. In fact, the Indian ruler Chandragupta Maurya created a new Indian state, the Mauryan Empire, in 324 B.C.E. (see Chapter 2) and drove out the Seleucid forces. His grandson Ashoka extended the empire to include most of India. A pious Buddhist, Ashoka sought to convert the remaining Greek communities in northwestern India to his religion.

The Seleucid rulers maintained relations with the Mauryan Empire. Trade was fostered, especially in such luxuries as spices and jewels. Seleucus also sent Greek and Macedonian ambassadors to the Mauryan court. Best known as these was Megasthenes, whose report on the people of India remained one of the West's best sources of information until the Middle Ages.

## Political Institutions

The Hellenistic monarchies created a semblance of stability for several centuries, even though Hellenistic kings refused to accept the status quo and periodically engaged in wars to alter it. At the same time, an underlying strain always existed between the new Greco-Macedonian ruling class and the native populations. Together these factors created a certain degree of tension that was never truly ended until the Roman state to the west stepped in and imposed a new order.

Although Alexander the Great had apparently planned to fuse Greeks and easterners—he used Persians as administrators, encouraged his soldiers to marry easterners, and did so himself—Hellenistic monarchs who succeeded him relied primarily on Greeks and Macedonians to form the new ruling class. Even those easterners who did advance to important administrative posts had learned Greek (all government business was transacted in Greek) and had become Hellenized in a cultural sense. The Greek ruling class was determined to maintain its privileged position.

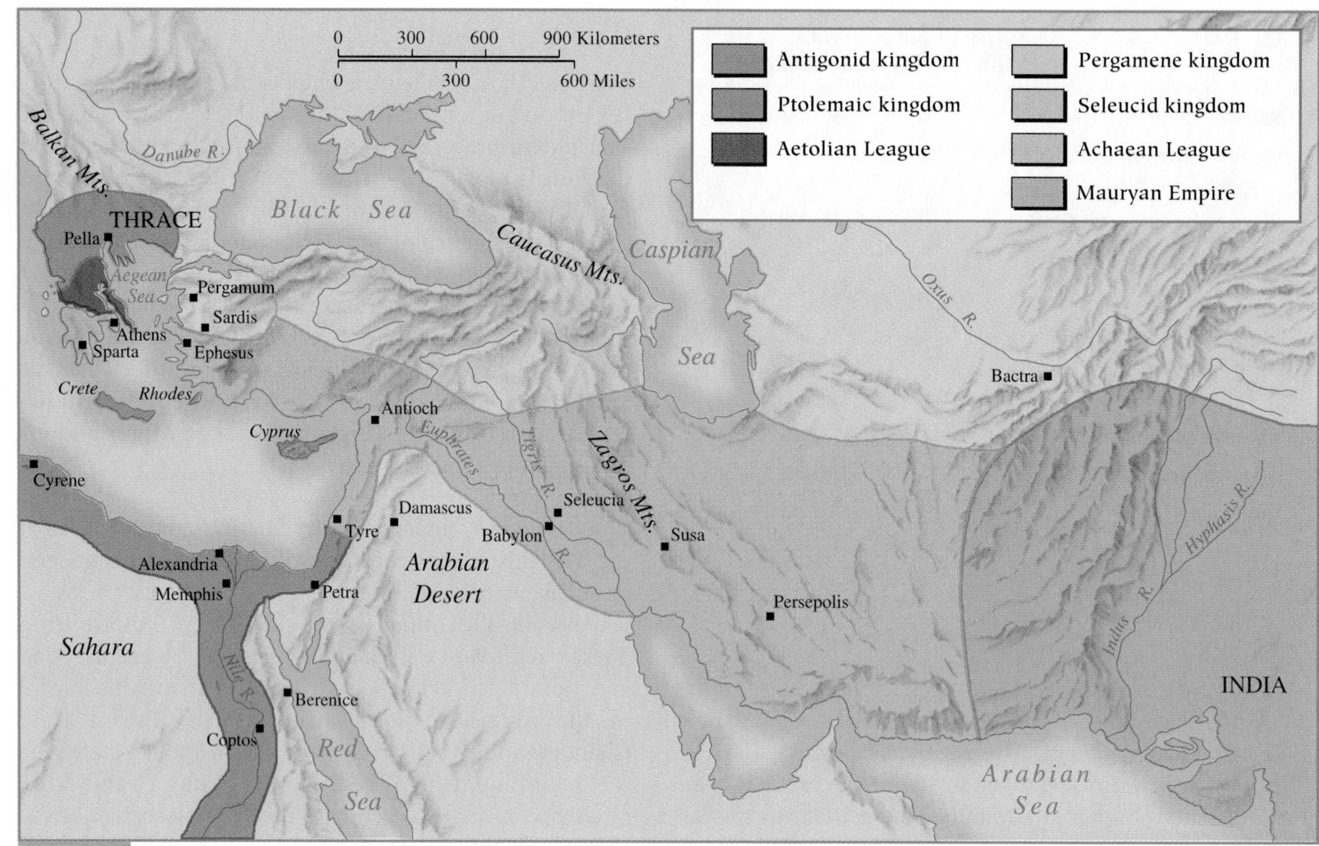


**MAP 4.3 The World of the Hellenistic Kingdoms.** Alexander died unexpectedly at the age of thirty-two and did not designate a successor. Upon his death, his generals struggled for power, eventually establishing four monarchies that spread Hellenistic culture and fostered trade and economic development. Which kingdom encompassed most of the old Persian Empire? **View an animated version of this map or related maps at http://history.wadsworth.com/duikerspielvogel05/**

## Hellenistic Cities

Cities played an especially important role in the Hellenistic kingdoms. Throughout his conquests, Alexander had founded a series of new cities and military settlements, and Hellenistic kings did likewise. The new population centers varied considerably in size and importance. Military settlements were meant to maintain order and might consist of only a few hundred men strongly dependent on the king. But there were also new independent cities with thousands of inhabitants. Alexandria in Egypt was the largest city in the Mediterranean region by the first century B.C.E. Seleucus was especially active in founding new cities, according to one ancient writer:

> The other kings have exulted in destroying existing cities; he, on the other hand, arranged to build cities which did not yet exist. He established so many . . . that they were enough to carry the names of towns in Macedonia as well as the names of those in his family. . . . One can go to Phoenicia to see his cities; one can go to Syria and see even more.[12]

Hellenistic rulers encouraged a massive spread of Greek colonists to the Middle East because of their intrinsic value to the new monarchies. Greeks (and Macedonians) provided not only recruits for the army but also a pool of civilian administrators and workers who contributed to economic development. Even architects, engineers, dramatists, and actors were in demand in the new Greek cities. Many Greeks and Macedonians were quick to see the advantages of moving to the new urban centers and gladly sought their fortunes in the Middle East. The Greek cities of the Hellenistic era were the chief agents in the spread of Greek culture in the Middle East—as far, in fact, as modern Afghanistan and India.

The Greeks' belief in their own cultural superiority provided an easy rationalization for their political dominance of the eastern cities. But Greek control of the new cities was also necessary because the kings frequently used the cities as instruments of government, enabling them to rule considerable territory without an extensive bureaucracy. At the same time, for security reasons, the Greeks needed the support of the kings. After all, the Hellenistic cities were islands of Greek culture in a sea of non-Greeks.

## The Importance of Trade

Agriculture was still of primary importance to both the native populations and the new Greek cities of the Hellenistic world. The Greek cities continued their old agrarian patterns. A well-defined citizen body owned land and worked it with the assistance of slaves. But these farms were isolated units in a vast area of land ultimately owned by the king or assigned to large estate owners and worked by native peasants dwelling in villages.

Commerce experienced considerable expansion in the Hellenistic era. Indeed, trading contacts linked much of the Hellenistic world. The decline in the number of political barriers encouraged more commercial traffic. Although Hellenistic monarchs still fought wars, the conquests of Alexander and the policies of his successors made possible greater trade between east and west. Two major trade routes connected the east with the Mediterranean. The central route was the major one and led by sea from India to the Persian Gulf, up the Tigris River to Seleucia on the Tigris. Overland routes from Seleucia then led to Antioch and Ephesus. A southern route wound its ways from India by sea but went around Arabia and up the Red Sea to Petra or later Berenice. Caravan routes then led overland to Coptos on the Nile, thence to Alexandria and the Mediterranean.

An incredible variety of products were traded: gold and silver from Spain; salt from Asia Minor; timber from Macedonia; ebony, gems, ivory, and spices from India; frankincense (used on altars) from Arabia; slaves from Thrace, Syria, and Asia Minor; fine wines from Syria and western Asia Minor; olive oil from Athens; and numerous exquisite foodstuffs, such as the famous prunes of Damascus. The greatest trade, however, was in the basic staple of life—grain.

## Social Life: New Opportunities for Women

One of the noticeable features of social life in the Hellenistic world was the emergence of new opportunities for women—at least, for upper-class women—especially in the economic realm. Documents show increasing numbers of women involved in managing slaves, selling property, and making loans. Even then, legal contracts in which women were involved had to include their official male guardians. Only in Sparta were women free to control their own economic affairs. Many Spartan women were noticeably wealthy; females owned 40 percent of Spartan land.

Spartan women, however, were an exception, especially on the Greek mainland. Women in Athens, for example, still remained highly restricted and supervised. Although a few philosophers welcomed female participation in men's affairs, many philosophers rejected equality between men and women and asserted that the traditional roles of wives and mothers were most satisfying for women.

But the opinions of philosophers did not prevent upper-class women from making gains in areas other than the economic sphere (see the box on p. 120). New possibilities for females arose when women in some areas of the Hellenistic world were allowed to pursue education in the traditional fields of literature, music, and even athletics. Education, then, provided new opportunities for women: female poets appeared in the third century, and there are instances of women involved in both scholarly and artistic activities.

The creation of the Hellenistic monarchies, which represented a considerable departure from the world of the city-state, also gave new scope to the role played by the monarchs' wives, the Hellenistic queens. In Macedonia, a pattern of alliances between mothers and sons provided openings for women to take an active role in politics, especially in political intrigue. In Egypt, opportunities for royal women were even greater because the Ptolemaic rulers reverted to an Egyptian custom of kings marrying their own sisters. Of the first eight Ptolemaic rulers, four wed their sisters. Ptolemy II and his sister-wife Arsinoë II were both worshiped as gods in their lifetimes. Arsinoë played an energetic role in government and was involved in the expansion of the Egyptian navy. She was also the first Egyptian queen whose portrait appeared on coins with that of her husband.

## Culture In The Hellenistic World

Although the Hellenistic kingdoms encompassed vast territories and many diverse peoples, the Greeks provided a sense of unity as a result of the diffusion of Greek culture throughout the Hellenistic world. The Hellenistic era was a period of considerable cultural accomplishment in many areas—literature, art, science, and philosophy. Although these achievements occurred throughout the Hellenistic world, certain centers, especially the great cities of Alexandria and Pergamum, stood out. In both cities, cultural developments were encouraged by the rulers themselves. Rich Hellenistic monarchs had considerable resources with which to patronize culture.

**New Directions in Literature and Art** The Hellenistic age produced an enormous quantity of literature, most of which has not survived. Hellenistic monarchs, who held literary talent in high esteem, subsidized writers on a grand scale. The Ptolemaic rulers of Egypt were particularly lavish. The combination of their largesse and a famous library with over 500,000 scrolls drew a host of scholars and authors to Alexandria, including a circle of poets. Theocritus (c. 315–250 B.C.E.), originally a native of the island of Sicily, wrote "little poems" or idylls dealing with erotic subjects, lovers' complaints, and pastoral themes expressing his love of nature and his appreciation of nature's beauties.

In the Hellenistic era, Athens remained the theatrical center of the Greek world. While little remained of tragedy, a New Comedy developed, which completely rejected political themes and sought only to entertain and amuse. The Athenian playwright Menander (c. 342–291 B.C.E.) was perhaps the best representative of New Comedy. Plots were simple: typically, a hero falls in love with a not-really-so-bad prostitute, who turns out eventually to be the long-lost daughter of a rich neighbor. The hero marries her, and they live happily ever after.

## A New Autonomy for Women

Upper-class women in Hellenistic society enjoyed noticeable gains, and even in the lives of ordinary women, a new assertiveness came to the fore despite the continuing domination of society by men. The first selection is taken from the letter of a wife to her husband, complaining about his failure to return home. In the second selection, a father complains that his daughter has abandoned him, contrary to an Egyptian law providing that children who have been properly raised should support their parents.

*What specific complaints are contained in each letter? What do these complaints reveal about some women in the Hellenistic world?*

### Letter from Isias to Hephaistion, 168 B.C.E.

If you are well and other things are going right, it would accord with the prayer that I make continually to the gods. I myself and the child and all the household are in good health and think of you always. When I received your letter from Horos, in which you announce that you are in detention in the Serapeum at Memphis, for the news that you are well I straightway thanked the gods, but about your not coming home, when all the others who had been secluded there have come, I am ill-pleased, because after having piloted myself and your child through such bad times and been driven to every extremity owing to the price of wheat, I thought that now at least, with you at home, I should enjoy some respite, whereas you have not even thought of coming home nor given any regard to our circumstances, remembering how I was in want of everything while you were still here, not to mention this long lapse of time and these critical days, during which you have sent us nothing. As, moreover, Horos who delivered the letter has brought news of your having been released from detention, I am thoroughly ill-pleased. Notwithstanding, as your mother also is annoyed, for her sake as well as for mine please return to the city, if nothing more pressing holds you back. You will do me a favor by taking care of your bodily health. Farewell.

### Letter from Ktesikles to King Ptolemy, 220 B.C.E.

I am wronged by Dionysios and by Nike my daughter. For though I raised her, my own daughter, and educated her and brought her to maturity, when I was stricken with bodily ill-health and was losing my eyesight, she was not minded to furnish me with any of the necessities of life. When I sought to obtain justice from her in Alexandria, she begged my pardon, and in the eighteenth year she swore me a written royal oath to give me each month twenty drachmas, which she was to earn by her own bodily labor. . . . But now corrupted by Dionysios, who is a comic actor, she does not do for me anything of what was in the written oath, despising my weakness and ill-health. I beg you, therefore, O king, not to allow me to be wronged by my daughter and by Dionysios the actor who corrupted her, but to order Diophanes the strategus [a provincial administrator] to summon them and hear us out; and if I am speaking the truth, let Diophanes deal with her corrupter as seems good to him and compel my daughter Nike to do justice to me. If this is done I shall no longer be wronged but by fleeing to you, O king, I shall obtain justice.

In addition to being patrons of literary talent, the Hellenistic monarchs were eager to spend their money to beautify and adorn the cities within their states. The founding of new cities and the rebuilding of old ones provided numerous opportunities for Greek architects and sculptors. The buildings of the Greek homeland—gymnasia, baths, theaters, and of course temples—lined the streets of these cities.

Both Hellenistic monarchs and rich citizens patronized sculptors. Thousands of statues, many paid for by the people honored, were erected in towns and cities all over the Hellenistic world. Hellenistic sculptors traveled throughout this world, attracted by the material rewards offered by wealthy patrons. As a result, Hellenistic sculpture was characterized by a considerable degree of uniformity. Hellenistic artistic styles even affected artists in India (see the comparative illustration on p. 121). While maintaining the technical skill of the classical period, Hellenistic sculptors moved away from the idealism of fifth-century classicism to a more emotional and realistic art, seen in numerous statues of old women, drunks, and little children at play.

**A Golden Age of Science** The Hellenistic era witnessed a more conscious separation of science from philosophy. In classical Greece, what we would call the physical and life sciences had been divisions of philosophical inquiry. Nevertheless, by the time of Aristotle, the Greeks had already established an important principle of scientific investigation, empirical research, or systematic observation as the basis for generalization. In the Hellenistic age, the sciences tended to be studied in their own right.

One of the traditional areas of Greek science was astronomy, and two Alexandrian scholars continued this exploration. Aristarchus of Samos (c. 310–230 B.C.E.) developed a *heliocentric* view of the universe, contending that the sun and the fixed stars remain stationary while the earth rotates around the sun in a circular orbit. He

The Art Archive/Kanellopoulos Museum Athens/Dagli Orti.

© Borromeo/Art Resource, NY

COMPARATIVE ILLUSTRATION

**Hellenistic Sculpture and a Greek-Style Buddha**

Greek architects and sculptors were highly valued throughout the Hellenistic world. Shown on the left is a terra-cotta statuette of a draped young woman, made as a tomb offering near Thebes, probably around 300 B.C.E. The incursion of Alexander into the western part of India resulted in some Greek cultural influences there, especially during the Hellenistic era. During the first century B.C.E., Indian sculptors in Gandhara, which is today part of Pakistan, began to create statues of the Buddha. The Buddhist Gandharan style combined Indian and Hellenistic artistic traditions, which is evident in the stone sculpture of Buddha on the right. Note the wavy hair topped by a bun tied with a ribbon, also a feature of earlier statues of Greek deities. This Buddha is also seen wearing a Greek-style toga.

also argued that the earth rotates around its own axis. This view was not widely accepted, and most scholars clung to the earlier *geocentric* view of the Greeks, which held that the earth was at the center of the universe. Another astronomer, Eratosthenes (c. 275–194 B.C.E.), determined that the earth was round and calculated the earth's circumference at 24,675 miles—within 200 miles of the actual figure.

A third Alexandrian scholar was Euclid, who lived around 300 B.C.E. He established a school in Alexandria but is primarily known for his work titled *Elements.* This was a systematic organization of the fundamental elements of geometry as they had already been worked out; it became the standard textbook of plane geometry and was used up to modern times.

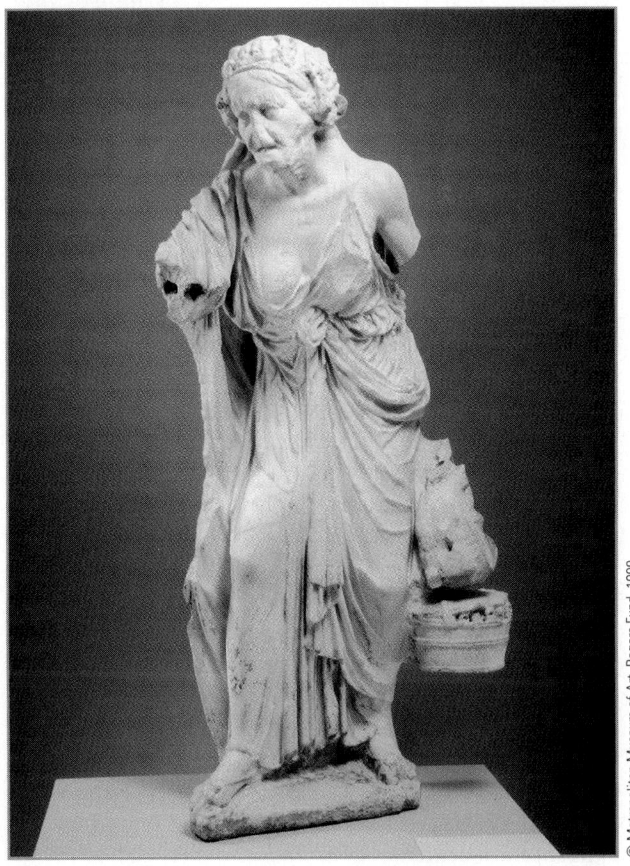

© Metropolitan Museum of Art, Rogers Fund, 1909

**Old Market Woman.** Hellenistic sculptors no longer tried to capture ideal beauty in their sculpture, a quest that characterized Greek classicism, but moved toward a more emotional and realistic art. This statue of an old market woman is typical of this new trend in art. She is seen carrying chickens and a basket of fruit. Old and haggard, mired in poverty, she struggles just to go on living.

## THE STOIC IDEAL OF HARMONY WITH GOD

The Stoic Cleanthes (331–232 B.C.E.) succeeded Zeno as head of this school of philosophy. One historian of Hellenistic civilization has called this work by Cleanthes the greatest religious hymn in Greece. Certainly, it demonstrates that Stoicism, unlike Epicureanism, did have an underlying spiritual foundation. This poem has been compared to the great psalms of the Hebrews.

*Based on Cleanthes' poem, what are some of the beliefs of the Stoics? How do they differ from Epicureanism?*

### Cleanthes, *Hymn to Zeus*

*Nothing occurs on the earth apart from you, O God,*
*nor in the heavenly regions nor on the sea, except*
*what bad men do in their folly; but you know*
*how to make the odd even, and to harmonize*
*what is dissonant; to you the alien is akin.*
*And so you have wrought together into one all*
*things that are good and bad,*
*So that there arises one eternal logos [rationale] of*
*all things,*
*Which all bad mortals shun and ignore,*
*Unhappy wretches, ever seeking the possession of*
*good things*
*They neither see nor hear the universal law of God,*
*By obeying which they might enjoy a happy life.*

By far the most famous scientist of the period was Archimedes (287–212 B.C.E.) of Syracuse. Archimedes was especially important for his work on the geometry of spheres and cylinders and for establishing the value of the mathematical constant pi. Archimedes was also a practical inventor. He may have devised the so-called Archimedean screw, used to pump water out of mines and to lift irrigation water, as well as a compound pulley for transporting heavy weights. During the Roman siege of Syracuse, he constructed a number of devices to thwart the attackers. According to Plutarch's account, the Romans became so frightened "that if they did but see a little rope or a piece of wood from the wall, instantly crying out, that there it was again, Archimedes was about to let fly some engine at them, they turned their backs and fled."[13] Archimedes' accomplishments inspired a wealth of semilegendary stories. Supposedly, he discovered specific gravity by observing the water he displaced in his bath and became so excited by his realization that he jumped out of the water and ran home naked, shouting, "Eureka!" ("I have found it!"). He is said to have emphasized the importance of levers by proclaiming to the king of Syracuse, "Give me a lever and a place to stand, and I will move the earth." The king was so impressed that he encouraged Archimedes to lower his sights and build defensive weapons instead.

**Philosophy: New Schools of Thought** While Alexandria and Pergamum became the renowned cultural centers of the Hellenistic world, Athens remained the prime center for philosophy. After Alexander the Great, the home of Socrates, Plato, and Aristotle continued to attract the most illustrious philosophers from the Greek world, who chose to establish their schools there. New schools of philosophical thought reinforced Athens's reputation as a philosophical center.

Epicurus (341–270 B.C.E.), the founder of **Epicureanism,** established a school in Athens near the end of the fourth century B.C.E. Epicurus believed that human beings were free to follow self-interest as a basic motivating force. Happiness was the goal of life, and the means to achieve it was the pursuit of pleasure, the only true good. But the pursuit of pleasure was not meant in a physical, hedonistic sense (which is what our word *epicurean* has come to mean). Pleasure was not satisfying one's desire in an active, gluttonous fashion but rather freedom from emotional turmoil, freedom from worry—the freedom that came from a mind at rest. To achieve this kind of pleasure, one had to free oneself from public affairs and politics. But this was not a renunciation of all social life, for to Epicurus, a life could be complete only when it was based on friendship. Epicurus' own life in Athens was an embodiment of his teachings. He and his friends created their own private community where they could pursue their ideal of true happiness.

Another school of thought was **Stoicism,** which became the most popular philosophy of the Hellenistic world and later flourished in the Roman Empire as well. It was the product of a teacher named Zeno (335–263 B.C.E.), who came to Athens and began to teach in a public colonnade known as the Painted Portico (the *Stoa Poikile*—hence Stoicism). Like Epicureanism, Stoicism was concerned with how individuals find happiness. But Stoics took a radically different approach to the problem. To them, happiness, the supreme good, could be found only by living in harmony with the divine will, by which people gained inner peace (see the box above). Life's problems could not disturb these people, and they could bear whatever life offered (hence our word *stoic*). Unlike Epicureans, Stoics did not believe in the need to separate oneself from the world and politics. Public service was regarded as noble, and the real Stoic was a good citizen and could even be a good government official.

Both Epicureanism and Stoicism focused primarily on human happiness, and their popularity would suggest a fundamental change in the Greek lifestyle. In the classical Greek world, the happiness of individuals and the meaning of life were closely associated with the life of the *polis*. One found fulfillment in the community. In the Hellenistic kingdoms, the sense that one could find satisfaction and fulfillment through life in the *polis* had weakened. People sought new philosophies that offered personal happiness, and in the cosmopolitan world of the Hellenistic states, with their mixture of peoples, a new openness to thoughts of universality could also emerge. For some people, Stoicism embodied this larger sense of community. The appeal of new philosophies in the Hellenistic era can also be explained by the apparent decline in certain aspects of traditional religion.

**Religion in the Hellenistic World** When the Greeks spread throughout the Hellenistic kingdoms, they took their gods with them. But over a period of time, there was a noticeable decline in the vitality of the traditional Greek religion, which left Greeks receptive to the numerous religious cults of the eastern world. The eastern religions that appealed most to Greeks, however, were the **mystery religions.** What was the source of their attraction?

Mystery cults, with their secret initiations and promises of individual salvation, were not new to the Greek world. But the Greeks of the Hellenistic era were also strongly influenced by eastern mystery cults, such as those of Egypt, which offered a distinct advantage over the Greek mystery religions. The latter had usually been connected to specific locations (such as Eleusis), which meant that a would-be initiate had to undertake a pilgrimage in order to participate in the rites. In contrast, the eastern mystery religions were readily available since temples to their gods and goddesses were located throughout the Greek cities of the east. All of the mystery religions were based on the same fundamental premises. Individuals could pursue a path to salvation and achieve eternal life by being initiated into a union with a savior god or goddess who had died and risen again.

The Egyptian cult of Isis was one of the most popular of the mystery religions. Isis was the goddess of women, marriage, and children; as one of her hymns states: "I am she whom women call goddess. I ordained that women should be loved by men: I brought wife and husband together, and invented the marriage contract. I ordained that women should bear children."[14] Isis was also portrayed as the giver of civilization, who had brought laws and letters to all humankind. The cult of Isis offered a precious commodity to its initiates—the promise of eternal life. In many ways, the cult of Isis and the other mystery religions of the Hellenistic era helped pave the way for Christianity.

## CONCLUSION

UNLIKE THE GREAT CENTRALIZED EMPIRES of the Persians and the Chinese, ancient Greece consisted of a large number of small, independent city-states, most of which had populations of only a few thousand. Despite the small size of their city-states, these ancient Greeks created a civilization that was the fountainhead of Western culture. Socrates, Plato, and Aristotle established the foundations of Western philosophy. Western literary forms are largely derived from Greek poetry and drama. Greek notions of harmony, proportion, and beauty have remained the touchstones for all subsequent Western art. A rational method of inquiry, so important to modern science, was conceived in ancient Greece. Many political terms are Greek in origin, and so are concepts of the rights and duties of citizenship, especially as they were conceived in Athens, the first great democracy. Especially during their classical period, the Greeks raised and debated the fundamental questions about the purpose of human existence, the structure of human society, and the nature of the universe that have concerned thinkers ever since.

All of these achievements came from a group of small city-states in ancient Greece. And yet there remains an element of tragedy about Greek civilization. For all of their brilliant accomplishments, the Greeks were unable to rise above the divisions and rivalries that caused them to fight each other and undermine their own civilization. Of course, their cultural contributions have outlived their political struggles. And the Hellenistic era, which emerged after the Greek city-states had lost their independence, made possible the spread of Greek ideas to larger areas.

The Hellenistic period was a vibrant one. New cities arose and flourished. New philosophical ideas captured the minds of many. Significant achievements were made in art, literature, and science. Greek culture spread throughout the Middle East and made an impact wherever it was carried. But serious problems remained. Hellenistic rulers continued to engage in inconclusive wars. Much of the formal culture was the special preserve of the Greek conquerors, whose attitude of superiority kept them largely separated from the native masses of the Hellenistic kingdoms. Although the Hellenistic world achieved a degree of political stability, by the late third century B.C.E. signs of decline were beginning to multiply. Some of the more farsighted perhaps realized the danger the growing power of Rome presented to the Hellenistic world. The Romans would ultimately inherit Alexander's empire and Greek culture, and we now turn to them to try to understand what made them such successful conquerors.

## TIMELINE

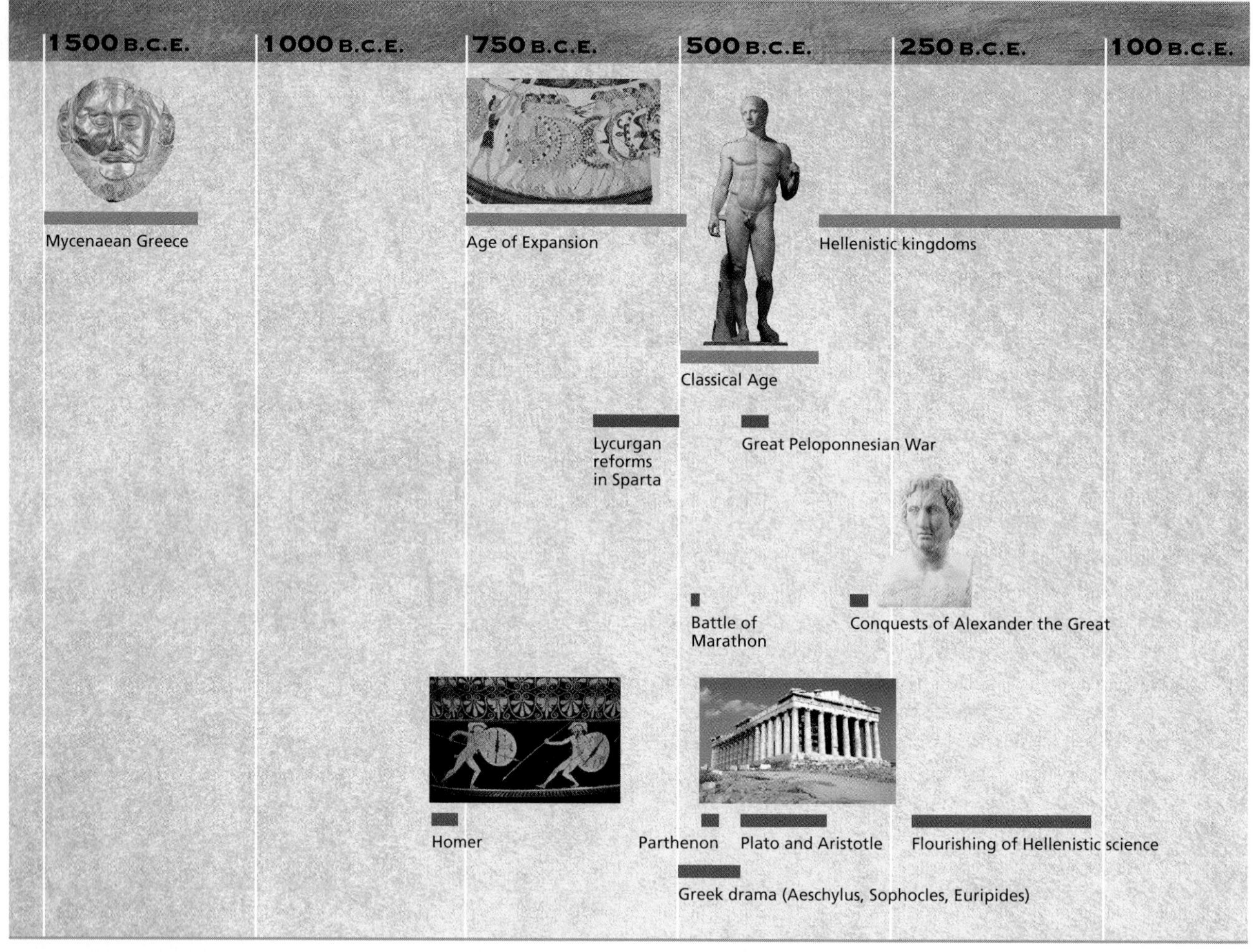


## CHAPTER NOTES

1. Homer, *Odyssey,* trans. E. V. Rieu (New York, 1946), p. 337.
2. Xenophon, *Symposium,* trans. O. J. Todd (New York, 1946), III, 5.
3. Homer, *Odyssey,* trans. E. V. Rieu (New York, 1959), pp. 290–291.
4. Quoted in T. R. Martin, *Ancient Greece* (New Haven, Conn., 1996), p. 62.
5. These words from Plutarch are quoted in E. Fantham et al., *Women in the Classical World* (New York, 1994), p. 64.
6. Thucydides, *The Peloponnesian War,* trans. R. Warner (New York, 1954), p. 24.
7. Sophocles, *Oedipus the King,* trans. D. Grene (Chicago, 1959), pp. 68–69.
8. Sophocles, *Antigone,* trans. D. Taylor (London, 1986), p. 146.
9. Plato, *The Republic,* trans. F. M. Cornford (New York, 1945), pp. 178–179.
10. Quotations from Aristotle are in S. Blundell, *Women in Ancient Greece* (Cambridge, Mass., 1995), pp. 106, 186.
11. Quoted in S. B. Pomeroy et al., *Ancient Greece: A Political, Social, and Cultural History* (Oxford, 1999), p. 390.
12. Quoted in G. Shipley, *The Greek World After Alexander, 323–30 B.C.* (London, 2000), p. 304.
13. Plutarch, *Life of Marcellus,* trans. J. Dryden (New York, n.d.), p. 378.
14. Quoted in W. W. Tarn, *Hellenistic Civilization* (London, 1930), p. 324.

## SUGGESTED READING

For a brief illustrated introduction to Greek history, see **J. Camp** and **E. Fisher, *The World of the Ancient Greeks*** (London, 2002). Good general introductions to Greek history include ***The Oxford History of the Classical World,*** ed. **J. Boardman, J. Griffin,** and **O. Murray** (Oxford, 1986), pp. 19–314; **T. R. Martin, *Ancient Greece*** (New Haven, Conn., 1996); **P. Cartledge, *The Cambridge Illustrated History of Ancient Greece*** (Cambridge, 1998); and **S. B. Pomeroy** et al., ***Ancient Greece: A Political, Social, and Cultural History*** (New York, 1998).

Early Greek history is examined in **O. Murray, *Early Greece,*** 2d ed. (Cambridge, Mass., 1993), and **J. L. Fitton, *The Discovery of the Greek Bronze Age*** (Cambridge, 1995). On colonization, see **J. Boardman, *The Greeks Overseas,*** rev. ed. (Baltimore, 1980). On tyranny, see **J. F. McGlew, *Tyranny and Political Culture in Ancient Greece*** (Ithaca, N.Y., 1993). On Sparta, see **P. Cartledge, *Spartan Reflections*** (Berkeley, Calif., 2001) and ***The Spartans*** (New York, 2003). On early Athens, see the still valuable **A. Jones, *Athenian Democracy*** (London, 1957), and **R. Osborne, *Demos*** (Oxford, 1985). The Persian Wars are examined in **P. Green, *The Greco-Persian Wars*** (Berkeley, Calif., 1996).

A general history of classical Greece can be found in **J. R. Davies, *Democracy and Classical Greece,*** 2nd ed. (Cambridge, Mass., 1993). Important works on Athens include **C. W. Fornara** and **L. J. Samons II,**

***Athens from Cleisthenes to Pericles*** (Berkeley, Calif., 1991); **D. Stockton, *The Classical Athenian Democracy*** (Oxford, 1990); and **D. Kagan, *Pericles of Athens and the Birth of Democracy*** (New York, 1991). On the development of the Athenian Empire, see **M. F. McGregor, *The Athenians and Their Empire*** (Vancouver, 1987). The best way to examine the Great Peloponnesian War is to read the work of Thucydides, ***History of the Peloponnesian War,*** trans. **R. Warner** (Harmondsworth, England, 1954). An excellent recent history is **D. Kagan, *The Peloponnesian War*** (New York, 2003).

A good brief study of Greek art is **J. Boardman, *Greek Art*** (London, 1985). On sculpture, see **A. Stewart, *Greek Sculpture: An Exploration*** (New Haven, Conn., 1990). A basic survey of architecture is **H. W. Lawrence, *Greek Architecture,*** rev. ed. (Harmondsworth, England, 1983). On Greek drama, see the general work by **J. De Romilly, *A Short History of Greek Literature*** (Chicago, 1985). On Greek philosophy, a detailed study is available in **W. K. C. Guthrie, *A History of Greek Philosophy,*** 6 vols. (Cambridge, 1962–1981). On Greek religion, see **J. N. Bremmer, *Greek Religion*** (Oxford, 1994). On athletic competitions, see **S. G. Miller, *Ancient Greek Athletics*** (New Haven, Conn., 2004).

On the family and women, see **C. B. Patterson, *The Family in Greek History*** (New York, 1998); **E. Fantham,** et al., ***Women in the Classical World*** (New York, 1994); and **S. Blundell, *Women in Ancient Greece*** (Cambridge, Mass., 1995).

The best general surveys of the Hellenistic era are **F. W. Walbank, *The Hellenistic World*** (Cambridge, Mass., 1993), and **G. Shipley, *The Greek World After Alexander, 323–30 B.C.*** (New York, 2000). For a good introduction to the early history of Macedonia, see **E. N. Borza, *In the Shadow of Olympus: The Emergence of Macedon*** (Princeton, N.J., 1990). Philip II of Macedonia is covered well in **N. Hammond** and **G. Griffith, *A History of Macedonia,*** vol. 2, 550–336 B.C. (Oxford, 1979). There are considerable differences of opinion on Alexander the Great. Good biographies include **R. L. Fox, *Alexander the Great*** (London, 1973); **P. Cartledge, *Alexander the Great*** (New York, 2004); **N. G. L. Hammond, *The Genius of Alexander the Great*** (Chapel Hill, N.C., 1997); **G. M. Rogers, *Alexander*** (New York, 2004); and **P. Green, *Alexander of Macedon*** (Berkeley, Calif., 1991).

The various Hellenistic monarchies can be examined in **N. G. L. Hammond** and **F. W. Walbank, *A History of Macedonia,*** vol. 3, 336–167 B.C. (Oxford, 1988); **S. Sherwin-White** and **A. Kuhrt, *From Samarkand to Sardis: A New Approach to the Seleucid Empire*** (Berkeley, Calif., 1993); and **N. Lewis, *Greeks in Ptolemaic Egypt*** (Oxford, 1986). On economic and social trends, see the classic and still indispensable **M. I. Rostovtzeff, *Social and Economic History of the Hellenistic World,*** 3 vols., 2d ed. (Oxford, 1953). Hellenistic women are examined in two works by **S. B. Pomeroy, *Goddesses, Whores, Wives, and Slaves: Women in Classical Antiquity*** (New York, 1975) and ***Women in Hellenistic Egypt*** (New York, 1984).

For a general introduction to Hellenistic culture, see **J. Onians, *Art and Thought in the Hellenistic Age*** (London, 1979). The best general survey of Hellenistic philosophy is **A. A. Long, *Hellenistic Philosophy: Stoics, Epicureans, Skeptics,*** 2d ed. (London, 1986). A superb work on Hellenistic science is **G. E. R. Lloyd, *Greek Science After Aristotle*** (London, 1973). On the entry of Rome into the Hellenistic world, see the basic work by **E. S. Gruen, *The Hellenistic World and the Coming of Rome,*** 2 vols. (Berkeley, Calif., 1984)

**History Now™**

**Enter *HistoryNow* using the access card that is available with this text. *HistoryNow* will assist you in understanding the content in this chapter with lesson plans generated for your needs, as well as provide you with a connection to the *Wadsworth World History Resource Center* (see description below for details).**

**WORLD HISTORY**
RESOURCE CENTER

**Enter the Resource Center using either your *HistoryNow* access card or your standalone access card for the *Wadsworth World History Resource Center.* Organized by topic, this website includes quizzes; images; over 350 primary source documents; interactive simulations; maps and timelines; movie explorations; and a wealth of other resources. You can read the following documents, and many more, at http://history.wadsworth.com/rc/world**

**Homer, *Odyssey,* Bk. 1**
**Plato, *Republic,* Bks. 5 and 6**

**Visit the World History Companion Web Site for chapter quizzes and more.**

**http://history.wadsworth.com/duikerspielvogel05/**

CHAPTER

# 5

# THE WORLD OF THE ROMANS

CHAPTER OUTLINE AND FOCUS QUESTIONS

**Early Rome and the Republic**

- What policies and institutions help explain the Romans' success in conquering Italy? How did Rome achieve its empire from 264 to 133 B.C.E., and what problems did Rome face as a result of its growing empire?

**The Roman Empire at Its Height**

- What were the chief features of the Roman Empire at its height in the second century C.E.?

**Crisis and the Late Empire**

- What reforms did Diocletian and Constantine institute, and to what extent were the reforms successful?

**Transformation of the Roman World: The Development of Christianity**

- What characteristics of Christianity enabled it to grow and ultimately to triumph?

**Comparison of the Roman and Han Empires**

- In what ways were the Roman Empire and the Han Chinese Empire similar, and in what ways were they different?

CRITICAL THINKING

- What did one historian mean when he said that the Romans became Christians and the Christians became Romans?

*Horatius defending the bridge as envisioned by Charles Le Brun, a seventeenth-century French painter*

ALTHOUGH THE ASSYRIANS, Persians, and Indians under the Mauryan dynasty had created empires, they were neither as large nor as well controlled as the Han Chinese and Roman Empires that flourished at the beginning of the first millennium C.E. These two were the most extensive empires the world had yet seen (the Han Empire, as we saw in Chapter 3, extended from Central Asia to the Pacific Ocean; the Roman Empire encompassed the lands around the Mediterranean as well as parts of the Middle East and western and central Europe).

Roman history is basically the remarkable story of how a group of Latin-speaking people who established a small community on a plain called Latium in central Italy went on to conquer all of Italy and then the entire Mediterranean world. Why were the Romans able to do this? Scholars do not really know all the answers, but the Romans had their own explanation. Early Roman history is filled with legendary tales of the heroes who made Rome great. One of the best known is the story of Horatius at the bridge. Threatened by attack from the neighboring Etruscans, Roman farmers abandoned their fields and moved into the city, where they would be protected by the walls. One weak point in the Roman defenses, however, was a wooden bridge over the Tiber River. Horatius was on guard at the bridge when a sudden assault by the Etruscans caused many Roman troops to throw down their weapons and flee. Horatius urged them to make a stand at the bridge behind him while he held the Etruscans back. Astonished at the sight of a single defender, the confused Etruscans threw their spears at Horatius, who caught them on his shield and barred the way. By the time the Etruscans had regrouped and were about to overwhelm the lone defender, the Roman soldiers brought down the bridge. When Horatius heard the bridge crash into the river behind him, he dived fully armed into the water and swam safely to the other side through a hail of arrows. Rome had been saved by the courageous act of a Roman who knew his duty and was determined to carry it out. Courage, duty, determination—these qualities would serve the many Romans who believed that it was their divine mission to rule nations and peoples. As one writer proclaimed: "By heaven's will my Rome shall be capital of the world."

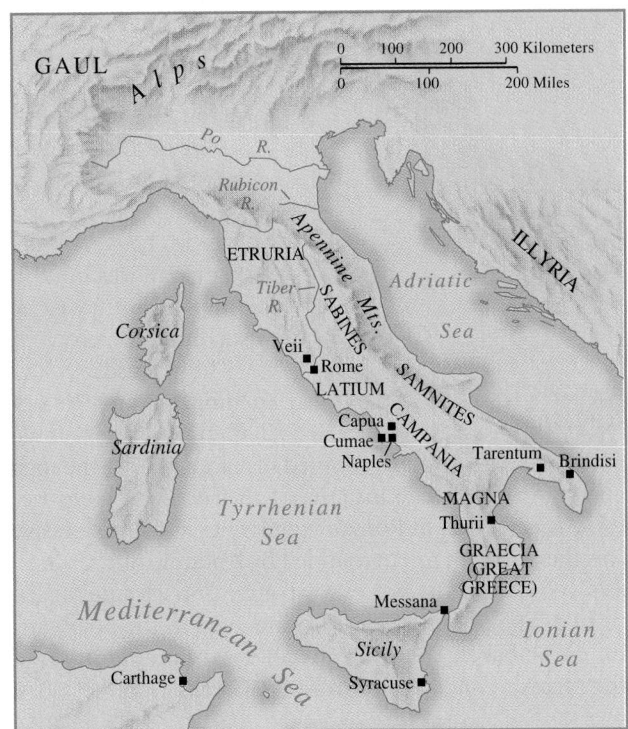


**MAP 5.1** **Ancient Italy.** Ancient Italy was home to several groups. Both the Etruscans in the north and the Greeks in the south had a major influence on the development of Rome. Once Rome conquered the Etruscans, Sabines, Samnites, and other local groups, what aspects of the Italian peninsula helped make it defensible against outside enemies? **View an animated version of this map or related maps at** http://history.wadsworth.com/duikerspielvogel05/

# Early Rome and the Republic

Italy is a peninsula extending about 750 miles from north to south (see Map 5.1). It is not very wide, however, averaging about 120 miles across. The Apennines form a ridge down the middle of Italy that divides west from east. Nevertheless, the peninsula has some fairly large fertile plains ideal for farming. Most important are the Po River valley in the north, probably the most fertile agricultural area; the plain of Latium, on which Rome was located; and Campania to the south of Latium. To the east of the Italian peninsula is the Adriatic Sea, and to the west, the Tyrrhenian Sea with the nearby large islands of Corsica and Sardinia. Sicily lies just west of the toe of the boot-shaped Italian peninsula.

Geography had an impact on Roman history. Although the Apennines bisected Italy, they were less rugged than the mountain ranges of Greece and did not divide the peninsula into many small isolated communities. Italy also possessed considerably more productive agricultural land than Greece, enabling it to support a large population. Rome's location was favorable from a geographical point of view. Located 18 miles inland on the Tiber River, Rome had access to the sea and yet was far enough inland to be safe from pirates. Built on seven hills, it was easily defended. Because the Tiber could be readily forded, Rome became a natural crossing point for north-south traffic in western Italy. All in all, Rome had a good central location in Italy from which to expand.

Moreover, the Italian peninsula juts into the Mediterranean, making it an important crossroads between the western and eastern portions of the region. Once Rome had unified Italy, involvement in Mediterranean affairs was natural. And after the Romans had conquered their Mediterranean empire, governing it was made considerably easier by Italy's central location.

## Early Rome

According to Roman legend, Rome was founded by the twin brothers Romulus and Remus in 753 B.C.E., and archaeologists have found that by that time, a village of huts had indeed been built on the tops of Rome's hills. The early Romans, basically a pastoral people, spoke Latin, which, like Greek, belongs to the Indo-European family of languages (see Table 1.2 in Chapter 1). The Roman historical tradition also maintained that early Rome (to 509 B.C.E.) had been under the control of seven kings and that two of the last three had been Etruscans, people who lived north of Rome in Etruria. Some historians believe that the king list may have historical accuracy. What is certain is that Rome did fall under the influence of the Etruscans for about a hundred years during the period of the kings and that by the beginning of the sixth century B.C.E., under Etruscan influence, Rome began to emerge as a city. The Etruscans were responsible for an outstanding building program. They constructed the first roadbed of the chief street through Rome, the Sacred Way, before 575 B.C.E. and oversaw the development of temples, markets, shops, streets, and houses. By 509 B.C.E., the traditionally accepted date when the monarchy was overthrown and a republican form of government

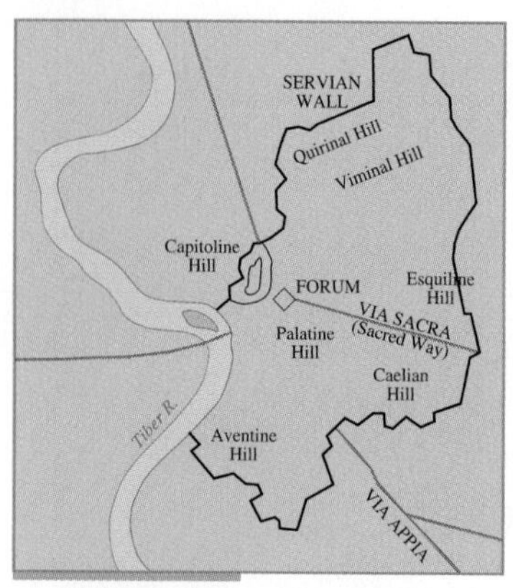


**The City of Rome**

established, a new Rome had emerged, essentially a result of the fusion of Etruscan and native Roman elements. After Rome had expanded over its seven hills and the valleys in between, the Servian Wall was built in the fourth century B.C.E. to surround the city.

The Etruscans had an impact on Roman civilization in ways large and small. The Romans adopted Etruscan dress—the toga and short cloak. The insignia of the Etruscan kings became the insignia of Roman magistrates. Most impressive was the *fasces,* an ax surrounded by a bundle of rods used as a symbol for the power to scourge and execute, hence to rule. The Romans were also indebted to the Etruscans for the alphabet. The Latin alphabet was a modification of the Etruscan one derived from the Greeks.

## The Roman Republic

The transition from monarchy to a republican government was not easy. Rome felt threatened by enemies from every direction and, in the process of meeting these threats, embarked on a military course that led to the conquest of the entire Italian peninsula.



**Etruscan Tomb Mural.** Like the Egyptians, the Etruscans filled their tombs with furniture, bowls, and other objects of daily life, as well as murals showing diversions experienced in life and awaiting the dead in the afterlife. Shown in this mural found in an Etruscan tomb at Tarquinia are servants and musicians at a banquet. This mural was painted in the first half of the fifth century B.C.E.

**The Roman Conquest of Italy** At the beginning of the Republic, Rome was surrounded by enemies, including the Latin communities on the plain of Latium. If we are to believe Livy, one of the chief ancient sources for the history of the early Roman Republic, Rome was engaged in almost continuous warfare with these enemies for the next hundred years. In his account, Livy provided a detailed narrative of Roman efforts. Many of his stories were legendary in character; writing in the first century B.C.E., he used such stories to teach Romans the moral values and virtues that had made Rome great. These included tenacity, duty, courage, and especially discipline (see the box on p. 129).

By 340 B.C.E., Rome had crushed the Latin states in Latium. During the next fifty years, the Romans waged a fierce struggle with the Samnites, a hill people from the central Apennines, some of whom had settled in Campania, south of Rome. Rome was again victorious. The conquest of the Samnites gave Rome considerable control over a large part of Italy and also brought it into direct contact with the Greek communities. The Greeks had arrived on the Italian peninsula in large numbers during the age of Greek colonization (750–550 B.C.E.; see Chapter 4). Initially, the Greeks settled in southern Italy and then crept around the coast and up the peninsula. They also occupied the eastern two-thirds of Sicily. So many Greeks settled in southern Italy that later Romans called it Magna Graecia, or "Great Greece."

The Greeks had much influence on Rome. They cultivated olives and grapes and provided artistic and cultural models through their sculpture, architecture, and literature. Soon after the conquest of the Samnites, the Romans were involved in hostilities with some of these Greek cities and by 267 B.C.E. had completed the conquest of southern Italy. After crushing the remaining Etruscan states to the north in 264 B.C.E., Rome had conquered all of Italy except the extreme north.

To rule Italy, the Romans devised the Roman Confederation. Under this system, Rome allowed some peoples—especially the Latins—to have full Roman citizenship. Most of the remaining communities were made allies. They remained free to run their own local affairs but were required to provide soldiers for Rome. Moreover, the Romans made it clear that loyal allies could improve their status and even have hope of becoming Roman citizens. The Romans had found a way to give conquered peoples a stake in Rome's success.

In the course of their expansion, the Romans had pursued consistent policies that help explain their success. The Romans were superb diplomats who excelled at making the correct diplomatic decisions. While firm and even cruel when

## Cincinnatus Saves Rome: A Roman Morality Tale

There is perhaps no better account of how the virtues of duty and simplicity enabled good Roman citizens to prevail during the travails of the fifth century B.C.E. than Livy's account of Cincinnatus. He was chosen dictator, supposedly in 457 B.C.E., to defend Rome against the attacks of the Aequi. The position of dictator was a temporary expedient used only in emergencies; the consuls would resign and a leader with unlimited power would be appointed for a limited period (usually six months). In this account, Cincinnatus did his duty, defeated the Aequi, and returned to his simple farm in just fifteen days.

*What values did Livy emphasize in his account of Cincinnatus? How important were those values to Rome's success? Why did Livy say he wrote his history? As a writer in the Augustan Age, would he have pleased or displeased Augustus with such a purpose?*

### Livy, *The Early History of Rome*

The city was thrown into a state of turmoil, and the general alarm was as great as if Rome herself were surrounded. Nautius was sent for, but it was quickly decided that he was not the man to inspire full confidence; the situation evidently called for a dictator, and, with no dissentient voice, Lucius Quinctius Cincinnatus was named for the post.

Now I would solicit the particular attention of those numerous people who imagine that money is everything in this world, and that rank and ability are inseparable from wealth: let them observe that Cincinnatus, the one man in whom Rome reposed all her hope of survival, was at that moment working a little three-acre farm . . . west of the Tiber, just opposite the spot where the shipyards are today. A mission from the city found him at work on his land—digging a ditch, maybe, or plowing. Greetings were exchanged, and he was asked—with a prayer for divine blessing on himself and his country—to put on his toga and hear the Senate's instructions. This naturally surprised him, and, asking if all were well, he told his wife Racilia to run to their cottage and fetch his toga. The toga was brought, and wiping the grimy sweat from his hands and face he put it on; at once the envoys from the city saluted him, with congratulations, as Dictator, invited him to enter Rome, and informed him of the terrible danger of Municius's army. A state vessel was waiting for him on the river, and on the city bank he was welcomed by his three sons who had come to meet him, then by other kinsmen and friends, and finally by nearly the whole body of senators. Closely attended by all these people and preceded by his lictors he was then escorted to his residence through streets lined with great crowds of common folk who, be it said, were by no means so pleased to see the new Dictator, as they thought his power excessive and dreaded the way in which he was likely to use it.

[Cincinnatus proceeds to raise an army, march out, and defeat the Aequi.]

In Rome the Senate was convened by Quintus Fabius the City Prefect, and a decree was passed inviting Cincinnatus to enter in triumph with his troops. The chariot he rode in was preceded by the enemy commanders and the military standards, and followed by his army loaded with its spoils. . . . Cincinnatus finally resigned after holding office for fifteen days, having originally accepted it for a period of six months.

**History Now™** To read more of Livy's writing, enter the *HistoryNow* documents area using the access card that is available for *World History*.

necessary—rebellions were crushed without mercy—they were also shrewd in extending their citizenship and allowing autonomy in domestic affairs. In addition, the Romans were not only good soldiers but also persistent ones. The loss of an army or a fleet did not cause them to quit but spurred them on to build new armies and new fleets. Finally, the Romans had a practical sense of strategy. As they conquered, they settled Romans and Latins in new communities outside Latium. By 264 B.C.E., the Romans had established fortified colonies at strategic locations throughout Italy. By building roads to these settlements and connecting them, the Romans created an impressive military and communications network that enabled them to rule effectively and efficiently (see the comparative illustration "Roman and Chinese Roads" on p. 130). By insisting on military service from its allies in the Roman confederation, Rome essentially mobilized the entire military manpower of Italy for its wars.

**The Roman State** After the overthrow of the monarchy, Roman nobles, eager to maintain their position of power, established a republican form of government. The chief executive officers of the Roman Republic were the **consuls** and **praetors.** Two consuls, chosen annually, administered the government and led the Roman army into battle. They possessed ***imperium,*** "the right to command." In 366 B.C.E., the office of praetor was created. The praetor also possessed *imperium* and could govern Rome when the consuls were away from the city and could also lead armies. The praetor's primary function, however, was the execution of justice. He was in charge of the civil law as it applied to Roman citizens. In 242 B.C.E., reflecting Rome's growth, another praetor was added to judge cases in which one or both people were noncitizens. The Roman state also had a number of administrative officials who handled specialized duties, such as the administration of financial affairs and supervision of the public games of Rome.

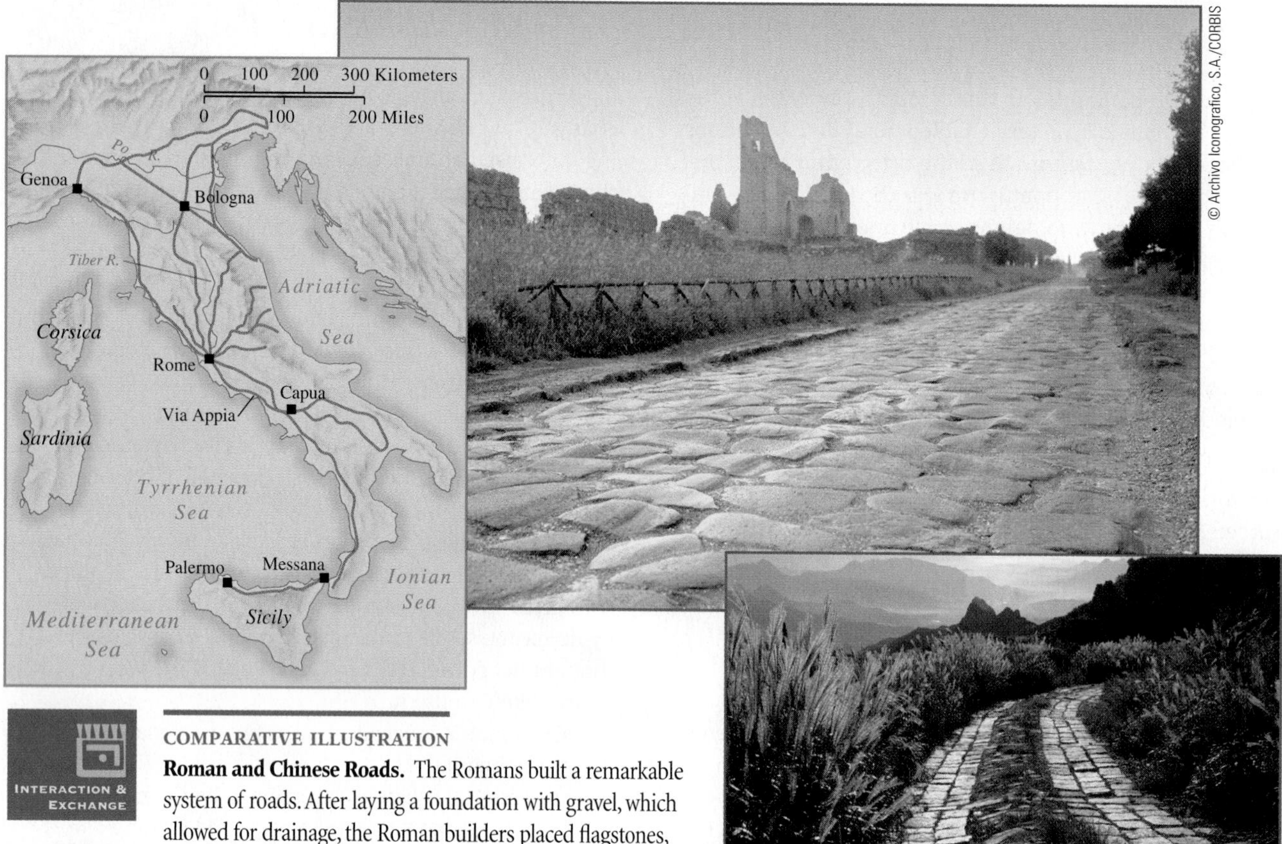






INTERACTION & EXCHANGE

COMPARATIVE ILLUSTRATION

**Roman and Chinese Roads.** The Romans built a remarkable system of roads. After laying a foundation with gravel, which allowed for drainage, the Roman builders placed flagstones, closely fitted together. Unlike other peoples who built similar kinds of roads, the Romans did not follow the contours of the land but made their roads as straight as possible to facilitate communications and transportation, especially for military purposes. Seen here is a view of the Via Appia (Appian Way), built in 312 B.C.E. under the leadership of the censor and consul Appius Claudius (Roman roads were often named after the great Roman families who encouraged their construction). The Via Appia (shown on the map) was meant to make it easy for Roman armies to march from Rome to the newly conquered city of Capua, a distance of 152 miles. Under the Empire, roads were extended to provinces throughout the Mediterranean, parts of western and eastern Europe, and into western Asia. By the beginning of the fourth century C.E., the Roman Empire contained 372 major roads covering 53,000 miles.

Like the Roman Empire, the Han Empire relied on roads constructed with stone slabs for the movement of military forces. The First Emperor of Qin was responsible for the construction of 4,350 miles of roads, and by the end of the second century C.E., China had almost 22,000 miles of roads. Although roads in both the Roman and Chinese empires were originally constructed for military purposes, they came to be used to facilitate communications and commercial traffic.

The Roman **senate** came to hold an especially important position in the Roman Republic. The senate or council of elders was a select group of about three hundred men who served for life. The senate could only advise the magistrates, but this advice of the senate was not taken lightly and by the third century B.C.E. had virtually the force of law.

The Roman Republic had a number of popular assemblies. By far the most important was the **centuriate assembly.** Organized by classes based on wealth, it was structured in such a way that the wealthiest citizens always had a majority. The centuriate assembly elected the chief magistrates and passed laws. Another assembly, the **council of the plebs,** came into being in 471 B.C.E.

The Roman Republic, then, witnessed the interplay of three major elements. Two consuls and later other elected officials served as magistrates and ran the state. An assembly of adult males (the centuriate assembly), controlled by the wealthiest citizens, elected these officials, while the senate, a small group of large landowners, advised them. The Roman state, then, was an aristocratic republic controlled by a relatively small group of privileged people.

**The Struggle of the Orders: Social Divisions in the Roman Republic** The most noticeable element in the social organization of early Rome was the division between two groups—the **patricians** and the **plebeians.** The patrician class in Rome consisted of families descended from the original senators appointed during the period of the kings. They were great landowners who constituted an aristocratic governing class. Only they could be consuls, other magistrates, and senators. Through their patronage of large numbers of dependent clients, they controlled the centuriate assembly and many other facets of Roman life. The plebeians constituted the considerably larger group of nonpatrician large landowners, less wealthy landholders, artisans, merchants, and small farmers. Although they, too, were citizens, they did not have the same rights as the patricians. Both patricians and plebeians could vote, but only the patricians could be elected to governmental offices. Both had the right to make legal contracts and marriages, but intermarriage between patricians and plebeians was forbidden. At the beginning of the fifth century B.C.E., the plebeians began a struggle to seek both political and social equality with the patricians.

The struggle between the patricians and plebeians dragged on for hundreds of years but led to success for the plebeians. A popular assembly for plebeians only, called the council of the plebs, was created in 471 B.C.E., and new officials, known as **tribunes of the plebs,** were given the power to protect plebeians against arrest by patrician magistrates. A new law allowed marriages between patricians and plebeians, and in the fourth century B.C.E., plebeians were permitted to become consuls. Finally, in 287 B.C.E., the council of the plebs received the right to pass laws for all Romans.

The struggle between the orders, then, had a significant impact on the development of the Roman state. Plebeians could now hold the highest offices of state, they could intermarry with the patricians, and they could pass laws binding on the entire Roman community. Theoretically, by 287 B.C.E., all Roman citizens were equal under the law, and all could strive for political office. But in reality, as a result of the right of intermarriage, a select number of patrician and plebeian families formed a new senatorial aristocracy that came to dominate the political offices. The Roman Republic had not become a democracy.

## The Roman Conquest of the Mediterranean (264–133 B.C.E.)

After their conquest of the Italian peninsula, the Romans found themselves face to face with a formidable Mediterranean power—Carthage. Founded on the coast of North Africa by Phoenicians around 800 B.C.E., Carthage had flourished and assembled an enormous empire in the western Mediterranean. By the third century B.C.E., the Carthaginian empire included the coast of northern Africa, southern Spain, Sardinia, Corsica, and western Sicily. With its monopoly of western Mediterranean trade, Carthage was the largest and richest state in the area. The presence of Carthaginians in Sicily made the Romans apprehensive about Carthaginian encroachment on the Italian coast. In 264 B.C.E., mutual suspicions drove the two powers into a lengthy struggle for control of the western Mediterranean (see Map 5.2).

**The Punic Wars** In the First Punic War (the Latin word for Phoenician was *punicus*), the Romans determined on the conquest of Sicily. The Romans—a land power—realized that they could not win the war without a navy and promptly developed a substantial naval fleet. After a long struggle, a Roman fleet defeated the Carthaginian navy off Sicily, and the war quickly came to an end. In 241 B.C.E., Carthage gave up all rights to Sicily and had to pay an indemnity to Rome. Sicily became the first Roman province.

Carthage vowed revenge and added new lands in Spain to compensate for the loss of Sicily. When the Romans encouraged one of Carthage's Spanish allies to revolt against Carthage, Hannibal, the greatest of the Carthaginian generals, struck back, beginning the Second Punic War (218–201 B.C.E.).

This time the Carthaginian strategy aimed at bringing the war home to the Romans and defeating them in their own backyard. Hannibal crossed the Alps with an army of thirty to forty thousand men and six thousand horses and elephants and inflicted a series of defeats on the Romans. At Cannae in 216 B.C.E., the Romans lost an army of almost forty thousand men. Rome seemed on the brink of disaster but refused to give up, raised yet another

**Roman Legionaries.** The Roman legionaries, famed for their courage and tenacity, made possible Roman domination of the Mediterranean Sea. At the time of the Punic Wars, the Roman legionaries wore chain-mail armor and plumed helmets and carried oval shields, as seen in this portrait of a legionary on the altar of Domitius Ahenobarbus. Heavy javelins and swords were their major weapons. This equipment remained standard until the time of Julius Caesar.

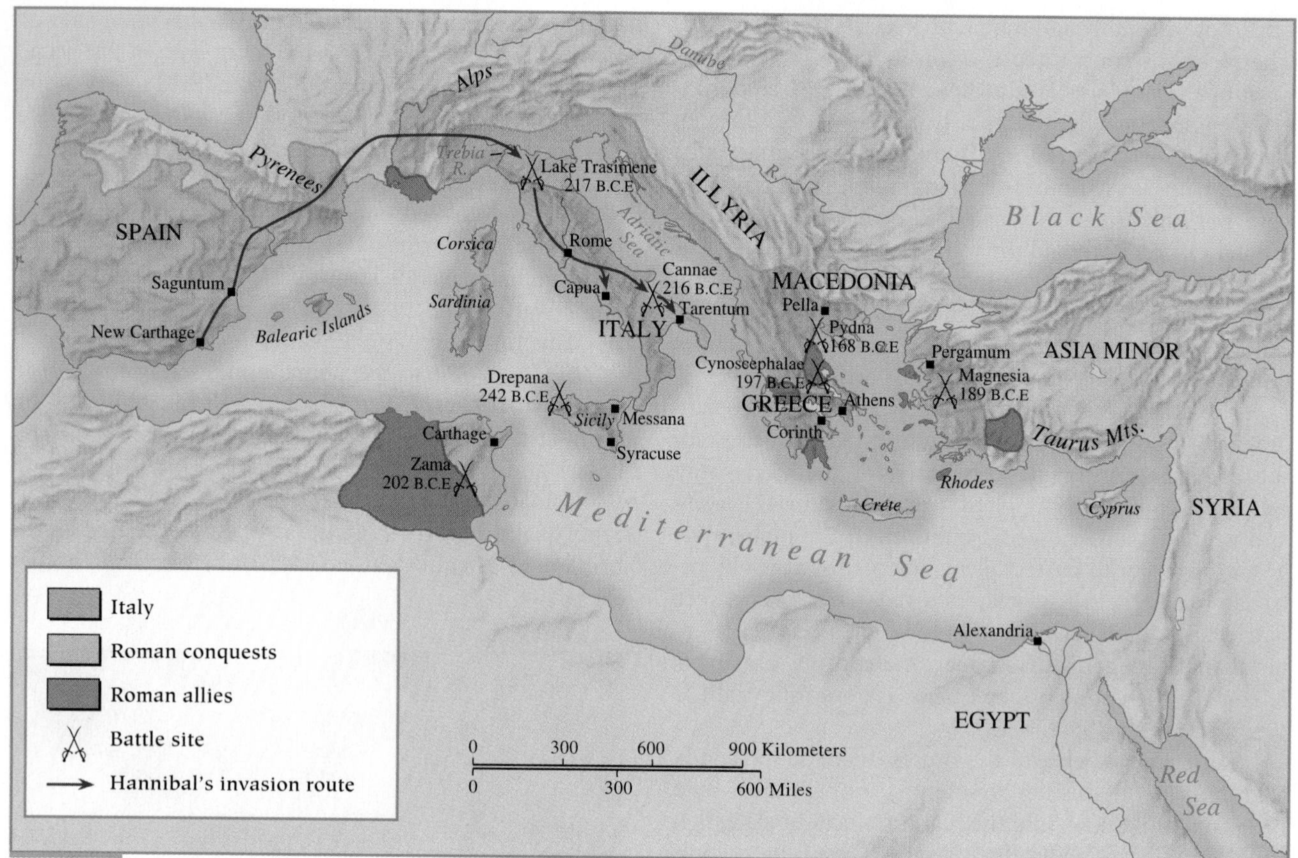


**MAP 5.2 Roman Conquests in the Mediterranean, 264–133 B.C.E.** Beginning with the Punic Wars, Rome expanded its holdings, first in the western Mediterranean at the expense of Carthage and later in Greece and western Asia Minor. ? What aspects of Mediterranean geography, combined with the territorial holdings and aspirations of Rome and the Carthaginians, made the Punic Wars more likely? **View an animated version of this map or related maps at** http://history.wadsworth.com/duikerspielvogel05/

army, and began to reconquer some of the Italian cities that had gone over to Hannibal's side. More important, the Romans pursued a strategy aimed at undermining the Carthaginian empire in Spain. By 206 B.C.E., the Romans had pushed the Carthaginians out of Spain.

The Romans then took the war directly to Carthage, forcing the Carthaginians to recall Hannibal from Italy. At the Battle of Zama in 202 B.C.E., the Romans decisively defeated Hannibal's forces, and the war was over. By the peace treaty signed in 201 B.C.E., Carthage lost Spain, which became another Roman province. Rome had become the dominant power in the western Mediterranean.

Fifty years later, the Romans fought their third and final struggle with Carthage. The Carthaginians had technically broken the peace treaty with Rome by going to war against one of Rome's North African allies who had been encroaching on Carthage's home territory. The Romans used this opportunity to carry out the complete destruction of Carthage in 146 B.C.E., a policy advocated by a number of Romans, especially the conservative politician Cato, who ended every speech he made to the senate with the words, "And I think Carthage must be destroyed" (see the box on p. 134). The territory of Carthage became a Roman province called Africa.

**The Eastern Mediterranean** During the Punic Wars, Rome had become acutely aware of the Hellenistic states of the eastern Mediterranean when the king of Macedonia made an alliance with Hannibal after the Roman defeat at Cannae. But Rome was preoccupied with the Carthaginians, and it was not until after the defeat of Carthage that Rome became involved in the world of Hellenistic politics as an advocate of the freedom of the Greek states. This support of the Greeks brought the Romans into conflict with both Macedonia and the kingdom of the Seleucids. Roman military victories and diplomatic negotiations rearranged the territorial boundaries of the Hellenistic kingdoms and brought the Greek states their freedom in 196 B.C.E. For fifty years, Rome tried to be a power broker in the affairs of the Greeks without assuming direct control of their lands. When these efforts failed, the Romans changed their policy.

**CHRONOLOGY The Roman Conquest of Italy and the Mediterranean**

| | |
|---|---|
| Rome crushes Latin revolt | 340 B.C.E. |
| Creation of the Roman confederation | 338 B.C.E. |
| Samnite Wars | 343–290 B.C.E. |
| First Punic War | 264–241 B.C.E. |
| Second Punic War | 218–201 B.C.E. |
| Battle of Cannae | 216 B.C.E. |
| Rome completes seizure of Spain | 206 B.C.E. |
| Battle of Zama | 202 B.C.E. |
| Third Punic War | 149–146 B.C.E. |
| Macedonia made a Roman province | 148 B.C.E. |
| Destruction of Carthage | 146 B.C.E. |
| Kingdom of Pergamum deeded to Rome | 133 B.C.E. |

In 148 B.C.E., Macedonia was made a Roman province, and when some of the Greek states rose in revolt against Rome's restrictive policies, Greece was placed under the control of the Roman governor of Macedonia. In 133 B.C.E., the king of Pergamum deeded his kingdom to Rome, giving Rome its first province in Asia. Rome was now master of the Mediterranean Sea.

**The Nature of Roman Imperialism** Rome's empire was built in three stages: the conquest of Italy, the conflict with Carthage and expansion into the western Mediterranean, and the involvement with and eventual domination of the Hellenistic kingdoms in the eastern Mediterranean. The Romans did not possess a master plan for the creation of an empire. Much of their expansion was opportunistic; once involved in a situation that threatened their security, the Romans did not hesitate to act. And the more they expanded, the more threats to their security appeared on the horizon, involving them in yet more conflicts. Indeed, the Romans liked to portray themselves as declaring war only for defensive reasons or to protect allies. That is only part of the story, however. It is likely, as some historians have recently suggested, that at some point a group of Roman aristocratic leaders emerged who favored expansion both for the glory it offered and for the economic benefits it provided. Certainly, by the second century B.C.E., aristocratic senators perceived new opportunities for lucrative foreign commands, enormous spoils of war, and an abundant supply of slave labor for their growing landed estates. By that same time, the destruction of Carthage indicated that Roman imperialism had become more arrogant and brutal as well. Rome's foreign success also had enormous repercussions for the internal development of the Roman Republic.

## The Decline and Fall of the Roman Republic (133–31 B.C.E.)

By the mid-second century B.C.E., Roman domination of the Mediterranean Sea was well established. Yet the process of creating an empire had weakened the internal stability of Rome. This led to a series of crises that plagued Rome for the next hundred years.

**Growing Inequality and Unrest** By the second century B.C.E., the senate had become the effective governing body of the Roman state. It consisted of some three hundred men, drawn primarily from the landed aristocracy; they remained senators for life and held the chief magistracies of the Republic. The senate directed the wars of the third and second centuries and took control of both foreign and domestic policy, including financial affairs.

Of course, these aristocrats formed only a tiny minority of the Roman people. The backbone of the Roman state and army had traditionally been the small farmers. But over time, many small farmers had found themselves unable to compete with large, wealthy landowners and had lost their lands. By taking over state-owned land and buying out small peasant owners, these landed aristocrats had developed large estates ***(latifundia)*** that used slave labor. Thus the rise of the *latifundia* contributed to a decline in the number of small farmers. Since the latter group traditionally provided the foundation of the Roman army, the number of men available for military service declined. Moreover, many of these small farmers drifted to the cities, especially Rome, forming a large class of landless poor.

Some aristocrats tried to remedy this growing economic and social crisis. Two brothers, Tiberius and Gaius Gracchus, came to believe that the underlying cause of Rome's problems was the decline of the small farmer. To help the landless poor, they bypassed the senate by having the council of the plebs pass land reform bills that called for the government to reclaim public land held by large landowners and distribute it to landless Romans. Many senators, themselves large landowners whose estates included large areas of public land, were furious. A group of senators took the law into their own hands and killed Tiberius in 133 B.C.E. Twelve years later, Gaius suffered the same fate. The attempts of the Gracchus brothers to bring reforms had opened the door to more instability and further violence. Changes in the Roman army soon brought even worse problems.

**A New Role for the Roman Army** In the closing years of the second century B.C.E., a Roman general named Marius began to recruit his armies in a new way. The Roman army had traditionally been a conscript army of small farmers who were landholders. Marius, who held the consulship from 104 to 100 B.C.E., recruited volunteers from both the urban and rural poor who possessed no property. These volunteers swore an oath of loyalty to the general, not the senate, thus inaugurating a professional-type

## The Destruction of Carthage

The Romans used a technical breach of Carthage's peace treaty with Rome to undertake a third and final war with Carthage (149–146 B.C.E.). Although Carthage posed no real threat to Rome's security, the Romans still remembered the traumatic experiences of the Second Punic War, when Hannibal had ravaged much of their homeland. The hard-liners gained the upper hand in the senate and called for the complete destruction of Carthage. The city was razed, the survivors sold into slavery, and the land turned into a province. In this passage, the historian Appian of Alexandria describes the final destruction of Carthage by the Romans under the command of Scipio Aemilianus.

*What does the description of Rome's destruction of Carthage reveal about the nature of Roman imperialism? What features seem more rhetorical than realistic? Why?*

### Appian, *Roman History*

Then came new scenes of horror. The fire spread and carried everything down, and the soldiers did not wait to destroy the buildings little by little, but pulled them all down together. So the crashing grew louder, and many fell with the stones into the midst dead. Others were seen still living, especially old men, women, and young children who had hidden in the inmost nooks of the houses, some of them wounded, some more or less burned, and uttering horrible cries. Still others, thrust out and falling from such a height with the stones, timbers, and fire, were torn asunder into all kinds of horrible shapes, crushed and mangled. Nor was this the end of their miseries, for the street cleaners, who were removing the rubbish with axes, mattocks, and boat hooks, and making the roads passable, tossed with these instruments the dead and the living together into holes in the ground, sweeping them along like sticks and stones or turning them over with their iron tools, and man was used for filling up a ditch. Some were thrown in head foremost, while their legs, sticking out of the ground, writhed a long time. Others fell with their feet downward and their heads above ground. Horses ran over them, crushing their faces and skulls, not purposely on the part of the riders, but in their headlong haste. Nor did the street cleaners either do these things on purpose; but the press of war, the glory of approaching victory, the rush of the soldiery, the confused noise of heralds and trumpeters all round, the tribunes and centurions changing guard and marching the cohorts hither and thither—all together made everybody frantic and heedless of the spectacle before their eyes.

Six days and nights were consumed in this kind of turmoil, the soldiers being changed so that they might not be worn out with toil, slaughter, want of sleep, and these horrid sights. . . .

Scipio, beholding this city, which had flourished 700 years from its foundation and had ruled over so many lands, islands, and seas, as rich in arms and fleets, elephants, and money as the mightiest empires, but far surpassing them in hardihood and high spirit . . . now come to its end in total destruction—Scipio, beholding this spectacle, is said to have shed tears and publicly lamented the fortune of the enemy. After meditating by himself a long time and reflecting on the inevitable fall of cities, nations, and empires, as well as of individuals, upon the fate of Troy, that once proud city, upon the fate of the Assyrian, the Median, and afterwards of the great Persian empire, and, most recently of all, of the splendid empire of Macedon, either voluntarily or otherwise the words of the poet [Homer, Iliad] escaped his lips:

*The day shall come in which our sacred Troy*
*And Priam, and the people over whom*
*Spear-bearing Priam rules, shall perish all.*

Being asked by Polybius in familiar conversation (for Polybius had been his tutor) what he meant by using these words, Polybius says that he did not hesitate frankly to name his own country, for whose fate he feared when he considered the mutability of human affairs. And Polybius wrote this down just as he heard it.

army that might no longer be subject to the state. Moreover, to recruit these men, a general would promise them land, forcing generals to play politics in order to get legislation passed that would provide the land for their veterans. Marius left a powerful legacy. He had created a new system of military recruitment that placed much power in the hands of the individual generals.

Lucius Cornelius Sulla was the next general to take advantage of the new military system. The senate had given him command of a war in Asia Minor, but when the council of the plebs tried to transfer command of this war to Marius, a civil war broke out. Sulla won and seized Rome itself in 82 B.C.E., conducting a reign of terror to wipe out all opposition. Then Sulla restored power to the hands of the senate and eliminated most of the powers of the popular assemblies. Sulla hoped that he had created a firm foundation for the traditional Republic governed by a powerful senate, but his real legacy was quite different from what he had intended. His example of using an army to seize power would prove most attractive to ambitious men.

**The Collapse of the Republic** For the next fifty years, Roman history was characterized by two important fea-

| **CHRONOLOGY The Decline and Fall of the Roman Republic** | |
|---|---|
| Reforms of Tiberius Gracchus133 b.c.e. | |
| Reforms of Gaius Gracchus | 123–121 B.C.E. |
| Marius: Consecutive consulships | 104–100 B.C.E. |
| Sulla as dictator | 82–79 B.C.E. |
| First Triumvirate (Caesar, Pompey, Crassus) | 60 B.C.E. |
| Caesar as dictator | 47–44 B.C.E. |
| Octavian defeats Antony at Actium | 31 B.C.E |

tures: the jostling for power by a number of powerful individuals and the civil wars generated by their conflicts. Three powerful individuals came to hold enormous military and political power—Crassus, Pompey, and Julius Caesar. Crassus, who was known as the richest man in Rome, had successfully put down a major slave rebellion. Pompey had returned from a successful military command in Spain in 71 B.C.E. and been hailed as a hero. Julius Caesar also had a military command in Spain. In 60 B.C.E., Caesar joined with Crassus and Pompey to form a coalition that historians call the First Triumvirate.

The combined wealth and power of these three men was enormous, enabling them to dominate the political scene and achieve their basic aims: Pompey received lands for his veterans and a command in Spain, Crassus was given a command in Syria, and Caesar was granted a special military command in Gaul (modern France). When Crassus was killed in battle in 53 B.C.E., his death left two powerful men with armies in direct competition. Caesar had conquered all of Gaul and gained fame, wealth, and military experience as well as an army of seasoned veterans who were loyal to him. When leading senators decided that Pompey would be less harmful to their cause and voted for Caesar to lay down his command and return as a private citizen to Rome, Caesar refused. He chose to keep his army and moved into Italy by crossing the Rubicon River, marching on Rome, and defeating Pompey and his allies, leaving Caesar in complete control of the Roman government.

Caesar was officially made **dictator** in 47 B.C.E. and three years later was named dictator for life. Realizing the need for reforms, he gave land to the poor and increased the size of the senate to nine hundred members. By filling it with many of his supporters and increasing the membership, he effectively weakened the power of the senate. He also reformed the calendar by introducing the Egyptian solar year of 365 days (with later changes in 1582, it became the basis of our own calendar). Caesar planned much more in the way of building projects and military adventures in the east, but in 44 B.C.E., a group of leading senators assassinated him (see the box on p. 136).

Within a few years after Caesar's death, two men had divided the Roman world between them—Octavian, Caesar's heir and grandnephew, taking the west and Antony, Caesar's ally and assistant, the east. But the empire of the Romans, large as it was, was still too small for two masters, and Octavian and Antony eventually came into conflict. Antony allied himself with the Egyptian queen Cleopatra VII, with whom, like Caesar before him, he fell deeply in love. At the Battle of Actium in Greece in 31 B.C.E., Octavian's forces smashed the army and navy of Antony and Cleopatra. Both fled to Egypt, where, according to the account of the Roman historian Florus, they committed suicide a year later:

> Antony was the first to commit suicide, by the sword. Cleopatra threw herself at Octavian's feet, and tried her best to attract his gaze: in vain, for his self-control was impervious to her beauty. It was not her life she was after, for that had already been granted, but a portion of her kingdom. When she realized this was hopeless and that she had been earmarked to feature in Octavian's triumph in Rome, she took advantage of her guard's carelessness to get herself into the mausoleum, as the royal tomb is called. Once there, she put on the royal robes which she was accustomed to wear, and lay down in a richly perfumed coffin beside her Antony. Then she applied poisonous snakes to her veins and slipped into death as though into a sleep.[1]

Octavian, at the age of thirty-two, stood supreme over the Roman world. The civil wars had ended. And so had the Republic.

**Caesar.** Conqueror of Gaul and member of the First Triumvirate, Julius Caesar is perhaps the best-known figure of the late Republic. Caesar became dictator of Rome in 47 B.C.E. and after his victories in the civil war was made dictator for life. Some members of the senate who resented his power assassinated him in 44 B.C.E. Pictured is a marble copy of the bust of Caesar.

## The Assassination of Julius Caesar

When it became apparent that Julius Caesar had no intention of restoring the Republic as they conceived it, about sixty senators, many of them his friends or pardoned enemies, formed a conspiracy to assassinate the dictator. It was led by Gaius Cassius and Marcus Brutus, who naively imagined that this act would restore the traditional Republic. The conspirators set the Ides of March (March 15), 44 B.C.E., as the date for the assassination. Caesar was in the midst of preparations for a campaign in the eastern part of the empire. Although informed that there was a plot against his life, he chose to disregard the warning. This account of Caesar's death is taken from his biography by the Greek writer Plutarch.

*What does the account of Caesar's assassination tell you about the character of Julius Caesar?*

### Plutarch, *Life of Caesar*

Fate, however, is to all appearance more unavoidable than unexpected. For many strange prodigies and apparitions are said to have been observed shortly before this event. . . . One finds it also related by many that a soothsayer bade him [Caesar] prepare for some great danger on the Ides of March. When this day was come, Caesar, as he went to the senate, met this soothsayer, and said to him by way of raillery, "The Ides of March are come," who answered him calmly, "Yes, they are come, but they are not past. . . ."

All these things might happen by chance. But the place which was destined for the scene of this murder, in which the senate met that day, was the same in which Pompey's statue stood, and was one of the edifices which Pompey had raised and dedicated with his theater to the use of the public, plainly showing that there was something of a supernatural influence which guided the action and ordered it to that particular place. Cassius, just before the act, is said to have looked toward Pompey's statue, and silently implored his assistance. . . . When Caesar entered, the senate stood up to show their respect to him, and of Brutus's confederates, some came about his chair and stood behind it, others met him, pretending to add their petitions to those of Tillius Cimber, in behalf of his brother, who was in exile; and they followed him with their joint applications till he came to his seat. When he was sat down, he refused to comply with their requests, and upon their urging him further began to reproach them severely for their importunities, when Tillius, laying hold of his robe with both his hands, pulled it down from his neck, which was the signal for the assault. Casca gave him the first cut in the neck, which was not mortal nor dangerous, as coming from one who at the beginning of such a bold action was probably very much disturbed; Caesar immediately turned about, and laid his hand upon the dagger and kept hold of it. And both of them at the same time cried out, he that received the blow, in Latin, "Vile Casca, what does this mean?" and he that gave it, in Greek to his brother, "Brother, help!" Upon this first onset, those who were not privy to the design were astonished, and their horror and amazement at what they saw were so great that they dared not fly nor assist Caesar, nor so much as speak a word. But those who came prepared for the business enclosed him on every side, with their naked daggers in their hands. Which way soever he turned he met with blows, and saw their swords leveled at his face and eyes, and was encompassed like a wild beast in the toils on every side. For it had been agreed they should each of them make a thrust at him, and flesh themselves with his blood: for which reason Brutus also gave him one stab in the groin. Some say that he fought and resisted all the rest, shifting his body to avoid the blows, and calling out for help, but that when he saw Brutus's sword drawn, he covered his face with his robe and submitted, letting himself fall, whether it were by chance or that he was pushed in that direction by his murderers, at the foot of the pedestal on which Pompey's statue stood, and which was thus wetted with his blood. So that Pompey himself seemed to have presided, as it were, over the revenge done upon his adversary, who lay here at his feet, and breathed out his soul through his multitude of wounds, for they say he received three-and-twenty. And the conspirators themselves were many of them wounded by each other, whilst they all leveled their blows at the same person.

**HistoryNow™** To read a full version of this document, enter the *HistoryNow* documents area using the access card that is available for *World History.*

# The Roman Empire at Its Height

With the victories of Octavian, peace finally settled on the Roman world. Although civil conflict still erupted occasionally, the new imperial state Octavian constructed experienced remarkable stability for the next two hundred years. The Romans imposed their peace on the largest empire established in antiquity.

## The Age of Augustus (31 B.C.E.–14 C.E.)

In 27 B.C.E., Octavian proclaimed the "restoration of the Republic." He understood that only traditional republican forms would satisfy the senatorial aristocracy. At the same time, Octavian was aware that the Republic could not be fully restored. Although he gave some power to the senate, in fact, Octavian became the first Roman emperor.

© Photo Vatican Museums

**Augustus.** Octavian, Caesar's adopted son, emerged victorious from the civil conflict that rocked the Republic after Caesar's assassination. The senate awarded him the title Augustus. This marble statue from Prima Porta, an idealistic portrait, is based on Greek rather than Roman models. The statue was meant to be a propaganda piece, depicting a youthful general addressing his troops. At the bottom stands Cupid, the son of Venus, goddess of love, meant to be a reminder that the Julians, Caesar's family, claimed descent from Venus, thus emphasizing the ruler's divine background.

The senate awarded him the title of Augustus—"the revered one"—a fitting title in view of his power, previously reserved for gods. Augustus proved highly popular, and his continuing control of the army afforded him great power. The senate gave Augustus the title of *imperator,* or commander in chief. *Imperator* is Latin for "emperor."

Augustus maintained a standing army of twenty-eight legions, or about 150,000 men (a legion was a military unit of about 5,000 troops). Only Roman citizens could be legionaries, while subject peoples could serve as auxiliary forces, which numbered around 130,000 under Augustus. Augustus was also responsible for setting up a **praetorian guard** of roughly 9,000 men who had the important task of guarding the person of the emperor. Eventually, the praetorian guard would play a weighty role in making and deposing emperors.

While claiming to have restored the Republic, Augustus inaugurated a new system for governing the provinces. Under the Republic, the senate had appointed the governors of the provinces. Now certain provinces were given to the emperor, who assigned deputies known as legates to govern them. The senate continued to name the governors of the remaining provinces, but the authority of Augustus enabled him to overrule the senatorial governors and establish a uniform imperial policy.

Augustus also stabilized the frontiers of the Roman Empire. He conquered the central and maritime Alps and then expanded Roman control of the Balkan peninsula up to the Danube River. His attempt to conquer Germany failed when three Roman legions led by a general named Varus were massacred in 9 C.E. by a coalition of German tribes. His defeats in Germany taught Augustus that Rome's power was not unlimited and also devastated him; for months he would beat his head on a door, shouting "Varus, give me back my legions!"

**Augustan Society** Roman society in the Early Roman Empire was characterized by a system of social stratification, inherited from the Republic, in which Roman citizens were divided into three basic classes: the senatorial, equestrian, and lower classes.

Augustus had accepted the senatorial order as a ruling class for the empire. Senators filled the chief magistracies of the Roman government, held the most important military posts, and governed the provinces. To belong to the senatorial order, one needed to possess property worth 1 million sesterces (an unskilled laborer in Rome received 3 sesterces a day; a Roman legionary, 900 sesterces a year in pay). The **equestrian** order was expanded under Augustus and given a share of power in the new imperial state. The equestrian order was open to all Roman citizens of good standing who possessed property valued at 400,000 sesterces. They, too, could now hold military and governmental offices, but the positions open to them were less important than those of the senatorial order.

Citizens not of the senatorial or equestrian orders belonged to the lower classes, who obviously constituted the overwhelming majority of the free citizens. The diminution of the power of the Roman assemblies ended whatever political power they possessed earlier in the Republic. Many of these people were provided with free grain and public spectacles to keep them from creating disturbances. Nevertheless, by gaining wealth and serving as lower officers in the Roman legions, it was sometimes possible for them to advance to the equestrian order.

Augustus died in 14 C.E. after dominating the Roman world for forty-five years. He had created a new order while placating those who yearned for the old by restoring traditional values, a fitting combination for a leader whose favorite maxim was "make haste slowly." By the time of his death, his new order was so well established that few agitated for an alternative. Indeed, as the Roman historian Tacitus pointed out, "Practically no one had ever seen truly Republican government.... Political equality was a thing of the past; all eyes watched for imperial commands."[2] The Republic was now only a memory—and given its last century of warfare, an unpleasant one at that. The new order was here to stay.

## The Early Empire (14–180)

There was no serious opposition to Augustus' choice of his stepson Tiberius as his successor. By his actions, Augustus established the Julio-Claudian dynasty; the next four successors of Augustus were related either to his own family or that of his wife, Livia.

Several major tendencies emerged during the rule of the Julio-Claudians (14–68 C.E.). In general, more and more of the responsibilities that Augustus had given to the senate tended to be taken over by the emperors, who also instituted an imperial bureaucracy, staffed by talented freedmen, to run the government on a daily basis. As the Julio-Claudian successors of Augustus acted more openly as real rulers rather than as "first citizens of the state," the opportunity for arbitrary and corrupt acts also increased. Nero (54–68) freely eliminated people he wanted out of the way, including his own mother, whom he had murdered. Without troops, the senators proved unable to oppose these excesses; however, Nero's extravagances did provoke a revolt of the Roman legions. Abandoned by his guards, Nero chose to commit suicide by stabbing himself in the throat after uttering his final words, "What an artist the world is losing in me."

**The Five Good Emperors (96–180)** Many historians see the ***Pax Romana*** (the Roman peace) and the prosperity it engendered as the chief benefits of Roman rule during the first and second centuries C.E. These benefits were especially noticeable during the reigns of the five so-called **good emperors.** These rulers treated the ruling classes with respect, cooperated with the senate, ended arbitrary executions, maintained peace throughout the empire, and supported generally beneficial domestic policies. Though absolute monarchs, they were known for their tolerance and diplomacy. By adopting capable men as their successors, the first four good emperors reduced the chances of succession problems.

Under the five good emperors, the powers of the emperor continued to be extended at the expense of the senate. Increasingly, imperial officials appointed and directed by the emperor took over the running of the government. The good emperors also extended the scope of imperial administration to include areas previously untouched by the imperial government. Trajan (98–117) implemented the establishment of a program that provided state funds to assist poor parents in raising and educating their children.

The good emperors were widely praised for their extensive building programs. Trajan and Hadrian (117–138) were especially active in constructing public works—aqueducts, bridges, roads, and harbor facilities—throughout the provinces and in Rome. Trajan built a new forum in Rome to provide a setting for his celebrated victory column. Hadrian's Pantheon, a temple of "all the gods," is one of the grandest ancient buildings surviving in Rome (see the illustration on p. 143).

**Frontiers and the Provinces** Although Trajan extended Roman rule into Dacia (modern Romania), Mesopotamia, and the Sinai peninsula (see Map 5.3), his successors recognized that the empire was overextended and returned to Augustus' policy of defensive imperialism. Hadrian withdrew Roman forces from much of Mesopotamia. Although he retained Dacia and Arabia, he went on the defensive in his frontier policy by reinforcing the fortifications along a line connecting the Rhine and Danube Rivers and building a defensive wall 80 miles long across northern Britain to keep the Scots out of Roman Britain. By the end of the second century, the Roman forces were established in permanent bases behind the frontiers. But when one frontier was attacked, troops had to be drawn from other frontiers, leaving them vulnerable to attack.

At its height in the second century, the Roman Empire was one of the greatest states the world had seen. It covered about 3.5 million square miles and had a population, like that of Han China, estimated at more than fifty million. While the emperors and the imperial administration provided a degree of unity, considerable leeway was given to local customs, and the privileges of Roman citizenship were extended to many people throughout the empire. In 212, the emperor Caracalla completed the process by giving Roman citizenship to every free inhabitant of the empire. Latin was the language of the western part of the empire, while Greek was used in the east. Roman culture spread to all parts of the empire and freely mixed with Greek culture, creating what has been called Greco-Roman civilization.

The administration and cultural life of the Roman Empire depended greatly on cities and towns. A provincial governor's staff was not large, so local city officials were expected to act as Roman agents in carrying out many government functions, especially those related to taxes. Most towns and cities were not large by modern standards. The largest was Rome, but there were also some large cities in the east: Alexandria in Egypt numbered over 300,000 inhabitants, Ephesus in Asia Minor had 200,000, and Antioch in Syria had around 150,000. In the west, cities were usually small, with only a few thousand inhabitants. Cities were important in the spread of Roman culture, law, and the Latin language, and they re-

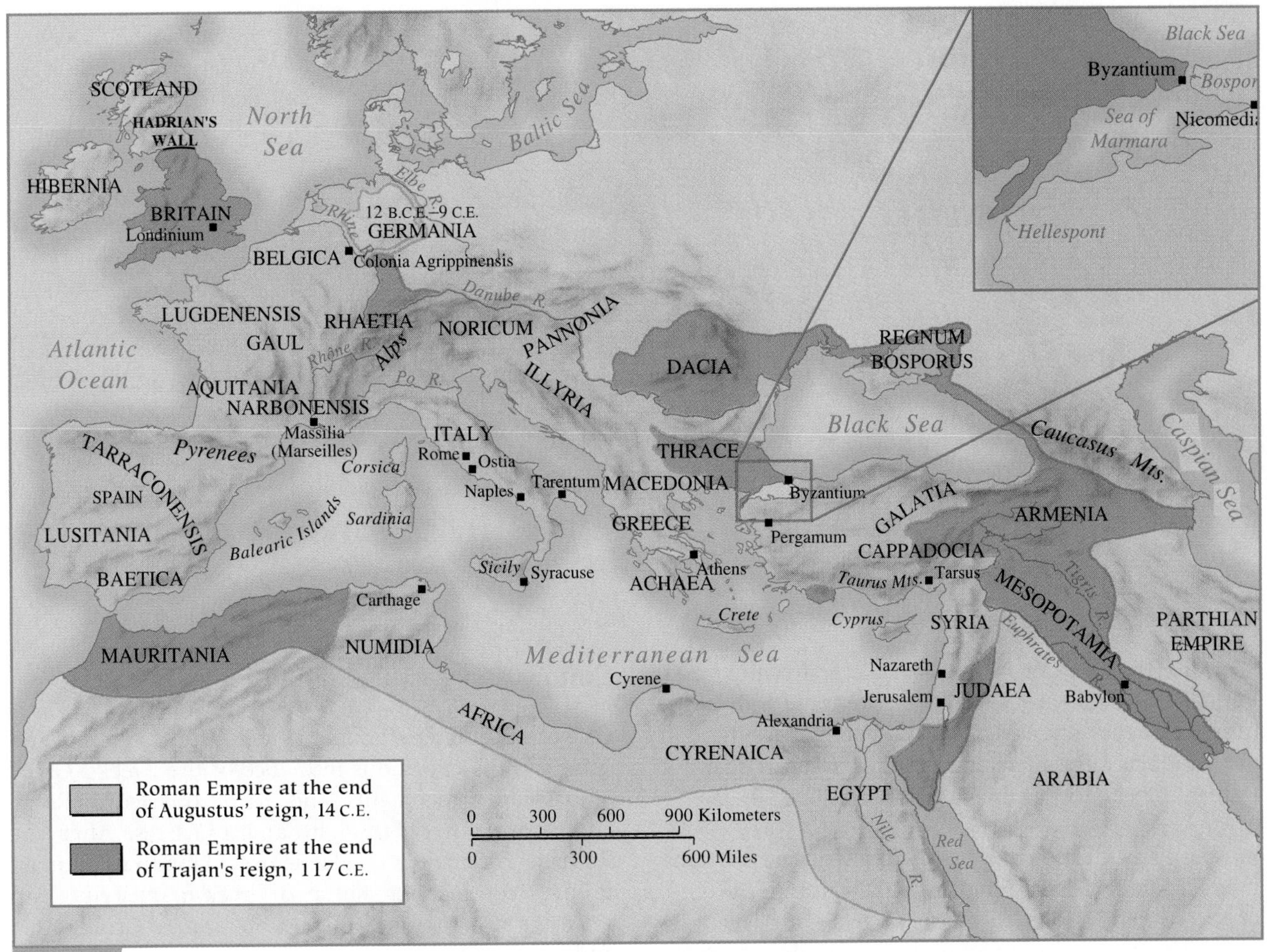


MAP 5.3 **The Roman Empire from Augustus to Trajan (14–117).** Augustus and later emperors continued the expansion of the Roman Empire, adding more resources but also increasing the tasks of administration and keeping the peace. Compare this map with Map 5.2. ? Which territories were conquered by Augustus, and which were added by the end of Trajan's reign? **View an animated version of this map or related maps at** http://history.wadsworth.com/duikerspielvogel05/

sembled one another with their temples, markets, amphitheaters, and other public buildings.

The process of Romanization in the provinces was reflected in significant changes in the governing classes of the empire. In the course of the first century, there was a noticeable decline in the number of senators from Italian families. By the end of the second century, Italian senators made up less than 50 percent of the total. Increasingly, the Roman senate was being recruited from wealthy provincial equestrian families. The provinces also provided many of the legionaries for the Roman army and, beginning with Trajan, supplied many of the emperors.

**Prosperity in the Early Empire: Trade** The Early Empire was a period of considerable prosperity. Internal peace resulted in unprecedented levels of trade. Merchants from all over the empire came to the chief Italian ports of Puteoli on the Bay of Naples and Ostia at the mouth of the Tiber. Moreover, the importation of large quantities of grain from Roman territories in northern Africa and Sicily to feed the populace of Rome and an incredible quantity of luxury items for the wealthy upper classes in the west led to a steady drain of gold and silver coins from Italy and the west to the eastern part of the empire.

Long-distance trade beyond the Roman frontiers also developed in the Early Empire. Developments in both the Roman and Chinese Empires helped foster the growth of this trade. Although both empires built roads chiefly for military purposes, the roads also came to be used to facilitate trade. Moreover, by creating large empires, the Romans and Chinese not only established internal stability but also pacified bordering territories, thus making traders less threatened by bandits. As a result, merchants fostered a network of trade routes that brought these two great empires into commercial contact.

Most important was the overland Silk Road, a regular caravan route between west and east (see Chapter 3). By the first century C.E., Chinese goods, including silk and lacquerware, were being sent into the eastern part of the Roman Empire, in southwestern Asia, where they were traded for woolen textiles, glass, and precious stones. Silk clothes were especially in demand by Rome's upper classes.

**Shipping Grain.** Trade was an important ingredient in the prosperity of the Early Roman Empire. This tomb painting from Ostia, the port of Rome at the mouth of the Tiber, shows workers loading grain onto the *Isis Giminiana,* a small merchant ship, for shipment upriver to Rome. The captain of the ship stands by the rudder. Next to him is Abascantus, the ship's owner.

After the takeover of Egypt in the first century C.E., Roman merchants also began an active trade with India, from where they received pepper and other spices used in the banquets of the wealthy. Even a trading post for Roman merchants was established in southern India.

**Prosperity in the Early Empire: Industry and Farming** Increased trade helped stimulate manufacturing. The cities of the east still produced the items made in Hellenistic times. The first two centuries of the empire also witnessed the high point of industrial development in Italy. Some industries became concentrated in certain areas, such as bronze work in Capua and pottery in Arretium in Etruria. Other industries, such as brick making, were pursued in rural areas as by-products of large landed estates.

Despite the profits from trade and commerce, agriculture remained the chief occupation of most people and the underlying basis of Roman prosperity. Although the *latifundia* still dominated agriculture, especially in southern and central Italy, small peasant farms persisted, particularly in Etruria and the Po valley. Although large estates concentrating on sheep and cattle raising used slaves, the lands of some *latifundia* were worked by free tenant farmers who paid rent in labor, produce, or sometimes cash.

The prosperity of the Roman world left an enormous gulf between rich and poor. The development of towns and cities, so important to the creation of any civilization, is based in large degree on the agricultural surpluses of the countryside. In ancient times, the margin of surplus produced by each farmer was relatively small. Therefore, the upper classes and urban populations had to be supported by the labor of a large number of agricultural producers who never found it easy to produce much more than they needed for themselves. In lean years, when there were no surpluses, the townspeople often took what they wanted, leaving little for the peasants.

## Culture and Society in the Roman World

One of the notable characteristics of Roman culture and society is the enormous influence of the Greeks. Greek ambassadors, merchants, and artists traveled to Rome and spread Greek thought and practices. After the Romans conquered the Hellenistic kingdoms, Roman military commanders shipped Greek manuscripts and artworks back to Rome. Rich Romans hired Greek tutors and sent their sons to Athens to study. As the Roman poet Horace said, "Captive Greece took captive her rude conqueror." Greek thought captivated Roman minds, and the Romans became willing transmitters of Greek culture—with resistance from some Romans who had nothing but contempt for Greek politics and feared that Greek notions would put an end to the old Roman values. Even those who favored Greek culture blamed the Greeks for Rome's new vices, including a taste for luxury and homosexual practices.

**Literature in the Republic** The Latin literature that first emerged in the third century B.C.E. was strongly influenced by Greek models, and it was not until the last century of the Republic that the Romans began to produce poetry in Latin using various Greek forms to express their own feelings about people, social and political life, and love. This evolution can be seen in the work of Catullus (c. 87–54 B.C.E.), the finest lyric poet Rome produced and one of the greatest in world literature.

Catullus became a master at adapting and refining Greek forms of poetry to express his emotions. He wrote poems on a variety of subjects, including political figures, social customs, the use of language, the death of his brother, and the travails of love. Catullus became infatuated with Clodia, the promiscuous wife of a provincial governor, and addressed a number of poems to her (he called her Lesbia), describing his passionate love and hatred for her (Clodia had many other lovers besides Catullus):

*You used to say that you wished to know only*
*Catullus, Lesbia, and wouldn't take even Jove*
*before me!*
*I didn't regard you just as my mistress then: I cherished you as a father does his sons or his daughters' husbands.*
*Now that I know you, I burn for you even more*
*fiercely, though I regard you as almost utterly*
*worthless.*
*How can that be, you ask? It's because such cruelty*
*forces lust to assume the shrunken place of*
*affection.*[3]

Catullus' ability to express in simple fashion his intense feelings and curiosity about himself and his world had a noticeable impact on later Latin poets.

The development of Roman prose was greatly aided by the practice of oratory. Romans had great respect for oratory because the ability to persuade people in public debate led to success in politics. Oratory was brought to perfection in a literary fashion by Cicero (106–43 B.C.E.), the best exemplar of the literary and intellectual interests of the senatorial elite of the late Republic and, indeed, the greatest prose writer of that period. For Cicero, oratory was not simply skillful speaking. An orator was a statesman, a man who achieved his highest goal by pursuing an active life in public affairs.

In his philosophical works, Cicero, more than anyone else, transmitted the classical intellectual heritage to the Western world. Cicero's original contributions to Western thought came in the field of politics. His works *On the Laws* and *On the Republic* provided fresh insights into political thought, including the need for a mixed constitution: "A moderate and well-balanced form of government which is a combination of the three simple good forms (monarchy, aristocracy, and democracy) is preferable even to monarchy."[4]

**Golden Age of Latin Literature** The high point of Latin literature was reached in the Age of Augustus, often called the golden age of Latin literature. The most distinguished poet of the Augustan age was Virgil (70–19 B.C.E.). The son of a small landholder in northern Italy, Virgil welcomed the rule of Augustus and wrote his greatest work in the emperor's honor. Virgil's masterpiece was *The Aeneid,* an epic poem clearly meant to rival the work of Homer. The connection between Troy and Rome is made in the poem when Aeneas, a hero of Troy, survives the destruction of Troy and eventually settles in Latium; hence Roman civilization is linked to Greek history. Aeneas is portrayed as the ideal Roman—his virtues are duty, piety, and faithfulness. Virgil's overall purpose was to show that Aeneas had fulfilled his mission to establish the Romans in Italy and thereby start Rome on its divine mission to rule the world.

*Let others fashion from bronze more lifelike,*
*breathing images–*
*For so they shall–and evoke living faces from marble;*
*Others excel as orators, others track with their*
*instruments*
*The planets circling in heaven and predict when*
*stars will appear.*
*But, Romans, never forget that government is your*
*medium!*
*Be this your art:–to practice men in the habit*
*of peace,*
*Generosity to the conquered, and firmness*
*against aggressors.*[5]

As Virgil expressed it, ruling was Rome's gift.

Ovid (43 B.C.E.–18 C.E.) was the last of the great poets of the golden age. He belonged to a youthful, privileged social group in Rome that liked to ridicule old Roman values. In keeping with the spirit of this group, Ovid wrote a series of frivolous love poems known as the *Amores.* Intended to entertain and shock, they achieved their goal. Another of Ovid's works was *The Art of Love.* This was essentially a takeoff on didactic poems. Whereas authors of earlier didactic poems had written guides to farming, hunting, or some such subject, Ovid's work was a handbook on the seduction of women (see the box on p. 142).

The most famous Latin prose work of the golden age was written by the historian Livy (59 B.C.E.–17 C.E.). Livy's masterpiece was the *History of Rome,* which covered the period from the foundation of the city to 9 B.C.E. Only 35 of the original 142 books have survived, although we do possess brief summaries of the whole work from other authors. Livy perceived history in terms of moral lessons. He stated in the preface:

> The study of history is the best medicine for a sick mind; for in history you have a record of the infinite variety of human experience plainly set out for all to see; and in that record you can find for yourself and your country both examples and warnings: fine things to take as models, base things, rotten through and through, to avoid.[6]

For Livy, human character was the determining factor in history.

**Roman Art** The Romans were also dependent on the Greeks for artistic inspiration. The Romans developed a taste for Greek statues, which they placed not only in public buildings but also in their private houses. Once demand outstripped the supply of original works, reproductions of Greek statues became fashionable. The Romans' own portrait sculpture was characterized by an intense realism that included even unpleasant physical

## Ovid and the Art of Love

Ovid has been called the last great poet of the Augustan golden age of literature. One of his most famous works was *The Art of Love,* a guidebook on the seduction of women. Unfortunately for Ovid, the work appeared at a time when Augustus was anxious to improve the morals of the Roman upper class. Augustus considered the poem offensive, and Ovid soon found himself in exile.

*What were Ovid's principles of love? Why do you think Augustus found* The Art of Love *so offensive?*

### Ovid, *The Art of Love*

Now I'll teach you how to captivate and hold the woman of your choice. This is the most important part of all my lessons. Lovers of every land, lend an attentive ear to my discourse; let goodwill warm your hearts, for I am going to fulfill the promises I made you.

First of all, be quite sure that there isn't a woman who cannot be won, and make up your mind that you will win her. Only you must prepare the ground. Sooner would the birds cease their song in the springtime, or the grasshopper be silent in the summer . . . than a woman resist the tender wooing of a youthful lover. . . .

Now the first thing you have to do is to get on good terms with the fair one's maid. She can make things easy for you. Find out whether she is fully in her mistress's confidence, and if she knows all about her secret dissipations. Leave no stone unturned to win her over. Once you have her on your side, the rest is easy. . . .

In the first place, it's best to send her a letter, just to pave the way. In it you should tell her how you dote on her; pay her pretty compliments and say all the nice things lovers always say. . . . Even the gods are moved by the voice of entreaty. And promise, promise, promise. Promises will cost you nothing. Everyone's a millionaire where promises are concerned. . . .

If she refuses your letter and sends it back unread, don't give up; hope for the best and try again. . . .

Don't let your hair stick up in tufts on your head; see that your hair and your beard are decently trimmed. See also that your nails are clean and nicely filed; don't have any hair growing out of your nostrils; take care that your breath is sweet, and don't go about reeking like a billy goat. All other toilet refinements leave to the women or to perverts. . . .

When you find yourself at a feast where the wine is flowing freely, and where a woman shares the same couch with you, pray to that god whose mysteries are celebrated during the night, that the wine may not overcloud your brain. 'Tis then you may easily hold converse with your mistress in hidden words whereof she will easily divine the meaning. . . .

By subtle flatteries you may be able to steal into her heart, even as the river insensibly overflows the banks which fringe it. Never cease to sing the praises of her face, her hair, her taper fingers and her dainty foot. . . .

Tears, too, are a mighty useful resource in the matter of love. They would melt a diamond. Make a point, therefore, of letting your mistress see your face all wet with tears. Howbeit, if you can't manage to squeeze out any tears–and they won't always flow just when you want them to–put your finger in your eyes.

details. Wall paintings and frescoes in the houses of the rich realistically depicted landscapes, portraits, and scenes from mythological stories.

The Romans excelled in architecture, a highly practical art. Although they continued to adapt Greek styles and made use of colonnades and rectangular structures, the Romans were also innovative. They made considerable use of curvilinear forms: the arch, vault, and dome. The Romans were also the first people in antiquity to use concrete on a massive scale. By combining concrete and curvilinear forms, they were able to construct massive buildings—public baths, such as those of Caracalla, and amphitheaters capable of seating fifty thousand spectators. These large buildings were made possible by Roman engineering skills. These same skills were put to use in constructing roads (the Romans built a network of 50,000 miles of roads throughout their empire), aqueducts (in Rome, almost a dozen aqueducts kept a population of one million supplied with water), and bridges.

**Roman Law** One of Rome's chief gifts to the Mediterranean world of its day and to later generations was its system of law. The Twelve Tables of 450 B.C.E. was Rome's first code of laws, but it was a product of a simple farming society and proved inadequate for later Roman needs. Nevertheless, from the Twelve Tables the Romans developed a system of civil law that applied to all Roman citizens. As Rome expanded, Romans became involved in problems between Romans and non-Romans as well as between two non-Romans. Although some of their rules of civil law could be used in these cases, special rules were often needed. These rules gave rise to a body of law known as the law of nations, defined by the Romans as "that part of the law which we apply both to ourselves and to foreigners." Under the influence of Stoicism (see Chapter 4), the Romans came to identify their law of nations with **natural law,** or universal law based on reason. This enabled them to establish standards of justice that applied to all people.

These standards of justice included principles that we would immediately recognize. A person was regarded as

© Michael S. Yamashita/CORBIS

© Fred Mayer/Magnum Photos

**The Pantheon.** Shown here is the Pantheon, one of Rome's greatest buildings. Constructed of brick, six kinds of concrete, and marble, it was a stunning example of the Romans' engineering skills. The outside porch of the Pantheon contained eighteen Corinthian granite columns, but it was the inside of the temple that amazed onlookers. The interior is a large circular space topped by a huge dome. A hole in the center of the roof was the only source of light. The dome, built up layer by layer, was made of concrete, weighing 10 million pounds. The walls holding the dome are almost 20 feet thick.

innocent until proved otherwise. People accused of wrongdoing were allowed to defend themselves before a judge. A judge was expected to weigh evidence carefully before arriving at a decision. These principles lived on long after the fall of the Roman Empire.

**The Roman Family** At the heart of the Roman social structure stood the family, headed by the ***paterfamilias***—the dominant male. The household also included the wife, sons with their wives and children, unmarried daughters, and slaves. A family was virtually a small state within the state, and the power of the *paterfamilias* was parallel to that of the state magistrates over the citizens. Like the Greeks, Roman males believed that the weakness of the female sex necessitated male guardians (see the box on p. 144). The *paterfamilias* exercised that authority; upon his death, sons or nearest male relatives assumed the role of guardians.

Fathers arranged the marriages of their daughters. In the Republic, women married "with legal control" passing from father to husband. By the mid-first century B.C.E., the dominant practice had changed to "without legal control," which meant that married daughters officially remained within the father's legal power. Since the fathers of most married women were dead, not being in the "legal control" of a husband entailed independent property rights that forceful women could translate into considerable power within the household and outside it.

Some parents in upper-class families provided education for their daughters. Some girls had private tutors, and others may have gone to primary schools. However, at the age when boys were entering secondary schools, girls were pushed into marriage. The legal minimum age for marriage was twelve, although fourteen was a more common age in practice. Although some Roman doctors warned that early pregnancies could be dangerous for young girls, early marriages persisted because women often died relatively young. A good example is Tullia, Cicero's beloved daughter. She was married at sixteen, widowed at twenty-two, remarried one year later, divorced at twenty-eight, remarried at twenty-nine, and divorced at thirty-three. She died at thirty-four.

By the second century C.E., significant changes were occurring in the Roman family. The *paterfamilias* no longer had absolute authority over his children; he could no longer sell them into slavery or have them put to death. Moreover, as noted, the husband's absolute authority over

## Cato the Elder on Women

During the Second Punic War, the Romans enacted the Oppian Law, which limited the amount of gold women could possess and restricted their dress and use of carriages. In 195 B.C.E., an attempt to repeal the law was made, and women demonstrated in the streets on behalf of this effort. According to the Roman historian Livy, the conservative Roman official Cato the Elder spoke against repeal and against the women favoring it. Although the words are probably not Cato's own, they do reflect a traditional male Roman attitude toward women.

*What particular actions on the part of the women protesting this law have angered Cato? What more general concerns does he have about Roman women? What does he believe is women's ultimate goal in regard to men?*

### Livy, *History of Rome*

"If each of us, citizens, had determined to assert his rights and dignity as a husband with respect to his own spouse, we should have less trouble with the sex as a whole; as it is, our liberty, destroyed at home by female violence, even here in the Forum is crushed and trodden underfoot, and because we have not kept them individually under control, we dread them collectively. . . . But from no class is there not the greatest danger if you permit them meetings and gatherings and secret consultations. . . .

"Our ancestors permitted no women to conduct even personal business without a guardian to intervene in her behalf; they wished them to be under the control of fathers, brothers, husbands; we (Heaven help us!) allow them now even to interfere in public affairs, yes, and to visit the Forum and our informal and formal sessions. What else are they doing now on the streets and at the corners except urging the bill of the tribunes and voting for the repeal of the law? Give loose rein to their uncontrollable nature and to this untamed creature and expect that they will themselves set bounds to their license; unless you act, this is the least of the things enjoined upon women by custom or law and to which they submit with a feeling of injustice. It is complete liberty or, rather, if we wish to speak the truth, complete license that they desire.

"If they win in this, what will they not attempt? Review all the laws with which your forefathers restrained their license and made them subject to their husbands; even with all these bonds you can scarcely control them. What of this? If you suffer them to seize these bonds one by one and wrench themselves free and finally to be placed on a parity with their husbands, do you think that you will be able to endure them? The moment they begin to be your equals, they will be your superiors. . . .

"Now they publicly address other women's husbands, and, what is more serious, they beg for a law and votes, and from sundry men they get what they ask. In matters affecting yourself, your property, your children, you, Sir, can be importuned; once the law has ceased to set a limit to your wife's expenditures you will never set it yourself. Do not think, citizens, that the situation which existed before the law was passed will ever return."

---

his wife also disappeared, and by the late second century, women were no longer required to have guardians.

Upper-class Roman women in the Early Empire had considerable freedom and independence. They had acquired the right to own, inherit, and dispose of property. Unlike the Greeks, Roman wives were not segregated from males in the home but were appreciated as enjoyable company and were at the center of household social life. Upper-class women could attend races, the theater, and events in the amphitheater, although in the latter two places they were forced to sit in separate female sections. Women could not participate in politics, but the Early Empire saw a number of important women who influenced politics through their husbands, including Livia, the wife of Augustus; Agrippina, the mother of Nero; and Plotina, the wife of Trajan.

**Slaves and Their Masters** Although slavery was a common institution throughout the ancient world, no people possessed more slaves or relied so much on slave labor as the Romans eventually did. The number of slaves increased dramatically in the last two centuries of the Republic as the empire was expanded through warfare. Dealers acquired slaves as prisoners of war, from pirates, and from trade outside Roman territory. But the number of slaves probably peaked in the Early Empire as the defensive imperial policies pursued after Augustus led to a decline in the supply of slaves from foreign conquest. Home-bred slaves then became the chief source.

Slaves were used in many ways in Roman society. The rich owned the most and the best. In the late Republic, it became a badge of prestige to be attended by many slaves. Greek slaves were in much demand as tutors, musicians, doctors, and artists. Many slaves of all nationalities were used as menial household workers, such as cooks, valets, waiters, cleaners, and gardeners. Roman businessmen would employ slaves as shop assistants or artisans. Slaves were also used as farm laborers; in fact, huge gangs of slaves worked the large landed estates under pitiful conditions. Cato the Elder argued that it was cheaper to work slaves to death and then replace them than to treat them favorably. In addition, the roads, aqueducts, and public buildings were constructed by contractors using slave labor. The total number of slaves is difficult to judge—estimates range from 20 to 35 percent of the population.

**A Roman Lady.** Roman women, especially those of the upper class, developed comparatively more freedom than women in classical Athens despite the persistent male belief that women required guardianship. This mural decoration was found in the remains of a villa destroyed by the eruption of Mount Vesuvius.

The treatment of Roman slaves varied. There are numerous instances of humane treatment by masters and situations where slaves even protected their owners from danger out of gratitude and esteem. But there are also examples of slaves murdering their owners, causing some Romans to live in unspoken fear of their slaves (see the box on p. 147). Slaves were also subject to severe punishments, torture, abuse, and hard labor that drove some to run away or even revolt against their owners. The Romans had stringent laws against aiding a runaway slave. The murder of a master by a slave might mean the execution of all the other household slaves.

Near the end of the second century B.C.E., large-scale slave revolts occurred in Sicily, where enormous gangs of slaves were subjected to horrible working conditions on large landed estates. Slaves were branded, beaten, fed inadequately, worked in chains, and housed at night in underground prisons. It took three years (135–132 B.C.E.) to crush a revolt of seventy thousand slaves, and the great revolt on Sicily (104–101 B.C.E.) involved most of the island and took a Roman army of seventeen thousand men to suppress. The most famous revolt on the Italian peninsula occurred in 73 B.C.E. Led by a Thracian gladiator named Spartacus, the revolt broke out in southern Italy and involved seventy thousand slaves. Spartacus managed to defeat several Roman armies before he was finally trapped and killed in southern Italy in 71 B.C.E. Six thousand of his followers were crucified, the traditional form of execution for slaves.

**Imperial Rome** At the center of the colossal Roman Empire was the ancient city of Rome (see Map 5.4). Truly a capital city, Rome had the largest population of any city in the empire—close to one million by the time of Augustus. Only Chang'an, the imperial capital of the Han Chinese Empire, had a comparable population during this time. For anyone with ambitions, Rome was the place to be. People from all over the empire resided there, with entire neighborhoods inhabited by specific groups, such as Greeks and Syrians.

An enormous gulf existed between rich and poor in the city of Rome. While the rich had comfortable villas, the poor lived in apartment blocks called *insulae,* which might be six stories high. Constructed of concrete, they were often poorly built and prone to collapse. The use of wooden beams in the floors and movable stoves, torches, candles, and lamps within the rooms for heat and light made the danger of fire a constant companion. Once started, fires were extremely difficult to put out. The famous conflagration of 64 C.E., which Nero was unjustly accused of starting, devastated a good part of the city. Besides the hazards of collapse and fire, living conditions were also poor. High rents forced entire families into one room. In the absence of plumbing and central heating, conditions were so uncomfortable that poorer Romans spent most of their time outdoors in the streets. Fortunately for these people, Rome boasted public buildings unequaled anywhere in the empire. Its temples, forums, markets, baths, theaters, triumphal arches, governmental buildings, and amphitheaters gave parts of the city an appearance of grandeur and magnificence.

Though the center of a great empire, Rome was also a great parasite. Beginning with Augustus, the emperors accepted responsibility for providing food for the urban populace, with about 200,000 people receiving free grain. Even with the free grain, conditions were grim for the poor.

In addition to food, entertainment was provided on a grand scale for the inhabitants of Rome. The poet Juvenal said of the Roman masses: "But nowadays, with no vote to sell, their motto is 'Couldn't care less.' Time was when their plebiscite elected generals, heads of state, commanders of legions: but now they've pulled in their horns, there are two things that concern them: Bread and Circuses."[7] Public spectacles were provided by the emperor and other state officials as part of the great festivals—most of them religious in origin—celebrated by the state. Over one hundred days a year were given over to these public holidays. The festivals included three major types of entertainment.

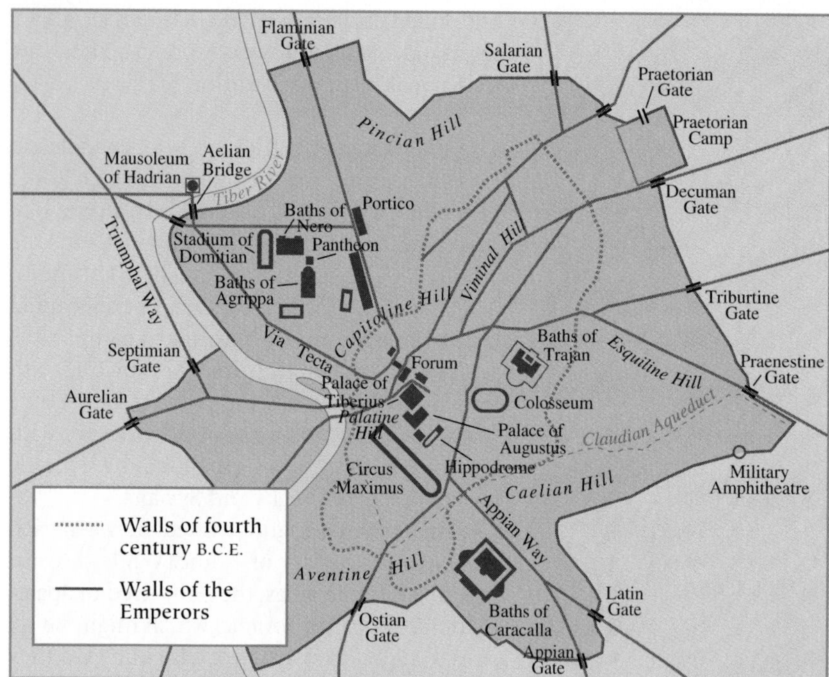


**MAP 5.4 Imperial Rome.** A large, overcrowded, and dirty city, Rome was the political, economic, social, and cultural hub of the Roman Empire. Squalid and desperate living conditions for the poor contrasted dramatically with the city's magnificent architectural works. ? How did roads from the outside enter Rome, and what might explain this? **View an animated version of this map or related maps at** http://history.wadsworth.com/duikerspielvogel05/

At the Circus Maximus, horse and chariot races attracted hundreds of thousands, while dramatic and other performances were held in theaters. But the most famous of all the public spectacles were the gladiatorial shows.

**The Gladiatorial Shows** The gladiatorial shows were an integral part of Roman society. They took place in amphitheaters, the first permanent one having been constructed at Rome in 29 B.C.E. Perhaps the most famous was the Flavian amphitheater, called the Colosseum, constructed at Rome to seat fifty thousand spectators. Amphitheaters were not limited to the city of Rome but were constructed throughout the empire. Considerable resources and ingenuity went into building them, especially in the arrangements for moving wild beasts efficiently into the arena. In most cities and towns, amphitheaters came to be the biggest buildings, rivaled only by the circuses for races and the public baths. Where a society invests its money gives an idea of its priorities. Since the amphitheater was the primary location for the gladiatorial games, it is fair to say that public slaughter was an important part of Roman culture.

**The Gladiatorial Games.** Although some gladiators were free men enticed by the possibility of rewards, most were condemned criminals, slaves, or prisoners of war who were trained in special schools. A great gladiator could win his freedom through the games. This mosaic, from the fourth century C.E., depicts different aspects of gladiatorial fighting and clearly shows the bloody nature of the gladiatorial games.

Gladiatorial games were held from dawn to dusk. Contests to the death between trained fighters formed the central focus of these games. Most gladiators were slaves or condemned criminals, although some free men lured by the hope of popularity and patronage by wealthy fans participated voluntarily. They were trained for combat in special gladiatorial schools.

Gladiatorial games included other forms of entertainment as well. Criminals of all ages and both sexes were sent into the arena without weapons to face certain death from wild animals who would tear them to pieces. Numerous kinds of animal contests were also staged: wild beasts against each other, such as bears against buffalo; staged hunts with men shooting safely from behind iron bars; and gladiators in the arena with bulls, tigers, and lions. Reportedly, five thousand beasts were killed in one day

## THE ROMAN FEAR OF SLAVES

The lowest stratum of the Roman population consisted of slaves. They were used extensively in households, at the court, as artisans in industrial enterprises, as business managers, and in numerous other ways. Although some historians have argued that slaves were treated more humanely during the Early Empire, these selections by the Roman historian Tacitus and the Roman statesman Pliny indicate that slaves still rebelled against their masters because of mistreatment. Many masters continued to live in fear of their slaves as witnessed by the saying, "As many enemies as you have slaves."

*What do these texts reveal about the practice of slavery in the Roman Empire? What were Roman attitudes toward the events discussed in them?*

### Tacitus, *The Annals of Imperial Rome*

Soon afterwards the City Prefect, Lucius Pedanius Secundus, was murdered by one of his slaves [61 C.E.]. Either Pedanius had refused to free the murderer after agreeing to a price, or the slave, in a homosexual infatuation, found competition from his master intolerable. After the murder, ancient custom required that every slave residing under the same roof must be executed. But a crowd gathered, eager to save so many innocent lives; and rioting began. The senate-house was besieged. Inside, there was feeling against excessive severity, but the majority opposed any change. Among the latter was Gaius Cassius Longinus, who when his turn came spoke as follows. . . .

"An ex-consul has been deliberately murdered by a slave in his own home. None of his fellow-slaves prevented or betrayed the murderer, though the senatorial decree threatening the whole household with execution still stands. Exempt them from the penalty if you like. But then, if the City Prefect was not important enough to be immune, who will be? Who will have enough slaves to protect him if Pedanius's four hundred were too few? Who can rely on his household's help if even fear for their own lives does not make them shield us?"

[The sentence of death was carried out.]

### Pliny the Younger to Acilius

This horrible affair demands more publicity than a letter—Larcius Macedo, a senator and ex-praetor, has fallen a victim to his own slaves. Admittedly he was a cruel and overbearing master, too ready to forget that his father had been a slave, or perhaps too keenly conscious of it. He was taking a bath in his house at Formiae when suddenly he found himself surrounded; one slave seized him by the throat while the others struck his face and hit him in the chest and stomach and—shocking to say—in his private parts. When they thought he was dead they threw him onto the hot pavement, to make sure he was not still alive. Whether unconscious or feigning to be so, he lay there motionless, thus making them believe that he was quite dead. Only then was he carried out, as if he had fainted with the heat, and received by his slaves who had remained faithful, while his concubines ran up, screaming frantically. Roused by their cries and revived by the cooler air he opened his eyes and made some movement to show that he was alive, it being now safe to do so. The guilty slaves fled, but most of them have been arrested and a search is being made for the others. Macedo was brought back to life with difficulty, but only for a few days; at least he died with the satisfaction of having revenged himself, for he lived to see the same punishment meted out as for murder. There you see the dangers, outrages, and insults to which we are exposed. No master can feel safe because he is kind and considerate; for it is their brutality, not their reasoning capacity, which leads slaves to murder masters..

**HistoryNow™** To read other works by Tacitus and Pliny, enter the *HistoryNow* documents area using the access card that is available for *World History.*

of games when the Emperor Titus inaugurated the Colosseum in 80 C.E.

These bloodthirsty spectacles were extremely popular with the Roman people. The Roman historian Tacitus said, "Few indeed are to be found who talk of any other subjects in their homes, and whenever we enter a classroom, what else is the conversation of the youths."[8] But the gladiatorial games served a purpose beyond mere entertainment. To the Romans, the games and the other forms of public entertainment fulfilled both a political and a social need. Certainly, they served to divert the idle masses from political unrest. It was said of Emperor Trajan that he understood that although the distribution of grain and money satisfied the individual, spectacles were necessary for the "contentment of the masses."

**Disaster in Southern Italy** Gladiatorial spectacles were contrived by humans, but the Roman Empire also experienced some spectacular natural disasters. One of the greatest was the eruption of Mount Vesuvius on August 24, 79 C.E. Although known to be a volcano, Vesuvius was thought to be extinct, its hillsides green with flourishing vineyards. Its eruption threw up thousands of tons of lava and ash. Toxic fumes killed many people, and the nearby city of Pompeii was quickly buried under volcanic ash. To the west, Herculaneum and other communities around the Bay of Naples were submerged beneath a mud flow (see the box on p. 148). Not for another 1,700 years were systematic excavations begun on the buried towns. The examination of their preserved remains have enabled archaeologists to reconstruct the everyday life and art of these Roman towns. Their discovery in the eighteenth

## The Eruption of Mount Vesuvius

Pliny the Younger, an upper-class Roman who rose to the position of governor of Bithynia in Asia Minor, wrote a letter to the Roman historian Tacitus, describing the death of his uncle, Pliny the Elder, as a result of the eruption of Mount Vesuvius. Pliny the Elder was the commander of a fleet at Miscenum. When the eruption occurred, his curiosity led him to take a detachment of his fleet to the scene. He landed at Stabiae, where he died from toxic fumes.

*What do you think were the reactions of upper-class Romans to this event? What do you think was the reaction of lower-class Romans?*

### Pliny, Letter to Cornelius Tacitus

Thank you for asking me to send you a description of my uncle's death so that you can leave an accurate account of it for posterity. . . . It is true that he perished in a catastrophe which destroyed the loveliest regions of the earth, a fate shared by whole cities and their people, and one so memorable that it is likely to make his name live for ever. . . .

My uncle was stationed at Misenum, in active command of the fleet. On 24 August, in the early afternoon, my mother drew his attention to a cloud of unusual size and appearance. . . . He called for his shoes and climbed up to a place which would give him the best view of the phenomenon. It was not clear at that distance from which mountain the cloud was rising (it was afterwards known to be Vesuvius); its general appearance can best be expressed as being like an umbrella pine, for it rose to a great height on a sort of trunk and then split off into branches, I imagine because it was thrust upwards by the first blast and then left unsupported as the pressure subsided, or else it was borne down by its own weight so that it spread out and gradually dispersed. In places it looked white, elsewhere blotched and dirty, according to the amount of soil and ashes it carried with it. My uncle's scholarly acumen saw at once that it was important enough for a closer inspection, and he ordered a boat to be made ready. . . .

[Unable to go farther by sea, he lands at Stabiae.]

Meanwhile on Mount Vesuvius broad sheets of fire and leaping flames blazed at several points, their bright glare emphasized by the darkness of night. My uncle tried to allay the fears of his companions by repeatedly declaring that these were nothing but bonfires left by the peasants in their terror, or else empty houses on fire in the districts thay had abandoned. . . .

They debated whether to stay indoors or take their chance in the open, for the buildings were now shaking with violent shocks, and seemed to be swaying to and fro as if they were torn from their foundations. Outside on the other hand, there was the danger of falling pumice-stones, even though these were light and porous; however, after comparing the risks they chose the latter. In my uncle's case one reason outweighed the other, but for the others it was a choice of fears. As a protection against falling objects they put pillows on their heads tied down with cloths.

Elsewhere there was daylight by this time, but they were still in darkness, blacker and denser than any ordinary night, which they relieved by lighting torches and various kinds of lamp. My uncle decided to go down to the shore and investigate on the spot the possibility of any escape by sea, but he found the waves still wild and dangerous. A sheet was spread on the ground for him to lie down, and he repeatedly asked for cold water to drink. Then the flames and smell of sulphur which gave warning of the approaching fire drove the others to take flight and roused him to stand up. He stood leaning on two slaves and then suddenly collapsed, I imagine because the dense fumes choked his breathing by blocking his windpipe which was constitutinally weak and narrow and often inflamed. When daylight returned on the 26th–two days after the last day he had seen–his body was found intact and uninjured, still fully clothed and looking more like sleep than death.

**History Now™** To read other works by Piny, enter the *HistoryNow* documents area using the access card that is available for *World History*.

century was an important force in stimulating both scholarly and public interest in classical antiquity and helped give rise to the Neoclassical style of that century.

# Crisis and the Late Empire

During the reign of Marcus Aurelius, the last of the five good emperors, a number of natural catastrophes struck Rome. To many Romans, these natural disasters seemed to portend an ominous future for Rome. New problems arose soon after the death of Marcus Aurelius in 180.

## Crisis in the Third Century

In the course of the third century, the Roman Empire came near to collapse. After a series of civil wars, Septimius Severus (193–211), who was born in North Africa and spoke Latin with an accent, used his legions to seize power. On his deathbed, Septimius Severus advised his sons, "Live in harmony, make the soldiers rich, and don't give a damn for anything else." His advice set the tone for the military monarchy that the Severans established. A new stability seemed at hand, but the increased power of the military led new military leaders to aspire to become emperor, and the military monarchy of the Severan rulers degenerated into military anarchy.

For the next fifty years (235–284), the empire was mired in the chaos of continual civil war. Contenders for the imperial throne found that bribing soldiers was an effective way to become emperor. In these five decades, there were twenty-two emperors, only two of whom did not meet a violent end. At the same time, the empire was beset by a series of invasions, no doubt encouraged by the internal turmoil. In the east, the Sassanid Persians made inroads into Roman territory. Germanic tribes also poured into the empire. The Goths overran the Balkans and moved into Greece and Asia Minor. The Franks advanced into Gaul and Spain. Not until the reign of Aurelian (270–275) were most of the boundaries restored.

Invasions, civil wars, and plague came close to causing an economic collapse of the Roman Empire in the third century. The population declined drastically, possibly by as much as one-third. There was a noticeable decline in trade and small industry. The labor shortage created by the plague affected both military recruiting and the economy. Farm production deteriorated significantly as fields were ravaged by Germanic tribes and even more often by the defending Roman armies. The monetary system began to show signs of collapse as a result of debased coinage and the beginnings of serious **inflation**. Armies were needed more than ever, but financial strains made it difficult to pay and enlist soldiers. By the mid-third century, the state had to rely on hiring Germans to fight under Roman commanders.

## The Late Roman Empire

At the end of the third century and beginning of the fourth, the Roman Empire gained a new lease on life through the efforts of two strong emperors, Diocletian and Constantine, who restored order and stability. The Roman Empire was virtually transformed into a new state: the so called Late Empire, which included a new governmental structure, a rigid economic and social system, and a new state religion—Christianity (see "Transformation of the Roman World: The Development of Christianity" later in this chapter).

**The Reforms of Diocletian and Constantine** Both Diocletian (284–305) and Constantine (306–337) expanded imperial control by strengthening and enlarging the administrative bureaucracies of the Roman Empire. Henceforth, civil and military bureaucracies were sharply separated. Each contained a hierarchy of officials who exercised control at the various levels. The emperor presided over both hierarchies of officials and served as the only link between them. New titles of nobility—such as *illustres* ("illustrious ones") and *illustrissimi* ("most illustrious ones")—were instituted to dignify the holders of positions in the civil and military bureaucracies.

Additional military reforms were also inaugurated. The army was enlarged, and mobile units were established that could be quickly moved to support frontier troops where the borders were threatened.

Constantine's biggest project was the construction of a new capital city in the east on the site of the Greek city of Byzantium on the shores of the Bosporus. Eventually renamed Constantinople (modern Istanbul), it was developed for defensive reasons: it had an excellent strategic location. Calling it his "New Rome," Constantine endowed the city with a forum, large palaces, and a vast amphitheater.

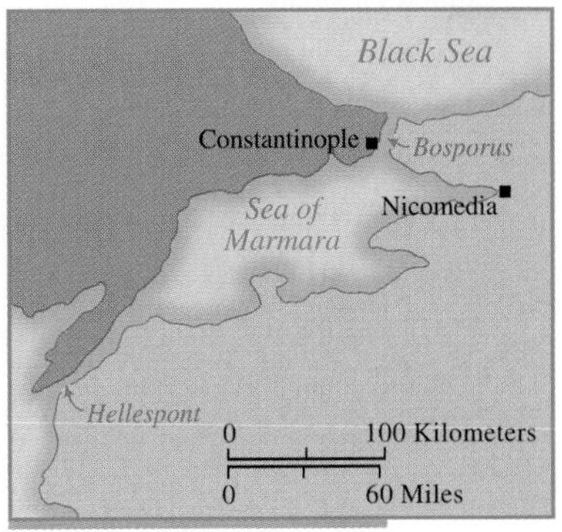

**Location of the "New Rome"**

The political and military reforms of Diocletian and Constantine greatly enlarged two institutions—the army and civil service—that drained most of the public funds. Though more revenues were needed to pay for the army and bureaucracy, the population was not growing, so the tax base could not be expanded. Diocletian and Constantine devised new economic and social policies to deal with these financial burdens, but like their political policies, these measures were all based on coercion and loss of individual freedom. To fight inflation, Diocletian resorted to issuing a price edict in 301 that established maximum wages and prices for the entire empire, but despite severe penalties, it was unenforceable and failed to work.

Coercion also came to form the underlying basis for numerous occupations in the Late Roman Empire. To ensure the tax base and keep the empire going despite the shortage of labor, the emperors issued edicts that forced people to remain in their designated vocations. Basic jobs, such as baker or shipper, became hereditary. Free tenant farmers continued to decline and soon found themselves bound to the land by large landowners who took advantage of depressed agricultural conditions to enlarge their landed estates.

In general, the economic and social policies of Diocletian and Constantine were based on an unprecedented degree of control and coercion. Though temporarily successful, such authoritarian policies in the long run stifled the very vitality the Late Empire needed to revive its sagging fortunes.

**The End of the Western Empire** Constantine had reunited the Roman Empire and restored a semblance of order. After his death, however, the empire continued to divide into western and eastern parts as fighting erupted on a regular basis between elements of the Roman army backing the claims of rival emperors. By 395, the western and eastern parts of the empire became virtually two independent states. In the course of the fifth century, while the empire in the east remained intact under the Roman emperor

| **CHRONOLOGY** The Late Empire—Chief Rulers and Events | |
|---|---|
| Military monarchy (Severan dynasty) | 193–235 |
| Military anarchy | 235–284 |
| Diocletian | 284–305 |
| Constantine | 306–337 |
| Edict of Milan | 313 |
| Theodosius "the Great" | 378–395 |
| Visigoths sack Rome | 410 |
| Vandals sack Rome | 455 |
| Romulus Augustulus is deposed | 476 |

in Constantinople (see "The Byzantine Empire" in Chapter 7), the administrative structure of the empire in the west collapsed and was replaced by an assortment of Germanic kingdoms. The process was a gradual one, beginning with the movement of Germans into the empire.

Although the Romans had established a series of political frontiers along the Rhine and Danube Rivers, Romans and Germans often came into contact across these boundaries. Until the fourth century, the empire had proved capable of absorbing these people without harm to its political structure. In the late fourth century, however, the Germanic tribes came under new pressure when the Huns, a fierce tribe of nomads from the steppes of Asia who may have been related to the Xiongnu, the invaders of the Han Empire in China, moved into the Black Sea region, possibly attracted by the riches of the empire to its south. One of the groups displaced by the Huns was the Visigoths, who moved south and west, crossed the Danube into Roman territory, and settled down as Roman allies. But the Visigoths soon revolted, and the Roman attempt to stop them at Adrianople in 378 led to a crushing defeat for Rome.

Increasing numbers of Germans now crossed the frontiers. In 410, the Visigoths sacked Rome. Vandals poured into southern Spain and Africa, Visigoths into Spain and Gaul. The Vandals crossed into Italy from North Africa and ravaged Rome again in 455. By the middle of the fifth century, the western provinces of the Roman Empire had been taken over by Germanic peoples who were in the process of setting up independent kingdoms. At the same time, a semblance of imperial authority remained in Rome, although the real power behind the throne tended to rest in the hands of important military officials known as masters of the soldiers. These military commanders controlled the government and dominated the imperial court. In 476, Odoacer, a new master of the soldiers, himself of German origin, deposed the Roman emperor, the boy Romulus Augustulus. To many historians, the deposition of Romulus signaled the end of the Roman Empire in the west. Of course, this is only a symbolic date, since much of direct imperial rule had already been lost in the course of the fifth century.

## Transformation of the Roman World: The Development of Christianity

The rise of Christianity marked a fundamental break with the dominant values of the Greco-Roman world. To understand the rise of Christianity, we must first examine both the religious environment of the Roman world and the Jewish background from which Christianity emerged.

### The Religious World of the Romans

Augustus had taken a number of steps to revive the Roman state religion, which had declined during the turmoil of the late Republic. The official state religion focused on the worship of a pantheon of Greco-Roman gods and goddesses, including Juno, the patron goddess of women; Minerva, the goddess of artisans; Mars, the god of war; and Jupiter Optimus Maximus ("best and greatest"), who became the patron deity of Rome and assumed a central place in the religious life of the city. The Romans believed that observance of ritual by state priests brought the Romans into a proper relationship with the gods and guaranteed security, peace, and prosperity. As Cicero, the first-century politician and writer, claimed, "We have overcome all the nations of the world, because we have realized that the world is directed and governed by the gods."[9]

The polytheistic Romans were extremely tolerant of other religions. They allowed the worship of native gods and goddesses throughout their provinces and even adopted some of the local gods. In addition, the imperial cult of Roma and Augustus was developed to bolster support for the emperors (see the comparative essay "Rulers and Gods" on p. 151). After Augustus, any dead emperors deified by the Roman senate were added to the official imperial cult.

The desire for a more emotional spiritual experience led many people to the mystery religions of the Hellenistic east, which flooded into the western Roman world during the Early Empire. The mystery religions promised their followers an entry into a higher world of reality and the promise of a future life superior to the present one. They also featured elaborate rituals with deep emotional appeal. By participating in their ceremonies and performing their rites, an adherent could achieve communion with spiritual beings and undergo purification that opened the door to life after death.

### The Jewish Background

In Hellenistic times, the Jewish people had been granted considerable independence by their Seleucid rulers (see Chapter 4). Roman involvement with the Jews began in

## COMPARATIVE ESSAY

# Rulers and Gods

All of the world's earliest civilizations believed that there was a close relationship between rulers and gods. In Egypt, pharaohs were considered gods whose role was to maintain the order and harmony of the universe in their own kingdom. In the words of an Egyptian hymn, "What is the king of Upper and Lower Egypt? He is a god by whose dealings one lives, the father and mother of all men, alone by himself, without an equal." In Mesopotamia, India, and China, rulers were thought to rule with divine assistance. Kings were often seen as rulers who derived their power from the gods and who were the agents or representatives of the gods. In ancient India, rulers claimed to be representatives of the gods because they were descended from Manu, the first man who had been made a king by Brahman, the chief god. Many Romans certainly believed that their success in creating an empire was a visible sign of divine favor.

Their supposed connection to the gods also caused rulers to seek divine aid in the affairs of the world. This led to the art of divination, or an organized method to discover the intentions of the gods. In Mesopotamian and Roman society, one form of divination involved the examination of the livers of sacrificed animals; features seen in the livers were interpreted to foretell events to come. The Chinese used oracle bones to receive advice from supernatural forces that were beyond the power of human beings. Questions to the gods were scratched on turtle shells or animal bones, which were then exposed to fire. Shamans then interpreted the meaning of the resulting cracks on the surface of the shells or bones as messages from supernatural forces. The Greeks divined the will of the gods by use of the oracle, a sacred shrine dedicated to a god or goddess who revealed the future in response to a question.

Underlying all of these divinatory practices was a belief in a supernatural universe, that is, a world in which divine forces were in charge and in which humans were dependent for their own well-being on those divine forces. It was not until the Scientific Revolution of the modern world that many people began to believe in a natural world that was not governed by spiritual forces.

Fitzwilliam Museum, University of Cambridge

**Vishnu.** Brahma the Creator, Shiva the Destroyer, and Vishnu the Preserver are the three chief Hindu gods of India. Vishnu is known as the Preserver because he mediates between Brahma and Shiva and is thus responsible for maintaining the stability of the universe.

63 B.C.E., and by 6 C.E., Judaea (which embraced the lands of the old Jewish kingdom of Judah) had been made a province and placed under the direction of a Roman procurator. But unrest continued, augmented by divisions among the Jews themselves. The Sadducees favored cooperation with the Romans. The Pharisees, although they wanted Judaea to be free from Roman control, did not advocate violent means to achieve this goal. The Essenes, as revealed in the Dead Sea Scrolls, a collection of documents first discovered in 1947, constituted a Jewish sect that lived in a religious community near the Dead Sea. They, like most other Jews, awaited a Messiah who would save Israel from oppression, usher in the kingdom of God, and establish a true paradise on earth. A fourth group, the Zealots, were militant extremists who advocated the violent overthrow of Roman rule. A Jewish revolt in 66 C.E. was crushed by the Romans four years later. The Jewish Temple in Jerusalem was destroyed, and Roman power once more stood supreme in Judaea.

## The Rise of Christianity

Jesus of Nazareth (c. 6 B.C.E.–29 C.E.) was a Palestinian Jew who grew up in Galilee, an important center of the militant Zealots. Jesus' message was simple. He reassured his fellow Jews that he did not plan to undermine their traditional religion: "Do not think that I have come to abolish the Law or the Prophets; I have not come to abolish them but to fulfill them."[10] According to Jesus, what was important was not strict adherence to the letter of the law and attention to rules and prohibitions but the transformation of the inner person: "So in everything, do to others what you would have them do to you, for this sums up the Law and the Prophets."[11] God's command was simple—to love God and one another: "Love the Lord your God with all your heart and with all your soul and with all your mind and with all your strength. The second is this: Love your neighbor as yourself."[12] In the Sermon on the Mount (see the box on p. 152), Jesus presented the ethical concepts—humility, charity, and

## Christian Ideals: The Sermon on the Mount

Christianity was simply one of many religions competing for attention in the Roman Empire during the first and second centuries. The rise of Christianity marked a fundamental break with the value system of the upper-class elites who dominated the world of classical antiquity. As these excerpts from the Sermon on the Mount in the Gospel of Saint Matthew illustrate, Christians emphasized humility, charity, brotherly love, and a belief in the inner being and a spiritual kingdom superior to this material world. These values and principles were not those of classical Greco-Roman civilization as exemplified in the words and deeds of its leaders.

*What were the ideals of early Christianity? How do they differ from the values and principles of classical Greco-Roman civilization? Compare this sermon to the Buddha's sermon on the Four Noble Truths from Chapter 2. How are they different? How are they similar?*

### The Gospel According to Saint Matthew

Now when he saw the crowds, he went up on a mountainside and sat down. His disciples came to him, and he began to teach them, saying:

*Blessed are the poor in spirit: for theirs is the kingdom of heaven.*
*Blessed are those who mourn: for they will be comforted.*
*Blessed are the meek: for they will inherit the earth.*
*Blessed are those who hunger and thirst for righteousness: for they will be filled.*
*Blessed are the merciful: for they will be shown mercy.*
*Blessed are the pure in heart: for they will see God.*
*Blessed are the peacemakers: for they will be called sons of God.*
*Blessed are those who are persecuted because of righteousness: for theirs is the kingdom of heaven. . . .*

You have heard that it was said, "Eye for eye, and tooth for tooth." But I tell you, Do not resist an evil person. If someone strikes you on the right cheek, turn to him the other also. . . .

You have heard that it was said, "Love your neighbor, and hate your enemy." But I tell you, Love your enemies and pray for those who persecute you. . . .

Do not store up for yourselves treasures on earth, where moth and rust destroy, and where thieves break in and steal. But store up for yourselves treasures in heaven, where moth and rust do not destroy, and where thieves do not break in and steal. For where your treasure is, there your heart will be also. . . .

No one can serve two masters. Either he will hate the one and love the other, or he will be devoted to the one and despise the other. You cannot serve both God and Money.

Therefore I tell you, do not worry about your life, what you will eat or drink; or about your body, what you will wear. Is not life more important than food, and the body more important than clothes? Look at the birds of the air; they do not sow or reap or store away in barns, and yet your heavenly Father feeds them. Are you not much more valuable than they? . . . So do not worry, saying, What shall we eat? or What shall we drink? or What shall we wear? For the pagans run after all these things, and your heavenly Father knows that you need them. But seek first his kingdom and his righteousness, and all these things will be given to you as well.

brotherly love—that would form the basis for the value system of medieval Western civilization.

Although some Jews welcomed Jesus as the Messiah who would save Israel from oppression and establish God's kingdom on earth, Jesus spoke of a heavenly kingdom, not an earthly one: "My kingdom is not of this world."[13] Consequently, he disappointed the radicals. On the other hand, conservative religious leaders believed Jesus was undermining respect for traditional Jewish religion. To the Roman authorities of Palestine and their local allies, the Nazarene was a potential revolutionary who might transform Jewish expectations of a messianic kingdom into a revolt against Rome. Therefore, Jesus found himself denounced on many sides and was given over to the Roman authorities. The procurator Pontius Pilate ordered his crucifixion. But that did not solve the problem. A few loyal followers of Jesus spread the story that Jesus had overcome death, had been resurrected, and had then ascended into heaven. The belief in Jesus' resurrection became an important tenet of Christian doctrine. Jesus was now hailed "the anointed one" (*Christos* in Greek), the Messiah who would return and usher in the kingdom of God on earth.

**The Importance of Paul** Christianity began, then, as a religious movement within Judaism. Although tradition holds that one of Jesus' disciples, Peter, founded the Christian church at Rome, the most important figure in early Christianity after Jesus was Paul of Tarsus (c. 5–c. 67). Paul believed that the message of Jesus should be

© Scala/Art Resource, NY

**Jesus and His Apostles.** Pictured is a fourth-century C.E. fresco from a Roman catacomb depicting Jesus and his apostles. Catacombs were underground cemeteries where early Christians buried their dead. Christian tradition holds that in times of imperial repression, Christians withdrew to the catacombs to pray and even hide.

preached not only to Jews but to Gentiles (non-Jews) as well. Paul was responsible for founding Christian communities throughout Asia Minor and along the shores of the Aegean.

Paul provided a universal foundation for the spread of Jesus' ideas. He taught that Jesus was, in effect, a savior-god, the son of God, who had come to earth to save all humans, who were basically sinners as a result of Adam's original sin of disobedience against God. By his death, Jesus had atoned for the sins of all humans and made possible their reconciliation with God and hence their salvation. By accepting Jesus as their savior, they too could be saved.

**The Spread of Christianity** Christianity spread slowly at first. Although the teachings of early Christianity were disseminated mostly by the preaching of convinced Christians, written materials also appeared. Among them were a series of letters or epistles written by Paul outlining Christian beliefs for different Christian communities. Some of Jesus' disciples may also have preserved some of the sayings of the master in writing and would have passed on personal memories that became the basis of the written gospels—the "good news" concerning Jesus—which were written down between 50 and 150 and attempted to give a record of Jesus' life and teachings; these texts formed the core of the New Testament.

Although Jerusalem was the first center of Christianity, destruction of the city by the Romans in 70 C.E. dispersed the Christians and left individual Christian churches with considerable independence. By 100, Christian churches had been established in most of the major cities of the east and in some places in the western part of the empire. Many early Christians came from the ranks of Hellenized Jews and the Greek-speaking populations of the east. But in the second and third centuries, an increasing number of followers came from Latin-speaking people. A Latin translation of the Greek New Testament that appeared soon after 200 aided this process.

Although some of the fundamental values of Christianity differed markedly from those of the Greco-Roman world, the Romans initially did not pay much attention to the Christians, whom they regarded at first as simply another sect of Judaism. The structure of the Roman Empire itself aided the growth of Christianity. Christian missionaries, including some of Jesus' original twelve apostles (disciples), used Roman roads to travel throughout the empire spreading their "good news."

**The Changing Roman View of Christianity** As the popular appeal of Christianity grew, the Roman attitude toward it began to change. The Romans were tolerant of other religions except when they threatened public order or public morals. Many Romans came to view Christians as harmful to the order of the Roman state. Since Christians held their meetings in secret and seemed to be connected to Christian groups in other areas, the government could view them as potentially dangerous to the state.

Some Romans felt that Christians were overly exclusive and hence harmful to the community and public order. The refusal of Christians to recognize other gods meant that they abstained from public festivals that honored these divinities. Finally, Christians refused to participate in the worship of the state gods and imperial cult. Since the Romans regarded these as important to the state, the Christians' refusal undermined the security of the state and hence constituted an act of treason, punishable by death. But to the Christians, who believed that there was only one real god, the worship of state gods and the emperors was idolatry and would endanger their own salvation.

Nevertheless, Roman persecution of Christians in the first and second centuries was only sporadic and local, never systematic. Persecution began during the reign of Nero. After the fire that destroyed much of Rome, the emperor used the Christians as scapegoats, accusing them of arson and hatred of the human race and subjecting them to cruel deaths in Rome. In the second century, Christians were largely ignored as harmless. By the end of the reigns of the five good emperors, Christians still represented a small minority, but one of considerable strength.

### The Triumph of Christianity

The sporadic persecution of Christians by the Romans in the first and second centuries had done little to stop the growth of Christianity and had in fact served to strengthen it as an institution in the second and third centuries by causing it to become more organized. Crucial to this change was the emerging role of the bishops, who began to assume more control over church communities. The Christian church was creating a well-defined hierarchical structure in which the bishops and clergy were salaried officers separate from the laity, or regular church members.

Christianity grew slowly in the first century, took root in the second, and by the third had spread widely. Why was Christianity able to attract so many followers? The Christian message had much to offer the Roman world. The promise of salvation, made possible by Jesus' death and resurrection, made a resounding impact on a world full of suffering and injustice. Christianity seemed to imbue life with a meaning and purpose beyond the simple material things of everyday reality. Second, Christianity seemed familiar. It was regarded as simply another mystery religion, offering immortality as the result of the sacrificial death of a savior-god. At the same time, it offered more than the other mystery religions did. Jesus had been a human figure, easy to relate to.

Finally, Christianity fulfilled the human need to belong. Christians formed communities bound to one another in which people could express their love by helping each other and offering assistance to the poor, sick, widows, and orphans. Christianity satisfied the need to belong in a way that the huge, impersonal, and remote Roman Empire never could.

Christianity proved attractive to all classes. The promise of eternal life was for all—rich, poor, aristocrats, slaves, men, and women. As Paul stated in his Epistle to the Colossians: "And [you] have put on the new self, which is being renewed in knowledge in the image of its Creator. Here there is no Greek nor Jew, circumcised or uncircumcised, barbarian, Scythian, slave or free, but Christ is all, and is in all."[14] Christianity emphasized a sense of spiritual equality for all people.

Many women, in fact, found that Christianity offered them new roles and new forms of companionship with other women. Christian women fostered the new religion in their homes and preached their convictions to other people in their towns and villages. Many also died for their faith. Perpetua (d. 203) was an aristocratic woman who converted to Christianity. Her pagan family begged her to renounce her new faith, but she refused. Arrested by the Roman authorities, she chose instead to die for her faith and was one of a group of Christians who were slaughtered by wild beasts in the arena at Carthage on March 7, 203.

As the Christian church became more organized, some emperors in the third century responded with more systematic persecutions, but their schemes failed to work. The last great persecution was at the beginning of the fourth century, but by that time Christianity had become too strong to be eradicated by force.

In the fourth century, Christianity prospered as never before after Constantine (306–337) became the first Christian emperor. Although he was not baptized until the end of his life, in 313 Constantine issued the Edict of Milan, officially tolerating the existence of Christianity. Under Theodosius "the Great" (378–395), it was made the official religion of the Roman Empire. Christianity had triumphed.

## Comparison of the Roman and Han Empires

At the beginning of the first millennium C.E., two great empires—the Roman Empire in the West and the Han Empire in the East—dominated large areas of the world. Although there was little contact between them, the Han Empire and the Roman Empire had some remarkable similarities. Both lasted for centuries, and both had remarkable success in establishing centralized control (see the comparative illustration on p. 155). They built elaborate systems of roads in order to rule efficiently and relied on provincial officials and especially towns and cities as local centers of administration. Architectural features found in the capital cities of Rome and Chang'an were also transferred on a smaller scale to provincial towns and cities. In both empires, settled conditions led to a high level of agricultural production that sustained large populations, estimated at between fifty and sixty million in each empire. Although both empires expanded into areas that had different languages, ethnic groups, and ways of life, they managed to carry their legal and political institutions, their technical skills, and their languages throughout their empires.

The Roman and Han Empires had similar social and economic structures. The family stood at the heart of the social structure, with the male head of the family as all-powerful. Duty, courage, obedience, and discipline were

© British Museum

© British Library

POLITICS & GOVERNMENT

COMPARATIVE ILLUSTRATION

**Emperors, West and East.** Two great empires with strong central government dominated much of the ancient world. Shown here are two emperors from these empires. The Roman emperor Hadrian, who ruled from 117 to 138, was the third of the five good emperors. He had been adopted by the emperor Trajan to serve as his successor. Hadrian was a strong and intelligent ruler who took his responsibilities seriously. Between 121 and 132, he visited all of the provinces in the empire. Liu Bang came from the peasant class but through his military prowess defeated all rivals in the civil wars that followed the death of the First Emperor of Qin. Liu Bang, who is known historically by his title of Han Gaozu, was the first emperor of the Han dynasty, which ruled China for four hundred years. He won the support of his subjects by reducing their tax burden. He was also responsible for bringing China back under central control but was killed in a frontier battle in 195 B.C.E.

values inculcated by the family that helped make the empires strong. The wealth of both societies also depended on agriculture. Although a free peasantry was a backbone of strength and stability in each, the gradual conversion of free peasants into tenant farmers by wealthy landowners was common to both societies and ultimately served to undermine the power of their imperial governments.

Of course, there were also significant differences. Social mobility was greater in Rome than in China, and merchants were more highly regarded and allowed more freedom in the West than in the East, as befitted a society in which commercial activity played such a vital role. Then, too, the dynastic principle in China added a strong element of stability. With the Mandate of Heaven, Chinese rulers had an authority to command, conferred by divine forces, that was easily passed on to other family members. Although Roman emperors were accorded divine status by the Roman senate after their death, accession to the Roman imperial throne depended less on dynastic principles than on naked military force. As a result, over a period of centuries, Chinese imperial authority was far more stable.

Despite the differences, one major inescapable similarity remains: both empires eventually faced overwhelming problems. Both suffered from overexpansion, and both fortified their long borders with walls, forts, and military garrisons to guard against invasions of nomadic peoples. Both empires were nevertheless eventually overcome by these peoples: the Han dynasty was weakened by the incursions of the Xiongnu, and the western Roman Empire eventually collapsed in the face of invasions by the Germanic peoples.

Nevertheless, one inescapable difference between these two contemporary empires also remained. Although the Han dynasty collapsed, the Chinese imperial tradition, as well as the class structure and set of values that sustained it, continued, and the Chinese Empire, under new dynasties, continued well into the twentieth century as a single political entity. In stark contrast, the Roman Empire collapsed and lived on only as an idea.

## CONCLUSION

Between 509 and 264 B.C.E., the Latin-speaking community of Rome expanded and brought about the union of almost all of Italy under its control. Even more dramatically, between 264 and 133 B.C.E., Rome expanded to the west and east and became master of the Mediterranean Sea and its surrounding territories, creating one of the largest empires in antiquity. Rome's republican institutions proved inadequate for the task of ruling an empire, however, and after a series of bloody civil wars, Octavian created a new order that would rule the empire in an orderly fashion. His successors established a Roman imperial state.

The Roman Empire experienced a lengthy period of peace and prosperity between 14 and 180. During this Pax Romana, trade flourished and the provinces were governed efficiently. In the course of the third century, however, the Roman Empire came near to collapse due to invasions, civil wars, and economic decline. Although the emperors Diocletian and Constantine brought new life to the so-called Late Empire, their efforts shored up the empire only temporarily. Beginning in 395, the empire divided into western and eastern parts, and in 476, the Roman Empire in the west came to an end.

Although the Roman Empire in the west collapsed and lived on only as an idea, Roman achievements were bequeathed to the future. The Romance languages of today (French, Italian, Spanish, Portuguese, and Romanian) are based on Latin. Western practices of impartial justice and trial by jury owe much to Roman law. As great builders, the Romans left monuments to their skills throughout Europe, some of which, such as aqueducts and roads, are still in use today. Aspects of Roman administrative practices survived in the Western world for centuries. The Romans also preserved the intellectual heritage of the Greco-Roman world of antiquity. Nevertheless, while many aspects of the Roman world would continue, the heirs of Rome created new civilizations—European, Islamic, and Byzantine—that would carry on yet another stage in the development of human society.

## TIMELINE

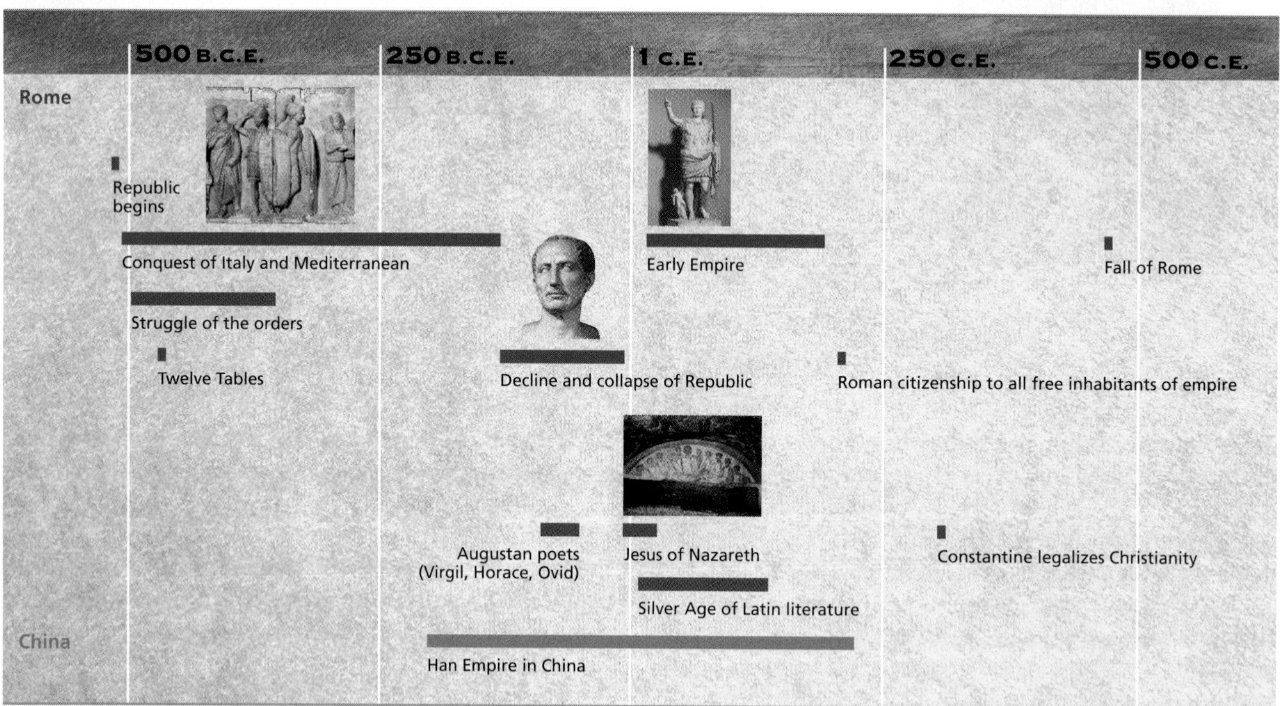


## CHAPTER NOTES

1. Florus, *Epitome of Roman History,* trans. E. S. Forster (Cambridge, Mass., 1961), IV, ii, 149–151.
2. Tacitus, *The Annals of Imperial Rome,* trans. M. Grant (New York, 1956), p. 31.
3. *The Poems of Catullus,* trans. C. Martin (Baltimore, 1990), p. 109.
4. Quoted in A. Everitt, *Cicero* (New York, 2001), p. 181.
5. Virgil, *The Aeneid,* trans. C. Day Lewis (Garden City, N.Y., 1952), p. 154.
6. Livy, *The Early History of Rome,* trans. A. de Sélincourt (New York, 1960), p. 18.
7. Juvenal, *The Sixteen Satires,* trans. P. Green (New York, 1967), sat. 10, p. 207.
8. Tacitus, *A Dialogue on Oratory, in The Complete Works of Tacitus,* trans. A. Church and W. Brodribb (New York, 1942), 29, p. 758.
9. Quoted in C. Starr, *Past and Future in Ancient History* (Lanham, Md., 1987), pp. 38–39.
10. Matthew 5:17.

11. Matthew 7:12.
12. Mark 12:30–31.
13. John 18:36.
14. Colossians 3:10–11.

## SUGGESTED READING

For a general account of Roman history, see **M.T. Boatwright, D. J. Gargola,** and **R. J. A. Talbert,** ***The Romans: From Village to Empire*** (New York, 2004). Good surveys of the Roman Republic include **M. H. Crawford, *The Roman Republic,*** 2d ed. (Cambridge, Mass., 1993); **H. H. Scullard, *History of the Roman World, 753-146 B.C.,*** 4th ed. (London, 1978); **M. Le Glay, J.-L. Voisin,** and **Y. Le Bohec, *A History of Rome,*** trans. **A. Nevill** (Oxford, 1996); and **A. Kamm, *The Romans*** (London, 1995). For an illustrated survey, see **G. Woolf,** ed., ***Cambridge Illustrated History of the Roman World*** (Cambridge, 2003). The history of early Rome is well covered in **T. J. Cornell, *The Beginnings of Rome: Italy and Rome from the Bronze Age to the Punic Wars (c. 1000–264 B.C.)*** (London, 1995).

Aspects of the Roman political structure can be studied in **R. E. Mitchell, *Patricians and Plebeians: The Origin of the Roman State*** (Ithaca, N.Y., 1990). Changes in Rome's economic life can be examined in **A. H. M. Jones, *The Roman Economy*** (Oxford, 1974). On the Roman social structure, see **G. Alfoeldy, *The Social History of Rome*** (London, 1985).

Accounts of Rome's expansion in the Mediterranean world are provided by **J.-M. David, *The Roman Conquest of Italy,*** trans. **A. Nevill** (Oxford, 1996), and **R. M. Errington, *The Dawn of Empire: Rome's Rise to World Power*** (Ithaca, N.Y., 1971). Especially important works on Roman expansion and imperialism include **W. V. Harris, *War and Imperialism in Republican Rome*** (Oxford, 1979), and **E. Badian, *Roman Imperialism in the Late Republic*** (Oxford, 1968). On Rome's struggle with Carthage, see **A. Goldsworthy, *The Punic Wars*** (New York, 2001).

An excellent account of basic problems in the late Republic can be found in **M. Beard** and **M. H. Crawford, *Rome in the Late Republic*** (London, 1984). The classic work on the fall of the Republic is **R. Syme, *The Roman Revolution*** (Oxford, 1960). Also valuable are **D. Shotter, *The Fall of the Roman Republic*** (London, 1994), and **E. Hildinger, *Swords Against the Senate: The Rise of the Roman Army and the Fall of the Republic*** (Cambridge, Mass., 2002).

Good surveys of the Early Roman Empire include **P. Garnsey** and **R. Saller, *The Roman Empire: Economy, Society and Culture*** (London, 1987); **C. Wells, *The Roman Empire,*** 2d ed. (London, 1992); and **M. Goodman, *The Roman World, 44 B.C.–A.D. 180*** (London, 1997). Studies of Roman emperors of the first and second centuries include **W. Eck, *The Age of Augustus,*** trans. **D. L. Schneider** (Oxford, 2003); **E. Champlin, *Nero*** (Cambridge, Mass., 2003); and **E. Speller, *Following Hadrian*** (Oxford, 2003).

The Roman army is examined in **A. Goldsworthy, *The Complete Roman Army*** (London, 2003). On the provinces and Roman foreign policy, see **E. N. Luttwak, *The Grand Strategy of the Roman Empire from the First Century A.D. to the Third*** (Baltimore, 1976), and **B. Isaac, *The Limits of Empire: The Roman Empire in the East*** (Oxford, 1990).

A good survey of Roman literature can be found in **R. M. Ogilvie, *Roman Literature and Society*** (Harmondsworth, England, 1980). On Roman art and architecture, see **R. Ling, *Roman Painting*** (New York, 1991); **D. E. Kleiner, *Roman Sculpture*** (New Haven, Conn., 1992); and **M. Wheeler, *Roman Art and Architecture*** (London, 1964). A general study of daily life in Rome is **F. Dupont, *Daily Life in Ancient Rome*** (Oxford, 1994). On the city of Rome, see **O. F. Robinson, *Ancient Rome: City Planning and Administration*** (New York, 1992). On the Roman family, see **S. Dixon, *The Roman Family*** (Baltimore, 1992). Roman women are examined in **S. B. Pomeroy, *Goddesses, Whores, Wives, and Slaves: Women in Classical Antiquity*** (New York, 1975), and **R. Baumann, *Women and Politics in Ancient Rome*** (New York, 1995). On slavery, see **K. R. Bradley, *Slavery and Society at Rome*** (New York, 1994). On the gladiators, see **T. Wiedemann, *Emperors and Gladiators*** (New York, 1992).

For a general introduction to early Christianity, see **J. Court** and **K. Court, *The New Testament World*** (Cambridge, 1990). Useful works on early Christianity include **W. A. Meeks, *The First Urban Christians*** (New Haven, Conn., 1983); **W. H. C. Frend, *The Rise of Christianity*** (Philadelphia, 1984); and **R. MacMullen, *Christianizing the Roman Empire*** (New Haven, Conn., 1984). For a detailed analysis of Christianity in the 30s and 40s of the first century C.E., see **J. D. Crossan, *The Birth of Christianity*** (New York, 1998). On Christian women, see **D. M. Scholer,** ed., ***Women in Early Christianity*** (New York, 1993), and **R. Kraemer, *Her Share of the Blessings: Women's Religion Among the Pagans, Jews and Christians in the Graeco-Roman World*** (Oxford, 1995).

On the Late Roman Empire, see **A. Cameron, *The Later Roman Empire*** (Cambridge, Mass., 1993). On the fourth century, see **M. Grant, *Constantine the Great: The Man and His Times*** (New York, 1993), and **T. D. Barnes, *The New Empire of Diocletian and Constantine*** (Cambridge, Mass., 1982). Studies analyzing the aristocratic circles, the barbarian invasions, and the military problem include **E. A. Thompson, *Romans and Barbarians*** (Madison, Wis., 1982); **A. Ferrill, *The Fall of the Roman Empire: The Military Explanation*** (London, 1986); and **J. M. O'Flynn, *Generalissimos of the Western Roman Empire*** (Edmonton, Canada, 1983). On the relationship between the Romans and the Germans, see **T. S. Burns, *Rome and the Barbarians, 100 B.C.–A.D. 400*** (Baltimore, 2003).

# Looking Ahead

**The immediate consequences** of the fall of Rome and the Han dynasty were a precipitous drop in world trade and a general decline of prosperity throughout the known world. But new societies eventually rose on the ashes of the ancient empires. Although many were different in key respects from those they replaced, they still carried the legacy of their predecessors. In the meantime, the forces that had been unleashed in the civilizations of antiquity sent out strands of influence that were laying the basis for new societies elsewhere in the world: south of the sahara in western and eastern Africa, where new societies were beginning to take shape; be-

**TIMELINE**

| | 6000 B.C.E. | 5000 B.C.E. | 4000 B.C.E. | 3000 B.C.E. | 2000 B.C.E. |
|---|---|---|---|---|---|
| Middle East | Agriculture and Neolithic towns | | | Sumerian civilization | |
| India | First agricultural settlements | | | Harappan civilization | |
| China |  | First settled agriculture | | | |
| Egypt and the Mediterranean | Agriculture in the Nile Valley | | | Flowering of Egyptian civilization | |

yond the Alps in central Europe, where the Germanic peoples were in the process of forming a new society; in southeastern Asia, where the influence of India and China was beginning to help shape new societies among the trading and agricultural societies in the region; and across the Sea of Japan in the Japanese islands, where native rulers would import Chinese ideas to form a new civilization uniquely their own. In the meantime, new civilizations were on the verge of creation across the oceans in the continents of North and South America.

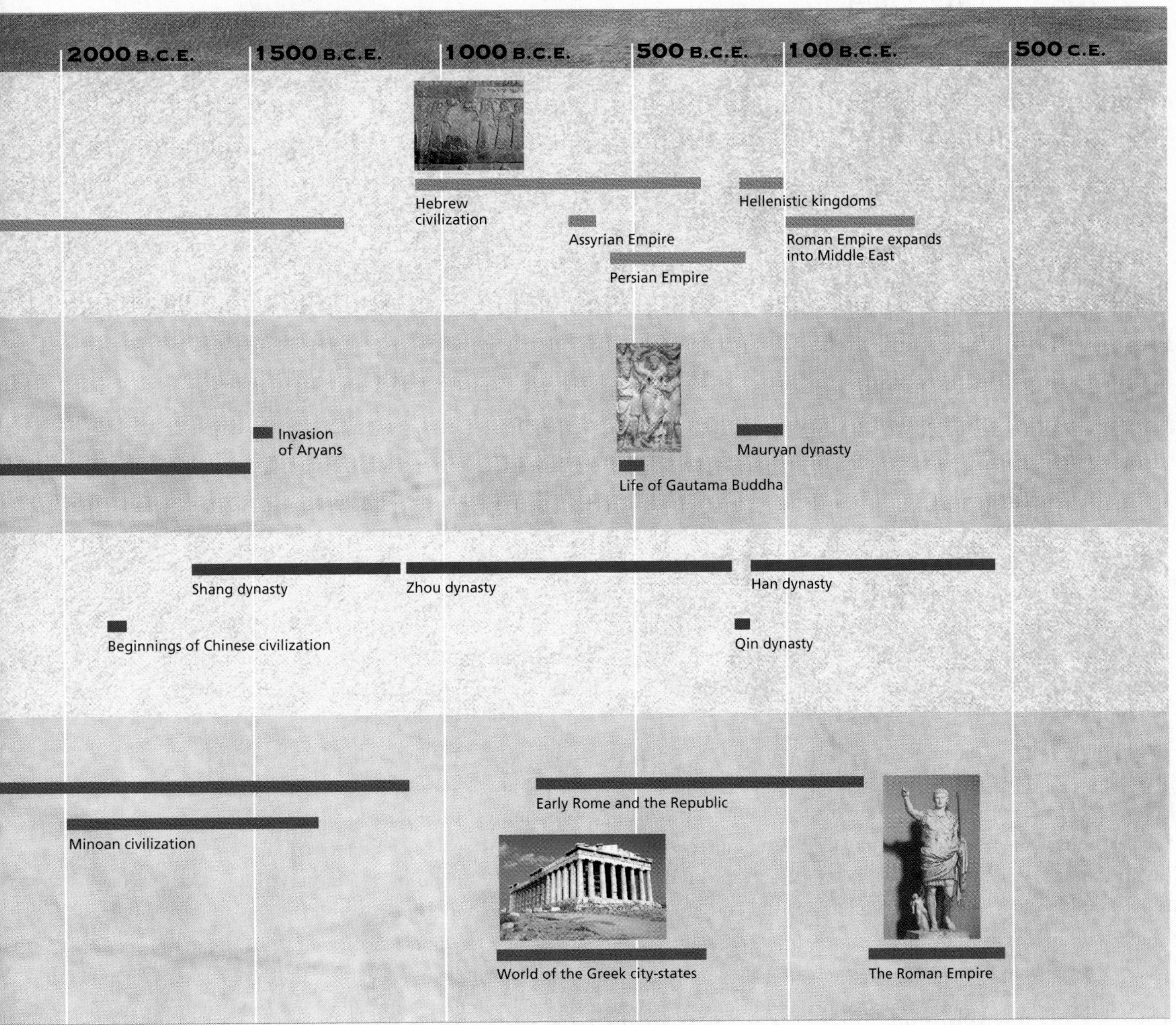

PART

# II

# NEW PATTERNS OF CIVILIZATION



BY THE BEGINNING of the first millennium C.E., the great states of the ancient world were in decline; some were even at the point of collapse. On the ruins of these ancient empires, new patterns of civilization began to take shape between 400 and 1500 C.E. In some cases, these new societies were built on the political and cultural foundations of their predecessors. The Tang dynasty in China and the Guptas in India both looked back to the ancient period to provide an ideological model for their own time. The Byzantine Empire carried on parts of the classical Greek tradition while also adopting the powerful creed of Christianity from the Roman Empire. In other cases, new states incorporated some elements of the former classical civilizations while heading in markedly different directions, as in the Arabic states in the Middle East and in the new European civilization of the Middle Ages. In Europe, the Renaissance of the fifteenth century brought an even greater revival of Greco-Roman culture.

During this period, a number of significant forces were at work in human society. The concept of civilization gradually spread from the heartland regions of the Middle East, the Mediterranean basin, the South Asian subcontinent, and China into new areas of the world–sub-Saharan Africa, central and western Europe, Southeast Asia, and even the islands of Japan, off the eastern edge of the Eurasian landmass. Across the oceans, unique but advanced civilizations began to take shape in isolation in the Americas. In the meantime, the vast migration of peoples continued, leading not only to bitter conflicts but also to increased interchanges of technology and ideas. The result was the transformation of separate and distinct cultures and civilizations into an increasingly complex and vast world system embracing not only technology and trade but also ideas and religious beliefs.

As had been the case during antiquity, the Middle East was the heart of this activity. The Arab Empire, which took shape after the death of Muhammad in the early seventh century, provided the key link in the revived trade routes through the region. Muslim traders–both Arab and Berber–opened contacts with West African societies south of the Sahara, while their ships followed the monsoon winds eastward as far as the Spice Islands in Southeast Asia. Nomads from Central Asia carried goods back and forth along the Silk Road between the Middle East and China. For the next several hundred years, the great cities of the Middle East–Mecca, Damascus, and Baghdad–became among the wealthiest in the known world.

Islam's contributions to the human experience during this period were cultural and technological as well as economic. Muslim philosophers preserved the works of the ancient Greeks for posterity, Muslim scientists and mathematicians made new discoveries about the nature of the universe and the human body, and Arab cartographers and historians mapped the known world and speculated about the fundamental forces in human society.

Metropolitan Museum of Art, Fletcher Fund, 1947, The A.W. Bahr Collection

But the Middle East was not the only or necessarily even the primary contributor to world trade and civilization during this period. While the Arab Empire became the linchpin of trade between the Mediterranean and eastern and southern Asia, a new center of primary importance in world trade was emerging in East Asia, focused on China. China had been a major participant in regional trade during the Han dynasty, when its silks were already being transported to Rome via Central Asia, but its role had declined after the fall of the Han. Now, with the rise of the great Tang and Song dynasties, China reemerged as a major commercial power in East Asia, trading by sea with Southeast Asia and Japan and by land with the nomadic peoples of Central Asia. Like the Middle East, China was also a prime source of new technology. From China came paper, printing, the compass, and gunpowder. The double-hulled Chinese junks that entered the Indian Ocean during the Ming dynasty were slow and cumbersome but extremely seaworthy and capable of carrying substantial quantities of goods over long distances. Many inventions arrived in Europe by way of India or the Middle East, and their Chinese origins were therefore unknown in the West.

Increasing trade on a regional or global basis also led to the exchange of ideas. Buddhism was brought to China by merchants, and Islam first arrived in sub-Saharan Africa and the Indonesian archipelago in the same manner. Merchants were not the only means by which religious and cultural ideas spread, however. Sometimes migration, conquest, or relatively peaceful processes played a part. The case of the Bantu-speaking peoples in Central Africa is apparently an example of peaceful expansion; and while Islam sometimes followed the path of Arab warriors, they rarely imposed their religion by force on the local population. In some instances, as with the Mongols, the conquerors made no effort to convert others to their own religions. By contrast, Christian monks, motivated by missionary fervor, converted many of the peoples of central and eastern Europe. Roman Catholic monks brought Latin Christianity to the Germanic and western Slavic peoples, and monks from the Byzantine Empire largely converted the southern and eastern Slavic populations to Eastern Orthodox Christianity.

Another characteristic of the period between 500 and 1500 C.E. was the almost constant migration of nomadic and seminomadic peoples. Dynamic forces in the Gobi Desert, Central Asia, the Arabian peninsula, and Central Africa provoked vast numbers of peoples to abandon their homelands and seek their livelihood elsewhere. Sometimes the migration was peaceful. More often, however, migration produced violent conflict and sometimes invasion and subjugation. As had been the case during antiquity, the most active source of migrants was Central Asia. The region later gave birth to the fearsome Mongols, whose armies advanced to the gates of central Europe and the conquest of China in the thirteenth century. Wherever they went, they left a train of enormous destruction and loss of life. Inadvertently, the Mongols were also the source of a new wave of epidemics that swept through much of Europe and the Middle East in the fourteenth century. The spread of the plague—known at the time as the Black Death—took much of the population of Europe to an early grave.

But there was another side to the era of nomadic expansion. Even the invasions of the Mongols—the "scourge of God," as Europeans of the thirteenth and fourteenth centuries called them—had constructive as well as destructive consequences. After their initial conquests, for a brief period of three generations, the Mongols provided an avenue for trade throughout the most extensive empire (known as the Pax Mongolica) the world had yet seen. ◆

CHAPTER

# THE AMERICAS

The Spanish conquest of the Aztecs

The Granger Collection, New York

## CHAPTER OUTLINE AND FOCUS QUESTIONS

### The Peopling of the Americas

- Who were the first Americans, and when and how did they come?

### Early Civilizations in Central America

- What were the main characteristics of religious belief in early Mesoamerica?

### The First Civilizations in South America

- What role did the environment play in the evolution of societies in the Americas?

### Stateless Societies in the Americas

- What were the main characteristics of stateless societies in the Americas, and how did they resemble and differ from the civilizations that arose there?

### CRITICAL THINKING

- In what ways were the early civilizations in the Americas similar to those in Part I, and in what ways were they unique?

IN AUGUST 1519, five hundred Spanish soldiers of fortune left their anchorage near the modern city of Veracruz on the Gulf of Mexico and began the long trek from the coast across the dusty plateau of Mexico to the capital of the Aztecs. At their head was Hernán Cortés, a Spanish conquistador who had just burned the ship on which he arrived to ensure that his followers would not launch a mutiny and sail back to Europe. In Tenochtitlán, the Aztec capital located at what is now Mexico City, Emperor Moctezuma received the news of the foreigners' presence and awaited their arrival with anticipation. According to Aztec legend, one of their ancestors, the godlike Quetzalcoatl, had left the area hundreds of years earlier, vowing to return one day to reclaim his heritage. Could this stranger with his band of men be Quetzalcoatl or his representative? When Cortés and his forces, now accompanied by a crowd of people they had encountered en route, reached the vicinity of Moctezuma's capital, the two men met face to face. With this encounter, the last barrier between the Old World and the previously unknown civilizations in the Western Hemisphere had been bridged, and a new era dawned.

# The Peopling of the Americas

The Aztecs were only the latest in a series of sophisticated societies that had sprung up at various locations in North and South America since human beings first crossed the Bering Strait several millennia earlier. Most of these early peoples, today often referred to as **Amerindians,** lived by hunting and fishing or by food gathering. But by the second millennium B.C.E., the first organized societies, based on the cultivation of agriculture, began to take root in Central and South America. One key area of development was on the plateau of central Mexico. Another was in the lowland regions along the Gulf of Mexico and extending into modern Guatemala. A third was in the central Andes Mountains, adjacent to the Pacific coast of South America. Others were just beginning to emerge in the river valleys and Great Plains of North America.

For the next two thousand years, these societies developed in isolation from their counterparts elsewhere in the world. This lack of contact with other human beings deprived them of access to technological and cultural developments taking place in Africa, Asia, and Europe. They did not know of the wheel, for example, and their written languages were rudimentary compared to equivalents in complex civilizations in other parts of the globe. But in other respects, their cultural achievements were the equal of those realized elsewhere. When the first European explorers arrived in the New World at the turn of the sixteenth century, they described much that they observed in glowing terms.

Unfortunately, one technological development that the peoples of America lacked was a knowledge of firearms. In a few short years, tiny bands of armed Spanish conquistadors were able to demolish the magnificent civilizations of the Aztecs, the Maya, and the Inka.

## The First Americans

When the first human beings arrived in the Western Hemisphere has long been a matter of dispute. In the centuries following the voyages of Christopher Columbus (1492–1504), speculation centered on the possibility that the first settlers to reach the American continents had crossed the Atlantic Ocean. Were they the lost tribes of Israel? Were they Phoenician seafarers from Carthage? Were they refugees from the legendary lost continent of Atlantis? In all cases, the assumption was that they were relatively recent arrivals.

By the mid-nineteenth century, under the influence of the new Darwinian concept of evolution, a new theory developed. It proposed that the peopling of America had taken place much earlier as a result of the migration of small communities across the Bering Strait. Recent evidence, including numerous physical similarities between some early Americans and contemporary peoples living in northeastern Asia, has confirmed this hypothesis. The debate on when the migrations began continues, however. The archaeologist Louis Leakey, one of the pioneers in the search for the origins of humankind in Africa, suggested that the first hominids may have arrived in America as long as 100,000 years ago. Others estimate that the first Americans were members of *Homo sapiens sapiens* who crossed from Asia by foot between 10,000 and 15,000 years ago in pursuit of herds of bison and caribou that moved into the area in search of grazing land at the end of the last ice age. A recently discovered site at Cactus Hill, in central Virginia, shows signs of human habitation as early as 15,000 years ago. Genetic evidence now suggests the possibility of an earlier date, perhaps as early as 29,000 years ago. And other recent discoveries indicate that some early settlers may have originally come from Africa rather than from Asia. The question has not yet been definitively answered.

Nevertheless, it is now generally accepted that human beings were living in the Americas at least 15,000 years ago. They gradually spread throughout the North American continent and had penetrated almost to the southern tip of South America by about 10,000 B.C.E. These first Americans were hunters and food gatherers who lived in small nomadic communities close to the source of their food supply. Although it is not known when agriculture was first practiced, beans and squash seeds have been found at sites that date back at least 8,000 years. The cultivation of maize (corn), and perhaps other crops as well, appears to have been under way as early as 5000 B.C.E. in the Tehuacán valley in central Mexico. A similar process may have been under way in the lowland regions near the modern city of Veracruz and in the Yucatán peninsula farther to the east. There, in the region that archaeologists call **Mesoamerica,** one of the first civilizations in the New World began to appear.

# Early Civilizations in Central America

The first signs of civilization in Mesoamerica appeared in the first millennium B.C.E., with the emergence of what is called Olmec culture in the hot and swampy lowlands along the coast of the Gulf of Mexico south of Veracruz (see Map 6.1). Olmec civilization was characterized by intensive agriculture along the muddy riverbanks in the area and by the carving of stone ornaments, tools, and monuments at sites such as San Lorenzo and La Venta. The site at La Venta includes a ceremonial precinct with a 30-foot-high earthen pyramid, the largest of its date in all Mesoamerica. The Olmec peoples organized a widespread trading network, carried on religious rituals, and devised an as yet undeciphered system of hieroglyphics that is similar in some respects to later Mayan writing (see "Mayan Hieroglyphs and Calendars" later in this chapter) and may be the ancestor of the first true writing systems in the New World.

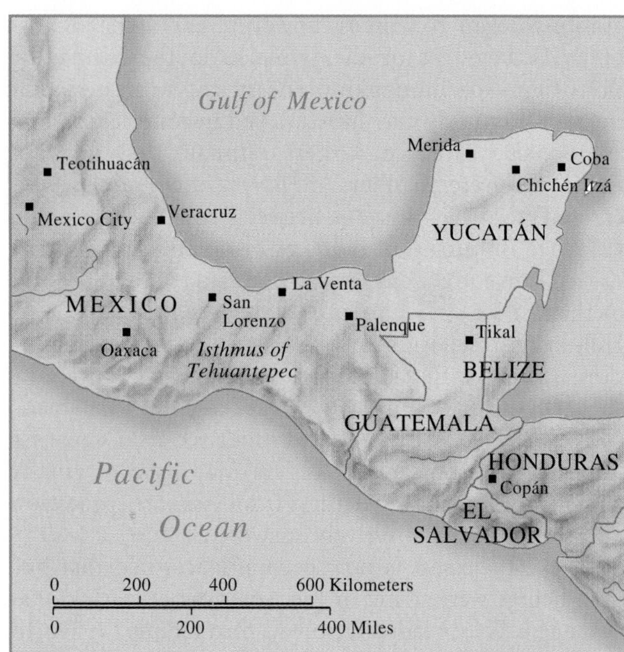


**MAP 6.1 The Heartland of Mesoamerica.** Mesoamerica was home to some of the first civilizations in the Western Hemisphere. This map shows the major urban settlements in the region. ? What areas were most associated with Olmec, Mayan, and Aztec culture? **View an animated version of this map or related maps at** http://history.wadsworth.com/duikerspielvogel05/

Olmec society apparently consisted of several classes, including a class of skilled artisans who produced a series of massive stone heads, some of which are more than 10 feet high. The Olmec peoples supported themselves primarily by cultivating crops, such as corn and beans, but also engaged in fishing and hunting. The Olmec apparently played a ceremonial game on a stone ball court, a ritual that would later be widely practiced throughout the region (see "The Maya" later in this chapter).

Eventually, Olmec civilization began to decline and apparently collapsed around the fourth century B.C.E. During its heyday, however, it extended from Mexico City to El Salvador and perhaps to the shores of the Pacific Ocean.

In the meantime, parallel developments were occurring at Monte Albán, on a hillside overlooking the modern city of Oaxaca, in central Mexico. Around the middle of the first millennium B.C.E., the Zapotec peoples created an extensive civilization that flourished for several hundred years in the highlands. Like the Olmec sites, Monte Albán contains a number of temples and pyramids, but they are located in much more awesome surroundings on a massive stone terrace atop a 1,200-foot-high mountain overlooking the Oaxaca valley. The majority of the population, estimated at about twenty thousand, dwelled on terraces cut into the sides of the mountain.

**The Grand Plaza at Monte Albán.** On the crest of a hilltop at Monte Albán, not far from the modern town of Oaxaca, the Zapotec peoples constructed this grand plaza around the seventh century C.E. In the vicinity are a palace, a ball court, three temple complexes, an observatory, and a majestic pyramid. As in other Mesoamerican cities like Teotihuacán, Tikal, Palenque, and Chichén Itzá, these religious sites functioned as immense stage sets where the entire community could observe and participate in the dramas and sacrificial rituals of their cultures. The use of poetry, music, and dance to dramatize human fears and hopes was a universal phenomenon in all ancient societies.

## Teotihuacán: America's First Metropolis

The first major metropolis in Mesoamerica was the city of Teotihuacán, capital of an early kingdom about 30 miles northeast of Mexico City that arose around the third century B.C.E. and flourished for nearly a millennium until it collapsed under mysterious circumstances about 800 C.E. Along the main thoroughfare were temples and palaces, all dominated by the massive Pyramid of the Sun (see the comparative illustration "The Pyramid" below), under which archaeologists have discovered the remains of sacrificial victims, probably put to death during the dedication of the structure. In the vicinity are the remains of a large market where goods from distant regions as well as agricultural produce grown by farmers in the vicinity were exchanged. The products traded included cacao, rubber, feathers, and various types of vegetables and meat. Pulque, a liquor extracted from the agave plant, was used in religious ceremonies. An obsidian mine nearby may explain the location of the city; obsidian is a volcanic glass that was prized in Mesoamerica for use in tools, mirrors, and the blades of sacrificial knives.

Most of the city consisted of one-story stucco apartment compounds; some were as large as 35,000 square feet, sufficient to house more than a hundred people. Each apartment was divided into several rooms, and the compounds were covered by flat roofs made of wooden beams, poles, and stucco. The compounds were separated by wide streets laid out on a rectangular grid and were entered through narrow alleys.

Living in the fertile Valley of Mexico, an upland plateau surrounded by magnificent snowcapped mountains, the inhabitants of Teotihuacán probably obtained the bulk of their wealth from agriculture.

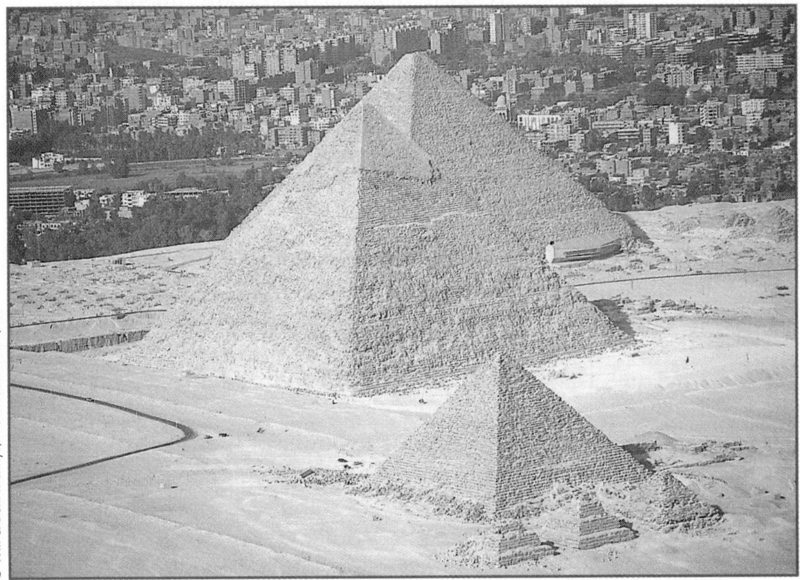

COMPARATIVE ILLUSTRATION

**The Pyramid.** The building of monumental structures known as pyramids was characteristic of a number of civilizations that arose in antiquity. The pyramid symbolized the linkage between the world of human beings and the realm of deities and was often used to house the tomb of a deceased ruler. Shown here are two prominent examples. The upper photo shows the pyramids of Giza, built in the third millennium B.C.E. and located near the modern city of Cairo. Shown below is the Pyramid of the Sun at Teotihuacán, erected in central Mexico in the fifth century C.E. Similar structures of various sizes were built throughout the Western Hemisphere. The concept of the pyramid was also widely applied in parts of Asia. Scholars still debate the technical aspects of constructing such pyramids.

At that time, the valley floor was filled with swampy lakes containing the water runoff from the surrounding mountains. The combination of fertile soil and adequate water combined to make the valley one of the richest farming areas in Mesoamerica.

Sometime during the eighth century, for unknown reasons, the wealth and power of the city began to decline, and eventually its ruling class departed, with the priests carrying stone images of local deities on their backs. The next two centuries were a time of troubles throughout the region as principalities fought over limited farmland. The problem was later compounded when peoples from surrounding areas, attracted by the rich farmlands, migrated into the Valley of Mexico and began to compete for territory with small city-states already established there. As the local population expanded, farmers began to engage in more intensive agriculture. They drained the lakes to build ***chinampas,*** swampy islands crisscrossed by canals that provided water for their crops and easy transportation to local markets for their excess produce.

## The Maya

Far to the east of the Valley of Mexico, another major civilization had arisen in the Yucatán peninsula. This was the civilization of the Maya, which was older and just as sophisticated as the society at Teotihuacán.

**Origins** Like the Aztecs and the inhabitants of Teotihuacán, the Maya trace their origins to the parent Olmec civilization in the lowlands along the Gulf of Mexico. It is not known when human beings first inhabited the Yucatán peninsula, but peoples contemporaneous with the Olmecs were already cultivating such crops as corn, yams, and manioc in the area during the first millennium B.C.E. As the population increased, an early civilization began to emerge along the Pacific coast directly to the south of the peninsula and in the highlands of modern Guatemala. Contacts were already established with the Olmecs to the west.

Since the area was a source for cacao trees and obsidian, the inhabitants soon developed relations with other early civilizations in the region. Cacao trees (whose name derives from the Mayan word *kakaw*) were the source of chocolate, which was used as a beverage by the upper classes, while cocoa beans, the fruit of the cacao tree, were used as currency in markets throughout the region.

As the population in the area increased, the inhabitants began to migrate into the central Yucatán peninsula to the north. The overcrowding forced farmers in the lowland areas to shift from slash-and-burn cultivation to swamp agriculture of the type practiced in the lake region of the Valley of Mexico. By the middle of the first millennium C.E., the entire area was honeycombed with a patchwork of small city-states competing for land and resources. The most important city-states were probably Tikal and Copán, but it is doubtful that any one was sufficiently powerful to dominate the area. The largest urban centers such as Tikal may have had 100,000 inhabitants at their height.

**Political Structures** The power of the rulers of the city-states was impressive. One of the monarchs at Copán—known to scholars as "18 Rabbit" from the hieroglyphs composing his name—ordered the construction of a grand palace requiring more than 30,000 person-days of labor. Around the ruler was a class of aristocrats whose wealth was probably based on the ownership of land farmed by their poorer relatives. Eventually, many of the aristocrats became priests or scribes at the royal court or adopted honored professions as sculptors or painters. As the society's wealth grew, so did the role of artisans and traders, who began to form a small middle class.

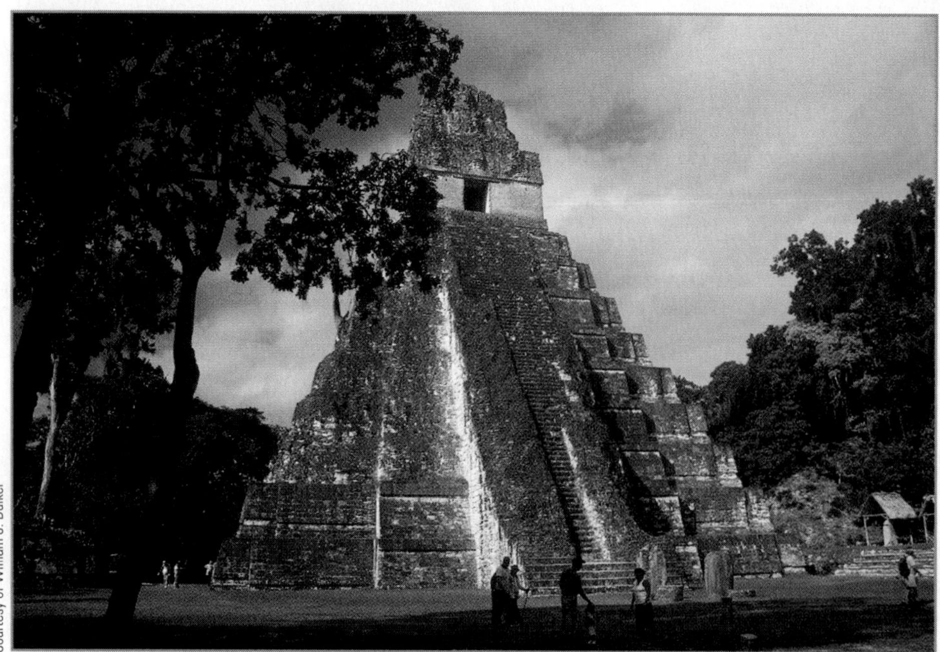

Courtesy of William J. Duiker

**Mayan Temple at Tikal.** This eighth-century temple, peering over the tree tops of a jungle at Tikal, represents the zenith of the engineering and artistry of the Mayan peoples. Erected to house the body of a ruler, such pyramidal tombs contained elaborate works of jade jewelry, polychrome ceramics, and intricate bone carvings depicting the ruler's life and various deities. This temple dominates a great plaza that is surrounded by a royal palace and various religious structures.

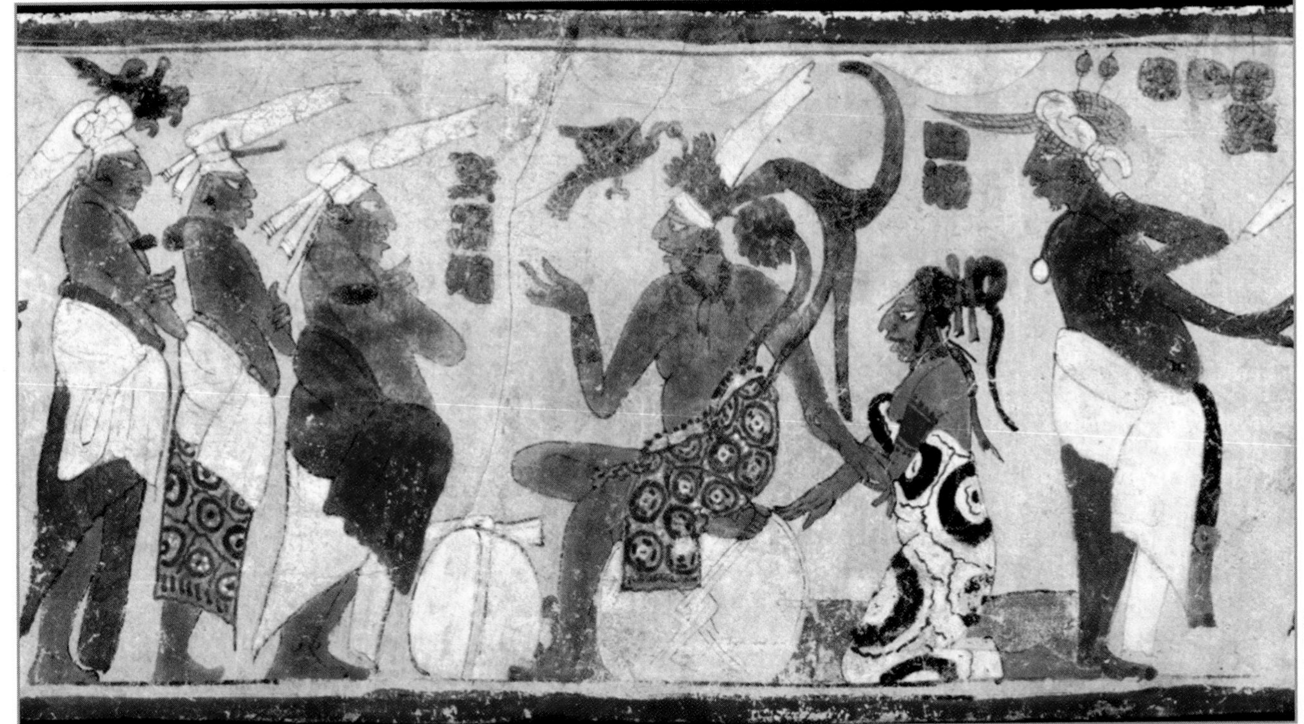

© Justin Kerr, 1997

**The Arranged Marriage.** The Maya recorded religious rites, as well as scenes of daily life, on polychrome clay vessels. Used in ritual ceremonies dedicated to the gods, these vessels contained a foamy chocolate beverage called *kakaw,* from which we derive the word *cacao,* the tree that produces the cocoa beans from which chocolate is made. The graphs accompanying the scenes normally refer to the cacao as well as the vessel's patron, most often the local lord. Here we see three men presenting an offering for an arranged marriage with a lord's daughter, who is shown kneeling behind her father. Mayan rulers often married their daughters to men of lower rank in order to elevate the latter's status and thereby guarantee their allegiance.

The majority of the population on the peninsula, however (estimated at roughly three million at the height of Mayan power), were farmers. They lived on their *chinampa* plots or on terraced hills in the highlands. Houses were built of adobe and thatch and probably resembled the houses of the majority of the population in the area today. There was a fairly clear-cut division of labor along gender lines. The men were responsible for fighting and hunting, the women for homemaking and the preparation of cornmeal, the staple food of much of the population.

Some noblewomen seem to have played important roles in both political and religious life. In the seventh century C.E., for example, Pacal became king of Palenque, one of the most powerful of the Mayan city-states, through the royal line of his mother and grandmother, thereby breaking the patrilineal descent twice. His mother ruled Palenque for three years and was the power behind the throne for her son's first twenty-five years of rule. Pacal legitimized his kingship by transforming his mother into a divine representation of the "first mother" goddess.

**Mayan Religion** Like some of the early religious beliefs in Asia and the Mediterranean, Mayan religion was polytheistic. Although the names were different, Mayan gods shared many of the characteristics of deities of nearby cultures. The supreme god was named Itzamna ("Lizard House"). Deities were ranked in order of importance and had human characteristics, as in ancient Greece and India. Some, like the jaguar god of night, were evil rather than good. Many of the nature deities may have been viewed as manifestations of one supreme godhead (see the box on p. 168). As at Teotihuacán, human sacrifice (normally by decapitation) was practiced to propitiate the heavenly forces. Scholars once believed that the Maya were a peaceful people who rarely engaged in violence. Now, however, it is thought that rivalry among Mayan city-states was endemic and often involved bloody clashes. Scenes from paintings and rock carvings depict a society preoccupied with war and the seizure of captives for sacrifice.

Physically, the Mayan cities were built around a ceremonial core dominated by a central pyramid surmounted by a shrine to the gods. Nearby were other temples, palaces, and a sacred ball court. Like many of their modern counterparts, Mayan cities suffered from urban sprawl, with separate suburbs for the poor and the middle class, and even strip malls stretched along transportation routes, where merchants hawked their wares to pedestrians passing by.

## The Creation of the World: A Mayan View

*Popul Vuh*, a sacred work of the ancient Maya, is an account of Mayan history and religious beliefs. No written version in the original Mayan script is extant, but shortly after the Spanish conquest, it was written down in Quiche (the spoken language of the Maya), using the Latin script, apparently from memory. This version was later translated into Spanish. The following excerpt from the opening lines of *Popul Vuh* recounts the Mayan myth of the creation.

*What similarities and differences do you see between this account of the beginning of the world and those of other ancient civilizations?*

### Popul Vuh: The Sacred Book of the Maya

This is the account of how all was in suspense, all calm, in silence; all motionless, still, and the expanse of the sky was empty.

This is the first account, the first narrative. There was neither man, nor animal, birds, fishes, crabs, trees, stones, caves, ravines, grasses, nor forests; there was only the sky.

The surface of the earth had not appeared. There was only the calm sea and the great expanse of the sky.

There was nothing brought together, nothing which could make a noise, nor anything which might move, or tremble, or could make noise in the sky.

There was nothing standing; only the calm water, the placid sea, alone and tranquil. Nothing existed.

There was only immobility and silence in the darkness, in the night. Only the Creator, the Maker, Tepeu, Gucumatz, the Forefathers, were in the water surrounded with light. They were hidden under green and blue feathers, and were therefore called Gucumatz. By nature they were great sages and great thinkers. In this manner the sky existed and also the Heart of Heaven, which is the name of God and thus He is called.

Then came the word. Tepeu and Gucumatz came together in the darkness, in the night, and Tepeu and Gucumatz talked together. They talked then, discussing and deliberating; they agreed, they united their words and their thoughts.

Then while they meditated, it became clear to them that when dawn would break, man must appear. Then they planned the creation, and the growth of the trees and the thickets and the birth of life and the creation of man. Thus it was arranged in the darkness and in the night by the Heart of Heaven who is called Huracan.

The first is called Caculha Huracan. The second is Chipi-Caculha. The third is Raxa-Caculha. And these three are the Heart of Heaven.

So it was that they made perfect the work, when they did it after thinking and meditating upon it.

**History Now™** To read more of *Popul Vuh*, enter the *HistoryNow* documents area using the access card that is available for *World History*.

The ball court was a rectangular space surrounded by vertical walls with metal rings through which the contestants attempted to drive a hard rubber ball. Although the rules of the game are only imperfectly understood, it apparently had religious significance, and the vanquished players were sacrificed in ceremonies held after the close of the game. Most of the players were men, although there may have been some women's teams. Similar courts have been found at sites throughout Central and South America, with the earliest, located near Veracruz, dating back to around 1500 B.C.E.

**Mayan Hieroglyphs and Calendars** In some ways, Mayan culture was more advanced than the later Aztec civilization in the Valley of Mexico. The Mayan writing system, which developed from the middle of the first millennium B.C.E., was much more sophisticated than the relatively primitive system used by the Aztecs (see the box on p. 169). Unfortunately, when the Spanish conquered the remains of Mayan civilization, they made no attempt to decipher the language with the assistance of natives familiar with the script. The Spanish bishop Diego de Landa, otherwise an astute and sympathetic observer of Mayan culture, remarked, "We found a large number of books in these characters and, as they contained nothing in which there were not to be seen superstition and lies of the devil, we burned them all, which they regretted to an amazing degree, and which caused them much affliction."[1]

The Mayan hieroglyphs remained undeciphered until scholars discovered that many passages contained symbols that recorded dates in the Mayan calendar. This calendar, which measures time back to a particular date in August 3114 B.C.E., required a sophisticated understanding of astronomical events and mathematics to compile. Starting with these known symbols as a foundation, modern scholars have gradually deciphered the script. Like the scripts of the Sumerians and ancient Egyptians, the Mayan hieroglyphs were both ideographic and phonetic and were becoming more phonetic as time passed.

One of the most important repositories of Mayan hieroglyphs is at Palenque, an archaeological site deep in the jungles in the neck of the Mexican peninsula, considerably to the west of the Yucatán (see Map 6.1). In a chamber located under the Temple of Inscriptions, archaeologists discovered a royal tomb and a massive limestone slab covered with hieroglyphs. By deciphering the message on the slab, archaeologists for the first time identified a historical figure in Mayan history. He was the ruler named Pacal, known

## A Sample of Mayan Writing

The Maya were the only Mesoamerican people to devise a complete written language. Like the Sumerian and Egyptian scripts, the Mayan system was composed of a mixture of ideographs and phonetic symbols, which were written in double columns to be read from left to right and top to bottom. The language was rudimentary in many ways. It had few adjectives or adverbs, and the numbering system used only three symbols: a shell for zero, a dot for one, and a bar for five.

During the classical era from 300 to 900 C.E., the Maya used the script to record dynastic statistics with deliberate precision, listing the date of the ruler's birth, his accession to power, and his marriage and death while highlighting victories in battle, the capture of prisoners, and ritual ceremonies. The symbols were carved on stone panels, stelae, and funerary urns or were painted with a brush on folding screen books made of bark paper; only four of these books from the late period remain extant today. A sample of Mayan hieroglyphs is shown below.

*How would you compare Mayan glyphs with the early forms of writing in Egypt, China, and Mesopotamia? Consider purpose, ease of writing, and potential for development into a purely phonetic system.*

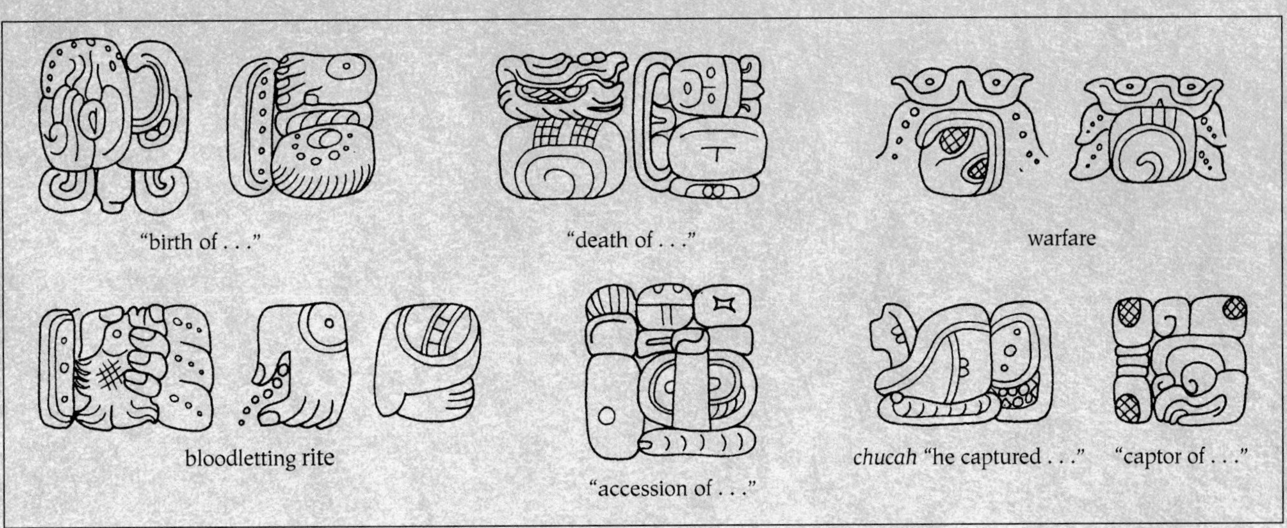


From *Atlas of Ancient America*, © Andromeda Oxford Limited, Oxford, England

Courtesy of William J. Duiker

**A Ball Court.** Throughout Mesoamerica, a dangerous game was played on ball courts such as this one. A large ball of solid rubber was propelled from the hip at such tremendous speed that players had to wear extensive padding. More than an athletic contest, the game had religious significance. The court is thought to have represented the cosmos and the ball the sun, and the losers were sacrificed to the gods in postgame ceremonies. The game is still played today in parts of Mexico.

© British Museum

**A Mayan Bloodletting Ceremony.** The Mayan elite drew blood at various ritual ceremonies. Here we see Lady Xok, the wife of a king of Yaxchilian, passing a rope pierced with thorns along her tongue in a bloodletting ritual. Above her, the king holds a flaming torch. This vibrant scene from an eighth-century C.E. palace lintel demonstrates the excellence of Mayan stone sculpture as well as the sophisticated weaving techniques shown in the queen's elegant gown.

from his glyph as "The Shield"; Pacal ordered the construction of the Temple of Inscriptions in the mid-seventh century, and it was his body that was buried in the tomb at the foot of the staircase leading down into the crypt.

As befits their intense interest in the passage of time, the Maya also had a sophisticated knowledge of astronomy and kept voluminous records of the movements of the heavenly bodies. There were practical reasons for their concern. The arrival of the planet Venus in the evening sky, for example, was a traditional time to prepare for war. The Maya also devised the so-called Long Count, a system of calculating time based on the lunar calendar that calls for the end of the current cycle of 5,200 years in the year (according to the Western solar-based Gregorian calendar) 2012.

**The Mystery of Mayan Decline** Sometime in the eighth or ninth century, the classical Mayan civilization in the central Yucatán peninsula began to decline. At Copán, for example, it ended abruptly in 822 C.E., when work on various stone sculptures ordered by the ruler suddenly ceased. The end of Palenque soon followed. Whether the decline was caused by overuse of the land, invasion, internal revolt, or a natural disaster such as a volcanic eruption is a question that has puzzled archaeologists for decades. Recent evidence supports the theory that overcultivation of the land due to a growing population gradually reduced crop yields. Another theory is that a long drought, which lasted for almost two centuries in the ninth and tenth centuries C.E., may have played a major role. We do know that the period was characterized by an increase in internecine war among the states and the rise of powerful nobles.

Whatever the case, cities like Tikal and Palenque were abandoned to the jungles, though newer urban centers in the northern part of the peninsula, like Uxmal and Chichén Itzá, survived and continued to prosper. According to local history, this latter area was taken over by peoples known as the Toltecs, led by a man known as Kukulcan ("Feathered Serpent"), who migrated to the peninsula from Tula in central Mexico sometime in the tenth century. Some scholars believe this flight was associated with the legend of the departure of Quetzalcoatl, the feathered serpent who promised that he would someday return to reclaim his homeland.

The Toltecs apparently controlled the upper peninsula from their capital at Chichén Itzá for several centuries, but this area was less fertile and more susceptible to drought than the earlier regions of Mayan settlement, and eventually they too declined. When the Spaniards arrived, the area was divided into a number of small principalities, and the cities, including Uxmal and Chichén Itzá, had been abandoned.

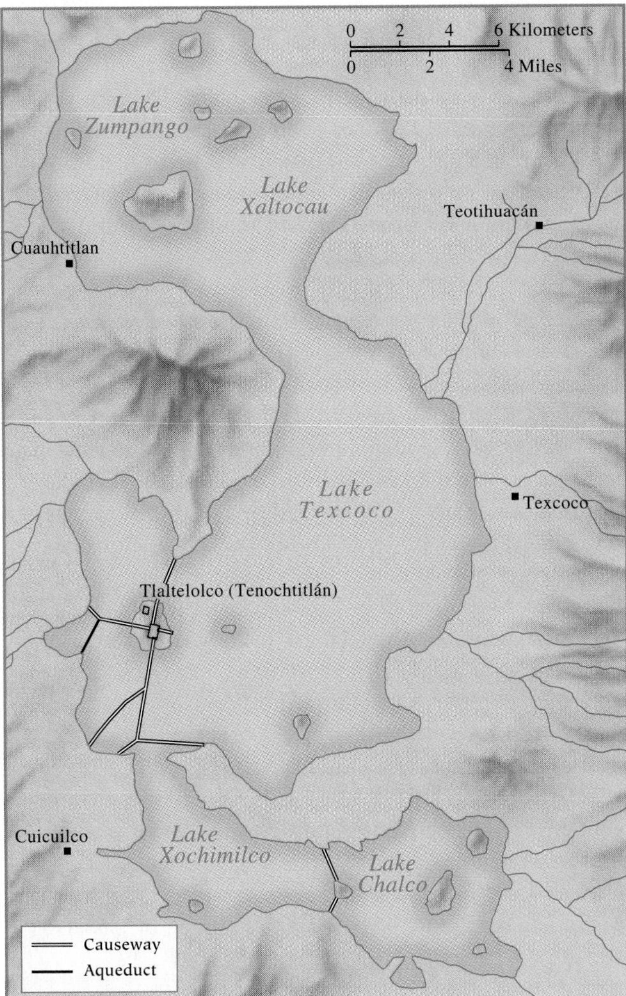


**MAP 6.2 The Valley of Mexico Under Aztec Rule.** The Aztecs were one of the most advanced peoples in pre-Columbian Central America. Their capital at Tlaltelolco was located at the site of modern-day Mexico City. Of the five lakes shown here, only Lake Texcoco remains today. ? What was the importance of Teotihuacán? **View an animated version of this map or related maps at** http://history.wadsworth.com/duikerspielvogel05/

**CHRONOLOGY Early America**

| | |
|---|---|
| Arrival of human beings in America | At least 15,000 years ago |
| First organized societies in the Andes | c. 6000 B.C.E. |
| Agriculture first practiced | c. 5000 B.C.E. |
| Rise of Olmec culture | First millennium B.C.E. |
| Origins of Mayan civilization | First millennium C.E. |
| Teotihuacán civilization | c. 300 B.C.E.–800 C.E. |
| Moche civilization | c. 150 C.E.–800 C.E. |
| Decline of the Maya | 800s |
| Civilization of Chimor | c. 1100–1450 |
| Migration of Mexica to Valley of Mexico | Late 1100s |
| Kingdom of the Aztecs | 1400s |
| Inka takeover in central Andes | 1400s |
| Arrival of Hernán Cortés in Mexico | 1519 |
| Pizarro's conquest of the Inca | 1532 |

## The Aztecs

Among the groups moving into the Valley of Mexico after the fall of Teotihuacán were the Mexica (pronounced "Maysheeka"). No one knows their origins, although folk legend held that their original homeland was an island in a lake called Aztlán. From that legendary homeland comes the name *Aztec*, by which they are known to the modern world. Sometime during the early twelfth century, the Aztecs left their original habitat and, carrying an image of their patron deity, Huitzilopochtli, began a lengthy migration that climaxed with their arrival in the Valley of Mexico sometime late in the century.

Less sophisticated than many of their neighbors, the Aztecs were at first forced to seek alliances with stronger city-states. They were excellent warriors, however, and (like Sparta in ancient Greece and the state of Qin in Zhou dynasty China) had become the leading city-state in the lake region by the early fifteenth century. Establishing their capital at Tenochtitlán, on an island in the middle of Lake Texcoco, they set out to bring the entire region under their domination (see Map 6.2).

For the remainder of the fifteenth century, the Aztecs consolidated their control over much of what is modern Mexico, from the Atlantic to the Pacific Ocean and as far south as the Guatemalan border. The new kingdom was not a centralized state but a collection of semiautonomous territories. To provide a unifying focus for the kingdom, the Aztecs promoted their patron god, Huitzilopochtli, as the guiding deity of the entire population, which now numbered several million.

**Politics** Like all great empires in ancient times, the Aztec state was authoritarian. Power was vested in the monarch, whose authority had both a divine and a secular character. The Aztec ruler claimed descent from the gods and served as an intermediary between the material and the metaphysical worlds. Unlike many of his counterparts in other ancient civilizations, however, the monarch did not obtain his position by a rigid law of succession. On the death of the ruler, his successor was selected from within the royal family by a small group of senior officials, who were also members of the family and were therefore eligible for the position. Once placed on the throne, the Aztec ruler was advised by a small council of lords, headed by a prime minister who served as the chief executive of the government, and a bureaucracy. Beyond the capital, the power of the central government was limited. Rulers of territories subject to the Aztecs were allowed considerable autonomy in return for paying tribute, in the form of

## MARKETS AND MERCHANDISE IN AZTEC MEXICO

One of our most valuable descriptions of Aztec civilization is *The Conquest of New Spain,* written by Bernal Díaz, a Spaniard who accompanied Hernán Cortés on his expedition to Mexico in 1519. In the following passage, Díaz describes the great market at Tenochtitlán.

*Which of the items offered for sale in this account might you expect to be available in a market in Asia, Africa, or Europe? What types of goods mentioned here appear to be unique to the Americas?*

### Bernal Díaz, *The Conquest of New Spain*

Let us begin with the dealers in gold, silver, and precious stones, feathers, cloaks, and embroidered goods, and male and female slaves who are also sold there. They bring as many slaves to be sold in that market as the Portuguese bring Negroes from Guinea. Some are brought there attached to long poles by means of collars round their necks to prevent them from escaping, but others are left loose. Next there were those who sold coarser cloth, and cotton goods and fabrics made of twisted thread, and there were chocolate merchants with their chocolate. In this way you could see every kind of merchandise to be found anywhere in New Spain, laid out in the same way as goods are laid out in my own district of Medina del Campo, a center for fairs, where each line of stalls has its own particular sort. So it was in this great market. There were those who sold sisal cloth and ropes and the sandals they wear on their feet, which are made from the same plant. All these were kept in one part of the market, in the place assigned to them, and in another part were skins of tigers and lions, otters, jackals, and deer, badgers, mountain cats, and other wild animals, some tanned and some untanned, and other classes of merchandise.

There were sellers of kidney beans and sage and other vegetables and herbs in another place, and in yet another they were selling fowls, and birds with great dewlaps, also rabbits, hares, deer, young ducks, little dogs, and other such creatures. Then there were the fruiterers; and the women who sold cooked food, flour and honey cake, and tripe, had their part of the market. Then came pottery of all kinds, from big water jars to little jugs, displayed in its own place, also honey, honey paste, and other sweets like nougat. Elsewhere they sold timber too, boards, cradles, beams, blocks, and benches, all in a quarter of their own.

Then there were the sellers of pitch pine for torches, and other things of that kind, and I must also mention, with all apologies, that they sold many canoe loads of human excrement, which they kept in the creeks near the market. This was for the manufacture of salt and the curing of skins, which they say cannot be done without it. I know that many gentlemen will laugh at this, but I assure them it is true. I may add that on all the roads they have shelters made of reeds or straw or grass so that they can retire when they wish to do so, and purge their bowels unseen by passersby, and also in order that their excrement shall not be lost.

goods or captives, to the central government. The most important government officials in the provinces were the tax collectors, who collected the tribute. They used the threat of military action against those who failed to carry out their tribute obligations and therefore, understandably, were not popular with the taxpayers. According to Bernal Díaz, a Spaniard who accompanied Hernán Cortés on his expedition to Tenochtitlán in 1519:

> All these towns complained about Montezuma [Moctezuma, the Aztec ruler at the time of the Cortés expedition] and his tax collectors, speaking in private so that the Mexican ambassadors should not hear them, however. They said these officials robbed them of all they possessed, and that if their wives and daughters were pretty they would violate them in front of their fathers and husbands and carry them away. They also said that the Mexicans [that is, the representatives from the capital] made the men work like slaves, compelling them to carry pine trunks and stone and firewood and maize overland and in canoes, and to perform other tasks, such as planting maize fields, and that they took away the people's lands as well for the service of their idols.[2]

**Social Structures** Positions in the government bureaucracy were the exclusive privilege of the hereditary nobility, all of whom traced their lineage to the founding family of the Aztec clan. Male children in noble families were sent to temple schools, where they were exposed to a harsh regimen of manual labor, military training, and memorization of information about Aztec society and religion. On reaching adulthood, they would select a career in the military service, the government bureaucracy, or the priesthood. As a reward for their services, senior officials received large estates from the government, and they alone had the right to hire communal labor.

The remainder of the population consisted of commoners, indentured workers, and slaves. Most indentured workers were landless laborers who contracted to work on the nobles' estates, while slaves served in the households of the wealthy. Slavery was not an inherited status, and the children of slaves were considered free citizens. Commoners might sell themselves into slavery when in debt and then later purchase their freedom.

The vast majority of the population were commoners. All commoners were members of large kinship groups called ***calpullis.*** Each *calpulli,* often consisting of as many as a thousand members, was headed by an elected chief, who ran its day-to-day affairs and served as an intermediary with the central government. Each

## Aztec Midwife Ritual Chants

Most Aztec women were burdened with time-consuming family chores, such as grinding corn into flour for tortillas and carrying heavy containers of water from local springs. Like their brothers, Aztec girls went to school, but rather than training for war, they learned spinning, weaving, and how to carry out family rituals. In the sixteenth century C.E., a Spanish priest, Bernardino de Sahagún, interviewed Aztec informants to compile a substantial account of traditional Aztec society. Here we read his narration of ritual chants used by midwives during childhood. For a boy, the highest honor was to shed blood in battle. For a girl, it was to offer herself to the work of domestic life. If a woman died in childbirth, however, she would be glorified as a "warrior woman." Compare the gender roles presented here with those of other ancient civilizations in preceding chapters.

*What does this document suggest as to the proper role to be played by a woman in Aztec society? How did the assigned roles for men and women in Mesoamerica compare with those that we have seen in other societies around the world?*

**Bernardino de Sahagún, *The Florentine Codex***

My precious son, my youngest one. . . . Heed, hearken: Thy home is not here, for thou art an eagle, thou art an ocelot. . . . Thou art the serpent, the bird of the lord of the near, of the nigh. Here is only the place of thy nest. Thou hast only been hatched here; thou hast only come, arrived. . . . Thou belongest out there. . . . Thou hast been sent into warfare. War is the desert, thy task. Thou shalt give drink, nourishment, food to the sun, the lord of the earth. . . . Perhaps thou wilt receive the gift, perhaps thou wilt merit death by the obsidian knife, the flowered death by the obsidian knife.

My beloved maiden. . . . Thou wilt be in the heart of the home, thou wilt go nowhere, thou wilt nowhere become a wanderer, thou becomest the banked fire, the hearth stones. Here our Lord planteth thee, burieth thee. And thou wilt become fatigued, thou wilt become tired, thou art to provide water, to grind maize, to drudge; thou art to sweat by the ashes, by the hearth.

*calpulli* was responsible for providing taxes (usually in the form of goods) and conscript labor to the state.

Each *calpulli* maintained its own temples and schools and administered the land held by the community. Farmland within the *calpulli* was held in common and could not be sold, although it could be inherited within the family. In the cities, each *calpulli* occupied a separate neighborhood, where its members often performed a particular function, such as metalworking, stonecutting, weaving, carpentry, or commerce. Apparently, a large proportion of the population engaged in some form of trade, at least in the densely populated Valley of Mexico, where an estimated half of the people lived in an urban environment. Many farmers brought their goods to the markets via the canals and sold them directly to retailers (see the box on p. 172).

The *calpulli* compounds themselves were divided into smaller family units. Individual families lived in small flat-roofed dwellings containing one or two rooms. Each house was separate from its neighbors and had direct access to the surrounding streets and canals. The houses of farmers living on the chinampas were set on raised dirt platforms built above the surrounding fields to prevent flooding.

Gender roles within the family were rigidly stratified. Male children were trained for war and were expected to serve in the army on reaching adulthood. Women were expected to work in the home, weave textiles, and raise children (see the box above), although like their brothers they were permitted to enter the priesthood. According to Bernal Díaz, a female deity presided over the rites of marriage. As in most traditional societies, chastity and obedience were desirable female characteristics. Although women in Aztec society enjoyed more legal rights than women in some traditional Old World civilizations, they were still not equal to men. Women were permitted to own and inherit property and to enter into contracts. Marriage was usually monogamous, although noble families sometimes practiced **polygyny** (having more than one wife at a time). Wedding partners were normally selected from within the lineage group but not the immediate family. As in most societies at the time, parents usually selected their child's spouse, often for purposes of political or social advancement.

Classes in Aztec society were rigidly stratified. Commoners were not permitted to enter the nobility, although some occasionally rose to senior positions in the army or the priesthood as the result of exemplary service. As in medieval Europe, such occupations often provided a route of upward mobility for ambitious commoners. A woman of noble standing would sometimes marry a commoner because the children of such a union would inherit her higher status, and she could expect to be treated better by her husband's family, who would be proud of the marriage relationship.

**Land Of The Feathered Serpent: Aztec Religion And Culture** The Aztecs, like their contemporaries throughout Mesoamerica, lived in an environment populated by a multitude of gods. Scholars have identified more than a hundred deities in the Aztec pantheon; some of them were nature spirits, like the rain god, Tlaloc, and some were patron deities, like the symbol of the Aztecs themselves, Huitzilopochtli. A supreme deity, called Ometeotl, represented the all-powerful and omnipresent forces of the heavens, but he was rather remote, and other gods, notably the feathered serpent Quetzalcoatl, had a more direct impact on the lives of the people. Representing the forces of creation, virtue, and learning and culture, Quetzalcoatl bears a distinct similarity to Shiva in Hindu belief. According to Aztec tradition, this godlike being had left his homeland in the Valley of Mexico in the tenth century, promising to return in triumph (see "The Mystery of Mayan Decline" earlier in this chapter).

Aztec cosmology was based on a belief in the existence of two worlds, the material and the divine. The earth was the material world and took the form of a flat disk surrounded by water on all sides. The divine world, which consisted of both heaven and hell, was the abode of the gods. Human beings could aspire to a form of heavenly salvation but first had to pass through a transitional stage, somewhat like Christian purgatory, before reaching their final destination, where the soul was finally freed from the body. To prepare for the final day of judgment, as well as to help them engage in proper behavior through life, all citizens underwent religious training at temple schools during adolescence and took part in various rituals throughout their lives. The most devout were encouraged to study for the priesthood. Once accepted, they served at temples ranging from local branches at the *calpulli* level to the highest shrines in the ceremonial precinct at Tenochtitlán. In some respects, however, Aztec society may have been undergoing a process of secularization. By late Aztec times, athletic contests at the ball court had apparently lost some of their religious significance. Gambling was increasingly common, and wagering over the results of the matches was widespread. One province reportedly sent sixteen thousand rubber balls to the capital city of Tenochtitlán as its annual tribute to the royal court.

Aztec religion contained a distinct element of fatalism that was inherent in the creation myth, which described an unceasing struggle between the forces of good and evil throughout the universe. This struggle led to the creation and destruction of four worlds, or suns. The world was now living in the time of the fifth sun. But that world, too, was destined to end with the destruction of this earth and all that is within it:

> *Even jade is shattered,*
> *Even gold is crushed,*
> *Even quetzal plumes are torn. . . .*
> *One does not live forever on this earth:*
> *We endure only for an instant!*[3]

In an effort to postpone the day of reckoning, the Aztecs practiced human sacrifice. The Aztecs believed that by appeasing the sun god, Huitzilopochtli, with sacrifices, they could delay the final destruction of their world. Victims were prepared for the ceremony through elaborate rituals and then brought to the holy shrine, where their hearts were ripped out of their chests and presented to the gods as a holy offering. It was an honor to be chosen for sacrifice, and captives were often used as sacrificial victims, since they represented valor, the trait the Aztecs prized most.

**Art and Culture** Like the art of the Olmecs, most Aztec architecture, art, and sculpture had religious significance. At the center of the capital city of Tenochtitlán was the sacred precinct, dominated by the massive pyramid dedicated to Huitzilopochtli and the rain god, Tlaloc. According to Bernal Díaz, at its base the pyramid was equal to the plots of six large European town houses and tapered from there to the top, which was surmounted by a platform containing shrines to the gods and an altar for performing human sacrifices. The entire pyramid was covered with brightly colored paintings and sculptures.

Although little Aztec painting survives, it was evidently of high quality. Bernal Díaz compared the best work with that of Michelangelo. Artisans worked with stone and with soft metals such as gold and silver, which they cast using the lost-wax technique. They did not have the knowledge for making implements in bronze or iron, however. Stoneworking consisted primarily of representations of the gods and bas-reliefs depicting religious ceremonies. Among the most famous is the massive disk called the Stone of the Sun, carved for use at the central pyramid at Tenochtitlán.

The Aztecs had devised a form of writing based on hieroglyphs that represented an object or a concept. The symbols had no phonetic significance and did not constitute a writing system as such but could give the sense of a message and were probably used by civilian or religious officials as notes or memorandums for their orations. Although many of the notes simply recorded dates in the complex calendar that had evolved since Olmec times, others provide insight into the daily lives of the Aztec peoples. A trained class of scribes carefully painted the notes on paper made from the inner bark of fig trees. Unfortunately, many of these notes were destroyed by the Spaniards as part of their effort to eradicate all aspects of Aztec religion and culture.

**The Destruction of Aztec Civilization** For a century, the Aztec kingdom dominated much of central Mexico from the Atlantic to the Pacific coast, and its influence penetrated as far south as present-day Guatemala. Most local officials had accepted the sovereignty of the king in Tenochtitlán, but in Tlaxcallan to the east, the authorities were restive under Aztec rule.

As noted at the start of this chapter, in 1519, a Spanish expedition under the command of Hernán Cortés landed at Veracruz, on the Gulf of Mexico. Marching to Tenochtitlán at the head of a small contingent of troops, Cortés received a friendly welcome from the Aztec monarch Moctezuma

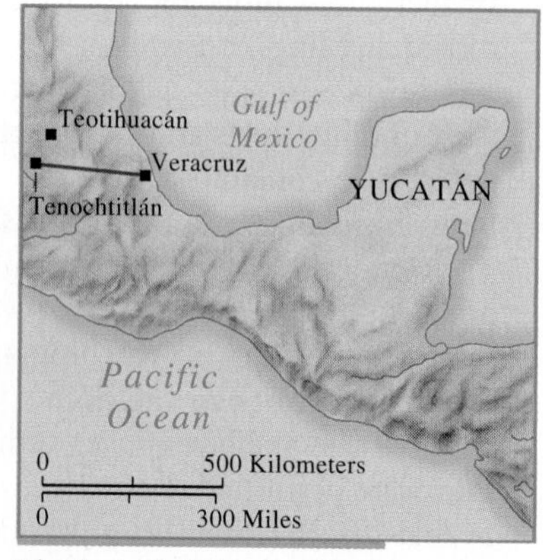


**The Arrival of Hernán Cortés in Mexico**

## Moctezuma's Greeting to Cortés

As his small party arrived in the Aztec capital of Tenochtitlán, Hernán Cortés was greeted by Emperor Moctezuma, who was under the impression that Cortés was the representative of Quetzalcoatl, the Aztec deity who had departed centuries earlier with a promise that he would one day return. In this letter to Queen Isabella of Spain, Cortés describes the welcoming ceremony and Moctezuma's opening address. As Moctezuma would soon discover, he had been deceived as to his visitor's identity and intentions.

*According to this letter, the Aztec rulers did not view themselves as divine. In what other civilizations that we have encountered in this book was this also the case?*

### Hernán Cortés, *Letter from Mexico*

Close to the city there is a wooden bridge ten paces wide across a breach in the causeway to allow the water to flow, as it rises and falls. . . .

After we had crossed this bridge, Moctezuma came to greet us and with him some two hundred lords, all barefoot and dressed in a different costume, but also very rich in their way and more so than the others. They came in two columns, pressed very close to the walls of the street, which is very wide and beautiful and so straight that you can see from one end to the other. It is two-thirds of a league long and has on both sides very good and big houses, both dwellings and temples.

[After an exchange of gifts, Moctezuma then] addressed me in the following way:

"Be assured that we shall obey you and hold you as our lord in place of that great sovereign of whom you speak; . . . I know full well of all that has happened to you from Puntunchan to here, and I also know how those of Cempoal and Tascalteca have told you much evil of me; believe only what you see with your eyes, for those are my enemies, and some were my vassals, and have rebelled against me at your coming and said those things to gain favor with you. I also know that they have told you the walls of my houses are made of gold, and that the floor mats in my rooms and other things in my household are likewise of gold, and that I was, and claimed to be, a god; and many other things besides. The houses as you see are of stone and lime and clay."

Then he raised his clothes and showed me his body, saying, as he grasped his arms and trunk with his hands, "See that I am of flesh and blood like you and all other men, and I am mortal and substantial. See how they have lied to you? It is true that I have some pieces of gold left to me by my ancestors; anything I might have shall be given to you whenever you ask. Now I shall go to other houses where I live, but here you shall be provided with all that you and your people require, and you shall receive no hurt, for you are in your own land and your own house."

Xocoyotzin (known also as Montezuma), who initially believed his visitor was a representative of Quetzalcoatl, the godlike "feathered serpent" (see the box above). The king and his subjects were astounded to see men on horseback, for the horse had disappeared from the Americas at least ten thousand years earlier.

The Granger Collection, New York

**The Spaniards Conquer a New World.** In attempting to subdue the Aztecs, the conquistadors relied on their superior weaponry. They also counted on the support of other Indian peoples, who were increasingly restive under Moctezuma's domination. Here we see two Spanish warriors and their Indian allies brandishing their steel weapons against the stones and arrows of the Aztecs. Having learned the value of mounted warfare from the Arabs during the Crusades (see Chapter 12), the Spaniards went to great lengths to bring horses to the Americas, suspending them in slings on their galleons to prevent injury. It is said that Cortés was more grieved by the death of a horse than by that of one of his warriors.

But tensions soon erupted between the Spaniards and the Aztecs, provoked in part by demands by Cortés that the Aztecs denounce their native beliefs and accept Christianity. When the Spanish took Moctezuma hostage and began to destroy Aztec religious shrines, the local population revolted and drove the invaders from the city (see the box on p. 176). Receiving assistance from the state of Tlaxcallan, Cortés managed to fight his way back into the city. Meanwhile the Aztecs were beginning to suffer the first effects of the diseases brought by the Europeans, which would eventually wipe out the majority of the local

## Face to Face

In this excerpt from a compilation of oral testimonials given to the Spanish friar Bernardino de Sahagún, Aztec observers describe the surprise attack by the conquistadors, who, fearing a revolt by the Mexicans, assaulted them first during a religious festival. Initially, the Spanish sought to destroy all evidence of Aztec religion—its manuscripts, artwork, and artifacts—in order to convert their new subjects to the Christian faith. Eventually, however, they realized that this effort could not succeed without an understanding of Aztec civilization. They thereupon initiated an enterprise to transcribe the local language, Nahuatl, into the Roman alphabet and to translate oral testimonials of Aztec history and culture into Spanish. This account of the brutal attack at Tenochtitlán from the Mexican point of view is the result.

*Why did the Spaniards launch their attack on the Aztecs? Is there any indication in this text whether the Spaniards' fears were justified?*

### Bernardino de Sahagún, *The Florentine Codex*

And when Moteucçoma went out to meet them at Huitzillan, thereupon he gave various things to the war leader, . . . . [and] he put flower wreaths on his head. Then he laid before him the golden necklaces, all the different things for greeting people. He ended by putting some of the necklaces on him.

Then [Cortés] said in reply to Moteucçoma, "Is it not you? Is it not you then? Moteucçoma?"

Moteucçoma said, "Yes, it is me." Thereupon he stood up straight, he stood up with their faces meeting. He bowed down deeply to him. He stretched as far as he could, standing stiffly. Addressing [Cortés], he said, ". . . And now it has come true, you have come. Be doubly welcomed, enter the land, go to enjoy your palace; rest your body. . . ."

[Cortés replied], "Let Moteucçoma be at ease, let him not be afraid, for we greatly esteem him. Now we are truly satisfied to see him in person and hear him, for until now we have greatly desired to see him and look upon his face. Well, now we have seen him, we have come to his homeland of Mexico. Bit by bit he will hear what we have to say."

Thereupon [the Spaniards} took [Moteucçoma] by the hand. They came along with him, stroking his hair to show their good feeling. And the Spaniards looked at him, each of them giving him a close look. . . .

When the festivity was being observed and there was dancing and singing, with voices raised in song, the singing was like the noise of waves breaking against the rocks. When it was time, when the moment had come for the Spaniards to do the killing, they came out equipped for battle. . . . They went into the temple courtyard to kill people. Those whose assignment it was to do the killing just went on foot, each with his metal sword and his leather shield, some of them iron-studded. Then they surrounded those who were dancing, going among the cylindrical drums. They struck a drummer's arms; both of his hands were severed. Then they struck his neck; his head landed far away. Then they stabbed everyone with iron lances and stuck them with iron swords. They stuck some in the belly, and then their entrails come spilling out. They split open the heads of some, they really cut their skulls to pieces, their skulls were cut up into little bits. . . .

And when it became known [what was happening], everyone cried out, "Mexica warriors, come running, get outfitted with devices, shields, and arrows, hurry, come running, the warriors are dying; they have died, perished, been annihilated, O Mexica warriors!" Thereupon there were war cries, shouting, and beating of hands against lips. The warriors quickly came outfitted, bunched together, carrying arrows and shields. Then the fighting began; they shot at them with barbed darts, spears, and tridents, and they hurled darts with broad obsidian points at them. A cloud of yellow reeds spread over the Spaniards.

population. In a battle that to many Aztecs must have seemed to symbolize the dying of the legendary fifth sun, the Aztecs were finally vanquished. Within months, their magnificent city and its temples, believed by the conquerors to be the work of Satan, had been destroyed.

# The First Civilizations in South America

South America is a vast continent, characterized by extremes in climate and geography. The north is dominated by the mighty Amazon River, which flows through dense tropical jungles carrying a larger flow of water than any other river system in the world (see Map 6.3). Farther to the south, the jungles are replaced by prairies and steppes stretching westward to the Andes Mountains, which extend the entire length of the continent, from the Isthmus of Panama to the Strait of Magellan. Along the Pacific coast, on the western slopes of the mountains, are some of the driest desert regions in the world.

South America has been inhabited by human beings for more than 12,000 years. Wall paintings discovered at the "cavern of the painted rock" in the Amazon region suggest that Stone Age peoples were living in the area at least 11,000 years ago, and a site at Monte Verde, along the

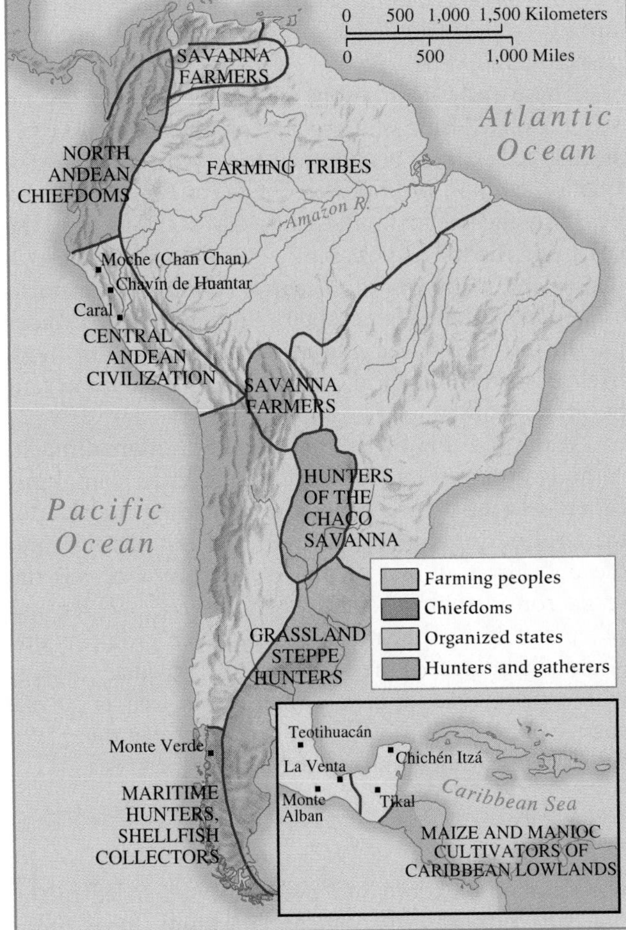


MAP 6.3 **Early Peoples and Cultures of Central and South America.** This map shows regions of early human settlements in Central and South America. Urban conglomerations appear in Mesoamerica (see inset) and along the western coast of South America. Why do you think urban centers appeared in these areas? **View an animated version of this map or related maps at** http://history.wadsworth.com/duikerspielvogel05/

central coast of Chile, has been dated to 10,500 B.C.E. Early peoples lived by hunting, fishing, and food gathering, but there are indications that irrigated farming was being practiced in the western slopes of the Andes Mountains over 4,000 years ago.

## Chavín de Huantar

By the third millennium B.C.E., complex societies had begun to emerge in the coastal regions of modern-day Peru and Ecuador. The first settlements were apparently located along the coast, but eventually farming communities began to appear in the river valleys flowing down from the Andes Mountains. Fish and agricultural products were traded to highland peoples for wool and salt.

By 2,500 B.C.E.—a thousand years earlier than the earliest known cities in Mesoamerica—the first urban settlements appeared. At Caral, an archaeological site located 14 miles inland from the coast, the remnants of a 4,500-year-old city sit on the crest of a 60-foot-high pyramid. The inhabitants engaged in farming but also provided cotton to fishing communities along the coast, who used the fiber to make fishnets.

This culture reached its height during the first millennium B.C.E. with the emergence of the Chavín style, named for a site near the modern city of Chavín de Huantar. The ceremonial precinct at the site contained an impressive stone temple complete with interior galleries, a stone-block ceiling, and a system of underground canals that probably channeled water into the temple complex for ceremonial purposes. The structure was surrounded by stone figures depicting various deities and two pyramids. Evidence of metallurgy has also been found, with objects made of copper and gold.

## Moche

Chavín society broke down by 200 B.C.E., but early in the first millennium C.E., another advanced civilization, comprising a total area of over 2,500 square miles, appeared in northern Peru, in the valley of the Moche River, which flows from the foothills of the Andes into the Pacific Ocean. The capital city, large enough in territory to contain over ten thousand people, was dominated by two massive adobe pyramids as much as 100 feet high. The largest, known as the Pyramid of the Moon, covered a total of 15 acres and was adorned with painted murals depicting battles, ritual sacrifices, and various local deities.

Artifacts found at Moche, especially the metalwork and stone and ceramic figures, exhibit a high quality of artisanship. They were imitated at river valley sites throughout the surrounding area, which suggests that the authority of the Moche rulers may have extended as far as 400 miles along the coast. The artifacts also indicate that the people at Moche, like those in Central America, were preoccupied with warfare. Paintings and pottery as well as other artifacts in stone, metal, and ceramics frequently portray warriors, prisoners, and sacrificial victims. The Moche were also fascinated by the heavens, and much of their art consisted of celestial symbols and astronomical constellations.

**Environmental Problems** The Moche River valley is extremely arid, receiving less than an inch of rain annually. The peoples in the area compensated by building a sophisticated irrigation system to carry water from the river to the parched fields. At its zenith, Moche culture was spectacular. By the eighth century C.E., however, the civilization was in a state of collapse, the irrigation canals had been abandoned, and the remaining population had abandoned the area and moved farther inland or suffered from severe malnutrition.

Courtesy of William J. Duiker

**Fantastic Creature Pot.** The elaborate pottery of the Moche valley artists provides an impressive visual record of the daily lives of the Peruvian peoples living in the sixth to ninth centuries C.E. Many of these colorful pots show scenes from everyday activities, such as hunting, fishing, weaving, cooking, and playing musical instruments. Others display religious ceremonies and sacrifice rituals. As illustrated in the fanged face of this fantastic creature, most probably a jaguar, these potters often blended the natural with the supernatural, which expressed the Moche worldview.

What had happened to bring Moche culture to this untimely end? Archaeologists speculate that environmental changes, perhaps brought on by changes in the water temperature known as **El Niño,** led to periods of drought and then to periodic flooding of coastal regions and the silting up of the irrigated fields (see the comparative essay, "History and the Environment," on p. 179).

Three hundred years later, a new power, the kingdom of Chimor, with its capital at Chan Chan, at the mouth of the Moche River, emerged in the area. Built almost entirely of adobe, Chan Chan housed an estimated thirty thousand residents in an area of over 12 square miles that included a number of palace compounds surrounded by walls nearly 30 feet high. One compound contained an intricate labyrinth that wound its way progressively inward until it ended in a central chamber, probably occupied by the ruler. Like the Moche before them, the people of Chimor relied on irrigation to funnel the water from the river into their fields. An elaborate system of canals brought the water through hundreds of miles of hilly terrain to the fields near the coast. Nevertheless, by the fifteenth century, Chimor, too, had disappeared, a victim of floods and a series of earthquakes that destroyed the intricate irrigation system that had been the basis of its survival.

These early civilizations in the Andes were by no means isolated from other societies in the region. As early as 2000 B.C.E., local peoples had been venturing into the Pacific Ocean on wind-powered rafts constructed of balsa wood. By the late first millennium C.E., seafarers from the coast of Ecuador had established a vast trading network that extended southward to central Peru and as far north as western Mexico, over 2,000 miles away. Items transported included jewelry, beads, and metal goods. In all likelihood, technological exchanges were an important by-product of the relationship.

Transportation by land, however, was more difficult. Although roads were constructed to facilitate communication between communities, the forbidding character of the terrain in the mountains was a serious obstacle, and the only draft animal on the entire continent was the llama, considerably less hardy than the cattle, horses, and water buffalo used in much of Asia. Such problems undoubtedly hampered the development of regular contacts with distant societies in the Americas, as well as the exchange of goods and ideas that had lubricated the rise of civilizations from China to the Mediterranean Sea.

## The Inka

The Chimor kingdom was eventually succeeded in the late fifteenth century by an invading force from the mountains far to the south. In the late fourteenth century, the Inka were a small community in the area of Cuzco, a city located at an altitude of 10,000 feet in the mountains of southern Peru. In the 1440s, however, under the leadership of their powerful ruler Pachakuti (sometimes called Pachacutec, or "he who transforms the world"), the Inka peoples launched a campaign of conquest that eventually brought the entire region under their authority. Under Pachakuti and his immediate successors, Topa Inka and Huayna Inka (the word *Inka* means "ruler"), the boundaries of the kingdom were extended as far as Ecuador, central Chile, and the edge of the Amazon basin.

**The Four Quarters: Inka Politics And Society** Pachakuti created a highly centralized state (see Map 6.4). With a stunning concern for mathematical precision, he divided his empire, called Tahuantinsuyu, or "the world of the four quarters," into provinces and districts. Each province contained about ten thousand residents (at least in theory) and was ruled by a governor related to the royal family. Excess inhabitants were transferred to other locations. The capital of Cuzco was divided into four quarters, or residential areas, and the social status and economic functions of the residents of each quarter were rigidly defined.

The state was built on forced labor. Often entire communities of workers were moved from one part of the country to another to open virgin lands or engage in massive construction projects. Under Pachakuti, the capital of

## COMPARATIVE ESSAY

# HISTORY AND THE ENVIRONMENT

In *The Decline and Fall of the Roman Empire,* published in 1788, the British historian Edward Gibbon raised a question that has fascinated historians ever since: What brought about the collapse of that once powerful civilization that dominated the Mediterranean region for over five centuries? Traditional explanations have centered on political or cultural factors, such as imperial overreach, moral decay, military weakness, or the impact of invasions. Recently, however, some historians have suggested that environmental factors, such as poisoning due to the use of lead water pipes and cups, the spread of malaria, or a lengthy drought in wheat-growing regions in North Africa, might have been at least contributory causes.

The current interest in the impact of the environment on the Roman Empire reflects a growing awareness among historians that environmental conditions may have been a key factor in the fate of several of the great societies in the ancient world. Climatic changes or natural disasters almost certainly led to the decline and collapse of civilization in the Indus River valley. In the Americas, massive flooding brought about by the El Niño effect (environmental conditions triggered by changes in water temperature in the Pacific Ocean) appears to be one possible cause for the collapse of the Moche civilizatin in what is today Peru, while drought and overcultivation of the land are often cited as reasons for the decline of the Maya in Mesoamerica.

Climatic changes continued to affect the fate of nations and peoples after the end of the classical era. Drought conditions and overuse of the land may have led to the gradual decline of Mesopotamia as a focal point of advanced civilization in the Middle East, while soil erosion and colder conditions doomed an early attempt by the Vikings to establish a foothold in Greenland and North America. Sometimes the problems were self-inflicted, as on Easter Island, a remote outpost in the Pacific Ocean, where Polynesian settlers migrating from the west about 900 C.E. so denuded the landscape that by the fifteenth century, what had been a reasonably stable and peaceful society had descended into civil war and cannibalism.

Climatic changes, of course, have not always been detrimental to the health and prosperity of human beings. A warming trend that took place at the end of the last ice age eventually made much of the world more habitable for farming peoples about 10,000 years ago. The effects of El Niño may be beneficial to people living in some areas and disastrous in others. But human misuse of land and water resources is always dangerous to settled societies, especially those living in fragile environments.

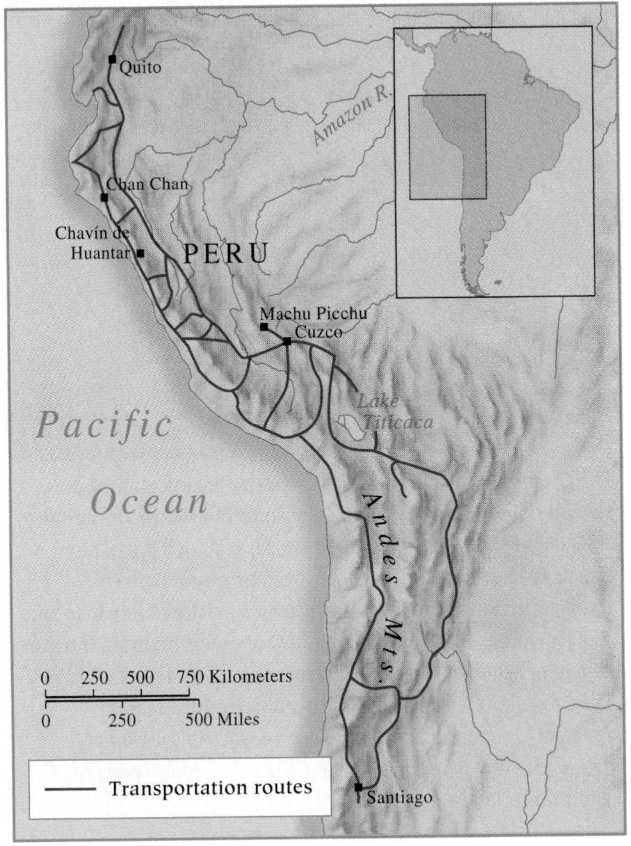


**MAP 6.4 The Inka Empire About 1500 C.E.** The Inka were the last civilization to flourish in South America prior to the arrival of the Spanish. The impressive system of roads constructed to facilitate communication shows the extent of Inka control throughout the Andes Mountains. **?** In what modern countries was the Inka state located? **View an animated version of this map or related maps at http://history.wadsworth.com/duikerspielvogel05/**

Cuzco was transformed from a city of mud and thatch into an imposing metropolis of stone. The walls, built of close-fitting stones without the use of mortar, were a wonder to early European visitors. The most impressive structure in the city was a temple dedicated to the sun. According to a Spanish observer, "All four walls of the temple were covered from top to bottom with plates and slabs of gold."[4] Equally impressive are the ruins of the abandoned city of Machu Picchu, built on a lofty hilltop far above the Urubamba River.

Another major construction project was a system of 24,800 miles of highways and roads that extended from the border of modern Colombia to a point south of modern Santiago, Chile. Two major roadways extended in a north-south direction, one through the Andes Mountains and the other along the coast, with connecting routes between

Courtesy of Carol C. Coffin

**Machu Picchu.** Situated in the Andes in modern Peru, Machu Picchu reflects the glory of Inka civilization. To farm such rugged terrain, the Inka constructed terraces and stone aqueducts. To span vast ravines, they built suspension bridges made of braided fiber and fastened them to stone abutments on the opposite banks. The most revered of the many temples and stone altars at Machu Picchu was the thronelike "hitching post of the sun," so called because of its close proximity to the sun god.

them. Rest houses and storage depots were placed along the roads. Suspension bridges made of braided fiber and fastened to stone abutments on opposite banks were built over ravines and waterways. Use of the highways was restricted to official and military purposes. Trained runners carried messages rapidly from one way station to another, enabling information to travel up to 140 miles in a single day.

In rural areas, the population lived mainly by farming. In the mountains, the most common form was terraced agriculture, watered by irrigation systems that carried precise amounts of water into the fields, which were planted with maize, potatoes, and other crops. The plots were tilled by collective labor regulated by the state. Like other aspects of Inka society, marriage was strictly regulated, and men and women were required to select a marriage partner from within the immediate tribal group. For women, there was one escape from a life of domestic servitude. Fortunate maidens were selected to serve as "chosen virgins" in temples throughout the country (see the box on p. 181). Noblewomen were eligible to compete for service in the Temple of the Sun at Cuzco, while commoners might hope to serve in temples in the provincial capitals. Punishment for breaking the vow of chastity was harsh, and few evidently took the risk.

**Inka Culture** Like many other civilizations in pre-Columbian Latin America, the Inka state was built on war. Soldiers for the 200,000-man Inka army, the largest and best

Courtesy of William J. Duiker

**The *Quipu*.** Not having a writing system, the Inka tallied the various data of their kingdom on strands of knotted yarn. Highly skilled and esteemed, official secretaries recorded population census data, crop and household inventories, government inspector reports, crime investigations, taxes, legal decisions and contracts, and all the official statistics of the realm by an intricate system of tying knots on a circular grouping of strings of yarn. The use of knotted yarn as a means of recording data was apparently not unique to the Inka. A passage in the Chinese classic *The Way of the Tao* declares, "Let the people revert to communication by knotted cords."

## Virgins with Red Cheeks

A letter from a Peruvian chief to King Philip III of Spain written four hundred years ago gives us a firsthand account of the nature of traditional Inkan society. The purpose of author Huaman Poma was both to justify the history and culture of the Inkan peoples and to record their sufferings under Spanish domination. In his letter, Poma describes Inkan daily life from birth to death in minute detail. He explains the different tasks assigned to men and women, beginning with their early education. Whereas boys were taught to watch the flocks and trap animals, girls were taught to dye, spin and weave cloth, and perform other domestic chores. Most interesting, perhaps, was the emphasis that the Inka placed on virginity, as is witnessed in the document presented here. The Inkan tradition of temple virgins is reminiscent of similar practices in ancient Rome, where young girls from noble families were chosen as priestesses to tend the sacred fire in the Temple of Vesta for thirty years. If one lost her virginity, she was condemned to be buried alive in an underground chamber.

*In this passage, one of the chief duties of a woman in Inkan society was to spin and weave. In what other traditional societies was textile making a woman's work? Why do you think this was the case?*

### Huaman Poma, *Letter to a King*

During the time of the Incas certain women, who were called *accla* or "the chosen," were destined for lifelong virginity. Mostly they were confined in houses and they belonged to one of two main categories, namely sacred virgins and common virgins.

The so-called "virgins with red cheeks" entered upon their duties at the age of twenty and were dedicated to the service of the Sun, the Moon, and the Day-Star. In their whole life they were never allowed to speak to a man.

The virgins of the Inca's own shrine of Huanacauri were known for their beauty as well as their chastity. The other principal shrines had similar girls in attendance. At the less important shrines there were the older virgins who occupied themselves with spinning and weaving the silklike clothes worn by their idols. There was a still lower class of virgins, over forty years of age and no longer very beautiful, who performed unimportant religious duties and worked in the fields or as ordinary seamstresses.

Daughters of noble families who had grown into old maids were adept at making girdles, headbands, string bags, and similar articles in the intervals of their pious observances.

Girls who had musical talent were selected to sing or play the flute and drum at Court, weddings and other ceremonies, and all the innumerable festivals of the Inca year.

There was yet another class of *accla* or "chosen," only some of whom kept their virginity and others not. These were the Inca's beautiful attendants and concubines, who were drawn from noble families and lived in his palaces. They made clothing for him out of material finer than taffeta or silk. They also prepared a maize spirit of extraordinary richness, which was matured for an entire month, and they cooked delicious dishes for the Inca. They also lay with him, but never with any other man.

armed in the region, were raised by universal male conscription. Military units were moved rapidly along the highway system and were housed in the rest houses located along the roadside. Since the Inka had no wheeled vehicles, supplies were carried on the backs of llamas. Once an area was placed under Inkan authority, the local inhabitants were instructed in the Quechua language, which became the lingua franca of the state, and were introduced to the state religion. The Inka had no writing system but kept records using a system of knotted strings called ***quipu,*** maintained by professionally trained officials, that were able to record all data of a numerical nature. What could not be recorded in such a manner was committed to memory and then recited when needed. The practice was apparently not invented by the Inka. Fragments of *quipu* have been found at Caral and dated at approximately 5,000 years ago.

As in the case of the Aztecs and the Maya, the lack of a fully developed writing system did not prevent the Inka from realizing a high level of cultural achievement. Most of what survives was recorded by the Spanish and consists of entertainment for the elites. The Inka had a highly developed tradition of court theater, including both tragic and comic works. There was also some poetry, composed in blank verse and often accompanied by music played on reed instruments.

**The Conquest Of The Inka** The Inka empire was still in existence when the first Spanish expeditions arrived in the central Andes. The leader of the Spanish invaders, Francisco Pizarro, was accompanied by only a few hundred companions, but like Cortés, he possessed steel weapons, gunpowder, and horses, none of which were familiar to his hosts. In the meantime, internal factionalism, combined with the onset of contagious diseases spread unknowingly by the Europeans, had weakened the ruling elite, and the empire fell rapidly to the Spanish forces in 1532. The last Inka ruler was tried by the Spaniards and executed. Pre-Columbian South America's greatest age was over.

# Stateless Societies in the Americas

Beyond Central America and the high ridges of the Andes Mountains, on the Great Plains of North America, along the Amazon River in South America, and on the islands of the Caribbean Sea, other communities of Amerindians were also beginning to master the art of agriculture and to build organized societies.

Although human beings had occupied much of the continent of North America during the early phase of human settlement, the switch to farming as a means of survival did not occur until the third millennium B.C.E. at the earliest, and not until much later in most areas of the continent. Until that time, most Amerindian communities lived by hunting, fishing, or foraging. As the supply of large animals began to diminish, they turned to smaller game and to fishing and foraging for wild plants, fruits, and nuts.

## The Eastern Woodlands

It was probably during the third millennium B.C.E.that peoples in the Eastern Woodlands (the land in eastern North America from the Great Lakes to the Gulf of Mexico) began to cultivate indigenous plants for food in a systematic way. As wild game and food became scarce, some communities began to place more emphasis on cultivating crops. This shift first occurred in the Mississippi River valley from Ohio, Indiana, and Illinois down to the Gulf of Mexico (see Map 6.5). Among the most commonly cultivated crops were maize, squash, beans, and various grasses.

As the population in the area increased, people began to congregate in villages, and sedentary communities began to develop in the alluvial lowlands, where the soil could be cultivated for many years at a time because of the nutrients deposited by the river water.

Village councils were established to adjudicate disputes, and in a few cases, several villages banded together under the authority of a local chieftain. Urban centers began to appear, some of them inhabited by ten thousand people or more. At the same time, regional trade increased. The people of the **Hopewell culture** in Ohio ranged from the shores of Lake Superior to the Appalachian Mountains and the Gulf of Mexico in search of metals, shells, obsidian, and manufactured items to support their economic needs and religious beliefs.

## Cahokia

At the site of Cahokia, near the modern city of East Saint Louis, Illinois, archaeologists found a burial mound more than 98 feet high with a base larger than that of the

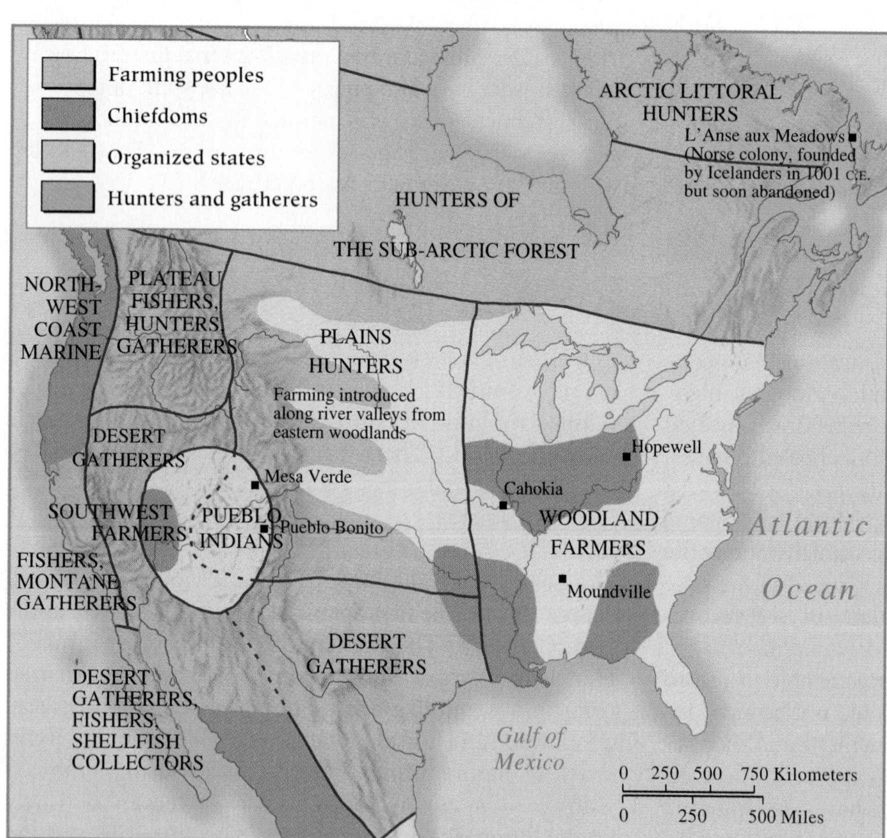


**MAP 6.5 Early Peoples and Cultures of North America.** This map shows regions of human settlement in pre-Columbian North America, including the short-lived Viking colony in Newfoundland. ? Where are the major urban centers located? **View an animated version of this map or related maps at** http://history.wadsworth.com/duikerspielvogel05/

Great Pyramid in Egypt. A hundred smaller mounds were also found in the vicinity. The town itself, which covered almost 300 acres and was surrounded by a wooden stockade, was apparently the administrative capital of much of the surrounding territory until its decline in the 1200s. With a population of over twenty thousand, it was reportedly the largest city in North America until Philadelphia surpassed that number in the early nineteenth century. Cahokia carried on extensive trade with other communities throughout the region, and there are some signs of regular contacts with the civilizations in Mesoamerica, such as the presence of ball courts in the Central American style. But wars were not uncommon, leading the Iroquois, who inhabited much of the modern states of Pennsylvania and New York as well as parts of southern Canada, to create a tribal alliance called the League of Iroquois.

## The "Ancient Ones": The Anasazi

West of the Mississippi River basin, most Amerindian peoples lived by hunting or food gathering. During the first millennium C.E., knowledge of agriculture gradually spread up the rivers to the Great Plains, and farming was practiced as far west as southwestern Colorado, where the Anasazi peoples (Navajo for "alien ancient ones") established an extensive agricultural community in an area extending from northern New Mexico and Arizona to southwestern Colorado and parts of southern Utah. Although they apparently never discovered the wheel or used beasts of burden, the Anasazi created a system of roads that facilitated an extensive exchange of technology, products, and ideas throughout the region. By the ninth century, they had mastered the art of irrigation, which allowed them to expand their productive efforts to squash and beans, and had established an important urban center at Chaco Canyon, in southern New Mexico, where they built a walled city with dozens of three-story adobe communal houses, called *pueblos,* with timbered roofs. Community religious functions were carried out in two large circular chambers called *kivas.* Clothing was made from hides or cotton cloth. At its height, Pueblo Bonito contained several hundred compounds housing several thousand residents.

In the mid-twelfth century, the Anasazi moved north to Mesa Verde, in southwestern Colorado. At first, they settled on top of the mesa, but eventually they expanded onto the cliffs of surrounding canyons.

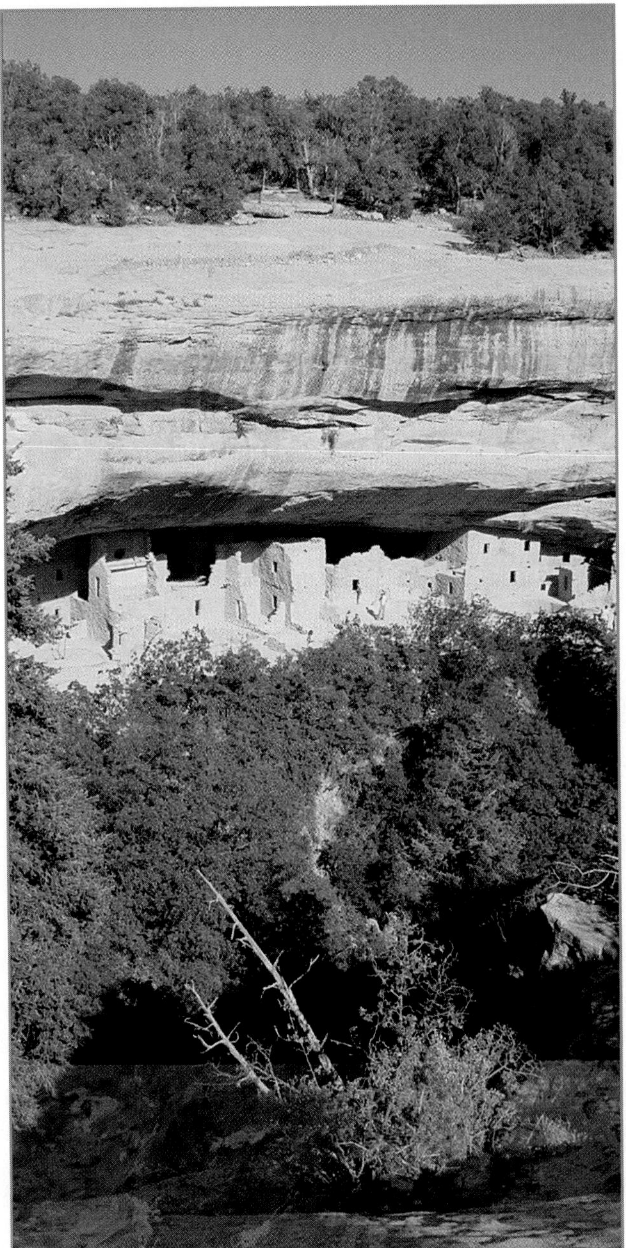
Courtesy of William J. Duiker

**Cliff Palace at Mesa Verde.** Mesa Verde is one of the best-developed sites of the Anasazi peoples in southwestern North America. At one time they were farmers who tilled the soil atop the mesas, but eventually they were forced to build their settlements in more protected locations. At Cliff Palace, shown here, adobe houses were hidden on the perpendicular face of the mesa. Access was achieved only by a perilous descent via indented finger- and toeholds on the rock face.

Sometime during the late thirteenth century, however, Mesa Verde was also abandoned, and the inhabitants migrated southward. Their descendants, the Zuni and the Hopi, now occupy pueblos in central Arizona and New Mexico. For years, archaeologists surmised that a severe drought was the cause of the migration, but new evidence has raised doubts that decreasing rainfall, by itself, was a sufficient explanation. An increase in internecine warfare, perhaps brought about by climatic changes, may also have played a role in the decision to relocate. Some archaeologists point to evidence that cannibalism was practiced at Pueblo Bonito and suggest that migrants from the south may have arrived in the area, provoking bitter rivalries within Anasazi society. In any event, with increasing aridity and the importation of the horse by the Spanish in the sixteenth century, hunting revived, and mounted nomads like the Apache and the Navajo came to dominate much of the Southwest.

## South America: The Arawak

East of the Andes Mountains in South America, other Amerindian societies were beginning to make the transition to agriculture. Perhaps the most prominent were the Arawak, a people living along the Orinoco River in modern Venezuela. Having begun to cultivate manioc (a tuber also known as *cassava* or *yuca,* the source of tapioca) along the banks of the river, they gradually migrated down to the coast and then proceeded to move eastward along the northern coast of the continent. Some occupied the islands of the Caribbean Sea. In their new island habitat, they lived by a mixture of fishing, hunting, and cultivating maize, beans, manioc, and squash, as well as other crops such as peanuts, peppers, and pineapples. As the population increased, a pattern of political organization above the village level appeared, along with recognizable social classes headed by a chieftain whose authority included control over the economy. The Arawak practiced human sacrifice, and some urban centers contained ball courts, suggesting the possibility of contacts with Mesoamerica.

In most such societies, where clear-cut class stratifications had not as yet taken place, men and women were considered of equal status. Men were responsible for hunting, warfare, and dealing with outsiders, while women were accountable for the crops, the distribution of food, maintaining the household, and bearing and raising the children. Their roles were complementary and were often viewed as a divine division of labor. In such cases, women in the stateless societies of North America held positions of greater respect than their counterparts in the river valley civilizations of the Old World.

## CONCLUSION

THE FIRST HUMAN BEINGS did not arrive in the Americas until quite late in the prehistorical period. For the next several millennia, their descendants were forced to respond to the challenges of the environment in total isolation from other parts of the world. Nevertheless, around 5000 B.C.E., farming settlements began to appear in river valleys and upland areas in both Central and South America. Not long afterward–as measured in historical time–organized communities located along the coast of the Gulf of Mexico and the western slopes of the central Andes Mountains embarked on the long march toward civilization. Along the same path, although perhaps somewhat less advanced in technological terms, were the emerging societies of North America, which were beginning to expand their commercial and cultural links with civilizations farther to the south and had already laid the foundations for future urbanization. Although the total number of people living in the Americas is a matter of debate, some scholars estimate a figure between ten and twenty million.

What is perhaps most striking about the developments in the New World is how closely the process paralleled that in the Old. Irrigated agriculture, long-distance trade, urbanization, and the development of a writing system were all hallmarks of the emergence of advanced societies of the classical type. One need only point to the awed comments of early Spanish visitors, who said that the cities of the Aztecs were the equal of Seville and the other great metropolitan centers of Spain.

In some respects, the societies that emerged in the Americas were not as advanced in technological terms as their counterparts elsewhere. They were not familiar with the process of smelting iron, for example, and they had not yet invented wheeled vehicles. Their writing systems, by comparison with those in the Old World, were still in their infancy. Several possible reasons have been advanced to explain this technological gap. Certainly geographic isolation–not only from people of other continents but also, in some cases, from each other–deprived them of the benefits of the diffusion of ideas that had assisted other societies in learning from their neighbors. In some ways, too, they were not as blessed by nature. As the sociologist Jared Diamond has pointed out, the Americas did not possess many indigenous varieties of edible grasses that could encourage hunter-gatherers to take up farming. Nor were there abundant large mammals that could easily be domesticated for food and transport. It was not until the arrival of the Europeans that such familiar attributes of civilization became widely available for human use in the Americas.[5]

At one time, scholars speculated that the societies of the Americas were largely peaceful and devoid of the widespread violence that plagued civilizations elsewhere. Recent evidence, however, suggests that the Amerindian peoples were every bit as addicted to warfare as those of the ancient empires of the Old World. Nevertheless, military prowess was of little help when the peoples of the Americas encountered the first visitors from overseas. The Europeans' advanced military technology and their mastery of horseback riding gave them a major advantage over the local population. Just as sedentary peoples in ancient Europe were often overwhelmed by nomads migrating westward from the steppes of Central Asia, so the armies of the Aztecs and the Inka were no match for the Spanish conquistadors, whose mobility on horseback had been increased through recent European contacts with Arab warriors in North Africa and the Middle East. Yet it should be noted that in the New World as in the Old, many of the first civilizations formed by the human species appear to have been brought to an end as much by environmental changes and disease as by war. In the next chapter, we shall return to the Old World, where new civilizations were in the process of replacing the ancient empires.

## TIMELINE

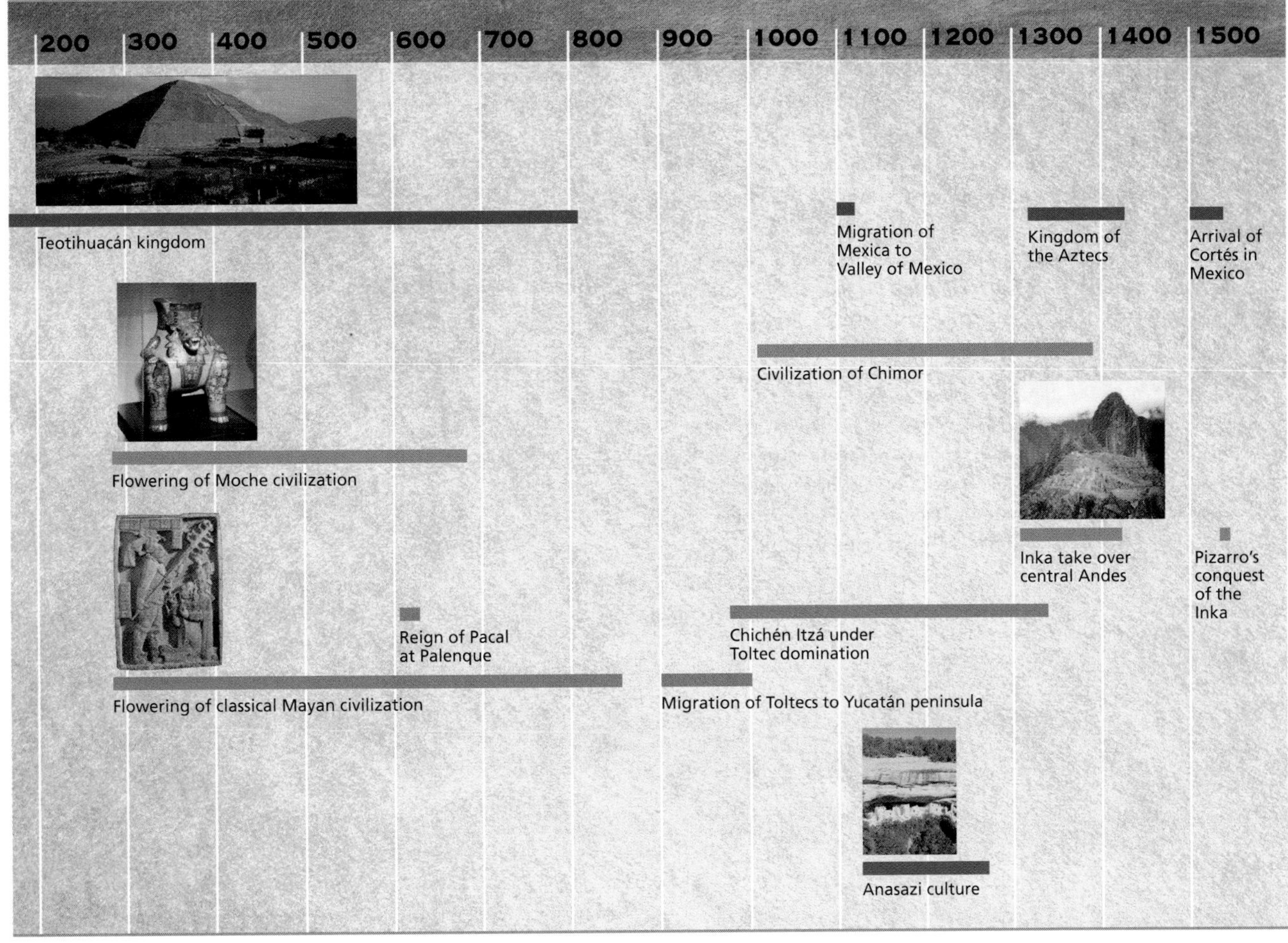


## CHAPTER NOTES

1. Quoted in S. Morley and G. W. Brainerd, *The Ancient Maya* (Stanford, Calif., 1983), p. 513.
2. B. Díaz, *The Conquest of New Spain* (Harmondsworth, England, 1975), p. 210.
3. Quoted in M. D. Coe, D. Snow, and E. P. Benson, *Atlas of Ancient America* (New York, 1988), p. 149.
4. G. de la Vega (El Inca), *Royal Commentaries of the Incas and General History of Peru,* pt. 1, trans. H. V. Livermore (Austin, Tex., 1966), p. 180.
5. J. Diamond, *Guns, Germs, and Steel: The Fates of Human Societies* (New York 1997), pp. 187–188.

## SUGGESTED READING

For a profusely illustrated and informative overview of the early civilizations of the Americas, see **M. D. Coe, D. Snow,** and **E. P. Benson, *Atlas of Ancient America*** (New York, 1988). The first arrival of human beings in the New World is discussed in **B. Fagan, *The Great Journey: The Peopling of Ancient America*** (London, 1987).

On Mayan civilization, see **D. Webster, *The Fall of the Ancient Maya: Solving the Mystery of the Maya Collapse*** (London, 2002). See also **M. D. Coe, *The Maya*** (London, 1993), and **J. Sabloff, *The New Archeology and the Ancient Maya*** (New York, 1990).

For an overview of Aztec civilization in Mexico, see **B. Fagan, *The Aztecs*** (New York, 1984). **S. D. Gillespie, *The Aztec Kings: The Construction of Rulership in Mexican History*** (Tucson, Ariz., 1989), is an imaginative effort to uncover the symbolic meaning in Aztec traditions. For a provocative study of religious traditions in a comparative context, see **B. Fagan, *From Black Land to Fifth Sun*** (Reading, Mass., 1998). On the Olmecs and the Zapotecs, see **E. P. Benson, *The Olmec and Their Neighbors*** (Washington, D.C., 1981); **M. D. Coe** and **R. A. Diehl, *In the Land of the Olmec*** (Austin, Tex., 1980); and **R. E. Blanton, *Monte Alban: Settlement Patterns at the Ancient Zapotec Capital*** (New York, 1978).

Much of our information about the lives of the peoples of ancient Central America comes from Spanish writers who visited or lived in the area during the sixteenth and seventeenth centuries. For the original Spanish conquest of Mexico, see **H. Cortés, *Letters from Mexico*** (New Haven, Conn., 1986), and **B. Díaz, *The Conquest of New Spain*** (Harmondsworth, England, 1975).

A worthy account of developments in South America is **G. Bawden, *The Moche*** (Oxford, 1996). On the Inka and their predecessors, see **R. W. Keatinge,** ed., ***Peruvian Prehistory: An Overview of Pre-Inca and Inca Society*** (Cambridge, 1988). The arrival of the Spanish is chronicled in **C. Howard, *Pizarro and the Conquest of Peru*** (New York, 1967).

On the art and culture of the ancient Americas, see **M. E. Miller, *Maya Art and Architecture*** (London, 1999); **E. Pasztory,**

*Pre-Columbian Art* (Cambridge, 1998); and **M. Léon-Portilla** and **E. Shorris,** ***In the Language of Kings*** (New York, 2001). Writing systems are discussed in **M. Coe,** ***Breaking the Maya Code*** (New York, 1992), and **G. Upton,** ***Signs of the Inka Quipu*** (Austin, Tex., 2003).

On social issues, see **L. Schele** and **D. Freidel,** ***A Forest of Kings: The Untold Story of the Ancient Maya*** (New York, 1990); **R. van Zantwijk,** ***The Aztec Arrangement: The Social History of Pre-Spanish Mexico*** (Norman, Okla., 1985); and **N. Shoemaker,** ***Negotiators of Change: Historical Perspectives on Native American Women*** (New York, 1995).

For a treatment of the role of the environment, see **B. Fagan,** ***Floods, Famine, and Emperors: El Niño and the Fate of Civilizations*** (New York, 1999).

## History Now™

**Enter *HistoryNow* using the access card that is available with this text. *HistoryNow* will assist you in understanding the content in this chapter with lesson plans generated for your needs, as well as provide you with a connection to the *Wadsworth World History Resource Center* (see description at right for details).**

## WORLD HISTORY RESOURCE CENTER

**Enter the Resource Center using either your *HistoryNow* access card or your standalone access card for the *Wadsworth World History Resource Center.* Organized by topic, this website includes quizzes; images; over 350 primary source documents; interactive simulations; maps and timelines; movie explorations; and a wealth of other resources. You can read the following documents, and many more, at** http://history.wadsworth.com/rc/world

Popul Voh

Visit the *World History* Companion Website for chapter quizzes and more.

http://history.wadsworth.com/duikerspielvogel05/

CHAPTER

# ISLAM AND BYZANTIUM

Muhammad rises to Heaven

British Library/Bridgeman Art Library

## CHAPTER OUTLINE AND FOCUS QUESTIONS

### The Rise of Islam

- What were the main tenets of Islam, and how does the religion compare with Judaism and Christianity?

### The Arab Empire and Its Successors

- Why did the Arabs undergo such a rapid expansion in the seventh and eighth centuries, and why were they so successful in creating an empire?

### Islamic Civilization

- What were the main features of Islamic society and culture during its era of early growth?

### The Byzantine Empire

- What were the main features of Byzantine civilization, and why did it follow a separate path from that taken by Christian societies in the West?

### CRITICAL THINKING

- In what ways did Byzantine and Islamic civilizations resemble and differ from each other? Was their relationship overall based on cooperation or conflict?

**IN THE YEAR 570**, in the Arabian city of Mecca, there was born a child named Muhammad whose life changed the course of world history. The son of a merchant, Muhammad grew to maturity in a time of transition. Old empires that had once ruled the entire Middle East were only a distant memory. The region was now divided into many separate states, and the people adhered to many different faiths.

According to tradition, the young Muhammad became deeply concerned at the corrupt and decadent society of his day and took to wandering in the hills outside the city to meditate on the conditions of his time. On one of these occasions, he experienced visions that he was convinced had been inspired by Allah. Muslims believe that this message had been conveyed to him by the angel Gabriel, who commanded Muhammad to preach the revelations that he would be given. Eventually, they would be transcribed into the holy book of Islam—the Qur'an—and provide inspiration to millions of people throughout the world.

Within a few decades of Muhammad's death, the Middle East was united once again. The initial triumph may have been primarily political and military, based on the transformative power of a dynamic new religion that inspired thousands of devotees to extend their faith to neighboring regions.

Islamic beliefs and culture exerted a powerful influence in all areas occupied by Arab armies. Initially, Arab beliefs and customs, as reflected through the prism of Muhammad's teachings, transformed the societies and cultures of the peoples living in the new empire. But eventually, the distinctive political and cultural forces that had long characterized the region began to reassert themselves. Factional struggles led to the decline and then the destruction of the empire.

Still, the Arab conquest left a powerful legacy that survived the decline of Arab political power. The ideological and emotional appeal of Islam remained strong throughout the Middle East and eventually extended into areas not occupied by Arab armies, such as the Indian subcontinent, Southeast Asia, and sub-Saharan Africa. ◇

# The Rise of Islam

The Arabs were a Semitic-speaking people of southwestern Asia with a long history. They were mentioned in Greek sources of the fifth century B.C.E. and even earlier in the Old Testament. The Greek historian Herodotus had applied the name *Arab* to the entire peninsula, calling it Arabia. In 106 B.C.E., the Romans extended their authority to the Arabian peninsula, transforming it into a province of their growing empire.

During Roman times, the region was inhabited primarily by the **Bedouin** Arabs, nomadic peoples who came originally from the northern part of the peninsula. Bedouin society was organized on a tribal basis. The ruling member of the tribe was called the ***sheikh*** and was selected from one of the leading families by a council of elders called the ***majlis.*** The *sheikh* ruled the tribe with the consent of the council. Each tribe was autonomous but felt a general sense of allegiance to the larger unity of all the clans in the region. In early times, the Bedouins had supported themselves primarily by sheepherding or by raiding passing caravans, but after the domestication of the camel during the second millennium B.C.E., the Bedouins began to participate in the caravan trade themselves and became major carriers of goods between the Persian Gulf and the Mediterranean Sea.

The Arabs of pre-Islamic times were polytheistic, with a supreme god known as Allah presiding over a community of spirits. It was a communal faith, involving all members of the tribe, and had no priesthood. Spirits were believed to inhabit natural objects, such as trees, rivers, and mountains, while the supreme deity was symbolized by a sacred stone. Each tribe possessed its own stone, but by the time of Muhammad, a massive black meteorite, housed in a central shrine called the Ka'aba in the commercial city of Mecca, had to come to possess especially sacred qualities.

## The Role of Muhammad

Into this world came Muhammad (also known as Mohammed), a man whose spiritual visions unified the Arab world (see Map 7.1) with a speed no one would have suspected possible. Born in Mecca to a merchant family and orphaned at the age of six, Muhammad (570–632) grew up to become a caravan manager and eventually married a rich widow, Khadija, who was also his employer. For several years, he lived in Mecca as a merchant but, according to tradition, was apparently troubled by the growing gap between the Bedouin values of honesty and generosity (he himself was a member of the local Hashemite clan of the Quraishi tribe) and the acquisitive behavior of the affluent commercial elites in the city. Deeply concerned, he began to visit the nearby hills to meditate in isolation. It was there that he encountered the angel Gabriel who commanded him to preach the revelations that he would be given.

It is said that Muhammad was acquainted with Jewish and Christian beliefs and came to believe that while Allah had already revealed himself in part through Moses and Jesus—and thus through the Hebraic and Christian traditions—the final revelations were now being given to him. Out of his revelations, which were eventually dictated to scribes, came the Qur'an ("recitation," also spelled Koran), the holy scriptures of Islam (*Islam* means "submission," implying submission to the will of Allah). The Qur'an contained the guidelines by which followers of Allah, known as

Mehmet Biber/Photo Researchers, Inc

**The Ka'aba in Mecca.** The Ka'aba, the shrine containing a black meteorite in the Arabian city of Mecca, is the most sacred site of the Islamic faith. Wherever Muslims pray, they are instructed to face Mecca; each thus becomes a spoke of the Ka'aba, the holy center of the wheel of Islam. If they are able to do so, all Muslims are encouraged to visit the Ka'aba at least once in their lifetime. Called the *hajj,* this pilgrimage to Mecca represents the ultimate in spiritual fulfillment.

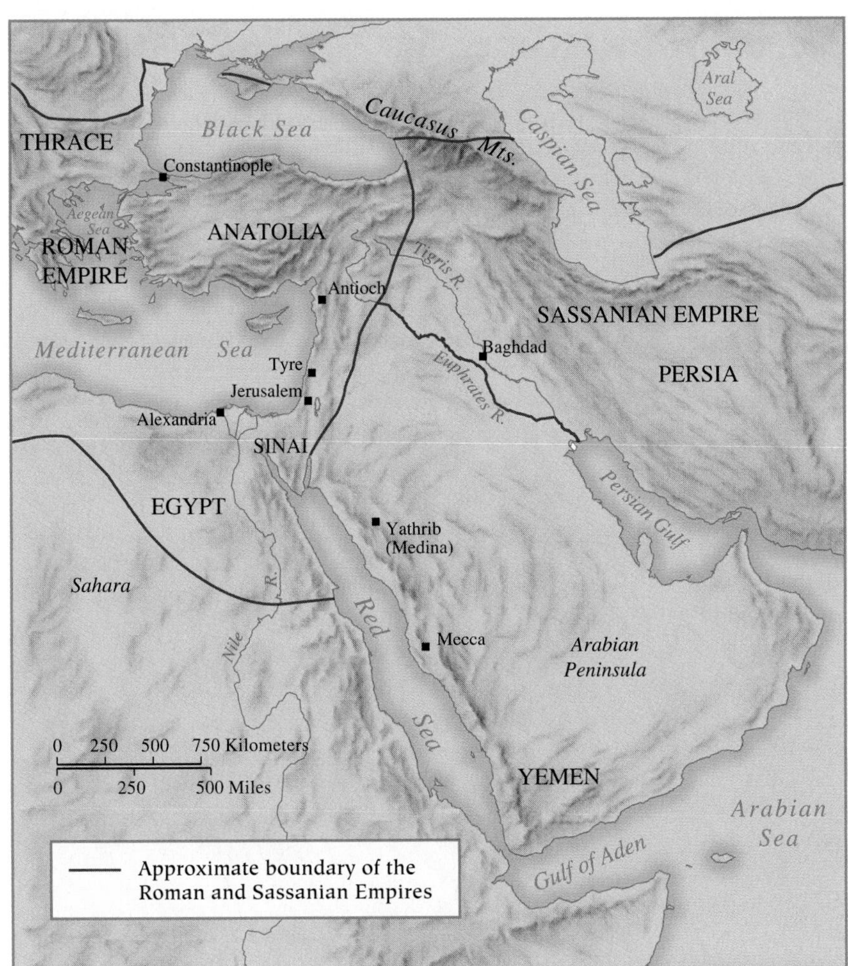


**MAP 7.1 The Middle East in the Time of Muhammad** When Islam began to spread throughout the Middle East in the early seventh century, the dominant states in the region were the Roman Empire in the eastern Mediterranean and the Sassanian Empire in Persia. What were the major territorial divisions existing at the time and the key sites connected to the rise of Islam? **View an animated version of this map or related maps at** http://history.wadsworth.com/duikerspielvogel05/

Muslims (practitioners of Islam), were to live. Like the Christians and the Jews, Muslims (also known as Moslems) were a "people of the Book," believers in a faith based on scripture.

Muslims believe that after returning home, Muhammad set out to comply with Gabriel's command by preaching to the residents of Mecca about his revelations. At first, many were convinced that he was a madman or a charlatan. Others were undoubtedly concerned that his vigorous attacks on traditional beliefs and the corrupt society around him could severely shake the social and political order. After three years of proselytizing, he had only thirty followers.

Discouraged, perhaps, by the systematic persecution of his followers, which was allegedly undertaken with a brutality reminiscent of the cruelties suffered by early Christians, as well as the failure of the Meccans to accept his message, in 622 Muhammad and some of his closest supporters (mostly from his own Hashemite clan) left the city and retreated north to the rival city of Yathrib, later renamed Medina, or "city of the Prophet." That flight, known in history as the **Hegira** (*Hijrah*), marks the first date on the official calendar of Islam. At Medina, Muhammad failed in his original purpose—to convert the Jewish community in Medina to his beliefs. But he was successful in winning support from many residents of the city as well as from Bedouins in the surrounding countryside. From this mixture, he formed the first Muslim community (the ***umma***). Returning to his birthplace at the head of a considerable military force, Muhammad conquered Mecca and converted the townspeople to the new faith. In 630, he made a symbolic visit to the Ka'aba, where he declared it a sacred shrine of Islam and ordered the destruction of the idols of the traditional faith. Two years later, Muhammad died, just as Islam was beginning to spread throughout the peninsula.

## The Teachings of Muhammad

Like Christianity and Judaism, Islam is monotheistic. Allah is the all-powerful being who created the universe and everything in it. Islam is also concerned with salvation and offers the hope of an afterlife. Those who hope to achieve it must subject themselves to the will of Allah. Unlike Christianity, Islam makes no claim to the divinity of its founder. Muhammad, like Abraham, Moses, and other figures of the Old Testament, was a prophet, but he was also a man like other men. Because, according to the Qur'an, earlier prophets had corrupted his revelations, Allah sent his complete revelation through Muhammad.

At the heart of Islam is the Qur'an, with its basic message that there is no God but Allah and Muhammad is his

## THE QUR'AN: THE PILGRIMAGE

The Qur'an is the sacred book of the Muslims, comparable to the Bible in Christianity. This selection from Sura 22, titled "Pilgrimage," discusses the importance of making a pilgrimage to Mecca, one of the Five Pillars of Islam. The pilgrim's final destination was the Ka'aba at Mecca, containing the Black Stone.

*What is the key purpose of undertaking a pilgrimage to Mecca? What is the historical importance of the sacred stone?*

### Qur'an, Sura 22: "Pilgrimage"

Exhort all men to make the pilgrimage. They will come to you on foot and on the backs of swift camels from every distant quarter; they will come to avail themselves of many a benefit, and to pronounce on the appointed days the name of God over the cattle which He has given them for food. Eat of their flesh, and feed the poor and the unfortunate.

Then let the pilgrims tidy themselves, make their vows, and circle the Ancient House. Such is God's commandment. He that reveres the sacred rites of God shall fare better in the sight of his Lord.

The flesh of cattle is lawful for you, except for that which has been specified before. Guard yourselves against the filth of idols; and avoid the utterance of falsehoods.

Dedicate yourselves to God, and serve none besides Him. The man who serves other deities besides God is like him who falls from heaven and is snatched by the birds or carried away by the wind to some far-off region. Even such is he.

He that reveres the offerings made to God shows the piety of his heart. Your cattle are useful to you in many ways until the time of their slaughter. Then they are offered for sacrifice at the Ancient House.

For every community We have ordained a ritual, that they may pronounce the name of God over the cattle which He has given them for food. Your God is one God; to Him surrender yourselves. Give good news to the humble, whose hearts are filled with awe at the mention of God; who endure adversity with fortitude, attend to their prayers, and give in alms from what We gave them.

We have made the camels a part of God's rites. They are of much use to you. Pronounce over them the name of God as you draw them up in line and slaughter them; and when they have fallen to the ground eat of their flesh and feed the uncomplaining beggar and the demanding supplicant. Thus have We subjected them to your service, so that you may give thanks.

Their flesh and blood does not reach God; it is your piety that reaches Him. Thus has He subjected them to your service, so that you may give glory to God for guiding you.

Give good news to the righteous. God will ward off evil from true believers. God does not love the treacherous and the thankless.

**HistoryNow™** To read a full version of the Qur'an, enter the *HistoryNow* documents area using the access card that is available for *World History.*

Prophet. Consisting of 114 *suras* (chapters) drawn together by a committee established after Muhammad's death, the Qur'an is not only the sacred book of Islam but also an ethical guidebook and a code of law and political theory combined.

As it evolved, Islam developed a number of fundamental tenets. At its heart lies the need to obey the will of Allah. This meant following a basic ethical code that consisted of what are popularly termed the **Five Pillars of Islam:** belief in Allah and Muhammad as his Prophet; standard prayer five times a day and public prayer on Friday at midday to worship Allah; observation of the holy month of **Ramadan,** including fasting from dawn to sunset; making a pilgrimage, if possible, to Mecca at least once in one's lifetime (see the box above); and giving alms (*zakat*) to the poor and unfortunate. The faithful who observed the law were guaranteed a place in an eternal paradise (a vision of a luxurious and cool garden shared by some versions of Eastern Christianity) with the sensuous delights so obviously lacking in the midst of the Arabian desert.

Islam was not just a set of religious beliefs but a way of life as well. After the death of Muhammad, Muslim scholars, known as the ***ulama,*** drew up a law code, called the ***Shari'a,*** to provide believers with a set of prescriptions to regulate their daily lives. Much of the *Shari'a* was drawn from existing legal regulations or from the ***Hadith,*** a collection of the sayings of the Prophet that was used to supplement the revelations contained in the holy scriptures.

Believers were subject to strict behavioral requirements. In addition to the Five Pillars, Muslims were forbidden to gamble, to eat pork, to drink alcoholic beverages, and to engage in dishonest behavior. Sexual mores were also strict. Contacts between unmarried men and women were discouraged, and ideally marriages were to be arranged by the parents. In accordance with Bedouin custom, polygyny was permitted, but Muhammad attempted to limit the practice by restricting males to four wives.

To what degree the traditional account of the exposition and inner meaning of the Qur'an can stand up to historical analysis is a matter of debate. The circumstances surrounding the life of Muhammad and his role in founding the religion of Islam, given the lack of verifiable evidence, remain highly speculative, and many Muslims are undoubtedly concerned that the consequences of rigorous examination might undercut key tenets of the Muslim faith. One of the problems connected with such an effort is that the earliest known ver-

British Library/Bridgeman Art Library

**Ascension of the Prophet Muhammad.** Shown here is an illustration of Muhammad's ascension to Heaven, as described in the Qur'an. Muhammad is veiled, in accordance with the accepted practice of not showing his facial features. Riding a celestial creature with the face of a woman, he arrives in Jerusalem to join Abraham, Jesus, and other prophets in prayer at the site of the Temple of Solomon. From there he ascends to Heaven to meet Allah, thus making the Dome of the Rock one of the sacred sites of the Muslim religion. Then Muhammad returned to Mecca, where he died in the year 632.

sions of the Qur'an available today do not contain the diacritical marks that modern Arabic uses to clarify meaning, thus leaving much of the sacred text ambiguous and open to varying interpretations.

# The Arab Empire and Its Successors

The death of Muhammad presented his followers with a dilemma. Although Muhammad had not claimed divine qualities, Muslims saw no separation between political and religious authority. Submission to the will of Allah meant submission to his Prophet Muhammad. According to the Qur'an, "Whoso obeyeth the messenger obeyeth Allah."[1] Muhammad's charismatic authority and political skills had been at the heart of his success. But Muslims have never agreed whether or not he named a successor, and although he had several daughters, he left no sons. In the male-oriented society of his day, who would lead the community of the faithful?

Shortly after Muhammad's death, a number of his closest followers selected Abu Bakr, a wealthy merchant from Medina who was Muhammad's father-in-law and one of his first supporters, as **caliph** (*khalifa,* literally "successor"). The caliph was the temporal leader of the Islamic community and was also considered, in general terms, to be a religious leader, or ***imam.*** Under Abu Bakr's prudent leadership, the movement succeeded in suppressing factional tendencies among some of the Bedouin tribes in the peninsula and began to direct its attention to wider fields. Muhammad had used the Arabic tribal custom of the *razzia* or raid in the struggle against his enemies. Now his successors turned to the same custom to expand the authority of the movement. The Qur'an called this activity "striving in the way of the Lord," or ***jihad.*** Although sometimes translated as "holy war," the term is ambiguous and has been subject to varying interpretations.

## Creation of an Empire

Once the Arabs had become unified under Muhammad's successor, they began directing outward against neighboring peoples the energy they had formerly directed against each other. The Byzantine and Sassanian Empires were the first to feel the strength of the newly united Arabs, now aroused to a peak of zeal by their common faith. At Yarmuk in 636, the Muslims defeated the Byzantine army. Four years later, they took possession of the Byzantine province of Syria. To the east, the Arabs defeated a Persian force in 637 and then went on to conquer the entire empire of the Sassanids by 650. In the meantime, Egypt and other areas of North Africa were also brought under Arab authority (see Chapter 8).

What accounts for this rapid expansion of the Arabs after the rise of Islam in the early seventh century? Historians have proposed various explanations, ranging from a prolonged drought on the Arabian peninsula to the desire of Islam's leaders to channel the energies of their new converts. Another hypothesis is that the expansion was deliberately planned by the ruling elites in Mecca to extend their trade routes and bring surplus-producing regions under their control. Whatever the case, Islam's ability to unify the Bedouin peoples certainly played a role. Although the Arab triumph was made substantially easier by the ongoing conflict between the Byzantine and Persian Empires, which had weakened both powers, the strength of the Bedouin armies should not be overlooked. Led by a series of brilliant generals, the Arabs put together a large, highly motivated army, whose valor was enhanced by the belief that Muslim warriors who died in battle were guaranteed a place in paradise.

Once the armies had prevailed, Arab administration of the conquered areas was generally tolerant. Sometimes, due

## A Pilgrimage to Mecca

The pilgrimage to Mecca, one of the Five Pillars of Islam, is the duty of every Muslim. Ibn Jubayr, a twelfth-century Spanish Muslim, left a description of his trip in his journal. The work is famous for its vivid and abundant detail. In this almost lyrical passage, Ibn Jubayr tells of reaching his final destination, the Ka'aba at Mecca, containing the Black Stone. The Qarmata were an extremist religious sect in ninth- and tenth-century Mesopotamia.

*What are the other Pillars of Islam? How does each tasks contribute to making a good Muslim?*

### Ibn Jubayr, *Travels*

The blessed Black Stone is encased in the corner [of the Ka'aba] facing east. The depth to which it penetrates it is not known, but it is said to extend two cubits into the wall. Its breadth is two-thirds of a span, its length one span and a finger joint. It has four pieces, joined together, and it is said that it was the Qarmata–may God curse them–who broke it. Its edges have been braced with a sheet of silver whose white shines brightly against the black sheen and polished brilliance of the Stone, presenting the observer a striking spectacle which will hold his gaze. The Stone, when kissed, has a softness and moistness which so enchants the mouth that he who puts his lips to it would wish them never to be removed. This is one of the special favors of Divine Providence, and it is enough that the Prophet–may God bless and preserve him–declare it to be a covenant of God on earth. May God profit us by the kissing and touching of it. By His favor may all who yearn fervently for it be brought to it. In the sound piece of the stone, to the right of him who presents himself to kiss it, is a small white spot that shines and appears like a mole on the blessed surface. Concerning this white mole, there is a tradition that he who looks upon it clears his vision, and when kissing it one should direct one's lips as closely as one can to the place of the mole.

to a shortage of trained Arab administrators, government was left to local officials. Conversion to Islam was generally voluntary in accordance with the maxim in the Qur'an that "there shall be no compulsion in religion."[2] Those who chose not to convert were required only to submit to Muslim rule and pay a head tax in return for exemption from military service, which was required of all Muslim males. Under such conditions, the local populations often welcomed Arab rule as preferable to Byzantine rule or that of the Sassanid dynasty in Persia. Furthermore, the simple and direct character of the new religion, as well as its egalitarian qualities (all people were viewed as equal in the eyes of Allah), were undoubtedly attractive to peoples throughout the region (see the box above).

## The Rise of the Umayyads

The main challenge to the growing empire came from within. Some of Muhammad's followers had not agreed with the selection of Abu Bakr as the first caliph and promoted the candidacy of Ali, Muhammad's cousin and son-in-law, as an alternative. Ali's claim was ignored by other leaders, however, and after Abu Bakr's death, the office was passed to Umar, another of Muhammad's followers. In 656, Umar's successor, Uthman, was assassinated, and Ali was finally selected for the position. But according to tradition, Ali's rivals were convinced that he had been implicated in the death of his predecessor, and a factional struggle broke out within the Muslim leadership. In 661, Ali himself was assassinated, and Mu'awiya, the governor of Syria and one of Ali's chief rivals, replaced him in office. Mu'awiya thereupon made the caliphate hereditary in his own family, called the Umayyads, who were a branch of the Quraishi clan. The new caliphate, with its capital at Damascus, remained in power for nearly a century.

The factional struggle within Islam did not bring an end to Arab expansion. At the beginning of the eighth century, new attacks were launched at both the western and the eastern ends of the Mediterranean world (see Map 7.2). Arab armies advanced across North Africa and conquered the Berbers, a primarily pastoral people living along the Mediterranean coast and in the mountains in the interior. Then, around 710, Arab forces, supplemented by Berber allies under their commander, Tariq, crossed the Strait of Gibraltar and occupied southern Spain. The Visigothic kingdom, already weakened by internecine warfare, quickly collapsed, and by 725, most of the Iberian peninsula had become a Muslim state with its center in Andalusia. Seven years later, an Arab force, making a foray into southern France, was defeated by the army of Charles Martel between Tours and Poitiers. Some historians think that internal exhaustion would have forced the invaders to retreat even without their defeat at the hands of the Franks. In any event, the Battle of Tours (or Poitiers) would be the high-water mark of Arab expansion in Europe.

In the meantime, in 717, another Muslim force had launched an attack on Constantinople with the hope of destroying the Byzantine Empire. But the Byzantines' use of Greek fire, a petroleum-based compound containing quicklime and sulfur, destroyed the Muslim fleet, thus saving the empire and indirectly Christian Europe, since the fall of Constantinople would have opened the door to an Arab invasion of eastern Europe. The Byzantine Empire and Islam now established an uneasy frontier in southern Asia Minor.

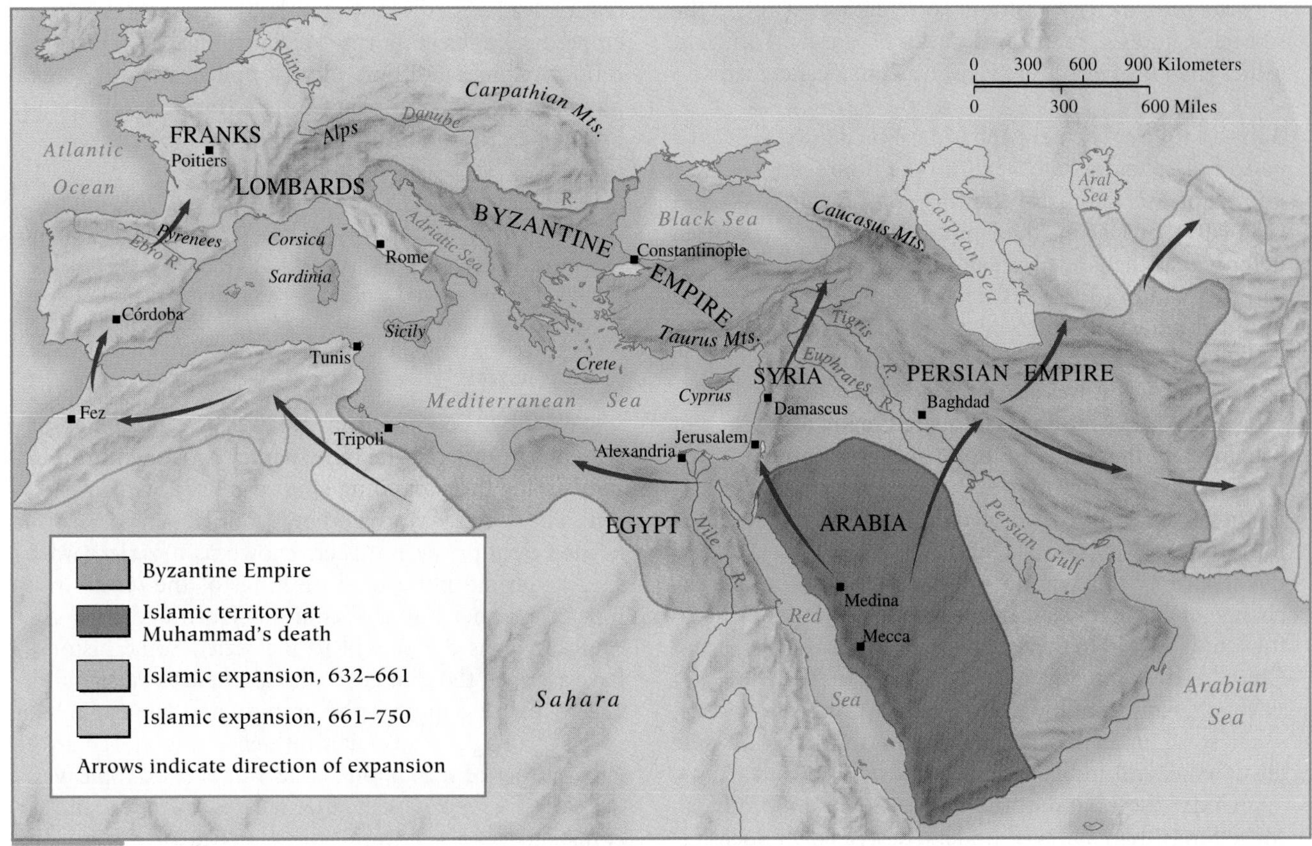


**MAP 7.2 The Expansion of Islam.** This map shows the expansion of the Islamic faith from its origins in the Arabian peninsula. Muhammad's followers carried the religion as far west as Spain and southern France and eastward to India and Southeast Asia. **?** In which of these areas is the Muslim faith still the dominant religion? **View an animated version of this map or related maps at http://history.wadsworth.com/duikerspielvogel05/**

## Succession Problems

Arab power also extended to the east, consolidating Islamic rule in Mesopotamia and Persia and northward into Central Asia. But factional disputes continued to plague the empire. Many Muslims of non-Arab extraction resented the favoritism shown by local administrators to Arabs. In some cases, resentment led to revolt, as in Iraq, where Ali's second son, Hussein, disputed the legitimacy of the Umayyads and incited his supporters—to be known in the future as **Shi'ites** (from the Arabic phrase *shi'at Ali*, "partisans of Ali")—to rise up against Umayyad rule in 680. Hussein's forces were defeated, but a schism between Shi'ite and **Sunni** (usually translated as "orthodox") Muslims had been created that continues to this day.

Umayyad rule, always (in historian Arthur Goldschmidt's words) "more political than pious," created resentment, not only in Mesopotamia, but also in North Africa, where Berber resistance continued, especially in the mountainous areas south of the coastal plains. According to critics, the Umayyads may have contributed to their own demise by their decadent behavior. One caliph allegedly swam in a pool of wine and then imbibed enough of the contents to lower the level significantly. Finally, in 750, a revolt led by Abu al-Abbas, a descendant of Muhammad's uncle, led to the overthrow of the Umayyads and the establishment of the Abbasid dynasty (750–1258) in what is now Iraq.

## The Abbasids

The Abbasid caliphs brought political, economic, and cultural change to the world of Islam. While seeking to implant their own version of religious orthodoxy, they tried to break down the distinctions between Arab and non-Arab Muslims. All Muslims were now allowed to hold both civil and military offices. This change helped open Islamic culture to the influences of the occupied civilizations. Many Arabs now began to intermarry with the peoples they had conquered. In many parts of the Islamic world, notably North Africa and the eastern Mediterranean, most Muslim converts began to consider themselves Arabs. In 762, the Abbasids built a new capital city at Baghdad, on the Tigris River far to the east of the Umayyad capital at Damascus. The new capital was strategically positioned to take advantage of river traffic to the Persian Gulf and also lay astride the caravan route from the Mediterranean to Central Asia. The move eastward allowed Persian influence to come to the fore, encouraging a new cultural orientation. Under the Abbasids, judges, merchants, and government officials, rather than warriors, were viewed as the ideal citizens.

**Abbasid Rule** The new Abbasid caliphate experienced a period of splendid rule well into the ninth century. Best known of the caliphs of the time was Harun al-Rashid (786–809), or Harun "the Upright," whose reign is often described as the golden age of the Abbasid caliphate. His son al-Ma'mun (813–833) was a patron of learning who founded an astronomical observatory and established a foundation for undertaking translations of classical Greek works. This was also a period of growing economic prosperity. The Arabs had conquered many of the richest provinces of the Roman Empire and now controlled the routes to the east (see Map 7.3). Baghdad became the center of an enormous commercial market that extended into Europe, Central Asia, and Africa, greatly adding to the wealth of the Islamic world and promoting an exchange of culture, ideas, and technology from one end of the known world to the other. Paper was introduced from China and eventually passed on to North Africa and Europe. Crops from India and Southeast Asia such as rice, sugar, sorghum, and cotton moved toward the west, while glass, wine, and indigo dye were introduced into China.

Under the Abbasids, the caliphs became more regal. More kings than spiritual leaders, described by such august phrases as the "caliph of God," they ruled by autocratic means, hardly distinguishable from the kings and emperors in neighboring civilizations. A thirteenth-century Chinese author, who compiled a world geography based on accounts by Chinese travelers, left the following description of one of the later caliphs:

> The king wears a turban of silk brocade and foreign cotton stuff [buckram]. On each new moon and full moon he puts on an eight-sided flat-topped headdress of pure gold, set with the most precious jewels in the world. His robe is of silk brocade and is bound around him with a jade girdle. On his feet he wears golden shoes. . . . The king's throne is set with pearls and precious stones, and the steps of the throne are covered with pure gold.[3]

As the caliph took on more of the trappings of a hereditary autocrat, the bureaucracy assisting him in administering the expanding empire grew more complex as well. The caliph was advised by a council (called a ***diwan***) headed by a prime minister, known as a ***vizier*** (*wazir*). The caliph did not attend meetings of the *diwan* in the normal manner but sat behind a screen and then communicated his divine will to the *vizier.* Some historians have ascribed the change in the caliphate to Persian influence, which permeated the empire after the capital was moved to Baghdad. Persian influence was indeed strong (the mother of the caliph al-Ma'mun, for example, was a Persian), but more likely, the increase in pomp and circumstance was a natural consequence of the growing power and prosperity of the empire.

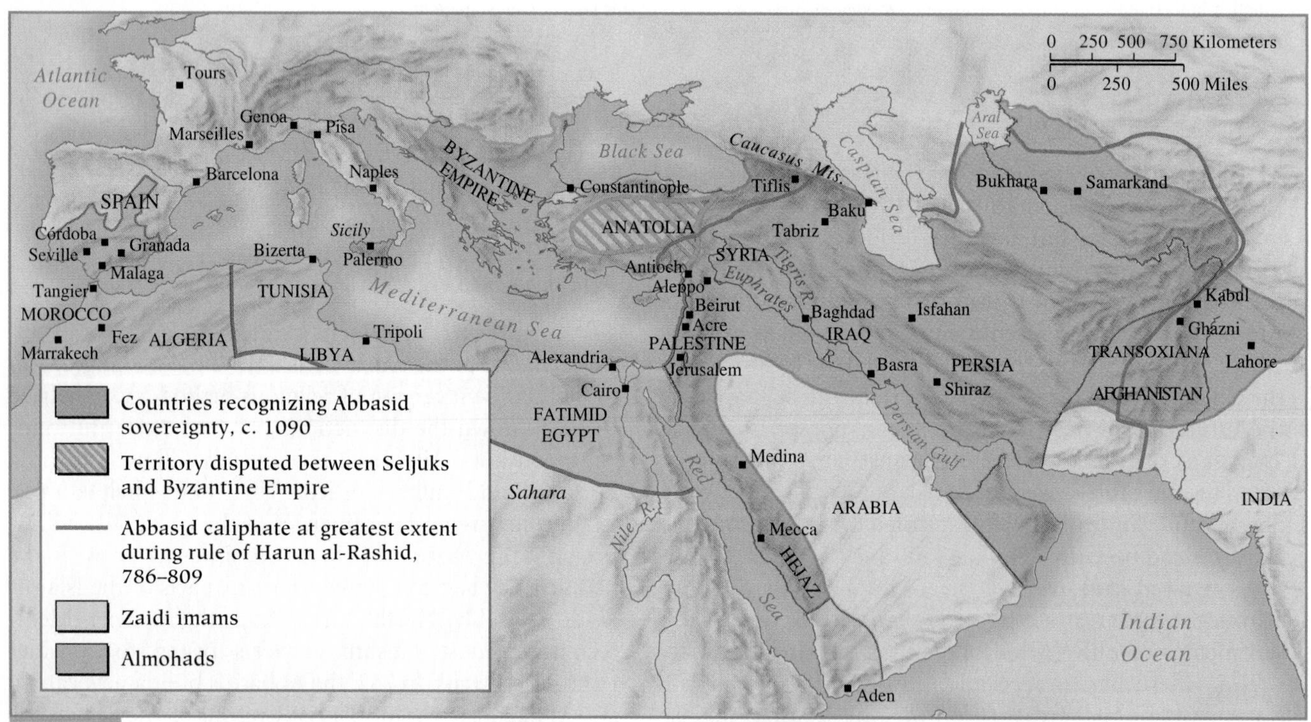


**MAP 7.3 The Abbasid Caliphate at the Height of Its Power.** The Abbasids arose in the eighth century as he defenders of the Muslim faith and established their capital at Baghdad. With its prowess as a trading state, the caliphate was the most powerful and extensive state in the region for several centuries. ? What were the major urban centers under the influence of Islam, as shown on this map?

**View an animated version of this map or related maps at** http://history.wadsworth.com/ duikerspielvogel05/

**Instability and Division** However, an element of instability lurked beneath the surface. The lack of spiritual authority may have weakened the caliphate in competition with its potential rivals, and disputes over succession were common. At Harun's death, the rivalry between his two sons, Amin and al-Ma'mun, led to civil war and the destruction of Baghdad. As described by the tenth-century Muslim historian al-Mas'udi, "Mansions were destroyed, most remarkable monuments obliterated; prices soared. . . . Brother turned his sword against brother, son against father, as some fought for Amin, others for Ma'mun. Houses and palaces fueled the flames; property was put to the sack."[4]

Wealth contributed to financial corruption. By awarding important positions to court favorites, the Abbasid caliphs began to undermine the foundations of their own power and eventually became mere figureheads. Under Harun al-Rashid, members of his Hashemite clan received large pensions from the state treasury, and his wife, Zubaida, reportedly spent huge sums while shopping on a pilgrimage to Mecca. One powerful family, the Barmakids, amassed vast wealth and power until Harun al-Rashid eliminated the entire clan in a fit of jealousy.

The life of luxury enjoyed by the caliph and other political and economic elites in Baghdad seemingly undermined the stern fiber of Arab society as well as the strict moral code of Islam. Strictures against sexual promiscuity were widely ignored, and caliphs were rumored to maintain thousands of concubines in their harems. Divorce was common, homosexuality was widely practiced, and alcohol was consumed in public despite Islamic law's prohibition against imbibing spirits.

The process of disintegration was accelerated by changes that were taking place within the armed forces and the bureaucracy of the empire. Given the shortage of qualified Arabs for key positions in the army and the administration, the caliphate began to recruit officials from among the non-Arab peoples in the empire, such as Persians and Turks from Central Asia. These people gradually became a dominant force in the army and administration.

Provincial rulers also began to break away from central control and establish their own independent dynasties. Already in the eighth century, a separate caliphate had been established in Spain when Abd al-Rahman of the Umayyad dynasty had fled there. In 756, he seized control of southern Spain and then expanded his power into the center of the peninsula. He took the title of ***emir,*** or commander, and set up the emirate of al-Andalus (the Arabic name for Spain) with its center at Córdoba. The rulers of al-Andalus developed a unique society in which all religions were tolerated. The court also supported writers and artists, creating a brillant and flourishing culture.

The fragmentation of the Islamic empire accelerated in the tenth century. Morocco became independent, and in 973, a new Shi'ite dynasty under the Fatimids was established in Egypt with its capital at Cairo. With increasing disarray in the empire, the Islamic world was held together only by the common commitment to the Arabic and the use of Qur'an as the prevailing means of communication.

## The Seljuk Turks

In the eleventh century, the Abbasid caliphate faced yet another serious threat in the form of the Seljuk Turks. The Seljuk Turks were a nomadic people from Central Asia who had converted to Islam and flourished as military mercenaries for the Abbasid caliphate, where they were known for their ability as mounted archers. Moving gradually into Iran and Armenia as the Abbasids weakened, the Seljuk Turks grew in number until by the eleventh century, they were able to occupy the eastern provinces of the Abbasid empire. In 1055, a Turkish leader captured Baghdad and assumed command of the empire with the title of **sultan** ("holder of power"). While the Abbasid caliph remained the chief representative of Sunni religious authority, the real military and political power of the state was in the hands of the Seljuk Turks. The latter did not establish their headquarters in Baghdad, which now entered a period of decline.

By the last quarter of the eleventh century, the Seljuks were exerting military pressure on Egypt and the Byzantine Empire. In 1071, when the Byzantines foolishly challenged the Turks, their army was routed at Manzikert, near Lake Van in eastern Turkey, and the victors took over most of the Anatolian peninsula (see Map 7.4). In dire straits, the Byzantine Empire turned to the west for help, setting in motion the papal pleas that led to the **Crusades** (see the next section).

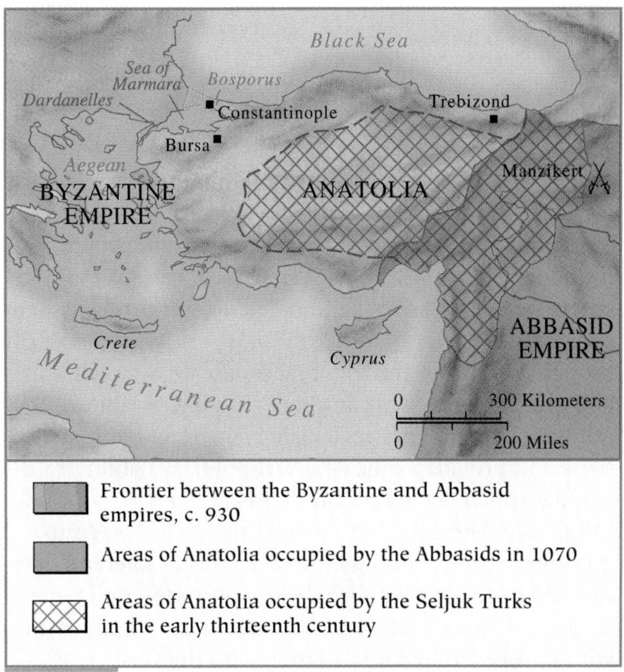


MAP 7.4 **The Turkish Occupation of Anatolia.** This map shows the expansion of Turkic-speaking peoples into the Anatolian peninsula in the tenth and eleventh centuries. The Ottoman Turks established their capital at Bursa in 1335 and eventually at Constantinople in 1453. ? What was at the time the major obstacle to Ottoman expansion into Europe? **View an animated version of this map or related maps at** http://history.wadsworth.com/duikerspielvogel05/

## The Crusades in Muslim Eyes

Usamah, an early-twelfth-century Muslim warrior and gentleman, had close associations with the crusaders. When he was ninety years old, he wrote his memoirs, including many entertaining observations on the crusaders, or "Franks" as he called them. Here Usamah is astounded at the Franks' rudeness to Muslims and at their assumption of cultural superiority.

*In what direction would the author be facing if he wished to pray to Mecca, as is required of a Muslim? Who were the "Franks," and where did the name originate?*

### Usamah, *Book of Reflections*

1. Everyone who is a fresh emigrant from the Frankish lands is ruder in character than those who have become acclimatized and have held long association with the Moslems. Here is an illustration of their rude character.

Whenever I visited Jerusalem I always entered the Aqsa Mosque, beside which stood a small mosque which the Franks had converted into a church. When I used to enter the Aqsa Mosque, which was occupied by the Templars [an order of crusading knights], who were my friends, the Templars would evacuate the little adjoining mosque so that I might pray in it. One day I entered this mosque, repeated the first formula, "Allah is great," and stood up in the act of praying, upon which one of the Franks rushed on me, got hold of me, and turned my face eastward, saying, "This is the way thou shouldst pray!" A group of Templars hastened to him, seized him, and repelled him from me. I resumed my prayer. The same man, while the others were otherwise busy, rushed once more on me and turned my face eastward, saying, "This is the way thou shouldst pray!" The Templars again came in to him and expelled him. They apologized to me, saying, "This is a stranger who has only recently arrived from the land of the Franks, and he has never before seen anyone praying except eastward." Thereupon I said to myself, "I have had enough prayer." So I went out, and have ever been surprised at the conduct of this devil of a man, at the change in the color of his face, his trembling, and his sentiment at the sight of one praying toward the qiblah.

2. In the army of King Fulk, son of Fulk, was a Frankish reverend knight who had just arrived from their land in order to make the holy pilgrimage and then return home. He was of my intimate fellowship and kept such constant company with me that he began to call me "my brother." Between us were mutual bonds of amity and friendship. When he resolved to return by sea to his homeland, he said to me:

"My brother, I am leaving for my country and I want thee to send with me thy son (my son, who was then fourteen years old, was at that time in my company) to our country, where he can see the knights and learn wisdom and chivalry. When he returns, he will be like a wise man."

Thus there fell upon my ears words which would never come out of the head of a sensible man; for even if my son were to be taken captive, his captivity could not bring him a worse misfortune than carrying him into the lands of the Franks.

In Europe, and undoubtedly within the Muslim world itself, the arrival of the Turks was regarded as a disaster. The Turks were viewed as barbarians who destroyed civilizations and oppressed populations. In fact, in many respects, Turkish rule in the Middle East was probably beneficial. Converted to Islam, the Turkish rulers temporarily brought an end to the fraternal squabbles between Sunni and Shi'ite Muslims while supporting the Sunnites. They put their energies into revitalizing Islamic law and institutions and provided much-needed political stability to the empire, which helped restore its former prosperity. Under Seljuk rule, Muslims began to organize themselves into autonomous brotherhoods, whose relatively tolerant practices characterized Islamic religious attitudes until the end of the nineteenth century, when increased competition with Europe led to confrontation with the West.

Seljuk political domination over the old Abbasid Empire, however, provoked resentment on the part of many Persian Shi'ites, who viewed the Turks as usurping foreigners who had betrayed the true faith of Islam. Among the regime's most feared enemies was Hasan al-Sabahh, a Cairo-trained Persian who formed a rebel group, popularly known as "assassins" (guardians), who for several decades terrorized government officials and other leading political and religious figures from their base in the mountains south of the Caspian Sea. Like their modern-day equivalents, the terrorist organization known as al-Qaeda, Sabahh's followers were highly motivated and were adept in infiltrating the enemy's camp in order to carry out their clandestine activities. The organization was finally eliminated by the invading Mongols in the thirteenth century.

## The Crusades

Just before the end of the eleventh century, the Byzantine emperor Alexius I desperately called for assistance from other Christian states in Europe to protect his empire against the invading Seljuk Turks. As part of his appeal, he said that the Muslims were desecrating Christian shrines in the Holy Land and also molesting Christian pilgrims en route to the shrines. In actuality, the Muslims had never threatened the shrines or cut off Christian access to them. But tension between Christendom and Islam was on the rise, and the Byzantine emperor's appeal received a ready response in Europe. Beginning in 1096 and continuing into the thirteenth century, a series of Christian raids on Islamic territories known as the Crusades brought the

Holy Land and adjacent areas on the Mediterranean coast from Antioch to the Sinai peninsula under Christian rule (see Chapter 12).

At first, Muslim rulers in the area were taken aback by the invading crusaders, whose armored cavalry presented a new challenge to local warriors, and their response was ineffectual. The Seljuk Turks by that time were preoccupied with events taking place farther to the east and took no action themselves. But in 1169, Sunni Muslims under the leadership of Saladin (Salah al-Din), vizier to the last Fatimid caliph, brought an end to the Fatimid dynasty. Proclaiming himself sultan, Saladin succeeded in establishing his control over both Egypt and Syria, thereby confronting the Christian states in the area with united Muslim power on two fronts. In 1187, Saladin's army invaded the kingdom of Jerusalem and destroyed the Christian forces concentrated there. Further operations reduced Christian occupation in the area to a handful of fortresses along the northern coast. Unlike the Christians, however, Saladin did not permit a massacre of the civilian population and even tolerated the continuation of Christian religious services in conquered territories. For a time, Christian occupation forces even carried on a lively trade relationship with Muslim communities in the region.

The Christians returned for another try a few years after the fall of Jerusalem, but the campaign succeeded only in securing some of the coastal cities. Although the Christians would retain a toehold on the coast for much of the thirteenth century (Acre, their last stronghold, fell to the Muslims in 1291), they were no longer a significant force in Middle Eastern affairs. In retrospect, the Crusades had only minimal importance in the history of the Middle East, although they may have served to unite the forces of Islam against the foreign invaders, thus creating a residue of distrust toward Christians that continues to resonate through the Islamic world today (see the box on p. 196). Far more important in their impact were the Mongols, a pastoral people who swept out of the Gobi Desert in the early thirteenth century to seize control over much of the known world (see Chapter 10). Beginning with the advances of Genghis Khan in northern China, Mongol armies later spread across Central Asia, and in 1258, under the leadership of Hulegu, brother of the more famous Khubilai Khan, they seized Persia and Mesopotamia, bringing an end to the caliphate at Baghdad.

### The Mongols

Unlike the Seljuk Turks, the Mongols were not Muslims, and they found it difficult to adapt to the settled conditions that they found in the major cities in the Middle East. Their treatment of the local population in conquered territories was brutal (according to one historian, after conquering a city, they wiped out not only entire families but also their household pets) and destructive to the economy. Cities were razed to the ground, and dams and other irrigation works were destroyed, reducing prosperous agricultural societies to the point of mass starvation. The Mongols advanced as far as the Red Sea, but their attempt to seize Egypt failed, in part because of the effective resistance posed by the Mamluks (a Turkish military class originally composed of slaves; sometimes written as Mamelukes), who had recently overthrown the administration set up by Saladin and seized power for themselves.

Eventually, the Mongol rulers in the Middle East began to take on the coloration of the peoples that they had conquered. Mongol elites converted to Islam, Persian influence became predominant at court, and the cities began to be rebuilt. By the fourteenth century, the Mongol empire began to split into separate kingdoms and then to disintegrate. In the meantime, however, the old Islamic empire originally established by the Arabs in the seventh and eighth centuries had come to an end. The new center of Islamic civilization was in Cairo, now about to promote a renaissance in Muslim culture under the sponsorship of the Mamluks.

To the north, another new force began to appear on the horizon with the rise of the Ottoman Turks on the Anatolian peninsula. In 1453, Sultan Mehmet II seized Constantinople and brought an end to the Byzantine Empire. Then the Ottomans began to turn their attention to the rest of the Middle East (see Chapter 15).

## Islamic Civilization

To be a Muslim is not simply to worship Allah but also to live according to his law as revealed in the Qur'an, which is viewed as fundamental and immutable doctrine, not to be revised by human beings.

As Allah has decreed, so must humans behave. Therefore, Islamic doctrine must be consulted to determine questions of politics, economic behavior, civil and criminal law, and social ethics. In Islamic society, there is no demarcation between church and state, between the sacred and the secular.

### The Wealth of Araby: Trade and Cities in the Middle East

As we have noted, this era was probably, overall, one of the most prosperous periods in the history of the Middle East. Trade flourished, not only in the Islamic world but also with China (now in a period of efflorescence during the era of the Tang and the Song dynasties—see Chapter 10), with the Byzantine Empire, and with the trading societies in Southeast Asia (see Chapter 9). Trade goods were carried both by ship and by the "fleets of the desert," the camel caravans that traversed the arid land from Morocco in the far west to the countries beyond the Caspian Sea. From West Africa came gold and slaves; from China, silk and porcelain; from East Africa, gold, ivory, and rhinoceros horn; and from the lands of South Asia, sandalwood, cotton, wheat, sugar, and spices. Within the empire, Egypt contributed grain; Iraq, linens, dates, and precious stones; Spain, leather goods, olives, and wine;

and western India, various textile goods. The exchange of goods was facilitated by the development of banking and the use of currency and letters of credit (see the comparative essay "Trade and Civilization" on p. 199).

Under these conditions, urban areas flourished. While the Abbasids were in power, Baghdad was probably the greatest city in the empire, but after the rise of the Fatimids in Egypt, the focus of trade shifted to Cairo, described by the traveler Leo Africanus as "one of the greatest and most famous cities in all the whole world, filled with stately and admirable palaces and colleges, and most sumptuous temples."[5] Other great commercial cities included Basra at the head of the Persian Gulf, Aden at the southern tip of the Arabian peninsula, Damascus in modern Syria, and Marrakech in Morocco. In the cities, the inhabitants were generally segregated by religion, with Muslims, Jews, and Christians living in separate neighborhoods. But all were equally subject to the most common threats to urban life—fire, flood, and disease.

The most impressive urban buildings were usually the palace for the caliph or the local governor and the great mosque. Houses were often constructed of stone or brick around a timber frame. The larger houses were often built around an interior courtyard, where the residents could retreat from the dust, noise, and heat of the city streets. Sometimes domestic animals such as goats or sheep would be stabled there. The houses of the wealthy were often multistoried, with balconies and windows covered with latticework to provide privacy for those inside. The poor in both urban and rural areas lived in simpler houses composed of clay or unfired bricks. The Bedouins lived in tents that could be dismantled and moved according to their needs.

**CHRONOLOGY Islam: The First Millennium**

| | |
|---|---|
| Life of Muhammad | 570–632 |
| Flight to Medina | 622 |
| Conquest of Mecca | 630 |
| Fall of Cairo | 640 |
| Defeat of Persians | 650 |
| Election of Ali to caliphate | 656 |
| Muslim entry into Spain | c. 710 |
| Abbasid caliphate | 750–1258 |
| Construction of city of Baghdad | 762 |
| Reign of Harun al-Rashid | 786–809 |
| Founding of Fatimid dynasty in Egypt | 973 |
| Capture of Baghdad by Seljuk Turks | 1055 |
| Seizure of Anatolia by Seljuk Turks | 1071 |
| First Crusade | 1096 |
| Saladin destroys Fatimid kingdom | 1169 |
| Fourth Crusade | 1204 |
| Mongols seize Baghdad | 1258 |
| Ottoman Turks capture Constantinople | 1453 |

Eating habits varied in accordance with economic standing and religious preference. Muslims did not eat pork, but those who could afford it often served other meats such as mutton, lamb, poultry, or fish. Fruit, spices, and various sweets were delicacies. The poor were generally forced to survive on boiled millet or peas with an occasional lump of meat or fat. Bread—white or whole meal—

British Library

© Michael Nicholson/CORBIS

COMPARATIVE ILLUSTRATION

**The Medieval Castle.** Beginning in the eighth century, Muslim rulers began to erect fortified stone castles in the desert. So impressed were the crusaders by the innovative defensive features they saw that they began to incorporate similar ideas into their own European castles, which had previously been made of wood. In twelfth-century Syria, the crusaders constructed the imposing citadel known as the Krak des Chevaliers (Castle of the Knights) on the foundation of a Muslim fort (right photo). This new model of a massive fortress of solid masonry spread to western Europe, as is evident in the castle shown in the left photo, built in the late thirteenth century in Wales.

## COMPARATIVE ESSAY

# TRADE AND CIVILIZATION

In 2002, archaeologists unearthed the site of an ancient Egyptian port city on the shores of the Red Sea. Established sometime during the first millennium B.C.E., the city of Berenike linked the Nile River valley with ports as far away as the island of Java in Southeast Asia. The discovery of Berenike is only the latest piece of evidence confirming the importance of interregional trade in the ancient world. The exchange of goods between far-flung societies became a powerful engine driving the rise of advanced civilizations throughout the ancient world. Raw materials such as copper, tin, and obsidian; items of daily necessity like salt, fish, and other foodstuffs; and luxury goods like gold, silk, and precious stones passed from one end of the Eurasian supercontinent to the other, across the desert from the Mediterranean Sea to sub-Saharan Africa, and throughout much of the Americas. Less well known but also important was the maritime trade that stretched from the Mediterranean across the Indian Ocean to port cities on the distant coasts of Southeast and East Asia.

During the first millennium C.E., the level of interdependence among human societies intensified as three major trade routes–across the Indian Ocean, along the Silk road, and by caravan across the Sahara–created the framework of a single trade system. The new global network was not only commercial but informational as well, transmitting technology and ideas, such as the emerging religions of Buddhism, Christianity, and Islam, to new destinations.

There was a close relationship between missionary activities and trade. Buddhist merchants first brought the teachings of Siddhartha Gautama to China, and Muslim traders carried Muhammad's words to Southeast Asia and sub-Saharan Africa. Indian traders carried Hindu beliefs and political institutions to Southeast Asia.

What caused the rapid expansion of trade during this period? One key factor was the introduction of technology to facilitate transportation. The development of the compass, improved techniques in mapmaking and shipbuilding, and greater knowledge of wind patterns all contributed to the expansion of maritime trade. Caravan trade, once carried by wheeled chariots or on the backs of oxen, now used the camel as the preferred beast of burden through the deserts of Africa, Central Asia, and the Middle East.

Another reason for the expansion of commerce during this period was the appearance of several multinational empires that created zones of stability and affluence in key areas of the Eurasian landmass. Most important were the emergence of the Abbasid empire in the Middle East and the rise of prosperity in China during the Tang and Song dynasties (see Chapter 10). The Mongol invasions in the thirteenth century temporarily disrupted the process but then created a new era of stability that fostered long-distance trade throughout the world.

could be found on tables throughout the region except in the deserts, where boiled grain was the staple food.

### Islamic Society

In some ways, Arab society was probably one of the most egalitarian of its time. Both the principles of Islam, which held that all were equal in the eyes of Allah, and the importance of trade to the prosperity of the state probably contributed to this egalitarianism. Although there was a fairly well defined upper class, consisting of the ruling families, senior officials, tribal elites, and the wealthiest merchants, there was no hereditary nobility as in many contemporary societies, and the merchants enjoyed a degree of respect that they did not receive in Europe, China, or India.

Though the Arab empire was more urbanized than most other societies at the time, the bulk of the population continued to live in the countryside and supported itself by farming or herding animals. During the early stages, most of the farmland was owned by independent peasants, but later some concentration of land in the hands of wealthy owners began to take place. In river valleys like the Tigris and Euphrates and the Nile, the majority of the farmers probably continued to be independent peasants.

Not all benefited from the high degree of social mobility in the Islamic world, however. Slavery was widespread. Since a Muslim could not be enslaved, the supply came from sub-Saharan Africa or from non-Islamic populations elsewhere in Asia. Most slaves were employed in the army (which was sometimes a road to power, as in the case of the Mamluks) or as domestic servants, who were sometimes permitted to purchase their freedom. The slaves who worked the large estates experienced the worst living conditions and rose in revolt on several occasions.

The Islamic principle of human equality also fell short, as in most other societies of its day, in the treatment of women. Although the Qur'an instructed men to treat women with respect, and women did have the right to own and inherit property, in general the male was dominant in Muslim society. Polygyny was permitted, and the right of divorce was in practice restricted to the husband, although some schools of legal thought permitted women to stipulate that their husband could have only one wife or to seek a separation in certain specific circumstances. Adultery and homosexuality were stringently forbidden (although such prohibitions were frequently ignored in practice), and Islamic custom required that women be cloistered in their homes (thus the

## "Draw Their Veils over Their Bosoms"

Prior to the Islamic era, many upper-class women greeted men on the street, entertained their husband's friends at home, went on pilgrimages to Mecca, and even accompanied their husbands to battle. Such women were neither veiled nor secluded. Muhammad, however, specified that his own wives, who (according to the Qur'an) were "not like any other women," should be modestly attired and should be addressed by men from behind a curtain. Over the centuries, Muslim theologians, fearful that female sexuality could threaten the established order, interpreted Muhammad's "modest attire" and his reference to curtains to mean segregated seclusion and body concealment for all Muslim women. In fact, one strict scholar in fourteenth-century Cairo went so far as to prescribe that ideally a woman should be allowed to leave her home only three times in her life: when entering her husband's home after marriage, after the death of parents, and after her own death.

In traditional Islamic societies, veiling and seclusion were more prevalent among urban women than among their rural counterparts. The latter, who worked in the fields and rarely saw people outside their extended family, were less restricted. In this excerpt from the Qur'an, women are instructed to "guard their modesty" and "draw veils over their bosoms." Nowhere in the Qur'an however, does it stipulate that women should be sequestered or covered from head to toe.

**Qur'an, Sura 24: "The Light"**

*And say to the believing women*
*That they should lower*
*Their gaze and guard*
*Their modesty: that they*
*Should not display their*
*Beauty and ornaments except*
*What [must ordinarily] appear*
*Thereof: that they should*
*Draw their veils over*
*Their bosoms and not display*
*Their beauty except*
*To their husbands, their fathers,*
*Their husbands' fathers, their sons,*
*Their husbands' sons,*
*Their brothers or their brothers' sons,*
*Or their sisters' sons,*
*Or their women, or the slaves*
*Whom their right hands*
*Possess, or male servants*
*Free of physical needs,*
*Or small children who*
*Have no sense of the shame*
*Of sex; and that they*
*Should not strike their feet*
*In order to draw attention*
*To their hidden ornaments.*

*How does the role of women in Islam compare with what we have seen in other traditional societies, such as India, China, and the Americas?*

**HistoryNow™** To read the Qur'an in its entirety, enter the *HistoryNow* documents area using the access card that is available for *World History.*

tradition of the harem) and prohibited from social contacts with males outside their own family. The custom of requiring women to cover virtually all parts of their body when appearing in public was common in urban areas and continues to be practiced in many Islamic societies today. It should be noted, however, that these customs owed more to traditional Arab practice than to Qur'anic law (see the box above).

## The Culture of Islam

The Arabs were truly heirs to many elements of the remaining Greco-Roman culture of the Roman Empire, and they assimilated Byzantine and Persian culture just as readily. In the eighth and ninth centuries, numerous Greek, Syrian, and Persian scientific and philosophical works were translated into Arabic and eventually found their way to Europe. As the chief language in the southern Mediterranean and the Middle East, Arabic became an international language. Later, Persian and Turkish also came to be important in administration and culture.

The spread of Islam led to the emergence of a new culture throughout the Arab empire. This was true in all fields of endeavor, from literature to art and architecture. But pre-Islamic traditions were not extinguished and frequently combined with Muslim motifs, resulting in creative works of great imagination and originality.

**Philosophy and Science** During the centuries following the rise of the Arab empire, it was the Islamic world that was most responsible for preserving and spreading the scientific and philosophical achievements of ancient civilizations. At a time when ancient Greek philosophy was largely unknown in Europe, key works by Aristotle, Plato, and other Greek philosophers were translated into Arabic and stored in a "house of wisdom" in Baghdad, where they were read and studied by Muslim scholars. Through the writings of the Spanish Muslim philosopher Ibn Rushd (known in the West as Averroës), many of these works eventually became known in Europe and influenced Christian thought. Texts on mathematics and linguistics were brought

© Giraudon/Art Resource, NY

**Preserving the Wisdom of the Greeks.** After the fall of the Roman Empire, the philosophical works of ancient Greece were virtually forgotten in Europe or were banned as heretical by the Byzantine Empire. It was thanks to Muslim scholars, who located copies at the magnificent library in Alexandria, Egypt, that many classical Greek writings survived. Here young Muslim scholars are being trained in the Greek language so that they can translate classical Greek writings into Arabic. Later they will be translated back into Western languages and serve as the catalyst for an intellectual revival in medieval and Renaissance Europe.

from India. The process was undoubtedly stimulated by the introduction of paper manufacturing from China in the eighth century. By the end of the century, the first paper factories had been established in Baghdad, and booksellers and libraries soon followed. The first paper mill in Europe appeared in the Pyrenees region of Spain in the twelfth century.

Although Islamic scholars are justly praised for preserving much of classical knowledge for the West, they also made considerable advances of their own. Nowhere is this more evident than in mathematics and the natural sciences. Islamic scholars adopted and passed on the numerical system of India, including the use of the zero, and a ninth-century Persian mathematician founded the mathematical discipline of algebra (*al-jābr*). In astronomy, Muslims set up an observatory at Baghdad to study the position of the stars. They were aware that the earth was round and in the ninth century produced a world map based on the tradition of the Greco-Roman astronomer Ptolemy.

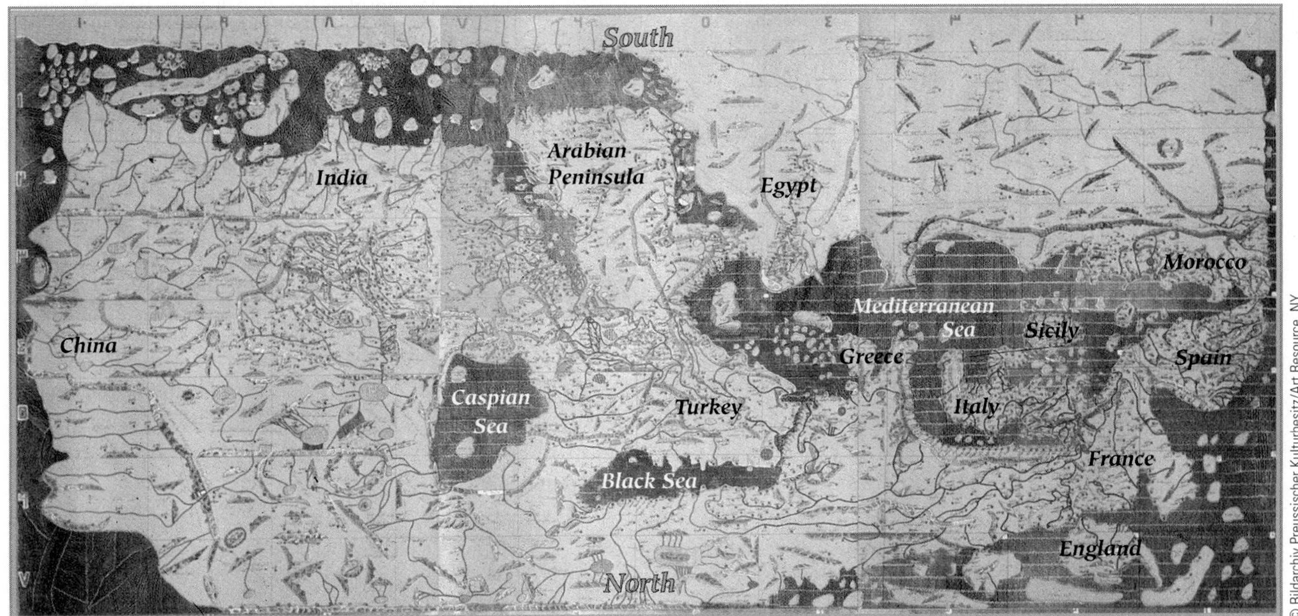


© Bildarchiv Preussischer Kulturbesitz/Art Resource, NY

**A Twelfth-Century Map of the World.** The twelfth-century Muslim geographer Al-Idrisi received his education in the Spanish city of Córdoba while it was under Islamic rule. Later he served at the court of the Norman king of Sicily, Roger II, where he created an atlas of the world based on Arab and European sources. According to Muslim practice at the time, north and south were inverted from modern practice. This map depicts the world as it was known at that time, stretching from the Spanish peninsula on the right to the civilization of China on the far left.

## LOVE FOR A CAMEL

Early Arabic poetry focused on simple pleasures, such as wine, women, song, and the faithful camel. This excerpt is from a longer work by the sixth-century Arab poet Tarafah. Tarafah was one of a group of seven poets called the "suspended ones." Their poems, having won a prize in an annual competition, were suspended on a wall for all to read.

*How does this poem celebrate the secular aspects of life?*

### The Ode of Tarafah

*Ah, but when grief assails me, straightway I ride it*
*off mounted on my swift, lean-flanked camel,*
*night and day racing, . . .*
*Her long neck is very erect when she lifts it up,*
*calling to mind the rudder of a Tigris-bound*
*vessel. Her skull is most like an anvil, the*
*junction of its two halves meeting together as*
*it might be on the edge of a file.*
*Her cheek is smooth as Syrian parchment, her split*
*lip a tanned hide of Yemen, its slit not bent*
*crooked; her eyes are a pair of mirrors, sheltering*
*in the caves of her brow-bones, the rock of a*
*pool's hollow, . . .*
*I am at her with the whip, and my she-camel quick-*
*ens pace what time the mirage of the burning*
*stone-tract shimmers; elegantly she steps, as a*
*slave-girl at a party will sway, showing her*
*master skirts of a trailing white gown.*
*I am not one that skulks fearfully among the*
*hilltops, but when the folk seek my succor I*
*gladly give it; if you look for me in the circle*
*of the folk you'll find me there, and if you*
*hunt me in the taverns there you'll catch me.*
*Come to me when you will, I'll pour you a flowing*
*cup, and if you don't need it, well, do without*
*and good luck to you!*
*Whenever the tribe is assembled you'll come upon*
*me at the summit of the noble House, the oft-*
*frequented; my boon-companions are white as*
*stars, and a singing-wench comes to us in her*
*striped gown or her saffron robe, wide the open-*
*ing of her collar, delicate her skin to my compan-*
*ions' fingers, tender her nakedness.*
*When we say, "Let's hear from you," she advances*
*to us chanting fluently, her glance languid, in*
*effortless song.*



Muslim scholars also made many new discoveries in optics and chemistry and, with the assistance of texts on anatomy by the ancient Greek physician Galen (c.180–200 C.E.), developed medicine as a distinctive field of scientific inquiry. Especially well known was Ibn Sina (980–1037). Known as Avicenna in the West, he compiled a medical encyclopedia that, among other things, emphasized the contagious nature of certain diseases and showed how they could be spread by contaminated water supplies. After its translation into Latin, Avicenna's work became a basic medical textbook for medieval European university students.

**Islamic Literature** Islam brought major changes to the literature of the Middle East. Muslims regarded the Qur'an as their greatest literary work, but pre-Islamic traditions continued to influence writers throughout the region.

The tradition of Arabic poetry was well established by the time of Muhammad. It extolled Bedouin tribal life, courage in battle, hunting, sports, and respect for the animals of the desert, especially the camel (see the box above). Because the Arabic language did not possess a written script until the fourth century C.E., poetry was originally passed on by memory. Later, in the eighth and ninth centuries, it was compiled in anthologies.

Pre-Muslim Persia also boasted a long literary tradition, most of it oral and written down in later centuries in the Arabic alphabet. The Persian poetic tradition remained strong under Islam. Rabe'a of Qozdar, Persia's first known woman poet, lived in the second half of the tenth century. Describing the suffering love brings, she wrote: "Beset with impatience I did not know / That the more one seeks to pull away, the tighter becomes the rope."[6]

In the West, the most famous works of Middle Eastern literature are undoubtedly the *Rubaiyat* of Omar Khayyam and *Tales from 1001 Nights* (also called *The Arabian Nights*). Paradoxically, these two works are not as popular with Middle Eastern readers. Both, in fact, were freely translated into Western languages for nineteenth-century European readers, who developed a taste for stories set in exotic foreign places.

Unfortunately, very little is known of the life or the poetry of the twelfth-century poet Omar Khayyam. Skeptical, reserved, and slightly contemptuous of his peers, he combined poetry with scientific works on mathematics and astronomy and a revision of the calendar that was more accurate than the Gregorian version devised in Europe hundreds of years later. Omar Khayyam did not write down his poems but composed them orally over wine with friends at a neighborhood tavern. They were recorded later by friends or scribes. Many poems attributed to him were actually written long after his death. Among them is the well-known couplet translated into English in the nineteenth century: "Here with a loaf of bread beneath the bough, / A flask of wine, a book of verse, and thou."

Omar Khayyam's poetry is simple and down to earth. Key themes are the impermanence of life, the impossibility of knowing God, and disbelief in an afterlife. Ironically, recent translations of his work appeal to modern attitudes of skepticism and minimalist simplicity that may make him even more popular in the West:

*In youth I studied for a little while;*
*Later I boasted of my mastery.*
*Yet this was all the lesson that I learned:*
*We come from dust, and with the wind are gone.*

*Of all the travelers on this endless road*
*No one returns to tell us where it leads,*
*There's little in this world but greed and need;*
*Leave nothing here, for you will not return. . . .*

*Since no one can be certain of tomorrow,*
*It's better not to fill the heart with care.*
*Drink wine by moonlight, darling, for the moon*
*Will shine long after this, and find us not.*[7]

Like Omar Khayyam's verse, *The Arabian Nights* was loosely translated into European languages and adapted to Western tastes. A composite of folktales, fables, and romances of Indian and indigenous origin, the stories interweave the natural with the supernatural. The earliest stories were told orally and were later transcribed, with many later additions, in Arabic and Persian versions. The famous story of Aladdin and the Magic Lamp, for example, was an eighteenth-century addition. Nevertheless, *The Arabian Nights* has entertained readers for centuries, allowing them to enter a land of wish fulfillment through extraordinary plots, sensuality, comic and tragic situations, and a cast of unforgettable characters.

Sadi (1210–1292), considered the Persian Shakespeare, remains to this day the favorite author in Iran. His *Rose Garden* is a collection of entertaining stories written in prose sprinkled with verse. He is also renowned for his sonnetlike love poems, which set a model for generations to come. Sadi was a master of the pithy maxim:

*A cat is a lion in catching mice*
*But a mouse in combat with a tiger.*

*He has found eternal happiness who lived a good life,*
*Because, after his end, good repute will keep his*
*name alive.*

*When thou fightest with anyone, consider*
*Whether thou wilt have to flee from him or he*
*from thee.*[8]

Some Arabic and Persian literature reflected the deep spiritual and ethical concerns of the Qur'an. Many writers, however, carried Islamic thought in novel directions. The thirteenth-century poet Rumi, for example, embraced **Sufism,** a form of religious belief that called for a mystical relationship between Allah and human beings (the term *Sufism* stems from the Arabic word for "wool," referring to the rough wool garments that its adherents wore). Converted to Sufism by a wandering dervish (dervishes, from the word for "poor" in Persian, sought to achieve a mystical union with Allah through dancing and chanting in an ecstatic trance), Rumi abandoned orthodox Islam to embrace God directly through ecstatic love. Realizing that love transcends intellect, he sought to reach God through a trance attained by the whirling dance of the dervish, set to mesmerizing music. As he twirled, the poet extemporized some of the most passionate lyrical verse ever conceived. His faith and art remain an important force in Islamic society today (see the box on p. 204).

The Islamic world also made a major contribution to historical writing, another discipline that was stimulated by the introduction of paper manufacturing. The first great Islamic historian was al-Mas'udi. Born in Baghdad in 896, he wrote about both the Muslim and the non-Muslim world, traveling widely in the process. His *Meadows of Gold* is the source of much of our knowledge about the golden age of the Abbasid caliphate. Translations of his work reveal a wide-ranging mind and a keen intellect, combined with a human touch that practitioners of the art in our century might find reason to emulate. Equaling al-Mas'udi in talent and reputation was the fourteenth-century historian Ibn Khaldun. Combining scholarship with government service, Ibn Khaldun was one of the first historians to attempt a philosophy of history.

**Islamic Art and Architecture** The art of Islam is a blend of Arab, Turkish, and Persian traditions. Although local influences can be discerned in Egypt, Anatolia, Spain, and other areas and the Mongols introduced an East Asian accent in the thirteenth century, for a long time Islamic art remained remarkably coherent over a wide area. First and foremost, the Arabs, with their new religion and their writing system, served as a unifying force. Fascinated by the mathematics and astronomy they inherited from the Romans or the Babylonians, they developed a sense of rhythm and abstraction that found expression in their use of repetitive geometric ornamentation. The Turks brought abstraction in figurative and nonfigurative designs, and the Persians added their lyrical poetical mysticism. Much Islamic painting, for example, consists of illustrations of Persian texts.

The ultimate expression of Islamic art is to be found in magnificent architectural monuments beginning in the late seventh century. The first great example is the Dome of the Rock, which was built in 691 to proclaim the spiritual and political legitimacy of the new religion

## The Passions of a Sufi Mystic

Sufism was an unorthodox form of Islam that flourished in many parts of the Muslim world. It preached the importance of a highly personal relationship between Allah and the individual believer. Sufi orders began to assume considerable influence by the thirteenth century, perhaps because of the disintegration of the Abbasid empire and the heightened instability throughout the Islamic world. Sufi missionaries played a major role in efforts to spread Islam to India and Central Asia. In this poem, the thirteenth-century Persian poet Rumi describes the mystical relationship achieved by means of passionate music and dance.

*How does this poem celebrate the spiritual side of life? Why might such writings be attacked as contrary to Islamic doctrine?*

### Rumi, *Call to the Dance*

*Come!*
*But don't join us without music.*
*We have a celebration here.*
*Rise and beat the drums.*

*We are Mansur who said "I am God!"*

*We are in ecstasy–*
*Drunk, but not from wine made of grapes.*

*Whatever your thoughts are about us,*
*We are far, far from them.*

*This is the night of the same*
*When we whirl to ecstasy.*

*There is light now,*
*There is light, there is light.*

*This is true love,*
*Which means farewell to the mind.*
*There is farewell today, farewell.*

*Tonight each flaming heart is a friend of music.*
*Longing for your lips,*
*My heart pours out of my mouth.*

*Hush!*
*You are made of feeling and thought and passion;*
*The rest is nothing but flesh and bone.*
*We are the soul of the world,*
*Not heavy or sagging like the body.*
*We are the spirit's treasure,*
*Not bound to this earth, to time or space.*

*How can they talk to us of prayer rugs and piety?*
*We are the hunter and the hunted,*
*Autumn and spring,*
*Night and day,*
*Visible and hidden.*
*Love is our mother.*
*We were born of Love.*

to the ancient world. Set in the sacred heart of Jerusalem on Muhammad's holy rock and touching both the Western Wall of the Jews and the oldest Christian church, the Dome of the Rock remains one of the most revered Islamic monuments. Constructed on Byzantine lines with an octagonal shape and marble columns and ornamentation, the interior reflects Persian motifs with mosaics of precious stones. Although rebuilt several times and incorporating influences from both East and West, this first monument to Islam represents the birth of a new art.

At first, desert Arabs, whether nomads or conquering armies, prayed in an open court, shaded along the *qibla* (the wall facing the holy city of Mecca) by a thatched roof supported by rows of palm trunks. There was also a ditch where the faithful could wash off the dust of the desert prior to prayer. As Islam became better established, enormous mosques were constructed, but they were still modeled on the open court, which would be surrounded on all four sides with pillars supporting a wooden roof over the prayer area facing the *qibla* wall. The largest mosque ever built, the Great Mosque of Samarra (848–852), covered 10 acres and contained 464 pillars in aisles surrounding the court. Set in the *qibla* wall was a niche, or ***mihrab,*** containing a decorated panel pointing to Mecca and representing Allah. Remains of the massive 30-foot-high outer wall still stand, but the most famous section of the Samarra mosque was its 90-foot-tall minaret, the tower accompanying a mosque from which the ***muezzin*** (crier) calls the faithful to prayer five times a day.

No discussion of mosques would be complete without mentioning the famous ninth-century mosque at Córdoba in southern Spain, which is still in remarkable condition. Its 514 columns supporting double horseshoe arches transform this architectural wonder into a unique forest of trees pointing upward, contributing to a light and airy effect. The unparalleled sumptuousness and elegance make the Córdoba mosque one of the wonders of world art, let alone Islamic art.

Since the Muslim religion combines spiritual and political power in one, palaces also reflected the glory of Islam. Beginning in the eighth century with the spectacular castles of Syria, the rulers constructed large brick domiciles reminiscent of Roman design, with protective walls, gates, and baths. With a central courtyard surrounded by two-story arcades and massive gate-towers,

Courtesy of William J.Duiker

© Nik Wheeler/Corbis

**The Recycled Mosque.** The Great Mosque at Córdoba was built on a site previously dedicated tothe Roman God Janus, which later boasted a Christian church built by the Visigoths. In the eighth century, the Muslims incorporated parts of the old church into the construction of their new mosque, aggrandizing it over the centuries. After the defeat of the Muslims, the mosque reverted to Christianity, and in 1523, a soaring cathedral sprouted from its spine (shown below). Inside, the mosque and the cathedral seem to blend well aesthetically, a prototype for harmonious religious coexistence. Throughout history, societies have destroyed past architectural wonders, robbing older marble glories to erect new marvels. It is rare and wonderful that the Great Mosque survived to vaunt its glittering dome in the *mihrab* chamber (shown in the inset above).

they resembled fortresses as much as palaces. Characteristic of such "desert palaces" was the gallery over the entrance gate, with holes through which boiling oil could be poured down on the heads of attacking forces. Unfortunately, none of these structures has survived.

The ultimate remaining Islamic palace is the fourteenth-century Alhambra in Spain. The extensive succession of courtyards, rooms, gardens, and fountains created a fairy-tale castle perched high above the city of Granada. Every inch of surface is decorated in intricate floral and semiabstract patterns; much of the decoration is done in carved plasterwork so fine that it resembles lace. The Lion Court in the center of the harem is world renowned for its lion fountain and surrounding arcade with elegant columns and carvings.

Since antiquity, one of the primary occupations of women has been the spinning and weaving of cloth to make clothing and other useful items for their families. In the Middle East, this skill reached an apogee in the art of the knotted woolen rug. Originating in the pre-Muslim era, rugs were initially used to insulate stone palaces against the cold as well as to warm shepherds' tents. Eventually they were applied to religious purposes, since every practicing Muslim is required to pray five times a day on clean ground. Small rugs served as prayer mats for individual use, while larger and more elaborate ones were given by rulers as rewards for political favors. Bedouins in the Arabian desert covered their sandy floors with rugs to create a cozy environment in their tents.

In villages throughout the Middle East, the art of rug weaving has been passed down from mother to daughter over the centuries. Small girls as young as four years old took part in the process by helping to spin and prepare the wool shorn from the family sheep. By the age of six, girls would begin their first rug, and before adolescence, their slender fingers would be producing fine carpets. Skilled artisanship represented an extra enticement to prospective bridegrooms, and rugs often became an important part of a woman's dowry to her future husband. After the wedding, the wife would continue to make rugs for home use, as well as for sale to augment the family income. Eventually, rugs began to be manufactured in workshops by professional artisans, who reproduced the designs from detailed painted diagrams.

Most decorations on the rugs, as well as on all forms of Islamic art, consisted of Arabic script and natural

Courtesy of William J. Duiker

**The Alhambra in Granada.** Islamic civilization reached its zenith with the fourteenth-century fairy-tale castle of Alhambra in southern Spain (below). Like the Hindus in India, the Muslims of the Middle East and Spain lived in a hot, dry climate, making water a highly prized commodity both literally and psychologically. The quiet, refreshing coolness of water became a vital component of Muslim architecture, displayed in gardens with fountains and reflecting pools such as this one at the Alhambra. Like the Hindus, Muslims wash prior to religious devotion and can be seen here performing ablutions in the courtyard of a sixteenth-century mosque in Istanbul (left).

Courtesy of William J. Duiker

**The Qur'an as Sculptured Design.** Muslim sculptors and artists, reflecting the official view that any visual representation of the prophet Muhammad was blasphemous, turned to geometric patterns, as well as to flowers and animals, as a means of fulfilling their creative urge. The predominant motif, however, was the reproduction of Qur'anic verses in the Arabic script. Calligraphy, which was almost as important in the Middle East as it was in traditional China, used the Arabic script to decorate all of the Islamic arts, from painting to pottery, tile and ironwork, and wall decorations such as this carved plaster panel in a courtyard of the Alhambra palace in Spain. Since a recitation from the Qur'an was an important component of the daily devotional activities for all practicing Muslims, elaborate scriptural panels such as this one perfectly blended the spiritual and the artistic realms.

Courtesy of William J. Duiker

plant and figurative motifs. Repeated continuously in naturalistic or semiabstract geometrical patterns called arabesques, these decorations completely covered the surface and left no area undecorated. This dense decor was also evident in brick, mosaic, and stucco ornamentation and culminated in the magnificent tile work of later centuries.

No representation of the Prophet Muhammad ever adorned a mosque, in painting or in any other art form. Although no passage of the Qur'an forbids representational painting, the *Hadith* warned against any attempt to imitate God through artistic creation or idolatry. From the time of the Dome of the Rock, no figurative representations appear in Islamic religious art.

Human beings and animals could still be represented in secular art, but relatively little survives from the early centuries aside from a very few wall paintings from the royal palaces. Although the Persians used calligraphy and art to decorate their books, the Arabs had no pictorial tradition of their own and only began to develop the art of book illustration in the late twelfth century to illustrate translations of Greek scientific works.

In the thirteenth century, a Mongol dynasty established at Tabriz, west of the Caspian Sea, offered the Middle East its first direct contact with the art of East Asia. Mongol painting, done in the Chinese manner with a full brush and expressing animated movement and intensity (see Chapter 10), freed Islamic painters from traditional confines and enabled them to experiment with new techniques.

# The Byzantine Empire

In the fourth century, a noticeable separation between the western and eastern parts of the Roman Empire began to develop. In the course of the fifth century, while the Germans moved into the western part of the empire and established various kingdoms, the Roman Empire in the east, centered on Constantinople, continued to prosper.

## The Reign of Justinian (527–565)

In the sixth century, the empire in the east came under the control of one of its most remarkable rulers, the emperor Justinian. As the nephew and heir of the previous emperor, Justinian had been well trained in imperial administration. He married Theodora, daughter of a lower-class circus trainer, who proved to be a remarkably strong-willed woman and played a crucial role in giving Justinian the determination to crush a revolt against his rule in 532. Justinian was determined to reestablish the Roman Empire in the entire Mediterranean world and began his attempt to reconquer the west within a year after the revolt had failed.

Justinian's army under Belisarius, probably the best general of the late Roman world, presented a formidable force. Belisarius sailed to North Africa and quickly destroyed the Vandals in two major battles. From North Africa, he led his forces onto the Italian peninsula after occupying Sicily in 535. But it was not until 552 that the Ostrogoths were finally defeated. Justinian appeared to have achieved his goals. He had restored the imperial

**The Emperor Justinian and His Court.** As the seat of Byzantine power in Italy, the town of Ravenna became adorned with examples of Byzantine art. The church of San Vitale at Ravenna contains some of the finest examples of sixth-century Byzantine mosaics, in which small pieces of colored glass were attached to the wall to form these figures and their surroundings. The emperor is seen as both head of state (he wears a jeweled crown and a purple robe) and head of the church (he carries a gold bowl symbolizing the body of Jesus).

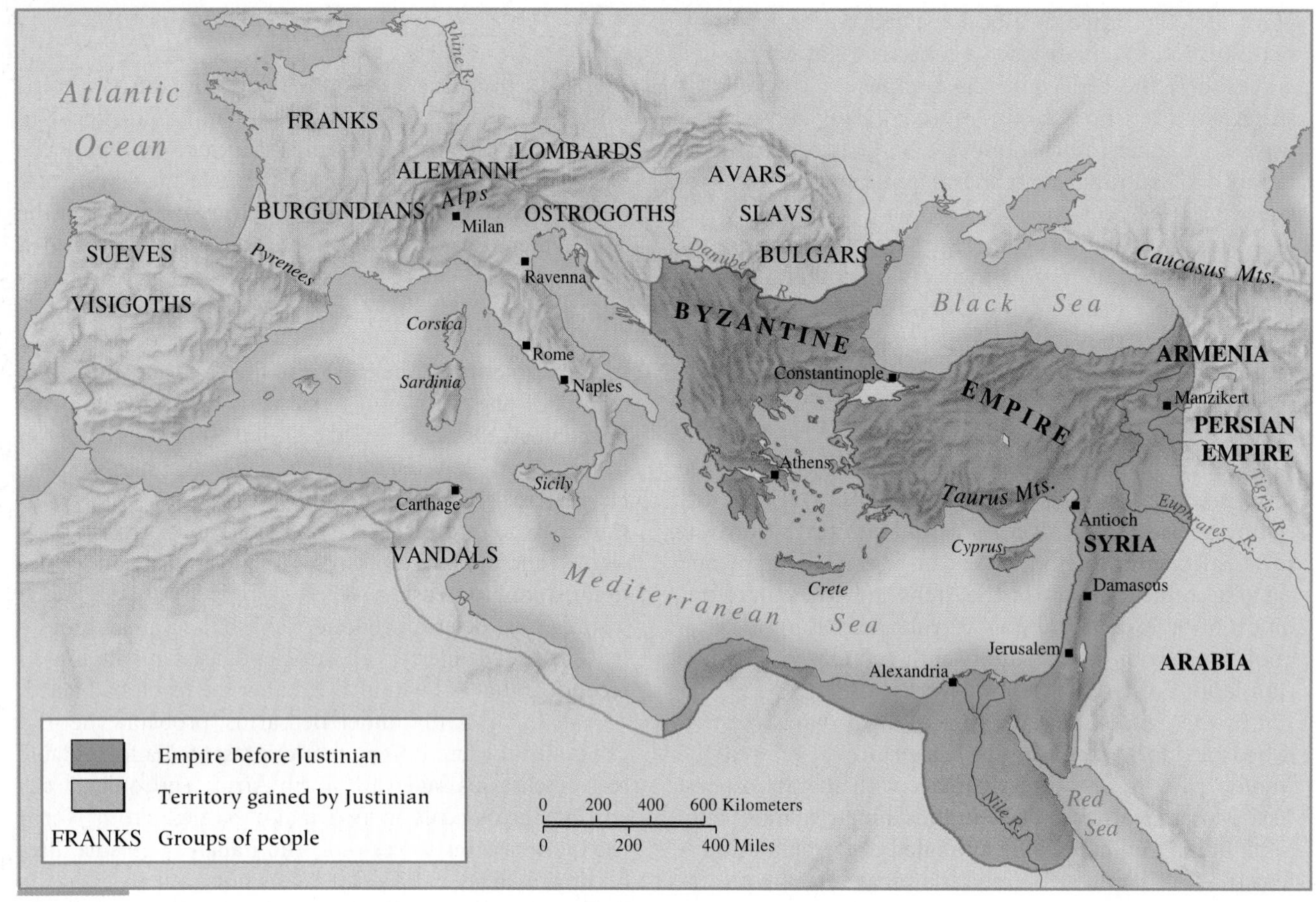


**MAP 7.5 The Byzantine Empire in the Time of Justinian.** The Byzantine emperor Justinian briefly restored much of the Mediterranean portion of the old Roman Empire. His general Belisarius quickly conquered the Vandals in North Africa but wrested Italy from the Ostrogoths only after a long and devastating struggle. ? Look back at Map 5.3. What former Roman territories lay outside Justinian's control? **View an animated version of this map or related maps at http://history .wadsworth.com/duikerspielvogel05/**

Mediterranean world; his empire included Italy, part of Spain, North Africa, Asia Minor, Palestine, and Syria (see Map 7.5). But the conquest of the western empire proved fleeting. Only three years after Justinian's death, another group of Germans known as the Lombards entered Italy. Although the eastern empire maintained the fiction of Italy as a province, its forces were limited to southern and central Italy, Sicily, and coastal areas, such as the territory around Ravenna.

**The Codification of Roman Law** Though his conquests proved short-lived, Justinian made a lasting contribution through his codification of Roman law. The eastern empire was heir to a vast quantity of materials connected to the development of Roman law. These included laws passed by the senate and assemblies, legal commentaries of jurists, decisions of praetors, and the edicts of emperors. Justinian had been thoroughly trained in imperial government and was well acquainted with Roman law. He wished to codify and simplify this mass of material.

To accomplish his goal, Justinian authorized the jurist Trebonian to make a systematic compilation of imperial edicts. The result was the Code of Law, the first part of the *Corpus Iuris Civilis* (Body of Civil Law), completed in 529. Four years later, two other parts of the *Corpus* appeared: the *Digest,* a compendium of writings of Roman jurists, and the *Institutes,* a brief summary of the chief principles of Roman law that could be used as a textbook on Roman law. The fourth part of the *Corpus* was the *Novels,* a compilation of the most important new edicts issued during Justinian's reign.

Justinian's codification of Roman law became the basis of imperial law in the Byzantine Empire until its end in 1453. More important, however, since it was written in Latin (it was in fact the last product of eastern Roman culture to be written in Latin, which was soon replaced by Greek), it was also eventually used in the West and became the basis of the legal system of all of continental Europe.

**Life in Constantinople: The Importance of Trade** After riots destroyed much of Constantinople in 532, Justinian rebuilt the city and gave it the appearance it would keep for almost a thousand years. With a population estimated in the hundreds of thousands, Constantinople was the largest city in Europe during the Middle Ages. It viewed itself as the center of an empire and a special Christian city.

Until the twelfth century, Constantinople was Europe's greatest commercial center. The city was the chief entrepôt for the exchange of products between West and East. Highly desired in Europe were the products of the East: silk from China, spices from Southeast Asia and India, jewelry and ivory from India (the latter used by artisans for church items), wheat and furs from southern Russia, and flax and honey from the Balkans. Many of these eastern goods were then shipped to the Mediterranean area and northern Europe. Despite the Germanic incursions, European trade did not entirely end.

Moreover, imported raw materials were used in Constantinople for local industries. During Justinian's reign, two Christian monks smuggled silkworms from China to begin a silk industry. The state had a monopoly on the production of silk cloth, and the workshops themselves were housed in Constantinople's royal palace complex. European demand for silk cloth made it the city's most lucrative product. It is interesting to note that the upper classes, including emperors and empresses, were not discouraged from making money through trade and manufacturing. Indeed, one empress even manufactured perfumes in her bedroom.

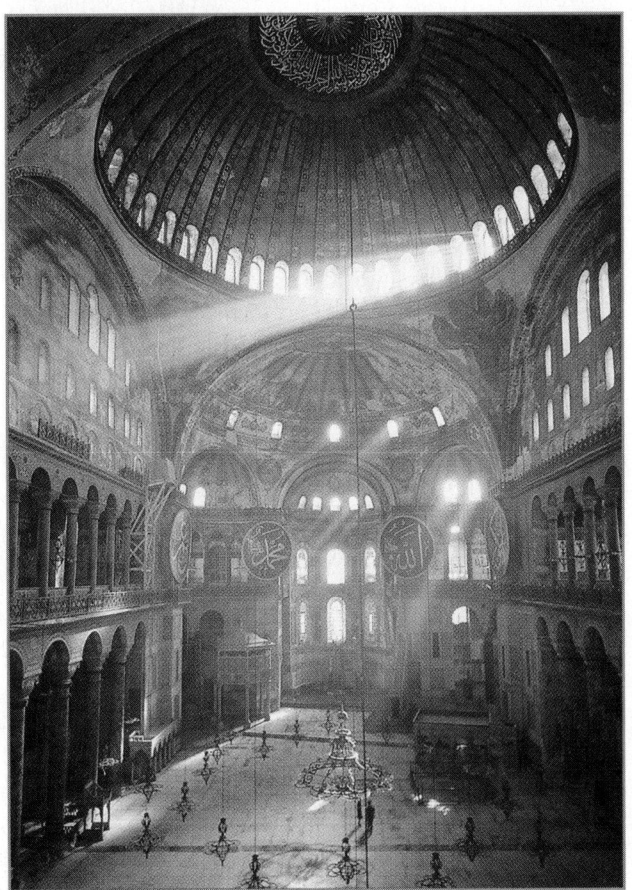



**Interior View of Hagia Sophia.** Pictured here is the interior of the Church of the Holy Wisdom in Constantinople (modern Istanbul), constructed under Justinian by Anthemius of Tralles and Isidore of Milan. Some of the stones used in the construction of the church had been plundered from the famous classical Temple of Diana, near Ephesus, in Turkey. This view gives an idea of how the windows around the base of the dome produced a special play of light within the cathedral. The pulpits and plaques bearing inscriptions from the Qur'an were introduced when the Turks converted this church to a mosque in the fifteenth century.

**The Emperor's Building Program** Much of Constantinople's appearance in the Early Middle Ages was due to Justinian's program of rebuilding in the sixth century. Earlier, Emperor Theodosius II (408–450) had constructed an enormous defensive wall to protect the city on its land side. The city was dominated by an immense palace complex, a huge arena known as the Hippodrome, and hundreds of churches. No residential district was particularly fashionable; palaces, tenements, and slums ranged alongside one another. Justinian added many new buildings. His public works projects included roads, bridges, walls, public baths, law courts, and colossal underground reservoirs to hold the city's water supply. He also built hospitals, schools, monasteries, and churches. Churches were his special passion, and in Constantinople alone he built or rebuilt thirty-four of them. His greatest achievement was the famous Hagia Sophia, the Church of the Holy Wisdom.

Completed in 537, Hagia Sophia was designed by two architects who may have been influenced by the dome-and- arch architecture of the Sassanid Persians. Justinian's builders did not use the simple, flat-roofed basilica of Western architecture. The center of Hagia Sophia consisted of four huge piers crowned by an enormous dome, which seemed to be floating in space. This effect was emphasized by Procopius, the court historian, who, at Justinian's request, wrote a treatise on the emperor's building projects: "From the lightness of the building, it does not appear to rest upon a solid foundation, but to cover the place beneath as though it were suspended from heaven by the fabled golden chain."[9] In part, this impression was created by putting forty-two windows around the base of the dome, which allowed an incredible play of light within the cathedral. Light served to remind the worshipers of God; as Procopius commented:

> Whoever enters there to worship perceives at once that it is not by any human strength or skill, but by the favor of God that this work has been perfected; his mind rises sublime to commune with God, feeling that He cannot be far off, but must especially love to dwell in the place which he has chosen; and this takes place not only when a man sees it for the first time, but it always makes the same impression upon him, as though he had never beheld it before.[10]

As darkness is illumined by invisible light, so too it was believed the world is illumined by invisible spirit.

The royal palace complex, Hagia Sophia, and the Hippodrome were the three greatest buildings in Constantinople. This last was a huge amphitheater, constructed of brick covered by marble, holding between forty and sixty thousand spectators. Although gladiator fights were held there, the main events were the chariot races; twenty-four would usually be presented in one day. The citizens of Constantinople were passionate fans of chariot racing. Successful charioteers were acclaimed as heroes and honored with public statues. Crowds in the Hippodrome also took on political significance. Being a member of the two chief factions of charioteers—the Blues or the Greens—was the only real outlet for political expression. Even emperors had to be aware of their demands and attitudes: the loss of a race in the Hippodrome frequently resulted in bloody riots, and rioting could threaten the emperor's power.

## From Eastern Roman to Byzantine Empire

Justinian's accomplishments had been spectacular, but when he died, he left the eastern Roman Empire with serious problems: too much distant territory to protect, an empty treasury, a smaller population after a plague, and renewed threats to the frontiers. During the reign of Heraclius (610–641), the empire faced attacks from the Persians to the east and the Slavs to the north.

The empire was left exhausted by these struggles. In the midst of them, it had developed a new system of defense by creating a new administrative unit, the *theme*, which combined civilian and military offices in the hands of the same person. Thus the civil governor was also the military leader of the area. Although this innovation helped the empire survive, it also fostered increased militarization. By the mid-seventh century, it had become apparent that a restored Mediterranean empire was simply beyond the resources of the eastern empire. A renewed series of external threats in the second half of the seventh century strengthened this development.

The most serious challenge to the eastern empire was presented by the rise of Islam, which, as noted earlier in the chapter, created a powerful new force that swept through the east. The defeat of the eastern Roman army at Yarmuk in 636 meant the loss of the provinces of Syria and Palestine. The Arabs also moved into the old Persian Empire and conquered it. The failed Arab attempt to besiege Constantinople in 717 left Arabs and eastern Roman forces facing each other along a frontier in southern Asia Minor.

Problems also arose along the northern frontier, especially in the Balkans, where an Asian people known as the Bulgars had arrived earlier in the sixth century. In 679, the Bulgars defeated the eastern Roman forces and took possession of the lower Danube valley, setting up a strong Bulgarian kingdom.

By the beginning of the eighth century, the eastern Roman Empire was greatly diminished in size, consisting only of the eastern Balkans and Asia Minor. It was now an eastern Mediterranean state. These external challenges had important internal repercussions as well. By the eighth century, the eastern Roman Empire had been transformed into what historians call the Byzantine Empire (sometimes referred to as Byzantium), a civilization with its own unique character that would last until 1453. (Constantinople was built on the site of an older city named Byzantium—hence the term *Byzantine*.)

**The Byzantine Empire, c. 750**

**The Byzantine Empire in the Eighth Century** The Byzantine Empire was a Greek state. Latin fell into disuse as Greek became not only the common language of the empire but its official language as well.

The Byzantine Empire was also a Christian state, built on a faith in Jesus that was shared by almost all its citizens. An enormous amount of artistic talent was poured into church construction, church ceremonies, and church decoration. Spiritual principles deeply permeated Byzantine art. The importance of religion to the Byzantines explains why theological disputes took on an exaggerated form. The most famous of these disputes, the so-called iconoclastic controversy, threatened the stability of the empire in the first half of the eighth century.

Beginning in the sixth century, the use of religious images, especially in the form of icons or pictures of sacred figures, became so widespread that charges of idolatry (the worship of images) began to be heard. The use of images or icons had been justified by the argument that icons were not worshiped but were simply used to help illiterate people understand their religion. This argument failed to stop the iconoclasts, as the opponents of icons were called.

**Iconoclasm** was not unique to the Byzantine Empire. In the neighboring Islamic empire, religious art did not include any physical representations of Muhammad. Iconoclasm would also play a role among some of the new religious groups that emerged in the Protestant Reformation in sixteenth-century Europe (see Chapter 14).

Beginning in 730, the Byzantine emperor Leo III (717–741) outlawed the use of icons. Strong resistance ensued, especially from monks. Leo III also used the iconoclastic controversy to add to the prestige of the patriarch of Constantinople, the highest church official in the east and second in dignity only to the bishop of Rome. The Roman popes were opposed to the iconoclastic edicts, and their opposition created considerable dissension between the popes and the Byzantine emperors. Late in the eighth century, the Byzantine rulers reversed their stand on the use of images, but not before considerable damage had been done to the unity of the Christian church. Although the final separation between Roman Catholicism and Greek Orthodoxy (as the Christian church in the Byzantine Empire was called) did not occur until 1054, the iconoclastic controversy was important in moving both sides in that direction.

The emperor occupied a crucial position in the Byzantine state. Portrayed as chosen by God, the Byzantine emperor was crowned in sacred ceremonies, and his subjects were expected to prostrate themselves in his presence. His power was considered absolute and was limited in practice only by deposition or assassination. Because the emperor appointed the patriarch, he also exercised control over both church and state. The Byzantines believed that God had commanded their state to preserve the true faith—Orthodox Christianity. Emperor, clergy, and civic officials were all bound together in service to this ideal. It can be said that spiritual values truly held the Byzantine state together.

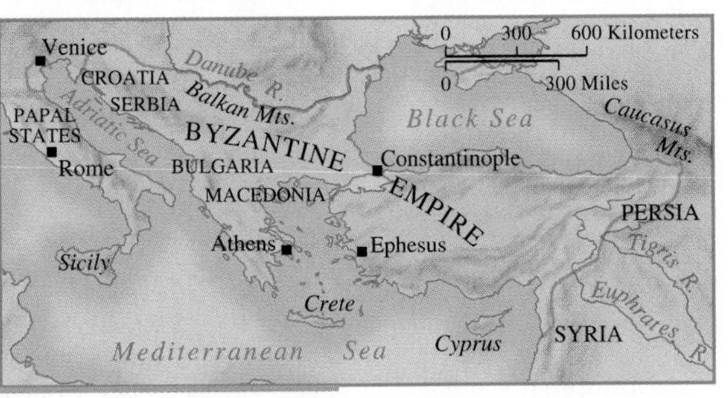

**The Byzantine Empire, 1025**

By 750, it was apparent that two of Rome's heirs, the Germanic kingdoms and the Byzantine Empire, were moving in different directions. Nevertheless, Byzantine influence on the medieval Western world was significant. The images of a Roman imperial state that continued to haunt the West had a living reality in the Byzantine state. The legal system of the West came to owe much to Justinian's codification of Roman law. In addition, the Byzantine Empire served in part as a buffer state, protecting the West for a long time from incursions from the east.

## The Zenith of Byzantine Civilization

In the seventh and eighth centuries, the Byzantine Empire had lost much of its territory to Slavs, Bulgars, and Muslims. By 750, the empire consisted only of Asia Minor, some lands in the Balkans, and the southern coast of Italy. Although Byzantium was beset with internal dissension and invasions in the ninth century, it was able to deal with them and not only endured but even expanded, reaching its high point in the tenth century, which some historians have called the golden age of Byzantine civilization.

During the reign of Michael III (842–867), the Byzantine Empire began to experience a revival. Iconoclasm was finally abolished in 843, and reforms were made in education, church life, the military, and the peasant economy. There was a noticeable intellectual renewal. But the Byzantine Empire under Michael was still plagued by persistent problems. The Bulgars mounted new attacks, and the Arabs continued to harass the empire. Moreover, a new church problem with political repercussions erupted over differences between the pope as leader of the western Christian church and the patriarch of Constantinople as leader of the eastern (or Orthodox) Christian church. Patriarch Photius condemned the pope as a heretic for accepting a revised form of the Nicene Creed stating that the Holy Spirit proceeded from the Father and the Son instead of "the Holy Spirit, who proceeds from the Father." A council of eastern bishops followed Photius' wishes and excommunicated the pope, creating the so-called Photian schism. Although the differences were later papered over, this controversy served to further the division between the eastern and western Christian churches.

**The Macedonian Dynasty** The problems that arose during Michael's reign were effectively dealt with by a new dynasty of Byzantine emperors known as the Macedonians (867–1056), who managed to hold off the external enemies, go over to the offensive, and reestablish domestic order. Supported by the church, the emperors thought of the Byzantine Empire as a continuation of the Christian Roman Empire of late antiquity. Although for diplomatic reasons they occasionally recognized the imperial titles of earlier western emperors, such as Charlemagne and Otto I, they still regarded them as little more than barbarian parvenus.

The Macedonian emperors could boast of a remarkable number of achievements in the late ninth and tenth centuries. They worked to strengthen the position of the free farmers, who felt threatened by the attempts of landed aristocrats to expand their estates at the farmers' expense. The emperors were well aware that the free farmers made up the rank and file of the Byzantine cavalry and provided the military strength of the empire. The Macedonian emperors also fostered a burst of economic prosperity by expanding trade relations with western Europe, especially by selling silks and metalwork. Thanks to this prosperity, the city of Constantinople flourished. Foreign visitors continued to be astounded by its size, wealth, and physical surroundings. To western Europeans, it was the stuff of legends and fables (see the box on p. 212).

In this period of prosperity, Byzantine cultural influence expanded due to the active missionary efforts of eastern Byzantine Christians. Eastern Orthodox Christianity was spread to eastern European peoples, such as the Bulgars and Serbs. Perhaps the greatest missionary success occurred when the prince of Kiev in Russia converted to Christianity in 987.

Under the Macedonian rulers, Byzantium enjoyed a strong civil service, talented emperors, and military advances. The Byzantine civil service was staffed by well-educated, competent aristocrats from Constantinople who oversaw the collection of taxes, domestic administration, and foreign policy. At the same time, the Macedonian dynasty produced some truly outstanding emperors skilled in administration and law, including Leo VI (886–912) and Basil II (976–1025). In the tenth century, competent emperors combined with a number of talented generals to mobilize the empire's military resources and take the offensive. The Bulgars were defeated, and both the eastern and western parts of Bulgaria were annexed to the empire. The Byzantines went on to add the

## A Western View of the Byzantine Empire

Bishop Liudprand of Cremona undertook diplomatic missions to Constantinople on behalf of two western kings, Berengar of Italy and Otto I of Germany. This selection is taken from his description of his mission to the Byzantine emperor Constantine VII in 949 as an envoy for Berengar, king of Italy from 950 until his overthrow by Otto I of Germany in 964. Liudprand had mixed feelings about Byzantium: admiration, yet also envy and hostility because of its superior wealth.

*What impressions of the Byzantine court do you receive from Liudprand's account? What is the modern meaning of the word* byzantine*? How does this account help explain the modern meaning of the word?*

### Liudprand of Cremona, *Antapodosis*

Next to the imperial residence at Constantinople there is a palace of remarkable size and beauty which the Greeks call Magnavra . . . the name being equivalent to "Fresh breeze." In order to receive some Spanish envoys, who had recently arrived, as well as myself . . . , Constantine gave orders that this palace should be got ready. . . .

Before the emperor's seat stood a tree, made of bronze gilded over, whose branches were filled with birds, also made of gilded bronze, which uttered different cries, each according to its varying species. The throne itself was so marvelously fashioned that at one moment it seemed a low structure, and at another it rose high into the air. It was of immense size and was guarded by lions, made either of bronze or of wood covered over with gold, who beat the ground with their tails and gave a dreadful roar with open mouth and quivering tongue. Leaning upon the shoulders of two eunuchs I was brought into the emperor's presence. At my approach the lions began to roar and the birds to cry out, each according to its kind; but I was neither terrified nor surprised, for I had previously made enquiry about all these things from people who were well acquainted with them. So after I had three times made obeisance to the emperor with my face upon the ground, I lifted my head, and behold! The man whom just before I had seen sitting on a moderately elevated seat had now changed his raiment and was sitting on the level of the ceiling. How it was done I could not imagine, unless perhaps he was lifted up by some such sort of device as we use for raising the timbers of a wine press. On that occasion he did not address me personally, . . . but by the intermediary of a secretary he enquired about Berengar's doings and asked after his health. I made a fitting reply and then, at a nod from the interpreter, left his presence and retired to my lodging.

It would give me some pleasure also to record here what I did then for Berengar. . . . The Spanish envoys . . . had brought handsome gifts from their masters to the emperor Constantine. I for my part had brought nothing from Berengar except a letter and that was full of lies. I was very greatly disturbed and shamed at this and began to consider anxiously what I had better do. In my doubt and perplexity it finally occurred to me that I might offer the gifts, which on my account I had brought for the emperor, as coming from Berengar, and trick out my humble present with fine words. I therefore presented him with nine excellent cuirasses, seven excellent shields with gilded bosses, two silver gilt cauldrons, some swords, spears, and spits, and what was more precious to the emperor than anything, four carzimasia; that being the Greek name for young eunuchs who have had both their testicles and their penis removed. This operation is performed by traders at Verdun, who take the boys into Spain and make a huge profit.

**HistoryNow™** To read more accounts by Liudprand, enter the *HistoryNow* documents area using the access card that is available for *World History.*

islands of Crete and Cyprus to the empire and defeat the Muslim forces in Syria, expanding the empire to the upper Euphrates. By the end of the reign of Basil II in 1025, the Byzantine Empire was the largest it had been since the beginning of the seventh century.

## New Challenges to the Byzantine Empire

The Macedonian dynasty of the tenth and eleventh centuries had restored much of the power of the Byzantine Empire; its incompetent successors, however, reversed most of the gains. After the Macedonian dynasty was extinguished in 1056, the empire was beset by internal struggles for power between ambitious military leaders and aristocratic families who bought the support of the great landowners of Anatolia by allowing them greater control over their peasants. This policy was self-destructive, however, because the peasant-warrior was an important source of military strength in the Byzantine state.

The growing division between the Catholic church of the West and the Eastern Orthodox church of the Byzantine Empire also weakened the Byzantine state. The Eastern Orthodox church was unwilling to accept the pope's claim that he was the sole head of the church. This dispute reached a climax in 1054 when Pope Leo IX and Patriarch Michael Cerularius, head of the Byzantine church, formally excommunicated each other, initiating a schism between the two great branches of Christianity that has not been healed to this day.

The Byzantine Empire faced external threats to its security as well. The greatest challenge came from the Seljuk Turks who had moved into Asia Minor—the heartland of the empire and its main source of food and manpower. After the Byzantine forces were disastrously defeated at

**CHRONOLOGY The Byzantine Empire**

| | |
|---|---|
| Justinian codifies Roman law | 529–533 |
| Reconquest of Italy by the Byzantines | 535–552 |
| Completion of Hagia Sophia | 537 |
| Attacks on the empire in reign of Heraclius | 610–641 |
| Arab defeat of Byzantines at Yarmuk | 636 |
| Defeat by the Bulgars; losses in the Balkans | 679 |
| Leo III and iconoclasm | 717–741 |
| Revival under Michael III | 842–867 |
| Macedonian dynasty | 867–1056 |
| Leo VI | 886–912 |
| Basil II | 976–1025 |
| Schism between Eastern Orthodox church and Catholic church | 1054 |
| Turkish defeat of Byzantines at Manzikert | 1071 |
| Revival under Alexius I Comnenus | 1081–1118 |
| Latin Empire of Constantinople | 1204–1261 |
| Revival of Byzantine Empire | 1261 |
| Fall of the empire | 1453 |

Manzikert by a Turkish army in 1071, the Turks advanced into Anatolia, where many peasants, already disgusted by their exploitation at the hands of Byzantine landowners, readily accepted Turkish control (see Map 7.4 on p. 195).

A new dynasty, however, soon breathed new life into the Byzantine Empire. The Comneni, under Alexius I Comnenus (1081–1118), were victorious on the Greek Adriatic coast against the Normans, defeated their enemies in the Balkans, and stopped the Turks in Anatolia. Lacking the resources to undertake additional campaigns against the Turks, Emperor Alexius I turned to the West for military assistance. The positive response to the emperor's request led to the Crusades. The Byzantine Empire lived to regret it.

## Impact of the Crusades

Ultimately, the Crusades had an enormous impact on the Byzantine Empire. In the First Crusade, the mostly French bands of crusading knights ignored their oath of allegiance and promises to Byzantine Emperor Alexis and organized their own crusader states in Palestine (see Chapter 12). Even more disastrous was the Fourth Crusade. On its way to Palestine, the crusading army became involved in a dispute over the succession to the Byzantine throne. The Venetian leaders of the Fourth Crusade saw an opportunity to neutralize their greatest commercial competitor, the Byzantine Empire. Diverted to Constantinopole, the crusaders sacked the great capital city in 1204 and set up the Latin Empire of Constantinople. Some parts of the Byzantine Empire managed to survive under Byzantine princes. In 1259, Michael Paleologus, a Greek military leader, took control of the kingdom of Nicaea in western Asia Minor and led a Byzantine army in recapturing Constantinople two years later.

The Byzantine Empire had been saved, but it was no longer a great Mediterranean power. The restored empire now consisted of the city of Constantinople and its surrounding territory along with some lands in Asia Minor. Though reduced in size, the empire limped along for another two centuries until its weakened condition finally enabled the Ottoman Turks to conquer it in 1453 (see Chapter 15).

## CONCLUSION

AFTER THE COLLAPSE of Roman power in the west, the eastern Roman Empire, centered on Constantinople, continued in the eastern Mediterranean and eventually emerged as the unique Christian civilization known as the Byzantine Empire, which flourished for hundreds of years. One of the greatest challenges to the Byzantine Empire, however, came from a new force–Islam–that blossomed in the Arabian peninsula and spread rapidly throughout the Middle East. In the eyes of some Europeans during the Middle Ages, the Arab empire was a malevolent force that posed a serious threat to the security of Christianity. Their fears were not entirely misplaced, for within half a century after the death of Islam's founder, Muhammad, Arab armies overran Christian states in North Africa and the Iberian peninsula, and Turkish Muslims moved eastward onto the fringes of the Indian subcontinent.

But although the teachings of Muhammad brought war and conquest to much of the known world, they also brought hope and a sense of political and economic stability to peoples throughout the region. Thus for many people in the medieval Mediterranean world, the arrival of Islam was a welcome event. Islam brought a code of law and a written language to societies that had previously not possessed them. Finally, by creating a revitalized trade network stretching from West Africa to East Asia, it established a vehicle for the exchange of technology and ideas that brought untold wealth to thousands and a better life to millions.

Like other empires in the region, the Arab empire did not last. It fell victim to a combination of internal and external pressures, and by the end of the thirteenth century, it was no more than a memory. But it left a powerful legacy in Islam, which remains one of the great religions of the world. In succeeding centuries, Islam began to penetrate into new areas beyond the edge of the Sahara and across the Indian Ocean into the islands of the Indonesian archipelago.

## TIMELINE

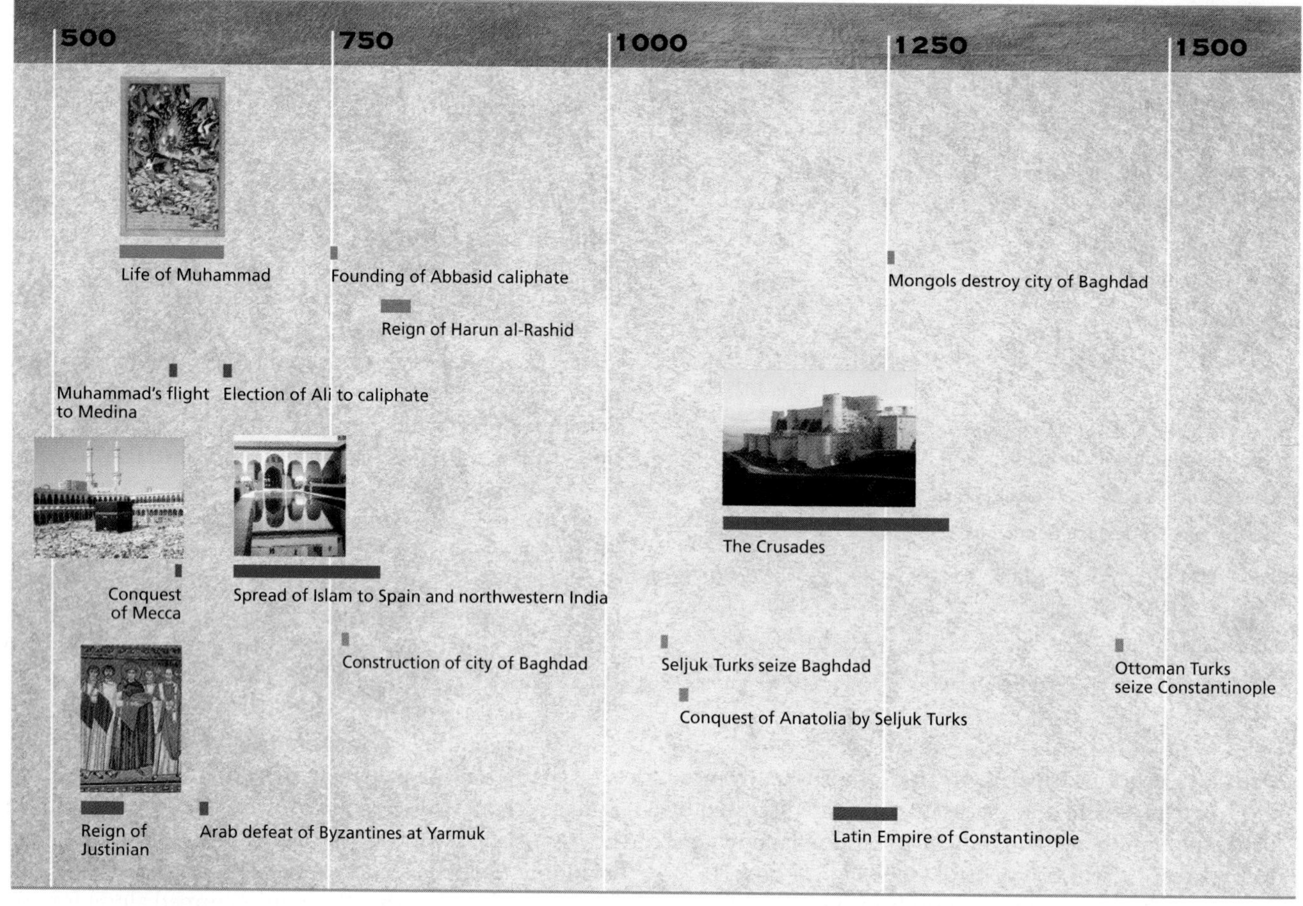


## CHAPTER NOTES

1. M. M. Pickthall, trans., *The Meaning of the Glorious Koran* (New York, 1953), p. 89.
2. Quoted in T. W. Lippman, *Understanding Islam: An Introduction to the Moslem World* (New York, 1982), p. 118.
3. F. Hirth and W. W. Rockhill, trans., *Chau Ju-kua: His Work on the Chinese and Arab Trade in the Twelfth and Thirteenth Centuries, Entitled Chu-fan-chi* (New York, 1966), p. 115.
4. al-Mas'udi, *The Meadows of Gold: The Abbasids,* ed. P. Lunde and C. Stone (London, 1989), p. 151.
5. L. Africanus, *The History and Description of Africa and of the Notable Things Therein Contained* (New York, n.d.), pp. 820–821.
6. E. Yarshater, ed., *Persian Literature* (Albany, N.Y., 1988), pp. 125–126.
7. Ibid., pp. 154–159.
8. E. Rehatsek, trans., *The Gulistan or Rose Garden of Sa'di* (New York, 1964), pp. 65, 67, 71.
9. Procopius, *Buildings of Justinian* (London, 1897), p. 9.
10. Ibid., p. 11.

## SUGGESTED READING

Standard works on the Arab empire and the rise of Islam include **T. W. Lippman, *Understanding Islam: An Introduction to the Moslem World*** (New York, 1982), and **G. E. Perry, *The Middle East: Fourteen Islamic Centuries,*** 2d ed. (Englewood Cliffs, N.J., 1992). For a more recent account, see **J. Bloom** and **S. Blair, *Islam: A Thousand Years of Faith and Power*** (New Haven, Conn., 2002).

Other worthwhile studies include **B. Lewis, *The Middle East: A Brief History of the Last 2,000 Years*** (New York, 1986); **K. Armstrong, *Islam: A Short History*** (New York, 2000); and **J. L. Esposito,** ed., ***The Oxford History of Islam*** (New York, 1999). For anthropological background, see **D. Bates** and **A. Rassam, *Peoples and Cultures of the Middle East*** (Englewood Cliffs, N.J., 1983).

On Islam, see **F. Denny, *An Introduction to Islam*** (New York, 1985), and **J. L. Esposito, *Islam: The Straight Path*** (New York, 1988). Among the various translations of the Qur'an, two of the best for the introductory student are **N. J. Dawood,** trans., ***The Koran*** (Harmondsworth, England, 1990), and **M. M. Pickthall,** trans., ***The Meaning of the Glorious Koran*** (New York, 1953). See also **R. W. Bulliet, *Conversion to Islam in the Medieval Period: An Essay in Quantitative History*** (Cambridge, 1979), and **K. Armstrong, *Muhammad: A Biography of the Prophet*** (San Francisco, 1993).

Specialized works on various historical periods are numerous. For a view of the Crusades from an Arab perspective, see **A. Maalouf, *The Crusades Through Arab Eyes*** (London, 1984), and **C. Hillenbrand, *The Crusades: Islamic Perspectives*** (New York, 2001). On the Mamluks, see **R. Irwin, *The Middle East in the Middle Ages: The Early Mamluk Sultanate, 1250–1382*** (Carbondale, Ill., 1986). In ***God of Battles: Christianity and Islam*** (Princeton, N.J., 1998),

**P. Partner** compares the expansionist tendencies of the two great religions. Also see **R. Fletcher, *The Cross and the Crescent: Christianity and Islam from Muhammad to the Reform*** (New York, 2005).

On the economy, see **E. Ashtor, *A Social and Economic History of the Near East in the Middle Ages*** (Berkeley, Calif., 1976); **K. N. Chaudhuri, *Asia Before Europe: Economy and Civilization of the Indian Ocean from the Rise of Islam to 1750*** (Cambridge, 1990); **C. Issawi, *The Middle East Economy: Decline and Recovery*** (Princeton, N.J., 1995); and **P. Crone, *Meccan Trade and the Rise of Islam*** (Princeton, N.J., 1987).

On women, see **F. Hussain**, ed., ***Muslim Women*** (New York, 1984); **G. Nashat** and **J. E. Tucker, *Women in the Middle East and North Africa*** (Bloomington, Ind., 1998); **S. S. Hughes** and **B. Hughes, *Women in World History,*** vol. 1 (London, 1995); and **L. Ahmed, *Women and Gender in Islam*** (New Haven, Conn., 1992).

For the best introduction to Islamic literature, consult **J. Kritzeck**, ed., ***Anthology of Islamic Literature*** (New York, 1964), with its concise commentaries and introduction. An excellent introduction to Persian literature can be found in **E. Yarshater, *Persian Literature*** (Albany, N.Y., 1988). For the student, **H. Haddawy,** trans., ***The Arabian Nights*** (New York, 1990), is the best version. It presents 271 "nights" in a clear and colorful style.

For the best introduction to Islamic art, consult the concise yet comprehensive work by **D. T. Rice, *Islamic Art,*** rev. ed. (London, 1975). Also see **J. Bloom** and **S. Blair, *Islamic Arts*** (London, 1997). For an excellent overview of world textiles, see **K. Wilson *A History of Textiles*** (Boulder, Colo. 1982).

Brief but good introductions to Byzantine history can be found in **J. Haldon, *Byzantium: A History*** (Charleston, S.C., 2000) and **W. Treadgold, *A Concise History of Byzantium*** (London, 2001). The best single political history is **G. Ostrogorsky, *A History of the Byzantine State,*** 2d ed. (New Brunswick, N.J., 1968). For a comprehensive survey of the Byzantine Empire, see **W. Treadgold, *A History of the Byzantine State and Society*** (Stanford, Calif., 1997). See also **C. Mango**, ed., ***The Oxford History of Byzantium*** (Oxford, 2002). On Justinian, see **J. Moorhead, *Justinian*** (London, 1995), and **J. A. S. Evans, *The Age of Justinian*** (New York, 1996). The role of the Christian church is discussed in **J. Hussey, *The Orthodox Church in the Byzantine Empire*** (Oxford, 1986)

## History Now™

**Enter *HistoryNow* using the access card that is available with this text. *HistoryNow* will assist you in understanding the content in this chapter with lesson plans generated for your needs, as well as provide you with a connection to the *Wadsworth World History Resource Center* (see description below for details).**

## WORLD HISTORY RESOURCE CENTER

**Enter the Resource Center using either your *HistoryNow* access card or your standalone access card for the *Wadsworth World History Resource Center.* Organized by topic, this website includes quizzes; images; over 350 primary source documents; interactive simulations; maps and timelines; movie explorations; and a wealth of other resources. You can read the following documents, and many more, at http://history.wadsworth.com/rc/world**

Muhammad's Last Sermon

Justinian's Code

Visit the *World History* Companion Website for chapter quizzes and more.

**http://history.wadsworth.com/duikerspielvogel05/**

CHAPTER

# EARLY CIVILIZATIONS IN AFRICA

*The Temple at Great Zimbabwe*

© Ariadne Van Zandbergen/Lonely Planet

## CHAPTER OUTLINE AND FOCUS QUESTIONS

### The Emergence of Civilization

- How did the advent of farming and pastoralism affect the various peoples of Africa in the classical era? How did the consequences of the agricultural revolution in Africa differ from those in other societies in Eurasia and America?

### The Coming of Islam

- What effects did the coming of Islam have on African religion, society, political structures, trade, and culture?

### States and Stateless Societies in Central and Southern Africa

- What role did migration play in the evolution of early African societies? How did the impact of these migrations compare with similar population movements elsewhere?

### African Society

- What role did lineage groups, women, and slavery play in African societies? Were there clear and distinct differences between African societies in various parts of the continent? If so, why?

### African Culture

- What are some of the chief characteristics of African sculpture and carvings, music, and architecture, and what purpose did these forms of creative expression serve in African society?

### CRITICAL THINKING

- With the exception of the Nile River valley, organized states did not emerge in the continent of Africa until much later than in many regions of the Eurasian supercontinent. Why do you think this was the case?

IN 1871, THE GERMAN EXPLORER Karl Mauch began to search southern Africa's central plateau for the colossal stone ruins of a legendary lost civilization. In late August, he found what he had been looking for. According to his diary: "Presently I stood before it and beheld a wall of a height of about 20 feet of granite bricks. Very close by there was a place where a kind of footpath led over rubble into the interior. Following this path I stumbled over masses of rubble and parts of walls and dense thickets. I stopped in front of a towerlike structure. Altogether it rose to a height of about 30 feet." Mauch was convinced that "a civilized nation must once have lived here." Like many other nineteenth-century Europeans, however, Mauch was equally convinced that the Africans who had lived there could never have built such splendid structures as the ones he had found at Great Zimbabwe. To Mauch and other archaeologists, Great Zimbabwe must have been the work of "a northern race closely akin to the Phoenician and Egyptian." It was not until the twentieth century that Europeans could overcome their prejudices and finally admit that Africans south of Egypt had also developed advanced civilizations with spectacular achievements.

The continent of Africa has played a central role in the long evolution of humankind. It was in Africa that the first hominids appeared more than three million years ago. It was probably in Africa that the immediate ancestors of modern human beings–*Homo sapiens*–emerged. The domestication of animals may have occurred first in Africa. Certainly, one of the first states appeared in Africa, in the Nile valley in the northeastern corner of the continent, in the form of the kingdom of the pharaohs. Recent evidence suggests that Egyptian civilization was significantly influenced by cultural developments taking place to the south, in Nubia, in modern Sudan.

After the decline of the Egyptian empire during the first millennium B.C.E., the focus of social change began to shift from the lower Nile valley to other areas of the continent: to West Africa, where a series of major trading states began to take part in the caravan trade with the Mediterranean through the vast wastes of the Sahara; to the region of the upper Nile River, where the states of Kush and Axum dominated trade for several centuries; and to the eastern coast from the Horn of Africa to the straits between the continent and the island of Madagascar, where African peoples began to play an active role in the commercial traffic in the Indian Ocean. In the meantime, a gradual movement of agricultural peoples brought Iron Age farming to the central portion of the continent, leading eventually to the creation of several states in the Congo River basin and the plateau region south of the Zambezi River.

The peoples of Africa, then, have played a significant role in the changing human experience since ancient times. Yet in many respects, that role was a distinctive one, a fact that continues to affect the fate of the continent in our own day. The landmass of Africa is so vast and its topography so diverse that communications within the continent and between Africans and peoples living elsewhere in the world have often been more difficult than in many neighboring regions. As a consequence, African societies are so disparate that generalizations about the nature of the peoples living on the continent are difficult to sustain. ◇

## The Emergence of Civilization

After Asia, Africa is the largest of the continents (see Map 8.1). It stretches nearly 5,000 miles from the Cape of Good Hope in the south to the Mediterranean in the north and extends a similar distance from Cape Verde on the west coast to the Horn of Africa on the Indian Ocean.

### The Land

Africa is as diverse as it is vast. The northern coast, washed by the Mediterranean Sea, is mountainous for much of its length. South of the mountains lies the greatest desert on earth, the Sahara, which stretches from the Atlantic to the Indian Ocean. To the east is the Nile River, heart of the ancient Egyptian civilization. Beyond that lies the Red Sea, separating Africa from Asia.

The Sahara acts as a great divide separating the northern coast from the rest of the continent. Africa south of the Sahara contains a number of major regions. In the west is the so-called hump of Africa, which juts like a massive shoulder into the Atlantic Ocean. Here the Sahara gradually gives way to grasslands in the interior and then to tropical rain forests along the coast. This region, dominated by the Niger River, is rich in natural resources and was the home of many ancient civilizations.

Far to the east, bordering the Indian Ocean, is a very different terrain of snowcapped mountains, upland plateaus, and lakes. Much of this region is grassland populated by wild beasts, which have given it the modern designation of Safari Country. Here, in the East African Rift valley in the lake district of modern Kenya, early hominids began their long trek toward civilization several million years ago.

Farther to the south lies the Congo basin, with its jungles watered by the mighty Congo River. The jungles of equatorial Africa then fade gradually into the hills, plateaus, and deserts of the south. This rich land contains some of the most valuable mineral resources known today.

It is not certain when agriculture was first practiced on the continent of Africa. Until recently, historians assumed that crops were first cultivated in the lower Nile valley (the northern part near the Mediterranean) about seven or eight thousand years ago, when wheat and barley were introduced, possibly from the Middle East. Eventually, as explained in Chapter 1, this area gave rise to the civilization of ancient Egypt.

### Kush

Recent evidence suggests that this hypothesis may need some revision. South of Egypt, near the junction of the White and the Blue Nile, is an area known historically as Nubia. Some archaeologists suggest that agriculture may have appeared first in Nubia rather than in the lower Nile valley. Stone Age farmers from Nubia may have begun to cultivate local crops such as sorghum and millet along the banks of the upper Nile (the southern part near the river's source) as early as the eleventh millennium B.C.E.

Recent archaeological finds also imply that the first true African kingdom may have been located in Nubia rather than in Egypt. A drawing on an incense burner dated to 3100 B.C.E. or earlier depicts a seated ruler with the falcon motif later adopted by the pharaohs of Egypt. Some scholars suggest that the Nubian concept of kingship may have spread to the north, past the cataracts along the Nile, where it eventually gave birth to the better-known civilization of Egypt.

Whatever the truth of such conjectures, it is clear that contacts between the upper and lower Nile had been established by the late third millennium B.C.E., when Egyptian merchants traveled to Nubia to obtain ivory, ebony, frankincense, and leopard skins. A few

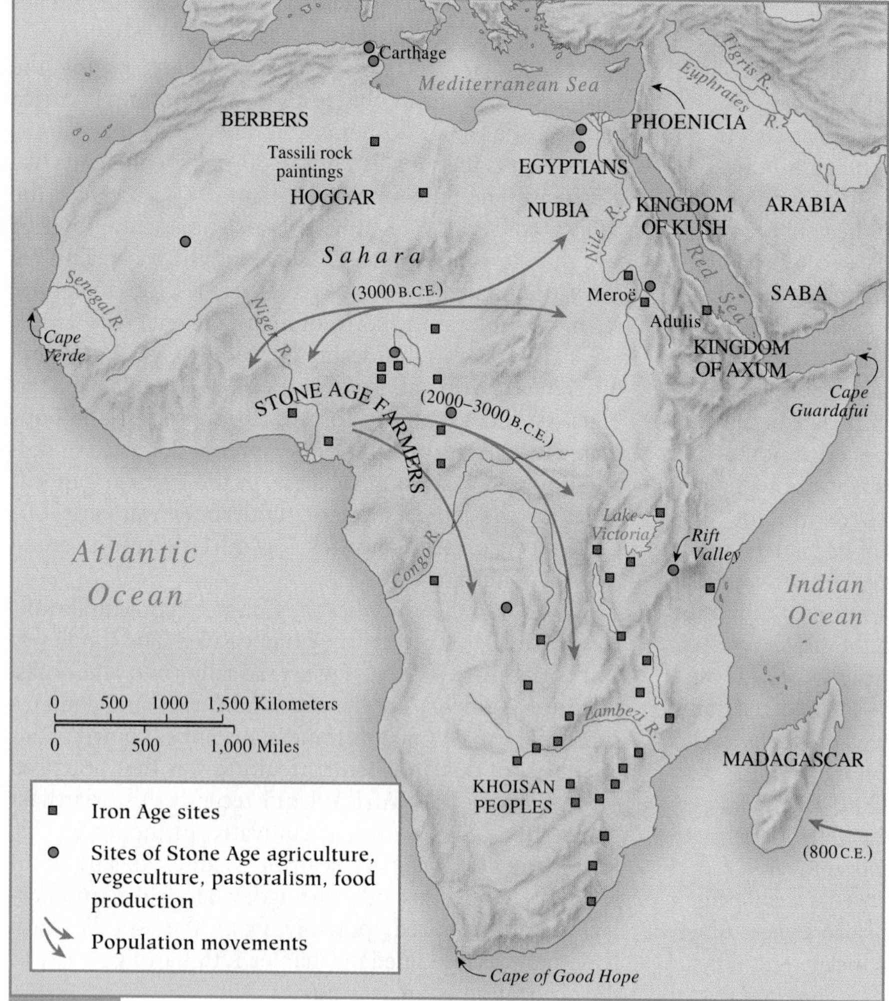


**MAP 8.1 Ancient Africa.** Modern human beings, known as *Homo sapiens,* first evolved on the continent of Africa. Some key sites of early human settlement are shown on this map. Which are the main river systems on the continent of Africa? **View an animated version of this map or related maps at** http://history.wadsworth.com/duikerspielvogel05/

centuries later, Nubia had become an Egyptian tributary. At the end of the second millennium B.C.E., Nubia profited from the disintegration of the Egyptian New Kingdom to become the independent state of Kush. Egyptian influence continued, however, as Kushite culture borrowed extensively from Egypt, including religious beliefs, the practice of interring kings in pyramids, and hieroglyphics.

Although its economy was probably founded primarily on agriculture and animal husbandry, Kush developed into a major trading state that endured for hundreds of years. Its commercial activities were stimulated by the discovery of iron ore in a floodplain near the river at Meroë. Strategically located at the point where a land route across the desert to the north intersected the Nile River, Meroë eventually became the capital of the state. In addition to iron products, Kush supplied goods from Central and East Africa, notably ivory, gold, ebony, and slaves (see the box on p. 220) to the Roman Empire, Arabia, and India. At first, goods were transported by donkey caravans to the point where the river north was navigable. By the last centuries of the first millennium B.C.E., however, the donkeys were being replaced by camels, newly introduced from the Arabian peninsula.

In the absence of extensive written records, confirmed evidence about the nature of Kushite society is limited, but it seems likely that it was predominantly urban. Initially, foreign trade was probably a monopoly of the state, but the presence of luxury goods in the numerous private tombs in the vicinity indicate that at one time material prosperity was relatively widespread. This suggests that commercial activities were being conducted by a substantial merchant class.

## Axum, Son of Saba

In the first millennium C.E., Kush declined and was eventually conquered by Axum, a new power located in the highlands of modern Ethiopia (see Map 8.2). Axum had been founded during the first millennium B.C.E., possibly by migrants from the kingdom of Saba (popularly known as Sheba) across the Red Sea on the southern tip of the Arabian peninsula. During antiquity, Saba was a major trading state, serving as a transit point for goods carried from South Asia into the lands surrounding the Mediterranean. Biblical sources credited the "queen of Sheba" with vast wealth and resources. In fact, much of that wealth had originated much farther to the east and passed through Saba en route to the countries adjacent to the Mediterranean.

When Saba declined, perhaps because of the desiccation of the Arabian Desert, Axum survived for centuries as an independent state (see the comparative illustration on p. 236). Like Saba, Axum owed much of its prosperity to its location on the commercial trade route between India and the Mediterranean, and Greek ships from the Ptolemaic kingdom in Egypt stopped regularly at the port of Adulis on the Red Sea. Axum exported ivory, frankincense, myrrh, and slaves, while its primary imports were textiles, metal goods, wine, and olive oil. For a time, Axum competed for control of the ivory trade with the neighboring state of Kush, and hunters from Axum armed with imported iron weapons scoured the entire region for elephants. Probably as a result of this compe-

## COMPARATIVE ESSAY

## The Migration of Peoples

About 50,000 years ago, a small band of *Homo sapiens sapiens* crossed the Sinai peninsula from Africa and began to spread out across the Eurasian supercontinent. Thus began a migration of peoples that continued with accelerating speed throughout the ancient era and beyond. By 40,000 B.C.E., their descendants had spread across Eurasia as far as China and eastern Siberia and had even settled the distant continent of Australia.

Who were these peoples, and what provoked their decision to change their habitat? Undoubtedly, the first migrants were foragers or hunters in search of wild game, but with the advent of agriculture and the domestication of animals about 12,000 years ago, other peoples began to migrate vast distances in search of fertile farming and pasturelands.

The ever-changing climate was undoubtedly a major factor driving the process. In the fourth millennium B.C.E., the drying up of rich pasturelands in the Sahara forced the local inhabitants to migrate eastward toward the Nile River valley and the grasslands of East Africa. At about the same time, Indo-European–speaking farming peoples left the region of the Black Sea and moved gradually into central Europe in search of new farmlands. They were eventually followed by nomadic groups from Central Asia who began to occupy lands along the frontiers of the Roman Empire, while other bands of nomads threatened the plains of northern China from the Gobi Desert. In the meantime, Bantu-speaking farmers migrated from the Niger River southward into the rain forests of Central Africa and beyond. Similar movements took place in Southeast Asia and the Americas.

This steady flow of migrating peoples often had a destabilizing effect on sedentary societies in their path. Nomadic incursions represented a constant menace to the security of China, Egypt, and the Roman Empire and ultimately brought them to an end. But this vast movement of peoples often had beneficial effects as well, spreading new technologies and means of livelihood. Although some migrants, like the Huns, came for plunder and left havoc in their wake, other groups, like the Celtic peoples and the Bantus, prospered in their new environment.

The most famous of all nomadic invasions represents a case in point. In the thirteenth century C.E., the Mongols left their homeland in the Gobi Desert, advancing westward into the Russian steppes and southward in China and Central Asia and leaving death and devastation in their wake. At the height of their empire, the Mongols controlled virtually all of Eurasia except its western and southern fringes, thus creating a zone of stability in which a global trade and informational network could thrive that stretched from China to the shores of the Mediterranean.

---

Mediterranean and the Red Sea. In that century, a Greek seafarer from Alexandria wrote an account of his travels down the coast from Cape Guardafui at the tip of the Horn of Africa to the Strait of Madagascar, thousands of miles to the south. Called the *Periplus*, this work provides generally accurate descriptions of the peoples and settlements along the African coast and the trade goods they supplied.

According to the *Periplus*, the port of Rhapta (possibly modern Dar es Salaam) was a commercial metropolis, exporting ivory, rhinoceros horn, and tortoise shell and importing glass, wine, grain, and metal goods such as weapons and tools. The identity of the peoples taking part in this trade is not clear, but it seems likely that the area was already inhabited by a mixture of local peoples and immigrants from the Arabian peninsula. Out of this mixture would eventually emerge an African-Arabian **Swahili** culture (see "East Africa: The Land of Zanj" later in this chapter) that continues to exist in coastal areas today. Beyond Rhapta was "unexplored ocean." Some contemporary observers believed that the Indian and Atlantic Oceans were connected. Others were convinced that the Indian Ocean was an enclosed sea and that the continent of Africa could not be circumnavigated.

Trade across the Indian Ocean and down the coast of East Africa, facilitated by the monsoon winds, would gradually become one of the most lucrative sources of commercial profit in the ancient and medieval worlds. Although the origins of the trade remain shrouded in mystery, traders eventually came by sea from as far away as the mainland of Southeast Asia. Early in the first millennium C.E., Malay peoples bringing cinnamon to the Middle East began to cross the Indian Ocean directly and landed on the southeastern coast of Africa. Eventually, a Malay settlement was established on the island of Madagascar, where the population is still of mixed Malay-African origin. Historians suspect that Malay immigrants were responsible for introducing such Southeast Asian foods as the banana and the yam to Africa. With its high yield and ability to grow in uncultivated rain forest, the banana often became the preferred crop of the Bantu peoples.

# The Coming of Islam

As we saw in Chapter 7, the rise of Islam during the first half of the seventh century C.E. had ramifications far beyond the Arabian peninsula. Arab armies swept across North Africa, incorporating it into the Arab empire and isolating the Christian state of Axum to the south. Although East Africa and West Africa south of the Sahara were not conquered by the Arab forces, Islam eventually penetrated these areas as well.

## African Religious Beliefs Before Islam

When Islam arrived, most African societies already had well-developed systems of religious beliefs. Like other aspects of African life, early African religious beliefs varied from place to place, but certain characteristics appear to have been shared by most African societies. One of these common features was **pantheism,** belief in a single creator god from whom all things came. Sometimes the creator god was accompanied by a whole pantheon of lesser deities. The Ashanti people of Ghana in West Africa believed in a supreme being called Nyame, whose sons were lesser gods. Each son served a different purpose: one was the rainmaker, another was the source of compassion, and a third was responsible for the sunshine. This heavenly hierarchy paralleled earthly arrangements: worship of Nyame was the exclusive preserve of the king through his priests; lesser officials and the common people worshiped Nyame's sons, who might intercede with their father on behalf of ordinary Africans.

Many African religions also shared a belief in a form of afterlife during which the soul floated in the atmosphere through eternity. Belief in an afterlife was closely connected to the importance of ancestors and the **lineage group**, or clan, in African society. Each lineage group could trace itself back to a founding ancestor or group of ancestors. These ancestral souls would not be extinguished as long as the lineage group continued to perform rituals in their name. The rituals could also benefit the lineage group on earth, for the ancestral souls, being closer to the gods, had the power to influence, for good or evil, the lives of their descendants.

Such beliefs were challenged but not always replaced by the arrival of Islam. In some ways, the tenets of Islam were in conflict with traditional African beliefs and customs. Although the concept of a single transcendent deity presented no problems in many African societies, Islam's rejection of spirit worship and a priestly class ran counter to the beliefs of many Africans and was often ignored in practice. Similarly, as various Muslim travelers observed, Islam's insistence on the separation of the sexes contrasted with the relatively informal relationships that prevailed in many African societies and was probably slow to take root. In the long run, imported ideas were synthesized with native beliefs to create a unique brand of Africanized Islam.

### CHRONOLOGY Early Africa

| | |
|---|---|
| Origins of agriculture in Africa | c. 7000 B.C.E. |
| Desiccation of the Sahara | Begins c. 5000 B.C.E. |
| Kingship appears in the Nile valley | c. 3100 B.C.E. |
| Kingdom of Kush in Nubia | c. 500 B.C.E. |
| Iron Age begins | c. sixth century B.C.E. |
| Beginnings of trans-Saharan trade | c. first millennium B.C.E. |
| Rise of Axum | First century C.E. |
| Conquest of Kush by Axum | Fourth century C.E. |
| Arrival of Bantus in East Africa | Early centuries C.E. |
| Arrival of Malays on Madagascar | Second century C.E. |
| Origins of Ghana | Fifth century C.E. |
| Arab takeover of lower Nile valley | 641 C.E. |
| Development of Swahili culture | c. first millennium C.E. |
| Spread of Islam across North Africa | Seventh century C.E. |
| Spread of Islam in Horn of Africa | Ninth century C.E. |
| Decline of Ghana | Twelfth century C.E. |
| Establishment of Zagwe dynasty in Ethiopia | c. 1150 |
| Rise of Mali | c. 1250 |
| Kingdom of Zimbabwe | c. 1300–c. 1450 |
| Portuguese ships explore West African coast | Mid-fifteenth century |

## The Arabs in North Africa

In 641, Arab forces advanced into Egypt, seized the delta of the Nile River, and brought two centuries of Byzantine rule to an end. To guard against attacks from the Byzantine fleet, the Arabs eventually built a new capital at Cairo, inland from the previous Byzantine capital of Alexandria, and began to consolidate their control over the entire region.

The Arab conquerors were probably welcomed by many of the local inhabitants, if not the majority. Although Egypt had been a thriving commercial center under the Byzantines, the average Egyptian had not shared in this prosperity. Tax rates were generally high, and Christians were subjected to periodic persecution by the Byzantines, who viewed the local Coptic faith and other sects in the area as heresies. Although the new rulers continued to obtain much of their revenue from taxing the local farming population, tax rates were generally lower than they had been under the corrupt Byzantine government, and conversion to Islam brought exemption from taxation. During the next generations, many Egyptians converted to the Muslim faith, but Islam did not move into the upper Nile valley until several hundred years later. As Islam spread southward, it was adopted by many lowland peoples, but it had less success in the mountains of Ethiopia, where Coptic Christianity continued to win adherents.

In the meantime, Arab rule was gradually being extended westward along the Mediterranean coast. When the Romans conquered Carthage in 146 B.C.E., they had called their new province Africa, thus introducing a name that would eventually be applied to the entire continent. After the fall of the Roman Empire, much of the area had reverted to the control of local Berber chieftains, but the Byzantines captured Carthage in the mid-sixth century C.E. In 690, the city was seized by the Arabs, who then began to extend their control over the entire area, which they called al-Maghrib ("the west").

At first, the local Berber peoples resisted their new conquerors. The Berbers were tough fighters, and for several generations, Arab rule was limited to the towns and lowland coastal areas. But Arab persistence eventually paid off, and by the early eighth century, the entire North African coast as far west as the Strait of Gibraltar was under Arab rule. The Arabs were now poised to cross the strait and expand into southern Europe and to push south beyond the fringes of the Sahara.

## The Kingdom of Ethiopia: A Christian Island in a Muslim Sea

By the end of the sixth century C.E., the kingdom of Axum, long a dominant force in the trade network through the Red Sea, was in a state of decline. Both overexploitation of farmland and a shift in trade routes away from the Red Sea to the Arabian peninsula and Persian Gulf contributed to this decline. By the beginning of the ninth century, the capital had been moved farther into the mountainous interior, and Axum was gradually transformed from a maritime power into an isolated agricultural society.

The rise of Islam on the Arabian peninsula hastened this process, as the Arab world increasingly began to serve as the focus of the regional trade passing through the area. By the eighth century, a number of Muslim trading states had been established on the African coast of the Red Sea, a development that contributed to the transformation of Axum into a landlocked society with primarily agricultural interests. At first, relations between Christian Axum and its Muslim neighbors were relatively peaceful, as the larger and more powerful Axumite kingdom attempted with some success to compel the coastal Islamic states to accept a tributary relationship. Axum's role in the local commercial network temporarily revived, and the area became a prime source for ivory, resins like frankincense and myrrh, and slaves. Slaves came primarily from the south, where Axum had been attempting to subjugate restive tribal peoples living in the Amharic plateau beyond its southern border.

Beginning in the twelfth century, however, relations between Axum and its neighbors deteriorated as the Muslim states along the coast began to move inland to gain control over the growing trade in slaves and ivory. Axum responded with force and at first had some success in reasserting its hegemony over the area. But in the early fourteenth century, the Muslim state of Adal, located at the juncture of the Indian Ocean and the Red Sea, launched a new attack on the Christian kingdom.

Axum also underwent significant internal change during this period. The Zagwe dynasty, which seized control of the country in the mid-twelfth century, centralized the government and extended the Christian faith throughout the kingdom, now known as Ethiopia. Military commanders or civilian officials who had personal or kinship ties with the royal court established vast landed estates to maintain security and facilitate the collection of taxes from the local population. In the meantime, Christian missionaries established monasteries and churches to propagate the faith in outlying areas. Close relations were reestablished with leaders of the Coptic church in Egypt and with Christian officials in the Holy Land. This process was continued by the Solomonids, who succeeded the Zagwe dynasty in 1270. But by the early fifteenth century, the state had become more deeply involved in an expanding conflict with Muslim Adal to the east, a conflict that lasted for over a century and gradually took on the characteristics of a holy war.

## East Africa: The Land of Zanj

The rise of Islam also had a lasting impact on the coast of East Africa, which the Greeks had called Azania and the Arabs called Zanj. During the seventh and eighth centuries, peoples from the Arabian peninsula and the Persian Gulf began to settle at ports along the coast and on the small islands offshore. Then, according to legend, in the middle of the tenth century, a Persian from the city of Shiraz sailed to the area with his six sons. As his small fleet stopped along the coast, each son disembarked on one of the coastal islands and founded a small community; these settlements eventually grew into important commercial centers such as Mombasa, Pemba, Zanzibar (literally, "the coast of Zanj"), and Kilwa.

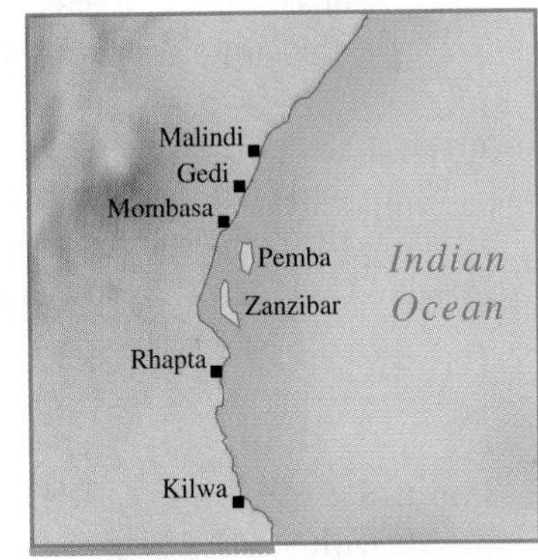

**The Swahili Coast**

Although the legend underestimates the degree to which the area had already become a major participant in local commerce as well as the role of the local inhabitants in the process, it does reflect the importance of Arab and Persian immigrants in the formation of a string of trading ports stretching from Mogadishu (today the capital of Somalia) in the north to Kilwa (south of present-day Dar es Salaam) in the south. Kilwa became especially important as it was near the southern limit for a ship hoping to complete the round-trip journey in a single season. Goods such as ivory, gold, and rhinoceros horn were exported across the Indian Ocean to countries as far away as China, while imports included iron goods, glassware, Indian textiles, and Chinese porcelain. Merchants in these cities often amassed considerable profit, as evidenced by their lavish stone palaces, some of which still stand in the modern cities of Mombasa and Zanzibar. Though now in ruins, Kilwa was one of the most magnificent cities of its day. The fourteenth-century Arab traveler Ibn Battuta described it as "amongst the most beautiful of cities and most elegantly built. All of it is of wood, and the ceilings of its houses are of al-dis [reeds]."[1] One particularly

## THE COAST OF ZANJ

From early times, the people living on the coast of East Africa took an active part in trade along the coast and across the Indian Ocean. The process began with the arrival of Arab traders early in the first millennium C.E. According to local legends, Arab merchants often married the daughters of the local chieftains and then received title to coastal territories as part of their wife's dowry. This description of the area was written by the Arab traveler al-Mas'udi, who visited the "land of Zanj" in 916.

*Why did Arab traders begin to settle along the coast of East Africa? What impact did the Arab presence have on the lives of the local population?*

### Al-Mas'udi in East Africa

The land of Zanj produces wild leopard skins. The people wear them as clothes, or export them to Muslim countries. They are the largest leopard skins and the most beautiful for making saddles. . . . They also export tortoise shell for making combs, for which ivory is likewise used. . . . The Zanj are settled in that area, which stretches as far as Sofala, which is the furthest limit of the land and the end of the voyages made from Oman and Siraf on the sea of Zanj. . . . The Zanj use the ox as a beast of burden, for they have no horses, mules or camels in their land. . . . There are many wild elephants in this land but no tame ones. The Zanj do not use them for war or anything else, but only hunt and kill them for their ivory. It is from this country that come tusks weighing fifty pounds and more. They usually go to Oman, and from there are sent to China and India. This is the chief trade route. . . .

The Zanj have an elegant language and men who preach in it. One of their holy men will often gather a crowd and exhort his hearers to please God in their lives and to be obedient to him. He explains the punishments that follow upon disobedience, and reminds them of their ancestors and kings of old. These people have no religious law: their kings rule by custom and by political expediency.

The Zanj eat bananas, which are as common among them as they are in India; but their staple food is millet and a plant called kalari which is pulled out of the earth like truffles. They also eat honey and meat. They have many islands where the coconut grows: its nuts are used as fruit by all the Zanj peoples. One of these islands, which is one or two days' sail from the coast, has a Muslim population and a royal family. This is the island of Kanbulu [thought to be modern Pemba].

impressive structure was the Husini Kubwa, a massive palace with vaulted roofs capped with domes and elaborate stone carvings, surrounding an inner courtyard. Ordinary townspeople and the residents in smaller towns did not live in such luxurious conditions, of course, but even so, affluent urban residents lived in spacious stone buildings, with indoor plumbing and consumer goods imported from as far away as China and southern Europe.

Most of the coastal states were self-governing, although sometimes several towns were grouped together under a single dominant authority. Government revenue came primarily from taxes imposed on commerce. Some trade went on between these coastal city-states and the peoples of the interior, who provided gold and iron, ivory, and various agricultural goods and animal products in return for textiles, manufactured articles, and weapons (see the box above). Relations apparently varied, and the coastal merchants sometimes resorted to force to obtain goods from the inland peoples. A Portuguese visitor recounted that "the men [of Mombasa] are oft-times at war and but seldom at peace with those of the mainland, and they carry on trade with them, bringing thence great store of honey, wax, and ivory."[2]

By the twelfth and thirteenth centuries, a mixed African-Arabian culture, eventually known as Swahili (from the Arabic *sahel*, meaning "coast"), began to emerge throughout the seaboard area. Intermarriage between the immigrants and the local population was common, although a distinct Arab community, made up primarily of merchants, persisted in many areas. The members of the ruling class were often of mixed heritage but usually traced their genealogy to Arab or Persian ancestors. By this time, too, many members of the ruling class had converted to Islam. Middle Eastern urban architectural styles and other aspects of Arab culture were implanted within a society still predominantly African. Arabic words and phrases were combined with Bantu grammatical structures to form a mixed language, also known as Swahili; it is the national language of Kenya and Tanzania today.

## The States of West Africa

During the eighth century, merchants from the Maghrib began to carry Muslim beliefs to the savanna areas south of the Sahara. At first, conversion took place on an individual basis rather than through official encouragement. The first rulers to convert to Islam were the royal family of Gao at the end of the tenth century. Five hundred years later, most of the population in the grasslands south of the Sahara had accepted Islam.

The expansion of Islam into West Africa had a major impact on the political system. By introducing Arabic as the first written language in the region and Muslim law codes and administrative practices from the Middle East, Islam provided local rulers with the tools to increase their authority and the efficiency of their governments. Moreover, as Islam gradually spread throughout the re-

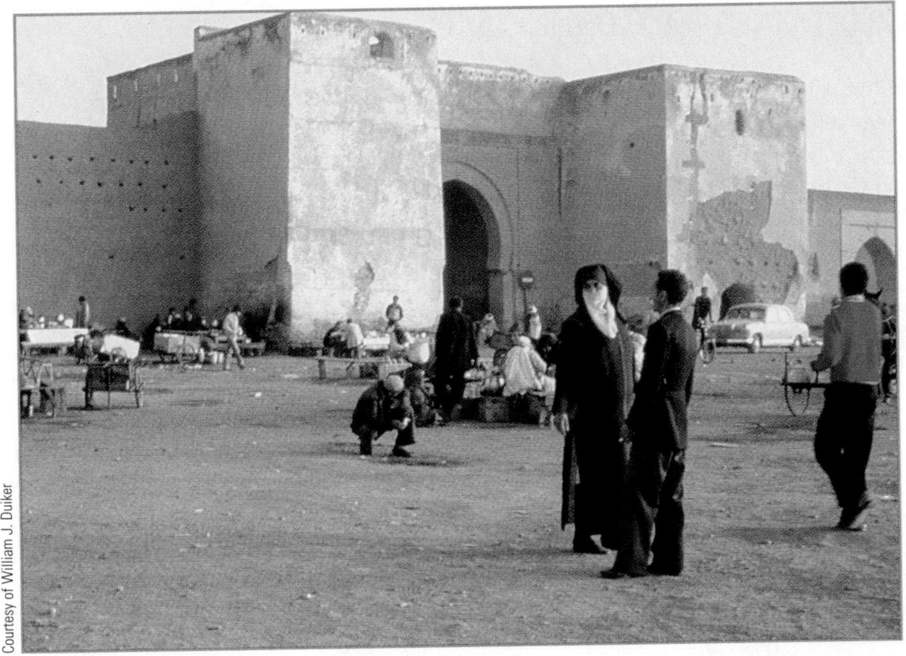


**The Great Gate at Marrakech.** The Moroccan city of Marrakech, founded in the ninth century C.E., was a major northern terminus of the trans-Saharan trade and one of the chief commercial centers in premodern Africa. Widely praised by such famous travelers as Ibn Battuta, the city was an architectural marvel in that all its major public buildings were constructed of red sandstone. Shown here is the Great Gate to the city, through which camel caravans passed en route to and from the vast desert. In the Berber language, Marrakech means "pass without making a noise," a reference to the need for caravan traders to be aware of the danger of thieves in the vicinity.

gion, a common religion united previously diverse peoples into a more coherent community.

When Islam arrived in the grasslands south of the Sahara, the region was beginning to undergo significant political and social change. A number of major trading states were in the making, and they eventually transformed the Sahara into one of the leading avenues of world trade, crisscrossed by caravan routes leading to destinations as far away as the Atlantic Ocean, the Mediterranean, and the Red Sea (see Map 8.3).

**Ghana** The first of these great commercial states was Ghana, which emerged in the fifth century C.E. in the upper Niger valley, a grassland region between the Sahara and the tropical forests along the West African coast. (The modern state of Ghana, which takes its name from the trading society under discussion here, is located in the forest region to the south.) The majority of the people in the area were Iron Age farmers living in villages under the authority of a local chieftain. Gradually, these local communities were united to form the kingdom of Ghana.

Although the people of the region had traditionally lived from agriculture, a primary reason for Ghana's growing importance was gold. The heartland of the state was located near one of the richest gold-producing areas in all of Africa. Ghanaian merchants transported the gold to Morocco, whence it was distributed throughout the known world. This trade began in ancient times, as the Greek historian Herodotus relates:

> The Carthaginians also tell us that they trade with a race of men who live in a part of Libya beyond the Pillars of Heracles [the Strait of Gibraltar]. On reaching this country, they unload their goods, arrange them tidily along the beach, and then, returning to their boats, raise a smoke. Seeing the smoke, the natives come

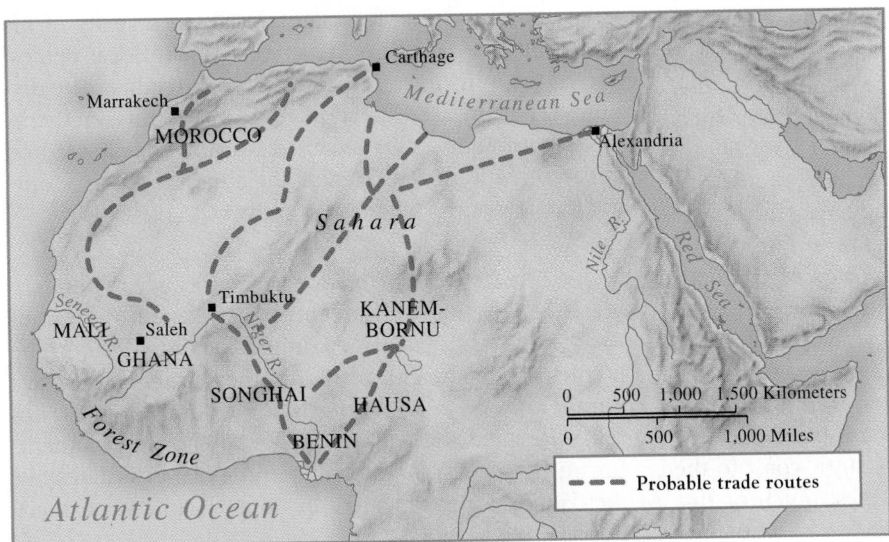


**MAP 8.3 Trans-Saharan Trade Routes.** Trade across the Sahara began during the first millennium B.C.E. With the arrival of the camel from the Middle East, trade expanded dramatically.
? What were the major cities involved in the trade, as shown on this map?
**View an animated version of this map or related maps at http://history.wadsworth.com/duikerspielvogel05/**

## Description of a Ghanaian Capital

After its first appearance in West Africa in the decades following the death of Muhammad, Islam competed with native African religions for followers. Eventually, several local rulers converted to the Muslim faith. This passage by the Arab geographer al-Bakri shows how both religions flourished side by side in the state of Ghana during the eleventh century.

*Why might an African ruler find it advantageous to adopt the Muslim faith? What kinds of changes would the adoption of Islam entail for the peoples living in West Africa?*

### Al-Bakri's Description of Ghana

The king's residence comprises a palace and conical huts, the whole surrounded by a fence like a wall. Around the royal town are huts and groves of thorn trees where live the magicians who control their religious rites. These groves, where they keep their idols and bury their kings, are protected by guards who permit no one to enter or find out what goes on in them.

None of those who belong to the imperial religion may wear tailored garments except the king himself and the heir-presumptive, his sister's son. The rest of the people wear wrappers of cotton, silk or brocade according to their means. Most of the men shave their beards and the women their heads. The king adorns himself with female ornaments around the neck and arms. On his head he wears gold-embroidered caps covered with turbans of finest cotton. He gives audience to the people for the redressing of grievances in a hut around which are placed 10 horses covered in golden cloth. Behind him stand 10 slaves carrying shields and swords mounted with gold. On his right are the sons of vassal kings, their heads plaited with gold and wearing costly garments. On the ground around him are seated his ministers, whilst the governor of the city sits before him. On guard at the door are dogs of fine pedigree, wearing collars adorned with gold and silver. The royal audience is announced by the beating of a drum, called daba, made out of a long piece of hollowed-out wood. When the people have gathered, his coreligionists draw near upon their knees sprinkling dust upon their heads as a sign of respect, whilst the Muslims clap hands as their form of greeting.

> down to the beach, place on the ground a certain quantity of gold in exchange for the goods, and go off again to a distance. The Carthaginians then come ashore and take a look at the gold; and if they think it represents a fair price for their wares, they collect it and go away; if, on the other hand, it seems too little, they go back aboard and wait, and the natives come and add to the gold until they are satisfied. There is perfect honesty on both sides; the Carthaginians never touch the gold until it equals in value what they have offered for sale, and the natives never touch the goods until the gold has been taken away.[3]

Later, Ghana became known to Arab-speaking peoples in North Africa as "the land of gold." Actually, the name was misleading, for the gold did not come from Ghana but from a neighboring people, who sold it to merchants from Ghana.

Eventually, other exports from Ghana found their way to the bazaars of the Mediterranean coast and beyond—ivory, ostrich feathers, hides, leather goods, and ultimately slaves. The origins of the slave trade in the area probably go back to the first millennium B.C.E., when Berber tribesmen seized African villagers in the regions south of the Sahara and sold them for profit to buyers in Europe and the Middle East. In return, Ghana imported metal goods (especially weapons), textiles, horses, and salt.

Much of the trade across the desert was still conducted by the nomadic Berbers, but Ghanaian merchants played an active role as intermediaries, trading tropical products such as bananas, kola nuts, and palm oil from the forest states of Guinea along the Atlantic coast to the south. By the eighth and ninth centuries, much of this trade was conducted by Muslim merchants, who purchased the goods from local traders (using iron and copper cash or cowrie shells from Southeast Asia as the primary means of exchange) and then sold them to Berbers, who carried them across the desert. The merchants who carried on this trade often became quite wealthy and lived in splendor in cities like Saleh, the capital of Ghana. So did the king, of course, who taxed the merchants as well as the farmers and the producers.

Like other West African kings, the king of Ghana ruled by divine right and was assisted by a hereditary aristocracy composed of the leading members of the prominent clans, who also served as district chiefs responsible for maintaining law and order and collecting taxes. The king was responsible for maintaining the security of his kingdom, serving as an intermediary with local deities, and functioning as the chief law officer to adjudicate disputes. The kings of Ghana did not convert to Islam themselves, although they welcomed Muslim merchants and apparently did not discourage their subjects from adopting the new faith (see the box above).

**Mali** The state of Ghana flourished for several hundred years, but by the twelfth century, weakened by ruinous wars with Berber tribesmen, it had begun to decline, and it collapsed at the end of the century. In its place rose a number of new trading societies, including large territorial states like Mali and Songhai in the west, Kanem-Bornu in the east, and small commercial city-states like the Hausa states, located in what is today northern Nigeria (see Map 8.4).

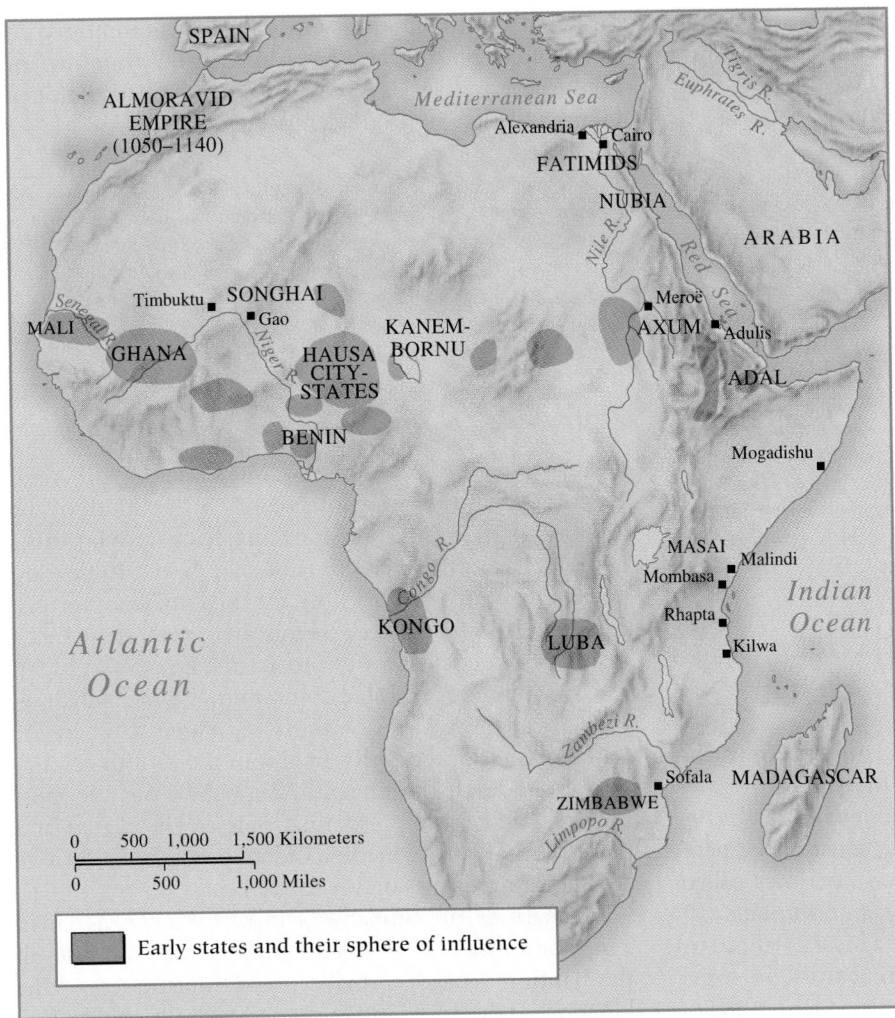


**MAP 8.4 The Emergence of States in Africa.** By the end of the first millennium C.E., organized states had begun to appear in various parts of Africa. What were some of the key states at the time, as shown on the map? **View an animated version of this map or related maps at** http://history .wadsworth.com/duikerspielvogel05/

The greatest of the states that emerged after the destruction of Ghana was Mali. Extending from the Atlantic coast inland as far as the trading cities of Timbuktu and Gao on the Niger River, Mali built its wealth and power on the gold trade. But the heartland of Mali was situated south of the Sahara in the savanna region, where sufficient moisture enabled farmers to grow such crops as sorghum, millet, and rice. The farmers lived in villages ruled by a local chieftain (called a *mansa*), who served as both religious and administrative leader and was responsible for forwarding tax revenues from the village to higher levels of government.

The primary wealth of the country was accumulated in the cities. Here lived the merchants, who were primarily of local origin, although many were now practicing Muslims. Commercial activities were taxed but were apparently so lucrative that both the merchants and the kings prospered. One of the most powerful kings of Mali was Mansa Musa (1312–1337), whose primary contribution to his people was probably not economic prosperity but the Muslim faith. Mansa Musa strongly encouraged the

Bibliothèque Nationale, Paris

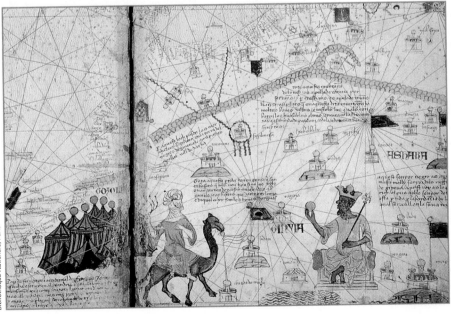

**Mansa Musa.** Mansa Musa, king of the West African state of Mali, was one of the richest and most powerful rulers of his day. During a famous pilgrimage to Mecca, he arrived in Cairo with a hundred camels laden with gold and gave away so much gold that its value depreciated there for several years. To promote the Islamic faith in his country, he bought homes in Cairo and Mecca to house pilgrims en route to the holy shrine, and he brought back to Mali a renowned Arab architect to build mosques in the trading centers of Gao and Timbuktu. His fame spread to Europe as well, evidenced by this Spanish map of 1375, which depicts Mansa Musa seated on his throne in Mali, holding an impressive gold nugget.

building of mosques and the study of the Qur'an in his kingdom and imported scholars and books to introduce his subjects to the message of Allah. One visitor from Europe, writing in the late fifteenth century, reported:

> The rich king of Timbuktu has many plates and scepters of gold, some whereof weigh 1,300 pounds; and he keeps a magnificent and well-furnished court. When he travels anywhere, he rides upon a camel which is led by some of his noblemen: and so he does likewise when he goes to warfare, and all his soldiers ride upon horses. . . . They often have skirmishes with those that refuse to pay tribute and, so many as they may take, they sell unto the merchants of Timbuktu. . . . Here are a great store of doctors, judges, priests and other learned men, that are bountifully maintained at the king's cost and charges. And hither are brought divers manuscripts of written books out of Barbary [North Africa] which are sold for more money than any other merchandise. The coin of Timbuktu is of gold without any stamp or superscription: but in matters of small value they use certain shells [cowrie shells] brought hither out of the kingdom of Persia.[4]

## States and Stateless Societies in Central and Southern Africa

In the southern half of the African continent, from the great basin of the Congo River to the Cape of Good Hope, states formed somewhat more slowly than in the north. Until the eleventh century C.E., most of the peoples in this region lived in what are sometimes called **stateless societies,** characterized by autonomous villages organized by clans and ruled by a local chieftain or clan head. Beginning in the eleventh century, in some parts of southern Africa, these independent villages gradually began to consolidate. Out of these groupings came the first states.

### The Congo River Valley

One area where this process occurred was the Congo River valley, where the combination of fertile land and nearby deposits of copper and iron enabled the inhabitants to enjoy an agricultural surplus and engage in regional commerce. Two new states in particular underwent this transition. Sometime during the fourteenth century, the kingdom of Luba was founded in the center of the continent, in a rich agricultural and fishing area near the shores of Lake Kisale. Luba had a relatively centralized government, in which the king appointed provincial governors, who were responsible for collecting tribute from the village chiefs. At about the same time, the kingdom of Kongo was formed just south of the mouth of the Congo River on the Atlantic coast.

These new states were primarily agricultural, although both had a thriving manufacturing sector and took an active part in the growing exchange of goods throughout the region. As time passed, both began to expand southward to absorb the mixed farming and pastoral peoples in the area of modern Angola. In the drier grassland area to the south, other small communities continued to support themselves by herding, hunting, or food gathering. A Portuguese sailor who encountered them in the late sixteenth century reported:

> These people are herdsmen and cultivators. . . . Their main crop is millet, which they grind between two stones or in wooden mortars to make flour. . . . Their wealth consists mainly in their huge number of dehorned cows. . . . They live together in small villages, in houses made of reed mats, which do not keep out the rain."[5]

### Zimbabwe

Farther to the east, the situation was somewhat different. In the grassland regions immediately to the south of the Zambezi River, a mixed economy involving farming, cattle herding, and commercial pursuits had begun to develop during the early centuries of the first millennium C.E. Characteristically, villages in this area were constructed inside walled enclosures to protect the animals at night. The most famous of these communities was Zimbabwe, located on the plateau of the same name between the Zambezi and Limpopo Rivers. From the twelfth century to the middle of the fifteenth, Zimbabwe was the most powerful and most prosperous state in the region and played a major role in the gold trade with the Swahili trading communities on the eastern coast.

The ruins of Zimbabwe's capital, known as Great Zimbabwe (the term *Zimbabwe* means "sacred house" in the Bantu language), provide a vivid illustration of the kingdom's power and influence. Strategically situated between substantial gold reserves to the west and a small

**Great Zimbabwe.** Situated on an important trade route and a center for cattle and agriculture, Great Zimbabwe was originally settled by pastoral peoples during the first millennium B.C.E. Later it became the capital of a prosperous state. Its 30-foot walls were the first in Africa to be constructed without the use of mortar. The walled palace shown here indicates why Great Zimbabwe is generally regarded as the most impressive archaeological site in southern Africa.

river leading to the coast, Great Zimbabwe was well placed to benefit from the expansion of trade between the coast and the interior. The town sits on a hill overlooking the river and is surrounded by stone walls, which enclosed an area large enough to hold over ten thousand residents. Like the Inka in South America (see Chapter 6), the local people stacked stone blocks without mortar to build their walls. The houses of the wealthy were built of cement on stone foundations, while those of the common people were of dried mud with thatched roofs. In the valley below is the royal palace, surrounded by a stone wall 30 feet high. Artifacts found at the site include household implements and ornaments made of gold and copper, as well as jewelry and even porcelain imported from China.

Most of the royal wealth probably came from two sources: the ownership of cattle and the king's ability to levy heavy taxes on the gold that passed through the kingdom en route to the coast. By the middle of the fifteenth century, however, the city was apparently abandoned, possibly because of environmental damage caused by overgrazing. With the decline of Zimbabwe, the focus of economic power began to shift northward to the valley of the Zambezi River.

### Southern Africa

South of the East African plateau and the Congo basin is a vast land of hills, grasslands, and arid desert stretching almost to the Cape of Good Hope at the tip of the continent. As Bantu-speaking farmers spread southward during the final centuries of the first millennium B.C.E., they began to encounter Stone Age peoples in the area who still lived primarily by hunting and foraging.

Available evidence suggests that early relations between these two peoples were relatively harmonious. Intermarriage between members of the two groups was apparently not unusual, and many of the hunter-gatherers were gradually absorbed into what became a dominantly Bantu-speaking pastoral and agricultural society that spread throughout much of southern Africa during the first millennium C.E.

**The Khoi and the San** Two such peoples were the Khoi and the San. The two were related because of their language, known as Khoisan, distinguished by the use of "clicking" sounds. The Khoi were herders, while the San were hunter-gatherers who lived in small family communities of twenty to twenty-five members throughout southern Africa from Namibia in the west to the Drakensberg Mountains near the southeastern coast. Scholars have learned about the early life of the San by interviewing their modern descendants and by studying rock paintings found in caves throughout the area. These multicolored paintings, which predate the coming of the Europeans, were drawn with a brush made of small feathers fastened to a reed. They depict various aspects of the San's lifestyle, including their hunting techniques and religious rituals.

## African Society

Drawing generalizations about social organization, cultural development, and daily life in traditional Africa is difficult because of the extreme diversity of the continent and its inhabitants. One-quarter of all the languages in the world are spoken in Africa, and five of the major language families are located there. Ethnic divisions are equally pronounced. Because many of these languages did not have a system of writing until fairly recently, historians must rely on accounts of the occasional visitor, such as al-Mas'udi and the famous fourteenth-century chronicler Ibn Battuta. Such travelers, however, tended to come into contact mostly with the wealthy and the powerful, leaving us to speculate about what life was like for ordinary Africans during this early period.

### Urban Life

African towns often began as fortified walled villages and gradually evolved into larger communities serving several purposes. Here, of course, were the center of government and the teeming markets filled with goods from distant regions. Here also were artisans skilled in metal- or woodworking, pottery making, and other crafts. Unlike the rural areas, where a village was usually composed of a single lineage group or clan, the towns drew their residents from several clans, although individual clans usually lived in their own compounds and were governed by their own clan heads.

In the states of West Africa, the focal point of the major towns was the royal precinct. The relationship between the ruler and the merchant class differed from the situation in most Asian societies, where the royal family and the aristocracy were largely isolated from the remainder of the population. In Africa, the chasm between the king and the common people was not so great. Often the ruler would hold an audience to allow people to voice their complaints or to welcome visitors from foreign countries. In the city-states of the East African coast as well, the ruler was frequently forced to share political power with a class of wealthy merchants and often, as in the case of the town of Kilwa, "did not possess more country than the city itself."[6]

This is not to say that the king was not elevated above all others in status. In wealthier states, the walls of the audience chamber would be covered with sheets of beaten silver and gold, and the king would be surrounded by hundreds of armed soldiers and some of his trusted advisers. Nevertheless, the symbiotic relationship between the ruler and merchant class served to reduce the gap between the king and his subjects. The relationship was mutually beneficial, since the merchants received honors and favors from the palace while the king's coffers were filled with taxes paid by the merchants. Certainly, it was to the benefit of the king to maintain law and order in his domain so that the merchants could ply their trade. As Ibn Battuta observed, among the good qualities of the peoples of West

**A "Lost City" in Africa.** Gedi was founded in the early thirteenth century and abandoned three hundred years later. Its romantic ruins suggest the grandeur of the Swahili civilization that once flourished along the eastern coast of Africa. Located 60 miles north of Mombasa, in present-day Kenya, Gedi once contained several thousand residents but was eventually abandoned after it was attacked by nomadic peoples from the north. Today the ruins of the town, surrounded by a 9-foot wall, seem dwarfed by towering baobab trees populated only by chattering monkeys. Shown here is the entrance to the palace, which probably served as the residence of the chief official in the town. Neighboring houses, constructed of coral stone, contain sumptuous rooms, with separate women's quarters and enclosed lavatories with urinal channels and double-sink washing benches. Artifacts found at the site came from as far away as Venice and China.

Courtesy of William J. Duiker

Africa was the prevalence of peace in the region. "The traveler is not afraid in it," he remarked, "nor is he who lives there in fear of the thief or of the robber by violence."[7]

## Village Life

The vast majority of Africans lived in small rural villages. Their identities were established by their membership in a nuclear family and a lineage group. At the basic level was the nuclear family of parents and preadult children; sometimes it included an elderly grandparent and other family dependents as well. They lived in small round huts constructed of packed mud and topped with a conical thatch roof. In most African societies, these nuclear family units would be combined into larger kinship communities known as households or lineage groups.

The lineage group was similar in many respects to the clan in China or the caste system in India in that it was normally based on kinship ties, although sometimes outsiders such as friends or other dependents may have been admitted to membership. Throughout the precolonial era, lineages served, in the words of one historian, as the "basic building blocks" of African society. The authority of the leading members of the lineage group was substantial. As in China, the elders had considerable power over the economic functions of the other people in the group, which provided mutual support for all members.

A village would usually be composed of a single lineage group, although some communities may have consisted of several unrelated families. At the head of the village was the familiar "big man," who was often assisted by a council of representatives of the various households in the community. Often the "big man" was believed to possess supernatural powers, and as the village grew in size and power, he might eventually be transformed into a local chieftain or monarch.

## The Role of Women

Although generalizations are risky, we can say that women were usually subordinate to men in Africa, as in most early societies. In some cases, they were valued for the work they could do or for their role in increasing the size of the lineage group. Polygyny was not uncommon, particularly in Muslim societies. Women often worked in the fields while the men of the village tended the cattle or went on hunting expeditions. In some communities, the women specialized in commercial activities. In one area in southern Africa, young girls were sent into the mines to extract gold because of their smaller physiques.

But there were some key differences between the role of women in Africa and elsewhere. In many African societies, lineage was **matrilinear** rather than **patrilinear.** In the words of Ibn Battuta during his travels in West Africa, "A man does not pass on inheritance except to the sons of his sister to the exclusion of his own sons."[8] He said he had never encountered this custom before except among the unbelievers of the Malabar coast in India. Women were often permitted to inherit property, and the husband was often expected to move into his wife's house.

Relations between the sexes were also sometimes more relaxed than in China or India, with none of the taboos characteristic of those societies. Again, in the words of Ibn Battuta, himself a Muslim:

> With regard to their women, they are not modest in the presence of men, they do not veil themselves in spite of their perseverance in the prayers. . . . The women there have friends and companions amongst men outside the prohibited degrees of marriage [i.e., other than brothers, fathers, etc.]. Likewise for the men, there are companions from amongst women outside the prohibited degrees. One of them would enter his house to find his wife with her companion and would not disapprove of that conduct.

## Women and Islam in North Africa

In Muslim societies in North Africa, as elsewhere, women were required to cover their bodies to avoid giving temptations to men, but Islam's puritanical insistence on the separation of the sexes contrasted with the relatively informal relationships that prevailed in many African societies. In this excerpt from *The History and Description of Africa,* Leo Africanus describes the customs along the Mediterranean coast of Africa. A resident of Spain of Muslim parentage who was captured by Christian corsairs in 1518 and later served under Pope Leo X, Leo Africanus undertook many visits to Africa.

*Which of the practices described here are dictated by the social regulations of Islam? Does the author approve of the behavior of African women as described in this passage?*

### Leo Africanus, *The History and Description of Africa*

Their women (according to the guise of that country) go very gorgeously attired: they wear linen gowns dyed black, with exceeding wide sleeves, over which sometimes they cast a mantle of the same color or of blue, the corners of which mantle are very [attractively] fastened about their shoulders with a fine silver clasp. Likewise they have rings hanging at their ears, which for the most part are made of silver; they wear many rings also upon their fingers. Moreover they usually wear about their thighs and ankles certain scarfs and rings, after the fashion of the Africans. They cover their faces with certain masks having only two holes for the eyes to peep out at. If any man chance to meet with them, they presently hide their faces, passing by him with silence, except it be some of their allies or kinsfolks; for unto them they always [uncover] their faces, neither is there any use of the said mask so long as they be in presence. These Arabians when they travel any journey (as they oftentimes do) they set their women upon certain saddles made handsomely of wicker for the same purpose, and fastened to their camel backs, neither be they anything too wide, but fit only for a woman to sit in. When they go to the wars each man carries his wife with him, to the end that she may cheer up her good man, and give him encouragement. Their damsels which are unmarried do usually paint their faces, breasts, arms, hands, and fingers with a kind of counterfeit color: which is accounted a most decent custom among them.

When Ibn Battuta asked an African acquaintance about these customs, the latter responded, "Women's companionship with men in our country is honorable and takes place in a good way: there is no suspicion about it. They are not like the women in your country." Ibn Battuta noted his astonishment at such a "thoughtless" answer and did not accept further invitations to visit his friend's house.[9]

Such informal attitudes toward the relationship between the sexes were not found everywhere in Africa and were probably curtailed as many Africans converted to Islam (see the box above). But it is a testimony to the tenacity of traditional customs that the relatively puritanical views about the role of women in society brought by Muslims from the Middle East made little impression even among Muslim families in West Africa.

## Slavery

African slavery is often associated with the period after 1500. Indeed, the slave trade did reach enormous proportions in the seventeenth and eighteenth centuries, when European slave ships transported millions of unfortunate victims abroad to Europe or the Americas (see Chapter 13).

Slavery did not originate with the coming of the Europeans, however. It had been practiced in Africa since ancient times and probably originated with prisoners of war who were forced into perpetual servitude. Slavery was common in ancient Egypt and became especially prevalent during the New Kingdom, when slaving expeditions brought back thousands of captives from the upper Nile to be used in labor gangs, for tribute, and even as human sacrifices.

Slavery persisted during the early period of state building, in the first and early second millennia C.E. Berber tribes may have regularly raided agricultural communities south of the Sahara for captives who were transported northward and eventually sold throughout the Mediterranean. Some were enrolled as soldiers, while others, often women, were used as domestic servants in the homes of the well-to-do. The use of captives for forced labor or for sale was apparently also common in African societies farther to the south and along the eastern coast.

Life was difficult for the average slave. The least fortunate were probably those who worked on plantations owned by the royal family or other wealthy landowners. Those pressed into service as soldiers were sometimes more fortunate, since in Muslim societies in the Middle East, they might at some point win their freedom. Many slaves were employed in the royal household or as domestic servants in private homes. In general, these slaves probably had the most tolerable existence. Although they were not ordinarily permitted to purchase their freedom, their living conditions were often decent and sometimes practically indistinguishable from those of the free individuals in the household. In some societies in North Africa, slaves reportedly made up as much as 75 percent of the entire population. Elsewhere, the percentage was much lower, in some cases less than 10 percent.

## African Culture

In early Africa, as in much of the rest of the world at the time, creative expression, whether in the form of painting, literature, or music, was above all a means of serving religion. Though to the uninitiated a wooden mask or the bronze and iron statuary of southern Nigeria is simply a work of art, to the artist it was often a means of expressing religious convictions. Some African historians reject the use of the term *art* to describe such artifacts because they were produced for religious rather than aesthetic purposes.

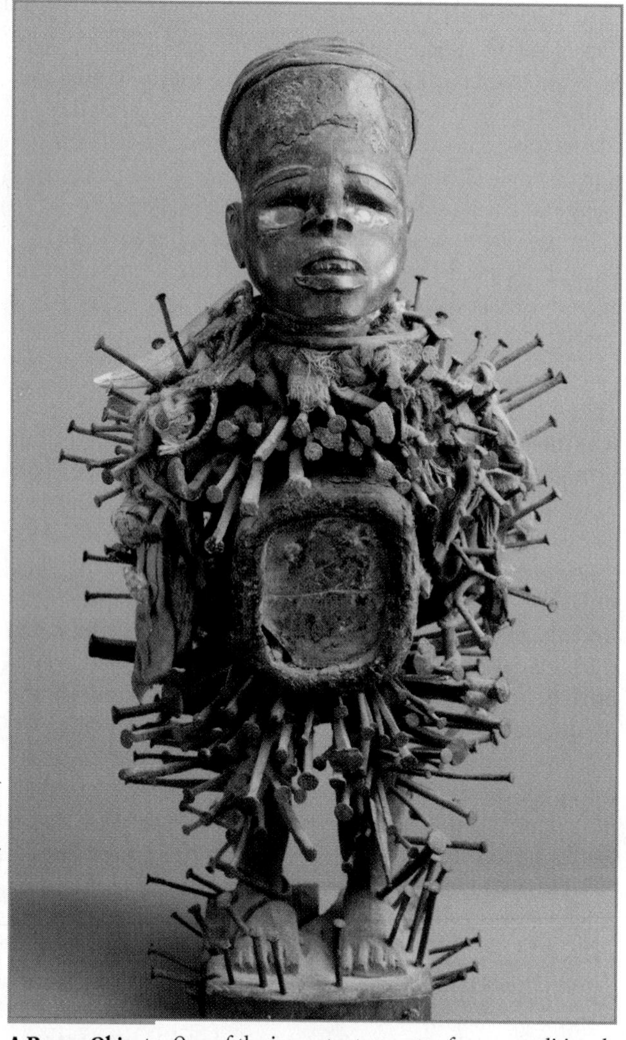

Carl Kaufman, Yale University Art Gallery

**A Power Object.** One of the important aspects of many traditional African religions is the close communion between the worlds of the living and the dead. The artifact shown here (known as a *nkisi*) is a sacred object used by the people of Kongo to harness the power of the spirits to solve problems encountered in their daily lives. Nails were driven into the object (normally a male statue or a two-headed dog) to arouse its inner spirits, who would be activated to identify the source of the problem and resolve it. Over the stomach of this artifact is a container for medicines to assist in the healing ritual.

### Painting and Sculpture

The earliest extant art forms in Africa are rock paintings. The most famous examples are in the Tassili Mountains in the central Sahara, where the earliest paintings may date back as far as 5000 B.C.E., though the majority are a millennium or so younger. Some of the later paintings depict the two-horse chariots used to transport goods prior to the introduction of the camel. Rock paintings are also found elsewhere in the continent, including the Nile valley and in eastern and southern Africa. Those of the San peoples of southern Africa are especially interesting for their illustrations of ritual ceremonies in which village shamans induce rain, propitiate the spirits, or cure illnesses.

More familiar, perhaps, are African wood carvings and sculpture. The remarkable statues, masks, and headdresses were carved from living trees, to the spirit of which the artists had made a sacrifice. These masks and headdresses were worn by costumed singers and dancers in performances to the various spirits, revealing the identification and intimacy of the African with the natural

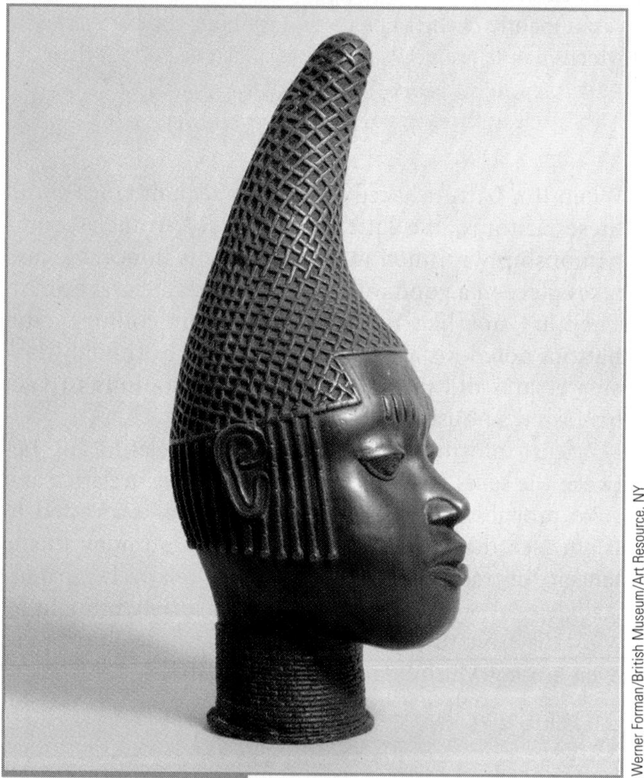

Werner Forman/British Museum/Art Resource, NY

**African Metalwork, Benin.** By 1500, the West African state of Benin had expanded into an extensive and powerful empire with a highly developed official court art, especially in metalwork. Rulers were commemorated with bronze, brass, and copper sculpture, such as the stunning head of a queen mother shown here. These pieces were intended as ancestral memorial portraits and were placed on the altar of the deceased ruler by his successor. The queen mother, who claimed a revered position in Benin culture, would have ordered several such artistic renderings. The delicate attention to detail and the graceful sense of movement of this head attest to the technical excellence and sophistication of Benin bronze casting.

world. In Mali, for example, the 3-foot-tall Ci Wara headdresses, one female, the other male, expressed meaning in performances that celebrated the mythical hero who had introduced agriculture.

Terra-cotta and metal figurines served a similar purpose. In the thirteenth and fourteenth centuries C.E., metal workers at Ife in what is now southern Nigeria produced handsome bronze and iron statues using the lost-wax method, in which melted wax is replaced in a mold by molten metal. The Ife sculptures may in turn have influenced artists in Benin, in West Africa, who produced equally impressive works in bronze during the same period. The Benin sculptures include bronze heads, relief plaques depicting life at court, ornaments, and figures of various animals.

Westerners once regarded African wood carvings and metal sculpture as a form of "primitive art," but the label is not appropriate. The metal sculpture of Benin, for example, is highly sophisticated, and some of the best works are considered masterpieces. Such artistic works were often created by artisans in the employ of the royal court.

## Music

Like sculpture and wood carving, African music and dance often served a religious function. With their characteristic heavy rhythmic beat, dances were a means of communicating with the spirits, and the frenzied movements that are often identified with African dance were intended to represent the spirits acting through humans.

African music during the traditional period varied to some degree from one society to another. A wide variety of instruments were used, including drums and other percussion instruments, xylophones, bells, horns and flutes, and stringed instruments like the fiddle, harp, and zither. Still, the music throughout the continent had sufficient common characteristics to justify a few generalizations. In the first place, a strong rhythmic pattern was an important feature of most African music, although the desired effect was achieved through a wide variety of means, including gourds, pots, bells, sticks beaten together, and hand clapping as well as drums.

Another important feature of African music was the integration of voice and instrument into a total musical experience. Musical instruments and the human voice were often woven together to tell a story, and instruments, such as the famous "talking drum," were often used to represent the voice. Choral music and individual voices were frequently used in a pattern of repetition and variation, sometimes known as "call and response." Through this technique, the audience participated in the music by uttering a single phrase over and over as a choral response to the changing call sung by the soloist. Sometimes instrumental music achieved a similar result.

Much music was produced in the context of social rituals, such as weddings and funerals, religious ceremonies, and official inaugurations. It could also serve an educational purpose by passing on to the young people information about the history and social traditions of the community. In the absence of written languages in sub-Saharan Africa (except for the Arabic script, used in Muslim societies in East and West Africa), music served as the primary means of transmitting folk legends and religious traditions from generation to generation. Storytelling, which was usually undertaken by a priestly class or a specialized class of storytellers, served a similar function.

## Architecture

No aspect of African artistic creativity is more varied than architecture. From the pyramids along the Nile to the ruins of Great Zimbabwe south of the Zambezi River, from the Moorish palaces at Zanzibar to the turreted mud mosques of West Africa, African architecture shows a striking diversity of approach and technique that is unmatched in other areas of creative endeavor.

The earliest surviving architectural form found in Africa is the pyramid. The Kushite kingdom at Meroë apparently adopted the pyramidal form from Egypt during the last centuries of the first millennium B.C.E. (see the photo on p. 219). Although used for the same purpose as their earlier counterparts at Giza, the pyramids at Meroë were distinctive in style; they were much smaller and were topped with a flat platform rather than rising to a point. Remains of temples with massive carved pillars at Meroë also reflect Egyptian influence.

Farther to the south, the kingdom of Axum was developing its own architectural traditions. Most distinctive were the carved stone pillars, known as stelae (see the comparative illustration on p. 236), that were used to mark the tombs of dead kings. Some stood as high as 100 feet. The advent of Christianity eventually had an impact on Axumite architecture. During the Zagwe dynasty in the twelfth and thirteenth centuries C.E., churches carved out of solid rock were constructed throughout the country. Stylistically, they combined indigenous techniques inherited from the pre-Christian period with elements borrowed from Christian churches in the Holy Land.

In West Africa, buildings constructed in stone were apparently a rarity until the emergence of states during the first millennium C.E. At that time, the royal palace, as well as other buildings of civic importance, were often built of stone or cement, while the houses of the majority of the population continued to be constructed of dried mud. On his visit to the state of Guinea on the West African coast, the sixteenth-century traveler Leo Africanus noted that the houses of the ruler and other elites were built of chalk with roofs of straw. Even then, however, well into the state-building period, mosques were often built of mud.

Along the east coast, the architecture of the elite tended to reflect Middle Eastern styles. In the coastal towns and islands from Mogadishu to Kilwa, the houses of the wealthy were built of stone and reflected Moorish (Spanish Muslim) influence. As elsewhere, the common people lived in huts of mud, thatch, or palm leaves (see the box on p. 237). Mosques were built of stone.

© Werner Forman/Art Resource, NY

© Réunion des Musées Nationaux/Art Resource, NY

© Borromeo/Art Resource, NY

ARTS & IDEAS

COMPARATIVE ILLUSTRATION

**The Stele.** A stele is a stone slab or pillar, usually decorated or inscribed, and placed upright. Stelae were often used to commemorate the accomplishments of a ruler or significant figure. Shown at the left is the tallest of the Axum stelae still standing, in present-day Ethiopia. The stone stelae in Axum in the fourth century B.C.E. marked the location of royal tombs with inscriptions commemorating the glories of the kings. An earlier famous stele, seen in the center, is that of Hammurabi (who ruled from 1792 to 1750 B.C.E.; see Chapter 1), which depicts Hammurabi standing in front of a seated god. Below the scene is an inscription of the Code of Hammurabi. A similar kind of stone pillar, shown at the right, was erected in India during the reign of Ashoka in the third century B.C.E. (see Chapter 2) to commemorate events in the life of the Buddha. Archaeologists have also found stelae in ancient China, Greece, and Mexico.

The most famous stone buildings in sub-Saharan Africa are those at Great Zimbabwe. Constructed without mortar, the outer wall and public buildings at Great Zimbabwe are an impressive monument to the architectural creativity of the peoples of the region.

## Literature

Literature in the sense of written works did not exist in sub-Saharan Africa during the early traditional period, except in regions where Islam had brought the Arabic script from the Middle East. But African societies compensated for the absence of a written language with a rich tradition of oral lore. The **bard,** or professional storyteller, was an ancient African institution by which history was transmitted orally from generation to generation. In many West African societies, bards were highly esteemed and served as counselors to kings as well as protectors of local tradition. Bards were revered for their oratory and singing skills, phenomenal memory, and astute interpretation of history. As one African scholar wrote, the death of a bard was equivalent to the burning of a library.

Bards served several necessary functions in society. They were chroniclers of history, preservers of social customs and proper conduct, and entertainers who possessed a monopoly over the playing of several musical instruments, which accompanied their narratives. Because of their unique position above normal society, bards often played the role of mediator between hostile families or clans in a community. They were also credited with possessing occult

## A Chinese View of Africa

This passage from Chau Ju-kua's thirteenth-century treatise on geography describes various aspects of life along the eastern coast of Africa in what is now Somalia, including the urban architecture. The author was an inspector of foreign trade in the city of Quanzhou (sometimes called Zayton) on the southern coast of China. His account was compiled from reports of seafarers. Note the varied uses that the local people make of a whale carcass.

*How does this passage compare with the earlier document by the Arab traveler al-Mas'di? What does it offer in terms of information about housing and consumption habits?*

### Chau Ju-kua on East Africa

The inhabitants of the Chung-li country [the Somali coast] go bareheaded and barefooted; they wrap themselves in cotton stuffs, but they dare not wear jackets, for the wearing of jackets and turbans is a privilege reserved to the ministers and the king's courtiers. The king lives in a brick house covered with glazed tiles, but the people live in huts made of palm leaves and covered with grass-thatched roofs. Their daily food consists of baked flour cakes, sheep's and camel's milk. There are great numbers of cattle, sheep, and camels. . . .

There are many sorcerers among them who are able to change themselves into birds, beasts, or aquatic animals, and by these means keep the ignorant people in a state of terror. If some of them in trading with some foreign ship have a quarrel, the sorcerers pronounce a charm over the ship so that it can neither go forward nor backward, and they only release the ship when it has settled the dispute. The government has formally forbidden this practice.

When one of the inhabitants dies, and they are about to bury him in his coffin, his kinsfolk from near and far come to condole. Each person, flourishing a sword in his hand, goes in and asks the mourners the cause of the person's death. If he was killed by the hand of man, each one says, we will revenge him on the murderer with these swords. Should the mourners reply that he was not killed by any one, but that he came to his end by the will of Heaven, they throw away their swords and break into violent wailing.

Every year there are driven on the coast a great many dead fish measuring two hundred feet in length and twenty feet through the body. The people do not eat the flesh of these fish, but they cut out their brains, marrow, and eyes, from which they get oil. They mix this oil with lime to caulk their boats, and use it also in lamps. The poor people use the ribs of these fish to make rafters, the backbones for door leaves, and they cut off vertebrae to make mortars with.

**The Mosque at Jenne, Mali.** With the opening of the gold fields south of Mali, in present-day Ghana, Jenne became an important trading center for gold. Shown here is its distinctive fourteenth-century mosque made of unbaked clay without reinforcements. The projecting timbers offer easy access for repairing the mud exterior, as was regularly required.

## A West African Oral Tradition

Like other great epics of world literature, the West African *Epic of Son-Jara* describes the ordeals of a male protagonist as he hurdles superhuman obstacles while fulfilling his heroic destiny. It is interesting, however, to observe the role played by women in the epic hero's calamitous journey. Although he is often opposed by evil witches and temptresses, he can also be assisted in the foiling of his foes by the courageous acts of a woman. Penelope in the *Odyssey* outwits her enemies, as does Sita in the Ramayana and Draupadi in the Mahabharata.

In this pivotal passage, Son-Jara's sister, Sugulun Kulunkan, offers to seduce his enemy Sumamuru in order to obtain the Manden secret, or magic spell, needed to control the kingdom of Mali. Sumamuru divulges his all-powerful secret and is rebuked by his mother; both son and mother then disown each other with the trenchant symbols of the slashed breast and cut cloth. After each line of verse recited by the bard, an assistant would respond with the endorsement "true." This practice is perhaps the distant ancestor of today's African American custom, called "call and response," of following each line of religious oratory with "Amen."

*What do you think the purpose of the call and response is in such epics? What effect does the technique have on the audience?*

### The Epic of Son-Jara

*Son-Jara's flesh-and-blood sister, Sugulun Kulunkan,*
*She said, "O Magan Son-Jara,*
*"One person cannot fight this war.*
*"Let me go seek Sumamuru.*
*"Were I then to reach him,*
*"To you I will deliver him,*
*"So that the folk of the Manden be yours,*
*"And all the Mandenland you shield."*
*Sugulun Kulunkan arose,*
*And went up to the gates of Sumamuru's fortress:*
. . .
*"Come open the gates, Susu Mountain Sumamuru!*
*"Come make me your bed companion!"*
*Sumamuru came to the gates:*
*"What manner of person are you?"*
*"It is I Sugulun Kulunkan!"*
*"Well, now, Sugulun Kulunkan,*
*"If you have come to trap me,*
*"To turn me over to some person,*
*"Know that none can ever vanquish me.*
*"I have found the Manden secret,*
*"And made the Manden sacrifice,*
*"And in five score millet stalks placed it,*
*"And buried them here in the earth.*
*"'Tis I who found the Manden secret,*
*"And made the Manden sacrifice,*
*"And in a red piebald bull did place it,*
*"And buried it here in the earth.*
*"Know that none can vanquish me.*
*"'Tis I who found the Manden secret*
*"And made a sacrifice to it,*
*"And in a pure white cock did place it.*
*"Were you to kill it,*
*"And uproot some barren groundnut plants,*
*"And strip them of their leaves,*
*"And spread them round the fortress,*
*"And uproot more barren peanut plants,*
*"And fling them into the fortress,*
*"Only then can I be vanquished."*
*His mother sprang forward at that:*
*"Heh! Susu Mountain Sumamuru!*
*"Never tell all to a woman,*
*"To a one-night woman!*
*"The woman is not safe, Sumamuru."*
*Sumamuru sprang towards his mother,*
*And came and seized his mother,*
*And slashed off her breast with a knife, magasi!*
*She went and got the old menstrual cloth.*
*"Ah! Sumamuru!" she swore.*
*"If your birth was ever a fact,*
*"I have cut your old menstrual cloth!"*

powers and could read divinations and give blessings and curses. Traditionally, bards also served as advisers to the king, sometimes inciting him to action (such as going to battle) through the passion of their poetry. When captured by the enemy, bards were often treated with respect and released or compelled to serve the victor with their art.

One of the most famous West African epics is *The Epic of Son-Jara.* Passed down orally by bards for more than seven hundred years, it relates the heroic exploits of Son-Jara (also known as Sunjata or Sundiata), the founder of Mali's empire and its ruler from 1230 to 1255. Although Mansa Musa is famous throughout the world because of his flamboyant pilgrimage to Mecca in the fourteenth century, Son-Jara is more celebrated in West Africa because of the dynamic and unbroken oral traditions of the West African peoples (see the box above).

In addition to the bards, women were appreciated for their storytelling talents, as well as for their role as purveyors of the moral values and religious beliefs of African societies. In societies that lacked a written tradition, women represented the glue that held the community together. Through the recitation of fables, proverbs, poems, and songs, mothers conditioned the communal bonding and moral fiber of succeeding generations in a way that was rarely encountered in the patriarchal societies of Europe, eastern and southern Asia, and the Middle East. Such activities were not only vital aspects of education in traditional Africa but also offered a welcome respite from the drudgery of everyday life and a spark to develop the imagination and artistic awareness of the young. Renowned for its many proverbs, Africa also offers the following: "A good story is like a garden carried in the pocket."

## CONCLUSION

**THANKS TO THE DEDICATED WORK** of a generation of archaeologists, anthropologists, and historians, we have a much better understanding of the evolution of human societies in Africa than we did a few decades ago. Intensive efforts by archaeologists have demonstrated beyond reasonable doubt that the first hominids lived there. Recent evidence suggests that farming may have been practiced in Africa more than twelve thousand years ago, and the concept of kingship may have originated not in Sumer or in Egypt but in the upper Nile valley as long ago as the fourth millennium B.C.E.

Less is known about more recent African history, partly because of the paucity of written records. Still, historians have established that the first civilizations had begun to take shape in sub-Saharan Africa by the first millennium C.E., while the continent as a whole was an active participant in emerging regional and global trade with the Mediterranean world and across the Indian Ocean.

Thus the peoples of Africa were not as isolated from the main currents of human history as was once assumed. Although the state-building process in sub-Saharan Africa was still in its early stages compared with the ancient civilizations of India, China, and Mesopotamia, in many respects these new states were as impressive and sophisticated as their counterparts elsewhere in the world.

In the fifteenth century, a new factor was added to the equation. Urged on by the tireless efforts of Prince Henry the Navigator, Portuguese fleets began to probe southward along the coast of West Africa. At first, their sponsors were in search of gold and slaves, but at the end of the century, Vasco da Gama's voyage around the Cape of Good Hope signaled Portugal's determination to dominate the commerce of the Indian Ocean in the future. The new situation posed a challenge to the peoples of Africa, whose nascent states and technology would be severely tested by the rapacious demands of the Europeans (see Chapter 13).

## TIMELINE

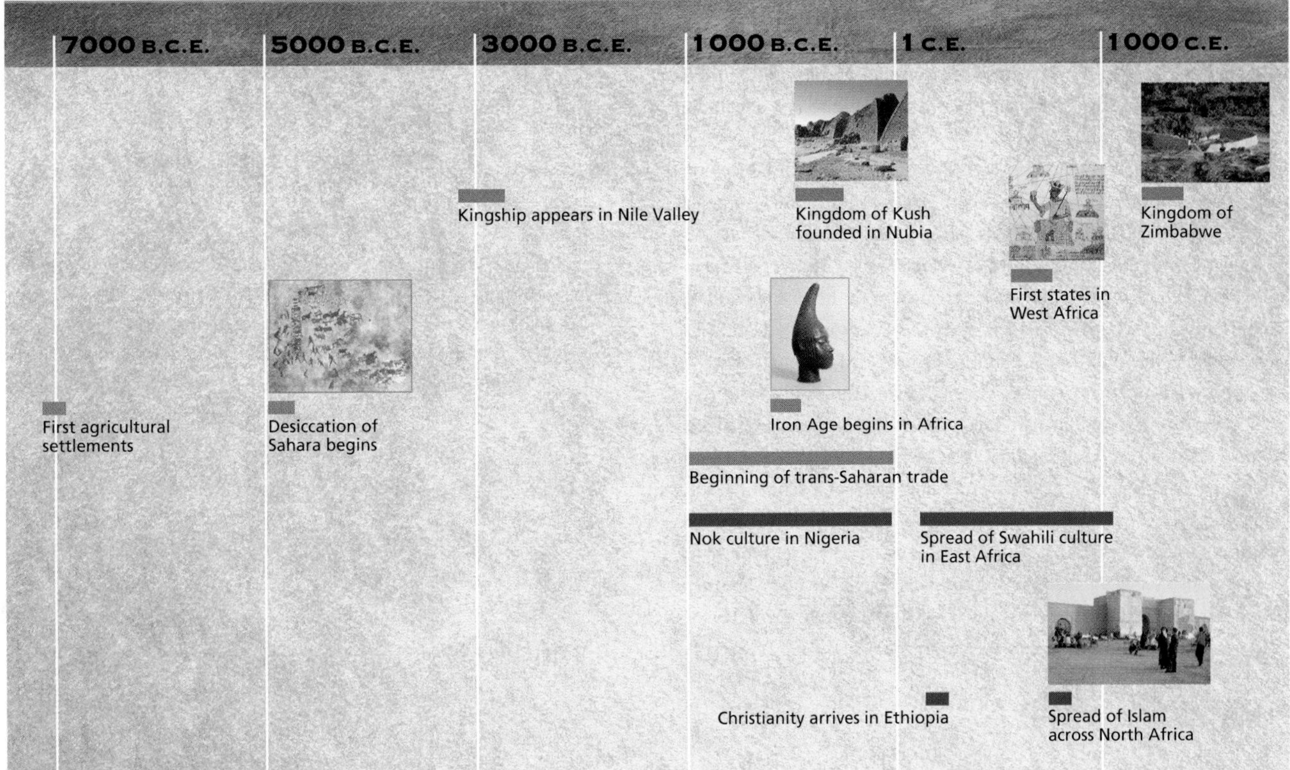

## CHAPTER NOTES

1. S. Hamdun and N. King, eds., *Ibn Battuta in Africa* (London, 1975), p. 19.
2. *The Book of Duarte Barbosa* (Nedeln, Liechtenstein, 1967), p. 28.
3. Herodotus, *The Histories,* trans. A. de Sélincourt (Baltimore, 1964), p. 307.
4. Quoted in M. Shinnie, *Ancient African Kingdoms* (London, 1965), p. 60.
5. C. R. Boxer, ed., *The Tragic History of the Sea, 1589–1622* (Cambridge, 1959), pp. 121–122.
6. Quoted in D. Nurse and T. Spear, *The Swahili: Reconstructing the History and Language of an African Society 800–1500* (Philadelphia, 1985), p. 84.
7. Hamdun and King, *Ibn Battuta in Africa,* p. 47.
8. Ibid., p. 28.
9. Ibid., pp. 28–30.

## SUGGESTED READING

In few areas of world history is scholarship advancing as rapidly as in African history. New information is constantly forcing archaeologists and historians to revise their assumptions about the early history of the continent. Standard texts therefore quickly become out-of-date as their conclusions are supplanted by new evidence.

Still, there are several worthwhile general surveys that provide a useful overview of the early period of African history. The dean of African historians, and certainly one of the most readable, is **B. Davidson.** For a sympathetic portrayal of the African people, see his ***African History*** (New York, 1968) and ***Lost Cities in Africa,*** rev. ed. (Boston, 1970). Other respected accounts are **R. Oliver** and **J. D. Fage, *A Short History of Africa*** (Middlesex, England, 1986), and **V. B. Khapoya, *The African Experience: An Introduction*** (Englewood Cliffs, N.J., 1994). For a readable treatment incorporating fairly recent evidence, see **K. Shillington, *History of Africa*** (New York, 1989). **R. O. Collins,** ed., ***Problems in African History: The Precolonial Centuries*** (New York, 1993), provides a useful collection of scholarly articles on key issues in precolonial Africa.

Specialized studies are beginning to appear with frequency on many areas of the continent. For a popular account of archaeological finds, see **B. Fagan, *New Treasures of the Past: Fresh Finds That Deepen Our Understanding of the Archaeology of Man*** (Leicester, England, 1987). For a more detailed treatment of the early period, see the multivolume ***General History of Africa,*** sponsored by UNESCO (Berkeley, Calif., 1998). **R. O. Collins** has provided a useful service with his ***African History in Documents,*** (Princeton, N.J., 1990). **C. Ehret, *An African Classical Age: Eastern and Southern Africa in World History, 1000 B.C. to 400 A.D.*** (Charlottesville, Va., 1998), applies historical linguistics to make up for the lack of documentary evidence in the precolonial era. **J. D. Clarke** and **S. A. Brandt,** eds., ***From Hunters to Farmers*** (Berkeley, Calif., 1984), takes an economic approach. Also see **D. A. Welsby, *The Kingdom of Kush: The Napataean Meroitic Empire*** (London, 1996), and **J. Middleton, *Swahili: An African Mercantile Civilization*** (New Haven, Conn., 1992). For a fascinating account of trans-Saharan trade, see **E. W. Bovill, *The Golden Trade of the Moors: West African Kingdoms in the Fourteenth Century,*** 2d ed. (Princeton, N.J., 1995). On the cultural background, see **R. Olaniyan,** ed., ***African History and Culture*** (Lagos, Nigeria, 1982), and **J. Vansina, *Paths in the Rainforest: Toward a History of Political Tradition in Equatorial Africa*** (Madison, Wis., 1990). Although there exist many editions of ***The Epic of Son-Jara,*** based on recitations of different bards, the most conclusive edition is by **F. D. Sisòkò,** translated and annotated by **J. W. Johnson** (Bloomington, Ind., 1992).

On East Africa, see **D. Nurse** and **T. Spear, *The Swahili: Reconstituting the History and Language of an African Society, 800–1500*** (Philadelphia, 1985). The maritime story is recounted with documents in **G. S. P. Freeman-Grenville, *The East African Coast: Select Documents from the First to the Earlier Nineteenth Century*** (Oxford, 1962). For the larger picture, see **K. N. Chaudhuri, *Trade and Civilization in the Indian Ocean: An Economic History from the Rise of Islam to 1750*** (Cambridge, 1985). On the early history of Ethiopia, see **S. Burstein,** ed., ***Ancient African Civilizations: Kush and Axum*** (Princeton, N.J., 1998).

For useful general surveys of southern Africa, see **N. Parsons, *A New History of Southern Africa*** (New York, 1983), and **K. Shillington, *A History of Southern Africa*** (Essex, England, 1987), a profusely illustrated account. For an excellent introduction to African art, see **M. B. Visond** et al., ***A History of Art in Africa*** (New York, 2001); **R. Hackett, *Art and Religion in Africa*** (London, 1996); and **F. Willet, *African Art,*** rev. ed. (New York, 1993).

### History Now™

**Enter *HistoryNow* using the access card that is available with this text. *HistoryNow* will assist you in understanding the content in this chapter with lesson plans generated for your needs, as well as provide you with a connection to the *Wadsworth World History Resource Center* (see description below for details).**

WORLD HISTORY RESOURCE CENTER

**Enter the Resource Center using either your *HistoryNow* access card or your standalone access card for the *Wadsworth World History Resource Center.* Organized by topic, this website includes quizzes; images; over 350 primary source documents; interactive simulations; maps and timelines; movie explorations; and a wealth of other resources. You can read the following documents, and many more, at http://history.wadsworth.com/rc/world**

An African story of the creation of humanity

A hymn to Mawari

Visit the *World History* Companion Website for chapter quizzes and more.

http://history.wadsworth.com/duikerspielvogel05/

CHAPTER

# THE EXPANSION OF CIVILIZATION IN SOUTHERN ASIA

© Thomas J. Abercrombie/National Geographic Image Collection

*One of the two massive carved statues of the Buddha formerly at Bamiyan*

## CHAPTER OUTLINE AND FOCUS QUESTIONS

### The Silk Road

- What were some of the chief destinations along the Silk Road, and what kinds of products and ideas traveled along the route?

### India After the Mauryas

- How did Buddhism change in the centuries after Siddhartha Gautama's death, and why did the religion ultimately decline in popularity in India?

### The Arrival of Islam

- What impact did Muslim rule have on Indian society? To what degree did the indigenous population convert to the new religion, and why?

### Society and Culture

- What are some of the most important cultural achievements of Indian civilization in the era between the Mauryas and Mughals?

### The Golden Region: Early Southeast Asia

- What were the main characteristics of Southeast Asian social and economic life, culture, and religion before 1500 C.E.?

## CRITICAL THINKING

- New religions had a significant impact on the social and cultural life of peoples living in southern Asia during the period covered in this chapter. What factors caused the spread of these religions in the first place? What changes occurred as a result of the introduction of these new faiths? Were the religions themselves affected by their spread into new regions of Asia?

WHILE TRAVELING from his native China to India along the Silk Route in the early fifth century C.E., the Buddhist monk Fa Xian stopped en route at a town called Bamiyan, a rest stop located deep in the mountains of what is today known as Afghanistan. At that time, Bamiyan was a major center of Buddhist studies, with dozens of temples and monasteries filled with students, all overlooked by two giant standing statues of the Buddha hewn directly out of the side of a massive cliff. Fa Xian was thrilled at the sight. "The law of Buddha," he remarked with satisfaction in his account of the experience, "is progressing and flourishing." He then continued southward to India, where he spent several years visiting Buddhists throughout the country. Because little of the literature from that period survives, Fa Xian's observations are a valuable resource for our knowledge of the daily lives of the Indian people.

The India that Fa Xian visited was no longer the unified land it had been under the Mauryan dynasty. The overthrow of the Mauryas in the early second century B.C.E. had been followed by several hundred years of disunity, when the subcontinent was divided into a number of separate kingdoms and principalities. The dominant force in the north was the Kushan state, established by Indo-European–speaking peoples who had been driven out of what is now China's Xinjiang province by the Xiongnu (see Chapter 3). The Kushans penetrated into the mountains north of the Indus River, where they eventually formed a kingdom with its capital at Bactria, not far from modern Kabul. Over the next two centuries, the Kushans expanded their supremacy along the Indus River and into the central Ganges valley.

Meanwhile, to the south, a number of kingdoms arose among the Dravidian peoples of the Deccan Plateau, which had been only partly under Mauryan rule. The most famous of these kingdoms was Chola (sometimes spelled Cola) on the southeastern coast. Chola developed into a major trading power and sent merchant fleets eastward across the Bay of Bengal, where they introduced Indian culture as well as Indian goods to the peoples of Southeast Asia. In the fourth century C.E., Chola was overthrown by the Pallavas, who ruled from their capital at Kanchipuram (known today as Kanchi), just southwest of modern Chennai (Madras), for the next four hundred years. ◇

## The Silk Road

The Kushan kingdom, with its power base beyond the Khyber Pass in modern Afghanistan, became the dominant political force in northern India in the centuries immediately after the fall of the Mauryas. Sitting astride the main trade routes across the northern half of the subcontinent, the Kushans thrived on the commerce that passed through the area (see Map 9.1). The bulk of that trade was between the Roman Empire and China and was transported along the route known as the Silk Road, one segment of which passed through the mountains northwest of India (see Chapter 10). From there, goods were shipped to Rome through the Persian Gulf or the Red Sea.

Trade between India and Europe had begun even before the rise of the Roman Empire, but it expanded rapidly in the first century C.E., when sailors mastered the pattern of the monsoon winds in the Indian Ocean (from the southwest in the summer and the northeast in the winter). Commerce between the Mediterranean and the Indian Ocean, as described in the *Periplus*, a first-century C.E. account by a Greek participant, was extensive and often profitable, and it resulted in the establishment of several small Roman settlements along the Indian coast. Rome imported ivory, indigo, textiles, precious stones, and pepper from India and silk from China. The Romans sometimes paid cash for these goods but also exported silver, wine, perfume, slaves, and glass and cloth from Egypt. Overall, Rome appears to have imported much more than it sold to the Far East, leading Emperor Tiberius to grumble that "the ladies and their baubles are transferring our money to foreigners."

The Silk Road was a conduit not only of material goods but also of technology and of ideas. The first Indian monks to visit China may have traveled over the road during the second century C.E. By the time of Fa Xian, Buddhist monks from China were beginning to arrive in increasing numbers to visit holy sites in India. The exchange of visits not only enriched the study of Buddhism in the two countries but also led to a fruitful exchange of ideas and technological advances in the realms of astronomy, mathematics, and linguistics. According to one scholar, the importation of Buddhist writings from India encouraged the development of printing in China, while the Chinese obtained lessons in health care from monks returned from the Asian subcontinent.

Indeed, the emergence of the Kushan kingdom as a major commercial power was due not only to its role as an intermediary in the Rome-China trade but also to the rising popularity of Buddhism. During the second century C.E., Kanishka, the greatest of the Kushan monarchs, began to patronize Buddhism. Under Kanishka and his successors, an intimate and mutually beneficial relationship was established between Buddhist monasteries and the local merchant community in thriving urban centers

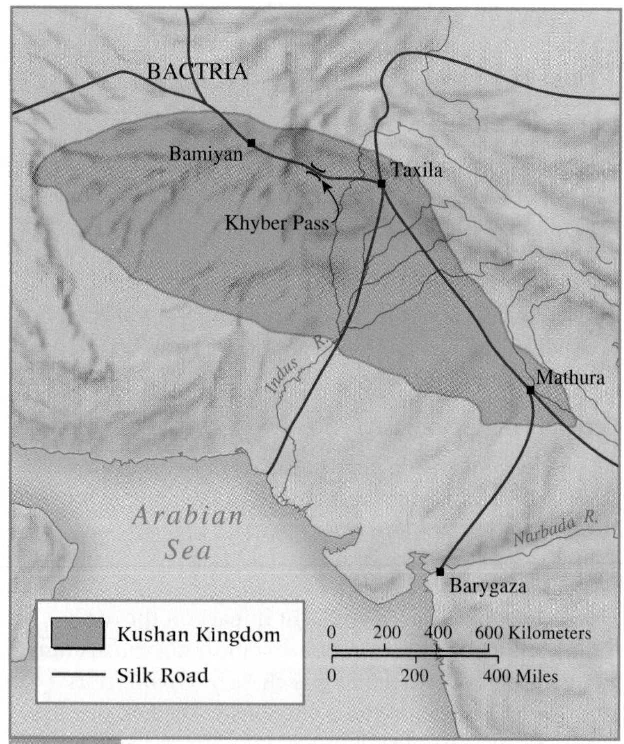


**MAP 9.1 The Kushan Kingdom and the Silk Road.** After the collapse of the Mauryan Empire, a new state formed by recent migrants from the north arose north of the Indus River valley. For the next four centuries, the Kushan kingdom played a major role in regional trade via the Silk Road until it declined in the third century C.E. ? What were the major products shipped along the Silk Road? To what degree was it a conduit for ideas and technology as well?

**View an animated version of this map or related maps at** http://history.wadsworth.com/duikerspielvogel05/

© Thomas J. Abercrombie/National Geographic Image Collection

© Kimbell Art Museum/CORBIS

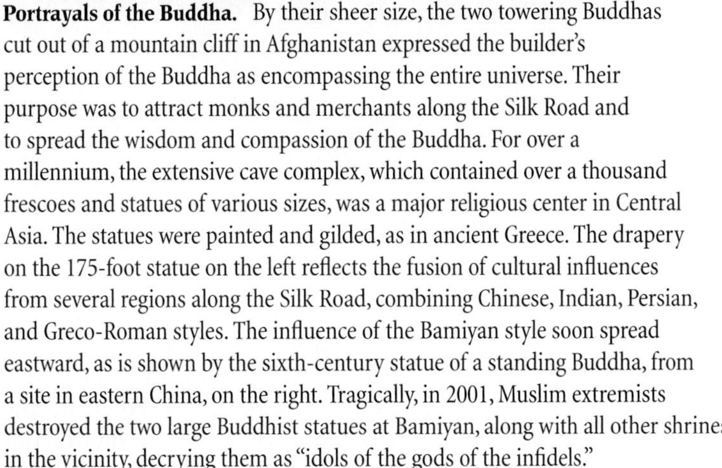

**Portrayals of the Buddha.** By their sheer size, the two towering Buddhas cut out of a mountain cliff in Afghanistan expressed the builder's perception of the Buddha as encompassing the entire universe. Their purpose was to attract monks and merchants along the Silk Road and to spread the wisdom and compassion of the Buddha. For over a millennium, the extensive cave complex, which contained over a thousand frescoes and statues of various sizes, was a major religious center in Central Asia. The statues were painted and gilded, as in ancient Greece. The drapery on the 175-foot statue on the left reflects the fusion of cultural influences from several regions along the Silk Road, combining Chinese, Indian, Persian, and Greco-Roman styles. The influence of the Bamiyan style soon spread eastward, as is shown by the sixth-century statue of a standing Buddha, from a site in eastern China, on the right. Tragically, in 2001, Muslim extremists destroyed the two large Buddhist statues at Bamiyan, along with all other shrines in the vicinity, decrying them as "idols of the gods of the infidels."

like Taxila and Varanasi. Merchants were eager to build stupas and donate money to monasteries in return for social prestige and the implied promise of a better life in this world or the hereafter.

For their part, the wealthy monasteries ceased to be simple communities where monks could find a refuge from the material cares of the world; instead they became major consumers of luxury goods provided by their affluent patrons. Monasteries and their inhabitants became increasingly involved in the economic life of society, and Buddhist architecture began to be richly decorated with precious stones and glass purchased from local merchants or imported from abroad. The process was very similar to the changes that would occur in the Christian church in medieval Europe.

It was from the Kushan kingdom that Buddhism began its long journey across the wastes of Central Asia to China and other societies in eastern Asia. As trade between the two regions increased, merchants and missionaries flowed from Bactria over the trade routes snaking through the mountains toward the northeast. At various stopping points on the trail, pilgrims erected statues and decorated mountain caves with magnificent frescoes depicting the life of the Buddha and his message to his followers. One of the most prominent of these centers was at Bamiyan, not far from modern-day Kabul, where believers carved two

## The Good Life in Medieval India

Much of what we know about life in medieval India comes from the accounts of Chinese missionaries who visited the subcontinent in search of documents recording the teachings of the Buddha. Here the Buddhist monk Fa Xian, who spent several years there in the fifth century C.E., reports on conditions in the kingdom of Mathura (Mo-tu-lo), a vassal state in western India that was part of the Gupta Empire. Although he could not have been pleased that the Gupta monarchs in India had adopted the Hindu faith, he found that the people were contented and prosperous except for the outcastes, whom he called Chandalas.

*To what degree do the practices described here appear to conform to the principles established by Siddhartha Gautama in his own teachings? Would political advisers such as Kautilya and the Chinese philosopher Mencius have approved of governmental policies?*

### Fa Xian, *The Travels of Fa Xian*

Going southeast from this somewhat less than 80 *joyanas,* we passed very many temples one after another, with some myriad of priests in them. Having passed these places, we arrived at a certain country. This country is called Mo-tu-lo. Once more we followed the Pu-na river. On the sides of the river, both right and left, are twenty *sangharamas,* with perhaps 3,000 priests. The law of Buddha is progressing and flourishing. Beyond the deserts are the countries of western India. The kings of these countries are all firm believers in the law of Buddha. They remove their caps of state when they make offerings to the priests. The members of the royal household and the chief ministers personally direct the food giving; when the distribution of food is over, they spread a carpet on the ground opposite the chief seat (the president's seat) and sit down before it. They dare not sit on couches in the presence of the priests. The rules relating to the almsgiving of kings have been handed down from the time of Buddha till now. Southward from this is the so-called middle country (Madhyadesa). The climate of this country is warm and equable, without frost or snow. The people are very well off, without poll tax or official restrictions. Only those who till the royal lands return a portion of profit of the land. If they desire to go, they go; if they like to stop, they stop. The kings govern without corporal punishment; criminals are fined, according to circumstances, lightly or heavily. Even in cases of repeated rebellion they only cut off the right hand. The king's personal attendants, who guard him on the right and left, have fixed salaries. Throughout the country the people kill no living thing nor drink wine, nor do they eat garlic or onions, with the exception of Chandalas only. The Chandalas are named "evil men" and dwell apart from others; if they enter a town or market, they sound a piece of wood in order to separate themselves; then men, knowing who they are, avoid coming in contact with them. In this country they do not keep swine nor fowls, and do not deal in cattle; they have no shambles [slaughterhouses] or wine shops in their marketplaces. In selling they use cowrie shells. The Chandalas only hunt and sell flesh.

mammoth statues of the Buddha out of a sheer sandstone cliff. According to the Chinese pilgrim Fa Xian (see the box above), when he visited the area in 400 C.E., over a thousand monks were attending a religious ceremony at the site.

# India After the Mauryas

The Kushan kingdom came to an end under uncertain conditions sometime in the third century C.E. In 320, a new state was established in the central Ganges valley by a local raja named Chandragupta (no relation to Chandragupta Maurya, the founder of the Mauryan dynasty). Chandragupta located his capital at Pataliputra, the site of the now decaying palace of the Mauryas. Under his successor Samudragupta, the territory under Gupta rule was extended into surrounding areas, and eventually the new kingdom became the dominant political force throughout northern India. It also established a loose suzerainty over the Dravidian state of Pallava to the south, thus becoming the greatest state in the subcontinent since the decline of the Mauryan Empire. Under a succession of powerful, efficient, and highly cultured monarchs, notably Samudragupta and Chandragupta II, India enjoyed a new "classical age" of civilization (see Map 9.2).

## The Gupta Dynasty: A New Golden Age?

The Gupta era was a time of prosperity and thriving commerce with China, Southeast Asia, and the Mediterranean. Great cities, notable for their temples and Buddhist monasteries as well as for their economic prosperity, rose along the main trade routes throughout the subcontinent. The religious trade also prospered, as pilgrims from across India and as far away as China came to visit the major religious centers.

As in the Mauryan Empire, much of the trade in the Gupta Empire was managed or regulated by the government. The Guptas owned mines and vast crown lands and

## CHRONOLOGY Medieval India

| | |
|---|---|
| Kushan kingdom | c. 150 B.C.E.–c. 200 C.E. |
| Gupta dynasty | 320–600s |
| Chandragupta I | 320–c. 330 |
| Samudragupta | c. 330–375 |
| Chandragupta II | 375–415 |
| Arrival of Fa Xian in India | c. 406 |
| First Buddhist temples at Ellora | Seventh century |
| Travels of Xuan Zang in India | 630–643 |
| Conquest of Sind by Arab armies | c. 711 |
| Mahmud of Ghazni | 997–1030 |
| Mongol invasion of northern India | 1221 |
| Delhi sultanate at peak | 1220 |
| Invasion of Tamerlane | 1398 |

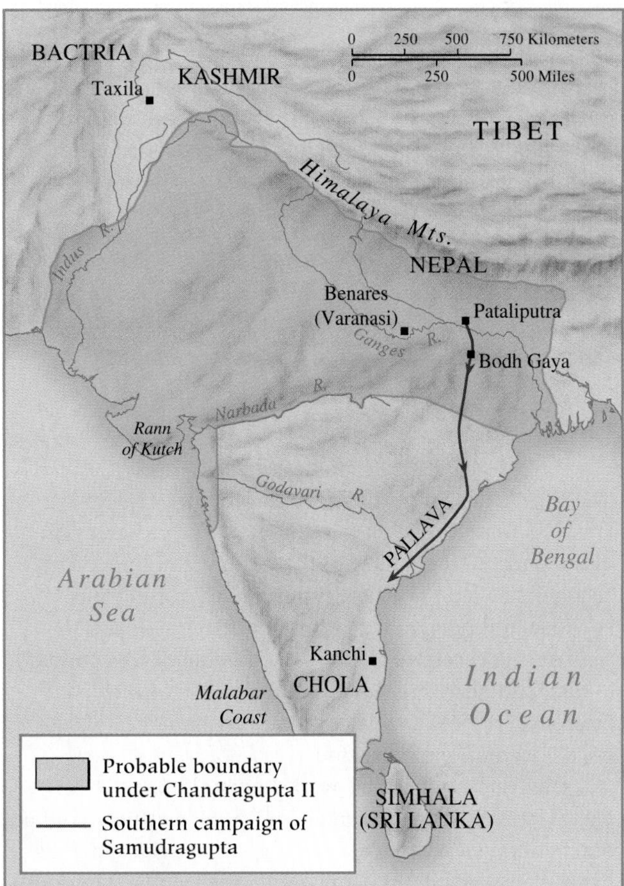


MAP 9.2 **The Gupta Empire.** The Gupta Empire was the only major state to arise in the Indian subcontinent during the first millennium C.E. The arrow traces the military campaign into southern India led by King Samudragupta. ? How did the Gupta empire differ in territorial extent from its great predecessor, the Mauryas? **View an animated version of this map or related maps at http://history.wadsworth.com/duikerspielvogel05/**

earned massive profits from their commercial dealings. But there was also a large private sector, dominated by great guilds that monopolized key sectors of the economy. A money economy had probably been in operation since the second century B.C.E., when copper and gold coins had been introduced from the Middle East. This in turn led to the development of banking. Nevertheless, there are indications that the circulation of coins was limited. The Chinese missionary Xuan Zang, who visited India early in the seventh century, remarked that most commercial transactions were conducted by barter.[1]

But the good fortunes of the Guptas proved to be relatively short-lived. Beginning in the late fifth century C.E., incursions by nomadic warriors from the northwest gradually reduced the power of the empire. Soon northern India was once more divided into myriad small kingdoms engaged in seemingly constant conflict.

## The Transformation of Buddhism

The Chinese pilgrims who traveled to India during the Gupta era found a Buddhism that had changed in a number of ways in the centuries since the time of Siddhartha Gautama. They also found a doctrine that was beginning to decline in popularity in the face of the rise of Hinduism.

The transformation in Buddhism had come about in part because the earliest written sources were transcribed two centuries after Siddhartha's death and in part because his message was reinterpreted as it became part of the everyday life of the people. Abstract concepts of a Nirvana that cannot be described began to be replaced, at least in the popular mind, with more concrete visions of heavenly salvation, and Siddhartha was increasingly regarded as a divinity rather than as a sage. The Buddha's teachings that all four classes were equal gave way to the familiar Brahmanic conviction that some people, by reason of previous reincarnations, were closer to Nirvana than others.

**Theravada** These developments led to a split in the movement. Purists emphasized what they insisted were the original teachings of the Buddha, describing themselves as the school of **Theravada,** or "the teachings of the elders." Followers of Theravada considered Buddhism a way of life, not a salvationist creed. Theravada stressed the importance of strict adherence to personal behavior and the quest for understanding as a means of release from the wheel of life.

**Mahayana** In the meantime, another interpretation of Buddhist doctrine was emerging in the northwest. Here Buddhist believers, perhaps hoping to compete with other salvationist faiths circulating in the region, began to promote the view that Nirvana could be achieved through devotion and not just through painstaking attention to one's behavior. According to advocates of this school, eventually to be known as **Mahayana** ("greater vehicle"), Theravada teachings were too demanding or

## THE EDUCATION OF A *BRAHMIN*

Although the seventh-century Chinese traveler Xuan Zang was a Buddhist, he faithfully recorded his impressions of the Hindu religion in his memoirs. Here he describes the education of a *brahmin,* the highest class in Indian society.

*How would you compare the educational practices described here with the training provided to young men in other traditional societies in Europe, Asia, and the Americas? What is distinctive, if anything, about the educational system in India?*

### Xuan Zang, *Records of Western Countries*

The Brahmans study the four *Veda Sastras.* The first is called *Shau* [longevity]; it relates to the preservation of life and the regulation of the natural condition. The second is called *Sse* [sacrifice]; it relates to the [rules of] sacrifice and prayer. The third is called *Ping* [peace or regulation]; it relates to decorum, casting of lots, military affairs, and army regulations. The fourth is called *Shue* [secret mysteries]; it relates to various branches of science, incantations, medicine.

The teachers [of these works] must themselves have closely studied the deep and secret principles they contain, and penetrated to their remotest meaning. They then explain their general sense, and guide their pupils in understanding the words that are difficult. They urge them on and skillfully conduct them. They add luster to their poor knowledge, and stimulate the desponding. If they find that their pupils are satisfied with their acquirements, and so wish to escape to attend to their worldly duties, then they use means to keep them in their power. When they have finished their education, and have attained thirty years of age, then their character is formed and their knowledge ripe. When they have secured an occupation they first of all thank their master for his attention. There are some, deeply versed in antiquity, who devote themselves to elegant studies, and live apart from the world, and retain the simplicity of their character. These rise above mundane presents, and are as insensible to renown as to the contempt of the world. Their name having spread afar, the rulers appreciate them highly, but are unable to draw them to the court. The chief of the country honors them on account of their [mental] gifts, and the people exalt their fame and render them universal homage. . . . They search for wisdom, relying on their own resources. Although they are possessed of large wealth, yet they will wander here and there to seek their subsistence. There are others who, whilst attaching value to letters, will yet without shame consume their fortunes in wandering about for pleasure, neglecting their duties. They squander their substance in costly food and clothing. Having no virtuous principle, and no desire to study, they are brought to disgrace, and their infamy is widely circulated.

too strict for ordinary people to follow and therefore favored the wealthy, who were more apt to have the time and resources to spend weeks or months away from their everyday occupations. Mahayana Buddhists referred to their rivals as **Hinayana,** or "lesser vehicle," because in Theravada fewer would reach enlightenment. Mahayana thus attempted to provide hope for the masses in their efforts to reach Nirvana, but to the followers of Theravada, it did so at the expense of an insistence on proper behavior.

To advocates of the Mahayana school, salvation could also come from the intercession of a **bodhisattva** ("he who possesses the essence of Buddhahood"). According to Mahayana beliefs, some individuals who had achieved *bodhi* and were thus eligible to enter the state of Nirvana after death chose instead, because of their great compassion, to remain on earth in spirit form to help all human beings achieve release from the life cycle. Followers of Theravada, who believed the concept of bodhisattva applied only to Siddhartha Gautama himself, denounced such ideas as "the teaching of demons." But to their proponents, such ideas extended the hope of salvation to the masses. Mahayana Buddhists revered the saintly individuals who, according to tradition, had become bodhisattvas at death and erected temples in their honor where the local population could pray and render offerings. The most famous bodhisattva was Avalokitesvara, a mythic figure whose name in Sanskrit means "Lord of Compassion." Perhaps because of the identification of Avalokitesvara with the concept of mercy, in China he was gradually transformed into a female figure known as Guan Yin (Kuan Yin).

A final distinguishing characteristic of Mahayana Buddhism was its reinterpretation of Buddhism as a religion rather than as a philosophy. Although Mahayana had philosophical aspects, its adherents increasingly regarded the Buddha as a divine figure, and an elaborate Buddhist cosmology developed. Nirvana was not a form of extinction but a true heaven with many rest stations along the way for the faithful.

Under Kushan rule, Mahayana achieved considerable popularity in northern India and for a while even made inroads in such Theravada strongholds as the island of Sri Lanka. But in the end, neither Mahayana nor Theravada was able to retain its popularity in Indian society. By the seventh century C.E., Theravada had declined rapidly on the subcontinent, although it retained its foothold in Sri

Lanka and across the Bay of Bengal in Southeast Asia, where it remained an influential force to modern times. Mahayana prospered in the northwest for centuries, but eventually it was supplanted by a revived Hinduism and later by a new arrival, Islam. But Mahayana too would find better fortunes abroad, as it was carried over the Silk Road or by sea to China and then to Korea and Japan (see Chapters 10 and 11). In all three countries, Buddhism has coexisted with Confucian doctrine and indigenous beliefs to the present.

### The Decline of Buddhism in India

Why was Buddhism unable to retain its popularity in its native India, although it became a major force elsewhere in Asia? Some have speculated that in denying the existence of the soul, Buddhism ran counter to traditional Hindu belief. Perhaps, too, one of Buddhism's strengths was also a weakness. In rejecting the class divisions that defined the Indian way of life, Buddhism appealed to those very groups who lacked an accepted place in Hindu society, such as the untouchables. But at the same time, it represented a threat to those with a higher status. Moreover, by emphasizing the responsibility of each person to seek an individual path to Nirvana, Buddhism undermined the strong social bonds of the Indian caste system.

Perhaps a final factor in the decline of Buddhism was the transformation of Brahmanism into a revised faith known as Hinduism. In its early development, Brahmanism had been highly elitist. Not only was observance of court ritual a monopoly of the *brahmin* class (see the box on p. 246), but the major route to individual salvation, asceticism, was hardly realistic for the average Indian. However, in the centuries after the fall of the Mauryas, a growing emphasis on devotion (***bhakti***) as a religious observance brought the possibility of improving one's *karma* by means of ritual acts within the reach of Indians of all classes. It seems likely that Hindu devotionalism rose precisely to combat the inroads of Buddhism and reduce the latter's appeal among the Indian population. The Chinese Buddhist missionary Fa Xian reported that mutual hostility between the Buddhists and the *brahmins* in the Gupta era was quite strong:

> Leaving the southern gate of the capital city, on the east side of the road is a place where Buddha once dwelt. Whilst here he bit [a piece from] the willow stick and fixed it in the earth; immediately it grew up seven feet high, neither more nor less. The unbelievers and Brahmans, filled with jealousy, cut it down and scattered the leaves far and wide, but yet it always sprang up again in the same place as before.[2]

For a while, Buddhism was probably able to stave off the Hindu challenge by its own salvationist creed of Mahayana, which also emphasized the role of devotion, but the days of Buddhism as a dominant faith in the subcontinent were numbered.

## The Arrival of Islam

While India was still undergoing a transition after the collapse of the Gupta Empire, a new and dynamic force in the form of Islam was arising in the Arabian peninsula to the west. As we have seen, during the seventh and eighth centuries, Arab armies carried the new faith westward to the Iberian peninsula and eastward across the arid wastelands of Persia and into the rugged mountains of the Hindu Kush. Islam first reached India through the Arabs in the eighth century, but a second onslaught in the tenth and eleventh centuries by Turkic-speaking converts had a more lasting effect.

Although Arab merchants had been active along the Indian coasts for centuries, Arab armies did not reach India until the early eighth century. When Indian pirates attacked Arab shipping near the delta of the Indus River, the Muslim ruler in Iraq demanded an apology from the ruler of Sind, a Hindu state in the Indus valley. When the latter refused, Muslim forces conquered lower Sind in 711 and then moved northward into the Punjab, bringing Arab rule into the frontier regions of the subcontinent for the first time.

### The Empire of Mahmud of Ghazni

For the next three centuries, Islam made no further advances into India. But a second phase began at the end of the tenth century with the rise of the state of Ghazni, located in the area of the old Kushan kingdom in present-day Afghanistan. The new kingdom was founded in 962 when Turkic-speaking slaves seized power from the Samanids, a Persian dynasty. When the founder of the new state died in 997, his son, Mahmud of Ghazni (997–1030), succeeded him. Brilliant and ambitious, Mahmud used his patrimony as a base of operations for sporadic forays against neighboring Hindu kingdoms to the southeast. Before his death in 1030, he was able to extend his rule throughout the upper Indus valley and as far south as the Indian Ocean (see Map 9.3). In wealth and cultural brilliance, his court at Ghazni rivaled that of the Abbasid dynasty in Baghdad. But his achievements had a dark side. Describing Mahmud's conquests in northwestern India, the contemporary historian al-Biruni wrote:

> Mahmud utterly ruined the prosperity of the country, and performed wonderful exploits by which the Hindus became like atoms scattered in all directions, and like a tale of old in the mouth of the people. Their scattered remains cherish, of course, the most inveterate aversion towards all Muslims. This is the reason, too, why Hindu sciences have retired far away from those parts of the country conquered by us, and have fled to places which our hand cannot yet reach, to Kashmir, Benares, and other places.[3]

Resistance against the advances of Mahmud and his successors into northern India was led by the Rajputs, aristocratic Hindu clans who were probably descended

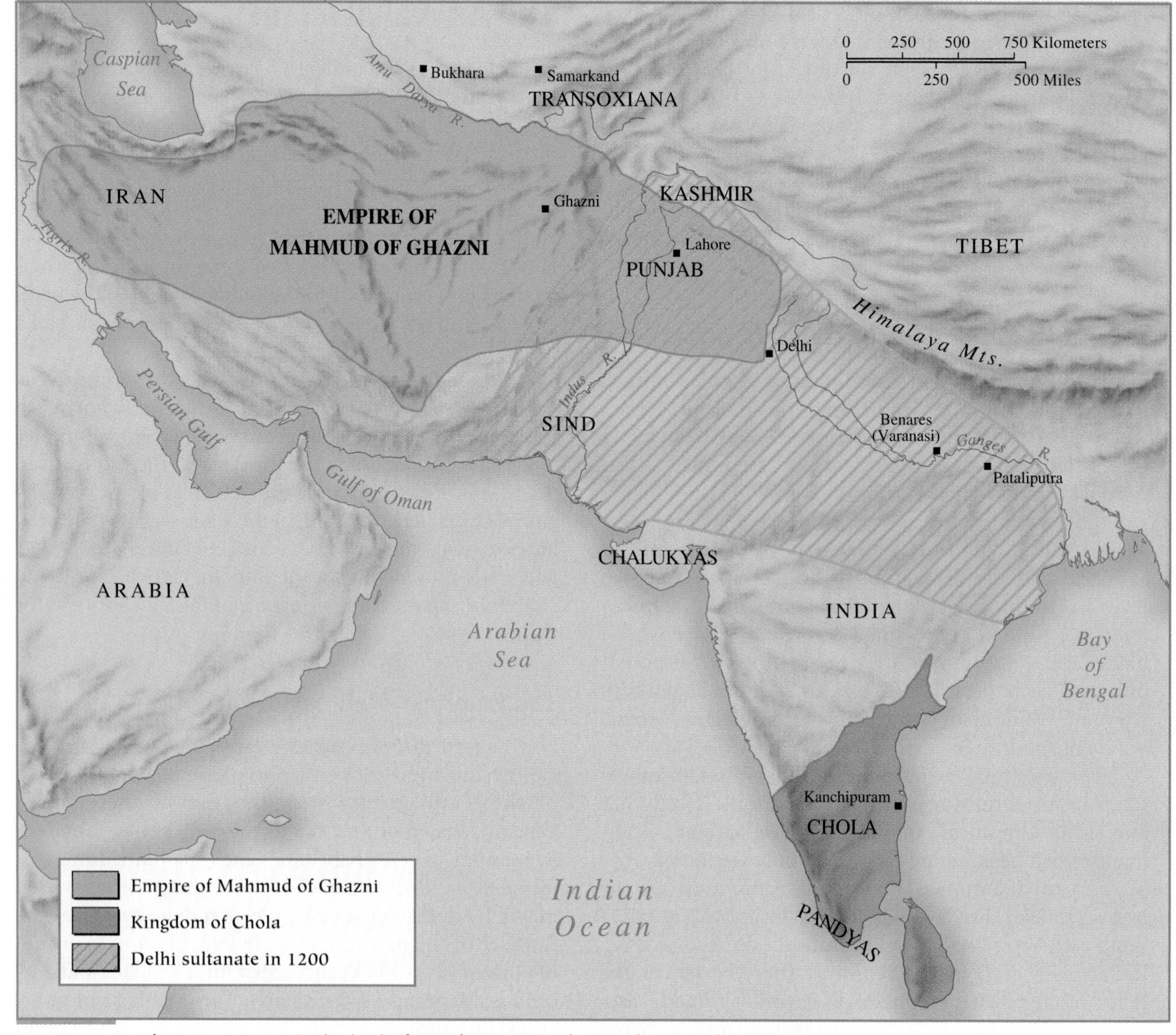


MAP 9.3 **India, 1000–1200.** Beginning in the tenth century, Turkic-speaking peoples invaded northwestern India and introduced Islam to the peoples in the area. Most famous was the empire of Mahmud of Ghazni. ? Which of the great trading states of southern India are located on the map?
**View an animated version of this map or related maps at** http://history.wadsworth.com/duikerspielvogel05/

from tribal groups that had penetrated into northwestern India from Central Asia in earlier centuries. The Rajputs possessed a strong military tradition and fought bravely, but their military tactics, based on infantry supported by elephants, were no match for the fearsome cavalry of the invaders, whose ability to strike with lightning speed contrasted sharply with the slow-footed forces of their adversaries. Moreover, the incessant squabbling among the Rajput leaders put them at a disadvantage against the single-minded intensity and religious fervor of Mahmud's armies. Although the power of Ghazni declined after his death, a successor state in the area resumed the advance in the late twelfth century, and by 1200, Muslim power, in the form of a new Delhi sultanate, had been extended over the entire plain of northern India.

## The Delhi Sultanate

South of the Ganges River valley, Muslim influence spread more slowly and in fact had little immediate impact. Muslim armies launched occasional forays into the Deccan Plateau, but at first they had little success, even though the area was divided among a number of warring kingdoms, including the Cholas along the eastern coast and the Pandyas far to the south.

One reason the Delhi sultanate failed to take advantage of the disarray of its rivals was the threat posed by the Mongols on the northwestern frontier (see Chapter 10). Mongol armies unleashed by the great tribal warrior Genghis Khan occupied Baghdad and destroyed the Abbasid caliphate in the 1250s, while other forces occupied the Punjab around Lahore, from which they threatened Delhi on several occasions. For the next half-century, the attention of the sultanate was focused on the Mongols. That threat finally declined in the early fourteenth century with the gradual breakup of the Mongol Empire, and a new Islamic state emerged in the form of the Tughluq dynasty (1320–1413), which extended its power into the Deccan Plateau. In praise of his sovereign, the Tughluq monarch Ala-ud-din, the poet Amir Khusrau exclaimed:

> *Happy be Hindustan, with its splendor of religion,*
> *Where Islamic law enjoys perfect honor and dignity;*
> *In learning Delhi now rivals Bukhara;*
> *Islam has been made manifest by the rulers.*
> *From Ghazni to the very shore of the ocean*
> *You see Islam in its glory.*[4]

Such happiness was not destined to endure, however. During the latter half of the fourteenth century, the Tughluq dynasty gradually fell into decline. In 1398, a new military force crossed the Indus River from the northwest, raided the capital of Delhi, and then withdrew. According to some contemporary historians, as many as 100,000 Hindu prisoners were massacred before the gates of the city. Such was India's first encounter with Tamerlane.

Courtesy of William J. Duiker

## Tamerlane

Tamerlane (b. 1330s), also known as Timur-i-lang (Timur the Lame), was the ruler of a Mongol khanate based in Samarkand to the north of the Pamir Mountains. His kingdom had been founded on the ruins of the Mongol Empire, which had begun to disintegrate as a result of succession struggles in the thirteenth century. Tamerlane, the son of a local aristocrat, seized power in Samarkand in 1369 and immediately launched a program of conquest. During the 1380s, he brought the entire region east of the Caspian Sea under his authority and then conquered Baghdad and occupied Mesopotamia (see Map 9.4). After his brief foray into northern India, he turned to the west and raided the Anatolian peninsula. Defeating the army of the Ottoman Turks, he advanced almost as far as the Bosporus before withdrawing. "The last of the great nomadic conquerors," as one recent historian described him, died in 1405 in the midst of a final military campaign.

The passing of Tamerlane removed a major menace from the diverse states of the Indian subcontinent. But the respite from external challenge was not a long one. By the end of the fifteenth century, two new challenges had appeared from beyond the horizon: the Mughals, a newly emerging nomadic power beyond the Khyber Pass in the north, and the Portuguese traders, who arrived by sea from the eastern coast of Africa in search of gold and spices. Both, in different ways, would exert a major impact on the later course of Indian civilization.

Courtesy of William J. Duiker

**Kutub Minar.** To commemorate their religious victory in 1192, the Muslim conquerors of northern India constructed a magnificent mosque on the site of Delhi's largest Hindu temple. Much of the material for the mosque came from twenty-seven local Hindu and Jain shrines (right). Adjacent to the mosque soars the Kutub Minar, symbol of the new conquering faith. Originally 238 feet high, the tower's inscription proclaimed its mission to cast the long shadow of God over the realm of the Hindus.

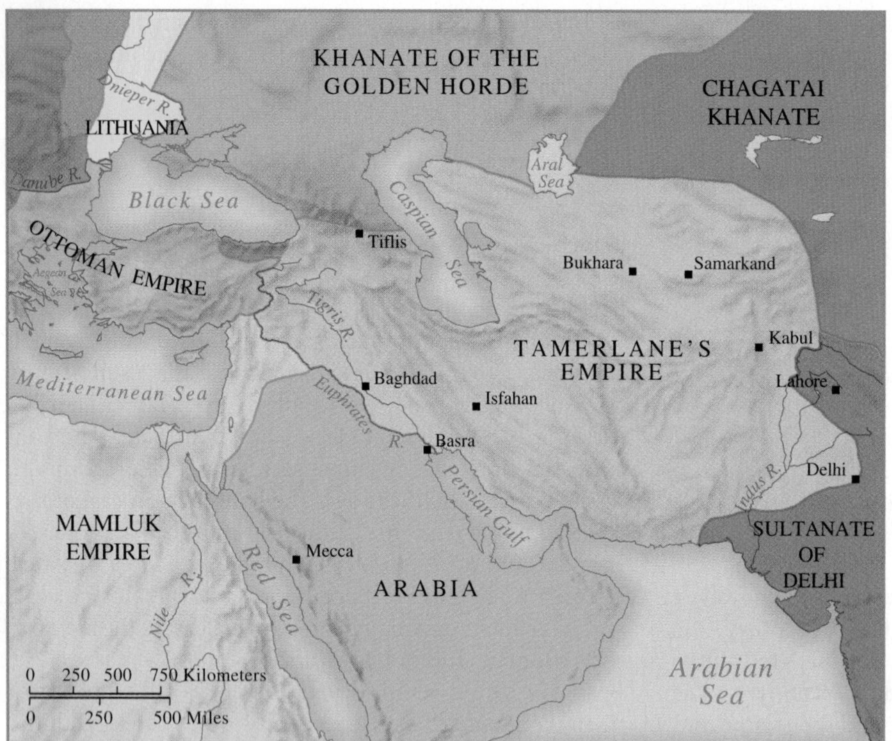


**MAP 9.4 The Empire of Tamerlane.** In the fourteenth century, Tamerlane, a feared conqueror of Mongolian extraction, established a short-lived empire in Central Asia with his capital at Samarkand. What parts of the Indian subcontinent were included in his empire?

**View an animated version of this map or related maps at** http://history.wadsworth.com/duikerspielvogel05/

Courtesy of William J. Duiker

**Samarkand, Gem of an Empire.** The city of Samarkand has a long history. Originating during the first millennium B.C.E. as a caravan stop on the Silk Road, it was later occupied by Alexander the Great, the Abbasids, and the Mongols before becoming the capital of Tamerlane's expanding empire. Tamerlane expended great sums in creating a city worthy of his own imperial ambitions. Shown here is the great square, known as the Registan. Site of a mosque, a library, and a Muslim university, all built in the exuberant Persian style, Samarkand was the jumping-off point for trade with China far to the east.

## Society and Culture

The establishment of Muslim rule over the northern parts of the subcontinent had a significant impact on the society and culture of the Indian people.

### Religion

Like their counterparts in other areas that came under Islamic rule, many Muslim rulers in India were relatively tolerant of other faiths and used peaceful means, if any, to encourage nonbelievers to convert to Islam. Even the more enlightened, however, could be fierce when their religious zeal was aroused. One ruler, on being informed that a Hindu fair had been held near Delhi, ordered the promoters of the event put to death. Hindu temples were razed, and mosques were erected in their place. Eventually, however, most Muslim rulers realized that not all Hindus could be converted and recognized the necessity of accepting what to them was an alien and repugnant religion. While Hindu religious practices were generally tolerated, non-Muslims were compelled to pay a tax to the state. Some Hindus likely

## THE ISLAMIC CONQUEST OF INDIA

One consequence of the Muslim conquest of northern India was the imposition of many Islamic customs on Hindu society. In this excerpt, the fourteenth-century Muslim historian Zia-ud-din Barani describes the attempt of one Muslim ruler, Ala-ud-din, to prevent the use of alcohol and gambling, two practices expressly forbidden in Muslim society. Ala-ud-din had seized power in Delhi from a rival in 1294.

*The ruler described here is a Muslim, establishing regulations for moral behavior in a predominantly Hindu society. Based on information available to you in Chapter 8, was a similar approach often adopted by Muslim rulers in African societies?*

### A Muslim Ruler Suppresses Hindu Practices

He forbade wine, beer, and intoxicating drugs to be used or sold; dicing, too, was prohibited. Vintners and beer sellers were turned out of the city, and the heavy taxes which had been levied from them were abolished. All the china and glass vessels of the Sultan's banqueting room were broken and thrown outside the gate of Badaun, where they formed a mound. Jars and casks of wine were emptied out there till they made mire as if it were the season of the rains. The Sultan himself entirely gave up wine parties. Self-respecting people at once followed his example; but the ne'er-do-wells went on making wine and spirits and hid the leather bottles in loads of hay or firewood and by various such tricks smuggled it into the city. Inspectors and gatekeepers and spies diligently sought to seize the contraband and the smugglers; and when seized the wine was given to the elephants, and the importers and sellers and drinkers [were] flogged and given short terms of imprisonment. So many were they, however, that holes had to be dug for their incarceration outside the great thoroughfare of the Badaun gate, and many of the wine bibbers died from the rigor of their confinement and others were taken out half-dead and were long in recovering their health. The terror of these holes deterred many from drinking. Those who could not give it up had to journey ten or twelve leagues to get a drink, for at half that distance, four or five leagues from Delhi, wine could not be publicly sold or drunk. The prevention of drinking proving very difficult, the Sultan enacted that people might distill and drink privately in their own homes, if drinking parties were not held and the liquor not sold. After the prohibition of drinking, conspiracies diminished.

converted to Islam to avoid paying the tax, but they were then expected to make the traditional charitable contribution required of Muslims in all Islamic societies.

Over time, millions of Hindus did turn to the Muslim faith. Some were individuals or groups in the employ of the Muslim ruling class, such as government officials, artisans, or merchants catering to the needs of the court. But many others were probably peasants from the *sudra* class or even untouchables who found in the egalitarian message of Islam a way of removing the stigma of low-class status in the Hindu social hierarchy.

Seldom have two major religions been so strikingly different. Where Hinduism tolerated a belief in the existence of several deities (although admittedly they were all considered by some to be manifestations of one supreme god), Islam was uncompromisingly monotheistic. Where Hinduism was hierarchical, Islam was egalitarian. Where Hinduism featured a priestly class to serve as an intermediary with the ultimate force of the universe, Islam permitted no one to come between believers and their god. Such differences contributed to the mutual hostility that developed between the adherents of the two faiths in the Indian subcontinent, but more mundane issues, such as the Muslim habit of eating beef and the idolatry and sexual frankness in Hindu art, were probably a greater source of antagonism at the popular level (see the box above).

In other cases, the two peoples borrowed from each other. Some Muslim rulers found the Indian idea of divine kingship appealing. In their turn, Hindu rajas learned by bitter experience the superiority of cavalry mounted on horses instead of elephants, the primary assault weapon in early India. Some upper-class Hindu males were attracted to the Muslim tradition of ***purdah*** and began to keep their women in seclusion (termed locally "behind the curtain") from everyday society. Hindu sources claimed that one reason for adopting the custom was to protect Hindu women from the roving eyes of foreigners. But it is likely that many Indian families adopted the practice for reasons of prestige or because they were convinced that *purdah* was a practical means of protecting female virtue. Adult Indian women had already begun to cover their heads with a scarf during the Gupta era.

All in all, Muslim rule probably did not have a significant impact on the lives of most Indian women (see the comparative essay, "Caste, Class, and Family," on p. 252). *Purdah* was practiced more commonly among high castes than among the lower castes. Though it was probably of little consolation, sexual relations in poor and low-class families were relatively egalitarian, as men and women worked together on press gangs or in the fields. Muslim customs apparently had little effect on the Hindu tradition of *sati* (widow burning). In fact, in many respects, Muslim women had more rights than

## COMPARATIVE ESSAY

# CASTE, CLASS, AND FAMILY

Why have men and women played such different roles throughout human history? Why have some societies historically adopted the nuclear family, while others preferred the joint family or the clan? Such questions are controversial and often subject to vigorous debate, yet they are crucial to our understanding of the human experience.

As we know, the first human beings practiced hunting and foraging, living in small bands composed of one or more lineage groups and moving from place to place in search of sustenance. Individual members of the community were assigned different economic and social roles—usually with men as the hunters and women as the food gatherers—but such roles were not rigidly defined. The concept of private property did not exist, and all members shared the goods possessed by the community according to need.

The agricultural revolution brought about dramatic changes in human social organizations. Although women, as food gatherers, may have been the first farmers, men—now increasingly deprived of their traditional role as hunters—began to replace them in the fields. As communities gradually adopted a sedentary lifestyle, women were increasingly assigned to domestic tasks in the home while raising the children. As farming communities grew in size and prosperity, vocational specialization and the concept of private property appeared, leading to the family as a legal entity and the emergence of a class system composed of elites, commoners, and slaves. Women were deemed inferior to men and placed in a subordinate status.

This trend toward job specialization and a rigid class system was less developed in pastoral societies, some of which still practiced a nomadic style of life and shared communal goods on a roughly equal basis within the community. Even within sedentary societies, there was considerable variety in the nature of social organizations. In some areas, the nuclear family consisted of parents and their dependent children. Other societies, however, adopted (either in theory or in practice) the idea of the joint family (ideally consisting of three generations of a family living under one roof) and sometimes even going a step further, linking several families under the larger grouping of the caste or the clan. Prominent examples of the latter tendency include India and China, although the degree to which such concepts conformed to reality is a matter of debate.

Such large social organizations, where they occurred, often established a rigid hierarchy of status within the community, including the subordination of women. On the other hand, they sometimes played a useful role in society, providing a safety net or a ladder of upward mobility for disadvantaged members of the group, as well as a form of stability in societies where legitimate and effective authority at the central level was lacking.

their Hindu counterparts. They had more property rights than Hindu women and were legally permitted to divorce under certain conditions and to remarry after the death of their husband. The primary role for Indian women in general, however, was to produce children. Sons were preferred over daughters, not only because they alone could conduct ancestral rights but also because a daughter was a financial liability. A daughter required that her father provide a costly dowry when she married, yet after the wedding, she would transfer her labor and assets to her husband's family. Still, women shared with men a position in the Indian religious pantheon. The cult of the mother-goddess, which had originated in the Harappan era, revived during the Gupta era stronger than ever. The Hindu female deity known as Devi was celebrated by both men and women as the source of cosmic power, bestower of wishes, and symbol of fertility.

Overall, the Muslims continued to view themselves as foreign conquerors and generally maintained a strict separation between the Muslim ruling class and the mass of the Hindu population. Although a few Hindus rose to important positions in the local bureaucracy, most high posts in the central government and the provinces were reserved for Muslims. Only with the founding of the Mughal dynasty was a serious effort undertaken to reconcile the differences.

One result of this effort was the religion of the Sikhs ("disciples"). Founded by the guru Nanak in the early sixteenth century in the Punjab, Sikhism attempted to integrate the best of the two faiths in a single religion. Sikhism originated in the devotionalist movement in Hinduism, which taught that God was the single true reality. All else is illusion. But Nanak rejected the Hindu tradition of asceticism and mortification of the flesh and, like Muhammad, taught his disciples to participate in the world. Sikhism achieved considerable popularity in northwestern India, where Islam and Hinduism confronted each other directly, and eventually evolved into a militant faith that fiercely protected its adherents against its two larger rivals. In the end, Sikhism did not reconcile Hinduism and Islam but provided an alternative to them.

One complication for both Muslims and Hindus as they tried to come to terms with the existence of a mixed society was the problem of class and caste. Could non-Hindus form castes, and if so, how were these castes related to the Hindu castes? Where did the Turkic-speaking elites who made up the ruling class in many of the Islamic states fit into the equation?

## Untouchables in South India

Some of the best descriptions of Indian society in the late medieval era came from European merchants and missionaries. The following passage was written by the Portuguese traveler Duarte Barbosa and describes an untouchable caste on the southwestern coast of India in the early sixteenth century. The Nayres mentioned in this excerpt were a higher caste in the region.

*Historians today evaluate documents such as this one with caution, since every observer approaches a society not his own from the perspective of his own experience and applying the values of his own society. That being the case, are there reasons to doubt the reliability of a report by a Christian on conditions in Hindu civilization?*

### Duarte Barbosa, *From the Land of Malabar*

And there is yet another caste of Heathen lower than these whom they call Poleas, who among all the rest are held to be accursed and excommunicated; they dwell in the fields and open campaigns [plots] in secret lurking places, whither folk of good caste never go save by mischance, and live in huts very strait and mean. They are tillers of rice with buffaloes and oxen. They never speak to the Nayres save from afar off, shouting so that they may hear them, and when they go along the roads they utter loud cries, that they may be let past, and whosoever hears them leaves the road, and stands in the wood till they have passed by; and if anyone, whether man or woman, touches them his kinsfolk slay him forthwith, and in vengeance therefore they slay Poleas until they weary without suffering any punishment. In certain months of the year they do their utmost to touch some Nayre woman by night as secretly as they can, and this only for the sake of doing evil. They go by in order to get into the houses of the Nayres to touch women, and during these months the women guard themselves carefully, and if they touch any woman, even though none have seen it, and there may be no witnesses, yet she declares it at once, crying out, and she will stay no longer in her house that her caste may not be destroyed; in general she flees to the house of some other low caste folk, and hides herself, that her kinsfolk may not slay her; and that thence she may help herself and be sold to foreigners, which is ofttimes done. And the manner of touching is this, even though no words are exchanged, they throw something at her, a stone or a stick, and if it touches her she is touched and ruined. These people are also great sorcerers and thieves; they are a very evil race.

The problem was resolved in a pragmatic manner that probably followed an earlier tradition of assimilating non-Hindu tribal groups into the system. Members of the Turkic ruling groups formed social groups that were roughly equivalent to the Hindu *brahmin* or *kshatriya* class. During the Delhi sultanate in the north, members of the local Rajput nobility who converted to Islam were occasionally permitted to join such class groupings. Ordinary Indians who converted to Islam also formed Muslim castes, although at a lower level on the social scale. Many who did so were probably artisans who converted en masse to obtain the privileges that conversion could bring.

In most of India, then, Muslim rule did not substantially disrupt the class and caste system. One perceptive European visitor in the early sixteenth century reported that in Malabar, along the southwestern coast, there were separate castes for fishing, pottery making, weaving, carpentry and metalworking, salt mining, sorcery, and labor on the plantations. There were separate castes for doing the laundry, one for the elite and the other for the common people (see the box above).

## Economy and Daily Life

India's landed and commercial elites lived in the cities, often in conditions of considerable opulence. The rulers, of course, possessed the most wealth. One maharaja of a relatively small state in southern India, for example, had over 100,000 soldiers in his pay along with nine hundred elephants and twenty thousand horses. Another maintained a thousand high-caste women to serve as sweepers of his palace. Each carried a broom and a brass basin containing a mixture of cow dung and water and followed him from one house to another, plastering the path where he was to tread. Most urban dwellers, of course, did not live in such style. Xuan Zang, the Chinese Buddhist missionary, left us a description of ordinary homes in seventh-century urban areas:

> Their houses are surrounded by low walls. . . . The earth being soft and muddy, the walls of the towns are mostly built of brick or tiles. The towers on the walls are constructed of wood or bamboo; the houses have balconies and belvederes, which are made of wood, with a coating of lime or mortar, and covered with tiles. The different buildings have the same form as those in China; rushes, or dry branches, or tiles, or boards are used for covering them. The walls are covered with lime and mud, mixed with cow's dung for purity. At different seasons they scatter flowers about. Such are some of their different customs.[5]

**Agriculture** The majority of India's population (estimated at slightly more than 100 million by the year 1000), however, lived on the land. Most were peasants who tilled small plots with a wooden plow pulled by oxen and paid a percentage of the harvest to their landlord. The landlord in turn forwarded part of the payment to the local ruler. In effect, the landlord functioned as a tax collector for the king, who retained ultimate ownership of all farmland in his domain. At best, most peasants lived at the subsistence level. At worst, they were forced into debt and fell victim to moneylenders who charged exorbitant rates of interest.

In the north and in the upland regions of the Deccan Plateau, the primary grain crops were wheat and barley. In the Ganges valley and the southern coastal plains, the main crop was rice. Vegetables were grown everywhere, and southern India produced many spices and fruits, sugarcane, and cotton. The cotton plant apparently originated in the Indus River valley and spread from there. Although some cotton was cultivated in Spain and North Africa by the eighth and ninth centuries, India remained the primary producer of cotton goods. Spices such as cinnamon, pepper, ginger, sandalwood, cardamom, and cumin were also major export products.

**Foreign Trade** Agriculture, of course, was not the only source of wealth in India. Since ancient times, the subcontinent had served as a major entrepôt for trade between the Middle East and the Pacific basin, as well as the source of other goods shipped throughout the known world. Although civil strife and piracy, heavy taxation of the business community by local rulers to finance their fratricidal wars, and increased customs duties between principalities may have contributed to a decline in internal trade, the level of foreign trade remained high, particularly in the Dravidian kingdoms in the south and along the northwestern coast, which were located along the traditional trade routes to the Middle East and the Mediterranean Sea. Much of this foreign trade was carried on by wealthy Hindu castes with close ties to the royal courts. But there were other participants as well, including such non-Hindu minorities as the Muslims, the Parsis, and the Jain community. The Parsis, expatriates from Persia who practiced the Zoroastrian religion, dominated banking and the textile industry in the cities bordering the Rann of Kutch. Later they would become a dominant economic force in the modern city of Mumbai (Bombay). The Jains became prominent in trade and manufacturing even though their faith emphasized simplicity and the rejection of materialism.

According to early European travelers, merchants often lived quite well. One Portuguese observer described the "Moorish" population in Bengal as follows:

> They have girdles of cloth, and over them silk scarves; they carry in their girdles daggers garnished with silver and gold, according to the rank of the person who carries them; on their fingers many rings set with rich jewels, and cotton turbans on their heads. They are luxurious, eat well and spend freely, and have many other extravagances as well. They bathe often in great tanks which they have in their houses. Everyone has three or four wives or as many as he can maintain. They keep them carefully shut up, and treat them very well, giving them great store of gold, silver and apparel of fine silk.[6]

Outside these relatively small, specialized trading communities, most manufacturing and commerce were in the hands of petty traders and artisans, who were generally limited to local markets. This failure to build on the promise of antiquity has led some historians to ask why India failed to produce an expansion of commerce and growth of cities similar to the developments that began in Europe during the High Middle Ages or even in China during the Song dynasty (see Chapter 10). Some have pointed to the traditionally low status of artisans and merchants in Indian society, symbolized by the comment in the *Arthasastra* that merchants were "thieves that are not called by the name of thief."[7] Yet commercial activities were frowned on in many areas in Europe throughout the Middle Ages, a fact that did not prevent the emergence of capitalist societies in much of the West.

Another factor may have been the monopoly on foreign trade held by the government in many areas of India. More important, perhaps, was the impact of the caste system, which reduced the ability of entrepreneurs to expand their activities and have dealings with other members of the commercial and manufacturing community. Successful artisans, for example, normally could not set up as merchants to market their products, nor could merchants compete for buyers outside their normal area of operations. The complex interlocking relationships among the various castes in a given region were a powerful factor inhibiting the development of a thriving commercial sector in medieval India.

## The Wonder of Indian Culture

The era between the Mauryas and the Mughals in India was a period of cultural evolution as Indian writers and artists built on the literary and artistic achievements of their predecessors. This is not to say, however, that Indian culture rested on its ancient laurels. To the contrary, it was an era of tremendous innovation in all fields of creative endeavor.

**Art and Architecture** At the end of antiquity, the primary forms of religious architecture were the Buddhist cave temples and monasteries. The next millennium witnessed the evolution of religious architecture from underground cavity to monumental structure.

The twenty-eight caves of Ajanta in the Deccan Plateau are one of India's greatest artistic achievements. They are as impressive for their sculpture and painting as for their architecture. Except for a few examples from the second century B.C.E., most of the caves were carved out of solid rock over an incredibly short period of eighteen years, from 460 to 478 C.E. (see the comparative illustration on p. 255). In contrast to the early unadorned temple halls, these temples were exuberantly decorated with ornate pillars, friezes, beamed ceilings, and statues of the Buddha and bodhisattvas. Several caves served as monasteries, which by then had been transformed from simple holes in the wall to large complexes with living apartments, halls, and shrines to the Buddha.

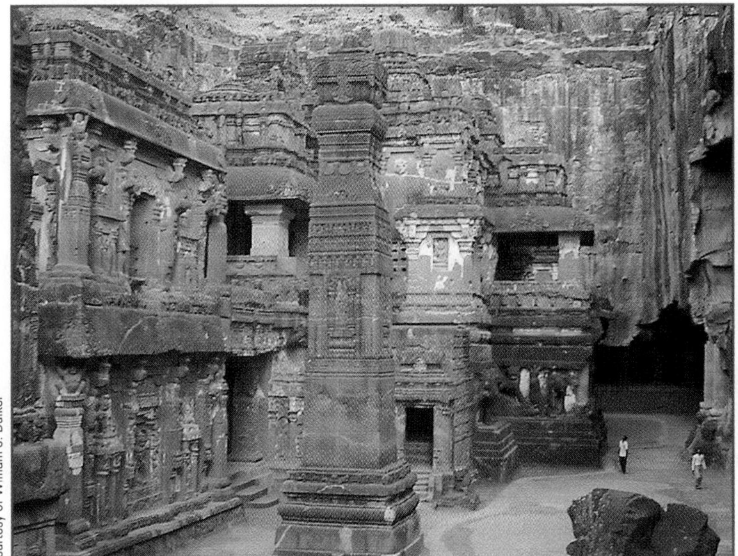
Courtesy of William J. Duiker

© Werner Forman/Art Resource, NY

ARTS & IDEAS

COMPARATIVE ILLUSTRATION

**Rock Architecture.** Along with the caves at Ajanta, one of the greatest examples of Indian rock architecture remains the eighth-century temple at Ellora, in central India, shown on the left. Named after Shiva's holy mountain in the Himalayas, the temple is approximately the size of the Parthenon in Athens but was literally carved out of a hillside. The builders dug nearly 100 feet straight down into the top of the mountain to isolate a single block of rock, removing in the process over 3 million cubic feet of stone. Unlike earlier rock-cut shrines, which had been constructed in the form of caves, the Ellora temple is open to the sky and filled with some of India's finest sculpture. The overall impression is one of massive grandeur.

This form of architecture also found expression in parts of Africa. In 1200 C.E., Christian monks in Ethiopia began to construct a remarkable series of eleven churches carved out of solid volcanic rock (right). After a 40-foot trench was formed by removing the bedrock, the central block of stone was hewed into the shape of a Greek cross; then it was hollowed out and decorated. These churches, which are still in use today, testify to the fervor of Ethiopian Christianity, which plays a major role in preserving the country's cultural and national identity.

All of the inner surfaces of the caves, including the ceilings, sculptures, walls, door frames, and pillars, were painted in vivid colors. Perhaps best known are the wall paintings, which illustrate the various lives and incarnations of the Buddha. These paintings are in an admirable state of preservation, making it possible to reconstruct the customs, dress, house interiors, and physical characteristics of the peoples of fifth-century India. The inner surfaces of the caves were covered with paintings executed in vivid colors and portraying the various lives and incarnations of the Buddha. Similar rock paintings, but focusing on secular subjects, can be found at Sigiriya, a fifth-century royal palace on the island of Sri Lanka.

Among the most impressive rock carvings in southern India are the cave temples at Mamallapuram (also known as Mahabalipuram), south of the modern city of Chennai (Madras). The sculpture, called *Descent of the Ganges River,* depicts the role played by Shiva in intercepting the heavenly waters of the Ganges and allowing them to fall gently on the earth. Mamallapuram also boasts an eighth-century shore temple, which is one of the earliest surviving freestanding structures in the subcontinent.

From the eighth century until the time of the Mughals, Indian architects built a multitude of magnificent Hindu temples, now constructed exclusively aboveground. Each temple consisted of a central shrine surmounted by a sizable tower, a hall for worshipers, a vestibule, and a porch, all set in a rectangular courtyard that might also contain other minor shrines. Temples became progressively more ornate until the eleventh century, when the sculpture began to dominate the structure itself. The towers became higher and the temple complexes more intricate, some becoming virtual walled compounds set one within the other and resembling towns in themselves.

Among the best examples of temple art are those in the eastern state of Orissa. The Sun Temple at Konarak, standing at the edge of the sea and covered with intricate carvings, is generally considered the masterpiece of its genre. Although now in ruins, the Sun Temple still boasts some of India's most memorable sculptures. Especially renowned are the twelve pairs of carved wheels; each is 10 feet high and represents one of the twelve signs of the zodiac.

The greatest example of medieval Hindu temple art, however, is probably Khajuraho. Of the original eighty-

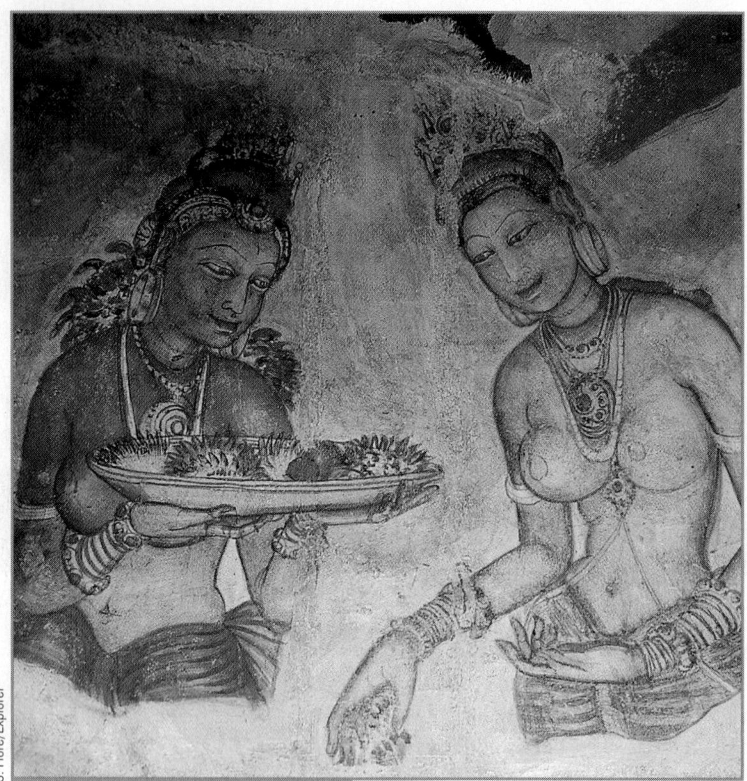
S. Fiore/Explorer

**Rock Paintings at Sigiriya, Sri Lanka.** Starting in the third century B.C.E., engineers on the island of Sri Lanka developed a sophisticated irrigation system consisting of dams, reservoirs, water tanks, and canals. One of the most impressive examples was built by the fifth century C.E. kingdom of Sigiriya, in the center of the island. The royal palace, perched for protective purposes on the summit of a 650-foot-high rock mesa, contains extensive water gardens, fountains, and swimming pools to provide royal entertainment. Portraits of serving girls from the king's harem, such as the one shown here, were painted high up along the cliff wall. Many such paintings were destroyed by Buddhist monks when they reclaimed the area after the king's sudden death. Fortunately, a few have survived to captivate viewers over the centuries.

five temples, dating from the tenth century, twenty-five remain standing today. All of the towers are buttressed at various levels on the sides, giving the whole a sense of unity and creating a vertical movement similar to Mount Kailasa in the Himalayas, sacred to Hindus. Everywhere the viewer is entertained by voluptuous temple dancers bringing life to the massive structures. One is removing a thorn from her foot, another is applying eye makeup, and yet another is wringing out her hair.

In the Deccan Plateau, a different style prevailed. The southern temple style was marked by massive oblong stone towers, some as much as 200 feet high. The towers were often covered with a profusion of sculpted figures and were visible for miles. The walls surrounding the temple complex were also surmounted with impressive gate towers, known as *gopuras*.

**Literature** During this period, Indian authors produced a prodigious number of written works, both religious and secular. Indian religious poetry was written in Sanskrit and also in the languages of southern India. As Hinduism was transformed from a contemplative to a more devotional religion, its poetry became more ardent and erotic and prompted a sense of divine ecstasy. Much of the religious verse extolled the lives and heroic acts of Shiva, Vishnu, Rama, and Krishna by repeating the same themes over and over, which is also a characteristic of Indian art. In the eighth century, a tradition of poet-saints inspired by intense mystical devotion to a deity emerged in southern India. Many were women who sought to escape the drudgery of domestic toil through an imagined sexual union with the god-lover. Such was the case for the twelfth-century mystic whose poem here expresses her sensuous joy in the physical-mystical union with her god:

*It was like a stream*
*running into the dry bed*
*of a lake,*
*like rain pouring on plants*
*parched to sticks.*
*It was like this world's pleasure*
*and the way to the other,*
*both walking towards me.*
*Seeing the feet of the master,*
*O lord white as jasmine*
*I was made worthwhile.*[8]

The great secular literature of traditional India was also written in Sanskrit in the form of poetry, drama, and prose. Some of the best medieval Indian poetry is found in single-stanza poems, which create an entire emotional scene in just four lines. Witness this poem by the poet Amaru:

*We'll see what comes of it, I thought,*
*and I hardened my heart against her.*
*What, won't the villain speak to me? she*
*thought, flying into a rage.*
*And there we stood, sedulously refusing to look one*
*another in the face,*
*Until at last I managed an unconvincing laugh,*
*and her tears robbed me of my resolution.*[9]

One of India's most famous authors was Kalidasa, who lived during the Gupta dynasty. Although little is known of him, including his dates, he probably wrote for the court of Chandragupta II (375–415 C.E.). Even today, Kalidasa's hundred-verse poem, *The Cloud Messenger,* remains one of the most popular Sanskrit poems.

In addition to being a poet, Kalidasa was also a great dramatist. He wrote three plays, all dramatic romances that blend the erotic with the heroic and the comic. *Shakuntala,* perhaps the best-known play in all Indian literature, tells the story of a king who, while out hunting, falls in love with the maiden Shakuntala. He asks her to

Marcello Bertinetti/Photo Researchers, Inc.

**Sculptural Decorations at Khajuraho.** This Hindu temple, one of the greatest in India, is literally covered with statues, both mortal and divine, depicted in erotic poses and thought to promote Hindu cosmology. Many represent the ideal couple or divine lovers, who symbolize the union of the worshipers with the deity, thus blending physical and spiritual beauty. Evolving from the traditional female earth spirit (see Chapter 2), women have been represented in Indian art as the sensuous bearers of fertility and prosperity. As a contemporary Indian text stated, "As a house without a wife, as frolic without a woman, so without the figure of woman the monument will be of inferior quality and will bear no fruit."

marry him and offers her a ring of betrothal but is suddenly recalled to his kingdom on urgent business. Shakuntala, who is pregnant, goes to him, but the king has been cursed by a hermit and no longer recognizes her. With the help of the gods, the king eventually does recall their love and is reunited with Shakuntala and their son.

Each of Kalidasa's plays is propelled by the magic powers of a goddess, and each ends in affirmation and unity. Another interesting aspect of Kalidasa's plays is that they combine several languages as well as poetry and prose. The language and form of the characters' speeches correspond to their position in the social hierarchy. Thus the king speaks in Sanskrit poetry, while the other characters in the play use prose in three different vernaculars of everyday life.

Kalidasa was one of the greatest Indian dramatists, but he was by no means the only one. Sanskrit plays typically contained one to ten acts. They were performed in theaters in the palaces or in court temples by troupes of actors of both sexes who were trained and supported by the royal family. The plots were usually taken from Indian legends of gods and kings. No scenery or props were used, but costumes and makeup were elaborate. The theaters had to be small because much of the drama was conveyed through intricate gestures and dance conventions. There were many different positions for various parts of the body, including one hundred for the hands alone.

Like poetry, prose developed in India from the Vedic period. The use of prose was well established by the sixth and seventh centuries C.E. This is truly astonishing considering that the novel did not appear until the tenth century in Japan and until the seventeenth century in Europe.

One of the greatest masters of Sanskrit prose was Dandin, who lived during the seventh century. In *The Ten Princes,* he created a fantastic and exciting world that fuses history and fiction. His keen powers of observation, details of low life, and humor give his writing considerable vitality. Witness the passage in which the mother of a courtesan describes the demanding education required for her most accomplished daughter (see the box on p. 258).

**Music** Another area of Indian creativity that developed during this era was music. Ancient Indian music had come from the chanting of the Vedic hymns and thus inevitably had a strong metaphysical and spiritual flavor. The actual physical vibrations of music (*nada*) were considered to be related to the spiritual world. An off-key or sloppy rendition of a sacred text could upset the harmony and balance of the entire universe.

In form, Indian classical music is based on a scale, called a *raga.* There are dozens, if not hundreds, of separate scales, which are grouped into separate categories depending on the time of day during which they are to be performed. The performers use a stringed instrument called a *sitar* and various types of wind instruments and drums. The performers select a basic *raga* and then are free to improvise the melodic structure and rhythm. A good performer never performs a particular *raga* the same way twice. As with jazz music in the West, the audience is concerned not so much with faithful reproduction as with the performer's creativity.

## THE EDUCATION OF A COURTESAN

The writings of the seventh-century author Dandin provide a lively portrait of Indian society. In this excerpt from his novel *The Ten Princes* are revealed the frustrations of a mother determined to mold her daughter into a wealthy courtesan, one who could assure herself and her family of a life of ease. Rather than focusing on attracting wealthy patrons, however, the daughter has preferred to share her charms with a handsome youth of no fortune.

*How would you define in a few words the advice given here on the training of a courtesan in medieval India? How has the daughter responded to this advice from her mother? Was she justified in her actions?*

### Dandin, *The Ten Princes*

At this point the mother lifted her hands, touched the earth with hair dappled with grey, lifted her head, and spoke: "Holy sir, this your maid-servant acquaints you with my own wrongdoing. And this wrongdoing of mine lay in the performance of my obvious duty. For obvious duty is as follows for the mother of a *fille de joie:* care of her daughter's person from the hour of birth; nourishment by a diet so regulated as to develop stateliness, vigor, complexion, intelligence, while harmonizing the humors, gastric calefaction, and secretions; not permitting her to see too much even of her father after the fifth year; festive ritual on birthdays and holy days; instruction in the arts of flirtation, both major and minor; thorough training in dance, song, instrumental music, acting, painting, also judgment of foods, perfumes, flowers, not forgetting writing and graceful speech; a conversational acquaintance with grammar, with logical inference and conclusion; profound skill in money-making, sport, and betting on cockfights or chess; assiduous use of go-betweens in the passages of coquetry; display of numerous well-dressed attendants at religious or secular celebrations; careful selection of teachers to insure success at unpremeditated vocal and other exhibitions; advertising on a national scale by a staff of trained specialists; publicity for beautymarks through astrologers and such; eulogistic mention in gatherings of men about town of her beauty, character, accomplishments, charm, and sweetness by hangers-on, gay dogs, buffoons, female religionists, and others; raising her price considerably when she has become an object of desire to young gentlemen; surrender to a lover of independent fortune, a philogynist or one intoxicated by seeing her charms, a gentlemen eminent for rank, figure, youth, money, vigor, purity, generosity, cleverness, gallantry, art, character, and sweetness of disposition; delivery, with gracious exaggeration of value received, to one less affluent, but highly virtuous and cultivated (the alternative is levying on his natural guardians, after informal union with such a gentleman); collection of bad debts by vamping judge and jury; mothering a lover's daughter; abstraction by ingenious tricks of money left in an admirer's possession after payment for periodical pleasures; steady quarreling with a defaulter or miser; stimulation of the spirit of generosity in an overthrifty adorer by the incentive of jealousy; repulse of the impecunious by biting speeches, by public taunts, by cutting his daughters, and by other embarrassing habits, as well as by simple contempt; continued clinging to the open-handed, the chivalrous, the blameless, the wealthy, with full consideration of the interrelated chances of money and misery.

"Besides, a courtesan should show readiness indeed, but no devotion to a lover; and, even if fond of him, she should not disobey mother or grandmother. In spite of all, the girl disregards her God-given vocation and has spent a whole month of amusement–at her own expense!–with a Brahman youth, a fellow from nowhere whose face is his fortune. Her snippiness has offended several perfectly solvent admirers and has pauperized her own family. And when I scolded her and told her: 'This is no kind of a scheme. This isn't pretty,' she was angry and took to the woods. And if she is obstinate, this whole family will stay right here and starve to death. There is nothing else to do." And the mother wept.

# The Golden Region: Early Southeast Asia

Between China and India lies the region that today is called Southeast Asia. It has two major components: a mainland region extending southward from the Chinese border down to the tip of the Malay peninsula and an extensive archipelago, most of which is part of present-day Indonesia and the Philippines. Travel between the islands and regions to the west, north, and east was not difficult, so Southeast Asia has historically served as a vast land bridge for the movement of peoples between China, the Indian subcontinent, and the more than 25,000 islands of the South Pacific.

Mainland Southeast Asia consists of several north-south mountain ranges, separated by river valleys that run in a southerly or southeasterly direction. During the first millennium C.E., two groups of migrants—the Thai from southwestern China and the Burmese from the Tibetan highlands—came down these valleys in search of new homelands, as earlier peoples had done before them. Once in Southeast Asia, most of these migrants settled in the fertile deltas of the rivers—the Irrawaddy and the Salween in Burma, the Chao Phraya in Thailand, and the Red River and the Mekong

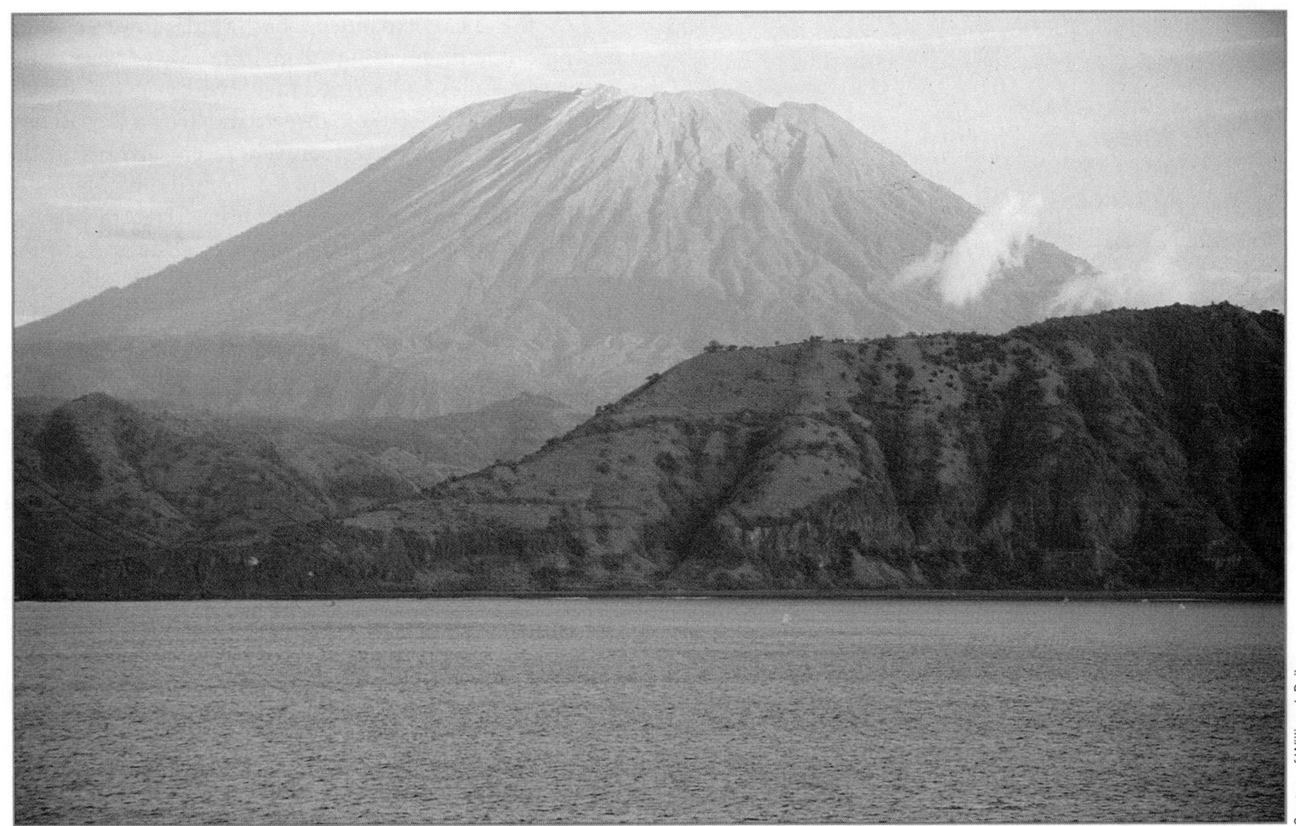


**The Mountain, in Myth and Reality.** In many traditional Asian societies, as in classical Greece, mountains were viewed as the abode of the gods, and temples were built in the shape of a mountain to create an earthly representation of a heavenly paradise. But mountains could hold dangers as well. Such is certainly the case with the Indonesian archipelago in Southeast Asia, an island chain formed by volcanic eruptions along a major fault line in the earth's crust. Shown here is beautiful Mount Agung, on the Indonesian island of Bali, still viewed as the local equivalent of sacred Mount Meru in India. In Balinese cosmology, the sea is the home of evil spirits, while humans occupy the profane world in between. An active volcano, Agung erupted in 1964, killing thousands of islanders in a cloud of volcanic ash.

in Vietnam—or in lowland areas in the islands to the south.

Although the river valleys facilitated north-south travel on the Southeast Asian mainland, movement between east and west was relatively difficult. The mountains are densely forested and often infested with malaria-carrying mosquitoes. Consequently, the lowland peoples in the river valleys were often isolated from each other and had only limited contacts with the upland peoples in the mountains. These geographical barriers may help explain why Southeast Asia is one of the few regions in Asia that was never unified under a single government.

Given Southeast Asia's location between China and India, it is not surprising that both civilizations influenced developments in the region. In 111 B.C.E., Vietnam was conquered by the Han dynasty and remained under Chinese control for more than a millennium; it will be discussed in Chapter 11. The Indian states never exerted much political control over Southeast Asia, but their influence was pervasive nevertheless. By the first centuries C.E., Indian merchants were sailing to Southeast Asia; they were soon followed by Buddhist and Hindu missionaries. Indian influence can be seen in many aspects of Southeast Asian culture, from political institutions to religion, architecture, language, and literature.

## Paddy Fields and Spices: The States of Southeast Asia

The traditional states of Southeast Asia can generally be divided between agricultural societies and trading societies. The distinction between farming and trade was a product of the environment. The agricultural societies—notably, Vietnam, Angkor in what is now Cambodia, and the Burmese state of Pagan—were situated in rich river deltas that were conducive to the development of a wet rice economy (see Map 9.5). Although all produced some goods for regional markets, none was tempted to turn to commerce as the prime source of national income. In fact, none was situated astride the main trade routes that crisscrossed the region.

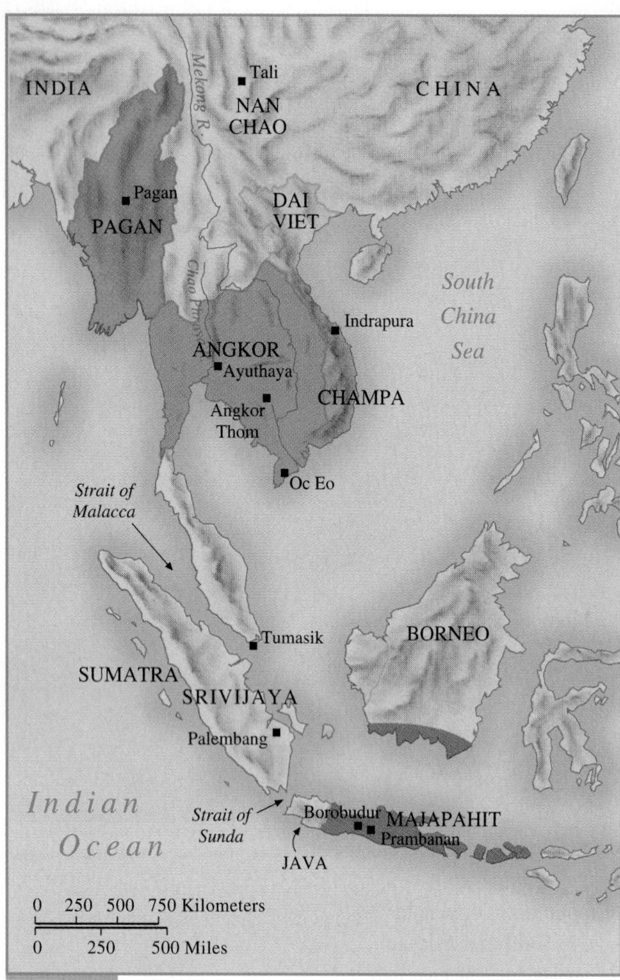


**MAP 9.5 Southeast Asia in the Thirteenth Century.** This map shows the major states that arose in Southeast Asia in the early second millennium C.E. Some, like Angkor and Dai Viet, were predominantly agricultural. Others, like Srivijaya and Champa, were commercial. **?** Which of these empires were soon to disappear?

**View an animated version of this map or related maps at** http://history .wadsworth.com/duikerspielvogel05/

**The Mainland States** The kingdom of Angkor, which took shape in the ninth century, was the most powerful state to emerge in mainland Southeast Asia before the sixteenth century (see the box on p. 261). The remains of its capital city, Angkor Thom, give a sense of the magnificence of Angkor civilization. The city formed a square 2 miles on each side. Its massive stone walls were several feet thick and were surrounded by a moat. Four main gates led into the city, which at its height had a substantial population. By the fourteenth century, however, Angkor had begun to decline, and in 1432, Angkor Thom was destroyed by the Thai, who had migrated into the region from southwestern China in the thirteenth century and established their capital at Ayuthaya, in lower Thailand, in 1351.

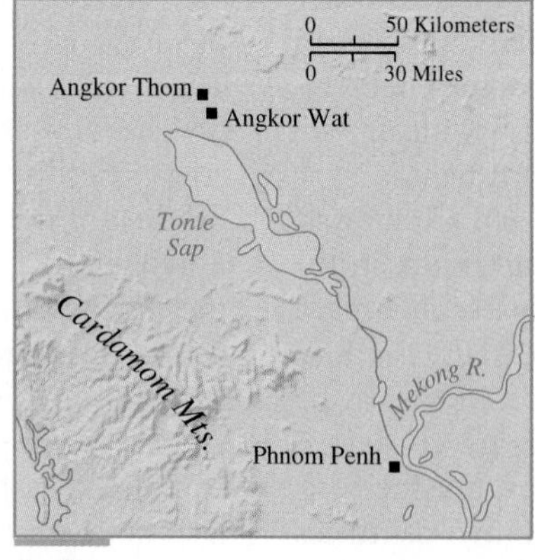


**Angkor**

As the Thai expanded southward, however, their main competition came from the west, where the Burmese peoples had formed their own agricultural society in the valleys of the Salween and Irrawaddy Rivers. Like the Thai, they were relatively recent arrivals in the area, having migrated southward from the highlands of Tibet beginning in the seventh century C.E. After subjugating weaker societies already living in the area, in the eleventh century they founded the first great Burmese state, the kingdom of Pagan. Like the Thai, they quickly converted to Buddhism and adopted Indian political institutions and culture. For a while, they were a major force in the western part of Southeast Asia, but attacks from the Mongols in the late thirteenth century (see Chapter 10) weakened Pagan, and the resulting vacuum may have benefited the Thai as they moved into areas occupied by Burmese migrants in the Chao Phraya valley.

**The Malay World** In the Malay peninsula and the Indonesian archipelago, a different pattern emerged. For centuries, this area had been linked to regional trade networks, and much of its wealth had come from the export of tropical products to China, India, and the Middle East. The vast majority of the inhabitants of the region were of Malay ethnic stock, a people who spread from their original homeland in southeastern China into island Southeast Asia and even to more distant locations in the South Pacific, such as Tahiti, Hawaii, and Easter Island.

Eventually, the islands of the Indonesian archipelago gave rise to two of the region's most notable trading societies—Srivijaya and Majapahit. Both were based in large part on spices. As the wealth of the Arab empire in the Middle East and then of western Europe increased, so did the demand for the products of East Asia. Merchant fleets from India and the Arabian peninsula sailed to the Indonesian islands to buy cloves, pepper, nutmeg, cinnamon, precious woods, and other exotic products coveted by the wealthy. In the eighth century, Srivijaya, located along the eastern coast of Sumatra, became a powerful commercial state that dominated the trade route passing through the Strait of Malacca, at that time the most convenient route from East Asia into the Indian Ocean. The rulers of Srivijaya had helped bring the route to prominence by controlling the pirates who had previously plagued shipping in the strait. Another inducement was Srivijaya's capital at Palembang, a deepwater port where sailors could wait out the change in the monsoon season before making their return voyage. In 1025, however, Chola, one of the kingdoms of southern India and a commercial rival of Srivijaya, inflicted a devastating defeat on the island kingdom. Although Srivijaya survived, it was unable to regain its former dominance, in part because

## THE KINGDOM OF ANGKOR

Angkor (known to the Chinese as Chen-la) was the greatest kingdom of its time in Southeast Asia. This passage, probably written in the thirteenth century by the Chinese port official Chau Ju-kua (see Chapter 8), includes a brief description of the capital city, Angkor Thom, which is still one of the great archaeological sites of the region. Angkor was already in decline when Chau Ju-kua described the kingdom, and the capital was abandoned soon afterward, in 1432.

*Because of the paucity of written records about Angkor society, documents such as this one by a Chinese source are important in providing knowledge about local conditions. What does this excerpt tell us about the political system, religious belief, and land use in thirteenth-century Angkor?*

### Chau Ju-kua, *Records of Foreign Nations*

The officials and the common people dwell in houses with sides of bamboo matting and thatched with reeds. Only the king resides in a palace of hewn stone. It has a granite lotus pond of extraordinary beauty with golden bridges, some three hundred odd feet long. The palace buildings are solidly built and richly ornamented. The throne on which the king sits is made of gharu wood and the seven precious substances; the dais is jewelled, with supports of veined wood [ebony?]; the screen [behind the throne] is of ivory.

When all the ministers of state have audience, they first make three full prostrations at the foot of the throne; they then kneel and remain thus, with hands crossed on their breasts, in a circle round the king, and discuss the affairs of state. When they have finished, they make another prostration and retire. . . .

[The people] are devout Buddhists. There are serving [in the temples] some three hundred foreign women; they dance and offer food to the Buddha. They are called *a-nan* or slave dancing girls.

As to their customs, lewdness is not considered criminal; theft is punished by cutting off a hand and a foot and by branding on the chest.

The incantations of the Buddhist and Taoist priests [of this country] have magical powers. Among the former those who wear yellow robes may marry, while those who dress in red lead ascetic lives in temples. The Taoists clothe themselves with leaves; they have a deity called P'o-to-li which they worship with great devotion.

[The people of this country] hold the right hand to be clean, the left unclean, so when they wish to mix their rice with any kind of meat broth, they use the right hand to do so and also to eat with.

The soil is rich and loamy; the fields have no bounds. Each one takes as much as he can cultivate. Rice and cereals are cheap; for every tael of lead one can buy two bushels of rice.

The native products comprise elephants' tusks, the *chan* and *su* [varieties of gharu wood], good yellow wax, kingfisher's feathers, . . . resin, foreign oils, ginger peel, gold-colored incense, . . . raw silk and cotton fabrics.

The foreign traders offer in exchange for these gold, silver, porcelainware, sugar, preserves, and vinegar.

the main trade route had shifted to the east, through the Strait of Sunda and directly out into the Indian Ocean. In the late thirteenth century, this shift in trade patterns led to the founding of the new kingdom of Majapahit on the island of Java. In the mid-fourteenth century, Majapahit succeeded in uniting most of the archipelago and perhaps even part of the Southeast Asian mainland under its rule (see the box on p. 262).

**The Role of India** Indian influence was evident in all of these societies to various degrees. Based on models from the Dravidian kingdoms of southern India, Southeast Asian kings were believed to possess special godlike qualities that set them apart from ordinary people. In some societies such as Angkor, the most prominent royal advisers constituted a *brahmin* class on the Indian model. In Pagan and Angkor, some division of the population into separate classes based on occupation and ethnic background seems to have occurred, although these divisions do not seem to have developed the rigidity of the Indian class system.

India also supplied Southeast Asians with a writing system. The societies of the region had no written scripts for their spoken languages before the arrival of the Indian merchants and missionaries. Indian phonetic symbols were borrowed and used to record the spoken language. Initially, Southeast Asian literature was written in the Indian Sanskrit but eventually came to be written in the local languages. Southeast Asian authors borrowed popular Indian themes, such as stories from the Buddhist scriptures and tales from the Ramayana.

A popular form of entertainment among the common people, the *wayang kulit*, or shadow play, may have come originally from India or possibly China, but it became a distinctive art form in Java and other islands of the Indonesian archipelago. In a shadow play, flat leather puppets were manipulated behind an illuminated screen while the narrator recited tales from the Indian classics. The plays were often accompanied by a gamelan, an orchestra composed primarily of percussion instruments such as gongs and drums that apparently originated in Java.

## THE LEGENDARY GRANDEUR OF MAJAPAHIT

The *Nagarkertagama,* written by the court poet Prapanca in 1365, was the national epic of the kingdom of Majapahit. This passage describes the relationship between the kingdom and neighboring countries in the region.

*What does this passage tell us about the nature of Majapahit and the qualities of its ruler? Is it as useful a description of Javanese society as, for example, those by the Chinese monks Fa Xian and Xuan Zang appearing earlier in this chapter?*

### Prapanca, *Nagarkertagama*

Such is the excellence of His Majesty the Prince who reigns at Majapahit as absolute monarch. His is praised like the moon in autumn, since he fills all the world with joy. The evil-doers are like the red lotus, the good—who love him wholeheartedly—are like the white lotus. His retinue, treasures, chariots, elephants, horses, etc., are [immeasurable] like the sea.

The land of Java is becoming more and more famous for its blessed state throughout the world. "Only Jambudwipa [India] and Java," so people say, "are mentioned for their superiority, good countries as they are, because of the multitude of men experienced in the doctrine . . . ; whatever 'work' turns up, they are very able to handle it."

First comes the Illustrious Brahmaraja, the excellent *brahmin,* an irreproachable, great poet and expert of the religious traditions; he has complete knowledge of the speculative as well as all the other philosophies, . . . the system of dialectical [logic], etc. And [then] the holy Shamana, very pious, virtuous, experienced in the Vedas and the six pure activities. And also the Illustrious Vishnu, powerful in Samaveda incantations, with which he aims to increase the country's prosperity.

For this reason all kinds of people have continually come from other countries, in multitudes. There are Jambudwipa, Kamboja [Cambodia], China, Yawana [Annam], Champa, Kannataka [in South China], etc., Goda [Gaur] and Siam—these are the places whence they come from. They come by ship with numerous merchants; monks and *brahmins* are the principal ones who as they come are regaled and are well pleased during their stay.

And in each month of Phalguna [February-March] His Majesty the Prince is honored and celebrated in his residence. Then the high state officials come from all over Java, the heads of districts, and the judicial officials . . . ; also the [people from] other islands, Bali, etc., all come with tributes so numerous that they are uninterrupted, to honor him. Traders and merchants fill the market in dense crowds with all their wares in great variety.

## Daily Life

Because of the diversity of ethnic backgrounds, religions, and cultures, making generalizations about daily life in Southeast Asia during the early historical period is difficult. Nevertheless, it appears that societies in the region did not always apply the social distinctions that prevailed in India. For example, although the local population, as elsewhere, was divided according to a variety of economic functions, the dividing lines between classes were not as rigid and imbued with religious significance as they were in the Indian subcontinent.

Courtesy of William J. Duiker

**Giant Heads of Easter Island.** When the Malay-Polynesian–speaking peoples spread out from their homeland into the islands of the Pacific, they eventually settled in areas as far distant as Hawaii and Easter Island. Some of these peoples first arrived on Easter Island in the fifth century C.E., and soon began to erect giant stone statues. It is thought that they were devised by rival chiefdoms for reasons of prestige. Moving them from the quarry (shown here) by rolling them on a bed of rounded logs resulted in the eventual devastation of the forests and the total erosion of the landscape, nearly wiping out the entire population.

**Social Structures** Still, traditional societies in Southeast Asia had some clearly hierarchical characteristics. At the top of the social ladder were the hereditary aristocrats, who monopolized both political power and economic wealth and enjoyed a borrowed aura of charisma by virtue of their proximity to the ruler. Most aristocrats lived in the major cities, which were the main source of power, wealth, and foreign influence. Beyond the major cities lived the mass of the population, composed of farmers, fishers, artisans, and merchants. In most Southeast Asian societies, the vast majority were probably rice farmers, living at a bare level of subsistence and paying heavy rents or taxes to a landlord or a local ruler.

The average Southeast Asian peasant was not actively engaged in commerce except as a consumer of various necessities. But accounts by foreign visitors indicate that in the Malay world, some were involved in growing or mining products for export, such as tropical food products, precious woods, tin, and precious gems. Most of the regional trade was carried on by local merchants, who purchased products from local growers and then transported them to the major port cities. During the early state-building era, roads were few and relatively primitive, so most of the trade was transported by small boats down rivers to the major ports along the coast. There the goods were loaded onto larger ships for delivery outside the region. Growers of export goods in areas near the coast were thus indirectly involved in the regional trade network but received few economic benefits from the relationship.

As we might expect from an area of such ethnic and cultural diversity, social structures differed significantly from country to country. In the Indianized states on the mainland, the tradition of a hereditary tribal aristocracy was probably accentuated by the Hindu practice of dividing the population into separate classes, called *varna* in imitation of the Indian model. In Angkor and Pagan, for example, the divisions were based on occupation or ethnic background. Some people were considered free subjects of the king, although there may have been legal restrictions against changing occupations. Others, however, may have been indentured to an employer. Each community was under a chieftain, who was in turn subordinated to a higher official responsible for passing on the tax revenues of each group to the central government.

In the kingdoms in the Malay peninsula and the Indonesian archipelago, social relations were generally less formal. Most of the people in the region, whether farmers, fishers, or artisans, lived in small *kampongs* (Malay for "villages") in wooden houses built on stilts to avoid flooding during the monsoon season. Some of the farmers were probably sharecroppers who paid a part of their harvest to a landlord, who was often a member of the aristocracy. But in other areas, the tradition of free farming was strong. In some cases, some of the poorer land belonged to the village as a collective unit and was assigned for use by the neediest families.

**Women and the Family** The women of Southeast Asia during this era have been described as the most fortunate in the world. Although most women worked side by side with men in the fields, as in Africa they often played an active role in trading activities. Not only did this lead to a higher literacy rate among women than among their male counterparts, but it also allowed them more financial

Clayton Fogel

**Angkor at War.** Whereas Angkor Wat was dedicated to Hindu mythology, the Bayon Temple in the nearby city of Angkor Thom was a Buddhist structure, erected when King Jayavarman converted to the new faith. The Bayon is known for its huge heads of the Boddhisattva of Mercy, but it also contains a series of extraordinary bas-reliefs, which illuminate the everyday life of thirteenth-century Cambodia. Shown here is the Angkor army heading into battle, with an infantry unit accompanied by the cavalry mounted on elephants, an unusual portrayal on a structure dedicated to the principle of nonviolence.

independence than their counterparts in China and India, a fact that was noticed by the Chinese traveler Zhou Daguan at the end of the thirteenth century: "In Cambodia it is the women who take charge of trade. For this reason a Chinese arriving in the country loses no time in getting himself a mate, for he will find her commercial instincts a great asset."[10]

Although, as elsewhere, warfare was normally part of the male domain, women sometimes played a role as bodyguards as well. According to Zhou Daguan, women were used to protect the royal family in Angkor, as well as in kingdoms located on the islands of Java and Sumatra. While there is no evidence that such female units ever engaged in battle, they did give rise to wondrous tales of "amazon" warriors in the writings of foreign travelers such as the fourteenth-century Muslim adventurer Ibn Battuta.

One reason for the enhanced status of women in traditional Southeast Asia is that the nuclear family was more common than the joint family system prevalent in China and the Indian subcontinent. Throughout the region, wealth in marriage was passed from the male to the female, in contrast to the dowry system applied in China and India. In most societies, virginity was usually not a valued commodity in brokering a marriage, and divorce proceedings could be initiated by either party. Still, most marriages were monogamous, and marital fidelity was taken seriously.

The relative availability of cultivable land in the region may help explain the absence of joint families. Joint families under patriarchal leadership tend to be found in areas where land is scarce and individual families must work together to conserve resources and maximize income. With the exception of a few crowded river valleys, few areas in Southeast Asia had a high population density per acre of cultivable land. Throughout most of the area, water was plentiful, and the land was relatively fertile. In parts of Indonesia, it was possible to survive by living off the produce of wild fruit trees—bananas, coconuts, mangoes, and a variety of other tropical fruits.

## World of the Spirits: Religious Belief

Indian religions also had a profound effect on Southeast Asia. Traditional religious beliefs in the region took the familiar form of spirit worship and animism that we have seen in other cultures. Southeast Asians believed that spirits dwelled in the mountains, rivers, streams, and other sacred places in their environment. Mountains were probably particularly sacred, since they were considered to be the abode of ancestral spirits, the place to which the souls of all the departed would retire after death.

When Hindu and Buddhist ideas began to penetrate the area early in the first millennium C.E., they exerted a strong appeal among local elites. Not only did the new doctrines offer a more convincing explanation of the nature of the cosmos, but they also provided local rulers with a means of enhancing their prestige and power and conferred an aura of legitimacy on their relations with their subjects. In the Javanese kingdoms and in Angkor, Hindu gods like Vishnu and Shiva provided a new and more sophisticated veneer for existing beliefs in nature deities and ancestral spirits. In Angkor, the king's duties included performing sacred rituals on the mountain in the capital city; in time, the ritual became a state cult uniting Hindu gods with local nature deities and ancestral spirits in a complex pantheon.

This state cult, financed by the royal court, eventually led to the construction of temples throughout the country. Many of these temples housed thousands of priests and retainers and amassed great wealth, including vast estates farmed by local peasants. It has been estimated that there were as many as 300,000 priests in Angkor at the height of its power. This vast wealth, which was often exempt from taxes, may be one explanation for the gradual decline of Angkor in the thirteenth and fourteenth centuries.

Initially, the spread of Hindu and Buddhist doctrines was essentially an elite phenomenon. Although the common people participated in the state cult and helped construct the temples, they did not give up their traditional beliefs in local deities and ancestral spirits. A major transformation began in the eleventh century, however, when Theravada Buddhism began to penetrate the mainland kingdom of Pagan from the island of Sri Lanka. From Pagan, it spread rapidly to other areas in Southeast Asia and eventually became the religion of the masses throughout the mainland west of the Annamite Mountains.

Theravada's appeal to the peoples of Southeast Asia is reminiscent of the original attraction of Buddhist thought centuries earlier on the Indian subcontinent. By teaching that individuals could seek Nirvana through their own actions rather than through the intercession of the ruler or a priest, Theravada was more accessible to the masses than the state cults promoted by the rulers. During the next centuries, Theravada gradually undermined the influence of state-supported religions and became the dominant faith in several mainland societies, including Burma, Thailand, Laos, and Cambodia. In the process, however, it was gradually appropriated by local rulers, who portrayed themselves as "immanent Buddhas," higher than ordinary mortals on the scale of human existence.

### CHRONOLOGY Early Southeast Asia

| | |
|---|---|
| Chinese conquest of Vietnam | 111 B.C.E. |
| Arrival of Burmese peoples | c. seventh century |
| Formation of Srivijaya | c. 670 |
| Construction of Borobudur | c. eighth century |
| Creation of Angkor kingdom | c. ninth century |
| Thai migrations into Southeast Asia | c. thirteenth century |
| Rise of Majapahit empire | 1292 |
| Fall of Angkor kingdom | 1432 |

**The Temple of Borobudur.** The colossal pyramid temple at Borobudur, on the island of Java, is one of the greatest Buddhist monuments. Constructed in the eighth century, it depicts the path to spiritual enlightenment in stone. Sculptures and relief portrayals of the life of the Buddha at the lower level depict the world of desire. At higher elevations, they give way to empty bell towers (see inset) and culminate at the summit with an empty and closed stupa, signifying the state of Nirvana. Shortly after it was built, Borobudur was abandoned as a new ruler switched his allegiance to Hinduism and ordered the erection of the Hindu temple of Prambanan nearby. Buried for a thousand years under volcanic ash and jungle, Borobudur was rediscovered in the nineteenth century and has recently been restored to its former splendor.

Theravada did not penetrate far into the Malay peninsula or the Indonesian island chain, perhaps because it entered Southeast Asia through Burma farther to the north. But the Malay world found its own popular alternative to state religions when Islam began to enter the area in the thirteenth and fourteenth centuries. Because Islam's expansion into Southeast Asia took place for the most part after 1500, its emergence as a major force in the region will be discussed later in the book.

Not surprisingly, Indian influence extended to the Buddhist and Hindu temples of Southeast Asia. Temple architecture reflecting Gupta or southern Indian styles began to appear in Southeast Asia during the first centuries C.E. Most famous is the Buddhist temple at Borobudur, in central Java. Begun in the late eighth century at the behest of a king of Sailendra (an agricultural kingdom based in eastern Java), Borobudur is a massive stupa with nine terraces. Sculpted on the sides of each terrace are bas-reliefs depicting the nine stages in the life of Siddhartha Gautama, from childhood to his final release from the chain of human existence. Surmounted by hollow bell-like towers containing representations of the Buddha and capped by a single stupa, the structure dominates the landscape for miles around.

Second only to Borobudur in technical excellence and even more massive in size are the ruins of the old capital city of Angkor Thom. The temple of Angkor Wat is the most famous and arguably the most beautiful of all the existing structures at Angkor Thom. Built on the model of the legendary Mount Meru (the home of the gods in Hindu tradition), it combines Indian architectural techniques with native inspiration in a structure of impressive delicacy and grace.

Courtesy of William J. Duiker

**Angkor Wat.** The Khmer rulers of Angkor constructed a number of remarkable temples and palaces. Devised as either Hindu or Buddhist shrines, the temples also reflected the power and sanctity of the king. This twelfth-century temple known as Angkor Wat is renowned both for its spectacular architecture and for the thousands of fine bas-reliefs relating Hindu legends and Khmer history. Most memorable are the heavenly dancing maidens and the royal processions with elephants and soldiers.

In existence for more than six hundred years, Angkor Thom serves as a bridge between the Hindu and Buddhist architectural styles. The last of its great temples, known as the Bayon, followed the earlier Hindu model but was topped with sculpted towers containing four-sided representations of a bodhisattva, searching, it is said, for souls to save. Shortly after the Bayon was built, Theravada Buddhist societies in Burma and Thailand began to create a new Buddhist architecture based on the concept of a massive stupa surmounted by a spire. Most famous, perhaps, is the Shwedagon Pagoda in Yangon (Rangoon), capital of modern Myanmar (Burma), which is covered with gold leaf contributed by devout Buddhists from around the country.

## CONCLUSION

During the more than fifteen hundred years from the fall of the Mauryas to the rise of the Mughals, Indian civilization faced a number of severe challenges. One challenge was primarily external and took the form of a continuous threat from beyond the mountains in the northwest. A second was generated by internal causes and stemmed from the tradition of factionalism and internal rivalry that had marked relations within the aristocracy since the Aryan invasion in the second millennium B.C.E. (see Chapter 2). Despite the abortive efforts of the Guptas, that tradition continued almost without interruption down to the founding of the Mughal Empire in the sixteenth century.

The third challenge was primarily cultural and appeared in the religious divisions between Hindus and Buddhists, and later between Hindus and Muslims, that took place throughout much of this period. It is a measure of the strength and resilience of Hindu tradition that it was able to surmount the challenge of Buddhism and by the late first millennium C.E. had managed to reassert its dominant position in Indian society. But that triumph was short-lived. Like so many other areas in the region of southern Asia, by 1000 C.E., it was now beset by a new challenge presented by nomadic forces from Central Asia. One result of the foreign conquest of northern India was the introduction of Islam into the region. As we shall see later, the new religion was about to become a serious rival to traditional beliefs among the Indian people.

During the same period that Indian civilization faced these challenges at home, it was having a profound impact on the emerging states of Southeast Asia. Situated at the crossroads between two oceans and two great civilizations, Southeast Asia has long served as a bridge linking peoples and cultures, and as complex societies began to develop in the area, it is not surprising that they were strongly influenced by the older civilizations of neighboring China and India. At the same time, the Southeast Asian peoples put their own unique stamp on the ideas that they adopted and eventually rejected those that were inappropriate to local conditions.

The result was a region characterized by an almost unparalleled cultural richness and diversity, reflecting influences from as far away as the Middle East yet preserving indigenous elements that were deeply rooted in the local culture. Unfortunately, that very diversity posed potential problems for the peoples of Southeast Asia as they faced a new challenge from beyond the horizon. We shall deal with that challenge when we return to the region later in the book. In the meantime, we must turn our attention to the other major civilization that spread its shadow over the societies of southern Asia—China.

## TIMELINE

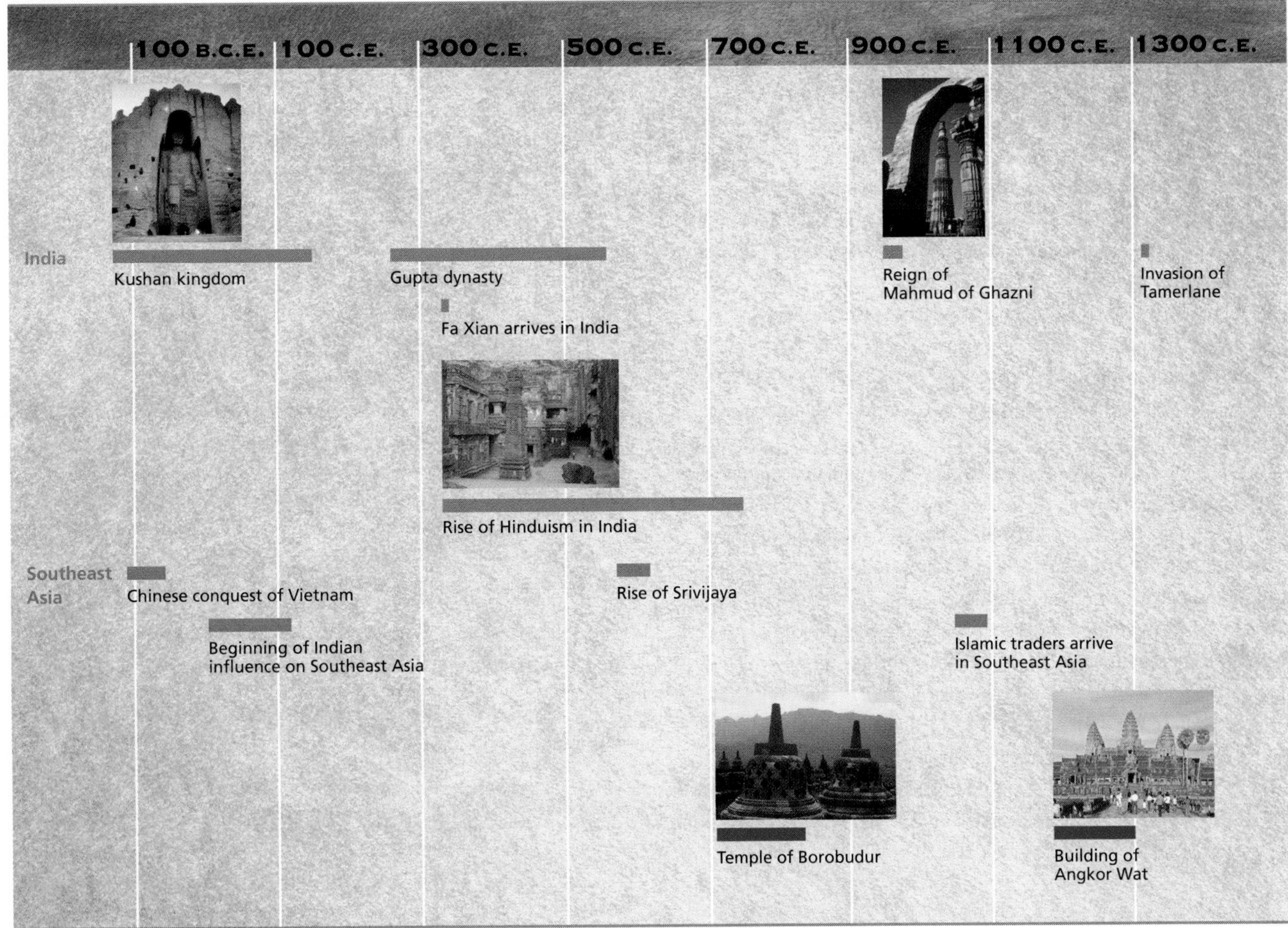

## CHAPTER NOTES

1. Hiuen Tsiang, *Si-Yu-Ki: Buddhist Records of the Western World,* trans. S. Beal (London, 1982), pp. 89–90.
2. "Fo-Kwo-Ki" (Travels of Fa Xian), ch. 20, p. 43, in ibid.
3. E. C. Sachau, *Alberoni's India* (London, 1914), vol. 1, p. 22.
4. Quoted in S. M. Ikram, *Muslim Civilization in India,* (New York, 1964), p. 68.
5. Hiuen Tsiang, *Si-Yu-Ki,* pp. 73–74.
6. D. Barbosa, *The Book of Duarte Barbosa* (Nedeln, Liechtenstein, 1967), pp. 147–148.
7. Quoted in R. Lannoy, *The Speaking Tree: A Study of Indian Culture and Society* (London, 1971), p. 232.
8. Quoted in S. Tharu and K. Lalita, *Women Writing in India,* vol. 1 (New York, 1991), p. 77.
9. Quoted in A. L. Basham, *The Wonder That Was India* (London, 1954), p. 426.
10. Quoted in S. Hughes and B. Hughes, *Women in World History,* vol. 1 (Armonk, N.Y., 1995), p. 217.

## SUGGESTED READING

The period from the decline of the Mauryas to the rise of the Mughals in India is not especially rich in terms of materials in English. Still, a number of the standard texts on Indian history contain useful sections on the period. Particularly good are **A. L. Basham, *The Wonder That Was India*** (London, 1954), and **S. Wolpert, *New History of India*** (New York, 1989).

A number of studies of Indian society and culture deal with this period. See, for example, **R. Lannoy, *The Speaking Tree*** (Oxford, 1971), for a sophisticated interpretation of Indian culture during the medieval period. On Buddhism, see **H. Nakamura, *Indian Buddhism: A Survey with Bibliographical Notes*** (Delhi, 1987), and **H. Akira, *A History of Indian Buddhism from Sakyamuni to Early Mahayana*** (Honolulu, 1990). For an interesting treatment of the Buddhist influence on commercial activities that is reminiscent of the role of Christianity in Europe, see **L. Xinru, *Ancient India and Ancient China: Trade and Religious Changes, A.D. 1–600*** (Delhi, 1988).

For a discussion of women's issues, see **S. Hughes** and **B. Hughes, *Women in World History,*** vol. 1 (Armonk, N.Y., 1995); **S. Tharu** and **K. Lalita, *Women Writing in India,*** vol. 1 (New York, 1991); and **V. Dehejia, *Devi: The Great Goddess*** (Washington, D.C., 1999).

The most comprehensive treatment of the Indian economy and, in particular, the regional trade throughout the Indian Ocean is **K. N. Chaudhuri, *Trade and Civilization in the Indian Ocean: An Economic History from the Rise of Islam to 1750*** (Cambridge, 1985), a groundbreaking comparative study. See also his more recent and massive ***Asia Before Europe: Economy and Civilization of the Indian Ocean from the Rise of Islam to 1750*** (Cambridge, 1990), which owes a considerable debt to F. Braudel's classical work on the Mediterranean region.

For an overview of events in Central Asia during this period, see **D. Christian, *Inner Eurasia from Prehistory to the Mongol Empire*** (Oxford, 1998), and **C. E. Bosworth, *The Later Ghaznavids: Splendor and Decay*** (New York, 1977). On the career of Tamerlane, see **B. F. Manz, *The Rise and Rule of Tamerlane*** (Cambridge, 1989).

For Indian art during the medieval period, see **S. Huntington, *The Art of Ancient India: Buddhist, Hindu, and Jain*** (New York, 1985), and **V. Dehejia, *Indian Art*** (London, 1997).

The early history of Southeast Asia is not as well documented as that of China or India. Except for Vietnam, where histories written in Chinese appeared shortly after the Chinese conquest, written materials on societies in the region are relatively sparse. Historians were therefore compelled to rely on stone inscriptions and the accounts of travelers and historians from other countries. As a result, the history of precolonial Southeast Asia was presented, as it were, from the outside looking in. For an overview of modern scholarship on the region, see **N. Tarling,** ed., ***The Cambridge History of Southeast Asia,*** vol. 1 (Cambridge, 1999).

Impressive advances are now being made in the field of prehistory. See **P. Bellwood, *Prehistory of the Indo-Malaysian Archipelago*** (Honolulu, 1997), and **C. Higham, *The Archaeology of Mainland Southeast Asia*** (Cambridge, 1989). Also see **C. Higham, *The Bronze Age of Southeast Asia*** (Cambridge, 1996).

The role of commerce has recently been highlighted as a key aspect in the development of the region. For two fascinating accounts, see **K. R. Hall, *Maritime Trade and State Development in Early Southeast Asia*** (Honolulu, 1985), and **A. Reid, *Southeast Asia in the Era of Commerce, 1450-1680: The Lands Below the Winds*** (New Haven, Conn., 1989). The latter is also quite useful on the role of women.

### History Now™

**Enter *HistoryNow* using the access card that is available with this text. *HistoryNow* will assist you in understanding the content in this chapter with lesson plans generated for your needs, as well as provide you with a connection to the *Wadsworth World History Resource Center* (see description below for details).**

### WORLD HISTORY RESOURCE CENTER

**Enter the Resource Center using either your *HistoryNow* access card or your standalone access card for the *Wadsworth World History Resource Center.* Organized by topic, this website includes quizzes; images; over 350 primary source documents; interactive simulations; maps and timelines; movie explorations; and a wealth of other resources. You can read the following documents, and many more, at http://history.wadsworth.com/rc/world**

Acts and Rewards of Devotion to the Buddha

The Buddhist Conception of the Intermediate State

Visit the *World History* Companion Website for chapter quizzes and more.

http://history.wadsworth.com/duikerspielvogel05/

CHAPTER

# 10

# THE FLOWERING OF TRADITIONAL CHINA

Metropolitan Museum of Art, Fletcher Fund, 1947, The A.W. Bahr Collection

*Detail of a Chinese scroll,* Spring Festival on the River

## CHAPTER OUTLINE AND FOCUS QUESTIONS

### China After the Han

- After the decline of the Han dynasty, China went through several centuries of internal division. Why do you think this occurred, and what impact did it have on Chinese society?

### China Reunified: The Sui, the Tang, and the Song

- What major changes in political structures and social and economic life occurred during the Sui, Tang, and Song dynasties?

### Explosion in Central Asia: The Mongol Empire

- Why were the Mongols able to amass an empire, and what were the main characteristics of their rule in China?

### The Ming Dynasty

- What were the chief initiatives taken by the early rulers of the Ming dynasty to enhance the role of China in the world? Why did the imperial court order the famous voyages of Zhenghe, and then why were they discontinued?

### In Search of the Way

- What roles did Buddhism, Daoism, and Neo-Confucianism play in Chinese intellectual life in the period between the Sui dynasty and the Ming?

### The Apogee of Chinese Culture

- What were the main achievements in Chinese literature and art in the period between the Tang dynasty and the Ming, and what technological innovations and intellectual developments contributed to these achievements?

### CRITICAL THINKING

- The civilization of ancient China fell under the onslaught of nomadic invasions, as had some of its counterparts elsewhere in the world. But China, unlike other classical empires, was later able to reconstitute itself on the same political and cultural foundations. How do you account for the difference?

ON HIS FIRST VISIT to the city, the traveler was mightily impressed. Its streets were so straight and wide that he could see through the city from one end to the other. Along the wide boulevards were beautiful palaces and inns in great profusion. The city was laid out in squares like a chessboard, and within each square were spacious courts and gardens. Truly, said the visitor, this must be one of the largest and wealthiest cities on earth–a city "planned out to a degree of precision and beauty impossible to describe."

The visitor was Marco Polo, and the city was Khanbaliq (later known as Beijing), capital of the Yuan dynasty (1279–1368) and one of the great urban centers of the Chinese Empire. Marco Polo was an Italian merchant who had traveled to China in the late thirteenth century and then served as an official at the court of Khubilai Khan. In later travels in China, Polo visited a number of other great cities, including the commercial hub of Ken-Zan-fu (Kaifeng) on the Yellow River. It is a city, he remarked,

> of great commerce, and eminent for its manufactures. Raw silk is produced in large quantities, and tissues of gold and every other kind of silk are woven there. At this place likewise they prepare every article necessary for the equipment of an army. All species of provisions are in abundance, and to be procured at a moderate price.[1]

Polo's diary, published after his return to Italy almost twenty years later, astonished readers with tales of this magnificent but unknown civilization far to the east.

When Marco Polo arrived, China was ruled by the Mongols, a nomadic people from Central Asia who had overthrown the Song (Sung) dynasty and assumed control of the Chinese Empire. The Yuan dynasty, as the Mongol rulers were called, was only one of a succession of dynasties to rule China after the collapse of the Han dynasty in the third century C.E. The end of the Han had led to a period of internal division and civil war that lasted nearly four hundred years and was aggravated by the threat posed by nomadic peoples from the north. This time of troubles ended in the early seventh century, however, when the dynamic Tang dynasty led China to some of its finest achievements.

To this point, Chinese history appeared to be following a pattern similar to that of India. There, as we have seen, the passing of the Mauryan dynasty in the second century B.C.E. unleashed a period of internal division that, except for the interval of the Guptas, lasted for several hundred years. It was not until the rise of the Mughal Empire in the early sixteenth century that unity returned to the subcontinent.

But China did not repeat the Indian experience. The Tang dynasty collapsed in 907, but after a brief interregnum, China was reunified under the Song, who ruled most of China for nearly three hundred years. The Song were in turn overthrown by the Mongols in the late thirteenth century, and they then gave way to a powerful new native dynasty, the Ming, in 1368. Dynasty followed dynasty, with periods of extraordinary cultural achievement alternating with periods of internal disorder, but in general Chinese society continued to build on the political and cultural foundations of the Zhou and the Han.

Chinese historians, viewing this vast process as it evolved over time, began to hypothesize that Chinese history was cyclical, driven by the dynamic interplay of the forces of good and evil, *yang* and *yin,* growth and decay. Beyond the forces of conflict and change lay the essential continuity of Chinese history, based on the timeless principles established by Confucius and other thinkers during the Zhou dynasty in antiquity. In actuality, this picture of a succession of dynasties, each seeking to replicate the glories of China's golden age under the early Zhou dynasty, disguises the reality that under the surface Chinese society was undergoing significant changes and bore scant resemblance to the kingdom that had been founded by the house of Zhou more than twenty centuries earlier. ◇

Courtesy of William J. Duiker

**The Big Goose Pagoda.** When the Buddhist pilgrim Xuan Zang returned to China from India in the mid-seventh century C.E., he settled in the capital of Chang'an, where, under orders from the Tang emperor, he began to translate Buddhist texts in his possession from Sanskrit into Chinese. The Big Goose Pagoda, shown here, was erected shortly afterward to house them. Originally known as the Pagoda of the Classics, the structure consists of seven stories and is over 240 feet tall.

## China After the Han

After the collapse of the Han dynasty at the beginning of the third century C.E., China fell into an extended period of division and civil war. Taking advantage of the absence of organized government in China, nomadic forces from the Gobi Desert penetrated south of the Great Wall and established their own rule over northern China. In the Yangtze valley and farther to the south, native Chinese rule was maintained, but constant civil war and instability led later historians to refer to the period as the "era of the six dynasties."

The collapse of the Han Empire had a marked effect on the Chinese psyche. The Confucian principles that emphasized hard work, the subordination of the individual to community interests, and belief in the essentially rational order of the universe came under severe challenge, and many Chinese began to turn to more messianic creeds that emphasized the supernatural or the promise of earthly or heavenly salvation. Intellectuals began to reject the stuffy moralism and complacency of State Confucianism and sought emotional satisfaction in hedonistic pursuits or philosophical Daoism (see the box on p. 271).

Eccentric behavior and a preference for philosophical Daoism became a common response to a corrupt age. A group of writers known as the "seven sages of the bamboo forest" exemplified the period. Among the best known

## A Daoist Critique of Confucianism

This document is a biting Daoist attack on the type of pompous and hypocritical Confucian "gentleman" who feigned high moral principles while secretly engaging in corrupt and licentious behavior. It was written during the chaotic period following the collapse of the Han dynasty, in the third century C.E.

*What were some of the key differences between the Daoist worldview and that of a follower of Confucius? Can you find any parallels with these views in Greek and Roman philosophy?*

### The Biography of a Great Man

What the world calls a gentleman [*chun-tzu*] is someone who is solely concerned with moral law [*fa*], and cultivates exclusively the rules of propriety [*li*]. His hand holds the emblem of jade [authority]; his foot follows the straight line of the rule. He likes to think that his actions set a permanent example; he likes to think that his words are everlasting models. In his youth, he has a reputation in the villages of his locality; in his later years, he is well known in the neighboring districts. Upward, he aspires to the dignity of the Three Dukes; downward, he does not disdain the post of governor of the nine provinces.

Have you ever seen the lice that inhabit a pair of trousers? They jump into the depths of the seams, hiding themselves in the cotton wadding, and believe they have a pleasant place to live. Walking, they do not risk going beyond the edge of the seam; moving, they are careful not to emerge from the trouser leg; and they think they have kept to the rules of etiquette. But when the trousers are ironed, the flames invade the hills, the fire spreads, the villages are set on fire and the towns burned down; then the lice that inhabit the trousers cannot escape.

What difference is there between the gentleman who lives within a narrow world and the lice that inhabit trouser legs?

was the poet Liu Ling, whose odd behavior is described in this oft-quoted passage:

> Liu Ling was an inveterate drinker and indulged himself to the full. Sometimes he stripped off his clothes and sat in his room stark naked. Some men saw him and rebuked him. Liu Ling said, "Heaven and earth are my dwelling, and my house is my trousers. Why are you all coming into my trousers?"[2]

But neither popular beliefs in the supernatural nor philosophical Daoism could satisfy deeper emotional needs or provide solace in time of sorrow or the hope of a better life in the hereafter. Buddhism filled that gap.

Buddhism was brought to China in the first or second century C.E., probably by missionaries and merchants traveling over the Silk Road. The concept of rebirth was probably unfamiliar to most Chinese, and the intellectual hairsplitting that often accompanied discussion of Buddha's message in India was too esoteric for Chinese tastes. Still, in the difficult years surrounding the decline of the Han dynasty, Buddhist ideas, especially those of the Mahayana school, began to find adherents among intellectuals and ordinary people alike. As Buddhism increased in popularity, it was frequently attacked by supporters of Confucianism and Daoism for its foreign origins. Some even claimed that Gautama Buddha had been a disciple of Lao Tzu. But such sniping did not halt the progress of Buddhism, and eventually the new faith was assimilated into Chinese culture, assisted by the efforts of such tireless advocates as the missionaries Fa Xian and Xuan Zang and the support of ruling elites in both northern and southern China (see "The Rise and Decline of Buddhism and Daoism" later in this chapter).

# China Reunified: The Sui, the Tang, and the Song

After nearly four centuries of internal division, China was unified once again in 581 when Yang Jian (Yang Chien), a member of a respected aristocratic family in northern China, founded a new dynasty, known as the Sui (581–618 C.E.). Yang Jian (who is also known by his reign title of Sui Wendi, or Sui Wen Ti) established his capital at the historic metropolis of Chang'an and began to extend his authority throughout the heartland of China.

## The Sui Dynasty

Like his predecessors, the new emperor sought to create a unifying ideology for the state to enhance its efficiency. But where Liu Bang, the founder of the Han dynasty, had adopted Confucianism as the official doctrine to hold the empire together, Yang Jian turned to Daoism and Buddhism. He founded monasteries for both doctrines in the capital and appointed Buddhist monks to key positions as political advisers.

Yang Jian was a builder as well as a conqueror, ordering the construction of a new canal from the capital to the confluence of the Wei and Yellow Rivers nearly 100 miles to the east. His son, Emperor Sui Yangdi (Sui Yang Ti), continued the process, and the 1,400-mile-long Grand Canal, linking the two great rivers of China, the Yellow and the Yangtze, was completed during his reign. The new canal facilitated the shipment of grain and other commodities from the rice-rich southern provinces to the densely populated north. The canal also served other purposes, such as speeding

COMPARATIVE ILLUSTRATION

**The Grand Canal.** Built over centuries, the Grand Canal is one of the wonders of China and a crucial conduit for carrying goods between northern and southern China. After the Song dynasty, when the region south of the Yangtze River became the heartland of the empire, the canal was used to carry rice and other agricultural products to the food-starved northern provinces. Many of the towns and cities located along the canal became famous for their wealth and cultural achievements. Among the most renowned was Suzhou, a center for silk manufacture, which is sometimes described as the "Venice of China" because of its many canals. Shown here on the top right is a classical example of a humpback bridge, crossing an arm of the canal in downtown Suzhou. The resemblance to the Bridge of Marvels in Venice (lower left), seems to be more than coincidental.

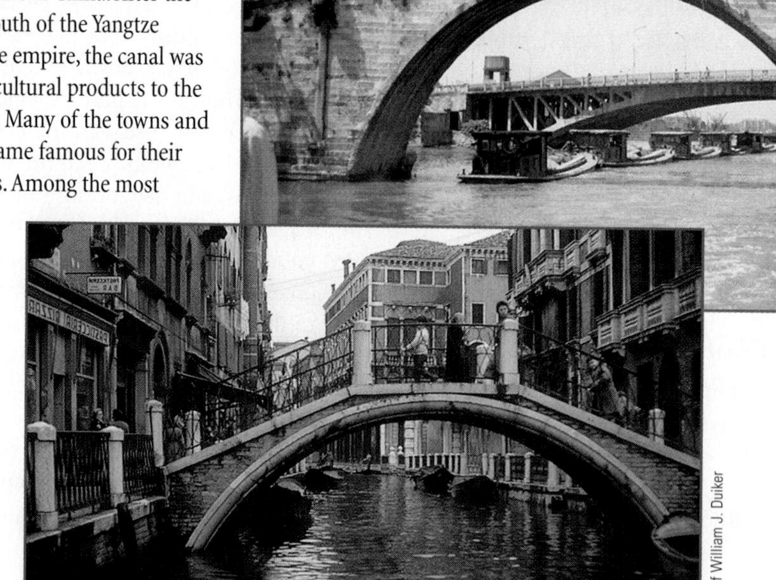

Courtesy of William J. Duiker

Courtesy of William J. Duiker

communications between the two regions and permitting the rapid dispatch of troops to troubled provinces. Sui Yangdi also used the canal as an imperial highway for inspecting his empire. One imperial procession from the capital to the central Yangtze region was described as follows:

> The emperor caused to be built dragon boats, . . . red battle cruisers, multi-decked transports, lesser vessels of bamboo slats. Boatmen hired from all the waterways . . . pulled the vessels by ropes of green silk on the imperial progress to Chiang-tu [Yangzhou]. The emperor rode in the dragon boat, and civil and military officials of the fifth grade and above rode in the multi-decked transports; those of the ninth grade and above were given the vessels of yellow bamboo. The boats followed one another poop to prow for more than 200 leagues [about 65 miles]. The prefectures and counties through which they passed were ordered to prepare to offer provisions. Those who made bountiful arrangements were given an additional office or title; those who fell short were given punishments up to the death penalty.[3]

Despite such efforts to project the majesty of the imperial personage, the Sui dynasty came to an end immediately after Sui Yangdi's death. The Sui emperor was a tyrannical ruler, and his expensive military campaigns aroused widespread unrest. After his return from a failed campaign against Korea in 618, the emperor was murdered in his palace. One of his generals, Li Yuan, took advantage of the instability that ensued and declared the foundation of a new dynasty, known as the Tang (T'ang). Building on the successes of its predecessor, the Tang lasted for three hundred years, until 907.

## The Tang Dynasty

Li Yuan ruled for a brief period and then was elbowed aside by his son, who assumed the reign title Tang Taizong (T'ang T'ai-tsung). Under his vigorous leadership, the Tang launched a program of internal renewal and external expansion that would make it one of the greatest dynasties in the long history of China (see Map 10.1). Under the Tang, the northwest was pacified and given the name of Xinjiang, or "new region." A long conflict with Tibet led for the first time to the extension of Chinese control over the vast and desolate plateau north of the Himalaya Mountains. The southern provinces below the Yangtze were fully assimilated into the Chinese Empire, and the imperial court established commercial and diplomatic relations with the states of Southeast Asia. With reason, China now claimed to be the foremost power in East Asia, and the emperor demanded fealty and tribute from all his fellow rulers beyond the frontier. Korea accepted tribute status and attempted to adopt the Chinese model, and the Japanese dispatched official missions to China to learn more about its customs and institutions (see Chapter 11).

Finally, the Tang dynasty witnessed a flowering of Chinese culture. Many modern observers feel that the era represents the apogee of Chinese creativity in poetry and sculpture. One reason for this explosion of culture was the influence of Buddhism, which affected art, literature, and philosophy, as well as religion and politics. Monaster-

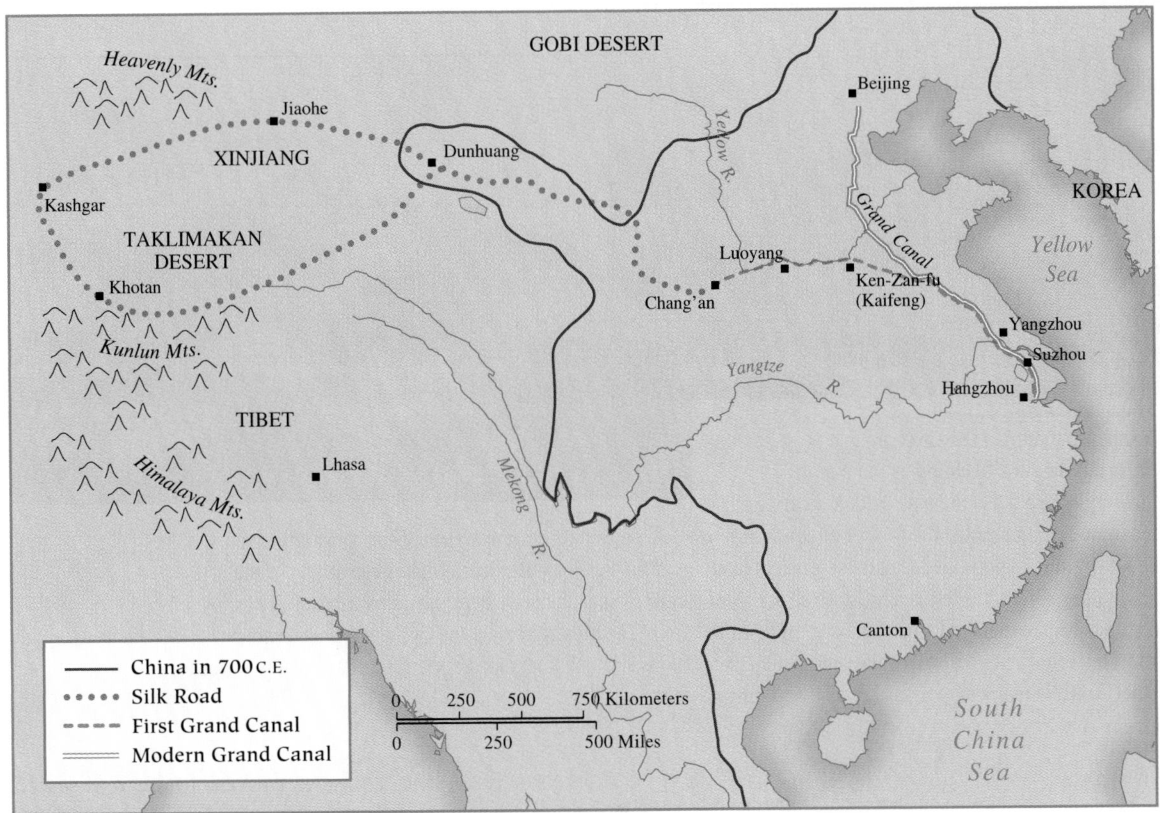


**MAP 10.1 China Under the Tang.** The era of the Tang dynasty was one of the greatest periods in the long history of China. Tang influence spread from heartland China into neighboring regions, including Central and Southeast Asia. Where are the Grand Canal and the Silk Road, as located on the map? **View an animated version of this map or related maps at** http://history.wadsworth.com/duikerspielvogel05/

ies sprang up throughout China, and (as under the Sui) Buddhist monks served as advisers at the Tang imperial court. The city of Chang'an, now restored to the glory it had known as the capital of the Han dynasty, once again became the seat of the empire. It was possibly the greatest city in the world of its time, with an estimated population of nearly two million. The city was filled with temples and palaces, and its markets teemed with goods from all over the known world (see the box on p. 275).

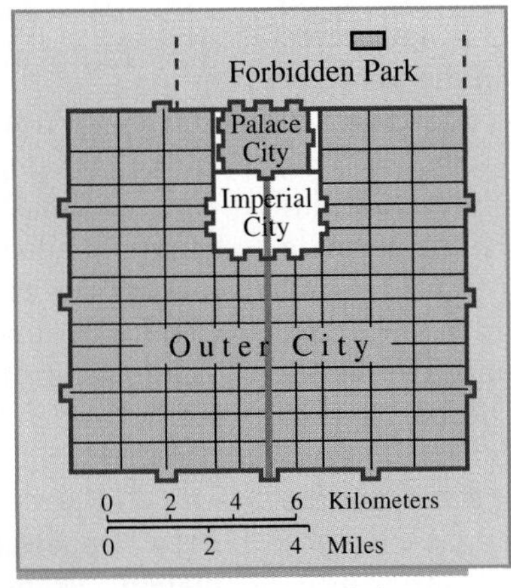


**Chang'an Under the Sui and the Tang**

But the Tang, like the Han, sowed the seeds of their own destruction. Tang rulers could not prevent the rise of internal forces that would ultimately weaken the dynasty and bring it to an end. Two ubiquitous problems were court intrigues and official corruption. Xuanzong (Hsuan Tsung, who reigned from 712 to 756), one of the great Tang emperors and a renowned patron of the arts, was dominated in later life by one of his favorite concubines, the beautiful Yang Guifei (Yang Kuei-fei). One of her protégés launched a rebellion in 755 and briefly seized power in the capital of Chang'an. The revolt was eventually suppressed, and Yang Guifei, who is viewed as one of the great villains of Chinese history, was put to death. But the Tang never fully recovered from the catastrophe. The loss of power by the central government led to increased influence by great landed families inside China and chronic instability along the northern and western frontiers, where local military commanders ruled virtually without central government interference. It was an eerie repetition of the final decades of the Han.

The end finally came in the early tenth century, when border troubles with northern nomadic peoples called the Khitan increased, leading to the final collapse of the dynasty in 907. The Tang had followed the classic strategy of "using a barbarian to oppose a barbarian" by allying with a trading people called the Uighurs (a Turkic-speaking people who had taken over many of the caravan routes along the Silk Road) against their old rivals. But yet another nomadic people called the Kirghiz defeated the Uighurs and then turned on the Tang government in its moment of weakness and overthrew it.

Courtesy of William J. Duiker

Courtesy of William J. Duiker

SCIENCE & TECHNOLOGY

COMPARATIVE ILLUSTRATION

**Early Agricultural Technology.** For centuries, farmers across the globe have adopted various techniques to guarantee the flow of adequate amounts of water to their crops. One of the most effective ways to irrigate fields in hilly regions is to construct terraces to channel the flow of water from higher elevations in the most effective manner. Shown on the left is a hillside terrace in northern China, an area where the cultivation of dry crops like oats and millet has been conducted since the sixth millennium B.C.E. The illustration on the right shows a terraced hillside in the southwestern corner of the Arabian peninsula. Excavations show that terraced agriculture has been practiced in mountainous parts of the peninsula for as long as five thousand years.

## The Song Dynasty

China slipped once again into chaos. This time, the period of foreign invasion and division was much shorter. In 960, a new dynasty, known as the Song (960–1279), rose to power. From the start, however, the Song (Sung) rulers encountered more problems than their predecessors. Although the founding emperor, Song Taizu (Sung T'ai-tsu), was able to co-opt many of the powerful military commanders whose rivalry had brought the Tang dynasty to an end, he was unable to reconquer the northwestern part of the country from the nomadic Khitan peoples. The emperor therefore established his capital farther to the east, at Kaifeng, where the Grand Canal intersected the Yellow River. Later, when pressures from the nomads in the north increased, the court was forced to move the capital even farther south, to Hangzhou (Hangchow), on the coast just south of the Yangtze River delta; the emperors who ruled from Hangzhou are known as the southern Song. The Song also lost control over Tibet. Despite its political and military weaknesses, the dynasty nevertheless ruled during a period of economic expansion, prosperity, and cultural achievement and is therefore considered among the more successful Chinese dynasties. The population of the empire had risen to an estimated forty million people, slightly more than that of the continent of Europe.

Yet the Song dynasty was never able to surmount the external challenge from the north, and that failure eventually brought about the end of the dynasty. During its final decades, the Song rulers were forced to pay tribute to the Jurchen peoples from Manchuria. In the early thirteenth century, the Song, ignoring precedent and the fate of the Tang, formed an alliance with the Mongols, a new and obscure nomadic people from the Gobi Desert. As under the Tang, the decision proved to be a disaster. Within a few years, the Mongols had become a much more serious threat to China than the Jurchen. After defeating the Jurchen, the Mongols turned their attention to the Song, advancing on Song territory from both the north and the west. By this time, the Song empire had been weakened by internal factionalism and a loss of tax revenues. After a series of river battles and sieges marked by the use of catapults and gunpowder, the Song were defeated, and the conquerors announced the creation of a new Yuan (Mongol) dynasty. Ironically, the Mongols had first learned about gunpowder from the Chinese.

## Political Structures: The Triumph of Confucianism

During the nearly seven hundred years from the Sui to the end of the Song, a mature political system based on principles originally established during the Qin and Han dynasties gradually emerged in China. After the Tang dynasty's brief flirtation with Buddhism, State Confucianism became the ideological cement that held the system together. The development of this system took several centuries, and it did not reach its height until the period of the Song dynasty.

**Equal Opportunity in China: The Civil Service Examination** At the apex of the government hierarchy was the **Grand Council,** assisted by a secretariat and a chancellery; it included representatives from all three authorities—civil, military, and censorate. Under the Grand Council was the Department of State Affairs, composed of ministries responsible for justice, military affairs, personnel,

## THE GOOD LIFE IN THE HIGH TANG

At the height of the Tang dynasty, China was at the apex of its power and magnificence. Here the Tang poet Du Fu (Tu Fu) describes a gala festival in the capital of Chang'an (Ch'ang-an) attended by the favored elite. The author's distaste for the spectacle of arrogance and waste is expressed in muted sarcasm.

*Why does the author of this poem appear to be so angry at the site of the festival he described here? Compare his feelings here with those he expresses in the short poem included in the box on p. 293*

**Du Fu, "A Poem"**

*Third day of the third month*
*The very air seems new*
*In Ch'ang-an along the water*
*Many beautiful girls . . .*
*Firm, plump contours,*
*Flesh and bone proportioned.*
*Dresses of gauze brocade*
*Mirror the end of spring*
*Peacocks crimped in thread of gold*
*Unicorns in silver. . . .*
*Some are kin to the imperial favorite*
*Among them the Lady of Kuo and the Lady*
*of Ch'in [Qin].*
*Camel-humps of purple meat*
*Brought in shining pans*
*The white meat of raw fish*
*Served on crystal platters*
*Don't tempt the sated palate.*
*All that is cut with fancy and*
*Prepared with care–left untouched.*
*Eunuchs, reins a-flying*
*Disturb no dust*
*Bring the "eight chef d'oeuvres"*
*From the palace kitchens.*
*Music of strings and pipes . . .*
*Accompanying the feasting*
*Moving the many guests*
*All of rank and importance.*
*Last comes a horseman*
*See him haughtily*
*Dismount near the screen*
*And step on the flowery carpet. . . .*
*The chancellor is so powerful*
*His mere touch will scorch*
*Watch you don't come near*
*Lest you displease him.*

public works, revenue, and rites (ritual). This department was in effect the equivalent of a modern cabinet.

The Tang dynasty adopted the practice of selecting bureaucrats through civil service examinations but was unable to curb the influence of the great aristocratic clans. The Song were more successful at limiting aristocratic control over the bureaucracy, in part because the power of the nobility had been irreparably weakened during the final years of the Tang dynasty and did not recover during the interregnum that followed its collapse.

One way of strengthening the power of the central administration was to make the civil service examination system the primary route to an official career. To reduce the power of the noble families, relatives of individuals serving in the imperial court, as well as eunuchs, were prohibited from taking the examinations. But if the Song rulers' objective was to make the bureaucracy more subservient to the court, they may have been disappointed. The rising professionalism of the bureaucracy, which numbered about ten thousand in the imperial capital, with an equal number at the local level, provided it with an esprit de corps and an influence that sometimes enabled it to resist the whims of individual emperors.

Under the Song, the examination system attained the form that it would retain in later centuries. In general, three levels of examinations were administered. The first was a qualifying examination given annually at the provincial capital. Candidates who succeeded in this first stage were considered qualified but normally were not given positions in the bureaucracy except at the local level. Many stopped at this level and accepted positions as village teachers to train other candidates. Candidates who wished to go on could take a second examination given at the capital every three years. Successful candidates could apply for an official position. Some went on to take the final examination, which was given in the imperial palace once every three years. Those who passed were eligible for high positions in the central bureaucracy or for appointments as district magistrates.

During the early Tang, the examinations included questions on Buddhist and Daoist as well as Confucian texts, but by Song times, examinations were based entirely on the Confucian classics. Candidates were expected to memorize passages and to be able to define the moral lessons they contained. The system guaranteed that successful candidates—and therefore officials—would have received a full dose of Confucian political and social ethics. Whether they followed those ethics, of course, was another matter. Many students complained about the rigors of memorization and the irrelevance of the process. Others brought crib notes into the examination hall (one enterprising candidate concealed an entire Confucian text in the lining of his cloak). One famous Tang scholar complained that if Mencius and other Confucian worthies

**A Young Chinese Bride and Her Dowry.** A Chinese bride had to leave her parental home for that of her husband, exchanging her filial allegiance to her in-laws. For this reason, the mother-son relationship would be the most important one in a Chinese woman's lifetime. With the expansion of the gentry class during the Song dynasty, young men who passed the civil service examination became the most sought-after marriage prospects, requiring that the families of young women offer a substantial dowry as an enticement to the groom's family. In this Persian miniature, a Chinese bride leads a procession along the Silk Road to marry a Turkish bridegroom, transporting her dowry of prized Chinese porcelain to her new home.

had lived in his own day, they would have refused to sit for the examinations.

The Song authorities ignored such criticisms, but they did open the system to more people by allowing all males except criminals or members of certain restricted occupations to take the examinations. To provide potential candidates with schooling, training academies were set up at the provincial and district level. Without such academies, only individuals fortunate enough to receive training in the classics in family-run schools would have had the expertise to pass the examinations. Such policies represented a considerable improvement over earlier times, when most candidates came from the ranks of the elite. According to one historian, more than half of the successful candidates during the mid-Song period came from families that had not previously had a successful candidate for at least three generations. In time, the majority of candidates came from the landed gentry, nonaristocratic landowners who controlled much of the wealth in the countryside. Because the gentry prized education and became the primary upholders of the Confucian tradition, they were often called the **scholar-gentry.**

But certain aspects of the system still prevented it from truly providing equal opportunity to all. In the first place, only males were eligible. Then again, the Song did not attempt to establish a system of universal elementary education. In practice, only those who had been given a basic education in the classics at home were able to enter the state-run academies and compete for a position in the bureaucracy. The poor had little chance.

Nor could the system guarantee an honest, efficient bureaucracy. Official arrogance, bureaucratic infighting, corruption, and legalistic interpretations of government regulations were as prevalent in medieval China as in bureaucracies the world over. Another problem was that officials were expected to use their positions to help their relatives. As we observed earlier, even Confucius held that filial duty transcends loyalty to the community. What is nepotism in Western eyes was simply proper behavior in China. Chinese rulers attempted to circumvent this problem by assigning officials outside their home region, but this policy met with only limited success.

Despite such weaknesses, the civil service examination system was an impressive achievement for its day and probably provided a more efficient government and more opportunity for upward mobility than were found in any other civilization of its time. Most Western governments, for example, began to recruit officials on the basis of merit only in the nineteenth century. Furthermore, by regulating the content of the examinations, the system helped provide China with a cultural uniformity lacking in empires elsewhere in Asia.

The court also attempted to curb official misbehavior through the censorate. Specially trained officials known as censors were assigned to investigate possible cases of official wrongdoing and report directly to the court. The censorate was supposed to be independent of outside pressures to ensure that its members would feel free to report wrongdoing wherever it occurred. In practice, censors who displeased high court officials were often removed or even subjected to more serious forms of punishment, which reduced the effectiveness of the system.

**Local Government** The Song dynasty maintained the local government institutions that it had inherited from its predecessors. At the base of the government pyramid was the district (or county), governed by a magistrate. The magistrate, assisted by his staff of three or four officials and several other menial employees, was responsible for maintaining law and order and collecting taxes within his jurisdiction. A district could exceed 100,000 people. Below the district was the basic unit of Chinese government, the village. Because villages were so numerous in China, the central government did not appoint an official at that level and allowed the villages to administer themselves. Village government was normally in the hands of a council of elders, usually assisted by a chief. The council, usually made up of the heads of influential families in the village, maintained the local irrigation and transportation network, adjudicated local disputes, organized and maintained a militia, and assisted in collecting taxes (usually paid in grain) and delivering them to the district magistrate.

As a rule, most Chinese had little involvement with government matters. When they had to deal with the government, they almost always turned to their village officials. Although the district magistrate was empowered to settle local civil disputes, most villagers preferred to resolve problems among themselves. It was expected that the magistrate and his staff would supplement their income by charging for such services, a practice that reduced the costs of the central government but also provided an opportunity for bribes, a problem that plagued the Chinese bureaucracy down to modern times.

## The Economy

During the long period between the Sui and the Song, the Chinese economy, like the government, grew considerably in size and complexity. China was still an agricultural society, but major changes were taking place within the economy and the social structure. The urban sector of the economy was becoming increasingly important, new social classes were beginning to appear, and the economic focus of the empire was beginning to shift from the Yellow River valley in the north to the Yangtze River valley in the center—a process that was encouraged both by the expansion of cultivation in the Yangtze delta and by the control exerted over the north by nomadic peoples during the Song.

**The Land Reform** The economic revival began shortly after the rise of the Tang. During the long period of internal division, land had become concentrated in the hands of aristocratic families, with most peasants reduced to serfdom or slavery. The early Tang tried to reduce the power of the landed nobility and maximize tax revenues by adopting the ancient "equal field" system, in which land was allocated to farmers for life in return for an annual tax payment and three weeks of conscript labor.

At first, the new system was vigorously enforced and led to increased rural prosperity and government revenue. But eventually, the rich and the politically influential learned to manipulate the system for their own benefit and accumulated huge tracts of land. The growing population, bolstered by a rise in food production and the extended period of social stability, also put steady pressure on the system. Finally, the government abandoned the effort to equalize landholdings and returned the land to private hands while attempting to prevent inequalities through the tax system. The failure to resolve the land problem contributed to the fall of the Tang dynasty in the early tenth century.

The Song tried to resolve the land problem by returning to the successful programs of the early Tang and reducing the power of the wealthy landed aristocrats. During the late eleventh century, the reformist official Wang Anshi (Wang An-shih) attempted to limit the size of landholdings through progressive land taxes and provided cheap credit to poor farmers to help them avoid bankruptcy. His reforms met with some success, but other developments probably contributed more to the general agricultural prosperity under the Song. These included the opening of new lands in the Yangtze River valley, improvements in irrigation techniques such as the chain pump (a circular chain of square pallets on a treadmill that enabled farmers to lift considerable amounts of water or mud to a higher level), and the introduction of a new strain of quick-growing rice from Southeast Asia, which permitted farmers in warmer regions to plant and harvest two crops each year.

**The Urban Economy** Major changes also took place in the Chinese urban economy, which witnessed a significant increase in trade and manufacturing. This process began under the Tang dynasty, but it was not entirely a product of deliberate state policy. In fact, early Tang rulers shared some of the traditional prejudice against commercial activities that had been prevalent under the Han and enacted a number of regulations that restricted trade. As under the Han, the state maintained monopolies over key commodities such as salt.

Despite the restrictive policies of the state, the urban sector grew steadily larger and more complex, helped by several new technological developments (see the comparative essay "The Spread of Technology" on p. 279). During the Tang, the Chinese mastered the art of manufacturing steel by mixing cast iron and wrought iron. The blast furnace was heated to a high temperature by burning coal, which had been used as a fuel in China from about the fourth century C.E. The resulting product was used in

**A Masterpiece of Social Documentation.** Besides being an artistic masterpiece, the Chinese scroll known as *Spring Festival on the River* is one of the most remarkable social documents of early-twelfth-century China. Nearly 33 feet long, it records in encyclopedic detail various aspects of Chinese society, from the imperial court down to the lowliest peasants, as they prepare for the spring festival. The viewer is expected to unfold the scroll slowly from right to left and linger on each segment as the scroll follows the path along the Yellow River to the Song capital of Kaifeng, at the time the most sophisticated city in the world.

the manufacture of swords, sickles, and even suits of armor. By the eleventh century, more than 35,000 tons of steel were being produced annually. The introduction of cotton offered new opportunities in textile manufacturing. Gunpowder was invented by the Chinese during the Tang dynasty and used primarily for explosives and a primitive flamethrower; it reached the West via the Arabs in the twelfth century.

**The Silk Road** The nature of trade was also changing. In the past, most long-distance trade had been undertaken by state monopoly. By the time of the Song, private commerce was being actively encouraged, and many merchants engaged in shipping as well as in wholesale and retail trade. Guilds began to appear, along with a new money economy. Paper currency began to be used in the eighth and ninth centuries. Credit (at first called "flying money") also made its first appearance during the Tang. With the increased circulation of paper money, banking began to develop as merchants found that strings of copper coins were too cumbersome for their increasingly complex operations. Unfortunately, early issues of paper currency were not backed by metal coinage and led to price inflation. Equally useful, if more prosaic, was the invention of the abacus, an early form of calculator that simplified the calculations needed for commercial transactions.

Long-distance trade, both overland and by sea, expanded under the Tang and the Song. Trade with countries and peoples to the west had been carried on for centuries (see Chapter 3), but it had declined dramatically between the fourth and sixth centuries C.E as a result of the collapse of the Han and Roman Empires. It began to revive with the rise of the Tang and the simultaneous unification of much of the Middle East under the Arabs. During the Tang era, the Silk Road revived and then reached its zenith. Much of the trade was carried by the Turkic-speaking Uighurs. During the Tang, Uighur caravans of two-humped Bactrian camels (a hardy variety native to Iran and regions to the northeast) carried goods back and forth between China and the countries of South Asia and the Middle East.

In actuality, the Silk Road was composed of a number of separate routes. The first to be used, probably because of the jade found in the mountains south of Khotan, ran along the southern rim of the Taklimakan Desert via Kashgar and thence through the Pamir Mountains into Bactria. The first Buddhist missionaries traveled this route from India to China. Eventually, however, this area began to dry up, and traders were forced to seek other routes. From a climatic standpoint, the best route for the Silk Road was to the north of the Tian Shan (Heavenly Mountains), where moisture-laden northwesterly winds created pastures where animals could graze. But the area was frequently infested by bandits who preyed on unwary travelers. Most caravans therefore followed the southern route, which passed along the northern fringes of the Taklimakan Desert to Kashgar and down into northwestern India. Travelers avoided the direct route through the desert (in the Uighur language, the name means "go in and you won't come out") and trudged from oasis to oasis along the southern slopes of the Tian Shan. The oases were created by the water runoff from winter snows in the mountains, which then dried up in the searing heat of the desert.

**The Maritime Route** The Silk Road was so hazardous that shipping goods by sea became increasingly popular. China had long been engaged in sea trade with other

## COMPARATIVE ESSAY

# THE SPREAD OF TECHNOLOGY

From the invention of stone tools and the discovery of fire to the introduction of agriculture and the writing system, mastery of technology has been a driving force in the history of human evolution. But why do some human societies appear to be much more advanced in their use of technology than others? People living on the island of New Guinea, for example, began cultivating local crops like taro and the banana as early as ten thousand years ago but never took the next steps toward creating a complex society until the arrival of Europeans many millennia later. Advanced societies had begun to emerge in the Western Hemisphere during the classical era, but none had discovered the use of the wheel or the smelting of metals for toolmaking. Writing was in its infancy there.

Technological advances appear to take place for two reasons: need and opportunity. Farming peoples throughout the world needed to control the flow of water, so in areas where water was scarce or unevenly distributed, they learned how to practice irrigation to make resources available throughout the region. Sometimes, however, opportunity strikes by accident (as in the legendary story of the Chinese princess who dropped a silkworm cocoon in her cup of hot tea) or when new technology is introduced from a neighboring region (as when the discovery of tin in Anatolia launched the Bronze Age throughout the Middle East).

The most important factor enabling societies to keep abreast of the latest advances in technology, it would appear, is participation in the global trade and communications network. In this respect, the relative ease of communications between the Mediterranean Sea and the Indus River valley represented a major advantage for the Abbasid Empire, since the peoples living there had rapid access to all the resources and technological advances in that part of the world. China was more isolated from such developments because of distance and the obstacle represented by the Himalaya Mountains. But because of its size and high level of cultural achievement, China was almost a continent in itself and was soon communicating with countries to the west via the Silk Road.

Societies that were not linked to his vast network were at an enormous disadvantage in keeping up with new developments in the field of technology. The peoples of New Guinea, at the far end of the Indonesian archipelago, had little or no contact with the outside world. In the Western Hemisphere, a trade network did begin to take shape between societies in the Andes and their counterparts in Mesoamerica. But because of difficulties in communication (see Chapter 6), contacts were more intermittent. As a result, technological developments taking place in distant Eurasia did not reach the Americas until the arrival of the conquistadors.

countries in the region, but most of the commerce was originally in the hands of Korean, Japanese, or Southeast Asian merchants. Chinese maritime trade, however, was stimulated by the invention of the compass and technical improvements in shipbuilding such as the widespread use of the sternpost rudder and the lug sail (which enabled ships to sail close to the wind). If Marco Polo's observations can be believed, by the thirteenth century, Chinese junks had multiple sails and weighed up to 2,000 tons, much more than contemporary ships in the West. The Chinese governor of Canton in the early twelfth century remarked:

> According to the government regulations concerning sea-going ships, the larger ones can carry several hundred men, and the smaller ones may have more than a hundred men on board. . . . The ship's pilots are acquainted with the configuration of the coasts; at night they steer by the stars, and in the daytime by the Sun. In dark weather they look at the south-pointing needle. They also use a line a hundred feet long with a hook at the end, which they let down to take samples of mud from the seabottom; by its appearance and smell they can determine their whereabouts.[4]

A wide variety of goods passed through Chinese ports. The Chinese exported tea, silk, and porcelain to the countries beyond the South China Sea, receiving exotic woods, precious stones, and various tropical goods in exchange. Seaports on the southern China coast exported sweet oranges, lemons, and peaches in return for grapes, walnuts, and pomegranates. Along the Silk Road to China came raw hides, furs, and horses. Chinese aristocrats, their appetite for material consumption stimulated by the affluence of Chinese society during much of the Tang and the Song periods, were fascinated by the exotic goods and the flora and the fauna of the desert and the tropical lands of the South Seas. The city of Chang'an became the eastern terminus of the Silk Road and perhaps the wealthiest city in the world during the Tang era. The major port of exit in southern China was Canton, where an estimated 100,000 merchants lived. Their activities were controlled by an imperial commissioner sent from the capital.

Some of this trade was a product of the tribute system, which the Chinese rulers used as an element of their foreign policy. The Chinese viewed the outside world as they viewed their own society—in a hierarchical manner. Rulers of smaller countries along the periphery were viewed as "younger brothers" of the Chinese emperor and owed fealty to him. Foreign rulers who accepted the relationship were required to pay tribute and to promise not to harbor enemies of the Chinese Empire. But the foreign rulers also benefited from the relationship. Not only did it

**CHRONOLOGY Medieval China**

| | |
|---|---|
| Arrival of Buddhism in China | c. first century C.E. |
| Fall of the Han dynasty | 220 C.E. |
| Sui dynasty | 581–618 |
| Tang dynasty | 618–907 |
| Li Bo (Li Po) and Du Fu (Tu Fu) | 700s |
| Emperor Xuanzong | 712–756 |
| Song dynasty | 960–1279 |
| Wang Anshi | 1021–1086 |
| Southern Song dynasty | 1127–1279 |
| Mongol conquest of China | 1279 |
| Reign of Khubilai Khan | 1260–1294 |
| Fall of the Yuan dynasty | 1368 |
| Ming dynasty | 1369–1644 |

confer legitimacy on them, but they often received magnificent gifts from their "elder brother" as a reward for good behavior. Merchants from their countries also gained access to the vast Chinese market.

## Society in Traditional China

These political and economic changes affected Chinese society during the Tang and Song era. For one thing, it became much more complex. Whereas previously China had been almost exclusively rural, with a small urban class of merchants, artisans, and workers almost entirely dependent on the state, the cities had now grown into an important, if statistically still insignificant, part of the population. Urban life, too, had changed. Cities were no longer primarily administrative centers dominated by officials and their families but now included a much broader mix of officials, merchants, artisans, touts, and entertainers. Unlike the situation in Europe, however, Chinese cities did not possess special privileges that protected their residents from the rapacity of the central government

In the countryside, equally significant changes were taking place as the relatively rigid demarcation between the landed aristocracy and the mass of the rural population gave way to a more complex mixture of landed gentry, free farmers, sharecroppers, and landless laborers. There was also a class of "base people," consisting of actors, butchers, and prostitutes, who possessed only limited legal rights and were not permitted to take the civil service examination.

**The Rise of the Gentry** Perhaps the most significant development was the rise of the landed gentry as the most influential force in Chinese society. The gentry class controlled much of the wealth in the rural areas and produced the majority of the candidates for the bureaucracy. By virtue of their possession of land and specialized knowledge of the Confucian classics, the gentry had replaced the aristocracy as the political and economic elite of Chinese society. Unlike the aristocracy, however, the gentry did not form an exclusive class separated by the accident of birth from the remainder of the population. Upward and downward mobility between the scholar-gentry class and the remainder of the population was not uncommon and may have been a key factor in the stability and longevity of the system. A position in the bureaucracy opened the doors to wealth and prestige for the individual and his family, but it was no guarantee of success, and the fortunes of individual families might experience a rapid rise and fall. The soaring ambitions and arrogance of China's landed gentry are vividly described in the following wish list set in poetry by a young bridegroom of the Tang dynasty:

*Chinese slaves to take charge of treasury and barn,*
*Foreign slaves to take care of my cattle and sheep.*
*Strong-legged slaves to run by saddle and stirrup*
*when I ride,*
*Powerful slaves to till the fields with might*
*and main,*
*Handsome slaves to play the harp and hand*
*the wine;*
*Slim-waisted slaves to sing me songs, and dance;*
*Dwarfs to hold the candle by my dining-couch.*[5]

For affluent Chinese in this era, life offered many more pleasures than had been available to their ancestors. There were new forms of entertainment, such as playing cards and chess (brought from India, although an early form had been invented in China during the Zhou dynasty); new forms of transportation, such as the paddle-wheel boat and horseback riding (made possible by the introduction of the stirrup); better means of communication (block printing was first invented in the eighth century C.E.); and new tastes for the palate introduced from lands beyond the frontier. Tea had been introduced from the Burmese frontier by monks as early as the Han dynasty, and brandy and other concentrated spirits produced by the distillation of alcohol made their appearance in the seventh century.

**Village China** The vast majority of the Chinese people still lived off the land in villages ranging in size from a few dozen residents to several thousand. The life of the farmers was bounded by their village. Although many communities were connected to the outside world by roads or rivers, the average Chinese rarely left the confines of their native village except for an occasional visit to a nearby market town. This isolation was psychological as well as physical, for most Chinese identified with their immediate environment and had difficulty envisioning themselves living beyond the bamboo hedges or mud walls that marked the limit of their horizon.

## THE SAINTLY MISS WU

The idea that a wife should sacrifice her wants to the needs of her husband and family was deeply embedded in traditional Chinese society. Widows in particular had few rights, and their remarriage was strongly condemned. In this account from a story by Hung Mai, a twelfth-century writer, the widowed Miss Wu wins the respect of the entire community by faithfully serving her mother-in-law.

*What is the moral of this story? How do the supernatural elements in the account strengthen the lesson intended by the author?*

### Hung Mai, *A Song Family Saga*

Miss Wu served her mother-in-law very filially. Her mother-in-law had an eye ailment and felt sorry for her daughter-in-law's solitary and poverty-stricken situation, so suggested that they call in a son-in-law for her and thereby get an adoptive heir. Miss Wu announced in tears, "A woman does not serve two husbands. I will support you. Don't talk this way." Her mother-in-law, seeing that she was determined, did not press her. Miss Wu did spinning, washing, sewing, cooking, and cleaning for her neighbors, earning perhaps a hundred cash a day, all of which she gave to her mother-in-law to cover the cost of firewood and food. If she was given any meat, she would wrap it up to take home. . . .

Once when her mother-in-law was cooking rice, a neighbor called to her, and to avoid overcooking the rice she dumped it into a pan. Owing to her bad eyes, however, she mistakenly put it in the dirty chamber pot. When Miss Wu returned and saw it, she did not say a word. She went to a neighbor to borrow some cooked rice for her mother-in-law and took the dirty rice and washed it to eat herself.

One day in the daytime neighbors saw [Miss Wu] ascending into the sky amid colored clouds. Startled, they told her mother-in-law, who said, "Don't be foolish. She just came back from pounding rice for someone, and is lying down on the bed. Go and look." They went to the room and peeked in and saw her sound asleep. Amazed, they left.

When Miss Wu woke up, her mother-in-law told her what happened, and she said, "I just dreamed of two young boys in blue clothes holding documents and riding on the clouds. They grabbed my clothes and said the Emperor of Heaven had summoned me. They took me to the gate of heaven and I was brought in to see the emperor, who was seated beside a balustrade. He said 'Although you are just a lowly ignorant village woman, you are able to serve your old mother-in-law sincerely and work hard. You really deserve respect.' He gave me a cup of aromatic wine and a string of cash, saying, 'I will supply you. From now on you will not need to work for others.' I bowed to thank him and came back, accompanied by the two boys. Then I woke up."

There was in fact a thousand cash on the bed, and the room was filled with a fragrance. They then realized that the neighbors' vision had been a spirit journey. From this point on even more people asked her to work for them, and she never refused. But the money that had been given to her she kept for her mother-in-law's use. Whatever they used promptly reappeared, so the thousand cash was never exhausted. The mother-in-law also regained her sight in both eyes.

An even more basic unit than the village in the lives of most Chinese, of course, was the family. The ideal was the joint family with at least three generations under one roof. Because of the heavy labor requirements of rice farming, the tradition of the joint family was especially prevalent in the south. When a son married, he was expected to bring his new wife back to live in his parents' home (see the box above). Often the parents added a new wing to the house for the new family. If a woman married, she went to live with her husband; women who did not marry remained in the home where they grew up.

Chinese village architecture reflected these traditions. Most family dwellings were simple, consisting of one or at most two rooms. They were usually constructed of dried mud, stone, or brick, depending on available materials and the prosperity of the family. Roofs were of thatch or tile, and the floors were usually of packed dirt. Large houses were often built in a square around an inner courtyard, thus guaranteeing privacy from the outside world.

Within the family unit, the eldest male theoretically ruled as an autocrat. He was responsible for presiding over ancestral rites at an altar, usually in the main room of the house. He had traditional legal rights over his wife, and if she did not provide him with a male heir, he was permitted to take a second wife. She, however, had no recourse to divorce. As the old saying went, "Marry a chicken, follow the chicken; marry a dog, follow the dog." Wealthy Chinese might keep concubines, who lived in a separate room in the house and sometimes competed with the legal wife for precedence.

In accordance with Confucian tradition, children were expected, above all, to obey their parents, who not only determined their children's careers but also selected their marriage partners. Filial piety was viewed as an absolute moral good, above virtually all other moral obligations. Even today, duty to one's parents is considered important in traditional Chinese families, and the tombstones of deceased Chinese are often decorated with tile paintings depicting the filial acts that they performed during their lifetime.

**Court Ladies Preparing Silk.** Since antiquity, human beings have fashioned textiles out of hemp, flax, wool, cotton, and silk. The Shang dynasty produced both hemp and silk cloth, while wool was prominent in the Middle East and Greece. Linen, woven in Egypt, was used by the Roman Empire to clothe its army. Fine Indian cotton was introduced to China along the Silk Road, just as Chinese satin was carried by Mongol warriors to Europe, where it was used for making banners. Sometimes the Chinese government demanded not only grain but also bolts of cloth as a tax from peasants. Silk, produced mostly by peasants as an agricultural by-product, was also woven, as seen here, by the elegant court ladies of the Song dynasty, and its use as a fabric was restricted to the elite classes until the nineteenth century.

**The Role of Women** The tradition of male superiority continued from ancient times into the medieval era, especially under the southern Song when it was reinforced by Neo-Confucianism. Female children were considered less desirable than males because they could not undertake heavy work in the fields or carry on the family traditions. Poor families often sold their daughters to wealthy villagers to serve as concubines, and female infanticide was not uncommon in times of famine to ensure there would be food for the remainder of the family. Concubines had few legal rights; female domestic servants, even fewer.

During the Song era, two new practices emerged that changed the equation for women seeking to obtain a successful marriage contract. First, a new form of dowry appeared. Whereas previously the prospective husband offered the bride's family a bride price, now the reverse became the norm, with the bride's parents paying the groom's family a dowry. With the prosperity that characterized Chinese society during much of the Song era, affluent parents sought to buy a satisfactory husband for their daughter, preferably one with a higher social standing and good prospects for an official career.

A second source of marital bait during the Song period was the promise of a bride with tiny bound feet. The process of **foot binding,** carried out on girls aged five to thirteen, was excruciatingly painful, since it bent and compressed the foot to half its normal size by imprisoning it in restrictive bandages. But the procedure was often performed by ambitious mothers intent on assuring their daughters of the best possible prospects for marriage. The zealous mother also wanted her daughter to possess a competitive edge in dealing with the other wives and concubines of her future husband. Bound feet represented submissiveness and self-discipline, two required attributes for the ideal Confucian wife.

Throughout northern China, foot binding became a common practice for women of all social classes. It was less common in southern China, where the cultivation of wet rice could not be carried out with bandaged feet; there it tended to be limited to the scholar-gentry class. Still, most Chinese women with bound feet contributed to the labor force to supplement the family income. Although foot binding was eventually prohibited, the practice lasted into the twentieth century, particularly in rural villages.

As in most traditional societies, there were exceptions to the low status of women in Chinese society. Women had substantial property rights and retained control over their dowries even after divorce or the death of the husband. Wives were frequently an influential force within the home, often handling the accounts and taking primary responsibility for raising the children. Some were active in politics. The outstanding example was Wu Zhao (c. 625–c. 706), popularly known as Empress Wu. Selected by Emperor Tang Taizong as a concubine, after his death she rose to a position of supreme power at court. At first, she was content to rule through her sons, but in 690, she declared herself empress of China. To bolster her claim of legitimacy, she cited a Buddhist *sutra* to the effect that a woman would rule the world seven hundred years after the death of Gautama Buddha. For her presumption, she has been vilified by later Chinese historians, but she was actually a quite capable ruler. She was responsible for giving meaning to the civil service examination system and was the first to select graduates of the examinations for the highest positions in government. During her last years, she reportedly fell under the influence of courtiers and was deposed in 705, when she was probably around eighty.

# Explosion in Central Asia: The Mongol Empire

The Mongols, who succeeded the Song as the rulers of China in 1279, rose to power in Asia with stunning rapidity. When Genghis Khan (also known as Chinggis Khan), the founder of Mongol greatness, was born, the Mongols were a relatively obscure pastoral people in the region of modern Mongolia. Like most of the nomadic peoples in the region, they were organized loosely into clans and tribes and even lacked a common name for themselves. Rivalry among the various tribes over pasture, livestock, and booty was intense and increased at the end of the twelfth century as a result of a growing population and the consequent overgrazing of pastures.

## The Creation of the Mongol Empire

Born in 1162, Genghis Khan (his original name was Temuchin, or Temujin) was the son of one of the more impoverished nobles of his tribe. While he was still a child, his father was murdered by a rival, and the youngster was temporarily forced to seek refuge in the wilderness. Nevertheless, through his prowess and the power of his personality, he gradually unified the Mongol tribes. In 1206, he was elected Genghis Khan ("universal ruler") at a massive tribal meeting. From that time on, he devoted himself to military pursuits. Mongol nomads were now forced to pay taxes and were subject to military conscription. "Man's highest joy," Genghis Khan reportedly remarked, "is in victory: to conquer one's enemies, to pursue them, to deprive them of their possessions, to make their beloved weep, to ride on their horses, and to embrace their wives and daughters."[6]

The army that Genghis Khan unleashed on the world was not exceptionally large—less than 130,000 men in 1227, at a time when the total Mongol population numbered between one and two million. But their mastery of military tactics set the Mongols apart from their rivals. Their tireless flying columns of mounted warriors surrounded their enemies and harassed them like cattle, luring them into pursuit, then ambushing them with flank attacks. John Plano Carpini, a contemporary Franciscan friar, described their tactics:

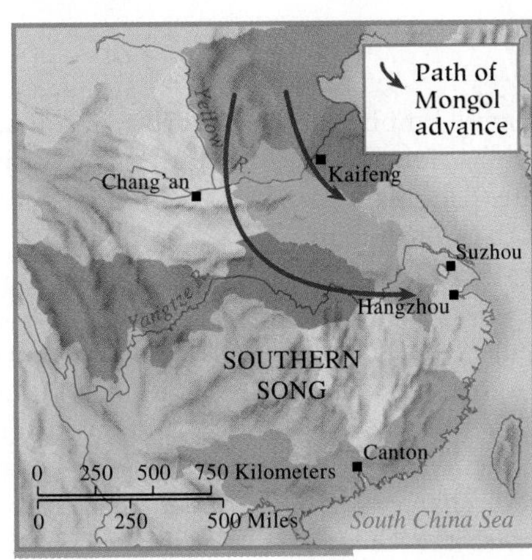


**The Mongol Conquest of China**

> As soon as they discover the enemy they charge and each one unleashes three or four arrows. If they see that they can't break him, they retreat in order to entice the enemy to pursue, thus luring him into an ambush prepared in advance. . . . Their military stratagems are numerous. At the moment of an enemy cavalry attack, they place prisoners and foreign auxiliaries in the forefront of their own position, while positioning the bulk of their own troops on the right and left wings to envelop the adversary, thus giving the enemy the impression that they are more numerous than in reality. If the adversary defends himself well, they open their ranks to let him pass through in flight, after which they launch in pursuit and kill as many as possible.[7]

In the years after the election of Temuchin as universal ruler, the Mongols, now in possession of a new type of compound bow, which added both power and distance, defeated tribal groups to their west and then turned their attention to the seminomadic non-Chinese kingdoms in northern China. There they discovered that their adversaries were armed with a weapon called a fire-lance, an early form of flamethrower. Gunpowder had been invented in China during the late Tang period, and by the early thirteenth century, a type of fire-lance had been developed that could spew out a combination of flame and projectiles that could travel 30 or 40 yards and inflict considerable damage on the enemy. By the end of the thirteenth century, the fire-lance had evolved into the much more effective hand-gun and cannon. These inventions came too late to save China from the Mongols, however, and were transmitted to Europe by the early fourteenth century by foreigners employed by the Mongol rulers of China.

While some Mongol armies were engaged in the conquest of northern China, others traveled farther afield and advanced as far as central Europe (see the box on p. 284). Only the death of the Great Khan may have prevented an all-out Mongol attack on western Europe. In 1231, the Mongols attacked Persia and then defeated the Abbasids at Baghdad in 1258 (see Chapter 7). Mongol forces attacked the Song from the west in the 1260s and finally defeated the remnants of the Song navy in 1279.

By then, the Mongol Empire was quite different from what it had been under its founder. Prior to the conquests of Genghis Khan, the Mongols had been purely nomadic. They spent their winters in the southern plains, where they found suitable pastures for their cattle, and traveled north in the summer to wooded areas where the water was sufficient. They lived in *yurts,* round tents covered with felt that were easily transported. For food, the Mongols depended on milk and meat from their herds and game from hunting.

To administer the new empire, Genghis Khan set up a capital city at Karakorum, in present-day Mongolia, but prohibited his fellow Mongols from practicing sedentary occupations or living in cities. But under his successors, Mongol aristocrats began to enter administrative positions, and commoners took up sedentary occupations as farmers or merchants. As one khan remarked, quoting his Chinese

## A Letter to the Pope

In 1243, Pope Innocent IV dispatched the Franciscan friar John Plano Carpini to the Mongol headquarters at Karakorum to appeal to the great khan Kuyuk to cease his attacks on Christians. After a considerable wait, Carpini was given the following reply, which could not have pleased the pope. The letter was discovered recently in the Vatican archives.

*Based on the account shown here, what message was the pope seeking to convey to the great khan in Karakorum? What is the nature of the latter's reply?*

### A Letter from Kuyuk Khan to Pope Innocent IV

By the power of the Eternal Heaven, We are the all-embracing Khan of all the Great Nations. It is our command:

This is a decree, sent to the great Pope that he may know and pay heed.

After holding counsel with the monarchs under your suzerainty, you have sent us an offer of subordination, which we have accepted from the hands of your envoy.

If you should act up to your word, then you, the great Pope, should come in person with the monarchs to pay us homage and we should thereupon instruct you concerning the commands of the Yasak.

Furthermore, you have said it would be well for us to become Christians. You write to me in person about this matter, and have addressed to me a request. This, your request, we cannot understand.

Furthermore, you have written me these words: "You have attacked all the territories of the Magyars and other Christians, at which I am astonished. Tell me, what was their crime?" These, your words, we likewise cannot understand. Jenghiz Khan and Ogatai Khakan revealed the commands of Heaven. But those whom you name would not believe the commands of Heaven. Those of whom you speak showed themselves highly presumptuous and slew our envoys. Therefore, in accordance with the commands of the Eternal Heaven the inhabitants of the aforesaid countries have been slain and annihilated. If not by the command of Heaven, how can anyone slay or conquer out of his own strength?

And when you say: "I am a Christian. I pray to God. I arraign and despise others," how do you know who is pleasing to God and to whom He allots His grace? How can you know it, that you speak such words?

Thanks to the power of the Eternal Heaven, all lands have been given to us from sunrise to sunset. How could anyone act other than in accordance with the commands of Heaven? Now your own upright heart must tell you: "We will become subject to you, and will place our powers at your disposal." You in person, at the head of the monarchs, all of you, without exception, must come to tender us service and pay us homage, then only will we recognize your submission. But if you do not obey the commands of Heaven, and run counter to our orders, we shall know that you are our foe.

That is what we have to tell you. If you fail to act in accordance therewith, how can we foresee what will happen to you? Heaven alone knows.

adviser, "Although you inherited the Chinese Empire on horseback, you cannot rule it from that position."[8]

The territorial nature of the empire also changed. Following tribal custom, at the death of the ruling khan, the territory was distributed among his heirs. Genghis Khan's empire was thus divided into several separate **khanates,** each under the autonomous rule of one of his sons by his principal wife (see Map 10.2). One of his sons was awarded the khanate of Chaghadai in Central Asia with its capital at Samarkand; another ruled Persia from the conquered city of Baghdad; a third took charge of the khanate of Kipchak (commonly known as the Golden Horde). But it was one of his grandsons, named Khubilai Khan (who ruled from 1260 to 1294), who completed the conquest of the Song and established a new Chinese dynasty, called the Yuan (from a phrase in the *Book of Changes* referring to the "original creative force" of the universe). Khubilai moved the capital of China northward to Khanbaliq ("city of the khan"), which was located on a major trunk route from the Great Wall to the plains of northern China. Later the city would be known by the Chinese name Beijing, or Peking ("northern capital").

## Mongol Rule in China

At first, China's new rulers exhibited impressive vitality. After a failed attempt to administer their conquest as they had ruled their own tribal society (some advisers reportedly even suggested that the plowed fields be transformed into pasture), Mongol rulers adapted to the Chinese political system and made use of local talents in the bureaucracy, although the highest positions were usually reserved for Mongols. The tripartite division of the administration into civilian, military, and censorate was retained, as were the six ministries. Eventually, even the civil service system was revived, as was the state cult of Confucius, although Khubilai Khan himself was a Buddhist. Some leading Mongols followed their ruler in converting to Buddhism, but most

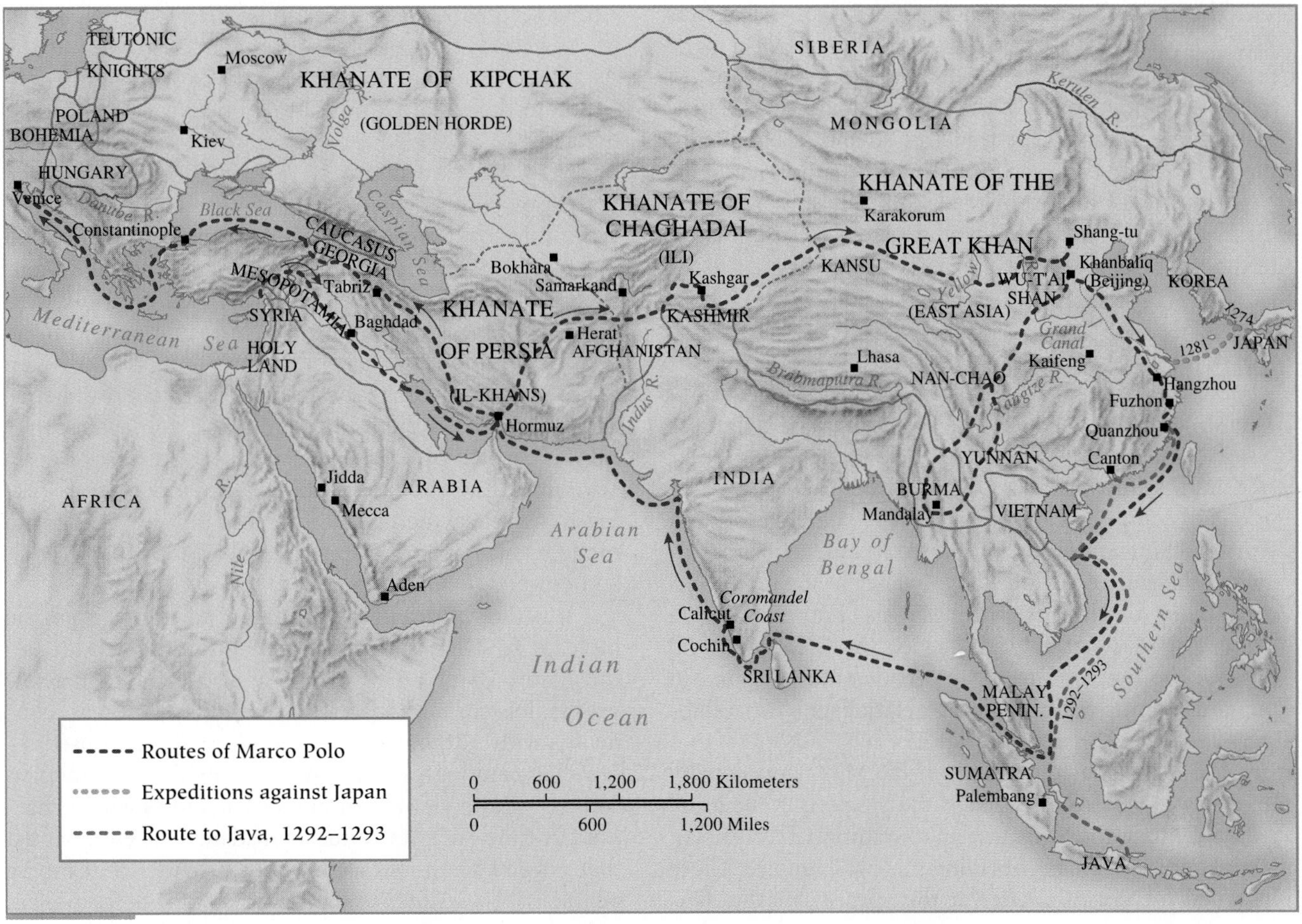

**MAP 10.2 Asia Under the Mongols.** This map shows the expansion of Mongol power throughout Eurasia in the thirteenth century. After the death of Genghis Kahn, the empire was divided into four separate khanates. ? In what modern-day countries were the four khanates located? **View an animated version of this map or related maps at http://history.wadsworth.com/duikerspielvogel05/**

commoners retained their traditional religion. In general, the Mongols remained apart as a separate class with their own laws.

The Mongols' greatest achievement may have been the prosperity they fostered. They continued the relatively tolerant economic policies of the southern Song, and by bringing the entire Eurasian landmass under a single rule, they encouraged long-distance trade, particularly along the Silk Road, now dominated by Muslim merchants from Central Asia. To promote trade, the Grand Canal was extended from the Yellow River to the capital. Adjacent to the canal, a paved highway was constructed that extended all the way from the Song capital of Hangzhou to its Mongol counterpart at Khanbaliq. According to the Italian merchant Marco Polo, who resided there during the reign of Khubilai Khan, the new capital was a magnificent city 24 miles in diameter where "so many pleasures may be found that one fancies himself to be in Paradise." The urban area was surrounded by thick walls of earth penetrated by twelve massive gates.

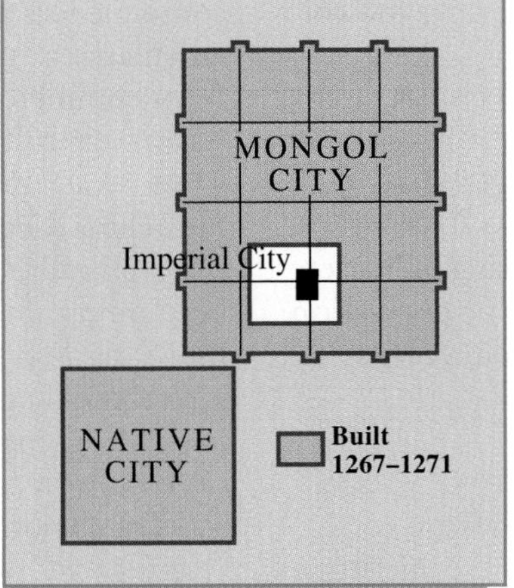


**Khanbaliq (Beijing) Under the Mongols**

## From the Yuan to the Ming

The Yuan eventually fell victim to the same fate that had afflicted other powerful dynasties in China. Excessive spending on foreign campaigns, inadequate tax revenues, factionalism and corruption at court and in the bureaucracy, and growing internal instability, brought about in part by a famine in central China in the 1340s, all contributed to the dynasty's demise. Khubilai Khan's successors lacked his administrative genius, and by the middle of the fourteenth century, the Yuan dynasty in China, like the Mongol khanates elsewhere in Central Asia, had fallen into a rapid decline.

The immediate instrument of Mongol defeat was Zhu Yuanzhang (Chu Yuan-chang), the son of a poor peasant in the lower Yangtze valley. After losing most of his family in the famine of the 1340s, Zhu became an itinerant monk and then the leader of a band of bandits. In the 1360s, unrest spread throughout the country, and after defeating a number of rivals, Zhu put an end to the disintegrating Yuan regime and declared the foundation of the new Ming ("bright") dynasty (1369–1644).

## The Ming Dynasty

The Ming inaugurated a new era of greatness in Chinese history. Under a series of strong rulers, China extended its rule into Mongolia and Central Asia. The Ming even briefly reconquered Vietnam, which, after a thousand years of Chinese rule, had reclaimed its independence following the collapse of the Tang dynasty in the tenth century. Along the northern frontier, the Emperor Yongle (Yung Lo; 1402–1424) strengthened the Great Wall and pacified the nomadic tribes that had troubled China in previous centuries. A tributary relationship was established with the Yi dynasty in Korea.

The internal achievements of the Ming were equally impressive. When they replaced the Mongols in the fourteenth century, the Ming turned to traditional Confucian institutions as a means of ruling their vast empire. These included the six ministries at the apex of the bureaucracy, the use of the civil service examinations to select members of the bureaucracy, and the division of the empire into provinces, districts, and counties. As before, Chinese villages were relatively autonomous, and local councils of elders continued to be responsible for adjudicating disputes, initiating local construction and irrigation projects, mustering a militia, and assessing and collecting taxes.

The society that was governed by this vast hierarchy of officials was a far cry from the predominantly agrarian society that had been ruled by the Han. In the burgeoning cities near the coast and along the Yangtze River valley, factories and workshops were vastly increasing the variety and output of their manufactured goods. The population had doubled, and new crops had been introduced, greatly expanding the food output of the empire.

### The Voyages of Zhenghe

In 1405, in a splendid display of Chinese maritime might, Emperor Yongle sent a fleet of Chinese trading ships under the eunuch admiral Zhenghe (Cheng Ho) through the Strait of Malacca and out into the Indian Ocean; there they traveled as far west as the east coast of Africa, stopping on the way at ports in South Asia. The size of the fleet was impressive: nearly 28,000 sailors on sixty-two ships, some of them junks larger by far than any other oceangoing vessels the world had yet seen. China seemed about to become a direct participant in the vast trade network that extended as far west as the Atlantic Ocean, thus culminating the process of opening China to the wider world that had begun with the Tang dynasty.

Why the expeditions were undertaken has been a matter of some debate. Some historians assume that economic profit was the main reason. Others point to Yongle's native curiosity and note that the voyage—and the six others that followed it—returned not only with goods but also with a plethora of information about the outside world as well as with some items unknown in China (the emperor was especially intrigued by the giraffes and placed them in the imperial zoo, where they were identified by soothsayers with the coming of good government). Others speculate that the emperor was seeking to ascertain the truth of rumors that his immediate predecessor, Emperor Jianwen (Chien Wen; 1398–1402), had escaped to Southeast Asia to live in exile.

Whatever the case, the voyages resulted in a dramatic increase in Chinese knowledge about the world and the nature of ocean travel. They also brought massive profits for their sponsors, including individuals connected with Admiral Zhenghe at court. This aroused resentment among conservatives within the bureaucracy, some of whom viewed commercial activities with a characteristic measure of Confucian disdain. One commented that an end to the voyages would provide the Chinese people with a respite "so that they can devote themselves to husbandry [agriculture] and schooling."

### An Inward Turn

Shortly after Yongle's death, the voyages were discontinued, never to be revived. The decision had long-term consequences and in the eyes of many modern historians marks a turning inward of the Chinese state, away from commerce and toward a more traditional emphasis on agriculture, away from the exotic lands to the south and toward the heartland of the country in the Yellow River valley.

Ironically, the move toward the Yellow River had been initiated by Yongle himself when he had decided to move the Ming capital from Nanjing, in central China, where the ships were built and the voyages launched, back to Beijing, where official eyes were firmly focused on the threat from beyond the Great Wall to the north. As a means of reducing that threat, Yongle ordered the resettlement of thousands of families from the rich Yangtze valley. The emperor had presumably not intended to set forces in motion that would divert the country from its growing contacts with the external world. After all, he had been the driving force behind Zhenghe's voyages. But the end result was a shift in the balance of power from central China, where it had been since the southern Song dynasty, back to northern China, where it had originated and would remain for the rest of the Ming era. China would not look outward again for over four centuries.

Why the Ming government discontinued Zhenghe's voyages and turned its attention back to domestic concerns has long been a matter of scholarly debate. Was it simply a consequence of court intrigues or the replacement of one emperor by another, or were there deeper issues involved? A recent theory that has gained wide attention even speculated that the Chinese fleets had not limited their explorations to the Indian Ocean but had actually circled the earth and discovered the existence of the Western Hemisphere. The voyages, and their abrupt discontinuance, remain one of the most fascinating enigmas in the history of China.

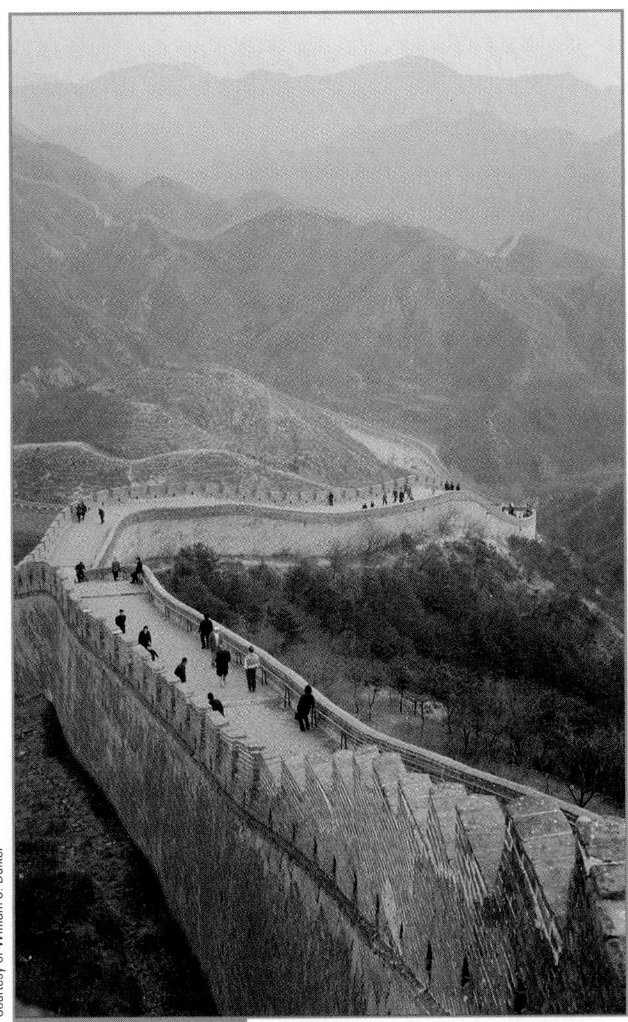

Courtesy of William J. Duiker

**The Great Wall of China.** Although the Great Wall is popularly believed to be over two thousand years old, the part of the wall that is most frequently visited by tourists was a reconstruction undertaken during the early Ming dynasty as a means of protection against invasion from the north. Part of that wall, which was built to protect the imperial capital of Beijing, is shown here.

# In Search of the Way

By the time of the Sui dynasty, Buddhism and Daoism had emerged as major rivals of Confucianism as the ruling ideology of the state. But during the last half of the Tang dynasty, Confucianism revived and once again became dominant at court, a position it would retain to the end of the dynastic period in the early twentieth century. Buddhist and Daoist beliefs, however, remained popular at the local level.

## The Rise and Decline of Buddhism and Daoism

As noted earlier, Buddhism arrived in China with merchants from India and found its first adherents among the merchant community and intellectuals intrigued by the new ideas. During the chaotic centuries following the collapse of the Han dynasty, Buddhism and Daoism appealed to those who were searching for more emotional and spiritual satisfaction than Confucianism could provide. Both faiths reached beyond the common people and found support among the ruling classes as well. There was even a small Christian church in the capital of Chang'an, introduced to China by Syrian merchants in the sixth century C.E.

**The Sinification of Buddhism** As Buddhism attracted more followers, it began to take on Chinese characteristics and divided into a number of separate sects. Some, like the ***Chan*** (*Zen* in Japanese) sect, called for mind training and a strict regimen as a means of seeking enlightenment, a technique that reflected Daoist ideas and appealed to many intellectuals (see the box on p. 288). Others, like the **Pure Land** sect, stressed the role of devotion, an approach that was more appealing to ordinary Chinese, who lacked the time and inclination for strict monastic discipline. Still others were mystical sects, like **Tantrism,** which emphasized the importance of magical symbols and ritual in seeking a preferred way to enlightenment. Some Buddhist groups, like their Daoist counterparts, had political objectives. The **White Lotus** sect, founded in 1133, often adopted the form of a rebel movement, seeking political reform or the overthrow of a dynasty and forecasting a new era when a "savior Buddha" would come to earth to herald the advent of a new age. Most believers, however, assimilated Buddhism into their daily lives, where it joined Confucian ideology and spirit worship as an element in the highly eclectic and tolerant Chinese worldview.

The burgeoning popularity of Buddhism continued into the early years of the Tang dynasty. Early Tang rulers lent their support to the Buddhist monasteries that had been established throughout the country. Buddhist scriptures were regularly included in the civil service examinations, and Buddhist and Daoist advisers replaced shamans and Confucian scholar-officials as advisers at court. But

## The Way of the Great Buddha

According to Buddhists, it is impossible to describe the state of Nirvana, which is sometimes depicted as an extinction of self. Yet Buddhist scholars found it difficult to avoid trying to interpret the term for their followers. The following passage by the Chinese monk Shen-Hui, one of the leading exponents of Chan Buddhism, dates from the eighth century and attempts to describe the means by which an individual may hope to seek enlightenment. There are clear similarities with philosophical Daoism.

*What are the similarities with philosophical Daoism expressed in this passage? Compare and contrast the views expressed here with the Neo-Confucian worldview.*

### Shen-Hui, *Elucidating the Doctrine*

"Absence of thought" is the doctrine.

"Absence of action" is the foundation.

True Emptiness is the substance.

And all wonderful things and beings are the function.

True Thusness is without thought; it cannot be known through conception and thought.

The True State is noncreated—can it be seen in matter and mind?

There is no thought except that of True Thusness.

There is no creation except that of the True State.

Abiding without abiding, forever abiding in Nirvana.

Acting without acting, immediately crossing to the Other Shore.

Thusness does not move, but its motion and functions are inexhaustible.

In every instant of thought, there is no seeking; the seeking itself is no thought.

Perfect wisdom is not achieved, and yet the Five Eyes all become pure and the Three Bodies are understood.

Great Enlightenment has no knowledge, and yet the Six Supernatural Powers of the Buddha are utilized and the Four Wisdoms of the Buddha are made great.

Thus we know that calmness is at the same time no calmness, wisdom at the same time no wisdom, and action at the same time no action.

The nature is equivalent to the void and the substance is identical with the Realm of Law.

In this way, the Six Perfections are completed.

None of the ways to arrive at Nirvana is wanting.

Thus we know that the ego and the dharmas are empty in reality and being and nonbeing are both obliterated.

The mind is originally without activity; the Way is always without thought.

No thought, no reflection, no seeking, no attainment;

No this, no that, no coming, no going.

With such reality one understands the True Insight [into previous and future mortal conditions and present mortal suffering].

With such a mind one penetrates the Eight Emancipations [through the eight stages of mental concentration].

By merits one accomplishes the Ten Powers of the Buddha.

History Now™ To read "Buddha Enters Nirvana," enter the *HistoryNow* documents area using the access card that is available for *World History.*

ultimately, Buddhism and Daoism lost favor at court and were increasingly subjected to official persecution. Part of the reason was xenophobia. Envious Daoists and Confucianists made a point of criticizing the foreign origins of Buddhist doctrines, which one prominent Confucian scholar characterized as nothing but "silly relics." To deflect such criticism, Buddhists attempted to make the doctrine more Chinese, equating the Indian concept of *dharma* (law) with the Chinese concept of *Dao* (the Way). Emperor Tang Taizong ordered the Buddhist monk Xuan Zang to translate Lao Tzu's classic, *The Way of the Dao,* into Sanskrit, reportedly to show visitors from India that China had its own equivalent to the Buddhist scriptures. But another reason for this change of heart may have been financial. The great Buddhist monasteries had accumulated thousands of acres of land and serfs that were exempt from paying taxes to the state. Such wealth contributed to the corruption of the monks and other Buddhist officials and in turn aroused popular resentment and official disapproval. As the state attempted to eliminate the great landholdings of the aristocracy, the large monasteries also attracted its attention. During the later Tang, countless temples and monasteries were destroyed, and over 100,000 monks were compelled to leave the monasteries and return to secular life.

**Buddhism Under Threat** There were probably deeper political and ideological reasons for the growing antagonism between Buddhism and the state. By preaching the illusory nature of the material world, Buddhism was denying the very essence of Confucian teachings—the necessity for filial piety and hard work. By encouraging young Chinese to abandon their rice fields and seek refuge and wisdom in the monasteries, Buddhism was undermining the foundation stones of Chinese society—the family unit and the work ethic. In the final analysis, Buddhism was incompatible with the activist element in Chinese society, an orientation that was most effectively expressed by State

© Art Archive/British Museum

**Cave Art at Dunhuang.** Dunhuang was a major rest stop on the eastern section of the Silk Road. Many merchants from Central Asia paused there while awaiting permission to travel on to the Tang capital at Chang'an. Before embarking on the last stage of their journey, some travelers endowed the creation of Buddhist frescoes and statuary in caves on a cliffside not far from their lodgings. Shown here is an eighth-century wall banner of the Buddha that shows distinct Indian influence. After the Muslim faith penetrated into the area, the caves were abandoned, not to be rediscovered until late in the nineteenth century.

Confucianism. In the competition with Confucianism for support by the state, Buddhism, like Daoism, was almost certain to lose, at least in the more this-worldly, secure, and prosperous milieu of late Tang and Song China. The two doctrines continued to win converts at the local level, but official support ceased. In the meantime, Buddhism was under attack in Central Asia as well. In the eighth century, the Uighur kingdom adopted **Manichaeanism,** an offshoot of the ancient Zoroastrian religion with some influence from Christianity. Manichaeanism spread rapidly throughout the area and may have been a reason for the European belief that a Christian king (the legendary Prester John) ruled somewhere in Asia. By the tenth century, Islam was beginning to move east along the Silk Road, posing a severe threat to both Manichaean and Buddhist centers in the area.

## Neo-Confucianism: The Investigation of Things

Into the vacuum left by the decline of Buddhism and Daoism stepped a revived Confucianism. But it was a Confucianism that had been significantly altered by its competition with Buddhist and Daoist teachings. Challenged by Buddhist and Daoist ideas about the nature of the universe, Confucian thinkers began to flesh out the spare metaphysical structure of classical Confucian doctrine with a set of sophisticated theories about the nature of the cosmos and humans' place in it. Although the origins of this effort can be traced to the early Tang period, it reached fruition during the intellectually prolific Song dynasty, when it became the dominant ideology of the state.

Courtesy of William J. Duiker

**Buddhist Sculpture at Longmen.** The Silk Road was an avenue for ideas as well as trade. Over the centuries, Christian, Buddhist, and Muslim teachings came to China across the sandy wastes of the Taklimakan Basin. In the seventh century, the Tang emperor Gaozong commissioned this massive temple carving as part of the large complex of cave art devoted to Buddha at Longmen in central China. Bold and grandiose in their construction, these statues reflect the glory of the Tang dynasty.

## A Confucian Wedding Ceremony

During the twelfth century, the philosopher Zhu Xi attempted to reinvigorate Confucian teachings in a contemporary setting that would be more accessible in its appeal to a broad audience. His goal was militantly Confucian, to combat both popular Buddhist doctrines and the superstitious practices of the common people. With his new moral code, Zhu Xi hoped to put Chinese society back on the Confucian track, with its emphasis on proper behavior. He therefore set forth the proper rituals required to carry out the special days that marked the lives of all Chinese: entry into adolescence, marriage, and funeral and ancestral rites. In the following excerpt, he prescribes the proper protocol for the Confucian wedding ceremony.

*What is the apparent purpose for describing proper etiquette as expressed in this passage? How does adherence to such rigid rituals contribute to becoming a good Confucian?*

### 4. Welcoming in Person

On the day before the wedding, the bride's family sends people to lay out the dowry furnishings in the groom's chamber. At dawn the groom's family sets places in the chamber. Meanwhile, the bride's family sets up places outside. As the sun goes down, the groom puts on full attire. After the presiding man makes a report at the offering hall, he pledges the groom and orders him to go to fetch the bride. The groom goes out and mounts his horse. When he gets to the bride's home he waits at his place. The presiding man of the bride's family makes a report at the offering hall, after which he pledges the bride and instructs her. Then he goes out to greet the groom. When the groom enters, he presents a goose. The duenna takes the girl out to climb into the conveyance. The groom mounts his horse and leads the way for the bridal vehicle. When they arrive at his house he leads the bride in and they take their seats. After the eating and drinking are done, the groom leaves the chamber. On reentering, he takes off his clothes and the candles are removed.

### 5. The Bride Is Presented to Her Parents-in-Law

The next day, having risen at dawn, the bride meets her parents-in-law, who entertain her. Then the bride is presented to the elders. If she is the wife of the eldest son, she serves food to her parents-in-law. Then the parents-in-law feast the bride.

### 6. Presentation at the Family Shrine

On the third day the presiding man takes the bride to be presented at the offering hall.

### 7. The Groom Is Presented to the Wife's Parents

The day after that the groom goes to see his wife's parents. Afterward he is presented to his wife's relatives. The bride's family entertains the groom, as in ordinary etiquette.

The fundamental purpose of **Neo-Confucianism,** as the new doctrine was called, was to unite the metaphysical speculations of Buddhism and Daoism with the pragmatic Confucian approach to society. In response to Buddhism and Daoism, Neo-Confucianism maintained that the world is real, not illusory, and that fulfillment comes from participation, not withdrawal.

The primary contributor to this intellectual effort was the philosopher Zhu Xi (Chu Hsi) (see the box above). Raised during the southern Song era, Zhu Xi accepted the division of the world into a material world and a transcendent world (called by Neo-Confucianists the **Supreme Ultimate,** or *Tai Ji*). The latter was roughly equivalent to the *Dao*, or Way, in classical Confucian philosophy. To Zhu Xi, this Supreme Ultimate was a set of abstract principles governed by the law of *yin* and *yang* and the five elements.

Human beings served as a link between the two halves of this bifurcated universe. Although human beings live in the material world, each individual has an identity that is linked with the Supreme Ultimate, and the goal of individual action is to transcend the material world in a Buddhist sense to achieve an essential identity with the Supreme Ultimate. According to Zhu Xi and his followers, the means of transcending the material world is self-cultivation, which is achieved by the "investigation of things."

**The School of Mind** During the remainder of the Song dynasty and into the early years of the Ming, Zhu Xi's ideas became the central core of Confucian ideology and a favorite source of questions for the civil service examinations. But during the mid-Ming era, his ideas came under attack from a Confucian scholar named Wang Yangming. Wang and his supporters disagreed with Zhu Xi's focus on learning through an investigation of the outside world and asserted that the correct way to transcend the material world was through an understanding of self. According to this so-called **School of Mind,** the mind and the universe were a single unit. Knowledge was thus intuitive rather than empirical and was obtained through internal self-searching rather than through an investigation of the outside world. The debate is reminiscent of a similar disagreement between followers of the ancient Greek philosophers Plato and Aristotle. Plato had argued that all knowledge comes from within, while Aristotle argued that knowledge resulted from an examination of the external world. Wang Yangming's ideas attracted many followers during the Ming dynasty, and the school briefly rivaled that of Zhu Xi in popularity among Confucian scholars. Nevertheless, it never won official acceptance, probably because it was too much like Buddhism in denying the importance of a life of participation and social action.

Neo-Confucianism remained the state doctrine until the end of the dynastic system in the twentieth century. Some historians have asked whether the doctrine can help explain why China failed to experience scientific and industrial revolutions of the sort that occurred in the West (see the comparative essay "The Scientific Revolution" in Chapter 17). In particular, it has been suggested that Neo-Confucianism tended to encourage an emphasis on the elucidation of moral principles rather than the expansion of scientific knowledge. Though the Chinese excelled in practical technology, inventing gunpowder, the compass (first used by seafarers during the Song dynasty), printing and paper, and cast iron, among other things, they had less interest in scientific theory. Their relative backwardness in mathematics is a good example. Chinese scholars had no knowledge of the principles of geometry and lagged behind other advanced civilizations in astronomy, physics, and optics. Until the Mongol era, they had no knowledge of Arabic numerals and lacked the concept of zero. Even after that time, they continued to use a cumbersome numbering system based on Chinese characters.

Furthermore, intellectual affairs in China continued to be dominated by the scholar-gentry, the chief upholders of Neo-Confucianism, who not only had little interest in the natural sciences or economic change but also viewed them as a threat to their own dominant status in Chinese society. The commercial middle class, who lacked social status and an independent position in society, had little say in intellectual matters. In contrast, in the West, an urban middle class emerged that was a source not only of wealth but also of social prestige, political power, and intellectual ideas. The impetus for the intellectual revolution in the West came from the members of the commercial bourgeoisie, who were interested in the conquest of nature and the development of technology. In China, however, the scholar-gentry continued to focus on the sources of human behavior and a correct understanding of the relationship between humankind and the universe. The result was an intellectual environment that valued continuity over change and tradition over innovation.

## The Apogee of Chinese Culture

The period between the Tang and the Ming dynasties was in many ways the great age of achievement in Chinese literature and art. Enriched by Buddhist and Daoist images and themes, Chinese poetry and painting reached the pinnacle of their creativity. Porcelain emerged as the highest form of Chinese ceramics, and sculpture flourished under the influence of styles imported from India and Central Asia.

### Literature

The development of Chinese literature was stimulated by two technological innovations: the invention of paper during the Han dynasty and the invention of woodblock printing during the Tang. At first, paper was used for clothing, wrapping material, toilet tissue, and even armor, but by the first century B.C.E., it was being used for writing as well.

In the seventh century C.E., the Chinese developed the technique of carving an entire page of text into a wooden block, inking it, and then pressing it onto a sheet of paper. Ordinarily, a text was printed on a long sheet of paper like a scroll. Then the paper was folded and stitched together to form a book. The earliest printed book known today is a Buddhist text published in 868 C.E.; it is more than 16 feet long. Although the Chinese eventually developed movable type as well, block printing continued to be used until relatively modern times because of the large number of Chinese characters needed to produce a lengthy text. Even with printing, books remained too expensive for most Chinese, but they did help popularize all forms of literary writing among the educated elite. Although literature was primarily a male occupation, a few women achieved prominence as a result of their creative prowess (see the box on p. 292).

During the post-Han era, historical writing and essays continued to be favorite forms of literary activity. Each dynasty produced an official dynastic history of its predecessor to elucidate sober maxims about the qualities of good and evil in human nature, and local gazetteers added to the general knowledge about the various regions. Encyclopedias brought together in a single location information and documents about all aspects of Chinese life.

**The Importance of Poetry** But it was in poetry, above all, that Chinese from the Tang to the Ming dynasties most effectively expressed their literary talents. Chinese poems celebrated the beauty of nature, the changes of the seasons, the joys of friendship and drink, sadness at the brevity of life, and old age and parting. Given the frequency of imperial banishment and the requirement that officials serve away from their home district, it is little wonder that separation was an important theme. Love poems existed, but were neither as intense as Western verse nor as sensual as Indian poetry.

The nature of the Chinese language imposed certain characteristics on Chinese poetry, the first being compactness. The most popular forms were four-line and eight-line poems, with five or seven words in each line. Because Chinese grammar does not rely on case or gender and makes no distinction between verb tenses, five-character Chinese poems were not only brief but often cryptic and ambiguous.

Two Tang poets, Li Bo (Li Po, sometimes known as Li Bai or Li Taibo) and Du Fu (Tu Fu), symbolized the genius of the era as well as the two most popular styles. Li Bo was a free spirit. His writing often centered on nature

## A PASSION FOR BOOKS

During the Song dynasty, upper-class Chinese women were often encouraged to learn to read in order to enhance their marriageability. They were discouraged from learning to write, however, since the ideal wife was expected to be reserved and modest in order to avoid attracting attention from those outside the family. A prominent exception to the rule was the woman writer Li Qingzhao (Li Ch'ing-chao, 1084–1151 C.E.). Although she was most appreciated for her poetry, this short prose passage, conveying her husband's passion for collecting books, offers rare details of daily life in twelfth-century China, as well as an intimate glimpse into their marriage. Chinese reverence for books, calligraphy, rubbings, and painting is movingly expressed in this excerpt, made all the more poignant by the knowledge that their magnificent collection was eventually destroyed by invading tribal peoples from the north.

*Compare the picture of a woman's role in society with that presented in the document on p. 281. Which do you think was more representative of conditions in traditional China?*

### Epilogue to Records on Metal and Stone

In 1101, in the first year of the Jian-zhong Reign, I came as a bride to the Zhao household. At that time my father was a division head in the Ministry of Rites, and my father-in-law, later a Grand Councilor, was an executive in the Ministry of Personnel. My husband was then twenty-one and a student in the Imperial Academy. In those days our two families, the Zhaos and the Lis, were not well-to-do and we were always frugal. On the first and fifteenth day of every month, my husband would get a short vacation from the Academy; he would "pawn some clothes" for five hundred cash and go to the market at Ziang-guo Temple, where he would buy fruit and rubbings of incriptions. When he brought these home, we would sit facing one another, rolling them out before us, examining and munching. And we thought ourselves persons [living in perfect contentment]. . . .

I happen to have an excellent memory, and every evening after we finished eating, we would sit in the hall called "Return Home" and make tea. Pointing to the heaps of books and histories, we would guess on which line of which page in which chapter of which book a certain passage could be found. Success in guessing determined who got to drink his or her tea first. Whenever I got it right, I would raise the teacup, laughing so hard that the tea would spill in my lap, and I would get up, not having been able to drink any of it at all. I would have been glad to grow old in such a world. Thus, even though we were living in anxiety, hardships, and poverty, our wills were not broken. . . .

In 1126, the first year of the Jing-kang Reign, my husband was governing Ze-chuan when we heard that the Jin Tartars were moving against the capital. He was in a daze, realizing that all those full trunks and overflowing chests, which he contemplated so lovingly and mournfully, would surely soon be his possessions no longer. In the third month of spring in 1127, the first year of the Jian-yan Reign, we hurried south for the funeral of his mother. Since we could not take the overabundance of our possessions with us, we first gave up the bulky printed volumes, the albums of paintings, and the most cumbersome of the vessels. Thus we reduced the size of the collection several times, and still we had fifteen cartloads of books. When we reached Dong-hai, it took a string of boats to ferry them all across the Huai, and again across the Yangzi to Jian-kang. In our old mansion in Qing-zhou we still had more than ten rooms of books and various items locked away, and we planned to have them all brought by boat the next year. But in the twelfth month Jin forces sacked Qing-zhou, and those ten or so rooms I spoke of were all reduced to ashes.

and shifted easily between moods of revelry and melancholy. Two of his best-known poems are "Resolution on Waking with a Hangover on a Spring Morning" and "Drinking Alone in Moonlight" (see the box on p. 293).

Where Li Bo was a carefree Daoist, Du Fu was a sober Confucian. His poems often dealt with historical issues or ethical themes, befitting a scholar-official living during the chaotic times of the late Tang era. Many of his works reflect a concern with social injustice and the plight of the unfortunate rarely to be found in the writings of his contemporaries (see the box on p. 293). Neither the poetry nor the prose of the great writers of the Tang and Song dynasties was written for or ever reached the majority of the Chinese population. The millions of Chinese peasants and artisans living in rural villages and market towns acquired their knowledge of Chinese history, Confucian moralisms, and even Buddhist scripture from stories, plays, and songs passed down by storytellers, wandering minstrels, and itinerant monks in a rich oral tradition.

**Popular Culture** By the Song dynasty, China had sixty million people, one million in Hangzhou alone. With the growth of cities came an increased demand for popular entertainment. Although the Tang dynasty had imposed a curfew on urban residents, the Song did not. The city gates and bridges were closed at dark, but food stalls and entertainment continued through the night. At fairgrounds throughout the year, one could find comedians, musicians, boxers, fencers, wrestlers, acrobats, puppets and marionettes, shadow plays, and especially storytellers.

## Two Tang Poets

Li Bo was one of the great poets of the Tang dynasty. The first selection is probably the best-known poem in China and has been memorized by schoolchildren for centuries. The second poem, "Drinking Alone in Moonlight," reflects the poet's carefree attitude toward life.

Du Fu, Li Bo's prime competitor as the greatest poet of the Tang dynasty, was often the more reflective of the two. In the final piece here, the poet has returned to his home in the capital after a rebellion against the dynasty has left the city in ruins.

*Historians often contrast these two famous poets in terms of their personalities and their approach to life. Can you see any differences in their points of view as conveyed in these short poems?*

### Li Bo, "Quiet Night Thoughts"

*Beside my bed the bright moonbeams bound*
*Almost as if there were frost on the ground.*
*Raising up, I gaze at the Mountain moon;*
*Lying back, I think of my old hometown.*

### Li Bo, "Drinking Alone in Moonlight"

*Among the flowers, with a jug of wine,*
*I drink all alone–no one to share.*
*Raising my cup, I welcome the moon.*
*And my shadow joins us, making a threesome.*
*Alas! the moon won't take part in the drinking,*
*And my shadow just does whatever I do.*
*But I'm friends for a while with the moon and*
*my shadow,*
*And we caper in revels well suited to spring.*
*As I sing the moon seems to sway back and forth;*
*As I dance my shadow goes flopping about.*
*As long as I'm sober we'll enjoy one another,*
*And when I get drunk, we'll go our own ways:*
*Forever committed to carefree play,*
*We'll all meet again in the Milky Way!*

### Du Fu, "Spring Prospect"

*The capital is taken. The hills and streams are left,*
*And with spring in the city the grass and trees*
*grown dense.*
*Mourning the times, the flowers trickle their tears;*
*Saddened with parting, the birds make my heart*
*flutter.*
*The army beacons have flamed for three months;*
*A letter from home would be worth ten thousand*
*in gold.*
*My white hairs I have anxiously scratched ever*
*shorter;*
*But such disarray! Even hairpins will do no good!*

Many of these arts had come from India centuries before and were now the favorite forms of amusement of the Chinese people.

**The Chinese Novel** During the Yuan dynasty, new forms of literary creativity, including popular theater and the novel, began to appear. The two most famous novels were *Romance of the Three Kingdoms* and *Tale of the Marshes*. The former had been told orally for centuries, appearing in written form during the Song as a scriptbook for storytellers. It was first printed in 1321 but was not published for mass consumption until 1522. Each new edition was altered in some way, making the final edition a composite effort of generations of the Chinese imagination. The plot recounts the power struggle that took place among competing groups after the fall of the Han dynasty. Packed with court intrigues, descriptions of peasant life, and gripping battles, *Romance of the Three Kingdoms* stands as a magnificent epic, China's counterpart to the Mahabharata.

*Tale of the Marshes* is an often violent tale of bandit heroes who at the end of the northern Song banded together to oppose government taxes and official oppression. They rob from those in power to share with the poor. *Tale of the Marshes* is the first prose fiction that describes the daily ordeal of ordinary Chinese people in their own language. Unlike the picaresque novel in the West, *Tale of the Marshes* does not limit itself to the exploits of one hero, offering instead 108 different story lines. This multitude of plots is a natural outgrowth of the tradition of the professional storyteller, who attempts to keep the audience's attention by recounting as many adventures as the market will bear.

## Art

Although painting flourished in China under the Han and reached a level of artistic excellence under the Tang, little remains from those periods. The painting of the Song and the Yuan, however, is considered the apogee of painting in traditional China.

Like literature, Chinese painting found part of its inspiration in Buddhist and Daoist sources. Some of the best surviving examples of the Tang period are the Buddhist wall paintings in the caves at Dunhuang, in Central Asia. These paintings were commissioned by Buddhist merchants who stopped at Dunhuang and, while awaiting permission to enter China, wished to give thanks for surviving the rigors of the Silk Road. The entrances to the caves were filled with stones after the tenth century, when Muslim zealots began to destroy Buddhist images throughout Central Asia, and have only recently been uncovered. Like the few surviving Tang scroll paintings, these wall paintings display a love of color and refinement that are reminiscent of styles in India and Persia.

Daoism ultimately had a greater influence than Buddhism on Chinese painting. From early times, Chinese artists removed themselves to the mountains to write and paint and find the *Dao,* or Way, in nature. In the fifth century, one Chinese painter, who was too old to travel, began to paint mountain scenes from memory and announced that depicting nature could function as a substitute for contemplating nature itself. Painting, he said, could be the means of realizing the *Dao.* This explains in part the emphasis on nature in traditional Chinese painting. The word for *landscape* in Chinese means "mountain-water," and the Daoist search for balance between earth and water, hard and soft, *yang* and *yin,* is at play in the tradition of Chinese painting. To enhance the effect, poems were added to the paintings, underscoring the fusion of poetry and painting in Chinese art. Many artists were proficient in both media, the poem inspiring the painting and vice versa.

To represent the totality of nature, Chinese artists attempted to reveal the quintessential forms of the landscape. Rather than depicting the actual realistic shape of a specific mountain, they tried to portray the idea of "mountain." Empty spaces were left in the paintings because in the Daoist vision, one cannot know the whole truth. Daoist influence was also evident in the tendency to portray human beings as insignificant in the midst of nature. In contrast to the focus on the human body and personality in Western art, Chinese art presented people as

**Emperor Ming-huang Traveling to Shu.**
Although the Tang dynasty was a prolific period in the development of Chinese painting, few examples have survived. Fortunately, the practice of copying the works of previous masters was a common tradition in China. Here we see an eleventh-century copy of an eighth-century painting depicting the precipitous journey of Emperor Ming-huang as he was driven by a revolt from the capital into the mountains of southwest China. Rather than portraying the bitterness of the emperor's precarious escape, however, the artist reflected the confidence and brillance of the Tang dynasty through cheerful color and an idyllic landscape.

tiny figures fishing in a small boat, meditating on a cliff, or wandering up a hillside trail, coexisting with but not dominating nature.

The Chinese displayed their paintings on long scrolls of silk or paper that were attached to a wooden cylindrical bar at the bottom. Varying in length from 3 to 20 feet, the paintings were unfolded slowly so that the eye could enjoy each segment, one after the other, beginning at the bottom with water or a village and moving upward into the hills to the mountain peaks and the sky.

By the tenth century, Chinese painters began to eliminate color from their paintings, preferring the challenge of capturing the distilled essence of the landscape in washes of black ink on white silk. Borrowing from calligraphy, now a sophisticated and revered art, they emphasized the brush stroke and created black-and-white landscapes characterized by a gravity of mood and dominated by overpowering mountains.

Other artists turned toward more expressionist and experimental painting. These so-called literati artists were scholars and administrators, highly educated and adept in music, poetry, and painting. Being scholars first and artists second, however, they believed that the purpose of painting was not representation but expression. No longer did painters wish to evoke the feeling of wandering in nature. Instead they tried to reveal to the viewer their own mind and feelings. Like many Western painters in the nineteenth and twentieth centuries, many of these artists were misunderstood by the public and painted only for themselves and one another.

Second only to painting in creativity was the field of ceramics, notably, the manufacture of porcelain. Made of fine clay baked at unusually high temperatures in a kiln, porcelain was first produced during the period after the fall of the Han and became popular during the Tang era. During the Song, porcelain came into its own. Most renowned perhaps are the celadons, in a delicate gray-green, but Song artists also excelled in other colors and techniques. As in painting, Song delicacy and grace contrasted with the bold and often crude styles popular under the Tang. The translucency of Chinese porcelain resulted from a technique that did not reach Europe until the eighteenth century. During the Yuan and the Ming, new styles appeared. Most notable is the cobalt blue-and-white porcelain usually identified with the Ming dynasty, which actually originated during the Yuan. The Ming also produced a multicolored porcelain—often in green, yellow, and red—covered with exotic designs.

Courtesy of William J. Duiker

**Tang Tomb Guardian.** During the Tang dynasty, well-to-do Chinese arranged for their tombs to be stocked with clay figures necessary to satisfy their every need in the afterlife. This practice provides the historian with a visual record of daily court life in imperial China. The more realistic the statue, the more insurance that the deceased would be well served by his musicians, his servants, his horses, and even his favorite dancing girls. Many tomb figures, such as camel drivers from Central Asia, Indian jugglers, and Syrian singers, illustrate the intermingling of peoples along the Silk Road. Shown here is a fierce tomb guardian, stomping on a demon. Painted in brilliant glazes, these ceramic figures are among the most impressive examples of Tang cultural achievement.

## CONCLUSION

**Traditionally, Chinese historians** believed that Chinese history tended to be cyclical. The pattern of history was marked by the rise and fall of great dynasties, interspersed with periods of internal division and foreign invasion. Underlying the waxing and waning of dynasties was the essential continuity of Chinese civilization.

This view of the dynamic forces of Chinese history was long accepted as valid by historians in China and in the West and led many to assert that Chinese history was unique and could not be placed in a European or universal framework. Whereas Western history was linear, leading steadily away from the past, China's always returned to its moorings and was rooted in the values and institutions of antiquity.

In recent years, however, this traditional view of a changeless China has come under increasing challenge from historians who see patterns of change that made the China of the late fifteenth century a very different place from the country that had existed at the rise of the Tang dynasty in 600. To these scholars, China had passed through its own version of the "middle ages" and was on the verge of beginning a linear evolution into a posttraditional society.

As we have seen, China at the beginning of the Ming had advanced in many ways since the end of the great Han dynasty over a thousand years earlier. The industrial and commercial sector had grown considerably in size, complexity, and technological capacity, while in the countryside the concentration of political and economic power in the hands of the aristocracy had been replaced by a more stable and more equitable mixture of landed gentry, freehold farmers, and sharecroppers. In addition, Chinese society had achieved a level of stability and social tranquillity that not only surpassed conditions during the final years of the Han but was the envy of observers from other lands, near and far. The civil service provided an avenue of upward mobility that was unavailable elsewhere in the world, and the state tolerated a diversity of beliefs that responded to the emotional needs and preferences of the Chinese people. In many respects, China's achievements were unsurpassed throughout the world and marked a major advance beyond the world of antiquity.

Yet there were also some key similarities between the China of the Ming and the China of late antiquity. Ming China was still a predominantly agrarian society, with wealth based primarily on the ownership of land. Commercial activities flourished but remained under a high level of government regulation and by no means represented a major proportion of the national income. China also remained a relatively centralized empire based on an official ideology that stressed the virtue of hard work, social conformity, and hierarchy. In foreign affairs, the long frontier struggle with the nomadic peoples along the northern and western frontiers continued unabated.

Thus the significant change that China experienced during its medieval era can probably be best described as change within continuity, an evolutionary working out of trends that had first become visible during the Han dynasty or even earlier. The result was a civilization that was the envy of its neighbors and of the world. It also influenced other states in the region, including Japan, Korea, and Vietnam. It is to these societies along the Chinese rimlands that we now turn.

## TIMELINE

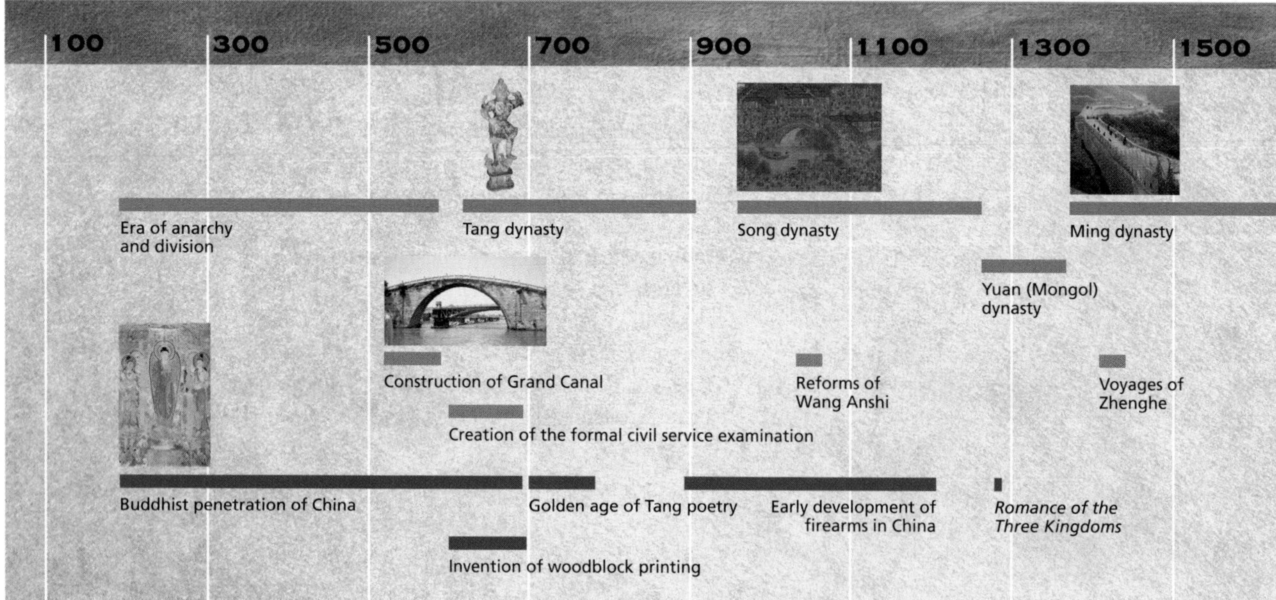

## CHAPTER NOTES

1. The *Travels of Marco Polo* (New York, n.d.), p. 128, 179.
2. Quoted in A. F. Wright, *Buddhism in Chinese History* (Stanford, Calif., 1959), p. 30.
3. Quoted in A. F. Wright, *The Sui Dynasty* (New York, 1978), p. 180.
4. Chu-yu, *P'ing-chow Table Talks,* quoted in R. Temple, *The Genius of China: 3,000 Years of Science, Discovery, and Invention* (New York, 1986), p. 150.
5. Quoted in E. H. Schafer, *The Golden Peaches of Samarkand: A Study of T'ang Exotics* (Berkeley, Calif., 1963), p. 43.
6. Quoted in J. K. Fairbank, E. O. Reischauer, and A. M. Craig, *East Asia: Tradition and Transformation* (Boston, 1973), p. 164.
7. Quoted in R. Grousset, *L'Empire des Steppes* (Paris, 1939), p. 285.
8. A. M. Khazanov, *Nomads and the Outside World* (Cambridge, 1983), p. 241.

## SUGGESTED READING

For an authoritative overview of the early imperial era in China, see **M. Elvin, *The Pattern of the Chinese Past*** (Stanford, Calif., 1973). A global perspective is presented in **S. A. M. Adshead, *China in World History*** (New York, 1988).

A vast body of material is available on almost all periods of early Chinese history. For the post-Han period, see **A. E. Dien,** ed., ***State and Society in Early Medieval China*** (Stanford, Calif., 1990); **F. Mote, *Imperial China*** (Cambridge, 1999); and **D. Twitchett** and **M. Loewe, *Cambridge History of China,*** vol. 3, ***Medieval China*** (Cambridge, 1986).

For a readable treatment of the brief but tempestuous Sui dynasty, see **A. F. Wright, *The Sui Dynasty*** (New York, 1978). The Song dynasty has been studied in considerable detail by historians. For an excellent interpretation, see **J. T. C. Liu, *China Turning Inward: Intellectual Changes in the Early Twelfth Century*** (Cambridge, Mass., 1988). Song problems with the northern frontier are chronicled in **Tao Jing-shen, *Two Sons of Heaven: Studies in Sung-Liao Relations*** (Tucson, Ariz., 1988).

There are a number of good studies on the Mongol period in Chinese history. See, for example, **W. A. Langlois, *China Under Mongol Rule*** (Princeton, N.J., 1981). **M. Rossabi, *Khubilai Khan: His Life and Times*** (Berkeley, Calif., 1988), is a good biography of the dynasty's greatest emperor, while **M. Rossabi,** ed., ***China Among Equals: The Middle Kingdom and Its Neighbors*** (Berkeley, Calif., 1983), deals with foreign affairs. For a provocative interpretation of Chinese relations with nomadic peoples, see **T. J. Barfield, *The Perilous Frontier: Nomadic Empires and China*** (Cambridge, 1989). An analytic account of the dynamics of nomadic society is **A. M. Khazanov, *Nomads and the Outside World*** (Cambridge, 1983).

The emergence of urban culture during this era is analyzed in **C. K. Heng, *Cities of Aristocrats and Bureaucrats: The Development of Medieval Chinese Cityscapes*** (Honolulu, 1999). For perspectives on China as viewed from the outside, see **J. Spence, *The Chan's Great Continent: China in a Western Mirror*** (New York, 1998). China's contacts with foreign cultures are discussed in **J. Waley-Cohen, *The Sextants of Beijing*** (New York, 1999). On the controversial belief that Chinese fleets circled the globe in the fifteenth century, see **G. Menzies, *1421: The Year China Discovered America*** (New York, 2002).

For an introduction to women's issues during this period, consult **P. B. Ebrey, *The Inner Quarters: Marriage and the Lives of Chinese Women in the Sung Period*** (Berkeley Calif., 1993); ***Chu Hsi's Family Rituals*** (Princeton, N.J., 1991); and ***"Women, Marriage, and the Family in Chinese History,"*** in **P. S. Ropp, *Heritage of China: Contemporary Perspectives on Chinese Civilization*** (Berkeley, Calif., 1990). For an overview of Chinese foot binding, see **C. F. Blake, *"Foot-Binding in Neo-Confucian China and the Appropriation of Female Labor," Signs* 19** (Spring 1994).

On Central Asia, two popular accounts are **J. Myrdal, *The Silk Road*** (New York, 1979), and **N. Marty, *The Silk Road*** (Methuen, Mass., 1987). A more interpretive approach is found in **S. A. M. Adshead, *Central Asia in World History*** (New York, 1993). See also **E. T. Grotenhuis,** ed., ***Along the Silk Road*** (Washington, D.C., 2002). Xuan Zang's journey to India is re-created in **R. Bernstein, *Ultimate Journey: Retracing the Path of an Ancient Buddhist Monk Who Crossed Asia in Search of Enlightenment*** (New York, 2000).

The classic work on Chinese literature is **Liu Wu-Chi, *An Introduction to Chinese Literature*** (Bloomington, Ind., 1966). Also consult the more recent and scholarly **S. Owen, *An Anthology of Chinese Literature: Beginnings to 1911*** (New York, 1996), and **V. Mair, *The Columbia Anthology of Traditional Chinese Literature*** (New York, 1994). For poetry, see **Liu Wu-Chi** and **I. Yucheng Lo, *Sunflower Splendor: Three Thousand Years of Chinese Poetry*** (Bloomington, Ind., 1975), and **S. Owen, *The Great Age of Chinese Poetry: The High T'ang*** (New Haven, Conn., 1981), the latter presenting poems in both Chinese and English.

For a comprehensive introduction to Chinese art, see the classic **M. Sullivan, *The Arts of China,*** 4th ed. (Berkeley, Calif., 1999); **M. Tregear, *Chinese Art,*** rev ed. (London, 1997); and **C. Clunas, *Art in China*** (Oxford, 1997). The standard introduction to Chinese painting can be found in **J. Cahill, *Chinese Painting*** (New York, 1985), and **Yang Xin** et al., ***Three Thousand Years of Chinese Painting*** (New Haven, Conn., 1997).

### History Now™

**Enter *HistoryNow* using the access card that is available with this text. *HistoryNow* will assist you in understanding the content in this chapter with lesson plans generated for your needs, as well as provide you with a connection to the *Wadsworth World History Resource Center* (see description below for details).**

### WORLD HISTORY RESOURCE CENTER

**Enter the Resource Center using either your *HistoryNow* access card or your standalone access card for the *Wadsworth World History Resource Center.* Organized by topic, this website includes quizzes; images; over 350 primary source documents; interactive simulations; maps and timelines; movie explorations; and a wealth of other resources. You can read the following documents, and many more, at http://history.wadsworth.com/rc/world**

Buddha Enters Nirvana

Dao De Jing, *Daoism*

Confucius, *The Doctrine of the Mean*

Visit the *World History* Companion Website for chapter quizzes and more.

http://history.wadsworth.com/duikerspielvogel05/

CHAPTER

# 11

# THE EAST ASIAN RIMLANDS: EARLY JAPAN, KOREA, AND VIETNAM

Vietnamese troops defending their homeland against Chinese invaders

Maurice Durand Collection, Yale University Library

## CHAPTER OUTLINE AND FOCUS QUESTIONS

### Japan: Land of the Rising Sun

- How did Japan's geographical location affect the course of its early history, and how did it influence the political structures and social institutions that arose there?

### Korea: Bridge to the East

- What were the main characteristics of economic and social life in early Korea?

### Vietnam: The Smaller Dragon

- What were the main developments in Vietnamese history before 1500? Why were the Vietnamese able to restore their national independence after a millennium of Chinese rule?

## CRITICAL THINKING

- How did Chinese civilization influence the societies that arose in Japan, Korea, and Vietnam during their early history?

WHEN THE EMPEROR FIRST laid his eyes on the rhinoceros horn, the elephant tusks, and the kingfisher plumes that had been brought to him from the land of Yueh, he knew that he must have more of them, so he ordered Commissioner T'u Sui to lead a vast army to extend his imperial authority over the small land to the south of his empire. The battle raged for three years, but the Yueh were not so easy to conquer. According to a Chinese account of the event, "The Yueh people entered the wilderness and lived there with the animals; none consented to be a slave of [Qin]. . . . [They] attacked by night, inflicting on them a great defeat and killing Commissioner T'u Sui."[1]

The date of the event described here was sometime in the late third century B.C.E., and the land of Yueh is today known as Vietnam. Although the Qin were eventually able to subdue their rebellious adversary, future Chinese dynasties would have similar difficulties in controlling the region, and in the tenth century C.E., the people of Yueh rose up once more and restored their independence. To this day, the relationship between China and Vietnam is an uneasy one, marked by alternating periods of cooperation and conflict.

The Qin emperor's disdainful attitude toward his small neighbor should not surprise us. During ancient times, China was the most technologically advanced society in East Asia. To the north and west were pastoral peoples whose military exploits were often impressive but whose political and cultural attainments were still limited, at least by comparison with the great river valley civilizations of the day. In inland areas south of the Yangtze River were scattered clumps of rice farmers and hill peoples, most of whom had not yet entered the era of state building and had little knowledge of the niceties of Confucian ethics. Along the fringes of Chinese civilization were a number of other agricultural societies that were beginning to follow a pattern of development similar to that of China, although somewhat later in time. One of these was the land of Yueh, where a relatively advanced agricultural civilization had been in existence for several hundred years before the area was finally conquered by the Han dynasty in the second century C.E. Another was in the islands of Japan, where an organized society was beginning to take shape just as Chinese administrators were attempting to consolidate imperial rule over the Vietnamese people. On the Korean peninsula, an advanced Neolithic society had already begun to develop a few centuries earlier.

All of these early agricultural societies were eventually influenced to some degree by their great neighbor, China. Vietnam remained under Chinese rule for a thousand years. Korea retained its separate existence but was long a tributary state of China and in many ways followed the cultural example of its larger patron. Only Japan retained both its political independence and its cultural uniqueness. Yet even the Japanese were strongly influenced by the glittering culture of their powerful neighbor, and today many Japanese institutions and customs still bear the imprint of several centuries of borrowing from China. In this chapter, we will take a closer look at these emerging societies along the Chinese rimlands and consider how their cultural achievements reflected or contrasted with those of the Chinese Empire. ◇

# Japan: Land of the Rising Sun

Geography accounts for many of the historical differences between Chinese and Japanese society. Whereas China is a continental civilization, Japan is an island country. It consists of four main islands (see Map 11.1): Hokkaido in the north, the main island of Honshu in the center, and the two smaller islands of Kyushu and Shikoku in the southwest. Its total land area is about 146,000 square miles, about the size of the state of Montana. Japan's main islands are at approximately the same latitude as the eastern seaboard of the United States.

Like the eastern United States, Japan is blessed with a temperate climate. It is slightly warmer on the east coast, which is washed by the Pacific Current sweeping up from the south, and has a number of natural harbors that provide protection from the winds and high waves of the Pacific Ocean. As a consequence, in recent times, the majority of the Japanese people have tended to live along the east coast, especially in the flat plains surrounding the cities of Tokyo, Osaka, and Kyoto. In these favorable environmental conditions, Japanese farmers have been able to harvest two crops of rice annually since early times.

By no means, however, is Japan an agricultural paradise. Like China, much of the country is mountainous, with only about 20 percent of the total land area suitable for cultivation. These mountains are of volcanic origin, since the Japanese islands are located at the juncture of the Asian and Pacific tectonic plates. This location is both an advantage and a disadvantage. Volcanic soils are extremely fertile, which helps explain the exceptionally high productivity of Japanese farmers. At the same time, the area is prone to earthquakes, such as the famous quake of 1923, which destroyed almost the entire city of Tokyo.

The fact that Japan is an island country has had a significant impact on Japanese history. As we have seen, the continental character of Chinese civilization, with its constant threat of invasion from the north, had a number of consequences for Chinese history. One effect was to make the Chinese more sensitive to the preservation of their culture from destruction at the hands of non-Chinese invaders. Proud of their own considerable cultural achievements and their dominant position throughout the region, the Chinese have traditionally been reluctant to dilute the purity of their culture with foreign innovations. Culture more than race is a determinant of the Chinese sense of identity.

By contrast, the island character of Japan probably had the effect of strengthening the Japanese sense of ethnic and cultural distinctiveness. Although the Japanese

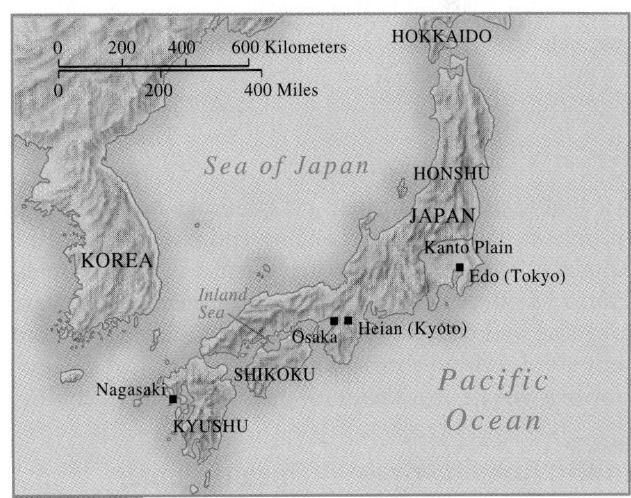


**MAP 11.1 Early Japan.** This map shows key cities in Japan during the early development of the Japanese state. ? What was the original heartland of Japanese civilization on the main island of Honshu? **View an animated version of this map or related maps at** http://history.wadsworth.com/duikerspielvogel05/

## THE EASTERN EXPEDITION OF EMPEROR JIMMU

Japanese myths maintained that the Japanese nation could be traced to the sun goddess Amaterasu, who was the ancestor of the founder of the Japanese imperial family, Emperor Jimmu. This passage from the *Nihon Shoki (The Chronicles of Japan)* describes the campaign in which the "divine warrior" Jimmu occupied the central plains of Japan, symbolizing the founding of the Japanese nation. Legend dates this migration to about 660 B.C.E., but modern historians believe that it took place much later (perhaps as late as the fourth century C.E.) and that the account of the "divine warrior" may represent an effort by Japanese chroniclers to find a local equivalent to the Sage Kings of prehistoric China.

*How does the author of this document justify the actions taken by Emperor Jimmu to defeat his enemies? What evidence does he present to demonstrate that Jimmu has the support of divine forces?*

### *The Chronicles of Japan*

Emperor Jimmu was forty-five years of age when he addressed the assemblage of his brothers and children: "Long ago, this central land of the Reed Plains was bequeathed to our imperial ancestors by the heavenly deities, Takamimusubi-no-Kami and Amaterasu Omikami. . . . However, the remote regions still do not enjoy the benefit of our imperial rule, with each town having its own master and each village its own chief. Each of them sets up his own boundaries and contends for supremacy against other masters and chiefs."

"I have heard from an old deity knowledgeable in the affairs of the land and sea that in the east there is a beautiful land encircled by blue mountains. This must be the land from which our great task of spreading our benevolent rule can begin, for it is indeed the center of the universe. . . . Let us go there, and make it our capital. . . ."

In the winter of that year . . . the Emperor personally led imperial princes and a naval force to embark on his eastern expedition. . . .

When Nagasunehiko heard of the expedition, he said: "The children of the heavenly deities are coming to rob me of my country." He immediately mobilized his troops and intercepted Jimmu's troops at the hill of Kusaka and engaged in a battle. . . . The imperial forces were unable to advance. Concerned with the reversal, the Emperor formulated a new divine plan and said to himself: "I am the descendant of the Sun Goddess, and it is against the way of heaven to face the sun in attacking my enemy. Therefore our forces must retreat to make a show of weakness. After making sacrifice to the deities of heaven and earth, we shall march with the sun on our backs. We shall trample down our enemies with the might of the sun. In this way, without staining our swords with blood, our enemies can be conquered." . . . So, he ordered the troops to retreat to the port of Kusaka and regroup there. . . .

[After withdrawing to Kusaka, the imperial forces sailed southward, landed at a port in the present-day Kita peninsula, and again advanced north toward Yamato.]

The precipitous mountains provided such effective barriers that the imperial forces were not able to advance into the interior, and there was no path they could tread. Then one night Amaterasu Omikami appeared to the Emperor in a dream: "I will send you the Yatagarasu, let it guide you through the land." The following day, indeed, the Yatagarasu appeared flying down from the great expanse of the sky. The Emperor said: "The coming of this bird signifies the fulfillment of my auspicious dream. How wonderful it is! Our imperial ancestor, Amaterasu Omikami, desires to help us in the founding of our empire."

**HistoryNow**™ To read more about Emperor Jimmu, enter the *HistoryNow* documents area using the access card that is available for *World History.*

view of themselves as the most ethnically homogeneous people in East Asia may not be entirely accurate (the modern Japanese probably represent a mix of peoples, much like their neighbors on the continent), their sense of racial and cultural homogeneity has enabled them to import ideas from abroad without worrying that the borrowings will destroy the uniqueness of their own culture.

## A Gift from the Gods: Prehistoric Japan

According to an ancient legend recorded in historical chronicles written in the eighth century C.E., the islands of Japan were formed as a result of the marriage of the god Izanagi and the goddess Izanami. After giving birth to Japan, Izanami gave birth to a sun goddess whose name was Amaterasu. A descendant of Amaterasu later descended to earth and became the founder of the Japanese nation. This Japanese creation myth is reminiscent of similar beliefs in other ancient societies, which often saw themselves as the product of a union of deities. What is interesting about the Japanese version is that it has survived into modern times as an explanation for the uniqueness of the Japanese people and the divinity of the Japanese emperor, who is still believed by some Japanese to be a direct descendant of the sun goddess Amaterasu (see the box above).

Modern scholars have a more prosaic explanation for the origins of Japanese civilization. According to archaeological evidence, the Japanese islands have been occupied by human beings for at least 100,000 years. The earliest known Neolithic inhabitants, known as the Jomon people from the cord pattern of their pottery, lived in the islands as much as 10,000 years ago. They lived by hunting, fishing, and food gathering and probably had not mastered the techniques of agriculture.

Agriculture probably first appeared in Japan sometime during the first millennium B.C.E., although some archaeologists believe that the Jomon people had already learned how to cultivate some food crops considerably earlier than that. About 400 B.C.E., rice cultivation was introduced, probably by immigrants from the mainland by way of the Korean peninsula. Until recently, historians believed that these immigrants drove out the existing inhabitants of the area and gave rise to the emerging Yayoi culture (named for the site near Tokyo where pottery from the period was found). It is now thought, however, that Yayoi culture was a product of a mixture between the Jomon people and the new arrivals, enriched by imports such as wet-rice agriculture, which had been brought by the immigrants from the mainland. In any event, it seems clear that the Yayoi peoples were the ancestors of the vast majority of present-day Japanese.

At first, the Yayoi lived primarily on the southern island of Kyushu, but eventually they moved northward onto the main island of Honshu, conquering, assimilating, or driving out the previous inhabitants of the area, some of whose descendants, known as the Ainu, still live in the northern islands. Finally, in the first centuries C.E., the Yayoi settled in the Yamato plain in the vicinity of the modern cities of Osaka and Kyoto. Japanese legend recounts the story of a "divine warrior" (in Japanese, *Jimmu*) who led his people eastward from the island of Kyushu to establish a kingdom in the Yamato plain (see the box on p. 300).

In central Honshu, the Yayoi set up a tribal society based on a number of clans, called ***uji***. Each *uji* was ruled by a hereditary chieftain, who provided protection to the local population in return for a proportion of the annual harvest. The population itself was divided between a small aristocratic class and the majority of the population, composed of rice farmers, artisans, and other household servants of the aristocrats. Yayoi society was highly decentralized, although eventually the chieftain of the dominant clan in the Yamato region, who claimed to be descended from the sun goddess Amaterasu, achieved a kind of titular primacy. There is no evidence, however, of a central ruler equivalent in power to the Chinese rulers of the Shang and the Zhou eras.

## The Rise of the Japanese State

Although the Japanese had been aware of China for centuries, they paid relatively little attention to their more advanced neighbor until the early seventh century, when the rise of the centralized and expansionistic Tang

Courtesy of William J. Duiker

Courtesy of William J. Duiker

Courtesy of William J. Duiker

SCIENCE & TECHNOLOGY

COMPARATIVE ILLUSTRATION

**The Longhouse.** Many early peoples built longhouses of wood and thatch to store their goods and carry on community activities. Many such structures were erected on heavy pilings to protect the interior from flooding, from insects, or from wild animals. On the left is a model of a sixth century C.E. warehouse in Osaka, Japan. The original was apparently used by local residents to store grain and other foodstuffs. In the center is the reconstruction of a similar structure built originally by Vikings in Denmark. The longhouses on the right are still occupied by families living on Nias, a small island off the coast of Sumatra. The outer walls were built to resemble the hulls of Dutch galleons that plied the seas near Nias during the seventeenth and eighteenth centuries.

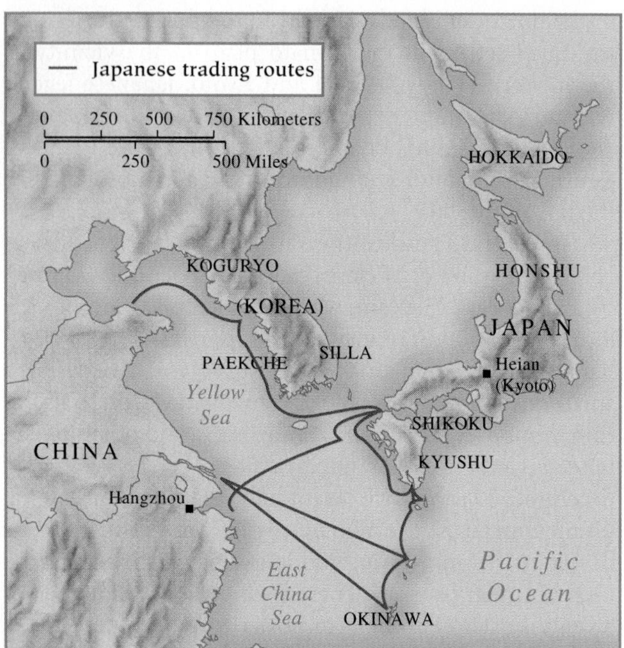


**MAP 11.2 Japan's Relations with China and Korea.** This map shows the Japanese islands at the time of the Yamato state. Maritime routes taken by Japanese traders and missionaries to China are indicated. What are the four major islands of Japan?

**View an animated version of this map or related maps at** http://history.wadsworth.com/duikerspielvogel05/

dynasty presented a challenge. The Tang began to meddle in the affairs of the Korean peninsula, conquering the southwestern coast and arousing anxiety in Japan. Yamato rulers attempted to deal with the potential threat posed by the Chinese in two ways. First, they sought alliances with the remaining Korean states. Second, they attempted to centralize their authority so that they could mount a more effective resistance in the event of a Chinese invasion. The key figure in this effort was Shotoku Taishi (572–622), a leading aristocrat in one of the dominant clans in the Yamato region. Prince Shotoku sent missions to the Tang capital of Chang'an to learn about the political institutions already in use in the relatively centralized Tang kingdom (see Map 11.2).

**Emulating the Chinese Model** Shotoku Taishi then launched a series of reforms to create a new system based roughly on the Chinese model. In the so-called seventeen-article constitution, he called for the creation of a centralized government under a supreme ruler and a merit system for selecting and ranking public officials (see the box on p. 303). His objective was to limit the powers of the hereditary nobility and enhance the prestige and authority of the Yamato ruler, who claimed divine status and was now emerging as the symbol of the unique character of the Japanese nation. In reality, there is evidence that places the origins of the Yamato clan on the Korean peninsula.

After Shotoku Taishi's death in 622, his successors continued to introduce reforms based on the Chinese model to make the government more efficient. In a series of so-called **Taika reforms** (*Taika* means "great change") that began in the mid-seventh century, the Grand Council of State was established, presiding over a cabinet of eight ministries. To the traditional six ministries of Tang China were added ministers representing the central secretariat and the imperial household. The territory of Japan was divided into administrative districts on the Chinese pattern. The rural village, composed ideally of fifty households, was the basic unit of government. The village chief was responsible for "the maintenance of the household registers, the assigning of the sowing of crops and the cultivation of mulberry trees, the prevention of offenses, and the requisitioning of taxes and forced labor." A law code was introduced, and a new tax system was established; now all farmland technically belonged to the state, so taxes were paid directly to the central government rather than through the local nobility, as had previously been the case.

As a result of their new acquaintance with China, the Japanese also developed a strong interest in Buddhism. Some of the first Japanese to travel to China during this period were Buddhist pilgrims hoping to learn more about the exciting new doctrine and bring back scriptures. Buddhism became quite popular among the aristocrats, who endowed wealthy monasteries that became active in Japanese politics. At first, the new faith did not penetrate to the masses, but eventually, popular sects such as the Pure Land sect, an import from China, won many adherents among the common people.

**The Nara Period** Initial efforts to build a new state modeled roughly after the Tang state were successful. After Shotoku Taishi's death in 622, political influence fell into the hands of the powerful Fujiwara clan, which managed to marry into the ruling family and continue the reforms Shotoku had begun. In 710, a new capital, laid out on a grid similar to the great Tang city of Chang'an, was established at Nara, on the eastern edge of the Yamato plain. The Yamato ruler began to use the title "son of Heaven" in the Chinese fashion. In deference to the allegedly divine character of the ruling family, the mandate remained in perpetuity in the imperial house rather than being bestowed on an individual who was selected by Heaven because of his talent and virtue, as was the case in China.

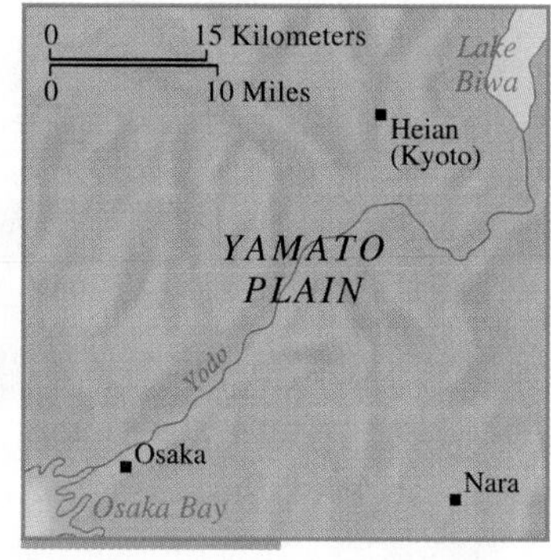


**The Yamato Plain**

Had these reforms succeeded, Japan might have followed the Chinese pattern and developed a centralized bureaucratic government. But as time passed, the central government proved unable to curb the power of the aristocracy. Unlike in Tang China, the civil service examinations in Japan were not open to all but were restricted to individuals of noble birth. Leading officials were awarded large tracts of land, and they and other powerful families

## THE SEVENTEEN-ARTICLE CONSTITUTION

The following excerpt from the *Nihon Shoki (The Chronicles of Japan)* is a passage from the seventeen-article constitution promulgated in 604 C.E. Although the opening section reflects Chinese influence in its emphasis on social harmony, there is also a strong focus on obedience and hierarchy. The constitution was put into practice during the reign of the famous Prince Shotoku.

*What are the key components in this first constitution in the history of Japan? To what degree do its provisions conform to Confucian principles in China?*

### The Chronicles of Japan

Summer, 4th month, 3rd day [12th year of Empress Suiko, 604 C.E.]. The Crown Prince personally drafted and promulgated a constitution consisting of seventeen articles, which are as follows:

I. Harmony is to be cherished, and opposition for opposition's sake must be avoided as a matter of principle. Men are often influenced by partisan feelings, except a few sagacious ones. Hence there are some who disobey their lords and fathers, or who dispute with their neighboring villages. If those above are harmonious and those below are cordial, their discussion will be guided by a spirit of conciliation, and reason shall naturally prevail. There will be nothing that cannot be accomplished.

II. With all our heart, revere the three treasures. The three treasures, consisting of Buddha, the Doctrine, and the Monastic Order, are the final refuge of the four generated beings, and are the supreme objects of worship in all countries. Can any man in any age ever fail to respect these teachings? Few men are utterly devoid of goodness, and men can be taught to follow the teachings. Unless they take refuge in the three treasures, there is no way of rectifying their misdeeds.

III. When an imperial command is given, obey it with reverence. The sovereign is likened to heaven, and his subjects are likened to earth. With heaven providing the cover and earth supporting it, the four seasons proceed in orderly fashion, giving sustenance to all that which is in nature. If earth attempts to overtake the functions of heaven, it destroys everything. . . . If there is no reverence shown to the imperial command, ruin will automatically result. . . .

VII. Every man must be given his clearly delineated responsibility. If a wise man is entrusted with office, the sound of praise arises. If a wicked man holds office, disturbances become frequent. . . . In all things, great or small, find the right man, and the country will be well governed. . . . In this manner, the state will be lasting and its sacerdotal functions will be free from danger.

were able to keep the taxes from the lands for themselves. Increasingly starved for revenue, the central government steadily lost power and influence.

**The Heian Period** In 794, the emperor moved the capital to his family's original power base at nearby Heian, on the site of present-day Kyoto. The new capital was laid out in the now familiar Chang'an checkerboard pattern, but on a larger scale than at Nara. Now increasingly self-confident, the rulers ceased to emulate the Tang and sent no more missions to Chang'an. At Heian, the emperor—as the royal line descended from the sun goddess was now styled—continued to rule in name, but actual power was in the hands of the Fujiwara clan, which had managed through intermarriage to link its fortunes closely with the imperial family. A senior member of the clan began to serve as regent (in practice, the chief executive of the government) for the emperor.

What was occurring was a return to the decentralization that had existed prior to Shotoku Taishi. The central government's attempts to impose taxes directly on the rice lands failed, and rural areas came under the control of powerful families whose wealth was based on the ownership of tax-exempt farmland (called *shoen*). To avoid paying taxes, peasants would often surrender their lands to a local aristocrat, who would then allow the peasants to cultivate the lands in return for the payment of rent. To obtain protection from government officials, these local aristocrats might in turn grant title of their lands to a more powerful aristocrat with influence at court. In return, these individuals would receive inheritable rights to a portion of the income from the estate.

With the decline of central power at Heian, local aristocrats tended to take justice into their own hands and increasingly used military force to protect their interests. A new class of military retainers called the **samurai** emerged whose purpose was to protect the security and property of their patron. They frequently drew their leaders from disappointed aristocratic office seekers, who thus began to occupy a prestigious position in local society, where they often served an administrative as well as a military function. The samurai lived a life of simplicity and self-sacrifice and were expected to maintain an intense and unquestioning loyalty to their lord (see the comparative essay "Feudal Orders Around the World" on p. 307). Bonds of loyalty were also quite strong among members of the samurai class, and homosexuality was common. Like the knights of medieval Europe, the samurai fought on horse-

**The Protective Dragon.** Viewing Heian culture as an era of decadent aristocratic excess, artists of the Kamakura period (1185–1333) strove to express spiritual purpose in their work. Illustrated narrative hand scrolls, for example, either dramatized the torments of hell or praised the lives of Buddhist saints. Here we see a colorful thirteenth-century painting that depicts a seventh-century Korean monk returning from his travels in China. At his departure from the dock, he rejected the love of a beautiful young woman because of his spiritual dedication. Brokenhearted, she plunges into the ocean, thus transforming herself into a dragon to guide him safely back to Korea. The woman was later recognized as a Buddhist saint whose sacrifice was deemed morally appropriate as a model for Japanese women of the era.

back (although a samurai carried a sword and a bow and arrows rather than lance and shield) and were supposed to live by a strict warrior code, known in Japan as **Bushido,** or "way of the warrior" (see the box on p. 308). As time went on, they became a major force and almost a surrogate government in much of the Japanese countryside.

**The Kamakura Shogunate and After** By the end of the twelfth century, as rivalries among noble families led to almost constant civil war, once again centralizing forces asserted themselves. This time the instrument was a powerful noble from a warrior clan named Minamoto Yoritomo (1142–1199), who defeated several rivals and set up his power base on the Kamakura peninsula, south of the modern city of Tokyo. To strengthen the state, he created a more centralized government (the ***bakufu,*** or "tent government") under a powerful military leader, known as the **shogun** (general). The shogun attempted to increase the powers of the central government while reducing rival aristocratic clans to vassal status. This **shogunate system,** in which the emperor was the titular authority while the shogun exercised actual power, served as the political system in Japan until the second half of the nineteenth century.

The system worked effectively, and it was fortunate that it did, because during the next century, Japan faced the most serious challenge it had confronted yet. The Mongols, who had destroyed the Song dynasty in China, were now attempting to assert their hegemony throughout all of Asia (see Chapter 10). In 1266, Emperor Khubilai Khan demanded tribute from Japan. When the Japanese refused, he invaded with an army of over 30,000 troops. Bad weather and difficult conditions forced a retreat, but the Mongols tried again in 1281. An army nearly 150,000 strong landed on the northern coast of Kyushu. The Japanese were able to contain them for two months until virtually the entire Mongol fleet was destroyed by a massive typhoon—a "divine wind" (*kamikaze*). Japan would not face a foreign invader again until American forces landed on the Japanese islands in the summer of 1945.

The resistance to the Mongols had put a heavy strain on the system, however, and in 1333, the Kamakura shogunate was overthrown by a coalition of powerful clans. A new shogun, supplied by the Ashikaga family, arose in Kyoto and attempted to continue the shogunate system. But the Ashikaga were unable to restore the centralized power of their predecessors. With the central government reduced to a shell, the power of the local landed aristocracy increased to an unprecedented degree. Heads of great noble families, now called **daimyo** ("great names"), controlled vast landed estates that owed no taxes to the government or to the court in Kyoto. As clan rivalries continued, the daimyo relied increasingly on the samurai for protection, and political power came into the hands of a loose coalition of noble families.

By the end of the fifteenth century, Japan was again close to anarchy. A disastrous civil conflict known as the Onin War (1467–1477) led to the virtual destruction of the capital city of Kyoto and the disintegration of the shogunate. With the disappearance of any central authority, powerful aristocrats in rural areas now seized total control over large territories and ruled as independent great lords. Territorial rivalries and claims of precedence led to almost constant warfare in this period of "warring states," as it is called (in obvious parallel with a similar era

**CHRONOLOGY Formation of the Japanese State**

| | |
|---|---|
| Shotoku Taishi | 572–622 |
| Era of Taika reforms | Mid-seventh century |
| Nara period | 710–784 |
| Heian (Kyoto) period | 794–1185 |
| Murasaki Shikibu | 978–c. 1016 |
| Minamoto Yoritomo | 1142–1199 |
| Kamakura shogunate | 1185–1333 |
| Mongol invasions | Late thirteenth century |
| Ashikaga period | 1333–1600 |
| Onin War | 1462–1477 |

during the Zhou dynasty in China). The trend back toward central authority did not begin until the last quarter of the sixteenth century.

## Economic and Social Structures

From the time the Yayoi culture was first established on the Japanese islands, Japan was a predominantly agrarian society. Although Japan lacked the spacious valleys and deltas of the river valley societies, its inhabitants were able to take advantage of their limited amount of tillable land and plentiful rainfall to create a society based on the cultivation of wet rice.

**Trade and Manufacturing** As in China, commerce was slow to develop in Japan. During ancient times, each *uji* had a local artisan class, composed of weavers, carpenters, and ironworkers, but trade was essentially local and was regulated by the local clan leaders. With the rise of the Yamato state, a money economy gradually began to develop, although most trade was still conducted through barter until the twelfth century, when metal coins introduced from China became more popular.

Trade and manufacturing began to develop more rapidly during the Kamakura period, with the appearance of trimonthly markets in the larger towns and the emergence of such industries as paper, iron casting, and porcelain. Foreign trade, mainly with Korea and China, began during the eleventh century. Japan exported raw materials, paintings, swords, and other manufactured items in return for silk, porcelain, books, and copper cash. Some Japanese traders were so aggressive in pressing their interests that authorities in China and Korea attempted to limit the number of Japanese commercial missions that could visit each year. Such restrictions were often ignored, however, and encouraged some Japanese traders to turn to piracy.

Significantly, manufacturing and commerce developed rapidly during the more decentralized period of the Ashikaga shogunate and the era of the warring states, perhaps because of the rapid growth in the wealth and autonomy of local daimyo families. Market towns, now operating on a full money economy, began to appear, (see the comparative illustration on p. 306) and local manufacturers formed guilds to protect their mutual interests. Sometimes local peasants would sell products made in their homes, such as clothing made of silk or hemp, household items, or food products, at the markets. In general, however, trade and manufacturing remained under the control of the local daimyo, who would often provide tax breaks to local guilds in return

**The Burning of the Palace.** The Kamakura era is represented in this action-packed thirteenth-century scene from the *Scroll of the Heiji Period,* which depicts the burning of a retired emperor's palace in the middle of the night. Servants and ladies of the court flee in vain from the massive flames. Confusion and violence reign. The determined faces of the samurai warriors only add to the ferocity of the attack.

Courtesy of the Tokyo National Museum

© Scala/Art Resource, NY

FAMILY & SOCIETY

COMPARATIVE ILLUSTRATION

**Urban Life in Medieval Japan and Europe.** Like Europe in the Middle Ages, medieval Japan was largely an agricultural society, but during their medieval periods, both began to develop trade and manufacturing in growing urban areas. Intraregional trade was transported by horse-drawn carts or by boats on rivers or along the coast. Portrayed at the top is a detail from a thirteenth-century scroll depicting the bustle and general confusion of the city of Edo (now Tokyo). On the bottom is a similar scene from a fourteenth-century painting by Ambrogio Lorenzetti. He portrays a street scene in Siena, Italy. In the street are donkeys loaded with goods, a goatherd driving his flock through the town, and two women from the country bringing their goods into the town. In the background, a shoemaker is at work in his shop, a teacher is instructing his students, a man is selling spices, and a tailor is cutting a piece of cloth.

for other benefits. Although Japan remained a primarily agricultural society, it was on the verge of a major advance in manufacturing.

**Daily Life** One of the first descriptions of the life of the Japanese people comes from a Chinese dynastic history from the third century C.E. It describes lords and peasants living in an agricultural society that was based on the cultivation of wet rice. Laws had been enacted to punish offenders, local trade was conducted in markets, and government granaries stored the grain that was paid as taxes (see the box on p. 309).

Life for the common people probably changed very little over the next several hundred years. Most were peasants, who worked on land owned by their lord or, in some cases, by the state or by Buddhist monasteries. By no means, however, were all peasants equal either economically or socially. Although in ancient times, all land was owned by the state and peasants working the land were taxed at an equal rate depending on the nature of the crop, after the Yamato era, variations began to develop. At the top were local officials, who were often well-to-do peasants. They were responsible for organizing collective labor services and collecting tax grain from the peasants and in turn were exempt from such obligations themselves.

The mass of the peasants were under the authority of these local officials. In general, peasants were free to dispose of their harvest as they saw fit after paying their tax quota, but in practical terms, their freedom was limited. Those who were unable to pay the tax sank to the level of ***genin,*** or landless laborers, who could be bought and sold by their proprietors like slaves along with the land on which they worked. Some fled to escape such a fate and attempted to survive by clearing plots of land in the mountains or by becoming bandits.

In addition to the *genin,* the bottom of the social scale was occupied by the ***eta,*** a class of hereditary slaves who were responsible for what were considered degrading oc-

## COMPARATIVE ESSAY

# FEUDAL ORDERS AROUND THE WORLD

When we use the word *feudalism,* we usually think of European knights on horseback clad in iron coats and armed with sword and lance. However, between 800 and 1500, a form of social organization that modern historians called feudalism developed in different parts of the world. By the term *feudalism,* these historians meant a decentralized political order in which local lords owed loyalty and provided military service to a king or more powerful lord. In Europe, a feudal order based on lords and vassals arose between 800 and 900 and flourished for the next four hundred years.

In Japan, a feudal order much like that found in Europe developed between 800 and 1500. By the end of the ninth century, powerful nobles in the countryside, while owing a loose loyalty to the Japanese emperor, began to exercise political and legal power in their own extensive lands. To protect their property and security, these nobles retained samurai, warriors who owed loyalty to the nobles and provided military service for them. Like knights in Europe, the samurai followed a warrior code and fought on horseback, clad in iron. However, they carried a sword and bow and arrow rather than a sword and lance.

In some respects, the political relationships among the Indian states beginning in the fifth century took on the character of the feudal system that emerged in Europe in the Middle Ages. Like medieval European lords, local Indian rajas were technically vassals of the king, but unlike in European feudalism, the relationship was not a contractual one. Still, the Indian model became highly complex, with "inner" and "outer" vassals, depending on their physical or political proximity to the king, and "greater" or "lesser" vassals, depending on their power and influence. As in Europe, the vassals themselves often had vassals.

In the Valley of Mexico, the Aztecs developed a political system between 1300 and 1500 that bore some similarities to the Japanese, Indian, and European feudal orders. Although the Aztec king was a powerful, authoritarian ruler, the local rulers of lands outside the capital city were allowed considerable freedom. However, they did pay tribute to the king and also provided him with military forces. Unlike the knights and samurai of Europe and Japan, however, Aztec warriors were armed with sharp knives made of stone and spears of wood fitted with razor-sharp blades cut from stone.

**Samurai.** During the Kamakura period, painters began to depict the adventures of the new warrior class. Here is an imposing mounted samurai warrior, the Japanese equivalent of the medieval knight in fief-holding Europe. Like his European counterpart, the samurai was supposed to live by a strict moral code and was expected to maintain an unquestioning loyalty to his liege lord. Above all, a samurai's life was one of simplicity and self-sacrifice.

cupations, such as curing leather and burying the dead. The origins of the *eta* are not entirely clear, but they probably were descendants of prisoners of war, criminals, or mountain dwellers who were not related to the dominant Yamato peoples. As we shall see, the *eta* are still a distinctive part of Japanese society, and although their full legal rights are guaranteed under the current constitution, discrimination against them is not uncommon.

Daily life for ordinary people in early Japan resembled that of their counterparts throughout much of Asia. The vast majority lived in small villages, several of which normally made up a single *shoen.* Housing was simple. Most lived in small two-room houses of timber, mud, or thatch, with dirt floors covered by straw or woven mats (the origin, perhaps, of the well-known *tatami,* or woven-mat floor, of more modern times). Their diet consisted of rice (if some was left after the payment of the grain tax), wild grasses, millet, roots, and some fish and birds. Life must have been difficult at best; as one eighth-century poet lamented:

*Here I lie on straw*
*Spread on bare earth,*
*With my parents at my pillow,*
*My wife and children at my feet,*
*All huddled in grief and tears.*
*No fire sends up smoke*
*At the cooking place,*
*And in the cauldron*
*A spider spins its web.*[2]

## JAPAN'S WARRIOR CLASS

The samurai was the Japanese equivalent of the medieval European knight. Like the latter, the samurai fought on horseback and was expected to adhere to a strict moral code. Although this passage comes from a document dating only to the 1500s, a distinct mounted warrior class had already begun to emerge in Japan as early as the tenth century. It shows the importance of hierarchy and duty in a society influenced by the doctrine of Confucius. Note the similarity with Krishna's discourse on the duties of an Indian warrior in Chapter 2.

*How would you compare the duties of the samurai with those of a knight in medieval Europe? Are his responsibilities closer to those of a Confucian "gentleman" in China?*

### The Way of the Samurai

The master once said: . . . Generation after generation men have taken their livelihood from tilling the soil, or devised and manufactured tools, or produced profit from mutual trade, so that peoples' needs were satisfied. Thus the occupations of farmer, artisan, and merchant necessarily grew up as complementary to one another. However, the samurai eats food without growing it, uses utensils without manufacturing them, and profits without buying or selling. . . . The samurai is one who does not cultivate, does not manufacture, and does not engage in trade, but it cannot be that he has no function at all as a samurai. . . .

If one deeply fixes his attention on what I have said and examines closely one's own function, it will become clear what the business of the samurai is. The business of the samurai consists in reflecting on his own station in life, in discharging loyal service to his master if he has one, in deepening his fidelity in associations with friends, and, with due consideration of his own position, in devoting himself to duty above all. . . . The samurai dispenses with the business of the farmer, artisan, and merchant and confines himself to practicing this Way; should there be someone in the three classes of the common people who transgresses against these moral principles, the samurai summarily punishes him and thus upholds proper moral principles in the land. . . . Outwardly he stands in physical readiness for any call to service, and inwardly he strives to fulfill the Way of the lord and subject, friend and friend, father and son, older and younger brother, and husband and wife. Within his heart he keeps to the ways of peace, but without he keeps his weapons ready for use. The three classes of the common people make him their teacher and respect him. By following his teachings, they are enabled to understand what is fundamental and what is secondary.

Herein lies the Way of the samurai, the means by which he earns his clothing, food, and shelter; and by which his heart is put at ease, and he is enabled to pay back at length his obligation to his lord and the kindness of his parents. Were there no such duty, it would be as though one were to steal the kindness of one's parents, greedily devour the income of one's master, and make one's whole life a career of robbery and brigandage. This would be very grievous.

**The Role of Women** Evidence about the relations between men and women in early Japan presents a mixed picture. The Chinese dynastic history reports that "in their meetings and daily living, there is no distinction between . . . men and women." It notes that a woman "adept in the ways of shamanism" had briefly ruled Japan in the third century C.E. But it also remarks that polygyny was common, with nobles normally having four or five wives and commoners two or three.[3] An eighth-century law code guaranteed the inheritance rights of women, and wives abandoned by their husbands were permitted to obtain a divorce and remarry. A husband could divorce his wife if she did not produce a male child, committed adultery, disobeyed her parents-in-law, talked too much, engaged in theft, was jealous, or had a serious illness.[4]

When Buddhism was introduced, women were initially relegated to a subordinate position in the new faith. Although they were permitted to take up monastic life—many widows entered a monastery at the death of their husbands—they were not permitted to visit Buddhist holy places, nor were they even (in the accepted wisdom) equal with men in the afterlife. One Buddhist commentary from the late thirteenth century said that a woman could not attain enlightenment because "her sin is grievous, and so she is not allowed to enter the lofty palace of the great Brahma, nor to look upon the clouds which hover over his ministers and people."[5] Other Buddhist scholars were more egalitarian: "Learning the Law of Buddha and achieving release from illusion have nothing to do with whether one happens to be a man or a woman."[6] Such views ultimately prevailed, and women were eventually allowed to participate fully in Buddhist activities in medieval Japan.

Although women did not possess the full legal and social rights of their male counterparts, they played an active role at various levels of Japanese society. Aristocratic women were prominent at court, and some, such as the author Lady Murasaki, became renowned for their artistic or literary talents (see the box on p. 310). Though few commoners could aspire to such prominence, women often appear in the scroll paintings of the period along with men, doing the spring planting, threshing and hulling the rice, and acting as carriers, peddlers, salespersons, and entertainers.

## LIFE IN THE LAND OF WA

Some of the earliest descriptions of Japan come from Chinese sources. The following passage from the *History of the Wei Dynasty* was written in the late third century C.E. The term *Wa* is a derogatory word meaning "dwarf" and was frequently used in China to refer to the Japanese people. The author of this passage, while remarking on the strange habits of the Japanese, writes without condescension.

*What does this document tell us about the nature of Japanese society in the third century C.E.? What does it tell us about the point of view of the author?*

### *History of the Wei Dynasty*

The people of Wa make their abode in the mountainous islands located in the middle of the ocean to the southeast of the Taifang prefecture. . . .

All men, old or young, are covered by tattoos. Japanese fishers revel in diving to catch fish and shell-fish. Tattoos are said to drive away large fish and water predators. They are considered an ornament. . . . Men allow their hair to cover both of their ears and wear head-bands. They wear loincloths wrapped around their bodies and seldom use stitches. Women gather their hair at the ends and tie it in a knot and then pin it to the top of their heads. They make their clothes in one piece, and cut an opening in the center for their heads. They plant wet-field rice, China-grass [a type of nettle], and mulberry trees. They raise cocoons and reel the silk off the cocoons. They produce clothing made of China-grass, of coarse silk, and of cotton. In their land, there are no cows, horses, tigers, leopards, sheep, or swan. They fight with halberds, shields, and wooden bows. . . . Their arrows are made of bamboo, and iron and bone points make up the arrowhead.

People . . . live long, some reaching one hundred years of age, and others to eighty or ninety years. Normally men of high echelon have four or five wives, and the plebeians may have two or three. When the law is violated, the light offender loses his wife and children by confiscation, and the grave offender has his household and kin exterminated. There are class distinctions within the nobility and the base, and some are vassals of others. There are mansions and granaries erected for the purpose of collecting taxes. . . .

When plebeians meet the high-echelon men on the road, they withdraw to the grassy area [side of the road] hesitantly. When they speak or are spoken to, they either crouch or kneel with both hands on the ground to show their respect. When responding they say "aye," which corresponds to our affirmative "yes."

## In Search of the Pure Land: Religion in Early Japan

In Japan, as elsewhere, religious belief began with the worship of nature spirits. Early Japanese worshiped spirits, called ***kami,*** who resided in trees, rivers and streams, and mountains. They also believed in ancestral spirits present in the atmosphere. In Japan, these beliefs eventually evolved into a kind of state religion called **Shinto** (the Sacred Way or the Way of the Gods) that is still practiced today. Shinto still serves as an ideological and emotional force that knits the Japanese into a single people and nation.

Shinto does not have a complex metaphysical superstructure or an elaborate moral code. It does require certain ritual acts, usually undertaken at a shrine, and a process of purification, which may have originated in primitive concerns about death, childbirth, illness, and menstruation. This traditional concern about physical purity may help explain the strong Japanese concern for personal cleanliness and the practice of denying women entrance to the holy places.

Another feature of Shinto is its stress on the beauty of nature and the importance of nature itself in Japanese life. Shinto shrines are usually located in places of exceptional beauty and are often dedicated to a nearby physical feature. As time passed, such primitive beliefs contributed to the characteristic Japanese love of nature. In this sense, early Shinto beliefs have been incorporated into the lives of all Japanese.

In time, Shinto evolved into a state doctrine that was linked with belief in the divinity of the emperor and the sacredness of the Japanese nation. A national shrine was established at Ise, north of the early capital of Nara, where the emperor annually paid tribute to the sun goddess. But although Shinto had evolved well beyond its primitive origins, like its counterparts elsewhere it could not satisfy all the religious and emotional needs of the Japanese people. For those needs, the Japanese turned to Buddhism.

As we have seen, Buddhism was introduced into Japan from China during the sixth century C.E. and had begun to spread beyond the court to the general population by the eighth century. As in China, most Japanese saw no contradiction between worshiping both the Buddha and their local nature gods, many of whom were considered to be later manifestations of the Buddha. Most of the Buddhist sects that had achieved popularity in China were established in Japan, and many of them attracted powerful patrons at court. Great monasteries were built that competed in wealth and influence with the noble families that had traditionally ruled the country.

## Seduction of the Akashi Lady

Out of the Japanese tradition of female introspective prose appeared one of the world's truly great novels, *The Tale of Genji,* written around the year 1000 by the diarist and court author Murasaki Shikibu, known as Lady Murasaki. It is even today revered for its artistic refinement and sensitivity and has influenced Japanese writing for a millennium. A panoramic portrayal of court life in tenth-century Japan, it traces the life and loves of the courtier Genji as he strives to remain in favor with those in power while at the same time pursuing his cult of love and beauty. Truly remarkable is the character of Genji himself, revealed to the reader through myriad psychological observations. In this excerpt, Genji has just seduced a lady at court and now feels misgivings at having betrayed his child bride. A *koto* is a Japanese stringed instrument similar to a zither.

*Why does this thousand-year-old passage speak to readers today with such a contemporary meaning?*

### Lady Murasaki, *The Tale of Genji*

A curtain string brushed against a koto, to tell him that she had been passing a quiet evening at her music.

"And will you not play for me on the koto of which I have heard so much?". . .

This lady had not been prepared for an incursion and could not cope with it. She fled to an inner room. How she could have contrived to bar it he could not tell, but it was very firmly barred indeed. Though he did not exactly force his way through, it is not to be imagined that he left matters as they were. Delicate, slender–she was almost too beautiful. Pleasure was mingled with pity at the thought that he was imposing himself upon her. She was even more pleasing than reports from afar had had her. The autumn night, usually so long, was over in a trice. Not wishing to be seen, he hurried out, leaving affectionate assurances behind.

Genji called in secret from time to time. The two houses being some distance apart, he feared being seen by fishers, who were known to relish a good rumor, and sometimes several days would elapse between his visits. . . .

Genji dreaded having Murasaki [his bride] learn of the affair. He still loved her more than anyone, and he did not want her to make even joking reference to it. She was a quiet, docile lady, but she had more than once been unhappy with him. Why, for the sake of brief pleasure, had he caused her pain? He wished it were all his to do over again. The sight of the Akashi lady only brought new longing for the other lady.

He got off a more earnest and affectionate letter than usual, at the end of which he said: "I am in anguish at the thought that, because of foolish occurrences for which I have been responsible but have had little heart, I might appear in a guise distasteful to you. There has been a strange, fleeting encounter. That I should volunteer this story will make you see, I hope, how little I wish to have secrets from you. Let the gods be my judges.

*"It was but the fisherman's brush with the salty sea pine.*
*Followed by a tide of tears of longing."*

Her reply was gentle and unreproachful, and at the end of it she said: "That you should have deigned to tell me a dreamlike story which you could not keep to yourself calls to mind numbers of earlier instances.

*"Naive of me, perhaps; yet we did make our vows.*
*And now see the waves that wash the Mountain of Waiting!"*

It was the one note of reproach in a quiet, undemanding letter. He found it hard to put down, and for some nights he stayed away from the house in the hills.

Perhaps the two most influential Buddhist sects were the **Pure Land** (Jodo) sect and **Zen** (in Chinese, Chan or Ch'an). The Pure Land sect, which taught that devotion alone could lead to enlightenment and release, was very popular among the common people, for whom monastic life was one of the few routes to upward mobility. Among the aristocracy, the most influential school was Zen, which exerted a significant impact on Japanese life and culture during the era of the warring states. In its emphasis on austerity, self-discipline, and communion with nature, Zen complemented many traditional beliefs in Japanese society and became an important component of the samurai warrior's code.

In Zen teachings, there were various ways to achieve enlightenment (***satori*** in Japanese). Some stressed that it could be achieved suddenly. One monk, for example, reportedly achieved *satori* by listening to the sound of a bamboo stick striking against roof tiles, another by carefully watching the opening of peach blossoms in the spring. But other practitioners, sometimes called adepts, said that enlightenment could come only through studying the scriptures and arduous self-discipline (known as *zazen,* or "seated Zen"). Seated Zen involved a lengthy process of meditation that cleansed the mind of all thoughts so that it could concentrate on the essential.

### Sources of Traditional Japanese Culture

Nowhere is the Japanese genius for blending indigenous and imported elements into an effective whole better demonstrated than in culture. In such widely diverse fields as art, architecture, sculpture, and literature, the Japanese from early times showed an impressive capacity

## A Sample of Linked Verse

One of the distinctive features of medieval Japanese literature was the technique of "linked verse." In a manner similar to haiku poetry today, such poems, known as *renga,* were written by groups of individuals who would join together to compose the poem, verse by verse. The following example, by three famous poets named Sogi, Shohaku, and Socho, is one of the most famous of the period.

*How do these Japanese poems differ from the poems produced in China during the Tang dynasty and quoted in Chapter 10?*

### The Three Poets at Minase

*Snow clinging to slope,* Sogi
*On mist-enshrouded mountains*
*At eveningtime.*
*In the distance flows* Shohaku
*Through plum-scented villages.*
*Willows cluster* Socho
*In the river breeze*
*As spring appears.*
*The sound of a boat being poled* Sogi
*In the clearness at dawn*
*Still the moon lingers* Shohaku
*As fog o'er-spreads*
*The night.*
*A frost-covered meadow;* Socho
*Autumn has drawn to a close.*
*Against the wishes* Sogi
*Of droning insects*
*The grasses wither.*

History Now™ To read more early Japanese poetry, enter the *HistoryNow* documents area using the access card that is available for *World History.*

to borrow selectively from abroad without destroying essential native elements.

Growing contact with China during the rise of the Yamato state stimulated Japanese artists. Missions sent to China and Korea during the seventh and eighth centuries returned with examples of Tang literature, sculpture, and painting, all of which influenced the Japanese.

**Literature** Borrowing from Chinese models was somewhat complicated, however, since the early Japanese had no writing system for recording their own spoken language and initially adopted the Chinese written language for writing. But resourceful Japanese soon began to adapt the Chinese written characters so that they could be used for recording the Japanese language. In some cases, Chinese characters were given Japanese pronunciations. But Chinese characters ordinarily could not be used to record Japanese words, which normally contain more than one syllable. Sometimes the Japanese simply used Chinese characters as phonetic symbols that were combined to form Japanese words. Later they simplified the characters into phonetic symbols that were used alongside Chinese characters. This hybrid system continues to be used today.

At first, most educated Japanese preferred to write in Chinese, and a court literature—consisting of essays, poetry, and official histories—appeared in the classical Chinese language. But spoken Japanese never totally disappeared among the educated classes and eventually became the instrument of a unique literature. With the lessening of Chinese cultural influence in the tenth century, Japanese verse resurfaced. Between the tenth and fifteenth centuries, twenty imperial anthologies of poetry were compiled. Initially, they were written primarily by courtiers, but with the fall of the Heian court and the rise of the warrior and merchant classes, all literate segments of society began to produce poetry.

Japanese poetry is unique. It expresses its themes in a simple form, a characteristic stemming from traditional Japanese aesthetics, Zen religion, and the language itself. The aim of the Japanese poet was to create a mood, perhaps the melancholic effect of gently falling cherry blossoms or leaves. With a few specific references, the poet suggested a whole world, just as Zen Buddhism sought enlightenment from a sudden perception. Poets often alluded to earlier poems by repeating their images with small changes, a technique that was viewed not as plagiarism but as an elaboration on the meaning of the earlier poem.

By the fourteenth century, the technique of the "linked verse" had become the most popular form of Japanese poetry. Known as *haiku,* it is composed of seventeen syllables divided into lines of five, seven, and five syllables. The poems usually focused on images from nature and the mutability of life. Often the poetry was written by several individuals alternately composing verses and linking them together into long sequences of hundreds and even thousands of lines (see the box above).

Poetry served a unique function at the Heian court, where it was the initial means of communication between lovers. By custom, aristocratic women were isolated from all contact with men outside their immediate family and spent their days hidden behind screens. Some amused themselves by writing poetry. When courtship began, poetic exchanges were the only means a woman had to attract her prospective lover, who would be enticed solely by her poetic art.

During the Heian period, male courtiers wrote in Chinese, believing that Chinese civilization was superior and worthy of emulation. Like the Chinese, they viewed prose fiction as "vulgar gossip." Nevertheless, from the ninth century to the twelfth, Japanese women were prolific writers of prose fiction in Japanese (see the box on p. 310). Excluded from school, they learned to read and write at home and wrote diaries and stories to pass the time. Some of the most talented women were invited to court as authors in residence.

In the increasingly pessimistic world of the warring states of Kamakura (1185–1333), Japanese novels typically focused on a solitary figure who is aloof from the refinements of the court and faces battle and possibly death. Another genre, that of the heroic war tale, came out of the new warrior class. These works described the military exploits of warriors, coupled with an overwhelming sense of sadness and loneliness.

The famous classical Japanese drama known as *No* also originated during this period. *No* developed out of a variety of entertainment forms, such as dancing and juggling, that were part of the native tradition or had been imported from China and other regions of Asia. The plots were normally based on stories from Japanese history or legend. Eventually, *No* evolved into a highly stylized drama in which the performers wore masks and danced to the accompaniment of instrumental music. Like much of Japanese culture, *No* was restrained, graceful, and refined.

**Art and Architecture** In art and architecture, as in literature, the Japanese pursued their interest in beauty, simplicity, and nature. To some degree, Japanese artists and architects were influenced by Chinese forms. As they became familiar with Chinese architecture, Japanese rulers and aristocrats tried to emulate the splendor of Tang civilization and began constructing their palaces and temples in Chinese style.

During the Heian period (794–1185), the search for beauty was reflected in various art forms, such as narrative hand scrolls, screens, sliding door panels, fans, and lacquer decoration. As in the case of literature, nature themes dominated, such as seashore scenes, a spring rain, moon and mist, or flowering wisteria and cherry blossoms. All were intended to evoke an emotional response on the part of the viewer. Japanese painting suggested the frail beauty of nature by presenting it on a smaller scale. The majestic mountain in a Chinese painting became a more intimate Japanese landscape with rolling hills and a rice field. Faces were rarely shown, and human drama was indicated by a woman lying prostrate or hiding her face in her sleeve. Tension was shown by two people talking at a great distance or with their backs to one another.

During the Kamakura period (1185–1333), the hand scroll with its physical realism and action-packed paintings of the new warrior class achieved great popularity. Reflecting these chaotic times, the art of portraiture flourished, and a scroll would include a full gallery of warriors and holy men in starkly realistic detail, including such unflattering features as stubble, worry lines on a forehead, and crooked teeth. Japanese sculptors also produced naturalistic wooden statues of generals, nobles, and saints. By far the most distinctive, however, were the fierce heavenly "guardian kings," who still intimidate the viewer today.

**Guardian Kings.** Larger than life and intimidating in its presence, this thirteenth-century wooden statue departs from the refined atmosphere of the Heian court and pulsates with the masculine energy of the Kamakura period. Placed strategically at the entrance to Buddhist shrines, guardian kings such as this one protected the temple and the faithful. In contrast to the refined atmosphere of the Fujiwara court, the Kamakura era was a warrior's world.

Zen Buddhism, an import from China in the thirteenth century, also influenced Japanese aesthetics. With its emphasis on immediate enlightenment without recourse to intellectual analysis and elaborate ritual, Zen reinforced the Japanese predilection for simplicity and self-discipline. During this era, Zen philosophy found expression in the Japanese garden, the tea ceremony, the art of flower arranging, pottery and ceramics, and miniature plant display (the famous ***bonsai,*** literally "pot scenery").

Landscapes served as an important means of expression in both Japanese art and architecture. Japanese gardens were initially modeled on Chinese examples. Early court texts during the Heian period emphasized the importance of including a stream or pond when creating a garden. The landscape surrounding the fourteenth-century Golden Pavilion in Kyoto displays a harmony of garden, water, and architecture that makes it one of the

Courtesy of William J. Duiker

© Charles Gupton, Tony Stone Images/Getty Images

**In the Garden.** In traditional China and Japan, gardens were meant to free the observer's mind of mundane concerns, offering spiritual refreshment in the quiet of nature. Chinese gardens were designed to reconstruct an orderly microcosm of nature, where the harassed Confucian official could find spiritual renewal. Wandering within a constantly changing perspective consisting of ponds, trees, rocks, and pavilions, he could imagine himself immersed in a monumental landscape. In this garden in Suzhou on the left, the rocks represent towering mountains to suggest the Daoist sense of withdrawal and eternity, reducing the viewer to a tiny speck in the grand flow of life.

In Japan, the traditional garden reflected the Zen Buddhist philosophy of simplicity, restraint, allusion, and tranquillity. In this garden at the Ryoanji temple in Kyoto, the rocks are meant to suggest mountains rising from a sea of pebbles. Such gardens served as an aid to meditation, inspiring the viewer to join with comrades in composing "linked verse" (see the box on p. 311).

treasures of the world. Because of the shortage of water in the city, later gardens concentrated on rock composition, using white pebbles to represent water.

Like the Japanese garden, the tea ceremony represents the fusion of Zen and aesthetics. Developed in the fifteenth century, it was practiced in a simple room devoid of external ornament except for a *tatami* floor, sliding doors, and an alcove with a writing desk and asymmetrical shelves. The participants could therefore focus completely on the activity of pouring and drinking tea. "Tea and Zen have the same flavor," goes the Japanese saying. Considered the ultimate symbol of spiritual deliverance, the tea ceremony had great aesthetic value and moral significance in traditional times as well as today.

Courtesy of William J. Duiker

**The Golden Pavilion in Kyoto.** The landscape surrounding the Golden Pavilion displays a harmony of garden, water, and architecture that makes it one of the treasures of the world. Constructed in the fourteenth century as a retreat for the shoguns to withdraw from their administrative chores, the pavilion is named for the gold foil that covered its exterior. Completely destroyed by an arsonist in 1950 as a protest against the commercialism of modern Buddhism, it was rebuilt and reopened in 1987. The use of water as a backdrop is especially noteworthy in Chinese and Japanese landscapes, as well as in the Middle East.

## Japan and the Chinese Model

Few societies in Asia have historically been as isolated as Japan. Cut off from the mainland by 120 miles of frequently turbulent ocean, the Japanese had only minimal contact with the outside world during most of their early development.

Whether this isolation was ultimately beneficial to Japanese society cannot be determined. On one hand, the lack of knowledge of developments taking place elsewhere probably delayed the process of change in Japan. On the other hand, the Japanese were spared the destructive invasions that afflicted other ancient civilizations. Certainly, once the Japanese became acquainted with Chinese culture at the height of the Tang era, they were quick to take advantage of the opportunity. In the space of a few decades, the young state adopted many aspects of Chinese society and culture and thereby introduced major changes into Japanese life.

Nevertheless, Japanese political institutions failed to follow all aspects of the Chinese pattern. Despite Prince Shotoku's effort to make effective use of the imperial traditions of Tang China, the decentralizing forces in Japanese society remained dominant throughout the period under discussion in this chapter. Adoption of the Confucian civil service examination did not lead to a breakdown of Japanese social divisions; instead, the examination was administered in a manner that preserved and strengthened them. Although Buddhist and Daoist doctrines made a significant contribution to Japanese religious practices, Shinto beliefs continued to play a major role in shaping the Japanese worldview.

Why Japan did not follow the Chinese road to centralized authority has been the subject of debate among historians. Some argue that the answer lies in differing cultural traditions, while others suggest that Chinese institutions and values were introduced too rapidly to be assimilated effectively by Japanese society. One factor may have been the absence of a foreign threat (except for the Mongols) in Japan. A recent view holds that diseases (such as smallpox and measles) imported inadvertently from China led to a marked decline in the population of the islands, reducing the food output and preventing the population from coalescing in more compact urban centers.

In any event, Japan was not the only society in Asia to assimilate ideas from abroad while at the same time preserving customs and institutions inherited from the past. Across the Sea of Japan to the west and several thousand miles to the southwest, other Asian peoples were embarked on a similar journey. We now turn to their experience.

# Korea: Bridge to the East

No society in East Asia was more strongly influenced by the Chinese model than Korea. Slightly larger than the state of Minnesota, the Korean peninsula was probably first settled by Altaic-speaking fishing and hunting peoples from neighboring Manchuria during the Neolithic Age. Because the area is relatively mountainous (only about one-fifth of the peninsula is adaptable to cultivation), farming was apparently not practiced until about 2000 B.C.E. The other aspect of Korea's geography that has profoundly affected its history is its proximity to both China and Japan.

In 109 B.C.E., the northern part of the peninsula came under direct Chinese rule. During the next several generations, the area was ruled by the Han dynasty, which divided the territory into provinces and introduced Chinese institutions. With the decline of the Han in the third century C.E., power gradually shifted to local tribal leaders, who drove out the Chinese administrators but continued to absorb Chinese cultural influence. Eventually, three separate kingdoms emerged on the peninsula: Koguryo in the north, Paekche in the southwest, and Silla in the southeast. The Japanese, who had recently established their own state on the Yamato plain, maintained a small colony on the southern coast.

Courtesy of the Korean Cultural Service Library

**Korean Royal Crown.** The Silla dynasty was renowned for the high quality of its gold, jewelry, crowns, and sword sheaths. Shown here is a jewel-inlaid royal crown of the fifth century C.E. that was excavated from a royal tomb in eastern Korea. Although much Silla artwork reflects Chinese influence, royal crowns located in Silla tombs often contain antlerlike motifs, reflecting the animistic traditions of Korea's pre-Chinese past. The comma-shaped jewels symbolize the king's Heaven-sanctioned authority on earth.

Courtesy of William J. Duiker

**Pulguksa Bell Tower.** Among the greatest architectural achievements on the Korean peninsula is the Pulguksa (Monastery of the Land of Buddha), built near Kyongju, the ancient capital of Silla, in the eighth century C.E. Shown here is the bell tower, located in the midst of beautiful parklands on the monastery grounds. Young Korean couples often come to this monastery after their weddings to be photographed in the stunning surroundings.

## The Three Kingdoms

From the fourth to the seventh centuries, the three kingdoms were bitter rivals for influence and territory on the peninsula. At the same time, all began to absorb Chinese political and cultural institutions. Chinese influence was most notable in Koguryo, where Buddhism was introduced in the late fourth century C.E. and the first Confucian academy on the peninsula was established in the capital at Pyongyang. All three kingdoms also appear to have accepted a tributary relationship with one or another of the squabbling states that emerged in China after the fall of the Han. The kingdom of Silla, less exposed than its two rivals to Chinese influence, was at first the weakest of the three, but eventually its greater internal cohesion—perhaps a consequence of the tenacity of its tribal traditions—enabled it to become the dominant power on the peninsula. Then the rulers of Silla forced the Chinese to withdraw from all but the area adjacent to the Yalu River. To pacify the haughty Chinese, Silla accepted tributary status under the Tang dynasty. The remaining Japanese colonies in the south were eliminated.



**Korea's Three Kingdoms**

With the country unified for the first time, the rulers of Silla attempted to use Chinese political institutions and ideology to forge a centralized state. Buddhism, now rising in popularity, became the state religion, and Korean monks followed the paths of their Japanese counterparts on journeys to the Middle Kingdom. Chinese architecture and art became dominant in the capital at Kyongju and other urban centers, and the written Chinese language became the official means of communication at court. But powerful aristocratic families, long dominant in the southeastern part of the peninsula, were still influential at court. They were able to prevent the adoption of the Tang civil service examination system and resisted the distribution of manorial lands to the poor. The failure to adopt the Chinese model was fatal. Squabbling among noble families steadily increased, and after the assassination of the king of Silla in 780, the country sank into civil war.

## The Flower Garden Scripture

By the eighth century, Buddhism had come to Korea from China, and like their counterparts in Christian Europe, Korean monks could accumulate merit toward salvation by copying the scriptures. In this passage, the eighth-century Master Yongi of Hwangyong monastery has volunteered to copy a scripture as a way of expressing gratitude for the love of his parents and assisting others in following the Buddhist Eightfold Way to wisdom. Note the careful attention to ritual as the process is brought to realization. This scripture, which was discovered in 1979, consisted of two scrolls of thirty white papers joined together, with characters in black ink. Each scroll was 45 feet long.

*What is the purpose of prescribing certain rituals for setting up this Buddhist scripture? Do you think precise regulations such as these have been prescribed in other religions as well?*

### An Eighth-Century Buddhist Scripture

The scripture is made as follows: First scented water is sprinkled around the roots of a paperbark mulberry tree to quicken its growth; the bark is then peeled and pounded to make paper with a clean surface. The copyists, the artisans who make the centerpiece of the scroll, and the painters who draw the images of buddhas and bodhisattvas all receive the bodhisattva ordination and observe abstinence. After relieving themselves, sleeping, eating, or drinking, they take a bath in scented water before returning to the work. Copyists are adorned with new pure garments, loose trousers, a coarse crown, and a deva crown. Two azure-clad boys sprinkle water on their heads and . . . azure-clad boys and musicians perform music. The processions to the copying site are headed by one who sprinkles scented water on their path, another who scatters flowers, a dharma master who carries a censer, and another dharma master who chants Buddhist verses. Each of the copyists carries incense and flowers and invokes the name of the Buddha as he progresses.

Upon reaching the site, all take refuge in the Three Jewels (the Buddha, the Dharma, and the Order), make three bows, and offer the *Flower Garland Scripture* and others to buddhas and bodhisattvas. Then they sit down and copy the scripture, make the centerpiece of the scroll, and paint the buddhas and bodhisattvas. Thus, azure-clad boys and musicians cleanse everything before a piece of relic is placed in the center.

Now I make a vow that the copied scripture will not break till the end of the future. . . . If all living beings rely on this scripture, they shall witness the Buddha, listen to his dharma, worship the relic, aspire to enlightenment without backsliding, cultivate the vows of the Universally Worthy Bodhisattva, and achieve Buddhahood.

## The Rise of the Koryo Dynasty

In the early tenth century, a new dynasty called Koryo (the root of the modern name of the country in English) arose in the north. The new kingdom adopted Chinese political institutions in an effort to strengthen its power and unify its territory. The civil service examination system was introduced in 958, but as in Japan, the bureaucracy continued to be dominated by influential aristocratic families.

The Koryo dynasty remained in power for four hundred years, protected from invasion by the absence of a strong dynasty in neighboring China. Under the Koryo, industry and commerce slowly began to develop, but as in China, agriculture was the prime source of wealth. In theory, all land was the property of the king, but in actuality, noble families controlled their holdings. The lands were worked by peasants who were subject to burdens similar to those of European serfs. At the bottom of society was a class of "base people" (*chonmin*), composed of slaves, artisans, and other specialized workers.

From a cultural point of view, the Koryo era was one of high achievement. Buddhist monasteries, run by sects introduced from China, including Pure Land and Zen (Chan), controlled vast territories, while their monks served as royal advisers at court. At first, Buddhist themes dominated in Korean art and sculpture, and the entire Tripitaka (the "three baskets," or sections, of the Buddhist canon) was printed using wooden blocks (see the box above). Eventually, however, with the appearance of landscape painting and porcelain, Confucian themes began to predominate.

## Under the Mongols

Like its predecessor in Silla, the kingdom of Koryo was unable to overcome the power of the nobility and the absence of a reliable tax base. In the thirteenth century, the Mongols seized the northern part of the country and assimilated it into the Yuan empire. The weakened kingdom of Koryo became a tributary of the great khan in Khanbaliq (see Chapter 10).

The era of Mongol rule was one of profound suffering for the Korean people, especially the thousands of peasants and artisans who were compelled to perform corvée labor to help build the ships in preparation for Khubilai Khan's invasion of Japan. On the positive side, the Mongols introduced many new ideas and technology from China and farther afield. The Koryo dynasty had managed to survive, but only by accepting

© Archivo Iconografico, S.A./CORBIS

Courtesy of William J. Duiker

**The Sokkuram Buddha.** As Buddhism spread from India to other parts of Asia, so did the representation of the Buddha in human form. From the first century C.E., statues of the Buddha began to absorb various cultural influences. Some early sculptures, marked by flowing draperies, reflected the Greco-Roman culture introduced to India during the era of Alexander the Great. Others were reminiscent of traditional male earth spirits, with broad shoulders and staring eyes. Under the Guptas, artists emphasized the Indian ideal of spiritual and bodily perfection.

As the faith spread along the Silk Road, representations of the Buddha began to reflect cultural influence from Persia and China, and eventually from Korea and Japan. Shown here is the eighth-century Sokkuram Buddha, created during the Silla dynasty. Unable to construct a structure similar to the cave temples in China and India because of the hardness of the rock in the nearby hills, Korean builders erected a small domed cave out of granite blocks and a wooden veranda (see inset). Today, pilgrims still climb the steep hill to pay homage to this powerful and serene Buddha, one of the finest in Asia.

Mongol authority, and when the power of the Mongols declined, the kingdom declined with it. With the rise to power of the Ming in China, Koryo collapsed, and power was seized by the military commander Yi Song-gye, who declared the founding of the new Yi dynasty in 1392. Once again, the Korean people were in charge of their own destiny.

## Vietnam: The Smaller Dragon

While the Korean people were attempting to establish their own identity in the shadow of the powerful Chinese empire, the peoples of Vietnam, on China's southern frontier, were trying to do the same. The Vietnamese (known as the Yueh in Chinese) began to practice irrigated agriculture in the flooded regions of the Red River delta at an early date and entered the Bronze Age sometime during the second millennium B.C.E. By about 200 B.C.E., a young state had begun to form in the area but immediately encountered the expanding power of the Qin empire (see Chapter 3). The Vietnamese were not easy to subdue, however, and the collapse of the Qin dynasty temporarily enabled them to preserve their independence. Nevertheless, a century later, they were absorbed into the Han empire.

At first, the Han were satisfied to rule the delta as an autonomous region under the administration of the local landed aristocracy. But Chinese taxes were oppressive, and in 39 C.E., a revolt led by the Trung Sisters (widows of local nobles who had been executed by the Chinese) briefly brought Han rule to an end. The Chinese soon suppressed the rebellion, however, and began to rule the area directly through officials dispatched from China. In time, however, these foreign officials began to intermarry with the local nobility and form a Sino-Vietnamese ruling class who, though trained in Chinese culture, began to identify with the cause of Vietnamese autonomy.

For nearly a thousand years, the Vietnamese were exposed to the art, architecture, literature, philosophy, and written language of China as the Chinese attempted to integrate the area culturally as well as politically and administratively into their empire. To all intents and purposes, the Red River delta, then known to the Chinese as the "pacified South" (Annam), became a part of China.

### The Rise of Great Viet

Despite the Chinese efforts to assimilate Vietnam, the Vietnamese sense of ethnic and cultural identity proved inextinguishable, and in the tenth century, the Viet-

Maurice Durand Collection, Yale University Library

**Defending the Homeland.** In the first century C.E., Trung Trac, the widow of a Vietnamese lord who had been executed for protesting against Chinese occupation policies, joined with her sister to launch a rebellion against Chinese rule. After temporary successes, the Trung sisters, shown here leading their troops against the occupying Han army, were captured by their adversaries and put to death. Despite their failure, the two later became cult figures in the pantheon of heroic figures, many of them women, who sought to restore Vietnamese independence.

namese took advantage of the collapse of the Tang dynasty in China to overthrow Chinese rule.

The new Vietnamese state, which called itself Dai Viet (Great Viet), became a dynamic new force on the Southeast Asian mainland. As the population of the Red River delta expanded, Dai Viet soon came into conflict with Champa, its neighbor to the south. Located along the central coast of modern Vietnam, Champa was a trading society based on Indian cultural traditions. Over the next several centuries, the two states fought on numerous occasions. By the end of the fifteenth century, Dai Viet had conquered Champa. The Vietnamese then resumed their march southward, establishing agricultural settlements in the newly conquered territory. By the seventeenth century, the Vietnamese had reached the Gulf of Siam.

The Vietnamese faced an even more serious challenge from the north. The Song dynasty in China, beset with its own problems on the northern frontier, eventually accepted the Dai Viet ruler's offer of tribute status (see the box on p. 319), but later dynasties attempted to reintegrate the Red River delta into the Chinese empire. The first effort was made in the late thirteenth century by the Mongols, who attempted on two occasions to conquer the Vietnamese. After a series of bloody battles, during which the Vietnamese displayed an impressive capacity for guerrilla warfare, the invaders were driven out. A little over a century later, the Ming dynasty tried again, and for twenty years Vietnam was once more under Chinese rule. In 1428, the Vietnamese evicted the Chinese again, but the experience had contributed to the strong sense of Vietnamese identity.

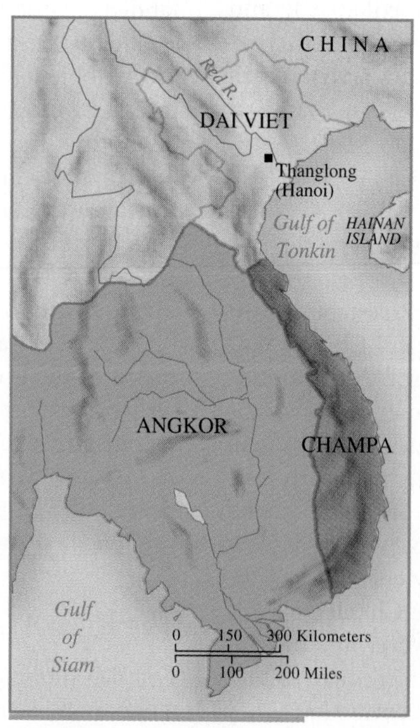


**The Kingdom of Dai Viet, 1100**

**The Chinese Legacy** Despite their stubborn resistance to Chinese rule, after the restoration of independence in the tenth century, Vietnamese rulers quickly discovered the convenience of the Confucian model in administering a river valley society and therefore attempted to follow Chinese practice in forming their own state. The ruler styled himself an emperor like his counterpart to the north (although he prudently termed himself a king in his direct dealings with the Chinese court), adopted Chinese court rituals, claimed the Mandate of Heaven, and arrogated to himself the same authority and privileges in his dealings with his subjects. But unlike a Chinese emperor, who had no particular symbolic role as defender of the Chinese people or Chinese culture, a Vietnamese monarch was viewed, above all, as the symbol and defender of Vietnamese independence.

Like their Chinese counterparts, Vietnamese rulers fought to preserve their authority from the challenges of powerful aristocratic families and turned to the Chinese bureaucratic model, including civil service examinations, as a means of doing so. Under the pressure of strong monarchs, the concept of merit eventually took hold, and the power of the landed aristocracy was weakened if not entirely broken. The Vietnamese adopted much of the Chinese administrative structure, including the six ministries, the censorate, and the various levels of provincial and local administration.

Another aspect of the Chinese legacy was the spread of Buddhist, Daoist, and Confucian ideas, which supplemented the Viets' traditional belief in nature spirits. Buddhist precepts became popular among the local population, who integrated the new faith into their existing belief system by founding Buddhist temples dedicated to the local village deity in the hope of guaranteeing an abundant harvest. Upper-class Vietnamese educated in the Confucian classics tended to follow the more agnostic Confucian doctrine, but some joined Buddhist monasteries. Daoism also flourished at all levels of society and, as in China, provided a structure for animistic beliefs and practices that still predominated at the village level.

During the early period of independence, Vietnamese culture also borrowed liberally from its larger neighbor. Educated Vietnamese tried

## A Plea to the Emperor

Like many other societies in premodern East and Southeast Asia, the kingdom of Vietnam regularly paid tribute to the imperial court in China. The arrangement was often beneficial to both sides, as the tributary states received a form of international recognition from the relationship, as well as trade privileges in the massive Chinese market. China, for its part, assured itself that neighboring areas would not harbor dissident elements hostile to its own security.

In this document, contained in a historical chronicle written by Le Tac in the fourteenth century, a claimant to the Vietnamese throne seeks recognition from the Song emperor while offering tribute to the Son of Heaven in China. Note the way in which the claimant, Le Hoan, founder of the early Le dynasty (980–1009), demeans the character of the Vietnamese people in comparison with the sophisticated ways of imperial China.

*What is the tribute system as described in this document? Does it provide benefits to both parties in the arrangement, and if so, how and why?*

### Le Tac, *Essay on Annam*

My ancestors have received favors from the Imperial Court. Living in a faraway country at a corner of the sea [Annam], they have been granted the seals of investiture for that barbarian area and have always paid to the Imperial ministers the tribute and respect they owed. But recently our House has been little favored by Heaven; however, the death of our ancestors has not prevented us from promptly delivering the tribute. . . .

But now the leadership of the country is in dispute and investiture has not yet been conferred by China. My father, Pou-ling, and my eldest brother, Lienn, formerly enjoyed the favors of the [Chinese] Empire, which endowed them with the titles and functions of office. They zealously and humbly protected their country, neither daring to appear lazy or negligent. . . . [But then] the good fortune of our House began to crumble. The mandarins [officials], the army, the people, the court elders, and members of my family, all . . . entreated me to lead the army. . . . My people, who are wild mountain-dwellers, have unpleasant and violent customs; they are a people who live in caves and have disorderly and impetuous habits. I feared that trouble would arise if I did not yield to their wishes. From prudence I therefore assumed power temporarily. . . . I hope that His Majesty will place my country among His other tributary states by granting me the investiture. He will instill peace in the heart of His little servant by allowing me to govern the patrimony my parents left me. Then shall I administer my barbarian and remote people. . . . I shall send tributes of precious stones and ivory, and before the Golden Gate I shall express my loyalty.

their hand at Chinese poetry, wrote dynastic histories in the Chinese style, and followed Chinese models in sculpture, architecture, and porcelain. Many of the notable buildings of the medieval period, such as the Temple of Literature and the famous One-Pillar Pagoda in Hanoi, are classic examples of Chinese architecture.

But there were signs that Vietnamese creativity would eventually transcend the bounds of Chinese cultural norms. Although most classical writing was undertaken in literary Chinese, the only form of literary expression deemed suitable by Confucian conservatives, an adaptation of Chinese written characters, called *chu nom* ("southern characters"), was devised to provide a written system for spoken Vietnamese. In use by the early ninth century, it eventually began to be used for the composition of essays and poetry in the Vietnamese language.

**Turtle Island, Hanoi.** Few sites in contemporary Vietnam reflect so graphically the complex historic relationship between the Vietnamese and the Chinese peoples. The island shown in this photograph is located on Returned Sword Lake in downtown Hanoi, the current capital of Vietnam. The lake owes its name to a legend that Le Loi, founder of the Le dynasty in the fifteenth century, had drawn a magic sword from the lake in order to achieve his great victory over Chinese occupation forces. Yet the temple that was later erected on a small island in the lake reflects the strong influence of Chinese styles on traditional Vietnamese architecture. After Le Loi's victory, the sword was returned to the water, and the Le dynasty accepted a tributary relationship to the Chinese emperor in Beijing.

Such pioneering efforts would lead in later centuries to the emergence of a vigorous national literature totally independent of Chinese forms.

## Society and Family Life

Vietnamese social institutions and customs were also strongly influenced by those of China. As in China, the introduction of a Confucian system and the adoption of civil service examinations undermined the role of the old landed aristocrats and led eventually to their replacement by the scholar-gentry class. Also as in China, the examinations were open to most males, regardless of family background, which opened the door to a degree of social mobility unknown in most of the states elsewhere in the region. Candidates for the bureaucracy read many of the same Confucian classics and absorbed the same ethical principles as their counterparts in China. At the same time, they were also exposed to the classic works of Vietnamese history, which strengthened their sense that Vietnam was a distinct culture similar to, but separate from, that of China.

The vast majority of the Vietnamese people, however, were peasants. Most were small landholders or sharecroppers who rented their plots from wealthier farmers, but large estates were rare due to the systematic efforts of the central government to prevent the rise of a powerful local landed elite.

Family life in Vietnam was similar in many respects to that in China. The Confucian concept of family took hold during the period of Chinese rule, along with the related concepts of filial piety and gender inequality. Perhaps the most striking difference between family traditions in China and Vietnam was that Vietnamese women possessed more rights both in practice and by law. Since ancient times, wives had been permitted to own property and initiate divorce proceedings. One consequence of Chinese rule was a growing emphasis on male dominance, but the tradition of women's rights was never totally extinguished and was legally recognized in a law code promulgated in 1460.

**CHRONOLOGY Early Korea and Vietnam**

| | |
|---|---|
| Chinese conquest of Korea and Vietnam | First century B.C.E. |
| Trung Sisters' Revolt | 39 C.E. |
| Foundation of Champa | 192 |
| Era of Three Kingdoms in Korea | Fourth–seventh centuries |
| Restoration of Vietnamese independence | 939 |
| Mongol invasion of Korea and Vietnam | 1257–1285 |
| Foundation of Yi dynasty in Korea | 1392 |
| Vietnamese conquest of Champa | 1471 |

Moreover, Vietnam had a strong historical tradition associating heroic women with the defense of the homeland. The Trung Sisters were the first but by no means the only example. In the following passage, a Vietnamese historian of the eighteenth century recounts their story:

> The imperial court was far away; local officials were greedy and oppressive. At that time the country of one hundred sons was the country of the women of Lord To. The ladies [the Trung Sisters] used the female arts against their irreconcilable foe; skirts and hairpins sang of patriotic righteousness, uttered a solemn oath at the inner door of the ladies' quarters, expelled the governor, and seized the capital. . . . Were they not grand heroines? . . . Our two ladies brought forward an army of all the people, and, establishing a royal court that settled affairs in the territories of the sixty-five strongholds, shook their skirts over the Hundred Yueh [the Vietnamese people].[7]

## CONCLUSION

THERE ARE SOME tantalizing similarities among the three countries we have examined in this chapter. All borrowed liberally from the Chinese model. At the same time, all adapted Chinese institutions and values to the conditions prevailing in their own societies. Though all expressed admiration and respect for China's achievement, all sought to keep Chinese power at a distance.

As an island nation, Japan was the most successful of the three in protecting its political sovereignty and its cultural identity. Both Korea and Vietnam were compelled on various occasions to defend their independence by force of arms. That experience may have shaped their strong sense of national distinctiveness, which we shall discuss further in a later chapter.

The appeal of Chinese institutions can undoubtedly be explained by the fact that Japan, Korea, and Vietnam were all agrarian societies, much like their larger neighbor. But it is undoubtedly significant that the aspect of Chinese political culture that was least amenable to adoption abroad was the civil service examination system. The Confucian concept of meritocracy ran directly counter to the strong aristocratic tradition that flourished in all three societies during their early stage of development. Even when the system was adopted, it was put to quite different uses. Only in Vietnam did the concept of merit eventually triumph over that of birth, as strong rulers of Dai Viet attempted to initiate the Chinese model as a means of creating a centralized system of government.

## TIMELINE

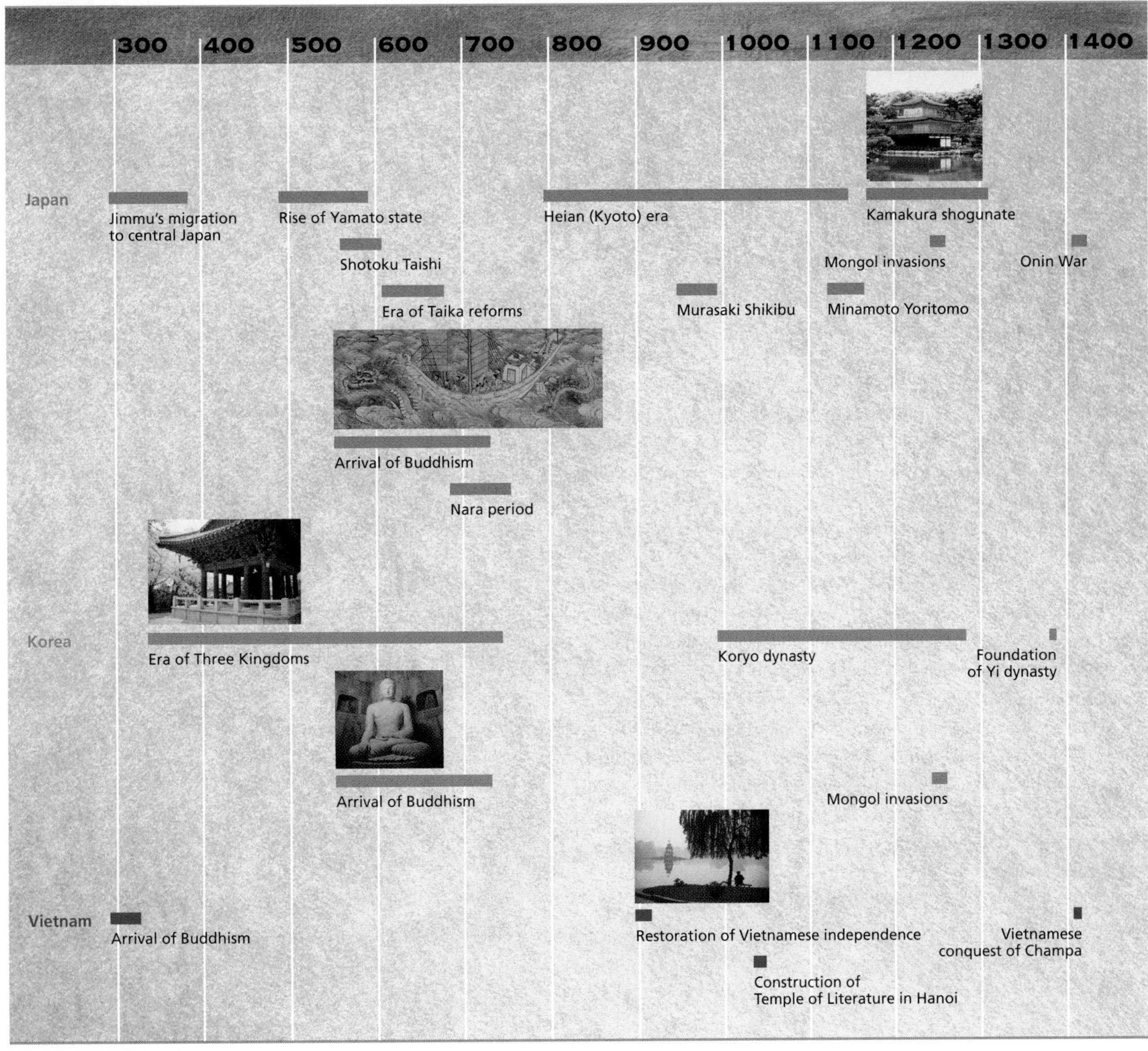


## CHAPTER NOTES

1. K. W. Taylor, *The Birth of Vietnam* (Berkeley, Calif., 1983), p. 18.
2. Quoted in D. J. Lu, *Sources of Japanese History,* vol. 1 (New York, 1974), p. 7.
3. From "The History of Wei," quoted in ibid., p. 10.
4. From "The Law of Households," quoted in ibid., p. 32.
5. From "On the Salvation of Women," quoted in ibid., p. 127.
6. Quoted in B. Ruch, "The Other Side of Culture in Medieval Japan," in K. Yamamura, ed., *The Cambridge History of Japan,* vol. 3, *Medieval Japan* (Cambridge, 1990), p. 506.
7. Quoted in Taylor, *Birth of Vietnam,* pp. 336–337.

## SUGGESTED READINGS

Some of the standard treatments of the rise of Japanese civilization appear in textbooks dealing with the early history of East Asia. Two of the best are **J. K. Fairbank, E. O. Reischauer,** and **A. M. Craig,** ***East Asia: Tradition and Transformation*** (Boston, 1973), and **C. Schirokauer,** ***A Brief History of Chinese and Japanese Civilizations*** (San Diego, Calif., 1989). For the latest scholarship on the early period, see the first three volumes of ***The Cambridge History of Japan,*** ed. **J. W. Hall, M. B. Jansen, M. Kanai,** and **D. Twitchett** (Cambridge, 1988).

The best available collections of documents on the early history of Japan are **D. J. Lu,** ed., ***Sources of Japanese History,*** vol. 1 (New York, 1974), and **W. T. de Bary** et al., eds., ***Sources of Japanese Tradition,*** vol. 1 (New York, 2001).

For specialized books on the early historical period, see **R. J. Pearson,** ed., ***Windows on the Japanese Past: Studies in Archaeology and Prehistory*** (Ann Arbor, Mich., 1986). **J. W. Hall,** ***Government and Local Power in Japan, 500–1700*** (Princeton, N.J., 1966), provides a detailed analysis of the development of Japanese political institutions. The relationship between disease and state building is analyzed in **W. W. Farris,** ***Population, Disease, and Land in Early Japan, 645–900*** (Cambridge, 1985). The Kamakura period is covered in **J. P. Mass**, ed., ***Court and Bakufu in Japan: Essays in Kamakura History*** (New Haven, Conn., 1982). See also **H. P. Varley, *The Onin War*** (New York, 1977). For Japanese Buddhism, see **W. T. de Bary**, ed., ***The Buddhist Tradition in India, China, and Japan*** (New York, 1972).

A concise and provocative introduction to women's issues during this period in Japan, as well as in other parts of the world, can be found in **S. S. Hughes** and **B. Hughes, *Women in World History*** (Armonk, N.Y., 1995). For a tenth-century account of daily life for women at the Japanese court, see **I. Morris**, trans. and ed., ***The Pillow Book of Sei Shonagon*** (New York, 1991). For the changes that took place from matrilocal and matrilineal marriages to a patriarchal society, consult **H. Tonomura, *"Black Hair and Red Trousers: Gendering the Flesh in Medieval Japan,"*** in ***American Historical Review*** 99 (1994).

The best introduction to Japanese literature for college students is still the concise and insightful **D. Keene, *Japanese Literature: An Introduction for Western Readers*** (London, 1953). The most comprehensive anthology is **Keene's *Anthology of Japanese Literature*** (New York, 1955), and the best history of Japanese literature, also by **Keene**, is ***Seeds in the Heart: Japanese Literature from Earlier Times to the Late Sixteenth Century*** (New York, 1993).

For the text of **Lady Murasaki's *Tale of Genji***, see the translation by **E. Seidensticker** (New York, 1976). The most accessible edition for college students is the same author's abridged Vintage Classics edition of 1990, which captures the spirit of the original in 360 pages.

For the most comprehensive introduction to Japanese art, consult **P. Mason, *History of Japanese Art*** (New York, 1993). Also see the concise **J. Stanley-Baker, *Japanese Art*** (London, 1984). For a stimulating text with magnificent illustrations, see **D. Elisseeff** and **V. Elisseeff, *Art of Japan*** (New York, 1985). See also **J. E. Kidder Jr., *The Art of Japan*** (London, 1985), for an insightful text accompanied by beautiful photographs.

For an informative and readable history of Korea, see **Lee Ki-baik, *A New History of Korea*** (Cambridge, 1984). **P. H. Lee**, ed., ***Sourcebook of Korean Civilization, vol. 1*** (New York, 1993), is a rich collection of documents dating from the period prior to the sixteenth century.

Vietnam often receives little attention in general studies of Southeast Asia because it was part of the Chinese empire for much of the traditional period. For a detailed investigation of the origins of Vietnamese civilization, see **K. W. Taylor, *The Birth of Vietnam*** (Berkeley, Calif., 1983). **T. Hodgkin, *Vietnam: The Revolutionary Path*** (New York, 1981), provides an overall survey of Vietnamese history to modern times.

## History Now™

**Enter *HistoryNow* using the access card that is available with this text. *HistoryNow* will assist you in understanding the content in this chapter with lesson plans generated for your needs, as well as provide you with a connection to the *Wadsworth World History Resource Center* (see description below for details).**

### World History Resource Center

**Enter the Resource Center using either your *HistoryNow* access card or your standalone access card for the *Wadsworth World History Resource Center*. Organized by topic, this website includes quizzes; images; over 350 primary source documents; interactive simulations; maps and timelines; movie explorations; and a wealth of other resources. You can read the following documents, and many more, at http://history.wadsworth.com/rc/world.**

Japanese Creation Myth
The Legend of King Onjo of Paekche
Story of the Trung Sisters

Visit the *World History* Companion Website for chapter quizzes and more.

**http://history.wadsworth.com/duikerspielvogel05/**

CHAPTER

# 12

# THE MAKING OF EUROPE

A medieval French manuscript illustration of the coronation of Charlemagne by Pope Leo III



## CHAPTER OUTLINE AND FOCUS QUESTIONS

### The Emergence of Europe in the Early Middle Ages

- What contributions did the Romans, the Christian church, and the Germanic peoples make to the new civilization that emerged in Europe after the collapse of the western Roman Empire?

### Europe in the High Middle Ages

- What roles did aristocrats, peasants, and townspeople play in medieval European civilization, and how did their lifestyles differ? How did cities in Europe compare to those in China and the Middle East?
- What were the main aspects of the political, economic, spiritual, and cultural revivals that took place in Europe during the High Middle Ages?

### Medieval Europe and the World

- In what ways did Europeans begin to relate to peoples in other parts of the world after 1000 C.E.?

### The Crises of the Late Middle Ages

- What problems did Europeans face during the fourteenth century, and what impact did they have on European economic, social, and religious life?

### Recovery: The Renaissance

- What were the main features of the Renaissance, and how did it differ from the Middle Ages?

### CRITICAL THINKING

- In what ways was the civilization that developed in Europe in the Middle Ages similar to those in China and the Middle East? How were they different?

IN 800, CHARLEMAGNE, the king of the Franks, journeyed to Rome to help Pope Leo III, head of the Catholic church, who was barely clinging to power in the face of rebellious Romans. On Christmas Day, Charlemagne and his family, attended by Romans and Franks, crowded into Saint Peter's Basilica to hear Mass. Quite unexpectedly, according to a Frankish writer, "as the king rose from praying before the tomb of the blessed apostle Peter, Pope Leo placed a golden crown on his head." The people in the church shouted, "Long life and victory to Charles Augustus, crowned by God the great and peace-loving Emperor of the Romans." Seemingly, the Roman Empire in the west had been reborn, and Charles had become the first Roman emperor since 476. But this "Roman emperor" was actually a German king, and he had been crowned by the head of the western Christian church. In truth, the coronation of Charlemagne was a sign not of the rebirth of the Roman Empire but of the emergence of a new European civilization that came into being in western Europe after the collapse of the western Roman Empire.

This new civilization–European civilization–was formed by the coming together of three major elements: the legacy of the Romans, the Christian church, and the Germanic peoples who moved in and settled the western empire. European civilization developed during a period that historians call the Middle Ages, or the medieval period, which lasted from about 500 to about 1500. To historians who first used the title, the Middle Ages was a middle period between the ancient world and the modern world. During the Early Middle Ages, from about 500 to 1000 C.E., the Roman world of the western empire was slowly transformed into a new Christian European society. ◇

# The Emergence of Europe in the Early Middle Ages

As we saw in Chapter 10, China descended into political chaos and civil wars after the end of the Han Empire, and it was almost four hundred years before a new imperial dynasty established political order. After the collapse of the western Roman Empire in the fifth century, it would also take hundreds of years to establish the foundations for a new society.

## The New Germanic Kingdoms

Germanic peoples had begun to move into the lands of the Roman Empire in the third century C.E., and by 500, the western Roman empire had been replaced politically by a series of successor states ruled by German kings. The fusion of Romans and Germans took different forms in the various Germanic kingdoms, although there were also similarities. Both the kingdom of the Ostrogoths in Italy and the kingdom of the Visigoths in Spain (see Map 12.1) favored coexistence between the Roman and German populations, both featured a warrior caste dominating a larger native population, and both continued to maintain much of the Roman structure of government while largely excluding Romans from power. Over a period of time, Germans and natives began to fuse. However, when the Roman armies abandoned Britain at the beginning of the fifth century, the Angles and Saxons, Germanic tribes from Denmark and northern Germany, moved in and settled there.

**The Kingdom of the Franks** Only one of the German states on the European continent proved long-lasting—the kingdom of the Franks. The establishment of a Frankish kingdom was the work of Clovis (c. 482–511), who became a Catholic Christian around 500. Clovis found that his conversion to Catholic Christianity gained him the support of the Roman Catholic church, as the Christian church in Rome had become known, which was only too eager to obtain the friendship of a major ruler in the Germanic states. By 510, Clovis had established a powerful new Frankish kingdom stretching from the Pyrenees in the west to German lands in the east (modern France and western Germany). After Clovis's death, however, as was the Frankish custom, his sons divided his newly created kingdom, and during the sixth and seventh centuries, the once-united Frankish kingdom came to be divided into three major areas: Neustria, Austrasia, and Burgundy.

**The Society of the Germanic Peoples** As Germans and Romans intermarried and began to create a new society, some of the social customs of the Germanic peoples came to play an important role. The crucial social bond among the Germanic peoples was the family, especially the extended family of husbands, wives, children, brothers, sisters, cousins, and grandparents. The German family structure was quite simple. Males were dominant and made all the important decisions. A woman obeyed her father until she married and then fell under the legal domination of her husband. For most women in the new Germanic kingdoms, their legal status reflected the material conditions of their lives. Most women had life expectancies of only thirty or forty years, and perhaps 15 percent of women died in their childbearing years, no doubt due to complications associated with childbirth. For most women, life consisted of domestic labor: providing food and clothing for the household, caring for the children, and assisting with farming chores.

The German conception of family affected the way Germanic law treated the problem of crime and punishment. In the Roman system, as in our own, a crime such as murder was considered an offense against society or the state and was handled by a court that heard evidence and arrived at a decision. Germanic law was personal. An injury by one person against another could lead to a blood feud in which the family of the injured party took revenge on the family of the wrongdoer. Feuds could lead to savage acts of revenge, such as hacking off hands or feet or gouging out eyes. Because this system could easily get out of control, an alternative system arose that made use of a fine called ***wergeld,*** which was the amount paid by a wrongdoer to the family of the person injured or killed. *Wergeld,* which means "money for a man," was the value of a person in monetary terms. That value varied considerably according to social status. An offense against a nobleman, for example, cost considerably more than one against a freeman or a slave.

Germanic law also provided a means of determining guilt: the ordeal. The ordeal was based on the idea of divine intervention: divine forces (whether pagan or Christian) would not allow an innocent person to be harmed (see the box on p. 326).

## The Role of the Christian Church

By the end of the fourth century, Christianity had become the predominant religion of the Roman Empire. As the official Roman state disintegrated, the Christian church

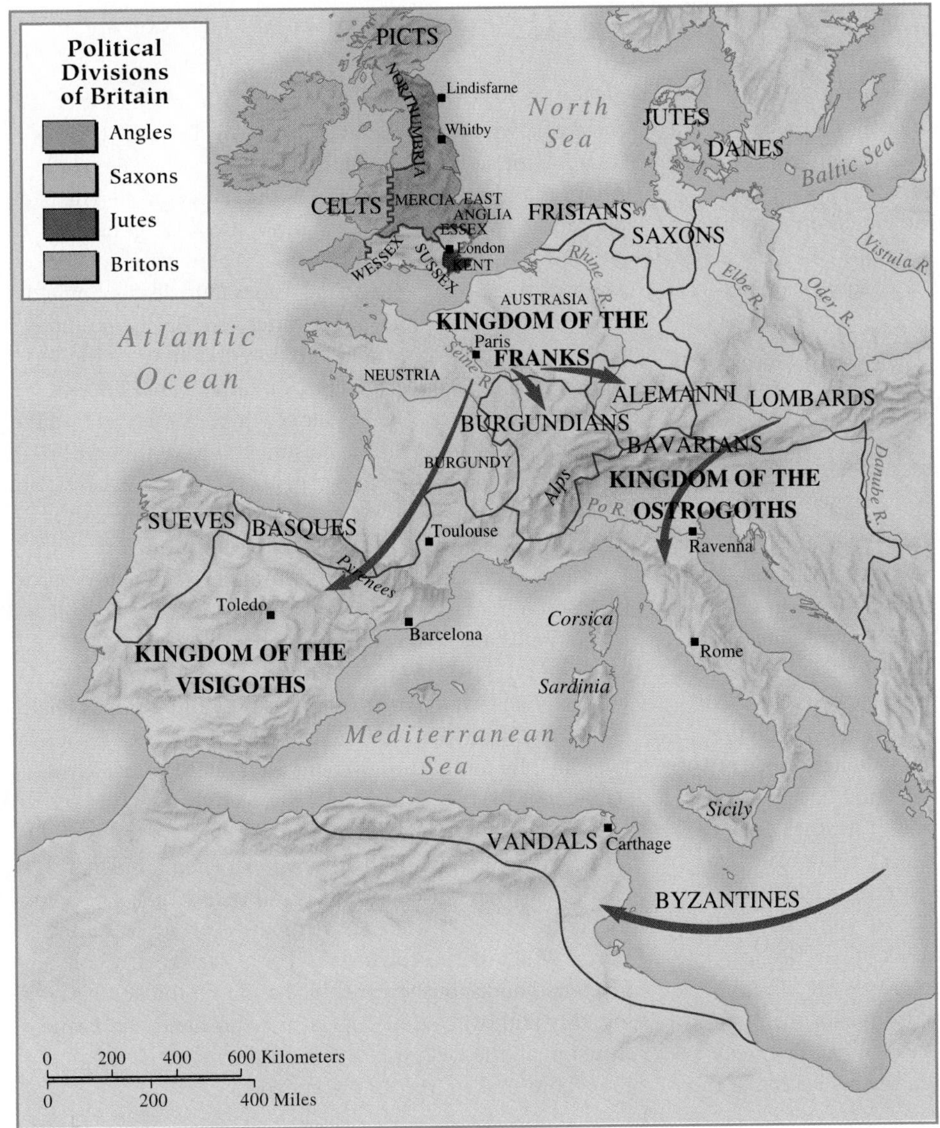


**MAP 12.1 The Germanic Kingdoms of the Old Western Empire.** The Germanic tribes filled the power vacuum caused by the demise of the Roman Empire, building states that blended elements of Germanic customs and laws with those of Roman culture, including large-scale conversions to Christianity. The Franks established the most durable of these Germanic states. ? How did the movements of Franks during this period correspond to the borders of present-day France? **View an animated version of this map or related maps at** http://history.wadsworth.com/duikerspielvogel05/

played an increasingly important role in the growth of the new European civilization.

**The Organization of the Church** By the fourth century, the Christian church had developed a system of government. The Christian community in each city was headed by a bishop, whose area of jurisdiction was known as a bishopric, or **diocese;** the bishoprics of each Roman province were joined together under the direction of an archbishop. The bishops of four great cities—Rome, Jerusalem, Alexandria, and Antioch—held positions of special power in church affairs because the churches in these cities all asserted that they had been founded by the original apostles sent out by Jesus. Soon, however, one of them—the bishop of Rome—claimed that he was the sole leader of the western Christian church. According to church tradition, Jesus had given the keys to the kingdom of heaven to Peter, who was considered the chief apostle and the first bishop of Rome. Subsequent bishops of Rome were considered Peter's successors and came to be known as popes (from the Latin word *papa,* meaning "father"). By the sixth century, popes had been successful in extending papal authority over the Christian church in the west and converting the pagan peoples of Germanic Europe. Their primary instrument of conversion was the monastic movement.

**The Monks and Their Missions** A **monk** (in Latin, *monachus,* meaning "someone who lives alone") was a man who sought to live a life divorced from the world, cut off from ordinary human society, in order to pursue an ideal of total dedication to God. As the monastic ideal spread, a new form of **monasticism** based on living together in a community soon became the dominant form. Saint Benedict (c. 480–c. 543), who founded a monastic house for which he wrote a set of rules, established the basic form of monastic life in the western Christian church

Benedict's rules divided each day into a series of activities, with primary emphasis on prayer and manual labor. Physical work of some kind was required of all monks for several hours a day because idleness was "the enemy of the soul." At the very heart of community practice was prayer, the proper "work of God." Although this included private meditation and reading, all monks gathered together seven times during the day for common prayer and chanting of psalms. The Benedictine life was a communal one. Monks ate, worked, slept, and worshiped together.

Each Benedictine monastery was strictly ruled by an **abbot,** or "father" of the monastery, who had complete authority over his fellow monks. Unquestioning obedience

## Germanic Customary Law: The Ordeal

In Germanic customary law, the ordeal was used as a means by which accused persons might clear themselves. Although the ordeal took different forms, all involved a physical trial of some sort, such as holding a red-hot iron. It was believed that God would protect the innocent and allow them to come through the ordeal unharmed. This sixth-century account by Gregory of Tours describes an ordeal by hot water.

*What was the purpose of the ordeal of hot water? What does it reveal about the nature of the society that used it?*

### Gregory of Tours, *An Ordeal of Hot Water* (c. 580)

An Arian presbyter disputing with a deacon of our religion made venomous assertions against the Son of God and the Holy Ghost, as is the habit of that sect [the Arians]. But when the deacon had discoursed a long time concerning the reasonableness of our faith and the heretic, blinded by the fog of unbelief, continued to reject the truth, . . . the former said: "Why weary ourselves with long discussions? Let acts approve the truth; let a kettle be heated over the fire and someone's ring be thrown into the boiling water. Let him who shall take it from the heated liquid be approved as a follower of the truth, and afterward let the other party be converted to the knowledge of the truth. And do you also understand, O heretic, that this our party will fulfill the conditions with the aid of the Holy Ghost; you shalt confess that there is no discordance, no dissimilarity in the Holy Trinity." The heretic consented to the proposition and they separated after appointing the next morning for the trial. But the fervor of faith in which the deacon had first made this suggestion began to cool through the instigation of the enemy. Rising with the dawn he bathed his arm in oil and smeared it with ointment. But nevertheless he made the round of the sacred places and called in prayer on the Lord. . . . About the third hour they met in the marketplace. The people came together to see the show. A fire was lighted, the kettle was placed upon it, and when it grew very hot the ring was thrown into the boiling water. The deacon invited the heretic to take it out of the water first. But he promptly refused, saying, "You who did propose this trial are the one to take it out." The deacon all of a tremble bared his arm. And when the heretic presbyter saw it besmeared with ointment he cried out: "With magic arts you have thought to protect yourself, that you have made use of these salves, but what you have done will not avail." While they were thus quarreling there came up a deacon from Ravenna named Iacinthus and inquired what the trouble was about. When he learned the truth he drew his arm out from under his robe at once and plunged his right hand into the kettle. Now the ring that had been thrown in was a little thing and very light so that it was thrown about by the water as chaff would be blown about by the wind; and searching for it a long time he found it after about an hour. Meanwhile the flame beneath the kettle blazed up mightily so that the greater heat might make it difficult for the ring to be followed by the hand; but the deacon extracted it at length and suffered no harm, protesting rather that at the bottom the kettle was cold while at the top it was just pleasantly warm. When the heretic beheld this he was greatly confused and audaciously thrust his hand into the kettle saying, "My faith will aid me." As soon as his hand had been thrust in all the flesh was boiled off the bones clear up to the elbow. And so the dispute ended.

to the will of the abbot was expected of every monk. Each Benedictine monastery held lands that enabled it to be a self-sustaining community, isolated from and independent of the world surrounding it. Within the monastery, however, monks were to fulfill their vow of poverty: "Let all things be common to all, as it is written, lest anyone should say that anything is his own."[1] Only men could be monks, but women, called **nuns,** also began to withdraw from the world to dedicate themselves to God.

Monasticism played an indispensable role in early medieval civilization. Monks became the new heroes of Christian civilization, and their dedication to God became the highest ideal of Christian life. They were the social workers of their communities: monks provided schools for the young, hospitality for travelers, and hospitals for the sick. Monks also copied Latin works and passed on the legacy of the ancient world to the new European civilization. Monasteries became centers of learning wherever they were located, and monks worked to spread Christianity to all of Europe.

Women played an important role in the monastic missionary movement and the conversion of the Germanic kingdoms. Some served as **abbesses** (an abbess was the head of a monastery or a convent for nuns); many abbesses came from aristocratic families, especially in Anglo-Saxon England. In the kingdom of Northumbria, for example, Saint Hilda founded the monastery of Whitby in 657. As abbess, she was responsible for making learning an important part of the life of the monastery.

## Charlemagne and the Carolingians

During the seventh and eighth centuries, as the kings of the Frankish kingdom gradually lost their power, the mayors of the palace—the chief officers of the king's household—assumed more control of the kingdom. One of these mayors, Pepin, finally took the logical step of assuming the kingship of the Frankish state for himself and his family. Upon his death in 768, his son came to the throne of the Frankish kingdom.

This new king was the dynamic and powerful ruler known to history as Charles the Great (768–814), or Charlemagne (from the Latin *Carolus Magnus*). He was determined and decisive, intelligent and inquisitive, a strong statesman, and a pious Christian. Himself unable to read or write, he was a wise patron of learning. In a series of military campaigns, he greatly expanded the territory he had inherited and created what came to be known as the Carolingian Empire. At its height, Charlemagne's empire covered much of western and central Europe; not until the time of Napoleon in the nineteenth century would an empire of its size be seen again in Europe (see the box on p. 328).

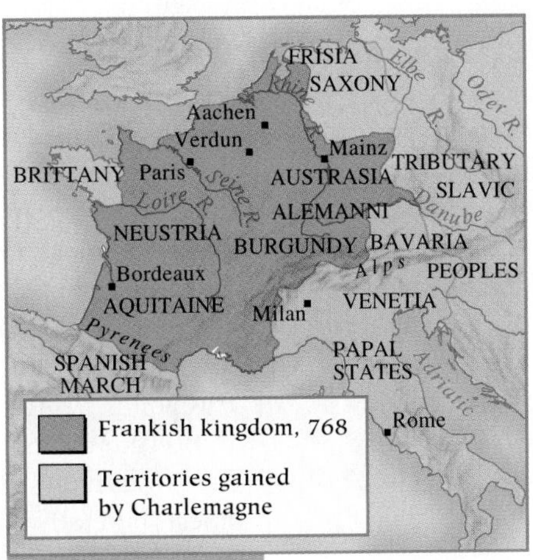

**Charlemagne's Empire**

Charlemagne continued the efforts of his father in organizing the Carolingian kingdom. Besides his household staff, Charlemagne's administration of the empire depended on the use of counts as the king's chief representatives in local areas. As an important check on the power of the counts, Charlemagne established the *missi dominici* ("messengers of the lord king"), two men who were sent out to local districts to ensure that the counts were executing the king's wishes.

As Charlemagne's power grew, so did his prestige as the most powerful Christian ruler; one monk even wrote that he ruled the "kingdom of Europe." In 800, Charlemagne acquired a new title: emperor of the Romans. Charlemagne's coronation as Roman emperor demonstrated the strength, even after three hundred years, of the concept of an enduring Roman Empire. More important, it symbolized the fusion of the Roman, Christian, and Germanic elements that formed the base of European civilization. A Germanic king had been crowned emperor of the Romans by the spiritual leader of western Christendom. A new civilization had emerged.

Granger Collection

**The Coronation of Charlemagne.** After rebellion in 799 forced Pope Leo III to seek refuge at Charlemagne's court, Charlemagne went to Rome to settle the affair. There, on Christmas Day 800, he was crowned emperor of the Romans by the pope. This manuscript illustration shows Leo III placing a crown on Charlemagne's head.

## The World of Lords and Vassals

The Carolingian Empire began to disintegrate soon after Charlemagne's death in 814, and less than thirty years later, in 843, it was divided among his grandsons into three major sections: the western Frankish lands, which formed the core of the eventual kingdom of France; the eastern lands, which eventually became Germany; and a "middle kingdom" extending from the North Sea to the Mediterranean. The territories of the middle kingdom became a source of incessant struggle between the other two Frankish rulers and their heirs. At the same time, powerful nobles gained even more power in their own local territories while the Carolingian rulers fought each other. Invasions in different parts of the old Carolingian world added to the process of disintegration.

**Invasions of the Ninth and Tenth Centuries** In the ninth and tenth centuries, western Europe was beset by a wave of invasions. Muslims attacked the southern coasts of Europe and sent raiding parties into southern France. The Magyars, a people from western Asia, moved into central Europe at the end of the ninth century and settled on the plains of Hungary, from where they made forays into western Europe. Finally crushed at the Battle of Lechfeld in Germany in 955, the Magyars converted to Christianity and settled down to create the kingdom of Hungary.

The most far-reaching attacks of the time came from the Northmen or Norsemen of Scandinavia, also known to us as the Vikings. The Vikings were warriors whose love of adventure and search for booty and new avenues of trade may have led them to invade other areas of Europe. Viking ships were the best of the period. Long and narrow with beautifully carved arched prows, the Viking "dragon ships" carried about fifty men. Their shallow draft

## The Achievements of Charlemagne

Einhard, the biographer of Charlemagne, was born in the valley of the Main River in Germany about 775. Raised and educated in the monastery of Fulda, an important center of learning, he arrived at the court of Charlemagne in 791 or 792. Although he did not achieve high office under Charlemagne, he served as private secretary to Louis the Pious, Charlemagne's son and successor. In this selection, Einhard discusses some of Charlemagne's accomplishments.

*How long did Einhard know Charlemagne? Does this excerpt reflect close, personal knowledge of the man, his court, and his works or hearsay and legend?*

### Einhard, *Life of Charlemagne*

Such are the wars, most skillfully planned and successfully fought, which this most powerful king waged during the forty-seven years of his reign. He so largely increased the Frank kingdom, which was already great and strong when he received it at his father's hands, that more than double its former territory was added to it. . . . He subdued all the wild and barbarous tribes dwelling in Germany between the Rhine and the Vistula, the Ocean and the Danube, all of which speak very much the same language, but differ widely from one another in customs and dress. . . .

He added to the glory of his reign by gaining the good will of several kings and nations; so close, indeed, was the alliance that he contracted with Alfonso, King of Galicia and Asturias, that the latter, when sending letters or ambassadors to Charles, invariably styled himself his man. . . . The Emperors of Constantinople [the Byzantine emperors] sought friendship and alliance with Charles by several embassies; and even when the Greeks [the Byzantines] suspected him of designing to take the empire from them, because of his assumption of the title Emperor, they made a close alliance with him, that he might have no cause of offense. In fact, the power of the Franks was always viewed with a jealous eye, whence the Greek proverb, "Have the Frank for your friend, but not for your neighbor."

This King, who showed himself so great in extending his empire and subduing foreign nations, and was constantly occupied with plans to that end, undertook also very many works calculated to adorn and benefit his kingdom, and brought several of them to completion. Among these, the most deserving of mention are the basilica of the Holy Mother of God at Aix-la-Chapelle [Aachen], built in the most admirable manner, and a bridge over the Rhine River at Mainz, half a mile long, the breadth of the river at this point. . . . Above all, sacred buildings were the object of his care throughout his whole kingdom; and whenever he found them falling to ruin from age, he commanded the priests and fathers who had charge of them to repair them, and made sure by commissioners that his instructions were obeyed. . . . Thus did Charles defend and increase as well as beautify his kingdom. . . .

He cherished with the greatest fervor and devotion the principles of the Christian religion, which had been instilled into him from infancy. Hence it was that he built the beautiful church at Aix-la-Chapelle, which he adorned with gold and silver and lamps, and with rails and doors of solid brass. He had the columns and marbles for this structure brought from Rome and Ravenna, for he could not find such as were suitable elsewhere. He was a constant worshiper at this church as long as his health permitted, going morning and evening, even after nightfall, besides attending mass. . . .

He was very forward in caring for the poor, so much so that he not only made a point of giving in his own country and his own kingdom, but when he discovered that there were Christians living in poverty in Syria, Egypt, and Africa, at Jerusalem, Alexandria, and Carthage, he had compassion on their wants, and used to send money over the seas to them. . . . He sent great and countless gifts to the popes, and throughout his whole reign the wish that he had nearest at heart was to reestablish the ancient authority of the city of Rome under his care and by his influence, and to defend and protect the Church of St. Peter, and to beautify and enrich it out of his own store above all other churches.

**HistoryNow™** To read a complete version of Einhard's *Life of Charlemagne*, enter the *HistoryNow* documents area using the access card that is available for *World History.*

enabled them to sail up European rivers and attack places at some distance inland. In the ninth century, Vikings sacked villages and towns, destroyed churches, and easily defeated small local armies. Viking attacks frightened people and led many a clergyman to plead with them to change their behavior and appease God's anger, as is revealed in this sermon in 1014 by an English archbishop:

> Things have not gone well now for a long time at home or abroad, but there has been devastation and persecution in every district again and again, and the English have been for a long time now completely defeated and too greatly disheartened through God's anger; and the pirates [Vikings] so strong with God's consent that often in battle one puts to flight ten, and sometimes less, sometimes more, all because of our sins. . . . We pay them continually and they humiliate us daily; they ravage and they burn, plunder, and rob and carry on board; and lo, what else is there in all these events except God's anger clear and visible over this people?[2]

By the mid-ninth century, the Northmen had begun to build winter settlements in different areas of Europe.

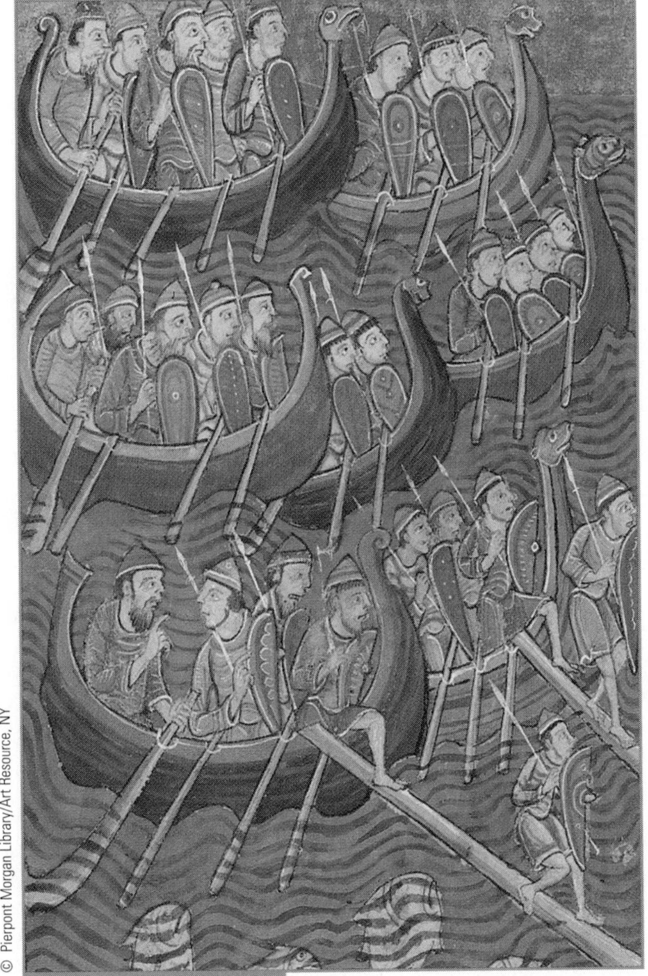

**The Vikings Attack England.** This illustration from an eleventh-century English manuscript depicts a group of armed Vikings invading England. Two ships have already reached the shore, and a few Vikings are shown walking down a long gangplank onto English soil. Also shown is a replica of a well-preserved Viking ship found at Oseberg, Norway. The Oseberg ship was one of the largest Viking ships in its day.

By 850, groups of Norsemen from Norway had settled in Ireland, and Danes occupied northeastern England by 878. Beginning in 911, the ruler of the western Frankish lands gave one band of Vikings land at the mouth of the Seine River, forming a section of France that came to be known as Normandy. This policy of settling the Vikings and converting them to Christianity was a deliberate one; by their conversion to Christianity, the Vikings were soon made a part of European civilization.

**The Development of Fief-Holding** The disintegration of central authority in the Carolingian world and the invasions by Muslims, Magyars, and Vikings led to the emergence of a new type of relationship between free individuals. When governments ceased to be able to defend their subjects, it became important to find some powerful lord who could offer protection in return for service. The contract sworn between a lord and his subordinate (known as a **vassal**) is the basis of a form of social organization that modern historians have called *feudalism.* But feudalism was never a cohesive system, and many historians today prefer to avoid using the term (see the comparative essay "Feudal Orders Around the World" on p. 307).

With the breakdown of royal governments, powerful nobles took control of large areas of land. They needed men to fight for them, so the practice arose of giving grants of land to vassals who in return would fight for their lord. The Frankish army had originally consisted of foot soldiers, dressed in coats of mail and armed with swords. But in the eighth century, a military change began to occur with the use of larger horses and the stirrup, which was introduced by nomadic horsemen from Asia. Earlier, horsemen had been throwers of spears. Now they came to be armored in coats of mail (the larger horse could carry the weight) and wielded long lances that enabled them to act as battering rams (the stirrup kept them on their horses). For almost five hundred years, warfare in Europe would be dominated by heavily armored cavalry, or *knights,* as they were called.

Of course, it was expensive to have a horse, armor, and weapons. It also took time and much practice to learn to wield these instruments skillfully from horseback.

Consequently, lords who wanted men to fight for them had to grant each vassal a piece of land that provided for the support of the vassal and his family. In return for the land, the vassal provided his lord with his fighting skills. Each needed the other. In the society of the Early Middle Ages, where there was little trade and wealth was based primarily on land, land became the most important gift a lord could give to a vassal in return for his loyalty and military service.

By the ninth century, the grant of land made to a vassal had become known as a **fief.** A fief was a piece of land held from the lord by a vassal in return for military service, but vassals who held such grants of land came to exercise rights of jurisdiction or political and legal authority within these fiefs. As the Carolingian world disintegrated politically under the impact of internal dissension and invasions, an increasing number of powerful lords arose who were now responsible for keeping order.

**The Practice of Fief-Holding** Fief-holding also became increasingly complicated with the development of **subinfeudation.** The vassals of a king, who were themselves great lords, might also have vassals who would owe them military service in return for a grant of land taken from their estates. Those vassals, in turn, might likewise have vassals, who at such a level would be simple knights with barely enough land to provide their equipment. The lord-vassal relationship, then, bound together both greater and lesser landowners. At all levels, the lord-vassal relationship was always an honorable relationship between free men and did not imply any sense of servitude.

Fief-holding came to be characterized by a set of practices that determined the relationship between a lord and his vassal. The major obligation of a vassal to his lord was to perform military service, usually about forty days a year. A vassal was also required to appear at his lord's court when summoned to give advice to the lord. He might also be asked to sit in judgment in a legal case, since the important vassals of a lord were peers and only they could judge each other. Finally, vassals were also responsible for aids, or financial payments to the lord on a number of occasions, among them the knighting of the lord's eldest son, the marriage of his eldest daughter, and the ransom of the lord's person if he were captured.

In turn, a lord had responsibilities toward his vassals. His major obligation was to protect his vassal, either by defending him militarily or by taking his side in a court of law. The lord was also responsible for the maintenance of the vassal, usually by granting him a fief.

**The Manorial System** The landholding class of nobles and knights contained a military elite whose ability to function as warriors depended on having the leisure time to pursue the arts of war. Landed estates, located on the fiefs given to a vassal by his lord and worked by a dependent peasant class, provided the economic sustenance that made this way of life possible. A **manor** was an agricultural estate operated by a lord and worked by peasants (see Map 12.2). Although a large class of free peasants continued to exist, increasing numbers of free peasants became **serfs**—persons bound to the land and required to provide labor services, pay rents, and be subject to the lord's jurisdiction. By the ninth century, probably 60 percent of the population of western Europe had become serfs.

Labor services consisted of working the lord's **demesne,** the land retained by the lord, which might consist of one-third to one-half of the cultivated lands scattered throughout the manor. The rest would be used by the peasants for themselves. Building barns and digging ditches were also part of the labor services. Serfs usually worked about three days a week for their lord and paid rents by giving the lord a share of every product they raised.

Serfs were legally bound to the lord's lands and could not leave without his permission. Although free to marry, serfs could not marry anyone outside their manor without the lord's approval. Moreover, lords sometimes exercised public rights or political authority on their lands, which gave them the right to try peasants in their own courts.

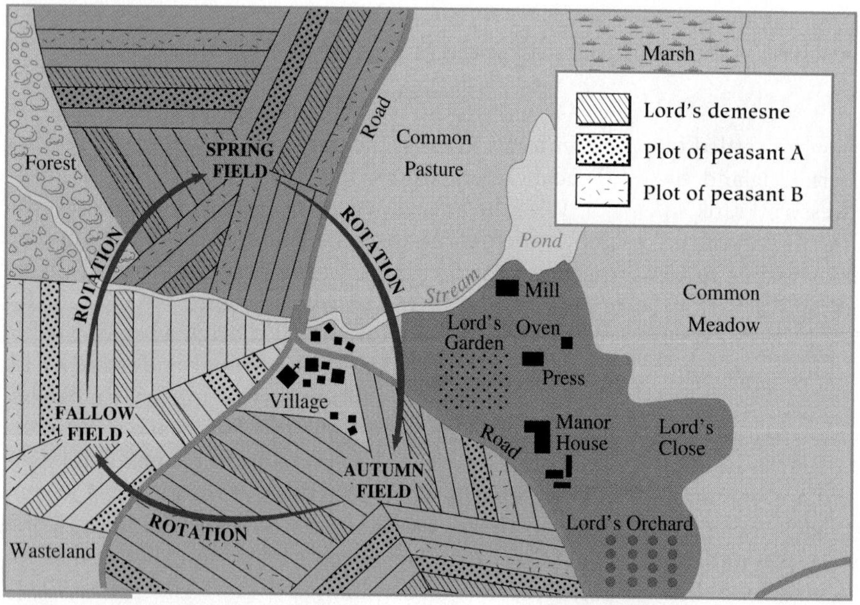

MAP 12.2 **A Typical Manor.** The manorial system created small, tightly knit communities in which peasants were economically and physically bound to their lord. Crops were rotated, with roughly one-third of the fields lying fallow at any one time, which helped replenish soil nutrients (see Chapter 9). How does the area of the lord's manor, other buildings, garden, and orchard compare to that of the peasant holdings in the village? **View an animated version of this map or related maps at** http://history.wadsworth.com/duikerspielvogel05/

## Europe in the High Middle Ages

The new European civilization that had emerged in the Early Middle Ages began to flourish in the High Middle Ages (1000–1300). New agricultural practices that increased the food supply spurred commercial and urban expansion. Both lords and vassals recovered from the invasions and internal dissension of the Early Middle Ages, and medieval kings began to exert a centralizing authority. The recovery of the Catholic church made it a forceful presence in every area of life. The High Middle Ages also gave birth to a cultural revival.

### Land and People

In the Early Middle Ages, Europe had a relatively small population of about 38 million, but in the High Middle Ages, the number of people nearly doubled to 74 million. What accounted for this dramatic increase? For one thing, conditions in Europe were more settled and more peaceful after the invasions of the Early Middle Ages had ended. For another, agricultural production surged after 1000.

**The New Agriculture** During the High Middle Ages, Europeans began to farm in new ways. An improvement in climate resulted in better growing conditions, but an important factor in increasing food production was the expansion of cultivated or arable land, accomplished by clearing forested areas. Peasants of the eleventh and twelfth centuries cut down trees and drained swamps until by the thirteenth century, Europeans had more acreage available for farming than at any time before or since.

Technological changes also furthered the development of farming. The Middle Ages saw an explosion of labor-saving devices, many of which were made from iron, which was mined in different areas of Europe. Iron was used to make scythes, axes, and hoes for use on farms as well as saws, hammers, and nails for building purposes. Iron was crucial in making the *carruca,* a heavy, wheeled plow with an iron plowshare pulled by teams of horses, which could turn over the heavy clay soil north of the Alps.

Besides using horsepower, the High Middle Ages harnessed the power of water and wind to do jobs formerly done by humans or animals. Located along streams, mills powered by water were used to grind grains and produce flour. Where rivers were lacking or not easily dammed, Europeans developed windmills to harness the power of the wind.

The shift from a two-field to a three-field system also contributed to the increase in food production (see the comparative illustration "The New Agriculture in the Medieval World" on p. 332). In the Early Middle Ages, peasants had planted one field while another of equal size was allowed to lie fallow to regain its fertility. Now estates were divided into three parts. One field was planted in the fall with winter grains, such as rye and wheat, while spring grains, such as oats or barley, and vegetables, such as peas or beans, were planted in the second field. The third was allowed to lie fallow. By rotating their use, only one-third rather than one-half of the land lay fallow at any time. The rotation of crops also kept the soil from being exhausted so quickly, and more crops could now be grown.

**Daily Life of the Peasantry** The lifestyle of the peasants was quite simple. Their cottages consisted of wood frames surrounded by sticks with the space between them filled with straw and rubble and then plastered over with clay. Roofs were simply thatched. The houses of poorer peasants consisted of a single room, but others had at least two rooms—a main room for cooking, eating, and other activities and another room for sleeping

Peasant women occupied an important but difficult position in manorial society. They were expected to carry and bear their children and at the same time fulfill their obligation to labor in the fields. Their ability to manage the household might determine whether a peasant family would starve or survive in difficult times.

Though simple, a peasant's daily diet was adequate when food was available. The staple of the peasant diet, and the medieval diet in general, was bread. Women made the dough for the bread at home and then brought their loaves to be baked in community ovens, which were owned by the lord of the manor. Peasant bread was highly nutritious, containing not only wheat and rye but also barley, millet, and oats, giving it a dark appearance and a very heavy, hard texture. Bread was supplemented by numerous vegetables from the household gardens, cheese from cow's or goat's milk, nuts and berries from woodlands, and fruits, such as apples, pears, and cherries. Chickens provided eggs and sometimes meat.

**The Nobility of the Middle Ages** In the High Middle Ages, European society, like that of Japan during the same period, was dominated by men whose chief concern was warfare. Like the Japanese samurai, many nobles loved war. As one nobleman wrote:

> *And well I like to hear the call of "Help" and see the*
> *wounded fall,*
> *Loudly for mercy praying,*
> *And see the dead, both great and small,*
> *Pierced by sharp spearheads one and all.*[3]

The men of war were the lords and vassals of medieval society.

The lords were the kings, dukes, counts, barons, and viscounts (and even bishops and archbishops) who had extensive landholdings and wielded considerable political influence. They formed an **aristocracy** or nobility of people who held real political, economic, and social power. Both the great lords and ordinary knights were warriors, and the institution of knighthood united them. But there were also social divisions among them based on extremes of wealth and landholdings.

Although aristocratic women could legally hold property, most women remained under the control of

COMPARATIVE ILLUSTRATION

**The New Agriculture in the Medieval World.** New agricultural methods and techniques in the Middle Ages enabled peasants in both Europe and China to increase food production. This general improvement in diet was a factor in supporting noticeably larger populations in both areas. At the bottom, a thirteenth-century illustration shows a group of English peasants harvesting grain. Overseeing their work is a bailiff, or manager, who supervised the work of the peasants. At the right, a twelfth-century painting shows Chinese peasants transplanting month-old seedlings from the nursery bed to their permanent field. Rice became the staple food in China.

Freer Gallery of Art, Smithsonian Institution, Washington, D.C.

Art Archive, London, from the collections of the British Library

men—their fathers until they married and their husbands after that. Nevertheless, these women had many opportunities for playing important roles. Because the lord was often away at war or at court, the lady of the castle had to manage the estate. Households could include large numbers of officials and servants, so this was no small responsibility. Maintaining the financial accounts alone took considerable financial knowledge. The lady of the castle was also responsible on a regular basis for overseeing the food supply and maintaining all the other supplies needed for the smooth operation of the household.

Although women were expected to be subservient to their husbands, there were many strong women who advised and sometimes even dominated their husbands. Perhaps most famous was Eleanor of Aquitaine (c. 1122–1204). Married to King Louis VII of France, Eleanor accompanied her husband on a Crusade, but her alleged affair with her uncle during the Crusade led Louis to have their marriage annulled. Eleanor then married Henry, duke of Normandy, who became King Henry II of England (1154–1189). She took an active role in politics, even assisting her sons in rebelling against Henry in 1173 and 1174.

## The New World of Trade and Cities

Medieval Europe was overwhelmingly an agrarian society, with most people living in small villages. In the eleventh and twelfth centuries, however, new elements were introduced that began to transform the economic foundation of European civilization: a revival of trade, the emergence of specialized craftspeople and artisans, and the growth and development of towns.

**The Revival of Trade** The revival of trade was a gradual process. During the chaotic conditions of the Early Middle Ages, large-scale trade had declined in western Europe except for Byzantine contacts with Italy and the Jewish traders who moved back and forth between the Muslim and Christian worlds. By the end of the tenth century, however, people were emerging in Europe with both the skills and the products for commercial activity. Cities in Italy took the lead in this revival of trade. Venice, for example, emerged as a town by the end of the eighth century, developed a mercantile fleet, and by the end of the tenth century had become the chief western trading center for Byzantine and Islamic commerce.

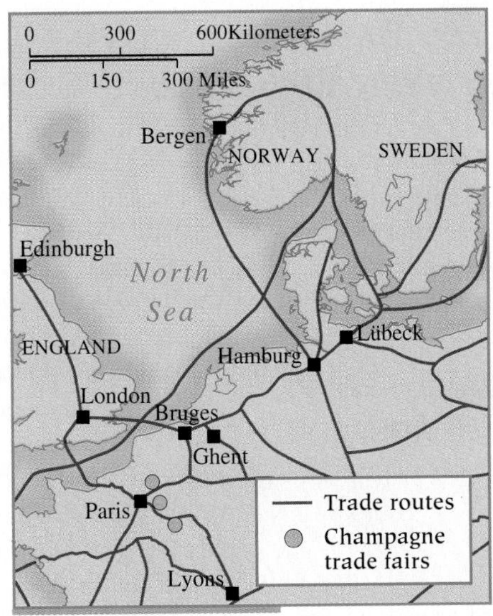

**Flanders as a Trade Center**

While the northern Italian cities were busy trading in the Mediterranean, the towns of Flanders were doing likewise in northern Europe. Flanders, the area along the coast of present-day Belgium and northern France, was known for its high-quality woolen cloth. The location of Flanders made it an ideal center for the traders of northern Europe. Merchants from England, Scandinavia, France, and Germany converged there to trade their goods for woolen cloth. Flanders prospered in the eleventh and twelfth centuries, and such Flemish towns as Bruges and Ghent became centers for the trade and manufacture of woolen cloth.

By the twelfth century, a regular exchange of goods had developed between Flanders and Italy, the two major centers of northern and southern European trade. To encourage this trade, the counts of Champagne in northern France devised a series of six fairs held annually in the chief towns of their territory. At these fairs, northern merchants brought the furs, woolen cloth, tin, and honey of northern Europe and exchanged them for the cloth and swords of northern Italy and the silks, sugar, and spices of the East.

As trade increased, both gold and silver came to be in demand at fairs and trading markets of all kinds. Slowly, a money economy began to emerge. New trading companies and banking firms were set up to manage the exchange and sale of goods. All of these new practices were part of the rise of **commercial capitalism,** an economic system in which people invested in trade and goods in order to make profits.

**Trade Outside Europe** In the High Middle Ages, Italian merchants became even more daring in their trade activities. They established trading posts in Cairo, Damascus, and a number of Black Sea ports, where they acquired spices, silks, jewelry, dyestuffs, and other goods brought by Muslim merchants from India, China, and Southeast Asia.

The spread of the Mongol Empire in the thirteenth century (see Chapter 10) also opened the door to Italian merchants in the markets of Central Asia, India, and China (see the box on p. 334). As nomads who relied on trade with settled communities, the Mongols maintained safe trade routes for merchants moving through their lands. Two Venetian merchants, the brothers Niccolò and Maffeo Polo, began to travel in the Mongol Empire around 1260.

The creation of the crusader states in Syria and Palestine in the twelfth and thirteenth centuries (discussed later in this chapter) was especially favorable to Italian merchants. In return for taking the crusaders to the east, Italian merchant fleets received trading concessions in Syria and Palestine. Venice, for example, who profited the most from this trade, was given a quarter, soon known as "a little Venice in the east," in Tyre on the coast of what is now Lebanon. Such quarters here and in other cities soon became bases for carrying on lucrative trade practices.

**The Growth of Cities** The revival of trade led to a revival of cities. Towns had greatly declined in the Early Middle Ages, especially in Europe north of the Alps. Old Roman cities continued to exist but had dwindled in size and population. With the revival of trade, merchants began to settle in these old cities, followed by craftspeople or artisans, people who on manors or elsewhere had developed skills and now saw an opportunity to ply their trade and make goods that could be sold by the merchants. In the course of the eleventh and twelfth centuries, the old Roman cities came alive with new populations and growth.

Beginning in the late tenth century, many new cities or towns were also founded, particularly in northern Europe. Usually, a group of merchants established a settlement near some fortified stronghold, such as a castle or monastery. (This explains why so many place names in Europe end in *borough, burgh, burg, or bourg,* all of which mean "fortress" or "walled enclosure.") Castles were particularly favored because they were generally located along trade routes; the lords of the castle also offered protection. If the settlement prospered and expanded, new walls were built to protect it.

Although lords wanted to treat towns and townspeople as they would their vassals and serfs, cities had totally different needs and a different perspective. Townspeople needed mobility to trade. Consequently, these merchants and artisans (who came to be called *burghers* or *bourgeois,* from the same root as *borough* and *burg*) needed their own unique laws to meet their requirements and were willing to pay for them. In many instances, lords and kings saw that they could also make money and were willing to sell to the townspeople the liberties they were beginning to demand, including the right to bequeath goods and sell property, freedom from any military obligation to the lord, and written urban laws that guaranteed their freedom. Some towns also obtained the right to govern themselves by choosing their own officials and administering their own courts of law.

## An Italian Banker Discusses Trading Between Europe And China

Working on behalf of a banking guild in Florence, Francesco Balducci Pegolotti journeyed to England and Cyprus. As a result of his contacts with many Italian merchants, he acquired considerable information about long-distance trade between Europe and China. In this account, written in 1340, he provides advice for Italian merchants.

*What were Francesco Pegolotti's impressions of China? Were they positive or negative? Explain your answer.*

**Francesco Balducci Pegolotti, *An Account Of Traders Between Europe And China***

In the first place, you must let your beard grow long and not shave. And at Tana [modern Rostov] you should furnish yourself with a guide. And you must not try to save money in the matter of guides by taking a bad one instead of a good one. For the additional wages of the good one will not cost you so much as you will save by having him. And besides the guide it will be well to take at least two good menservants who are acquainted with the Turkish tongue. . . .

The road you travel from Tana to China is perfectly safe, whether by day or night, according to what the merchants say who have used it. Only if the merchant, in going or coming, should die upon the road, everything belonging to him will become the possession of the lord in the country in which he dies. . . . And in like manner if he dies in China. . . .

China is a province which contains a multitude of cities and towns. Among others there is one in particular, that is to say the capital city, to which many merchants are attracted, and in which there is a vast amount of trade; and this city is called Khanbaliq [modern Beijing]. And the said city has a circuit of one hundred miles, and is all full of people and houses. . . .

Whatever silver the merchants may carry with them as far as China, the emperor of China will take from them and put into his treasury. And to merchants who thus bring silver they give that paper money of theirs in exchange . . . and with this money you can readily buy silk and all other merchandise that you have a desire to buy. And all the people of the country are bound to receive it. And yet you shall not pay a higher price for your goods because your money is of paper.

Where townspeople experienced difficulties in obtaining privileges, they often swore an oath, forming an association called a **commune,** and resorted to force against their lay or ecclesiastical lords. Communes made their first appearance in northern Italy, in towns that were governed by their bishops, who were used by the emperors as their chief administrators. In the eleventh century, city residents swore communal associations with the bishops' noble vassals and overthrew the authority of the bishops by force. Communes took over the rights of government and created new offices for self-rule. Although communes were also sworn in northern Europe, townspeople did not have the support of rural nobles, and revolts against lay lords were usually suppressed. When they succeeded, communes received the right to choose their own officials and run their own cities. Unlike the towns in Italy, however, where the decline of the emperor's authority ensured that the northern Italian cities could function as self-governing republics, towns in France and England, like their counterparts in the Islamic and Chinese empires, did not become independent city-states but remained ultimately subject to royal authority.

Medieval cities in Europe, then, possessed varying degrees of self-government, depending on the amount of control retained over them by the lord or king in whose territory they were located. Nevertheless, all towns, regardless of the degree of outside control, evolved institutions of government for running the affairs of the community. Only males who were born in the city or had lived there for a particular length of time were defined as citizens. In many cities, these citizens elected members of a city council who served as judges and city officials and passed laws.

Medieval cities remained relatively small in comparison to either ancient or modern cities. A large trading city would number about 5,000 inhabitants. By 1200, London was the largest city in England with 30,000 people. Otherwise, north of the Alps, only a few great urban centers of commerce, such as Bruges and Ghent, had a population close to 40,000. Italian cities tended to be larger, with Venice, Florence, Genoa, Milan, and Naples numbering almost 100,000. Even the largest European city, however, seemed small alongside the Byzantine capital of Constantinople or the Arab cities of Damascus, Baghdad, and Cairo.

**Daily Life in the Medieval City** Medieval towns were surrounded by stone walls that were expensive to build, so the space within was precious. Consequently, most medieval cities featured narrow, winding streets with houses crowded against each other and second and third stories extending out over the streets. Because dwellings were built mostly of wood before the fourteenth century and candles and wood fires were used for light and heat, fire was a constant threat. Medieval cities burned rapidly once a fire started.

Most of the people who lived in cities were merchants involved in trade and artisans engaged in manufacturing a wide range of goods, such as cloth, metalwork, shoes,

Bibliothèque Nationale, Paris

**Shops in a Medieval Town.** Most urban residents were merchants involved in trade and artisans who manufactured a wide variety of products. Master craftsmen had their workshops in the ground-level rooms of their houses. In this illustration, two well-dressed burghers are touring the shopping district of a French town. Tailors, furriers, a barber, and a grocer (from left to right) are visible at work in their shops.

and leather goods. Generally, merchants and artisans had their own sections within a city. The merchant area included warehouses, inns, and taverns. Artisan sections were usually divided along craft lines. From the twelfth century on, craftspeople began to organize themselves into **guilds**, and by the thirteenth century, there were individual guilds for virtually every craft. Each craft had its own street where its activity was pursued.

The physical environment of medieval cities was not pleasant. They were dirty and smelled of animal and human wastes deposited in backyard privies or on the streets. The rivers in most cities were polluted with wastes, especially from the tanning and animal-slaughtering industries. Because of the pollution, cities did not use the rivers for drinking water but relied instead on wells.

Private and public baths also existed in medieval towns. Paris, for example, had thirty-two public baths for men and women. City laws did not allow lepers and people with "bad reputations" to use them. This did not, however, prevent public baths from being known for permissiveness due to public nudity. One contemporary commented on what occurred in public bathhouses: "Shameful things. Men make a point of staying all night in the public baths and women at the break of day come in and through 'ignorance' find themselves in the men's rooms."[4]

In medieval cities, women, in addition to supervising the household, purchasing food and preparing meals, raising the children, and managing the family finances, were also often expected to help their husbands in their trades. Some women also developed their own trades to earn extra money. When some master craftspeople died, their widows even carried on their trades. Some women in medieval towns were thus able to lead lives of considerable independence.

## Evolution of the European Kingdoms

The recovery and growth of European civilization in the High Middle Ages also affected the state. Although lords and vassals seemed forever mired in endless petty conflicts, some medieval kings inaugurated the process of developing new kinds of monarchical states that were based on the centralization of power rather than the decentralized political order that was characteristic of fief-holding. By the thirteenth century, European monarchs were solidifying their governmental institutions in pursuit of greater power.

**England in the High Middle Ages** On October 14, 1066, an army of heavily armed knights under William of Normandy landed on the coast of England and soundly defeated King Harold and his Anglo-Saxon foot soldiers. William was crowned king of England at Christmastime in London and then began the process of combining Anglo-Saxon and Norman institutions to create a new England. Many of the Norman knights were given parcels of land that they held as fiefs from the new English king. William made all nobles swear an oath of loyalty to him as sole ruler of England and insisted that all people owed loyalty to the king. All in all, William of Normandy established a strong, centralized monarchy.

In the twelfth century, the power of the English monarchy was greatly enlarged during the reign of Henry II (1154–1189). The new king was particularly successful in strengthening the power of the royal courts. Henry expanded the number of criminal cases to be tried in the king's court and also devised means for taking property cases from local courts to the royal courts. Henry's goals were clear: expanding the power of the royal courts expanded the king's power and, of course, brought revenues into his coffers. Moreover, since the royal courts were now found throughout England, a body of **common law** (law that was common to the whole kingdom) began to replace the different law codes that often varied from place to place.

Many English nobles came to resent the growth of the king's power and rose in rebellion during the reign of King John (1199–1216). At Runnymeade in 1215, John was forced to seal the Magna Carta (Great Charter) guaranteeing feudal liberties. Feudal custom had always recognized that the relationship between king and vassals was based on mutual rights and obligations. Magna Carta gave written recognition to that fact and was used in later years to support the idea that a monarch's power was limited.

During the reign of Edward I (1272–1307), an institution of great importance in the development of representative government—the English Parliament—

also emerged. Originally, the word *parliament* was applied to meetings of the king's Great Council, in which the greater barons and chief prelates of the church met with the king's judges and principal advisers to deal with judicial affairs. But in his need for money, Edward I in 1295 invited two knights from every county and two residents from each town to meet with the Great Council to consent to new taxes. This was the first Parliament.

The English Parliament, then, came to be composed of two knights from every county and two burgesses from every borough as well as the barons and ecclesiastical lords. Eventually, barons and church lords formed the House of Lords; knights and burgesses, the House of Commons. The Parliaments of Edward I approved taxes, discussed politics, passed laws, and handled judicial business. The law of the realm was beginning to be determined not by the king alone but by the king in consultation with representatives of various groups that constituted the community.

**Growth of the French Kingdom** In 843, the Carolingian Empire had been divided into three major sections. The western Frankish lands formed the core of the eventual kingdom of France. In 987, after the death of the last Carolingian king, the western Frankish nobles chose Hugh Capet as the new king, thus establishing the Capetian dynasty of French kings. Although they carried the title of kings, the Capetians had little real power. They controlled as the royal domain only the lands around Paris known as the Île-de-France. As kings of France, the Capetians were formally the overlords of the great lords of France, such as the dukes of Normandy, Brittany, Burgundy, and Aquitaine. In reality, however, many of the dukes were considerably more powerful than the Capetian kings.

The reign of King Philip II Augustus (1180–1223) was an important turning point in the growth of the French monarchy. Philip II waged war against the Plantagenet rulers of England, who also ruled the French territories of Normandy, Maine, Anjou, and Aquitaine,

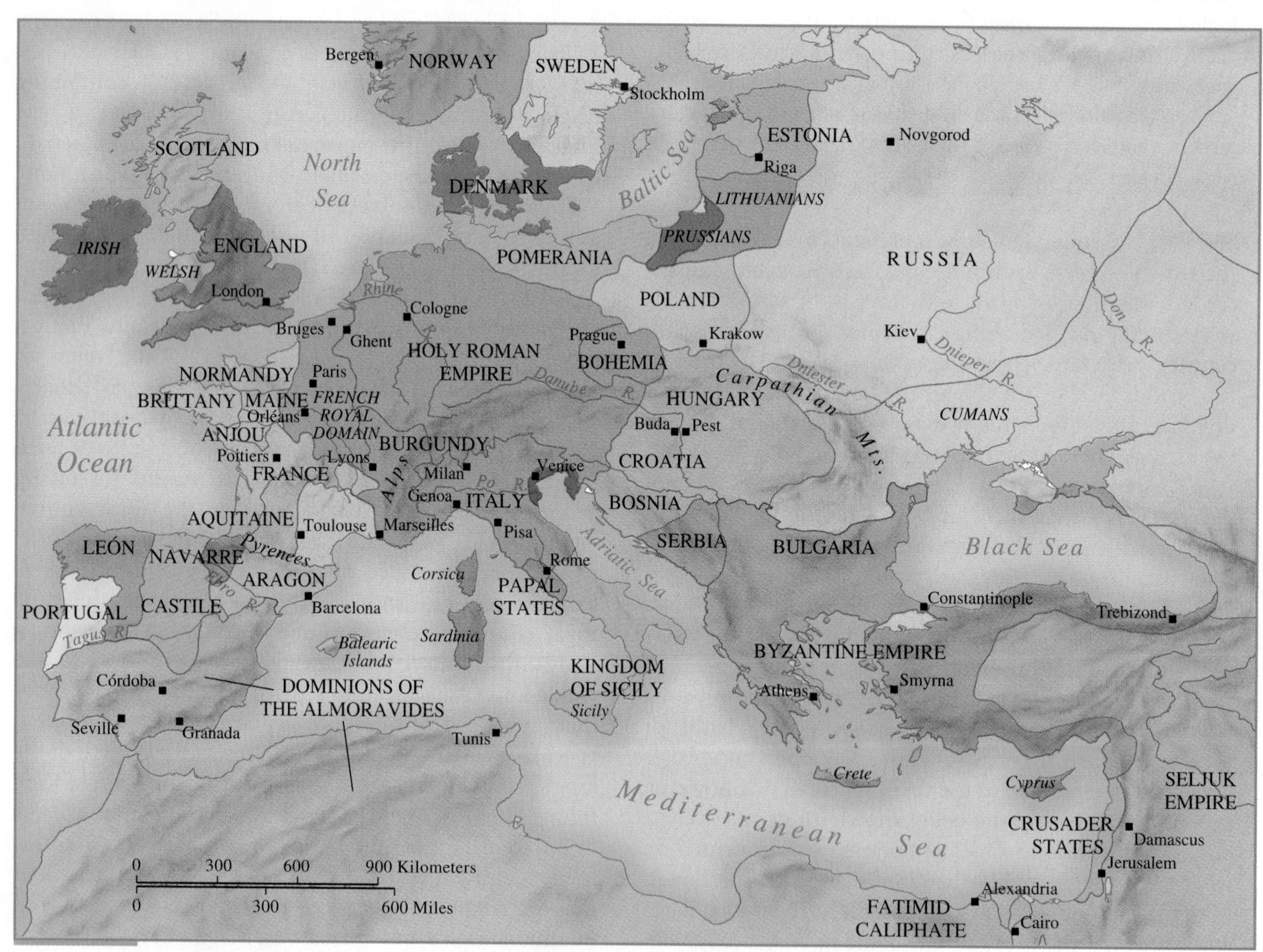


**MAP 12.3 Europe in the High Middle Ages.** Although the nobility dominated much of European society in the High Middle Ages, kings began the process of extending their power in more effective ways, creating the monarchies that would form the European states. Which were the strongest monarchical states by 1300? Why? **View an animated version of this map or related maps at http://history.wadsworth.com/duikerspielvogel05/**

and was successful in gaining control of most of these territories, thus enlarging the power of the French monarchy (see Map 12.3). To administer justice and collect royal revenues in his new territories, Philip appointed new royal officials, thus inaugurating a French royal bureaucracy in the thirteenth century.

Capetian rulers after Philip II continued to add lands to the royal domain. Philip IV the Fair (1285–1314) was especially effective in strengthening the French monarchy. He reinforced the royal bureaucracy and also brought a French parliament into being by asking representatives of the three estates, or classes—the clergy (first estate), the nobles (second estate), and the townspeople (third estate)—to meet with him. They did so in 1302, inaugurating the Estates-General, the first French parliament, although it had little real power. By the end of the thirteenth century, France was the largest, wealthiest, and best-governed monarchical state in Europe.

**The Lands of the Holy Roman Empire** In the tenth century, the powerful dukes of the Saxons became kings of the eastern Frankish kingdom (or Germany, as it came to be called). The best known of the Saxon kings of Germany was Otto I (936–973), who intervened in Italian politics and for his efforts was crowned by the pope in 962 as emperor of the Romans, reviving a title that had not been used since the time of Charlemagne.

As leaders of a new Roman empire, the German kings attempted to rule both German and Italian lands. Frederick I (1152–1190) and Frederick II (1212–1250) tried to create a new kind of empire. Previous German rulers had focused on building a strong German kingdom to which Italy might be added as an appendage. Frederick I, however, planned to get his chief revenues from Italy as the center of a "holy empire," as he called it (hence the name Holy Roman Empire). But his attempt to conquer northern Italy ran into severe opposition from the pope and the cities of northern Italy. An alliance of these north Italian cities and the pope defeated the forces of Emperor Frederick I in 1176.

The main goal of Frederick II was the establishment of a strong centralized state in Italy. However, he too became involved in a deadly struggle with the popes in the north Italian cities. Frederick waged a bitter struggle, winning many battles but ultimately losing the war.

The struggle between popes and emperors had dire consequences for the Holy Roman Empire. By spending their time fighting in Italy, the German emperors left Germany in the hands of powerful German lords who ignored the emperor and created their own independent kingdoms. This ensured that the German monarchy would remain weak and incapable of maintaining a centralized monarchical state; thus the German Holy Roman Emperor had no real power over either Germany or Italy. Unlike France and England, neither Germany nor Italy had a centralized national monarchy in the Middle Ages. Both Germany and Italy consisted of many small, independent states, a situation that changed little until the nineteenth century.

**The Slavic Peoples of Central and Eastern Europe** The Slavic peoples were originally a single people in central Europe, but they gradually divided into three major groups: the western, southern, and eastern Slavs (see Map 12.4). The western Slavs eventually formed the Polish and Bohemian kingdoms. German Christian missionaries converted both the Czechs in Bohemia and the Slavs in Poland by the tenth century. The non-Slavic kingdom of Hungary, which emerged after the Magyars settled down after their defeat in 955, was also converted to Christianity

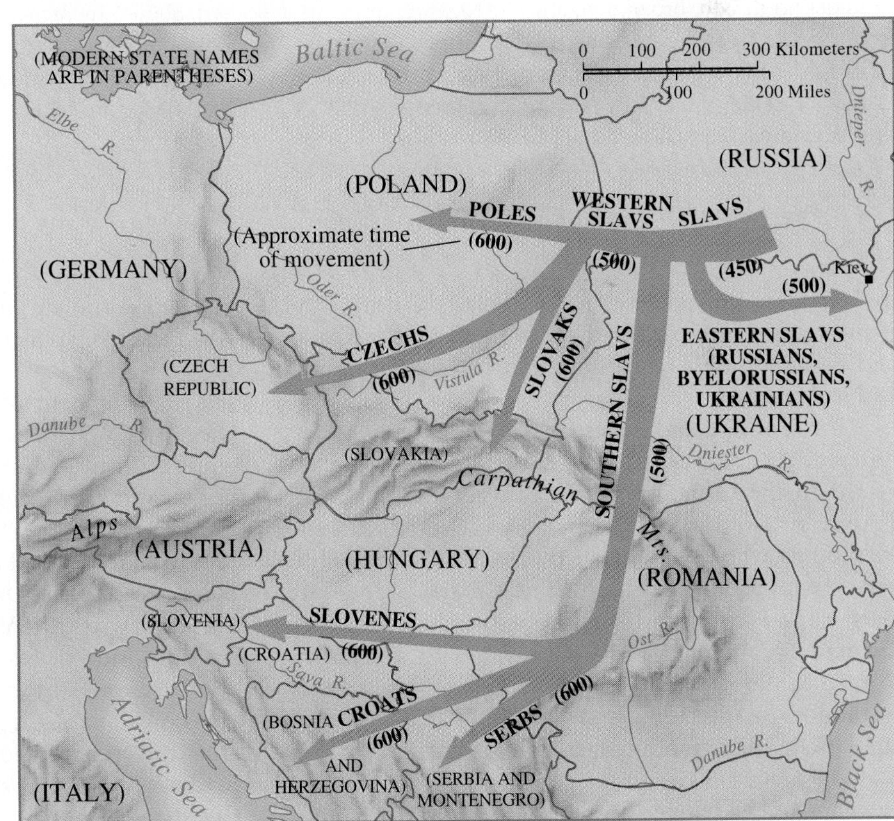


**MAP 12.4 The Migrations of the Slavs.** Originally from east-central Europe, the Slavic people broke into three groups. The western Slavs converted to Catholic Christianity, while most of the eastern Slavs and southern Slavs, under the influence of the Byzantine Empire, embraced the Eastern Orthodox faith. ? What connections do these Slavic migrations have with what we today characterize as eastern Europe? **View an animated version of this map or related maps at http://history.wadsworth.com/ duikerspielvogel05/**

## A Muslim's Description of the Rus

Despite the difficulties that travel presented, early medieval civilization did witness some contact among the various cultures. This might occur through trade, diplomacy, or the conquest and migration of peoples. This document is a description of the Swedish Rus, who eventually merged with the native Slavic peoples to form the principality of Kiev, commonly regarded as the first Russian state. It was written by Ibn Fadlan, a Muslim diplomat sent from Baghdad in 921 to a settlement on the Volga River. His comments on the filthiness of the Rus reflect the Muslim preoccupation with cleanliness.

*What was Ibn Fadlan's impression of the Rus? Why do you think he was so critical of their behavior?*

### Ibn Fadlan, Description of the Rus

I saw the Rus folk when they arrived on their trading mission and settled at the river Atul (Volga). Never had I seen people of more perfect physique. They are tall as date palms, and reddish in color. They wear neither coat nor kaftan, but each man carried a cape which covers one half of his body, leaving one hand free. No one is ever parted from his axe, sword, and knife. Their swords are Frankish in design, broad, flat, and fluted. Each man has a number of trees, figures, and the like from the fingernails to the neck. Each woman carried on her bosom a container made of iron, silver, copper, or gold–its size and substance depending on her man's wealth.

They [the Rus] are the filthiest of God's creatures. They do not wash after discharging their natural functions, neither do they wash their hands after meals. They are as lousy as donkeys. They arrive from their distant lands and lay their ships alongside the banks of the Atul, which is a great river, and there they build big houses on its shores. Ten or twenty of them may live together in one house, and each of them has a couch of his own where he sits and diverts himself with the pretty slave girls whom he had brought along for sale. He will make love with one of them while a comrade looks on; sometimes they indulge in a communal orgy, and, if a customer should turn up to buy a girl, the Rus man will not let her go till he has finished with her.

They wash their hands and faces every day in incredibly filthy water. Every morning the girl brings her master a large bowl of water in which he washes his hands and face and hair, then blows his nose into it and spits into it. When he has finished the girl takes the bowl to his neighbor–who repeats the performance. Thus the bowl goes the rounds of the entire household. . . .

If one of the Rus folk falls sick they put him in a tent by himself and leave bread and water for him. They do not visit him, however, or speak to him, especially if he is a serf. Should he recover he rejoins the others; if he dies they burn him. But if he happens to be a serf they leave him for the dogs and vultures to devour. If they catch a robber they hang him to a tree until he is torn to shreds by wind and weather.

by German missionaries. The Poles, Czechs, and Hungarians all accepted Catholic or western Christianity and became closely tied to the Roman Catholic church and its Latin culture.

The southern and eastern Slavic populations took a different path: the Slavic peoples of Moravia were converted to the Orthodox Christianity of the Byzantine Empire by two Byzantine missionary brothers, Cyril and Methodius, who began their activities in 863. The southern Slavic peoples included the Croats, Serbs, and Bulgarians. For the most part, they too embraced eastern Orthodoxy, although the Croats came to accept the Roman Catholic church. The acceptance of Eastern Orthodoxy by the Serbs and Bulgarians tied their cultural life to the Byzantine state.

The eastern Slavic peoples, from whom the modern Russians and Ukrainians are descended, had settled in the territory of present-day Ukraine and European Russia. There, beginning in the late eighth century, they began to encounter Swedish Vikings who moved down the extensive network of rivers into the lands of the eastern Slavs in search of booty and new trade routes (see the box above). These Vikings built trading settlements and eventually came to dominate the native peoples, who called them "the Rus," from which the name *Russia* is derived.

**The Development of Russia** A Viking leader named Oleg (c. 873–913) settled in Kiev at the beginning of the tenth century and created the Rus state known as the principality of Kiev. His successors extended their control over the eastern Slavs and expanded the territory of Kiev until it included the territory between the Baltic and Black Seas and the Danube and Volga Rivers. By marrying Slavic wives, the Viking ruling class was gradually assimilated into the Slavic population.

The growth of the principality of Kiev attracted religious missionaries, especially from the Byzantine Empire. One Rus ruler, Vladimir (c. 980–1015), married the Byzantine emperor's sister and officially accepted Christianity for himself and his people in 987. From the end of the tenth century, Byzantine Christianity became the model for Russian religious life.

The Kievan Rus state prospered and reached its high point in the first half of the eleventh century. But civil wars and new invasions by Asian nomads caused the principality of Kiev to collapse, and the sack of Kiev by

| CHRONOLOGY The European Kingdoms | |
|---|---|
| England | |
| Norman Conquest | 1066 |
| William the Conqueror | 1066–1087 |
| Henry II | 1154–1189 |
| John | 1199–1216 |
| Magna Carta | 1215 |
| Edward I | 1272–1307 |
| First Parliament | 1295 |
| France | |
| Philip II Augustus | 1180–1223 |
| Philip IV | 1285–1314 |
| First Estates-General | 1302 |
| Germany and the Empire | |
| Otto I | 936–973 |
| Frederick I | 1152–1190 |
| Northern Italian cities defeat Frederick | 1176 |
| Frederick II | 1212–1250 |
| The Eastern World | |
| Mongol conquest of Russia | 1230s |
| Alexander Nevsky, prince of Novgorod | c. 1220–1263 |

north Russian princes in 1169 brought an end to the first Russian state. That first Russian state had remained closely tied to the Byzantine Empire, not to the new Europe. In the thirteenth century, the Mongols conquered Russia and cut it off even more from Europe.

The Mongols had exploded onto the scene in the thirteenth century, moving east into China and west into the Middle East and central Europe. Although they conquered Russia, they were not numerous enough to settle the vast Russian lands. They occupied only part of Russia but required Russian princes to pay tribute to them. One Russian prince soon emerged as more powerful than the others. Alexander Nevsky, prince of Novgorod, defeated a German invading army in northwestern Russia in 1242. His cooperation with the Mongols won him their favor. The khan, leader of the western part of the Mongol Empire, rewarded Alexander Nevsky with the title of grand-prince, enabling his descendants to become the princes of Moscow and eventually leaders of all Russia.

## Christianity and Medieval Civilization

Christianity was an integral part of the fabric of European society and the consciousness of Europe. Papal directives affected the actions of kings and princes alike, and Christian teachings and practices touched the lives of all Europeans.

**The Papal Monarchy** Since the fifth century, the popes of the Catholic church had reigned supreme over church affairs. They had also come to exercise control over the territories in central Italy that came to be known as the Papal States, which kept the popes involved in political matters, often at the expense of their spiritual obligations. At the same time, the church became increasingly entangled in the evolving feudal relationships. High officials of the church, such as bishops and abbots, came to hold their offices as fiefs from nobles. As vassals, they were obliged to carry out the usual duties, including military service. Of course, lords assumed the right to choose their vassals and thus came to appoint bishops and abbots. Because lords often chose their vassals from other noble families for political reasons, these bishops and abbots were often worldly figures who cared little about their spiritual responsibilities.

By the eleventh century, church leaders realized the need to free the church from the interference of lords in the appointment of church officials. **Lay investiture** was the practice by which secular rulers both chose nominees to church offices and invested them with the symbols of their office. Pope Gregory VII (1073–1085) decided to fight this practice. Gregory claimed that he, as pope, was God's "vicar on earth" and that the pope's authority extended over all of Christendom, including its rulers. In 1075, he issued a decree forbidding high-ranking clerics from receiving their investiture from lay leaders.

Gregory soon found himself in conflict with the king of Germany over his actions. King Henry IV (1056–1106) of Germany was also a determined man who had appointed high-ranking clerics, especially bishops, as his vassals in order to use them as administrators. Henry had no intention of obeying a decree that challenged the very heart of his administration.

The struggle between Henry IV and Gregory VII, which is known as the Investiture Controversy, was one of the great conflicts between church and state in the High Middle Ages. It dragged on until a new German king and a new pope reached a compromise in 1122 called the Concordat of Worms. Under this agreement, a bishop in Germany was first elected by church officials. After election, the nominee paid homage to the king as his lord, who then invested him with the symbols of temporal office. A representative of the pope, however, then invested the new bishop with the symbols of his spiritual office.

**The Church Supreme** The popes of the twelfth century did not abandon the reform ideals of Pope Gregory VII, but they were more inclined to consolidate their power and build a strong administrative system. During the papacy of Pope Innocent III (1198–1216), the Catholic church reached the height of its power. At the beginning of his pontificate, in a letter to a priest, the pope made a clear statement of his views on papal supremacy:

> As God, the creator of the universe, set two great lights in the firmament of heaven, the greater light to rule the day, and the lesser light to rule the night, so He set two great dignities in the firmament of the universal church, . . . the greater to rule

the day, that is, souls, and the lesser to rule the night, that is, bodies. These dignities are the papal authority and the royal power. And just as the moon gets her light from the sun, and is inferior to the sun . . . so the royal power gets the splendor of its dignity from the papal authority.[5]

Innocent III's actions were those of a man who believed that he, the pope, was the supreme judge of European affairs. To achieve his political ends, he did not hesitate to use the spiritual weapons at his command, especially the **interdict,** which forbade priests to dispense the **sacraments** of the church in the hope that the people, deprived of the comforts of religion, would exert pressure against their ruler. Apparently Pope Innocent's interdicts worked: for example, one of them forced the king of France, Philip Augustus, to take back his wife and queen after Philip had tried to have his marriage annulled.

**New Religious Orders and New Spiritual Ideals** Between 1050 and 1150, a wave of religious enthusiasm seized Europe, leading to a spectacular growth in the number of monasteries and the emergence of new monastic orders. Most important was the Cistercian order, founded in 1098 by a group of monks dissatisfied with the moral degeneration and lack of strict discipline at their own Benedictine monastery. The Cistercians were strict. They ate a simple diet and possessed only a single robe apiece. More time for prayer and manual labor was provided by shortening the number of hours spent at religious services. The Cistercians played a major role in developing a new, activist spiritual model for twelfth-century Europe. A Benedictine monk often spent hours in prayer to honor God. The Cistercian ideal had a different emphasis: "Arise, soldier of Christ, arise! Get up off the ground and return to the battle from which you have fled! Fight more boldly after your flight, and triumph in glory!"[6] These were the words of Saint Bernard of Clairvaux (1090–1153), who more than any other person embodied the new spiritual ideal of Cistercian monasticism (see the box on p. 341).

Women were also actively involved in the spiritual movements of the age. The number of women joining religious houses grew dramatically in the High Middle Ages. Most nuns were from the ranks of the landed aristocracy. Convents were convenient for families unable or unwilling to find husbands for their daughters and for aristocratic women who did not wish to marry. Female intellectuals found them a haven for their activities. Most of the learned women of the Middle Ages were nuns.

In the thirteenth century, two new religious orders emerged that had a profound impact on the lives of ordinary people. Like their founder, Saint Francis of Assisi (1182–1226), the Franciscans lived among the people, preaching repentance and aiding the poor. Their calls for a return to the simplicity and poverty of the early church, reinforced by their own example, were especially effective and made them very popular.

The dominican order arose out of the desire of a Spanish priest, Dominic de Guzmán (1170–1221), to defend church teachings from **heresy**—beliefs contrary to official church doctrine. Unlike Francis, Dominic was an intellectual who was appalled by the growth of heresy. He came to believe that a new religious order of men who lived lives of poverty but were learned and capable of preaching effectively would best be able to attack heresy. The Dominicans became especially well known for their roles as the inquisitors of the papal Inquisition.

The Holy Office, as the papal Inquisition was formally called, was a court that had been established by the church to find and try heretics. Anyone accused of heresy who refused to confess was considered guilty and was turned over to the state for execution. So also were relapsed heretics—those who confessed, did penance, and then reverted to heresy again. Most heretics, however, were put in prison or made to do various forms of penance. To the Christians of the thirteenth century, who believed that there was only one path to salvation, heresy was a crime against God and against humanity. In their minds, force should be used to save souls from damnation.



**A Group of Nuns.** Although still viewed by the medieval church as inferior to men, women were as susceptible to the spiritual fervor of the twelfth century as men, and female monasticism grew accordingly. This miniature shows a group of Flemish nuns listening to the preaching of an abbot, Gilles li Muisis. The nun wearing a white robe at the far left is a novice.

## A Miracle of Saint Bernard

Saint Bernard of Clairvaux has been called "the most widely respected holy man of the twelfth century." He was an outstanding preacher, wholly dedicated to the service of God. His reputation reportedly influenced many young men to join the Cistercian order. He also inspired a myriad of stories dealing with his miracles.

*What two miracles occur in this excerpt from the life of Saint Bernard? What does this document reveal about popular religious practices during the Middle Ages?*

### A Miracle of Saint Bernard

A certain monk, departing from his monastery . . . , threw off his habit, and returned to the world at the persuasion of the Devil. And he took a certain parish living; for he was a priest. Because sin is punished with sin, the deserter from his Order lapsed into the vice of lechery. He took a concubine to live with him, as in fact is done by many, and by her he had children.

But as God is merciful and does not wish anyone to perish, it happened that many years after, the blessed abbot [Saint Bernard] was passing through the village in which this same monk was living, and went to stay at his house. The renegade monk recognized him, and received him very reverently, and waited on him devoutly . . . but as yet the abbot did not recognize him.

On the morrow, the holy man said Matins and prepared to be off. But as he could not speak to the priest, since he had got up and gone to the church for Matins, he said to the priest's son "Go, give this message to your master." Now the boy had been born dumb. He obeyed the command and feeling in himself the power of him who had given it, he ran to his father and uttered the words of the Holy Father clearly and exactly. His father, on hearing his son's voice for the first time, wept for joy, and made him repeat the same words . . . and he asked what the abbot had done to him. "He did nothing to me," said the boy, "except to say, 'Go and say this to your father.'"

At so evident a miracle the priest repented, and hastened after the holy man and fell at his feet saying, "My Lord and Father, I was your monk so-and-so, and at such-and-such a time I ran away from your monastery. I ask your Paternity to allow me to return with you to the monastery, for in your coming God has visited my heart." The saint replied unto him, "Wait for me here, and I will come back quickly when I have done my business, and I will take you with me." But the priest, fearing death (which he had not done before), answered, "Lord, I am afraid of dying before then." But the saint replied, "Know this for certain, that if you die in this condition, and in this resolve, you will find yourself a monk before God."

The saint [eventually] returned and heard that the priest had recently died and been buried. He ordered the tomb to be opened. And when they asked him what he wanted to do, he said, "I want to see if he is lying as a monk or a clerk in his tomb." "As a clerk," they said; "we buried him in his secular habit." But when they had dug up the earth, they found that he was not in the clothes in which they had buried him; but he appeared in all points, tonsure and habit, as a monk. And they all praised God.

**HistoryNow™** To read two accounts of the early career of Saint Bernard, enter the *HistoryNow* documents area using the access card that is available for *World History.*

## The Culture of the High Middle Ages

The High Middle Ages was a time of extraordinary intellectual and artistic vitality. It witnessed the birth of universities and a building spree that left Europe bedecked with churches and cathedrals.

**The Rise of Universities** The university as we know it—with faculty, students, and degrees—was a product of the High Middle Ages. The word *university* is derived from the Latin word *universitas,* meaning a corporation or guild, and referred to either a corporation of teachers or a corporation of students. Medieval universities were educational guilds or corporations that produced educated and trained individuals.

The first European university appeared in Bologna, Italy, where a great teacher named Irnerius (1088–1125), who taught Roman law, attracted students from all over Europe. Most of them were laymen, usually older individuals who were administrators for kings and princes and were eager to learn more about law to apply it in their own jobs. To protect themselves, students at Bologna formed a guild or *universitas,* which was recognized by Emperor Frederick Barbarossa and given a charter in 1158. Kings, popes, and princes soon competed to found new universities, and by the end of the Middle Ages, there were eighty universities in Europe, most of them in England, France, Italy, and Germany.

University students (all men—women did not attend universities in the Middle Ages) began their studies with the traditional **liberal arts** curriculum, which consisted of grammar, rhetoric, logic, arithmetic, geometry, music, and astronomy. Teaching was done by the lecture method. The word *lecture* is derived from the Latin verb for "read." Before the development of the printing press in the fifteenth century, books were expensive and few students could afford them, so teachers read from a basic text (such as a collection of laws if the subject was law) and then added their explanations. No exams were given after a series of lectures, but when a student applied for a degree, he was given a comprehensive oral examination by a committee of teachers. The exam was taken after a four-

or six-year period of study. The first degree a student could earn was a bachelor of arts; later he might receive a master of arts degree.

After completing the liberal arts curriculum, a student could go on to study law, medicine, or theology. This last was the most highly regarded subject at the medieval university. The study of any of these three disciplines could take a decade or more. A student who passed his final oral examinations was granted a doctor's degree, which officially enabled him to teach his subject. Students who received degrees from medieval universities could pursue other careers besides teaching that proved to be much more lucrative. A law degree was necessary for those who wished to serve as advisers to kings and princes. The growing administrative bureaucracies of popes and kings also demanded a supply of clerks with a university education who could keep records and draw up official documents. Universities provided the teachers, administrators, lawyers, and doctors for medieval society.

**The Development of Scholasticism** The importance of Christianity in medieval society made it certain that theology would play a central role in the European intellectual world. Theology, the formal study of religion, was "queen of the sciences" in the new universities.

Beginning in the eleventh century, the effort to apply reason or logical analysis to the church's basic theological doctrines had a significant impact on the study of theology. The word ***scholasticism*** is used to refer to the philosophical and theological system of the medieval schools. Scholasticism tried to reconcile faith and reason, to demonstrate that what was accepted on faith was in harmony with what could be learned by reason.

The overriding task of scholasticism was to harmonize Christian teachings with the work of the Greek philosopher Aristotle. In the twelfth century, due largely to the work of Muslim and Jewish scholars in Spain, western Europe was introduced to a large number of Greek scientific and philosophical works, including the works of Aristotle. However, Aristotle's works threw many theologians into consternation. Aristotle was so highly regarded that he was called "the philosopher," yet he had arrived at his conclusions by rational thought, not by faith, and some of his doctrines contradicted the teachings of the church. The most famous attempt to reconcile Aristotle and the doctrines of Christianity was that of Saint Thomas Aquinas.

Thomas Aquinas (1225–1274) is best known for his *Summa Theologica* (*A Summa of Theology*—a summa was a compendium of knowledge that attempted to bring together all the received learning of the preceding centuries on a given subject). Aquinas' masterpiece was organized according to the dialectical method of the scholastics. Aquinas first posed a question, cited sources that offered opposing opinions on the question, and then resolved the matter by arriving at his own conclusions. In this fashion, Aquinas raised and discussed some six hundred articles.

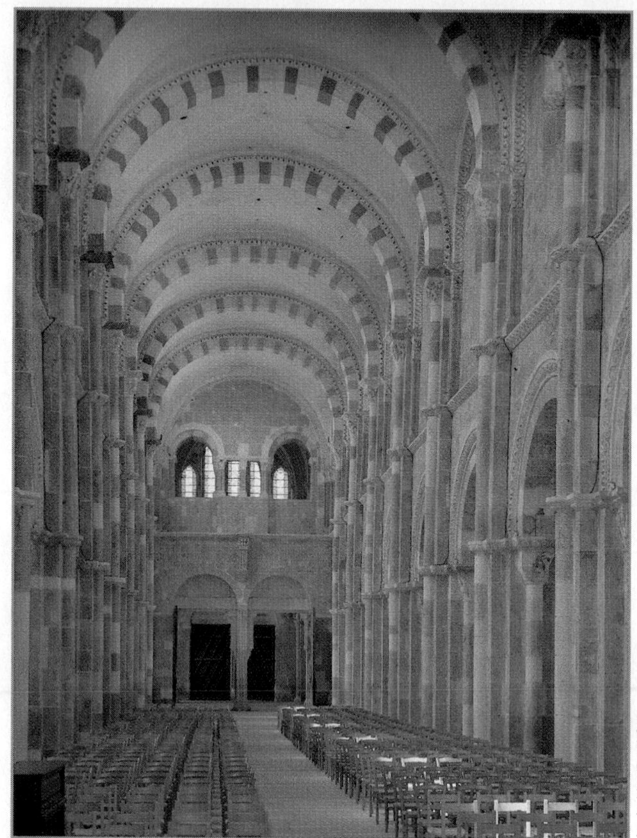

Art Archive/Dagli Orti

**Barrel Vaulting.** The eleventh and twelfth centuries witnessed an enormous amount of church construction. Utilizing the basilica shape, master builders replaced flat wooden roofs with long, round stone vaults, known as barrel vaults. As this illustration of a Romanesque church in Vienne, France, indicates, the barrel vault limited the size of a church and left little room in the walls for windows.

Aquinas' reputation derives from his masterful attempt to reconcile faith and reason. He took it for granted that there were truths derived by reason and truths derived by faith. He was certain, however, that the two truths could not be in conflict. The natural mind, unaided by faith, could arrive at truths concerning the physical universe. Without the help of God's grace, however, reason alone could not grasp spiritual truths, such as the Trinity (the manifestation of God in three separate yet identical persons—Father, Son, and Holy Spirit) or the Incarnation (Jesus' simultanteous identity as God and human).

**Romanesque Architecture** The eleventh and twelfth centuries witnessed an explosion of building, both private and public. The construction of castles and churches absorbed most of the surplus resources of medieval society and at the same time reflected its basic preoccupations, God and warfare. The churches were by far the most conspicuous of the public buildings.

The cathedrals of the eleventh and twelfth centuries were built in the **Romanesque** style, prominent examples of which can be found in Germany, France, and

Spain. Romanesque churches were normally built in the basilica shape used in the construction of churches in the Late Roman Empire. Basilicas were rectangular churches with flat wooden roofs. Romanesque builders made a significant innovation by replacing the flat wooden roof with a long, round stone vault called a barrel vault or a cross vault where two barrel vaults intersected. Although barrel and cross vaults were technically difficult to create, they were considered aesthetically more pleasing than flat wooden roofs and were also less apt to catch fire.

Because stone roofs were extremely heavy, Romanesque churches required massive pillars and walls to hold them up. This left little space for windows, and Romanesque churches were correspondingly dark on the inside. Their massive walls and pillars gave Romanesque churches a sense of solidity and almost the impression of a fortress.

**The Gothic Cathedral** Begun in the twelfth century and brought to perfection in the thirteenth, the **Gothic** cathedral remains one of the greatest artistic triumphs of the High Middle Ages. Soaring skyward, as if to reach heaven, it was a fitting symbol for medieval people's preoccupation with God.

Two fundamental innovations of the twelfth century made Gothic cathedrals possible. The combination of ribbed vaults and pointed arches replaced the barrel vault of Romanesque churches and enabled builders to make Gothic churches higher than Romanesque ones. The use of pointed arches and ribbed vaults created an impression of upward movement, a sense of weightless upward thrust that implied the energy of God. Another technical innovation, the flying buttress, a heavy arched pier of stone built onto the outside of the walls, made it possible to distribute the weight of the church's vaulted ceilings outward and down and thus eliminate the heavy walls used in Romanesque churches to hold the weight of the massive barrel vaults. Thus Gothic cathedrals could be built with thin walls containing magnificent stained-glass windows, which created a play of light inside that varied with the sun at different times of the day. The extensive use of colored light in Gothic cathedrals was not accidental but was executed by people who believed that natural light was a symbol of the divine light of God.

The first fully Gothic church was the abbey of Saint-Denis near Paris, inspired by its famous Abbot Suger (1122–1151) and built between 1140 and 1150. By the mid-thirteenth century, French Gothic architecture, most brilliantly executed in cathedrals in Paris (Notre-Dame), Reims, Amiens, and Chartres, had spread to virtually all of Europe.

A Gothic cathedral was the work of the entire community. All classes contributed to its construction. Master masons, who were both architects and engineers, designed them, and stonemasons and other craftspeople were paid a daily wage and provided the skilled labor to build them. A Gothic cathedral symbolized the chief preoccupation of a medieval Christian community, its dedication to a spiritual ideal. As we have observed before, the largest buildings of an era reflect the values of its society. The Gothic cathedral, with its towers soaring toward heaven, gave witness to an age when a spiritual impulse underlay most aspects of its existence.

**The Gothic Cathedral.** The Gothic cathedral was one of the great artistic triumphs of the High Middle Ages. Seen here is the cathedral of Notre-Dame in Paris. Begun in 1163, it was not completed until the beginning of the fourteenth century.

## Medieval Europe and the World

As it developed, European civilization remained largely confined to its home continent. Some Europeans, especially merchants, had contacts with parts of Asia and Africa, and Viking explorers even reached the eastern fringes of North America in the tenth and eleventh centuries. But at the end of the eleventh century, Europeans began their first concerted attempt to expand beyond the frontiers of Europe by conquering the land of Palestine.

## THE SIEGE OF JERUSALEM: CHRISTIAN AND MUSLIM PERSPECTIVES

During the First Crusade, Christian knights laid siege to Jerusalem in June 1099. The first excerpt is taken from an account by Fulcher of Chartres, who accompanied the crusaders to the Holy Land. The second selection is by a Muslim writer, Ibn al-Athir, whose account of the First Crusade can be found in his history of the Muslim world.

*How do these two accounts differ? What was the fate of the Muslims in Jerusalem?*

### Fulcher of Chartres, *Chronicle of the First Crusade*

Then the Franks entered the city magnificently at the noonday hour on Friday, the day of the week when Christ redeemed the whole world on the cross. With trumpets sounding and with everything in an uproar, exclaiming: "Help, God!" they vigorously pushed into the city, and straightway raised the banner on the top of the wall. All the heathen, completely terrified, changed their boldness to swift flight through the narrow streets of the quarters. The more quickly they fled, the more quickly they were put to flight.

Count Raymond and his men, who were bravely assailing the city in another section, did not perceive this until they saw the Saracens [Muslims] jumping from the top of the wall. Seeing this, they joyfully ran to the city as quickly as they could, and helped the others pursue and kill the wicked enemy.

Then some, both Arabs and Ethiopians, fled into the Tower of David; others shut themselves in the Temple of the Lord and of Solomon, where in the halls a very great attack was made on them. Nowhere was there a place where the Saracens could escape swordsmen.

On the top of Solomon's Temple, to which they had climbed in fleeing, many were shot to death with arrows and cast down headlong from the roof. Within this Temple, about ten thousand were beheaded. If you had been there, your feet would have been stained up to the ankles with the blood of the slain. What more shall I tell? Not one of them was allowed to live. They did not spare the women and children.

### Account of Ibn al-Athir

In fact Jerusalem was taken from the north on the morning of Friday 22 Sha'ban 492/15 July 1099. The population was put to the sword by the Franks, who pillaged the area for a week. A band of Muslims barricaded themselves into the Oratory of David and fought on for several days. They were granted their lives in return for surrendering. The Franks honored their word, and the group left by night for Ascalon. In the Masjid al-Aqsa the Franks slaughtered more than 70,000 people, among them a large number of Imams and Muslim scholars, devout and ascetic men who had left their homelands to live lives of pious seclusion in the Holy Place. The Franks stripped the Dome of the Rock of more than forty silver candelabra, each of them weighing 3,600 drams, and a great silver lamp weighing forty-four Syrian pounds, as well as a hundred and fifty smaller candelabra and more than twenty gold ones, and a great deal more booty. Refugees from Syria reached Baghdad in Ramadan, among them the qadi Abu sa'd al-Harawi. They told the Caliph's ministers a story that wrung their hearts and brought tears to their eyes. On Friday they went to the Cathedral Mosque and begged for help, weeping so that their hearers wept with them as they described the sufferings of the Muslims in the Holy City: the men killed, the women and children taken prisoner, the homes pillaged. Because of the terrible hardships they had suffered, they were allowed to break the fast.

**History Now™** To read a number of accounts of the Siege of Jerusalem, enter the *HistoryNow* documents area using the access card that is available for *World History.*

## The First Crusades

The Crusades were based on the idea of a holy war against the infidels or unbelievers. The wrath of Christians was directed against the Muslims, and at the end of the eleventh century, Christian Europe found itself with a glorious opportunity to attack them. The immediate impetus for the Crusades came when the Byzantine emperor, Alexius I, asked Pope Urban II for help against the Seljuk Turks, who were Muslims. The pope saw a golden opportunity to provide papal leadership for a great cause: to rally the warriors of Europe for the liberation of Jerusalem and the Holy Land (Palestine) from the infidel. At the Council of Clermont in southern France near the end of 1095, Urban II challenged Christians to take up their weapons and join in a holy war to recover the Holy Land. The pope promised remission of sins: "All who die by the way, whether by land or by sea, or in battle against the pagans, shall have immediate remission of sins. This I grant them through the power of God with which I am invested."[7] The enthusiastic crowd cried out in response: "It is the will of God, it is the will of God."

Three organized crusading bands of noble warriors, most of them French, made their way eastward. The crusading army probably numbered several thousand cavalry and as many as ten thousand infantry. After the capture of Antioch in 1098, much of the crusading host proceeded down the Palestinian coast, evading the well-defended coastal cities, and reached Jerusalem in June 1099. After a five-week siege, the Holy City was taken amid a horrible massacre of the inhabitants—men, women, and children (see the box above).

After further conquest of Palestinian lands, the crusaders ignored the wishes of the Byzantine emperor and organized four Latin crusader states. Because the crusader kingdoms were surrounded by Muslims hostile to them, they grew increasingly dependent on the Italian commercial cities for supplies from Europe. Some Italian cities, such as Genoa, Pisa, and above all Venice, grew rich and powerful in the process.

But it was not easy for the crusader kingdoms to maintain themselves. Already by the 1120s, the Muslims had begun to strike back. The fall of one of the Latin kingdoms in 1144 led to renewed calls for another Crusade, especially from the monastic firebrand Saint Bernard of Clairvaux. He exclaimed, "Now, on account of our sins, the enemies of the cross have begun to show their faces. . . . What are you doing, you servants of the cross? Will you throw to the dogs that which is most holy? Will you cast pearls before swine?"[8] Bernard even managed to enlist two powerful rulers, but their Second Crusade proved to be a total failure.

The Third Crusade was a reaction to the fall of the Holy City of Jerusalem in 1187 to the Muslim forces under Saladin. Now all of Christendom was ablaze with calls for a new Crusade. Three major monarchs agreed to lead their forces in person: Emperor Frederick Barbarossa of Germany (1152–1190), Richard I the Lionhearted of England (1189–1199), and Philip II Augustus, king of France (1180–1223). Some of the crusaders finally arrived in the East by 1189 only to encounter problems. Frederick Barbarossa drowned while swimming in a local river, and his army quickly disintegrated. The English and French arrived by sea and met with success against the coastal cities, where they had the support of their fleets, but when they moved inland, they failed miserably. Eventually, after Philip went home, Richard the Lionhearted negotiated a settlement whereby Saladin agreed to allow Christian pilgrims free access to Jerusalem.

### The Later Crusades

After the death of Saladin in 1193, Pope Innocent III initiated the Fourth Crusade. On its way to the East, the crusading army became involved in a dispute over the succession to the Byzantine throne. The Venetian leaders of the Fourth Crusade saw an opportunity to neutralize their greatest commercial competitor, the Byzantine Empire. Diverted to Constantinople, the crusaders sacked the great capital city of Byzantium in 1204 and set up the new Latin Empire of Constantinople. Not until 1261 did a Byzantine army recapture Constantinople. In the meantime, additional Crusades were undertaken to reconquer the Holy Land. All of them were largely disasters, and by the end of the thirteenth century, the European military effort to capture Palestine was recognized as a complete failure.

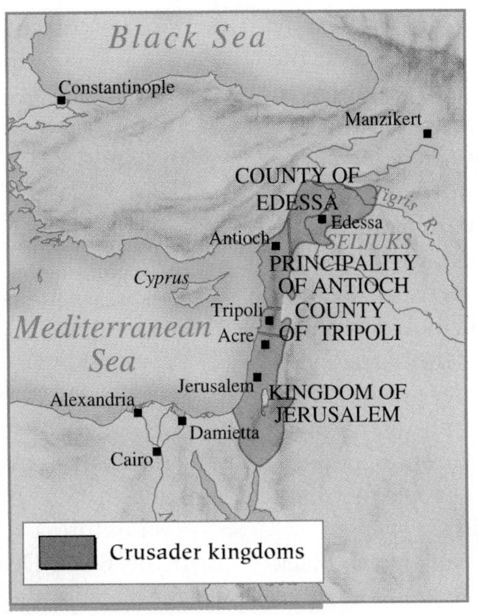

**Crusader Kingdoms in Palestine**

**CHRONOLOGY The Crusades**

| | |
|---|---|
| Urban's call for a Crusade at Clermont | 1095 |
| First Crusade | 1096–1099 |
| Second Crusade | 1147–1149 |
| Saladin's conquest of Jerusalem | 1187 |
| Third Crusade | 1189–1192 |
| Fourth Crusade—sack of Constantinople | 1204 |
| Latin Empire of Constantinople | 1204–1261 |

## The Crises of the Late Middle Ages

At the beginning of the fourteenth century, changes in weather patterns in Europe ushered in what has been called a "little ice age." Shortened growing seasons and disastrous weather conditions, including heavy storms and constant rain, led to widespread famine and hunger. Soon an even greater catastrophe struck.

### The Black Death

The **Black Death** of the mid-fourteenth century was the most devastating natural disaster in European history, ravaging Europe's population and causing economic, social, political, and cultural upheaval. Contemporary chroniclers lamented how parents abandoned their children; one related the words: "Oh father, why have you abandoned me? . . . Mother, where have you gone?"[9]

Bubonic plague was the most common and most important form of plague in the diffusion of the Black Death and was spread by black rats infested with fleas who were host to the deadly bacterium *Yersinia pestis.* This great plague originated in Asia. After disappearing from Europe and the Middle East in the Middle Ages, bubonic plague continued to haunt areas of southwestern China. Rats accompanying Mongol troops spread the plague into central and northwestern China and into Central Asia in the mid-thirteenth century. From there, trading caravans brought the plague to Caffa, on the Black Sea, in 1346 (see the comparative essay "The Role of Disease" on p. 346).

## COMPARATIVE ESSAY

# THE ROLE OF DISEASE

When Hernán Cortés and his fellow conquistadors arrived in Mesoamerica in 1519, the local inhabitants were frightened of the horses and the firearms that accompanied the Spaniards. What they did not know was that the most dangerous enemies brought by these strange new arrivals were invisible—the disease-bearing microbes that would soon kill them by the millions.

Diseases have been the scourge of animal species since the dawn of prehistory, making the lives of human beings, in the words of the English philosopher Thomas Hobbes, "nasty, brutish, and short." With the increasing sophistication of forensic evidence, archaeologists today are able to determine from recently discovered human remains that our immediate ancestors were plaqued by such familiar ailments as anemia, arthritis, tuberculosis, and malaria.

With the explosive growth of the human population brought about by the agricultural revolution, the problems posed by the presence of disease intensified. As people began to congregate in villages and cities, bacteria settled in their piles of refuse and were carried by lice in their clothing. The domestication of animals made humans more vulnerable to diseases carried by their livestock. As population density increased, the danger of widespread epidemics increased with it.

As time went on, succeeding generations gradually developed a partial or complete immunity to many of these diseases, which became chronic rather than fatal to their victims, as occurred with malaria in parts of Africa, for example, and chickenpox in the Americas. But when a disease was introduced to a particular society that had not previously been exposed to it, the consequences were often fatal. The most dramatic example was the famous Black Death, the plague that ravaged Europe and China during the fourteenth century, killing up to one-half of the inhabitants in the affected regions. Smallpox had the same impact in the Americas after the arrival of Christopher Columbus, and malaria was fatal to many Europeans on their arrival in West Africa.

How were these diseases transmitted? In most instances, they followed the trade routes. Such was the case with the Black Death, which was initially carried by fleas living in the saddlebags of Mongol warriors as they advanced toward Europe in the thirteenth and fourteenth centuries and thereafter by rats in the holds of cargo ships. Smallpox and other diseases were brought to the Americas by the conquistadors. Epidemics, then, are a price that humans pay for having developed the network of rapid communications that has accompanied the evolution of human society.

The plague reached Europe in October 1347 when Genoese merchants brought it from Caffa to the island of Sicily off the coast of Italy. It quickly spread to southern Italy, and to southern France by the end of the year (see Map 12.5). Diffusion of the Black Death followed commercial trade routes. In 1348, it spread through Spain, France, and the Low Countries and into Germany. By the end of that year, it had moved to England, ravaging it in 1349. By the end of 1349, the plague had reached northern Europe and Scandinavia. Eastern Europe and Russia were affected by 1351.

Mortality figures for the Black Death were incredibly high. Especially hard hit were Italy's crowded cities, where 50 to 60 percent of the people died. One citizen of Florence wrote, "A great many breathed their last in the public streets, day and night; a large number perished in their homes, and it was only by the stench of their decaying bodies that they proclaimed their deaths to their neighbors. Everywhere the city was teeming with corpses."[10] In England and Germany, entire villages simply disappeared. It has been estimated that out of a total European population of 75 million, as many as 38 million people may have died of the plague between 1347 and 1351.

The attempt of contemporaries to explain the Black Death and mitigate its harshness led to extreme sorts of behavior. To many, either the plague had been sent by God as a punishment for humans' sins, or it had been caused by the devil. Some, known as the flagellants, resorted to extreme measures to gain God's forgiveness. Groups of flagellants, both men and women, wandered from town to town, flogging each other with whips to beg the forgiveness of a God who, they felt, had sent the plague to punish humans for their sinful ways. One contemporary chronicler described their activities:

> The penitents went about, coming first out of Germany. They were men who did public penance and scourged themselves with whips of hard knotted leather with little iron spikes. Some made themselves bleed very badly between the shoulder blades and some foolish women had cloths ready to catch the blood and smear it on their eyes, saying it was miraculous blood. While they were doing penance, they sang very mournful songs about the nativity and the passion of Our Lord. The object of this penance was to put a stop to the mortality, for in that time . . . at least a third of all the people in the world died.[11]

The flagellants created mass hysteria wherever they went, and authorities worked overtime to crush the movement.

An outbreak of virulent anti-Semitism also accompanied the Black Death. Jews were accused of causing the plague by poisoning town wells. The worst **pogroms** (massacres) against this minority were carried out in Germany,

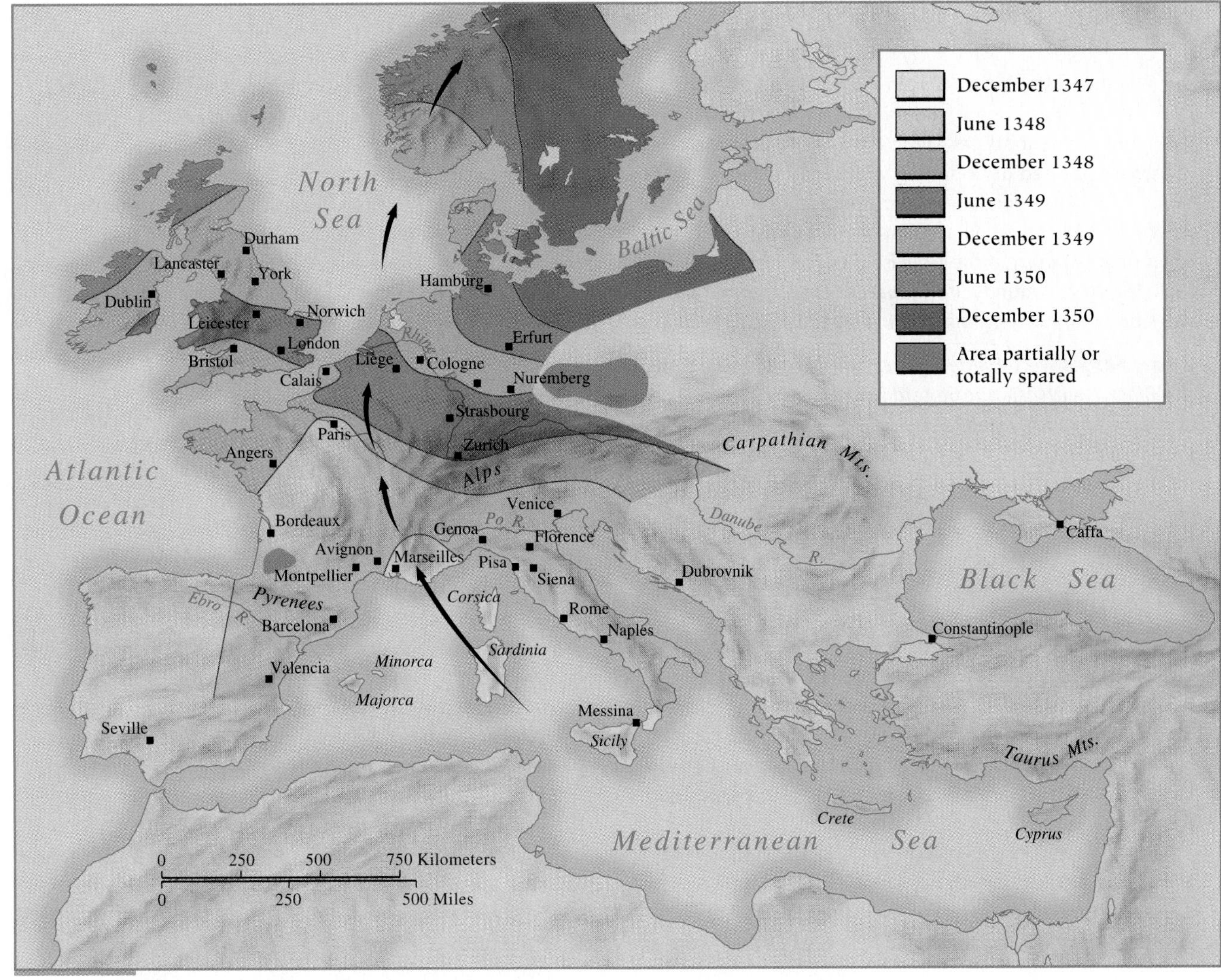


**MAP 12.5** **Spread of the Black Death.** The plague entered Europe in Sicily in 1347 and within three years had killed between one-quarter and one-half of the population. Outbreaks continued into the early eighteenth century, and it took Europe two hundred years to return to the population level it had before the Black Death. ? Is there a general pattern between distance from Sicily and the elapsed time before a region was infected with the plague? **View an animated version of this map or related maps at** http://history.wadsworth.com/duikerspielvogel05/

where more than sixty major Jewish communities had been exterminated by 1351 (see the box on p. 348). Many Jews fled eastward to Russia and especially to Poland, where the king offered them protection. Eastern Europe became home to large Jewish communities.

## Economic Dislocation and Social Upheaval

The death of so many people in the fourteenth century also had severe economic consequences. Trade declined, and some industries suffered greatly. Florence's woolens industry, one of the giants, had produced 70,000 to 80,000 pieces of cloth in 1338; in 1378, it was yielding only 24,000 pieces.

Both peasants and noble landlords were also affected. A shortage of workers caused a dramatic rise in the price of labor, while the decline in the number of people lowered the demand for food, resulting in falling prices. Landlords were now paying more for labor at the same time that their rental income was declining. Concurrently, the decline in the number of peasants after the Black Death made it easier for some to convert their labor services to rent, thus freeing them from serfdom. But there were limits to how much the peasants could advance. They faced the same economic hurdles as the lords, who also attempted to impose wage restrictions and reinstate old forms of labor service. New governmental taxes also hurt. Peasant complaints became widespread and soon gave rise to rural revolts.

Although the peasant revolts sometimes resulted in short-term gains for the participants, the uprisings were relatively easily crushed and their gains quickly lost. Accustomed to ruling, the established classes easily combined and stifled dissent. Nevertheless, the revolts of the

## A Medieval Holocaust: The Cremation of the Strasbourg Jews

In their attempt to explain the widespread horrors of the Black Death, medieval Christian communities looked for scapegoats. As at the time of the Crusades, the Jews were accused of poisoning wells and hence spreading the plague. This selection by a contemporary chronicler, written in 1349, gives an account of how Christians in the town of Strasbourg in the Holy Roman Empire dealt with their Jewish community. It is apparent that financial gain was also an important factor in killing the Jews.

*What charges were made against the Jews in regard to the Black Death? Can it be said that these charges were economically motivated? Why or why not? Why did the anti-Semitism of towns such as Strasbourg lead to the establishment of large Jewish populations in eastern Europe?*

### Jacob von Königshofen, "The Cremation of the Strasbourg Jews"

In the year 1349 there occurred the greatest epidemic that ever happened. Death went from one end of the earth to the other. . . . And from what this epidemic came, all wise teachers and physicians could only say that it was God's will. . . . This epidemic also came to Strasbourg in the summer of the above-mentioned year, and it is estimated that about sixteen thousand people died.

In the matter of this plague the Jews throughout the world were reviled and accused in all lands of having caused it through the poison which they are said to have put into the water and the wells–that is what they were accused of–and for this reason the Jews were burnt all the way from the Mediterranean into Germany. . . .

[The account then goes on to discuss the situation of the Jews in the city of Strasbourg.]

On Saturday . . . they burnt the Jews on a wooden platform in their cemetery. There were about two thousand people of them. Those who wanted to baptize themselves were spared. [Some say that about a thousand accepted baptism.] Many small children were taken out of the fire and baptized against the will of their fathers and mothers. And everything that was owed to the Jews was canceled, and the Jews had to surrender all pledges and notes that they had taken for debts. The council, however, took the cash that the Jews possessed and divided it among the workingmen proportionately. The money was indeed the thing that killed the Jews. If they had been poor and if the feudal lords had not been in debt to them, they would not have been burnt. . . .

Thus were the Jews burnt at Strasbourg, and in the same year in all the cities of the Rhine, whether Free Cities or Imperial Cities or cities belonging to the lords. In some towns they burnt the Jews after a trial; in others, without a trial. In some cities the Jews themselves set fire to their houses and cremated themselves.

It was decided in Strasbourg that no Jew should enter the city for a hundred years, but before twenty years had passed, the council and magistrates agreed that they ought to admit the Jews again into the city for twenty years. And so the Jews came back again to Strasbourg in the year 1368 after the birth of our Lord.

fourteenth century had introduced a new element to European life; henceforth, social unrest would be a characteristic of European history.

## Political Instability

Famine, plague, economic turmoil, and social upheaval were not the only problems of the fourteenth century. War and political instability must also be added to the list. Of all the struggles that ensued in the fourteenth century, the Hundred Years' War was the most violent.

**The Hundred Years' War** In the thirteenth century, England still held one small possession in France known as the duchy of Gascony. As duke of Gascony, the English king pledged loyalty as a vassal to the French king, but when King Philip VI of France (1328–1350) seized Gascony in 1337, the duke of Gascony—King Edward III of England (1327–1377)—declared war on Philip.

The war began in a burst of knightly enthusiasm. The French army of 1337 still relied largely on heavily armed noble cavalrymen, who looked with contempt on foot soldiers and crossbowmen, whom they regarded as social inferiors. The English, too, used heavily armed cavalry, but they relied even more on large numbers of paid foot soldiers. Armed with pikes, many of these soldiers had also adopted the longbow, invented by the Welsh. The longbow had greater striking power, longer range, and more rapid speed of fire then the crossbow.

The first major battle of the war occurred in 1346 at Crécy, just south of Flanders. The larger French army followed no battle plan but simply attacked the English lines in a disorderly fashion. The arrows of the English archers decimated the French cavalry. As the chronicler Froissart described it, "[with their longbows] the English continued to shoot into the thickest part of the crowd, wasting none of their arrows. They impaled or wounded horses and riders, who fell to the ground in great distress, unable to get up again without the help of several men."[12] It was a stunning victory for the English and the foot soldier.

The Battle of Crécy was not decisive, however. The English simply did not possess the resources to subjugate all of France, but they continued to try. The English king, Henry V (1413–1422), was especially eager to achieve vic-

Bibliothèque Nationale, Paris, Bridgeman Art Library

**The Battle of Crécy.** This fifteenth-century manuscript illustration depicts the Battle of Crécy, the first of several military disasters suffered by the French in the Hundred Years' War, and shows why the English preferred the longbow to the crossbow. At the left, the French crossbowmen stop shooting and prime their weapons by cranking the handle, while English archers continue to shoot their longbows (a skilled archer could launch ten arrows a minute).

tory. At the Battle of Agincourt in 1415, the heavy, armor-plated French knights attempted to attack across a field turned to mud by heavy rain; the result was a disastrous French defeat and the death of fifteen hundred French nobles. The English were masters of northern France.

The seemingly hopeless French cause fell into the hands of the dauphin Charles, the heir to the throne, who governed the southern two-thirds of French lands. Charles's cause seemed doomed until a French peasant woman quite unexpectedly saved the timid monarch. Born in 1412, the daughter of well-to-do peasants, Joan of Arc was a deeply religious person who came to believe that her favorite saints had commanded her to free France. In February 1429, Joan made her way to the dauphin's court and persuaded Charles to allow her to accompany a French army to Orléans. Apparently inspired by the faith of the peasant girl known as "the Maid of Orléans," the French armies found new confidence in themselves and liberated the city. Joan had brought the war to a decisive turning point.

But she did not live to see the war concluded. Captured in 1430, Joan was turned over by the English to the Inquisition on charges of witchcraft. In the fifteenth century, spiritual visions were thought to be inspired by either God or the devil. Joan was condemned to death as a heretic and burned at the stake in 1431. To the end, as the flames rose up around her, she declared "that her voices came from God and had not deceived her." Twenty-five years later, a new ecclesiastical court exonerated her of these charges, and five centuries later, in 1920, she was made a saint of the Roman Catholic church.

Joan of Arc's accomplishments proved decisive. Although the war dragged on for another two decades, defeats of English armies in Normandy and Aquitaine led to French victory by 1453. Important to the French success was the use of the cannon, a new weapon made possible by the invention of gunpowder. The Chinese had invented gunpower in the eleventh century and devised a simple cannon by the thirteenth century. The Mongols greatly improved this technology, developing more accurate cannons and cannonballs; both spread to the Middle East in the thirteenth century and to Europe by the fourteenth. The use of gunpowder eventually brought drastic changes to European warfare by making castles, city walls, and armored knights obsolete.

**Political Disintegration** By the fourteenth century, the feudal order had begun to break down. With money from taxes, kings could now hire professional soldiers, who tended to be more reliable than feudal knights anyway. Fourteenth-century kings had their own problems as well. Many dynasties in Europe were unable to produce male heirs, while the founders of new dynasties had to fight for their positions as groups of nobles, trying to gain advantages for themselves, supported opposing candidates. Rulers encountered financial problems too. Hiring professional soldiers left them always short of cash, adding yet another element of uncertainty and confusion to fourteenth-century politics.

## The Decline of the Church

The papacy of the Roman Catholic church reached the height of its power in the thirteenth century. But problems in the fourteenth century led to a serious decline for the church. By that time, the monarchies of Europe were no longer willing to accept papal claims of temporal supremacy, as is evident in the struggle between Pope Boniface VIII (1294–1303) and King Philip IV (1285–1314) of France. In his desire to acquire new revenues, Philip expressed the right to tax the clergy of France, but Boniface VIII claimed that the clergy of any state could not pay taxes to their secular ruler without the pope's consent. In no uncertain terms he argued that popes were supreme over both the church and the state (see the box on p. 350).

Philip IV refused to accept the pope's position and sent a small contingent of French forces to capture Boniface and bring him back to France for trial. The pope escaped but soon died from the shock of his experience.

## Boniface VIII's Defense of Papal Supremacy

One of the most remarkable documents of the fourteenth century was the exaggerated statement of papal supremacy issued by Pope Boniface VIII in 1302 in the heat of his conflict with the French king Philip IV. Ironically, this strongest statement ever made of papal supremacy was issued at a time when the rising power of the secular monarchies made it increasingly difficult for the premises to be accepted. Not long after issuing it, Boniface was taken prisoner by the French. Although he was freed by his fellow Italians, the humiliation of his defeat brought his death a short time later.

*What claims does Boniface VIII make in* Unam Sanctam*? To what extent are these claims a logical continuation of the development of the papacy in the Middle Ages? If you were a monarch, why would you object to these claims?*

### Pope Boniface VIII, *Unam Sanctam*

We are compelled, our faith urging us, to believe and to hold–and we do firmly believe and simply confess–that there is one holy catholic and apostolic church, outside of which there is neither salvation nor remission of sins. . . . In this church there is one Lord, one faith, and one baptism. . . . Therefore, of this one and only church there is one body and one head . . . Christ, namely, and the vicar of Christ, St. Peter, and the successor of Peter. For the Lord himself said to Peter, feed my sheep. . . .

We are told by the word of the gospel that in this His fold there are two swords–a spiritual, namely, and a temporal. . . . Both swords, the spiritual and the material, therefore, are in the power of the church; the one, indeed, to be wielded for the church, the other by the church; the one by the hand of the priest, the other by the hand of kings and knights, but at the will and sufferance of the priest. One sword, moreover, ought to be under the other, and the temporal authority to be subjected to the spiritual. . . .

Therefore if the earthly power err it shall be judged by the spiritual power; but if the lesser spiritual power err, by the greater. But if the greatest, it can be judged by God alone, not by man, the apostle bearing witness. A spiritual man judges all things, but he himself is judged by no one. This authority, moreover, even though it is given to man and exercised through man, is not human but rather divine, being given by divine lips to Peter and founded on a rock for him and his successors through Christ himself whom he has confessed; the Lord himself saying to Peter: "Whatsoever thou shalt bind, etc." Whoever, therefore, resists this power thus ordained by God, resists the ordination of God. . . .

Indeed, we declare, announce, and define that it is altogether necessary to salvation for every human creature to be subject to the Roman pontiff.

**HistoryNow™** To read another of Boniface VIII's writings, enter the *HistoryNow* documents area using the access card that is available for *World History.*

To ensure his position and avoid any future papal threat, Philip IV engineered the election of a Frenchman, Clement V (1305–1314), as pope. Using the excuse of turbulence in the city of Rome, the new pope took up residence in Avignon on the east bank of the Rhone River.

From 1305 to 1377, the popes resided in Avignon, leading to an increase in antipapal sentiment. The city of Rome was the traditional capital of the universal church. The pope was the bishop of Rome, and it was unseemly that the head of the Catholic church should reside in Avignon instead of Rome. Moreover, the splendor in which the pope and cardinals were living in Avignon led to highly vocal criticism of both clergy and papacy. At last, Pope Gregory XI, perceiving the disastrous decline in papal prestige, returned to Rome in 1377.

**The Great Schism and Cries for Reform** Gregory XI (1370–1378) died in Rome the spring after his return. When the college of cardinals met to elect a new pope, the citizens of Rome, fearful that the French majority would choose another Frenchman who would move the papacy back to Avignon, threatened that the cardinals would not leave Rome alive unless a Roman or an Italian were elected pope. Wisely, the terrified cardinals duly elected the Italian archbishop of Bari as Pope Urban VI (1378–1389). Five months later, a group of dissenting cardinals—the French ones—declared Urban's election invalid and chose one of their number, a Frenchman, who took the title of Clement VII and promptly returned to Avignon. Because Urban remained in Rome, there were now two popes, beginning what has been called the Great Schism of the church.

The Great Schism divided Europe. France and its allies supported the pope in Avignon, whereas France's enemy England and its allies supported the pope in Rome. The Great Schism was also damaging to the faith of Christian believers. The pope was widely believed to be the true leader of Christendom; when both lines of popes denounced the other as the Antichrist, people's faith in the papacy and the church were undermined. Finally, a church council met at Constance, Switzerland, in 1417. After the competing popes resigned or were deposed, a new pope was elected who was acceptable to all parties.

By the mid-fifteenth century, as a result of these crises, the church had lost much of its temporal power. Even worse, the papacy and the church had also lost much of their moral prestige.

## Recovery: The Renaissance

People who lived in Italy between 1350 and 1550 or so believed that they were witnessing a rebirth of classical antiquity—the world of the Greeks and Romans. To them, this marked a new age, which historians later called the **Renaissance** (French for "rebirth") and viewed as a distinct period of European history, which began in Italy and then spread to the rest of Europe.

Renaissance Italy was largely an urban society. The city-states became the centers of Italian political, economic, and social life. Within this new urban society, a secular spirit emerged as increasing wealth created new possibilities for the enjoyment of worldly things.

The Renaissance was also an age of recovery from the disasters of the fourteenth century, including the Black Death, political disorder, and economic recession. In pursuing that recovery, Italian intellectuals became intensely interested in the glories of their own past, the Greco-Roman culture of antiquity.

A new view of human beings emerged as people in the Italian Renaissance began to emphasize individual ability. The fifteenth-century Florentine architect Leon Battista Alberti expressed the new philosophy succinctly: "Men can do all things if they will."[13] This high regard for human worth and for individual potentiality gave rise to a new social ideal of the well-rounded personality or "universal person" (*l'uomo universale*) who was capable of achievements in many areas of life.

### The Intellectual Renaissance

The emergence and growth of individualism and secularism as characteristics of the Italian Renaissance are most noticeable in the intellectual and artistic realms. The most important literary movement associated with the Renaissance is humanism.

**Renaissance humanism** was an intellectual movement based on the study of the classics, the literary works of Greece and Rome. Humanists studied the liberal arts—grammar, rhetoric, poetry, moral philosophy or ethics, and history—all based on the writings of ancient Greek and Roman authors. We call these subjects the humanities.

Petrarch (1304–1374), who has often been called the father of Italian Renaissance humanism, did more than any other individual in the fourteenth century to foster its development. Petrarch sought to find forgotten Latin manuscripts and set in motion a ransacking of monastic libraries throughout Europe. He also began the humanist emphasis on the use of pure classical Latin. Humanists used the works of Cicero as a model for prose and those of Virgil for poetry. As Petrarch said, "Christ is my God; Cicero is the prince of the language."

In Florence, the humanist movement took a new direction at the beginning of the fifteenth century. Fourteenth-century humanists such as Petrarch had described the intellectual life as one of solitude. They rejected family and a life of action in the community. However, the humanists who worked as secretaries for the city council of Florence took a new interest in civic life. They came to believe that it was the duty of an intellectual to live an active life for one's state. Humanists came to believe that their study of the humanities should be put to the service of the state. It is no accident that humanists served as secretaries in Italian city-states or at courts of princes or popes.

Also evident in the humanism of the first half of the fifteenth century was a growing interest in classical Greek civilization. One of the first Italian humanists to gain a thorough knowledge of Greek was Leonardo Bruni, who became an enthusiastic pupil of the Byzantine scholar Manuel Chrysoloras, who taught in Florence from 1396 to 1400.

### The Artistic Renaissance

Renaissance artists sought to imitate nature in their works of art. Their search for naturalism became an end in itself: to persuade onlookers of the reality of the object or event they were portraying. At the same time, the new artistic standards reflected the new attitude of mind in which human beings became the focus of attention, the "center and measure of all things," as one artist proclaimed.

The frescoes by Masaccio (1401–1428) in Florence have long been regarded as the first masterpieces of Early Renaissance art. With his use of monumental figures, a more realistic relationship between figures and landscape, and the visual representation of the laws of perspective, a new realistic style of painting was born. Onlookers became aware of a world of reality that appeared to be a continuation of their own.

This new Renaissance style was absorbed and modified by other Florentine painters in the fifteenth century. Especially important were two major developments. One emphasized the technical side of painting—understanding the laws of perspective and the geometrical organization of outdoor space and light. The second development was the investigation of movement and anatomical structure. The realistic portrayal of the human nude became one of the foremost preoccupations of Italian Renaissance artists.

A new style in architecture also emerged when Filippo Brunelleschi (1377–1446), inspired by Roman models, created an interior in the Church of San Lorenzo in Florence that was very different from that of the great medieval cathedrals. San Lorenzo's classical columns, rounded arches, and coffered ceiling created an environment that did not overwhelm the worshippers physically and psychologically, as Gothic cathedrals did, but comforted them as a space created to fit human, not divine, measurements. Like painters and sculptors, Renaissance architects sought to reflect a human-centered world.

By the end of the fifteenth century, Italian artists had mastered the new techniques for scientific observation of the world around them and were now ready to move into new forms of creative expression. This marked the shift

**Brunelleschi, Interior of San Lorenzo.** Cosimo de' Medici contributed massive amounts of money to the rebuilding of the church of San Lorenzo. As seen in this view of the nave and choir of the church, Brunelleschi's architectural designs were based on the basilica plan borrowed by early Christians from pagan Rome. San Lorenzo's simplicity, evident in its rows of slender Corinthian columns, created a human-centered space.

to the High Renaissance, which was dominated by the work of three artistic giants, Leonardo da Vinci (1452–1519), Raphael (1483–1520), and Michelangelo (1475–1564). Leonardo carried on the fifteenth-century experimental tradition by studying everything and even dissecting human bodies in order to see how nature worked. But Leonardo stressed the need to advance beyond such realism and initiated the High Renaissance's preoccupation with the idealization of nature, an attempt to generalize from realistic portrayal to an ideal form.

At twenty-five, Raphael was already regarded as one of Italy's best painters. He was acclaimed for his numerous madonnas, in which he attempted to achieve an ideal of beauty far surpassing human standards. He is well known for his frescoes in the Vatican Palace, which reveal a world of balance, harmony, and order—the underlying principles of the art of the classical world of Greece and Rome.

Michelangelo, an accomplished painter, sculptor, and architect, was fiercely driven by a desire to create, and he worked with great passion and energy on a remarkable number of projects. Michelangelo was influenced by Neoplatonism, especially evident in his figures on the ceiling of the Sistine Chapel. These muscular figures reveal an ideal type of human being with perfect proportions. In good Neoplatonic fashion, their beauty is meant to be a reflection of divine beauty; the more beautiful the body, the more God-like the figure. Another manifestation of Michelangelo's search for ideal beauty was his *David,* a colossal marble statue commissioned by the government of Florence in 1501 and completed in 1504.

**Leonardo da Vinci, *The Last Supper.*** Leonardo da Vinci was the impetus behind the High Renaissance concern for the idealization of nature, moving from a realistic portrayal of the human figure to an idealized form. Evident in Leonardo's *Last Supper* is his effort to depict a person's character and inner nature by the use of gesture and movement. Unfortunately, Leonardo used an experimental technique in this fresco, which soon led to its physical deterioration.

**Michelangelo, *David.*** This statue of David, cut from an 18-foot-high piece of marble, exalts the beauty of the human body and is a fitting symbol of the Italian Renaissance's affirmation of human power. Completed in 1504, *David* was moved by Florentine authorities to a special location in front of the Palazzo Vecchio, the seat of the Florentine government.

## The State in the Renaissance

In the second half of the fifteenth century, attempts were made to reestablish the centralized power of monarchical governments after the political disasters of the fourteenth century. Some historians called these states the "new monarchies," especially those of France, England, and Spain (see Map 12.6).

**The Italian States** The Italian states provided the earliest examples of state building in the fifteenth century. During the Middle Ages, Italy had failed to develop a centralized territorial state, and by the fifteenth century, five major powers dominated the Italian peninsula: the duchy of Milan, the republics of Florence and Venice, the Papal States, and the kingdom of Naples.

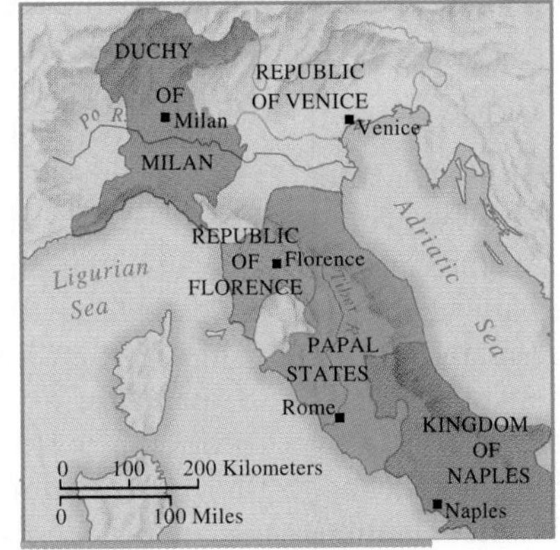


**Italian States in the Middle Ages**

Milan, Florence, and Venice proved especially adept at building strong, centralized states. Under a series of dukes, Milan became a highly centralized territorial state in which the rulers devised systems of taxation that generated enormous revenues for the government. The maritime republic of Venice remained an extremely stable political entity governed by a small oligarchy of merchant-aristocrats. Its commercial empire brought in vast revenues and gave it the status of an international power. In Florence, Cosimo de' Medici took control of the merchant oligarchy in 1434. Through lavish patronage and careful courting of political allies, he and his family dominated the city at a time when Florence was the center of the cultural Renaissance.

As strong as these Italian states became, they still could not compete with the powerful monarchical states to the north and west. Beginning in 1494, Italy became a battlefield for the great power struggle between the French and Spanish monarchies, a conflict that led to Spanish domination of Italy in the sixteenth century.

**Western Europe** The Hundred Years' War left France prostrate. But it had also engendered a certain degree of French national feeling toward a common enemy that the kings could use to reestablish monarchical power. The development of a French territorial state was greatly advanced by King Louis XI (1461–1483), known as the Spider because of his wily and devious ways. Louis strengthened the use of the ***taille***—an annual direct tax usually on land or property—as a permanent tax imposed by royal authority, giving him a sound, regular source of income, which created the foundations of a strong French monarchy.

The Hundred Years' War had also strongly affected the English. The cost of the war in its final years and the losses to the labor force strained the English economy. At the end of the war, England faced even greater turmoil when a civil war, known as the War of the Roses, erupted and aristocratic factions fought over the monarchy until 1485, when Henry Tudor established a new dynasty.

As the first Tudor king, Henry VII (1485–1509) worked to establish a strong monarchical government. Henry ended the petty wars of the nobility by abolishing their private armies. He was also very thrifty. By not overburdening the nobility and the middle class with taxes, Henry won their favor, and they provided him much support.

Spain, too, experienced the growth of a strong national monarchy by the end of the fifteenth century. During the Middle Ages, several independent Christian kingdoms had emerged in the course of the long reconquest of the Iberian peninsula from the Muslims. Two of the strongest were Aragon and Castile. When Isabella of Castile (1474–1504) married Ferdinand of Aragon (1479–1516) in 1469, it was a major step toward unifying

**MAP 12.6 Europe in the Second Half of the Fifteenth Century.** By the second half of the fifteenth century, states in western Europe, particularly France, Spain, and England, had begun the process of modern state building. With varying success, they reined in the power of the church and nobles, increased the ability to levy taxes, and established effective government bureaucracies. **?** What aspects of Europe's political boundaries help explain why France and the Holy Roman Empire were often at war with each other?

**View an animated version of this map or related maps at** http://history .wadsworth.com/duikerspielvogel05/

Spain. The two rulers worked to strengthen royal control of government. They filled the royal council, which supervised the administration of the government, with middle-class lawyers. Trained in Roman law, these officials operated on the belief that the monarchy embodied the power of the state. Ferdinand and Isabella also reorganized the military forces of Spain, making the new Spanish army the best in Europe by the sixteenth century.

**Central and Eastern Europe** Unlike France, England, and Spain, the Holy Roman Empire failed to develop a strong monarchical authority. The failure of the German emperors in the thirteenth century ended any chance of centralized monarchical authority, and Germany became a land of hundreds of virtually independent states. After 1438, the position of Holy Roman emperor was held by members of the Habsburg dynasty. Having gradually acquired a number of possessions along the Danube, known collectively as Austria, the house of Habsburg had become one of the wealthiest landholders in the empire and by the mid-fifteenth century had begun to play an important role in European affairs.

In eastern Europe, rulers struggled to achieve the centralization of the territorial states. Religious differences troubled the area, as Roman Catholics, Eastern Orthodox Christians, and other groups, including the Mongols, confronted each other. In Poland, the nobles gained the upper hand and established the right to elect their kings, a policy that drastically weakened royal authority.

Since the thirteenth century, Russia had been under the domination of the Mongols. Gradually, the princes of Moscow rose to prominence by using their close relationship to the Mongol khans to increase their wealth and expand their possessions. During the reign of the great Prince Ivan III (1462–1505), a new Russian state was born. Ivan annexed other Russian principalities and took advantage of dissension among the Mongols to throw off their yoke by 1480.

## CONCLUSION

THE COLLAPSE OF THE HAN dynasty in China in the third century C.E. led to nearly four centuries of internal chaos. The fall of the Roman Empire in the fifth century brought a quite different result as three new civilizations emerged out of the collapse of Roman power in the Mediterranean. Islam emerged in the Middle East. The eastern part of the old Roman Empire, increasingly Greek in culture, continued to survive as the Christian Byzantine Empire. And a new Christian European civilization was establishing its roots in the west.

The coronation of Charlemagne, the descendant of a Germanic tribe converted to Christianity, as Roman emperor in 800 symbolized the fusion of the three chief components of the new European civilization: the German tribes, the Roman legacy, and the Christian church. Charlemagne's Carolingian Empire fostered the idea of a distinct European identity, which has led one recent historian to call him a "father of Europe."[14] With the disintegration of that empire, power fell into the hands of many different lords, who came to constitute a powerful group of nobles that dominated the political, economic, and social life of Europe. But quietly and surely, within this world of castles and private power, kings gradually began to extend their public power and laid the foundations for the European kingdoms that in one form or another have dominated European politics ever since.

European civilization began to flourish in the High Middle Ages. The revival of trade, the expansion of towns and cities, and the development of a money economy did not mean the end of a predominantly rural European society, but they did open the door to new ways to make a living and new opportunities for people to expand and enrich their lives. At the same time, the High Middle Ages also gave birth to an intellectual and spiritual revival that transformed European society.

Fourteenth-century Europe was challenged by an overwhelming number of disintegrative forces, but European society proved remarkably resilient. Elements of recovery in the age of the Renaissance made the fifteenth century a period of significant artistic, intellectual, and political change in Europe. By the second half of the fifteenth century, the growth of strong, centralized monarchical states made possible the dramatic expansion of Europe into other parts of the world.

## TIMELINE

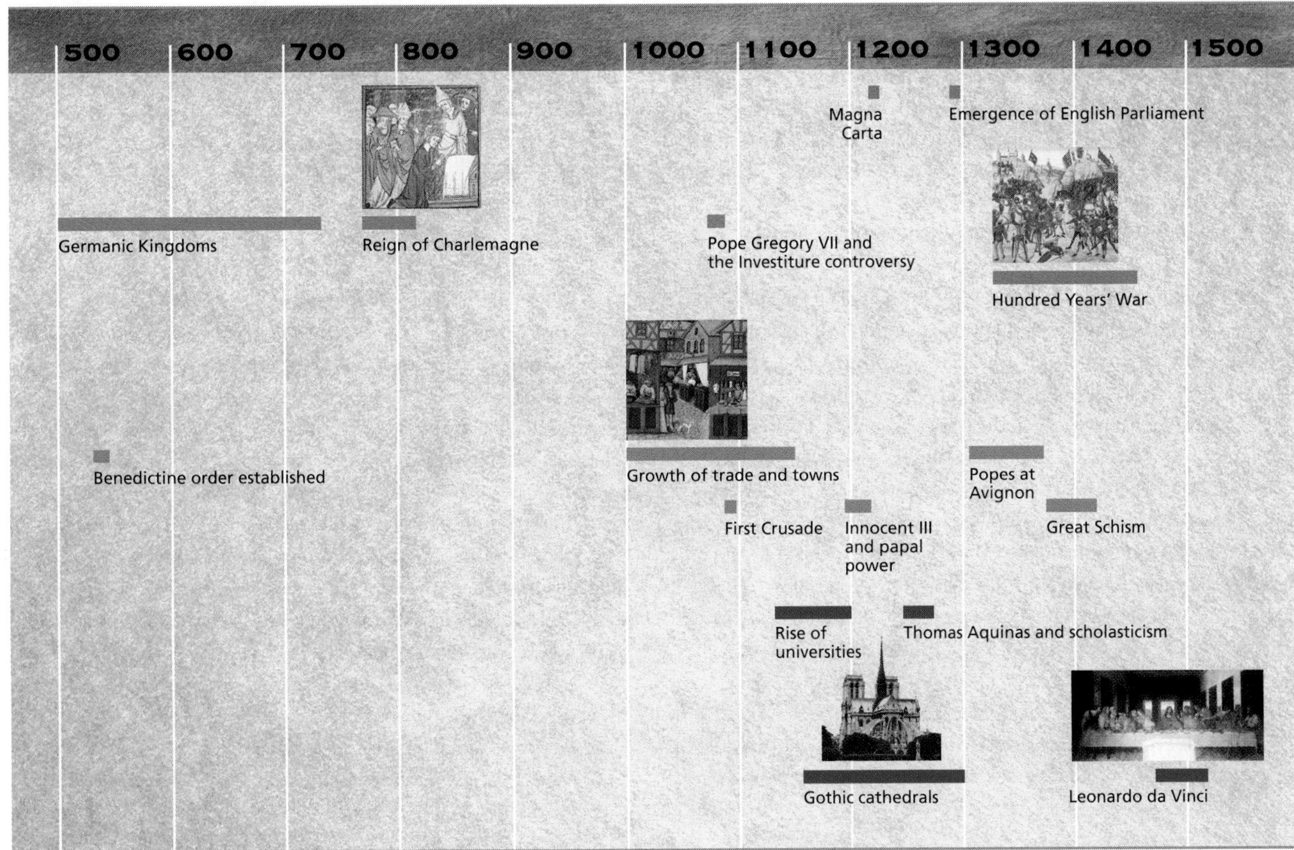

## CHAPTER NOTES

1. Quoted in N. F. Cantor, ed., *The Medieval World, 300–1300* (New York, 1963), p. 104.
2. Quoted in S. Keynes, "The Vikings in England, c. 790–1016," in P. Sawyer, ed., *The Oxford Illustrated History of the Vikings* (Oxford, 1997), p. 81.
3. Quoted in M. Perry, J. Peden, and T. von Laue, *Sources of the Western Tradition,* vol. 1 (Boston, 1987), p. 218.
4. Quoted in J. Gimpel, *The Medieval Machine* (Harmondsworth, England, 1977), p. 92.
5. O. J. Thatcher and E. H. McNeal, eds., *A Source Book for Medieval History* (New York, 1905), p. 208.
6. Quoted in R. H. C. Davis, *A History of Medieval Europe from Constantine to Saint Louis,* 2d ed. (New York, 1988), p. 252.
7. Thatcher and McNeal, *Source Book for Medieval History,* p. 517.
8. Quoted in H. E. Mayer, *The Crusades,* trans. J. Gillingham (New York, 1972), pp. 99–100.
9. Quoted in D. J. Herlihy, *The Black Death and the Transformation of the West,* ed. S. K. Cohn Jr. (Cambridge, Mass., 1997), p. 9.
10. G. Boccaccio, *The Decameron,* trans. F. Winwar (New York, 1955), p. xiii.
11. J. Froissart, *Chronicles,* ed. and trans. G. Brereton (Harmondsworth, England, 1968), p. 111.
12. Ibid., p. 89.
13. Quoted in J. Burckhardt, *The Civilization of the Renaissance in Italy,* trans. S. G. C. Middlemore (London, 1960), p. 81.
14. A. Barbero, *Charlemagne: Father of a Continent,* trans. A. Cameron (Berkeley, Calif., 2004), p. 4.

## SUGGESTED READING

For general histories of the Middle Ages, see **E. Peters, *Europe and the Middle Ages,*** 2d ed. (Englewood Cliffs, N.J., 1989); **D. Nicholas, *The Evolution of the Medieval World: Society, Government, and Thought in Europe, 312–1500*** (London, 1993); and **B. Rosenwein, *A Short History of the Middle Ages*** (Orchard Park, N.Y., 2002). A brief history of the Early Middle Ages can be found in **R. Collins, *Early Medieval Europe, 300–1000*** (New York, 1991). For a good collection of essays, see **R. McKitterick,** ed., ***Early Middle Ages: Europe, 400–1000*** (Oxford, 2001).

Carolingian Europe is examined in **P. Riche, *The Carolingians: A Family Who Forged Europe*** (Philadelphia, 1993). On Charlemagne, see **A. Barbero, *Charlemagne: Father of a Continent,*** trans. **A. Cameron** (Berkeley, Calif., 2004).

Two introductory works on fief-holding are **J. R. Strayer, *Feudalism*** (Princeton, N.J., 1985), and the classic work by **M. Bloch, *Feudal Society*** (London, 1961). For an important revisionist view, see **S. Reynolds, *Fiefs and Vassals*** (Oxford, 1994).

For a good introduction to the High Middle Ages, see **W. C. Jordan, *Europe in the High Middle Ages*** (New York, 2003); **J. H. Mundy, *Europe in the High Middle Ages, 1150–1309,*** 3d ed. (New York, 1999); and **M. Barber, *The Two Cities: Medieval Europe, 1050–1320*** (London, 1992).

On economic conditions in the Middle Ages, see **N. J. G. Pounds, *An Economic History of Medieval Europe*** (New York, 1974). Urban history is covered in **D. Nicholas, *The Growth of the Medieval City: From Late Antiquity to the Early Fourteenth Century*** (New York, 1997). On women in general, see **D. J. Herlihy, *Opera Muliebria: Women and Work in Medieval Europe*** (New York, 1990). On peasant life, see **R. Fossier, *Peasant Life in the Medieval West*** (New York, 1988).

There are numerous works on the various medieval states. On England, see **R. Frame, *The Political Development of the British Isles, 1100–1400*** (Oxford, 1990). On Germany, see **H. Fuhrmann, *Germany in the High Middle Ages, c. 1050–1250*** (Cambridge, 1986), an excellent account, and **B. Arnold, *Princes and Territories in Medieval Germany*** (Cambridge, 1991). On France, see **J. Dunbabib, *France in the Making, 843–1180*** (Oxford, 1985). On Italy, see **D. J. Herlihy, *Cities and Society in Medieval Italy*** (London, 1980). On eastern Europe, see **N. Davies, *God's Playground: A History of Poland,*** vol. 1 (Oxford, 1981), and **S. Franklin** and **J. Shephard, *The Emergence of Rus, 750–1200*** (New York, 1996).

For a general survey of Christianity in the Middle Ages, see **J. H. Lynch, *The Medieval Church: A Brief History*** (London, 1992). For a superb introduction to early Christianity, see **P. Brown, *The Rise of Western Christendom: Triumph and Adversity, A.D. 200–1000,*** 2d ed. (Oxford, 2002). On the papacy in the High Middle Ages, see **I. S. Robinson, *The Papacy*** (Cambridge, 1990). The papacy of Innocent III is covered in **J. E. Sayers, *Innocent III, Leader of Europe, 1198–1216*** (New York, 1994). Works on monasticism include **C. H. Lawrence, *Medieval Monasticism*** (London, 1984), a good general account, and **H. Leyser, *Hermits and the New Monasticism*** (London, 1984). A general study of the church in the fourteenth century is **F. P. Oakley, *The Western Church in the Later Middle Ages*** (Ithaca, N.Y., 1980).

On medieval intellectual life, see **M. L. Colish, *Medieval Foundations of the Western Intellectual Tradition, 400–1400*** (New Haven, Conn., 1997). A good introduction to Romanesque style is **A. Petzold, *Romanesque Art*** (New York, 1995). On the Gothic movement, see **M. Camille, *Gothic Art: Glorious Visions*** (New York, 1996), and **C. Wilson, *The Gothic Cathedral*** (London, 1990).

Two general surveys on the Crusades are **H. E. Mayer, *The Crusades,*** 2d ed. (New York, 1988), and **J. Riley-Smith, *The Crusades: A Short History*** (New Haven, Conn., 1987). On the First Crusade, see **T. Asbridge, *The First Crusade: A New History*** (Oxford, 2004).

On the Black Death, see **J. Kelly, *The Great Mortality*** (New York, 2005); and **D. J. Herlihy, *The Black Death and the Transformation of the West,*** ed. S. K. Cohn Jr. (Cambridge, Mass., 1997).

A worthy account of the Hundred Years' War is **A. Curry, *The Hundred Years' War*** (New York, 1993). On Joan of Arc, see **M. Warner, *Joan of Arc: The Image of Female Heroism*** (New York, 1981).

General works on the Renaissance in Europe include **P. Burke, *The European Renaissance: Centres and Peripheries*** (Oxford, 1998), and **J. R. Hale, *The Civilization of Europe in the Renaissance*** (New York, 1994). For beautifully illustrated introductions to the Renaissance, see **G. Holmes, *Renaissance*** (New York, 1996), and **M. Aston,** ed., ***The Panorama of the Renaissance*** (New York, 1996).

A brief introduction to Renaissance humanism can be found in **C. G. Nauert Jr., *Humanism and the Culture of Renaissance Europe***

(Cambridge, 1995). Good surveys of Renaissance art include **R. Turner, *Renaissance Florence: The Invention of a New Art*** (New York, 1997), and **F. Hartt, *History of Italian Renaissance Art,*** 4th ed. (Englewood Cliffs, N.J., 1994).

For a general work on the political development of Europe in the Renaissance, see **J. H. Shennan, *The Origins of the Modern European State, 1450–1725*** (London, 1974). The best overall study of the Italian states is **L. Martines, *Power and Imagination: City-States in Renaissance Italy*** (New York, 1979).

### History Now™

**Enter *HistoryNow* using the access card that is available with this text. *HistoryNow* will assist you in understanding the content in this chapter with lesson plans generated for your needs, as well as provide you with a connection to the *Wadsworth World History Resource Center* (see the following description for details).**

### World History Resource Center

**Enter the Resource Center using either your *HistoryNow* access card or your standalone access card for the *Wadsworth World History Resource Center.* Organized by topic, this website includes quizzes; images; over 350 primary source documents; interactive simulations; maps and timelines; movie explorations; and a wealth of other resources. You can read the following documents, and many more, at http://history.wadsworth.com/rc/world**

Grant of an Estate to the Monks of Saint-Denis
Thomas Aquinas, *Summa Theologica*
The Hundred Years' War in the High Court of Parlement

Visit the *World History* Companion Website for chapter quizzes and more.

http://history.wadsworth.com/duikerspielvogel05/

# Looking Ahead

The millennium following the destruction of the ancient empires brought about enormous changes in human society. During the era of Mongol expansion, there was widespread death and suffering throughout the known world. At the same time, the world had witnessed a significant expansion in the technological and material capacity of human societies and in the depth of contact among them. The era of widespread peace

**TIMELINE**

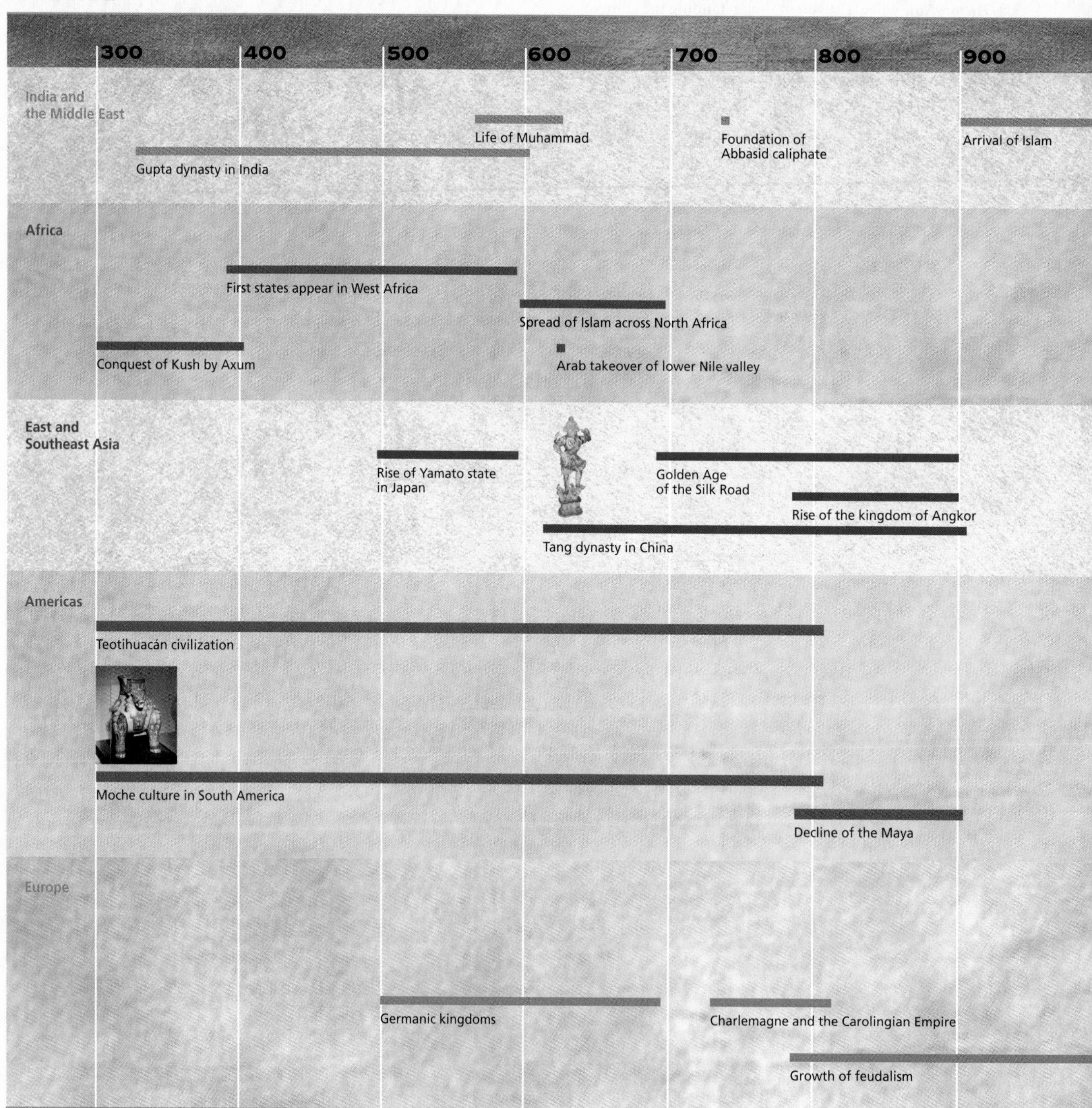

brought about as the result of the Mongol conquests also inaugurated what one scholar has described as the "idea of the unified conceptualization of the globe," creating a "basic information circuit" that spread commodities, ideas, and inventions from one end of the Eurasian supercontinent to the other. The way was prepared for a new stage of world history.

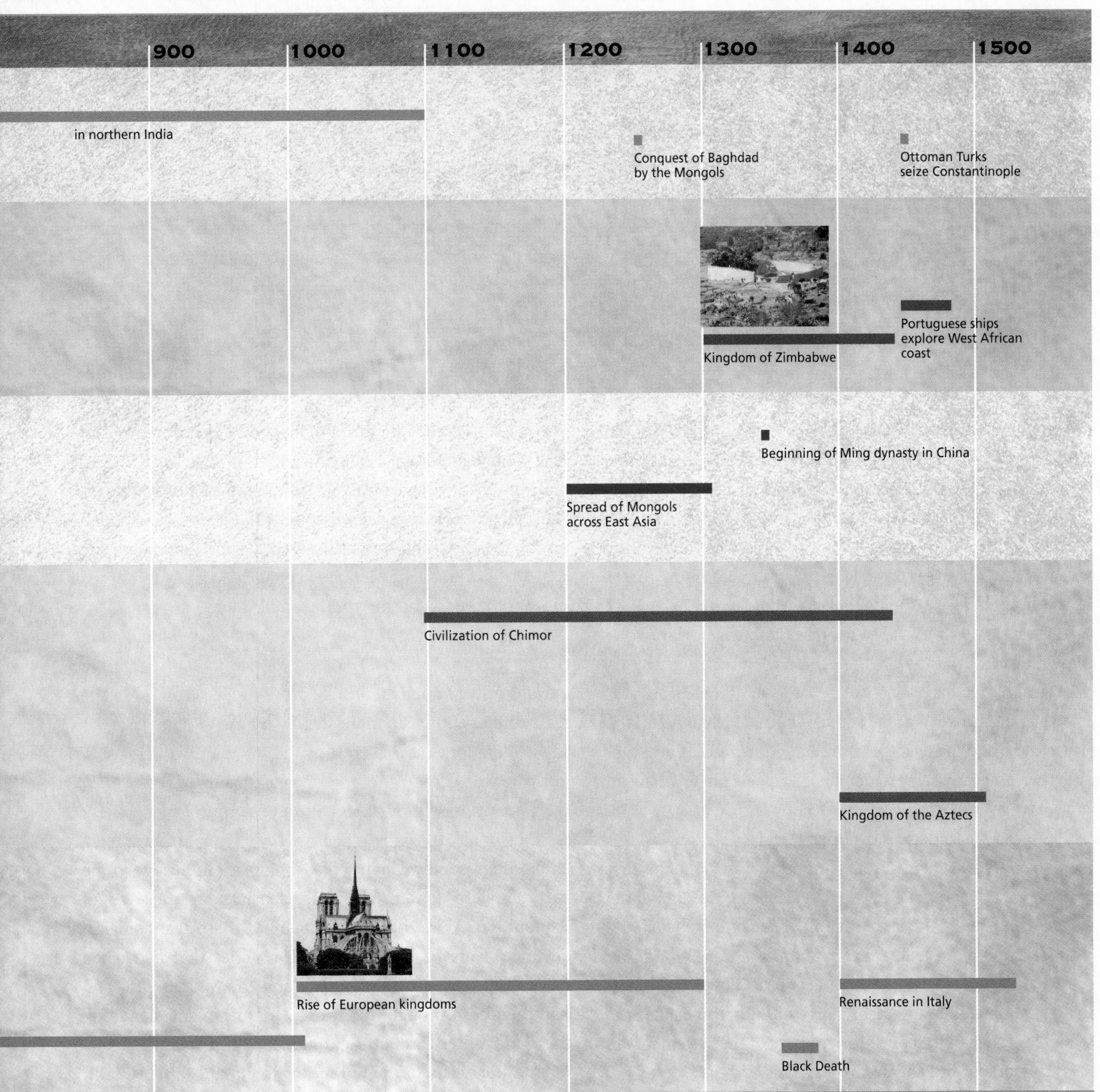

PART

# III

# THE EMERGENCE OF NEW WORLD PATTERNS (1500–1800)



HISTORIANS OFTEN REFER to the period from the sixteenth through eighteenth centuries as the early modern era. During these years, several factors were at work that created the conditions of our own time.

From a global perspective, perhaps the most noteworthy event of the period was the extension of the maritime trade network throughout the entire populated world. The Chinese had inaugurated the process with their groundbreaking voyages to East Africa in the early fifteenth century, but the primary instrument of that expansion was a resurgent Europe, which exploded onto the world scene with the initial explorations of the Portuguese and the Spanish at the end of the fifteenth century and then gradually came to dominate shipping on international trade routes during the next three centuries.

Some contemporary historians argue that it was this sudden burst of energy from Europe that created the first truly global economic network. According to Immanuel Wallerstein, one of the leading proponents of this theory, the Age of Exploration led to the creation of a new "world system" characterized by the emergence of global trade networks dominated by the rising force of European capitalism, which now began to scour the periphery of the system for access to markets and cheap raw materials.

Some historians, however, qualify Wallerstein's view and point to the Mongol expansion beginning in the thirteenth century or even to the rise of the Arab empire in the Middle East a few centuries earlier as signs of the creation of a global communications network enabling goods and ideas to travel from one end of the Eurasian supercontinent to the other.

Whatever the truth of this debate, there are still many reasons for considering the end of the fifteenth century as a crucial date in world history. In the most basic sense, it marked the end of the long isolation of the Western Hemisphere from the rest of the inhabited world. In so doing, it led to the creation of the first truly global network of ideas and commodities, which would introduce plants, ideas, and (unfortunately) many new diseases to all humanity (see the comparative essay in Chapter 13). Second, the period gave birth to a stunning increase in trade and manufacturing that stimulated major economic changes not only in Europe but in other parts of the world as well.

The period from 1500 to 1800, then, was an incubation period for the modern world and the launching pad for an era of Western domination that would reach fruition in the nineteenth century. To understand why the West emerged as the leading force in the world at that time, it is necessary to grasp what factors were at work in Europe and why they were absent in other major civilizations around the globe.

Historians have identified improvements in navigation, shipbuilding, and weaponry that took place in Europe in the early modern era as essential elements in the Age of Exploration. As we have seen, many of these technological advances were based on earlier discoveries that had taken place elsewhere–in China, India, and the Middle East–and had then been brought to Europe on Muslim ships or along the trade routes through Central Asia. But it was the capacity and the desire of the Europeans to enhance their wealth

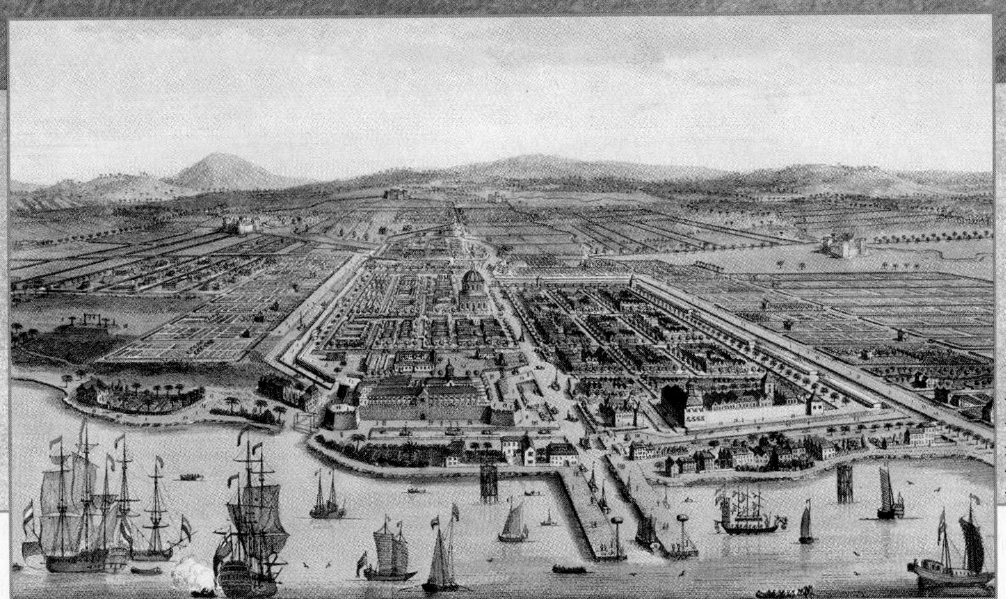


and power by making practical use of the discoveries of others that was the significant factor in the equation and enabled them to dominate international sea lanes and create vast colonial empires in the New World.

European expansion was not fueled solely by economic considerations, however. As had been the case with the rise of Islam in the seventh and eighth centuries, religion played a major role in motivating the European Age of Exploration in the early modern era. Although Christianity was by no means a new religion in the sixteenth century (as Islam had been at the moment of Arab expansion), the world of Christendom was in the midst of a major period of conflict with the forces of Islam, a rivalry that had been exacerbated by the conquest of the Byzantine Empire by the Ottoman Turks in 1453.

Although the claims of Portuguese and Spanish adventurers that their activities were motivated primarily by a desire to bring the word of God to non-Christian peoples undoubtedly included a considerable measure of self-delusion and hypocrisy, there seems no reason to doubt that religious motives played a meaningful part in the European Age of Exploration. Religious motives were perhaps less evident in the activities of the non-Catholic powers that entered the competition beginning in the seventeenth century. English and Dutch merchants and officials were more inclined to be motivated purely by the pursuit of economic profit.

Conditions in many areas of Asia were less conducive to these economic and political developments. In China, a centralized monarchy continued to rely on a prosperous agricultural sector as the economic foundation of the empire. In Japan, power was centralized under the powerful Tokugawa shogunate, and the era of peace and stability that ensued saw an increase in manufacturing and commercial activity. But Japanese elites, after initially expressing interest in the outside world, abruptly shut the door on European trade and ideas in an effort to protect the "land of the gods" from external contamination.

In India and the Middle East, commerce and manufacturing had played a vital role in the life of societies since the emergence of the Indian Ocean trade network in the first centuries C.E. But beginning in the eleventh century, the area had suffered through an extended period of political instability, marked by invasions by nomadic peoples from Central Asia. The violence of the period and the local rulers' lack of experience in promoting maritime commerce had a severe depressing effect on urban manufacturing and commerce.

In the early modern era, then, Europe was best placed to take advantage of the technological innovations that had become increasingly available throughout the Old World. It possessed the political stability, the capital, and a "modernizing elite" that spurred efforts to wrest the greatest benefit from the new conditions. Where other regions were still beset by internal obstacles or had deliberately turned inward to seek their destiny, Europe now turned outward to seek a new and dominant position in the world. Nevertheless, significant changes were taking place in other parts of the world as well and many of these changes had relatively little to do with the situation in the West. As we shall see, the impact of European expansion on the rest of the world was still limited at the end of the eighteenth century. While European political authority was firmly established in a few key areas, such as the Spice Islands and Latin America, traditional societies remained relatively intact in most regions of Africa and Asia. And processes at work in these societies were often operating independently of events in Europe and would later give birth to forces that acted to restrict or shape the Western impact. One of these forces was the progressive emergence of centralized states, some of them built on the concept of ethnic unity. ◆

CHAPTER

# 13

# NEW ENCOUNTERS: THE CREATION OF A WORLD MARKET

*The port of Calicut in the mid-1500s*

Courtesy of the Beinecke Rare Book and Manuscript Library

## CHAPTER OUTLINE AND FOCUS QUESTIONS

### An Age of Exploration and Expansion

- Why did Europeans begin to embark on voyages of exploration at the end of the fifteenth century?

### The Portuguese Maritime Empire

- Why were the Portuguese so successful in taking over the spice trade?

### Spanish Conquests in the "New World"

- How did Portugal and Spain acquire their overseas empires, and how did their methods differ?

### The Impact of European Expansion

- What were some of the consequences of the arrival of the European traders and missionaries for the peoples of Asia, Africa, and the Americas?

### Africa in Transition

- What were the main features of the African slave trade, and what effects did European participation have on traditional practices?

### Southeast Asia in the Era of the Spice Trade

- What were the main characteristics of Southeast Asian societies, and how were they affected by the coming of Islam and the Europeans?

### CRITICAL THINKING

- Christopher Columbus has recently become a controversial figure in world history. Why do you think this is so, and how would you evaluate his contribution to the modern world?

WHEN, IN THE SPRING OF 1498, the Portuguese fleet arrived at the town of Calicut (now known as Kozhikode), on the western coast of India, fleet commander Vasco da Gama ordered a landing party to go ashore to contact the local authorities. The first to greet them, a Muslim merchant from Tunisia, said, "May the Devil take thee! What brought thee hither?" "Christians and spices," replied the visitors. "A lucky venture, a lucky venture," replied the Muslim. "Plenty of rubies, plenty of emeralds! You owe great thanks to God, for having brought you to a country holding such riches!"[1]

Such words undoubtedly delighted the Portuguese, who sent a landing party ashore and concluded that the local population appeared to be Christians. Although it later turned out that they were mistaken–the local faith was a form of Hinduism–their spirits were probably not seriously dampened, for God was undoubtedly less important than gold and glory to sailors like themselves who had gone through considerable hardship to become the first Europeans since the ancient Greeks to sail across the Indian Ocean. They left two months later with a cargo of spices and the determination to return soon with a second and larger fleet.

Vasco da Gama's maiden voyage to India inaugurated an extended period of European expansion into Asia, led by merchant adventurers and missionaries, that lasted several hundred years and had effects that are still felt today. Eventually, it resulted in a Western takeover of existing trade routes in the Indian Ocean and the establishment of colonies throughout Asia, Africa, and Latin America. So complete did Western dominance seem that some historians assumed that the peoples of the non-Western world were mere passive recipients in this process, absorbing and assimilating the advanced knowledge of the West and offering nothing in return. Historians writing about the period after 1500 often talked metaphorically about the "impact of the West" and the "response" of non-Western peoples.

That image of impact and response, however, is not an entirely accurate description of what took place between the end of the fifteenth century and the end of the eighteenth. Although European rule was firmly established in Latin America and the island regions of Southeast Asia, traditional governments and institutions elsewhere remained largely intact and in some areas, notably South Asia and the Middle East, displayed considerable vitality. Moreover, although da Gama and his contemporaries are deservedly famous for their contribution to a new era of maritime commerce that circled the globe, they were not alone in extending the world trade network and transporting goods and ideas from one end of the earth to the other. As we have seen in Chapter 10, Chinese fleets had roamed the Indian Ocean for several years during the early fifteenth century, before the Ming dynasty in Beijing reversed its policy and brought an end to Chinese involvement with the outside world. Islam, too, was on the march, blazing new trails into Southeast Asia and across the Sahara to the civilizations that flourished along the banks of the Niger River. In this chapter, we turn our attention to the stunning expansion in the scope and volume of commercial and cultural contacts that took place in the generations preceding and following da Gama's historic voyage to India, as well as to the factors that brought about this expansion. ◇

# An Age of Exploration and Expansion

The voyage of Vasco da Gama has customarily been seen as a crucial step in the opening of trade routes to the East. In the sense that the voyage was a harbinger of future European participation in the spice trade, this view undoubtedly has merit. In fact, however, as has been pointed out in earlier chapters, the Indian Ocean had been a busy thoroughfare for centuries. The spice trade had been carried on by sea in the region since the days of the legendary Queen of Sheba, and Chinese junks had sailed to the area in search of cloves and nutmeg since the Tang dynasty (see Chapter 10).

## Islam and the Spice Trade

By the fourteenth century, a growing percentage of the spice trade was being transported in Muslim ships sailing from ports in India or the Middle East. Muslims, either Arabs or Indian converts, had taken part in the Indian Ocean trade for centuries, and by the thirteenth century, Islam had established a presence in seaports on the islands of Sumatra and Java and was gradually moving inland. In 1292, the Venetian traveler Marco Polo observed that Muslims were engaging in missionary activity in northern Sumatra: "This kingdom is so much frequented by the Saracen merchants that they have converted the natives to the Law of Mahomet—I mean the townspeople only, for the hill people live for all the world like beasts, and eat human flesh, as well as other kinds of flesh, clean or unclean."[2]

But the major impact of Islam came in the early fifteenth century with the rise of the new sultanate at Malacca, whose founder was a Muslim convert. With its strategic location astride the strait of the same name (see Map 13.1), Malacca "is a city that was made for commerce; . . . the trade and commerce between the different nations for a thousand leagues on every hand must come to Malacca,"[3] said a sixteenth-century Portuguese visitor. Within a few years, Malacca had become the leading power in the region.

Unfortunately for the Muslim traders who had come to Southeast Asia for the spice trade, others would also covet that trade. Although China's interest in the area would soon come to an end, the arrival of da Gama's fleet was a sure sign that others would soon follow. Southeast Asia was on the verge of a new era in which outside forces would compete aggressively to exploit the region's vast riches.

## A New Player: Europe

For almost a millennium, Catholic Europe had been confined to one area. Its one major attempt to expand beyond those frontiers, the Crusades, had largely failed. Of course, Europe had never completely lost contact with the outside world: the goods of Asia and Africa made their way into medieval castles, the works of Muslim philosophers were read in medieval universities, and the Vikings in the ninth and tenth centuries had even explored the eastern fringes of North America. Nevertheless, Europe's contacts with non-European civilizations remained limited until the fifteenth century, when Europeans began to embark on a remarkable series of overseas journeys. What prompted European seafarers to undertake such dangerous voyages to the ends of the earth?

Europeans had long been attracted to the East. In the Middle Ages, myths and legends of an exotic land of great riches and magic were widespread. Although Muslim control of Central Asia cut Europe off from the countries farther east, the Mongol conquests in the thirteenth century had reopened the doors. The most famous medieval

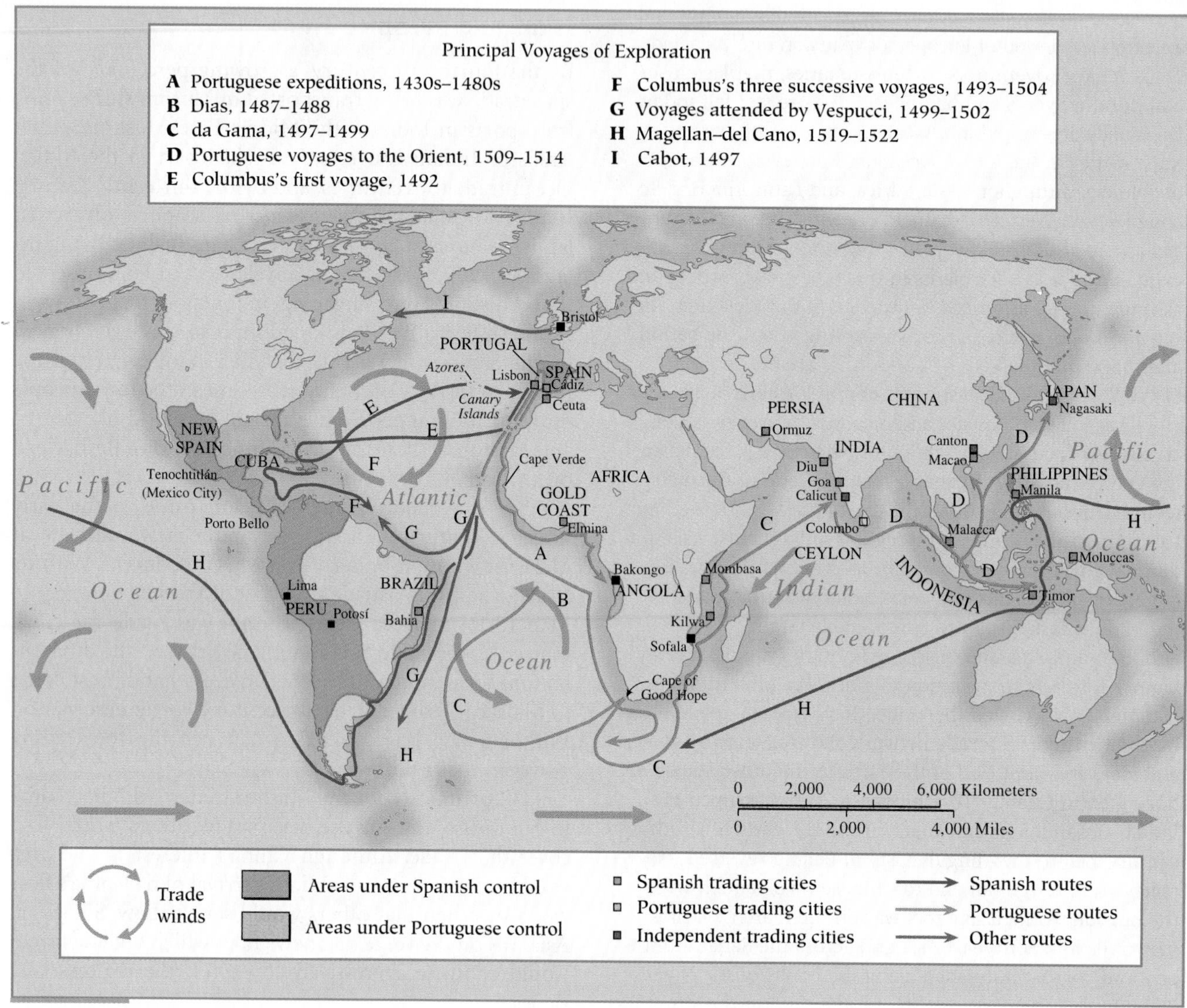


**MAP 13.1 European Voyages and Possessions in the Sixteenth and Seventeenth Centuries.** This map indicates the most important voyages launched by Europeans during their momentous Age of Exploration in the sixteenth and seventeenth centuries. ? How did the prevailing wind patterns assist European explorers in their voyages throughout the world? **View an animated version of this map or related maps at** http://history.wadsworth.com/duikerspielvogel05/

travelers to the East were the Polos of Venice. In 1271, the brothers Nicolò and Maffeo Polo, merchants from Venice, accompanied by Nicolò's son Marco, undertook the lengthy journey to the court of the great Mongol ruler Khubilai Khan (see Chapter 10). As one of the Great Khan's ambassadors, Marco reportedly traveled to Japan as well and did not return to Italy until 1295. An account of his experiences, the *Travels,* proved to be the most informative of all the descriptions of Asia by medieval European travelers. Others, like the Franciscan friar John Plano Carpini, had preceded the Polos, but in the fourteenth century the conquests of the Ottoman Turks and then the breakup of the Mongol Empire reduced Western traffic to the East. With the closing of the overland routes, a number of people in Europe became interested in the possibility of reaching Asia by sea. Christopher Columbus had a copy of Marco Polo's *Travels* in his possession when he began to envision his epoch-making voyage across the Atlantic Ocean.

**The Motives** An economic motive thus looms large in Renaissance European expansion (see Chapter 12). The rise of capitalism in Europe was undoubtedly a powerful spur to the process. Merchants, adventurers, and government officials had high hopes of finding precious metals and expanding the areas of trade, especially for the spices of the East. Spices continued to be transported to Europe via Arab intermediaries but were outrageously expensive. Adventurous Europeans did not hesitate to express their desire to share in the wealth. As one Spanish conquistador explained, he and his kind went to the New World to "serve God and His Majesty, to give light to those who were in darkness, and to grow rich, as all men desire to do."[4]

This statement expresses another major reason for the overseas voyages—religious zeal. A crusading mentality was particularly strong in Portugal and Spain, where the Muslims had largely been driven out in the Middle Ages. Contemporaries of Prince Henry the Navigator of Portugal said that he was motivated by "his great desire to make increase in the faith of our Lord Jesus Christ and to bring him all the souls that should be saved." The naval academy established by the prince to promote overseas exploration was subsidized in part by a militantly anti-Muslim Christian brotherhood. Although most scholars believe that the religious motive was secondary to economic considerations, it would be foolish to overlook the genuine desire on the part of both explorers and conquistadors, let alone missionaries, to convert the heathen to Christianity. Hernán Cortés, the conqueror of Mexico, asked his Spanish rulers if it was not their duty to ensure that the native Mexicans "are introduced into and instructed in the holy Catholic faith."[5] Spiritual and secular affairs were closely intertwined in the sixteenth century. No doubt, grandeur and glory as well as plain intellectual curiosity and a spirit of adventure also played some role in European expansion.

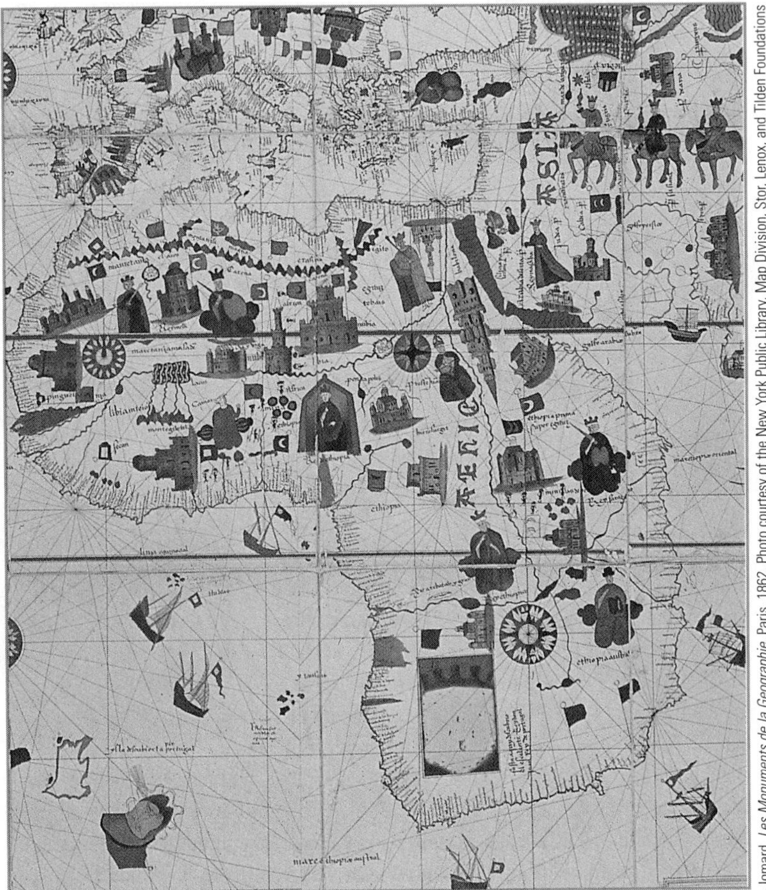

Jomard, *Les Monuments de la Geographie*, Paris, 1862, Photo courtesy of the New York Public Library, Map Division, Stor, Lenox, and Tilden Foundations

**A Sixteenth-Century Map of Africa.** Advances in mapmaking also contributed to the European Age of Exploration. Here a section of a world map by the early-sixteenth-century Spanish cartographer Juan de la Cosa shows the continent of Africa. Note the drawing of the legendary Prester John, mentioned in Chapter 8, at the right, and the Portuguese caravels with their lateen sails in the South Atlantic Ocean.

**The Means** If "God, glory, and gold" were the primary motives, what made the voyages possible? First of all, the expansion of Europe was a state enterprise, tied to the growth of centralized monarchies during the Renaissance. By the second half of the fifteenth century, European monarchies had increased both their authority and their resources and were in a position to turn their energies beyond their borders. That meant the invasion of Italy for France, but for Portugal, a state not strong enough to pursue power in Europe, it meant going abroad. The Spanish scene was more complex, since the Spanish monarchy was strong enough by the sixteenth century to pursue power both on the Continent and beyond.

At the same time, by the end of the fifteenth century, European states had a level of knowledge and technology that enabled them to achieve a regular series of voyages beyond Europe. Although the highly schematic and symbolic medieval maps were of little help to sailors, the ***portolani,*** detailed charts made by medieval navigators and mathematicians in the thirteenth and fourteenth centuries, were more useful. With details on coastal contours, distances between ports, and compass readings, they proved of great value for voyages in European waters. But because the *portolani* were drawn on a flat scale and took no account of the curvature of the earth, they were of little use for longer overseas voyages. Only when seafarers began to venture beyond the coasts of Europe did they begin to accumulate information about the actual shape of the earth. By the end of the fifteenth century, cartography had developed to the point that Europeans possessed fairly accurate maps of the known world.

In addition, Europeans had developed remarkably seaworthy ships as well as new navigational techniques. European shipmakers had mastered the use of the sternpost rudder (an import from China) and had learned how to combine the use of triangular lateen sails with a square rig. With these innovations, they could construct ships mobile enough to sail against the wind and engage in naval warfare and also large enough to mount heavy cannons and carry a substantial amount of goods over long distances. Previously, sailors had used a quadrant and their knowledge of the position of the polestar to ascertain their latitude. Below the equator, however, this technique was useless. Only with the assistance of new navigational aids such as the compass (a Chinese invention) and the astrolabe (an astronomical instrument reportedly devised by Arab sailors, used to measure the altitude of the sun and the stars above the horizon) were they able to explore the high seas with confidence.

Courtesy of William J. Duiker

National Maritime Museum, Greenwich, England

**European Warships During the Age of Exploration.** Prior to the fifteenth century, most European ships were either small craft with lateen sails used in the Mediterranean or slow, unwieldy square-rigged vessels operating in the North Atlantic. By the sixteenth century, European naval architects began to build ships that combined the maneuverability and speed offered by lateen sails (widely used by sailors in the Indian Ocean) with the carrying capacity and seaworthiness of the square-riggers. For a century, caravels (left) were the feared "sea-raiders" of the oceans. Eventually, as naval technology progressed, European warships developed in size and firepower, as the illustration of Portuguese carracks on the right shows.

A final spur to exploration was the growing knowledge of the wind patterns in the Atlantic Ocean (see Map 13.1). The first European fleets sailing southward along the coast of West Africa had found their efforts to return hindered by the strong winds that blew steadily from the north along the coast. By the late fifteenth century, however, sailors had learned to tack out into the ocean, where they were able to catch westerly winds in the vicinity of the Azores that brought them back to the coast of western Europe. Christopher Columbus used this technique in his voyages to the Americas, and others relied on their new knowledge of the winds to round the continent of Africa in search of spices.

## The Portuguese Maritime Empire

Portugal took the lead when it began exploring the coast of Africa under the sponsorship of Prince Henry the Navigator (1394–1460). Prince Henry had three objectives: finding a Christian kingdom with which to ally against the Muslims, acquiring new trade opportunities for Portugal, and extending Christianity. In 1419, he founded a school for navigators on the southwestern coast of Portugal. Shortly thereafter, Portuguese fleets began probing southward along the western coast of Africa in search of gold, which had for centuries been carried northward from south of the Atlas Mountains in central Morocco. In 1441, Portuguese ships reached the Senegal River, just north of Cape Verde, and brought home a cargo of black Africans, most of whom were sold as slaves to wealthy buyers elsewhere in Europe. Within a few years, about a thousand slaves a year were shipped from the area back to Lisbon. Inadvertently, the Portuguese had found a way to circumvent the traditional trans-Saharan slave route from Central Africa to the Mediterranean.

Continuing southward, in 1471 the Portuguese discovered a new source of gold along the southern coast of the hump of West Africa (an area that would henceforth be known to Europeans as the Gold Coast). A few years later, they established contact with the state of Bakongo, near the mouth of the Congo River in Central Africa, and with the inland state of Benin, north of the Gold Coast. To facilitate trade in gold, ivory, and slaves (not all slaves were brought back to Lisbon; some were bartered to local merchants for gold), the Portuguese leased land from local rulers and built stone forts along the coast.

### The Portuguese in India

Hearing reports of a route to India around the southern tip of Africa, Portuguese sea captains continued their probing. In 1487, Bartolomeu Dias took advantage of westerly winds in the South Atlantic to round the Cape of Good Hope, but he feared a mutiny from his crew and returned home without continuing onward. Ten years later, a fleet under the command of Vasco da Gama rounded the cape and stopped at several ports controlled by Muslim merchants along the coast of East Africa, including Sofala, Kilwa, and Mombasa. Then, having located a Muslim navigator who was familiar with seafaring in the region, da Gama's fleet crossed the Arabian Sea and arrived off the port of Calicut on the southwestern coast of India, on May 18, 1498. The Portuguese crown had sponsored da Gama's voyage with the clear objective of destroying the Muslim monopoly over the spice trade, a monopoly that had been intensified by the Ottoman conquest of Constantinople in 1453 (see Chapter 15). Calicut was a major entrepôt on the long route from the Spice Islands to the Mediterranean Sea, but the ill-informed Europeans believed it was the source of the spices themselves. They had also heard there was a Christian community in the area, supposedly established by the apostle Thomas in the first century C.E.

The Portuguese did not find any Christians, but they did find the spices. Although he lost two ships en route, da Gama's remaining vessels returned to Europe with their holds filled with ginger and cinnamon, a cargo that earned the investors a profit of several thousand percent.

Courtesy of William J. Duiker

Courtesy of William J. Duiker

Courtesy of Claire L. Duiker

COMPARATIVE ILLUSTRATION

**Western Religions in Asia.** In the century after the arrival of the first European explorers, missionaries joined their contemporaries on voyages to spread the Gospel of Jesus Christ, and communities of Christians began to form in coastal areas throughout the continents of Africa and Asia. Shown upper right is Saint Francis Church, the oldest Christian church in India. First erected by the Portuguese in 1503, it was later renovated by the Dutch and still reflects a combination of Iberian and Dutch architectural styles. At the lower right is the Catholic Cathedral in the enclave of Goa, once the headquarters of the Portuguese maritime empire. There is also a small Jewish community in Cochin that traces its roots back over one thousand years. The doorway to the Jewish section of the city still exists (see above left).

## The Portuguese Conquest of Malacca

In 1511, a Portuguese fleet led by Afonso de Albuquerque attacked the Muslim sultanate at Malacca, on the west coast of the Malay peninsula. Occupation of the port gave the Portuguese control over the strategic Strait of Malacca and the route to the Spice Islands. In this passage, Albuquerque tells his men the reasons for the attack. Note that he sees control of Malacca as a way to reduce the power of the Muslim world. The relevance of economic wealth to military power continues to underlie conflicts among nations today. The Pacific War in the 1940s, for example, began as a result of a conflict over control of the rich resources of Southeast Asia.

*What reasons does the author advance to justify his decision to launch an attack on Malacca? How might the ruler of Malacca respond to these reasons?*

### *The Commentaries of the Great Afonso de Albuquerque, Second Viceroy of India*

Although there be many reasons which I could allege in favor of our taking this city and building a fortress therein to maintain possession of it, two only will I mention to you, on this occasion. . . .

The first is the great service which we shall perform to Our Lord in casting the Moors out of this country. . . . If we can only achieve the task before us, it will result in the Moors resigning India altogether to our rule, for the greater part of them—or perhaps all of them—live upon the trade of this country and are become great and rich, and lords of extensive treasures. . . . For when we were committing ourselves to the business of cruising in the Straits [of the Red Sea], where the King of Portugal had often ordered me to go (for it was there that His Highness considered we could cut down the commerce which the Moors of Cairo, of Mecca, and of Judah, carry on with these parts), Our Lord for his service thought right to lead us hither, for when Malacca is taken the places on the Straits must be shut up, and they will never more be able to introduce their spiceries into those places.

And the other reason is the additional service which we shall render to the King D. Manuel in taking this city, because it is the headquarters of all the spiceries and drugs which the Moors carry every year hence to the Straits without our being able to prevent them from so doing; but if we deprive them of this their ancient market there, there does not remain for them a single port, nor a single situation, so commodious in the whole of these parts, where they can carry on their trade in these things. . . . I hold it as very certain that if we take this trade of Malacca away out of their hands, Cairo and Mecca are entirely ruined, and to Venice will no spiceries be conveyed except that which her merchants go and buy in Portugal.

## The Search for Spices

During the next years, the Portuguese set out to gain control of the spice trade. In 1510, Admiral Afonso de Albuquerque established his headquarters at Goa, on the western coast of India south of present-day Mumbai (Bombay). From there, the Portuguese raided Arab shippers, provoking the following comment from an Arab source: "[The Portuguese] took about seven vessels, killing those on board and making some prisoner. This was their first action, may God curse them."[6] In 1511, Albuquerque attacked Malacca itself.

For Albuquerque, control of Malacca would serve two purposes. It could help destroy the Arab spice trade network by blocking passage through the Strait of Malacca, and it could also provide the Portuguese with a way station en route to the Spice Islands and other points east (see the box above). After a short but bloody battle, the Portuguese seized the city and put the local Arab population to the sword. They then proceeded to erect the normal accouterments of the day—a fort, a factory (a common term at the time for a warehouse), and a church.

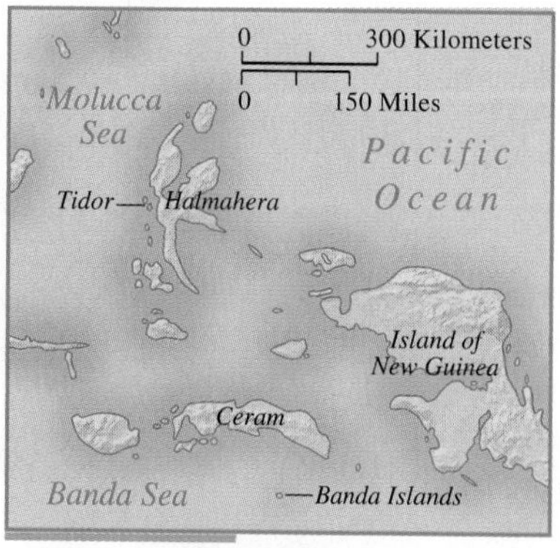

**The Spice Islands**

From Malacca, the Portuguese launched expeditions farther east, to China and the Moluccas, then known as the Spice Islands. There they signed a treaty with a local sultan for the purchase and export of cloves to the European market. Within a few years, they had managed to seize control of the spice trade from Muslim traders and had garnered substantial profits for the Portuguese monarchy.

Why were the Portuguese so successful? Basically, their success was a matter of guns and seamanship. The first Portuguese fleet to arrive in Indian waters was relatively modest in size. It consisted of three ships and twenty guns, a force sufficient for self-defense and intimidation but not for serious military operations. Sixteenth-century Portuguese fleets were more heavily armed and were capable of inflicting severe defeats if necessary on local naval and land forces. The Portuguese by no means possessed a monopoly on the use of firearms and explosives, but they used the maneuverability of their light ships to maintain their distance while

**CHRONOLOGY The Spice Trade**

| | |
|---|---|
| Vasco da Gama lands at Calicut in southwestern India | 1498 |
| Portuguese seize Malacca | 1511 |
| Portuguese ships land in southern China | 1514 |
| Magellan's voyage around the world | 1519–1522 |
| East India Company established | 1600 |
| Vereenigde Oost-Indische Compagnie (VOC) established | 1602 |
| English arrive at Surat in northwestern India | 1608 |
| Dutch fort established at Batavia | 1619 |
| Dutch seize Malacca from the Portuguese | 1641 |
| Burmese sack of Ayuthaya | 1767 |
| British seize Malacca from the Dutch | 1795 |

bombarding the enemy with their powerful cannons. Such tactics gave them a military superiority over lightly armed rivals that they were able to exploit until the arrival of other European forces several decades later.

## Spanish Conquests in the "New World"

While the Portuguese were seeking access to the spice trade of the Indies by sailing eastward through the Indian Ocean, the Spanish attempted to reach the same destination by sailing westward across the Atlantic. Although the Spanish came to overseas discovery and exploration later than the Portuguese, their greater resources enabled them to establish a far grander overseas empire.

### The Voyages

An important figure in the history of Spanish exploration was an Italian from Genoa, Christopher Columbus (1451–1506). Knowledgeable Europeans were aware that the world was round but had little understanding of its circumference or the extent of the continent of Asia. Convinced that the circumference of the earth was smaller than contemporaries believed and that Asia was larger, Columbus felt that Asia could be reached by sailing due west instead of eastward around Africa. After being rejected by the Portuguese, he persuaded Queen Isabella of Spain to finance his exploratory expedition, which reached the Americas in October 1492 and explored the coastline of Cuba and the northern shores of the neighboring island of Hispaniola. Columbus believed that he had reached Asia and in three subsequent voyages (1493, 1498, and 1502) sought in vain to find a route through the outer islands to the Asian mainland. In his four voyages, Columbus reached all the major islands of the Caribbean, which he called the Indies, as well as Honduras in Central America.

Although Columbus clung to his belief until his death, other explorers soon realized that he had discovered a new frontier altogether. State-sponsored explorers joined the race to the New World. A Venetian seafarer, John Cabot, explored the New England coastline of the Americas under a license from King Henry VII of England. The continent of South America was discovered accidentally by the Portuguese sea captain Pedro Cabral in 1500. Amerigo Vespucci, a Florentine, accompanied several voyages and wrote a series of letters describing the geography of the New World. The publication of these letters led to the use of the name "America" (after Amerigo) for the new lands.

**Columbus Landing in the New World.** In the log that he wrote during his first voyage to the Americas, Christopher Columbus noted that the peoples of the New World were intelligent and friendly, and relations between them and the Spanish were amicable at first. Later, however, the conquistadors began to mistreat the local people. Here is a somewhat imaginative painting of the first encounter from a European perspective. Note the upturned eyes of Columbus and several of his companions, suggesting that their motives were spiritual rather than material.

## The Conquests

The newly discovered territories were referred to as the New World, even though they possessed flourishing civilizations populated by millions of people when the Europeans arrived. But the Americas were new to the Europeans, who quickly saw opportunities for conquest and exploitation. The Spanish, in particular, were interested because in 1494 the Treaty of Tordesillas had divided the newly discovered world into separate Portuguese and Spanish spheres of influence. Thereafter, the route east around the Cape of Good Hope was to be reserved for the Portuguese, while the route across the Atlantic (except for the eastern hump of South America) was assigned to Spain. The Spanish **conquistadors** were a hardy lot of mostly upper-class individuals motivated by a typical sixteenth-century blend of glory, greed, and religious crusading zeal. Although sanctioned by the Castilian crown, these groups were financed and outfitted privately, not by the government.

Their superior weapons, organizational skills, and determination brought the conquistadors incredible success. Beginning in 1519 with a small band of men, Hernán Cortés took three years to overthrow the mighty Aztec empire in central Mexico, led by the chieftain Moctezuma (see Chapter 6). By 1550, the Spanish had gained control of northern Mexico. Between 1531 and 1536, another expedition, led by a hardened and somewhat corrupt soldier, Francisco Pizarro (1470–1541), took control of the Inca empire high in the Peruvian Andes. The Spanish conquests were undoubtedly facilitated by the previous arrival of European diseases, which had decimated the local population. Although it took another three decades before the western part of Latin America was brought under Spanish control (the Portuguese took over Brazil), already by 1535, the Spanish had created a system of colonial administration that made the New World an extension of the old—at least in European eyes.

**CHRONOLOGY Spanish Activities in the Americas**

| | |
|---|---|
| Christopher Columbus's first voyage to the Americas | 1492 |
| Last voyages of Columbus | 1502–1504 |
| Spanish conquest of Mexico | 1519–1522 |
| Francisco Pizarro's conquest of the Inka | 1531–1536 |

## Governing the Empire

Spanish policy toward the inhabitants of the New World, whom the Europeans called Indians, was a combination of confusion, misguided paternalism, and cruel exploitation. Confusion arose over the nature of the Indians. Unsure whether these strange creatures were "full men" or not, Spanish doctors of law debated how to fit them into currently existing European legal patterns. While the conquistadors made decisions based on expediency and their own interests, Queen Isabella declared the Indians to be subjects of Castile and instituted the **encomienda** system, which permitted the conquering Spaniards to collect tribute from the natives and use them as laborers. In return, the holders of an *encomienda* were supposed to protect the Indians and supervise their spiritual and material needs. In practice, this meant that the settlers were free to implement the system as they pleased. Three thousand miles from Spain, Spanish settlers largely ignored their government and brutally used the Indians to pursue their own

**Havana, Spain's Lifeline to the New World.** After the conquest of Mexico by Hernán Cortés, trade between Spain and its new possession flourished. Spanish navigators soon discovered that the Bay of Havana, on the north shore of the island of Cuba, was an ideal stopping point for fleets en route to and from the New World, and a city sprang up along the banks of its harbor. To protect the population from the ravages of enemy fleets—notably the English—Spanish authorities erected a number of fortifications along the coast near the city. The tower on the left is part of El Moro castle, an early fortification located at the entrance to the bay. It has long served as a visual symbol of the city of Havana.

## Las Casas and the Spanish Treatment of the American Natives

Bartolomé de Las Casas (1474–1566) was a Dominican monk who participated in the conquest of Cuba and received land and Indians in return for his efforts. But in 1514, he underwent a radical transformation that led him to believe that the Indians had been cruelly mistreated by his fellow Spaniards. He spent the remaining years of his life (he lived to the age of ninety-two) fighting for the Indians. This section is taken from his most influential work, *Brevísima Relación de la Destrucción de las Indias,* known to English readers as *The Tears of the Indians.* This work was largely responsible for the legend of the Spanish as inherently "cruel and murderous fanatics." Many scholars today feel that Las Casas may have exaggerated his account to shock his contemporaries into action.

*What forms of cruelty does the author mention in this document? Compare this account with that recorded in the box on p. 382*

### Bartolomé de Las Casas, *The Tears of the Indians*

There is nothing more detestable or more cruel than the tyranny which the Spaniards use toward the Indians for the getting of pearl. Surely the infernal torments cannot much exceed the anguish that they endure, by reason of that way of cruelty; for they put them under water some four or five ells deep, where they are forced without any liberty of respiration, to gather up the shells wherein the Pearls are; sometimes they come up again with nets full of shells to take breath, but if they stay any while to rest themselves, immediately comes a hangman row'd in a little boat, who as soon as he hath well beaten them, drags them again to their labor. Their food is nothing but filth, and the very same that contains the Pearl, with small portion of that bread which that Country affords; in the first whereof there is little nourishment; and as for the latter, it is made with great difficulty, besides that they have not enough of that neither for sustenance; they lie upon the ground in fetters, lest they should run away; and many times they are drown'd in this labor, and are never seen again till they swim upon the top of the waves; oftentimes they also are devoured by certain sea monsters, that are frequent in those seas. Consider whether this hard usage of the poor creatures be consistent with the precepts which God commands concerning charity to our neighbor, by those that cast them so undeservedly into the dangers of a cruel death, causing them to perish without any remorse or pity, or allowing them the benefit of the Sacraments, or the knowledge of Religion; it being impossible for them to live any time under the water; and this death is so much the more painful, by reason that by the coarctation of the breast, while the lungs strive to do their office, the vital parts are so afflicted that they die vomiting the blood out of their mouths. Their hair also, which is by nature black, is hereby changed and made of the same color with that of the sea Wolves; their bodies are also so besprinkled with the froth of the sea, that they appear rather like monsters than men.

economic interests. Indians were put to work on sugar plantations and in the lucrative gold and silver mines. Forced labor, starvation, and especially disease took a fearful toll of Indian lives. With little or no natural resistance to European diseases, the Indians of America were ravaged by smallpox, measles, and typhus brought by the explorers and the conquistadors. Although scholarly estimates of native populations vary drastically, a reasonable guess is that at least half of the natives died of European diseases. On Hispaniola alone, out of an initial population of 100,000 natives when Columbus arrived in 1493, only 300 Indians survived by 1570. In 1542, largely in response to the publications of Bartolomé de Las Casas, a Dominican monk who championed the Indians (see the box above), the government abolished the *encomienda* system and provided more protection for the natives.

A board of trade known as the *Casa de Contratactión* supervised all economic matters related to the New World, but the chief organ of colonial administration was the Council of the Indies. The council nominated colonial viceroys, oversaw their activities, and kept an eye on ecclesiastical affairs in the colonies. Spanish possessions in the New World were initially divided between New Spain (Mexico, Central America, and the Caribbean islands), with its center in Mexico City, and Peru (western South America), with its capital at Lima. Each area was governed by a viceroy who served as the king's chief civil and military officer and was aided by advisory groups called *audiencias,* which also functioned as supreme judicial bodies.

By papal agreement, the Catholic monarchs of Spain were given extensive rights over ecclesiastical affairs in the New World. They could nominate church officials, build churches, collect fees, and supervise the various religious orders that conducted missionary activities. Catholic monks had remarkable success converting and baptizing hundreds of thousands of Indians in the early years of the conquest. Soon after the missionaries came the establishment of dioceses, parishes, schools, and hospitals—all the trappings of a European society.

## An Aztec's Lament

In an earlier chapter, we observed the Spanish conquest of Mexico from the point of view of the invaders. Here we present an Aztec account. Aztec memoirs of the battle were collected by the Spanish a few years after the seizure of Tenochtitlán and were later translated from the original Nahuatl into Spanish or other European languages. In this passage, an Aztec observer describes the enormous sense of sorrow he felt at the tragedy that had befallen his compatriots. Note that the writer concludes that the defeat was ordained by the "Giver of Life" because of his displeasure with the Aztec people.

*How would you characterize the attitude expressed here as a response to the destruction of Aztec culture? Does it display an emotion of anger or of resignation? How has Aztec religion played a role in defining that response?*

### Flowers and Songs of Sorrow

*Nothing but flowers and songs of sorrow*
*are left in Mexico and Tlatelolco,*
*where once we saw warriors and wise men.*

*We know it is true*
*that we must perish,*
*for we are mortal men.*
*You, the Giver of Life,*
*you have ordained it.*

*We wander here and there*
*in our desolate poverty.*
*We are mortal men.*
*We have seen bloodshed and pain*
*where once we saw beauty and valor.*

*We are crushed to the ground;*
*we lie in ruins.*
*There is nothing but grief and suffering*
*in Mexico and Tlatelolco,*
*where once we saw beauty and valor.*

*Have you grown weary of your servants?*
*Are you angry with your servants,*
*O Giver of Life?*

# The Impact of European Expansion

The arrival of the Europeans had an enormous impact on both the conquerors and the conquered and has recently been labelled by historians the **Columbian Exchange**. The native American civilizations, which (as we discussed in Chapter 6) had their own unique qualities and a degree of sophistication rarely appreciated by the conquerors, were virtually destroyed, while the native populations were ravaged by diseases introduced by the Europeans. Ancient social and political structures were ripped up and replaced by European institutions, religion, language, and culture (see the box above).

How does one evaluate the psychological impact of colonization on the colonizers? The relatively easy European success in dominating native peoples undoubtedly reinforced the conviction of Europeans in the inherent superiority of their civilization. The Scientific Revolution of the seventeenth century, to be followed by the era of imperialism two centuries later, then served to strengthen the Eurocentric perspective that has long pervaded Western civilization in its relationship with the rest of the world.

European expansion also affected the conquerors in the economic arena. Wherever they went in the Americas, Europeans sought gold and silver. One Aztec observer commented that the Spanish conquerors "longed and lusted for gold. Their bodies swelled with greed, and their hunger was ravenous; they hungered like pigs for that gold."[7] Rich silver deposits were found and exploited in Mexico and southern Peru (modern Bolivia). When the mines at Potosí in Peru were opened in 1545, the value of precious metals imported into Europe quadrupled. It has been estimated that between 1503 and 1650, some 35 million pounds of silver and over 400,000 pounds of gold entered the port of Seville, fueling a price revolution that affected the Spanish economy.

But gold and silver were only two of the products sent to Europe from the New World. Into Seville flowed sugar, dyes, cotton, vanilla, and hides from livestock raised on the South American pampas. New agricultural products native to the Americas, such as potatoes, coffee, corn, manioc, and tobacco, were also imported (see the comparative essay "The Columbian Exchange" on p. 374). Because of its trading posts in Asia, Portugal soon challenged the Italian states as the chief entry point of the eastern trade in spices, jewels, silk, carpets, ivory, leather, and perfumes, although the Venetians clung tenaciously to a portion of the spice trade until they lost out to the Dutch in the seventeenth century. Economic historians believe that the increase in the volume and area of European trade and the rise in fluid capital due to this expansion were crucial factors in producing a new era of commercial capitalism that represented the first step toward the world economy that has characterized the modern era (see Map 13.2).

European expansion, which was in part a product of European rivalries, also deepened those rivalries and increased the tensions among European states. Bitter conflicts arose over the cargoes coming from the New World and Asia. Although the Spanish and Portuguese

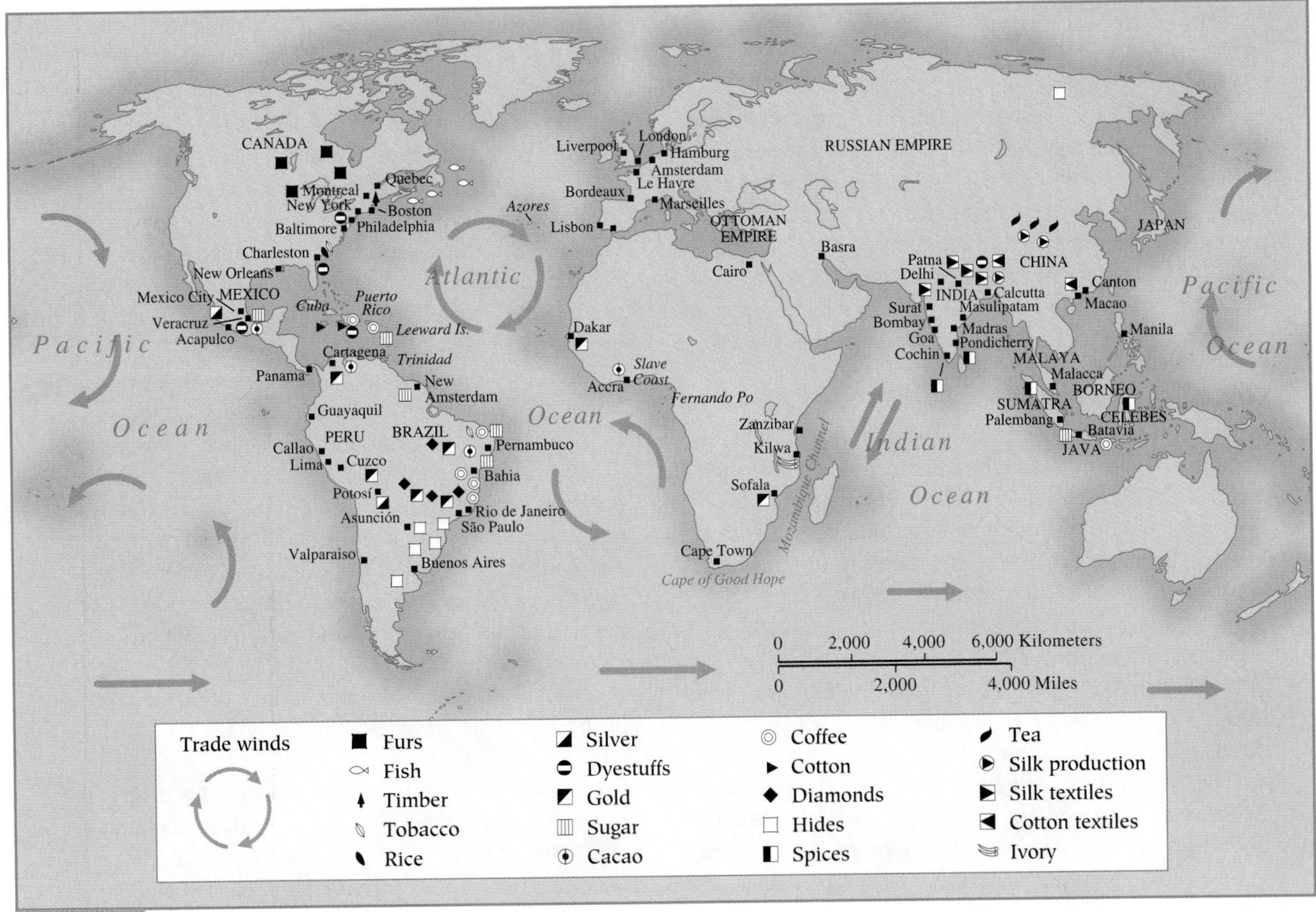


**MAP 13.2 The Pattern of World Trade from the Sixteenth Through Eighteenth Centuries.** This map shows the major products that were traded by European merchants throughout the world during the era of European exploration. Prevailing wind patterns in the oceans are shown on the map. ? What were the primary sources of gold and silver, so sought after by Columbus and his successors? **View an animated version of this map or related maps at** http://history.wadsworth.com/duikerspielvogel05/

were first in the competition, by the end of the sixteenth century, new competitors were entering the scene and beginning to challenge the dominance of the Iberian powers. The first to arrive were the English and the Dutch.

Why did Europeans risk their lives to explore new lands far from friendly shores? For some, expansion

Photos courtesy of William J. Duiker

**Manioc, Food for the Millions.** One of the plants native to the Americas that European adventurers would take back to the Old World was manioc (also known as cassava or yuca). A tuber like the potato, manioc is a prolific crop that grows well in poor, dry soils, but it lacks the high nutrient value of grain crops such as wheat and rice and for that reason never became popular in Europe (except as the source of tapioca). It was introduced to Africa in the seventeenth century and eventually became a staple food for up to one-third of the population of the continent. Shown here (inset) is a manioc plant growing in East Africa.

## COMPARATIVE ESSAY

# THE COLUMBIAN EXCHANGE

In the Western world, the discovery of the Americas has traditionally been viewed essentially in a positive sense, as the first step in a process that expanded the global trade network and eventually led to economic well-being and the spread of civilization throughout the world. In recent years, however, that view has come under sharp attack from some observers, who claim that for the peoples of the New World, the primary legacy of the European conquest was not improved living standards but harsh colonial exploitation and the spread of pestilential diseases that decimated the local population. The brunt of such criticism has been directed at Christopher Columbus, one of the chief initiators of the discovery and conquest of the Americas. Taking issue with the prevailing image of Columbus as a heroic figure in world history, critics view him as a symbol of Spanish colonial repression and a prime mover in the virtual extinction of the peoples and cultures of the New World.

There is no doubt that the record of the European conquistadors in the Western Hemisphere leaves much to be desired, and certainly the voyages of Columbus were not of universal benefit to his contemporaries or to the generations later to come. They not only resulted in the destruction of vibrant civilizations that were evolving in the Americas but also led ultimately to the enslavement of millions of Africans, who were separated from their families and shipped to a new world in conditions of inhuman bestiality.

But to focus solely on the evils that were committed in the name of civilization misses a larger point and distorts the historical realities of the era. The age of European expansion that began with Prince Henry the Navigator and Christopher Columbus was only the latest in a series of population movements that included the spread of nomadic peoples across Central Asia and the expansion of Islam from the Middle East after the death of the prophet Muhammad. In fact, the migration of peoples in search of survival and a better livelihood has been a central theme in the evolution of the human race since the dawn of prehistory. Virtually all of them involved acts of unimaginable cruelty and the forcible displacement of peoples and societies.

Even more important, it seems clear that the consequences of such population movements are too complex to be summed up in moral or ideological simplifications. The European expansion into the Americas, for example, not only brought the destruction of cultures and dangerous new diseases but also initiated the exchange of plant and animal species that have ultimately been of widespread benefit to peoples throughout the globe. The introduction of the horse, cow, and various grain crops vastly increased food productivity in the New World. The cultivation of corn, manioc, and the potato, all of them products of the Americas, have had the same effect in Asia, Africa, and Europe.

Christopher Columbus was a man of his time, with many of the character traits and prejudices common to his era. Whether he was hero or a villain is a matter of debate. That he and his contemporaries played a key role in the emergence of the modern world is a matter of which there can be no doubt.

From the Collections of the Library of Congress

**Massacre of the Indians.** This sixteenth-century engraving is an imaginative treatment of what was probably an all-too-common occurrence as the Spanish attempted to enslave the American peoples and convert them to Christianity.

abroad brought hopes for land, riches, and social advancement. One Spaniard commented in 1572 that many "poor young men" left Spain for Mexico, where they might hope to acquire landed estates and call themselves "gentlemen." Although some wives accompanied their husbands abroad, many ordinary European women found new opportunities for marriage in the New World because of the lack of white women. In the violence-prone world of early Spanish America, a number of women also found themselves rich after their husbands were killed unexpectedly. In one area of Central America, women owned about 25 percent of the landed estates by 1700.

## New Rivals

Portugal's efforts to dominate the trade of the Indian Ocean were never totally successful. The Portuguese lacked both the numbers and the wealth to overcome local resistance and colonize the Asian regions. Moreover, their massive investments in ships and laborers for their empire (hundreds of ships and hundreds of thousands of workers in shipyards and overseas bases) proved very costly. Only half of the ships involved in the India trade survived for a second journey. Disease, shipwreck, and battles took a heavy toll of life. The empire was simply

Courtesy of William J. Duiker

**Passage to the Unknown.** During its historic first voyage around the world in the early sixteenth century, Ferdinand Magellan's fleet sailed through this passage near the southern tip of South America. Now known as the Strait of Magellan, this channel between the mainland and the island of Tierra del Fuego remains to sailors one of the most terrifying in the world, with 100-miles-per-hour winds gusting regularly through the narrow passage between the Pacific and Atlantic Oceans.

too large and Portugal too small to maintain it, and by the end of the century, the Portuguese were being severely challenged by rivals.

**Europe and Asia** The Spanish had established themselves in Asia in the early 1520s, when Ferdinand Magellan, seeking a western route to the Spice Islands across the Pacific Ocean, had sailed around Cape Horn, at the southern tip of South America, crossed the Pacific, and landed on the island of Cebu in the Philippine Islands. Although Magellan and some forty of his crew were killed in a skirmish with the local population, one of the two remaining ships, now under the command of the Spanish navigator Sebastian del Cano, sailed on to Tidor, in the Moluccas, and thence around the world via the Cape of Good Hope. In the words of a contemporary historian, they arrived in Cádiz "with precious cargo and fifteen men surviving out of a fleet of five sail."[8]

As it turned out, the Spanish could not follow up on Magellan's accomplishment, and in 1529 they sold their rights in Tidor to the Portuguese. But Magellan's voyage was not a total loss. In the absence of concerted resistance from the local population, the Spanish managed to consolidate their control over the Philippines, which eventually became a major Spanish base in the carrying trade across the Pacific. Spanish galleons carried silk and other luxury goods to Acapulco in exchange for silver from the mines of Mexico.

The primary threat to the Portuguese toehold in Southeast Asia, however, came from the English and the Dutch, both of whom were now strongly influenced by mercantilist theory (see Chapter 14). In 1591, the first English expedition to the Indies through the Indian Ocean arrived in London with a cargo of pepper. Nine years later, a private joint-stock company, the East India Company, was founded to provide a stable source of capital for future voyages. In 1608, an English fleet landed at Surat, on the northwestern coast of India. Eventually, a commercial treaty was signed, and a permanent English representative was assigned to the Mughal imperial court. Trade with Southeast Asia soon followed.

The Dutch were quick to follow suit. Dutch sailors had managed to obtain Portuguese maps of the Indian coast, and the first Dutch fleet arrived in India in 1595. In 1602, the Dutch East India Company was established under government sponsorship and was soon actively competing with the English and the Portuguese in the region.

0 100 Kilometers
0 100 Miles
Strait of Magellan
Atlantic Ocean
Tierra del Fuego
Pacific Ocean
Beagle Channel
Cape Horn

**Cape Horn and the Strait of Magellan**

Bibliothèque Nationale, Paris

**A Pepper Plantation.** During the Age of Exploration, pepper was one of the most sought-after spices by European adventurers. Unlike cloves and nutmeg, it was found elsewhere in Asia as well as in the Indonesian archipelago. Shown here is a French pepper plantation in southern India. Eventually, the French were driven out of the Indian subcontinent by the British and retained only a few tiny enclaves along the coast.

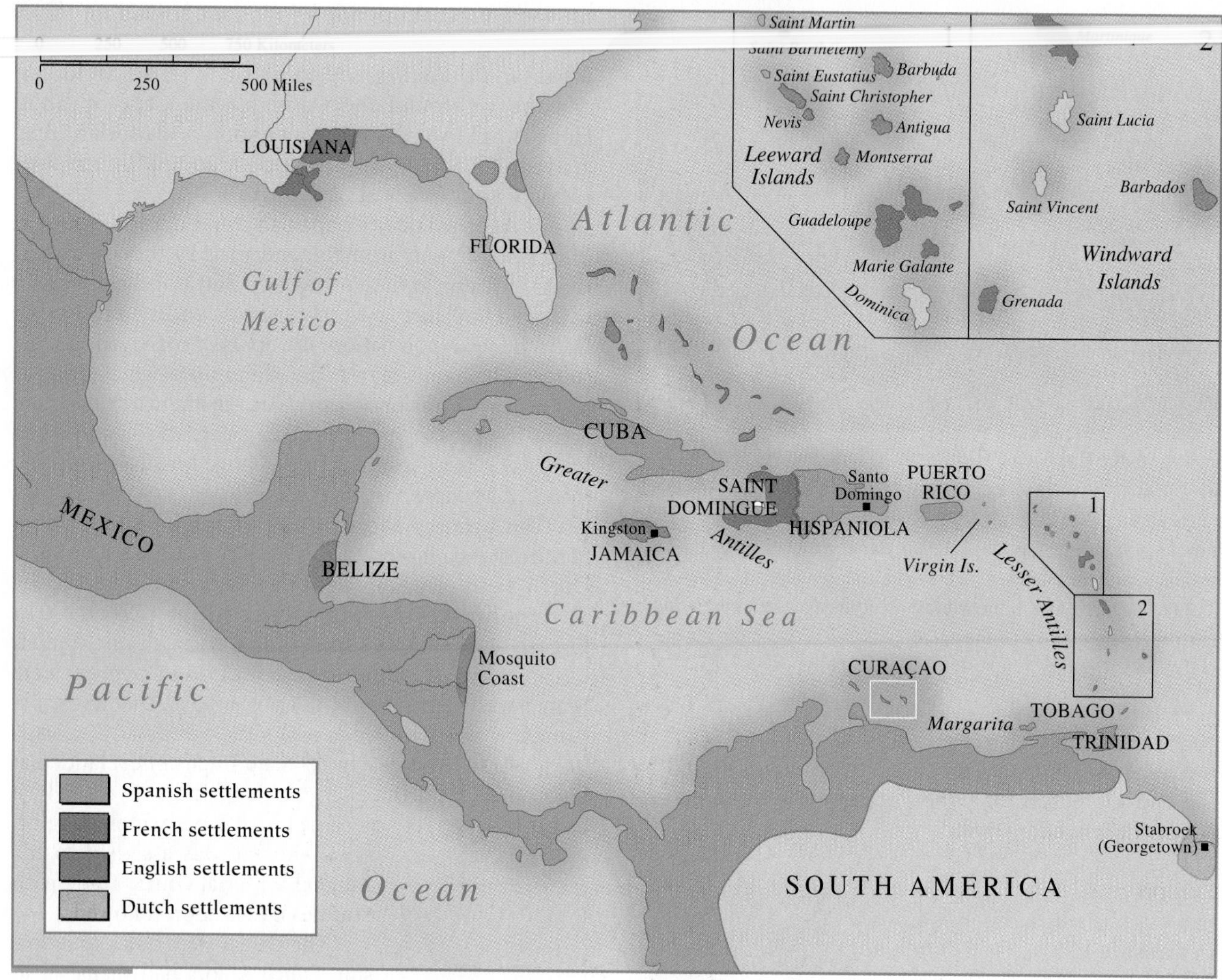


MAP 13.3 **European Possessions in the West Indies.** After the first voyage of Christopher Columbus, other European adventurers followed on his trail, seeking their share of the alleged riches of the New World.

? Where were the major settlements established by European countries in the sixteenth century?

**View an animated version of this map or related maps at** http://history.wadsworth .com/duikerspielvogel05/

**Europeans in the Americas** The Dutch, the French, and the English also began to make inroads on Spanish and Portuguese possessions in the Americas. War and steady pressure from their Dutch and English rivals eroded Portuguese trade in both the West and the East, although Portugal continued to profit from its large colonial empire in Brazil. A formal administration system had been instituted in Brazil in 1549, and Portuguese migrants had established massive plantations there to produce sugar for export to the Old World. The Spanish also maintained an enormous South American empire, but Spain's importance as a commercial power declined rapidly in the seventeenth century because of a drop in the output of the silver mines, the poverty of the Spanish monarchy, and the stifling hand of the Spanish aristocracy as well as the pressure of its English rival.

The Dutch formed their own Dutch West India Company in 1621 to compete with Spanish and Portuguese interests in the Americas. But although it made some inroads in Portuguese Brazil and the Caribbean, the company's profits were never large enough to compensate for the expenditures. Dutch settlements were also established on the North American continent. The mainland colony of New Netherlands stretched from the mouth of the Hudson River as far north as Albany, New York. In the meantime, French colonies appeared in the Lesser Antilles, and in Louisiana, at the mouth of the Mississippi River (see Map 13.3).

In the second half of the seventeenth century, however, rivalry and years of warfare with the English and the French (who had also become active in North America) brought the decline of the Dutch commercial empire in the New World. In 1664, the English seized the colony of New Netherlands and renamed it New York, and the Dutch West India Company soon went bankrupt. In 1663, Canada became the property of the French crown and was administered like a French province. But the French failed to provide adequate men or money, allowing their continental wars to take precedence over the conquest of the North American continent. By the early eighteenth century, the French began to cede some of their American possessions to their English rival.

The English, meanwhile, had proceeded to create a colonial empire in the New World along the Atlantic seaboard of North America. The failure of the Virginia Company made it evident that colonizing American lands was not necessarily conducive to quick profits. But the desire to escape from religious oppression combined with economic interests did make successful colonization possible, as the Massachusetts Bay Company demonstrated. The Massachusetts colony had only four thousand settlers in its early years, but by 1660 their number had swelled to forty thousand. Although the English had established control over most of the eastern seaboard by the end of the seventeenth century, the North American colonies still remained of minor significance to the English economy.

## Africa in Transition

Although the primary objective of the Portuguese in rounding the Cape of Good Hope was to find a sea route to the Spice Islands, they soon discovered that profits were to be made en route, along the eastern coast of Africa.

### The Portuguese in Africa

In the early sixteenth century, a Portuguese fleet commanded by Francisco de Almeida seized a number of East African port cities, including Kilwa, Sofala, and Mombasa, and built forts along the coast in an effort to control the trade in the area. Above all, the Portuguese wanted to monopolize the trade in gold, which was mined by Bantu workers in the hills along the upper Zambezi River and then shipped to Sofala on the coast (see Chapter 8). For centuries, the gold trade had been monopolized by local Shona peoples at Zimbabwe. In the fifteenth century, it had come under the control of a Shona dynasty known as the Mwene Metapa.

The Mwene Metapa had originally controlled the region south of the Zambezi River and may have been the builders of the impressive city known today as Great Zimbabwe, but sometime in the fifteenth century, they moved northeastward to the valley of the Zambezi. Here they encountered the arriving Portuguese, who had begun to move inland to gain access to the lucrative gold trade and had established ports on the Zambezi River. The Portuguese opened treaty relations with the Mwene Metapa, and Jesuit priests were eventually posted to the court in 1561. At first, the Mwene Metapa found the Europeans useful as an ally against local rivals, but by the end of the sixteenth century, the Portuguese had established a protectorate and forced the local ruler to grant title to large tracts of land to European officials and private individuals living in the area. Eventually, those lands would be integrated into the colony of Mozambique. The Portuguese, however, lacked the personnel, the capital, and the expertise to dominate local trade, and in the late seventeenth century, a vassal of the Mwene Metapa succeeded in driving them from the plateau; his descendants maintained control of the area for the next two hundred years.

Courtesy of William J. Duiker

Courtesy of William J. Duiker

INTERACTION & EXCHANGE

COMPARATIVE ILLUSTRATION

**Fort Jesus at Mombasa.** Mombasa, a port city on the eastern coast of Africa, was a jumping-off point for the Portuguese as they explored the lands bordering on the Indian Ocean. Erected in the early sixteenth century atop a bluff overlooking the harbor, Fort Jesus remained an imposing symbol of European power until 1698, when the Portuguese were expelled by the Arabs. Portuguese soldiers painted the graffiti of caravels in the harbor (see inset) while the fort was under siege by Arab forces, perhaps dreaming of an escape to their faraway home.

North of the Zambezi River, Bantu peoples were coming under pressure not only from the Portuguese but also from pastoralists migrating southward from the southern Sudan. The latter were frequently aggressive and began to occupy the rift valley and parts of the lake district that had previously been controlled by Bantu farmers. In some cases, the conflict between farmers and pastoralists was fairly clear-cut. In Rwanda and Burundi, immediately west of Lake Victoria, farming Hutu peoples (Bantu speakers) defended their hilltop communities against roving Tutsi pastoralists occupying the surrounding lowlands.

## The Dutch in South Africa

The first Europeans to settle in southern Africa were the Dutch. After an unsuccessful attempt to seize the Portuguese settlement on the island of Mozambique off the East African coast, in 1652 the Dutch set up a way station at the Cape of Good Hope to serve as a base for their fleets en route to the East Indies. At first, the new settlement was meant simply to provide food and other provisions to Dutch ships, but eventually it developed into a permanent colony. Dutch farmers, known as Boers and speaking a Dutch dialect that evolved into Afrikaans, began to settle in the sparsely occupied areas outside the city of Cape Town. The temperate climate and the absence of tropical diseases made the territory near the cape practically the only land south of the Sahara that the Europeans found suitable for habitation.

## The Kingdom of Songhai

West Africa had been penetrated from across the Sahara since ancient times, and contact undoubtedly increased after the establishment of Muslim control over the Mediterranean coastal regions. Muslim traders crossed the desert carrying Islamic values, political culture, and legal traditions along with their goods. The early stage of state formation had culminated with the kingdom of Mali, symbolized by the renowned Mansa Musa, whose pilgrimage to Mecca in the fourteenth century had left an indelible impression on observers (see Chapter 8).

After Mali's decline, it was succeeded by the kingdom of Songhai. Under King Askia Mohammed (1493–1528), the leader of a pro-Islamic faction who had seized power from members of the original founding family, the state increasingly relied on Islamic institutions and ideology to strengthen national unity and centralize authority (see the box on p. 379). Askia Mohammed himself embarked on a pilgrimage to Mecca and was recognized by the caliph of Cairo as the Muslim ruler of the Niger River valley. On his return from Mecca, he tried to revive Timbuktu as a major center of Islamic learning but had little success in converting his subjects. He did preside over a significant increase in trans-Saharan trade, which provided a steady source of income to Songhai and other kingdoms in the region. Despite the efforts of Askia Mohammed and his successors, centrifugal forces within Songhai eventually led to its breakup after his death.

The period of Songhai's decline was also a time of increased contact with Europeans. The English, the French, and the Dutch all became active in the West African trade in the mid-sixteenth century. The Dutch, in particular, encroached on the Portuguese spheres of influence. During the mid-seventeenth century, the Dutch seized a number of Portuguese forts along the West African coast while at the same time taking over the bulk of the Portuguese trade across the Indian Ocean.

**CHRONOLOGY The Penetration of Africa**

| | |
|---|---|
| Life of Prince Henry the Navigator | 1394–1460 |
| Portuguese ships reach the Senegal River | 1441 |
| Bartolomeu Dias sails around the tip of Africa | 1487 |
| First Portuguese sugar plantation at São Tomé | 1490 |
| First boatload of slaves to the Americas | 1518 |
| Dutch way station established at Cape of Good Hope | 1652 |
| Ashanti kingdom established in West Africa | 1680 |
| Portuguese expelled from Mombasa | 1728 |

## The Slave Trade

The European exploration of the African coastline had little apparent significance for most peoples living in the interior of the continent, except for a few who engaged in direct or indirect trade with the foreigners. But for peoples living on or near the coast, the impact was often great indeed. As the trade in slaves increased during the sixteenth through eighteenth centuries, thousands, and then millions, were removed from their homes and forcibly exported to plantations in the New World.

**Origins of Slavery in Africa** Traffic in slaves had existed for centuries before the arrival of Portuguese fleets along African shores. West African states like the kingdoms of Mali and Songhai routinely used slaves (mostly captured in battles with neighboring rivals) as agricultural laborers. In East Africa and the upper Nile valley, slavery had been practiced since ancient times and continued at a fairly steady level during the fifteenth century, with the major trade routes snaking across the Sahara and up the Nile River. The primary market for African slaves was the Middle East, where most were used as domestic servants. Slavery also existed in many European countries, where a few slaves from Africa or war captives from the regions north of the Black Sea were used for domestic purposes or as agricultural workers in the lands adjacent to the Mediterranean.

## King of Songhai

*The Epic of Askia Mohammed* is an oral history passed down through generations of West Africans. It relates the heroic deeds of the famous monarch who led the kingdom of Songhai to the zenith of its power in the early sixteenth century. In the epic, the young hero, called Mamar Kassaye, becomes chieftain by killing his evil uncle Si (Sonni Ali Ber, who ruled Songhai from 1463 to 1492). Once in power, Mamar consolidated the expanding Songhai kingdom and ruled it until his death in 1528. He was revered for his piety, his patronage of scholarship at Timbuktu, and his celebrated pilgrimage to Mecca. The following passage describes his assumption of power and the means he used to convert his subjects to Islam.

*How does the chieftain in this story seek to convert his subjects to the Muslim faith? Compare his technique with that used by the ruler Ala-ud-din in India, as recorded in Chapter 10.*

### The Epic of Askia Mohammed

*His father gave him a white stallion, really white,*
*really, really, really, really, really, really, really*
*white like, like percale.*
*He gave him all the things necessary.*
*He gave him two lances.*
*He gave him a saber, which he wore.*
*He gave him a shield.*
*He bid him good-bye.*

. . .

*The horse gallops swiftly, swiftly, swiftly, swiftly,*
*swiftly, swiftly he is approaching.*
*He comes into view suddenly, leaning forward on*
*his mount.*
*Until, until, until, until, until, until, until he touches*
*the prayer skin of his uncle, then he reins his*
*horse there.*

. . .

*As he approaches the prayer skin of his uncle,*
*He reins his horse.*
*He unslung his lance, and pierced his uncle with it*
*until the lance touched the prayer skin.*
*Until the spear went all the way to the prayer skin.*

. . .

*They took away the body, and Mamar came to sit*
*down on the prayer skin of his uncle.*
*They prayed.*
*They took away the body to bury it.*
*That is how Mamar took the chieftaincy.*

. . .

*He ruled then, he ruled, he ruled, he ruled, he converted.*
*Throughout Mamar's reign, what he did was*
*to convert people.*
*Any village that he hears is trying to resist,*
*That is not going to submit,*
*He gets up and destroys the village.*
*If the village accepts, he makes them pray.*
*If they resist, he conquers the village, he burns the*
*village.*
*Mamar made them convert, Mamar made them con-*
*vert, Mamar made them convert.*
*Until, until, until, until, until, until he got up and*
*said he would go to Mecca.*

. . .

*They build a mosque before his arrival.*
*When he arrives, he and his people,*
*He teaches the villagers prayers from the Koran.*
*He makes them pray.*
*They–they learn how to pray.*
*After that, in the morning, he continues on.*
*Every village that follows his orders, that accepts his*
*wishes,*
*He conquers them, he moves on.*
*Every village that refuses his demand,*
*He conquers it, he burns it, he moves on.*
*Until the day–Mamar did that until, until, until, un-*
*til the day he arrived at the Red Sea.*

At first, the Portuguese simply replaced European slaves with African ones. During the second half of the fifteenth century, about a thousand slaves were taken to Portugal each year; the vast majority were apparently destined to serve as domestic servants for affluent families throughout Europe. But the discovery of the New World in the 1490s and the subsequent planting of sugarcane in South America and the islands of the Caribbean changed the situation. Cane sugar was native to Indonesia and had first been introduced to Europeans from the Middle East during the Crusades. By the fifteenth century, it was grown (often by slaves from Africa or the region of the Black Sea) in modest amounts on Cyprus, Sicily, and southern regions of the Iberian peninsula. But when the Ottoman Empire seized much of the eastern Mediterranean (see Chapter 15), the Europeans needed to seek out new areas suitable for cultivation. In 1490, the Portuguese established sugar plantations worked by African laborers at São Tomé, an island in the Bay of Biafra off the central coast of Africa. Demand increased as sugar gradually replaced honey as a sweetener, especially in northern Europe.

But the primary impetus to the sugar industry came from the colonization of the Americas. During the sixteenth century, plantations were established along the eastern coast of Brazil and on several islands in the Caribbean. Because the cultivation of cane sugar is an arduous process demanding both skill and large quantities of labor, the new plantations required more workers than

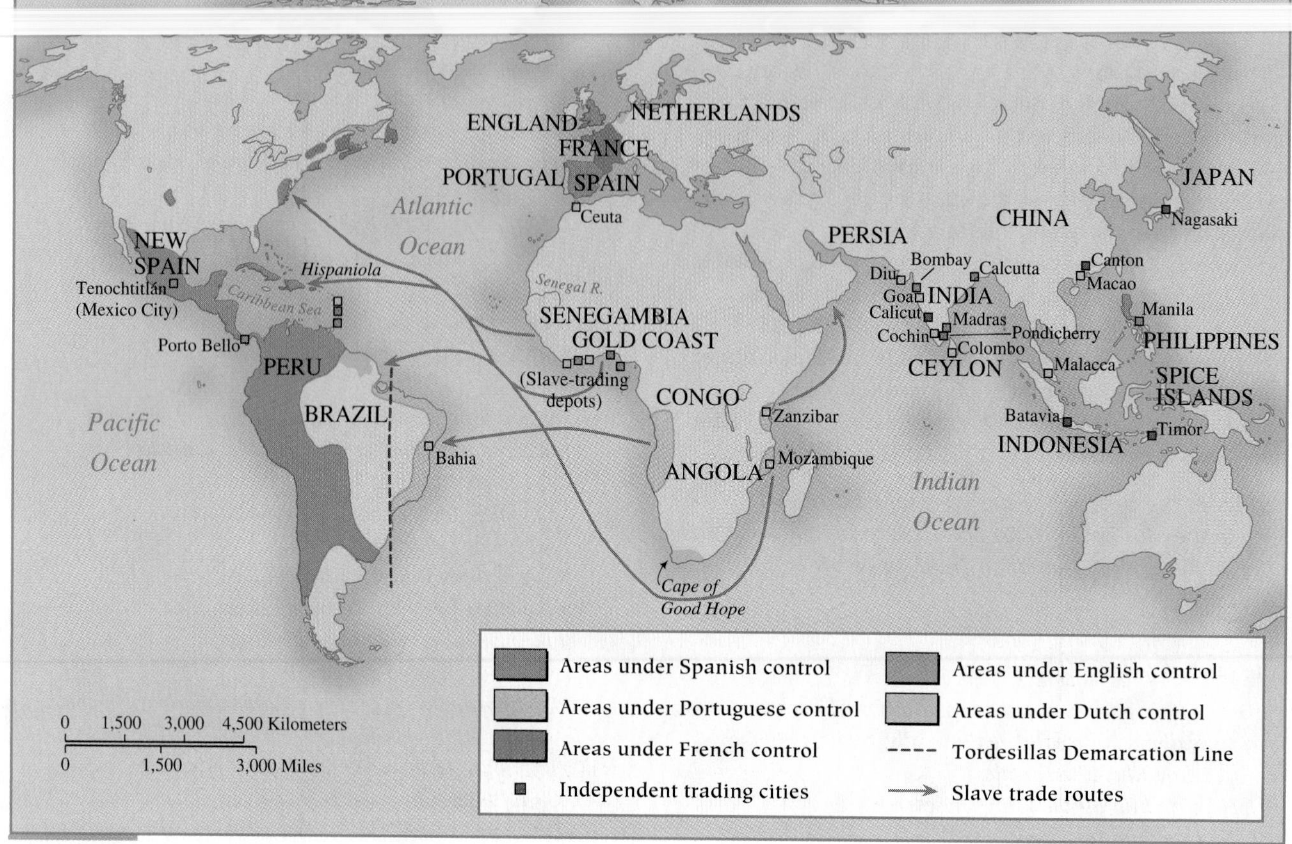


**MAP 13.4 The Slave Trade.** Beginning in the sixteenth century, the trade in African slaves to the New World became a major source of profit to European merchants. This map traces the routes taken by slave trading ships, as well as the territories and ports of call of European powers in the seventeenth century. ? What were the major destinations for the slave trade? **View an animated version of this map or related maps at** http://history.wadsworth.com/duikerspielvogel05/

could be provided by the native population in the New World, many of whom had died of diseases imported from the Old World. Since the climate and soil of much of West Africa were not especially conducive to the cultivation of sugar, African slaves began to be shipped to Brazil and the Caribbean to work on the plantations. The first were sent from Portugal, but in 1518, a Spanish ship carried the first boatload of African slaves directly from Africa to the New World.

**Growth of the Slave Trade** During the next two centuries, the trade in slaves increased by massive proportions (see Map 13.4). An estimated 275,000 enslaved Africans were exported to other countries during the sixteenth century, with 2,000 going annually to the Americas alone. During the next century, the total climbed to over a million and jumped to six million in the eighteenth century, when the trade spread from West and Central Africa to East Africa. Even during the nineteenth century, when Great Britain and a number of other European countries attempted to end the slave trade, nearly two million were exported. It has been estimated that altogether as many as ten million African slaves were transported to the Americas between the early sixteenth and the late nineteenth centuries. As many as two million were exported to other areas during the same period.

**The Middle Passage** One reason for these astonishing numbers, of course, was the tragically high death rate. In what is often called the **Middle Passage,** the arduous voyage from Africa to the Americas, losses were frequently appalling. Although figures on the number of slaves who died on the journey are almost entirely speculative, during the first shipments, up to one-third of the human cargo may have died of disease or malnourishment. Even among crew members, mortality rates were sometimes as high as one in four. Later merchants became more efficient and reduced losses to about 10 percent. Still, the future slaves were treated in an inhumane manner, chained together in the holds of ships reeking with the stench of human waste and diseases carried by vermin.

Ironically, African slaves who survived the brutal voyage fared somewhat better than whites after their arrival. Mortality rates for Europeans in the West Indies, in fact, were ten to twenty times higher than in Europe, and death rates for those newly arrived in the islands averaged more

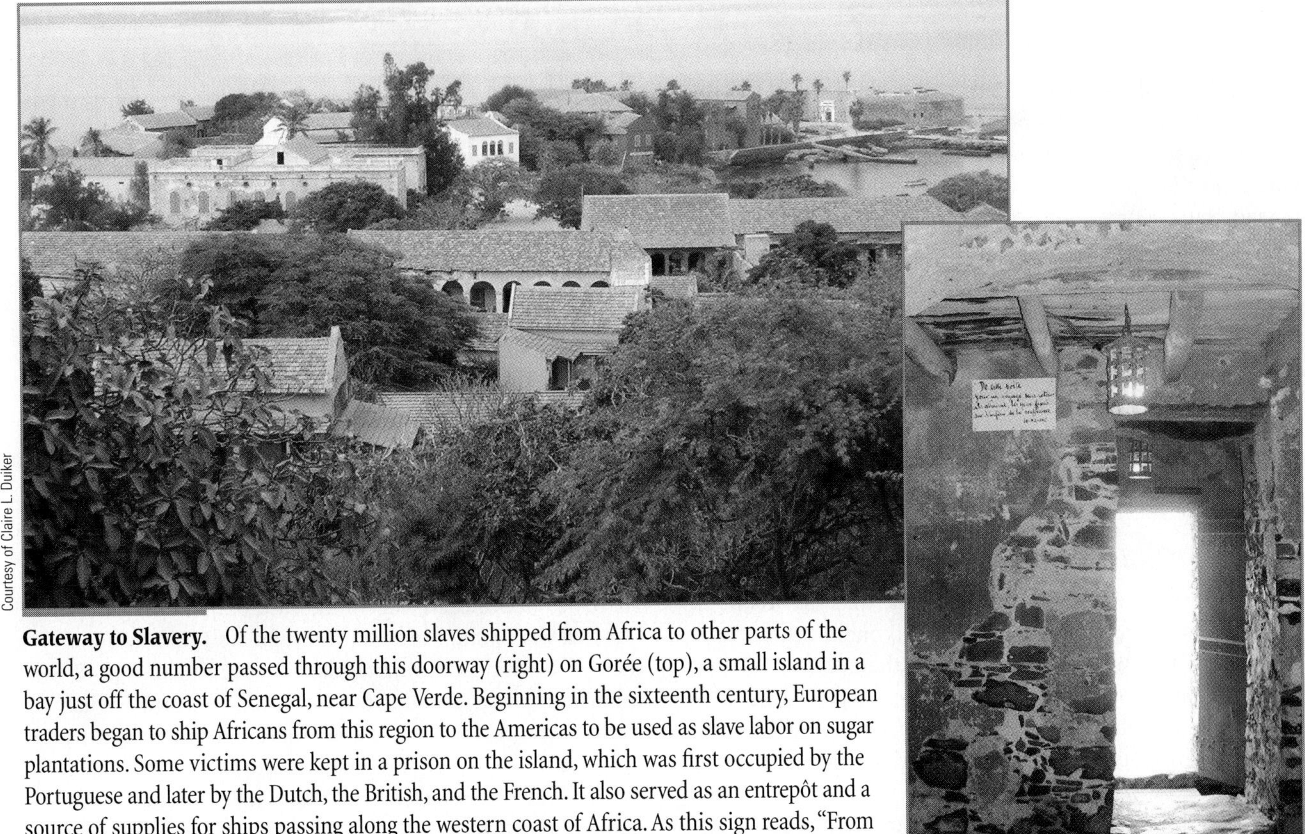

Courtesy of Claire L. Duiker

Courtesy of Claire L. Duiker

**Gateway to Slavery.** Of the twenty million slaves shipped from Africa to other parts of the world, a good number passed through this doorway (right) on Gorée (top), a small island in a bay just off the coast of Senegal, near Cape Verde. Beginning in the sixteenth century, European traders began to ship Africans from this region to the Americas to be used as slave labor on sugar plantations. Some victims were kept in a prison on the island, which was first occupied by the Portuguese and later by the Dutch, the British, and the French. It also served as an entrepôt and a source of supplies for ships passing along the western coast of Africa. As this sign reads, "From this door, they would embark on a voyage with no return, eyes fixed on an infinity of suffering."

than 125 per 1,000 annually. But the figure for Africans, many of whom had developed at least a partial immunity from yellow fever, was only about 30 per 1,000.

The reason for these staggering death rates was clearly more than maltreatment, although that was certainly a factor. As we have seen, the transmission of diseases from one continent to another brought high death rates among those lacking immunity. African slaves were somewhat less susceptible to European diseases than the American Indian populations. Indeed, they seem to have possessed a degree of immunity, perhaps because their ancestors had developed antibodies to "white people's diseases" owing to the trans-Saharan trade. The Africans would not have had immunity to native American diseases, however.

The mortality rates, of course, were higher for immigrants than for those born in the New World, who as children gradually developed at least a partial immunity to many of the more fatal diseases. Death rates for native-born slaves tended to be significantly lower than for recent arrivals, which raises the question of why the slave population did not begin to rise after the initial impact of settlement had worn off. The answer appears to be a matter of economics. In the first place, only half as many women were enslaved as men, birthrates for women living in slavery were low, and infant mortality was high. In the second place, as long as the price of slaves was low, many slave owners in the West Indies apparently believed that purchasing a new slave was less expensive than raising a child from birth to working age at adolescence. After the price of slaves began to rise during the eighteenth century, plantation owners started to devote more efforts to replenishing the supply of workers by natural means.

**Sources of Slaves** Slaves were obtained by traditional means. Before the coming of the Europeans in the fifteenth century, most slaves in Africa were prisoners or war captives or had inherited their status. Many served as domestic servants or as wageless workers for the local ruler, and some were permitted to purchase their freedom under certain conditions. When Europeans first began to take part in the slave trade, they would normally purchase slaves from local African merchants at the infamous slave markets in exchange for gold, guns, or other European manufactured goods such as textiles or copper or iron utensils (see the box on p. 382). At first, local slave traders obtained their supply from immediately surrounding regions, but as demand increased, they had to move farther inland to find their victims. In a few cases, local rulers became concerned about the impact of the slave trade on the political and social well-being of their societies. In a letter to the king of Portugal in 1526, King Affonso of Bakongo (Congo) complained that "so great, Sire, is the corruption and licentiousness that our country is being completely depopulated."[9] As a general rule, however, local monarchs viewed the slave trade as a source of income, and many launched forays against defenseless villages in search of unsuspecting victims.

## A Slave Market in Africa

Traffic in slaves had been carried on in Africa since the kingdom of the pharaohs in ancient Egypt. But the slave trade increased dramatically after the arrival of European ships off the coast of West Africa. The following passage by a Dutch observer describes a slave market in Africa and the conditions on the ships that carried the slaves to the New World. Note the difference in tone between this account and the far more critical views expressed in Chapter 22.

*What is the author's overall point of view with respect to the institution of slavery? Does he justify the practice? How does he compare Dutch behavior with that of other European countries involved?*

### Slavery in Africa: A Firsthand Report

Not a few in our country fondly imagine that parents here sell their children, men their wives, and one brother the other. But those who think so deceive themselves, for this never happens on any other account but that of necessity, or some great crime; most of the slaves that are offered to us are prisoners of war, who are sold by the victors as their booty.

When these slaves come to Fida, they are put in prison all together; and when we treat concerning buying them, they are brought out into a large plain. There, by our surgeons, whose province it is, they are thoroughly examined, even to the smallest member, and that naked too, both men and women, without the least distinction or modesty. Those that are approved as good are set on one side; and the lame or faulty are set by as invalids. . . .

The invalids and the maimed being thrown out, . . . the remainder are numbered, and it is entered who delivered them. In the meanwhile, a burning iron, with the arms or name of the companies, lies in the fire, with which ours are marked on the breast. This is done that we may distinguish them from the slaves of the English, French, or others (which are also marked with their mark), and to prevent the Negroes exchanging them for worse, at which they have a good hand.

I doubt not but this trade seems very barbarous to you, but since it is followed by mere necessity, it must go on; but we take all possible care that they are not burned too hard, especially the women, who are more tender than the men.

When we have agreed with the owners of the slaves, they are returned to their prison. There from that time forward they are kept at our charge, costing us two pence a day a slave; which serves to subsist them, like our criminals, on bread and water. To save charges, we send them on board our ships at the very first opportunity, before which their masters strip them of all they have on their backs so that they come aboard stark naked, women as well as men. In this condition they are obliged to continue, if the master of the ship is not so charitable (which he commonly is) as to bestow something on them to cover their nakedness.

You would really wonder to see how these slaves live on board, for though their number sometimes amounts to six or seven hundred, yet by the careful management of our masters of ships, they are so regulated that it seems incredible. And in this particular our nation exceeds all other Europeans, for the French, Portuguese and English slave ships are always foul and stinking; on the contrary, ours are for the most part clean and neat.

The slaves are fed three times a day with indifferent good victuals, and much better than they eat in their own country. Their lodging place is divided into two parts, one of which is appointed for the men, the other for the women, each sex being kept apart. Here they lie as close together as it is possible for them to be crowded.

We are sometimes sufficiently plagued with a parcel of slaves which come from a far inland country who very innocently persuade one another that we buy them only to fatten and afterward eat them as a delicacy. When we are so unhappy as to be pestered with many of this sort, they resolve and agree together (and bring over the rest to their party) to run away from the ship, kill the Europeans, and set the vessel ashore, by which means they design to free themselves from being our food.

I have twice met with this misfortune; and the first time proved very unlucky to me, I not in the least suspecting it, but the uproar was quashed by the master of the ship and myself by causing the abettor to be shot through the head, after which all was quiet.

Historians once thought that Europeans controlled the terms of the slave trade and were able to obtain victims at bargain prices. Recently, however, it has become clear that African intermediaries—private merchants, local elites, and trading state monopolies—were very active in the process and were often able to dictate the price, volume, and availability of slaves to European purchasers. The majority of the slaves sold to European buyers were males; females, who were in great demand in Africa and on the trans-Saharan trade, tended to be reserved for those markets. The slave merchants were often paid in various types of imported goods, including East Asian textiles (highly desired for their bright colors and durability), furniture, and other manufactured products. Until the end of the seventeenth century, the Portuguese preferred gold to slaves and would sometimes pay for the gold by selling slaves to African kingdoms that were short of labor. In fact, not until the beginning of the eighteenth century did slaves surpass gold and ivory as the continent's leading exports.

**The Effects of the Slave Trade** The effects of the slave trade varied from area to area. It might be assumed that apart from the tragic effects on the lives of individual victims and their families, the practice would have led to the depopulation of vast areas of the continent. This did occur in some areas, notably in modern Angola, south of the Congo River basin, and in thinly populated areas in East Africa, but it was less true in West Africa. There high birthrates were often able to counterbalance the loss of able-bodied adults, and the introduction of new crops from the New World, such as maize, peanuts, and manioc, led to an increase in food production that made it possible to support a larger population. One of the many cruel ironies of history is that while the institution of slavery was a tragedy for many, it benefited others.

Still, there is no denying the reality that from a moral point of view, the slave trade represented a tragic loss for millions of Africans, not only for the individual victims but also for their families. One of the more poignant aspects of the trade is that as many as 20 percent of those sold to European slavers were children, a statistic that may be partly explained by the fact that many European countries had enacted regulations that permitted more children than adults to be transported aboard the ships.

How did Europeans justify cruelty of such epidemic proportions? In some cases, they rationalized that slave traders were only carrying on a tradition that had existed for centuries throughout the Mediterranean and African world. In others, they eased their consciences by noting that slaves brought from Africa would now be exposed to the Christian faith and would be able to replace American Indian workers, many of whom were considered too physically fragile for the heavy human labor involved in cutting sugarcane.

## Political and Social Structures in a Changing Continent

Of course, the Western economic penetration of Africa had other dislocating effects. As in other parts of the non-Western world, the importation of manufactured goods from Europe undermined the foundations of local cottage industry and impoverished countless families. The demand for slaves and the introduction of firearms intensified political instability and civil strife. At the same time, the impact of the Europeans should not be exaggerated. Only in a few isolated areas, such as South Africa and Mozambique, were permanent European settlements established. Elsewhere, at the insistence of African rulers and merchants, European influence generally did not penetrate beyond the coastal regions.

Nevertheless, inland areas were often affected by events taking place elsewhere. In the western Sahara, for example, the diversion of trade routes toward the coast led to the weakening of the old Songhai trading empire and its eventual conquest by a vigorous new Moroccan dynasty in the late sixteenth century. Morocco had long hoped to expand its influence into the Sahara in order to seize control over the commerce in gold and salt, and in 1590, Moroccan forces defeated Songhai's army at Gao, on the Niger River, and then occupied the great caravan center of Timbuktu. Even after the departure of the invaders, Songhai was beyond recovery, and the next two centuries were marked by civil disorder among tribal groups and intense competition between Muslims in the cities and towns and adherents of traditional African religions in rural areas.

European influence had a more direct impact along the coast of West Africa, especially in the vicinity of European forts such as Dakar and Sierra Leone, but no European colonies were established there before 1800. Most of the numerous African states in the area from Cape Verde to the delta of the Niger River were sufficiently strong to resist Western encroachments, and they often allied with each other to force European purchasers to respect their monopoly over trading operations. Some, like the powerful Ashanti kingdom, established in 1680 on the Gold Coast, profited substantially from the rise in seaborne commerce. Some states, particularly along the so-called Slave Coast, in what is now Dahomey and Togo, or in the densely populated Niger River delta, took an active part in the slave trade. The demands of slavery and the temptations of economic profit, however, also contributed to the increase in conflict among the states in the area.

This was especially true in the region of the Congo River, where Portuguese activities eventually led to the splintering of the Bakongo empire and two centuries of rivalry and internal strife among the successor states in the area. A similar pattern developed in East Africa, where Portuguese activities led to the decline and eventual collapse of the Mwene Metapa. Northward along the coast, in present-day Kenya and Tanzania, African rulers, assisted by Arab forces from Oman and Muscat in the Arabian peninsula, expelled the Portuguese from Mombasa in 1728. Swahili culture now regained some of the dynamism it had possessed before the arrival of Vasco da Gama and his successors. But with much shipping now diverted southward to the route around the Cape of Good Hope, the commerce of the area never completely recovered and was increasingly dependent on the export of slaves and ivory obtained through contacts with African states in the interior.

# Southeast Asia in the Era of the Spice Trade

In Southeast Asia, the encounter with the West that began with the arrival of Portuguese fleets in the Indian Ocean at the end of the fifteenth century eventually resulted in the breakdown of traditional societies and the advent of colonial rule. The process was a gradual one, however. By 1700, although the Dutch retained their hold on the islands, Europeans had generally abandoned the Southeast Asian mainland. As we will see in a later chapter, though, the mainland's reprieve was only temporary.

## The Arrival of the West

As we have seen, the Spanish soon followed the Portuguese into Southeast Asia. By the seventeenth century, the Dutch, English, and French had begun to join the scramble for rights to the lucrative spice trade.

Within a short time, the Dutch, through the aggressive and well-financed Dutch East India Company (Vereenigde Oost-Indische Compagnie, or VOC, which possessed ten times the capital of the English East India Company), had not only succeeded in elbowing their rivals out of the spice trade but had also begun to consolidate their political and military control over the area. On the island of Java, where they established a fort at Batavia (today's Jakarta) in 1619 (see the comparative illustration below), the Dutch found that it was necessary to bring the inland regions under their control to protect their position. Rather than establishing a formal colony, however, they tried to rule as much as possible through the local landed aristocracy. On Java and the neighboring island of Sumatra, the VOC established pepper plantations, which soon became the source of massive profits for Dutch mer-

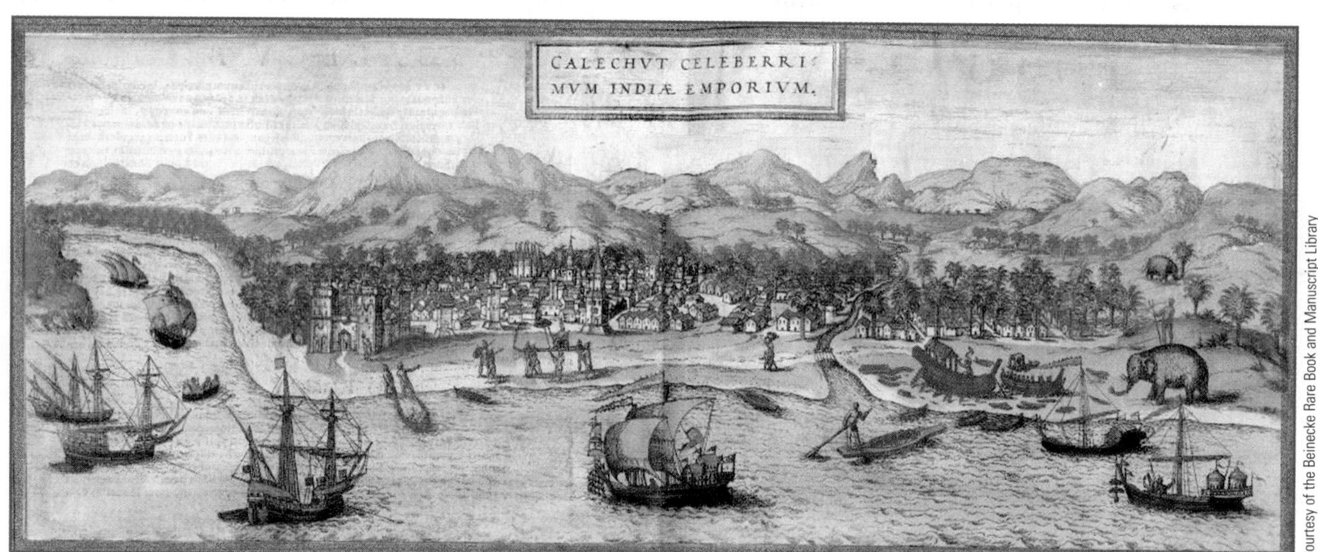

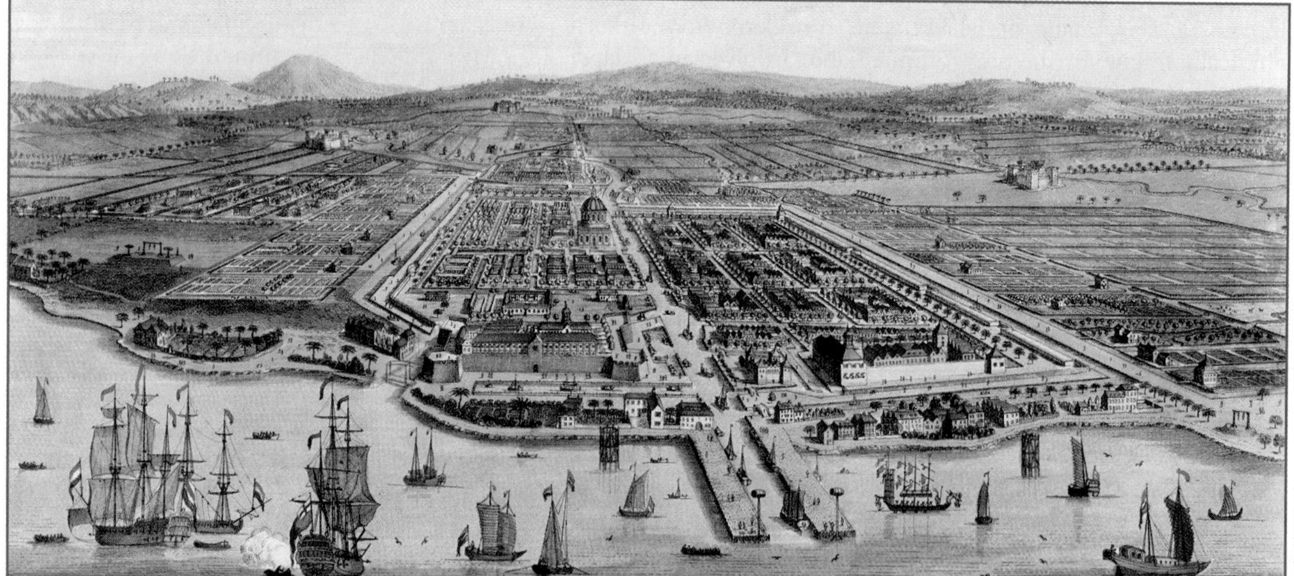

Art Archive, London

COMPARATIVE ILLUSTRATION

**Europe in Asia.** As Europeans began to move into parts of Asia, they reproduced many of the physical surroundings of their homeland in the port cities they built there. This is evident in comparing these two scenes. The etching of the port at Calicut, India (upper figure), reveals many architectural details brought by the Portuguese in the 1500s. The lower figure is a seventeenth-century view of Batavia, which the Dutch built as their headquarters on the northern coast of Java in 1619. Eventually, the canals of Batavia became breeding grounds for malaria-bearing mosquitos, forcing the Dutch to move a few miles to the south, the site of modern-day Jakarta.

chants in Amsterdam. Elsewhere they attempted to monopolize the clove trade by limiting cultivation of the crop to one island. By the end of the eighteenth century, the Dutch had succeeded in bringing almost the entire Indonesian archipelago under their control.

The arrival of the Europeans had somewhat less impact on mainland Southeast Asia, where cohesive monarchies in Burma (modern Myanmar), Thailand, and Vietnam resisted foreign encroachment. In addition, the coveted spices did not thrive on the mainland, so the Europeans' efforts there were far less determined than in the islands. The Portuguese did establish limited trade relations with several mainland states, including the Thai kingdom at Ayuthaya, Burma, Vietnam, and the remnants of the old Angkor kingdom in Cambodia. By the early seventeenth century, other nations had followed and had begun to compete actively for trade and missionary privileges. As was the case elsewhere, the Europeans soon became involved in local factional disputes as a means of obtaining political and economic advantages. In Burma, the English and the French supported rival groups in the internal struggles of the monarchy until a new dynasty emerged and threw the foreigners out. A similar process took place at Ayuthaya, where the French were forced to evacuate the area in the late seventeenth century.

In Vietnam, the arrival of Western merchants and missionaries coincided with a period of internal conflict among ruling groups in the country. After their arrival in the mid-seventeenth century, the European powers characteristically began to intervene in local politics, with the Portuguese and the Dutch supporting rival factions. By the end of the century, when it became clear that economic opportunities were limited, most European states abandoned their factories (trading stations) in the area. French missionaries attempted to remain, but their efforts were hampered by the local authorities, who viewed the Catholic insistence that converts give their primary loyalty to the pope as a threat to the legal status and prestige of the Vietnamese emperor (see the box on p. 386).

## State and Society in Precolonial Southeast Asia

Between 1400 and 1800, Southeast Asia experienced the last flowering of traditional culture before the advent of European rule in the nineteenth century. Although the coming of the Europeans had an immediate and direct impact in some areas, notably the Philippines and parts of the Malay world, in most areas Western influence was still relatively limited. Europeans occasionally dabbled in local politics and modified regional trade patterns, but they generally were not a decisive factor in the evolution of local political or social systems.

Nevertheless, Southeast Asian societies were changing in several subtle ways—in their trade patterns, their means of livelihood, and their religious beliefs. In some ways, these changes accentuated the differences between individual states in the region. Yet beneath these differences was an underlying commonality of life for most people. Despite the diversity of cultures and religious beliefs in the area, Southeast Asians were in most respects closer to each other than they were to peoples outside the region. For the most part, the states and peoples of Southeast Asia were still in control of their own destiny.

**Religion and Kingship** During the early modern era, both Buddhism and Islam became well established in Southeast Asia, and Christianity began to attract some converts, especially in the Philippines. Buddhism was dominant in lowland areas on the mainland, from Burma to Vietnam. At first, Muslim influence was felt mainly on the Malay peninsula and along the northern coasts of Java and Sumatra, where local merchants encountered their Muslim counterparts from foreign lands on a regular basis. At the same time, traditional religious beliefs continued to survive, especially in inland areas, where the local populations either ignored the new doctrines or integrated them into their traditional forms of spirit worship. Buddhists in rural Burma and Thailand, for example, might also believe in nature spirits. On Java and Sumatra, where Islam was slow to

**The Thai Capital at Ayuthaya.** The longest-lasting Thai capital was at Ayuthaya, which was one of the finest cities in Asia from the fourteenth century to the eighteenth. After the Burmese invasion in 1767, most of Ayuthaya's inhabitants were killed, and all official Thai records were destroyed. Here the remains of some Buddhist stupas, erected in a ceremonial precinct in the center of the city, remind us of the greatness of Thai civilization.

In 1681, King Louis XIV of France wrote a letter to the "king of Tonkin" (the Trinh family head, then acting as viceroy to the Vietnamese ruler) requesting permission for Christian missionaries to proselytize in Vietnam. The latter politely declined the request on the grounds that such activity was prohibited by ancient custom. In fact, Christian missionaries had been active in Vietnam for years, and their intervention in local politics had aroused the anger of the court in Hanoi.

*Compare the response given here to Louis XIV's request to the answer given to the pope by the Mongol emperor Kuyuk Khan in 1244, presented in the box on page 284 Which do you believe was the more conciliatory?*

## A Letter to the King of Tonkin from Louis XIV

Most high, most excellent, most mighty, and most magnanimous Prince, our very dear and good friend, may it please God to increase your greatness with a happy end!

We hear from our subjects who were in your Realm what protection you accorded them. We appreciate this all the more since we have for you all the esteem that one can have for a prince as illustrious through his military valor as he is commendable for the justice which he exercises in his Realm. We have even been informed that you have not been satisfied to extend this general protection to our subjects but, in particular, that you gave effective proofs of it to Messrs. Deydier and de Bourges. We would have wished that they might have been able to recognize all the favors they received from you by having presents worthy of you offered you; but since the war which we have had for several years, in which all of Europe had banded together against us, prevented our vessels from going to the Indies, at the present time, when we are at peace after having gained many victories and expanded our Realm through the conquest of several important places, we have immediately given orders to the Royal Company to establish itself in your kingdom as soon as possible, and have commanded Messrs. Deydier and de Bourges to remain with you in order to maintain a good relationship between our subjects and yours, also to warn us on occasions that might present themselves when we might be able to give you proofs of our esteem and of our wish to concur with your satisfaction as well as with your best interests.

By way of initial proof, we have given orders to have brought to you some presents which we believe might be agreeable to you. But the one thing in the world which we desire most, both for you and for your Realm, would be to obtain for your subjects who have already embraced the law of the only true God of heaven and earth, the freedom to profess it, since this law is the highest, the noblest, the most sacred, and especially the most suitable to have kings reign absolutely over the people.

We are even quite convinced that, if you knew the truths and the maxims which it teaches, you would give first of all to your subjects the glorious example of embracing it. We wish you this incomparable blessing together with a long and happy reign, and we pray God that it may please Him to augment your greatness with the happiest of endings.

Written at Saint-Germain-en-Laye, the 10th day of January, 1681,

Your very dear and good friend,
Louis

## Answer from the King of Tonkin to Louis XIV

The King of Tonkin sends to the King of France a letter to express to him his best sentiments, saying that he was happy to learn that fidelity is a durable good of man and that justice is the most important of things. Consequently practicing of fidelity and justice cannot but yield good results. Indeed, though France and our Kingdom differ as to mountains, rivers, and boundaries, if fidelity and justice reign among our villages, our conduct will express all of our good feelings and contain precious gifts. Your communication, which comes from a country which is a thousand leagues away, and which proceeds from the heart as a testimony of your sincerity, merits repeated consideration and infinite praise. Politeness toward strangers is nothing unusual in our country. There is not a stranger who is not well received by us. How then could we refuse a man from France, which is the most celebrated among the kingdoms of the world and which for love of us wishes to frequent us and bring us merchandise? These feelings of fidelity and justice are truly worthy to be applauded. As regards your wish that we should cooperate in propagating your religion, we do not dare to permit it, for there is an ancient custom, introduced by edicts, which formally forbids it. Now, edicts are promulgated only to be carried out faithfully; without fidelity nothing is stable. How could we disdain a well-established custom to satisfy a private friendship? . . .

We beg you to understand well that this is our communication concerning our mutual acquaintance. This then is my letter. We send you herewith a modest gift, which we offer you with a glad heart.

This letter was written at the beginning of winter and on a beautiful day.

## THE TIMELY END OF SULTAN ZAINAL-'ABIDIN

Acheh, (modern Aceh), on the northern tip of the island of Sumatra, was one of the first areas in Southeast Asia to be converted to Islam. This passage from the *History of Acheh* describes the cruel habits of Sultan Zainal-'Abidin, who ruled in the early seventeenth century. Note the understated way in which the author describes his deposition.

*How does the author of this document regard the overthrow of the sovereign of Acheh? Would such an action be approved according to political principles in other Asian countries, such as India and China? What about Europe?*

### *History of Acheh*

Then Sultan Seri'Alam was deposed and Sultan Zainal was installed.

The former had occupied the throne for one year before passing away. He passed away in the year 995 [1617 C.E.]. . . .

After the kingdom of Acheh Dar as-Salam and all its subject territories had been handed over to Sultan Zainal-'Abidin, he would always go out on to the arena and would have rutting elephants as well as ones which were not rutting charge each other, and as a result several people were gored to death by them, and the Bunga Setangkai palace was rammed and then collapsed in ruins together with its annexes. . . . He would order men to beat each other and to duel with staves and shields, and would order Achehnese champion fencers to compete with Indian ones, so that several of the Achehnese and Indian fencers were killed and some were wounded. . . .

If the Sultan were holding audience in a certain place all the chiefs were instructed to sit in homage in the hot sun or in the rain without distinction between the good or the evil. . . .

When the chiefs noticed these habits of the Sultan, and observed that they were growing worse day by day, they said to each other, "What should we do about our lord, for if his oppression of us is like this while he is still young, what will it be like when he is older? According to us, if he continues to be ruler everything will certainly fall in ruins about our ears." Then Sharif al-Muluk Maharaja Lela said, "If that is how it is, it would be best for us to depose our lord the Sultan."

After the chiefs had reached agreement on this matter, one evening the Sultan summoned persons to recite texts in praise of God, and the chiefs were summoned along with them. On that occasion they were reciting texts in the Friday annex. The Sultan was then put on an elephant and was taken to Makota' Alam [where he was put to death]. . . . The Sultan had occupied the throne for two years when he passed away. He passed away in the year 997. In that same year Sultan' Ala ad-Din Ri'ayat Shah Marhum Sayyid al-Mukkamil was installed.

penetrate into the interior, the result was a division between devout Muslims in the cities and essentially animist peasants in the rural villages that persists to this day.

Both Buddhism and Islam brought other changes in their train—temple education for Buddhists and schools for Islamic scholars and new religious and moral restrictions on human behavior such as refraining from eating pork and drinking wine for Muslims (though some foreign Muslims complained that the latter rule was not always followed). Because Islam discouraged the traditional tattooing of the body, Muslim converts turned to the technique of decorating textiles called *batik.*

Buddhism and Islam also helped shape Southeast Asian political institutions. As the political systems began to mature, they evolved into four main types: Buddhist kings, Javanese kings, Islamic sultans, and Vietnamese emperors (for the case of Vietnam, which was strongly influenced by China, see Chapter 11). In each case, institutions and concepts imported from abroad were adapted to local circumstances.

The Buddhist style of kingship took shape between the eleventh and the fifteenth centuries, as Theravada Buddhism spread throughout the area. It became the predominant political system in the Buddhist states of mainland Southeast Asia—Burma, Ayuthaya, Laos, and Cambodia. Perhaps the dominant feature of the Buddhist model was the godlike character of the monarch, who was considered by virtue of his karma to be innately superior to other human beings and served as a link between human society and the cosmos. Court rituals stressed the sacred character of the monarch, and even the palace was modeled after the symbolic design of the Hindu universe. In its center was an architectural rendering of sacred Mount Meru, the legendary home of the gods.

The Javanese model was a blend of Buddhist and Islamic political traditions. Like their Buddhist counterparts, Javanese monarchs possessed a sacred quality and maintained the balance between the sacred and the material world, but as Islam penetrated the Indonesian islands in the fifteenth and sixteenth centuries, the monarchs began to lose their semidivine quality.

The Islamic model was found mainly on the Malay peninsula and along the coast of the Indonesian archipelago. In this pattern, the head of state was a sultan, who was viewed as a mortal, although he still possessed some magical qualities. The sultan served as a defender of the faith and staffed his bureaucracy mainly with aristocrats, but he also frequently relied on the Muslim community of scholars—the *ulama*—and was expected, at least in theory, to rule according to the *Shari'a* (see the box above).

As Europeans began to explore new parts of the world beginning in the fifteenth century, they were convinced that it was their duty to introduce civilized ways to the heathen peoples of Asia, Africa, and the Americas. Such was the message of Spanish captain Vasco Núñez one September morning in 1513, when from a hill on the Isthmus of Panama he first laid eyes on the Pacific Ocean. Two centuries later, however, the intrepid British explorer James Cook, during his last visit to the island of Tahiti in 1777, expressed in his private journal his growing doubts that Europeans had brought lasting benefits to the Polynesian islanders. Such disagreements over the alleged benefits of Western civilization to non-Western peoples would continue to spark debate during the centuries that followed and remain with us today (see the comparative essay "Imperialism: the Balance Sheet" in Chapter 20).

*Why does James Cook express his regret that the peoples of Tahiti had been exposed to European influence? How might Captain Núñez have wished to respond?*

### Gonzalo Fernández de Ovieda, *Historia General y Natural de las Indias*

On Tuesday, the twenty-fifth of September of the year 1513, at ten o'clock in the morning, Captain Vasco Núñez, having gone ahead of his company, climbed a hill with a bare summit, and from the top of this hill saw the South Sea. Of all the Christians in his company, he was the first to see it. He turned back toward his people, full of joy, lifting his hands and his eyes to Heaven, praising Jesus Christ and his glorious Mother the Virgin, Our Lady. Then he fell upon his knees on the ground and gave great thanks to God for the mercy He had shown him, in allowing him to discover that sea, and thereby to render so great a service to God and to the most serene Catholic Kings of Castile, our sovereigns. . . .

And he told all the people with him to kneel also, to give the same thanks to God, and to beg Him fervently to allow them to see and discover the secrets and great riches of that sea and coast, for the greater glory and increase of the Christian faith, for the conversion of the Indians, natives of those southern regions, and for the fame and prosperity of the royal throne of Castile and of its sovereigns present and to come. All the people cheerfully and willingly did as they were bidden; and the Captain made them fell a big tree and make from it a tall cross, which they erected in that same place, at the top of the hill from which the South Sea had first been seen. And they all sang together the hymn of the glorious holy fathers of the Church, Ambrose and Augustine, led by a devout priest Andrés de Vera, who was with them, saying with tears of joyful devotion *Te Deum laudamus, Te Dominum confitemur.*

### Journal of Captain James Cook

I cannot avoid expressing it as my real opinion that it would have been far better for these poor people never to have known our superiority in the accommodations and arts that make life comfortable, than after once knowing it, to be again left and abandoned in their original incapacity of improvement. Indeed they cannot be restored to that happy mediocrity in which they lived before we discovered them, if the intercourse between us should be discontinued. It seems to me that it has become, in a manner, incumbent on the Europeans to visit them once in three or four years, in order to supply them with those conveniences which we have introduced among them, and have given them a predilection for. The want of such occasional supplies will, probably, be felt very heavily by them, when it may be too late to go back to their old, less perfect, contrivances, which they now despise, and have discontinued since the introduction of ours. For, by the time that the iron tools, of which they are now possessed, are worn out, they will have almost lost the knowledge of their own. A stone hatchet is, at present, as rare a thing amongst them, as an iron one was eight years ago, and a chisel of bone or stone is not to be seen.

**The Economy** During the early period of European penetration, the economy of most Southeast Asian societies was based on agriculture, as it had been for thousands of years. Still, by the sixteenth century, commerce was beginning to affect daily life, especially in the cities that were beginning to proliferate along the coasts or on navigable rivers. In part, this was because agriculture itself was becoming more commercialized as cash crops like sugar and spices replaced subsistence farming of rice or other cereals in some areas.

Regional and interregional trade were already expanding before the coming of the Europeans. The central geographical location of Southeast Asia enabled it to become a focal point in a widespread trading network. Spices, of course, were the mainstay of the interregional trade, but Southeast Asia exchanged other products as well. The region exported tin (mined in Malaya since the tenth century), copper, gold, tropical fruits and other agricultural products, cloth, gems, and luxury goods in exchange for manufactured goods, ceramics, and high-quality textiles such as silk from China. Although on balance the region was an importer of manufactured goods, it produced some high-quality goods of its own. The ceramics of Vietnam and Thailand, though not made with the high-temperature firing techniques used in China, were still of good quality. The Portuguese traveler Duarte Barbosa observed that the Javanese were skilled cabinetmakers, weapons manufacturers, shipbuilders, and locksmiths. The royal courts were both the main producers and the primary consumers of luxury goods, most of which were produced by highly skilled slaves in the employ of the court.

In general, Southeast Asians probably enjoyed a somewhat higher living standard than their contemporaries elsewhere in Asia. Although most of the population was poor by modern Western standards, hunger was not a widespread problem. Several factors help explain this relative prosperity. In the first place, most of Southeast Asia has been blessed with a salubrious climate. The uniformly high temperatures and the abundant rainfall enable as many as two or even three crops to be grown each year. Second, although the soil in some areas is poor, the alluvial deltas on the mainland are fertile, and the volcanoes of Indonesia periodically spew forth rich volcanic ash that renews the mineral resources of the soil of Sumatra and Java. Finally, with some exceptions, most of Southeast Asia was relatively thinly populated. According to one estimate, the population of the entire region in 1600 was about twenty million, or about 14 persons per square mile, well below levels elsewhere in Asia. Only in a few areas such as the Red River delta in northern Vietnam was overpopulation a serious problem.

**Society** Social institutions tended to be fairly homogeneous throughout Southeast Asia. Compared with China and India, there was little social stratification, and the nuclear family predominated. In general, women fared better in the region than anywhere else in Asia. Daughters often had the same inheritance rights as sons, and family property was held jointly between husband and wife. Wives were often permitted to divorce their husbands, and monogamy was the rule rather than the exception. In some cases, the family of the groom provided the dowry in marriage, and married couples often went to live in the wife's village. Although women were usually restricted to specialized work, such as making ceramics, weaving, or transplanting the rice seedlings into the main paddy fields, and rarely possessed legal rights equal to those of men, they enjoyed a comparatively high degree of freedom and status in most societies in the region and, as we saw in Chapter 9, were sometimes involved in commerce. In the Indonesian islands, for example, women apparently devised a simple fourteen-character alphabet based on the Indian script to record their business transactions. This written language was often passed on to their daughters, while their sons were trained to read sacred works in religious schools.

## CONCLUSION

During the Fifteenth century, Europeans burst onto the world scene. Beginning with the seemingly modest ventures of the Portuguese ships that sailed southward along the West African coast, the process accelerated with the epoch-making voyages of Christopher Columbus to the Americas and Vasco da Gama to the Indian Ocean in the 1490s. Soon a number of other European states had entered the fray, and by the end of the eighteenth century, they had created a global trade network dominated by Western ships and Western power that distributed foodstuffs, textile goods, spices, and precious minerals from one end of the globe to the other (see Map 13.2).

In less than three hundred years, the European Age of Exploration changed the face of the world. In some areas, such as the Americas and the Spice Islands, it led to the destruction of indigenous civilizations and the establishment of European colonies. In others, as in Africa, South Asia, and mainland Southeast Asia, it left native regimes intact but had a strong impact on local societies and regional trade patterns. In some areas, it led to the irreversible decline in traditional institutions and values, setting in motion a corrosive process that has not been reversed to this day (see the box on p. 388).

Ever since, many observers have viewed the process in a favorable light. Not only did the Age of Exploration expand world trade and foster the exchange of new crops and discoveries between the Old World and the New, but it also introduced Christianity to "heathen peoples" around the globe. Many modern historians, however, have been much more critical, concluding that European activities during the sixteenth, seventeenth, and eighteenth centuries created a "tributary mode of production" based on European profits from unequal terms of trade that foreshadowed the exploitative relationship characteristic of the later colonial period (see Chapter 20).

Some scholars have questioned that contention, however, and argue that although Western commercial operations had a significant impact on global trade patterns, they did not—at least not before the nineteenth century—freeze out non-European participants. Muslim merchants, for example, were long able to evade European efforts to eliminate them from the spice trade, and the trans-

European merchant shipping along the West African coast. In some cases, the European presence may even have encouraged new economic activity, as in the Indian subcontinent (see Chapter 15).

By the same token, the Age of Exploration did not, as some have claimed, usher in an era of Western dominance over the rest of the world. In the Middle East, powerful empires continued to hold sway over the lands washed by the Muslim faith. Beyond the Himalayas, Chinese emperors in their new northern capital of Beijing retained proud dominion over all the vast territory of continental East Asia. We shall deal with these regions, and how they confronted the challenges of a changing world, in the next two chapters.

## TIMELINE

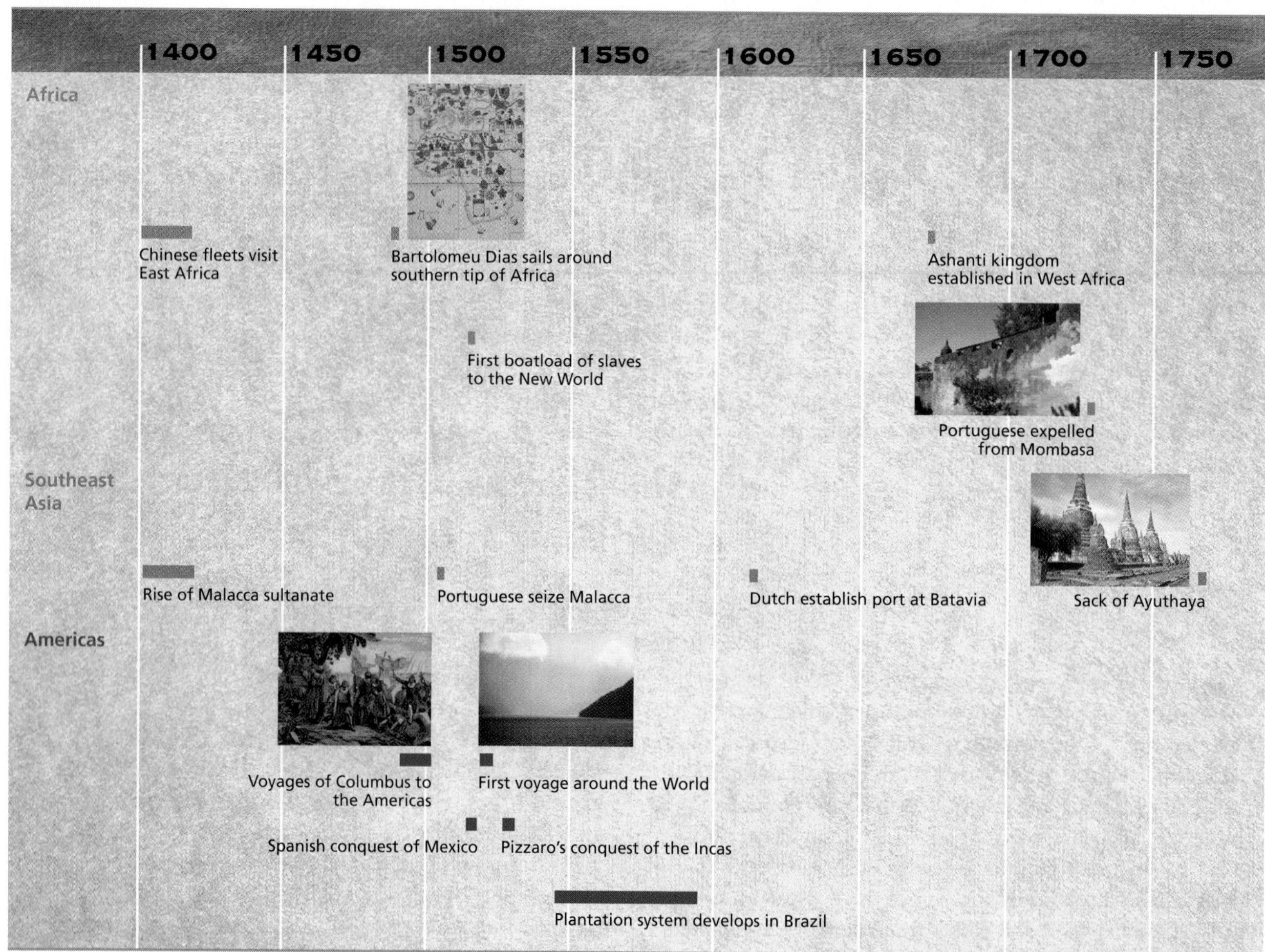


## CHAPTER NOTES

1. *A Journal of the First Voyage of Vasco da Gama* (London, 1898), cited in J. H. Parry, *The European Reconnaissance: Selected Documents* (New York, 1968), p. 82.
2. H. J. Benda and J. A. Larkin, eds., *The World of Southeast Asia: Selected Historical Readings* (New York, 1967), p. 13.
3. Parry, *European Reconnaissance,* quoting from A. Cortesão, *The Summa Oriental of Tomé Pires* (London, 1944), vol. 2, pp. 283, 287.
4. Quoted in J. H. Parry, *The Age of Reconnaissance: Discovery, Exploration, and Settlement, 1450 to 1650* (New York, 1963), p. 33.
5. Quoted in R. B. Reed, "The Expansion of Europe," in R. DeMolen, ed., *The Meaning of the Renaissance and Reformation* (Boston, 1974), p. 308.
6. K. N. Chaudhuri, *Trade and Civilization in the Indian Ocean: An Economic History from the Rise of Islam to 1750* (Cambridge, 1985), p. 65.
7. Quoted in M. Leon-Portilla, ed., *The Broken Spears: The Aztec Account of the Conquest of Mexico* (Boston, 1969), p. 51.
8. Quoted in Parry, *Age of Reconnaissance,* pp. 176–177.
9. Quoted in B. Davidson, *Africa in History: Themes and Outlines* (London, 1968), p. 137.

## SUGGESTED READING

On the technological aspects of European expansion, see **C. M. Cipolla, *Guns, Sails, and Empires: Technological Innovation and the Early Phases of European Expansion, 1400–1700*** (New York, 1965); **F. Fernandez-Armesto**, ed., ***The Times Atlas of World Exploration*** (New York, 1991); and **R. C. Smith, *Vanguard of Empire: Ships of Exploration in the Age of Columbus*** (Oxford, 1993); also see **A. Pagden, *Lords of All the World: Ideologies of Empire in Spain, Britain, and France, c. 1500–c. 1800*** (New Haven, Conn., 1995). For an overview on the impact of European expansion in the Indian Ocean, see **K. N. Chaudhuri, *Trade and Civilization in the Indian Ocean: An Economic History from the Rise of Islam to 1750*** (Cambridge, 1985). For a series of stimulating essays reflecting modern scholarship, see **J. D. Tracy, *The Rise of Merchant Empires: Long-Distance Trade in the Early Modern World, 1350–1750*** (Cambridge, 1990).

On European expansion in the Americas, see **S. E. Morison, *The European Discovery of America: The Southern Voyages, 1492–1616*** (New York, 1974). A gripping work on the conquistadors is **H. Thomas, *Conquest: Montezuma, Cortés, and the Fall of Old Mexico*** (New York, 1993). The human effects of the interaction of New and Old World cultures are examined thoughtfully in **A. W. Crosby, *The Columbian Exchange: Biological and Cultural Consequences of 1492*** (Westport, Conn., 1972).

On Portuguese expansion, the fundamental work is **C. R. Boxer, *The Portuguese Seaborne Empire, 1415–1825*** (New York, 1969). On the Dutch, see **J. I. Israel, *Dutch Primacy in World Trade, 1585–1740*** (Oxford, 1989). British activities are chronicled in **S. Sen, *Empire of Free Trade: The East India and the Making of the Colonial Marketplace*** (Philadelphia, 1998), and **Anthony Wild's** elegant work ***The East India Company: Trade and Conquest from 1600*** (New York, 2000).

The effects of European trade in Southeast Asia are discussed in **A. Reid, *Southeast Asia in the Age of Commerce, 1450–1680*** (New Haven, Conn., 1989). On the spice trade, see **A. Dalby, *Dangerous Tastes: The Story of Spices*** (Berkeley, Calif., 2000) and **J. Turner, *Spice: The History of a Temptation*** (New York, 2004).

On the African slave trade, the standard work is **P. Curtin, *The African Slave Trade: A Census*** (Madison, Wis., 1969). For more recent treatments, see **P. Lovejoy, *Transformations in Slavery: A History of Slavery in Africa*** (1983), and **P. Manning, *Slavery and African Life*** (Cambridge, 1990); **H. Thomas, *The Slave Trade*** (New York, 1997), provides a useful overview. Also see **C. Palmer, *Human Cargoes: The British Slave Trade to Spanish America, 1700-1739*** (Urbana, Ill., 1981), and **K. F. Kiple, *The Caribbean Slave: A Biological History*** (Cambridge, 1984).

For a brief introduction to women's experiences during the Age of Exploration and global trade, see **S. Hughes** and **B. Hughes, *Women in World History, vol. 2*** (Armonk, N.Y., 1997). For a more theoretical discussion of violence and gender in the early modern period, consult **R. Trexler, *Sex and Conquest: Gendered Violence, Political Order, and the European Conquest of the Americas*** (Ithaca, N.Y., 1995). The native American female experience with the European encounter is presented in **R. Gutierrez, *When Jesus Came the Corn Mothers Went Away: Marriage, Sexuality and Power in New Mexico, 1500–1846*** (Stanford, Calif., 1991), and **K. Anderson, *Chain Her by One Foot: The Subjugation of Women in Seventeenth-Century New France*** (London, 1991).

### HistoryNow™

**Enter *HistoryNow* using the access card that is available with this text. *HistoryNow* will assist you in understanding the content in this chapter with lesson plans generated for your needs, as well as provide you with a connection to the *Wadsworth World History Resource Center* (see description below for details).**

### WORLD HISTORY RESOURCE CENTER

**Enter the Resource Center using either your *HistoryNow* access card or your standalone access card for the *Wadsworth World History Resource Center.* Organized by topic, this website includes quizzes; images; over 350 primary source documents; interactive simulations; maps and timelines; movie explorations; and a wealth of other resources. You can read the following documents, and many more, at http://history.wadsworth.com/rc/world**

Vasco da Gama, "Round Africa to India"
Hans Mayr, "The Voyages and Acts of Dom Francisco"
Fra Soncino, "Regarding John Cabot's First Voyage"

Visit the *World History* Companion Website for chapter quizzes and more.

http://history.wadsworth.com/duikerspielvogel05/

CHAPTER

# 14

# EUROPE TRANSFORMED: REFORM AND STATE BUILDING

A sixteenth-century engraving of Martin Luther in front of Charles V at the Diet of Worms



## CHAPTER OUTLINE AND FOCUS QUESTIONS

### The Reformation of the Sixteenth Century

- What were the main tenets of Lutheranism, Calvinism, and Anabaptism, and how did they differ from each other and from Catholicism?

### Europe in Crisis, 1560–1650

- Why is the period between 1560 and 1650 in Europe called an age of crisis, and how did the turmoil contribute to the artistic developments of the period?

### Response to Crisis: The Practice of Absolutism

- What was absolutism, and what were the main characteristics of the absolute monarchies that emerged in France, Prussia, Austria, and Russia?

### England and Limited Monarchy

- How and why did England avoid the path of absolutism?

### The Flourishing of European Culture

- How did the artistic and literary achievements of this era reflect the political and economic developments of the period?

## CRITICAL THINKING

- What was the relationship between European overseas expansion (as seen in Chapter 13) and political, economic, and social developments in Europe?

ON APRIL 18, 1520, A LOWLY MONK stood before the emperor and princes of Germany in the city of Worms. He had been called before this august gathering to answer charges of heresy, charges that could threaten his very life. The monk was confronted with a pile of his books and asked if he wished to defend them all or reject a part. Courageously, Martin Luther defended them all and asked to be shown where any part was in error on the basis of "Scripture and plain reason." The emperor was outraged by Luther's response and made his own position clear the next day: "Not only I, but you of this noble German nation, would be forever disgraced if by our negligence not only heresy but the very suspicion of heresy were to survive. After having heard yesterday the obstinate defense of Luther, I regret that I have so long delayed in proceeding against him and his false teaching. I will have no more to do with him." Luther's appearance at Worms set the stage for a serious challenge to the authority of the Catholic church. This was by no means the first crisis in the church's fifteen-hundred-year history, but its consequences were more far-reaching than anyone at Worms in 1520 could have imagined.

After the disintegrative patterns of the fourteenth century, Europe began a remarkable recovery that encompassed a revival of arts and letters in the fifteenth century, known as the Renaissance, and a religious renaissance in the sixteenth century, known as the Reformation. The religious division of Europe (Catholics versus Protestants) that was a result of the Reformation was instrumental in beginning a series of wars that dominated much of European history from 1560 to 1650 and exacerbated the economic and social crises that were besetting the region.

One of the responses to the crises of the seventeenth century was a search for order. The most general trend was an extension of monarchical power as a stablizing force. This development, which historians have called absolutism or absolute monarchy, was most evident in France during the flamboyant reign of Louis XIV, regarded by some as the perfect embodiment of an absolute monarch.

But absolutism was not the only response to the search for order in the seventeenth century. Other states, such as England, reacted very differently to domestic crisis, and another very different system emerged where monarchs were limited by the power of their representative assemblies. Absolute and limited monarchy were the two poles of seventeenth-century state building. ◇

# The Reformation of the Sixteenth Century

The **Protestant Reformation** is the name given to the religious reform movement that divided the western Christian church into Catholic and Protestant groups. Although Martin Luther began the Reformation in the early sixteenth century, several earlier developments had set the stage for religious change.

## Background to the Reformation

Changes in the fifteenth century—the age of the Renaissance—helped prepare the way for the dramatic upheavals in sixteenth-century Europe.

**The Growth of State Power** In the first half of the fifteenth century, European states had continued the disintegrative patterns of the previous century. In the second half of the fifteenth century, however, recovery had set in, and attempts had been made to reestablish the centralized power of monarchical governments. To characterize the results, some historians have used the label "Renaissance states"; others have spoken of the **"new monarchies,"** especially those of France, England, and Spain at the end of the fifteenth century (see Chapter 12).

Although appropriate, the term *new monarch* can also be misleading. What was new about these Renaissance monarchs was their concentration of royal authority, their attempts to suppress the nobility, their efforts to control the church in their lands, and their desire to obtain new sources of revenue in order to increase royal power and enhance the military forces at their disposal. Like the rulers of fifteenth-century Italian states, the Renaissance monarchs were often crafty men obsessed with the acquisition and expansion of political power. Of course, none of these characteristics was entirely new; a number of medieval monarchs, especially in the thirteenth century, had also exhibited them. Nevertheless, the Renaissance period does mark the further extension of royal centralized authority.

No one gave better expression to the Renaissance preoccupation with political power than Niccolò Machiavelli (1469–1527), an Italian who wrote *The Prince* (1513), one of the most influential works on political power in the Western world. Machiavelli's major concerns in *The Prince* were the acquisition, maintenance, and expansion of political power as the means to restore and maintain order in his time. In the Middle Ages, many political theorists stressed the ethical side of a prince's activity—how a ruler ought to behave based on Christian moral principles. Machiavelli bluntly contradicted this approach: "For the gap between how people actually behave and how they ought to behave is so great that anyone who ignores everyday reality in order to live up to an ideal will soon discover he had been taught how to destroy himself, not how to preserve himself."[1] Machiavelli considered his approach far more realistic than that of his medieval forebears. Political activity, therefore, could not be restricted by moral considerations. The prince acts on behalf of the state and for the sake of the state must be willing to let his conscience sleep. Machiavelli was among the first Western thinkers to abandon morality as the basis for the analysis of political activity. The same emphasis on the ends justifying the means, or on achieving results regardless of the methods employed, had in fact been expressed a thousand years earlier by a court official in India named Kautilya in his treatise on politics, the *Arthasastra* (see Chapter 2).

**Social Changes in the Renaissance** Social changes in the fifteenth century also had an impact on the Reformation of the sixteenth century. After the severe economic reversals and social upheavals of the fourteenth century, the European economy gradually recovered as manufacturing and trade increased in volume. The Italians and especially the Venetians expanded their wealthy commercial empire, rivaled only by the increasingly powerful Hanseatic League, a commercial and military alliance of north German coastal towns. Not until the sixteenth century, when overseas discoveries gave new importance to the states facing the Atlantic, did the Italian city-states begin to suffer from the competitive advantages of the more powerful national territorial states.

As noted in Chapter 12, society in the Middle Ages was divided into three estates: the clergy, or first estate, whose preeminence was grounded in the belief that people should be guided to spiritual ends; the nobility, or second estate, whose privileges rested on the principle that

Staatliche Landesbildstelle Hamburg

**Harbor Scene at Hamburg.** Hamburg was a founding member of the Hanseatic League. This illustration from a fifteenth-century treatise on the laws of Hamburg shows a busy port with ships of all sizes. At the left, a crane is used to unload barrels. In the building at the right, customs officials collect their dues. Merchants and townspeople are shown talking at dockside.

nobles provided security and justice for society; and the peasants and inhabitants of the towns and cities, the third estate. Although this social order continued into the Renaissance, some changes also became evident.

Throughout much of Europe, the landholding nobles faced declining real incomes during most of the fourteenth and fifteenth centuries. Many members of the old nobility survived, however, and new blood also infused its ranks. By 1500, the nobles, old and new, who constituted between 2 and 3 percent of the population in most countries, managed to dominate society, as they had done in the Middle Ages, holding important political posts and serving as advisers to the king.

Except in the heavily urban areas of northern Italy and Flanders, peasants made up the overwhelming mass of the third estate—they constituted 85 to 90 percent of the total European population. Serfdom decreased as the manorial system continued its decline. Increasingly, the labor dues owed by a peasant to his lord were converted into rents paid in money. By 1500, especially in western Europe, more and more peasants were becoming legally free. At the same time, peasants in many areas resented their social superiors and sought a greater share of the benefits coming from their labor. In the sixteenth century, the grievances of peasants, especially in Germany, led many of them to support religious reform movements.

The remainder of the third estate were inhabitants of towns and cities, originally merchants and artisans. But by the fifteenth century, the Renaissance town or city had become more complex. At the top of urban society were the patricians, whose wealth from capitalistic enterprises in trade, industry, and banking enabled them to dominate their urban communities economically, socially, and politically. Below them were the petty burghers—the shopkeepers, artisans, guildmasters, and guildsmen—who were largely concerned with providing goods and services for local consumption. Below these two groups were the propertyless workers earning pitiful wages and the unemployed, living squalid and miserable lives. These poor city-dwellers constituted 30 to 40 percent of the urban population. The pitiful conditions of the lower groups in urban society often led them to support calls for radical religious reform in the sixteenth century.

**The Impact of Printing** The Renaissance witnessed the development of printing, which made an immediate impact on European intellectual life and thought. Printing from hand-carved wooden blocks had been done in the West since the twelfth century and in China even before that. What was new in the fifteenth century in Europe was multiple printing with movable metal type. The development of printing from movable type was a gradual process that culminated sometime between 1445 and 1450; Johannes Gutenberg of Mainz played an important role in bringing the process to completion. Gutenberg's Bible, completed in 1455 or 1456, was the first true book produced from movable type.

By 1500, there were more than a thousand printers in Europe, who collectively had published almost forty thousand titles (between eight and ten million copies). Probably half of these books were religious—Bibles and biblical commentaries, books of devotion, and sermons. Next in importance were the Latin and Greek classics, medieval grammars, legal handbooks, and works on philosophy.

The printing of books encouraged the development of scholarly research and the desire to attain knowledge. Printing also stimulated the development of an ever-expanding lay reading public, a development that had an enormous impact on European society. Indeed, without the printing press, the new religious ideas of the Reformation would never have spread as rapidly as they did in the sixteenth century. Moreover, printing allowed European civilization to compete for the first time with the civilization of China.

**Prelude to Reformation** During the second half of the fifteenth century, the new classical learning of the Italian Renaissance spread to the European countries north of the Alps and spawned a movement called **Christian humanism** or **northern Renaissance humanism,** whose major goal was the reform of Christendom. The Christian humanists believed in the ability of human beings to reason and improve themselves and thought that through education in the sources of classical, and especially Christian, antiquity, they could instill an inner piety or an inward religious feeling that would bring about a reform of the church and society. To change society, they must first change the human beings who compose it.

The most influential of all the Christian humanists was Desiderius Erasmus (1466–1536), who formulated and popularized the reform program of Christian humanism. He called his conception of religion "the philosophy of Christ," by which he meant that Christianity should be a guiding philosophy for the direction of daily life rather than the system of dogmatic beliefs and practices that the medieval church seemed to stress. In other words, he emphasized inner piety and deemphasized the external forms of religion (such as the sacraments, pilgrimages, fasts, and relics). To Erasmus, the reform of the church meant spreading an understanding of the philosophy of Jesus Christ, providing enlightened education in the sources of early Christianity, and criticizing the abuses in the church. No doubt his work helped prepare the way for the Reformation; as contemporaries proclaimed, "Erasmus laid the egg that Luther hatched."

**Church and Religion on the Eve of the Reformation** Corruption in the Catholic church was another factor that encouraged people to want reform. Between 1450 and 1520, a series of popes—called the Renaissance popes—failed to meet the church's spiritual needs. The popes were supposed to be the spiritual leaders of the Catholic church, but as leaders of the Papal States, they were all too often involved in worldly interests. Julius II (1503–1513), the fiery "warrior-pope," personally led armies against his enemies, much to the disgust of pious Christians, who viewed the pope as a spiritual leader. As one intellectual wrote, "How, O bishop standing in the room of the Apostles, dare you teach the people the things that pertain to war?" Many high church officials were also concerned with money and used their church offices as opportunities to advance their careers and their wealth, and many ordinary parish priests seemed ignorant of their spiritual duties.

While the leaders of the church were failing to meet their responsibilities, ordinary people were clamoring for meaningful religious expression and certainty of salvation. As a result, for some the process of salvation became almost mechanical. Collections of **relics** grew as more and more people sought certainty of salvation through veneration of these relics. Frederick the Wise, elector of Saxony and Martin Luther's prince, had amassed over five thousand relics to which were attached **indulgences** that could reduce one's time in purgatory by 1,443 years. (An indulgence is a remission, after death, of all or part of the punishment due to sin.)

## Martin Luther and the Reformation in Germany

Martin Luther was a monk and a professor at the University of Wittenberg, where he lectured on the Bible. Probably sometime between 1513 and 1516, through his study of the Bible, he arrived at an answer to a problem—the assurance of salvation—that had disturbed him since his entry into the monastery.

Catholic doctrine had emphasized that both faith and good works were required of a Christian to achieve personal salvation. In Luther's eyes, human beings, weak and powerless in the sight of an almighty God, could never do enough good works to merit salvation. Through his study of the Bible, Luther came to believe that humans are not saved through their good works but through faith in the promises of God, made possible by the sacrifice of Jesus on the cross. This doctrine of salvation, or justification by grace through faith alone, became the primary doctrine of

## Luther and the Ninety-Five Theses

To most historians, the publication of Luther's Ninety-Five Theses marks the beginning of the Reformation. To Luther, they were simply a response to what he considered blatant abuses committed by sellers of indulgences. Although written in Latin, the theses were soon translated into German and disseminated widely across Germany. They made an immense impression on Germans already dissatisfied with the ecclesiastical and financial policies of the papacy.

*What are the major ideas of Luther's Ninety-Five Theses? Why did they have such a strong appeal in Germany?*

### Martin Luther, Selections from the Ninety-Five Theses

5. The Pope has neither the will nor the power to remit any penalties beyond those he has imposed either at his own discretion or by canon law.
20. Therefore the Pope, by his plenary remission of all penalties, does not mean "all" in the absolute sense, but only those imposed by himself.
21. Hence those preachers of Indulgences are wrong when they say that a man is absolved and saved from every penalty by the Pope's Indulgences.
27. It is mere human talk to preach that the soul flies out [of purgatory] immediately [when] the money clinks in the collection box.
28. It is certainly possible that when the money clinks in the collection box greed and avarice can increase; but the intercession of the Church depends on the will of God alone.
50. Christians should be taught that, if the Pope knew the exactions of the preachers of Indulgences, he would rather have the basilica of St. Peter reduced to ashes than built with the skin, flesh, and bones of his sheep [the indulgences that so distressed Luther were being sold to raise money for the construction of the new St. Peter's Basilica in Rome].
81. This wanton preaching of pardons makes it difficult even for learned men to redeem respect due to the Pope from the slanders or at least the shrewd questionings of the laity.
82. For example: "Why does not the Pope empty purgatory for the sake of most holy love and the supreme need of souls? This would be the most righteous of reasons, if he can redeem innumerable souls for sordid money with which to build a basilica, the most trivial of reasons."
86. Again: "Since the Pope's wealth is larger than that of the crassest Crassi of our time, why does he not build this one basilica of St. Peter with his own money, rather than with that of the faithful poor?"
90. To suppress these most conscientious questionings of the laity by authority only, instead of refuting them by reason, is to expose the Church and the Pope to the ridicule of their enemies, and to make Christian people unhappy.
94. Christians should be exhorted to seek earnestly to follow Christ, their Head, through penalties, deaths, and hells.
95. And let them thus be more confident of entering heaven through many tribulations rather than through a false assurance of peace.

**History Now™** To read a full version of this document, enter the *HistoryNow* documents area using the access card that is available for *World History.*

the Protestant Reformation (**justification by faith** is the act by which a person is made deserving of salvation). Because Luther had arrived at this doctrine from his study of the Bible, the Bible became for Luther as for all other Protestants the chief guide to religious truth.

Luther did not see himself as a rebel, but he was greatly upset by the widespread selling of indulgences. Especially offensive in his eyes was the monk Johann Tetzel, who hawked indulgences with the slogan: "As soon as the coin in the coffer [money box] rings, the soul from purgatory springs." Greatly angered, he issued in 1517 a stunning indictment of the abuses in the sale of indulgences, known as the Ninety-Five Theses (see the box above). Thousands of copies were printed and quickly spread to all parts of Germany.

By 1520, Luther had begun to move toward a more definite break with the Catholic church and called on the German princes to overthrow the papacy in Germany and establish a reformed German church. Through all his calls for change, Luther expounded more and more on his new doctrine of salvation. It is faith alone, he said, not good works, that justifies and brings salvation through Christ.

Unable to accept Luther's ideas, the church excommunicated him in January 1521. He had also been summoned in 1520 to appear before the imperial diet or Reichstag of the Holy Roman Empire, convened by the newly elected Emperor Charles V (1519–1556). Ordered to recant the heresies he had espoused, Luther refused and made the famous reply that became the battle cry of the Reformation:

> Unless I am convicted by Scripture and plain reason—I do not accept the authority of popes and councils, for they have contradicted each other—my conscience is captive to the Word of God. I cannot and I will not recant anything, for to go against conscience is neither right nor safe. Here I stand, I cannot do otherwise. God help me. Amen.[2]

Members of the Reichstag were outraged and demanded that Luther be captured and delivered to the emperor. But

Luther's ruler, Elector Frederick of Saxony, stepped in and protected him.

During the next few years, Luther's religious movement became a revolution. Luther was able to gain the support of many of the German rulers among the three hundred or so states that made up the Holy Roman Empire. These rulers quickly took control of the churches in their territories. The Lutheran churches in Germany (and later in Scandinavia) quickly became territorial or state churches in which the state supervised the affairs of the church. As part of the development of these state-dominated churches, Luther also instituted new religious services to replace the Catholic Mass. These focused on Bible reading, preaching of the word of God, and song. Following his own denunciation of clerical celibacy, Luther married a former nun, Katherina von Bora, in 1525. His union provided a model of married and family life for the new Protestant minister.

**Politics and Religion in the German Reformation** From its very beginning, the fate of Luther's movement was closely tied to political affairs. In 1519, Charles I, king of Spain and the grandson of Emperor Maximilian, was elected Holy Roman Emperor as Charles V. Charles V ruled over an immense empire, consisting of Spain and its overseas possessions, the traditional Austrian Habsburg lands, Bohemia, Hungary, the Low Countries, and the kingdom of Naples in southern Italy. Politically, Charles wanted to maintain his enormous empire; religiously, he hoped to preserve the unity of his empire in the Catholic faith. However, a number of problems kept him preoccupied and cost him both his dream and his health.

Moreover, the internal political situation in the Holy Roman Empire was not in Charles's favor. Although all the German states owed loyalty to the emperor, in the Middle Ages these states had become quite independent of imperial authority. By the time Charles V was able to bring military forces to Germany in 1546, Lutheranism had become well established and the Lutheran princes were well organized. Unable to defeat them, Charles was forced to negotiate a truce. An end to religious warfare in Germany came in 1555 with the Peace of Augsburg. The division of Christianity was formally acknowledged; Lutheran states were to have the same legal rights as Catholic states. Although the German states were now free to choose between Catholicism and Lutheranism, the peace settlement did not recognize the principle of religious toleration for individuals. The right of each German ruler to determine the religion of his subjects was accepted, but not the right of the subjects to choose their own religion.

## The Spread of the Protestant Reformation

With the Peace of Augsburg, what had at first been merely feared was now certain: the ideal of Christian unity was forever lost. The rapid spread of new Protestant groups made this a certainty.

**Calvin and Calvinism** John Calvin (1509–1564) was educated in his native France but after his conversion to Protestantism was forced to flee to the safety of Switzerland. In 1536, he published the first edition of the *Institutes of the Christian Religion,* a masterful synthesis of Protestant thought that immediately secured Calvin's reputation as one of the new leaders of Protestantism.

On most important doctrines, Calvin stood very close to Luther. He adhered to the doctrine of justification by faith alone to explain how humans achieved salvation. But Calvin also placed much emphasis on the absolute sovereignty of God or the all-powerful nature of God—what Calvin called the "power, grace, and glory of God." One of the ideas derived from his emphasis on the

**Luther Versus the Pope.** In the 1520s, after Luther's return to Wittenberg, his teachings began to spread rapidly, ending ultimately in a reform movement supported by state authorities. Pamphlets containing picturesque woodcuts were important in the spread of Luther's ideas. In the woodcut shown here, the crucified Jesus attends Luther's service on the left, while on the right the pope is at a table selling indulgences.

absolute sovereignty of God—**predestination**—gave a unique cast to Calvin's teachings. This "eternal decree," as Calvin called it, meant that God had predestined some people to be saved (the elect) and others to be damned (the reprobate). According to Calvin, "He has once for all determined, both whom He would admit to salvation, and whom He would condemn to destruction."[3] Although Calvin stressed that there could be no absolute certainty of salvation, his followers did not always make this distinction. The practical psychological effect of predestination was to give later Calvinists an unshakable conviction that they were doing God's work on earth, making Calvinism a dynamic and activist faith.

In 1536, Calvin began working to reform the city of Geneva. He was able to fashion a tightly organized church order that employed both clergy and laymen in the service of the church. The Consistory, a special body for enforcing moral discipline, functioned as a court to oversee the moral life, daily behavior, and doctrinal orthodoxy of Genevans and to admonish and correct deviants. Citizens in Geneva were punished for such varied "crimes" as dancing, singing obscene songs, drunkenness, swearing, and playing cards.

Calvin's success in Geneva enabled the city to become a vibrant center of Protestantism. Following Calvin's lead, missionaries trained in Geneva were sent to all parts of Europe. Calvinism became established in France, the Netherlands, Scotland, and central and eastern Europe, and by the mid-sixteenth century, Calvin's Geneva stood as the fortress of the Reformation.

**John Calvin.** After a conversion experience, John Calvin abandoned his life as a humanist and became a reformer. In 1536, Calvin began working to reform the city of Geneva, where he remained until his death in 1564. This sixteenth-century portrait of Calvin pictures him near the end of his life.

**The English Reformation** The English Reformation was rooted in politics, not religion. King Henry VIII (1509–1547) had a strong desire to divorce his first wife, Catherine of Aragon, with whom the king had a daughter, Mary, but no male heir. He wanted to marry Anne Boleyn, with whom the king had fallen in love. Impatient with the pope's unwillingness to grant him an annulment of his marriage, Henry turned to England's own church courts. As archbishop of Canterbury and head of the highest church court in England, Thomas Cranmer ruled in May 1533 that the king's marriage to Catherine was "absolutely void." At the beginning of June, Anne was crowned queen, and three months later a child was born, a girl (the future queen Elizabeth I), much to the king's disappointment.

In 1534, at Henry's request, Parliament moved to finalize the break of the Church of England with Rome. The Act of Supremacy of 1534 declared that the king was "the only supreme head on earth of the Church of England," a position that gave him control of doctrine, clerical appointments, and discipline. Although Henry VIII had broken with the papacy, little change occurred in matters of doctrine, theology, and ceremony. Some of his supporters, including Archbishop Cranmer, sought a religious reformation as well as an administrative one, but Henry was unyielding. But he died in 1547 and was succeeded by his son, the underage and sickly Edward VI (1547–1553), and during Edward's reign, Cranmer and others inclined toward Protestant doctrines were able to move the Church of England (or Anglican church) in a more Protestant direction. New acts of Parliament gave the clergy the right to marry and created a new Protestant church service.

Edward VI was succeeded by Mary (1553–1558), a Catholic who attempted to return England to Catholicism. Her actions aroused much anger, however, especially when "bloody Mary" burned more than three hundred Protestant heretics. By the end of Mary's reign, England was more Protestant than it had been at the beginning.

**The Anabaptists** The Anabaptists were the radical reformers of the Protestant Reformation. To Anabaptists, the true Christian church was a voluntary association of believers who had undergone spiritual rebirth and had then been baptized into the church. Anabaptists advocated adult rather than infant baptism. They also wanted to return to the practices and spirit of early Christianity and considered all believers to be equal. Each church

## A Protestant Woman

In the initial zeal of the Protestant Reformation, women were frequently allowed to play unusual roles. Catherine Zell of Germany (c. 1497–1562) first preached beside her husband in 1527. After the death of her two children, she devoted the rest of her life to helping her husband and their Anabaptist faith. This selection is taken from one of her letters to a young Lutheran minister who had criticized her activities.

*What new ideas did Catherine Zell bring to the Reformation? Why did people react so strongly against them?*

### Catherine Zell to Ludwig Rabus of Memmingen

I, Catherine Zell, wife of the late lamented Mathew Zell, who served in Strasbourg, where I was born and reared and still live, wish you peace and enhancement in God's grace. . . .

From my earliest years I turned to the Lord, who taught and guided me, and I have at all times, in accordance with my understanding and His grace, embraced the interests of His church and earnestly sought Jesus. Even in youth this brought me the regard and affection of clergymen and others much concerned with the church, which is why the pious Mathew Zell wanted me as a companion in marriage; and I, in turn, to serve the glory of Christ, gave devotion and help to my husband, both in his ministry and in keeping his house. . . . Ever since I was ten years old I have been a student and a sort of church mother, much given to attending sermons. I have loved and frequented the company of learned men, and I conversed much with them, not about dancing, masquerades, and worldly pleasures but about the kingdom of God. . . .

Consider the poor Anabaptists, who are so furiously and ferociously persecuted. Must the authorities everywhere be incited against them, as the hunter drives his dog against wild animals? Against those who acknowledge Christ the Lord in very much the same way we do and over which we broke with the papacy? Just because they cannot agree with us on lesser things, is this any reason to persecute them and in them Christ, in whom they fervently believe and have often professed in misery, in prison, and under the torments of fire and water?

Governments may punish criminals, but they should not force and govern belief, which is a matter for the heart and conscience not for temporal authorities. . . . When the authorities pursue one, they soon bring forth tears, and towns and villages are emptied.

chose its own minister, who might be any member of the community since all Christians were considered priests (though women were often excluded).

Finally, unlike the Catholics and other Protestants, most Anabaptists believed in the complete separation of church and state. Government was to be excluded from the realm of religion and could not exercise political jurisdiction over real Christians. Anabaptists refused to hold political office or bear arms because many took the commandment "Thou shall not kill" literally. Their political beliefs as much as their religious beliefs caused the Anabaptists to be regarded as dangerous radicals who threatened the very fabric of sixteenth-century society. Indeed, the chief thing Protestants and Catholics could agree on was the need to persecute Anabaptists.

## The Social Impact of the Protestant Reformation

The Protestants were especially important in developing a new view of the family (see the comparative essay on p. 401). Because Protestantism had eliminated any idea of special holiness for celibacy and had abolished both monasticism and a celibate clergy, the family could be placed at the center of human life, and a new stress on "mutual love between man and wife" could be extolled.

But were doctrine and reality the same? Most often, reality reflected the traditional roles of husband as the ruler and wife as the obedient servant whose chief duty was to please her husband. Luther stated it clearly:

> The rule remains with the husband, and the wife is compelled to obey him by God's command. He rules the home and the state, wages war, defends his possessions, tills the soil, builds, plants, etc. The woman on the other hand is like a nail driven into the wall . . . so the wife should stay at home and look after the affairs of the household, as one who has been deprived of the ability of administering those affairs that are outside and that concern the state. She does not go beyond her most personal duties.[4]

Obedience to her husband was not a wife's only role; her other important duty was to bear children. To Calvin and Luther, this function of women was part of the divine plan, and for most Protestant women, family life was their only destiny (see the box above). Overall, the Protestant Reformation did not noticeably alter women's subordinate place in society.

## The Catholic Reformation

By the mid-sixteenth century, Lutheranism had become established in Germany and Scandinavia and Calvinism in Scotland, Switzerland, France, the Netherlands, and eastern Europe. In England, the split from Rome had resulted in the

**MAP 14.1 Catholics and Protestants in Europe by 1560.** The Reformation continued to evolve beyond the basic split of the Lutherans from the Catholics. Several Protestant sects broke away from the teachings of Martin Luther, each with a separate creed and different ways of worship. In England, Henry VIII broke with the Catholic church for political and dynastic reasons. **?** Which areas of Europe were solidly Catholic, which were solidly Lutheran, and which were neither?

**View an animated version of this map or related maps at** http://history.wadsworth.com/duikerspielvogel05/

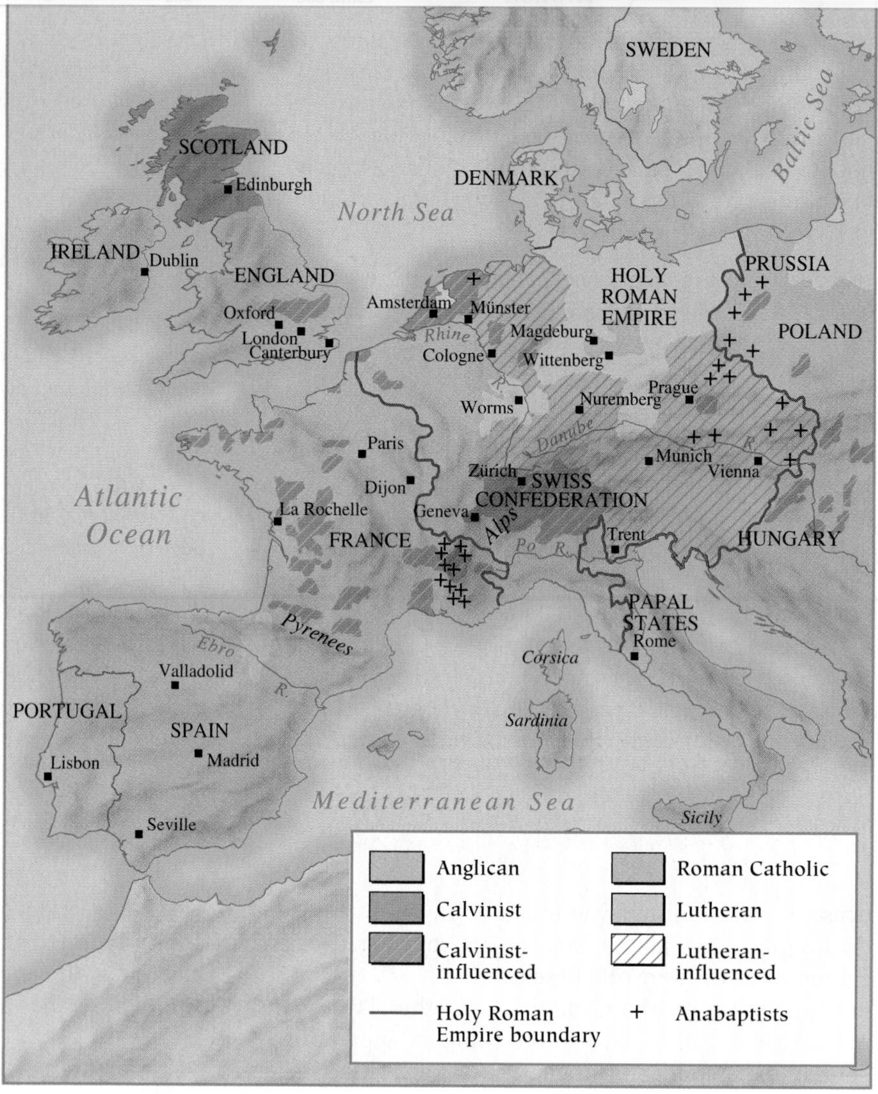


creation of a national church. The situation in Europe did not look particularly favorable to the Roman Catholic church (see Map 14.1). However, the Catholic church also underwent a revitalization in the sixteenth century, giving it new strength. There were three chief pillars of the **Catholic Reformation:** the Jesuits, a reformed papacy, and the Council of Trent.

**The Society of Jesus** The Society of Jesus, known as the Jesuits, was founded by a Spanish nobleman, Ignatius of Loyola (1491–1556). Loyola gathered together a small group of individuals who were recognized as a religious order by the pope in 1540. The new order was grounded on the principles of absolute obedience to the papacy, a strict hierarchical order for the society, the use of education to achieve its goals, and a dedication to engage in "conflict for God." A special vow of absolute obedience to the pope made the Jesuits an important instrument for papal policy. Jesuit missionaries proved singularly successful in restoring Catholicism to parts of Germany and eastern Europe.

Another prominent Jesuit activity was the propagation of the Catholic faith among non-Christians. Francis Xavier (1506–1552), one of the original members of the Society of Jesus, carried the message of Catholic Christianity to the East. After converting tens of thousands in India, he traveled to Malacca and the Moluccas before finally reaching Japan in 1549. He spoke highly of the Japanese: "They are a people of excellent morals—good in general and not malicious."[5] Thousands of Japanese, especially in the southernmost islands, became Christians. In 1552, Xavier set out for China but died of fever before he reached the mainland.

Although conversion efforts in Japan proved short-lived, Jesuit activity in China, especially that of the Italian Matteo Ricci, was more long-lasting. Recognizing the

COMPARATIVE ESSAY

## MARRIAGE IN THE EARLY MODERN WORLD

Marriage is an ancient institution. In China, mythical stories about the beginnings of Chinese civilization maintain that the rites of marriage began with the primordial couple Fuxi and Nugun and that these rites actually preceded such discoveries as fire, farming, and medicine. In the early modern world, family and marriage were inseparable and at the center of all civilizations.

In the early modern period, the family was still at the heart of Europe's social organization. For the most part, people still thought of the family in traditional terms, as a patriarchal institution with the husband dominating his wife and children. The upper classes in particular were still concerned for the family as a "house," an association whose collective interests were more important than those of its individual members. Parents (especially the fathers) still generally selected marriage partners for their children, based on the interests of the family. One French noble responded to his son's inquiry about his upcoming marriage, "Mind your own business." Details were worked out well in advance, sometimes when children were only two or three years old, and reinforced by a legally binding contract. The important aspect of the contract was the size of the dowry, money presented by the wife's family to the husband upon marriage. The dowry could involve large sums and was expected of all families.

Arranged marriages were not unique to Europe but were common throughout the world. In China, marriages were normally arranged for the benefit of the family, often by a go-between, and the groom and bride were usually not consulted. Frequently, they did not meet until the marriage ceremony. Love was obviously not a reason for marriage and in fact was often viewed as a distraction because it took the married couple's attention away from their chief responsibility to the larger family unit. In Japan, marriages too were arranged, often by the heads of dominant families in rural areas, and the new wife moved in with the family of her husband. In India, not only were marriages arranged, but it was not uncommon for women to be married before the age of ten. In colonial Latin America, parents also determined the choice of a spouse and often chose a dwelling for the couple as well. The process of selection was frequently complicated by the need for the lower classes to present gifts to powerful landlords who dominated their regions in order to gain their permission to marry. These nobles often stopped unmarried women from marrying in order to keep them as servants.

Arranged marriages were the logical result of a social system in which men dominated and women's primary role was to bear children, manage the household, and work in the field. Not until the nineteenth century did a feminist movement emerge in Europe to improve the rights of women. By the beginning of the twentieth century, that movement had spread to other parts of the world. The New Culture Movement in China, for example, advocated the free choice of spouses. Despite the progress that has been made throughout the world in allowing people to choose their spouses, there are still some places, especially in rural areas, where families are still active in the choice of marriage partners.

Chinese pride in their own culture, the Jesuits attempted to draw parallels between Christian and Confucian concepts and to show the similarities between Christian morality and Confucian ethics. For their part, the missionaries were much impressed with many aspects of Chinese civilization, and reports of their experiences heightened European curiosity about this great society on the other side of the world.

**Ignatius of Loyola.** The Jesuits became the most important new religious order of the Catholic Reformation. Shown here in a sixteenth-century painting by an unknown artist is Ignatius of Loyola, founder of the Society of Jesus. Loyola is seen kneeling before Pope Paul III, who officially recognized the Jesuits in 1540.

**A Reformed Papacy** A reformed papacy was another important factor in the development of the Catholic Reformation. The involvement of Renaissance popes in dubious finances and Italian political and military affairs had created numerous sources of corruption. It took the jolt of the Protestant Reformation to bring about serious reform. Pope Paul III (1534–1549) perceived the need for change and took the audacious step of appointing a reform commission to ascertain the church's ills. The commission's report in 1537 blamed the church's problems on the corrupt policies of popes and cardinals. It was also Paul III who formally recognized the Jesuits and began the Council of Trent.

**The Council of Trent** In March 1545, a group of high church officials met in the city of Trent on the border between Germany and Italy and initiated the Council of Trent, which met intermittently from 1545 to 1563 in three major sessions. The final decrees of the Council of Trent reaffirmed traditional Catholic teachings in opposition to Protestant beliefs. Scripture and tradition were affirmed as equal authorities in religious matters; only the church could interpret Scripture. Both faith and good works were declared necessary for salvation. Belief in purgatory and in the use of indulgences was strengthened, although the selling of indulgences was prohibited.

After the Council of Trent, the Roman Catholic church possessed a clear body of doctrine and a unified church under the acknowledged supremacy of the popes. The Roman Catholic church had become one Christian denomination among many. With a new spirit of confidence, the Catholic church entered a militant phase, as well prepared as the Calvinists to do battle for the Lord. An era of religious warfare was about to unfold.

| CHRONOLOGY Key Events of the Reformation Era | |
|---|---|
| Luther's Ninety-Five Theses | 1517 |
| Excommunication of Luther | 1521 |
| Act of Supremacy in England | 1534 |
| Pontificate of Paul III | 1534–1549 |
| John Calvin's *Institutes of the Christian Religion* | 1536 |
| Jesuits recognized as a religious order | 1540 |
| Council of Trent | 1545–1563 |
| Peace of Augsburg | 1555 |

# Europe in Crisis, 1560–1650

Between 1560 and 1650, Europe experienced religious wars, revolutions and constitutional crises, economic and social disintegration, and a witchcraft craze. It was truly an age of crisis.

## Politics and the Wars of Religion in the Sixteenth Century

By 1560, Calvinism and Catholicism had become militant religions dedicated to spreading the word of God as they interpreted it. Although their struggle for the minds and hearts of Europeans was at the heart of the religious wars of the sixteenth century, economic, social, and political forces also played an important role in these conflicts.

**The French Wars of Religion (1562–1598)** Religion was central to the French civil wars of the sixteenth century. The growth of Calvinism had led to persecution by the French kings, but the latter did little to stop the spread of Calvinism. Huguenots (as the French Calvinists were called) constituted only about 7 percent of the population, but 40 to 50 percent of the French nobility became Huguenots, including the house of Bourbon, which stood next to the Valois in the royal line of succession. The conversion of so many nobles made the Huguenots a potentially dangerous political threat to monarchical power. Still, the Calvinist minority was greatly outnumbered by the Catholic majority, and the Valois monarchy was staunchly Catholic.

The religious issue was not the only factor that contributed to the French civil wars. Towns and provinces, which had long resisted the growing power of monarchical centralization, were only too willing to join a revolt against the monarchy. So were the nobles, and the fact that so many of them were Calvinists created an important base of opposition to the crown.

For thirty years, battles raged in France between Catholic and Calvinist parties. Finally, in 1589, Henry of Navarre, the political leader of the Huguenots and a member of the Bourbon dynasty, succeeded to the throne as Henry IV (1589–1610). Realizing, however, that he would never be accepted by Catholic France, Henry converted to Catholicism. With his coronation in 1594, the Wars of Religion had finally come to an end. The Edict of Nantes in 1598 solved the religious problem by acknowledging Catholicism as the official religion of France while guaranteeing the Huguenots the right to worship and to enjoy all political privileges, including the holding of public offices.

**Philip II and Militant Catholicism** The greatest advocate of militant Catholicism in the second half of the sixteenth century was King Philip II of Spain (1556–1598), the son and heir of Charles V. Philip's reign ushered in an age of Spanish greatness, both politically and culturally. Philip II had inherited from his father Spain, the Netherlands, and possessions in Italy and the New World. To strengthen his control, Philip insisted on strict conformity to Catholicism and strong, monarchical authority. Achieving the latter was not an easy task, because each of the lands of his empire had its own structure of government.

The Catholic faith was crucial to the Spanish people and their ruler. Driven by a heritage of crusading fervor, Spain saw itself as a nation of people chosen by God to save Catholic Christianity from the Protestant heretics. Philip II, the "most Catholic king," became the champion of Catholicism throughout Europe. Spain's leadership of a "holy league" against Turkish encroachments in the Mediterranean resulted in a stunning victory over the Turkish fleet in the Battle of Lepanto in 1571. But Philip's problems with the Netherlands and the English Queen Elizabeth led to his greatest misfortunes.

Philip's attempt to strengthen his control in the Spanish Netherlands, which consisted of seventeen provinces (modern Netherlands and Belgium), soon led to a revolt. The nobles, who stood to lose the most politically, strongly opposed Philip's efforts. Religion also became a major catalyst for rebellion when Philip attempted to crush Calvinism. Violence erupted in 1566, and the revolt became organized, especially in the northern provinces, where the Dutch, under the leadership of William of Nassau, the prince of Orange, offered growing resistance. The struggle dragged on for decades until 1609, when a twelve-year truce ended the war, virtually recognizing the independence of the northern provinces. These seven northern provinces, which called themselves the United Provinces of the Netherlands, became the core of the modern Dutch state.

To most Europeans, Spain still seemed the greatest power of the age at the beginning of the seventeenth century, but the reality was quite different. The Spanish treasury was empty, the armed forces were obsolescent, and the government was inefficient. Spain continued to play the role of a great power, but real power had shifted to England.

**The England of Elizabeth** When Elizabeth Tudor, the daughter of Henry VIII and Anne Boleyn, ascended the throne in 1558, England was home to fewer than four million people. Yet during her reign, the small island kingdom became leader of the Protestant nations of Europe and laid the foundations for a world empire.

Intelligent, cautious, and self-confident, Elizabeth moved quickly to solve the difficult religious problem she inherited from her half-sister, Queen Mary. Elizabeth's religious policy was based on moderation and compromise. She repealed the Catholic laws of Mary's reign, and a new Act of Supremacy designated Elizabeth as "the only supreme governor" of both church and state. The Church of England under Elizabeth was basically Protestant, but it was of a moderate bent that kept most people satisfied.

Caution and moderation also dictated Elizabeth's foreign policy. Gradually, however, Elizabeth was drawn

Courtesy of J. K. Wingfield Digby, Sherborne Castle, England

**Procession of Queen Elizabeth I.** Intelligent and learned, Elizabeth Tudor was familiar with Latin and Greek and spoke several European languages. Served by able administrators, Elizabeth ruled for nearly forty-five years and generally avoided open military action against any major power. This picture, painted near the end of her reign, shows the queen in a ceremonial procession.

into conflict with Spain. Having resisted for years the idea of invading England as too impractical, Philip II of Spain was finally persuaded to do so by advisers who assured him that the people of England would rise against their queen when the Spaniards arrived. A successful invasion of England would mean the overthrow of heresy and the return of England to Catholicism. Philip ordered preparations for a fleet of warships, the *Armada,* to spearhead the invasion of England.

The Armada was a disaster. The Spanish fleet that finally set sail had neither the ships nor the manpower that Philip had planned to send. Battered by a number of encounters with the English, the Spanish fleet sailed back to Spain by a northward route around Scotland and Ireland, where it was further pounded by storms. Although the English and Spanish would continue their war for another sixteen years, the defeat of the Armada guaranteed for the time being that England would remain a Protestant country.

## Economic and Social Crises

The period of European history from 1560 to 1650 witnessed severe economic and social crises as well as political upheaval. Economic contraction began to be evident in some parts of Europe by the 1620s. In the 1630s and 1640s, as imports of silver from the Americas declined, economic recession intensified, especially in the Mediterranean area. Once the industrial and financial center of Europe in the age of the Renaissance, Italy was now becoming an economic backwater.

**Population Decline** Population trends of the sixteenth and seventeenth centuries also reveal Europe's worsening conditions. The population of Europe increased from 60 million in 1500 to 85 million by 1600, the first major recovery of European population since the devastation of the Black Death in the mid-fourteenth century. However, records also indicate a decline of the population by 1650, especially in central and southern Europe. Europe's longtime adversaries—war, famine, and plague—continued to affect population levels. Europe's entry into another "little ice age" after the middle of the sixteenth century, when average temperatures fell, affected harvests and gave rise to food shortages. Europe's problems created social tensions, some of which became manifested in an obsession with witches.

**Witchcraft Mania** Hysteria over witchcraft affected the lives of many Europeans in the sixteenth and seventeenth centuries. Perhaps more than 100,000 people were prosecuted throughout Europe on charges of witchcraft. As more and more people were brought to trial, the fear of witches, as well as the fear of being accused of witchcraft, escalated to frightening levels (see the box on p. 405).

Common people—usually those who were poor and without property—were more likely to be accused of witchcraft. Indeed, where lists are given, those mentioned most often are milkmaids, peasant women, and servant girls. In the witchcraft trials of the sixteenth and seventeenth centuries, more than 75 percent of the accused were women, most of them single or widowed and many over fifty years old.

That women should be the chief victims of witchcraft trials was hardly accidental. Nicholas Rémy, a witchcraft judge in France in the 1590s, found it "not unreasonable that this scum of humanity, i.e., witches, should be drawn chiefly from the feminine sex." To another judge, it came as no surprise that witches would confess to sexual experiences with Satan: "The Devil uses them so, because he knows that women love carnal pleasures, and he means to bind them to his allegiance by such agreeable provocations."[6]

By the mid-seventeenth century, the witchcraft hysteria had begun to subside. As governments grew stronger, fewer magistrates were willing to accept the unsettling and divisive conditions generated by the trials of witches. Moreover, by the end of the seventeenth and beginning of the eighteenth centuries, more and more people were questioning altogether their old attitudes toward religion and found it especially contrary to reason to believe in the old view of a world haunted by evil spirits.

**Economic Trends in the Seventeenth Century** In the course of the seventeenth century, new economic trends also emerged. **Mercantilism** is the name historians apply to the set of economic tendencies that came to dominate economic practices in the seventeenth century. According to the mercantilists, the prosperity of a nation depended on a plentiful supply of bullion (gold and silver). For this reason, it was desirable to achieve a favorable balance of trade in which goods exported were of greater value than those imported, promoting an influx of gold and silver payments that would increase the quantity of bullion. Furthermore, to encourage exports, governments should stimulate and protect export industries and trade by granting trade monopolies, encouraging investment in new industries through subsidies, importing foreign artisans, and improving transportation systems by building roads, bridges, and canals. By placing high tariffs on foreign goods, they could reduce imports and prevent them from competing with domestic industries. Colonies were also deemed valuable as sources of raw materials and markets for finished goods.

Mercantilist theory on the role of colonies was matched in practice by Europe's overseas expansion. With the development of colonies and trading posts in the Americas and the East, Europeans embarked on an adventure in international commerce in the seventeenth century. Although some historians speak of a nascent world economy, we should remember that local, regional, and intra-European trade still predominated. At the end of the seventeenth century, for example, English imports totaled 360,000 tons, but only 5,000 tons came from the East Indies. What made the

# A Witchcraft Trial in France

Persecutions for witchcraft reached their high point in the sixteenth and seventeenth centuries, when tens of thousands of people were brought to trial. In this excerpt from the minutes of a trial in France in 1652, we can see why the accused witch stood little chance of exonerating herself.

*Why were women, particularly older women, especially vulnerable to accusations of witchcraft? What "proofs" are offered here that Suzanne Gaudry had consorted with the devil? What does this account tell us about the spread of witchcraft persecutions in the seventeenth century?*

## The Trial of Suzanne Gaudry

28 May, 1652. . . . Interrogation of Suzanne Gaudry, prisoner at the court of Rieux. . . . During interrogations on May 28 and May 29, the prisoner confessed to a number of activities involving the devil.

### Deliberation of the Court–June 3, 1652

The undersigned advocates of the Court have seen these interrogations and answers. They say that the aforementioned Suzanne Gaudry confesses that she is a witch, that she had given herself to the devil, that she had renounced God, Lent, and baptism, that she has been marked on the shoulder, that she has cohabited with the devil and that she has been to the dances, confessing only to have cast a spell upon and caused to die a beast of Philippe Cornié. . . .

### Third Interrogation, June 27

This prisoner being led into the chamber, she was examined to know if things were not as she had said and confessed at the beginning of her imprisonment.

–Answers no, and that what she has said was done so by force.

Pressed to say the truth, that otherwise she would be subjected to torture, having pointed out to her that her aunt was burned for this same subject.

–Answers that she is not a witch. . . .

She was placed in the hands of the officer in charge of torture, throwing herself on her knees, struggling to cry, uttering several exclamations, without being able, nevertheless, to shed a tear. Saying at every moment that she is not a witch.

### The Torture

On this same day, being at the place of torture.

This prisoner, before being strapped down, was admonished to maintain herself in her first confessions and to renounce her lover.

–Says that she denies everything she has said, and that she has no lover. Feeling herself being strapped down, says that she is not a witch, while struggling to cry . . . and upon being asked why she confessed to being one, said that she was forced to say it.

Told that she was not forced, that on the contrary she declared herself to be a witch without any threat.

–Says that she confessed it and that she is not a witch, and being a little stretched [on the rack] screams ceaselessly that she is not a witch.

Asked if she did not confess that she had been a witch for twenty-six years.

–Says that she said it, that she retracts it, crying that she is not a witch.

Asked if she did not make Philippe Cornié's horse die, as she confessed.

–Answers no, crying Jesus-Maria, that she is not a witch.

The mark having been probed by the officer, in the presence of Doctor Bouchain, it was adjudged by the aforesaid doctor and officer truly to be the mark of the devil.

Being more tightly stretched upon the torture rack, urged to maintain her confessions.

–Said that it was true that she is a witch and that she would maintain what she had said.

Asked how long she has been in subjugation to the devil.

–Answers that it was twenty years ago that the devil appeared to her, being in her lodgings in the form of a man dressed in a little cowhide and black breeches. . . .

### Verdict

July 9, 1652. In the light of the interrogations, answers, and investigations made into the charge against Suzanne Gaudry, . . . seeing by her own confessions that she is said to have made a pact with the devil, received the mark from him, . . . and that following this, she had renounced God, Lent, and baptism and had let herself be known carnally by him, in which she received satisfaction. Also, seeing that she is said to have been a part of nocturnal carols and dances.

For expiation of which the advice of the undersigned is that the office of Rieux can legitimately condemn the aforesaid Suzanne Gaudry to death, tying her to a gallows, and strangling her to death, then burning her body and burying it here in the environs of the woods.

transoceanic trade rewarding, however, was not the volume but the value of its goods. Dutch, English, and French merchants were bringing back products that were still consumed largely by the wealthy but were beginning to make their way into the lives of artisans and merchants. Pepper and spices from the Indies, West Indian and Brazilian sugar, and Asian coffee and tea were becoming more readily available to European consumers.

The commercial expansion of the sixteenth and seventeenth centuries was made easier by new forms of commercial organization, especially the **joint-stock company.** Individuals bought shares in a company and received dividends on their investment while a board of directors ran the company and made the important business decisions. The return on investments could be spectacular. During its first ten years, investors received 30 percent annually on their money from the Dutch East India Company, which opened the Spice Islands and Southeast Asia to Dutch activity. The joint-stock company made it easier to raise large amounts of capital for world trading ventures.

Despite the growth of commercial capitalism, most of the European economy still depended on an agricultural system that had experienced few changes since the thirteenth century. At least 80 percent of Europeans still worked on the land. Almost all of the peasants of western Europe were free of serfdom, although many still owed a variety of feudal dues to the nobility. Despite the expanding markets and rising prices, European peasants saw little or no improvement in their lot as they faced increased rents and fees and higher taxes imposed by the state.

**CHRONOLOGY Europe in Crisis, 1560–1650: Key Events**

| | |
|---|---|
| Reign of Philip II | 1556–1598 |
| French Wars of Religion | 1562–1598 |
| Outbreak of revolt in the Netherlands | 1566 |
| Spanish Armada | 1588 |
| Edict of Nantes | 1598 |
| Twelve-year truce between Spain and the Netherlands | 1609 |
| Thirty Years' War | 1618–1648 |
| Peace of Westphalia | 1648 |

## Seventeenth-Century Crises: Revolution and War

During the first half of the seventeenth century, a series of rebellions and civil wars rocked the domestic stability of many European governments. A devastating war that affected much of Europe also added to the sense of crisis.

**The Thirty Years' War (1618–1648)** The Thirty Years' War began in 1618 in the Germanic lands of the Holy Roman Empire as a struggle between Catholic forces, led by the Habsburg Holy Roman Emperors, and Protestant—primarily Calvinist—nobles in Bohemia who rebelled against Habsburg authority (see Map 14.2). What began as a struggle over religious issues soon became a wider conflict perpetuated by political motivations as both minor and major European powers—Denmark, Sweden, France, and Spain—entered the war. The competition for European leadership between the Bourbon dynasty of France and the Habsburg dynasties of Spain and the Holy Roman Empire was an especially important factor. Nevertheless, most of the battles were fought on German soil (see the box on p. 408).

The war in Germany was officially ended in 1648 by the Peace of Westphalia, which proclaimed that all German states, including the Calvinist ones, were free to determine their own religion. The major contenders gained new territories, and France emerged as the dominant nation in Europe. The more than three hundred entities that made up the Holy Roman Empire were recognized as independent states, and each was given the power to conduct its own foreign policy; this brought an end to the Holy Roman Empire and ensured German disunity for another two hundred years. The Peace of Westphalia made it clear that political motives, not religious convictions, had become the guiding force in public affairs.

**A Military Revolution?** By the seventeenth century, war played an increasingly important role in European affairs. Military power was considered essential to a ruler's reputation and power; thus the pressure to build an effective military machine was intense. Some historians believe that the changes that occurred in the science of warfare between 1560 and 1650 warrant the title of military revolution.

Medieval warfare, with its mounted knights and supplementary archers, had been transformed in the Renaissance by the employment of infantry armed with pikes and halberds and arranged in massed rectangles known as squadrons or battalions. The use of firearms required adjustments to the size and shape of the massed infantry and made the calvary less effective.

It was Gustavus Adolphus, the king of Sweden, who developed the first standing army of conscripts, notable for the flexibility of its tactics. The infantry brigades of Gustavus's army were composed of equal numbers of musketeers and pikemen, standing six men deep. They employed the salvo, in which all rows of the infantry fired at once instead of row by row. These salvos of fire, which cut up the massed ranks of the opposing infantry squadrons, were followed by a pike charge, giving the infantry a primarily offensive deployment. Gustavus also used the cavalry in a more mobile fashion. After shooting a pistol volley, they charged the enemy with their swords. Additional flexibility was obtained by using lighter artillery pieces that were more easily moved during battle. All of these charges required coordination, careful train-

**MAP 14.2 Europe in the Seventeenth Century.** This map shows Europe at the time of the Thirty Years' War (1618–1648). Although the struggle began in Bohemia and much of the fighting took place in the Germanic lands of the Holy Roman Empire, the conflict became a Europe-wide struggle. ? Compare this map with Map 14.1. Which countries engaged in the war were predominantly Protestant, which were Catholic, and which were mixed? **View an animated version of this map or related maps at** http://history.wadsworth.com/duikerspielvogel05/

ing, and better discipline, forcing rulers to move away from undisciplined mercenary forces.

Military changes between 1560 and 1650 included increased use of firearms and cannons, greater flexibility and mobility in tactics, and better-disciplined and better-trained armies. These innovations necessitated standing armies, based partly on conscription, which grew ever larger and more expensive as the seventeenth century progressed. Such armies could be maintained only by levying heavier taxes, making war an economic burden and an ever more important part of the early modern European state. The creation of large bureaucracies to supervise the military resources of the state led to a growth in the power of state governments.

# Response to Crisis: The Practice of Absolutism

Many people responded to the crises of the seventeenth century by searching for order. An increase in monarchical power became an obvious means for achieving stability. The result was what historians have called **absolutism** or absolute monarchy. Absolutism meant that the sovereign power or ultimate authority in the state rested in the hands of a king who claimed to rule by divine right—the idea that kings received their power from God and were responsible to no one but God. Late-sixteenth-century political theorists believed that sovereign power consisted

## The Face of War in the Seventeenth Century

We have a firsthand account of the face of war in Germany from a picaresque novel called *Simplicius Simplicissimus,* written by Jakob von Grimmelshausen. The author's experiences as a soldier in the Thirty Years' War give his descriptions of the effect of the war on ordinary people a certain vividness and reality. This selection describes the fate of a peasant farm, an experience all too familiar to thousands of German peasants between 1618 and 1648.

*What does this document reveal about the effect of war on ordinary Europeans?*

### Jakob von Grimmelshausen, *Simplicius Simplicissimus*

The first thing these horsemen did in the nice back rooms of the house was to put in their horses. Then everyone took up a special job, one having to do with death and destruction. Although some began butchering, heating water, and rendering lard, as if to prepare for a banquet, others raced through the house, ransacking upstairs and down; not even the privy chamber was safe, as if the golden fleece of Jason might be hidden there. Still others bundled up big packs of cloth, household goods, and clothes, as if they wanted to hold a rummage sale somewhere. What they did not intend to take along they broke and spoiled. Some ran their swords into the hay and straw, as if there hadn't been hogs enough to stick. Some shook the feathers out of beds and put bacon slabs, hams, and other stuff in the ticking, as if they might sleep better on these. Others knocked down the hearth and broke the windows, as if announcing an everlasting summer. They flattened out copper and pewter dishes and baled the ruined goods. They burned up bedsteads, tables, chairs, and benches, though there were yards and yards of dry firewood outside the kitchen. Jars and crocks, pots and casseroles all were broken, either because they preferred their meat broiled or because they thought they'd eat only one meal with us. In the barn, the hired girl was handled so roughly that she was unable to walk away, I am ashamed to report. They stretched the hired man out flat on the ground, stuck a wooden wedge in his mouth to keep it open, and emptied a milk bucket full of stinking manure drippings down his throat; they called it a Swedish cocktail. He didn't relish it and made a very wry face. By this means they forced him to take a raiding party to some other place where they carried off men and cattle and brought them to our farm. Among those were my father, mother, and [sister] Ursula.

Then they used thumbscrews, which they cleverly made out of their pistols, to torture the peasants, as if they wanted to burn witches. Though he had confessed to nothing as yet, they put one of the captured hayseeds in the bake-oven and lighted a fire in it. They put a rope around someone else's head and tightened it like a tourniquet until blood came out of his mouth, nose, and ears. In short, every soldier had his favorite method of making life miserable for peasants, and every peasant had his own misery. My father was, as I thought, particularly lucky because he confessed with a laugh what others were forced to say in pain and martyrdom. No doubt because he was the head of the household, he was shown special consideration; they put him close to a fire, tied him by his hands and legs, and rubbed damp salt on the bottoms of his feet. Our old nanny goat had to lick it off and this so tickled my father that he could have burst laughing. This seemed so clever and entertaining to me—I had never seen or heard my father laugh so long—that I joined him in laughter, to keep him company or perhaps to cover up my ignorance. In the midst of such glee he told them the whereabouts of hidden treasure much richer in gold, pearls, and jewelry than might have been expected on a farm.

I can't say much about the captured wives, hired girls, and daughters because the soldiers didn't let me watch their doings. But I do remember hearing pitiful screams from various dark corners and I guess that my mother and our Ursula had it no better than the rest.



of the authority to make laws, levy taxes, administer justice, control the state's administrative system, and determine foreign policy.

## France Under Louis XIV

France during the reign of Louis XIV (1661–1715) has traditionally been regarded as the best example of the practice of absolute or **divine-right monarchy** in the seventeenth century. French culture, language, and manners reached into all levels of European society. French diplomacy and wars overwhelmed the political affairs of western and central Europe. The court of Louis XIV seemed to be imitated everywhere in Europe (see the comparative illustration on p. 409).

**Political Institutions** One of the keys to Louis's power was his control of the central policy-making machinery of government because it was part of his own court and household. The royal court located at Versailles served

© Réunion des Musées Nationaux/Art Resource, NY

© Metropolitan Museum of Art, Rogers Fund, 1942

POLITICS & GOVERNMENT

COMPARATIVE ILLUSTRATION

**Sun Kings, West and East.** At the end of the seventeenth century, two powerful rulers dominated their kingdoms. Both monarchs ruled states that dominated the affairs of the regions around them. And both rulers saw themselves as favored by divine authority—Louis XIV as a divine-right monarch and Kangxi as possessing the mandate of Heaven. Thus both rulers saw themselves not as divine beings but as divinely ordained beings whose job was to govern organized societies. On the left, Louis XIV, who ruled France from 1643 to 1715, is seen in a portrait by Hyacinth Rigaud that captures the king's sense of royal dignity and grandeur. On the right, Kangxi, who ruled China from 1661 to 1722, is seen in a nineteenth-century portrait that shows the ruler seated in majesty on his imperial throne.

three purposes simultaneously: it was the personal household of the king, the location of central governmental machinery, and the place where powerful subjects came to find favors and offices for themselves and their clients. The greatest danger to Louis's personal rule came from the very high nobles and princes of the blood (the royal princes), who considered it their natural role to assert the policy-making role of royal ministers. Louis eliminated this threat by removing them from the royal council, the chief administrative body of the king, and enticing them to his court, where he could keep them preoccupied with court life and out of politics. Instead of the high nobility and royal princes, Louis relied for his ministers on nobles who came from relatively new aristocratic families. His ministers were expected to be subservient: "I had no intention of sharing my authority with them," Louis said.

Louis's domination of his ministers and secretaries gave him control of the central policy-making machinery of government and thus authority over the traditional areas of monarchical power: the formulation of foreign policy, the making of war and peace, the assertion of the secular power of the crown against any religious authority, and the ability to levy taxes to fulfill these functions. However, Louis had considerably less success with the internal administration of the kingdom. The traditional groups and institutions of French society—the nobles, officials, town councils, guilds, and representative estates in some provinces—were simply too powerful for the king to have direct control over the lives of his subjects. As a result, the control of the central government over the provinces and the people was carried out largely by the careful bribery of the important people to see that the king's policies were executed.

© Giraudon/Art Resource, NY

**Interior of Versailles: The Hall of Mirrors.** Pictured here is the exquisite Hall of Mirrors in King Louis XIV's palace at Versailles. Located on the second floor, the hall overlooks the park below. Hundreds of mirrors were placed on the wall opposite the windows to create an illusion of even greater width. Careful planning went into every detail of the interior decoration. Even doorknobs were specially designed to reflect the magnificence of Versailles.

**The Economy and the Military** The cost of building palaces, maintaining his court, and pursuing his wars made finances a crucial issue for Louis XIV. He was most fortunate in having the services of Jean-Baptiste Colbert (1619–1683) as controller general of finances. Colbert sought to increase the wealth and power of France by general adherence to mercantilism, which focused on the role of the state, believing that state intervention in the economy was desirable for the sake of the national good. To decrease imports and increase exports, Colbert granted subsidies to individuals who established new industries. To improve communications and the transportation of goods internally, he built roads and canals. To decrease imports directly, Colbert raised tariffs on foreign goods.

The increase in royal power that Louis pursued led the king to develop a professional army numbering 100,000 men in peacetime and 400,000 in time of war. To achieve the prestige and military glory befitting an absolute king as well as to ensure the domination of his Bourbon dynasty over European affairs, Louis waged four wars between 1667 and 1713. His ambitions roused much of Europe to form coalitions that were determined to prevent the certain destruction of the European balance of power by Bourbon hegemony. Although Louis added some territory to France's northeastern frontier and established a member of his own Bourbon dynasty on the throne of Spain, he also left France impoverished and surrounded by enemies.

## Absolutism in Central and Eastern Europe

During the seventeenth century, a development of great importance for the modern Western world took place with the appearance in central and eastern Europe of three new powers: Prussia, Austria, and Russia.

**Prussia** Frederick William the Great Elector (1640–1688) laid the foundation for the Prussian state. Realizing that the land he had inherited, known as Brandenburg-Prussia, was a small, open territory with no natural frontiers for defense, Frederick William built an army of forty thousand men, making it the fourth largest in Europe. To sustain the army, Frederick William established the General War Commissariat to levy taxes for the army and oversee its growth. The Commissariat soon evolved into an agency for civil government as well. The new bureaucratic machine became the elector's chief instrument to govern the state. Many of its officials were members of the Prussian landed aristocracy, the Junkers, who also served as officers in the all-important army.

In 1701, Frederick William's son Frederick officially gained the title of king. Elector Frederick III became King Frederick I, and Brandenburg-Prussia simply Prussia. In the eighteenth century, Prussia emerged as a great power in Europe.

## PETER THE GREAT DEALS WITH A REBELLION

During his first visit to the West, in 1697–1698, Peter received word that the Streltsy, an elite military unit stationed in Moscow, had revolted against his authority. Peter hurried home and crushed the revolt in a very savage fashion. This selection is taken from an Austrian account of how Peter dealt with the rebels.

*How did Peter the Great deal with the revolt of the Streltsy? What does his approach to this problem tell us about the tsar?*

### Peter and the Streltsy

How sharp was the pain, how great the indignation, to which the tsar's Majesty was mightily moved, when he knew of the rebellion of the Streltsy, betraying openly a mind panting for vengeance! He was still tarrying at Vienna, quite full of the desire of setting out for Italy; but, fervid as was his curiosity of rambling abroad, it was, nevertheless, speedily extinguished on the announcement of the troubles that had broken out in the bowels of his realm. Going immediately to Lefort . . . , he thus indignantly broke out: "Tell me, Francis, how I can reach Moscow by the shortest way, in a brief space, so that I may wreak vengeance on this great perfidy of my people, with punishments worthy of their abominable crime. Not one of them shall escape with impunity. Around my royal city, which, with their impious efforts, they planned to destroy, I will have gibbets and gallows set upon the walls and ramparts, and each and every one of them will I put to a direful death." Nor did he long delay the plan for his justly excited wrath; he took the quick post, as his ambassador suggested, and in four weeks' time he had got over about three hundred miles without accident, and arrived the 4th of September, 1698–a monarch for the well disposed, but an avenger for the wicked.

His first anxiety after his arrival was about the rebellion–in what it consisted, what the insurgents meant, who dared to instigate such a crime. And as nobody could answer accurately upon all points, and some pleaded their own ignorance, others the obstinacy of the Streltsy, he began to have suspicions of everybody's loyalty. . . . No day, holy or profane, were the inquisitors idle; every day was deemed fit and lawful for torturing. There were as many scourges as there were accused, and every inquisitor was a butcher. . . . The whole month of October was spent in lacerating the backs of culprits with the knout and with flames; no day were those that were left alive exempt from scourging or scorching; or else they were broken upon the wheel, or driven to the gibbet, or slain with the ax. . . .

To prove to all people how holy and inviolable are those walls of the city which the Streltsy rashly meditated scaling in a sudden assault, beams were run out from all the embrasures in the walls near the gates, in each of which two rebels were hanged. This day beheld about two hundred and fifty die that death. There are few cities fortified with as many palisades as Moscow has given gibbets to her guardian Streltsy.

**Austria** The Austrian Habsburgs had long played a significant role in European politics as Holy Roman Emperors. By the end of the Thirty Years' War, the Habsburg hopes of creating an empire in Germany had been dashed. In the seventeenth century, the house of Austria created a new empire in eastern and southeastern Europe.

The nucleus of the new Austrian Empire remained the traditional Austrian hereditary possessions: Lower and Upper Austria, Carinthia, Carniola, Styria, and Tyrol. To these had been added the kingdom of Bohemia and parts of northwestern Hungary. After the defeat of the Turks in 1687 (see Chapter 15), Austria took control of all of Hungary, Transylvania, Croatia, and Slovenia, thus establishing the Austrian Empire in southeastern Europe. By the beginning of the eighteenth century, the house of Austria had assembled an empire of considerable size.

The Austrian monarchy, however, never became a highly centralized, absolutist state, primarily because it contained so many different national groups. The Austrian Empire remained a collection of territories held together by the Habsburg emperor, who was archduke of Austria, king of Bohemia, and king of Hungary. Each of these regions, however, had its own laws and political life.

**From Muscovy to Russia** A new Russian state had emerged in the fifteenth century under the leadership of the principality of Muscovy and its grand dukes. In the sixteenth century, Ivan IV (1533–1584) became the first ruler to take the title of *tsar* (the Russian word for *Caesar*). Ivan expanded the territories of Russia eastward and crushed the power of the Russian nobility. He was known as Ivan the Terrible because of his ruthless deeds, among them stabbing his son to death in a heated argument. When Ivan's dynasty came to an end in 1598, it was followed by a period of anarchy that did not end until the Zemsky Sobor (national assembly) chose Michael Romanov as the new tsar, establishing a dynasty that lasted until 1917. One of its most prominent members was Peter the Great.

Peter the Great (1689–1725) was an unusual character. A towering, strong man at 6 feet 9 inches tall, Peter enjoyed a low kind of humor—belching contests and crude jokes—and vicious punishments, including floggings, impalings, and roastings (see the box above). Peter got a firsthand view of the West when he made a trip there in 1697–1698 and returned to Russia with a firm determination to westernize or Europeanize Russia. He was especially eager to borrow European technology in order to give him the army and navy he needed to make Russia a great power.

As could be expected, one of his first priorities was the reorganization of the army and the creation of a navy. Employing both Russians and Europeans as officers, he conscripted peasants for twenty-five-year stints of service to build a standing army of 210,000 men. Peter has also been given credit for forming the first Russian navy.

To impose the rule of the central government more effectively throughout the land, Peter divided Russia into provinces. Although he hoped to create a "police state," by which he meant a well-ordered community governed in accordance with law, few of his bureaucrats shared his concept of duty to the state. Peter hoped for a sense of civic duty, but his own forceful personality created an atmosphere of fear that prevented it.

The object of Peter's domestic reforms was to make Russia into a great state and military power. His primary goal was to "open a window to the west," meaning an ice-free port easily accessible to Europe. This could only be achieved on the Baltic, but at that time, the Baltic coast was controlled by Sweden, the most important power in northern Europe. A long and hard-fought war with Sweden won Peter the lands he sought. In 1703, Peter began the construction of a new city, Saint Petersburg, his window to the west and a symbol that Russia was looking westward to Europe. Under Peter, Russia became a great military power and, by his death in 1725, an important European state.

# England and Limited Monarchy

Not all states were absolutist in the seventeenth century. One of the most prominent examples of resistance to absolute monarchy came in England, where king and Parliament struggled to determine the roles each should play in governing England.

## Conflict Between King and Parliament

With the death of Queen Elizabeth I in 1603, the Tudor dynasty became extinct, and the Stuart line of rulers was inaugurated with the accession to the throne of Elizabeth's cousin, King James VI of Scotland, who became James I (1603–1625) of England. James espoused the divine right of kings, a viewpoint that alienated Parliament, which had grown accustomed under the Tudors to act on the premise that monarch and Parliament together ruled England as a "balanced polity." Then, too, the Puritans—Protestants within the Anglican church who, inspired by Calvinist theology, wished to eliminate every trace of Roman Catholicism from the Church of England—were alienated by the king's strong defense of the Anglican church. Much of England's gentry, mostly well-to-do landowners, had become Puritans, and this Puritan gentry formed an important and substantial part of the House of Commons, the lower house of Parliament. It was not wise to alienate these men.

The conflict that had begun during the reign of James came to a head during the reign of his son Charles I (1625–1649). Charles also believed in divine-right monarchy, and religious differences also added to the hostility between Charles I and Parliament. The attempt of Charles to impose more ritual on the Anglican church struck the Puritans as a return to Catholic practices. When Charles tried to force the Puritans to accept his religious policies, thousands of them went off to the "howling wildernesses" of America.

## Civil War and Commonwealth

Grievances mounted until England finally slipped into a civil war (1642–1648) won by the parliamentary forces, due largely to the New Model Army of Oliver Cromwell, the only real military genius of the war. The New Model Army was composed primarily of more extreme Puritans known as the Independents, who, in typical Calvinist fashion, believed they were doing battle for God. As Cromwell wrote in one of his military reports, "Sir, this is none other but the hand of God; and to Him alone belongs the glory." We might give some credit to Cromwell; his soldiers were well trained in the new military tactics of the seventeenth century.

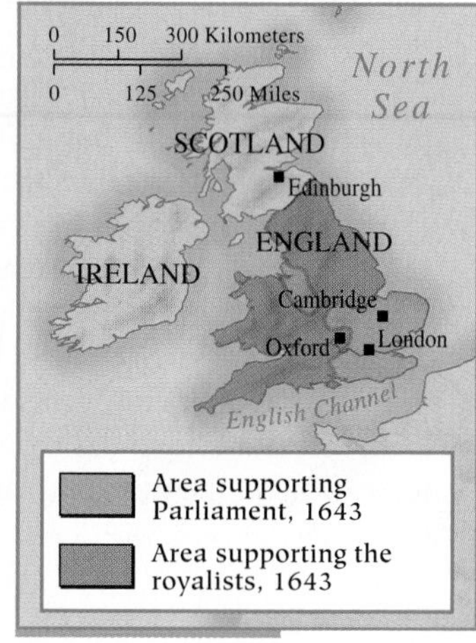

**Civil War in England**

After the execution of Charles I on January 30, 1649, Parliament abolished the monarchy and the House of Lords and proclaimed England a republic or commonwealth. But Cromwell and his army, unable to work effectively with Parliament, dispersed it by force and established a military dictatorship. After Cromwell's death in 1658, the army decided that military rule was no longer feasible and restored the monarchy in the person of Charles II, the son of Charles I.

## Restoration and a Glorious Revolution

Charles was sympathetic to Catholicism, and Parliament's suspicions were aroused in 1672 when Charles took the audacious step of issuing the Declaration of Indulgence, which suspended the laws that Parliament had passed against Catholics and Puritans after the restoration of the monarchy. Parliament forced the king to suspend the declaration.

The accession of James II (1685–1688) to the crown virtually guaranteed a new constitutional crisis for England. An open and devout Catholic, his attempt to further Catholic interests made religion once more a primary cause of conflict between king and Parliament.

| CHRONOLOGY Absolute and Limited Monarchy | |
|---|---|
| France | |
| Louis XIV | 1643–1715 |
| Brandenburg-Prussia | |
| Frederick William the Great Elector | 1640–1688 |
| Elector Frederick III (King Frederick I) | 1688–1713 |
| Russia | |
| Ivan IV the Terrible | 1533–1584 |
| Peter the Great | 1689–1725 |
| First trip to the West | 1697–1698 |
| Construction of Saint Petersburg begins | 1703 |
| England | |
| Civil wars | 1642–1648 |
| Commonwealth | 1649–1653 |
| Charles II | 1660–1685 |
| Declaration of Indulgence | 1672 |
| James II | 1685–1688 |
| Glorious Revolution | 1688 |
| Bill of Rights | 1689 |

Robert Walker, *Oliver Cromwell*, 1649, courtesy of the National Portrait Gallery, London

**Oliver Cromwell.** Oliver Cromwell was a dedicated Puritan who helped form the New Model Army and defeat the forces supporting King Charles I. Unable to work with Parliament, he came to rely on military force to rule England. Cromwell is pictured here in 1649, on the eve of his military campaign in Ireland.

James named Catholics to high positions in the government, army, navy, and universities. Parliamentary outcries against James's policies stopped short of rebellion because members knew that he was an old man and that his successors were his Protestant daughters Mary and Anne, born to his first wife. But on June 10, 1688, a son was born to James II's second wife, also a Catholic. Suddenly the specter of a Catholic hereditary monarchy loomed large. A group of prominent English noblemen invited the Dutch chief executive, William of Orange, husband of James's daughter Mary, to invade England. William and Mary raised an army and invaded England while James, his wife, and their infant son fled to France. With little bloodshed, England had undergone its "Glorious Revolution."

In January 1689, Parliament offered the throne to William and Mary, who accepted it along with the provisions of a bill of rights (see the box on p. 414). The Bill of Rights affirmed Parliament's right to make laws and levy taxes. The rights of citizens to keep arms and have a jury trial were also confirmed. By deposing one king and establishing another, Parliament had destroyed the divine-right theory of kingship (William was, after all, king by grace of Parliament, not God) and asserted its right to participate in the government. Parliament did not have complete control of the government, but it now had the right to participate in affairs of state. Over the next century, it would gradually prove to be the real authority in the English system of **limited (constitutional) monarchy.**

# The Flourishing of European Culture

Despite religious wars and the growth of absolutism, European culture continued to flourish. The era was blessed with a number of prominent artists and writers.

## Art: The Baroque

The artistic movement known as the **Baroque** dominated the Western artistic world for a century and a half. The Baroque began in Italy in the last quarter of the sixteenth century and spread to the rest of Europe and Latin America. Baroque artists sought to harmonize the classical ideals of Renaissance art with the spiritual feelings of the sixteenth-century religious revival. In large part, Baroque art and architecture reflected the search for power that was characteristic of much of the seventeenth century. Baroque churches and palaces featured richly ornamented facades, sweeping staircases, and an overall splendor meant to impress people. Kings and princes wanted not only their subjects but also other kings and princes to be in awe of their power.

Baroque painting was known for its use of dramatic effects to arouse the emotions, especially evident in the works of Peter Paul Rubens (1577–1640), a prolific artist

## The Bill of Rights

In 1688, the English experienced a bloodless revolution in which the Stuart king James II was replaced by Mary, James's daughter, and her husband, William of Orange. After William and Mary had assumed power, Parliament passed a Bill of Rights that specified the rights of Parliament and laid the foundation for a constitutional monarchy.

*How did the Bill of Rights lay the foundation for a constitutional monarchy in England?*

### The Bill of Rights

Whereas the said late King James II having abdicated the government, and the throne being thereby vacant, his Highness the prince of Orange (whom it hath pleased Almighty God to make the glorious instrument of delivering this kingdom from popery and arbitrary power) did (by the device of the lords spiritual and temporal, and diverse principal persons of the Commons) cause letters to be written to the lords spiritual and temporal, being Protestants, and other letters to the several counties, cities, universities, boroughs, and Cinque Ports, for the choosing of such persons to represent them, as were of right to be sent to parliament, to meet and sit at Westminster upon the two and twentieth day of January, in this year 1689, in order to such an establishment as that their religion, laws, and liberties might not again be in danger of being subverted; upon which letters elections have been accordingly made.

And thereupon the said lords spiritual and temporal and Commons, pursuant to their respective letters and elections, being now assembled in a full and free representation of this nation, taking into their most serious consideration the best means for attaining the ends aforesaid, do in the first place (as their ancestors in like case have usually done), for the vindication and assertion of their ancient rights and liberties, declare:

1. That the pretended power of suspending laws, or the execution of laws, by regal authority, without consent of parliament is illegal.
2. That the pretended power of dispensing with the laws, or the execution of law by regal authority, as it hath been assumed and exercised of late, is illegal.
3. That the commission for erecting the late court of commissioners for ecclesiastical causes, and all other commissions and courts of like nature, are illegal and pernicious.
4. That levying money for or to the use of the crown by pretense of prerogative, without grant of parliament, for longer time or in other manner than the same is or shall be granted, is illegal.
5. That it is the right of the subjects to petition the king, and all commitments and prosecutions for such petitioning are illegal.
6. That the raising or keeping a standing army within the kingdom in time of peace, unless it be with consent of parliament, is against law.
7. That the subjects which are Protestants may have arms for their defense suitable to their conditions, and as allowed by law.
8. That election of members of parliament ought to be free.
9. That the freedom of speech, and debates or proceedings in parliament, ought not to be impeached or questioned in any court or place out of parliament.
10. That excessive bail ought not to be required, nor excessive fines imposed, nor cruel and unusual punishments inflicted.
11. That jurors ought to be duly impaneled and returned, and jurors which pass upon men in trials for high treason ought to be freeholders.
12. That all grants and promises of fines and forfeitures of particular persons before conviction are illegal and void.
13. And that for redress of all grievances, and for the amending, strengthening, and preserving of the laws, parliament ought to be held frequently.

History Now™ To read a full version of this document, enter the *HistoryNow* documents area using the access card that is available for *World History*.

and an important figure in the spread of the Baroque from Italy to other parts of Europe. In his artistic masterpieces, bodies in violent motion, heavily fleshed nudes, a dramatic use of light and shadow, and rich sensuous pigments converge to express intense emotions.

Perhaps the greatest figure of the Baroque was the Italian architect and sculptor Gian Lorenzo Bernini (1598–1680), who completed Saint Peter's Basilica at the Vatican and designed the vast colonnade enclosing the piazza in front of it. Action, exuberance, profusion, and dramatic effects mark the work of Bernini in the interior of Saint Peter's, where his *Throne of Saint Peter* hovers in midair, held by the hands of the four great doctors of the Catholic church. Above the chair, rays of golden light drive a mass of clouds and angels toward the spectator. In his most striking sculptural work, the *Ecstasy of Saint Theresa*, Bernini depicts a moment of mystical experience in the life of the sixteenth-century Spanish saint. The elegant draperies and the expression on her face create a sensuously real portrayal of physical ecstasy.

## Art: Dutch Realism

The supremacy of Dutch commerce in the seventeenth century was paralleled by a brilliant flowering of Dutch painting. Wealthy patricians and burghers of Dutch urban society commissioned works of art for their guild halls, town halls, and private dwellings. The interests of this burgher society were reflected in the subject matter of many Dutch paintings: portraits of themselves, group portraits of their military companies and guilds, landscapes, seascapes, genre scenes, still lifes, and the interiors of their residences. Neither classical nor Baroque, Dutch painters were primarily interested in the realistic portrayal of secular everyday life.

This interest in painting scenes of everyday life is evident in the work of Judith Leyster (c. 1609–1660), who established her own independent painting career, a remarkable occurrence in seventeenth-century Europe. Leyster became the first female member of the painting Guild of Saint Luke in Haarlem, which enabled her to set up her own workshop and take on three male pupils. Musicians playing their instruments, women sewing, children laughing while playing games, and actors performing all form the subject matter of Leyster's portrayals of everyday Dutch life. But she was also capable of introspection, as is evident in her *Self-Portrait.*

## A Golden Age of Literature in England

In England, writing for the stage reached new heights between 1580 and 1640. The golden age of English literature is often called the Elizabethan Era because much of the English cultural flowering occurred during Elizabeth's reign. Elizbethan literature exhibits the exuberance and pride associated with English exploits under Queen Elizabeth (see the box on p. 416). Of all the forms of Elizabethan literature, none expressed the energy and intellectual versatility of the era better than drama. And no

**Peter Paul Rubens, *The Landing of Marie de' Medici at Marseilles.*** The Flemish painter Peter Paul Rubens played a key role in spreading the Baroque style from Italy to other parts of Europe. In *The Landing of Marie de' Medici at Marseilles,* Rubens made a dramatic use of light and color, bodies in motion, and luxurious nudes to heighten the emotional intensity of the scene. This was one of a cycle of twenty-one paintings dedicated to the queen mother of France.

**Gian Lorenzo Bernini, *Ecstasy of Saint Theresa.*** One of the great artists of the Baroque period was the Italian sculptor and architect Gian Lorenzo Bernini. The *Ecstasy of Saint Theresa,* created for the Cornaro Chapel in the Church of Santa Maria della Vittoria in Rome, was one of Bernini's most famous pieces of sculpture. Bernini sought to convey visually Theresa's own description of the mystical experience when an angel supposedly pierced her heart repeatedly with a golden arrow.

## William Shakespeare: In Praise of England

William Shakespeare is one of the most famous playwrights in the Western world. He was a universal genius, outclassing all others in his psychological insights, depth of characterization, imaginative skills, and versatility. His historical plays reflected the patriotic enthusiasm of the English in the Elizabethan Era, as this excerpt from *Richard II* illustrates.

*Why is William Shakespeare aptly described as not merely a playwright but a "complete man of the theater"? Which countries might Shakespeare have meant to suggest by the phrase "the envy of less happier lands"?*

### William Shakespeare, *Richard II*

*This royal throne of kings, this sceptered isle,*
*This earth of majesty, this seat of Mars,*
*This other Eden, demi-Paradise,*
*This fortress built by Nature for herself*
*Against infection and the hand of war,*
*This happy breed of men, this little world,*
*This precious stone set in the silver sea,*
*Which serves it in the office of a wall*
*Or as a moat defensive to a house*
*Against the envy of less happier lands–*
*This blessed plot, this earth, this realm, this England,*
*This nurse, this teeming womb of royal kings,*
*Feared by their breed and famous by their birth,*
*Renowned for their deeds as far from home,*
*For Christian service and true chivalry,*
*As is the sepulcher in stubborn Jewry [the Holy Sepulcher in Jerusalem among the steadfast Jewish people]*
*Of the world's ransom, blessed Mary's Son–*
*This land of such dear souls, this dear dear land,*
*Dear for her reputation through the world,*
*Is now leased out, I die pronouncing it,*
*Like a tenement or pelting farm.*
*England, bound in with the triumphant sea,*
*Whose rocky shore beats back the envious siege*
*Of watery Neptune, is now bound in with shame,*
*With inky blots and rotten parchment bonds.*
*That England, that was wont to conquer others,*
*Hath made a shameful conquest of itself.*
*Ah, would the scandal vanish with my life,*
*How happy then were my ensuing death!*

dramatist is more famous or more accomplished than William Shakespeare (1564–1614).

Shakespeare was a "complete man of the theater." Although best known for writing plays, he was also an actor and a shareholder in the chief acting company of the time, the Lord Chamberlain's Company, which played in various London theaters. Shakespeare is to this day hailed as a genius. A master of the English language, he imbued its words with power and majesty. And his technical proficiency was matched by incredible insight into human psychology. Whether writing tragedies or comedies, Shakespeare exhibited a remarkable understanding of the human condition.

National Gallery of Art, Washington, D.C., gift of Mr. and Mrs. Robert Woods Bliss

**Judith Leyster, *Self Portrait.*** Although Judith Leyster was a well-known artist to her Dutch contemporaries, her fame diminished soon after her death. In the late nineteenth century, however, a Dutch art historian rediscovered her work. In her *Self-Portrait*, painted in 1635, she is seen pausing in her work in front of one of the scenes of daily life that made her such a popular artist in her own day.

## CONCLUSION

In Chapter 13, we observed how the movement of Europeans outside of Europe began to change the shape of world history. But what had made this development possible? After all, the religious division of Europe had led to almost a hundred years of religious warfare complicated by serious political, economic, and social issues—the worst series of wars and civil wars since the collapse of the western Roman Empire—before Europeans finally admitted that they would have to tolerate different ways to worship God.

At the same time, the concept of a united Christendom, held as an ideal since the Middle Ages, had been irrevocably destroyed by the religious wars, enabling a system of nation-states to emerge in which power politics took on increasing significance. Within those states slowly emerged some of the machinery that made possible a growing centralization of power. In absolutist states, strong monarchs with the assistance of their aristocracies took the lead in promoting greater centralization. In all the major European states, a growing concern for power led to larger armies and greater conflict, stronger economies, and more powerful governments. From a global point of view, Europeans—with their strong governments, prosperous economies, and strengthened military forces—were beginning to dominate other parts of the world, leading to a growing belief in the superiority of their civilization.

Yet despite Europeans' increasing domination of global trade markets, they had not achieved their goal of diminishing the power of Islam, first pursued during the Crusades. In fact, as we shall see in the next chapter, in the midst of European expansion and exploration, three new and powerful Muslim empires were taking shape in the Middle East and South Asia.

## TIMELINE

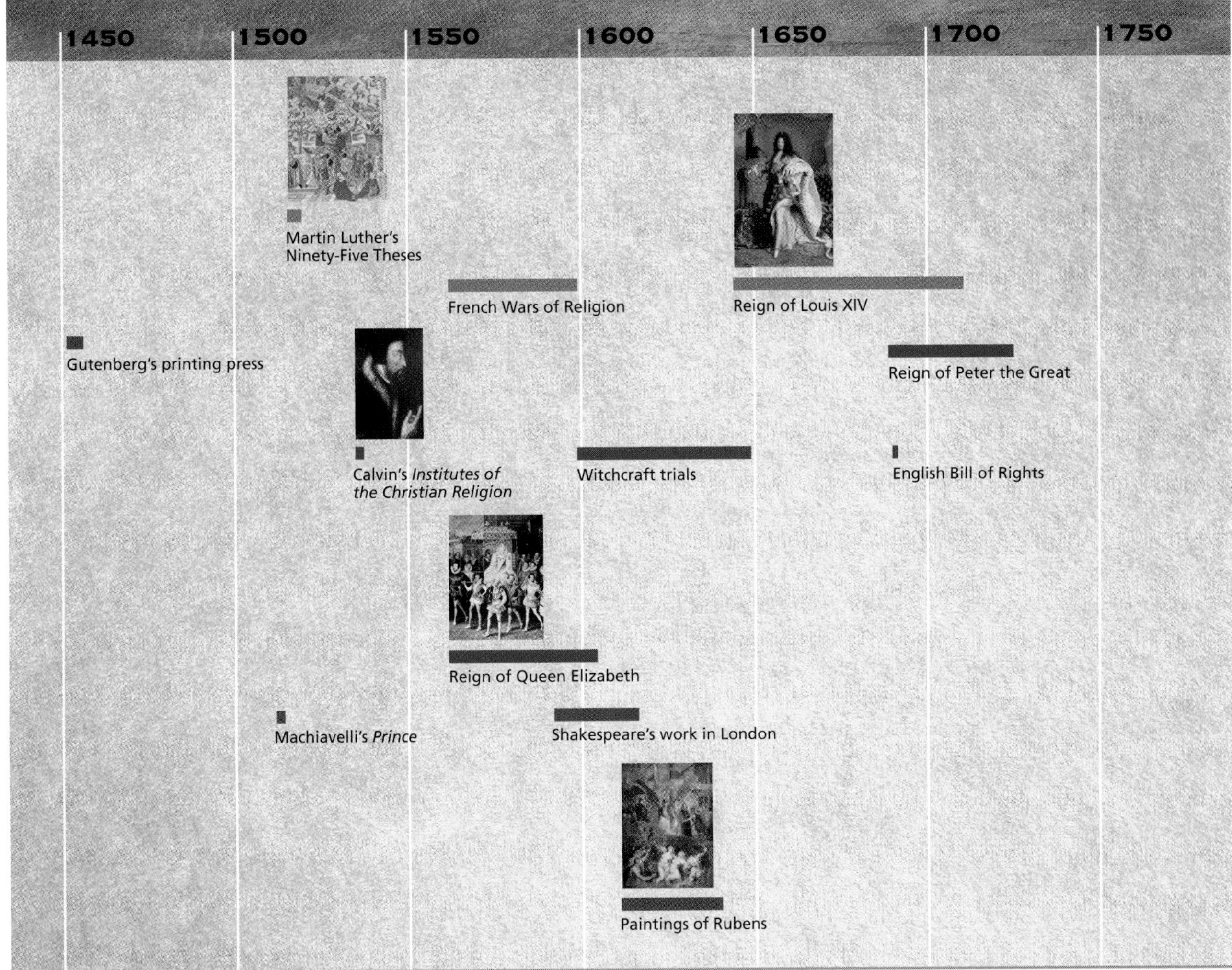

## CHAPTER NOTES

1. N. Machiavelli, *The Prince*, trans. D. Wootton (Indianapolis, Ind., 1995), p. 48.
2. Quoted in R. Bainton, *Here I Stand: A Life of Martin Luther* (New York, 1950), p. 144.
3. J. Calvin, *Institutes of the Christian Religion*, trans. J. Allen (Philadelphia, 1936), vol. 1, p. 228; vol. 2, p. 181.
4. Quoted in B. S. Anderson and J. P. Zinsser, *A History of Their Own: Women in Europe from Prehistory to the Present* (New York, 1988), vol. 1, p. 259.
5. Quoted in J. O'Malley, *The First Jesuits* (Cambridge, Mass., 1993), p. 76.
6. Quoted in J. Klaits, *Servants of Satan: The Age of Witch Hunts* (Bloomington, Ind., 1985), p. 68.

## SUGGESTED READING

Basic surveys of the Reformation period include **H. J. Grimm, *The Reformation Era, 1500–1650,*** 2d ed. (New York, 1973); **D. L. Jensen, *Reformation Europe,*** 2d ed. (Lexington, Mass., 1990); **J. D. Tracy, *Europe's Reformations, 1450–1650*** (Oxford, 1999); **D. MacCulloch, *The Reformation*** (New York, 2003); and **C. Lindberg, *The European Reformations*** (Cambridge, Mass., 1996). Also see the interesting and useful book by **S. Ozment, *Protestants: The Birth of a Revolution*** (New York, 1992).

The classic account of Martin Luther's life is **R. Bainton, *Here I Stand: A Life of Martin Luther*** (New York, 1950). More recent works include **J. M. Kittelson, *Luther the Reformer: The Story of the Man and His Career*** (Minneapolis, Minn., 1986), and **H. A. Oberman, *Luther: Man Between God and the Devil*** (New York, 1992). See also the brief biography by **M. Marty, *Martin Luther*** (New York, 2004). On the role of Charles V, see **W. Maltby, *The Reign of Charles V*** (New York, 2002). The most comprehensive account of the various groups and individuals who are called Anabaptist is **G. H. Williams, *The Radical Reformation,*** 2d ed. (Kirksville, Mo., 1992). A good survey of the English Reformation is **A. G. Dickens, *The English Reformation,*** 2d ed. (New York, 1989). On John Calvin, see **A. McGrath, *A Life of John Calvin: A Study in the Shaping of Western Culture*** (Cambridge, Mass., 1990), and **W. J. Bouwsma, *John Calvin*** (New York, 1988).

On the impact of the Reformation on the family, see **J. F. Harrington, *Reordering Marriage and Society in Reformation Germany*** (New York, 1995). A good introduction to the Catholic Reformation can be found in **R. P. Hsia, *The World of Catholic Renewal, 1540–1770*** (Cambridge, 1998).

On the French Wars of Religion, see **M. P. Holt, *The French Wars of Religion, 1562–1629*** (New York, 1995), and **R. J. Knecht, *The French Wars of Religion, 1559–1598,*** 2d ed. (New York, 1996). A good biography of Philip II is **G. Parker, *Philip II,*** 3d ed. (Chicago, 1995). Elizabeth's reign can be examined in **C. Haigh, *Elizabeth I,*** 2d ed. (New York, 1998). On the Thirty Years' War, see **R. G. Asch, *The Thirty Years' War: The Holy Roman Empire and Europe, 1618–1648*** (New York, 1997).

Witchcraft hysteria can be examined in **B. P. Levack, *The Witch-Hunt in Early Modern Europe*** (London, 1987).

For a brief account of seventeenth-century French history, see **J. B. Collins, *The State in Early Modern France*** (Cambridge, 1995). A solid and very readable biography of Louis XIV is **J. Levi, *Louis XIV*** (New York, 2004). For a brief study, see **P. R. Campbell, *Louis XIV, 1661–1715*** (London, 1993). On the creation of an Austrian state, see **P. S. Fichtner, *The Habsburg Monarchy, 1490–1848*** (New York, 2003). See **P. H. Wilson, *Absolutism in Central Europe*** (New York, 2000), on both Prussia and Austria. Works on Peter the Great include **M. S. Anderson, *Peter the Great,*** 2d ed. (New York, 1995), and **L. Hughes, *Russia in the Age of Peter the Great*** (New Haven, Conn., 1998). On England, see **M. A. Kishlansky, *A Monarchy Transformed*** (London, 1996) on the English Revolution, and **W. A. Speck, *The Revolution of 1688*** (Oxford, 1988).

For a general survey of Baroque culture, see **J. S. Held, *Seventeenth and Eighteenth Century Art: Baroque Painting, Sculpture, Architecture*** (New York, 1971). The literature on Shakespeare is enormous. For a biography, see **A. L. Rowse, *The Life of Shakespeare*** (New York, 1963).

### History Now™

**Enter *HistoryNow* using the access card that is available with this text. *HistoryNow* will assist you in understanding the content in this chapter with lesson plans generated for your needs, as well as provide you with a connection to the *Wadsworth World History Resource Center* (see description below for details).**

### WORLD HISTORY RESOURCE CENTER

**Enter the Resource Center using either your *HistoryNow* access card or your standalone access card for the *Wadsworth World History Resource Center.* Organized by topic, this website includes quizzes; images; over 350 primary source documents; interactive simulations; maps and timelines; movie explorations; and a wealth of other resources. You can read the following documents, and many more, at http://history.wadsworth.com/rc/world**

Niccolò Machiavelli, *The Prince,* selected chapters

Erasmus and Luther, "On Free Will and Salvation"

Saint-Simone, "The Daily Ritual of the King and His Courtiers"

Visit the *World History* Companion Website for chapter quizzes and more.

http://history.wadsworth.com/duikerspielvogel05/

SCIENCE & TECHNOLOGY

"War,
Ferna
been
Impr
course of events."
situation in the M
century, when the
of warfare and gav
that stood at the h
But it could as eas
when potential ad
reaching across oc

One crucial as
in the nature of w
and arrow to the a
superior instrume
tage against a poo
possession of iron
invading Hyksos t
nium B.C.E.

Mobility is ano
second millennium
ized the art of war
River valley in nort
stirrup enabled mo
technique applied v
devastated civilizat

was that they wer
and therefore owe
tan. Other military
were thus loyal to

The Janissary
changes in warfar
in the late fourtee
the new technolog
(see the compara
above). The tradit
outmoded and wa
with muskets. Thu
infantry who serv
palace and as a me
Balkans. With his
the famous Battle
hegemony in the a

## Expansion of th

Under Murad's s
Ottomans advanc
slaughtered the flo
on the Danube. A

CHAPTER

# 15

# THE MUSLIM EMPIRES

## CHAPTER OUTLINE AND FOCUS QUESTIONS

### The Ottoman Empire

- What was the ethnic composition of the Ottoman Empire, and how did the government of the sultan administer such a diverse population? How did Ottoman policy in this regard compare with that applied in Europe and Asia?

### The Safavids

- What role did women play in each of the Muslim empires? Compare Safavid policy toward women with that followed in other parts of the world.

### The Grandeur of the Mughals

- Why are the Ottoman, Safavid, and Mughal Empires sometimes called "gunpowder empires," and in what ways were they similar?

### CRITICAL THINKING

- What were the main characteristics of each of the Muslim empires, and in what ways did they resemble each other? How are they distinct from their European counterparts?

*The Battle of Mohács*

THE OTTOMAN ARMY, led by Sultan Suleyman the Magnificent, arrived at Mohács, on the plains of Hungary, on an August morning in 1526. The Turkish force numbered about 100,000 men, and in its baggage were three hundred new long-range cannons. Facing them was a somewhat larger European force, clothed in heavy armor but armed with only one hundred older cannons.

The battle began at noon and was over in two hours. The flower of Hungarian cavalry had been destroyed, and twenty thousand foot soldiers had drowned in a nearby swamp. The Ottomans had lost fewer than two hundred men. Two weeks later, they seized the Hungarian capital at Buda and prepared to lay siege to the nearby Austrian city of Vienna. Europe was in a panic. It was to be the high point of Turkish expansion in Europe.

In launching their Age of Exploration, European rulers had hoped that by controlling global markets, they could cripple the power of Islam and reduce its threat to the security of Europe. But the dream of Christian nations to expand their influence around the globe at the expense of their great Muslim rival had not been achieved. On the contrary, the Muslim world, which seemed to have entered a period of decline with the collapse of the Abbasid

executed (strangled with a silk bowstring) or later imprisoned. Heirs to the throne were assigned as provincial governors to provide them with experience.

**The Harem** The heart of the sultan's power was in the Topkapi Palace in the center of Istanbul. Topkapi (meaning "cannon gate") was constructed in 1459 by Mehmet II and served as an administrative center as well as the private residence of the sultan and his family. Eventually, it had a staff of twenty thousand employees. The private domain of the sultan was called the **harem** ("sacred place"). Here he resided with his concubines. Normally, a sultan did not marry but chose several concubines as his favorites; they were accorded this status after they gave birth to sons. When a son became a sultan, his mother became known as the queen mother and served as adviser to the throne. This tradition, initiated by the influential wife of Suleyman the Magnificent, often resulted in considerable authority for the queen mother in the affairs of state.

Members of the harem, like the Janissaries, were often of slave origin and formed an elite element in Ottoman society. Since the enslavement of Muslims was forbidden, slaves were taken among non-Islamic peoples. Some concubines were prisoners selected for the position, while others were purchased or offered to the sultan as gifts. They were then trained and educated like the Janissaries in a system called *devshirme* ("collection"). *Devshirme* had originated in the practice of requiring local clan leaders to provide prisoners to the sultan as part of their tax obligation. Talented males were given special training for eventual placement in military or administrative positions, while their female counterparts were trained for service in the harem, with instruction in reading, the Qur'an, sewing and embroidery, and musical performance. They were ranked according to their status, and some were permitted to leave the harem to marry officials. If they were later divorced, they were sometimes allowed to return to the harem.

Unique to the Ottoman Empire from the fifteenth century onward was the exclusive use of slaves to reproduce its royal heirs. Contrary to myth, few of the women of the imperial harem were used for sexual purposes, as the majority were relatives of the sultan's extended family—sisters, daughters, widowed mothers, and in-laws, with their own personal slaves and entourage. Contemporary European observers compared the atmosphere in the Topkapi harem to a Christian nunnery, with its hierarchical organization, enforced chastity, and rule of silence.

Because of their proximity to the sultan, the women of the harem often wielded so much political power that the era has been called "the sultanate of women." Queen mothers administered the imperial household and engaged in diplomatic relations with other countries while controlling the marital alliances of their daughters with senior civilian and military officials or members of other royal families in the region. One princess was married

Topkapi Palace Museum/Bridgeman Art Library

**Recruitment of the Children.** The Ottoman Empire, like its Chinese counterpart, sought to recruit its officials on the basis of merit. Through the system called *devshirme* ("collection"), youthful candidates were selected from the non-Muslim population in villages throughout the empire. In this painting, an imperial officer is counting coins to pay for the children's travel expenses to Istanbul, where they will undergo extensive academic and military training. Note the concern of two of the mothers and a priest as they question the official, who undoubtedly underwent the process himself as a child. As they leave their family and friends, the children carry their worldly possessions in bags slung over their shoulders.

seven separate times from the age of two after her previous husbands died either in battle or by execution.

**Administration of the Government** The sultan ruled through an imperial council that met four days a week and was chaired by the chief minister known as the grand vezir (*wazir,* sometimes rendered in English as *vizier*). The sultan often attended behind a screen, whence he could privately indicate his desires to the grand vezir. The latter presided over the imperial bureaucracy. Like the palace guard, the bureaucrats were not an exclusive group but were chosen at least partly by merit from a palace school for training officials. Most officials were Muslims by birth, but some talented Janissaries became

## COMPARATIVE ESSAY

## THE CHANGING FACE OF WAR

"War," as the renowned French historian Fernand Braudel once observed, "has always been a matter of arms and techniques. Improved techniques can radically alter the course of events." Braudel's remark was directed to the situation in the Mediterranean region during the sixteenth century, when the adoption of artillery changed the face of warfare and gave enormous advantages to the countries that stood at the head of the new technological revolution. But it could as easily have been applied to the present day, when potential adversaries possess weapons capable of reaching across oceans and continents.

One crucial aspect of military superiority, of course, lies in the nature of weaponry. From the invention of the bow and arrow to the advent of the atomic era, the possession of superior instruments of war has provided a distinct advantage against a poorly armed enemy. It was at least partly the possession of iron weapons, for example, that enabled the invading Hyksos to conquer Egypt during the first millennium B.C.E.

Mobility is another factor of vital importance. During the second millennium B.C.E., horse-drawn chariots revolutionized the art of war from the Mediterranean Sea to the Yellow River valley in northern China. Later, the invention of the stirrup enabled mounted warriors to shoot from horseback, a technique applied with great effect by the Mongols as they devastated civilizations across the Eurasian supercontinent.

To protect themselves from marauding warriors, settled societies began to erect massive walls around their cities and fortresses. That in turn led to the invention of siege weapons like the catapult and the battering ram. The Mongols allegedly even came up with an early form of chemical warfare, hurling human bodies infected with the plague into the bastions of their enemies.

The invention of explosives launched the next great revolution in warfare. First used as a weapon of war by the Tang dynasty in China, explosives were brought to the West by the Turks, who used them with great effectiveness in the fifteenth century against the Byzantine Empire. But the Europeans quickly mastered the new technology and took it to new heights, inventing hand-held firearms and mounting iron cannons on their warships. The latter represented a significant advantage to European fleets as they began to compete with rivals for control of the Indian and Pacific Oceans.

The twentieth century saw revolutionary new developments in the art of warfare, from armed vehicles to airplanes and on to the nuclear age. But as weapons grow ever more fearsome, they are more risky to use, resulting in the paradox of the Vietnam War, when lightly armed Viet Cong guerrilla units were able to fight the world's mightiest army to a virtual standstill. As the Chinese military strategist Sun Tzu had long ago observed, victory in war often goes to the smartest, not the strongest.

---

was that they were directly subordinated to the sultanate and therefore owed their loyalty to the person of the sultan. Other military forces were organized by the beys and were thus loyal to their local tribal leaders.

The Janissary corps also represented a response to changes in warfare. As the knowledge of firearms spread in the late fourteenth century, the Turks began to master the new technology, including siege cannons and muskets (see the comparative essay "The Changing Face of War above). The traditional nomadic cavalry charge was now outmoded and was superseded by infantry forces armed with muskets. Thus the Janissaries provided a well-armed infantry who served both as an elite guard to protect the palace and as a means of extending Turkish control in the Balkans. With his new forces, Murad defeated the Serbs at the famous Battle of Kosovo in 1389 and ended Serbian hegemony in the area.

### Expansion of the Empire

Under Murad's successor, Bayazid I (1389–1402), the Ottomans advanced northward, annexed Bulgaria, and slaughtered the flower of French cavalry at a major battle on the Danube. A defeat at the hands of the Mongol warrior Tamerlane (see Chapter 9) in 1402 proved to be only a temporary setback. When Mehmet II (1451–1481) succeeded to the throne, he was determined to capture Constantinople. Already in control of the Dardanelles, he ordered the construction of a major fortress on the Bosporus just north of the city, which put the Turks in a position to strangle the Byzantines.

**The Fall of Constantinople** The last Byzantine emperor desperately called for help from the Europeans, but only the Genoese came to his defense. With eighty thousand troops ranged against only seven thousand defenders, Mehmet laid siege to Constantinople in 1453. In their attack on the city, the Turks made use of massive cannons with 26-foot barrels that could launch stone balls weighing up to 1,200 pounds each. The Byzantines stretched heavy chains across the Golden Horn, the inlet that forms the city's harbor, to prevent a naval attack from the north and prepared to make their final stand behind the 13-mile-long wall along the western edge of the city. But Mehmet's forces seized the tip of the peninsula north of the Golden Horn and then dragged their ships overland across the peninsula from the Bosporus and put them into the water behind the chains.

## THE FALL OF CONSTANTINOPLE

Few events in the history of the Ottoman Empire are more dramatic than the conquest of Constantinople in 1453. In this excerpt, the conquest is described by Kritovoulos, a Greek who later served in the Ottoman administration. Although the author did not witness the conquest itself, he was apparently well informed about the event and provides us with a vivid description.

*What was the strategy used by the Turkish forces to seize the city of Constantinople? What was the significance of their victory for the future of the region?*

### Kritovoulos, *Life of Mehmed the Conqueror*

So saying, he [the Sultan] led them himself. And they, with a shout on the run and with a fearsome yell, went on ahead of the Sultan, pressing on up to the palisade. After a long and bitter struggle they hurled back the Romans [Byzantines] from there and climbed by force up the palisade. They dashed some of their foe down into the ditch between the great wall and the palisade, which was deep and hard to get out of, and they killed them there. The rest they drove back to the gate.

He had opened this gate in the great wall, so as to go easily over to the palisade. Now there was a great struggle there and great slaughter among those stationed there, for they were attacked by the heavy infantry and not a few others in irregular formation, who had been attracted from many points by the shouting. There the Emperor Constantine [Constantine XIII Paleologus], with all who were with him, fell in gallant combat.

The heavy infantry were already streaming through the little gate into the City, and others had rushed in through the breach in the great wall. Then all the rest of the army, with a rush and a roar, poured in brilliantly and scattered all over the City. And the Sultan stood before the great wall, where the standard also was and the ensigns, and watched the proceedings. The day was already breaking. . . .

The soldiers fell on them [the citizens] with anger and great wrath. For one thing, they were actuated by the hardships of the siege. For another, some foolish people had hurled taunts and curses at them from the battlements all through the siege. Now, in general they killed so as to frighten all the City, and to terrorize and enslave all by the slaughter.

When they had had enough of murder, and the City was reduced to slavery, some of the troops turned to the mansions of the mighty, by bands and companies and divisions, for plunder and spoil. Others went to the robbing of churches, and others dispersed to the simple homes of the common people, stealing, robbing, plundering, killing, insulting, taking and enslaving men, women, and children, old and young, priests, monks–in short, every age and class. . . .

After this the Sultan entered the City and looked about to see its great size, its situation, its grandeur and beauty, its teeming population, its loveliness, and the costliness of its churches and public buildings and of the private houses and community houses and those of the officials. . . . When he saw what a large number had been killed, and the ruin of the buildings, and the wholesale ruin and destruction of the City, he was filled with compassion and repented not a little at the destruction and plundering. Tears fell from his eyes as he groaned deeply and passionately: "What a city we have given over to plunder and destruction." . . .

As for the great City of Constantine, raised to a great height of glory and dominion and wealth in its own times, overshadowing to an infinite degree all the cities around it, renowned for its glory, wealth, authority, power, and greatness, and all its other qualities, it thus came to its end.

**History Now**™ To read a full version of this document, enter the *HistoryNow* documents area using the access card that is available for *World History*.

Finally, the walls were breached; the Byzantine emperor died in the final battle (see the box above). Mehmet II, standing before the palace of the emperor, paused to reflect on the passing nature of human glory. But it was not long before he and the Ottomans were again on the march.

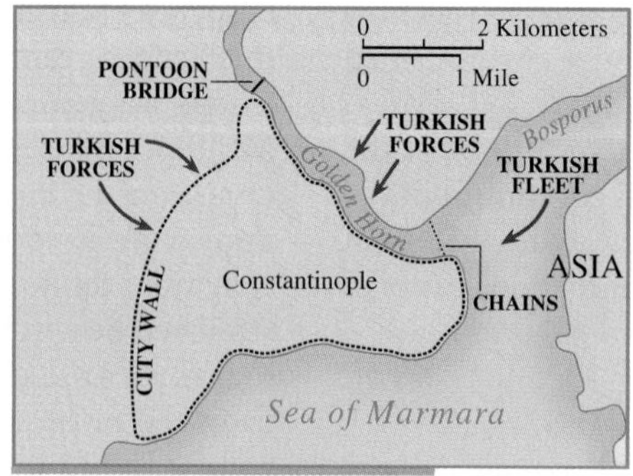

**The Fall of Constantinople, 1453**

**The Advance into Western Asia and Africa** With their new capital at Constantinople, renamed Istanbul, the Ottoman Turks had become a dominant force in the Balkans and the Anatolian peninsula. They now began to advance to the east against the Shi'ite kingdom of the Safavids in Persia (see "The Safavids" later in this chapter), which had been promoting rebellion among the Anatolian tribal population and disrupting Turkish trade through the Middle East. After defeating the Safavids at a major battle in 1514, Emperor Selim I (1512–1520) consolidated Turkish control over Mesopotamia and then turned his attention to the Mamluks in Egypt, who had failed to support the Ottomans in their struggle against the Safavids. The Mamluks were defeated in Syria in 1516; Cairo fell a year later. Now controlling several of

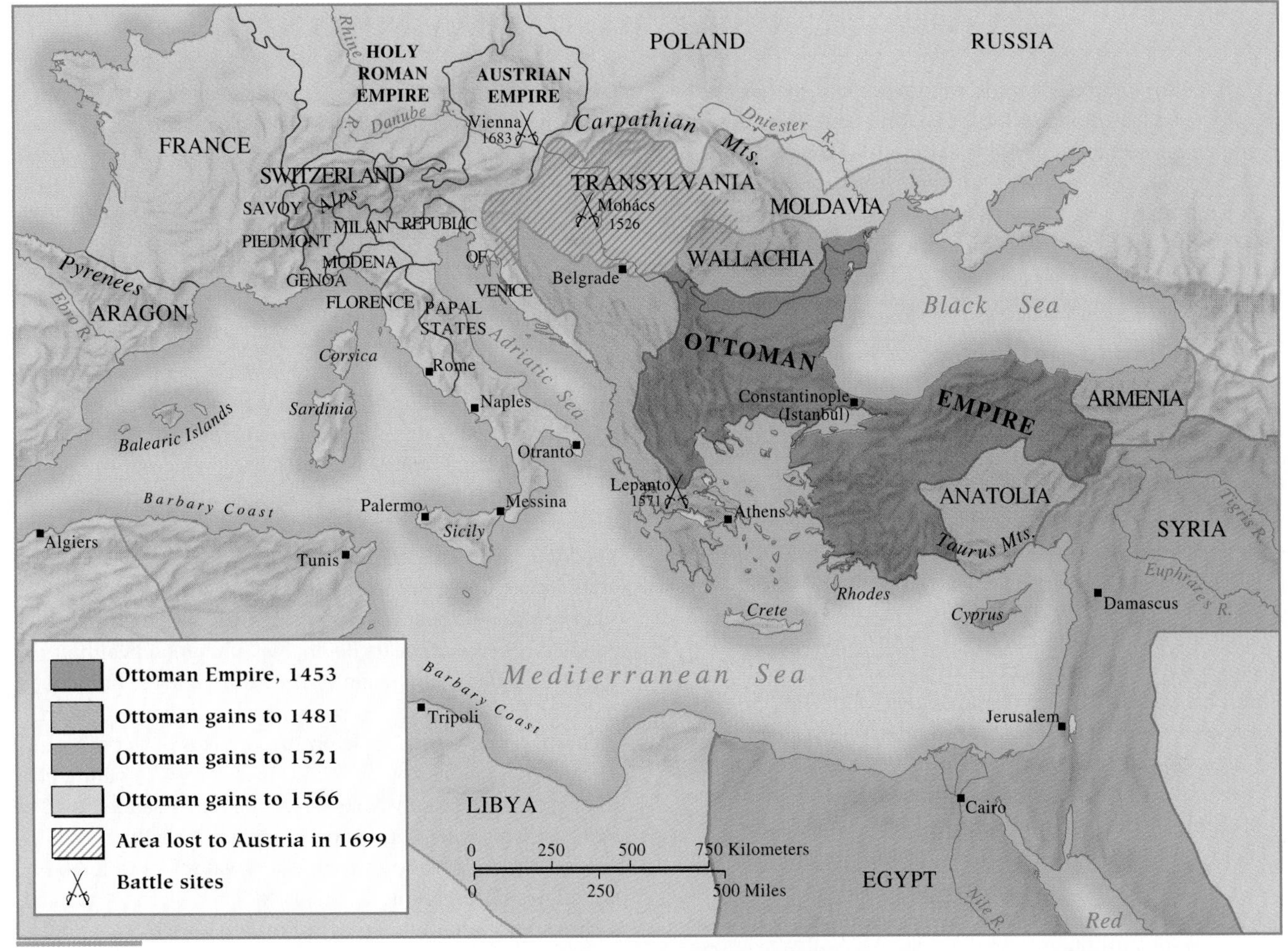


**MAP 15.1 The Ottoman Empire.** This map shows the territorial growth of the Ottoman Empire from the eve of the conquest of Constantinople in 1453 to the end of the seventeenth century, when a defeat at the hands of Austria led to the loss of a substantial portion of central Europe. ? Where did the Ottomans come from? **View an animated version of this map or related maps at** http://history.wadsworth.com/duikerspielvogel05/

the holy cities of Islam, including Jerusalem, Mecca, and Medina, Selim declared himself the new caliph, or successor to Muhammad. During the next few years, Turkish armies and fleets advanced westward along the African coast, occupying Tripoli, Tunis, and Algeria and eventually penetrating almost to the Strait of Gibraltar (see Map 15.1). In their advance, the invaders had taken advantage of the progressive disintegration of the Nasrid dynasty in Morocco, which had been in decline for decades and had lost its last foothold on the European continent when Granada fell to Spain in 1492.

The impact of Turkish rule on the peoples of North Africa was relatively light. Like their predecessors, the Turks were Muslims, and they preferred where possible to administer their conquered regions through local rulers. Central government direction was achieved through appointed *pashas* who collected taxes (and then paid a fixed percentage as tribute to the central government), maintained law and order, and were directly responsible to Istanbul. The Turks ruled from coastal cities like Algiers, Tunis, and Tripoli and made no attempt to control the interior beyond maintaining the trade routes through the Sahara to the trading centers along the Niger River. Meanwhile, local pirates along the Barbary Coast—the northern coast of Africa from Egypt to the Atlantic Ocean—competed with their Christian rivals in raiding the shipping that passed through the Mediterranean.

By the seventeenth century, the links between the imperial court in Istanbul and its appointed representatives in the Turkish regencies in North Africa had begun to decline. Some of the pashas were dethroned by local elites, while others, such as the bey of Tunis, became hereditary rulers. Even Egypt, whose agricultural wealth and control over the route to the Red Sea made it the most important country in the area to the Turks, gradually became autonomous under a new official class of Janissaries. Many of them became wealthy landowners by exploiting their official function to collect tax revenues far in excess of what they had to remit to Istanbul. In the early eighteenth century, the Mamluks returned to power, although the

## A Portrait of Suleyman the Magnificent

Suleyman the Magnificent was perhaps the greatest of all Ottoman sultans. Like King Louis XIV of France and Emperor Kangxi of China, he presided over his domain at the peak of its military and cultural achievement. This description of him was written by Ghislain de Busbecq, the Habsburg ambassador to Constantinople. Busbecq observed Suleyman at first hand and, as this excerpt indicates, was highly impressed by the Turkish ruler.

*What were the main achievements of Suleyman that caused him to be called "the Magnificent"? Is this description the work of an admirer or a critic? Why?*

### Ghislain de Busbecq, *The Turkish Letters*

The Sultan was seated on a rather low sofa, no more than a foot from the ground and spread with many costly coverlets and cushions embroidered with exquisite work. Near him were his bow and arrows. His expression, as I have said, is anything but smiling, and has a sternness which, though sad, is full of majesty. On our arrival we were introduced into his presence by his chamberlains, who held our arms—a practice which has always been observed since a Croatian sought an interview and murdered the Sultan Amurath in a revenge for the slaughter of his master, Marcus the Despot of Serbia. After going through the pretense of kissing his hand, we were led to the wall facing him backwards, so as not to turn our backs or any part of them toward him. He then listened to the recital of my message, but, as it did not correspond with his expectations (for the demands of my imperial master [the Habsburg emperor Ferdinand I] were full of dignity and independence, and, therefore, far from acceptable to one who thought that his slightest wishes ought to be obeyed) he assumed an expression of disdain, and merely answered "Giusel, Giusel," that is, "Well, Well." We were then dismissed to our lodging. . . .

You will probably wish me to describe the impression which Suleyman made upon me. He is beginning to feel the weight of years, but his dignity of demeanor and his general physical appearance are worthy of the ruler of so vast an empire. He has always been frugal and temperate, and was so even in his youth, when he might have erred without incurring blame in the eyes of the Turks. Even in his earlier years he did not indulge in wine or in those unnatural vices to which the Turks are often addicted. Even his bitterest critics can find nothing more serious to allege against him than his undue submission to his wife and its result in his somewhat precipitate action in putting Mustapha [his firstborn son, by another wife] to death, which is generally imputed to her employment of love potions and incantations. It is generally agreed that, ever since he promoted her to the rank of his lawful wife, he has possessed no concubines, although there is no law to prevent his doing so. He is a strict guardian of his religion and its ceremonies, being not less desirous of upholding his faith than of extending his dominions. For his age—he has almost reached his sixtieth year—he enjoys quite good health, though his bad complexion may be due to some hidden malady; and indeed it is generally believed that he has an incurable ulcer or gangrene on his leg. This defect of complexion he remedies by painting his face with a coating of red powder, when he wishes departing ambassadors to take with them a strong impression of his good health; for he fancies that it contributes to inspire greater fear in foreign potentates if they think that he is well and strong. I noticed a clear indication of this practice on the present occasion; for his appearance when he received me in the final audience was very different from that which he presented when he gave me an interview on my arrival.

**HistoryNow**™ To read a related document, enter the *HistoryNow* documents area using the access card that is available for *World History.*

Turkish government managed to retain some control by means of a viceroy appointed from Istanbul.

**Turkish Expansion in Europe** After their conquest of Constantinople in 1453, the Ottoman Turks tried to complete their conquest of the Balkans, where they had been established since the fourteenth century. Although they were successful in taking the Romanian territory of Wallachia in 1476, the resistance of the Hungarians initially kept the Turks from advancing up the Danube valley. From 1480 to 1520, internal problems and the need to consolidate their eastern frontiers kept the Turks from any further attacks on Europe.

Suleyman I the Magnificent (1520–1566; see the box above), however, brought the Turks back to Europe's attention. Advancing up the Danube, the Turks seized Belgrade in 1521 and won a major victory over the Hungarians at the Battle of Mohács on the Danube in 1526. Subsequently, the Turks overran most of Hungary, moved into Austria, and advanced as far as Vienna, where they were finally repulsed in 1529. At the same time, they extended their power into the western Mediterranean and threatened to turn it into a Turkish lake until a large Turkish fleet was destroyed by the Spanish at Lepanto in 1571 (see the comparative illustration on p. 425). Despite the defeat, the Turks continued to hold nominal suzerainty over the southern shores of the Mediterranean.

Although Europeans frequently called for new Christian Crusades against the "infidel" Turks, the

© Ancient Art & Architecture

AREPHOT/ORONOZ

SCIENCE & TECHNOLOGY

COMPARATIVE ILLUSTRATION

**Commemorating Victory, from Mohács to Lepanto.** In 1526, the Ottoman army won an important victory over European forces at Mohács, on the plains of Hungary. Less than half a century later, the Ottoman advance was halted at Lepanto, off the coast of Greece, where a Turkish fleet met defeat at the hands of the Europeans. Both victories reflected the importance of modern technology. Not surprisingly, both battles were commemorated in important paintings by the victors. On the left, Ottoman forces advance against their adversaries at Mohács; on the right, the victorious European fleet arrives at Messina, a port city on the island of Sicily.

Ottoman Empire was by the beginning of the seventeenth century being treated like any other European power by European rulers seeking alliances and trade concessions. During the first half of the seventeenth century, the Ottoman Empire was a "sleeping giant." Involved in domestic bloodletting and heavily threatened by a challenge from Persia, the Ottomans were content with the status quo in eastern Europe. But under a new line of **grand vezirs** in the second half of the seventeenth century, the Ottoman Empire again took the offensive. By mid-1683, the Ottomans had marched through the Hungarian plain and laid siege to Vienna. Repulsed by a mixed army of Austrians, Poles, Bavarians, and Saxons, the Turks retreated and were pushed out of Hungary by a new European coalition. Although they retained the core of their empire, the Ottoman Turks would never again be a threat to Europe. The Turkish empire held together for the rest of the seventeenth and the eighteenth centuries, but it faced new challenges from the ever-growing Austrian Empire in southeastern Europe and the new Russian giant to the north.

## The Nature of Turkish Rule

Like other Muslim empires in Persia and India, the Ottoman political system was the result of the evolution of tribal institutions into a sedentary empire. At the apex of the Ottoman system was the sultan, who was the supreme authority in both a political and a military sense. The origins of this system can be traced back to the bey, who was only a tribal leader, a first among equals, who could claim loyalty from his chiefs so long as he could provide booty and grazing lands for his subordinates. Disputes were settled by tribal law; Muslim laws were secondary. Tribal leaders collected taxes—or booty—from areas under their control and sent one-fifth on to the bey. Both administrative and military power were centralized under the bey, and the capital was wherever the bey and his administration happened to be.

**The Role of the Sultan** But the rise of empire brought about changes and an adaptation to Byzantine traditions of rule. The status and prestige of the sultan now increased relative to the subordinate tribal leaders, and the position took on the trappings of imperial rule. Court rituals were inherited from the Byzantines and Persians, and a centralized administrative system was adopted that increasingly isolated the sultan in his palace. The position of the sultan was hereditary, with a son, although not necessarily the eldest, always succeeding the father. This practice led to chronic succession struggles upon the death of individual sultans, and the losers were often executed (strangled with a silk bowstring) or later imprisoned. Heirs to the throne were assigned as provincial governors to provide them with experience.

**The Harem** The heart of the sultan's power was in the Topkapi Palace in the center of Istanbul. Topkapi (meaning "cannon gate") was constructed in 1459 by Mehmet II and served as an administrative center as well as the private residence of the sultan and his family. Eventually, it had a staff of twenty thousand employees. The private domain of the sultan was called the **harem** ("sacred place"). Here he resided with his concubines. Normally, a sultan did not marry but chose several concubines as his favorites; they were accorded this status after they gave birth to sons. When a son became a sultan, his mother became known as the queen mother and served as adviser to the throne. This tradition, initiated by the influential wife of Suleyman the Magnificent, often resulted in considerable authority for the queen mother in the affairs of state.

Members of the harem, like the Janissaries, were often of slave origin and formed an elite element in Ottoman society. Since the enslavement of Muslims was forbidden, slaves were taken among non-Islamic peoples. Some concubines were prisoners selected for the position, while others were purchased or offered to the sultan as gifts. They were then trained and educated like the Janissaries in a system called *devshirme* ("collection"). *Devshirme* had originated in the practice of requiring local clan leaders to provide prisoners to the sultan as part of their tax obligation. Talented males were given special training for eventual placement in military or administrative positions, while their female counterparts were trained for service in the harem, with instruction in reading, the Qur'an, sewing and embroidery, and musical performance. They were ranked according to their status, and some were permitted to leave the harem to marry officials. If they were later divorced, they were sometimes allowed to return to the harem.

Unique to the Ottoman Empire from the fifteenth century onward was the exclusive use of slaves to reproduce its royal heirs. Contrary to myth, few of the women of the imperial harem were used for sexual purposes, as the majority were relatives of the sultan's extended family—sisters, daughters, widowed mothers, and in-laws, with their own personal slaves and entourage. Contemporary European observers compared the atmosphere in the Topkapi harem to a Christian nunnery, with its hierarchical organization, enforced chastity, and rule of silence.

Because of their proximity to the sultan, the women of the harem often wielded so much political power that the era has been called "the sultanate of women." Queen mothers administered the imperial household and engaged in diplomatic relations with other countries while controlling the marital alliances of their daughters with senior civilian and military officials or members of other royal families in the region. One princess was married seven separate times from the age of two after her previous husbands died either in battle or by execution.

Topkapi Palace Museum/Bridgeman Art Library

**Recruitment of the Children.** The Ottoman Empire, like its Chinese counterpart, sought to recruit its officials on the basis of merit. Through the system called *devshirme* ("collection"), youthful candidates were selected from the non-Muslim population in villages throughout the empire. In this painting, an imperial officer is counting coins to pay for the children's travel expenses to Istanbul, where they will undergo extensive academic and military training. Note the concern of two of the mothers and a priest as they question the official, who undoubtedly underwent the process himself as a child. As they leave their family and friends, the children carry their worldly possessions in bags slung over their shoulders.

**Administration of the Government** The sultan ruled through an imperial council that met four days a week and was chaired by the chief minister known as the grand vezir (*wazir,* sometimes rendered in English as *vizier*). The sultan often attended behind a screen, whence he could privately indicate his desires to the grand vezir. The latter presided over the imperial bureaucracy. Like the palace guard, the bureaucrats were not an exclusive group but were chosen at least partly by merit from a palace school for training officials. Most officials were Muslims by birth, but some talented Janissaries became

**CHRONOLOGY The Ottoman Empire**

| | |
|---|---|
| Reign of Osman I | 1280–1326 |
| Ottoman Turks first cross the Bosporus | 1345 |
| Murad I consolidates Turkish power in the Balkans | 1360 |
| Ottomans defeat Serbian army at Kosovo | 1389 |
| Tamerlane defeats Ottoman army at Ankara | 1402 |
| Rule of Mehmet II (the Conqueror) | 1451–1481 |
| Turkish conquest of Constantinople | 1453 |
| Turks defeat Mamluks in Syria and seize Cairo | 1516–1517 |
| Reign of Suleyman I (the Magnificent) | 1520–1566 |
| Defeat of Hungarians at Battle of Mohács | 1526 |
| Defeat of Turks at Vienna | 1529 |
| Battle of Lepanto | 1571 |

senior members of the bureaucracy, and almost all the later grand vezirs came from the *devshirme* system.

Local administration during the imperial period was a product of Turkish tribal tradition and was similar in some respects to fief-holding in Europe. The empire was divided into provinces and districts governed by officials who, like their tribal predecessors, combined both civil and military functions. They were assisted by bureaucrats trained in the palace school in Istanbul. Senior officials were assigned land in fief by the sultan and were then responsible for collecting taxes and supplying armies to the empire. These lands were then farmed out to the local cavalry elite called the ***sipahis,*** who exacted a tax from all peasants in their fiefdoms for their salary. These local officials were not hereditary aristocrats, but sons often inherited their fathers' landholdings, and the vast majority were descendants of the beys who had served as tribal elites during the preimperial period.

## Religion and Society in the Ottoman World

Like most Turkic-speaking peoples in the Anatolian peninsula and throughout the Middle East, the Ottoman ruling elites were Sunni Muslims. Ottoman sultans had claimed the title of caliph ("defender of the faith") since the early sixteenth century and thus theoretically were responsible for guiding the flock and maintaining Islamic law, the *Shari'a.* In practice, the sultan assigned these duties to a supreme religious authority, who administered the law and maintained a system of schools for educating Muslims.

Islamic law and customs were applied to all Muslims in the empire. Like their rulers, most Turkic-speaking people were Sunni Muslims, but some communities were attracted to Sufism (see Chapter 7) or other heterodox doctrines. The government tolerated such activities so long as their practitioners remained loyal to the empire, but in the early sixteenth century, unrest among these groups—some of whom converted to the Shi'ite version of Islamic doctrine—outraged the conservative *ulama* and eventually led to war against the Safavids (see "The Safavids" later in this chapter).

**The Treatment of Minorities** Non-Muslims—mostly Orthodox Christians (Greeks and Slavs), Jews, and Armenian Christians—formed a significant minority within the empire, which treated them with relative tolerance. Non-Muslims were compelled to pay a head tax (because of their exemption from military service), and they were permitted to practice their religion or convert to Islam, although Muslims were prohibited from adopting another faith. Most of the population in European areas of the empire remained Christian, but in some places, such as the territory now called Bosnia, substantial numbers converted to Islam.

Each religious group within the empire was organized as an administrative unit called a ***millet*** ("nation" or "community"). Each group, including the Muslims themselves, had its own patriarch or grand rabbi who dealt as an intermediary with the government and administered the community according to its own laws. The leaders of the individual nations were responsible to the sultan and his officials for the behavior of the subjects under their care and collected taxes for transmission to the government. Each nation established its own system of justice, set its own educational policies, and provided welfare for the needy.

Nomadic peoples were placed in a separate "nation" and were subject to their own regulations and laws. They were divided into the traditional nomadic classifications of tribes, clans, and "tents" (individual families) and were governed by their hereditary chiefs, the beys. As we have seen, the beys were responsible for administration and for collecting taxes for the state.

**Social Classes** The subjects of the Ottoman Empire were also divided by occupation and place of residence. In addition to the ruling class, there were four main occupational groups: peasants, artisans, merchants, and pastoral peoples. The first three were classified as "urban" residents. Peasants tilled land that was leased to them by the state (ultimate ownership of all land resided with the sultan), but the land was deeded to them, so they were able to pass it along to their heirs. They were not allowed to sell the land and thus in practice were forced to remain on the soil. Taxes were based on the amount of land the peasants possessed and were paid to the local *sipahis,* who held the district in fief.

Artisans were organized according to craft guilds. Each guild, headed by a council of elders, was responsible not only for dealing with the governmental authorities but also for providing financial services, social security, and training for its members. Outside the ruling elite, merchants were the most priviliged class in Ottoman society.

They were largely exempt from government regulations and taxes and were therefore able in many cases to amass large fortunes. Charging interest was technically illegal under Islamic law, but the rules were often ignored in practice. In the absence of regulations, merchants often established monopolies and charged high prices, which caused them to be bitterly resented by other subjects of the empire.

**The Position of Women** Technically, women in the Ottoman Empire were subject to the same restrictions that afflicted their counterparts in other Muslim societies, but their position was ameliorated to some degree by various factors. In the first place, non-Muslims were subject to the laws and customs of their own religions; thus Orthodox Christian, Jewish, and Armenian Christian women were spared some of the restrictions applied to their Muslim sisters. In the second place, Islamic laws as applied in the Ottoman Empire defined the legal position of women comparatively tolerantly. Women were permitted to own and inherit property, including their dowries. They could not be forced into marriage and in certain cases were permitted to seek a divorce. As we have seen, women often exercised considerable influence in the palace and in a few instances even served as senior officials, such as governors of provinces. The relatively tolerant attitude toward women in Ottoman-held territories has been ascribed by some to Turkish tribal traditions, which took a more egalitarian view of sex roles than the sedentary societies of the region did.

## The Ottomans in Decline

The Ottoman Empire reached its zenith under Suleyman the Magnificent, often known as Suleyman Kanuni, or "the lawgiver," who launched the conquest of Hungary. But Suleyman also sowed the seeds of the empire's eventual decline. He executed his two most able sons on suspicion of factionalism and was succeeded by Selim II (the Sot, or "the drunken sultan"), the only surviving son.

By the seventeenth century, signs of internal rot had begun to appear, although the first loss of imperial territory did not occur until 1699, at the Battle of Carlowitz. Apparently, a number of factors were involved. In the first place, the administrative system inherited from the tribal period began to break down. Although the *devshirme* system of training officials continued to function, *devshirme* graduates were now permitted to marry and inherit property and to enroll their sons in the palace corps. Thus they were gradually transformed from a meritocratic administrative elite into a privileged and often degenerate hereditary caste. Local administrators were corrupted and taxes rose as the central bureaucracy lost its links with rural areas. The imperial treasury was depleted by constant wars, and transport and communications were neglected. Interest in science and technology, once a hallmark of the Arab empire, was in decline. In addition, the empire was increasingly beset by economic difficulties, caused by the diversion of trade routes away from the eastern Mediterranean and the price inflation brought about by the influx of cheap American silver.

Another sign of change within the empire was the increasing degree of material affluence and the impact of Western ideas and customs. Sophisticated officials and merchants began to mimic the habits and lifestyles of their European counterparts, dressing in the European fashion, purchasing Western furniture and art objects, and ignoring Muslim strictures against the consumption of alcohol and sexual activities outside marriage. During the sixteenth and early seventeenth centuries, coffee and tobacco were introduced into polite Ottoman society, and cafés for the consumption of both began to appear in the major cities (see the box on p. 430). One sultan in the early seventeenth century issued a decree prohibiting the consumption of both coffee and tobacco, arguing (correctly, no doubt) that many cafés were nests of antigovernment intrigue. He even began to wander incognito through the streets of Istanbul at night. Any of his subjects detected in immoral or illegal acts were summarily executed and their bodies left on the streets as an example to others.

There were also signs of a decline in competence within the ruling family. Whereas the first sultans reigned twenty-seven years on average, later ones averaged only thirteen years. The throne now went to the oldest surviving male, while his rivals were kept secluded in a latticed cage and thus had no governmental experience if they succeeded to rule. Later sultans also became less involved in government, and more power flowed to the office of the grand vezir (called the **Sublime Porte**) or to eunuchs and members of the harem. Palace intrigue increased as a result.

## Ottoman Art

The Ottoman sultans were enthusiastic patrons of the arts and maintained large ateliers of artisans and artists, primarily at the Topkapi Palace in Istanbul but also in other important cities of the vast empire. The period from Mehmet II in the fifteenth century to the early eighteenth century witnessed the flourishing of pottery, rugs, silk and other textiles, jewelry, arms and armor, and calligraphy. All adorned the palaces of the new rulers, testifying to their opulence and exquisite taste. The artists came from all parts of the realm and beyond. Besides Turks, there were Persians, Greeks, Armenians, Hungarians, and Italians, all vying for the esteem and generous rewards of the sultans and fearing that losing favor might mean losing their heads! In the second half of the sixteenth century, Istanbul alone listed over 150 craft guilds, ample proof of the artistic activity of the era.

**Architecture** By far the greatest contribution of the Ottoman Empire to world art was its architecture, especially the magnificent mosques of the second half of the sixteenth century. Traditionally, prayer halls in mosques were subdivided by numerous pillars that supported small individual domes, creating a private, forestlike atmosphere.

Robert Harding Picture Library; photo: Robert Frerck

Courtesy of William J. Duiker

**The Suleymaniye Mosque, Istanbul.** The magnificent mosques built under the patronage of Suleyman the Magnificent are a great legacy of the Ottoman Empire and a fitting supplement to Santa Sophia (Hagia Sophia) Cathedral, built by the Byzantine emperor Justinian in the sixth century C.E. Towering under a central dome, these mosques seem to defy gravity, and, like European Gothic cathedrals, convey a sense of weightlessness. The Suleymaniye Mosque is one of the most impressive and most graceful in Istanbul. A far cry from the seventh-century desert mosques constructed of palm trunks, the Ottoman mosques stand among the architectural wonders of the world. Under the massive dome, the interior of the Suleymaniye Mosque offers a quiet refuge for prayer and reflection, bathed in muted sunlight and the warmth of plush carpets, as shown in the inset photo.

The Turks, however, modeled their new mosques on the open floor plan of the Byzantine church of Santa Sophia (completed in 537), which had been turned into a mosque by Mehmet II, and began to push the pillars toward the outer wall to create a prayer hall with an uninterrupted central area under one large dome. With this plan, large numbers of believers could worship in unison in accordance with Muslim preference. By the mid-sixteenth century, the greatest of all Ottoman architects, Sinan, began erecting the first of his eighty-one mosques with an uncluttered prayer area. Each was topped by an imposing dome, and often, as at Edirne, the entire building was framed with four towering narrow minarets. By emphasizing its vertical lines, the minarets camouflaged the massive stone bulk of the structure and gave it a feeling of incredible lightness. These four graceful minarets would find new expression sixty years later in India's white marble Taj Mahal (see "Mughal Culture" later in this chapter).

The lightness of the exterior was reinforced in the mosque's interior by the soaring height of the dome and the numerous windows. Added to this were delicate plasterwork and tile decoration that transformed the mosque into a monumental oasis of spirituality, opulence, and power. Sinan's masterpieces, such as the Suleymaniye and the Blue Mosque of Istanbul, were always part of a large socioreligious compound that included a library, school, hospital, mausoleums, and even bazaars, all of equally magnificent construction.

Earlier, the thirteenth-century Seljuk Turks of Anatolia had created beautiful tile decorations with two-color mosaics. Now Ottoman artists invented a new glazed tile art with painted flowers and geometrical designs in brilliant blue, green, yellow, and their own secret "tomato red." Entire walls, both interior and exterior, were covered with the painted tiles, which adorned palaces as well as mosques. Produced at Iznik (the old Nicaea), the distinctive tiles and pottery were in great demand; the city's ateliers boasted more than three hundred artisans in the late sixteenth century.

**Textiles** The sixteenth century also witnessed the flourishing of textiles and rugs. The Byzantine emperor Justinian had introduced the cultivation of silkworms to the West in the sixth century, and the silk industry resurfaced under the Ottomans. Its capital was at Bursa, where factories produced silks for wall hangings, soft covers, and especially court costumes. Perhaps even more famous than Turkish silk are the rugs. But whereas silks were produced under the patronage of the sultans, rugs were a peasant industry. Each village boasted its own distinctive design and color scheme for the rugs it produced.

## A Turkish Discourse on Coffee

Coffee was first introduced to Turkey from the Arabian peninsula in the mid-sixteenth century and allegedly came to Europe during the Turkish seige of Vienna in 1527. The following account was written by Katib Chelebi, a seventeenth-century Turkish author who, among other things, compiled an extensive encyclopedia and bibliography. Here, in *The Balance of Truth,* he describes how coffee entered the empire and the problems it caused for public morality. (In the Muslim world, as in Europe and later in colonial America, the drinking of coffee was associated with coffeehouses, where rebellious elements often gathered to promote antigovernment activities.) Chelebi died in Istanbul in 1657, reportedly while drinking a cup of coffee.

*Why do you think coffee became identified as a dangerous substance in the Ottoman Empire? Were the authorities successful in suppressing its consumption?*

### Katib Chelebi, *The Balance of Truth*

[Coffee] originated in Yemen and has spread, like tobacco, over the world. Certain sheikhs, who lived with their dervishes in the mountains of Yemen, used to crush and eat the berries . . . of a certain tree. Some would roast them and drink their water. Coffee is a cold dry food, suited to the ascetic life and sedative of lust. . . .

It came to Asia Minor by sea, about 1543, and met with a hostile reception, fetwas [decrees] being delivered against it. For they said, Apart from its being roasted, the fact that it is drunk in gatherings, passed from hand to hand, is suggestive of loose living. It is related of Abul-Suud Efendi that he had holes bored in the ships that brought it, plunging their cargoes of coffee into the sea. But these strictures and prohibitions availed nothing. . . . One coffeehouse was opened after another, and men would gather together, with great eagerness and enthusiasm, to drink. Drug addicts in particular, finding it a life-giving thing, which increased their pleasure, were willing to die for a cup.

Storytellers and musicians diverted the people from their employments, and working for one's living fell into disfavor. Moreover the people, from prince to beggar, amused themselves with knifing one another. Toward the end of 1633, the late Ghazi Gultan Murad, becoming aware of the situation, promulgated an edict, out of regard and compassion for the people, to this effect: Coffeehouses throughout the Guarded Domains shall be dismantled and not opened hereafter. Since then, the coffeehouses of the capital have been as desolate as the heart of the ignorant. . . . But in cities and towns outside Istanbul, they are opened just as before. As has been said above, such things do not admit of a perpetual ban.

# The Safavids

After the collapse of the empire of Tamerlane in the early fifteenth century, the area extending from Persia into Central Asia lapsed into anarchy. The Uzbeks, Turkic-speaking peoples from Central Asia, were the chief political and military force in the area. From their capital at Bokhara, they maintained a semblance of control over the highly fluid tribal alignments until the emergence of the Safavid dynasty in Persia at the beginning of the sixteenth century.

## The Rise of the Safavids

The Safavid dynasty was founded by Shah Ismail (1487–1524), the descendant of a sheikh called Safi al-Din (thus the name Safavid), who traced his origins to Ali, the fourth imam of the Muslim faith. In the early fourteenth century, Safi had been the leader of a community of Turkic-speaking tribespeople in Azerbaijan, near the Caspian Sea. Safi's community was only one of many Sufi mystical religious groups throughout the area. In time, the doctrine spread among nomadic groups throughout the Middle East and was transformed into the more activist Shi'ite heresy. Its adherents were known as "red heads" because of their distinctive red cap with twelve folds, meant to symbolize allegiance to the twelve imams of the Shi'ite faith.

In 1501, Ismail's forces seized much of the lands of modern Iran and Iraq and proclaimed himself the shah of a new Persian state. Baghdad was subdued in 1508 and the Uzbeks in Bokhara shortly thereafter. Ismail now sent Shi'ite preachers into Anatolia to proselytize and promote rebellion among Turkish tribal peoples in the Ottoman Empire. In retaliation, the Ottoman sultan, Selim I, advanced against the Safavids in Iran and won a major battle near Tabriz in 1514. But Selim could not maintain control of the area, and Ismail regained Tabriz a few years later.

The Ottomans returned to the attack in the 1580s and forced the new Safavid shah, Abbas I (1587–1629), to sign a punitive peace in which much territory was lost. The capital was subsequently moved from Tabriz in the northwest to Isfahan in the south. Still, it was under Shah Abbas that the Safavids reached the zenith of their glory. He established a system similar to the Janissaries in Turkey to train administrators to replace the traditional warrior elite. He also used the period of peace to strengthen his army, now armed with modern weapons, and in the early seventeenth century he attempted to regain the lost territories. Although he had some initial success, war resumed in the 1620s, and a lasting peace was not achieved until 1638 (see Map 15.2).

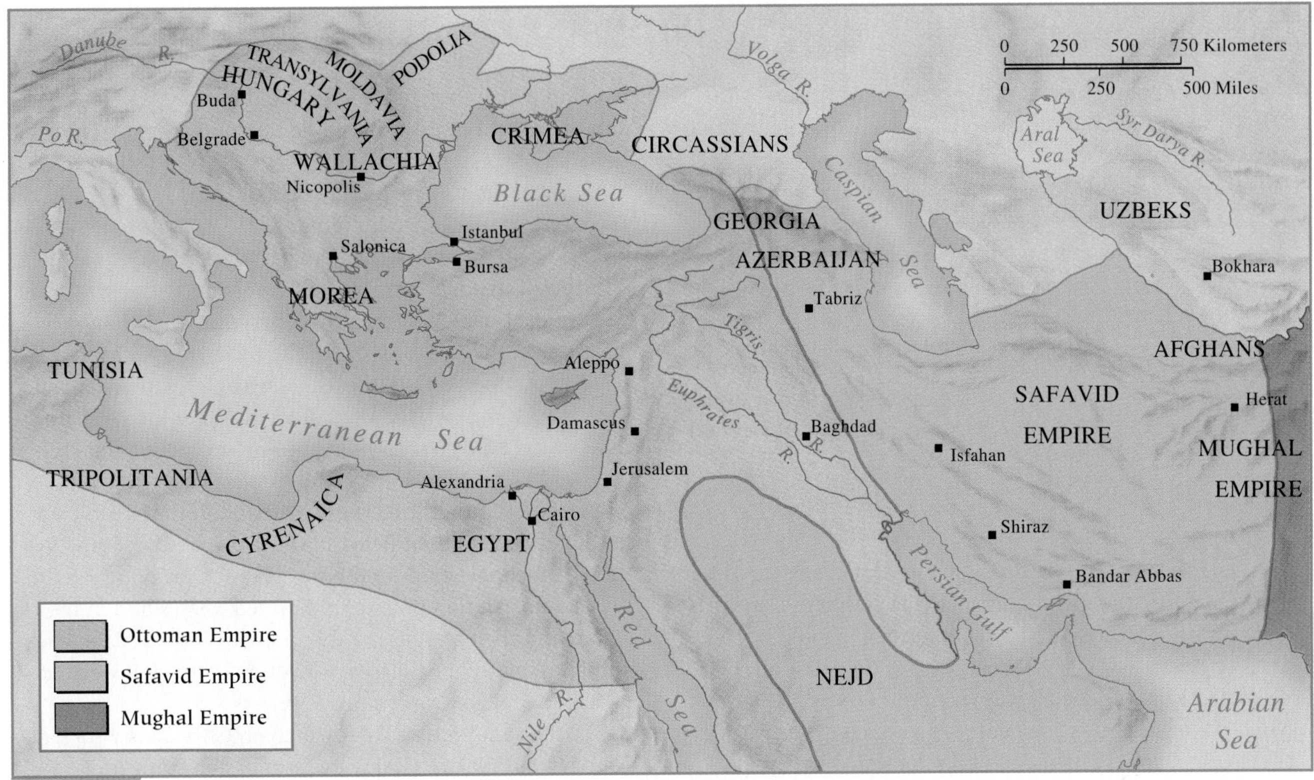


**MAP 15.2 The Ottoman and Safavid Empires, c. 1683.** During the seventeenth century, the two empires contested vigorously for hegemony in the eastern Mediterranean and the Middle East. This map shows the territories controlled by each state in the late seventeenth century. ? What were the key cities in the two empires? **View an animated version of this map or related maps at** http://history.wadsworth.com/duikerspielvogel05/

## Decline of the Dynasty

Abbas the Great had managed to strengthen the dynasty significantly, and for a time after his death in 1629, it remained stable and vigorous. But succession conflicts plagued the dynasty. Partly as a result, the power of the more militant Shi'ites began to increase at court and in Safavid society at large. The intellectual freedom that had characterized the empire at its height was curtailed under the pressure of religious orthodoxy, and Iranian women, who had enjoyed considerable freedom and influence during the early empire, were forced to withdraw into seclusion and behind the veil. Meanwhile, attempts to suppress the religious beliefs of minorities led to increased popular unrest. In the early eighteenth century, Afghan warriors took advantage of local revolts to seize the capital of Isfahan, forcing the remnants of the Safavid ruling family to retreat to Azerbaijan, their original homeland. The Ottomans seized territories along the western border. Eventually, order was restored by the military adventurer Nadir Shah Afshar, who launched an extended series of campaigns that restored the country's borders and even occupied the Mughal capital of Delhi (see "Twilight of the Mughals" later in this chapter). After his death, the Zand dynasty ruled until the end of the eighteenth century.

## Safavid Politics and Society

Like the Ottoman Empire, Iran under the Safavids was a mixed society. The Safavids had come to power with the support of nomadic Turkic-speaking tribal groups, and leading elements from those groups retained considerable influence within the empire. But the majority of the population were Iranian; most of them were farmers or townspeople, with attitudes inherited from the relatively sophisticated and urbanized culture of pre-Safavid Iran. Faced with the problem of integrating unruly Turkic-speaking tribal peoples with the sedentary Persian-speaking population of the urban areas, the Safavids used the Shi'ite faith as a unifying force (see the box on p. 432). The shah himself acquired an almost divine quality and claimed to be the spiritual leader of all Islam. Shi'ism was declared the state religion.

Although there was a landed aristocracy, aristocratic power and influence were firmly controlled by strong-minded shahs, who confiscated aristocratic estates when possible and brought them under the control of the crown. Appointment to senior positions in the bureaucracy was by merit rather than birth. To avoid encouraging competition between Turkish and non-Turkish elements, Shah Abbas I hired a number of foreigners from neighboring countries for positions in his government.

## The Religious Zeal of Shah Abbas the Great

Shah Abbas I, probably the greatest of the Safavid rulers, expanded the borders of his empire into areas of the southern Caucasus inhabited by Christians and other non-Muslim peoples. After Persian control was assured, he instructed that the local population be urged to convert to Islam for its own protection and the glory of God. In this passage, his biographer, the Persian historian Eskander Beg Monshi, recounts the story of that effort.

*How do the efforts to convert nonbelievers to Islam compare with similar programs by Muslim rulers in India, as described in Chapter 9? What is the author's point of view on the matter?*

### The Conversion of a Number of Christians to Islam

This year the Shah decreed that those Armenians and other Christians who had been settled in [the southern Caucasus] and had been given agricultural land there should be invited to become Muslims. Life in this world is fraught with vicissitudes, and the Shah was concerned lest, in a period when the authority of the central government was weak, these Christians . . . might be subjected to attack by the neighboring Lor tribes (who are naturally given to causing injury and mischief), and their women and children carried off into captivity. In the areas in which these Christian groups resided, it was the Shah's purpose that the places of worship which they had built should become mosques, and the muezzin's call should be heard in them, so that these Christians might assume the guise of Muslims, and their future status accordingly be assured. . . .

Some of the Christians, guided by God's grace, embraced Islam voluntarily; others found it difficult to abandon their Christian faith and felt revulsion at the idea. They were encouraged by their monks and priests to remain steadfast in their faith. After a little pressure had been applied to the monks and priests, however, they desisted, and these Christians saw no alternative but to embrace Islam, though they did so with reluctance. The women and children embraced Islam with great enthusiasm, vying with one another in their eagerness to abandon their Christian faith and declare their belief in the unity of God. Some five thousand people embraced Islam. As each group made the Muslim declaration of faith, it received instruction in the Koran and the principles of the religious law of Islam, and all bibles and other Christian devotional material were collected and taken away from the priests.

In the same way, all the Armenian Christians who had been moved to [the area] were also forcibly converted to Islam. . . . Most people embraced Islam with sincerity, but some felt an aversion to making the Muslim profession of faith. True knowledge lies with God! May God reward the Shah for his action with long life and prosperity!

The Safavid shahs took a direct interest in the economy and actively engaged in commercial and manufacturing activities, although there was also a large and affluent urban bourgeoisie. Like the Ottoman sultan, one shah regularly traveled the city streets incognito to check on the honesty of his subjects. When he discovered that a baker and a butcher were overcharging for their products, he had the baker cooked in his own oven and the butcher roasted on a spit. The road system was reportedly quite poor, but most goods traveled by caravan. The government provided accommodations for weary travelers and, at least in times of strong rulers, kept the roads relatively clear of thieves and bandits.

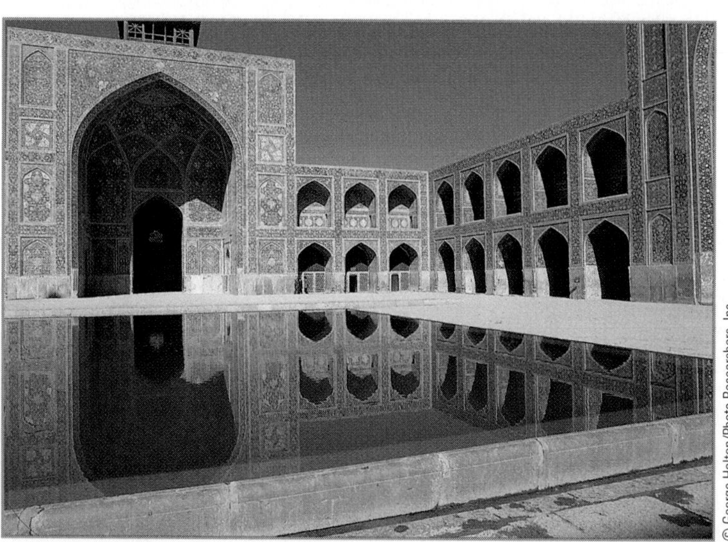

© George Holton/Photo Researchers, Inc.

**The Royal Academy of Isfahan.** Along with institutions such as libraries and hospitals, theological schools were often included in the mosque compound. One of the most sumptuous was the Royal Academy of Isfahan, built by the shah of Persia the early eighteenth century. This view shows the large courtyard surrounded by arcades of student rooms, reminiscent of the arrangement of monks' cells in European cloisters.

## CHRONOLOGY The Safavids

| | |
|---|---|
| Ismail seizes Iran and Iraq and becomes shah of Persia | 1501 |
| Ismail conquers Baghdad and defeats Uzbeks | 1508 |
| Reign of Shah Abbas I | 1587–1629 |
| Truce achieved between Ottomans and Safavids | 1638 |
| Collapse of Safavid Empire | 1723 |

At its height, Safavid Iran was a worthy successor of the great Persian empires of the past, although it was probably not as wealthy as its neighbors to the east and west, the Mughals and the Ottomans. Hemmed in by the seapower of the Europeans to the south and by the land power of the Ottomans to the west, the Safavids had no navy and were forced to divert overland trade with Europe through southern Russia to avoid an Ottoman blockade. Still, the brocades, carpets, and leather goods of Iran were highly prized throughout the world. A school of philosophy that sought truth in a fusion of rationalist and intuitive methods flourished in the sixteenth and seventeenth centuries, and Safavid science, medicine, and mathematics were the equal of other societies in the region.

## Safavid Art and Literature

Persia witnessed an extraordinary flowering of the arts during the reign of Shah Abbas I. His new capital, Isfahan, was a grandiose planned city with wide visual perspectives and a sense of order almost unique in the region. Shah Abbas ordered his architects to position his palaces, mosques, and bazaars around a massive rectangular polo ground. Much of the original city is still in good condition and remains the gem of modern Iran. The immense mosques are richly decorated with elaborate blue tiles. The palaces are delicate structures with unusual slender wooden columns. These architectural wonders of Isfahan epitomize the grandeur, delicacy, and color that defined the Safavid golden age. To adorn the splendid buildings, Safavid artisans created imaginative metalwork, tile decorations, and original and delicate glass vessels. The ceramics of the period, imitating Chinese prototypes of celadon or blue-and-white Ming design, largely ignored traditional Persian designs.

The greatest area of productivity, however, was in textiles. Silk weaving based on new techniques became a national industry. The silks depicted birds, animals, and flowers in a brilliant mass of color with silver and gold threads. Above all, carpet weaving flourished, stimulated by the great demand for Persian carpets in the West. Still highly prized all over the world, these seventeenth-century carpets reflect the grandeur and artistry of the Safavid dynasty.

The long tradition of Persian painting continued in the Safavid era but changed from paintings to line drawings and from landscape scenes to portraits, mostly of young ladies, boys, lovers, or dervishes. Although some Persian artists studied in Rome, Safavid art was little influenced by the West. Riza-i-Abassi, the most famous artist of this period, created exquisite works on simple naturalistic subjects, such as an ox plowing, hunters, or lovers. Soft colors, delicacy, and flowing movement were the dominant characteristics of the painting of this era.

British Library, London

**An Older Man Watches Girls Bathing.** By the late fifteenth century, miniature painting in Persia began to exhibit new vitality under the influence of the renowned artist Bihzad. Rather than painting scenes in the tradition of an idealized or dreamlike world, Bihzad sought to portray ordinary people in their everyday lives, highlighting their individual features and gestures while they bathed, cooked a meal, or climbed a ladder while constructing a palace. Although Islamic custom forbade the painting of nude women, the subject of this miniature, taken from a contemporary poem, offered the artist an opportunity to portray an older man watching young girls romping energetically in their bath.

### The Mughal Conquest of Northern India

Babur, the founder of the great Mughal dynasty, began his career by allying with one Indian prince against another and then turned on his ally to put himself in power, a tactic that had been used by the Ottomans and the Mongols before him (see Chapter 10). In this excerpt from his memoirs, Babur describes his triumph over the powerful army of his Indian enemy, the Sultan Ibrâhim.

*What did the Mughals have in common with the Ottomans and the Mongols as they expanded their empires? Why do you think these tactics were successful?*

**Babur, *Memoirs***

They made one or two very poor charges on our right and left divisions. My troops making use of their bows, plied them with arrows, and drove them in upon their center. The troops on the right and the left of their center, being huddled together in one place, such confusion ensued, that the enemy, while totally unable to advance, found also no road by which they could flee. The sun had mounted spear-high when the onset of battle began, and the combat lasted till midday, when the enemy were completely broken and routed, and my friends victorious and exulting. By the grace and mercy of Almighty God, this arduous undertaking was rendered easy for me, and this mighty army, in the space of half a day, laid in the dust. Five or six thousand men were discovered lying slain, in one spot, near Ibrâhim. We reckoned that the number lying slain, in different parts of this field of battle, amounted to fifteen or sixteen thousand men. On reaching Agra, we found, from the accounts of the natives of Hindustân, that forty or fifty thousand men had fallen in this field. After routing the enemy, we continued the pursuit, slaughtering, and making them prisoners. . . .

It was now afternoon prayers when Tahir Taberi, the younger brother of Khalîfeh, having found Ibrâhim lying dead amidst a number of slain, cut off his head, and brought it in. . . .

In consideration of my confidence in Divine aid, the Most High God did not suffer the distress and hardships that I had undergone to be thrown away, but defeated my formidable enemy, and made me the conqueror of the noble country of Hindustân. This success I do not ascribe to my own strength, nor did this good fortune flow from my own efforts, but from the fountain of the favor and mercy of God.

# The Grandeur of the Mughals

In retrospect, the period from the sixteenth to eighteenth centuries can be viewed both as a high point of traditional culture in India and as the first stage of perhaps its greatest challenge. The era began with the creation of one of the subcontinent's greatest empires, that of the Mughals. Mughal rulers, although foreigners and Muslims like many of their immediate predecessors, nevertheless brought India to a peak of political power and cultural achievement. For the first time since the Mauryan dynasty, the entire subcontinent was united under a single government, with a common culture that inspired admiration and envy throughout the entire region.

## The Mughal Dynasty: A "Gunpowder Empire"?

When the Portuguese fleet led by Vasco da Gama arrived at the port of Calicut in the spring of 1498 (see Chapter 13), the Indian subcontinent was still divided into a number of Hindu and Muslim kingdoms. But it was on the verge of a new era of unity that would be brought about by a foreign dynasty called the Mughals. Like so many recent rulers of northern India, the founders of the Mughal Empire were not natives of India but came from the mountainous region north of the Ganges River. The founder of the dynasty, known to history as Babur (1483–1530), had an illustrious pedigree. His father was descended from the great Asian conqueror Tamerlane, his mother from the Mongol conqueror Genghis Khan.

Babur had inherited a fragment of Tamerlane's empire in an upland valley of the Syr Darya River (see Map 15.2). Driven south by the rising power of the Uzbeks and then the Safavid dynasty in Persia, Babur and his warriors seized Kabul in 1504 and, thirteen years later, crossed the Khyber Pass into India.

Following a pattern that we have seen before, Babur began his rise to power by offering to help an ailing dynasty against its opponents. Although his own forces were far smaller than those of his adversaries, he possessed advanced weapons, including artillery, and used them to great effect. His use of mobile cavalry was particularly successful against the massed forces, supplemented by mounted elephants, of his enemy. In 1526, with only twelve thousand troops against an enemy force nearly ten times that size, Babur captured Delhi and established his power in the plains of northern India (see the box above). Over the next several years, he continued his conquests in northern India until his death in 1530 at the age of forty-seven.

Babur's success was due in part to his vigor and his charismatic personality, which earned him the undying loyalty of his followers. His son and successor Humayun (1530–1556), was, in the words of one British historian, "intelligent but lazy." Whether or not this is a fair characterization, Humayun clearly lacked the will to consolidate his father's conquests and the personality to inspire loy-

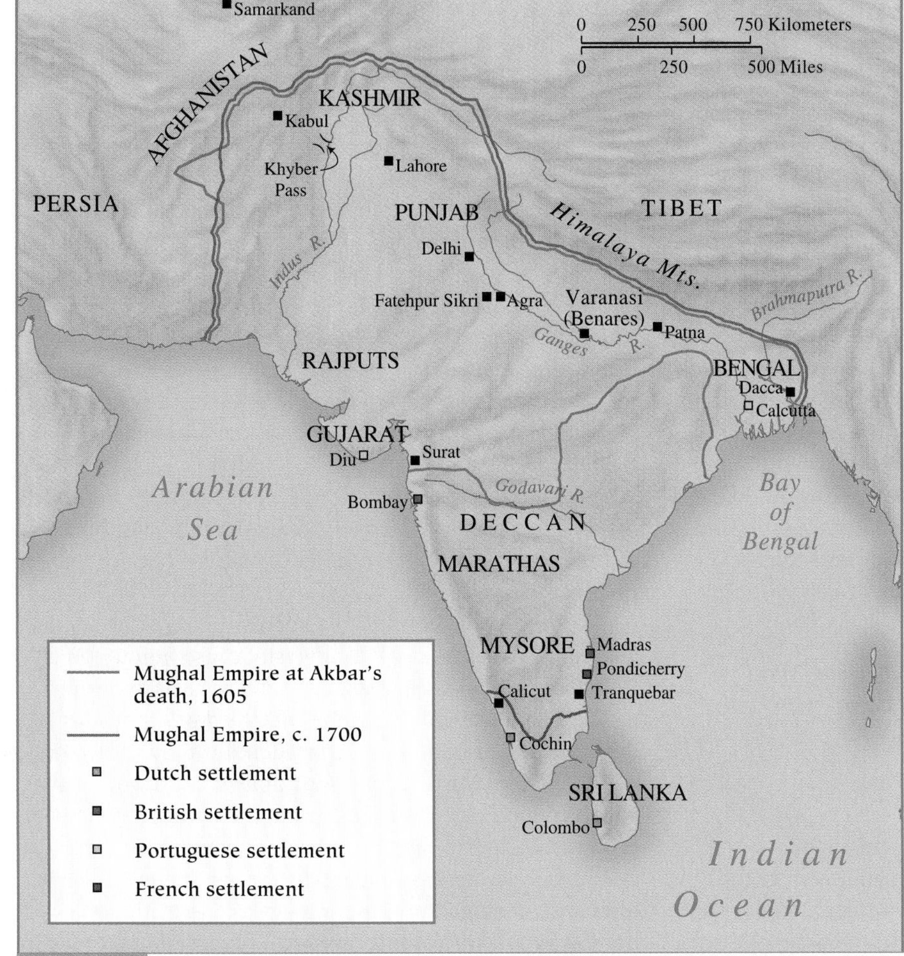


**MAP 15.3 The Mughal Empire.** This map indicates the expansion of the Mughal Empire from the death of Akbar in 1605 to the rule of Aurangzeb at the end of the seventeenth century. **?** In which cities on the map were European settlements located? **View an animated version of this map or related maps at** http://history.wadsworth.com/duikerspielvogel05/

alty among his subjects. In 1540, he was forced to flee to Persia, where he lived in exile for sixteen years. Finally, with the aid of the Safavid shah of Persia, he returned to India and reconquered Delhi in 1555 but died the following year in a household accident, reportedly from injuries suffered in a fall after smoking a pipeful of opium.

Humayun was succeeded by his son Akbar (1556–1605). Born while his father was living in exile, Akbar was only fourteen when he mounted the throne. Illiterate but highly intelligent and industrious, Akbar set out to extend his domain, then limited to Punjab and the upper Ganges River valley. "A monarch," he remarked, "should be ever intent on conquest, otherwise his neighbors rise in arms against him. The army should be exercised in warfare, lest from want of training they become self-indulgent."[1] By the end of his life, he had brought Mughal rule to most of the subcontinent, from the Himalaya Mountains to the Godavari River in central India and from Kashmir to the mouths of the Brahmaputra and the Ganges. In so doing, Akbar had created the greatest Indian empire since the Mauryan dynasty nearly two thousand years earlier. Some historians believe Akbar's success was due to the use of heavy artillery, which enabled his armies to besiege and subdue the traditional stone fortresses of his rivals. This "gunpowder empire" thesis has been challenged by the historian Douglas Streusand, who argues that the Mughals used "the carrot and the stick" to extend their authority, relying not just on heavy artillery but also on other forms of siege warfare and the offer of negotiations. Whatever the case, the end result was an empire that appeared highly centralized from the outside but was actually a collection of semiautonomous principalities ruled by provincial elites and linked together by the overarching majesty of the Mughal emperor (see Map 15.3).

## Akbar and Indo-Muslim Civilization

Although Akbar was probably the greatest of the conquering Mughal monarchs, like his famous predecessor Ashoka, he is best known for the humane character of his rule. Above all, he accepted the diversity of Indian society and took steps to reconcile his Muslim and Hindu subjects.

**Religion** Though raised an orthodox Muslim, Akbar had been exposed to other beliefs during his childhood and had little patience with the pedantic views of Muslim scholars at court. As emperor, he displayed a keen interest in other religions, not only tolerating Hindu practices in his own domains but also welcoming the expression of Christian views by his Jesuit advisers. Akbar put his policy of religious tolerance into practice by taking a Hindu princess as one of his wives, and the success of this marriage may well have had an effect on his religious convictions. He patronized classical Indian arts and architecture and abolished many of the restrictions faced by Hindus in a Muslim-dominated society.

During his later years, Akbar became steadily more hostile to Islam. To the dismay of many Muslims at court, he sponsored a new form of worship called the Divine Faith *(Din-i-Ilahi),* which combined characteristics of several religions with a central belief in the infallibility of all deci-

## A Religion Fit for a King

Emperor Akbar's attempt to create a new form of religion, known as the "Divine Faith," was partly a product of his inquisitive mind. But it was also influenced by Akbar's long friendship with Abu'l Fazl Allami, a courtier who introduced the young emperor to the Shi'ite tradition that each generation produced an individual *(imam)* who possessed a "divine light" capable of interpreting the holy scriptures. One of the sources of this Muslim theory was the Greek philosopher Plato's idea of a "philosopher king," who in his wisdom could provide humanity with an infallible guide in affairs of religion, morality, and statecraft. Akbar, of course, found the idea appealing, since it provided support for his efforts to reform religious practices in the empire. Abu'l Fazl, however, had made many enemies with his advice and was assassinated at the order of Akbar's son and successor, Jahangir, in 1602. The following excerpt is from Abu'l Fazl's writings on the subject.

*In this account, what role does the Mughal emperor play in promoting public morality? What tactics must he apply to bring about success in his efforts?*

### Abu'l Fazl, *Institutes of Akbar*

Royalty is a light emanating from God, and a ray from the sun, the illuminator of the universe, the argument of the book of perfection, the receptacle of all virtues. Modern language calls this light the divine light, and the tongue of antiquity called it the sublime halo. It is communicated by God to kings without the intermediate assistance of anyone, and men, in the presence of it, bend the forehead of praise toward the ground of submission.

Again, many excellent qualities flow from the possession of this light:

1. *A paternal love toward the subjects.* Thousands find rest in the love of the king, and sectarian differences do not raise the dust of strife. In his wisdom, the king will understand the spirit of the age, and shape his plans accordingly.

2. *A large heart.* The sight of anything disagreeable does not unsettle him, nor is want of discrimination for him a source of disappointment. His courage steps in. His divine firmness gives him the power of requittal, nor does the high position of an offender interfere with it. The wishes of great and small are attended to, and their claims meet with no delay at his hands.

3. *A daily increasing trust in God.* When he performs an action, he considers God as the real doer of it [and himself as the medium] so that a conflict of motives can produce no disturbance.

4. *Prayer and devotion.* The success of his plans will not lead him to neglect, nor will adversity cause him to forget God and madly trust in man. He puts the reins of desire into the hands of reason; in the wide field of his desires he does not permit himself to be trodden down by restlessness; neither will he waste his precious time in seeking after that which is improper. He makes wrath, the tryant, pay homage to wisdom, so that blind rage may not get the upper hand, and inconsiderateness overstep the proper limits. . . . He is forever searching after those who speak the truth and is not displeased with words that seem bitter but are, in reality, sweet. He considers the nature of the words and the rank of the speaker. He is not content with not committing violence, but he must see that no injustice is done within his realm.

sions reached by the emperor (see the box above). Some historians have maintained that Akbar totally abandoned Islam and adopted a Persian model of imperial divinity. But others have pointed out that the emperor was claiming only divine guidance, not divine status, and suggest that the new ideology was designed to cement the loyalty of officials to the person of the monarch. Whatever the case, the new faith aroused deep hostility in Muslim circles and rapidly vanished after his death.

**Society and the Economy** Akbar also extended his innovations to the empire's administration. Although the upper ranks of the government continued to be dominated by nonnative Muslims, a substantial proportion of lower-ranking officials were Hindus, and a few Hindus were appointed to positions of importance. At first, most officials were paid salaries, but later they were ordinarily assigned sections of agricultural land for their temporary use; they kept a portion of the taxes paid by the local peasants in lieu of a salary. These local officials, known as ***zamindars,*** were expected to forward the rest of the taxes from the lands under their control to the central government. *Zamindars* often recruited a number of military and civilian retainers and accumulated considerable power in their localities.

The same tolerance that marked Akbar's attitude toward religion and administration extended to the Mughal legal system. While Muslims were subject to the Islamic codes (the *Shari'a*), Hindu law (the *Dharmashastra*) applied to areas settled by Hindus, who after 1579 were no longer required to pay the hated *jizya*, or poll tax on non-Muslims. Punishments for crime were relatively mild, at least by the standards of the day, and justice was administered in a relatively impartial and efficient manner.

Overall, Akbar's reign was a time of peace and prosperity. Although all Indian peasants were required to pay about one-third of their annual harvest to the state through the *zamindars*, the system was applied fairly, and when drought struck in the 1590s, the taxes were reduced or even suspended altogether. Thanks to a long period of relative peace and political stability, commerce and manufacturing flourished. Foreign trade, in particular, thrived as Indian goods, notably textiles, tropical food products, spices, and precious stones, were exported in exchange for gold and silver. Tariffs on imports were low. Much of the foreign commerce was handled by Arab traders, since the Indians, like their Mughal rulers, did not care for travel by sea. Internal trade, however, was dominated by large merchant castes, who also were active in banking and handicrafts.

## Twilight of the Mughals

Akbar died in 1605 and was succeeded by his son Jahangir (1605–1628). During the early years of his reign, Jahangir continued to strengthen central control over the vast empire. Eventually, however, his grip began to weaken (according to his memoirs, he "only wanted a bottle of wine and a piece of meat to make merry"), and the court fell under the influence of one of his wives, the Persian-born Nur Jahan (see the box on p. 438). The empress took advantage of her position to enrich her own family and arranged for her niece Mumtaz Mahal to marry her husband's third son and ultimate successor, Shah Jahan. When Shah Jahan succeeded to the throne in 1628, he quickly demonstrated the single-minded quality of his grandfather (albeit in a much more brutal manner), ordering the assassination of all of his rivals in order to secure his position.

**Jahangir the Magnificent.** In 1615, the British ambassador to the Mughal court presented an official portrait of King James I to Shah Jahangir, who returned the favor with a portrait of himself. Thus was established a long tradition of exchanging paintings between the two empires. As it turned out, the practice altered the art of Mughal portraiture, which previously had shown the emperor in action poses, hunting, at official functions, or in battle. Henceforth, portraits of the ruler followed European practice by proclaiming the opulence and spiritual power of the empire. In this painting, Jahangir has chosen spiritual over earthly power by offering a book to a sheikh while ignoring the Ottoman sultan, King James I, and the Hindu artist who painted the picture. Even the cherubs, a European artifice, are dazzled by the shah's divine character, which is further demonstrated by an enormous halo.

**The Reign of Shah Jahan** During a reign of three decades, Shah Jahan maintained the system established by his predecessors while expanding the boundaries of the empire by successful campaigns in the Deccan Plateau and against Samarkand, north of the Hindu Kush. But Shah Jahan's rule was marred by his failure to deal with the growing domestic problems. He had inherited a nearly empty treasury because of Empress Nur Jahan's penchant for luxury and ambitious charity projects. Though the majority of his subjects lived in grinding poverty, Shah Jahan's frequent military campaigns and expensive building projects put a heavy strain on the imperial finances and compelled him to raise taxes. At the same time, the government did little to improve rural conditions. In a country where transport was primitive (it often took three months to travel the 600 miles between Patna, in the middle of the Ganges River valley, and Delhi) and drought conditions frequent, the dynasty made few efforts to increase agricultural efficiency or to improve the roads or the irrigation network. A Dutch merchant in Gujarat described conditions during a famine in the mid-seventeenth century:

> As the famine increased, men abandoned towns and villages and wandered helplessly. It was easy to recognize their condition: eyes sunk deep in head, lips pale and covered with slime, the skin hard, with the bones showing through, the belly nothing but a pouch hanging down empty, knuckles and kneecaps showing prominently. One would cry and howl for hunger, while another lay stretched on the ground dying in misery; wherever you went, you saw nothing but corpses.[2]

In 1648, Shah Jahan moved his capital from Agra to Delhi and built the famous Red Fort in his new capital city. But he is best known for the Taj Mahal in Agra, widely considered to be the most beautiful building in India, if not in the entire world (see p. 442). The story is a romantic one—that the Taj was built by the emperor in memory of his wife Mumtaz Mahal, who had died giving birth to her thirteenth child at the age of thirty-nine. But the story has a less attractive side: the expense of the building, which employed twenty thousand masons over twenty years, forced the government to raise agricultural taxes, further impoverishing many Indian peasants.

## The Power Behind the Throne

During his reign as Mughal emperor, Jahangir (1605–1628) was addicted to alcohol and opium. Because of his weakened condition, his Persian wife, Nur Jahan, began to rule on his behalf. She also groomed his young son Khurram to rule as the future emperor Shah Jahan and arranged for him to marry her own niece, Mumtaz Mahal, thereby cementing her influence over two successive Mughal rulers. During this period, Nur Jahan was the de facto ruler of India, exerting her influence in both internal and foreign affairs during an era of peace and prosperity. Although the extent of her influence was often criticized at court, her performance impressed many European observers, as these remarks by two English visitors attest.

*Compare the role of Nur Jahan in this document to those of other female political figures in such areas as China, Africa, and Europe. What do they all have in common?*

### Nur Jahan, *Empress of Mughal India*

If anyone with a request to make at Court obtains an audience or is allowed to speak, the King hears him indeed, but will give no definite answer of Yes or No, referring him promptly to Asaf Khan, who in the same way will dispose of no important matter without communicating with his sister, the Queen, and who regulates his attitude in such a way that the authority of neither of them may be diminished. Anyone then who obtains a favour must thank them for it, and not the King. . . .

Her abilities were uncommon; for she rendered herself absolute, in a government in which women are thought incapable of bearing any part. Their power, it is true, is sometimes exerted in the harem; but, like the virtues of the magnet, it is silent and unperceived. Nur Jahan stood forth in public; she broke through all restraint and custom, and acquired power by her own address, more than by the weakness of Jahangir. . . .

Her former and present supporters have been well rewarded, so that now most of the men who are near the King owe their promotion to her, and are consequently under . . . obligations to her. . . . Many misunderstandings result, for the King's orders or grants of appointments, etc., are not certainties, being of no value until they have been approved by the Queen.

**History Now™** To read a related document, enter the *HistoryNow* documents area using the access card that is available for *World History.*

**Rule of Aurangzeb** Succession struggles returned to haunt the dynasty in the mid-1650s when Shah Jahan's illness led to a struggle for power between his sons Dara Shikoh and Aurangzeb. Dara Shikoh was described by his contemporaries as progressive and humane, although possessed of a violent temper and a strong sense of mysticism. But he apparently lacked political acumen and was outmaneuvered by Aurangzeb (1658–1707), who had Dara Shikoh put to death and then imprisoned his father in the fort at Agra.

Aurangzeb is one of the most controversial individuals in the history of India. A man of high principle, he attempted to eliminate many of what he considered to be India's social evils, prohibiting the immolation of widows on their husband's funeral pyre *(sati)*, the castration of eunuchs, and the exaction of illegal taxes. With less success, he tried to forbid gambling, drinking, and prostitution. But Aurangzeb, a devout and somewhat doctrinaire Muslim, also adopted a number of measures that reversed the policies of religious tolerance established by his predecessors. The building of new Hindu temples was prohibited and the Hindu poll tax was restored. Forced conversions to Islam were resumed, and non-Muslims were driven from the court. Aurangzeb's heavy-handed religious policies led to considerable domestic unrest and to a revival of Hindu fervor during the last years of his reign. A number of revolts also broke out against imperial authority.

**Decline of the Mughals** During the eighteenth century, Mughal power was threatened from both within and without. Fueled by the growing power and autonomy of the local gentry and merchants, rebellious groups in provinces throughout the empire, from the Deccan to the Punjab, began to reassert local authority and reduce the power of the Mughal emperor to that of a "tinsel sovereign." Increasingly divided, India was vulnerable to attack from abroad. In 1739, Delhi was sacked by the Persians, who left it in ashes and carried off its splendid Peacock Throne.

A number of obvious reasons for the virtual collapse of the Mughal Empire can be identified, including the draining of the imperial treasury and the decline in competence of the Mughal rulers. By 1700, the Europeans, who at first were no more than an irritant, had begun to seize control of regional trade routes and to meddle in the internal politics of the subcontinent.

It should be noted, however, that even at its height under Akbar, the empire was less a centralized state than a loosely knit collection of heterogeneous principalities held together by the authority of the throne, which tried to combine Persian concepts of kingship with the Indian

## The Capture of Port Hoogly

In 1632, the Mughal ruler, Shah Jahan, ordered an attack on the city of Hoogly, a fortified Portuguese trading post on the northeastern coast of India. For the Portuguese, who had profited from half a century of triangular trade between India, China, and various countries in the Middle East and Southeast Asia, the loss of Hoogly at the hands of the Mughals hastened the decline of their influence in the region. Presented here are two contemporary versions of the battle. The first, from the *Padshahnama (Book of Kings),* relates the course of events from the Mughal point of view. The second account is by John Cabral, a Jesuit missionary who was resident in Hoogly at the time.

*How do these two accounts of the Battle of Hoogly differ? Is there any way to reconcile the two into a single account?*

### The *Padshahnama*

During the reign of the Bengalis, a group of Frankish [European] merchants . . . settled in a place one *kos* from Satgaon on the banks of the [?] and, on the pretext that they needed a place for trading, they received permission from the Bengalis to construct a few edifices. Over time, due to the indifference of the governors of Bengal, many Franks gathered there and built dwellings of the utmost splendor and strength, fortified with cannons, guns, and other instruments of war. It was not long before it became a large settlement and was named Hoogly. . . . The Franks' ships trafficked at this port, and commerce was established, causing the market at the port of Satgaon to slump. . . . Of the peasants of those places, they converted some to Christianity by force and others through greed and sent them off to Europe in their ships. . . .

Since the improper actions of the Christians of Hoogly Port toward the Muslims was accurately reflected in the mirror of the mind of the Emperor before his accession to the throne, when the imperial banners cast their shadows over Bengal, and inasmuch as he was always inclined to propagate the true religion and eliminate infidelity, it was decided that when he gained control over this region he would eradicate the corruption of these abominators from the realm.

### John Cabral, *Travels of Sebastian Manrique, 1629–1649*

Hugli continued at peace all the time of the great King Jahangir. For, as this Prince, by what he showed, was more attached to Christ than to Mohammad and was a Moor in name and dress only. . . . Sultan Khurram was in everything unlike his father, especially as regards the latter's leaning towards Christianity. . . . He declared himself the mortal enemy of the Christian name and the restorer of the law of Mohammad. . . . He sent a firman [order] to the Viceroy of Bengal, commanding him without reply or delay, to march upon the Bandel of Hugli and put it to fire and the sword. He added that, in doing so, he would render a signal service to God, to Mohammad, and to him. . . .

Consequently, on a Friday, September 24, 1632, . . . all the people [the Portuguese] embarked with the utmost secrecy. . . . Learning what was going on, and wishing to be able to boast that they had taken Hugli by storm, they [the imperialists] made a general attack on the Bandel by Saturday noon. They began by setting fire to a mine, but lost in it more men than we. Finally, however, they were masters of the Bandel.

tradition of decentralized power. Decline set in when centrifugal forces gradually began to predominate over centripetal ones.

Ironically, one element in this process was the very success of the system, which led to the rapid expansion of wealth and autonomous power at the local level. As local elites increased their wealth and influence, they became less willing to accept the authority and financial demands from Delhi. The reassertion of Muslim orthodoxy under Aurangzeb and his successors simply exacerbated the problem. This process was hastened by the growing European military and economic presence along the periphery of the empire.

## The Impact of Western Power in India

As we have seen, the first Europeans to arrive were the Portuguese. Although they established a virtual monopoly over regional trade in the Indian Ocean, they did not aggressively seek to penetrate the interior of the subcontinent. The situation changed at the end of the sixteenth century, when the English and the Dutch entered the scene. Soon both powers were in active competition with Portugal, and with each other, for trading privileges in the region (see the box above).

Penetration of the new market was not easy. When the first English fleet arrived at Surat, a thriving port on the northwestern coast of India, in 1608, its request for trading privileges was rejected by Emperor Jahangir, at the suggestion of the Portuguese advisers already in residence at the imperial court. Needing lightweight Indian cloth to trade for spices in the East Indies, the English persisted, and in 1616, they were finally permitted to install their own ambassador at the imperial court in Agra. Three years later, the first English factory was established at Surat.

During the next several decades, the English presence in India steadily increased as Mughal power [illegible] by mid-century, additional English factories had been established at Fort William (now the great city of Calcutta, recently renamed Kolkata) on the Hoogly River near the Bay of Bengal and at Madras (now known as Chennai) on the southeastern coast. From there, English ships carried Indian-made cotton goods to the East Indies, where they were bartered for spices, which were shipped back to England. Tensions between local authorities and the English over the payment of taxes led to a short war in 1686. The English were briefly expelled, but after differences were patched up, Aurangzeb permitted them to return.

English success in India attracted rivals, including the Dutch and the French. The Dutch abandoned their interests to concentrate on the spice trade in the middle of the seventeenth century, but the French were more persistent and established factories of their own. For a brief period, under the ambitious empire builder Joseph François Dupleix, the French competed successfully with the British. But the military genius of Sir Robert Clive, an aggressive British administrator and empire builder who eventually became the chief representative of the East India Company in the subcontinent, and the refusal of the French government to provide financial support for Dupleix's efforts eventually left the French with only their fort at Pondicherry and a handful of small territories on the southeastern coast.

In the meantime, Clive began to consolidate British control in Bengal, where the local ruler had attacked Fort William and imprisoned the local British population in the infamous Black Hole of Calcutta (an underground prison for holding the prisoners, many of whom died in captivity). In 1757, a small British force numbering about three thousand defeated a Mughal-led army over ten times that size in the Battle of Plassey. As part of the spoils of victory, the British East India Company exacted from the now-decrepit Mughal court the authority to collect taxes from extensive lands in the area surrounding Calcutta. Less than ten years later, British forces seized the reigning Mughal emperor in a skirmish at Buxar, and the British began to consolidate their economic and administrative control over Indian territory through the surrogate power of the now powerless Mughal court (see Map 15.4).

To officials of the East India Company, the expansion of their authority into the interior of the subcontinent probably seemed like a simple commercial decision, a move designed to seek guaranteed revenues to pay for the increasingly expensive military operations in India. To historians, it marks a major step in the gradual transfer of all of the Indian subcontinent to the British East India Company and later, in 1858, to the British crown. The process was more haphazard than deliberate. Under a new governor general, Warren Hastings, the British attempted to consolidate areas under their control and defeat such rivals as the rising Hindu Marathas, who exploited the decline of the Mughals to expand their own empire in Maharashtra.

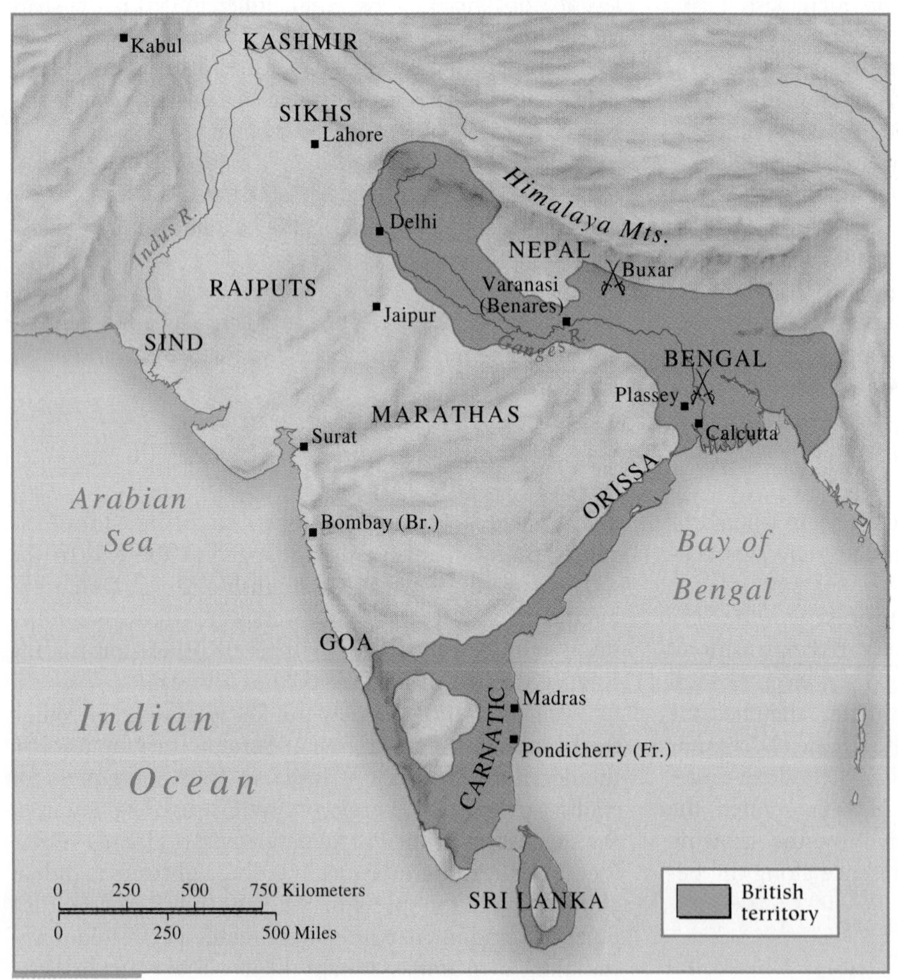


**MAP 15.4 India in 1805.** By the early nineteenth century, virtually all of the Indian subcontinent had fallen under British domination. The extent of British territory, with prominent cities and major geographical terms indicated, is shown here. ? Where was the capital of the Mughal Empire? **View an animated version of this map or related maps at** http://history.wadsworth.com/duikerspielvogel05/

**Economic Difficulties** The company's takeover of vast landholdings, notably in the eastern Indian states of Orissa and Bengal, may have been a windfall for enterprising British officials, but it was a disaster for the Indian economy. In the first place, it resulted in the transfer of capital from the local

**CHRONOLOGY The Mughal Era**

| | |
|---|---|
| Arrival of Vasco da Gama at Calicut | 1498 |
| Babur seizes Delhi | 1526 |
| Death of Babur | 1530 |
| Humayun recovers throne in Delhi | 1555 |
| Death of Humayun and accession of Akbar | 1556 |
| First Jesuit mission to Agra | 1580 |
| Death of Akbar and accession of Jahangir | 1605 |
| Arrival of English at Surat | 1608 |
| Reign of Emperor Shah Jahan | 1628–1657 |
| Foundation of English fort at Madras | 1639 |
| Aurangzeb succeeds to the throne | 1658 |
| Bombay ceded to England | 1661 |
| Death of Aurangzeb | 1707 |
| French capture Madras | 1746 |
| Battle of Plassey | 1757 |

Indian aristocracy to company officials, most of whom sent their profits back to Britain. Second, it hastened the destruction of once healthy local industries, because British goods such as machine-made textiles were imported duty-free into India to compete against local products. Finally, British expansion hurt the peasants. As the British took over the administration of the land tax, they also applied British law, which allowed the lands of those unable to pay the tax to be confiscated. In the 1770s, a series of massive famines led to the death of an estimated one-third of the population in the areas under company administration. The British government attempted to resolve the problem by assigning tax lands to the local revenue collectors *(zamindars)* in the hope of transforming them into English-style rural gentry, but many collectors themselves fell into bankruptcy and sold their lands to absentee bankers while the now landless peasants remained in abject poverty. It was hardly an auspicious beginning to "civilized" British rule.

**Resistance to the British** As a result of such problems, Britain's rise to power in India did not go unchallenged. Astute Indian commanders avoided pitched battles with the well-armed British troops but harassed and ambushed them in the manner of guerrillas in our time. Said Haidar Ali, one of Britain's primary rivals for control in southern India:

> You will in time understand my mode of warfare. Shall I risk my cavalry which cost a thousand rupees each horse, against your cannon ball which cost two pice? No! I will march your troops until their legs swell to the size of their bodies. You shall not have a blade of grass, nor a drop of water. I will hear of you every time your drum beats, but you shall not know where I am once a month. I will give your army battle, but it must be when I please, and not when you choose.[3]

Unfortunately for India, not all its commanders were as astute as Haidar Ali. In the last years of the eighteenth century, when the East India Company's authority came into the capable hands of Lord Cornwallis and his successor, Lord Mornington, the future marquess of Wellesley, the stage was set for the final consolidation of British rule over the subcontinent.

## Society Under the Mughals

The Mughals were the last of the great traditional Indian dynasties. Like so many of their predecessors since the fall of the Guptas nearly a thousand years before, the Mughals were Muslims. But like the Ottoman Turks, the best Mughal rulers did not simply impose Islamic institutions and beliefs on the predominantly Hindu population; they combined Muslim with Hindu and even Persian concepts and cultural values in a unique social and cultural synthesis that still today seems to epitomize the greatness of Indian civilization.

**The Position of Women** Whether Mughal rule had much effect on the lives of ordinary Indians seems somewhat problematic. The treatment of women is a good example. Women had traditionally played an active role in Mongol tribal society—many actually fought on the battlefield alongside the men—and Babur and his successors often relied on the women in their families for political advice. Women from aristocratic families were often awarded honorific titles, received salaries, and were permitted to own land and engage in business. Women at court sometimes received an education, and Emperor Akbar reportedly established a girls' school at Fatehpur Sikri to provide teachers for his own daughters. Aristocratic women often expressed their creative talents by writing poetry, painting, or playing music. Women of all castes were adept at spinning thread, either for their own use or to sell to weavers to augment the family income. Weaving was carried out in home production units by all the members of the subcaste weaving families. They sold simple cloth to local villages and fine cotton, silk, and wool to the Mughal court. By Akbar's rule, in fact, the textile manufacturing was of such high quality and so well established that India sold cloth to much of the world: Arabia, the coast of East Africa, Egypt, Southeast Asia, and Europe.

To a certain degree, these Mughal attitudes toward women may have had an impact on Indian society. Women were allowed to inherit land, and some even possessed *zamindar* rights. Women from mercantile castes sometimes took an active role in business activities. At the same time, however, as Muslims, the Mughals subjected women to certain restrictions under Islamic law. On the whole, these Mughal practices coincided with and even accentuated existing tendencies in Indian society. The Muslim practice of isolating women and preventing them from associating with men outside the home (*purdah*) was adopted by many upper-class Hindus as a means of enhancing their status or protecting their women from unwelcome advances by Muslims in positions of authority. In other ways, Hindu practices were unaffected. The

**Muslims and Hindus** For their part, Hindus sometimes attempted to defend themselves and their religious practices against the efforts of some Mughal monarchs to impose the Islamic religion and Islamic mores on the indigenous population. In some cases, despite official prohibitions, Hindu men forcibly married Muslim women and then converted them to the native faith, while converts to Islam normally lost all of their inheritance rights within the Indian family. Government orders to destroy Hindu temples were often ignored by local officials, sometimes as the result of bribery or intimidation. Sometimes Indian practices had an influence on the Mughal elites, as many Mughal chieftains married Indian women and adopted Indian forms of dress.

**The Economy** Long-term stability led to increasing commercialization and the spread of wealth to new groups within Indian society. The Mughal era saw the emergence of an affluent landed gentry and a prosperous merchant class. Members of prestigious castes from the pre-Mughal period reaped many of the benefits of the increasing wealth, but some of these changes transcended caste boundaries and led to the emergence of new groups who achieved status and wealth on the basis of economic

with the foreigners. For a time, that relationship often worked to the Indians' benefit. Later, as we shall see, they would have cause to regret the arrangement.

## Mughal Culture

The era of the Mughals was one of synthesis in culture as well as in politics and religion. The Mughals combined Islamic themes with Persian and indigenous motifs to produce a unique style that enriched and embellished Indian art and culture. The Mughal emperors were zealous patrons of the arts and enticed painters, poets, and artisans from as far away as the Mediterranean. Apparently, the generosity of the Mughals made it difficult to refuse a trip to India. It was said that they would reward a poet with his weight in gold.

**Architecture** Undoubtedly, the Mughals' most visible achievement was in architecture. Here they integrated Persian and Indian styles in a new and sometimes breathtakingly beautiful form best symbolized by the Taj Mahal, built by the emperor Shah Jahan in the mid-seventeenth century. Although the human and economic cost of the Taj tarnishes the romantic legend of its construction, there is no denying the beauty of the building. It had evolved from a style that

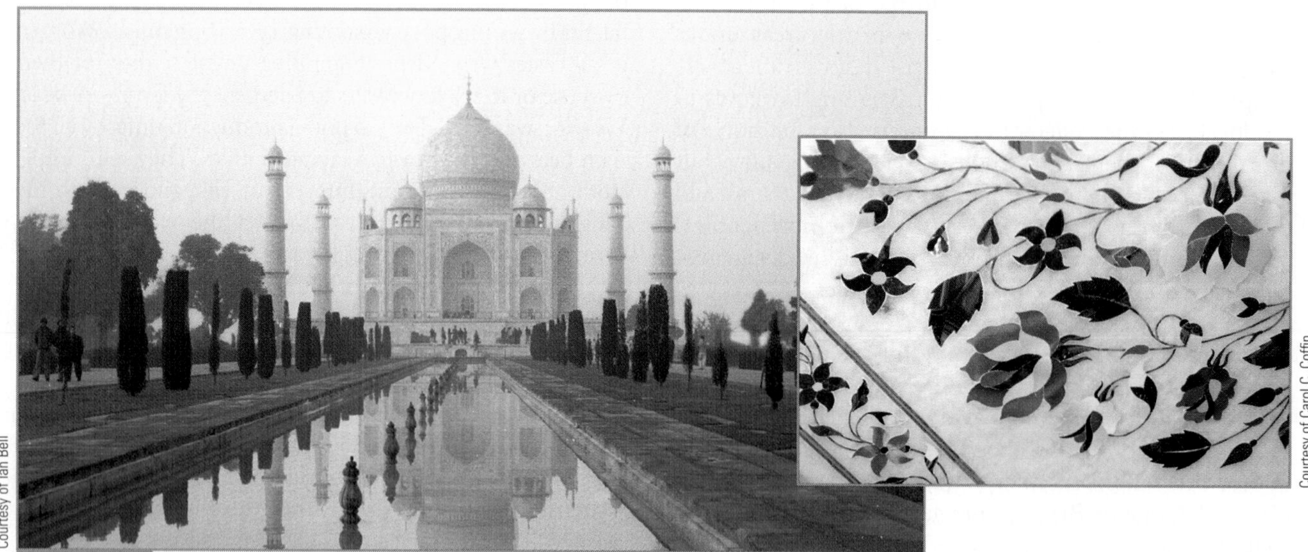

Courtesy of Ian Bell

Courtesy of Carol C. Coffin

**The Taj Mahal.** The Taj Mahal, completed in 1653, was built by the Mughal emperor Shah Jahan as a tomb to glorify the memory of his beloved wife. Raised on a marble platform above the Jumna River, the Taj is dramatically framed by contrasting twin red sandstone mosques, magnificent gardens, and a long reflecting pool that mirrors and magnifies its beauty. The effect is one of monumental size, near blinding brilliance, and delicate lightness, a startling contrast to the heavier and more masculine Baroque style then popular in Europe. The inset offers an example of the exquisite inlay of precious stones that adorns the facade.

**Fatehpur Sikri.** In gratitude to a Sufi mystic who had correctly forecast the birth of his son, Akbar chose the mystic's village of Sikri as the site for his new palace and capital city. Completed at great speed in 1586, the splendid city, which was built of red sandstone and measured 2 miles long and a mile wide, was soon abandoned because of an inadequate water supply. Its elaborate palaces, mosque, reflecting pools and courtyards, harems, and impressive victory gate all testify to the elegance and greatness of Akbar's reign.

originated several decades earlier with the tomb of Humayun, which was built by his widow in Agra in 1565 during the reign of Akbar.

Humayun's mausoleum had combined Persian and Islamic motifs in a square building finished in red sandstone and topped with a dome. The style was repeated in a number of other buildings erected throughout the empire, but the Taj brought the style to perfection. Working with a model created by his Persian architect, Shah Jahan raised the dome and replaced the red sandstone with brilliant white marble. The entire exterior and interior surface is decorated with cut-stone geometrical patterns, delicate black stone tracery, or intricate inlay of colored precious stones in floral and Qur'anic arabesques. The technique of creating dazzling floral mosaics of lapis lazuli, malachite, carnelian, turquoise, and mother-of-pearl may have been introduced by Italian artists at the Mughal court. Shah Jahan had intended to erect a similar building in black marble across the river for his own remains, but the plans were abandoned after he was deposed by his son Aurangzeb. Shah Jahan spent his last years imprisoned in a room in the Red Fort at Agra; from his windows, he could see the beautiful memorial to his beloved wife.

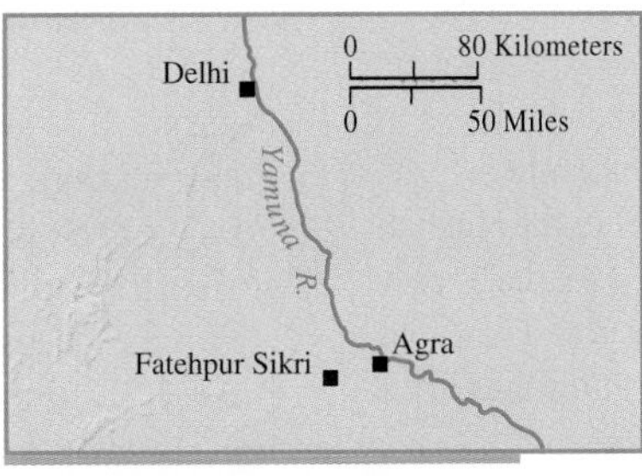


**Central India Under the Mughals**

The Taj was by no means the only magnificent building erected during the Mughal era. Akbar, who, in the words of a contemporary, "dresses the work of his mind and heart in the garment of stone and clay," was the first of the great Mughal builders. His first palace at Agra, the Red Fort, was begun in 1565. A few years later, he ordered the construction of a new palace at Fatehpur Sikri, 26 miles to the west. The new palace was built in honor of a Sufi mystic who had correctly forecast the birth of a son to the emperor. In gratitude, Akbar decided to build a new capital city and palace on the site of the mystic's home. Over a period of fifteen years, from 1571 to 1586, a magnificent new city in red sandstone was constructed. Although the city was abandoned before completion and now stands almost untouched, it is a popular destination for tourists and pilgrims.

**Painting** The other major artistic achievement of the Mughal period was painting. Painting had never been one of the great attainments of Indian culture due in part to a technological difficulty. Paper was not introduced to India from Persia until the latter part of the fourteenth century, so traditionally painting had been done on palm

**The Fall of Port Hoogly.** The art of the illustrated manuscript reached its zenith in the ateliers of prestigious artists at the Mughal court. Combining Persian and Indian motifs with a Western use of perspective, Indian artists produced paintings of exceptional quality. Following a long tradition in the region, Mughal rulers commissioned elaborate illustrated histories to commemorate key events during their reigns. Shown here is a scene from the Mughal victory over the Portuguese at Port Hoogly in 1632 (see the box on p. 439). The artist not only presents the action on a grand scale but offers details of Portuguese-style architecture and Europeans in plumed hats. Shah Jahan (in a green jacket in the foreground), backed by a cannon barrage, leads his troops in battle.

leaves, which had severely hampered artistic creativity. By the fifteenth century, Indian painting had made the transition from palm leaf to paper, and the new medium eventually stimulated a burst of creativity, particularly in the genre of miniatures, or book illustrations.

As in so many other areas of endeavor, painting in Mughal India resulted from the blending of two cultures. While living in exile, Emperor Humayun had learned to admire Persian miniatures. On his return to India in 1555, he invited two Persian masters to live in his palace and introduce the technique to his adopted land. His successor, Akbar, appreciated the new style and popularized it with his patronage. He established a state workshop at Fatehpur Sikri for two hundred artists, mostly Hindus, who worked under the guidance of the Persian masters to create the Mughal school of painting.

The "Akbar style" combined Persian with Indian motifs, such as the use of extended space and the portrayal of physical human action, characteristics not usually seen in Persian art. Akbar also apparently encouraged the imitation of European art forms, including the portrayal of Christian subjects, the use of perspective, lifelike portraits, and the shading of colors in the Renaissance style. The depiction of the human figure in Mughal painting outraged orthodox Muslims at court, but Akbar argued that the painter, "in sketching anything that has life . . . must come to feel that he cannot bestow individuality upon his work, and is thus forced to think of God, the Giver of Life, and will thus increase in knowledge."[4]

Painting during Akbar's reign followed the trend toward realism and historical narrative that had originated in the Ottoman Empire. For example, Akbar had the illustrated *Book of Akbar* made to record his military exploits and court activities. Many of these paintings of Akbar's life portray him in action in his real world. After his death, his son and grandson continued the patronage of the arts.

**Literature** The development of Indian literature was held back by the absence of printing, which was not introduced until the end of the Mughal era. Literary works were inscribed by calligraphers, and one historian has estimated that the library of Agra contained more than 24,000 volumes. Poetry, in particular, flourished under the Mughals, who established poet laureates at court. Poems were written in the Persian style and in the Persian language. In fact, Persian became the official language of the court until the sack of Delhi in 1739. At the time, the Indians' anger at their conquerors led them to adopt Urdu as the new language for the court and for poetry. By that time, Indian verse on the Persian model had already lost its original vitality and simplicity and had become more artificial in the manner of court literature everywhere.

Another aspect of the long Mughal reign was a Hindu revival of devotional literature, much of it dedicated to Krishna and Rama. The retelling of the Ramayana in the vernacular, beginning in the southern Tamil languages in the eleventh century and spreading slowly northward, culminated in the sixteenth-century Hindi version by the great poet Tulsidas (1532–1623). His *Ramcaritmanas* presents the devotional story with a deified Rama and Sita. Tulsidas's genius was in combining the conflicting cults of Vishnu and Shiva into a unified and overwhelming love for the divine, which he expressed in some of the most moving of all Indian poetry. The *Ramcaritmanas* has eclipsed its two-thousand-year-old Sanskrit ancestor in popularity and even became the basis of an Indian television series in the late 1980s.

## CONCLUSION

THE THREE EMPIRES that we have discussed in this chapter exhibit a number of striking similarities. First of all, they were Muslim in their religious affiliation, although the Safavids were Shi'ite rather than Sunni, a distinction that often led to mutual tensions and conflict. More important, perhaps, they were all of nomadic origin, and the political and social institutions that they adopted carried the imprint of their preimperial past. Once they achieved imperial power, however, all three ruling dynasties displayed an impressive capacity to administer a large empire and brought a degree of stability to peoples who had all too often lived in conditions of internal division and war.

Another similarity is that the mastery of the techniques of modern warfare, including the use of firearms, played a central role in all three empires' ability to overcome their rivals and rise to regional hegemony. Some scholars have therefore labeled them "gunpowder empires" in the belief that technical prowess in the art of warfare was a key element in their success. Although that is undoubtedly true, we should not forget that other factors, such as dynamic leadership, political acumen, and the possession of an ardent following motivated by religious zeal, were at least equally important in their drive to power and ability to retain it. Weapons by themselves do not an empire make.

The rise of these powerful Muslim states coincided with the opening period of European expansion at the end of the fifteenth century and the beginning of the sixteenth. The military and political talents of these empires helped protect much of the Muslim world from the resurgent forces of Christianity. To the contrary, the Ottoman Turks carried their empire into the heart of Christian Europe and briefly reached the gates of the great city of Vienna. By the end of the eighteenth century, however, the Safavid dynasty had imploded, and the powerful Mughal Empire was in a state of virtual collapse. Only the Ottoman Empire was still functioning. Yet it too had lost much of its early expansionistic vigor and was showing signs of internal decay.

The reasons for the decline of these empires have inspired considerable debate among historians. One factor was undoubtedly the expansion of European power into the Indian Ocean and the Middle East. But internal causes were probably more important in the long run. All three empires experienced growing factionalism within the ruling elite, incompetence within the palace, and the emergence of divisive forces in the empire at large–factors that have marked the passing of traditional empires since early times. Climate change (the region was reportedly hotter and drier after the beginning of the seventeenth century) may have been a contributing factor. Paradoxically, one of the greatest strengths of these empires–their mastery of gunpowder–may have simultaneously been a serious weakness in that it allowed them to develop a complacent sense of security. With little incentive to turn their attention to new developments in science and technology, they were increasingly vulnerable to attack by the advanced nations of the West. The weakening of the gunpowder empires created a political vacuum into which the dynamic and competitive forces of European capitalism were quick to enter.

The gunpowder empires, however, were not the only states in the Old World that were able to resist the first outward thrust of European expansion. Farther to the east, the mature civilizations in China and Japan successfully faced a similar challenge from Western merchants and missionaries. Unlike their counterparts in South Asia and the Middle East, as the nineteenth century dawned, they continued to thrive.

## CHAPTER NOTES

1. Quoted in V. A. Smith, *The Oxford History of India* (Oxford, 1967), p. 341.
2. Quoted in M. Edwardes, *A History of India: From the Earliest Times to the Present Day* (London, 1961), p. 188.
3. Quoted in ibid., p. 220.
4. Quoted in R. C. Craven, *Indian Art: A Concise History* (New York, 1976), p. 205.

## SUGGESTED READING

The most complete general survey of the Ottoman Empire is **S. J. Shaw, *History of the Ottoman Empire and Modern Turkey*** (Cambridge, 1976). Shaw is difficult reading but informative on administrative matters. A more readable albeit less definitive account is ***Lord Kinross, The Ottoman Centuries: The Rise and Fall of the Ottoman Empire*** (New York, 1977), which is larded with human-interest stories.

For a dramatic account of the conquest of Constantinople in 1453, see **S. Runciman, *The Fall of Constantinople, 1453*** (Cambridge, 1965). The life of Mehmet II is chronicled in **F. Babinger, *Mehmed the Conqueror and His Time,*** trans. **R. Manheim** (Princeton, N.J., 1979). On Suleyman the Magnificent, see **R. Merriman, *Suleiman the Magnificent, 1520–1566*** (Cambridge, 1944). On the Safavids, see **R. M. Savory, *Iran Under the Safavids*** (Cambridge, 1980), and **E. B. Monshi, *History of Shah Abbas the Great,*** 2 vols. (Boulder, Colo., 1978).

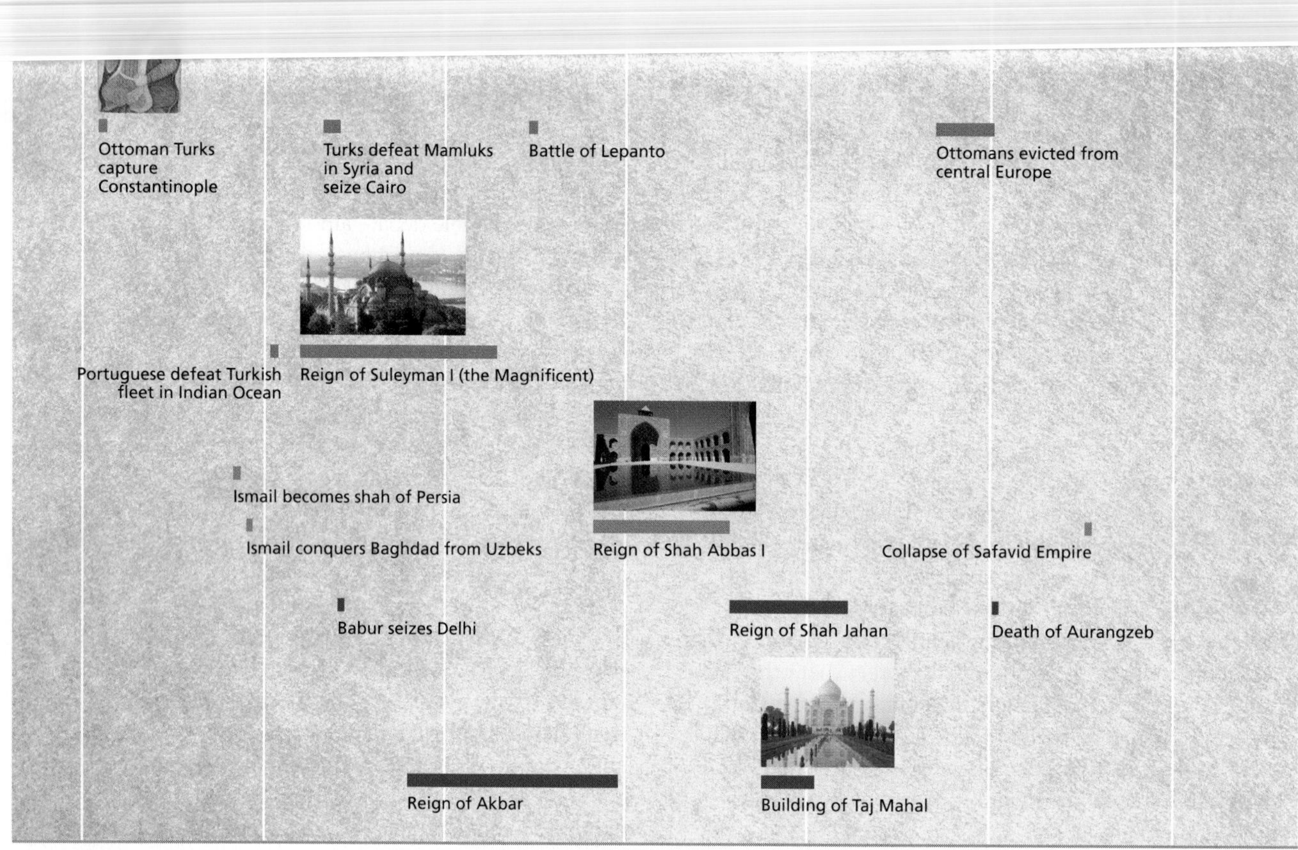


For an overview of the Mughal era, see **S. Wolpert, *New History of India*** (New York, 1989). A more dramatic account for the general reader is **W. Hansen, *The Peacock Throne: The Drama of Mogul India*** (New York, 1972).

There are a number of specialized works on various aspects of the period. For a treatment of the Mughal era in the context of Islamic rule in India, see **S. M. Ikram, *Muslim Civilization in India*** (New York, 1964). The concept of "gunpowder empires" is persuasively analyzed in **D. E. Streusand, *The Formation of the Mughal Empire*** (Delhi, 1989). Economic issues predominate in much recent scholarship. For example, **S. Subrahmanyan, *The Political Economy of Commerce: Southern India, 1500–1650*** (Cambridge, 1990), focuses on the interaction between internal and external trade in southern India during the early stages of the period. The Mughal Empire is analyzed in a broad Central Asian context in **R. C. Foltz, *Mughal India and Central Asia*** (Karachi, 1998). Finally, **K. N. Chaudhuri, *Trade and Civilization in the Indian Ocean: An Economic History from the Rise of Islam to 1750*** (Cambridge, 1985), views Indian commerce in the perspective of the regional trade network throughout the Indian Ocean.

For treatments of all three Muslim empires in a comparative context, see **J. J. Kissling** et al., ***The Last Great Muslim Empires*** (Princeton, N.J., 1996), and **M. G. S. Hodgson, *Rethinking World History: Essays on Europe, Islam, and World History*** (Cambridge, 1993).

For an introduction to the women of the Ottoman and Mughal Empires, see **S. Hughes** and **B. Hughes, *Women in World History,*** vol. 2 (Armonk, N.Y., 1997). For a more detailed presentation of women in the imperial harem, consult **L. P. Peirce, *"Beyond Harem Walls: Ottoman Royal Women and the Exercise of Power,"*** in ***Gendered Domains: Rethinking Public and Private in Women's History***, ed. **D. O. Helly** and **S. M. Reverby** (Ithaca, N.Y., 1992), and **L. P. Peirce, *The Imperial Harem: Women and Sovereignty in the Ottoman Empire*** (Oxford, 1993). The fascinating story of the royal woman who played an important role behind the scenes is found in **E. B. Findly,** ***Nur Jahan: Empress of Mughal India*** (Oxford, 1993).

On the art of this era, see **R. C. Craven,** ***Indian Art: A Concise History,*** rev. ed. (New York, 1997); **J. Bloom** and **S. Blair,** ***Islamic Arts*** (London, 1997); **M. C. Beach,** ***The Imperial Image*** (Washington, D.C., 1981); **M. C. Beach** and **E. Koch,** ***King of the World: The Padshahnama*** (London, 1997); and **M. Hattstein** and **P. Delius,** ***Islam: Art and Architecture*** (Konigswinter, Germany, 2004).

### History Now™

**Enter *HistoryNow* using the access card that is available with this text. *HistoryNow* will assist you in understanding the content in this chapter with lesson plans generated for your needs, as well as provide you with a connection to the *Wadsworth World History Resource Center* (see the following description for details).**

### WORLD HISTORY RESOURCE CENTER

**Enter the Resource Center using either your *HistoryNow* access card or your standalone access card for the *Wadsworth World History Resource Center.* Organized by topic, this website includes quizzes; images; over 350 primary source documents; interactive simulations; maps and timelines; movie explorations; and a wealth of other resources. You can read the following documents, and many more, at http://history.wadsworth.com/rc/world**

Lady Mary Wortley Montagu, "Dining with the Sultana"
Travels of Ibn Battuta
Classical Persian Poetry

Visit the *World History* Companion Website for chapter quizzes and more.

http://history.wadsworth.com/duikerspielvogel05/

CHAPTER 16

# THE EAST ASIAN WORLD

*Emperor Kangxi*

© Metropolitan Museum of Art, Rogers Fund, 1942

## CHAPTER OUTLINE AND FOCUS QUESTIONS

### China at Its Apex

- Why were the Manchus so successful at establishing a foreign dynasty in China, and what were the main characteristics of Manchu rule?

### Changing China

- How did the economy and society change during the Ming and Qing eras, and to what degree did these changes seem to be leading toward an industrial revolution on the European model?

### Tokugawa Japan

- How did the society and economy of Japan change during the Tokugawa era, and how did Japanese culture reflect those changes?

### Korea: The Hermit Kingdom

- To what degree did developments in Korea during this period reflect conditions in China and Japan? What were the most unique aspects of Korean civilization?

### CRITICAL THINKING

- How did China and Japan respond to the coming of the Europeans, and what explains the differences? What impact did European contacts have on these two East Asian civilizations through the end of the eighteenth century?

IN DECEMBER 1717, Emperor Kangxi returned from a hunting trip north of the Great Wall and began to suffer from dizzy spells. Conscious of his approaching date with mortality—he was now nearly seventy years of age—the emperor called together his sons and leading government officials in the imperial palace and issued an edict summing up his ideas on the art of statecraft. Rulers, he declared, should be sincere in their reverence for Heaven's laws as the fundamental strategy for governing the country. Among those laws were the following: show concern for the welfare of the people, practice diligence, protect the state from its enemies, choose able advisers, and strike a careful balance between leniency and strictness, principle and expedience. That, he concluded, was all there was to it.[1]

Any potential successor to the throne would be well advised to attend to the emperor's advice. Kangxi was not only one of the longest-reigning of all Chinese rulers but also one of its wisest. His era was one of peace and prosperity, and after half a century of rule, the empire was now at the zenith of its power and influence. As his life approached its end, Heaven must indeed have been pleased at the quality of his stewardship.

As for the emperor's edict, it clearly reflected the genius of Confucian teachings at their best and has a timeless quality that applies to our age as well as to the Golden Age of the Qing dynasty.

Kangxi reigned during one of the most glorious eras in the long history of China. Under the Ming (1369–1644) and the early Qing (1644–1911) dynasties, the empire expanded its borders to a degree not seen since the Han and the Tang. Chinese culture was the envy of its neighbors and earned the admiration of many European visitors, including Jesuit priests and Enlightenment philosophes.

On the surface, China appeared to be an unchanging society patterned after the Confucian vision of a "golden age" in the remote past. This indeed was the image presented by China's rulers, who referred constantly to tradition as a model for imperial institutions and cultural values. Although few observers could have been aware of it at the time, however, China was changing–and rather rapidly.

A similar process was under way in neighboring Japan. A vigorous new shogunate called the Tokugawa rose to power in the early seventeenth century and managed to revitalize the traditional system in a somewhat more centralized form that enabled it to survive for another 250 years. But major structural changes were taking place in Japanese society, and by the nineteenth century, tensions were growing as the gap between theory and reality widened.

One of the many factors involved in the quickening pace of change in both countries was contact with the West, which began with the arrival of Portuguese ships in Chinese and Japanese ports in the first half of the sixteenth century. The Ming and the Tokugawa initially opened their doors to European trade and missionary activity. Later, however, Chinese and Japanese rulers became concerned about the corrosive effects of Western ideas and practices and attempted to protect their traditional societies from external intrusion. But neither could forever resist the importunities of Western trading nations, and when the doors to the West were finally reopened in the mid-nineteenth century, both societies were ripe for radical change. ◇

# China at Its Apex

In 1514, a Portuguese fleet dropped anchor off the coast of China, just south of the Pearl River estuary and present-day Hong Kong. It was the first direct contact between the Chinese Empire and the West since the arrival of the Venetian adventurer Marco Polo two centuries earlier, and it opened an era that would eventually change the face of China and, indeed, all the world.

## From the Ming to the Qing

Marco Polo had reported on the magnificence of China after visiting Beijing during the reign of Khubilai Khan, the great Mongol ruler. By the time the Portuguese fleet arrived off the coast of China, of course, the Mongol Empire had long since disappeared. It had gradually weakened after the death of Khubilai Khan and was finally overthrown in 1368 by a massive peasant rebellion under the leadership of Zhu Yuanzhang, who had declared himself the founding emperor of a new Ming (Bright) dynasty and assumed the reign title of Ming Hongwu (Ming Hung Wu, or Ming Martial Emperor).

As we have seen, the Ming inaugurated a period of territorial expansion westward into Central Asia and southward into Vietnam while consolidating control over China's vast heartland. At the same time, the dynasty sponsored a series of voyages that spread Chinese influence far into the Indian Ocean. Then suddenly the voyages were discontinued and the dynasty turned its attention to domestic concerns (see Chapter 10).

**First Contacts with the West** Despite the Ming's retreat from active participation in maritime trade, when the Portuguese arrived in 1514, China was in command of a vast empire that stretched from the steppes of Central Asia to the China Sea, from the Gobi Desert to the tropical rain forests of Southeast Asia. From the lofty perspective of the imperial throne in Beijing, the Europeans could only have seemed like an unusually exotic form of barbarian to be placed within the familiar framework of the tributary system, the hierarchical arrangement in which rulers of all other countries were regarded as "younger brothers" of the Son of Heaven. Indeed, the bellicose and uncultured behavior of the Portuguese so outraged Chinese officials that they expelled the Europeans, but after further negotiations, the Portuguese were permitted to occupy the tiny territory of Macao, a foothold they would retain until the end of the twentieth century.

Initially, the arrival of the Europeans did not have much impact on Chinese society. Direct trade between Europe and China was limited, and Portuguese ships became involved in the regional trade network, carrying silk to Japan in return for Japanese silver. Eventually, the Spanish also began to participate, using the Philippines as an anchor in the galleon trade between China and the great silver mines in the Americas.

More influential than trade, perhaps, were the ideas introduced by Christian missionaries. Among the most active and the most effective were highly educated Jesuits, who were familiar with European philosophical and scientific developments. Recognizing the Chinese pride in their own culture, the Jesuits attempted to draw parallels between Christian and Confucian concepts (for example, they identified the Western concept of God with the Chinese character for Heaven) and to show the similarities between Christian morality and Confucian ethics. European inventions such as the clock, the prism, and various astronomical and musical instruments impressed Chinese officials, hitherto deeply imbued with a sense of the superiority of Chinese civilization, and helped

## The Art of Printing

Europeans obtained much of their early information about China from the Jesuits who served at the Ming court in the sixteenth and seventeenth centuries. Clerics such as the Italian Matteo Ricci (1552–1610) found much to admire in Chinese civilization. Here Ricci expresses a keen interest in Chinese printing methods, which at that time were well in advance of the techniques used in the West. Later Christian missionaries expressed strong interest in Confucian philosophy and Chinese ideas of statecraft.

*How did the Chinese method of printing differ from that developed in Europe at that time? What were its advantages?*

### Matteo Ricci, *The Diary of Matthew Ricci*

The art of printing was practiced in China at a date somewhat earlier than that assigned to the beginning of printing in Europe, which was about 1405. It is quite certain that the Chinese knew the art of printing at least five centuries ago, and some of them assert that printing was known to their people before the beginning of the Christian era, about 50 B.C. Their method of printing differs widely from that employed in Europe, and our method would be quite impracticable for them because of the exceedingly large number of Chinese characters and symbols. . . .

Their method of making printed books is quite ingenious. The text is written in ink, with a brush made of very fine hair, on a sheet of paper which is inverted and pasted on a wooden tablet. When the paper has become thoroughly dry, its surface is scraped off quickly and with great skill, until nothing but a fine tissue bearing the characters remains on the wooden tablet. Then, with a steel graver, the workman cuts away the surface following the outlines of the characters until these alone stand out in low relief. From such a block a skilled printer can make copies with incredible speed, turning out as many as fifteen hundred copies in a single day. . . . This scheme of engraving wooden blocks is well adapted for the large and complex nature of the Chinese characters, but I do not think it would lend itself very aptly to our European type, which could hardly be engraved upon wood because of its small dimensions.

Their method of printing has one decided advantage, namely, that once these tablets are made, they can be preserved and used for making changes in the text as often as one wishes. Additions and subtractions can also be made as the tablets can be readily patched. . . . We have derived great benefit from this method of Chinese printing, as we employ the domestic help in our homes to strike off copies of the books on religious and scientific subjects which we translate into Chinese from the languages in which they were written originally. In truth, the whole method is so simple that one is tempted to try it for himself after once having watched the process. The simplicity of Chinese printing is what accounts for the exceedingly large numbers of books in circulation here and the ridiculously low prices at which they are sold.

**History Now™** To read a memorial to Matteo Ricci, enter the *HistoryNow* documents area using the access card that is available for *World History.*

Western ideas win acceptance at court. An elderly Chinese scholar expressed his wonder at the miracle of eyeglasses:

*White glass from across the Western Seas*
*Is imported through Macao:*
*Fashioned into lenses big as coins,*
*They encompass the eyes in a double frame.*
*I put them on–it suddenly becomes clear;*
*I can see the very tips of things!*
*And read fine print by the dim-lit window*
*Just like in my youth.*[2]

For their part, the missionaries were much impressed with many aspects of Chinese civilization, and reports of their experiences heightened European curiosity about this great society on the other side of the world (see the box above).

**The Ming Brought to Earth** During the late sixteenth century, the Ming began to decline as a series of weak rulers led to an era of corruption, concentration of land ownership, and ultimately peasant rebellions and tribal unrest along the northern frontier. The inflow of vast amounts of foreign silver led to an alarming increase in inflation. Then the arrival of the English and the Dutch disrupted the silver trade; silver imports plummeted, severely straining the Chinese economy by raising the value of the metal relative to that of copper. Crop yields declined due to harsh weather—linked to the "little ice age" of the early seventeenth century—and the resulting scarcity reduced the ability of the government to provide food in times of imminent starvation. High taxes, provoked in part by increased official corruption, led to peasant unrest and worker violence in urban areas. A folk song of the period, addressed to the "Lord of Heaven," complained,

*Old skymaster,*
*You're getting on, your ears are deaf, your eyes are gone.*
*Can't see people, can't hear words.*
*Glory for those who kill and burn;*
*For those who fast and read the scriptures,*
*Starvation.*
*Fall down, old master sky, how can you be so high?*
*How can you be so high? Come down to earth.*[3]

As always, internal problems were accompanied by unrest along the northern frontier. Following long precedent, the Ming had attempted to pacify the frontier tribes by forging alliances with them, arranging marriages between them and the local aristocracy, and granting trade privileges. One of the alliances was with the Manchus (also known as the Jurchen), the descendants of peoples who had briefly established a kingdom in northern China during the early thirteenth century. The Manchus, a mixed agricultural and hunting people, lived northeast of the Great Wall in the area known today as Manchuria.

At first, the Manchus were satisfied with consolidating their territory and made little effort to extend their rule south of the Great Wall. But during the first decades of the seventeenth century, the problems of the Ming dynasty began to come to a head. A major epidemic devastated the population in many areas of the country. The suffering brought on by the epidemic helped spark a vast peasant revolt led by Li Zicheng (Li Tzu-ch'eng, 1604–1651). Li was a postal worker in central China who had been dismissed from his job as part of a cost-saving measure by the imperial court, now increasingly preoccupied by tribal attacks along the frontier (see Map 16.1). In the 1630s, Li managed to extend the revolt throughout the country and finally occupied the capital of Beijing in 1644. The last Ming emperor committed suicide by hanging himself from a tree in the palace gardens.

But Li was unable to hold his conquest. The overthrow of the Ming dynasty presented a great temptation to the Manchus. With the assistance of many military commanders who had deserted from the Ming, the Manchu's conquered Beijing. Li Zicheng's army disintegrated, and the Manchus declared the creation of a new dynasty with the reign title of the Qing (Ch'ing, or Pure). Once again, China was under foreign rule.

## The Greatness of the Qing

The accession of the Manchus to power in Beijing was not universally applauded. Their ruthless policies and insensitivity to Chinese customs soon provoked resistance. Some Ming loyalists fled to Southeast Asia, but others continued their resistance to the new rulers from inside the country. To make it easier to identify the rebels, the government ordered all Chinese to adopt Manchu dress and hairstyles. All Chinese males were to shave their foreheads and braid their hair into a queue; those who refused were to be executed. As a popular saying put it, "Lose your hair or lose your head."[4]

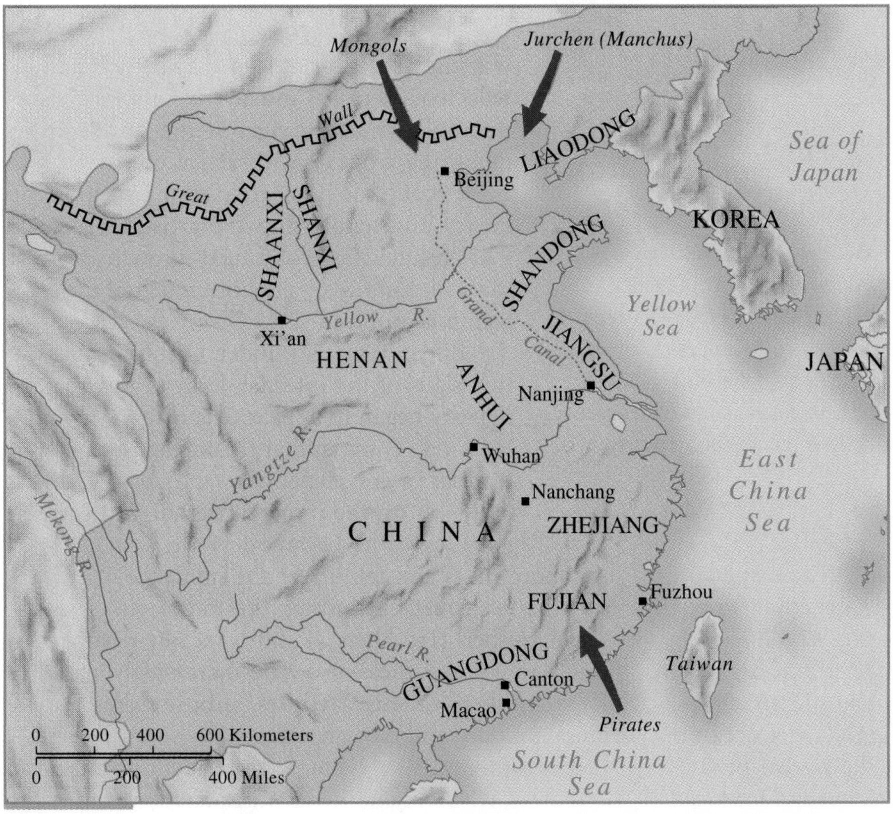

But the Manchus eventually proved to be more adept at adapting to Chinese conditions than their predecessors, the Mongols. Unlike the latter, who had tried to impose their own methods of ruling, the Manchus adopted the Chinese political system (although, as we shall see, they retained their distinct position within it) and were gradually accepted by most Chinese as the legitimate rulers of the country.

Like all of China's great dynasties, the Qing was blessed with a series of strong early rulers who pacified the country, rectified many of the most obvious social and economic inequities, and restored peace and prosperity. For the Ming dynasty, these strong emperors had been Hongwu and Yongle; under the Qing, they would be Kangxi (K'ang Hsi) and Qianlong (Ch'ien Lung). The two Qing monarchs ruled China for well over a century, from the middle of the seventeenth century to the end of the eighteenth, and were responsible for much of the greatness of Manchu China.

**MAP 16.1 China and Its Enemies During the Late Ming Era.** During the seventeenth century, the Ming dynasty faced challenges on two fronts, from China's traditional adversaries—nomadic groups north of the Great Wall—and from new arrivals—European merchants—who had begun to press for trading privileges along the southern coast. ? How do these threats differ from those faced by previous dynasties in China? **View an animated version of this map or related maps at http://history.wadsworth.com/duikerspielvogel05/**

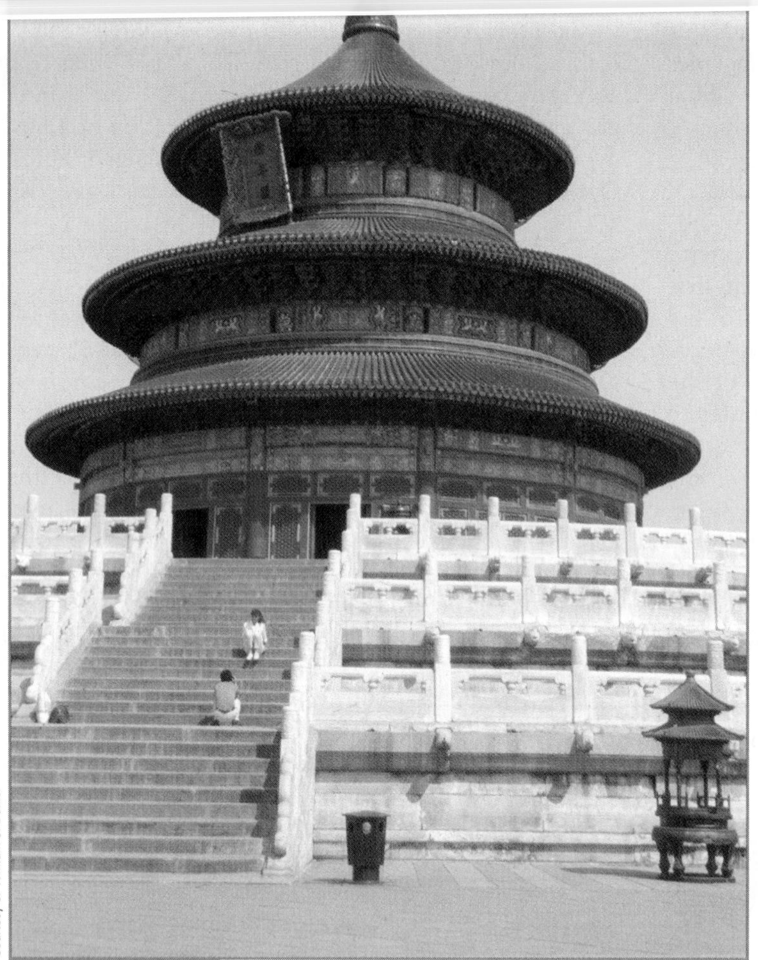


**The Temple of Heaven.** This temple, located in the capital city of Beijing, is one of the most important historical structures in China. Built in 1420 at the order of the Ming emperor Yongle, it served as the location for the emperor's annual ceremony appealing to Heaven for a good harvest. As a symbol of their efforts to continue the imperial traditions, the Manchu emperors embraced the practice as well. Yongle's temple burned to the ground in 1889 but was immediately rebuilt according to the original design.

**The Reign of Kangxi** Kangxi (1661–1722) was arguably the greatest ruler in Chinese history. Ascending to the throne at the age of seven, he was blessed with diligence, political astuteness, and a strong character and began to take charge of Qing administration while still an adolescent. During the six decades of his reign, Kangxi not only stabilized imperial rule by pacifying the restive peoples along the northern and western frontiers but also managed to make the dynasty acceptable to the general population. As an active patron of arts and letters, he cultivated the support of scholars through a number of major projects.

During Kangxi's reign, the activities of the Western missionaries, Dominicans and Franciscans as well as Jesuits, reached their height. An intellectually curious ruler like the Mughal emperor Akbar, Kangxi was quite tolerant of the Christians, and several Jesuit missionaries became influential at court. Several hundred court officials converted to Christianity, as did an estimated 300,000 ordinary Chinese. But the Christian effort was ultimately undermined by squabbling among the Western religious orders over the Jesuit policy of accommodating local beliefs and practices in order to facilitate conversion. The Jesuits had acquiesced to the emperor's insistence that traditional Confucian rituals such as ancestor veneration were civil ceremonies and thus could be undertaken by Christian converts. Jealous Dominicans and Franciscans complained to the pope, who issued an edict ordering all missionaries and converts to conform to the official orthodoxy set forth in Europe. At first, Kangxi attempted to resolve the problem by appealing directly to the Vatican, but the pope was uncompromising. After Kangxi's death, his successor began to suppress Christian activities throughout China.

**The Reign of Qianlong** Kangxi's achievements were carried on by his successors, Yongzheng (Yung Cheng, 1722–1736) and Qianlong (1736–1795). Like Kangxi, Qianlong was known for his diligence, tolerance, and intellectual curiosity, and he too combined vigorous military action against the unruly tribes along the frontier with active efforts to promote economic prosperity, administrative efficiency, and scholarship and artistic excellence. The result was continued growth for the Manchu Empire throughout much of the eighteenth century.

But it was also under Qianlong that the first signs of the internal decay of the Manchu dynasty began to appear. The clues were familiar ones. Qing military campaigns along the frontier were expensive and placed heavy demands on the imperial treasury. As the emperor aged, he became less astute in selecting his subordinates and fell under the influence of corrupt elements at court, including the notorious Manchu official Heshen (Ho Shen). Funds officially destined for military or other official use were increasingly siphoned off to Heshen or his favorites, arousing resentment among military and civilian officials.

Corruption at the center led inevitably to unrest in rural areas, where higher taxes, bureaucratic venality, and rising pressure on the land because of the growing population had produced economic hardship. The heart of the unrest was in central China, where discontented peasants who had recently been settled on infertile land launched a revolt known as the White Lotus Rebellion (1796–1804). The revolt was eventually suppressed but at great expense.

## Sixteen Confucian Commandments

Although the Qing dynasty was of foreign origin, its rulers found Confucian maxims convenient for maintaining the social order. In 1670, the great emperor Kangxi issued the Sacred Edict to popularize Confucian values among the common people. The edict was read publicly at periodic intervals in every village in the country and set the standard for behavior throughout the empire. Note the similarities and differences with the Japanese decree on p. 469 later in this chapter.

*In what ways does this set of commandments conform to the principles of State Confucianism? How do these standards compare with those being applied in Japan?*

### Kangxi's Sacred Edict

1. Esteem most highly filial piety and brotherly submission, in order to give due importance to the social relations.
2. Behave with generosity toward your kindred, in order to illustrate harmony and benignity.
3. Cultivate peace and concord in your neighborhoods, in order to prevent quarrels and litigations.
4. Recognize the importance of husbandry and the culture of the mulberry tree, in order to ensure a sufficiency of clothing and food.
5. Show that you prize moderation and economy, in order to prevent the lavish waste of your means.
6. Give weight to colleges and schools, in order to make correct the practice of the scholar.
7. Extirpate strange principles, in order to exalt the correct doctrine.
8. Lecture on the laws, in order to warn the ignorant and obstinate.
9. Elucidate propriety and yielding courtesy, in order to make manners and customs good.
10. Labor diligently at your proper callings, in order to stabilize the will of the people.
11. Instruct sons and younger brothers, in order to prevent them from doing what is wrong.
12. Put a stop to false accusations, in order to preserve the honest and good.
13. Warn against sheltering deserters, in order to avoid being involved in their punishment.
14. Fully remit your taxes, in order to avoid being pressed for payment.
15. Unite in hundreds and tithing, in order to put an end to thefts and robbery.
16. Remove enmity and anger, in order to show the importance due to the person and life.

**Qing Politics** One reason for the success of the Manchus was their ability to adapt to their new environment. They retained the Ming political system with relatively few changes. They also tried to establish their legitimacy as China's rightful rulers by stressing their devotion to the principles of Confucianism. Emperor Kangxi ostentatiously studied the Confucian classics and issued a "sacred edict" that proclaimed to the entire empire the importance of the moral values established by the master (see the box above).

Still, the Manchus, like the Mongols, were ethnically, linguistically, and culturally distinct from their subject population. The Qing attempted to cope with this reality by adopting a two-pronged strategy. On the one hand, the Manchus, representing less than 2 percent of the entire population, were legally defined as distinct from everyone else in China. The Manchu nobles retained their aristocratic privileges, while their economic base was protected by extensive landholdings and revenues provided from the state treasury. Other Manchus were assigned farmland and organized into military units, called **banners,** which were stationed as separate units in various strategic positions throughout China. These "bannermen" were the primary fighting force of the empire. Ethnic Chinese were prohibited from settling in Manchuria and were still compelled to wear their hair in a queue as a sign of submission to the ruling dynasty.

But while the Qing attempted to protect their distinct identity within an alien society, they also recognized the need to bring ethnic Chinese into the top ranks of imperial administration. Their solution was to create a system, known as **dyarchy,** in which all important administrative positions were shared equally by Chinese and Manchus. Of the six members of the grand secretariat, three were Manchu and three were Chinese. Each of the six ministries had an equal number of Chinese and Manchu members, and Manchus and Chinese also shared responsibilities at the provincial level. Below the provinces, Chinese were dominant. Although the system did not work perfectly, the Manchus' willingness to share power did win over the allegiance of many Chinese. Meanwhile, the Manchus themselves, despite official efforts to preserve their separate language and culture, were increasingly assimilated into Chinese civilization.

The new rulers also tinkered with the civil service examination system. In an effort to make it more equitable, quotas were established for each major ethnic group and each province to prevent the positions from being monopolized by candidates from certain provinces in central China that had traditionally produced large numbers of officials (see the box on p. 454). In practice, however, the examination system probably became less equitable during the Manchu era because increasingly positions were assigned to candidates who had purchased their degree

## A Last Will and Testament

The Ming dynasty official Yang Jisheng is remembered by historians of China primarily for his admirable courage in speaking out against the corruption of powerful forces at the imperial court. The reward for his courage was torture and eventual execution. On learning of his fate, Yang wrote from prison to his family on how to comport themselves in a proper Confucian manner. His "Final Instructions," as they were to be known, would be widely circulated during the late Ming and early Qing dynasties as a model for managing family affairs.

First, he pleaded with his wife not to commit suicide after his execution, a common practice at the time to proclaim a widow's fidelity and chastity. Unfortunately, on the day of his execution, she hanged herself in the town marketplace. Second, he advised his two sons to devote themselves to studying for the civil service examination in preparation for a prestigious official career. Following the common practice of his day, he counseled them to focus on memorization of text rather than on absorbing the inner message of the classics, a widely followed tendency that reduced the essential teachings of Confucius and his followers to a dry scholasticism.

*How does the author of this letter advise his sons to prepare for a career in the bureaucracy? How does he use his own official career as an example of proper behavior?*

### Yang Jisheng, "Final Instructions"

**To the Wife**

My only regret will be that my two sons are both young. In studying they have both made progress, and in the future they will both succeed. I only fear that [my death will] adversely affect their [future]. My one daughter is not yet married; without someone to teach, guide, and take care of her, I am afraid she will be ridiculed. If I should happen to die, I leave you behind to teach and guide my sons and daughter into adulthood. If each is able to complete their household and establish their objectives, then it will be as if I am still alive . . . .

[My concubine] Erzhen is still young and moreover has no children. After I have died, see that she marries someone else. Give her an allotment of clothing and jewelry. . . . You must not have her stay at home and maintain widowhood. . . .

As for second elder sister and fourth elder sister, I'd like you always to look after them. As for fifth elder sister and sixth elder sister, when our father's concubine dies you should also become close to them. . . . The remaining household affairs I am sure you will deal with well.

**To the Sons**

You two are young in years. I fear that if you come to the notice of slick, sleazy people, they will try to tempt and defraud you. Some will ask you to dinner, some will tempt you to gamble, some will present you with objects you desire, some will tempt you with beautiful women. As soon as you enter their snare, you will suffer losses to them. Not only will the patrimony be completely dissipated, they'll also keep you from becoming a proper person. . . .

Preparing for the examinations is simply a matter of memorizing a great deal and composing a great deal. From the basic classics of the *Four Books,* memorize one thousand selections and read one hundred essays, one hundred policy inquiries, fifty declarations, and eighty judgments. If you have extra energy, read one hundred selections from the Five Classics and one hundred sections of better ancient prose. Every day compose one section of text, and every month write three essays and two policy inquiries. It is crucial to remember that you must not pass a single day without a teacher. If you have no teacher, then you have no strictness and no fear. . . . If you pass the local examinations or become a *jinshi* [obtain a doctorate], considering my bitter [experiences] it is best if you do not become an official. If you do become an official, you must be upright and honest, loyal and trustworthy, wholeheartedly serving the country to the best of your ability.

rather than competing through the system. Moreover, positions were becoming harder to obtain because their number did not rise fast enough to match the unprecedented increase in population under Qing rule.

**China on the Eve of the Western Onslaught** In some ways, China was at the height of its power and glory in the mid-eighteenth century. But as we have seen, it was also during this period that the first signs of the decay of the Qing dynasty began to appear.

Unfortunately for China, the decline of the Qing occurred just as China's modest relationship with the West was about to give way to a new era of military confrontation and increased pressure for trade. The first problems came in the north, where Russian traders seeking skins and furs began to penetrate the region between Siberian Russia and Manchuria. Earlier the Ming dynasty had attempted to deal with the Russians by the traditional method of placing them in a tributary relationship and playing them off against other non-Chinese groups in the area. But the tsar refused to play by Chinese rules. His envoys to Beijing ignored the tribute system and refused to perform the kowtow (the ritual of prostration and touching the forehead to the ground), the classical symbol of fealty demanded of all foreign ambassadors to the Chinese court. Formal diplomatic relations were finally established in 1689, when the Treaty of Nerchinsk (negotiated with the aid of Jesuit missionaries resident at the

**CHRONOLOGY China During the Early Modern Era**

| | |
|---|---|
| Portuguese arrive in southern China | 1514 |
| Matteo Ricci arrives in China | 1601 |
| Li Zicheng occupies Beijing | 1644 |
| Manchus seize China | 1644 |
| Reign of Kangxi | 1661–1722 |
| Treaty of Nerchinsk | 1689 |
| First English trading post at Canton | 1699 |
| Reign of Qianlong | 1736–1795 |
| Lord Macartney's mission to China | 1793 |
| White Lotus Rebellion | 1796–1804 |

Qing court) settled the boundary dispute and provided for regular trade between the two countries. Through such arrangements, the Manchus were able not only to pacify the northern frontier but also to extend their rule over Xinjiang and Tibet to the west and southwest (see Map 16.2). In the meantime, tributary relations were established with such neighboring countries as Korea, Burma, Vietnam, and Ayuthaya.

Dealing with the foreigners who arrived by sea was more difficult. By the end of the seventeenth century, the English had replaced the Portuguese as the dominant force in European trade. Operating through the East India Company, which served as both a trading unit and the administrator of English territories in Asia, the English established their first trading post at Canton in 1699. Over the next decades, trade with China, notably the export of tea and silk to England, increased rapidly. To limit

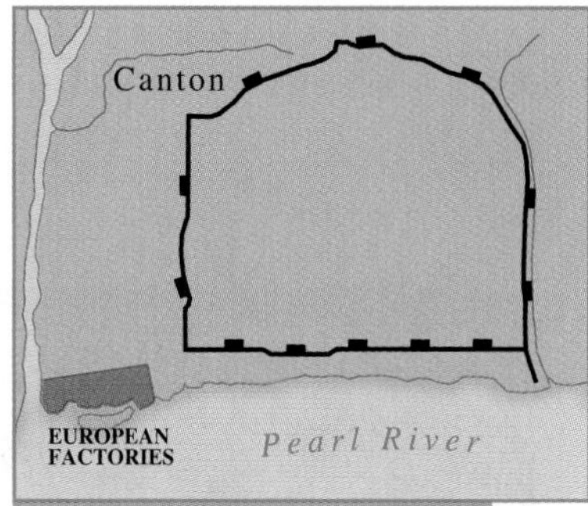


**Canton in the Eighteenth Century**

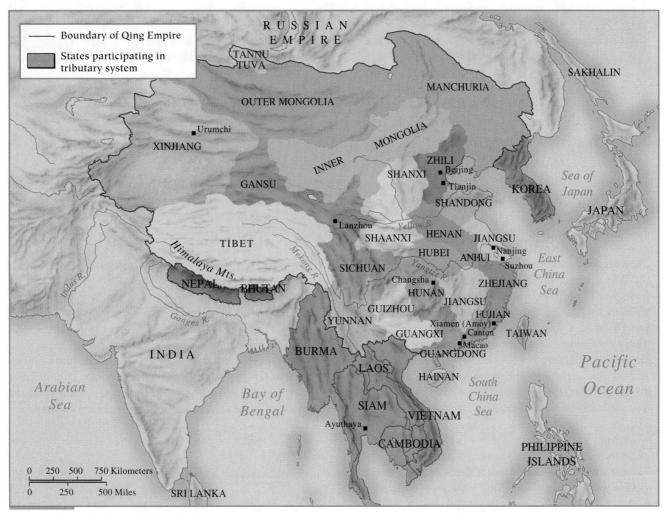

**MAP 16.2 The Qing Empire in the Eighteenth Century.** The boundaries of the Chinese Empire at the height of the Qing dynasty in the eighteenth century are shown on this map. What areas were linked in tributary status to the Chinese empire? **View an animated version of this map or related maps at** http://history.wadsworth.com/duikerspielvogel05/

Art Archive/Marine Museum Stockholm/Dagli Orti (A)

**European Warehouses at Canton.** Aggravated by the growing presence of foreigners in the eighteenth century, the Chinese court severely restricted the movement of European traders in China. They were permitted to live only in a compound near Canton during the seven months of the trading season and could go into the city only three times a month. In this painting, the Dutch and British flags fly over the warehouses and residences of the foreign community, while Chinese sampans and junks sit anchored in the river.

contact between Chinese and Europeans, the Qing licensed Chinese trading firms at Canton to be the exclusive conduit for trade with the West. Eventually, the Qing confined the Europeans to a small island just outside the city walls and permitted them to reside there only from October through March.

For a while, the British tolerated this system, which brought considerable profit to the East India Company and its shareholders. But by the end of the eighteenth century, the British had begun to demand access to other cities along the Chinese coast and that the country be opened to British manufactured goods. The British government and traders alike were restive at the uneven balance of trade between the two countries, which forced the British to ship vast amounts of silver bullion to China in exchange for its silk, porcelain, and tea. In 1793, a mission under Lord Macartney visited Beijing to press for liberalization of trade restrictions. A compromise was reached on the kowtow (Macartney was permitted to bend on one knee, as was the British custom), but Qianlong expressed no interest in British manufactured products (see the box on p. 457). An exasperated Macartney compared the Chinese Empire to "an old, crazy, first-rate man-of-war" that had once awed its neighbors "merely by her bulk and appearance" but was now destined under incompetent leadership to be "dashed to pieces on the shore."[5] With his contemptuous dismissal of the British request, the emperor had inadvertently sowed the seeds for a century of humiliation.

## Changing China

During the Ming and Qing dynasties, China remained a predominantly agricultural society; nearly 85 percent of its people were farmers. But although most Chinese still lived in rural villages, the economy was undergoing a number of changes that have led some historians to suggest that China, under other circumstances, might have experienced an industrial revolution as in the West. In this view, the arrival of Western imperialism in the nineteenth century not only failed to stimulate economic change but may actually have hindered it.

### The Population Explosion

In the first place, the center of gravity was continuing to shift steadily from the north to the south. In the early centuries of Chinese civilization, the bulk of the population had been located along the Yellow River. Smaller settlements were located along the Yangtze and in the mountainous re-

## The Tribute System in Action

In 1793, the British emissary Lord Macartney visited the Qing Empire to request the opening of formal diplomatic and trading relations between his country and China. Emperor Qianlong's reply, addressed to King George III of Britain, illustrates how the imperial court in Beijing viewed the world. King George could not have been pleased. The document provides a good example of the complacency with which the Celestial Empire viewed the world beyond its borders.

*What reasons does the emperor give for refusing Macartney's request to have a permanent British ambassador in Beijing? How does the tribute system differ from the principles of international relations as practiced in the West?*

### A Decree of Emperor Qianlong

An Imperial Edict to the King of England: You, O King, are so inclined toward our civilization that you have sent a special envoy across the seas to bring to our Court your memorial of congratulations on the occasion of my birthday and to present your native products as an expression of your thoughtfulness. On perusing your memorial, so simply worded and sincerely conceived, I am impressed by your genuine respectfulness and friendliness and greatly pleased.

As to the request made in your memorial, O King, to send one of your nationals to stay at the Celestial Court to take care of your country's trade with China, this is not in harmony with the state system of our dynasty and will definitely not be permitted. Traditionally people of the European nations who wished to render some service under the Celestial Court have been permitted to come to the capital. But after their arrival they are obliged to wear Chinese court costumes, are placed in a certain residence, and are never allowed to return to their own countries. This is the established rule of the Celestial Dynasty with which presumably you, O King, are familiar. Now you, O King, wish to send one of your nationals to live in the capital, but he is not like the Europeans who come to Peking as Chinese employees, live there, and never return home again, nor can he be allowed to go and come and maintain any correspondence. This is indeed a useless undertaking.

Moreover the territory under the control of the Celestial Court is very large and wide. There are well-established regulations governing tributary envoys from the outer states to Peking [Beijing], giving them provisions (of food and traveling expenses) by our post-houses and limiting their going and coming. There has never been a precedent for letting them do whatever they like. Now if you, O King, wish to have a representative in Peking, his language will be unintelligible and his dress different from the regulations; there is no place to accommodate him. . . .

The Celestial Court has pacified and possessed the territory within the four seas. Its sole aim is to do its utmost to achieve good government and to manage political affairs, attaching no value to strange jewels and precious objects. The various articles presented by you, O King, this time are accepted by my special order to the office in charge of such functions in consideration of the offerings having come from a long distance with sincere good wishes. As a matter of fact, the virtue and prestige of the Celestial Dynasty having spread far and wide, the kings of the myriad nations come by land and sea with all sorts of precious things. Consequently there is nothing we lack, as your principal envoy and others have themselves observed. We have never set much store on strange or ingenious objects, nor do we need any more of your country's manufactures. . . .

gions of the south, but the administrative and economic center of gravity was clearly in the north. By the Song period, however, that emphasis had already begun to shift drastically as a result of climatic changes, deforestation, and continuing pressure from nomads in the Gobi Desert. By the early Qing, the economic breadbasket of China was located along the Yangtze River or in the mountains to the south. One concrete indication of this shift occurred during the Ming dynasty, when Emperor Yongle ordered the renovation of the Grand Canal to facilitate the shipment of rice from the Yangtze delta to the food-starved north.

Moreover, the population was beginning to increase rapidly. For centuries, China's population had remained within a range of 50 to 100 million, rising in times of peace and prosperity and falling in periods of foreign invasion and internal anarchy. During the Ming and the early Qing, however, the population increased from an estimated 70 to 80 million in 1390 to over 300 million at the end of the eighteenth century. There were probably several reasons for this population increase: the relatively long period of peace and stability under the early Qing; the introduction of new crops from the Americas, including peanuts, sweet potatoes, and maize; and the planting of a new species of faster-growing rice from Southeast Asia (see the comparative essay "The Population Explosion" on p. 458).

Of course, this population increase meant much greater pressure on the land, smaller farms, and a razor-thin margin of safety in case of climatic disaster. The imperial court attempted to deal with the problem through a variety of means, most notably by preventing the concentration of land in the hands of wealthy landowners. Nevertheless, by the eighteenth century, almost all the land that could be irrigated was already under cultivation, and the problems of rural hunger and landlessness became increasingly serious.

## Population Explosion

experienced a dramatic growth in population. In Europe, the population grew from 120 million people to almost 200 million by 1800; China, from less than 200 million to 300 million during the same period.

Four factors were important in causing this population explosion. First, better growing conditions, made possible by an improvement in climate, affected wide areas of the world and enabled people to produce more food. Summers in both China and Europe were warmer beginning in the early eighteenth century. Second, by the eighteenth century, people had begun to develop immunities to the epidemic diseases that had caused widespread loss of life between 1500 and 1700. The increase in travel by ship after 1500 had led to devastating epidemics. For example, the arrival of Europeans in Mexico led to smallpox, measles, and chickenpox among a native population that had no immunities to European diseases. In 1500, between 11 and 20 million people lived in the area of Mexico; by 1650, only 1.5 million remained. Gradually, however, people developed immunities to these diseases.

A third factor in the population increase came from new food sources. As a result of the Columbian exchange (see the box on p. 374) American food crops, such as corn, potatoes, and sweet potatoes,

species of rice from Southeast Asia that had a shorter harvest cycle than that of existing varieties. These new foods provided additional sources of nutrition that enabled more people to live for a longer time. At the same time, land development and canal building in the eighteenth century also enabled government authorities to move food supplies to areas threatened with crop failure and famine.

Finally, the use of new weapons based on gunpowder allowed states to control larger territories and ensure a new degree of order. The early rulers of the Qing dynasty, for example, pacified the Chinese Empire and ensured a long period of peace and stability. Absolute monarchs achieved similar goals in a number of European states. Less violence led to fewer deaths at the same time that an increase in food supplies and a decrease in deaths from diseases were occurring, thus making possible in the eighteenth century the beginning of the world population explosion that persists to this day.

Werner Forman Archive

**Festival of the Yam.** The spread of a few major food crops made possible new sources of nutrition to feed more people. The importance of the yam to the Ashanti people of West Africa is evident in this celebration of a yam festival at harvest time in 1817.

## Seeds of Industrialization

Another change that took place during the early modern period in China was the steady growth of manufacturing and commerce. Taking advantage of the long era of peace and prosperity, merchants and manufacturers began to expand their operations beyond their immediate provinces. Commercial networks began to operate on a regional and sometimes even a national basis as trade in silk, metal and wood products, porcelain, cotton goods, and cash crops like cotton and tobacco developed rapidly. Foreign trade also expanded as Chinese merchants set up extensive contacts with countries in Southeast Asia.

Although this rise in industrial and commercial activity resembles the changes occurring in western Europe, China and Europe differed in several key ways. In the first place, members of the bourgeoisie in China were not as independent as their European counterparts. In China, trade and manufacturing remained under the firm control of the state. In addition, political and social prejudices against commercial activity remained strong. Reflecting an ancient preference for agriculture over manufacturing and trade, the state levied heavy taxes on manufacturing and commerce while attempting to keep agricultural taxes low.

One of the consequences of these differences was a growing technological gap between China and Europe. The Chinese reaction to European clockmaking techniques provides an example. In the early seventeenth century, the Jesuit Matteo Ricci introduced advanced European clocks driven by weights or springs. The emperor was fascinated and found the clocks more reliable than Chinese methods of keeping time. Over the next decades, European timepieces became a popular novelty at court, but the Chinese expressed little curiosity about the technology involved, provoking one European to remark that playthings like cuckoo clocks "will be received here with much greater interest than scientific instruments or *objets d'art*."[6]

City of Suzhou, China

**Shopping for Souvenirs in Suzhou.** Chinese block-print artists never obtained the status and popularity of their counterparts in Japan, since elite artists in Qing China considered such paintings an inferior genre. Chinese commercial artists, however, were more receptive to the technique, borrowing the use of perspective from the West, as seen in this eighteenth-century print of Suzhou. A busy port and a favorite tourist destination, Suzhou attracted urban Chinese who were eager to collect printed scenes of cities, beautiful women, or illustrated themes from Chinese literature in a fashionable and exotic style.

## Daily Life in Qing China

Despite the changes in the economy, daily life in China under the Ming and early Qing dynasties continued to follow traditional patterns.

**The Family** As in earlier periods, Chinese society was organized around the family. As before, the ideal family unit in Qing China was the joint family, in which as many as three or even four generations lived under the same roof. When sons married, they brought their wives to live with them in the family homestead. Prosperous families would add a separate section to the house to accommodate the new family unit. Unmarried daughters would also remain in the house. Aging parents and grandparents remained under the same roof until they died and were cared for by younger members of the household. This ideal did not always correspond to reality, however, since many families did not possess sufficient land to support a large household. One historian has estimated that only about 40 percent of Chinese families actually lived in joint families.

The family retained its importance in early Qing times for much the same reasons as in earlier times. As a labor-intensive society based primarily on the cultivation of rice, China needed large families to help with the harvest and to provide security for parents too old to work in the fields. Sons were particularly prized, not only because they had strong backs but also because they would raise their own families under the parental roof. With few opportunities for employment outside the family, sons had little choice but to remain with their parents and help on the land. Within the family, the oldest male was king, and his wishes theoretically had to be obeyed by all family members. These values were reiterated in Emperor Kangxi's Sacred Edict, which listed filial piety and loyalty to the family as its first two maxims (see the box on p. 453).

For many Chinese, the effects of these values were most apparent in the choice of a marriage partner. Marriages were normally arranged for the benefit of the family, often by a go-between, and the groom and bride were usually not consulted. Frequently, they did not meet until the marriage ceremony. Under such conditions, love was clearly a secondary consideration. In fact, it was often viewed as detrimental, since it inevitably distracted the attention of the husband and wife from their primary responsibility to the larger family unit.

Although this emphasis on filial piety might seem to represent a blatant disregard for individual rights, the obligations were not all on the side of the children. The father was expected to provide support for his wife and children and, like the ruler, was supposed to treat those in his care with respect and compassion. All too often, however, the male head of the family was able to exact his privileges without performing his responsibilities in return.

Beyond the joint family was the clan. Sometimes called a lineage, a clan was an extended kinship unit consisting of dozens or even hundreds of joint and nuclear families linked together by a clan council of elders and a variety of other common social and religious functions. The clan served a number of useful purposes. Some clans possessed lands that could be rented out to poorer families, or richer families within the clan might provide land for the poor. Since there was no general state-supported educational system, sons of poor families might be invited to study in a school established in the home of a more prosperous relative. If the young man succeeded in becoming an official, he would be expected to provide favors and prestige for the clan as a whole.

Like joint families, clans were not universal, and millions of Chinese had none. The clans apparently originated in the great landed families of the Tang period and managed to survive despite periodic efforts by the imperial court to weaken and destroy them. In many cases, clan solidarity was weakened by intralineage conflicts or differing levels of status and economic achievement. Nevertheless, in the early modern period, they were still an influential force at the local level and were particularly prevalent in the south.

## A Chinese Woman Artist

During the early Qing era, increasing numbers of women from gentry families became skilled painters, studying in the privacy of their homes, as they were not expected to practice their art in public. Some were taught by other family members or by distant relatives, who were referred to as the "teachers of the inner chambers." Often a shared interest in art created a strong bond between a married couple, as witnessed here in this son's account of his mother's artistic venture.

*Why is the career of Chen Shu an unusual one in Qing China? How does her son explain the reasons why she was permitted to paint?*

### Chen Shu, *View from the Jade Terrace*

As a child she learned to read by asking the boys of her clan to pass along what they learned in school. Her strict mother initially frowned on such unfeminine conduct and forbade her to take time away from her needlework to practice with the brush. Undeterred, Chen Shu one day made a copy of a famous painting hanging on the wall of her father's study. For this she was beaten, but a god intervened by appearing to her mother in a dream and saying: "I have given your daughter a brush. Someday she will be famous. How can you forbid it?" This tale served to underscore the idea that Chen Shu was destined for great achievement and perhaps was used to explain her devotion to pursuits regarded by some as unnecessary, even undesirable, for women.

Chen Shu married into the Qian family . . . becoming the second wife of Qian Lunguang. Qian did not distinguish himself as an official, but he did earn a modest reputation as a calligrapher and poet. Shared artistic interests were a part of the couple's relationship, and Qian occasionally added poetic inscriptions to Chen's paintings. . . .

The Qian family associated with some of the leading scholars of the area and took pleasure in entertaining guests, evidently in a manner beyond the family's means. To defray the costs of these gatherings, Chen Shu pawned her clothing and sold her jewelry and paintings. . . .

The shape of Chen Shu's artistic career was determined by her primary roles as wife and mother. From the 1680s through the first decade of the seventeenth century, much of her time was devoted to caring for her four children . . . , parents-in-law, and mother. . . . Chen Shu undoubtedly continued to paint during these busy years, but her last three decades seem to have been her most productive; her surviving dated paintings were executed between 1700 and 1735.

In 1721 Qian Chenqun, her eldest son, . . . received an appointment to the Hanlin Academy. . . . When her son asked the [imperial] court's permission to visit her in 1735, she nobly insisted that he stay at his post and . . . set out to join him in the capital. . . . She was then seventy-five years old. . . . Late in the spring of the following year she died in Beijing. . . .

In the course of his successful career under the Qianlong emperor, Qian Chenqun frequently presented paintings by his mother to the throne. The emperor received Chen Shu's works with pleasure and wrote on many of them with his characteristic lack of restraint.

**The Role of Women** In traditional China, the role of women had always been inferior to that of men. A sixteenth-century Spanish visitor to South China observed that Chinese women were "very secluded and virtuous, and it was a very rare thing for us to see a woman in the cities and large towns, unless it was an old crone."[7] Women were more visible, he said, in rural areas, where they frequently could be seen working in the fields.

The concept of female inferiority had deep roots in Chinese history. This view was embodied in the belief that only a male would carry on sacred family rituals and that men alone had the talent to govern others. Only males could aspire to a career in government or scholarship. Within the family system, the wife was clearly subordinated to the husband. Legally, she could not divorce her husband or inherit property. The husband, however, could divorce his wife if she did not produce male heirs, or he could take a second wife as well as a concubine for his pleasure. A widow suffered especially, because she had to either raise her children on a single income or fight off her former husband's greedy relatives, who would coerce her to remarry since, according to the law, they would then inherit all of her previous property and her original dowry.

Female children were less desirable because of their limited physical strength and because their parents would be required to pay a dowry to the parents of their future husband. Female children normally did not receive an education, and in times of scarcity when food was in short supply, daughters might even be put to death.

Though women were clearly inferior to men in theory, this was not always the case in practice. Capable women often compensated for their legal inferiority by playing a strong role within the family. Women were often in charge of educating the children and handled the family budget. Some privileged women also received training in the Confucian classics, although their schooling was generally for a shorter time and less rigorous than that of their male counterparts. A few produced significant works of art and poetry (see the box above).

All in all, however, life for women in traditional China was undoubtedly difficult. In Chinese novels, women were treated as scullery maids or love objects. They were frequently under the domination of both their husband and their mother-in-law, and in some cases the bullying was so brutal that suicide seemed to be the only way out.

## Cultural Developments

During the late Ming and the early Qing dynasties, traditional culture in China reached new heights of achievement. With the rise of a wealthy urban class, the demand for art, porcelain, textiles, and literature was at a premium.

**The Rise of the Chinese Novel** During the Ming dynasty, a new form of literature arose that eventually evolved into the modern Chinese novel. Although considered less respectable than poetry and nonfiction prose, these groundbreaking works (often written anonymously or under pseudonyms) were enormously popular, especially among well-to-do urban dwellers.

Written in a colloquial style, the new fiction was characterized by a realism that resulted in vivid portraits of Chinese society. Many of the stories sympathized with society's downtrodden—often helpless maidens—and dealt with such crucial issues as love, money, marriage, and power. Adding to the realism were sexually explicit passages that depicted the private side of Chinese life. Readers delighted in sensuous tales that, no matter how pornographic, always professed a moral lesson; the villains were punished and the virtuous rewarded. During the more puritanical Qing era, a number of the more erotic works were censored or banned and found refuge in Japan, where several have recently been rediscovered by scholars.

*Gold Vase Plum,* known in English translation as *The Golden Lotus,* presents a cutting exposé of the decadent aspects of late Ming society. Considered by many the first realistic social novel—preceding its European counterparts by two centuries—*The Golden Lotus* depicts the depraved life of a wealthy landlord who cruelly manipulates those around him for sex, money, and power. In a rare exception in Chinese fiction, the villain is not punished for his evil ways; justice is served instead by the misfortunes that befall his descendants.

*The Dream of the Red Chamber* is generally considered China's most distinguished popular novel. Published in 1791, some 150 years after *The Golden Lotus,* it tells of the tragic love between two young people caught in the financial and moral disintegration of a powerful Chinese clan. The hero and the heroine, both sensitive and spoiled, represent the inevitable decline of the Chia family and come to an equally inevitable tragic end, she in death and he in an unhappy marriage to another.

**The Art of the Ming and the Qing** During the Ming and the early Qing, China produced its last outpouring of traditional artistic brilliance. Although most of the creative work was modeled on past examples, the art of this period is impressive for its technical perfection and breathtaking quantity.

In architecture, the most outstanding example is the Imperial City in Beijing. Building on the remnants of the palace of the Yuan dynasty, the Ming emperor Yongle ordered renovations when he returned the capital to Beijing in 1421. Succeeding emperors continued to add to the palace, but the basic design has not changed since the Ming era. Surrounded by high walls, the immense compound is divided into a maze of private apartments and offices and

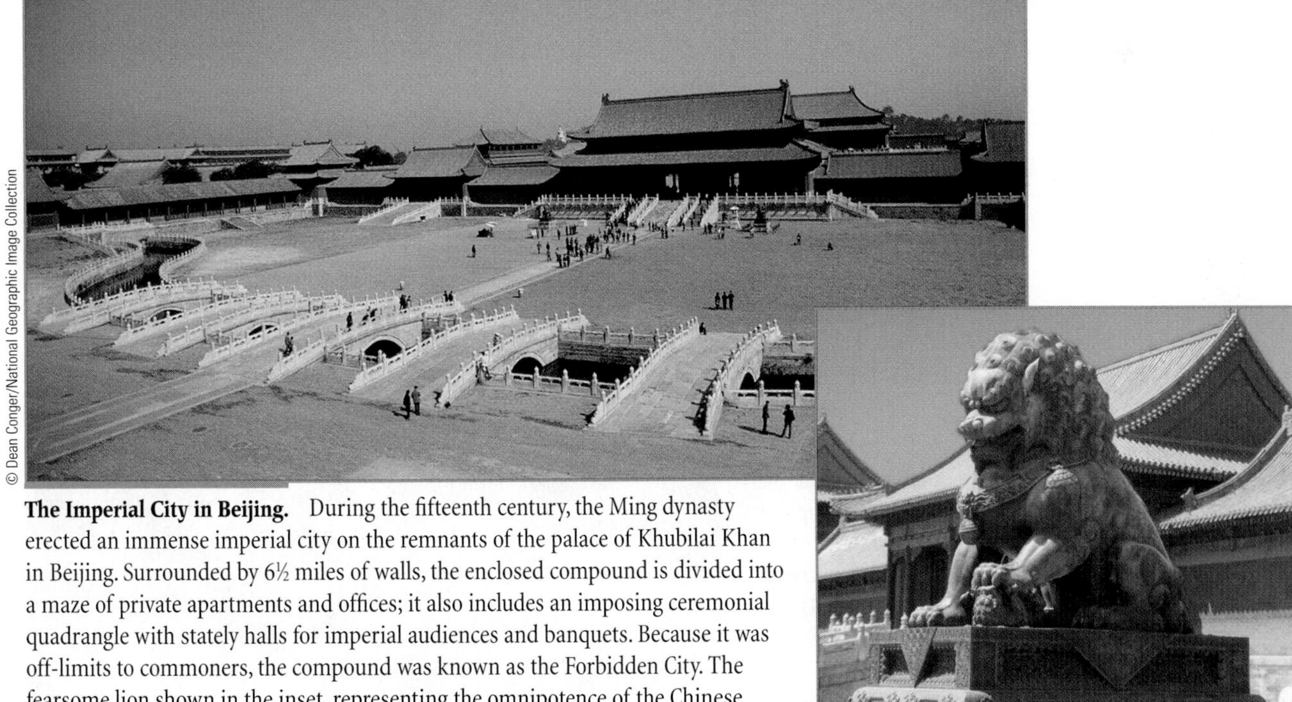





**The Imperial City in Beijing.** During the fifteenth century, the Ming dynasty erected an immense imperial city on the remnants of the palace of Khubilai Khan in Beijing. Surrounded by 6½ miles of walls, the enclosed compound is divided into a maze of private apartments and offices; it also includes an imposing ceremonial quadrangle with stately halls for imperial audiences and banquets. Because it was off-limits to commoners, the compound was known as the Forbidden City. The fearsome lion shown in the inset, representing the omnipotence of the Chinese Empire, guards the entrance to the private apartments of the palace.

**Beijing Under the Ming and the Manchus, 1400–1911**

an imposing rectangular quadrangle with a series of stately halls for imperial audiences and banquets. The grandiose scale, richly carved marble, spacious gardens, and graceful upturned roofs also contribute to the splendor of the "Forbidden City."

The decorative arts flourished in this period, especially the intricately carved lacquerware and the boldly shaped and colored cloisonné, a type of enamelwork in which colored areas are separated by thin metal bands. Silk production reached its zenith, and the best-quality silks were highly prized in Europe, where chinoiserie, as Chinese art of all kinds was called, was in vogue. Perhaps the most famous of all the achievements of the Ming era was its blue-and-white porcelain, still prized by collectors throughout the world. Of unsurpassed luminosity, this porcelain was used by Ming emperors to promote the prestige of their opulent and powerful empire. One variety caused such a sensation in the Netherlands that the Dutch began to manufacture their own blue-and-white porcelain at a new factory set up in Delft.

During the Qing dynasty, artists produced great quantities of paintings, mostly for home consumption. The wealthy city of Yangzhou on the Grand Canal emerged as an active artistic center. Inside the Forbidden City in Beijing, court painters worked alongside Jesuit artists and experimented with Western techniques. European art, however, did not greatly influence Chinese painting at this time; some dismissed it as mere "craftsmanship." Scholarly painters and the literati totally rejected foreign techniques and became obsessed with traditional Chinese styles. As a result, Qing painting became progressively more repetitive and stale. Ironically, the Qing dynasty thus represents both the apogee of traditional Chinese art and the beginning of its decline.

# Tokugawa Japan

At the end of the fifteenth century, the traditional Japanese system was at a point of near anarchy. With the decline in the authority of the Ashikaga shogunate at Kyoto, clan rivalries had exploded into an era of warring states similar to the period of the same name in Zhou dynasty China. Even at the local level, power was frequently diffuse. The typical daimyo (great lord) domain had often become little more than a coalition of fief-holders held together by a loose allegiance to the manor lord. Prince Shotoku's dream of a united Japan appeared to be only a distant memory (see Chapter 11). In actuality, Japan was on the verge of an extended era of national unification and peace under the rule of its greatest shogunate, the Tokugawa.

## The Three Great Unifiers

The process began in the mid-sixteenth century with the emergence of three very powerful political figures, Oda Nobunaga (1568–1582), Toyotomi Hideyoshi (1582–1598), and Tokugawa Ieyasu (1598–1616). In 1568, Oda Nobunaga, the son of a samurai and a military commander under the Ashikaga shogunate, seized the imperial capital of Kyoto and placed the reigning shogun under his

Courtesy of William J. Duiker

**World-Class China Ware.** Ming porcelain was noted throughout the world for its delicate blue-and-white floral decorations. The blue coloring was produced with cobalt that had originally been brought from the Middle East along the Silk Road and was known in China as "Mohammedan blue." In the early seventeenth century, the first Ming ware arrived in the Netherlands, where it was called *kraak* because it had been loaded on two Portuguese ships known as carracks seized by the Dutch fleet. It took Dutch artisans over a century to learn how to produce a porcelain as fine as the examples brought from China.

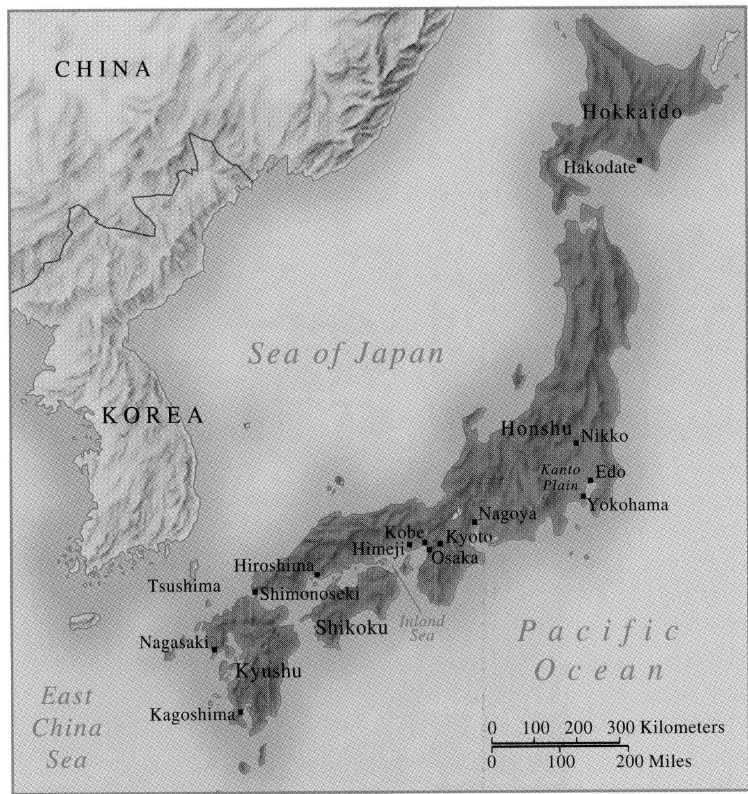


**MAP 16.3** **Tokugawa Japan.** This map shows the Japanese islands during the long era of the Tokugawa shogunate. Key cities, including the shogun's capital of Edo, are shown. ? Where was the imperial court located? **View an animated version of this map or related maps at** http://history.wadsworth.com/ duikerspielvogel05/

domination. During the next few years, the brutal and ambitious Nobunaga attempted to consolidate his rule throughout the central plains by defeating his rivals and suppressing the power of the Buddhist estates, but he was killed by one of his generals in 1582 before the process was complete. He was succeeded by Toyotomi Hideyoshi, a farmer's son who had worked his way up through the ranks to become a military commander. Originally lacking a family name of his own, he eventually adopted the name Toyotomi ("abundant provider") to embellish his reputation for improving the material standards of his domain. Hideyoshi located his capital at Osaka, where he built a castle to accommodate his headquarters, and gradually extended his power outward to the southern islands of Shikoku and Kyushu (see Map 16.3). By 1590, he had persuaded most of the daimyo on the Japanese islands to accept his authority and created a national currency. Then he invaded Korea in an abortive effort to export his rule to the Asian mainland.

Despite their efforts, however, neither Nobunaga nor Hideyoshi was able to eliminate the power of the local daimyo. Both were compelled to form alliances with some daimyo in order to destroy other more powerful rivals. At the conclusion of his conquests in 1590, Toyotomi Hideyoshi could claim to be the supreme proprietor of all registered lands in areas under his authority. But he then reassigned those lands as fiefs to the local daimyo, who declared their allegiance to him. The daimyo in turn began to pacify the countryside, carrying out extensive "sword hunts" to disarm the population and attracting samurai to their service. The Japanese tradition of decentralized rule had not been overcome.

After Hideyoshi's death in 1598, Tokugawa Ieyasu, the powerful daimyo of Edo (modern Tokyo), moved to fill the vacuum. Neither Hideyoshi nor Oda Nobunaga had claimed the title of shogun, but Ieyasu named himself shogun in 1603, initiating the most powerful and long-lasting of all Japanese shogunates. The Tokugawa rulers completed the restoration of central authority begun by Nobunaga and Hideyoshi and remained in power until 1868, when a war dismantled the entire system. As a contemporary phrased it, "Oda pounds the national rice cake, Hideyoshi kneads it, and in the end Ieyasu sits down and eats it."[8]

## Opening to the West

The unification of Japan took place almost simultaneously with the coming of the Europeans. Portuguese traders sailing in a Chinese junk that may have been blown off course by a typhoon had landed on the islands in 1543. Within a few years, Portuguese ships were stopping at Japanese ports on a regular basis to take part in the regional trade between Japan, China, and Southeast Asia. The first Jesuit missionary, Francis Xavier, arrived in 1549.

Initially, the visitors were welcomed. The curious Japanese (the Japanese were "very desirous of knowledge," said Francis Xavier) were fascinated by tobacco, clocks, spectacles, and other European goods, and local daimyo were interested in purchasing all types of European weapons and armaments (see the box on p. 465). Oda Nobunaga and Toyotomi Hideyoshi found the new firearms helpful in defeating their enemies and unifying the islands. The effect on Japanese military architecture was particularly striking as local lords began to erect castles on the European model. Many of these castles, such as Hideyoshi's castle at Osaka, still exist today.

The missionaries also had some success. Though confused by misleading translations of sacred concepts in both cultures (Francis Xavier was notoriously poor at learning foreign languages), they converted a number of local daimyo, some of whom may have been motivated in part by the desire for commercial profits. By the end of the sixteenth century, thousands of Japanese in the southernmost islands of Kyushu and Shikoku had become Christians. One converted daimyo ceded the superb natural harbor of the modern city of Nagasaki to the Society of Jesus, which proceeded to use the new settlement for

Courtesy of William J. Duiker

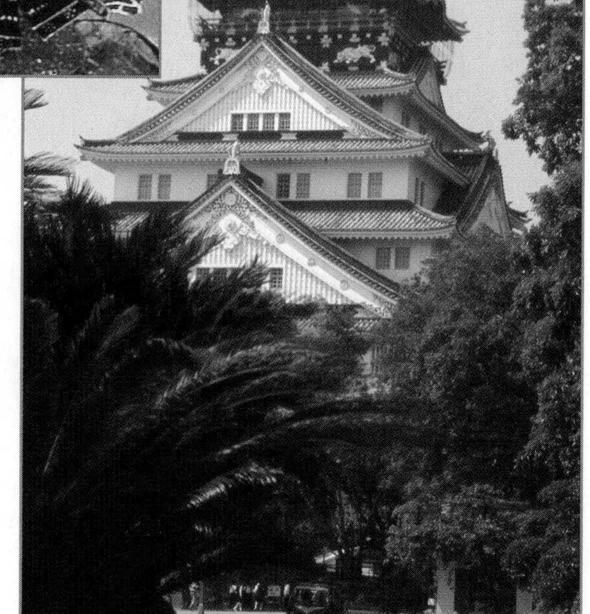

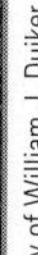

Courtesy of William J. Duiker

**The Siege of Osaka Castle.** In imitation of European castle architecture, the Japanese perfected a new type of fortress-palace in the early seventeenth century. Strategically placed high on a hilltop, constructed of heavy stone with tiny windows, and fortified by numerous watchtowers and massive walls, these strongholds were impregnable to arrows and catapults. They served as a residence for the local daimyo, while the castle compound also housed his army and contained the seat of the local government. Osaka Castle (on the right) was built by Hideyoshi essentially as a massive stage set to proclaim his power and grandeur. In 1615, the powerful warlord Tokugawa Ieyasu seized the castle, as shown in the screen painting above. The family's control over Japan lasted nearly 250 years. Note the presence of firearms, introduced by the Europeans half a century earlier.

Collection Musée Guimet, Paris, photo © Michael Holford, London

**Arrival of the Portuguese at Nagasaki.** Portuguese traders, dressed in billowing pantaloons and broad-brimmed hats, landed in Japan by accident in 1543. In a few years, they were arriving regularly, taking part in a regional trade network between Japan, China, and Southeast Asia. In these panels done in black lacquer and gold leaf, we see a late-sixteenth-century Japanese interpretation of the first Portuguese landing at Nagasaki.

## A Present for Lord Tokitaka

The Portuguese introduced firearms to Japan in the sixteenth century, and Japanese warriors were quick to explore the possibilities of these new weapons. In this passage, the daimyo of a small island off the southern tip of Japan receives an explanation of how to use the new weapons and is fascinated by the results. Note how Lord Tokitaka attempts to understand the procedures in terms of traditional Daoist beliefs.

*How does Lord Tokitaka use Daoist concepts to explain something unfamiliar to him? What impact did the introduction of firearms have on Japanese society at the time?*

### The Japanese Discover Firearms

"There are two leaders among the traders, the one called Murashusa, and the other Christian Mota. In their hands they carried something two or three feet long, straight on the outside with a passage inside, and made of a heavy substance. The inner passage runs through it although it is closed at the end. At its side there is an aperture which is the passageway for fire. Its shape defies comparison with anything I know. To use it, fill it with powder and small lead pellets. Set up a small . . . target on a bank. Grip the object in your hand, compose your body, and closing one eye, apply fire to the aperture. Then the pellet hits the target squarely. The explosion is like lightning and the report like thunder. Bystanders must cover their ears. . . . This thing with one blow can smash a mountain of silver and a wall of iron. If one sought to do mischief in another man's domain and he was touched by it, he would lose his life instantly. Needless to say this is also true for the deer and stag that ravage the plants in the fields."

Lord Tokitaka saw it and thought it was the wonder of wonders. He did not know its name at first nor the details of its use. Then someone called it "iron-arms," although it was not known whether the Chinese called it so, or whether it was so called only on our island. Thus, one day, Tokitaka spoke to the two alien leaders through an interpreter: "Incapable though I am, I should like to learn about it." Whereupon, the chiefs answered, also through an interpreter: "If you wish to learn about it, we shall teach you its mysteries." Tokitaka then asked, "What is its secret?" The chief replied: "The secret is to put your mind aright and close one eye." Tokitaka said: "The ancient sages have often taught how to set one's mind aright, and I have learned something of it. If the mind is not set aright, there will be no logic for what we say or do. Thus, I understand what you say about setting our minds aright. However, will it not impair our vision for objects at a distance if we close an eye? Why should we close an eye?" To which the chiefs replied: "That is because concentration is important in everything. When one concentrates, a broad vision is not necessary. To close an eye is not to dim one's eyesight but rather to project one's concentration farther. You should know this." Delighted, Tokitaka said: "That corresponds to what Lao Tzu has said, 'Good sight means seeing what is very small.' "

That year the festival day of the Ninth Month fell on the day of the Metal and the Boar. Thus, one fine morning the weapon was filled with powder and lead pellets, a target was set up more than a hundred paces away, and fire was applied to the weapon. At first the people were astonished; then they became frightened. But in the end they all said in unison: "We should like to learn!" Disregarding the high price of the arms, Tokitaka purchased from the aliens two pieces of the firearms for his family treasure. As for the art of grinding, sifting, and mixing of the powder, Tokitaka let his retainer, Shinokawa Shoshiro, learn it. Tokitaka occupied himself, morning and night, and without rest in handling the arms. As a result, he was able to convert the misses of his early experiments into hits–a hundred hits in a hundred attempts.

both missionary and trading purposes. But papal claims to the loyalty of all Japanese Christians and the European habit of intervening in local politics soon began to arouse suspicion in official circles. Missionaries added to the problem by deliberately destroying local idols and shrines and turning some temples into Christian schools or churches.

**Expulsion of the Christians** Inevitably, the local authorities reacted. In 1587, Toyotomi Hideyoshi issued an edict prohibiting further Christian activities within his domains. Japan, he declared, was "the land of the Gods," and the destruction of shrines by the foreigners was "something unheard of in previous ages." To "corrupt and stir up the lower classes" to commit such sacrileges, he declared, was "outrageous."[9] The parties responsible (the Jesuits) were ordered to leave the country within twenty days. Hideyoshi was careful to distinguish missionary from trading activities, however, and merchants were permitted to continue their operations (see the box on p. 466).

The Jesuits protested the expulsion, and eventually Hideyoshi relented, permitting them to continue proselytizing so long as they were discreet. But he refused to repeal the edicts, and when the aggressive activities of newly arrived Spanish Franciscans aroused his ire, he ordered the execution of nine missionaries and a number of their Japanese converts. When the missionaries continued to interfere in local politics (some even tried to incite the daimyo in the southern islands against the shogunate government in Edo), Tokugawa Ieyasu completed the process by ordering the eviction of all missionaries in 1612. The persecution of Japanese Christians intensified,

## TOYOTOMI HIDEYOSHI EXPELS THE MISSIONARIES

[illegible] missionaries in sixteenth-century Japan began to interfere in local politics and criticize traditional religious practices, Toyotomi Hideyoshi issued an edict calling for their expulsion. In this letter to the Portuguese viceroy in Asia, Hideyoshi explains his decision. Note his conviction that Buddhists, Confucianists, and followers of Shinto all believe in the same God and his criticism of Christianity for rejecting all other faiths.

*What reason does Hideyoshi give for prohibiting the practice of Christianity in Japan? How do his religious beliefs, as expressed in this document, differ from those of other religions like Christianity and Islam?*

### Toyotomi Hideyoshi, Letter to the Viceroy of the Indies

Ours is the land of the Gods, and God is mind. Everything in nature comes into existence because of mind. Without God there can be no spirituality. Without God there can be no way. God rules in times of prosperity as in times of decline. God is positive and negative and unfathomable. Thus, God is the root and source of all existence. This God is spoken of by Buddhism in India, Confucianism in China, and Shinto in Japan. To know Shinto is to know Buddhism as well as Confucianism.

As long as man lives in this world, Humanity will be a basic principle. Were it not for Humanity and Righteousness the sovereign would not be a sovereign, nor a minister of a state a minister. It is through the practice of Humanity and Righteousness that the foundations of our relationships between sovereign and minister, parent and child, and husband and wife are established. If you are interested in the profound philosophy of God and Buddha, request an explanation and it will be given to you. In your land one doctrine is taught to the exclusion of others, and you are not yet informed of the [Confucian] philosophy of Humanity and Righteousness. Thus there is no respect for God and Buddha and no distinction between sovereign and ministers. Through heresies you intend to destroy the righteous law. Hereafter, do not expound, in ignorance of right and wrong, unreasonable and wanton doctrines. A few years ago the so-called Fathers came to my country seeking to bewitch our men and women, both of the laity and clergy. At that time punishment was administered to them, and it will be repeated if they should return to our domain to propagate their faith. It will not matter what sect or denomination they represent—they shall be destroyed. It will then be too late to repent. If you entertain any desire of establishing amity with this land, the seas have been rid of the pirate menace, and merchants are permitted to come and go. Remember this.

leading to an abortive revolt by Christian peasants on the island of Kyushu in 1637, which was bloodily suppressed.

At first, Japanese authorities hoped to maintain commercial relations with European countries even while suppressing the Western religion, but eventually they decided to prohibit foreign trade altogether and closed the two major foreign factories on the island of Hirado and at Nagasaki. The sole remaining opening to the West was at Deshima Island in Nagasaki harbor, where a small Dutch community was permitted to engage in limited trade with Japan (the Dutch, unlike the Portuguese and the Spanish, had not allowed missionary activities to interfere with their commercial interests). Dutch ships were permitted to dock at Nagasaki harbor only once a year and, after close inspection, were allowed to remain for two or three months. Conditions on the island of Deshima itself were quite confining: the Dutch physician Engelbert Kaempfer complained that the Dutch lived in "almost perpetual imprisonment."[10] Nor were the Japanese free to engage in foreign trade. A small amount of commerce took place with China, but Japanese subjects of the shogunate were forbidden to leave the country on penalty of death.

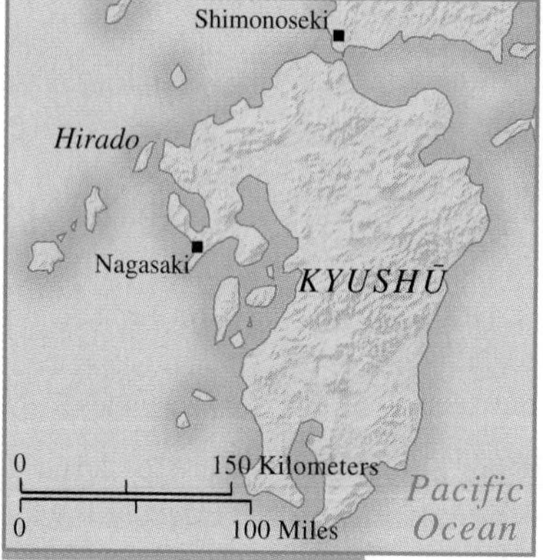

Nagasaki and Hirado Island

## The Tokugawa "Great Peace"

Once in power, the Tokugawa attempted to strengthen the system that had governed Japan for over three hundred years. They followed precedent in ruling through the *bakufu,* composed now of a coalition of daimyo, and a council of elders. But the system was more centralized than it had been previously. Now the shogunate government played a dual role. It set national policy on behalf of the emperor in Kyoto while simultaneously governing the shogun's own domain, which included about one-quarter of the national territory as well as the three great cities of Edo, Kyoto, and Osaka. As before, the state was divided into separate territories, called domains *(han),* which were ruled by a total of about 250 individual daimyo lords. The daimyo were themselves divided into two types: the *fudai* (inside) daimyo, who were mostly small daimyo directly subordinate to the shogunate, and the *tozama* (outside) daimyo, who were larger and more in-

### CHRONOLOGY Japan and Korea During the Early Modern Era

| | |
|---|---|
| First phonetic alphabet in Korea | Fifteenth century |
| Portuguese merchants arrive in Japan | 1543 |
| Francis Xavier arrives in Japan | 1549 |
| Rule of Oda Nobunaga | 1568–1582 |
| Seizure of Kyoto | 1568 |
| Rule of Toyotomi Hideyoshi | 1582–1598 |
| Edict prohibiting Christianity in Japan | 1587 |
| Occupation of Korea | 1592–1598 |
| Rule of Tokugawa Ieyasu | 1598–1616 |
| Creation of Tokugawa shogunate | 1603 |
| Dutch granted permission to trade at Nagasaki | 1609 |
| Order evicting Christian missionaries | 1612 |
| Yi dynasty of Korea declares fealty to China | 1630s |
| Christian uprising suppressed | 1637 |
| Dutch post at Nagasaki transferred to Hirado | 1641 |

dependent lords usually more distant from the center of shogunate power in Edo.

**Daimyo and Samurai** In theory, the daimyo were essentially autonomous, since they were able to support themselves from taxes on their lands (the shogunate received its own revenues from its extensive landholdings). In actuality, the shogunate was able to guarantee daimyo loyalties by compelling daimyo lords to maintain two residences, one in their own domains and the other at Edo, and to leave their families in Edo as hostages for the daimyo's good behavior. Keeping up two residences also placed the Japanese nobility in a difficult economic position. Some were able to defray the high costs by concentrating on cash crops such as sugar, fish, and forestry products, but most were rice producers, and their revenues remained roughly the same throughout the period. The daimyo were also able to protect their economic interests by depriving their samurai retainers of their proprietary rights over the land and transforming them into salaried officials. The fief thus became a stipend, and the personal relationship between the daimyo and his retainers gradually gave way to a bureaucratic authority.

The Tokugawa also tinkered with the social system by limiting the size of the samurai class and reclassifying samurai who supported themselves by tilling the land as commoners. In fact, with the long period of peace brought about by Tokugawa rule, the samurai gradually ceased to be a warrior class and were required to live in the castle towns. As a gesture to their glorious past, samurai were still permitted to wear their two swords, and a rigid separation was maintained between persons of samurai status and the nonaristocratic segment of the population. The Jesuit missionary Francis Xavier observed that "on no account would a poverty-stricken gentleman marry with someone outside the gentry, even if he were given great sums to do so."[11]

**Seeds of Capitalism** The long period of peace under the Tokugawa shogunate made possible a dramatic rise in commerce and manufacturing, especially in the growing cities. By the mid-eighteenth century, Edo, with a population of more than one million, was one of the largest cities in the world. The growth of trade and industry was stimulated by a rising standard of living—driven in part by technological advances in agriculture and an expansion of arable land—and the voracious appetites of the aristocrats for new products. The daimyo's need for income also contributed as many of them began to promote the sale of local goods from their domains, such as textiles, forestry products, sugar, and sake (fermented rice wine).

Most of this commercial expansion took place in the major cities and the castle towns, where the merchants and artisans lived along with the samurai, who were clustered in neighborhoods surrounding the daimyo's castle. Banking flourished and paper money became the normal medium of exchange in commercial transactions. Merchants formed guilds not only to control market conditions but also to facilitate government control and the collection of taxes. Under the benign if somewhat contemptuous supervision of Japan's noble rulers, a Japanese merchant class gradually began to emerge from the shadows to play a significant role in the life of the Japanese nation. Some historians view the Tokugawa era as the first stage in the rise of an indigenous form of capitalism, based loosely on the Western model.

Eventually, the increased pace of industrial activity spread beyond the cities into rural areas. As in Great Britain, cotton was a major factor. Cotton had been introduced to China during the Song dynasty and had spread to Korea and Japan shortly thereafter. Traditionally, however, cotton cloth had been too expensive for the common people, who instead wore clothing made of hemp. Imports increased during the sixteenth century, however, when cotton cloth began to be used for uniforms, matchlock fuses, and sails. Eventually, technological advances reduced the cost, and specialized communities for producing cotton cloth began to appear in the countryside and were gradually transformed into towns. By the eighteenth century, cotton had firmly replaced hemp as the cloth of choice for most Japanese.

Not everyone benefited from the economic changes of the seventeenth and eighteenth centuries, however, notably the samurai, who were barred by tradition and prejudice from commercial activities. Although some profited from their transformation into a managerial class on the daimyo domains, most still relied on their revenues from rice lands, which were often insufficient to cover their rising expenses; consequently, they fell heavily into debt. Others were released from servitude to their lord and became "masterless samurai." Occasionally, these unemployed warriors (known as **ronin**, or "wave men") revolted or plotted against the local authorities. In one episode, made famous in song and story as the "Forty-Seven Ronin," the masterless samurai of a local lord who had been forced to commit suicide by a shogunate official later assassinated the official in revenge. Although their act received wide popular acclaim, the *ronin* were later forced to take their own lives.

**Land Problems** The effects of economic developments on the rural population during the Tokugawa era are harder to estimate. Some farm families benefited by exploiting the growing demand for cash crops. But not all prospered. Most peasants continued to rely on rice cultivation and were whipsawed between declining profits and rising costs and taxes (as daimyo expenses increased, land taxes often took up to 50 percent of the annual harvest). Many were forced to become tenants or to work as wage laborers on the farms of wealthy neighbors or in village industries. When rural conditions in some areas became desperate, peasant revolts erupted. According to one estimate, nearly seven thousand disturbances took place during the Tokugawa era. In general, though, the rural unrest was probably motivated less by a decline in the standard of living than by local factors and a new sense of peasant assertiveness. Peasant disturbances became a more or less routine means of protesting against rising taxes and official corruption or of demanding "benevolence" from the manor lord in times of climatic disaster.

Some Japanese historians, influenced by a Marxist view of history, have interpreted such evidence as an indication that the Tokugawa economic system was exploitative, with feudal aristocrats oppressing powerless peasants. Recent scholars, however, have tended to adopt a more balanced view, maintaining that both agriculture and manufacturing and commerce experienced extensive growth. Some point out that although the population doubled in the seventeenth century, a relatively low rate for the time period, so did the amount of cultivable land, while agricultural technology made significant advances.

The relatively low rate of population growth probably meant that Japanese peasants were spared the kind of land hunger that many of their counterparts in China faced. Recent evidence indicates that the primary reasons for the relatively low rate of population growth were late marriage, abortion, and infanticide. As Honda Toshiaki, a late-eighteenth-century demographer, described:

> Aware that if they have many children they will not have any property to leave them, [husbands and wives] confer and decide that rather than rear children who in later years will have great difficulty in making a decent living, it is better to take precautions before they are born and not add another mouth to feed. If they do have a child, they secretly destroy it, calling the process by the euphemism of "thinning out."[12]

## Life in the Village

The changes that took place during the Tokugawa era had a major impact on the lives of ordinary Japanese. In some respects, the result was an increase in the power of the central government at the village level. The shogunate increasingly relied on Confucian maxims advocating obedience and hierarchy to enhance its authority with the general population. Decrees from the *bakufu* instructed the peasants on all aspects of their lives, including their eating habits and their behavior (see the box on p. 469). At the same time, the increased power of the government led to more autonomy from the local daimyo for the peasants. Villages now had more control over their local affairs and were responsible to the central government as much as to the nearby manor lord, although land taxes were still paid to the daimyo.

At the same time, the Tokugawa era saw the emergence of the nuclear family *(ie)* as the basic unit in Japanese society. In previous times, Japanese peasants had few legal rights. Most were too poor to keep their conjugal family unit intact or to pass property on to their children. Many lived at the manorial residence or worked as servants in the households of more affluent villagers. Now, with farm income on the rise, the nuclear family took on the same form as in China, although without the joint family concept. The Japanese system of inheritance was based on primogeniture. Family property was passed on to the eldest son, although younger sons often received land from their parents to set up their own families after marriage.

**The Role of Women** Another result of the changes under the Tokugawa was that women were somewhat more restricted than they had been previously. The rights of females were especially restricted in the samurai class, where Confucian values were highly influential. Male heads of households had broad authority over property, marriage, and divorce; wives were expected to obey their husbands on pain of death. Males often took concubines or homosexual partners, while females were expected to remain chaste. The male offspring of samurai parents studied the Confucian classics in schools established by the daimyo, while females were reared at home, where only the fortunate might receive a rudimentary training in reading and writing Chinese characters. Some women, however, became accomplished poets and painters since, in aristocratic circles, female literacy was prized for enhancing the refinement, social graces, and moral virtue of the home. Under the Tokugawa, it was the obligation of the wife in elite families to reflect her husband's rank and status through a strict code of comportment and dress.

Women were similarly at a disadvantage among the common people. Marriages were arranged, and as in China, the new wife moved in with the family of her husband. A wife who did not meet the expectations of her spouse or his family was likely to be divorced. Still, gender relations were more egalitarian than among the nobility.

## Keeping to the Straight and Narrow in Tokugawa Japan

Like the Qing dynasty in China, the Tokugawa shoguns attempted to keep their subjects in line with decrees that carefully prescribed all kinds of behavior. As this decree, which was circulated in all Japanese villages, shows, the *bakufu* sought to be the moral instructor as well as the guardian and protector of the Japanese people.

*Compare these maxims with the commandments issued by Qing Emperor Kangxi earlier in this chapter (see the box on p. 453). What do they explain about the nature of politics in Tokugawa Japan?*

### Maxims for Peasant Behavior

1. Young people are forbidden to congregate in great numbers.
2. Entertainments unsuited to peasants, such as playing the samisen or reciting ballad dramas, are forbidden.
3. Staging sumo matches is forbidden for the next five years.
4. The edict on frugality issued by the *han* at the end of last year must be observed.
5. Social relations in the village must be conducted harmoniously.
6. If a person has to leave the village for business or pleasure, that person must return by ten at night.
7. Father and son are forbidden to stay overnight at another person's house. An exception is to be made if it is to nurse a sick person.
8. Corvée [obligatory labor] assigned by the *han* must be performed faithfully.
9. Children who practice filial piety must be rewarded.
10. One must never get drunk and cause trouble for others.
11. Peasants who farm especially diligently must be rewarded.
12. Peasants who neglect farm work and cultivate their paddies and upland fields in a slovenly and careless fashion must be punished.
13. The boundary lines of paddy and upland fields must not be changed arbitrarily.
14. Recognition must be accorded to peasants who contribute greatly to village political affairs.
15. Fights and quarrels are forbidden in the village.
16. The deteriorating customs and morals of the village must be rectified.
17. Peasants who are suffering from poverty must be identified and helped.
18. This village has a proud history compared to other villages, but in recent years bad times have come upon us. Everyone must rise at six in the morning, cut grass, and work hard to revitalize the village.
19. The punishments to be meted out to violators of the village code and gifts to be awarded the deserving are to be decided during the last assembly meeting of the year.

Women were generally valued as childbearers and homemakers, and both sexes worked in the fields. Coeducational schools were established in villages and market towns, and about one-quarter of the students were female. Poor families, however, often put infant daughters to death or sold them into prostitution and the "floating world" of entertainment (see "The Literature of the New Middle Class" later in this chapter). During the late Tokugawa era, peasant women became more outspoken and active in social protests and in some cases played a major role in provoking demonstrations against government exactions or exploitative acts by landlords or merchants.

Such attitudes toward women operated within the context of the increasingly rigid stratification of Japanese society. Deeply conservative in their social policies, the Tokugawa rulers established strict legal distinctions between the four main classes in Japan (warriors, artisans, peasants, and merchants). Intermarriage between classes was forbidden in theory, although sometimes the prohibitions were ignored in practice. Below these classes were Japan's outcasts, the ***eta.*** Formerly, they were permitted to escape their status, at least in theory. The Tokugawa made their status hereditary and enacted severe discriminatory laws against them, regulating their place of residence, their dress, and even their hairstyles.

## Tokugawa Culture

Under the Tokugawa, the tensions between the old society and the emerging new one were starkly reflected in the arena of culture. On the one hand, the classical culture, influenced by Confucian themes, Buddhist quietism, and the samurai warrior tradition, continued to flourish under the patronage of the shogunate. On the other, a vital new set of cultural values began to appear, especially in the cities. This innovative era witnessed the rise of popular literature written by and for the townspeople. With the development of woodblock printing in the early seventeenth century, literature became available to the common people, literacy levels rose, and lending libraries increased the accessibility of the printed word. In contrast to the previous mood of doom and gloom, the new prose was cheerful and even frivolous, its primary aim being to divert and amuse.

**The Literature of the New Middle Class** The best examples of this new urban fiction are the works of Saikaku (1642–1693), considered one of Japan's finest novelists. Saikaku's greatest novel, *Five Women Who Loved Love*, relates the amorous exploits of five women of the merchant class. Based partly on real-life experiences, it broke from the Confucian ethic of wifely fidelity to her husband and portrayed women who were willing to die for love—and all but one eventually did. Despite the tragic circumstances, the tone of the novel is upbeat and sometimes comic, and the author's wry comments prevent the reader from becoming emotionally involved with the heroines' misfortunes. In addition to heterosexual novels for the merchant class, Saikaku wrote of homosexual liaisons among the samurai.

In the theater, the rise of *Kabuki* threatened the long dominance of the *No* play, replacing the somewhat restrained and elegant thematic and stylistic approach of the classical drama with a new emphasis on violence, music, and dramatic gestures. Significantly, the new drama emerged not from the rarefied world of the court but from the new world of entertainment and amusement (see the comparative illustration on p. 471). Its very commercial success, however, led to difficulties with the government, which periodically attempted to restrict or even suppress it. Early *Kabuki* was often performed by prostitutes, and shogunate officials, fearing that such activities could have a corrupting effect on the nation's morals, prohibited women from appearing on the stage; at the same time, they attempted to create a new professional class of male actors to impersonate female characters on stage. The decree had a mixed effect, however, because it encouraged homosexual activities, which had been popular among the samurai and in Buddhist monasteries since medieval times. Yet the use of male actors also promoted a greater emphasis on physical activities such as acrobatics and swordplay and furthered the evolution of *Kabuki* into a mature dramatic art.

In contrast to the popular literature of the Tokugawa period, poetry persevered in its more serious tradition. Although linked verse, so popular in the fourteenth and fifteenth centuries, found a more lighthearted expression in the sixteenth century, the most exquisite poetry was produced in the seventeenth century by the greatest of all Japanese poets, Basho (1644–1694). He was concerned with the search for the meaning of existence and the poetic expression of his experience. Basho's genius lies in his sudden juxtaposition of a general or eternal condition with an immediate perception, an electrical spark that instantly reveals a moment of truth. With his love of Daoism and Zen Buddhism, Basho found answers to his quest for the meaning of life in nature, and his poems are grounded in seasonal imagery. The following are among his most famous poems:

> *The ancient pond*
> *A frog leaps in*
> *The sound of the water.*

> *On the withered branch*
> *A crow has alighted—*
> *The end of autumn.*

His last poem, dictated to a disciple only three days prior to his death, succinctly expressed his frustration with the unfinished business of life:

> *On a journey, ailing–*
> *my dreams roam about*
> *on a withered moor.*

Like all great artists, Basho made his poems seem effortless and simple. He speaks directly to everyone, everywhere.

**Tokugawa Art** Art also reflected the dynamism and changes in Japanese culture under the Tokugawa regime. The shogun's order that all daimyo and their families live every other year in Edo set off a burst of building as provincial rulers competed to erect the most magnificent mansion. Furthermore, the shoguns themselves constructed splendid castles adorned with sumptuous, almost ostentatious decor and furnishings. And the prosperity of the newly rising merchant class added fuel to the fire. Japanese paintings, architecture, textiles, and ceramics all flourished during this affluent era.

Court painters filled magnificent multipaneled screens with gold foil, which was also used to cover walls and even ceilings. This lavish use of gold foil mirrored the grandeur of the new Japanese rulers but also served a prac-

McGill University School of Architecture

**The Katsura Imperial Villa.** Built for an imperial prince in the early seventeenth century, the Katsura villa in Kyoto, with its illusion of artlessness, is considered one of the masterpieces of Japanese architecture. The palace complex, along with its gardens, was inspired by a palace in *The Tale of Genji,* which was still considered a cultural ideal. Once Tokugawa Ieyasu had established his shogunate in Edo and began to consolidate his authority, he proclaimed a ban on the construction of new fortified castles such as the one built by Hideyoshi in Osaka. Subsequent palaces would resemble the Katsura model, with low buildings made of wood and no fortifications. The interior reflected the etiquette of a highly hierarchical society, with formalized spaces and different floor levels in the reception hall. Such measures ensured that vassals would be positioned at a lower level to demonstrate respect and obedience to their lord.

© Art Institute of Chicago, Clarence Buckingham Collection

COMPARATIVE ILLUSTRATION

**Popular Culture: East and West**

By the eighteenth century, a popular culture distinct from the elite culture of the nobility was beginning to emerge in the urban worlds of both the East and the West. At the left is a scene from the "floating world," as the pleasure district in Edo, Japan, was called. Seen here are courtesans, storytellers, jesters, and various other entertainers. Below is a scene from the celebration of Carnival on the Piazza Sante Croce in Florence, Italy. Carnival was a period of festivities before Lent, mostly celebrated in Roman Catholic countries. Carnival became an occasion for indulgence in food, drink, games, and practical jokes.

© Scala/Art Resource, NY

tical purpose: it reflected light in the dark castle rooms, where windows were kept small for defensive purposes. In contrast to the almost gaudy splendors of court painting, however, some Japanese artists of the late sixteenth century returned to the tradition of black ink wash. No longer copying the Chinese, these masterpieces expressed Japanese themes and techniques. In *Pine Forest* by Tohaku, a pair of six-panel screens depicting pine trees, 85 percent of the paper is left blank, suggesting mist and the quiet of an autumn dawn.

Although Japan was isolated from the Western world during much of the Tokugawa era, Japanese art was enriched by ideas from other cultures. Japanese pottery makers borrowed both techniques and designs from Korea to produce handsome ceramics. The passion for "Dutch learning" inspired Japanese to study Western medicine, astronomy, and languages and also led to experimentation with oil painting and Western ideas of perspective and the interplay of light and dark. Some painters depicted the "southern barbarians," with their strange ships and costumes, large noses, and plumed hats. Europeans desired Japanese lacquerware and metalwork, inlaid with ivory and mother-of-pearl, and especially the ceramics, which were now as highly prized as those of the Chinese.

Perhaps the most famous of all Japanese art of the Tokugawa era is the woodblock print. Genre painting, or representations of daily life, began in the sixteenth century and found its new mass-produced form in the eighteenth-century woodblock print. The now literate mercantile class was eager for illustrated texts of the amusing and bawdy tales that had circulated in oral tradition. At first, these prints were done in black and white,

**One of the Fifty-Three Stations Along the Tokaido Road.** This block print by the famous Japanese artist Hiroshige shows the movement of goods along the main trunk road stretching from Kyoto to Edo in mid-nineteenth-century Japan. With gentle humor, Hiroshige portrayed in a series of color paintings the customs of travelers passing through various post stations along the east-coast road. These romantic and somewhat fanciful scenes, very popular at the time, evoke an idyllic past, filling today's viewer with nostalgia for the old Japan.



but later they included vibrant colors. The self-confidence of the age is dramatically captured in these prints, which represent a collective self-portrait of the late Tokugawa urban classes. Some prints depict entire city blocks filled with people, trades, and festivals, while others show the interiors of houses; thus they provide us with excellent visual documentation of the times. Others portray the "floating world" of the entertainment quarter, with scenes of carefree revelers enjoying the pleasures of life.

One of the most renowned of the numerous block-print artists was Utamaro (1754–1806), who painted erotic and sardonic women in everyday poses, such as walking down the street, cooking, or drying their bodies after a bath. Hokusai (1760–1849) was famous for *Thirty-Six Views of Mount Fuji,* a new and bold interpretation of the Japanese landscape. Finally, Ando Hiroshige (1797–1858) developed the genre of the travelogue print in his *Fifty-Three Stations of the Tokaido Road,* which presented ordinary scenes of daily life, both in the country and in the cities, all enveloped in a lyrical, quiet mood.

Why did a new popular culture begin to appear in Tokugawa Japan while traditional values continued to prevail in neighboring China? One factor was the rapid growth of the cities as the main point of convergence for all the dynamic forces taking place in Japanese society. But other factors may have been at work as well. Despite the patent efforts of the Tokugawa rulers to promote traditional Confucian values, Confucian doctrine had historically occupied a relatively weak position in Japanese society. In China, the scholar-gentry class served as the defenders and propagators of traditional orthodoxy, but the samurai, who were steeped in warrior values and had little exposure to Confucian learning, did not play a similar role in Japan. Tokugawa policies also contributed. Whereas the scholar-gentry class in Qing China continued to reside in the villages, serving as members of the local council or as instructors in local schools, the samurai class in Japan was deliberately isolated from the remainder of the population by government fiat and class privilege. The result was an ideological and cultural vacuum that would eventually be filled by the growing population of merchants and artisans in the major cities.

## Korea: The Hermit Kingdom

While Japan was gradually moving away from its agrarian origins, the Yi dynasty in Korea was attempting to pattern its own society on the Chinese model. The dynasty had been founded by the military commander Yi Song Gye in the late fourteenth century and immediately set out to establish close political and cultural relations with the Ming dynasty. From their new capital at Seoul, located on the Han River in the center of the peninsula, the Yi rulers accepted a tributary relationship with their powerful neighbor and engaged in the wholesale adoption of Chinese institutions and values. As in China, the civil service examinations tested candidates on their knowledge of the Confucian classics, and success was viewed as an essential step toward upward mobility.

There were differences, however. As in Japan, the dynasty continued to restrict entry into the bureaucracy to members of the aristocratic class, known in Korea as the *yangban* (or "two groups," the civilian and military). At the same time, the peasantry remained in serflike conditions, working on government estates or on the manor holdings of the landed elite. A class of slaves *(chonmin)* labored on government plantations or served in certain occupations, such as butchers and entertainers, considered beneath the dignity of other groups in the population.

Eventually, Korean society began to show signs of independence from Chinese orthodoxy. In the fifteenth century, a phonetic alphabet for writing the Korean spoken language *(hangul)* was devised. Although it was initially held in contempt by the elites and used primarily as a teaching device, eventually it became the medium for private correspondence and the publishing of fiction for a popular audience. At the same time, changes were taking place in the economy, where rising agricultural production contributed to a population increase and the appear-

Courtesy of William J. Duiker

**Seoul Palace Pagoda.** When the Yi dynasty came into power in the late fourteenth century, it established its capital at Seoul on the Han River. There it constructed a new palace. Korean public architecture was highly influenced by the Chinese classical model, as the multitiered pagoda on the palace grounds attests.

ance of a small urban industrial and commercial sector, and in society, where the long domination of the *yangban* class began to weaken. As their numbers increased and their power and influence declined, some *yangban* became merchants or even moved into the ranks of the peasantry, further blurring the distinction between the aristocratic class and the common people.

In general, Korean rulers tried to keep the country isolated from the outside world, but they were not always successful. The Japanese invasion under Toyotomi Hideyoshi in the late sixteenth century had a disastrous impact on Korean society. A Manchu force invaded northern Korea in the 1630s and eventually compelled the Yi dynasty to grant allegiance to the new imperial government in Beijing. Korea was relatively untouched by the arrival of European merchants and missionaries, although information about Christianity was brought to the peninsula by Koreans returning from tribute missions to China, and a small Catholic community was established there in the late eighteenth century.

## CONCLUSION

When Christopher Columbus sailed from southern Spain in his three ships in August 1492, he was seeking a route to China and Japan. He did not find it, but others soon did. In 1514, Portuguese ships arrived on the coast of southern China. Thirty years later, a small contingent of Portuguese merchants became the first Europeans to set foot on the islands of Japan.

At first the new arrivals were welcomed, if only as curiosities. Eventually, several European nations established trade relations with China and Japan, and Christian missionaries of various religious orders were active in both countries and in Korea as well. But their success was short-lived. Europeans eventually began to be perceived as detrimental to law and order, and during the seventeenth century, the majority of the foreign merchants and missionaries were evicted from all three countries. From that time until the middle of the nineteenth century, China, Japan, and Korea were relatively little affected by events taking place beyond their borders.

That fact deluded many observers into the assumption that the societies of East Asia were essentially stagnant, characterized by agrarian institutions and values reminiscent of those of the feudal era in Europe. As we have seen, however, that picture is misleading, for all three countries were changing and by the early nineteenth century were quite different from what they had been three centuries earlier.

Ironically, these changes were especially marked in Tokugawa Japan, an allegedly "closed country," where traditional classes and institutions were under increasing strain, not only from the emergence of a new merchant class but also from the centralizing tendencies of the powerful Tokugawa shogunate. Some historians have seen strong parallels between Tokugawa Japan and early modern Europe, which gave birth to centralized empires and a strong merchant class during the same period. The image of the monarchy is reflected in a song sung at the shrine of Toyotomi Hideyoshi in Kyoto:

*Who's that*
*Holding over four hundred provinces*
*In the palm of his hand*
*And entertaining at a tea-party?*
*It's His Highness*
*So mighty, so impressive!*[13]

By the beginning of the nineteenth century, then, powerful tensions, reflecting a growing gap between ideal and reality, were at work in both Chinese and Japanese society. Under these conditions, both countries were soon forced to face a new challenge from the aggressive power of an industrializing Europe.

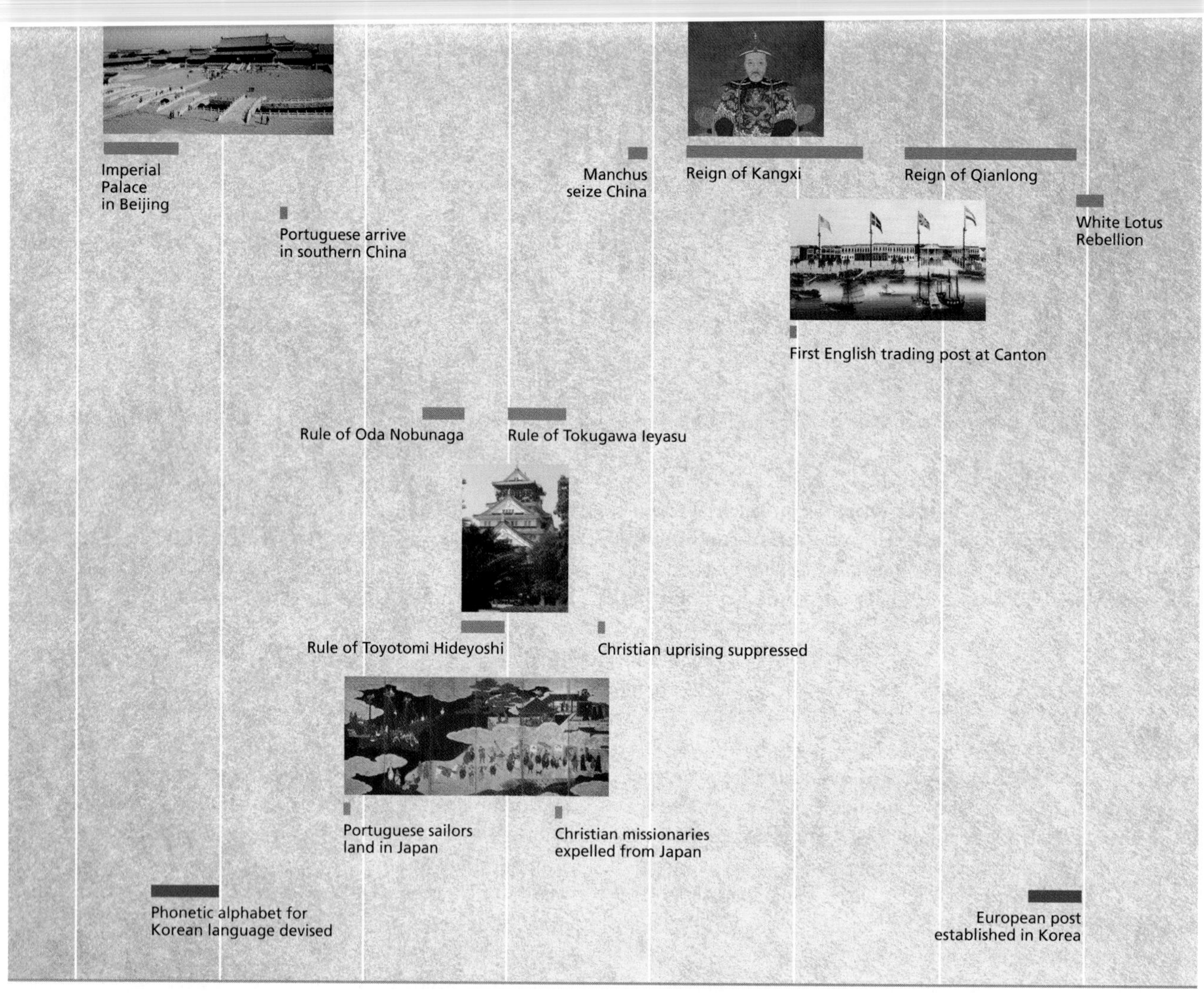


## CHAPTER NOTES

1. J. D. Spence, *Emperor of China: Self-Portrait of K'ang Hsi* (New York, 1974), pp. 143–144.
2. Quoted in R. Strassberg, *The World of K'ang Shang-jen: A Man of Letters in Early Ch'ing China* (New York, 1983), p. 275.
3. Quoted in F. Wakeman Jr., *The Great Enterprise: The Manchu Reconstruction of Imperial Order in Seventeenth-Century China* (Berkeley, Calif., 1985), p. 16.
4. L. Struve, *The Southern Ming, 1644–1662* (New Haven, Conn., 1984), p. 61.
5. J. L. Cranmer-Byng, *An Embassy to China: Lord Macartney's Journal, 1793–1794* (London, 1912), p. 340.
6. Quoted in D. J. Boorstin, *The Discoverers: A History of Man's Search to Know His World and Himself* (New York, 1983), p. 63.
7. Quoted in C. R. Boxer, ed., *South China in the Sixteenth Century* (London, 1953), p. 265.
8. Quoted in C. Nakane and S. Oishi, eds., *Tokugawa Japan* (Tokyo, 1990), p. 14.
9. Quoted in J. Elisonas, "Christianity and the Daimyo," in J. W. Hall, ed., *The Cambridge History of Japan,* vol. 4 (Cambridge, 1991), p. 360.
10. E. Kaempfer, *The History of Japan: Together with a Description of the Kingdom of Siam, 1690–1692,* vol. 2 (Glasgow, 1906), pp. 173–174.
11. Quoted in J. H. Parry, *European Reconnaissance: Selected Documents* (New York, 1968), p. 144.
12. Quoted in D. Keene, *The Japanese Discovery of Europe, 1720–1830,* rev. ed. (Stanford, Calif., 1969), p. 114.
13. Quoted in R. Tsunda et al., *Sources of Japanese Tradition* (New York, 1964), p. 313.

## SUGGESTED READING

For a general overview of this period in East Asian history, see volumes 8 and 9 of **F. W. Mote** and **D. Twitchett**, eds., ***The Cambridge History of China*** (Cambridge, 1976), and **J. W. Hall,** ed., ***The Cambridge History of Japan,*** vol. 4 (Cambridge, 1991).

For information on Chinese voyages into the Indian Ocean, see **P. Snow, *The Star Raft: China's Encounter with Africa*** (Ithaca, N.Y., 1988). Also see **Ma Huan, *Ying-hai Sheng-lan: The Overall Survey of the Ocean's Shores*** (Bangkok, 1996), an ocean survey by a fifteenth-century Chinese cataloger.

On the late Ming, see **J. D. Spence, *The Search for Modern China*** (New York, 1990), and **L. Struve, *The Southern Ming, 1644–1662*** (New Haven, Conn., 1984). On the rise of the Qing, see **F. Wakeman Jr., *The Great Enterprise: The Manchu Reconstruction of Imperial Order in Seventeenth-Century China*** (Berkeley, Calif., 1985). On Kangxi, see **J. D. Spence, *Emperor of China: Self-Portrait of K'ang Hsi*** (New York, 1974). Social issues are discussed in **S. Naquin** and **E. Rawski, *Chinese Society in the Eighteenth Century*** (New Haven, Conn., 1987). Also see **J. D. Spence** and **J. Wills,** eds., ***From Ming to Ch'ing*** (New Haven, Conn., 1979). For a very interesting account of Jesuit missionary experiences in China, see **L. J. Gallagher,** ed. and trans., ***China in the Sixteenth Century: The Journals of Matthew Ricci, 1583–1616*** (New York, 1953). For brief biographies of Ming-Qing luminaries such as Wang Yangming, Zheng Chenggong, and Emperor Qianlong, see **J. E. Wills** Jr., ***Mountains of Fame: Portraits in Chinese History*** (Princeton, N.J., 1994).

The best surveys of Chinese literature are **S. Owen, *An Anthology of Chinese Literature: Beginnings to 1911*** (New York, 1996), and **V. Mair, *The Columbia Anthology of Traditional Chinese Literature*** (New York, 1994). For a comprehensive introduction to the Chinese art of this period, see **M. Sullivan, *The Arts of China,*** 4th ed. (Berkeley, Calif., 1999), and **C. Clunas, *Art in China*** (Oxford, 1997). For the best introduction to the painting of this era, see **J. Cahill, *Chinese Painting*** (New York, 1977).

On Japan before the rise of the Tokugawa, see **J. W. Hall** et al., eds., ***Japan Before Tokugawa: Political Consolidation and Economic Growth*** (Princeton, N.J., 1981), and **G. Elison** and **B. L. Smith,** eds., ***Warlords, Artists, and Commoners: Japan in the Sixteenth Century*** (Honolulu, 1981). See also **M. E. Berry, *Hideyoshi*** (Cambridge, Mass., 1982), the first biography of this fascinating figure in Japanese history. On early Christian activities, see **G. Elison, *Deus Destroyed: The Image of Christianity in Early Modern Japan*** (Cambridge, Mass., 1973). Buddhism is dealt with in **N. McMullin, *Buddhism and the State in Sixteenth Century Japan*** (Princeton, N.J., 1984).

On the Tokugawa era, see **H. Bolitho, *Treasures Among Men: The Fudai Daimyo in Tokugawa Japan*** (New Haven, Conn., 1974), and **R. B. Toby, *State and Diplomacy in Early Modern Japan: Asia in the Development of the Tokugawa Bakufu*** (Princeton, N.J., 1984). See also **C. I. Mulhern,** ed., ***Heroic with Grace: Legendary Women of Japan*** (Armonk, N.Y., 1991). Three other worthwhile studies are **S. Vlastos, *Peasant Protests and Uprisings in Tokugawa Japan*** (Berkeley, Calif., 1986); **H. Ooms, *Tokugawa Ideology: Early Constructs, 1570–1680*** (Princeton, N.J., 1985); and **C. Nakane,** ed., ***Tokugawa Japan: The Social and Economic Antecedents of Modern Japan*** (Tokyo, 1990).

For a brief introduction to women in the Ming and Qing dynasties as well as the Tokugawa era, see **S. Hughes** and **B. Hughes, *Women in World History,*** vol. 2 (Armonk, N.Y., 1997), and **S. Mann** and **Y. Cheng,** eds, ***Under Confucian Eyes: Writings on Gender in Chinese History*** (Berkeley, Calif., 2001). On women's literacy in seventeenth-century China, see **D. Ko, *Teachers of the Inner Chambers: Women and Culture in Seventeenth Century China*** (Stanford, Calif., 1994). Most valuable is the collection of articles edited by **G. L. Bernstein, *Re-Creating Japanese Women, 1600–1945*** (Berkeley, Calif., 1991).

Of specific interest to Japanese literature of the Tokugawa era is **D. Keene,** ***World Within Walls: Japanese Literature of the Pre-Modern Era, 1600–1867*** (New York, 1976). For an introduction to Basho's life, poems, and criticism, consult the stimulating ***Basho and His Interpreters: Selected Hokku with Commentary*** (Stanford, Calif., 1991), by **M. Ueda.**

For the most comprehensive and accessible overview of Japanese art, see **P. Mason, *Japanese Art*** (New York, 1993). For a concise introduction to Japanese art of the Tokugawa era, see **J. Stanley-Baker, *Japanese Art*** (London, 1984).

## HistoryNow™

**Enter *HistoryNow* using the access card that is available with this text. *HistoryNow* will assist you in understanding the content in this chapter with lesson plans generated for your needs, as well as provide you with a connection to the *Wadsworth World History Resource Center* (see description below for details).**

**WORLD HISTORY**
RESOURCE CENTER

**Enter the Resource Center using either your *HistoryNow* access card or your standalone access card for the *Wadsworth World History Resource Center.* Organized by topic, this website includes quizzes; images; over 350 primary source documents; interactive simulations; maps and timelines; movie explorations; and a wealth of other resources. You can read the following documents, and many more, at http://history.wadsworth.com/rc/world**

*The Dream of the Red Chamber*
Honda Toshiaki, "A Secret Plan for Government, 1798"

Visit the *World History* Companion Website for chapter quizzes and more.

**http://history.wadsworth.com/duikerspielvogel05/**

CHAPTER

# 17

# THE WEST ON THE EVE OF A NEW WORLD ORDER

The storming of the Bastille



## CHAPTER OUTLINE AND FOCUS QUESTIONS

### Toward a New Heaven and a New Earth: An Intellectual Revolution in the West

- Who were the leading figures of the Scientific Revolution and the Enlightenment, and what were their main contributions?

### Economic Changes and the Social Order

- What changes occurred in the European economy in the eighteenth century, and to what degree were these changes reflected in social patterns?

### Colonial Empires and Revolution in the Western Hemisphere

- How did Spain and Portugal administer their American colonies, and what were the main characteristics of Latin American society in the eighteenth century?

### Toward a New Political Order and Global Conflict

- What do historians mean by the term *enlightened absolutism,* and to what degree did eighteenth-century Prussia, Austria, and Russia exhibit its characteristics?

### The French Revolution

- What were the causes, the main events, and the results of the French Revolution?

### The Age of Napoleon

- Which aspects of the French Revolution did Napoleon preserve, and which did he destroy?

## CRITICAL THINKING

- In what ways were the American Revolution, the French Revolution, and the seventeenth-century English revolutions alike? In what ways were they different?

**ON THE MORNING OF JULY 14, 1789,** a Parisian mob of some eight thousand men and women in search of weapons streamed toward the Bastille, a royal armory filled with arms and ammunition. The Bastille was also a state prison, and although it held only seven prisoners at the time, in the eyes of these angry Parisians, it was a glaring symbol of the government's despotic policies. It was defended by the marquis de Launay and a small garrison of 114 men. The attack on the Bastille began in earnest in the early afternoon, and after three hours of fighting, de Launay and the garrison surrendered. Angered by the loss of ninety-eight protesters, the victors beat de Launay to death, cut off his head, and carried it aloft in triumph through the streets of Paris. When King Louis XVI was told the news of the fall of the Bastille by the duc de La Rochefoucauld-Liancourt, he exclaimed, "Why, this is a revolt." "No, Sire," replied the duke. "It is a revolution."

The French Revolution was a key factor in the emergence of a new world order. Historians have often portrayed the eighteenth century as the final phase of Europe's old order, before the violent upheaval and reordering of society associated with the French Revolution. The old order—still largely agrarian, dominated by kings and landed aristocrats, and grounded in privileges for nobles, clergy, towns, and provinces–seemed to continue a basic pattern that had prevailed in Europe since medieval times. However, just as a new intellectual order based on rationalism and secularism was emerging in Europe, demographic, economic, social, and political patterns were beginning to change in ways that proclaimed the emergence of a modern new order.

The French Revolution demolished the institutions of the old regime and established a new order based on individual rights, representative institutions, and a concept of loyalty to the nation rather than to the monarch. The revolutionary upheavals of the era, especially in France, created new liberal and national political ideals, summarized in the French revolutionary slogan, "Liberty, Equality, Fraternity," that transformed France and then spread to other European countries and the rest of the world. ◇

## Toward a New Heaven and a New Earth: An Intellectual Revolution in the West

In the seventeenth century, a group of scientists set the Western world on a new path known as the **Scientific Revolution,** which brought to Europeans a new way of viewing the universe and their place in it. The Scientific Revolution affected only a small number of Europe's educated elite. But in the eighteenth century, this changed dramatically as a group of intellectuals popularized the ideas of the Scientific Revolution and used them to undertake a dramatic reexamination of all aspects of life. The widespread impact of these ideas on their society has caused historians ever since to call the eighteenth century in Europe the Age of Enlightenment.

### The Scientific Revolution

The Scientific Revolution ultimately challenged conceptions and beliefs about the nature of the external world that had become dominant by the Late Middle Ages.

**Toward a New Heaven: A Revolution in Astronomy** The philosophers of the Middle Ages had used the ideas of Aristotle, Ptolemy (the greatest astronomer of antiquity, who lived in the second century C.E.), and Christianity to form the Ptolemaic or **geocentric theory** of the universe. In this conception, the universe was seen as a series of concentric spheres with a fixed or motionless earth at its center. Composed of material substance, the earth was imperfect and constantly changing. The spheres that surrounded the earth were made of a crystalline, transparent substance and moved in circular orbits around the earth. The heavenly bodies, which numbered ten in 1500, were pure orbs of light, embedded in the moving, concentric spheres. Working outward from the earth, the first eight spheres contained the moon, Mercury, Venus, the sun, Mars, Jupiter, Saturn, and the fixed stars. The ninth sphere imparted to the eighth sphere of the fixed stars its daily motion, while the tenth sphere was frequently described as the prime mover that moved itself and imparted motion to the other spheres. Beyond the tenth sphere was the Empyrean Heaven—the location of God and all the saved souls. God and the saved souls were at one end of the universe, then, and humans were at the center. They had power over the earth, but their real purpose was to achieve salvation.

Nicholas Copernicus (1473–1543), a native of Poland, was a mathematician who felt that Ptolemy's geocentric system failed to accord with the observed motions of the heavenly bodies and hoped that his **heliocentric** (sun-centered) **theory** would offer a more accurate explanation. Copernicus argued that the sun was motionless at the center of the universe. The planets revolved around the sun in the order of Mercury, Venus, the earth, Mars, Jupiter, and Saturn. The moon, however, revolved around the earth. Moreover, what appeared to be the movement of the sun around the earth was really explained by the daily rotation of the earth on its axis and the journey of the earth around the sun each year. But Copernicus did not reject the idea that the heavenly spheres moved in circular orbits.

The next step in destroying the geocentric conception and supporting the Copernican system was taken by Johannes Kepler (1571–1630). A brilliant German mathematician and astronomer, Kepler arrived at laws of planetary motion that confirmed Copernicus's heliocentric theory. In his first law, however, he contradicted Copernicus by showing that the orbits of the planets around the sun were not circular but elliptical, with the sun at one focus of the ellipse rather than at the center.

Kepler's work destroyed the basic structure of the Ptolemaic system. People could now think in new terms of the actual paths of planets revolving around the sun in elliptical orbits. But important questions remained unanswered. For example, what were the planets made of? An Italian scientist achieved the next important breakthrough to a new cosmology by answering that question.

Galileo Galilei (1564–1642) taught mathematics and was the first European to make systematic observations of the heavens by means of a telescope, inaugurating a new age in astronomy. Galileo turned his telescope to the skies and made a remarkable series of discoveries: mountains on the moon, four moons revolving around Jupiter, and sunspots. Galileo's observations seemed to destroy yet another aspect of the traditional cosmology in that the universe seemed to be composed of material similar to that of earth rather than a perfect and unchanging substance.

Galileo's revelations, published in *The Starry Messenger* in 1610, made Europeans aware of a new picture of the universe. But the Catholic church condemned Copernicanism and ordered Galileo to abandon the Copernican thesis. The church attacked the Copernican system because it threatened not only Scripture but also an entire conception of the universe. The heavens were no longer a spiritual world but a world of matter.

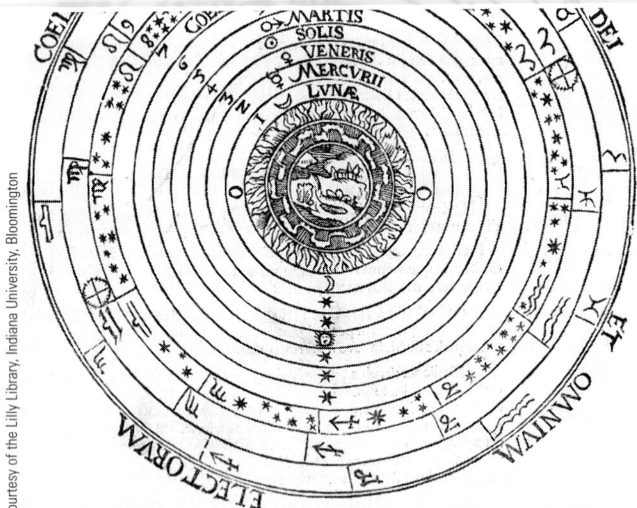


Courtesy of the Lilly Library, Indiana University, Bloomington

**Medieval Conception of the Universe.** As this sixteenth-century illustration shows, the medieval cosmological view placed the earth at the center of the universe, surrounded by a series of concentric spheres. The earth was imperfect and constantly changing, while the heavenly bodies that surrounded it were perfect and incorruptible. Beyond the tenth and final sphere was heaven, where God and all the saved souls were located. (The circles read, from the center outward: 1. Moon, 2. Mercury, 3. Venus, 4. Sun, 5. Mars, 6. Jupiter, 7. Saturn, 8. Firmament (of the Stars), 9. Crystalline Sphere, 10. Prime Mover, and at the end, Empyrean Heaven—Home of God and all the Elect, that is, saved souls.)

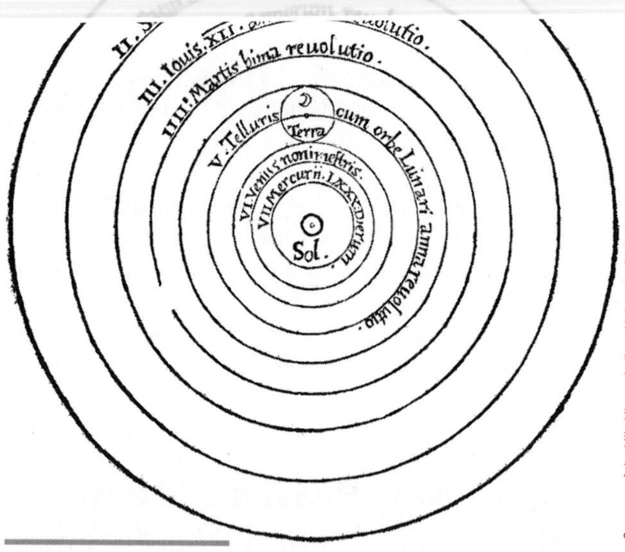


Courtesy of the Lilly Library, Indiana University, Bloomington

**The Copernican System.** The Copernican system was presented in *On the Revolutions of the Heavenly Spheres,* published shortly before Copernicus's death. As shown in this illustration from the first edition of the book, Copernicus maintained that the sun was the center of the universe while the planets, including the earth, revolved around it. Moreover, the earth rotated daily on its axis. (The circles read, from the outside in: 1. Immobile Sphere of the Fixed Stars, 2. Saturn, orbit of 30 years, 3. Jupiter, orbit of 12 years, 4. Mars, orbit of 2 years, 5. Earth, with the moon, orbit of one year, 6. Venus, 7. Mercury, orbit of 80 days, 8. Sun.)

By the 1630s and 1640s, most astronomers had come to accept the new heliocentric conception of the universe. Nevertheless, the problem of explaining motion in the universe and tying together the ideas of Copernicus, Galileo, and Kepler had not yet been done. This would be the work of an Englishman who has long been considered the greatest genius of the Scientific Revolution.

Born in 1642, Isaac Newton taught at Cambridge University, where he wrote his major work, *Mathematical Principles of Natural Philosophy,* known simply as the *Principia* by the first word of its Latin title. In the first book of the *Principia,* Newton defined the three laws of motion that govern the planetary bodies, as well as objects on earth. Crucial to his whole argument was the universal law of gravitation, which explained why the planetary bodies did not go off in straight lines but continued in elliptical orbits about the sun. In mathematical terms, Newton explained that every object in the universe is attracted to every other object by a force called gravity.

Newton had demonstrated that one mathematically proven universal law could explain all motion in the universe. At the same time, the Newtonian synthesis created a new cosmology in which the universe was seen as one huge, regulated machine that operated according to natural laws in absolute time, space, and motion. Newton's **world-machine** concept dominated the modern worldview until the twentieth century, when Albert Einstein's concept of relativity created a new picture of the universe.

**Toward a New Earth: Descartes and Rationalism** The new conception of the universe contained in the cosmological revolution of the sixteenth and seventeenth centuries inevitably had an impact on the Western view of humankind. Nowhere is this more evident than in the work of the French philosopher René Descartes (1596–1650). The starting point for Descartes's new system was doubt. As Descartes explained at the beginning of his most famous work, *Discourse on Method,* written in 1637, he decided to set aside all that he had learned and begin again. One fact seemed to Descartes beyond doubt—his own existence:

> But I immediately became aware that while I was thus disposed to think that all was false, it was absolutely necessary that I who thus thought should be something; and noting that this truth *I think, therefore I am,* was so steadfast and so assured that the suppositions of the skeptics, to whatever extreme they might all be carried, could not avail to shake it, I concluded that I might without scruple accept it as being the first principle of the philosophy I was seeking.[1]

## COMPARATIVE ESSAY

# The Scientific Revolution

When Catholic missionaries began to arrive in China during the sixteenth century, they marveled at the sophistication of Chinese civilization and its many accomplishments, including wood-block printing and the civil service examination system. In turn, their hosts were impressed with European inventions such as the spring-driven clock and eyeglasses.

It is no surprise that the visitors from the West were impressed with what they saw in China, for that country had long been at the forefront of human achievement. From now on, however, Europe would take the lead in the advance of science and technology, a phenomenon that would ultimately result in bringing about the Industrial Revolution and beginning a transformation of human society that would lay the foundations of the modern world.

Why did Europe suddenly become the engine for rapid global change in the seventeenth and eighteenth centuries? One fact was the change in the European worldview, the shift from a metaphysical to a materialist perspective and the growing inclination among European intellectuals to question first principles. Whereas in China, for example, the "investigation of things" proposed by Song dynasty thinkers had been put to the use of analyzing and confirming principles first established by Confucius and his contemporaries, empirical scientists in early modern Europe rejected received religious ideas, developed a new conception of the universe, and sought ways to improve material conditions around them.

Why were European thinkers more interested in practical applications of their discoveries than their counterparts elsewhere? No doubt the literate mercantile and propertied elites of Europe were attracted to the new science because it offered new ways to exploit resources for profit. Some of the early scientists made it easier for these groups to accept the new ideas by showing how they could be applied directly to specific industrial and technological needs. Galileo, for example, consciously sought an alliance between science and the material interests of the educated elite when he assured his listeners that the science of mechanics would be quite useful "when it becomes necessary to build bridges or other structures over water, something occurring mainly in affairs of great importance."

A final factor can be attributed to political changes that were beginning to take place in Europe during this period. Many European states enlarged their bureaucratic machinery and consolidated their governments in order to collect the revenues and amass the armies needed to compete militarily with rivals. Political leaders desperately sought ways to enhance their wealth and power and grasped eagerly at whatever tools were available to guarantee their survival and prosperity.

With this emphasis on the mind, Descartes asserted that he would accept only things that his reason said were true.

From his first postulate, Descartes deduced an additional principle, the separation of mind and matter. Descartes argued that since "the mind cannot be doubted but the body and material world can, the two must be radically different." From this came an absolute dualism between mind and matter, or what has also been called **Cartesian dualism.** Using mind or human reason and its best instrument, mathematics, humans can understand the material world because it is pure mechanism, a machine that is governed by its own physical laws because it was created by God—the great geometrician.

Descartes's separation of mind and matter allowed scientists to view matter as dead or inert, as something that was totally separate from themselves and could be investigated independently by reason. The split between mind and body led Westerners to equate their identity with mind and reason rather than with the whole organism. Descartes has rightly been called the father of modern **rationalism.**

**Europe, China, and Scientific Revolutions** An interesting question that arises is why the Scientific Revolution occurred in Europe and not in China. In the Middle Ages, China had been the most technologically advanced civilization in the world. After 1500, that distinction passed to the West (see the comparative essay "The Scientific Revolution" above). Historians are not sure why. Some have compared the sense of order in Chinese society to the competitive spirit existing in Europe. Others have emphasized China's ideological viewpoint that favored living in harmony with nature rather than trying to dominate it. One historian has even suggested that China's civil service system drew the "best and the brightest" into government service, to the detriment of other occupations.

## Background to the Enlightenment

The impetus for political and social change in the eighteenth century stemmed in part from the **Enlightenment.** The Enlightenment was a movement of intellectuals who were greatly impressed with the accomplishments of the Scientific Revolution. When they used the word *reason*—one of their favorite words—they were advocating the application of the scientific method to the understanding of all life. All institutions and all systems of thought were subject to the rational, scientific way of thinking if people would only free themselves from the shackles of past, worthless traditions, especially religious ones. If Isaac Newton could discover the natural laws regulating the world of nature, they too, by using reason, could find the laws that governed human society. This belief in turn led them to hope that they could make progress toward a better society than the one they had inherited. *Reason, natural law, hope, progress*—these were the buzzwords in the heady atmosphere of eighteenth-century Europe.

Major sources of inspiration for the Enlightenment were two Englishmen, Isaac Newton and John Locke. Newton contended that the world and everything in it worked like a giant machine. Enchanted by the grand design of this world-machine, the intellectuals of the Enlightenment were convinced that by following Newton's rules of reasoning, they could discover the natural laws that governed politics, economics, justice, and religion.

John Locke's theory of knowledge also made a great impact. In his *Essay Concerning Human Understanding,* written in 1690, Locke denied the existence of innate ideas and argued instead that every person was born with a *tabula rasa,* a blank mind:

> Let us then suppose the mind to be, as we say, white paper, void of all characters, without any ideas. How comes it to be furnished? Whence comes it by that vast store which the busy and boundless fancy of man has painted on it with an almost endless variety? Whence has it all the materials of reason and knowledge? To this I answer, in one word, from experience. . . . Our observation, employed either about external sensible objects or about the internal operations of our minds perceived and reflected on by ourselves, is that which supplies our understanding with all the materials of thinking.[2]

By denying innate ideas, Locke's philosophy implied that people were molded by their environment, by whatever they perceived through their senses from their surrounding world. By changing the environment and subjecting people to proper influences, they could be changed and a new society created. And how should the environment be changed? Newton had paved the way: reason enabled enlightened people to discover the natural laws to which all institutions should conform.

## The Philosophes and Their Ideas

The intellectuals of the Enlightenment were known by the French term ***philosophes,*** although they were not all French and few were philosophers in the strict sense of the term. They were literary people, professors, journalists, economists, political scientists, and above all, social reformers. They came from both the nobility and the middle class, and a few even stemmed from lower-middle-class origins. Although it was a truly international and cosmopolitan movement, the Enlightenment also enhanced the dominant role being played by French culture; Paris was its recognized capital. Most of the leaders of the Enlightenment were French. The French philosophes, in turn, affected intellectuals elsewhere and created a movement that touched the entire Western world, including the British and Spanish colonies in America (see Map 17.1).

To the philosophes, the role of philosophy was not just to discuss the world but to change it. To the philosophes, reason was a scientific method, and it relied on an appeal to facts. A spirit of rational criticism was to be applied to everything, including religion and politics. Spanning almost a century, the Enlightenment evolved with each succeeding generation, becoming more radical as new thinkers built on the contributions of their predecessors. A few individuals, however, dominated the landscape so completely that we can gain insight into the core ideas of the philosophes by focusing on the three French giants—Montesquieu, Voltaire, and Diderot.

**Montesquieu** Charles de Secondat, the baron de Montesquieu (1689–1755), came from the French nobility. His most famous work, *The Spirit of the Laws,* was published in 1748. In this comparative study of governments, Montesquieu attempted to apply the scientific method to the social and political arena to ascertain the "natural laws" governing the social and political relationships of human beings. Montesquieu distinguished three basic kinds of governments: republic, monarchy, and despotism.

Montesquieu used England as an example of monarchy, and it was his analysis of England's constitution that led to his most lasting contribution to political thought—the importance of checks and balances achieved by means of a **separation of powers.** He believed that England's system, with its separate executive, legislative, and judicial powers that served to limit and control each other, provided the greatest freedom and security for a state. The translation of his work into English two years after publication ensured its being read by American political leaders, who eventually incorporated its principles into the U.S. Constitution.

**Voltaire** The greatest figure of the Enlightenment was François-Marie Arouet, known simply as Voltaire (1694–1778). Son of a prosperous middle-class family from Paris, he studied law, although he achieved his first success as a playwright. Voltaire was a prolific author and wrote an almost endless stream of pamphlets, novels, plays, letters, philosophical essays, and histories.

Voltaire was especially well known for his criticism of traditional religion and his strong attachment to the ideal of religious toleration (see the box on p. 482). As he grew older, Voltaire became ever more strident in his denunciations. "Crush the infamous thing," he thundered repeatedly—the infamous thing being religious fanaticism, intolerance, and superstition.

Throughout his life, Voltaire championed not only religious tolerance but also **deism,** a religious outlook shared by most other philosophes. Deism was built on the

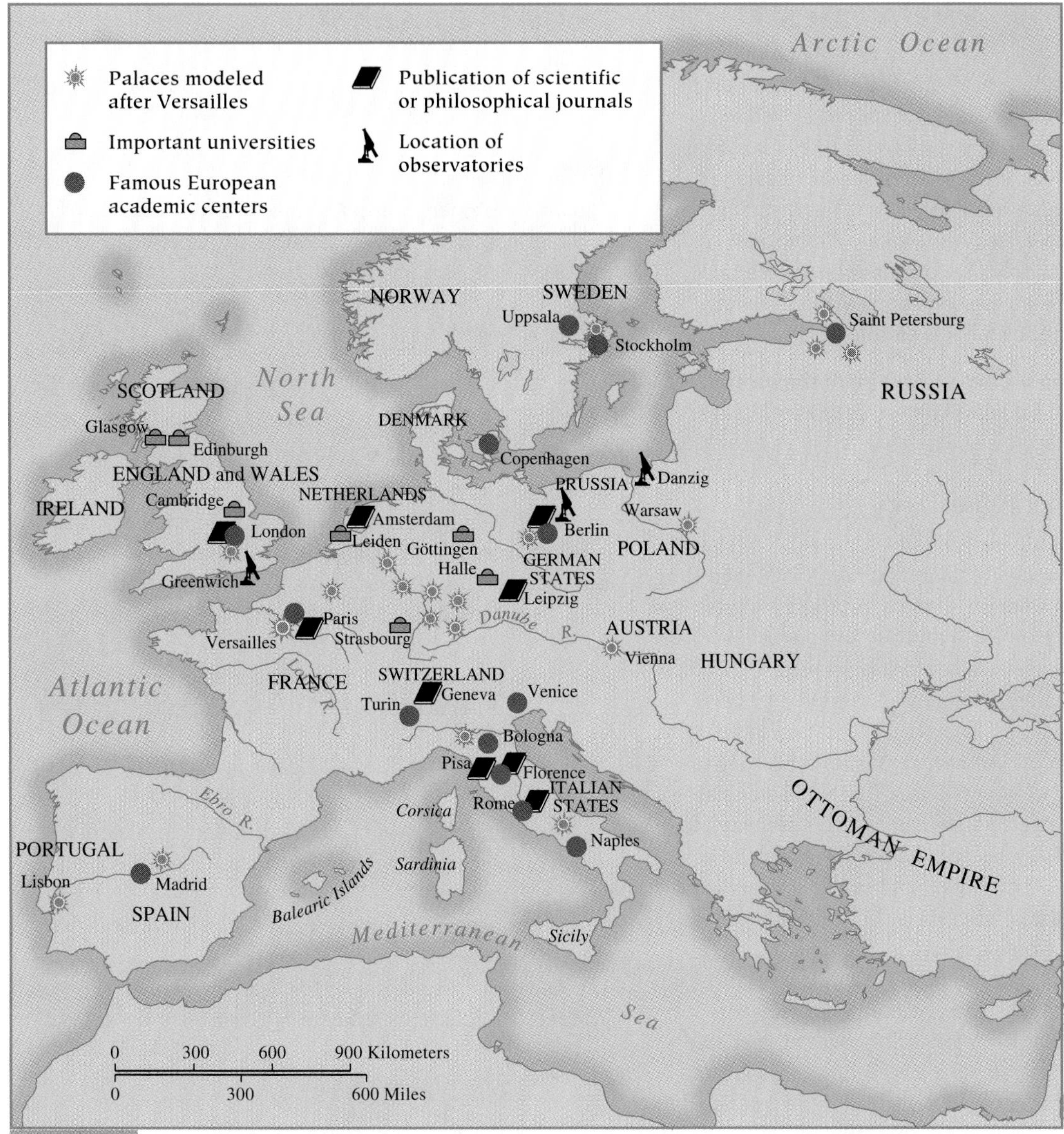


**MAP 17.1 The Enlightenment in Europe.** "Have the courage to use your own intelligence!" The words of the German philosopher Immanuel Kant epitomize the role of the individual in using reason to understand all aspects of life—the natural world and the sphere of human nature, behavior, and institutions. ? Which countries or regions were at the center of the Enlightenment, and what reasons could account for peripheral regions being less involved? **View an animated version of this map or related maps at** http://history.wadsworth.com/duikerspielvogel05/

Newtonian world-machine, which implied the existence of a mechanic (God) who had created the universe. To Voltaire and most other philosophes, the universe was like a clock, and God was the clockmaker who had created it, set it in motion, and allowed it to run according to its own natural laws.

**Diderot** Denis Diderot (1713–1784) was the son of a skilled craftsman from eastern France who became a writer so that he could be free to study and read in many subjects and languages. One of Diderot's favorite topics was Christianity, which he condemned as fanatical and unreasonable. Of all religions, Christianity, he averred, was the worst, "the most absurd and the most atrocious in its dogma."

Diderot's most famous contribution to the Enlightenment was the *Encyclopedia, or Classified Dictionary of the Sciences, Arts, and Trades,* a twenty-eight-volume compendium of knowledge that he edited and referred to as the "great work of his life." Its purpose, according to Diderot, was to "change the general way of thinking." It did precisely that in becoming a major weapon of the philosophes' crusade against the old French society. The contributors included many philosophes who attacked

## THE ATTACK ON RELIGIOUS INTOLERANCE

Although Voltaire's ideas on religion were not original, his lucid prose, biting satire, and clever wit caused his works to be widely read and all the more influential. These two selections present different sides of Voltaire's attack on religious intolerance. The first is from his straightforward treatise *The Ignorant Philosopher,* and the second is from his only real literary masterpiece, the novel *Candide,* where he uses humor to make the same fundamental point about religious intolerance.

*Compare the two approaches of Voltaire to the problem of religious intolerance. Do you think one is more effective? Why?*

### Voltaire, *The Ignorant Philosopher*

The contagion of fanaticism then still subsists. . . . The author of the Treatise upon Toleration has not mentioned the shocking executions wherein so many unhappy victims perished in the valleys of Piedmont. He has passed over in silence the massacre of six hundred inhabitants of Valtelina, men, women, and children, who were murdered by the Catholics in the month of September, 1620. I will not say it was with the consent and assistance of the archbishop of Milan, Charles Borome, who was made a saint. Some passionate writers have averred this fact, which I am very far from believing; but I say, there is scarce any city or borough in Europe where blood has not been spilt for religious quarrels; I say, that the human species has been perceptibly diminished because women and girls were massacred as well as men; I say, that Europe would have had a third larger population if there had been no theological disputes. In fine, I say, that so far from forgetting these abominable times, we should frequently take a view of them, to inspire an eternal horror for them; and that it is for our age to make reparation by toleration, for this long collection of crimes, which has taken place through the want of toleration, during sixteen barbarous centuries.

Let it not then be said, that there are no traces left of that shocking barbarism, of the want of toleration; they are still everywhere to be met with, even in those countries that are esteemed the most humane. The Lutheran and Calvinist preachers, were they masters, would, perhaps, be as little inclined to pity, as obdurate, as insolent as they upbraid their antagonists with being.

### Voltaire, *Candide*

At last [Candide] approached a man who had just been addressing a big audience for a whole hour on the subject of charity. The orator peered at him and said:

"What is your business here? Do you support the Good Old Cause?"

"There is no effect without a cause," replied Candide modestly. "All things are necessarily connected and arranged for the best. It was my fate to be driven from Lady Cunégonde's presence and made to run the gauntlet, and now I have to beg my bread until I can earn it. Things could not have happened otherwise."

"Do you believe that the Pope is Antichrist, my friend?" said the minister.

"I have never heard anyone say so," replied Candide; "but whether he is or he isn't, I want some food."

"You don't deserve to eat," said the other. "Be off with you, you villain, you wretch! Don't come near me again or you'll suffer for it."

The minister's wife looked out of the window at that moment, and seeing a man who was not sure that the Pope was Antichrist, emptied over his head a chamber pot, which shows to what lengths ladies are driven by religious zeal.

**HistoryNow™** To read a related document, enter the *HistoryNow* documents area using the access card that is available for *World History.*

religious intolerance and advocated a program for social, legal, and political improvements that would lead to a society that was more cosmopolitan, more tolerant, more humane, and more reasonable. The *Encyclopedia* was sold to doctors, clergymen, teachers, lawyers, and even military officers, thus spreading the ideas of the Enlightenment.

**Toward a New "Science of Man"** The Enlightenment belief that Newton's scientific methods could be used to discover the natural laws underlying all areas of human life led to the emergence in the eighteenth century of what the philosophes called a "science of man," or what we would call the social sciences. In a number of areas, such as economics, politics, and education, the philosophes arrived at natural laws that they believed governed human actions.

Adam Smith (1723–1790) has been viewed as one of the founders of the modern discipline of economics. Smith believed that individuals should be free to pursue their own economic self-interest. Through the actions of these individuals, all society would ultimately benefit. Consequently, the state should in no way interrupt the free play of natural economic forces by government regulations on the economy but should leave it alone, a doctrine that subsequently became known as ***laissez-faire*** (French for "leave it alone").

**A London Coffeehouse.** Coffeehouses first appeared in the major cities of the Ottoman Empire in the sixteenth century, where they were often associated with antigovernment activity. They spread quickly throughout Europe and by the beginning of the eighteenth century had become a means for spreading Enlightenment ideas. In addition to drinking coffee, patrons of coffeehouses could read magazines and newspapers, exchange ideas, play chess, smoke, and even engage in business transactions. In this scene from a London coffeehouse of 1705, well-attired gentlemen make bids on commodities.

Smith gave to government only three basic functions: it should protect society from invasion (army), defend its citizens from injustice (police), and keep up certain public works, such as roads and canals, that private individuals could not afford.

**The Later Enlightenment** By the late 1760s, a new generation of philosophes who had grown up with the worldview of the Enlightenment began to move beyond their predecessors' beliefs. Most famous was Jean-Jacques Rousseau (1712–1778), whose political beliefs were presented in two major works. In his *Discourse on the Origins of the Inequality of Mankind,* Rousseau argued that people had adopted laws and governors in order to preserve their private property. In the process, they had become enslaved by government. What, then, should people do to regain their freedom? In his celebrated treatise *The Social Contract,* published in 1762, Rousseau found an answer in the concept of the social contract whereby an entire society agreed to be governed by its general will. Each individual might have a particular will contrary to the general will, but if the individual put his particular will (self-interest) above the general will, he should be forced to abide by the general will. "This means nothing less than that he will be forced to be free," said Rousseau, because the general will was not only political but also ethical; it represented what the entire community ought to do.

Another influential treatise by Rousseau was his novel *Émile,* one of the Enlightenment's most important works on education. Rousseau's fundamental concern was that education should foster, rather than restrict, children's natural instincts. Rousseau's own experiences had shown him the importance of the emotions. What he sought was a balance between heart and mind, between emotion and reason.

But Rousseau did not necessarily practice what he preached. His own children were sent to orphanages, where many children died at a young age. Rousseau also viewed women as "naturally" different from men. In Rousseau's *Émile,* Sophie, Émile's intended wife, was educated for her role as wife and mother by learning obedience and the nurturing skills that would enable her to provide loving care for her husband and children. Not everyone in the eighteenth century, however, agreed with Rousseau.

**The "Woman Question" in the Enlightenment** For centuries, many male intellectuals had argued that the nature of women made them inferior to men and made male domination of women necessary and right. In the Scientific Revolution, however, some women had made notable contributions. Maria Winkelmann in Germany, for example, was an outstanding practicing astronomer. Nevertheless, when she applied for a position as assistant astronomer at the Berlin Academy, for which she was highly qualified, she was denied the post by the academy's members, who feared that it would establish a precedent by hiring a woman ("mouths would gape"). Winkelmann's difficulties with the Berlin Academy reflect the obstacles women faced in being accepted in scientific work, which was considered a male preserve.

Female thinkers in the eighteenth century disagreed with this attitude and provided suggestions for improving the conditions of women. The strongest statement for the rights of women was advanced by the English writer Mary Wollstonecraft (1759–1797), viewed by many as the founder of modern European **feminism.**

In her *Vindication of the Rights of Women,* written in 1792, Wollstonecraft pointed out two contradictions in the views of women held by such Enlightenment thinkers as Rousseau. To argue that women must obey men, she said, was contrary to the beliefs of the same individuals that a system based on the arbitrary power of monarchs over their subjects or slave owners over their slaves was wrong. The subjection of women to men was equally wrong. In addition, she argued that the Enlightenment was based on an ideal of reason innate in all human beings. If women have reason, then they too are entitled to the same rights that men have in education and in economic and political life (see the box on p. 485).

## Culture in an Enlightened Age

Although the Baroque style that had dominated the seventeenth century continued to be popular, by the 1730s, a new style affecting decoration and architecture known as **Rococo** had spread throughout Europe. Unlike the Baroque, which stressed power, grandeur, and movement, Rococo emphasized grace, charm, and gentle action. Rococo rejected strict geometrical patterns and had a fondness for curves; it liked to follow the wandering lines of natural objects, such as seashells and flowers. It made much use of interlaced designs colored in gold with delicate contours and graceful arcs. Highly secular, its lightness and charm spoke of the pursuit of pleasure, happiness, and love.

Some of Rococo's appeal is evident already in the work of Antoine Watteau (1684–1721), whose lyrical views of aristocratic life, refined, sensual, and civilized, with gentlemen and ladies in elegant dress, revealed a world of upper-class pleasure and joy. Underneath that exterior, however, was an element of sadness as the artist revealed the fragility and transitory nature of pleasure, love, and life.

Another aspect of Rococo was that its decorative work could easily be paired with Baroque architecture. The palace at Versailles had made an enormous impact on Europe. "Keeping up with the Bourbons" became important as European rulers built grandiose palaces. While imitating Versailles in size, they were not so much modeled after the French classical style as they were after the seventeenth-century Italian Baroque, as modified by a series of brilliant German and Austrian sculptor-architects. This Baroque-Rococo architectural style typified eighteenth century palaces and church buildings, and often the same architects designed both. This is evident in the work of one of the greatest architects of the eighteenth-century, Balthasar Neumann (1687–1753). One of Neumann's masterpieces was the pilgrimage church of the Vierzehnheiligen (The Fourteen Saints) in southern Germany. Secular and spiritual merge in its lavish and fanciful ornamentation; light, bright colors; and elaborate, rich detail.

**High Culture** Historians have grown accustomed to distinguishing between a civilization's high culture and its popular culture. **High culture** is the literary and artistic culture of the educated and wealthy ruling classes; **popular culture** is the written and unwritten culture of the masses, most of which has traditionally been passed down orally.

**Antoine Watteau, *Return from Cythera.*** Antoine Watteau was one of the most gifted painters in eighteenth-century France. His portrayal of aristocratic life reveals a world of elegance, wealth, and pleasure. In this painting, which is considered his masterpiece, Watteau depicts a group of aristocratic lovers about to depart the island of Cythera, where they have paid homage to Venus, the goddess of love. Luxuriously dressed, they move from the woodlands to a golden barge that is waiting to take them from the island.

## The Rights of Women

Mary Wollstonecraft responded to an unhappy childhood in a large family by seeking to lead an independent life. Few occupations were available for middle-class women in her day, but she survived by working as a teacher, chaperone, and governess to aristocratic children. All the while, she wrote and developed her ideas on the rights of women. This excerpt is taken from her *Vindication of the Rights of Woman,* written in 1792. This work led to her reputation as the foremost British feminist thinker of the eighteenth century.

*What picture does the author paint of the women of her day? Why are they in such a deplorable state? How does Wollstonecraft suggest that both women and men are at fault for the "slavish" situation of females?*

### Mary Wollstonecraft, *Vindication of the Rights of Woman*

It is a melancholy truth—yet such is the blessed effect of civilization—the most respectable women are the most oppressed; and, unless they have understandings far superior to the common run of understandings, taking in both sexes, they must, from being treated like contemptible beings, become contemptible. How many women thus waste life away the prey of discontent, who might have practiced as physicians, regulated a farm, managed a shop, and stood erect, supported by their own industry, instead of hanging their heads surcharged with the dew of sensibility, that consumes the beauty to which it at first gave luster. . . .

Proud of their weakness, however, [women] must always be protected, guarded from care, and all the rough toils that dignify the mind. If this be the fiat of fate, if they will make themselves insignificant and contemptible, sweetly to waste "life away," let them not expect to be valued when their beauty fades, for it is the fate of the fairest flowers to be admired and pulled to pieces by the careless hand that plucked them. In how many ways do I wish, from the purest benevolence, to impress this truth on my sex; yet I fear that they will not listen to a truth that dear-bought experience has brought home to many an agitated bosom, nor willingly resign the privileges of rank and sex for the privileges of humanity, to which those have no claim who do not discharge its duties. . . .

Would men but generously snap our chains, and be content with rational fellowship instead of slavish obedience, they would find us more observant daughters, more affectionate sisters, more faithful wives, and more reasonable mothers—in a word, better citizens. We should then love them with true affection, because we should learn to respect ourselves; and the peace of mind of a worthy man would not be interrupted by the idle vanity of his wife.

History Now™ To read a full version of this document, enter the *HistoryNow* documents area using the access card that is available for *World History.*

By the eighteenth century, the two forms were beginning to blend, owing to the expansion of both the reading public and publishing. Whereas French publishers issued three hundred titles in 1750, about sixteen hundred were being published yearly in the 1780s. Although many of these titles were still geared for small groups of the educated elite, many were also directed to the new reading public of the middle classes, which included women and even urban artisans.

An important aspect of the growth of publishing and reading in the eighteenth century was the development of magazines for the general public. Great Britain saw 25

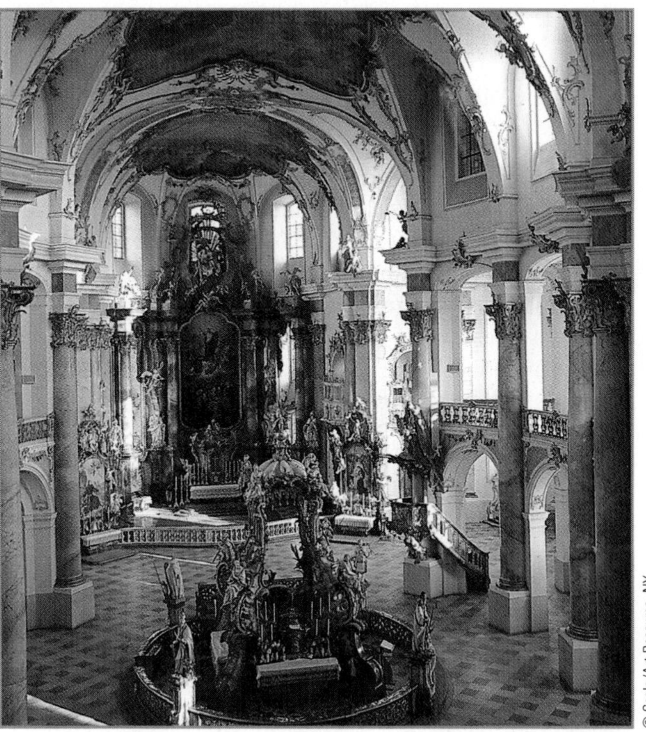



**Vierzehnheiligen, Interior View.** Pictured here is the interior of the Vierzehnheiligen, the pilgrimage church in southern Germany designed by Balthasar Neumann. Elaborate detail, blazing light, rich colors, and opulent decoration were combined to create a work of stunning beauty. The pilgrim in search of holiness is struck by an incredible richness of detail. Persuaded by joy rather than fear, the believer is lifted toward heaven on a cloud of rapture.

different periodicals published in 1700, 103 in 1760, 158 in 1780. Along with magazines came daily newspapers. The first was printed in London in 1702, but by 1780, thirty-seven other English towns had their own newspapers.

**Popular Culture** The distinguishing characteristic of popular culture is its collective nature. Group activity was especially common in the *festival,* a broad name used to cover a variety of celebrations: community festivals in Catholic Europe that celebrated the feast day of the local patron saint; annual festivals, such as Christmas and Easter, that go back to medieval Christianity; and the ultimate festival, Carnival, which was celebrated in the Mediterranean world of Spain, Italy, and France as well as in Germany and Austria.

Carnival began after Christmas and lasted until the start of Lent, the forty-day period of fasting and purification leading up to Easter. Because during Lent people were expected to abstain from meat, sex, and most recreations, Carnival was a time of great indulgence when heavy consumption of food and drink were the norm. It was a time of intense sexual activity as well. Songs with double meanings that would ordinarily be considered offensive could be sung publicly at this time of year. A float of Florentine "keymakers," for example, sang this ditty to the ladies: "Our tools are fine, new and useful. We always carry them with us. They are good for anything. If you want to touch them, you can."[3]

## Economic Changes and the Social Order

The eighteenth century in Europe witnessed the beginning of economic changes that ultimately had a strong impact on the rest of the world.

### New Economic Patterns

Europe's population began to grow around 1750 and continued to increase steadily. The total European population was probably around 120 million in 1700, 140 million in 1750, and 190 million in 1790. A falling death rate was perhaps the most important reason for this population growth. Of great significance in lowering death rates was the disappearance of bubonic plague, but so was diet. More plentiful food and better transportation of food supplies led to improved nutrition and relief from devastating famines.

More plentiful food was in part a result of improvements in agricultural practices and methods in the eighteenth century, especially in Britain, parts of France, and the Low Countries. Food production increased as more land was farmed, yields per acre increased, and climate improved. Climatologists believe that the "little ice age" of the seventeenth century declined in the eighteenth, especially evident in moderate summers that provided more ideal growing conditions. Also important to the increased yields was the cultivation of new vegetables, including two important American crops, the potato and maize (Indian corn). Both had been brought to Europe from the Americas in the sixteenth century.

In European industry in the eighteenth century, the most important product was textiles, most of which were still produced by master artisans in guild workshops. But a shift in textile production to the countryside was spreading to many rural areas of Europe by the "putting-out" or "domestic" system in which a merchant-capitalist entrepreneur bought the raw materials, mostly wool and flax, and "put them out" to rural workers who spun the raw material into yarn and then wove it into cloth on simple looms. Capitalist-entrepreneurs sold the finished product, made a profit, and used it to purchase materials to manufacture more. This system became known as the **cottage industry** because the spinners and weavers did their work on spinning wheels and looms in their own cottages.

In the eighteenth century, overseas trade boomed. Some historians speak of the emergence of a true global economy, pointing to the patterns of trade that interlocked Europe, Africa, the East, and the Americas (see Map 17.2). One such pattern involved the influx of gold and silver into Spain from its colonial American empire. Much of this gold and silver made its way to Britain, France, and the Netherlands in return for manufactured goods. British, Dutch, and French merchants in turn used their profits to buy tea, spices, silk, and cotton goods from China and India to sell in Europe. Another important source of trading activity involved the plantations of the Western Hemisphere. The plantations were worked by African slaves and produced tobacco, cotton, coffee, and sugar, all products in demand by Europeans. In a third pattern of trade, British merchant ships carried British manufactured goods to Africa, where they were traded for cargos of slaves, which were then shipped to Virginia and paid for by tobacco, which was in turn shipped back to Britain, where it was processed and then sold in Germany for cash.

Commercial capitalism created enormous prosperity for some European countries. By 1700, Spain, Portugal, and the Dutch Republic, which had earlier monopolized overseas trade, found themselves increasingly overshadowed by France and England, which built enormously profitable colonial empires in the course of the eighteenth century. After the French lost the Seven Years' War in 1763, Britain emerged as the world's strongest overseas trading nation, and London became the world's greatest port.

### European Society in the Eighteenth Century

The pattern of Europe's social organization, first established in the Middle Ages, continued well into the eighteenth century. Society was still divided into the traditional "orders" or "estates" determined by heredity.

Because society was still mostly rural in the eighteenth century, the peasantry constituted the largest social

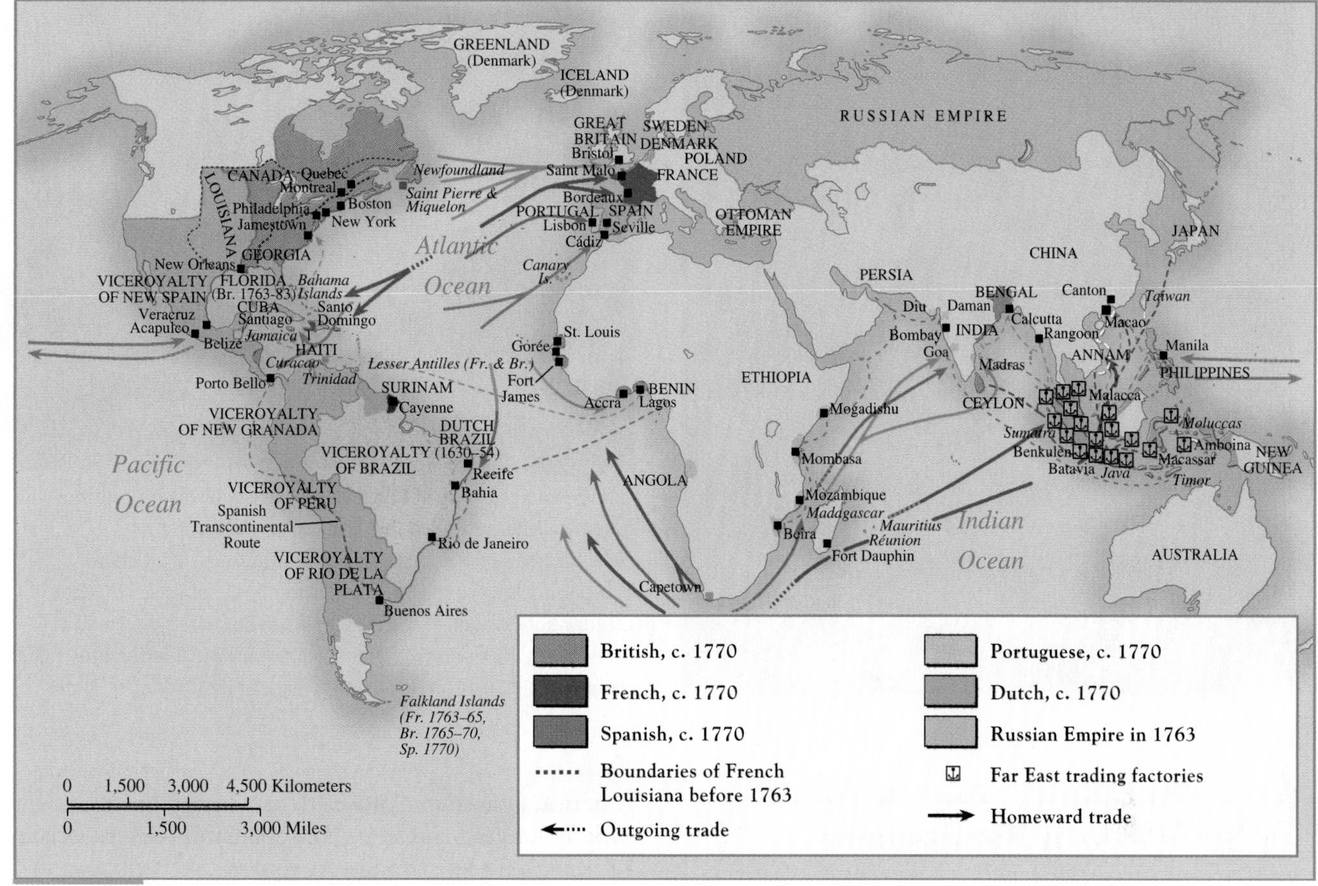


**MAP 17.2 Global Trade Patterns of the European States in the Eighteenth Century.** New patterns of trade interlocked Europe, Africa, the East, and the Americas. Dutch, English, French, Spanish, and Portuguese colonies were established in North and South America, and the ships of these nations participated in the trade routes across the Atlantic, Pacific, and Indian Oceans. ? With what regions did Britain conduct most of its trade? **View an animated version of this map or related maps at** http://history.wadsworth.com/duikerspielvogel05/

group, about 85 percent of Europe's population. There were rather wide differences within this group, however, especially between free peasants and serfs. In eastern Germany, eastern Europe, and Russia, serfs remained tied to the lands of their noble landlords. In contrast, peasants in Britain, northern Italy, the Low Countries, Spain, most of France, and some areas of western Germany were largely free.

The nobles, who constituted only 2 to 3 percent of the European population, played a dominating role in society. Being born a noble automatically guaranteed a place at the top of the social order, with all its attendant special privileges and rights. Nobles, for example, were exempt from many forms of taxation. Since medieval times, landed aristocrats had functioned as military officers, and eighteenth-century nobles held most of the important offices in the administrative machinery of state and controlled much of the life of their local districts.

Townspeople were still a distinct minority of the total population except in the Dutch Republic, Britain, and parts of Italy. At the end of the eighteenth century, about one-sixth of the French population lived in towns of two thousand people or more. The biggest city in Europe was London, with a million inhabitants; Paris was a little more than half that size.

Many cities in western and even central Europe had a long tradition of **patrician** oligarchies that continued to control their communities by dominating town and city councils. Just below the patricians stood an upper crust of the middle classes: nonnoble officeholders, financiers and bankers, merchants, wealthy ***rentiers*** who lived off their investments, and important professionals, including lawyers. Another large urban group was the lower middle class, made up of master artisans, shopkeepers, and small traders. Below them were the laborers or working classes and a large group of unskilled workers who served as servants, maids, and cooks at pitifully low wages.

Collection of the Earl of Pembroke, Wilton House, Wilts., UK/Bridgeman Art Library

© Erich Lessing/Art Resource, NY

**The Aristocratic Way of Life.** The eighteenth-century country house in Britain fulfilled the desire of aristocrats for both elegance and greater privacy. The painting above by Richard Wilson shows a typical English country house of the eighteenth century, surrounded by a simple and serene landscape. Thomas Gainsborough's *Conversation in the Park,* shown at left, captures the relaxed life of two aristocrats in the park of their country estate.

# Colonial Empires and Revolution in the Western Hemisphere

The colonial empires in the Western Hemisphere were an integral part of the European economy in the eighteenth century and became entangled in the conflicts of the European states. Nevertheless, the colonies of Latin America and British North America were developing along lines that sometimes differed significantly from those of Europe.

## The Society of Latin America

In the sixteenth century, Portugal came to dominate Brazil while Spain established a colonial empire in the New World that included Central America, most of South America, and parts of North America. Within the lands of Central and South America, a new civilization arose that we have come to call Latin America (see Map 17.3).

Latin America was a multiracial society. Already by 1501, Spanish rulers allowed intermarriage between Europeans and native American Indians, whose offspring became known as ***mestizos.*** In addition, over a period of three centuries, possibly as many as eight million African slaves were brought to Spanish and Portuguese America to work the plantations. **Mulattoes**—the offspring of Africans and whites—joined mestizos and descendants of whites, Africans, and native Indians to produce a unique multiracial society in Latin America.

**The Economic Foundations** Both the Portuguese and the Spanish sought to profit from their colonies in Latin America. One source of wealth came from the abundant supplies of gold and silver. The Spaniards were especially successful, finding supplies of gold in the Caribbean and New Granada (Colombia) and silver in Mexico and the viceroyalty of Peru. Most of the gold and silver was sent to Europe, and little remained in the New World to benefit the people whose labor had produced it.

Although the pursuit of gold and silver offered prospects of fantastic financial rewards, agriculture proved to be a more abiding and more rewarding source of prosperity for Latin America. A noticeable feature of Latin American agriculture was the dominant role of the large landowner. Both Spanish and Portuguese landowners created immense estates, which left the Indians either to work as **peons**—native peasants permanently dependent on the landowners—on their estates or as poor farmers on marginal lands. This system of large landowners and dependent peasants has remained one of the persistent features of Latin American society. By the eighteenth century, both Spanish and Portuguese landowners were producing primarily for sale abroad.

Trade was another avenue for the economic exploitation of the American colonies. Latin American colonies became sources of raw materials for Spain and Portugal as gold, silver, sugar, tobacco, diamonds, animal hides, and a number of other natural products made their way to Europe. In turn, the mother countries supplied their colonists with manufactured goods. Both Spain and Portugal closely regulated the trade of their American colonies to keep others out, but both the British and the French became too powerful to be excluded from this lucrative Latin American market.

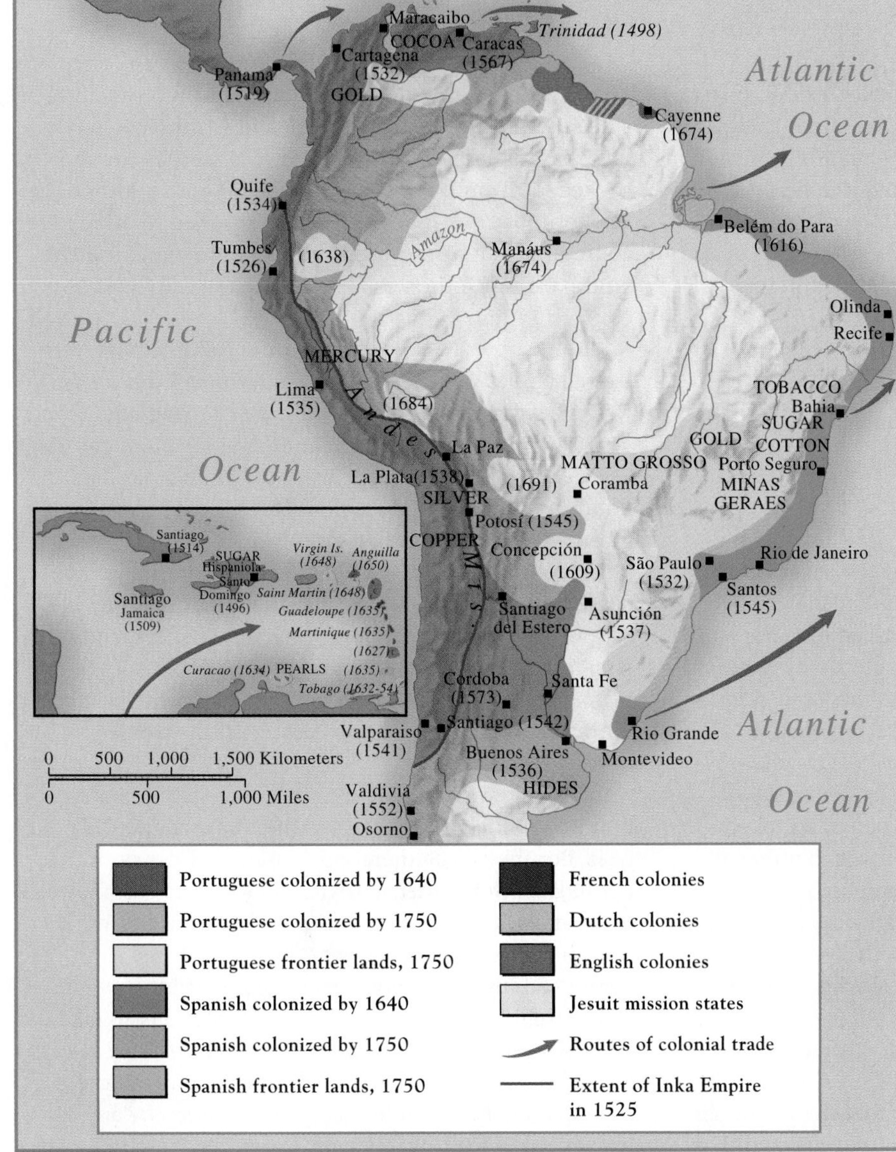


**MAP 17.3 Latin America in the Eighteenth Century.** In the eighteenth century, Latin America was largely the colonial preserve of the Spanish, although Portugal continued to dominate Brazil. The Latin American colonies supplied the Spanish and Portuguese with gold, silver, sugar, tobacco, cotton, and animal hides. **?** How do you explain the ability of Europeans to dominate such large areas of Latin America? **View an animated version of this map or related maps at** http://history.wadsworth.com/duikerspielvogel05/

**The State and the Church in Colonial Latin America** Portuguese Brazil and Spanish America were colonial empires that lasted over three hundred years. The difficulties of communication and travel between the Americas and Europe made the attempts of the Spanish and Portuguese monarchs to provide close regulation of their empires virtually impossible, which left colonial officials in Latin America with much autonomy in implementing imperial policies. However, the Iberians tried to keep the most important posts of colonial government in the hands of Europeans.

Beginning in the mid-sixteenth century, the Portuguese monarchy began to assert its control over Brazil by establishing the position of governor-general. The governor-general (later called a **viceroy**) developed a bureaucracy but had at best only loose control over the captains-general, who were responsible for governing the districts into which Brazil was divided.

To rule his American empire, the king of Spain appointed viceroys, the first of which was established for New Spain (Mexico) in 1535. Another viceroy was appointed for Peru in 1543. In the eighteenth century, two additional viceroyalties—New Granada and La Plata—were added. Viceroyalties were in turn subdivided into smaller units. All of the major government positions were held by Spaniards. For **creoles**—American-born descendants of Europeans—the chief opportunity to hold a government post was in city councils.

From the beginning of their conquest of lands in the Western Hemisphere, Spanish and Portuguese rulers were determined to Christianize the indigenous peoples. This policy gave the Catholic church an important role to play in the Americas—a role that added considerably to church power. Catholic missionaries fanned out to different parts of the Spanish Empire. To facilitate their efforts, missionaries brought Indians together into villages where the natives could be converted, taught trades, and encouraged to grow crops (see the box on p. 490). Their missions enabled missionaries to control the lives of the Indians and keep them docile.

The Catholic church built hospitals, orphanages, and schools that instructed Indian students in the rudiments of reading, writing, and arithmetic. The church also provided outlets for women other than marriage. Nunneries were places of prayer and quiet contemplation, but women in religious orders, many of them of aristocratic background, often lived well and operated outside their establishments by running schools and hospitals. Indeed, one of these nuns, Sor Juana Inés de la Cruz (1651–1695), was one of seventeenth-century Latin America's best-known literary figures. She wrote poetry and prose and urged that women be educated.

## The Missions

In 1609, two Jesuit priests embarked on a missionary ... with the Guarani Indians in eastern Paraguay. Eventually the Jesuits established more than thirty missions in the region. Well organized and zealous, the Jesuits transformed their missions into profitable business activities. This description of a Jesuit mission in Paraguay was written by Félix de Azara, a Spanish soldier and scientist.

*How were the missions organized to enable missionaries to control many aspects of the Indians' lives? Why was this deemed necessary?*

### Félix de Azara, *Description and History of Paraguay and Rio de la Plata*

Having spoken of the towns founded by the Jesuit fathers, and of the manner in which they were founded, I shall discuss the government which they established in them. . . . In each town resided two priests, a curate and a subcurate, who had certain assigned functions. The subcurate was charged with all the spiritual tasks, and the curate with every kind of temporal responsibility. . . .

The curate allowed no one to work for personal gain; he compelled everyone, without distinction of age or sex, to work for the community, and he himself saw to it that all were equally fed and dressed. For this purpose the curates placed in storehouses all the fruits of agriculture and the products of industry, selling in the Spanish towns their surplus of cotton, cloth, tobacco, vegetables, skins, and wood, transporting them in their own boats down the nearest rivers, and returning with implements and whatever else was required.

From the foregoing one may infer that the curate disposed of the surplus funds of the Indian towns, and that no Indian could aspire to own private property. This deprived them of any incentive to use reason or talent, since the most industrious, able, and worthy person had the same food, clothing, and pleasures as the most wicked, dull, and indolent. It also follows that although this form of government was well designed to enrich the communities it also caused the Indian to work at a languid pace, since the wealth of his community was of no concern to him.

It must be said that although the Jesuit fathers were supreme in all respects, they employed their authority with a mildness and a restraint that command admiration. They supplied everyone with abundant food and clothing. They compelled the men to work only half a day, and did not drive them to produce more. Even their labor was given a festive air, for they went in procession to the fields, to the sound of music . . . and the music did not cease until they had returned in the same way they had set out. They gave them many holidays, dances, and tournaments, dressing the actors and the members of the municipal councils in gold or silver tissue and the most costly European garments, but they permitted the women to act only as spectators.

They likewise forbade the women to sew; this occupation was restricted to the musicians, sacristans, and acolytes. But they made them spin cotton; and the cloth that the Indians wove, after satisfying their own needs, they sold together with the surplus cotton in the Spanish towns, as they did with the tobacco, vegetables, wood, and skins. The curate and his companion, or subcurate, had their own plain dwellings, and they never left them except to take the air in the great enclosed yard of their college. They never walked through the streets of the town or entered the house of any Indian or let themselves be seen by any woman—or indeed, by any man, except for those indispensable few through whom they issued their orders.

## British North America

In the eighteenth century, Spanish power in the New World was increasingly challenged by the British. (The United Kingdom of Great Britain came into existence in 1707, when the governments of England and Scotland were united; the term *British* came into use to refer to both English and Scots.) In eighteenth-century Britain, the king or queen and Parliament shared power, with Parliament gradually gaining the upper hand. The monarch chose ministers who were responsible to the crown and who set policy and guided Parliament. Parliament had the power to make laws, levy taxes, pass budgets, and indirectly influence the monarch's ministers.

Growing trade and industry led to a growing middle class in Britain that favored expansion of trade and world empire. These people found a spokesman in William Pitt the Elder, who became prime minister in 1757 and expanded the British Empire by acquiring Canada and India in the Seven Years' War.

**The American Revolution** At the end of the Seven Years' War in 1763, Great Britain had become the world's greatest colonial power. In North America, Britain controlled Canada and the lands east of the Mississippi. After the Seven Years' War, British policy makers sought to obtain new revenues from the colonies to pay for British army expenses in defending the colonists. An attempt to levy new taxes by the Stamp Act of 1765 led to riots and the law's quick repeal.

The Americans and the British had different conceptions of empire. The British envisioned a single empire

**Sor Juana Inés de la Cruz.** Nunneries in colonial Latin America gave women—especially upper-class women—some opportunity for intellectual activity. As a woman, Juana Inés de la Cruz was denied admission to the University of Mexico. Consequently, she entered a convent, where she wrote poetry and plays until her superiors forced her to focus on less worldly activities.

with Parliament as the supreme authority throughout. The Americans, in contrast, had their own representative assemblies. They believed that neither king nor Parliament should interfere in their internal affairs and that no tax could be levied without the consent of their own assemblies.

Crisis followed crisis in the 1770s until 1776, when the colonists decided to declare their independence from the British Empire. On July 4, 1776, the Second Continental Congress approved a declaration of independence written by Thomas Jefferson. A stirring political document, the Declaration of Independence affirmed the Enlightenment's natural rights of "life, liberty, and the pursuit of happiness" and declared the colonies to be "free and independent states absolved from all allegiance to the British crown." The war for American independence had formally begun.

Of great importance to the colonies' cause was their support by foreign countries who were eager to gain revenge for earlier defeats at the hands of the British. French officers and soldiers served in the American Continental Army under George Washington as commander in chief. When the British army of General Cornwallis was forced to surrender to a combined American and French army and French fleet under Washington at Yorktown in 1781, the British decided to call it quits. The Treaty of Paris, signed in 1783, recognized the independence of the American colonies and granted the Americans control of the territory from the Appalachians to the Mississippi River.

**Birth of a New Nation** The thirteen American colonies had gained their independence, but a fear of concentrated power and concern for their own interests caused them to have little enthusiasm for establishing a united nation with a strong central government, and so the Articles of Confederation, ratified in 1781, did not create one. A movement for a different form of national government soon arose. In the summer of 1787, fifty-five delegates attended a convention in Philadelphia to revise the Articles of Confederation. The convention's delegates—wealthy, politically experienced, and well educated—rejected revision and decided instead to devise a new constitution.

The proposed United States Constitution established a central government distinct from and superior to governments of the individual states. The central or federal government was divided into three branches, each with some power to check the functioning of the others. A president would serve as the chief executive with the power to execute laws, veto the legislature's acts, supervise foreign affairs, and direct military forces. Legislative power was vested in the second branch of government, a bicameral legislature composed of the Senate, elected by the state legislatures, and the House of Representatives, elected directly by the people. A supreme court and other courts "as deemed necessary" by Congress provided the third branch of government. They would enforce the Constitution as the "supreme law of the land."

The Constitution was approved by the states—by a slim margin. Important to its success was a promise to add a bill of rights to the Constitution as the new government's first piece of business. Accordingly, in March 1789, the new Congress enacted the first ten amendments to the Constitution, ever since known as the Bill of Rights. These guaranteed freedom of religion, speech, press, petition, and assembly, as well as the right to bear arms, protection against unreasonable searches and arrests, trial by jury, due process of law, and protection of property rights. Many of these rights were derived from the **natural rights** philosophy of the eighteenth-century philosophes and the American colonists. Is it any wonder that many European intellectuals saw the American Revolution as the embodiment of the Enlightenment's political dreams?

## Toward a New Political Order and Global Conflict

There is no doubt that Enlightenment thought had some impact on the political development of European states in the eighteenth century. The philosophes believed in natural rights, which were thought to be privileges that ought not to be withheld from any person. These natural rights included equality before the law, freedom of religious worship, freedom of speech and press, and the right to assemble, hold property, and pursue happiness.

But how were these natural rights to be established and preserved? Most philosophes believed that people needed to be ruled by an enlightened ruler. What, however, made rulers enlightened? They must allow religious toleration, freedom of speech and press, and the rights of private property. They must foster the arts, sciences, and education. Above all, they must obey the laws and enforce them fairly for all subjects. Only strong monarchs seemed capable of overcoming vested interests and effecting the reforms society needed. Reforms then should come from above (from absolute rulers) rather than from below (from the people).

Many historians once assumed that a new type of monarchy emerged in the later eighteenth century, which they called *enlightened despotism* or **enlightened absolutism.** Monarchs such as Frederick II of Prussia, Catherine the Great of Russia, and Joseph II of Austria supposedly followed the advice of the philosophes and ruled by enlightened principles. Recently, however, scholars have questioned the usefulness of the concept of enlightened absolutism. We can determine the extent to which it can be applied by examining the major "enlightened absolutists" of the late eighteenth century.

### Prussia: The Army and the Bureaucracy

Frederick II, known as Frederick the Great (1740–1786), was one of the best-educated and most cultured monarchs of the eighteenth century. He was well versed in Enlightenment thought and even invited Voltaire to live at his court for several years. A believer in the king as the "first servant of the state," Frederick the Great was a conscientious ruler who enlarged the Prussian army (to 200,000 men) and kept a strict watch over the bureaucracy. The Prussian army, because of its size and excellent reputation, was the most important institution in the state. Its officers, who were members of the nobility or landed aristocracy, had a strong sense of service to the king or state. As Prussian nobles, they believed in duty, obedience, and sacrifice. The bureaucracy also had its own code in which the supreme values were obedience, honor, and service to the king as the highest duty.

For a time, Frederick seemed quite willing to make enlightened reforms. He abolished the use of torture except in treason and murder cases and also granted limited freedom of speech and press, as well as complete religious toleration. However, he kept Prussia's rigid social structure and serfdom intact and avoided any additional reforms.

### The Austrian Empire of the Habsburgs

The Austrian Empire had become one of the great European states by the beginning of the eighteenth century. Yet it was difficult to rule because it was a sprawling conglomerate of nationalities, languages, religions, and cultures (see Map 17.4). Empress Maria Theresa (1740–1780) managed to make administrative reforms that helped centralize the Austrian Empire, but they were done for practical reasons—to strengthen the power of the Habsburg state—and were accompanied by an enlargement and modernization of the armed forces. Maria Theresa remained staunchly conservative and was not open to the wider reform calls of the philosophes. But her successor was.

Joseph II (1780–1790) believed in the need to sweep away anything standing in the path of reason. As he said, "I have made Philosophy the lawmaker of my empire; her logical applications are going to transform Austria." Joseph's reform program was far-reaching. He abolished serfdom, abrogated the death penalty, and established the principle of equality of all before the law. Joseph produced drastic religious reforms as well, including complete religious toleration.

Joseph's reform program proved overwhelming for Austria, however. He alienated the nobility by freeing the serfs and alienated the church by his attacks on the monastic establishment. Joseph realized his failure when he wrote the epitaph for his own gravestone: "Here lies Joseph II, who was unfortunate in everything that he undertook." His successors undid many of his reforms.

### Russia Under Catherine the Great

Catherine II the Great (1762–1796) was an intelligent woman who was familiar with the works of the philosophes and seemed to favor enlightened reforms.

**CHRONOLOGY Enlightened Absolutism in Eighteenth-Century Europe**

| | |
|---|---|
| **Prussia** | |
| **Frederick II the Great** | **1740–1786** |
| **Austrian Empire** | |
| **Maria Theresa** | **1740–1780** |
| **Joseph II** | **1780–1790** |
| **Russia** | |
| **Peter III** | **1762** |
| **Catherine II the Great** | **1762–1796** |
| **Pugachev's rebellion** | **1773–1775** |
| **Charter of the Nobility** | **1785** |

**MAP 17.4 Europe in 1763.** By the middle of the eighteenth century, five major powers dominated Europe—Prussia, Austria, Russia, Britain, and France. Each sought to enhance its power both domestically, through a bureaucracy that collected taxes and ran the military, and internationally, by capturing territory or preventing other powers from capturing territory. ? Given the distribution of Prussian and Habsburg holdings, in what areas of Europe were they most likely to compete for land and power? **View an animated version of this map or related maps at** http://history.wadsworth.com/duikerspielvogel05/

She invited the French philosophe Diderot to Russia and, when he arrived, urged him to speak frankly "as man to man." He did, outlining a far-reaching program of political and financial reform. But Catherine was skeptical about impractical theories, which, she said, "would have turned everything in my kingdom upside down." She did consider the idea of a new law code that would recognize the principle of the equality of all people in the eyes of the law. But in the end she did nothing, knowing that her success depended on the support of the Russian nobility. In 1785, she gave the nobles a charter that exempted them from taxes.

Catherine's policy of favoring the landed nobility led to even worse conditions for the Russian peasants and a rebellion. Led by an illiterate Cossack, Emelyan Pugachev, the rebellion spread across southern Russia. But the rebellion soon faltered. Pugachev was captured, tortured, and executed. The rebellion collapsed completely, and Catherine responded with even greater measures against the peasantry.

Above all, Catherine proved a worthy successor to Peter the Great in her policies of territorial expansion westward into Poland and southward to the Black Sea. Russia spread southward by defeating the Turks. Russian expansion westward occurred at the expense of neighboring Poland. In three partitions of Poland, Russia gained about 50 percent of Polish territory.

## Enlightened Absolutism Reconsidered

Of the rulers we have discussed, only Joseph II sought truly radical changes based on Enlightenment ideas. Both Frederick II and Catherine II liked to talk about enlightened reforms, and they even attempted some. But the policies of neither seemed seriously affected by Enlightenment thought. Necessities of state and maintenance of the existing system took precedence over reform. Indeed, many historians maintain that Joseph, Frederick, and Catherine were all primarily guided by a concern for the power and well-being of their states. In the final analysis, heightened state power was used to create armies and wage wars to gain more power.

It would be foolish, however, to overlook the fact that the ability of enlightened rulers to make reforms was also limited by political and social realities. Everywhere in Europe, the hereditary aristocracy was still the most powerful class in society. Enlightened reforms were often limited to administrative and judicial measures that did not seriously undermine the powerful interests of the European nobility. As the chief beneficiaries of a system based on traditional rights and privileges for their class, they were not willing to support a political ideology that trumpeted the principle of equal rights for all. The first serious challenge to their supremacy would come in the French Revolution, an event that blew open the door to the modern world of politics.

**Robert Clive in India.** Robert Clive was the leader of the army of the British East India Company. He had been commanded to fight the ruler of Bengal in order to gain trading privileges. To make his job easier, Clive arranged a meeting with Mir Jaffier, the commander of Bengal's army, in order to win him over to the British side. Although not present at the meeting, British artist Francis Hayman imaginatively re-created the scene in this 1760 painting.

## Changing Patterns of War: Global Confrontation

The philosophes condemned war as a foolish waste of life and resources in stupid quarrels of no value to humankind. Despite their words, the rivalry among states that led to costly struggles remained unchanged in the European world of the eighteenth century. Europe consisted of a number of self-governing, individual states that were chiefly guided by the self-interest of the ruler. And as Frederick the Great of Prussia said, "The fundamental rule of governments is the principle of extending their territories."

By far the most dramatic confrontation occurred in the Seven Years' War. Although it began in Europe, it soon turned into a global conflict fought in Europe, India, and North America. In Europe, the British and Prussians fought the Austrians, Russians, and French. With his superb army and military skill, Frederick the Great of Prussia was able for some time to defeat the Austrian, French, and Russian armies. Eventually, however, his forces were gradually worn down and faced utter defeat until a new Russian tsar withdrew Russian troops from the conflict. A stalemate ensued, ending the European conflict in 1763.

The struggle between Britain and France in the rest of the world had more decisive results. In India, local rulers allied with British and French troops fought a number of battles. Ultimately, the British under Robert Clive won out, not because they had better forces but because they were more persistent. By the Treaty of Paris in 1763, the French withdrew and left India to the British.

The greatest conflicts of the Seven Years' War took place in North America, where it was known as the French and Indian War. French North America (Canada and Louisiana) was thinly populated and run by the French government as a vast trading area. British North America had come to consist of thirteen colonies on the eastern coast of the present United States. These were thickly populated, containing about 1.5 million people by 1750, and were also prosperous.

British and French rivalry led to a number of confrontations. The French had more troops in North America but less naval support. The defeat of French fleets in 1759 left the French unable to reinforce their garrisons. That year, British forces under General Wolfe defeated the French under General Montcalm on the Plains of Abraham, outside Quebec. The British went on to seize Montreal, the Great Lakes area, and the Ohio valley. The French were forced to make peace. By the Treaty of Paris, they ceded Canada and the lands east of the Mississippi to England. Their ally Spain transferred Spanish Florida to British control; in return, the French gave their Louisiana territory to the Spanish. By 1763, Great Britain had become the world's greatest colonial power. The loss of France's empire was soon followed by an even greater internal upheaval.

## The French Revolution

The year 1789 witnessed two far-reaching events, the beginning of a new United States of America under its revamped Constitution and the eruption of the French Revolution. Compared to the American Revolution a decade earlier, the French Revolution was more complex, more violent, and far more radical in its attempt to reconstruct both a new political and a new social order.

### Background to the French Revolution

The root causes of the French Revolution must be sought in the condition of French society. Before the Revolution, France was a society grounded in privilege and inequality. Its population of 27 million was divided, as it had been since the Middle Ages, into three orders or estates.

**Social Structure of the Old Regime** The first estate consisted of the clergy and numbered about 130,000 people who owned approximately 10 percent of the land. Clergy were exempt from the *taille,* France's chief tax. Clergy were also radically divided: the higher clergy, stemming from aristocratic families, shared the interests of the nobility, while the parish priests were often poor and from the class of commoners.

The second estate was the nobility, composed of about 350,000 people who owned about 25 to 30 percent of the land. The nobility had continued to play an important and even crucial role in French society in the eighteenth century, holding many of the leading positions in the government, the military, the law courts, and the higher church offices. The nobles sought to expand their power at the expense of the monarchy and to maintain their control over positions in the military, church, and government. Moreover, the possession of privileges remained a hallmark of the nobility. Common to all nobles were tax exemptions, especially from the *taille.*

The third estate, or the commoners of society, constituted the overwhelming majority of the French population. They were divided by vast differences in occupation, level of education, and wealth. The peasants, who alone constituted 75 to 80 percent of the total population, were by far the largest segment of the third estate. They owned about 35 to 40 percent of the land, although their landholdings varied from area to area and over half had little or no land on which to survive. Serfdom no longer existed on any large scale in France, but French peasants still had obligations to their local landlords that they deeply resented. These "relics of feudalism," or aristocratic privileges, were obligations that survived from an earlier age and included the payment of fees for the use of village facilities, such as the flour mill, community oven, and winepress.

Another part of the third estate consisted of skilled craftspeople, shopkeepers, and other wage earners in the cities. In the eighteenth century, a rise in consumer prices greater than the increase in wages left these urban groups with a noticeable decline in purchasing power. Their daily struggle for survival led many of these people to play an important role in the Revolution, especially in Paris.

About 8 percent of the population, or 2.3 million people, constituted the bourgeoisie or middle class, who owned about 20 to 25 percent of the land. This group included merchants, industrialists, and bankers who controlled the resources of trade, manufacturing, and finance and benefited from the economic prosperity after 1730. The bourgeoisie also included professional people—lawyers, holders of public offices, doctors, and writers. Many members of the bourgeoisie had their own set of grievances because they were often excluded from the social and political privileges monopolized by nobles.

Moreover, the new political ideas of the Enlightenment proved attractive to both the aristocracy and the bourgeoisie. Both elites, long accustomed to a new socioeconomic reality based on wealth and economic achievement, were increasingly frustrated by a monarchical system resting on privileges and on an old and rigid social order based on the concept of estates. The opposition of these elites to the **old order** led them ultimately to drastic action against the monarchical **old regime.** In a real sense, the Revolution had its origins in political grievances.

**Other Problems Facing the French Monarchy** The inability of the French monarchy to deal with new social realities was exacerbated by specific problems in the 1780s. Although France had enjoyed fifty years of economic expansion, bad harvests in 1787 and 1788 and the beginnings of a manufacturing depression resulted in food shortages, rising prices for food and other goods, and unemployment in the cities. The number of poor, estimated at almost one-third of the population, reached crisis proportions on the eve of the Revolution.

The immediate cause of the French Revolution was the near collapse of government finances. Costly wars and royal extravagance drove French governmental expenditures ever higher. On the verge of a complete financial collapse, the government of Louis XVI (1774–1792) was finally forced to call a meeting of the Estates-General, the French parliamentary body that had not met since 1614. The Estates-General consisted of representatives from the three orders of French society. In the elections for the Estates-General, the government had ruled that the third estate should get double representation (it did, after all, constitute 97 percent of the population). Consequently, while both the first estate (the clergy) and the second estate (the nobility) had about three hundred delegates each, the third estate had almost six hundred representatives, most of whom were lawyers from French towns.

## From Estates-General to National Assembly

The Estates-General opened at Versailles on May 5, 1789. It was troubled from the start with the question of whether voting should be by order or by head (each delegate having one vote). Traditionally, each order would vote as a group and have one vote. That meant that the first and second estates could outvote the third estate two to one. The third estate demanded that each deputy have one vote. With the assistance of liberal nobles and clerics, that would give the third estate a majority. When the first estate declared in favor of voting by order, the third estate responded dramatically. On June 17, 1789, the third estate declared itself the "National Assembly" and decided to draw up a constitution. This was the first step in the French Revolution because the third estate had no legal right to act as the National Assembly. But this audacious act was soon in jeopardy, as the king sided with the first estate and threatened to dissolve the Estates-General. Louis XVI now prepared to use force.

The common people, however, saved the third estate from the king's forces. On July 14, a mob of Parisians stormed the Bastille, a royal armory, and proceeded to dismantle it, brick by brick. Louis XVI was soon informed that the royal troops were unreliable. Louis's acceptance of that reality signaled the collapse of royal authority; the king could no longer enforce his will.

At the same time, popular revolts broke out throughout France, both in the cities and in the countryside (see the comparative illustration below). Behind the popular uprising was a growing resentment of the entire landholding system, with its fees and obligations. The fall of the Bastille and the king's apparent capitulation to the demands of the third estate now led peasants to take matters into their own hands. The peasant rebellions that occurred throughout France had a great impact on the National Assembly meeting at Versailles.

## Destruction of the Old Regime

One of the first acts of the National Assembly was to abolish the rights of landlords and the fiscal exemptions of nobles, clergy, towns, and provinces. Three weeks later, the National Assembly adopted the Declaration of the Rights of Man and the Citizen (see the box on p. 498). This charter of basic liberties proclaimed freedom and equal rights for all men and access to public office based on talent. All citizens were to have the right to take part in the legislative process. Freedom of speech and the press were coupled with the outlawing of arbitrary arrests.

The declaration also raised another important issue. Did its ideal of equal rights for "all men" also include women? Many deputies insisted that it did, provided that, as one said, "women do not hope to exercise political rights and functions." Olympe de Gouges, a playwright, refused to accept this exclusion of women from political rights. Echoing the words of the official declaration, she penned the Declaration of the Rights of Woman and the Female Citizen, in which she insisted that women should have all

Art Archive/School of Oriental and African Studies/Eileen Tweedy

Musée de la Révolution Française, Vizille, France/Visual Arts Library, London/Bridgeman Art Library

POLITICS & GOVERNMENT

COMPARATIVE ILLUSTRATION

**Revolution and Revolt in France and China.** Both France and China experienced revolutionary upheaval at the end of the eighteenth century and well into the nineteenth century. In both countries, common people often played an important role. At the right is a scene from the storming of the Bastille in 1789. This early success ultimately led to the overthrow of the monarchy. At the bottom is a scene from one of the struggles during the Taiping Rebellion, a major peasant revolt in the mid-nineteenth century in China. Above, an imperial Chinese army is shown recapturing the city of Nanjing from Taiping rebels in 1864.

the same rights as men (see the box on p. 499). The National Assembly ignored her demands.

Because the Catholic church was seen as an important pillar of the old order, it too was reformed. Most of the lands of the church were seized. The new Civil Constitution of the Clergy was put into effect. Both bishops and priests were to be elected by the people and paid by the state. The Catholic church, still an important institution in the life of the French people, now became an enemy of the Revolution.

By 1791, the National Assembly had finally completed a new constitution that established a limited constitutional monarchy. There was still a monarch (now called "king of the French"), but the new Legislative Assembly was to make the laws. The Legislative Assembly, in which sovereign power was vested, was to sit for two years and consist of 745 representatives chosen by an indirect system of election that preserved power in the hands of the more affluent members of society. A small group of fifty thousand electors chose the deputies.

By 1791, the old order had been destroyed. However, many people—including Catholic priests, nobles, lower classes hurt by a rise in the cost of living, peasants who remained opposed to dues that had still not been abandoned, and political clubs like the Jacobins who offered more radical solutions to France's problems—opposed the new order. The king also made things difficult for the new government when he sought to flee France in June 1791 and almost succeeded before being recognized, captured, and brought back to Paris. In this unsettled situation, under a discredited and seemingly disloyal monarch, the new Legislative Assembly held its first session in October 1791. France's relations with the rest of Europe soon led to Louis's downfall.

On August 27, 1791, the monarchs of Austria and Prussia, fearing that revolution would spread to their countries, invited other European monarchs to use force to reestablish monarchical authority in France. The French fared badly in the initial fighting in the spring of 1792, and a frantic search for scapegoats began. As one observer noted, "Everywhere you hear the cry that the king is betraying us, the generals are betraying us, that nobody is to be trusted; . . . that Paris will be taken in six weeks by the Austrians. . . . We are on a volcano ready to spout flames."[4] Defeats in war coupled with economic shortages in the spring led to renewed political demonstrations, especially against the king. In August 1792, radical political groups in Paris took the king captive and forced the Legislative Assembly to suspend the monarchy and call for a national convention, chosen on the basis of universal male suffrage, to decide on the future form of government. The French Revolution was about to enter a more radical stage.

## The Radical Revolution

In September 1792, the newly elected National Convention began its sessions. Dominated by lawyers and other professionals, two-thirds of its deputies were under forty-five, and almost all had gained political experience as a result of the Revolution. Almost all distrusted the king. As a result, the convention's first step on September 21 was to abolish the monarchy and establish a republic. On January 21, 1793, the king was executed, and the destruction of the old regime was complete. But the execution of the king created new enemies for the Revolution both at home and abroad.

In Paris, the local government, known as the Commune, whose leaders came from the working classes, favored radical change and put constant pressure on the convention, pushing it to ever more radical positions. Moreover, peasants in the west and inhabitants of the major provincial cities refused to accept the authority of the convention.

A foreign crisis also loomed large. By the beginning of 1793, after the king had been executed, most of Europe—an informal coalition of Austria, Prussia, Spain,

**Women Patriots.** Women played a variety of roles in the events of the French Revolution. This picture shows a women's patriotic club discussing the decrees of the National Convention, an indication that some women became highly politicized by the upheavals of the Revolution.

and the Citizen was adopted in August 1789 by the National Assembly. The declaration affirmed that "men are born and remain free and equal in rights," that governments must protect these natural rights, and that political power is derived from the people.

*What "natural rights" does this document proclaim? To what extent was the document influenced by the writings of the philosophes? What similarities exist between this French document and the American Declaration of Independence? Why do such parallels exist?*

### Declaration of the Rights of Man and the Citizen

The representatives of the French people, organized as a national assembly, considering that ignorance, neglect, and scorn of the rights of man are the sole causes of public misfortunes and of corruption of governments, have resolved to display in a solemn declaration the natural, inalienable, and sacred rights of man, so that this declaration, constantly in the presence of all members of society, will continually remind them of their rights and their duties. . . . Consequently, the National Assembly recognizes and declares, in the presence and under the auspices of the Supreme Being, the following rights of man and citizen:

1. Men are born and remain free and equal in rights; social distinctions can be established only for the common benefit.
2. The aim of every political association is the conservation of the natural and imprescriptible rights of man; these rights are liberty, property, security, and resistance to oppression.
4. Liberty consists in being able to do anything that does not harm another person. . . .
6. The law is the expression of the general will; all citizens have the right to concur personally or through their representatives in its formation; it must be the same for all, whether it protects or punishes. All citizens being equal in its eyes are equally admissible to all honors, positions, and public employments, according to their capabilities and without other distinctions than those of their virtues and talents.
7. No man can be accused, arrested, or detained except in cases determined by the law, and according to the forms which it has prescribed. . . .
10. No one may be disturbed because of his opinions, even religious, provided that their public demonstration does not disturb the public order established by law.
11. The free communication of thoughts and opinions is one of the most precious rights of man: every citizen can therefore freely speak, write, and print. . . .
14. Citizens have the right to determine for themselves or through their representatives the need for taxation of the public, to consent to it freely, to investigate its use, and to determine its rate, basis, collection, and duration. . . .
16. Any society in which guarantees of rights are not assured nor the separation of powers determined has no constitution.

**History Now™** To read a full version of this document, enter the *HistoryNow* documents area using the access card that is available for *World History.*

Portugal, Britain, the Dutch Republic, and even Russia—aligned militarily against France. Grossly overextended, the French armies began to experience reverses, and by late spring, France was threatened with invasion.

**A Nation in Arms** To meet these crises, the convention gave broad powers to an executive committee of twelve known as the Committee of Public Safety, which came to be dominated by Maximilien Robespierre. For a twelve-month period, from 1793 to 1794, the Committee of Public Safety took control of France. To save the Republic from its foreign foes, the committee decreed a universal mobilization of the nation on August 23, 1793:

> Young men will fight, young men are called to conquer. Married men will forge arms, transport military baggage and guns and will prepare food supplies. Women, who at long last are to take their rightful place in the revolution and follow their true destiny, will forget their futile tasks: their delicate hands will work at making clothes for soldiers; they will make tents and they will extend their tender care to shelters where the defenders of the *Patrie* [nation] will receive the help that their wounds require. Children will make lint of old cloth. It is for them that we are fighting: children, those beings destined to gather all the fruits of the revolution, will raise their pure hands toward the skies. And old men, performing their missions again, as of yore, will be guided to the public squares of the cities where they will kindle the courage of young warriors and preach the doctrines of hate for kings and the unity of the Republic.[5]

In less than a year, the French revolutionary government had raised an army of 650,000 and by 1795 had pushed the allies back across the Rhine and even conquered the Austrian Netherlands.

The French revolutionary army was an important step in the creation of modern **nationalism.** Previously, wars had been fought between governments or ruling dynasties

## Declaration of the Rights of Woman and the Female Citizen

Olympe de Gouges (the pen name used by Marie Gouze) was a butcher's daughter who wrote plays and pamphlets. She argued that the Declaration of the Rights of Man and the Citizen did not apply to women and composed her own Declaration of the Rights of Woman.

*What rights for women does this document enunciate? To what extent have women in the Western world achieved these rights?*

### Declaration of the Rights of Woman and the Female Citizen

Mothers, daughters, sisters and representatives of the nation demand to be constituted into a national assembly. Believing that ignorance, omission, or scorn for the rights of woman are the only causes of public misfortunes and of the corruption of governments, the women have resolved to set forth in a solemn declaration the natural, inalienable, and sacred rights of woman in order that this declaration, constantly exposed before all the members of the society, will ceaselessly remind them of their rights and duties. . . .

Consequently, the sex that is as superior in beauty as it is in courage during the sufferings of maternity recognizes and declares in the presence and under the auspices of the Supreme Being, the following Rights of Woman and of Female Citizens.

1. Woman is born free and lives equal to man in her rights. Social distinctions can be based only on the common utility.
2. The purpose of any political association is the conservation of the natural and imprescriptible rights of woman and man; these rights are liberty, property, security, and especially resistance to oppression.
3. The principle of all sovereignty rests essentially with the nation, which is nothing but the union of woman and man; no body and no individual can exercise any authority which does not come expressly from [the nation].
4. Liberty and justice consist of restoring all that belongs to others; thus, the only limits on the exercise of the natural rights of woman are perpetual male tyranny; these limits are to be reformed by the laws of nature and reason. . . .
6. The law must be the expression of the general will; all female and male citizens must contribute either personally or through their representatives to its formation; it must be the same for all: male and female citizens, being equal in the eyes of the law, must be equally admitted to all honors, positions, and public employment according to their capacity and without other distinctions besides those of their virtues and talents.
7. No woman is an exception; she is accused, arrested, and detained in cases determined by law. . . .
10. No one is to be disquieted for his very basic opinions; woman has the right to mount the scaffold; she must equally have the right to mount the rostrum, provided that her demonstrations do not disturb the legally established public order.
11. The free communication of thoughts and opinions is one of the most precious rights of woman, since that liberty assured the recognition of children by their fathers. . . .
14. Female and male citizens have the right to verify, either by themselves or through their representatives, the necessity of the public contribution. This can only apply to women if they are granted an equal share, not only of wealth, but also of public administration, and in the determination of the proportion, the base, the collection, and the duration of the tax. . . .
16. No society has a constitution without the guarantee of rights and the separation of powers; the constitution is null if the majority of individuals comprising the nation have not cooperated in drafting it.

by relatively small armies of professional soldiers. The new French army was the creation of a "people's" government; its wars were now "people's" wars. The entire nation was to be involved in the war. But when dynastic wars became people's wars, warfare increased in ferocity and lack of restraint. The wars of the French revolutionary era opened the door to the total war of the modern world.

**Reign of Terror** To meet the domestic crisis, the National Convention and the Committee of Public Safety launched the Reign of Terror. Revolutionary courts were instituted to protect the Republic from its internal enemies. In the course of nine months, sixteen thousand people were officially killed under the blade of the guillotine—a revolutionary device designed for the quick and efficient separation of heads from bodies (see the box on p. 500).

Revolutionary armies were set up to bring recalcitrant cities and districts back under the control of the National Convention. The Committee of Public Safety decided to make an example of Lyons, which had defied the authority of the National Convention. By April 1794, some 1,880 citizens of Lyons had been executed. When the guillotine proved too slow, cannon fire was used to blow condemned men into open graves. A German observed:

> Whole ranges of houses, always the most handsome, burnt. The churches, convents, and all the dwellings of the former

## Justice in the Reign of Terror

The Reign of Terror created a repressive environment in which revolutionary courts often acted quickly to condemn traitors to the revolutionary cause. In this account, an English visitor describes the court, the procession to the scene of execution, and the final execution procedure.

*How were the condemned taken to the executioner? How did this serve to inflame the crowds? How were people executed? Why?*

### J. G. Milligen, *The Revolutionary Tribunal* (Paris, October 1793)

In the center of the hall, under a statue of Justice, holding scales in one hand, and a sword in the other, sat Dumas, the President, with the other judges. Under them were seated the public accuser, Fourquier-Tinville, and his scribes. . . . To the right were benches on which the accused were placed in several rows, and *gendarmes* with carbines and fixed bayonets by their sides. To the left was the jury.

Never can I forget the mournful appearance of these funereal processions to the place of execution. The march was opened by a detachment of mounted *gendarmes*–the carts followed; they were the same carts as those that are used in Paris for carrying wood; four boards were placed across them for seats, and on each board sat two, and sometimes three victims; their hands were tied behind their backs, and the constant jostling of the cart made them nod their heads up and down, to the great amusement of the spectators. On the front of the cart stood Samson, the executioner, or one of his sons or assistants; *gendarmes* on foot marched by the side; then followed a hackney, in which was the reporting clerk, whose duty it was to witness the execution, and then return to the public accuser's office to report the execution of what they called the law.

The process of execution was also a sad and heart-rending spectacle. In the middle of the Place de la Revolution was erected a guillotine, in front of a colossal statue of Liberty, represented seated on a rock, a cap on her head, a spear in her hand, the other reposing on a shield. On one side of the scaffold were drawn out a sufficient number of carts, with large baskets painted red, to receive the heads and bodies of the victims. Those bearing the condemned moved on slowly to the foot of the guillotine; the culprits were led out in turn, and if necessary, supported by two of the executioner's assistants, but their assistance was rarely required. Most of these unfortunates ascended the scaffold with a determined step–many of them looked up firmly on the menacing instrument of death, beholding for the last time the rays of the glorious sun, beaming on the polished axe: and I have seen some young men actually dance a few steps before they went up to be strapped to the perpendicular plane, which was then tilted to a horizontal plane in a moment, and ran on the grooves until the neck was secured and closed in by a moving board, when the head passed through what was called, in derision, "the republican toilet seat"; the weighty knife was then dropped with a heavy fall; and, with incredible dexterity and rapidity, two executioners tossed the body into the basket, while another threw the head after it.

**History Now™** To read a related document, enter the *HistoryNow* documents area using the access card that is available for *World History.*

> patricians were in ruins. When I came to the guillotine, the blood of those who had been executed a few hours beforehand was still running in the street. . . . I said to a group of [radicals] that it would be decent to clear away all this human blood. Why should it be cleared? one of them said to me. It's the blood of aristocrats and rebels. The dogs should lick it up.[6]

**Equality and Slavery: Revolution in Haiti** Early in the French Revolution, the desire for equality led to a discussion of what to do about slavery. A club called Friends of the Blacks advocated the abolition of slavery, which was achieved in France in September 1791. However, French planters in the West Indies, who profited greatly from the use of slaves on their sugar plantations, opposed the abolition of slavery in the French colonies. When the National Convention came to power, the issue was revisited, and on February 4, 1794, guided by ideals of equality, the government abolished slavery in the colonies.

Cuba
West Indies
Hispaniola
SAINT DOMINGUE (Fr.)
(Sp.)
Santo Domingo
Puerto Rico
Atlantic Ocean
0 150 300 Kilometers
0 75 150 Miles

**Revolt in Saint Domingue**

In one French colony, slaves had already rebelled for their freedom. In 1791, black slaves in the French sugar colony of Saint Domingue (the western third of the island of Hispaniola), inspired by the ideals of the revolution occurring in France, revolted against French plantation owners. Led by Toussaint L'Ouverture (1746–1803), a son of African slaves, over 100,000 black slaves rose in revolt and seized control of all of Hispaniola. Later, an army sent by Napoleon captured L'Ouverture, who died in captivity in France. But the French soldiers, weakened by disease, soon succumbed to the slave forces. On January 1, 1804, the western part of Hispaniola, now called Haiti, announced its freedom and became the first independent state in Latin America. One of the French revolutionary ideals had triumphed abroad.

## Reaction and the Directory

By the summer of 1794, the French had been successful on the battlefield against their foreign foes, making the Terror less necessary. But the Terror continued because Robespierre, who had become a figure of power and authority, became obsessed with purifying the body politic of all the corrupt. Many deputies in the National Convention were fearful, however, that they were not safe while Robespierre was free to act and gathered enough votes to condemn him. Robespierre was guillotined on July 28, 1794.

After the death of Robespierre, a reaction set in as more moderate middle-class leaders took control. The Reign of Terror came to a halt, and the National Convention reduced the power of the Committee of Public Safety. In addition, a new constitution was drafted in August 1795 that reflected the desire for a stability that did not sacrifice the ideals of 1789. Five directors—the Directory—acted as the executive authority.

The period of the Revolution under the government of the Directory (1795–1799) was an era of stagnation and corruption. At the same time, the Directory faced political enemies from both the left and the right of the political spectrum. On the right, royalists who wanted to restore the monarchy continued their agitation. On the left, radical hopes of power were revived by continuing economic problems. Battered from both sides, unable to solve the country's economic problems, and still carrying on the wars inherited from the Committee of Public Safety, the Directory increasingly relied on the military to maintain its power. This led to a coup d'état in 1799 in which the popular military general Napoleon Bonaparte seized power.

**CHRONOLOGY The French Revolution**

| | |
|---|---|
| Meeting of Estates-General | May 5, 1789 |
| Formation of National Assembly | June 17, 1789 |
| Fall of the Bastille | July 14, 1789 |
| Declaration of the Rights of Man and the Citizen | August 26, 1789 |
| Civil Constitution of the Clergy | July 12, 1790 |
| Flight of the king | June 20–21, 1791 |
| Attack on the royal palace | August 10, 1792 |
| Abolition of the monarchy | September 21, 1792 |
| Execution of the king | January 21, 1793 |
| Levy-in-mass | August 23, 1793 |
| Execution of Robespierre | July 28, 1794 |
| Adoption of Constitution of 1795 and the Directory | August 22, 1795 |

# The Age of Napoleon

Napoleon dominated both French and European history from 1799 to 1815. He was born in 1769 in Corsica shortly after France had annexed the island. The young Napoleon Bonaparte was sent to France to study in one of the new military schools and was a lieutenant when the Revolution broke out in 1789. The Revolution and the European war that followed gave him new opportunities, and Napoleon rose quickly through the ranks. In 1794, at the age of only twenty-five, he was made a brigadier general by the Committee of Public Safety. Two years later, he commanded the French armies in Italy, where he won a series of victories and returned to France as a conquering hero (see the box on p. 502). After a disastrous expedition to Egypt, Napoleon returned to Paris, where he participated in the coup that gave him control of France. He was only thirty years old.

After the coup of 1799, a new form of the Republic—called the Consulate—was proclaimed in which Napoleon, as first consul, controlled the entire executive authority of government. He had overwhelming influence over the legislature, appointed members of the administrative bureaucracy, commanded the army, and conducted foreign affairs. In 1802, Napoleon was made consul for life, and in 1804, he returned France to monarchy when he had himself crowned as Emperor Napoleon I.

## Domestic Policies

One of Napoleon's first domestic policies was to establish peace with the oldest and most implacable enemy of the Revolution, the Catholic church. In 1801, Napoleon arranged a concordat with the pope that recognized Catholicism as the religion of a majority of the French people. In return, the pope agreed not to raise the question of the church lands confiscated in the Revolution. As a result of the concordat, the Catholic church was no longer an enemy of the French government, and those who had acquired church lands during the Revolution were assured that they would not be stripped of them, an assurance that made them supporters of the Napoleonic regime.

Napoleon's most enduring domestic achievement was his codification of the laws. Before the Revolution, France had some three hundred local legal systems. During the Revolution, efforts were made to prepare a single code of laws for the entire nation, but it remained for Napoleon to bring the work to completion in the famous Civil Code. This preserved most of the revolutionary gains by recognizing the principle of the equality of all citizens before the law, the abolition of serfdom and feudalism, and religious toleration. Property rights were also protected.

At the same time, the Civil Code strictly curtailed the rights of some people. During the radical phase of the

## Napoleon and Psychological Warfare

In 1796, at the age of twenty-seven, Napoleon Bonaparte was given command of the French army [illegible] His use of speed, deception, and surprise to overwhelm his opponents is well known. In this selection from a proclamation to his troops in Italy, Napoleon also appears as a master of psychological warfare.

*What themes did Napoleon use to play upon the emotions of his troops and inspire them to greater efforts? Do you think Napoleon believed these words? Why or why not?*

### Napoleon Bonaparte, Proclamation to French Troops in Italy (April 26, 1796)

Soldiers:

In a fortnight you have won six victories, taken twenty-one standards [flags of military units], fifty-five pieces of artillery, several strong positions, and conquered the richest part of Piedmont [in northern Italy]; you have captured 15,000 prisoners and killed or wounded more than 10,000 men. . . . You have won battles without cannon, crossed rivers without bridges, made forced marches without shoes, camped without brandy and often without bread. Soldiers of liberty, only republican troops could have endured what you have endured. Soldiers, you have our thanks! The [illegible]

The two armies which but recently attacked you with audacity are fleeing before you in terror; the wicked men who laughed at your misery and rejoiced at the thought of the triumphs of your enemies are confounded and trembling.

But, soldiers, as yet you have done nothing compared with what remains to be done. . . . Undoubtedly the greatest obstacles have been overcome; but you still have battles to fight, cities to capture, rivers to cross. Is there one among you whose courage is abating? No. . . . All of you are consumed with a desire to extend the glory of the French people; all of you long to humiliate those arrogant kings who dare to contemplate placing us in fetters; all of you desire to dictate a glorious peace, one which will indemnify the *Patrie* for the immense sacrifices it has made; all of you wish to be able to say with pride as you return to your villages, "I was with the victorious army of Italy!"

**HistoryNow**™ To read a related document, enter the *HistoryNow* documents area using the access card that is available for *World History*.

French Revolution, new laws had made divorce an easy process for both husbands and wives and allowed sons and daughters to inherit property equally. Napoleon's Civil Code undid these laws. Divorce was still allowed but was made more difficult for women to obtain. Women were now "less equal than men" in other ways as well. When they married, their property came under the control of their husbands.

Napoleon also developed a powerful, centralized administrative machine and worked hard to develop a bureaucracy of capable officials. Early on, the regime showed that it cared little whether the expertise of officials had been acquired in royal or revolutionary bureaucracies. Promotion, whether in civil or military offices, was to be based not on rank or birth but on ability only. This principle of a government career open to talent was, of course, what many bourgeois had wanted before the Revolution.

In his domestic policies, then, Napoleon both destroyed and preserved aspects of the Revolution. Liberty had been replaced by an initially benevolent despotism that grew increasingly arbitrary as the demands of war overwhelmed Napoleon and the French. The Civil Code, however, preserved the equality of all citizens before the law. The concept of careers open to talent was also a gain of the Revolution that Napoleon preserved.

## Napoleon's Empire

When Napoleon became consul in 1799, France was at war with a second European coalition of Russia, Great Britain, and Austria. Napoleon realized the need for a pause and made a peace treaty in 1802. But war was renewed in 1803 with Britain, who was soon joined by Austria, Russia, and Prussia in the Third Coalition. In a series of battles from 1805 to 1807, Napoleon's Grand Army defeated the Austrian, Prussian, and Russian armies, giving Napoleon the opportunity to create a new European order.

**The Grand Empire** From 1807 to 1812, Napoleon was the master of Europe. His Grand Empire was composed of three major parts: the French Empire, dependent states, and allied states (see Map 17.5). Dependent states were kingdoms under the rule of Napoleon's relatives; these came to include Spain, the Netherlands, the kingdom of Italy, the Swiss Republic, the Grand Duchy of Warsaw, and the Confederation of the Rhine (a union of all German states except Austria and Prussia). Allied states were those defeated by Napoleon and forced to join his struggle against Britain; these included Prussia, Austria, Russia, and Sweden.

Within his empire, Napoleon sought acceptance of certain revolutionary principles, including legal equality,

**The Coronation of Napoleon.** In 1804, Napoleon restored monarchy to France when he had himself crowned as emperor. In the coronation scene painted by Jacques-Louis David, Napoleon is shown crowning his wife, the empress Josephine, while the pope looks on. The painting shows Napoleon's mother seated in the box in the background, even though she was not at the ceremony.

religious toleration, and economic freedom. In the inner core and dependent states of his Grand Empire, Napoleon tried to destroy the old order. Nobility and clergy everywhere in these states lost their special privileges. He decreed equality of opportunity with offices open to talent, equality before the law, and religious toleration. This spread of French revolutionary principles was an important factor in the development of liberal traditions in these countries.

Napoleon hoped that his Grand Empire would last for centuries; it collapsed almost as rapidly as it had been formed. As long as Britain ruled the waves, it was not subject to military attack. Napoleon hoped to invade Britain, but he could not overcome the British navy's decisive defeat of a combined French-Spanish fleet at Trafalgar in 1805. To defeat Britain, Napoleon turned to his **Continental System.** An alliance put into effect between 1806 and 1808, it attempted to prevent British goods from reaching the European continent in order to weaken Britain economically and destroy its capacity to wage war. But the Continental System failed. Allied states resented it; some began to cheat and others to resist.

Napoleon also encountered new sources of opposition. His conquests made the French hated oppressors and aroused the patriotism of the conquered people. A Spanish uprising against Napoleon's rule, aided by British support, kept a French force of 200,000 pinned down for years.

**The Fall of Napoleon** The beginning of Napoleon's downfall came in 1812 with his invasion of Russia. The refusal of the Russians to remain in the Continental System left Napoleon with little choice. Although aware of the risks in invading such a huge country, he also knew that if the Russians were allowed to challenge the Continental System unopposed, others would soon follow suit. In June 1812, he led his Grand Army of more than 600,000 men into Russia. Napoleon's hopes for victory depended on quickly defeating the Russian armies, but the Russian forces retreated and refused to give battle, torching their own villages and countryside to keep Napoleon's army from finding food. When the Russians did stop to fight at Borodino, Napoleon's forces won an indecisive and costly victory. When the remaining troops of the Grand Army arrived in Moscow, they

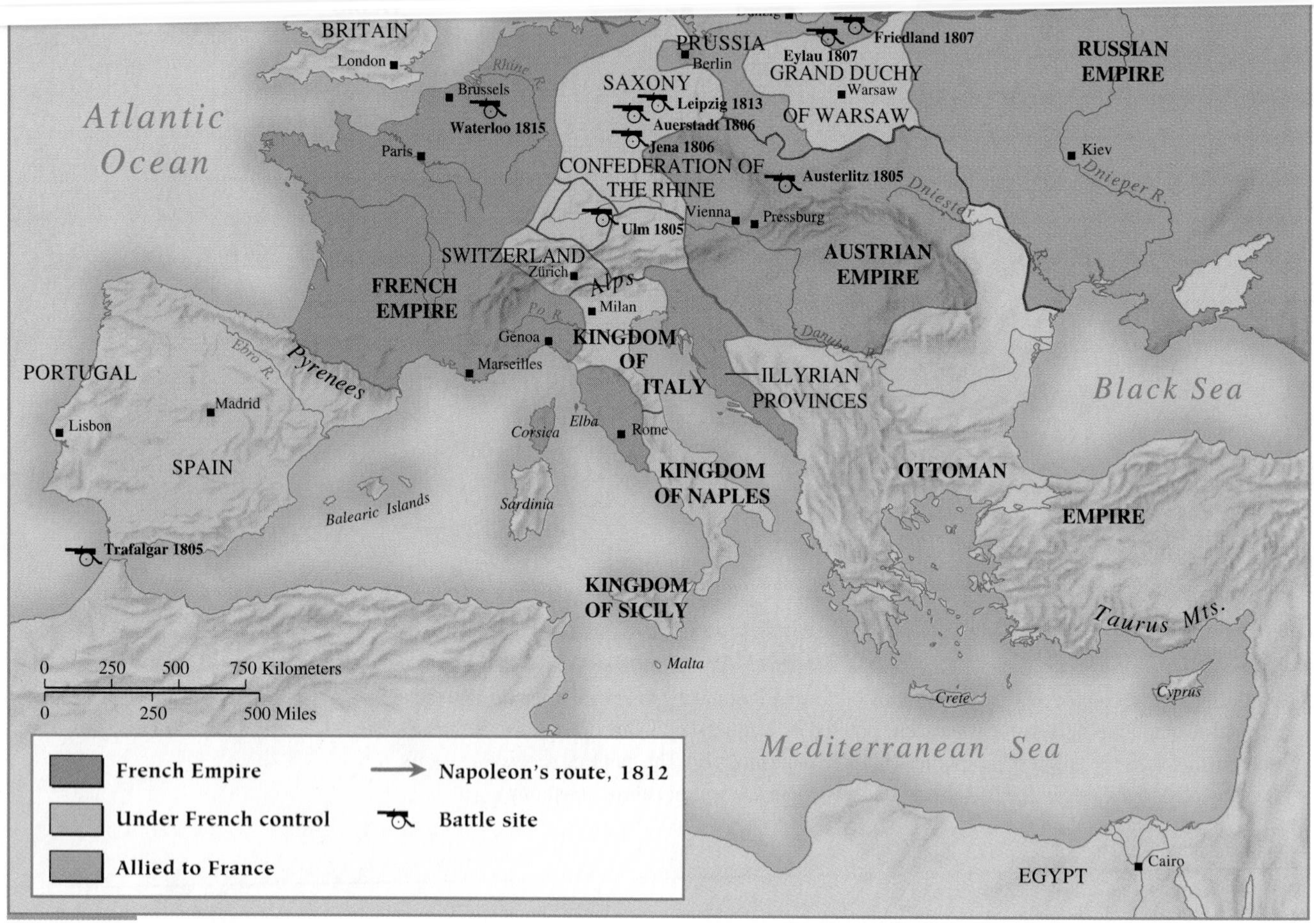


**MAP 17.5 Napoleon's Grand Empire.** Napoleon's Grand Army won a series of victories against Britain, Austria, Prussia, and Russia that gave the French emperor full or partial control over much of Europe by 1807. ? On the Continent, what is the overall relationship between distance from France and degree of French control, and how can you account for this? **View an animated version of this map or related maps at http://history.wadsworth.com/duikerspielvogel05/**

found the city ablaze. Lacking food and supplies, Napoleon abandoned Moscow late in October and made a retreat across Russia in terrible winter conditions. Only 40,000 of the original 600,000 men managed to arrive back in Poland in January 1813.

This military disaster led other European states to rise up and attack the crippled French army. Paris was captured in March 1814, and Napoleon was sent into exile on the island of Elba, off the coast of Italy. Meanwhile, the Bourbon monarchy was restored in the person of Louis XVIII, the Count of Provence, brother of the executed king. (Louis XVII, son of Louis XVI, had died in prison at age ten.) Napoleon, bored on Elba, slipped back into France. When troops were sent to capture him, Napoleon opened his coat and addressed them: "Soldiers of the 5th regiment, I am your Emperor. . . . If there is a man among you would kill his Emperor, here I am!" No one fired a shot. Shouting *"Vive l'Empereur! Vive l'Empereur!"* the troops went over to his side, and Napoleon entered Paris in triumph on March 20, 1815.

The powers that had defeated him pledged once more to fight him. Having decided to strike first at his enemies, Napoleon raised yet another army and moved to attack the allied forces stationed in what is now Belgium. At Waterloo on June 18, Napoleon met a combined British and Prussian army under the duke of Wellington and suffered a bloody defeat. This time, the victorious allies exiled him to Saint Helena, a small, forsaken island in the South Atlantic. Only Napoleon's memory continued to haunt French political life.

## CONCLUSION

THE SCIENTIFIC REVOLUTION was a major turning point in modern civilization. With a new conception of the universe came a new conception of humankind and the belief that by using reason alone people could understand and dominate the world of nature. In combination with the eighteenth-century Enlightenment, the Scientific Revolution gave the West an intellectual boost that contributed to the increased confidence of Western civilization. Europeans–with their strong governments, prosperous economies, and strengthened military forces–began to dominate other parts of the world, leading to a growing belief in the superiority of their civilization.

Everywhere in Europe at the beginning of the eighteenth century, the old order remained strong. Monarchs sought to enlarge their bureaucracies to raise taxes to support the large standing armies that had originated in the seventeenth century. The existence of five great powers, with two of them (France and England) embattled in the East and in the Western Hemisphere, ushered in a new scale of conflict; the Seven Years' War can legitimately be viewed as the first world war. Throughout Europe, increased demands for taxes to support these conflicts led to attacks on the privileged orders and a desire for change not met by the ruling monarchs. The inability of that old order to deal meaningfully with this desire for change led to a revolutionary outburst at the end of the eighteenth century that brought the old order to an end.

The revolutionary era of the late eighteenth century was a time of dramatic political transformations. Revolutionary upheavals, beginning in North America and continuing in France, spurred movements for political liberty and equality. The documents promulgated by these revolutions, the Declaration of Independence and the Declaration of the Rights of Man and the Citizen, embodied the fundamental ideas of the Enlightenment and created a liberal political agenda based on a belief in popular sovereignty–the people as the source of political power–and the principles of liberty and equality. Liberty meant, in theory, freedom from arbitrary power as well as the freedom to think, write, and worship as one chose. Equality meant equality in rights and equality of opportunity based on talent rather than wealth or status at birth. In practice, equality remained limited; property owners had greater opportunities for voting and office holding, and women were still not treated as the equals of men.

The French Revolution set in motion a modern revolutionary concept. No one had foreseen or consciously planned the upheaval that began in 1789, but thereafter, radicals and revolutionaries knew that mass uprisings by the common people could overthrow unwanted elitist governments. For these people, the French Revolution became a symbol of hope; for those who feared such changes, it became a symbol of dread. The French Revolution became the classical political and social model for revolution. At the same time, the liberal and national political ideals created by the Revolution dominated the political landscape for well over a century. A new era had begun, and the world would never be the same.

## CHAPTER NOTES

1. R. Descartes, *Philosophical Writing*, ed. and trans. N. K. Smith (New York, 1958), pp 118–119.
2. J. Locke, *An Essay Concerning Human Understanding* (New York, 1964), pp. 89–90.
3. Quoted in P. Burke, *Popular Culture in Early Modern Europe*, rev. ed. (New York, 1994), p. 186.
4. Quoted in W. Doyle, *The Oxford History of the French Revolution* (Oxford, 1989), p. 184.
5. Quoted in L. Gershoy, *The Era of the French Revolution* (Princeton, N.J., 1957), p. 157.
6. Quoted in Doyle, *The Oxford History of the French Revolution*, p. 254.

## SUGGESTED READING

Three general surveys of the Scientific Revolution are **J. R. Jacob, *The Scientific Revolution: Aspirations and Achievements, 1500–1700*** (Atlantic Highlands, N.J., 1998); **S. Shapin, *The Scientific Revolution*** (Chicago, 1996); and **J. Henry, *The Scientific Revolution and the Origins of Modern Science*** (New York, 1997).

Good introductions to the Enlightenment can be found in **U. Im Hof, *The Enlightenment*** (Oxford, 1994); **D. Goodman, *The Republic of Letters: A Cultural History of the French Enlightenment*** (Ithaca, N.Y., 1994); and **D. Outram, *The Enlightenment*** (Cambridge, 1995). On the social history of the Enlightenment, see **T. Munck, *The Enlightenment: A Comparative Social History, 1721–1794*** (London, 2000). On women in the eighteenth century, see **N. Z. Davis** and **A. Farge**, eds., ***A History of Women: Renaissance and Enlightenment Paradoxes*** (Cambridge, Mass., 1993), and **O. Hufton, *The Prospect Before Her: A History of Women in Western Europe, 1500–1800*** (New York, 1998).

On the European nobility in the eighteenth century, see **J. Dewald, *The European Nobility, 1400–1800*** (Cambridge, 1996). On European cities, see **J. de Vries, *European Urbanization, 1500–1800*** (Cambridge, Mass., 1984). The warfare of this period is examined in **M. S. Anderson, *War and Society in Europe of the Old Regime, 1615–1789*** (New York, 1988).

TIMELINE

1600 | 1650 | 1700 | 1750 | 1800 | 1850

Reign of Frederick the Great

Seven Years' War

American Declaration of Independence

Storming of the Bastille

Work of Descartes

Work of Isaac Newton

Diderot, *Encyclopedia*

Reign of Terror in France

Napoleon becomes emperor

Rousseau, *The Social Contract*

Work of Sor Juana Inéz de la Cruz

Work of Watteau

Reform program of Joseph II

Battle of Waterloo

For a brief survey of Latin America, see **E. B. Burns, *Latin America: A Concise Interpretative History,*** 4th ed. (Englewood Cliffs, N.J., 1986). A more detailed work on colonial Latin American history is **J. Lockhardt** and **S. B. Schwartz, *Early Latin America: A History of Colonial Spanish America and Brazil*** (New York, 1983). A history of the revolutionary era in America can be found in **C. Bonwick, *The American Revolution*** (Charlottesville, Va., 1991). The importance of ideology is treated in **G. Wood, *The Radicalism of the American Revolution*** (New York, 1992).

On enlightened absolutism, see **H. M. Scott**, ed., ***Enlightened Absolutism: Reform and Reformers in Later Eighteenth-Century Europe*** (Ann Arbor, Mich., 1990). Good biographies of some of Europe's monarchs include **R. Asprey, *Frederick the Great: The Magnificent Enigma*** (New York, 1986); **I. De Madariaga, *Catherine the Great: A Short History*** (New Haven, Conn., 1990); and **T. C. W. Blanning, *Joseph II*** (New York, 1994).

A well written, up-to-date introduction to the French Revolution can be found in **W. Doyle, *The Oxford History of the French Revolution*** (Oxford, 1989). On the entire revolutionary and Napoleonic eras, see **O. Connelly, *The French Revolution and Napoleonic Era,*** 3d ed. (Fort Worth, Tex., 2000), and **D. M. G. Sutherland, *France, 1789-1815: Revolution and Counter-Revolution*** (London, 1985). Two brief works are **A. Forrest, *The French Revolution*** (Oxford, 1995), and **J. M. Roberts, *The French Revolution,*** 2d ed. (New York, 1997).

On the early years of the Revolution, see **T. Tackett, *Becoming a Revolutionary*** (Princeton, N.J., 1996), and **N. Hampson, *Prelude to Terror*** (Oxford, 1988). For interesting insight into Louis XVI and French society, see **T. Tackett, *When the King Took Flight*** (Cambridge, Mass., 2003). Important works on the radical stage of the French Revolution include **N. Hampson, *The Terror in the French Revolution*** (London, 1981); **R. R. Palmer, *Twelve Who Ruled*** (Princeton, N.J., 1965), a classic; and **R. Cobb, *The People's Armies*** (London, 1987). The importance of the revolutionary wars in the radical stage of the Revolution is underscored in **T. C. W. Blanning, *The French Revolutionary Wars, 1787–1802*** (New York, 1996). On the role of women in revolutionary France, see **O. Hufton, *Women and the Limits of Citizenship in the French Revolution*** (Toronto, 1992), and **J. Landes, *Women and the Public Sphere in the Age of the French Revolution*** (Ithaca, N.Y., 1988). On Napoleon, see **S. Englund, *Napoleon: A Political Life*** (New York, 2004); **G. J. Ellis, *Napoleon*** (New York, 1997); and the massive biographies by **F. J. McLynn, *Napoleon: A Biography*** (London, 1997), and **A. Schom, *Napoleon Bonaparte*** (New York, 1997).

**History Now™**

Enter *HistoryNow* using the access card that is available with this text. *HistoryNow* will assist you in understanding the content in this chapter with lesson plans generated for your needs, as well as provide you with a connection to the *Wadsworth World History Resource Center* (see description below for details).

**WORLD HISTORY**
RESOURCE CENTER

Enter the Resource Center using either your *HistoryNow* access card or your standalone access card for the *Wadsworth World History Resource Center.* Organized by topic, this website includes quizzes; images; over 350 primary source documents; interactive simulations; maps and timelines; movie explorations; and a wealth of other resources. You can read the following documents, and many more, at http://history.wadsworth.com/rc/world

Jean-Jacques Rousseau, *The Social Contract*

Edmund Burke, *Reflections on the Revolution in France*

Baron von Stein, contemporary account of the Prussian victory over Napoleon's army

Visit the *World History* Companion Website for chapter quizzes and more.

http://history.wadsworth.com/duikerspielvogel05/

# Looking Ahead

**Within the centralized states** at the end of the eighteenth century, the steady growth of a commercial and manufacturing sector was beginning to create the conditions for a future industrial revolution. A number of Asian societies had made technological advances during this period and witnessed the emergence of a more visible and articulate urban bourgeoisie. For the moment, however, such forces were mere portents for the future, not

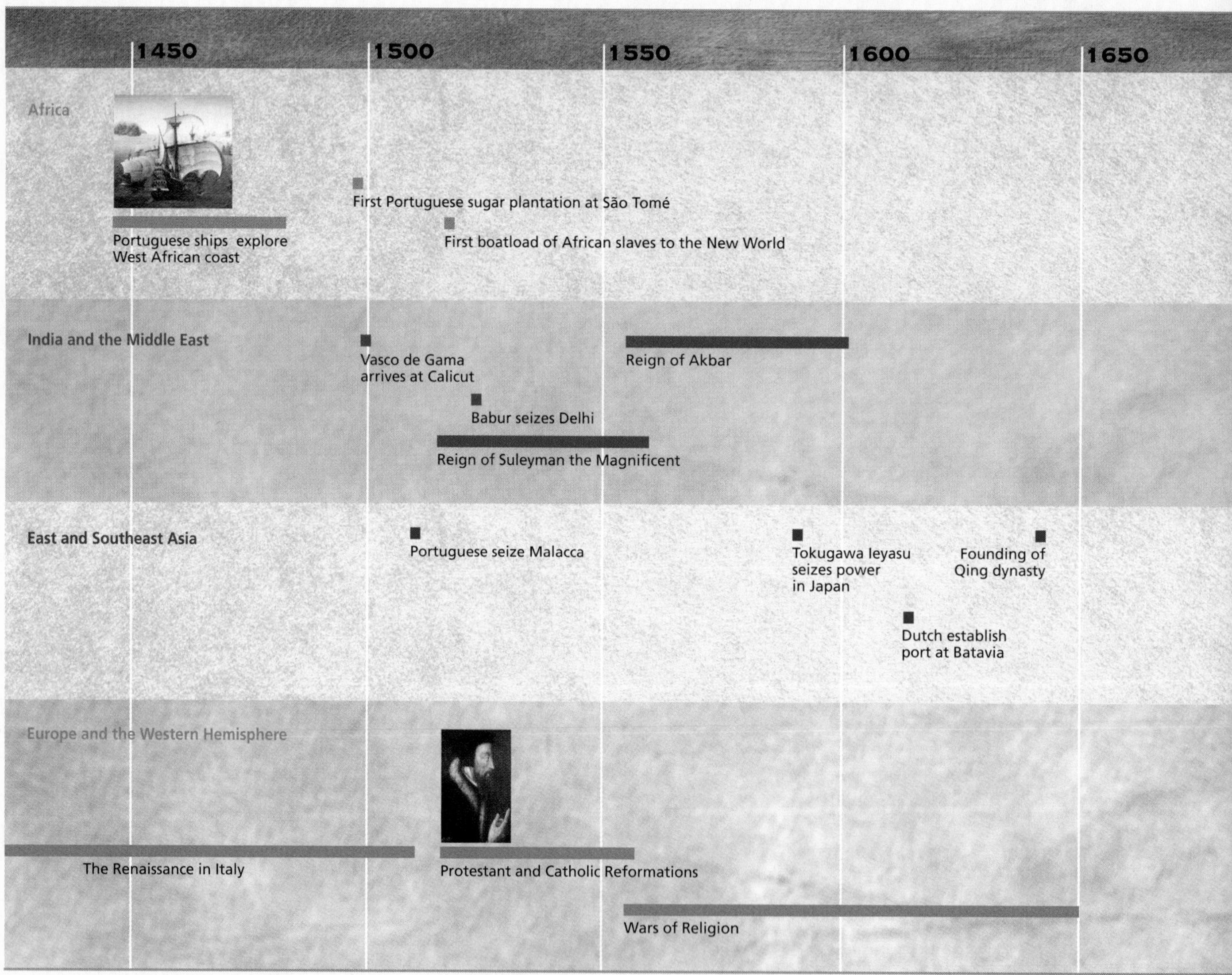

signs of an imminent industrial revolution. At the beginning of the nineteenth century, the primary fact of life for most Asian and African societies was the expansionist power of an industrializing and ever more aggressive Europe. The power and ambition of the West provided an immediate challenge to the independence and destiny of societies throughout the rest of the world. The nature of that challenge will be the subject of our next section.

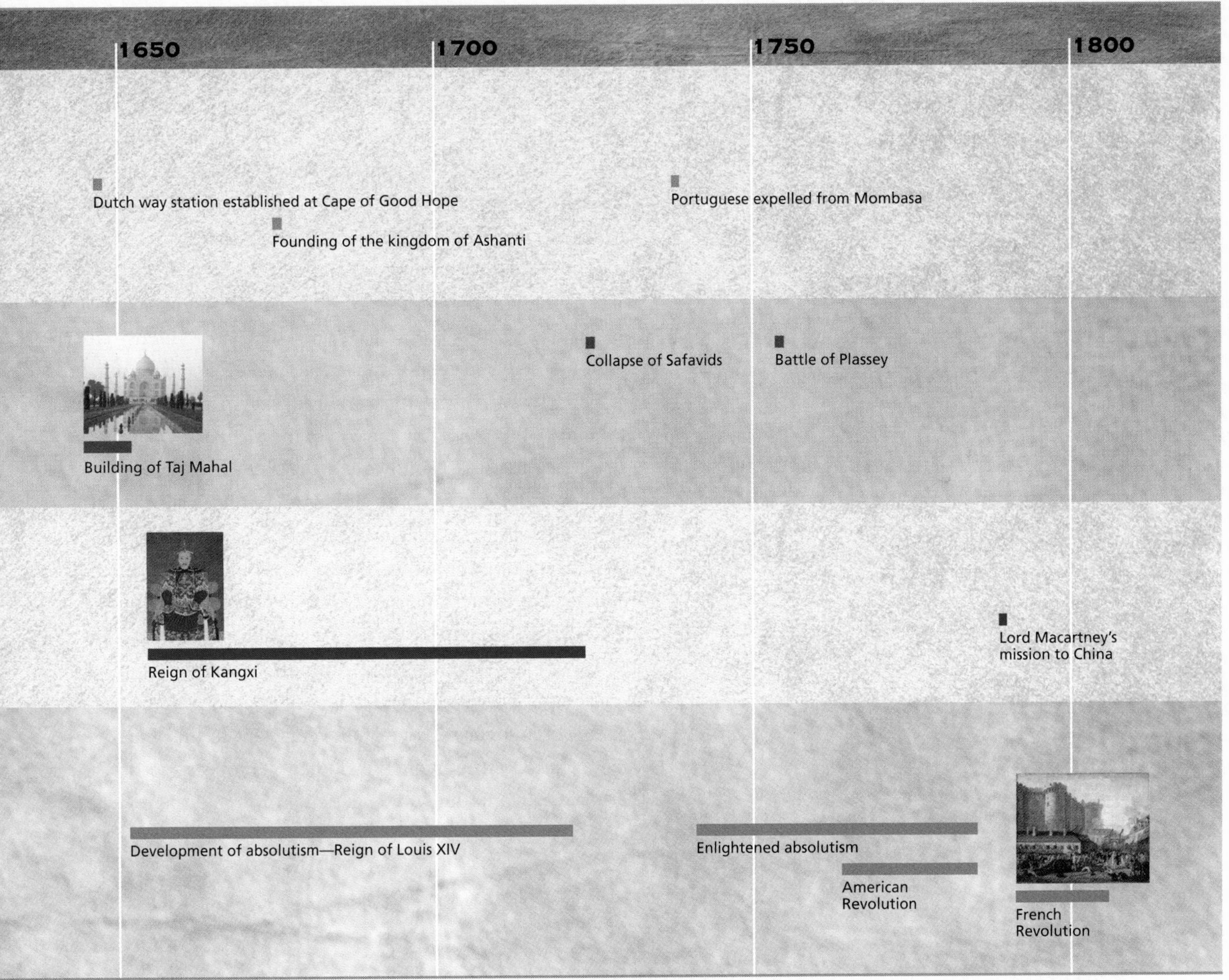

PART

# IV

# MODERN PATTERNS OF WORLD HISTORY (1800–1945)



THE PERIOD OF WORLD HISTORY from 1800 to 1945 was characterized, above all, by two major developments: the growth of industrialization and Western domination of the world. The two developments were, of course, interconnected. The Industrial Revolution became one of the major forces of change in the nineteenth century as it led Western civilization into the industrial era that has characterized the modern world. Beginning in Britain, it spread to the Continent and the Western Hemisphere in the course of the nineteenth century. At the same time, the Industrial Revolution created the technological means, including new weapons, by which the West achieved domination of much of the rest of the world by the end of the nineteenth century.

Europeans had begun to explore the world in the fifteenth century, but even as late as 1870, they had not yet completely penetrated North America, South America, Australia, or most of Africa. In Asia and Africa, with few exceptions, the Western presence was limited to trading posts. Between 1870 and 1914, Western civilization expanded into the rest of the Americas and Australia, while the bulk of Africa and Asia was divided into European colonies or spheres of influence. Two major events explain this remarkable expansion: the migration of many Europeans to other parts of the world due to population growth and the revival

V and A Picture Library

of imperialism, which was made possible by the West's technological advancement. Beginning in the 1880s, European states began an intense scramble for overseas territory. This revival of imperialism—the "new imperialism," some have called it—led Europeans to carve up Asia and Africa.

What was the overall economic effect of imperialism on the subject peoples? For most of the population in colonial areas, Western domination was rarely beneficial and often destructive. Although a limited number of merchants, large landowners, and traditional hereditary elites undoubtedly prospered under the umbrella of the expanding imperialistic economic order, the majority of colonial peoples, urban and rural alike, probably suffered considerable hardship as a result of the policies adopted by their foreign rulers.

Some historians point out, however, that for all the inequities of the colonial system, there was a positive side to the experience as well. The expansion of markets and the beginnings of a modern transportation and communications network, while bringing few immediate benefits to the colonial peoples, offered considerable promise for future economic growth. At the same time, the introduction of new ways of looking at human freedom and the relationship between the individual and society set the stage for a reevaluation of such ideas after the restoration of independence following World War II.

Perhaps the Western concept that had the most immediate impact on the era was the rise of nationalism. Like the Industrial Revolution, the idea of nationalism originated in eighteenth-century Europe, where it was a product of the secularization of the age and the experiences of the French revolutionary and Napoleonic eras. Although the concept provided the basis for a new sense of community and the rise of the modern nation-state, it also gave birth to ethnic tensions and hatred that resulted in bitter disputes and civil strife and contributed to the competition that eventually erupted into world war. Nevertheless, colonial peoples soon learned the power of nationalism, and in the twentieth century, nationalism would become a powerful force in the rest of the world as nationalist revolutions moved through Asia, Africa, and the Middle East. Moreover, the exhaustive struggles of two world wars sapped the power of the European states, and the colonial powers no longer had the energy or the wealth to maintain their colonial empires after World War II. ◆

CHAPTER

# 18

# THE BEGINNINGS OF MODERNIZATION: INDUSTRIALIZATION AND NATIONALISM, 1800–1870

A meeting of the Congress of Vienna

© Scala/Art Resource, NY

## CHAPTER OUTLINE AND FOCUS QUESTIONS

### The Industrial Revolution and Its Impact

- What were the basic features of the new industrial system created by the Industrial Revolution, and what effects did the new system have on urban life, social classes, family life, and standards of living?

### Reaction and Revolution: The Growth of Nationalism

- What were the major ideas associated with conservatism, liberalism, and nationalism, and what role did each ideology play in Europe and Latin America between 1800 and 1870?
- What were the causes of the revolutions of 1848, and why did these revolutions fail?

### National Unification and the National State, 1848–1871

- What actions did Cavour and Bismarck take to bring about unification in Germany and Italy, respectively, and what role did war play in their efforts?

### Cultural Life: Romanticism and Realism in the Western World

- What were the main characteristics of Romanticism and Realism?

### CRITICAL THINKING

- In what ways were the intellectual and artistic developments of the age related to the development of industrialization and the growth of nationalism?

IN SEPTEMBER 1814, hundreds of foreigners began to converge on Vienna, the capital city of the Austrian Empire. Many were members of European royalty–kings, archdukes, princes, and their wives–accompanied by their diplomatic advisers and scores of servants. Their congenial host was the Austrian emperor, Francis I, who never tired of regaling Vienna's guests with concerts, glittering balls, sumptuous feasts, and innumerable hunting parties. One participant remembered, "Eating, fireworks, public illuminations. For eight or ten days, I haven't been able to work at all. What a life!" Of course, not every waking hour was spent in pleasure during this gathering of notables, known to history as the Congress of Vienna. These people were also representatives of all the states that had fought Napoleon, and their real business was to arrange a final peace settlement after almost a decade of war. On June 8, 1815, they finally completed their task.

The forces of upheaval unleashed during the French revolutionary and Napoleonic wars were temporarily quieted in 1815 as rulers sought to restore stability by reestablishing much of the old order to a Europe ravaged by war. But the Western world had been changed, and it would not readily go back to the old system. New ideologies of change, especially liberalism and nationalism, products of the upheaval initiated in France, had become too powerful to be contained. The forces of change called forth revolts that periodically shook the West and culminated in a spate of revolutions in 1848. Some of the revolutions and revolutionaries were successful; most were not. And yet by 1870, many of the goals sought by the liberals and nationalists during the first half of the nineteenth century seemed to have been achieved. National unity became a reality in Italy and Germany, and many Western states developed parliamentary features.

During the late eighteenth and early nineteenth centuries, another revolution–an industrial one–transformed the economic and social structure of Europe and spawned the industrial era that has characterized modern world history. ◇

# The Industrial Revolution and Its Impact

The Industrial Revolution triggered an enormous leap in industrial production. Coal and steam replaced wind and water as new sources of energy and power to drive labor-saving machines. In turn, these machines called for new ways of organizing human labor as factories replaced workshops and home workrooms. During the Industrial Revolution, Europe shifted from an economy based on agriculture and handicrafts to an economy based on manufacturing by machines and automated factories.

Although it took decades for the Industrial Revolution to spread, it was truly revolutionary in the way it fundamentally changed the world. Large numbers of people moved from the countryside to cities to work in the new factories. The creation of a wealthy industrial middle class and a huge industrial working class substantially transformed traditional social relationships. Finally, the Industrial Revolution fundamentally altered how people related to nature, ultimately creating an environmental crisis that in the twentieth century was finally recognized as a danger to human existence itself.

## The Industrial Revolution in Great Britain

Although the Industrial Revolution evolved over a period of time, historians generally agree that it began in Britain sometime after 1750.

**Origins** A number of factors or conditions coalesced in Britain to produce the Industrial Revolution. Improvements in agricultural practices in the eighteenth century led to a significant increase in food production. British agriculture could now feed more people at lower prices with less labor; even ordinary British families did not have to use most of their income to buy food, giving them the wherewithal to purchase manufactured goods. At the same time, the rapid population growth in the second half of the eighteenth century provided a pool of surplus labor for the new factories of the emerging British industry.

Britain also had a ready supply of capital for investment in the new industrial machines and the factories that were needed to house them. In addition to profits from trade and the cottage industry, Britain possessed an effective central bank and well-developed, flexible credit facilities. But capital is only part of the story. Britain had a fair number of individuals who were interested in making profits if the opportunity presented itself. No doubt the English revolutions of the seventeenth century had helped create an environment in Britain, unlike that of the absolutist states on the Continent, where political power rested in the hands of a progressive group of people who favored innovation in economic matters.

Britain also had ample supplies of important mineral resources, such as coal and iron ore, needed in the manufacturing process. It was also small, and the relatively short distances made transportation nonproblematic. Britain's government, too, played a significant role in the process of industrialization. Parliament contributed to the favorable business climate by providing a stable government and passing laws that protected private property.

Finally, the many markets of the Commonwealth gave British industrialists a ready outlet for their manufactured goods. British exports quadrupled from 1660 to 1760. In the course of its eighteenth-century wars and conquests, Great Britain had assembled a vast colonial empire at the expense of its leading rivals, the Dutch Republic and France. A crucial factor in Britain's successful industrialization was the ability to produce cheaply the articles in greatest demand. The traditional methods of the cottage industry could not keep up with the growing demand for cotton clothes throughout Britain and its vast colonial empire. This problem led British cloth manufacturers to seek and accept the new methods of manufacturing that a series of inventions provided. In so doing, these individuals ignited the Industrial Revolution.

**Changes in Textile Production** The invention of the flying shuttle made weaving on a loom faster and enabled weavers to double their output. This created shortages of yarn until James Hargreaves's spinning jenny, perfected by 1768, allowed spinners to produce yarn in greater quantities. Edmund Cartwright's loom, powered by water and invented in 1787, allowed the weaving of cloth to catch up with the spinning of yarn. It was now more efficient to bring workers to the machines and organize their labor collectively in factories located next to rivers and streams, the sources of power for these early machines.

What pushed the cotton industry to even greater heights of productivity was the invention of the steam engine. In the 1760s, a Scottish engineer, James Watt (1736–1819), built an engine powered by steam that could pump water from mines three times as quickly as previous engines. In 1782, Watt developed a rotary engine that could turn a shaft and thus drive machinery. Steam power could now be applied to spinning and weaving cotton, and before long, cotton mills using steam engines were multiplying across Britain. Fired by coal, these steam engines could be located anywhere.

The new boost given to cotton textile production by technological changes became readily apparent. In 1760, Britain had imported 2.5 million pounds of raw cotton, which was farmed out to cottage industries. In 1787, the British imported 22 million pounds of cotton; most of it was spun on machines, some powered by water in large mills. By 1840, some 366 million pounds of cotton—now Britain's most important product in value—were being imported. By this time, most cotton industry employees worked in factories, and British cotton goods were sold everywhere in the world.

**Other Technological Changes** The British iron industry was radically transformed during the Industrial Revolution. Britain had always had large resources of iron ore, but at the beginning of the eighteenth century, the basic process of producing iron had changed little since the Middle Ages and still depended heavily on charcoal. A better quality of iron came into being in the 1780s when Henry Cort developed a system called puddling, in which coke, which was derived from coal, was used to burn away impurities in pig iron (crude iron) and produce an iron of high quality. A boom then ensued in the British iron industry. In 1740, Britain produced 17,000 tons of iron; by the 1840s, over 2 million tons; and by 1852, almost 3 million tons, more than the rest of the world combined.

The new high-quality wrought iron was in turn used to build new machines and ultimately new industries. In 1804, Richard Trevithick pioneered the first steam-powered locomotive on an industrial rail line in southern Wales. It pulled 10 tons of ore and seventy people at 5 miles per hour. Better locomotives soon followed. Engines built by George Stephenson and his son proved superior, and it was Stephenson's *Rocket* that was used on the first public railway line, which opened in 1830, stretching 32 miles from Liverpool to Manchester. *Rocket* sped along at 16 miles per hour. Within twenty years, locomotives had reached 50 miles per hour, an incredible speed to contemporary travelers. By 1840, Britain had almost 6,000 miles of railroads.

The railroad was an important contribution to the success and maturing of the Industrial Revolution. Railway construction created new job opportunities, especially for farm laborers and peasants who had long been accustomed to finding work outside their local villages. Perhaps most important, the proliferation of a cheaper and faster means of transportation had a ripple effect on the growth of the industrial economy. As the prices of goods fell, markets grew larger; increased sales meant more factories and more machinery, thereby reinforcing the self-sustaining aspect of the Industrial Revolution, a fundamental break with the traditional European economy. Continuous, self-sustaining economic growth came to be accepted as a fundamental characteristic of the new economy.

**The Industrial Factory** Another visible symbol of the Industrial Revolution was the factory (see the comparative illustration on p. 515). From its beginning, the factory created a new labor system. Factory owners wanted to use their new machines constantly. Workers were therefore obliged to work regular hours and in shifts to keep the machines producing at a steady rate. Early factory workers, however, came from rural areas, where they were used to a different pace of life. Peasant farmers worked hard, especially at harvest time, but they were also used to periods of inactivity.

Early factory owners therefore had to create a system of work discipline in which employees became accustomed to working regular hours and doing the same work over and over. Of course, such work was boring, and factory owners resorted to tough methods to accomplish their goals. They issued minute and detailed factory regulations (see the box on p. 516). For example, adult workers were fined for a wide variety of minor infractions, such as being a few minutes late for work, and dismissed for more serious misdoings, especially drunkenness, which set a bad example for younger workers and also courted disaster in the midst of dangerous machinery. Employers found that dismissals and fines worked well for adult employees; in a time when great population growth had

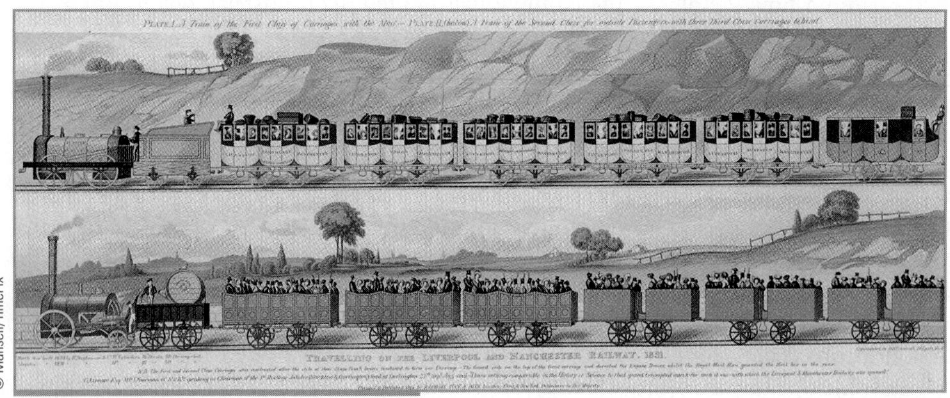



**Railroad Line from Liverpool to Manchester.** The railroad line from Liverpool to Manchester, first opened in 1830, relied on steam locomotives. As is evident in this illustration, carrying passengers was the railroad's main business. First-class passengers rode in covered cars, second- and third-class passengers in open cars.

© CORBIS

Laurie Platt Whitney, Inc.

SCIENCE & TECHNOLOGY

COMPARATIVE ILLUSTRATION

**Textile Factories, West and East.** The development of the factory changed the relationship between workers and employers as workers were encouraged to adjust to a new system of discipline that forced them to work regular hours under close supervision. At the top is an 1851 illustration that shows women working in a British cotton factory. The factory system came later to the rest of the world than it did in Britain. Shown at the bottom is one of the earliest industrial factories in Japan, the Tomioka silk factory, built in the 1870s. Note that although women are doing the work in both factories, the managers are men.

produced large masses of unskilled labor, dismissal meant disaster. Children were less likely to understand the implications of dismissal, so they were sometimes disciplined more directly—often by beating. As the nineteenth century progressed, the second and third generations of workers came to view a regular workweek as a natural way of life.

By the mid-nineteenth century, Great Britain had become the world's first and richest industrial nation. Britain was the "workshop, banker, and trader of the world." It produced one-half of the world's coal and manufactured goods; its cotton industry alone in 1850 was equal in size to the industries of all other European countries combined.

## The Spread of Industrialization

From Great Britain, industrialization spread to the Continental countries of Europe and the United States at different times and speeds during the nineteenth century. First to be industrialized on the Continent were Belgium, France, and the German states (see Map 18.1).

**Industrialization on the Continent** In 1815, Belgium, France, and the German states were still largely agrarian. Although they had experienced developments similar to those of Britain in the eighteenth century, these countries did not share Britain's move into new industrial directions in the 1770s and 1780s because they lacked some of the advantages that had made Britain's Industrial Revolution possible. Lack of good roads and problems with river transit made transportation difficult. Customs barriers along state boundaries increased the costs and prices of goods. Moreover, Continental entrepreneurs were generally less enterprising than their British counterparts and tended to adhere to traditional business attitudes, including an unwillingness to take risks in investment. Consequently, industrialization on the Continent faced numerous hurdles, and as it proceeded in earnest after 1815, it did so along lines that were somewhat different from Britain's.

Lack of technical knowledge was initially a major obstacle to industrialization. But the Continental countries possessed an advantage here; they could simply borrow British techniques and practices. Gradually, the Continent achieved technological independence as local people learned all the skills their British teachers had to offer. Even more important, however, Continental countries, especially France and the German states, began to establish a wide range of technical schools to train engineers and mechanics.

That government played an important role in this regard brings us to a second difference between British and Continental industrialization. Governments in most of the Continental countries were accustomed to playing a significant role in economic affairs. Furthering the development of industrialization was a logical extension of that attitude. For example, the governments awarded grants to inventors and provided funds to build roads, canals, and railroads. By 1850, a network of iron rails had spread across Europe.

## DISCIPLINE IN THE NEW FACTORIES

Workers in the new factories of the Industrial Revolution had been accustomed to a lifestyle free of overseers. Unlike the cottages, where workers spun thread and wove cloth in their own rhythm and time, the factories demanded a new, rigorous discipline geared to the requirements of the machines. This selection is taken from a set of rules for a factory in Berlin in 1844. They were typical of company rules everywhere the factory system had been established.

*What impact did factories have on the lives of workers? To what extent have such "rules" determined much of modern industrial life?*

### Factory Rules, Foundry and Engineering Works, Royal Overseas Trading Company

In every large works, and in the coordination of any large number of workmen, good order and harmony must be looked upon as the fundamentals of success, and therefore the following rules shall be strictly observed.

1. The normal working day begins at all seasons at 6 A.M. precisely and ends, after the usual break of half an hour for breakfast, an hour for dinner, and half an hour for tea, at 7 P.M., and it shall be strictly observed. . . .
2. Workers arriving 2 minutes late shall lose half an hour's wages; whoever is more than 2 minutes late may not start work until after the next break, or at least shall lose his wages until then. Any disputes about the correct time shall be settled by the clock mounted above the gatekeeper's lodge. . . .
3. No workman, whether employed by time or piece, may leave before the end of the working day, without having first received permission from the overseer and having given his name to the gate keeper. Omission of these two actions shall lead to a fine of ten silver groschen payable to the sick fund.
4. Repeated irregular arrival at work shall lead to dismissal. This shall also apply to those who are found idling by an official or overseer, and refuse to obey their order to resume work. . . .
6. No worker may leave his place of work otherwise than for reasons connected with his work.
7. All conversation with fellow-workers is prohibited; if any worker requires information about his work, he must turn to the overseer, or to the particular fellow-worker designated for the purpose.
8. Smoking in the workshops or in the yard is prohibited during working hours; anyone caught smoking shall be fined five silver groschen for the sick fund for every such offense. . . .
10. Natural functions must be performed at the appropriate places, and whoever is found soiling walls, fences, squares, etc., and similarly, whoever is found washing his face and hands in the workshop and not in the places assigned for the purpose, shall be fined five silver groschen for the sick fund. . . .
12. It goes without saying that all overseers and officials of the firm shall be obeyed without question, and shall be treated with due deference. Disobedience will be punished by dismissal.
13. Immediate dismissal shall also be the fate of anyone found drunk in any of the workshops. . . .
14. Every workman is obliged to report to his superiors any acts of dishonesty or embezzlement on the part of his fellow workmen. If he omits to do so, and it is shown after subsequent discovery of a misdemeanor that he knew about it at the time, he shall be liable to be taken to court as an accessory after the fact and the wage due to him shall be retained as punishment.

**HistoryNow**™ To read a related document, enter the *HistoryNow* documents area using the access card that is available for *World History.*

A third significant difference between British and Continental industrialization was the role of the **joint-stock investment bank** on the Continent. Such banks pooled the savings of thousands of small and large investors, creating a supply of capital that could then be plowed back into industry. These investments were essential to Continental industrialization. By starting with less expensive machines, the British had been able to industrialize largely through the private capital of successful individuals who reinvested their profits. On the Continent, advanced industrial machines necessitated large amounts of capital; joint-stock industrial banks provided it.

**The Industrial Revolution in the United States** The Industrial Revolution also transformed the new nation in North America, the United States. In 1800, six out of every seven American workers were farmers, and there were no cities with more than 100,000 people. By 1860, however, the population had sextupled to 30 million people, larger than Great Britain; nine U.S. cities had populations over 100,000; and only 50 percent of American workers were farmers.

In sharp contrast to Britain, the United States was a large country. Thousands of miles of roads and canals were built linking east and west. The steamboat facilitated trans-

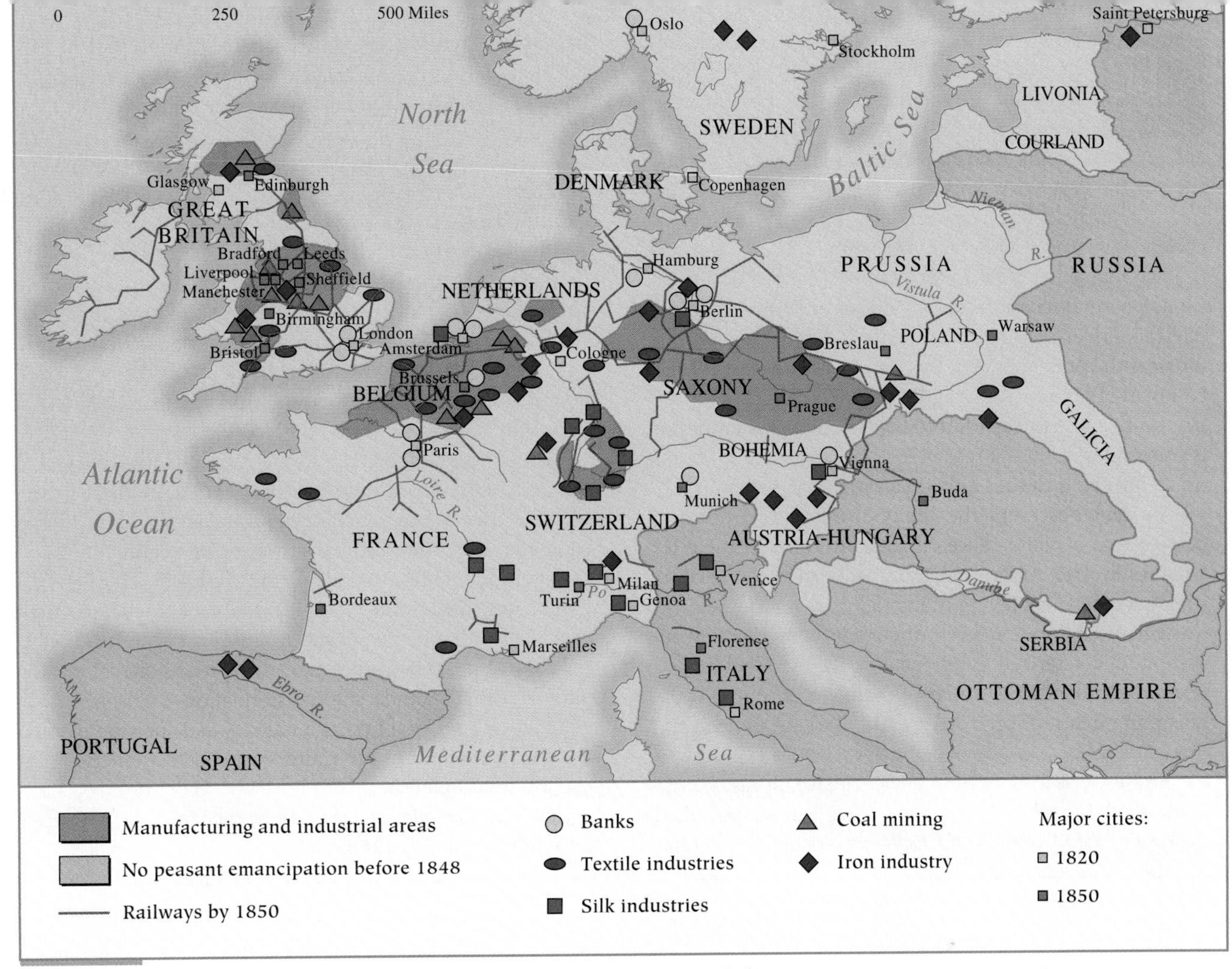


**MAP 18.1 The Industrialization of Europe by 1850.** Great Britain was Europe's first industrialized country; however, by the middle of the nineteenth century, several regions on the Continent had made significant advances in industrialization, especially in Belgium, France, and the German states. ? What reasons could explain why coal mining and iron industries are densely clustered in manufacturing and industrial areas? **View an animated version of this map or related maps at** http://history.wadsworth.com/duikerspielvogel05/

portation on the Great Lakes, Atlantic coastal waters, and rivers. Most important in the development of an American transportation system was the railroad. Beginning with 100 miles in 1830, by 1860 there were over 27,000 miles of railroad track covering the United States. This transportation revolution turned the United States into a single massive market for the manufactured goods of the Northeast, the early center of American industrialization.

Labor for the growing number of factories in this area came primarily from rural New England. Many of the workers in the new textile and shoe factories of the region were women, often accounting for more than 80 percent of the labor force. Factory owners sometimes sought entire families, including children, to work in their mills; one mill owner ran this advertisement in a newspaper in Utica, New York: "Wanted: A few sober and industrious families of at least five children each, over the age of eight years, are wanted at the Cotton Factory in Whitestown. Widows with large families would do well to attend this notice."

## Limiting the Spread of Industrialization in the Rest of the World

Before 1870, the industrialization that was transforming western and central Europe and the United States did not extend in any significant way to the rest of the world (see the comparative essay "The Industrial Revolution" on p. 518). Even in eastern Europe, industrialization lagged far behind. Russia, for example, was still largely rural and agricultural, ruled by an autocratic regime that preferred to keep the peasants in serfdom.

Why some societies were able to embark on the road to industrialization during the nineteenth century and others were not has long been debated. Some historians have found an answer in the cultural characteristics of individual societies, such as the Protestant work ethic in parts of Europe or the tradition of social discipline and class hierarchy in Japan. Others have placed more emphasis on practical reasons. To the historian Peter Stearns, for example, the availability of capital, natural resources, a network of trade relations, and navigable rivers all helped stimulate industrial growth in nineteenth-century Britain. By contrast, the lack of an urban market for agricultural goods (which reduced the landowner's incentives to introduce mechanized farming) is sometimes cited as a reason for China's failure to set out on its own path toward industrialization.

To some observers, the ability of western European countries to exploit the wealth and resources of their colonies in Asia, Africa, and Latin America was crucial to their success in achieving industrial prowess. In their view, the Age of Exploration led to the creation of a new "world system" characterized by the emergence of global trade networks, propelled by the rising force of European capitalism in pursuit of precious metals, markets, and cheap raw materials.

These views are not mutually exclusive. In his recent book titled *The Great Divergence: China, Europe, and the Making of the Modern World Economy,* Kenneth Pomeranz has argued that access to coal resources and to the cheap raw materials of the Americas were both assets for Great Britain as it became the first to enter the industrial age.

Clearly there is no single answer to this controversy. Whatever the case, the advent of the industrial age had a number of lasting consequences for the world at large. On the one hand, the material wealth of the nations that successfully passed through the process increased significantly. In many cases, the creation of advanced industrial societies strengthened democratic institutions and led to a higher standard of living for the majority of the population. It also helped reduce class barriers and bring about the emancipation of women from many of the legal and social restrictions that had characterized the previous era.

On the other hand, not all the consequences of the Industrial Revolution were beneficial. In the industrializing societies themselves, rapid economic change often led to widening disparities in the distribution of wealth and a sense of rootlessness and alienation among much of the population. While some societies were able to manage these problems with a degree of success, others experienced a breakdown of social values and widespread political instability. In the meantime, the transformation of Europe into a giant factory sucking up raw materials and spewing manufactured goods out to the entire world had a wrenching impact on traditional societies whose own economic, social, and cultural foundations were forever changed by absorption into the new world order.

In other parts of the world where they had established control (see Chapter 20), newly industrialized European states pursued a deliberate policy of preventing the growth of mechanized industry. A good example is India. In the eighteenth century, India had become one of the world's greatest exporters of cotton cloth produced by hand labor. In the first half of the nineteenth century, much of India fell under the control of the British East India Company. With British control came inexpensive British factory-produced textiles, and soon thousands of Indian spinners and hand-loom weavers were unemployed. British policy encouraged Indians to export their raw materials while buying British-made goods. India provides an excellent example of how some of the rapidly industrializing nations of Europe worked to thwart the spread of the Industrial Revolution to their colonial dominions.

## Social Impact of the Industrial Revolution

Eventually, the Industrial Revolution revolutionized the social life of Europe and the world. This change was already evident in the first half of the nineteenth century in the growth of cities and emergence of new social classes.

**Population Growth and Urbanization** Population had begun to increase in the eighteenth century, but the pace accelerated dramatically in the nineteenth century. In 1750, the total European population stood at an estimated 140 million; by 1850, it had almost doubled to 266 million. The key to the expansion of population was the decline in death rates evident throughout Europe. Wars and major epidemic diseases, such as plague and smallpox, became less frequent, which led to a drop in the number of deaths. Thanks to the increase in the food supply, more people were better fed and more resistant to disease.

Throughout Europe, cities and towns grew rapidly in the first half of the nineteenth century, a phenomenon related to industrialization. By 1850, especially in Great Britain and Belgium, cities were rapidly becoming home for many industries. With the steam engine, factory owners could locate their manufacturing plants in urban centers, where they had ready access to transportation facilities and large numbers of new arrivals from the country looking for work.

In 1800, Great Britain had one major city, London, with a population of one million, and six cities with populations between 50,000 and 100,000. Fifty years later, London's population had swelled to 2,363,000, and there were nine cities over 100,000 and eighteen cities with populations between 50,000 and 100,000. Over 50 percent of the British population lived in towns and cities by 1850. Urban populations also grew on the Continent, but at a less frenzied pace.

The dramatic growth of cities in the first half of the nineteenth century produced miserable living conditions for many of the inhabitants. Located in the center of most industrial towns were the row houses of the industrial workers. Rooms were not large and were frequently overcrowded, as a government report of 1838 in Britain revealed: "I entered several of the tenements. In one of them, on the ground floor, I found six persons occupying a very small room, two in bed, ill with fever. In the room above this were two more persons in one bed, ill with fever." Another report said, "There were 63 families where there were at least five persons to one bed; and there were some in which even six were packed in one bed, lying at the top and bottom—children and adults."[1]

Sanitary conditions in these towns were appalling; sewers and open drains were common on city streets: "In the center of this street is a gutter, into which the refuse of animal and vegetable matters of all kinds, the dirty water from the washing of clothes and of the houses, are all poured, and there they stagnate and putrefy."[2] Unable to deal with human wastes, cities in the early industrial era smelled horrible and were extraordinarily unhealthy. Towns and cities were fundamentally death traps. As deaths outnumbered births in most large cities in the first half of the nineteenth century, only a constant influx of people from the country kept them alive and growing.

**The Industrial Middle Class** The rise of industrial capitalism produced a new kind of middle class. The bourgeoisie was not new; it had existed since the emergence of cities in the Middle Ages. Originally, the bourgeois or burgher was simply a town dweller, active as a merchant, official, artisan, lawyer, or man of letters. Because many of these people lived comfortable lives, the term took on a certain cachet. And so as other people began to accumulate wealth, the term *bourgeois* came to be applied to people involved in commerce, industry, and banking as well as professionals such as teachers, physicians, and government officials, regardless of where they lived.

The new industrial middle class was made up of the people who constructed the factories, purchased the machines, and figured out where the markets were (see the box on p. 520). Their qualities included resourcefulness, single-mindedness, resolution, initiative, vision, ambition, and often, of course, greed. As Jedediah Strutt, a cotton manufacturer said, "Getting of money . . . is the main business of the life of men."

Members of the industrial middle class sought to reduce the barriers between themselves and the landed elite, but it is clear that they tried at the same time to separate themselves from the laboring classes below them. The working class was actually a mixture of different groups in the first half of the nineteenth century, but in the course of that century, factory workers would form an industrial **proletariat** that constituted a majority of the working class.

**The Industrial Working Class** Early industrial workers faced wretched working conditions. Work shifts ranged from twelve to sixteen hours a day, six days a week, with a half hour for lunch and dinner. There was no security of employment and no minimum wage. The worst conditions were in the cotton mills, where temperatures were especially debilitating. One report noted that "in the cotton-spinning work, these creatures are kept, fourteen hours in each day, locked up, summer and winter, in a heat of from eighty to eighty-four degrees." Mills were also dirty, dusty, and unhealthy.

Conditions in the coal mines were also harsh. Although steam-powered engines were used to lift coal from the mines to the top, inside the mines, men still bore the burden of digging the coal out while horses, mules, women, and children hauled coal carts on rails to the lift. Dangerous conditions, including cave-ins, explosions, and gas fumes, were a way of life. The cramped conditions in the mines—tunnels were often only 3 or 4 feet high—and their constant dampness led to deformed bodies and ruined lungs.

Both children and women worked in large numbers in early factories and mines. Children had been an important part of the family economy in preindustrial times, working in the fields or carding and spinning wool at home. In the Industrial Revolution, however, child labor was exploited more than ever (see the box on p. 521). The owners of cotton factories found child labor very helpful. Children had

**Women in the Mines.** Both women and children were often employed in the early factories and mines of the nineteenth century. As is evident in this illustration of a woman dragging a cart loaded with coal behind her, they often worked under very trying conditions.

In the nineteenth century, a new industrial middle class in Great Britain took the lead in creating the Industrial Revolution. Japan did not begin to industrialize until after 1870 (see Chapter 21). There, too, an industrial middle class emerged, although there were also important differences in the attitudes of business leaders in Britain and Japan. Some of these differences can be seen in these documents. The first is an excerpt from *Self-Help,* first published in 1859, a book by Samuel Smiles, a writer who espoused the belief that people succeed through "individual industry, energy, and uprightness." The two additional selections are by Shibuzawa Eiichi, a Japanese industrialist who supervised textile factories. Although he began his business career in 1873, he did not write his autobiography, the source of his first excerpt, until 1927.

*What do you think are the major similarities and differences between the business attitudes of Samuel Smiles and Shibuzawa Eiichi? How do you explain the differences?*

### Samuel Smiles, *Self-Help*

"Heaven helps those who help themselves" is a well-worn maxim, embodying in a small compass the results of vast human experience. The spirit of self-help is the root of all genuine growth in the individual; and, exhibited in the lives of many, it constitutes the true source of national vigor and strength. Help from without is often enfeebling in its effects, but help from within invariably invigorates. Whatever is done for men or classes, to a certain extent takes away the stimulus and necessity of doing for themselves; and where men are subjected to overguidance and overgovernment, the inevitable tendency is to render them comparatively helpless. . . .

National progress is the sum of individual industry, energy, and uprightness, as national decay is of individual idleness, selfishness, and vice. What we are accustomed to decry as great social evils, will, for the most part, be found to be only the outgrowth of our own perverted life; and though we may endeavor to cut them down and extirpate them by means of law, they will only spring up again with fresh luxuriance in some other form, unless the individual conditions of human life and character are radically improved. If this view be correct, then it follows that the highest patriotism and philanthrophy consist, not so much in altering laws and modifying institutions as in helping and stimulating men to elevate and improve themselves by their own free and independent action as individuals. . . .

Many popular books have been written for the purpose of communicating to the public the grand secret of making money. But there is no secret whatever about it, as the proverbs of every nation abundantly testify. . . . "A penny saved is a penny gained."—"Diligence is the mother of goodluck."—"No pains no gains."—"No sweat no sweet."—"Sloth, the Key of poverty."—"work, and thou shalt have."—"He who will not work, neither shall he eat."—"The world is his, who has patience and industry."

### Shibuzawa Eiichi, *Autobiography*

I . . . felt that it was necessary to raise the social standing of those who engaged in commerce and industry. By way of setting an example, I began studying and practicing the teachings of the *Analects of Confucius.* It contains teachings first enunciated more than twenty-four hundred years ago. Yet it supplies the ultimate in practical ethics for all of us to follow in our daily living. It has many golden rules for businessmen. For example, there is a saying: "Wealth and respect are what men desire, but unless a right way is followed, they cannot be obtained; poverty and lowly position are what men despise, but unless a right way is found, one cannot leave that status once reaching it." It shows very clearly how a businessman must act in this world.

### Shibuzawa Eiichi on Progress

One must beware of the tendency of some to argue that it is through individualism or egoism that the State and society can progress most rapidly. They claim that under individualism, each individual competes with the others, and progress results from this competition. But this is to see merely the advantages and ignore the disadvantages, and I cannot support such a theory. Society exists, and a State has been founded. Although people desire to rise to positions of wealth and honor, the social order and the tranquility of the State will be disrupted if this is done egoistically. Men should not do battle in competition with their fellow men. Therefore, I believe that in order to get along together in society and serve the State, we must by all means abandon this idea of independence and self-reliance and reject egoism completely.

a particular delicate touch as spinners of cotton. Their smaller size made it easier for them to move under machines to gather loose cotton. Moreover, children were more easily trained to do factory work. Above all, children represented a cheap supply of labor. In 1821, about half of the British population was under twenty years of age. Hence children made up an abundant supply of labor, and they were paid only about one-sixth to one-third of what a man was paid. In the cotton factories in 1838, children under eighteen made up 29 percent of the total workforce; children as young as seven worked twelve to fifteen hours per day, six days a week, in cotton mills.

By 1830, women and children made up two-thirds of the cotton industry's labor. However, as the number of children employed declined under the Factory Act of 1833, their places were taken by women, who came to

## CHILD LABOR: DISCIPLINE IN THE TEXTILE MILLS

Child labor was not new, but in the early Industrial Revolution it was exploited more systematically. These selections are taken from the Report of Sadler's Committee, which was commissioned in 1832 to inquire into the condition of child factory workers.

*What kind of working conditions did children face in the mills during the early Industrial Revolution? Why were they beaten?*

### How They Kept the Children Awake

It is a very frequent thing at Mr. Marshall's [at Shrewsbury] where the least children were employed (for there were plenty working at six years of age), for Mr. Horseman to start the mill earlier in the morning than he formerly did; and provided a child should be drowsy, the overlooker walks round the room with a stick in his hand, and he touches that child on the shoulder, and says, "Come here." In a corner of the room there is an iron cistern; it is filled with water; he takes this boy, and takes him up by the legs, and dips him over head in the cistern, and sends him to work for the remainder of the day. . . .

What means were taken to keep the children to their work?—Sometimes they would tap them over the head, or nip them over the nose, or give them a pinch of snuff, or throw water in their faces, or pull them off where they were, and job them about to keep them waking.

### The Sadistic Overlooker

Samuel Downe, age 29, factory worker living near Leeds; at the age of about ten began work at Mr. Marshall's mill at Shrewsbury, where the customary hours when work was brisk were generally 5 A.M. to 8 P.M., sometimes from 5:30 A.M. to 8 or 9:

What means were taken to keep the children awake and vigilant, especially at the termination of such a day's labour as you have described?—There was generally a blow or a box, or a tap with a strap, or sometimes the hand.

Have you yourself been strapped?—Yes, most severely, till I could not bear to sit upon a chair without having pillows, and through that I left. I was strapped both on my own legs, and then I was put upon a man's back, and then strapped and buckled with two straps to an iron pillar, and flogged, and all by one overlooker; after that he took a piece of tow, and twisted it in the shape of a cord, and put it in my mouth, and tied it behind my head.

He gagged you?—Yes; and then he ordered me to run round a part of the machinery where he was overlooker, and he stood at one end, and every time I came there he struck me with a stick, which I believe was an ash plant, and which he generally carried in his hand, and sometimes he hit me, and sometimes he did not; and one of the men in the room came and begged me off, and that he let me go, and not beat me any more, and consequently he did.

You have been beaten with extraordinary severity?—Yes, I was beaten so that I had not power to cry at all, or hardly speak at one time. What age were you at that time?—Between 10 and 11.

**History Now™** To read a related document, enter the *HistoryNow* documents area using the access card that is available for *World History.*

dominate the labor forces of the early factories. Women made up 50 percent of the labor force in textile (cotton and woolen) factories before 1870. They were mostly unskilled labor and were paid half or less of what men received.

Laws that limited the work hours of children and women also led to a new pattern of work based on a separation of work and home. Men were expected to be responsible for the primary work obligations, while women assumed daily control of the family and performed low-paying jobs such as laundry work that could be done in the home. Domestic industry made it possible for women to continue their contributions to family survival.

**Efforts at Change** In the first half of the nineteenth century, the pitiful conditions found in the slums, mines, and factories of the Industrial Revolution gave rise to efforts for change. One of them was a movement known as **socialism.** The term eventually became associated with a Marxist analysis of human society (see Chapter 19), but early socialism was largely the product of intellectuals who believed in the equality of all people and wanted to replace competition with cooperation in industry. To later socialists, especially the followers of Karl Marx, such ideas were merely impractical dreams, and with contempt they labeled these theorists **utopian socialists.** The term has lasted to this day.

Robert Owen, a British cotton manufacturer, was one such utopian socialist. He believed that humans would show their true natural goodness if they lived in a cooperative environment. At New Lanark in Scotland, he transformed a squalid factory town into a flourishing, healthy community. But when he tried to create such a cooperative community at New Harmony, Indiana, in the United States in the 1820s, fighting within the community eventually destroyed his dream.

Another movement for change was the formation of labor organizations to gain decent wages and working conditions. Known as **trade unions,** these new associations were formed by skilled workers in a number of new industries, including ironworkers and coal miners. Some trade unions were even willing to strike (refuse to work) to gain their goal of winning improvements for the members of their own trades. In the 1820s and 1830s, the union movement began to focus on the creation of national unions. The largest and most successful of these unions in Britain was the Amalgamated Society of Engineers, formed in 1851. Its provision of generous unemployment benefits in return for a small weekly payment was precisely the kind of practical gains these trade unions sought.

## Reaction and Revolution: The Growth of Nationalism

After the defeat of Napoleon, European rulers moved to restore much of the old order. This was the goal of the great powers—Great Britain, Austria, Prussia, and Russia—when they met at the Congress of Vienna in September 1814 to arrange a final peace settlement after the Napoleonic wars. The leader of the congress was the Austrian foreign minister, Prince Klemens von Metternich (1773–1859), who claimed that he was guided at Vienna by the **principle of legitimacy.** To reestablish peace and stability in Europe, he considered it necessary to restore the legitimate monarchs who would preserve traditional institutions. This had already been done in France with the restoration of the Bourbon monarchy, but the principle of legitimacy was in fact largely ignored elsewhere; the great powers all grabbed land to add to their states (see Map 18.2).

The peace arrangements of 1815 were but the beginning of a conservative reaction determined to contain the liberal and nationalist forces unleashed by the French Revolution. Metternich and his kind were representatives of the ideology known as **conservatism.** Most conservatives favored obedience to political authority, believed that organized religion was crucial to social order, hated revolutionary upheavals, and were unwilling to accept either the liberal demands for civil liberties and representative governments or the nationalistic aspirations generated by the French revolutionary era. After 1815, the political philosophy of conservatism was supported by hereditary monarchs, government bureaucracies, landowning aristocracies, and revived churches, be they Protestant or Catholic. The conservative forces were dominant after 1815.

One method used by the great powers to maintain the new status quo they had constructed was the Concert of Europe, according to which Great Britain, Russia, Prussia, and Austria (and later France) agreed to meet pe-

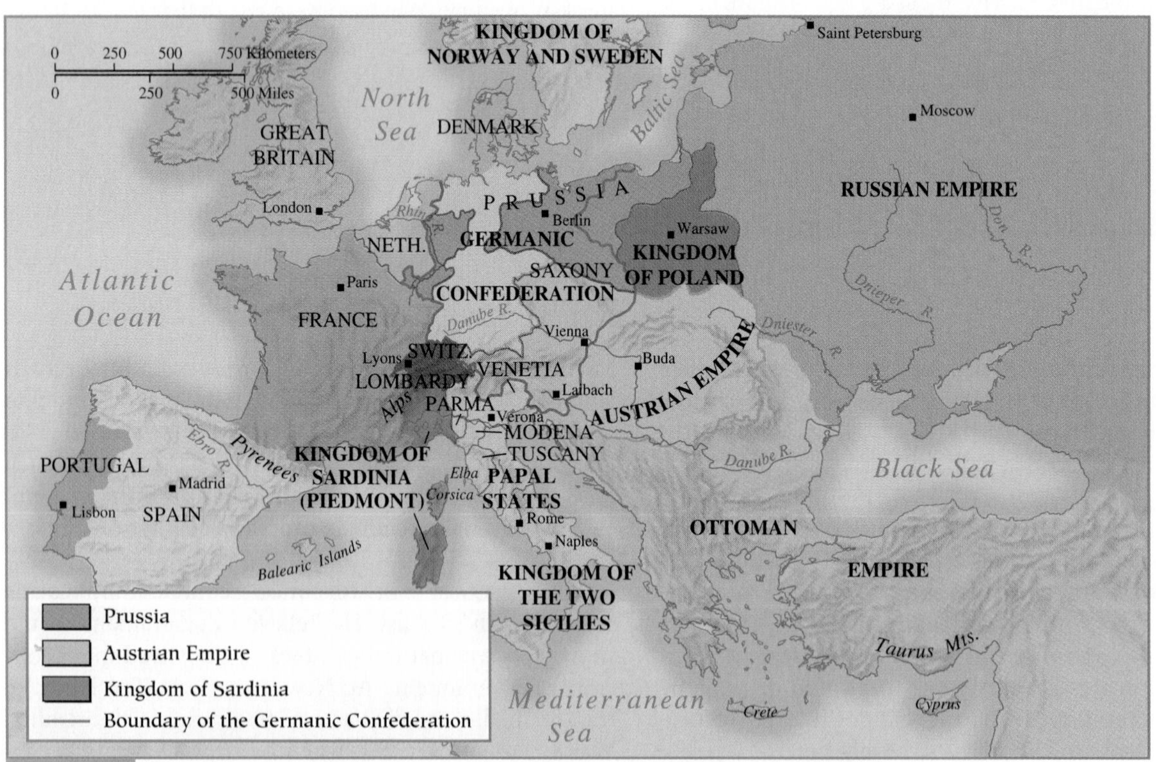

**MAP 18.2 Europe After the Congress of Vienna, 1815.** The Congress of Vienna imposed order on Europe based on the principles of monarchical government and a balance of power. Monarchs were restored in France, Spain, and other states recently under Napoleon's control, and much territory changed hands, often at the expense of small and weak states. ? How did Europe's major powers manipulate territory to decrease the probability that France could again threaten the Continent's stability? **View an animated version of this map or related maps at** http://history.wadsworth.com/duikerspielvogel05/

riodically in conferences to take steps that would maintain the peace in Europe. Eventually, the great powers adopted a **principle of intervention,** asserting the right to send armies into countries where there were revolutions to restore legitimate monarchs to their thrones.

## Forces for Change

After 1815, conservative governments throughout Europe worked to maintain the old order. However, powerful forces for change—liberalism and nationalism—were also at work. **Liberalism** owed much to the Enlightenment of the eighteenth century and the American and French Revolutions at the end of that century; it was based on the idea that people should be as free from restraint as possible.

Politically, liberals came to hold a common set of beliefs. Chief among them was the protection of civil liberties, or the basic rights of all people, which included equality before the law; freedom of assembly, speech, and the press; and freedom from arbitrary arrest. All of these freedoms should be guaranteed by a written document, such as the American Bill of Rights or the French Declaration of the Rights of Man and the Citizen. In addition to religious toleration for all, most liberals advocated separation of church and state. Liberals also demanded the right of peaceful opposition to the government in and out of parliament and the making of laws by a representative assembly (legislature) elected by qualified voters. Many liberals believed, then, in a constitutional monarchy or constitutional state with limits on the powers of government in order to prevent despotism and in written constitutions that would guarantee these rights. Liberals were not democrats, however. They thought that the right to vote and hold office should be open only to men who owned property. As a political philosophy, liberalism was adopted by middle-class men, especially the industrial bourgeoisie, who favored voting rights for themselves so that they could share power with the landowning classes.

**Nationalism** was an even more powerful ideology for change in the nineteenth century. Nationalism arose out of an awareness of being part of a community that has common institutions, traditions, language, and customs. This community is called a nation, and the primary political loyalty of individuals would be to the nation. Nationalism did not become a popular force for change until the French Revolution. From then on, nationalists came to believe that each nationality should have its own government. Thus the Germans, who were not united, wanted national unity in a German nation-state with one central government. Subject peoples, such as the Hungarians, wanted the right to establish their own autonomy rather than be subject to a German minority in the multinational Austrian Empire.

Nationalism, then, was a threat to the existing political order. A united Germany, for example, would upset the balance of power established at Vienna in 1815. At the same time, an independent Hungarian state would mean the breakup of the Austrian Empire. Because many European states were multinational, conservatives tried hard to repress the radical threat of nationalism.

At the same time, in the first half of the nineteenth century, nationalism and liberalism became strong allies. Most liberals believed that liberty could be realized only by peoples who ruled themselves. Many nationalists believed that once each people obtained its own state, all nations could be linked together into a broader community of all humanity. In fact, the nationalism that later triumphed in the second half of the nineteenth century—a new, loud, chauvinistic nationalism—divided people rather than unifying them as the new national states became embroiled in bitter competition (see Chapter 19).

## The Revolutions of 1848

The conservative order dominated much of Europe after 1815, but the forces of liberalism and nationalism, first generated by the French Revolution, continued to grow as that second great revolution, the Industrial Revolution, expanded and brought new groups of people who wanted change. In 1848, these forces for change erupted.

Revolution in France was the spark for revolution in other countries. A severe industrial and agricultural depression beginning in 1846 brought hardship in France to the lower middle class, workers, and peasants, while the government's persistent refusal to extend the suffrage angered the disfranchised members of the middle class. When the government of King Louis-Philippe (1830–1848) refused to make changes, opposition grew and finally overthrew the monarchy on February 24, 1848. A group of moderate and radical republicans established a provisional government and called for the election by universal male suffrage of a "constituent assembly" that would draw up a new constitution.

The new constitution, ratified on November 4, 1848, established a republic (the Second Republic) with a single legislature elected to three-year terms by universal male suffrage and a president, also elected by universal male suffrage to a four-year term. In the elections for the presidency held in December 1848, Charles Louis Napoleon Bonaparte, the nephew of the famous ruler, won a resounding victory. Within four years, President Napoleon would become Emperor Napoleon and establish an authoritarian regime.

**Revolution in Central Europe** News of the 1848 revolution in France led to upheaval in central Europe as well (see the box on p. 524). The Vienna settlement in 1815 had recognized the existence of thirty-eight sovereign states (called the Germanic Confederation) in what had once been the Holy Roman Empire. Austria and Prussia were the two great powers in terms of size and might; the other states varied considerably. In 1848, cries for change caused many German rulers to promise constitutions, a

## Revolutionary Excitement: Carl Schurz and the Revolution of 1848 in Germany

The excitement with which German liberals and nationalists received the news of the 1848 revolution in France and their own expectations for Germany are well captured in this selection from the *Reminiscences of Carl Schurz.* Schurz (1829–1906) made his way to the United States after the failure of the German revolution and eventually became a U.S. senator.

*How did the fervent desire expressed by Schurz for "German unity" and the founding of a great national German Empire express itself in nineteenth-century German history?*

### Carl Schurz, *Reminiscences*

One morning, toward the end of February, 1848, I sat quietly in my attic-chamber, working hard at my tragedy of "Ulrich von Hutten" [a sixteenth-century German humanist and knight], when suddenly a friend rushed breathlessly into the room, exclaiming: "What, you sitting here! Do you not know what has happened?"

"No; what?"

"The French have driven away Louis Philippe and proclaimed the republic."

I threw down my pen—and that was the end of "Ulrich von Hutten." I never touched the manuscript again. We tore down the stairs, into the street, to the market-square, the accustomed meeting-place for all the student societies after their midday dinner. Although it was still forenoon, the market was already crowded with young men talking excitedly. There was no shouting, no noise, only agitated conversation. What did we want there? This probably no one knew. But since the French had driven away Louis Philippe and proclaimed the republic, something of course must happen here, too. . . . We were dominated by a vague feeling as if a great outbreak of elemental forces had begun, as if an earthquake was impending of which we had felt the first shock, and we instinctively crowded together. . . .

The next morning there were the usual lectures to be attended. But how profitless! The voice of the professor sounded like a monotonous drone coming from far away. What he had to say did not seem to concern us. The pen that should have taken notes remained idle. At last we closed with a sigh the notebook and went away, impelled by a feeling that now we had something more important to do—to devote ourselves to the affairs of the fatherland. And this we did by seeking as quickly as possible again the company of our friends, in order to discuss what had happened and what was to come. In these conversations, excited as they were, certain ideas and catchwords worked themselves to the surface, which expressed more or less the feelings of the people. Now had arrived in Germany the day for the establishment of "German Unity," and the founding of a great, powerful national German Empire. In the first line the convocation of a national parliament. Then the demands for civil rights and liberties, free speech, free press, the right of free assembly, equality before the law, a freely elected representation of the people with legislative power, responsibility of ministers, self-government of the communes, the right of the people to carry arms, the formation of a civic guard with elective officers, and so on—in short, that which was called a "constitutional form of government on a broad democratic basis." Republican ideas were at first only sparingly expressed. But the word democracy was soon on all tongues, and many, too, thought it a matter of course that if the princes should try to withhold from the people the rights and liberties demanded, force would take the place of mere petition. Of course the regeneration of the fatherland must, if possible, be accomplished by peaceable means. . . . Like many of my friends, I was dominated by the feeling that at last the great opportunity had arrived for giving to the German people the liberty which was their birthright and to the German fatherland its unity and greatness, and that it was now the first duty of every German to do and to sacrifice everything for this sacred object.

free press, jury trials, and other liberal reforms. In Prussia, King Frederick William IV (1840–1861) agreed to establish a new constitution and work for a united Germany.

The promise of unity reverberated throughout all the German states as governments allowed elections by universal male suffrage for deputies to an all-German parliament called the Frankfurt Assembly. Its purpose was to fulfill a liberal and nationalist dream—the preparation of a constitution for a new united Germany. But the Frankfurt Assembly failed to achieve its goal. The members had no real means of compelling the German rulers to accept the constitution they had drawn up. German unification was not achieved; the revolution had failed.

The Austrian Empire needed only the news of the revolution in Paris to erupt in flames in March 1848. The Austrian Empire was a multinational state, a collection of at least eleven ethnically distinct peoples, including Germans, Czechs, Magyars (Hungarians), Slovaks, Romanians, Serbians, and Italians, who had pledged their loyalty to the Habsburg emperor. The Germans, though only a quarter of the population, were economically dominant and played a leading role in governing Austria. The Hungarians, however, wanted their own legislature. In March, demonstrations in Buda, Prague, and Vienna led to the dismissal of Metternich, the Austrian foreign minister and the arch-

**Austrian Students in the Revolutionary Civil Guard.** In 1848, revolutionary fervor swept the European continent and toppled governments in France, central Europe, and Italy. In the Austrian Empire, students joined the revolutionary civil guard in taking control of Vienna and forcing the Austrian emperor to call a constituent assembly to draft a liberal constitution.

symbol of the conservative order, who fled abroad. In Vienna, revolutionary forces took control of the capital and demanded a liberal constitution. Hungary was given its own legislature and a separate national army. In Bohemia, the Czechs began to clamor for their own government as well.

Austrian officials had made concessions to appease the revolutionaries, but they were determined to reestablish firm control. As in the German states, they were increasingly encouraged by the divisions between radical and moderate revolutionaries and played on the middle-class fear of a working-class social revolution. In June 1848, Austrian military forces ruthlessly suppressed the Czech rebels in Prague. By the end of October, radical rebels had been crushed in Vienna, but it was only with the assistance of a Russian army of 140,000 men that the Hungarian revolution was finally put down in 1849. The revolutions in the Austrian Empire had failed.

**Revolts in the Italian States** So did revolutions in Italy. The Congress of Vienna had established nine states in Italy, including the kingdom of Sardinia in the north, ruled by the house of Savoy; the kingdom of the Two Sicilies (Naples and Sicily); the Papal States; a handful of small duchies; and the important northern provinces of Lombardy and Venetia, which were now part of the Austrian Empire. Italy was largely under Austrian domination, but a new movement for Italian unity known as Young Italy led to initially successful revolts in 1848. Within a year, however, the Austrians had reestablished complete control over Lombardy and Venetia, and the old order also prevailed in the rest of Italy.

Throughout Europe in 1848, popular revolutions had led to liberal constitutions and liberal governments. Moderate, middle-class liberals and radical workers soon divided over their aims, however, and the failure of the revolutionaries to stay united soon led to the reestablishment of authoritarian regimes. In other parts of the Western world, revolutions took somewhat different directions.

## Independence and the Development of the National State in Latin America

By the end of the eighteenth century, the ideas of the Enlightenment and the new political ideals stemming from the successful revolution in North America were beginning to influence the creole elites (descendants of Europeans who became permanent inhabitants of Latin America). The principles of the equality of all people in the eyes of the law, free trade, and a free press proved very attractive. Sons of creoles, such as Simón Bolívar and José de San Martín, who became leaders of the independence movement, even went to European universities, where they imbibed the ideas of the Enlightenment. These Latin American elites, joined by a growing class of merchants, especially resented the domination of their trade by Spain and Portugal.

**Nationalistic Revolts in Latin America** The creole elites soon began to use their new ideas to denounce the rule of the Iberian monarchs and the peninsulars (Spanish and Portuguese officials who resided in Latin America for political and economic gain). When Napoleon Bonaparte toppled the monarchies of Spain and Portugal, the authority of the Spaniards and Portuguese in their colonial empires was weakened, and between 1807 and 1825, a series of revolts enabled most of Latin America to become independent.

Beginning in 1810, Mexico, too, experienced a revolt, fueled initially by the desire of the creole elites to overthrow the rule of the peninsulars. The first real hero of Mexican independence was Miguel Hidalgo y Costilla, a parish priest in a small village about 100 miles from Mexico City. Hidalgo had studied the French Revolution and roused the local Indians and mestizos to free themselves from the Spanish: "My children, this day comes to us as a new dispensation. Are you ready to receive it? Will you be free? Will you make the effort to recover from the hated Spaniards the lands stolen from your forefathers three hundred years ago?"[3] It was September 16, 1810, and a crowd of Indians and mestizos, armed with clubs, machetes, and a few guns, quickly formed a mob army to attack the Spaniards. But Hidalgo was not a good organizer, and his forces were soon crushed. A military court sentenced Hidalgo to death, but his memory lived on. In fact, September 16, the first day of the uprising, is celebrated as Mexico's Independence Day.

The participation of Indians and mestizos in Mexico's revolt against Spanish control frightened both creoles and peninsulars. Fearful of the masses, they cooperated in defeating the popular revolutionary forces. The elites—both creoles and peninsulars—then decided to overthrow Spanish rule as a way of preserving their own power. They selected a creole military leader, Augustín de Iturbide, as their leader and the first emperor of Mexico in 1821.

Independence movements elsewhere in Latin America were the work of elites—primarily creoles—who overthrew Spanish rule and created new governments that they could dominate. The masses of people—Indians, blacks, mestizos, and mulattoes—gained little from the revolts. José de San Martín (1778–1850) of Argentina and Simón Bolívar (1783–1830) of Venezuela, leaders of the independence movement, were both members of the creole elite, and both were hailed as the liberators of South America.

By 1810, the forces of San Martín had freed Argentina from Spanish authority. Bolívar led the bitter struggle for independence in Venezuela and then went on to liberate New Grenada (Colombia) and Ecuador. San Martín believed that the Spaniards must be removed from all of South America if any nation was to be free. In January 1817, he led his forces over the high Andes Mountains, an amazing feat in itself. Two-thirds of their pack mules and horses died during the difficult journey. Many of the soldiers suffered from lack of oxygen and severe cold while crossing mountain passes that were more than 2 miles above sea level. The arrival of San Martín's forces in Chile completely surprised the Spaniards, whose forces were routed at the battle of Chacabuco on February 12, 1817. In 1821, San Martín moved on to Lima, Peru, the center of Spanish authority.

Convinced that he was unable to complete the liberation of Peru, San Martín welcomed the arrival of Bolívar and his forces. The liberator of Venezuela took on the task of crushing the last significant Spanish army at Ayacucho on December 9, 1824. By then, Peru, Uruguay, Paraguay, Colombia, Venezuela, Argentina, Bolivia, and Chile had all become free states (see Map 18.3). In 1823, the Central American states became independent and in 1838–1839 divided into five republics (Guatemala, El Salvador, Honduras, Costa Rica, and Nicaragua). Earlier, in 1822, the prince regent of Brazil had declared Brazil's independence from Portugal.

**The Difficulties of Nation Building** The new Latin American nations faced a number of serious problems. The wars for independence had themselves resulted in a staggering loss of population, property, and livestock; at the same time, disputes arose between nations over their precise boundaries. Poor transportation and communication systems also made national unity difficult.

The new nations of Latin America began with republican governments, but they had had no experience in ruling themselves. Soon after independence, strong leaders known as ***caudillos*** came to power. They ruled chiefly by military force and were usually supported by the landed elites. Many kept the new national states together. Sometimes they were also modernizers who built roads, canals, ports, and schools. Others were destructive, such as Antonio de Santa Anna, who, in ruling Mexico from 1829 to 1855, misused state funds, created chaos, and lost some of Mexico's territory to the United States.

Although political independence brought economic independence, old patterns were hard to extinguish. Instead of Spain and Portugal, Great Britain now dominated the Latin American economy. Old trade patterns soon reemerged. Because Latin America served as a source of raw materials and foodstuffs for the industrializing nations of Europe and North America, exports, especially of wheat, tobacco, wool, sugar, coffee, and hides, to the North Atlantic countries increased no-

**José de San Martín.** José de San Martín of Argentina was one of the famous leaders of the Latin American independence movement. His forces liberated Argentina, Chile, and Peru from Spanish authority. In this painting by Theodore Géricault, San Martín is shown leading his troops at the Battle of Chacabuco in Chile in 1817.

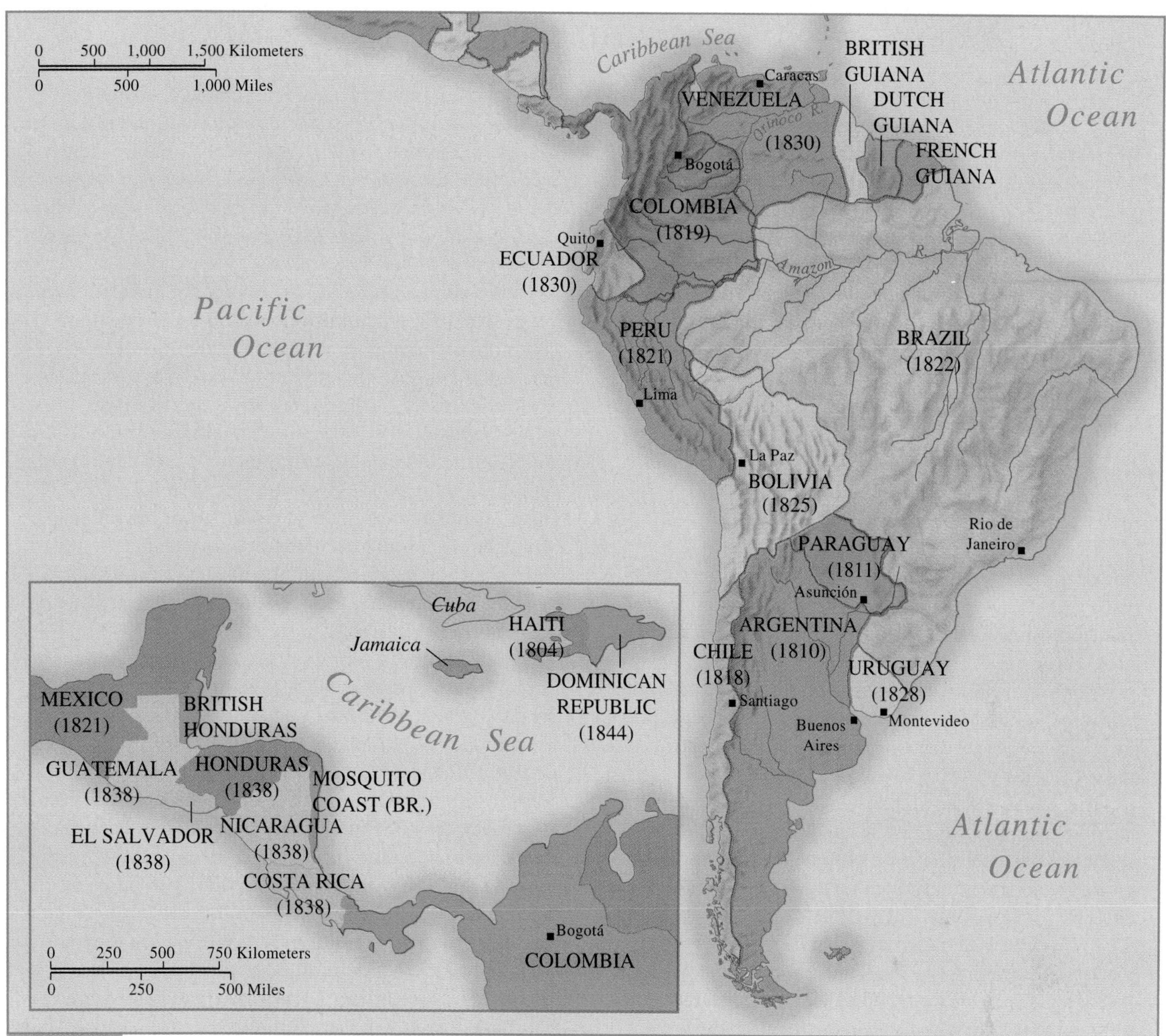


**MAP 18.3 Latin America in the First Half of the Nineteenth Century.** Latin American colonies took advantage of Spain's weakness during the Napoleonic wars to fight for independence, beginning with Argentina in 1810 and spreading throughout the region over the next decade with the help of leaders like Simón Bolívar and José de San Martín. ? How many South American countries are sources of rivers that feed the Amazon, and roughly what percentage of the continent is contained within the Amazon's watershed? **View an animated version of this map or related maps at** http://history.wadsworth.com/duikerspielvogel05/

ticeably. At the same time, the importation of finished consumer goods, especially textiles, also grew and caused a decline in industrial production in Latin America. For Latin America, the emphasis on the export of raw materials and the import of finished products ensured the ongoing domination of the Latin American economy by foreigners.

A fundamental underlying problem for all of the new Latin American nations was the persistent domination of society by the landed elites. Large estates remained the persistent fact of Latin America's economic and social life (see the box on p. 528). By 1848, for example, the Sánchez Navarro family in Mexico possessed seventeen estates comprising 16 million acres. Estates were often so large that they could not be farmed efficiently.

Land remained the basis of wealth, social prestige, and political power throughout the nineteenth century. Landed elites ran governments, controlled courts, and kept a system of inexpensive labor. These landowners made enormous profits growing single, specialized crops for export, such as coffee, while the masses, unable to have land to grow basic food crops, endured dire poverty.

## A Radical Critique of the Land Problem in Mexico

The domination of Mexico by elites who owned large estates remained a serious problem throughout the nineteenth century. Conservatives, of course, favored the great estates as the foundation stones of their own political power, while even liberals shied away from any extremist attack on property rights. Nevertheless, there were some strong voices of protest, as this excerpt from a speech delivered in 1857 by the social liberal Ponciano Arriaga demonstrates. Arriaga's appeal went unheeded; conservatives called him a "communist."

*What serious problems were engendered by ownership of large estates in Latin American politics? How did such holdings determine the structure of Latin American societies?*

### Ponciano Arriaga, Speech to the Constitutional Convention of 1856–1857

One of the most deeply rooted evils of our country–an evil that merits the close attention of legislators when they frame our fundamental law–is the monstrous division of landed property.

While a few individuals possess immense areas of uncultivated land that could support millions of people, the great majority of Mexicans languish in a terrible poverty and are denied property, homes, and work. . . .

There are Mexican landowners who occupy (if one can give that name to a purely imaginary act) an extent of land greater than the areas of some of our sovereign states, greater even than that of one of several European states.

In this vast area, much of which lies idle, deserted, abandoned, awaiting the arms and labor of men, live four or five million Mexicans who know no other industry than agriculture, yet are without land or the means to work it, and who cannot emigrate in the hope of bettering their fortunes. They must either vegetate in idleness, turn to banditry, or accept the yoke of a landed monopolist who subjects them to intolerable conditions of life. . . .

How can a hungry, naked, miserable people practice popular government? How can we proclaim the equal rights of men and leave the majority of the nation in conditions worse than those of helots or pariahs? How can we condemn slavery in words, while the lot of most of our fellow citizens is more grievous than that of the black slaves of Cuba or the United States? . . .

With some honorable exceptions, the rich landowners of Mexico, or the administrators who represent them, resemble the feudal lords of the Middle Ages. On his seignorial land, . . . the landowner makes and executes laws, administers justice and exercises civil power, imposes taxes and fines, has his own jails and irons, metes out punishments and tortures, monopolizes commerce, and forbids the conduct without his permission of any business but that of the estate. The judges or officials who exercise on the hacienda the powers attached to public authority are usually the master's servants or tenants, his retainers, incapable of enforcing any law but the will of the master.

An astounding variety of devices are employed to exploit the peons or tenants, to turn a profit from their sweat and labor. They are compelled to work without pay even on days traditionally set aside for rest. They must accept rotten seeds or sick animals whose cost is charged to their miserable wages. They must pay enormous parish fees that bear no relation to the scale of fees that the owner or majordomo has arranged beforehand with the parish priest. They must make all their purchases on the hacienda, using tokens or paper money that do not circulate elsewhere. At certain seasons of the year they are assigned articles of poor quality, whose price is set by the owner or majordomo, constituting a debt which they can never repay. They are forbidden to use pastures and woods, firewood and water, or even the wild fruit of the fields, save with the express permission of the master. In fine, they are subject to a completely unlimited and irresponsible power

## Nationalism in the Balkans: The Ottoman Empire and the Eastern Question

The Ottoman Empire had long been in control of much of southeastern Europe (an area known as the Balkans). In the first half of the nineteenth century, a number of states in the Balkans sought to free themselves from the Ottomans. Serbia, for example, won its autonomy in 1817. As the Ottoman Empire began to decline and authority over its outlying territories in southeastern Europe waned, European governments began to take an active interest in its disintegration. The "Eastern Question," as it came to be called, troubled European diplomats throughout the nineteenth century. Russia's proximity to the Ottoman Empire and the religious bonds between the Russians and the Greek Orthodox Christians in Turkish-dominated southeastern Europe naturally gave Russia special opportunities to enlarge its sphere of influence. The Austrian Empire feared Russian ambitions and had its own interest in the apparent demise of the Ottoman Empire. France and Britain were interested in commercial opportunities and naval bases in the eastern Mediterranean.

In 1821, the Greeks revolted against their Turkish masters. Although subject to Muslim control for four hundred

**Florence Nightingale.** Florence Nightingale is shown caring for wounded British soldiers following a battle in September 1854 in which the allies had defeated the Russians. After a British journalist, W. H. Russell, issued a scathing denunciation of the quality of medical care afforded to wounded British soldiers, the British government allowed Nightingale to take a group of nurses to the Crimean warfront. Through her efforts in the Crimean War, Nightingale helped make nursing an admirable profession for middle-class women.

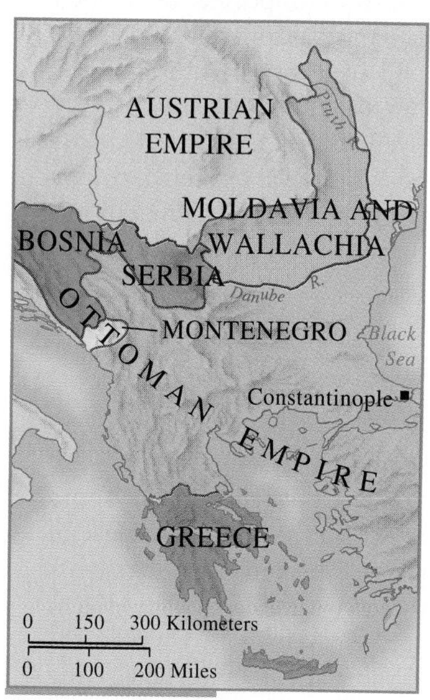


**The Balkans in 1830**

years, the Greeks had been allowed to maintain their language and their Greek Orthodox faith. The Greek revolt was soon transformed into a noble cause by an outpouring of European sentiment for the Greeks' struggle. In 1827, a combined British and French fleet went to Greece and defeated a large Turkish fleet. A year later, Russia declared war on the Ottoman Empire. In 1829, the Turks agreed to allow Russia, France, and Britain to decide the fate of Greece, and one year later, the three powers declared Greece an independent kingdom.

**The Crimean War** The Crimean War was another episode in the story of the Eastern Question. In 1853, war had erupted again between the Russians and Turks over Russian demands for the right to protect Christian shrines in Palestine, a privilege that had already been extended to the French. When the Turks refused, the Russians invaded Turkish Moldavia and Wallachia. Failure to resolve the problem by negotiations led the Turks to declare war on Russia on October 4, 1853. In the following year, on March 28, Great Britain and France, fearful that the Russians would gain at the expense of the disintegrating Ottoman Empire, declared war on Russia.

The Crimean War was poorly planned and poorly fought. Britain and France decided on an attack on Russia's Crimean peninsula in the Black Sea. After a long siege and at a terrible cost in troops on both sides, the main Russian fortress of Sevastopol fell in September 1855, and the Russians soon sued for peace. By the Treaty of Paris, signed in March 1856, Russia was forced to give up Bessarabia at the mouth of the Danube and accept the neutrality of the Black Sea. In addition, the Danubian principalities of Moldavia and Wallachia were placed under the protection of all the great powers.

The Crimean War proved costly to both sides. More than 250,000 soldiers died in the war, 60 percent of them from disease (especially cholera). Even more would have died on the British side if it had not been for the efforts of Florence Nightingale (1820–1910). Her insistence on strict sanitary conditions saved many lives and helped make nursing a profession of trained, middle-class women.

The Crimean War destroyed the Concert of Europe. Austria and Russia, the two chief powers maintaining the status quo in the first half of the nineteenth century, were now enemies because of Austria's unwillingness to support Russia in the war. Russia, defeated and humiliated by the obvious failure of its armies, withdrew from European affairs for the next two decades. Great Britain, disillusioned by its role in the war, also pulled back from Continental affairs. Austria, paying the price for its neutrality, was now without friends among the great powers. This new international situation opened the door for the unification of Italy and Germany.

0 250 500 750 Kilometers
0 250 500 Miles
Dniester R.
Dnieper R.
MOLDAVIA
BESSARABIA
WALLACHIA
Danube R.
Black Sea
Sevastopol
Seige of Sevastopol September 1854
Russian attack
Sinope
Constantinople
Dardanelles 1853
Anglo-French attack
Gallipoli April 1854
OTTOMAN EMPIRE

**The Crimean War**

# National Unification and the National State, 1848–1871

The revolutions of 1848 had failed, but within twenty-five years, many of the goals sought by liberals and nationalists during the first half of the nineteenth century were achieved. Italy and Germany became nations, and many European states were led by constitutional monarchs.

**CHRONOLOGY The Unification of Italy**

| | |
|---|---|
| Victor Emmanuel II | 1849–1878 |
| Count Cavour becomes prime minister of Piedmont | 1852 |
| Garibaldi's invasion of the Two Sicilies | 1860 |
| Kingdom of Italy is proclaimed | March 17, 1861 |
| Italy's annexation of Venetia | 1866 |
| Italy's annexation of Rome | 1870 |

## The Unification of Italy

The Italians were the first people to benefit from the breakdown of the Concert of Europe. In 1850, Austria was still the dominant power on the Italian peninsula. After the failure of the revolution of 1848–1849, more and more Italians looked to the northern Italian state of Piedmont, ruled by the royal house of Savoy, as their best hope to achieve the unification of Italy. It was, however, doubtful that the little state could provide the leadership needed to unify Italy until King Victor Emmanuel II (1849–1878) named Count Camillo di Cavour (1810–1861) prime minister in 1852.

As prime minister, Cavour pursued a policy of economic expansion that increased government revenues and enabled Piedmont to equip a large army. Cavour, however, knew that Piedmont's army was not strong enough to beat the Austrians; consequently, he made an alliance with the French emperor Louis Napoleon and then provoked the Austrians into invading Piedmont in 1859. After French armies defeated the Austrians, a peace settlement gave the French Nice and Savoy, which they had been promised for making the alliance, and Lombardy went to Piedmont. Cavour's success caused nationalists in some northern Italian states (Parma, Modena, and Tuscany) to overthrow their governments and join Piedmont.

Meanwhile, in southern Italy, Giuseppe Garibaldi (1807–1882), a dedicated Italian patriot, raised an army of a thousand volunteers called the Red Shirts because of the color of their uniforms. Garibaldi's forces swept through Sicily and then crossed over to the mainland and began a victorious march up the Italian peninsula (see the box on p. 532). Naples, and with it the kingdom of the Two Sicilies, fell in early September. Ever the patriot, Garibaldi chose to turn over his conquests to Cavour's Piedmontese forces. On March 17, 1861, the new kingdom of Italy was proclaimed under a centralized government subordinated to the control of Piedmont and King Victor Emmanuel II (1861–1878) of the house of Savoy.

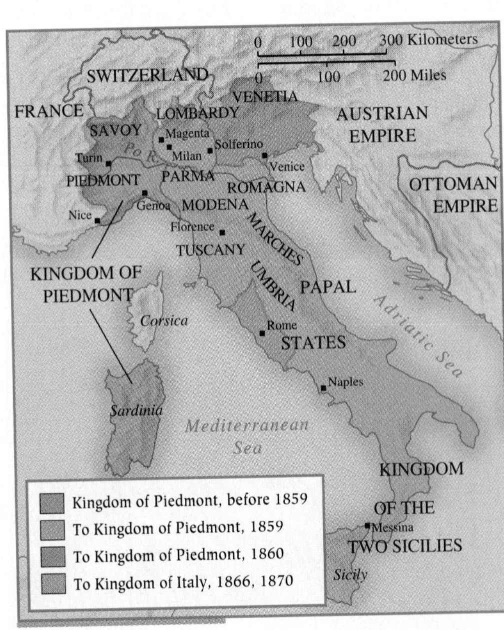


**The Unification of Italy**

The task of unification was not yet complete, however. Venetia in the north was still held by Austria, and Rome was under papal control, supported by French troops. In the Austro-Prussian War of 1866, the new Italian state became an ally of Prussia. Although the Italian army was defeated by the Austrians, Prussia's victory left the Italians with Venetia. In 1870, the Franco-Prussian War resulted in the withdrawal of French troops from Rome. The Italian army then annexed the city on September 20, 1870, and Rome became the new capital of the united Italian state.

## The Unification of Germany

After the failure of the Frankfurt Assembly to achieve German unification in 1848–1849, more and more Germans looked to Prussia for leadership in the cause of German unification. Prussia had become a strong, prosperous, and authoritarian state, with the Prussian king in firm control of both government and the army. In the 1860s, King William I (1861–1888) attempted to enlarge and strengthen the Prussian army. When the Prussian legislature refused to levy new taxes for the proposed military changes, William appointed a new prime minister, Count Otto von Bismarck (1815–1898). Bismarck ignored the legislative opposition to the military reforms, arguing instead that "Germany does not look to Prussia's liberalism but to her power. . . . Not by speeches and majorities will the great questions of the day be decided—that was the mistake of 1848–1849—but by iron and blood."[4] Bismarck collected the taxes, reorganized the

**CHRONOLOGY The Unification of Germany**

| | |
|---|---|
| King William I of Prussia | 1861–1888 |
| Danish War | 1864 |
| Austro-Prussian War | 1866 |
| Franco-Prussian War | 1870–1871 |
| German Empire is proclaimed | January 18, 1871 |

**The Unification of Germany.** Under Prussian leadership, a new German empire was proclaimed on January 18, 1871, in the Hall of Mirrors in the palace at Versailles. King William of Prussia became Emperor William I of the Second German Empire. Otto von Bismarck, the man who had been so instrumental in creating the new German state, is shown here, resplendently attired in his white uniform, standing at the foot of the throne.

army anyway, and governed Prussia by simply ignoring parliament. In the meantime, opposition to his domestic policy determined Bismarck on an active foreign policy, which led to war and German unification. Bismarck has often been portrayed as the ultimate realist, the foremost nineteenth-century practitioner of ***Realpolitik***—the "politics of reality."

After defeating Denmark with Austrian help in 1864 and gaining control over the duchies of Schleswig and Holstein, Bismarck created friction with the Austrians and goaded them into a war on June 14, 1866. The Austrians were barely defeated at Königgrätz on July 3, but Prussia now organized the German states north of the Main River into the North German Confederation. The southern German states, largely Catholic, remained independent but signed military alliances with Prussia due to their fear of France, their western neighbor.

Prussia now dominated all of northern Germany. However, problems with France soon arose. Bismark realized that France would never be content with a strong German state to its east because of the potential threat to French security. In 1870, Prussia and France became embroiled in a dispute over the candidacy of a relative of the Prussian king for the throne of Spain. Bismarck manipulated the misunderstandings between the French and Prussians to goad the French into declaring war on Prussia on July 15, 1870. The southern German states honored their military alliances with Prussia and joined the war effort against the French. The Prussian armies advanced into France, and at Sedan, on September 2, 1870, captured an entire French army and Napoleon III himself. Paris capitulated on January 28, 1871. France had to pay an indemnity of 5 billion francs (about $1 billion) and give up the provinces of Alsace and Lorraine to the new German state, a loss that left the French burning for revenge.

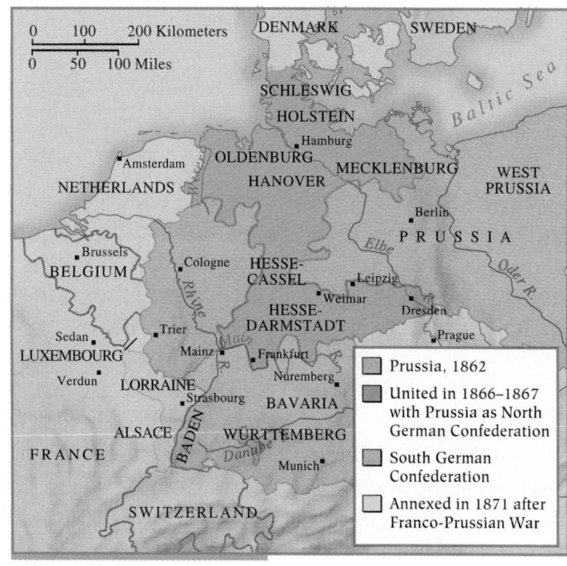


**The Unification of Germany**

Even before the war had ended, the southern German states had agreed to enter the North German Confederation. On January 18, 1871, in the Hall of Mirrors in Louis XIV's palace at Versailles, William I was proclaimed kaiser or emperor of the Second German Empire (the first was the medieval Holy Roman Empire). German unity had been achieved by the Prussian monarchy and the Prussian army. The Prussian leadership of German unification meant the triumph of authoritarian, militaristic values over liberal, constitutional sentiments in the development of the new German state. With its industrial resources and military might, the new state had become the strongest power on the Continent. A new European balance of power was at hand.

## GARIBALDI AND ROMANTIC NATIONALISM

Giuseppe Garibaldi was one of the more colorful figures involved in the unification of Italy. Accompanied by only a thousand of his famous Red Shirts, the Italian soldier of fortune left Genoa on the night of May 5, 1860, for an invasion of the kingdom of the Two Sicilies. The ragged band entered Palermo, the chief city on the island of Sicily, on May 31. This selection is taken from an account by a correspondent for the *Times* of London, the Hungarian-born Nandor Eber.

*This article from the London* Times *is the first newspaper primary source document to appear in this textbook. How does this new source of information reflect the growth of an industrial middle class?*

### *Times,* June 13, 1860

Palermo, May 31—Anyone in search of violent emotions cannot do better than set off at once for Palermo. However blasé he may be, or however milk-and-water his blood, I promise it will be stirred up. He will be carried away by the tide of popular feeling. . . .

In the afternoon Garibaldi made a tour of inspection round the town. I was there, but find it really impossible to give you a faint idea of the manner in which he was received everywhere. It was one of those triumphs which seem to be almost too much for a man. . . . The popular idol, Garibaldi, in his red flannel shirt, with a loose colored handkerchief round his neck, and his worn "wide-awake" [a soft-brimmed felt hat], was walking on foot among those cheering, laughing, crying, mad thousands; and all his few followers could do was to prevent him from being bodily carried off the ground. The people threw themselves forward to kiss his hands, or, at least, to touch the hem of his garment, as if it contained the panacea for all their past and perhaps coming suffering. Children were brought up, and mothers asked on their knees for his blessing; and all this while the object of this idolatry was calm and smiling as when in the deadliest fire, taking up the children and kissing them, trying to quiet the crowd, stopping at every moment to hear a long complaint of houses burned and property sacked by the retreating soldiers, giving good advice, comforting, and promising that all damages should be paid for. . . .

One might write volumes of horrors on the vandalism already committed, for every one of the hundred ruins has its story of brutality and inhumanity. . . . In these small houses a dense population is crowded together even in ordinary times. A shell falling on one, and crushing and burying the inmates, was sufficient to make people abandon the neighboring one and take refuge a little further on, shutting themselves up in the cellars. When the Royalists retired they set fire to those of the houses which had escaped the shells, and numbers were thus burned alive in their hiding places. . . .

If you can stand the exhalation, try and go inside the ruins, for it is only there that you will see what the thing means and you will not have to search long before you stumble over the remains of a human body, a leg sticking out here, an arm there, a black face staring at you a little further on. You are startled by a rustle. You look round and see half a dozen gorged rats scampering off in all directions, or you see a dog trying to make his escape over the ruins. . . . I only wonder that the sign of these scenes does not convert every man in the town into a tiger and every woman into a fury. But these people have been so long ground down and demoralized that their nature seems to have lost the power of reaction.

**HistoryNow™** To read a related document, enter the *HistoryNow* documents area using the access card that is available for *World History.*

## Nationalism and Reform: The European National State at Mid-Century

While European affairs were dominated by the unification of Italy and Germany, other states in the Western world were also undergoing change.

**Great Britain** Unlike the nations on the Continent, Great Britain managed to avoid the revolutionary upheavals of the first half of the nineteenth century. In the early part of the century, Britain was governed by the aristocratic landowning classes that dominated both houses of Parliament. But in 1832, to avoid the turmoil on the Continent, Parliament passed a reform bill that increased the number of male voters, chiefly members of the industrial middle class. By joining the industrial middle class to the landed interest in ruling Britain, Britain avoided revolution in 1848.

Another reason for Britain's stability was its continuing economic growth. After 1850, middle-class prosperity was at last coupled with some improvements for the working classes as real wages for laborers increased over 25 percent between 1850 and 1870. The British sense of national pride was well represented in Queen Victoria (1837–1901), whose sense of duty and moral respectability reflected the attitudes of her age, which has ever since been known as the Victorian Age.

In the 1850s and 1860s, the liberal parliamentary system of Britain also made both social and political reforms that enabled the country to remain stable. Although the Whigs (now called the Liberals), who had been responsible for the Reform Act of 1832, talked about passing additional reform legislation, it was actually the Tories (now called the Conservatives) who carried it through. Under the leadership of Benjamin Disraeli (1804–1881), the Tory leader in Parliament, the Reform Act of 1867 added an important step in the democratization of Britain. The number of voters increased from one million to slightly over two million. At the same time, the extension of the right to vote had an important by-product as it forced the Liberals and Conservatives to organize carefully in order to manipulate the electorate. Party discipline intensified, and the rivalry between the Liberals and Conservatives became a regular feature of parliamentary life.

**France** Events in France after the revolution of 1848 moved toward the restoration of monarchy. Four years after his election as president, Louis Napoleon returned to the people to ask for the restoration of the empire. Ninety-seven percent responded in the affirmative, and on December 2, 1852, Louis Napoleon assumed the title of Napoleon III (the first Napoleon had abdicated in favor of his son, Napoleon II, on April 6, 1814). The Second Empire had begun.

The first five years of Napoleon III's reign were a spectacular success. He took many steps to expand industrial growth. Government subsidies helped foster the rapid construction of railroads as well as harbors, roads, and canals. The major French railway lines were completed during Napoleon's reign, and iron production tripled. In the midst of this economic expansion, Napoleon III also undertook a vast reconstruction of the city of Paris. The medieval Paris of narrow streets and old city walls was destroyed and replaced by a modern Paris of broad boulevards, spacious buildings, circular plazas, public squares, an underground sewage system, a new public water supply, and gas streetlights.

In the 1860s, as opposition to his rule began to mount, Napoleon III liberalized his regime. He gave the Legislative Corps more say in affairs of state, including debate over the budget. Liberalization policies worked initially; in a plebiscite in May 1870 on whether to accept a new constitution that might have inaugurated a parliamentary regime, the French people gave Napoleon another resounding victory. This triumph was short-lived, however. War with Prussia in 1870 brought Napoleon's ouster, and a republic was proclaimed.

**The Austrian Empire** Although nationalism was a major force in nineteenth-century Europe, one of the region's most powerful states, the Austrian Empire, managed to frustrate the desire of its numerous ethnic groups for self-determination. After the Habsburg rulers had crushed the revolutions of 1848–1849, they restored centralized, autocratic government to the empire. But Austria's defeat at the hands of the Prussians in 1866 forced the Austrians to deal with the fiercely nationalistic Hungarians.

The result was the negotiated ***Ausgleich,*** or Compromise, of 1867, which created the Dual Monarchy of Austria-Hungary. Each part of the empire now had its own constitution, its own legislature, its own governmental bureaucracy, and its own capital (Vienna for Austria and Buda for Hungary). Holding the two states together were a single monarch—Francis Joseph (1848–1916) was emperor of Austria and king of Hungary—and a common army, foreign policy, and system of finances. The *Ausgleich* did not, however, satisfy the other nationalities that made up the Austro-Hungarian Empire.

**Russia** At the beginning of the nineteenth century, Russia was overwhelmingly rural, agricultural, and autocratic. The Russian tsar was still regarded as a divine-right monarch with unlimited power. The Russian imperial autocracy, based on soldiers, secret police, and repression, had withstood the revolutionary fervor of the first half of the nineteenth century. However, defeat in the Crimean War in 1856 led even staunch conservatives to realize that Russia was falling hopelessly behind the western European powers. Tsar Alexander II (1855–1881) decided to make serious reforms.

Serfdom was the most burdensome problem in tsarist Russia. On March 3, 1861, Alexander issued his emancipation edict (see the box on p. 534). Peasants were now free to own property and marry as they chose. But the system of land redistribution instituted after emancipation was not particularly favorable to them. The government provided land for the peasants by purchasing it from the landlords, but the landowners often chose to keep the best parcels. The Russian peasants soon found that they had inadequate amounts of arable land to support themselves.

Nor were the peasants completely free. The state compensated the landowners for the land given to the peasants, but the peasants were expected to repay the state in long-term installments. To ensure that the payments were made, peasants were subjected to the authority of their *mir,* or village commune, which was collectively responsible for the land payments to the government. And since the village communes were responsible for the payments, they were reluctant to allow peasants to leave their land. Emancipation, then, led not to a free, landowning peasantry along the Western model but to an unhappy, land-starved peasantry that largely followed the old ways of agricultural production.

Alexander II attempted other reforms as well, but he soon found that he could please no one. Reformers wanted more and rapid change; conservatives thought that the tsar was attempting to undermine the basic institutions of Russian society. When one group of radicals assassinated Alexander II in 1881, his son and successor, Alexander III, turned against reform and returned to the traditional methods of repression.

## Emancipation: Serfs and Slaves

Although overall their histories have been quite different, Russia and the United States shared a common feature in the 1860s. They were the only states in the Western world that still had large enslaved populations (the Russian serfs were virtually slaves). The leaders of both countries issued emancipation proclamations within two years of each other. The first excerpt is taken from the imperial decree of March 3, 1861, which freed the Russian serfs. The second excerpt is from Abraham Lincoln's Emancipation Proclamation, issued on January 1, 1863.

*What changes did Tsar Alexander II's emancipation of the serfs initiate in Russia? What effect did Lincoln's Emancipation Proclamation have on the southern "armed rebellion"? What reasons does each leader give for his action?*

### Alexander II's Imperial Decree, March 3, 1861

By the grace of God, we, Alexander II, Emperor and Autocrat of all the Russias, King of Poland, Grand Duke of Finland, etc., to all our faithful subjects, make known:

Called by Divine Providence and by the sacred right of inheritance to the throne of our ancestors, we took a vow in our innermost heart to respond to the mission which is intrusted to us as to surround with our affection and our Imperial solicitude all our faithful subjects of every rank and of every condition, from the warrior, who nobly bears arms for the defense of the country, to the humble artisan devoted to the works of industry; from the official in the career of the high offices of the State to the laborer whose plough furrows the soil. . . .

We thus came to the conviction that the work of a serious improvement of the condition of the peasants was a sacred inheritance bequeathed to us by our ancestors, a mission which, in the course of events, Divine Providence called upon us to fulfill. . . .

In virtue of the new dispositions above mentioned, the peasants attached to the soil will be invested within a term fixed by the law with all the rights of free cultivators. . . .

At the same time, they are granted the right of purchasing their close, and, with the consent of the proprietors, they may acquire in full property the arable lands and other appurtenances which are allotted to them as a permanent holding. By the acquisition in full property of the quantity of land fixed, the peasants are free from their obligations toward the proprietors for land thus purchased, and they enter definitely into the condition of free peasant-landholders.

### Lincoln's Emancipation Proclamation, January 1, 1863

Now therefore, I, Abraham Lincoln, President of the United States, by virtue of the power in me vested as Commander-in-Chief of the Army and Navy of the United States in time of actual armed rebellion against the authority and government of the United States, and as a fit and necessary war measure for suppressing such rebellion, do, on this 1st day of January, A.D. 1863, and in accordance with my purpose to do so, . . . order and designate as the States and parts of States wherein the people thereof, respectively, are this day in rebellion against the United States the following, to wit:

Arkansas, Texas, Louisiana, . . . Mississippi, Alabama, Florida, Georgia, South Carolina, North Carolina, and Virginia . . .

And by virtue of the power for the purpose aforesaid, I do order and declare that all persons held as slaves within said designated States and parts of States are, and henceforward shall be free; and that the Executive Government of the United States, including the military and naval authorities thereof, will recognize and maintain the freedom of said persons.

## The Growth of the United States

The U.S. Constitution, ratified in 1789, committed the United States to two of the major forces of the first half of the nineteenth century, liberalism and nationalism. The election of Andrew Jackson (1767–1845) as president in 1828 opened a new era in American politics. Jacksonian democracy introduced mass democratic politics when property qualifications for voting were dropped. By the 1830s, suffrage had been extended to almost all adult white males.

By the mid-nineteenth century, the issue of slavery had become a threat to American national unity. Like the North, the South had grown dramatically in population during the first half of the nineteenth century. However, the South's economy was based on growing cotton on plantations, chiefly by slave labor. Although new slave imports had been barred in 1808, there were four million African American slaves in the South by 1860—four times the number sixty years earlier. The cotton economy and plantation-based slavery were related, and the South was determined to maintain them. In the North, many people feared the spread of slavery into western territories.

As polarization over the issue of slavery intensified, compromise became less feasible. When Abraham Lincoln (1809–1865), who had said in a speech in Illinois in 1858 that "this government cannot endure permanently half slave and half free," was elected president in November 1860, the die was cast. Lincoln carried only 2 of the 1,109 counties in the South. In February 1861,

**CHRONOLOGY Developments in the Western Hemisphere**

| | |
|---|---|
| **Latin America** | |
| Revolution in Mexico | 1810 |
| Bolívar and San Martín free most of South America | 1810–1824 |
| Augustín de Iturbide becomes emperor of Mexico | 1821 |
| Brazil gains independence from Portugal | 1822 |
| **United States** | |
| Election of Andrew Jackson | 1828 |
| Election of Abraham Lincoln | 1860 |
| Civil War | 1861–1865 |
| Lincoln's Emancipation Proclamation | 1863 |
| **Canada** | |
| Rebellions | 1837–1838 |
| United Provinces of Canada | 1840 |
| Dominion of Canada | 1867 |

seven Southern states formed a rival nation, the Confederate States of America, and in April, fighting erupted between North and South.

The American Civil War (1861–1865) was an extraordinarily bloody struggle. Over 600,000 soldiers died, either in battle or from deadly infectious diseases spawned by filthy camp conditions. Over a period of four years, the Union (Northern) states mobilized their superior assets and gradually wore down the South. Moreover, what had begun as a war to save the Union became a war against slavery. On January 1, 1863, Lincoln's Emancipation Proclamation made most of the nation's slaves "forever free" (see the box on p. 534). The surrender of Confederate forces on April 9, 1865, confirmed that the United States would once again be "one nation, indivisible."

### The Emergence of a Canadian Nation

By the Treaty of Paris in 1763, Canada—or New France, as it was called—passed into the hands of the British. By 1800, most Canadians favored more autonomy, although differences existed among the colonists on the form this autonomy should take. Upper Canada (now Ontario) was predominantly English-speaking, while Lower Canada (now Quebec) was dominated by French Canadians. Increased immigration to Canada in the early nineteenth century also fueled the desire for self-government. After two short rebellions against the government broke out in Upper and Lower Canada in 1837 and 1838, the British moved toward change. In 1840, the British Parliament formally joined Upper and Lower Canada into the United Provinces of Canada, without granting self-government.

The head of Upper Canada's Conservative Party, John Macdonald, became an avid apostle for self-government. Fearful of U.S. designs on Canada, the British government finally capitulated to Macdonald's campaign, and in 1867, Parliament passed the British North American Act, which established a Canadian nation—the Dominion of Canada—with its own constitution. Macdonald became the first prime minister. Although Canada now possessed a parliamentary system and ruled itself, foreign affairs still remained the preserve of the British government.

## Cultural Life: Romanticism and Realism in the Western World

At the end of the eighteenth century, a new intellectual movement known as **Romanticism** emerged to challenge the ideas of the Enlightenment. The Enlightenment stressed reason as the chief means for discovering truth. Although the Romantics by no means disparaged reason, they tried to balance its use by stressing the importance of feeling, emotion, and imagination as sources of knowing.

### The Characteristics of Romanticism

Romantic writers emphasized emotion and sentiment and believed that these inner feelings were understandable only to the person experiencing them. In their novels, Romantic writers created figures who were often misunderstood and rejected by society but who continued to believe in their own worth through their inner feelings.

Many Romantics also possessed a passionate interest in the past. They revived medieval Gothic architecture and left European countrysides adorned with pseudo-medieval castles and cities bedecked with grandiose neo-Gothic cathedrals, city halls, and parliamentary buildings. Literature, too, reflected this historical consciousness. The novels of Walter Scott (1771–1832) became European best-sellers in the first half of the nineteenth century. *Ivanhoe,* in which Scott sought to evoke the clash between Saxon and Norman knights in medieval England, became one of his most popular works.

Many Romantics had a deep attraction to the exotic and unfamiliar. In an exaggerated form, this preoccupation gave rise to so-called **Gothic literature,** chillingly evident in Mary Shelley's *Frankenstein* and Edgar Allen Poe's short stories of horror (see the box on p. 538). Some Romantics even brought the unusual into their own lives by seeking extraordinary states of experience in drug-induced altered states of consciousness by experimenting with cocaine, opium, and hashish.

To the Romantics, poetry ranked above all other literary forms as the direct expression of the soul. Romantic poetry gave full expression to one of the most important characteristics of Romanticism: love of nature, especially evident in the poetry of William Wordsworth (1770–1850), the foremost Romantic prophet of nature. His experience of nature was almost mystical as he claimed to receive "authentic tidings of invisible things":

*One impulse from a vernal wood*
*May teach you more of man,*
*Of Moral Evil and of good,*
*Than all the sages can.*[5]

Romantics believed that nature served as a mirror into which humans could look to learn about themselves.

Like the literary arts, the visual arts were also deeply affected by Romanticism. To Romantic artists, all artistic expression was a reflection of the artist's inner feelings; a painting should mirror the artist's vision of the world and be the instrument of his own imagination.

The early life experiences of Caspar David Friedrich (1774–1840) left him with a lifelong preoccupation with God and nature. Friedrich painted landscapes with an interest that transcended the mere presentation of natural details. His portrayals of mountains shrouded in mist, gnarled trees bathed in moonlight, and the stark ruins of monasteries surrounded by withered trees all conveyed a feeling of mystery and mysticism. For Friedrich, nature was a manifestation of divine life, as is evident in *Man and Woman Gazing at the Moon.* To Friedrich, the artistic process depended on the use of an unrestricted imagination that could only be achieved through inner vision.

**Caspar David Friedrich, *Man and Woman Gazing at the Moon.*** The German artist Caspar David Friedrich sought to express in painting his own mystical view of nature. "The divine is everywhere," he once wrote, "even in a grain of sand." In this painting, a couple is shown from the back gazing at the moon. They are overwhelmed by the powerful presence of nature and the immensity of the universe.

Eugène Delacroix (1798–1863) was one of the most famous French exponents of the Romantic school of painting. Delacroix visited North Africa in 1832 and was strongly impressed by its vibrant colors and the brilliant dress of the people. His paintings came to exhibit two primary characteristics, a fascination with the exotic and a passion for color. Both are apparent in his *Women of Algiers.* Significant for its use of light and its patches of interrelated color, this portrayal of the world of harem concubines in exotic Algeria was considered somewhat scandalous in the early nineteenth century. In Delacroix, theatricality and movement combined with a daring use of color. Many of his works reflect his own belief that "a painting should be a feast to the eye."

## A New Age of Science

The Scientific Revolution had created a modern, rational approach to the study of the natural world, but even in the eighteenth century, these intellectual developments had remained the preserve of an educated elite and resulted in few practical benefits. With the Industrial Revolution, however, came a renewed interest in basic scientific research. By the 1830s, new scientific discoveries had led to many practical benefits that caused science to have an ever-greater impact on European life.

In biology, the Frenchman Louis Pasteur (1822–1895) came up with the germ theory of disease, which had enormous practical applications in the development of modern scientific medical practices. In chemistry, the Russian Dmitri Mendeleev (1834–1907) in the 1860s classified all the material elements then known on the basis of their atomic weights and provided the systematic foundation for the periodic law. The Briton Michael Faraday (1791–1867) put together a primitive generator that laid the foundation for the use of electricity.

The popularity of scientific and technological achievement produced a widespread acceptance of the **scientific method** as the only path to objective truth and objective reality. This undermined the faith of many people in religious revelation. It is no accident that the nineteenth century was an age of increasing **secularization,** evident in the belief that truth was to be found in the concrete material existence of human beings. No one did more to create a picture of humans as material beings that were simply part of the natural world than Charles Darwin.

In 1859, Charles Darwin (1809–1882) published *On the Origin of Species by Means of Natural Selection.* The basic idea of this book was that all plants and animals had each evolved over a long period of time from earlier and simpler forms of life, a principle known as **organic evolution.** Darwin was important in explaining how this natural process worked. In every species, he argued, "many more individuals of each species are born than can possibly survive." This results in a "struggle for existence." Darwin believed that some organisms were more adaptable to the environment than others, a process that Darwin called **natural selection.** Those that were naturally selected for survival ("survival of the fit") reproduced and thrived. The unfit did not and became extinct. The fit who survived passed on small variations that enhanced their survival until, from Darwin's point of view, a new separate species emerged. In *The Descent of Man,* published in 1871, he argued for the animal origins of human beings: "Man is the co-descendant with other mammals of a common progenitor." Humans were not an exception to the rule governing other species.

**Eugène Delacroix, *Women of Algiers.*** Also characteristic of Romanticism was its love of the exotic and unfamiliar. In his *Women of Algiers,* Delacroix reflected this fascination with the exotic in this portrayal of harem concubines from North Africa in which the clothes and jewelry of the women combine with their calm facial expressions to create an atmosphere of peaceful sensuality. At the same time, Delacroix's painting reflects his preoccupation with light and color.

## Realism in Literature and Art

The word **Realism** was first employed in 1850 to describe a new style of painting and soon spread to literature. The literary Realists of the mid-nineteenth century rejected Romanticism. They wanted to deal with ordinary characters from actual life rather than Romantic heroes in exotic settings. They also sought to avoid emotional language by using close observation and precise description, an approach that led them to write novels rather than poems.

The leading novelist of the 1850s and 1860s, the Frenchman Gustave Flaubert (1821–1880), perfected the Realist novel. His *Madame Bovary* (1857) was a straightforward description of barren and sordid provincial life in France. Emma Bovary is trapped in a marriage to a drab provincial doctor. Impelled by the images of romantic love she has read about in novels, she seeks the same thing for herself in adulterous love affairs. Unfulfilled, she is ultimately driven to suicide, unrepentant to the end for her lifestyle.

In art, too, Realism became dominant after 1850. Realist art demonstrated three major characteristics: a desire to depict the everyday life of ordinary people, whether peasants, workers, or prostitutes; an attempt at photographic realism; and an interest in the natural environment. The French became leaders in Realist painting.

Gustave Courbet (1819–1877), the most famous artist of the Realist school, reveled in realistic portrayals of everyday life. His subjects were factory workers, peasants, and the wives of saloonkeepers. "I have never seen either angels or goddesses, so I am not interested in painting them," he exclaimed. One of his famous works, *The Stonebreakers,* painted in 1849, shows two road workers engaged in the deadening work of breaking stones to build a road. This representation of human misery was a scandal to those who objected to Courbet's "cult of ugliness."

## GOTHIC LITERATURE: EDGAR ALLAN POE

American writers and poets made significant contributions to the movement of Romanticism. Although Edgar Allan Poe (1809–1849) was influenced by the German Romantic school of mystery and horror, many literary historians give him the credit for pioneering the modern short story. This selection from the conclusion of "The Fall of the House of Usher" gives a feeling for the nature of so-called Gothic literature.

*What were the aesthetic aims of Gothic literature? How did it come to be called "Gothic"? How did its values relate to those of the Romantic movement as a whole?*

### Edgar Allan Poe, "The Fall of the House of Usher"

No sooner had these syllables passed my lips, than—as if a shield of brass had indeed, at the moment, fallen heavily upon a floor of silver—I became aware of a distinct, hollow, metallic, and clangorous, yet apparently muffled, reverberation. Completely unnerved, I leaped to my feet; but the measured rocking movement of Usher was undisturbed. I rushed to the chair in which he sat. His eyes were bent fixedly before him, and throughout his whole countenance there reigned a stony rigidity. But, as I placed my hand upon his shoulder, there came a strong shudder over his whole person; a sickly smile quivered about his lips; and I saw that he spoke in a low, hurried, and gibbering murmur, as if unconscious of my presence. Bending closely over him, I at length drank in the hideous import of his words.

"Not hear it?—yes, I hear it, and *have* heard it. Long-long-long-many minutes, many hours, many days, have I heard it—yet I dared not—oh, pity me, miserable wretch that I am!—I dared not—I *dared* not speak! *We have put her living in the tomb!* Said I not that my senses were acute? I *now* tell you that I heard her first feeble movements in the hollow coffin. I heard them—many, many days ago—yet I dared not—*I dared not speak!* And now—to-night— . . . the rending of her coffin, and the grating of the iron hinges of her prison, and her struggles within the coppered archway of the vault! Oh whither shall I fly? Will she not be here anon? Is she not hurrying to upbraid me for my haste? Have I not heard her footstep on the stair? Do I not distinguish that heavy and horrible beating of her heart? MADMAN!"—here he sprang furiously to his feet, and shrieked out his syllables, as if in the effort he were giving up his soul—"MADMAN! I TELL YOU THAT SHE NOW STANDS WITHOUT THE DOOR!"

As if in the superhuman energy of his utterance there had been found the potency of a spell, the huge antique panels to which the speaker pointed threw slowly back, upon the instant, their ponderous and ebony jaws. It was the work of the rushing gust—but then without those doors there DID stand the lofty and enshrouded figure of the lady Madeline of Usher. There was blood upon her white robes, and the evidence of some bitter struggle upon every portion of her emaciated frame. For a moment she remained trembling and reeling to and fro upon the threshold, then, with a low moaning cry, fell heavily inward upon the person of her brother, and in her violent and now final death-agonies, bore him to the floor a corpse, and a victim to the terrors he had anticipated.

**Gustave Courbet, *The Stonebreakers.*** Realism, largely developed by French painters, aimed at a lifelike portrayal of the daily activities of ordinary people. Gustave Courbet was the most famous of the Realist artists. As is evident in *The Stonebreakers*, he sought to portray things as they really appear. He shows an old road builder and his young assistant in their tattered clothes, engrossed in their dreary work of breaking stones to construct a road.

## CONCLUSION

**BETWEEN 1800 AND 1870,** the forces unleashed by two revolutions—the French Revolution and the Industrial Revolution—led to Western global dominance by the end of the nineteenth century. The Industrial Revolution seemed to prove to Europeans the underlying assumption of the Scientific Revolution of the seventeenth century—that human beings were capable of dominating nature. By rationally manipulating the material environment for human benefit, people could achieve new levels of material prosperity and produce machines not dreamed of in their wildest imaginings. Some of these new machines included weapons of war that enabled the Western world to devastate and control non-Western civilizations.

In 1815, a conservative order had been reestablished throughout Europe, but the revolutionary waves in Latin America and Europe in the first half of the nineteenth century made it clear that the ideologies of liberalism and nationalism, unleashed by the French Revolution and now reinforced by the spread of industrialization, were still alive and active in the Western world. Between 1850 and 1871, the national state became the focus of people's loyalty. Wars, both foreign and civil, were fought to create unified nation-states, and both wars and changing political alignments served as catalysts for domestic reforms that made the nation-state the center of attention. Liberal nationalists had believed that unified nation-states would preserve individual rights and lead to a greater community of peoples. But the new nationalism of the late nineteenth century, loud and chauvinistic, did not unify peoples but divided them instead as the new national states became embroiled in bitter competition after 1870.

Many people, however, were hardly aware of nationalism's dangers in 1870. The spread of industrialization and the growing popularity of science and technology were sources of optimism, not pessimism. After the revolutionary and military upheavals of the mid-century decades, many Westerners believed that they stood on the verge of a new age of progress.

## CHAPTER NOTES

1. Quotations in E. R. Pike, *Human Documents of the Industrial Revolution in Britain* (London, 1966), pp. 314, 343.
2. Ibid., p. 315.
3. Quoted in H. Herring, *A History of Latin America* (New York, 1961), p. 255.
4. Quoted in L. L. Snyder, ed., *Documents of German History* (New Brunswick, N.J., 1958), p. 202.
5. W. Wordsworth, "The Tables Turned," *Poems of Wordsworth*, ed. M. Arnold (London, 1963), p. 138.

## SUGGESTED READING

For a good survey of the entire nineteenth century, see **R. Gildea, *Barricades and Borders: Europe, 1800–1914,*** 2d ed. (Oxford, 1996). Also valuable is **M. S. Anderson, *The Ascendancy of Europe, 1815–1914,*** 2d ed. (London, 1985). The well-written work by **D. Landes, *The Unbound Prometheus: Technological Change and Industrial Development in Western Europe from 1750 to the Present*** (Cambridge, 1969), is still a good introduction to the Industrial Revolution. Also of value is **D. Fisher, *The Industrial Revolution*** (New York, 1992). There is a good collection of articles in **M. Teich** and **R. Porter,** eds., ***The Industrial Revolution in National Context: Europe and the USA*** (Cambridge, 1996). For a broader perspective, see **P. Stearns, *The Industrial Revolution in World History*** (Boulder, Colo., 1993). On the role of the British, see **K. Morgan, *The Birth of Industrial Britain: Economic Change, 1750–1850*** (London, 1999).

On the social impact of the Industrial Revolution, see **P. Pilbeam, *The Middle Classes in Europe, 1789–1914*** (Basingstoke, England, 1990); **T. Koditschek, *Class Formation and Urban Industrial Society*** (New York, 1990); and **F. Crouzet, *The First Industrialists: The Problems of Origins*** (Cambridge, 1985), on British entrepreneurs. **G. Himmelfarb, *The Idea of Poverty: England in the Early Industrial Age*** (New York, 1984), traces the concepts of poverty and poor from the mid-eighteenth century to the mid-nineteenth century. A classic work on female labor patterns is **L. A. Tilly** and **J. W. Scott, *Women, Work, and Family*** (New York, 1978). See also **J. Lown, *Women and Industrialization: Gender at Work in Nineteenth-Century England*** (Minneapolis, Minn., 1990). For a global approach to the modern economy, see **K. Pomeranz, *The Great Deliverance: China, Europe, and the Making of the Modern World Economy*** (Princeton, N.J., 2002).

For a survey of the period 1814–1848, see **M. Broers, *Europe After Napoleon: Revolution, Reaction, and Romanticism, 1814–1848*** (New York, 1996). There are some useful books on individual countries that cover more than this chapter. These include **R. Magraw, *France, 1815–1914: The Bourgeois Century*** (London, 1983); **D. Saunders, *Russia in the Age of Reaction and Reform, 1801–1881*** (London, 1992); **J. J. Sheehan, *German History, 1770–1866*** (New York, 1989); **N. McCord, *British History, 1815–1906*** (New York, 1991); and **A. Sked, *The Decline and Fall of the Habsburg Empire, 1815–1918*** (London, 1989). The best introduction to the revolutions of 1848 is **J. Sperber, *The European Revolutions, 1848–1851*** (New York, 1994).

For a comprehensive survey of Latin American history, see **E. Williamson, *The Penguin History of Latin America*** (London, 1992). On the revolts in Latin America, see **J. Lynch, *The Spanish American Revolutions, 1808–1826*** (New York, 1973). A good survey of nineteenth-century developments can be found in **D. Bushnell** and **N. Macaulay, *The Emergence of Latin America in the Nineteenth Century*** (Oxford, 1988). For a detailed account of the Ottoman Empire in the nineteenth century, see **S. Shaw, *History of the Ottoman Empire and Modern Turkey,*** vol. 2 (Cambridge, 1977).

The unification of Italy can be examined in **D. M. Smith, *Victor Emmanuel, Cavour and the Risorgimento*** (London, 1971), and **H. Hearder, *Cavour*** (New York, 1994). The unification of Germany

TIMELINE

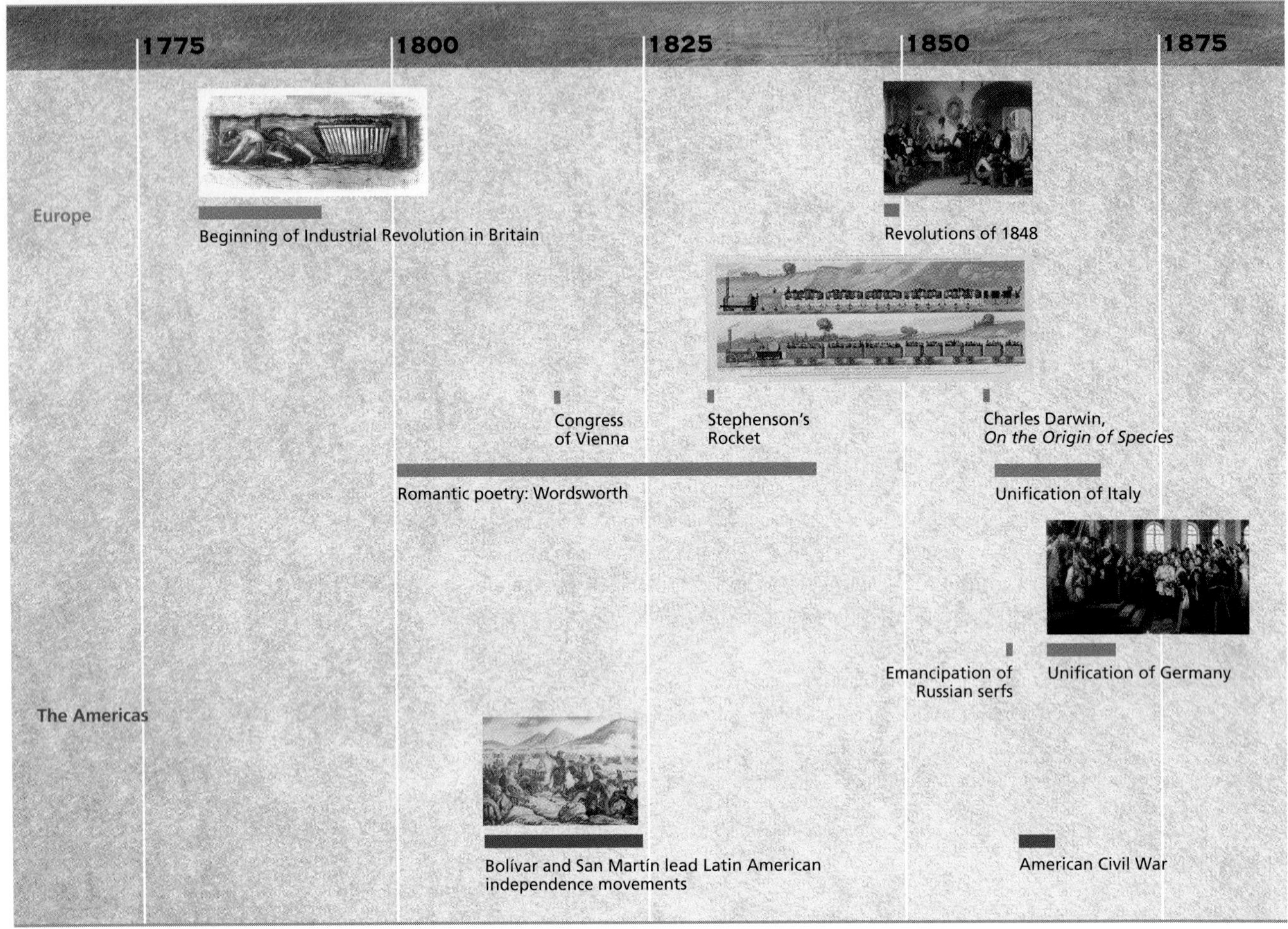


can be pursued first in two good biographies of Bismarck, **E. Crankshaw, *Bismarck*** (New York, 1981), and **E. Feuchtwanger, *Bismarck*** (London, 2002). See also the brief study by **B. Waller, *Bismarck,*** 2d ed. (Oxford, 1997). For a good introduction to the French Second Empire, see **A. Plessis, *The Rise and Fall of the Second Empire, 1852–1871,*** trans. J. Mandelbaum (New York, 1985). Louis Napoleon's role can be examined in **J. F. McMillan, *Napoleon III*** (New York, 1991). On the emancipation of the Russian serfs, see **D. Field, *The End of Serfdom: Nobility and Bureaucracy in Russia, 1855–1861*** (Cambridge, 1976). The evolution of British political parties in mid-century is examined in **H. J. Hanham, *Elections and Party Management: Politics in the Time of Disraeli and Gladstone,*** 2d ed. (London, 1978). A good one-volume survey of the Civil War can be found in **P. J. Parish, *The American Civil War*** (New York, 1975). For a general history of Canada, see **C. Brown,** ed., ***The Illustrated History of Canada*** (Toronto, 1991).

For an introduction to the intellectual changes of the nine-teenth century, see **O. Chadwick, *The Secularization of the European Mind in the Nineteenth Century*** (Cambridge, 1975). A beautifully illustrated introduction to Romanticism can be found in **H. Honour, *Romanticism*** (New York, 1979). On the ideas of the Romantics, see **M. Cranston, *The Romantic Movement*** (Oxford, 1994). For an introduction to the arts, see **W. Vaughan, *Romanticism and Art*** (New York, 1994). A detailed biography of Darwin can be found in **J. Bowlby, *Charles Darwin: A Biography*** (London, 1990). On Realism, **J. Malpas, *Realism*** (Cambridge, 1997), is a good introduction.

**History Now™**

**Enter *HistoryNow* using the access card that is available with this text. *HistoryNow* will assist you in understanding the content in this chapter with lesson plans generated for your needs, as well as provide you with a connection to the *Wadsworth World History Resource Center* (see description below for details).**

**WORLD HISTORY**
RESOURCE CENTER

**Enter the Resource Center using either your *HistoryNow* access card or your standalone access card for the *Wadsworth World History Resource Center.* Organized by topic, this website includes quizzes; images; over 350 primary source documents; interactive simulations; maps and timelines; movie explorations; and a wealth of other resources. You can read the following documents, and many more, at http://history.wadsworth.com/rc/world**

Thomas Malthus, *An Essay on the Principle of Population*
The Chartist Petition
Guiseppe Mazzini, excerpts from *The Duties of Man*

Visit the *World History* Companion Website for chapter quizzes and more.

http://history.wadsworth.com/duikerspielvogel05/

CHAPTER

# 19

# The Emergence of Mass Society in the Western World

Swimmers gather in front of concession stands at Coney Island



## CHAPTER OUTLINE AND FOCUS QUESTIONS

### The Growth of Industrial Prosperity

- What was the Second Industrial Revolution, and what effects did it have on economic and social life?
- What were the main ideas of Karl Marx, and what role did they play in politics and the union movement in the late nineteenth and early twentieth centuries?

### The Emergence of Mass Society

- What is meant by the term *mass society,* and what were its main characteristics?

### The National State

- What general political trends were evident in the nations of western Europe in the late nineteenth and early twentieth centuries, and to what degree were those trends also apparent in the nations of Latin America, North America, and central and eastern Europe?

### Toward the Modern Consciousness: Intellectual and Cultural Developments

- What intellectual and cultural developments in the late nineteenth and early twentieth centuries "opened the way to a modern consciousness," and how did this consciousness differ from earlier worldviews?

## CRITICAL THINKING

- What was the relationship between economic, social, political, intellectual, and cultural developments between 1871 and 1914?

AFTER 1870, NEW WORK PATTERNS in the Western world established the "weekend" as a distinct time of recreation and fun, while new forms of mass transportation–railroads and streetcars–enabled even workers to make brief excursions to amusement parks. Coney Island was only 8 miles from central New York City; Blackpool in England was a short train ride from nearby industrial towns. With their Ferris wheels and other daring rides that threw young men and women together, amusement parks offered a whole new world of entertainment. Thanks to the railroad, seaside resorts, once the preserve of the wealthy, also became accessible to more people for weekend visits, much to the disgust of one upper-class regular, who complained about the new "day-trippers": "They swarm upon the beach, wandering listlessly about with apparently no other aim than to get a mouthful of fresh air." Enterprising entrepreneurs in resorts like Blackpool welcomed the masses of new visitors, however, and built piers laden with food, drink, and entertainment to serve them.

Mass leisure was but one aspect of the new mass society that emerged in the West during the decades leading up to 1914. Those decades marked a dynamic age of material prosperity in the West. The new industries, new sources of energy, and new goods of the Second Industrial Revolution transformed the human environment and led people to believe that their material progress reflected human progress. Scientific and technological achievements, many naively believed, would improve the human condition and solve all problems. The doctrine of progress became an article of faith.

The rapid economic changes of the nineteenth century led to the emergence of mass society in the Western world. Mass society meant improvements for the lower classes, who benefited from the extension of voting rights, a better standard of living, and universal education. The coming of mass society also created new roles for the governments of European nation-states, which now fostered national loyalty, created mass armies by conscription, and took more responsibility for public health and housing measures in their cities. Within many of these nation-states, the growth of the middle class had led to the triumph of liberal practices: constitutional governments, parliaments, and principles of equality. The period after 1870 also witnessed the growth of political democracy as the right to vote was extended to all adult males; women would still have to fight for the same political rights. With political democracy came a new mass politics that would become a regular feature of the twentieth century.

The period between 1870 and 1914 was also a time of great tension as imperialist adventures, international rivalries, and cultural uncertainties disturbed the apparent calm. Europeans engaged in a race for colonies that greatly intensified existing antagonisms among European states, and the creation of mass conscript armies and enormous military establishments served to heighten tensions among the major powers. At the same time, despite the appearance of progress, Western philosophers, writers, and artists were exploring modern cultural expressions that questioned traditional ideas and values and increasingly provoked a crisis of confidence. ◇

Fotomas Index

**An Age of Progress.** The Second Industrial Revolution led many Europeans to believe that most human problems would be solved by scientific achievements. This illustration is from a special issue of the *Illustrated London News* celebrating the Diamond Jubilee of Queen Victoria in 1897. On the left are scenes from 1837, when Victoria came to the British throne; on the right are scenes from 1897. The vivid contrast underscored the magazine's conclusion: "The most striking . . . evidence of progress during the reign is the ever increasing speed which the discoveries of physical science have forced into everyday life. Steam and electricity have conquered time and space to a greater extent during the last sixty years than all the preceding six hundred years witnessed."

# The Growth of Industrial Prosperity

At the heart of Europe's belief in progress between 1870 and 1914 was the stunning material growth produced by what historians have called the Second Industrial Revolution.

## New Products

The first major change in industrial development after 1870 was the substitution of steel for iron. New methods for shaping steel made it useful in the construction of lighter, smaller, and faster machines and engines as well as railways, ships, and armaments. In 1860, Great Britain, France, Germany, and Belgium produced 125,000 tons of steel; by 1913, the total was 32 million tons.

Electricity was a major new form of energy that could be easily converted into other forms—such as heat, light, and motion—and moved relatively effortlessly through space by means of transmitting wires. In the 1870s, the first commercially practical generators of electrical current were developed, and by 1910, hydroelectric power stations and coal-fired steam-generating plants enabled homes and factories in whole neighborhoods to be tied in to a single, common source of power.

Electricity spawned a number of inventions. The light bulb, developed independently by the American Thomas Edison and the Briton Joseph Swan, permitted homes and cities to be illuminated by electric lights. A revolution in communications began when Alexander Graham Bell invented the telephone in 1876 and Guglielmo Marconi sent the first radio waves across the Atlantic in 1901. By the 1880s, electricity-powered streetcars and subways had appeared in major Euro-

## The Department Store and the Beginnings of Mass Consumerism

Domestic markets were especially important for the sale of the goods being turned out by Europe's increasing number of industrial plants. New techniques of mass marketing arose to encourage the sale of the new consumer goods. The Parisians pioneered in the development of the department store, and this selection is taken from a contemporary's account of the growth of these stores in the French capital city.

*Did the invention of department stores respond to or create the new "consumer ethic" in industrialized societies? What was this new twentieth-century ethic? According to Lavasseur, what were the positive effects of department stores on Parisian society?*

### E. Lavasseur, On Parisian Department Stores, 1907

It was in the reign of Louis-Philippe [1830–1848] that department stores for fashion goods and dresses, extending to material and other clothing, began to be distinguished. The type was already one of the notable developments of the Second Empire; it became one of the most important ones of the Third Republic. These stores have increased in number and several of them have become extremely large. Combining in their different departments all articles of clothing, toilet articles, furniture and many other ranges of goods, it is their special object so to combine all commodities as to attract and satisfy customers who will find conveniently together an assortment of a mass of articles corresponding to all their various needs. They attract customers by permanent display, by free entry into the shops, by periodic exhibitions, by special sales, by fixed prices, and by their ability to deliver the goods purchased to customers' homes, in Paris and to the provinces. Turning themselves into direct intermediaries between the producer and the consumer, even producing sometimes some of their articles in their own workshops, buying at lowest prices because of their large orders and because they are in a position to profit from bargains, working with large sums, and selling to most of their customers for cash only, they can transmit these benefits in lowered selling prices. They can even decide to sell at a loss, as an advertisement or to get rid of out-of-date fashions. Taking 5–6 per cent on 100 million [francs] brings them in more than 20 per cent would bring to a firm doing a turnover of 50,000 francs.

The success of these department stores is only possible thanks to the volume of their business, and this volume needs considerable capital and a very large turnover. Now capital, having become abundant, is freely combined nowadays in large enterprises, although French capital has the reputation of being more wary of the risks of industry than of State or railway securities. On the other hand, the large urban agglomerations, the ease with which goods can be transported by the railways, the diffusion of some comforts to strata below the middle classes, have all favored these developments.

As example we may cite some figures relating to these stores. . . .

*Le Louvre,* dating to the time of the extension of the rue de Rivoli under the Second Empire [1855], did in 1893 a business of 120 million at a profit of 6.4 per cent. *Le Bon-Marché,* which was a small shop when Mr. Boucicaut entered it in 1852, already did a business of 20 million at the end of the Empire [1870]. During the republic its new buildings were erected; Mme. Boucicaut turned it by her will into a kind of cooperative society, with shares and an ingenious organization; turnover reached 150 million in 1893, leaving a profit of 5 per cent. . . .

According to the tax records of 1891, these stores in Paris, numbering 12, employed 1,708 persons and were rated on their site values at 2,159,000 francs; the largest had then 542 employees. These same stores had, in 1901, 9,784 employees; one of them over 2,000 and another over 1,600; their site value has doubled (4,089,000 francs).

pean cities. Electricity also transformed the factory. Conveyor belts, cranes, machines, and machine tools could all be powered by electricity and located anywhere. Thanks to electricity, all countries could now enter the industrial age.

The development of the internal combustion engine, fired by oil and gasoline, provided a new source of power in transportation and gave rise to ocean liners as well as to the airplane and the automobile. In 1900, world production stood at 9,000 cars, but an American, Henry Ford, revolutionized the automotive industry with the mass production of the Model T. By 1916, Ford's factories were producing 735,000 cars a year. In 1903, at Kitty Hawk, North Carolina, brothers Orville and Wilbur Wright made the first flight in a fixed-wing airplane. In 1919, the first regular passenger air service was established.

## New Patterns

Industrial production grew rapidly at this time because of the greatly increased sales of manufactured goods. An increase in real wages for workers after 1870, combined with lower prices for manufactured goods because of reduced transportation costs, made it easier for Europeans to buy consumer products. In the cities, the first department stores began to sell a whole new range of consumer goods made possible by the development of the steel and electrical industries (see the box above). The desire to own sewing machines, clocks, bicycles, electric lights, and typewriters was rapidly generating a new consumer ethic that has been a crucial part of the modern economy.

Not all nations benefited from the Second Industrial Revolution. Between 1870 and 1914, Germany replaced Great Britain as the industrial leader of Europe. Moreover, by 1900, Europe was divided into two economic zones. Great Britain, Belgium, France, the Netherlands, Germany, the western part of the Austro-Hungarian Empire, and northern Italy constituted an advanced industrialized core that had a high standard of living, decent systems of transportation, and relatively healthy and educated peoples (see Map 19.1). Another part of Europe, the backward and little industrialized area to the south and east, consisting of southern Italy, most of Austria-Hungary, Spain, Portugal, the Balkan kingdoms, and Russia, was still largely agricultural and relegated by the industrial countries to the function of providing food and raw materials.

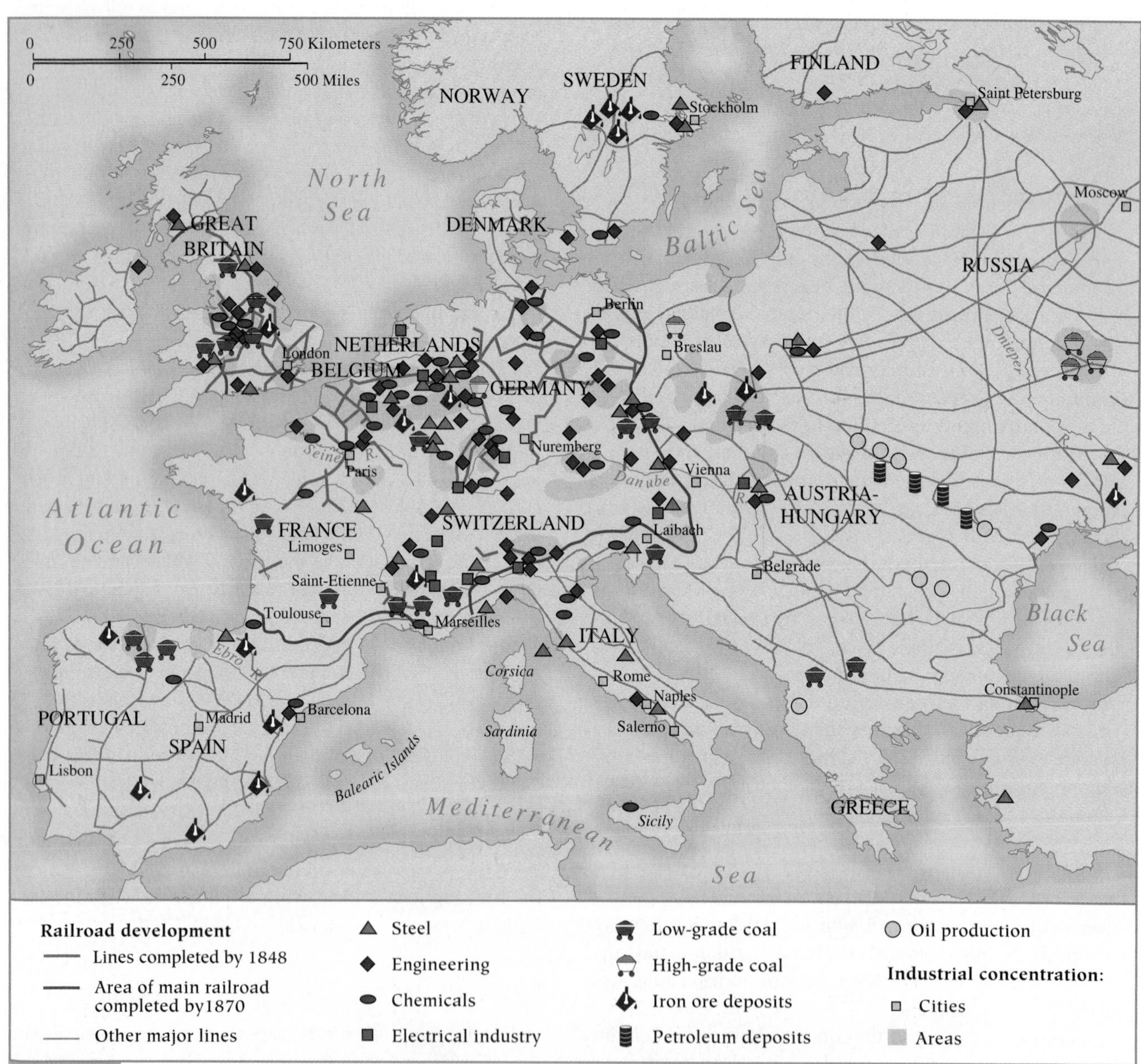


MAP 19.1 **The Industrial Regions of Europe at the End of the Nineteenth Century.** By the end of the nineteenth century, the Second Industrial Revolution—in steelmaking, electricity, petroleum, and chemicals—had spurred substantial economic growth and prosperity in western and central Europe; it also sparked economic and political competition between Great Britain and Germany. ? Look back at Map 18.1. What parts of Europe not industrialized in 1850 had become industrialized in the ensuing decades? **View an animated version of this map or related maps at** http://history.wadsworth.com/duikerspielvogel05/

## Toward a World Economy

The economic developments of the late nineteenth century, combined with the transportation revolution that saw the growth of marine transport and railroads, fostered a true world economy. By 1900, Europeans were receiving beef and wool from Argentina and Australia, coffee from Brazil, nitrates from Chile, iron ore from Algeria, and sugar from Java. European capital was also invested abroad to develop railways, mines, electrical power plants, and banks. High rates of return, such as 11.3 percent on Latin American banking shares that were floated in London, provided plenty of incentive for investors. Of course, foreign countries also provided markets for the surplus manufactured goods of Europe. With its capital, industries, and military might, Europe dominated the world economy by the beginning of the twentieth century.

## The Spread of Industrialization

At the same time, after 1870, industrialization began to spread beyond western and central Europe and North America. Especially noticeable was its rapid development, fostered by governments, in Russia and Japan. A surge of industrialization began in Russia in the 1890s under the guiding hand of Sergei Witte, the minister for finance. Witte pushed the government toward a program of massive railroad construction. By 1900, some 35,000 miles of track had been laid. Witte's program also made possible the rapid growth of a modern steel and coal industry, making Russia by 1900 the fourth-largest producer of steel, behind the United States, Germany, and Great Britain. Russia was also turning out half of the world's production of oil.

In Japan, the imperial government took the lead in promoting industry (see Chapter 21). The government financed industries, built railroads, brought foreign experts to train Japanese employees in new industrial techniques, and instituted a universal educational system based on applied science. By the end of the nineteenth century, Japan had developed key industries in tea, silk, armaments, and shipbuilding.

## Women and Work: New Job Opportunities

During the course of the nineteenth century, working-class organizations persisted in the belief that women should remain at home to bear and nurture children and not be allowed in the industrial workforce. Working-class men argued that keeping women out of the factories would ensure the moral and physical well-being of families. In reality, however, if their husbands were unemployed, women had to do low-wage work or labor part time in sweatshops to support their families.

The Second Industrial Revolution opened the door to new jobs for women. The development of larger industrial plants and the expansion of government services created a variety of service or white-collar jobs. The increased demand for white-collar workers at relatively low wages coupled with a shortage of male workers led employers to hire women. Big businesses and retail shops needed clerks, typists, secretaries, file clerks, and salesclerks. The expansion of government services opened opportunities for women to be secretaries and telephone operators and to take jobs in health and social services. Compulsory education necessitated more teachers, while the development of modern hospital services opened the way for an increase in nurses.

Many of the new white-collar jobs were far from exciting. The work was routine and, except for teaching and nursing, required few skills beyond basic literacy. Nevertheless, these jobs had distinct advantages for many women. For some middle-class women, the new jobs offered freedom from the domestic patterns expected of them. Moreover, because middle-class women did not receive an education comparable to that of men, they were limited in the careers they could pursue. Thus they found it easier to fill the jobs at the lower end of middle-class occupations, such as teaching and civil service jobs, especially in the post office. Most of the new white-collar jobs, however, were filled by working-class women who saw the job as an opportunity to escape from the physical labor of the lower-class world.

## Organizing the Working Classes

The desire to improve their working and living conditions led many industrial workers to form socialist political parties and socialist labor unions. These emerged after 1870, but the theory that made them possible had been developed more than two decades earlier in the work of Karl Marx. **Marxism** made its first appearance on the eve of the revolutions of 1848 with the publication of a short treatise titled *The Communist Manifesto,* written by two Germans, Karl Marx (1818–1883) and Friedrich Engels (1820–1895).

**Marxist Theory** Marx and Engels began their treatise with the statement that "the history of all hitherto existing society is the history of class struggles." Throughout history, then, oppressor and oppressed have "stood in constant opposition to one another."[1] One group of people—the oppressors—owned the means of production and thus had the power to control government and society. Indeed, government itself was but an instrument of the ruling class. The other group, which depended on the owners of the means of production, were the oppressed.

In the industrialized societies of Marx's day, the **class struggle** continued. According to Marx and Engels, "Society as a whole is more and more splitting up into two great hostile camps, into two great classes directly facing each other: Bourgeoisie and Proletariat." Marx predicted that the struggle between the bourgeoisie and the proletariat would finally break into open revolution, "where the violent overthrow of the bourgeoisie lays the foundation for the sway of the proletariat." The fall of

## The Classless Society

In *The Communist Manifesto,* Karl Marx and Friedrich Engels projected as the end product of the struggle between the bourgeoisie and the proletariat the creation of a classless society. In this selection, they discuss the steps by which that classless society would be reached.

*How did Marx and Engels define the proletariat? The bourgeoisie? Why did Marxists come to believe that this distinction was paramount for understanding history? For shaping the future?*

### Karl Marx and Friedrich Engels, *The Communist Manifesto*

We have seen . . ., that the first step in the revolution by the working class is to raise the proletariat to the position of ruling class. . . . The proletariat will use its political supremacy to wrest, by degrees, all capital from the bourgeoisie, to centralize all instruments of production in the hands of the State, i.e., of the proletariat organized as the ruling class; and to increase the total of productive forces as rapidly as possible.

Of course, in the beginning, this cannot be effected except by means of despotic inroads on the rights of property, and on the conditions of bourgeois production; by means of measures, therefore, which appear economically insufficient and untenable, but which, in the course of the movement, outstrip themselves, necessitate further inroads upon the old social order, and are unavoidable as a means of entirely revolutionizing the mode of production.

These measures will of course be different in different countries.

Nevertheless, in the most advanced countries, the following will be pretty generally applicable:

1. Abolition of property in land and application of all rents of land to public purposes.
2. A heavy progressive or graduated income tax.
3. Abolition of all right of inheritance. . . .
5. Centralization of credit in the hands of the State, by means of a national bank with State capital and an exclusive monopoly.
6. Centralization of the means of communication and transport in the hands of the State.
7. Extension of factories and instruments of production owned by the State. . . .
8. Equal liability of all to labor. Establishment of industrial armies, especially for agriculture.
9. Combination of agriculture with manufacturing industries; gradual abolition of the distinction between town and country, by a more equable distribution of the population over the country.
10. Free education for all children in public schools. Abolition of children's factory labor in its present form. . . .

When, in the course of development, class distinctions have disappeared, and all production has been concentrated in the whole nation, the public power will lose its political character. Political power, properly so called, is merely the organized power of one class for oppressing another. If the proletariat during its contest with the bourgeoisie is compelled, by the force of circumstances, to organize itself as a class, if, by means of a revolution, it makes itself the ruling class, and, as such, sweeps away by force the old conditions of production, then it will, along with these conditions, have swept away the conditions for the existence of class antagonisms and of classes generally, and will thereby have abolished its own supremacy as a class.

In place of the old bourgeois society, with its classes and class antagonisms, we shall have an association, in which the free development of each is the condition for the free development of all.

the bourgeoisie "and the victory of the proletariat are equally inevitable."[2] For a while, the proletariat would form a dictatorship in order to organize the means of production. However, the end result would be a classless society, since classes themselves arose from the economic differences that have been abolished; the state—itself an instrument of the bourgeois interests—would wither away (see the box above).

**Socialist Parties** In time, Marx's ideas were picked up by working-class leaders who formed socialist parties. Most important was the German Social Democratic Party (SPD), which emerged in 1875 and espoused revolutionary Marxist rhetoric while organizing itself as a mass political party competing in elections for the Reichstag (the lower house of parliament). Once in the Reichstag, SPD delegates sought to pass legislation to improve the condition of the working class. Despite government efforts to destroy it, the SPD continued to grow. When it received four million votes in the 1912 elections, it became the largest party in Germany.

Socialist parties emerged in other European states, although not with the kind of success achieved by the German Social Democrats. In 1889, leaders of the various socialist parties formed the Second International, an association of national socialist groups that would fight against capitalism worldwide. (The First International had failed in 1872.) The Second International took some coordinated actions—May Day (May 1), for example, was made an international labor holiday—but differences often wreaked havoc at the organization's congresses.

Verein für Geschichte der Arbeiterbewegung, Vienna

**"Proletarians of the World, Unite!"** To improve their working and living conditions, many industrial workers, inspired by the ideas of Karl Marx, joined working-class or socialist parties. Pictured here is a socialist-sponsored poster that proclaims in German the closing words of *The Communist Manifesto:* "Proletarians of the World, Unite!"

**Revisionism and Trade Unions** Marxist parties divided over the issue of **revisionism.** Pure Marxists believed in the imminent collapse of capitalism and the need for socialist ownership of the means of production. But others, called revisionists, rejected **revolutionary socialism** and argued that workers must organize mass political parties and work together with other progressive elements to gain reform. Having won the right to vote, workers were in a better position than ever to achieve their aims through democratic channels. Evolution by democratic means, not revolution, would achieve the desired goal of socialism.

Another force working for evolutionary rather than revolutionary socialism was the development of trade unions. In Great Britain, unions won the right to strike in the 1870s. Soon after, the masses of workers in factories were organized into trade unions in order to use the instrument of the strike. By 1900, there were two million workers in British trade unions; by 1914, there were almost four million. Trade unions in the rest of Europe had varying degrees of success, but by the outbreak of World War I, they had made considerable progress in bettering both the living and the working conditions of the laboring classes.

## The Emergence of Mass Society

The rapid economic and social changes of the nineteenth century led to the emergence of **mass society** by the century's end. For the lower classes, mass society brought voting rights, an improved standard of living, and access to education. However, mass society also made possible the development of organizations that manipulated the populations of the nation-states. To understand this mass society, we need to examine some aspects of its structure.

### The New Urban Environment

One of the most important consequences of industrialization and the population explosion of the nineteenth century was urbanization. In the course of the nineteenth century, more and more people came to live in cities. In 1800, city-dwellers constituted 40 percent of the population in Britain, 25 percent in France and Germany, and only 10 percent in eastern Europe. By 1914, urban residents had increased to 80 percent of the population in Britain, 45 percent in France, 60 percent in Germany, and 30 percent in eastern Europe. The size of cities also expanded dramatically, especially in industrialized countries. Between 1800 and 1900, London's population grew from 960,000 to 6.5 million and Berlin's from 172,000 to 2.7 million.

Urban populations grew faster than the general population primarily because of the vast migration from rural areas to cities. People were driven by sheer economic necessity—unemployment and physical want—from the countryside to the city. But cities also grew faster in the second half of the nineteenth century because health and living conditions were improving as reformers and city officials used new technology to ameliorate the urban landscape. In the 1840s, a number of urban reformers had pointed to filthy living conditions as the primary cause of epidemic diseases and urged sanitary reforms to correct the problem. Following the advice of reformers, city governments set up boards of health to improve the quality of housing. New building regulations required running water and an internal drainage system for all new buildings. For the first time in Western history, the role of municipal governments had been expanded to include detailed regulations for the improvement of the living conditions of urban dwellers.

Essential to the public health of the modern European city was the ability to bring in clean water and to expel sewage. The problem of fresh water was solved by a system of dams and reservoirs that stored the water and aqueducts and tunnels that carried it from the countryside to the city and into individual dwellings. Gas heaters in the 1860s, and later electric heaters, made regular hot

## The Housing Venture of Octavia Hill

Octavia Hill was a practical-minded British housing reformer who believed that workers and their families were entitled to happy homes. At the same time, she was convinced that the poor needed guidance and encouragement, not charity. In this selection, she describes her housing venture.

*Did Octavia Hill's housing venture create financial returns for her initial investment? What benefits did her tenants receive in turn? What feelings and beliefs about the lower classes are evident in Hill's account?*

### Octavia Hill, *Homes of the London Poor*

About four years ago I was put in possession of three houses in one of the worst courts of Marylebone. Six other houses were bought subsequently. All were crowded with inmates.

The first thing to be done was to put them in decent tenantable order. The set last purchased was a row of cottages facing a bit of desolate ground, occupied with wretched, dilapidated cowsheds, manure heaps, old timber, and rubbish of every description. The houses were in a most deplorable condition–the plaster was dropping from the walls; on one staircase a pail was placed to catch the rain that fell through the roof. All the staircases were perfectly dark; the banisters were gone, having been burnt as firewood by tenants. The grates, with large holes in them, were falling forward into the rooms. The washhouse, full of lumber belonging to the landlord, was locked up; thus the inhabitants had to wash clothes, as well as to cook, eat and sleep in their small rooms. The dustbin, standing in the front part of the houses, was accessible to the whole neighbourhood, and boys often dragged from it quantities of unseemly objects and spread them over the court. The state of the drainage was in keeping with everything else. The pavement of the backyard was all broken up, and great puddles stood in it, so that the damp crept up the outer walls. . . .

As soon as I entered into possession, each family had an opportunity of doing better: those who would not pay, or who led clearly immoral lives, were ejected. The rooms they vacated were cleansed; the tenants who showed signs of improvement moved into them, and thus, in turn, an opportunity was obtained for having each room distempered and papered. The drains were put in order, a large slate cistern was fixed, the wash-house was cleared of its lumber, and thrown open on stated days to each tenant in turn. The roof, the plaster, the woodwork was repaired; the staircase walls were distempered; new grates were fixed; the layers of paper and rag (black with age) were torn from the windows, and glass was put in; out of 192 panes only eight were found unbroken. The yard and footpath were paved.

The rooms, as a rule, were re-let at the same prices at which they had been let before; but tenants with large families were counselled to take two rooms, and for these much less was charged than if let singly: this plan I continue to pursue. Incoming tenants are not allowed to take a decidedly insufficient quantity of room, and no subletting is permitted. . . .

The pecuniary result has been very satisfactory. Five per cent has been paid on all the capital invested. A fund for the repayment of capital is accumulating. A liberal allowance has been made for repairs. . . .

My tenants are mostly of a class far below that of mechanics. They are, indeed, of the very poor. And yet, although the gifts they have received have been next to nothing, none of the families who have passed under my care during the whole four years have continued in what is called "distress," except such as have been unwilling to exert themselves. Those who will not exert the necessary self-control cannot avail themselves of the means of livelihood held out to them. But, for those who are willing, some small assistance in the form of work has, from time to time, been provided–not much, but sufficient to keep them from want or despair.

baths available to many people. The treatment of sewage was also improved by laying mammoth underground pipes that carried raw sewage far from the city for disposal. In the late 1860s, a number of German cities began to construct sewer systems. The city of Frankfurt, for example, began its program after a lengthy public campaign enlivened by the slogan "From the Toilet to the River in Half an Hour."

Middle-class reformers also focused on the housing needs of the working class. Overcrowded, disease-ridden slums were viewed as dangerous not only to physical health but also to the political and moral health of the entire nation. V. A. Huber, the foremost early German housing reformer, wrote in 1861, "Certainly it would not be too much to say that the home is the communal embodiment of family life. Thus the purity of the dwelling is almost as important for the family as is the cleanliness of the body for the individual."[3] To Huber, good housing was a prerequisite for stable family life, and without stable family life, society would fall apart.

Early efforts to attack the housing problem emphasized the middle-class, liberal belief in the power of private, or free, enterprise. Reformers such as Huber believed that the construction of model dwellings renting at a reasonable price would force other private landlords to elevate their housing standards. A fine example of this approach was the work of Octavia Hill (see the box above). As the number and size of cities continued to mushroom, governments by the 1880s concluded that private enterprise could not solve the housing crisis. In 1890, a British law empowered local town councils to construct cheap housing for the working classes. Similar activity was set in motion in Germany. More and more, governments were stepping into areas of activity that they would not have touched earlier.

## The Social Structure of Mass Society

At the top of European society stood a wealthy elite, constituting but 5 percent of the population while controlling between 30 and 40 percent of the wealth. In the course of the nineteenth century, landed aristocrats had joined with the most successful industrialists, bankers, and merchants (the wealthy upper-middle class) to form a new elite. Members of this elite, whether aristocratic or middle-class in background, assumed leadership roles in government bureaucracies and military hierarchies. Marriage also united the two groups. Daughters of business tycoons gained titles, while aristocratic heirs gained new sources of cash. When the American Consuelo Vanderbilt married the duke of Marlborough, the new duchess brought $10 million to her husband.

The middle classes consisted of a variety of groups. Below the upper middle class was a group that included lawyers, doctors, and members of the civil service, as well as business managers, engineers, architects, accountants, and chemists benefiting from industrial expansion. Beneath this solid and comfortable middle group was a lower middle class of small shopkeepers, traders, manufacturers, and prosperous peasants.

Standing between the lower middle class and the lower classes were new groups of white-collar workers who were the product of the Second Industrial Revolution—the salespeople, bookkeepers, bank tellers, telephone operators, and secretaries. Though often paid little more than skilled laborers, these white-collar workers were committed to middle-class ideals.

The middle classes shared a certain lifestyle, the values of which dominated much of nineteenth-century society. The members of the middle class were especially active in preaching their worldview to their children and to the upper and lower classes of their society. This was especially evident in Victorian Britain, often considered a model of middle-class society. The European middle classes believed in hard work, which was open to everyone and guaranteed to have positive results. They were also regular churchgoers who believed in the good conduct associated with traditional Christian morality. The middle class was concerned with propriety, the right way of doing things, which gave rise to an incessant stream of books aimed at the middle-class market with such titles as *The Habits of Good Society* or *Don't: A Manual of Mistakes and Improprieties More or Less Prevalent in Conduct and Speech.*

Below the middle classes on the social scale were the working classes, who constituted almost 80 percent of the European population. Many of them were landholding peasants, agricultural laborers, and sharecroppers, especially in eastern Europe. The urban working class consisted of many different groups, including skilled artisans in such traditional trades as cabinetmaking, printing, and the making of jewelry, along with semiskilled laborers, who included such people as carpenters, bricklayers, and many factory workers. At the bottom of the urban working class stood the largest group of workers, the unskilled laborers. They included day laborers, who worked irregularly for very low wages, and large numbers of domestic servants, most of whom were women.

Urban workers did experience a real betterment in the material conditions of their lives after 1870. A rise in real wages, accompanied by a decline in many consumer costs, especially in the 1880s and 1890s, made it possible for workers to buy not only food and housing but also more clothes and even leisure at the same time that strikes and labor agitation were providing shorter workdays (no more than ten hours) and Saturday afternoons off.

CORBIS

**Working-Class Housing in London.** Although urban workers experienced some improvements in the material conditions of their lives after 1870, working-class housing remained drab and depressing. This 1912 photograph of working-class housing in the East End of London shows rows of similar-looking buildings on treeless streets. Most often, these buildings had no gardens or green areas.

## The Experiences of Women

In the nineteenth century, women remained legally inferior, economically dependent, and largely defined by family and household roles. Many women still aspired to the ideal of femininity popularized by writers and poets. Alfred Lord Tennyson's poem *The Princess* expressed it well:

> *Man for the field and woman for the hearth:*
> *Man for the sword and for the needle she:*
> *Man with the head and woman with the heart:*
> *Man to command and woman to obey;*
> *All else confusion.*

This traditional characterization of the sexes, based on gender-defined social roles, was elevated to the status of universal male and female attributes in the nineteenth century, due largely to the impact of the Industrial Revolution on the family. As the chief family wage earners, men worked outside the home for pay, while women were left with the care of the family, for which they were paid nothing.

**Marriage and the Family** For most of the nineteenth century, marriage was viewed as the only honorable career available to most women. Although the middle class glorified the ideal of domesticity, for most women marriage was a matter of economic necessity. The lack of meaningful work and the lower wages paid to women for their work made it difficult for single women to earn a living. Most women chose to marry.

Birthrates also dropped significantly in the nineteenth century. The most significant development in the modern family was the decline in the number of offspring born to the average woman. While some historians attribute increased birth control to more widespread use of coitus interruptus, or male withdrawal before ejaculation, others have emphasized female control of family size through abortion and even infanticide or abandonment. That a change in attitude occurred was apparent in the development of a movement to increase awareness of birth control methods. Europe's first birth control clinic, founded by Dr. Aletta Jacob, opened in Amsterdam in 1882.

The family was the central institution of middle-class life. Men provided the family income while women focused on household and child care. The use of domestic servants in many middle-class homes, made possible by an abundant supply of cheap labor, reduced the amount of time middle-class women had to spend on household work. At the same time, by reducing the number of children in the family, mothers could devote more time to child care and domestic leisure.

The middle-class family fostered an ideal of togetherness. The Victorians created the family Christmas with its yule log, Christmas tree, songs, and exchange of gifts. In the United States, Fourth of July celebrations changed from drunken revels to family picnics by the 1850s.

Women in working-class families were more accustomed to hard work. Daughters in working-class families were expected to work until they married; even after marriage, they often did piecework at home to help support the family. For the children of the working classes, childhood was over by the age of nine or ten when they became apprentices or were employed in odd jobs.

Between 1890 and 1914, however, family patterns among the working class began to change. High-paying jobs in heavy industry and improvements in the standard of living made it possible for working-class families to depend on the income of husbands and the wages of grown children. By the early twentieth century, some working-class mothers could afford to stay at home, following the pattern of middle-class women. At the same time, working-class families also aspired to buy new consumer products, such as sewing machines, clocks, bicycles, and cast-iron stoves.

These working-class families also followed the middle classes in limiting the size of their families. Children began to be viewed as dependents rather than wage earners as child labor laws and compulsory education took children out of the workforce and into schools. At the same time, strikes and labor agitation led to laws that re-

Harrogate Museums and Art Gallery, North Yorkshire, UK/Bridgeman Art Library

**A Middle-Class Family.** Nineteenth-century middle-class moralists considered the family the fundamental pillar of a healthy society. The family was a crucial institution in middle-class life, and togetherness constituted one of the important ideals of the middle-class family. This painting by William P. Frith, titled *Many Happy Returns of the Day*, shows a family birthday celebration for a little girl in which grandparents, parents, and children take part. The servant at the left holds the presents for the little girl.

duced work hours to ten per day by 1900 and eliminated work on Saturday afternoons, which enabled working-class parents to devote more attention to their children and develop deeper emotional ties with them.

**The Movement for Women's Rights** In the 1830s, a number of women in the United States and Europe, who worked together in several reform movements, argued for the right of women to divorce and own property. These early efforts were not particularly successful, however. For example, women did not gain the right to their own property until 1870 in Britain, 1900 in Germany, and 1907 in France.

Custody and property rights were only a beginning for the women's movement, however. Some middle- and upper-middle-class women gained access to higher education, while others sought entry into occupations dominated by men. The first to fall was teaching. As medical training was largely closed to women, they sought alternatives in the development of nursing. An upper-class nursing pioneer in Germany was Amalie Sieveking (1794–1859), who founded the Female Association for the Care of the Poor and Sick in Hamburg. As she explained, "To me, at least as important were the benefits which [work with the poor] seemed to promise for those of my sisters who would join me in such a work of charity. The higher interests of my sex were close to my heart."[4] Sieveking's work was followed by the more famous British nurse, Florence Nightingale, whose efforts during the Crimean War (1854–1856), combined with those of Clara Barton in the American Civil War (1861–1865), transformed nursing into a profession of trained, middle-class "women in white."

By the 1840s and 1850s, the movement for women's rights had entered the political arena with the call for equal political rights. Many feminists believed that the right to vote was the key to all other reforms to improve the position of women. **Suffragists** had one basic aim: the right of women to full citizenship in the nation-state.

The British women's movement was the most vocal and active in Europe. Emmeline Pankhurst (1858–1928) and her daughters, Christabel and Sylvia, founded the Women's Social and Political Union in 1903, which enrolled mostly middle- and upper-class women. Pankhurst's organization realized the value of the media and used unusual publicity stunts to call attention to its demands. Derisively labeled "suffragettes" by male politicians, its members pelted government officials with eggs, chained themselves to lampposts, smashed the windows of department stores on fashionable shopping streets, burned railroad cars, and went on hunger strikes in jail.

Before World War I, the demands for women's rights were being heard throughout Europe and the United States, although only in Norway and some American states did women actually receive the right to vote before 1914. It would take the dramatic upheaval of World War I before male-dominated governments capitulated on this basic issue.

Women reformers also took on issues besides suffrage. In many countries, women supported peace movements. Bertha von Suttner (1843–1914) became head of the Austrian Peace Society and protested against the growing arms race of the 1890s. Her novel *Lay Down Your Arms* became a best-seller and brought her the Nobel Peace Prize in 1905. Lower-class women also took up the cause of peace. A group of women workers marched in Vienna in 1911 and demanded, "We want an end to armaments, to the means of murder, and we want these millions to be spent on the needs of the people."

Bertha von Suttner was but one example of the "new women" who were becoming more prominent at the turn of the century. These women rejected traditional feminine roles (see the box on p. 552) and sought new freedom outside the household and new roles other than those of wife and mother.

## Education in an Age of Mass Society

Universal education was a product of the mass society of the late nineteenth and early twentieth centuries. Education in the early nineteenth century was primarily for the elite or the wealthier middle class, but after 1870, most Western governments began to offer at least primary education to both boys and girls between the ages of six and twelve. States also assumed responsibility for better training of teachers by establishing teacher-training schools. By the beginning of the twentieth century, many European states, especially in northern and western Europe, provided state-financed primary schools, salaried and trained teachers, and free, compulsory elementary education.

Why did Western nations make this commitment to **mass education?** One reason was industrialization. The new firms of the Second Industrial Revolution demanded skilled labor. Both boys and girls with an elementary education had new possibilities of jobs beyond their villages or small towns, including white-collar jobs in railways and subways, post offices, banking and shipping firms, teaching, and nursing. Mass education furnished the trained workers industrialists needed. For most students, elementary education led to apprenticeship and a job.

The chief motive for mass education, however, was political. The increase in suffrage created the need for a more educated electorate. Even more important, however, mass compulsory education instilled patriotism and nationalized the masses, providing an opportunity for even greater national integration. As people lost their ties to local regions and even to religion, nationalism supplied a new faith. The use of a single national language created greater national unity than loyalty to a ruler did (see the comparative essay "The Rise of Nationalism" on p. 553).

## Advice to Women: Be Independent

Although a majority of women probably followed the nineteenth-century middle-class ideal of women as keepers of the household and nurturers of husband and children, an increasing number of women fought for the rights of women. This selection is taken from Act III of Henrik Ibsen's play *A Doll's House* (1879), in which the character Nora Helmer declares her independence from her husband's control over her life.

*In Ibsen's play, what challenges does Nora Helmer make to the prevailing view of the proper role and behavior of wives? Why is her husband so shocked? Why did Ibsen title this play* A Doll's House?

### Henrik Ibsen, *A Doll's House*

Nora: (Pause) Does anything strike you as we sit here?

Helmer: What should strike me?

Nora: We've been married eight years; does it not strike you that this is the first time we two, you and I, man and wife, have talked together seriously?

Helmer: Seriously? What do you mean, *seriously?*

Nora: For eight whole years, and more—ever since the day we first met—we have never exchanged one serious word about serious things. . . .

Helmer: Why, my dearest Nora, what have you to do with serious things?

Nora: There we have it! You have never understood me. I've had great injustice done to me, Torvald; first by father, then by you.

Helmer: What! Your father and me? We, who have loved you more than all the world?

Nora *(Shaking her head):* You have never loved me. You just found it amusing to think you were in love with me.

Helmer: Nora! What a thing to say!

Nora: Yes, it's true, Torvald. When I was living at home with father, he told me his opinions and mine were the same. If I had different opinions, I said nothing about them, because he would not have liked it. He used to call me his doll-child and played with me as I played with my dolls. Then I came to live in your house.

Helmer: What a way to speak of our marriage!

Nora *(Undisturbed):* I mean that I passed from father's hands into yours. You arranged everything to your taste and I got the same tastes as you; or pretended to—I don't know which—both, perhaps; sometimes one, sometimes the other. When I look back on it now, I seem to have been living here like a beggar, on hand-outs. I lived by performing tricks for you, Torvald. But that was how you wanted it. You and father have done me a great wrong. It is your fault that my life has come to naught.

Helmer: Why, Nora, how unreasonable and ungrateful! Haven't you been happy here?

Nora: No, never. I thought I was, but I never was.

Helmer: Not—not happy! . . .

Nora: I must stand quite alone if I am ever to know myself and my surroundings; so I cannot stay with you.

Helmer: Nora! Nora!

Nora: I am going at once. I daresay [my friend] Christina will take me in for tonight.

Helmer: You are mad! I shall not allow it! I forbid it!

Nora: It's no use your forbidding me anything now. I shall take with me only what belongs to me; from you I will accept nothing, either now or later.

Helmer: This is madness!

Nora: Tomorrow I shall go home—I mean to what was my home. It will be easier for me to find a job there.

Helmer: Oh, in your blind inexperience—

Nora: I must try to gain experience, Torvald.

Helmer: Forsake your home, your husband, your children! And you don't consider what the world will say.

Nora: I can't pay attention to that. I only know that I must do it.

Helmer: This is monstrous! Can you forsake your holiest duties?

Nora: What do you consider my holiest duties?

Helmer: Need I tell you that? Your duties to your husband and children.

Nora: I have other duties equally sacred.

Helmer: Impossible! What do you mean?

Nora: My duties toward myself.

Helmer: Before all else you are a wife and a mother.

Nora: That I no longer believe. Before all else I believe I am a human being, just as much as you are—or at least that I should try to become one. I know that most people agree with you, Torvald, and that they say so in books. But I can no longer be satisfied with what most people say and what is in books. I must think things out for myself and try to get clear about them.

Compulsory elementary education created a demand for teachers, and most of them were women. Many men viewed the teaching of children as an extension of women's "natural role" as nurturers of children. Moreover, females were paid lower salaries, in itself a considerable incentive for governments to encourage the establishment of teacher-training institutes for women. The first female colleges were teacher-training schools. It was not until the beginning of the twentieth century that women were permitted to enter the male-dominated universities.

The most immediate result of mass education was an increase in literacy. In Germany, Great Britain, France, and the Scandinavian countries, adult illiteracy was virtu-

## COMPARATIVE ESSAY

# The Rise of Nationalism

Like the Industrial Revolution, the concept of nationalism originated in eighteenth-century Europe, where it was the product of a variety of factors, including the spread of printing and the replacement of Latin with vernacular languages, the secularization of the age, and the experience of the French revolutionary and Napoleonic eras. The French were the first to show what a nation in arms could accomplish, but peoples conquered by Napoleon soon created their own national armies. At the beginning of the nineteenth century, peoples who had previously focused their identity on a locality or a region, on loyalty to a monarch or to a particular religious faith, now shifted their political allegiance to the idea of a nation, based on ethnic, linguistic, or cultural factors. The idea of the nation had explosive consequences: by the end of the first two decades of the twentieth century, the three largest multiethnic states in the world–Imperial Russia, Austria-Hungary, and the Ottoman Empire–had all given way to a number of individual nation-states.

The idea of establishing political boundaries on the basis of ethnicity, language, or culture had a broad appeal throughout Western civilization, but it had unintended consequences. Although the concept provided the basis for a new sense of community that was tied to liberal thought in the first half of the nineteenth century, it also gave birth to ethnic tensions and hatred in the second half of the century that resulted in bitter disputes and contributed to the competition between nation-states that eventually erupted into world war. Governments, following the lead of the radical government in Paris during the French Revolution, took full advantage of the rise of a strong national consciousness and transformed war from the sport of kings into a matter of national honor and commitment. Universal schooling enabled states to arouse patriotic enthusiasm and create national unity. Most soldiers who joyfully went to war in 1914 were convinced that their nation's cause was just.

But if the concept of nationalism was initially the product of conditions in modern Europe, it soon spread to other parts of the world. Although a few societies, such as Vietnam, had already developed a strong sense of national identity, most of the peoples living in Asia and Africa lived in multiethnic and multireligious communities and were not yet ripe for the spirit of nationalism. As we shall see, the first attempts to resist European colonial rule were thus often based on religious or ethnic identity, rather than on the concept of denied nationhood. But the imperialist powers, who at first benefited from the lack of political cohesion among their colonial subjects, eventually reaped what they had sown. As the colonial peoples became familiar with Western concepts of democracy and self-determination, they too began to manifest a sense of common purpose that helped knit together the different elements in their societies to oppose colonial regimes and create the conditions for the emergence of future nations. For good or ill, the concept of nationalism had now achieved global proportions. We shall explore such issues, and their consequences, in greater detail in the chapters that follow.

ally eliminated by 1900. Where there was less schooling, the story was quite different. Adult illiteracy rates were 79 percent in Serbia, 78 percent in Romania, and 79 percent in Russia.

## Leisure in an Age of Mass Society

With the Industrial Revolution came new forms of leisure. Work and leisure became opposites as leisure came to be viewed as what people do for fun when they are not at work. The new leisure hours created by the industrial system—evening hours after work, weekends, and later a week or two in the summer—largely determined the contours of the new **mass leisure.**

New technology created novel experiences for leisure, such as the Ferris wheel at amusement parks, while the subways and streetcars of the 1880s meant that even the working classes were no longer dependent on neighborhood facilities but could make their way to athletic games, amusement parks, and dance halls. Railroads could take people to the beaches on weekends.

By the late nineteenth century, team sports had also developed into another important form of mass leisure. Unlike the old rural games, they were no longer chaotic and spontaneous activities but became strictly organized with sets of rules and officials to enforce them. These rules were the products of organized athletic groups, such as the English Football Association (1863) and the American Bowling Congress (1895). The development of urban transportation systems made possible the construction of stadiums where thousands could attend, making mass spectator sports into a big business.

The new forms of popular leisure drew mass audiences and mostly served to provide entertainment and distract people from the realities of their work lives. The new mass leisure was quite different from earlier forms of popular culture. Festivals and fairs had been based on an ethos of active community participation, whereas the new forms of mass leisure were standardized for largely passive audiences. Amusement parks and professional sports teams were, after all, big businesses organized to make profits.

**A Women's College.** Women were largely excluded from male-dominated universities before 1900. Consequently, the demand of women for higher education led to the establishment of women's colleges, most of which were primarily teacher-training schools. This photograph shows a group of women in an astronomy class at Vassar College in the United States in 1878. Maria Mitchell, a famous astronomer, was head of the department.

## The National State

Throughout much of the Western world by 1870, the national state had become the focus of people's loyalties and the arena for political activity. Only in Russia, eastern Europe, Austria-Hungary, and Ireland did national groups still struggle for independence.

### Tradition and Change in Latin America

After 1870, Latin America began to experience an era of rapid economic growth based to a large extent on the export of a few basic items, such as wheat and beef from Argentina, coffee from Brazil, nitrates from Chile, coffee and bananas from Central America, and sugar and silver from Peru. These foodstuffs and raw materials were exchanged for finished goods—textiles, machines, and luxury goods—from Europe and the United States. Despite their economic growth, Latin American nations remained economic colonies of Western nations.

Old patterns also still largely prevailed in society. Rural elites dominated their estates and their workers. Although slavery was abolished by 1888, former slaves and their descendants were at the bottom of their society. The Indians remained poverty-stricken.

One result of the new prosperity that came from increased exports was growth in the middle sectors of Latin American society—lawyers, merchants, shopkeepers, businesspeople, schoolteachers, professors, bureaucrats, and military officers. These middle sectors, which made up only 5 to 10 percent of the population, depending on the country, were hardly large enough in numbers to consititute a true middle class. Nevertheless, after 1900, the middle sectors continued to expand. They lived in the cities, sought education and decent incomes, and increasingly saw the United States as the model to emulate, especially in regard to industrialization and education.

As Latin American export economies boomed, the working class expanded, which in turn led to the growth of labor unions, especially after 1914. Radical unions often advocated the use of the general strike as an instrument for change. By and large, however, the governing elites succeeded in stifling the political influence of the working class by restricting workers' right to vote. The need for industrial labor also led Latin American countries to encourage immigration from Europe. Between 1880 and 1914, three million Europeans, primarily Italians and Spaniards, settled in Argentina. Over 100,000 Europeans, mostly Italian, Portuguese, and Spanish, arrived in Brazil each year between 1891 and 1900.

### Political Change in Latin America

Latin America also experienced a political transformation after 1870. Large landowners began to take a more direct interest in national politics, sometimes expressed by a direct involvement in governing. In Argentina and Chile, for example, landholding elites controlled the governments, and although they produced constitutions similar to those of the United States and Europe, they were careful to ensure their power by regulating voting rights.

In some countries, large landowners made use of dictators to maintain the interests of the ruling elite. Porfirio Díaz, who ruled Mexico from 1876 to 1910, established a conservative, centralized government with the support of the army, foreign capitalists, large landowners, and the

**Emiliano Zapata.** The inability of Francisco Madero to carry out far-reaching reforms led to a more radical upheaval in the Mexican countryside. Emiliano Zapata led a band of Indians in a revolt against the large landowners of southern Mexico and issued his own demands for land reform.

Catholic church. But there were forces for change in Mexico that led to a revolution in 1910.

During Díaz's dictatorial regime, the real wages of the working class had declined. Moreover, 95 percent of the rural population owned no land, while about a thousand families owned almost all of Mexico. When a liberal landowner, Francisco Madero, forced Díaz from power, he opened the door to a wider revolution. Madero's ineffectiveness triggered a demand for agrarian reform led by Emiliano Zapata, who aroused the masses of landless peasants and began to seize the haciendas of the wealthy landholders (see the box on p. 556). The ensuing revolution caused untold destruction to the Mexican economy. Finally, a new constitution in 1917 established a strong presidency, initiated land reform policies, established limits on foreign investors, and set an agenda for social welfare for workers. The revolution also led to an outpouring of nationalistic pride. Intellectuals and artists in particular sought to capture what was unique about Mexico, with special emphasis on its Indian past. As the Mexican minister of education said, "Tired, disgusted of all this copied civilization, . . . we wish to cease being Europe's spiritual colonies."

By this time, a new power had begun to wield its influence over Latin America. At the beginning of the twentieth century, the United States, which had begun to emerge as a great world power, increasingly interfered in the affairs of its southern neighbors. As a result of the Spanish-American War (1898), Cuba became an American protectorate, and Puerto Rico was annexed outright. American investments in Latin America soon followed; so did American resolve to protect these investments. Between 1898 and 1934, U.S. military forces were sent to Cuba, Mexico, Guatemala, Honduras, Nicaragua, Panama, Colombia, Haiti, and the Dominican Republic to protect American interests. Some expeditions remained for many years; U.S. Marines were in Haiti from 1915 to 1934, and Nicaragua was occupied from 1909 to 1933. At the same time, the United States became the chief foreign investor in Latin America.

## The Rise of the United States

Four years of bloody civil war had preserved American national unity, but the old South had been destroyed. Between 1860 and World War I, the United States made the shift from an agrarian to a mighty industrial nation. American heavy industry stood unchallenged in 1900. In that year, the Carnegie Steel Company alone produced more steel than Great Britain's entire steel industry. Industrialization also led to urbanization. Whereas 20 percent of Americans lived in cities in 1860, over 40 percent did in 1900.

By 1900, the United States had become the world's richest nation and its greatest industrial power. Yet serious questions remained about the quality of American life. In 1890, the richest 9 percent of Americans owned an incredible 71 percent of the wealth. Labor unrest over unsafe working conditions, strict work discipline, and periodic cycles of devastating unemployment led workers to organize. By the turn of the century, one national organization, the American Federation of Labor, emerged as labor's dominant voice. Its lack of real power, however, is reflected in its membership figures. In 1900, it represented only one of every twelve American industrial workers.

During the Progressive Era after 1900, the reform of many features of American life became a primary issue. Under President Theodore Roosevelt (1901–1909), the federal government began to regulate corrupt industrial practices. President Woodrow Wilson (1913–1921) was responsible for the implementation of a graduated federal income tax. Like European states, the United States was moving slowly into policies that extended the functions of the state.

**The United States as a World Power** At the end of the nineteenth century, the United States began to expand abroad. The Samoan Islands in the Pacific became the

## Zapata and Land Reform

Emiliano Zapata was a sharecropper on a sugar plantation in Morelos, a mountainous state in southern Mexico. Using the slogan "Land and Liberty," Zapata formed a guerrilla band of Indians and led them in revolt against the haciendas of southern Mexico, burning the houses and sugar refineries. Convinced that the new president of Mexico, Francisco Madero, would not go far enough with land reform, Zapata issued his own plan, the Plan of Ayala, from which these excerpts are taken.

*Why did the hacienda system and its abuses prompt Zapata to issue the Plan of Ayala? Why did both his origins and this proposal endear him to the common and poor people of Mexico?*

### The Plan of Ayala

The Liberating Plan of the sons of the State of Morelos, members of the insurgent army that demands the . . . reforms that it judges convenient and necessary for the welfare of the Mexican Nation.

We, the undersigned, constituted as a Revolutionary Junta, in order to maintain and obtain the fulfillment of the promises made by the revolution of November 20, 1910, solemnly proclaim in the face of the civilized world . . . , so that it may judge us, the principles that we have formulated in order to destroy the tyranny that oppresses us. . . .

1. Considering that the President of the Republic, Don Francisco I. Madero, has made a bloody mockery of Effective Suffrage by . . . entering into an infamous alliance with the . . . enemies of the Revolution that he proclaimed, in order to forge the chains of a new dictatorship more hateful and terrible than that of Porfirio Díaz. . . . For these reasons we declare the said Francisco I. Madero unfit to carry out the promises of the Revolution of which he was the author. . . .
4. The Revolutionary Junta of the State of Morelos formally proclaims to the Mexican people: That it endorses the Plan of San Luis Potosí [Madero's revolutionary plan] with the additions stated below for the benefit of the oppressed peoples, and that it will defend its principles until victory or death. . . .
6. As an additional part of the plan we proclaim, be it known: that the lands, woods, and waters usurped . . . through tyranny and venal justice henceforth belong to the towns or citizens who have corresponding titles to those properties, of which they were despoiled by the bad faith of our oppressors. They shall retain possession of the said properties at all costs, arms in hand. The usurpers who think they have a right to the said lands may state their claims before special tribunals to be established upon the triumph of the Revolution.
7. Since the immense majority of Mexican towns and citizens own nothing but the ground on which they stand and endure a miserable existence, denied the opportunity to improve their social condition or to devote themselves to industry or agriculture because a few individuals monopolize the lands, woods, and waters—for these reasons the great estates shall be expropriated, with indemnification to the owners of one-third of such monopolies, in order that the towns and citizens of Mexico may obtain colonies, town sites, and arable lands. Thus the welfare of the Mexican people shall be promoted in all respects.
8. The properties of those [landowners] who directly or indirectly oppose the present Plan shall be seized by the nation, and two thirds of their value shall be used for war indemnities and pensions for the widows and orphans of the soldiers who may perish in the struggle for this Plan.

first important American colony; the Hawaiian Islands were the next to fall. By 1887, American settlers had gained control of the sugar industry on the Hawaiian Islands. As more Americans settled in Hawaii, they sought to gain political power. When Queen Liliuokalani tried to strengthen the power of the monarchy in order to keep the islands for the native peoples, the American government sent U.S. Marines to "protect" American lives. The queen was deposed, and Hawaii was annexed by the United States in 1898.

The American defeat of Spain in the Spanish-American War in 1898 encouraged Americans to extend their empire by acquiring Cuba, Puerto Rico, Guam, and the Philippines. Although the Filipinos hoped for independence, the Americans refused to grant it. As President McKinley said, the United States had the duty "to educate the Filipinos and uplift and Christianize them," a remarkable statement in view of the fact that most of them had been Roman Catholics for centuries. It took three years and sixty thousand troops to pacify the Philippines and establish American control. By the beginning of the twentieth century, the United States had become another Western imperialist power.

### The Growth of Canada

Canada, too, faced problems of national unity between 1870 and 1914. At the beginning of 1870, the Dominion of Canada had only four provinces: Quebec, Ontario, Nova Scotia, and New Brunswick. With the addition of two more provinces in 1871—Manitoba and British Columbia—the Dominion of Canada now extended from the Atlantic Ocean to the Pacific. As the first prime minister, John Macdonald (1815–1891) moved to strengthen Canadian unity. He pushed for the construction of a transcontinental railroad, which was finally completed in 1885 and opened the western lands to industrial and commercial development. This also led to the incorporation of two more provinces—Alberta and Saskatchewan—in 1905 into the Dominion of Canada.

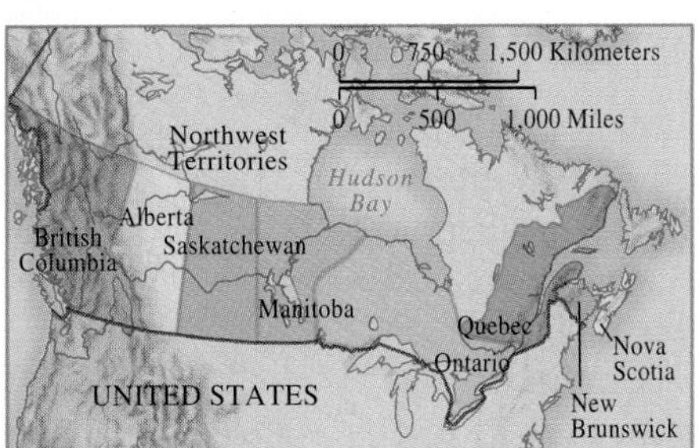

**Canada, 1914**

Real unity was difficult to achieve, however, because of the distrust between the English-speaking majority and the French-speaking Canadians, living primarily in Quebec. Wilfred Laurier, who became the first French Canadian prime minister in 1896, was able to reconcile Canada's two major groups and resolve the issue of separate schools for French Canadians. During Laurier's administration, industrialization boomed, especially the production of textiles, furniture, and railway equipment. Hundreds of thousands of immigrants, primarily from central and eastern Europe, also flowed into Canada. Many settled on lands in the west, thus helping populate Canada's vast territories.

## Europe

Within the major European states, considerable progress was made in achieving such liberal practices as constitutions and parliaments, but it was largely in western European states that **mass politics** became a reality. Reforms encouraged the expansion of political democracy through voting rights for men and the creation of mass political parties. At the same time, however, these latter developments were strongly resisted in parts of Europe where the old political forces remained strong.

**Western Europe: The Growth of Political Democracy** By 1871, Great Britain had a functioning two-party parliamentary system. For fifty years, the Liberals and Conservatives alternated in power at regular intervals, although they also shared some common features. Both were dominated by a ruling class made up of a coalition of aristocratic landowners frequently involved in industrial and financial activities and upper-middle-class businesspeople. And both competed with each other in supporting legislation that expanded the right to vote. By 1918, all males over twenty-one and women over thirty could vote. Political democracy was soon accompanied by social welfare measures for the working class.

The growth of trade unions, which advocated more radical change of the economic system, and the emergence in 1900 of the Labour Party, which dedicated itself to workers' interests, caused the Liberals, who held the government from 1906 to 1914, to realize that they would have to create a program of social welfare or lose the support of the workers. Therefore, they voted for a series of social reforms. The National Insurance Act of 1911 provided benefits for workers in case of sickness and unemployment, to be paid for by compulsory contributions from workers, employers, and the state. Additional legislation provided a small pension for Britons over age seventy and compensation for those injured in accidents while at work. While the benefits of the program and tax increases were both modest, they were the first hesitant steps toward the future British welfare state.

In France, the confusion that ensued after the collapse of the Second Empire finally ended in 1875 when an improvised constitution established a republican form of government. This constitution established a bicameral legislature, with an upper house, the Senate, elected indirectly and a lower house, the Chamber of Deputies, chosen by universal male suffrage. The powers of the president, selected by the legislature to be the executive of the government for a term of seven years, were deliberately left vague. The premier (or prime minister) led the government, and he and his ministers were responsible not to the president but to the Chamber of Deputies.

The Constitution of 1875, intended only as a stopgap measure, solidified the republic—the Third Republic—which lasted sixty-five years. France's parliamentary system was weak, however, because the existence of a dozen political parties forced the premier to depend on a coalition of parties to stay in power. The Third Republic was notorious for its changes of government. Nevertheless, by 1914, the republic commanded the loyalty of most French people.

By 1870, Italy had emerged as a geographically united state with pretensions to great power status. Its internal weaknesses, however, gave that claim a particularly hollow ring. Sectional differences—a poverty-stricken south and an industrializing north—thwarted any sense of national unity. Chronic turmoil between labor and industry undermined the social fabric. The Italian government was unable to deal effectively with these problems because of the extensive corruption among government officials and the lack of stability created by ever-changing government coalitions.

**Central and Eastern Europe: Persistence of the Old Order** The constitution of the new imperial Germany begun by Bismarck in 1871 provided for a bicameral legislature. The lower house of the German parliament, the Reichstag, was elected on the basis of universal male suffrage, but it did not have ministerial responsibility. Ministers of government, among whom the most important was the chancellor, were responsible not to the parliament but to the emperor. The emperor also commanded the armed forces and controlled foreign policy and internal administration.

During the reign of Emperor William II (1888–1918), the new imperial Germany begun by Bismarck continued as an "authoritarian, conservative, military-bureaucratic power state." By the end of William's reign, Germany had become the strongest military and industrial power on the Continent. More than 50 percent of German workers had jobs in industry, while only 30 percent of the workforce was still in agriculture. Urban centers had mushroomed in number and size. These rapid changes helped produce a society torn between modernization and traditionalism. With the expansion of industry and cities came demands for true democracy. Conservative forces, especially the landowning nobility and representatives of heavy industry, two of the powerful ruling groups in Germany, tried to block it by supporting William II's activist foreign policy of finding Germany's "place in the sun." Expansion abroad, they believed, would divert people's attention from the yearning for democracy at home.

The tensions in German society created by the conflict between modernization and traditionalism were also manifested in a new, radicalized, right-wing politics. A number of nationalist pressure groups arose to support nationalistic goals. Antisocialist and antiliberal, such groups as the Pan-German League stressed strong German nationalism and advocated imperialism as a tool to overcome social divisions and unite all classes. They also denounced the Jews as the destroyers of the German national community, fueling the flames of **anti-Semitism** (see "Anti-Semitism" later in this chapter).

After the creation of the Dual Monarchy of Austria-Hungary in 1867, the Austrian part received a constitution that theoretically established a parliamentary system. However, Emperor Francis Joseph (1848–1916) largely ignored parliament, ruling by decree when parliament was not in session.

The problem of the various nationalities remained a difficult one. The German minority that governed Austria felt increasingly threatened by the Czechs, Poles, and other Slavic groups within the empire. The granting of universal male suffrage in 1907 served only to exacerbate the problem when nationalities that had played no role in the government now agitated in the parliament for autonomy. This led prime ministers after 1900 to ignore the parliament and rely increasingly on imperial emergency decrees to govern. On the eve of World War I, the Austro-Hungarian Empire was as far away as ever from solving its minorities problem.

By 1870, Russia was witnessing an increasing number of reform movements. Intellectuals known as **Westernizers** believed that Western ways were the solutions to Russia's problems and advocated the creation of parliamentary institutions and a policy of industrialization. Westernizers, however, were opposed by **Slavophiles,** who maintained that Russia's tsarist system, peasant villages, and Orthodox religious faith were superior to any Western ideals. Other Russians rejected both the Westernizers and Slavophiles and called for a more radical approach to reform. Among these were the **anarchists,** who believed that small groups of well-trained fanatical revolutionaries could perpetrate so much violence that the state and all its institutions would disintegrate. Anarchist revolutionaries considered assassination as their primary instrument of terror, and one group was successful in killing Tsar Alexander II in 1881.

For the anarchists, this act had unexpected repercussions. Alexander III (1881–1894), the son and successor of the assassinated tsar, was now convinced that his father's attempts at reform had been a mistake, and he lost no time in persecuting both reformers and revolutionaries. When Alexander III died, his weak son and successor, Nicholas II (1894–1917), began his rule with his father's conviction that the absolute power of the tsars should be preserved: "I shall maintain the principle of autocracy just as firmly and unflinchingly as did my unforgettable father."[5] But conditions were changing, especially with the growth of industrialization.

Industrialization progressed rapidly in Russia after 1890, and with it came factories, an industrial working

## CHRONOLOGY The National State, 1870–1914

| | |
|---|---|
| **Great Britain** | |
| Formation of Labour Party | 1900 |
| National Insurance Act | 1911 |
| **France** | |
| Republican constitution (Third Republic) | 1875 |
| **Germany** | |
| Bismarck as chancellor | 1871–1890 |
| Emperor William II | 1888–1918 |
| **Austria-Hungary** | |
| Emperor Francis Joseph | 1848–1916 |
| **Russia** | |
| Tsar Alexander III | 1881–1894 |
| Tsar Nicholas II | 1894–1917 |
| First Congress of Social Democratic Party | 1898 |
| Russo-Japanese War | 1904–1905 |
| Revolution | 1905 |
| **Latin America** | |
| Rule of Porfirio Díaz in Mexico | 1876–1910 |
| Mexican Revolution begins | 1910 |
| **United States** | |
| Spanish-American War | 1898 |
| Theodore Roosevelt | 1901–1909 |
| Woodrow Wilson | 1913–1921 |
| **Canada** | |
| Transcontinental railroad | 1885 |
| Wilfred Laurier as prime minister | 1896 |

class, and the development of socialist parties, although repression in Russia soon forced them to go underground and turn revolutionary. The Marxist Social Democratic Party, for example, held its first congress in Minsk in 1898, but the arrest of its leaders caused the next one to be held in Brussels in 1903, attended by Russian émigrés. The Social Revolutionaries worked to overthrow the tsarist autocracy and establish peasant socialism. The growing opposition to the tsarist regime finally exploded into revolution in 1905.

The defeat of the Russians by the Japanese in 1904–1905 encouraged antigovernment groups to rebel against the tsarist regime. Nicholas II granted civil liberties and agreed to create a legislative assembly, the Duma, elected directly by a broad franchise. But real constitutional monarchy proved short-lived. Already by 1907, the tsar had curtailed the power of the Duma and relied again on the army and bureaucracy to rule Russia.

## International Rivalries and the Winds of War

Between 1871 and 1914, Europeans experienced a long period of peace. There were wars (including wars of conquest in the non-Western world), but none involved the great powers. However, Europe endured a series of crises that might easily have led to war. Until 1890, Bismarck, the chancellor of Germany, exercised a restraining influence on Europeans. He realized that the emergence in 1871 of a unified Germany as the most powerful state on the Continent had upset the balance of power established at Vienna in 1815 (see Map 19.2). Fearful of a possible anti-German alliance between France and Russia and

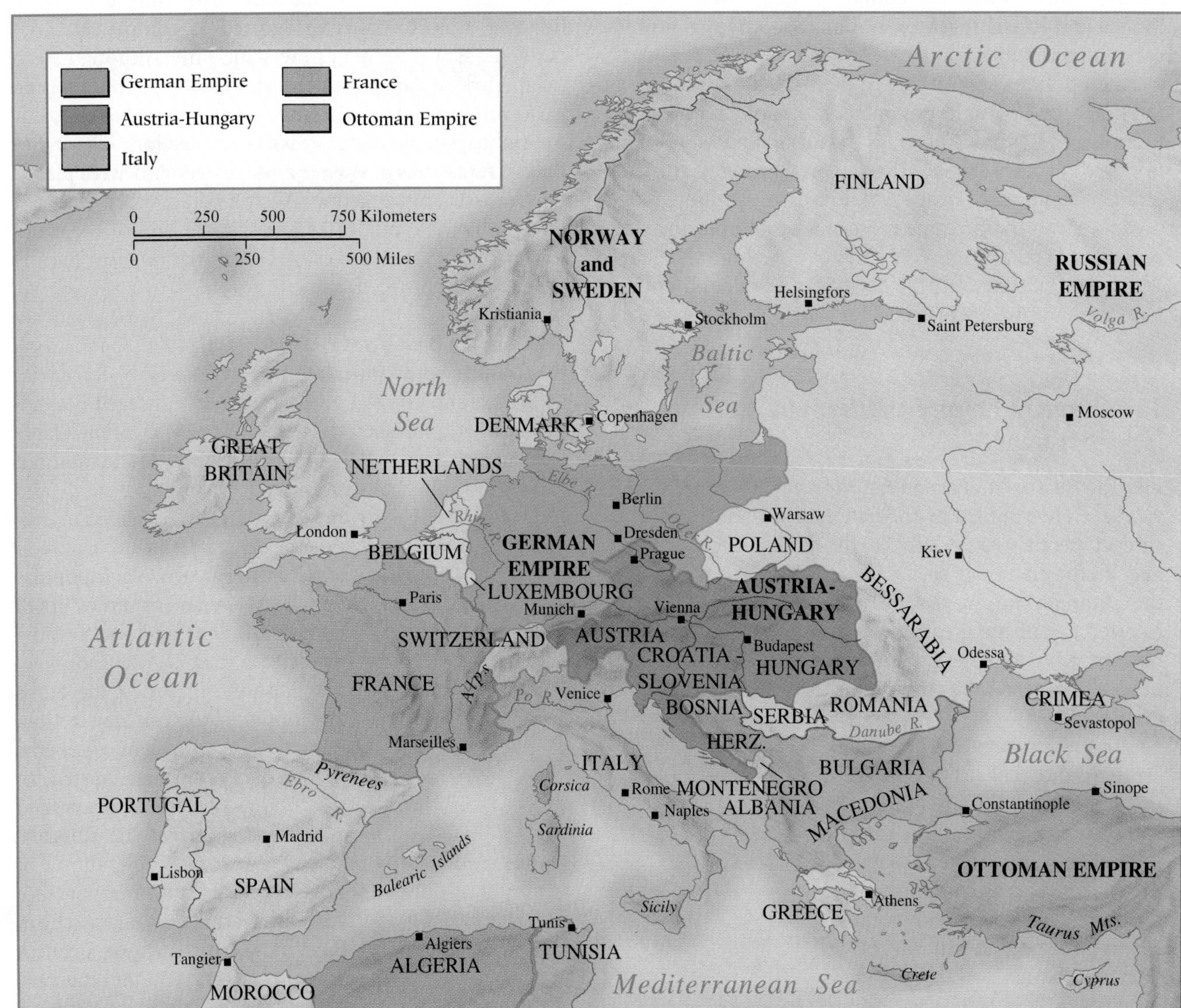


**MAP 19.2 Europe in 1871.** German unification in 1871 upset the balance of power established at Vienna in 1815 and eventually led to a realignment of European alliances. By 1907, Europe was divided into two opposing camps: the Triple Entente of Great Britain, Russia, and France and the Triple Alliance of Germany, Austria-Hungary, and Italy. ? How was Germany affected by the formation of the Triple Entente? **View an animated version of this map or related maps at** http://history.wadsworth.com/duikerspielvogel05/

possibly even Austria, Bismarck made a defensive alliance with Austria in 1879. Both powers agreed to support each other in the event of an attack by Russia. In 1882, this German-Austrian alliance was enlarged with the entrance of Italy, angry with the French over conflicting colonial ambitions in North Africa. The Triple Alliance of 1882 committed Germany, Austria-Hungary, and Italy to unite in their defense against France. Bismarck also signed a separate treaty with Russia.

When Emperor William II cashiered Bismarck in 1890 and took over direction of Germany's foreign policy, he embarked on an activist foreign policy dedicated to enhancing German power by finding, as he put it, Germany's rightful "place in the sun." One of his changes in Bismarck's foreign policy was to drop the treaty with Russia, which he viewed as being at odds with Germany's alliance with Austria. The ending of the alliance brought France and Russia together, and in 1894, the two powers concluded a military alliance. During the next ten years, German policies abroad caused the British to draw closer to France. By 1907, a loose confederation of Great Britain, France, and Russia—known as the Triple Entente—stood opposed to the Triple Alliance of Germany, Austria-Hungary, and Italy. Europe was now divided into two opposing camps that became more and more inflexible and unwilling to compromise. A series of crises in the Balkans between 1908 and 1913 over the remnants of the Ottoman Empire set the stage for World War I.

**CHRONOLOGY European Diplomacy, 1870–1914**

| | |
|---|---|
| Triple Alliance: Germany, Austria-Hungary, and Italy | 1882 |
| Military alliance: Russia and France | 1894 |
| Entente Cordiale: France and Britain | 1904 |
| Triple Entente: France, Britain, and Russia | 1907 |
| First Balkan War | 1912 |
| Second Balkan War | 1913 |

## The Ottoman Empire and Nationalism in the Balkans

Like the Austro-Hungarian Empire, the Ottoman Empire was severely troubled by the nationalist aspirations of its subject peoples, especially in the Balkans. Corruption and inefficiency had so weakened the Ottoman Empire that only the interference of the great European powers, who were fearful of each other's designs on the empire, kept it alive.

In the course of the nineteenth century, the Balkan provinces of the Ottoman Empire gradually gained their freedom, although the rivalry in the region between Austria and Russia complicated the process. Serbia had already received a large degree of autonomy in 1829, although it remained a province of the Ottoman Empire until 1878. Greece became an independent kingdom in 1830 after its successful revolt. By the Treaty of Adrianople in 1829, Russia received a protectorate over the principalities of Moldavia and Wallachia but was forced to give them up after the Crimean War. In 1861, Moldavia and Wallachia were merged into the state of Romania. Not until Russia's defeat of the Ottoman Empire in 1878, however, was Romania recognized as completely independent, as was Serbia at the same time. Although freed from Turkish rule, Montenegro was placed under an Austrian protectorate, while Bulgaria achieved autonomous status under Russian protection. The other Balkan territories of Bosnia and Herzegovina were placed under Austrian protection; Austria could occupy but not annex them. Despite these gains, at the end of the nineteenth century, the forces of Balkan nationalism had by no means been stilled.

**The Balkans in 1913**

**Crises in the Balkans, 1908–1913** In 1908, Austria took the drastic step of annexing the Slavic-speaking territories of Bosnia and Herzegovina. Serbia was outraged because the annexation dashed the Serbs' hopes of creating a large Serbian kingdom that would include most of the southern Slavs. But the Austrians had annexed Bosnia and Herzegovina explicitly to prevent that eventuality. The creation of a large Serbia would be a threat to the unity of their empire with its large Slavic population. The Russians, as protectors of their fellow Slavs and also desiring to increase their own authority in the Balkans, supported the Serbs and opposed the Austrian action. Backed by the Russians, the Serbs prepared for war against Austria. At this point, William II intervened and demanded that the Russians accept Austria's annexation of Bosnia and Herzegovina or face war with Germany. Weakened from their defeat in the Russo-Japanese War in 1904–1905, the Russians backed down but vowed revenge. Two wars between the Balkan states in 1912–1913 further embittered the inhabitants of the region and generated more tensions among the great powers.

Serbia's desire to create a large Serbian kingdom remained unfulfilled. In frustration, Serbian nationalists blamed the Austrians. Austria-Hungary was convinced that Serbia was a mortal threat to its empire and must at some point be crushed. As Serbia's chief supporters, the Russians were determined not to back down again in the event of a confrontation with Austria or Germany in the Balkans. The allies of Austria-Hungary and Russia were also determined to be more supportive of their respective allies in another crisis. By the beginning of 1914, two armed camps viewed each other with suspicion.

## Toward The Modern Consciousness: Intellectual And Cultural Developments

Before 1914, many people in the Western world continued to believe in the values and ideals that had been generated by the Scientific Revolution and the Enlightenment. The idea that human beings could improve themselves and achieve a better society seemed to be proved by a rising standard of living, urban comforts, and mass education. Such products of modern technology as electric lights and automobiles reinforced the popular prestige of science. It was easy to think that the human mind could make sense of the universe. Between 1870 and 1914, radically new ideas challenged these optimistic views and opened the way to a modern consciousness.

AP/Wide World Photos

**Marie Curie.** Marie Curie was born in Warsaw, Poland, but studied at the University of Paris, where she received degrees in both physics and mathematics. She was the first woman to win two Nobel Prizes, one in 1903 in physics and another in chemistry in 1911. She is shown here in her Paris laboratory in 1921. She died of leukemia, a result of her laboratory work with radioactivity.

### A New Physics

Science was one of the chief pillars underlying the optimistic and rationalistic view of the world that many Westerners shared in the nineteenth century. Supposedly based on hard facts and cold reason, science offered a certainty of belief in the orderliness of nature that was comforting to many people for whom traditional religious beliefs no longer had much meaning. Many naively believed that the application of already known scientific laws would give humanity a complete understanding of the physical world and an accurate picture of reality. The new physics dramatically altered that perspective.

Throughout much of the nineteenth century, Westerners adhered to the mechanical conception of the universe postulated by the classical physics of Isaac Newton. In this perspective, the universe was viewed as a giant machine in which time, space, and matter were objective realities that existed independently of the people observing them. Matter was thought to be composed of indivisible and solid material bodies called atoms.

These views were first seriously questioned at the end of the nineteenth century. The French scientist Marie Curie (1867–1934) and her husband, Pierre (1859–1906), discovered that an element called radium gave off rays of radiation that apparently came from within the atom itself. Atoms were not simply hard, material bodies but small worlds containing such subatomic particles as electrons and protons, which behaved in seemingly random and inexplicable fashion.

Building on this work, in 1900 a Berlin physicist, Max Planck (1858–1947), rejected the belief that a heated body radiates energy in a steady stream but maintained instead that it did so discontinuously, in irregular packets of energy that he called "quanta." The quantum theory raised fundamental questions about the subatomic realm of the atom. By 1900, the old view of atoms as the basic building blocks of the material world was being seriously questioned.

Albert Einstein (1879–1955), a German-born patent officer working in Switzerland, pushed these new theories into new terrain. In 1905, Einstein published a paper titled "The Electro-Dynamics of Moving Bodies" that contained his special theory of relativity. According to **relativity theory,** space and time are not absolute but relative to the observer, and both are interwoven into what Einstein called a four-dimensional space-time continuum. Neither space nor time had an existence independent of human experience. As Einstein later explained simply to a

## Freud and the Concept of Repression

Freud's psychoanalytical theories resulted from his attempt to understand the world of the unconscious. This excerpt is taken from a lecture given in 1909 in which Freud describes how he arrived at his theory of the role of repression. Although Freud valued science and reason, his theories of the unconscious produced a new image of the human being as governed less by reason than by irrational forces.

*According to Freud, how did he discover the existence of repression? What function does repression perform?*

### Sigmund Freud, *Five Lectures on Psychoanalysis*

I did not abandon [the technique of encouraging patients to reveal forgotten experiences], however, before the observations I made during my use of it afforded me decisive evidence. I found confirmation of the fact that the forgotten memories were not lost. They were in the patient's possession and were ready to emerge in association to what was still known by him; but there was some force that prevented them from becoming conscious and compelled them to remain unconscious. The existence of this force could be assumed with certainty, since one became aware of an effort corresponding to it if, in opposition to it, one tried to introduce the unconscious memories into the patient's consciousness. The force which was maintaining the pathological condition became apparent in the form of resistance on the part of the patient.

It was on this idea of resistance, then, that I based my view of the course of psychical events in hysteria. In order to effect a recovery, it had proved necessary to remove these resistances. Starting out from the mechanism of cure, it now became possible to construct quite definite ideas of the origin of the illness. The same forces which, in the form of resistance, were now offering opposition to the forgotten material's being made conscious, must formerly have brought about the forgetting and must have pushed the pathogenic experiences in question out of consciousness. I gave the name of "repression" to this hypothetical process, and I considered that it was proved by the undeniable existence of resistance.

The further question could then be raised as to what these forces were and what the determinants were of the repression in which we now recognized the pathogenic mechanism of hysteria. A comparative study of the pathogenic situations which we had come to know through the cathartic procedure made it possible to answer this question. All these experiences had involved the emergence of a wishful impulse which was in sharp contrast to the subject's other wishes and which proved incompatible with the ethical and aesthetic standards of his personality. There had been a short conflict, and the end of this internal struggle was that the idea which had appeared before consciousness as the vehicle of this irreconcilable wish fell a victim to repression, was pushed out of consciousness with all its attached memories, and was forgotten. Thus the incompatibility of the wish in question with the patient's ego was the motive for the repression; the subject's ethical and other standards were the repressing forces. An acceptance of the incompatible wishful impulse or a prolongation of the conflict would have produced a high degree of unpleasure; this unpleasure was avoided by means of repression, which was thus revealed as one of the devices serving to protect the mental personality.

**History Now™** To read excerpts from Freud's *Interpretation of Dreams,* enter the *HistoryNow* documents area using the access card that is available for *World History.*

journalist, "It was formerly believed that if all material things disappeared out of the universe, time and space would be left. According to the relativity theory, however, time and space disappear together with the things."[6] Moreover, matter and energy reflected the relativity of time and space. Einstein concluded that matter was nothing but another form of energy. His epochal formula $E = mc^2$—indicating that the energy of each particle of matter is equivalent to its mass times the square of the velocity of light—was the key theory explaining the vast energies contained within the atom. It led to the atomic age.

## Sigmund Freud and Psychoanalysis

At the turn of the twentieth century, the Viennese physician Sigmund Freud (1856–1939) advanced a series of theories that undermined optimism about the rational nature of the human mind. Freud's thought, like the new physics, added to the uncertainties of the age. His major ideas were published in 1900 in *The Interpretation of Dreams.*

According to Freud, human behavior was strongly determined by the unconscious, by past experiences and internal forces of which people were largely oblivious. For Freud, human behavior was no longer truly rational but rather instinctive or irrational. He argued that painful and unsettling experiences were blotted from conscious awareness but still continued to influence behavior since they had become part of the unconscious (see the box above). Repression began in childhood. Freud devised a method, known as **psychoanalysis,** by which a psychotherapist and patient could probe deeply into the memory in order to retrace the chain of repression all the way back to its childhood origins. By making the conscious mind aware of the unconscious and its repressed contents, the patient's psychic conflict was resolved.

## Social Darwinism and Racism

In the second half of the nineteenth century, scientific theories were sometimes wrongly applied to achieve other ends. For example, the application of Charles Darwin's principle of organic evolution to the social order came to be known as **social Darwinism,** the belief that societies were organisms that evolved through time from a struggle with their environment. Progress came from the "struggle for survival," as the "fit"—the strong—advanced while the weak declined.

Darwin's ideas were also applied to human society in an even more radical way by rabid nationalists and racists. In their pursuit of national greatness, extreme nationalists often insisted that nations, too, were engaged in a struggle for existence in which only the fittest survived. The German general Friedrich von Bernhardi argued in 1907, "War is a biological necessity of the first importance, . . . since without it an unhealthy development will follow, which excludes every advancement of the race, and therefore all real civilization. 'War is the father of all things.'"[7]

Perhaps nowhere was the combination of extreme nationalism and racism more evident or more dangerous than in Germany. One of the chief propagandists of German racism was Houston Stewart Chamberlain (1855–1927), a Briton who became a German citizen. According to Chamberlain, modern-day Germans were the only pure successors of the **Aryans,** who were portrayed as the true and original founders of Western culture. The Aryan race, under German leadership, must be prepared to fight for Western civilization and save it from the destructive assaults of such lower races as Jews, Negroes, and Orientals. Chamberlain singled out the Jews as the racial enemy who wanted to destroy the Aryan race.

**Anti-Semitism** Anti-Semitism had a long history in European civilization, but in the nineteenth century, as a result of the ideals of the Enlightenment and the French Revolution, Jews were increasingly granted legal equality in many European countries. Many Jews now left the ghetto and became assimilated into the cultures around them. Many became successful as bankers, lawyers, scientists, scholars, journalists, and stage performers.

These achievements represent only one side of the picture, however. In Germany and Austria during the 1880s and 1890s, conservatives founded right-wing anti-Jewish parties that used anti-Semitism to win the votes of traditional lower-middle-class groups who felt threatened by the new economic forces of the times. However, the worst treatment of Jews at the turn of the century occurred in eastern Europe, where 72 percent of the world's Jewish population lived. Russian Jews were forced to live in certain regions of the country, and persecutions and pogroms were widespread. Hundreds of thousands of Jews decided to emigrate to escape the persecution.

Many Jews went to the United States, although some moved to Palestine, which soon became the focus of a Jewish nationalist movement called **Zionism.** For many Jews, Palestine, the land of ancient Israel, had long been the land of their dreams. A key figure in the growth of political Zionism was Theodore Herzl (1860–1904), who predicted in his book *The Jewish State,* "The Jews who wish it will have their state" (see the box on p. 564).

Settlement in Palestine was difficult, however, because it was then part of the Ottoman Empire, which was opposed to Jewish immigration. Despite the problems, however, the first Zionist Congress, which met in Switzerland in 1897, proclaimed as its aim the creation of a "home in Palestine secured by public law" for the Jewish people. In 1900, around a thousand Jews migrated to Palestine, and the trickle rose to about three thousand a year between 1904 and 1914, keeping the Zionist dream alive.

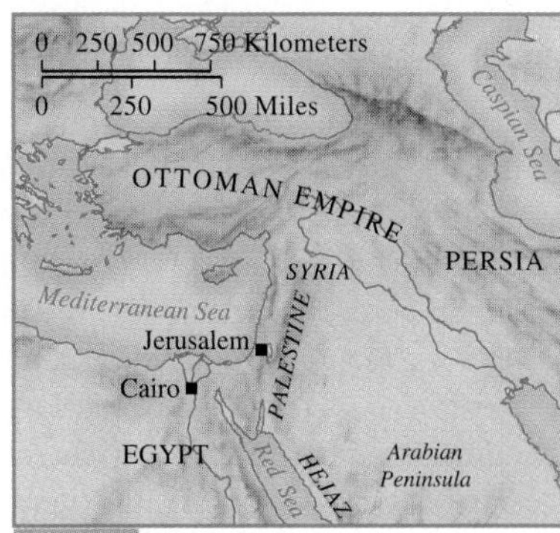

**Palestine**

## The Culture of Modernity

The revolution in physics and psychology was paralleled by a revolution in literature and the arts. Before 1914, writers and artists were rebelling against the traditional literary and artistic styles that had dominated European cultural life since the Renaissance. The changes that they produced have since been called **Modernism.**

At the beginning of the twentieth century, a group of writers known as the Symbolists caused a literary revolution. Primarily interested in writing poetry and strongly influenced by the ideas of Freud, the Symbolists believed that an objective knowledge of the world was impossible (see the box on p. 565). The external world was not real but only a collection of symbols that reflected the true reality of the individual human mind. Art, they believed, should function for its own sake instead of serving, criticizing, or seeking to understand society.

The period from 1870 to 1914 was one of the most fertile in the history of art. Since the Renaissance, the task of artists had been to represent reality as accurately as possible. By the late nineteenth century, artists were seeking new forms of expression. The preamble to modern painting can be found in **Impressionism,** a movement that originated in France in the 1870s when a group of artists rejected the studios and museums and went out into the countryside to

## THE VOICE OF ZIONISM: THEODOR HERZL AND THE JEWISH STATE

The Austrian Jewish journalist Theodor Herzl wrote *The Jewish State* in the summer of 1895 in Paris while he was covering the Dreyfus case for his Vienna newspaper. (Alfred Dreyfus, a French army officer who was also Jewish, was wrongly convicted of selling military secrets. Although he was later exonerated, the case revealed the depth of anti-Semitism in France.) In several weeks, during a period of feverish composition, he set about to analyze the fundamental causes of anti-Semitism and devise a solution to the "Jewish problem." In this selection, he discusses two of his major conclusions.

*Why did Herzl believe that Palestine was necessary for Jews? How does he seek to gain the acceptance of the Turkish sultan and the Christian nations of Europe?*

### Theodor Herzl, *The Jewish State*

I do not intend to arouse sympathetic emotions on our behalf. That would be a foolish, futile, and undignified proceeding. I shall content myself with putting the following questions to the Jews: Is it true that, in countries where we live in perceptible numbers, the position of Jewish lawyers, doctors, technicians, teachers, and employees of all descriptions becomes daily more intolerable? True, that the Jewish middle classes are seriously threatened? True, that the passions of the mob are incited against our wealthy people? True, that our poor endure greater sufferings than any other proletariat?

I think that this external pressure makes itself felt everywhere. In our economically upper classes it causes discomfort, in our middle classes continual and grave anxieties, in our lower classes absolute despair.

Everything tends, in fact, to one and the same conclusion, which is clearly enunciated in that classic Berlin phrase: "Juden 'raus!" (Out with the Jews!)

I shall now put the Jewish Question in the curtest possible form: Are we to "get out" now? And if so, to what place? Or, may we yet remain? And if so, how long?

Let us first settle the point of staying where we are. Can we hope for better days, can we possess our souls in patience, can we wait in pious resignation till the princes and peoples of this earth are more mercifully disposed toward us? I say that we cannot hope for a change in the current of feeling. And why not? . . . The nations in whose midst Jews live are all, either covertly or openly, Anti-Semitic. . . .

The whole plan is in its essence perfectly simple, as it must necessarily be if it is to come within the comprehension of all.

Let the sovereignty be granted us over a portion of the globe large enough to satisfy the rightful requirements of a nation; the rest we shall manage for ourselves.

The creation of a new State is neither ridiculous nor impossible. We have in our day witnessed the process in connection with nations which were not in the bulk of the middle class, but poorer, less educated, and consequently weaker than ourselves. The Governments of all countries scourged by Anti-Semitism will be keenly interested in assisting us to obtain the sovereignty we want. . . .

Palestine is our ever memorable historic home. The very name of Palestine would attract our people with a force of marvelous potency. Supposing his Majesty the Sultan were to give us Palestine, we could in return undertake to regulate the whole finances of Turkey. We should there form a portion of the rampart of Europe against Asia, an outpost of civilization as opposed to barbarism. We should as a neutral State remain in contact with all Europe, which would have to guarantee our existence. The sanctuaries of Christendom would be safeguarded by assigning to them an extraterritorial status such as is well known to the law of nations. We should form a guard of honor about these sanctuaries, answering for the fulfillment of this duty with our existence. This guard of honor would be the great symbol of the solution of the Jewish Question after eighteen centuries of Jewish suffering.

paint nature directly. Camille Pissarro (1830–1903), one of Impressionism's founders, expressed what they sought:

> Precise drawing is dry and hampers the impression of the whole, it destroys all sensations. Do not define too closely the outlines of things; it is the brush stroke of the right value and color which should produce the drawing. . . . Work at the same time upon sky, water, branches, ground, keeping everything going on an equal basis and unceasingly rework until you have got it. . . . Don't proceed according to rules and principles, but paint what you observe and feel. Paint generously and unhesitatingly, for it is best not to lose the first impression.[8]

An important Impressionist painter was Berthe Morisot (1841–1895), who believed that women had a special vision, which was, as she said, "more delicate than that of men." She made use of lighter colors and flowing brush strokes (see the comparative illustration on p. 566). Near the end of her life, she lamented the refusal of men to take her work seriously: "I don't think there has ever been a man who treated a woman as an equal, and that's all I would have asked, for I know I'm worth as much as they."[9]

In the 1880s, a new movement known as **Post-Impressionism** arose in France and soon spread to other European countries. A famous Post-Impressionist was the tortured and tragic figure Vincent van Gogh (1853–1890). For van Gogh, art was a spiritual experi-

## Symbolist Poetry: Art for Art's Sake

The Symbolist movement was an important foundation for Modernism. The Symbolists believed that the working of the mind was the proper study of literature. Arthur Rimbaud was one of Symbolism's leading practitioners in France. Although his verses seem to have little real meaning, they were not meant to describe the external world precisely but rather to enchant the mind. Art was not meant for the masses but only for "art's sake." Rimbaud wrote, "By the alchemy of the words, I noted the inexpressible. I fixed giddiness."

*How does the poem by Rimbaud reflect the Symbolist movement? What parallels do you perceive between Symbolist poetry and Impressionist painting?*

### Arthur Rimbaud, *The Drunken Boat*

*As I floated down impassable rivers,*
*I felt the boatmen no longer guiding me:*
*After them came redskins who with war cries*
*Nailed them naked to the painted poles.*

*I was oblivious to the crew,*
*I who bore Flemish wheat and English cotton.*
*When the racket was finished with my boatmen,*
*The waters let me drift my own free way.*

*In the tide's furious pounding,*
*I, the other winter, emptier than children's minds,*
*I sailed! And the unmoored peninsulas*
*Have not suffered more triumphant turmoils.*

*The tempest blessed my maritime watches.*
*Lighter than a cork I danced on the waves,*
*Those eternal rollers of victims,*
*Ten nights, without regretting the lantern-foolish eye!*

*Sweeter than the bite of sour apples to a child,*
*The green water seeped through my wooden hull,*
*Rinsed me of blue wine stains and vomit,*
*Broke apart grappling iron and rudder.*

*And then I bathed myself in the poetry*
*Of the star-sprayed milk-white sea,*
*Devouring the azure greens; where, pale*
*And ravished, a pensive drowned one sometimes floats;*

*Where, suddenly staining the blueness, frenzies*
*And slows rhythms in the blazing of day,*
*Stronger than alcohol, vaster than our lyres,*
*The russet bitterness of love ferments. . . .*

*I have dreamed of the green night bedazzled with*
*snow,*
*A kiss climbing slowly to the eyes of the sea,*
*The flow of unforgettable sap,*
*And the yellow-blue waking of singing phosphorous!*

*Long months I have followed, like maddened cattle,*
*The surge assaulting the rocks*
*Without dreaming that the Virgin's luminous feet*
*Could force a muzzle on the panting ocean!*

*I have struck against the shores of incredible*
*Floridas*
*Mixing panther-eyed flowers like human skins!*
*Rainbows stretched like bridle reins*
*Under the ocean's horizon, toward sea-green troops! . . .*

ence. He was especially interested in color and believed that it could act as its own form of language. Van Gogh maintained that artists should paint what they feel.

By the beginning of the twentieth century, the belief that the task of art was to represent "reality" had lost much of its meaning. By that time, the new psychology and the new physics had made it evident that many people were not sure what constituted reality anyway. Then, too, the growth of photography gave artists another reason to reject Realism. Invented in the 1830s, photography became popular and widespread after George Eastman created the first Kodak camera in 1888 for the mass market. What was the point of an artist's doing what the camera did better? Unlike the camera, which could only mirror reality, artists could create reality. Like the Symbolist writers of the time, artists sought meaning in individual consciousness.

By 1905, one of the most important figures in modern art was just beginning his career. Pablo Picasso (1881–1973) was from Spain but settled in Paris in 1904. Picasso was extremely flexible and painted in a remarkable variety of styles. He was instrumental in the development of a new style called **Cubism** that used geometrical designs as visual stimuli to re-create reality in the viewer's mind.

The modern artist's flight from "visual reality" reached a high point in 1910 with the beginning of **abstract painting.** A Russian who worked in Germany, Wassily Kandinsky (1866–1944) was one of the founders of abstract painting. As is evident in his *Painting with White Border*, Kandinsky sought to avoid representation altogether. He believed that art should speak directly to the soul. To do so, it must avoid any

ARTS & IDEAS

COMPARATIVE ILLUSTRATION

**Painting—West and East.** Berthe Morisot, the first female painter to join the Impressionists, developed her own unique style. Her gentle colors and strong use of pastels are especially evident in *Young Girl by the Window,* seen at the left. The French Impressionist style also spread abroad. One of the most outstanding Japanese artists of the time was Kuroda Seiki (1866–1924), who returned from nine years in Paris to open a Western-style school of painting in Tokyo. Shown at the right is his *By the Lake,* painted in 1897, an excellent example of the fusion of contemporary French Impressionist painting with the Japanese tradition of courtesan prints.

reference to visual reality and concentrate on line and color.

Modernism in the arts revolutionized architecture and architectural practices. A new principle known as **functionalism** motivated this revolution. Functionalism meant that buildings, like the products of machines, should be "functional" or useful, fulfilling the purpose for which they were constructed. Art and engineering were to be unified, and all unnecessary ornamentation was to be stripped away.

**Vincent van Gogh, *The Starry Night.*** The Dutch painter Vincent van Gogh was a major figure among the Post-Impressionists. His originality and power of expression made a strong impact on his artistic successors. In *The Starry Night,* van Gogh's subjective vision was given full play as the dynamic swirling forms of the heavens above overwhelmed the village below. The heavens seem alive with a mysterious spiritual force.

**Pablo Picasso, *Les Demoiselles d'Avignon*.** Pablo Picasso, a major pioneer and activist of modern art, experimented with a remarkable variety of modern styles. *Les Demoiselles d'Avignon* was the first great example of Cubism, which one art historian called "the first style of this [twentieth] century to break radically with the past." Geometrical shapes replace traditional forms, forcing the viewer to re-create reality in his or her own mind. The head at the upper right of the painting reflects Picasso's attraction to aspects of African art, as is evident from the Congo mask included at the right.

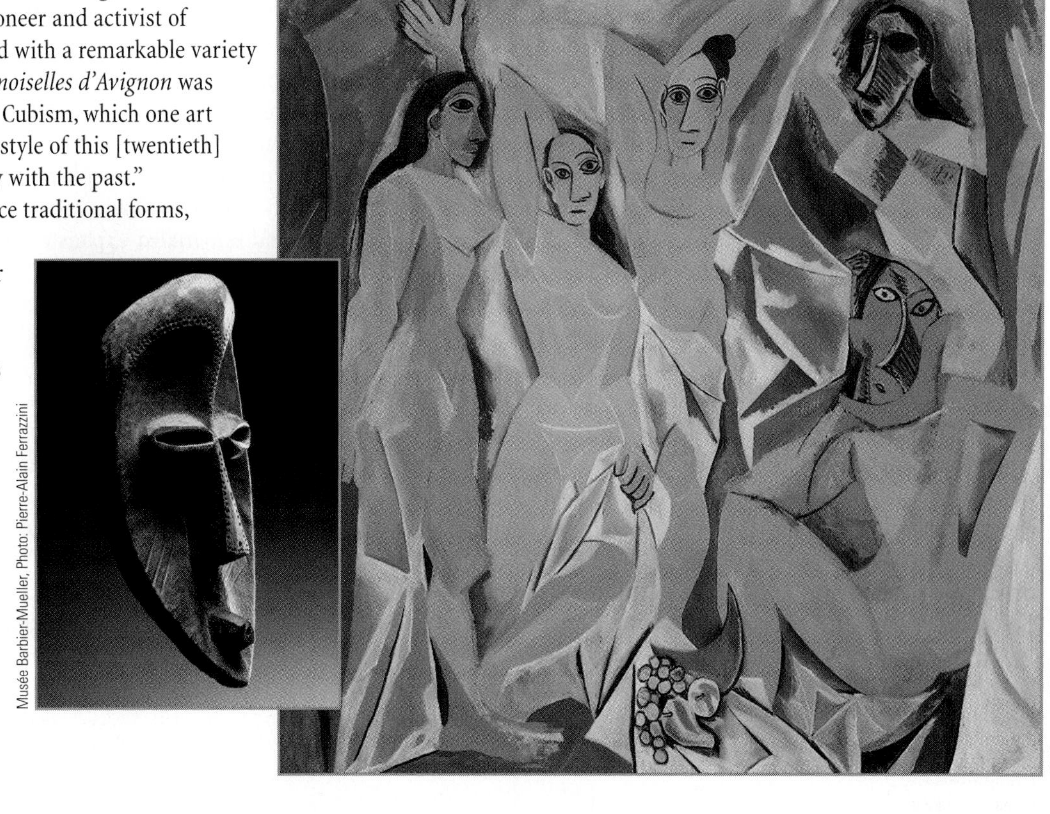





The United States was a leader in these pioneering architectural designs. Unprecedented urban growth and the absence of restrictive architectural traditions allowed for new building methods, especially in the relatively new city of Chicago. The Chicago School of the 1890s, led by Louis H. Sullivan (1856–1924), used reinforced concrete, steel frames, and electric elevators to build skyscrapers virtually free of external ornamentation. One of Sullivan's most successful pupils was Frank Lloyd Wright (1869–1959), who became known for innovative designs in domestic architecture. Wright's private houses, built chiefly for wealthy patrons, featured geometrical structures with long lines, overhanging roofs, and severe planes of brick and stone. The interiors were open spaces and included cathedral ceilings and built-in furniture and lighting. Wright pioneered the modern American house.



**Wassily Kandinsky, Composition VIII, No. 2 (Painting with White Border).** One of the founders of abstract painting was the Russian Wassily Kandinsky, who sought to eliminate representation altogether by focusing on color and avoiding any resemblance to visual reality. In *Painting with White Border,* Kandinsky used color "to send light into the darkness of men's hearts." He believed that color, like music, could fulfill a spiritual goal of appealing directly to the human being.

## CONCLUSION

**Between 1870 and 1914,** the national state began to expand its functions beyond all previous limits. Fearful of the growth of socialism and trade unions, governments attempted to appease the working masses by adopting such **social insurance** measures as protection against accidents, illness, and old age. These social welfare measures were narrow in scope and limited in benefits before 1914. Moreover, they failed to halt the growth of socialism. Nevertheless, they signaled a new direction for state action to benefit the mass of its citizens.

This extension of state functions took place in an atmosphere of increased national loyalty. After 1870, nation-states increasingly sought to solidify the social order and win the active loyalty and support of their citizens by deliberately cultivating national feelings. Yet this policy contained potentially great dangers. Nations had discovered once again that imperialistic adventures and military successes could arouse nationalistic passions and smother domestic political unrest. But they also found—belatedly in 1914—that nationalistic feelings could also lead to intense international rivalries that made war almost inevitable.

What many Europeans liked to call their "age of progress" between 1870 and 1914 was also an era of anxiety. Frenzied imperialist expansion had created vast European empires and **spheres of influence** around the globe. This feverish competition for colonies, however, had markedly increased the antagonisms among the European states. At the same time, the Western treatment of native peoples as racial inferiors caused educated, non-Western elites in these colonies to initiate movements for national independence. Before these movements could be successful, however, the power that Europeans had achieved through their mass armies and technological superiority had to be weakened. The Europeans inadvertently accomplished this task for their colonial subjects by demolishing their own civilization on the battlegrounds of Europe in World War I and World War II.

## TIMELINE

1870 | 1880 | 1890 | 1900 | 1910 | 1920

Beginning of Third Republic in France

Triple Alliance

Mexican Revolution begins

Triple Entente

Beginning of German Social Democratic Party

Women's Social and Political Union founded in Britain

Bell invents the telephone

Emergence of mass newspapers

Marie Curie wins first Nobel Prize

Mass production of Ford's Model T

Impressionism

Freud, *The Interpretation of Dreams*

Beginning of abstract painting

Einstein's special theory of relativity

## CHAPTER NOTES

1. K. Marx and F. Engels, *The Communist Manifesto* (Harmondsworth, England, 1967), p. 80. Originally published in 1848.
2. Ibid., pp. 91, 94.
3. Quoted in N. Bullock and J. Read, *The Movement for Housing Reform in Germany and France, 1840–1914* (Cambridge, 1985), p. 42.
4. Quoted in C. M. Prelinger, "Prelude to Consciousness: Amalie Sieveking and the Female Association for the Care of the Poor and the Sick," in J. C. Fout, ed., *German Women in the Nineteenth Century: A Social History* (New York, 1984), p. 119.
5. Quoted in S. Galai, *The Liberation Movement in Russia, 1900–1905* (Cambridge, 1973), p. 26.
6. Quoted in A. E. E. McKenzie, *The Major Achievements of Science* (New York, 1960), vol. 1, p. 310.
7. F. von Bernhardi, *Germany and the Next War,* trans. A. H. Powles (New York, 1914), pp. 18–19.
8. Quoted in J. Rewald, *History of Impressionism* (New York, 1961), pp. 456–458.
9. Quoted in A. Higonnet, *Berthe Morisot's Images of Women* (Cambridge, Mass., 1992), p. 19.

## SUGGESTED READING

The subject of the Second Industrial Revolution is well covered in **D. Landes, *The Unbound Prometheus,*** cited in Chapter 18. For a fundamental survey of European industrialization, see **A. S. Milward** and **S. B. Saul, *The Development of the Economies of Continental Europe, 1850–1914*** (Cambridge, Mass., 1977). The impact of the new technology on European thought is imaginatively discussed in **S. Kern, *The Culture of Time and Space, 1880–1918*** (Cambridge, Mass., 1983).

On Marx, there is the standard work by **D. McLellan, *Karl Marx: His Life and Thought*** (New York, 1974). For an introduction to international socialism, see **A. Lindemann, *A History of European Socialism*** (New Haven, Conn., 1983).

For a good introduction to housing reform on the Continent, see **N. Bullock** and **J. Read, *The Movement for Housing Reform in Germany and France, 1840–1914*** (Cambridge, 1985). An interesting work on aristocratic life is **D. Cannadine, *The Decline and Fall of the British Aristocracy*** (New Haven, Conn., 1990). On the middle classes, see **P. Pilbeam, *The Middle Classes in Europe, 1789–1914*** (Basingstoke, England, 1990), and **R. Magraw, *A History of the French Working Class*** (Cambridge, Mass., 1992). On the working classes, see **L. Berlanstein, *The Working People of Paris, 1871–1914*** (Baltimore, 1984). There are good overviews of women's experiences in the nineteenth century in **B. Smith, *Changing Lives: Women in European History Since 1700*** (Lexington, Mass., 1989), and **M. J. Boxer** and **J. H. Quataert,** eds., ***Connecting Spheres: Women in the Western World, 1500 to the Present*** (Oxford, 1987). The world of women's work is examined in **L. A. Tilly** and **J. W. Scott, *Women, Work, and Family*** (New York, 1978). The rise of feminism is examined in **J. Rendall, *The Origins of Modern Feminism: Women in Britain, France and the United States*** (London, 1985). For a new perspective on domestic life, see **J. Flanders, *Inside the Victorian Home: A Portrait of Domestic Life in Victorian England*** (New York, 2004). On various aspects of education, see **M. J. Maynes, *Schooling in Western Europe: A Social History*** (Albany, N.Y., 1985), and **J. S. Hurt, *Elementary Schooling and the Working Classes, 1860–1918*** (London, 1979). A concise and well-presented survey of leisure patterns is **G. Cross, *A Social History of Leisure Since 1600*** (State College, Pa., 1989).

The domestic politics of the period can be examined in the general works listed in the bibliography for Chapter 18. There are also specialized works on aspects of each country's history. On Britain, see **D. Read, *The Age of Urban Democracy: England, 1868–1914*** (New York, 1994). For a detailed examination of French history from 1871 to 1914, see **J.-M. Mayeur** and **M. Reberioux, *The Third Republic from Its Origins to the Great War, 1871–1914*** (Cambridge, 1984). On Germany, see **W. J. Mommsen, *Imperial Germany, 1867–1918*** (New York, 1995), and **V. R. Berghahn, *Imperial Germany, 1871–1914*** (Providence, R.I., 1995). On the nationalities problem in the Austro-Hungarian Empire, see **R. Kann, *The Multinational Empire: Nationalism and National Reform in the Habsburg Monarchy, 1848–1918,*** 2 vols. (New York, 1950). On aspects of Russian history, see **H. Rogger, *Russia in the Age of Modernization and Revolution, 1881–1917*** (London, 1983), and **A. Ascher, *The Revolution of 1905: Russia in Disarray*** (New York, 1988). On the United States, see **D. Cashman, *America in the Gilded Age: From the Death of Lincoln to the Rise of Theodore Roosevelt*** (New York, 1984), and **J. W. Chambers, *The Tyranny of Change: America in the Progressive Era, 1900–1917*** (New York, 1980). On Latin American economic developments, see **B. Albert, *South America and the World Economy from Independence to 1930*** (London, 1983). For a comprehensive examination of the Mexican Revolution, see **A. Knight, *The Mexican Revolution,*** 2 vols. (Cambridge, 1986). Two fundamental works on the diplomatic history of the period are by **W. L. Langer, *European Alliances and Alignments,*** 2d ed. (New York, 1966), and ***The Diplomacy of Imperialism,*** 2d ed. (New York, 1965).

A well-regarded study of Freud is **P. Gay, *Freud: A Life for Our Time*** (New York, 1988). Modern anti-Semitism is covered in **A. S. Lindemann, *Esau's Tears: Modern Anti-Semitism and the Rise of the Jews*** (New York, 1997). European racism is analyzed in **G. L. Mosse, *Toward the Final Solution*** (New York, 1980). For a recent biography of Theodor Herzl, see **J. Kornberg, *Theodor Herzl: From Assimilation to Zionism*** (London, 1993). Very valuable on modern art are **M. Powell-Jones, *Impressionism*** (London, 1994); **G. Crepaldi, *The Impressionists*** (New York, 2002); **B. Denvir, *Post-Impressionism*** (New York, 1992); and **T. Parsons, *Post-Impressionism: The Rise of Modern Art*** (London, 1992).

**History Now™**

Enter *HistoryNow* using the access card that is available with this text. *HistoryNow* will assist you in understanding the content in this chapter with lesson plans generated for your needs, as well as provide you with a connection to the *Wadsworth World History Resource Center* (see description at right for details).

**WORLD HISTORY RESOURCE CENTER**

Enter the Resource Center using either your *HistoryNow* access card or your standalone access card for the *Wadsworth World History Resource Center.* Organized by topic, this website includes quizzes; images; over 350 primary source documents; interactive simulations; maps and timelines; movie explorations; and a wealth of other resources. You can read the following documents, and many more, at http://history.wadsworth.com/rc/world

Karl Marx and Friedrich Engels, *The Communist Manifesto*

Visit the *World History* Companion Website for chapter quizzes and more.

http://history.wadsworth.com/duikerspielvogel05/

CHAPTER

# 20

# THE HIGH TIDE OF IMPERIALISM

*Establishing British rule in Africa*



## CHAPTER OUTLINE AND FOCUS QUESTIONS

### The Spread of Colonial Rule

- What were the causes of the new imperialism of the nineteenth century, and how did it differ from European expansion in earlier periods?

### The Colonial System

- What types of administrative systems did the various colonial powers establish in their colonies, and how did these systems reflect the general philosophy of colonialism?

### The Emergence of Anticolonialism

- How did the subject peoples respond to colonialism, and what role did nationalism play in their response?

### CRITICAL THINKING

- What were the consequences of the new imperialism of the nineteenth century for the colonies and the colonial powers? How do you feel the imperialist countries should be evaluated in terms of their motives and stated objectives?

IN 1877, THE YOUNG British empire builder Cecil Rhodes drew up his last will and testament. He bequeathed his fortune, achieved as a diamond magnate in South Africa, to two of his close friends and acquaintances. He also instructed them to use the inheritance to form a secret society with the aim of bringing about "the extension of British rule throughout the world, the perfecting of a system of emigration from the United Kingdom . . . especially the occupation by British settlers of the entire continent of Africa, the Holy Land, the valley of the Euphrates, the Islands of Cyprus and Candia [Crete], the whole of South America. . . . The ultimate recovery of the United States of America as an integral part of the British Empire . . . then finally the foundation of so great a power as to hereafter render wars impossible and promote the best interests of humanity."[1]

Preposterous as such ideas sound today, they serve as a graphic reminder of the hubris that characterized the worldview of Rhodes and many of his contemporaries during the age of imperialism, as well as the complex union of moral concern and vaulting ambition that motivated their actions on the world stage.

Through their efforts, Western colonialism spread throughout much of the non-Western world during the nineteenth and early twentieth centuries. Spurred by the demands of the Industrial Revolution, a few powerful Western states–notably, Great Britain, France, Germany, Russia, and the United States–competed avariciously for consumer markets and raw materials for their expanding economies. By the end of the nineteenth century, virtually all of the traditional societies in Asia and Africa were under direct or indirect colonial rule. As the new century began, the Western imprint on Asian and African societies, for better or for worse, appeared to be a permanent feature of the political and cultural landscape. ◇

## The Spread of Colonial Rule

In the nineteenth century, a new phase of Western expansion into Asia and Africa began. Whereas European aims in the East before 1800 could be summed up in Vasco da Gama's famous phrase "Christians and spices," now a new relationship took shape as European nations began to view Asian and African societies as sources of industrial raw materials and as markets for Western manufactured goods. No longer were Western gold and silver exchanged for cloves, pepper, tea, silk, and porcelain. Now the prodigious output of European factories was sent to Africa and Asia in return for oil, tin, rubber, and the other resources needed to fuel the Western industrial machine.

### The Motives

The reason for this change, of course, was the Industrial Revolution, which began in England in the late eighteenth century and spread to the Continent a few decades later. Now industrializing countries in the West needed vital raw materials that were not available at home, as well as a reliable market for the goods produced in their factories. The latter factor became increasingly crucial as producers began to discover that their home markets could not always absorb domestic output, and thus they had to export their manufactures to make a profit. When consumer demand lagged, economic depression threatened.

As Western economic expansion into Asia and Africa gathered strength during the nineteenth century, it became fashionable to call the process **imperialism.** Although the term *imperialism* has other meanings, in this instance it referred to the efforts of capitalist states in the West to seize markets, cheap raw materials, and lucrative avenues for investment in the countries beyond Western civilization. In this interpretation, the primary motives behind the Western expansion were economic. The best-known promoter of this view was the British political economist John A. Hobson, who published a major analysis titled *Imperialism: A Study* in 1902. In this influential book, Hobson maintained that modern imperialism was a direct consequence of the modern industrial economy.

As in the earlier phase of Western expansion, however, the issue was not simply an economic one. As Hobson himself conceded, economic concerns were inevitably tinged with political overtones and with questions of national grandeur and moral purpose as well. In the minds of nineteenth-century Europeans, economic wealth, national status, and political power went hand in hand with the possession of a colonial empire. To global strategists, colonies brought tangible benefits in the world of balance-of-power politics as well as economic profits, and many nations became involved in the pursuit of colonies as much to gain advantage over their rivals as to acquire territory for its own sake.

The relationship between colonialism and national survival was expressed directly in a speech by the French politician Jules Ferry in 1885. A policy of "containment or abstinence," he warned, would set France on "the broad road to decadence" and initiate its decline into a "third- or fourth-rate power." British imperialists, convinced by the theory of social Darwinism that in the struggle between nations, only the fit are victorious and survive, agreed. As the British professor of mathematics Karl Pearson argued in 1900, "The path of progress is strewn with the wrecks of nations; traces are everywhere to be seen of the [slaughtered remains] of inferior races. . . . Yet these dead people are, in very truth, the stepping stones on which mankind has arisen to the higher intellectual and deeper emotional life of today."[2]

For some, colonialism had a moral purpose, whether to promote Christianity or to build a better world. The British colonial official Henry Curzon declared that the British empire "was under Providence, the greatest instrument for good that the world has seen." To Cecil Rhodes, the most famous empire builder of his day, the extraction of material wealth from the colonies was only a secondary matter. "My ruling purpose," he remarked, "is the extension of the British Empire."[3] That British Empire, on which, as the saying went, "the sun never set," was the envy of its rivals and was viewed as the primary source of British global dominance during the second half of the nineteenth century.

### The Tactics

With the change in European motives for colonization came a corresponding shift in tactics. Earlier, when their economic interests were more limited, European states had generally been satisfied to deal with existing independent states rather than attempting to establish direct control over vast territories. There had been exceptions where state power at the local level was at the point of collapse (as in India), where European economic interests were especially intense (as in Latin America and the East Indies), or where there was no centralized authority (as in North

Africa had been limited to controlling the regional trade network and establishing a few footholds where the foreigners could carry on trade and missionary activity.

After 1800, the demands of industrialization in Europe created a new set of dynamics. Maintaining access to industrial raw materials such as oil and rubber and setting up reliable markets for European manufactured products required more extensive control over colonial territories. As competition for colonies increased, the colonial powers sought to solidify their hold over their territories to protect them from attack by their rivals. During the last two decades of the nineteenth century, the quest for colonies became a scramble as all the major European states, now joined by the United States and Japan, engaged in a global land grab. In many cases, economic interests were secondary to security concerns or the requirements of national prestige. In Africa, for example, the British engaged in a struggle with their rivals to protect their interests in the Suez Canal and the Red Sea. In Southeast Asia, the United States seized the Philippines from Spain at least partly to keep them out of the hands of the Japanese, and the French took over Indochina for fear that it would otherwise be occupied by Germany, Japan, or the United States.

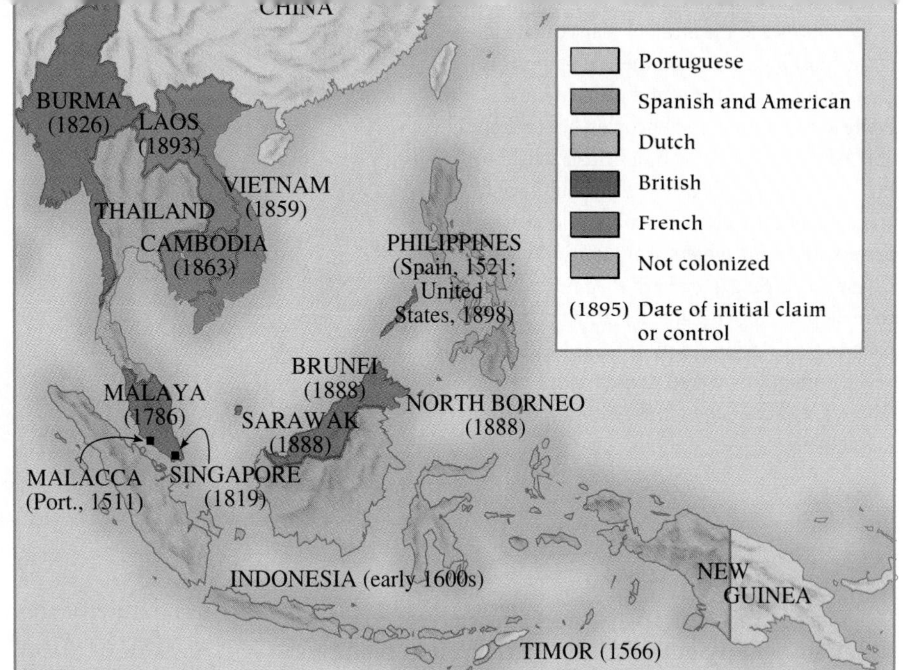


**MAP 20.1 Colonial Southeast Asia.** This map shows the spread of European colonial rule into Southeast Asia from the sixteenth century to the end of the nineteenth. Malacca, initially seized by the Portuguese in 1511, was taken by the Dutch in the seventeenth century and then by the British one hundred years later. ? What was the importance of Malacca? **View an animated version of this map or related maps at** http://history.wadsworth.com/duikerspielvogel05/

By 1900, almost all the societies of Africa and Asia were either under full colonial rule or, as in the case of China and the Ottoman Empire, at a point of virtual collapse. Only a handful of states, such as Japan in East Asia, Thailand in Southeast Asia, Afghanistan and Persia in the Middle East, and mountainous Ethiopia in East Africa, managed to escape internal disintegration or subjection to colonial rule. For the most part, the exceptions were the result of good fortune rather than design. Thailand escaped subjugation primarily because officials in London and Paris found it more convenient to transform the country into a buffer state than to fight over it. Ethiopia and Afghanistan survived due to their remote location and mountainous terrain. Only Japan managed to avoid the common fate through a concerted strategy of political and economic reform.

## "Opportunity in the Orient": The Colonial Takeover in Southeast Asia

In 1800, only two societies in Southeast Asia were under effective colonial rule: the Spanish Philippines and the Dutch East Indies. During the nineteenth century, however, European interest in Southeast Asia increased rapidly, and by 1900, virtually the entire area was under colonial rule (see Map 20.1). The process began after the Napoleonic Wars, when the British, by agreement with the Dutch, abandoned their claims to territorial possessions in the East Indies in return for a free hand in the Malay peninsula. In 1819, the colonial administrator Stamford Raffles founded a new British colony on the island of Singapore at the tip of the peninsula. When the invention of steam power enabled merchant ships to save time and distance by passing through the Strait of Malacca rather than sailing with the westerlies across the southern Indian Ocean, Singapore became a major stopping point for traffic en route to and from China and other commercial centers in the region.

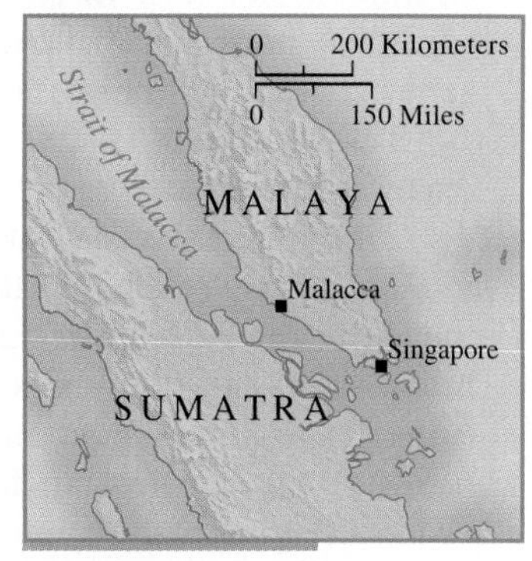


**The Malay Peninsula**

British turned what was once a pirate lair located at the entrance to the Strait of Malacca into one of the most important commercial seaports in Asia. By the end of the century, Singapore was home to a rich mixture of peoples, both European and Asian. This painting by a British artist in the 1890s graphically displays the multiracial character of the colony as strollers, rickshaw drivers, and lamplighters share space along the Esplanade, in Singapore harbor. Almost all colonial port cities became a melting pot of peoples from various parts of the world. Many of the immigrants served as merchants, urban laborers, and craftsmen in the new imperial marketplace.

During the next few decades, the pace of European penetration into Southeast Asia accelerated as the British established control over Burma, arousing fears in France that its British rival might soon establish a monopoly of trade in South China. The French still maintained a clandestine missionary organization in Vietnam despite harsh persecution by the local authorities, who viewed Christianity as a threat to Confucian doctrine. In 1857, the French government decided to force the Vietnamese to accept French protection. A naval attack launched a year later was not a total success, but the French eventually forced the Nguyen dynasty in Vietnam to cede territories in the Mekong River delta. A generation later, French rule was extended over the remainder of the country. By 1900 French seizure of neighboring Cambodia and Laos had led to the creation of the French-ruled Indochinese Union.

After the French conquest of Indochina, Thailand was the only remaining independent state on the Southeast Asian mainland. Under the astute leadership of two remarkable rulers, King Mongkut and his son, King Chulalongkorn, the Thai attempted to introduce Western learning and maintain relations with the major European powers without undermining internal stability or inviting an imperialist attack. In 1896, the British and the French agreed to preserve Thailand as an independent buffer zone between their possessions in Southeast Asia.

The final piece in the colonial edifice in Southeast Asia was put in place in 1898, when U.S. naval forces under Commodore George Dewey defeated the Spanish fleet in Manila Bay. President William McKinley agonized over the fate of the Philippines but ultimately decided that the moral thing to do was to turn the islands into an American colony to prevent them from falling into the hands of the Japanese. In fact, the Americans (like the Spanish before them) found the islands convenient as a jumping-off point for the China trade (see Chapter 21). The mixture of moral idealism and the desire for profit was reflected in a speech given in the Senate in January 1900 by Senator Albert Beveridge of Indiana:

> Mr. President, the times call for candor. The Philippines are ours forever, "territory belonging to the United States," as the Constitution calls them. And just beyond the Philippines are China's illimitable markets. We will not retreat from either. . . . We will not renounce our part in the mission of our race, trustee, under God, of the civilization of the world. And we will move forward to our work, not howling out regrets like slaves whipped to their burdens, but with gratitude for a task worthy of our strength, and thanksgiving to Almighty God that He has marked us as His chosen people, henceforth to lead in the regeneration of the world.[4]

Not all Filipinos agreed with Senator Beveridge's portrayal of the situation. Under the leadership of Emilio Aguinaldo, guerrilla forces fought bitterly against U.S. troops to establish their independence from both Spain and the United States. But America's first war against guerrilla forces in Asia was a success, and the bulk of the resistance collapsed in 1901. President McKinley had his stepping-stone to the rich markets of China.

## Empire Building in Africa

Up to the beginning of the nineteenth century, the relatively limited nature of European economic interests in Africa had provided little temptation for the penetration of the interior or the political takeover of the coastal areas. The slave trade, the main source of European profit during the eighteenth century, could be carried on by using African rulers and merchants as intermediaries. Disease, political instability, the lack of transportation, and the generally unhealthy climate all deterred the Europeans from more extensive efforts in Africa.

**The Growing European Presence in West Africa** As the new century dawned, the slave trade itself was in a state of decline. One reason was the growing sense of outrage among humanitarians in several European countries over the purchase, sale, and exploitation of human beings. Dutch merchants effectively ceased trafficking in slaves in 1795, and the Danes stopped in 1803. A few years later, the slave trade was declared illegal in both Great Britain and the United States. The British began to apply pressure on other nations to follow suit, and most did so after the end of the Napoleonic Wars in 1815, leaving only Portugal and Spain as practitioners of the trade south of the equator. In the meantime, the demand for slaves began to decline in the Western Hemisphere, and by the 1880s, slavery had been abolished in all major countries of the world. It continued to exist, although at a reduced rate, along the Swahili Coast of East Africa.

Economic as well as humanitarian interests contributed to the end of the slave trade. The cost of slaves had begun to rise after the middle of the eighteenth century, and the growth of the slave population reduced the need for additional labor on the plantations in the Americas. The British, with some reluctant assistance from France and the United States, added to the costs by actively using their navy to capture slave ships and free the occupants. When slavery was abolished in the United States in 1863 and in Cuba and Brazil seventeen years later, the slave trade across the Atlantic was effectively brought to an end.

As the slave trade in the Atlantic declined during the first half of the nineteenth century, European interest in what was sometimes called "legitimate trade" in natural resources increased. Exports of peanuts, timber, hides, and palm oil from West Africa increased substantially during the first decades of the century, while imports of textile goods and other manufactured products rose.

Stimulated by growing commercial interests in the area, European governments began to push for a more permanent presence along the coast. During the first decades of the nineteenth century, the British established settlements along the Gold Coast and in Sierra Leone, where they set up agricultural plantations for freed slaves who had returned from the Western Hemisphere or had been liberated by British ships while en route to the Americas. A similar haven for ex-slaves was developed with the assistance of the United States in Liberia. The French occupied the area around the Senegal River near Cape Verde, where they attempted to develop peanut plantations (see Map 20.2).

The growing European presence in West Africa led to the emergence of a new class of Africans educated in Western culture and often employed by Europeans. Many became Christians, and some studied in European or American universities. At the same time, the European presence inevitably led to increasing tensions with African governments in the area. British efforts to increase trade with Ashanti led to conflict in the 1820s, but British influence in the area intensified in later

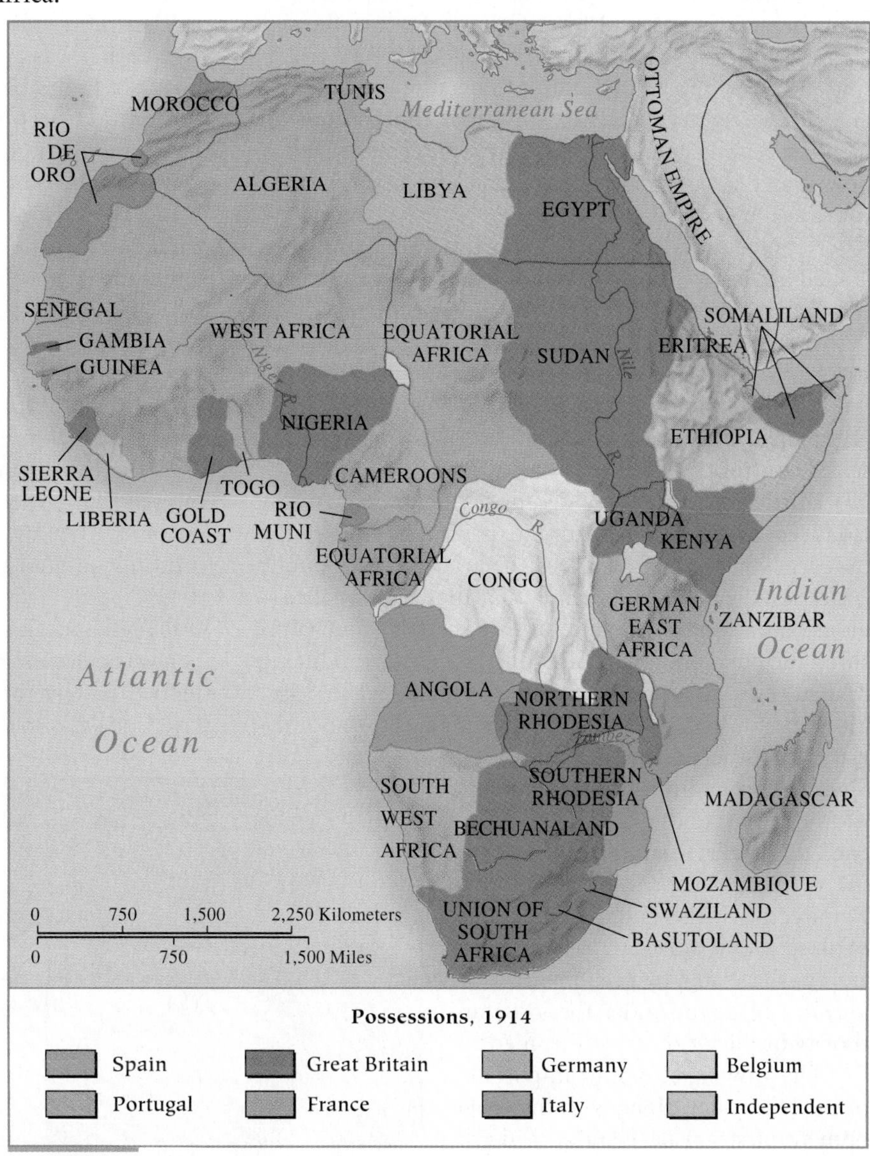


**MAP 20.2** **Africa in 1914.** By the beginning of 1900, virtually all of Africa was under some form of European rule. The territorial divisions established by colonial powers on the continent of Africa on the eve of World War I are shown here. Which European countries possessed the most colonies in Africa? **View an animated version of this map or related maps at** http://history.wadsworth.com/duikerspielvogel05/

decades. Most African states, especially those with a fairly high degree of political integration, were able to maintain their independence from this creeping European encroachment, called "informal empire" by some historians, but the prospects for the future were ominous. When local groups attempted to organize to protect their interests, the British stepped in and annexed the coastal states as the British colony of Gold Coast in 1874. At about the same time, the British extended an informal protectorate over warring ethnic groups in the Niger delta.

**Imperialist Shadow over the Nile** A similar process was under way in the Nile valley. There had long been interest in shortening the trade route to the East by digging a canal across the low, swampy isthmus separating the Mediterranean from the Red Sea. The Turks had considered constructing a canal from Cairo to Suez in the sixteenth century, as had the French king Louis XIV a century later, but the French did nothing about it until the end of the eighteenth century. At that time, Napoleon planned a military takeover of Egypt to cement French power in the eastern Mediterranean and open a faster route to India.

Napoleon's plan proved abortive. French troops landed in Egypt in 1798 and toppled the ramshackle Mamluk regime in Cairo, but the British counterattacked, destroying the French fleet and eventually forcing the French to evacuate in disarray. The British restored the Mamluks to power, but in 1805, Muhammad Ali, an Ottoman army officer of Turkish or Albanian extraction, seized control.

During the next three decades, Muhammad Ali introduced a series of reforms to bring Egypt into the modern world. He modernized the army, set up a public educational system (supplementing the traditional religious education provided in Muslim schools), and sponsored the creation of a small industrial sector producing refined sugar, textiles, munitions, and even ships. Muhammad Ali also extended Egyptian authority southward into the Sudan and across the Sinai peninsula into Arabia, Syria, and northern Iraq and even briefly threatened to seize Istanbul itself. To prevent the possible collapse of the Ottoman Empire, the British and the French recognized Muhammad Ali as the hereditary **pasha** (later to be known as the *khedive*) of Egypt under the loose authority of the Ottoman government.

The growing economic importance of the Nile valley, along with the development of steam navigation, made the heretofore visionary plans for a Suez canal more urgent. In 1854, the French entrepreneur Ferdinand de Lesseps signed a contract to begin construction of the canal, and it was completed in 1869. The project brought little immediate benefit to Egypt, however. The construction not only cost thousands of lives but also left the Egyptian government deep in debt, forcing it to depend increasingly on foreign financial support. When an army revolt against growing foreign influence broke out in 1881, the British stepped in to protect their investment (they had bought Egypt's canal company shares in 1875) and establish an informal protectorate that would last until World War I.

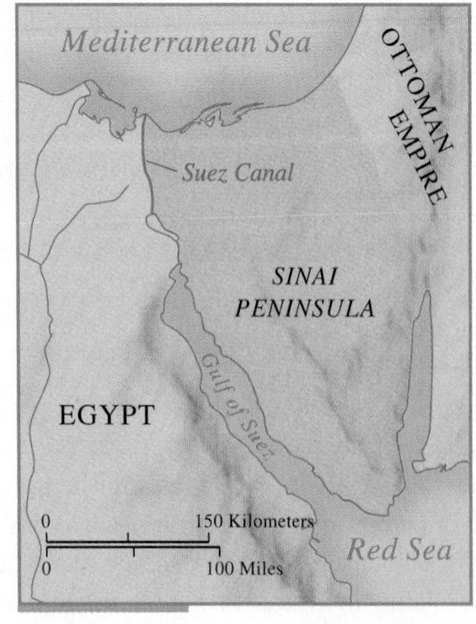

**The Suez Canal**

Rising discontent in the Sudan added to Egypt's growing internal problems. In 1881, the Muslim cleric Muhammad Ahmad, known as the Mahdi (in Arabic, the "rightly guided one"), led a religious revolt that brought much of the upper Nile under his control. The famous British general Charles Gordon, who had earlier commanded Manchu armies fighting against the Taiping Rebellion in China (see Chapter 21), led a military force to Khartoum to restore Egyptian authority, but his besieged army was captured in 1885 by the Mahdi's troops, thirty-six hours before a British rescue mission reached Khartoum. Gordon himself died in the battle, which became one of the most dramatic news stories of the last quarter of the century.

The weakening of Turkish rule in the Nile valley had a parallel farther to the west, where local viceroys in Tripoli, Tunis, and Algiers had begun to establish their autonomy. In 1830, the French, on the pretext of protecting European shipping in the Mediterranean from pirates, seized the area surrounding Algiers and integrated it into the French Empire. By the mid-1850s, more than 150,000 Europeans had settled in the fertile region adjacent to the coast. In 1881, the French imposed a protectorate on neighboring Tunisia. Only Tripoli and Cyrenaica (the Ottoman provinces that comprise modern Libya) remained under Turkish rule until the Italians seized them in 1911–1912.

**Arab Merchants and European Missionaries in East Africa** As always, events in East Africa followed their own distinctive pattern of development. Whereas the Atlantic slave trade was in decline, demand for slaves was increasing on the other side of the continent due to the growth of plantation agriculture in the region and on the islands off the coast. The French introduced sugar to the island of Réunion early in the century, and plantations of cloves (introduced from the Moluccas in the eighteenth century) were established under Omani Arab ownership on the island of Zanzibar. Zanzibar itself became the major shipping port along the entire east coast during the early nineteenth century, and the sultan of Oman, who had reasserted Arab suzerainty over the region in the aftermath of the collapse of Portuguese authority, established his capital at Zanzibar in 1840.

Bildarchiv Preussische Kulturbesitz, Berlin/Art Resource, NY

**The Opening of the Suez Canal.** The Suez Canal, which connected the Mediterranean and the Red Seas, was constructed under the direction of the French promoter Ferdinand de Lesseps. Still in use today, the canal is Egypt's greatest revenue producer. This sketch shows the ceremonial passage of the first ships through the canal in 1869. Note the combination of sail and steam power, reflecting the transition to coal-powered ships in the mid-nineteenth century.

From Zanzibar, Arab merchants fanned out into the interior plateaus in search of slaves, ivory (known as "white gold"), and other local products. The competition for slaves spread as far as Lake Victoria and the lower Sudan as traders from the north launched their own raids to obtain conscripts for the Egyptian army. The khedive sent General Charles Gordon to Uganda to stop the practice, but in the absence of alternative sources of income, local merchants could not easily be persuaded to give up a lucrative occupation.

The tenacity of the slave trade in East Africa—Zanzibar had now become the largest slave market in Africa—was undoubtedly a major reason for the rise of Western interest and Christian missionary activity in the region during the middle of the century. The most renowned missionary was the Scottish doctor David Livingstone, who arrived in Africa in 1841. Because Livingstone spent much of his time exploring the interior of the continent, discovering Victoria Falls in the process, he was occasionally criticized for being more explorer than missionary. But Livingstone was convinced that it was his divinely appointed task to bring Christianity to the far reaches of the continent, and his passionate opposition to slavery did far more to win public support for the abolitionist cause than did the efforts of any other figure of his generation. Public outcries provoked the British to redouble their efforts to bring the slave trade in East Africa to an end, and in 1873, the slave market at Zanzibar

© Bojan Brecelj/CORBIS

**Legacy of Shame.** By the mid-nineteenth century, most European nations had prohibited the trade in African slaves, but slavery continued to exist in East Africa under the sponsorship of the sultan of Zanzibar. When the Scottish missionary David Livingstone witnessed a slave raid near Lake Tanganyika in 1871, he wrote, "It gave me the impression of being in Hell." Despite his efforts, the practice was not eradicated until well into the next century. Shown here are domestic slaves on the island of Zanzibar under the baton of a supervisor. The photograph was taken about 1890.

convinced that missionary work and economic development had to go hand in hand, pleading to his fellow Europeans to introduce the "three C's" (Christianity, commerce, and civilization) to the continent. How much easier such a task would be if African peoples were under benevolent European rule!

There were more prosaic reasons as well. Advances in Western technology and European superiority in firearms made it easier than ever for a small European force to defeat superior numbers. Furthermore, life expectancy for Europeans living in Africa had improved. With the discovery that quinine (extracted from the bark of the cinchona tree) could provide partial immunity from the ravages of malaria, the mortality rate for Europeans living in Africa dropped dramatically in the 1840s. By the end of the century, European residents in tropical Africa faced only slightly higher risks of death by disease than individuals living in Europe.

Under these circumstances, King Leopold of Belgium used missionary activities as an excuse to claim vast territories in the Congo River basin (Belgium, he said, as "a small country, with a small people," needed a colony to enhance its image).[6] This set off a desperate race among European nations to stake claims throughout sub-Saharan Africa. Leopold ended up with the territories south of the Congo River, while France occupied areas to the north (Leopold bequeathed the Congo to Belgium on his death). Meanwhile, on the eastern side of the continent, Germany (through the activities of an ambitious missionary and with the agreement of the British, who needed German support against the French) annexed the colony of Tanganyika. To avert the possibility of violent clashes among the great powers, the German chancellor, Otto von Bismarck, convened a conference in Berlin in 1884 to set ground rules for future annexations of African territory by European nations. The conference combined high-minded resolutions with a hard-headed recognition of practical interests. The delegates called for free commerce in the Congo and along the Niger River as well as for further efforts to end the slave trade. At the same time, the participants recognized the inevitability of the imperialist dynamic, agreeing only that future annexations of African territory should not be given international recognition until effective occupation had been demonstrated. No African delegates were present.

The Berlin Conference had been convened to avert war and reduce tensions among European nations competing for the spoils of Africa. It proved reasonably successful at achieving the first objective but less so at the second. During the next few years, African territories were annexed without provoking a major confrontation between the Western powers, but in the late 1890s, Britain and France reached the brink of conflict at Fashoda, a small town on the Nile River in the Sudan. The French had been advancing eastward across the Sahara with the transparent objective of controlling the regions around the upper Nile. In 1898, British and Egyptian troops seized the Sudan from successors of the Mahdi and then marched southward to head off the French. After a tense face-off at Fashoda, the French government backed down, and British authority over the area was secured. Except for the Mediterranean littoral and their small possessions of Djibouti and a portion of the Somali coast, the French were restricted to equatorial Africa.

Ironically, the only major clash between Europeans over Africa took place in southern Africa, where competition among the powers was almost nonexistent. The discovery of gold and diamonds in the Boer republic of the Transvaal was the source of the problem. Clashes between the Afrikaner population and foreign (mainly British) miners and developers led to an attempt by Cecil Rhodes, prime minister of the Cape Colony and a prominent entrepreneur in the area, to subvert the Transvaal and bring it under British rule. In 1899, the so-called Boer War broke out between Britain and the Transvaal, which was backed by its fellow republic, the Orange Free State. Guerrilla resistance by the Boers was fierce, but the vastly superior forces of the British were able to prevail by 1902. To compensate the defeated Afrikaner population for the loss of independence, the British government agreed that only whites would vote in the now essentially self-governing colony. The Boers were placated, but the brutalities committed during the war (the British introduced an institution later to be known as the concentration camp) created bitterness on both sides that continued to fester through future decades.

### CHRONOLOGY Imperialism in Africa

| | |
|---|---|
| **Dutch abolish slave trade in Africa** | **1795** |
| **Napoleonic invasion of Egypt** | **1798** |
| **Slave trade declared illegal in Great Britain** | **1808** |
| **Boers' Great Trek in southern Africa** | **1830s** |
| **French seize Algeria** | **1830** |
| **Sultan of Oman establishes capital at Zanzibar** | **1840** |
| **David Livingstone arrives in Africa** | **1841** |
| **Slavery abolished in the United States** | **1863** |
| **Completion of Suez Canal** | **1869** |
| **Zanzibar slave market closed** | **1873** |
| **British establish Gold Coast colony** | **1874** |
| **British establish informal protectorate over Egypt** | **1881** |
| **Berlin Conference on Africa** | **1884** |
| **Charles Gordon killed at Khartoum** | **1885** |
| **Confrontation at Fashoda** | **1898** |
| **Boer War** | **1899–1902** |
| **Union of South Africa established** | **1910** |

## The Colonial System

Now that they had control of most of the world, what did the colonial powers do with it? As we have seen, their primary objective was to exploit the natural resources of the subject areas and to open up markets for manufactured goods and capital investment from the mother country. In some cases, that goal could be realized in cooperation with local political elites, whose loyalty could be earned, or purchased, by economic rewards or by confirming them in their positions of authority and status in a new colonial setting. Sometimes, however, this policy of **indirect rule** was not feasible because local leaders refused to cooperate with their colonial masters or even actively resisted the foreign conquest. In such cases, the local elites were removed from power and replaced with a new set of officials recruited from the mother country.

In general, the societies most likely to actively resist colonial conquest were those with a long tradition of national cohesion and independence, such as Burma and Vietnam in Asia and the African Muslim states in northern Nigeria and Morocco. In those areas, the colonial powers tended to dispense with local collaborators and govern directly. In parts of Africa, the Indian subcontinent, and the Malay peninsula, where the local authorities, for whatever reason, were willing to collaborate with the imperialist powers, indirect rule was more common.

The distinctions between **direct rule** and indirect rule were not merely academic and often had fateful consequences for the peoples involved. Where colonial powers encountered resistance and were forced to overthrow local political elites, they often adopted policies designed to eradicate the source of resistance and destroy the traditional culture. Such policies often had quite corrosive effects on the indigenous societies and provoked resentment and resistance that not only marked the colonial relationship but even affected relations after the restoration of national independence. The bitter struggles after World War II in Algeria, the Dutch East Indies, and Vietnam can be ascribed in part to that phenomenon.

### The Philosophy of Colonialism

To justify their rule, the colonial powers appealed in part to the time-honored maxim of "might makes right." By the end of the nineteenth century, that attitude received pseudoscientific validation from the concept of social Darwinism, which maintained that only societies that moved aggressively to adapt to changing circumstances would survive and prosper in a world governed by the Darwinian law of "survival of the fittest."

Some people, however, were uncomfortable with such a brutal view of the law of nature and sought a moral justification that appeared to benefit the victim. Here again, as we have seen, the concept of social Darwinism pointed the way. By bringing the benefits of Western democracy, capitalism, and Christianity to the tradition-ridden societies of Africa and Asia, the colonial powers were enabling primitive peoples to adapt to the challenges of the modern world. Buttressed by such comforting theories, sensitive Western minds could ignore the brutal aspects of colonialism and persuade themselves that in the long run the results would be beneficial for both sides. Few were as adept at describing the "civilizing mission" of colonialism as the French administrator and twice governor-general of French Indochina Albert Sarraut. While admitting that colonialism was originally an "act of force" undertaken for commercial profit, he insisted that by redistributing the wealth of the earth, the colonial process would result in a better life for all:

> Is it just, is it legitimate that such [an uneven distribution of resources] should be indefinitely prolonged? . . . No! . . . Humanity is distributed throughout the globe. No race, no people has the right or power to isolate itself egotistically from the movements and necessities of universal life.[7]

But what about the possibility that historically and culturally the societies of Asia and Africa were fundamentally different from those of the West and could not, or would not, be persuaded to transform themselves along Western lines? Was the human condition universal, or were human beings so shaped by their history and geographical environment that their civilizations would inevitably remain distinct? In that case, a policy of cultural transformation could not be expected to succeed and could even lead to disaster.

**Assimilation and Association** In fact, colonial theorists never decided this issue one way or the other. The French, who were most inclined to philosophize about the problem, adopted the terms **assimilation** (which implied an effort to transform colonial societies in the Western image) and **association** (implying collaboration with local elites while leaving local traditions alone) to describe the two alternatives and then proceeded to vacillate between them. French policy in Indochina, for example, began as one of association but switched to assimilation under pressure from those who felt that colonial powers owed a debt to their subject peoples. But assimilation (which in any case was never accepted as feasible or desirable by many colonial officials) aroused resentment among the local population, many of whom opposed the destruction of their native traditions. In the end, the French abandoned the attempt to justify their presence and fell back on a policy of ruling by force of arms.

Other colonial powers had little interest in the issue. The British, whether out of a sense of pragmatism or one of racial superiority, refused to entertain the possibility of assimilation and treated their subject peoples as culturally and racially distinct. In formulating a colonial policy for the Philippines, the United States adopted a policy of assimilation in theory but did not always put it into practice.

To many of the colonial peoples, such questions must have appeared academic, since the primary objectives of all the colonial states were economic exploitation and the retention of power. Like the British soldier in Kipling's poem "On the Road to Mandalay," all too many Westerners living in the colonies believed that the Great Lord Buddha was nothing but a "bloomin' idol made of mud."

**Colonialism in Action** In practice, colonialism in India, Southeast Asia, and Africa exhibited many similarities but also some differences. Some of these variations can be traced to political or social differences among the colonial powers themselves. The French, for example, often tried to impose a centralized administrative system on their colonies that mirrored the system in use in France, while the British sometimes attempted to transform local aristocrats into the equivalent of the landed gentry at home in Britain. Other differences stemmed from conditions in the colonies themselves and the colonizers' aspirations for them. For instance, the Western powers believed that their economic interests were far more limited in Africa than elsewhere and therefore treated their African colonies somewhat differently than those in India or Southeast Asia.

## India Under the British Raj

By 1800, the once glorious empire of the Mughals had been reduced by British military power to a shadow of its former greatness. During the next few decades, the British sought to consolidate their control over the Indian subcontinent, expanding from their base areas along the coast into the interior. Some territories were taken over directly, first by the East India Company and later by the British crown; others were ruled indirectly through their local maharajas and rajas.

**Benefits of British Rule** Not all of the effects of British rule were bad. British governance over the subcontinent brought order and stability to a society that had been rent by civil war. By the early nineteenth century, British control had been consolidated and led to a relatively honest and efficient government that in many respects operated to the benefit of the average Indian. One of the benefits of the period was the heightened attention given to education. Through the efforts of the British administrator Thomas Babington Macaulay, a new school system was established to train the children of Indian elites, and the British civil service examination was introduced (see the box on p. 583). The instruction of young girls also expanded, with the primary purpose of making them better wives and mothers for the educated male population. The admission of the first Indian woman to a Madras medical college, for example, occurred in 1875.

Courtesy of William J. Duiker

**Gateway to India?** Built in the Roman imperial style by the British to commemorate the visit to India of King George V and Queen Mary in 1911, the Gateway of India was erected at the water's edge in the harbor of Bombay, India's greatest port city. For thousands of British citizens arriving in India, the Gateway of India was the first view of their new home and a symbol of the power and majesty of the British raj. Only a few dozen yards away was the luxurious Taj Mahal Hotel. Constructed in the popular Anglo-Indian style, it was built to house European visitors upon their arrival in India.

## INDIAN IN BLOOD, ENGLISH IN TASTE AND INTELLECT

Thomas Babington Macaulay (1800–1859) was named a member of the Supreme Council of India in the early 1830s. In that capacity, he was responsible for drawing up a new educational policy for British subjects in the area. In his *Minute on Education,* he considered the claims of English and various local languages to become the vehicle for educational training and decided in favor of the former. It is better, he argued, to teach Indian elites about Western civilization so as "to form a class who may be interpreters between us and the millions whom we govern; a class of persons, Indian in blood and color, but English in taste, in opinions, in morals, and in intellect." Later Macaulay became a prominent historian. The debate over the relative benefits of English and the various Indian languages continues today.

*How does the author of this document justify the teaching of the English language? Do you find his arguments persuasive? How might a critic respond?*

### Thomas Babington Macaulay, *Minute on Education*

We have a fund to be employed as government shall direct for the intellectual improvement of the people of this country. The simple question is, what is the most useful way of employing it?

All parties seem to be agreed on one point, that the dialects commonly spoken among the natives of this part of India contain neither literary or scientific information, and are, moreover so poor and rude that, until they are enriched from some other quarter, it will not be easy to translate any valuable work into them. . . .

What, then, shall the language [of education] be? One half of the Committee maintain that it should be the English. The other half strongly recommend the Arabic and Sanskrit. The whole question seems to me to be, which language is the best worth knowing?

I have no knowledge of either Sanskrit or Arabic—but I have done what I could to form a correct estimate of their value. I have read translations of the most celebrated Arabic and Sanskrit works. I have conversed both here and at home with men distinguished by their proficiency in the Eastern tongues. I am quite ready to take the Oriental learning at the valuation of the Orientalists themselves. I have never found one among them who could deny that a single shelf of a good European library was worth the whole native literature of India and Arabia. . . .

It is, I believe, no exaggeration to say, that all the historical information which has been collected from all the books written in the Sanskrit language is less valuable than what may be found in the most paltry abridgments used at preparatory schools in England. In every branch of physical or moral philosophy the relative position of the two nations is nearly the same.

**History Now™** To read a full version of this document, enter the *HistoryNow* documents area using the access card that is available for *World History.*

British rule also brought an end to some of the more inhumane aspects of Indian tradition. The practice of *sati* was outlawed, and widows were legally permitted to remarry. The British also attempted to put an end to the endemic brigandage (known as *thuggee,* which gave rise to the English word *thug*) that had plagued travelers in India since time immemorial. Railroads, the telegraph, and the postal service were introduced to India shortly after they appeared in Great Britain itself. Work began on the main highway from Calcutta to Delhi in 1839 (see Map 20.4), and the first rail network was opened in 1853. A new penal code based on the British model was adopted, and health and sanitation conditions were improved.

**The Cost of Colonialism** But the Indian people paid a high price for the peace and stability brought by the British **raj** (from the Indian *raja,* or prince). Perhaps the most flagrant cost was economic. While British entrepreneurs and a small percentage of the Indian population attached to the imperial system reaped financial benefits from British rule, it brought hardship to millions of others in both the cities and the rural areas. The introduction of British textiles put thousands of Bengali women out of work and severely damaged the local textile industry.

In rural areas, the British introduced the *zamindar* system (see Chapter 15) in the misguided expectation that it would both facilitate the collection of agricultural taxes and create a new landed gentry, who could, as in Britain, become the conservative foundation of imperial rule. But the local gentry took advantage of this new authority to increase taxes and force the less fortunate peasants to become tenants or lose their land entirely. When rural unrest threatened, the government passed legislation protecting farmers against eviction and unreasonable rent increases, but this measure had little effect outside the southern provinces, where it had originally been enacted. Similarly, British officials made few efforts during the nineteenth century to introduce democratic institutions or values to the Indian people. As one senior political figure remarked in Parliament in 1898, democratic institutions "can no more be carried to India by Englishmen . . . than they can carry ice in their luggage."[8]

British colonialism was also remiss in bringing the benefits of modern science and technology to India. Some limited forms of industrialization took place, notably in the manufacturing of textiles and jute (used in making rope). The first textile mill opened in 1856. Seventy years later, there were eighty mills in the city of Bombay alone.

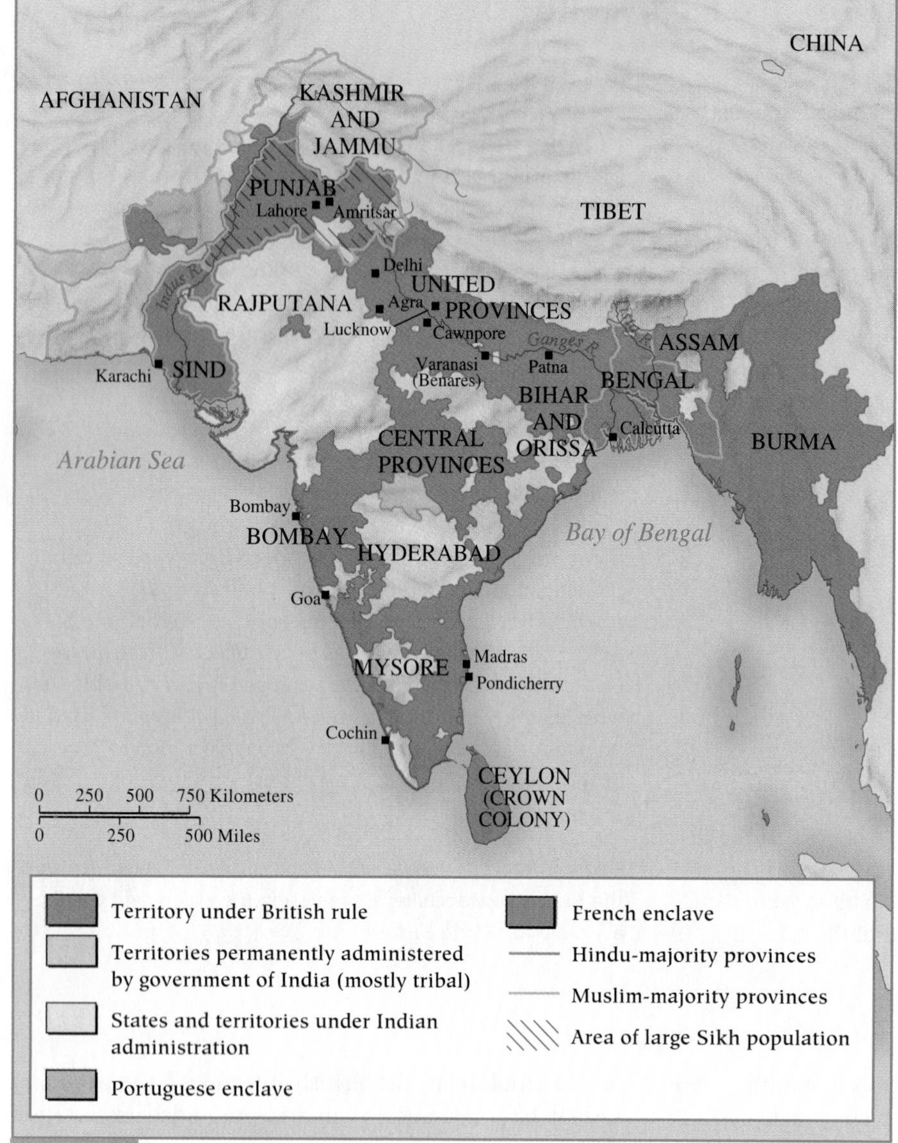


**MAP 20.4 India Under British Rule, 1805–1931.** This map shows the different forms of rule that the British applied in India under their control. ? Where are the major cities of the subcontinent located? **View an animated version of this map or related maps at** http://history.wadsworth.com/duikerspielvogel05/

Nevertheless, the lack of local capital and the advantages given to British imports prevented the emergence of other vital new commercial and manufacturing operations.

Foreign rule also had a psychological effect on the Indian people. Although many British colonial officials sincerely tried to improve the lot of the people under their charge, British arrogance and contempt for native tradition cut deeply into the pride of many Indians, especially those of high caste, who were accustomed to a position of superior status in India. Educated Indians trained in the Anglo-Indian school system for a career in the civil service, as well as Eurasians born to mixed marriages, often imitated the behavior and dress of their rulers, speaking English, eating Western food, and taking up European leisure activities, but many rightfully wondered where their true cultural loyalties lay (see the comparative illustration on p. 587). This cultural collision was poignantly described in the novel *A Passage to India* by the British writer E. M. Forster, which relates the story of a visiting Englishwoman who becomes interested in the Indian way of life, much to the dismay of the local European community.

## Colonial Regimes in Southeast Asia

In Southeast Asia, economic profit was the immediate and primary aim of colonial enterprise. For that purpose, colonial powers tried wherever possible to work with local elites to facilitate the exploitation of natural resources. Indirect rule reduced the cost of training European administrators and had a less corrosive impact on the local culture. In the Dutch East Indies, for example, officials of the Dutch East India Company (VOC) entrusted local administration to the indigenous landed aristocracy, who maintained law and order and collected taxes in return for a payment from the VOC (see the box on p. 586). The British followed a similar practice in Malaya. While establishing direct rule over the crucial commercial centers of Singapore and Malacca, the British allowed local Muslim rulers to maintain princely power in the interior of the peninsula.

**Administration and Education** Indirect rule, however convenient and inexpensive, was not always feasible. In some instances, local resistance to the colonial conquest made such a policy impossible. In Burma, the staunch opposition of the monarchy and other traditionalist forces caused the British to abolish the monarchy and administer the country directly through their colonial government in India. In Indochina, the French used both direct and indirect means. They imposed direct rule on the southern provinces in the Mekong delta but governed the north as a protectorate, with the emperor retaining titular authority from his palace in Huê. The

**The Company Resident and His Puppet.** The British of the East India Company gradually replaced the sovereigns of the once independent Indian states with puppet rulers who carried out the company's policies. Here we see the company's resident dominating a procession in Tanjore in 1825, while the Indian ruler, Sarabhoji, follows like an obedient shadow. As a boy, Sarabhoji had been educated by European tutors and had filled his life and home with English books and furnishings.

French adopted a similar policy in Cambodia and Laos, where local rulers were left in charge with French advisers to counsel them.

Whatever method was used, colonial regimes in Southeast Asia, as elsewhere, were slow to create democratic institutions. The first legislative councils and assemblies were composed almost exclusively of European residents in the colony. The first representatives from the indigenous population were wealthy and conservative in their political views. When Southeast Asians complained, colonial officials gradually and reluctantly began to broaden the franchise. Albert Sarraut advised patience in awaiting the full benefits of colonial policy: "I will treat you like my younger brothers, but do not forget that I am the older brother. I will slowly give you the dignity of humanity."[9]

Colonial officials were also slow to adopt educational reforms. Although the introduction of Western education was one of the justifications of colonialism, colonial officials soon discovered that educating native elites could backfire. Often there were few jobs for highly trained lawyers, engineers, and architects in colonial societies, leading to the threat of an indigestible mass of unemployed intellectuals who would take out their frustrations on the colonial regime. Educational opportunities for the common people were even harder to come by. In French-controlled Vietnam in 1917, only 3,000 of the 23,000 villages in the country had a public school. The French had opened a university in Hanoi, but it was immediately closed as a result of student demonstrations. As one French official noted in voicing his opposition to increasing the number of schools in Vietnam, educating the natives meant not "one coolie less, but one rebel more."

**Economic Development** Colonial powers were equally reluctant to take up the "white man's burden" in the area of economic development. As we have seen, their primary goals were to secure a source of cheap raw materials and to maintain markets for manufactured goods. Such objectives would be undermined by the emergence of advanced industrial economies. So colonial policy concentrated on the export of raw materials—teakwood from

## The Effects of Dutch Colonialism in Java

Eduard Douwes Dekker was a Dutch colonial official who served in the East Indies for nearly twenty years. In 1860, he published a critique of the Dutch colonial system that had an impact in the Netherlands similar to that of Harriet Beecher Stowe's *Uncle Tom's Cabin* in the United States. In the following excerpt from his book *Max Havelaar, or Coffee Auctions of the Dutch Trading Company,* Douwes Dekker described the system as it was applied on the island of Java, in the Indonesian archipelago.

*According to the author, what was the impact of Dutch colonial policies on Javanese peasants? How might a colonial official respond to the criticism?*

### Eduard Douwes Dekker, *Max Havelaar*

The Javanese is by nature a husbandman; the ground whereon he is born, which gives much for little labor, allures him to it, and, above all things, he devotes his whole heart and soul to the cultivating of his rice fields, in which he is very clever. He grows up in the midst of his sawahs [rice fields] . . . ; when still very young, he accompanies his father to the field, where he helps him in his labor with plow and spade, in constructing dams and drains to irrigate his fields; he counts his years by harvests; he estimates time by the color of the blades in his field; he is at home amongst the companions who cut paddy with him; he chooses his wife amongst the girls of the dessah [village], who every evening tread the rice with joyous songs. The possession of a few buffaloes for plowing is the ideal of his dreams. The cultivation of rice is in Java what the vintage is in the Rhine provinces and in the south of France. But there came foreigners from the West, who made themselves masters of the country. They wished to profit by the fertility of the soil, and ordered the native to devote a part of his time and labor to the cultivation of other things which should produce higher profits in the markets of Europe. To persuade the lower orders to do so, they had only to follow a very simple policy. The Javanese obeys his chiefs; to win the chiefs, it was only necessary to give them a part of the gain,—and success was complete.

To be convinced of the success of that policy we need only consider the immense quantity of Javanese products sold in Holland; and we shall also be convinced of its injustice, for, if anybody should ask if the husbandman himself gets a reward in proportion to that quantity, then I must give a negative answer. The Government compels him to cultivate certain products on his ground; it punishes him if he sells what he has produced to any purchaser but itself; and it fixes the price actually paid. The expenses of transport to Europe through a privileged trading company are high; the money paid to the chiefs for encouragement increases the prime cost; and because the entire trade must produce profit, that profit cannot be got in any other way than by paying the Javanese just enough to keep him from starving, which would lessen the producing power of the nation.

Burma; rubber and tin from Malaya; spices, tea and coffee, and palm oil from the East Indies; and sugar and copra (coconut meat) from the Philippines.

In some Southeast Asian colonial societies, a measure of industrial development did take place to meet the needs of the European population and local elites. Major manufacturing cities like Rangoon in lower Burma, Batavia on the island of Java, and Saigon in French Indochina grew rapidly. Although the local middle class benefited from the increased economic activity, most large industrial and commercial establishments were owned and managed by Europeans or, in some cases, by Indian or Chinese merchants. In Saigon, for example, even the production of *nuoc mam,* the traditional Vietnamese fish sauce, was under Chinese ownership. In most cities, foreigners controlled banking, major manufacturing activities, and the import-export trade. The natives were more apt to work in a family business, in factory or assembly plants, or as peddlers, day laborers, or rickshaw pullers—in other words, at less profitable and less capital-intensive businesses.

**Colonialism and the Countryside** Despite the growth of an urban economy, the vast majority of people in the colonial societies continued to farm the land. Many continued to live by subsistence agriculture, but the colonial policy of emphasizing cash crops for export also led to the creation of a form of plantation agriculture in which peasants were recruited to work as wage laborers on rubber and tea plantations owned by Europeans. To maintain a competitive edge, the plantation owners kept the wages of their workers at poverty level. Many plantation workers were "shanghaied" (the English term originated from the practice of recruiting laborers, often from the docks and streets of Shanghai, by unscrupulous means such as the use of force, alcohol, or drugs) to work on plantations, where conditions were often so inhumane that thousands died. High taxes, enacted by colonial governments to pay for administrative costs or improvements in the local infrastructure, were a heavy burden for poor peasants.

The situation was made even more difficult by the steady growth of the population. Peasants in Asia had always had large families on the assumption that a high proportion of their children would die in infancy. But improved sanitation and medical treatment resulted in lower rates of infant mortality and a staggering increase in population. The population of the island of Java, for

**CHRONOLOGY Imperialism in Asia**

| | |
|---|---|
| Stamford Raffles arrives in Singapore | 1819 |
| British attack lower Burma | 1826 |
| British rail network opened in northern India | 1853 |
| Sepoy Rebellion | 1857 |
| French attack Vietnam | 1858 |
| Indian National Congress established | 1885 |
| British and French agree to neutralize Thailand | 1896 |
| Commodore Dewey defeats Spanish fleet in Manila Bay | 1898 |

example, increased from about a million in the precolonial era to about 40 million at the end of the nineteenth century. Under these conditions, the rural areas could no longer support the growing populations, and many young people fled to the cities to seek jobs in factories or shops. The migratory pattern gave rise to squatter settlements in the suburbs of the major cities.

As in India, colonial rule did bring some benefits to Southeast Asia. It led to the beginnings of a modern economic infrastructure and to what is sometimes called a "modernizing elite" dedicated to the creation of an advanced industrialized society. The development of an export market helped create an entrepreneurial class in rural areas. This happened, for example, on the outer islands of the Dutch East Indies (such as Borneo and Sumatra), where small growers of rubber trees, palm trees for oil, coffee, tea, and spices began to share in the profits of the colonial enterprise.

A balanced assessment of the colonial legacy in Southeast Asia must take into account that the early stages of industrialization are difficult in any society. Even in western Europe, industrialization led to the creation of an impoverished and powerless proletariat, urban slums, and displaced peasants driven from the land. In much of Europe and Japan, however, the bulk of the population eventually enjoyed better material conditions as the profits from manufacturing and plantation agriculture were reinvested in the national economy and gave rise to increased consumer demand. In contrast, in Southeast Asia, most of the profits were repatriated to the colonial mother country, while displaced peasants fleeing to cities like Rangoon, Batavia, and Saigon found little opportunity for employment. Many were left with seasonal employment, with one foot on the farm and one in the factory. The old world was being destroyed, while the new one had yet to be born.

Durand Collection of Vietnamese Art, Yale University Library

British Library, Oriental and India Office Collections

COMPARATIVE ILLUSTRATION

**Cultural Influences—East and West.** When Europeans moved into Asia in the nineteenth century, some Asians began to imitate European customs for prestige or social advancement. Seen at left, for example, is a young Vietnamese during the 1920s dressed in Western sports clothes, learning to lift weights. Sometimes, however, the cultural influence went the other way. At right, an English nabob, as European residents in India were often called, apes the manner of an Indian aristocrat, complete with harem and hookah, the Indian water pipe. The paintings on the wall, however, are in the European style.

Courtesy of William J. Duiker

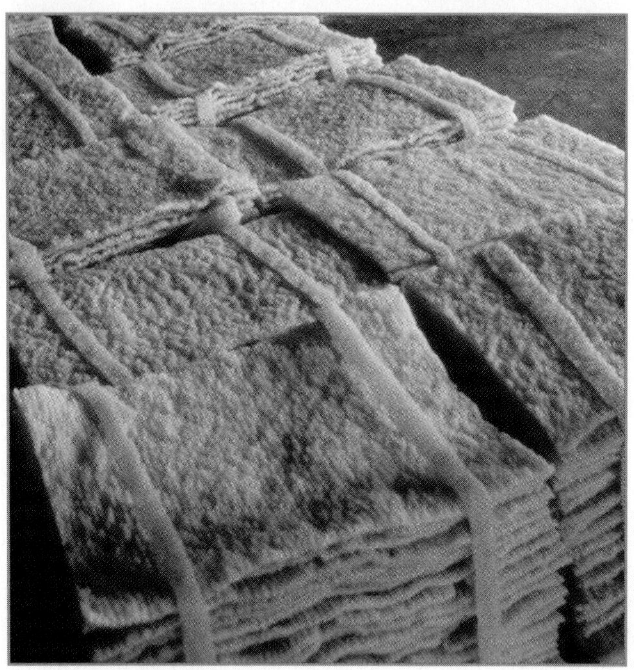
Courtesy of William J. Duiker

**A Rubber Plantation.** Natural rubber was one of the most important cash crops in European colonies in Asia. Rubber trees, native to the Amazon River basin in Brazil, were eventually transplanted to Southeast Asia, where they became a major source of profit. Workers on the plantations received few benefits, however. Once the sap of the tree (known as latex and shown on the left) was extracted, it was hardened and pressed into sheets (right photo) and then sent to Europe for refining.

## Colonialism in Africa

Colonialism had similar consequences in Africa, although with some changes in emphasis. As we have seen, European economic interests were more limited in Africa than elsewhere. Having seized the continent in what could almost be described as a fit of hysteria, the European powers had to decide what to do with it. With economic concerns relatively limited except for isolated areas like the gold mines in the Transvaal and copper deposits in the Belgian Congo, interest in Africa declined, and most European governments settled down to govern their new territories with the least effort and expense possible. In many cases, this meant a form of indirect rule similar to what the British used in the princely states in India. The British with their tradition of decentralized government at home were especially prone to adopt this approach.

**Indirect Rule** In the minds of British administrators, the stated goal of indirect rule was to preserve African political traditions. The desire to limit cost and inconvenience was one reason for this approach, but it may also have been due to the conviction that Africans were inherently inferior to the white race and thus incapable of adopting European customs and institutions. In any event, indirect rule entailed relying to the greatest extent possible on existing political elites and institutions. Initially, in some areas the British simply asked a local ruler to formally accept British authority and to fly the Union Jack over official buildings. Sometimes it was the Africans who did the bidding, as in the case of the African leaders in Cameroons who wrote to Queen Victoria:

> We *wish* to have your laws in our towns. We want to have every *fashion* altered; also we will do according to your Consul's *word*. Plenty wars here in our country. Plenty murder and plenty idol worshippers. Perhaps these *lines* of our writing will *look* to you as an *idle* tale.
>
> We have *spoken* to the English consul plenty times about having an English *government* here. We never have answer from you, so we wish to write you *ourselves*.[10]

Nigeria offers a typical example of British indirect rule. British officials maintained the central administration, but local authority was assigned to native chiefs, with British district officers serving as intermediaries with the central administration. Where a local aristocracy did not exist, the British assigned administrative responsibility to clan heads from communities in the vicinity. The local authorities were expected to maintain law and order and to collect taxes from the native population. As a general rule, indigenous customs were left undisturbed, although the institution of slavery was abolished (see the box on p. 590). A dual legal system was instituted that applied African laws to Africans and European laws to foreigners.

One advantage of such an administrative system was that it did not severely disrupt local customs and institutions. Nevertheless, it had several undesirable consequences. In the first place, it was essentially a fraud, since all major decisions were made by the British administra-

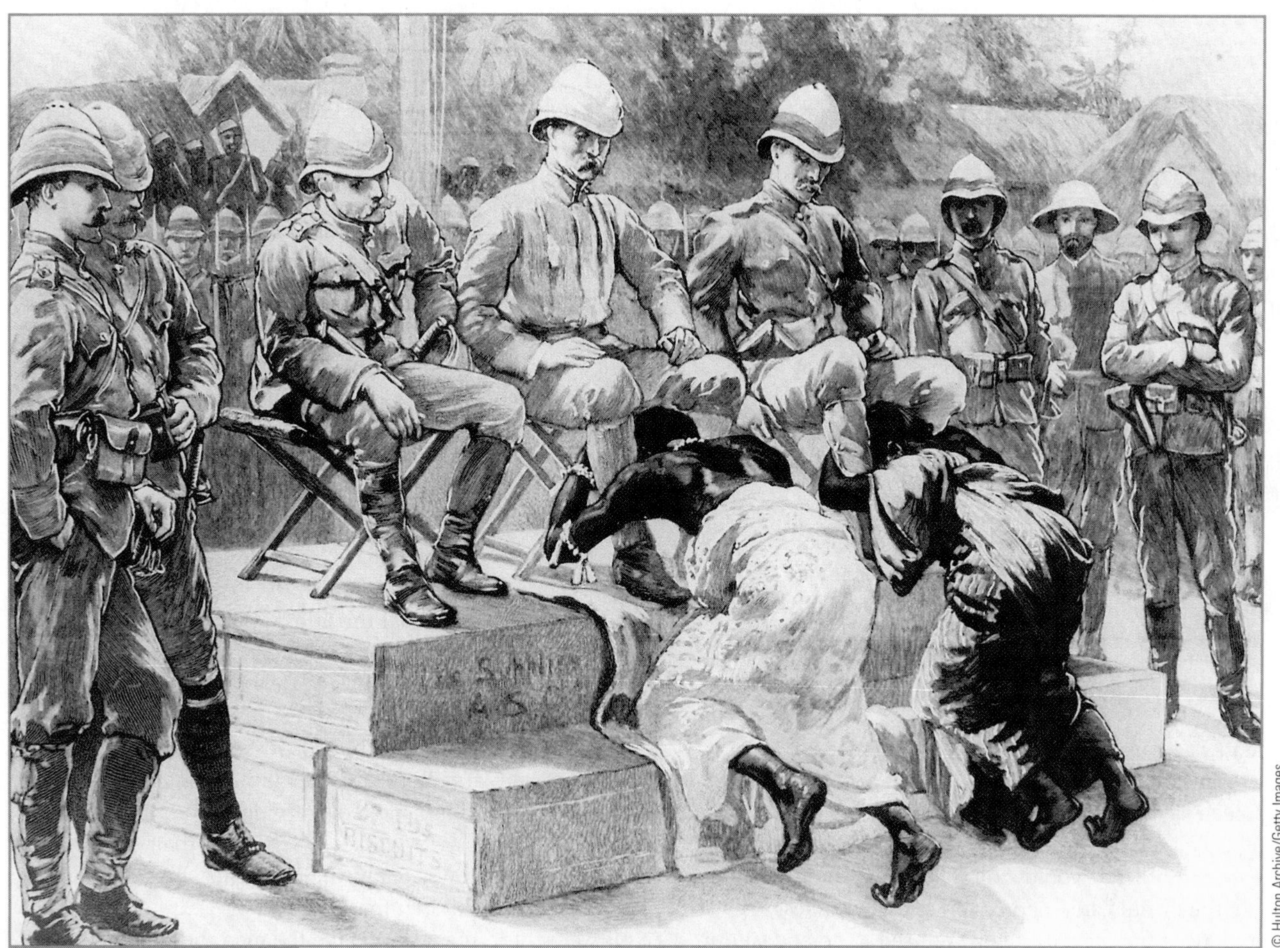




**Revere the Conquering Heroes.** European colonial officials were quick to place themselves at the top of the political and social hierarchy in their conquered territories. Here British officials accept the submission of the Ashanti king and queen, according to African custom, in 1896.

tors while the native authorities served primarily as a mechanism for enforcing those decisions. Moreover, indirect rule served to perpetuate the autocratic system often in use prior to colonial takeover. It was official policy to inculcate respect for authority in areas under British rule, and there was a natural tendency to view the local aristocracy as the African equivalent of the British ruling class. Such a policy provided few opportunities for ambitious and talented young Africans from outside the traditional elite and thus sowed the seeds for class tensions after the restoration of independence in the twentieth century.

**The British in East Africa** The situation was somewhat different in East Africa, especially in Kenya, which had a relatively large European population attracted by the temperate climate in the central highlands. The local government had encouraged white settlers to migrate to the area as a means of promoting economic development and encouraging financial self-sufficiency. To attract Europeans, fertile farmlands in the central highlands were reserved for European settlement, while, as in South Africa, specified reserve lands were set aside for Africans. The presence of a substantial European minority (although, in fact, they represented only about 1 percent of the entire population) had an impact on Kenya's political development. The white settlers actively sought self-government and dominion status similar to that granted to such former British possessions as Canada and Australia. The British government, however, was not willing to run the risk of provoking racial tensions with the African majority and agreed only to establish separate government organs for the European and African populations.

**British Rule in South Africa** The British used a different system in southern Africa, where there was a high percentage of European settlers. The situation was further complicated by the division between English-speaking and Afrikaner elements within the European population. In 1910, the British agreed to the creation of the independent Union of South Africa, which combined the old Cape Colony and Natal with the Boer republics. The new union adopted a representative government, but only for the European population, while the African reserves of Basutoland (now Lesotho), Bechuanaland (now Botswana), and Swaziland were subordinated directly to the crown. The union was now free to manage its own domestic

## "THERE'S A EUROPEAN, THERE'S A EUROPEAN!"

Most Africans living outside the port cities had little idea of what to expect from the arrival of the white man and the new colonial authority. Thanks to these memoirs, recounted a half-century later by an African woman from northern Nigeria, we are offered an intimate glimpse into the arrival of the British at the end of the nineteenth century. It is interesting to note that slavery among Africans was still a long-established tradition in the area. In a later passage, the woman remarks that her family lost income from the flight of its slaves, but the loss was offset by a reduction in taxes that African farmers had traditionally been compelled to pay to fill the pockets of local officials and chiefs.

*Why did the Fulani and the Habe peoples respond in different ways to the arrival of the Europeans? How did the Europeans affect the institution of slavery in the area?*

### Baba, A Hausa Woman of Nigeria

When I was a maiden the Europeans first arrived. Ever since we were quite small the *malams* [Muslim scholars] had been saying that the Europeans would come with a thing called a train, they would come with a thing called a motor-car. . . . They would stop wars, they would repair the world, they would stop oppression and lawlessness, we should live at peace with them. We used to go and sit quietly and listen to the prophecies. . . .

I remember when a European came to Karo on a horse, and some of his foot soldiers went into the town. Everyone came out to look at them. . . . Everyone at Karo ran away—"There's a European, there's a European!" . . .

At that time Yusufu was the [Fulani] king of Kano. He did not like the Europeans, he did not wish them, he would not sign their treaty. Then he saw that perforce he would have to agree, so he did. We Habe wanted them to come, it was the Fulani who did not like it. When the Europeans came the Habe saw that if you worked for them they paid you for it, they didn't say, like the Fulani, "Commoner, give me this! Commoner, bring me that!" Yes, the Habe wanted them. . . .

The Europeans said that there were to be no more slaves; if someone said "Slave!" you could complain to the *alkali* [judge] who would punish the master who said it, the judge said, "That is what the Europeans have decreed." . . . When slavery was stopped, nothing much happened at our *rinji* [the farm where their slaves lived] except that some slaves whom we had bought in the market ran away. Our own father went to his farm and worked, he and his son took up their large hoes. . . . They farmed guineacorn and millet and groundnuts and everything; before this they had supervised the slaves' work—now they did their own. When the midday food was ready, the women of the compound would give us children the food, one of us drew water, and off we went to the farm to take the men their food at the foot of a tree.

affairs and possessed considerable autonomy in foreign relations. Formal British rule was also extended to the remaining lands south of the Zambezi River, which were eventually divided into the territories of Northern and Southern Rhodesia. Southern Rhodesia attracted many British immigrants, and in 1922, after a popular referendum, it became a crown colony (see the box on p. 591).

**Direct Rule** Most other European nations governed their African possessions through a form of direct rule. The prototype was the French system, which reflected the centralized administrative system introduced in France itself by Napoleon. As in the British colonies, at the top of the pyramid was a French official, usually known as the governor-general, who was appointed from Paris and governed with the aid of a bureaucracy in the capital city. At the provincial level, French commissioners were assigned to deal with local administrators, but the latter were required to be conversant in French and could be transferred to a new position at the needs of the central government.

Moreover, the French ideal was to assimilate their African subjects into French culture rather than preserving their native traditions. Africans were eligible to run for office and to serve in the French National Assembly, and a few were appointed to high positions in the colonial administration. Such policies reflected the relative absence of racist attitudes in French society, as well as the conviction among the French of the superiority of Gallic culture and their revolutionary belief in the universality of human nature.

After World War I, European colonial policy in Africa entered a new and more formal phase. The colonial administrative network was extended to a greater degree into outlying areas, where it was represented by a district official and defended by a small native army under European command. Greater attention was given to improving social services, including education, medicine and sanitation, and communications. The colonial system was now viewed more formally as a moral and social responsibility, a "sacred trust" to be maintained by the civilized countries until the Africans became capable of self-government. More emphasis was placed on economic development and on the exploitation of natural resources to provide the colonies with the means of achieving self-sufficiency. More Africans were now serving in colonial administrations, although relatively few were placed in positions of responsibility. On the other hand, race

# The Ndebele Rebellion

As British forces advanced northward from the Cape Colony toward the Zambezi River in the 1890s, they overran the Ndebele people, who occupied rich lands in the region near the site of the ruins of Great Zimbabwe. Angered by British brutality, Ndebele warriors revolted in 1896 to throw off their oppressors. Despite the Ndebele's great superiority in numbers, British units possessed the feared Maxim gun, which mowed down African attackers by the hundreds. Faced with defeat, the Ndebele king, Lobengula, fled into the hills and committed suicide. In the following account, a survivor describes the conflict.

*Compare this account with that of the Hausa women from Nigeria in the document on p. 590. What factors might account for the differences?*

### Ndansi Kumalo, *A Personal Account*

We surrendered to the white people and were told to go back to our homes and live our usual lives and attend to our crops. But the white men sent native police who did abominable things; they were cruel and assaulted a lot of our people and helped themselves to our cattle and goats. . . . They interfered with our wives and molested them. . . . We thought it best to fight and die rather than bear it. . . .

We knew that we had very little chance because their weapons were so much superior to ours. But we meant to fight to the last, feeling that even if we could not beat them we might at least kill a few of them and so have some sort of revenge. . . .

I remember a fight . . . when we charged the white men. There were some hundreds of us; the white men also were many. We charged them at close quarters: we thought we had a good chance to kill them but the Maxims were too much for us. . . . Many of our people were killed in this fight. . . .

We were still fighting when we heard that [Cecil] Rhodes was coming and wanted to make peace with us. It was best to come to terms he said, and not go shedding blood like this on both sides. . . . So peace was made. Many of our people had been killed, and now we began to die of starvation; and then came the rinderpest and the cattle that were still left to us perished. We could not help thinking that all these dreadful things were brought by the white people.

**Serving the White Ruler.** Although European governments claimed to be carrying out the civilizing mission in Africa, all too often the local population was forced to labor in degrading conditions to serve the economic interests of the occupying power. Here African workers are depicted as they transport goods for a European merchant.

## The Civilizing Mission in Egypt

In many parts of the colonial world, European occupation served to sharpen class divisions in traditional societies. Such was the case in Egypt, where the British protectorate, established in the early 1880s, benefited many elites, who profited from the introduction of Western culture. Ordinary Egyptians, less inclined to adopt foreign ways, seldom profited from the European presence. In response, British administrators showed little patience for their subjects who failed to recognize the superiority of Western civilization. This view found expression in the words of the governor-general, Lord Cromer, who remarked in exasperation, "The mind of the Oriental, . . . like his picturesque streets, is eminently wanting in symmetry. His reasoning is of the most slipshod description." Cromer was especially irritated at the local treatment of women, arguing that the seclusion of women and the wearing of the veil were the chief causes of Islamic backwardness.

Such views were echoed by some Egyptian elites, who were utterly seduced by Western culture and embraced the colonialists' condemnation of native ways. The French-educated lawyer Qassim Amin was one example. His book, *The Liberation of Women,* published in 1899 and excerpted here, precipitated a heated debate between those who considered Western nations the liberators of Islam and those who reviled them as oppressors.

**Qassim Amin, *The Liberation of Women***

European civilization advances with the speed of steam and electricity, and has even overspilled to every part of the globe so that there is not an inch that he [European man] has not trodden underfoot. Any place he goes he takes control of its resources . . . and turns them into profit . . . and if he does harm to the original inhabitants, it is only that he pursues happiness in this world and seeks it wherever he may find it . . . . For the most part he uses his intellect, but when circumstances require it, he deploys force. He does not seek glory from his possessions and colonies, for he has enough of this through his intellectual achievements and scientific inventions. What drives the Englishman to dwell in India and the French in Algeria. . . . is profit and the desire to acquire resources in countries where the inhabitants do not know their value or how to profit from them.

When they encounter savages they eliminate them or drive them from the land, as happened in America . . . and is happening now in Africa. . . . When they encounter a nation like ours, with a degree of civilization, with a past, and a religion . . . and customs and . . . institutions . . . they deal with its inhabitants kindly. But they do soon acquire its most valuable resources, because they have greater wealth and intellect and knowledge and force. . . . [The veil constitued] a huge barrier between woman and her elevation, and consequently a barrier between the nation and its advance.

*Why does the author believe that Western culture would be beneficial to Egyptian society? How might a critic of colonialism respond?*

HistoryNow™ To read Cromer's "Why Britain Acquired Egypt in 1882," enter the *HistoryNow* documents area using the access card that is available for *World History.*

consciousness probably increased during this period. Segregated clubs, schools, and churches were established as more European officials brought their wives and began to raise families in the colonies.

At the same time, the establishment of colonial rule often had the effect of reducing the rights and the status of women in Africa. African women had traditionally benefited from the prestige of matrilineal systems and were empowered by their traditional role as the primary agricultural producer in their community. Under colonialism, European settlers not only took the best land for themselves but also, in introducing new agricultural techniques, tended to deal exclusively with males, encouraging the latter to develop lucrative cash crops, while women were restricted to traditional farming methods. Whereas African men applied chemical fertilizer to the fields, women used manure. While men began to use bicycles, and eventually trucks, to transport goods, women still carried their goods on their heads, a practice that continues today.

# The Emergence of Anticolonialism

Thus far we have looked at the colonial experience primarily from the point of view of the colonial powers. Equally important is the way the subject peoples reacted to the experience. From the perspective of nearly half a century, it seems clear that their primary response was to turn to nationalism.

## Stirrings of Nationhood

As we have seen, nationalism refers to a state of mind rising out of an awareness of being part of a community that possesses common institutions, traditions, language, and customs (see the comparative essay "The Rise of Nationalism" in Chapter 19). Few nations in the world today meet such criteria. Most modern states contain a variety of ethnic, religious, and linguistic communities, each with its own sense of cultural and national identity. Should Canada, for example, which includes peoples of French, English, and Native American heritage, be considered a nation? Another question is how nationalism differs from other forms of tribal, religious, or linguistic affiliation. Should every group that resists assimilation into a larger cultural unity be called nationalist?

Such questions complicate the study of nationalism even in Europe and North America and make agreement on a definition elusive. They create even greater dilemmas in discussing Asia and Africa, where most societies are deeply divided by ethnic, linguistic, and religious differences and the very term *nationalism* is a foreign concept imported from the West (see the box on p. 595). Prior to the colonial era, most traditional societies in Africa and Asia were formed on the basis of religious beliefs, tribal loyalties, or devotion to hereditary monarchies. Although individuals in some countries may have identified themselves as members of a particular national group, others viewed themselves as subjects of a king, members of a tribe, or adherents to a particular religion.

The advent of European colonialism brought the consciousness of modern nationhood to many of the societies of Asia and Africa. The creation of European colonies with defined borders and a powerful central government led to the weakening of tribal and village ties and a significant reorientation in the individual's sense of political identity. The introduction of Western ideas of citizenship and representative government produced a new sense of participation in the affairs of government. At the same time, the appearance of a new elite class based not on hereditary privilege or religious sanction but on alleged racial or cultural superiority aroused a shared sense of resentment among the subject peoples, who felt a common commitment to the creation of an independent society. By the first quarter of the twentieth century, political movements dedicated to the overthrow of colonial rule had arisen throughout much of the non-Western world.

Modern nationalism, then, was a product of colonialism and, in a sense, a reaction to it. But a sense of nationhood does not emerge full-blown in a given society. The rise of modern nationalism is a process that begins among a few members of the educated elite (most commonly among articulate professionals such as lawyers, teachers, journalists, and doctors) and then spreads only gradually to the mass of the population. Even after national independence has been realized, as we shall see, it is often questionable whether a mature sense of nationhood has been created.

## Traditional Resistance: A Precursor to Nationalism

The beginnings of modern nationalism can be found in the initial resistance by the indigenous peoples to the colonial conquest. Although, strictly speaking, such resistance was not "nationalist" because it was essentially motivated by the desire to defend traditional institutions, it did reflect a primitive concept of nationhood in that it aimed at protecting the homeland from the invader; later patriotic groups have often hailed early resistance movements as the precursors of twentieth-century nationalist movements. Thus traditional resistance to colonial conquest may logically be viewed as the first stage in the development of modern nationalism.

Such resistance took various forms. For the most part, it was led by the existing ruling class. In the Ashanti kingdom in Africa and in Burma and Vietnam in Southeast Asia, resistance to Western domination was initially directed by the imperial courts. In some cases, traditionalists continued to oppose foreign conquest even after resistance had collapsed at the center. In India, Tipu Sultan resisted the British in the Deccan after the collapse of the Mughal dynasty. Similarly, after the decrepit monarchy in Vietnam had bowed to French pressure, a number of civilian and military officials set up an organization called Can Vuong (literally "save the king") and continued their resistance without imperial sanction (see the box on p. 595).

The first stirrings of nationalism in India took place in the early nineteenth century with the search for a renewed sense of cultural identity. In 1828, Ram Mohan Roy, a *brahmin* from Bengal, founded the Brahmo Samaj (Society of Brahma). Roy probably had no intention of promoting Indian national independence but created the new organization as a means of helping his fellow religionists defend the Hindu religion against verbal attacks by their British acquaintances. Roy was by no means a hidebound traditionalist. He opposed such practices as *sati* and recognized the benefit of introducing the best aspects of European culture into Indian society.

Sometimes traditional resistance to Western penetration went beyond elite circles. Most commonly, it appeared in the form of peasant revolts. Rural rebellions were not uncommon in traditional Asian societies as a means of expressing peasant discontent with high taxes, official corruption, rising rural debt, and famine in the countryside. Under colonialism, rural conditions often deteriorated as population density increased and peasants were driven off the land to make way for plantation agriculture. Angry peasants then vented their frustration at the foreign invaders. For example, in Burma, the Buddhist monk Saya San led a peasant uprising against the British many years after they had completed their takeover. Similar forms of unrest occurred in various parts of India, where *zamindars* and rural villagers alike resisted government attempts to increase tax revenues. Yet another peasant uprising took place in Algeria in 1840.

**The Sepoy Rebellion** Sometimes the resentment had a religious basis, as in the Sudan, where the revolt led by the Mahdi had strong Islamic overtones, although it was initially provoked by Turkish misrule in Egypt. More significant than Roy's Brahmo Samaj in its impact on British

Emile Duboc, 35 mois de campagne en Chine, au Tonkin (1882–885)

**The Pagoda of Torments.** In their zeal to carry out their civilizing mission, colonial officials in Asia often had little patience for the physical remnants of traditional culture in the territories under their authority. Here French officials in formal tropical attire inspect an ancient Confucian temple in the old capital city of Hanoi, Vietnam. Not long afterward, the building, like many others of the precolonial era, was demolished. Such arrogant acts aroused strong hostility among the local population.

policy was the famous Sepoy Rebellion of 1857 in India. The **sepoys** (derived from the Turkish *sipahi,* a cavalryman or soldier) were native troops hired by the East India Company to protect British interests in the region. Unrest within Indian units of the colonial army had been common since early in the century, when it had been sparked by economic issues, religious sensitivities, or nascent anticolonial sentiment. Such attitudes intensified in the mid-1850s when the British instituted a new policy of shipping Indian troops abroad—a practice that exposed Hindus to pollution by foreigners. In 1857, tension erupted when the British adopted the new Enfield rifle for use by sepoy infantrymen. The new weapon was a muzzle loader that used paper cartridges covered with animal fat and lard; because the cartridge had to be bitten off, it broke strictures against high-class Hindus' eating animal products and Muslim prohibitions against eating pork. Protests among sepoy units in northern India turned into a full-scale mutiny, supported by uprisings in rural districts in various parts of the country. But the revolt lacked clear goals, and rivalries between Hindus and Muslims and discord among the leaders within each community prevented coordination of operations. Although Indian troops often fought bravely and outnumbered the British six to one, they were poorly organized, and the British forces (supplemented in many cases by sepoy troops) suppressed the rebellion.

Still, the revolt frightened the British and led to a number of major reforms. The proportion of native troops relative to those from Great Britain was reduced, and precedence was given to ethnic groups likely to be loyal to the British, such as the Sikhs of Punjab and the Gurkhas, an upland people from Nepal in the Himalaya Mountains. To avoid religious conflicts, ethnic groups were spread throughout the service rather than assigned to special units. The British also decided to suppress the final remnants of the hapless Mughal dynasty, which had supported the mutiny, and turned responsibility for the administration of the subcontinent over to the crown.

## To Resist or Not to Resist

How to respond to the imposition of colonial rule was sometimes an excruciating problem for political elites in many Asian countries, since resistance often seemed futile while simply adding to the suffering of the indigenous population. Hoang Cao Khai and Phan Dinh Phung were members of the Confucian scholar-gentry from the same village in Vietnam. Yet they reacted in dramatically different ways to the French conquest of their country. Their exchange of letters, reproduced below, illustrates the dilemmas they faced.

*Explain briefly the reasons advanced by each writer to justify his actions. Which argument do you believe would earn more support from contemporaries? Why?*

### Hoang Cao Khai's Letter to Phan Dinh Phung

Soon, it will be seventeen years since we ventured upon different paths of life. How sweet was our friendship when we both lived in our village. . . . At the time when the capital was lost and after the royal carriage had departed, you courageously answered the appeals of the King by raising the banner of righteousness. It was certainly the only thing to do in those circumstances. No one will question that.

But now the situation has changed and even those without intelligence or education have concluded that nothing remains to be saved. How is it that you, a man of vast understanding, do not realize this? . . . You are determined to do whatever you deem righteous. . . . But though you have no thoughts for your own person or for your own fate, you should at least attend to the sufferings of the population of a whole region. . . .

Until now your actions have undoubtedly accorded with your loyalty. May I ask however what sin our people have committed to deserve so much hardship? I would understand your resistance, did you involve but your family for the benefit of a large number. As of now, hundreds of families are subject to grief; how do you have the heart to fight on? I venture to predict that, should you pursue your struggle, not only will the population of our village be destroyed but our entire country will be transformed into a sea of blood and a mountain of bones. It is my hope that men of your superior morality and honesty will pause a while to appraise the situation.

### Reply of Phan Dinh Phung to Hoang Cao Khai

In your letter, you revealed to me the causes of calamities and of happiness. You showed me clearly where advantages and disadvantages lie. All of which sufficed to indicate that your anxious concern was not only for my own security but also for the peace and order of our entire region. I understood plainly your sincere arguments.

I have concluded that if our country has survived these past thousand years when its territory was not large, its army not strong, its wealth not great, it was because the relationships between king and subjects, fathers and children, have always been regulated by the five moral obligations. In the past, the Han, the Sung, the Yuan, the Ming time and again dreamt of annexing our country and of dividing it up into prefectures and districts within the Chinese administrative system. But never were they able to realize their dream. Ah! if even China, which shares a common border with our territory, and is a thousand times more powerful than Vietnam, could not rely upon her strength to swallow us, it was surely because the destiny of our country had been willed by Heaven itself.

The French, separated from our country until the present day by I do not know how many thousand miles, have crossed the oceans to come to our country. Wherever they came, they acted like a storm, so much so that the Emperor had to flee. The whole country was cast into disorder. Our rivers and our mountains have been annexed by them at a stroke and turned into a foreign territory.

Moreover, if our region has suffered to such an extent, it was not only from the misfortunes of war. You must realize that wherever the French go, there flock around them groups of petty men who offer plans and tricks to gain the enemy's confidence. . . . They use every expedient to squeeze the people out of their possessions. That is how hundreds of misdeeds, thousands of offenses have been perpetrated. How can the French not be aware of all the suffering that the rural population has had to endure? Under these circumstances, is it surprising that families should be disrupted and the people scattered?

My friend, if you are troubled about our people, then I advise you to place yourself in my position and to think about the circumstances in which I live. You will understand naturally and see clearly that I do not need to add anything else.

Like the Sepoy Rebellion, traditional resistance movements usually met with little success. Peasants armed with pikes and spears were no match for Western armies possessing the most terrifying weapons then known to human society. In a few cases, such as the revolt of the Mahdi at Khartoum, the natives were able to defeat the invaders temporarily. But such successes were rare, and the late nineteenth century witnessed the seemingly inexorable march of the Western powers, armed with the Gatling gun (the first rapid-fire weapon and the precursor of the modern machine gun), to mastery of the globe.

## COMPARATIVE ESSAY

# IMPERIALISM: THE BALANCE SHEET

Few periods of history are as controversial among scholars and casual observers as the era of imperialism. To defenders of the colonial enterprise like the poet Rudyard Kipling, imperialism was the "white man's burden," a disagreeable but necessary phase in the evolution of human society, lifting up the toiling races from tradition to modernity and bringing an end to poverty, famine, and disease (see the box on p. 579).

Critics took exception to such views, portraying imperialism as a tragedy of major proportions. The insatiable drive of the advanced economic powers for access to raw materials and markets created an exploitative environment that transformed the vast majority of colonial peoples into a permanent underclass, while restricting the benefits of modern technology to a privileged few. Kipling's "white man's burden" was dismissed as a hypocritical gesture to hoodwink the naive and salve the guilty feelings of those who recognized imperialism for what it was—a savage act of rape.

Defenders of the colonial experiment sometimes concede that there were gross inequities in the colonial system but point out that there was a positive side to the experience as well. The expansion of markets and the beginnings of a modern transportation and communications network, while bringing few immediate benefits to the colonial peoples, laid the groundwork for future economic growth. At the same time, the introduction of new ways of looking at human freedom, the relationship between the individual and society, and democratic principles set the stage for the adoption of such ideas after the restoration of independence following World War II. Finally, the colonial experience offered a new approach to the traditional relationship between men and women. Although colonial rule was by no means uniformly beneficial to the position of women in African and Asian societies, growing awareness of the struggle by women in the West to seek equality offered their counterparts in the colonial territories a weapon to fight against the long-standing barriers of custom and legal discrimination.

How, then, are we to draw up a final balance sheet on the era of Western imperialism? Although both sides have good points to make, perhaps the critics have the best of the argument. While sometimes the colonial authorities did provide the beginnings of an infrastructure that could eventually serve as the foundation of an advanced industrial society, all too often they sought to prevent the rise of industrial and commercial sectors in their colonies that might provide competition to producers in the home country. Sophisticated, age-old societies that could have been left to respond to the technological revolution in their own way were thus squeezed dry of precious national resources under the false guise of a "civilizing mission." As the sociologist Clifford Geertz remarked in his book *Agricultural Involution: The Processes of Ecological Change in Indonesia,* the tragedy is not that the colonial peoples suffered through the colonial era but that they suffered for nothing.

## CONCLUSION

**BY THE FIRST QUARTER** of the twentieth century, virtually all of Africa and a good part of South and Southeast Asia were under some form of colonial rule. With the advent of the age of imperialism, a global economy was finally established, and the domination of Western civilization over those of Africa and Asia appeared to be complete.

Defenders of colonialism argue that the system was a necessary if painful stage in the evolution of human societies. Critics, however, charge that the Western colonial powers were driven by an insatiable lust for profits (see the comparative essay "Imperialism: The Balance Sheet" above). They dismiss the Western civilizing mission as a fig leaf to cover naked greed and reject the notion that imperialism played a salutary role in hastening the adjustment of traditional societies to the demands of industrial civilization. In the blunt words of two Western critics of imperialism: "Why is Africa (or for that matter Latin America and much of Asia) so poor? . . . The answer is very brief: we have made it poor."[11]

Between these two irreconcilable views, where does the truth lie? This chapter has contended that neither extreme position is justified. In fact, the consequences of colonialism have been more complex than either its defenders or its critics would have us believe. While the colonial peoples received little immediate benefit from the imposition of foreign rule, overall the imperialist era brought about a vast expansion of the international trade network and created at least the potential for societies throughout Africa and Asia to play an active and rewarding role in the new global economic arena. If, as the historian William McNeill believes, the introduction of new technology through cross-cultural encounters is the driving force of change in world history, then Western imperialism, whatever its faults, served a useful purpose in opening the door to such change, much as the rise of the Arab empire and the Mongol invasions hastened the process of global economic development in an earlier time.

Still, the critics have a point. Although colonialism did introduce the peoples of Asia and Africa to new technology and the expanding economic marketplace, it was unnecessarily brutal in its application and all too often failed to realize the exalted claims and objectives of its promoters. Existing economic networks—often potentially valuable as a foundation for later economic development—were ruthlessly swept aside in the interests of providing markets for Western manufactured goods. Potential sources of native industrialization were nipped in the bud to avoid competition for factories in Amsterdam, London, Pittsburgh, or Manchester. Training in Western democratic ideals and practices was ignored out of fear that the recipients might use them as weapons against the ruling authorities.

The fundamental weakness of colonialism, then, was that it was ultimately based on the self-interests of the citizens of the colonial powers. Where those interests collided with the needs of the colonial peoples, those of the former always triumphed. However sincerely the David Livingstones, Albert Sarrauts, and William McKinleys of the world were convinced of the rightness of their civilizing mission, the ultimate result was to deprive the colonial peoples of the right to make their own choices about their own destiny.

In one area of Asia, the spreading tide of imperialism did not result in the establishment of formal Western colonial control. In East Asia, the traditional societies of China and Japan were buffeted by the winds of Western expansionism during the nineteenth century but successfully resisted foreign conquest. In the next chapter, we will see how they managed to retain their independence while attempting to cope with the demands of a changing world.

## TIMELINE

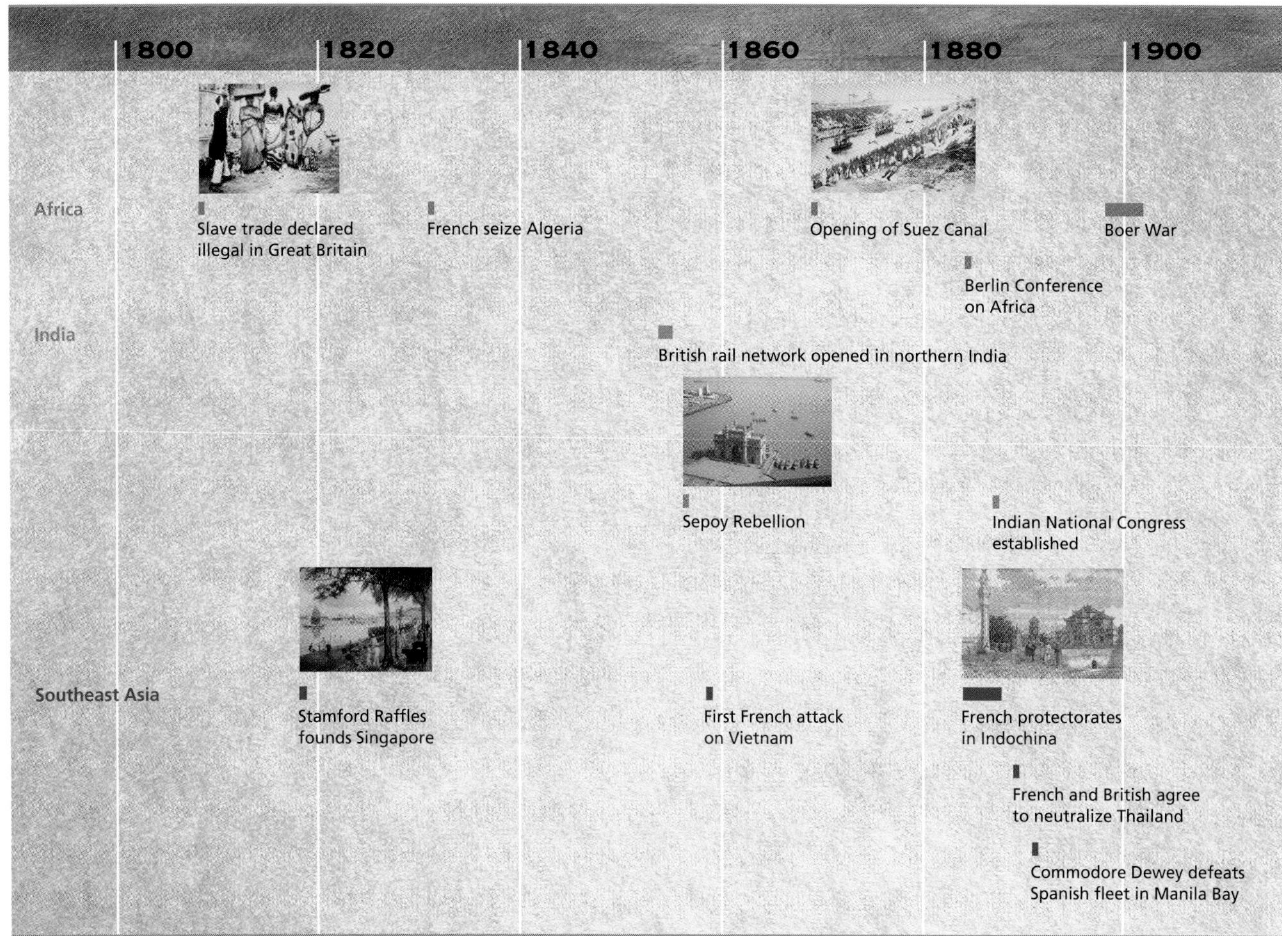

## CHAPTER NOTES

1. Quoted in J. G. Lockhart and C. M. Wodehouse, *Rhodes* (1963), pp. 69–70.
2. K. Pearson, *National Life from the Standpoint of Science* (London, 1905), p. 184.
3. Quoted in H. Braunschwig, *French Colonialism, 1871–1914* (London, 1961), p. 80.
4. Quoted in R. Bartlett, ed., *The Record of American Diplomacy: Documents and Readings in the History of American Foreign Relations* (New York, 1952), p. 385.
5. Quoted in J. Iliffe, *Africans: The History of a Continent* (Cambridge, 1995), p. 124.
6. Quoted in T. Pakenham, *The Scramble for Africa* (New York, 1991), p. 13.
7. Quoted in G. Garros, *Forceries Humaines* (Paris, 1926), p. 21.
8. Cited in B. Schwartz's review of D. Cannadine's *Ornamentalism: How the British Saw Their Empire, Atlantic,* November 2001, p. 135.
9. Quoted in L. Roubaud, *Vietnam: La Tragédie Indochinoise* (Paris, 1926), p. 80.
10. Quoted in Pakenham, *Scramble for Africa,* p. 182, citing a letter to Queen Victoria dated August 7, 1879.
11. Quoted in P. C. W. Gutkind and I. Wallerstein, eds., *The Political Economy of Contemporary Africa* (Beverly Hills, Calif., 1976), p. 14.

## SUGGESTED READING

There are a number of good works on the subject of imperialism and colonialism. For a study that directly focuses on the question of whether colonialism was beneficial to subject peoples, see **D. K. Fieldhouse, *The West and the Third World: Trade, Colonialism, Dependence, and Development*** (Oxford, 1999). Also see **W. Baumgart, *Imperialism: The Idea and Reality of British and French Colonial Expansion, 1880–1914*** (Oxford, 1982), and **D. B. Abernathy, *Global Dominance: European Overseas Empires, 1415–1980*** (New Haven, Conn., 2000). On technology, see **D. R. Headrick, *The Tentacles of Progress: Technology Transfer in the Age of Imperialism, 1850–1940*** (Oxford, 1988). For a defense of the British imperial mission, see **N. Ferguson, *Empire: The Rise and Demise of the British World Order*** (New York, 2003).

On the imperialist age in Africa, above all see **R. Robinson** and **J. Gallagher, *Africa and the Victorians: The Official Mind of Imperialism*** (London, 1961). Also see **B. Vandervoort, *Wars of Imperial Conquest in Africa, 1830–1914*** (Bloomington, Ind., 1998), and two works by **T. Pakenham, *The Scramble for Africa*** (New York, 1991) and ***The Boer War*** (London, 1979). On southern Africa, see **J. Guy, *The Destruction of the Zulu Kingdom*** (London, 1979), and **D. Nenoon** and **B. Nyeko, *Southern Africa Since 1800*** (London, 1984). Also informative is **R. O. Collins,** ed., ***Historical Problems of Imperial Africa*** (Princeton, N.J., 1994).

For an overview of the British takeover and administration of India, see **S. Wolpert, *A New History of India*** (New York, 1989). **C. A. Bayly, *Indian Society and the Making of the British Empire*** (Cambridge, 1988), is a scholarly analysis of the impact of British conquest on the Indian economy. Also see **A. Wild's** elegant ***East India Company: Trade and Conquest from 1600*** (New York, 2000). For a comparative approach, see **R. Murphey, *The Outsiders: The Western Experience in China and India*** (Ann Arbor, Mich., 1977). In a provocative work, ***Ornamentalism: How the British Saw Their Empire*** (Oxford, 2000), **D. Cannadine** argues that it was class and not race that motivated British policy in the subcontinent.

General studies of the colonial period in Southeast Asia are rare because most authors focus on specific areas. For some stimulating essays on a variety of aspects of the topic, see ***Continuity and Change in Southeast Asia: Collected Journal Articles of Harry J. Benda*** (New Haven, Conn., 1972). For an overview by several authors, see **N. Tarling,** ed., ***The Cambridge History of Southeast Asia,*** vol. 3 (Cambridge, 1992).

For an introduction to the effects of colonialism on women in Africa and Asia, see **S. Hughes** and **B. Hughes, *Women in World History,*** vol. 2 (Armonk, N.Y., 1997). Also consult the classic by **E. Boserup, *Women's Role in Economic Development*** (London, 1970); **J. Taylor, *The Social World of Batavia*** (Madison, Wis., 1983); and **L. Ahmed, *Women and Gender in Islam*** (New Haven, Conn., 1992).

## HistoryNow™

**Enter *HistoryNow* using the access card that is available with this text. *HistoryNow* will assist you in understanding the content in this chapter with lesson plans generated for your needs, as well as provide you with a connection to the *Wadsworth World History Resource Center* (see description below for details).**

### WORLD HISTORY RESOURCE CENTER

**Enter the Resource Center using either your *HistoryNow* access card or your standalone access card for the *Wadsworth World History Resource Center.* Organized by topic, this website includes quizzes; images; over 350 primary source documents; interactive simulations; maps and timelines; movie explorations; and a wealth of other resources. You can read the following documents, and many more, at http://history.wadsworth.com/rc/world**

J. A. Hobson, *Imperialism: A Study*

Henry Morton Stanley, *How I Found Livingstone*

Visit the *World History* Companion Website for chapter quizzes and more.

http://history.wadsworth.com/duikerspielvogel05/

CHAPTER

# 21

# SHADOWS OVER THE PACIFIC: EAST ASIA UNDER CHALLENGE

National Maritime Museum, London

*The Opium War begins*

## CHAPTER OUTLINE AND FOCUS QUESTIONS

### The Decline of the Manchus

- Why did the Qing dynasty decline and ultimately collapse, and what role did the Western powers play in this process?

### Chinese Society in Transition

- What political, economic, and social reforms were instituted by the Qing dynasty during its final decades, and why were they not more successful in reversing the decline of Manchu rule?

### A Rich Country and a Strong State: The Rise of Modern Japan

- To what degree was the Meiji Restoration a "revolution," and to what degree did it succeed in transforming Japan?

### CRITICAL THINKING

- How did China and Japan each respond to Western pressures in the nineteenth century, and what implication did their different responses have for each nation's history?

THE BRITISH EMISSARY Lord Macartney had arrived in Beijing in 1793 with a caravan loaded with six hundred cases of gifts for the emperor. Flags and banners provided by the Chinese proclaimed in Chinese characters that the visitor was an "ambassador bearing tribute from the country of England." But the tribute was in vain, for Macartney's request for an increase in trade between the two countries was flatly rejected, and he left Beijing in October with nothing to show for his efforts. Not until half a century later would the Qing dynasty–at the point of a gun–agree to the British demand for an expansion of commercial ties.

In fact, the Chinese emperor Qianlong had responded to the requests of his visitor with polite but poorly disguised condescension. To Macartney's proposal that a British ambassador be stationed in the capital of Beijing, the emperor replied that such a request was "not in harmony with the state system of our dynasty and will definitely not be permitted". As for the British envoy's suggestion that regular trade relations be established between the two countries, that proposal was also rejected. We receive all sorts of precious things, replied the Celestial Emperor, as gifts from the myriad nations. "Consequently," he added, "there is nothing we lack, as your principal envoy and others have themselves observed. We have never set much store on strange or ingenious objects, nor do we need more of your country's manufactures."

Historians have often viewed the failure of the Macartney mission as a reflection of the disdain of Chinese rulers toward their counterparts in other countries and their serene confidence in the superiority of Chinese civilization in a world inhabited by barbarians. If that was the case, Qianlong's confidence was misplaced, for as the eighteenth century came to an end, the country faced a growing challenge from the escalating power and ambitions of the West. When insistent British demands for the right to carry out trade and missionary activities in China were rejected, Britain resorted to force and in the Opium War, which broke out in 1839, gave Manchu troops a sound thrashing. A humiliated China was finally forced to open its doors. ◇

## The Decline of the Manchus

In 1800, the Qing (Ch'ing) or Manchu dynasty was at the height of its power. China had experienced a long period of peace and prosperity under the rule of two great emperors, Kangxi and Qianlong. Its borders were secure, and its culture and intellectual achievements were the envy of the world. Its rulers, hidden behind the walls of the Forbidden City in Beijing, had every reason to describe their patrimony as the "Central Kingdom." But a little over a century later, humiliated and harassed by the black ships and big guns of the Western powers, the Qing dynasty, the last in a series that had endured for more than two thousand years, collapsed in the dust (see Map 21.1).

Historians once assumed that the primary reason for the rapid decline and fall of the Manchu dynasty was the intense pressure applied to a proud but somewhat complacent traditional society by the modern West. Now, however, most historians believe that internal changes played a major role in the dynasty's collapse and point out that at least some of the problems suffered by the Manchus during the nineteenth century were self-inflicted.

Both explanations have some validity. Like so many of its predecessors, after an extended period of growth, the Qing dynasty began to suffer from the familiar dynastic ills of official corruption, peasant unrest, and incompetence at court. Such weaknesses were probably exacerbated by the rapid growth in population. The long era of peace and stability, the introduction of new crops from the Americas, and the cultivation of new, fast-ripening strains of rice enabled the Chinese population to double between 1550 and 1800. The population continued to grow, reaching the unprecedented level of 400 million by the end of the nineteenth century. Even without the irritating presence of the Western powers, the Manchus were probably destined to repeat the fate of their imperial predecessors. The ships, guns, and ideas of the foreigners simply highlighted the growing weakness of the Manchu dynasty and likely hastened its demise. In doing so, Western imperialism still exerted an indelible impact on the history of modern China—but as a contributing, not a causal, factor.

### Opium and Rebellion

By 1800, Westerners had been in contact with China for more than two hundred years, but after an initial period of flourishing relations, Western traders had been limited to a small commercial outlet at Canton. This arrangement was not acceptable to the British, however. Not only did they chafe at being restricted to a tiny enclave, but the growing British appetite for Chinese tea created a severe balance-of-payments problem. After the failure of the Macartney mission in 1793, another mission, led by Lord Amherst, arrived in China in 1816. But it too achieved little except to worsen the already strained relations between the two countries. The British solution was opium. A product more addictive than tea, opium was grown in northeastern India and then shipped to China. Opium had been grown in southwestern China for several hundred years but had been used primarily for medicinal purposes. Now, as imports increased, popular demand for the product in southern China became insatiable despite an official prohibition on its use. Soon bullion was flowing out of the Chinese imperial treasury into the pockets of British merchants.

The Chinese became concerned and tried to negotiate. In 1839, Lin Zexu (Lin Tse-hsu; 1785–1850), a Chinese official appointed by the court to curtail the opium trade, appealed to Queen Victoria on both moral and practical grounds and threatened to prohibit the sale of rhubarb (widely used as a laxative in nineteenth-century Europe) to Great Britain if she did not respond (see the box on p. 602). But moral principles, then as now, paled before the lure of commercial profits, and the British continued to promote the opium trade, arguing that if the Chinese did not want the opium, they did not have to buy it. Lin Zexu attacked on three fronts, imposing penalties on smokers, arresting dealers, and seizing supplies from importers as they attempted to smuggle the drug into China. The last tactic caused his downfall. When he blockaded the foreign factory area in Canton to force traders to hand over their remaining chests of opium, the British government, claiming that it could not permit British subjects "to be exposed to insult and injustice," launched a naval expedition to punish the Manchus and force the court to open China to foreign trade.[1]

**The Opium War** The Opium War (1839–1842) lasted three years and demonstrated the superiority of British firepower and military tactics (including the use of a shallow-draft steamboat that effectively harassed Chinese coastal defenses). British warships destroyed Chinese coastal and

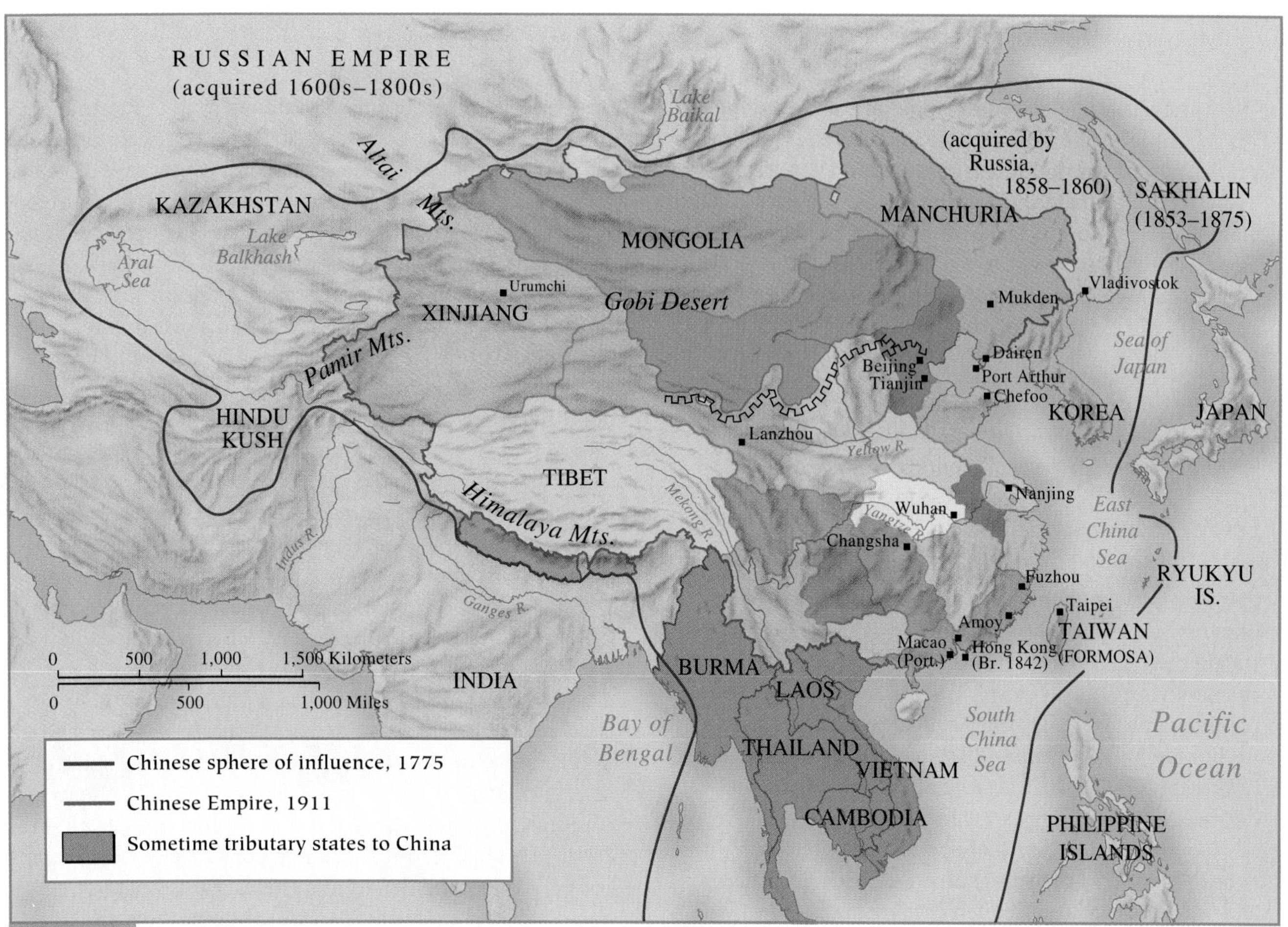


MAP 21.1 **The Qing Empire.** Shown here is the Qing Empire at its height of power in the late eighteenth century, together with its shrunken boundaries at the moment of dissolution in 1911.
? Where are China's tributary states on the map? **View an animated version of this map or related maps at** http://history.wadsworth.com/duikerspielvogel05/

river forts and seized the offshore island of Chusan, not far from the mouth of the Yangtze River. When a British fleet sailed virtually unopposed up the Yangtze to Nanjing and cut off the supply of "tribute grain" from southern to northern China, the Qing finally agreed to British terms. In the Treaty of Nanjing in 1842, the Chinese agreed to open five coastal ports to British trade, limit tariffs on imported British goods, grant extraterritorial rights to British citizens in China, and pay a substantial indemnity to cover the costs of the war. China also agreed to cede the island of Hong Kong (dismissed by a senior British official as a "barren rock") to Great Britain. Nothing was said in the treaty about the opium trade, which continued unabated until it was brought under control through Chinese government efforts in the early twentieth century.

Although the Opium War has traditionally been considered the beginning of modern Chinese history, it is unlikely that many Chinese at the time would have seen it that way. This was not the first time that a ruling dynasty had been forced to make concessions to foreigners, and the opening of five coastal ports to the British hardly constituted a serious threat to the security of the empire. Although a few concerned Chinese argued that the court should learn more about European civilization, others contended that China had nothing to learn from the barbarians and that borrowing foreign ways would undercut the purity of Confucian civilization.

For the time being, the Manchus attempted to deal with the problem in the traditional way of playing the foreigners off against each other. Concessions granted to the British were offered to other Western nations, including the United States, and soon thriving foreign concession areas were operating in treaty ports along the southern Chinese coast from Canton to Shanghai.

**The Taiping Rebellion** In the meantime, the Qing court's failure to deal with pressing internal economic problems led to a major peasant revolt that shook the foundations of the empire. On the surface, the Taiping (T'ai p'ing) Rebellion owed something to the Western incursion; the leader of the uprising, Hong Xiuquan (Hung Hsiu-ch'uan), a failed examination candidate, was a Christian convert who viewed

## A Letter of Advice to the Queen

Lin Zexu was the Chinese imperial commissioner in Canton at the time of the Opium War. Prior to the conflict, he attempted to use reason and the threat of retaliation to persuade the British to cease importing opium illegally into southern China. The following excerpt is from a letter that he wrote to Queen Victoria. In it, he appeals to her conscience while showing the condescension that the Chinese traditionally displayed to the rulers of other countries.

*How does the imperial commissioner seek to persuade Queen Victoria to prohibit the sale of opium in China? To what degree are his arguments persuasive?*

### Lin Zexu, Letter to Queen Victoria

The kings of your honorable country by a tradition handed down from generation to generation have always been noted for their politeness and submissiveness. . . . Privately we are delighted with the way in which the honorable rulers of your country deeply understand the grand principles and are grateful for the Celestial grace. . . . The profit from trade has been enjoyed by them continuously for two hundred years. This is the source from which your country has become known for its wealth.

But after a long period of commercial intercourse, there appear among the crowd of barbarians both good persons and bad, unevenly. Consequently there are those who smuggle opium to seduce the Chinese people and so cause the spread of the poison to all provinces. . . .

The wealth of China is used to profit the barbarians. That is to say, the great profit made by barbarians is all taken from the rightful share of China. By what right do they then in return use the poisonous drug to injure the Chinese people? . . . Let us ask, where is your conscience? I have heard that the smoking of opium is very strictly forbidden by your country; that is because the harm caused by opium is clearly understood. Since it is not permitted to do harm to your own country, then even less should you let it be passed on to the harm of other countries–how much less to China! Of all that China exports to foreign countries, there is not a single thing which is not beneficial to people. . . . Is there a single article from China which has done any harm to foreign countries? Take tea and rhubarb, for example; the foreign countries cannot get along for a single day without them. . . . On the other hand, articles coming from the outside to China can only be used as toys. We can take them or get along without them. Nevertheless our Celestial Court lets tea, silk, and other goods be shipped without limit and circulated everywhere without begrudging it in the slightest. This is for no other reason but to share the benefit with the people of the whole world. . . .

May you, O King, check your wicked and sift your vicious people before they come to China, in order to guarantee the peace of your nation, to show further the sincerity of your politeness and submissiveness, and to let the two countries enjoy together the blessings of peace. . . . After receiving this dispatch will you immediately give us a prompt reply regarding the details and circumstances of your cutting off the opium traffic. Be sure not to put this off.

**History Now**™ To read a full version of this document, enter the *HistoryNow* documents area using the access card that is available for *World History.*

himself as a younger brother of Jesus and hoped to establish what he referred to as a "Heavenly Kingdom of Supreme Peace" in China. But there were many local causes as well. The rapid increase in population forced millions of peasants to eke out a living as sharecroppers or landless laborers. Official corruption and incompetence led to the whipsaw of increased taxes and a decline in government services; even the Grand Canal was allowed to silt up, hindering the shipment of grain. In 1853, the rebels seized the old Ming capital of Nanjing, but that proved to be the rebellion's high-water mark. Plagued by factionalism, the rebellion gradually lost momentum until it was finally suppressed in 1864.

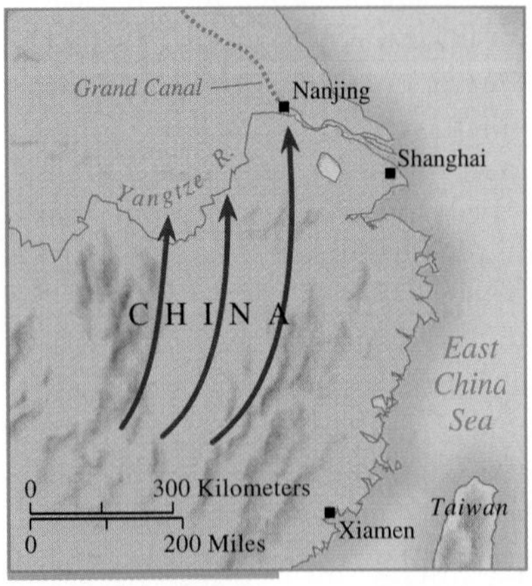

**The Taiping Rebellion**

One reason for the dynasty's failure to deal effectively with the internal unrest was its continuing difficulties with the Western imperialists. In 1856, the British and the French, still smarting from trade restrictions and limitations on their missionary activities, launched a new series of attacks against China and seized Beijing in 1860. As punishment, British troops destroyed the imperial summer palace just outside the city. In the ensuing Treaty of Tianjin (Tientsin), the Qing agreed to humiliating new concessions: the legalization of the opium trade, the opening of additional ports to foreign trade, and the cession of the peninsula of Kowloon (opposite the island of Hong Kong) to the British (see Map 21.2). Additional territories in the north were ceded to Russia.

**The Opium War.** The Opium War, waged between China and Great Britain between 1839 and 1842, was China's first conflict with a European power. Lacking modern military technology, the Chinese suffered a humiliating defeat. In this painting, heavily armed British steamships destroy unwieldy Chinese junks along the Chinese coast. China's humiliation at sea was a legacy of its rulers' lack of interest in maritime matters since the middle of the fifteenth century, when Chinese junks were among the most advanced sailing ships in the world.

National Maritime Museum, London

## Efforts at Reform

By the late 1870s, the old dynasty was well on the road to internal disintegration. In fending off the Taiping Rebellion, the Manchus had been compelled to rely for support on armed forces under regional command. After quelling the revolt, many of these regional commanders refused to disband their units and, with the support of the local gentry, continued to collect local taxes for their own use. The dreaded pattern of imperial breakdown, so familiar in Chinese history, was beginning to appear once again.

In its weakened state, the court finally began to listen to the appeals of reform-minded officials, who called for a new policy of what they called **self-strengthening,** in which Western technology would be adopted while Confucian principles and institutions were maintained intact. This policy, popularly known by its slogan "East for Essence, West for Practical Use," remained the guiding standard for Chinese foreign and domestic policy for nearly a quarter of a century. Some even called for reforms in education and in China's hallowed political institutions (see the box on p. 604). Pointing to the power and prosperity of Great Britain, the journalist Wang Tao (Wang T'ao; 1828–1897) remarked, "The real strength of England . . . lies in the fact that there is a sympathetic understanding between the governing and the governed, a close relationship between the ruler and the people. . . . My observation is that the daily domestic political life of England actually embodies the traditional ideals of our ancient Golden Age."[2] Such democratic ideas were too radical for most

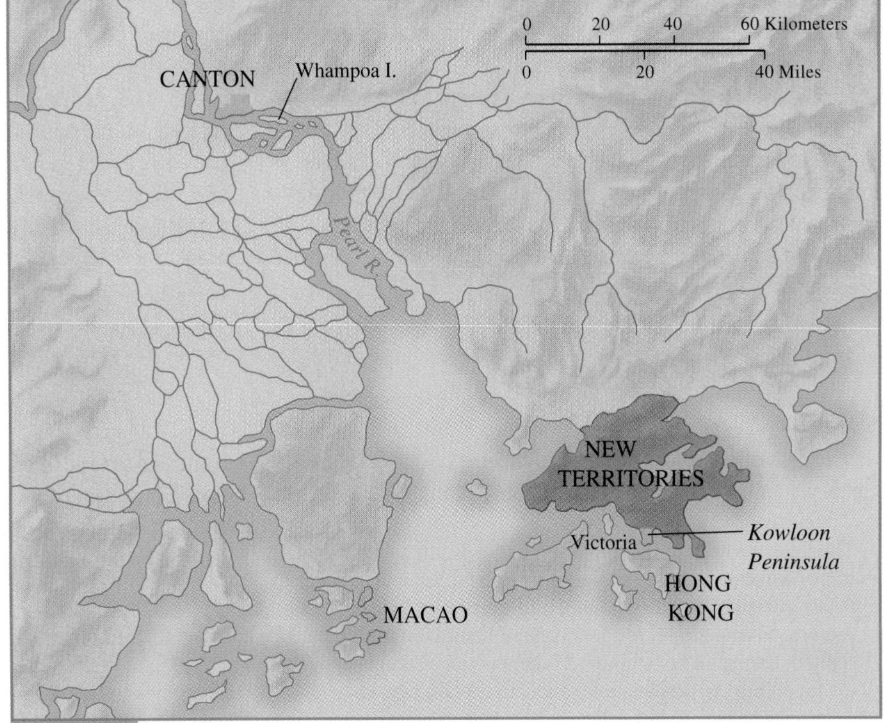


**MAP 21.2 Canton and Hong Kong.** This map shows the estuary of the Pearl River in southern China, an important area of early contact between China and Europe. ? What was the importance of Canton? **View an animated version of this map or related maps at http://history.wadsworth.com/duikerspielvogel05/**

## An Appeal for Change in China

After the humiliating defeat at the hands of the British in the Opium War, a few Chinese intellectuals began to argue that China must change its ways in order to survive. Among such reformist thinkers was the journalist and author Wang Tao. After a trip to Europe in the late 1860s, Wang returned to China convinced of the technological superiority of the West and the need for his country to adopt reforms to enable it to compete effectively in a changing world. He had only limited success in persuading his contemporaries of the need for dramatic change. Many Chinese were undoubtedly reluctant to believe his claim that China was not the Middle Kingdom or "all under Heaven" but only one nation among many in a rapidly changing world.

*What kinds of arguments did the author of this document use to persuade the reader to accept his point of view? Do you agree that Confucius would have found Wang Tao's arguments persuasive?*

### Wang Tao on Reform

I know that within a hundred years China will adopt all Western methods and excel in them. For though both are vessels, a sailboat differs in speed from a steamship; though both are vehicles, a horse-drawn carriage cannot cover the same distance as a locomotive train. Among weapons, the power of the bow and arrow, sword and spear, cannot be compared with that of firearms; and of firearms, the old types do not have the same effect as the new. Although it be the same piece of work, there is a difference in the ease with which it can be done by machine and by human labor. When new methods do not exist, people will not think of changes; but when there are new instruments, to copy them is certainly possible. Even if the Westerners should give no guidance, the Chinese must surely exert themselves to the utmost of their ingenuity and resources on these things.

Alas! People all understand the past, but they are ignorant of the future. Only scholars whose thoughts run deep and far can grasp the trends. As the mind of Heaven changes above, so do human affairs below. Heaven opens the minds of the Westerners and bestows upon them intelligence and wisdom. Their techniques and skills develop without bound. They sail eastward and gather in China. This constitutes an unprecedented situation in history, and a tremendous change in the world. The foreign nations come from afar with their superior techniques, contemptuous of us in our deficiencies. They show off their prowess and indulge in insults and oppression; they also fight among themselves. Under these circumstances, how can we not think of making changes? . . .

If China does not make any change at this time, how can she be on a par with the great nations of Europe, and compare with them in power and strength? Nevertheless, the path of reform is beset with difficulties. What the Western countries have today are regarded as of no worth by those who arrogantly refuse to pay attention. Their argument is that we should use our own laws to govern the empire, for that is the Way of our sages. They do not know that the Way of the sages is valued only because it can make proper accommodations according to the times. If Confucius lived today, we may be certain that he would not cling to antiquity and oppose making changes. . . .

But how is this to be done? First, the method of recruiting civil servants should be changed. The examination essays, coming down to the present, have gone from bad to worse and should be discarded. And yet we are still using them to select civil servants.

Second, the method of training soldiers should be changed. Now our army units and naval forces have only names registered on books, but no actual persons enrolled. The authorities consider our troops unreliable and so they recuit militia who, however, can be assembled but cannot be disbanded. . . . The arms of the Manchu banners and the ships of the naval forces should all be changed. . . . If they continue to hold on to their old ways and make no plans for change, it may be called "using untrained people to fight," which is no different from driving them to their deaths.

reformers, however. One of the leading court officials of the day, Zhang Zhidong (Chang Chih-tung), countered:

> The doctrine of people's rights will bring us not a single benefit but a hundred evils. Are we going to establish a parliament? . . . Even supposing the confused and clamorous people are assembled in one house, for every one of them who is clear-sighted, there will be a hundred others whose vision is beclouded; they will converse at random and talk as if in a dream—what use will it be?[3]

For the time being, Zhang Zhidong's arguments won the day. During the last quarter of the century, the Manchus attempted to modernize their military establishment and build up an industrial base without disturbing the essential elements of traditional Chinese civilization. Railroads, weapons arsenals, and shipyards were built, but the value system remained essentially unchanged.

## The Climax of Imperialism

In the end, the results spoke for themselves. During the last two decades of the nineteenth century, the European penetration of China, both political and military, intensified. Rapacious imperialists began to bite off the outer edges of the Qing Empire. The Gobi Desert north of the Great Wall, Central Asia, and Tibet, all inhabited by non-Chinese peo-

Courtesy of Claire L. Duiker

**The Potala Palace in Tibet.** Tibet was among the most distant appendages of the Qing dynasty. Once a powerful kingdom on the western edge of imperial China, Tibet was peopled by an ethnic group who practiced a distinct form of Buddhism. When Manchu power declined at the end of the nineteenth century, the Tibetans sought to restore their independence. The leading religious figure in Tibetan Buddhism was the Dalai Lama, who lived in this building, constructed in the seventeenth century in the capital of Lhasa.

ples and never fully assimilated into the Chinese Empire, were gradually lost. In the north and northwest, the main beneficiary was Russia, which took advantage of the dynasty's weakness to force the cession of territories north of the Amur River in Siberia. In Tibet, competition between Russia and Great Britain prevented either power from seizing the territory outright but at the same time enabled Tibetan authorities to revive local autonomy never recognized by the Chinese. In the south, British and French advances in mainland Southeast Asia removed Burma and Vietnam from their traditional vassal relationship to the Manchu court. Even more ominous were the foreign spheres of influence in the Chinese heartland, where local commanders were willing to sell exclusive commercial, railroad-building, or mining privileges.

The breakup of the Manchu dynasty accelerated at the end of the nineteenth century. In 1894, the Qing went to war with Japan over Japanese incursions into the Korean peninsula, which threatened China's long-held suzerainty over the area (see "Joining the Imperialist Club" later in this chapter). To the surprise of many observers, the Chinese were roundly defeated, confirming to some critics the devastating failure of the policy of self-strengthening by halfway measures. The disintegration of China accelerated in 1897, when Germany, a new entry in the race for spoils in East Asia, used the pretext of the murder of two German missionaries by Chinese rioters to demand the cession of territories in the Shandong (Shantung) peninsula. The approval of the demand by the imperial court set off a scramble for territory by other interested powers (see Map 21.3). Russia now

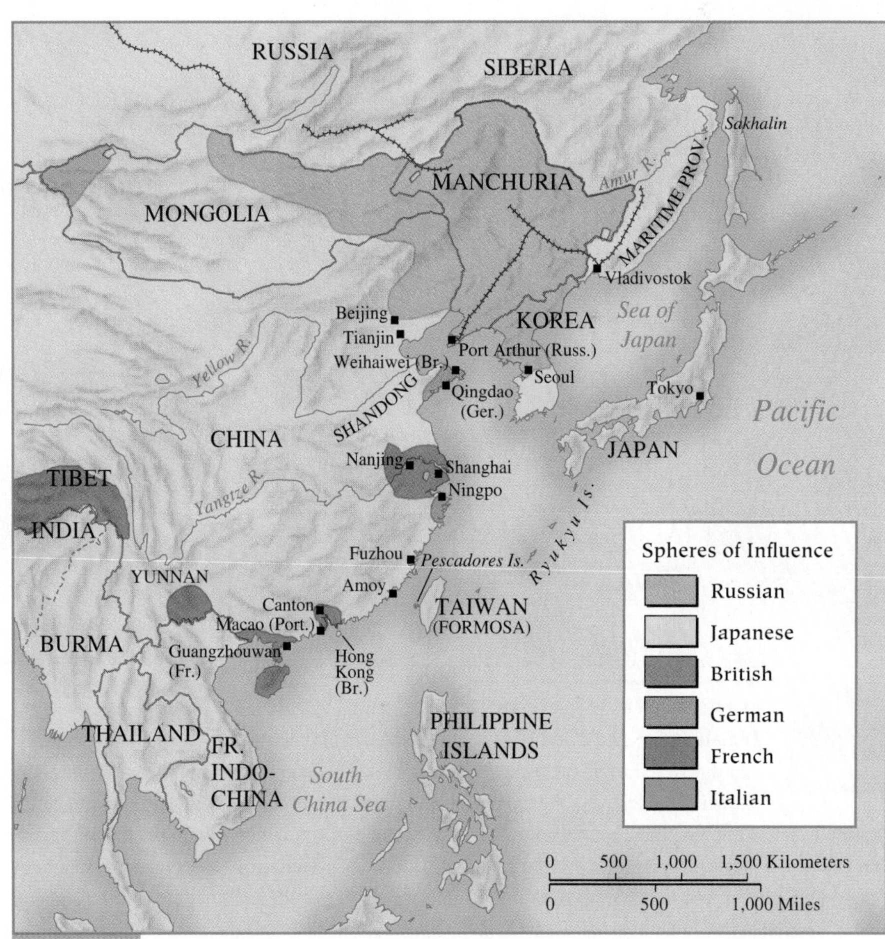


**MAP 21.3 Foreign Possessions and Spheres of Influence About 1900.** At the end of the nineteenth century, China was being carved up like a melon by foreign imperialist powers. ? Which of the areas marked on the map were removed from Chinese control during the nineteenth century? **View an animated version of this map or related maps at http://history.wadsworth.com/ duikerspielvogel05/**

demanded the Liaodong peninsula with its ice-free port at Port Arthur, and Great Britain weighed in with a request for a coaling station in northern China and obtained a 100-year lease on the so-called New Territories on the mainland adjacent to Hong Kong island.

The government responded to the challenge with yet another effort at reform. In the spring of 1898, an outspoken advocate of change, the progressive Confucian scholar Kang Youwei (K'ang Yu-wei), won the support of the young Guangxu (Kuang Hsu) emperor for a comprehensive reform program patterned after recent measures in Japan. Without change, Kang argued, China would perish. During the next several weeks, the emperor issued edicts calling for major political, administrative, and educational reforms. Not surprisingly, Kang's proposals were opposed by many conservatives, who saw little advantage and much risk in copying the West. More important, the new program was opposed by the emperor's aunt, the Empress Dowager Cixi (Tz'u Hsi), the real power at court (see the comparative illustration below). Cixi had begun her political career as a concubine to an earlier emperor. After his death, she became a dominant force at court and in 1878 placed her infant nephew, the future Guangxu emperor, on the throne. For two decades, she ruled in his name as regent. Cixi interpreted Guangxu's action as a British-supported effort to reduce her influence at court. With the aid of conservatives in the army, she arrested and executed several of the reformers and had the em-

Freer Gallery of Art, Smithsonian Institution, Washington, DC

National Portrait Gallery, London

POLITICS & GOVERNMENT

COMPARATIVE ILLUSTRATION

**Female Rulers—East and West.** Two prominent female rulers in the late nineteenth century were Empress Dowager Cixi of China and Queen Victoria of Great Britain. Cixi, shown at the left, was the most powerful figure in late-nineteenth-century China. Originally a concubine at the imperial court, she later placed her young nephew on the throne and dominated the political scene for a quarter of a century, until her death in 1908. Conservative in her views, she staunchly resisted her advisers' suggestions for changes to help China face the challenge posed by the West. Note the long fingernails, a symbol of the privileged class, in this photograph taken in her final years. Queen Victoria, shown at the right, had the longest reign in British history (1837–1901). During her reign, the British Empire reached the height of its power, but by this time the monarchy was increasingly less relevant in Britain's liberal parliamentary system of government. Nevertheless, Victoria's sense of duty and moral responsibility reflected the attitudes of her age, which has ever since been known as the Victorian Age.

peror incarcerated in the palace. Kang Youwei succeeded in fleeing abroad. With Cixi's palace coup, the so-called One Hundred Days of reform came to an end.

**Opening the Door** During the next two years, foreign pressure on the dynasty intensified. With encouragement from the British, who hoped to avert a total collapse of the Manchu Empire, U.S. Secretary of State John Hay presented the other imperialist powers with a proposal to ensure equal economic access to the China market for all states. Hay also suggested that all powers join together to guarantee the territorial and administrative integrity of the Chinese Empire. Though probably motivated more by the United States' preference for open markets than by a benevolent wish to protect China, the so-called **Open Door Notes** did have the practical effect of reducing the imperialist hysteria over access to the China market. That hysteria, a product of decades of mythologizing among Western commercial interests about the 400 million Chinese customers, had accelerated at the end of the century as fear of China's imminent collapse increased. The "gentlemen's agreement" about the Open Door (it was not a treaty, merely a pious and nonbinding expression of intent) served to deflate fears in Britain, France, Germany, and Russia that other powers would take advantage of China's weakness to dominate the China market.

**Justice or Mercy? Uncle Sam Decides.** In the summer of 1900, Chinese rebels called Boxers besieged Western embassies in the imperial capital of Beijing. Western nations, including the United States, dispatched troops to North China to rescue their compatriots. In the cartoon, which appeared in a contemporary American newsmagazine, China figuratively seeks pardon from a stern Uncle Sam.

**The Boxer Rebellion** In the long run, then, the Open Door policy was a positive step that brought a measure of sanity to imperialist behavior in East Asia. Unfortunately, it came too late to stop the domestic explosion known as the Boxer Rebellion. The Boxers, so-called because of the physical exercises they performed (which closely resembled the more martial forms of tai chi), were members of a secret society operating primarily in rural areas in northern China. Provoked by a damaging drought and high unemployment caused in part by foreign economic activity (the introduction of railroads and steamships, for example, undercut the livelihood of barge workers on the rivers and canals), the Boxers attacked foreign residents and besieged the foreign legation quarter in Beijing until the foreigners were rescued by an international expeditionary force in the late summer of 1900. As punishment, the foreign troops destroyed a number of temples in the capital suburbs, and the Chinese government was compelled to pay a heavy indemnity to the foreign governments involved in suppressing the uprising.

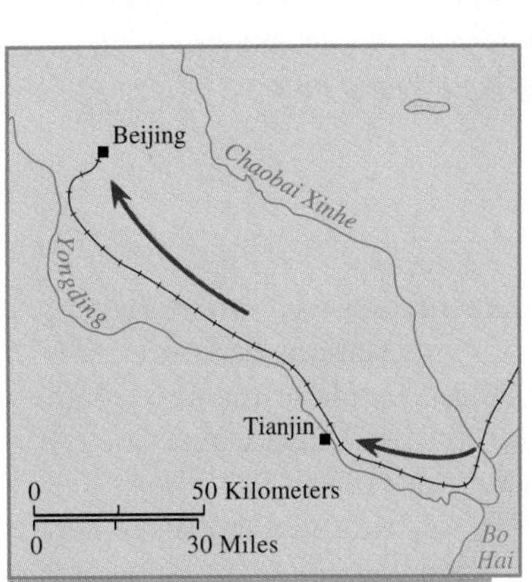


**The International Expeditionary Force Advances to Beijing to Suppress the Boxers**

## Collapse of the Old Order

During the next few years, the old dynasty tried desperately to reform itself. The empress dowager, who had long resisted change, now embraced a number of reforms. The venerable civil service examination system was replaced by a new educational system based on the Western model. In 1905, a commission was formed to study constitutional changes; over the next few years, legislative assemblies were established at the provincial level, and elections for a national assembly were held in 1910.

Such moves helped shore up the dynasty temporarily, but history shows that the most dangerous period for an authoritarian system is when it begins to reform itself, because change breeds instability and performance rarely matches rising expectations. Such was the case in China. The emerging provincial elite, composed of merchants, professionals, and reform-minded gentry, soon became impatient with the slow pace of political change and were disillusioned to find that the new assemblies were intended to be primarily advisory rather than legislative. The government also alienated influential elements by financing railway development projects through foreign firms rather than local investors. The reforms also had

## Program for a New China

In 1905, Sun Yat-sen united a number of anti-Manchu groups into a single patriotic organization called the Revolutionary Alliance (Tongmenghui). The new organization eventually formed the core of his Guomindang, or Nationalist Party. This excerpt is from the organization's manifesto, published in 1905 in Tokyo. Note that Sun believed that the Chinese people were not ready for democracy and required a period of tutelage to prepare them for the final era of constitutional political government. This was a formula that would be adopted by many other political leaders in Asia and Africa after World War II.

*How do Sun Yat-sen's proposals compare with those advanced by Wang Tao earlier in this chapter? Can Sun be described as a Chinese nationalist?*

### Sun Yat-sen, Manifesto for the Tongmenghui

By order of the Military Government, . . . the Commander-in-Chief of the Chinese National Army proclaims the purposes and platform of the Military Government to the people of the nation:

Therefore we proclaim to the world in utmost sincerity the outline of the present revolution and the fundamental plan for the future administration of the nation.

1. *Drive out the Tartars:* The Manchus of today were originally the eastern barbarians beyond the Great Wall. They frequently caused border troubles during the Ming dynasty; then when China was in a disturbed state they came inside Shanhaikuan, conquered China, and enslaved our Chinese people. . . . The extreme cruelties and tyrannies of the Manchu government have now reached their limit. With the righteous army poised against them, we will overthrow that government, and restore our sovereign rights.
2. *Restore China:* China is the China of the Chinese. The government of China should be in the hands of the Chinese. After driving out the Tartars we must restore our national state. . . .
3. *Establish the Republic:* Now our revolution is based on equality, in order to establish a republican government. All our people are equal and all enjoy political rights. . . .
4. *Equalize land ownership:* The good fortune of civilization is to be shared equally by all the people of the nation. We should improve our social and economic organization, and assess the value of all the land in the country. Its present price shall be received by the owner, but all increases in value resulting from reform and social improvements after the revolution shall belong to the state, to be shared by all the people, in order to create a socialist state, where each family within the empire can be well supported, each person satisfied, and no one fail to secure employment. . . .

The above four points will be carried out in three steps in due order. The first period is government by military law. When the righteous army has arisen, various places will join the cause. . . . Evils like the oppression of the government, the greed and graft of officials, . . . the cruelty of tortures and penalties, the tyranny of tax collections, the humiliation of the queue [the requirement that all Chinese males braid their hair]—shall all be exterminated together with the Manchu rule. Evils in social customs, such as the keeping of slaves, the cruelty of foot binding, the spread of the poison of opium, should also all be prohibited. . . .

The second period is that of government by a provisional constitution. When military law is lifted in each *hsien* [district], the Military Government shall return the right of self-government to the local people. . . .

The third period will be government under the constitution. Six years after the provisional constitution has been enforced a constitution shall be made. The military and administrative powers of the Military Government shall be annulled; the people shall elect the president, and elect the members of parliament to organize the parliament.

**History Now™** To read Sun Yat-sen's *Fundamentals of National Reconstruction,* enter the *HistoryNow* documents area using the access card that is available for *World History.*

little meaning for peasants, artisans, miners, and transportation workers, whose living conditions were being eroded by rising taxes and official venality. Rising rural unrest, as yet poorly organized and often centered on secret societies such as the Boxers, was an ominous sign of deep-seated resentment to which the dynasty would not, or could not, respond.

**The Rise of Sun Yat-sen** To China's reformist elite, such signs of social discontent were a threat to be avoided. To its tiny revolutionary movement, they were a harbinger of promise. The first physical manifestations of future revolution appeared during the last decade of the nineteenth century with the formation of the Revive China Society by the young radical Sun Yat-sen (1866–1925). Born in a village south of Canton, Sun was educated in Hawaii and returned to China to practice medicine. Soon he turned his full attention to the ills of Chinese society.

At first, Sun's efforts yielded few positive results, but in a convention in Tokyo in 1905, he managed to unite

## CHRONOLOGY China in the Era of Imperialism

| | |
|---|---|
| Lord Macartney's mission to China | 1793 |
| Opium War | 1839–1842 |
| Taiping rebels seize Nanjing | 1853 |
| Taiping Rebellion suppressed | 1864 |
| Cixi becomes regent for nephew, the Guangxu emperor | 1878 |
| Sino-Japanese War | 1894–1895 |
| One Hundred Days reform | 1898 |
| Open Door policy | 1899 |
| Boxer Rebellion | 1900 |
| Commission to study constitution formed | 1905 |
| Deaths of Cixi and the Guangxu emperor | 1908 |
| Revolution in China | 1911 |

**Sun Yat-sen, Father of Modern China.** The son of a peasant in southern China, Sun Yat-sen rose to become a prominent revolutionary and the founder of the first Chinese republic. This photograph shows Sun as he assumed office as provisional president in January 1912. Shortly thereafter, he was forced to resign in favor of General Yuan Shikai, who moved the capital from Nanjing to Beijing.

radical groups from across China in the so-called Revolutionary Alliance (Tongmenghui, or T'ung Meng Hui). The new organization's program was based on Sun's "three people's principles" of nationalism (meaning primarily the elimination of Manchu rule over China), democracy, and people's livelihood. It called for a three-stage process beginning with a military takeover and ending with a constitutional democracy (see the box on p. 608). Although the new organization was small and relatively inexperienced, it benefited from rising popular discontent.

**The Revolution of 1911** In October 1911, Sun's followers launched an uprising in the industrial center of Wuhan, in central China. With Sun traveling in the United States, the insurrection lacked leadership, but the decrepit government's inability to react quickly encouraged political forces at the provincial level to take measures into their own hands. The dynasty was now in a state of virtual collapse: the empress dowager had died in 1908, one day after her nephew; the throne was now occupied by China's "last emperor," the infant Puyi (P'u Yi). Sun's party had neither the military strength nor the political base necessary to seize the initiative, however, and was forced to turn to a representative of the old order, General Yuan Shikai (Yuan Shih-k'ai). A prominent figure in military circles since the beginning of the century, Yuan had been placed in charge of the imperial forces sent to suppress the rebellion, but now he abandoned the Manchus and acted on his own behalf. In negotiations with representatives of Sun Yat-sen's party (Sun himself had arrived in China in January 1912), he agreed to serve as president of a new Chinese republic. The old dynasty and the age-old system that it had attempted to preserve were no more.

Although the dynasty was gone, Sun and his followers were unable to consolidate their gains. The program of the Revolutionary Alliance was based on Western liberal democratic principles aimed at the urban middle class. That class and program had provided the foundation for the capitalist democratic revolutions in western Europe and North America in the late eighteenth and nineteenth centuries, but the middle class in China was still too small to form the basis for a new political order. The vast majority of the Chinese people still lived on the land. Sun had hoped to win their support with a land reform program, but few peasants had participated in the 1911 revolution. In failing to create new institutions and values to provide a framework for a changing society, the events of 1911 were less a revolution than a collapse of the old order. Weakened by imperialism and its own internal weaknesses, the old dynasty had come to an abrupt end before new political and social forces were ready to fill the vacuum.

What China had experienced was part of a historical process that was bringing down traditional empires across the globe, both in regions threatened by Western imperialism and in Europe itself, where tsarist Russia, the Austro-Hungarian Empire, and the Ottoman Empire all came to an end within a few years after the collapse of the Qing. The circumstances of their demise were not all the same. The Austro-Hungarian Empire, for example, was dismembered by the victorious allies after World War I, and the fate of tsarist Russia was directly linked to that conflict. Still, all four regimes shared the responsibility for their common fate in that they had failed to meet the challenges posed by the times. All had responded to the forces of industrialization and popular participation in the political process with hesitation and reluctance, and their attempts at reform were too little and too late. All paid the supreme price for their folly.

## Chinese Society in Transition

The growing Western presence in China during the late nineteenth and early twentieth centuries obviously had a major impact on Chinese society; hence many historians have asserted that the arrival of the Europeans shook China out of centuries of slumber and launched it on the road to revolutionary change. In fact, when the European economic penetration began to accelerate in the mid-nineteenth century, Chinese society was already in a state of transition. The growth of industry and trade was particularly noticeable in the cities, where a national market for such commodities as oil, copper, salt, tea, and porcelain had developed. The foundation of an infrastructure more conducive to the rise of a money economy appeared to be in place. In the countryside, new crops introduced from abroad significantly increased food production and aided population growth. The Chinese economy had never been more productive or more complex.

### Obstacles to Industrialization

Whether these changes by themselves would eventually have led to an industrial revolution and the rise of a capitalist society on the Western model in the absence of Western intervention is a question that historians cannot answer. Certainly, a number of obstacles would have made it difficult for China to embark on the Western path if it had wished to do so.

Although industrial production was on the rise, it was still based almost entirely on traditional methods. There was no uniform system of weights and measures, and the banking system was still primitive by European standards. The use of paper money, invented by the Chinese centuries earlier, had essentially been abandoned. The transportation system, which had been neglected since the end of the Yuan dynasty, was increasingly chaotic. There were few paved roads, and the Grand Canal, long the most efficient means of carrying goods from north to south, was silting up. As a result, merchants had to rely more and more on the coastal route, where they faced increasing competition from foreign shipping.

Although foreign concession areas in the coastal cities provided a conduit for the importation of Western technology and modern manufacturing methods, the Chinese borrowed less than they might have. Foreign manufacturing enterprises could not legally operate in China until the last decade of the nineteenth century, and their methods had little influence beyond the concession areas. Chinese efforts to imitate Western methods, notably in shipbuilding and weapons manufacture, were dominated by the government and often suffered from mismanagement.

Equally serious problems persisted in the countryside. The rapid increase in population had led to smaller plots and burgeoning numbers of tenant farmers. Whether per capita consumption of food was on the decline is not clear from the available evidence, but apparently rice as a staple of the diet was increasingly being replaced by less nutritious foods. Some farmers benefited from switching to commercial agriculture to supply the markets of the growing coastal cities, but the shift entailed a sizable investment. Many farmers went so deeply into debt that they eventually lost their land. In the meantime, the traditional patron-client relationship was frayed as landlords moved to the cities to take advantage of the glittering urban lifestyle.

Most important, perhaps, was that the Qing dynasty was still locked into a traditional mind-set that discouraged commercial activities and prized the time-honored virtues of agrarian society. China also lacked the European tradition of a vigorous and self-confident merchant class based in cities that were autonomous or even independent of the feudal political leader in the surrounding areas.

### The Impact of Imperialism

In any event, the advent of the imperialist era in the second half of the nineteenth century made such questions academic; imperialism created serious distortions in the local economy that resulted in massive changes in Chinese society during the twentieth century. Whether the Western intrusion was beneficial or harmful is debated to this day. The Western presence undoubtedly accelerated the development of the Chinese economy in some ways: the introduction of modern means of production, transport, and communications; the creation of an export market; and the steady integration of the Chinese market into the nineteenth-century global economy. To many Westerners at the time, it was self-evident that such changes would ultimately benefit the Chinese people (see the comparative essay “Imperialism and the Global Environment” on p. 611). Western civilization represented the most advanced stage of human development. By supplying (in the catch phrase of the day) “oil for the lamps of China,” it was providing a backward society with an opportunity to move up a notch or two on the ladder of human evolution.

Not everyone agreed. The Russian Marxist Vladimir Lenin contended that Western imperialism actually hindered the process of structural change in

## COMPARATIVE ESSAY

# Imperialism and the Global Environment

Beginning in the 1870s, European states engaged in an intense scramble for overseas territory. This "new imperialism" led Europeans to carve up Asia and Africa and create colonial empires. Within these empires, European states exercised complete political control over the indigenous societies and redrew political boundaries to meet their needs. In Africa, for example, in drawing the boundaries that separated one colony from another (boundaries that often became the boundaries of the modern countries of Africa), Europeans paid no attention to the existing political divisions; they often divided distinctive communities between colonies or made two communities that were hostile to each other members of the same colony.

In similar fashion, Europeans paid little or no heed to the economic needs of their colonial subjects but instead set up the economies of their empires to meet their own needs in the world market. In the process, Europeans often dramatically altered the global environment, a transformation that was made visible in a variety of ways. Westerners built railways and ports, erected telegraph lines, drilled for oil, and dug mines for gold, tin, iron ore, and copper. All of these projects transformed and often scarred the natural landscape.

Landscapes, however, were even more dramatically altered by Europe's demand for cash food crops. Throughout vast regions of Africa and Asia, tropical forests were felled to make way for plantations that cultivated crops that could be exported for sale. In Ceylon (modern Sri Lanka) and India, the British cut down vast tropical forests to plant row upon row of tea bushes. The Dutch razed forests in the East Indies to plant cinchona trees imported from Peru. (Quinine, derived from the trees' bark, dramatically reduced the death rate for malaria and made it possible for Europeans to live more securely in the tropical regions of Africa and Asia.) In Indochina, the French replaced extensive forests with sugar and coffee plantations. Native workers, who were usually paid pitiful wages by their European overseers, provided the labor for all of these vast plantations.

In many areas, precious farmland was turned over to the cultivation of cash crops. In the Dutch East Indies, farmers were forced to plow up some of their rice fields to make way for the cultivation of sugar. In West Africa, overplanting of cash crops damaged fragile grasslands and turned parts of the Sahel into a wasteland.

European states, however, greatly profited from this transformed environment. In *Agriculture in the Tropics: An Elementary Treatise,* written in 1909, the British botanist John Christopher Willis expressed his thoughts on this European policy:

> Whether planting in the tropics will always continue to be under European management is another question, but the northern powers will not permit that the rich and as yet comparatively undeveloped countries of the tropics should be entirely wasted by being devoted merely to the supply of the food and clothing wants of their own people, when they can also supply the wants of the colder zones in so many indispensable products.

In Willis's eyes, the imperialist transformation of the environments of Asia and Africa to serve European needs was entirely justified.

Archive Photos/Popperfoto

**Picking Tea Leaves in Ceylon.** In this 1900 photograph, women pick tea leaves for shipment abroad on a plantation in Ceylon (Sri Lanka). The British cut down vast stands of tropical forests in Ceylon and India to grow tea to satisfy demand back home.

preindustrial societies because it thwarted the rise of a local industrial and commercial sector in order to maintain colonies and semicolonies as a market for Western manufactured goods and a source of cheap labor and materials. Fellow Marxists in China such as Mao Zedong (see Chapter 23) later took up Lenin's charge and asserted that if the West had not intervened, China would have found its own road to capitalism and thence to socialism and communism.

Many historians today would say that the answer was a little of both. By shaking China out of its traditional mind-set, imperialism accelerated the process of change that had begun in the late Ming and early Qing periods and forced the Chinese to adopt new ways of thinking and acting. At the same time, China paid a heavy price in the destruction of its local industry while many of the profits flowed abroad. Although the Industrial Revolution is a painful process whenever and wherever it occurs, the

Chinese found the experience doubly painful because it was foisted on China from the outside.

## Daily Life

At the beginning of the nineteenth century, daily life for most Chinese was not substantially different from what it had been for centuries. Most were farmers, living in thousands of villages in rice fields and on hillsides throughout the countryside. Their lives were governed by the harvest cycle, village custom, and family ritual. Their roles in society were firmly fixed by the time-honored principles of Confucian social ethics. Male children, at least the more fortunate ones, were educated in the Confucian classics, while females remained in the home or in the fields. All children were expected to obey their parents, wives to submit to their husbands.

A visitor to China a hundred years later would have seen a very different society, although still recognizably Chinese. Change was most striking in the coastal cities, where the educated and affluent had been visibly affected by the growing Western cultural presence. Confucian social institutions and behavioral norms were declining rapidly in influence, while those of Europe and North America were on the ascendant. Change was much less noticeable in the countryside, but even there, the customary bonds had been dangerously frayed by the rapidly changing times.

Some of the change can be traced to the educational system. During the nineteenth century, the importance of a Confucian education steadily declined as up to half of the degree holders had purchased their degrees. After 1906, when the government abolished the civil service examinations, a Confucian education ceased to be the key to a successful career, and Western-style education became more desirable. The old dynasty attempted to modernize by establishing an educational system on the Western model with universal education at the elementary level. Such plans had some effect in the cities, where public schools, missionary schools, and other private institutions educated a new generation of Chinese with little knowledge of or respect for the past.

**Changing Roles for Women** The status of women was also in transition. During the mid-Qing era, women were expected to remain in the home. Their status as useless sex objects was painfully symbolized by the practice of foot binding, a custom that had probably originated among court entertainers in the Tang dynasty and later spread to the common people. By the mid-nineteenth century, more than half of all adult women probably had bound feet.

During the second half of the nineteenth century, signs of change began to appear. Women began to seek employment in factories—notably in cotton mills and in the silk industry, established in Shanghai in the 1890s. Some women were active in dissident activities, such as the Taiping Rebellion and the Boxer movement, and a few fought beside men in the 1911 revolution. Qiu Jin, a well-known female revolutionary, wrote a manifesto calling for women's liberation and then organized a revolt against the Manchu government, only to be captured and executed at the age of thirty-two in 1907.

By the end of the century, educational opportunities for women began to appear for the first time. Christian missionaries began to open girls' schools, mainly in the foreign concession areas. Although only a relatively small number of women were educated in these schools, they had a significant impact on Chinese society as progressive intellectuals began to argue that ignorant women produced ignorant children. In 1905, the court announced its intention to open public schools for girls, but few such schools ever materialized. Private schools for girls were established in some urban areas. The government also began to take steps to discourage the practice of foot binding, initially with only minimal success.

Courtesy of Peabody Essex Museum

**Women with Bound Feet.** To provide the best possible marriage for their daughters, upper-class families began to perform footbinding during the Song dynasty. Eventually the practice spread to all social classes in China. Although small feet were supposed to denote a woman of leisure, most Chinese women with bound feet contributed to the labor force, working mainly in textiles and handicrafts to supplement the family income. Here we see five women with bound feet sorting tea leaves in Shanghai.

# A Rich Country and a Strong State: The Rise of Modern Japan

By the beginning of the nineteenth century, the Tokugawa shogunate had ruled the Japanese islands for two hundred years. It had revitalized the old governmental system, which had virtually disintegrated under its predecessors. It had driven out the foreign traders and missionaries and isolated the country from virtually all contacts with the outside world. The Tokugawa maintained formal relations only with Korea, although informal trading links with Dutch and Chinese merchants continued at Nagasaki. Isolation, however, did not mean stagnation. Although the vast majority of Japanese still depended on agriculture for their livelihood, a vigorous manufacturing and commercial sector had begun to emerge during the long period of peace and prosperity. As a result, Japanese society had begun to undergo deep-seated changes, and traditional class distinctions were becoming blurred. Eventually, these changes would end Tokugawa rule and destroy the traditional feudal system.

Some historians speculate that the Tokugawa system was beginning to come apart, just as the medieval order in Europe had started to disintegrate at the beginning of the Renaissance. Factionalism and corruption plagued the central bureaucracy, while rural unrest, provoked by a series of poor harvests brought about by bad weather, swept the countryside. Farmers fled to the towns, where anger was already rising as a result of declining agricultural incomes and shrinking stipends for the samurai. Many of the samurai lashed out at the perceived incompetence and corruption of the government. In response, the *bakufu* became increasingly rigid, persecuting its critics and attempting to force fleeing peasants to return to their lands. The government also intensified its efforts to maintain the nation's isolation from the outside world, driving away foreign ships that were beginning to prowl along the Japanese coast in increasing numbers.

## An End to Isolation

To the Western powers, the continued isolation of Japanese society was an affront and a challenge. Driven by the growing rivalry among themselves and convinced that the expansion of trade on a global basis would benefit all nations, Western nations began to approach Japan in the hope of opening up the hermit kingdom to foreign economic interests.

The first to succeed was the United States. American steamships crossing the northern Pacific needed a fueling station before going on to China and other ports in the area. In the summer of 1853, an American fleet of four warships under Commodore Matthew C. Perry arrived in Edo (now Tokyo) Bay with a letter from President Millard Fillmore asking for the opening of foreign relations between the two countries (see the box on p. 614). A few months later, Perry returned with a larger fleet for an answer. In his absence, Japanese officials had debated the issue. Some argued that contacts with the West would be both politically and morally disadvantageous to Japan, while others pointed to U.S. military superiority and recommended concessions. For the shogunate in Edo, the black guns of Perry's ships proved decisive, and Japan agreed to the Treaty of Kanagawa, which provided for the return of shipwrecked American sailors, the opening of two ports, and the establishment of a U.S. consulate on Japanese soil. In 1858, U.S. consul Townsend Harris negotiated a more elaborate commercial treaty calling for the opening of several ports to U.S. trade and residence, the exchange of ministers, and the granting of extraterritorial privileges for U.S. residents in Japan. Similar treaties were soon signed with several European nations.

Boehringer Collection, Mariners' Museum, Newport News, VA

**Swift as a Swimming Dragon.** When Commodore Perry arrived in Tokyo Bay with a small fleet of U.S. warships in July 1853, the size, speed, and armaments of the "black ships" frightened Japanese onlookers and undoubtedly contributed to the willingness of the Tokugawa shogunate to seek a compromise with the foreigners. One Japanese artist, who had probably never before seen a modern steamship, recorded his impression of the visitors in this imaginative painting.

## A Letter to the Shogun

When Commodore Matthew Perry arrived in Tokyo Bay on his first visit to Japan, in July 1853, he carried a letter from the president of the United States, Millard Fillmore. The letter requested that trade relations between the two countries be established. The United States was already becoming a major participant in the race for the East Asian market. Little did the president know how momentous the occasion was or with what eagerness the Japanese would eventually respond to the challenge.

*Why did President Fillmore want to establish relations with Japan? Why were Japanese leaders reluctant to do so?*

### A Letter from the President of the United States

Millard Fillmore
President of the United States of America

To His Imperial Majesty,
The Emperor of Japan

Great and Good Friend!
I send you this public letter by Commodore Matthew C. Perry, an officer of the highest rank in the Navy of the United States, and commander of the squadron now visiting your Imperial Majesty's dominions.

I have directed Commodore Perry to assure your Imperial Majesty that I entertain the kindest feelings towards your Majesty's person and government; and that I have no other object in sending him to Japan, but to propose to your Imperial Majesty that the United States and Japan should live in friendship, and have commercial intercourse with each other. The constitution and laws of the United States forbid all interference with the religious or political concerns of other nations. I have particularly charged Commodore Perry to abstain from every act which could possibly disturb the tranquillity of your Imperial Majesty's dominions.

The United States of America reach from ocean to ocean, and our territory of Oregon and state of California lie directly opposite to the dominions of your Imperial Majesty. Our steamships can go from California to Japan in eighteen days. . . .

Japan is also a rich and fertile country, and produces many very valuable articles. . . . I am desirous that our two countries should trade with each other, for the benefit both of Japan and the United States.

We know that the ancient laws of your Imperial Majesty's government do not allow of foreign trade except with the Dutch. But as the state of the world changes, and new governments are formed, it seems to be wise from time to time to make new laws. . . . If your Imperial Majesty were so far to change the ancient laws as to allow a free trade between the two countries, it would be extremely beneficial to both. . . .

Many of our ships pass every year from California to China; and great numbers of our people pursue the whale fishery near the shores of Japan. It sometimes happens in stormy weather that one of our ships is wrecked on your Imperial Majesty's shores. In all such cases we ask and expect, that our unfortunate people should be treated with kindness, and that their property should be protected, till we can send a vessel and bring them away. . . .

May the Almighty have your Imperial Majesty in his great and holy keeping! . . .

Your Good Friend,
Millard Fillmore

**HistoryNow**™ To read Commodore Perry's "When We Landed in Japan," enter the *HistoryNow* documents area using the access card that is available for *World History.*

The decision to open relations with the Western barbarians was highly unpopular in some quarters, particularly in regions distant from the shogunate headquarters in Edo. Resistance was especially strong in two of the key outside daimyo territories in the south, Satsuma and Choshu, both of which had strong military traditions. In 1863, the "Sat-Cho" alliance forced the hapless shogun to promise to end relations with the West. The shogun eventually reneged on the agreement, but the rebellious groups soon disclosed their own weakness. When Choshu troops fired on Western ships in the Strait of Shimonoseki, the Westerners fired back and destroyed the Choshu fortifications. The incident convinced the rebellious samurai of the need to strengthen their own military and intensified their unwillingness to give in to the West. Having strengthened their influence at the imperial court in Kyoto, they demanded the shogun's resignation and the restoration of the emperor's power. In January 1868, rebel armies attacked the shogun's palace in Kyoto and proclaimed the restored authority of the emperor. After a few weeks, resistance collapsed, and the venerable shogunate system was brought to an end.

## The Meiji Restoration

Although the victory of the Sat-Cho faction had appeared on the surface to be a triumph of tradition over change, the new leaders soon realized that Japan must modernize to survive. Accordingly, they embarked on a policy of comprehensive reform that would lay the foundations of a modern industrial nation within a generation.

## Program for Reform in Japan

In the spring of 1868, the reformers drew up a program for transforming Japanese society along Western lines in the post-Tokugawa era. Though vague in its essentials, the Charter Oath is a good indication of the plans that were carried out during the Meiji Restoration. Compare this program with the Declaration of the Rights of Man and the Citizen drafted at the time of the French Revolution and discussed in Chapter 17.

*Do these basic principles all conform to the basic concepts of liberal democracy as practiced in Western societies? To what degree did the Meiji political system put them into effect? How did the Meiji constitution differ from those in the West?*

### The Charter Oath of Emperor Meiji

By this oath we set up as our aim the establishment of the national weal on a broad basis and the framing of a constitution and laws.

1. Deliberative assemblies shall be widely established and all matters decided by public discussion.
2. All classes, high and low, shall unite in vigorously carrying out the administration of affairs of state.
3. The common people, no less than the civil and military officials, shall each be allowed to pursue his own calling so that there may be no discontent.
4. Evil customs of the past shall be broken off and everything based upon the just laws of Nature.
5. Knowledge shall be sought throughout the world so as to strengthen the foundations of imperial rule.

The symbol of the new era was the young emperor himself, who had taken the reign name Meiji ("enlightened rule") on ascending the throne after the death of his father in 1867. Although the post-Tokugawa period was termed a "restoration," the Meiji ruler, who shared the modernist outlook of the Sat-Cho group, was controlled by the new leadership just as the shogunate had controlled his predecessors. In tacit recognition of the real source of political power, the new capital was located at Edo (now renamed Tokyo, "eastern capital"), and the imperial court was moved to the shogun's palace in the center of the city.

**The Transformation of Japanese Politics** Once in power, the new leaders launched a comprehensive reform of Japanese political, social, economic, and cultural institutions and values. They moved first to abolish the remnants of the old order and strengthen executive power in their hands. To undercut the power of the daimyo, hereditary privileges were abolished in 1871, and the great lords lost title to their lands. As compensation, they were given government bonds and were named governors of the territories formerly under their control. The samurai, comprising about 8 percent of the total population, received a lump-sum payment to replace their traditional stipends, but they were forbidden to wear the sword, the symbol of their hereditary status.

The Meiji modernizers also set out to create a modern political system on the Western model. In the Charter Oath of 1868, the new leaders promised to create a new deliberative assembly within the framework of continued imperial rule (see the box above). Although senior positions in the new government were given to the daimyo, the key posts were dominated by modernizing samurai, eventually to be known as the ***genro,*** or elder statesmen, from the Sat-Cho clique.

During the next two decades, the Meiji government undertook a systematic study of Western political systems. A constitutional commission under Prince Ito Hirobumi traveled to several Western countries, including Great Britain, Germany, Russia, and the United States, to study their political systems. As the process evolved, a number of factions appeared, each representing different political ideas. The most prominent were the Liberal Party and the Progressive Party. The Liberal Party favored political reform on the Western liberal democratic model with supreme authority vested in the parliament as the representative of the people. The Progressive Party called for the distribution of power between the legislative and executive branches, with a slight nod to the latter. There was also an imperial party, which advocated the retention of supreme authority exclusively in the hands of the emperor.

**The Constitution of 1890** During the 1870s and 1880s, these factions competed for preeminence. In the end, the Progressives emerged victorious. The Meiji Constitution, which was adopted in 1890, was based on the Bismarckian model with authority vested in the executive branch; the imperialist faction was pacified by the statement that the constitution was the gift of the emperor. Members of the cabinet were to be handpicked by the Meiji oligarchs. The upper house of parliament was to be appointed and have equal legislative powers with the lower house, called the Diet, whose members would be elected. The core ideology of the state was called the ***kokutai*** (national polity), which embodied (although in very imprecise form) the concept of the uniqueness of the Japanese system based on the supreme authority of the emperor.

The result was a system that was democratic in form but despotic in practice, modern in appearance but still traditional in that power remained in the hands of a ruling oligarchy. The system permitted the traditional ruling class to retain its influence and economic power while acquiescing in the emergence of new institutions and values.

**Meiji Economics** With the end of the daimyo domains, the government needed to establish a new system of land ownership that would transform the mass of the rural population from indentured serfs into citizens. To do so, it enacted a land reform program that redefined the domain lands as the private property of the tillers while compensating the previous owner with government bonds. One reason for the new policy was that the government needed operating revenues. At the time, public funds came mainly from customs fees, which were limited by agreement with the foreign powers to 5 percent of the value of the product. To remedy the problem, the Meiji leaders added a new agriculture tax, which was set at an annual rate of 3 percent of the estimated value of the land. The new tax proved to be a lucrative and dependable source of income for the government, but it was onerous for the farmers, who had previously paid a fixed percentage of their harvest to the landowner. As a result, in bad years, many taxpaying peasants were unable to pay their taxes and were forced to sell their lands to wealthy neighbors. Eventually, the government reduced the tax to 2.5 percent of the land value. Still, by the end of the century, about 40 percent of all farmers were tenants.

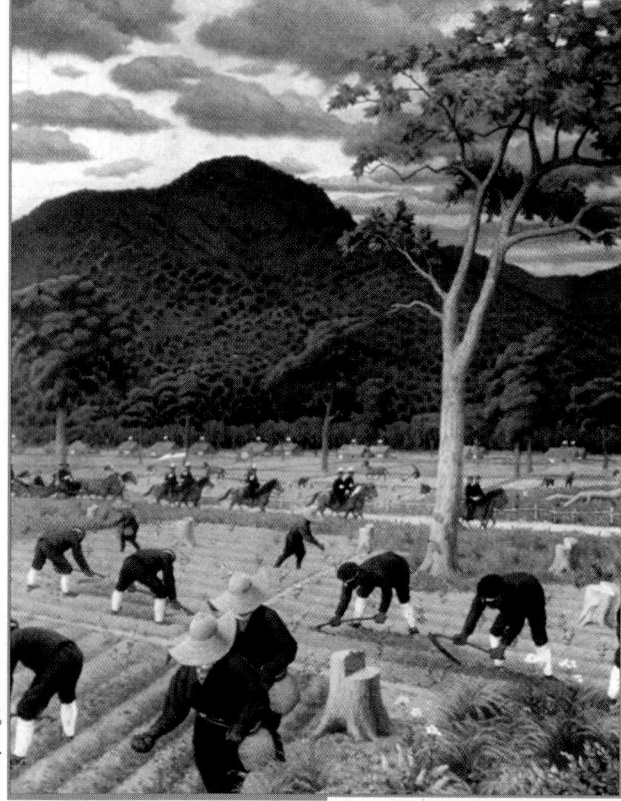


**The Emperor Inspects His Domain.** A crucial challenge for the Japanese government during the Meiji era was to find employment for the traditional warrior class in a time of peace and social transformation. One method was to assign a house and a plot of land to members of the samurai class in order to enable them to support themselves in a changing economy. In this painting from the 1880s, Emperor Meiji inspects a farm colony set up for samurai on the northern island of Hokkaido. The workers are wearing modern military uniforms, although they are engaged in traditional farm labor. The practice of showing the imperial face in public was an innovation introduced by Emperor Meiji that earned him the affection of his subjects.

With its budget needs secured, the government turned to the promotion of industry with the basic objective of guaranteeing Japan's survival against the challenge of Western imperialism. Building on the small but growing industrial economy that existed under the Tokugawa, the Meiji reformers provided a massive stimulus to Japan's industrial revolution. The government provided financial subsidies to needy industries, training, foreign advisers, improved transport and communications, and a universal educational system emphasizing applied science. In contrast to China, Japan was able to achieve results with minimum reliance on foreign capital. Although the first railroad—built in 1872—was financed by a loan from Great Britain, future projects were all backed by local funds. The foreign currency holdings came largely from tea and silk, which were exported in significant quantities during the latter half of the nineteenth century.

During the late Meiji era, Japan's industrial sector began to grow. Besides tea and silk, other key industries were weaponry, shipbuilding, and sake (fermented rice wine). From the start, the distinctive feature of the Meiji model was the intimate relationship between government and private business in terms of operations and regulations. Once an individual enterprise or industry was on its feet (or, sometimes, when it had ceased to make a profit), it was turned over entirely to private ownership, although the government often continued to play some role even after its direct involvement in management was terminated. Historians have explained the process:

> [The Meiji government] pioneered many industrial fields and sponsored the development of others, attempting to cajole businessmen into new and risky kinds of endeavor, helping assemble the necessary capital, forcing weak companies to merge into stronger units, and providing private entrepreneurs with aid and privileges of a sort that would be corrupt favoritism today. All this was in keeping with Tokugawa traditions that business operated under the tolerance and patronage of government. Some of the political leaders even played a dual role in politics and business.[4]

From the workers' perspective, the Meiji reforms had a less attractive side. As we have seen, the new land tax provided the funds to subsidize the growth of the industrial sector, but it imposed severe hardships on the rural population, many of whom abandoned their farms and fled to the cities, where they provided an abundant source of cheap labor for Japanese industry. As in Europe during the early decades of the Industrial Revolution, workers toiled for long hours in the coal mines and textile mills, often under horrendous conditions. Reportedly, coal miners employed on a small island in Nagasaki harbor worked naked in temperatures up to 130 degrees Fahrenheit. If they tried to escape, they were shot.

**Building a Modern Social Structure** By the late Tokugawa era, the rigidly hierarchical social order was showing signs of disintegration. Rich merchants were buying their way into the ranks of the samurai, and Japanese of all classes were beginning to abandon their rice fields and move into the growing cities. Nevertheless, community and hierarchy still formed the basis of Japanese society. The lives of all Japanese were determined by their membership in various social groups—the family, the village, and their social class. Membership in a particular social class determined a person's occupation and social relationships with others. Women in particular were constrained by the "three obediences" imposed on their sex: child to father, wife to husband, and widow to son. Husbands could easily obtain a divorce, but wives could not (one regulation allegedly decreed that a husband could divorce his spouse if she drank too much tea or talked too much). Marriages were arranged, and the average age at marriage for females was sixteen years. Females did not share inheritance rights with males, and few received any education outside the family.

The Meiji reformers dismantled much of the traditional social system in Japan. With the abolition of hereditary rights in 1871, the legal restrictions of the past were brought to an end with a single stroke. Special privileges for the aristocracy were abolished, as were the legal restrictions on the *eta,* the traditional slave class (numbering about 400,000 in the 1870s). Another key focus of the reformers was the army. The Sat-Cho reformers had been struck by the weakness of the Japanese forces in clashes with Western powers and embarked on a major program to create a military force that could compete in the modern world. The old feudal army based on the traditional warrior class was abolished, and an imperial army based on universal conscription was formed in 1871. For many rural males, the army became a route of upward mobility.

Education also underwent major changes. The Meiji leaders recognized the need for universal education including technical subjects, and after a few years of experimenting, they adopted the American model of a three-tiered system culminating in a series of universities and specialized institutes. In the meantime, they sent bright students to study abroad and brought foreign scholars to Japan to teach in the new schools, where much of the content was inspired by Western models. In another break with tradition, women for the first time were given an opportunity to get an education (see the box on p. 618).

Western influence was evident elsewhere as well. Western fashions became the rage in elite circles, and the ministers of the first Meiji government were known as the "dancing cabinet" because of their addiction to Western-style ballroom dancing. Young people, increasingly exposed to Western culture and values, began to imitate the clothing styles, eating habits, and social practices of their European and American counterparts. They even took up American sports when baseball was introduced.

**Traditional Values and Women's Rights** The self-proclaimed transformation of Japan into a "modern society," however, by no means detached the country entirely from its traditional moorings. Although an educational order in 1872 increased the percentage of Japanese women exposed to public education, conservatives soon began to impose restrictions and bring about a return to more traditional social relationships. The importance of traditional values was underlined by the Imperial Rescript on Education in 1890 (see the box on p. 619). Displayed in every school and recited by the students, it stressed the Confucian virtues of filial piety, patriotism, and loyalty to the family and community. Traditional values were given a firm legal basis in the Constitution of 1890, which restricted the franchise to males and defined individual liberties as "subject to the limitations imposed by law," and by the Civil Code of 1898, which deemphasized individual rights and essentially placed women within the context of their role in the family.

By the end of the nineteenth century, however, changes were under way as women began to play a crucial role in their nation's effort to modernize. Urged by their parents to augment the family income, as well as by the government to fulfill their patriotic duty, young girls were sent en masse to work in textile mills. From 1894 to 1912, women represented 60 percent of the Japanese labor force. Thanks to them, by 1914, Japan was the world's leading exporter of silk and dominated cotton manufacturing. If it had not been for the export revenues earned from textile exports, Japan might not have been able to develop its heavy industry and military prowess without an infusion of foreign capital.

Japanese women received few rewards, however, for their contribution to the nation. In 1900, new regulations prohibited women from joining political organizations or attending public meetings. Beginning in 1905, a group of independent-minded women petitioned the Japanese parliament to rescind this restriction, but it was not repealed until 1922.

## Joining the Imperialist Club

Traditionally, Japan had not been an expansionist country. As we have seen, except for sporadic forays against Korea, the Japanese had generally been satisfied to remain on their home islands and had even deliberately isolated themselves from their neighbors during the Tokugawa era. Now, however, the Japanese did not just imitate the domestic policies of their Western mentors; they also emulated the Western approach to foreign affairs. This is perhaps not surprising. The Japanese regarded themselves as particularly vulnerable in the world economic arena. Their territory was small, lacking in resources, and

## "In the Beginning, We Were the Sun"

One aspect of Western thought that the Meiji reformers did not seek to imitate was the idea of sexual equality. Although Japanese women sometimes tried to be "modern" like their male counterparts, Japanese society as a whole continued to treat women differently, as had been the case during the Tokugawa era. In 1911, a young woman named Hiratsuka Raicho founded a journal named *Seito (Blue Stockings)* to promote the liberation of women in Japan. The goal of the new movement was to encourage women to develop their own latent talents, rather than to demand legal changes in Japanese society. The following document is the proclamation that was issued at the creation of the Seito Society. Compare it to Mary Wollstonecraft's discussion of the rights of women in Chapter 17.

*What, in the author's view, was necessary to bring about the liberation of women in Meiji Japan? Were her proposals similar to those set forth by her counterparts in the West?*

### Hiratsuka Raicho, Proclamation at the Founding of the Seito Society

Freedom and Liberation! Oftentimes we have heard the term "liberation of women." But what is it then? Are we not seriously misunderstanding the term freedom or liberation? Even if we call the problem the liberation of women, are there not many other issues involved? Assuming that women are freed from external oppression, liberated from constraint, given the so-called higher education, employed in various occupations, given franchise, and provided an opportunity to be independent from the protection of their parents and husbands, and to be freed from the little confinement of their homes, can all of these be called liberation of women? They may provide proper surroundings and opportunities to let us fulfill the true goal of liberation. Yet they remain merely the means, and do not represent our goal or ideals.

However, I am unlike many intellectuals in Japan who suggest that higher education is not necessary for women. Men and women are endowed by nature to have equal faculties. Therefore, it is odd to assume that one of the sexes requires education while the other does not. This may be tolerated in a given country and in a given age, but it is fundamentally a very unsound proposition.

I bemoan the facts that there is only one private college for women in Japan, and that there is no tolerance on man's part to permit entrance of women into many universities maintained for men. However, what benefit is there when the intellectual level of women becomes similar to that of men? Men seek knowledge in order to escape from their lack of wisdom and lack of enlightenment. They want to free themselves. . . . Yet multifarious thought can darken true wisdom, and lead men away from nature. . . .

Now, what is the true liberation which I am seeking? It is none other than to provide an opportunity for women to develop fully their hidden talents and hidden abilities. We must remove all the hindrances that stand in the way of women's development, whether they be external oppression or lack of knowledge. And above and beyond these factors, we must realize that we are the masters in possession of great talents, for we are the bodies which enshrine the great talents.

densely populated, and they had no natural outlet for expansion. To observant Japanese, the lessons of history were clear. Western nations had amassed wealth and power not only because of their democratic systems and high level of education but also because of their colonies.

The Japanese began their program of territorial expansion close to home (see Map 21.4). In 1874, the Japanese claimed compensation from China for fifty-four sailors from the Ryukyu Islands who had been killed by aborigines on the island of Taiwan and sent a Japanese fleet to Taiwan to punish the perpetrators. When the Qing dynasty evaded responsibility for the incident while agreeing to pay an indemnity to Japan to cover the cost of the expedition, it weakened its claim to ownership of the island of Taiwan. Japan was then able to claim suzerainty over the Ryukyu Islands, long tributary to the Chinese Empire. Two years later, Japanese naval pressure forced Korea to open three ports to Japanese commerce.

Korea had long followed Japan's example and attempted to isolate itself from outside contact except for periodic tribute missions to China. Christian missionaries, mostly Chinese or French, were vigorously persecuted. But Korea's problems were basically internal. In the early 1860s, a peasant revolt, inspired in part by the Taiping Rebellion in China, caused considerable devastation before being crushed in 1864. In succeeding years, the Yi dynasty sought to strengthen the country by returning to traditional values and fending off outside intrusion, but rural poverty and official corruption remained rampant. A U.S. fleet, following the example of Commodore Perry in Japan, sought to open the country in 1871 but was driven off with considerable loss of life.

Korea's most persistent suitor, however, was Japan, which was determined to bring an end to Korea's dependency status with China and modernize it along Japanese lines. In 1876, the two countries signed an agreement opening three treaty ports to Japanese commerce in return for Japanese recognition of Korean independence. During the 1880s, Sino-Japanese rivalry over Korea intensified. China supported conservatives at the Korean court, while Japan promoted a more radical faction that was determined to break loose from lingering Chinese influence.

## The Rules of Good Citizenship in Meiji Japan

After seizing power from the Tokugawa shogunate in 1868, the new Japanese leaders turned their attention to the creation of a new political system that would bring the country into the modern world. After exploring various systems in use in the West, a constitutional commission decided to adopt the system used in imperial Germany because of its paternalistic character. To promote civic virtue and obedience among the citizenry, the government then drafted an imperial rescript that was to be taught to every schoolchild in the country. The rescript instructed all children to obey their sovereign and place the interests of the community and the state above their own personal desires.

### Imperial Rescript on Education, 1890

Know ye, Our subjects:

Our Imperial Ancestors have founded Our Empire on a basis broad and everlasting, and have deeply and firmly implanted virtue. Our subjects ever united in loyalty and filial piety have from generation to generation illustrated the beauty thereof. This is the glory of the fundamental character of Our Empire, and herein also lies the source of Our education. Ye, Our subjects, be filial to your parents, affectionate to your brothers and sisters, as husbands and wives be harmonious, as friends true; bear yourselves in modesty and moderation; extend your benevolence to all; pursue learning and cultivate arts, and thereby develop intellectual faculties and perfect moral powers; furthermore, advance public good and promote common interests; always respect the Constitution and observe the laws; should emergency arise, offer yourselves to the State; and thus guard and maintain the prosperity of Our Imperial Throne coeval with heaven and earth. So shall ye not only be Our good and faithful subjects, but render illustrious the best traditions of your forefathers.

*What, according to this document, was the primary purpose of education in Meiji Japan? How did these goals compare with those in China and the West?*

When a new peasant rebellion broke out in Korea in 1894, China and Japan intervened on opposite sides. During the war, the Japanese navy destroyed the Chinese fleet and seized the Manchurian city of Port Arthur (see the box on p. 622). In the Treaty of Shimonoseki, the Manchus were forced to recognize the independence of Korea and cede Taiwan and the Liaodong peninsula with its strategic naval base at Port Arthur to Japan.

Shortly thereafter, under pressure from the European powers, the Japanese returned the Liaodong peninsula to China, but in the early twentieth century, they went back on the offensive. Rivalry with Russia over influence in Korea led to increasingly strained relations between the two countries. In 1904, Japan launched a surprise attack on the Russian naval base at Port Arthur, which Russia had taken from China in 1898. The Japanese armed forces were weaker, but Russia faced difficult logistical problems along its new Trans-Siberian Railway and severe political instability at home. In 1905, after Japanese warships sank almost the entire Russian fleet off the coast of Korea, the Russians agreed to a humiliating peace, ceding the strategically located Liaodong peninsula back to Japan, as well as southern Sakhalin and the Kurile Islands. Russia also agreed to abandon its political and economic influence in Korea and southern Manchuria, which now came increasingly under Japanese control. The Japanese victory stunned the world, including the colonial peoples of Southeast Asia, who now began to realize that the white race was not necessarily invincible.

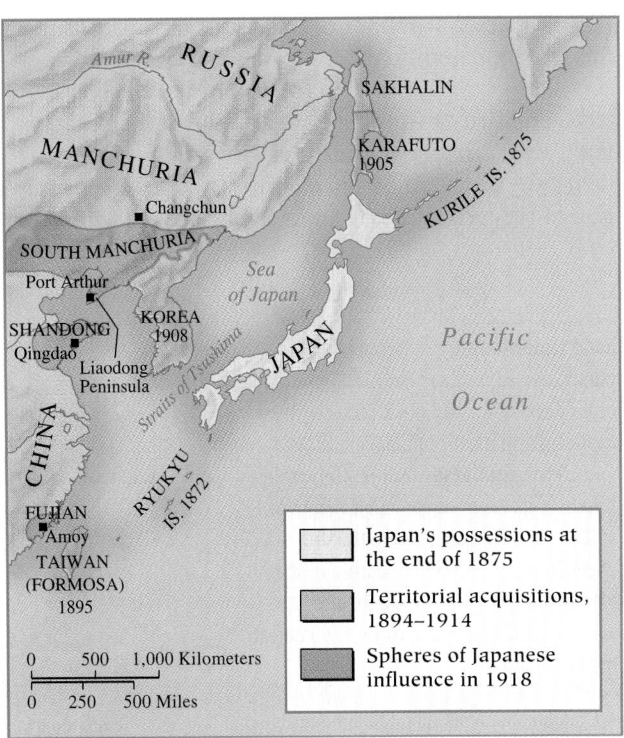


**MAP 21.4 Japanese Overseas Expansion During the Meiji Era.** Beginning in the late nineteenth century, Japan ventured beyond its home islands and became an imperialist power. The extent of Japanese colonial expansion through World War I is shown here. ? Which parts of imperial China were now under Japanese influence? **View an animated version of this map or related maps at** http://history.wadsworth.com/duikerspielvogel05/

During the next few years, the Japanese consolidated their position in northeastern Asia, annexing Korea in 1908 as an integral part of Japan. When the Koreans protested the seizure, Japanese reprisals resulted in thousands of deaths. The United States was the first nation to recognize the annexation, in return for Tokyo's declaration of respect for U.S. authority in the Philippines and Japanese acceptance of the principles of the Open Door. But mutual suspicion between the two countries was growing, sparked in part by U.S. efforts to restrict immigration from all Asian countries. President Theodore Roosevelt, who mediated the Russo-Japanese War, had aroused the anger of many Japanese by turning down a Japanese demand for reparations from Russia. In turn, some Americans began to fear the rise of a "yellow peril" manifested by Japanese expansion in East Asia.

**CHRONOLOGY Japan and Korea in the Era of Imperialism**

| | |
|---|---|
| Commodore Perry arrives in Tokyo Bay | 1853 |
| Townsend Harris Treaty | 1858 |
| Fall of Tokugawa Shogunate | 1868 |
| U.S. fleet fails to open Korea | 1871 |
| Feudal titles abolished | 1871 |
| Imperial army formed | 1871 |
| Meiji Constitution adopted | 1890 |
| Imperial Rescript on Education | 1890 |
| Treaty of Shimonoseki awards Taiwan to Japan | 1895 |
| Russo-Japanese War | 1904–1905 |
| Korea annexed | 1908 |

## Japanese Culture in Transition

The wave of Western technology and ideas that entered Japan in the second half of the nineteenth century greatly altered the shape of traditional Japanese culture. Literature in particular was affected as European models eclipsed the repetitive and frivolous tales of the Tokugawa era. Dazzled by this "new" literature, Japanese authors began translating and imitating the imported models. Experimenting with Western verse, Japanese poets were at first influenced primarily by the British but eventually adopted such French styles as Symbolism, Dadaism, and Surrealism, although some traditional poetry was still composed.

As the Japanese invited technicians, engineers, architects, and artists from Europe and the United States to teach their "modern" skills to a generation of eager students, the Meiji era became a time of massive consumption of Western artistic techniques and styles. Japanese architects and artists created huge buildings of steel and reinforced concrete adorned with Greek columns and cupolas, oil paintings reflecting the European concern with depth perception and shading, and bronze sculptures of secular subjects. All expressed the individual creator's emotional and aesthetic preferences.

Cultural exchange also went the other way as Japanese arts and crafts, porcelains, textiles, fans, folding screens, and wood-block prints became the vogue in Europe and North America. Japanese art influenced Western painters such as Vincent van Gogh, Edgar Degas, and James Whistler, who experimented with flatter compositional perspectives and unusual poses. Japanese gardens, with their exquisite attention to the positioning of rocks and falling water, became especially popular in the United States.

**Total Humiliation.** Whereas China had persevered in hiding behind the grandeur of its past, Japan had embraced the West, modernizing itself politically, militarily, and culturally. China's humiliation at the hands of its newly imperialist neighbor is evident in this scene, where the differences in dress and body posture of the officials negotiating the treaty after the war reflect China's disastrous 1895 defeat by the Japanese.

© Seitoku Kinen Kaigakan hekigashu, 1932, Meiji Jingu, Hosankai

**The Emperor Reviews His Fleet.** In 1868, reformist elements overthrew the Tokugawa shogunate and launched an era of rapid modernization in Japanese society. Emperor Meiji, who had mounted the throne the previous year, became the symbol of his nation's effort to transform itself along Western lines. Although according to tradition the emperor played no military role in Japanese society, Emperor Meiji is shown here surveying a parade of warships in 1905 following the Japanese victory over Imperial Russia. On the right is Admiral Togo, who had commanded the fleet in its stunning victory over Russian naval forces in the Sea of Japan.

After the initial period of mass absorption of Western art, a national reaction occurred at the end of the nineteenth century as many artists returned to pre-Meiji techniques. In 1889, the Tokyo School of Fine Arts (today the Tokyo National University of Fine Arts and Music) was founded to promote traditional Japanese art. Over the next several decades, Japanese art underwent a dynamic resurgence, reflecting the nation's emergence as a prosperous and powerful state. While some Japanese artists attempted to synthesize native and foreign techniques, others returned to past artistic traditions for inspiration.

In architecture, Japan's split personality revealed itself most effectively in the Diet building. As the home of the new Japanese parliament, it was supposed to reflect both progress and the nation and culture of Japan. For half a century, conflicting views over the priority of these concepts delayed its construction. After a number of proposals were rejected, the government held a competition in 1919, but none of the designs won general approval. Finally, in 1936 the government decided on the final design, which followed neither traditional styles nor European architecture of the period.

## The Meiji Restoration: A Revolution from Above

Japan's transformation from a feudal, agrarian society to an industrializing, technologically advanced society in little more than half a century has frequently been described by outside observers (if not by the Japanese themselves) in almost miraculous terms. Some historians have questioned this characterization, pointing out that the achievements of the Meiji leaders were spotty. In *Japan's Emergence as a Modern State,* the Canadian historian E. H. Norman lamented that the Meiji Restoration was an "incomplete revolution" because it had not ended the economic and social inequities of feudal society or enabled the common people to participate fully in the governing process. Although the *genro* were enlightened in many respects, they were also despotic and elitist, and the distribution of wealth remained as unequal as it had been under the old system.[5]

These criticisms are persuasive, although they could also be applied to most other societies going through the early stages of industrialization. In any event, from an economic perspective, the Meiji Restoration was one of the great success stories of modern times. Not only did the Meiji leaders put Japan firmly on the path to economic and political development, but they also managed to remove the unequal treaty provisions that had been imposed at mid-century. Japanese achievements are especially impressive when compared with the difficulties experienced by China, which was not only unable to realize significant changes in its traditional society but had not even reached a consensus on the need for doing so. Japan's achievements more closely resemble those of Europe, but whereas the West needed a century and a half to achieve a significant level of industrial development, the Japanese realized it in forty years.

One of the distinctive features of Japan's transition from a traditional to a modern society during the Meiji era was that it took place for the most part without violence or the kind of social or political revolution that occurred in so many other countries. The Meiji Restoration, which began the process, has been called a "revolution from above," a comprehensive restructuring of Japanese society by its own ruling group.

Technically, of course, the Meiji Restoration was not a revolution, since it was not violent and did not result in the displacement of one ruling class by another. The existing elites undertook to carry out a series of major reforms that transformed society but left their own

## Two Views of the World

During the nineteenth century, China's hierarchical way of looking at the outside world came under severe challenge, not only from European countries avid for new territories in Asia but also from the rising power of Japan, which accepted the Western view that a colonial empire was the key to national greatness. Japan's first objective was Korea, long a dependency of China, and in 1894, the competition between China and Japan in the peninsula led to war. The following declarations of war by the rulers of the two countries are revealing. Note the Chinese use of the derogatory term *wojen* ("dwarf people") in referring to the Japanese.

*Compare these two statements in terms of the worldviews of China and Japan at the end of the nineteenth century. Which point of view do you find to be more persuasive?*

### Declaration of War Against China

Korea is an independent state. She was first introduced into the family of nations by the advice and guidance of Japan. It has, however, been China's habit to designate Korea as her dependency, and both openly and secretly to interfere with her domestic affairs. At the time of the recent insurrection in Korea, China despatched troops thither, alleging that her purpose was to afford a succor to her dependent state. We, in virtue of the treaty concluded with Korea in 1882, and looking to possible emergencies, caused a military force to be sent to that country.

Wishing to procure for Korea freedom from the calamity of perpetual disturbance, and thereby to maintain the peace of the East in general, Japan invited China's cooperation for the accomplishment of the object. But China, advancing various pretexts, declined Japan's proposal. . . . Such conduct on the part of China is not only a direct injury to the rights and interests of this Empire, but also a menace to the permanent peace and tranquility of the Orient. . . . In this situation, . . . we find it impossible to avoid a formal declaration of war against China.

### Declaration of War Against Japan

Korea has been our tributary for the past two hundred odd years. She has given us tribute all this time, which is a matter known to the world. For the past dozen years or so Korea has been troubled by repeated insurrections and we, in sympathy with our small tributary, have as repeatedly sent succor to her aid. . . . This year another rebellion was begun in Korea, and the King repeatedly asked again for aid from us to put down the rebellion. We then ordered Li Hung-chang to send troops to Korea; and they having barely reached Yashan the rebels immediately scattered. But the *Wojen,* without any cause whatever, suddenly sent their troops to Korea, and entered Seoul, the capital of Korea, reinforcing them constantly until they have exceeded ten thousand men. In the meantime the Japanese forced the Korean king to change his system of government, showing a disposition every way of bullying the Koreans. . . .

As Japan has violated the treaties and not observed international laws, and is now running rampant with her false and treacherous actions commencing hostilities herself, and laying herself open to condemnation by the various powers at large, we therefore desire to make it known to the world that we have always followed the paths of philanthropy and perfect justice throughout the whole complications, while the *Wojen,* on the other hand, have broken all the laws of nations and treaties which it passes our patience to bear with. Hence we commanded Li Hung-chang to give strict orders to our various armies to hasten with all speed to root the *Wojen* out of their lairs.

---

power intact. In the words of one historian, it was "a kind of amalgamation, in which the enterprising, adaptable, or lucky individuals of the old privileged classes [were] for most practical purposes tied up with those individuals of the old submerged classes, who, probably through the same gifts, were able to rise." In that respect, the Meiji Restoration resembles the American Revolution more than the French Revolution; it was a "conservative revolution" that resulted in gradual change rather than rapid and violent change.[6]

**Sources of Japanese Uniqueness** The differences between the Japanese response to the West and that of China and many other nations in the region have sparked considerable debate among students of comparative history, and a number of explanations have been offered. Some have argued that Japan's success was partly due to good fortune. Lacking abundant natural resources, it was exposed to less pressure from the West than many of its neighbors. That argument is problematic, however, and would probably not have been accepted by Japanese observers at the time. Nor does it explain why nations under considerably less pressure, such as Laos and Nepal, did not advance even more quickly. All in all, the luck hypothesis is not very persuasive.

Some explanations have already been suggested in this book. Japan's unique geographical position in Asia was certainly a factor. China, a continental nation with a heterogeneous ethnic composition, was distinguished from its neighbors by its Confucian culture. By contrast, Japan was an island nation, ethnically and linguistically homogeneous, and had never been conquered. Unlike the Chinese or many

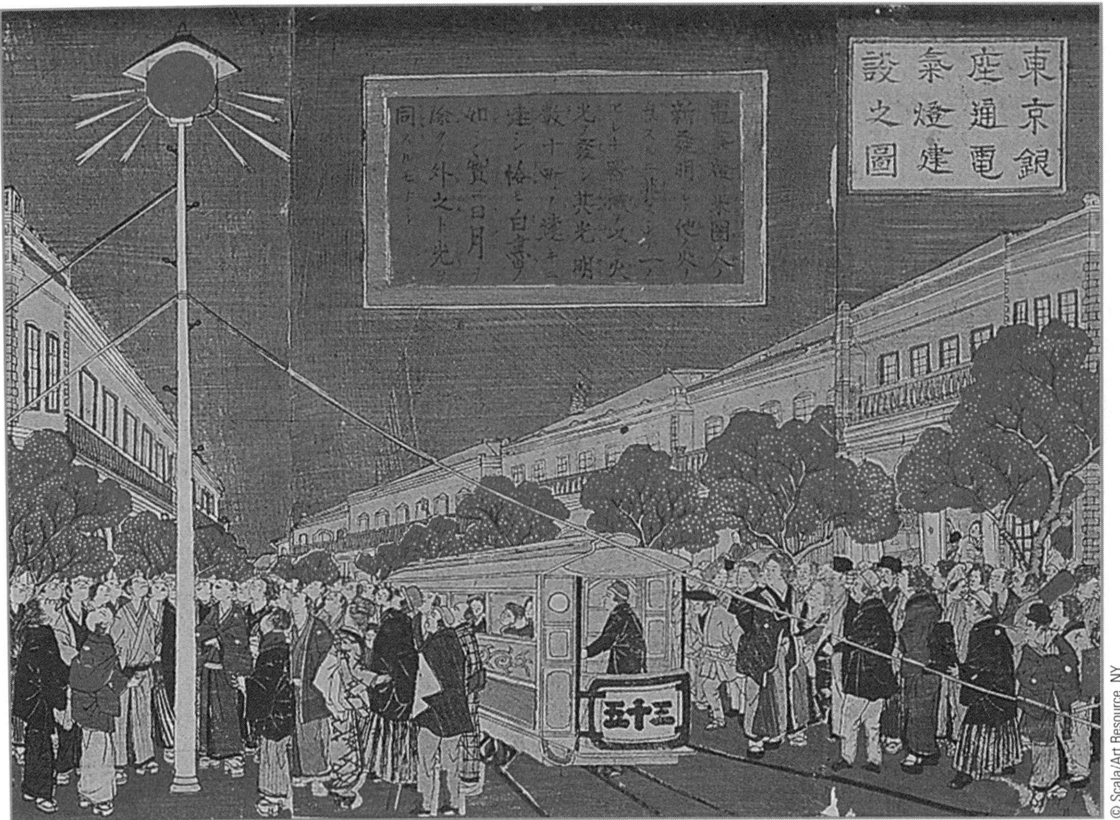



**The Ginza in Downtown Tokyo.** This 1877 wood-block print shows the Ginza, a major commercial thoroughfare in downtown Tokyo, with modern brick buildings, rickshaws, and a horse-drawn streetcar. The centerpiece and focus of public attention is a new electric streetlight. In combining traditional form with modern content, this painting symbolizes the unique ability of the Japanese to borrow ideas from abroad while preserving much of the essence of their traditional culture.

other peoples in the region, the Japanese had little to fear from cultural change in terms of its effect on their national identity. If Confucian culture, with all its accouterments, was what defined the Chinese gentleman, his Japanese counterpart, in the familiar image, could discard his sword and kimono and don a modern military uniform or a Western business suit and still feel comfortable in both worlds.

Whatever the case, as the historian W. G. Beasley has noted, the Meiji Restoration was possible because aristocratic and capitalist elements managed to work together in a common effort to bring about national wealth and power. The nature of the Japanese value system, with its emphasis on practicality and military achievement, may also have contributed. Finally, the Meiji also benefited from the fact that the pace of urbanization and commercial and industrial development had already begun to quicken under the Tokugawa. Japan, it was said, was ripe for change, and nothing could have been more suitable as an antidote for the collapsing old system than the Western emphasis on wealth and power. It was a classic example of challenge and response.

**Fusing East and West** The final product was an amalgam of old and new, native and foreign, forming a new civilization that was still uniquely Japanese. There were some undesirable consequences, however. Because Meiji politics was essentially despotic, Japanese leaders were able to fuse key traditional elements such as the warrior ethic and the concept of feudal loyalty with the dynamics of modern industrial capitalism to create a state totally dedicated to the possession of material wealth and national power. This combination of *kokutai* and capitalism, which one scholar has described as a form of "Asian fascism," was highly effective but explosive in its international manifestation. Like modern Germany, which also entered the industrial age directly from feudalism, Japan eventually engaged in a policy of repression at home and expansion abroad in order to achieve its national objectives. In Japan, as in Germany, it took defeat in war to disconnect the drive for national development from the feudal ethic and bring about the transformation to a pluralistic society dedicated to living in peace and cooperation with its neighbors.

## CONCLUSION

**Few areas of the world** resisted the Western incursion as stubbornly and effectively as East Asia. Although military, political, and economic pressure by the European powers was relatively intense during this era, two of the main states in the area were able to retain their independence, while the third—Korea—was temporarily absorbed by one of its larger neighbors. Why the Chinese and the Japanese were able to prevent a total political and military takeover by foreign powers is an interesting question. One key reason was that both had a long history as well-defined states with a strong sense of national community and territorial cohesion. Although China had frequently been conquered, it had retained its sense of unique culture and identity. Geography, too, was in its favor. As a continental nation, China was able to survive partly because of its sheer size. Japan possessed the advantage of an island location.

Even more striking, however, is the different way in which the two states attempted to deal with the challenge. While the Japanese chose to face the problem in a pragmatic manner, borrowing foreign ideas and institutions that appeared to be of value and at the same time not in conflict with traditional attitudes and customs, China agonized over the issue for half a century while conservative elements fought a desperate battle to retain a maximum of the traditional heritage intact.

This chapter has discussed some of the possible reasons for those differences. In retrospect, it is difficult to avoid the conclusion that the Japanese approach was the more effective one. Whereas the Meiji leaders were able to set in motion an orderly transition from a traditional to an advanced society, in China the old system collapsed in disorder, leaving chaotic conditions that were still not rectified a generation later. China would pay a heavy price for its failure to respond coherently to the challenge.

But the Japanese "revolution from above" was by no means an unalloyed success. Ambitious efforts by Japanese leaders to carve out a share in the spoils of empire led to escalating conflict with China as well as with rival Western powers and in the early 1940s to global war. We will deal with that issue in Chapter 24. Meanwhile, in Europe, a combination of old rivalries and the effects of the Industrial Revolution were leading to a bitter regional conflict that eventually engulfed the entire world.

## TIMELINE

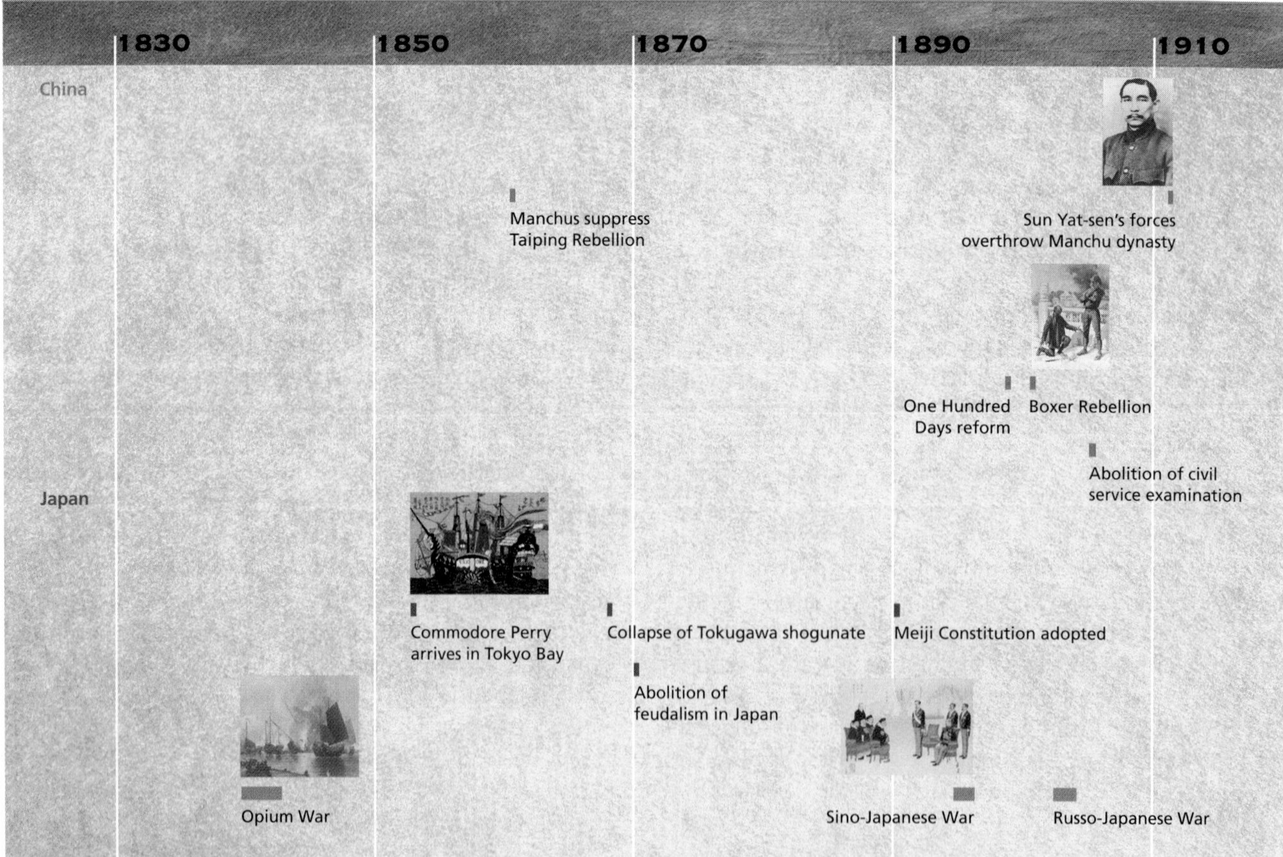

## CHAPTER NOTES

1. H. B. Morse, *The International Relations of the Chinese Empire* (London, 1910–1918), vol. 2, p. 622.
2. Quoted in S. Teng and J. K. Fairbank, eds., *China's Response to the West: A Documentary Survey, 1839–1923* (New York, 1970), p. 140.
3. Ibid., p. 167.
4. J. K. Fairbank, A. M. Craig, and E. O. Reischauer, *East Asia: Tradition and Transformation* (Boston, 1973), p. 514.
5. Quoted in J. W. Dower, ed., *The Origins of the Modern Japanese State: Selected Writings of E. H. Norman* (New York, 1975), p. 13.
6. C. Brinton, *The Anatomy of Revolution* (New York, 1965), quoted in W. G. Beasley, *The Meiji Restoration* (Stanford, Calif., 1972), p. 423.

## SUGGESTED READING

For a general overview of modern Chinese history, see **I. C. Y. Hsu, *The Rise of Modern China*** (Oxford, 1990). Also see **J. Spence's** stimulating work ***The Search for Modern China*** (New York, 1990).

On the Taiping Rebellion, see **J. Spence, *God's Chinese Son: The Taiping Heavenly Kingdom of Hong Xiuquan*** (New York, 1996). Social issues are dealt with in **E. S. Rawski, *The Last Emperors: A Social History of Qing Imperial Institutions*** (Berkeley, Calif., 1998). On the Manchus' attitude toward modernization, see **D. Pong, *Shen Pao-chen and China's Modernization in the Nineteenth Century*** (New York, 1994).

Sun Yat-sen's career is explored in **M. C. Bergère, *Sun Yat-sen***, trans. **J. Lloyd** (Stanford, Calif., 2000). **S. Seagraves' *Dragon Lady: The Life and Legend of the Last Empress of China*** (New York, 1992) is a revisionist treatment of Empress Dowager Cixi. On the Boxer Rebellion, the definitive work is **J. Esherick, *The Origins of the Boxer Uprising*** (Berkeley, Calif., 1987). Also see **D. Preston, *The Boxer Rebellion: The Dramatic Story of China's War on Foreigners That Shook the World in the Summer of 1900*** (Berkeley, Calif., 2001).

The Meiji period of modern Japan is covered in **M. B. Jansen**, ed., ***The Emergence of Meiji Japan*** (Cambridge, 1995). Also see **D. Keene, *Emperor of Japan: Meiji and His World, 1852–1912*** (New York, 2000). See also **C. Gluck, *Japan's Modern Myths: Ideology in the Late Meiji Period*** (Princeton, N. J., 1985). On the economy, see **R. Smethurst, *Agricultural Development and Tenancy Disputes in Japan, 1870–1940*** (Princeton, N.J., 1986), and **M. Hane, *Peasants, Rebels, and Outcastes: The Underside of Modern Japan*** (New York, 1982). To understand the role of the samurai in the Meiji Revolution, see **E. Ikegami, *The Taming of the Samurai: Honorific Individualism and the Making of Modern Japan*** (Cambridge, 1995).

On the international scene, **W. Lafeber, *The Clash: U.S.–Japanese Relations Throughout History*** (New York, 1997), is a good source of information. Also see **M. Peattie** and **R. Myers, *The Japanese Colonial Empire, 1895–1945*** (Princeton, N. J., 1984). The best introduction to Japanese art is **P. Mason, *History of Japanese Art*** (New York, 1993). See also **J. S. Baker's** concise ***Japanese Art*** (London, 1984).

CHAPTER

# 22

# THE BEGINNING OF THE TWENTIETH-CENTURY CRISIS: WAR AND REVOLUTION

British troops wait for the signal to attack



## CHAPTER OUTLINE AND FOCUS QUESTIONS

### The Road to World War I

- What were the long-range and immediate causes of World War I?

### The Great War

- Why did the course of World War I turn out to be so different from what the belligerents had expected? How did World War I affect the belligerents' governmental and political institutions, economic affairs, and social life?

### War and Revolution

- What were the causes of the Russian Revolution of 1917, and why did the Bolsheviks prevail in the civil war and gain control of Russia?

### The Futile Search for Stability

- What crises did Europe and the United States face in the interwar years?

### In Pursuit of a New Reality: Cultural and Intellectual Trends

- How did the cultural and intellectual trends of the interwar years reflect the crises of the interwar years as well as the experience of World War I?

## CRITICAL THINKING

- What was the relationship between World War I and the Russian Revolution?

ON JULY 1, 1916, BRITISH and French infantry forces attacked German defensive lines along a 25-mile front near the Somme River in France. Each soldier carried almost 70 pounds of equipment, making it "impossible to move much quicker than a slow walk." German machine guns soon opened fire: "We were able to see our comrades move forward in an attempt to cross No-Man's-Land, only to be mown down like meadow grass," recalled one British soldier. "I felt sick at the sight of this carnage and remember weeping." In one day, more than 21,000 British soldiers died. After six months of fighting, the British had advanced 5 miles; one million British, French, and German soldiers had been killed or wounded.

Philip Gibbs, an English war correspondent, described what he saw in the German trenches that the British forces overran: "Victory! . . . Some of the German dead were young boys, too young to be killed for old men's crimes, and others might have been old or young. One could not tell because they had no faces, and were just masses of raw flesh in rags of uniforms. Legs and arms lay separate without any bodies thereabout."

World War I (1914–1918) was the defining event of the twentieth-century Western world. Overwhelmed by the scale of its battles, the extent of its casualties, and its impact on all facets of life, contemporaries referred to it simply as the "Great War." The Great War was all the more disturbing to Europeans because it came after what many believed to have been an age of progress. Material prosperity and a fervid belief in scientific and technological advancement had convinced many people that the world stood on the verge of creating the utopia that humans had dreamed of for centuries. The historian Arnold Toynbee expressed what the pre–World War I era had meant to his generation:

> [We had expected] that life throughout the world would become more rational, more humane, and more democratic and that, slowly, but surely, political democracy would produce greater social justice. We had also expected that the progress of science and technology would make mankind richer, and that this increasing wealth would gradually spread from a minority to a majority. We had expected that all this would happen peacefully. In fact we thought that mankind's course was set for an earthly paradise.[1]

After 1918, it was no longer possible to maintain naive illusions about the progress of Western civilization. As World War I was followed by revolutionary upheavals, the mass murder machines of totalitarian regimes, and the destructiveness of World War II, it became all too apparent that instead of a utopia, Western civilization had become a nightmare. World War I and the revolutions it spawned can properly be seen as the first stage in the crisis of the twentieth century. ◇

# The Road to World War I

On June 28, 1914, the heir to the Austrian throne, the Archduke Francis Ferdinand, was assassinated in the Bosnian city of Sarajevo. Although this event precipitated the confrontation between Austria and Serbia that led to World War I, underlying forces had been propelling Europeans toward armed conflict for a long time.

## Nationalism and Internal Dissent

The system of nation-states that had emerged in Europe in the second half of the nineteenth century (see Map 22.1) had led to severe competition. Rivalries over colonies and trade intensified during a frenzied imperialist expansion, while the division of Europe's great powers into two loose alliances (Germany, Austria, and Italy; France, Great Britain, and Russia) only added to the tensions. The series of crises that tested these alliances in the 1900s and early 1910s had left European states embittered, eager for revenge, and willing to revert to war as an acceptable way to preserve the power of their national states.

The growth of nationalism in the nineteenth century had yet another serious consequence. Not all ethnic groups had achieved the goal of nationhood. Slavic minorities in the Balkans and the polyglot Habsburg Empire, for example, still dreamed of creating their own national states. So did the Irish in the British Empire and the Poles in the Russian Empire.

National aspirations, however, were not the only source of internal strife at the beginning of the twentieth century. Socialist labor movements had grown more powerful and were increasingly inclined to use strikes, even violent ones, to achieve their goals. Some conservative leaders, alarmed at the increase in labor strife and class division, even feared that European nations were on the verge of revolution. Did these statesmen opt for war in 1914 because they believed that "prosecuting an active foreign policy," as some Austrian leaders expressed it, would smother "internal troubles"? Some historians have argued that the desire to suppress internal disorder may have encouraged some leaders to take the plunge into war in 1914.

## Militarism

The growth of large mass armies after 1900 not only heightened the existing tensions in Europe but also made it inevitable that if war did come, it would be extremely destructive. **Conscription**—obligatory military service—had been established as a regular practice in most Western countries before 1914 (the United States and Britain were major exceptions). European military machines had doubled in size between 1890 and 1914. With its 1.3 million men, the Russian army had grown to be the largest, but the French and Germans were not far behind, with 900,000 each. The British, Italian, and Austrian armies numbered between 250,000 and 500,000 soldiers.

**Militarism,** however, involved more than just large armies. As armies grew, so did the influence of military leaders, who drew up vast and complex plans for quickly mobilizing millions of men and enormous quantities of supplies in the event of war. Fearful that changing these plans would cause chaos in the armed forces, military leaders insisted that the plans could not be altered. In the crises during the summer of 1914, the generals' lack of flexibility forced European political leaders to make decisions for military instead of political reasons.

## The Outbreak of War: Summer 1914

Militarism, nationalism, and the desire to stifle internal dissent may all have played a role in the coming of World War I, but the decisions made by European leaders in the summer of 1914 directly precipitated the conflict. It was another crisis in the Balkans that forced this predicament on Europe's statesmen.

As we have seen, states in southeastern Europe had struggled to free themselves from Ottoman rule in the course of the nineteenth and early twentieth centuries.

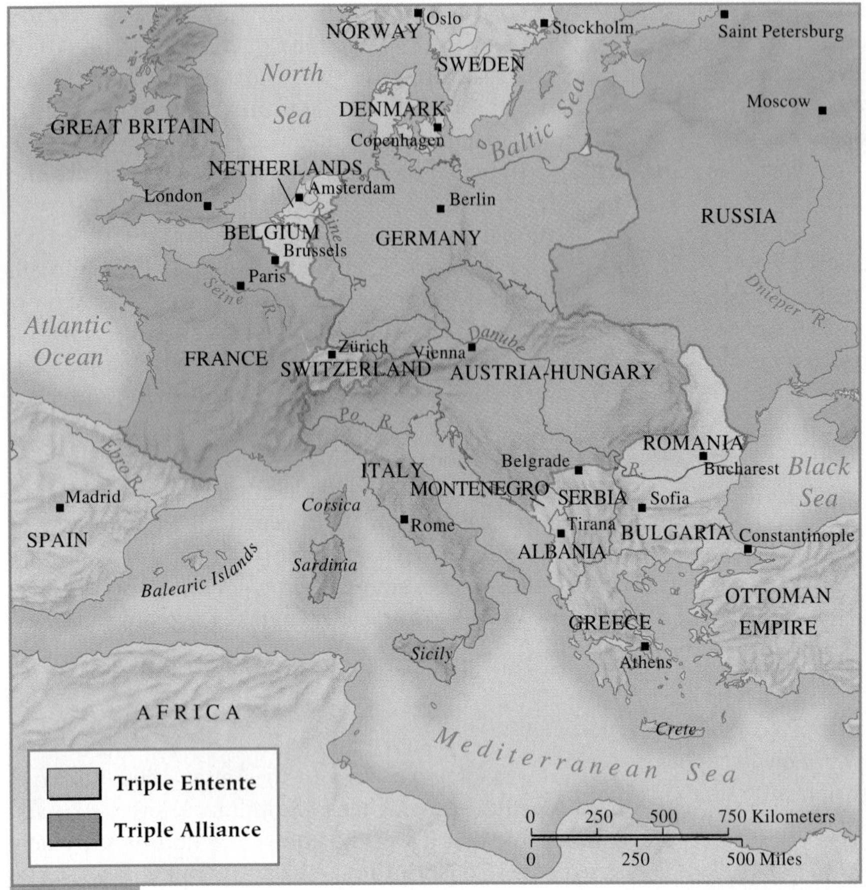


**MAP 22.1 Europe in 1914.** By 1914, two alliances dominated Europe: the Triple Entente of Britain, France, and Russia and the Triple Alliance of Germany, Austria-Hungary, and Italy. Russia sought to bolster fellow Slavs in Serbia, whereas Austria-Hungary was intent on increasing its power in the Balkans and thwarting Serbia's ambitions. Thus the Balkans became the flash point for World War I. **?** Which nonaligned nations were positioned between the two alliances? **View an animated version of this map or related maps at** http://history.wadsworth.com/duikerspielvogel05/

But the rivalry between Austria-Hungary and Russia for domination of these new states created serious tensions in the region. By 1914, Serbia, supported by Russia, was determined to create a large, independent Slavic state in the Balkans, while Austria, which had its own Slavic minorities to contend with, was equally set on preventing that possibility. Many Europeans perceived the inherent dangers in this combination of Serbian ambition bolstered by Russian hatred of Austria and the Austrian conviction that Serbia's success would mean the end of its empire. The British ambassador to Vienna wrote in 1913:

> Serbia will some day set Europe by the ears, and bring about a universal war on the Continent. . . . I cannot tell you how exasperated people are getting here at the continual worry which that little country causes to Austria under encouragement from Russia. . . . It will be lucky if Europe succeeds in avoiding war as a result of the present crisis. The next time a Serbian crisis arises . . . , I feel sure that Austria-Hungary will refuse to admit of any Russian interference in the dispute and that she will proceed to settle her differences with her little neighbor by herself.[2]

It was against this backdrop of mutual distrust and hatred that the events of the summer of 1914 were played out.

**The Assassination of Francis Ferdinand** The assassination of the Austrian Archduke Francis Ferdinand and his wife, Sophia, on June 28, 1914, was carried out by a Bosnian activist who worked for the Black Hand, a Serbian terrorist organization dedicated to the creation of a pan-Slavic kingdom. Although the Austrian government did not know whether the Serbian government had been directly involved in the archduke's assassination, it saw an opportunity to "render Serbia innocuous once and for all by a display of force," as the Austrian foreign minister put it. Fearful of Russian intervention on Serbia's behalf, Austrian leaders sought the backing of their German allies. Emperor William II and his chancellor gave their assurance that Austria-Hungary could rely on Germany's "full support," even if "matters went to the length of a war between Austria-Hungary and Russia."

Strengthened by German support, Austrian leaders issued an ultimatum to Serbia on July 23 in which they made such extreme demands that Serbia had little choice but to reject some of them in order to preserve its sovereignty. Austria then declared war on Serbia on July 28. Still smarting from its humiliation in the Bosnian crisis of 1908, Russia was determined to support Serbia's cause. On July 28, Tsar Nicholas II ordered partial mobilization of the Russian army against Austria. The Russian General Staff informed the tsar that their mobilization plans were based on a war against both Germany and Austria simultaneously. They could not execute partial mobilization without creating chaos in the army. Consequently, the Russian government ordered full mobilization of the Russian army on July 29, knowing that the Germans would consider this an act of war against them (see the box on p. 629). Germany reacted quickly. It issued an ultimatum that Russia must halt its mobilization within twelve hours. When the Russians ignored it, Germany declared war on Russia on August 1.

**Impact of the Schlieffen Plan** At this stage of the conflict, German war plans determined whether or not France would become involved in the war. Under the guidance of General Alfred von Schlieffen, chief of staff from 1891 to

## "You Have to Bear the Responsibility for War or Peace"

After Austria declared war on Serbia on July 28, 1914, Russian support of Serbia and German support of Austria threatened to escalate the conflict in the Balkans into a wider war. As we can see in these last-minute telegrams between the Russians and Germans, neither side was able to accept the other's line of reasoning.

*Do you think that these "sincere and devoted" friends and cousins, Emperor William II and Tsar Nicholas II, could have prevented World War I? Was Emperor William II correct when he said in his telegram of July 30 that the tsar alone would "have to bear the responsibility for war or peace"?*

### Communications Between Berlin and Saint Petersburg on the Eve of World War I

**Emperor William II to Tsar Nicholas II, July 28, 10:45 P.M.**

I have heard with the greatest anxiety of the impression which is caused by the action of Austria-Hungary against Servia [Serbia]. The inscrupulous agitation which has been going on for years in Servia has led to the revolting crime of which Archduke Franz Ferdinand has become a victim. The spirit which made the Servians murder their own King and his consort still dominates that country. Doubtless You will agree with me that both of us, You as well as I, and all other sovereigns, have a common interest to insist that all those who are responsible for this horrible murder shall suffer their deserved punishment. . . .

Your most sincere and devoted friend and cousin

*(Signed)* WILHELM

**Tsar Nicholas II to Emperor William II, July 29, 1 P.M.**

I am glad that you are back in Germany. In this serious moment I ask You earnestly to help me. An ignominious war has been declared against a weak country and in Russia the indignation which I fully share is tremendous. I fear that very soon I shall be unable to resist the pressure exercised upon me and that I shall be forced to take measures which will lead to war. To prevent a calamity as a European war would be, I urge You in the name of our old friendship to do all in Your power to restrain Your ally from going too far.

*(Signed)* NICOLAS

**Emperor William II to Tsar Nicholas II, July 29, 6:30 P.M.**

I have received Your telegram and I share Your desire for the conservation of peace. However: I cannot—as I told You in my first telegram—consider the action of Austria-Hungary as an "ignominious war." Austria-Hungary knows from experience that the promises of Servia as long as they are merely on paper are entirely unreliable. . . . I believe that a direct understanding is possible and desirable between Your Government and Vienna, an understanding which—as I have already telegraphed You—my Government endeavors to aid with all possible effort. Naturally military measures by Russia, which might be construed as a menace by Austria-Hungary, would accelerate a calamity which both of us desire to avoid and would undermine my position as mediator which—upon Your appeal to my friendship and aid—I willingly accepted.

*(Signed)* WILHELM

**Emperor William II to Tsar Nicholas II, July 30, 1 A.M.**

My Ambassador has instructions to direct the attention of Your Government to the dangers and serious consequences of a mobilization. I have told You the same in my last telegram. Austria-Hungary has mobilized only against Servia, and only a part of her army. If Russia, as seems to be the case, according to Your advice and that of Your Government, mobilizes against Austria-Hungary, the part of the mediator with which You have entrusted me in such friendly manner and which I have accepted upon Your express desire, is threatened if not made impossible. The entire weight of decision now rests upon Your shoulders; You have to bear the responsibility for war or peace.

*(Signed)* WILHELM

**German Chancellor to German Ambassador at Saint Petersburg, July 31, URGENT**

In spite of negotiations still pending and although we have up to this hour made no preparations for mobilization, Russia has mobilized her entire army and navy, hence also against us. On account of these Russian measures, we have been forced, for the safety of the country, to proclaim the threatening state of war, which does not yet imply mobilization. Mobilization, however, is bound to follow if Russia does not stop every measure of war against us and against Austria-Hungary within 12 hours, and notifies us definitely to this effect. Please to communicate this at once to M. Sazonoff and wire hour of communication.

1905, the German General Staff had devised a military plan based on the assumption of a two-front war with France and Russia because the two powers had formed a military alliance in 1894. The Schlieffen Plan called for a minimal troop deployment against Russia while most of the German army would make a rapid invasion of France before Russia could become effective in the east or before the British could cross the English Channel to help France. This meant invading France by advancing through neutral Belgium, with its level coastal plain on which the army

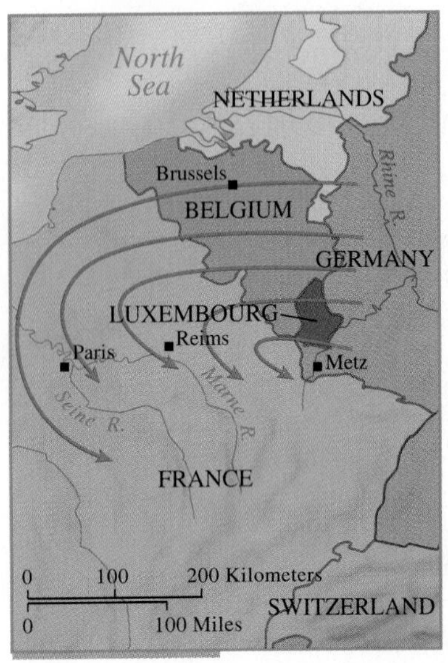


**The Schlieffen Plan**

could move faster than on the rougher terrain to the southeast. After the planned quick defeat of the French, the German army expected to redeploy to the east against Russia. Under the Schlieffen Plan, Germany could not mobilize its troops solely against Russia and therefore declared war on France on August 3 after it had issued an ultimatum to Belgium on August 2 demanding the right of German troops to pass through Belgian territory. On August 4, Great Britain declared war on Germany, officially over this violation of Belgian neutrality but in fact over the British desire to maintain world power. As one British diplomat argued, if Germany and Austria were to win the war, "what would be the position of a friendless England?" By August 4, all the great powers of Europe were at war.

## The Great War

Before 1914, many political leaders had become convinced that war involved so many political and economic risks that it was not worth fighting. Others had believed that "rational" diplomats could control any situation and prevent the outbreak of war. At the beginning of August 1914, both of these prewar illusions were shattered, but the new illusions that replaced them soon proved to be equally foolish.

### 1914–1915: Illusions and Stalemate

Europeans went to war in 1914 with remarkable enthusiasm (see the box on p. 631). Government propaganda had been successful in stirring up national antagonisms before the war. Now in August 1914, the urgent pleas of governments for defense against aggressors fell on receptive ears in every belligerent nation. Most people seemed genuinely convinced that their nation's cause was just. A new set of illusions also fed the enthusiasm for war. In August 1914, almost everyone believed that the war would be over in a few weeks. People were reminded that all *European* wars since 1815 had ended in a matter of weeks, thus conveniently overlooking the American Civil War (1861–1865), which was a better prototype for World War I. Both the soldiers who exuberantly boarded the trains for the war front in August 1914 and the jubilant citizens who bombarded them with flowers as they departed believed that the warriors would be home by Christmas.

German hopes for a quick end to the war rested on a military gamble. The Schlieffen Plan had called for the German army to make a vast encircling movement through Belgium into northern France that would sweep around Paris and encircle most of the French army. But the plan suffered a major defect from the beginning; it called for a strong right flank for the encircling of Paris, but German military leaders, concerned by a Russian invasion in the east, had moved forces from the right flank to strengthen the German army in the east.

As a result, the German advance was halted only 20 miles from Paris at the First Battle of the Marne (September 6–10). The war quickly turned into a stalemate as neither the Germans nor the French could dislodge the other from the trenches they had begun to dig for shelter. Two lines of trenches soon extended from the English Channel to the frontiers of Switzerland (see Map 22.2). The Western Front had become bogged down in **trench warfare,** which kept both sides immobilized in virtually the same positions for four years.

**The Excitement of War.** World War I was greeted with incredible enthusiasm. Each of the major belligerents was convinced of the rightness of its cause, thus proving the power of nationalism. Even socialists supported their governments rather than maintaining the solidarity of the working classes regardless of nationality. Everywhere in Europe, jubilant civilians sent their troops off to war with joyous fervor, as is evident in this photograph of French troops marching off to war. The belief that the soldiers would be home by Christmas proved to be a pathetic illusion.

## THE EXCITEMENT OF WAR

The incredible outpouring of patriotic enthusiasm that greeted the declaration of war at the beginning of August 1914 demonstrated the power that nationalistic feeling had attained at the beginning of the twentieth century. Many Europeans seemingly believed that the war had given them a higher purpose, a renewed dedication to the greatness of their nations. These selections are taken from three sources: the autobiography of Stefan Zweig, an Austrian writer; the memoirs of Robert Graves, a British writer; and a letter by a German soldier, Walter Limmer, to his parents.

*After reading these three selections, what do you think it is about war that creates such feelings of patriotism and enthusiasm? Why do you think peace was a less effective unifier of countries? Is this still true today?*

### Stefan Zweig, *The World of Yesterday*

The next morning I was in Austria. In every station placards had been put up announcing general mobilization. The trains were filled with fresh recruits, banners were flying, music sounded, and in Vienna I found the entire city in a tumult. . . . There were parades in the street, flags, ribbons, and music burst forth everywhere, young recruits were marching triumphantly, their faces lighting up at the cheering. . . .

And to be truthful, I must acknowledge that there was a majestic, rapturous, and even seductive something in this first outbreak of the people from which one could escape only with difficulty. And in spite of all my hatred and aversion for war, I should not like to have missed the memory of those days. As never before, thousands and hundreds of thousands felt what they should have felt in peace time, that they belonged together. A city of two million, a country of nearly fifty million, in that hour felt that they were participating in world history, in a moment which would never recur, and that each one was called upon to cast his infinitesimal self into the glowing mass, there to be purified of all selfishness. All differences of class, rank, and language were flooded over at that moment by the rushing feeling of fraternity. . . .

What did the great mass know of war in 1914, after nearly half a century of peace? They did not know war, they had hardly given it a thought. It had become legendary, and distance had made it seem romantic and heroic. They still saw it in the perspective of their school readers and of paintings in museums; brilliant cavalry attacks in glittering uniforms, the fatal shot always straight through the heart, the entire campaign a resounding march of victory—"We'll be home at Christmas," the recruits shouted laughingly to their mothers in August of 1914. . . . A rapid excursion into the romantic, a wild, manly adventure—that is how the war of 1914 was painted in the imagination of the simple man, and the younger people were honestly afraid that they might miss this most wonderful and exciting experience of their lives; that is why they hurried and thronged to the colors, and that is why they shouted and sang in the trains that carried them to the slaughter; wildly and feverishly the red wave of blood coursed through the veins of the entire nation.

### Robert Graves, *Goodbye to All That*

I had just finished with Charterhouse and gone up to Harlech, when England declared war on Germany. A day or two later I decided to enlist. In the first place, though the papers predicted only a very short war—over by Christmas at the outside—I hoped that it might last long enough to delay my going to Oxford in October, which I dreaded. Nor did I work out the possibilities of getting actively engaged in the fighting, expecting garrison service at home, while the regular forces were away. In the second place, I was outraged to read of the German's cynical violation of Belgian neutrality. Though I discounted perhaps twenty per cent of the atrocity details as wartime exaggeration, that was not, of course, sufficient.

### Walter Limmer, Letter to His Parents

In any case I mean to go into this business. . . . That is the simple duty of every one of us. And this feeling is universal among the soldiers, especially since the night when England's declaration of war was announced in the barracks. We none of us got to sleep till three o'clock in the morning, we were so full of excitement, fury, and enthusiasm. It is a joy to go to the Front with such comrades. We are bound to be victorious! Nothing else is possible in the face of such determination to win.

**HistoryNow**™ To read an opposing point of view by Rosa Luxembourg, enter the *HistoryNow* documents area using the access card that is available for *World History.*

In contrast to the Western Front, the war in the east was marked by much more mobility, although the cost in lives was equally enormous. At the beginning of the war, the Russian army moved into eastern Germany but was decisively defeated at the Battles of Tannenberg on August 30 and the Masurian Lakes on September 15. The Russians were no longer a threat to German territory.

The Austrians, Germany's allies, fared less well initially. They had been defeated by the Russians in Galicia and thrown out of Serbia as well. To make matters worse, the Italians betrayed the Germans and Austrians and entered the war on the Allied side by attacking Austria in May 1915. By this time, the Germans had come to the aid of the Austrians. A German-

**MAP 22.2 World War I, 1914–1918.** This map shows how greatly the Western and Eastern Fronts of World War I differed. After initial German gains in the west, the war became bogged down in trench warfare, with little change in the battle lines between 1914 and 1918. The Eastern Front was marked by considerable mobility, with battle lines shifting by hundreds of miles. ? How do you explain the difference in the two fronts? **View an animated version of this map or related maps at http://history.wadsworth.com/duikerspielvogel05/**

Austrian army defeated and routed the Russian army in Galicia and pushed the Russians back 300 miles into their own territory. Russian casualties stood at 2.5 million killed, captured, or wounded; the Russians had almost been knocked out of the war. Buoyed by their success, the Germans and Austrians, joined by the Bulgarians in September 1915, attacked and eliminated Serbia from the war.

## 1916–1917: The Great Slaughter

The successes in the east enabled the Germans to move back to the offensive in the west. The early trenches dug in 1914, stretching from the English Channel to the frontiers of Switzerland, had by now become elaborate systems of defense. Both lines of trenches were protected by barbed-wire entanglements 3 to 5 feet high and 90 feet wide, concrete machine-gun nests, and mortar batteries, supported farther back by heavy artillery. Troops lived in holes in the ground, separated from each other by a "no-man's land."

The unexpected development of trench warfare on the Western Front baffled military leaders, who had been trained to fight wars of movement and maneuver. Periodically the high command on either side would order an offensive that would begin with an artillery barrage to flatten the enemy's barbed wire and leave the enemy in a state of shock. After "softening up" the enemy in this fashion, a mass of soldiers would climb out of their trenches with fixed bayonets and hope to work their way toward the enemy trenches. The attacks rarely worked, as the machine gun put hordes of men advancing unprotected across

## The Reality of War: Trench Warfare

The romantic illusion about the excitement and adventure of war that filled the minds of so many young men who marched off to battle quickly disintegrated after a short time in the trenches on the Western Front. This description of trench warfare is taken from the most famous novel that emerged from World War I, Erich Maria Remarque's *All Quiet on the Western Front,* written in 1929. Remarque had fought in the trenches in France.

*What is causing the "madness and despair" Remarque describes in the trenches? Why does the recruit in this scene apparently go insane?*

### Erich Maria Remarque, *All Quiet on the Western Front*

We wake up in the middle of the night. The earth booms. Heavy fire is falling on us. We crouch into corners. We distinguish shells of every calibre.

Each man lays hold of his things and looks again every minute to reassure himself that they are still there. The dugout heaves, the night roars and flashes. We look at each other in the momentary flashes of light, and with pale faces and pressed lips shake our heads.

Every man is aware of the heavy shells tearing down the parapet, rooting up the embankment and demolishing the upper layers of concrete. . . . Already by morning a few of the recruits are green and vomiting. They are too inexperienced. . . .

The bombardment does not diminish. It is falling in the rear too. As far as one can see it spouts fountains of mud and iron. A wide belt is being raked.

The attack does not come, but the bombardment continues. Slowly we become mute. Hardly a man speaks. We cannot make ourselves understood.

Our trench is almost gone. At many places it is only eighteen inches high; it is broken by holes, and craters, and mountains of earth. A shell lands square in front of our post. At once it is dark. We are buried and must dig ourselves out. . . .

Towards morning, while it is still dark, there is some excitement. Through the entrance rushes in a swarm of fleeing rats that try to storm the walls. Torches light up the confusion. Everyone yells and curses and slaughters. The madness and despair of many hours unloads itself in this outburst. Faces are distorted, arms strike out, the beasts scream; we just stop in time to avoid attacking one another. . . .

Suddenly it howls and flashes terrifically, the dugout cracks in all its joints under a direct hit, fortunately only a light one that the concrete blocks are able to withstand. It rings metallically; the walls reel; rifles, helmets, earth, mud, and dust fly everywhere. Sulfur fumes pour in. . . . The recruit starts to rave again and two others follow suit. One jumps up and rushes out, we have trouble with the other two. I start after the one who escapes and wonder whether to shoot him in the leg—then it shrieks again; I fling myself down and when I stand up the wall of the trench is plastered with smoking splinters, lumps of flesh, and bits of uniform. I scramble back.

The first recruit seems actually to have gone insane. He butts his head against the wall like a goat. We must try tonight to take him to the rear. Meanwhile we bind him, but so that in case of attack he can be released.

Suddenly the nearer explosions cease. The shelling continues but it has lifted and falls behind us; our trench is free. We seize the hand grenades, pitch them out in front of the dugout, and jump after them. The bombardment has stopped and a heavy barrage now falls behind us. The attack has come.

No one would believe that in this howling waste there could still be men; but steel helmets now appear on all sides out of the trench, and fifty yards from us a machine gun is already in position and barking.

The wire entanglements are torn to pieces. Yet they offer some obstacle. We see the storm troops coming. Our artillery opens fire. Machine guns rattle, rifles crack. The charge works its way across. Haie and Kropp begin with the hand grenades. They throw as fast as they can; others pass them, the handles with the strings already pulled. Haie throws seventy-five yards, Kropp sixty; it has been measured; the distance is important. The enemy as they run cannot do much before they are within forty yards.

We recognize the distorted faces, the smooth helmets: they are French. They have already suffered heavily when they reach the remnants of the barbed-wire entanglements. A whole line has gone down before our machine guns; then we have a lot of stoppages and they come nearer.

I see one of them, his face upturned, fall into a wire cradle. His body collapses, his hands remain suspended as though he were praying. Then his body drops clean away and only his hands with the stumps of his arms, shot off, now hang in the wire.

open fields at a severe disadvantage. In 1916 and 1917, millions of young men were sacrificed in the search for the elusive breakthrough. In ten months at Verdun, 700,000 men lost their lives over a few miles of terrain.

Warfare in the trenches of the Western Front produced unimaginable horrors (see the box above). Battlefields were hellish landscapes of barbed wire, shell holes, mud, and injured and dying men. The introduction of poison gas in 1915 produced new forms of injuries, as one British writer described them:

> I wish those people who write so glibly about this being a holy war could see a case of mustard gas . . . could see the poor things burnt and blistered all over with great mustard-coloured suppurating blisters with blind eyes all sticky . . . and stuck

**The Horrors of War.** The slaughter of millions of men in the trenches of World War I created unimaginable horrors for the participants. For the sake of survival, many soldiers learned to harden themselves against the stench of decomposing bodies and the sight of bodies horribly dismembered by artillery barrages.

> together, and always fighting for breath, with voices a mere whisper, saying that their throats are closing and they know they will choke.[3]

Soldiers in the trenches also lived with the persistent presence of death. Since combat went on for months, soldiers had to carry on in the midst of countless bodies of dead men or the remains of men dismembered by artillery barrages. Many soldiers remembered the stench of decomposing bodies and the swarms of rats that grew fat in the trenches.

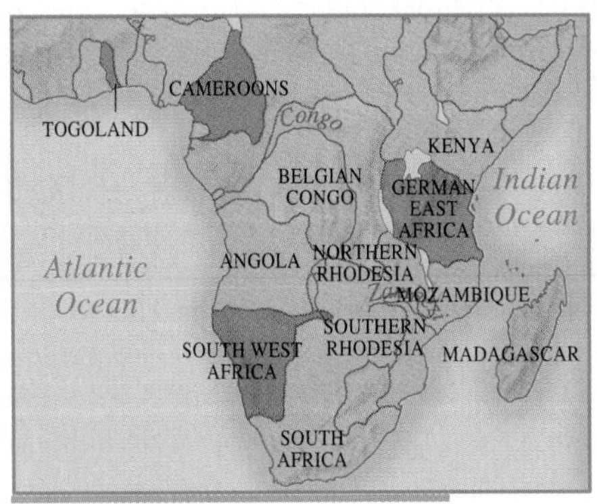


**German Possessions in Africa, 1914**

## The Widening of the War

As another response to the stalemate on the Western Front, both sides looked for new allies who might provide a winning advantage. The Ottoman Empire had already come into the war on Germany's side in August 1914. Russia, Great Britain, and France declared war on the Ottoman Empire in November. Although the Allies attempted to open a Balkan front by landing forces at Gallipoli, southwest of Constantinople, in April 1915, the entry of Bulgaria into the war on the side of the Central Powers (as Germany, Austria-Hungary, and the Ottoman Empire were called) and a disastrous campaign at Gallipoli caused them to withdraw. The Italians, as we have seen, also entered the war on the Allied side after France and Britain promised to further their acquisition of Austrian territory. In the long run, however, Italian military incompetence forced the Allies to come to the assistance of Italy.

**A Global Conflict** The war that originated in Europe rapidly became a world conflict (see the comparative illustration on p. 635). In the Middle East, a British officer who came to be known as Lawrence of Arabia (1888–1935) incited Arab princes to revolt against their Ottoman overlords in 1917. In 1918, British forces from Egypt destroyed the rest of the Ottoman Empire in the Middle East. For their Middle East campaigns, the British mobilized forces from India, Australia, and New Zealand.

In 1914, Germany possessed four colonies in Africa: Togoland, Cameroons, South West Africa, and German East Africa. British and French forces quickly occupied Togoland in West Africa, but Cameroons was not taken until 1916. British and white African forces invaded South West Africa in 1914 and forced the Germans to surrender in July 1915. The Allied campaign in East Africa proved more difficult and costly, and it was not until 1918 that the German forces surrendered there.

In these battles, Allied governments drew mainly on African soldiers, but some states, especially France, also recruited African troops to fight in Europe. The French drafted more than 170,000 West African soldiers. While some served as garrison forces in North Africa, many of the West African troops fought in the trenches on the Western front. About 80,000 Africans were killed or injured in Europe. They were often at a distinct disadvantage due to the unfamiliar terrain and climate.

Hundreds of thousands of Africans were also used for labor, especially for carrying supplies and building roads and bridges. In East Africa, both sides drafted African laborers as carriers for their armies. Disease and starvation caused by neglect led to the death of more than 100,000 of these laborers. In East Asia, thousands of Chinese and Indochinese also worked as laborers in European factories.

In East Asia and the Pacific, Japan joined the Allies on August 23, 1914, primarily to seize control of German territories in Asia. The Japanese took possession of German territories in China, as well as the German-occupied Marshall, Mariana, and Caroline Islands. The decision to

© Bettmann/CORBIS

COMPARATIVE ILLUSTRATION

**Soldiers from Around the World.** Although World War I began in Europe, it soon became a global conflict fought in different areas of the world and with soldiers from all parts of the world. France, especially, recruited troops from its African colonies to fight in Europe. The photo at the top shows French African troops fighting in the trenches on the Western Front. About eighty thousand Africans were killed or injured in Europe. The photo at the bottom shows a group of German soldiers in their machine-gun nest on the Western Front.

reward Japan for its cooperation eventually created difficulties in China (see Chapter 23). New Zealand and Australia quickly joined the Japanese in conquering the German-held parts of New Guinea and the Bismarck Archipelago.

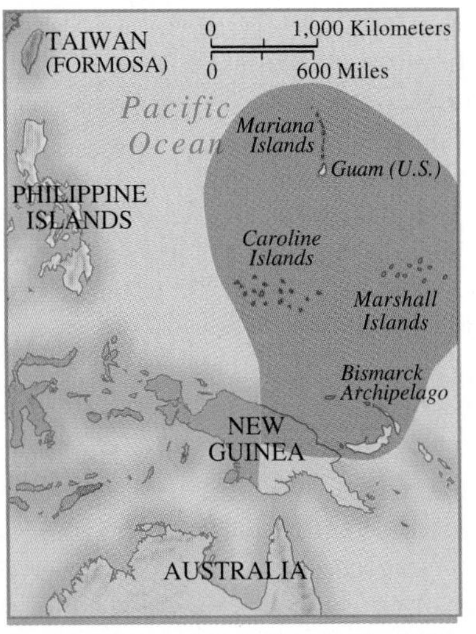


**German Possessions in the Pacific, 1914**

**Entry of the United States** Most important to the Allied cause was the entry of the United States into the war. The impetus for American involvement grew out of the naval conflict between Germany and Great Britain. Britain used its superior naval power to maximum effect by imposing a naval blockade on Germany. Germany retaliated with a counter blockade enforced by submarine warfare. Strong American protests over the German sinking of passenger liners, especially the British ship *Lusitania* on May 7, 1915, in which more than a hundred Americans lost their lives, forced the German government to suspend unrestricted submarine warfare in September 1915 to avoid further antagonizing the Americans.

In January 1917, however, eager to break the deadlock in the war, the Germans decided on another military gamble by returning to unrestricted submarine warfare. German naval officers convinced Emperor William II that the use of unrestricted submarine warfare could starve the British into submission within five months, before the Americans could act. The return to unrestricted submarine warfare brought the United States into the war on April 6, 1917. Although American troops did not arrive in Europe in large numbers until 1918, the entry of the United States into the war in 1917 gave the Allied Powers a psychological boost when they needed it.

The year 1917 had not been a good year for them. Allied offensives on the Western Front were disastrously defeated. The Italian armies were smashed in October, and in November a revolution in Russia (see "The Russian Revolution" later in this chapter) led to Russia's withdrawal from the war and left Germany free to concentrate entirely on the Western Front. The cause of the Central Powers looked favorable, although war weariness in the Ottoman Empire, Bulgaria, Austria-Hungary, and Germany was beginning to take its toll. The home front was rapidly becoming a cause for as much concern as the war front.

## The Home Front: The Impact of Total War

The prolongation of World War I made it a **total war** that affected the lives of all citizens, however remote they might be from the battlefields. The need to organize masses of men and matériel for years of combat (Germany alone had 5.5 million men in active units in 1916) led to increased centralization of government powers, economic regimentation, and manipulation of public opinion to keep the war effort going.

### Political Centralization and Economic Regimentation

Because the war was expected to be short, little thought had been given to economic considerations or long-term wartime needs. Governments had to respond quickly, however, when the war machines failed to achieve their knockout blows and made ever-greater demands for men and matériel. To meet these needs, governments expanded their powers. Countries drafted tens of millions of young men for that elusive breakthrough to victory.

Throughout Europe, wartime governments expanded their powers over their economies. Free market capitalistic systems were temporarily shelved as governments experimented with price, wage, and rent controls, rationed food supplies and materials, and nationalized transportation systems and industries. In effect, to mobilize all national resources for the war effort, European nations had moved toward planned economies directed by government agencies. Under total war mobilization, the distinction between soldiers at war and civilians at home was narrowed. In the view of political leaders, all citizens constituted a national army dedicated to victory. As the American president, Woodrow Wilson, expressed it, the men and women "who remain to till the soil and man the factories are no less a part of the army than the men beneath the battle flags."

### Public Order and Public Opinion

As the Great War dragged on and casualties grew worse, the patriotic enthusiasm that had marked the early stages of the conflict waned. By 1916, there were numerous signs that civilian morale was beginning to crack under the pressure of total war. War governments, however, fought back against the growing opposition to the war. Authoritarian regimes, such as those of Germany, Russia, and Austria-Hungary, had always relied on force to subdue their populations, but under the pressures of the war, even parliamentary regimes resorted to an expansion of police powers to stifle internal dissent. At the very beginning of the war, the British Parliament passed the Defense of the Realm Act (DORA), which allowed the public authorities to arrest dissenters as traitors. Newspapers were censored, and sometimes their publication was even suspended. In France, government authorities began in 1917 to suppress basic civil liberties.

Wartime governments made active use of propaganda to arouse enthusiasm for the war. At first, public officials needed to do little to achieve this goal. The British and French, for example, exaggerated German atrocities in Belgium and found that their citizens were only too willing to believe these accounts. But as the war dragged on and morale sagged, governments were forced to devise new techniques for stimulating enthusiasm. In one British recruiting poster, for example, a small daughter asked her

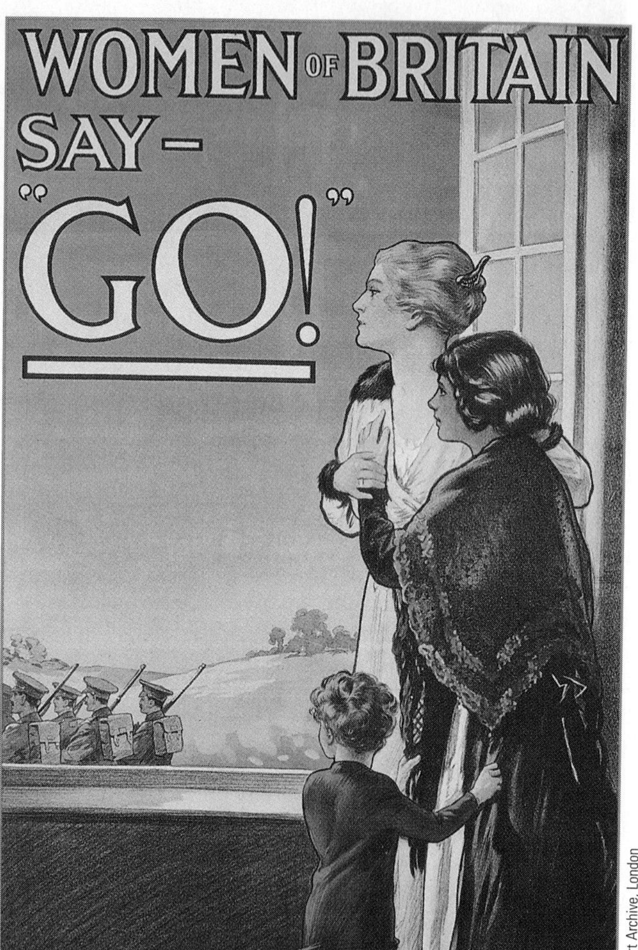


**British Recruiting Poster.** As the conflict persisted month after month, governments resorted to active propaganda campaigns to generate enthusiasm for the war. In this British recruiting poster, the government tried to pressure men into volunteering for military service. By 1916, the British were forced to adopt compulsory military service.

## Women in the Factories

During World War I, women were called on to assume new job responsibilities, including factory work. In this selection, Naomi Loughnan, a young, upper-middle-class woman, describes the experiences in a munitions plant that considerably broadened her perspective on life.

*The two groups Naomi Loughnan observes closely in this passage are men and lower-class women. What has she learned about these groups while working in the munitions factory? What did she learn about herself?*

### Naomi Loughnan, "Munition Work"

We little thought when we first put on our overalls and caps and enlisted in the Munition Army how much more inspiring our life was to be than we had dared to hope. Though we munition workers sacrifice our ease, we gain a life worth living. Our long days are filled with interest, and with the zest of doing work for our country in the grand cause of Freedom. As we handle the weapons of war we are learning great lessons of life. In the busy, noisy workshops we come face to face with every kind of class, and each one of these classes has something to learn from the others. . . .

Engineering mankind is possessed of the unshakable opinion that no woman can have the mechanical sense. If one of us asks humbly why such and such an alteration is not made to prevent this or that drawback to a machine, she is told, with a superior smile, that a man has worked her machine before her for years, and that therefore if there were any improvement possible it would have been made. As long as we do exactly what we are told and do not attempt to use our brains, we give entire satisfaction, and are treated as nice, good children. Any swerving from the easy path prepared for us by our males arouses the most scathing contempt in their manly bosoms. . . . Women have, however, proved that their entry into the munition world has increased the output. Employers who forget things personal in their patriotic desire for large results are enthusiastic over the success of women in the shops. But their workmen have to be handled with the utmost tenderness and caution lest they should actually imagine it was being suggested that women could do their work equally well, given equal conditions of training–at least where muscle is not the driving force. . . .

The coming of the mixed classes of women into the factory is slowly but surely having an educative effect upon the men. "Language" is almost unconsciously becoming subdued. There are fiery exceptions, who make our hair stand up on end under our close-fitting caps, but a sharp rebuke or a look of horror will often straighten out the most savage. . . . It is grievous to hear the girls also swearing and using disgusting language. Shoulder to shoulder with the children of the slums, the upper classes are having their eyes opened at last to the awful conditions among which their sisters have dwelt. Foul language, immorality, and many other evils are but the natural outcome of overcrowding and bitter poverty. . . . Sometimes disgust will overcome us, but we are learning with painful clarity that the fault is not theirs whose actions disgust us, but must be placed to the discredit of those other classes who have allowed the continued existence of conditions which generate the things from which we shrink appalled.

father, "Daddy, what did YOU do in the Great War?" while her younger brother played with toy soldiers and cannons.

Total war made a significant impact on European society, most visibly by bringing an end to unemployment. The withdrawal of millions of men from the labor market to fight, combined with the heightened demand for wartime products, led to jobs for everyone able to work.

**Women in the War Effort** World War I also opened new roles for women. Because so many men went off to fight at the front, women were called on to assume jobs and responsibilities that had not been available to them before. Overall, the number of women employed in Britain who held new jobs or replaced men rose by 1,345,000. Women were also now employed in jobs that had been considered "beyond the capacity of women." These included such occupations as chimney sweeps, truck drivers, farm laborers, and factory workers in heavy industry (see the box above). In Germany, 38 percent of the workers in the Krupp Armaments works in 1918 were women. Nevertheless, despite the noticeable increase in women's wages that resulted from government regulations, women's industrial wages were still not equal to men's wages by the end of the war.

Even worse, women's place in the workforce was far from secure. Both men and women seemed to assume that many of the new jobs for women were only temporary, an expectation quite evident in the British poem "War Girls," written in 1916:

*There's the girl who clips your ticket for the train,*
*And the girl who speeds the lift from floor to floor,*
*There's the girl who does a milk-round in the rain,*
*And the girl who calls for orders at your door.*
*Strong, sensible, and fit,*
*They're out to show their grit,*
*And tackle jobs with energy and knack.*
*No longer caged and penned up,*
*They're going to keep their end up*
*Till the khaki soldier boys come marching back.*[4]

At the end of the war, governments moved quickly to remove women from the jobs they had encouraged them to take earlier. By 1919, there were 650,000 unemployed women in Britain, and wages for women who were still employed were lowered. The work benefits for women from World War I seemed to be short-lived as demobilized men returned to the job market.

Nevertheless, in some countries the role played by women in the wartime economies did have a positive impact on the women's movement for social and political emancipation. The most obvious gain was the right to vote, given to women in Germany and Austria immediately after the war (in Britain a few months earlier). Contemporary media, however, tended to focus on the more noticeable yet in some ways more superficial social emancipation of upper- and middle-class women. In ever-larger numbers, these young women took jobs, had their own apartments, and showed their new independence by smoking in public and wearing shorter dresses, cosmetics, and new hairstyles.

## War and Revolution

By 1917, total war was creating serious domestic turmoil in all of the European belligerent states. Only one, however, experienced the kind of complete collapse that others were predicting might happen throughout Europe. Out of Russia's collapse came the Russian Revolution.

### The Russian Revolution

After the Revolution of 1905 had failed to bring any substantial changes to Russia, Tsar Nicholas II relied on the army and bureaucracy to uphold his regime. But World War I magnified Russia's problems and severely challenged the tsarist government. The tsar, possessed of a strong sense of moral duty to his country, was the only European monarch to take personal charge of the armed forces despite a lack of training for such an awesome responsibility. Russian industry was unable to produce the weapons needed for the army. Ill-led and ill-armed, Russian armies suffered incredible losses. Between 1914 and 1916, two million soldiers were killed, and another four to six million were wounded or captured.

The tsarist government was unprepared for the tasks that it faced in 1914. Even conservative aristocrats were appalled by the incompetent and inefficient bureaucracy of the political and military system. In the meantime, Tsar Nicholas II was increasingly insulated from events by his German-born wife, Alexandra, a well-educated woman who had fallen under the influence of Rasputin, a Siberian peasant whom the tsarina regarded as a holy man because he alone seemed able to stop the bleeding of her hemophiliac son, Alexis. Rasputin's influence made him a power behind the throne, and he did not hesitate to interfere in government affairs. As the leadership at the top experienced a series of military and economic disasters, the middle class, aristocrats, peasants, soldiers, and workers grew more and more disenchanted with the tsarist regime. Even conservative aristocrats who supported the monarchy felt the need to do something to reverse the deteriorating situation. For a start, they assassinated Rasputin in December 1916. By then it was too late to save the monarchy, and its fall came quickly.

**The March Revolution** At the beginning of March 1917, a series of strikes broke out in the capital city of Petrograd (formerly Saint Petersburg). Here the actions of working-class women helped change the course of Russian history. Weeks earlier, the government had introduced bread rationing in the capital city after the price of bread had skyrocketed. Many of the women who stood in the lines waiting for bread were also factory workers who had put in twelve-hour days. The Russian government had become aware of the volatile situation in the capital from a police report:

> Mothers of families, exhausted by endless standing in line at stores, distraught over their half-starving and sick children, are today perhaps closer to revolution than [the liberal opposition leaders] and of course they are a great deal more dangerous because they are the combustible material for which only a single spark is needed to burst into flame.[5]

On March 8, a day celebrated since 1910 as International Women's Day, about ten thousand Petrograd women marched through the city chanting "Peace and Bread" and "Down with Autocracy." Soon the women were joined by other workers, and together they called for a general strike that succeeded in shutting down all the factories in the city two days later. The tsarina wrote to Nicholas at the battlefront that "this is a hooligan movement. If the weather were very cold they would all probably stay at home." Believing his wife, Nicholas II responded to his military commanders, "I command you tomorrow to stop the disorders in the capital, which are unacceptable in the difficult time of war with Germany and Austria."[6] The troops were ordered to disperse the crowds, by shooting them if necessary. Initially the troops did so, but soon significant numbers of the soldiers joined the demonstrators. The Duma or legislative body, which the tsar had tried to dissolve, met anyway and on March 12 declared that it was assuming governmental responsibility. It established a provisional government on March 15; the tsar abdicated the same day.

The Provisional Government, headed by Alexander Kerensky (1881–1970) decided to carry on the war to preserve Russia's honor—a major blunder because it satisfied neither the workers nor the peasants, who above all wanted an end to the war. The Provisional Government also faced another authority, the **soviets,** or councils of workers' and soldiers' deputies. The Petrograd soviet had been formed in March 1917; at the same time, soviets sprang up spontaneously in army units, factory towns, and rural areas. The soviets represented the more radical interests of the lower classes and were largely composed of socialists of various kinds. Among them was the

**The Women's March in Petrograd.** After the imposition of bread rationing in Petrograd, ten thousand women engaged in mass demonstrations and demanded "Peace and Bread" for the families of soldiers. This photograph shows the women marching through the streets of Petrograd on March 8, 1917.

Marxist Social Democratic Party, which had formed in 1898 but divided in 1903 into two factions known as the Mensheviks and the Bolsheviks. The Mensheviks wanted the Social Democrats to be a mass electoral socialist party based on a Western model.

**Lenin and the Bolshevik Revolution** The Bolsheviks were a small faction of Russian Social Democrats who had come under the leadership of Vladimir Ulianov, known to the world as Lenin (1870–1924). Trained as a lawyer, in 1887, he turned into a dedicated enemy of tsarist Russia when his older brother was executed for planning to assassinate the tsar. Arrested for his revolutionary activity, Lenin was shipped to prison in Siberia. After his release, he chose to go into exile in Switzerland and eventually assumed the leadership of the Bolshevik wing of the Russian Social Democratic Party. Under Lenin's direction, the Bolsheviks became a party dedicated to violent revolution. He believed that only a revolution could destroy the capitalist system and that a "vanguard" of activists must form a small party of well-disciplined professional revolutionaries to accomplish the task. Between 1900 and 1917, Lenin spent most of his time in Switzerland. When the Provisional Government was formed in March 1917, he believed that an opportunity for the Bolsheviks to seize power had come. Just weeks later, with the connivance of the German High Command, who hoped to create disorder in Russia, Lenin was shipped to Russia in a sealed train by way of Finland.

Lenin's arrival in Russia opened a new stage of the Russian Revolution. Lenin maintained that the soviets of soldiers, workers, and peasants were ready-made instruments of power. The Bolsheviks must work toward gaining control of these groups and then use them to overthrow the Provisional Government. At the same time, Bolshevik propaganda must seek mass support through promises geared to the needs of the people: an end to the war, redistribution of all land to the peasants, the transfer of factories and industries from capitalists to committees of workers, and the relegation of government power from the Provisional Government to the soviets. Three simple slogans summed up the Bolshevik program: "Peace, Land, Bread," "Worker Control of Production," and "All Power to the Soviets."

By the end of October, the Bolsheviks had achieved a slight majority in the Petrograd and Moscow soviets. The number of party members had also grown, from 50,000 to 240,000. With Leon Trotsky (1877–1940), a fervid revolutionary, as chairman of the Petrograd soviet, Lenin and the Bolsheviks were in a position to seize power in the name of the soviets. During the night of November 6, pro-soviet and pro-Bolshevik forces took control of Petrograd; the Provisional Government quickly collapsed, with little bloodshed. The following night, the all-Russian Congress of Soviets, representing local soviets from all over the country, affirmed the transfer of power. At the second session, the night of November 8, Lenin announced the new Soviet government, the Council of People's Commissars, with himself as its head (see the box on p. 640).

But the Bolsheviks, soon renamed the Communists, still had a long way to go. For one thing, Lenin had promised peace, and that, he realized, was not an easy task

## Soldier and Peasant Voices

In 1917, Russia experienced a cataclysmic upheaval as two revolutions overthrew the tsarist regime and then the provisional government that replaced it. Peasants, workers, and soldiers poured out their thoughts and feelings on these events, some of them supporting the Bolsheviks and others denouncing the Bolsheviks for betraying their socialist revolution. These selections are taken from two letters, the first from a soldier and the second from a peasant. Both are addressed to Bolshevik leaders.

*What arguments do both of the writers of these letters use against Lenin and the Bolsheviks? Why do they feel so betrayed by the Bolsheviks?*

### Letter from a Soldier in Leningrad to Lenin, January 6, 1918

Bastard! What the hell are you doing? How long are you going to keep on degrading the Russian people? After all, it's because of you they killed the former minister . . . and so many other innocent victims. Because of you, they might kill even other former ministers belonging to the [Socialist Revolutionary] party because you call them counterrevolutionaries and even monarchists. . . . And you, you Bolshevik gang leader hired either by Nicholas II or by Wilhelm II, are waging this pogrom propaganda against men who may have done time with you in exile.

Scoundrel! A curse on you from the politically conscious Russian proletariat, the conscious ones and not the kind who are following you–that is, the Red Guards, the tally clerks, who, when they are called to military service, all hide at the factories and now are killing . . . practically their own father, the way the soldiers did in 1905 when they killed their own, or the way the police and gendarmes did in [1917]. That's who they're more like. They're not pursuing the ideas of socialism because they don't understand them (if they did they wouldn't act this way) but because they get paid a good salary both at the factory and in the Red Guards. But not all the workers are like that–there are very politically aware ones and the soldiers–again not all of them–are like that but only former policemen, constables, gendarmes and the very very ignorant ones who under the old regime tramped with hay on one foot and straw on the other because they couldn't tell their right foot from their left and they are pursuing not the ideas of socialism that you advocate but to be able to lie on their cots in the barracks and do absolutely nothing not even to be asked to sweep the floor, which is already piled with several inches of filth. And so the entire proletariat of Russia is following you, but count fewer than are against you, but they are only physically or rather technically stronger than the majority, and that is what you're abusing when you disbanded the Constituent Assembly the way Nicholas II disbanded the Duma. You point out that counterrevolutionaries gathered there. You lie, scoundrel, there wasn't a single counterrevolutionary and if there was then it was you, the Bolsheviks, which you proved by your actions when you encroached on the gains of the revolution: you are shutting down newspapers, even socialist ones, arresting socialists, committing violence and deceiving the people; you promised loads but did none of it.

### Letter from a Peasant to the Bolshevik Leaders, January 10, 1918

To You!

Rulers, plunderers, rapists, destroyers, usurpers, oppressors of Mother Russia, citizens Lenin, Trotsky, Uritsky, Zinoviev, Spiridonova, Antonov, Lunacharsky, Krylenko, and Co. [leaders of the Bolshevik party]:

Allow me to ask you how long you are going to go on degrading Russia's millions, its tormented and exhausted people. Instead of peace, you signed an armistice with the enemy, and this gave our opponent a painful advantage, and you declared war on Russia. You moved the troops you had tricked to the Russian-Russian front and started a fratricidal war. Your mercenary Red Guards are looting, murdering, and raping everywhere they go. A fire has consumed all our dear Mother Russia. Rail transport is idle, as are the plants and factories; the entire population has woken up to find itself in the most pathetic situation, without bread or kerosene or any of the other essentials, unclothed or unshod in unheated houses. In short: hungry and cold. . . . You have strangled the entire press, and freedom with it, you have wiped out the best freedom fighters, you have destroyed all Russia. Think it over, you butchers, you hirelings of the Kaiser [William II]. Isn't your turn about up, too? For all you are doing, we, politically aware Great Russians, are sending you butchers, you hirelings of the Kaiser, our curse. May you be damned, you accursed one, you bloodthirsty butchers, you hirelings of the Kaiser–don't think you're in the clear, because the Russian people will sober up and that will be the end of you. I'm writing in red ink to show that you are bloodthirsty. . . . I'm writing these curses, a great Russian native of Orel Province, peasant of Mtsensk Uezd.

because of the humiliating losses of Russian territory that it would entail. There was no real choice, however. On March 3, 1918, Lenin signed the Treaty of Brest-Litovsk with Germany and gave up eastern Poland, the Ukraine, Finland, and the Baltic provinces. To his critics, Lenin argued that it made no difference because the spread of socialist revolution throughout Europe would make the treaty largely irrelevant. In any case, he had promised peace to the Russian people, but real peace did not come, for the country soon sank into civil war.

**Civil War** There was great opposition to the new Communist regime, not only from groups loyal to the tsar but also from bourgeois and aristocratic liberals and anti-Leninist socialists. In addition, thousands of Allied troops were eventually sent to different parts of Russia in the hope of bringing Russia back into the war.

Between 1918 and 1921, the Red (Bolshevik) Army was forced to fight on many fronts. The first serious threat to the Bolsheviks came from Siberia, where White (anti-Bolshevik) forces attacked westward and advanced almost to the Volga River before being stopped. Attacks also came from the Ukrainians in the southeast and from the Baltic regions. In mid-1919, White forces swept through the Ukraine and advanced almost to Moscow. By 1920, the major White forces had been defeated and the Ukraine retaken. The next year, the Communist regime regained control over the independent nationalist governments in the Caucasus: Georgia, Russian Armenia, and Azerbaijan.

The royal family was yet another victim of the civil war. After the tsar had abdicated, he, his wife, and their five children had been taken into captivity. They were moved in August 1917 to Tobolsk in Siberia and in April 1918 to Ekaterinburg, a mining town in the Urals. On the night of July 16, members of the local soviet murdered the tsar and his family and burned their bodies in a nearby mine shaft.

**CHRONOLOGY The Russian Revolution**

| | |
|---|---|
| | 1916 |
| Murder of Rasputin | December |
| | 1917 |
| March of women in Petrograd | March 8 |
| General strike in Petrograd | March 10 |
| Establishment of Provisional Government | March 12 |
| Tsar Nicholas II abdicates | March 15 |
| Formation of Petrograd soviet | March |
| Lenin arrives in Russia | April 3 |
| Bolsheviks gain majority in Petrograd soviet | October |
| Bolsheviks overthrow Provisional Government | November 6–7 |
| | 1918 |
| Treaty of Brest-Litovsk | March 3 |
| Murder of royal family | July 16 |
| Civil war | 1918–1921 |

How had Lenin and the Bolsheviks triumphed over what seemed at one time to be overwhelming forces? For one thing, the Red Army became a well-disciplined and formidable fighting force, largely due to the organizational genius of Leon Trotsky. As commissar of war, Trotsky reinstated the draft and insisted on rigid discipline;

© Brown Brothers

© Underwood & Underwood/CORBIS

**Lenin and Trotsky.** Vladimir Lenin and Leon Trotsky were important figures in the success of the Bolsheviks in seizing power in Russia. On the left, Lenin is seen addressing a rally in Moscow in 1917. On the right, Trotsky, who became commissar of war in the new regime, is shown haranguing his troops.

soldiers who deserted or refused to obey orders were summarily executed.

The disunity of the anti-Communist forces seriously weakened the efforts of the Whites. Political differences created distrust among the Whites and prevented them from cooperating effectively with each other. Some Whites insisted on restoring the tsarist regime, while others understood that only a more liberal democratic program had any chance of success. It was difficult enough to achieve military cooperation; political differences made it virtually impossible.

The Whites' inability to agree on a common goal was in sharp contrast to the Communists' single-minded sense of purpose. Inspired by their vision of a new socialist order, the Communists had the advantage of possessing the determination that comes from revolutionary fervor and revolutionary convictions.

The Communists also succeeded in translating their revolutionary faith into practical instruments of power. A policy of **war communism,** for example, was used to ensure regular supplies for the Red Army. War communism included the nationalization of banks and most industries, the forcible requisition of grain from peasants, and the centralization of state power under Bolshevik control. Another Bolshevik instrument was "revolutionary terror." A new Red secret police, known as the Cheka, instituted the Red Terror, aimed at nothing less than the destruction of all opponents of the new regime.

Finally, the intervention of foreign armies enabled the Communists to appeal to the powerful force of Russian patriotism. Although the Allied Powers had intervened initially in Russia to encourage the Russians to remain in the war, the end of the war on November 11, 1918, had made that purpose inconsequential. Nevertheless, Allied troops remained, and even more were sent, as Allied countries did not hide their anti-Bolshevik feelings. At one point, over 100,000 foreign troops, mostly Japanese, British, American, and French, were stationed on Russian soil. This intervention by the Allies enabled the Communist government to appeal to patriotic Russians to fight the attempts of foreigners to control their country.

By 1921, the Communists were in control of Russia. In the course of the civil war, the Bolshevik regime had also transformed Russia into a bureaucratically centralized state dominated by a single party. It was also a state that was largely hostile to the Allied Powers who had sought to assist the Bolsheviks' enemies in the civil war. To most historians, the Russian Revolution is unthinkable without the total war of World War I, for only the collapse of Russia made it possible for a radical minority like the Bolsheviks to seize the reins of power. In turn, the Russian Revolution had an impact on the course of World War I.

## The Last Year of the War

For Germany, the withdrawal of the Russians from the war in March 1918 offered renewed hope for a favorable end to the war. The victory over Russia persuaded Erich von Ludendorff (1865–1937), who guided German military operations, and most German leaders to make one final military gamble—a grand offensive in the west to break the military stalemate. The German attack was launched in March and lasted into July, but an Allied counterattack, supported by the arrival of 140,000 fresh American troops, defeated the Germans at the Second Battle of the Marne on July 18. Ludendorff's gamble had failed. With the arrival of two million more American troops on the Continent, Allied forces began to advance steadily toward Germany.

On September 29, 1918, General Ludendorff informed German leaders that the war was lost and demanded that the government sue for peace at once. When German officials discovered, however, that the Allies were unwilling to make peace with the autocratic imperial government, reforms were instituted to create a liberal government. But these constitutional reforms came too late for the exhausted and angry German people. On November 3, naval units in Kiel mutinied, and within days, councils of workers and soldiers were forming throughout northern Germany and taking over the supervision of civilian and military administrations. William II capitulated to public pressure and abdicated on November 9, and the Socialists under Friedrich Ebert (1871–1925) announced the establishment of a republic. Two days later, on November 11, 1918, the new German government agreed to an armistice. The war was over.

### CHRONOLOGY World War I

| | |
|---|---|
| | **1914** |
| **Battle of Tannenberg** | **August 26–30** |
| **First Battle of the Marne** | **September 6–10** |
| **Battle of Masurian Lakes** | **September 15** |
| | **1915** |
| **Battle of Gallipoli begins** | **April 25** |
| **Italy declares war on Austria-Hungary** | **May 23** |
| | **1916** |
| **Battle of Verdun** | **February 21–December 18** |
| | **1917** |
| **United States enters the war** | **April 6** |
| | **1918** |
| **Last German offensive** | **March 21–July 18** |
| **Second Battle of the Marne** | **July 18** |
| **Allied counteroffensive** | **July 18–November 10** |
| **Armistice between Allies and Germany** | **November 11** |

**The Casualties of the War** World War I devastated European civilization. Between 8 and 9 million soldiers died on the battlefields; another 22 million were wounded. Many of those who survived later died from war injuries or lived on without arms or legs or with other forms of mutilation. The birthrate in many European countries declined noticeably as a result of the death or maiming of so many young men. World War I also created a "lost generation" of war veterans who had become inured to violence and who would later band together in support of Mussolini and Hitler in their tyrannical bids for power.

Nor did the killing affect only soldiers. Untold numbers of civilians died from war injuries or starvation. In 1915, after an Armenian uprising against the Ottoman government, the government retaliated with fury by killing Armenian men and expelling women and children. Within seven months, 600,000 Armenians had been killed, and 500,000 had been deported. Of the latter, 400,000 died while marching through the deserts and swamps of Syria and Mesopotamia. By September 1915, an estimated one million Armenians were dead, the victims of genocide.

## The Peace Settlement

In January 1919, the delegations of twenty-seven victorious Allied nations gathered in Paris to conclude a final settlement of the Great War. Over a period of years, the reasons for fighting World War I had been transformed from selfish national interests to idealistic principles.

**The Big Four at Paris.** Shown here are the Big Four at the Paris Peace Conference: David Lloyd George of Britain, Vittorio Orlando of Italy, Georges Clemenceau of France, and Woodrow Wilson of the United States. Although Italy was considered one of the Big Four powers, Britain, France, and the United States (the Big Three) made the major decisions at the peace conference.

**Peace Aims** No one expressed these principles better than U.S. President Woodrow Wilson. Wilson's proposals for a truly just and lasting peace included "open covenants of peace, openly arrived at" instead of secret diplomacy; the reduction of national armaments to a "point consistent with domestic safety"; and the self-determination of people so that "all well-defined national aspirations shall be accorded the utmost satisfaction." Wilson characterized World War I as a people's war waged against "absolutism and militarism," which could be eradicated only by creating democratic governments and a "general association of nations" that would guarantee the "political independence and territorial integrity to great and small states alike" (see the box on p. 644). As the spokesman for a new world order based on democracy and international cooperation, Wilson was enthusiastically cheered by many Europeans when he arrived in Europe for the peace conference, held at the palace of Versailles.

Wilson soon found, however, that more practical motives guided other states at the peace table. The secret treaties and agreements that had been made before the war could not be totally ignored, even if they did conflict with the principle of self-determination enunciated by Wilson. National interests also complicated the deliberations of the Paris Peace Conference. David Lloyd George, prime minister of Great Britain, had won a decisive electoral victory in December 1918 on a platform of making the Germans pay for this dreadful war.

France's approach to peace was determined primarily by considerations of national security. To Georges Clemenceau, the feisty premier of France who had led his country to victory, the French people had borne the brunt of German aggression. They deserved revenge and security against future German aggression.

The most important decisions at the Paris Peace Conference were made by Wilson, Clemenceau, and Lloyd George. Italy was considered one of the so-called Big Four powers but played a much less important role than the other three countries. Germany, of course, was not invited to attend, and Russia could not because of its civil war.

In view of the many conflicting demands at Versailles, it was inevitable that the Big Three would quarrel. Wilson was determined to create a "league of nations" to prevent future wars. Clemenceau and Lloyd George were equally determined to punish Germany. In the end, only compromise made it possible to achieve a peace settlement. Wilson's wish that the creation of an international peacekeeping organization be the first order of business was granted, and on January 25, 1919, the conference adopted the principle of the League of Nations. In return, Wilson agreed to make compromises on territorial arrangements to guarantee the establishment

## The Voice of Peacemaking: Woodrow Wilson

"We are fighting for the liberty, the self-government, and the undictated development of all peoples." When the Allied powers met in Paris in January 1919, it soon became apparent that the victors had different opinions on the kind of peace they expected. These excerpts are from the speeches of Woodrow Wilson in which the American president presented his idealistic goals for a peace based on justice and reconciliation.

*What principles and goals did President Wilson establish for the Paris Peace Conference? In view of the horrors of World War I, were these goals realistic?*

### May 26, 1917

We are fighting for the liberty, the self-government, and the undictated development of all peoples, and every feature of the settlement that concludes this war must be conceived and executed for that purpose. Wrongs must first be righted and then adequate safeguards must be created to prevent their being committed again. . . .

No people must be forced under sovereignty under which it does not wish to live. No territory must change hands except for the purpose of securing those who inhabit it a fair chance of life and liberty. No indemnities must be insisted on except those that constitute payment for manifest wrongs done. No readjustments of power must be made except such as will tend to secure the future peace of the world and the future welfare and happiness of its peoples.

And then the free peoples of the world must draw together in some common covenant, some genuine and practical cooperation that will in effect combine their force to secure peace and justice in the dealings of nations with one another.

### April 6, 1918

We are ready, whenever the final reckoning is made, to be just to the German people, deal fairly with the German power, as with all others. There can be no difference between peoples in the final judgment, if it is indeed to be a righteous judgment. To propose anything but justice, even-handed and dispassionate justice, to Germany at any time, whatever the outcome of the war, would be to renounce and dishonor our own cause. For we ask nothing that we are not willing to accord.

### January 3, 1919

Our task at Paris is to organize the friendship of the world, to see to it that all the moral forces that make for right and justice and liberty are united and are given a vital organization to which the peoples of the world will readily and gladly respond. In other words, our task is no less colossal than this, to set up a new international psychology, to have a new atmosphere.

**History Now™** To read the Treaty of Versailles, enter the *HistoryNow* documents area using the access card that is available for *World History.*

of the League, believing that a functioning League could later rectify bad arrangements. Clemenceau also compromised to obtain some guarantees for French security. He renounced France's desire for a separate Rhineland and instead accepted a defensive alliance with Great Britain and the United States. Both states pledged to help France if it were attacked by Germany.

**The Treaty of Versailles** The final peace settlement consisted of five separate treaties with the defeated nations—Germany, Austria, Hungary, Bulgaria, and Turkey. The Treaty of Versailles with Germany, signed on June 28, 1919, was by far the most important one. The Germans considered it a harsh peace and were particularly unhappy with Article 231, the so-called **War Guilt Clause,** which declared Germany (and Austria) responsible for starting the war and ordered Germany to pay **reparations** for all the damage to which the Allied governments and their people were subjected as a result of the war "imposed upon them by the aggression of Germany and her allies."

The military and territorial provisions of the treaty also rankled Germans. Germany had to lower its army to 100,000 men, reduce its navy, and eliminate its air force. German territorial losses included the return of Alsace and Lorraine to France and sections of Prussia to the new Polish state (see Map 22.3). German land west and as far as 30 miles east of the Rhine was established as a demilitarized zone and stripped of all armaments or fortifications to serve as a barrier to any future German military moves westward against France. Outraged by the "dictated peace," the new German government complained but accepted the treaty.

**The Other Peace Treaties** The separate peace treaties made with the other Central Powers extensively redrew the map of eastern Europe. Many of these changes merely ratified what the war had already accomplished. Both the German and Russian empires lost considerable territory in eastern Europe, and the Austro-Hungarian Empire disappeared altogether. New nation-states emerged from the lands of these three empires: Finland, Latvia, Estonia, Lithuania, Poland, Czechoslovakia, Austria, and Hungary. Territorial rearrangements were also made in the Balkans. Romania acquired additional lands from Russia, Hungary, and Bulgaria. Serbia formed

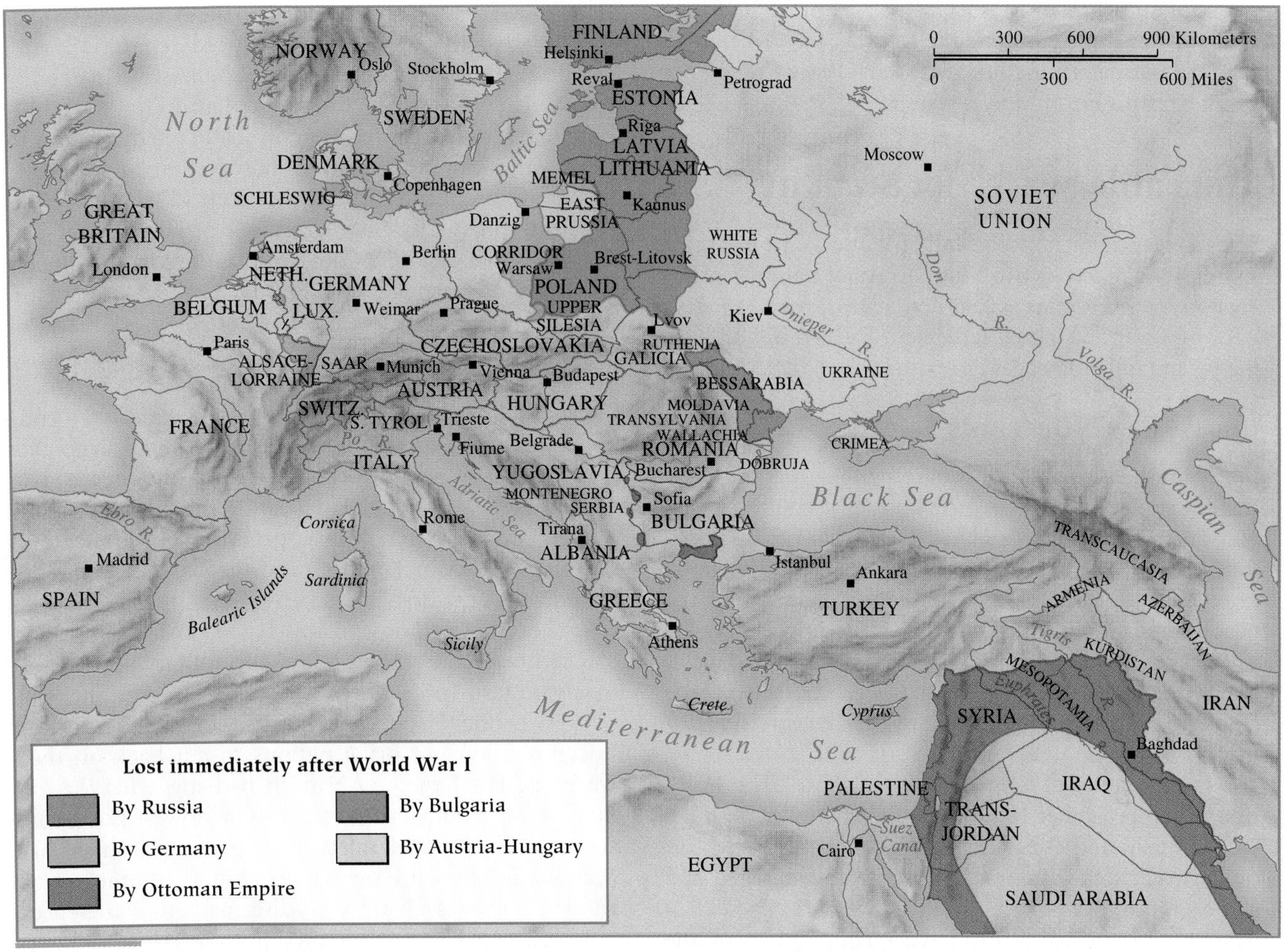

**MAP 22.3 Territorial Changes in Europe and the Middle East After World War I.** The victorious Allies met in Paris to determine the shape and nature of postwar Europe. At the urging of U.S. President Woodrow Wilson, many nationalist aspirations of former imperial subjects were realized with the creation of several new countries from the prewar territory of Austria-Hungary, Germany, Russia, and the Ottoman Empire. ? What new countries emerged in Europe and the Middle East? **View an animated version of this map or related maps at** http://history.wadsworth.com/duikerspielvogel05/

the nucleus of a new southern Slavic kingdom, later called Yugoslavia, which united Serbs, Croats, and Slovenes under a single monarch.

Although the Paris Peace Conference was supposedly guided by the principle of self-determination, the mixtures of peoples in eastern Europe made it impossible to draw boundaries along neat ethnic lines. As a result of compromises, virtually every eastern European state was left with a minorities problem that could lead to future conflicts. Germans in Poland; Hungarians, Poles, and Germans in Czechoslovakia; Hungarians in Romania; and the combination of Serbs, Croats, Slovenes, Macedonians, and Albanians in Yugoslavia all became sources of later conflict.

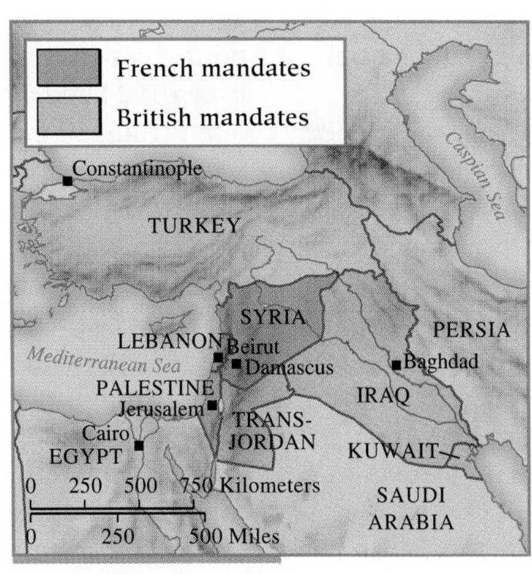


**The Middle East in 1919**

Yet another centuries-old empire, the Ottoman Empire, was dismembered by the peace settlement after the war. To gain Arab support against the Ottoman Turks during the war, the Western Allies had promised to recognize the independence of Arab states in the Middle Eastern lands of the Ottoman Empire. But the imperialist habits of Western nations died hard. After the war, France was given control of Lebanon and Syria, while Britain received Iraq and Palestine. Officially, both acquisitions were called **mandates.** Since Woodrow Wilson had opposed the outright annexation of colonial territories by the Allies, the peace settlement had created a system of mandates whereby a nation officially administered a territory on behalf of the League of Nations. The system of mandates could not hide the fact that the principle of national self-determination at the Paris Peace Conference was largely for Europeans.

## The Futile Search for Stability

The peace settlement at the end of World War I had tried to fulfill the nineteenth-century dream of nationalism by creating new boundaries and new states. From its inception, however, this peace settlement had left nations unhappy and only too eager to revise it.

### Uneasy Peace, Uncertain Security

President Woodrow Wilson had recognized that the peace treaties contained unwise provisions that could serve as new causes for conflicts and had placed many of his hopes for the future in the League of Nations. The League, however, was not particularly effective in maintaining the peace. The failure of the United States to join the League in a backlash of isolationist sentiment undermined its effectiveness from the beginning. Moreover, the League could use only economic sanctions to halt aggression.

**The French Policy of Coercion (1919–1924)** The weakness of the League of Nations and the failure of both the United States and Great Britain to honor their defensive military alliances with France left France embittered and alone. France's search for security between 1919 and 1924 was founded primarily on a strict enforcement of the Treaty of Versailles. This tough policy toward Germany began with the issue of the reparations payments that the Germans were supposed to make to compensate for war damage. In April 1921, the Allied Reparations Commission settled on a sum of 132 billion marks ($33 billion), payable in annual installments of 2.5 billion (gold) marks. The new German republic made its first payment in 1921, but by the following year, facing financial problems, the Germans announced that they were unable to pay more. Outraged, the French government sent troops to occupy the Ruhr valley, Germany's chief industrial and mining center. Because the Germans would not pay reparations, the French would collect reparations in kind by operating and using the Ruhr's mines and factories.

Both Germany and France suffered from the French occupation of the Ruhr. The German government adopted a policy of passive resistance to French occupation that was largely financed by printing more paper money. This only intensified the inflationary pressures that had begun in Germany toward the end of the war. The German mark became worthless, and economic disaster fueled political upheavals. All the nations, including France, were happy to cooperate with the American suggestion for a new conference of experts to reassess the reparations problem.

**The Hopeful Years (1924–1929)** In August 1924, an international commission produced a new plan for reparations. The Dawes Plan, named after the American banker who chaired the commission, reduced reparations and stabilized Germany's payments on the basis of its ability to pay. The Dawes Plan also granted an initial $200 million loan for German recovery, which opened the door to heavy American investments in Europe that helped create an era of European prosperity between 1924 and 1929.

With prosperity came a new age of European diplomacy. A spirit of cooperation was fostered by the foreign ministers of Germany and France, Gustav Stresemann and Aristide Briand, who concluded the Treaty of Locarno in 1925. This guaranteed Germany's new western borders with France and Belgium. Although Germany's new eastern borders with Poland were conspicuously absent from the agreement, the Locarno pact was viewed by many as the beginning of a new era of European peace. On the day after the pact was concluded, the *New York Times* proclaimed, "France and Germany Ban War Forever," and the *London Times* declared, "Peace at Last."[7]

The spirit of Locarno was based on little real substance, however. Germany lacked the military power to alter its western borders even if it wanted to. And the issue of disarmament soon proved that even the spirit of Locarno could not bring nations to cut back on their weapons. The League of Nations had suggested the "reduction of national armaments to the lowest point consistent with national safety." Germany, of course, had been disarmed with the expectation that other states would do likewise. Numerous disarmament conferences, however, failed to achieve anything substantial as states were unwilling to trust their security to anyone but their own military forces.

### The Great Depression

After World War I, most European states hoped to return to the liberal ideal of a private-enterprise, market economy largely free of state intervention. But the war had vastly strengthened business cartels and labor unions, making some government regulation of these powerful organizations necessary. At the same time, reparations and war debts had severely damaged the postwar international economy, making the prosperity that did occur between 1924 and 1929 at best a fragile one and the dream of returning to the liberal ideal of a self-regulating market economy merely an illusion. What destroyed the concept altogether was the Great Depression.

**Causes** Two factors played a major role in the coming of the Great Depression: a downturn in domestic economies and an international financial crisis created by the collapse of the American stock market in 1929. Already in the mid-1920s, prices for agricultural goods were beginning to decline rapidly due to overproduction of basic commodities such as wheat. In 1925, states in central and eastern Europe began to impose tariffs to close their markets to other countries' goods. An increase in the use of oil

**The Great Depression: Bread Lines in Paris.** The Great Depression devastated the European economy and had serious political repercussions. Because of its more balanced economy, France did not feel the effects of the depression as quickly as other European countries. By 1931, however, even France was experiencing lines of unemployed people at free-food centers.

and hydroelectricity led to a slump in the coal industry even before 1929.

In addition to these domestic economic troubles, much of the European prosperity between 1924 and 1929 had been built on American bank loans to Germany. In 1928, American investors had begun to pull money out of Germany in order to invest in the booming New York stock market. The crash of the U.S. stock market in October 1929 led panicky American investors to withdraw even more of their funds from Germany and other European markets. The withdrawal of funds seriously weakened the banks of Germany and other central European states. The Credit-Anstalt, Vienna's most prestigious bank, collapsed on May 31, 1931. By that time, trade was slowing down, industrialists were cutting back production, and unemployment was increasing as the ripple effects of international bank failures had a devastating impact on domestic economies.

**Repercussions** Economic depression was by no means a new phenomenon in European history. But the depth of the economic downturn after 1929 fully justifies the Great Depression label. During 1932, the worst year of the downturn, one British worker in four was unemployed, and six million workers, or 40 percent of the German labor force, were out of work. Between 1929 and 1932, industrial production plummeted almost 50 percent in the United States and nearly as much in Germany. Unemployed and homeless people filled the streets of cities throughout the advanced industrial world (see the box on p. 648).

The economic crisis also had unexpected social repercussions. Women were often able to secure low-paying jobs as servants, housecleaners, or laundresses, while many men remained unemployed, either begging on the streets or remaining at home to do household tasks. This reversal of traditional gender roles caused resentment on the part of many unemployed men, opening them to the shrill cries of demagogues with simple solutions to the economic crisis. In addition, high unemployment rates among young males often led them to join gangs that gathered in parks or other public places, creating fear among local residents.

Governments seemed powerless to deal with the crisis. The classical liberal remedy for depression, a deflationary policy of balanced budgets, which involved cutting costs by lowering wages and raising tariffs to exclude other countries' goods from home markets, only served to worsen the economic crisis and cause even greater mass discontent. This in turn led to serious political repercussions. Increased government activity in the economy was one reaction. Another effect was a renewed interest in Marxist doctrines. Hadn't Marx predicted that capitalism would destroy itself through overproduction? Communism took on new popularity, especially with workers and intellectuals. Finally, the Great Depression increased the attractiveness of simplistic dictatorial solutions, especially from a new movement known as fascism. Everywhere, democracy seemed on the defensive in the 1930s.

## The Democratic States

After World War I, Great Britain went through a period of serious economic difficulties. During the war, Britain had lost many of the markets for its industrial products, especially to the United States and Japan. The postwar decline of such staple industries as coal, steel, and textiles led to a rise in unemployment, which reached the two million mark in 1921. But Britain soon rebounded and from 1925 to 1929 experienced an era of renewed prosperity, even though unemployment remained at the startling level of 10 percent.

**Great Britain** By 1929, Britain faced the growing effects of the Great Depression. The Labour Party, which had become the largest party in Britain, failed to solve the nation's

## The Great Depression: Unemployed and Homeless in Germany

In 1932, Germany had six million unemployed workers, many of them wandering aimlessly about the country, begging for food and seeking shelter in city lodging houses for the homeless. The Great Depression was an important factor in the rise to power of Adolf Hitler and the Nazis. This selection presents a description of the unemployed homeless in 1932.

*Why did Hauser compare the scene he describes from 1932 with the years of 1917 and 1918? Why does he compare the hungry men with animals?*

### Heinrich Hauser, "With Germany's Unemployed"

An almost unbroken chain of homeless men extends the whole length of the great Hamburg-Berlin highway. . . . All the highways in Germany over which I have traveled this year presented the same aspect. . . .

Most of the hikers paid no attention to me. They walked separately or in small groups, with their eyes on the ground. And they had the queer, stumbling gait of barefooted people, for their shoes were slung over their shoulders. Some of them were guild members–carpenters . . . milkmen . . . and bricklayers . . . but they were in a minority. Far more numerous were those whom one could assign to no special profession or craft–unskilled young people, for the most part, who had been unable to find a place for themselves in any city or town in Germany, and who had never had a job and never expected to have one. There was something else that had never been seen before–whole families that had piled all their goods into baby carriages and wheelbarrows that they were pushing along as they plodded forward in dumb despair. It was a whole nation on the march.

I saw them–and this was the strongest impression that the year 1932 left with me–I saw them, gathered into groups of fifty or a hundred men, attacking fields of potatoes. I saw them digging up the potatoes and throwing them into sacks while the farmer who owned the field watched them in despair and the local policeman looked on gloomily from the distance. I saw them staggering toward the lights of the city as night fell, with their sacks on their backs. What did it remind me of? Of the War, of the worst periods of starvation in 1917 and 1918, but even then people paid for the potatoes. . . .

I saw that the individual can know what is happening only by personal experience. I know what it is to be a tramp. I know what cold and hunger are. . . . But there are two things that I have only recently experienced–begging and spending the night in a municipal lodging house.

I entered the huge Berlin municipal lodging house in a northern quarter of the city. . . .

Distribution of spoons, distribution of enameled-ware bowls with the words "Property of the City of Berlin" written on their sides. Then the meal itself. A big kettle is carried in. Men with yellow smocks have brought it in, and men with yellow smocks ladle out the food. These men, too, are homeless and they have been expressly picked by the establishment and given free food and lodging and a little pocket money in exchange for their work about the house.

Where have I seen this kind of food distribution before? In a prison that I once helped to guard in the winter of 1919 during the German civil war. There was the same hunger then, the same trembling, anxious expectation of rations. Now the men are standing in a long row, dressed in their plain nightshirts that reach to the ground, and the noise of their shuffling feet is like the noise of big wild animals walking up and down the stone floor of their cages before feeding time. The men lean far over the kettle so that the warm steam from the food envelops them, and they hold out their bowls as if begging and whisper to the attendant, "Give me a real helping. Give me a little more." A piece of bread is handed out with every bowl.

My next recollection is sitting at table in another room on a crowded bench that is like a seat in a fourth-class railway carriage. Hundreds of hungry mouths make an enormous noise eating their food. The men sit bent over their food like animals who feel that someone is going to take it away from them. They hold their bowl with their left arm partway around it, so that nobody can take it away, and they also protect it with their other elbow and with their head and mouth, while they move the spoon as fast as they can between their mouth and the bowl.

History Now™ To read about World War I rationing in Germany, enter the *HistoryNow* documents area using the access card that is available for *World History.*

economic problem and fell from power in 1931. A national government (a coalition of Liberals and Conservatives) claimed credit for bringing Britain out of the worst stages of the depression, primarily by using the traditional policies of balanced budgets and protective tariffs. British politicians had largely ignored the new ideas of a Cambridge economist, John Maynard Keynes (1883–1946), who published his *General Theory of Employment, Interest, and Money* in 1936. He condemned the traditional view that in a free economy, depressions should be left to work themselves out and argued instead that unemployment stemmed not from overproduction but from a decline in demand and that demand could be increased by putting people back to work constructing highways and public buildings, even if governments had to go into debt to pay for these works, a concept known as **deficit spending.**

**France** After the defeat of Germany, France had become the strongest power on the European continent. Its greatest need was to rebuild the devastated areas of northern and eastern France. However, no French government seemed capable of solving France's financial problems between 1921 and 1926. Like other European countries, though, France did experience a period of relative prosperity between 1926 and 1929.

Because it had a more balanced economy than other nations, France did not begin to feel the full effects of the Great Depression until 1932. Economic instability soon had political repercussions. During a nineteen-month period in 1932 and 1933, six different cabinets were formed as France faced political chaos. Finally, in June 1936, a coalition of leftist parties—Socialists and Radicals—formed a Popular Front government.

Although the Popular Front initiated a program for workers that consisted of the right of collective bargaining, a forty-hour workweek, two-week paid vacations, and minimum wages, its policies failed to solve the problems of the depression. By 1938, the French were experiencing a serious decline of confidence in their political system.

**Germany** After the imperial Germany of William II had come to an end in 1918 with Germany's defeat in World War I, a German democratic state known as the Weimar Republic was established. From the very start, the Weimar Republic was plagued by problems. It had no truly outstanding political leaders, and in 1925, Paul von Hindenburg, a World War I military hero, was elected president at the age of seventy-seven. Hindenburg was a traditional military man, monarchist in sentiment, who at heart was not in favor of the republic he had been elected to serve.

The Weimar Republic also faced serious economic difficulties. Germany experienced runaway inflation in 1922 and 1923; widows, orphans, the retired elderly, army officers, teachers, civil servants, and others who lived on fixed incomes all watched their monthly stipends become worthless and their lifetime savings evaporate. Their economic losses increasingly pushed the middle class to the rightist parties that were hostile to the republic. To make matters worse, after a period of prosperity from 1924 to 1929, Germany faced the Great Depression. Unemployment increased to 3 million in March 1930 and 4.4 million by December of the same year. The depression paved the way for the rise of extremist parties.

**United States** After Germany, no Western nation was more affected by the Great Depression than the United States. By 1932, U.S. industrial production fell to half what it had been in 1929. By 1933, there were fifteen million unemployed. Under these circumstances, the Democratic presidential candidate, Franklin Delano Roosevelt (1882–1945), was able to win a landslide electoral victory in 1932. He and his advisers pursued a policy of active government intervention in the economy that came to be known as the New Deal, which included a stepped-up program of public works. The Works Progress Administration (WPA), a government organization established in 1935, employed two to three million people building bridges, roads, post offices, and airports. The Roosevelt administration was also responsible for new social legislation that launched the American welfare state. In 1935, the Social Security Act created a system of old-age pensions and unemployment insurance.

The New Deal provided some social reform measures that perhaps averted the possibility of social revolution in the United States. It did not, however, solve the unemployment problems of the Great Depression. In May 1937, during what was considered a period of full recovery, American unemployment still stood at seven million. Only World War II and the subsequent growth of the armaments industry brought American workers back to full employment.

## Socialism in Soviet Russia

With their victory in the civil war in 1920, Bolshevik leaders could now turn to the challenging task of building the first socialist society in a world dominated by their capitalist enemies. But the civil war had taken an enormous toll of life. During the civil war, Lenin had pursued a policy of war communism, but once the war was over, peasants began to sabotage the program by hoarding food. Added to this problem was drought, which caused a great famine between 1920 and 1922 that claimed as many as five million lives. Industrial collapse paralleled the agricultural disaster. By 1921, industrial output was only 20 percent of its 1913 levels. Russia was exhausted. A peasant banner proclaimed, "Down with Lenin and horseflesh, Bring back the Tsar and pork." As Leon Trotsky said, "The country, and the government with it, were at the very edge of the abyss."[8]

**New Policies** In March 1921, Lenin pulled Russia back from the abyss by adopting his **New Economic Policy** (NEP), a modified version of the old capitalist system. Forced requisitioning of food from the peasants was halted, and peasants were now allowed to sell their produce openly. Retail stores and small industries that employed fewer than twenty employees could now operate under private ownership, although heavy industry, banking, utilities, and mines remained in the hands of the government.

In 1922, Lenin and the Communists formally created a new state called the Union of Soviet Socialist Republics, known as the USSR by its initials or the Soviet Union by its shortened form. Already by that year, a revived market and a good harvest had brought the famine to an end; Soviet agricultural production climbed to 75 percent of its prewar level. Overall, the NEP had saved the nation from complete economic disaster even though Lenin and other leading Communists intended it to be only a temporary, tactical retreat from the goals of communism.

The new government also introduced a number of social changes. Alexandra Kollontai (1872–1952), who had become a supporter of revolutionary socialism while in exile in Switzerland, took the lead in pushing a Bolshevik program for women's rights and social welfare reforms. As minister of social welfare, she tried to provide health care for women and children by establishing Palaces for the Protection of Maternity and Children. Between 1918 and 1920, the new regime issued a series of reforms that made marriage a civil act, legalized divorce, decreed the equality of men and women, and permitted abortions. Kollontai was also instrumental in establishing an agency within the Communist Party known as Zhenotdel that sent men and women to all parts of the Russian Empire to explain the new social order. In the provinces in the east, Zhenotdel members were often brutally murdered by angry men who objected to any kind of liberation for their wives and daughters. Much to Kollontai's disappointment, many of these early Communist social reforms were also undone as the Communists came to face more pressing matters, including survival of the new regime.

**The Struggle for Power** Lenin's death in 1924 inaugurated a struggle for power among the seven members of the Politburo, the institution that had become the leading organ of the party. The Politburo was severely divided over the future direction of the nation. The Left, led by Leon Trotsky, wanted to end the NEP and launch the nation on the path of rapid industrialization, primarily at the expense of the peasantry. This same group wanted to continue the revolution, believing that the survival of the Russian Revolution ultimately depended on the spread of communism abroad. Another group in the Politburo, called the Right, rejected the cause of world revolution and wanted to concentrate instead on constructing a socialist state. The members of this group also favored a continuation of Lenin's NEP because they believed that too rapid industrialization would harm the living standards of the peasantry.

These ideological divisions were underscored by an intense personal rivalry between Leon Trotsky and Joseph Stalin. In 1924, Trotsky held the post of commissar of war and was the leading spokesman for the Left in the Politburo. Joseph Stalin (1879–1953) was content to hold the dull bureaucratic job of party general secretary, while other Politburo members held party positions that enabled them to display their brilliant oratorical abilities. Stalin was skillful in avoiding allegiance to either the Left or the Right factions in the Politburo. He was also a good organizer (his fellow Bolsheviks called him "Comrade Card-Index"), and the other members of the Politburo soon found that the position of party secretary was really the most important in the party hierarchy. Stalin used his post as party general secretary to gain complete control of the Communist Party. Trotsky was expelled from the party in 1927. By 1929, Stalin had succeeded in eliminating the Old Bolsheviks of the revolutionary era from the Politburo and establishing a dictatorship so powerful that the Russian tsars of old would have been envious.

## In Pursuit of a New Reality: Cultural and Intellectual Trends

Four years of devastating war left many Europeans with a profound sense of despair and a conviction that something was dreadfully wrong with Western values. The Great Depression only added to the desolation left behind by World War I.

Political and economic uncertainties were paralleled by social innovations. World War I had served to break down many traditional middle-class attitudes, especially toward sexuality. In the 1920s, women's physical appearance changed dramatically. Short skirts, short hair, the use of cosmetics that were once thought to be the preserve of prostitutes, and the new practice of suntanning gave

**Hannah Höch, *Cut with the Kitchen Knife Dada Through the Last Weimar Beer Belly Cultural Epoch of Germany.*** Hannah Höch, a prominent figure in the postwar Dada movement, used photomontage to create images that reflected on women's issues. In *Cut with the Kitchen Knife,* she combined pictures of German political leaders with sports stars, Dada artists, and scenes from urban life. One major theme emerged: the confrontation between the anti-Dada world of German political leaders and the Dada world of revolutionary ideals. Höch associated women with Dada and the new world.

COMPARATIVE ESSAY

## A Revolution in the Arts

The period between 1880 and 1930 witnessed a revolution in the arts throughout Western civilization. Fueled in part by developments in physics and psychology, artists and writers rebelled against the traditional belief that the task of art was to represent "reality" and experimented with innovative new techniques in order to approach reality from a totally fresh perspective. Their daring break with the past reflected both the exhilaration of an age propelled by technological discoveries and a fascination with the unconscious contents of the human mind.

From Impressionism and Expressionism to Cubism, abstract art, Dadaism, and Surrealism, painters seemed intoxicated with the belief that their canvases would help reveal the radically changing world. Especially after the cataclysm of World War I, which shattered the image of a rational society, artists sought an absolute freedom of expression, confident that art could redefine humanity in the midst of chaos. Other arts soon followed their lead: James Joyce turned prose on its head by focusing on his characters' innermost thoughts; Arnold Schönberg created atonal music by using a scale composed of twelve notes independent of any tonal key; and Le Corbusier launched a revolution in architecture by using concrete slabs to make "machines for living."

This revolutionary spirit is exemplified by Pablo Picasso's canvas *Les Demoiselles d'Avignon,* painted in 1907 (see the illustration on p. 567). Picasso used geometrical designs to create a new reality and appropriated other cultural resources in the desire to revitalize Western art. Reflecting the prevailing European view that African masks were primitive oddities, Picasso ignored the cultural and religious significance of such carvings. Although some African observers charged that Picasso had exploited African culture just as European governments had exploited their colonies, Picasso had succeeded in helping revitalize Western art.

Another illustration of the revolutionary approach to art was the decision by the French artist Marcel Duchamp to enter a porcelain urinal in a 1917 art exhibit held in New York City. By signing it and giving it the title "Fountain," Duchamp proclaimed that he had transformed the urinal into a work of art. His "ready-mades" (as such art would henceforth be labeled) declared that art was whatever the artist proclaimed as art. The Dadaist Kurt Schwitters brought together postage stamps, old handbills, streetcar tickets, newspaper scraps, and pieces of cardboard to form his works of art.

Such intentionally irreverent acts were a slap in the face of the established art world and demystified the nearly sacred reverence that had traditionally been attached to works of art. Essentially, Duchamp, Schwitters, and others claimed that anything under the sun could be selected as a work of art because the mental choice itself equaled the act of artistic creation. Therefore, art need not be a manual construct; it need only be a mental conceptualization. This liberating concept opened the floodgates of the art world, causing the new century to swim in this free-flowing, exploratory torrent.

women a new image. This change in physical appearance, which stressed more exposure of a woman's body, was also accompanied by frank discussions of sexual matters. In 1926, the Dutch physician Theodor van de Velde published *Ideal Marriage: Its Physiology and Technique.* Translated into a number of languages, it became an international best-seller. Van de Velde described female and male anatomy, discussed birth control techniques, and glorified sexual pleasure in marriage.

## Nightmares and New Visions

Uncertainty also pervaded the cultural and intellectual achievements of the interwar years. Postwar artistic trends were largely a working out of the implications of prewar developments. Abstract painting, for example, became ever more popular as many pioneering artists of the early twentieth century matured between the two world wars (see the comparative essay above). In addition, prewar fascination with the absurd and the unconscious contents of the mind seemed even more appropriate after the nightmare landscapes of World War I battlefronts. This gave rise to both the Dada movement and Surrealism.

**The Dada Movement** **Dadaism** attempted to enshrine the purposelessness of life. Tristan Tzara (1896–1945), a Romanian-French poet and one of the founders of Dadaism, expressed the Dadaist contempt for the Western tradition in a lecture in 1922: "The acts of life have no beginning or end. Everything happens in a completely idiotic way. . . . Like everything in life, Dada is useless." Revolted by the insanity of life, the Dadaists tried to give it expression by creating anti-art. The 1918 Berlin Dada Manifesto maintained that "Dada is the international expression of our times, the great rebellion of artistic movements." Many Dadaists took pieces of junk (wire, string, rags, scraps of newspaper, nails, washers) and assembled them into collages, believing that they were transforming the refuse of their culture into art.

In the hands of Hannah Höch (1889–1978), Dada became an instrument to comment on women's roles in the

## Hesse and the Unconscious

The novels of Hermann Hesse made a strong impact on young people, first in Germany in the 1920s and then in the United States in the 1960s after they had been translated into English. Many of these young people shared Hesse's fascination with the unconscious and his dislike of modern industrial civilization. This excerpt from *Demian* spoke directly to many of them.

*How does Hesse's interest in the unconscious appear in this excerpt? Why was a dislike of mechanized society particularly intense after World War I?*

### Hermann Hesse, *Demian*

The following spring I was to leave the preparatory school and enter a university. I was still undecided, however, as to where and what I was to study. I had grown a thin mustache, I was a full-grown man, and yet I was completely helpless and without a goal in life. Only one thing was certain: the voice within me, the dream image. I felt the duty to follow this voice blindly wherever it might lead me. But it was difficult and each day I rebelled against it anew. Perhaps I was mad, as I thought at moments; perhaps I was not like other men? But I was able to do the same things the others did; with a little effort and industry I could read Plato, was able to solve problems in trigonometry or follow a chemical analysis. There was only one thing I could not do: wrest the dark secret goal from myself and keep it before me as others did who knew exactly what they wanted to be—professors, lawyers, doctors, artists, however long this would take them and whatever difficulties and advantages this decision would bear in its wake. This I could not do. Perhaps I would become something similar, but how was I to know? Perhaps I would have to continue my search for years on end and would not become anything, and would not reach a goal. Perhaps I would reach this goal but it would turn out to be an evil, dangerous, horrible one?

I wanted only to try to live in accord with the promptings which came from my true self. Why was that so very difficult?

new mass culture. Höch was the only female member of the Berlin Dada Club, which featured the use of photomontage. Her work was part of the first Dada show in Berlin in 1920. In *Dada Dance,* she seemed to criticize the "new woman" by making fun of the way women were inclined to follow fashion trends. In other works, however, she projected positive images of the modern woman and expressed a keen interest in new freedoms for women.

**Surrealism and Modern Architecture** Perhaps more important as an artistic movement was **Surrealism,** which sought a reality beyond the material, sensible world and

**Salvador Dalí, *The Persistence of Memory.*** Surrealism was another important artistic movement between the wars. Influenced by the theories of Freudian psychology, Surrealists sought to reveal the world of the unconscious, or the "greater reality" that they believed existed beyond the world of physical appearances. As is evident in this painting, Salvador Dalí sought to portray the world of dreams by painting recognizable objects in unrecognizable relationships.

found it in the world of the unconscious through the portrayal of fantasies, dreams, or nightmares. Employing logic to convey the illogical, the Surrealists created disturbing and evocative images. The Spaniard Salvador Dalí (1904–1989) became the high priest of Surrealism and in his mature phase became a master of representational Surrealism. In *The Persistence of Memory,* Dalí portrayed recognizable objects divorced from their normal context. By placing these objects into unrecognizable relationships, Dalí created a disturbing world in which the irrational had become tangible.

The move to functionalism in modern architecture also became more widespread in the 1920s and 1930s. Especially important in the spread of functionalism was the Bauhaus school of art, architecture, and design, founded in 1919 at Weimar, Germany, by the Berlin architect Walter Gropius. The Bauhaus teaching staff was made up of architects, artists, and designers. They worked together to combine the study of fine arts (painting and sculpture) with the applied arts (printing, weaving, and furniture making). Gropius urged his followers to foster a new union of arts and crafts in order to create the buildings and objects of the future.

## Probing the Unconscious

The interest in the unconscious, evident in Surrealism, was also apparent in the new literary techniques that emerged in the 1920s. One of its most apparent manifestations was in the "stream of consciousness" technique, in which the writer presented an interior monologue, or a report of the innermost thoughts of each character. One example of this genre was written by the Irish exile James Joyce (1882–1941). His *Ulysses,* published in 1922, told the story of one day in the life of ordinary people in Dublin by following the flow of their inner dialogue. Disconnected ramblings and veiled allusions pervade Joyce's work.

The German writer Hermann Hesse (1877–1962) dealt with the unconscious in a considerably different fashion. His novels reflected the influence of both Carl Jung's psychological theories and Eastern religions and focused among other things on the spiritual loneliness of modern human beings in a mechanized urban society. *Demian* was a psychoanalytic study of incest, and *Steppenwolf* mirrored the psychological confusion of modern existence. Hesse's novels made a large impact on German youth in the 1920s (see the box on p. 652). He won the Nobel Prize for literature in 1946.

For much of the Western world, the best way to find (or escape) reality was in the field of mass entertainment. The 1930s represented the heyday of the Hollywood studio system, which in the single year of 1937 turned out nearly six hundred feature films. Supplementing the movies were cheap paperbacks and radio, which brought sports, soap operas, and popular music to the masses.

Mass forms of communication and entertainment were not new. But the increased size of audiences and the ability of radio and cinema, unlike the printed word, to provide an immediate mass experience did add new dimensions to mass culture. Favorite film actors and actresses became stars whose lives then became subject to public adoration and scrutiny. Sensuous actresses such as Marlene Dietrich, whose appearance in the early sound film *The Blue Angel* catapulted her to fame, projected new images of women's sexuality.

## CONCLUSION

**WORLD WAR I SHATTERED** the liberal, rational society of late-nineteenth- and early-twentieth-century Europe. The incredible destruction and the death of almost ten million people undermined the whole idea of progress. New propaganda techniques had manipulated entire populations into sustaining their involvement in a meaningless slaughter.

World War I was a total war and involved an unprecedented mobilization of resources and populations and increased government centralization of power over the lives of its citizens. Civil liberties, such as freedom of the press, speech, assembly, and movement, were circumscribed in the name of national security. The war made the practice of strong central authority a way of life.

The turmoil wrought by World War I seemed to open the door to even greater insecurity. Revolutions in Russia and the Middle East dismembered old empires and created new states that gave rise to unexpected problems. Expectations that Europe and the world would return to normalcy were soon dashed by the failure to achieve a lasting peace, economic collapse, and the rise of authoritarian governments that not only restricted individual freedoms but sought even greater control over the lives of their subjects in order to manipulate and guide them to achieve the goals of their totalitarian regimes.

Finally, World War I ended the age of European hegemony over world affairs. By demolishing their own civilization on the battlegrounds of Europe in World War I, Europeans inadvertently encouraged the subject peoples of their vast colonial empires to initiate movements for national independence. In the next chapter, we examine some of those movements.

## TIMELINE

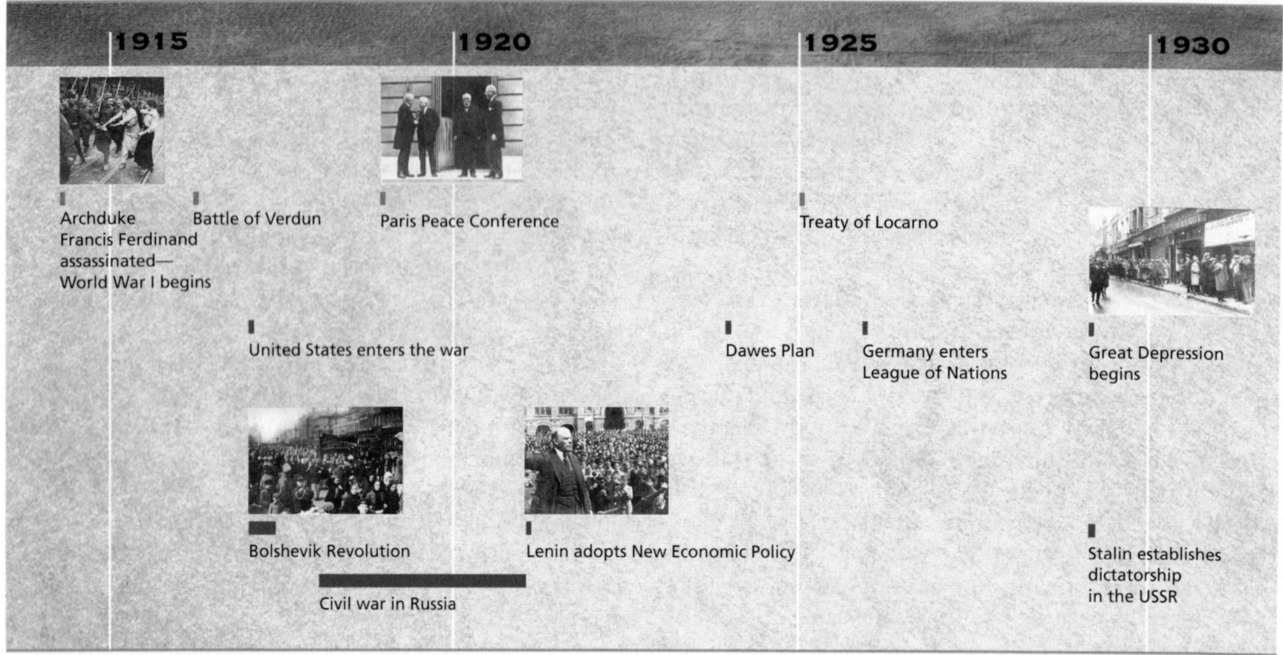


## CHAPTER NOTES

1. A. Toynbee, *Surviving the Future* (New York, 1971), pp. 106–107.
2. Quoted in J. Remak, "1914—The Third Balkan War: Origins Reconsidered," *Journal of Modern History* 43 (1971): 364–365.
3. Quoted in J. M. Winter, *The Experience of World War I* (New York, 1989), p. 142.
4. Quoted in C. W. Reilly, ed., *Scars upon My Heart: Women's Poetry and Verse of the First World War* (London, 1981), p. 90.
5. Quoted in W. M. Mandel, *Soviet Women* (Garden City, N.Y., 1975), p. 43.
6. Quoted in M. D. Steinberg, *Voices of Revolution, 1917* (New Haven, Conn., 2001), p. 55.
7. Quoted in R. Paxton, *Europe in the Twentieth Century,* 2d ed. (San Diego, Calif., 1985), p. 237.
8. Quoted in I. Howe, ed., *The Basic Writings of Trotsky* (London, 1963), p. 162.

## SUGGESTED READING

The historical literature on the causes of World War I is vast. A good starting point is the work by **J. Joll, *The Origins of the First World War,*** 2d ed. (London, 1992). The belief that Germany was primarily responsible for the war was argued vigorously by the German scholar **F. Fischer** in ***Germany's Aims in the First World War*** (New York, 1967), ***World Power or Decline: The Controversy over Germany's Aims in World War I*** (New York, 1974), and ***War of Illusions: German Policies from 1911 to 1914*** (New York, 1975). On the events leading to war, see **D. Fromkin, *Europe's Last Summer: Who Started the Great War in 1914?*** (New York, 2004). On the role of militarism, see **D. Hermann, *The Arming of Europe and the Making of the First World War*** (New York, 1997).

The best account of World War I is now **H. Strachan, *The First World War*** (New York, 2004). Strachan has also completed the first volume of a massive three-volume study of World War I, ***The First World War, vol. 1*** (New York, 2003). See also **J. Keegan, *An Illustrated History of the First World War*** (New York, 2001). Two other worthy accounts are **M. Gilbert, *The First World War*** (New York, 1994), and the lavishly illustrated book by **J. M. Winter, *The Experience of World War I*** (New York, 1989). See also the brief work by **N. Heyman, *World War I*** (Westport, Conn., 1997). There is an excellent collection of articles in **H. Strachan, *The Oxford Illustrated History of the First World War*** (New York, 1998). The nature of trench warfare is examined in **T. Ashworth, *Trench Warfare, 1914–1918: The Live-and-Let-Live System*** (London, 1980). The war at sea is studied in **R. Hough, *The Great War at Sea, 1914–18*** (Oxford, 1983). For an interesting perspective on World War I and the beginnings of the modern world, see **M. Eksteins, *Rites of Spring: The Great War and the Birth of the Modern Age*** (Boston, 1989). For a new interpretation, see **D. Stevenson, *Cataclysm: The First World War as Political Tragedy*** (New York, 2004).

On the role of women in World War I, see **G. Braybon, *Women Workers in the First World War: The British Experience*** (London, 1981); **J. M. Winter** and **R. M. Wall,** eds., ***The Upheaval of War: Family, Work and Welfare in Europe, 1914–1918*** (Cambridge, 1988); and **G. Braybon** and **P. Summerfield, *Women's Experiences in Two World Wars*** (London, 1987).

The role of war aims in shaping the peace settlement is examined in **V. H. Rothwell, *British War Aims and Peace Diplomacy, 1914–1918*** (Oxford, 1971), and **D. R. Stevenson, *French War Aims Against Germany, 1914–1919*** (New York, 1982).

A good introduction to the Russian Revolution can be found in **R. A. Wade, *The Russian Revolution, 1917*** (Cambridge, 2000), and

**S. Fitzpatrick,** ***The Russian Revolution, 1917–1932,*** 2d ed. (New York, 1994). See also **R. Pipes,** ***The Russian Revolution*** (New York, 1990). For a study that puts the Russian Revolution into the context of World War I, see **P. Holquist,** ***Making War, Forging Revolution*** (Cambridge, Mass., 2002). There is a good analysis as well as a good collection of the thoughts and experiences of ordinary Russian people in 1917 in **M. D. Steinberg,** ***Voices of Revolution, 1917*** (New Haven, Conn., 2001). On Lenin, see **R. Service,** ***Lenin: A Biography*** (Cambridge, Mass., 2000). On social reforms, see **W. Goldman,** ***Women, the State, and Revolution*** (Cambridge, 1993). A comprehensive study of the Russian civil war is **W. B. Lincoln,** ***Red Victory: A History of the Russian Civil War*** (New York, 1989).

World War I and the Russian Revolution are also well covered in two good general surveys, **R. Paxton,** ***Europe in the Twentieth Century,*** 2d ed. (San Diego, 1985), and **A. Rudhart,** ***Twentieth-Century Europe*** (Englewood Cliffs, N.J., 1986).

For a general introduction to the interwar period, see **M. Kitchen,** ***Europe Between the Wars*** (London, 1988). On European security issues after the Peace of Paris, see **S. Marks,** ***The Illusion of Peace: Europe's International Relations, 1918–1933*** (New York, 1976). The Locarno agreements are well examined in **J. Jacobson,** ***Locarno Diplomacy*** (Princeton, N.J., 1972). The best study on the problem of reparations is **M. Trachtenberg,** ***Reparations in World Politics*** (New York, 1980), which paints a more positive view of French policies. The "return to normalcy" after the war is analyzed in **C. S. Maier,** ***Recasting Bourgeois Europe: Stabilization in France, Germany, and Italy in the Decade After World War I*** (Princeton, N.J., 1975). Also valuable is **D. P. Silverman,** ***Reconstructing Europe After the Great War*** (Cambridge, Mass., 1982). On the Great Depression, see **C. P. Kindleberger,** ***The World in Depression, 1929–39,*** rev. ed. (Berkeley, Calif., 1986). On Weimar Germany, see **P. Bookbinder,** ***Weimar Germany*** (New York, 1996), and **R. Henig,** ***The Weimar Republic, 1919–1933*** (New York, 1998), a brief study.

## HistoryNow™

**Enter *HistoryNow* using the access card that is available with this text. *HistoryNow* will assist you in understanding the content in this chapter with lesson plans generated for your needs, as well as provide you with a connection to the *Wadsworth World History Resource Center* (see description below for details).**

**WORLD HISTORY**
RESOURCE CENTER

**Enter the Resource Center using either your *HistoryNow* access card or your standalone access card for the *Wadsworth World History Resource Center.* Organized by topic, this website includes quizzes; images; over 350 primary source documents; interactive simulations; maps and timelines; movie explorations; and a wealth of other resources. You can read the following documents, and many more, at http://history.wadsworth.com/rc/world**

Samuel Williamson, *The Origins of World War I*

World War I poetry

Visit the *World History* Companion Website for chapter quizzes and more.

http://history.wadsworth.com/duikerspielvogel05/

CHAPTER

# 23

# NATIONALISM, REVOLUTION, AND DICTATORSHIP: AFRICA, ASIA, AND LATIN AMERICA FROM 1919 TO 1939

## CHAPTER OUTLINE AND FOCUS QUESTIONS

### The Rise of Nationalism

- What were the various stages in the rise of nationalist movements in Asia, Africa, and the Middle East, and what problems did they face?

### Revolution in China

- What problems did China encounter between the two world wars, and what solutions did the Nationalists and the Communists propose to solve them?

### Japan Between the Wars

- How did Japan address the problems of nation-building in the first decades of the twentieth century, and why did democratic institutions not take hold more effectively?

### Nationalism and Dictatorship in Latin America

- What problems did the nations of Latin America face in the interwar years? To what degree were they a consequence of foreign influence?

## CRITICAL THINKING

- What were the various stages in the rise of nationalist movements in Asia, Africa, and the Middle East after World War I, and how did they differ from one region to the other?

AP/Wide World Photos

*Nehru confers with Mahatma Gandhi, the "Soul of India"*

IN 1930, MOHANDAS GANDHI, the sixty-one-year-old leader of the nonviolent movement for Indian independence from British rule, began a march to the sea with seventy-eight followers. Their destination was Dandi, a little coastal town some 240 miles away. The group covered about 12 miles a day. As they went, Gandhi preached his doctrine of nonviolent resistance to British rule in every village he passed through: "Civil disobedience is the inherent right of a citizen. He dare not give it up without ceasing to be a man." By the time he reached Dandi, twenty-four days later, his small group had become a nonviolent army of thousands. When they arrived at Dandi, Gandhi picked up a pinch of salt from the sand. All along the coast, thousands did likewise, openly breaking British laws that prohibited Indians from making their own salt. The British had long profited from their monopoly on the making and sale of salt, an item much in demand in a tropical country. By their simple acts of disobedience, Gandhi and the Indian people had taken a bold step on their long march to independence.

The salt march was but one of many nonviolent activities that Mohandas Gandhi undertook between World War I and World War II to win India's goal of national independence from British rule. World War I had not only deeply affected the lives of Europeans, but it had also undermined the prestige of Western civilization in the minds of many observers in the rest of the world. When Europeans devastated their own civilization on the battlefields of Europe, the subject peoples of their vast colonial empires were quick to understand what it meant. In Africa and Asia, movements for national independence began to take shape. Some were inspired by the nationalist and liberal movements of the West, while others began to look toward the new Marxist model provided by the victory of the Communists in the Soviet Union, who soon worked to spread their revolutionary vision to African and Asian societies. In the Middle East, World War I ended the rule of the Ottoman Empire and led to the creation of new states, some of which adopted Western features. For some Latin American countries, the fascist dictatorships of Italy and Germany provided models for change. ◇

## The Rise of Nationalism

Although the West had emerged from World War I relatively intact, its political and social foundations and its self-confidence had been severely undermined. Within Europe, doubts about the future viability of Western civilization were widespread, especially among the intellectual elite. These doubts were quick to reach the attention of perceptive observers in Asia and Africa and contributed to a rising tide of unrest against Western political domination throughout the colonial and semicolonial world. That unrest took a variety of forms but was most notably displayed in increasing worker activism, rural protest, and a rising sense of national fervor among anticolonialist intellectuals. In areas of Asia, Africa, and Latin America where independent states had successfully resisted the Western onslaught, the discontent fostered by the war and later by the Great Depression led to a loss of confidence in democratic institutions and the rise of political dictatorships.

### Modern Nationalism

The first stage of resistance to the West in Asia and Africa had met with humiliation and failure and must have confirmed many Westerners' conviction that colonial peoples lacked both the strength and the know-how to create modern states and govern their own destinies. In fact, the process was just beginning. The next phase—the rise of modern nationalism—began to take shape at the beginning of the twentieth century and was the product of the convergence of several factors. The primary source of anticolonialist sentiment was a new urban middle class of westernized intellectuals. In many cases, these merchants, petty functionaries, clerks, students, and professionals had been educated in Western-style schools. A few had spent time in the West. Many spoke Western languages, wore Western clothes, and worked in occupations connected with the colonial regime. Some even wrote in the languages of their colonial masters.

The results were paradoxical. On the one hand, this "new class" admired Western culture and sometimes harbored a deep sense of contempt for traditional ways. On the other hand, many strongly resented the foreigners and their arrogant contempt for colonial peoples. Though eager to introduce Western ideas and institutions into their own society, these intellectuals were dismayed at the gap between ideal and reality, theory and practice, in colonial policy. Although Western political thought exalted democracy, equality, and individual freedom, democratic institutions were primitive or nonexistent in the colonies.

Equality in economic opportunity and social life was also noticeably lacking. Normally, the middle classes did not suffer in the same manner as impoverished peasants or menial workers on sugar or rubber plantations, but they, too, had complaints. They were usually relegated to low-level jobs in the government or business and paid less than Europeans in similar positions. The superiority of the Europeans was expressed in a variety of ways, including "whites only" clubs and the use of the familiar form of the language (normally used by adults to children) when addressing the natives.

Under these conditions, many of the new urban educated class were very ambivalent toward their colonial masters and the civilization that they represented. Out of this mixture of hopes and resentments emerged the first stirrings of modern nationalism in Asia and Africa. During the first quarter of the century, in colonial and semicolonial societies from the Suez Canal to the shores of the Pacific Ocean, educated native peoples began to organize political parties and movements seeking reforms or the end of foreign rule and the restoration of independence.

**Religion and Nationalism** At first, many of the leaders of these movements did not focus clearly on the idea of nationhood but tried to defend native economic interests or religious beliefs. In Burma, for example, the first expression of modern nationalism came from students at the University of Rangoon, who protested against official persecution of the Buddhist religion and British lack of respect for local religious traditions. Adopting the name Thakin (a polite term in the Burmese language meaning "lord" or "master," thus emphasizing their demand for the right to rule themselves), they protested against British arrogance and failure to observe local customs in Buddhist temples (such as failing to remove their footwear). Only in the 1930s did the Thakins begin to focus specifically on national independence.

In the Dutch East Indies, the Sarekat Islam (Islamic Association) began as a self-help society among Muslim merchants to fight against domination of the local economy by Chinese interests. Eventually, activist elements began to realize that the source of the problem was not the Chinese merchants but the colonial presence, and in the 1920s, Sarekat Islam was transformed into a new

## The Dilemma of the Intellectual

Sutan Sjahrir (1909–1966) was a prominent leader of the Indonesian nationalist movement who briefly served as prime minister of the Republic of Indonesia in the 1950s. Like many Western-educated Asian intellectuals, he was tortured by the realization that by education and outlook he was closer to his colonial masters—in his case, the Dutch—than to his own people. He wrote the following passage in a letter to his wife in 1935 and later included it in his book *Out of Exile.*

*Why does the author feel estranged from his native culture? What is his answer to the challenges faced by his country in coming to terms with the modern world?*

### Sutan Sjahrir, *Out of Exile*

Am I perhaps estranged from my people? . . . Why are the things that contain beauty for them and arouse their gentler emotions only senseless and displeasing for me? In reality, the spiritual gap between my people and me is certainly no greater than that between an intellectual in Holland . . . and the undeveloped people of Holland. . . . The difference is rather . . . that the intellectual in Holland does not feel this gap because there is a portion–even a fairly large portion–of his own people on approximately the same intellectual level as himself. . . .

This is what we lack here. Not only is the number of intellectuals in this country smaller in proportion to the total population–in fact, very much smaller–but in addition, the few who are here do not constitute any single entity in spiritual outlook, or in any spiritual life or single culture whatsoever. . . . It is for them so much more difficult than for the intellectuals in Holland. In Holland they build–both consciously and unconsciously–on what is already there. . . . Even if they oppose it, they do so as a method of application or as a starting point.

In our country this is not the case. Here there has been no spiritual or cultural life, and no intellectual progress for centuries. There are the much-praised Eastern art forms but what are these except bare rudiments from a feudal culture that cannot possibly provide a dynamic fulcrum for people of the twentieth century? . . . Our spiritual needs are needs of the twentieth century; our problems and our views are of the twentieth century. Our inclination is no longer toward the mystical, but toward reality, clarity, and objectivity. . . .

We intellectuals here are much closer to Europe or America than we are to the Borobudur or Mahabharata or to the primitive Islamic culture of Java and Sumatra. . . .

So, it seems, the problem stands in principle. It is seldom put forth by us in this light, and instead most of us search unconsciously for a synthesis that will leave us internally tranquil. We want to have both Western science and Eastern philosophy, the Eastern "spirit," in the culture. But what is this Eastern spirit? It is, they say, the sense of the higher, of spirituality, of the eternal and religious, as opposed to the materialism of the West. I have heard this countless times, but it has never convinced me.

organization, the Nationalist Party of Indonesia (PNI), that focused on national independence. Like the Thakins in Burma, this party would eventually lead the country to independence after World War II.

**Independence or Modernization? The Nationalist Quandary** Building a new nation, however, requires more than a shared sense of grievances against the foreign invader. A host of other issues also had to be resolved. Soon patriots throughout the colonial world were engaged in a lively and sometimes acrimonious debate over such questions as whether independence or modernization should be their primary objective. The answer depended in part on how the colonial regime was perceived. If it was viewed as a source of needed reforms in a traditional society, a gradualist approach made sense. But if it was seen primarily as an impediment to change, the first priority was to bring it to an end. The vast majority of patriotic individuals were convinced that to survive, their societies must adopt much of the Western way of life; yet many were equally determined that the local culture would not, and should not, become a carbon copy of the West. What was the national identity, after all, if it did not incorporate some elements from the traditional way of life?

Another reason for using traditional values was to provide ideological symbols that the common people could understand and would rally around. Though aware that they needed to enlist the mass of the population in the common struggle, most urban intellectuals had difficulty communicating with the teeming population in the countryside who did not understand such complicated and unfamiliar concepts as democracy and nationhood. As the Indonesian intellectual Sutan Sjahrir lamented, many westernized intellectuals had more in common with their colonial rulers than with the native population in the rural villages (see the box above). As one French colonial official remarked in some surprise to a Vietnamese reformist, "Why, Monsieur, you are more French than I am!"

## Gandhi and the Indian National Congress

Nowhere in the colonial world were these issues debated more vigorously than in India. Before the Sepoy Rebellion (see Chapter 20), Indian consciousness had focused primarily on the question of religious identity. But in the latter half of the nineteenth century, a stronger sense of national consciousness began to arise, provoked by the conservative policies and racial arrogance of the British colonial authorities.

The first Indian nationalists were upper-class and educated. Many of them were from urban areas such as Bombay, Madras, and Calcutta. Some were trained in law and were members of the civil service. At first, many tended to prefer reform to revolution and believed that India needed modernization before it could handle the problems of independence. An exponent of this view was Gopal Gokhale (1866–1915), a moderate nationalist who hoped that he could convince the British to bring about needed reforms in Indian society. Gokhale and other like-minded reformists did have some effect. In the 1880s, the government introduced a measure of self-government for the first time. All too often, however, such efforts were sabotaged by local British officials.

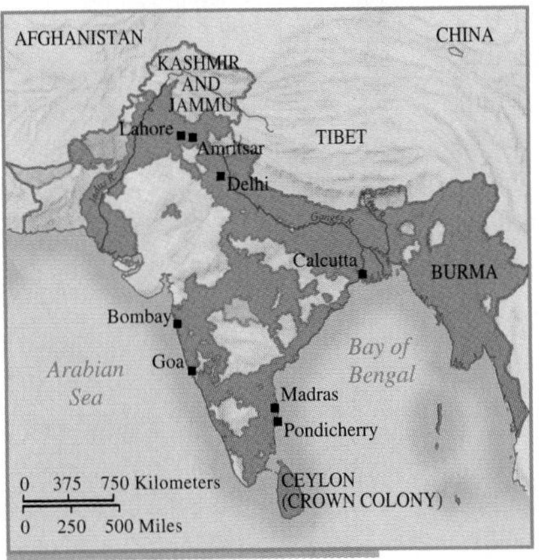

**British India Between the Wars**

The slow pace of reform convinced many Indian nationalists that relying on British benevolence was futile. In 1885, a small group of Indians, with some British participation, met in Bombay to form the Indian National Congress (INC). They hoped to speak for all India, but most were high-caste English-trained Hindus. Like their reformist predecessors, members of the INC did not demand immediate independence and accepted the need for reforms to end traditional abuses like child marriage and *sati.* At the same time, they called for an Indian share in the governing process and more spending on economic development and less on military campaigns along the frontier. The British responded with a few concessions, but change was glacially slow. As impatient members of the INC became disillusioned, the radicals split off and formed the New Party, which called for the use of terrorism and violence to achieve national independence.

The INC also had difficulty reconciling religious differences within its ranks. The stated goal of the INC was to seek self-determination for all Indians regardless of class or religious affiliation, but many of its leaders were Hindu and inevitably reflected Hindu concerns. In the first decade of the twentieth century, the separate Muslim League was created to represent the interests of the millions of Muslims in Indian society.

**Nonviolent Resistance** In 1915, a young Hindu lawyer returned from South Africa to become active in the INC. He transformed the movement and galvanized India's struggle for independence and identity. Mohandas Gandhi was born in 1869 in Gujarat, in western India, the son of a government minister. In the late nineteenth century, he studied in London and became a lawyer. In 1893, he went to South Africa to work in a law firm serving Indian émigrés working as laborers there. He soon became aware of the racial prejudice and exploitation experienced by Indians living in the territory and tried to organize them to protect their interests.

On his return to India, Gandhi immediately became active in the independence movement. Using his experience in South Africa, he set up a movement based on nonviolent resistance (the Hindi term was ***satyagraha,*** "hold fast to the truth") to try to force the British to improve the lot of the poor and grant independence to India. His goal was twofold: to convert the British to his views while simultaneously strengthening the unity and sense of self-respect of his compatriots. Gandhi was particularly concerned about the plight of the millions of untouchables, whom he called *harijans,* or "children of God." When the British attempted to suppress dissent, he called on his followers to refuse to obey British regulations. He began to manufacture his own clothes (Gandhi now dressed in a simple *dhoti* made of coarse homespun cotton) and adopted the spinning wheel as a symbol of Indian resistance to imports of British textiles.

Gandhi, now increasingly known as India's "Great Soul" *(Mahatma),* organized mass protests to achieve his aims, but in 1919 they got out of hand and led to violence and British reprisals. British troops killed hundreds of unarmed protesters in the enclosed square in the city of Amritsar in northwestern India. When the protests spread, Gandhi was horrified at the violence and briefly retreated from active politics. Nevertheless, he was arrested for his role in the protests and spent several years in prison.

Gandhi combined his anticolonial activities with an appeal to the spiritual instincts of all Indians. Though he had been born and raised a Hindu, his universalist approach to the idea of God transcended individual religion, although it was shaped by the historical themes of Hindu belief. At a speech given in London in September 1931, he expressed his view of the nature of God as "an indefinable mysterious power that pervades everything . . . , an unseen power which makes itself felt and yet defies all proof."[1]

While Gandhi was in prison, the political situation continued to evolve. In 1921, the British passed the Government of India Act, transforming the heretofore advisory Legislative Council into a bicameral parliament, two-thirds of whose members would be elected. Similar bodies were created at the provincial level. In a stroke, five million Indians were enfranchised. But such reforms were no longer enough for many members of the INC, who wanted to push aggressively for full independence. The British exacerbated the situation by increasing the

**Nehru and Gandhi.** Mahatma Gandhi (on the right), India's "Great Soul," became the emotional leader of India's struggle for independence from British colonial rule. Unlike many other nationalist leaders, Gandhi rejected the materialistic culture of the West and urged his followers to return to the native traditions of the Indian village. To illustrate his point, Gandhi dressed in the simple Indian *dhoti* rather than in the Western fashion favored by many of his colleagues. With Gandhi, Jawaharlal Nehru (on the left) was a leading figure in the Indian struggle for independence. Unlike Gandhi, however, his goal was to transform India into a modern industrial society. After independence in 1947, he became the nation's prime minister until his death in 1964.

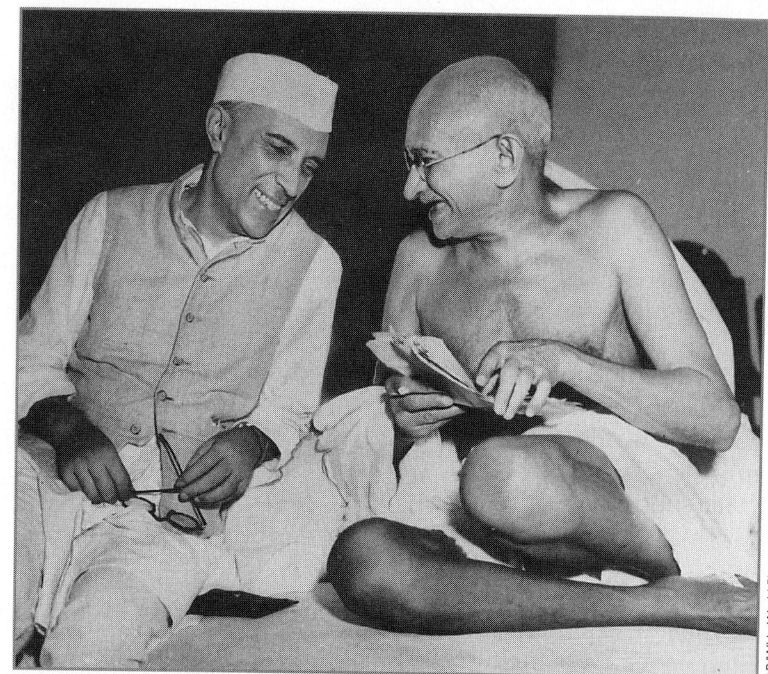

AP/Wide World Photos

salt tax and prohibiting the Indian people from manufacturing or harvesting their own salt. Gandhi, now released from prison, returned to his earlier policy of **civil disobedience** by openly joining several dozen supporters in a 200-mile walk to the sea, where he picked up a lump of salt and urged Indians to ignore the law. Gandhi and many other members of the INC were arrested.

Indian women were active in the movement. The first organizations to promote women's rights had been established in the early years of the century, and they quickly became involved in a variety of efforts to bring about social reforms. Women accounted for about twenty thousand, or nearly 10 percent, of people arrested and jailed for taking part in demonstrations during the interwar period. Women marched, picketed foreign shops, and promoted the spinning and wearing of homemade cloth. By the 1930s, women's associations were actively promoting a number of reforms, including women's education, the introduction of birth control devices, the abolition of child marriage, and universal suffrage. In 1929, the Sarda Act raised the minimum age of marriage to fourteen.

**New Leaders and New Problems** In the 1930s, a new figure entered the movement in the person of Jawaharlal Nehru (1889–1964), son of an earlier INC leader. Educated in the law in Great Britain and a *brahmin* by birth, Nehru personified the new Anglo-Indian politician: secular, rational, upper-class, and intellectual. In fact, he appeared to be everything that Gandhi was not. With his emergence, the independence movement embarked on two paths, religious and secular, native and Western, traditional and modern. The dual character of the INC leadership may well have strengthened the movement by bringing together the two primary impulses behind the desire for independence: elite nationalism and the primal force of Indian traditionalism. But it portended trouble for the nation's new leadership in defining India's future path in the contemporary world. In the meantime, Muslim discontent with Hindu dominance over the INC was increasing. In 1940, the Muslim League called for the creation of a separate Muslim state of Pakistan ("land of the pure") in the northwest (see the box on p. 661). As communal strife between Hindus and Muslims increased, many Indians came to realize with sorrow (and some British colonialists with satisfaction) that British rule was all that stood between peace and civil war.

## The Nationalist Revolt in the Middle East

In the Middle East, as in Europe, World War I hastened the collapse of old empires. The Ottoman Empire, which had dominated the eastern Mediterranean since the seizure of Constantinople in 1453, had been growing steadily weaker since the end of the eighteenth century, troubled by rising governmental corruption, a decline in the effectiveness of the sultans, and the loss of considerable territory in the Balkans and southwestern Russia. In North Africa, Ottoman authority, tenuous at best, had disintegrated in the nineteenth century, enabling the French to seize Algeria and Tunisia and the British to establish a protectorate over the Nile River valley.

**Decline of the Ottoman Empire** Reformist elements in Istanbul, to be sure, had tried from time to time to resist the trend, but military defeats continued: Greece declared its independence, and Ottoman power declined steadily in the Middle East. A rising sense of nationality among Serbs, Armenians, and other minority peoples threatened the internal stability and cohesion of the empire. In the 1870s, a new generation of Ottoman reformers seized power in Istanbul and pushed through a constitution

## A Call for a Muslim State

Mohammed Iqbal, a well-known Muslim poet in colonial India, was also a prominent advocate of the creation of a separate state for Muslims in South Asia. In this passage from an address he presented to the All-India Muslim League in December 1930, he explained the rationale for his proposal.

*Why does the author believe that a separate state for Muslims in India will be required? How does he attempt to persuade non-Muslims that this will be to their benefit as well?*

### Mohammed Iqbal, Speech to the All-India Muslim League

It cannot be denied that Islam, regarded as an ethical ideal plus a certain kind of polity—by which expression I mean a social structure regulated by a legal system and animated by a specific ethical ideal—has been the chief formative factor in the life history of the Muslims of India. It has furnished those basic emotions and loyalties which gradually unify scattered individuals and groups and finally transform them into a well-defined people. Indeed it is no exaggeration to say that India is perhaps the only country in the world where Islam, as a people-building force, has worked at its best. In India, as elsewhere, the structure of Islam as a society is almost entirely due to the working of Islam as a culture inspired by a specific ethical ideal. What I mean to say is that Muslim society, with its remarkable homogeneity and inner unity, has grown to be what it is under the pressure of the laws and institutions associated with the culture of Islam.

Communalism in its higher aspect, then, is indispensable to the formation of a harmonious whole in a country like India. The units of Indian society are not territorial as in European countries. India is a continent of human groups belonging to different religions. Their behavior is not at all determined by a common race consciousness. Even the Hindus do not form a homogeneous group. The principle of European democracy cannot be applied to India without recognizing the fact of communal groups. The Muslim demand for the creation of a Muslim India within India is, therefore, perfectly justified.

The idea need not alarm the Hindus or the British. India is the greatest Muslim country in the world. The life of Islam, as a cultural force, in this country very largely depends on its centralization in a specified territory. This centralization of the most living portion of the Muslims of India, whose military and police service has, notwithstanding unfair treatment from the British, made the British rule possible in this country, will eventually solve the problem of India as well as of Asia. It will intensify their sense of responsibility and deepen their patriotic feeling. Thus possessing full opportunity of development within the body politic of India, the northwest India Muslims will prove the best defenders of India against a foreign invasion, be the invasion one of ideas or of bayonets. . . .

I therefore demand the formation of a consolidated Muslim State in the best interests of India and Islam. For India it means security and peace resulting from an internal balance of power; for Islam an opportunity to rid itself of the stamp that Arabian imperialism was forced to give it, to mobilize its law, its education, its culture, and to bring them into closer contact with its own original spirit and with the spirit of modern times.

aimed at forming a legislative assembly that would represent all the peoples in the state. But the sultan they placed on the throne suspended the new charter and attempted to rule by traditional authoritarian means.

By the end of the nineteenth century, the defunct 1876 constitution had become a symbol of change for reformist elements, now grouped together under the common name **Young Turks** (undoubtedly borrowed from the Young Italy nationalist movement earlier in the century). They found support in the Ottoman army and administration and among Turks living in exile. In 1908, the Young Turks forced the sultan to restore the constitution, and he was removed from power the following year.

But the Young Turks had appeared at a moment of extreme fragility for the empire. Internal rebellions, combined with Austrian annexations of Ottoman territories in the Balkans, undermined support for the new government and provoked the army to step in. With most minorities from the old empire now removed from Istanbul's authority, many ethnic Turks began to embrace a new concept of a Turkish state based on Turkish nationality.

The final blow to the old empire came in World War I, when the Ottoman government allied with Germany in the hope of driving the British from Egypt and restoring Ottoman rule over the Nile valley. In response, the British declared an official protectorate over Egypt and, aided by the efforts of the dashing if eccentric British adventurer T. E. Lawrence (popularly known as Lawrence of Arabia), sought to undermine Ottoman rule in the Arabian peninsula by encouraging Arab nationalists there. In 1916, the local governor of Mecca, encouraged by the British, declared Arabia independent from Ottoman rule, while British troops, advancing from Egypt, seized Palestine. In October 1918, having suffered more than 300,000 casualties during the war, the Ottoman Empire negotiated an armistice with the Allied Powers.

**Mustafa Kemal and the Modernization of Turkey** During the next few years, the tottering empire began to fall apart as the British and the French made plans to divide up Ottoman territories in the Middle East and the Greeks won Allied approval to seize the western parts of the Anatolian peninsula for their dream of re-creating the substance of the old Byzantine Empire. The impending collapse energized key elements in Turkey under the leadership of a war hero, Colonel Mustafa Kemal (1881–1938), who had commanded Turkish forces in their defense of the Dardanelles against a British invasion during World War I. Now he resigned from the army and convoked a national congress that called for an elected government and the preservation of the remaining territories of the old empire in a new republic of Turkey. Establishing his capital at Ankara, Kemal's forces drove the Greeks from the Anatolian peninsula and persuaded the British to agree to a new treaty. In 1923, the last of the Ottoman sultans fled the country, which was now declared a Turkish republic. The Ottoman Empire had come to an end.

**Mustafa Kemal Atatürk.** The war hero Mustafa Kemal took the initiative in creating the republic of Turkey. As president of the new republic, Atatürk ("Father Turk," as he came to be called) worked hard to transform Turkey into a modern secular state by restructuring the economy, adopting Western dress, and breaking the powerful hold of Islamic traditions. He is now reviled by Muslim fundamentalists for his opposition to an Islamic state.

During the next few years, President Mustafa Kemal (now popularly known as Atatürk, or "Father Turk") attempted to transform Turkey into a modern secular republic. The trappings of a democratic system were put in place, centered on an elected Grand National Assembly, but the president was relatively intolerant of opposition and harshly suppressed critics of his rule. Turkish nationalism was emphasized, and the Turkish language, now written in the Roman alphabet, was shorn of many of its Arabic elements. Popular education was emphasized, old aristocratic titles like *pasha* and *bey* were abolished, and all Turkish citizens were given family names in the European style.

Atatürk also took steps to modernize the economy, overseeing the establishment of a light industrial sector producing textiles, glass, paper, and cement and instituting a five-year plan on the Soviet model to provide for state direction over the economy. Atatürk was no admirer of Soviet communism, however, and the Turkish economy can be better described as a form of state capitalism. He also encouraged the modernization of the agricultural sector through the establishment of training institutions and model farms, but such reforms had relatively little effect on the nation's predominantly conservative peasantry.

Perhaps the most significant aspect of Atatürk's reform program was his attempt to break the power of the Islamic clerics and transform Turkey into a secular state. The caliphate was formally abolished in 1924 (see the box on p. 663), and *Shari'a* (Islamic law) was replaced by a revised version of the Swiss law code. The fez (the brimless cap worn by Turkish Muslims) was abolished, and women were discouraged from wearing the traditional Islamic veil. Women received the right to vote in 1934 and were legally guaranteed equal rights with men in all aspects of marriage and inheritance. Education and the professions were now open to citizens of both sexes, and some women even began to participate in politics. All citizens were given the right to convert to another religion at will. Finally, Atatürk attempted to break the waning power of the various religious orders of Islam, abolishing all monasteries and brotherhoods.

The legacy of Mustafa Kemal Atatürk was enormous. Although not all of his reforms were widely accepted in practice, especially by devout Muslims, most of the changes he introduced were retained after his death in 1938. In virtually every respect, the Turkish republic was the product of his determined efforts to create a modern Turkish nation.

**Modernization in Iran** In the meantime, a similar process was under way in Persia. Under the Qajar dynasty (1794–1925), the country had not been very successful in resisting Russian advances in the Caucasus or resolving its domestic problems. To secure themselves from foreign in-

## Mustafa Kemal's Case against the Caliphate

As part of his plan to transform Turkey into a modern society, Mustafa Kemal Atatürk proposed bringing an end to the caliphate, which had been in the hands of Ottoman sultans since the formation of the empire. In the following passage from a speech to the National Assembly, he gives his reasons.

*When and why was the caliphate system first established? Why does Mustafa Kemal believe that it no longer meets the needs of the Turkish people?*

### Atatürk's Speech to the Assembly, October 1924

The monarch designated under the title of Caliph was to guide the affairs of [all] Muslim peoples and to secure the execution of the religious prescriptions which would best correspond to their worldly interests. He was to defend the rights of all Muslims and concentrate all the affairs of the Muslim world in his hands with effective authority.

The sovereign entitled Caliph was to maintain justice among the three hundred million Muslims on the terrestrial globe, to safeguard the rights of these peoples, to prevent any event that could encroach upon order and security, and confront every attack which the Muslims would be called upon to encounter from the side of other nations. It was to be part of his attributes to preserve by all means the welfare and spiritual development of Islam. . . .

If the Caliph and Caliphate, as they maintained, were to be invested with a dignity embracing the whole of Islam, ought they not to have realized in all justice that a crushing burden would be imposed on Turkey, on her existence; her entire resources and all her forces would be placed at the disposal of the Caliph? . . .

For centuries our nation was guided under the influence of these erroneous ideas. But what has been the result of it? Everywhere they have lost millions of men. "Do you know," I asked, "how many sons of Anatolia have perished in the scorching deserts of the Yemen? Do you know the losses we have suffered in holding Syria and Egypt and in maintaining our position in Africa? And do you see what has come out of it? Do you know?

"Those who favor the idea of placing the means at the disposal of the Caliph to brave the whole world and the power to administer the affairs of the whole of Islam must not appeal to the population of Anatolia alone but to the great Muslim agglomerations which are eight or ten times as rich in men.

"New Turkey, the people of New Turkey, have no reason to think of anything else but their own existence and their own welfare. She has nothing more to give away to others."

**HistoryNow™** To read Atatürk's "Address to the Turkish Yash," enter the *HistoryNow* documents area using the access card that is available for *World History.*

fluence, the shahs moved the capital from Tabriz to Tehran, in a mountainous area just south of the Caspian Sea. During the mid-nineteenth century, one modernizing shah attempted to introduce political and economic reforms but was impeded by resistance from tribal and religious—predominantly Shi'ite—forces. To buttress its rule, the dynasty turned increasingly to Russia and Great Britain to protect itself from its own people.

Eventually, the growing foreign presence led to the rise of a native Persian nationalist movement. Its efforts were largely directed against Russian advances in the northwest and the growing European influence in the small modern industrial sector, the profits from which left the country or disappeared into the hands of the dynasty's ruling elite. Supported actively by Shi'ite religious leaders, opposition to the regime rose steadily among both peasants and merchants in the cities, and in 1906, popular pressures forced the reigning shah to grant a constitution on the Western model. It was an eerie foretaste of the revolution of 1979 (see Chapter 28).

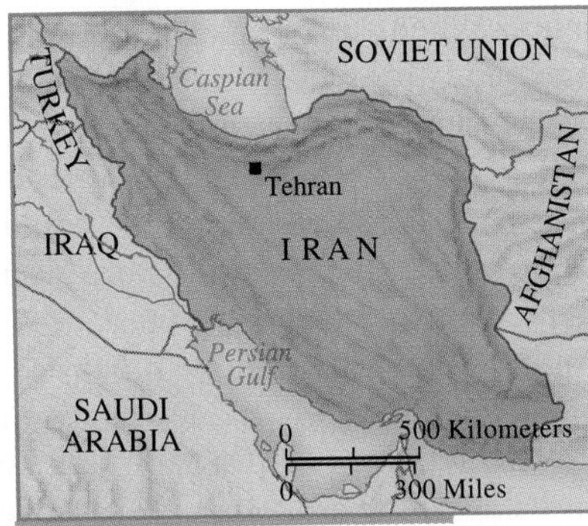


**Iran Under the Pahlavi Dynasty**

As in the Ottoman Empire and Manchu China, however, the modernizers had moved too soon, before their power base was secure. With the support of the Russians and the British, the shah was able to retain control, while the two foreign powers began to divide the country into separate spheres of influence. One reason for the growing foreign presence in Persia was the discovery of oil reserves in the southern part of the country in 1908. Within a few years, oil exports increased rapidly, with the bulk of the profits going into the pockets of British investors.

In 1921, an officer in the Persian army by the name of Reza Khan (1878–1944) led a mutiny that seized power in Tehran. The new ruler's original intention had been to establish a republic, but resistance from traditional forces impeded his efforts, and in 1925 the new Pahlavi dynasty, with Reza Khan as shah, replaced the now defunct Qajar dynasty. During the next few years, Reza Khan attempted to follow the example of Atatürk in Turkey, introducing a number of reforms to strengthen the central government, modernize

**The Impact of Oil.** Oil discoveries early in the twentieth century began to bring wealth to Persia. Shown here are workers building an oil derrick in Persia (later renamed Iran).

the civilian and military bureaucracy, and establish a modern economic infrastructure. He also officially changed the name of the nation to Iran.

Unlike Atatürk, Reza Khan did not attempt to destroy the power of Islamic beliefs, but he did encourage the establishment of a Western-style educational system and forbade women to wear the veil in public. Women continued to be exploited, however. As in the case of the textile industry in Meiji Japan (see Chapter 21), it was the intensive labor of Iranian women in the carpet industry that provided major export earnings—second only to oil—in the interwar period. To strengthen the sense of Persian nationalism and reduce the power of Islam, Reza Khan attempted to popularize the symbols and beliefs of pre-Islamic times. Like his Qajar predecessors, however, he was hindered by strong foreign influence. When the Soviet Union and Great Britain decided to send troops into the country during World War II, he resigned in protest and died three years later.

**Nation-Building in Iraq** One other consequence of the collapse of the Ottoman Empire was the emergence of a new political entity along the Tigris and Euphrates Rivers, once the heartland of ancient empires. Lacking defensible borders and sharply divided along ethnic and religious lines—a Shi'ite majority in rural areas was balanced by a vocal Sunni minority in the cities and a largely Kurdish population in the northern mountains—the area had been under Ottoman rule since the seventeenth century. With the advent of World War I, the lowland area from Baghdad southward to the Persian Gulf was occupied by British forces, who hoped to protect oil-producing regions in neighboring Persia from a German takeover.

Although the British claimed to have arrived as liberators, in 1920 the country now known as Iraq was placed under British control as a mandate of the League of Nations. Civil unrest and growing anti-Western sentiment rapidly dispelled any possible plans for the emergence of an independent government, and in 1921, after the suppression of resistance forces, the country was placed under the titular authority of King Faisal of Syria, a descendant of Muhammad. The latter relied for support primarily on the politically more sophisticated urban Sunni population, although they represented less than a quarter of the population. The discovery of oil near Kirkuk in 1927 increased the value of the area to the British, who granted formal independence to the country in 1932, although British advisers retained a strong influence over the fragile government.

**The Rise of Arab Nationalism and the Problem of Palestine** As we have seen, the Arab uprising during World War I helped bring about the demise of the Ottoman Empire. Unrest against Ottoman rule had existed in the Arabian peninsula since the eighteenth century, when the Wahhabi revolt attempted to drive out the outside influences and cleanse Islam of corrupt practices that had developed in past centuries. The revolt was eventually suppressed, but Wahhabi influence persisted.

World War I offered an opportunity for the Arabs to throw off the shackles of Ottoman rule—but what would replace them? The Arabs were not a nation but an idea, a loose collection of peoples who often did not see eye to eye on matters that affected their community. Disagreement over what constitutes an Arab has plagued generations of political leaders who have sought unsuccessfully to knit together the disparate peoples of the region into a single Arab nation.

When the Arab leaders in Mecca declared their independence from Ottoman rule in 1916, they had hoped for British support, but they were to be sorely disappointed. At the close of the war, the British and French agreed to create a number of mandates in the area under the general supervision of the League of Nations. Iraq and Trans-Jordan were assigned to the British; Syria and Lebanon (the two areas were separated so that Christian peoples in Lebanon could be placed under Christian administration) were given to the French.

The land of Palestine—once the home of the Jews but now inhabited primarily by Muslim Palestinians—became a separate mandate. According to the Balfour Declaration, issued by the British foreign secretary Lord Balfour in November 1917, Palestine was to be a national

**CHRONOLOGY The Middle East Between the Wars**

| | |
|---|---|
| Balfour Declaration on Palestine | 1917 |
| British mandate In Iraq | 1920 |
| Reza Khan seizes power in Persia | 1921 |
| End of Ottoman Empire and establishment of a republic in Turkey | 1923 |
| Rule of Mustafa Kemal Atatürk in Turkey | 1923–1938 |
| Beginning of Pahlavi dynasty in Iran | 1925 |
| Establishment of kingdom of Saudi Arabia | 1932 |

home for the Jews. The declaration was ambiguous on the legal status of the territory and promised that the decision would not undermine the rights of the non-Jewish peoples currently living in the area. But Arab nationalists were incensed. How could a national home for the Jewish people be established in a territory where 90 percent of the population was Muslim?

In the early 1920s, a leader of the Wahhabi movement, Ibn Saud (1880–1953), united Arab tribes in the northern part of the Arabian peninsula and drove out the remnants of Ottoman rule. Ibn Saud was a descendant of the family that had led the Wahhabi revolt in the eighteenth century. Devout and gifted, he won broad support among Arab tribal peoples and established the kingdom of Saudi Arabia throughout much of the peninsula in 1932.

At first, his new kingdom, consisting essentially of the vast wastes of central Arabia, was desperately poor. Its financial resources were limited to the income from Muslim pilgrims visiting the holy sites in Mecca and Medina. But during the 1930s, American companies began to explore for oil, and in 1938, Standard Oil made a successful strike at Dhahran, on the Persian Gulf. Soon an Arabian-American oil conglomerate, popularly called Aramco, was established, and the isolated kingdom was suddenly inundated by Western oilmen and untold wealth.

In the meantime, Jewish settlers began to arrive in Palestine in response to the promises made in the Balfour Declaration. As tensions between the new arrivals and existing Muslim residents began to escalate, the British tried to restrict Jewish immigration into the territory and rejected the concept of a separate state. They also created a separate emirate of Trans-Jordan out of the eastern section of Palestine. After World War II, it would become the independent kingdom of Jordan. The stage was set for the conflicts that would take place in the region after World War II.

## Nationalism and Revolution in Asia and Africa

Before the Russian Revolution, to most intellectuals in Asia and Africa, "westernization" referred to the capitalist democratic civilization of western Europe and the United States, not the doctrine of social revolution developed by Karl Marx. Until 1917, Marxism was regarded as a utopian idea rather than a concrete system of government. Moreover, to many intellectuals, Marxism appeared to have little relevance to conditions in Asia and Africa. Marxist doctrine, after all, declared that a communist society would arise only from the ashes of an advanced capitalism that had already passed through the Industrial Revolution. From the perspective of Marxist historical analysis, most societies in Asia and Africa were still at the feudal stage of development; they lacked the economic conditions and political awareness to achieve a socialist revolution that would bring the working class to power. Finally, the Marxist view of nationalism and religion had little appeal to many patriotic intellectuals in the non-Western world. Marx believed that nationhood and religion were essentially false ideas that diverted the attention of the oppressed masses from the critical issues of class struggle and, in his phrase, the exploitation of one person by another. Instead, Marx stressed an "internationalist"

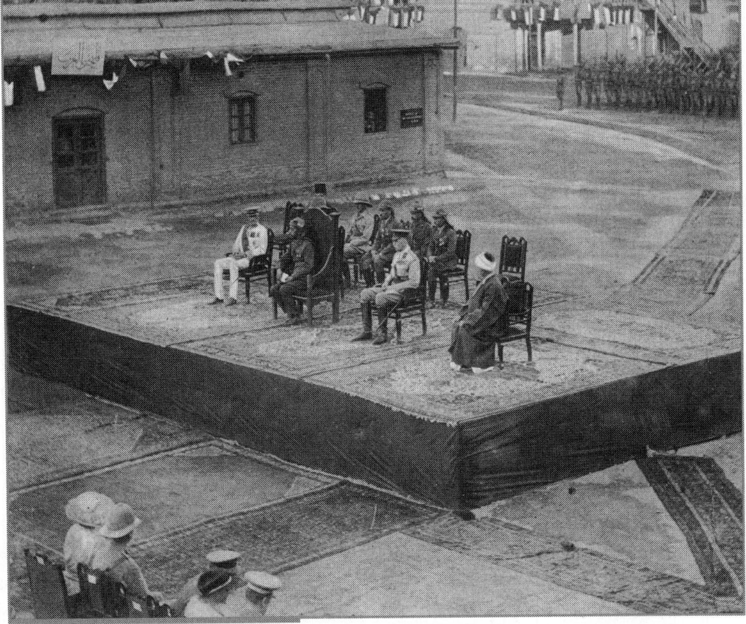



**An Exercise in Nation-Building.** When the Ottoman Empire collapsed after World War I, the victorious Allied powers struggled to pick up the pieces and establish several fledgling new nations in the Middle East. It was a daunting task, given the ethnic diversity and the lack of any tradition of statehood in the area. Nowhere was the problem more acute than in Mesopotamia, where a British mandate—to be called Iraq—was created in 1921. Lacking a royal family with roots in the area, the British authorities selected Amir Faisal, a descendant of Muhammad, as constitutional monarch, although he had never visited the region. Shown here is the installation ceremony, held in August 1921. King Faisal, flanked by two British officials, is seated second from the left while a band plays the British anthem "God Save the King."

Agence Vietnamienne d'Information, Hanoi

**Vanguard of Revolution.** Through the Communist International (Comintern for short), with its headquarters in Moscow, the Soviet Union sought to direct the activities of Communist parties throughout the world. Revolutionaries from all areas of the globe received training at the agency's famous "Stalin School" and then were sent back to their home countries to promote insurrections against the established governments.

During the 1920s and 1930s, much of the focus of the Comintern was on the promotion of revolt in colonial territories. Shown here are a group of delegates who attended the seventh congress of the organization, held in Moscow in 1935. The Vietnamese revolutionary Ho Chi Minh is in the top row, third from the left. Note that several delegates have covered their faces in order to disguise their identities.

outlook based on class consciousness and the eventual creation of a classless society with no artificial divisions based on culture, nation, or religion.

For these reasons, many patriotic non-Western intellectuals initially found Marxism to be both irrelevant and unappealing. That situation began to change after the Russian Revolution in 1917. The rise to power of Lenin's Bolsheviks demonstrated that a revolutionary party espousing Marxist principles could overturn a corrupt, outdated system and launch a new experiment dedicated to ending human inequality and achieving a paradise on earth. In 1920, Lenin proposed a new revolutionary strategy designed to relate Marxist doctrine and practice to non-Western societies. His reasons were not entirely altruistic. Soviet Russia, surrounded by capitalist powers, desperately needed allies in its struggle to survive in a hostile world.

**Lenin and the East** To Lenin, the anticolonial movements emerging in North Africa, Asia, and the Middle East after World War I were natural allies of the beleaguered new regime in Moscow. In the spring of 1913, he had written, "Was it so long ago that China was considered typical of the lands that had been standing still for centuries? Today China is a land of seething political activity, the scene of a virile social movement and of a democratic upsurge."[2] Similar conditions, he added, were spreading the democratic revolution to other parts of Asia—to Turkey, Persia, and China. Ferment was on the rise even in British India. Lenin was convinced that only the ability of the imperialist powers to find markets, raw materials, and sources of capital investment in the non-Western world kept capitalism alive. If the tentacles of capitalist influence in Asia and Africa could be severed, imperialism would weaken and collapse.

Establishing such an alliance was not easy, however. Most nationalist leaders in colonial countries belonged to the urban middle class, and many abhorred the idea of a comprehensive revolution to create a totally egalitarian society. In addition, many still adhered to traditional religious beliefs and were opposed to the atheistic principles of classical Marxism.

Since it was unrealistic to expect bourgeois nationalist support for social revolution, Lenin sought a compromise by which Communist parties could be organized among the working classes in the preindustrial societies of Asia and Africa. These parties would then forge informal alliances with existing middle-class parties to struggle against the common enemies of feudal reaction (the remnants of the traditional ruling class) and Western imperialism. Such an alliance, of course, could not be permanent because many bourgeois nationalists in Asia and Africa would reject an egalitarian, classless society. Once the imperialists had been overthrown, therefore, the Communist parties would turn against their erstwhile nationalist partners to seize power on their own and carry out the socialist revolution. Lenin thus proposed a two-stage revolution: an initial "national democratic" stage followed by a "proletarian socialist" stage.

Lenin's strategy became a major element in Soviet foreign policy in the 1920s. Soviet agents fanned out across the world to carry Marxism beyond the boundaries of industrial Europe. The primary instrument of this effort was the **Communist International,** or **Comintern** for short. Formed in 1919 at Lenin's prodding, the Comintern was a worldwide organization of Communist parties dedicated to the advancement of world revolution. At its headquarters in Moscow, agents from around the world were trained in the precepts of world communism and then sent back to their countries to form Marxist parties and promote the cause of social revolution. By the end of the 1920s, almost every colonial or semicolonial society in Asia had a party based on Marxist principles. The Soviets had less success in the Middle East, where Marxist ideology appealed mainly to minorities such as Jews and Armenians in the cities, or in black Africa, where Soviet strategists in any case did not feel conditions were sufficiently advanced for the creation of Communist organizations.

**The Appeal of Communism** According to Marxist doctrine, the rank and file of Communist parties should be urban factory workers alienated from capitalist society by inhuman working conditions. In practice, many of the leaders even in European Communist parties tended to be urban intellectuals or members of the lower middle class (in Marxist parlance, the "petty bourgeoisie"). That phenomenon was even more true in the non-Western world, where most early Marxists were rootless intellectuals. Some were probably drawn into the movement for patriotic reasons and saw Marxist doctrine as a new, more effective means of modernizing their societies and removing the colonial exploiters (see the box on p. 668). Others were attracted by the message of egalitarian communism and the utopian dream of a classless society. For those who had lost their faith in traditional religion, communism often served as a new secular ideology, dealing not with the hereafter but with the here and now or, indeed, with a remote future when the state would wither away and the "classless society" would replace the lost truth of traditional faiths.

Of course, the new doctrine's appeal was not the same in all non-Western societies. In Confucian societies such as China and Vietnam, where traditional belief systems had been badly discredited by their failure to counter the Western challenge, communism had an immediate impact and rapidly became a major factor in the anticolonial movement. In Buddhist and Muslim societies, where traditional religion remained strong and actually became a cohesive factor in the resistance movement, communism had less success. To maximize their appeal and minimize potential conflict with traditional ideas, Communist parties frequently attempted to adapt Marxist doctrine to indigenous values and institutions. In the Middle East, for example, the Ba'ath Party in Syria adopted a hybrid socialism combining Marxism with Arab nationalism. In Africa, radical intellectuals talked vaguely of a uniquely "African road to socialism."

The degree to which these parties were successful in establishing alliances with nationalist parties and building a solid base of support among the mass of the population also varied from place to place. In some instances, the Communists were briefly able to establish a cooperative relationship with the bourgeois parties. The most famous example was the alliance between the Chinese Communist Party and Sun Yat-sen's Nationalist Party (discussed in the next section). In the Dutch East Indies, the Indonesian Communist Party (known as the PKI) allied with the middle-class nationalist group Sarekat Islam but later broke loose in an effort to organize its own mass movement among the poor peasants. In French Indochina, Vietnamese Communists organized by the Moscow-trained revolutionary Ho Chi Minh sought at first to cooperate with bourgeois nationalist parties against the colonial regime, but these efforts were abandoned in 1928 when the Comintern, reacting to Chiang Kai-shek's betrayal of the alliance with the Chinese Communist Party, declared that Communist parties should restrict their recruiting efforts to the most revolutionary elements in society—notably, the urban intellectuals and the working class. Harassed by colonial authorities and saddled with strategic directions from Moscow that often had little relevance to local conditions, Communist parties in most colonial societies had little success in the 1930s and failed to build a secure base of support among the mass of the population.

## Revolution in China

Overall, revolutionary Marxism had its greatest impact in China, where a group of young radicals, including several faculty and staff members from Peking University, founded the Chinese Communist Party (CCP) in 1921. The rise of the CCP was a consequence of the failed revolution of 1911. When political forces are too weak or too divided to consolidate their power during a period of instability, the military usually steps in to fill the vacuum. In China, Sun Yat-sen and his colleagues had accepted General Yuan Shikai (Yuan Shih-k'ai) as president of the new Chinese republic in 1911 because they lacked the military force to compete with his control over the army. Moreover, many feared, perhaps rightly, that if the revolt lapsed into chaos, the Western powers would intervene and the last shreds of Chinese sovereignty would be lost. But some had misgivings about Yuan's intentions. As one remarked in a letter to a friend, "We don't know whether he will be a George Washington or a Napoleon."

## THE PATH OF LIBERATION

In 1919, the Vietnamese revolutionary Ho Chi Minh (1890–1969) was living in exile in France, where he first became acquainted with the new revolutionary experiment in Bolshevik Russia. He became a leader of the Vietnamese Communist movement. In the following passage, written in 1960, he reminisces about his reasons for becoming a Communist. The Second International mentioned in the text was an organization created in 1889 by moderate socialists who pursued their goal by parliamentary means. Lenin created the Third International, or Comintern, in 1919 to promote violent revolution.

*Why does Ho Chi Minh believe that the Third International was the key to the liberation of the colonial peoples? What were the essential elements of Lenin's strategy for bringing that about?*

### Ho Chi Minh, "The Path Which Led Me to Leninism"

After World War I, I made my living in Paris, now as a retoucher at a photographer's, now as a painter of "Chinese antiquities" (made in France!). I would distribute leaflets denouncing the crimes committed by the French colonialists in Vietnam.

At that time, I supported the October Revolution only instinctively, not yet grasping all its historic importance. I loved and admired Lenin because he was a great patriot who liberated his compatriots; until then, I had read none of his books.

The reason for my joining the French Socialist Party was that these "ladies and gentlemen"—as I called my comrades at that moment—had shown their sympathy toward me, toward the struggle of the oppressed peoples. But I understood neither what was a party, a trade union, nor what was Socialism nor Communism.

Heated discussions were then taking place in the branches of the Socialist Party, about the question whether the Socialist Party should remain in the Second International, should a Second-and-a-Half International be founded, or should the Socialist Party join Lenin's Third International? I attended the meetings regularly, twice or three times a week, and attentively listened to the discussion. First, I could not understand thoroughly. Why were the discussions so heated? Either with the Second, Second-and-a-Half, or Third International, the revolution could be waged. What was the use of arguing then? As for the First International, what had become of it?

What I wanted most to know—and this precisely was not debated in the meetings—was: which International sides with the peoples of colonial countries?

I raised this question—the most important in my opinion—in a meeting. Some comrades answered: It is the Third, not the Second International. And a comrade gave me Lenin's "Thesis on the national and colonial questions," published by *l'Humanité,* to read.

There were political terms difficult to understand in this thesis. But by dint of reading it again and again, finally I could grasp the main part of it. What emotion, enthusiasm, clear-sightedness, and confidence it instilled in me! I was overjoyed to tears. Though sitting alone in my room, I shouted aloud as if addressing large crowds: "Dear martyrs, compatriots! This is what we need, this is the path to our liberation!"

After that, I had entire confidence in Lenin, in the Third International.

As it turned out, he was neither. Understanding little of the new ideas sweeping into China from the West, Yuan ruled in a traditional manner, reviving Confucian rituals and institutions and eventually trying to found a new imperial dynasty. Yuan's dictatorial inclinations rapidly led to clashes with Sun's party, now renamed the *Guomindang* (*Kuomintang*), or Nationalist Party. When Yuan dissolved the new parliament, the Nationalists launched a rebellion. When it failed, Sun Yat-sen fled to Japan.

Yuan was strong enough to brush off the challenge from the revolutionary forces but not to turn back the clock of history. He died in 1916 (apparently of natural causes, although legend holds that his heart was broken by growing popular resistance to his imperial pretensions) and was succeeded by one of his military subordinates. For the next several years, China slipped into semianarchy as the power of the central government disintegrated and military warlords seized power in the provinces.

## Mr. Science and Mr. Democracy: The New Culture Movement

Although the failure of the 1911 revolution was a clear sign that China was not yet ready for radical change, discontent with existing conditions continued to rise in various sectors of Chinese society. The most vocal protests came from radical intellectuals, who opposed Yuan Shikai's conservative rule but were now convinced that political change could not take place until the Chinese people were more familiar with trends in the outside world. Braving the displeasure of Yuan and his successors, progressive intellectuals at Peking University launched the **New Culture Movement,** aimed at abolishing the remnants of the old system and introducing Western values and institutions into China. Using the classrooms of China's most prestigious university as well as the pages of newly established progressive magazines and newspapers,

YMCA of the USA Archives, University of Minnesota Libraries

Courtesy of William J. Duiker

**Student Demonstrations in Beijing.** On May 4, 1919, students gathered at the Gate of Heavenly Peace in Beijing to protest against the Japanese takeover of the Shandong peninsula after World War I (left photo). The event triggered the famous May Fourth Movement, which highlighted the demand of progressive forces in China for political and social reforms. Eighty years to the day later, the event was repeated as students and their supporters gathered in the same spot to demand democracy and an end to official corruption in China. A portrait of the deceased Communist Leader Mao Zedong looks down in seeming disdain (right photo).

the intellectuals introduced a bewildering mix of new ideas, from the philosophy of Friedrich Nietszche and Bertrand Russell to the educational views of the American John Dewey and the feminist plays of Henrik Ibsen. As such ideas flooded into China, they stirred up a new generation of educated Chinese youth, who chanted "Down with Confucius and sons" and talked of a new era dominated by "Mr. Sai" (Mr. Science) and "Mr. De" (Mr. Democracy). No one was a greater defender of free thought and speech than the chancellor of Peking University, Cai Yuanpei (Ts'ai Yüan-p'ei):

> So far as theoretical ideas are concerned, I follow the principles of "freedom of thought" and an attitude of broad tolerance in accordance with the practice of universities the world over. . . . Regardless of what school of thought a person may adhere to, so long as that person's ideas are justified and conform to reason and have not been passed by through the process of natural selection, although there may be controversy, such ideas have a right to be presented.[3]

The problem was that appeals for American-style democracy and women's liberation had little relevance to Chinese peasants, most of whom were still illiterate and concerned above all with survival. Consequently, the New Culture Movement did not win widespread support outside the urban areas. It certainly earned the distrust of conservative military officers, one of whom threatened to lob artillery shells into Peking University to destroy the poisonous new ideas and their advocates.

Discontent among intellectuals, however, was soon joined by the rising chorus of public protest against Japan's efforts to expand its influence on the mainland. During the first decade of the twentieth century, Japan had taken advantage of the Qing's decline to extend its domination over Manchuria and Korea (see Chapter 21). In 1915, the Japanese government insisted that Yuan Shikai accept a series of twenty-one demands that would have given Japan a virtual protectorate over the Chinese government and economy. Yuan was able to fend off the most far-reaching Japanese demands by arousing popular outrage in China, but at the Paris Peace Conference four years later, Japan received Germany's sphere of influence in Shandong Province as a reward for its support of the Allied cause in World War I. On hearing that the Chinese government had accepted the decision, on May 4, 1919, patriotic students, supported by other sectors of the urban population, demonstrated in Beijing and other major cities of the country. Although this May Fourth Movement did not lead to the restoration of Shandong, it did alert a substantial part of the politically literate population to the threat to national survival and the incompetence of the warlord government.

## The Nationalist-Communist Alliance

By 1920, central authority had almost ceased to exist in China. Two competing political forces now began to emerge from the chaos. One was Sun Yat-sen's Nationalist Party. Driven from the political arena seven years earlier by Yuan Shikai, the party now reestablished itself on the mainland by making an alliance with the warlord ruler of Guangdong (Kwangtung) Province in southern China. From Canton, Sun sought international assistance to carry out his national revolution. The other was the CCP. Following Lenin's strategy, Comintern agents soon advised the new party to link up with the more experienced Nationalists. Sun Yat-sen needed the expertise and the diplomatic support that the Soviet Union could provide because his anti-imperialist rhetoric had alienated many

Western powers; one English-language newspaper in Shanghai remarked, "All his life, all his influence, are devoted to ideas which keep China in turmoil, and it is utterly undesirable that he should be allowed to prosecute those aims here."[4] In 1923, the two parties formed an alliance to oppose the warlords and drive the imperialist powers out of China.

For three years, with the assistance of a Comintern mission in Canton, the two parties submerged their mutual suspicions and mobilized and trained a revolutionary army to march north and seize control over China. The so-called Northern Expedition began in the summer of 1926 (see Map 23.1). By the following spring, revolutionary forces were in control of all Chinese territory south of the Yangtze River, including the major river ports of Wuhan and Shanghai. But tensions between the two parties now surfaced. Sun Yat-sen had died of cancer in 1925 and was succeeded as head of the Nationalist Party by his military subordinate, Chiang Kai-shek. Chiang feigned support for the alliance with the Communists but actually planned to destroy them. In April 1927, he struck against the Communists and their supporters in Shanghai, killing thousands. After the massacre, most of the Communist leaders went into hiding in the city, where they attempted to revive the movement in its traditional base among the urban working class. Some party members, however, led by the young Communist organizer Mao Zedong (Mao Tse-tung), fled to the hilly areas south of the Yangtze River.

Unlike most CCP leaders, Mao was convinced that the Chinese revolution must be based on the impoverished peasants in the countryside. The son of a prosperous peasant, Mao had helped organize a peasant movement in southern China during the early 1920s and then served as an agitator in rural villages in his native province of Hunan during the Northern Expedition in the fall of 1926. At that time, he wrote a famous report to the party leadership suggesting that the CCP support peasant demands for a land revolution (see the box on p. 671). But his superiors refused, fearing that such radical policies would destroy the alliance with the Nationalists.

**CHRONOLOGY Revolution in China**

| | |
|---|---|
| May Fourth demonstrations | 1919 |
| Formation of Chinese Communist Party | 1921 |
| Northern Expedition | 1926–1928 |
| Establishment of Nanjing Republic | 1928 |
| Long March | 1934–1935 |

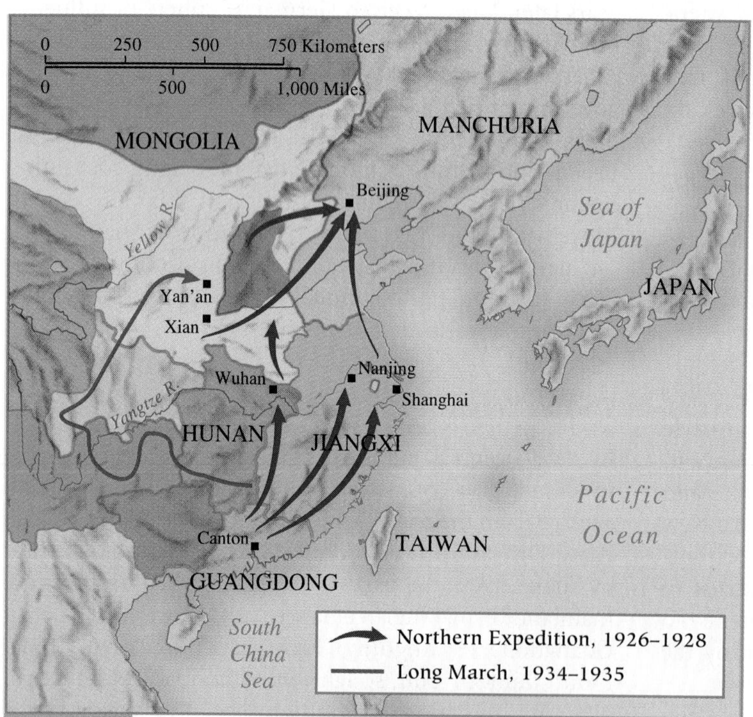


**MAP 23.1 The Northern Expedition and the Long March.** This map shows the routes taken by the combined Nationalist-Communist forces during the Northern Expedition of 1926–1928. The thinner arrow indicates the route taken by Communist units during the Long March led by Mao Zedong. ? Where did Mao establish his new headquarters? **View an animated version of this map or related maps at http://history.wadsworth.com/duikerspielvogel05/**

## The Nanjing Republic

In 1928, Chiang Kai-shek founded a new Chinese republic at Nanjing, and over the next three years, he managed to reunify China by a combination of military operations and inducements (known as "silver bullets") to various northern warlords to join his movement. He also attempted to put an end to the Communists, rooting them out of their urban base in Shanghai and their rural redoubt in the rugged hills of Jiangxi (Kiangsi) Province. He succeeded in the first task in 1931, when most party leaders were forced to flee Shanghai for Mao's base in southern China. Three years later, using their superior military strength, Chiang's troops surrounded the Communist base in Jiangxi, inducing Mao's young People's Liberation Army (PLA) to abandon its guerrilla lair and embark on the famous Long March, an arduous journey of thousands of miles on foot through mountains, marshes, and deserts to the small provincial town of Yan'an (Yenan) 200 miles north of the city of Xian in the dusty hills of northern China (see Map 23.1). Of the ninety thousand who embarked on the journey in October 1934, only ten thousand arrived in Yan'an a year later. Contemporary observers

## A Call for Revolt

In the fall of 1926, Nationalist and Communist forces moved north from Canton on their Northern Expedition in an effort to defeat the warlords. The young Communist Mao Zedong accompanied revolutionary troops into his home province of Hunan, where he submitted a report to the CCP Central Committee calling for a massive peasant revolt against the ruling order. The report shows his confidence that peasants could play an active role in the Chinese revolution despite the skepticism of many of his colleagues.

*Why does Mao Zedong believe that rural peasants could help bring about a social revolution in China? How does his vision compare with the reality of the Bolshevik Revolution in Russia?*

### Mao Zedong, "The Peasant Movement in Hunan"

During my recent visit to Hunan I made a firsthand investigation of conditions. . . . In a very short time, . . . several hundred million peasants will rise like a mighty storm, . . . a force so swift and violent that no power, however great, will be able to hold it back. They will smash all the trammels that bind them and rush forward along the road to liberation. They will sweep all the imperialists, warlords, corrupt officials, local tyrants, and evil gentry into their graves. Every revolutionary party and every revolutionary comrade will be put to the test, to be accepted or rejected as they decide. There are three alternatives. To march at their head and lead them? To trail behind them, gesticulating and criticizing? Or to stand in their way and oppose them? Every Chinese is free to choose, but events will force you to make the choice quickly.

The main targets of attack by the peasants are the local tyrants, the evil gentry and the lawless landlords, but in passing they also hit out against patriarchal ideas and institutions, against the corrupt officials in the cities and against bad practices and customs in the rural areas. . . . As a result, the privileges which the feudal landlords enjoyed for thousands of years are being shattered to pieces. . . . With the collapse of the power of the landlords, the peasant associations have now become the sole organs of authority, and the popular slogan "All power to the peasant associations" has become a reality.

The peasants' revolt disturbed the gentry's sweet dreams. When the news from the countryside reached the cities, it caused immediate uproar among the gentry. . . . From the middle social strata upwards to the Kuomintang right-wingers, there was not a single person who did not sum up the whole business in the phrase, "It's terrible!" . . . Even quite progressive people said, "Though terrible, it is inevitable in a revolution." In short, nobody could altogether deny the word "terrible." But . . . the fact is that the great peasant masses have risen to fulfill their historic mission. . . . What the peasants are doing is absolutely right; what they are doing is fine! "It's fine!" is the theory of the peasants and of all other revolutionaries. Every revolutionary comrade should know that the national revolution requires a great change in the countryside. The Revolution of 1911 did not bring about this change, hence its failure. This change is now taking place, and it is an important factor for the completion of the revolution. Every revolutionary comrade must support it, or he will be taking the stand of counterrevolution.

**History Now™** To read several documents by Mao Zedong, enter the *HistoryNow* documents area using the access card that is available for *World History*.

must have thought that the Communist threat to the Nanjing regime had been averted forever.

Meanwhile, Chiang was trying to build a new nation. When the Nanjing republic was established in 1928, Chiang publicly declared his commitment to Sun Yat-sen's Three People's Principles. In a program announced in 1918, Sun had written about the all-important second stage of "political tutelage":

> China . . . needs a republican government just as a boy needs school. As a schoolboy must have good teachers and helpful friends, so the Chinese people, being for the first time under republican rule, must have a farsighted revolutionary government for their training. This calls for the period of political tutelage, which is a necessary transitional stage from monarchy to republicanism. Without this, disorder will be unavoidable.[5]

In keeping with Sun's program, Chiang announced a period of political indoctrination to prepare the Chinese people for a final stage of constitutional government. In the meantime, the Nationalists would use their dictatorial power to carry out a land reform program and modernize the urban industrial sector.

But it would take more than paper plans to create a new China. Years of neglect and civil war had severely frayed the political, economic, and social fabric of the nation. There were faint signs of an impending industrial revolution in the major urban centers, but most of the people in the countryside, drained by warlord exactions and civil strife, were still grindingly poor and overwhelmingly illiterate. A Westernized middle class had begun to emerge in the cities and formed much of the natural constituency of the Nanjing government. But this new westernized elite, preoccupied with bourgeois values of individual advancement and material accumulation, had few links with the peasants in the countryside or the rickshaw

David King Collection, London

© Earl Leaf/Rapho

POLITICS & GOVERNMENT

COMPARATIVE ILLUSTRATION

**Communist Leaders in China and the Soviet Union.** In 1934, Mao Zedong led his bedraggled forces on the famous Long March from southern China to a new location at Yan'an, in the hills just south of the Gobi Desert. In the photo at the right, Chairman Mao (on the left) and Zhu De, one of his generals, pose outside the Chinese Communist Party's new headquarters. By this time, Mao had become the leader of the communist movement, although the Communists did not take complete control of China until 1949. Joseph Stalin had become leader of the Communist Party in the Soviet Union in 1928 and within a year had established a powerful dictatorship over the entire country. In the picture above, from 1933, Stalin is signing what is supposedly a death warrant. As the terror increased in the late 1930s, Stalin signed such lists every day.

drivers "running in this world of suffering," in the poignant words of a Chinese poet. In an expressive phrase, some critics dismissed Chiang and his chief followers as "banana Chinese"—yellow on the outside, white on the inside.

**The Best of East and West** Chiang was aware of the difficulty of introducing exotic foreign ideas into a society still culturally conservative. While building a modern industrial sector, he attempted to synthesize modern Western ideas with traditional Confucian values of hard work, obedience, and moral integrity. In the officially promoted New Life Movement, sponsored by his Wellesley-educated wife, Mei-ling Soong, Chiang sought to propagate traditional Confucian social ethics such as integrity, propriety, and righteousness while rejecting what he considered the excessive individualism and material greed of Western capitalism.

Unfortunately for Chiang, Confucian ideas—at least in their institutional form—had been widely discredited by the failure of the traditional system to solve China's growing problems. With only a tenuous hold over the Chinese provinces (the Nanjing government had total control over only a handful of provinces in the Yangtze valley), a growing Japanese threat in the north, and a world suffering from the Great Depression, Chiang made little progress with his program. Lacking the political sensitivity of Sun Yat-sen and fearing Communist influence, Chiang repressed all opposition and censored free expression, thereby alienating many intellectuals and political moderates. Since the urban middle class and landed gentry were his natural political constituency, he shunned programs that would lead to a redistribution of wealth. A land reform program was enacted in 1930 but had little effect.

Chiang Kai-shek's government had little more success in promoting industrial development. During the decade of precarious peace following the Northern Expedition, industrial growth averaged only about 1 percent annually. Much of the national wealth was in the hands of the senior officials and close subordinates of the ruling elite. Military expenses consumed half the budget, and distressingly little was devoted to social and economic development.

The new government, then, had little success in dealing with China's deep-seated economic and social problems. The deadly combination of internal disintegration and foreign pressure now began to coincide with the virtual collapse of the global economic order during the

COMPARATIVE ESSAY

## Out of the Doll's House

In Henrik Ibsen's play *A Doll's House,* published in 1879, Nora Helmer informs her husband, Torvald, that she will no longer accept his control over her life and announces her intention to leave home to start her life anew. When the outraged Torvald cites her sacred duties as wife and mother, Nora replies that she has other duties just as sacred, those to herself. "I can no longer content myself with what most people say," she declares. "I must think over things for myself and get to understand them."

To Ibsen's contemporaries, such remarks were revolutionary. In nineteenth-century Europe, the traditional characterization of the sexes, based on gender-defined social roles, had been elevated to the status of a universal law. As the family wage earners, men were expected to go off to work, while women were assigned the responsibility of caring for home and family. Women were advised to accept their lot and play their role as effectively and as gracefully as possible.

The ideal, however, did not always match reality. With the advent of the Industrial Revolution, many women, especially those from the lower classes, were driven by the need for supplemental income to seek employment outside the home, often in the form of menial labor. Some women, inspired by the ideals of human dignity and freedom expressed during the Enlightenment and the French Revolution, began to protest against a tradition of female inferiority that had long kept them in a "doll's house" of male domination and to claim equal rights before the law.

The movement to liberate women from the iron cage of legal and social inferiority first began to gain ground in English-speaking countries like Great Britain and the United States, but it gradually spread to the continent of Europe and then to colonial areas in Africa and Asia. By the first decades of the twentieth century, women's liberation movements were under way in parts of North Africa, the Middle East, and East Asia, voicing a growing demand for access to education, equal treatment before the law, and the right to vote.

Progress, however, was often agonizingly slow, especially in societies where age-old traditional values had not yet been undermined by the corrosive force of the Industrial Revolution. In many colonial societies, the effort to improve the condition of women was subordinated to the goal of gaining national independence. In some instances, women's liberation movements were led by educated elites who failed to include the concerns of working-class women in their agendas. Colonialism, too, was a double-edged sword, as the sexist bias of European officials combined with indigenous traditions of male superiority to marginalize women even further. As men moved to the cities to exploit opportunities provided by the new colonial administration, women were left to cope with their traditional responsibilities in the villages, often without the safety net of male support that had sustained them during the precolonial era.

---

Great Depression and the rise of militant political forces in Japan determined to extend Japanese influence and power in an unstable Asia. These forces and the turmoil they unleashed will be examined in the next chapter.

## "Down with Confucius and Sons": Economic, Social, and Cultural Change in Republican China

The transformation of the old order that had commenced at the end of the Qing era continued into the period of the early Chinese republic. The industrial sector continued to grow, albeit slowly. Although about 75 percent of all industrial production was still craft-produced in the early 1930s, mechanization was gradually beginning to replace manual labor in a number of traditional industries, notably in the manufacture of textile goods. Traditional Chinese exports, such as silk and tea, were hit hard by the Great Depression, however, and manufacturing suffered a decline during the 1930s. It is difficult to gauge conditions in the countryside during the early republican era, but there is no doubt that farmers were often victimized by high taxes imposed by local warlords and the endemic political and social conflict.

**Social Changes** Social changes followed shifts in the economy and the political culture. By 1915, the assault on the old system and values by educated youth was intense. The main focus of the attack was the Confucian concept of the family—in particular, filial piety and the subordination of women (see the comparative essay "Out of the Doll's House" above). Young people demanded the right to choose their own mates and their own careers. Inspired by a visit to China of the American women's advocate Margaret Sanger in 1922, women demanded rights and opportunities equal to those enjoyed by men. More broadly, progressives called for an end to the concept of duty to the community and praised the Western individualist ethos. The popular short story writer Lu Xun (Lu Hsun) criticized the Confucian concept of family as a "man-eating" system that degraded humanity. In a famous short story titled "Diary of a Madman," the protagonist remarks:

> I remember when I was four or five years old, sitting in the cool of the hall, my brother told me that if a man's parents were ill,

## An Arranged Marriage

Under Western influence, Chinese social customs changed dramatically for many urban elites in the interwar years. A vocal women's movement, inspired in part by translations of Henrik Ibsen's play *A Doll's House*, campaigned aggressively for universal suffrage and an end to sexual discrimination. Some progressives called for free choice in marriage and divorce and even for free love. By the 1930s, the government had taken some steps to free women from patriarchal marriage constraints and realize sexual equality. But life was generally unaffected in the villages, where traditional patterns held sway. This often created severe tensions between older and younger generations, as this passage by the popular twentieth-century novelist Ba Jin shows.

*Why does Chueh-hsin comply with the wishes of his father in the matter of his marriage? Why were arranged marriages so prevalent in traditional China?*

### Ba Jin, *Family*

Brought up with loving care, after studying with a private tutor for a number of years, Chueh-hsin entered middle school. One of the school's best students, he graduated four years later at the top of his class. He was very interested in physics and chemistry and hoped to study abroad, in Germany. His mind was full of beautiful dreams. At that time he was the envy of his classmates.

In his fourth year at middle school, he lost his mother. His father later married again, this time to a younger woman who had been his mother's cousin. Chueh-hsin was aware of his loss, for he knew full well that nothing could replace the love of a mother. But her death left no irreparable wound in his heart; he was able to console himself with rosy dreams of his future. Moreover, he had someone who understood him and could comfort him–his pretty cousin Mei, "mei" for "plum blossom."

But then, one day, his dreams were shattered, cruelly and bitterly shattered. The evening he returned home carrying his diploma, the plaudits of his teachers and friends still ringing in his ears, his father called him into his room and said:

"Now that you've graduated, I want to arrange your marriage. Your grandfather is looking forward to having a great-grandson, and I, too, would like to be able to hold a grandson in my arms. You're old enough to be married; I won't feel easy until I fulfill my obligation to find you a wife. Although I didn't accumulate much money in my years away from home as an official, still I've put by enough for us to get along on. My health isn't what it used to be; I'm thinking of spending my time at home and having you help me run the household affairs. All the more reason you'll be needing a wife. I've already arranged a match with the Li family. The thirteenth of next month is a good day. We'll announce the engagement then. You can be married within the year. . . ."

Chueh-hsin did not utter a word of protest, nor did such a thought ever occur to him. He merely nodded to indicate his compliance with his father's wishes. But after he returned to his own room, and shut the door, he threw himself down on his bed, covered his head with the quilt and wept. He wept for his broken dreams.

He was deeply in love with Mei, but now his father had chosen another, a girl he had never seen, and said that he must marry within the year. What's more, his hopes of continuing his studies had burst like a bubble. It was a terrible shock to Chueh-hsin. His future was finished, his beautiful dreams shattered.

He cried his disappointment and bitterness. But the door was closed and Chueh-hsin's head was beneath the bedding. No one knew. He did not fight back, he never thought of resisting. He only bemoaned his fate. But he accepted it. He complied with his father's will without a trace of resentment. But in his heart he wept for himself, wept for the girl he adored–Mei, his "plum blossom."

---

> he should cut off a piece of his flesh and boil it for them if he wanted to be considered a good son. I have only just realized that I have been living all these years in a place where for four thousand years they have been eating human flesh.[6]

Such criticisms did have some beneficial results. During the early republic, the tyranny of the old family system began to decline, at least in urban areas, under the impact of economic changes and the urgings of the New Culture intellectuals. Women began to escape their cloistered existence and seek education and employment alongside their male contemporaries. Free choice in marriage and a more relaxed attitude toward sex became commonplace among affluent families in the cities, where the teenage children of Westernized elites aped the clothing, social habits, and musical tastes of their contemporaries in Europe and the United States.

But as a rule, the new individualism and women's rights did not penetrate to the textile factories, where over a million women worked in slave labor conditions, or to the villages, where traditional attitudes and customs held sway. Arranged marriages continued to be the rule rather than the exception, and concubinage remained common. According to a survey taken in the 1930s, well over two-thirds of the marriages even among urban couples had been arranged by their parents (see the box above), and in one rural area, only 3 out of 170 villagers interviewed had even heard of the idea of "modern marriage." Even the tradition of binding the feet of female children continued despite efforts by the Nationalist government to eradicate the practice.

**A New Culture?** Nowhere was the struggle between traditional and modern more visible than in the field of culture. Beginning with the New Culture era, radical reformists criticized traditional culture as the symbol and instrument of feudal oppression that must be entirely eradicated before a new China could stand with dignity in the modern world. During the 1920s and 1930s, Western literature and art became highly popular, especially among the urban middle class. Traditional culture continued to prevail among more conservative elements, and some intellectuals argued for a new art that would synthesize the best of Chinese and foreign culture. But the most creative artists were interested in imitating foreign trends, while traditionalists were more concerned with preservation.

Literature in particular was influenced by foreign ideas as Western genres like the novel and the short story attracted a growing audience. Although most Chinese novels written after World War I dealt with Chinese subjects, they reflected the Western tendency toward social realism and often dealt with the new westernized middle class (Mao Dun's *Midnight,* for example, describes the changing mores of Shanghai's urban elites) or the disintegration of the traditional Confucian family (Ba Jin's famous novel *Family* is an example). Most of China's modern authors displayed a clear contempt for the past.

# Japan Between the Wars

During the first two decades of the twentieth century, Japan made remarkable progress toward the creation of an advanced society on the Western model. The political system based on the Meiji Constitution of 1890 began to evolve along Western pluralistic lines, and a multiparty system took shape, while the economic and social reforms launched during the Meiji era led to increasing prosperity and the development of a modern industrial and commercial sector. Optimists had reason to hope that Japan was on the road to becoming a full-fledged democracy.

## Experiment in Democracy

During the first quarter of the twentieth century, the Japanese political system appeared to evolve significantly toward the Western democratic model. Political parties expanded their popular following and became increasingly competitive, and universal male suffrage was instituted in the 1920s. Individual pressure groups began to appear in Japanese society, along with an independent press and a bill of rights. The influence of the old ruling oligarchy, the *genro,* had not yet been significantly challenged, however, nor had that of its ideological foundation, the *kokutai* (see Chapter 21).

These fragile democratic institutions were able to survive throughout the 1920s (often called the era of Taisho democracy, from the reign title of the ruling emperor). During that period, the military budget was reduced, and a suffrage bill enacted in 1925 granted the vote to all Japanese males, thus continuing the process of democratization begun earlier in the century. Women remained disenfranchised, but women's associations gained increasing visibility during the 1920s, and many women were active in the labor movement and in campaigning for various social reforms.

But the era was also marked by growing social turmoil, and two opposing forces within the system were gearing up to challenge the prevailing wisdom. On the left, a Marxist labor movement, which reflected the tensions within the working class and the increasing radicalism among the rural poor, began to take shape in the early 1920s in response to growing economic difficulties. Attempts to suppress labor disturbances led to further radicalization. On the right, ultranationalist groups called for a rejection of Western models of development and a more militant approach to realizing national objectives. In 1919, the radical nationalist Kita Ikki called for a military takeover and the establishment of a new system bearing strong resemblance to what would later be called National Socialism in Germany.

**Swinging to the Latest Tunes.** Whereas women of the old regime were swathed in colorful floor-length kimonos, elaborate coiffures, and traditional Japanese sandals, in the early 1930s many young Japanese adopted Western dress and leisure pursuits. Here we see young women with bobbed hair, short skirts, and high heels, performing the latest dances with young men in Western suits to the syncopation of a swinging brass band.

## In Search of Old Japan

Japanese authors produced a host of superb works in the early twentieth century. Many authors blended Western psychology with Japanese sensibility in novels of yearning for old Japan. Here the novelist Junichiro Tanizaki recalls the charm of an island as yet untouched and unpolluted by modernization.

*How did Japanese politicians in the interwar years make use of such sentiments to achieve their own political goals?*

### Junichiro Tanizaki, *Some Prefer Nettles*

The island of Awaji showed not very large on the map, and its harbor very possibly consisted of but this one road. You go straight down, the inn manager had said, till you come out at the river, and the theater is in the flats beyond. The rows of houses therefore most probably ended at the river. This may have been the seat of some minor baron a century ago—even then it could hardly have been imposing enough to be called a castle town—and it had probably changed little since. A modern coating goes no farther than the large cities that are a country's arteries, and there are not many such cities anywhere. In an old country with a long tradition, China and Europe as well as Japan—any country, in fact, except a very new one like the United States—the smaller cities, left aside by the flow of civilization, retain the flavor of an earlier day until they are overtaken by catastrophe.

This little harbor, for instance: it had its electric wires and poles, its painted billboards, and here and there a display window, but one could ignore them and find on every side townsmen's houses that might have come from an illustration to a seventeenth-century novel. The earthen walls covered to the eaves with white plaster, the projecting lattice fronts with their solid, generous slats of wood, the heavy tiled roofs held down by round ridge-tiles, the shop signs—"Lacquer," "Soy," "Oil"—in fading letters on fine hardwood grounds, and inside, beyond earth-floored entrances, the shop names printed on dark-blue half-curtains—it was not the old man's remark this time but every detail brought back—how vividly!—the mood and air of old Japan. Kaname felt as if he were being drunk up into the scene, as if he were losing himself in the clean white walls and the brilliant blue sky. Those walls were a little like the sash around O-hisa's waist: their first luster had disappeared in long years under the fresh sea winds and rains, and bright though they were, their brightness was tempered by a certain reserve, a soft austerity.

Kaname felt a deep repose come over him. "These old houses are so dark you have no idea what's inside."

"Partly it's because the road is so bright." The old man had come up beside them. "The ground here seems almost white."

Kaname thought of the faces of the ancients in the dusk behind their shop curtains. Here on this street people with faces like theater dolls must have passed lives like stage lives. The world of the plays—of O-yumi, Jurobei of Awa, the pilgrim O-tsuru, and the rest—must have been just such a town as this. And wasn't O-hisa a part of it? Fifty years ago, a hundred years ago, a woman like her, dressed in the same kimono, was perhaps going down this same street in the spring sun, lunch in hand, on her way to the theater beyond the river. Or perhaps, behind one of these latticed fronts, she was playing "Snow" on her koto. O-hisa was a shade left behind by another age.

This cultural conflict between old and new, native and foreign, was reflected in literature. Japanese self-confidence had been somewhat restored after the victories over China and Russia, and this resurgence sparked a great age of creativity in the early twentieth century. Now more adept at handling European literary forms, Japanese writers blended Western psychology with Japanese sensibility in exquisite novels reeking with nostalgia for the old Japan. A well-known example is Junichiro Tanizaki's *Some Prefer Nettles*, published in 1928, which delicately juxtaposes the positive aspects of both traditional and modern Japan (see the box above). By the 1930s, however, military censorship increasingly inhibited free literary expression. Many authors continued to write privately, producing works that reflected the gloom of the era. This attitude is perhaps best exemplified by Shiga Naoya's novel *A Dark Night's Journey*, written during the early 1930s and capturing a sense of the approaching global catastrophe. It is regarded as the masterpiece of modern Japanese literature.

## A *Zaibatsu* Economy

Japan also continued to make impressive progress in economic development. Spurred by rising domestic demand as well as continued government investment in the economy, the production of raw materials tripled between 1900 and 1930, and industrial production increased more than twelvefold. Much of the increase went into exports, and Western manufacturers began to complain about increasing competition from the Japanese.

As often happens, rapid industrialization was accompanied by some hardship and rising social tensions. In the Meiji model, various manufacturing processes were concentrated in a single enterprise, the ***zaibatsu,*** or financial clique. Some of these firms were existing merchant companies, such as Mitsui and Sumitomo, that had the capital and the foresight to move into new areas of opportunity. Others were formed by enterprising samurai, who used their status and experience in management to good account in a new environment. Whatever their origins, these firms gradually developed, often with official encouragement, into large conglomerates that controlled a major segment of the Japanese economy. By 1937, the four largest *zaibatsu* (Mitsui, Mitsubishi, Sumitomo, and Yasuda) controlled 21 percent of the banking industry, 26 percent of mining, 35 percent of shipbuilding, 38 percent of commercial shipping, and more than 60 percent of paper manufacturing and insurance.

This concentration of power and wealth in a few major industrial combines created problems in Japanese society. In the first place, it resulted in the emergence of a dual economy: on the one hand, a modern industry characterized by up-to-date methods and massive government subsidies, and on the other, a traditional manufacturing sector characterized by conservative methods and small-scale production techniques.

Concentration of wealth also led to growing economic inequalities. As we have seen, economic growth had been achieved at the expense of the peasants, many of whom fled to the cities to escape rural poverty. That labor surplus benefited the industrial sector, but the urban proletariat was still poorly paid and ill-housed. Rampant inflation in the price of rice led to food riots shortly after World War I. A rapid increase in population (the total population of the Japanese islands increased from an estimated 43 million in 1900 to 73 million in 1940) led to food shortages and the threat of rising unemployment. In the meantime, those left on the farm continued to suffer. As late as the beginning of World War II, an estimated one-half of all Japanese farmers were tenants.

### Shidehara Diplomacy

A final problem for Japanese leaders in the post-Meiji era was the familiar colonial dilemma of finding sources of raw materials and foreign markets for the nation's manufactured goods. Until World War I, Japan had dealt with the problem by seizing territories such as Taiwan, Korea, and southern Manchuria and transforming them into colonies or protectorates of the growing Japanese empire. That policy had succeeded brilliantly, but it had also begun to arouse the concern and in some cases the hostility of the Western nations. China was also becoming apprehensive; as we have seen, Japanese demands for Shandong Province at the Paris Peace Conference in 1919 aroused massive protests in major Chinese cities.

The United States was especially concerned about Japanese aggressiveness. Although the United States had been less active than some European states in pursuing colonies in the Pacific, it had a strong interest in keeping the area open for U.S. commercial activities. In 1922, in Washington, D.C., the United States convened a major conference of nations with interests in the Pacific to discuss problems of regional security. The Washington Conference led to agreements on several issues, but the major accomplishment was a nine-power treaty recognizing the territorial integrity of China and the Open Door. The other participants induced Japan to accept these provisions by accepting its special position in Manchuria.

During the remainder of the 1920s, Japanese governments attempted to play by the rules laid down at the Washington Conference. Known as Shidehara diplomacy, after the foreign minister (and later prime minister) who attempted to carry it out, this policy sought to use diplomatic and economic means to realize Japanese interests in Asia. But this approach came under severe pressure as Japanese industrialists began to move into new areas, such as heavy industry, chemicals, mining, and the manufacturing of appliances and automobiles. Because such industries desperately needed resources not found in abundance locally, the Japanese government came under increasing pressure to find new sources abroad.

**The Rise of Militant Nationalism** In the early 1930s, with the onset of the Great Depression and growing tensions in the international arena, nationalist forces rose to dominance in the government. The changes that occurred in the 1930s were not in the constitution or the institutional structure, which remained essentially intact, but in the composition and attitudes of the ruling group. Party leaders during the 1920s had attempted to realize Japanese aspirations within the existing global political and economic framework. The dominant elements in the government in the 1930s, a mixture of military officers and ultranationalist politicians, were convinced that the diplomacy of the 1920s had failed and advocated a more aggressive approach to protecting national interests in a brutal and competitive world (see Chapter 24).

Historians argue over whether Taisho democracy was merely a fragile period of comparative liberalization within a framework dominated by the Meiji vision of empire and *kokutai* or whether the militant nationalism of the 1930s was an aberration brought on by the depression, which caused the emerging Japanese democracy to wilt. Perhaps both contentions contain a little truth. A process of democratization was taking place in Japan during the first decades of the twentieth century, but without shaking the essential core of the Meiji concept of the state. When the "liberal" approach of the 1920s failed to solve the problems of the day, the shift toward a more aggressive approach was inevitable.

## Nationalism and Dictatorship in Latin America

Although the nations of Latin America played little role in World War I, that conflict nevertheless exerted an impact on the region, especially on its economy. By the end of the 1920s, the region was also strongly influenced by another event of global proportions—the Great Depression.

## The Economy and the United States

At the beginning of the twentieth century, virtually all of Latin America, except for the three Guianas, British Honduras, and some of the Caribbean Islands, had achieved independence. The economy of the region (see Map 23.2) was based largely on the export of foodstuffs and raw materials. Some countries relied on exports of only one or two products. Argentina, for example, exported primarily beef and wheat; Chile, nitrates and copper; Brazil and the Caribbean nations, sugar; and the Central American states, bananas. A few reaped large profits from these exports, but for the majority of the population, the returns were meager.

World War I led to a decline in European investment in Latin America and a rise in the U.S. role in the local economies. By the late 1920s, the United States had replaced Great Britain as the foremost source of investment in Latin America. Unlike the British, however, U.S. investors put their funds directly into production enterprises, causing large segments of the area's export industries to fall into American hands. A number of Central American states, for example, were popularly labeled "banana republics" because of the power and influence of the U.S.-owned United Fruit Company. American firms also dominated the copper mining industry in Chile and Peru and the oil industry in Mexico, Peru, and Bolivia.

Increasing economic power reinforced the traditionally high level of U.S. political influence in Latin America. This influence was especially evident in Central America and the Caribbean, regions that many Americans considered their backyard and thus vital to U.S. national security. The growing U.S. presence in the region provoked hostility and a growing national consciousness among Latin Americans, who viewed the United States as an aggressive imperialist power. Some charged that Washington worked to keep ruthless dictators, such as Juan Vicente Gómez of Venezuela and Fulgencio Batista of Cuba, in power in order to preserve U.S. economic influence; sometimes the United States even intervened militarily. In a bid to improve relations with Latin American countries, President Franklin D. Roosevelt in 1935 promulgated the **Good Neighbor policy** (see the box on p. 679), which rejected the use of U.S. military force in the region. To underscore his sincerity, Roosevelt ordered the withdrawal of U.S. marines from the island nation of Haiti in 1936. For the first time in thirty years, there were no U.S. occupation troops in Latin America.

Because so many Latin American nations depended for their livelihood on the export of raw materials and food products, the Great Depression of the 1930s was a disaster for the region. The total value of Latin American exports in 1930 was

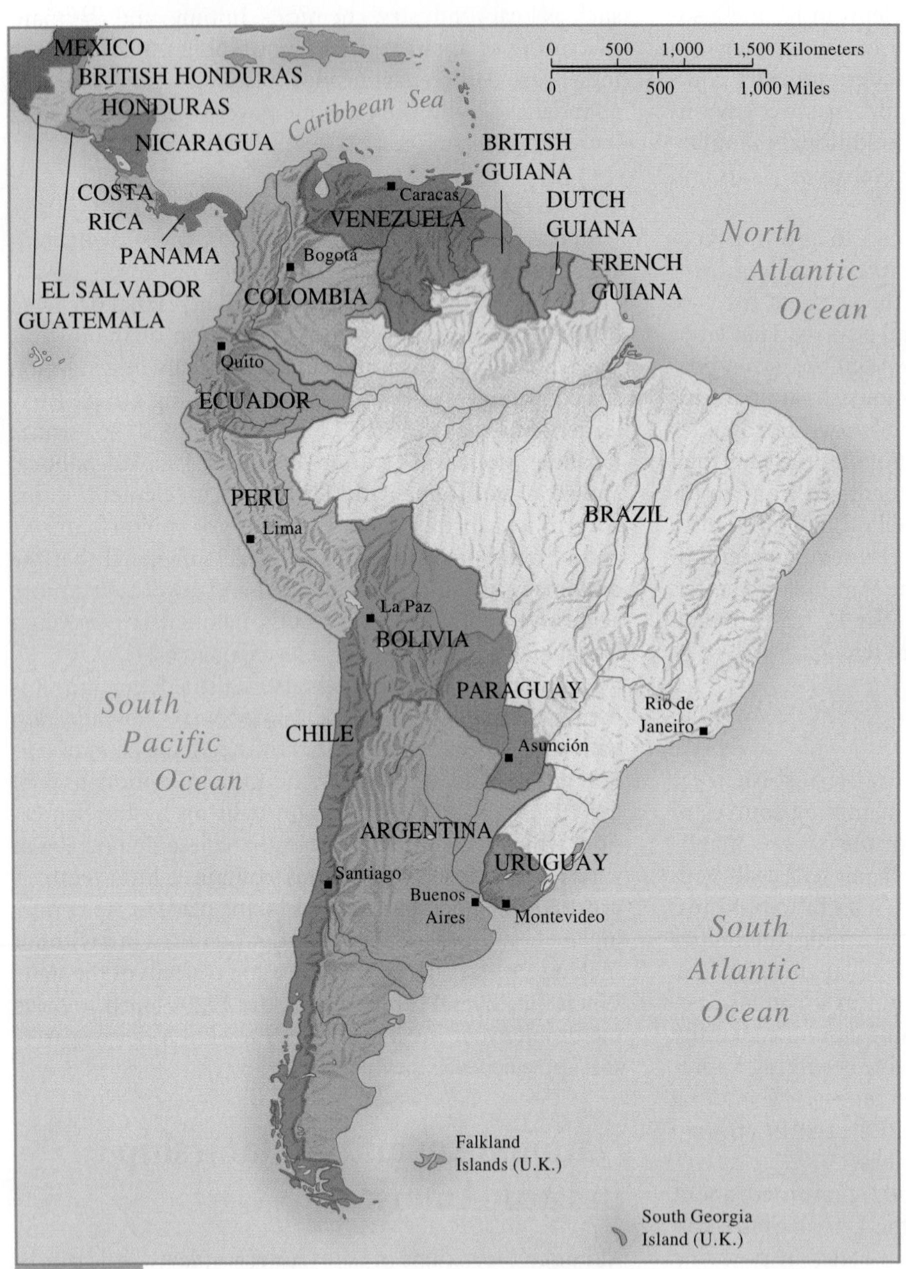


**MAP 23.2 Latin America in the First Half of the Twentieth Century.** Shown here are the boundaries dividing the countries of Latin America after the independence movements of the nineteenth century. Which areas remained under European rule? **View an animated version of this map or related maps at** http://history.wadsworth.com/duikerspielvogel05/

## A Pledge of Cooperation

During the first three decades of the twentieth century, the United States intervened periodically in the affairs of various countries of Latin America to protect the lives of its citizens and its growing economic interests. By the late 1920s, that policy had aroused considerable resentment on the part of governments throughout the region. In August 1936, U.S. President Franklin D. Roosevelt attempted to allay such concerns by announcing the Good Neighbor policy toward other nations in the hemisphere. Excerpts of his speech follow.

*What were the key features of Roosevelt's Good Neighbor Policy and how did it differ from past U.S. policy in Latin America?*

### Roosevelt's Good Neighbor Policy

Long before I returned to Washington as President of the United States, I had made up my mind that . . . the United States could best serve the cause of peaceful humanity by setting an example. That was why on the 4th of March, 1933, I made the following declaration:

> In the field of world policy I would dedicate this nation to the policy of the good neighbor–the neighbor who resolutely respects himself and because he does so, respects the rights of others–the neighbor who respects his obligations and respects the sanctity of his agreements in and with a world of neighbors.

In the whole of the Western Hemisphere our good neighbor policy had produced results that are especially heartening. . . . The American republics to the south of us have been ready always to cooperate with the United States on a basis of equality and mutual respect, but before we inaugurated the good neighbor policy there was among them resentment and fear, because certain administrations in Washington had slighted their national pride and their sovereign rights.

In pursuance of the good neighbor policy, and because in my younger days I had learned many lessons in the hard school of experience, I stated that the United States was opposed definitely to armed intervention.

We have negotiated a Pan-American convention embodying the principles of nonintervention. We have abandoned the Platt amendment which gave us the right to intervene in the internal affairs of the Republic of Cuba. We have withdrawn American marines from Haiti. We have signed a new treaty which places our relations with Panama on a mutually satisfactory basis. We have undertaken a series of trade agreements with other American countries to our mutual commercial profit. . . .

Throughout the Americas the spirit of the good neighbor is a practical and living fact. The twenty-one American republics are not only living together in friendship and in peace; they are united in the determination so to remain.

only half the figure for the previous five years. Spurred by the decline in foreign revenues, Latin American governments began to encourage the development of new industries. In some cases—the steel industry in Chile and Brazil, the oil industry in Argentina and Mexico—government investment made up for the absence of local sources of capital.

## The Move to Authoritarianism

During the late nineteenth century, most governments in Latin America had been increasingly dominated by landed or military elites, who controlled the mass of the population—mostly impoverished peasants—by the blatant use of military force. This trend toward authoritarianism increased during the 1930s as domestic instability caused by the effects of the Great Depression led to the creation of military dictatorships throughout the region. This trend was especially evident in Argentina, Brazil, and Mexico—three countries that together possessed more than half of the land and wealth of Latin America.

**Argentina** Political domination by an elite minority often had disastrous effects. The government of Argentina, controlled by landowners who had benefited from the export of beef and wheat, was slow to recognize the growing importance of establishing a local industrial base. In 1916, Hipólito Irigoyen (1852–1933), head of the Radical Party, was elected president on a program to improve conditions for the middle and lower classes. Little was achieved, however, as the party became increasingly corrupt and drew closer to the large landowners. In 1930, the army overthrew Irigoyen's government and reestablished the power of the landed class. But their efforts to return to the previous export economy and suppress the growing influence of labor unions failed, and in 1946 General Juan Perón—claiming the support of the *descamisados* ("shirtless ones")—seized sole power (see Chapter 27).

**Brazil** Brazil followed a similar path. In 1889, the army overthrew the Brazilian monarchy, installed by Portugal years before, and established a republic. But it was dominated by landed elites, many of whom had grown wealthy through their ownership of coffee plantations. By 1900, three-quarters of the world's coffee was grown in Brazil. As in Argentina, the ruling oligarchy ignored the importance of establishing an urban industrial base. When the Great Depression ravaged profits from coffee exports, a wealthy rancher, Getúlio Vargas (1883–1954), seized power and ruled the country as president from 1930 to

1945. At first, Vargas sought to appease workers by declaring an eight-hour workday and a minimum wage, but, influenced by the apparent success of fascist regimes in Europe, he ruled by increasingly autocratic means and relied on a police force that used torture to silence his opponents. His industrial policy was relatively enlightened, however, and by the end of World War II, Brazil had become Latin America's major industrial power. In 1945, the army, fearing that Vargas might prolong his power illegally after calling for new elections, forced him to resign.

**Mexico** Mexico, in the years after World War I, was not an authoritarian state, but neither was it democratic. The Mexican Revolution at the beginning of the twentieth century had been the first significant effort in Latin American history to overturn the system of large estates and improve the living standards of the masses (see Chapter 19). Out of the political revolution emerged a relatively stable political order. The revolution, however, was democratic in form only, as the official political party, known as the Institutional Revolutionary Party (PRI), controlled the levers of power throughout society. Every six years, PRI bosses chose the party's presidential candidate, who was then dutifully elected by the people.

The situation began to change with the election of Lázaro Cárdenas (1895–1970) as president in 1934. Cárdenas won wide popularity with the peasants by ordering the redistribution of 44 million acres of land controlled by landed elites. He also won popular support by adopting a stronger stand against the United States, seizing control over the oil industry, which had hitherto been dominated by major U.S. oil companies. Alluding to the Good Neighbor policy, President Roosevelt refused to intervene, and eventually Mexico agreed to compensate U.S. oil companies for their lost property. It then set up PEMEX, a state administered organization, to run the oil industry.

**CHRONOLOGY Latin America Between the Wars**

| | |
|---|---|
| Hipólito Irigoyen becomes president of Argentina | 1916 |
| Argentinian military overthrows Irigoyen | 1930 |
| Rule of Getúlio Vargas in Brazil | 1930–1945 |
| Presidency of Lázaro Cárdenas in Mexico | 1934–1940 |
| Beginning of Good Neighbor policy | 1935 |

## Latin American Culture

During the early twentieth century, modern European artistic and literary movements began to penetrate Latin America. In major cities, such as Buenos Aires and São Paulo, wealthy elites supported avant-garde trends, but other artists returned from abroad to adapt modern techniques to their native roots.

For many artists and writers, their work provided a means of promoting the emergence of a new national essence. An example was the Mexican muralist Diego Rivera (1886–1957). Rivera had studied in Europe, where he was influenced by fresco painting in Italy. After his return to Mexico, where the government provided financial support for the painting of murals on public buildings, he began to produce a monumental style of mural art that served two purposes: to illustrate the national past by portraying Aztec legends as well as Mexican festivals and folk customs and to promote a political message in favor of realizing the social goals of the Mexican Revolution. Rivera's murals can be found in such diverse locations as the Ministry of Education and the Social Security Hospital in Mexico City and the chapel of the Agricultural School at Chapingo.

**Getúlio Vargas.** The man at left is Getúlio Vargas, a rancher and lawyer who turned to politics and became president of Brazil after a military coup in 1930. Vargas's New State imitated some of the features of Fascist Italy and Nazi Germany, including the creation of a popular militia under party control called the "Blue Shirts."

**Struggle for the Banner.** Like Diego Rivera, David Alfaro Siqueiros (1896–1974) painted on public buildings large murals that celebrated the Mexican Revolution and the workers' and peasants' struggle for freedom. Beginning in the 1930s, Siqueiros expressed sympathy for the exploited and downtrodden peoples of Mexico in dramatic frescoes such as this one. He painted similar murals in Uruguay, Argentina, and Brazil and was once expelled from the United States, where his political art and views were considered too radical.

## CONCLUSION

THE TURMOIL brought about by World War I not only resulted in the destruction of several of the major Western empires and a redrawing of the map of Europe but also opened the door to political and social upheavals elsewhere in the world. In the Middle East, the decline and fall of the Ottoman Empire led to the creation of the secular republic of Turkey. The state of Saudi Arabia emerged in the Arabian peninsula, and Palestine became a source of tension between newly arrived Jewish settlers and longtime Muslim residents.

Other parts of Asia and Africa also witnessed the rise of movements for national independence. In Africa, these movements were spearheaded by native leaders educated in Europe or the United States. In India, Gandhi and his campaign of civil disobedience played a crucial role in his country's bid to be free of British rule. Communist movements also began to emerge in Asian societies as radical elements sought new methods of bringing about the overthrow of Western imperialism. Japan continued to follow its own path to modernization, which, although successful from an economic point of view, took a menacing turn during the 1930s.

Between 1919 and 1939, China experienced a dramatic struggle to establish a modern nation. Two dynamic political organizations—the Nationalists and the Communists—competed for legitimacy as the rightful heirs of the old order. At first, they formed an alliance in an effort to defeat their common adversaries, but cooperation ultimately turned to conflict. The Nationalists under Chiang Kai-shek emerged supreme, but Chiang found it difficult to control the remnants of the warlord regime in China, while the Great Depression undermined his efforts to build an industrial nation.

During the interwar years, the nations of Latin America faced severe economic problems because of their dependence on exports. Increasing U.S. investments in Latin America contributed to growing hostility against the powerful neighbor to the north. The Great Depression forced the region to begin developing new industries, but it also led to the rise of authoritarian governments, some of them modeled after the fascist regimes of Italy and Germany.

By demolishing the remnants of their old civilization on the battlefields of World War I, Europeans had inadvertently encouraged the subject peoples of their vast colonial empires to begin their own movements for national independence. The process was by no means completed in the two decades following the Treaty of Versailles, but the bonds of imperial rule had been severely strained. Once Europeans began to weaken themselves in the even more destructive conflict of World War II, the hopes of African and Asian peoples for national independence and freedom could at last be realized. It is to that devastating world conflict that we must now turn.

## TIMELINE

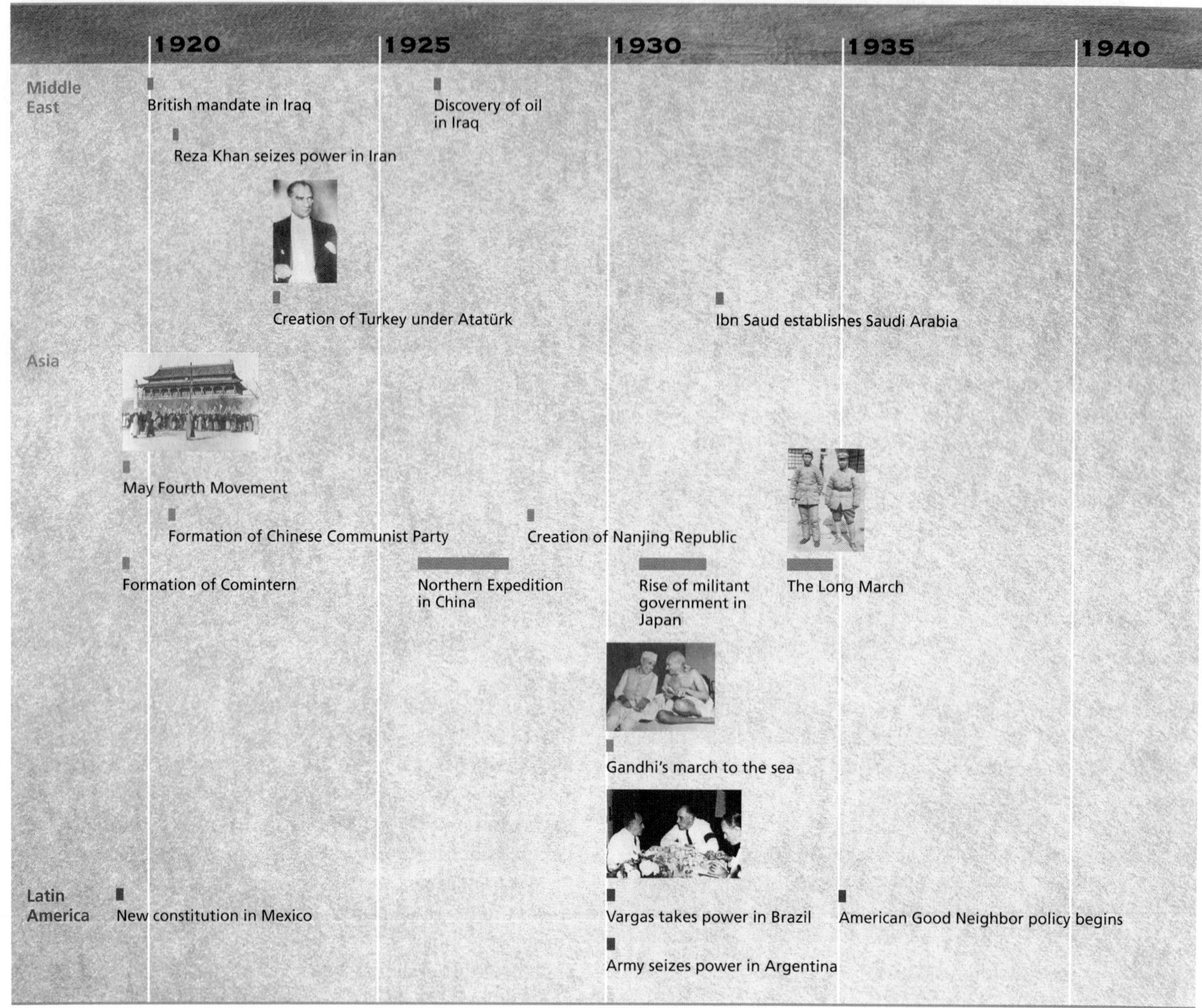


## CHAPTER NOTES

1. Speech delivered in London, September 1931, while attending the first Roundtable Conference.
2. V. I. Lenin, "The Awakening of Asia," *in The Awakening of Asia: Selected Essays* (New York, 1963–1968), p. 22.
3. Ts'ai Yuan-p'ei, "Ta Lin Ch'in-nan Han," in *Ts'ai Yuan-p'ei Hsien-sheng Ch'uan-chi* [Collected Works of Mr. Ts'ai Yuan-p'ei] (Taipei, 1968), pp. 1057–1058.
4. Quoted in N. R. Clifford, *Spoilt Children of Empire: Westerners in Shanghai and the Chinese Revolution of the 1920s* (Hanover, N.H., 1991), p. 93.
5. Quoted in W. T. de Bary et al., eds., *Sources of Chinese Tradition* (New York, 1963), p. 783.
6. Lu Xun, "Diary of a Madman," *in Selected Works of Lu Hsun* (Beijing, 1957), vol. 1, p. 20.

## SUGGESTED READING

The classic study of nationalism in the non-Western world is **R. Emerson, *From Empire to Nation*** (Boston, 1960). For a more recent approach, see **B. Anderson, *Imagined Communities: Reflections on the Origin and Spread of Nationalism*** (London, 1983). On nationalism in India, see **S. Wolpert, *Congress and Indian Nationalism: The Pre-Independence Phase*** (New York, 1988). Also see **P. Chatterjee, *The Nation and Its Fragments: Colonial and Postcolonial Histories*** (Princeton, N.J., 1993), and **E. Gellner, *Nations and Nationalism*** (Ithaca, N.Y., 1994).

There have been a number of studies of Mahatma Gandhi and his ideas. See, for example, **J. M. Brown, *Gandhi: Prisoner of Hope*** (New Haven, Conn., 1989), and **D. Dalton, *Mahatma Gandhi: Nonviolent Power in Action*** (New York, 1995). For a study of Nehru, see **J. M. Brown, *Nehru*** (New York, 2000).

For a general survey of events in the Middle East in the interwar era, see **H. M. Sachar, *The Emergence of the Middle East, 1914–1924*** (New York, 1969). For more specialized studies, see **I. Gershoni** et al., ***Egypt, Islam, and the Arabs: The Search for Egyptian Nationhood*** (Oxford, 1993), and **W. Laqueur, *A History of Zionism: From the French Revolution to the Establishment of the State of Israel*** (New York, 1996). The role of Atatürk is examined in **A. Mango, *Atatürk: The Biography of the Founder of Modern Turkey*** (New York, 2000). The Palestinian issue is dealt with in **B. Morris, *Righteous Victims: The Palestinian Conflict, 1880–2000.*** (New York, 2001). On the founding of Iraq, see **S. Mackey, *The Reckoning: Iraq and the Legacy of Saddam Hussein*** (New York, 2002). Nascent nationalist movements in Africa are discussed in **R. Collins, *Historical Problems of Imperial Africa*** (Princeton, 1994).

On the early republic in China, see **L. Yu-sheng, *The Crisis of Chinese Consciousness: Radical Antitraditionalism in the May Fourth Era*** (Madison, Wis., 1979). The rise of the Chinese Communist Party is discussed in **A. Dirlik, *The Origins of Chinese Communism*** (Oxford, 1989). There are a number of biographies of Mao Zedong. A readable and informative one is **S. Schram, *Mao Tse-tung: A Political Biography*** (Baltimore, 1966). Also see **J. D. Spence, *Mao Zedong: A Penguin Life*** (New York, 1999). For an inside account of the Chinese Communist movement by a sympathetic Western journalist, see **E. Snow, *Red Star over China*** (New York, 1938). On Chiang Kai-shek, see **J. Fenby, *Generalissimo: Chiang Kai-shek and the China He Lost*** (New York, 2003). For a discussion of the role of ideology and nationalism in early-twentieth-century China, see **J. Fitzgerald, *Awakening China: Politics, Culture, and Class in the Nationalist Revolution*** (Stanford, Calif., 1997). On the interwar era in Japan, see **P. Duus**, ed., ***The Cambridge History of Japan,*** vol. 6 (Cambridge, 1989).

For an overview of Latin American history in the 1920s and 1930s, see **E. Williamson, *The Penguin History of Latin America*** (Harmondsworth, England, 1992). On U.S.–Latin American relations, see the classic study by **B. Wood, *The Making of the Good Neighbor Policy*** (New York, 1960). On Argentina, Brazil, and Mexico, see **D. Rock, *Argentina, 1516–1982*** (London, 1986); **E. B. Burns, *A History of Brazil,*** 2d ed. (New York, 1980); and **M. C. Meyer** and **W. L. Sherman, *The Course of Mexican History,*** 3d ed. (New York, 1987). On Getúlio Vargas, see **R. Bourne, *Getúlio Vargas of Brazil, 1883–1954: Sphinx of the Pampas*** (London, 1974). On culture, see **J. Franco, *The Modern Culture of Latin America: Society and the Artist*** (Harmondsworth, England, 1970).

For a general introduction to the women's movement during this era, consult **C. Johnson-Odim** and **M. Strobel**, eds., ***Restoring Women to History*** (Bloomington, Ind., 1999). For collections of essays concerning African women, see **C. Robertson** and **I. Berger, *Women and Class in Africa*** (New York, 1986), and **S. Stichter** and **J. I. Parparti,** eds., ***Patriarchy and Class: African Women in the Home and Workforce*** (Boulder, Colo., 1988). To follow the women's movement in India, see **S. Tharu** and **K. Lalita, *Women Writing in India,*** vol. 2 (New York, 1993). For Japan, see **S. Sievers, *Flowers in Salt: The Beginnings of Feminist Consciousness in Modern Japan*** (Stanford, Calif., 1983).

CHAPTER

# 24

# THE CRISIS DEEPENS: WORLD WAR II

© Time Life Pictures/Getty Images

*Adolf Hitler salutes military leaders and soldiers during a military rally*

## CHAPTER OUTLINE AND FOCUS QUESTIONS

### Retreat from Democracy: Dictatorial Regimes

- What are the characteristics of totalitarian states, and to what degree were these characteristics present in Fascist Italy, Nazi Germany, and Stalinist Russia? To what extent, if any, was Japan a totalitarian state?

### The Path to War

- What were the underlying causes of World War II, and what specific steps taken by Nazi Germany and Japan led to war?

### World War II

- What were the main events of World War II in Europe and Asia?

### The New Order

- What was the nature of the new orders that Germany and Japan attempted to establish in the territories they occupied?

### The Home Front

- What were conditions like on the home front for the major belligerents in World War II?

### Aftermath: Toward the Cold War

- How did the Allies' visions of the postwar world differ, and how did these differences contribute to the emergence of the Cold War?

### CRITICAL THINKING

- What was the relationship between World War I and World War II, and what were the differences in the ways the wars were fought?

ON FEBRUARY 3, 1933, only four days after he had been appointed chancellor of Germany, Adolf Hitler met secretly with Germany's leading generals. He revealed to them his desire to remove the "cancer of democracy," create a new authoritarian leadership, and forge a new domestic unity. All Germans would need to realize that "only a struggle can save us and that everything else must be subordinated to this idea." Youth especially must be trained and their wills strengthened "to fight with all means." Since Germany's living space was too small for its people, Hitler said, Germany must rearm and prepare for "the conquest of new living space in the east and its ruthless Germanization." Even before he had consolidated his power, Adolf Hitler had a clear vision of his goals, and their implementation meant another war.

World War II in Europe was clearly Hitler's war. Although other countries may have helped make the war possible by not resisting Hitler's Germany earlier, it was Nazi Germany's actions that made World War II inevitable.

But it was more than just Hitler's war. World War II was in fact two separate and parallel conflicts, one provoked by the ambitions of Germany in Europe and the other by the ambitions of Japan in Asia. Around the same time that Hitler was consolidating his power in the early 1930s, the United States and major European nations raised their tariff rates against Japanese imports in a desperate effort to protect local businesses and jobs. In response, militant groups in Tokyo began to argue that Japan must obtain by violent action what it could not secure by peaceful means. By 1941, when the United States became embroiled in both wars, the two had merged into a single global conflict.

Although World War I had been described as a total war, World War II was even more so and was fought on a scale unheard of in history. Almost everyone in the warring countries was involved in one way or another: as soldiers; as workers in wartime industries; as ordinary citizens subject to invading armies, military occupation, or bombing raids; as refugees; or as victims of mass extermination. The world had never witnessed such widespread human-induced death and destruction. ◇

## Retreat from Democracy: Dictatorial Regimes

The rise of dictatorial regimes in the 1930s had a great deal to do with the coming of World War II. By 1939, only two major states in Europe, France and Great Britain, remained democratic. Italy and Germany had succumbed to the political movement called fascism, and Soviet Russia under Stalin moved toward repressive totalitarianism. A host of other European states and Latin American countries adopted authoritarian structures of different kinds, while a militarist regime in Japan moved that country down the path of war.

The dictatorial regimes between the wars assumed both old and new forms. Dictatorship was not new, but the modern **totalitarian state** was. The totalitarian regimes, best exemplified by Stalinist Russia and Nazi Germany, greatly extended the functions and power of the central state. The modern totalitarian state went beyond the ideal of passive obedience expected in a traditional dictatorship or authoritarian monarchy. The new "total states" expected the active loyalty and commitment of citizens to the regime's goals, whether they be war, a socialist society, or a thousand-year Reich. They used modern mass propaganda techniques and high-speed communications to conquer the minds and hearts of their subjects. The total state sought to control not only the economic, political, and social aspects of life but the intellectual and cultural aspects as well.

The modern totalitarian state was to be led by a single leader and a single party. It ruthlessly rejected the liberal ideal of limited government power and constitutional guarantees of individual freedoms. Indeed, individual freedom was to be subordinated to the collective will of the masses, organized and determined for them by the leader or leaders. Modern technology also gave total states unprecedented police controls to force their wishes on their subjects.

### The Birth of Fascism

In the early 1920s, Benito Mussolini bestowed on Italy the first fascist movement in Europe. Mussolini (1883–1945) began his political career as a socialist, but in 1919, he established a new political group, the *Fascio di Combattimento* (League of Combat), which won support from middle-class industrialists fearful of working-class agitation and large landowners who objected to agricultural strikes. Mussolini also perceived that Italians were angry over Italy's failure to receive more territorial acquisitions after World War I. In 1920 and 1921, bands of armed Fascists called ***squadristi*** were formed and turned loose in attacks on socialist offices and newspapers. The movement gained momentum as Mussolini's nationalist rhetoric and the middle-class fear of socialism, communist revolution, and disorder made the Fascists seem more and more attractive. On October 29, 1922, after Mussolini and the Fascists threatened to march on Rome if they were not given power, King Victor Emmanuel (1900–1946) capitulated and made Mussolini prime minister of Italy.

By 1926, Mussolini had established the institutional framework for a Fascist dictatorship. Press laws gave the government the right to suspend any publications that fostered disrespect for the Catholic church, the monarchy, or the state. The prime minister was made "head of government" with the power to legislate by decree. A law empowered the police to arrest and confine anybody for both nonpolitical and political crimes without pressing charges. The government was given the power to dissolve political and cultural associations. In 1926, all anti-Fascist parties were outlawed, and a secret police force was established. By the end of the year, Mussolini ruled Italy as *Il Duce*, the leader.

Mussolini conceived of the Fascist state as totalitarian: "Fascism is totalitarian, and the Fascist State, the synthesis and unity of all values, interprets, develops and gives strength to the whole life of the people."[1] Mussolini did try to create a police state, but it was not very effective. Police activities in Italy were never as repressive, efficient, or savage as those of Nazi Germany. Likewise, the Italian Fascists' attempt to exercise control over all forms of mass media, including newspapers, radio, and cinema, in order to use propaganda as an instrument to integrate the masses into the state, was rarely effective. Most commonly, Fascist propaganda was disseminated through simple slogans, such as "Mussolini is always right," plastered on walls all over Italy.

Mussolini and the Fascists also attempted to mold Italians into a single-minded community by developing Fascist organizations. Because the secondary schools maintained considerable freedom from Fascist control,

AP/Wide World Photos

**Mussolini—The Iron *Duce*.** One of Mussolini's favorite images of himself was that of the iron *Duce*—the strong leader who is always right. Consequently, he was often seen in military-style uniforms and military poses. This photograph shows Mussolini in one of his numerous uniforms with his Black Shirt bodyguards giving the Fascist salute.

the regime relied more and more on the activities of youth organizations, known as the Young Fascists, to indoctrinate the young people of the nation in Fascist ideals, especially those of discipline and preparation for war.

The Fascists portrayed the family as the pillar of the state and women as the basic foundation of the family. "Woman into the home" became the Fascist slogan. Women were to be homemakers and baby producers, "their natural and fundamental mission in life," according to Mussolini, for population growth was viewed as an indicator of national strength. Employment outside the home was an impediment distracting from conception: "It forms an independence and consequent physical and moral habits contrary to child bearing."[2]

Despite the instruments of repression, the use of propaganda, and the creation of numerous Fascist organizations, Mussolini never achieved the degree of totalitarian control attained in Hitler's Germany or Stalin's Soviet Union. Mussolini and the Fascist Party did not completely destroy the old power structure. Some institutions, including the Catholic church, the armed forces, and the monarchy, were never absorbed into the Fascist state and managed to maintain their independence. In all areas of Italian life under Mussolini and the Fascists, there was a noticeable dichotomy between Fascist ideals and practice. The Italian Fascists promised much but actually delivered considerably less, and they were soon overshadowed by a much more powerful fascist movement to the north.

## Hitler and Nazi Germany

In 1923, a small south German rightist party known as the Nazis, led by an obscure Austrian rabble-rouser named Adolf Hitler, created a stir when it tried to seize power in southern Germany in conscious imitation of Mussolini's march on Rome in 1922. Although the attempt failed, Hitler and the Nazis achieved sudden national prominence. Within ten years, they had taken over complete power.

**Hitler and the Early Nazi Party** At the end of World War I, after four years of service on the Western Front, Adolf Hitler went to Munich and decided to enter politics. In 1919, he joined the obscure German Workers' Party, one of a number of right-wing extreme nationalist parties in Munich. By the summer of 1921, he had assumed control of the party, which he renamed the National Socialist German Workers' Party (NSDAP), or Nazi for short. Hitler worked assiduously to develop the party into a mass political movement with flags, badges, uniforms, its own newspaper, and its own police force or party militia known as the SA, the *Sturmabteilung,* or Storm Troops. The SA was used to defend the party in meeting halls and break up the meetings of other parties. Hitler's own oratorical skills were largely responsible for attracting an increasing number of followers. By 1923, the party had grown from its early hundreds into a membership of 55,000, of whom 15,000 served in the SA.

Overconfident, Hitler staged an armed uprising against the government in Munich in November 1923. The so-called Beer Hall Putsch was quickly crushed, and Hitler was sentenced to prison. During his brief stay in jail, he wrote *Mein Kampf (My Struggle),* an autobiographical account of his movement and its underlying ideology. Extreme German nationalism, virulent anti-Semitism, and anticommunism are linked together by a social Darwinian theory of struggle that stresses the right of superior nations to *Lebensraum* (living space) through expansion and the right of superior individuals to secure authoritarian leadership over the masses.

During his imprisonment, Hitler also came to the realization that the Nazis would have to come to power by constitutional means, not by overthrowing the Weimar Republic. This implied the formation of a mass political party that would actively compete for votes with the other political parties. After his release from prison, Hitler reorganized the Nazi Party on a regional basis and expanded it to all parts of Germany. By 1929, the Nazis had a national party organization.

**The Rise to Power** By 1932, the Nazi Party had 800,000 members and had become the largest party in the Reichstag. Germany's economic difficulties were a crucial factor in the Nazis' rise to power. Unemployment rose dramatically, from just over four million in 1931 to six million by the winter of 1932. The economic and psychological impact of the Great Depression made extremist parties promising dramatic quick fixes more attractive. The Nazis maintained that they stood above classes and parties. Hitler vowed to create a new Germany free of class differences and party infighting. His appeal to national pride, national honor, and traditional militarism struck chords of emotion in his listeners. A schoolteacher in Hamburg said after attending one of Hitler's rallies: "When the speech was over, there was roaring enthusiasm and applause. . . . Then he went—How many look up to him with touching faith as their saviour, their deliverer from unbearable distress."[3]

Increasingly, the right-wing elites of Germany—the industrial magnates, landed aristocrats, military establishment, and higher bureaucrats—came to see Hitler as the man who had the mass support to establish a right-wing, authoritarian regime that would save Germany and their privileged positions from a communist takeover. Under pressure, since the Nazi Party had the largest share of seats in the Reichstag, President Paul von Hindenburg agreed to allow Hitler to become chancellor (on January 30, 1933) and create a new government.

Within two months, Hitler had laid the foundations for the Nazis' complete control over Germany. The crowning step in Hitler's "legal seizure" of power came on March 23, when the Reichstag passed the Enabling Act by a two-thirds vote. This legislation, which empowered the government to dispense with constitutional forms for four years while it issued laws that dealt with the country's problems, provided the legal basis for Hitler's subsequent acts. In effect, Hitler became a dictator appointed by the parliamentary body itself.

With their new source of power, the Nazis acted quickly to coordinate all institutions under Nazi control. The civil service was purged of Jews and democratic elements, concentration camps were established for opponents of the new regime, the autonomy of the federal states was eliminated, trade unions were dissolved, and all political parties except the Nazis were abolished. By the end of the summer of 1933, within seven months of being appointed chancellor, Hitler and the Nazis had established the foundations for a totalitarian state. When Hindenburg died on August 2, 1934, the office of Reich president was abolished, and Hitler became sole ruler of Germany. Public officials and soldiers were all required to take a personal oath of loyalty to Hitler as the "*Führer* (leader) of the German Reich and people."

**The Nazi State, 1933–1939** Having smashed the parliamentary state, Hitler now felt that the real task was at hand: to develop the "total state." Hitler's goal was the development of an "Aryan" racial state that would dominate Europe and possibly the world for generations to come. That required a movement in which the German people would be actively involved, not passively cowed by force. Hitler stated:

> We must develop organizations in which an individual's entire life can take place. Then every activity and every need of every individual will be regulated by the collectivity represented by the party. There is no longer any arbitrary will; there are no longer any free realms in which the individual belongs to himself. . . . The time of personal happiness is over.[4]

The Nazis pursued the creation of this totalitarian state in a variety of ways.

Mass demonstrations and spectacles were employed to integrate the German nation into a collective fellowship and to mobilize it as an instrument for Hitler's policies (see the box on p. 689). These mass demonstrations, especially the Nuremberg party rallies that were held every September, combined the symbolism of a religious service with the merriment of a popular amusement. They had great appeal and usually evoked mass enthusiasm and excitement.

The apparatus of Hitler's total state had some confusing features. One usually thinks of Nazi Germany as having an all-powerful government that maintained absolute control and order. In truth, Nazi Germany was the scene of almost constant personal and institutional conflict, which resulted in administrative chaos. Struggle characterized relationships within the party, within the state, and between party and state. Hitler, of course, remained the ultimate decision maker and absolute ruler.

In the economic sphere, Hitler and the Nazis also established control. Although the regime pursued the use of public works projects and "pump-priming" grants to private construction firms to foster employment and end the depression, there is little doubt that rearmament contributed far more to solving the unemployment problem. Unemployment, which had stood at 6 million in 1932, dropped to 2.6 million in 1934 and less than 500,000 in 1937. The regime claimed full credit for solving Germany's economic woes, and this was an important factor in convincing many Germans to accept the new regime, despite its excesses.

For Germans who needed coercion, the Nazi total state had its instruments of terror and repression. Especially important were the *Schutzstaffel* (guard squadrons), known simply as the SS. Originally created as Hitler's personal bodyguard, the SS, under the direction of Heinrich Himmler (1900–1945), came to control all of the regular and secret police forces. Himmler and the SS functioned on the basis of two principles: terror and ideology. Terror included the instruments of repression and murder: the secret police, criminal police, concentration camps, and later the execution squads and death camps for the extermination of the Jews. For Himmler, the SS was a crusading order whose primary goal was to further the Aryan master race.

Other institutions, such as the Catholic and Protestant churches, primary and secondary schools, and universities, were also brought under the control of the Nazi totalitarian state. Nazi professional organizations and leagues were formed for civil servants, teachers, women, farmers, doctors, and lawyers. Since the early indoctrination of youth would create the foundation for a strong totalitarian state for the future, youth organizations—the *Hitler Jugend* (Hitler Youth) and its female counterpart, the *Bund deutscher Mädel* (League of German Maidens)—were given special attention. The oath required of Hitler Youth members demonstrates the degree of dedication expected of youth in the Nazi state: "In the presence of this blood banner, which represents our Führer, I swear to devote all my energies and my strength to the savior of our country, Adolf Hitler. I am willing and ready to give up my life for him, so help me God."

### CHRONOLOGY The Totalitarian States

| | |
|---|---|
| **Fascist Italy** | |
| Creation of Fascist Party | 1919 |
| Mussolini is made prime minister | 1922 (October 29) |
| Establishment of Fascist dictatorship | 1926 |
| **Nazi Germany** | |
| Hitler as Munich politician | 1919–1923 |
| Beer Hall Putsch | 1923 |
| Hitler is made chancellor | 1933 (January 30) |
| Enabling Act | 1933 (March 23) |
| Hindenburg dies; Hitler as sole ruler | 1934 (August 2) |
| Nuremberg laws | 1935 |
| *Kristallnacht* | 1938 (November 9–10) |
| **Soviet Union** | |
| First five-year plan begins | 1928 |
| Stalin's purges | 1936–1938 |

Hugo Jaeger, Life Magazine, © TimePix

**The Nazi Mass Spectacle.** Hitler and the Nazis made clever use of mass spectacles to rally the German people behind the Nazi regime. These mass demonstrations evoked intense enthusiasm, as is evident in this photograph of Hitler arriving at the Bückeberg near Hamelin for the Harvest Festival in 1937. Almost one million people were present for the celebration.

## Propaganda and Mass Meetings in Nazi Germany

Propaganda and mass rallies were two of the chief instruments that Hitler used to prepare the German people for the tasks he set before them. In the first selection, taken from *Mein Kampf,* Hitler explains the psychological importance of mass meetings in creating support for a political movement. In the second excerpt, taken from his speech to a crowd at Nuremberg, he describes the kind of mystical bond he hoped to create through his mass rallies.

*In Hitler's view, what do mass meetings accomplish for his movement? How do mass rallies further the development of nationalism?*

### Adolf Hitler, *Mein Kampf*

The mass meeting is also necessary for the reason that in it the individual, who at first, while becoming a supporter of a young movement, feels lonely and easily succumbs to the fear of being alone, for the first time gets the picture of a larger community, which in most people has a strengthening, encouraging effect. . . . When from his little workshop or big factory, in which he feels very small, he steps for the first time into a mass meeting and has thousands and thousands of people of the same opinions around him, when, as a seeker, he is swept away by three or four thousand others into the mighty effect of suggestive intoxication and enthusiasm, when the visible success and agreement of thousands confirm to him the rightness of the new doctrine and for the first time arouse doubt in the truth of his previous conviction–then he himself has succumbed to the magic influence of what we designate as "mass suggestion." The will, the longing, and also the power of thousands are accumulated in every individual. The man who enters such a meeting doubting and wavering leaves it inwardly reinforced: he has become a link in the community.

### Adolf Hitler, Speech at the Nuremberg Party Rally, 1936

Do we not feel once again in this hour the miracle that brought us together? Once you heard the voice of a man, and it struck deep into your hearts; it awakened you, and you followed this voice. Year after year you went after it, though him who had spoken you never even saw. You heard only a voice, and you followed it. When we meet each other here, the wonder of our coming together fills us all. Not every one of you sees me, and I do not see every one of you. But I feel you, and you feel me. It is the belief in our people that has made us small men great, that has made us poor men rich, that has made brave and courageous men out of us wavering, spiritless, timid folk; this belief made us see our road when we were astray; it joined us together into one whole! . . . You come, that . . . you may, once in a while, gain the feeling that now we are together; we are with him and he with us, and we are now Germany!

**HistoryNow™** To read more works of Adolf Hitler, enter the *HistoryNow* documents area using the access card that is available for *World History.*

The creation of the Nazi total state also had an impact on women. Women played a crucial role in the Aryan racial state as bearers of the children who would bring about the triumph of the Aryan race. To the Nazis, the differences between men and women were natural: men were warriors and political leaders, while women were destined to be wives and mothers.

Nazi ideas determined employment opportunities for women. The Nazis hoped to drive women out of certain areas of the labor market, including heavy industry or other jobs that might hinder women from bearing healthy children. Certain professions, including university teaching, medicine, and law, were also considered inappropriate for women, especially married women. Instead the Nazis encouraged women to pursue professional occupations that had direct practical application, such as social work and nursing. The Nazi regime pushed its campaign against working women with such poster slogans as "Get hold of pots and pans and broom and you'll sooner find a groom!"

The Nazi total state was intended to be an Aryan racial state. From its beginning, the Nazi Party reflected Hitler's strong anti-Semitic beliefs. In September 1935, the Nazis announced new racial laws at the annual party rally in Nuremberg. These "Nuremberg laws" excluded German Jews from German citizenship and forbade marriages and extramarital relations between Jews and German citizens. The "Nuremberg laws" essentially separated Jews from the Germans politically, socially, and legally and were the natural extension of Hitler's stress on the creation of a pure Aryan race.

A more violent phase of anti-Jewish activity took place in 1938 and 1939, initiated on November 9–10, 1938, by the infamous *Kristallnacht,* or night of shattered glass. The assassination of a secretary in the German embassy in Paris became the pretext for a Nazi-led rampage against the Jews in which synagogues were burned, seven thousand Jewish businesses were destroyed, and at least one hundred Jews were killed. Moreover, twenty thousand Jewish males were rounded up and sent to concentration camps. Jews were barred from all public buildings and prohibited from owning, managing, or working in any retail store. Finally, under the direction of the SS, Jews were encouraged to "emigrate from Germany."

## The Formation of Collective Farms

Accompanying the rapid industrialization of the Soviet Union was the collectivization of agriculture, a feat that involved nothing less than transforming Russia's 26 million family farms into 250,000 collective farms (*kolkhozes*). This selection provides a firsthand account of how the process worked.

*What was the purpose of collectivizing Soviet agriculture? According to Belov, why did the peasants of his village assault the Party representatives? What was the result of their protest?*

### Max Belov, *The History of a Collective Farm*

General collectivization in our village was brought about in the following manner: Two representatives of the [Communist] Party arrived in the village. All the inhabitants were summoned by the ringing of the church bell to a meeting at which the policy of general collectivization was announced. . . . The upshot was that although the meeting lasted two days, from the viewpoint of the Party representatives nothing was accomplished.

After this setback the Party representatives divided the village into two sections and worked each one separately. Two more officials were sent to reinforce the first two. A meeting of our section of the village was held in a stable which had previously belonged to a kulak [wealthy farmer]. The meeting dragged on until dark. Suddenly someone threw a brick at the lamp, and in the dark the peasants began to beat the Party representatives, who jumped out the window and escaped from the village barely alive. The following day seven people were arrested. The militia was called in and stayed in the village until the peasants, realizing their helplessness, calmed down. . . .

By the end of 1930 there were two kolkhozes in our village. Though at first these collectives embraced at most only 70 percent of the peasant households, in the months that followed they gradually absorbed more and more of them.

In these kolkhozes the great bulk of the land was held and worked communally, but each peasant household owned a house of some sort, a small plot of ground and perhaps some livestock. All the members of the kolkhoz were required to work on the kolkhoz a certain number of days each month; the rest of the time they were allowed to work on their own holdings. They derived their income partly from what they grew on their garden strips and partly from their work in the kolkhoz.

When the harvest was over, and after the farm had met its obligations to the state and to various special funds (for insurance, seed, etc.) and had sold on the market whatever undesignated produce was left, the remaining produce and the farm's monetary income were divided among the kolkhoz members according to the number of "labor days" each one had contributed to the farm's work. . . . It was in 1930 that the kolkhoz members first received their portions out of the "communal kettle." After they had received their earnings, at the rate of 1 kilogram of grain and 55 kopecks per labor day, one of them remarked, "You will live, but you will be very, very thin."

In the spring of 1931 a tractor worked the fields of the kolkhoz for the first time. The tractor was "capable of plowing every kind of hard soil and virgin sod," as Party representatives told us at the meeting in celebration of its arrival. The peasants did not then know that these "steel horses" would carry away a good part of the harvest in return for their work. . . .

By late 1932 more than 80 percent of the peasant households . . . had been collectivized. . . . That year the peasants harvested a good crop and had hopes that the calculations would work out to their advantage and would help strengthen them economically. These hopes were in vain. The kolkhoz workers received only 200 grams of flour per labor day for the first half of the year; the remaining grain, including the seed fund, was taken by the government. The peasants were told that industrialization of the country, then in full swing, demanded grain and sacrifices from them.

## The Stalinist Era in the Soviet Union

Stalin made a significant shift in economic policy in 1928 when he launched his first five-year plan. Its real goal was nothing less than the transformation of the agrarian Soviet Union into an industrial country virtually overnight. Instead of producing consumer goods, the first five-year plan emphasized maximum production of capital goods and armaments and succeeded in quadrupling the production of heavy machinery and doubling oil production. Between 1928 and 1937, during the first two five-year plans, steel production increased from 4 million to 18 million tons per year.

Rapid industrialization was accompanied by an equally rapid collectivization of agriculture. Stalin believed that the capital needs for industrial growth could be met by creating agricultural surpluses through eliminating private farms and pushing people into collective farms (see the box above). By eliminating private property, a communist ideal would also be achieved.

By 1934, Russia's 26 million family farms had been collectivized into 250,000 units. This was done at tremendous cost, since Stalin did not hesitate to starve the peasants, especially in the Ukraine, to gain their compliance with the policy of collectivization. Stalin himself supposedly told Winston Churchill during World War II that ten million peasants died in the artificially created famines of 1932 and 1933. The only concession Stalin made to the peasants was to allow each household to have one tiny, privately owned garden plot.

There were additional costs to Stalin's program of rapid industrialization, however. To achieve his goals, Stalin strengthened the party bureaucracy under his control. Anyone who resisted was sent into forced labor camps in Siberia. Stalin's desire for sole control of decision making also led to purges of the Old Bolsheviks. Between 1936 and 1938, the most prominent Old Bolsheviks were put on trial and condemned to death. During this same time, Stalin undertook a purge of army officers, diplomats, union officials, party members, intellectuals, and numerous ordinary citizens. One old woman was sent to Siberia for saying, "If people prayed, they would work better." Estimates are that eight million Russians were arrested; millions died in Siberian forced-labor camps. This gave Stalin the distinction of being one of the greatest mass murderers in human history. The Stalinist bloodbath made what some Western intellectuals had hailed as the "new civilization" much less attractive by the late 1930s.

Disturbed by a rapidly declining birthrate, Stalin also reversed much of the permissive social legislation of the early 1920s. Advocating complete equality of rights for women, the Communists had made divorce and abortion easy to obtain while also encouraging women to work outside the home and to set their own moral standards. After Stalin came to power, the family was praised as a miniature collective in which parents were responsible for inculcating values of duty, discipline, and hard work. Abortion was outlawed, and divorced fathers who failed to support their children were fined heavily.

### The Rise of Militarism in Japan

The rise of militarism in Japan resulted not from a seizure of power by a new political party but from the growing influence of militant forces at the top of the political hierarchy. During the 1920s, a multiparty system based on democratic practices appearing to be emerging. Two relatively moderate political parties, the Minseito and the Seiyukai, dominated the legislature and took turns providing executive leadership in the cabinet. Nevertheless, the political system was probably weaker than it seemed at the time. Both of the major parties were deeply dependent on campaign contributions from powerful corporations, and conservative forces connected to the military or the old landed aristocracy were still highly influential behind the scenes. As in the Weimar Republic in Germany during the same period, the actual power base of modern political forces was weak, and politicians unwittingly undermined the fragile system by engaging in bitter attacks on each other.

In the early 1930s, the growing confrontation with China in Manchuria, combined with the onset of the Great Depression, brought an end to the fragile stability of the immediate postwar years. The depression had a disastrous effect on Japan. The value of Japanese exports dropped by 50 percent from 1929 to 1931, and wages dropped nearly as much. Hardest hit were farmers as the price of rice and other staple food crops plummeted.

During the early 1930s, civilian cabinets managed to cope with the economic challenges presented by the depression. By abandoning the gold standard, Prime Minister Inukai Tsuyoshi was able to lower the price of Japanese goods on the world market, and exports climbed back to earlier levels. But the political parties were no longer able to stem the growing influence of militant nationalist elements.

In May 1932, Tsuyoshi was assassinated by right-wing extremists. He was succeeded by a moderate, Admiral Saito Makoto, but extremist patriotic societies composed of ultranationalists began to terrorize opponents, assassinating businessmen and public figures identified with the Shidehara policy of conciliation toward the outside world (see Chapter 23). Some, like the publicist Kita Ikki, were convinced that the parliamentary system had been corrupted by materialism and Western values and should be replaced by a system that would return to traditional Japanese values and imperial authority. His message, "Asia for the Asians," had not won widespread support during the relatively prosperous 1920s but increased in popularity after the Great Depression, which convinced many Japanese that capitalism was unsuitable for Japan. These same people advocated the use of military force to create a self-sufficient Japan that would acquire the resources and raw materials it needed by controlling East Asia.

During the mid-1930s, the influence of the military and extreme nationalists over the government steadily increased. Minorities and left-wing elements were persecuted, and moderates were intimidated into silence. Terrorists tried for their part in assassination attempts portrayed themselves as selfless patriots and received light sentences. Japan continued to hold national elections, and moderate candidates continued to receive substantial popular support, but the cabinets were dominated by the military or advocates of Japanese expansionism. In February 1936, junior army officers led a coup, briefly occupying the Diet building and other key government installations in Tokyo and assassinating several members of the cabinet. The ringleaders were quickly tried and convicted of treason, but under conditions that further strengthened the influence of the military.

## The Path to War

Only twenty years after the war to end war, the world plunged back into the nightmare of total war. The efforts at collective security in the 1920s—the League of Nations, the attempts at disarmament, the pacts and treaties—all proved meaningless in view of the growth of Nazi Germany and the rise of Japan.

## The Path to War in Europe

World War II in Europe had its beginnings in the ideas of Adolf Hitler, who believed that only Aryans were capable of building a great civilization. But to Hitler, the Germans, the leading group of Aryans, were threatened from the east by a large mass of inferior peoples, the Slavs, who had learned to use German weapons and technology. Germany needed more land to support a larger population and be a great power. Already in the 1920s, in the second volume of *Mein Kampf,* Hitler had indicated where a National Socialist regime would find this land: "And so we National Socialists . . . take up where we broke off six hundred years ago. We stop the endless German movement to the south and west, and turn our gaze toward the land in the east. . . . If we speak of soil in Europe today, we can primarily have in mind only Russia and her vassal border states."[5] Once Russia had been conquered, its land could be resettled by German peasants while the Slavic population could be used as slave labor to build the Aryan racial state that would dominate Europe for a thousand years. Hitler's conclusion was apparent: Germany must prepare for its inevitable war with the Soviet Union.

**A Diplomatic Revolution: Scrapping the Treaty of Versailles** When Hitler became chancellor on January 30, 1933, Germany's situation in Europe seemed weak. The Versailles treaty had created a demilitarized zone on Germany's western border that would allow the French to move into the heavily industrialized parts of Germany in the event of war. To Germany's east, the smaller states, such as Poland and Czechoslovakia, had defensive treaties with France. The Versailles treaty had also limited Germany's army to 100,000 troops with no air force and only a small navy.

Posing as a man of peace in his public speeches, Hitler emphasized that Germany wished only to revise the unfair provisions of Versailles by peaceful means and achieve Germany's rightful place among the European states. On March 9, 1935, he announced the creation of a new air force and one week later the introduction of a military draft that would expand Germany's army from 100,000 to 550,000 troops. Hitler's unilateral repudiation of the Versailles treaty brought a swift reaction, as France, Great Britain, and Italy condemned Germany's action and warned against future aggressive steps. But nothing concrete was done.

On March 7, 1936, buoyed by his conviction that the Western democracies had no intention of using force to maintain the Treaty of Versailles, Hitler sent German troops into the demilitarized Rhineland. According to the Versailles treaty, the French had the right to use force against any violation of the demilitarized Rhineland. But France would not act without British support, and the British viewed the occupation of German territory by German troops as reasonable action by a dissatisfied power. The London *Times* noted that the Germans were only "going into their own back garden."

**Hitler Arrives in Vienna.** By threatening to invade Austria, Hitler forced the Austrian government to capitulate to his wishes. Austria was annexed to Germany. Shown here is the triumphal arrival of Hitler in Vienna on March 13, 1938. Seated in the car to Hitler's right is Arthur Seyss-Inquart, Hitler's new handpicked governor of Austria.

Meanwhile, Hitler gained new allies. In October 1935, Benito Mussolini had committed Fascist Italy to imperial expansion by invading Ethiopia. Angered by French and British opposition to his invasion, Mussolini welcomed Hitler's support and began to draw closer to the German dictator he had once called a buffoon. The joint intervention of Germany and Italy on behalf of General Francisco Franco in the Spanish Civil War in 1936 also drew the two nations closer. In October 1936, Mussolini and Hitler concluded an agreement that recognized their common political and economic interests, and one month later, Mussolini referred publicly to the new Rome-Berlin Axis. Also in November, Germany and Japan (the rising military power in the Far East) concluded the Anti-Comintern Pact and agreed to maintain a common front against communism.

By the end of 1936, Hitler and Nazi Germany had achieved a "diplomatic revolution" in Europe. The Treaty of Versailles had been virtually scrapped, and Germany was once more a "world power," as Hitler proclaimed. Hitler was convinced that neither the French nor the British would provide much opposition to his plans and decided in 1938 to move on Austria. By threaten-

## THE MUNICH CONFERENCE

At the Munich Conference, the leaders of France and Great Britain capitulated to Hitler's demands on Czechoslovakia. While the British prime minister, Neville Chamberlain, defended his actions at Munich as necessary for peace, another British statesman, Winston Churchill, characterized the settlement at Munich as "a disaster of the first magnitude."

*What were the opposing views of Churchill and Chamberlain on the Munich Conference? With whom do you agree? Why?*

### Winston Churchill, Speech to the House of Commons (October 5, 1938)

I will begin by saying what everybody would like to ignore or forget but which must nevertheless be stated, namely, that we have sustained a total and unmitigated defeat, and that France has suffered even more than we have. . . . The utmost my right honorable Friend the Prime Minister . . . has been able to gain for Czechoslovakia and in the matters which were in dispute has been that the German dictator, instead of snatching his victuals from the table, has been content to have them served to him course by course. . . . And I will say this, that I believe the Czechs, left to themselves and told they were going to get no help from the Western Powers, would have been able to make better terms than they have got. . . .

We are in the presence of a disaster of the first magnitude which has befallen Great Britain and France. Do not let us blind ourselves to that. . . .

And do not suppose that this is the end. This is only the beginning of the reckoning. This is only the first sip, the first foretaste of a bitter cup which will be proffered to us year by year unless by a supreme recovery of moral health and martial vigor, we arise again and take our stand for freedom as in the olden time.

### Neville Chamberlain, Speech to the House of Commons (October 6, 1938)

That is my answer to those who say that we should have told Germany weeks ago that, if her army crossed the border of Czechoslovakia, we should be at war with her. We had no treaty obligations and no legal obligations to Czechoslovakia. . . . When we were convinced, as we became convinced, that nothing any longer would keep the Sudetenland within the Czechoslovakian State, we urged the Czech Government as strongly as we could to agree to the cession of territory, and to agree promptly. . . . It was a hard decision for anyone who loved his country to take, but to accuse us of having by that advice betrayed the Czechoslovakian State is simply preposterous. What we did was to save her from annihilation and give her a chance of new life as a new State, which involves the loss of territory and fortifications, but may perhaps enable her to enjoy in the future and develop a national existence under a neutrality and security comparable to that which we see in Switzerland today. Therefore, I think the Government deserve the approval of this House for their conduct of affairs in this recent crisis, which has saved Czechoslovakia from destruction and Europe from Armageddon.

**HistoryNow™** To read more wartime speeches of Churchill and Chamberlain, enter the *HistoryNow* documents area using the access card that is available for *World History.*

ing Austria with invasion, Hitler coerced the Austrian chancellor into putting Austrian Nazis in charge of the government. The new government promptly invited German troops to enter Austria and assist in maintaining law and order. One day later, on March 13, 1938, after his triumphal return to his native land, Hitler formally annexed Austria to Germany. Great Britain's ready acknowledgment of Hitler's action only increased the German dictator's contempt for Western weakness.

**The Takeover of Czechoslovakia** The annexation of Austria improved Germany's strategic position in central Europe and put Germany in position for Hitler's next objective—the destruction of Czechoslovakia. This goal might have seemed unrealistic since democratic Czechoslovakia was quite prepared to defend itself and was well supported by pacts with France and the Soviet Union. Hitler believed, however, that France and Britain would not use force to defend Czechoslovakia.

He was right again. On September 15, 1938, Hitler demanded the cession of the Sudetenland (an area in northwestern Czechoslovakia that was inhabited largely by ethnic Germans) to Germany and expressed his willingness to risk "world war" to achieve his objective. Instead of objecting, the British, French, Germans, and Italians—at a hastily arranged conference at Munich—reached an agreement that essentially met all of Hitler's demands. German troops were allowed to occupy the Sudetenland as the Czechs, abandoned by their Western allies and the Soviet Union, stood by helplessly. The Munich Conference was the high point of Western **appeasement** of Hitler. When Neville Chamberlain, the British prime minister, returned to England from Munich, he boasted that the Munich agreement meant "peace for our time." Hitler had promised Chamberlain that he had made his last demand. Like scores of German politicians before him, Chamberlain had believed Hitler's promises (see the box above).

**Poland** In fact, Munich confirmed Hitler's perception that the Western democracies were weak and would not fight. Increasingly, Hitler was convinced of his own infallibility, and he had by no means been satisfied at Munich. In March 1939, Germany occupied the Czech lands (Bohemia and Moravia) while the Slovaks, with his encouragement, declared their independence of the Czechs and became a puppet state (Slovakia) of Nazi Germany. On the evening of March 15, 1939, Hitler triumphantly declared in Prague that he would be known as the greatest German of them all.

At last, the Western states realized that they had to react vigorously to the Nazi threat. Hitler's continued naked aggression made clear that his promises were worthless. When he began to demand the return to Germany of Danzig, which had been made a free city by the Treaty of Versailles to serve as a seaport for Poland, Britain recognized the danger and offered to protect Poland in the event of war. At the same time, both France and Britain realized that among the European powers, only the Soviet Union was powerful enough to help contain Nazi aggression and so began political and military negotiations with Stalin. Their distrust of Soviet communism, however, made an alliance unlikely.

Meanwhile, Hitler pressed on in the belief that Britain and France would not really fight over Poland. To preclude an alliance between the western European states and the Soviet Union, which would create the danger of a two-front war, Hitler, ever the opportunist, negotiated his own nonaggression pact with Stalin and shocked the world with its announcement, on August 23, 1939. The treaty with the Soviet Union gave Hitler the freedom to attack Poland. He told his generals: "Now Poland is in the position in which I wanted her. . . . I am only afraid that at the last moment some swine or other will yet submit to me a plan for mediation."[6] He need not have worried. On September 1, German forces invaded Poland; two days later, Britain and France declared war on Germany. Europe was again at war.

## The Path to War in Asia

In September 1931, on the pretext that the Chinese had attacked a Japanese railway near Mukden (the "Mukden incident" had actually been carried out by Japanese saboteurs), Japanese military units seized Manchuria. Japanese officials in Tokyo were divided over the wisdom of the takeover, but the moderates were unable to control the army. Eventually, worldwide protests against the Japanese action led the League of Nations to send an investigative commission to Manchuria. When the commission issued a report condemning the seizure, Japan withdrew from the League. Over the next several years, the Japanese consolidated their hold on Manchuria, renaming it Manchukuo and placing it under the titular authority of the former Chinese emperor and now Japanese puppet Pu Yi. Japan now began to expand into northern China.

Not all politicians in Tokyo agreed with this aggressive policy, but right-wing terrorists assassinated some of the key critics and intimidated others into silence. By the mid-1930s, militants connected with the government and the armed forces were effectively in control of Japanese politics. The United States refused to recognize the Japanese takeover of Manchuria but was unwilling to threaten the use of force. Instead the Americans attempted to appease Japan in the hope of encouraging Japanese moderates. As a senior U.S. diplomat with long experience in Asia warned in a memorandum to the president:

> Utter defeat of Japan would be no blessing to the Far East or to the world. It would merely create a new set of stresses, and substitute for Japan the [Soviet Union] as the successor to Imperial

**A Japanese Victory in China.** After consolidating its authority over Manchuria, Japan began to expand into northern China. Direct hostilities between Japanese and Chinese forces began in 1937. By 1939, Japan had conquered most of eastern China. This photograph shows victorious Japanese soldiers amid the ruins of the railway station in Hankou, which became China's temporary capital after the fall of Nanjing.

## Japan's Justification for Expansion

Advocates of Japanese expansion justified their proposals by claiming both economic necessity and moral imperatives. Note the familiar combination of motives in this passage written by an extremist military leader in the late 1930s.

*What arguments does Hashimoto Kingoro make in favor of territorial expansion? What is his reaction to the condemnation of western European nations?*

### Hashimoto Kingoro on the Need for Emigration and Expansion

We have already said that there are only three ways left to Japan to escape from the pressure of surplus population. We are like a great crowd of people packed into a small and narrow room, and there are only three doors through which we might escape, namely emigration, advance into world markets, and expansion of territory. The first door, emigration, has been barred to us by the anti-Japanese immigration policies of other countries. The second door, advance into world markets, is being pushed shut by tariff barriers and the abrogation of commercial treaties. What should Japan do when two of the three doors have been closed against her?

It is quite natural that Japan should rush upon the last remaining door.

It may sound dangerous when we speak of territorial expansion, but the territorial expansion of which we speak does not in any sense of the word involve the occupation of the possessions of other countries, the planting of the Japanese flag thereon, and the declaration of their annexation to Japan. It is just that since the Powers have suppressed the circulation of Japanese materials and merchandise abroad, we are looking for some place overseas where Japanese capital, Japanese skills and Japanese labor can have free play, free from the oppression of the white race.

We would be satisfied with just this much. What moral right do the world powers who have themselves closed to us the two doors of emigration and advance into world markets have to criticize Japan's attempt to rush out of the third and last door?

If they do not approve of this, they should open the doors which they have closed against us and permit the free movement overseas of Japanese emigrants and merchandise. . . .

At the time of the Manchurian incident, the entire world joined in criticism of Japan. They said that Japan was an untrustworthy nation. They said that she had recklessly brought cannon and machine guns into Manchuria, which was the territory of another country, flown airplanes over it, and finally occupied it. But the military action taken by Japan was not in the least a selfish one. Moreover, we do not recall ever having taken so much as an inch of territory belonging to another nation. The result of this incident was the establishment of the splendid new nation of Manchuria. The Powers are still discussing whether or not to recognize this new nation, but regardless of whether or not other nations recognize her, the Manchurian empire has already been established, and now, seven years after its creation, the empire is further consolidating its foundations with the aid of its friend, Japan.

And if it is still protested that our actions in Manchuria were excessively violent, we may wish to ask the white race just which country it was that sent warships and troops to India, South Africa, and Australia and slaughtered innocent natives, bound their hands and feet with iron chains, lashed their backs with iron whips, proclaimed these territories as their own, and still continues to hold them to this very day.

Russia—as a contestant (and at least an equally unscrupulous and dangerous one) for the mastery of the East. Nobody except perhaps Russia would gain from our victory in such a war."[7]

**Japanese Aggression in China** For the moment, the prime victim of Japanese aggression was China. Chiang Kai-shek attempted to avoid a confrontation with Japan so that he could deal with the Communists, whom he considered the greater threat. When clashes between Chinese and Japanese troops broke out, he sought to appease the Japanese by granting them the authority to administer areas in northern China. But as Japan moved steadily southward, popular protests in Chinese cities against Japanese aggression intensified. In December 1936, Chiang was briefly kidnapped by military forces commanded by General Zhang Xueliang, who compelled him to end his military efforts against the Communists in Yan'an and form a new united front against the Japanese. After Chinese and Japanese forces clashed at Marco Polo Bridge, south of Beijing, in July 1937, China refused to apologize, and hostilities spread.

Japan had not planned to declare war on China, but neither side would compromise, and the 1937 incident eventually turned into a major conflict. The Japanese advanced up the Yangtze River valley and seized the Chinese capital of Nanjing in December, but Chiang Kai-shek refused to capitulate and moved his government upriver to Hankou. When the Japanese seized that city, he moved on to Chongqing, in remote Sichuan province. Japanese strategists had hoped to force Chiang to join a Japanese-dominated New Order in East Asia, comprising Japan, Manchuria, and China. This was part of a larger plan to seize Soviet Siberia with its rich resources and create a new "Monroe Doctrine for Asia" under which Japan would guide its Asian neighbors on the path to development and prosperity (see the box above). After all, who better to instruct Asian societies on modernization than the one Asian country that had already achieved it?

**Advance to the South** During the late 1930s, Japan began to cooperate with Nazi Germany on the assumption that the two countries would ultimately launch a joint attack on the Soviet Union and divide up its resources between them. But when Germany surprised the world by signing a nonaggression pact with the Soviets in August 1939, Japanese strategists were compelled to reevaluate their long-term objectives. Japan was not strong enough to defeat the Soviet Union alone, as a small but bitter border war along the Siberian frontier near Manchuria had amply demonstrated. So the Japanese began to shift their sights southward to the vast resources of Southeast Asia—the oil of the Dutch East Indies, the rubber and tin of Malaya, and the rice of Burma and Indochina.

A move southward, of course, would risk war with the European colonial powers and the United States. Japan's attack on China in the summer of 1937 had already aroused strong criticism abroad, particularly from the United States, where President Franklin Roosevelt threatened to "quarantine" the aggressors after Japanese military units bombed an American naval ship operating in China. Public fear of involvement forced the president to draw back, but when Japan suddenly demanded the right to occupy airfields and exploit economic resources in French Indochina in the summer of 1940, the United States warned the Japanese that it would cut off the sale of oil and scrap iron unless Japan withdrew from the area and returned to its borders of 1931.

The Japanese viewed the American threat of retaliation as an obstacle to their long-term objectives. Japan badly needed oil and scrap iron from the United States. Should they be cut off, Japan would have to find them elsewhere. The Japanese were thus caught in a vise. To obtain guaranteed access to natural resources that were necessary to fuel the Japanese military machine, Japan must risk being cut off from its current source of raw materials that would be needed in case of a conflict. After much debate, the Japanese decided to launch a surprise attack on American and European colonies in Southeast Asia in the hope of a quick victory that would evict the United States from the region.

**CHRONOLOGY The Path to War, 1931–1939**

| | |
|---|---|
| Japan seizes Manchuria | September 1931 |
| Hitler becomes chancellor | January 30, 1933 |
| Hitler announces a German air force | March 9, 1935 |
| Hitler announces military conscription | March 16, 1935 |
| Mussolini invades Ethiopia | October 1935 |
| Hitler occupies demilitarized Rhineland | March 7, 1936 |
| Mussolini and Hitler intervene in Spanish Civil War | 1936 |
| Rome-Berlin Axis | October 1936 |
| Anti-Comintern Pact (Japan and Germany) | November 1936 |
| Japan invades China | July 1937 |
| Germany annexes Austria | March 13, 1938 |
| Munich Conference: Sudetenland goes to Germany | September 29, 1938 |
| Germany occupies the rest of Czechoslovakia | March 1939 |
| German-Soviet Nonaggression Pact | August 23, 1939 |
| Germany invades Poland | September 1, 1939 |
| Britain and France declare war on Germany | September 3, 1939 |

# World War II

Unleashing a *Blitzkrieg*, or "lightning war," Hitler stunned Europe with the speed and efficiency of the German attack. Armored columns or panzer divisions (a panzer division was a strike force of about three hundred tanks and accompanying forces and supplies) supported by airplanes broke quickly through Polish lines and encircled the bewildered Polish troops. Conventional infantry units then moved in to hold the newly conquered territory. Within four weeks, Poland had surrendered. On September 28, 1939, Germany and the Soviet Union officially divided Poland between them.

## Europe at War

Although Hitler's hopes to avoid a war with the western European states were dashed when France and Britain declared war on September 3, he was confident that he could control the situation. After a winter of waiting (called the "phony war"), Hitler resumed the war on April 9, 1940, with another *Blitzkrieg*, against Denmark and Norway (see Map 24.1). One month later, on May 10, the Germans launched their attack on the Netherlands, Belgium, and France. The main assault through Luxembourg and the Ardennes forest was completely unexpected by the French and British forces. German panzer divisions broke through the weak French defensive positions there and raced across northern France, splitting the Allied armies and trapping French troops and the entire British army on the beaches of Dunkirk. Only by heroic efforts did the British succeed in a gigantic evacuation of 330,000 Allied (mostly British) troops. The French capitulated on June 22. German armies occupied about three-fifths of France, while the French hero of World War I, Marshal Henri Pétain (1856–1951), established an authoritarian regime (known as Vichy France) over the remainder. Germany was now in control of western and central Europe, but Britain had still not been defeated.

**The Problem of Britain** As Hitler realized, an amphibious invasion of Britain would be possible only if Germany gained control of the air. At the beginning of

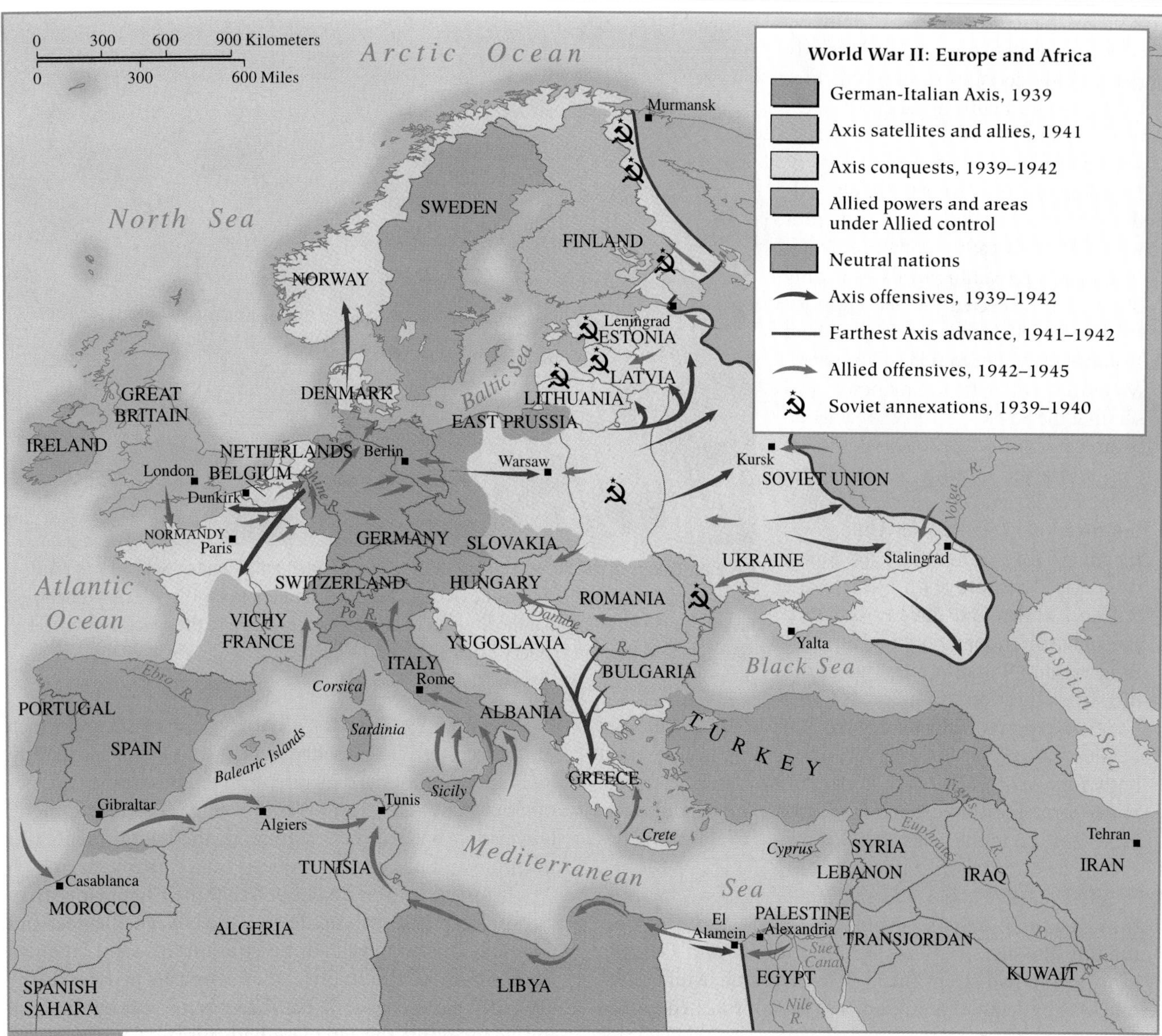


**MAP 24.1 World War II in Europe and North Africa.** With its fast and effective military, Germany quickly overwhelmed much of western Europe. However, Hitler overestimated his country's capabilities and underestimated those of his foes. By late 1942, his invasion of the Soviet Union was failing, and the United States had become a major factor in the war. The Allies successfully invaded Italy in 1943 and France in 1944. ? Which countries were neutral, and how did geography help make their neutrality an option? **View an animated version of this map or related maps at** http://history.wadsworth.com/duikerspielvogel05/

August 1940, the *Luftwaffe* (the German air force) launched a major offensive against British air and naval bases, harbors, communication centers, and war industries. The British fought back doggedly, supported by an effective radar system that gave them early warning of German attacks. Nevertheless, the British air force suffered critical losses by the end of August and was probably saved by a change in Hitler's strategy. In September, in retaliation for a British attack on Berlin, Hitler ordered a shift from military targets to massive bombing of British cities to break British morale. The British rebuilt their air strength quickly and were soon inflicting major losses on *Luftwaffe* bombers. By the end of September, Germany had lost the Battle of Britain, and the invasion of Britain had to be postponed.

At this point, Hitler pursued the possibility of a Mediterranean strategy, which would involve capturing Egypt and the Suez Canal and closing the Mediterranean to British ships, thereby shutting off Britain's supply of oil. Hitler's commitment to the Mediterranean was never wholehearted, however. His initial plan was to let the Italians defeat the British in North Africa, but this strategy failed when the British routed the Italian army. Although Hitler then sent German troops to the North

African theater of war, his primary concern lay elsewhere; he had already reached the decision to fulfill his lifetime obsession with the acquisition of territory in the east.

**Invasion of the Soviet Union** Although he had no desire for a two-front war, Hitler became convinced that Britain was remaining in the war only because it expected Soviet support. If the Soviet Union were smashed, Britain's last hope would be eliminated. Moreover, Hitler had convinced himself that the Soviet Union, with what he regarded as its Jewish-Bolshevik leadership and a pitiful army, could be defeated quickly and decisively. Although the invasion of the Soviet Union was scheduled for spring 1941, the attack was delayed because of problems in the Balkans. Hitler had already obtained the political cooperation of Hungary, Bulgaria, and Romania, but Mussolini's disastrous invasion of Greece in October 1940 exposed Hitler's southern flank to British air bases in Greece. To secure his Balkan flank, German troops seized both Yugoslavia and Greece in April 1941. Now reassured, Hitler turned to the east and invaded the Soviet Union on June 22, 1941, in the belief that the Soviets could still be decisively defeated before winter set in.

AKG London

**German Troops in the Soviet Union.** At first, the German attack on the Soviet Union was enormously successful, leading one German general to remark in his diary, "It is probably no overstatement to say that the Russian campaign has been won in the space of two weeks." Shown here is German artillery firing on Soviet positions.

The massive attack stretched out along an 1,800-mile front. German troops advanced rapidly, capturing two million Russian soldiers. By November, one German army group had swept through the Ukraine, while a second was besieging Leningrad; a third approached within 25 miles of Moscow, the Russian capital. An early winter and unexpected Soviet resistance, however, brought a halt to the German advance. For the first time in the war, German armies had been stopped. A counterattack in December 1941 by a Soviet army supposedly exhausted by Nazi victories came as an ominous ending to the year for the Germans. By that time, another of Hitler's decisions—the declaration of war on the United States—probably made his defeat inevitable and turned another European conflict into a global war.

## Japan at War

On December 7, 1941, Japanese carrier-based aircraft attacked the U.S. naval base at Pearl Harbor in the Hawaiian Islands. The same day, other units launched assaults on the Philippines and began advancing toward the British colony of Malaya (see Map 24.2). Shortly thereafter, Japanese forces invaded the Dutch East Indies and occupied a number of islands in the Pacific Ocean. In some cases, as on the Bataan peninsula and the island of Corregidor in the Philippines, resistance was fierce, but by the spring of 1942, almost all of Southeast Asia and much of the western Pacific had fallen into Japanese hands. Japan then announced its intention to liberate the colonies of Southeast Asia from Western rule. For the moment, however, it needed the resources of the region for its war machine and placed its conquests on a wartime basis.

Japanese leaders had hoped that their lightning strike at American bases would destroy the U.S. Pacific fleet and persuade the Roosevelt administration to accept Japanese domination of the Pacific. The American people, in the eyes of Japanese leaders, had been made soft by material indulgence. But the Japanese had miscalculated. The attack on Pearl Harbor galvanized American opinion and won broad support for Roosevelt's war policy. The United States now joined with European nations and Nationalist China in a combined effort to defeat Japan and bring an end to its hegemony in the Pacific. Believing the American involvement in the Pacific would render the United States ineffective in the European theater of war, Hitler declared war on the United States four days after Pearl Harbor.

## The Turning Point of the War, 1942–1943

The entry of the United States into the war created a coalition (the Grand Alliance) that ultimately defeated the Axis Powers (Germany, Italy, and Japan). Nevertheless, the three major Allies—Britain, the United States, and the Soviet Union—had to overcome mutual suspicions before they could operate as an effective alliance. Two factors aided that process. First, Hitler's declaration of war on the United States made it easier for the Americans to accept the British and Russian contention

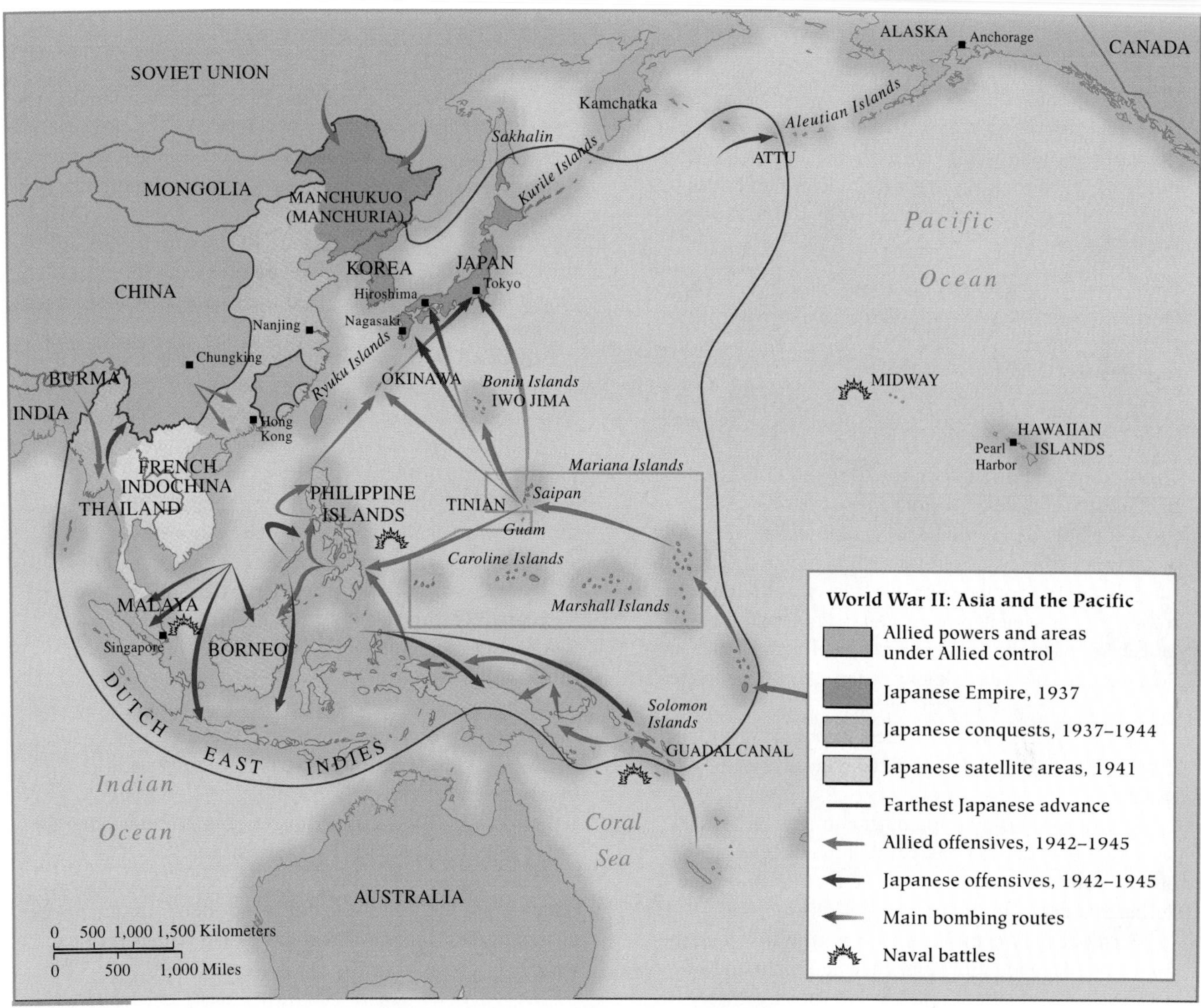


**MAP 24.2 World War II in Asia and the Pacific.** In 1937, Japan invaded northern China, beginning its effort to create a "Great East Asia Co-Prosperity Sphere." Further expansion induced America to end iron and oil sales to Japan. Deciding that war with the United States was inevitable, Japan engineered a surprise attack on Pearl Harbor. Why was control of the islands in the western Pacific of great importance both to the Japanese and to the Allies? **View an animated version of this map or related maps at** http://history.wadsworth.com/duikerspielvogel05/

that the defeat of Germany should be the first priority of the United States. For that reason, the United States, under its lend-lease program (which had begun before U.S. entry into the war), sent large amounts of military aid, including $50 billion worth of trucks, planes, and other arms, to the British and the Soviets. Also important to the alliance was the tacit agreement of the three chief Allies to stress military operations while ignoring political differences and larger strategic issues concerning any postwar settlement. At the beginning of 1943, the Allies agreed to fight until the Axis Powers surrendered unconditionally. Although this principle of **unconditional surrender** prevented a repeat of the mistake of World War I, which was ended in 1918 with an armistice rather than a total victory, it likely discouraged dissident Germans and Japanese from overthrowing their governments in order to arrange a negotiated peace. At the same time, it did have the effect of cementing the Grand Alliance by making it nearly impossible for Hitler to divide his foes.

Defeat, however, was far from Hitler's mind at the beginning of 1942. As Japanese forces advanced into Southeast Asia and the Pacific after crippling the American naval fleet at Pearl Harbor, Hitler and his European allies continued the war in Europe against Britain and the Soviet Union. Until the fall of 1942, it appeared that the Germans might still prevail on the battlefield. Reinforcements in North Africa enabled the Afrika Korps under General Erwin Rommel to break through the British defenses in Egypt and advance toward Alexandria. In the spring of 1942, a renewed German

## A German Soldier at Stalingrad

The Soviet victory at Stalingrad was a major turning point in World War II. This excerpt comes from the diary of a German soldier who fought and died in the Battle of Stalingrad. His dreams of victory and a return home with medals are soon dashed by the realities of Soviet resistance.

*What does this soldier believe about the Führer? Why? What has been the source of his information? Why is the battle for Stalingrad considered a major turning point in World War II?*

### Diary of a German Soldier

Today, after we'd had a bath, the company commander told us that if our future operations are as successful, we'll soon reach the Volga, take Stalingrad, and then the war will inevitably soon be over. Perhaps we'll be home by Christmas.

*July 29.* The company commander says the Russian troops are completely broken, and cannot hold out any longer. To reach the Volga and take Stalingrad is not so difficult for us. The Führer knows where the Russians' weak point is. Victory is not far away. . . .

*August 10.* The Führer's orders were read out to us. He expects victory of us. We are all convinced that they can't stop us.

*August 12.* This morning outstanding soldiers were presented with decorations. . . . Will I really go back to Elsa without a decoration? I believe that for Stalingrad the Führer will decorate even me. . . .

*September 4.* We are being sent northward along the front toward Stalingrad. We marched all night and by dawn had reached Voroponovo Station. We can already see the smoking town. It's a happy thought that the end of the war is getting nearer. That's what everyone is saying. . . .

*September 8.* Two days of nonstop fighting. The Russians are defending themselves with insane stubbornness. Our regiment has lost many men. . . .

*September 16.* Our battalion, plus tanks, is attacking the [grain storage] elevator, from which smoke is pouring—the grain in it is burning; the Russians seem to have set light to it themselves. Barbarism. The battalion is suffering heavy losses. . . .

*October 10.* The Russians are so close to us that our planes cannot bomb them. We are preparing for a decisive attack. The Führer has ordered the whole of Stalingrad to be taken as rapidly as possible. . . .

*October 22.* Our regiment has failed to break into the factory. We have lost many men; every time you move you have to jump over bodies. . . .

*November 10.* A letter from Elsa today. Everyone expects us home for Christmas. In Germany everyone believes we already hold Stalingrad. How wrong they are. If they could only see what Stalingrad has done to our army. . . .

*November 21.* The Russians have gone over to the offensive along the whole front. Fierce fighting is going on. So, there it is—the Volga, victory, and soon home to our families! We shall obviously be seeing them next in the other world.

*November 29.* We are encircled. It was announced this morning that the Führer has said: "The army can trust me to do everything necessary to ensure supplies and rapidly break the encirclement."

*December 3.* We are on hunger rations and waiting for the rescue that the Führer promised. . . .

*December 14.* Everybody is racked with hunger. Frozen potatoes are the best meal, but to get them out of the ice-covered ground under fire from Russian bullets is not so easy. . . .

*December 26.* The horses have already been eaten. I would eat a cat; they say its meat is also tasty. The soldiers look like corpses or lunatics, looking for something to put in their mouths. They no longer take cover from Russian shells; they haven't the strength to walk, run away, and hide. A curse on this war!

offensive in the Soviet Union led to the capture of the entire Crimea, causing Hitler to boast in August 1942:

> As the next step, we are going to advance south of the Caucasus and then help the rebels in Iran and Iraq against the English. Another thrust will be directed along the Caspian Sea toward Afghanistan and India. Then the English will run out of oil. In two years we'll be on the borders of India. Twenty to thirty elite German divisions will do. Then the British Empire will collapse.[8]

But this would be Hitler's last optimistic outburst. By the fall of 1942, the war had turned against the Germans.

**North Africa and the Eastern Front** In North Africa, British forces had stopped Rommel's troops at El Alamein in the summer of 1942 and then forced them back across the desert. In November 1942, British and American forces invaded French North Africa and forced the German and Italian troops to surrender in May 1943. On the Eastern Front, the turning point of the war occurred at Stalingrad. After the capture of the Crimea, Hitler's generals wanted him to concentrate on the Caucasus and its oil fields, but Hitler decided that Stalingrad, a major industrial center on the Volga, should be taken first. Between November 1942 and February 1943, German troops were stopped, then encircled, and finally forced to surrender on February 2, 1943 (see the box above). The entire German Sixth Army of 300,000 men was lost. By February 1943, German forces in Russia were back to

**CHRONOLOGY The Course of World War II**

| | |
|---|---|
| Germany and the Soviet Union divide Poland | September 28, 1939 |
| *Blitzkrieg* against Denmark and Norway | April 1940 |
| *Blitzkrieg* against Belgium, Netherlands, and France | May 1940 |
| France surrenders | June 22, 1940 |
| Battle of Britain | Fall 1940 |
| Nazi seizure of Yugoslavia and Greece | April 1941 |
| Germany invades the Soviet Union | June 22, 1941 |
| Japanese attack on Pearl Harbor | December 7, 1941 |
| Battle of the Coral Sea | May 7–8, 1942 |
| Battle of Midway Island | June 4, 1942 |
| Allied invasion of North Africa | November 1942 |
| German surrender at Stalingrad | February 2, 1943 |
| Axis forces surrender in North Africa | May 1943 |
| Battle of Kursk | July 5–12, 1943 |
| Invasion of mainland Italy | September 1943 |
| Allied invasion of France | June 6, 1944 |
| Hitler commits suicide | April 30, 1945 |
| Germany surrenders | May 7, 1945 |
| Atomic bomb dropped on Hiroshima | August 6, 1945 |
| Japan surrenders | August 14, 1945 |

their positions of June 1942. By the spring of 1943, long before Allied troops returned to the European continent, even Hitler knew that the Germans would not defeat the Soviet Union.

**Asia** The tide of battle in the Far East also turned dramatically in 1942. In the Battle of the Coral Sea on May 7 and 8, 1942, American naval forces stopped the Japanese advance and temporarily relieved Australia of the threat of invasion. On June 4, at the Battle of Midway Island, American carrier planes destroyed all four of the attacking Japanese aircraft carriers and established American naval superiority in the Pacific. By the fall of 1942, Allied forces were beginning to gather for offensive operations into southern China from Burma, through the Dutch East Indies by a process of "island hopping" by troops commanded by the American general Douglas MacArthur, and across the Pacific with a combination of U.S. Army, Marine, and Navy attacks on Japanese-held islands. After a series of bitter engagements in the waters of the Solomon Islands from August to November 1942, Japanese fortunes began to fade.

## The Last Years of the War

By the beginning of 1943, the tide of battle had turned against Germany, Italy, and Japan. After the Axis forces had surrendered in Tunisia on May 13, 1943, the Allies crossed the Mediterranean and carried the war to Italy. After taking Sicily, Allied troops began the invasion of mainland Italy in September. In the meantime, after the ouster and arrest of Benito Mussolini, a new Italian government offered to surrender to Allied forces. But Mussolini was liberated by the Germans in a daring raid and then set up as the head of a puppet German state in northern Italy while German troops moved in and occupied much of Italy. The new defensive lines established by the Germans in the hills south of Rome were so effective that the Allied advance up the Italian peninsula was a painstaking affair accompanied by heavy casualties. Rome did not fall to the Allies until June 4, 1944. By that time, the Italian war had assumed a secondary role anyway as the Allies prepared to open their long-awaited "second front" in western Europe.

**Allied Advances in Europe** Since the autumn of 1943, the Allies had been planning a cross-channel invasion of France from Britain. Under the direction of the American general Dwight D. Eisenhower (1890–1969), the Allies landed five assault divisions on the beaches of Normandy on June 6, 1944, in history's greatest naval invasion. An initially indecisive German response enabled the Allied forces to establish a beachhead. Within three months, they had landed two million men and a half-million vehicles that pushed inland and broke through German defensive lines.

After the breakout, Allied troops moved south and east and liberated Paris by the end of August. By March 1945, they had crossed the Rhine River and advanced farther into Germany. At the end of April 1945, Allied armies in northern Germany moved toward the Elbe River, where they finally linked up with the Soviets. The Soviets had come a long way since the Battle of Stalingrad in 1943. In the summer of 1943, Hitler gambled on taking the offensive by making use of newly developed heavy tanks. German forces were soundly defeated by the Soviets at the Battle of Kursk (July 5–12), the greatest tank battle of World War II. Soviet forces now began a relentless advance westward. The Soviets had reoccupied the Ukraine by the end of 1943 and lifted the siege of Leningrad and moved into the Baltic states by the beginning of 1944. Advancing along a northern front, Soviet troops occupied Warsaw in January 1945 and entered Berlin in April. Meanwhile, Soviet troops along a southern front swept through Hungary, Romania, and Bulgaria.

In January 1945, Hitler had moved into a bunker 55 feet under Berlin to direct the final stages of the war. In his final political testament, Hitler, consistent to the end in his rabid anti-Semitism, blamed the Jews for the war: "Above all I charge the leaders of the nation and those under them to scrupulous observance of the laws of race and to merciless opposition to the universal poisoner of all peoples, international Jewry."[9] Hitler committed suicide on April 30, two days after Mussolini had been shot by partisan Italian forces. On May 7, German commanders surrendered. The war in Europe was over.

© Mainichi Shimbun, Tokyo

**Refugees Flee Yokohama.** American bombing attacks on Japanese cities began in earnest in November 1944. Built of flimsy materials, Japan's crowded cities were soon devastated by these air raids. This photograph shows a homeless family fleeing Yokohama, a shelter for refugees until American bombers devastated the city on May 29, 1945.

**Defeat of Japan** The war in Asia continued. Beginning in 1943, American forces had gone on the offensive and advanced their way, slowly at times, across the Pacific. American forces took an increasing toll of enemy resources, especially at sea and in the air. As Allied military power drew inexorably closer to the main Japanese islands in the first months of 1945, President Harry Truman, who had succeeded to the presidency on the death of Franklin Roosevelt in April, had an excruciatingly difficult decision to make. Should he use atomic weapons (at the time, only two bombs were available, and their effectiveness had not been demonstrated) to bring the war to an end without the necessity of an Allied invasion of the Japanese homeland? As the world knows, Truman answered that question in the affirmative. The first bomb was dropped on the city of Hiroshima on August 6. Truman then called on Japan to surrender or expect a "rain of ruin from the air." When the Japanese did not respond, a second bomb was dropped on Nagasaki. Japan surrendered unconditionally on August 14. World War II, in which seventeen million men died in battle and perhaps eighteen million civilians perished as well (some estimate total losses at fifty million), was finally over.

# The New Order

The initial victories of the Germans and the Japanese gave them the opportunity to create new orders in Europe and Asia. Although both countries presented positive images of these new orders for publicity purposes, in practice both followed policies of ruthless domination of their subject peoples.

## The New Order in Europe

After the German victories, Nazi propagandists created glowing images of a **Nazi New Order** in Europe based on "equal chances" for all nations and an integrated economic community. This was not Hitler's conception of a European New Order. He saw the Europe he had conquered simply as subject to German domination. Only the Germans, he once said, "can really organize Europe."

**The Nazi Empire** The Nazi empire stretched across continental Europe from the English Channel in the west to the outskirts of Moscow in the east. In no way was this empire organized systematically or governed efficiently. Nazi-occupied Europe was organized in one of two ways.

## Hitler's Plans for a New Order in the East

Hitler's nightly monologues to his postdinner guests, which were recorded by the Führer's private secretary, Martin Bormann, reveal much about the New Order he wished to create. On the evening of October 17, 1941, Hitler expressed his views on what the Germans would do with their newly conquered territories in the east.

*What were Hitler's plans for the conquered eastern territories and the peoples who inhabited these lands? Concerning eastern Europeans, do you believe Hitler's statements that "we don't hate them" and "we are guided only by reason"? What motivations do you see behind this monologue?*

### *Hitler's Secret Conversations,* October 17, 1941

In comparison with the beauties accumulated in Central Germany, the new territories in the East seem to us like a desert. . . . This Russian desert, we shall populate it. . . . We'll take away its character of an Asiatic steppe; we'll Europeanize it. With this object, we have undertaken the construction of roads that will lead to the southernmost point of the Crimea and to the Caucasus. These roads will be studded along their whole length with German towns, and around these towns our colonists will settle.

As for the two or three million men whom we need to accomplish this task, we'll find them quicker than we think. They'll come from Germany, Scandinavia, the Western countries, and America. I shall no longer be here to see all that, but in twenty years the Ukraine will already be a home for twenty million inhabitants besides the natives. In three hundred years, the country will be one of the loveliest gardens in the world.

As for the natives, we'll have to screen them carefully. The Jew, that destroyer, we shall drive out. . . . We shan't settle in the Russian towns, and we'll let them fall to pieces without intervening. And, above all, no remorse on this subject! We're not going to play at children's nurses; we're absolutely without obligations as far as these people are concerned. To struggle against the hovels, chase away the fleas, provide German teachers, bring out newspapers—very little of that for us! We'll confine ourselves, perhaps, to setting up a radio transmitter, under our control. For the rest, let them know just enough to understand our highway signs, so that they won't get themselves run over by our vehicles. . . . There's only one duty: to Germanize this country by the immigration of Germans, and to look upon the natives as Redskins. If these people had defeated us, Heaven have mercy! But we don't hate them. That sentiment is unknown to us. We are guided only by reason. . . .

All those who have the feeling for Europe can join in our work.

In this business I shall go straight ahead, cold-bloodedly. What they may think about me, at this juncture, is to me a matter of complete indifference. I don't see why a German who eats a piece of bread should torment himself with the idea that the soil that produces this bread has been won by the sword.

Some areas, such as western Poland, were directly annexed by Nazi Germany and made into German provinces. Most of occupied Europe was administered by German military or civilian officials in combination with varying degrees of indirect control from collaborationist regimes.

Racial considerations played an important role in how conquered peoples were treated. German civil administrations were established in Norway, Denmark, and the Netherlands because the Nazis considered their peoples Aryan, racially kin to the Germans and hence worthy of more lenient treatment. "Inferior" Latin peoples, such as the occupied French, were given military administrations. By 1943, however, as Nazi losses continued to multiply, all the occupied territories of northern and western Europe were ruthlessly exploited for material goods and manpower for Germany's labor needs.

**Plans for an Aryan Racial Empire** Because the conquered lands in the east contained the living space for German expansion and were populated in Nazi eyes by racially inferior Slavic peoples, Nazi administration there was considerably more ruthless. Hitler's racial ideology and his plans for an Aryan racial empire were so important to him that he and the Nazis began to implement their racial program soon after the conquest of Poland. Heinrich Himmler, a strong believer in Nazi racial ideology and the leader of the SS, was put in charge of German resettlement plans in the east. Himmler's task was to evacuate the inferior Slavic peoples and replace them with Germans, a policy first applied to the new German provinces created from the lands of western Poland. One million Poles were uprooted and dumped in southern Poland. Hundreds of thousands of ethnic Germans (descendants of Germans who had migrated decades earlier from Germany to different parts of southern and eastern Europe) were encouraged to colonize designated areas in Poland. By 1942, two million ethnic Germans had been settled in Poland.

The invasion of the Soviet Union inflated Nazi visions of German colonization in the east. Hitler spoke to his intimate circle of a colossal project of social engineering after the war, in which Poles, Ukrainians, and Russians would become slave labor while German peasants settled on the abandoned lands and Germanized them (see the box above). Nazis involved in this kind of planning were well aware of the human costs. Himmler told a gathering of SS officers that although the destruction of thirty million Slavs was a prerequisite for German plans in the east, "whether nations live in prosperity or starve to death interests me only insofar as we need them as slaves for our culture. Otherwise it is of no interest."[10]

**Use of Foreign Workers** Labor shortages in Germany led to a policy of ruthless mobilization of foreign labor for Germany. After the invasion of the Soviet Union, the four million Russian prisoners of war captured by the Germans along with more than two million workers conscripted in France became a major source of heavy labor, but it was wasted by allowing more than three million of them to die from neglect. In 1942, a special office was created to recruit labor for German farms and industries. By the summer of 1944, seven million foreign workers were laboring in Germany, constituting 20 percent of Germany's labor force. At the same time, another seven million workers were supplying forced labor in their own countries on farms, in industries, and even in military camps. Forced labor, however, often proved counterproductive because it created economic chaos in occupied countries and disrupted industrial production that could have helped Germany. The brutal character of Germany's recruitment policies often led more and more people to resist the Nazi occupation forces.

## The Holocaust

No aspect of the Nazi New Order was more terrifying than the deliberate attempt to exterminate the Jewish people of Europe. Racial struggle was a key element in Hitler's ideology and meant to him a clearly defined conflict of opposites: the Aryans, creators of human cultural development, against the Jews, parasites who were trying to destroy the Aryans. By the beginning of 1939, Nazi policy focused on promoting the "emigration" of German Jews from Germany. Once the war began in September 1939, the so-called Jewish problem took on new dimensions. For a while there was discussion of the Madagascar Plan, which aspired to the mass shipment of Jews to the African island of Madagascar. When war contingencies made this plan impractical, an even more drastic policy was conceived.

**The SS and the *Einsatzgruppen*** Himmler and the SS organization shared Hitler's racial ideology. The SS was given responsibility for what the Nazis called their **Final Solution** to the Jewish problem—the annihilation of the Jewish people. Reinhard Heydrich (1904–1942), head of the SS's Security Service, was given administrative responsibility for the Final Solution. After defeating Poland, Heydrich ordered the special strike forces (***Einsatzgruppen***) that he had created to round up all Polish Jews and concentrate them in ghettos established in a number of Polish cities.

In June 1941, the *Einsatzgruppen* were given new responsibilities as mobile killing units. These SS death squads followed the regular army's advance into the Soviet Union. Their job was to round up Jews in the villages and execute and bury them in mass graves, often giant pits dug by the victims themselves before they were shot. Such constant killing produced morale problems among the SS executioners. During a visit to Minsk in the Soviet Union, Himmler tried to build morale by pointing out that "he would not like it if Germans did such a thing gladly. But their conscience was in no way impaired, for they were soldiers who had to carry out every order unconditionally. He alone had responsibility before God and Hitler for everything that was happening, . . . and he was acting from a deep understanding of the necessity for this operation."[11]

Library of Congress

**The Holocaust: Activities of the *Einsatzgruppen*.** The activities of the mobile killing units known as the *Einsatzgruppen* were the first stage in the mass exterminations of the Holocaust. This picture shows the execution of a Jew by a member of one of these SS killing squads. Onlookers include members of the German Army, the German Labor Service, and even Hitler Youth. When it became apparent that this method of killing was inefficient, it was replaced by the death camps.

**The Death Camps** Although it has been estimated that as many as one million Jews were killed by the *Einsatzgruppen,* this approach to solving the Jewish problem was soon perceived as inadequate. So the Nazis opted for the systematic annihilation of the European Jewish population in death camps. The plan was simple: Jews from countries occupied by Germany (or sympathetic to Germany) would be rounded up, packed like cattle into freight trains, and shipped to Poland, where six extermination centers were built for this purpose. The largest and most famous was Auschwitz-Birkenau. Medical technicians chose Zyklon B (the commercial name for hydrogen cyanide) as the most effective gas for quickly killing large numbers of people in gas chambers designed to look like shower rooms to facilitate the cooperation of the victims. After gassing, the corpses would be burned in specially built crematoria.

By the spring of 1942, the death camps were in operation. Although initial priority was given to the elimination of the ghettos in Poland, by the summer of 1942, Jews were also being shipped from France, Belgium, and the Netherlands. Even as the Allies were making significant advances in 1944, Jews were being shipped from Greece and Hungary. These shipments depended on the cooperation of Germany's Transport Ministry, but despite desperate military needs, the Final Solution had priority in using railroad cars for the transportation of Jews to death camps.

A harrowing experience awaited the Jews when they arrived at one of the six death camps. Rudolf Höss, commandant at Auschwitz-Birkenau, described it:

> We had two SS doctors on duty at Auschwitz to examine the incoming transports of prisoners. The prisoners would be marched by one of the doctors, who would make spot decisions as they walked by. Those who were fit for work were sent into the camp. Others were sent immediately to the extermination plants. Children of tender years were invariably exterminated since by reason of their youth they were unable to work. . . . At Auschwitz we endeavored to fool the victims into thinking that they were to go through a delousing process. Of course, frequently they realized our true intentions and we sometimes had riots and difficulties due to that fact.[12]

About 30 percent of the arrivals at Auschwitz were sent to a labor camp, while the remainder went to the gas chambers (see the box on p. 706). After they had been gassed, the bodies were burned in the crematoria. The victims' goods and even their bodies were used for economic gain. Women's hair was cut off, collected, and turned into mattresses or cloth. Some inmates were also subjected to cruel and painful "medical" experiments. The Germans killed between five and six million Jews, over three million of them in the death camps. About 90 percent of the Jewish populations of Poland, the Baltic countries, and Germany were exterminated. Overall, the Holocaust was responsible for the death of nearly two out of every three European Jews.

**The Other Holocaust** The Nazis were also responsible for another Holocaust, the death by shooting, starvation, or overwork of at least another nine to ten million people. Because the Nazis also considered the Gypsies of Europe (like the Jews) a race containing alien blood, they were systematically rounded up for extermination. About 40 percent of Europe's one million Gypsies were killed in the death camps. The leading elements of the "subhuman" Slavic peoples—the clergy, intelligentsia, civil leaders, judges, and lawyers—were arrested and deliberately killed. Probably an additional four million Poles, Ukrainians, and Byelorussians lost their lives as slave laborers for Nazi Germany, and three to four million Soviet prisoners of war were killed in captivity. The Nazis also singled out homosexuals for persecution, and thousands lost their lives in concentration camps.

## The New Order in Asia

Once the takeover was completed, Japanese war policy in the occupied areas in Asia became essentially defensive, as Japan hoped to use its new possessions to meet its burgeoning needs for raw materials, such as tin, oil, and rubber, and also as an outlet for Japanese manufactured goods. To provide an organizational structure for the arrangement, Japanese leaders set up the Great East-Asia Co-Prosperity Sphere, a self-sufficient economic community designed to provide mutual benefits to the occupied areas and the home country (see the box on p. 707). The Ministry for Great East Asia, staffed by civilians, was established in Tokyo in October 1942 to handle arrangements between Japan and the conquered territories.

**Japanese Policies** The Japanese conquest of Southeast Asia had been accomplished under the slogan "Asia for the Asiatics," and many Japanese probably sincerely believed that their government was bringing about the liberation of the Southeast Asian peoples from European colonial rule. Japanese officials in the occupied territories quickly made contact with anticolonialist elements and promised that independent governments would be established under Japanese tutelage. Such governments were eventually established in Burma, the Dutch East Indies, Vietnam, and the Philippines.

In fact, however, real power rested with the Japanese military authorities in each territory, and the local Japanese military command was directly subordinated to the army general staff in Tokyo. The economic resources of the colonies were exploited for the benefit of the Japanese war machine, while natives were recruited to serve in local military units or conscripted to work on public works projects. In some cases, the people living in the occupied areas were subjected to severe hardships. In Indochina, for example, forced requisitions of rice by the local Japanese authorities for shipment abroad created a food shortage that caused the starvation of over a million Vietnamese in 1944 and 1945.

## THE HOLOCAUST: THE CAMP COMMANDANT AND THE CAMP VICTIMS

The systematic annihilation of millions of men, women, and children in extermination camps makes the Holocaust one of the most horrifying events in history. The first document is taken from an account by Rudolf Höss, commandant of the extermination camp at Auschwitz-Birkenau. In the second document, a French doctor explains what happened at one of the crematoria described by Höss.

*What "equipment" does Höss describe? What process does the French doctor describe? Is there any sympathy for the victims in either account? Why or why not? How could such a horrifying process have been allowed to occur? Who was held responsible after the war? Was this sufficient?*

### Commandant Höss Describes the Equipment

The two large crematoria, Nos. I and II, were built during the winter of 1942–43. . . . Each . . . could cremate c. 2,000 corpses within twenty-four hours. . . . Crematoria I and II both had underground undressing and gassing rooms which could be completely ventilated. The corpses were brought up to the ovens on the floor above by lift. The gas chambers could hold c. 3,000 people.

The firm of Topf had calculated that the two smaller crematoria, III and IV, would each be able to cremate 1,500 corpses within twenty-four hours. However, owing to the wartime shortage of materials, the builders were obliged to economize, and so the undressing rooms and gassing rooms were built above ground and the ovens were of a less solid construction. But it soon became apparent that the flimsy construction of these two four-retort ovens was not up to the demands made on it. No. III ceased operating altogether after a short time and later was no longer used. No. IV had to be repeatedly shut down since after a short period in operation of 4–6 weeks, the ovens and chimneys had burnt out. The victims of the gassing were mainly burnt in pits behind crematorium IV.

The largest number of people gassed and cremated within twenty-four hours was somewhat over 9,000.

### A French Doctor Describes the Victims

It is mid-day, when a long line of women, children, and old people enter the yard. The senior official in charge . . . climbs on a bench to tell them that they are going to have a bath and that afterward they will get a drink of hot coffee. They all undress in the yard. . . . The doors are opened and an indescribable jostling begins. The first people to enter the gas chamber begin to draw back. They sense the death which awaits them. The SS men put an end to this pushing and shoving with blows from their rifle butts beating the heads of the horrified women who are desperately hugging their children. The massive oak double doors are shut. For two endless minutes one can hear banging on the walls and screams which are no longer human. And then—not a sound. Five minutes later the doors are opened. The corpses, squashed together and distorted, fall out like a waterfall. . . . The bodies, which are still warm, pass through the hands of the hairdresser, who cuts their hair, and the dentist, who pulls out their gold teeth. . . . One more transport has just been processed through No. IV crematorium.

The Japanese planned to implant a new moral and social order as well as a new political and economic order in the occupied areas. Occupation policy stressed traditional values such as obedience, community spirit, filial piety, and discipline that reflected the prevailing political and cultural bias in Japan, while supposedly Western values such as materialism, liberalism, and individualism were strongly discouraged. To promote this New Order, occupation authorities gave particular support to local religious organizations but discouraged the formation of formal political parties.

**Resentment and Resistance** At first, many Southeast Asian nationalists took Japanese promises at face value and agreed to cooperate with their new masters. In Burma, an independent government was established in 1943 and subsequently declared war on the Allies. But as the exploitative nature of Japanese occupation policies became increasingly clear, sentiment turned against the New Order. Japanese officials sometimes unwittingly provoked resentment by their arrogance and contempt for local customs. In the Dutch East Indies, for example, Indonesians were required to bow in the direction of Tokyo and recognize the divinity of the Japanese emperor, practices that were repugnant to Muslims. In Burma, Buddhist pagodas were sometimes used as military latrines.

Like German soldiers in occupied Europe, Japanese military forces often had little respect for the lives of their subject peoples. In their conquest of Nanjing, China, in 1937, Japanese soldiers had spent several days in killing, raping, and looting. Almost 800,000 Koreans were sent overseas, most of them as forced laborers, to Japan. Tens of thousands of women from Korea and the Philippines were forced to serve as "comfort women" (prostitutes) for Japanese troops. In construction projects to help their war effort, the Japanese also made extensive use of labor forces composed of both prisoners of war and local peoples. In building the Burma-Thailand railway in 1943, for example, the Japanese used 61,000 Australian, British, and Dutch prisoners of war and almost 300,000 workers from Burma, Malaya, Thailand, and the Dutch East Indies. An

## Japan's Plan for Asia

The Japanese objective in World War II was to create a vast Great East-Asia Co-Prosperity Sphere to provide Japan with needed raw materials and a market for its exports. The following passage is from a secret document produced by a high-level government committee in January 1942.

*What were Japan's proposals for a Japanese-led Asia? How did the government committee that produced this document distinguish between "Occidental individualism and materialism" and "the Imperial Way"? From the evidence of this document, were individualism and materialism a part of the Imperial Way?*

### Draft Plan for the Establishment of the Great East-Asia Co-Prosperity Sphere

*The Plan.* The Japanese empire is a manifestation of morality and its special characteristic is the propagation of the Imperial Way. It is necessary to foster the increased power of the empire, to cause East Asia to return to its original form of independence and co-prosperity by shaking off the yoke of Europe and America, and to let its countries and peoples develop their respective abilities in peaceful cooperation and secure livelihood.

*The Form of East Asiatic Independence and Co-Prosperity.* The states, their citizens, and resources, comprised in those areas pertaining to the Pacific, Central Asia, and the Indian Oceans formed into one general union are to be established as an autonomous zone of peaceful living and common prosperity on behalf of the peoples of the nations of East Asia. The area including Japan, Manchuria, North China, lower Yangtze River, and the Russian Maritime Province, forms the nucleus of the East Asiatic Union. The Japanese empire possesses a duty as the leader of the East Asiatic Union.

The above purpose presupposes the inevitable emancipation or independence of Eastern Siberia, China, Indo-China, the South Seas, Australia, and India. . . .

*Outline of East Asiatic Administration.* It is intended that the unification of Japan, Manchoukuo, and China in neighborly friendship be realized by the settlement of the Sino-Japanese problems through the crushing of hostile influences in the Chinese interior, and through the construction of a new China. . . . Aggressive American and British influences in East Asia shall be driven out of the area of Indo-China and the South Seas, and this area should be brought into our defense sphere. The war with Britain and America shall be prosecuted for that purpose. . . .

### Chapter 3: Political Construction

*Basic Plan.* The realization of the great ideal of constructing Greater East Asia Co-Prosperity requires not only the complete prosecution of the current Greater East Asia War but also presupposes another great war in the future. . . .

The following are the basic principles for the political construction of East Asia. . . .

The desires of the peoples in the sphere for their independence shall be respected, and endeavors shall be made for their fulfillment, but proper and suitable forms of government shall be decided for them in consideration of military and economic requirements and of the historical, political, and cultural elements peculiar to each area.

It must also be noted that the independence of various peoples of East Asia should be based on the idea of constructing East Asia as "independent countries existing within the New Order of East Asia" and that this conception differs from an independence based on the idea of liberalism and national self-determination. . . .

Western individualism and materialism shall be rejected, and a moral worldview, the basic principle of whose morality shall be the Imperial Way, shall be established. The ultimate object to be achieved is not exploitation but co-prosperity and mutual help, not competitive conflict but mutual assistance and mild peace, not a formal view of equality but a view of order based on righteous classification, not an idea of rights but an idea of service, and not several worldviews but one unified worldview.

inadequate diet and appalling work conditions in an unhealthy climate led to the deaths of 12,000 Allied prisoners of war and 90,000 native workers by the time the railway was completed.

Such Japanese behavior created a dilemma for many nationalists, who had no desire to see the return of the colonial powers. Some turned against the Japanese, while others lapsed into inactivity. Indonesian patriots tried to have it both ways, feigning support for Japan while attempting to sabotage the Japanese administration. In French Indochina, Ho Chi Minh's Indochinese Communist Party established contacts with American military units in southern China and agreed to provide information on Japanese troop movements and rescue downed American fliers in the area. In Malaya, where Japanese treatment of ethnic Chinese residents was especially harsh, many joined a guerrilla movement against the occupying forces. By the end of the war, little support remained in the region for the erstwhile "liberators."

# The Home Front

World War II was even more of a total war than World War I. Fighting was much more widespread and covered most of the planet. Economic mobilization was more

**Germany** In August 1914, Germans had enthusiastically cheered their soldiers marching off to war. In September 1939, the streets were quiet. Many Germans were apathetic or, even worse for the Nazi regime, had a foreboding of disaster. Hitler was very aware of the importance of the home front. He believed that the collapse of the home front in World War I had caused Germany's defeat, and in his determination to avoid a repetition of that experience, he adopted economic policies that may indeed have cost Germany the war.

To maintain the morale of the home front during the first two years of the war, Hitler refused to cut the production of consumer goods or increase the production of armaments. *Blitzkrieg* allowed the Germans to win quick victories, after which they believed they could plunder the food and raw materials of the conquered countries to avoid diverting resources away from the civilian economy. After German defeats on the Russian front and the American entry into the war, the economic situation changed. Early in 1942, Hitler finally ordered a massive increase in armaments production and in the size of the army. Hitler's architect, Albert Speer, was made minister for armaments and munitions in 1942. By eliminating waste and rationalizing procedures, Speer was able to triple the production of armaments between 1942 and 1943 despite the intense Allied air raids. Speer's urgent plea for a total mobilization of resources for the war effort went unheeded, however. Hitler, fearful of civilian morale problems that would undermine the home front, refused any dramatic cuts in the production of consumer goods. A total mobilization of the economy was not implemented until 1944, when schools, theaters, and cafés were closed and Speer was finally permitted to use all remaining resources for the production of a few basic military items. By that time, it was in vain. Total war mobilization in July 1944 was too little too late to save Germany from defeat.

The war caused a reversal in Nazi attitudes toward women. Nazi resistance to female employment declined as the war progressed and more and more men were called up for military service. Nazi magazines now proclaimed, "We see the woman as the eternal mother of our people, but also as the working and fighting comrade of the man."[14] But the number of women working in industry, agriculture, commerce, and domestic service increased only slightly. The total number of employed women in September 1944 was 14.9 million, compared to 14.6 million in May 1939. Many women, especially those of the middle class, resisted regular employment, particularly in factories. Even the introduction of labor conscription for women in January 1943 failed to achieve much as women found ingenious ways to avoid the regulations.

**Japan** In Japan, society was placed on a wartime footing even before the attack on Pearl Harbor. A conscription law was passed in 1938, and economic resources were placed under strict government control. Two years later, all political parties were merged into the Imperial Rule Assistance Association. Labor unions were dissolved, and education and culture were purged of all "corrupt" Western ideas in favor of traditional values emphasizing the divinity of the emperor and the higher spirituality of Japanese civilization. During the war, individual rights were severely curtailed as the entire population was harnessed to the needs of the war effort. Traditional habits of obedience and hierarchy were emphasized to encourage citizens to sacrifice their resources, and sometimes their lives, for the national cause. Especially important was the code of Bushido, or the way of the warrior, the old code of morality of the samurai, who had played a prominent military role in medieval and early modern Japanese history. The code of Bushido was revived during the nationalistic fervor of the 1930s. Based on an ideal of loyalty and service, the code emphasized the obligation to honor and defend emperor, country, and family and to sacrifice one's life if one failed in this sacred mission. The system culminated in the final years of the war, when young Japanese were encouraged to volunteer en masse to serve as pilots in the suicide missions (known as *kamikaze*, or "divine wind") against American fighting ships.

Women's rights, too, were to be sacrificed to the greater national cause. Already by 1937, Japanese women were being exhorted to fulfill their patriotic duty by bearing more children and by espousing the slogans of the Greater Japanese Women's Association. However, Japan was extremely reluctant to mobilize women on behalf of the war effort. General Hideki Tojo, prime minister from 1941 to 1944, opposed female employment, arguing that "the weakening of the family system would be the weakening of the nation. . . . We are able to do our duties only because we have wives and mothers at home."[15] Female employment increased during the war, but only in areas, such as the textile industry and farming, where women had traditionally worked. Instead of using women to meet labor shortages, the Japanese government brought in Korean and Chinese laborers.

## The Bombing of Cities

Bombing was used in World War II against nonhuman military targets, against enemy troops, and against civilian populations. The bombing of civilians made World War II as devastating for noncombatants as it was for frontline soldiers. A small number of bombing raids in the last year of World War I had given rise to the argument, crystallized in 1930 by the Italian general Giulio Douhet, that the public outcry in reaction to the bombing of civilian populations would be an effective way to coerce governments into making peace. Consequently, European air forces began to develop long-range bombers in the 1930s.

***Luftwaffe* Attacks** The first sustained use of civilian bombing contradicted Douhet's theory. Beginning in early September, the German *Luftwaffe* subjected London and many other British cities and towns to nightly air

© J.R. Eyerman/Time Life Pictures/Getty Images

The Herald and Evening Times Picture Library, © SMG Newspapers Ltd.

COMPARATIVE ILLUSTRATION

**The Bombing of Civilians—East and West.** World War II was the most destructive war in world history, not only for frontline soldiers but for civilians at home as well. The most devastating bombing of civilians came near the end of World War II when the United States dropped atomic bombs on the Japanese cities of Hiroshima and Nagasaki. At the left is a view of Hiroshima after the bombing that shows the incredible devastation produced by the atomic bomb. The picture at the right shows a street in Clydebank, near Glasgow in Scotland, the day after the city was bombed by the Germans in March 1941. Only seven of the city's twelve thousand houses were left undamaged; 35,000 of the 47,000 inhabitants became homeless overnight.

raids, making the Blitz (as the British called the German air raids) a national experience. Londoners took the first heavy blows and set the standard for the rest of the British population by keeping up their spirits. But London morale was helped by the fact that German raids were widely dispersed over a very large city. Smaller communities were more directly affected by the devastation. On November 14, 1940, for example, the *Luftwaffe* destroyed hundreds of shops and 100 acres of the city center of Coventry. The destruction of smaller cities did produce morale problems as rumors of social collapse spread quickly in these communities (see the comparative illustration above). Nevertheless, morale was soon restored. War production in these areas, in any case, seems to have been little affected by the raids.

**The Bombing of Germany** The British failed to learn from their own experience, however, and soon retaliated by bombing Germany. Prime Minister Winston Churchill (1874–1965) and his advisers believed that destroying German communities would break civilian morale and bring victory. Major bombing raids began in 1942 under the direction of Arthur Harris, the wartime leader of the British air force's Bomber Command, which was rearmed with four-engine heavy bombers capable of taking the war into the center of occupied Europe. On May 31, 1942, Cologne became the first German city to be subjected to an attack by a thousand bombers.

The entry of the Americans into the war produced a new bombing strategy. American planes flew daytime missions aimed at the precision bombing of transportation facilities and wartime industries, while the British Bomber Command continued nighttime saturation bombing of all German cities with populations over 100,000. Bombing raids added an element of terror to circumstances already made difficult by growing shortages of food, clothing, and fuel. Germans especially feared the incendiary bombs, which set off firestorms that swept destructive paths through the cities. Four raids on Hamburg in August 1943 produced temperatures of 1,800 degrees Fahrenheit, obliterated half the city's buildings, and killed 50,000 civilians. The ferocious bombing of Dresden for three days in 1945 (February 13–15) created a firestorm that may have killed as many as 100,000 inhabitants and refugees. Even some Allied leaders began to criticize what they saw as the unnecessary terror bombing of German cities.

Germany suffered enormously from the Allied bombing raids. Millions of buildings were destroyed, and possibly half a million civilians died from the raids. Nevertheless, it is highly unlikely that Allied bombing sapped the morale of the German people. Instead,

Germans, whether pro-Nazi or anti-Nazi, fought on stubbornly, often driven simply by a desire to live. Nor did the bombing destroy Germany's industrial capacity. The Allied Strategic Bombing survey revealed that the production of war materials actually increased between 1942 and 1944. Even in 1944 and 1945, Allied raids cut German armaments production by only 7 percent. Nevertheless, the widespread destruction of transportation systems and fuel supplies made it extremely difficult for the new materials to reach the German military.

**The Bombing of Japan: The Atomic Bomb** In Japan, the bombing of civilians reached a new level with the use of the first atomic bomb. Japan was especially vulnerable to air raids because its air force had been virtually destroyed in the course of the war and its crowded cities were built of flimsy materials. Attacks on Japanese cities by the new American B-29 Superfortresses, the biggest bombers of the war, began in June 1944. By the summer of 1945, many of Japan's industries had been destroyed, along with one-fourth of its dwellings. After the Japanese government decreed the mobilization of all people between the ages of thirteen and sixty into the People's Volunteer Corps, President Truman and his advisers feared that Japanese fanaticism might mean a million American casualties. This concern led them to drop the atomic bomb on Hiroshima (August 6) and Nagasaki (August 9). The destruction was incredible. Of 76,000 buildings near the center of the explosion in Hiroshima, 70,000 were flattened, and 140,000 of the city's 400,000 inhabitants died by the end of 1945. By the end of 1950, another 50,000 had perished from the effects of radiation. The dropping of the first atomic bomb introduced the world to the nuclear age.

In the years following the end of the war, Truman's decision to approve the use of nuclear weapons to compel Japan to surrender was harshly criticized, not only for causing thousands of civilian casualties but also for introducing a frightening new weapon that could threaten the survival of the human race. Some have even charged that Truman's real purpose in ordering the nuclear strikes was to intimidate the Soviet Union. Defenders of the decision argue that the human costs of invading the Japanese home islands would have been infinitely higher had the bombs not been dropped, and the Soviet Union would have had ample time to consolidate its control over Manchuria.

## Aftermath: Toward the Cold War

The total victory of the Allies in World War II was not followed by a real peace but by the beginnings of a new conflict known as the **Cold War,** which dominated world politics until the end of the 1980s. The origins of the Cold War stemmed from the military, political, and ideological differences, especially between the Soviet Union and the United States, that became apparent at the Allied war conferences held in the last years of the war. Although Allied leaders were mostly preoccupied with how to end the war, they were also strongly motivated by differing, and often conflicting, visions of the postwar world.

Stalin, Roosevelt, and Churchill, the leaders of the Big Three of the Grand Alliance, met at Tehran, the capital of Iran, in November 1943 to decide the future course of the war. Their major tactical decision concerned the final assault on Germany. Stalin and Roosevelt argued successfully for an American-British invasion of the Continent through France, which they scheduled for the spring of 1944. The acceptance of this plan had important consequences. It meant that Soviet and British-American forces would meet in defeated Germany along a north-south dividing line and that eastern Europe would most likely be liberated by Soviet forces. The Allies also agreed to a partition of postwar Germany until denazification could take place.

### The Yalta Conference

By the time of the conference at Yalta in southern Russia in February 1945, the defeat of Germany was a foregone conclusion. The Western powers, which had earlier believed that the Soviets were in a weak position, now faced the reality of eleven million Red Army soldiers taking possession of eastern and central Europe. Like Churchill, Stalin was still operating under the notion of spheres of influence. He was deeply suspicious of the Western powers and desired a buffer to protect the Soviet Union from possible future Western aggression. At the same time, however, Stalin was eager to obtain economically important resources and strategic military positions. Roosevelt by this time was moving away from the notion of spheres of influence toward the more Wilsonian ideal of self-determination. He called for "the end of the system of unilateral action, exclusive alliances, and spheres of influence." The Grand Alliance approved a declaration on liberated Europe. This was a pledge to assist liberated Europe in the creation of "democratic institutions of their own choice." Liberated countries were to hold free elections to determine their political systems.

At Yalta, Roosevelt sought Soviet military help against Japan. The atomic bomb was not yet assured, and American military planners feared the possibility of heavy losses in amphibious assaults on the Japanese home islands. Roosevelt therefore agreed to Stalin's price for military assistance against Japan: possession of Sakhalin and the Kurile Islands, as well as two warm-water ports and railroad rights in Manchuria.

The creation of the United Nations was a major American concern at Yalta. Roosevelt hoped to ensure the participation of the Big Three powers in a postwar international organization before difficult issues divided them into hostile camps. After a number of compromises, both Churchill and Stalin accepted Roosevelt's plans for a United Nations organization and set the first meeting for San Francisco in April 1945.

The issues of Germany and eastern Europe were treated less decisively. The Big Three reaffirmed that Germany must surrender unconditionally and created four occupation zones (see Map 24.3). German reparations were set at $20 billion. A compromise was also worked out in regard to Poland. Stalin agreed to free elections in the future to determine a new government. But the issue of free elections in eastern Europe caused a serious rift between the Soviets and the Americans. The principle was that eastern European governments would be freely elected, but they were also supposed to be pro-Soviet. As Churchill expressed it, "The Poles will have their future in their own hands, with the single limitation that they must honestly follow in harmony with their allies, a policy friendly to Russia."[16] This attempt to reconcile two irreconcilable goals was doomed to failure, as soon became evident at the next conference of the Big Three powers.

## The Potsdam Conference

Even before the conference at Potsdam took place in July 1945, Western relations with the Soviets were deteriorating rapidly. The Grand Alliance had been a collaboration of necessity in which ideological incompatibility had been subordinated to the pragmatic concerns of the war. The Allies' only common aim was the defeat of Nazism. Once this aim had been accomplished, the many differences that antagonized East-West relations came to the surface.

The Potsdam conference of July 1945 consequently began under a cloud of mistrust. Roosevelt had died on April 12 and had been succeeded as president by Harry Truman. During the conference, Truman received word that the atomic bomb had been successfully tested. Some historians have argued that this knowledge resulted in Truman's stiffened resolve against the Soviets. Whatever the reasons, there was a new coolness in the relations between the Soviets and Americans. At Potsdam, Truman demanded free elections throughout eastern Europe. Stalin responded, "A freely elected government in any of these east European countries would be anti-Soviet, and that we cannot allow."[17] After a bitterly fought and devastating war, Stalin sought absolute military security. To him, it could be gained only by the presence of Communist states in eastern Europe. Free elections might result in governments hostile to the Soviets. By the middle of 1945, only an invasion by Western forces could undo developments in eastern Europe, and after the world's most destructive conflict had ended, few people favored such a policy.

As the war slowly receded into the past, the reality of conflicting ideologies had reappeared. Many in the West interpreted Soviet policy as part of a worldwide Communist conspiracy. The Soviets viewed Western, especially American, policy as nothing less than global capitalist expansionism or, in Leninist terms, economic imperialism. Vyacheslav Molotov, the Russian foreign minister, referred to the Americans as "insatiable imperialists" and "war-mongering groups of adventurers."[18] In

Art Archive, London

**The Victorious Allied Leaders at Yalta.** Even before World War II ended, the leaders of the Big Three of the Grand Alliance—Churchill, Roosevelt, and Stalin (shown from left to right)—met in wartime conferences to plan the final assault on Germany and negotiate the outlines of the postwar settlement. At the Yalta meeting (February 5–11, 1945), the three leaders concentrated on postwar issues. The American president, who died two months later, appeared timeworn at Yalta.

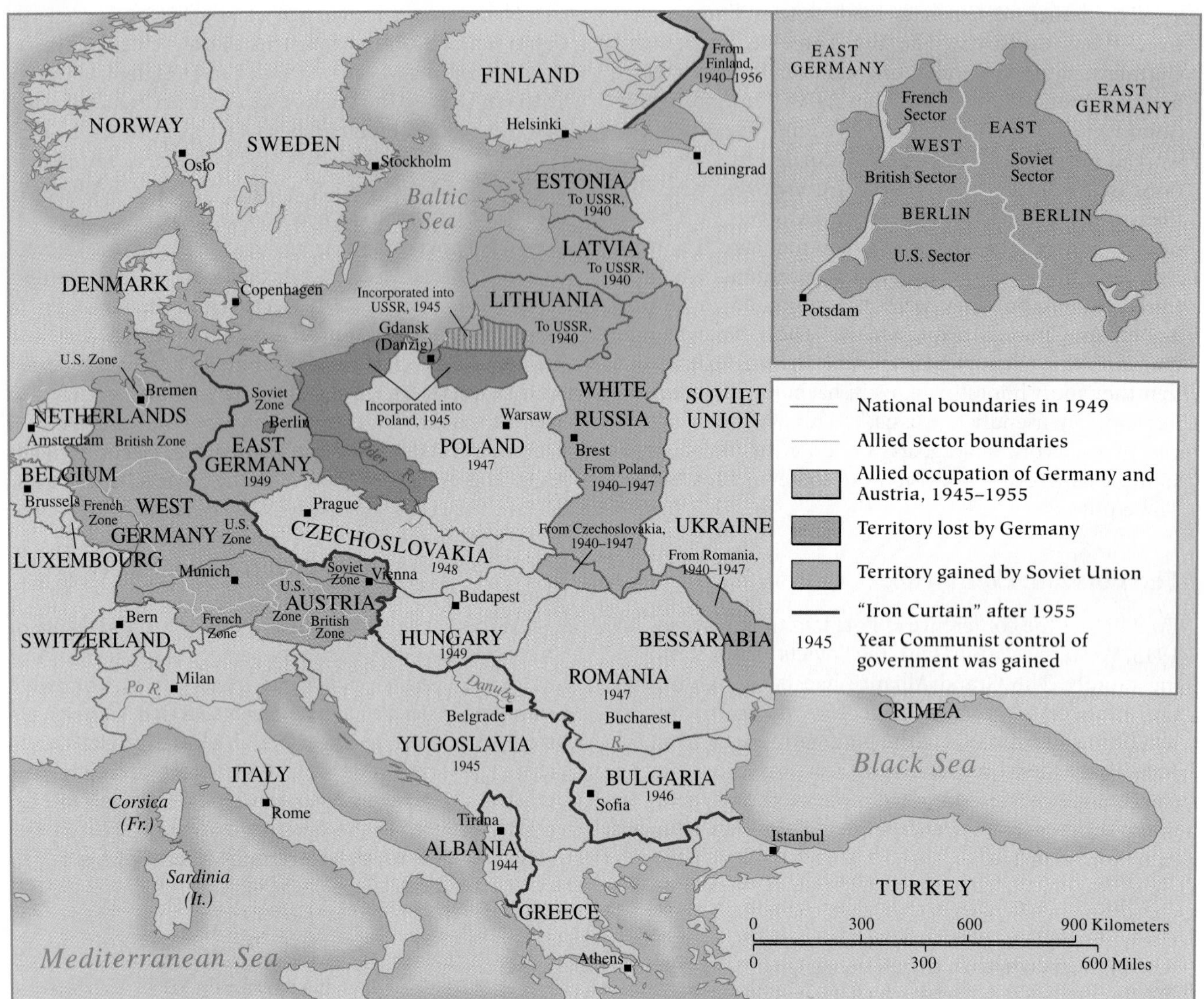


**MAP 24.3 Territorial Changes in Europe After World War II.** In the last months of World War II, the Red Army occupied much of eastern Europe. Stalin sought pro-Soviet satellite states in the region as a buffer against future invasions from western Europe, whereas Britain and the United States wanted democratically elected governments. Soviet military control of the territory settled the question.
? Which country gained the greatest territory at the expense of Germany? **View an animated version of this map or related maps at** http://history.wadsworth.com/duikerspielvogel05/

March 1946, in a speech to an American audience, the former British prime minister Winston Churchill declared that "an iron curtain" had "descended across the continent," dividing Europe into two hostile camps. Stalin branded Churchill's speech a "call to war with the Soviet Union." Only months after the world's most devastating conflict had ended, the world seemed once again to be bitterly divided.

## CONCLUSION

**WORLD WAR II** was the most devastating total war in human history. Germany, Italy, and Japan had been utterly defeated. Perhaps as many as fifty million people—soldiers and civilians—had been killed in six years. In Asia and Europe, cities had been reduced to rubble, and millions of people faced starvation as once fertile lands stood neglected or wasted. Untold millions of people had become refugees.

What were the underlying causes of the war? One direct cause of the conflict was the effort by two rising capitalist powers, Germany and Japan, to make up for their relatively late arrival on the scene to carve out their own global empires. Key elements in both countries had resented the agreements reached after the end of World War I that divided the world in a manner favorable to their rivals and hoped to overturn them at the earliest opportunity. Neither Germany nor Japan possessed a strong tradition of political pluralism; to the contrary, in both countries, the legacy of a feudal past marked by a strong military tradition still wielded a strong influence over the political system and the mind-set of the entire population. It is no surprise that under the impact of the Great Depression, which had severe effects in both countries, fragile democratic institutions were soon overwhelmed by militant forces determined to enhance national wealth and power.

Whatever the causes of World War II, the consequences were soon to be evident. European hegemony over the world was at an end, and two new superpowers had emerged to take its place. Even before the last battles had been fought, the United States and the Soviet Union had arrived at different visions of the postwar world. No sooner had the war ended than their differences created a new and potentially even more devastating conflict known as the Cold War. And even though Europeans seemed merely pawns in the struggle between the two superpowers, they managed to stage a remarkable recovery of their own civilization. In Asia, defeated Japan made a miraculous economic recovery, and an era of European domination finally came to an end.

**TIMELINE**

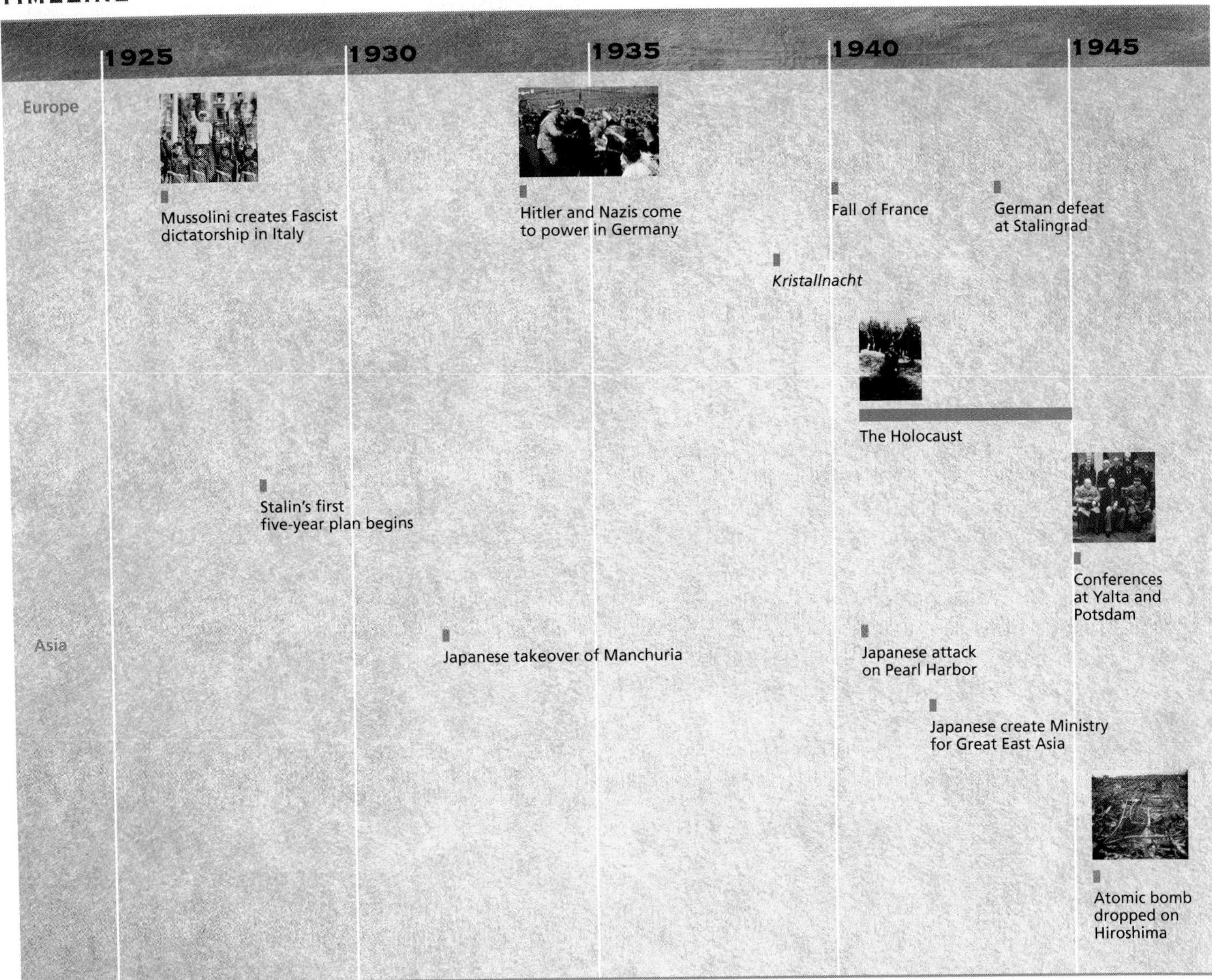

## CHAPTER NOTES

1. B. Mussolini, "The Doctrine of Fascism," in A. Lyttleton, ed., *Italian Fascisms from Pareto to Gentile* (London, 1973), p. 42.
2. Quoted in A. De Grand, "Women Under Italian Fascism," "*Historical Journal* 19 (1976): 958–959.
3. Quoted in J. J. Spielvogel, *Hitler and Nazi Germary: A History,* 5th ed. (Upper Saddle River, N.J., 2005), p. 60.
4. Quoted in J. Fest, *Hitler,* trans. R. Winston and C. Winston (New York, 1974), p. 418.
5. A. Hitler, *Mein Kampf,* trans. R. Manheim (Boston, 1971), p. 654.
6. *Documents on German Foreign Policy* (London, 1956), Series D, vol. 7, p. 204.
7. Memorandum by John Van Antwerp MacMurray, quoted in A. Waldron, *How the Peace Was Lost: The 1935 Memorandum* (Stanford, Calif., 1992), p. 5.
8. Quoted in A. Speer, *Spandau,* trans. R. Winston and C. Winston (New York, 1976), p. 50.
9. *Nazi Conspiracy and Aggression* (Washington, D.C., 1946), vol. 6, p. 262.
10. International Military Tribunal, *Trial of the Major War Criminals* (Nuremberg, 1947–1949), vol. 22, p. 480.
11. Quoted in R. Hilberg, *The Destruction of the European Jews,* rev. ed. (New York, 1985), vol. 1, pp. 332–333.
12. *Nazi Conspiracy and Aggression,* vol. 6, p. 789.
13. Quoted in J. Campbell, *The Experience of World War II* (New York, 1989), p. 170.
14. Quoted in C. Koonz, "Mothers in the Fatherland: Women in Nazi Germany," in R. Bridenthal and C. Koonz, eds., *Becoming Visible: Women in European History* (Boston, 1977), p. 466.
15. Quoted in Campbell, *Experience of World War II,* p. 143.
16. Quoted in N. Graebner, *Cold War Diplomacy, 1945–1960* (Princeton, N.J., 1962), p. 117.
17. Ibid.
18. Quoted in W. Loth, *The Division of the World, 1941–1955* (New York, 1988), p. 81.

## SUGGESTED READING

For a general study of fascism, see **S. G. Payne, *A History of Fascism*** (Madison, Wis., 1996), and **R. O. Paxton, *The Anatomy of Fascism*** (New York, 2004). The best biography of Mussolini is **R. J. B. Bosworth, *Mussolini*** (London, 2002). Two brief but excellent surveys of Fascist Italy are **A. Cassels, *Fascist Italy,*** 2nd ed. (Arlington Heights, Ill., 1985), and **J. Whittam, *Fascist Italy*** (New York, 1995).

Two brief but sound surveys of Nazi Germany are **J. J. Spielvogel, *Hitler and Nazi Germany: A History,*** 5th ed. (Upper Saddle River, N.J., 2005), and **J. Dülffer, *Nazi Germany, 1933–1945*** (New York, 1996). The best biographies of Hitler are **A. Bullock, *Hitler: A Study in Tyranny*** (New York, 1964); **J. Fest, *Hitler,*** trans. **R. Winston** and **C. Winston** (New York, 1974); and **I. Kershaw, *Hitler, 1889–1936: Hubris*** (New York, 1999), and ***Hitler: Nemesis*** (New York, 2000). Two works that examine the enormous literature on Hitler are **J. Lukacs, *The Hitler of History*** (New York, 1997), and **R. Rosenbaum, *Explaining Hitler*** (New York, 1998). On the rise of the Nazis to power, see **R. J. Evans *The Coming of the Third Reich*** (New York, 2004), the first volume in a projected three-volume history of Nazi Germany. Basic studies of the SS include **R. Koehl, *The Black Corps: The Structure and Power Struggles of the Nazi SS*** (Madison, Wis., 1983), and **H. Krausnick** and **M. Broszat, *Anatomy of the SS State*** (London, 1970). On women, see **C. Koonz, *Mothers in the Fatherland: Women, the Family, and Nazi Politics*** (New York, 1987). The Hitler Youth is examined in **M. Kater, *The Hitler Youth*** (New York, 2004). On Nazi anti-Jewish policies between 1933 and 1939, see **S. Friedländer, *Nazi Germany and the Jews,*** vol. 1, ***The Years of Persecution, 1933–1939*** (New York, 1997).

The collectivization of agriculture in the Soviet Union is examined in **S. Fitzpatrick, *Stalin's Peasants: Resistance and Survival in the Russian Village After Collectivization*** (New York, 1995). Industrialization is covered in **H. Kuromiya, *Stalin's Industrial Revolution: Politics and Workers, 1928–1932*** (New York, 1988). Stalin's purges are examined in **R. Conquest, *The Great Terror: A Reassessment*** (New York, 1990). On Stalin himself, see **R. Service, *Stalin: A Biography*** (Cambridge, Mass., 2004), and **R. W. Thurston, *Life and Terror in Stalin's Russia, 1934–1941*** (New Haven, Conn., 1996).

A basic study of Germany's foreign policy from 1933 to 1939 can be found in **G. Weinberg, *The Foreign Policy of Hitler's Germany: Diplomatic Revolution in Europe, 1933–36*** (Chicago, 1970), and ***The Foreign Policy of Hitler's Germany: Starting World War II, 1937–1939*** (Chicago, 1980). Japan's march to war is examined in **A. Iriye, *The Origins of the Second World War in Asia and the Pacific*** (London, 1987).

General works on World War II include **M. K. Dziewanowski, *War at Any Price: World War II in Europe, 1939–1945,*** 2d ed. (Englewood Cliffs, N.J., 1991); the comprehensive study by **G. Weinberg, *A World at Arms: A Global History of World War II*** (Cambridge, 1994); and **J. Campbell, *The Experience of World War II*** (New York, 1989). On Hitler as a military leader, see **R. Lewin, *Hitler's Mistakes*** (New York, 1986). On battles, see **J. Keegan, *The Second World War*** (New York, 1990).

Excellent studies of the Holocaust include **R. Hilberg, *The Destruction of the European Jews,*** rev. ed., 3 vols. (New York, 1985), and **L. Yahil, *The Holocaust*** (New York, 1990). For brief studies, see **J. Fischel, *The Holocaust*** (Westport, Conn., 1998), and **D. Dwork** and **R. J. van Pelt, *Holocaust: A History*** (New York, 2002). A good overview of the scholarship on the Holocaust is **M. Marrus, *The Holocaust in History*** (New York, 1987). Other Nazi atrocities are examined is **B. Wytwycky, *The Other Holocaust*** (Washington, D.C., 1980).

General studies on the impact of total war include **J. Costello, *Love, Sex and War: Changing Values, 1939–1945*** (London, 1985); **P. Summerfield, *Women Workers in the Second World War: Production and Patriarchy in Conflict*** (London, 1984); and **M. R. Marrus, *The Unwanted: European Refugees in the Twentieth Century*** (New York, 1985). On the home front in Germany, see **E. R. Beck, *Under the Bombs: The German Home Front, 1942–1945*** (Lexington, Ky., 1986), and **M. Kitchen, *Nazi Germany at War*** (New York, 1995). The Soviet Union during the war is examined in **M. Harrison, *Soviet Planning in Peace and War, 1938–1945*** (Cambridge, 1985). On the American home front, see the collection of essays in **K. P. O'Brien** and **L. H. Parsons, *The Home-Front War: World War II and American Society*** (Westport, Conn., 1995). The Japanese home front is examined in **T. R. H. Havens, *The Valley of Darkness: The Japanese People and World War Two*** (New York, 1978).

On the destruction of Germany by bombing raids, see **H. Rumpf, *The Bombing of Germany*** (London, 1963). The German bombing of Britain is covered in **T. Harrisson, *Living Through the Blitz*** (London, 1985). On Hiroshima, see **A. Chisholm, *Faces of Hiroshima*** (London, 1985).

On the emergence of the Cold War, see **W. Loth, *The Division of the World, 1941–1955*** (New York, 1988). On the wartime summit conferences, see **H. Feis, *Churchill, Roosevelt, Stalin: The War They Waged and the Peace They Sought,*** 2d ed. (Princeton, N.J., 1967), and **D. Clemens, *Yalta*** (New York, 1970).

## HistoryNow™

**Enter *HistoryNow* using the access card that is available with this text. *HistoryNow* will assist you in understanding the content in this chapter with lesson plans generated for your needs, as well as provide you with a connection to the *Wadsworth World History Resource Center* (see description below for details).**

### WORLD HISTORY RESOURCE CENTER

**Enter the Resource Center using either your *HistoryNow* access card or your standalone access card for the *Wadsworth World History Resource Center.* Organized by topic, this website includes quizzes; images; over 350 primary source documents; interactive simulations; maps and timelines; movie explorations; and a wealth of other resources. You can read the following documents, and many more, at http://history.wadsworth.com/rc/world**

Franklin D. Roosevelt, "Four Freedoms" Speech

Wannsee Conference, Minutes of Discussion on the "Final Solution"

Visit the *World History* Companion Website for chapter quizzes and more.

http://history.wadsworth.com/duikerspielvogel05/

# Looking Ahead

How are we to draw up a final balance sheet on the era of Western imperialism? To its defenders, it was a necessary stage in the evolution of the human race, a flawed but essentially humanitarian effort to provide the backward peoples of Africa and Asia with a boost up the ladder of evolution. To its critics, it was a tragedy of major proportions. The insatiable drive of the advanced economic powers for access to raw materials and markets resulted in the widespread destruction of traditional cultures and created an exploitative environment that transformed the vast majority of colonial peoples into a permanent underclass while restricting the benefits of modern technology to a privileged few. Sophisticated, age-old societies that should have been left to respond to the technological revolution in their own way were subjected to foreign rule and squeezed dry of precious

**TIMELINE**

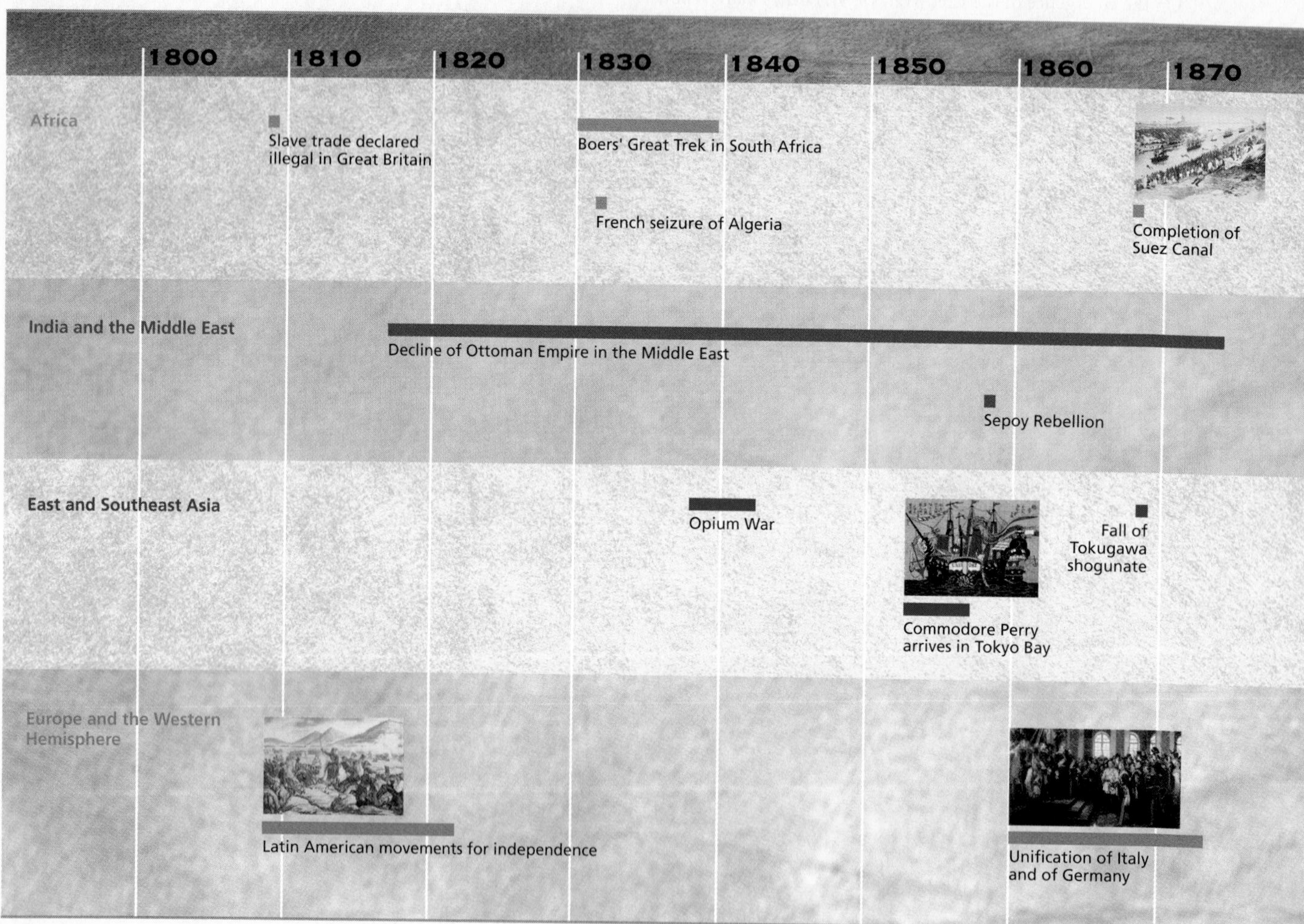

national resources under the guise of the "civilizing mission."

In this debate, the critics surely have the best argument. All in all, the colonial experience was brutal, and its benefits accrued almost entirely to citizens of the ruling power. The argument that the Western societies had a "white man's burden" to civilize the world was all too often a hypocritical gesture to salve the guilty feelings of those who recognized imperialism for what it was—a savage act of rape.

But although the experience was a painful one, human societies were able to survive it and earn a second chance to make better use of the stunning promise of the industrial era. How they have fared in that effort will be the subject of the final section of this book.

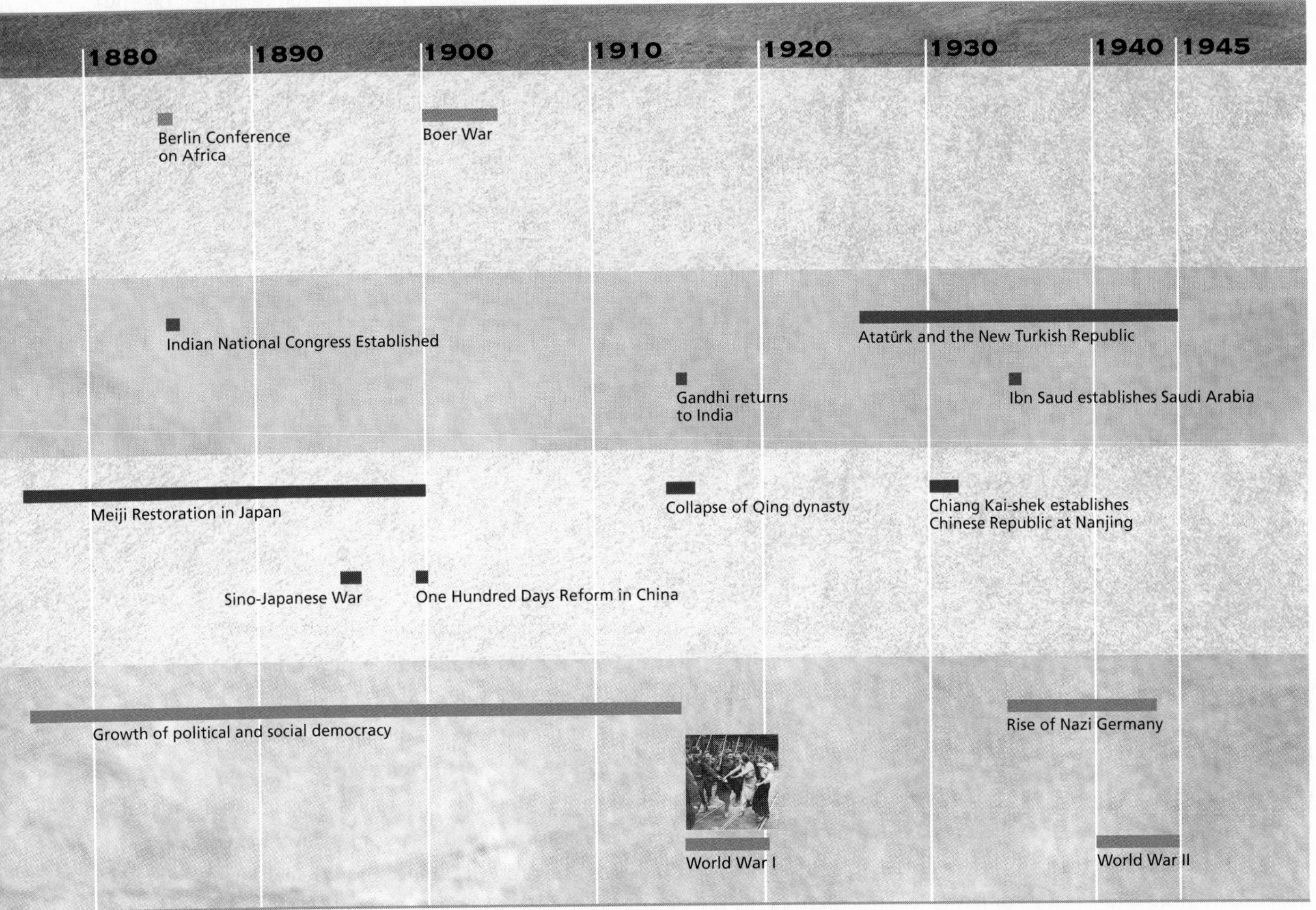

PART

# V

# TOWARD A GLOBAL CIVILIZATION? THE WORLD SINCE 1945



AS WORLD WAR II came to an end, the survivors of that bloody struggle could afford to face the future with a cautious optimism. Europeans might hope that the bitter rivalry that had marked relations among the Western powers would finally be put to an end and that the wartime alliance of the United States, Great Britain, and the Soviet Union could be maintained into the postwar era.

More than sixty years later, these hopes have been only partly realized. In the decades following the war, the Western capitalist nations managed to recover from the economic depression that had led into World War II and advanced to a level of economic prosperity never seen before. The bloody conflicts that had erupted among European nations during the first half of the twentieth century came to an end, and Germany and Japan were fully integrated into the world community.

At the same time, the prospects for a stable, peaceful world and an end to balance-of-power politics were hampered by the emergence of the grueling and sometimes tense ideological struggle between the socialist and capitalist camps, a competition headed by the only remaining great powers, the Soviet Union and the United States.

In the shadow of this rivalry, the Western European states made a remarkable economic recovery and reached untold levels of prosperity. In Eastern Europe, Soviet domination, both politically and economically, seemed so complete that many doubted it could ever be undone. But communism had never developed deep roots in Eastern Europe, and when, in the late 1980s, Soviet leader Mikhail Gorbachev indicated that his government would no longer pursue military intervention, Eastern European states acted quickly to establish their freedom and adopt new economic structures based on Western models.

Outside the West, the peoples of Africa and Asia had their own reasons for optimism as World War II came to a close. In the Atlantic Charter, Franklin Roosevelt and Winston Churchill had set forth a joint declaration of their peace aims calling for the self-determination of all peoples and self-government and sovereign rights for all nations that had been deprived of them.

As it turned out, some colonial powers were reluctant to divest themselves of their colonies. Still, World War II had severely undermined the stability of the colonial order, and by the end of the 1940s, most colonies in Asia had received their independence. Africa followed a decade or two later.

Broadly speaking, the leaders of these newly liberated countries set forth three goals at the outset of independence. They wanted to throw off the shackles of Western economic domination and ensure material prosperity for all of their citizens. They wanted to introduce new political institutions that would enhance the right of self-determination of their peoples. And they wanted to develop a sense of common nationhood within the population and establish secure territorial boundaries. Most opted to follow a capitalist or a moderately socialist path toward economic development. In a few cases—most notably in China and Vietnam—revolutionary leaders opted for the communist mode of development.

Regardless of the path chosen, most of the results were often disappointing. Much of Africa and Asia remained economically dependent on the advanced industrial nations Some societies faced severe problems of urban and rural poverty.

What had happened to tarnish the bright dream of economic affluence? During the late 1950s and early 1960s, one school of thought was dominant among scholars and gov-

Courtesy of William J. Duiker

ernment officials in the United States. Known as modernization theory, this school took the view that the problems faced by the newly independent countries were a consequence of the difficult transition from a traditional to a modern society. Modernization theorists were convinced that agrarian countries were destined to follow the path of the West toward the creation of modern industrial societies but would need time as well as substantial amounts of economic and technological assistance from the West to complete the journey.

Eventually, modernization theory began to come under attack from a new generation of younger scholars. In their view, the responsibility for continued economic underdevelopment in the developing world lay not with the countries themselves but with their continued domination by the ex-colonial powers. In this view, known as dependency theory, the countries of Asia, Africa, and Latin America were the victims of the international marketplace, which charged high prices for the manufactured goods of the West while dooming preindustrial countries to low prices for their own raw material exports. Efforts by such countries to build up their own industrial sectors and move into the stage of self-sustaining growth were hampered by foreign control—through European- and American-owned corporations—over many of their resources. To end this "neocolonial" relationship, the dependency theory advocates argued, developing societies should reduce their economic ties with the West and practice a policy of economic self-reliance, thereby taking control over their own destinies.

Leaders of African and Asian countries also encountered problems creating new political cultures responsive to the needs of their citizens. At first, most accepted the concept of democracy as the defining theme of that culture. Within a decade, however, democratic systems throughout the developing world were replaced by military dictatorships or one-party governments that redefined the concept of democracy to fit their own preferences. It was clear that the difficulties in building democratic political institutions in developing societies had been underestimated.

The problem of establishing a common national identity has in some ways been the most daunting of all the challenges facing the new nations of Asia and Africa. Many of these new states were a composite of a wide variety of ethnic, religious, and linguistic groups who found it difficult to agree on common symbols of nationalism. Problems of establishing an official language and delineating territorial boundaries left over from the colonial era created difficulties in many countries. Internal conflicts spawned by deep-rooted historical and ethnic hatreds have proliferated throughout the world, leading to a vast new movement of people across state boundaries equal to any that has occurred since the great population migrations of the thirteenth and fourteenth centuries.

The introduction of Western cultural values and customs has also had a destabilizing effect in many areas. Although such ideas are welcomed by some groups, they are firmly resisted by others. Where Western influence has the effect of undermining traditional customs and religious beliefs, it often provokes violent hostility and sparks tension and even conflict within individual societies. Much of the anger recently directed at the United States in Muslim countries has undoubtedly been generated by such feelings.

Nonetheless, social and political attitudes are changing rapidly in many Asian and African countries as new economic circumstances have led to a more secular worldview, a decline in traditional hierarchical relations, and a more open attitude toward sexual practices. In part, these changes have been a consequence of the influence of Western music, movies, and television. But they are also a product of the growth of an affluent middle class in many societies of Asia and Africa.

Today we live not only in a world economy but in a world society, where a revolution in the Middle East can cause a rise in the price of oil in the United States and a change in social behavior in Malaysia and Indonesia, where the collapse of an empire in Asia can send shock waves as far as Hanoi and Havana, and where a terrorist attack in New York City or London can disrupt financial markets around the world. ◆

CHAPTER

# 25

# IN THE GRIP OF THE COLD WAR: THE BREAKDOWN OF THE YALTA SYSTEM

Art Archive, London

Churchill, Roosevelt, and Stalin at Yalta

## CHAPTER OUTLINE AND FOCUS QUESTIONS

### The Collapse of the Grand Alliance

- Why were the United States and the Soviet Union suspicious of each other after World War II, and what events between 1945 and 1949 heightened the tensions between the two nations?

### Cold War in Asia

- How and why did Mao Zedong and the Communists come to power in China, and what were the Cold War implications of their triumph?

### From Confrontation to Coexistence

- What events led to the era of coexistence in the 1960s, and to what degree did each side contribute to the reduction in international tensions?

### An Era of Equivalence

- Why did the Cold War briefly flare up again in the 1980s, and why did it come to a definitive end at the end of the decade?

### CRITICAL THINKING

- How have historians answered the question of whether the United States or the Soviet Union bears the primary responsibility for the Cold War, and what evidence can be presented on each side of the issue?

"OUR MEETING HERE in the Crimea has reaffirmed our common determination to maintain and strengthen in the peace to come that unity of purpose and of action which has made victory possible and certain for the United Nations in this war. We believe that this is a sacred obligation which our Governments owe to our peoples and to all the peoples of the world."[1]

With these ringing words, drafted at the Yalta Conference in February 1945, U.S. President Franklin D. Roosevelt, Soviet leader Joseph Stalin, and British Prime Minister Winston Churchill affirmed their common hope that the Grand Alliance that had been victorious in World War II could be sustained into the postwar era. Only through continuing and growing cooperation and understanding among the three Allies, the statement asserted, could a secure and lasting peace be realized that, in the words of the Atlantic Charter, would "afford assurance that all the men in all the lands may live out their lives in freedom from fear and want."

Roosevelt hoped that the decisions reached at Yalta would provide the basis for a stable peace in the postwar era. Allied occupation forces–American, British, and French in the west and Soviet in the east–were to bring about the end of Axis administration and to organize the free election of democratic governments throughout Europe. To foster mutual trust and an end to the suspicions that had marked relations between the capitalist world and the Soviet Union prior to the war, Roosevelt tried to reassure Stalin that Moscow's legitimate territorial aspirations and genuine security needs would be adequately met in a durable peace settlement.

However, this was not to be. Within months after the German surrender, the mutual trust among the Allies–if it had ever truly existed–rapidly disintegrated, and the dream of a stable peace was replaced by the specter of a potential nuclear holocaust. The United Nations, envisioned by its founders as a mechanism for adjudicating international disputes, became mired in partisan bickering. As the Cold War between Moscow and Washington intensified, Europe was divided into two armed camps, while the two superpowers, glaring at each other across a deep ideological divide, held the survival of the entire world in their hands. ◇

## The Collapse of the Grand Alliance

When World War II finally ended, Soviet military forces occupied all of Eastern Europe and the Balkans (except Greece, Albania, and Yugoslavia), while U.S. and other Allied forces secured the western part of the Continent. Roosevelt had assumed that free elections, administered promptly by "democratic and peace-loving forces," would lead to democratic governments responsive to the local population. But it soon became clear that the Soviet Union interpreted the Yalta agreement differently. When Soviet occupation authorities began forming a new Polish government, Stalin refused to accept the Polish government-in-exile—headquartered in London during the war and composed primarily of landed aristocrats who harbored a deep distrust of the Soviet Union—and instead set up a government composed of Communists who had spent the war in Moscow. Roosevelt complained to Stalin but eventually agreed to a compromise whereby two members of the London government were included in the new Communist regime. A week later, Roosevelt was dead of a cerebral hemorrhage, emboldening Stalin to do pretty much as he pleased.

### Soviet Domination of Eastern Europe

Similar developments took place in all of the states occupied by Soviet troops. Coalitions of all political parties (except fascist or right-wing parties) were formed to run the government, but within a year or two, the Communist Party in each coalition had assumed the lion's share of power. It was then a short step to the establishment of one-party Communist governments. Between 1945 and 1947, Communist governments became firmly entrenched in East Germany, Bulgaria, Romania, Poland, and Hungary. In Czechoslovakia, with its strong tradition of democratic institutions, the Communists did not achieve their goals until 1948. After the Czech elections of 1946, the Communist Party shared control of the government with the non-Communist parties. When it appeared that the latter might win new elections early in 1948, the Communists seized control of the government on February 25. All other parties were dissolved, and the Communist leader Klement Gottwald became the new president of Czechoslovakia.

**Eastern Europe in 1946**

Yugoslavia was a notable exception to the pattern of Soviet dominance in Eastern Europe. The Communist Party there had led resistance to the Nazis during the war and easily assumed power when the war ended. Josip Broz, known as Tito (1892–1980), the leader of the Communist resistance movement, appeared to be a loyal Stalinist. After the war, however, he moved to establish an independent Communist state. Stalin hoped to take control of Yugoslavia, but Tito refused to capitulate to Stalin's demands and gained the support of the people (and some sympathy in the West) by portraying the struggle as one of Yugoslav national freedom. In 1958, the Yugoslav party congress asserted that Yugoslav Communists did not see themselves as deviating from communism, only from Stalinism. They considered their more decentralized system, in which workers managed themselves and local communes exercised some political power, closer to the Marxist-Leninist ideal.

To Stalin (who had once boasted, "I will shake my little finger, and there will be no more Tito"), the creation of pliant pro-Soviet regimes throughout Eastern Europe may simply have represented his interpretation of the Yalta peace agreement and a reward for sacrifices suffered during the war, satisfying Moscow's aspirations for a buffer zone against the capitalist West. If the Soviet leader had any intention of promoting future Communist revolutions in Western Europe—and there is some indication that he did—such developments would have to await the appearance of a new capitalist crisis a decade or more into the future. As Stalin undoubtedly recalled, Lenin had always maintained that revolutions come in waves.

### Descent of the Iron Curtain

To the United States, however, the Soviet takeover of Eastern Europe represented an ominous development that threatened Roosevelt's vision of a durable peace. Public suspicion of Soviet intentions grew rapidly, especially among the millions of Americans

© CORBIS

**A Call to Arms.** In March 1946, former British prime minister Winston Churchill gave a speech before a college audience in Fulton, Missouri, that electrified the world. Soviet occupation of the countries of Eastern Europe, he declared, had divided the Continent into two conflicting halves, separated by an "iron curtain." Churchill's speech has often been described as the opening salvo in the Cold War, and Moscow responded by labeling the speech "reactionary" and "unconvincing." In the photo, Churchill, with President Harry Truman behind him, prepares to give his address.

who still had relatives living in Eastern Europe. Winston Churchill was quick to put such fears into words. In a highly publicized speech at Westminster College in Fulton, Missouri, in March 1946, the former British prime minister declared that an "iron curtain" had "descended across the Continent," dividing Germany and Europe itself into two hostile camps. Stalin responded by branding Churchill's speech a "call to war with the Soviet Union." But he need not have worried. Although public opinion in the United States placed increasing pressure on Roosevelt's successor, Harry S. Truman (1884–1972), to devise an effective strategy to counter Soviet advances abroad, the American people were in no mood for another war.

## The Truman Doctrine

A civil war in Greece created another potential arena for confrontation between the superpowers and an opportunity for the Truman administration to take a stand. Communist guerrilla forces supported by Tito's Yugoslavia had taken up arms against the pro-Western government in Athens. Great Britain had initially assumed primary responsibility for promoting postwar reconstruction in the eastern Mediterranean, but in 1947, continuing economic problems caused the British to withdraw from the active role they had been playing in both Greece and Turkey. President Truman, alarmed by British weakness and the possibility of Soviet expansion into the eastern Mediterranean, responded with the Truman Doctrine (see the box on p. 725), which said in essence that the United States would provide money to countries that claimed they were threatened by communist expansion. If the Soviets were not stopped in Greece, the Truman argument ran, then the United States would have to face the spread of communism throughout the free world. As Dean Acheson, the U.S. secretary of state, explained, "Like apples in a barrel infected by disease, the corruption of Greece would infect Iran and all the East . . . likewise Africa . . . Italy . . . France. . . . Not since Rome and Carthage has there been such a polarization of power on this earth."[2]

The U.S. suspicion that Moscow was actively supporting the insurgent movement in Greece turned out to be unfounded. Stalin was apparently unhappy with Tito's promoting the conflict, not only because he suspected that the latter was attempting to create his own sphere of influence in the Balkans but also because it risked provoking a direct confrontation between the United States and the Soviet Union.

## The Marshall Plan

The proclamation of the Truman Doctrine was followed in June 1947 by the European Recovery Program, better known as the Marshall Plan, which provided $13 billion for the economic recovery of war-torn Europe. Underlying the program was the belief that communist aggression fed off economic turmoil. General George C. Marshall noted in a speech at Harvard University, "Our policy is not directed against any country or doctrine but against hunger, poverty, desperation, and chaos."[3]

From the Soviet perspective, the Marshall Plan was capitalist imperialism, a thinly veiled attempt to buy the support of the smaller European countries "in return for the relinquishing . . . of their economic and later also their political independence."[4] A Soviet spokesperson described the United States as the "main force in the imperialist camp," whose ultimate goal was "the strengthening of imperialism, preparation for a new imperialist war, a

## THE TRUMAN DOCTRINE

By 1947, the battle lines in the Cold War had been clearly drawn. This excerpt is taken from a speech by President Harry Truman to the U.S. Congress in which he justified his request for aid to Greece and Turkey. Truman expressed the urgent need to contain the expansion of communism. Compare this statement with that of Soviet leader Leonid Brezhnev cited on p. 744.

*How did President Truman defend his request for aid to Greece and Turkey? What role did this decision play in intensifying the Cold War?*

### Truman's Speech to Congress, March 12, 1947

The peoples of a number of countries of the world have recently had totalitarian regimes forced upon them against their will. The Government of the United States has made frequent protests against coercion and intimidation, in violation of the Yalta agreement, in Poland, Rumania, and Bulgaria. I must also state that in a number of other countries there have been similar developments.

At the present moment in world history nearly every nation must choose between alternative ways of life. The choice is too often not a free one.

One way of life is based upon the will of the majority, and is distinguished by free institutions, representative government, free elections, guarantees of individual liberty, freedom of speech and religion, and freedom from political oppression.

The second way of life is based upon the will of a minority forcibly imposed upon the majority. It relies upon terror and oppression, a controlled press and radio, fixed elections, and the suppression of personal freedoms.

I believe that it must be the policy of the United States to support free peoples who are resisting attempted subjugation by armed minorities or by outside pressures.

I believe that we must assist free people to work out their own destinies in their own way.

I believe that our help should be primarily through economic and financial aid, which is essential to economic stability and orderly political processes. . . . I therefore ask the Congress for assistance to Greece and Turkey in the amount of $400,000,000.

**HistoryNow™** To read a full version of the Truman Doctrine, enter the *HistoryNow* documents area using the access card that is available for *World History.*

struggle against socialism and democracy, and the support of reactionary and antidemocratic, pro-fascist regimes and movements." Although the Marshall Plan was open to the Soviet Union and its Eastern European satellite states, they refused to participate. The Soviets were in no position to compete financially with the United States, however, and could do little to counter the Marshall Plan except tighten their control in Eastern Europe.

## Europe Divided

By 1947, the split in Europe between east and west had become a fact of life. At the end of World War II, the United States had favored a quick end to its commitments in Europe. But American fears of Soviet aims caused the United States to play an increasingly important role in European affairs. In an article in *Foreign Affairs* in July 1947, George Kennan, a well-known U.S. diplomat with much knowledge of Soviet affairs, advocated a policy of **containment** against further aggressive Soviet moves. Kennan favored the "adroit and vigilant application of counter-force at a series of constantly shifting geographical and political points, corresponding to the shifts and maneuvers of Soviet policy." When the Soviets blockaded Berlin in 1948, containment of the Soviet Union became formal U.S. policy.

**The Berlin Airlift** The fate of Germany had become a source of heated contention between East and West. Aside from **denazification** and the partitioning of Germany (and Berlin) into four occupied zones, the Allied powers had agreed on little with regard to the conquered nation. Even denazification proceeded differently in the various zones of occupation. The Americans and British proceeded methodically—the British had tried two million cases by 1948—while the Soviets (and French) went after major criminals and allowed lesser officials to go free. The Soviet Union, hardest hit by the war, took reparations from Germany by pillaging German industry. The technology-starved Soviets dismantled and removed to Russia 380 factories from the western zones of Berlin before transferring their control to the Western powers. By the summer of 1946, two hundred chemical, paper, and textile factories in the East German zone had likewise been shipped to the Soviet Union. At the same time, the

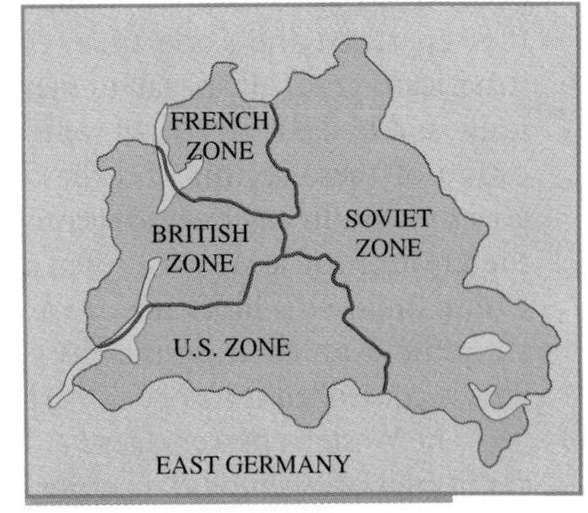

**Berlin at the Start of the Cold War**

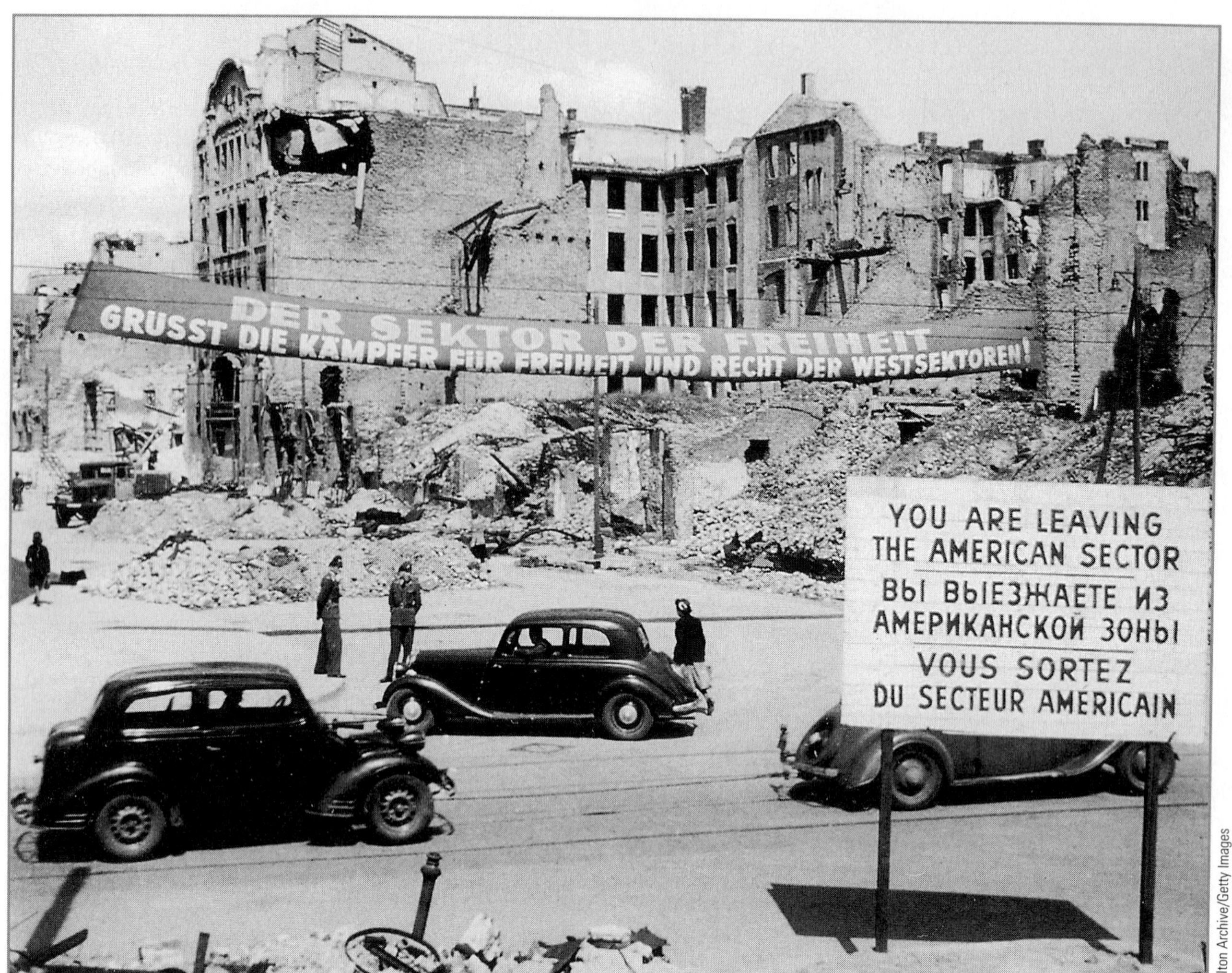



**A City Divided.** In 1948, U.S. planes airlifted supplies into Berlin to break the blockade that Soviet troops had imposed to isolate the city. Shown here is "Checkpoint Charlie," located at the boundary between the U.S. and Soviet zones of Berlin, just as Soviet roadblocks are about to be removed. The banner at the entrance to the Soviet sector reads, ironically, "The sector of freedom greets the fighters for freedom and right of the Western sectors."

German Communist Party was reestablished, under the control of Walter Ulbricht (1893–1973), and was soon in charge of the political reconstruction of the Soviet zone in eastern Germany.

Although the foreign ministers of the four occupying powers kept meeting in an attempt to arrive at a final peace treaty with Germany, they moved further and further apart. At the same time, the British, French, and Americans gradually began to merge their zones economically and by February 1948 were making plans for unification of these sectors and the formation of a national government. In an effort to secure all of Berlin and to halt the creation of a West German government, the Soviet Union imposed a blockade of West Berlin that prevented all traffic from entering the city's western zones through Soviet-controlled territory in East Germany.

The Western powers faced a dilemma.Direct military confrontation seemed dangerous, and no one wished to risk World War III. Therefore, an attempt to break through the blockade with tanks and trucks was ruled out. The solution was to deliver supplies for the city's inhabitants by plane. At its peak, the Berlin Airlift flew 13,000 tons of supplies daily into Berlin. The Soviets, also not wanting war, did not interfere and finally lifted the blockade in May 1949. The blockade of Berlin had severely increased tensions between the United States and the Soviet Union and brought the separation of Germany into two states. The Federal Republic of Germany was formally created from the three Western zones in September 1949, and a month later, the separate German Democratic Republic (GDR) was established in East Germany. Berlin remained a divided city and the source of much contention between East and West.

**Cold War Alliances** The search for security in the new world of the Cold War also led to the formation of military alliances. The North Atlantic Treaty Organization (NATO) was formed in April 1949 when Belgium,

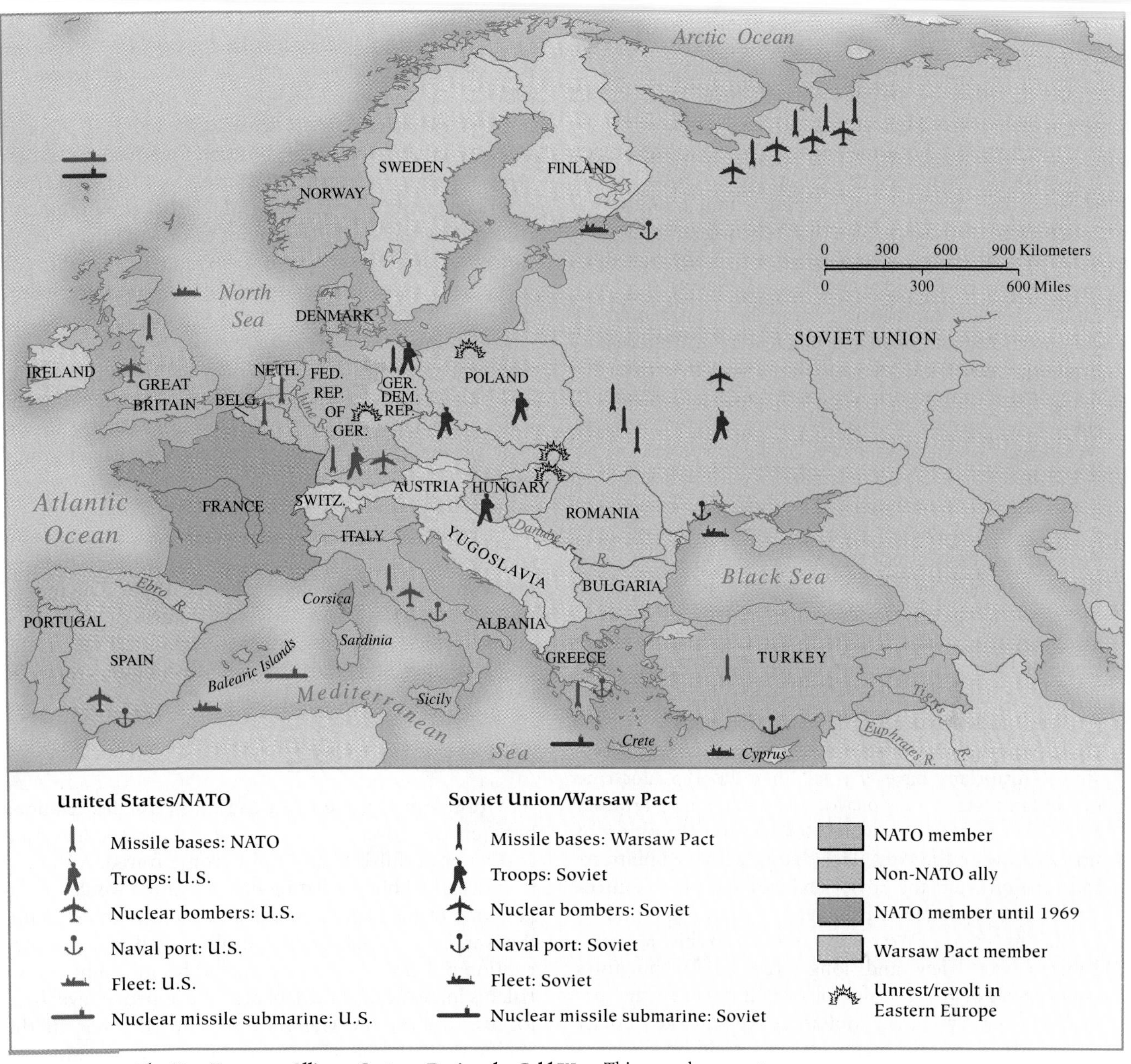


**MAP 25.1 The New European Alliance Systems During the Cold War.** This map shows postwar Europe as it was divided during the Cold War into two contending power blocs, the NATO alliance and the Warsaw Pact. Major military and naval bases are indicated by symbols on the map. ? Where on the map was the so-called "Iron Curtain"? **View an animated version of this map or related maps at** http://history.wadsworth.com/duikerspielvogel05/

Luxembourg, the Netherlands, France, Britain, Italy, Denmark, Norway, Portugal, and Iceland signed a treaty with the United States and Canada. All the powers agreed to provide mutual assistance if any one of them was attacked. A few years later, West Germany and Turkey joined NATO.

The Eastern European states soon followed suit. In 1949, they formed the Council for Mutual Economic Assistance (COMECON) for economic cooperation. Then, in 1955, Albania, Bulgaria, Czechoslovakia, East Germany, Hungary, Poland, Romania, and the Soviet Union organized a formal military alliance, the Warsaw Pact. Once again, Europe was tragically divided into hostile alliance systems (see Map 25.1).

**Who Started the Cold War?** There has been considerable historical debate over who bears responsibility for starting the Cold War. In the 1950s, most scholars in the West assumed that the bulk of the blame must fall on the shoulders of Stalin, whose determination to impose Soviet rule on Eastern Europe snuffed out hopes for freedom and self-determination there and aroused justifiable fears of communist expansion in the West. During the next decade, however, revisionist historians—influenced in part by aggressive U.S. policies in Southeast Asia—began to argue that the fault lay primarily in Washington, where Truman and his anticommunist advisers abandoned the precepts of Yalta and sought to encircle the Soviet Union with a tier of pliant U.S. client states.

In retrospect, both the United States and the Soviet Union took some unwise steps at the end of World War II. However, both nations were working within a framework conditioned by the past. The rivalry between the two superpowers ultimately stemmed from their different historical perspectives and their irreconcilable political ambitions. Intense competition for political and military supremacy had long been a regular feature of Western civilization. The United States and the Soviet Union were the heirs of that European tradition of power politics, and it should not surprise us that two such different systems would seek to extend their way of life to the rest of the world. Because of its need to secure its western border, the Soviet Union was not prepared to give up the advantages it had gained in Eastern Europe from Germany's defeat. But neither were Western leaders prepared to accept without protest the establishment of a system of Soviet satellites that not only threatened the security of Western Europe but also deeply offended Western sensibilities because of its blatant disregard of the Western concept of human rights.

This does not necessarily mean that both sides bear equal responsibility for starting the Cold War. Some revisionist historians have claimed that the U.S. doctrine of containment was a provocative action that aroused Stalin's suspicions and drove Moscow into a position of hostility toward the West. This charge lacks credibility. As information from the Soviet archives and other sources has become available, it is increasingly clear that Stalin's suspicions of the West were rooted in his Marxist-Leninist worldview and long predated Washington's enunciation of the doctrine of containment. As his foreign minister, Vyacheslav Molotov, once remarked, Soviet policy was inherently aggressive and would be triggered whenever the opportunity offered. Although Stalin apparently had no master plan to advance Soviet power into Western Europe, he was probably prepared to make every effort to do so once the next revolutionary wave arrived. Western leaders were fully justified in reacting to this possibility by strengthening their own lines of defense. On the other hand, a case can be made that in deciding to respond to the Soviet challenge in a primarily military manner, Western leaders overreacted to the situation and virtually guaranteed that the Cold War would be transformed into an arms race that could conceivably result in a new and uniquely destructive war.

## Cold War In Asia

The Cold War was somewhat slower to make its appearance in Asia. At Yalta, Stalin formally agreed to enter the Pacific War against Japan three months after the close of the conflict with Germany. As a reward for Soviet participation in the struggle against Japan, Roosevelt promised that Moscow would be granted "preeminent interests" in Manchuria (interests reminiscent of those possessed by imperial Russia prior to its defeat at the hands of Japan in 1904–1905) and the establishment of a Soviet naval base at Port Arthur. In return, Stalin promised to sign a treaty of alliance with the Republic of China, thus implicitly committing the Soviet Union not to provide the Chinese Communists with support in a possible future civil war. Although many observers would later question Stalin's sincerity in making such a commitment to the vocally anti-Communist Chiang Kai-shek, in Moscow the decision probably had a logic of its own. Stalin had no particular liking for the independent-minded Mao Zedong and indeed did not anticipate a Communist victory in any civil war in China. Only an agreement with Chiang could provide the Soviet Union with a strategically vital economic and political presence in northern China.

Despite these commitments, the Allied agreements soon broke down, and East Asia was sucked into the vortex of the Cold War by the end of the 1940s. The root of the problem lay in the underlying weakness of the Chiang regime, which threatened to create a political vacuum in East Asia that both Moscow and Washington would be tempted to fill.

### The Chinese Civil War

As World War II came to an end in the Pacific, relations between the government of Chiang Kai-shek in China and its powerful U.S. ally had become frayed. Although Roosevelt had hoped that republican China would be the keystone of his plan for peace and stability in Asia after the war, U.S. officials became disillusioned with the corruption of Chiang's government and his unwillingness to risk his forces against the Japanese (he hoped to save them for use against the Communists after the war in the Pacific ended), and China was no longer the focus of Washington's close attention as the war came to a close. Nevertheless, U.S. military and economic aid to China had been substantial, and at war's end, the new Truman administration still hoped that it could rely on Chiang to support U.S. postwar goals in the region.

While Chiang Kai-shek wrestled with Japanese aggression and problems of national development, the Communists were building up their strength in northern China. To enlarge their political base, they carried out a "mass line" policy (from the masses to the masses), reducing land rents and confiscating the lands of wealthy landlords. By the end of World War II, twenty to thirty million Chinese were living under the administration of the Communists, and their People's Liberation Army (PLA) included nearly one million troops.

As the war came to an end, world attention began to focus on the prospects for renewed civil strife in China. Members of a U.S. liaison team stationed in Yan'an were impressed by the performance of the Communists, and

Jack Wiles, *Life Magazine* © 1945 TimePix

**Chiang Kai-shek and Mao Zedong Exchange a Toast.** After World War II, the United States sent General George C. Marshall to China in an effort to prevent civil war between Chiang Kai-shek's government and the Communists. Marshall's initial success was symbolized by this toast between Chiang (at the right) and Mao. But suspicion ran too deep, and soon conflict ensued, leading to a Communist victory in 1949. Chiang's government retreated to the island of Taiwan.

some recommended that the United States should support them or at least remain neutral in a possible conflict between Communists and Nationalists for control of China. The Truman administration, though skeptical of Chiang's ability to forge a strong and prosperous country, was increasingly concerned about the spread of communism in Europe and tried to find a peaceful solution through the formation of a coalition government of all parties in China.

**The Communist Triumph** The effort failed. By 1946, full-scale war between the Nationalist government, now reinstalled in Nanjing, and the Communists resumed. Now Chiang Kai-shek's errors came home to roost. In the countryside, millions of peasants, attracted to the Communists by promises of land and social justice, flocked to serve in Mao Zedong's PLA. In the cities, middle-class Chinese, normally hostile to communism, were alienated by Chiang's brutal suppression of all dissent and his government's inability to slow the ruinous rate of inflation or solve the economic problems it caused. With morale dropping in the cities, Chiang's troops began to defect to the Communists. Sometimes whole divisions, officers as well as ordinary soldiers, changed sides. By 1948, the PLA was advancing south out of Manchuria and had encircled Beijing. Communist troops took the old imperial capital, crossed the Yangtze the following spring, and occupied the commercial hub of Shanghai (see Map 25.2). During the next few months, Chiang's government and two million of his followers fled to Taiwan, which the Japanese had returned to Chinese control after World War II.

The Truman administration reacted to the spread of Communist power in China with acute discomfort. Washington had no desire to see a Communist government on the mainland, but it had little confidence in Chiang Kai-shek's ability to realize Roosevelt's dream of a strong, united, and prosperous China. In December 1945, President Truman sent General George C. Marshall to China in a last-ditch effort to bring about a peaceful settlement, but anti-Communist elements in the Republic of China resisted U.S. efforts to create a coalition government with the Chinese Communist Party (CCP). During the next two years, the United States gave limited military support to Chiang's regime but refused to commit U.S. power to guarantee its survival. The administration's hands-off policy deeply angered many members of Congress, who charged that the White House was "soft on communism" and declared further that Roosevelt had betrayed Chiang Kai-shek at Yalta by granting privileges in Manchuria to the Soviet Union. In their view, Soviet troops had hindered the dispatch of Chiang's forces to the area and provided the PLA with weapons to use against its rivals.

In later years, sources in both Moscow and Beijing suggested that the Soviet Union gave little assistance to the CCP in its struggle against the Nanjing regime. In fact, Stalin periodically advised Mao against undertaking the effort. Although Communist forces undoubtedly received some assistance from Soviet occupation troops in Manchuria, their victory ultimately stemmed from conditions inside China, not from the intervention of outside powers. So indeed argued the Truman administration in 1949, when it issued a white paper that placed most of the

across the 38th parallel with the aim of unifying Korea under a single, noncommunist government.

President Truman worried that by approaching the Chinese border at the Yalu River, the UN troops could trigger Chinese intervention, but MacArthur assured him that China would not respond. In November, however, Chinese "volunteer" forces intervened in force on the side of North Korea and drove the UN troops southward in disarray. A static defense line was eventually established near the original dividing line at the 38th parallel (see Map 25.3), although the war continued.

To many Americans, the Chinese intervention in Korea was clear evidence that China intended to promote communism throughout Asia, and recent evidence suggests that Mao was convinced that a revolutionary wave was on the rise in Asia. In fact, however, China's decision to enter the war was probably motivated in large part by the fear that hostile U.S. forces might be stationed on the Chinese frontier and perhaps even launch an attack across the border. MacArthur intensified such fears by calling publicly for air attacks on Manchurian cities in preparation for an attack on Communist China.

In any case, the outbreak of the Korean War was particularly unfortunate for China. Immediately after the invasion, President Truman dispatched the U.S. Seventh Fleet to the Taiwan Strait to prevent a possible Chinese invasion of Taiwan. Even more unfortunate, the invasion hardened Western attitudes against the new Chinese government and led to China's isolation from the major capitalist powers for two decades. The United States continued to support the Nationalist government in Taiwan as the only legal representative of the Chinese people and supported its occupation of China's seat on the UN Security Council. As a result, China was cut off from all forms of economic and technological assistance and was forced to rely almost entirely on the Soviet Union, with which it had signed a pact of friendship and cooperation in early 1950.

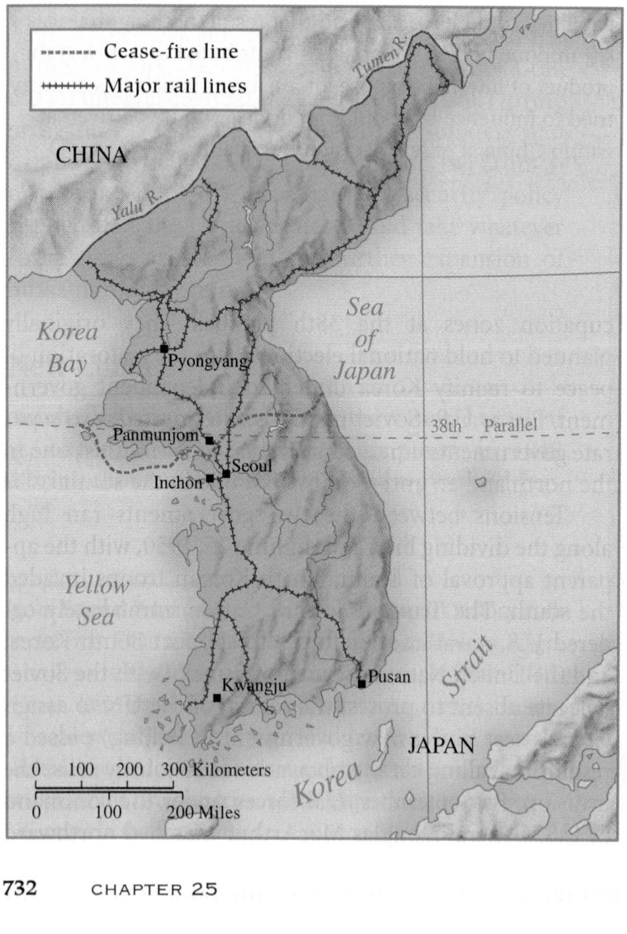

## Conflict in Indochina

During the mid-1950s, China sought to build contacts with the nonsocialist world. A cease-fire agreement brought the Korean War to an end in July 1953, and China signaled its desire to live in peaceful coexistence with other independent countries in the region. But a relatively minor conflict now began to intensify on China's southern flank, in French Indochina. The struggle had begun after World War II, when Ho Chi Minh's Indochinese Communist Party, at the head of a multiparty nationalist alliance called the Vietminh Front, seized power in northern and central Vietnam after the surrender of imperial Japan. After abortive negotiations between Ho's government and the returning French, war broke out in December 1946. French forces occupied the cities and the densely populated lowlands, while the Vietminh took refuge in the mountains.

For three years, the Vietminh gradually increased in size and effectiveness. What had begun as an anticolonial struggle by Ho's Vietminh Front against the French after World War II became entangled in the Cold War in the early 1950s, when both the United States and the new Communist government in China began to intervene in the conflict to promote their own national security objectives. China began to provide military assistance to the Vietminh to protect its own borders from hostile forces. The Americans supported the French but pressured the French government to prepare for an eventual transition to non-Communist governments in Vietnam, Laos, and Cambodia.

At the Geneva Conference in 1954, with the French public tired of fighting the "dirty war" in Indochina, the French agreed to a peace settlement with the Vietminh. Vietnam was temporarily divided into a northern Communist half (known as the Democratic Republic of Vietnam) and a non-Communist southern half based in Saigon (eventually to be known as the Republic of



**MAP 25.3 The Korean Peninsula.** In January 1950, North Korean forces crossed the 38th parallel in a sudden invasion of the south. Shown here is the cease-fire line that brought an end to the war in 1953. Major railroad lines are also shown. What is the importance of the Yalu River? **View an animated version of this map or related maps at** http://history.wadsworth.com/duikerspielvogel05/

© Black Star

**Ho Chi Minh Plans an Attack on the French.** Unlike many peoples in Southeast Asia, the Vietnamese had to fight for their independence after World War II. That fight was led by the talented Communist leader Ho Chi Minh. In this photograph, Ho (in the center), assisted by his chief strategist, Vo Nguyen Giap (at the far right), plans an attack on French positions in Vietnam.

Vietnam). A demilitarized zone separated the two at the 17th parallel. Elections were to be held in two years to create a unified government. Cambodia and Laos were both declared independent under neutral governments.

China had played an active role in bringing about the settlement and clearly hoped that it would reduce tensions in the area, but subsequent efforts to improve relations between China and the United States foundered on the issue of Taiwan. In the fall of 1954, the United States signed a mutual security treaty with the Republic of China guaranteeing U.S. military support in case of an invasion of Taiwan. When Beijing demanded U.S. withdrawal from Taiwan as the price for improved relations, diplomatic talks between the two countries collapsed.



**Indochina After 1954**

## From Confrontation To Coexistence

The decade of the 1950s opened with the world teetering on the edge of a nuclear holocaust. The Soviet Union had detonated its first nuclear device in 1949, and the two blocs—capitalist and socialist—viewed each other across an ideological divide that grew increasingly bitter with each passing year. Yet as the decade drew to a close, a measure of sanity crept into the Cold War, and the leaders of the major world powers began to seek ways to coexist in a peaceful and stable world (see Map 25.4).

The first clear sign of change occurred after Stalin's death in early 1953. His successor, Georgy Malenkov (1902–1988), openly hoped to improve relations with the Western powers in order to reduce defense expenditures and shift government spending to growing consumer needs. Nikita Khrushchev (1894–1971), who replaced Malenkov in 1955, continued his predecessor's efforts to reduce tensions with the West and improve the living standards of the Soviet people.

In an adroit public relations touch, Khrushchev promoted an appeal for a policy of **peaceful coexistence** with the West. In 1955, he surprisingly agreed to negotiate an end to the postwar occupation of Austria by the victorious allies and allow the creation of a neutral country with strong cultural and economic ties with the West. He also called for a reduction in defense expenditures and reduced the size of the Soviet armed forces.

### Ferment in Eastern Europe

At first, Western leaders were suspicious of Khrushchev's motives, especially in light of events that were taking place in Eastern Europe. The key to security along the western frontier of the Soviet Union was the string of Eastern European satellite states that had been assembled in the aftermath of World War II (see Map 25.1). Once Communist domination had been assured, a series of "little Stalins" put into power by Moscow instituted Soviet-type five-year plans that emphasized heavy industry rather than consumer goods, the collectivization of agriculture, and the nationalization of industry. They also appropriated the political tactics that Stalin had perfected in the Soviet Union, eliminating all non-Communist parties and establishing the classical institutions of repression—the secret police and military forces. Dissidents were

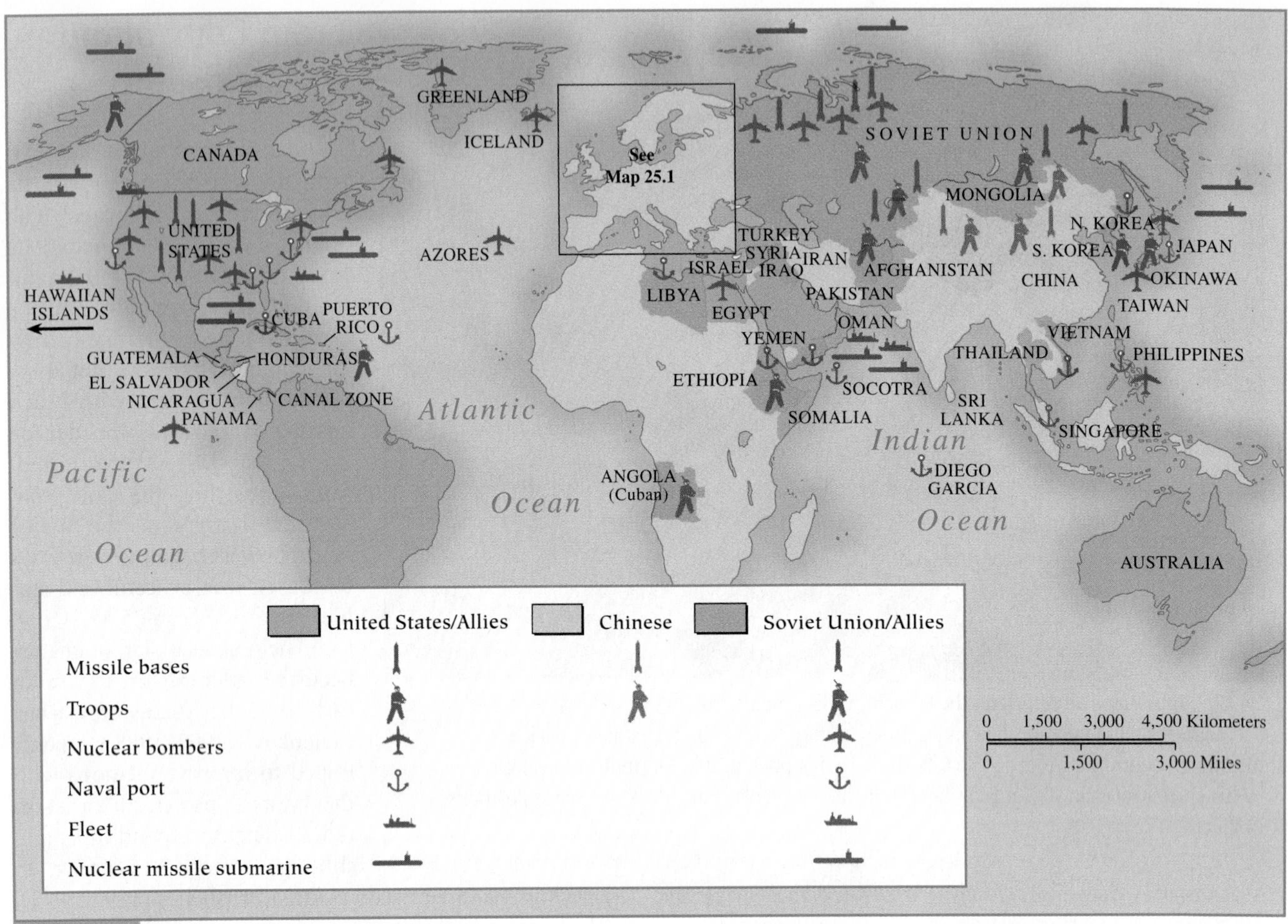


**MAP 25.4 The Global Cold War.** This map indicates the location of major military bases and missile sites possessed by the contending power blocs throughout the world at the height of the Cold War. **?** Which continents are the most heavily armed? **View an animated version of this map or related maps at** http://history.wadsworth.com/duikerspielvogel05/

tracked down and thrown into prison, and "national Communists" who resisted total subservience to the Soviet Union were charged with treason in mass show trials and executed.

Despite these repressive efforts, discontent became increasingly evident in several Eastern European countries. Hungary, Poland, and Romania harbored bitter memories of past Russian domination and suspected that Stalin, under the guise of proletarian internationalism, was seeking to revive the empire of the Romanovs. For the vast majority of peoples in Eastern Europe, the imposition of the so-called people's democracies (a term invented by Moscow to define a society in the early stage of socialist transition) resulted in economic hardship and severe threats to the most basic political liberties. The first indications of unrest appeared in East Berlin, where popular riots broke out against Communist rule in 1953. The riots eventually subsided, but the virus had spread to neighboring countries.

In Poland, public demonstrations against an increase in food prices in 1956 escalated into widespread protests against the regime's economic policies, restrictions on the freedom of Catholics to practice their religion, and the continued presence of Soviet troops (as called for by the Warsaw Pact) on Polish soil. In a desperate effort to defuse the unrest, the party leader stepped down and was replaced by Wladyslaw Gomulka (1905–1982), a popular figure who had previously been demoted for his "nationalist" tendencies. When Gomulka took steps to ease the crisis, Khrushchev flew to Warsaw to warn him against adopting policies that could undermine the political dominance of the party and weaken security links with the Soviet Union. Ultimately, Poland agreed to remain in the Warsaw Pact and to maintain the sanctity of party rule; in return, Gomulka was authorized to adopt domestic reforms, such as easing restrictions on religious practice and ending the policy of forced collectivization in rural areas.

**The Hungarian Revolution** The developments in Poland sent shock waves throughout the region. The impact was strongest in neighboring Hungary, where the methods of the local "little Stalin," Matyas Rakosi, were so brutal that he had been summoned to Moscow for a lecture. In late October 1956, student-led popular riots broke out in the capital of Budapest and soon spread to

AP/Wide World Photos

**How the Mighty Have Fallen.** In the fall of 1956, Hungarian freedom fighters rose up against Communist domination of their country in the short-lived Hungarian revolution. Their actions threatened Soviet hegemony in Eastern Europe, however, and in late October, Soviet leader Nikita Khrushchev dispatched troops to quell the uprising. In the meantime, the Hungarian people had voiced their discontent by toppling a gigantic statue of Joseph Stalin in the capital of Budapest. Statues of the Soviet dictator had been erected in all the Soviet satellites after World War II. ("W.C." identifies a public toilet in European countries.)

other towns and villages throughout the country. Rakosi was forced to resign and was replaced by Imre Nagy (1896–1958), a national Communist who attempted to satisfy popular demands without arousing the anger of Moscow. Unlike Gomulka, however, Nagy was unable to contain the zeal of leading members of the protest movement, who sought major political reforms and the withdrawal of Hungary from the Warsaw Pact. On November 1, Nagy promised free elections, which, given the mood of the country, would probably have brought an end to Communist rule. After a brief moment of uncertainty, Moscow decided on firm action. Soviet troops, recently withdrawn at Nagy's request, returned to Budapest and installed a new government under the more pliant party leader János Kádár (1912–1989). While Kádár rescinded many of Nagy's measures, Nagy sought refuge in the Yugoslav embassy. A few weeks later, he left the embassy under the promise of safety but was quickly arrested, convicted of treason, and executed.

**Different Roads to Socialism** The dramatic events in Poland and Hungary graphically demonstrated the vulnerability of the Soviet satellite system in Eastern Europe, and many observers throughout the world anticipated that the United States would intervene on behalf of the freedom fighters in Hungary. After all, the Eisenhower administration had promised that it would "roll back" communism, and radio broadcasts by the U.S.-sponsored Radio Liberty and Radio Free Europe had encouraged the peoples of Eastern Europe to rise up against Soviet domination. In reality, Washington was well aware that U.S. intervention could lead to nuclear war and limited itself to protests against Soviet brutality in crushing the uprising.

The year of discontent was not without consequences, however. Soviet leaders now recognized that Moscow could maintain control over its satellites in Eastern Europe only by granting them the leeway to adopt domestic policies appropriate to local conditions. Khrushchev had already embarked on this path in 1955 when he assured Tito that there were "different roads to socialism." Some Eastern European Communist leaders now took Khrushchev at his word and adopted reform programs to make socialism more palatable to their subject populations. Even Kádár, derisively labeled the "butcher of Budapest," managed to preserve many of Nagy's reforms to allow a measure of capitalist incentive and freedom of expression in Hungary.

The easing of Stalinist-style terror in some of Moscow's client states in Eastern Europe was accompanied by a new crisis over Berlin. The Soviet Union had launched its first intercontinental ballistic missile (ICBM) in August 1957, arousing U.S. fears of a missile gap between the United States and the Soviet Union. Khrushchev attempted to take advantage of the U.S. frenzy over missiles to solve the problem of West Berlin, which had remained a "Western island" of prosperity inside the relatively poverty-stricken state of East Germany. Many East Germans sought to escape to West Germany by fleeing through West Berlin, a serious blot on the credibility of the GDR and a potential source of instability in East-West relations. In November 1958, Khrushchev announced that unless the West removed its forces from West Berlin within six months, he would turn over control of the access routes to the East Germans. Unwilling to accept an ultimatum that would have abandoned West Berlin to the Communists, President Dwight D. Eisenhower and the West stood firm, and Khrushchev eventually backed down.

Despite such periodic crises in East-West relations, there were tantalizing signs that an era of true peaceful coexistence between the two power blocs could be achieved. In the late 1950s, the United States and the Soviet Union initiated a cultural exchange program. While the Leningrad Ballet appeared at theaters in the United States, Benny Goodman and the film *West Side Story* played in Moscow. In 1958, Khrushchev visited the United States and had a brief but friendly encounter with President Eisenhower at the presidential retreat in northern Maryland.

## Rivalry in the Third World

Yet Khrushchev could rarely avoid the temptation to gain an advantage over the United States in the competition for influence throughout the world, and this resulted in an unstable relationship between the two superpowers. Moscow also took every opportunity to promote its interests at the United Nations and in the Third World, as the unaligned countries of Asia, Africa, and Latin America were now popularly called. Unlike Stalin, Khrushchev viewed the

AP/Wide World Photos

**The Kitchen Debate.** During the late 1950s, the United States and the Soviet Union sought to defuse Cold War tensions by encouraging cultural exchanges between the two countries. On one occasion, U.S. Vice President Richard M. Nixon visited Moscow in conjunction with the arrival of an exhibit to introduce U.S. culture and society to the Soviet people. Here Nixon lectures Soviet Communist Party chief Nikita Khrushchev on the technology of the U.S. kitchen. To Nixon's left is future Soviet president Leonid Brezhnev.

dismantling of colonial regimes in the area as a potential advantage for the Soviet Union and sought especially to exploit the deep suspicions of the United States in Latin America. To improve Soviet influence in such areas, Khrushchev established alliances with key Third World leaders such as Sukarno in Indonesia, Gamel Abdul Nasser in Egypt, Jawaharlal Nehru in India, and Fidel Castro in Cuba (see Chapter 28). In January 1961, just as John F. Kennedy assumed the U.S. presidency, Khrushchev unnerved the new president at an informal summit meeting in Vienna by declaring that the Soviet Union would provide active support to national liberation movements throughout the world. There were rising fears in Washington of Soviet meddling in such sensitive trouble spots as Southeast Asia, Central Africa, and the Caribbean.

**The Cuban Missile Crisis** The Cold War confrontation between the United States and the Soviet Union reached frightening levels during the Cuban Missile Crisis. In 1959, a left-wing revolutionary named Fidel Castro (b. 1927) overthrew the Cuban dictator Fulgencio Batista and established a Soviet-supported totalitarian regime. After the utter failure of a U.S.-supported attempt to overthrow Castro's regime in 1961 (known as the "Bay of Pigs" incident), the Soviet Union decided to place nuclear missiles in Cuba in 1962. The United States was not prepared to allow nuclear weapons within striking distance of the American mainland, even though it had placed some of its own nuclear weapons in Turkey, within range of the Soviet Union. Khrushchev was quick to point out that "your rockets are in Turkey. You are worried by Cuba . . . because it is 90 miles from the American coast. But Turkey is next to us."[5] When U.S. intelligence discovered that a Soviet fleet carrying missiles was indeed heading to Cuba, President Kennedy decided to blockade Cuba and prevent the fleet from reaching its destination. This approach to the problem had the

© Bettman/CORBIS

**John F. Kennedy and the Cuban Missile Crisis.** During the Cuban Missile Crisis, the United States and the Soviet Union came frighteningly close to a direct nuclear confrontation. This photograph shows President John F. Kennedy meeting with his cabinet and advisers during the Cuban crisis in October 1962. At Kennedy's left is Robert McNamara, the secretary of defense, and to his right is Dean Rusk, the secretary of state.

## The Cuban Missile Crisis from Khrushchev's Perspective

The Cuban Missile Crisis was one of the sobering experiences of the Cold War. It led the two superpowers to seek new ways to lessen the tensions between them. This version of the events is taken from the memoirs of Nikita Khrushchev.

*Why, according to his memoirs, did Nikita Khrushchev decide to place missiles in Cuba? Why did he agree to remove them later?*

### Khrushchev Remembers

I will explain what the Caribbean crisis of October 1962 was all about. . . . At the time that Fidel Castro led his revolution to victory and entered Havana with his troops, we had no idea what political course his regime would follow. . . . All the while the Americans had been watching Castro closely. At first they thought that the capitalist underpinnings of the Cuban economy would remain intact. So by the time Castro announced that he was going to put Cuba on the road toward Socialism, the Americans had already missed their chance to do anything about it by simply exerting their influence: there were no longer any forces left which could be organized to fight on America's behalf in Cuba. That left only one alternative–invasion! . . .

After Castro's crushing victory over the counterrevolutionaries we intensified our military aid to Cuba. . . . We were sure that the Americans would never reconcile themselves to the existence of Castro's Cuba. They feared, as much as we hoped, that a Socialist Cuba might become a magnet that would attract other Latin American countries to Socialism. . . . It was clear to me that we might very well lose Cuba if we didn't take some decisive steps in her defense. . . . We had to think up some way of confronting America with more than words. We had to establish a tangible and effective deterrent to American interference in the Caribbean. But what exactly? The logical answer was missiles. We knew that American missiles were aimed against us in Turkey and Italy, to say nothing of West Germany. . . . My thinking went like this: if we installed the missiles secretly and then if the United States discovered the missiles were there after they were already poised and ready to strike, the Americans would think twice before trying to liquidate our installations by military means. . . . I want to make one thing absolutely clear: when we put our ballistic missiles in Cuba we had no desire to start a war. On the contrary, our principal aim was only to deter America from starting a war. . . .

President Kennedy issued an ultimatum, demanding that we remove our missiles and bombers from Cuba. . . . We sent the Americans a note saying that we agreed to remove our missiles and bombers on the condition that the President give us his assurance that there would be no invasion of Cuba by the forces of the United States or anybody else. Finally Kennedy gave in and agreed to make a statement giving us such an assurance. . . . It had been, to say the least, an interesting and challenging situation. The two most powerful nations of the world had been squared off against each other, each with its finger on the button. You'd have thought that war was inevitable. But both sides showed that if the desire to avoid war is strong enough, even the most pressing dispute can be solved by compromise. And a compromise over Cuba was indeed found. The episode ended in a triumph of common sense. . . . It was a great victory for us, though, that we had been able to extract from Kennedy a promise that neither America nor any of her allies would invade Cuba. . . . The Caribbean crisis was a triumph of Soviet foreign policy and a personal triumph in my own career as a statesman and as a member of the collective leadership. We achieved, I would say, a spectacular success without having to fire a single shot!

**History Now™** To read several documents related to the Cuban Missile Crisis, enter the *HistoryNow* documents area using the access card that is available for *World History.*

benefit of delaying confrontation and giving the two sides time to find a peaceful solution. Although hard-liners on both sides were reluctant to compromise, Khrushchev eventually agreed to turn back the fleet if Kennedy pledged not to invade Cuba (see the box above). In a conciliatory letter to Kennedy, Khrushchev wrote:

> We and you ought not to pull on the ends of the rope in which you have tied the knot of war, because the more the two of us pull, the tighter that knot will be tied. And a moment may come when that knot will be tied too tight that even he who tied it will not have the strength to untie it. . . . Let us not only relax the forces pulling on the ends of the rope; let us take measures to untie that knot. We are ready for this.[6]

The intense feeling that the world might have been annihilated in a few days had a profound influence on both sides. A hotline between Moscow and Washington was installed in 1963 to expedite communications between the two superpowers in time of crisis. In the same year, the two powers agreed to ban nuclear tests in the atmosphere, a step that served to lessen the tensions between the two nations.

## The Sino-Soviet Dispute

Nikita Khrushchev had launched his slogan of peaceful coexistence as a means of improving relations with the capitalist powers; ironically, one result of the campaign

## A Plea for Peaceful Coexistence

The Soviet leader Vladimir Lenin had contended that war between the socialist and imperialist camps was inevitable because the imperialists would never give up without a fight. That assumption had probably guided the thoughts of Joseph Stalin, who told colleagues shortly after World War II that a new war would break out in fifteen to twenty years. But Stalin's successor, Nikita Khrushchev, feared that a new world conflict could result in a nuclear holocaust and contended that the two sides must learn to coexist, although peaceful competition would continue. In this speech given in Beijing in 1959, Khrushchev attempted to persuade the Chinese to accept his views. But Chinese leaders argued that the "imperialist nature" of the United States would never change and warned that they would not accept any peace agreement in which they had no part.

*Why does Nikita Khrushchev feel that a conflict between the socialist and capitalist camps is no longer necessary, as Lenin had predicted?*

### Khrushchev's Speech to the Chinese, 1959

Comrades! Socialism brings to the people peace—that greatest blessing. The greater the strength of the camp of socialism grows, the greater will be its possibilities for successfully defending the cause of peace on this earth. The forces of socialism are already so great that real possibilities are being created for excluding war as a means of solving international disputes. . . .

When I spoke with President Eisenhower—and I have just returned from the United States of America—I got the impression that the President of the U.S.A.—and not a few people support him—understands the need to relax international tension. . . .

There is only one way of preserving peace—that is the road of peaceful coexistence of states with different social systems. The question stands thus: either peaceful coexistence or war with its catastrophic consequences. Now, with the present relation of forces between socialism and capitalism being in favor of socialism, he who would continue the "cold war" is moving towards his own destruction. . . .

Already in the first years of the Soviet power the great Lenin defined the general line of our foreign policy as being directed towards the peaceful coexistence of states with different social systems. For a long time, the ruling circles of the Western Powers rejected these truly humane principles. Nevertheless the principles of peaceful coexistence made their way into the hearts of the vast majority of mankind. . . .

It is not at all because capitalism is still strong that the socialist countries speak out against war, and for peaceful coexistence. No, we have no need of war at all. If the people do not want it, even such a noble and progressive system as socialism cannot be imposed by force of arms. The socialist countries therefore, while carrying through a consistently peace-loving policy, concentrate their efforts on peaceful construction; they fire the hearts of men by the force of their example in building socialism, and thus lead them to follow in their footsteps. The question of when this or that country will take the path to socialism is decided by its own people. This, for us, is the holy of holies.

was to undermine Moscow's ties with its close ally China. During Stalin's lifetime, Beijing had accepted the Soviet Union as the acknowledged leader of the socialist camp. After Stalin's death, however, relations began to deteriorate. Part of the reason may have been Mao Zedong's contention that he, as the most experienced Marxist leader, should now be acknowledged as the most authoritative voice within the socialist community. But another determining factor was that just as Soviet policies were moving toward moderation, China's were becoming more radical.

Several other issues were involved, including territorial disputes along the Sino-Soviet border and China's unhappiness with limited Soviet economic assistance. But the key sources of disagreement involved ideology and the Cold War. Chinese leaders were convinced that the successes of the Soviet space program confirmed that the socialists were now technologically superior to the capitalists (the East Wind, trumpeted the Chinese official press, had now triumphed over the West Wind), and they urged Khrushchev to go on the offensive to promote world revolution. Specifically, China wanted Soviet assistance in retaking Taiwan from Chiang Kai-shek. But Khrushchev was trying to improve relations with the West and rejected Chinese demands for support against Taiwan (see the box above).

By the end of the 1950s, the Soviet Union had begun to remove its advisers from China, and in 1961, the dispute broke into the open. Increasingly isolated, China voiced its hostility to what Mao described as the "urban industrialized countries" (which included the Soviet Union) and portrayed itself as the leader of the "rural underdeveloped countries" of Asia, Africa, and Latin America in a global struggle against imperialist oppression. In effect, China had applied Mao Zedong's concept of people's war in an international framework.

### The Second Indochina War

China's radicalism was intensified in the early 1960s by the outbreak of renewed war in Indochina. The Eisenhower administration had opposed the peace settlement at

## Combating the Americans

In December 1960, the National Front for the Liberation of South Vietnam, or NLF, was born. Composed of political and social leaders opposed to the anti-Communist government of Ngo Dinh Diem in South Vietnam, it operated under the direction of the Vietnam Workers' Party in North Vietnam and served as the formal representative of revolutionary forces in the South throughout the remainder of the Vietnam War. When, in the spring of 1965, President Lyndon Johnson began to dispatch U.S. combat troops to Vietnam to prevent a Communist victory there, the NLF issued the following declaration.

*How does the NLF justify its claim to represent the legitimate aspirations of the people of South Vietnam? How do you believe the Johnson administration would respond?*

### Statement of the National Liberation Front of South Vietnam

American imperialist aggression against South Vietnam and interference in its internal affairs have now continued for more than ten years. More American troops and supplies, including missile units, Marines, B-57 strategic bombers, and mercenaries from South Korea, Taiwan, the Philippines, Australia, Malaysia, etc., have been brought to South Vietnam. . . .

The Saigon puppet regime, paid servant of the United States, is guilty of the most heinous crimes. These despicable traitors, these boot-lickers of American imperialism, have brought the enemy into our country. They have brought to South Vietnam armed forces of the United States and its satellites to kill our compatriots, occupy and ravage our sacred soil and enslave our people.

The Vietnamese, the peoples of all Indo-China and Southeast Asia, supporters of peace and justice in every part of the world, have raised their voice in angry protest against this criminal unprovoked aggression of the United States imperialists.

In the present extremely grave situation, the South Vietnam National Liberation Front considers it necessary to proclaim anew its firm and unswerving determination to resist the U.S. imperialists and fight for the salvation of our country. . . . [It] will continue to rely chiefly on its own forces and potentialities, but it is prepared to accept any assistance, moral and material, including arms and other military equipment, from all the socialist countries, from nationalist countries, from international organizations, and from the peace-loving peoples of the world.

Geneva in 1954, which divided Vietnam temporarily into two separate regroupment zones, specifically because the provision for future national elections opened up the possibility that the entire country would come under Communist rule. But Eisenhower had been unwilling to introduce U.S. military forces to continue the conflict without the full support of the British and the French, who preferred to seek a negotiated settlement. In the end, Washington promised not to break the provisions of the agreement but refused to commit itself to the results.

During the next several months, the United States began to provide aid to a new government in South Vietnam. Under the leadership of the anti-Communist politician Ngo Dinh Diem, the South Vietnamese government began to root out dissidents. With the tacit approval of the United States, Diem refused to hold the national elections called for by the Geneva Accords. It was widely anticipated, even in Washington, that the Communists would win such elections. In 1959, Ho Chi Minh, despairing of the peaceful unification of the country under Communist rule, decided to promote revolutionary war in the south.

By 1963, South Vietnam was on the verge of collapse. Diem's autocratic methods and inattention to severe economic inequality had alienated much of the population, and revolutionary forces, popularly known as the Viet Cong (Vietnamese Communists) and supported by the Communist government in the North, expanded their influence throughout much of the country. In the fall of 1963, with the approval of the Kennedy administration, senior military officers overthrew the Diem regime. But factionalism kept the new military leadership from reinvigorating the struggle against the insurgent forces, and the situation in South Vietnam grew worse. By early 1965, the Viet Cong, whose ranks were now swelled by military units infiltrating from North Vietnam, were on the verge of seizing control of the entire country. In March, President Lyndon Johnson decided to send U.S. combat troops to South Vietnam to prevent a total defeat for the anticommunist government in Saigon (see the box above).

**The Role of China** Chinese leaders observed the gradual escalation of the conflict in South Vietnam with mixed feelings. They were undoubtedly pleased to have a firm Communist ally—one that had in many ways followed the path of Mao Zedong—just beyond their southern frontier. Yet they were concerned that renewed bloodshed in South Vietnam might enmesh China in a new conflict with the United States. Nor did they welcome the specter of a powerful and ambitious united Vietnam, which might wish to extend its influence throughout mainland Southeast Asia, an area that Beijing considered its own backyard.

Chinese leaders therefore tiptoed delicately through the minefield of the Indochina conflict. As the war escalated in 1964 and 1965, Beijing publicly announced that the Chinese people fully supported their comrades seeking

## A Manual for Revolutionaries

In the 1920s, Mao Zedong (Mao Tse-tung) formulated his theory of people's war, which held that in preindustrial societies, revolution could be more readily fomented in the countryside than in the cities. Forty years later, Lin Biao, Mao's colleague and the minister of defense, placed the concept in an international framework, arguing that the rural nations of the world (led, of course, by China) would defeat the industrialized "urban" nations (represented by the United States and the Soviet Union). This is an excerpt from the article in which Lin Biao presented his thesis. His message was also intended as a signal to North Vietnamese leaders not to escalate the conflict in South Vietnam to a point that might involve a direct confrontation with the United States.

*What are the key elements in Lin Biao's strategy to promote global revolution? How might this advice be interpreted by China's ally in North Vietnam?*

### Lin Biao, "Long Live the Victory of People's War"

Many countries and peoples in Asia, Africa, and Latin America are now being subjected to aggression and enslavement on a serious scale by the imperialists headed by the United States and their lackeys. The basic political and economic conditions in many of these countries have many similarities to those that prevailed in old China. As in China, the peasant question is extremely important in these regions. The peasants constitute the main force of the national-democratic revolution against the imperialists and their lackeys. In committing aggression against these countries, the imperialists usually begin by seizing the big cities and the main lines of communication. But they are unable to bring the vast countryside completely under their control. The countryside, and the countryside alone, can provide the broad areas in which the revolutionaries can maneuver freely. The countryside, and the countryside alone, can provide the revolutionary basis from which the revolutionaries can go forward to final victory. Precisely for this reason, Mao Tse-tung's theory of establishing revolutionary base areas in the rural districts and encircling the cities from the countryside is attracting more and more attention among the people in these regions.

Taking the entire globe, if North America and Western Europe can be called "the cities of the world," then Asia, Africa, and Latin America constitute "the rural areas of the world." Since World War II, the proletarian revolutionary movement has for various reasons been temporarily held back in the North American and West European capitalist countries, while the people's revolutionary movement in Asia, Africa, and Latin America has been growing vigorously. In a sense, the contemporary world revolution also presents a picture of the encirclement of cities by the rural areas. In the final analysis, the whole cause of world revolution hinges on the revolutionary struggles of the Asian, African, and Latin American peoples, who make up the overwhelming majority of the world's population. The socialist countries should regard it as their internationalist duty to support the people's revolutionary struggles in Asia, Africa, and Latin America. . . .

Ours is the epoch in which world capitalism and imperialism are heading for their doom and communism is marching to victory. Comrade Mao Tse-tung's theory of people's war is not only a product of the Chinese revolution, but has also the characteristic of our epoch. The new experience gained in the people's revolutionary struggles in various countries since World War II has provided continuous evidence that Mao Tse-tung's thought is a common asset of the revolutionary people of the whole world. This is the great international significance of the thought of Mao Tse-tung.

national liberation but privately assured Washington that China would not directly enter the conflict unless U.S. forces threatened its southern border. Beijing also refused to cooperate fully with Moscow in shipping Soviet goods to North Vietnam through Chinese territory (see the box above).

Despite its dismay at the lack of full support from China, the Communist government in North Vietnam responded to U.S. escalation by infiltrating more of its own regular force troops into the south, and by 1968, the war had reached a stalemate (see the comparative illustration on p. 741). The Communists were not strong enough to overthrow the government in Saigon, whose weakness was shielded by the presence of half a million U.S. troops, but President Johnson was reluctant to engage in all-out war on North Vietnam for fear of provoking a global nuclear conflict. In the fall, after the Communist-led Tet offensive undermined claims of progress in Washington and aroused intense antiwar protests in the United States, peace negotiations began in Paris.

Richard Nixon came into the White House in 1969 on a pledge to bring an honorable end to the Vietnam War. With U.S. public opinion sharply divided on the issue, he began to withdraw U.S. troops while continuing to hold peace talks in Paris. But the centerpiece of his strategy was to improve relations with China and thus undercut Chinese support for the North Vietnamese war effort. During the 1960s, relations between Moscow and Beijing had reached a point of extreme tension, and thousands of troops were stationed on both sides of their long common frontier. To intimidate their Communist rivals, Soviet sources hinted that they might launch a preemp-

© Hoang Mai

© AP / Wide World Photos

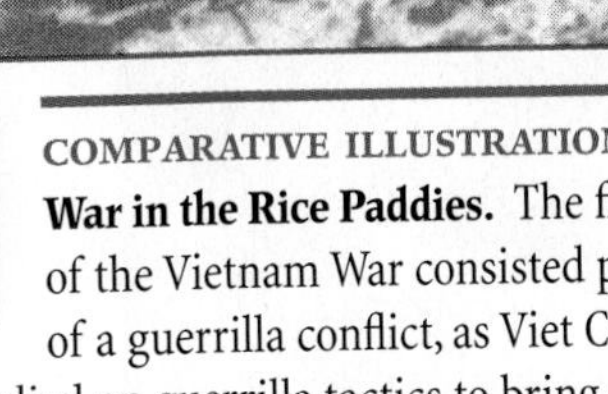

POLITICS & GOVERNMENT

COMPARATIVE ILLUSTRATION

**War in the Rice Paddies.** The first stage of the Vietnam War consisted primarily of a guerrilla conflict, as Viet Cong insurgents relied on guerrilla tactics to bring down the U.S.-supported government in Saigon. In 1965, however, President Lyndon Johnson ordered U. S. combat troops into South Vietnam (right photo) in a desperate bid to prevent a Communist victory in that beleaguered country. The Communist government in Hanoi responded in kind, sending its own regular forces down the Ho Chi Minh Trail to confront U.S. troops on the battlefield. On the left, North Vietnamese troops storm the U.S. marine base at Khe Sanh, near the demilitarized zone, in 1968, the most violent year of the war.

tive strike to destroy Chinese nuclear facilities in Xinjiang. Sensing an opportunity to split the two onetime allies, Nixon sent his emissary Henry Kissinger on a secret trip to China. Responding to assurances that the United States was determined to withdraw from Indochina and hoped to improve relations with the mainland regime, Chinese leaders invited President Nixon to visit China in early 1972. Nixon accepted, and the two sides agreed to set aside their differences over Taiwan to pursue a better mutual relationship.

**The Fall of Saigon** Incensed at the apparent betrayal by their close allies, North Vietnamese leaders decided to seek a peaceful settlement of the war in the south. In January 1973, a peace treaty was signed in Paris calling for the removal of all U.S. forces from South Vietnam. In return, the Communists agreed to halt military operations and to engage in negotiations to resolve their differences with the Saigon regime. But negotiations between north and south over the political settlement soon broke down, and in early 1975, the Communists resumed the offensive. At the end of April, under a massive assault by North Vietnamese military forces, the South Vietnamese government surrendered. A year later, the country was unified under Communist rule.

The Communist victory in Vietnam was a severe humiliation for the United States, but its strategic impact was limited because of the new relationship with China. During the next decade, Sino-American relations continued to improve. In 1979, diplomatic ties were established between the two countries under an arrangement whereby the United States renounced its mutual security treaty with the Republic of China in return for a pledge from China to seek reunification with Taiwan by peaceful means (see the box on p. 743). By the end of the 1970s, China and the United States had forged a "strategic relationship" in which they would cooperate against the common threat of Soviet hegemony in Asia.

Why had the United States failed to achieve its objective of preventing a Communist victory in Vietnam? One leading member of the Johnson administration later commented that Washington had underestimated the determination of its adversary in Hanoi and overestimated the patience of the American people. Deeper reflection suggests, however, that another factor was equally important: the United States had overestimated the ability of its client state in South Vietnam to defend itself against a disciplined adversary. In subsequent years, it became a crucial lesson to the Americans on the perils of nation-building.

AP/Wide World Photos

**A Bridge Across the Cold War Divide.** In January 1972, U.S. President Richard Nixon startled the world by visiting mainland China and beginning the long process of restoring normal relations between the two countries. Despite Nixon's reputation as a devout anti-Communist, the visit was a success as the two sides agreed to put aside their most bitter differences in an effort to reduce tensions in Asia. Here Nixon and Chinese leader Mao Zedong exchange a historic handshake in Beijing.

## An Era of Equivalence

When the Johnson administration sent U.S. combat troops to South Vietnam in 1965, Washington's main concern was with Beijing, not Moscow. By the mid-1960s, U.S. officials viewed the Soviet Union as an essentially conservative power, more concerned with protecting its vast empire than with expanding its borders. In fact, U.S.policy makers periodically sought Soviet assistance in seeking a peaceful settlement of the Vietnam War. So long as Khrushchev was in power, they found a receptive ear in Moscow. Khrushchev was firmly dedicated to promoting peaceful coexistence (at least on his terms) and sternly advised the North Vietnamese against a resumption of revolutionary war in South Vietnam.

After October 1964, when Khrushchev was replaced by a new leadership headed by party chief Leonid Brezhnev (1906–1982) and Prime Minister Alexei Kosygin (1904–1980), Soviet attitudes about Vietnam became more ambivalent. On the one hand, the new Soviet leaders had no desire to see the Vietnam conflict poison relations between the great powers. On the other hand, Moscow was eager to demonstrate its support for the North Vietnamese to deflect Chinese charges that the Soviet Union had betrayed the interests of the oppressed peoples of the world. As a result, Soviet officials publicly voiced sympathy for the U.S. predicament in Vietnam but put no pressure on their allies to bring an end to the war. Indeed, the Soviet Union became Hanoi's main supplier of advanced military equipment in the final years of the war.

## A New Beginning in Sino-American Relations

On January 1, 1979, the United States and the People's Republic of China agreed to establish diplomatic relations. It was the first time that the two countries had exchanged diplomatic representatives since 1949, when the Communist Party seized control of the mainland from Chiang Kai-shek's Nationalist government. To achieve their new relationship, both Beijing and Washington had to place several contentious issues on the back burner—notably, the continued existence of the Republic of China on the island of Taiwan. Note how the two statements carefully describe that issue to reflect their distinct points of view.

*What are the key differences between these two statements with regard to the situation on the island of Taiwan? Given these differences, why did China and the United States decide to resume diplomatic relations?*

### Statement of the United States of America

As of January 1, 1979, the United States of America recognizes the People's Republic of China as the sole legal government of China. On the same date, the People's Republic of China accords similar recognition to the United States of America. The United States thereby establishes diplomatic relations with the People's Republic of China.

On that same date, January 1, 1979, the United States of America will notify Taiwan that it is terminating diplomatic relations and that the Mutual Defense Treaty between the United States and the Republic of China is being terminated in accordance with the provisions of the Treaty. The United States also states that it will be withdrawing its remaining military personnel from Taiwan within four months.

In the future, the American people and the people of Taiwan will maintain commercial, cultural and other relations without official government representation and without diplomatic relations.

The Administration will seek adjustments to our laws and regulations to permit the maintenance of commercial, cultural and other non-governmental relationships in the new circumstances that will exist after normalization.

The United States is confident that the people of Taiwan face a peaceful and prosperous future. The United States continues to have an interest in the peaceful resolution of the Taiwan issue and expects that the Taiwan issue will be settled peacefully by the Chinese themselves.

The United States believes that the establishment of diplomatic relations with the People's Republic will contribute to the welfare of the American people, to the stability of Asia where the United States has major security and economic interests and to the peace of the entire world.

### Statement of the People's Republic of China

As of January 1, 1979, the People's Republic of China and the United States of America recognize each other and establish diplomatic relations, thereby ending the prolonged abnormal relationship between them. This is a historic event in Sino-U.S. relations.

As is known to all, the Government of the People's Republic of China is the sole legal government of China and Taiwan is a part of China. The question of Taiwan was the crucial issue obstructing the normalization of relations between China and the United States. It has now been resolved between the two countries in the spirit of the Shanghai Communiqué and through their joint efforts, thus enabling the normalization of relations so ardently desired by the people of the two countries. As for the way of bringing Taiwan back to the embrace of the motherland and reunifying the country, it is entirely China's internal affair.

At the invitation of the U.S. Government, Teng Hsiao-ping [Deng Xiaoping], vice-premier of the State Council of the People's Republic of China, will pay an official visit to the United States in January 1979, with a view to further promoting the friendship between the two peoples and good relations between the two countries.

## The Brezhnev Doctrine

In the meantime, new Cold War tensions were brewing in Eastern Europe, where discontent with Stalinist policies began to emerge in Czechoslovakia. The latter had not shared in the thaw of the mid-1950s and remained under the rule of the hard-liner Antonin Novotny (1904–1975), who had been placed in power by Stalin himself. By the late 1960s, however, Novotny's policies had led to widespread popular alienation, and in 1968, with the support of intellectuals and reformist party members, Alexander Dubček (1921–1992) was elected first secretary of the Communist Party. He immediately attempted to create what was popularly called "socialism with a human face," relaxing restrictions on freedom of speech and the press and the right to travel abroad. Economic reforms were announced, and party control over all aspects of society was reduced. A period of euphoria erupted that came to be known as the "Prague Spring."

It proved to be short-lived. Encouraged by Dubček's actions, some Czechs called for more far-reaching

## The Brezhnev Doctrine

In the summer of 1968, when the new Communist Party leaders in Czechoslovakia were seriously considering proposals for reforming the totalitarian system there, the Warsaw Pact nations met under the leadership of Soviet party chief Leonid Brezhnev to assess the threat to the socialist camp. Shortly after, military forces of several Soviet bloc nations entered Czechoslovakia and imposed a new government subservient to Moscow. The move was justified by the spirit of "proletarian internationalism" and was widely viewed as a warning to China and other socialist states not to stray too far from Marxist-Leninist orthodoxy, as interpreted by the Soviet Union. But Moscow's actions also raised tensions in the Cold War.

*How does Leonid Brezhnev justify the Soviet decision to invade Czechoslovakia? To what degree do you find his arguments persuasive?*

### A Letter to the Central Committee of the Communist Party of Czechoslovakia

Dear comrades!

On behalf of the Central Committees of the Communist and Workers' Parties of Bulgaria, Hungary, the German Democratic Republic, Poland, and the Soviet Union, we address ourselves to you with this letter, prompted by a feeling of sincere friendship based on the principles of Marxism-Leninism and proletarian internationalism and by the concern of our common affairs for strengthening the positions of socialism and the security of the socialist community of nations.

The development of events in your country evokes in us deep anxiety. It is our firm conviction that the offensive of the reactionary forces, backed by imperialists, against your Party and the foundations of the social system in the Czechoslovak Socialist Republic, threatens to push your country off the road of socialism and that consequently it jeopardizes the interests of the entire socialist system. . .

We neither had nor have any intention of interfering in such affairs as are strictly the internal business of your Party and your state, nor of violating the principles of respect, independence, and equality in the relations among the Communist Parties and socialist countries. . . .

At the same time we cannot agree to have hostile forces push your country from the road of socialism and create a threat of severing Czechoslovakia from the socialist community. . . . This is the common cause of our countries, which have joined in the Warsaw Treaty to ensure independence, peace, and security in Europe, and to set up an insurmountable barrier against the intrigues of the imperialist forces, against aggression and revenge. . . . We shall never agree to have imperialism, using peaceful or non-peaceful methods, making a gap from the inside or from the outside in the socialist system, and changing in imperialism's favor the correlation of forces in Europe. . . .

That is why we believe that a decisive rebuff of the anti-communist forces, and decisive efforts for the preservation of the socialist system in Czechoslovakia are not only your task but ours as well. . . .

We express the conviction that the Communist Party of Czechoslovakia, conscious of its responsibility, will take the necessary steps to block the path of reaction. In this struggle you can count on the solidarity and all-round assistance of the fraternal socialist countries.

Warsaw, July 15, 1968.

reforms, including neutrality and withdrawal from the Soviet bloc. To forestall the spread of this "spring fever," the Soviet Red Army, supported by troops from other Warsaw Pact states, invaded Czechoslovakia in August 1968 and crushed the reform movement. Gustav Husak (1913–1991), a committed Stalinist, replaced Dubček and restored the old order, while Moscow attempted to justify its action by issuing the so-called Brezhnev Doctrine (see the box above).

In East Germany, as well, Stalinist policies continued to hold sway. The ruling Communist government in East Germany, led by Walter Ulbricht, had consolidated its position in the early 1950s and became a faithful Soviet satellite. Industry was nationalized and agriculture collectivized. After the 1953 workers' revolt was crushed by Soviet tanks, a steady flight of East Germans to West Germany ensued, primarily through the city of Berlin. This exodus of mostly skilled laborers ("Soon only party chief Ulbricht will be left," remarked one Soviet observer sardonically) created economic problems and in 1961 led the East German government to erect a wall separating East Berlin from West Berlin, as well as even more fearsome barriers along the entire border with West Germany.

After building the Berlin Wall, East Germany succeeded in developing the strongest economy among the Soviet Union's Eastern European satellites. In 1971, Ulbricht was succeeded by Erich Honecker (1912–1994), a party hard-liner. Propaganda increased, and the use of the Stasi, the secret police, became a hallmark of Honecker's virtual dictatorship. Honecker ruled unchallenged for the next eighteen years.

## An Era of Détente

Still, under Brezhnev and Kosygin, the Soviet Union continued to pursue peaceful coexistence with the West and adopted a generally cautious posture in foreign affairs. By the early 1970s, a new age in Soviet-American relations had emerged, often referred to by the French term ***détente,*** meaning a reduction of tensions between the two sides. One symbol of the new relationship was the Antiballistic Missile (ABM) Treaty, often called SALT I (for Strategic Arms Limitation Talks), signed in 1972, in which the two nations agreed to limit the size of their ABM systems.

Washington's objective in pursuing the treaty was to make it unlikely that either superpower could win a nuclear exchange by launching a preemptive strike against the other. U.S. officials believed that a policy of "equivalence," in which there was a roughly equal power balance on each side, was the best way to avoid a nuclear confrontation. Détente was pursued in other ways as well. When President Nixon took office in 1969, he sought to increase trade and cultural contacts with the Soviet Union. His purpose was to set up a series of "linkages" in U.S.-Soviet relations that would persuade Moscow of the economic and social benefits of maintaining good relations with the West.

A symbol of that new relationship was the Helsinki Agreement. Signed in 1975 by the United States, Canada, and all European nations on both sides of the Iron Curtain, these accords recognized all borders in Europe that had been established since the end of World War II, thereby formally acknowledging for the first time the Soviet sphere of influence in Eastern Europe. The Helsinki Agreement also committed the signatories to recognize and protect the human rights of their citizens, a clear effort by the Western states to improve the performance of the Soviet Union and its allies in that arena.

**CHRONOLOGY The Cold War to 1980**

| | |
|---|---|
| Truman Doctrine | 1947 |
| Formation of NATO | 1949 |
| Soviet Union explodes first nuclear device | 1949 |
| Communists come to power in China | 1949 |
| Nationalist government retreats to Taiwan | 1949 |
| Korean War | 1950–1953 |
| Geneva Conference ends Indochina War | 1954 (July 21) |
| Warsaw Pact created | 1955 |
| Khrushchev calls for peaceful coexistence | 1956 |
| Sino-Soviet dispute breaks into the open | 1961 |
| Cuban Missile Crisis | 1962 |
| SALT I treaty signed | 1972 |
| Nixon's visit to China | 1972 |
| Fall of South Vietnam | 1975 |
| Soviet invasion of Afghanistan | 1979 |

## Renewed Tensions in the Third World

Protection of human rights became one of the major foreign policy goals of the next U.S. president, Jimmy Carter (b. 1924). Ironically, just at the point when U.S. involvement in Vietnam came to an end and relations with China began to improve, U.S.-Soviet relations began to sour, for several reasons. Some Americans had become increasingly concerned about aggressive new tendencies in Soviet foreign policy. The first indication came in Africa. Soviet influence was on the rise in Somalia, across the Red Sea from South Yemen, and later in neighboring Ethiopia. In Angola, once a colony of Portugal, an insurgent movement supported by Cuban troops came to power. In 1979, Soviet troops were sent across the border into Afghanistan to protect a newly installed Marxist regime facing internal resistance from fundamentalist Muslims. Some observers suspected that the ultimate objective of the Soviet advance into hitherto neutral Afghanistan was to extend Soviet power into the oil fields of the Persian Gulf. To deter such a possibility, the White House promulgated the Carter Doctrine, which stated that the United States would use its military power, if necessary, to safeguard Western access to the oil reserves in the Middle East. In fact, sources in Moscow later disclosed that the Soviet advance had little to do with the oil of the Persian Gulf but was an effort to increase Soviet influence in a region increasingly beset by Islamic fervor. Soviet officials feared that Islamic activism could spread to the Muslim populations in the Soviet republics in Central Asia and were confident that the United States was too distracted by the **"Vietnam syndrome"** (the public fear of U.S. involvement in another Vietnam-type conflict) to respond.

Another reason for the growing suspicion of the Soviet Union in the United States was that some U.S. defense analysts began to charge that the Soviet Union had rejected the policy of equivalence and was seeking strategic superiority in nuclear weapons. Accordingly, they argued for a substantial increase in U.S. defense spending. Such charges, combined with evidence of Soviet efforts in Africa and the Middle East and reports of the persecution of Jews and dissidents in the Soviet Union, helped undermine public support for détente in the United States. These changing attitudes were reflected in the failure of the Carter administration to obtain congressional approval of a new arms limitation agreement (SALT II), signed with the Soviet Union in 1979.

## Countering the Evil Empire

The early years of the administration of President Ronald Reagan (1911–2004) witnessed a return to the harsh rhetoric, if not all of the harsh practices, of the Cold War. President Reagan's anti-Communist credentials were well known. In a speech given shortly after his election in 1980, he referred to the Soviet Union as an "evil empire" and frequently voiced his suspicion of its motives in foreign affairs. In an effort to eliminate perceived Soviet advantages in strategic weaponry, the White House began a military

## COMPARATIVE ESSAY

# One World, One Environment

A crucial factor that is affecting the evolution of society and the global economy in the early twenty-first century is growing concern over the impact of industrialization on the earth's environment. Humans have always caused some harm to their natural surroundings, but never has the danger of significant ecological damage been as extensive as during the past century. The effects of chemicals introduced into the atmosphere or into rivers, lakes, and oceans have increasingly threatened the health and well-being of all living species.

For many years, the main focus of environmental concern was in the developed countries of the West, where industrial effluents, automobile exhaust, and the use of artificial fertilizers and insecticides led to urban smog, extensive damage to crops and wildlife, and a major reduction of the ozone layer in the upper atmosphere. In recent years, the problem has spread elsewhere. China's headlong rush to industrialization has resulted in major ecological damage in that country. Industrial smog has created almost unlivable conditions in many cities in Asia, while hillsides denuded of their forests have caused severe problems of erosion and destruction of farmlands. Destruction of the rain forest is a growing problem in many parts of the world, notably in Brazil and Indonesia. With the forest cover throughout the earth rapidly disappearing, there is less plant life to perform the crucial process of reducing carbon dioxide levels in the atmosphere.

**Destruction of the Environment.** This stunted tree has been killed by acid rain, a combination of sulfuric and nitric acids mixed with moisture in the air. Entire forests of trees killed by acid rain are becoming common sights in Canada, the United States, and northern Europe.

One of the few beneficial consequences of such incidents has been a growing international consensus that environmental concerns have taken on a truly global character. Although the danger of global warming—allegedly caused by the release, as a result of industrialization, of hothouse gases into the atmosphere—has not yet been definitively proved, it has become a source of sufficient concern to bring about an international conference on the subject in Kyoto, Japan, in December 1997. If, as many scientists predict, worldwide temperatures should continue to increase, the rise in sea levels could pose a significant threat to low-lying islands and coastal areas throughout the world, while climatic change could lead to severe droughts or excessive rainfall in cultivated areas.

It is one thing to recognize a problem, however, and another to solve it. So far, cooperative efforts among nations to alleviate environmental problems have all too often been hindered by economic forces or by political, ethnic, and religious disputes. The 1997 conference on global warming, for example, was marked by bitter disagreement over the degree to which developing countries should share the burden of cleaning up the environment. As a result, it achieved few concrete results. The fact is, few nations have been willing to take unilateral action that might pose an obstacle to economic development plans or lead to a rise in unemployment. In 2001, President George W. Bush refused to sign the Kyoto Agreement on the grounds that it discriminated against advanced Western countries.

buildup that stimulated a renewed arms race. In 1982, the Reagan administration introduced the nuclear-tipped cruise missile, whose ability to fly at low altitudes made it difficult to detect by enemy radar. Reagan also became an ardent exponent of the Strategic Defense Initiative (SDI), nicknamed "**Star Wars.**" Its purposes were to create a space shield that could destroy incoming missiles and to force Moscow into an arms race that it could not hope to win.

The Reagan administration also adopted a more activist, if not confrontational, stance in the Third World. That attitude was most directly demonstrated in Central America, where the revolutionary Sandinista regime had been established in Nicaragua after the overthrow of the Somoza dictatorship in 1979. Charging that the Sandinista regime was supporting a guerrilla insurgency movement in nearby El Salvador, the Reagan administration began to provide material aid to the government in El Salvador while simultaneously supporting an anticommunist guerrilla movement (the **Contras**) in Nicaragua. Though the administration insisted that it was countering the spread of communism in the Western Hemisphere, its Central American policy aroused considerable controversy in Congress, where some members charged that growing U.S. involvement could lead to a repeat of the nation's bitter experience in Vietnam.

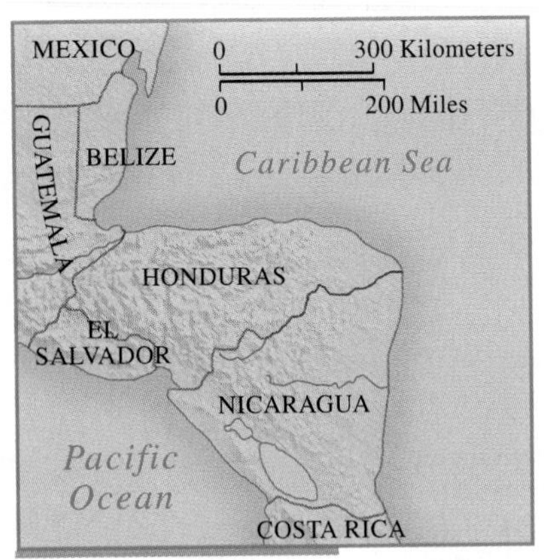

**Northern Central America**

The Reagan administration also took the offensive in other areas. By providing military support to the anti- Soviet insurgents in Afghanistan, the White House helped maintain a Vietnam-like war in Afghanistan that would embed the Soviet Union in its own quagmire. Like the Vietnam War, the conflict in Afghanistan resulted in heavy casualties and demonstrated that the influence of a superpower was limited in the face of strong nationalist, guerrilla-type opposition.

## CONCLUSION

**AT THE END OF WORLD WAR II,** a new conflict erupted in Europe as the new superpowers, the United States and the Soviet Union, began to compete for political domination. This ideological division soon spread to the rest of the world as the United States fought in Korea and Vietnam to prevent the spread of communism, promoted by the new Maoist government in China, while the Soviet Union used its influence to prop up pro-Soviet regimes in Asia, Africa, and Latin America.

Thus what had begun as a confrontation across the great divide of the Iron Curtain in Europe eventually took on global significance. As a result, both Moscow and Washington became entangled in areas that in themselves had little importance in terms of national security interests. To make matters worse, U.S. policy makers all too often applied the lessons of World War II (the so-called **Munich syndrome,** according to which efforts to appease an aggressor only encourage his appetite for conquest) to crisis points in the Third World, where conditions were not remotely comparable.

By the 1980s, however, there were tantalizing signs of a thaw in the Cold War. China and the United States, each hoping to gain leverage with Moscow, had agreed to establish diplomatic relations. Freed from its concerns over Beijing's open support of revolutions in the Third World, the United States decided to withdraw from South Vietnam, and the war there came to an end without involving the great powers in a dangerous confrontation. Although Washington and Moscow continued to compete for advantage all over the world, both sides gradually came to realize that the struggle for domination could best be carried out in the political and economic arenas rather than on the battlefield. If so, world leaders could begin to turn the focus of their attention from ideological confrontation to other issues of common human concern, such as world hunger, and the environment (see the comparative essay "One World, One Environment" on p. 746).

## CHAPTER NOTES

1. Quoted in *Department of State Bulletin,* February 11, 1945, pp. 213–216.
2. Quoted in J. M. Jones, *The Fifteen Weeks (February 21–June 5, 1947),* 2d ed. (New York, 1964), pp. 140–141.
3. Quoted in W. Laqueur, *Europe in Our Time* (New York, 1992), p. 111.
4. Quoted in W. Loth, *The Division of the World, 1941–1955* (New York, 1988), pp. 160–161.
5. Quoted in P. Lane, *Europe Since 1945: An Introduction* (Totowa, N.J., 1985), p. 248.
6. Quoted in R. F. Kennedy, *Thirteen Days: A Memoir of the Cuban Missile Crisis* (New York, 1969), pp. 89–90.

## TIMELINE

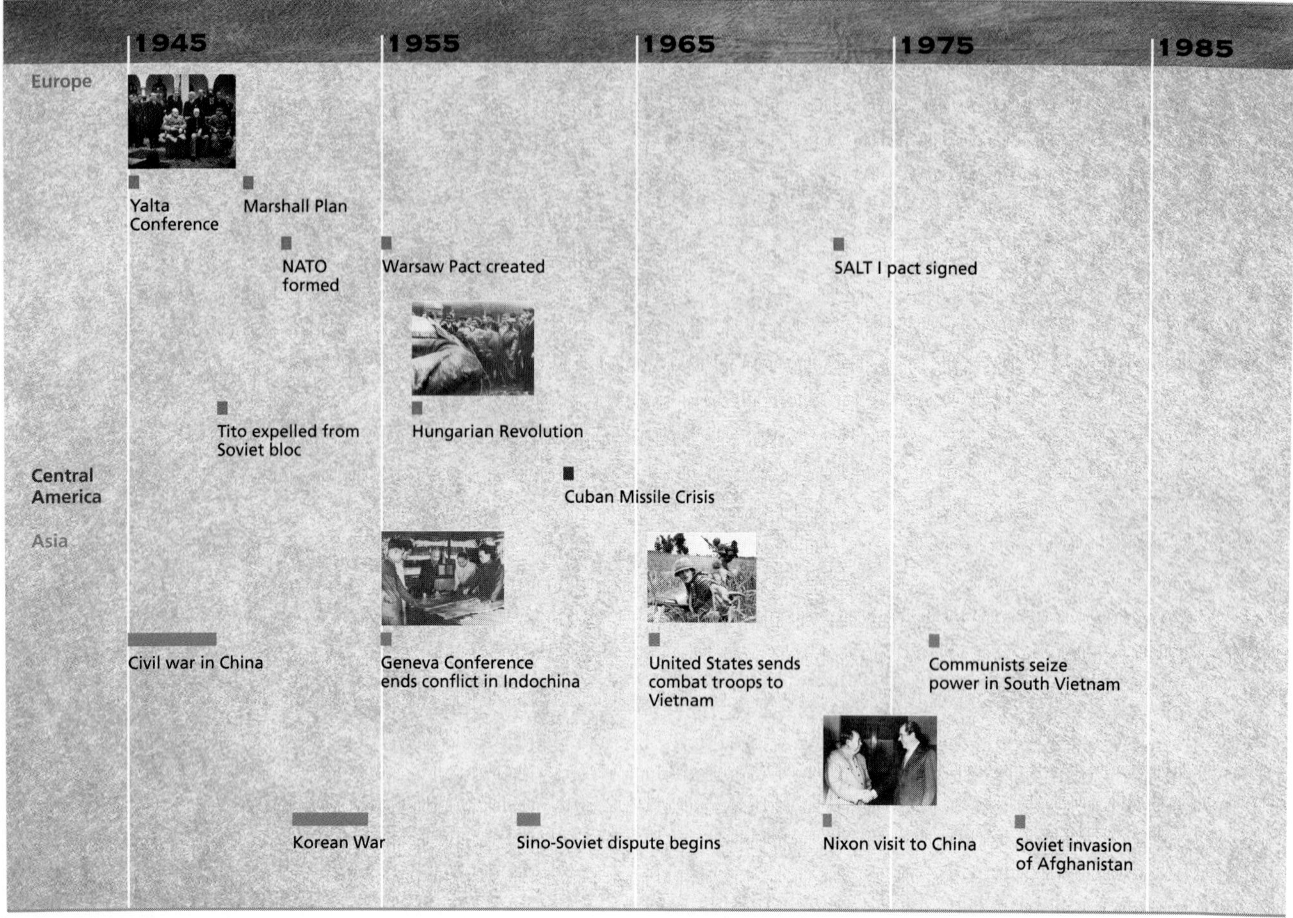


## SUGGESTED READING

There is a detailed literature on the Cold War. Two general accounts are **R. B. Levering, *The Cold War, 1945–1972*** (Arlington Heights, Ill., 1982), and **B. A. Weisberger, *Cold War, Cold Peace: The United States and Russia Since 1945*** (New York, 1984). Two works that maintain that the Soviet Union was chiefly responsible for the Cold War are **H. Feis, *From Trust to Terror: The Onset of the Cold War, 1945–1950*** (New York, 1970), and **A. Ulam, *The Rivals: America and Russia Since World War II*** (New York, 1971). Revisionist studies on the Cold War have emphasized U.S. responsibility for the Cold War, especially its global aspects. These works include **J. Kolko** and **G. Kolko, *The Limits of Power: The World and United States Foreign Policy, 1945–1954*** (New York, 1972); **W. La Feber, *America, Russia, and the Cold War, 1945–1966,*** 2d ed. (New York, 1972); and **M. Sherwin, *A World Destroyed: The Atomic Bomb and the Grand Alliance*** (New York, 1975). For a critique of the revisionist studies, see **R. L. Maddox, *The New Left and the Origins of the Cold War*** (Princeton, N.J., 1973). **R. Garthoff, *Détente and Confrontation: American-Soviet Relations from Nixon to Reagan*** (Washington, D.C., 1985), provides a detailed analysis of U.S.-Soviet relations in the 1970s and 1980s. For a highly competent retrospective analysis of the Cold War era, see **J. L. Gaddis, *We Now Know: Rethinking Cold War History*** (Oxford, 1997). For the perspective of a veteran journalist, see **M. Frankel, *High Noon in the Cold War: Kennedy, Khrushchev, and the Cuban Missile Crisis*** (New York, 2004).

A number of studies of the early stages of the Cold War have been based on documents unavailable until the late 1980s or early 1990s. See, for example, **O. A. Westad, *Cold War and Revolution: Soviet-American Rivalry and the Origins of the Chinese Civil War*** (New York, 1993); **D. A. Mayers, *Cracking the Monolith: U.S. Policy Against the Sino-Soviet Alliance, 1949–1955*** (Baton Rouge, La., 1986); and **Chen Jian, *China's Road to the Korean War: The Making of the Sino-American Confrontation*** (New York, 1994). **S. Goncharov, J. W. Lewis,** and **Xue Litai, *Uncertain Partners: Stalin, Mao, and the Korean War*** (Stanford, Calif., 1993), provides a fascinating view of the war from several perspectives.

For important studies of Soviet foreign policy, see **A. B. Ulam, *Expansion and Coexistence: Soviet Foreign Policy, 1917–1973,*** 2d ed. (New York, 1974), and ***Dangerous Relations: The Soviet Union in World Politics, 1970–1982*** (New York, 1983). The effects of the Cold War on Germany are examined in **J. H. Backer, *The Decision to***

***Divide Germany: American Foreign Policy in Transition*** (Durham, N.C., 1978). On atomic diplomacy in the Cold War, see **G. F. Herken, *The Winning Weapon: The Atomic Bomb in the Cold War, 1945–1950*** (New York, 1981). For a good introduction to the arms race, see **E. M. Bottome, *The Balance of Terror: A Guide to the Arms Race,*** rev. ed. (Boston, 1986).

There are several surveys of Chinese foreign policy since the Communist rise to power. For one important account, see **Chen Jian, *Mao's China and the Cold War*** (Chapel Hill, N.C., 2001). On Sino-U.S. relations, see **H. Harding, *A Fragile Relationship: The United States and China Since 1972*** (Washington, D.C., 1992), and **W. Burr,** ed., ***The Kissinger Transcripts: The Top-Secret Talks with Beijing and Moscow*** (New York, 1998). On Chinese policy in Korea, see **Shu Guang Zhang, *Mao's Military Romanticism: China and the Korean War*** (Lawrence, Kans., 2001), and **Xiaobing Li** et al., ***Mao's Generals Remember Korea*** (Lawrence, Kans., 2001). On Sino-Vietnamese relations, see **Ang Cheng Guan, *Vietnamese Communists' Relations with China and the Second Indochina Conflict*** (Jefferson, N.C., 1997).

**History Now™**

**Enter *HistoryNow* using the access card that is available with this text. *HistoryNow* will assist you in understanding the content in this chapter with lesson plans generated for your needs, as well as provide you with a connection to the *Wadsworth World History Resource Center* (see description below for details).**

**WORLD HISTORY RESOURCE CENTER**

**Enter the Resource Center using either your *HistoryNow* access card or your standalone access card for the *Wadsworth World History Resource Center.* Organized by topic, this website includes quizzes; images; over 350 primary source documents; interactive simulations; maps and timelines; movie explorations; and a wealth of other resources. You can read the following documents, and many more, at http://history.wadsworth.com/rc/world**

Charles Maier on the Cold War
Winston Churchill's Iron Curtain speech
John F. Kennedy, Address on the Cuban Missile Crisis

Visit the *World History* Companion Website for chapter quizzes and more.

http://history.wadsworth.com/duikerspielvogel05/

CHAPTER

# 26

# BRAVE NEW WORLD: COMMUNISM ON TRIAL

## CHAPTER OUTLINE AND FOCUS QUESTIONS

### The Postwar Soviet Union

- How did Nikita Khrushchev change the system that the Soviet dictator Joseph Stalin had put in place before his death in 1953? What were Khrushchev's criticisms of his predecessor?

### The Disintegration of the Soviet Empire

- What were the key components of *perestroika*, which Mikhail Gorbachev espoused during the 1980s? Why were they unsuccessful in preventing the collapse of the Soviet Union?

### The East Is Red: China Under Communism

- What were Mao Zedong's chief goals for China, and what policies did he institute to try to achieve them?

### "Serve the People": Chinese Society Under Communism

- What significant political, economic, and social changes have taken place in China since the death of Mao Zedong?

### CRITICAL THINKING

- Why has Communism survived in China but failed in Eastern Europe and Russia? Compare conditions in China today with those in countries that have abandoned the communist system elsewhere in the world. Are Chinese leaders justified in claiming that without party leadership, the country would fall into chaos?

Courtesy of William J. Duiker

*Shopping in Moscow*

ACCORDING TO KARL MARX, capitalism is a system that involves the exploitation of man by man; under socialism, it is the other way around. That wry joke was typical of popular humor in post–World War II Moscow, where the dreams of a future utopia had faded in the grim reality of life in the Soviet Union.

For the average Soviet citizen after World War II, few images better displayed the shortcomings of the Soviet system than the sight of people queuing up in a long line outside an official state store selling consumer goods. Because the command economy was so inefficient, items of daily use were chronically in such short supply that when a particular item became available, people often lined up immediately to buy several for themselves and their friends. Sometimes, if they saw a line forming, people would automatically join the queue without even knowing what item was available for purchase!

Despite the evident weaknesses of the centralized Soviet economy, the Communist monopoly on power seemed secure, as did Moscow's hold over its client states in Eastern Europe. In fact, for three decades after the end of World War II, the Soviet Empire appeared to be a permanent feature of the international landscape. But by the early 1980s, it had become clear that there were cracks in the Kremlin wall. The Soviet economy was stagnant, the minority nationalities were restive, and Eastern European leaders were increasingly emboldened to test the waters of the global capitalist marketplace. In the United States, the newly elected president, Ronald Reagan, boldly predicted the imminent collapse of the "evil empire."

Although many observers questioned his remarks at the time, they soon seemed uncannily clairvoyant. Within a span of less than three years (1989–1991), the Soviet Union ceased to exist as a nation as Russia and other former Soviet republics declared their separate independence, Communist regimes in Eastern Europe were toppled, and the long-standing division of postwar Europe came to an end. Although Communist parties survived the demise of the system and showed signs of renewed vigor in some countries in the region, their monopoly is gone, and they must now compete with other parties for power.

The fate of communism in China has been quite different. Despite some turbulence, communism has survived in China, even as that nation takes giant strides toward becoming an economic superpower. Yet as China's leaders struggle to bring the nation into the modern age, many of the essential principles of Marxist-Leninist dogma have been tacitly abandoned, and cynicism among the nation's youth is widespread. Whether communism will continue to provide a usable framework for the challenges that lie ahead remains an open question. ◇

## The Postwar Soviet Union

World War II had left the Soviet Union as one of the world's two superpowers and its leader, Joseph Stalin, in a position of strength. He and his Soviet colleagues were now in control of a vast empire (see Map 26.1) that included Eastern Europe, much of the Balkans, and new territory gained from Japan in East Asia.

### From Stalin to Khrushchev

World War II devastated the Soviet Union. Twenty million citizens lost their lives, and cities such as Kiev, Kharkov, and Leningrad suffered enormous physical destruction. As the lands that had been occupied by the German forces were liberated, the Soviet government turned its attention to restoring their economic structures. Nevertheless, in 1945, agricultural production was only 60 percent and steel output only 50 percent of prewar levels. The Soviet people faced incredibly difficult conditions: they worked longer hours; they ate less; they were ill-housed and poorly clothed.

**Stalinism in Action** In the immediate postwar years, the Soviet Union removed goods and materials from occupied Germany and extorted valuable raw materials from its satellite states in Eastern Europe. More important, however, to create a new industrial base, Stalin returned to the method he had used in the 1930s—the extraction of development capital from Soviet labor. Working hard for little pay and for precious few consumer goods, Soviet laborers were expected to produce goods for export with little in return for themselves. The incoming capital from abroad could then be used to purchase machinery and Western technology. The loss of millions of men in the war meant that much of this tremendous workload fell on Soviet women, who performed almost 40 percent of the heavy manual labor.

The pace of economic recovery in the Soviet Union was impressive. By 1947, industrial production had attained 1939 levels; three years later, it had surpassed those levels by 40 percent. New power plants, canals, and giant factories were built, and industrial enterprises and oil fields were established in Siberia and Soviet Central Asia. Stalin's new five-year plan, announced in 1946, reached its goals in less than five years.

Although Stalin's economic recovery policy was successful in promoting growth in heavy industry, primarily for the benefit of the military, consumer goods remained scarce. The development of thermonuclear weapons, MIG fighter planes, and the first space satellite (*Sputnik*) in the 1950s may have elevated the Soviet state's reputation as a world power abroad, but domestically, the Soviet people were shortchanged. Heavy industry grew at a rate three times that of personal consumption. Moreover, the housing shortage was acute, with living conditions especially difficult in the overcrowded cities.

When World War II ended in 1945, Stalin had been in power for more than fifteen years. During that time, he had removed all opposition to his rule and emerged as the undisputed master of the Soviet Union. Political terror enforced by several hundred thousand secret police ensured that he would remain in power. By the late 1940s, there were an estimated nine million Soviet citizens in Siberian concentration camps.

Increasingly distrustful of competitors, Stalin exercised sole authority and pitted his subordinates against each other. His morbid suspicions extended to even his closest colleagues. In 1948, Andrei Zhdanov, his presumed successor and head of the Leningrad party organization, died under mysterious circumstances, but almost certainly at Stalin's order. Within weeks, the Leningrad party organization was purged of several top leaders, many of whom were charged with traitorous connections with Western intelligence agencies. In succeeding years, Stalin directed his suspicion at other members of the inner circle, including Foreign Minister Vyacheslav Molotov.

Known as "Old Stone Butt" in the West for his stubborn defense of Soviet security interests, Molotov had been Stalin's loyal lieutenant since the early years of Stalin's rise to power. Now Stalin distrusted Molotov and had his Jewish wife placed in a Siberian concentration camp. Stalin's colleagues became completely cowed. As he remarked mockingly on one occasion, "When I die, the imperialists will strangle all of you like a litter of kittens."[1]

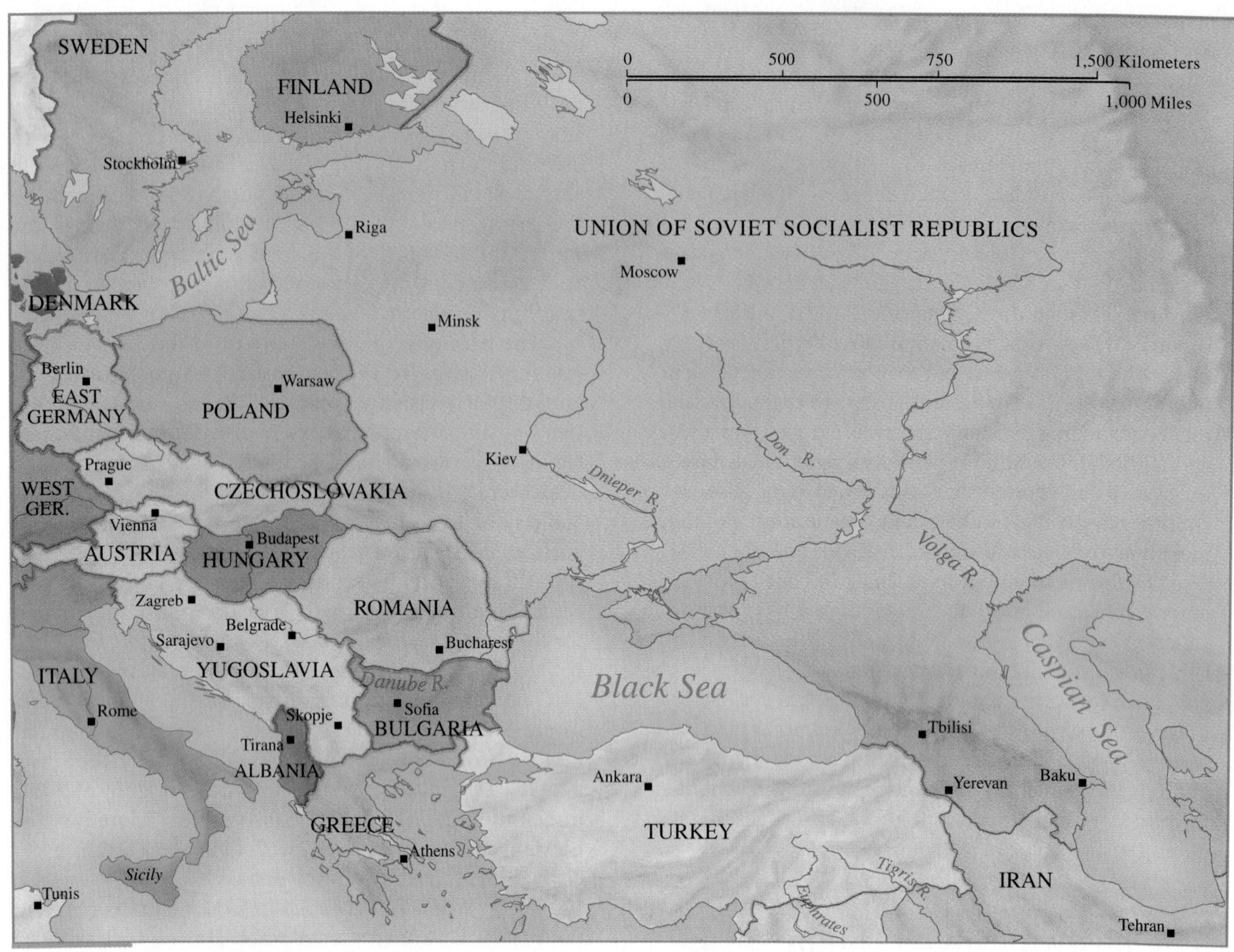


**MAP 26.1** **Eastern Europe and the Soviet Union.** After World War II, the boundaries of Eastern Europe were redrawn as a result of Allied agreements reached at the Tehran and Yalta conferences. This map shows the new boundaries that were established throughout the region, placing Soviet power at the center of Europe. ? How had the boundaries changed from the prewar era? **View an animated version of this map or related maps at** http://history.wadsworth.com/duikerspielvogel05/

Stalin died in 1953 and, after some bitter infighting within the party leadership, was succeeded by Georgy Malenkov, a veteran administrator and ambitious member of the Politburo (the party's governing body). Malenkov came to power with a clear agenda. In foreign affairs, he hoped to promote an easing of Cold War tensions and improve relations with the Western powers. For Moscow's Eastern European allies, he advocated a "new course" in their mutual relations and a decline in Stalinist methods of rule. Inside the Soviet Union, he hoped to reduce defense expenditures and improve the standard of living. Such goals were laudable and probably had the support of the majority of the Russian people, but they did not necessarily appeal to key groups including the army, the Communist Party, the managerial elite, and the security services (now known as the Committee on Government Security, or KGB). Malenkov was soon removed from his position, and power shifted to his rival, the new party general secretary, Nikita Khrushchev.

**The Rise and Fall of Khrushchev** During the struggle for power with Malenkov, Khrushchev had outmaneuvered his rival by calling for heightened defense expenditures and a continuing emphasis on heavy industry. Once in power, however, Khrushchev showed the political dexterity displayed by many an American politician and reversed his priorities. He now resumed the efforts of his predecessor to reduce tensions with the West and boost the standard of living of the Russian people. He moved vigorously to improve the performance of the Soviet economy and revitalize Soviet society. By nature, Khrushchev was a man of enormous energy and an innovator. In an attempt to release the stranglehold of the central bureaucracy over the national economy, he abolished dozens of government ministries and split up the party and government apparatus. Khrushchev also attempted to rejuvenate the stagnant agricultural sector, long the Achilles' heel of the Soviet economy. He attempted to spur production by increasing profit incentives and

Courtesy of William J. Duiker

**The Portals of Doom.** Perhaps the most feared location in the Soviet Union was Lyubyanka Prison, an ornate prerevolutionary building in the heart of Moscow. Taken over by the Bolsheviks after the 1917 revolution, it became the headquarters of the Soviet secret police, the Cheka, later to be known as the KGB. It was here that many Soviet citizens accused of "counterrevolutionary acts" were imprisoned and executed. The figure on the pedestal is Felix Dzerzhinsky, first director of Cheka. After the disintegration of the Soviet Union, the statue was removed.

opened "virgin lands" in Soviet Kazakhstan to bring thousands of acres of new land under cultivation.

Like any innovator, Khrushchev had to overcome the inherently conservative instincts of the Soviet bureaucracy, as well as of the mass of the Soviet population. His plan to remove the "dead hand" of the state, however laudable in intent, alienated much of the Soviet official class, and his effort to split the party angered those who saw it as the central force in the Soviet system. Khrushchev's agricultural schemes inspired similar opposition. Although the Kazakhstan wheat lands would eventually demonstrate their importance, progress was slow, and his effort to persuade Russians to eat more corn (an idea he had apparently picked up during a visit to the United States) earned him the mocking nickname "Cornman." Disappointing agricultural production, combined with high military spending, hurt the Soviet economy. The industrial growth rate, which had soared in the early 1950s, now declined dramatically, from 13 percent in 1953 to 7.5 percent in 1964.

Khrushchev was probably best known for his policy of **destalinization.** Khrushchev had risen in the party hierarchy as a Stalin protégé, but he had been deeply disturbed by his mentor's excesses and, once in a position of authority, moved to excise the Stalinist legacy from Soviet society. The campaign began at the Twentieth National Congress of the Communist Party in February 1956, when Khrushchev gave a long speech in private criticizing some of Stalin's major shortcomings. The speech had apparently not been intended for public distribution, but it was quickly leaked to the Western press and created a sensation throughout the world (see the box on p. 754). During the next few years, Khrushchev encouraged more freedom for writers, artists, and composers, arguing that "readers should be given the chance to make their own judgments" about the acceptability of controversial literature and that "police measures shouldn't be used."[2] Under Khrushchev's instructions, thousands of prisoners were released from concentration camps.

Khrushchev's personality, however, did not endear him to higher Soviet officials, who frowned at his tendency to crack jokes and play the clown. Nor were the higher members of the party bureaucracy pleased when Khrushchev tried to curb their privileges. Foreign policy failures further damaged Khrushchev's reputation among his colleagues. His plan to place missiles in Cuba was the final straw (see Chapter 25). While he was away on vacation in 1964, a special meeting of the Soviet Politburo voted him out of office (because of "deteriorating health") and forced him into retirement. Although a team of leaders succeeded him, real power came into the hands of Leonid Brezhnev (1906–1982), the "trusted" supporter of Khrushchev who had engineered his downfall.

## The Brezhnev Years (1964–1982)

The ouster of Nikita Khrushchev in October 1964 vividly demonstrated the challenges that would be encountered by any leader sufficiently bold to try to reform the Soviet system. In democratic countries, pressure on the government

## Khrushchev Denounces Stalin

Three years after Stalin's death, the new Soviet premier, Nikita Khrushchev, addressed the Twentieth Congress of the Communist Party and denounced the former Soviet dictator for his crimes. This denunciation was the beginning of a policy of destalinization.

*What were the key charges that Khrushchev made against his predecessor, Joseph Stalin? Can it be said that Khrushchev corrected these problems?*

### Khrushchev Addresses the Twentieth Party Congress, February 1956

Comrades, . . . quite a lot has been said about the cult of the individual and about its harmful consequences. . . . The cult of the person of Stalin . . . became at a certain specific stage the source of a whole series of exceedingly serious and grave perversions of Party principles, of Party democracy, of revolutionary legality.

Stalin absolutely did not tolerate collegiality in leadership and in work and . . . practiced brutal violence, not only toward everything which opposed him, but also toward that which seemed to his capricious and despotic character, contrary to his concepts.

Stalin abandoned the method of ideological struggle for that of administrative violence, mass repressions and terror. . . . Arbitrary behavior by one person encouraged and permitted arbitrariness in others. Mass arrests and deportations of many thousands of people, execution without trial and without normal investigation created conditions of insecurity, fear, and even desperation.

Stalin showed in a whole series of cases his intolerance, his brutality, and his abuse of power. . . . He often chose the path of repression and annihilation, not only against actual enemies, but also against individuals who had not committed any crimes against the Party and the Soviet government. . . .

Many Party, Soviet, and economic activists who were branded in 1937–8 as "enemies" were actually never enemies, spies, wreckers, and so on, but were always honest communists; they were only so stigmatized, and often, no longer able to bear barbaric tortures, they charged themselves (at the order of the investigative judges-falsifiers) with all kinds of grave and unlikely crimes.

This was the result of the abuse of power by Stalin, who began to use mass terror against the Party cadres. . . . Stalin put the Party and the NKVD [the Soviet police agency] up to the use of mass terror when the exploiting classes had been liquidated in our country and when there were no serious reasons for the use of extraordinary mass terror. The terror was directed . . . against the honest workers of the Party and the Soviet state. . . .

Stalin was a very distrustful man, sickly, suspicious. . . . Everywhere and in everything he saw "enemies," "two-facers," and "spies." Possessing unlimited power, he indulged in great willfulness and choked a person morally and physically. A situation was created where one could not express one's own will. When Stalin said that one or another would be arrested, it was necessary to accept on faith that he was an "enemy of the people." What proofs were offered? The confession of the arrested. . . . How is it possible that a person confesses to crimes that he had not committed? Only in one way—because of application of physical methods of pressuring him, tortures, bringing him to a state of unconsciousness, deprivation of his judgment, taking away of his human dignity.

**HistoryNow™** To read more of Khrushchev's speech, enter the *HistoryNow* documents area using the access card that is available for *World History*.

comes from various sources in society at large—the business community and labor unions, innumerable interest groups, and, of course, the general public. In the Soviet Union, pressure on government and party leaders originated from sources essentially operating inside the system—the government bureaucracy, the party apparatus, the KGB, and the armed forces.

Leonid Brezhnev, the new party chief, was undoubtedly aware of these realities of Soviet politics, and his long tenure in power was marked, above all, by the desire to avoid changes that might provoke instability, either at home or abroad. Brezhnev was himself a product of the Soviet system. He had entered the ranks of the party leadership under Stalin, and although he was not a particularly avid believer in party ideology—indeed, there were innumerable stories about his addiction to "bourgeois pleasures," including expensive country houses and fast cars (many of them gifts from foreign leaders)—he was no partisan of reform.

Still, Brezhnev sought stability in the domestic arena. He and his prime minister, Alexei Kosygin, undertook what might be described as a program of "de-Khrushchevization," returning the responsibility for long-term planning to the central ministries and reuniting the Communist Party apparatus. Despite some cautious attempts to stimulate the stagnant farm sector, there was no effort to revise the basic collective system. In the industrial sector, the regime launched a series of reforms designed to give factory managers (themselves employees of the state) more responsibility for setting prices, wages, and production quotas. These "Kosygin reforms" had little effect, however, because they were stubbornly resisted by the bureaucracy and were adopted by relatively few enterprises in the vast state-owned industrial sector.

**A Controlled Society** Brezhnev also initiated a significant retreat from Khrushchev's policy of destalinization. Criticism of the "Great Leader" had angered conservatives both within the party hierarchy and among the public at large, many of whom still revered Stalin as a hero and a defender of Russia against Nazi Germany. Many influential figures in the Kremlin feared that destalinization could lead to internal instability and a decline in public trust in the legitimacy of party leadership—the hallowed "dictatorship of the proletariat." Early in Brezhnev's reign, Stalin's reputation began to revive. Although his alleged shortcomings were not totally ignored, he was now described in the official press as "an outstanding party leader" who had been primarily responsible for the successes achieved by the Soviet Union.

The regime also adopted a more restrictive policy toward dissidents in Soviet society. Critics of the Soviet system, such as the physicist Andrei Sakharov, were harassed and arrested or, like the famous writer Alexander Solzhenitsyn, forced to leave the country. There was also a qualified return to the anti-Semitic policies and attitudes that had marked the Stalin era. Such indications of renewed repression aroused concern in the West and were instrumental in the inclusion of a statement on human rights in the 1975 Helsinki Agreement (see Chapter 25).

Free expression was also restricted. The media were controlled by the state and presented only what the state wanted people to hear. The two major newspapers, *Pravda* ("Truth") and *Izvestia* ("News"), were the agents of the party and the government, respectively. Cynics joked that there was no news in *Pravda* and no truth in *Izvestia*. According to Western journalists, airplane accidents in the Soviet Union were rarely publicized, on the grounds that they would raise questions about the quality of the Soviet airline industry. The government made strenuous efforts to prevent the Soviet people from exposure to harmful foreign ideas, especially modern art, literature, and rock music. When the Summer Olympic Games were held in Moscow in 1980, Soviet newspapers advised citizens to keep their children indoors to keep them from being polluted with "bourgeois" ideas passed on by foreign visitors.

For citizens of Western democracies, such a political atmosphere would seem highly oppressive, but for the Russian people, an emphasis on law and order was an accepted aspect of everyday life inherited from the tsarist period. Conformity was the rule in virtually every corner of Soviet society, from the educational system (characterized at all levels by rote memorization and political indoctrination) to child rearing (it was forbidden, for example, to be left-handed) and even to yearly vacations (most workers took their vacations at resorts run by their employer, where the daily schedule of activities was highly regimented). Young Americans studying in the Soviet Union reported that their Soviet friends were often shocked to hear U.S. citizens criticizing their own president.

**A Stagnant Economy** Soviet leaders also failed to achieve their objective of revitalizing the national economy. Whereas growth rates during the early Khrushchev era had been impressive (prompting Khrushchev during a 1956 reception at the Kremlin to chortle, "We will bury you"), under Brezhnev industrial growth declined to an annual rate of less than 4 percent in the early 1970s and less than 3 percent in the period from 1975 to 1980. Successes in the agricultural sector were equally meager. Grain production rose from less than 90 million tons in the early 1950s to nearly 200 million tons in the 1970s but then stagnated at that level.

One of the primary problems with the Soviet economy was the absence of incentives. Salary structures offered little reward for hard labor and extraordinary achievement. Pay differentials operated in a much narrower range than in most Western societies, and there was little danger of being dismissed. According to the Soviet constitution, every Soviet citizen was guaranteed an opportunity to work.

There were, of course, some exceptions to this general rule. Athletic achievement was highly prized, and a gymnast of Olympic stature would receive great rewards in the form of prestige and lifestyle. Senior officials did not receive high salaries but were provided with countless perquisites, such as access to foreign goods, official automobiles with a chauffeurs, and entry into prestigious institutions of higher learning for their children. For the elite, it was *blat* (influence) that most often differentiated them from the rest of the population. The average citizen, however, had little material incentive to produce beyond the minimum acceptable level. It is hardly surprising that per capita productivity was only about half that realized in most capitalist countries. At the same time, the rudeness of clerks and waiters became legendary.

The problem of incentives existed at the managerial level as well, where centralized planning discouraged initiative and innovation. Factory managers, for example, were assigned monthly and annual quotas by the Gosplan (the "state plan," drawn up by the central planning commission). Because state-owned factories faced little or no competition, managers did not care whether their products were competitive in terms of price and quality, so long as the quota was attained. One of the key complaints of Soviet citizens was the low quality of domestic consumer goods. Knowledgeable consumers quickly discovered that products manufactured at the end of the month were often of lower quality (because factory workers had to rush to meet their quotas) and attempted to avoid purchasing them.

Often consumer goods were simply unavailable. Soviet citizens automatically got in line when they saw a queue forming in front of a store because they never knew when something might be available again. When they reached the head of the line, most would purchase several of the same item in order to swap with their friends and neighbors. A popular joke at the time was that a Soviet inventor had managed to produce an airplane that was

Courtesy of William J. Duiker

**Queuing Up.** Because of the policy of state control over the economy, the availability of goods in the Soviet Union was a consequence not of market factors but of decisions made by government bureaucrats. As a result, needed goods were often in short supply. When Soviet citizens heard that a shipment of a particular product had arrived at a state store, they queued up to buy it. Here shoppers line up in front of a state-run store selling dinnerware in Moscow.

cheap enough to be purchased by every citizen. Everyone was delighted because now when they heard that there was a sale of a particular item anywhere in the country, they would be able to fly in and buy it. This "queue psychology," of course, was a time-consuming process and inevitably served to reduce the per capita rate of productivity.

Soviet citizens often tried to overcome the shortcomings of the system by resorting to the black market. Private economic activities, of course, were illegal, but many workers took to moonlighting to augment their meager salaries. An employee in a state-run appliance store, for example, would promise to repair a customer's television set on his own time in return for a payment "under the table." Otherwise, servicing of the set might require several weeks. Knowledgeable observers estimated that as much as one-third of the entire Soviet economy operated outside the legal system.

Another major obstacle to economic growth was inadequate technology. Except in the area of national defense, the overall level of Soviet technology was not comparable to that of the West or the advanced industrial societies of East Asia. Part of the problem, of course, stemmed from the issues already described. With no competition, factory managers had little incentive to improve the quality of their products. But another reason was the high priority assigned to defense. The military sector regularly received the most resources from the government and attracted the cream of the country's scientific talent.

**An Aging Leadership** Such problems would be intimidating for any government; they were particularly so for the elderly generation of party leaders surrounding Leonid Brezhnev, many of whom were cautious to a fault. Though some undoubtedly recognized the need for reform and innovation, they were paralyzed by the fear of instability and change. The problem worsened during the late 1970s when Brezhnev's health began to deteriorate.

Brezhnev died in November 1982 and was succeeded by Yuri Andropov (1914–1984), a party veteran and head of the Soviet secret services. During his brief tenure as party chief, Andropov was a vocal advocate of reform, but most of his initiatives were limited to the familiar nostrums of punishment for wrongdoers and moral exhortations to Soviet citizens to work harder. At the same time, material incentives were still officially discouraged and generally ineffective. Andropov had been ailing when he was selected to succeed Brezhnev as party chief, and when he died after only a few months in office, little had been done to change the system. He was succeeded, in turn, by a mediocre party stalwart, the elderly Konstantin

Chernenko (1911–1985). With the Soviet system in crisis, Moscow seemed stuck in a time warp. As one concerned observer told an American journalist, "I had a sense of foreboding, like before a storm. That there was something brewing in people and there would be a time when they would say, 'That's it. We can't go on living like this. We can't. We need to redo everything.'"[3]

## Cultural Expression in the Soviet Bloc

In his occasional musings about the future communist utopia, Karl Marx had predicted that a new, classless society would replace the exploitative and hierarchical systems of feudalism and capitalism. Workers would engage in productive activities and share equally in the fruits of their labor. In their free time, they would produce a new, advanced culture, proletarian in character and egalitarian in content.

The reality in the post–World War II Soviet Union and Eastern Europe was somewhat different. Under Stalin, the Soviet cultural scene was a wasteland. Beginning in 1946, a series of government decrees made all forms of literary and scientific expression dependent on the state. All Soviet culture was expected to follow the party line. Historians, philosophers, and social scientists all grew accustomed to quoting Marx, Lenin, and, above all, Stalin as their chief authorities. Novels and plays, too, were supposed to portray Communist heroes and their efforts to create a better society. No criticism of existing social conditions was permitted. Even distinguished composers such as Dmitry Shostakovich were compelled to heed Stalin's criticisms, including his view that contemporary Western music was nothing but a "mishmash." Some areas of intellectual activity were virtually abolished; the science of genetics disappeared, and few movies were made during Stalin's final years.

Stalin's death brought a modest respite from cultural repression. Writers and artists banned during the Stalin years were again allowed to publish. Still, Soviet authorities, including Khrushchev, were reluctant to allow cultural freedom to move far beyond official Soviet ideology.

These restrictions, however, did not prevent the emergence of some significant Soviet literature, although authors paid a heavy price if they alienated the Soviet authorities. Boris Pasternak (1890–1960), who began his literary career as a poet, won the Nobel Prize in 1958 for his celebrated novel *Doctor Zhivago,* written between 1945 and 1956 and published in Italy in 1957. But the Soviet government condemned Pasternak's anti-Soviet tendencies, banned the novel, and would not allow him to accept the prize. The author had alienated the authorities by describing a society scarred by the excesses of Bolshevik revolutionary zeal.

Alexander Solzhenitsyn (b. 1918) caused an even greater furor than Pasternak. Solzhenitsyn had spent eight years in forced labor camps for criticizing Stalin, and his novel *One Day in the Life of Ivan Denisovich,* which won him the Nobel Prize in 1970, was an account of life in those camps (see the box on p. 758). Khrushchev allowed the book's publication as part of his destalinization campaign. Solzhenitsyn then wrote *The Gulag Archipelago,* a detailed indictment of the whole system of Soviet oppression. Soviet authorities denounced Solzhenitsyn's efforts to inform the world of Soviet crimes against humanity and expelled him from the Soviet Union in 1973.

Courtesy of William J. Duiker

**Stalinist Heroic: An Example of Socialist Realism.** Under Stalin and his successors, art was assigned the task of indoctrinating the Soviet population on the public virtues, such as hard work, loyalty to the state, and patriotism. Grandiose statuary erected to commemorate the heroic efforts of the Red Army during World War II appeared in every Soviet city. Here is an example in Minsk, today the capital of Belarus.

Exile abroad rather than imprisonment in forced labor camps was perhaps a sign of modest progress. But even the limited freedom that had arisen during the Khrushchev years was rejected after his fall from power. Cultural controls were reimposed, destalinization was halted, and authors were again sent to labor camps for expressing outlawed ideas. These restrictive policies continued until the late 1980s.

In the Eastern European satellites, cultural freedom varied considerably from country to country. In Poland, intellectuals had access to Western publications as well as greater freedom to travel to the West. Hungarian and Yugoslav Communists, too, tolerated a certain level of intellectual activity that was not liked but at least not prohibited. Elsewhere, intellectuals were forced to conform to the regime's demands. After the Soviet invasion of Czechoslovakia in 1968 (see Chapter 25), Czech Communists pursued a policy of strict cultural control.

The socialist camp also experienced the many facets of modern popular culture. By the early 1970s, there were 28 million television sets in the Soviet Union, although state authorities controlled the content of the programs that the Soviet people watched. Tourism, too, made inroads into the Communist world as state-run industries provided vacation time and governments established resorts for workers on the Black Sea and Adriatic

## One Day in the Life of Ivan Denisovich

On November 20, 1962, a Soviet magazine published a work by Alexander Solzhenitsyn that created a literary and political furor. The short novel related one day in the life of its chief character, Ivan Denisovich, at a Siberian concentration camp, to which he had been sentenced at the end of World War II for supposedly spying for the Germans while a Soviet soldier. This excerpt narrates the daily journey from the prison camp to a work project through the 17 degrees-below-zero cold of Siberia. Many Soviets identified with Ivan as a symbol of the suffering they had endured under Stalin.

*What was the purpose of the author in writing this literary work? How did it contribute to Khrushchev's destalinization program?*

### Alexander Solzhenitsyn, *One Day in the Life of Ivan Denisovich*

There were escort guards all over the place. They flung a semicircle around the column on its way to the power station, their machine guns sticking out and pointing right at your face. And there were guards with gray dogs. One dog bared its fangs as if laughing at the prisoners. The escorts all wore short sheepskins, except for half a dozen whose coats trailed the ground. The long sheepskins were interchangeable: they were worn by anyone whose turn had come to man the watchtowers.

And once again as they brought the squads together the escort recounted the entire power-station column by fives. . . .

Out beyond the camp boundary the intense cold, accompanied by a headwind, stung even Shukhov's face, which was used to every kind of unpleasantness. Realizing that he would have the wind in his face all the way to the power station, he decided to make use of his bit of rag. To meet the contingency of a headwind he, like many other prisoners, had got himself a cloth with a long tape on each end. The prisoners admitted that these helped a bit. Shukhov covered his face up to the eyes, brought the tapes around below his ears, and fastened the ends together at the back of his neck. Then he covered his nape with the flap of his hat and raised his coat collar. The next thing was to pull the front flap of the hat down into his brow. Thus in front only his eyes remained unprotected. He fixed his coat tightly at the waist with the rope. Now everything was in order except for his hands, which were already stiff with cold (his mittens were worthless). He rubbed them, he clapped them together, for he knew that in a moment he'd have to put them behind his back and keep them there for the entire march.

The chief of the escort guard recited the "morning prayer," which every prisoner was heartily sick of:

"Attention, prisoners. Marching orders must be strictly obeyed. Keep to your ranks. No hurrying, keep a steady pace. No talking. Keep your eyes fixed ahead and your hands behind your backs. A step to right or left is considered an attempt to escape and the escort has orders to shoot without warning. Leading guards, on the double."

The two guards in the lead of the escort must have set out along the road. The column heaved forward, shoulders swaying, and the escorts, some twenty paces to the right and left of the column, each man at a distance of ten paces from the next, machine guns held at the ready, set off too.

coasts. In Poland, the number of vacationers who used holiday retreats increased from 700,000 in 1960 to 2.8 million in 1972.

Spectator sports became a large industry and were also highly politicized as a result of Cold War divisions. "Each new victory," one party leader stated, "is a victory for the Soviet form of society and the socialist sport system; it provides irrefutable proof of the superiority of socialist culture over the decaying culture of the capitalist states."[4] Accordingly, the state provided money for the construction of gymnasiums and training camps and portrayed athletes as superheroes.

## Social Changes in the Soviet Union and Eastern Europe

The imposition of Marxist systems in Eastern Europe had far-reaching social consequences. Most Eastern European countries made the change from peasant societies to modern, industrialized economies. In Bulgaria, for example, 80 percent of the labor force was engaged in agriculture in 1950, but only 20 percent was still working there in 1980. Although the Soviet Union and its Eastern European satellites never achieved the high standards of living of the West, they did experience some improvement. In 1960, the average real income of Polish peasants was four times higher than before World War II. Consumer goods also became more widely available. In East Germany, only 17 percent of families had television sets in 1960, but 75 percent had acquired them by 1972.

According to Marxist doctrine, state control of industry and the elimination of private property were supposed to lead to a classless society. Although that ideal was never achieved, it did have important social consequences. For one thing, traditional ruling classes were stripped of their special status after 1945. The Potocki family in Poland, for example, which had owned 9 million acres of land before the war, lost all of its possessions, and family members were reduced to the ranks of common laborers.

**Education** The desire to create a classless society led to noticeable changes in education. In some countries, laws mandated quota systems based on class. In East Germany, for example, 50 percent of the students in secondary schools had to be children of workers and peasants. The sons of manual workers constituted 53 percent of university students in Yugoslavia in 1964 and 40 percent in East Germany, compared to only 15 percent in Italy and 5.3 percent in West Germany. Social mobility also increased. In Poland in 1961, half of all white-collar workers came from blue-collar families. A significant number of judges, professors, and industrial managers stemmed from working-class backgrounds.

Education became crucial in preparing for new jobs in the communist system and led to higher enrollments in both secondary schools and universities. In Czechoslovakia, for example, the number of students in secondary schools tripled between 1945 and 1970, and the number of university students quadrupled between the 1930s and the 1960s. The type of education that students received also changed. In Hungary before World War II, 40 percent of students studied law, 9 percent engineering and technology, and 5 percent agriculture. In 1970, 35 percent were in engineering and technology, 9 percent in agriculture, and only 4 percent in law.

By the 1970s, the new managers of society, regardless of class background, realized the importance of higher education and used their power to gain special privileges for their children. By 1971, 60 percent of the children of white-collar workers attended university, and even though blue-collar families constituted 60 percent of the population, only 36 percent of their children attended institutions of higher learning. Even East Germany dropped its requirement that 50 percent of secondary students had to be the offspring of workers and peasants.

**The New Elite** This shift in educational preferences demonstrates yet another aspect of the social structure in the communist world: the emergence of a new privileged class, made up of members of the Communist Party, state officials, high-ranking officers in the military and the secret police, and a few special professional groups. The new elite not only possessed political power but also received special privileges, including the right to purchase high-quality goods in special stores (in Czechoslovakia, the elite could obtain organically grown produce not available to anyone else), paid vacations at special resorts, access to good housing and superior medical services, and advantages in education and jobs for their children. In 1980, in one Soviet province, 70 percent of Communist Party members came from the families of managers, technicians, and government and party bureaucrats.

Ideals of equality did not include women. Men dominated the leadership positions of the Communist parties. Women did have greater opportunities in the workforce and even in the professions, however. In the Soviet Union, women comprised 51 percent of the labor force in 1980; by the mid-1980s, they constituted 50 percent of the engineers, 80 percent of the doctors, and 75 percent of the teachers and teachers' aides. But many of these were low-paying jobs; most female doctors, for example, worked in primary care and were paid less than skilled machinists. The chief administrators in hospitals and schools were still men.

Moreover, although women made up nearly half of the workforce, they were never freed of their traditional roles in the home (see the box on p. 760). Most women confronted what came to be known as the "double shift." After working eight hours in their jobs, they came home to face the housework and care of the children. They might spend two hours a day in long lines at a number of stores waiting to buy food and clothes. Because of the housing situation, they were forced to use kitchens that were shared by a number of families.

Nearly three-quarters of a century after the Bolshevik Revolution, then, the Marxist dream of an advanced, egalitarian society was as far away as ever. Although in some respects conditions in the socialist camp were better than before World War II, many problems and inequities were as intransigent as ever.

## The Disintegration of the Soviet Empire

On the death of Konstantin Chernenko in 1985, party leaders selected a talented and youthful Soviet official, Mikhail Gorbachev, to succeed him. The new Soviet leader had shown early signs of promise. Born into a peasant family in 1931, Gorbachev combined farmwork with school and received the Order of the Red Banner for his agricultural efforts. This award and his good school record enabled him to study law at the University of Moscow. After receiving his law degree in 1955, he returned to his native southern Russia, where he eventually became first secretary of the Communist Party in the city of Stavropol (he had joined the party in 1952) and then first secretary of the regional party committee. In 1978, Gorbachev was made a member of the party's Central Committee in Moscow. Two years later, he became a full member of the ruling Politburo and secretary of the Central Committee.

During the early 1980s, Gorbachev began to realize the immensity of Soviet problems and the crucial need to transform the system. During a visit to Canada in 1983, he discovered to his astonishment that Canadian farmers worked hard on their own initiative. "We'll never have this for fifty years," he reportedly remarked.[5] On his return to Moscow, he set up a number of committees to evaluate the situation and recommend measures to improve the system.

## "It's So Difficult to Be a Woman Here"

One of the major problems for Soviet women was the balancing of work and family roles, a problem noticeably ignored by authorities. This excerpt is taken from a series of interviews of thirteen women in Moscow conducted in the late 1970s by Swedish investigators. As is evident in this interview with Anna, a young wife and mother, these Soviet women took pride in their achievements but were also frustrated with their lives. It is hardly surprising that the conflicting pressures on women between the demands of the family and the state's push for industrialization would result in a drop in birthrates and a change in family structure.

*How does this passage reflect the role of women in the Soviet Union? It what sense is that role different from that of women in the West?*

### Moscow Women: Interview with Anna

[Anna is twenty-one and married, has a three-month-old daughter, and lives with her husband and daughter in a one-room apartment with a balcony and a large bathroom. Anna works as a hairdresser; her husband is an unemployed writer.]

*Are there other kinds of jobs dominated by women?* Of course! Preschool teachers are exclusively women. Also beauticians. But I guess that's about all. Here women work in every profession, from tractor drivers to engineers. But I think there ought to be more jobs specifically for women so that there are *some* differences. In this century women have to be equal to men. Now women wear pants, have short hair, and hold important jobs, just like men. There are almost no differences left. Except in the home.

*Do women and men have the same goal in life?* Of course. Women want to get out of the house and have careers, just the same as men do. It gives women a lot of advantages, higher wages, and so on. In that sense we have the same goal, but socially I don't think so. The family is, after all, more important for a woman. A man can live without a family; all he needs is for a woman to come from time to time to clean for him and do his laundry. He sleeps with her if he feels like it. Of course, a woman can adopt this lifestyle, but I still think that most women want their own home, family, children. From time immemorial, women's instincts have been rooted in taking care of their families, tending to their husbands, sewing, washing—all the household chores. Men are supposed to provide for the family; women should keep the home fires burning. This is so deeply ingrained in women that there's no way of changing it.

*Whose career do you think is the most important?* The man's, naturally. The family is often broken up because women don't follow their men when they move where they can get a job. That was the case of my in-laws. They don't live together any longer because my father-in-law worked for a long time as far away as Smolensk. He lived alone, without his family, and then, of course, it was only natural that things turned out the way they did. It's hard for a man to live without his family when he's used to being taken care of all the time. Of course there are men who can endure, who continue to be faithful, etc., but for most men it isn't easy. For that reason I think a woman ought to go where her husband does. . . .

That's the way it is. Women have certain obligations, men others. One has to understand that at an early age. Girls have to learn to take care of a household and help at home. Boys too, but not as much as girls. Boys ought to be with their fathers and learn how to do masculine chores. . . .

It's so difficult to be a woman here. With emancipation, we lead such abnormal, twisted lives, because women have to work the same as men do. As a result, women have very little time for themselves to work on their femininity.

## The Gorbachev Era

With his election as party general secretary in 1985, Gorbachev seemed intent on taking earlier reforms to their logical conclusions. The cornerstone of his program was ***perestroika,*** or "restructuring." At first it meant only a reordering of economic policy, as Gorbachev called for the beginning of a market economy with limited free enterprise and some private property. Initial economic reforms were difficult to implement, however. Radicals demanded decisive measures; conservatives feared that rapid changes would be too painful. In his attempt to achieve compromise, Gorbachev often pursued partial liberalization, which satisfied neither faction and also failed to work, producing only more discontent.

Gorbachev soon perceived that in the Soviet system, the economic sphere was intimately tied to the social and political spheres. Any efforts to reform the economy without political or social reform would be doomed to failure. One of the most important instruments of *perestroika* was ***glasnost,*** or "openness." Soviet citizens and officials were encouraged to discuss openly the strengths and weaknesses of the Soviet Union. This policy could be seen in *Pravda*, the official newspaper of the Communist Party, where news of disasters such as the nuclear accident at Chernobyl in 1986 and collisions of ships in the Black Sea began to appear. This more liberal approach was soon extended to include reports of official corruption, sloppy factory work, and protests against government policy. The arts also benefited from the new policy as previously banned works were now published and motion pictures were allowed to depict negative aspects of Soviet life. Music based on Western styles, such as jazz and rock, could now be performed

Courtesy of William J. Duiker

**Something Old, Something New.** Under Soviet rule, church weddings were declared illegal and marriage became a simple civil ceremony, lacking the ritual solemnity that religious sanctions had previously provided. With the disintegration of the Soviet Union in 1991, many people began to return to prerevolutionary practices. Here newlyweds in the Ukrainian port city of Odessa celebrate their marriage ties in the traditional manner.

openly. Religious activities, long banned by the government, were once again tolerated.

Political reforms were equally revolutionary. In June 1987, the principle of two-candidate elections was introduced; previously, voters had been presented with only one candidate. Most dissidents, including Andrei Sakharov, who had spent years in internal exile, were released. At the Communist Party conference in 1988, Gorbachev called for the creation of a new Soviet parliament, the Congress of People's Deputies, whose members were to be chosen in competitive elections. It convened in 1989, the first such meeting in the nation since 1918. Because of its size, the Congress chose a Supreme Soviet of 450 members to deal with day-to-day activities. The revolutionary nature of Gorbachev's political reforms was evident in Sakharov's rise from dissident to elected member of the Congress of People's Deputies. As a leader of the dissident deputies, Sakharov called for an end to the Communist monopoly of power and, on December 11, 1989, the day he died, urged the creation of a new, noncommunist party. Early in 1990, Gorbachev legalized the formation of other political parties and struck out Article 6 of the Soviet Constitution, which guaranteed the "leading role" of the Communist Party. Hitherto, the position of first secretary of the party was the most important post in the Soviet Union, but as the Communist Party became less closely associated with the state, the powers of this office diminished. Gorbachev attempted to consolidate his power by creating a new state presidency and in March 1990 became the Soviet Union's first president.

**The Beginning of the End** One of Gorbachev's most serious problems stemmed from the nature of the Soviet Union. The Union of Soviet Socialist Republics was a truly multiethnic country, containing 92 nationalities and 112 recognized languages. Previously, the iron hand of the Communist Party, centered in Moscow, had kept a lid on the centuries-old ethnic tensions that had periodically erupted throughout the history of the region. As Gorbachev released this iron grip, tensions resurfaced, a by-product of *glasnost* that Gorbachev had not anticipated. Ethnic groups took advantage of the new openness to protest what they perceived to be ethnically motivated slights. As violence erupted, the Soviet army, in disarray since the Soviet intervention in Afghanistan in 1979, had difficulty controlling the situation. In some cases, independence movements and ethnic causes became linked, as in Azerbaijan, where the National Front became the spokesgroup for the Muslim Azerbaijanis in the conflict with Christian Armenians.

The period from 1988 to 1990 witnessed the emergence of nationalist movements throughout the republics of the Soviet Union. Often motivated by ethnic concerns, many of them called for sovereignty of the republics and independence from Russian-based rule centered in Moscow. Such movements sprang up first in Georgia in late 1988 and then in Latvia, Estonia, Moldavia, Uzbekistan, Azerbaijan, and Lithuania.

In December 1989, the Communist Party of Lithuania declared itself independent of the Communist Party of the Soviet Union. Gorbachev made it clear that he supported self-determination but not secession, which he believed would be detrimental to the Soviet Union. Nevertheless, on March 11, 1990, the Lithuanian Supreme Council unilaterally declared Lithuania independent. Its formal name was now the Lithuanian Republic; the adjectives Soviet and Socialist had been dropped. On March 15, the Soviet Congress of People's Deputies, though recognizing a general right to secede from the Union of Soviet Socialist Republics, declared the Lithuanian declaration null and void, insisting that proper procedures must be followed before secession would be acceptable.

**Twilight of Empire** During 1990 and 1991, Gorbachev struggled to deal with Lithuania and the other problems unleashed by his reforms. On the one hand, he tried to appease the conservative forces who complained about the growing disorder within the Soviet Union. On the other hand, he tried to accommodate the liberal forces, especially those in the Soviet republics, who increasingly favored a new kind of decentralized Soviet federation. Gorbachev especially labored to cooperate more closely with Boris Yeltsin (b. 1931), elected president of the Russian Republic in June 1991.

By 1991, conservatives within the army, government, KGB, and military industries had grown increasingly worried about the possible dissolution of the Soviet Union and its impact on their own fortunes. On August 19, 1991, a group of these discontented rightists arrested Gorbachev and attempted to seize power. Gorbachev's unwillingness to work with the conspirators and the

**MAP 26.2 Eastern Europe and the former Soviet Union.** After the disintegration of the Soviet Union in 1991, several onetime Soviet republics declared their independence. This map shows the new configuration of the states that emerged in the 1990s from the former Soviet Union. The breakaway region of Chechnya is indicated on the map. ? What new nations have appeared from the old Soviet Union since the end of the Cold War? **View an animated version of this map or related maps at** http://history.wadsworth.com/duikerspielvogel05/

brave resistance in Moscow of Yeltsin and thousands of Russians who had grown accustomed to their new liberties caused the coup to disintegrate rapidly. The actions of these right-wing plotters served to accelerate the very process they had hoped to stop—the disintegration of the Soviet Union.

Despite desperate pleas from Gorbachev, the Soviet republics soon opted for complete independence. Ukraine voted for independence on December 1, 1991. A week later, the leaders of Russia, Ukraine, and Belarus announced that the Soviet Union had "ceased to exist" and would be replaced by a "commonwealth of independent states." Gorbachev resigned on December 25, 1991, and turned over his responsibilities as commander in chief to Boris Yeltsin, the president of Russia. By the end of 1991, one of the largest empires in world history had come to an end, and a new era had begun in its lands (see Map 26.2).

## The New Russia: From Empire to Nation

Within Russia, a new power struggle soon ensued. Yeltsin, a onetime engineer from Sverdlovsk who had been dismissed from the Politburo in 1987 for radicalism, was committed to introducing a free market economy as quickly as possible. In December 1991, the Congress of People's Deputies granted Yeltsin temporary power to rule by decree. But former Communist Party members and their allies in the Congress were opposed to many of Yeltsin's economic reforms and tried to place new limits on his powers. Yeltsin fought back. After winning a vote of confidence, both in himself and in his economic reforms, on April 25, 1993, Yeltsin pushed ahead with plans for a new Russian constitution that would abolish the Congress of People's Deputies, create a two-chamber parliament, and establish a strong presidency.

Nevertheless, the conflict between Yeltsin and the Congress continued and turned violent. On September 21, Yeltsin issued a decree dissolving the Congress of People's Deputies and scheduling new parliamentary elections for December. A hard-line parliamentary minority resisted and even took the offensive, urging supporters to take over government offices and the central television station. On October 4, Yeltsin responded by ordering military forces to storm the parliament building and arrest hard-line opponents. Yeltsin used his victory to consolidate his power; at the same time, he remained committed to holding new parliamentary elections on December 12.

During the mid-1990s, Yeltsin was able to maintain a precarious grip on power while seeking to implement reforms that would place Russia on a firm course toward a pluralistic political system and a market economy. But the new post-Communist Russia remained as fragile as ever. Burgeoning economic inequality and rampant corruption aroused widespread criticism and shook the confidence of the Russian people in the superiority of the capitalist system over the one that existed under Communist rule. A nagging war in the Caucasus—where the people of Chechnya have resolutely sought national independence from Russia—drained the government budget and exposed the decrepit state of the once vaunted Red Army. In presidential elections held in 1996, Yeltsin was reelected, but the rising popularity of a revived Communist Party and the growing strength of nationalist elements, combined with Yeltsin's precarious health, raised serious questions about the future of the country.

What derailed Yeltsin's plan to transform Soviet society? To some critics, Yeltsin tried to achieve too much too fast. Between 1991 and 1995, state firms that had previously provided about 80 percent of all industrial production and employment had been privatized, while the price of goods (previously subject to government regulation) was opened up to market forces. Only agriculture, where the decision to privatize collective farms had little impact in rural areas, was left substantially untouched. The immediate results were disastrous: industrial output dropped by over a third, while unemployment levels and prices rose dramatically. Many Russian workers and soldiers were not paid their salaries for months on end, and many social services came to an abrupt halt.

There were other problems as well. With the harsh official and ideological constraints of the Soviet system suddenly removed, corruption—labeled by one observer "criminal gang capitalism"—became rampant, and the government often appeared inept in coping with the complexities of a market economy. Few Russians seemed to grasp the realities of modern capitalism and understandably reacted to the inevitable transition pains from the old system by placing all the blame at the foot of the new one. The fact is, Yeltsin attempted to change the structure of the Soviet system without due regard to the necessity of changing the mentality of the people as well. The result was a high level of disenchantment. A new joke circulated among the Russian people: "We know now that everything they told us about communism was false. And everything they told us about capitalism was true."

**The Putin Era** At the end of 1999, Yeltsin suddenly resigned his office and was replaced by Vladimir Putin (b. 1952), a former member of the KGB. Putin vowed to bring an end to the rampant corruption and inexperience that permeated Russian political culture and to strengthen the role of the central government in managing the affairs of state. During succeeding months, his proposal to centralize power in the hands of the federal government in Moscow was given approval by the parliament; in early 2001, he presented a new plan to regulate political parties, which numbered more than fifty at the beginning of the decade.

Putin also vowed to bring the breakaway state of Chechnya back under Russian authority and to assume a more assertive role in international affairs. The new president took advantage of growing public anger at Western plans to expand the NATO alliance into Eastern Europe, as well as aggressive actions by NATO countries against Serbia in the Balkans (see Chapter 27), to restore Russia's position as an influential force in the world. To assuage national pride, he entered negotiations with such former republics of the old Soviet Union as Belarus and Ukraine to tighten forms of mutual political and economic cooperation.

Pride in the recent achievements of the Russian nation, however, is hard to come by these days. Not only have the boundaries of the old Soviet empire shrunk by one-third, but the living standards of the Russian people have declined as well. According to recent statistics, mortality rates have risen by an estimated 40 percent in the last three decades, and the national population is predicted to decline by almost fifty million in the next half-century. Since the early 1980s, marriage rates have declined by over 30 percent, and the rate of divorce has increased by a similar measure. For the Russian people, there is very little good news these days.

Courtesy of William J. Duiker

**Ghosts of Soviet Olympic Glory.** A poignant legacy of the collapse of the Soviet Union is reflected in this abandoned skating rink and ski jump in Almaty, Kazakhstan. It was in this rink and on the adjacent ski jump in the mountains of Central Asia that the Soviet Union trained its best athletes to win international competitions for gold medals and glory during the Cold War. Here we sense the ghosts of former skaters, subsidized darlings of the Soviet Empire, as they attempt the difficult triple jump.

### COMPARATIVE ESSAY

## Family and Society in an Era of Change

It is one of the paradoxes of the modern world that at a time of political stability and economic prosperity for many people in the advanced capitalist societies, public cynicism about the system is increasingly widespread. Alienation and drug use are at dangerously high levels, and the rate of criminal activities in most areas remains much higher than in the immediate postwar era.

Although the reasons advanced to explain this paradox vary widely, many observers place the responsibility for many contemporary social problems on the decline of the traditional family system. There has been a steady rise in the percentage of illegitimate births and single-parent families in countries throughout the Western world. In the United States, approximately half of all marriages end in divorce. Even in two-parent families, more and more parents work full time, leaving the children to fend for themselves on their return from school. In many countries in Europe, the birthrate has dropped to alarming levels, leading to a severe labor shortage that is attracting a rising number of immigrants from other parts of the world.

Observers point to several factors as an explanation for these conditions: the growing emphasis in advanced capitalist states on an individualistic lifestyle devoted to instant gratification, a phenomenon promoted vigorously by the advertising media; the rise of the feminist movement, which has freed women from the servitude imposed on their predecessors, but at the expense of removing them from full-time responsibility for the care of the next generation; and the increasing mobility of contemporary life, which disrupts traditional family ties and creates a sense of rootlessness and impersonality in the individual's relationship to the surrounding environment.

This phenomenon is not unique to Western civilization. The traditional nuclear family is also under attack in many societies around the world. Even in East Asia, where the Confucian tradition of family solidarity has been endlessly touted as a major factor in the region's economic success, the incidence of divorce and illegitimate births is on the rise, as is the percentage of women in the workforce. Older citizens frequently complain that the Asian youth of today are too materialistic, faddish, and steeped in the individualistic values of the West. Such criticisms are now voiced in mainland China as well as in the capitalist societies around its perimeter (see Chapter 29).

In societies less exposed to the individualist lifestyle portrayed so prominently in Western culture, traditional attitudes about the family continue to hold sway. In the Middle East, governmental and religious figures seek to prevent the Western media from undermining accepted mores. Success is sometimes elusive, however, as the situation in Iran demonstrates. Despite the zealous guardians of Islamic morality, many young Iranians are clamoring for the individual freedoms that have been denied to them since the Islamic revolution took place over two decades ago (see Chapter 28).

President Putin has attempted to deal with the chronic problems in Russian society by centralizing his control over the system, and by silencing critics—notably in the Russian media. Such moves have aroused unease among many observers in the West and provoked the United States to warn him against derailing the trend toward democratic institutions and practices in the old Soviet bloc. But there is a widespread sense of unease in Russia today about the decline of social order—marked by a rising incidence of alcoholism, sexual promiscuity, criminal activities, and the disintegration of the traditional family system (see the comparative essay "Family and Society in an Era of Change" above) in post-Soviet Russia—and many of Putin's compatriots express sympathy with his attempt to restore a sense of pride and discipline in Russian society. He was not alone in expressing the view in the spring of 2005 that the breakup of the Soviet Union was a national tragedy.

## Eastern Europe: From Satellites to Sovereign Nations

The disintegration of the Soviet Union had an immediate impact on its neighbors to the west. First to respond, as in 1956, was Poland, where popular protests at high food prices had erupted in the early 1980s, leading to the rise of an independent labor movement called Solidarity. Led by Lech Walesa (b. 1943), Solidarity rapidly became an influential force for change and a threat to the government's monopoly of power. The union was outlawed in 1981, but martial law did not solve Poland's serious economic problems, and in 1988, the Communist government bowed to the inevitable and permitted free national elections to take place, resulting in the election of Walesa as president of Poland in December 1990. Unlike the situation in 1956, when Khrushchev had intervened to prevent the collapse of the Soviet satellite system in Eastern Europe, in the late 1980s, Moscow—inspired by Gorbachev's policy of encouraging "new thinking" to improve relations with the Western powers—took no action to reverse the verdict in Warsaw.

In Hungary, as in Poland, the process of transition had begun many years previously. After crushing the Hungarian revolution of 1956, the Communist government of János Kádár had tried to assuage popular opinion by enacting a series of far-reaching economic reforms (labeled "communism with a capitalist face-lift"), but as the 1980s progressed, the economy sagged, and in 1989, the regime permitted the formation of opposition political parties, leading eventually to the formation of a noncommunist coalition government in elections held in March 1990.

The transition in Czechoslovakia was more abrupt. After Soviet troops crushed the Prague Spring in 1968, hard-line Communists under Gustav Husak followed a policy of massive repression to maintain their power. In 1977, dissident intellectuals formed an organization called Charter 77 as a vehicle for protest against violations of human rights. Regardless of the repressive atmosphere, dissident activities continued to grow during the 1980s, and when massive demonstrations broke out in several major cities in 1989, President Husak's government, lacking any real popular support, collapsed. At the end of December, he was replaced by Václav Havel, a dissident playwright who had been a leading figure in Charter 77.

But the most dramatic events took place in East Germany, where a persistent economic slump and the ongoing oppressiveness of the regime of Erich Honecker led to a flight of refugees and mass demonstrations against the regime in the summer and fall of 1989. Capitulating to popular pressure, the Communist government opened its entire border with the West. The Berlin Wall, the most tangible symbol of the Cold War, became the site of a massive celebration, and most of it was dismantled by joyful Germans from both sides of the border. In March 1990, free elections led to the formation of a noncommunist government that rapidly carried out a program of political and economic reunification with West Germany.

The dissolution of the Soviet Union and its satellite system in Eastern Europe brought a dramatic end to the Cold War. By the beginning of the 1990s, a generation of global rivalry between two ideological systems had come to a close, and world leaders turned their attention to the construction of what U.S. President George H. W. Bush called the New World Order. But what sort of new order would it be?

**CHRONOLOGY The Soviet Bloc and its Demise**

| | |
|---|---|
| Death of Joseph Stalin | 1953 |
| Rise of Nikita Khrushchev | 1955 |
| Destalinization speech | 1956 |
| Removal of Khrushchev | 1964 |
| The Brezhnev Era | 1964–1982 |
| Rule of Andropov and Chernenko | 1982–1985 |
| Gorbachev comes to power in Soviet Union | 1985 |
| Collapse of Communist governments in Eastern Europe | 1989 |
| Disintegration of Soviet Union | 1991 |
| Presidency of Boris Yeltsin in Russia | 1991–1999 |
| Vladimir Putin elected president of Russia | 2000 |

# The East is Red: China Under Communism

In the fall of 1949, China was at peace for the first time in twelve years. The newly victorious Communist Party, under the leadership of its chairman, Mao Zedong, turned its attention to consolidating its power base and healing the wounds of war. Its long-term goal was to construct a socialist society, but its leaders realized that popular support for the revolution was based on the party's platform of honest government, land reform, social justice, and peace rather than on the utopian goal of a classless society. Accordingly, the new regime followed Soviet precedent in adopting a moderate program of political and economic recovery known as New Democracy.

## New Democracy

With **New Democracy**—patterned roughly after Lenin's New Economic Policy in Soviet Russia in the 1920s (see Chapter 22)—the new Chinese leadership tacitly recognized that time and extensive indoctrination would be needed to convince the Chinese people of the superiority of socialism. In the meantime, the party would rely on capitalist profit incentives to spur productivity. Manufacturing and commercial firms were permitted to remain under private ownership, although with stringent government regulations. To win the support of the poorer peasants, who made up the majority of the population, a land redistribution program was adopted, but the collectivization of agriculture was postponed.

In a number of key respects, New Democracy was a success. About two-thirds of the peasant households in the country received land and thus had reason to be grateful to the new regime. Spurred by official tolerance for capitalist activities and the end of internal conflict, the national economy began to rebound, although agricultural production still lagged behind both official targets and the growing population, which was increasing at an annual rate of more than 2 percent. But not all benefited. In the course of carrying out land redistribution, thousands if not millions of landlords and rich farmers lost their lands, their personal property, their freedom, and sometimes their lives. Many of those who died were tried and convicted of "crimes against the people" in tribunals

## Land Reform in Action

One of the great achievements of the new Communist regime in China was the land reform program, which resulted in the distribution of farmland to almost two-thirds of the rural population. The program consequently won the gratitude of millions of Chinese. But it also had a dark side as local land reform tribunals routinely convicted "wicked landlords" of crimes against the people and then put them to death. The following passage, written by a foreign observer, describes the process in one village.

*What was the purpose of the Communist Party in carrying out land reform in China? How did the tactics employed here support that strategy?*

### Revolution in a Chinese Village

T'ien-ming [a Party cadre] called all the active young cadres and the militiamen of Long Bow [village] together and announced to them the policy of the county government, which was to confront all enemy collaborators and their backers at public meetings, expose their crimes, and turn them over to the county authorities for punishment. He proposed that they start with Kuo Te-yu, the puppet village head. Having moved the group to anger with a description of Te-yu's crimes, T'ien-ming reviewed the painful life led by the poor peasants during the occupation and recalled how hard they had all worked and how as soon as they harvested all the grain the puppet officials, backed by army bayonets, took what they wanted, turned over huge quantities to the Japanese devils, forced the peasants to haul it away, and flogged those who refused.

As the silent crowd contracted toward the spot where the accused man stood, T'ien-ming stepped forward. . . . "This is our chance. Remember how we were oppressed. The traitors seized our property. They beat us and kicked us. . . .

"Let us speak out the bitter memories. Let us see that the blood debt is repaid. . . ."

He paused for a moment. The peasants were listening to every word but gave no sign as to how they felt. . . .

"Come now, who has evidence against this man?"

Again there was silence.

Kuei-ts'ai, the new vice-chairman of the village, found it intolerable. He jumped up [and] struck Kuo Te-yu on the jaw with the back of his hand. "Tell the meeting how much you stole," he demanded.

The blow jarred the ragged crowd. It was as if an electric spark had tensed every muscle. Not in living memory had any peasant ever struck an official. . . .

The people in the square waited fascinated as if watching a play. They did not realize that in order for the plot to unfold they themselves had to mount the stage and speak out what was on their minds.

That evening T'ien-ming and Kuei-ts'ai called together the small groups of poor peasants from various parts of the village and sought to learn what it was that was really holding them back. *They soon found the root of the trouble was fear* of the old established political forces, and their military backers. The old reluctance to move against the power of the gentry, the fear of ultimate defeat and terrible reprisal that had been seared into the consciousness of so many generations, lay like a cloud over the peasants' minds and hearts.

Emboldened by T'ien-ming's words, other peasants began to speak out. They recalled what Te-yu had done to them personally. Several vowed to speak up and accuse him the next morning. After the meeting broke up, the passage of time worked its own leaven. In many a hovel and tumbledown house talk continued well past midnight. Some people were so excited they did not sleep at all. . . .

On the following day the meeting was livelier by far. It began with a sharp argument as to who would make the first accusation, and T'ien-ming found it difficult to keep order. Before Te-yu had a chance to reply to any questions, a crowd of young men, among whom were several militiamen, surged forward ready to beat him.

set up under official sponsorship in towns and villages around the country. As Mao himself later conceded, many were innocent of any crime, but in the eyes of the party, their deaths were necessary to destroy the power of the landed gentry in the countryside (see the box above).

## The Transition to Socialism

Originally, party leaders intended to follow the Leninist formula of delaying the building of a fully socialist society until China had a sufficient industrial base to permit the mechanization of agriculture. In 1953, they launched the nation's first five-year plan (patterned after similar Soviet plans), which called for substantial increases in industrial output. Lenin had believed that mechanization would induce Russian peasants to join collective farms, which, because of their greater size and efficiency, could better afford to purchase expensive farm machinery. But the difficulty of providing tractors and reapers for millions of rural villages eventually convinced Mao that it would take years, if not decades, for China's infant industrial base to meet the needs of a modernizing agricultural sector. He therefore decided to begin collectivization immediately, in the hope that collective farms would increase food production and release land, labor, and capital for the industrial sector. Accordingly, beginning in 1955, virtually all private farmland was collectivized (although peasant families were allowed to retain small private plots), and most businesses and industries were nationalized.

Collectivization was achieved without provoking the massive peasant unrest that had taken place in the Soviet Union during the 1930s, perhaps because the Chinese government followed a policy of persuasion rather than compulsion (Mao Zedong remarked that Stalin had "drained the pond to catch the fish") and because the Communist land redistribution program had already earned the support of millions of rural Chinese. But the hoped-for production increases did not materialize, and in 1958, at Mao's insistent urging, party leaders approved a more radical program known as the **Great Leap Forward.** Existing rural collectives, normally the size of a traditional village, were combined into vast "people's communes," each containing more than thirty thousand people. These communes were to be responsible for all administrative and economic tasks at the local level. The party's official slogan promised "Hard work for a few years, happiness for a thousand."[7]

Some party members were concerned that this ambitious program would threaten the government's rural base of support, but Mao argued that Chinese peasants were naturally revolutionary in spirit. The Chinese rural masses, he said, are

> first of all, poor, and secondly, blank. That may seem like a bad thing, but it is really a good thing. Poor people want change, want to do things, want revolution. A clean sheet of paper has no blotches, and so the newest and most beautiful words can be written on it, the newest and most beautiful pictures can be painted on it.[8]

Those words, of course, were *socialism* and *communism.*

The communes were a disaster. Administrative bottlenecks, bad weather, and peasant resistance to the new system (which, among other things, attempted to eliminate work incentives and destroy the traditional family as the basic unit of Chinese society) combined to drive food production downward, and over the next few years, as many as fifteen million people may have died of starvation. Many peasants were reportedly reduced to eating the bark off trees and in some cases allowing infants to starve. In 1960, the experiment was essentially abandoned. Although the commune structure was retained, ownership and management were returned to the collective level. Mao was severely criticized by some of his more pragmatic colleagues (one remarked bitingly that "one cannot reach Heaven in a single step"), provoking him to complain that he had been relegated to the sidelines "like a Buddha on a shelf."

## The Great Proletarian Cultural Revolution

But Mao was not yet ready to abandon either his power or his dream of a totally egalitarian society. In 1966, he returned to the attack, mobilizing discontented youth and disgruntled party members into revolutionary units known as Red Guards, who were urged to take to the streets to cleanse Chinese society—from local schools and factories to government ministries in Beijing—of impure elements who (in Mao's mind, at least) were guilty of "taking the capitalist road." Supported by his wife, Jiang Qing, and other radical party figures, Mao launched China on a new forced march toward communism.

The so-called **Great Proletarian Cultural Revolution** (meaning a great revolution to create a proletarian culture) lasted for ten years, from 1966 to 1976. Some Western observers interpreted it as a simple power struggle between Mao Zedong and some of his key rivals such as Liu Shaoqi (Liu Shao-ch'i), Mao's designated successor, and Deng Xiaoping (Teng Hsiao-p'ing), the party's general secretary. Both were removed from their positions, and Liu later died, allegedly of torture, in a Chinese prison. But real policy disagreements were involved. Mao and his supporters feared that capitalist values and the remnants of "feudalist" Confucian ideas would undermine ideological fervor and betray the revolutionary cause. He was convinced that only an atmosphere of **uninterrupted revolution** could enable the Chinese to overcome the lethargy of the past and achieve the final stage of utopian communism. "I care not," he once wrote, "that the winds blow and the waves beat. It is better than standing idly in a courtyard."

His opponents argued for a more pragmatic strategy that gave priority to nation-building over the ultimate communist goal of spiritual transformation. But with Mao's supporters now in power, the party carried out vast economic and educational reforms that virtually eliminated any remaining profit incentives, established a new school system that emphasized "Mao Zedong thought," and stressed practical education at the elementary level at the expense of specialized training in science and the humanities in the universities. School learning was discouraged as a legacy of capitalism, and Mao's famous *Little Red Book* (officially, *Quotations of Chairman Mao Zedong,* a slim volume of Maoist aphorisms to encourage good behavior and revolutionary zeal) was hailed as the most important source of knowledge in all areas.

The radicals' efforts to destroy all vestiges of traditional society were reminiscent of the Reign of Terror in revolutionary France, when the Jacobins sought to destroy organized religion and even created a new revolutionary calendar. Red Guards rampaged through the country attempting to eradicate the "four olds" (old thought, old culture, old customs, and old habits). They destroyed temples and religious sculptures; they tore down street signs and replaced them with new ones carrying revolutionary names. At one point, the city of Shanghai even ordered that the significance of colors in stoplights be changed so that red (the revolutionary color) would indicate that traffic could move.

But a mood of revolutionary ferment and enthusiasm is difficult to sustain. Key groups, including bureaucrats, urban professionals, and many military officers, did not share Mao's belief in the benefits of uninterrupted revolution and constant turmoil. Many were alienated by

© Private Collection/Bridgeman Art Library

**Hail the Great Helmsman!** During the Great Proletarian Cultural Revolution, Chinese art was restricted to topics that promoted revolution and the thoughts of Chairman Mao Zedong. All the knowledge that the true revolutionary required was to be found in Mao's *Little Red Book,* a collection of his sayings on proper revolutionary behavior. In this painting, Chairman Mao stands among his admirers, who wave copies of the book as a symbol of their total devotion to him and his vision of a future China.

the arbitrary actions of the Red Guards, who indiscriminately accused and brutalized their victims in a society where legal safeguards had almost entirely vanished (see the box on p. 769). Inevitably, the sense of anarchy and uncertainty caused popular support for the movement to erode, and when the end came with Mao's death in 1976, the vast majority of the population may well have welcomed its demise.

Personal accounts by young Chinese who took part in the Cultural Revolution show that their initial enthusiasm often turned to disillusionment. In *Son of the Revolution,* Liang Heng tells how at first he helped friends organize Red Guard groups: "I thought it was a great idea. We would be following Chairman Mao just like the grown-ups, and Father would be proud of me. I suppose I too resented the teachers who had controlled and criticized me for so long, and I looked forward to a little revenge."[9] Later he had reason to repent. His sister ran off to join the local Red Guard group. Prior to her departure, she denounced her mother and the rest of her family as "rightists" and enemies of the revolution. Their home was regularly raided by Red Guards, and their father was severely beaten and tortured for having three neckties and "Western shirts." Books, paintings, and writings were piled in the center of the floor and burned before his eyes. On leaving, a few of the Red Guards helped themselves to his monthly salary and his transistor radio.

## From Mao to Deng

Mao Zedong died in September 1976 at the age of eighty-three. After a short but bitter succession struggle, the pragmatists led by Deng Xiaoping seized power from the radicals and formally brought the Cultural Revolution to an end. Mao's widow, Jiang Qing, and three other radicals (derisively called the "Gang of Four" by their opponents) were placed on trial and sentenced to death or to long prison terms. The egalitarian policies of the previous decade were reversed, and a new program emphasizing economic modernization was introduced.

Under the leadership of Deng Xiaoping, who placed his supporters in key positions throughout the party and the government, attention focused on what were called the **Four Modernizations:** industry, agriculture, technology, and national defense. Deng had been a leader of the faction that opposed Mao's program of rapid socialist transformation, and during the Cultural Revolution, he had been forced to perform menial labor to "sincerely correct his errors." But Deng continued to espouse the pragmatic approach and reportedly once remarked, "Black cat, white cat, what does it matter so long as it catches the mice?" Under the program of Four Modernizations, many of the restrictions against private activities and profit incentives were eliminated, and people were encouraged to work hard to benefit themselves and Chinese society. The familiar slogan "Serve the people" was replaced by a new one repugnant to the tenets of Mao Zedong thought: "Create wealth for the people."

Crucial to the program's success was the government's ability to attract foreign technology and capital. For more than two decades, China had been isolated from technological advances taking place elsewhere in the world. Now, to make up for lost time, the government abandoned its policy of self-reliance and sought to improve relations with the rest of the world. It encouraged foreign investment and sent thousands of students and specialists abroad to study capitalist techniques.

By adopting this pragmatic approach in the years after 1976, China made great strides in ending its chronic problems of poverty and underdevelopment. Per capita income roughly doubled during the 1980s; housing, education, and sanitation improved; and both agricultural and industrial output skyrocketed.

But critics, both Chinese and foreign, complained that Deng's program had failed to achieve a "fifth modernization": democracy. Official sources denied such charges and spoke proudly of restoring "socialist legality" by doing away with the arbitrary punishments applied during the Cultural Revolution. Deng himself encouraged the Chinese people to speak out against earlier ex-

## Make Revolution!

In 1966, Mao Zedong unleashed the power of revolution on China. Rebellious youth in the form of Red Guards rampaged through all levels of society, exposing anti-Maoist elements, suspected "capitalist roaders," and those identified with the previous ruling class. In this poignant excerpt, Nien Cheng, the widow of an official of Chiang Kai-shek's regime, describes a visit by Red Guards to her home during the height of the Cultural Revolution.

*How do the tactics of the Red Guards compare with those employed by land reform cadres in the box on p. 766? To what degree did they succeed in remaking the character of the Chinese people?*

### Nien Cheng, *Life and Death in Shanghai*

Suddenly the doorbell began to ring incessantly. At the same time, there was furious pounding of many firsts on my front gate, accompanied by the confused sound of hysterical voices shouting slogans. The cacophony told me that the time of waiting was over and that I must face the threat of the Red Guards and the destruction of my home. . . .

Outside, the sound of voices became louder. "Open the gate! Open the gate! Are you all dead? Whey don't you open the gate?" Someone was swearing and kicking the wooden gate. The horn of the truck was blasting too. . . .

I stood up to put the book on the shelf. A copy of the Constitution of the People's Republic caught my eye. Taking it in my hand and picking up the bunch of keys I had ready on my desk, I went downstairs.

At the same moment, the Red Guards pushed open the front door and entered the house. There were thirty or forty senior high school students, aged between fifteen and twenty, led by two men and one woman much older.

The leading Red Guard, a gangling youth with angry eyes, stepped forward and said to me, "We are the Red Guards. We have come to take revolutionary action against you!"

Though I knew it was futile, I held up the copy of the Constitution and said calmly, "It's against the Constitution of the People's Republic of China to enter a private house without a search warrant."

The young man snatched the document out of my hand and threw it on the floor. With his eyes blazing, he said, "The Constitution is abolished. It was a document written by the Revisionists within the Communist Party. We recognize only the teachings of our Great Leader Chairman Mao." . . .

Another young man used a stick to smash the mirror hanging over the blackwood chest facing the front door.

Mounting the stairs, I was astonished to see several Red Guards taking pieces of my porcelain collection out of their padded boxes. One young man had arranged a set of four Kangxi wine cups in a row on the floor and was stepping on them. I was just in time to hear the crunch of delicate porcelain under the sole of his shoe. The sound pierced my heart. Impulsively I leapt forward and caught his leg just as he raised his foot to crush the next cup. He toppled. We fell in a heap together. . . . The other Red Guards dropped what they were doing and gathered around us, shouting at me angrily for interfering in their revolutionary activities.

The young man whose revolutionary work of destruction I had interrupted said angrily, "You shut up! These things belong to the old culture. They are the useless toys of the feudal emperors and the modern capitalist class and have no significance to us, the proletarian class. They cannot be compared to cameras and binoculars, which are useful for our struggle in time of war. Our Great Leader Chairman Mao taught us, 'If we do not destroy, we cannot establish.' The old culture must be destroyed to make way for the new socialist culture."

cesses. In the late 1970s, ordinary citizens pasted "big character posters" criticizing the abuses of the past on the so-called Democracy Wall near Tiananmen Square in downtown Beijing.

Yet it soon became clear that the new leaders would not tolerate any direct criticism of the Communist Party or of Marxist-Leninist ideology. Dissidents were suppressed, and some were sentenced to long prison terms. Among them was the well-known astrophysicist Fang Lizhi (Fang Li-chih), who spoke out publicly against official corruption and the continuing influence of Marxist-Leninist concepts in post-Mao China, telling an audience in Hong Kong that "China will not be able to modernize if it does not break the shackles of Maoist and Stalinist-style socialism." Fang immediately felt the weight of official displeasure. He was refused permission to travel abroad, and articles that he submitted to official periodicals were rejected.

The problem began to intensify in the late 1980s as more Chinese began to study abroad and more information about Western society reached educated individuals inside the country. Rising expectations aroused by the economic improvements of the early 1980s led to increasing pressure from students and other urban residents for better living conditions, relaxed restrictions on study abroad, and increased freedom to select employment after graduation.

## Incident at Tiananmen Square

As long as economic conditions for the majority of Chinese were improving, other classes did not share the students' discontent, and the government was able to isolate them from other elements in society. But in the late 1980s, an overheated economy led to rising inflation and

**Punishing China's Enemies During the Cultural Revolution.** The Cultural Revolution, which began in 1966, was a massive effort by Mao Zedong and his radical supporters to eliminate rival elements within the Chinese Communist party and the government. Accused of being "capitalist roaders," such individuals were subjected to public criticism and removed from their positions. Some were imprisoned or executed. Here Red Guards parade a victim wearing a dunce cap through the streets of Beijing.

growing discontent among salaried workers, especially in the cities. At the same time, corruption, nepotism, and favored treatment for senior officials and party members were provoking increasing criticism. In May 1989, student protesters carried placards demanding "Science and Democracy" (reminiscent of the slogan of the May Fourth Movement, whose seventieth anniversary was celebrated in the spring of 1989), an end to official corruption, and the resignation of China's aging party leadership (see the comparative illustration on p. 771). These demands received widespread support from the urban population (although notably less in rural areas) and led to massive demonstrations in Tiananmen Square (see the box on p. 772).

The demonstrations divided the Chinese leaders. Reformist elements around party general secretary Zhao Ziyang were sympathetic to the protesters, but veteran leaders such as Deng Xiaoping saw the student demands for more democracy as a disguised call for an end to Communist Party rule. After some hesitation, the government sent tanks and troops into Tiananmen Square to crush the demonstrators. Dissidents were arrested, and the regime once again began to stress ideological purity and socialist values. Although the crackdown provoked widespread criticism abroad, Chinese leaders insisted that economic reforms could only take place in conditions of party leadership and political stability.

Deng Xiaoping and other aging party leaders turned to the army to protect their base of power and suppress what they described as "counterrevolutionary elements." Deng was undoubtedly counting on the fact that many Chinese, particularly in rural areas, feared a recurrence of the disorder of the Cultural Revolution and craved economic prosperity more than political reform. In the months following the confrontation, the government issued new regulations requiring courses on Marxist-Leninist ideology in the schools, sought out dissidents within the intellectual community, and made it clear that while economic reforms would continue, the CCP's monopoly of power would not be allowed to decay. Harsh punishments were imposed on those accused of undermining the Communist system and supporting its enemies abroad.

COMPARATIVE ILLUSTRATION

**Student Rebellions in France and China.** University students played an important role in revolutionary upheavals in the late 1960s in France and in the late 1980s in Eastern Europe and China. The discontent of university students in France exploded in the late 1960s in a series of student revolts. At the left is a scene from a student revolt in 1968. The photograph shows the barricades that students erected by overturning cars on a Parisian street on the morning of May 11 during the height of the revolt. The demonstrations that erupted in Beijing's Tiananmen Square in the spring of 1989 spread rapidly to other parts of China. Seen at the right is a group of students from a high school who are marching to the city of Guilin to display their own determination to take part in the reform of Chinese society.

## From Marx to Confucius?

In the 1990s, the government began to nurture urban support by reducing the rate of inflation and guaranteeing the availability of consumer goods in great demand among the rising middle class. Under Deng Xiaoping's successor, Jiang Zemin (b. 1926), who occupied the positions of both party chief and president of China, the government promoted rapid economic growth while cracking down harshly on political dissent. That policy paid dividends in bringing about a perceptible decline in alienation among the population in the cities. Industrial production continued to increase rapidly, leading to predictions that China would become one of the economic superpowers of the twenty-first century. But discontent in rural areas began to increase, as lagging farm income, high taxes, and official corruption sparked resentment in the countryside.

Partly out of fear that such developments could undermine the socialist system and the rule of the CCP, conservative leaders attempted to curb Western influence and restore faith in Marxism-Leninism. In what may be a tacit recognition that Marxist exhortations were no longer an effective means of enforcing social discipline, the party turned to Confucianism as an antidote. Ceremonies celebrating the birth of Confucius now received official sanction, and the virtues promoted by the master, such as righteousness, propriety, and filial piety, were widely cited as an antidote to the tide of antisocial behavior. An article in the official newspaper *People's Daily* asserted that the spiritual crisis in contemporary Western culture stemmed from the incompatibility between science and the Christian religion. The solution, the author maintained, was Confucianism, "a nonreligious humanism that can provide the basis for morals and the value of life." Because a culture combining science and Confucianism was taking shape in East Asia, he asserted, "it will thrive particularly well in the next century and will replace modern and contemporary Western culture."[10]

In the world arena, China now relies on the spirit of nationalism to achieve its goals, conducting an independent foreign policy and playing an increasingly active role in the region. To some of its neighbors, including Japan, India, and Russia, China's new posture is cause for disquiet and gives rise to suspicions that it is once again preparing to flex its muscle as in the imperial era. The first example of this new attitude took place as early as 1979, when Chinese forces briefly invaded Vietnam as punishment for the Vietnamese occupation of neighboring Cambodia. In the 1990s, China aroused concern in the region by claiming sole ownership over the Spratly Islands in the South China Sea and over Diaoyu Island (also claimed by Japan) near Taiwan (see Map 26.3).

To Chinese leaders, however, such actions simply represent legitimate efforts to resume China's rightful role in the affairs of the region. After a century of humiliation at the hands of the Western powers and neighboring Japan, the nation, in Mao's famous words of 1949, "has stood up" and no one will be permitted to

## STUDENTS APPEAL FOR DEMOCRACY

In the spring of 1989, thousands of students gathered in Tiananmen Square in downtown Beijing to provide moral support to their many compatriots who had gone on a hunger strike in an effort to compel the Chinese government to reduce the level of official corruption and enact democratic reforms, opening the political process to the Chinese people. The statement that follows was printed on flyers and distributed to participants and passersby on May 17, 1989, to explain the goals of the movement.

*What were the key demands of the protesters in Tiananmen Square? Were they approved by the Chinese government?*

### "Why Do We Have to Undergo a Hunger Strike?"

By 2:00 P.M. today, the hunger strike carried out by the petition group in Tiananmen Square has been under way for 96 hours. By this morning, more than 600 participants have fainted. When these democracy fighters were lifted into the ambulances, no one who was present was not moved to tears.

Our petition group now undergoing the hunger strike demands that at a minimum the government agree to the following two points:

1. To engage on a sincere and equal basis in a dialogue with the "higher education dialogue group." In addition, to broadcast the actual dialogue in its entirety. We absolutely refuse to agree to a partial broadcast, to empty gestures, or to fabrications that dupe the people.
2. To evaluate in a fair and realistic way the patriotic democratic movement. Discard the label of "trouble-making" and redress the reputation of the patriotic democratic movement.

It is our view that the request for a dialogue between the people's government and the people is not an unreasonable one. Our party always follows the principle of seeking truths from actual facts. It is therefore only natural that the evaluation of this patriotic democratic movement should be done in accordance with the principle of seeking truths from actual facts.

Our classmates who are going through the hunger strike are the good sons and daughters of the people! One by one, they have fallen. In the meantime, our "public servants" are completely unmoved. Please, let us ask where your conscience is.

humiliate it again. For the moment, at least, a fervent patriotism seems to be on the rise in China, actively promoted by the party as a means of holding the country together. Pride in the achievement of national sports teams is intense, and two young authors recently achieved wide acclaim with the publication of their book *The China That Can Say No,* a response to criticism of the country in the United States and Europe. The decision by the International Olympic Committee to award the 2008 Summer Games to Beijing led to widespread celebration throughout the country.

Pumping up the spirit of patriotism is not a solution of all problems. Unrest is growing among China's national minorities: in Xinjiang, where restless Muslim peoples are observing with curiosity the emergence of independent Islamic states in Central Asia, and in Tibet, where the official policy of quelling separation has led to the violent suppression of Tibetan culture and an influx of thousands of ethnic Chinese immigrants. In the meantime, the Falun Gong religious movement, which the government has attempted to suppress as a potentially serious threat to its authority, is an additional indication that with the disintegration of the old Maoist utopia, the Chinese people will need more than a pallid version of Marxism-Leninism or a revived Confucianism to fill the gap.

Whether the current leadership will be able to prevent further erosion of the party's power and prestige is unclear. In the short term, efforts to slow the process of change may succeed because many Chinese are understandably fearful of punishment and concerned for their careers. And high economic growth rates can sometimes obscure a multitude of problems as many individuals will opt to chase the fruits of materialism rather than the less tangible benefits of personal freedom. But in the long run, the party leadership must resolve the contradiction between political authoritarianism and economic prosperity. One is reminded of Chiang Kai-shek's failed attempt during the 1930s to revive Confucian ethics as a standard of behavior for modern China: dead ideologies cannot be revived by decree.

New leaders installed in 2002 and 2003 appear to recognize the challenge. Hu Jintao (b. 1943), who replaced Jiang Zemin as CCP general secretary and head of state, appears to recognize the need for further reforms to open up Chinese society and bridge the yawning gap between rich and poor. In recent years, the government has shown a growing tolerance for the public exchange of ideas, which has surfaced with the proliferation of bookstores, avant-garde theater, experimental art exhibits, and the Internet. In 2005, an estimated 27 percent of all Chinese citizens possessed a cell phone.

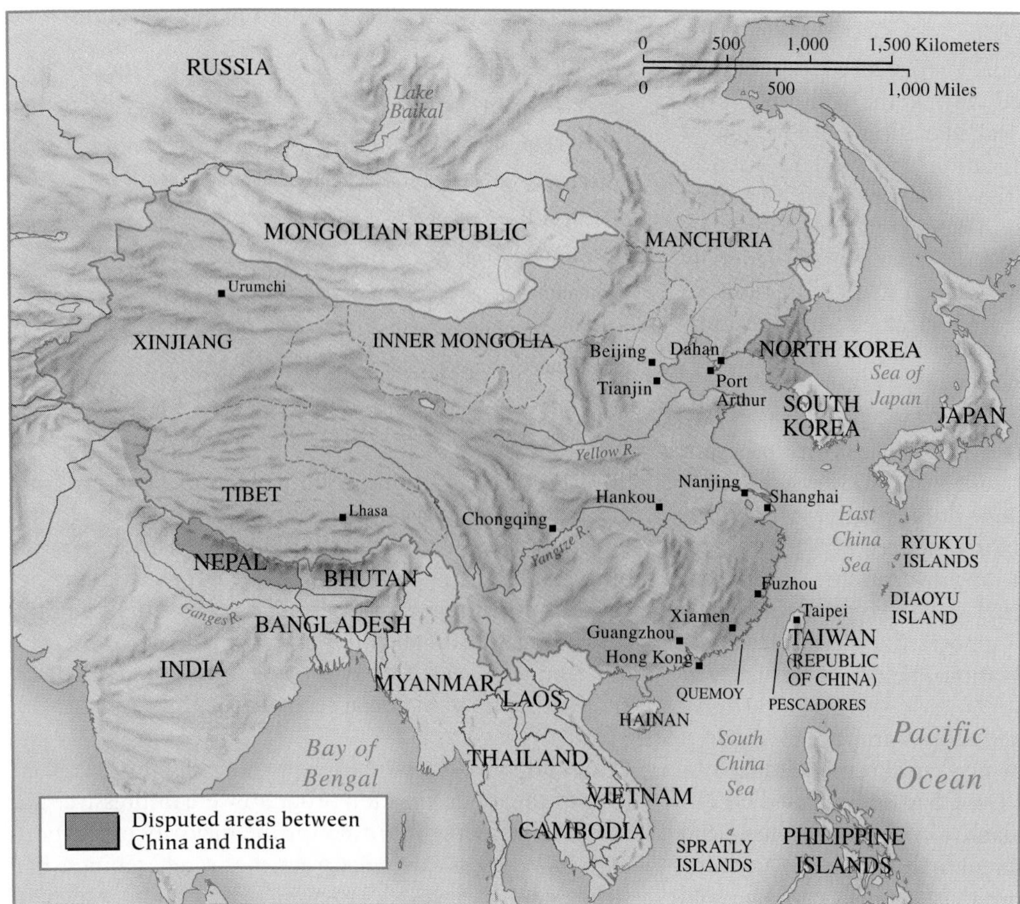


**MAP 26.3 The People's Republic of China.** This map shows China's current boundaries. Major regions are indicated in capital letters. Areas in dispute are shown by darker shading. ? In which regions are there movements against Chinese rule? **View an animated version of this map or related maps at** http://history.wadsworth.com/duikerspielvogel05/

## "Serve the People": Chinese Society Under Communism

When the Communist Party came to power in 1949, Chinese leaders made it clear that their policies would differ from the Soviet model in one key respect. Whereas the Bolsheviks had distrusted nonrevolutionary elements in Russia and relied almost exclusively on the use of force to achieve their objectives, the CCP sought to win support from the mass of the population by carrying out reforms that could win popular support. This "mass line" policy, as it was known, worked fairly well until the late 1950s, when Mao and his radical allies adopted policies such as the Great Leap Forward that began to alienate much of the population. Ideological purity was valued over expertise in building an advanced and prosperous society.

### Economics in Command

When he came to power in the late 1970s, Deng Xiaoping recognized the need to restore credibility to a system on the verge of breakdown, and hoped that rapid economic growth would satisfy the Chinese people and prevent them from demanding political reforms. The post-Mao leaders clearly placed economic performance over ideological purity. To stimulate the stagnant industrial sector, which had been under state control since the end of the New Democracy era, they reduced bureaucratic controls over state industries and allowed local managers to have more say over prices, salaries, and quality control. Productivity was encouraged by permitting bonuses for extra effort, a policy that had been discouraged during the Cultural Revolution. The regime also tolerated the emergence of a small private sector. Unemployed youth were encouraged to set up restaurants, bicycle or radio repair shops, and handicraft shops on their own initiative.

Finally, the regime opened up the country to foreign investment and technology. Special economic zones were established in urban centers near the coast (ironically, many were located in the old nineteenth-century treaty ports), where lucrative concessions were offered to encourage foreign firms to build factories. The tourist industry was encouraged, and students were sent abroad to study.

The new leaders especially stressed educational reform. The system adopted during the Cultural Revolution, emphasizing practical education and ideology at the expense of higher education and modern science, was rapidly abandoned (the *Little Red Book* was even withdrawn from circulation and could no longer be found on bookshelves), and a new system based generally on the Western model was instituted. Admission to higher education was based on success in merit examinations, and courses on science and mathematics received high priority.

**CHRONOLOGY China Under Communist Rule**

| | |
|---|---|
| New Democracy | 1949–1955 |
| Era of Collectivization | 1955–1958 |
| Great Leap Forward | 1958–1960 |
| Great Proletarian Cultural Revolution | 1966–1976 |
| Death of Mao Zedong | 1976 |
| Era of Deng Xiaoping | 1978–1997 |
| Tiananmen Square incident | 1989 |
| Presidency of Jiang Zemin | 1993–2002 |
| Hu Jintao becomes president | 2002 |

**Agricultural Reform** No economic reform program could succeed unless it included the countryside. Three decades of socialism had done little to increase food production or to lay the basis for a modern agricultural sector. China, with a population now numbering one billion, could still barely feed itself. Peasants had little incentive to work and few opportunities to increase production through mechanization, the use of fertilizer, or better irrigation.

Under Deng Xiaoping, agricultural policy made a rapid about-face. Under the new **rural responsibility system,** adopted shortly after Deng had consolidated his authority, collectives leased land to peasant families, who paid a quota in the form of rent to the collective. Anything produced on the land above that payment could be sold on the private market or consumed. To soak up excess labor in the villages, the government encouraged the formation of so-called sideline industries, a modern equivalent of the traditional cottage industries in premodern China. Peasants raised fish or shrimp, made consumer goods, and even assembled living room furniture and appliances for sale to their newly affluent compatriots.

The reform program had a striking effect on rural production. Grain production increased rapidly, and farm income doubled during the 1980s. Yet it also created problems. In the first place, income at the village level became more unequal as some enterprising farmers (known locally as "ten-thousand-dollar households") earned profits several times those realized by their less fortunate or less industrious neighbors. When some farmers discovered that they could earn more by growing cash crops or other specialized commodities, they devoted less land to rice and other grain crops, thus threatening to reduce the supply of China's most crucial staple. Finally, the agricultural policy threatened to undermine the government's population control program, which party leaders viewed as crucial to the success of the Four Modernizations.

Since a misguided period in the mid-1950s when Mao Zedong had argued that more labor would result in higher productivity, China had been attempting to limit its population growth. By 1970, the government had launched a stringent family planning program—including education, incentives, and penalties for noncompliance—to persuade the Chinese people to limit themselves to one child per family. The program did have some success, and population growth was reduced drastically in the early 1980s. The rural responsibility system, however, undermined the program because it encouraged farm families to pay the penalties for having additional children in the belief that their labor would increase family income and provide the parents with a form of social security for their old age.

**Evaluating the Four Modernizations** Still, the overall effects of the modernization program were impressive. The standard of living improved for the majority of the population. Whereas a decade earlier, the average Chinese had struggled to earn enough to buy a bicycle, radio, watch, or washing machine, by the late 1980s, many were beginning to purchase videocassette recorders, refrigerators, and color television sets. Yet the rapid growth of the economy created its own problems: inflationary pressures, greed, envy, increased corruption, and—most dangerous of all for the regime—rising expectations. Young people in particular resented restrictions on employment (most young people in China are still required to accept the jobs that are offered to them by the government or school officials) and opportunities to study abroad. Disillusionment ran high, especially in the cities, where lavish living by officials and rising prices for goods aroused widespread alienation and cynicism.

During the 1990s, growth rates in the industrial sector continued to be high as domestic capital became increasingly available to compete with the growing presence of foreign enterprises. The government finally recognized the need to close down inefficient state enterprises, and by the end of the decade, the private sector, with official encouragement, accounted for over 10 percent of the gross domestic product. A stock market opened, and China's prowess in the international marketplace improved dramatically.

But as Chinese leaders now discovered, rapid economic change never comes without cost. The closing of state-run factories has led to the dismissal of millions of workers each year, and the private sector, although growing at over 20 percent annually, is unable to absorb them all. Discontent has been growing in the countryside

© Courtesy of William J. Duiker

**Nanjing Road: A Consumer's Paradise.** Shanghai has become China's most affluent city, its forest of shimmering skyscrapers testifying to the phenomenal expansion of the Chinese economy in recent years. Nanjing Road, seen here, is one long avenue of towering banks, office buildings, hotels, and luxurious department stores. Along with these competing Chinese commercial signs, the ubiquitous American enterprises, such as KFC, Pepsi-Cola, and McDonald's, vie for the attention of the fashionably dressed Shanghainese as they shop for the latest styles.

as well, where a grain surplus has cut into farm incomes (the government tried to increase the official purchase price for grain but rescinded the order when it became too expensive). China's recent entrance into the World Trade Organization may help the national economy as a whole, but is less likely to benefit farmers, who must now face the challenge of cheap foreign food imports. Millions of rural Chinese have left for the big cities, where many of them are unable to find steady employment and are forced to live in squalid conditions in crowded tenements

© Vittoriano Rastelli/CORBIS

**Downtown Beijing.** Deng Xiaoping's policy of Four Modernizations had a dramatic visual effect on the capital city of Beijing, as evidenced by this photo of skyscrapers thrusting up beyond the walls of the fifteenth-century Imperial City. Many of these buildings are apartment houses for the capital city's growing population, most of them migrants from the countryside looking for employment.

or in the sprawling suburbs. Millions of others remain on the farm but attempt to maximize their income by producing for the market or by increasing the size of their families.

Another factor hindering China's rush to economic advancement is the impact on the environment. With the rising population, fertile land is in increasingly short supply (China, with twice the population, now has only two-thirds as much irrigable land as it had in 1950). Soil erosion is a major problem, especially in the north, where the desert is encroaching on farmlands. Water is also a problem. A massive dam project now under way in the Yangtze River valley has sparked protests from environmentalists, as well as from local peoples forced to migrate from the area. The rate of air pollution is ten times the level in the United States, contributing to growing health concerns. Chinese leaders now face the uncomfortable reality that the pains of industrialization are not exclusive to capitalist countries.

## Social Problems

At the root of Marxist-Leninist ideology is the idea of building a new citizen free from the prejudices, ignorance, and superstition of the "feudal" era and the capitalist desire for self-gratification. This new citizen would be characterized not only by a sense of racial and sexual equality but also by the selfless desire to contribute his or her utmost for the good of all.

**Women and the Family** From the very start, the Chinese Communist government intended to bring an end to the Confucian legacy in modern China. Women were given the vote and encouraged to become active in the political process. At the local level, an increasing number of women became active in the CCP and in collective organizations. In 1950, a new marriage law guaranteed women equal rights with men. Most important, perhaps, it permitted women for the first time to initiate divorce proceedings against their husbands. Within a year, nearly one million divorces had been granted.

The regime also undertook to destroy the influence of the traditional family system. To the Communists, loyalty to the family, a crucial element in the Confucian social order, undercut loyalty to the state and to the dictatorship of the proletariat.

At first, however, the new government moved carefully to avoid alienating its supporters in the countryside unnecessarily. When collective farms were established in the mid-1950s, payment for hours worked in the form of ration coupons was made not to the individual but to the family head, thus maintaining the traditionally dominant position of the patriarch. When people's communes were established in the late 1950s, payments went to the individual.

During the political radicalism of the Great Leap Forward, children were encouraged to report to the authorities any comments by their parents that criticized the system. Such practices continued during the Cultural Revolution, when children were expected to tell on their parents, students on their teachers, and employees on their superiors. Some have suggested that Mao deliberately encouraged such practices to bring an end to the traditional "politics of dependency." According to this theory, historically the famous "five relationships" forced individuals to swallow their anger and frustration and accept the hierarchical norms established by Confucian ethics (known in Chinese as "to eat bitterness"). By encouraging the oppressed elements in society—the young, the female, and the poor—to voice their bitterness, Mao was hoping to break the tradition of dependency. Such denunciations had been issued against landlords and other "local tyrants" in the land reform tribunals of the late 1940s and early 1950s. Later, during the Cultural Revolution, they were applied to other authority figures in Chinese society.

**Lifestyle Changes** The post-Mao era brought a decisive shift away from revolutionary utopianism and back toward the pragmatic approach to nation building. For most people, it meant improved living conditions and a qualified return to family traditions. For the first time, millions of Chinese saw the prospect of a house or an urban apartment with a washing machine, television set, and indoor plumbing. Young people whose parents had given them patriotic names such as Build the Country, Protect Mao Zedong, and Assist Korea began to choose more elegant and cosmopolitan names for their own children. Some names, such as Surplus Grain or Bring a Younger Brother, expressed hope for the future.

The new attitudes were also reflected in physical appearance. For a generation after the civil war, clothing had been restricted to the traditional baggy "Mao suit" in olive drab or dark blue, but by the 1980s, young people craved such fashionable Western items as designer jeans, trendy sneakers, and sweat suits (or reasonable facsimiles). Cosmetic surgery to create a more buxom figure or a more Western facial look became increasingly common among affluent young women in the cities. Many had the epicanthic fold over their eyelids removed or their noses enlarged—a curious decision in view of the tradition of referring derogatorily to foreigners as "big noses."

Religious practices and beliefs also changed. As the government became more tolerant, some Chinese began returning to the traditional Buddhist faith or to folk religions, and Buddhist and Taoist temples were once again crowded with worshipers. Despite official efforts to suppress its more evangelical forms, Christianity became increasingly popular; like the "rice Christians" (persons who supposedly converted for economic reasons) of the past, many viewed it as a symbol of success and cosmopolitanism.

As with all social changes, China's reintegration into the outside world has had a price. Arranged marriages, nepotism, and mistreatment of females (for example, under the one-child rule, parents reportedly killed female infants to regain the possibility of having a son) have come back, although such behavior likely survived under the cloak of revolutionary purity for a generation. Materialistic attitudes are prevalent among young people, along with a corresponding cynicism about politics and the CCP. Expensive weddings are now increasingly common, and bribery and favoritism are all too frequent. Crime of all types, including an apparently growing incidence of prostitution and sex crimes against women, appears to be on the rise. To discourage sexual abuse, the government now seeks to provide free legal services for women living in rural areas.

There is also a price to pay for the trend toward privatization. Under the Maoist system, the elderly and the sick were provided with retirement benefits and health care by the state or by the collective organizations. Under current conditions, with the latter no longer playing such a social role and more workers operating in the private sector, the safety net has been removed. The government recently attempted to fill the gap by enacting a social security law, but because of lack of funds, eligibility is limited primarily to individuals in the urban sector of the economy. Those living in the countryside—who still represent 60 percent of the population—are essentially left to their own devices.

Courtesy of William J. Duiker

**A Street Calligrapher.** During the Great Proletarian Cultural Revolution, all aspects of traditional culture were forbidden. Only items with revolutionary themes were permitted to be created or displayed. This elderly Chinese gentleman, a calligrapher by profession, had been prohibited from practicing his craft for two decades until the post-Mao era in the 1980s. He then resumed his career at a roadside stand on a residential street in Beijing.

## China's Changing Culture

The rise to power of the Communists in 1949 added a new dimension to the debate over the future of culture in China. The new leaders rejected the Western attitude of "art for art's sake" and, like their Soviet counterparts, viewed culture as an important instrument of indoctrination. The standard would no longer be aesthetic quality or the personal preference of the artist but "art for life's sake," whereby culture would serve the interests of socialism.

At first, the new emphasis on socialist realism did not entirely extinguish the influence of traditional culture. Mao and his colleagues tolerated—and even encouraged—efforts by artists to synthesize traditional ideas with socialist concepts and Western techniques. During the Cultural Revolution, however, all forms of traditional culture came to be viewed as reactionary. Socialist realism became the only acceptable standard in literature, art, and music. All forms of traditional expression were forbidden.

Nowhere were the dilemmas of the new order more challenging than in literature. In the heady afterglow of the Communist victory, many progressive writers supported the new regime and enthusiastically embraced Mao's exhortation to create a new Chinese literature for the edification of the masses. But in the harsher climate of the 1960s, many writers were criticized by the party for their excessive individualism and admiration for Western culture. Such writers either toed the new line and suppressed their doubts or were jailed and silenced (see the box on p. 778).

After Mao's death, Chinese culture was finally released from the shackles of socialist realism. In painting, where for a decade the only acceptable standard for excellence was praise for the party and its policies, the new permissiveness led to a revival of interest in both traditional and Western forms. Although some painters continued to blend Eastern and Western styles, others imitated trends from abroad, experimenting with a wide range of previously prohibited art styles, including Cubism and abstract painting.

In the late 1980s, two avant-garde art exhibits shocked the Chinese public and provoked the wrath of the party. An exhibition of nude paintings, the first ever held in China, attracted many viewers but reportedly offended the modesty of many Chinese. The second was an exhibit presenting the works of various schools of modern and postmodern art. The event resulted in considerable commentary and some expressions of public hostility. After a Communist critic lambasted the works as promiscuous and ideologically reactionary, the government declared that henceforth it would regulate all art exhibits.

The limits of freedom of expression were most apparent in literature. During the early 1980s, party leaders encouraged Chinese writers to express their views on the mistakes of the past, and a new "literature of the wounded" began to describe the brutal and arbitrary character of the Cultural Revolution. One of the most prominent writers was Bai Hua, whose script for the film *Bitter*

## CONCLUSION

**For four decades** after the end of World War II, the world's two superpowers competed for global hegemony. The Cold War became the dominant feature on the international scene and determined the internal politics of many countries around the world as well.

By the early 1980s, some of the tension had gone out of the conflict as it appeared that both Moscow and Washington had learned to tolerate the other's existence. Skeptical minds even suspected that both countries drew benefits from their mutual rivalry and saw it as an advantage in carrying on their relations with friends and allies. Few suspected that the Cold War, which had long seemed a permanent feature of world politics, was about to come to an end.

What brought about the collapse of the Soviet Empire? Some observers argue that the ambitious defense policies adopted by the Reagan administration forced Moscow into an arms race it could not afford, which ultimately led to a collapse of the Soviet economy. Others suggest that Soviet problems were more deep-rooted and would have ended in the disintegration of the Soviet Union even without outside stimulation. Both arguments have some validity, but the latter is surely closer to the mark. For years, if not decades, leaders in the Kremlin had disguised or ignored the massive inefficiencies of the Soviet system. In the 1980s, the perceptive Mikhail Gorbachev tried to save the system by instituting radical reforms. By then, however, it was too late.

Why has communism survived in China, albeit in a substantially altered form, when it failed in Eastern Europe and the Soviet Union? One of the primary factors is probably cultural. Although the doctrine of Marxism-Leninism originated in Europe, many of its main precepts, such as the primacy of the community over the individual and the denial of the concept of private property, run counter to trends in Western civilization. This inherent conflict is especially evident in the societies of central Europe, which were strongly influenced by Enlightenment philosophy and the Industrial Revolution. These forces were weaker in the countries farther to the east, but both had begun to penetrate tsarist Russia by the end of the nineteenth century.

By contrast, Marxism-Leninism found a more receptive climate in China and other countries in the region influenced by Confucian tradition. In its political culture, the Communist system exhibits many of the same characteristics as traditional Confucianism–a single truth, an elite governing class, and an emphasis on obedience to the community and its governing representatives–while feudal attitudes regarding female inferiority, loyalty to the family, and bureaucratic arrogance are hard to break. On the surface, China today bears a number of uncanny similarities to the China of the past.

Yet these similarities should not blind us to the real changes that are taking place in Chinese society today. Although the youthful protesters in Tiananmen Square were comparable in some respects to the reformist elements of the early republic, the China of today is fundamentally different from that of the early twentieth century. Literacy rates and the standard of living are far higher, the pressures of outside powers are less threatening, and China has entered its own industrial and technological revolution. For many Chinese, independent talk radio and the Internet are a greater source of news and views than are the official media. Where Sun Yat-sen, Chiang Kai-shek, and even Mao Zedong broke their lances on the rocks of centuries of tradition, poverty, and ignorance, China's present leaders rule a country much more aware of the world and its place in it.

## CHAPTER NOTES

1. Quoted in V. Zubok and C. Pleshakov, *Inside the Kremlin's Cold War: From Stalin to Khrushchev* (Cambridge, Mass., 1996), p. 166.
2. N. Khrushchev, *Khrushchev Remembers*, trans. S. Talbott (Boston, 1970), p. 77.
3. Quoted in H. Smith, *The New Russians* (New York, 1990), p. 30.
4. Quoted in F. B. Tipton and R. Aldrich, *An Economic and Social History of Europe from 1939 to the Present* (Baltimore, 1987), p. 193.
5. Quoted in H. Smith, *New Russians*, p. 74.
6. *New York Times*, May 7, 1992.
7. Quoted in S. Karnow, *Mao and China: Inside China's Cultural Revolution* (New York, 1972), p. 95.
8. Quoted from an article by Mao in the June 1, 1958, issue of the journal *Red Flag* in S. R. Schram, *The Political Thought of Mao Tse-tung* (New York, 1963), p. 253.
9. Liang Heng and J. Shapiro, *Son of the Revolution* (New York, 1983).
10. Quoted in F. Ching, "Confucius, the New Saviour," *Far Eastern Economic Review*, November 10, 1994, p. 37.
11. Quoted in J. Spence, *Chinese Roundabout: Essays in History and Culture* (New York, 1992), p. 285.

## SUGGESTED READING

For a general view of modern Russia, see **M. Malia, *Russia Under Western Eyes*** (Cambridge, Mass., 1999). On the Khrushchev years, see **E. Crankshaw, *Khrushchev: A Career*** (New York, 1966). For the final years of the Soviet era, see **S. F. Cohen, *Rethinking the Soviet Experience*** (New York, 1985); **R. J. Hill, *The Soviet Union: Politics, Economics, and Society***, 2d ed. (London, 1989); **M. Lewin, *The Gorbachev Phenomenon*** (Berkeley, Calif., 1988); **G. Hosking, *The***

## TIMELINE

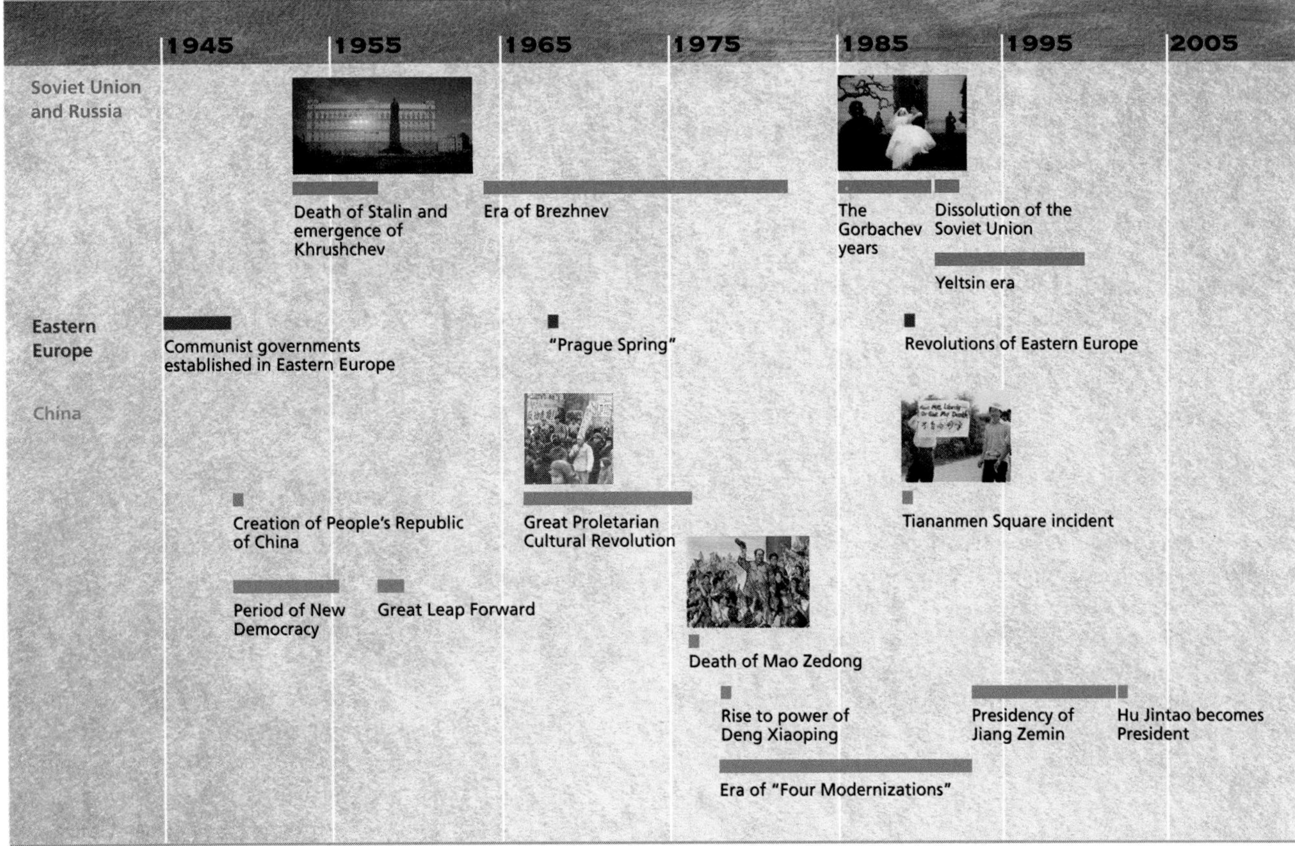


***Awakening of the Soviet Union*** (London, 1990); and **S. White, *Gorbachev and After*** (Cambridge, 1991). For an inquiry into the reasons for the Soviet collapse, see **R. Conquest, *Reflections on a Ravaged Century*** (New York, 1999), and **R. Strayer, *Why Did the Soviet Union Collapse? Understanding Historical Change*** (New York, 1998). On economic conditions in post-Soviet Russia, see **J. Blasi, M. Kroumova,** and **D. Kruse, *Kremlin Capitalism: The Privatization of the Russian Economy*** (Ithaca, N.Y., 1997).

For a general study of the Soviet satellites in Eastern Europe, see **S. Fischer-Galati, *Eastern Europe in the 1980s*** (London, 1981). The unique path of Yugoslavia is examined in **L. J. Cohen** and **P. Warwick, *Political Cohesion in a Fragile Mosaic: The Yugoslav Experience*** (Boulder, Colo., 1983). On East Germany, see **C. B. Scharf, *Politics and Change in East Germany*** (Boulder, Colo., 1984). Additional studies on the recent history of these countries include **T. G. Ash, *The Polish Revolution: Solidarity*** (New York, 1984); **B. Kovrig, *Communism in Hungary from Kun to Kádár*** (Stanford, Calif., 1979); **T. G. Ash, *The Magic Lantern: The Revolution of '89 Witnessed in Warsaw, Budapest, Berlin, and Prague*** (New York, 1990); **M. Shafir, *Romania: Politics, Economics and Society*** (London, 1985); **E. Biberaj, *Albania: A Socialist Maverick*** (Boulder, Colo., 1990); and **S. Ramet, *Nationalism and Federalism in Yugoslavia*** (Bloomington, Ind., 1992).

A number of useful surveys deal with China after World War II. The most comprehensive treatment of the Communist period is **M. Meisner, *Mao's China and After: A History of the People's Republic*** (New York, 1986). For shorter accounts of the period, see **J. Grasso** et al., ***Modernization and Revolution in China*** (Armonk, N.Y., 1991), and **C. Dietrich, *People's China: A Brief History*** (New York, 1986). For documents, see **M. Selden,** ed., ***The People's Republic of China: A Documentary History of Revolutionary Change*** (New York, 1978).

There are countless specialized studies on various aspects of the Communist period in China. The Cultural Revolution is treated dramatically in **S. Karnow, *Mao and China: Inside China's Cultural Revolution*** (New York, 1972). For individual accounts of the impact of the revolution on people's lives, see the celebrated book by **Nien Cheng, *Life and Death in Shanghai*** (New York, 1986), and **Liang Heng** and **J. Shapiro, *After the Revolution*** (New York, 1986).

For the early post-Mao period, see **O. Schell, *To Get Rich Is Glorious*** (New York, 1986), and the sequel, ***Discos and Democracy: China in the Throes of Reform*** (New York, 1988). The 1989 demonstrations and their aftermath are chronicled in **L. Feigon's** eyewitness account, ***China Rising: The Meaning of Tiananmen*** (Chicago, 1990), and **D. Morrison, *Massacre in Beijing*** (New York, 1989). For commentary by Chinese dissidents, see **Liu Binyan, *China's Crisis, China's Hope*** (Cambridge, 1990), and **Fang Lizhi, *Bringing Down the Great Wall: Writings on Science, Culture, and Democracy in China*** (New York, 1991). Documentary material relating to the events of 1989 are chronicled in **A. J. Nathan** and **P. Link**, eds., ***The Tiananmen Papers*** (New York, 2001). Subsequent events are analyzed in **J. Fewsmith, *China Since Tiananmen: The Politics of Transition*** (Cambridge, 2001).

For a comprehensive introduction to twentieth-century Chinese literature, consult **E. Widmer** and **D. Der-Wei Wang**, eds., ***From May Fourth to June Fourth: Fiction and Film in Twentieth-Century China*** (Cambridge, Mass., 1993), and **J. Lau** and **H. Goldblatt, *The Columbia Anthology of Modern Chinese Literature*** (New York, 1995). To witness daily life in the mid-1980s, see **Z. Xinxin** and **S. Ye, *Chinese Lives: An Oral History of Contemporary China*** (New York, 1987). An excellent survey of Chinese women writers is found in **M. S. Duke**, ed., ***Modern Chinese Women Writers: Critical Appraisals*** (Armonk, N.Y., 1989). See the interesting chapters on Ding Ling and her contemporaries in **J. Spence, *The Gate of Heavenly Peace*** (New York, 1981). For the most comprehensive analysis of twentieth-century Chinese art, consult **M. Sullivan, *Arts and Artists of Twentieth-Century China*** (Berkeley, Calif., 1996).

For a discussion of the women's movement in China during this period, see **J. Stacey, *Patriarchy and Socialist Revolution in China*** (Berkeley, Calif., 1983), and **M. Wolf, *Revolution Postponed: Women in Contemporary China*** (Stamford, Conn., 1985). Gender issues are treated in **B. Entwistle** and **G. E. Henderson**, eds., ***Redrawing Boundaries: Work, Households, and Gender in China*** (Berkeley, Calif., 2000). To follow the firsthand account of a Chinese woman revolutionary, read **Y. Daiyun** and **C. Wakeman, *To the Storm: The Odyssey of a Revolutionary Chinese Woman***

**History Now™**

**Enter *HistoryNow* using the access card that is available with this text. *HistoryNow* will assist you in understanding the content in this chapter with lesson plans generated for your needs, as well as provide you with a connection to the *Wadsworth World History Resource Center* (see description below for details).**

**WORLD HISTORY RESOURCE CENTER**

**Enter the Resource Center using either your *HistoryNow* access card or your standalone access card for the *Wadsworth World History Resource Center.* Organized by topic, this website includes quizzes; images; over 350 primary source documents; interactive simulations; maps and timelines; movie explorations; and a wealth of other resources. You can read the following documents, and many more, at http://history.wadsworth.com/rc/world**

Mikhail Gorbachev, "On the End of the Cold War"

Lin Piao, "The Nature of People's War"

Visit the *World History* Companion Website for chapter quizzes and more.

http://history.wadsworth.com/duikerspielvogel05/

CHAPTER

# 27

# EUROPE AND THE WESTERN HEMISPHERE SINCE 1945

© Bettman/CORBIS

*Children play amid the ruins of Warsaw, Poland, at the end of World War II*

## CHAPTER OUTLINE AND FOCUS QUESTIONS

### Recovery and Renewal in Europe

- What problems have the nations of Western Europe faced since 1945, and what steps have they taken to try to solve these problems?

### Emergence of the Superpower: The United States

- What political, social, and economic changes has the United States experienced since 1945?

### The Development of Canada

- What political, social, and economic developments has Canada experienced since 1945?

### Latin America Since 1945

- What problems have the nations of Latin America faced since 1945, and what role has Marxist ideology played in their efforts to solve these problems?

### Society and Culture in the Western World

- What major social, cultural, and intellectual developments have occurred in Western Europe and North America since 1945?

### CRITICAL THINKING

- What are the similarities and differences between the major political, economic, and social developments in the first half of the twentieth century and in the second half of the century?

THE END OF WORLD WAR II in Europe had been met with great joy. One visitor in Moscow reported: "I looked out of the window [at 2 A.M.]; almost everywhere there were lights in the windows–people were staying awake. Everyone embraced everyone else; someone sobbed aloud." But after the victory parades and celebrations, Europeans awoke to a devastating realization: their civilization was in ruins. Almost forty million people (both soldiers and civilians) had been killed over the last six years. Massive air raids and artillery bombardments had reduced many of the great cities of Europe to heaps of rubble. The Polish capital of Warsaw had been almost completely obliterated. An American general described Berlin: "Wherever we looked, we saw desolation. It was like a city of the dead. Suffering and shock were visible in every face. Dead bodies still remained in canals and lakes and were being dug out from under bomb debris." Millions of Europeans faced starvation as grain harvests were only half of what they had been in 1939. Millions were also homeless.

Yet by 1970, Europe had not only recovered from the devastating effects of World War II but had experienced an economic resurgence that seemed nothing less than miraculous. Economic growth and virtually full employment continued so long that the first postwar recession, in 1973, came as a shock. It was short-lived, however, and economic growth resumed. After the collapse of Communist governments in the revolutions of 1989, a number of Eastern European states sought to create market economies and join the military and economic unions first formed by Western European states.

The most significant factor after 1945 was the emergence of the United States as the world's richest and most powerful nation. American prosperity reached new heights in the two decades after World War II, but a series of economic and social problems–including racial division and staggering budget deficits–left an imposing array of difficulties.

Latin America, to the south of the United States, had its own unique heritage. Although some Latin Americans in the nineteenth century had looked to the United States as a model for their own development, in the twentieth century many attacked the United States for its military and economic domination of their countries. And even though they had escaped the turmoil of World War II, many Latin American countries struggled with economic and political instability in the postwar years.

As the West adjusted from Cold War to post–Cold War realities, other changes were also shaping the Western outlook. The demographic face of European countries changed as massive numbers of immigrants created more ethnically diverse populations. New artistic and intellectual currents, the continued advance of science and technology, the coming to grips with environmental problems, the surge of the women's liberation movement–all spoke of a vibrant, ever-changing world. At the same time, a devastating series of terrorist attacks made the Western world vividly aware of its vulnerability to international terrorism. ◇

## Recovery and Renewal in Europe

All the nations of Europe faced similar problems at the end of World War II. Above all, they needed to rebuild their shattered economies. Within a few years after the defeat of Germany and Italy, an incredible economic revival brought renewed growth to Western Europe.

### Western Europe: The Triumph of Democracy

With the economic aid of the Marshall Plan, the countries of Western Europe recovered relatively rapidly from the devastation of World War II. Between the early 1950s and late 1970s, industrial production surpassed all previous records, and Western Europe experienced virtually full employment.

**France: From de Gaulle to New Uncertainties** The history of France for nearly a quarter century after the war was dominated by one man—Charles de Gaulle (1890–1970). The creation of the Fourth Republic, with a parliamentary system based on parties that de Gaulle considered weak, led him to withdraw for a while from politics. However, in 1958, frightened by the bitter divisions within France caused by the Algerian crisis (see Chapter 28), the panic-stricken leaders of the Fourth Republic offered to let de Gaulle take over the government and revise the constitution.

De Gaulle's constitution for the Fifth Republic greatly enhanced the power of the office of president, who now had the right to choose the prime minister, dissolve parliament, and supervise both defense and foreign policy. Once elected to that office, de Gaulle sought to return France to a position of great power. With that goal in mind, he invested heavily in the nuclear arms race. France exploded its first nuclear bomb in 1960. Nevertheless, de Gaulle did not really achieve his ambitious goals; in truth, France was too small for such global ambitions.

During de Gaulle's presidency, the French gross domestic product experienced an annual increase of 5.5 percent, greater than that of the United States. France became a major industrial producer and exporter, particularly in such areas as automobiles and armaments. But the expansion of traditional industries, such as coal, steel, and railroads, which had all been nationalized, led to large government deficits. The cost of living rose faster in France than in the rest of Europe. Increased dissatisfaction led in May 1968 to a series of student protests, followed by a general strike by the labor unions. Although he restored order, de Gaulle became discouraged, resigned from office in April 1969, and died the next year.

**Charles de Gaulle.** As president, Charles de Gaulle sought to revive the greatness of the French nation. He is shown here dressed in his military uniform participating in a formal state ceremony

The worsening of France's economic situation in the 1970s brought a shift to the left politically. By 1981, the Socialists had become the dominant party in the National Assembly, and the Socialist leader, François Mitterrand (1916–1995), was elected president. Mitterrand passed a number of measures to aid workers: a higher minimum wage, expanded social benefits, a mandatory fifth week of paid vacation for salaried workers, and a thirty-nine-hour workweek. The victory of the Socialists led them to enact some of their more radical reforms: the government nationalized the steel industry, major banks, the space and electronics industries, and important insurance firms.

The Socialist policies, however, largely failed to work, and within three years, a decline in support for the Socialists caused the Mitterrand government to reprivatize portions of the economy. But France's economic decline continued. In 1993, French unemployment stood at 10.6 percent, and in the elections in March of that year, the Socialists won only 28 percent of the vote; a coalition of conservative parties ended up with 80 percent of the seats. The move to the right was strengthened when the conservative mayor of Paris, Jacques Chirac (b. 1932), was elected president in May 1995. Chirac pursued a plan of sending illegal immigrants back to their home countries and, after his reelection in 2002, strongly opposed the 2003 U.S. invasion of Iraq.

**From West Germany to One Germany** As noted in Chapter 25, the three Western zones of Germany were unified as the Federal Republic of Germany in 1949. Konrad Adenauer (1876–1967), the leader of the Christian Democratic Union (CDU), served as chancellor from 1949 to 1963 and became the Federal Republic's "founding hero." Adenauer sought respect for postwar Germany by cooperating with the United States and the other Western European nations.

Adenauer's chancellorship is largely associated with the resurrection of the West German economy, even today regarded as a modern miracle. Although West Germany had only 52 percent of the territory of prewar Germany, by 1955 the West German gross domestic product exceeded that of prewar Germany. Real wages doubled between 1950 and 1965. Unemployment fell from 8 percent in 1950 to 0.4 percent in 1965.

After the Adenauer era, German voters moved politically from the center-right of the Christian Democrats to center-left politics; in 1969, the Social Democrats became the leading party. The first Social Democratic chancellor was Willy Brandt (1913–1992), who was especially successful with his "opening toward the east" (known as *Ostpolitik*), for which he received the Nobel Peace Prize in 1972. On March 19, 1971, Brandt worked out the details of a treaty with East Germany (the former Russian zone) that led to greater cultural, personal, and economic contacts between West and East Germany.

In 1982, the Christian Democratic Union of Helmut Kohl (b. 1930) formed a new center-right government. Kohl was a clever politician who benefited greatly from an economic boom in the mid-1980s and the 1989 revolution in East Germany, which led in 1990 to the long-awaited reunification of the two Germanies, making the new Germany, with its 79 million people, the leading power in Europe.

But the excitement over reunification soon dissipated as new problems arose. All too soon, the realization set in that the revitalization of eastern Germany would take far more money than was originally thought, and Kohl's government was soon forced to face the politically undesirable task of raising taxes substantially. Moreover, the virtual collapse of the economy in eastern Germany led to extremely high levels of unemployment and severe discontent. One of the responses was a return to power for the Social Democrats under the leadership of Gerhard Schroeder (b. 1944). Although Schroeder had little success with Germany's economic woes, the Social Democrats were continued in power in elections held in 2002.

**The Decline of Great Britain** The end of World War II left Britain with massive economic problems. In elections held immediately after the war, the Labour Party overwhelmingly defeated Churchill's Conservatives. Labour had promised far-reaching reforms, particularly in the area of social welfare, and in a country with a tremendous shortage of consumer goods and housing, its platform was quite appealing. The new Labour government under Clement Attlee (1883–1967) proceeded to turn Britain into a modern **welfare state.**

The process began with the nationalization of the Bank of England, the coal and steel industries, public transportation, and public utilities, such as electricity and gas. In 1946, the new government established a comprehensive social security program and nationalized medical insurance, thereby enabling the state to subsidize the unemployed, the sick, and the aged. The health act established a system of **socialized medicine** that forced doctors and dentists to work with state hospitals, although private practice could be maintained. The British welfare state became the norm for most European nations after the war.

Continuing economic problems, however, brought the Conservatives back into power from 1951 to 1964. Although the British economy had recovered from the war, its slow rate of recovery reflected a long-term economic decline. As a result of World War II, Britain had lost much of its prewar revenues from abroad but was left with a burden of debt from its many international commitments. At the same time, as the influence of the United States and the Soviet Union continued to rise, Britain's ability to play the role of a world power declined substantially. Between 1964 and 1979, Conservatives and Labour alternated in power, but neither party was able to heal Britain's ailing economy.

In 1979, the Conservatives returned to power under Margaret Thatcher (b. 1925), who became the first woman prime minister in British history (see the box on

**Margaret Thatcher.** Great Britain's first female prime minister, Margaret Thatcher was a strong leader who dominated British politics in the 1980s. This picture of Thatcher was taken at the Chelsea Flower Show in May 1990. Six months later, a revolt within her own party caused her to resign as prime minister.

| CHRONOLOGY Western Europe | |
|---|---|
| Welfare state emerges in Great Britain | 1946 |
| Konrad Adenauer becomes chancellor of West Germany | 1949 |
| Charles de Gaulle reassumes power in France | 1958 |
| Student protests in France | 1968 |
| Willy Brandt becomes chancellor of West Germany | 1969 |
| Margaret Thatcher becomes prime minister of Great Britain | 1979 |
| François Mitterrand becomes president of France | 1981 |
| Helmut Kohl becomes chancellor of West Germany | 1982 |
| Reelection of Mitterrand | 1988 |
| Reunification of Germany | 1990 |
| Conservative victory in France | 1993 |
| Election of Chirac | 1995 |
| Labour Party victory in Great Britain | 1997 |
| Social Democratic victory in Germany | 1998 |
| Reelection of Chirac | 2002 |

p. 787). Thatcher pledged to lower taxes, reduce government bureaucracy, limit social welfare, restrict union power, and end inflation. The "Iron Lady," as she was called, did break the power of the labor unions. Although she did not eliminate the basic components of the social welfare system, she used austerity measures to control inflation. "Thatcherism," as her economic policy was termed, improved the British economic situation, but at a price. The south of England, for example, prospered, but the old industrial areas of the Midlands and north declined and were beset by high unemployment, poverty, and sporadic violence.

Thatcher dominated British politics in the 1980s. But in 1990, Labour's fortunes revived when Thatcher's government attempted to replace local property taxes with a flat-rate tax payable by every adult to a local authority. Many British citizens argued that this was nothing more than a poll tax that would allow the rich to get away with paying the same rate as the poor. In 1990, after antitax riots broke out, Thatcher's popularity plummeted, and a revolt within her own party forced her to resign as prime minister. She was replaced by John Major (b. 1943), but his government failed to capture the imagination of most Britons. In new elections on May 1, 1997, the Labour Party won a landslide victory. The new prime minister, Tony Blair (b. 1953), was a moderate whose youthful energy immediately instilled a new vigor on the political scene. Blair was one of the major leaders in forming an international coalition against terrorism after the terrorist attack on the United States in 2001. Four years later, his support of the U.S. war in Iraq when a majority of Britons opposed it caused his popularity to decline.

## Eastern Europe After Communism

The fall of Communist governments in Eastern Europe during the revolutions of 1989 brought a wave of euphoria. The new structures meant an end to a postwar European order that had been imposed on unwilling peoples by the victorious forces of the Soviet Union (see Chapter 25). In 1989 and 1990, new governments throughout Eastern Europe worked diligently to scrap the remnants of the old system and introduce the democratic procedures and market systems they believed would revitalize their scarred lands. But this process proved to be neither simple nor easy.

Nevertheless, by the beginning of the twenty-first century, many of these states, especially Poland and the Czech Republic, were making a successful transition to both free markets and democracy. In Poland, Aleksander Kwasniewski, although a former Communist, was elected president in November 1995 and pushed Poland toward an increasingly prosperous free market economy. His success brought his reelection in October 2000. In Czechoslovakia, the shift to noncommunist rule was complicated by old problems, especially ethnic issues. Czechs and Slovaks disagreed over the makeup of the new state but were able to agree to a peaceful division of the country. On January 1, 1993, Czechoslovakia split into the Czech Republic and Slovakia. Václav Havel was elected the first

## MARGARET THATCHER: ENTERING A MAN'S WORLD

In 1979, Margaret Thatcher became the first woman to serve as Britain's prime minister. In this excerpt from her autobiography, Thatcher describes how she was interviewed by Conservative Party officials when they first considered her as a possible candidate for Parliament. Thatcher ran for Parliament for the first time in 1950; she lost but increased the Conservative vote total in the district by 50 percent over the previous election.

*In this account, is Margaret Thatcher's being a woman more important to her or to others? Why would this disparity exist?*

### Margaret Thatcher, *The Path to Power*

And, as always with me, there was politics. I immediately joined the Conservative Association and threw myself into the usual round of Party activities. In particular, I thoroughly enjoyed what was called the "'39–'45" discussion group, where Conservatives of the war generation met to exchange views and argue about the political topics of the day. . . . It was as a representative of the Oxford University Graduate Conservative Association (OUGCA) that I went to the Llandudno Conservative Party Conference in October 1948.

It had originally been intended that I should speak at the Conference, seconding an OUGCA motion deploring the abolition of university seats. At that time universities had separate representation in Parliament, and graduates had the right to vote in their universities as well as in the constituency where they lived. (I supported separate university representation, but not the principle that graduates should have more than one vote. . . .) It would have been my first Conference speech, but in the end the seconder chosen was a City man, because the City seats were also to be abolished.

My disappointment at this was, however, very quickly overcome and in a most unexpected way. After one of the debates, I found myself engaged in one of those speculative conversations which young people have about their future prospects. An Oxford friend, John Grant, said he supposed that one day I would like to be a Member of Parliament. "Well, yes," I replied, "but there's not much hope of that. The chances of my being selected are just nil at the moment." I might have added that with no private income of my own there was no way I could have afforded to be an MP on the salary then available. I had not even tried to get on the Party's list of approved candidates.

Later in the day, John Grant happened to be sitting next to the Chairman of the Dartford Conservative Association, John Miller. The Association was in search of a candidate. I learned afterwards that the conversation went something like this: "I understand that you're still looking for a candidate at Dartford?" . . .

"That's right. Any suggestions?"

"Well, there's a young woman, Margaret Roberts, that you might look at. She's very good."

"Oh, but Dartford is a real industrial stronghold. I don't think a woman would do at all."

"Well, you know best of course. But why not just look at her?"

And they did. I was invited to have lunch with John Miller and his wife, Phee, and the Dartford Woman's Chairman, Mrs. Fletcher, on the Saturday on Llandudno Pier. Presumably, and in spite of any reservations about the suitability of a woman candidate for their seat, they liked what they saw. I certainly got on well with them. . . .

I did not hear from Dartford until December, when I was asked to attend an interview at Palace Chambers, Bridge Street. . . . Very few outside the political arena know just how nerve-racking such occasions are. The interviewee who is not nervous and tense is very likely to perform badly: for, as any chemist will tell you, the adrenaline needs to flow if one is to perform at one's best. . . .

I found myself short-listed, and was asked to go to Dartford itself for a further interview. . . . As one of five would-be candidates, I had to give a fifteen-minute speech and answer questions for a further ten minutes.

It was the questions which were more likely to cause me trouble. There was a good deal of suspicion of woman candidates, particularly in what was regarded as a tough industrial seat like Dartford. This was quite definitely a man's world into which not just angels feared to tread. . . .

The most reliable sign that a political occasion has gone well is that you have enjoyed it. I enjoyed that evening at Dartford, and the outcome justified my confidence. I was selected.

History Now™ To read Margaret Thatcher on Christianity and wealth, enter the *HistoryNow* documents area using the access card that is available for *World History.*

president of the new Czech Republic, which soon became one of Eastern Europe's most prosperous and politically stable countries.

The revival of the post–Cold War Eastern European states was evident in their desire to join both NATO and the European Union, the two major Cold War institutions of Western European unity. In 1997, Poland, the Czech Republic, and Hungary became full members of NATO. (on the European Union, see "The Unification of Europe" on p. 789).

**The Disintegration of Yugoslavia** From its beginning in 1919, Yugoslavia had been an artificial creation. After World War II, the dictatorial Marshal Tito had managed to hold together the six disparate republics and two autonomous provinces that made up the country. After his death in 1980, no strong leader emerged, and eventually Yugoslavia was caught up in the reform movements sweeping through Eastern Europe.

After negotiations among the six republics failed, Slovenia and Croatia declared their independence in June 1991. This action was opposed by Slobodan Milošević, the leader of the province of Serbia. He asserted that these republics could only be independent if new border arrangements were made to accommodate the Serb minorities in those republics who did not want to live outside the boundaries of Serbia. Serbian forces attacked both new states; although unsuccessful against Slovenia, they captured one-third of Croatia's territory.

The international recognition in 1992 of independent Slovenia and Croatia and soon thereafter Macedonia and Bosnia and Herzegovina did not deter the Serbs, who now turned their guns on Bosnia. By mid-1993, Serbian forces had acquired 70 percent of Bosnian territory. The Serbian policy of **ethnic cleansing**—killing or forcibly removing Bosnian Muslims from their lands—revived memories of Nazi atrocities in World War II. This account by one Muslim survivor from the town of Srebrenica is eerily reminiscent of the activities of the Nazi *Einsatzgruppen* (See Chapter 24):

> When the truck stopped, they told us to get off in groups of five. We immediately heard shooting next to the trucks. . . . About ten Serbs with automatic rifles told us to lie down on the ground face first. As we were getting down, they started to shoot, and I fell into a pile of corpses. I felt hot liquid running down my face. I realized that I was only grazed. As they continued to shoot more groups, I kept on squeezing myself in between dead bodies.[1]

Almost eight thousand men and boys were killed by the Serbian massacre at Srebrenica. Nevertheless, despite worldwide outrage, European governments failed to take a forceful stand against the Serbs' actions, leaving the Muslim population of Bosnia in desperate straits. At last, as the fighting spread, European nations and the United States began to intervene to stop the bloodshed, and in the fall of 1995, a fragile cease-fire agreement was reached. An international peacekeeping force was stationed in the area to maintain tranquillity.

Peace in Bosnia, however, did not bring peace to Yugoslavia. A new war erupted in 1999 over Kosovo,

AP/Wide World Photos

**The War in Bosnia.** By mid-1993, irregular Serbian forces had overrun much of Bosnia and Herzegovina amid scenes of untold suffering. This photograph shows a woman running past the bodies of victims of a mortar attack on Sarajevo on August 21, 1992. Three mortar rounds landed, killing at least three people.

which had been made an autonomous province within the Serbian republic by Tito in 1974. Kosovo's inhabitants were mainly ethnic Albanians. But the province was also home to a Serbian minority In 1989, Yugoslav president Milosěvić stripped Kosovo of its autonomous status. Four years later, some groups of ethnic Albanians founded the Kosovo Liberation Army (KLA) and began a campaign against Serbian rule in Kosovo. When Serb forces began to massacre ethnic Albanians in an effort to crush the KLA, the United States and its NATO allies mounted a bombing campaign that forced Milosěvić to stop. In the fall elections of 2000, Milosěvić himself was ousted from power and he was later put on trial by an international tribunal for war crimes against humanity for his ethnic cleansing policies throughout Yugoslavia's disintegration.

The fate of Bosnia and Kosovo has not yet been finally determined. In Bosnia, thirty thousand NATO troops remain, trying to keep the peace. In Kosovo, NATO military forces were brought in to maintain an uneasy peace while United Nations officials worked to set up democratic institutions. In 2004, the last political vestige of Yugoslavia ceased to exist when the new national government under Vojislav Kostunica officially renamed the truncated country Serbia and Montenegro.

## The Unification of Europe

As we saw in Chapter 25, the divisions created by the Cold War led the nations of Western Europe to seek military security by forming the North Atlantic Treaty Organization (NATO) in 1949. The destructiveness of two world wars, however, caused many thoughtful Europeans to consider the need for some additional form of unity.

In 1957, France, West Germany, the Benelux countries (Belgium, the Netherlands, and Luxembourg), and Italy signed the Treaty of Rome, which created the European Economic Community (EEC). The EEC eliminated customs barriers for the six member nations and created a large free-trade area protected from the rest of the world by a common external tariff. All the member nations benefited economically. In 1973, Great Britain, Ireland, and Denmark gained membership in what now was called the European Community (EC). Greece joined in 1981, followed by Spain and Portugal in 1986. In 1995, Austria, Finland, and Sweden also became members of the EC.

**The European Union** The European Community was an economic union, not a political one. By 2000, the EC contained 370 million people and constituted the world's largest single trading entity, transacting one-fourth of the world's commerce. In the 1980s and 1990s, the EC moved toward even greater economic integration. The Treaty on European Union, which went into effect on January 1, 1994, turned the European Community into the European Union, a true economic and monetary union of all EC members. One of its first goals was achieved in 1999 with the introduction of a common currency, the euro. On January 1, 2002, the euro officially replaced twelve national currencies.

In addition to having a single internal market for those twelve members and a common currency, the EU also established a common agricultural policy, in which subsidies were provided to farmers to enable them to sell their goods competitively on the world market. The end of national passports gave millions of Europeans greater flexibility in travel. The European Union has been less successful in setting common foreign policy goals, primarily because individual nations still see foreign policy as a national priority and are reluctant to give up this power to a single overriding institution. However, the EU did create a military force of sixty thousand, chiefly used for humanitarian and peacekeeping purposes. Indeed, the focus of the EU is on peaceful conflict resolution, not making war.

But as successful as the European Union has been, problems exist. Europeans are often divided on the European Union. Some oppose it because the official representatives of the EU are not democratically accountable to the people. Moreover, many Europeans do not see themselves as "Europeans" but remain committed to a national identity. Despite these problems, in a poll taken in the fall of 2001, 54 percent of Europeans said that membership in the EU was a "good thing."

**Toward a United Europe** At the beginning of the twenty-first century, the EU established a new goal: to incorporate into the union the states of eastern and southeastern Europe. Many of these states were considerably poorer than the current members, which raised the possibility that adding these nations might weaken the EU itself. To lessen the danger, EU members established a set of qualifications that focus on demonstrating a commitment both to market capitalism and to democracy, including not only the rule of law but also respect for minorities and human rights. Hence joining the EU might well add to the stability of these nations and make the dream of a united Europe a reality. In May 2004, the European Union took the plunge and added ten new members: Cyprus, the Czech Republic, Estonia, Hungary, Latvia, Lithuania, Malta, Poland, Slovakia, and Slovenia, thus enlarging the population of the EU to 455 million peoples (see Map 27.1).

# Emergence of the Superpower: The United States

At the end of World War II, the United States emerged as one of the world's two superpowers. As its Cold War confrontation with the Soviet Union intensified, the United States directed much of its energy toward combating the spread of communism throughout the world. With the collapse of the Soviet Union at the beginning of the 1990s, the United States became the world's foremost military power.

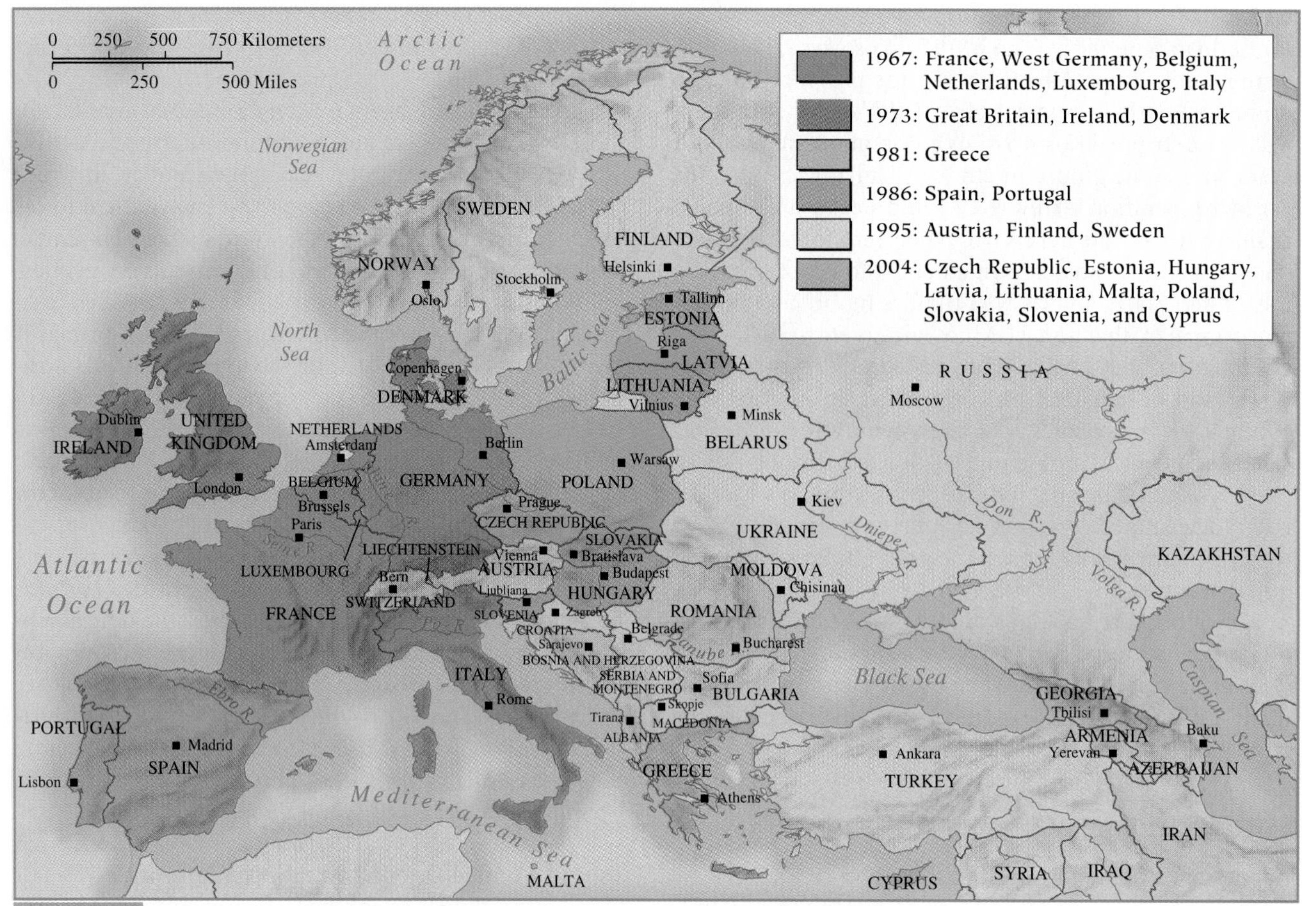


**MAP 27.1 European Union, 2004.** Beginning in 1957 as the European Economic Community, also known as the Common Market, the union of European states seeking to integrate their economies has gradually grown from six members to twenty-five in 2004. The European Union has achieved two major goals—the creation of a single internal market and a common currency—although it has been less successful at working toward common political and foreign policy goals. What additional nations do you think will eventually join the European Union? **View an animated version of this map or related maps at** http://history.wadsworth.com/duikerspielvogel05/

## American Politics and Society Through the Vietnam Era

Franklin Roosevelt's New Deal of the 1930s initiated a basic transformation of American society that included a dramatic increase in the role and power of the federal government, the rise of organized labor as a significant force in the economy and politics, a commitment to the welfare state, a grudging acceptance of ethnic minorities, and a willingness to experiment with deficit spending as a means of spurring the economy. The New Deal in American politics was bolstered by the election of Democratic presidents—Harry S. Truman in 1948, John F. Kennedy in 1960, and Lyndon B. Johnson in 1964. Even the election of a Republican president, Dwight D. Eisenhower, in 1952 and 1956 did not significantly alter the fundamental direction of the New Deal. As Eisenhower stated in 1954, "Should any political party attempt to abolish Social Security and eliminate labor laws and farm programs, you would not hear of that party again in our political history."

The economic boom after World War II fueled confidence in the American way of life. A shortage of consumer goods during the war left Americans with both surplus income and the desire to purchase these goods after the war. Then, too, the development of organized labor enabled more and more workers to get the wage increases that spurred the growth of the domestic market. Between 1945 and 1973, real wages grew an average of 3 percent a year, the most prolonged advance in U.S. history.

Starting in the 1960s, problems that had been glossed over earlier came to the fore. The decade began on a youthful and optimistic note when John F. Kennedy (1917–1963), age forty-three, became the youngest elected president in the history of the United States and the first one born in the twentieth century. His own administration, cut short by an assassin's bullet on

© Bob Adelman/Magnum Photos

**The Civil Rights Movement.** In the early 1960s, Martin Luther King Jr. and his Southern Christian Leadership Conference organized a variety of activities to pursue the goal of racial equality. He is shown here with his wife, Coretta (right), and Rosa Parks and Ralph Abernathy (far left) leading a march in 1965 against racial discrimination. He was assassinated three years later.

November 22, 1963, focused primarily on foreign affairs. Kennedy's successor, Lyndon B. Johnson (1908–1973), who won a new term as president in a landslide in 1964, used his stunning mandate to pursue the growth of the welfare state begun in the New Deal. Johnson's programs included health care for the elderly and the War on Poverty, to be fought with food stamps and the Job Corps.

Johnson's other domestic passion was achieving equal rights for black Americans. In August 1963, the eloquent Martin Luther King Jr. (1929–1968), a Baptist minister and leader of a growing movement for racial equality, led the March on Washington for Jobs and Freedom to dramatize black Americans' desire for treatment no different from that accorded to whites. This march and King's impassioned plea for racial equality (see the box on p. 792) had an electrifying effect on the American people. President Johnson pursued the cause of civil rights. As a result of his initiative, Congress enacted the Civil Rights Act of 1964, which created the machinery to end segregation and discrimination in the workplace and in public accommodations. The Voting Rights Act the following year eliminated obstacles to black participation in elections in southern states. But laws alone could not guarantee the "Great Society" that Johnson envisioned, and soon the administration faced bitter social unrest.

In the North and the West, blacks had had voting rights for many years, but local patterns of segregation resulted in considerably higher unemployment rates for blacks (and Hispanics) than for whites and left blacks segregated in huge urban ghettos. It was in these ghettos that radical black nationalist leaders, such as Malcolm X of the Black Muslims, attracted more attention with their calls for militant action than the nonviolent appeals of Martin Luther King. In the summer of 1965, race riots erupted in the Watts district of Los Angeles that led to thirty-four deaths and the destruction of over one thousand buildings. When King was assassinated in 1968, more than one hundred cities erupted in rioting, including Washington, D.C., the nation's capital. The combination of riots and extremist comments by radical black leaders led to a "white backlash" and a severe racial division of America.

Antiwar protests also divided the American people after President Johnson committed American troops to a costly war in Vietnam (see Chapter 25). Teach-ins, sit-ins, and the occupations of university buildings alternated with more radical demonstrations that increasingly led to violence. The killing of four student protesters at Kent State University in 1970 by the Ohio National Guard shocked both activists and ordinary Americans, and thereafter the vehemence of the antiwar movement began to subside. But the combination of antiwar demonstrations and riots in the cities caused many people to call for "law and order," an appeal used by Richard Nixon (1913–1994), the Republican presidential candidate in 1968. With Nixon's election in 1968, a shift to the right in American politics had begun.

## The Shift Rightward After 1973

Nixon eventually ended American involvement in Vietnam by gradually withdrawing American troops. Politically, he pursued a "southern strategy," carefully calculating that "law and order" issues would appeal to southern whites. The Republican strategy, however, also gained support among white Democrats in northern cities, where court-mandated busing of students to distant neighborhoods to achieve racial integration of the public schools had provoked a white backlash.

As president, Nixon was paranoid about conspiracies and resorted to subversive methods of gaining political intelligence on his political opponents. Nixon's zeal led to the Watergate scandal—a botched attempt to plant listening devices in the Democratic National Headquarters and the ensuing cover-up. Although Nixon repeatedly denied involvement in the affair, secret tapes he made of his own conversations in the White House revealed otherwise. On August 9, 1974, Nixon resigned in disgrace, an act

## "I Have a Dream"

In the spring of 1963, a bomb attack on a church that killed four African American children and the brutal fashion in which police handled black demonstrators brought the nation's attention to the policies of racial segregation in Birmingham, Alabama. A few months later, on August 28, 1963, Martin Luther King Jr. led a march on Washington, D.C., and gave an inspired speech at the Lincoln Memorial that catalyzed the civil rights movement.

*Martin Luther King Jr. was known as a highly skilled and moving orator. What are some of the rhetorically effective elements in this speech?*

### Martin Luther King Jr., "I Have a Dream"

I am happy to join with you today in what will go down in history as the greatest demonstration for freedom in the history of our nation.

Five score years ago, a great American, in whose symbolic shadow we stand today, signed the Emancipation Proclamation. This momentous decree came as a great beacon light of hope to millions of Negro slaves, who had been seared in the flames of withering injustice. It came as a joyous daybreak to end the long night of their captivity.

But one hundred years later, the Negro still is not free; one hundred years later, the life of the Negro is still sadly crippled by the manacles of segregation and the chains of discrimination; one hundred years later, the Negro lives on a lonely island of poverty in the midst of a vast ocean of material prosperity; one hundred years later, the Negro is still languished in the corners of American society and finds himself in exile in his own land. . . .

So we've come here today to dramatize a shameful condition. In a sense we've come to our nation's capital to cash a check. When the architects of our republic wrote the magnificent words of the Constitution and the Declaration of Independence, they were signing a promissory note to which every American was to fall heir. This note was the promise that all men, yes, black men as well as white men, would be guaranteed the unalienable rights of life, liberty, and the pursuit of happiness.

It is obvious today that America has defaulted on this promissory note in so far as her citizens of color are concerned. Instead of honoring this sacred obligation, America has given the Negro people a bad check, a check which has come back marked "insufficient funds." But we refuse to believe that the bank of justice is bankrupt. . . .

We have also come to this hallowed spot to remind America of the fierce urgency of now. This is no time to engage in the luxury of cooling off or to take the tranquilizing drug of gradualism. Now is the time to make real the promises of democracy; now is the time to rise from the dark and desolate valley of segregation to the sunlit path of racial justice; now is the time to lift our nation from the quicksands of racial injustice to the solid rock of brotherhood; now is the time to make justice a reality for all of God's children. It would be fatal for the nation to overlook the urgency of the moment. . . .

I say to you today, my friends, so even though we face the difficulties of today and tomorrow, I still have a dream. It is a dream deeply rooted in the American dream. I have a dream that one day this nation will rise up and live out the true meaning of its creed, "We hold these truths to be self-evident, that all men are created equal." I have a dream that one day on the red hills of Georgia, sons of former slaves and the sons of former slave owners will be able to sit down together at the table of brotherhood. . . . I have a dream that my four little children will one day live in a nation where they will not be judged by the color of their skin, but by the content of their character. . . .

This is our hope. This is the faith that I go back to the South with. With this faith we will be able to hew out of the mountain of despair a stone of hope. With this faith we will be able to transform the jangling discords of our nation into a beautiful symphony of brotherhood. With this faith we will be able to work together, to pray together, to struggle together, to go to jail together, to stand up for freedom together, knowing that we will be free one day. And this will be the day. This will be the day when all of God's children will be able to sing with new meaning, "My country 'tis of thee, sweet land of liberty, of thee I sing. Land where my father died, land of the pilgrims' pride, from every mountainside, let freedom ring." And if America is to be a great nation, this must become true. . . .

And when this happens, and when we allow freedom to ring, when we let it ring from every village and every hamlet, from every state and every city, we will be able to speed up that day when all of God's children, black men and white men, Jews and Gentiles, Protestants and Catholics, will be able to join hands and sing in the words of the old Negro spiritual: "Free at last. Free at last. Thank God Almighty, we are free at last."

that saved him from almost certain impeachment and conviction.

After Watergate, American domestic politics focused on economic issues. Gerald Ford (b. 1913) became president when Nixon resigned, only to lose in the 1976 election to the former governor of Georgia, Jimmy Carter (b. 1924), who campaigned as an outsider against the Washington establishment. By 1980, the Carter administration faced two devastating problems. High inflation and a decline in average weekly earnings were causing a perceptible drop in American living standards. At the same time, a crisis abroad had erupted when fifty-three

Americans were taken hostage by the Iranian government of Ayatollah Khomeini and held for nearly fifteen months (see Chapter 28). Carter's inability to gain the release of the American hostages led to perceptions at home that he was a weak president. His overwhelming loss to Ronald Reagan (1911–2004) in the election of 1980 brought forward the chief exponent of right-wing Republican policies.

The Reagan Revolution, as it has been called, sent U.S. policy in a number of new directions. Reversing decades of changes, Reagan cut back on the welfare state by decreasing spending on food stamps, school lunch programs, and job programs. At the same time, his administration fostered the largest peacetime military buildup in American history. Total federal spending rose from $631 billion in 1981 to over $1 trillion by 1986. But instead of raising taxes to pay for the new expenditures, Reagan convinced Congress that massive tax cuts would supposedly stimulate rapid economic growth and produce new revenues. Reagan's policies seemed to work in the short run as the United States experienced an economic upturn that lasted until the end of the 1980s. But the administration's spending policies also produced record government deficits, which loomed as an obstacle to long-term growth. In the 1970s, the total deficit was $420 billion; Reagan's budget deficits were three times that amount.

The inability of Reagan's successor, George H. W. Bush (b. 1924), to deal with the deficit problem, coupled with an economic downturn, led to the election of a Democrat, Bill Clinton, in November 1992. The new president was a southerner who claimed to be a new Democrat—one who favored a number of the Republican policies of the 1980s. This was a clear indication that the rightward drift in American politics was by no means ended by this Democratic victory. In fact, Clinton's reelection in 1996 was due in part to his adoption of conservative policies.

President Clinton's political fortunes were aided considerably by a lengthy economic revival. A steady reduction in the annual government budget deficit strengthened confidence in the performance of the national economy. Much of Clinton's second term, however, was overshadowed by charges of misconduct stemming from the president's affair with Monica Lewinsky, a White House intern. After a bitter partisan struggle, the U.S. Senate acquitted the president on two articles of impeachment brought by the House of Representatives. But Clinton's problems helped the Republican candidate, George W. Bush, win the presidential election in 2000. Although Bush lost the popular vote to Al Gore, he narrowly won the electoral vote after a highly controversial victory in the state of Florida.

The first four years of Bush's administration were largely occupied with the war on terrorism and the U.S.-led war on Iraq, launched in 2003. The Office of Homeland Security was established after the 2001 terrorist assaults to help protect the United States from future terrorist acts. At the same time, Bush pushed tax cuts through Congress that mainly favored the wealthy and helped produce deficits surpassing even those of the Reagan years. Environmentalists were especially disturbed by the Bush administration's efforts to weaken environmental laws and alter regulations to benefit American corporations. In November 2004, after a divisive political campaign, Bush was narrowly elected to a second term.

## The Development of Canada

Canada's development in the postwar years paralleled that of the United States. For twenty-five years after World War II, Canada experienced extraordinary economic prosperity as it set out on a path of industrial development. Canada had always had a strong export economy based on its abundant natural resources. Now it also developed electronic, aircraft, nuclear, and chemical engineering industries on a large scale. Much of the Canadian growth, however, was financed by capital from the United States, which resulted in American ownership of Canadian businesses. Though many Canadians welcomed the economic growth, others feared American economic domination of Canada and its resources.

A notable feature of Canada's postwar history has been its close relationship with the United States. In addition to fears of economic domination, Canadians have also worried about playing a subordinate role politically and militarily to the neighboring superpower. Canada agreed to join NATO in 1949 and even sent military contingents to fight in Korea the following year. But to avoid subordination to the United States or any other great power, Canada has consistently and actively supported the United Nations. Nevertheless, concerns about the United States have not kept Canada from maintaining a special relationship with its southern neighbor.

For three decades after 1945, the Liberal Party largely dominated Canadian politics and created Canada's welfare state by enacting a national social security system (the Canada Pension Plan) and a national health insurance program. The most prominent Liberal government was that of Pierre Trudeau (1919–2000), who came to power in 1968. A French Canadian, Trudeau did not harbor separatist sentiments and was dedicated to Canada's federal union. In 1968, his government passed the Official Languages Act, which created a bilingual federal civil service and encouraged the growth of French culture and language in Canada. Although Trudeau's government vigorously pushed an industrialization program, high inflation and Trudeau's efforts to impose the will of the federal government on the powerful provincial governments alienated voters and weakened his government.

Economic recession in the early 1980s brought Brian Mulroney (b. 1939), leader of the Progressive Conservative Party, to power in 1984. Mulroney's government sought greater privatization of Canada's state-run corporations and negotiated a free-trade agreement with the

United States. Bitterly resented by many Canadians, the agreement cost Mulroney's government much of its popularity. In 1993, the ruling Conservatives were overwhelmingly defeated, and the Liberal leader, Jean Chrétien (b. 1934), became prime minister. Chrétien's conservative fiscal policies, combined with strong economic growth, enabled his government to have a budgetary surplus by the late 1990s and led to another Liberal victory in the elections of 1997. In 2003, Chrétien retired and was replaced by Paul Martin.

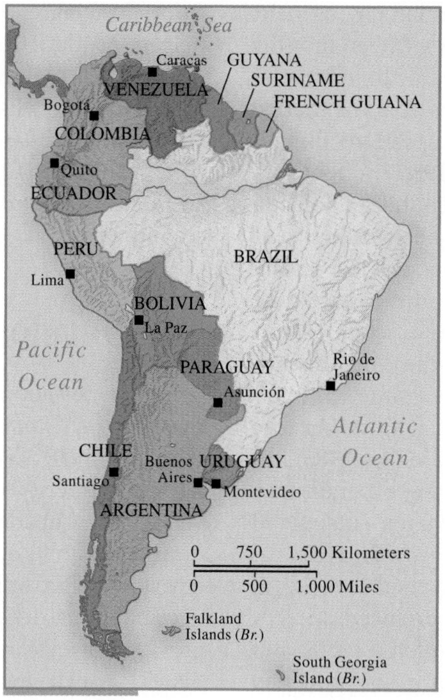

**South America**

The government also faced an ongoing crisis over the French-speaking province of Quebec. In the late 1960s, the Parti Québécois, headed by René Lévesque, campaigned on a platform of Quebec's secession from the Canadian confederation. In 1970, the party won 24 percent of the popular vote in Quebec's provincial elections. To pursue their dream of separation, some underground separatist groups even used terrorist bombings and kidnapped two prominent government officials. In 1976, the Parti Québécois won Quebec's provincial elections and in 1980 called for a referendum that would enable the provincial government to negotiate Quebec's independence from the rest of Canada. Voters in Quebec narrowly rejected the plan in 1995, however, and debate over the province's future continues to divide Canada.

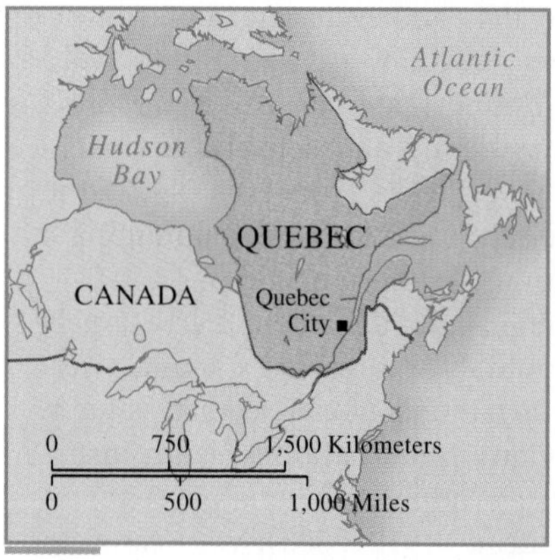

**Quebec**

## Latin America Since 1945

The Great Depression of the 1930s had caused a political instability in many Latin American countries that led to military coups and militaristic regimes (see Chapter 23). But the depression also led Latin America to move from a traditional to a modern economic structure. Since the nineteenth century, Latin Americans had exported raw materials, especially minerals and foodstuffs, while buying the manufactured goods of the industrialized countries in Europe and the United States. As a result of the depression, however, exports were cut in half, and the revenues available to buy manufactured goods declined. This encouraged many Latin American countries to develop industries to produce goods that were formerly imported. Due to a shortage of capital in the private sector, governments often invested in the new industries, thus leading, for example, to government-run steel industries in Chile and Brazil and oil industries in Argentina and Mexico.

By the 1960s, however, Latin American countries still found themselves dependent on the United States, Europe, and now Japan, especially for the advanced technology needed for modern industries. Because of the great poverty in many Latin American countries, domestic markets were limited in size, and many Latin American countries failed to find markets abroad for their products. These failures led to instability and a new reliance on military regimes, especially to curb the power of the new industrial middle class and working classes, which had increased in size and power as a result of industrialization. In the 1960s, repressive military regimes in Chile, Brazil, and Argentina abolished political parties and repeatedly returned to export-import economies financed by foreigners. They also invited multinational companies to come in. The companies that accepted the invitation wanted primarily to take advantage of Latin America's raw materials and abundant supply of cheap labor, which only contributed to the ongoing dependency of Latin America on the industrially developed nations.

In the 1970s, Latin American regimes grew even more dependent on maintaining their failing economies by borrowing from abroad, especially from banks in Europe and the United States. Between 1970 and 1982, debt to foreigners increased from $27 billion to $315 billion. By 1982, a number of governments announced that they could no longer pay interest on their debts to foreign banks, and their economies began to crumble.

In the 1980s, the debt crisis was paralleled by a movement toward democracy. In part, some military leaders were simply unwilling to deal with the monstrous debt problems. At the same time, many people realized that military power without popular consent was incapable of providing a strong state. Then, too, there was a swelling of popular support for basic rights and free and fair elections. By the mid-1980s, democratic regimes were in place everywhere except Cuba, some of the Central American states, Chile, and Paraguay.

The United States has also played an important role in Latin America since 1945. The United States had intervened militarily in Latin American affairs for years, particularly in Central America and the Caribbean, a region considered its "backyard" and thus of strategic importance. Beginning in the 1920s, the United States had replaced Britain as the foremost investor in Latin America. Unlike the British, however, American investors put funds directly into production enterprises so that large segments of Latin America's export industries fell into American hands. The American-owned United Fruit Company turned a number of Central American nations into "banana republics," while American companies gained control of the copper-mining industry in Chile and Peru and the oil industry in Mexico, Peru, and Bolivia. The control of these industries by American investors reinforced a growing nationalist consciousness against America as a neo-imperialist power.

**Central America**

But the United States had also tried to pursue a new relationship with Latin America. In 1948, the nations of the Western Hemisphere formed the Organization of American States (OAS), which was intended to eliminate unilateral action by one state within the internal or external affairs of any other state. But as the Cold War between the United States and the Soviet Union intensified, American policy makers grew anxious about the possibility of Communist regimes arising in Central America and the Caribbean and returned to a policy of unilateral action when they believed that Soviet agents were attempting to establish Communist governments. Especially after the success of Castro in Cuba (see the next section), the desire of the United States to prevent "another Cuba" largely determined American policy toward Latin America until the collapse of the Cold War in the 1990s. The United States provided massive military aid to anti-Communist regimes, regardless of their nature.

## The Threat of Marxist Revolutions

Until the 1960s, Marxism played little role in the politics of Latin America. The success of Fidel Castro in Cuba and his espousal of Marxism, however, opened the door for other Marxist movements that aimed to gain the support of peasants and industrial workers and bring radical change to Latin America.

**The Cuban Revolution** A dictatorship, headed by Fulgencio Batista (1901–1973) and closely tied economically to U.S. investors, had ruled Cuba since 1934. A strong opposition movement to Batista's government developed, led by Fidel Castro (b. 1926) and assisted by Ernesto "Ché" Guevara (1928-1967), an Argentinian who believed in the need for revolutionary upheaval (see the box on p. 796). When their initial assaults brought little success, Castro's forces turned to guerrilla warfare. Batista's regime responded with such brutality that he alienated his own supporters. The dictator fled in December 1958, and Castro's revolutionaries seized Havana on January 1, 1959.

Relations between Cuba and the United States quickly deteriorated when the Soviet Union early in 1960 agreed to buy Cuban sugar and provide $100 million in credits. On March 17, 1960, President Eisenhower directed the Central Intelligence Agency (CIA) to "organize the training of Cuban exiles, mainly in Guatemala, against a possible future day when they might return to their homeland."[2] Arms from Eastern Europe began to arrive in Cuba, the United States cut its purchases of Cuban sugar, and the Cuban government nationalized U.S. companies and banks. In October 1960, the United States declared a trade embargo of Cuba, which drove Castro closer to the Soviet Union. In December 1960, Castro declared himself a Marxist.

On January 3, 1961, the United States broke diplomatic relations with Cuba. The new U.S. president, John F. Kennedy, supported a coup attempt against Castro's government, but the landing of fourteen hundred CIA-assisted Cuban exiles in Cuba at the Bay of Pigs on April 17, 1961, turned into a military disaster. The Soviets then attempted to place nuclear missiles in the country, an act that led to a showdown with the United States (see Chapter 25). As its part of the bargain to defuse the missile crisis, the United States agreed not to invade Cuba.

**Fidel Castro.** On January 1, 1959, a band of revolutionaries led by Fidel Castro overthrew the authoritarian government of Fulgencio Batista. Castro is shown here in 1957, surrounded by some of his followers at a secret base near the Cuban coast.

## Castro's Revolutionary Ideals

On July 26, 1953, Fidel Castro and a small group of supporters launched an ill-fated attack on the Moncada Barracks in Santiago de Cuba. Castro was arrested and put on trial. This excerpt is taken from his defense speech, in which he discussed the goals of the revolutionaries.

*What did Fidel Castro intend to accomplish by his revolution in Cuba? On whose behalf did he fight this revolution?*

### Fidel Castro, "History Will Absolve Me"

I stated that the second consideration on which we based our chances for success was one of social order because we were assured of the people's support. When we speak of the people we do not mean the comfortable ones, the conservative elements of the nation, who welcome any regime of oppression, any dictatorship, and despotism, prostrating themselves before the master of the moment until they grind their foreheads into the ground. When we speak of struggle, the people means the vast unredeemed masses, to whom all make promises and whom all deceive; we mean the people who yearn for a better, more dignified, and more just nation; who are moved by ancestral aspirations of justice, for they have suffered injustice and mockery, generation after generation; who long for great and wise changes in all aspects of their life; people, who, to attain these changes, are ready to give even the very last breath of their lives–when they believe in something or in someone, especially when they believe in themselves.

In the brief of this cause there must be recorded the five revolutionary laws that would have been proclaimed immediately after the capture of the Moncada barracks and would have been broadcast to the nation by radio. . . .

The First Revolutionary Law would have returned power to the people and proclaimed the Constitution of 1940 the supreme Law of the land, until such time as the people should decide to modify or change it. . . .

The Second Revolutionary Law would have granted property, not mortgageable and not transferable, to all planters, subplanters, lessees, partners, and squatters who hold parcels of five or less *caballerias* [tract of land, about 33 acres] of land, and the state would indemnify the former owners on the basis of the rental which they would have received for these parcels over a period of ten years.

The Third Revolutionary Law would have granted workers and employees the right to share 30 percent of the profits of all the large industrial, mercantile, and mining enterprises, including the sugar mills. . . .

The Fourth Revolutionary Law would have granted all planters the right to share 55 percent of the sugar production and a minimum quota of forty thousand *arrobas* [25 pounds] for all small planters who have been established for three or more years.

The Fifth Revolutionay Law would have ordered the confiscation of all holdings and ill-gotten gains of those who had committed frauds during previous regimes, as well as the holdings and ill-gotten gains of all their legatees and heirs. . . .

Furthermore, it was to be declared that the Cuban policy in the Americas would be one of close solidarity with the democratic people of this continent, and that those politically persecuted by bloody tyrants oppressing our sister nations would find generous asylum, brotherhood, and bread in [Cuba]. Not the persecution, hunger, and treason that they find today. Cuba should be the bulwark of liberty and not a shameful link in the chain of despotism.

But the missile crisis affected Cuba in another way as well. Castro realized that the Soviet Union had been unreliable. If revolutionary Cuba was to be secure, the Cubans would have to instigate social revolution in the rest of Latin America. Castro judged Bolivia, Haiti, Venezuela, Colombia, Paraguay, and a number of Central American states to be especially open to radical revolution. He believed that once guerrilla wars were launched, peasants would flock to the movement and overthrow the old regimes. Guevara began a guerrilla war in Bolivia but was caught and killed by the Bolivian army in the fall of 1967. The Cuban strategy had failed.

Nevertheless, within Cuba, Castro's socialist revolution proceeded, with mixed results. The Cuban Revolution did secure some social gains for its people, especially in health care and education. The regime provided free medical services for all citizens, and the population's health improved noticeably. Illiteracy was wiped out by developing new schools and establishing teacher-training institutes that tripled the number of teachers within ten years. The theoretical equality of women in Marxist thought was put into practice in Cuba by new laws. One such law was the family code, which stated that husband and wife were equally responsible for the economic support of the family and household, as well as for child care. Such laws led to improvements but fell short of creating full equality for women.

Eschewing rapid industrialization, Castro encouraged agricultural diversification, but the Cuban economy continued to rely on the production and sale of sugar. Economic problems forced the Castro regime to depend on Soviet subsidies and the purchase of Cuban sugar by Soviet bloc countries. After the collapse of these Communist regimes in 1989, Cuba lost their support. Although economic conditions in Cuba have steadily declined, Castro manages to remain in power.

**Chile's Marxist Adventure** Another challenge to U.S. influence in Latin America came in 1970 when the Marxist Salvador Allende (1908–1973) was elected president of Chile and attempted to create a socialist society by constitutional means. Chile suffered from a number of economic problems. Wealth was concentrated in the hands of large landowners and a few large corporations. Inflation, foreign debts, and a decline in the mining industry (copper exports accounted for 80 percent of Chile's export income) caused untold difficulties. Right-wing control of the government failed to achieve any solutions, especially since foreign investments were allowed to expand. There was already growing resentment of U.S. corporations, especially Anaconda and Kennecott, which controlled the copper industry.

In the 1970 elections, a split in the moderate forces enabled Allende to become president of Chile as head of a coalition of Socialists, Communists, and Catholic radicals. Allende increased the wages of industrial workers and began to move toward socialism by nationalizing the largest domestic and foreign-owned corporations. Nationalization of the copper industry—essentially without compensation for the owners—caused the Nixon administration to cut off all aid to Chile, creating serious problems for the Chilean economy. At the same time, the government offered only halfhearted resistance to radical workers who were beginning to take control of the landed estates.

In response, the upper and middle classes began to organize strikes against the government (with support from the American CIA). Allende attempted to stop the disorder by bringing three military officers into his cabinet. They succeeded in ending the strikes, but when Allende's coalition increased its vote in the congressional elections of March 1973, the Chilean army, under the direction of General Augusto Pinochet (b. 1915), decided on a coup d'état. In September 1973, Allende and thousands of his supporters were killed. Contrary to the expectations of many right-wing politicians, the military remained in power and set up a dictatorship. The regime moved quickly to outlaw all political parties and restore many nationalized imdustries to their original owners. The regime's horrible abuses of human rights led to growing unrest against the government in the mid-1980s.

In 1989, free elections produced a new president, Patricio Aylwin, who advocated free market economics. Despite some economic improvement, unemployment remained high. Early in 2004, Chile entered into a free-trade agreement with the United States in the hopes of boosting economic growth.

**Nicaragua: From the Somozas to the Sandinistas** The United States had intervened in Nicaraguan domestic affairs in the early twentieth century, and U.S. marines even remained there for long periods of time. After the leader of the U.S.-supported National Guard, Anastasio Somoza, seized control of the government in 1937, his family remained in power for forty-three years. U.S. support for the Somoza military regime enabled the family to overcome its opponents while enriching themselves at the expense of the state.

Opposition to the regime finally arose from Marxist guerrilla forces known as the Sandinista National Liberation Front. By mid-1979, military victories by the Sandinistas left them in virtual control of the country. Inheriting a poverty-stricken nation, the Sandinistas organized a provisional government aligned with the Soviet Union. The Reagan and Bush administrations, believing that Central America faced the danger of another Communist state, financed Contra rebels in a guerrilla war against the Sandinista government. The Contra war and an American economic embargo damaged the Nicaraguan economy and undermined support for the Sandinistas. In 1990, they agreed to free elections and lost to a coalition headed by Violeta Barrios de Chamorro (b. 1929). Nevertheless, the Sandinistas remained the strongest single party in Nicaragua.

## Nationalism and the Military: The Examples of Argentina and Brazil

The military became the power brokers of twentieth-century Latin America. Especially in the 1960s and 1970s, Latin American armies portrayed themselves as the guardians of national honor and orderly progress.

**Argentina** Juan Perón first rose to prominence as a member of the military regime that had seized power in Argentina in 1943. As labor secretary in the military government, he used his position to curry favor with the workers. But as Perón grew more popular, other army officers began to fear his power and arrested him. An uprising by workers forced the officers to back down, and in 1946, Perón was elected president.

To please his chief supporters—labor and the urban middle class—Perón pursued a policy of increased industrialization. At the same time, he sought to free Argentina from foreign investors. The government bought the railways; took over the banking, insurance, shipping, and communications industries; and assumed regulation of imports and exports. But Perón's regime was also authoritarian. His wife, Eva Perón, organized women's groups to support the government, while Perón created fascist gangs, modeled after Hitler's Brown Shirts, that used violence to intimidate his opponents. But growing corruption in the Perón government and the alienation of more and more people by the regime's excesses encouraged the military to overthrow him in September 1955. Perón went into exile in Spain.

Overwhelmed by problems, however, military leaders eventually decided to allow Juan Perón to return. Reelected president in September 1973, Perón died a year later. In 1976, the military installed a new regime. Tolerating no opposition, the military leaders encouraged the "disappearance" of their opponents. Perhaps thirty thousand people, including six thousand leftists, were killed as a result.

But economic problems remained. To divert people's attention, the military regime invaded the Falkland Islands off the coast of Argentina in April 1982. Great Britain, which had controlled the islands since the nineteenth century, sent ships and troops to defend the islands. When the Argentine forces surrendered to the British in July, angry Argentinians denounced the military regime. The loss discredited the military and opened the door to civilian rule. In 1983, Raúl Alfonsín of the Radical Party was elected president and tried to restore democratic practices. In elections in 1989, the Peronist Carlos Saúl Menem (b. 1930) won. This peaceful transfer of power gave hope that Argentina was moving on a democratic path. Despite problems of foreign debt and inflation, the government of President Nestor Kirchner has witnessed economic growth since 2003.

**CHRONOLOGY Latin America**

| | |
|---|---|
| Juan Perón becomes president of Argentina | 1946 |
| Creation of Organization of American States | 1948 |
| Castro's forces seize Cuba | 1959 |
| Bay of Pigs invasion | 1961 |
| Cuban Missile Crisis | 1962 |
| Death of Ché Guevara in Bolivia | 1967 |
| Presidency of Luis Echeverría in Mexico | 1970–1976 |
| Overthrow of Salvador Allende in Chile | 1973 |
| Perón returns to power | 1973 |
| Presidency of José López Portillo in Mexico | 1976–1982 |
| Sandinistas establish provisional government in Nicaragua | 1979 |
| Falklands War | 1982 |
| Election of Carlos Salinas in Mexico | 1988 |
| Election of Carlos Menem in Argentina | 1989 |
| Election of Vicente Fox in Mexico | 2000 |
| Election of Luiz Inacio Lula da Silva in Brazil | 2002 |

**Brazil** After the military put an end to the authoritarian regime of Getúlio Vargas in 1945, Brazil established a republic. Over the next two decades, various democratically elected presidents (including Vargas himself) struggled to solve Brazil's economic problems, especially its soaring inflation, with little success. Finally, in the spring of 1964, the military decided to intervene and took over the government.

Unlike previous interventions by military leaders in politics, this time the armed forces remained in direct control of the country for twenty years. The military set course on a new economic direction, cutting back somewhat on state control of the economy and emphasizing market forces. Beginning in 1968, the new policies seemed to work, and Brazil experienced an "economic miracle" as it moved into self-sustaining economic growth, generally the hallmark of a modern economy. Economic growth also included the economic exploitation of the Amazon basin, which the regime opened to farming; some believe the corresponding destruction of the extensive Amazon rain forests, which is still going on, poses a threat to the ecological balance not only of Brazil but of the earth itself. Rapid economic growth had additional drawbacks. Ordinary Brazilians hardly benefited as the gulf between rich and poor, always wide, grew even wider. In 1960, the wealthiest 10 percent of Brazil's population received 40 percent of the nation's income; in 1980, they received 51 percent. Then, too, rapid development led to an inflation rate of 100 percent a year, while an enormous foreign debt added to the problems. By the early 1980s, the economic miracle was turning into an economic nightmare. Overwhelmed, the generals retreated and opened the door for a return to democracy in 1985.

© CORBIS

**The Peróns.** Elected president of Argentina in 1946, Juan Perón soon established an authoritarian regime that nationalized some of Argentina's basic industries and organized fascist gangs to overwhelm its opponents. He is shown here with his wife, Eva, during the inauguration ceremonies initiating his second term as president, in 1952.

The new democratic government faced herculean obstacles—a massive foreign debt, runaway inflation, and a lack of social consensus. Nevertheless, by the 1990s, some stability was maintained as Brazil became committed to democratic elections. The continuing gulf between rich and poor helped lead to the election of Luiz Inacio

## Student Revolt in Mexico

Growing conflict between government authorities and university students in Mexico came to a violent and bloody climax on October 2, 1968, when army troops killed and wounded large numbers of students in Mexico City. This excerpt is taken from an account of the events by the student National Strike Council.

*Why did the Mexican army attack this peaceful student protest? Do you think that the timing of the Olympic Games in Mexico City was a factor? How does this event compare with what happened at Kent State University in 1970 and with the 1989 student protests in Tiananmen Square?*

### National Strike Council, Events of October 2–3

After an hour and a half of a peaceful meeting attended by ten thousand people and witnessed by scores of domestic and foreign reporters, a helicopter gave the army the signal to attack by dropping flares into the crowd. Simultaneously, the plaza was surrounded and attacked by members of the army and all police forces, using weapons of every caliber, up to 9 mm.

The local papers have given the following information about the attack, confirmed by firsthand witnesses:

1. Numerous secret policemen had infiltrated the meeting in order to attack it from within, with orders to kill. They were known to each other by the use of a white handkerchief tied around their right hands. . . .
3. High caliber weaponry and expansion bullets were used. Seven hours after the massacre began, tanks cleaned up the residential buildings of Nonoalco-Tlaltelolco with short cannon blasts and machine-gun fire.
4. On the morning of October 3, the apartments of supposedly guilty individuals were still being searched, without a search warrant.
5. Doctors in the emergency wards of the city hospitals were under extreme pressure, being forced to forgo attention to the victims until they had been interrogated and placed under guard. Various interns who attended the demonstration for the purpose of giving medical aid had since disappeared.
6. The results of this brutal military operation include hundreds of dead (including women and children), thousands of wounded, an unwarranted search of all the apartments in the area, and thousands of violent arrests. Those arrested were taken to various illegal locations, such as Military Camp No. 1. It should be added that members of the National Strike Council who were captured were stripped and herded into a small archaeological excavation at Tlaltelolco, converted for the moment into a dungeon. Some of them were put up against a wall and shot.
7. Onesimo Mason, the general who directed the operation, praised the preparedness of his men, in contrast to the obvious lack of preparedness on the part of the students.

All this has occurred only ten days before the start of the Olympics. The repression is expected to become even greater after the Games, in view of the fact that national public opinion and the protest from the provinces are unified against a regime whose only interest lies in demonstrating its power to control.

Already individual liberties have been suspended, and restricted zones have been created where all vehicles are searched at gunpoint and personal identification is demanded. The Secretary of Defense declared that the friendly disposition of the regime will solve the conflict.

WE ARE NOT AGAINST THE OLYMPIC GAMES. WELCOME TO MEXICO.

Lula da Silva in 2002, who has pursued a policy of increased trade.

## The Mexican Way

During the 1950s and 1960s, Mexico's ruling party (the Institutional Revolutionary Party, or PRI) focused on a balanced industrial program. Fifteen years of steady economic growth combined with low inflation and real gains in wages for more and more people made those years seem a "golden age" in Mexico's economic development. But at the end of the 1960s, the true nature of Mexico's domination by one party became apparent with the student protest movement. On October 2, 1968, a demonstration of university students in Tlaltelolco Square in Mexico City was met by police forces, who opened fire and killed hundreds of students (see the box above). Leaders of the PRI became concerned about the need to change the system.

The next two presidents, Luis Echeverría (1970–1976) and José López Portillo (1976–1982), introduced political reforms. Rules for the registration of political parties were eased, making their growth more likely, and greater freedom of debate in the press and universities was allowed. But economic problems continued to trouble Mexico. In the late 1970s, vast new reserves of oil were discovered. As the sale of oil abroad increased dramatically, the government became even more dependent on oil revenues. When world oil prices dropped in the mid-1980s, Mexico was no longer able to make payments on its foreign debt, which had reached $80 billion in 1982. The government was forced to adopt new economic policies, including the increased sale of public-owned companies to private parties.

The debt crisis and rising unemployment increased dissatisfaction with the government, which was especially evident in the 1988 election, when the PRI's choice for president, Carlos Salinas, who was expected to win in a landslide, won by only a 50.3 percent majority. Increasing dissatisfaction with the government's economic policies finally led to the unthinkable: in 2000, Vicente Fox defeated the PRI candidate for the presidency. Despite high hopes, Fox's presidency has failed to deal with police corruption and bureaucratic inefficiency in the government.

## Society and Culture in the Western World

Socially, culturally, and intellectually, the Western world during the second half of the twentieth century was marked by much diversity, although many trends represented a continuation of prewar modern developments.

### The Emergence of a New Society

During the postwar era, such products of new technologies as computers, television, jet planes, contraceptive devices, and new surgical techniques all dramatically and quickly altered the pace and nature of human life. The rapid changes in postwar society were fueled by scientific advances and rapid economic growth. Called a technocratic society by some and the **consumer society** by others, postwar Western society was characterized by a changing social structure and new movements for change.

The structure of European society was altered after 1945. Especially noticeable were the changes in the middle class. Such traditional middle-class groups as businesspeople and professionals in law, medicine, and the universities were greatly augmented by a new group of managers and technicians as large companies and government agencies employed increasing numbers of white-collar supervisory and administrative personnel. Whether in Eastern or Western Europe, the new managers and experts were very much alike. Everywhere their positions depended on specialized knowledge acquired from some form of higher education. Everywhere they focused on the effective administration of their corporations.

**A Society of Consumers** Changes also occurred among the traditional lower classes. Especially noticeable was the dramatic shift of people from rural to urban areas. The number of people in agriculture declined drastically; by the 1950s, the number of farmers throughout most of Europe had dropped by 50 percent. Nor did the size of the industrial working class expand. In West Germany, industrial workers made up 48 percent of the labor force throughout the 1950s and 1960s. Thereafter, the number of industrial workers began to dwindle as the number of white-collar service employees increased. At the same time, a substantial increase in their real wages enabled the working classes to aspire to the consumption patterns of the middle class. Buying on the installment plan, which was introduced in the 1930s, became widespread beginning in the 1950s and gave workers a chance to imitate the middle class by buying such products as televisions, washing machines, refrigerators, vacuum cleaners, and stereos. But the most visible symbol of mass consumerism was the automobile. Before World War II, cars were reserved mostly for the European upper classes. In 1948, there were 5 million cars in all of Europe, but by 1957, the number had tripled. By the 1960s, there were almost 45 million cars.

Rising incomes, combined with shorter working hours, created an even greater market for mass leisure activities. Between 1900 and 1980, the workweek was reduced from sixty hours to a little more than forty hours, and the number of paid holidays increased. All aspects of popular culture—music, sports, media—became commercialized and offered opportunities for leisure activities.

Another very visible symbol of mass leisure was the growth of tourism. Before World War II, most persons who traveled for pleasure were from the upper and middle classes. After the war, the combination of more vacation time, increased prosperity, and the flexibility provided by package tours with their lower rates and budget-priced accommodations enabled millions to expand their travel possibilities.

**Student Protests** Social change was also evident in new educational patterns and student revolts. Before World War II, higher education had remained largely the preserve of Europe's wealthier classes. After the war, European states began to foster greater equality of opportunity in higher education by eliminating fees, and universities experienced an influx of students from the middle and lower classes. Enrollments grew dramatically; in France, 4.5 percent of young people went to a university in 1950. By 1965, the figure had increased to 14.5 percent.

But there were problems. Overcrowded classrooms, professors who paid little attention to students, administrators who acted in an authoritarian fashion, and an education that to many seemed irrelevant to the modern age led to an outburst of student revolts in the late 1960s. In part, these were an extension of the anti–Vietnam War protests in American universities in the mid-1960s. Perhaps the most famous student revolt occurred in France in 1968. It erupted at the University of Nanterre outside Paris but soon spread to the Sorbonne, the main campus of the University of Paris (see the illustration in Chapter 26 on p. 771). French students demanded a greater voice in the administration of the university, took over buildings, and then expanded the scale of their protests by inviting workers to support them. Half of France's workforce went on strike in May 1968. After the Gaullist government instituted a hefty wage hike, the workers returned to work, and the police repressed the remaining student protesters.

There were several reasons for the student radicalism. Some students were genuinely motivated by a desire to reform the university. Others were protesting the Vietnam War, which they viewed as a product of Western imperialism. They also attacked other aspects of Western society, such as its materialism, and expressed concern about becoming cogs in the large and impersonal bureaucratic jungles of the modern world. For many students, the calls for democratic decision making within the universities were a reflection of their deeper concerns about the direction of Western society.

## The Permissive Society

The **permissive society** was yet another label critics applied to the new society of postwar Europe. World War I had seen the first significant crack in the rigid code of manners and morals of the nineteenth century. Subsequently, the 1920s had witnessed experimentation with drugs, the appearance of hard-core pornography, and a new sexual freedom (police in Berlin, for example, issued cards that permitted female and male homosexual prostitutes to practice their trade). But these indications of a new attitude appeared mostly in major cities and touched only small numbers of people. After World War II, changes in manners and morals were far more extensive and far more noticeable.

Sweden took the lead in the propagation of the so-called sexual revolution of the 1960s, but the rest of Europe and the United States soon followed. Sex education in the schools and the decriminalization of homosexuality were but two aspects of Sweden's liberal legislation. The introduction of the birth control pill, which became widely available by the mid-1960s, gave people more freedom in sexual behavior. Meanwhile, sexually explicit movies, plays, and books broke new ground in the treatment of once hidden subjects. Cities like Amsterdam, which allowed open prostitution and the public sale of hard-core pornography, attracted thousands of curious tourists.

The new standards were evident in the breakdown of the traditional family. Divorce rates increased dramatically, especially in the 1960s, while the incidence of premarital and extramarital sexual experiences also rose substantially. A survey in the Netherlands in 1968 revealed that 78 percent of men and 86 percent of women had participated in extramarital sex.

The 1960s also saw the emergence of a drug culture. Marijuana, though illegal, was widely used among college and university students. For young people more interested in higher levels of consciousness, Timothy Leary, who had done research at Harvard on the psychedelic effects of LSD (lysergic acid diethylamide), became the high priest of hallucinogenic experiences.

New attitudes toward sex and the use of drugs were only two manifestations of a growing youth movement in the 1960s that questioned authority and fostered rebellion against the older generation. Spurred on by opposition to the Vietnam War and a growing political consciousness, the youth rebellion became a full-fledged protest movement by the second half of the 1960s (see the box on p. 802).

**The "Love-In."** In the 1960s, a number of outdoor public festivals for young people combined music, drugs, and sex. Flamboyant dress, face painting, free-form dancing, and illegal drugs were vital ingredients in creating an atmosphere dedicated to "love and peace." Shown here is a "love-in" that was held on the grounds of an English country estate in the Summer of Love, 1967.

## Women in the Postwar Western World

Despite their enormous contributions to the war effort, women at the end of World War II were removed from the workforce to free up jobs for the soldiers returning home. After the horrors of war, people seemed willing for a while to return to traditional family practices. Female participation in the workforce declined, and birthrates began to rise, creating a "baby boom." This increase in the birthrate, however, did not last, and birthrates—and hence the size of families—began to decline by the early 1960s. Largely responsible for this

## "The Times They Are a-Changin'": The Music of Youthful Protest

In the 1960s, the lyrics of rock music reflected the rebellious mood of many young people. Bob Dylan (b. 1941), who became a vastly influential performer and recording artist, expressed the feelings of the younger generation. His song "The Times They Are a-Changin'," released in 1964, has been called an "anthem for the protest movement."

*What caused the student campus revolts of the 1960s? What and whom does Dylan identify in this song as the problem?*

### Bob Dylan, "The Times They Are a-Changin'"

*Come gather 'round people*
*Wherever you roam*
*And admit that the waters*
*Around you have grown*
*And accept it that soon*
*You'll be drenched to the bone*
*If your time to you*
*Is worth savin'*
*Then you better start swimmin'*
*Or you'll sink like a stone*
*For the times they are a-changin'*

*Come writers and critics*
*Who prophesize with your pen*
*And keep your eyes wide*
*The chance won't come again*
*And don't speak too soon*
*For the wheel's still in spin*
*And there's no tellin' who*
*That it's namin'*
*For the loser now*
*Will be later to win*
*For the times they are a-changin'*

*Come senators, congressmen*
*Please heed the call*
*Don't stand in the doorway*
*Don't block up the hall*
*For he that gets hurt*
*Will be he who has stalled*
*There's a battle outside*
*And it is ragin'*
*It'll soon shake your windows*
*And rattle your walls*
*For the times they are a-changin'*

*Come mothers and fathers*
*Throughout the land*
*And don't criticize*
*What you can't understand*
*Your sons and your daughters*
*Are beyond your command*
*Your old road*
*Is rapidly agin'*
*Please get out of the new one*
*If you can't lend your hand*
*For the times they are a-changin'*

*The line it is drawn*
*The curse it is cast*
*The slow one now*
*Will later be fast*
*As the present now*
*Will later be past*
*The order is*
*Rapidly fadin'*
*And the first one now*
*Will later be last*
*For the times they are a-changin'*

decline was the widespread practice of birth control. Invented in the nineteenth century, the condom was already in wide use, but the development in the 1960s of oral contraceptives, known as birth control pills, provided a reliable means of birth control that quickly spread to all Western countries.

The trend toward smaller families contributed to changes in women's employment in both Europe and the United States, primarily because women now needed to devote far fewer years to rearing children. That led to a large increase in the number of married women in the workforce. At the beginning of the twentieth century, even working-class wives tended to stay at home if they could afford to do so. In the postwar period, this was no longer the case. In the United States, for example, married women made up about 15 percent of the female labor force in 1900; by 1970, their number had increased to 62 percent.

But the increased number of women in the workforce did not change some old patterns. Working-class women in particular still earned salaries lower than those of men performing equivalent work. In the 1960s, women earned only 60 percent of men's wages in Britain, 50 percent in France, and 63 percent in West Germany. In addition, women still tended to enter traditionally female jobs. As one Swedish woman guidance counselor remarked in 1975: "Every girl now thinks in terms of a job. This is progress. They want children, but they don't pin their hopes on marriage. They don't intend to be housewives for some future husband. But there has been no change in their vocational choices."[3] Many European women also still faced the double burden of earning income on the one hand and raising a family and maintaining the household on the other. Such inequalities led increasing numbers of women to rebel.

**The Feminist Movement: The Search for Liberation** The participation of women in World Wars I and II helped them achieve one of the major aims of the nineteenth-century feminist movement—the right to vote. Already after World War I, many governments acknowledged the contributions of women to the war effort by granting them the right to vote. Sweden, Great Britain, Germany, Poland, Hungary, Austria, and Czechoslovakia did so in 1918, followed by the United States in 1920. Women in France and Italy did not obtain the right to vote until 1945. After World War II, European women tended to fall back into the traditional roles expected of them, and little was heard of feminist concerns. But by the late 1960s, women began to assert their rights again and speak as feminists. Along with the student upheavals of the late 1960s came renewed interest in feminism, or the **women's liberation movement,** as it was now called. Increasingly, women protested that the acquisition of political and legal equality had not brought true equality with men:

> We are economically oppressed: in jobs we do full work for half pay; in the home we do unpaid work full-time. We are commercially exploited by advertisement, television, and the press; legally we often have only the status of children. We are brought up to feel inadequate, educated to narrower horizons than men. This is our specific oppression as women. It is as women that we are, therefore, organizing.[4]

These were the words of a British Women's Liberation Workshop in 1969.

Of great importance to the emergence of the postwar women's liberation movement was the work of a French woman, Simone de Beauvoir (1908–1986). Born into a Catholic middle-class family and educated at the Sorbonne in Paris, de Beauvoir supported herself as a teacher and later as a novelist and writer. De Beauvoir believed that she lived a "liberated" life for a twentieth-century European woman, but for all her freedom, she still came to perceive that as a woman she faced limits that men did not. In 1949, she published her highly influential work *The Second Sex,* in which she argued that as a result of male-dominated societies, women had been defined by their differences from men and consequently received second-class status (see the box on p. 804).

Another important influence in the growth of a women's movement in the 1960s came from Betty Friedan (b. 1921). A journalist and the mother of three children, Friedan grew increasingly uneasy with her attempt to fulfill the traditional role of the "ideal housewife and mother." In 1963, she published *The Feminine Mystique,* in which she analyzed the problems of middle-class American women in the 1950s and argued that women were being denied equality with men. *The Feminine Mystique* became a best-seller and made Friedan a celebrity.

**Transformation in Women's Lives** To ensure the natural replacement of a country's population, women need to produce an average of 2.1 children each. Many European countries fell short of this mark; their populations stopped growing in the 1960s, and the trend has continued since then. By the 1990s, among the nations of the European Union, the average number of children per woman of childbearing age was 1.4. Spain's rate, 1.15 in 2002, was among the lowest in the world.

At the same time, the number of women in the workforce has continued to rise. In Britain, for example, the number of women in the labor force went from 32 percent to 44 percent between 1970 and 1990. Moreover, women have entered new employment areas. Greater access to universities and professional schools enabled women to take jobs in law, medicine, government, business, and education. In the Soviet Union, for example, about 70 percent of doctors and teachers were women. Nevertheless,

AP/Wide World Photos

**Women's Liberation Movement.** In the late 1960s, as women began once again to assert their rights, a revived women's liberation movement emerged. Feminists in the movement maintained that women themselves must alter the conditions of their lives. During this women's liberation rally, some women climbed the statue of Admiral Farragut in Washington, D.C., to exhibit their signs.

## The Voice of the Women's Liberation Movement

Simone de Beauvoir was an important figure in the emergence of the postwar women's liberation movement. This excerpt is taken from her book *The Second Sex,* in which she argued that women have been forced into a position subordinate to men.

*What did Simone de Beauvoir mean by the "second sex"? By "the Other"? What is the difference between being a "thing" and having an "authentic existence"? According to the author, how do women fall prey to the former?*

### Simone de Beauvoir, *The Second Sex*

Now, woman has always been man's dependent, if not his slave; the two sexes have never shared the world in equality. And even today woman is heavily handicapped, though her situation is beginning to change. Almost nowhere is her legal status the same as man's, and frequently it is much to her disadvantage. Even when her rights are legally recognized in the abstract, long-standing custom prevents their full expression in the mores. In the economic sphere men and women can almost be said to make up two castes; other things being equal, the former hold the better jobs, get higher wages, and have more opportunity for success than their new competitors. In industry and politics men have a great many more positions and they monopolize the most important posts. In addition to all this, they enjoy a traditional prestige that the education of children tends in every way to support, for the present enshrines the past—and in the past all history has been made by men. At the present time, when women are beginning to take part in the affairs of the world, it is still a world that belongs to men—they have no doubt of it at all and women have scarcely any. To decline to be the *Other,* to refuse to be a party to a deal—this would be for women to renounce all the advantages conferred upon them by their alliance with the superior caste. Man-the-sovereign will provide woman-the-liege with material protection and will undertake the moral justification of her existence; thus she can evade at once both economic risk and the metaphysical risk of a liberty in which ends and aims must be contrived without assistance. Indeed, along with the ethical urge of each individual to affirm his subjective existence, there is also the temptation to forgo liberty and become a thing. This is an inauspicious road, for he who takes it—passive, lost, ruined—becomes henceforth the creature of another's will, frustrated in his transcendence and deprived of every value. But it is an easy road; on it one avoids the strain involved in undertaking an authentic existence. When man makes of woman the *Other,* he may, then, expect her to manifest deep-seated tendencies toward complicity. Thus, woman may fail to lay claim to the status of subject because she lacks definite resources, because she feels the necessary bond that ties her to man regardless of reciprocity, and because she is often very well pleased with her role as the *Other.*

Now, what peculiarly signalizes the situation of woman is that she—a free and autonomous being like all human creatures—nevertheless finds herself living in a world where men compel her to assume the status of the *Other.*

economic inequality still often prevailed; women received lower wages than men for comparable work and received fewer promotions to management positions.

Feminists in the women's liberation movement came to believe that women themselves must transform the fundamental conditions of their lives. Women sought and gained a measure of control over their own bodies by seeking to legalize both contraception and abortion. In the 1960s and 1970s, hundreds of thousands of European women worked to repeal laws that prohibited contraception and abortion and began to meet with success. Even in Catholic countries, where the church remained strongly opposed to both procedures, legislation allowing contraception and abortion was passed in the 1970s and 1980s.

As more women became activists, they also became involved in new issues. In the 1980s and 1990s, women faculty in universities concentrated on developing new cultural attitudes through the new academic field of women's studies. Courses in women's studies, which stressed the role and contributions of women in history, mushroomed in colleges and universities on both sides of the Atlantic.

Other women began to try to affect the political environment by allying with the antinuclear movement. In 1981, a group of women in Britain protested American nuclear missiles by chaining themselves to the fence of an American military base. Thousands more joined in creating a peace camp around the military compound. Enthusiasm ran high; one participant said, "I'll never forget that feeling; it'll live with me forever. . . . As we walked round, and we clasped hands . . . it was for women; it was for peace; it was for the world."[5]

Some women joined the ecological movement. As one German writer who was concerned with environmental issues said, it is women "who must give birth to children, willingly or unwillingly, in this polluted world of ours." Especially prominent was the number of women members in the Green Party in Germany (see "The Environment and the Green Movements" later in this chapter).

Women in the West have also reached out to work with women from the rest of the world in international conferences to change the conditions of their lives. Between 1975 and 1995, the United Nations held conferences in Mexico City, Copenhagen, Nairobi, and Beijing.

These meetings made clear the differences between women from Western and non-Western countries. Whereas women from Western countries spoke about political, economic, cultural, and sexual rights, women from developing countries in Latin America, Africa, and Asia focused their attention on bringing an end to the violence, hunger, and disease that haunt their lives. Despite these differences, these meetings made it clear how women in both developed and developing nations were organizing to make people aware of women's issues.

## The Growth of Terrorism

Acts of terror by individuals and groups opposed to governments became a frightening aspect of modern Western society. During the late 1970s and early 1980s, small bands of terrorists used assassination, indiscriminate killing of civilians, the taking of hostages, and the hijacking of airplanes to draw attention to their demands or to destabilize governments in the hope of achieving their political goals. Terrorist acts garnered considerable media attention. When Palestinian terrorists kidnapped and killed eleven Israeli athletes at the Munich Olympic Games in 1972, hundreds of millions of people watched the drama unfold on television. Indeed, some observers believe that media exposure has been an important catalyst for some terrorist groups.

Motivations for terrorist acts varied considerably. Left- and right-wing terrorist groups flourished in the late 1970s and early 1980s, but terrorist acts also stemmed from militant nationalists who wished to create separatist states. Most prominent was the Irish Republican Army (IRA), which resorted to vicious attacks against the ruling government and innocent civilians in Northern Ireland.

Although left- and right-wing terrorist activities declined in Europe in the 1980s, international terrorism remained rather commonplace. Angered over the loss of their territory to Israel, some militant Palestinians responded with a policy of terrorist attacks against Israel's supporters. Palestinian terrorists operated throughout European countries, attacking both Europeans and American tourists; Palestinian terrorists massacred vacationers at airports in Rome and Vienna in 1985. State-sponsored terrorism was often an integral part of international terrorism. Militant governments, especially in Iran, Libya, and Syria, assisted terrorist organizations that made attacks on Europeans and Americans. On December 21, 1988, Pan American flight 103 from Frankfurt to New York exploded over Lockerbie, Scotland, killing all 259 passengers and crew members. A massive investigation finally revealed that the bomb responsible for the explosion had been planted by two Libyan terrorists.

**Terrorist Attack On The United States** One of the most destructive acts of terrorism occurred on September 11, 2001, in the United States. Terrorists hijacked four commercial jet airplanes after takeoff from Boston, Newark, and Washington, D.C. The hijackers flew two of the airplanes directly into the towers of the World Trade Center in New York City, causing these buildings, as well as a number of surrounding buildings, to collapse. A third hijacked plane slammed into the Pentagon near Washington, D.C. The fourth plane, apparently headed for Washington, crashed instead in an isolated area of Pennsylvania. In total, nearly three thousand people were killed, including everyone aboard the four airliners.

These coordinated acts of terror were carried out by hijackers connected to an international terrorist organization known as al-Qaeda (see the comparative illustration on p. 806), run by Osama bin Laden. A native of Saudi Arabia of Yemeni extraction, bin Laden used an inherited fortune to set up terrorist training camps in Afghanistan, under the protection of the nation's militant fundamentalist Islamic rulers known as the Taliban.

U.S. President George W. Bush vowed to wage a lengthy and thorough war on terrorism and worked to create a coalition of nations to assist in ridding the world of al-Qaeda and other terrorist groups. Within weeks of the attack on America, United States and NATO air forces began bombing Taliban-controlled command centers, airfields, and al-Qaeda hiding places in Afghanistan. On the ground, Afghan forces, assisted by U.S. special forces, pushed the Taliban out and gained control of the country by the end of November. A democratic multiethnic government was installed but faced problems in 2003 and 2004 (see Chapter 28) from revived Taliban activity.

**The West and Islam** One of the major sources of terrorist activity against the West, especially the United States, has come from some parts of the Muslim world. No doubt, the ongoing Israeli-Palestinian conflict, in which the United States has steadfastly supported Israel, helped give rise to anti-Western and especially anti-U.S. feeling among many Muslims. In 1979, a revolution in Iraq that led to the overthrow of the shah and the creation of a new Islamic government also fed anti-Western sentiment (see Chapter 28).

The involvement of the United States in the liberation of Kuwait in the Persian Gulf War in 1991 also had unexpected consequences in the relationship of Islam and the West. During that war, United States forces were stationed in Saudi Arabia, the location of many sacred Islamic sites. The presence of American forces was considered an affront to Islam by certain anti-Western Islamic groups, especially that of Osama bin Laden and his followers. These anti-Western attitudes came to be shared by a number of Islamic groups in other parts of the world.

The U.S. attack on Iraq in 2003 has further inflamed some Islamic groups against the West. Although there was no evidence of a relationship between al-Qaeda terrorists and the regime of Iraqi dictator Saddam Hussein, this claim was one of the excuses used by the United States to launch a preemptive war against Iraq. Although many

AP/Wide World Photos

AP/Wide World Photos

POLITICS & GOVERNMENT

COMPARATIVE ILLUSTRATION

**International Terrorism.** International terrorism had become commonplace by the start of the twenty-first century. At the left is a picture of a hijacked U.S. airliner about to hit one of the twin towers of the World Trade Center in New York City while smoke billows from the site of the first such attack on September 11, 2001. This devastating plot was carried out by an international terrorist group known as al-Qaeda. Seen at the right is a scene from another al-Qaeda attack on October 12, 2002, the bombing of two nightclubs in Bali, a popular resort in Indonesia. Almost two hundred people, including Indonesians, Australians, Canadians, French, and Britons were killed, and more than one hundred others were injured.

Iraqis welcomed the overthrow of Saddam Hussein, the death of innocent civilians and the torturing of prisoners by American soldiers in prisons in Iraq served to deepen anti-American sentiment in the Arab world.

## Guest Workers and Immigrants

As the economies of the Western European countries revived in the 1950s and 1960s, a severe labor shortage forced them to rely on foreign workers. Thousands of Turks and eastern and southern Europeans came to Germany, North Africans to France, and people from the Caribbean, India, and Pakistan to Great Britain. Overall, there were probably fifteen million guest workers in Europe in the 1980s.

Although these workers were necessary for economic reasons, their presence created social and political problems for their host countries. Their concentration in certain cities and even certain sections of those cities often created tensions with the local native populations. Foreign workers constituted almost one-fifth of the population in the German cities of Frankfurt, Munich, and Stuttgart. Having become settled in their new countries, many were unwilling to leave, even after the end of the postwar boom in the early 1970s led to mass unemployment.

In the 1980s, the problem of foreign workers was intensified by an influx of other refugees, especially to West Germany, which had liberal immigration laws that permitted people seeking asylum from political persecution to enter the country. During the 1970s and 1980s, West Germany absorbed over a million refugees from Eastern Europe and East Germany. In 1986 alone, 200,000 political refugees from Pakistan, Bangladesh, and Sri Lanka entered the country.

This great influx of foreigners, many of them nonwhite, strained not only the social services of European countries but also the patience of native residents who opposed making their countries ethnically diverse. Antiforeign sentiment, increased by growing unemployment, was encouraged by new right-wing political parties that catered to people's complaints. Thus the National Front in France, organized by Jean-Marie Le Pen, and the Republican Party in Germany, led by Franz Schönhuber, a former SS officer, advocated restricting all new immigration and limiting the assimilation of settled immigrants. Much more frightening, however, have been the organized campaigns of violence, especially against African and Asian immigrants, by radical right-wing groups.

Even nations that have been especially tolerant in opening their borders to immigrants and seekers of asylum are changing their policies. In the Netherlands, 19 percent of the people have a foreign background, representing almost 180 nationalities. In 2004, however, the Dutch government passed tough new immigration laws, including a requirement that newcomers pass a Dutch language and culture test before being admitted to the Netherlands.

## The Environment and the Green Movements

Beginning in the 1970s, environmentalism became a serious item on the European political agenda. By that time, serious ecological problems had become all too apparent. Air pollution, produced by nitrogen oxide and sulfur dioxide emissions from road vehicles, power plants, and industrial factories, was causing respiratory illnesses and having corrosive effects on buildings and monuments. Many rivers, lakes, and seas had become so polluted that they posed serious health risks. Dying forests and disappearing wildlife alarmed more and more people. The opening of Eastern Europe after the revolutions of 1989 brought to the world's attention the incredible environmental destruction of that region caused by unfettered industrial pollution.

Environmental concerns forced the major political parties in Europe to advocate new regulations for the protection of the environment. The Soviet nuclear power disaster at Chernobyl in the Ukraine in 1986 made Europeans even more aware of potential environmental hazards, and 1987 was touted as the "year of the environment." Many European states established government ministries to oversee environmental issues.

Growing ecological awareness also gave rise to Green movements and Green Parties that emerged throughout Europe in the 1970s. Most visible was the Green Party in Germany, which was officially organized in 1979 and had by 1987 elected forty-two delegates to the West German parliament. Green Parties also competed successfully in Sweden, Austria, and Switzerland.

Although the Green movements and parties have played an important role in making people aware of ecological problems, they have not supplanted the traditional political parties, as some political analysts in the mid-1980s forecast. For one thing, the coalitions that made up the Greens found it difficult to agree on all issues and tended to splinter into different cliques. Moreover, traditional political parties have co-opted the environmental issues of the Greens. By the 1990s, more and more European governments were beginning to sponsor projects to safeguard the environment and clean up the worst sources of pollution.

## Western Culture Since 1945

Intellectually and culturally, the Western world since World War II has been notable for its diversity and innovation. Especially since 1970, new directions have led some observers to speak of a postmodern cultural world.

**Postwar Literature** The most original trend in postwar literature was known as the Theater of the Absurd. Its most famous proponent was the Irishman Samuel Beckett (1906–1990), who lived in France. In Beckett's play *Waiting for Godot* (1952), the action on the stage is not drawn from real life. Two men talk as they wait for someone with whom they may or may not have an appointment. No background information on the two men is provided. During the course of the play, nothing seems to happen. The audience is never told if the action in front of them is real or unreal. Unlike traditional theater, suspense is maintained not by having the audience wonder what is going to happen next but by having them wonder what is happening now.

The Theater of the Absurd reflected its time. The postwar period was a time of disillusionment with fixed ideological beliefs in politics or religion. The same disillusionment that inspired the **existentialism** of Albert Camus (1913–1960) and Jean-Paul Sartre (1905–1980), with its sense of the world's meaninglessness, underscored the bleak worldview of absurdist drama and literature. The beginning point of the existentialism of Sartre and Camus was the absence of God in the universe. Although the death of God was tragic, it meant that humans had no preordained destiny and were utterly alone in the universe, with no future and no hope. As Camus expressed it:

> A world that can be explained even with bad reasons is a familiar world. But, on the other hand, in a universe suddenly divested of illusions and lights, man feels an alien, a stranger. His exile is without remedy since he is deprived of the memory of a lost home or the hope of a promised land. This divorce between man and his life, the actor and his setting, is properly the feeling of absurdity.[6]

According to Camus, then, the world was absurd and without meaning; humans, too, are without meaning and purpose. Reduced to despair and depression, humans have but one ground of hope—themselves.

**Postmodernism** The term *postmodern* covers a variety of intellectual and artistic styles and ways of thinking prominent since the 1970s. In the broadest sense, **postmodernism** rejects the modern Western belief in an objective truth and instead focuses on the relative nature of reality and knowledge.

While existentialism wrestled with notions of meaning and existence, a group of French philosophers in the 1960s attempted to understand how meaning and knowledge operate through the study of language and signs. **Poststructuralism** or **deconstruction,** formulated by Jacques Derrida (1930–2004), holds that culture is created and can therefore be analyzed in a variety of ways, according to the manner in which people create their own meaning. Hence there is no fixed truth or universal meaning.

Michel Foucault (1926–1984) drew on Derrida to explore relationships of power. Believing that "power is exercised rather than possessed," Foucault argued that the diffusion of power and oppression marks all relationships. For example, any act of teaching entails components of assertion and submission, as the student adopts the ideas of the person in power. Therefore, all norms are culturally produced and entail some degree of power struggle.

Postmodernism was also evident in literature. In the Western world, the best examples were found in Latin America, in a literary style called "magic realism," and in Central and Eastern Europe. Magic realism combined realistic events with dreamlike or fantastic backgrounds. One of the finest examples of magic realism can be found in the novel *One Hundred Years of Solitude*, written by a Colombian, Gabriel García Márquez (b. 1928), who won the Nobel Prize for literature in 1982. The novel is the story of the fictional town of Macondo as seen by several generations of the Buendias, its founding family. The author slips back and forth between fact and fantasy. Villagers are not surprised when a local priest rises into the air and floats. However, when wandering gypsies introduce these villagers to magnets, telescopes, and magnifying glasses, the villagers are dumbfounded by what they see as magic. According to the author, fantasy and fact depend on one's point of view.

The other center of Postmodernism was in Central and Eastern Europe, especially in the work of Milan Kundera (b. 1929) of Czechoslovakia. Like the magic realists of Latin America, Kundera also blended fantasy with realism. Unlike the magic realists, Kundera used fantasy to examine moral issues and remained optimistic about the human condition. Indeed, in his first novel, *The Unbearable Lightness of Being*, published in 1984, Kundera does not despair because of the political repression that he so aptly describes in his native land but allows his characters to use love as a way to a better life. The human spirit can be diminished but not destroyed.

## Trends in Art

Following the war, the United States dominated the art world, much as it did the world of popular culture. New York City replaced Paris as the artistic center of the West. The Guggenheim Museum, the Museum of Modern Art, and the Whitney Museum of Modern Art, together with New York's numerous art galleries, promoted modern art and helped determine artistic tastes throughout much of the world. One of the styles that became synonymous with the emergence of the New York art scene was **Abstract Expressionism.**

Dubbed "action painting" by one critic, Abstract Expressionism was energetic and spontaneous, qualities evident in the enormous canvases of Jackson Pollock (1912–1956). In such works as *Lavender Mist* (1950) paint seems to explode, enveloping the viewer with emotion and movement. Pollock's swirling forms and seemingly chaotic patterns broke all conventions of form and structure. His drip paintings, with their total abstraction, were extremely influential with other artists, and he eventually became a celebrity. Inspired by Native American sand painters, Pollock painted with the canvas on the floor. He explained, "On the floor I am more at ease. I feel nearer, more a part of the painting, since this way I can walk around it, work from four sides and be literally *in* the painting. When I am in the painting, I am not aware of what I am doing. There is pure harmony."

The early 1960s saw the emergence of Pop Art, which took images of popular culture and transformed them into works of fine art. Andy Warhol (1930–1987), who began as an advertising illustrator, was the most famous of the pop artists. Warhol adapted images from commercial art, such as cans of Campbell's soup, and photographs of such celebrities as Marilyn Monroe. Other artists drew their inspiration from comic strips. Derived from mass culture, these works were mass-produced and deliberately "of the moment," expressing the fleeting whims of popular culture.

Postmodernism's eclectric commingling of past tradition with Modernist innovation became increasingly evident in architecture. Robert Venturi argued that architects should look as much to the commercial strips of Las Vegas as to the historical styles of the past for inspiration.

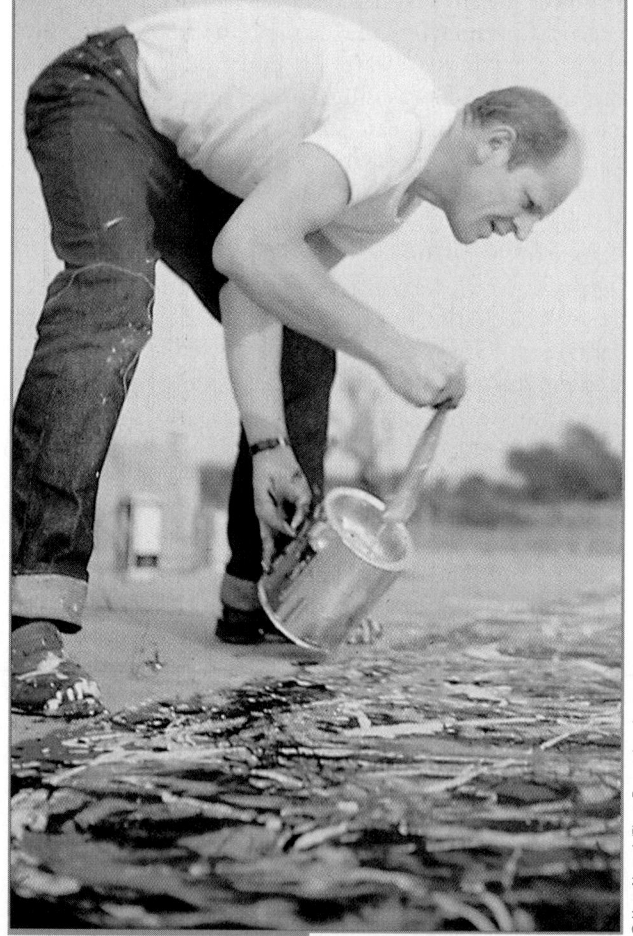



**Jackson Pollock Does a Painting.** One of the best-known practitioners of Abstract Expressionism, which was at the center of the artistic mainstream after World War II, was the American Jackson Pollock, who achieved his ideal of total abstraction in his drip paintings. He is shown here at work in his Long Island studio. Pollock found it easier to cover his large canvases with exploding patterns of color when he put them on the floor.

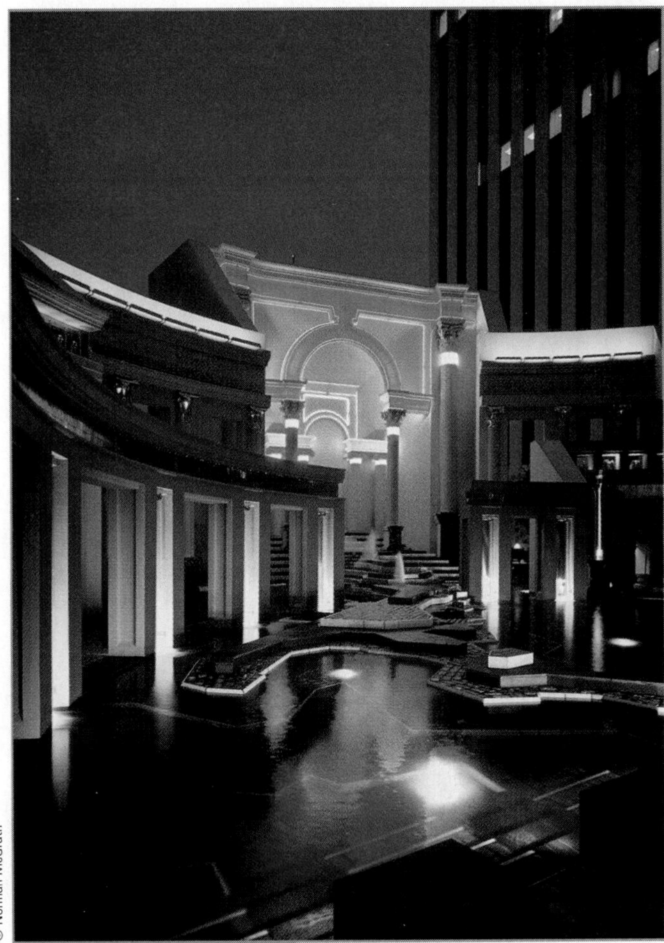
© Norman McGrath

**Charles Moore, *Piazza d'Italia.*** Dedicated to the Italian communities of New Orleans, *Piazza d'Italia* includes a schematic map of Italy on its pavement. The architect, Charles Moore, combined elements from Italy's rich cultural past, such as Roman columns and Renaissance Baroque colonnades, with modern materials like neon lighting and stainless steel to create an eclectic Postmodern plaza.

One example is provided by Charles Moore. His *Piazza d'Italia* (1976–1980) in New Orleans is an outdoor plaza that combines classical Roman columns with stainless steel and neon lights. This blending of modern-day materials with historical references distinguished the Postmodern architecture of the late 1970s and 1980s from the Modernist glass box.

## The World of Science and Technology

Many of the scientific and technological achievements since World War II have revolutionized people's lives. During World War II, university scientists were recruited to work for their governments and develop new weapons and practical instruments of war. British physicists played a crucial role in the development of an improved radar system that helped defeat the German air force in the Battle of Britain in 1940. German scientists created self-propelled rockets as well as jet airplanes to keep Hitler's hopes alive for a miraculous turnaround in the war. The computer, too, was a wartime creation. The British mathematician Alan Turing designed a primitive computer to assist British intelligence in breaking the secret codes of German ciphering machines. The most famous product of wartime scientific research was the atomic bomb, created by a team of American and European scientists under the guidance of the physicist J. Robert Oppenheimer. Many wartime devices were created for destructive purposes, but computers and breakthrough technologies such as nuclear energy were soon adapted for peacetime uses.

The sponsorship of research by governments and the military during World War II created a new scientific model. Science had become very complex, and only large organizations with teams of scientists, huge laboratories, and complicated equipment could undertake large-scale scientific projects. The requisite facilities were so expensive that they could be provided only by governments or large corporations.

There was no more stunning example of how the new scientific establishment operated than the space race of the 1960s. The announcement by the Soviets in 1957 that they had sent the first space satellite, *Sputnik,* into orbit around the earth spurred the United States to launch an ambitious project to land a manned spacecraft on the moon within a decade. Massive amounts of government money financed the scientific research and technological advances that attained this goal in 1969.

In 2004, two vehicles sent by the National Aeronautics and Space Administration (NASA) arrived on the planet Mars. These Mars rovers, called *Spirit* and *Opportunity,* landed three weeks apart on different parts of the planet. Both contained instruments that determine the chemical content of rocks. Based on the minerals found in Mars rocks, NASA scientists were able to conclude that the now barren planet once had generous supplies of water. NASA plans additional missions to Mars to help prepare for the eventual landing of humans on the planet.

The postwar alliance of science and technology led to an accelerated rate of change that became a fact of life in Western society (see the comparative essay, "From the Industrial Age to the Technological Age" on p. 810). One product of this alliance—the computer—may yet prove to be the most revolutionary of all the technological inventions of the twentieth century. Early computers, which required thousands of vacuum tubes to function, were large and hot and took up considerable space. The development of the transistor and then the silicon chip produced a revolutionary new approach to computer design. With the invention in 1971 of the microprocessor, a machine that combines the equivalent of thousands of transistors on a single, tiny silicon chip, the road was open for the development of the personal computer. By the 1990s, the personal computer had become a regular fixture in businesses, schools, and homes. The Internet—the world's largest computer

## COMPARATIVE ESSAY

### From the Industrial Age to the Technological Age

SCIENCE & TECHNOLOGY

As many observers have noted, a key aspect of the world economy is that it is in the process of transition to what has been called a "postindustrial age," characterized by a system that is not only increasingly global in scope but also increasingly technology-intensive in character. Since World War II, a stunning array of technological changes—especially in transportation, communications, space exploration, medicine, and agriculture—have transformed the world in which we live. Technological changes have also raised new questions and concerns as well as unexpected results. Some scientists have worried that genetic engineering might result accidentally in new strains of deadly bacteria that cannot be controlled outside the laboratory. Some doctors have recently raised the alarm that the overuse of antibiotics has created supergerms that are resistant to antibiotic treatment. The Technological Revolution has also led to the development of more advanced methods of destruction. Most frightening have been nuclear weapons.

The transition to a technology-intensive postindustrial world, which the futurologist Alvin Toffler has dubbed the Third Wave (the first two being the Agricultural and Industrial Revolutions), has produced difficulties for people in many walks of life—for blue-collar workers, whose high wages price them out of the market as firms begin to move their factories abroad; for the poor and uneducated, who lack the technical skills to handle complex tasks in the contemporary economy; and even for some members of the middle class, who have been fired or forced into retirement as their employers seek to reduce payrolls or outsource jobs to compete in the global marketplace.

It is now increasingly clear that the Technological Revolution, like the Industrial Revolution that preceded it, will entail enormous consequences and may ultimately give birth to a new era of social and political instability. The success of advanced capitalist states in the post–World War II era has been built on a broad consensus on the importance of two propositions: (1) the need for high levels of government investment in education, communications, and transportation as a means of meeting the challenges of continued economic growth and technological innovation and (2) the desirability of cooperative efforts in the international arena as a means of maintaining open markets for the free exchange of goods.

In the new century, these assumptions are increasingly under attack as citizens refuse to support education and oppose the formation of trading alliances to promote the free movement of goods and labor across national borders. The breakdown of the public consensus that brought modern capitalism to a pinnacle of achievement raises serious questions about the likelihood that the coming challenges of the Third Wave can be successfully met without a growing measure of political and social tension.

network—provides millions of people around the world with quick access to immense quantities of information, as well as rapid communication and commercial transactions. By 2000, an estimated 500 million people were using the Internet.

Despite the marvels produced by science and technology, some people came to question the underlying assumption of this alliance—that scientific knowledge gave human beings the ability to manipulate the environment for their benefit. They maintained that some technological advances had far-reaching side effects damaging to the environment. The chemical fertilizers, for example, that were touted for producing larger crops wreaked havoc with the ecological balance of streams, rivers, and woodlands. *Small Is Beautiful,* written by the British economist E. F. Schumacher (1911–1977), was a fundamental critique of the dangers of the new science and technology (see the box on p. 811).

## Varieties of Religious Life

Existentialism was one response to the despair generated by the apparent collapse of civilized values in the twentieth century. A revival of religion was another. Ever since the Enlightenment of the eighteenth century, Christianity had been on the defensive. But in the twentieth century, a number of religious leaders attempted to bring new life to Christianity.

In the Catholic church, attempts at religious renewal came from two charismatic popes—John XXIII and John Paul II. Pope John XXIII (1881–1963) reigned as pope for only a short time (1958–1963) but sparked a dramatic revival of Catholicism when he summoned the twenty-first ecumenical council of the Catholic church. Known as Vatican Council II, it liberalized a number of Catholic practices. The Mass was henceforth to be celebrated in the vernacular languages rather than Latin. New avenues of communication with other Christian faiths were also opened for the first time since the Reformation.

John Paul II (1920–2005), who had been the archbishop of Krakow in Poland before his elevation to the papacy in 1978, was the first non-Italian to be elected pope since the sixteenth century. Although he alienated a number of people by reasserting traditional Catholic teaching on such issues as birth control, women in the priesthood, and clerical celibacy, John Paul's numerous travels around the world helped strengthen the Catholic church throughout the non-Western world. A strong be-

## Small Is Beautiful: The Limits of Modern Technology

Although science and technology have produced an amazing array of achievements in the postwar world, some voices have been raised in criticism of their sometimes destructive aspects. In 1975, in his book *Small Is Beautiful,* the British economist E. F. Schumacher examined the effects modern industrial technology has had on the earth's resources.

*According to Schumacher, under what illusion are modern humans living? What three irreplaceable things does he suggest people are consuming without noticing? What is "technology with a human face"? How does the author suggest this might transform modern life? Are Schumacher's ideas Postmodern? Why or why not?*

### E. F. Schumacher, *Small Is Beautiful*

Is it not evident that our current methods of production are already eating into the very substance of industrial man? To many people this is not at all evident. Now that we have solved the problem of production, they say, have we ever had it so good? Are we not better fed, better clothed, and better housed than ever before—and better educated? Of course we are: most, but by no means all, of us: in the rich countries. But this is not what I mean by "substance." The substance of [humankind] cannot be measured by Gross National Product. Perhaps it cannot be measured at all, except for certain symptoms of loss. However, this is not the place to go into the statistics of these symptoms, such as crime, drug addiction, vandalism, mental breakdown, rebellion, and so forth. Statistics never prove anything.

I started by saying that one of the most fateful errors of our age is the belief that the problem of production has been solved. This illusion, I suggested, is mainly due to our inability to recognize that the modern industrial system, with all its intellectual sophistication, consumes the very basis on which it has been erected. To use the language of the economist, it lives on irreplaceable capital which it cheerfully treats as income. I specified three categories of such capital: fossil fuels, the tolerance margins of nature, and the human substance. Even if some readers should refuse to accept all three parts of my argument, I suggest that any one of them suffices to make my case.

And what is my case? Simply that our most important task is to get off our present collision course. And who is there to tackle such a task? I think every one of us. . . . To talk about the future is useful only if it leads to action *now.* And what can we do *now,* while we are still in the position of "never having had it so good"? To say the least . . . we must thoroughly understand the problem and begin to see the possibility of evolving a new lifestyle, with new methods of production and new patterns of consumption: a lifestyle designed for permanence. To give only three preliminary examples: in agriculture and horticulture, we can interest ourselves in the perfection of production methods which are biologically sound, build up soil fertility, and produce health, beauty, and permanence. Productivity will then look after itself. In industry, we can interest ourselves in the evolution of small-scale technology, relatively nonviolent technology, "technology with a human face," so that people have a chance to enjoy themselves while they are working, instead of working solely for their pay packet and hoping, usually forlornly, for enjoyment solely during their leisure time.

---

liever in social justice, the charismatic John Paul II was a powerful figure reminding Europeans of their spiritual heritage and the need to temper the pursuit of materialism with spiritual concerns.

**Fundamentalism** Despite the revival of religion after World War II, church attendance in Europe and the United States declined dramatically in the 1960s and 1970s as a result of growing secular attitudes. Yet even though the numbers of regular churchgoers in established Protestant and Catholic churches continued to decline, the number of fundamentalist churches and churchgoers has been growing, especially in the United States.

**Fundamentalism** was originally a movement within Protestantism that arose early in the twentieth century. Its goal was to maintain a strict traditional interpretation of the Bible and the Christian faith, especially in opposition to the theory of Darwinian evolution and secularism. In the 1980s and 1990s, fundamentalists became involved in a struggle against such nontheistic belief systems as secular humanism and communism, as well as legalized abortion and homosexuality. Especially in the United States, fundamentalists organized politically to elect candidates who supported their views. This so-called Christian right played an influential role in electing Ronald Reagan and both George Bushes to the presidency.

**The Growth of Islam** Fundamentalism, however, was not unique to Protestantism. In Islam, the term *fundamentalism* is used to refer to a return to traditional Islamic values, especially in opposition to a perceived weakening of moral strictures due to the corrupting influence of Western ideas and practices. After the Iranian revolution of 1979, the term was also applied to militant Islamic movements, such as the Taliban in Afghanistan, who favored militant action against Western influence.

Despite wariness about Islamic radicalism in the aftermath of the September 11, 2001, terrorist attacks on the United States, Islam is growing in both Europe and the United States, thanks primarily to the migration of people from Muslim countries. Muslim communities became established in France, Germany, Britain, Italy, and Spain during the 1980s and 1990s, and they built mosques for religious worship and religious education.

## The Explosion of Popular Culture

Popular culture in the twentieth century, especially since World War II, has played an important role in helping Western people define themselves. It also reflects the economic system that supports it, for this system manufactures, distributes, and sells the images that people consume as popular culture. Modern popular culture is therefore an integral part of the mass consumer society in which it has emerged.

The United States has been the most influential force in shaping popular culture in the West and, to a lesser degree, the rest of the world. Through movies, music, advertising, and television, the United States has spread its particular form of consumerism and the American dream around the globe. Already in 1923, the New York *Morning Post* noted that "the film is to America what the flag was once to Britain. By its means Uncle Sam may hope some day . . . to Americanize the world."[7] In movies, television, and popular music, the impact of American popular culture on the Western world is apparent.

Motion pictures were the primary vehicle for the diffusion of American popular culture in the years immediately following the war and continued to dominate both European and American markets in the next decades. Although developed in the 1930s, television did not become readily available until the late 1940s. By 1954, there were 32 million sets in the United States as television became the centerpiece of middle-class life. In the 1960s, as television spread around the world, American networks exported their products to Europe and developing countries at extraordinarily low prices.

The United States has also dominated popular music since the end of World War II. Jazz, blues, rhythm and blues, rap, rock and roll, and hip-hop have been by far the most popular music forms in the Western world—and much of the non-Western world—during this time. All of them originated in the United States, and all are rooted in African American musical innovations. As these forms spread to the rest of the world, they inspired local artists, who then transformed the music in their own way.

The introduction of the video music channel MTV in the early 1980s radically changed the music scene by making image as important as sound in the selling of records. Artists like Michael Jackson and Madonna became superstars by treating the music video as an art form. Rather than merely a recorded performance, many videos were short films involving elaborate staging and special effects set to music. Technological advances became prevalent in the music of the 1980s with the advent of the synthesizer, an electronic piano that produced computerized sounds.

Sports have become a major product of both popular culture and the leisure industry. The development of satellite television and various electronic breakthroughs helped make sports a global phenomenon. The Olympic Games could now be broadcast around the world instantly from anyplace on earth. Sports became a cheap form of entertainment for consumers as spectators did not have to leave their homes to watch athletic competitions. As sports television revenue escalated, many sports came to receive the bulk of their yearly revenue from television contracts.

As sports assumed a prominent position in the social life of the world, the pressures and rewards to not just compete but win intensified. Fueled by advertising endorsements, the scientific study of sport led to aerodynamic helmets for cyclists, skin-tight bodysuits for skiers and swimmers, and improved nutritional practices in all sports. Such technological advances, however, have increased the manner in which athletes might break the rules. From steroids to blood doping, some have used medical supplements to illegally enhance their conditioning. Mandatory drug testing in the Olympics, Tour de France, and World Cup attempts to level the playing field and avoid repercussions such as occurred when reports of steroid abuse prompted a governmental investigation of major-league baseball in the United States.

## CONCLUSION

WESTERN EUROPE BECAME a new community in the 1950s and 1960s as a remarkable economic recovery fostered a new optimism. Western European states became accustomed to political democracy, and with the development of the European Community, many of them began to move toward economic unity. But nagging economic problems, new ethnic divisions, resentment and violence toward immigrants, environmental degradation, and the inability to work together to stop a civil war in their own backyard have all indicated that what had been seen as a glorious new path for Europe in the 1950s and 1960s had become laden with pitfalls by the end of the century.

In the Western Hemisphere, the United States and Canada built prosperous economies and relatively stable communities in the 1950s, but there too, new problems, including ethnic, racial, and linguistic differences, along with economic difficulties, have dampened the optimism of earlier decades. While some Latin American nations shared in the economic growth of the 1950s and 1960s, it was not matched by political stability. Only in the 1980s did democratic governments begin to replace oppressive military regimes with any consistency.

Western societies after 1945 were also participants in an era of rapidly changing international relationships. While Latin American countries struggled to find a new relationship with the colossus to the north, European states reluctantly let go of their colonial empires. Between 1947 and 1962, virtually every colony in the world achieved independence. Although some colonial powers willingly relinquished their control, others, especially the French, had to be driven out by national wars of liberation. Decolonization was a difficult and even bitter process, but as we shall see in the final chapters, it created a new world as the non-Western states ended the long-held ascendancy of the Western nations.

## TIMELINE

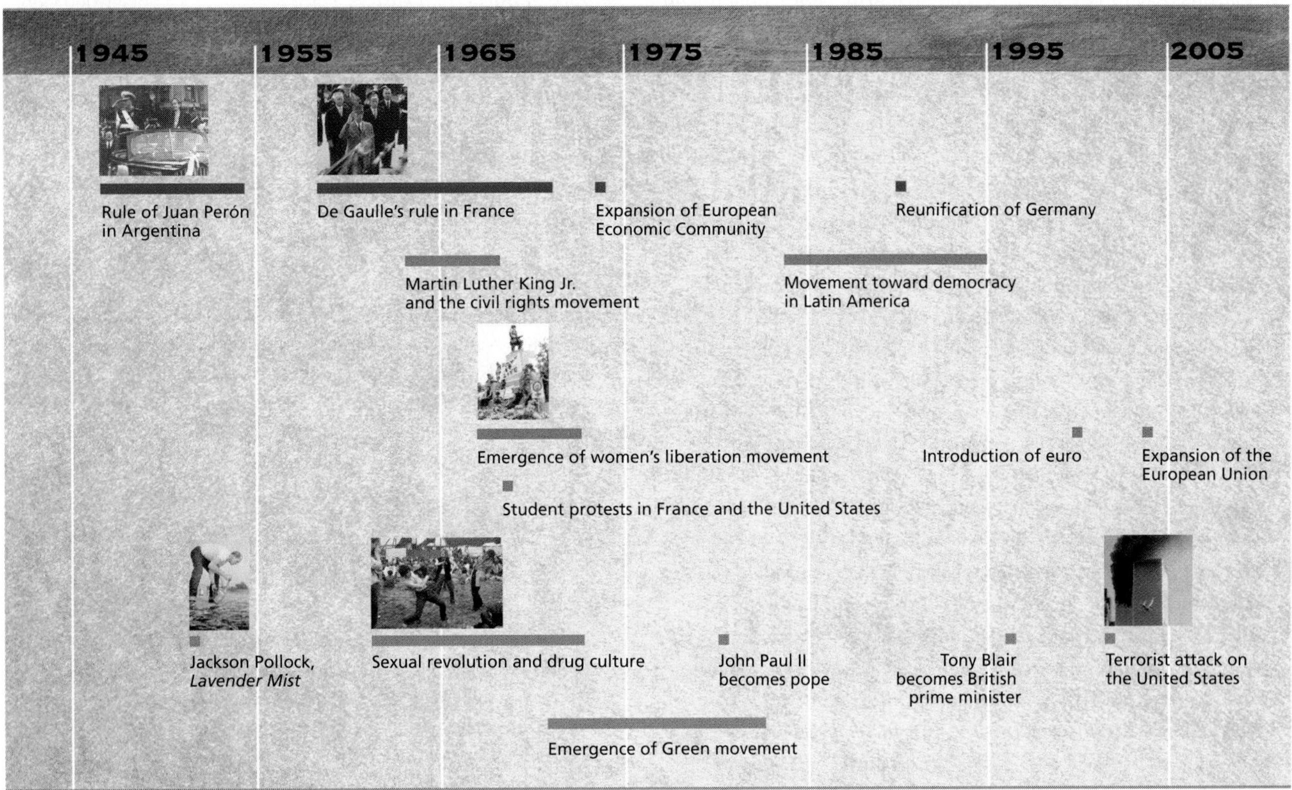


## CHAPTER NOTES

1. Quoted in W. I. Hitchcock, *The Struggle for Europe: The Turbulent History of a Divided Continent, 1945–2002* (New York, 2003), pp. 399–400.
2. D. D. Eisenhower, *The White House Years: Waging Peace, 1956–1961* (Garden City, N.Y., 1965), p. 533.
3. Quoted in H. Scott, *Sweden's "Right to Be Human"—Sex-Role Equality: The Goal and the Reality* (London, 1982), p. 125.
4. Quoted in M. Rowe et al., *Spare Rib Reader* (Harmondsworth, England, 1982), p. 574.
5. Quoted in R. Bridenthal, "Women in the New Europe," in R. Bridenthal, S. M. Stuard, and M. E. Wiesner, eds., *Becoming Visible: Women in European History,* 3d ed. (Boston, 1998), pp. 564–565.
6. Quoted in H. Grosshans, *The Search for Modern Europe* (Boston, 1970), p. 421.
7. Quoted in R. Maltby, ed., *Passing Parade: A History of Popular Culture in the Twentieth Century* (New York, 1989), p. 11.

## SUGGESTED READINGS

For a well-written survey on Europe since 1945, see **W. I. Hitchcock, *The Struggle for Europe: The Turbulent History of a Divided Continent, 1945–2002*** (New York, 2002). See also **W. Laqueur, *Europe in Our Time*** (New York, 1992). The rebuilding of postwar Europe is examined in **D. W. Ellwood, *Rebuilding Europe: Western Europe, America, and Postwar Reconstruction*** (London, 1992). On the building of common institutions in Western Europe, see **S. Henig, *The Uniting of Europe: From Discord to Concord*** (London, 1997). For a survey of West Germany, see **H. A. Turner, *Germany from Partition***

***to Reunification*** (New Haven, Conn., 1992). France under de Gaulle is examined in **A. Shennan, *De Gaulle*** (New York, 1993), and **D. J. Mahoney, *De Gaulle: Statesmanship, Grandeur, and Modern Democracy*** (Westport, Conn., 1996). On Britain, see **K. O. Morgan, *The People's Peace: British History, 1945–1990*** (Oxford, 1992). On the recent history of these countries, see **E. J. Evans, *Thatcher and Thatcherism*** (New York, 1997); **S. Baumann-Reynolds, *François Mitterrand*** (Westport, Conn., 1995); and **K. Jarausch, *The Rush to German Unity*** (New York, 1994).

For a general survey of American history, see **Stephan Thernstrom, *A History of the American People,*** 2d ed. (San Diego, Calif., 1989). The Truman administration is covered in **R. J. Donovan, *Tumultuous Years: The Presidency of Harry S. Truman*** (New York, 1977). On the Eisenhower years, see **S. Ambrose, *Eisenhower: The President*** (New York, 1984). **D. J. Garrow, *Martin Luther King Jr. and the Southern Christian Leadership Conference*** (New York, 1986), discusses the emergence of the civil rights movement. On the turbulent decade of the 1960s, see **W. O'Neill, *Coming Apart: An Informal History of America in the 1960s*** (Chicago, 1971). On Nixon and Watergate, see **J. A. Lukas, *Nightmare: The Underside of the Nixon Years*** (New York, 1976). Works on more recent events include **B. Glad, *Jimmy Carter: From Plains to the White House*** (New York, 1980), and **G. Wills, *Reagan's America: Innocents at Home*** (New York, 1987). On Canadian history, see **R. Bothwell, I. Drummond,** and **J. English, *Canada Since 1945*** (Toronto, 1981).

For general surveys of Latin American history, see **E. B. Burns, *Latin America: A Concise Interpretive Survey,*** 4th ed. (Englewood Cliffs, N.J., 1986), and **E. Williamson, *The Penguin History of Latin America*** (London, 1992). The twentieth century is the focus of **T. E. Skidmore** and **P. H. Smith, *Modern Latin America,*** 3d ed. (New York, 1992). On the role of the military, see **A. Rouquié, *The Military and the State in Latin America*** (Berkeley, Calif., 1987). Works on other countries examined in this chapter include **L. A. Pérez, *Cuba: Between Reform and Revolution*** (New York, 1988); **B. Loveman, *Chile: The Legacy of Hispanic Capitalism,*** 2d ed. (New York, 1988); **J. A. Booth, *The End and the Beginning: The Nicaraguan Revolution*** (Boulder, Colo., 1985); **J. A. Page, *Perón: A Biography*** (New York, 1983); **D. Rock, *Argentina, 1516–1987: From Spanish Colonization to Alfonsn,*** 2d ed. (Berkeley, Calif., 1987); **E. B. Burns, *A History of Brazil,*** 2d ed. (New York, 1980); **R. Da Matta, *Carnivals, Rogues, and Heroes: An Interpretation of the Brazilian Dilemma*** (Notre Dame, Ind., 1991); and **M. C. Meyer** and **W. L. Sherman, *The Course of Mexican History,*** 4th ed. (New York, 1991).

The student revolts of the late 1960s are put into a broader context in **D. Caute, *The Year of the Barricades: A Journey Through 1968*** (New York, 1988). On the turbulent 1960s, see **A. Marwick, *The Sixties: Social and Cultural Transformation in Britain, France, Italy, and the United States*** (Oxford, 1999). On the women's liberation movement, see **D. Bouchier, *The Feminist Challenge: The Movement for Women's Liberation in Britain and the United States*** (New York, 1983); **D. Meyer, *Sex and Power: The Rise of Women in America, Russia, Sweden, and Italy*** (Middletown, Conn., 1987); **T. Keefe, *Simone de Beauvoir*** (New York, 1998); and **C. Duchen, *Women's Rights and Women's Lives in France, 1944–1968*** (New York, 1994). On the sexual revolution, see **D. Allyn, *Make Love, Not War—The Sexual Revolution: An Unfettered History*** (New York, 2000). On terrorism, see **W. Laqueur, *Terrorism,*** 2d ed. (New York, 1988). The problems of guest workers and immigrants are examined in **J. Miller, *Foreign Workers in Western Europe*** (London, 1981). On the development of the Green Parties, see **M. O'Neill, *Green Parties and Political Change in Contemporary Europe*** (Aldershot, England, 1997).

For a general view of postwar thought, see **R. N. Stromberg, *European Intellectual History Since 1789,*** 5th ed. (Englewood Cliffs, N.J., 1990). On the arts, see **A. Marwick, *Arts in the West Since 1945*** (Oxford, 2002). The space race is examined in **W. A. McDougall, *The Heavens and the Earth: A Political History of the Space Age*** (New York, 1984). There is an excellent survey of twentieth-century popular culture in **R. Maltby,** ed., ***Passing Parade: A History of Popular Culture in the Twentieth Century*** (New York, 1989)

**History Now™**

**Enter *HistoryNow* using the access card that is available with this text. *HistoryNow* will assist you in understanding the content in this chapter with lesson plans generated for your needs, as well as provide you with a connection to the *Wadsworth World History Resource Center* (see description below for details).**

**WORLD HISTORY**
RESOURCE CENTER

**Enter the Resource Center using either your *HistoryNow* access card or your standalone access card for the *Wadsworth World History Resource Center.* Organized by topic, this website includes quizzes; images; over 350 primary source documents; interactive simulations; maps and timelines; movie explorations; and a wealth of other resources. You can read the following documents, and many more, at http://history.wadsworth.com/rc/world**

Vanoos speeches by Ronald Reagan
Joint speech on counterterrorism by George W. Bush and Vladimir Putin

Visit the *World History* Companion Website for chapter quizzes and more.

**http://history.wadsworth.com/duikerspielvogel05/**

CHAPTER

# 28

# CHALLENGES OF NATION-BUILDING IN AFRICA AND THE MIDDLE EAST

© Herbert M. Cole

*The African community: soul of a continent*

## CHAPTER OUTLINE AND FOCUS QUESTIONS

### *Uhuru:* The Struggle for Independence in Africa

- What role did nationalist movements play in the transition to independence in Africa, and how did such movements differ from their counterparts elsewhere?

### The Era of Independence

- How have dreams clashed with realities in the independent nations of Africa, and how have African governments sought to meet these challenges?

### Continuity and Change in Modern African Societies

- How did the colonial era and the rise of independent states affect the lives and the role of women in African societies? How does that role compare with other parts of the contemporary world?

### Crescent of Conflict

- What political and economic problems have the nations of the Middle East faced since the end of World War II, and to what degree have they managed to resolve those problems?

### Society and Culture in the Contemporary Middle East

- How have religious issues affected economic, social, and cultural conditions in the Middle East in recent decades?

### CRITICAL THINKING

- What factors can be advanced to explain the chronic instability and internal conflict that have characterized conditions in Africa and the Middle East since World War II?

AT THE END OF WORLD WAR II, many societies in Asia and Africa had already been exposed to over half a century of colonial rule. Although Europeans complacently assumed that colonialism was a necessary evil in the process of introducing civilization to backward peoples around the globe, many Asians and Africans disagreed. Some even argued that the Western drive for political hegemony and economic profit, far from being a panacea for the world's ills, was a plague that threatened ultimately to destroy human civilization.

Such views were especially prevalent in the Middle East, where many Muslims viewed Western materialist culture as a threat to the fundamental principles of Islam. They were also common in Africa, where some intellectuals argued that it was the obligation of the peoples of that continent to use their own humanistic and spiritual qualities—as symbolized in the traditional village community—to help save the human race. Few were more outspoken in their contempt for Western culture than the Ghanaian official Michael Francis Dei-Anang. In *Whither Bound Africa,* written in 1946, he scathingly unmasked the pretensions of Western superiority:

*Forward! To what?*
*The Slums, where man is dumped upon man,*
*Where penury*
*And misery*
*Have made their hapless homes,*
*And all is dark and drear?*
*Forward! To what?*
*The factory*
*To grind hard hours*
*In an inhuman mill,*
*In one long ceaseless spell?*
*Forward! To what?*
*To the reeking round*
*Of medieval crimes,*
*Where the greedy hawks*
*of Aryan stock*
*Prey with bombs and guns*
*On men of lesser breed?*
*Forward to CIVILIZATION!*[1]

To Africans like Dei-Anang, the new Africa that emerged from imperialist rule had a duty to seek new ways of resolving the problems of humanity.

In the three decades following the end of World War II, the peoples of Africa and the Middle East were gradually liberated from the formal trappings of European colonialism. But the transition to independence has not been an unalloyed success in either region. In both cases, the legacy of colonialism in the form of political inexperience and continued European economic domination has frustrated the ability of the leaders of the emerging new states to achieve political stability. At the same time, arbitrary boundaries imposed by the colonial powers, combined with ethnic and religious divisions, have led to bitter conflicts that have posed a severe obstacle to the dream of solidarity and cooperation in forging a common destiny. Today, these new regions, although blessed with enormous potential, are among the most volatile and conflict-ridden areas in the world. ◇

## *Uhuru:* The Struggle for Independence in Africa

After World War II, Europeans reluctantly recognized that the end result of colonial rule in Africa would be African self-government, if not full independence. Accordingly, the African population would have to be trained to handle the responsibilities of representative government. In many cases, however, relatively little had been done to prepare the local population for self-rule. Early in the colonial era, during the late nineteenth century, African administrators had held influential positions in several British colonies, and one even served as governor of the Gold Coast. But with the formal institution of colonial rule, senior positions were reserved for the British, although local authority remained in the hands of native rulers.

After World War II, most British colonies introduced reforms that increased the representation of the local population. Members of legislative and executive councils were increasingly chosen through elections, and Africans came to constitute a majority of these bodies. Elected councils at the local level were introduced in the 1950s to reduce the power of the tribal chiefs and clan heads, who had controlled local government under indirect rule. An exception was South Africa, where European domination continued. In the Union of South Africa, the franchise was restricted to whites except in the former territory of the Cape Colony, where persons of mixed ancestry had enjoyed the right to vote since the mid-nineteenth century. Black Africans did win some limited electoral rights in Northern and Southern Rhodesia (now Zambia and Zimbabwe), although whites generally dominated the political scene.

A similar process of political liberalization was taking place in the French colonies. At first, the French tried to assimilate the African peoples into French culture. By the 1920s, however, racist beliefs in Western cultural superiority and the tenacity of traditional beliefs and practices among Africans had somewhat discredited this ideal. The French therefore substituted a more limited program of assimilating African elites into Western culture and using them as administrators at the local level as a link to the remainder of the population.

### The Colonial Legacy

As in Asia, colonial rule had a mixed impact on the societies and peoples of Africa. The Western presence brought a number of short-term and long-term benefits to Africa, such as improved transportation and communication facilities, and in a few areas laid the foundation for a modern industrial and commercial sector. Improved sanitation and medical care increased life expectancy. The introduction of selective elements of Western political systems laid the basis for the gradual creation of democratic societies.

Yet the benefits of westernization were distributed very unequally, and the vast majority of Africans found their lives little improved, if at all. Only South Africa and French-held Algeria, for example, developed modern industrial sectors, extensive railroad networks, and modern communications systems. In both countries, European settlers were numerous, most investment capital for industrial ventures was European, and whites comprised almost the entire professional and managerial class. Members of the native population were generally restricted to unskilled or semiskilled jobs at wages less than one-fifth those enjoyed by Europeans.

Many colonies concentrated on export crops—peanuts in Senegal and Gambia, cotton in Egypt and

Uganda, coffee in Kenya, palm oil and cocoa products in the Gold Coast. Here the benefits of development were somewhat more widespread. In some cases, the crops were grown on plantations, which were usually owned by Europeans. But plantation agriculture was not always suitable in Africa, and much farming was done by free or tenant farmers. In some areas, where land ownership was traditionally vested in the community, the land was owned and leased by the corporate village. The vast majority of the profits from the exports, however, accrued to Europeans or to merchants from other foreign countries, such as India and the Arab emirates.

While a fortunate few benefited from the increase in exports, the vast majority of Africans continued to be subsistence farmers growing food for their own consumption. The gap was particularly wide in places like Kenya, where the best lands had been reserved for European settlers to make the colony self-sufficient. As in other parts of the world, the early stages of the Industrial Revolution were especially painful for the rural population, and ordinary subsistence farmers reaped few benefits from colonial rule. To make matters worse, in some areas—notably in West Africa—the cultivation of cash crops eroded the fragile soil base and turned farmland into desert.

## The Rise of Nationalism

Political organizations for African rights did not arise until after World War I, and then only in a few areas, such as British-ruled Kenya and the Gold Coast. At first, organizations such as the National Congress of British West Africa (formed in 1919 in the Gold Coast) and Jomo Kenyatta's Kikuyu Central Association focused on improving living conditions in the colonies rather than on national independence. After World War II, however, following the example of independence movements elsewhere, these groups became organized political parties with independence as their objective. In the Gold Coast, Kwame Nkrumah (1909–1972) led the Convention People's Party, the first formal political party in black Africa. In the late 1940s, Jomo Kenyatta (1894–1978) founded the Kenya African National Union (KANU), which focused on economic issues but had an implied political agenda as well.

For the most part, these political activities were basically nonviolent and were led by Western-educated African intellectuals. Their constituents were primarily urban professionals, merchants, and members of labor unions. But the demand for independence was not entirely restricted to the cities. In Kenya, for example, the widely publicized Mau Mau movement among the Kikuyu people used terrorism as an essential element of its program to achieve ***uhuru*** (Swahili for "freedom") from the British. Although most of the violence was directed against other Africans—only about 100 Europeans were killed in the violence, compared with an estimated 1,700 Africans who lost their lives at the hands of the rebels—the specter of Mau Mau terrorism alarmed the European population and convinced the British government in 1959 to promise eventual independence.

A similar process was occurring in Egypt, which had been a protectorate of Great Britain (and under loose Turkish suzerainty until the breakup of the Ottoman Empire) since the 1880s. National consciousness had existed in Egypt since well before the colonial takeover, and members of the legislative council were calling for independence even before World War I. In 1918, a formal political party called the Wafd was formed to promote Egyptian independence. The intellectuals were opposed as much to the local palace government as to the British, however, and in 1952, an army coup overthrew King Farouk and established an independent republic.

In areas such as South Africa and Algeria, where the political system was dominated by European settlers, the transition to independence was more complicated. In South Africa, political activity by local Africans began with the formation of the African National Congress (ANC) in 1912. Initially, the ANC was dominated by Western-oriented intellectuals and had little mass support. Its goal was to achieve economic and political reforms, including full equality for educated Africans, within the framework of the existing system. But the ANC's efforts met with little success, while conservative white parties managed to stiffen the segregation laws. In response, the ANC became increasingly radicalized, and by the 1950s, the prospects for a violent confrontation were growing.

In Algeria, resistance to French rule by Berbers and Arabs in rural areas had never ceased. After World War II, urban agitation intensified, leading to a widespread rebellion against colonial rule in the mid-1950s. At first, the French government tried to maintain its authority in Algeria, which was considered an integral part of metropolitan France. But when Charles de Gaulle became president in 1958, he reversed French policy, and Algeria became independent under President Ahmad Ben Bella (b. 1918) in 1962. The armed struggle in Algeria hastened the transition to statehood in its neighbors as well. Tunisia won its independence in 1956 after some urban agitation and rural unrest but retained close ties with Paris. The French attempted to suppress the nationalist movement in Morocco by sending Sultan Muhammad V into exile, but the effort failed, and in 1956 he returned as the ruler of the independent state of Morocco.

Most black African nations achieved their independence in the late 1950s and 1960s, beginning with the Gold Coast, now renamed Ghana, in 1957 (see Map 28.1). Nigeria, the Belgian Congo (renamed Zaire and then the Democratic Republic of the Congo), Kenya, Tanganyika (later, when joined with Zanzibar, renamed Tanzania), and several other countries soon followed. Most of the French colonies agreed to accept independence within the framework of de Gaulle's French Community. By the late 1960s, only parts of southern Africa and the Portuguese possessions of Mozambique and Angola remained under European rule.

Independence came later to Africa than to most of Asia. Several factors help explain the delay. For one thing, colonialism was established in Africa somewhat later than in most areas of Asia, and the inevitable reaction from the local population was consequently delayed. Furthermore, with the exception of a few areas in West Africa and along the Mediterranean, coherent states with a strong sense of cultural, ethnic, and linguistic unity did not exist in most of Africa. Most traditional states, such as Ashanti in West Africa, Songhai in the southern Sahara, and Bakongo in the Congo basin, were collections of heterogeneous peoples with little sense of national or cultural identity. Even after colonies were established, the European powers often practiced a policy of "divide and rule," while the British encouraged political decentralization by retaining the authority of the traditional native chieftains. It is hardly surprising that when opposition to colonial rule emerged, unity was difficult to achieve.

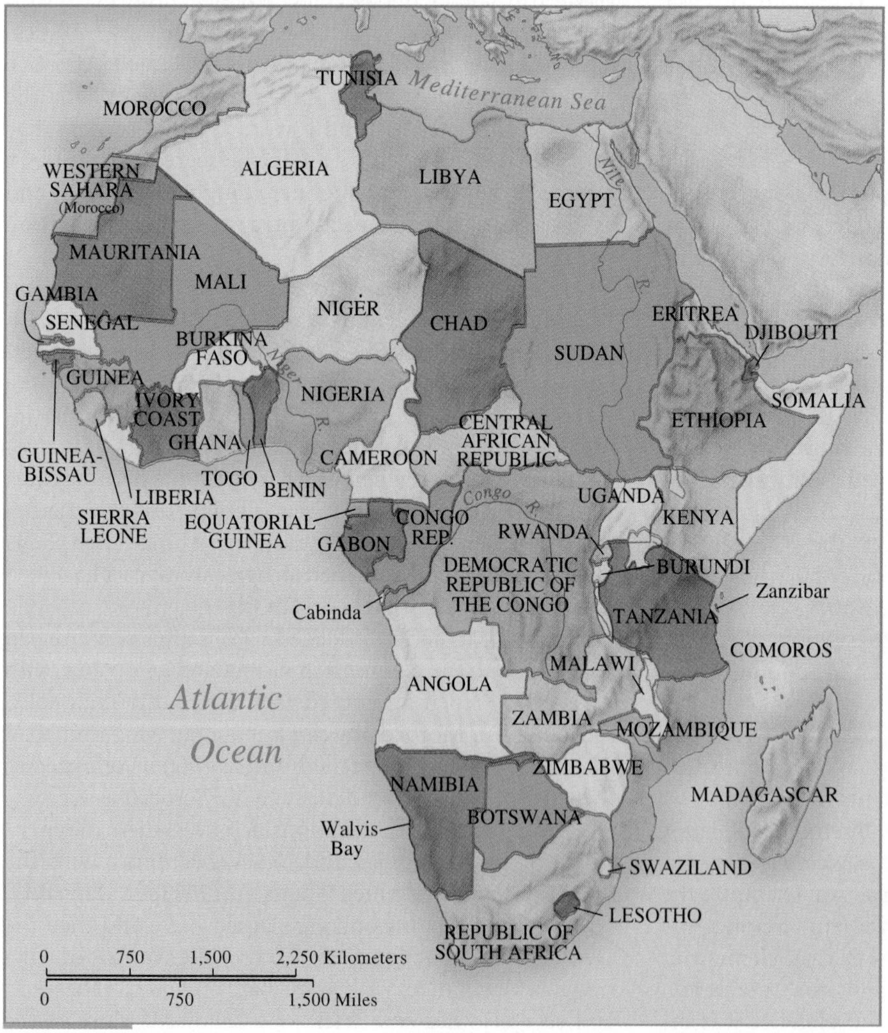

# The Era of Independence

The newly independent African states faced intimidating challenges. Like the new states in South and Southeast Asia, they had been profoundly affected by colonial rule. Yet the experience had been highly unsatisfactory in most respects. Although Western political institutions, values, and technology had been introduced, at least in the cities, the exposure to European civilization had been superficial at best for most Africans and tragic for many. At the outset of independence, most African societies were still primarily agrarian and traditional, and their modern sectors depended mainly on imports from the West.

## Pan-Africanism and Nationalism: The Destiny of Africa

Like the leaders of the new states in South and Southeast Asia, most African leaders came from the urban middle class. They had studied in Europe or the United States and spoke and read European languages. Although most were profoundly critical of colonial policies, they appeared to accept the relevance of the Western model to Africa and gave at least lip service to Western democratic values.

Their views on economics were somewhat more diverse. Some, like Jomo Kenyatta of Kenya and General Mobutu Sese Seko (1930–1998) of Zaire, were advocates of Western-style capitalism. Others, like Julius Nyerere (b. 1922) of Tanzania, Kwame Nkrumah of Ghana, and Sékou Touré (1922–1984) of Guinea, preferred an "African form of socialism," which bore scant resemblance to the Marxist-Leninist socialism practiced in the Soviet Union. According to its advocates, it was descended from traditional communal practices in precolonial Africa.

Like the leaders of other developing countries, the new political leaders in Africa were highly nationalistic and generally accepted the colonial boundaries. But as we have seen, these boundaries were artificial creations of the colonial powers. Virtually all of the new states included widely diverse ethnic, linguistic, and territorial groups. Zaire, for example, was composed of more than two

**MAP 28.1 Modern Africa.** This map shows the division of independent states in Africa today. **?** Which is the most populated nation on the continent? **View an animated version of this map or related maps at** http://history.wadsworth.com/duikerspielvogel05/

## Toward African Unity

In May 1963, the leaders of thirty-two African states met in Addis Ababa, the capital of Ethiopia, to discuss the creation of an organization that would represent the interests of all the newly independent countries of Africa. The result was the Organization of African Unity. An excerpt from its charter is presented here. Although the organization did not realize all of the aspirations of its founders, it provided a useful forum for the discussion and resolution of its members' common problems. In 2001, it was replaced by the new African Union, which was designed to bring about increased cooperation among the states on the continent.

*What are the key objectives expressed in this charter? To what degree have they been achieved?*

### Charter of the Organization of African Unity

We, the Heads of African States and Governments assembled in the City of Addis Ababa, Ethiopia;

CONVINCED that it is the inalienable right of all people to control their own destiny;

CONSCIOUS of the fact that freedom, equality, justice, and dignity are essential objectives for the achievement of the legitimate aspirations of the African peoples;

CONSCIOUS of our responsibility to harness the natural and human resources of our continent for the total advancement of our peoples in spheres of human endeavor;

INSPIRED by a common determination to promote understanding among our peoples and cooperation among our States in response to the aspirations of our peoples for brotherhood and solidarity, in a larger unity transcending ethnic and national differences;

CONVINCED that, in order to translate this determination into a dynamic force in the cause of human progress, conditions for peace and security must be established and maintained;

DETERMINED to safeguard and consolidate the hard-won independence as well as the sovereignty and territorial integrity of our States, and to fight against neocolonialism in all its forms;

DEDICATED to the general progress of Africa; . . .

DESIROUS that all African States should henceforth unite so that the welfare and well-being of their peoples can be assured;

RESOLVED to reinforce the links between our states by establishing and strengthening common institutions;

HAVE agreed to the present Charter.

History Now™ To read the full version of this document, enter the *HistoryNow* documents area using the access card that is available for *World History.*

hundred territorial groups speaking seventy-five different languages.

A number of leaders—including Nkrumah of Ghana, Touré of Guinea, and Kenyatta of Kenya—were enticed by the dream of **pan-Africanism,** a concept of continental unity that transcended national boundaries. Nkrumah in particular hoped that a pan-African union could be established that would unite all of the new countries of the continent in a broader community. His dream achieved concrete manifestation in the Organization of African Unity (OAU), which was founded in Addis Ababa in 1963 (see the box above).

Pan-Africanism originated among African intellectuals during the first half of the twentieth century. A basic element was the belief in **negritude** (blackness)—the conviction that there was a distinctive "African personality" that owed nothing to Western materialism and provided a common sense of destiny for all black African peoples. According to Aimé Césaire, a West Indian of African descent and a leading ideologist of the movement, whereas Western civilization prized rational thought and material achievement, African culture emphasized emotional expression and a common sense of humanity.

The concept of negritude was in part a natural defensive response to the social Darwinist concepts of Western racial superiority and African inferiority that were popular in Europe and the United States during the early years of the twentieth century. At the same time, it was stimulated by growing self-doubt among many European intellectuals after World War I, who feared that Western civilization was on a path of self-destruction.

Negritude had more appeal to Africans from French colonies than to those from British possessions. Yet it also found adherents in the British colonies, as well as in the United States and elsewhere in the Americas. African American intellectuals such as W. E. B. Du Bois and the Jamaican politician Marcus Garvey attempted to promote a "black renaissance" by popularizing the idea of a distinct African personality.

## Dream and Reality: Political and Economic Conditions in Independent Africa

The program of the OAU called for an Africa based on freedom, equality, justice, and dignity and on the unity, solidarity, prosperity, and territorial integrity of African

## Stealing the Nation's Riches

After 1965, African novelists transferred their anger from the foreign oppressor to their own national leaders, deploring their greed, corruption, and inhumanity. One of the most pessimistic expressions of this betrayal of newly independent Africa is found in *The Beautiful Ones Are Not Yet Born,* a novel published by the Ghanaian author Ayi Kwei Armah in 1968. The author decried the government of Kwame Nkrumah and was unimpressed with the rumors of a military coup, which, he predicted, would simply replace the present regime with a new despot and his entourage of "fat men." Ghana today has made significant progress in reducing the level of corruption.

*According to the author of this passage, who is to blame for conditions in his country? Did the charter of the OAU (see the box on p. 819) make provisions for dealing with this situation?*

### Ayi Kwei Armah, *The Beautiful Ones Are Not Yet Born*

The net had been made in the special Ghanaian way that allowed the really big corrupt people to pass through it. A net to catch only the small, dispensable fellows, trying in their anguished blindness to leap and to attain the gleam and the comfort the only way these things could be done. And the big ones floated free, like all the slogans. End bribery and corruption. Build Socialism. Equality. Shit. A man would just have to make up his mind that there was never going to be anything but despair, and there would be no way of escaping it. . . .

In the life of the nation itself, maybe nothing really new would happen. New men would take into their hands the power to steal the nation's riches and to use it for their own satisfaction. That, of course, was to be expected. New people would use the country's power to get rid of men and women who talked a language that did not flatter them. There would be nothing different in that. That would only be a continuation of the Ghanaian way of life. But here was the real change. The individual man of power now shivering, his head filled with the fear of the vengeance of those he had wronged. For him everything was going to change. And for those like him who had grown greasy and fat singing the praises of their chief, for those who had been getting themselves ready for the enjoyment of hoped-for favors, there would be long days of pain ahead. The flatterers with their new white Mercedes cars would have to find ways of burying old words. For those who had come directly against the old power, there would be much happiness. But for the nation itself there would only be a change of embezzlers and a change of the hunters and the hunted. A pitiful shrinking of the world from those days Teacher still looked back to, when the single mind was filled with the hopes of a whole people. A pitiful shrinking, to days when all the powerful could think of was to use the power of a whole people to fill their own paunches. Endless days, same days, stretching into the future with no end anywhere in sight.

states. It did not take long for reality to set in. Vast disparities in education and income made it hard to establish democracy in much of Africa. Expectations that independence would lead to stable political structures based on "one person, one vote" were soon disappointed as the initial phase of pluralistic governments gave way to a series of military regimes and one-party states. Between 1957 and 1982, more than seventy leaders of African countries were overthrown by violence.

**Problems of Independence** Hopes that independence would inaugurate an era of economic prosperity and equality were similarly dashed. Part of the problem could be (and was) ascribed to the lingering effects of colonialism. Most new countries in Africa were dependent on the export of a single crop or natural resource. When prices fluctuated or dropped, these countries were at the mercy of the vagaries of the international market. In several cases, the resources were still controlled by foreigners, leading to the charge that colonialism had been succeeded by **neocolonialism,** in which Western domination was maintained by economic rather than political or military means. To make matters worse, most African states had to import technology and manufactured goods from the West, and the prices of those goods rose more rapidly than those of the export products.

The new states also contributed to their own problems. Treasury funds were squandered on military equipment or expensive consumer goods rather than applied to building up the infrastructure to support and sustain an industrial economy. Corruption, a painful reality throughout the modern world, became almost a way of life in Africa as bribery became necessary to obtain even the most basic services (see the box above).

Finally, population growth, which has hindered economic growth in the new nations of Asia and Africa more than any other factor, crippled efforts to create modern economies. In recent decades, annual population growth has averaged nearly 3 percent throughout Africa, the highest rate of any continent. Drought conditions and the inexorable spread of the Sahara (a result of *desertification,* caused partly by overcultivation of the land) led to wide-

Ajasi Alama; Problems of Transport at Weya Rural Area; 2005. Zimbabwe Artists Project

Courtesy of Claire L. Duiker

**Problems of Transport.** The lack of efficient transportation is a serious problem in the developing world, especially in rural areas. In this painting by an artist from Zimbabwe, we see villagers trudging the long distance to the Weya Clinic. One pregnant woman, who was being pushed to the clinic in a wheelbarrow, is being assisted in her delivery by the roadside. Some villagers travel to town on a pick-up truck, while others watch the overcrowded bus pass them by. Although some artists in contemporary Africa continue to utilize traditional themes and techniques, this painting is an example of a new compositional African style, with painted figures resembling appliqué cutouts in bright colors. On the right side we see a typically overloaded bus in Senegal.

spread hunger and starvation, first in West African countries such as Niger and Mali and then in Ethiopia, Somalia, and the Sudan.

One factor that has begun to temper the rate of population growth is disease. In recent years, the prevalence of HIV and AIDS in Africa has reached epidemic proportions. Three of every four AIDS cases reported around the world are on the continent of Africa. If the disease is not curtailed, it will eventually reduce population growth on the continent—but at an enormous price in terms of human suffering.

Poverty is endemic in Africa, particularly among the three-quarters of the population still living off the land. Urban areas have grown tremendously, but as in much of Asia, most are surrounded by massive squatter settlements of rural peoples who had fled to the cities in search of a better life. The expansion of the cities has overwhelmed fragile transportation and sanitation systems and led to rising pollution and perpetual traffic jams, while millions are forced to live without running water and electricity. Meanwhile, the fortunate few (all too often government officials on the take) live the high life and emulate the consumerism of the West (in a particularly expressive phrase, the rich in many East African countries are known as *wabenzi*, or Mercedes-Benz people).

In "Pedestrian, to Passing Benz-Man," the Kenyan poet Albert Ojuka voiced the popular discontent with economic inequality:

*You man, lifted gently*
*out of the poverty and suffering*
*we so recently shared; I say–*
*why splash the muddy puddle on to*
*my bare legs, as if, still unsatisfied*
*with your seated opulence*
*you must sully the unwashed*
*with your diesel-smoke and mud-water*
*and force him to buy, beyond his means*
*a bar of soap from your shop?*
*a few years back we shared a master*
*today you have none, while I have*
*exchanged a parasite for something worse.*
*But maybe a few years is too long a time.*[2]

It is a lament still voiced today.

**The Search for Community** Finally, Africans have been disappointed that the dream of a united Africa has not been realized. No one skewered the pretensions of the apostles of negritude better than the Ugandan poet Taban Lo Liyong. In his poem "Negritude Is Crying over Spilt Milk," he observed:

*Strange mules called Negritude*
*and African Personality*
*Overran the terrain*
*And kicked wisdom down*
*Or above our heads.*

*Politicians quite unaware*
*How low we are*
*On the ladder universal*
*Decided to halt the race*
*And embrace the niches sure*
*Where we were stuck for the moment.*[3]

But while some criticize the tendency to pursue what Taban called the "vanishing exotica" of the past, most Africans feel a shared sense of continuing victimization at the hands of the West and are convinced that independence has not ended Western interference in and domination of African affairs. Many African leaders were angered when Western powers led by the United States conspired to overthrow the radical politician Patrice Lumumba in Zaire in the early 1960s. The episode reinforced their desire to form the OAU as a means of reducing Western influence. But aside from agreeing to adopt a neutral stance during the Cold War, African states have had difficulty achieving a united position on many issues, and their disagreements have left the region vulnerable to external influence and even led to conflict. During the late 1980s and early 1990s, border disputes festered in many areas of the continent and in some cases—as with Morocco and a rebel movement in the Western Sahara and between Kenya and Uganda—flared into outright war.

Even within many African nations, the concept of nationhood has been undermined by the renascent force of regionalism or tribalism. Nigeria, with the largest population on the continent, was rent by civil strife during the late 1960s when dissident Ibo groups in the southeast attempted unsuccessfully to form the independent state of Biafra. Another force undermining nationalism in Africa has been pan-Islamism. Its prime exponent in Africa was the Egyptian president Gamal Abdul Nasser. After Nasser's death in 1970, the torch of Islamic unity in Africa was carried by the Libyan president Muammar Qadhafi, whose ambitions to create a greater Muslim nation in the Sahara under his authority led to conflict with neighboring Chad. The Islamic resurgence also surfaced in Ethiopia, where Muslim tribespeople in Eritrea rebelled against the Marxist regime of Colonel Mengistu in Addis Ababa. More recently, it has flared up in Nigeria and other nations of West Africa, where divisions between Muslims and Christians have erupted into violence.

## The Search for Solutions

While the problems of nation-building mentioned so far have to one degree or another afflicted all of the emerging states of Africa throughout the continent, each has sought to deal with the challenge in its own way, and sometimes with strikingly different consequences. Despite all its shared difficulties, Africa today remains one of the most diverse regions on the globe.

**Tanzania: An African Route to Socialism** Concern over the dangers of economic inequality inspired a number of African leaders to restrict foreign investment and nationalize the major industries and utilities while promoting democratic ideals and values. Julius Nyerere of Tanzania was the most consistent, promoting the ideals of socialism and self-reliance through his Arusha Declaration of 1967 (see the box on p. 823). Taking advantage of his powerful political influence, Nyerere placed limitations on income and established village collectives to avoid the corrosive effects of economic inequality and government corruption. Sympathetic foreign countries provided considerable economic aid to assist the experiment, and many observers noted that levels of corruption, political instability, and ethnic strife were lower in Tanzania than in many other African countries. Unfortunately, corruption has increased in recent years, while political elements on the island of Zanzibar, citing the stagnation brought by two decades of socialism, are agitating for autonomy or even total separation from the mainland. Tanzania also has poor soil, inadequate rainfall, and limited resources, all of which have contributed to its slow growth and continuing rural and urban poverty.

In 1985, Nyerere voluntarily retired from the presidency. In his farewell speech, he confessed that he had failed to achieve many of his ambitious goals to create a socialist society in Africa. In particular, he admitted that his plan to collectivize the traditional private farm *(shamba)* had run into strong resistance from conservative peasants. "You can socialize what is not traditional," he remarked. "The *shamba* can't be socialized." But Nyerere insisted that many of his policies had succeeded in improving social and economic conditions, and he argued that the only real solution was to consolidate the multitude of small countries in the region into a larger East African Federation.

**Kenya: The Perils of Capitalism** The countries that opted for capitalism faced their own dilemmas. Neighboring Kenya, blessed with better soil in the highlands, a local tradition of aggressive commerce, and a residue of European settlers, welcomed foreign investment and profit incentives. The results have been mixed. Kenya has a strong current of indigenous African capitalism and a substantial middle class, mostly based in the capital, Nairobi. But landlessness, unemployment, and income inequities are high, even by African standards (almost

## Socialism Is Not Racialism

At Arusha, Tanzania, in 1967, Julius Nyerere, the nation's president, set forth the principles for building a socialist society. Nyerere made it clear that he was talking about an African style of socialism, which would put ownership of his country's wealth into the hands of the people rather than into the hands of foreign capitalists. Since then, Tanzania has taken a socialist approach to economic development. The results have been mixed: the country is not wealthy, but there are few extremes of rich and poor.

*According to Julius Nyerere, why is socialism appropriate for the new nations of Africa? How would you compare his vision of socialism with that practiced in the Soviet Union and China?*

### Julius Nyerere, The Arusha Declaration

The Arusha Declaration and the actions relating to public ownership were all concerned with ensuring that we can build socialism in our country. The nationalization and the taking of a controlling interest in many firms were a necessary part of our determination to organize our society in such a way that our efforts benefit all our people and that there is no exploitation of one man by another.

Yet these actions do not in themselves create socialism. . . . The basis of socialism is a belief in the oneness of man and the common historical destiny of mankind. Its basis, in other words, is human equality.

Acceptance of this principle is absolutely fundamental to socialism. The justification of socialism is Man—not the State, not the flag. Socialism is not for the benefit of black men, nor brown men, nor white men, nor yellow men. The purpose of socialism is the service of man, regardless of color, size, shape, skill, ability, or anything else. . . .

Socialism has nothing to do with race, nor with country of origin. In fact any intelligent man, whether he is a socialist or not, realizes that there are socialists in capitalist countries—and from capitalist countries. Very often such socialists come to work in newly independent and avowedly socialist countries like Tanzania because they are frustrated in their capitalist homeland. . . .

Neither is it sensible for a socialist to talk as if all capitalists are devils. It is one thing to dislike the capitalist system and to try and frustrate people's capitalist desires. But it would be as stupid for us to assume that capitalists have horns as it is for people in Western Europe to assume that we in Tanzania have become devils.

In fact the leaders in the capitalist countries have now begun to realize that communists are human beings like themselves—that they are not devils. . . . It would be very absurd if we react to the stupidity they are growing out of and become equally stupid ourselves in the opposite direction! We have to recognize in our words and our actions that capitalists are human beings as much as socialists. They may be wrong; indeed by dedicating ourselves to socialism we are saying that they are. But our task is to make it impossible for capitalism to dominate us.

---

one-fifth of the country's thirty million people are squatters, and unemployment is currently estimated at 45 percent). The rate of population growth—more than 3 percent annually—is one of the highest in the world. Eighty percent of the population remains rural, and 40 percent live below the poverty line. The result has been widespread unrest in a country formerly admired for its successful development.

Kenya's problems have been exacerbated by chronic disputes between disparate ethnic groups and a simmering tension in relations between farmers and pastoralists. For many years, the country maintained a fragile political stability under the dictatorial rule of President Daniel arap Moi, one of the most authoritarian of African leaders. Plagued by charges of corruption, Moi finally agreed to retire in 2002.

**Angola and Ethiopia: Experiments in Marxism** Beginning in the mid-1970s, a few African nations decided to adopt Soviet-style Marxism-Leninism. In Angola and Ethiopia, Marxist parties followed the Soviet model and attempted to create fully socialist societies with the assistance of Soviet experts and Cuban troops and advisers. Economically, the results were disappointing, and both countries faced severe internal opposition. In Ethiopia, the revolt by Muslim tribal peoples in the province of Eritrea led to the fall of the Marxist leader Mengistu and his regime in 1990 and the eventual independence of Eritrea. A similar revolt erupted against the government in Angola, with the rebel group UNITA controlling much of the rural population and for a time threatening the capital city, Luanda. With the death of the rebel leader Julius Savimbi in 2002, the revolt finally appeared to be at an end.

**South Africa: An End to Apartheid** Perhaps Africa's greatest success story is in South Africa, where the white government—which long maintained a policy of racial segregation (**apartheid**) and restricted black sovereignty to a series of small "Bantustans" in relatively infertile areas of the country—finally accepted the inevitability of African involvement in the political process and the national economy. In 1990, the government of President F. W. de Klerk (b. 1936) released African National Congress leader Nelson Mandela (b. 1918) from prison, where he had been held since 1964. In 1993, the two leaders agreed to hold democratic national elections the following spring. In the meantime,

**Performing a Ritual Dance.** For many Africans, the focus of their historical identity lies not in the big cities but in the countless small communities that dot the landscape of their continent. Yet within that traditional concept lies the source of bitter conflict, in the long-standing tension between cattle herders such as the Masai and the Fulani and the cultivators of the soil, many of them members of the Kikuyu language family. Shown here is a pastoral community in northern Kenya performing a traditional ritual dance. Desiccation of the savanna grasslands has forced many such communities to migrate southward, where they compete for precious lands with indigenous farmers. Conflicts over land—often exacerbated by religious differences—threaten the precarious stability of many African nations.

ANC representatives agreed to take part in a transitional coalition government with de Klerk's National Party. Those elections resulted in a substantial majority for the ANC, and Mandela became president.

In May 1996, a new constitution was approved, calling for a multiracial state. The National Party immediately went into opposition, claiming that the new charter did not adequately provide for joint decision making by members of the coalition. The third group in the coalition government, the Zulu-based Inkatha Freedom Party, agreed to remain within the government, but rivalry between the ANC and Zulu elites intensified. Zulu chief Mangosuthu Buthelezi, drawing on the growing force of Zulu nationalism, began to invoke the memory of the great nineteenth-century Zulu ruler Shaka in a possible bid at future independence.

In 1999, a major step toward political stability was taken when Nelson Mandela stepped down from the presidency, to be replaced by his long-time disciple Thabo Mbeki. The new president faced a number of intimidating problems, including rising unemployment, widespread lawlessness, chronic corruption, and an ominous flight of capital and professional personnel from the country. Mbeki's conservative economic policies earned the support of some white voters and the country's new black elite but has provoked criticism from labor union groups, who contend that the benefits of the new black leadership are not seeping down to the poor. Government promises to carry out an extensive land reform program—aimed at providing farmland to the nation's forty million black farmers—have not been fulfilled, provoking some squatters to seize unused private lands near Johannesburg.

Still, South Africa remains the wealthiest and most industrialized state in Africa and the best hope that a multiracial society can succeed on the continent. The country's black elite now number nearly one-quarter of its wealthiest households, compared with only 9 percent in 1991.

**Nigeria: A Nation Divided** If the situation in South Africa provides grounds for modest optimism, the situation in Nigeria provides reason for serious concern. Africa's largest country in terms of population and one of its wealthiest because of substantial oil reserves, Nigeria had for many years been in the grip of military strongmen. During his rule, General Sani Abacha ruthlessly suppressed all opposition and in late 1995 ordered the execution of a writer despite widespread protests from human rights groups abroad. Ken Saro-Wiwa had criticized environmental damage caused by foreign interests in southern Nigeria, but the regime's major concern was his sup-

Courtesy of William J. Duiker

Courtesy of William J. Duiker

**Cape Town: A Tale of Two Cities.** First settled by the Dutch in the seventeenth century, Cape Town has long been the most modern city in Africa, as well as one of its most beautiful. Situated at the foot of scenic Table Mountain, its business and financial center has long been dominated by Europeans (see left photo). Despite the abolition of apartheid in the 1990s, much of Cape Town's black population still resides in the crowded "townships" located along the fringes of the city, as shown in the right photo.

port for separatist activities in the area that had launched the Biafran insurrection in the late 1960s. Abacha died in 1998, and national elections led to the creation of a civilian government under Olusegun Obasanjo. Civilian leadership has not been a panacea for Nigeria's problems, however. In early 2000, religious riots between Christians and Muslims broke out in several northern cities as a result of the decision by provincial officials to apply Islamic law throughout their jurisdictions.

The dispute between Muslims and Christians in Nigeria is a contemporary variant of the traditional tensions that have existed between farmers and pastoralists throughout recorded history. Muslim cattle herders, migrating southward to escape the increasing desiccation of the grasslands south of the Sahara, compete for precious land with indigenous—primarily Christian—farmers. Often the confrontation leads to outbreaks of violence with strong religious and ethnic overtones. Although President Obasanjo has sought to defuse the crisis, the dispute threatens the fragile unity of Africa's most populous country.

The religious tensions that erupted in Nigeria have spilled over into neighboring states. In the Ivory Coast, the death of President Houphouet-Boigny in 1993 led to an outbreak of long-simmering resentment between Christians in the south and recently arrived Muslim immigrants in the north. National elections held in the fall of 2000, resulting in the election of a Christian president, were marked by sporadic violence and widespread charges of voting irregularities. In the meantime, pressure to apply *Shari'a* is spreading to Nigeria's northern neighbor, Niger, where the government has opposed Islamic law on the grounds that it would unsettle the country. Christian churches have been attacked, and bars and brothels have been sacked and burned to the ground.

A similar faultline between farmers and pastoralists has been at the root of the lengthy civil war that has been raging in the Sudan. Conflict between Muslim pastoralists—supported by the central government in Khartoum—and predominantly Christian black farmers in the southern part of the country was finally brought to an end in 2004, but new outbreaks of violence have erupted in western Darfur province, leading to reports of widespread starvation among the local villagers. At first, women singers, known as *hakamah,* chanted songs of bravery to inspire their Muslim brethren onto victory. Later they were persuaded to change their lyrics and to entreat their compatriots to bring an end to the bloodshed.

**Central Africa: Cauldron of Conflict** The most tragic situation is in the Central African states of Rwanda and Burundi, where a chronic conflict between the minority Tutsis and the Hutu majority has led to a bitter civil war, with thousands of refugees fleeing to the neighboring Congo. In another classic example of conflict between pastoral and farming peoples, the nomadic Tutsis, supported by the colonial Belgian government, had long dominated the sedentary Hutu population. It was the attempt of the Bantu-speaking Hutus to bring an end to Tutsi domination that initiated the most recent conflicts, marked by massacres on both sides. In the meantime, the presence of large numbers of foreign troops and refugees intensified centrifugal forces inside Zaire, where General Mobutu Sese Seko had long ruled with an iron hand. In 1997, military forces led by Mobutu's longtime opponent Lauren Kabila managed to topple the general's corrupt government. Once in power, Kabila renamed the country the Democratic Republic of the Congo and promised a return to democratic practices. The new government systematically suppressed political dissent, however, and in January 2001, Kabila was assassinated, to be succeeded by his son. Peace talks to end the conflict began that fall, but fighting continued.

**The Good News** Not all the news in Africa has been bad. Stagnant economies have led to the collapse of one-party regimes and the emergence of fragile democracies in several countries. Dictatorships were brought to an end in Ethiopia, Liberia, and Somalia, although in each case the fall of the regime was later followed by political instability or civil war. In Senegal, national elections held in the summer of 2000 brought an end to four decades of rule by the once-dominant Socialist Party. The new president, Abdoulaye Wade, is a staunch advocate of promoting development throughout Africa on the capitalist model. Perhaps the most notorious dictator was Idi Amin of Uganda, who led a military coup against Prime Minister Milton Obote in 1971. After ruling by terror and brutal repression of dissident elements, he was finally deposed in 1979. In recent years, stability has returned to the country, which in May 1996 had its first presidential election in more than fifteen years. In Eritrea, a popular Islamic government is gradually rebuilding the country and has signed a cease-fire agreement to bring an end to its bitter border conflict with Ethiopia.

**The African Union: A Glimmer of Hope** It is clear that African societies have not yet begun to surmount the challenges they have faced since independence. Most African states are still poor and their populations illiterate. But a significant part of the problem is that the nation-state system is not particularly well suited to the African continent. Africans must find better ways to cooperate with each other and to protect and promote their own interests. A first step in that direction was taken in 1991, when the OAU agreed to establish the African Economic Community (AEC). In 2001, the OAU was replaced by the African Union, which is intended to provide greater political and economic integration throughout the continent on the pattern of the European Union (see Chapter 27). The new organization has already sought to mediate several of the conflicts in the region.

As Africa evolves, it is useful to remember that economic and political change is often an agonizingly slow and painful process. Introduced to industrialization and concepts of Western democracy only a century ago, African societies are still groping for ways to graft Western political institutions and economic practices onto a native structure still significantly influenced by traditional values and attitudes. As one African writer recently observed, it is easy to be cynical in Africa because changes in political regimes have had little effect on people's livelihood. Still, he said, "let us welcome the wind of change. This, after all, is a continent of winds. The trick is to keep hope burning, like a candle protected from the wind."[4]

**CHRONOLOGY Modern Africa**

| | |
|---|---|
| Statehood for Ghana | 1957 |
| Algeria gains independence from France | 1962 |
| Formation of the Organization for African Unity | 1963 |
| Zimbabwe gains independence | 1980 |
| Release of ANC chairman Nelson Mandela from prison | 1990 |
| Nelson Mandela elected president of South Africa | 1994 |
| Civil War in Central Africa | 1996–2000 |
| Olusegun Obasanjo elected president of Nigeria | 1999 |

## Continuity and Change in Modern African Societies

In general, the impact of the West has been greater on urban and educated Africans and more limited on their rural and illiterate compatriots. After all, the colonial presence was first and most firmly established in the cities. Many cities, including Dakar, Lagos, Johannesburg, Cape Town, Brazzaville, and Nairobi, are direct products of the colonial experience. Most African cities today look like their counterparts elsewhere in the world. They have high-rise buildings, blocks of residential apartments, wide boulevards, neon lights, movie theaters, and traffic jams.

### Education

The educational system has been the primary means of introducing Western values and culture. In the precolonial era, formal schools did not really exist in Africa except for parochial schools in Christian Ethiopia and academies to train young males in Islamic doctrine and law in Muslim societies in North and West Africa. For the average African, education took place at the home or in the village courtyard and stressed socialization and vocational training. Traditional education in Africa was not necessarily inferior to that in Europe. Social values and customs were transmitted to the young by storytellers, often village elders, who could gain considerable prestige through their performance.

Europeans introduced modern Western education into Africa in the nineteenth century. At first, the schools concentrated on vocational training, with some instruction in European languages and Western civilization. Eventually, pressure from Africans led to the introduction of professional training, and the first institutes of higher learning were established in the early twentieth century.

With independence, African countries established their own state-run schools. The emphasis was on the primary level, but high schools and universities were established in major cities. The basic objectives have been to introduce vocational training and improve literacy rates. Unfortunately, both funding and trained teachers are scarce in most countries, and few rural areas have schools. As a result, illiteracy remains high, estimated at about 70 percent of the population across the continent. There has been a perceptible shift toward education in the vernacular languages. In West Africa, only about one in four adults is conversant in a Western language.

One interesting vehicle for popular education that emerged during the transition to independence in Nigeria was the Onitsha Market pamphlet. These pamphlets were "how-to" books advising readers on how to succeed in a rapidly changing Africa. They tended to be short, inexpensive, and humorous, with flashy covers to attract the potential buyer's attention. One, titled *The Nigerian Bachelor's Guide,* sold forty thousand copies. Unfortunately, the Onitsha Market and the pamphlet tradition were destroyed during the Nigerian civil war of the late 1960s, but they undoubtedly played an important role during a crucial period in the country's history. Recently, Onitsha has become the largest producer of video movies in sub-Saharan Africa. Most of them provide escapist entertainment—horror films and the like.

## Rural Life

Outside the major cities, where about three-quarters of the continent's inhabitants live, Western influence has had less of an impact. Millions of people throughout Africa (as in Asia) live much as their ancestors did, in thatch huts without modern plumbing and electricity (see the comparative illustration below); they farm or hunt by traditional methods, practice time-honored family rituals, and believe in the traditional deities. Even here, however, change is taking place. Slavery has been eliminated, for the most part, although there have been persistent reports of raids by slave traders on defenseless villages in the southern Sudan. Economic need, though, has brought about massive migrations as some leave to work on plantations, others move to the cities, and still others flee to refugee camps to escape starvation.

## African Women

One of the consequences of colonialism and independence has been a change in the relationship between men and women. In precolonial Africa, as in traditional societies in Asia, men and women had distinctly different roles. Women in sub-Saharan Africa, however, generally did not live under the severe legal and social disabilities that we have seen in such societies as China and India. Their role, it has been said, was "complementary rather than subordinate to that of men."[5]

Within the family, wives normally showed a degree of deference to their husbands, and polygamy was not unusual. But because society was usually arranged on communal lines, property was often held in common, and production tasks were divided on a cooperative rather than hierarchical basis. The status of women tended to rise as they moved through the life cycle. Women became more important as they reared children; in old age, they often became eligible to serve in senior roles within the family,

Courtesy of William J. Duiker

Courtesy of William J. Duiker

COMPARATIVE ILLUSTRATION

**Traditional Patterns in the Countryside.** In different parts of the world, many people continue to follow patterns of living that are centuries old. In Africa, the houses of rural peoples are often constructed from a wooden frame woven from poles and branches, known as wattle, daubed with mud and then covered with a thatched roof. At the left is a scene from a Kenyan village not far from the Indian Ocean, where a young man is applying mud to the wall of his future house. The photo at the right shows a village in India, where housing styles and village customs have changed little since they were first described by Portuguese travelers in the sixteenth century. Note the thatched roofs and the mud-and-straw walls plastered with dung used in constructing these houses, reminiscent of those found in Africa.

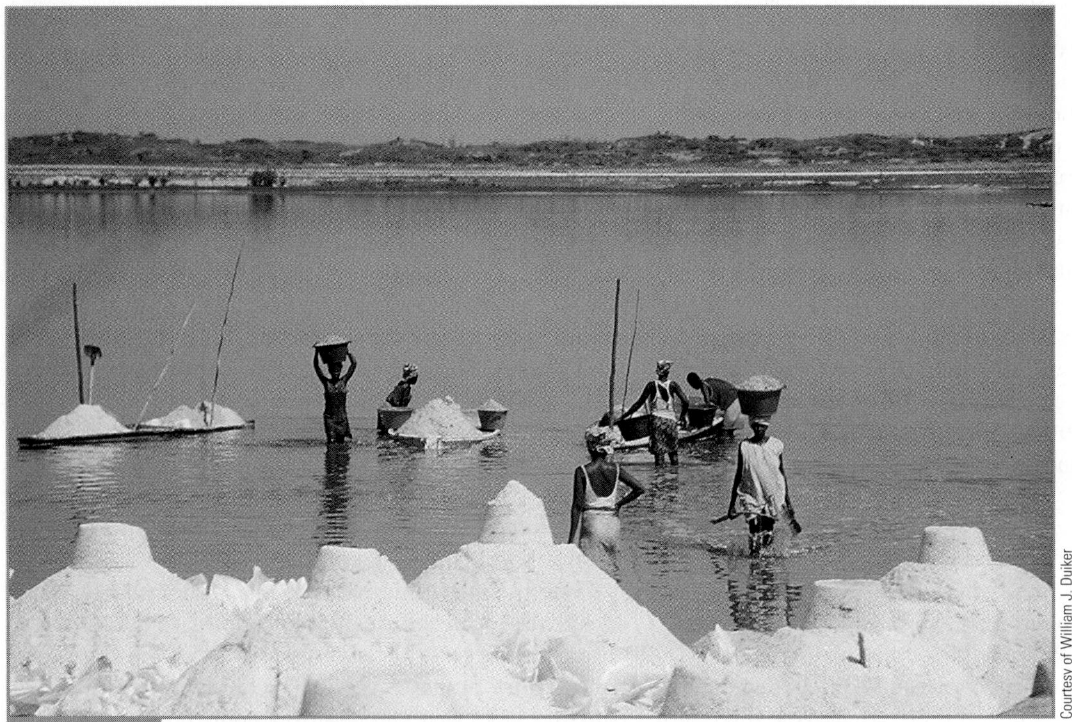
Courtesy of William J. Duiker

**Salt of the Earth.** During the precolonial era, many West African societies were forced to import salt from Mediterranean countries in exchange for tropical products and gold. Today the people of Senegal satisfy their domestic needs by mining salt deposits contained in lakes like this one in the interior of the country. These lakes are the remnants of vast seas that covered the region of the Sahara in prehistoric times. Note that it is women who are doing much of the heavy labor while men occupy the managerial positions.

lineage, or village. In some societies, such as the Ashanti kingdom in West Africa, women such as the queen mother were eligible to hold senior political positions.

Sexual relationships changed profoundly during the colonial era, sometimes in ways that could justly be described as beneficial. Colonial governments attempted to bring an end to forced marriage, bodily mutilation such as clitoridectomy, and polygamy. Missionaries introduced women to Western education and encouraged them to organize themselves to defend their interests.

But the new system had some unfavorable consequences as well. Like men, women now became a labor resource. As African males were taken from the villages to serve as forced labor on construction projects, the traditional division of labor was disrupted, and women were forced to play a more prominent role in the economy. At the same time, their role in the broader society was constricted. In British colonies, Victorian attitudes of sexual repression and female subordination led to restrictions on women's freedom, and the positions in government they had formerly held were closed to them.

**Gender Roles** Independence also had a significant impact on gender roles in African society. Almost without exception, the new governments established the principle of sexual equality and permitted women to vote and run for political office. Yet as elsewhere, women continue to operate at a disability in a world dominated by males. Politics remains a male preserve, and although a few professions, such as teaching, child care, and clerical work, are dominated by women, most African women are employed in menial positions such as agricultural labor, factory work, and retail trade or as domestics. Education is open to all at the elementary level, but women comprise less than 20 percent of students at the upper levels in most African societies today.

In rural areas, where traditional attitudes continue to exert a strong influence, individuals may still be subordinated to communalism. In some societies, female genital mutilation, the traditional rite of passage for a young girl's transit to womanhood, is still widely practiced. Polygamy is also not uncommon, and arranged marriages are still the rule rather than the exception. The dichotomy between rural and urban values can lead to acute tensions. Many African villagers regard the cities as the fount of evil, decadence, and corruption. Women in particular have suffered from the tension between the pull of the city and the village. As men are drawn to the cities in search of employment and excitement, their wives and girlfriends are left behind, both literally and figuratively, in the native village.

**Urban Women** Not surprisingly, women have made the greatest strides in the cities. Most urban women, like men, now marry on the basis of personal choice, although a significant minority are still willing to accept their parents' choice. After marriage, African women appear to occupy a more equal position than their counterparts in most Asian countries. Each marriage partner tends to maintain a separate income, and women often have the right to possess property separate from their husbands. While many wives still defer to their husbands in the traditional manner, others are like the woman in Abioseh Nicol's story "A Truly Married Woman," who, after years of living as a common-law wife with her husband, is finally able to provide the price and finalize the marriage. After the wedding, she declares, "For twelve years I have got up every morning at five to make tea for you and breakfast. Now I am a truly married woman [and] you must treat me with a little more respect. You are now my husband and not a lover. Get up and make yourself a cup of tea."[6]

Within the cities, there is a growing feminist movement, but it is firmly based on conditions in the local environment. Many African women writers, for example, opt for a brand of African feminism much like that of Ama Ata Aidoo, a Ghanaian novelist, whose ultimate objective is to free African society as a whole, not just its female inhabitants. After receiving her education at a girls' school in the Gold Coast and attending Stanford University in the United States, she embarked on a writing career. Every African woman and every man, she insists, "should be a feminist, especially if they believe that Africans should take charge of our land, its wealth, our lives, and the burden of our development. Because it is not possible to advocate independence for our continent without also believing that African women must have the best that the environment can offer."[7]

## African Culture

Inevitably, the tension between traditional and modern, native and foreign, and individual and communal that has permeated contemporary African society has spilled over into culture. In general, in the visual arts and music, utility and ritual have given way to pleasure and decoration. In the process, Africans have been affected to a certain extent by foreign influences but have retained their distinctive characteristics. Wood carving, metalwork, painting, and sculpture, for example, have preserved their traditional forms but are now increasingly adapted to serve the tourist industry and the export market.

**Literature** No area of African culture has been so strongly affected by political and social events as literature. Except for Muslim areas in North and East Africa, precolonial Africans did not have a written literature, although their tradition of oral storytelling served as a rich repository of history, custom, and folk culture. The first written literature in the vernacular or in European languages emerged during the nineteenth century in the form of novels, poetry, and drama.

Angry at the negative portrayal of Africa in Western literature (see the box on p. 830), African authors initially wrote primarily for a European audience as a means of establishing black dignity and purpose. Embracing the ideals of negritude, many glorified the emotional and communal aspects of the traditional African experience. The Nigerian Chinua Achebe is considered the first major African novelist to write in the English language. In his writings, he attempted to interpret African history from a native perspective and to forge a new sense of African identity. In his trailblazing novel *Things Fall Apart* (1958), he recounted the story of a Nigerian who refused to submit to the new British order and eventually committed suicide. Criticizing his contemporaries who accepted foreign rule, the protagonist lamented that the white man "has put a knife on the things that held us together and we have fallen apart."

In recent decades, the African novel has taken a dramatic turn, shifting its focus from the brutality of the foreign oppressor to the shortcomings of the new native leadership. Having gained independence, African politicians were portrayed as mimicking and even outdoing the injustices committed by their colonial predecessors. A prominent example of this genre is the work of the Kenyan Ngugi Wa Thiong'o (b. 1938). His first novel, *A Grain of Wheat,* takes place on the eve of *uhuru,* or independence. Although it mocks local British society for its racism, snobbishness, and superficiality, its chief interest lies in its unsentimental and even unflattering portrayal of ordinary Kenyans in their daily struggle for survival.

Like most of his predecessors, Ngugi initially wrote in English, but he eventually decided to write in his native Kikuyu as a means of broadening his readership. For that reason, perhaps, in the late 1970s, he was placed under house arrest for writing subversive literature. There, he secretly wrote *Devil on the Cross,* which urged his compatriots to overthrow the ruling government. Published in 1980, the book sold widely and was eventually read aloud by storytellers throughout Kenyan society. Fearing an attempt on his life, Ngugi has since lived in exile.

Many of Ngugi's contemporaries have followed his lead and focused their frustration on the failure of the continent's new leadership to carry out the goals of independence. One of the most outstanding is the Nigerian Wole Soyinka (b. 1934). His novel *The Interpreters* (1965) lambasted the corruption and hypocrisy of Nigerian politics. Succeeding novels and plays have continued that tradition, resulting in a Nobel Prize for literature in 1986. In 1994, however, Soyinka barely managed to escape arrest, and he now lives abroad. In a protest against the brutality of the Abacha regime in Nigeria, he published from exile a harsh exposé of the crisis. His book, *The Open Sore of a Continent,* placed the primary responsibility for failure not on Nigeria's long list of dictators but on the very concept of the modern nation-state, which was introduced into Africa arbitrarily by Europeans. A nation, he contends, can only emerge from below, as the expression of the moral and political will of the local inhabitants; it cannot be imposed artificially from above.

## AFRICA: DARK OR RADIANT CONTINENT?

Colonialism camouflaged its economic objectives under the cloak of a "civilizing mission," which in Africa was aimed at illuminating the so-called Dark Continent with Europe's brilliant civilization. In 1899, the Polish-born English author Joseph Conrad fictionalized his harrowing journey up the Congo River in the novella *Heart of Darkness.* Expressing views from his Victorian perspective, he portrayed an Africa that was incomprehensible, irrational, sensual, and therefore threatening. Conrad, however, was shocked by the horrific exploitation of the peoples of the Belgian Congo, presenting them with a compassion rarely seen during the heyday of imperialism.

Over the years, Conrad's work has provoked much debate, and many African writers have been prompted to counter his vision by reaffirming the dignity and purpose of the African people. One of the first to do so was the Guinean author Camara Laye (1928–1980), who in 1954 composed a brilliant novel, *The Radiance of the King,* which can be viewed as the mirror image of Conrad's *Heart of Darkness.* In Laye's work, another European protagonist undertakes a journey into the impenetrable heart of Africa. This time, however, he is enlightened by the process, thereby obtaining self-knowledge and ultimately salvation.

*Compare these two passages in terms of their depiction of the continent of Africa. Is Laye making a response to Conrad? If so, what is it?*

### Joseph Conrad, *Heart of Darkness*

We penetrated deeper and deeper into the heart of darkness. It was very quiet there. At night sometimes the roll of drums behind the curtain of trees would run up the river and remain sustained faintly, as if hovering in the air high over our heads, till the first break of day. Whether it meant war, peace, or prayer we could not tell. . . . But suddenly, as we struggled round a bend, there would be a glimpse of rush walls, of peaked grass-roofs, a burst of yells, a whirl of black limbs, a mass of hands clapping, of feet stamping, of bodies swaying, of eyes rolling, under the droop of heavy and motionless foliage. The steamer toiled along slowly on the edge of a black and incomprehensible frenzy. The prehistoric man was cursing us, praying to us, welcoming us—who could tell? We were cut off from the comprehension of our surroundings; we glided past like phantoms, wondering and secretly appalled, as sane men would be before an enthusiastic outbreak in a madhouse. . . .

It was unearthly, and the men were—No, they were not inhuman. Well, you know, that was the worst of it—this suspicion of their not being inhuman. It would come slowly to one. They howled and leaped, and spun, and made horrid faces; but what thrilled you was just the thought of their humanity—like yours—the thought of your remote kinship with this wild and passionate uproar. Ugly. Yes, it was ugly enough; but if you were man enough you would admit to yourself that there was in you just the faintest trace of a response to the terrible frankness of that noise, a dim suspicion of there being a meaning in it which you—you so remote from the night of first ages—could comprehend. And why not? The mind of man is capable of anything—because everything is in it, all the past as well as all the future. What was there after all? Joy, fear, sorrow, devotion, valour, rage—who can tell?—but truth—truth stripped of its cloak of time.

### Camara Laye, *The Radiance of the King*

"I enjoy life . . . ," thought Clarence. "If I filed my teeth like the people of Aziana, no one could see any difference between me and them." There was, of course, the difference in pigmentation in the skin. But what difference did that make? "It's the soul that matters," he kept telling himself. "And in that respect I am exactly as they are." . . .

But where was this radiance coming from? Clarence got up and went to the right-hand window, from which this radiance seemed to be streaming. . . .

He saw the king. And then he knew where the extraordinary radiance was coming from. . . .

And he had the feeling that all was lost. But had he not already lost everything? . . . He would remain for ever chained to the South, chained to his hut, chained to everything he had so thoughtlessly abandoned himself to. His solitude seemed to him so heavy, it burdened him with such a great weight of sorrow that his heart seemed about to break. . . .

But at that very moment the king turned his head, turned it imperceptibly, and his glance fell upon Clarence. . . .

"Yes, no one is as base as I, as naked as I," he thought. "And you, lord, you are willing to rest your eyes upon me!" Or was it because of his very nakedness? . . . "Because of your very nakedness!" the look seemed to say. "That terrifying void that is within you and which opens to receive me; your hunger which calls to my hunger; your very baseness which did not exist until I gave it leave; and the great shame you feel. . . ."

When he had come before the king, when he stood in the great radiance of the king, still ravaged by the tongue of fire, but alive still, and living only through the touch of that fire, Clarence fell upon his knees, for it seemed to him that he was finally at the end of his seeking, and at the end of all seekings.

A number of Africa's most prominent writers today are women. Traditionally, African women were valued for their talents as storytellers, but writing was strongly discouraged by both traditional and colonial authorities on the grounds that women should occupy themselves with their domestic obligations. In recent years, however, a number of women have emerged as prominent writers of African fiction. Two examples are Buchi Emecheta (b. 1940) of Nigeria and Ama Ata Aidoo (b. 1942) of Ghana. Beginning with *Second Class Citizen* (1975), which chronicled the breakdown of her own marriage, Emecheta has published numerous works exploring the role of women in contemporary African society and decrying the practice of polygamy. Ama Ata Aidoo has focused on the identity of today's African women and the changing relations between men and women in society. In her novel *Changes: A Love Story* (1991), she chronicles the lives of three women, none presented as a victim but all caught up in the struggle for survival and happiness.

**Music** Contemporary African music also reflects a hybridization or fusion with Western culture. Having traveled to the New World via the slave trade centuries earlier, African drum beats evolved into North American jazz and Latin American dance rhythms, only to return to reenergize African music. In fact, today music is one of Africans' most effective weapons for social and political protest. Easily accessible to all, African music, whether Afro-beat in Nigeria, *rai* in Algeria, or *reggae* in Benin, represents the "weapon of the future," contemporary musicians say; "it helped free Nelson Mandela" and "will put Africa back on the map." Censored by all the African dictatorial regimes, these courageous musicians persist in their struggle against corruption, what one singer calls the second slavery, "the cancer that is eating away at the system." Their voices echo the chorus "Together we can build a nation, / Because Africa has brains, youth, knowledge."[8]

## Gathered at the Beach

Nowhere in the developing world is the dilemma of continuity and change more agonizing than in Africa. Mesmerized by the spectacle of Western affluence yet repulsed by the bloody trail from slavery to World War II and the atomic bombs over Hiroshima and Nagasaki, African intellectuals have been torn between the dual images of Western materialism and African negritude.

What is the destiny of Africa? Some Africans still yearn for the dreams embodied in the program of the OAU. Novelist Ngugi Wa Thiong'o calls for "an internationalization of all the democratic and social struggles for human equality, justice, peace, and progress."[9] Some African political leaders, however, have apparently discarded the democratic ideal and turned their attention to what is sometimes called the "East Asian model," based on the Confucian tenet of subordination of the individual to the community as the guiding principle of national development (see Chapter 29). Whether African political culture today is well placed to imitate the strategy adopted by the fast-growing nations of East Asia—who in any event are now encountering problems of their own—is questionable. Like all peoples, Africans must ultimately find their own solutions within the context of their own traditions, not by seeking to imitate the example of others.

For the average African, of course, such intellectual dilemmas pale before the daily challenge of survival. But the fundamental gap between the traditional village and the modern metropolis is perhaps wider in Africa than anywhere else in the world and may well be harder to bridge. The solution is not yet visible.

In the meantime, writes the Ghanaian author George Awoonor-Williams, all Africans are exiles:

*The return is tedious*
*And the exiled souls gathered at the beach*
*Arguing and deciding their future*
*Should they return home*
*And face the fences the termites had eaten*
*And see the dunghill that has mounted their*
*birthplace? . . .*
*The final strokes will land them on forgotten shores*
*They committed the impiety of self-deceit*
*Slashed, cut and wounded their souls*
*And left the mangled remainder in manacles.*

*The moon, the moon is our father's spirit*
*At the stars entrance the night revellers gather*
*To sell their chatter and inhuman sweat to the*
*gateman*
*And shuffle their feet in agonies of birth.*
*Lost souls, lost souls, lost souls, that are*
*Still at the gate.*[10]

# Crescent of Conflict

"We Muslims are of one family even though we live under different governments and in various regions."[11] So said Ayatollah Ruholla Khomeini, the Islamic religious figure and leader of the 1979 revolution that overthrew the shah in Iran. The ayatollah's remark was not just a pious wish by a religious mystic but an accurate reflection of one crucial aspect of the political dynamics in the region.

If the concept of negritude (blackness) represents an alternative to the system of nation-states in Africa, in the Middle East a similar role has been played by the forces of militant Islam. In both regions, a yearning for a sense of community beyond national borders tugs at the emotions and intellect of their inhabitants and counteracts the dynamic pull of nationalism that has provoked political turmoil and conflict in much of the rest of the world.

A dramatic example of the powerful force of pan-Islamic sentiment took place on September 11, 2001, when Muslim militants hijacked four U.S. airliners and turned them into missiles aimed at the center of world capitalism (see Chapter 27). Although the headquarters of the terrorist network that carried out the attack—

## The Roots of Terrorism

In the weeks and months following the terrorist attack on September 11, 2001, commentators throughout the world voiced their views on the roots of the attack and how to prevent a recurrence. In many Muslim countries, horror at the violence was balanced by a conviction that the problem could not be solved simply by seeking out the perpetrators and destroying their terrorist network. Rather, terrorism was a consequence of contemporary conditions throughout much of the Arab world and could only be resolved by political and economic means. Such was the view of the author of the following editorial, published a few days following the attack in *El Watan,* an independent newspaper in Algiers, the capital of Algeria. Algerian society had been shattered by terrorist activities committed by Islamic militants for over a decade.

*According to the author of this passage, who is to blame for the conditions that led to the attack on the World Trade Center? To what degree does the Western world share responsibility?*

### Algeria: Rethinking the Variables

Even if the U.S. military kills Bin Laden and decimates his forces, international terrorism will be only weakened, not destroyed. Experts agree on this point, and some assert that if Bin Laden dies a martyr, his name will act as a stimulus for terrorist movements around the world that won't hesitate to commit further spectacular attacks.

And so as the fear and anger fade, a growing chorus of voices is calling for a comprehensive approach to terrorism, the fruit of intensive thought about its deepest nature. The first conclusion will involve the responsibility of the Western world, which throughout history has allowed religious fundamentalism to thrive when it served Western interests.

Thus, the West unconditionally backed the monarchies of the Gulf, a breeding ground of fundamentalism, because of their oil resources, while at the same time lending blinkered support to Israel's expansionist policies. Against the will of their people, Arab and Muslim leaders have been coddled by the West, spurring popular anger to fever pitch during the Gulf War.

Resentment, widespread in the Arab world by the end of the 20th century, has been exploited by the fundamentalists, who have channeled it into a "holy war" (jihad) against the West. The West, and notably the United States, has learned nothing from all this. Worse, the West has aggravated frustrations the world over by canonizing laissez-faire economics, whose centerpiece—globalization—heralds the systematic impoverishment of billions of people.

But it would be hasty to blame the West alone for terrorism. Both governments and movements in the Arab-Muslim world have sought to impose their religious dogma everywhere by means of systematic terror perpetrated by fanatical groups. Their aim is to create Afghan-type states. Algeria is the clearest case in point.

known as al-Qaeda—was located in Afghanistan, the militants themselves came from several different Muslim states, primarily Saudi Arabia. In the months that followed, support for al-Qaeda and its mysterious leader, Osama bin Laden, intensified throughout the Muslim world. To many observers, it was clear that bin Laden and his cohorts had tapped into a wellspring of hostility and resentment directed at much of the Western world (see the box above).

What were the sources of Muslim anger? In a speech released on videotape shortly after the attack, bin Laden declared that the attacks were a response to the "humiliation and disgrace" inflicted on the Islamic world for over eighty years, a period dating back to the end of World War I. For the Middle East, the period between the two world wars was an era of transition. With the fall of the Ottoman and Persian Empires, new modernizing regimes emerged in Turkey and Iran, and a more traditionalist but fiercely independent government was established in Saudi Arabia. Elsewhere, European influence continued to be strong; the British and French had mandates in Syria, Lebanon, Jordan, and Palestine, and British influence persisted in Iraq, in southern Arabia, and throughout the Nile valley. **Pan-Arabism** was on the rise, but it lacked focus and coherence.

During World War II, the region became the cockpit of European rivalries, as it had been during World War I. The region was more significant to the warring powers than previously because of the growing importance of oil and the Suez Canal's position as a vital sea route. For a brief period, the German Afrika Korps threatened to seize Egypt and the Suez Canal, but British troops defeated the German forces at El Alamein, west of Alexandria, in 1942. From that time until the end of the war, the entire region from the Mediterranean Sea eastward was under secure Allied occupation.

## The Question of Palestine

As in other areas of Asia, the end of World War II led to the emergence of a number of independent states. Jordan, Lebanon, and Syria, all European mandates before the war, became independent. Egypt, Iran, and Iraq, though still under a degree of Western influence, became increasingly autonomous. Sympathy for the idea of Arab unity led to the formation of the Arab League in 1945, but different points of view among its members prevented it from achieving anything of substance.

The one issue on which all Arab states in the area could agree was the question of Palestine. As tensions between Jews and Arabs in that mandate intensified during the 1930s, the British attempted to limit Jewish immigration into the area and firmly rejected proposals for independence, despite the promise made in the 1917 Balfour Declaration (see Chapter 23). After World War II, the Zionists turned for support to the United States, and in March 1948, the Truman administration approved the concept of an independent Jewish state, even though only about one-third of the local residents were Jews. In May, the new state of Israel was formally established.

To its Arab neighbors, the new state represented a betrayal of the interests of the Palestinian people, 90 percent of whom were Muslim, and a flagrant disregard for the conditions set out in the Balfour Declaration. Outraged at the lack of Western support for Muslim interests in the area, several Arab countries invaded the new Jewish state. The invasion did not succeed because of internal divisions among the Arabs, but both sides remained bitter, and the Arab states refused to recognize Israel.

The war had other lasting consequences as well, because it led to the exodus of thousands of Palestinian refugees into neighboring Muslim states. Jordan, which had become independent under its Hashemite ruler, was now flooded by the arrival of one million urban Palestinians in a country occupied by half a million Bedouins. To the north, the state of Lebanon had been created to provide the local Christian community with a country of their own, but the arrival of the Palestinian refugees upset the delicate balance between Christians and Muslims. In any event, the creation of Lebanon had angered the Syrians, who had lost it as well as other territories to Turkey as a result of European decisions before and after the war.

## Nasser and Pan-Arabism

The dispute over Palestine placed Egypt in an uncomfortable position. Technically, Egypt was not an Arab state. King Farouk, who had acceded to power in 1936, had frequently declared support for the Arab cause, but the Egyptian people were not Bedouins and shared little of the culture of the peoples across the Red Sea. Nevertheless, Farouk committed Egyptian armies to the disastrous war against Israel.

In 1952, King Farouk, whose corrupt habits had severely eroded his early popularity, was overthrown by a military coup engineered by young military officers. The real force behind the scenes was Colonel Gamal Abdul Nasser (1918–1970), the son of a minor government functionary who, like many of his fellow officers, had been angered by the army's inadequate preparation for the war against Israel four years earlier. In 1953, the monarchy was replaced by a republic.

In 1954, Nasser seized power in his own right and immediately instituted a land reform program. He also adopted a policy of neutrality in foreign affairs and expressed sympathy for the Arab cause. The British presence had rankled many Egyptians for years, for even after granting Egypt independence, Britain had retained control over the Suez Canal to protect its route to the Indian Ocean. In 1956, Nasser suddenly nationalized the Suez Canal Company, which had been under British and French administration. Seeing a threat to their route to the Indian Ocean, the British and the French launched a joint attack on Egypt to protect their investment. They were joined by Israel, whose leaders had grown exasperated at sporadic Arab commando raids on Israeli territory and now decided to strike back. But the Eisenhower administration in the United States, concerned that the attack smacked of a revival of colonialism, supported Nasser and brought about the withdrawal of foreign forces from Egypt and of Israeli troops from the Sinai peninsula (see the box on p. 834).

**The United Arab Republic** Nasser now turned to pan-Arabism. Egypt had won approval from other states in the area for its successful eviction of the British and the French from the Suez Canal and for its sponsorship of efforts to replace Israel by an independent Palestinian state. In 1958, Egypt united with Syria as the United Arab Republic (UAR). The union had been proposed by the Ba'ath Party, which advocated the unity of all Arab states in a new socialist society. In 1957, the Ba'ath Party assumed power in Syria and opened talks with Egypt on a union between the two countries, which took place in March 1958 following a plebiscite. Nasser was named president of the new state.

Egypt and Syria hoped that the union would eventually include all Arab states, but other Arab leaders, including the young King Hussein of Jordan and the kings of Iraq and Saudi Arabia, were suspicious. The latter two in particular feared pan-Arabism on the reasonable assumption that they would be asked to share their vast oil revenues with the poorer states of the Middle East. Indeed, in Nasser's view, through Arab unity, this wealth could be used to improve the standard of living in the area. To achieve a more equitable division of the wealth of the region, natural resources and major industries would be nationalized; central planning would guarantee that resources were exploited efficiently, but private enterprise would continue at the local level.

In the end, however, Nasser's determination to extend state control over the economy brought an end to the UAR. When the government announced the nationalization of a large number of industries and utilities in 1961, a military coup overthrew the Ba'ath leaders in Damascus, and the new authorities declared that Syria would end its relationship with Egypt.

The breakup of the UAR did not necessarily end Nasser's dream of pan-Arabism. In 1962, Algeria finally received its independence from France and, under its new

## The Suez Canal Belongs to Egypt!

The Suez Canal was built between 1854 and 1869, using mainly French capital and Egyptian labor, under the direction of the French promoter Ferdinand de Lesseps. It was managed by a Paris-based limited liability corporation, called the Suez Canal Company, under a ninety-nine-year lease. Over time, the canal came to symbolize colonial exploitation in the minds of many Egyptians. In this excerpt from a speech given in July 1956, President Nasser declared that it was time for the canal to be owned and managed by Egyptians. The decision led to a brief invasion by Great Britain and France, but under pressure, the European powers backed down, and Nasser got his way.

*How does President Nasser justify his claim of Egyptian ownership of the Suez Canal? What was the result of the seizure?*

### Nasser's Speech Nationalizing the Suez Canal Company

The Suez Canal is an Egyptian canal built as a result of great sacrifices. The Suez Canal Company is an Egyptian company that was expropriated from Egypt by the British, who, since the canal was dug, have been obtaining the profits of the Company. . . . And yet the Suez Canal Company is an Egyptian limited liability company. The annual Canal revenue is 35 million Egyptian pounds. From this sum Egypt—which lost 120,000 workers in digging the Canal—takes one million pounds from the Company. . . .

It is a shame when the blood of peoples is sucked, and it is no shame that we should borrow for construction. We will not allow the past to be repeated again, but we will cancel the past by restoring our rights in the Suez Canal. . . . We will build the High Dam, and we will obtain our rights. We will build it as we wish, and we are determined to do so. The 35 million pounds which the Company collects each year will be collected by us. . . . When we build the High Dam, we will be building the dam of prestige, freedom, and dignity, and we will be putting an end to the dams of humiliation. . . .

Now that the rights have been restored to their people after one hundred years, we are achieving true liberation. The Suez Canal Company was a state within a state, depending on the conspiracies of imperialism and its supporters. The Canal was built for the sake of Egypt, but it was a source of exploitation. There is no shame in being poor, but it is a shame to suck blood. Today we restore these rights, and I declare in the name of the Egyptian people that we will protect these rights with our blood and soul. . . .

The people will stand united as one man to resist imperialist acts of treachery. . . . When we restore all our rights, we shall become stronger and our production will increase. At this moment, some of your brethren, the sons of Egypt, are now taking over the Egyptian Suez Canal Company and directing it. We have taken this decision to restore part of the glories of the past and to safeguard our national dignity and pride. May God bless you and guide you in the path of righteousness.

president, Ahmad Ben Bella, established close relations with Egypt, as did a new republic in Yemen. During the mid-1960s, Egypt took the lead in promoting Arab unity against Israel. At a meeting of Arab leaders held in Jerusalem in 1964, the Palestine Liberation Organization (PLO) was set up under Egyptian sponsorship to represent the interests of the Palestinians. According to the charter of the PLO, only the Palestinian people (and thus not Jewish immigrants from abroad) had the right to form a state in the old British mandate. A guerrilla movement called al-Fatah, led by the dissident PLO figure Yasir Arafat (1929–2004), began to launch terrorist attacks on Israeli territory, prompting the Israeli government to raid PLO bases in Jordan in 1966.

## The Arab-Israeli Dispute

Growing Arab hostility was a constant threat to the security of Israel. In the years after independence, Israeli leaders dedicated themselves to creating a Jewish homeland. Aided by reparations paid by the postwar German government and private funds provided by Jews living abroad, notably in the United States, the government attempted to build a democratic and modern state that would be a magnet for Jews throughout the world and a symbol of Jewish achievement.

Ensuring the survival of the tiny state surrounded by antagonistic Arab neighbors was a considerable challenge, made more difficult by divisions within the Israeli population. Some were immigrants from Europe, while others came from the Middle East. Some were secular and even socialist in their views, while others were politically and religiously conservative. The state was also home to Christians as well as Muslim Palestinians who had not fled to other countries. To balance these diverse interests, Israel established a parliament, called the Knesset, on the European model, with proportional representation based on the number of votes each party received in the general election. The parties were so numerous that none ever received a majority of votes, and all governments had to be formed from a coalition of several parties. As a result, moderate secular leaders such as longtime prime minister David Ben Gurion had to cater to more marginal parties composed of conservative religious groups.

During the late 1950s and 1960s, the dispute between Israel and other states in the Middle East intensified. Essentially alone except for the sympathy of the United States and a handful of Western European countries, Israel adopted a policy of determined resistance to and immediate retaliation against alleged PLO and Arab provocations. By the spring of 1967, relations between Israel and its Arab neighbors had deteriorated as Nasser attempted to improve his standing in the Arab world by imposing a blockade against Israeli commerce through the Gulf of Aqaba.

**The Six-Day War** Concerned that it might be isolated, and lacking firm support from Western powers (who had originally guaranteed Israel the freedom to use the Gulf of Aqaba), in June 1967, Israel suddenly launched air strikes against Egypt and several of its Arab neighbors. Israeli armies then broke the blockade at the head of the Gulf of Aqaba and occupied the Sinai peninsula. Other Israeli forces attacked Jordanian territory on the West Bank of the Jordan River (Jordan's King Hussein had recently signed an alliance with Egypt and placed his army under Egyptian command), occupied the whole of Jerusalem, and seized Syrian military positions in the Golan Heights, along the Israeli-Syrian border (see Map 28.2).

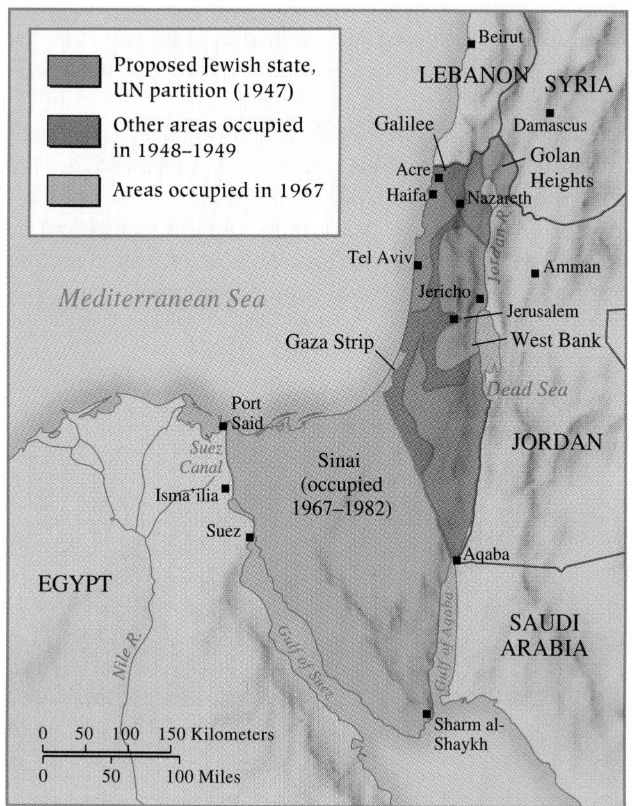


**MAP 28.2 Israel and Its Neighbors.** This map shows the evolution of the state of Israel since its founding in 1948. Areas occupied by Israel after the Six-Day War in 1967 are indicated in green. ? What is the significance of the West Bank? **View an animated version of this map or related maps at** http://history.wadsworth.com/duikerspielvogel05/

Despite limited Soviet support for Egypt and Syria, in a war lasting only six days, Israel had mocked Nasser's pretensions of Arab unity and tripled the size of its territory, thus enhancing its precarious security. But the new Israel aroused even more bitter hostility among the Arabs and added one million Palestinians inside its borders, most of them on the West Bank of the Jordan River.

During the next few years, the focus of the Arab-Israeli dispute shifted as Arab states demanded the return of the occupied territories. Meanwhile, many Israelis argued that the new lands improved the security of the beleaguered state and should be retained. Concerned that the dispute might lead to a confrontation between the superpowers, with the Soviet Union backing the Arabs, the Nixon administration tried to achieve a peace settlement. The peace effort received a mild stimulus when Nasser died of a heart attack in September 1970 and was succeeded by his vice president, ex-general Anwar al-Sadat (1918–1981). Sadat soon showed himself to be more pragmatic than his predecessor, dropping the now irrelevant name United Arab Republic in favor of the Arab Republic of Egypt and replacing Nasser's socialist policies with a new strategy based on free enterprise and encouragement of Western investment. He also agreed to sign a peace treaty with Israel on condition that Israel withdraw to its pre-1967 frontiers. Concerned that other Arab countries would refuse to make peace and take advantage of its presumed weakness, Israel refused.

Rebuffed in his offer of peace, smarting from criticism of his moderate stand from other Arab leaders, and increasingly concerned over Israeli plans to build permanent Jewish settlements in the occupied territories, Sadat attempted once again to renew Arab unity through a new confrontation with Israel. On Yom Kippur (the Jewish Day of Atonement), an Israeli national holiday, Egyptian forces suddenly launched an air and artillery attack on Israeli positions in the Sinai just east of the Suez Canal. Syrian armies attacked Israeli positions in the Golan Heights. After early Arab successes, the Israelis managed to recoup some of their losses on both fronts. As a superpower confrontation between the United States and the Soviet Union loomed, a cease-fire was finally reached. The focus of tension, however, now switched to Lebanon, where many Palestinians had found refuge and the PLO had set up its headquarters. Rising tension along the border was compounded by increasingly hostile disputes between Christians and Muslims over control of the capital, Beirut.

**The Camp David Agreement** After his election as U.S. president in 1976, Jimmy Carter began to press for a compromise peace based on Israel's return of occupied Arab territories and Arab recognition of the state of Israel. In September 1978, Sadat and Israeli prime minister Menachem Begin (1913–1992) met with Carter at Camp David, the presidential retreat in Maryland. Israel agreed to withdraw from the Sinai but not from other occupied territories unless it was recognized by other Arab countries.

The promise of the Camp David agreement was not fulfilled. One reason was the assassination of Sadat by Islamic militants in October 1981. But there were deeper causes, including the continued unwillingness of many Arab governments to recognize Israel and the Israeli government's encouragement of Jewish settlements on the occupied West Bank.

**The PLO and the *Intifada*** During the early 1980s, the militancy of the Palestinians increased, leading to rising unrest, popularly labeled the ***intifada*** (uprising), among PLO supporters living inside Israel. To control the situation, a new Israeli government under Prime Minister Itzhak Shamir invaded southern Lebanon to destroy PLO commando bases near the Israeli border. The invasion provoked international condemnation and further destabilized the perilous balance between Muslims and Christians in Lebanon. As the 1990s began, U.S.-sponsored peace talks opened between Israel and a number of its neighbors. The first major breakthrough came in 1993, when Israel and the PLO reached an agreement calling for Palestinian autonomy in selected areas of Israel in return for PLO recognition of the legitimacy of the Israeli state.

Progress in implementing the agreement, however, was slow. Terrorist attacks by Palestinian militants resulted in heavy casualties and shook the confidence of many Jewish citizens that their security needs could be protected under the agreement. At the same time, Jewish residents of the West Bank resisted the extension of Palestinian authority in the area. In November 1995, Prime Minister Yitzhak Rabin was assassinated by an Israeli opponent of the accords. National elections held a few months later led to the formation of a new government under Benjamin Netanyahu, which adopted a tougher stance in negotiations with the Palestinian Authority under Yasir Arafat. When Netanyahu was replaced by a new Labour government under Prime Minister Ehud Barak, the latter promised to revitalize the peace process. Negotiations continued with the PLO and also got under way with Syria over a peace settlement in Lebanon and the possible return of the Golan Heights. But in late 2000, peace talks broke down over the future of the city of Jerusalem, leading to massive riots by Palestinians and the election of a new and more hard-line Israeli prime minister, former defense minister Ariel Sharon. Sharon's ascent to leadership was accompanied by a rash of suicide attacks by Palestinians against Israeli targets, an intensive Israeli military crackdown on suspected terrorist sites inside Palestinian territory, and a dramatic increase in bloodshed on both sides. The death of Yasir Arafat in 2004 and his replacement by the Palestinian moderate Mahmoud Abbas raised modest hopes for progress in peace talks, but key issues remain unresolved, including the future status of Jerusalem and Jewish settlements in the occupied territories.

### CHRONOLOGY The Arab-Israeli Dispute

| | |
|---|---|
| Formation of the state of Israel | 1948 |
| Founding of the Palestine Liberation Organization | 1964 |
| Six-Day War between Arab states and Israel | 1967 |
| Yom Kippur War between Arab states and Israel | 1973 |
| Camp David accords | 1978 |
| Israeli forces invade Lebanon | 1982 |
| Agreement on Palestinian autonomy | 1994 |
| Assassination of Yitzhak Rabin | 1995 |
| Peace talks between Israel and Syria begin | 1999 |
| Election of Ariel Sharon as prime minister of Israel | 2000 |

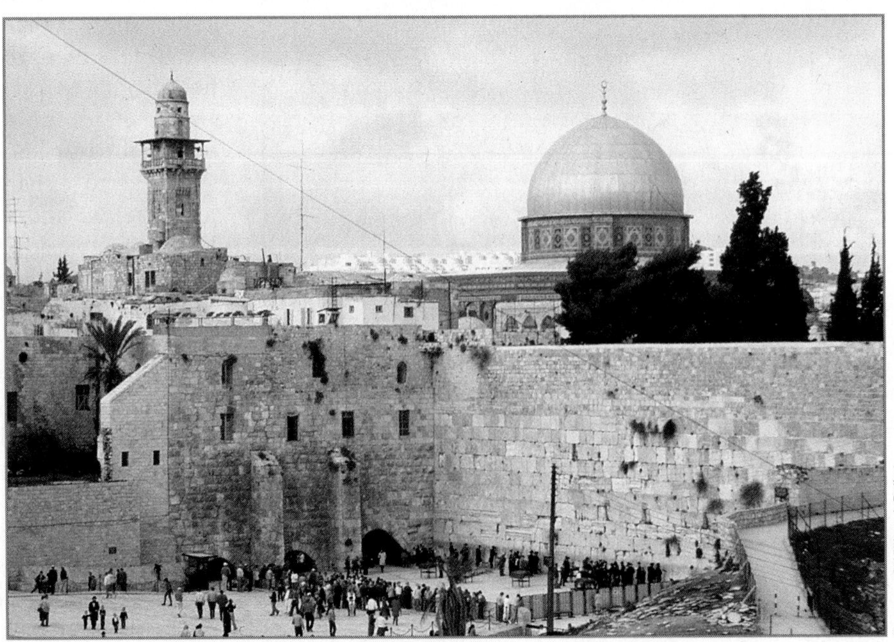

Courtesy of William J. Duiker

**The Temple Mount at Jerusalem.** The Temple Mount is one of the most sacred spots in the city of Jerusalem. Originally, it was the site of a temple built during the reign of Solomon, king of the Jews, about 1000 B.C.E. The Western Wall of the temple is shown in the foreground. Beyond the wall is the Dome of the Rock complex, built on the place from which Muslims believe that Muhammad ascended to heaven. Sacred to both Judaism and Islam, the Temple Mount is now a major bone of contention between Muslims and Jews and a prime obstacle to a final settlement of the Arab-Israeli dispute.

## Revolution in Iran

The Arab-Israeli dispute also provoked an international oil crisis. In 1960, a number of oil-producing states formed the Organization of Petroleum Exporting Countries (OPEC) to gain control over oil prices, but the organization was not recognized by the foreign oil companies. During the 1973 Yom Kippur War, some OPEC nations announced significant increases in the price of oil to foreign countries. The price hikes were accompanied by an apparent oil shortage and created serious economic problems in the United States and Europe as well as in the Third World. They also proved to be a boon to oil-exporting countries, such as Libya, now under the leadership of the militantly anti-Western Colonel Muammar Qadhafi (b. 1942).

One of the key oil-exporting countries was Iran. Under the leadership of Shah Mohammad Reza Pahlavi (1919–1980), who had taken over from his father in 1941, Iran had become one of the richest countries in the Middle East. Although relations with the West had occasionally been fragile (especially after the prime minister attempted to nationalize the oil industry in 1951), during the next twenty years Iran became a prime ally of the United States in the Middle East. With encouragement from the United States, which hoped that Iran could become a force for stability in the Persian Gulf, the shah attempted to carry through a series of social and economic reforms to transform the country into the most advanced in the region.

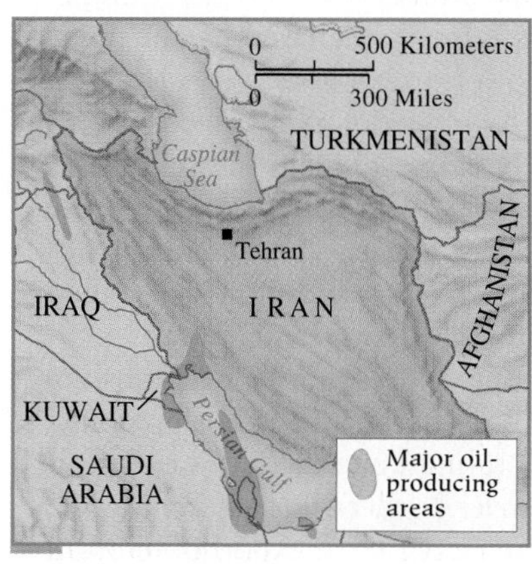


**Iran**

Statistical evidence suggests that his efforts were succeeding. Per capita income increased dramatically, literacy rates improved, a modern communications infrastructure took shape, and an affluent middle class emerged in the capital of Tehran. Under the surface, however, trouble was brewing. Despite an ambitious land reform program, many peasants were still landless, unemployment among intellectuals was dangerously high, and the urban middle class was squeezed by high inflation. Housing costs had skyrocketed, provoked in part by the massive influx of foreigners attracted by oil money.

**The Fall of the Shah** Some of the unrest took the form of religious discontent as millions of devout Muslims looked with distaste at a new Iranian civilization based on greed, sexual license, and material accumulation. Religious conservatives opposed rampant government corruption, the ostentation of the shah's court, and the extension of voting rights to women. Some opposition elements resorted to terrorism against wealthy Iranians or foreign residents in an attempt to provoke social and political disorder. In response, the shah's U.S.-trained security police, the *Savak,* imprisoned and sometimes tortured thousands of dissidents.

Leading the opposition was Ayatollah Ruholla Khomeini (1900–1989), an austere Shi'ite cleric who had been exiled to Iraq and then to France because of his outspoken opposition to the shah's regime. From Paris, Khomeini continued his attacks in print, on television, and in radio broadcasts. By the late 1970s, large numbers of Iranians—especially Shi'ite Muslims, whose approach to religion is sometimes more mystical and messianic than that of their Sunni counterparts—began to respond to Khomeini's diatribes against the "satanic regime," and demonstrations by his supporters were repressed with ferocity by the police. But workers' strikes grew in intensity. In 1979, the government collapsed and was replaced by a hastily formed Islamic republic headed by the returning Ayatollah Khomeini. The new government, dominated by Shi'ite clergy, immediately began to introduce traditional Islamic law. A new reign of terror ensued as supporters of the shah were rounded up and executed.

Though much of the outside world focused on the U.S. embassy in Tehran, where militants held a number of foreign hostages, the Iranian Revolution involved much more. In the eyes of the ayatollah and his followers, the United States was "the great Satan," the powerful protector of Israel and enemy of Muslims everywhere. Furthermore, it was responsible for the corruption of Iranian society under the shah. With economic conditions in Iran rapidly deteriorating, the Islamic revolutionary government finally agreed to free the hostages in return for the release of Iranian assets in the United States.

During the next few years, the intensity of the Iranian Revolution moderated slightly as the government displayed a modest tolerance for a loosening of clerical control over freedom of expression and social activities. But rising criticism of rampant official corruption and a high rate of inflation sparked a new wave of government repression in the mid-1990s; newspapers were censored, the universities were purged of disloyal or "un-Islamic" elements, and religious militants raided private homes in search of blasphemous activities.

In 1997, a moderate Muslim cleric, Mohammad Khatemi, was elected president of Iran. Khatemi's victory reflected a growing desire among many Iranians for a more pluralistic society open to the outside world. He promoted reforms in a number of areas, including a relaxation of press censorship, leading to the emergence of several reformist newspapers and magazines, as well as a loosening of dress codes and restrictions on women's activities. After reelection in August 2001, he vowed to continue his reformist efforts. In the days following the terrorist attacks on the United States on September 11, he declared publicly that Muslims must reject terrorism as a tool in promoting Islam. But conservative clerics, anxious to contain the longing for

**Iranian Women Practicing Soccer.** Despite the restriction of having to cover their bodies in public, young Iranian women play soccer and other sports, attend schools and universities, and partake in other activities of the modern world. Here we see young women playing a game of soccer in their black-hooded garments. Although they rarely did so before the Islamic Revolution, today about two million Iranian women take part in sports.



personal freedom that was increasing among younger Iranians, struck back by curtailing freedom of the press and defying parliamentary legislation that they considered destructive of the purity of the Islamic state. Although student protests erupted into the streets in 2003, hard-liners continued to reject proposals to expand civil rights and limit the power of the clerics.

## Crisis in the Gulf

Although much of the Iranians' anger was directed against the United States during the early phases of the revolution, Iran had equally hated enemies closer to home. To the north, the immense power of the Soviet Union, driven by atheistic communism, was viewed as a modern version of the Russian threat of previous centuries. To the west was a militant and hostile Iraq, now under the leadership of the ambitious Saddam Hussein (b. 1937). Iraq had just passed through a turbulent period. The monarchy had been overthrown by a military coup in 1958, but conflicts within the military ruling junta led to chronic instability, and in 1979 Colonel Saddam Hussein, a prominent member of the local Ba'athist party, seized power on his own.

**The Vision of Saddam Hussein** Saddam Hussein was a fervent believer in the creation of a single Arab state in the Middle East and soon began to persecute non-Arab elements in Iraq, including Persians and Kurds. He then turned his sights to territorial expansion to the east.

Iraq and Iran had long had an uneasy relationship, fueled by religious differences (Iranian Islam is predominantly Shi'ite, while the ruling caste in Iraq was Sunni) and a perennial dispute over borderlands adjacent to the Persian Gulf, the vital waterway for the export of oil from both countries. Like several of its neighbors, Iraq had long dreamed of unifying the Arabs but had been hindered by internal factions and suspicion among its neighbors.

During the mid-1970s, Iran gave some support to a Kurdish rebellion in the mountains of Iraq. In 1975, the

**Raid on Tikrit.** Although the U.S.-led coalition won a rapid and relatively bloodless victory in Iraq in 2003, the transition to peace has been more complex as resistance forces, supplemented by Islamic militants from abroad, have launched periodic attacks on occupation troops, as well as on Iraqis who cooperate with them, in an effort to destabilize the situation. Here U.S. infantry units carry out a raid on Tikrit, once a stronghold of support for the Saddam Hussein regime.

government of the shah agreed to stop aiding the rebels in return for territorial concessions at the head of the Gulf. Five years later, however, the Kurdish revolt had been suppressed.

Saddam Hussein now saw his opportunity; accusing Iran of violating the territorial agreement, he launched an attack on his neighbor. The war was a bloody one and lasted for nearly ten years. Poison gas was used against civilians, and children were employed to clear minefields. Finally, with both sides virtually exhausted, a cease-fire was arranged in the fall of 1988.

The bitter conflict with Iran had not slaked Saddam Hussein's appetite for territorial expansion. In early August 1990, Iraqi military forces suddenly moved across the border and occupied the small neighboring country of Kuwait at the head of the Gulf. The immediate pretext was the claim that Kuwait was pumping oil from fields inside Iraqi territory. Baghdad was also angry over the Kuwaiti government's demand for repayment of loans it had made to Iraq during the war with Iran. But the underlying reason was Iraq's contention that Kuwait was legally a part of Iraq. Kuwait had been part of the Ottoman Empire until the beginning of the twentieth century, when the local prince had agreed to place his patrimony under British protection. When Iraq became independent in 1932, it claimed the area on the grounds that the state of Kuwait had been created by British imperialism, but opposition from major Western powers and other countries in the region, who feared the consequences of a "greater Iraq," prevented an Iraqi takeover.

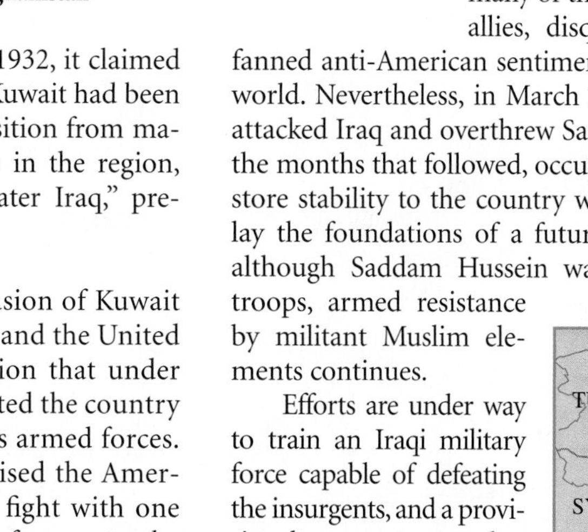

**Afghanistan**

**Operation Desert Storm** The Iraqi invasion of Kuwait in 1990 sparked an international outcry, and the United States assembled a multinational coalition that under the name Operation Desert Storm liberated the country and destroyed a substantial part of Iraq's armed forces. President George H. W. Bush had promised the American people that U.S. troops would not fight with one hand tied behind their backs (a clear reference to the Vietnam War), but the allied forces did not occupy Baghdad at the end of the war out of fear that doing so would cause a breakup of the country, an eventuality that would operate to the benefit of Iran. The allies hoped instead that Saddam's regime would be ousted by an internal revolt. In the meantime, harsh economic sanctions were imposed on the Iraqi government as the condition for peace. The anticipated overthrow of Saddam Hussein did not materialize, however, and his tireless efforts to evade the conditions of the ceasefire continued to bedevil U.S. President Bill Clinton and his successor, George W. Bush.

## Conflicts in Afghanistan and Iraq

The terrorist attacks launched against U.S. cities in September 2001 added a new dimension to the Middle Eastern equation. After the failure of the Soviet Union to quell the rebellion in Afghanistan during the 1980s, a fundamentalist Muslim group known as the Taliban, supported covertly by the United States, seized power in Kabul and ruled the country with a fanaticism reminiscent of the Cultural Revolution in China. Backed by conservative religious forces in Pakistan, the Taliban provided a base of operations for Osama bin Laden's al-Qaeda terrorist network. After the attacks of September 11, a coalition of forces led by the United States overthrew the Taliban and attempted to build a new and moderate government. But the country's history of bitter internecine warfare among various tribal groups represents a severe challenge to those efforts.

In the meantime, the Bush administration, charging that Iraqi dictator Saddam Hussein not only had provided support to bin Laden's terrorist organization but also sought to develop weapons of mass destruction, threatened to invade Iraq and remove him from power. The plan, widely debated in the media and opposed by many of the United States' traditional allies, disquieted Arab leaders and fanned anti-American sentiment throughout the Muslim world. Nevertheless, in March 2003, American-led forces attacked Iraq and overthrew Saddam Hussein's regime. In the months that followed, occupation forces sought to restore stability to the country while setting forth plans to lay the foundations of a future democratic society. But although Saddam Hussein was later captured by U.S. troops, armed resistance by militant Muslim elements continues.

Efforts are under way to train an Iraqi military force capable of defeating the insurgents, and a provisional government has been formed, the embryo of a future pro-Western state that could serve as an emblem of democracy in the Middle East. Squabbling among Sunni, Shi'ite, and Kurdish elements within the country, however, is a vivid reminder that a similar effort by the British eighty years earlier ended without success.

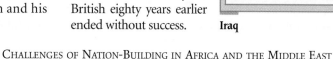

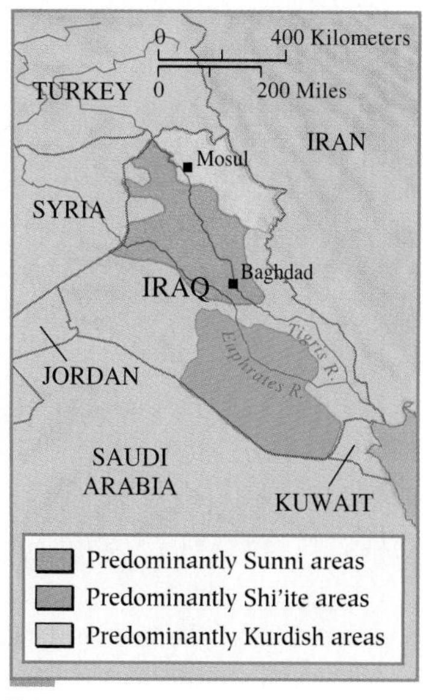

**Iraq**

# Society and Culture in the Contemporary Middle East

To many seasoned observers, U.S. plans in Iraq seem unrealistic, since democratic values are not deeply rooted in the region. Feudal rulers remain in power, notably on the Arabian peninsula. The kings of Saudi Arabia, for example, continue to rule by traditional precepts and, citing the distinctive character of Muslim political institutions, have been reluctant to establish representative political institutions. As a general rule, these rulers maintain and even enforce the strict observance of traditional customs. Religious police in Saudi Arabia are responsible for enforcing the Muslim dress code, maintaining the prohibition against alcohol, and making sure offices close during the time for prayer.

## Varieties of Government

In some societies, traditional authority has been replaced by charismatic one-party rule or military dictatorships. Nasser's Egypt was a single-party state where the leader won political power by the force of his presence or personality. The regimes of Ayatollah Khomeini in Iran, Muammar Qadhafi in Libya, and Saddam Hussein in Iraq can also trace much of their power to the personal appeal of the leader.

In other states, however, charismatic rule has given way to modernizing bureaucratic regimes. Examples include the governments of Syria, Yemen, Turkey, and Egypt since Nasser, where Anwar al-Sadat and his successor, Hosni Mubarak, focused on performance. Sometimes the authoritarian character of the regimes has been modified by some democratic tendencies, especially in Turkey, where free elections and the sharing of power have become more prevalent in recent years. A few Arab nations, such as Bahrain, Kuwait, and Jordan, have even engaged in limited forms of democratic experimentation.

Only in Israel, however, are democratic institutions firmly established. The Israeli system suffers from the proliferation of minor parties, some of which are able to dictate policy because their support is essential to keeping a coalition government in power. In recent years, divisions between religious conservatives and secular elements within the Jewish community have become increasingly sharp. Nevertheless, the government generally reflects the popular will, and power is transferred by peaceful and constitutional means.

## The Economics of Oil

Few areas exhibit a greater disparity of individual and national wealth than the Middle East. While millions live in abject poverty, a fortunate few rank among the wealthiest people in the world. For example, the annual per capita income in Egypt is about $600 (in U.S. dollars), whereas in the tiny states of Kuwait and the United Arab Emirates, it is nearly $20,000. The primary reason for this disparity is oil. Unfortunately for most of the peoples of the region, oil

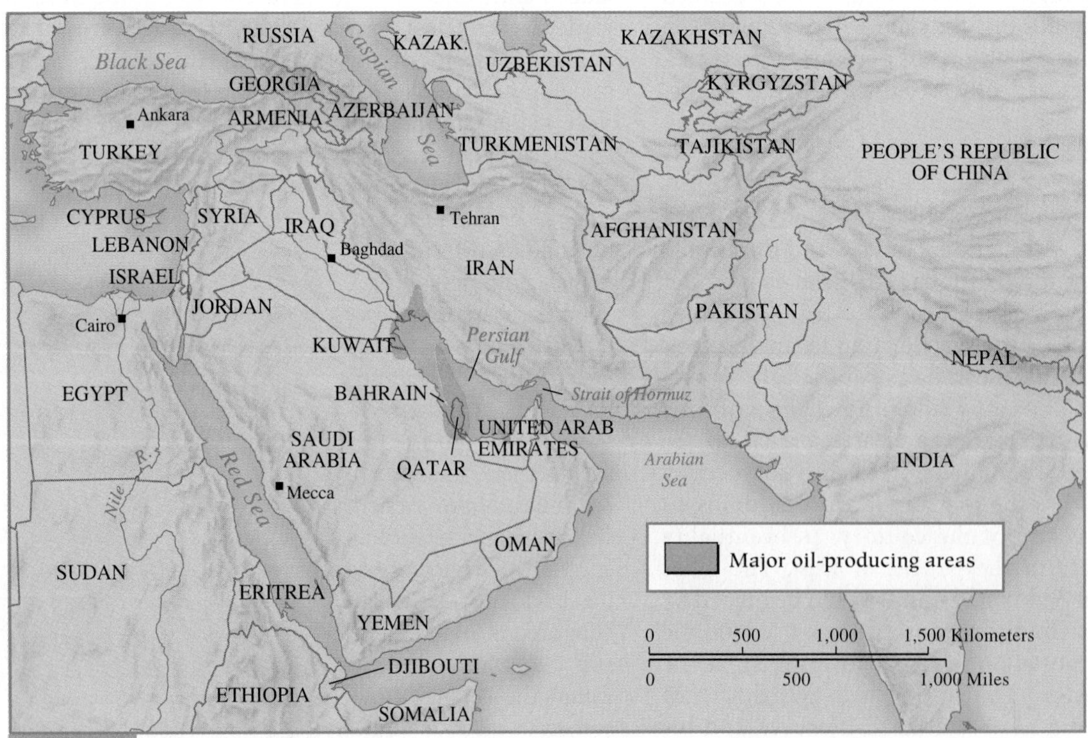


**MAP 28.3 The Modern Middle East.** Shown here are the boundaries dividing the independent states in the contemporary Middle East. ? Which are the major oil-producing countries? **View an animated version of this map or related maps at** http://history.wadsworth.com/duikerspielvogel05/

**CHRONOLOGY The Modern Middle East**

| | |
|---|---|
| King Farouk overthrown in Egypt | 1952 |
| Egypt nationalizes the Suez Canal | 1956 |
| Formation of the United Arab Republic | 1958 |
| Six-Day War between Arab states and Israel | 1967 |
| First oil crisis | 1973 |
| Yom Kippur War between Arab states and Israel | 1973 |
| Iranian Revolution | 1979 |
| Iran-Iraq War begins | 1980 |
| Israeli forces invade Lebanon | 1982 |
| Iraqi invasion of Kuwait | 1990 |
| Persian Gulf War | 1991 |
| Peace talks between Israel and Syria begin | 1999 |
| Reformists win parliamentary majority in Iran | 2000 |
| Al-Qaeda terrorist attack on the United States | 2001 |
| U.S.-led forces invade Iraq | 2003 |

reserves are distributed unevenly and all too often are located in areas where the population density is low (see Map 28.3). Egypt and Turkey, with more than fifty million inhabitants apiece, have almost no oil reserves. The combined population of Kuwait, the United Arab Emirates, and Saudi Arabia is well under ten million people. This disparity in wealth inspired Nasser's quest for Arab unity but has also posed a major obstacle to that unity.

The importance of petroleum has obviously been a boon to several of the states in the region, but it has been an unreliable one. Because of violent fluctuations in the price of oil, the income of oil-producing states has varied considerably. The spectacular increase in oil prices during the 1970s, when members of OPEC were able to raise the price of a barrel of oil from about \$3 to \$30, was not sustained, forcing a number of oil-producing countries to scale back their economic development plans.

**Economics and Islam** Not surprisingly, considering their different resources and political systems, the states of the Middle East have adopted diverse approaches to the problem of developing strong and stable economies. Some, like Nasser in Egypt and the leaders of the Ba'ath Party in Syria, attempted to create a form of Arab socialism, favoring a high level of government involvement in the economy to relieve the inequities of the free enterprise system. Others turned to the Western capitalist model to maximize growth while using taxes or massive development projects to build a modern infrastructure, redistribute wealth, and maintain political stability and economic opportunity for all.

Whatever their approach, all the states have attempted to develop their economies in accordance with Islamic beliefs. Although the Qur'an has little to say about economics and can be variously interpreted as capitalist or socialist, it is clear in its opposition to charging interest and in its concern for the material welfare of the Muslim community, the *umma*. How these goals are to be achieved is a matter of interpretation.

Socialist theories of economic development such as Nasser's were often suggested as a way to promote economic growth while meeting the requirements of Islamic doctrine. State intervention in the economic sector would bring about rapid development, while land redistribution and the nationalization or regulation of industry would minimize the harsh inequities of the marketplace. In general, however, the socialist approach has had little success, and most governments, including those of Egypt and Syria, eventually shifted to a more free enterprise approach while encouraging foreign investment to compensate for a lack of capital or technology.

**Agricultural Policies** Although the amount of arable land is relatively small, most countries in the Middle East rely to a certain degree on farming to supply food for their growing populations. Much of the fertile land was owned by wealthy absentee landlords, but land reform programs in several countries have attempted to alleviate this problem.

The most comprehensive and probably the most successful land reform program was instituted in Egypt, where Nasser and his successors managed to reassign nearly a quarter of all cultivable lands by limiting the amount a single individual could hold. Similar programs in Iran, Iraq, Libya, and Syria generally had less effect. After the 1979 revolution in Iran, many farmers seized lands forcibly from the landlords, creating questions of ownership that the revolutionary government has tried with minimal success to resolve.

Agricultural productivity throughout the region has been plagued by the lack of water. With populations growing at more than 2 percent annually on average in the Middle East (more than 3 percent in some countries), several governments have tried to increase the amount of water available for irrigation. Many attempts have been sabotaged by government ineptitude, political disagreements, and territorial conflicts, however. The best-known example is the Aswan Dam, which was built by Soviet engineers in the 1950s. The project was designed to control the flow of water throughout the Nile valley, but it has had a number of undesirable environmental consequences. Today, the dearth of water in the region is reaching crisis proportions.

**Migratory Workers** Another way governments have attempted to deal with rapid population growth is to encourage emigration. Oil-producing states with small populations, such as Saudi Arabia and the United Arab Emirates, have imported labor from other countries in the region, mostly to work in the oil fields. By the mid-1980s, more than 40 percent of the population in those states was composed of foreign nationals, who often sent the bulk of their salaries back to their families in their home countries. The decline in oil revenues in the mid-1980s, however, has forced several governments to take measures to stabilize or reduce the migrant population. After the Iraqi invasion in 1990, Kuwait, for example, expelled all Palestinians and restricted migrant workers from other countries to a three-year stay.

**Challenges to Democracy** The economies of the Middle Eastern countries, then, are in a state of flux. Political and military conflicts have exacerbated economic problems such as water use, which have in turn compounded political issues. For example, disputes between Israel and its neighbors over water rights and between Iraq and its neighbors over the exploitation of the Tigris and Euphrates Rivers have caused serious tensions in recent years. In Saudi Arabia, declining oil revenues combined with the evidence of corruption among Saudi elites have aroused a deep sense of anger and support for radical politics among some segments of the populace.

What explains the failure of democratic institutions and values to take root in the contemporary Middle East? Some observers attribute the cause to the willingness of Western governments to coddle dictatorships as a means of preserving their access to the vast oil reserves located on the Arabian peninsula. Others ascribe it to deep-seated factors embedded in the history and culture of the region or in the religion of Islam itself. As Bashar al-Assad, the president of Syria, remarked, he would tolerate only "positive criticism" of his policies. "We have to have our own democracy to match our history and culture," he said, "arising from the needs of our people and our reality."[12]

Whatever the cause, critics charge that the lack of personal freedom has aroused a level of popular discontent that local governments seek to deflect—often with great success—onto the West (see the box on p. 844). For their part, Middle Eastern political leaders undoubtedly fear that greater popular participation in the affairs of state could radicalize local politics and threaten the precarious stability of many states in the region. Current efforts by the Bush administration in the United States to promote a wave of democracy throughout the Middle East, however laudatory, represent an enormous gamble on the future stability of the region.

## The Islamic Revival

In recent years, many developments in the Middle East have been described in terms of a resurgence of traditional values and customs in response to Western influence. Indeed, some conservative religious forces in the area have consciously attempted to replace foreign culture and values with allegedly "pure" Islamic forms of belief and behavior.

But the Islamic revival is not a simple dichotomy between traditional and modern, native and foreign, or irrational and rational. In the first place, many Muslims in the Middle East still believe that Islamic values and modern ways are not incompatible and may even be mutually reinforcing. Second, the resurgence of what are sometimes called "fundamentalist" Islamic groups may, in a Middle Eastern context, appear to be a rational and practical response to destabilizing forces, such as corruption and hedonism, and self-destructive practices, such as drunkenness, prostitution, and the use of drugs. Finally, the reassertion of Islamic values is seen as a means of es-

**Answering the Call of the *Muezzin.*** With the renewed fervor of Muslims in the world today, scenes such as this one in Kuwait exemplify the adherents' humble submission to God. Required to pray five times a day—at dawn, noon, mid-afternoon, sunset, and early evening—a Muslim, after ritual ablutions, prostrates himself facing Mecca to proclaim, "There is no god but Allah, and Muhammad is his prophet." Responding to the call of the *muezzin,* which today is often a recorded message from the minaret of a mosque, the faithful can perform their prayers in a few minutes, wherever they are, at home or in any public place. There are an estimated 1.3 billion Muslims in the world today, 175 million of whom are in Indonesia, 105 million in India, and 15 million in Europe.

tablishing a cultural identity and fighting off the onslaught of Western ideas.

**Modernist Islam** Initially, many Muslim intellectuals responded to Western influence by trying to create a "modernized" set of Islamic beliefs and practices that would not clash with the demands of the twentieth century. This process took place to some degree in most Islamic societies, but it was especially prevalent in Turkey, Egypt, and Iran. Mustafa Kemal Atatürk embraced the strategy when he attempted to secularize the Islamic religion in the new Turkish republic. The Turkish model was followed by Shah Reza Khan and his son Mohammad Reza Pahlavi in Iran and then by Nasser in postwar Egypt, all of whom attempted to honor Islamic values while asserting the primacy of other issues such as political and economic development. Religion, in effect, had become the handmaiden of political power, national identity, and economic prosperity.

These secularizing trends were particularly noticeable among the political, intellectual, and economic elites in urban areas. They had less influence in the countryside, among the poor, and among devout elements within the clergy. Many of the clerics believed that Western influence in the cities had given birth to political and economic corruption, sexual promiscuity, hedonism, individualism, and the prevalence of alcohol, pornography, and drugs. Although such practices had long existed in the Middle East, they were now far more visible and socially acceptable.

This reaction intensified after World War I, when the Western presence increased. In 1928, devout Muslims in Egypt formed the Muslim Brotherhood as a means of promoting personal piety. Later the movement began to take a more activist approach, including the use of terrorism by a radical minority. Despite Nasser's surface commitment to Islamic ideals and Arab unity, some Egyptians were fiercely opposed to his policies and regarded his vision of Arab socialism as a betrayal of Islamic principles. Nasser reacted harshly and executed a number of his leading opponents.

**Return to Tradition** The movement to return to traditional practices reached its zenith in Iran under Ayatollah Khomeini. It is not surprising that Iran took the lead in light of its long tradition of ideological purity within the Shi'ite sect as well as the uncompromisingly secular character of the shah's reforms in the postwar era. In Iran today, traditional Islamic beliefs are all-pervasive and extend into education, clothing styles, social practices, and the legal system. In recent years, for example, Iranian women have been heavily fined or even flogged for violating the Islamic dress code.

The cultural and social effects of the Iranian Revolution were profound as Iranian ideas spread throughout the area. In Algeria, the political influence of fundamentalist Islamic groups grew substantially and enabled them to win a stunning victory in the national elections in 1992. When the military stepped in to cancel the second round of elections and crack down on the militants, the latter responded with a campaign of terrorism against moderates that claimed thousands of lives.

A similar trend emerged in Egypt, where militant groups such as the Muslim Brotherhood engaged in terrorism, including the assassination of President Anwar al-Sadat and attacks on foreign tourists, who are considered carriers of corrupt Western influence.

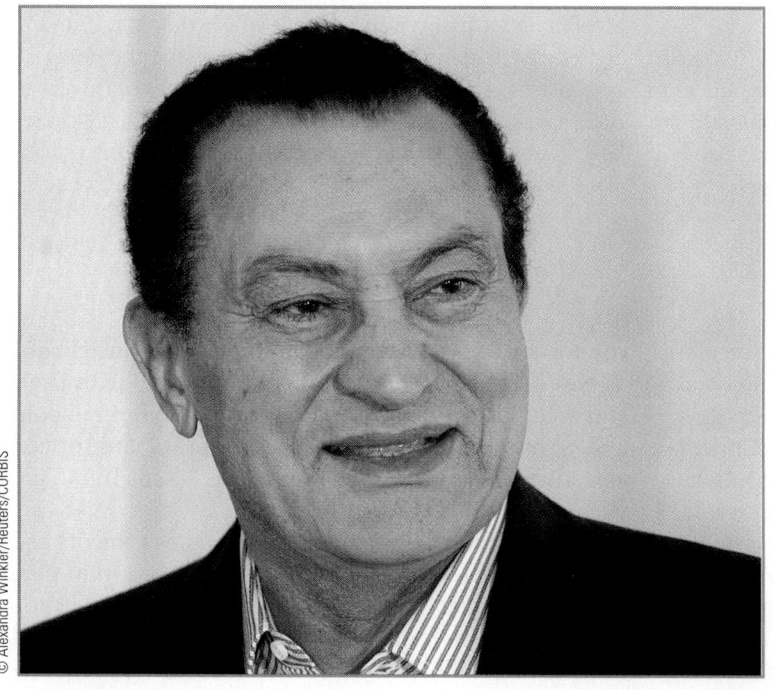

© Alexandra Winkler/Reuters/CORBIS

**Hosni Mubarak of Egypt.** Hosni Mubarak (b. 1929) has been president of Egypt since the death of his predecessor Anwar al-Sadat in 1981. One of the most prominent political figures in the contemporary Middle East, Mubarak personifies the dilemmas of a Muslim leader in seeking to bring about democratic reforms in his society. Although Egypt has historically been one of the most tolerant of Muslim societies, in recent years traditionalist elements have energetically sought to impose their values, sometimes by the use of violence. To preserve social order, Mubarak has catered to pressures from conservative Muslim elements while cracking down harshly on terrorist activities.

## Islam and Democracy

One of George W. Bush's key objectives in launching the invasion of Iraq in 2003 was to promote the emergence of democratic states throughout the Middle East. According to U.S. officials, one of the ultimate causes of the formation of terrorist movements in Muslim societies is the prevalence in such countries of dictatorial governments that do not serve the interests of their citizens. According to the Pakistani author of this editorial, the problem lies as much with the actions of Western countries as it does with political attitudes in the Muslim world.

*How does the author answer the charge that democracy and Islam are incompatible? To what degree is the West responsible for problems in the Middle East?*

### M. J. Akbar, "Linking Islam to Dictatorship"

Let us examine a central canard, that Islam and democracy are incompatible. This is an absurdity. There is nothing Islamic or un-Islamic about democracy. Democracy is the outcome of a political process, not a religious process.

It is glibly suggested that "every" Muslim country is a dictatorship, but the four largest Muslim populations of the world—in Indonesia, India, Bangladesh, and Turkey—vote to change governments. Pakistan could easily have been on this list.

Voting does not make these Muslims less or more religious. There are dictators among Muslims just as there are dictators among Christians, Buddhists, and Hindus (check out Nepal). . . . Christian Latin America has seen ugly forms of dictatorship, as has Christian Africa.

What is unique to the Muslim world is not the absence of democracy but the fact that in 1918, after the defeat of the Ottoman Empire, every single Muslim in the world lived under foreign subjugation.

Every single one, from Indonesia to Morocco via Turkey. The Turks threw out their invaders within a few years under the great leadership of Kemal Atatürk, but the transition to self-rule in other Muslim countries was slow, uncertain, and full of traps planted by the world's preeminent powers.

The West, in the shape of Britain, France, or America, was never interested in democracy when a helpful dictator or king would serve. When people got a chance to express their wish, it was only logical that they would ask for popular rule. It was the street that brought Mossadegh to power in Iran and drove the shah of Iran to tearful exile in Rome. Who brought the shah of Iran and autocracy back to Iran? The CIA.

If Iranian democracy had been permitted a chance in 1953, there would have been no uprising led by Ayatollah Khomeini in 1979. In other countries, where the struggle for independence was long and brutal, as in Algeria and Indonesia, the militias who had fought the war institutionalized army authority. In other instances, civilian heroes confused their own well-being with national health. They became regressive dictators. Once again, there was nothing Islamic about it.

Muslim countries will become democracies, too, because it is the finest form of modern governance. But it will be a process interrupted by bloody experience as the street wrenches power from usurpers.

Democracy has happened in Turkey. It has happened in Bangladesh. It is happening in Indonesia. It almost happened in Pakistan, and the opportunity will return. Democracy takes time in the most encouraging environments.

Democracy has become the latest rationale for the occupation of Iraq. . . . Granted, democracy is always preferable to tyranny no matter how it comes. But Iraqis are not dupes. They will take democracy and place it at the service of nationalism. A decade ago, America was careless about the definition of victory. Today it is careless about the definition of democracy.

There is uncertainity and apprehension across the Muslim nations: uncertainty about where they stand, and apprehension about both American power and the repugnant use of terrorism that in turn invites the exercise of American power. There is also anger that a legitimate cause like that of Palestine can get buried in the debris of confusion. Muslims do not see Palestinians as terrorists.

Even in Turkey, generally considered the most secular of Islamic societies, a militant political group, known as the Islamic Welfare Party, took power in a coalition government formed in 1996. The new prime minister, Necmettin Erbakan, adopted a pro-Arab stance in foreign affairs and threatened to reduce the country's economic and political ties to Europe. Worried moderates voiced their concern that the secular legacy of Kemal Atatürk was being eroded, and eventually Erbakan agreed to resign under heavy pressure from the military. Rejected in its application for membership in the European Union and uncomfortable with the militancy of its Arab neighbors, Turkey has established a security relationship with Israel and seeks close ties with the United States. But religious and economic discontent lies just beneath the surface, and Atatürk's own legacy, known as "Kemalism," has come under close scrutiny by critics.

Throughout the Middle East, even governments and individuals who do not support efforts to return to pure Islamic principles have adjusted their behavior and beliefs in subtle ways (see the comparative essay "Religion and Society" on p. 845). In Egypt, for example, the government

## COMPARATIVE ESSAY

# Religion and Society

Religion & Philosophy

The nineteenth and twentieth centuries witnessed a steady trend toward the secularization of society as people increasingly turned from religion to science for an explanation of natural phenomena and for answers to the challenges of everyday life.

In recent years, however, the trend has reversed, as religious faith in all its guises appears to be in a state of revival in much of the world. Although the percentage of people attending religious services on a regular basis or professing firm religious convictions has been dropping steadily in many countries, the intensity of religious belief appears to be growing among the faithful. This phenomenon has been widely publicized in the United States, where the evangelical movement has become a significant force in politics and an influential factor in defining many social issues. But it has also occurred in Latin America, where a drop in membership in the Roman Catholic church has been offset by significant increases in the popularity of evangelical Protestant sects. In the Muslim world, the influence of traditional Islam has been steadily on the rise, not only in the Middle East but also in non-Arab countries like Malaysia and Indonesia (see Chapter 29). Even in Russia and China, where half a century of Communist government sought to eradicate religion as the "opiate of the people," the popularity of religion is growing.

One major reason for the increasing popularity of religion in contemporary life is the desire to counter the widespread sense of malaise brought on by the absence of any sense of meaning and purpose in life—a purpose that religious faith provides. For many evangelical Christians in the United States, for example, the adoption of a Christian lifestyle is seen as a necessary prerequisite for resolving problems of crime, drugs, and social alienation. It is likely that a similar phenomenon is present with other religions and in other parts of the world.

Historical evidence suggests, however, that although religious fervor may serve to enhance the sense of community and commitment among believers, it can have a highly divisive impact on society as a whole, as the examples of Northern Ireland, Yugoslavia, and the Middle East vividly attest. Even if less dramatically, as in the United States, Latin America, and Africa, religion not only unites but also divides, and it will be a continuing task for religious leaders of all faiths to promote tolerance for peoples of other persuasions.

Another challenge for contemporary religion is to find ways to coexist with expanding scientific knowledge. Influential figures in the evangelical movement in the United States, for example, not only support a conservative social agenda but also express a growing suspicion of the role of technology and science in the contemporary world. Similar views are often expressed by significant factions in other world religions. Although fear over the impact of science on contemporary life is widespread, efforts to turn the clock back to a mythical golden age are not likely to succeed in the face of powerful forces for change set in motion by advances in scientific knowledge.

now encourages television programs devoted to religion in preference to comedies and adventure shows imported from the West, and alcohol is discouraged or at least consumed more discreetly. On the other hand, criticism of strict government censorship is on the rise in Iran, and the recent election of a moderate majority in the Iranian parliament may undercut the domination of all aspects of social and cultural life by fundamentalist clerics.

## The Role of Women

Nowhere have the fault lines between tradition and modernity within Muslim societies in the Middle East been so sharp as in the ongoing debate over the role of women. At the beginning of the twentieth century, women's place in Middle Eastern society had changed little since the death of the prophet Muhammad. Women were secluded in their homes and had few legal, political, or social rights.

During the first decades of the twentieth century, advocates of modernist views began to contend that Islamic doctrine was not inherently opposed to women's rights. To modernists, Islamic traditions such as female seclusion, wearing the veil, and even polygamy were actually pre-Islamic folk traditions that had been tolerated in the early Islamic era and continued to be practiced in later centuries. Such views had considerable impact on a number of Middle Eastern societies, including Turkey and Iran. As we have seen, greater rights for women was a crucial element in the social revolution promoted by Kemal Atatürk in Turkey. In Iran, Shah Reza Khan and his son granted female suffrage and encouraged the education of women. In Egypt, a vocal feminist movement arose in educated women's circles in Cairo as early as the 1920s. With the exception of Orthodox religious communities, women in Israel have achieved substantial equality with men and are active in politics, the professions, and even the armed forces. Golda Meir (1898–1978), prime minister of Israel from 1969 to 1974, became an international symbol of the ability of women to be world leaders.

In recent years, a more traditional view of women's role has tended to prevail in many Middle Eastern countries. Attacks by religious conservatives on the growing role of women contributed to the emotions underlying the Iranian Revolution of 1979. Iranian women were

## Keeping the Camel out of the Tent

"Almighty God created sexual desire in ten parts; then he gave nine parts to women and one to men." So pronounced Ali, Muhammad's son-in-law, as he explained why women are held morally responsible as the instigators of sexual intercourse. Consequently, over the centuries, Islamic women have been secluded, veiled, and in many cases genitally mutilated in order to safeguard male virtue. Women are forbidden to look directly at, speak to, or touch a man prior to marriage. Even today, they are often sequestered at home or limited to strictly segregated areas away from all male contact. Women normally pray at home or in an enclosed antechamber of the mosque so that their physical presence will not disturb men's spiritual concentration.

Especially limiting today are the laws governing women's behavior in Saudi Arabia. Schooling for girls has never been compulsory because fathers believe that "educating women is like allowing the nose of the camel into the tent; eventually the beast will edge in and take up all the room inside." The country did not establish its first girls' school until 1956. The following description of Saudi women is from *Nine Parts Desire: The Hidden World of Islamic Women,* by the journalist Geraldine Brooks.

*According to the author of this passage, do women in Saudi Arabia have an opportunity to receive an education? To what degree do they take an advantage of it?*

### Geraldine Brooks, *Nine Parts Desire*

Women were first admitted to university in Saudi Arabia in 1962, and all women's colleges remain strictly segregated. Lecture rooms come equipped with closed-circuit TVs and telephones, so women students can listen to a male professor and question him by phone, without having to contaminate themselves by being seen by him. When the first dozen women graduated from university in 1973, they were devastated to find that their names hadn't been printed on the commencement program. The old tradition, that it dishonors women to mention them, was depriving them of recognition they believed they'd earned. The women and their families protested, so a separate program was printed and a segregated graduation ceremony was held for the students' female relatives. . . .

But while the opening of women's universities widened access to higher learning for women, it also made the educational experience much shallower. Before 1962, many progressive Saudi families had sent their daughters abroad for education. They had returned to the kingdom not only with a degree but with experience of the outside world. . . . Now a whole generation of Saudi women have completed their education entirely within the country. . . .

Lack of opportunity for education abroad means that Saudi women are trapped in the confines of an education system that still lags men's. Subjects such as geology and petroleum engineering–tickets to influential jobs in Saudi Arabia's oil economy–remain closed to women. . . . Few women's colleges have their own libraries, and libraries shared with men's schools are either entirely off limits to women or open to them only one day per week. . . .

But women and men sit the same degree examinations. Professors quietly acknowledge the women's scores routinely outstrip the men's. "It's no surprise," said one woman professor. "Look at their lives. The boys have their cars, they can spend the evenings cruising the streets with their friends, sitting in cafés, buying black-market alcohol and drinking all night. What do the girls have? Four walls and their books. For them, education is everything."

instructed to wear the veil and to dress modestly in public. Films produced in postrevolutionary Iran rarely featured women, and when they did, physical contact between men and women was prohibited. The events in Iran had repercussions in secular Muslim societies such as Egypt, Turkey, and far-off Malaysia, where women began to dress more modestly in public and criticism of open sexuality in the media became increasingly frequent.

The most conservative nation by far remains Saudi Arabia, where women are not only segregated and expected to wear the veil in public, but are also restricted in education and forbidden to drive automobiles (see the box above). Still, women's rights have been extended in a few countries. In 1999, women obtained the right to vote in Kuwait, and they have been granted an equal right with their husbands to seek a divorce in Egypt. Even in Iran, women have many freedoms that they lacked before the twentieth century; for example, they can receive military training, vote, practice birth control, and publish fiction. Most important, today nearly 60 percent of university entrants in Iran are women. Recently, supporters of the moderate president Mohammed Khatemi have proposed that women be permitted to play a greater role in the political process. Some have even gone on the offensive to promote their cause. In Morocco, sociologist Fatima Mernissi has studied the sacred texts to demonstrate how Islam's male establishment has distorted the Prophet's message over the centuries as a political weapon to dominate women and keep them behind locked doors.

## Literature and Art

As in other areas of Asia and Africa, the encounter with the West in the nineteenth and twentieth centuries stimulated a cultural renaissance in the Middle East. Muslim authors translated Western works into Arabic and Persian and began to experiment with new literary forms.

**National Literatures** Iran has produced one of the most prominent national literatures in the contemporary Middle East. Since World War II, Iranian literature has been hampered somewhat by political considerations, since it has been expected to serve first the Pahlavi monarchy and then the Islamic republic. Nevertheless, Iranian writers are among the most prolific in the region and often write in prose, which has finally been accepted as the equal of poetry. Perhaps the most outstanding Iranian author of the twentieth century was the short story writer Sadeq Hedayat. Hedayat was obsessed with the frailty and absurdity of life and wrote with compassion about the problems of ordinary human beings. Frustrated and disillusioned at the government's suppression of individual liberties, he committed suicide in 1951. Like Japan's Mishima Yukio, Hedayat later became a cult figure among his country's youth.

Despite the male-oriented character of Iranian society, many of the new writers have been women. Since the revolution, the veil and the *chador,* an all-enveloping cloak, have become the central metaphor in Iranian women's writing. Those who favor body covering praise it as the last bastion of defense against Western cultural imperialism. Behind the veil, the Islamic woman can breathe freely, unpolluted by foreign exploitation and moral corruption. Other Iranian women, however, consider the veil and *chador* a "mobile prison" or an oppressive anachronism from the Dark Ages. As one writer, Sousan Azadi, expressed it, "As I pulled the chador over me, I felt a heaviness descending over me. I was hidden and in hiding. There was nothing visible left of Sousan Azadi. I felt like an animal of the light suddenly trapped in a cave. I was just another faceless Moslem woman carrying a whole inner world hidden inside the *chador.*"[13] Whether or not they accept the veil, women writers are a vital part of contemporary Iranian literature, addressing all aspects of social issues.

Like Iran, Egypt in the twentieth century has experienced a flowering of literature accelerated by the establishment of the Egyptian republic in the early 1950s. The most illustrious contemporary Egyptian writer is Naguib Mahfouz, who won the Nobel Prize for literature in 1988. His *Cairo Trilogy* (1952) chronicles three generations of a merchant family in Cairo during the tumultuous years between the world wars. Mahfouz is particularly adept at blending panoramic historical events with the intimate lives of ordinary human beings. Unlike many other modern writers, his message is essentially optimistic and reflects his hope that religion and science can work together for the overall betterment of humankind. No woman writer has played a more active role in exposing the physical and psychological grievances of Egyptian women than Nawal el-Saadawi. Since publication of her explosive book *The Hidden Face of Eve* (1980), she has battled against the injustices of religious fundamentalism and a male-dominated society, even enduring imprisonment for promoting her cause.

Although Israeli literature arises from a totally different tradition from that of its neighbors, it shares with them certain contemporary characteristics and a concern for ordinary human beings. Early writers identified with the aspirations of the new nation, trying to find a sense of order in the new reality, voicing terrors from the past and hopes for the future. Some contemporary Israeli authors, however, have refused to serve as standard-bearers for Zionism and are speaking out on sensitive national issues. The internationally renowned novelist Amos Oz, for example, is a vocal supporter of peace with the Palestinians. Oz is a member of Peace Now and the author of a political tract titled *Israel, Palestine, and Peace.* In a 2002 interview, Oz accused both Ariel Sharon and Yasir Arafat of being "immovable, handcuffed to the past and to each other."[14] With the Arabs feeling victimized by colonialism and the Jews by Nazi Germany, each side believes that it alone is the rightful proprietor of ancient Palestine. For Oz, the only solution is compromise, which, however unsatisfactory for both sides, is preferable to mutual self-destruction.

As in other areas of the developing world, the reading of books has drastically declined in the Middle East, eclipsed by television and other forms of popular entertainment and discouraged by poverty and by government censorship reflecting political control or religious conservatism. The old maxim that "Cairo writes, Beirut publishes, and Baghdad reads" is no longer true. In Egypt, where even *The Tales from the 1001 Nights* is banned, the government censors most new fiction, while in Iraq, severe inflation has made the purchase price of books prohibitive. Another problem stems from the fact that the one common language of the Middle East—classical Arabic—is not conducive to expressing contemporary life, since it is as old-fashioned as Shakespearean English. Yet if they choose to write in their national Arabic dialects, authors greatly restrict their audience within the region.

**Art and Music** Like literature, the art of the modern Middle East has been profoundly influenced by its exposure to Western culture. At first, artists tended to imitate Western models, but later they began to experiment with national styles, returning to earlier forms for inspiration. Some emulated the writers in returning to the village to depict peasants and shepherds, but others followed international trends and attempted to express the alienation and disillusionment that characterize so much of modern life.

The popular music of the contemporary Middle East has also been strongly influenced by that of the modern West, but to different degrees in different countries. In Israel, many contemporary young rock stars voice lyrics as irreverent toward the traditions of their elders as those of Europe and the United States. One idol of many Israeli young people, the rock star Aviv Ghefen, declares himself "a person of no values," and his music carries a shock value that attacks the country's political and social shibboleths. The rock music popular among Palestinians, on the other hand, makes greater use of Arab musical motifs and is closely tied to a political message. One recording, "The Song of the Engineer," lauds Yehia Ayash, a Palestinian accused of manufacturing many of the explosive devices used in terrorist attacks on Israeli citizens. The lyrics have their own shock value: "Spread the flame of revolution. Your explosive will wipe the enemy out, like a volcano, a torch, a banner." When one Palestinian rock leader from the Gaza Strip was asked why his group employed a musical style that originated in the West, he explained, "For us, this is a tool like any other. Young people in Gaza like our music, they listen to us, they buy our cassettes, and so they spread our message."

## CONCLUSION

The Middle East, like the continent of Africa, is one of the most unstable regions in the world today. In part, this turbulence is due to the continued interference of outsiders attracted by the massive oil reserves under the parched wastes of the Arabian peninsula and in the vicinity of the Persian Gulf. Oil is indeed both a blessing and a curse to the peoples of the region.

Another factor contributing to the volatility of the Middle East is the tug-of-war between the sense of ethnic identity in the form of nationalism and the intense longing to be part of a broader Islamic community, a dream that dates back to the time of the prophet Muhammad.

The desire to create that community–a vision threatened by the presence of the alien state of Israel–inspired Gamal Abdul Nasser in the 1950s and Ayatollah Khomeini in the 1970s and 1980s and probably motivates many of the actions of Osama bin Laden and other less radical Islamic purists today.

A final reason for the turmoil currently affecting the Middle East is the intense debate over the role of religion in civil society. Although efforts in various Muslim countries to return to an allegedly purer form of Islam appear harsh and even repugnant to many observers, it is important to note that Muslim societies are not alone in deploring the sense of moral decline that is now allegedly taking place in societies throughout the world. Nor are they alone in advocating a restoration of traditional religious values as a means of reversing the trend. Movements dedicated to such purposes are appearing in many other societies (including Israel and the United States) and can be viewed as an understandable reaction to the rapid and often bewildering changes taking place in the contemporary world. Not infrequently, members of such groups turn to violence as a means of making their point.

Whatever the reasons, it is clear that a deep-seated sense of anger is surging through much of the Islamic world today, an anger that transcends specific issues like the situation in Iraq or the Arab-Israeli dispute. Although economic privation and political oppression are undoubtedly important factors, the roots of Muslim resentment, as the historian Bernard Lewis has pointed out, lie in a historical sense of humiliation at the hands of a Western colonialism that first emerged centuries ago, when the Arab hegemony in the Mediterranean region was replaced by European domination, and culminated early in the twentieth century, when much of the Middle East was occupied by Western colonial regimes. Today the world is reaping the harvest of that long-cultivated bitterness, and the consequences cannot be foreseen.

## CHAPTER NOTES


1. Quoted in G.-C. M. Mutiso, *Socio-Political Thought in African Literature* (New York, 1974), p. 117.
2. A. Ojuka, "Pedestrian, to Passing Benz-Man," quoted in A. Roscoe, *Uhuru's Fire: African Literature East to South* (Cambridge, 1977), p. 103.
3. Taban Lo Liyong, "Student's Lament," quoted in Roscoe, *Uhuru's Fire*, pp. 120–121.
4. D. Agbee, quoted in *World Press Review*, August 1991, p. 16.
5. K. Little, *African Women in Towns: An Aspect of Africa's Social Revolution* (Cambridge, 1973), p. 6.
6. A. Nicol, *A Truly Married Woman and Other Stories* (London, 1965), p. 12.
7. A. Ata Aidoo, *No Sweetness Here* (New York, 1995), p. 136.
8. G. Médioni, "Stand Up, Africa!" *World Press Review*, July 2002, p. 34.
9. Ngugi Wa Thiong'o, *Decolonising the Mind: The Politics of Language in African Literature* (Portsmouth, N.H., 1986), p. 103.
10. G. Awoonor-Williams, *Rediscovery and Other Poems* (Ibadan, Nigeria, 1964), quoted in Mutiso, pp. 81-82.
11. Quoted in R. R. Andersen, R. F. Seibert, and J. G. Wagner, *Politics and Change in the Middle East: Sources of Conflict and Accommodation*, 4th ed. (Englewood Cliffs, N.J., 1982), p. 51.
12. Susan Sachs, "Assad Looks at Syria's Economy in Inaugural Talk," in *New York Times*, July 18, 2000.
13. S. Azadi, with A. Ferrante, *Out of Iran* (London, 1987), p. 223.
14. A. Oz, *Jim Lehrer NewsHour, PBS*, January 23, 2002.

## TIMELINE

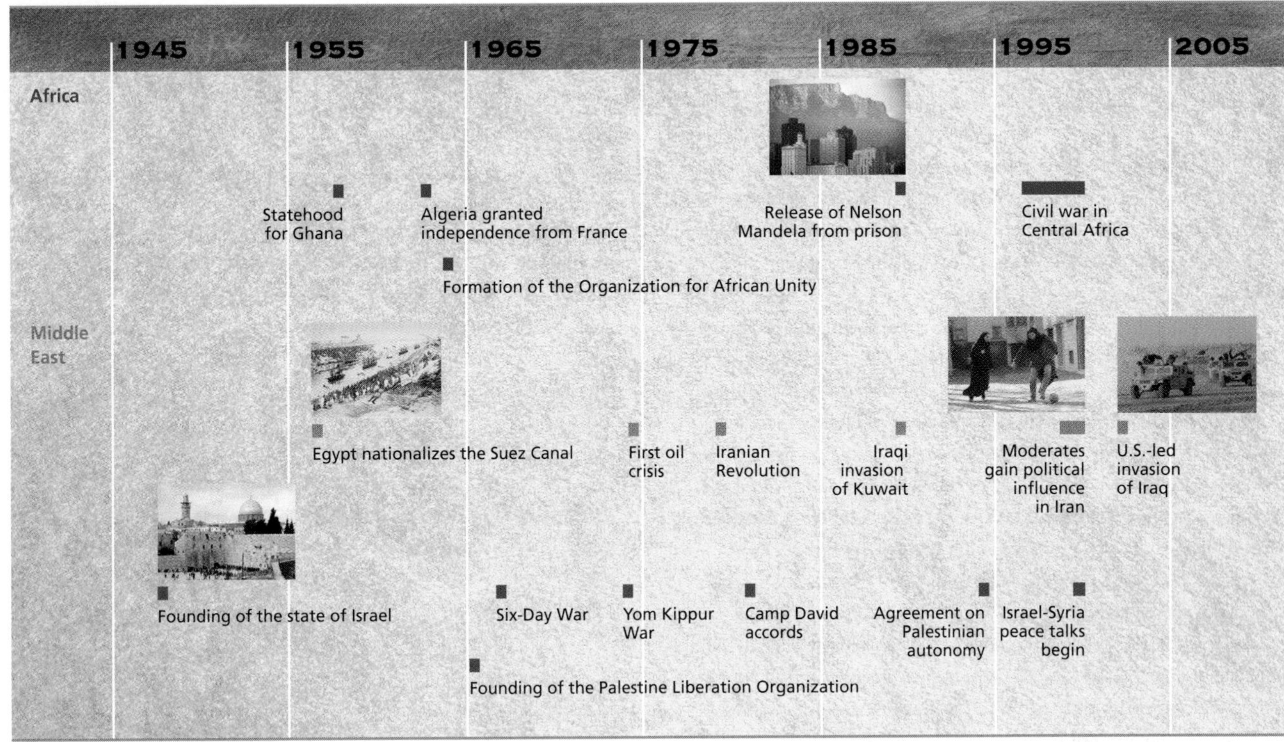


## SUGGESTED READING

For a general survey of contemporary African history, see **R. Oliver, *The African Experience*** (New York, 1992), which contains interesting essays on a variety of themes, and **K. Shillington, *History of Africa*** (New York, 1989), which takes a chronological and geographical approach and includes excellent maps and illustrations.

Two excellent treatments by preeminent historians of the African continent are **B. Davidson, *Africa in History: Themes and Outlines*,** rev. ed. (New York, 1991), and **P. Curtin** et al., ***African History*** (London, 1995). Also see **H. French, *A Continent for the Taking: The Tragedy and Hope of Africa*** (New York, 2004).

On nationalist movements, see **P. Gifford** and **W. R. Louis,** eds., ***The Transfer of Power in Africa*** (New Haven, Conn., 1982), and **J. D. Hargreaves, *Decolonisation in Africa*** (London, 1988). Also see **D. Birmingham, *Kwame Nkrumah: The Father of African Nationalism*** (Athens, Ohio, 1998). For a poignant analysis of the hidden costs of nation building, see **N. F. Mostert, *The Epic of South Africa's Creation and the Tragedy of the Xhosa People*** (London, 1992). Also see **A. Mazrui** and **M. Tidy, *Nationalism and New States in Africa*** (Portsmouth, N.H., 1984), and **S. Decalo, *Coups and Army Rule in Africa*** (New Haven, Conn., 1990).

For a survey of economic conditions in Africa, see ***Sub-Saharan Africa: From Crisis to Sustainable Growth*** (Washington, D.C., 1989), issued by the World Bank. Also see **A. O'Connor, *The African City*** (London, 1983), and **J. Illiffe, *The African Poor*** (Cambridge, 1983).

For a survey of African literature, see **O. Owomoyela,** ed., ***A History of Twentieth-Century African Literatures*** (Lincoln, Nebr., 1993); **M. J. Hay, *African Novels in the Classroom*** (Boulder, Colo., 2000); and **M. J. Daymond** et al., eds. ***Women Writing Africa: The Southern Region*** (New York, 2003). On art, see **S. L. Kasfir, *Contemporary African Art*** (London, 1999).

For interesting analyses of women's issues in the Africa of this time frame, see **S. B. Stichter** and **J. L. Parpart,** eds., ***Patriarchy and Class: African Women in the Home and the Workforce*** (Boulder, Colo., 1988), and **M. Kevane, *Women and Development in Africa: How Gender Works*** (Boulder, Colo., 2004).

For contrasting views on the reasons for Africa's current difficulties, see **J. Marah, *The African People in the Global Village: An Introduction to Pan-African Studies*** (Lanham, Md., 1998), and **G. Ayittey, *Africa in Chaos*** (New York, 1998).

Good general surveys of the modern Middle East include **A. Goldschmidt Jr., *A Concise History of the Middle East*** (Boulder, Colo., 1991), and **G. E. Perry, *The Middle East: Fourteen Islamic Centuries*** (Elizabeth, N.J., 1992).

On Israel and the Palestinian question, see **D. Ross, *The Missing Peace: The Inside Story of the Fight for Middle East Peace*** (New York, 2004). On Jerusalem, see **B. Wasserstein, *Divided Jerusalem: The Struggle for the Holy City*** (New Haven, Conn., 2000).

The issue of oil is examined in **G. Luciani, *The Oil Companies and the Arab World*** (New York, 1984), and **P. Odell, *Oil and World Power*** (New York, 1986). Also see **M. H. Kerr** and **E. S. Yassin,** eds., ***Rich and Poor States in the Middle East: Egypt and the New Arab Order*** (Boulder, Colo., 1985).

On the Iranian Revolution, see **S. Bakash, *The Reign of the Ayatollahs*** (New York, 1984), and **B. Rubin, *Iran Since the***

***Revolution*** (Boulder, Colo., 1985). On Ayatollah Khomeini's role and ideas, see **H. Algar, *Islam and Revolution: The Writings and Declarations of Imam Khomeini*** (Berkeley, Calif., 1981). The Iran-Iraq War is discussed in **C. Davies,** ed., ***After the War: Iran, Iraq and the Arab Gulf*** (Chichester, England, 1990), and **S. C. Pelletiere, *The Iran-Iraq War: Chaos in a Vacuum*** (New York, 1992).

For historical perspective on the invasion of Iraq, see **J. Kendell, *Iraq's Unruly Century*** (New York, 2003). **R. Khalidi's *Resurrecting Empire: Western Footprints and America's Perilous Path in the Middle East*** (Boston, 2003), is a critical look at U. S. policy in the region.

On the politics of the Middle East, see **J. A. Bill** and **R. Springborg, *Politics in the Middle East*** (London, 1990), and **R. R. Anderson, R. F. Seibert,** and **J. G. Wagner, *Politics and Change in the Middle East: Sources of Conflict and Accommodation*** (Englewood Cliffs, N.J., 1993). For expert analysis on the current situation in the region, see **B. Lewis, *What Went Wrong? Western Impact and Middle Eastern Response*** (Oxford, 2001), and **P. L. Bergen, *Holy War, Inc.: Inside the Secret World of Osama bin Laden*** (New York, 2001).

Two excellent surveys of women in Islam from pre-Islamic society to the present are **L. Ahmed, *Women and Gender in Islam: Historical Roots of a Modern Debate*** (New Haven, Conn., 1993), and **G. Nashat** and **J. E. Tucker, *Women in the Middle East and North Africa*** (Bloomington, Ind., 1999). Also consult **M. Afkhami** and **E. Friedl, *In the Eye of the Storm: Women in Post-Revolutionary Iran*** (Syracuse, N.Y., 1994), and **W. Wiebke, *Women in Islam*** (Princeton, N.J., 1995).

For a scholarly but accessible overview of Arabic literature, see **M. M. Badawi, *A Short History of Modern Arab Literature*** (Oxford, 1993). For Iranian literature, see **S. Sullivan** and **F. Milani, *Stories by Iranian Women Since the Revolution*** (Austin, Tex., 1991), and **M. M. Khorrami** and **S. Vatanabadi,** eds., ***A Feast in the Mirror: Short Stories by Contemporary Iranian Women*** (Boulder, Colo., 2000).

## History Now™

**Enter *HistoryNow* using the access card that is available with this text. *HistoryNow* will assist you in understanding the content in this chapter with lesson plans generated for your needs, as well as provide you with a connection to the *Wadsworth World History Resource Center* (see description below for details).**

## WORLD HISTORY RESOURCE CENTER

**Enter the Resource Center using either your *HistoryNow* access card or your standalone access card for the *Wadsworth World History Resource Center.* Organized by topic, this website includes quizzes; images; over 350 primary source documents; interactive simulations; maps and timelines; movie explorations; and a wealth of other resources. You can read the following documents, and many more, at http://history.wadsworth.com/rc/world**

A. L. Geyer, "The Case for Apartheid"

Speeches by Nelson Mandela

Visit the *World History* Companion Website for chapter quizzes and more.

**http://history.wadsworth.com/duikerspielvogel05/**

CHAPTER

# 29

# TOWARD THE PACIFIC CENTURY?

## CHAPTER OUTLINE AND FOCUS QUESTIONS

### South Asia

- How did Mahatma Gandhi's and Jawaharlal Nehru's goals for India differ, and what role has each leader's views played in shaping modern India?

### Southeast Asia

- What kinds of problems have the nations of Southeast Asia faced since 1945, and how have they attempted to solve these problems?

### East Asia

- How did the Allied occupation after World War II change Japan's political and economic institutions, and what remained unchanged?

### CRITICAL THINKING

- What factors have contributed to the economic successes achieved by Japan and the "Little Tigers" in recent years? Have the nations of South and Southeast Asia achieved the same results?

Courtesy of William J. Duiker

*Hong Kong: symbol of the Pacific century*

**FIRST-TIME VISITORS** to the Malaysian capital of Kuala Lumpur are astonished to observe a pair of twin towers thrusting up above the surrounding buildings into the clouds. The Petronas Towers rise 1,483 feet from ground level, leading to claims by Malaysian officials that they are the world's tallest buildings, at least for the time being.

More than an architectural achievement, the towers announced the emergence of Southeast Asia as a major player on the international scene. It is probably no accident that the foundations were laid on the site of the Selangor Cricket Club, symbol of colonial hegemony in Southeast Asia. "These towers," commented one local official, "will do wonders for Asia's self-esteem and confidence, which I think is very important, and which I think at this moment are at the point of takeoff."[1]

The Petronas Towers in Kuala Lumpur are only one symbol of the emergence of Asia as a major player in global politics in the century now unfolding. Several other cities in the region, including Hong Kong, Singapore, Tokyo, and Shanghai, have become major capitals of finance and monuments of economic prowess, rivaling traditional centers like New York, London, Berlin, and Paris. Together, they herald the opening of what has been called "the Pacific Century." ◇

## South Asia

In 1947, nearly two centuries of British colonial rule came to an end when two new independent nations, India and Pakistan, came into being. Under British authority, the subcontinent of South Asia had been linked ever more closely to the global capitalist economy. Yet as in other areas of Asia and Africa, the experience brought only limited benefits to the local peoples; little industrial development took place, and the bulk of the profits went into the pockets of Western entrepeneurs.

For half a century, nationalist forces had been seeking reforms in colonial policy and the eventual overthrow of colonial power. But the peoples of South Asia did not regain their independence until after World War II.

### The End of the British Raj

During the 1930s, the nationalist movement in India was severely shaken by factional disagreements between Hindus and Muslims. The outbreak of World War II subdued these sectarian clashes, but they erupted again after the war ended in 1945. Battles between Hindus and Muslims broke out in several cities, and Mohammed Ali Jinnah, leader of the Muslim League, demanded the creation of a separate state for each. Meanwhile, the Labour Party, which had long been critical of the British colonial legacy on both moral and economic grounds, had come to power in Britain, and the new prime minister, Clement Attlee, announced that power would be transferred to "responsible Indian hands" by June 1948.

But the imminence of independence did not dampen communal strife. As riots escalated, the British reluctantly accepted the inevitability of partition and declared that on August 15, 1947, two independent nations—Hindu India and Muslim Pakistan—would be established. Pakistan would be divided between the main area of Muslim habitation in the Indus River valley in the west and a separate territory in east Bengal 2,000 miles to the east. Although Mahatma Gandhi warned that partition would provoke "an orgy of blood,"[2] he was increasingly regarded as a figure of the past, and his views were ignored.

The British instructed the rulers in the princely states to choose which nation they would join by August 15, but problems arose in predominantly Hindu Hyderabad, where the governor was a Muslim, and the mountainous province of Jammu and Kashmir, usually referred to simply as Kashmir, where a Hindu prince ruled over a Muslim population. After independence was declared, the flight of millions of Hindus and Muslims across the borders led to violence and the death of more than a million people. One of the casualties was Gandhi, who was assassinated on January 30, 1948, as he was going to morning prayer. The assassin, a Hindu militant, was apparently motivated by Gandhi's opposition to a strictly Hindu India.

### Independent India

With independence, the Indian National Congress, now renamed the Congress Party, moved from opposition to the responsibility of power under Jawaharlal Nehru, the new prime minister. The prospect must have been intimidating. The vast majority of India's 400 million people were poor and illiterate. The new nation encompassed a bewildering number of ethnic groups and fourteen major languages. Although Congress leaders spoke bravely of building a new nation, Indian society still bore the scars of past wars and divisions.

The government's first problem was to resolve disputes left over from the transition period. The rulers of Hyderabad and Kashmir had both followed their own preferences rather than the wishes of their subject populations. Nehru was determined to include both states within India. In 1948, Indian troops invaded Hyderabad and annexed the area. India was also able to seize most of Kashmir, but at the cost of creating an intractable problem that has poisoned relations with Pakistan to the present day.

**An Experiment in Democratic Socialism** Under Nehru's leadership, India adopted a political system on the British model, with a figurehead president and a parliamentary form of government. A number of political parties operated legally, but the Congress Party, with its enormous prestige and charismatic leadership, was dominant at both the central and local levels.

Nehru had been influenced by British socialism and patterned his economic policy roughly after the program of the British Labour Party. The state took over ownership of the major industries and resources, transportation, and utilities, while private enterprise was permitted at the local and retail levels. Farmland remained in private hands, but rural cooperatives were officially encouraged. The government also sought to avoid excessive dependence on foreign investment and technological assistance. All businesses were required by law to have majority Indian ownership.

In other respects, Nehru was a devotee of Western materialism. He was convinced that to succeed, India must industrialize. In advocating industrialization, Nehru departed sharply from Gandhi, who believed that materialism was morally corrupting and that only simplicity and nonviolence (as represented by the traditional Indian village and the symbolic spinning wheel) could save India, and the world itself, from self-destruction (see the box on p. 854).

The primary themes of Nehru's foreign policy were anticolonialism and antiracism. Under his guidance, India took a neutral stance in the Cold War and sought to provide leadership to all newly independent nations in Asia, Africa, and Latin America. India's neutrality put it at odds with the United States, which during the 1950s was

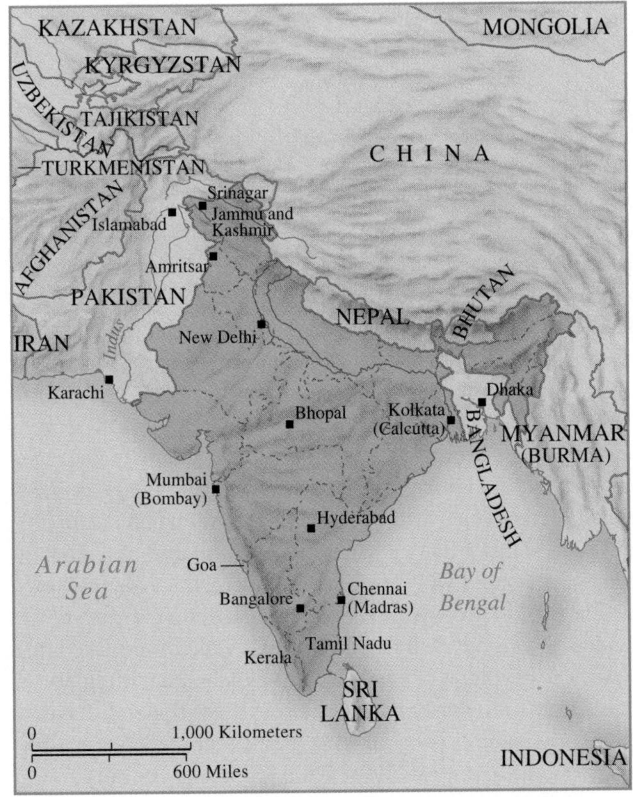


**MAP 29.1 Modern South Asia.** This map shows the boundaries of all the states in contemporary South Asia. India, the largest in area and population, is highlighted by darker shading. ? Which of the countries on this map have a Muslim majority? **View an animated version of this map or related maps at** http://history.wadsworth.com/duikerspielvogel05/

trying to mobilize all nations against what it viewed as the menace of international communism.

Relations with Pakistan continued to be troubled. India refused to consider Pakistan's claim to Kashmir, even though the majority of the population there was Muslim. Tension between the two countries persisted, erupting into war in 1965. In 1971, when riots against the Pakistani government broke out in East Pakistan, India intervened on the side of East Pakistan, which declared its independence as the new nation of Bangladesh (see Map 29.1).

**The Post-Nehru Era** Nehru's death in 1964 aroused concern that Indian democracy was dependent on the Nehru mystique. When his successor, a Congress Party veteran, died in 1966, Congress leaders selected Nehru's daughter, Indira Gandhi (no relation to Mahatma Gandhi), as the new prime minister. Gandhi was inexperienced in politics, but she quickly showed the steely determination of her father.

Like Nehru, Gandhi embraced democratic socialism and a policy of neutrality in foreign affairs, but she was more activist than her father. To combat rural poverty, she nationalized banks, provided loans to peasants on easy terms, built low-cost housing, distributed land to the landless, and introduced electoral reforms to enfranchise the poor.

Gandhi was especially worried by India's growing population and in an effort to curb the growth rate adopted a policy of enforced sterilization. This policy proved unpopular, however, and, along with growing official corruption and Gandhi's authoritarian tactics, led to her defeat in the general election of 1975, the first time the Congress Party had failed to win a majority at the national level.

Courtesy of William J. Duiker

**India's Hope, India's Sorrow.** In India, as in many other societies in Southern Asia, overpopulation is a serious obstacle to economic development. The problem is particularly serious in large cities where thousands of poor children are forced into begging or prostitution. Shown here are a few of the thousands of street children in the commercial hub of Mumbai (Bombay). With the Indian economy experiencing rapid growth, the national government is aggressively addressing the issue of poverty.

## Two Visions for India

Although Jawaharlal Nehru and Mohandas Gandhi agreed on their desire for an independent India, their visions of the future of their homeland were dramatically different. Nehru favored industrialization to build material prosperity, whereas Gandhi praised the simple virtues of manual labor. The first excerpt is from a speech by Nehru; the second is from a letter written by Gandhi to Nehru.

*What are the key differences between these two views on the future of India? Why do you think Nehru's proposals triumphed over those of Mahatma Gandhi?*

### Nehru's Socialist Creed

I am convinced that the only key to the solution of the world's problems and of India's problems lies in socialism, and when I use this word I do so not in a vague humanitarian way but in the scientific economic sense. . . . I see no way of ending the poverty, the vast unemployment, the degradation and the subjection of the Indian people except through socialism. That involves vast and revolutionary changes in our political and social structure, the ending of vested interests in land and industry, as well as the feudal and autocratic Indian states system. That means the ending of private property, except in a restricted sense, and the replacement of the present profit system by a higher ideal of cooperative service. . . . In short, it means a new civilization, radically different from the present capitalist order. Some glimpse we can have of this new civilization in the territories of the USSR. Much has happened there which has pained me greatly and with which I disagree, but I look upon that great and fascinating unfolding of a new order and a new civilization as the most promising feature of our dismal age.

### Mohandas Gandhi, A Letter to Jawaharlal Nehru

I believe that if India, and through India the world, is to achieve real freedom, then sooner or later we shall have to go and live in the villages—in huts, not in palaces. Millions of people can never live in cities and palaces in comfort and peace. Nor can they do so by killing one another, that is, by resorting to violence and untruth. . . . We can have the vision of . . . truth and nonviolence only in the simplicity of the villages. That simplicity resides in the spinning wheel and what is implied by the spinning wheel. . . .

You will not be able to understand me if you think that I am talking about the villages of today. My ideal village still exists only in my imagination. . . . In this village of my dreams the villager will not be dull—he will be all awareness. He will not live like an animal in filth and darkness. Men and women will live in freedom, prepared to face the whole world. There will be no plague, no cholera, and no smallpox. Nobody will be allowed to be idle or to wallow in luxury. Everyone will have to do body labor. Granting all this, I can still envisage a number of things that will have to be organized on a large scale. Perhaps there will even be railways and also post and telegraph offices. I do not know what things there will be or will not be. Nor am I bothered about it. If I can make sure of the essential thing, other things will follow in due course. But if I give up the essential thing, I give up everything.

History Now™ To read more of Nehru's writings, enter the *HistoryNow* documents area using the access card that is available for *World History.*

A minority government of procapitalist parties was formed, but within two years, Gandhi was back in power. She now faced a new challenge, however, in the rise of religious strife. The most dangerous situation was in the Punjab, located in the border regions between India and Pakistan, where militant Sikhs were demanding autonomy or even independence from India. Gandhi did not shrink from a confrontation and attacked Sikh rebels hiding in their Golden Temple in the city of Amritsar. The incident aroused widespread anger among the Sikh community, and in 1984, Sikh members of Gandhi's personal bodyguard assassinated her.

By now, Congress politicians were convinced that the party could not remain in power without a member of the Nehru family at the helm. Gandhi's son Rajiv, a commercial airline pilot with little interest in politics, was persuaded to replace his mother as prime minister. Rajiv lacked the strong ideological and political convictions of his mother and grandfather and allowed a greater role for private enterprise. But his government was criticized for cronyism, inefficiency, and corruption, as well as insensitivity to the poor.

Rajiv Gandhi also sought to play a role in regional affairs, mediating a dispute between the government in Sri Lanka and Tamil rebels (known as the "Elam Tigers") who were ethnically related to the majority population in southern India. The decision cost him his life: while campaigning for reelection in 1991, he was assassinated by a member of the Tiger organization. India faced the future without a member of the Nehru family as prime minister.

During the early 1990s, Congress remained the leading party, but the powerful hold it had once had on the Indian electorate was gone. New parties, such as the militantly Hindu Bharata Janata Party (BJP), actively vied with Congress for control of the central and state governments. Growing political instability at the center was accompanied by rising tensions between Hindus and Muslims.

When a coalition government formed under Congress leadership collapsed, the BJP, under Prime Minister A. B. Vajpayee, ascended to power and played on Hindu sensibilities to build its political base. The new government based its success on an aggressive program of privatization in the industrial and commercial sectors and made a major effort to support the nation's small but growing technological base. But BJP leaders had underestimated the discontent of India's less affluent citizens (an estimated 350 million Indians earn less than one U.S. dollar a day), and in the spring of 2004, a stunning defeat in national elections forced the Vajpayee government to resign. The Congress Party returned to power at the head of a coalition government based on a commitment to maintain economic growth while carrying out reforms in rural areas.

**CHRONOLOGY South Asia**

| | |
|---|---|
| India and Pakistan become independent | 1947 |
| Assassination of Mahatma Gandhi | 1948 |
| Death of Jawaharlal Nehru | 1964 |
| Indo-Pakistani War | 1965 |
| Indira Gandhi elected prime minister | 1966 |
| Bangladesh declares its independence | 1971 |
| Assassination of Indira Gandhi | 1984 |
| Rajiv Gandhi assassinated | 1991 |
| Destruction of mosque at Ayodhya | 1992 |
| Benazir Bhutto removed from power in Pakistan | 1997 |
| Military coup overthrows civilian government in Pakistan | 1999 |
| U.S.-led forces oust Taliban in Afghanistan | 2001 |
| Congress Party returns to power in India | 2004 |

## The Land of the Pure: Pakistan Since Independence

When in August 1947, Pakistan achieved independence, it was, unlike its neighbor India, in all respects a new nation, based on religious conviction rather than historical or ethnic tradition. The unique state consisted of two separate territories 2,000 miles apart. West Pakistan, including the Indus River basin and the West Punjab, was perennially short of water and was populated by dry crop farmers and peoples of the steppe. East Pakistan was made up of the marshy deltas of the Ganges and Brahmaputra Rivers. Densely populated with rice farmers, it was the home of the artistic and intellectual Bengalis.

Even though the new state was an essentially Muslim society, its first years were marked by intense internal conflicts over religious, linguistic, and regional issues. Mohammed Ali Jinnah's vision of a democratic state that would assure freedom of religion and equal treatment for all was opposed by those who advocated a state based on Islamic principles.

Even more dangerous was the division between east and west. Many in East Pakistan felt that the government, based in the west, ignored their needs. In 1952, riots erupted in East Pakistan over the government's decision to adopt Urdu, a language derived from Hindi and used by Muslims in northern India, as the national language of the entire country. Most East Pakistanis spoke Bengali, an unrelated language. Tensions persisted, and in March 1971, East Pakistan declared its independence as the new nation of Bangladesh. Pakistani troops attempted to restore central government authority in the capital of Dhaka, but rebel forces supported by India went on the offensive, and the government bowed to the inevitable and recognized independent Bangladesh.

The breakup of the union between East and West Pakistan undermined the fragile authority of the military regime that had ruled Pakistan since 1958 and led to its replacement by a civilian government under Zulfikar Ali Bhutto. But now religious tensions came to the fore, despite a new constitution that made a number of key concessions to conservative Muslims. In 1977, a new military government under General Zia Ul Ha'q came to power with a commitment to make Pakistan a truly Islamic state. Islamic law became the basis for social behavior as well as for the legal system. Laws governing the consumption of alcohol and the role of women were tightened in accordance with strict Muslim beliefs. But after Zia was killed in a plane crash, Pakistanis elected Benazir Bhutto, the daughter of Zulfikar Ali Bhutto and a supporter of secularism who had been educated in the United States. She too was removed from power by a military regime, in 1990, on charges of incompetence and corruption. Reelected in 1993, she attempted to crack down on opposition forces but was removed once again amid renewed charges of official corruption. Her successor soon came under fire for the same reason and in 1999 was ousted by a military coup led by General Pervaiz Musharraf, who promised to restore political stability and honest government.

In September 2001, Pakistan became the focus of international attention when a coalition of forces arrived in Afghanistan to overthrow the Taliban regime and destroy the al-Qaeda terrorist network. Despite considerable support for the Taliban among the local population, President Musharraf pledged his help in bringing terrorists to justice. He also promised to return his country to the secular principles espoused by Mohammed Ali Jinnah. His situation was complicated by renewed tensions with India over Kashmir and a series of violent clashes between Muslims and Hindus in India. In 2003, however, relations began to improve as both sides promised to seek a peaceful solution to the Kashmir dispute.

## Poverty and Pluralism in South Asia

The leaders of the new states that emerged in South Asia after World War II faced a number of problems. The peoples of South Asia were still overwhelmingly poor and illiterate, while the sectarian, ethnic, and cultural divisions that had plagued Indian society for centuries had not dissipated.

**The Politics of Communalism** Perhaps the most sincere effort to create democratic instititutions was in India, where the new constitution called for social justice, liberty, equality of status and opportunity, and brotherhood. All citizens were guaranteed protection from discrimination on the grounds of religious belief, race, caste, sex, or place of birth.

In theory, then, India became a full-fledged democracy on the British parliamentary model. In actuality, a number of distinctive characteristics made the system less than fully democratic in the Western sense but may also have enabled it to survive. As we have seen, India became in essence a one-party state. By leading the independence movement, the Congress Party had amassed massive public support, which enabled it to retain its preeminent position in Indian politics for three decades. The party also avoided being identified as a party exclusively for the Hindu majority by including prominent non-Hindus among its leaders and favoring measures to protect minority groups such as Sikhs and Muslims from discrimination.

After Nehru's death in 1964, however, problems emerged that had been disguised by his adept maneuvering. Part of the problem was the familiar one of a party too long in power. Party officials became complacent and all too easily fell prey to the temptations of corruption and pork-barrel politics.

Another problem was **communalism.** Beneath the surface unity of the new republic lay age-old ethnic, linguistic, and religious divisions. Because of India's vast size and complex history, no national language had ever emerged. Hindi was the most prevalent, but it was the native language of less than one-third of the population. During the colonial period, English had served as the official language of government, and many non-Hindi speakers suggested making it the official language. But English was spoken only by the educated elite, and it represented an affront to national pride. Eventually, India recognized fourteen official tongues, making the parliament sometimes sound like the Tower of Babel.

Divisiveness increased after Nehru's death, and under his successors, official corruption grew. Only the lack of appeal of its rivals and the Nehru family charisma carried on by his daughter Indira Gandhi kept the party in power. But she was unable to prevent the progressive disintegration of the party's power base at the state level, where regional or ideological parties won the allegiance of voters by exploiting ethnic or social revolutionary themes.

During the 1980s, religious tensions began to intensify, not only among Sikhs in the northwest but also between Hindus and Muslims. As we have seen, Gandhi's uncompromising approach to Sikh separatism led to her assassination in 1984. Under her son, Rajiv Gandhi, Hindu militants at Ayodhya, in northern India, demanded the destruction of a mosque built on the alleged site of King Rama's birthplace, where a Hindu temple had previously existed. In 1992, Hindu demonstrators destroyed the mosque and erected a temporary temple at the site, provoking clashes between Hindus and Muslims throughout the country. In protest, rioters in neighboring Pakistan destroyed a number of Hindu shrines in that country.

In recent years, communal divisions have intensified, as militant Hindu groups agitate for a state that caters to the Hindu majority, now numbering more than 700 million people. In the spring of 2002, violence between Hindus and Muslims flared up again over plans by Hindu activists to build a permanent temple to Rama at the site of the destroyed mosque at Ayodhya. In the meantime, some textbooks have been rewritten to reflect a more "Hinduized" version of history, including the contention that the Indus valley civilization was founded by Aryan peoples.

**The Economy** Nehru's answer to the social and economic inequality that had long afflicted the subcontinent was socialism. He instituted a series of five-year plans, which led to the creation of a relatively large and reasonably efficient industrial sector, centered on steel, vehicles, and textiles. Industrial production almost tripled between 1950 and 1965, and per capita income rose by 50 percent between 1950 and 1980, although it was still less than \$300 (in U.S. dollars).

By the 1970s, however, industrial growth had slowed. The lack of modern infrastructure was a problem, as was the rising price of oil, most of which had to be imported. The relative weakness of the state-owned sector, which grew at an annual rate of only about 2 percent in the 1950s and 1960s, versus 5 percent for the private sector, also became a serious obstacle.

India's major economic weakness, however, was in agriculture. At independence, mechanization was almost unknown, fertilizer was rarely used, and most farms were small and uneconomical because of the Hindu tradition of dividing the land equally among all male children. As a result, the vast majority of the Indian people lived in conditions of abject poverty. Landless laborers outnumbered landowners by almost two to one. The government attempted to relieve the problem by redistributing land to the poor, limiting the size of landholdings, and encouraging farmers to form voluntary cooperatives. But all three programs ran into widespread opposition and apathy.

Another problem was overpopulation. Even before independence, the country had had difficulty supporting its people. In the 1950s and 1960s, the population grew by more than 2 percent annually, twice the nineteenth-century rate. Beginning in the 1960s, the Indian government sought to curb population growth.

Indira Gandhi instituted a program combining monetary rewards and compulsory sterilization. Males who had fathered too many children were sometimes forced to undergo a vasectomy. Popular resistance undermined the program, however, and the goals were scaled back in the 1970s. As a result, India has made little progress in holding down its burgeoning population, now estimated at more than one billion. One factor in the continued growth has been a decline in the death rate, especially the rate of infant mortality. Nevertheless, as a result of media popularization and better government programs, the trend today, even in poor rural villages, is toward smaller families. The average number of children a woman bears has been reduced from six in 1950 to three today. As has occurred elsewhere, the decline in family size began among the educated and is gradually spreading throughout Indian society.

The so-called **green revolution** that began in the 1960s helped reduce the severity of the population problem. The introduction of more productive, disease-resistant strains of rice and wheat doubled grain production between 1960 and 1980. But the green revolution also increased rural inequality. Only the wealthier farmers were able to purchase the necessary fertilizer, while poor peasants were often driven off the land. Millions fled to the cities, where they lived in vast slums, working at menial jobs or even begging for a living.

After the death of Indira Gandhi in 1984, her son Rajiv proved more receptive to foreign investment and a greater role for the private sector in the economy. India began to export more manufactured goods, including computer software. The pace of change has accelerated under Rajiv Gandhi's successors, who have continued to transfer state-run industries to private hands. These policies have stimulated the growth of a prosperous new middle class, now estimated at more than 100 million. Consumerism has soared, and sales of television sets, automobiles, videocassette recorders, and telephones have increased dramatically. Equally important, Western imports are being replaced by new products manufactured in India with Indian brand names.

One consequence of India's entrance into the industrial age is the emergence of a small but vibrant technological sector that provides many important services to the world's advanced nations. The city of Bangalore in South India has become an important technological center, benefiting from low wages and the presence of skilled labor with proficiency in the English language.

Nevertheless, Nehru's dream of a socialist society remains strong. State-owned enterprises still produce about half of all domestic goods, and high tariffs continue to stifle imports. Nationalist parties have played on the widespread fear of foreign economic influence to force the cancellation of some contracts and the relocation of some foreign firms. A combination of religious and environmental groups attempted unsuccessfully to prevent Kentucky Fried Chicken from establishing outlets in major Indian cities (see the box on p. 858). The fast-food invasion has led to a phenomenon occurring all over Asia: the growing incidence of obesity among children.

As in the industrialized countries of the West, economic growth has been accompanied by environmental damage. Water and air pollution has led to illness and death for many people, and an environmental movement has emerged. Some critics, reflecting the traditional anti-imperialist attitude of Indian intellectuals, blame Western capitalist corporations for the problem, as in the highly publicized case of leakage from a foreign-owned chemical plant at Bhopal. Much of the problem, however, comes from state-owned factories erected with Soviet aid. And not all the environmental damage can be ascribed to industrialization. The Ganges River is so polluted by human overuse that it is risky for Hindu believers to bathe in it.

Moreover, many Indians have not benefited from the new prosperity. Nearly one-third of the population lives below the national poverty line. Millions continue to live in urban slums, such as the famous "City of Joy" in Kolkata (Calcutta), and most farm families remain desperately poor. Despite the socialist rhetoric of India's leaders, the inequality of wealth in India is as pronounced as it is in capitalist nations in the West. Indeed, India has been described as two nations: an educated urban India of 100 million people surrounded by more than nine times that many impoverished peasants in the countryside.

**Caste, Class, and Gender** Drawing generalizations about the life of the average Indian is difficult because of ethnic, religious, and caste differences, which are compounded by the vast gulf between town and country.

Courtesy of William J. Duiker

**Fetching Water at the Village Well.** The scarcity of water will surely become one of the planet's most crucial problems in the twenty-first century. It will affect all nations, developed and developing, rich and poor. Although many Indians live with an inadequate water supply, these women are fortunate to have a well in their village. More typical is the image of the Indian woman, dressed in a colorful *sari,* children encircling her as she walks to her distant home, carrying a heavy pail of water on her head.

## Say No to McDonald's and KFC!

One of the consequences of Rajiv Gandhi's decision to deregulate the Indian economy has been an increase in the presence of foreign corporations, including U.S. fast-food restaurant chains. Their arrival set off a storm of protest in India: from environmentalists concerned that raising grain for chickens is an inefficient use of land, from religious activists angry at the killing of animals for food, and from nationalists anxious to protect the domestic market from foreign competition. Fast-food restaurants now represent a growing niche in Indian society, but most cater to local tastes, avoiding beef products and offering many vegetarian dishes, such as the Veg Pizza McPuff. The author of this piece, which appeared in the *Hindustan Times,* was Maneka Gandhi, a daughter-in-law of Indira Gandhi and a onetime minister of the environment who has emerged as a prominent rival of Congress Party president Sonia Gandhi.

*Why does the author of this article oppose the introduction of fast-food restaurants in India? Do you think her complaints apply in the United States as well?*

### Why India Doesn't Need Fast Food

India's decision to allow Pepsi Foods Ltd. to open 60 restaurants in India—30 each of Pizza Hut and Kentucky Fried Chicken—marks the first entry of multinational, meat-based junk-food chains into India. If this is allowed to happen, at least a dozen other similar chains will very quickly arrive, including the infamous McDonald's.

The implications of allowing junk-food chains into India are quite stark. As the name denotes, the foods served at Kentucky Fried Chicken (KFC) are chicken-based and fried. This is the worst combination possible for the body and can create a host of health problems, including obesity, high cholesterol, heart ailments, and many kinds of cancer. Pizza Hut products are a combination of white flour, cheese, and meat—again, a combination likely to cause disease. . . .

Then there is the issue of the environmental impact of junk-food chains. Modern meat production involves misuse of crops, water, energy, and grazing areas. In addition, animal agriculture produces surprisingly large amounts of air and water pollution.

KFC and Pizza Hut insist that their chickens be fed corn and soybeans. Consider the diversion of grain for this purpose. As the outlets of KFC and Pizza Hut increase in number, the poultry industry will buy up more and more corn to feed the chickens, which means that the corn will quickly disappear from the villages, and its increased price will place it out of reach for the common man. Turning corn into junk chicken is like turning gold into mud. . . .

It is already shameful that, in a country plagued by famine and flood, we divert 37 percent of our arable land to growing animal fodder. Were all of that grain to be consumed directly by humans, it would nourish five times as many people as it does after being converted into meat, milk, and eggs. . . .

Of course, it is not just the KFC and Pizza Hut chains of Pepsi Foods Ltd. that will cause all of this damage. Once we open India up by allowing these chains, dozens more will be eagerly waiting to come in. Each city in America has an average of 5,000 junk-food restaurants. Is that what we want for India?

Although the constitution of 1950 guaranteed equal treatment and opportunity for all, regardless of class and caste, and prohibited discrimination based on untouchability, prejudice is hard to eliminate. Untouchability persists, particularly in the villages, where *harijans,* now called ***dalits,*** still perform menial tasks and are often denied fundamental human rights.

In general, urban Indians appear less conscious of caste distinctions. Material wealth rather than caste identity is increasingly defining status. Still, color consciousness based on the age-old distinctions between upper-class and lower-class Indians remains strong. Class-conscious Hindus still express a distinct preference for light-skinned marital partners.

In recent years, low-class Indians (who represent more than 80 percent of the voting public) have begun to demand affirmative action to relieve their disabilities and give them a more equal share in the national wealth. But opponents of such measures are often not reluctant to fight back. Phoolan Devi, known as the "bandit queen," spent several years in jail for taking part in the murder of twenty men from a landowning caste who had allegedly gang-raped her when she was an adolescent. Her campaign for office during the 1996 elections was the occasion of violent arguments between supporters and opponents, and she was assassinated in 2001.

In few societies was the life of women more restricted than in traditional India. Hindu favoritism toward men was compounded by the Muslim custom of *purdah* to create a society in which males were dominant in virtually all aspects of life. Females received no education and had no inheritance rights. They were restricted to the home and tied to their husbands for life. Widows were expected to shave their heads and engage in a life of religious meditation or even to immolate themselves on their husband's funeral pyre *(sati).*

After independence, India's leaders sought to equalize treatment of the sexes. The constitution expressly forbade discrimination based on sex and called for equal pay for equal work. Laws prohibited child marriage, *sati,* and the

## A Critique of Western Feminism

Organized efforts to protect the rights of women have been under way in India since the 1970s, when the Progressive Organization for Women (POW) instituted a campaign against sexual harassment and other forms of discrimination against women in Indian society. Like many of their counterparts in other parts of Asia and Africa, however, many activists for women's rights in India are critical of Western feminism, charging that it is irrelevant to their own realities. Although Indian feminists feel a bond with their sisters all over the world, they insist on resolving Indian problems with Indian solutions. The author of this editorial is Madhu Kishwar, founder and editor of a women's journal in New Delhi.

*What are the author's criticisms of Western feminism? What differences between Indian and American society explain her attitude?*

### Finding Indian Solutions to Women's Problems

Western feminism, exported to India and many other Third World countries in recent decades, has brought with it serious problems.

As products of a more homogenized culture, most Western feminists assume women's aspirations the world over must be quite similar. Yet a person's idea of a good life and her aspirations are closely related to what is valued in her particular society. This applies to feminism itself. An offshoot of individualism and liberalism, it posits that each individual is responsible primarily to herself. . . .

In societies like India, most of us find it difficult to tune in to this extreme individualism. For instance, most Indian women are unwilling to assert rights in a way that estranges them not just from their family but also from their larger community. . . .

This isn't slavery to social opinion. Rather, many of us believe life is a poor thing if our own dear ones don't honor and celebrate our rights, if our freedom cuts us off from others. In our culture, both men and women are taught to value the interests of our families more than our self-interest. . . .

Cultural issues aside, my most fundamental reservation regarding feminism is that it has strengthened the tendency among India's Western-educated elites to adopt the statist authoritarian route to social reform. The characteristic feminist response to most social issues affecting women–in the workplace, in the media, in the home–is to demand more and more stringent laws. . . .

But dearly held and deeply cherished cultural norms cannot be changed simply by applying the instruments of state repression through legal punishment. Social reform is too complex and important a matter to be left to the police and courts. The best of laws will tend to fail if social opinion is contrary to them. Therefore, the statist route of using laws as a substitute for creating a new social consensus about women's rights tends to be counterproductive.

payment of a dowry by the bride's family. Women were encouraged to attend school and enter the labor market.

Such laws, along with the dynamics of economic and social change, have had a major impact on the lives of many Indian women. Middle-class women in urban areas are much more likely to seek employment outside the home, and many hold managerial and professional positions. Some Indian women, however, choose to play a dual role—a modern one in their work and in the marketplace and a more submissive, traditional one at home (see the box above).

Nothing more strikingly indicates the changing role of women in South Asia than the fact that in recent years, three of the major countries in the area—India, Pakistan, and Sri Lanka—have had women prime ministers. It is worthy of mention, however, that all three—Indira Gandhi, Benazir Bhutto, and Srimivao Bandaranaike—came from prominent political families and owed their initial success to a husband or father who had served as prime minister before them.

Like other aspects of life, the role of women has changed much less in rural areas. In the early 1960s, many villagers still practiced the institution of *purdah.* Female children are still much less likely to receive an education. The overall literacy rate in India today is less than 40 percent, but it is undoubtedly much lower among women. Laws relating to dowry, child marriage, and inheritance are routinely ignored in the countryside. There have been a few highly publicized cases of *sati,* although undoubtedly more women die of mistreatment at the hands of their husband or of other members of his family. In a few instances, widows have been forcibly thrown on the funeral pyre by their in-laws.

Perhaps the most tragic aspect of continued sexual discrimination in India is the high mortality rate among girls. One-quarter of the female children born in India die before the age of fifteen as a result of neglect or even infanticide. Others are aborted before birth after gender-detection examinations.

## South Asian Art and Literature Since Independence

Recent decades have witnessed a prodigious outpouring of literature in India. Most works have been written in one of the Indian languages and have not been translated into a foreign tongue. Fortunately, however, many authors choose to write in English. Known as Indo-Anglian literature, such works are written primarily for the Indian elite or for foreign audiences. For that reason, some critics charge that Indo-Anglian literature lacks authenticity.

Because of the vast quantity of works published (India is currently the third-largest publisher of English-language books in the world), only a few of the most prominent fiction writers can be mentioned here. Anita Desai (b. 1937) was one of the first prominent female writers in contemporary India. Her writing focuses on the struggle of Indian women to achieve a degree of independence. In her first novel, *Cry, the Peacock,* the heroine finally seeks liberation by murdering her husband, preferring freedom at any cost to remaining a captive of traditional society.

The best-known female writer in South Asia today is Taslima Nasrin (b. 1962) of Bangladesh. She first became famous when she was sentenced to death for her novel *Shame* (1993), in which she criticized official persecution of the Hindu minority. An outspoken feminist, she is critical of Islam for obstructing human progress and women's equality. She now lives in exile in Europe.

The most controversial writer in India today is Salman Rushdie (b. 1947). In *Midnight's Children,* published in 1980, the author linked his protagonist, born on the night of independence, to the history of modern India, its achievements and its frustrations. Like his contemporaries Günter Grass and Gabriel García Márquez, Rushdie used the technique of magical realism to jolt his audience into a recognition of the inhumanity of modern society and the need to develop a sense of moral concern for the fate of the Indian people and for the world as a whole.

Rushdie's later novels have tackled such problems as religious intolerance, political tyranny, social injustice, and greed and corruption. His attack on Islamic fundamentalism in *The Satanic Verses* (1988) won plaudits from literary critics but provoked widespread criticism among Muslims, including a death sentence by Ayatollah Khomeini in Iran. *The Moor's Last Sigh* (1995), which focuses on the alleged excesses of Hindu nationalism, has been banned in India.

Like Chinese and Japanese artists, Indian artists have agonized over how best to paint with a modern yet indigenous mode of expression. During the colonial period, Indian art went in several directions at once. One school of painters favored traditional themes; another experimented with a colorful primitivism founded on folk art. Many Indian artists painted representational social art extolling the suffering and silent dignity of India's impoverished millions. After 1960, however, most Indian artists adopted abstract art as their medium. Surrealism in particular, with its emphasis on spontaneity and the unconscious, appeared closer to the Hindu tradition of favoring intuition over reason. Yet Indian artists are still struggling to find the ideal way to be both modern and Indian.

Courtesy of William J. Duiker

**No Room in Paradise?** The color and diversity of popular Hinduism are nowhere more fully displayed than on the *gopuram,* or gate tower, of the modern Hindu temple. The celestial figures shown here in rich profusion are located on the tower surmounting the entrance gate of a temple devoted to Shiva in the southern Indian city of Chennai (Madras). Depicting the various Hindu myths, each deity appeals to the needs and devotion of the believers. Often depicted as couples, these gods and goddesses represent the ideal physical and spiritual union, which is to be emulated by the faithful.

### Gandhi's Vision

Indian society looks increasingly Western in form, if not in content. As in a number of other Asian and African societies, the distinction between traditional and modern, or native and westernized, sometimes seems to be a simple dichotomy between rural and urban. The major cities appear modern and westernized, but the villages have changed little since precolonial days.

Yet traditional practices appear to be more resilient in India than in many other societies, and the result is often a synthesis rather than a clash between conflicting institutions and values. Unlike China, India has not rejected its past but merely adjusted it to meet the needs of the present. Clothing styles in the streets, where the *sari* and *dhoti* continue to be popular; religious practices in the temples; and social relationships in the home all testify to the importance of tradition in India.

One disadvantage of the eclectic approach, which seeks to blend the old and the new rather than choosing one over the other, is that sometimes contrasting traditions cannot be reconciled. In his book *India: A Wounded Civilization,* V. S. Naipaul, a West Indian of Indian descent, charged that Mahatma Gandhi's glorification of poverty and the simple Indian village was an obstacle to efforts to overcome the poverty, ignorance, and degradation of India's past and build a prosperous modern society. Gandhi's vision of a spiritual India, Naipaul complained, was a balm for defeatism and an excuse for failure.

Certainly, India faces a difficult dilemma. To build a democratic, prosperous society, the Indian people must discard many of their traditional convictions and customs. Belief in inherent caste distinctions is incompatible with the democratic belief in equality before the law. These traditional beliefs also undercut the work ethic and the modern sentiment of nationalism.

So long as Indians accept their fate as predetermined, they will find it difficult to change their environment and create a new society. Yet their traditional beliefs provide a measure of identity and solace often lacking in other societies, where such traditional spiritual underpinnings have eroded. Destroying India's traditional means of coping with a disagreeable reality without changing that reality would be cruel indeed.

## Southeast Asia

As we have seen in Chapter 24, Japanese wartime occupation had a great impact on attitudes among the peoples of Southeast Asia. It demonstrated the vulnerability of colonial rule in the region and showed that an Asian power could defeat Europeans. The Allied governments themselves also contributed—sometimes unwittingly—to rising aspirations for independence by promising self-determination for all peoples at the end of the war. Although Winston Churchill later said that the Atlantic Charter did not apply to the colonial peoples, it would be difficult to put the genie back in the bottle again.

Some did not try. In July 1946, the United States granted total independence to the Philippines. The Americans maintained a military presence on the islands, however, and U.S. citizens retained economic and commercial interests in the new country.

The British, too, under the Labour Party, were willing to bring an end to a century of imperialism in the region. In 1948, the Union of Burma received its independence. Malaya's turn came in 1957, after a Communist guerrilla movement had been suppressed.

The French and the Dutch, however, both regarded their colonies in the region as economic necessities as well as symbols of national grandeur and refused to turn them over to nationalist movements at the end of the war. The Dutch attempted to suppress a rebellion in the East Indies led by Sukarno, leader of the Indonesian Nationalist Party. But the United States, which feared a Communist victory there, pressured the Dutch to grant independence to Sukarno and his non-Communist forces, and in 1950 the Dutch finally agreed to recognize the new Republic of Indonesia.

The situation was somewhat different in Vietnam, where the Communists seized power throughout most of the country. After the French refused to recognize the new government and reimposed their rule, war broke out in December 1946. At the time it was only an anticolonial war, but it would soon become much more (see Chapter 25).

### The Era of Independent States

Many of the leaders of the newly independent states in Southeast Asia (see Map 29.2) admired Western political institutions and hoped to adapt them to their own countries. New constitutions were patterned on Western democratic models, and multiparty political systems quickly sprang into operation.

**The Search for a New Political Culture** By the 1960s, most of these budding experiments in pluralist democracy had been abandoned or were under serious threat. Some had been replaced by military or one-party autocratic regimes. In Burma, a moderate government based on the British parliamentary system and dedicated to Buddhism and nonviolent Marxism had given way to a military government. In Thailand, too, the military now ruled. In the Philippines, President Ferdinand Marcos discarded democratic restraints and established his own centralized control. In South Vietnam, Ngo Dinh Diem and his successors paid lip service to the Western democratic model but ruled by authoritarian means.

One problem faced by most of these states was that independence had not brought material prosperity or ended economic inequality and the domination of the local economies by foreign interests. Most economies in the region were still characterized by tiny industrial sectors;

**MAP 29.2 Modern Southeast Asia.** Shown here are the countries that comprise contemporary Southeast Asia. The major islands that make up the Republic of Indonesia are indicated in italics. ? Where is the new nation of East Timor? **View an animated version of this map or related maps at http://history.wadsworth.com/duikerspielvogel05/**

they lacked technology, educational resources, capital investment, and leaders trained in developmental skills.

The presence of widespread ethnic, linguistic, cultural, and economic differences also made the transition to Western-style democracy difficult. In Malaya, for example, the majority Malays—most of whom were farmers—feared economic and political domination by the local Chinese minority, who were much more experienced in industry and commerce. In 1961, the Federation of Malaya, whose ruling party was dominated by Malays, integrated former British possessions on the island of Borneo into the new Union of Malaysia in a move to increase the non-Chinese proportion of the country's population. Yet periodic conflicts persisted as the Malaysian government attempted to guarantee Malay control over politics and a larger role in the economy.

The most publicized example of a failed experiment in democracy was in Indonesia. In 1950, the new leaders drew up a constitution creating a parliamentary system under a titular presidency. Sukarno was elected the first president. A spellbinding orator, Sukarno played a major role in creating a sense of national identity among the disparate peoples of the Indonesian archipelago (see the box on p. 863).

In the late 1950s, Sukarno, exasperated at the incessant maneuvering among devout Muslims, Communists, and the army, dissolved the constitution and attempted to rule on his own through what he called **guided democracy.** As he described it, guided democracy was closer to Indonesian traditions and superior to the Western variety. The weakness of the latter was that it allowed the majority to dominate the minority, whereas guided democracy would reconcile different opinions and points of view in a government operated by consensus. Highly suspicious of the West, Sukarno nationalized foreign-owned enterprises and sought economic aid from China and the Soviet Union while relying for domestic support on the Indonesian Communist Party.

## The Golden Throat of President Sukarno

President Sukarno of Indonesia was a spellbinding speaker and a charismatic leader of his nation's struggle for independence. These two excerpts are from speeches in which Sukarno promoted two of his favorite projects: Indonesian nationalism and "guided democracy." The force that would guide Indonesia, of course, was to be Sukarno himself.

*Is Sukarno correct in declaring that Indonesia is as large as the United States? What are his criticisms of Western democracy?*

### Sukarno on Indonesian Greatness

What was Indonesia in 1945? What was our nation then? It was only two things, only two things. A flag and a song. That is all. (Pause, finger held up as afterthought.) But no, I have omitted the main ingredient. I have missed the most important thing of all. I have left out the burning fire of freedom and independence in the breast and heart of every Indonesian. That is the most important thing—this is the vital chord—the spirit of our people, the spirit and determination to be free. This was our nation in 1945—the spirit of our people!

And what are we today? We are a great nation. We are bigger than Poland. We are bigger than Turkey. We have more people than Australia, than Canada, we are bigger in area and have more people than Japan. In population now we are the fifth-largest country in the world. In area, we are even bigger than the United States of America. The American Ambassador, who is here with us, admits this. Of course, he points out that we have a lot of water in between our thousands of islands. But I say to him—America has a lot of mountains and deserts, too!

### Sukarno on Guided Democracy

Indonesia's democracy is not liberal democracy. Indonesian democracy is not the democracy of the world of Montaigne or Voltaire. Indonesia's democracy is not à la America, Indonesia's democracy is not the Soviet—NO! Indonesia's democracy is the democracy which is implanted in the breasts of the Indonesian people, and it is that which I have tried to dig up again, and have put forward as an offering to you. . . . If you, especially the undergraduates, are still clinging to and being borne along the democracy made in England, or democracy made in France, or democracy made in America, or democracy made in Russia, you will become a nation of copyists!

**HistoryNow™** To read President Sukarno's opening speech at the Bandung Conference, enter the *HistoryNow* documents area using the access card that is available for *World History.*

The army and conservative Muslims resented Sukarno's increasing reliance on the Communists, and the Muslims were further upset by his refusal to consider a state based on Islamic principles. In 1965, military officers launched a coup d'état that provoked a mass popular uprising, which resulted in the slaughter of several hundred thousand suspected Communists, many of whom were overseas Chinese, long distrusted by the Muslim majority. In 1967, a military government under General Suharto was installed.

The new government made no pretensions of reverting to democratic rule, but it did restore good relations with the West and sought foreign investment to repair the country's ravaged economy. But it also found it difficult to placate Muslim demands for an Islamic state. In a few areas, including western Sumatra, militant Muslims took up arms against the state.

The one country in Southeast Asia that explicitly rejected the Western model was North Vietnam. Its leaders opted for the Stalinist pattern of national development, based on Communist Party rule and socialist forms of ownership. In 1958, stimulated by the success of collectivization in neighboring China, the government launched a three-year plan to lay the foundation for a socialist society. Collective farms were established, and all industry and commerce above the family level were nationalized.

**Recent Trends Toward Democracy** In recent years, some Southeast Asian societies have shown signs of evolving toward more democratic forms. In the Philippines, the dictatorial regime of Ferdinand Marcos was overthrown by a massive public uprising in 1986 and replaced by a democratically elected government under President Corazon Aquino, the widow of a popular politician assassinated a few years earlier. Aquino was unable to resolve many of the country's chronic economic and social difficulties, however, and political stability remains elusive; one of her successors, Joseph Estrada, a former actor, was forced to resign on the charge of corruption, and Muslims in the southern island of Mindanao have mounted a terrorist campaign in their effort to obtain autonomy or independence.

In other nations, the results have also been mixed. Although Malaysia is a practicing democracy, tensions persist between Malays and Chinese as well as between secular and orthodox Muslims who seek to create an Islamic state. In neighboring Thailand, the military has found it expedient to hold national elections for civilian governments, but the danger of a military takeover is never far beneath the surface.

In Indonesia, difficult economic conditions caused by a financial crisis in 1997 (see the next section), combined with popular anger against the Suharto government (several members of his family had reportedly used their positions to amass considerable wealth), led to violent street riots and demands for his resignation. Forced to step down in the spring of 1998, Suharto was replaced by his deputy B. J. Habibie, who called for the establishment of a national assembly to select a new government based on popular aspirations. The assembly selected a moderate Muslim leader as president, but he was charged with corruption and incompetence and was replaced in 2001 by his vice president, Sukarno's daughter, Megawati Sukarnoputri.

The new government faced a severe challenge, not only from the economic crisis but also from dissident elements seeking autonomy or even separation from the republic. Under pressure from the international community, Indonesia agreed to grant independence to the onetime Portuguese colony of East Timor, where the majority of the people are Roman Catholics. But violence provoked by pro-Indonesian militia units forced many refugees to flee the country. Religious tensions have also erupted between Muslims and Christians elsewhere in the archipelago, and Muslim rebels in western Sumatra continue to agitate for a new state based on strict adherence to fundamentalist Islam.

In direct elections held in 2004, General Susilo Yudhyono defeated Megawati Sukarnoputri and ascended to the presidency. The new chief executive promised a new era of political stability, honest government, and economic reform but faces a number of severe challenges. Concerned about high wages and the risk of terrorism, a number of foreign firms have relocated their factories elsewhere in Asia, forcing thousands of workers to return to the countryside. Pressure from traditional Muslims to abandon the nation's secular tradition and move toward the creation of an Islamic state continues to grow. That the country was able to hold democratic elections in the midst of such tensions holds some promise for the future.

Elsewhere in the region, progress toward democracy has been mixed. In Vietnam, the trend has been toward a greater popular role in the governing process. Elections for the unicameral parliament are more open than in the past. The government remains suspicious of Western-style democracy, however, and represses any opposition to the Communist Party's guiding role over the state.

Only in Burma (now renamed Myanmar), where the military has been in complete control since the early 1960s, have the forces of greater popular participation been virtually silenced. Even there, however, the power of the ruling regime of General Ne Win (1911–2003), known as SLORC, has been vocally challenged by Aung San Huu Kyi (b. 1952), the admired daughter of one of the heroes of the country's struggle for national liberation after World War II.

**Increasing Prosperity and Financial Crisis** The trend toward more representative systems of government has been due in part to increasing prosperity and the growth of an affluent and educated middle class. Although Indonesia, Burma, and the three Indochinese states are still overwhelmingly agrarian, Malaysia and Thailand have been undergoing relatively rapid economic development.

In the late summer of 1997, however, these economic gains were threatened and popular faith in the ultimate benefits of globalization was shaken as a financial crisis swept through the region. The crisis was triggered by a number of problems, including growing budget deficits caused by excessive government expenditures on ambitious development projects, irresponsible lending and investment practices by financial institutions, and an overvaluation of local currencies relative to the U.S. dollar. An underlying cause of these problems was the prevalence of backroom deals between politicians and business leaders that temporarily enriched both groups at the cost of eventual economic dislocation.

Courtesy of William J. Duiker

**Soccer, a Global Obsession.** Professional soccer has become the most popular sport in the world. It offers a diversion from daily drudgery and promotes intense patriotism as each nation supports its team. Moreover, children the world over enjoy playing soccer, even when there are no playing fields in the vicinity. Shown here is a match held in an ancestral Chinese temple in Hoi An, Vietnam.

**CHRONOLOGY Southeast Asia**

| | |
|---|---|
| August Revolution in Vietnam | 1945 |
| Philippines become independent | 1946 |
| Beginning of Franco-Vietminh War | 1946 |
| Burma becomes independent | 1948 |
| Recognition of the Republic of Indonesia | 1950 |
| Malaya becomes independent | 1957 |
| Beginning of Sukarno's "guided democracy" in Indonesia | 1959 |
| Military seizes power in Indonesia | 1965 |
| Foundation of ASEAN | 1967 |
| Fall of Saigon to North Vietnamese forces | 1975 |
| Vietnamese invade Cambodia | 1978 |
| Corazon Aquino elected president in the Philippines | 1986 |
| United Nations forces arrive in Cambodia | 1991 |
| Vietnam becomes a member of ASEAN | 1996 |
| Islamic and student protests in Indonesia | 1996–1997 |
| Suharto steps down as president of Indonesia | 1998 |
| Tsunami causes widespread death and destruction throughout the region | 2004 |

As local currencies plummeted in value, the International Monetary Fund agreed to provide assistance, but only on the condition that the governments concerned permit greater transparency in their economic systems and allow market forces to operate more freely, even at the price of bankruptcies and the loss of jobs. By the early 2000s, there were signs that the economies in the region had weathered the crisis and were beginning to recover. The massive tsunami that struck in December 2004 was another setback, as well as a human tragedy of enormous proportions.

## Regional Conflict and Cooperation: The Rise of ASEAN

In addition to their continuing internal challenges, Southeast Asian states have been hampered by serious tensions among themselves. Some of these tensions were a consequence of historical rivalries and territorial disputes that had been submerged during the long era of colonial rule. Cambodia, for example, has bickered with both of its neighbors, Thailand and Vietnam, over mutual frontiers drawn up originally by the French for their own convenience.

After the reunification of Vietnam under Communist rule in 1975, the lingering border dispute between Cambodia and Vietnam erupted again. In April 1975, a brutal revolutionary regime under the leadership of the Khmer Rouge dictator Pol Pot came to power in Cambodia and proceeded to carry out the massacre of more than one million Cambodians. Then, claiming that vast territories in the Mekong delta had been seized from Cambodia by the Vietnamese in previous centuries, the Khmer Rouge regime launched attacks across the common border. In response, Vietnamese forces invaded Cambodia in December 1978 and installed a pro-Hanoi regime in Phnom Penh. Fearful of Vietnam's increasing power in the region, China launched a brief attack on Vietnam to demonstrate its displeasure.

The outbreak of war among the erstwhile Communist allies aroused the concern of other countries in the neighborhood. In 1967, several non-Communist countries had

Courtesy of William J. Duiker

**Holocaust in Cambodia.** When the Khmer Rouge seized power in Cambodia in April 1975, they immediately emptied the capital of Phnom Penh and systematically began to eliminate opposition elements throughout the country. Thousands were tortured in the infamous Tuol Sleng prison and then marched out to the countryside, where they were massacred. Their bodies were thrown into massive pits. The succeeding government disinterred the remains, which are now displayed at an outdoor museum on the site.

established the Association of Southeast Asian Nations (ASEAN). Composed of Indonesia, Malaysia, Thailand, Singapore, and the Philippines, ASEAN at first concentrated on cooperative social and economic endeavors, but after the end of the Vietnam War, it cooperated with other states in an effort to force the Vietnamese to withdraw. In 1991, the Vietnamese finally withdrew, and a new government was formed in Phnom Penh.

The growth of ASEAN from a weak collection of diverse states into a stronger organization whose members cooperate militarily and politically has helped provide the nations of Southeast Asia with a more cohesive voice to represent their interests on the world stage. They will need it, for disagreements with Western countries over global economic issues and the rising power of China will present major challenges in coming years. That Vietnam was admitted into ASEAN in 1996 should provide both Hanoi and its neighbors with greater leverage in dealing with their powerful neighbor to the north.

## Daily Life: Town and Country in Contemporary Southeast Asia

The urban-rural dichotomy observed in India is also found in Southeast Asia, where the cities resemble those in the West while the countryside often appears little changed from precolonial days. In cities such as Bangkok, Manila, and Jakarta, broad boulevards lined with skyscrapers alternate with muddy lanes passing through neighborhoods packed with wooden shacks topped by thatch or rusty tin roofs. Nevertheless, in recent decades, millions of Southeast Asians have fled to these urban slums. Although most available jobs are menial, the pay is better than in the villages.

**The Urban Impact** The urban migrants change not only their physical surroundings but their attitudes and values as well. Sometimes the move leads to a decline in traditional beliefs. Belief in the existence of nature and ancestral spirits, for example, has declined among the urban populations of Southeast Asia. In Thailand, Buddhism has come under pressure from the rising influence of materialism, although temple schools still educate thousands of rural youths whose families cannot afford the cost of public education.

Nevertheless, Buddhist, Muslim, and Confucian beliefs remain strong, even in cosmopolitan cities such as Bangkok, Jakarta, and Singapore. This preference for the traditional also shows up in lifestyle. Native dress—or an eclectic blend of Asian and Western dress—is still common. Traditional music, art, theater, and dance remain popular, although Western rock music has become fashionable among the young, and Indonesian filmmakers complain that Western films are beginning to dominate the market.

The increasing inroads made by Western culture have caused anxiety in some countries (see the comparative illustration below). In Malaysia, for example, fundamentalist Muslims criticize the prevalence of pornography, hedonism, drugs, and alcohol in Western culture and have tried to limit their presence in their own country. The Malaysian government has attempted to limit the number of U.S. en-

Courtesy of William J. Duiker

© Jim Whitmer Photography

COMPARATIVE ILLUSTRATION

**Exchange of Foods—East and West.** The McDonald's fast-food chain has become a prime symbol of U.S. cultural influence throughout the world. Popular with young people, it is often the target of attacks from those who criticize the impact that American values have had on traditional cultures, from Europe to East Asia. Some especially focus on the health problems that will arise from the typical American junk-food diet. At the left, we see a giant statue of Ronald McDonald welcoming young Indonesians to a restaurant in the capital city of Jakarta. At the same time, Eastern foods and eating styles have also made an enormous impact on the Western world, where they are appreciated by some for their nutritional value and health benefits, as well as for their exotic flavors. Seen at the right is a Chinese restaurant in the city of Amsterdam.

tertainment programs shown on local television stations and has replaced them with shows on traditional themes.

**The Role of Women** One of the most significant changes that has taken place in Southeast Asia in recent decades is in the role of women in society. In general, women in the region have historically faced fewer restrictions on their activities and enjoyed a higher status than women elsewhere in Asia. Nevertheless, they were not the equal of men in every respect.With independence, Southeast Asian women gained new rights. Virtually all of the constitutions adopted by the newly independent states granted women full legal and political rights, including the right to work. Today, women have increased opportunities for education and have entered careers previously reserved for men. Women have become more active in politics, and as we have seen, some have served as heads of state.

Yet women are not truly equal to men in any country in Southeast Asia. Sometimes the distinction is simply a matter of custom. In Vietnam, women are legally equal to men, yet until recently no women had served in the Communist Party's ruling Politburo. In Thailand, Malaysia, and Indonesia, women rarely hold senior positions in government service or in the boardrooms of major corporations. Similar restrictions apply in Myanmar, although Aung San Huu Kyi is the leading figure in the democratic opposition movement.

Sometimes, too, women's rights have been undermined by a social or religious backlash. The revival of Islamic fundamentalism has had an especially strong impact in Malaysia, where Malay women are expected to cover their bodies and wear the traditional Muslim headdress. Even in non-Muslim countries, women are still expected to behave demurely and exercise discretion in all contacts with the opposite sex.

## Cultural Trends

In most countries in Southeast Asia, writers, artists, and composers are attempting to synthesize international styles and themes with local tradition and experience. The novel has become increasingly popular as writers seek to find the best medium to encapsulate the dramatic changes that have taken place in the region in recent decades.

The best-known writer in postwar Indonesia—at least to readers abroad—is Pramoedya Toer. Born in 1925 in eastern Java, he joined the Indonesian nationalist movement in his early twenties. Arrested in 1965 on the charge of being a Communist, he spent the next several years in prison. While incarcerated, he began writing his four-volume *Buru Quartet,* which recounts in fictional form the story of the struggle of the Indonesian people for freedom from colonial rule and the autocratic regimes of the independence period. He remains under house arrest in Java today, and his novels are forbidden to circulate in Indonesia.

Among the most talented of contemporary Vietnamese novelists is Duong Thu Huong (b. 1947). A member of the Vietnamese Communist Party who served on the front lines during the Sino-Vietnamese war in 1979, she later became outspoken in her criticism of the party's failure to carry out democratic reforms and was briefly imprisoned in 1991. Undaunted by official pressure, she has written several novels that express the horrors experienced by guerrilla fighters during the Vietnam War and the cruel injustices perpetrated by the regime in the cause of building socialism.

## A Region in Flux

Today, the Western image of a Southeast Asia mired in the Vietnam conflict and the tensions of the Cold War has become a memory. In ASEAN, the states in the region have created the framework for a regional organization that can serve their common political, economic, technological, and security interests. A few members of ASEAN are already on the road to advanced development.

To be sure, there are continuing signs of trouble. The recent financial crisis has aroused serious political unrest in Indonesia and has the potential to create similar problems elsewhere. There are disquieting signs that al-Qaeda has established a presence in the region. Myanmar remains isolated and appears mired in a state of chronic underdevelopment and brutal military rule. The three states of Indochina remain potentially unstable and have not yet

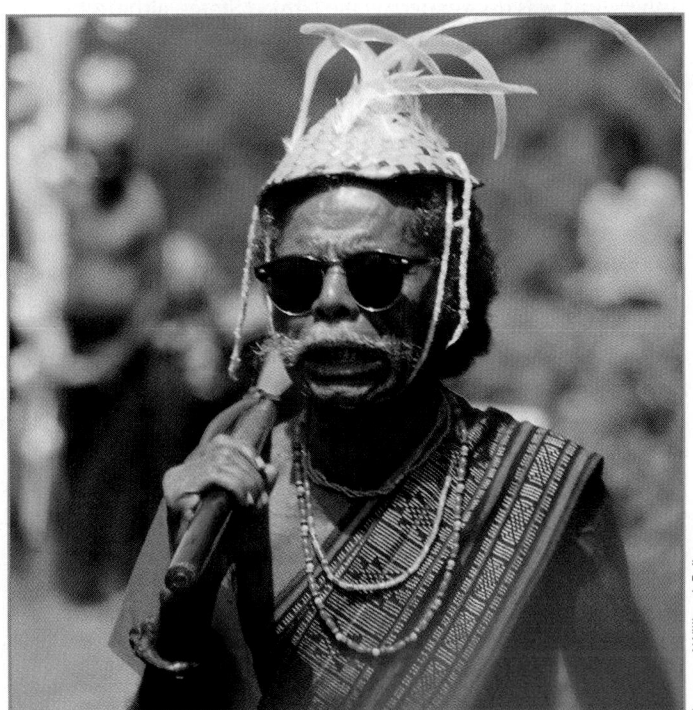

Courtesy of William J. Duiker

**One World, One Fashion.** One of the negative aspects of tourism is the eroding of distinctive ethnic cultures, even in previously less traveled areas. Nevertheless, fashions from other lands often seem exotic and enticing. This village chief from Flores, a remote island in the Indonesian archipelago, seems very proud of his designer sunglasses.

been fully integrated into the region as a whole. All things considered, however, the situation is more promising today than would have seemed possible a generation ago.

## East Asia

In August 1945, Japan was in ruins, its cities destroyed, its vast Asian empire in ashes, its land occupied by a foreign army. Half a century later, Japan had emerged as the second-greatest industrial power in the world, democratic in form and content and a source of stability throughout the region. Japan's achievement spawned a number of Asian imitators. Known as the "Little Tigers," the four industrializing societies of Taiwan, Hong Kong, Singapore, and South Korea achieved considerable success by following the path originally charted by Japan. Along with Japan, they became economic powerhouses and ranked among the world's top twenty trading nations. Other nations in Asia and elsewhere took note and began to adopt the Japanese formula. It is no wonder that observers relentlessly heralded the coming of the Pacific Century.

**General MacArthur and Emperor Hirohito.** After the end of World War II, U.S. General Douglas MacArthur was appointed supreme commander of the Allied powers. In that capacity, he directed U.S. policy during the occupation of Japan from 1945 to 1950. Here MacArthur stands side by side with Emperor Hirohito of Japan. Note the cultural and attitudinal differences of the two leaders expressed by their contrasting body language.

### The Japanese Miracle: The Transformation of Modern Japan

For five years after the end of the war in the Pacific, Japan was governed by an Allied administration under the command of U.S. General Douglas MacArthur. The occupation regime was dominated by the United States, although the country was technically administered by a new Japanese government. As commander of the occupation administration, MacArthur was responsible for demilitarizing Japanese society, destroying the Japanese war machine, trying Japanese civilian and military officials charged with war crimes, and laying the foundations of postwar Japanese society (see the box on p. 869).

One of the sturdy pillars of Japanese militarism had been the giant business cartels, known as *zaibatsu* (see Chapter 23). Allied policy was designed to break up the *zaibatsu* into smaller units in the belief that corporate concentration not only hindered competition but was inherently undemocratic and conducive to political authoritarianism. Occupation planners also intended to promote the formation of independent labor unions, to lessen the power of the state over the economy, and to provide a mouthpiece for downtrodden Japanese workers. Economic inequality in rural areas was to be reduced by a comprehensive land reform program that would turn the land over to the people who farmed it. Finally, the educational system was to be remodeled along American lines so that it would turn out independent individuals rather than automatons subject to manipulation by the state.

The Allied program was an ambitious and even audacious plan to remake Japanese society and has been justly praised for its clear-sighted vision and altruistic motives. Parts of the program, such as the constitution, the land reforms, and the educational system, succeeded brilliantly. But as other concerns began to intervene, changes or compromises were made that were not always successful. In particular, with the rise of Cold War sentiment in the United States in the late 1940s, the goal of decentralizing the Japanese economy gave way to the desire to make Japan a key partner in the effort to defend East Asia against international communism. Convinced of the need to promote economic recovery in Japan, U.S. policy makers began to show more tolerance for the *zaibatsu*. Concerned at growing radicalism within the new labor movement, U.S. occupation authorities placed less emphasis on the independence of the labor unions.

Cold War concerns also affected U.S. foreign relations with Japan. On September 8, 1951, the United States and other former belligerent nations signed a peace treaty restoring Japanese independence. In turn, Japan renounced any claim to such former colonies or territories as Taiwan, Korea, and southern Sakhalin and the Kurile Islands (see Map 29.3). On the same day, Japan and the

## The Emperor Is Not Divine

At the close of World War II, the United States agreed that Japan could retain the emperor, but only on condition that he renounce his divinity. When the governments of Great Britain and the Soviet Union advocated that Hirohito be tried as a war criminal, General Douglas MacArthur, the supreme commander of Allied occupation forces in Japan, argued that the emperor had a greater grasp of democratic principles than most other Japanese and that his presence was vital to the success of Allied occupation policy. That recommendation was upheld. On New Year's Day, 1946, the emperor issued a rescript denying his divinity. To many Japanese of the era, however, he remained a divine figure.

*How does the rescript justify the denial of imperial divinity? Why was the emperor considered divine in the first place?*

### Hirohito, Rescript on Divinity

In greeting the New Year, we recall to mind that the Emperor Meiji proclaimed as the basis of our national policy the five clauses of the Charter at the beginning of the Meiji era. . . .

The proclamation is evident in its significance and high in its ideals. We wish to make this oath anew and restore the country to stand on its own feet again. We have to reaffirm the principles embodied in the Charter and proceed unflinchingly towards elimination of misguided practices of the past; and keeping in close touch with the desires of the people, we will construct a new Japan through thoroughly being pacific, the officials and the people alike, obtaining rich culture and advancing the standard of living of the people.

The devastation of war inflicted upon our cities, the miseries of the destitute, the stagnation of trade, shortage of food, and the great and growing number of the unemployed are indeed heart-rending, but if the nation is firmly united in its resolve to face the present ordeal and to see civilization consistently in peace, a bright future will undoubtedly be ours, not only for our country but for the whole of humanity. . . .

We stand by the people and we wish always to share with them in their moments of joys and sorrows. The ties between us and our people have always stood upon mutual trust and affection. They do not depend upon mere legends and myths. They are not predicated on the false conception that the Emperor is divine and that the Japanese people are superior to other races and fated to rule the world.

Our Government should make every effort to alleviate their trials and tribulations. At the same time, we trust that the people will rise to the occasion and will strive courageously for the solution of their outstanding difficulties and for the development of industry and culture. Acting upon a consciousness of solidarity and of mutual aid and broad tolerance in their civil life, they will prove themselves worthy of their best tradition. By their supreme endeavors in that direction, they will be able to render their substantial contribution to the welfare and advancement of mankind.

The resolution for the year should be made at the beginning of the year. We expect our people to join us in all exertions looking to accomplishment of this great undertaking with an indomitable spirit.

United States signed a defensive alliance and agreed that the latter could maintain military bases on the Japanese islands. Japan was now formally independent but in a new dependency relationship with the United States. A provision in the new constitution renounced war as an instrument of national policy and prohibited the raising of an army. Thus by the early 1950s, Japan had regained partial control over its destiny.

**Politics and Government** The Allied occupation administrators started with the conviction that Japanese expansionism was directly linked to the institutional and ideological foundations of the Meiji Constitution. Accordingly, they set out to change Japanese politics into something closer to the pluralistic model used in most Western nations. Yet a number of characteristics of the postwar Japanese political system reflected the tenacity of the traditional political culture. Although Japan had a multiparty system with two major parties, the Liberal Democrats and the Socialists, in practice there was a "government party" and a permanent opposition—the Liberal Democrats were not voted out of office for thirty years. Many of the leading Liberal Democrats controlled factions on a patron-client basis, and decisions on key issues, such as who should assume the prime ministership, were reached by a modern equivalent of the Meiji oligarchs.

That tradition changed suddenly in 1993 when the ruling Liberal Democrats, shaken by persistent reports of corruption and cronyism between politicians and business interests, failed to win a majority of seats in parliamentary elections. Mirohiro Hosokawa, the leader of one of several newly formed parties, was elected prime minister. The new coalition government, however, quickly split into feuding factions, and in 1995, the Liberal Democrats returned to power. Successive prime ministers proved unable to carry out promised reforms, and in 2001, Junichiro Koizumi, a former minister of health and welfare, was elected prime minister. He too promised far-reaching reforms to make the political system more responsive to the challenge facing the country—so far with little success.

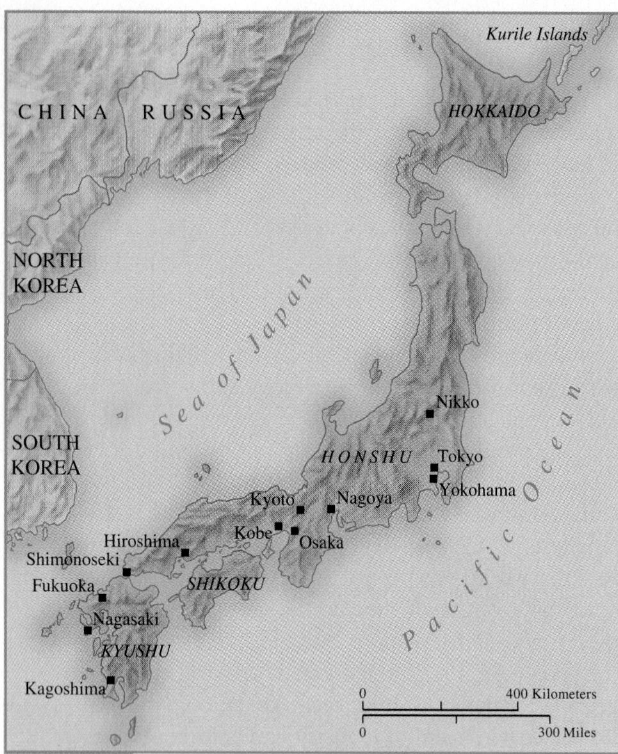


**MAP 29.3 Modern Japan.** Shown here are the four main islands that comprise the contemporary state of Japan. Which is the largest? **View an animated version of this map or related maps at** http://history.wadsworth.com/duikerspielvogel05/

These challenges include not only curbing persistent political corruption but also reducing the government's involvement in the economy. Since the Meiji period, the government has played an active role in mediating management-labor disputes, establishing price and wage policies, and subsidizing vital industries and enterprises producing goods for export. This government intervention in the economy was once cited as a key reason for the efficiency of Japanese industry and the emergence of the country as an industrial giant.

In recent years, however, as the economy remained mired in recession, the government's actions have increasingly come under fire. Japanese firms now argue that deregulation is needed to enable them to innovate to keep up with the competition. Such reforms, however, have been resisted by powerful government ministries.

Last but certainly not least, minorities such as the *eta* (now known as the **Burakumin**) and Korean residents in Japan continue to be subjected to legal and social discrimination. For years, official sources were reluctant to divulge growing evidence that thousands of Korean women were conscripted to serve as prostitutes (euphemistically called "comfort women") for Japanese soldiers during the war, and many Koreans living in Japan contend that such prejudicial attitudes continue to exist. Representatives of the "comfort women" have demanded both financial compensation and a formal letter of apology from the Japanese government for the treatment they received during the Pacific War. Negotiations over the issue are under way.

The issue of Japan's behavior during World War II has been especially sensitive. During the 1990s, critics at home and abroad charged that textbooks printed under the guidance of the Ministry of Education did not adequately discuss the atrocities committed by the Japanese government and armed forces during World War II. Other Asian governments were incensed at Tokyo's failure to accept responsibility for that behavior and demanded a formal apology. The government expressed remorse, but only in the context of the aggressive actions of all colonial powers during the imperialist era. In the view of many Japanese, the actions of their government during the Pacific War were a form of self-defense. Although fear of the potential revival of Japanese militarism is still strong in the region, the United States has not shared this concern and applauded Japan's decision to enhance its self-defense forces to deal with potential disturbances in the region. The issue has provoked vigorous debate in Japan, where some observers have argued that their country should adopt a more assertive stance toward the United States and play a larger role in Asian affairs.

Japan has carried out an increasingly independent foreign policy in recent years and has succeeded in maintaining amicable relations with virtually all nations. Its only serious dispute is with Russia, which has consistently refused Japan's request for the return of four islands in the Kurile chain, near the northern Japanese island of Hokkaido.

**The Economy** Nowhere are the changes in postwar Japan so visible as in the economic sector, where Japan developed into a major industrial and technological power in the space of a century, surpassing such advanced Western societies as Germany, France, and Great Britain.

Although this "Japanese miracle" has often been described as beginning after the war as a result of the Allied reforms, in fact Japanese economic growth began much earlier, with the Meiji reforms, which helped transform Japan from an autocratic society based on semifeudal institutions into an advanced capitalist democracy.

As noted, the officials of the Allied occupation identified the Meiji economic system with centralized power and the rise of Japanese militarism. Accordingly, they set out to break up the *zaibatsu* and decentralize Japanese industry and commerce. But with the rise of Cold War tensions, the policy was scaled back. Looser ties between companies were still allowed, and a new type of informal relationship, sometimes called the ***keiretsu,*** or "interlocking arrangement," began to take shape. Through such arrangements among suppliers, wholesalers, retailers, and financial institutions, the *zaibatsu* system was reconstituted under a new name.

The occupation administration had more success with its program to reform the agricultural system. Half of the population still lived on farms, and half of all farmers were still tenants. Under the land reform program, all lands owned by absentee landlords and all cultivated landholdings over an established maximum were sold on easy credit terms to the tenants. The program created a strong class of yeoman farmers, and tenants declined to about 10 percent of the rural population.

During the next fifty years, Japan re-created the stunning results of the Meiji era. In 1950, the Japanese gross domestic product was about one-third that of Great Britain or France. Today, it is larger than both put together and well over half that of the United States. Japan is the greatest exporting nation in the world, and its per capita income equals or surpasses that of most advanced Western states.

Explanations for Japan's success have tended to fall into two major categories. Some analysts point to cultural factors: the Japanese are naturally group-oriented and find it easy to cooperate with one another. Traditionally hardworking and frugal, they are more inclined to save than to consume, a trait that boosts the savings rate and labor productivity. Like all Confucian societies, the Japanese value education, and consequently the labor force is highly skilled. The literacy rate is almost 100 percent, and a significantly higher proportion of the population graduates from high school than in most advanced nations of the West.

Other observers give more practical reasons for Japan's success. Paradoxically, Japan benefited from the total destruction of its industrial base during World War II, because it did not have the antiquated plants that held back many industries in the United States. Secure under U.S. protection, Japan spends less than 1 percent of its gross domestic product on national defense, whereas the United States spends more than 5 percent. The Japanese government has actively promoted business interests. Some critics have charged that Japan has gone beyond promotion to unfair trade practices, subsidizing exports through the Ministry of International Trade and Industry (MITI), dumping goods at prices below cost to break into a foreign market, maintaining an artificially low standard of living at home to encourage exports, and unduly restricting imports from other countries.

There is some truth on both sides of the argument. Many of the practical steps Japan took were possible precisely because of the cultural factors described here. The tradition of loyalty to the firm, for example, derives from the communal tradition in Japanese society. The concept of sacrificing one's personal interests to those of the state, though not necessarily rooted in the traditional period, was certainly fostered by the *genro* oligarchy during the Meiji era.

**A Miracle Tarnished** In recent years, the Japanese economy has run into serious difficulties, raising the question as to whether the vaunted Japanese model is as appealing as many observers earlier declared. A rise in the value of the yen hurt exports and burst the bubble of investment by Japanese banks that had taken place under the umbrella of government protection. Lacking a domestic market equivalent in size to the United States, in the 1990s the Japanese economy slipped into a recession that continues today.

These economic difficulties have placed heavy pressure on some of the vaunted features of the Japanese economy. The tradition of lifetime employment created a bloated white-collar workforce and has made downsizing difficult. Today, job security is on the decline as increasing numbers of workers are being laid off. A disproportionate burden has fallen on women, who lack seniority and continue to suffer from various forms of discrimination in the workplace. In the meantime, many older Japanese have seen their savings diminish, while retirement programs are increasingly strained by the demands of a rapidly aging population.

A final change is that slowly but inexorably, the Japanese market is beginning to open up to international competition. Foreign automakers are winning a growing share of the domestic market, and the government—concerned at the prospect of food shortages—has committed itself to facilitating the importation of rice from abroad. Greater exposure to foreign competition may improve the performance of Japanese manufacturers. In recent years, Japanese consumers have become increasingly critical of the quality of some domestic products, provoking one cabinet minister to complain about "sloppiness and complacency" among Japanese firms (the scandal in the United States over defects in Firestone tires, produced by the Japanese tiremaker Bridgestone, is a case in point). One apparent reason for the country's recent quality problems is the cost-cutting measures adopted by Japanese companies to meet the challenges from abroad.

**A Society in Transition** During the occupation, Allied planners set out to change social characteristics that they believed had contributed to Japanese aggressiveness before and during World War II. The new educational system removed all references to filial piety, patriotism, and loyalty to the emperor while emphasizing the individualistic values of Western civilization. The new constitution and a revised civil code eliminated remaining legal restrictions on women's rights to obtain a divorce, hold a job, or change their domicile. Women were guaranteed the right to vote and were encouraged to enter politics.

Such efforts to remake Japanese behavior through legislation were only partially successful. During the past sixty years, Japan has unquestionably become a more individualistic and egalitarian society. At the same time, many of the distinctive characteristics of traditional Japanese society have persisted into the present day, although in somewhat altered form. The emphasis on loyalty to the group and community relationships, for example, is reflected in the strength of corporate loyalties in contemporary Japan, although, as we have seen, the attitude has eroded in recent years.

Emphasis on the work ethic also remains strong. The tradition of hard work is taught at a young age. Japanese students attend school 240 days a year, compared to 180

## Growing Up in Japan

Japanese schoolchildren are exposed to a much more regimented environment than U.S. children experience. Most Japanese schoolchildren, for example, wear black-and-white uniforms to school. These regulations are examples of rules adopted by middle school systems in various parts of Japan. The Ministry of Education in Tokyo concluded that these regulations were excessive, but they are probably typical.

*What is the apparent purpose of these regulations? Why does Japan appear to place more restrictions on adolescent behavior?*

### School Regulations, Japanese Style

1. Boys' hair should not touch the eyebrows, the ears, or the top of the collar.
2. No one should have a permanent wave, or dye his or her hair. Girls should not wear ribbons or accessories in their hair. Hair dryers should not be used.
3. School uniform skirts should be ____ centimeters above the ground, no more and no less (differs by school and region).
4. Keep your uniform clean and pressed at all times. Girls' middy blouses should have two buttons on the back collar. Boys' pant cuffs should be of the prescribed width. No more than 12 eyelets should be on shoes. The number of buttons on a shirt and tucks in a shirt are also prescribed.
5. Wear your school badge at all times. It should be positioned exactly.
6. Going to school in the morning, wear your book bag strap on the right shoulder; in the afternoon on the way home, wear it on the left shoulder. Your book case thickness, filled and unfilled, is also prescribed.
7. Girls should wear only regulation white underpants of 100% cotton.
8. When you raise your hand to be called on, your arm should extend forward and up at the angle prescribed in your handbook.
9. Your own route to and from school is marked in your student rule handbook; carefully observe which side of each street you are to use on the way to and from school.
10. After school you are to go directly home, unless your parent has written a note permitting you to go to another location. Permission will not be granted by the school unless this other location is a suitable one. You must not go to coffee shops. You must be home by ____ o'clock.
11. It is not permitted to drive or ride a motorcycle, or to have a license to drive one.
12. Before and after school, no matter where you are, you represent our school, so you should behave in ways we can all be proud of.

days in the United States, and homework assignments tend to be more extensive. The results are impressive: Japanese schoolchildren consistently earn higher scores on achievement tests than children in other advanced countries. At the same time, this devotion to success has often been accompanied by bullying by teachers and what Americans might consider an oppressive sense of conformity (see the box above).

Most young Japanese endure enormous pressures from society, school, and family. Ironically, once students have been accepted into college, the amount of work assigned tends to decrease, because graduates of the best universities are virtually guaranteed lucrative employment offers. Nevertheless, the early training instills an attitude of deference to group interests that persists throughout life.

By all accounts, independent thinking is on the increase in Japan. In some cases, it leads to antisocial behavior, such as crime or membership in a teenage gang. Crime rates, while well below those in the United States, have risen dramatically in recent years, leading Prime Minister Koizumi to lament that Japan is not "the world's safest country" anymore.[3] Antisocial feeling, however, is usually expressed in more indirect ways, such as the recent fashion among young people of dyeing their hair brown (known in Japanese as "tea hair"). Because the practice is banned in many schools and generally frowned upon by the older generation (one police chief dumped a pitcher of beer on a student with brown hair whom he noticed in a bar), many young Japanese dye their hair as a gesture of independence. When seeking employment or getting married, however, they return their hair to its natural color.

One of the more tenacious legacies of the past in Japanese society is sexual inequality. Although women are now legally protected against discrimination in employment, very few have reached senior levels in business, education, or politics. Women now comprise nearly 50 percent of the workforce, but most are in retail or service occupations, and their average salary is only about half that of men. Less than 10 percent of managerial workers in Japan are women, compared to nearly half in the United States. There is a feminist movement in Japan, but it has none of the vigor and mass support of its counterpart in the United States.

Japan's welfare system also differs profoundly from its Western counterparts. Applicants are required to seek assistance first from their own families, and the physically able are ineligible for government aid. As a result, less than 1 percent of the population receives welfare benefits, compared with more than 10 percent who receive some form of assistance in the United States.

Traditionally, it was the responsibility of the eldest child in a Japanese family to care for aging parents, but that system is beginning to break down because of limited housing space and the growing tendency of working-age women to seek jobs in the marketplace. The proportion of Japanese over sixty-five years of age who live with their children has dropped from 80 percent in 1970 to around 50 percent today. At the same time, public and private pension plans are under increasing financial pressure, partly because of a low birthrate and a graying population. Japan today has the highest proportion of people over age sixty-five of any industrialized country in the world—17 percent of the country's total population of about 130 million.

© Barry Cronin Newsmakers/Getty Images

**Cool *Otaku* Fashion Teens.** Fashion-conscious teenagers have become Japan's most dedicated consumers. With the economy in the doldrums and real estate costs soaring, many young people live with their families well into their twenties, using the money saved to purchase the latest styles in clothing. Avid readers of fashion magazines, these *otaku* ("obsessed") teenagers—heirs of Japan's long affluence—pay exorbitant prices for hip-hop outfits, platform shoes, and layered dresses.

Unlike most other advanced countries with similar problems, however, Japan has been reluctant to increase the rate of immigration into the country. Immigrants comprise only 1 percent of the total population, and most are descendants of Koreans and Chinese who settled in Japan before World War II.

Whether the unique character of modern Japan will endure is unclear. Confidence in the Japanese "economic miracle" has been shaken by the recent downturn, and there are indications of a growing tendency toward hedonism and individualism among Japanese youth. Older Japanese frequently complain that the younger generation lacks their sense of loyalty and willingness to sacrifice.

**Religion** When Japan was opened to the West in the nineteenth century, many Japanese became convinced of the superiority of foreign ideas and institutions and were especially interested in Western religion and culture. Although Christian converts were few, numbering less than 1 percent of the population, the influence of Christianity was out of proportion to the size of the community. Many intellectuals during the Meiji era were impressed by the emotional commitment shown by missionaries in Japan and viewed Christianity as a contemporary version of Confucianism.

Today, Japan includes almost 1.5 million Christians, along with 93 million Buddhists. Many Japanese also follow Shinto, no longer identified with reverence for the emperor and the state. As in the West, increasing urbanization has led to a decline in the practice of organized religion, although evangelical sects have proliferated in recent years. The largest and best-known sect is Soka Gakkai, a lay Buddhist organization that has attracted millions of followers and formed its own political party, the Komeito. Zen Buddhism retains its popularity, and some businesspeople seek to use Zen techniques to learn how to focus on willpower as a means of outwitting a competitor. The head of one Zen monastery, however, has publicly apologized for the sect's role in promoting fanatical patriotism in the military before World War II.

**Japanese Culture** Western literature, art, and music have had a major impact on Japanese society. After World War II, many of the writers who had been active before the war resurfaced, but now their writing reflected demoralization. Many were attracted to existentialism, and some turned to hedonism and nihilism. For these disillusioned authors, defeat was compounded by fear of the Americanization of postwar Japan. One of the best examples of this attitude was the novelist Yukio Mishima, who led a crusade to stem the tide of what he described as America's "universal and uniform 'Coca-Colonization'" of the world in general and Japan in particular.[4] Mishima's ritual suicide in 1970 was the subject of widespread speculation and transformed him into a cult figure.

One of Japan's most serious-minded contemporary authors is Kenzaburo Oe (b. 1935). His work, rewarded with a Nobel Prize for literature in 1994, presents Japan's ongoing quest for modern identity and purpose. His characters reflect the spiritual anguish precipitated by the collapse of the imperial Japanese tradition and the subsequent adoption of Western culture—a trend that Oe contends has culminated in unabashed materialism, cultural decline, and a moral void. Yet unlike Mishima, Oe does not wish to reinstill the imperial traditions of the past but rather seeks to regain spiritual meaning by retrieving the sense of communality and innocence found in rural Japan.

A recent phenomenon is the so-called industrial novel, which lays bare the vicious infighting and pressure tactics that characterize Japanese business today. Another popular genre is the "art-manga," or literary cartoon. Manga has become popular in the United States, especially in the form of adventure stories appealing to young girls.

Other aspects of Japanese culture have also been influenced by Western ideas, although without the intense preoccupation with synthesis that is evident in literature. Western music is very popular in Japan, and scores of Japanese classical musicians have succeeded in the West. Even rap music has gained a foothold among Japanese youth, although without the association with sex, drugs, and violence that it has in the United States. Although some of the lyrics betray an attitude of modest revolt against the uptight world of Japanese society, most lack any such connotations. An example is the rap song "Street Life":

> *Now's the time to hip-hop,*
> *Everybody's crazy about rap,*
> *Hey, hey, you all, listen up,*
> *Listen to my rap and cheer up.*

As one singer remarked, "We've been very fortunate, and we don't want to bother our Moms and Dads. So we don't sing songs that would disturb parents."[5]

There are some signs that under the surface, the tension between traditional and modern is exacting a price. As novelists such as Mishima and Oe feared, the growing focus on material possessions and the decline of traditional religious beliefs have left a spiritual void. Some young people have reacted to the emptiness of their lives by joining religious cults such as Aum Shinri Kyo, which came to world attention in 1995 when members of the organization carried out a poison gas attack on the Tokyo subway that killed several people.

## The Little Tigers

The success of postwar Japan in meeting the challenge from the capitalist West soon caught the eye of other Asian nations. By the 1980s, several smaller states in the region, known collectively as the Little Tigers, had successively followed the Japanese example.

**South Korea: A Peninsula Divided** While the world was focused on the economic miracle occurring on the Japanese islands, another miracle of sorts was taking place across the Sea of Japan on the Asian mainland. In 1953, the Korean peninsula was exhausted from three years of bitter fraternal war, a conflict that took the lives of an estimated four million Koreans on both sides of the 38th parallel and turned as much as one-quarter of the population into refugees. Although a cease-fire was signed in July 1953, it was a fragile peace that left two heavily armed and mutually hostile countries facing each other suspiciously.

North of the truce line was the People's Republic of Korea (PRK), a police state under the dictatorial rule of the Communist leader Kim Il Sung (1912–1994). To the south was the Republic of Korea, under the equally autocratic President Syngman Rhee (1875–1965), a fierce anti-Communist who had led the resistance to the northern invasion. But many Koreans resented Rhee's reliance on the wealthy landlord class. After several years of harsh rule, marked by government corruption, fraudulent elections, and police brutality, demonstrations broke out in the capital city of Seoul in the spring of 1960 and forced him into retirement.

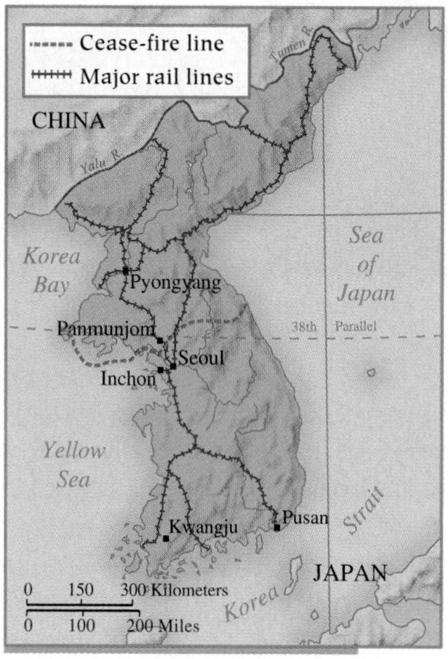

**The Korean Peninsula Since 1953**

The Rhee era was followed by a brief period of multiparty democratic government, but in 1961, a coup d'état placed General Chung Hee Park (1917–1979) in power. The new regime promulgated a new constitution, and in 1963, Park was elected president of a civilian government. He set out to foster recovery of the economy from decades of foreign occupation and civil war. Because the private sector had been relatively weak under Japanese rule, the government played an active role in the process by instituting a series of five-year plans that targeted specific industries for development, promoted exports, and funded infrastructure development. Under a land reform program, large landowners were required to sell all their farmland above 7.4 acres to their tenants at low prices.

The program was a solid success. Benefiting from the Confucian principles of thrift, respect for education, and hard work, as well as from Japanese capital and technology, South Korea gradually emerged as a major industrial power in East Asia. The economic growth rate rose from less than 5 percent annually in the 1950s to an average of 9 percent under Chung Hee Park. The largest corporations—including Samsung, Daewoo, and Hyundai—were transformed into massive conglomerates called ***chaebol,*** the Korean equivalent of the *zaibatsu* of prewar Japan. Taking advantage of relatively low wages and a stunningly high rate of saving, Korean businesses began to compete actively with the Japanese for export markets in Asia and throughout the world. Per capita income also increased dramatically, from less than $90 (in U.S. dollars) annually in 1960 to $1,560 (twice that of Communist North Korea) twenty years later.

But like many other countries in the region, South Korea was slow to develop democratic principles. Although his government functioned with the trappings of democracy, Park continued to rule by autocratic means and suppressed all forms of dissidence. In 1979, Park was assassinated. But after a brief interregnum of democratic rule, in 1980 a new military government under General Chun Doo Hwan seized power. The new regime was as authoritarian as its predecessors, but opposition to autocratic rule had now spread to much of the urban population.

With Chun under increasing pressure from the United States to moderate the oppressive character of his rule, national elections were finally held in 1989. The successful candidate was succeeded by another elected president, Kim Young Sam, in 1992. Kim promised to make South Korea "a freer and more mature democracy" and attempted to crack down on the influence of the giant *chaebols,* which were accused of giving massive bribes in return for favors from government officials. He also initiated contacts with the Communist regime in the PRK on possible steps toward eventual reunification of the peninsula.

But the nation's problems were more serious than the endemic problem of corruption. A growing trade deficit, combined with a declining growth rate, led to increased unemployment and bankruptcy. After the Asian financial crisis emerged in 1997, economic conditions worsened, leading to the election of a longtime opposition figure, Kim Dae Jung, to the presidency. But although the new leader promised drastic reforms, his regime too was charged with corruption and incompetence. In the meantime, relations with North Korea, now under the dictorial rule of Kim Il Sung's son Kim Jong Il and on the verge of becoming a nuclear power, remain tense.

**Taiwan: The Other China** South Korea was not the only rising industrial power trying to imitate the success of the Japanese in East Asia. To the south on the island of Taiwan, the Republic of China began to do the same.

After retreating to Taiwan following their defeat by the Communists, Chiang Kai-shek and his followers established a new capital at Taipei. The government, which continued to refer to itself as the Republic of China (ROC), contended that it remained the legitimate representative of the Chinese people and that it would eventually return in triumph to the mainland.

The Nationalists had much more success on Taiwan than they had achieved on the mainland. In the relatively safe and stable environment provided by a security treaty with the United States, signed in 1954, the ROC was able to concentrate on economic growth without worrying about a Communist invasion.

The government moved rapidly to create a solid agricultural base. A land reform program led to the reduction of rents, and landholdings over 3 acres were purchased by the government and resold to the tenants at reasonable prices. At the same time, local manufacturing and commerce were strongly encouraged. By the 1970s, Taiwan had become one of the most dynamic industrial economies in East Asia. The government played a major role in the process, targeting strategic industries for support and investing in infrastructure. At the same time, as in Japan, the government stressed the importance of private enterprise and encouraged foreign investment and a high rate of internal savings.

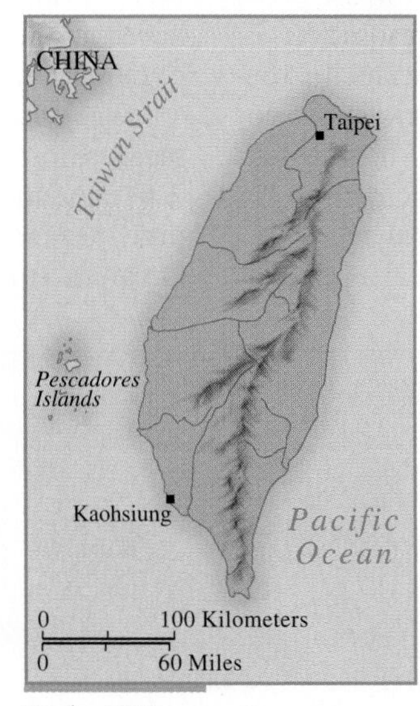

**Modern Taiwan**

In contrast to the Communist regime in the People's Republic of China (PRC), the ROC actively maintained Chinese tradition, promoting respect for Confucius and the ethical principles of the past, such as hard work, frugality, and filial piety. Although there was some corruption in both the government and the private sector, income differentials between the wealthy and the poor were generally less than elsewhere in the region, and the overall standard of living increased substantially. Health and sanitation improved, literacy rates were quite high, and an active family planning program reduced the rate of population growth. Nevertheless, the total population on the island increased from about seven million in 1945 to about twenty million in the mid-1980s.

Increasing prosperity, however, did not lead to the democratization of the political process. The Nationalists continued to rule by emergency decree and refused to permit the formation of opposition political parties on the ground that the danger of invasion from the mainland had not subsided. Some friction developed between the mainlanders, who numbered about two million and were dominant in the government, and the native Taiwanese (mostly ethnic Chinese whose ancestors had emigrated to the island during the Qing dynasty). By the 1980s, however, these fissures in Taiwanese society had begun to diminish; by then, an ever-higher proportion of the population had been born on the island and identified themselves as Taiwanese.

After the death of Chiang Kai-shek in 1975, the ROC slowly began to move toward a more representative form of government, including elections and legal opposition parties. A national election in 1992 resulted in a bare majority for the Nationalists over strong opposition from the Democratic Progressive Party (DPP). But political liberalization had its dangers; some members of the DPP began to agitate for an independent Republic of Taiwan, a possibility that aroused concern within the Nationalist government in Taipei and frenzied hostility on the mainland. The election of DPP leader Chen Shuibian as ROC president in March 2000 angered Beijing, which threatened to invade Taiwan should the island continue to delay unification with the mainland.

Whether Taiwan will remain an independent state or be united with the mainland is impossible to predict. The

## To Those Living in Glass Houses

Kishore Mahbubani is permanent secretary in the Ministry of Foreign Affairs in Singapore. Previously, he served as his country's ambassador to the United Nations. In this 1994 article, adapted from a piece in the *Washington Quarterly*, the author advises his audience to stop lecturing Asian societies on the issue of human rights and focus attention instead on problems in the United States. In his view, today the countries of the West have much to learn from their counterparts in East Asia. This viewpoint is shared by many other observers, political leaders, and foreign affairs specialists in the region.

*What are the author's criticisms of Western civilization? How does he justify the "Asian" approach to politics?*

### Kishore Mahbubani, "Go East, Young Man"

In a major reversal of a pattern lasting centuries, many Western societies, including the U.S., are doing some major things fundamentally wrong, while a growing number of East Asian societies are doing the same things right. The results are most evident in the economic sphere. In purchasing power parity terms, East Asia's gross domestic product is already larger than that of either the U.S. or European community. Such economic prosperity, contrary to American belief, results not just from free-market arrangements but also from the right social and political choices. . . .

In most Asian eyes, the evidence of real social decay in the U.S. is clear and palpable. Since 1960, the U.S. population has grown by 41%. In the same period, there has been a 560% increase in violent crimes, a 419% increase in illegitimate births, a 400% increase in divorce rates, a 300% increase in children living in single-parent homes, a more than 200% increase in teenage suicide rates, and a drop of almost 80 points in [SAT] scores. A clear American paradox is that a society that places such a high premium on freedom has effectively reduced the physical freedom of most Americans, especially those who live in large cities. They live in heavily fortified homes, think twice before taking an evening stroll around their neighborhoods, and feel increasingly threatened by random violence when they are outside.

To any Asian, it is obvious that the breakdown of the family and social order in the U.S. owes itself to a mindless ideology that maintains that the freedom of a small number of individuals who are known to pose a threat to society (criminals, terrorists, street gang members, drug dealers) should not be constrained (for example, through detention without trial), even if to do so would enhance the freedom of the majority. . . . This belief is purely and simply a gross violation of common sense.

My hope is that Americans will come to visit East Asia in greater numbers. When they do, they will come to realize that their society has swung much too much in one direction: liberating the individual while imprisoning society. The relatively strong and stable family and social institutions of East Asia will appear more appealing. And as Americans experience the freedom of walking on city streets in Asia, they may begin to understand that freedom can also result from greater social order and discipline. Perhaps the best advice to give to a young American is: "Go East, Young Man."

United States continues to provide defensive military assistance to the Taiwanese armed forces and has made it clear that it supports self-determination for the people of Taiwan and that it expects the final resolution of the Chinese civil war to be by peaceful means. In the meantime, economic and cultural contacts between Taiwan and the mainland are steadily increasing. However, the Taiwanese have shown no inclination to accept the PRC's offer of "one country, two systems," under which the ROC would accept the PRC as the legitimate government of China in return for autonomous control over the affairs of Taiwan.

**Singapore and Hong Kong: The Littlest Tigers** The smallest but by no means least successful of the Little Tigers are Singapore and Hong Kong. Both are essentially city-states, with large populations densely packed into small territories. Singapore, once a British colony and briefly a part of the state of Malaysia, is now an independent nation. Hong Kong was a British colony until it was returned to PRC control in 1997. In recent years, both have emerged as industrial powerhouses, with standards of living well above those of their neighbors.

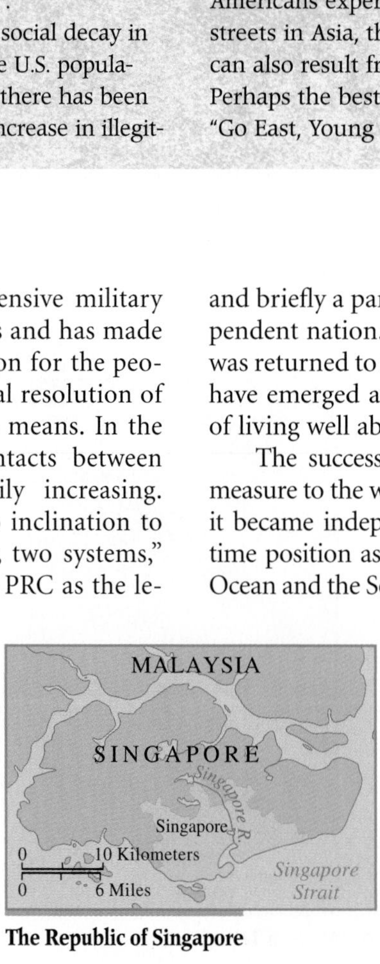

The Republic of Singapore

The success of Singapore must be ascribed in good measure to the will and energy of its political leaders. When it became independent in August 1965, Singapore's long-time position as an entrepôt for trade between the Indian Ocean and the South China Sea was on the wane. With only 618 square miles of territory, much of it marshland and tropical jungle, Singapore had little to offer but the frugality and industriousness of its predominantly overseas Chinese population.

Within a decade, Singapore's role and reputation had dramatically changed. Under the leadership of Prime Minister Lee Kuan-yew (b. 1923), once the firebrand leader of the radical People's Action Party, the government cultivated an attractive business climate while engaging in massive public works projects to feed, house, and educate its two million citizens. The major components of success have been shipbuilding, oil refineries, tourism, electronics, and finance—the city-state has become the banking hub of the entire region.

**You *Can* Take It with You.** While wealthy Chinese in traditional China buried clay models of personal possessions to accompany the departed to the next world, ordinary people burned paper effigies, which were transported to the afterlife by means of the rising smoke. This custom survives in many Chinese communities today, as this photograph taken in modern-day Singapore demonstrates. Some merchants make their living by manufacturing paper replicas of elaborate houses such as seen here, often featuring such embellishments as television sets, elegant furniture, and even Mercedes automobiles.

Like South Korea and Taiwan, Singapore relied on a combination of government planning, entrepreneurial spirit, export promotion, high productivity, and an exceptionally high rate of saving to achieve industrial growth rates of nearly 10 percent annually during the last quarter of the twentieth century. In recent years, however, the rate of growth has dropped dramatically, due primarily to increasing competition from China.

As in the other Little Tigers, an authoritarian political system has guaranteed a stable environment for economic growth. Until his retirement in 1990, Lee Kuan-yew and his People's Action Party dominated Singapore politics, and opposition elements were intimidated into silence or arrested. The prime minister openly declared that the Western model of pluralist democracy was not appropriate for Singapore and lauded the Meiji model of centralized development (see the box on p. 876). Confucian values of thrift, hard work, and obedience to authority have been promoted as the ideology of the state. The government has had a passion for cleanliness and at one time even undertook a campaign to persuade its citizens to flush the public urinals. In 1989, the local *Straits Times,* a mouthpiece of the government, published a photograph of a man walking sheepishly from a row of urinals. The caption read "Caught without a flush: Mr. Amar Mohamed leaving the Lucky Plaza [a local shopping center] toilet without flushing the urinal."[6]

But economic success has begun to undermine the authoritarian foundations of the system as a more sophisticated citizenry voices aspirations for more political freedoms and an end to government paternalism. Lee Kuan-yew's successor, Goh Chok Tong, promised a "kinder, gentler" Singapore, and political restrictions on individual behavior are gradually being relaxed. There is reason for optimism that a more pluralistic political system will gradually emerge.

The future of Hong Kong is not so clear-cut. As in Singapore, sensible government policies and the hard work of its people have enabled Hong Kong to thrive. At first, the prosperity of the colony depended on a plentiful supply of cheap labor. Inundated with refugees from the mainland during the 1950s and 1960s, the population of Hong Kong burgeoned to more than six million. More recently, Hong Kong has benefited from increased tourism, manufacturing, and the growing economic prosperity of neighboring Guangdong province, the most prosperous region of the PRC. Unlike the other societies discussed in this chapter, Hong Kong has relied on an unbridled free market system rather than active state intervention in the economy. At the same time, by allocating substantial funds for transportation, sanitation, education, and public housing, the government has created favorable conditions for economic development.

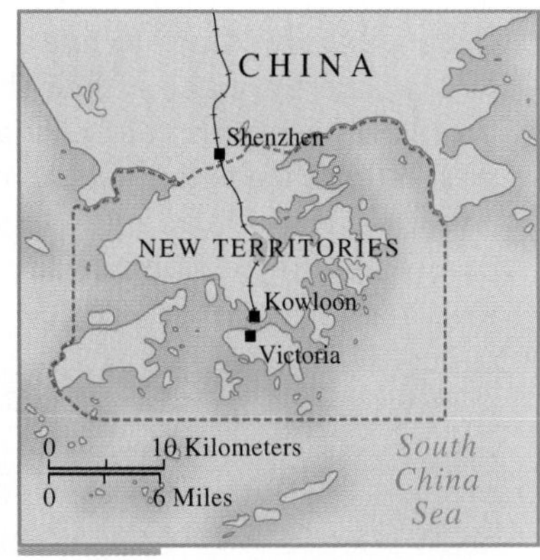


**Hong Kong**

When Britain's ninety-nine-year lease on the New Territories, the foodbasket of the colony, expired on July 1, 1997, Hong Kong returned to mainland authority. Although the Chinese promised the British that for fifty years the people of Hong Kong would live under a capitalist system and be essentially self-governing, recent statements by Chinese leaders have raised questions about the degree of autonomy Hong Kong will continue to receive under Chinese rule (see the box on p. 878).

## Return to the Motherland

After lengthy negotiations, in December 1984, China and Great Britain agreed that on July 1, 1997, Hong Kong would return to Chinese sovereignty. Key sections of the agreement are included here. In succeeding years, authorities of the two countries held further negotiations. Some of the discussions raised questions in the minds of residents of Hong Kong as to whether their individual liberties would indeed be respected after the colony's return to China.

*What restrictions does this document place on the autonomy of Hong Kong? How does the system in Hong Kong differ from that on the mainland of China?*

### The Joint Declaration on Hong Kong

The Hong Kong Special Administrative Region will be directly under the authority of the Central People's Government of the People's Republic of China. The Hong Kong Special Administrative Region will enjoy a high degree of autonomy, except in foreign and defense affairs, which are the responsibility of the Central People's Government.

The Hong Kong Special Administrative Region will be vested with executive, legislative, and independent judicial power, including that of final adjudication. The laws currently in force in Hong Kong will remain basically unchanged.

The Government of the Hong Kong Special Administrative Region will be composed of local inhabitants. The chief executive will be appointed by the Central People's Government on the basis of the results of elections or consultations to be held locally. Principal officials will be nominated by the chief executive of the Hong Kong Special Administrative Region for appointment by the Central People's Government. . . .

The current social and economic systems in Hong Kong will remain unchanged, and so will the lifestyle. Rights and freedoms, including those of the person, of speech, of the press, of assembly, of association, of travel, of movement, of correspondence, of strike, of choice of occupation, of academic research, and of religious belief will be ensured by law. . . . Private property, ownership of enterprises, legitimate right of inheritance, and foreign investment will be protected by law.

## On the Margins of Asia: Postwar Australia and New Zealand

Geographically, Australia and New Zealand are not part of Asia, and throughout their short history, both countries have identified culturally and politically with the West rather than with their Pacific Rim neighbors. Their political institutions and values are derived from Europe, and their economies resemble those of the advanced countries of the world rather than the preindustrial societies of much of Southeast Asia. Both are currently members of the British Commonwealth and of the U.S.-led ANZUS alliance (Australia, New Zealand, and the United States).

Yet trends in recent years have been drawing both states, especially Australia, closer to Asia. In the first place, immigration from East and Southeast Asia has increased rapidly. More than one-half of current immigrants into

Courtesy of William J. Duiker

**The Hong Kong Skyline.** Hong Kong reverted to Chinese sovereignty in 1997 after a century of British rule. To commemorate the occasion, the imposing Conference Center, shown here in the foreground, was built on reclaimed shoreland in Hong Kong harbor. The center is surrounded by the gleaming modern skyscrapers of the city of Victoria, with Victoria Peak in the background. The Star Ferry, long a fixture for local residents, plies its way between the island and the peninsula of Kowloon.

**CHRONOLOGY Japan and the Little Tigers Since World War II**

| | |
|---|---|
| End of World War II in the Pacific | 1945 |
| Chiang Kai-shek retreats to Taiwan | 1949 |
| End of U.S. occupation of Japan | 1950 |
| Korean War | 1950–1953 |
| United States–Republic of China security treaty | 1954 |
| Syngman Rhee overthrown in South Korea | 1960 |
| Rise to power of Chung Hee Park in South Korea | 1961 |
| Independence of Republic of Singapore | 1965 |
| Death of Chiang Kai-shek | 1975 |
| Chung Hee Park assassinated | 1979 |
| End of United States–Republic of China security treaty | 1979 |
| Students riot in South Korea | 1987 |
| First free general elections on Taiwan | 1992 |
| Election of Kim Young Sam as president in South Korea | 1992 |
| Return of Hong Kong to Chinese control | 1997 |
| Financial crisis hits the region | 1997 |
| Chen Shuibian elected president of Taiwan | 2000 |
| Junichiro Koizumi elected prime minister in Japan | 2001 |

Australia come from East Asia, and about 7 percent of the population of about 18 million people is now of Asian descent. In New Zealand, residents of Asian descent represent only about 3 percent of the population of 3.5 million, but about 12 percent of the population are Maoris, Polynesian peoples who settled on the islands about a thousand years ago. Second, trade relations with Asia are increasing rapidly. About 60 percent of Australia's export markets today are in East Asia, and the region is the source of about one-half of its imports. Asian trade with New Zealand is also on the increase.

At the same time, the links that bind both countries to Great Britain and the United States have been loosening. There are moves under way in Australia and New Zealand to withdraw from the British Commonwealth, although the outcome at this point appears far from certain. Although security ties with the United States remain important, the Australian government is seeking to establish closer ties with the ASEAN alliance. Farther removed from Asia both physically and psychologically, New Zealand assigns less importance to its security treaty with the United States and has been vocally critical of U.S. nuclear policies in the region.

Whether Australia and New Zealand will ever become an integral part of the Asia-Pacific region is uncertain. Cultural differences stemming from the European origins of the majority of the population in both countries hinder mutual understanding on both sides of the divide, and many ASEAN leaders express reluctance to accept the two countries as full members of the alliance. But economic and geographical realities act as a powerful force, and should the Pacific region continue on its current course toward economic prosperity and political stability, the role of Australia and New Zealand will assume greater significance.

## Explaining the East Asian Miracle

What explains the striking ability of Japan and the four Little Tigers to transform themselves into export-oriented societies capable of competing with the advanced nations of Europe and the Western Hemisphere? As we have noted, there are two contrasting explanations. Some point to the traditional character traits of Confucian societies, such as thrift, a work ethic, respect for education, and obedience to authority. Others place more emphasis on deliberate steps taken by government and economic leaders to meet the political, economic, and social challenges faced by their societies.

There is no reason to doubt that cultural factors have contributed to the economic success of these societies. Habits such as frugality, industriousness, and subordination of individual desires have all played a role in their governments' ability to concentrate on the collective interest. Whether such values should be specifically identified with Confucianism, however, is a matter of debate. After all, until recently, mainland China did not share in the economic success of its neighbors despite a long tradition of espousing Confucian values. In fact, some historians in recent years have maintained that it was precisely those Confucian values that hindered China's early response to the challenge of the West.

The key factor, it appears, is the emergence of a political elite that focuses on maximizing the productive capacity of a given society. The creative talents of the Chinese people were not efficiently utilized until Deng Xiaoping launched his program of Four Modernizations in the late 1970s. The same situation applied in neighboring areas while they were under European or Japanese colonial rule (although Japanese colonialism did lead to the creation of an infrastructure more conducive to later development than was the case in European colonies). Only when a "modernizing elite" took charge and began to place a high priority on economic development were the stunning advances of recent decades achieved.

Another common factor is that Japan and its emulators were operating within a regional framework highly conducive to rapid economic development. The Little Tigers received substantial inputs of capital and technology from the advanced nations of the West—Taiwan and South Korea from the United States, Hong Kong and Singapore from Britain. Japan relied to a greater degree on its own efforts but received a significant advantage by being placed under the U.S. security umbrella and guaranteed access to markets and sources of raw materials in a region dominated by U.S. naval power.

## COMPARATIVE ESSAY

# GLOBAL VILLAGE OR CLASH OF CIVILIZATIONS?

As the Cold War came to an end in the early 1990s, statesmen, scholars, and political pundits began to forecast the emergence of a "new world order." One hypothesis was that the decline of communism signaled that the industrial capitalist democracies of the West had triumphed in the world of ideas and were now poised to remake the rest of the world in their own image.

Not all agreed with this optimistic view of the world situation. In *The Clash of Civilizations and the Remaking of the World Order,* the historian Samuel P. Huntington suggested that the post–Cold War era, far from marking the triumph of the Western idea, would be characterized by increased global fragmentation and a "clash of civilizations" based on ethnic, cultural, or religious differences. According to Huntington, the coming decades may see a world dominated by disputing cultural blocs in East Asia, Western Europe and the United States, Eurasia, and the Middle East. The dream of a universal order—a global village—dominated by Western values, he concludes, is a fantasy.

Events in recent years have lent some support to Huntington's hypothesis. The collapse of the Soviet Union led to the emergence of an atmosphere of conflict and tension all along the perimeter of the old Soviet empire. More recently, the terrorist attack on the United States in September 2001 set the advanced nations of the West and much of the Muslim world on a collision course. As for the new economic order—now enshrined as official policy in Western capitals—public anger at the impact of globalization has reached disturbing levels in many countries, leading to a growing demand for self-protection and group identity in an impersonal and rapidly changing world.

Are we then headed toward Huntington's prediction of multiple power blocs divided by religion and culture? His thesis is indeed a useful corrective to the complacent tendency of many observers to view Western civilization as the zenith of human achievement. On the other hand, by dividing the world into competing cultural blocs, Huntington has underestimated the centrifugal forces at work in the various regions of the world. As the industrial and technological revolutions spread across the face of the earth, their impact is measurably stronger in some societies than in others, thus intensifying historical rivalries in a given region while establishing links between individual societies and counterparts in other parts of the world. In recent years, for example, Japan has had more in common with the United States than with its traditional neighbors, China and Korea.

The most likely scenario for the next few decades, then, is more complex than either the global village hypothesis or its rival, the clash of civilizations. The world of the twenty-first century will be characterized by simultaneous trends toward globalization and fragmentation as the thrust of technology and information transforms societies and gives rise to counterreactions among societies seeking to preserve a group identity and a sense of meaning and purpose in a confusing world.

## CONCLUSION

THE RISE OF ASIA as a crucial factor in the global economic order has sparked widespread debate, and sometimes concern, in major world capitals. Some observers see major Asian states like China, Japan, and even India as future competitors with advanced Western nations (see the comparative essay "Global Village or Clash of Civilizations" above), an observation made more ominous in recent years by the outsourcing of jobs to the region.

To some observers, the economic achievements of the nations of the western Pacific have come at a high price, in the form of political authoritarianism and a lack of attention to human rights. Until recently, government repression of opposition has been common in many of these nations. In addition, the rights of national minorities and women are often still limited in comparison with the advanced nations of the West. Recent developments such as the financial crisis of 1997 and the long economic downturn in Japan have also somewhat tarnished the image of the "Asian miracle," raising concern that some of the factors that contributed to economic success in prior years are now making it difficult for governments to develop open and accountable financial systems.

Still, it should be kept in mind that progress in political pluralism and human rights has not always been easy to achieve in the West and even now frequently fails to match expectations. A look at the historical record suggests that political pluralism is often a by-product of economic growth and that political values and institutions evolve in response to changing social conditions. A rising standard of living and increased social mobility should go far toward enhancing political freedom and promoting social justice in the countries bordering the western Pacific.

The efforts of these nations to find a way to accommodate traditional and modern, native and foreign, raise a final question. As we have seen, Mahatma Gandhi believed that materialism is ultimately a dead end. In light of contemporary concerns about the emptiness of life in the West and the self-destructiveness of material culture, can his message be ignored?

## TIMELINE

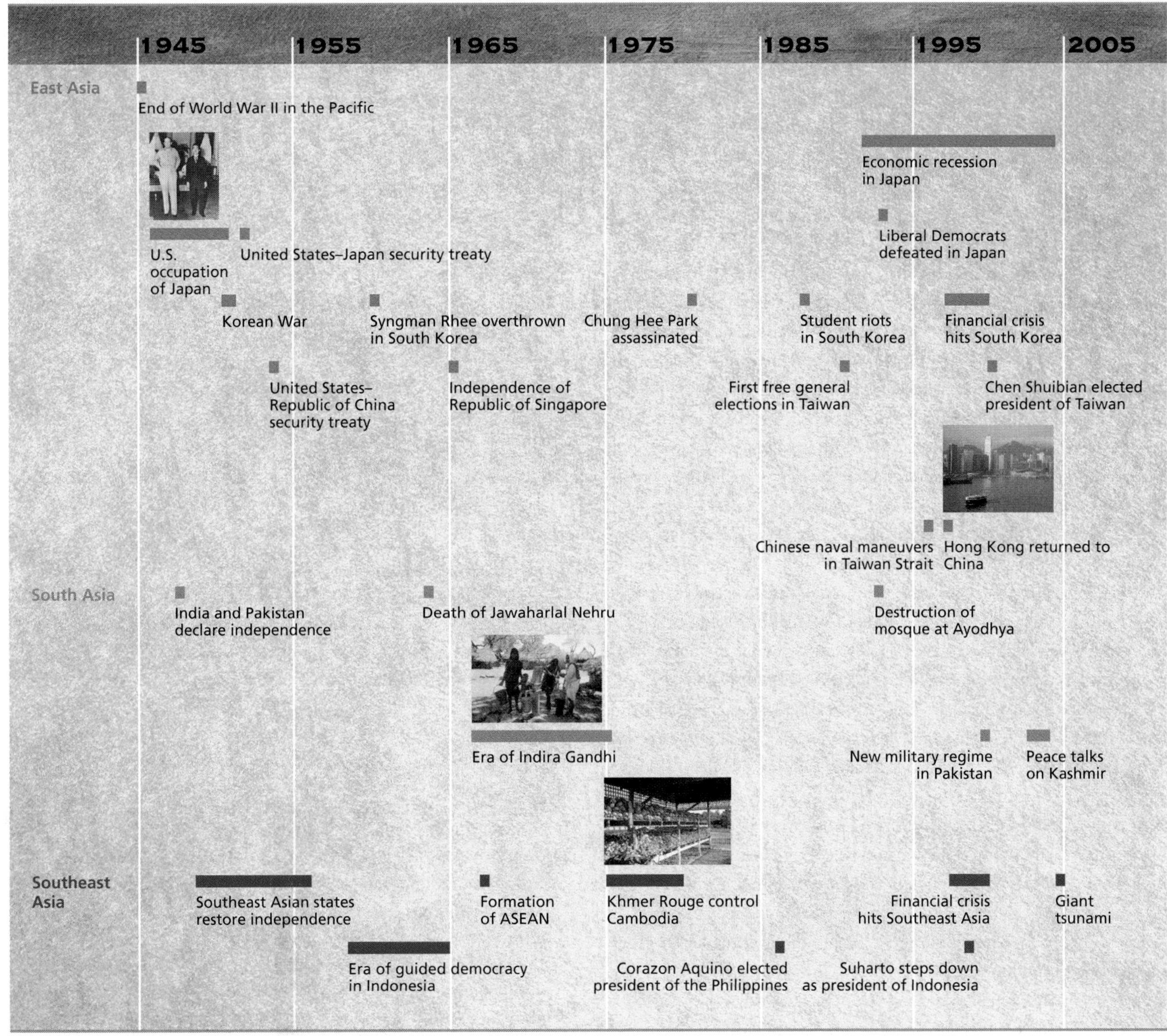


## CHAPTER NOTES

1. *New York Times,* May 2, 1996.
2. Quoted in L. Collins and D. Lapierre, *Freedom at Midnight* (New York, 1975), p. 252.
3. *New York Times,* September 6, 2003.
4. Y. Mishima and G. Bownas, eds., *New Writing in Japan* (Harmondsworth, England, 1972), p. 16.
5. *New York Times,* January 29, 1996.
6. S. Seser, "A Reporter at Large," *New Yorker,* January 13, 1992, p. 44.

## SUGGESTED READING

For a survey of postwar Indian history, see **S. Wolpert, *A New History of India*** (New York, 1989). Also see **P. Brass, *The New Cambridge History of India: The Politics of Independence*** (Cambridge, 1990), and **S. Tharoor, *India: From Midnight to the Millennium*** (New York, 1997). On India's founding father, see **J. Brown, *Nehru: A Political Life*** (New Haven, Conn., 2003). The life and career of Indira Gandhi have been well chronicled. Two fine biographies are **T. Ali, *An Indian Dynasty: The Story of the Nehru-Gandhi Family*** (New York, 1985), and **K. Frank, *Indira: The Life of Indira Nehru Gandhi*** (New York, 2000). On Pakistan, see **O. B. Jones, *Pakistan: Eye of the Storm*** (New Haven, Conn., 2002). Also of interest is **C. Baxter, *Bangladesh: From a Nation to a State*** (Boulder, Colo., 1997).

On Indian literature, see **D. Ray** and **A. Singh,** eds., ***India: An Anthology of Contemporary Writing*** (Athens, Ohio, 1983). See also **S. Tharu** and **K. Lalita,** eds., ***Women Writing in India,*** vol. 2 (New York, 1993).

There are a number of standard surveys of the history of modern Southeast Asia. Unfortunately, many of them are now out of date because of the changes that have taken place in the region since the end of the Vietnam War. For an introduction with a strong emphasis on recent events, see **D. R. Sar Desai, *Southeast Asia: Past and Present,*** 2d ed. (Boulder, Colo., 1989). For a more scholarly approach, see **D. J. Steinberg,** ed., ***In Search of Southeast Asia,*** 2d ed. (New York, 1985).

For a broader perspective on Indonesian society and culture, see **T. Friend, *Indonesian Destinies*** (Cambridge, Mass., 2003). For a political perspective on the Suharto years, see **M. Vatiokis, *Indonesian Politics Under Suharto*** (London, 1993). The rise of terrorism in the region is discussed in **Z. Abuza, *Militant Islam in Southeast Asia: Crucible of Terror*** (Boulder, Colo., 2003). Also see **C. Christie, *A Modern History of Southeast Asia: Decolonization, Nationalism and Separatism*** (London, 1996).

For an overview of women's issues in contemporary South and Southeast Asia, consult **B. Ramusack** and **S. Sievers, *Women in Asia*** (Bloomington, Ind., 1999). Articles that focus on the socioeconomic problems of women in India in the 1980s are found in **M. Kishwar** and **R. Vanita**, eds., ***In Search of Answers: Indian Women's Voices from Manushi*** (London, 1991). **K. Bhasin, R. Menon,** and **N. S. Khan**, eds., ***Against All Odds: Essays on Women, Religion and Development from India and Pakistan*** (New Delhi, 1994), explores fundamentalist conservatism among both Hindu and Muslim women. Of interest on Southeast Asian women's issues are **W. Williams, *Japanese Lives: Women and Men in Modern Indonesian Society*** (New Brunswick, N.J., 1991), and **C. B. N. Chin, *In Service and Servitude: Foreign Female Domestic Workers and the Malaysian "Modernity" Project*** (New York, 1998).

For a balanced treatment of all issues relating to postwar Japan, see **J. McLain, *Japan: A Modern History*** (New York, 2001). For a more journalistic approach that raises questions about the future of democracy in Japan, see **I. Buruma, *Inventing Japan*** (New York, 2002). For a topical approach with a strong emphasis on economic and social matters, **J. E. Hunter, *The Emergence of Modern Japan: An Introductory History Since 1853*** (London, 1989), is excellent. For an extensive analysis of Japan's adjustment to the Allied occupation, see **J. W. Dower, *Embracing Defeat: Japan in the Wake of World War II*** (New York, 1999). Political dissent and its consequences are dealt with in **N. Fields, *In the Realm of the Dying Emperor*** (New York, 1991).

Japanese social issues have often been examined from an economic perspective as foreign observers try to discover the reasons for the nation's economic success. **C. Nakane, *Japanese Society*** (Harmondsworth, England, 1979) provides a scholarly treatment, while **R. J. Hendry, *Understanding Japanese Society*** (Beckenham, England, 1987), is more accessible. For a more local treatment, see **R. P. Dore, *Shinohata: A Portrait of a Japanese Village*** (New York, 1978), and **T. C. Bestor, *Neighborhood Tokyo*** (Stanford, Calif., 1989). **T. Heymann, *On an Average Day in Japan*** (New York, 1992), provides an interesting statistical comparison of Japanese and American society. On the role of women in modern Japan, see **D. Robins-Mowry, *The Hidden Sun: Women of Modern Japan*** (Boulder, Colo., 1983), and **N. Bornoff, *Pink Samurai: Love, Marriage, and Sex in Contemporary Japan*** (New York, 1991).

On the four Little Tigers and their economic development, see **E. F. Vogel, *The Four Little Dragons: The Spread of Industrialization in East Asia*** (Cambridge, Mass., 1991); **J. W. Morley**, ed., ***Driven by Growth: Political Change in the Asia-Pacific Region*** (Armonk, N.Y., 1992); and **J. Woronoff, *Asia's Miracle Economies*** (New York, 1986). For an interesting collection of articles on the role of Confucian ideology in promoting economic growth, see **Hung-chao Tai**, ed., ***Confucianism and Economic Development*** (Washington, D.C., 1989). For individual treatments of the Little Tigers, see **Hak-kyu Sohn, *Authoritarianism and Opposition in South Korea*** (London, 1989); **D. F. Simon, *Taiwan: Beyond the Economic Miracle*** (Armonk, N.Y., 1992); **Lee Kuan Yew, *From Third World to First: The Singapore Story, 1965–2000*** (New York, 2000); and **K. Rafferty, *City on the Rocks: Hong Kong's Uncertain Future*** (London, 1991). Also see **M. Rubinstein, *Taiwan: A New History*** (New York, 2001).

**History Now™**

**Enter *HistoryNow* using the access card that is available with this text. *HistoryNow* will assist you in understanding the content in this chapter with lesson plans generated for your needs, as well as provide you with a connection to the *Wadsworth World History Resource Center* (see description below for details).**

**WORLD HISTORY RESOURCE CENTER**

**Enter the Resource Center using either your *HistoryNow* access card or your standalone access card for the *Wadsworth World History Resource Center.* Organized by topic, this website includes quizzes; images; over 350 primary source documents; interactive simulations; maps and timelines; movie explorations; and a wealth of other resources. You can read the following documents, and many more, at http://history.wadsworth.com/rc/world**

The Manila Accord

Declaration of Pakistan and India on Jammu and Kashmir

Visit the *World History* Companion Website for chapter quizzes and more.

http://history.wadsworth.com/duikerspielvogel05/

# Looking Ahead

**Even as the world** becomes more global in culture and interdependent in its mutual relations, centrifugal forces are at work attempting to redefine the political, cultural, and ethnic ways in which it is divided. Such efforts are often disruptive and can sometimes work against measures to enhance our human destiny. But they also represent an integral part of human character and human history and cannot be suppressed in the relentless drive to create a world society. In his crusade against the "Coca-Colonization" of the world, the Japanese novelist Yukio Mishima was expressing a fear that is shared today by millions throughout the world, as Walt Disney, rock music, and McDonald's relentlessly erode the boundaries that separate one culture and people from another. What will result from this concern is as yet unclear. The Technological Revolution is proceeding at a dizzying speed that can carry information, ideas, and images around the world in seconds.

What is already apparent is that technological advances will have an enormous impact on human society in coming generations. Although many of these consequences may be welcome, others represent a serious

**TIMELINE**

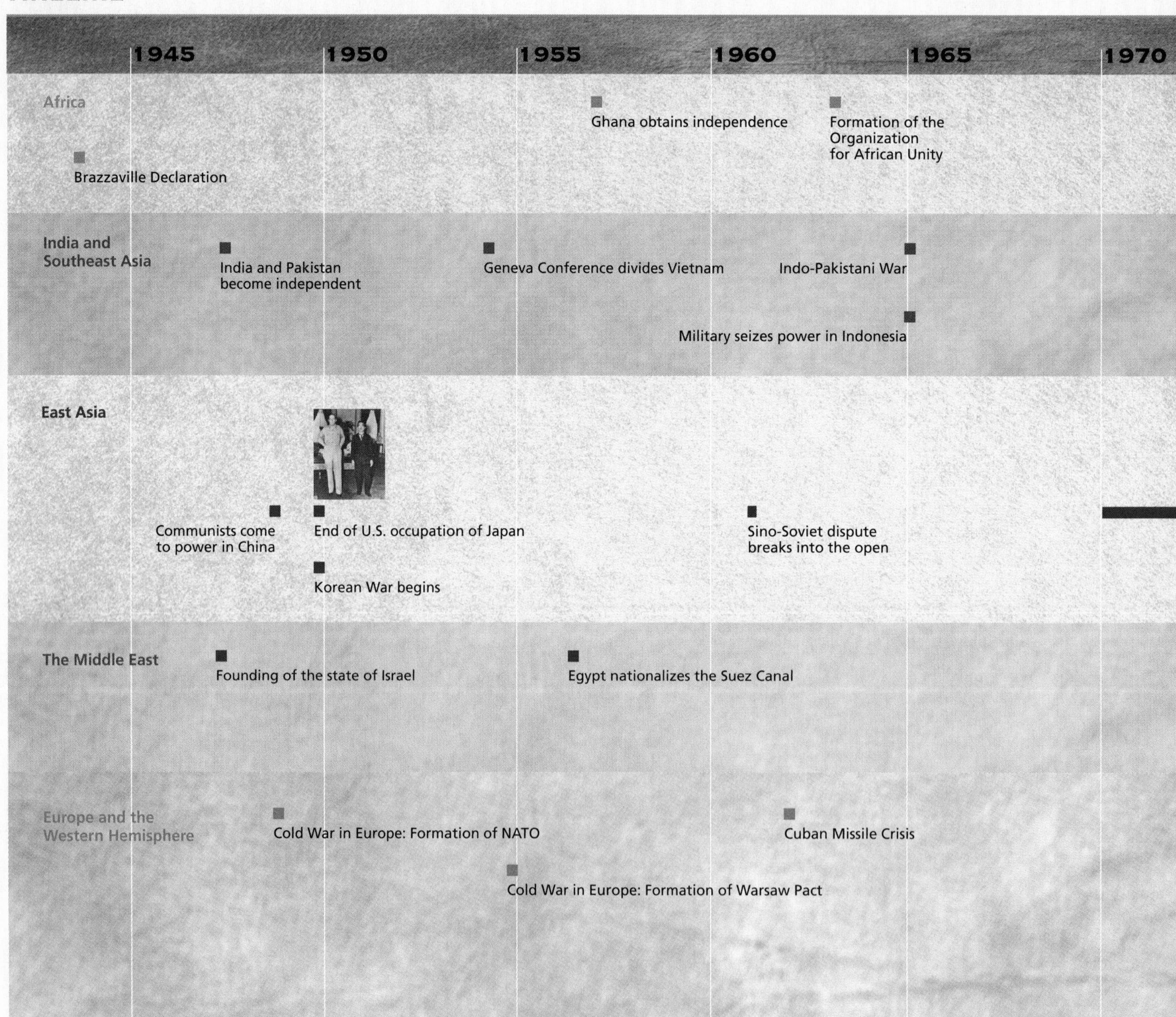

challenge, as individuals raised on television, video games, and the computer find less and less time for human relationships or creative activities. To some, the only antidote to the sense of confusion and alienation afflicting contemporary life is to reject the scientific outlook, with its secularizing implications, and return to religious faith. Others hope that a combination of scientific knowledge and spiritual revival can spark a renewal that will enable people to deal constructively with contemporary alienation and confusion.

There are already initial signs that as the common dangers posed by environmental damage, overpopulation, and scarcity of resources become even more apparent, societies around the world will find ample reason to turn their attention from cultural differences to the demands of global interdependence. The greatest challenge of the twenty-first century may be to reconcile the drive for individual and group identity with the common needs of the human community.

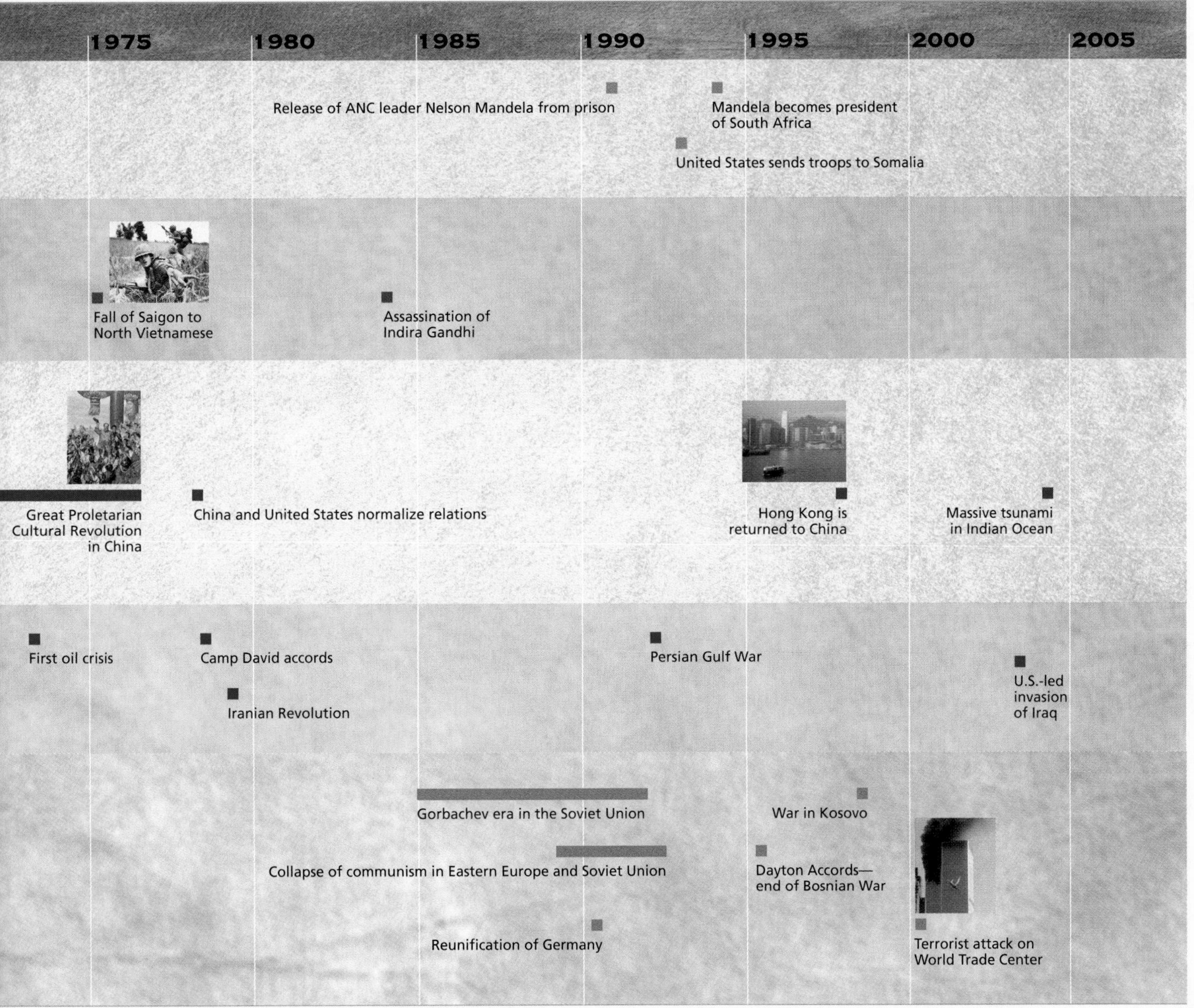

# Glossary

**absolutism** a form of government where the sovereign power or ultimate authority rested in the hands of a monarch who claimed to rule by divine right and was therefore responsible only to God.

**Abstract Expressionism** a post–World War II artistic movement that broke with all conventions of form and structure in favor of total abstraction.

**Agricultural (Neolithic) Revolution** the shift from hunting animals and gathering plants for sustenance to producing food by systematic agriculture that occurred gradually between 10,000 and 4000 B.C.E. (the Neolithic or "New Stone" Age).

**agricultural revolution** the application of new agricultural techniques that allowed for a large increase in productivity in the eighteenth century.

**Amerindian** earliest inhabitants of North and South America. Original theories suggested migration from Siberia across the Bering Land Bridge; more recent evidence suggests migration also occurred by sea from regions of the South Pacific to South America.

**anarchism** a political theory that holds that all governments and existing social institutions are unnecessary and advocates a society based on voluntary cooperation.

**ANC** the African National Congress. Founded in 1912, it was the beginning of political activity by South African blacks. Banned by politically dominant European whites in 1960, it was not officially "unbanned" until 1990. It is now the official majority party of the South African government.

**Analects** the body of writing containing conversations between Confucius and his disciples that preserves his worldly wisdom and pragmatic philosophies.

**anti-Semitism** hostility toward or discrimination against Jews.

**apartheid** the system of racial segregation practiced in the Republic of South Africa until the 1990s, which involved political, legal, and economic discrimination against nonwhites.

**appeasement** the policy, followed by the European nations in the 1930s, of accepting Hitler's annexation of Austria and Czechoslovakia in the belief that meeting his demands would assure peace and stability.

**Aramaic** A Semitic language dominant in the Middle East in the first century B.C.E.; still in use in small regions of the Middle East and southern Asia.

**Arianism** a Christian heresy that taught that Jesus was inferior to God. Though condemned by the Council of Nicaea in 325, Arianism was adopted by many of the Germanic peoples who entered the Roman Empire over the next centuries.

**aristocracy** a class of hereditary nobility in medieval Europe; a warrior class who shared a distinctive lifestyle based on the institution of knighthood, although there were social divisions within the group based on extremes of wealth.

**Arthasastra** an early Indian political treatise that sets forth many fundamental aspects of the relationship of rulers and their subjects. It has been compared to Machiavelli's well-known book, *The Prince,* and has provided principles upon which many aspects of social organization have developed in the region.

**Aryans** Indo–European-speaking nomads who entered India from the Central Asian steppes between 1500 and 1000 B.C.E. and greatly affected Indian society, notably by establishing the caste system. The term was later adopted by German Nazis to describe their racial ideal.

**asceticism** a lifestyle involving the denial of worldly pleasures. Predominantly associated with Hindu, Buddhist, or Christian religions, adherents perceive their practices as a path to greater spitiuality.

**ASEAN** the Association for the Southeast Asian Nations formed in 1967 to promote the prosperity and political stability of its member nations. Currently Brunei, Indonesia, Laos, Malaysia, Myanmar, the Philippines, Singapore, Thailand, and Vietnam are members. Other countries in the region participate as "observer" members.

**Ausgleich** the "Compromise" of 1867 that created the dual monarchy of Austria-Hungary. Austria and Hungary each had its own capital, constitution, and legislative assembly, but were united under one monarch.

**authoritarian state** a state that has a dictatorial government and some other trappings of a totalitarian state, but does not demand that the masses be actively involved in the regime's goals as totalitarian states do.

**auxiliaries** troops enlisted from the subject peoples of the Roman Empire to supplement the regular legions composed of Roman citizens.

**bakufu** the centralized government set up in Japan in the twelfth century. See shogunate system.

**balance of power** a distribution of power among several states such that no single nation can dominate or interfere with the interests of another.

**Banners** Originally established in 1639 by the Qing empire, the Eight Banners were administrative divisions into which all Manchu families were placed. Banners quickly evolved into the basis of Manchu military organization with each required to raise and support a prescribed number of troops.

**Bao-jia system** the Chinese practice, reportedly originated by the Qin dynasty in the third century B.C.E., of organizing families into groups of five or ten to exercise mutual control and surveillance and reduce loyalty to the family.

**Baroque** a style that dominated Western painting, sculpture, architecture and music from about 1580 to 1730, generally characterized by elaborate ornamentation and dramatic effects. Important practitioners included Bernini, Rubens, Handel, and Bach.

**Bedouins** nomadic tribes originally from northern Arabia, who became important traders after the domestication of the camel during the first millennium B.C.E. Early converts to Islam, their values and practices deeply affected Muhammad.

**benefice** in the Christian church, a position, such as a bishopric, that consisted of both a sacred office and the right of the holder to the annual revenues from the position.

**Berbers** an ethnic group indigenous to western North Africa.

**bey** a provincial governor in the Ottoman Empire.

**bhakti** in Hinduism, devotion as a means of religious observance open to all persons regardless of class.

***bodhi*** Wisdom. Sometimes described as complete awareness of the true nature of the universe.

**bicameral legislature** a legislature with two houses.

**Black Death** the outbreak of plague (mostly bubonic) in the mid-fourteenth century that killed from 25 to 50 percent of Europe's population.

***Blitzkrieg*** "lightning war." A war conducted with great speed and force, as in Germany's advance at the beginning of World War II.

**bodhisattvas** in some schools of Buddhism, individuals who have achieved enlightenment but, because of their great compassion, have chosen to renounce Nirvana and to remain on earth in spirit form to help all human beings achieve release from reincarnation.

**Bolsheviks** a small faction of the Russian Social Democratic Party who were led by Lenin and dedicated to violent revolution; seized power in Russia in 1917 and were subsequently renamed the Communists.

***bonsai*** Originating in China in the first millenium B.C.E. and known there as *penzai,* it was imported to Japan between 700–900 C.E. Bonsai combines patience and artistry in the cultivation of stunted trees and shrubs to create exquisite nature scenes in miniature.

**boyars** the Russian nobility.

***Brahman*** The Hindu word roughly equivalent to God; the Divine basis of all being; regarded as the source and sum of the cosmos.

***brahmin*** A member of the Hindu priestly caste or class; literally "one who has realized or attempts to realize Brahman." Traditionally, duties of a brahmin include studying Hindu religious scriptures and transmitting them to others orally. The priests of Hindu temples are brahmin.

**Brezhnev Doctrine** the doctrine, enunciated by Leonid Brezhnev, that the Soviet Union had a right to intervene if socialism was threatened in another socialist state; used to justify the use of Soviet troops in Czechoslovakia in 1968.

**Buddhism** A religion and philosophy based on the teachings of Siddhartha Gautama in about 500 B.C.E. Principally practiced in China, India, and other parts of Asia, Buddhism has 360 million followers and is considered a major world releigion.

**Burakumin** A Japanese minority similar to dalits (or untouchables) in Indian culture. Past and current discrimination has resulted in lower educational attainment and socioeconomic status for members of this group. Movements with objectives ranging from "liberation" to integration have tried over the years to change this situation.

**Bushido** The code of conduct observed by samurai warriors; comparable to the European concept of chilvalry.

**caliph** the secular leader of the Islamic community.

**calpulli** In Aztec society, a kinship group, often of a thousand or more, which served as an intermediary with the central government, providing taxes and conscript labor to the state.

**capital** material wealth used or available for use in the production of more wealth.

**caste system** a system of rigid social hierarchcy in which all members of that society are assigned by birth to specific "ranks," and inherit specific roles and privileges.

**cartel** a combination of independent commercial enterprises that work together to control prices and limit competition.

**Cartesian dualism** Descartes's principle of the separation of mind and matter (and mind and body) that enabled scientists to view matter as something separate from themselves that could be investigated by reason.

**caudillos** strong leaders in nineteenth-century Latin America, who were usually supported by the landed elites and ruled chiefly by military force, though some were popular; they included both modernizers and destructive dictators.

**censorate** one of the three primary Chinese ministries, originally established in the Qin dynasty, whose inspectors surveyed the efficiency of officials throughout the system.

**chaebol** a South Korean business structure similar to the Japanese keiretsu.

***Chan Buddhism*** a Chinese sect (Zen in Japanese) influenced by Daoist ideas, which called for mind training and a strict regimen as a means of seeking enlightenment.

**chansons de geste** a form of vernacular literature in the High Middle Ages that consisted of heroic epics focusing on the deeds of warriors.

***chinampas*** in Mesoamerica, artifical islands crisscrossed by canals that provided water for crops and easy transportation to local markets.

**chivalry** the ideal of civilized behavior that emerged among the nobility in the eleventh and twelfth centuries under the influence of the church; a code of ethics knights were expected to uphold.

**Christian (northern) humanism** an intellectual movement in northern Europe in the late fifteenth and early sixteenth centuries that combined the interest in the classics of the Italian Renaissance with an interest in the sources of early Christianity, including the New Testament and the writings of the church fathers.

**civic humanism** an intellectual movement of the Italian Renaissance that saw Cicero, who was both an intellectual and a statesman, as the ideal and held that humanists should be involved in government and use their rhetorical training in the service of the state.

**civil rights** the basic rights of citizens including equality before the law, freedom of speech and press, and freedom from arbitrary arrest.

**civil service examination** an elaborate Chinese system of selecting bureaucrats on merit, first introduced in 165 C.E., developed by the Tang dynasty in the seventh century C.E. and refined under the Song dynasty; later adopted in Vietnam and with less success in Japan and Korea. It contributed to efficient government, upward mobility, and cultural uniformity.

**class struggle** the basis of the Marxist analysis of history, which says that the owners of the means of production have always oppressed the workers and predicts an inevitable revolution. See Marxism.

**Cold War** the ideological conflict between the Soviet Union and the United States after World War II.

**collective farms** large farms created in the Soviet Union by Stalin by combining many small holdings into one large farm worked by the peasants under government supervision.

**collective security** the use of an international army raised by an association of nations to deter aggression and keep the peace.

**coloni** free tenant farmers who worked as sharecroppers on the large estates of the Roman Empire (singular: *colonus*).

**Comintern** a worldwide organization of Communist parties, founded by Lenin in 1919, dedicated to the advancement of world revolution; also known as the Third International.

**common law** law common to the entire kingdom of England; imposed by the king's courts beginning in the twelfth century to replace the customary law used in county and feudal courts that varied from place to place.

**commune** in medieval Europe, an association of townspeople bound together by a sworn oath for the purpose of obtaining basic liberties from the lord of the territory in which the town was located; also, the self-governing town after receiving its liberties.

**communalism** in South Asia, the tendency of people to band together in mutually antagonistic social sub-groups; elsewhere used to describe unifying trends in the larger community.

**conciliarism** a movement in fourteenth- and fifteenth-century Europe that held that final authority in spiritual matters resided with a general church council, not the pope; emerged in response to the Avignon papacy and the Great Schism and used to justify the summoning of the Council of Constance (1414–1418).

**condottieri** leaders of bands of mercenary soldiers in Renaissance Italy who sold their services to the highest bidder.

**Confucianism** a system of thought based on the teachings of Confucius (551–479 B.C.E.) that developed into the ruling ideology of the Chinese state. See Neo-Confucianism.

**conquistadors** "conquerors." Leaders in the Spanish conquests in the Americas, especially Mexico and Peru, in the sixteenth century.

**conscription** a military draft.

**conservatism** an ideology based on tradition and social stability that favored the maintenance of established institutions, organized religion, and obedience to authority and resisted change, especially abrupt change.

**consuls** the chief executive officers of the Roman Republic. Two were chosen annually to administer the government and lead the army in battle.

**consumer society** a term applied to Western society after World War II as the working classes adopted the consumption patterns of the middle class and installment plans, credit cards, and easy credit made consumer goods such as appliances and automobiles widely available.

**containment** a policy adopted by the United States in the Cold War. Its goal was to use whatever means, short of all-out war, to limit Soviet expansion.

**Continental System** Napoleon's effort to bar British goods from the Continent in the hope of weakening Britain's economy and destroying its capacity to wage war.

**Contras** in Nicaragua in the 1980s, an anti-Sandinista guerrilla movement supported by the U.S. Reagan administration.

**Coptic** a form of Christianity, originally Egyptian, that has thrived in Ethiopia since the fourth century C.E.

**cosmopolitanism** the quality of being sophisticated and having wide international experience.

**cottage industry** a system of textile manufacturing in which spinners and weavers worked at home in their cottages using raw materials supplied to them by capitalist entrepreneurs.

**Crusade** in the Middle Ages, a military campaign in defense of Christendom.

**cultural relativism** the belief that no culture is superior to another because culture is a matter of custom, not reason, and derives its meaning from the group holding it.

**cuneiform** "wedge-shaped." A system of writing developed by the Sumerians that consisted of wedge-shaped impressions made by a reed stylus on clay tablets.

**daimyo** prominent Japanese families who provided allegiance to the local shogun in exchange for protection; similar to vassals in Europe.

***dalits*** commonly referred to as untouchables; the lowest level of Indian society, technically outside the caste system and considered less than human; renamed harijans ("children of God") by Gandhi, they remain the object of discrimination despite affirmative action programs.

***Dao*** a Chinese philosophical concept, literally "The Way," central to both Confucianism and Daoism, that describes the behavior proper to each member of society; somewhat similar to the Indian concept of dharma.

**Daoism** a Chinese philosophy traditionally ascribed to the perhaps legendary Lao Tzu, which holds that acceptance and spontaneity are the keys to harmonious interaction with the universal order; an alternative to Confucianism.

**decolonization** the process of becoming free of colonial status and achieving statehood; occurred in most of the world's colonies between 1947 and 1962.

**deism** belief in God as the creator of the universe who, after setting it in motion, ceased to have any direct involvement in it and allowed it to run according to its own natural laws.

**deficit spending** the concept, developed by John Maynard Keynes in the 1930s, that in times of economic depression governments should stimulate demand by hiring people to do public works, such as building highways, even if this increased public debt.

**demesne** the part of a manor retained under the direct control of the lord and worked by the serfs as part of their labor services.

**denazification** after World War II, the Allied policy of rooting out any traces of Nazism in German society by bringing prominent Nazis to trial for war crimes and purging any known Nazis from political office.

**depression** a very severe, protracted economic downturn with high levels of unemployment.

**destalinization** the policy of denouncing and undoing the most repressive aspects of Stalin's regime; begun by Nikita Khrushchev in 1956.

**détente** the relaxation of tension between the Soviet Union and the United States that occurred in the 1970s.

***devshirme*** in the Ottoman Empire, a system (literally, "collection") of training talented children to be administrators or members of the sultan's harem; originally meritocratic, by the seventeenth century, it degenerated into a hereditary caste.

**dharma** in Hinduism and Buddhism, the law that governs the universe, and specifically human behavior.

**dialectic** logic, one of the seven liberal arts that made up the medieval curriculum. In Marxist thought, the process by which all change occurs through the clash of antagonistic elements.

**Diaspora** the scattering of Jews throughout the ancient world after the Babylonian captivity in the sixth century B.C.E.

**dictator** in the Roman Republic, an official granted unlimited power to run the state for a short period of time, usually six months, during an emergency.

**diocese** the area under the jurisdiction of a Christian bishop; based originally on Roman administrative districts.

**direct representation** a system of choosing delegates to a representative assembly in which citizens vote directly for the delegates who will represent them.

**divination** the practice of seeking to foretell future events by interpreting divine signs, which could appear in various forms, such as in entrails of animals, in patterns in smoke, or in dreams.

**divine-right monarchy** a monarchy based on the belief that monarchs receive their power directly from God and are responsible to no one except God.

**domino theory** the belief that if the Communists succeeded in Vietnam, other countries in Southeast and East Asia would also fall (like dominoes) to communism; a justification for the U.S. intervention in Vietnam.

**dualism** the belief that the universe is dominated by two opposing forces, one good and the other evil.

**dyarchy** during the Qing dynasty in China, a system in which all important national and provincial admininstrative positions were shared equally by Chinese and Manchus, which helped to consolidate both Manchu rule and their assimilation.

**dynastic state** a state where the maintenance and expansion of the interests of the ruling family is the primary consideration.

**economic imperialism** the process in which banks and corporations from developed nations invest in underdeveloped regions and establish a major presence there in the hope of making high profits; not necessarily the same as colonial expansion in that businesses invest where they can make a profit, which may not be in their own nation's colonies.

**El Niño** periodic changes in water temperature at the surface of the Pacific Ocean, which can lead to major environmental changes and may have led to the collapse of the Moche civilization in what is now Peru.

***emir*** "commander" (Arabic), used by Muslim rulers in southern Spain and elsewhere.

**empiricism** the practice of relying on observation and experiment.

**enclosure movement** in the eighteenth century, the fencing in of the old open fields, combining many small holdings into larger units that could be farmed more efficiently.

***encomienda*** a grant from the Spanish monarch to colonial conquistadors; see *encomienda system.*

**encomienda system** the system by which Spain first governed its American colonies. Holders of an encomienda were supposed to protect the Indians as well as using them as laborers and collecting tribute but in practice exploited them.

**encyclical** a letter from the pope to all the bishops of the Roman Catholic church.

**enlightened absolutism** an absolute monarchy where the ruler follows the principles of the Enlightenment by introducing reforms for the improvement of society, allowing freedom of speech and the press, permitting religious toleration, expanding education, and ruling in accordance with the laws.

**Enlightenment** an eighteenth-century intellectual movement, led by the philosophes, that stressed the application of reason and the scientific method to all aspects of life.

**entrepreneur** one who organizes, operates, and assumes the risk in a business venture in the expectation of making a profit.

**Epicureanism** a philosophy founded by Epicurus in the fourth century C.E. that taught that happiness (freedom from emotional turmoil) could be achieved through the pursuit of pleasure (intellectual rather than sensual pleasure).

**equestrians** a group of extremely wealthy men in the late Roman Republic who were effectively barred from high office, but sought political power commensurate with their wealth; called equestrians because many had gotten their start as cavalry officers (*equites*).

***eta*** in feudal Japan, a class of hereditary slaves who were responsible for what were considered degrading occupations, such as curing leather and burying the dead.

**ethnic cleansing** the policy of killing or forcibly removing people of another ethnic group; used by the Serbs against Bosnian Muslims in the 1990s.

**eucharist** a Christian sacrament in which consecrated bread and wine are consumed in celebration of Jesus' Last Supper; also called the Lord's Supper or communion.

**eunuch** a man whose testicles have been removed; a standard feature of the Chinese imperial system, the Ottoman Empire, and the Mughal Dynasty, among others.

**evolutionary socialism** a socialist doctrine espoused by Eduard Bernstein who argued that socialists should stress cooperation and evolution to attain power by democratic means rather than by conflict and revolution.

**fascism** an ideology or movement that exalts the nation above the individual and calls for a centralized government with a dictatorial leader, economic and social regimentation, and forcible suppression of opposition; in particular, the ideology of Mussolini's Fascist regime in Italy.

**feminism** the belief in the social, political, and economic equality of the sexes; also, organized activity to advance women's rights.

**fief** a landed estate granted to a vassal in exchange for military services.

**filial piety** in traditional China, in particular, a hierarchical system in which every family member has his or her place, subordinate to a patriarch who has in turn reciprocal responsibilities.

**Final Solution** the physical extermination of the Jewish people by the Nazis during World War II.

**five pillars of Islam** the core requirements of the faith, observation of which would lead to paradise: belief in Allah and his Prophet Muhammad; prescribed prayers; observation of Ramadan; pilgrimage to Mecca; and giving alms to the poor.

**five relationships** in traditional China, the hierarchical interpersonal associations considered crucial to social order, within the family, between friends, and with the king.

**folk culture** the traditional arts and crafts, literature, music, and other customs of the people; something that people make, as opposed to modern popular culture, which is something people buy.

**foot binding** an extremely painful process, common in China throughout the second millenium C.E., that compressed girls' feet to half their natural size, representing submissiveness and self-discipline, which were considered necessary attributes for an ideal wife.

**four modernizations** the slogan for radical reforms of Chinese industry, agriculture, technology, and national defense, instituted by Deng Xiaoping after his accession to power in the late 1970s.

**free trade** the unrestricted international exchange of goods with low or no tariffs.

**fundamentalism** a movement that emphasizes rigid adherence to basic religious principles; often used to describe evangelical Christianity, it also characterizes the practices of Islamic conservatives.

**general strike** a strike by all or most workers in an economy; espoused by Georges Sorel as the heroic action that could be used to inspire the workers to destroy capitalist society.

***genin*** landless laborers in feudal Japan, who were effectively slaves.

**gentry** well-to-do English landowners below the level of the nobility; played an important role in the English Civil War of the seventeenth century.

**geocentric theory** the idea that the earth is at the center of the universe and that the sun and other celestial objects revolve around the earth.

**glasnost** "openness." Mikhail Gorbachev's policy of encouraging Soviet citizens to openly discuss the strengths and weaknesses of the Soviet Union.

***Gleichschaltung*** the coordination of all government institutions under Nazi control in Germany from 1933.

**global civilization** human society considered as a single world-wide entity, in which local differences are less important than overall similarities.

**good emperors** the five emperors who ruled from 96 to 180 (Nerva, Trajan, Hadrian, Antoninus Pius, and Marcus Aurelius), a period of peace and prosperity for the Roman Empire.

**Grand Council** the top of the government hierarchy in the Song dynasty in China.

**grand vezir** (*also*, vizier) the chief executive in the Ottoman Empire, under the sultan.

**Great Leap Forward** a short-lived, radical experiment in China, started in 1958, which created vast rural communes and attempted to replace the family as the fundamental social unit.

**Great Proletarian Cultural Revolution** an attempt to destroy all vestiges of tradition in China, in order to create a totally egalitarian society; launched by Mao Zedong in 1966, it became virtually anarchic and lasted only until Mao's death in 1976.

**Great Schism** the crisis in the late medieval church when there were first two and then three popes; ended by the Council of Constance (1414–1418).

**green revolution** the introduction of technological agriculture, especially in India in the 1960s, which increased food production substantially but also exacerbated rural inequality because only the wealthier farmers could afford fertilizer.

**guest workers** foreign workers working temporarily in European countries.

**guided democracy** the name given by President Sukarno of Indonesia in the late 1950s to his style of government, which theoretically operated by consensus.

**guild** an association of people with common interests and concerns, especially people working in the same craft. In medieval Europe, guilds came to control much of the production process and to restrict entry into various trades.

**guru** teacher, especially in the Hindu, Buddhist and Sikh religious traditions, where it is an important honorific.

**gymnasium** in classical Greece, a place for athletics; in the Hellenistic Age, a secondary school with a curriculum centered on music, physical exercise, and literature.

***Hadith*** a collection of the sayings of the Prophet Muhammad, used to supplement the revelations contained in the Qur'an.

**Hanseatic League** a commercial and military alliance of north German coastal towns, increasingly powerful in the fifteenth century C.E.

**harem** the private domain of a ruler such as the sultan in the Ottoman Empire or the caliph of Baghdad, generally large and mostly inhabited by the extended family.

**Hegira** the flight of Muhammad from Mecca to Medina in 622, which marks the first date on the official calendar of Islam.

**heliocentric theory** the idea that the sun (not the earth) is at the center of the universe.

**Hellenistic** literally, "to imitate the Greeks"; the era after the death of Alexander the Great when Greek culture spread into the Near East and blended with the culture of that region.

**helots** serfs in ancient Sparta, who were permanently bound to the land that they worked for their Spartan masters.

**heresy** the holding of religious doctrines different from the official teachings of the church.

**Hermeticism** an intellectual movement beginning in the fifteenth century that taught that divinity is embodied in all aspects of nature; included works on alchemy and magic as well as theology and philosophy. The tradition continued into the seventeenth century and influenced many of the leading figures of the Scientific Revolution.

**hetairai** highly sophisticated courtesans in ancient Athens who offered intellectual and musical entertainment as well as sex.

**hieroglyphics** a highly pictorial system of writing most often associated with ancient Egypt. Also used (with different "pictographs") by other ancient peoples such as the Mayans.

**high culture** the literary and artistic culture of the educated and wealthy ruling classes.

**Hinayana** the scornful name for Theravada Buddhism ("lesser vehicle") used by devotees of Mahayana Buddhism.

**Hinduism** the main religion in India, it emphasizes reincarnation, based on the results of the previous life, and the desirability of escaping this cycle. Its various forms feature both asceticism and the pleasures of ordinary life, and encompass a multitude of gods as different manifestations of one ultimate reality.

**Holocaust** the mass slaughter of European Jews by the Nazis during World War II.

**Hopewell culture** a Native American society that flourished from about 200 B.C.E. to 400 C.E., noted for large burial mounds and extensive manufacture. Largely based in Ohio, its traders ranged as far as the Gulf of Mexico.

**hoplites** heavily armed infantry soldiers used in ancient Greece in a phalanx formation.

**Huguenots** French Calvinists.

**humanism** an intellectual movement in Renaissance Italy based upon the study of the Greek and Roman classics.

**Hundred Schools** (of philosophy) in China around the third century B.C.E., a wide-ranging debate over the nature of human beings, society, and the universe. The Schools included Legalism and Daoism, as well as Confucianism.

**hydraulic society** a society organized around a large irrigation system.

**iconoclasm** an eighth-century Byzantine movement against the use of icons (pictures of sacred figures), which was condemned as idolatry.

**ideology** a political philosophy such as conservatism or liberalism.

***imam*** an Islamic religious leader; some traditions say there is only one per generation, others use the term more broadly.

**imperialism** the policy of extending one nation's power either by conquest or by establishing direct or indirect economic or cultural authority over another. Generally driven by economic self-interest, it can also be motivated by a sincere (if often misguided) sense of moral obligation.

**imperium** "the right to command." In the Roman Republic, the chief executive officers (consuls and praetors) possessed the *imperium;* a military commander was an *imperator.* In the Roman Empire, the title *imperator,* or emperor, came to be used for the ruler.

**indirect representation** a system of choosing delegates to a representative assembly in which citizens do not choose the delegates directly but instead vote for electors who choose the delegates.

**indirect rule** a colonial policy of foreign rule in cooperation with local political elites; implemented in much of India and Malaya, and parts of Africa, it was not feasible where resistance was greater.

**individualism** emphasis on and interest in the unique traits of each person.

**indulgence** the remission of part or all of the temporal punishment in purgatory due to sin; granted for charitable contributions and other good deeds. Indulgences became a regular practice of the Christian church in the High Middle Ages, and their abuse was instrumental in sparking Luther's reform movement in the sixteenth century.

**infanticide** the practice of killing infants.

**inflation** a sustained rise in the price level.

***intifada*** the "uprising" of Palestinians living under Israeli control, especially in the 1980s and 1990s.

**intendants** royal officials in seventeenth-century France who were sent into the provinces to execute the orders of the central government.

**intervention, principle of** the idea, after the Congress of Vienna, that the great powers of Europe had the right to send armies into countries experiencing revolution to restore legitimate monarchs to their thrones.

**Islam** the religion derived from the revelations of Muhammad, the Prophet of Allah; literally, "submission" (to the will of Allah); also the culture and civilization based upon the faith.

**isolationism** a foreign policy in which a nation refrains from making alliances or engaging actively in international affairs.

**Jainism** an Indian religion, founded in the fifth century B.C.E., which stresses extreme simplicity.

**Janissaries** an elite core of eight thousand troops personally loyal to the sultan of the Ottoman Empire.

***jati*** a kinship group, the basic social organization of traditional Indian society, to some extent specialized by occupation.

**jihad** In Islam, "striving in the way of the Lord." The term is ambiguous and has been subject to varying interpretations, from the practice of conducting raids against local neighbors to the conduct of "holy war" against unbelievers.

**joint-stock company** a company or association that raises capital by selling shares to individuals who receive dividends on their investment while a board of directors runs the company.

**joint-stock investment bank** a bank created by selling shares of stock to investors. Such banks potentially have access to much more capital than do private banks owned by one or a few individuals.

**Jomon** the earliest known Neolithic inhabitants of Japan, named for the cord pattern of their pottery.

**justification by faith** the primary doctrine of the Protestant Reformation; taught that humans are saved not through good works, but by the grace of God, bestowed freely through the sacrifice of Jesus.

***Kabuki*** a form of Japanese theater which developed in the seventeenth century C.E.; originally disreputable, it became a highly stylized art form.

**kami** spirits who were worshiped in early Japan, and resided in trees, rivers and streams. See Shinto.

***karma*** a fundamental concept in Hindu (and later Buddhist, Jain, and Sikh) philosophy, that rebirth in a future life is determined by actions in this or other lives; the word refers to the entire process, to the individual's actions, and also to the cumulative result of those actions, for instance a store of good or bad karma.

**keiretsu** a type of powerful industrial or financial conglomerate that emerged in post–World War II Japan following the abolition of zaibatsu.

**khanates** Mongol kingdoms, in particular the subdivisions of Genghis Khan's empire ruled by his heirs.

***kokutai*** the core ideology of the Japanese state, particularly during the Meiji Restoration, stressing the uniqueness of the Japanese system and the supreme authority of the emperor.

**kolkhoz** a collective farm in the Soviet Union, in which the great bulk of the land was held and worked communally. Between 1928 and 1934, 250,000 kolkhozes replaced 26 million family farms.

***kshatriya*** originally, the warrior class of Aryan society in India; ranked below (sometimes equal to) brahmins, in modern times often government workers or soldiers.

**laissez-faire** "to let alone." An economic doctrine that holds that an economy is best served when the government does not interfere but allows the economy to self-regulate according to the forces of supply and demand.

**latifundia** large landed estates in the Roman Empire (singular: *latifundium*).

**lay investiture** the practice in which a layperson chose a bishop and invested him with the symbols of both his temporal office and his spiritual office; led to the Investiture Controversy, which was ended by compromise in the Concordat of Worms in 1122.

***Lebensraum*** "living space." The doctrine, adopted by Hitler, that a nation's power depends on the amount of land it occupies; thus, a nation must expand to be strong.

**Legalism** a Chinese philosophy that argued that human beings were by nature evil and would follow the correct path only if coerced by harsh laws and stiff punishments. Adopted as official ideology by the Qin dynasty, it was later rejected but remained influential.

**legitimacy, principle of** the idea that after the Napoleonic wars peace could best be reestablished in Europe by restoring legitimate monarchs who would preserve traditional institutions; guided Metternich at the Congress of Vienna.

**Leninism** Lenin's revision of Marxism that held that Russia need not experience a bourgeois revolution before it could move toward socialism.

**liberal arts** the seven areas of study that formed the basis of education in medieval and early modern Europe. Following Boethius and other late Roman authors, they consisted of grammar, rhetoric, and dialectic or logic (the *trivium*) and arithmetic, geometry, astronomy, and music (the *quadrivium*).

**liberalism** an ideology based on the belief that people should be as free from restraint as possible. Economic liberalism is the idea that the government should not interfere in the workings of the economy. Political liberalism is the idea that there should be restraints on the exercise of power so that people can enjoy basic civil rights in a constitutional state with a representative assembly.

**limited liability** the principle that shareholders in a joint-stock corporation can be held responsible for the corporation's debts only up to the amount they have invested.

**limited (constitutional) monarchy** a system of government in which the monarch is limited by a representative assembly and by the duty to rule in accordance with the laws of the land.

**lineage group** the descendants of a common ancestor; relatives, often as opposed to immediate family.

**Longshan** a Neolithic society from near the Yellow River in China, sometimes identified by its black pottery.

**maharaja** originally, a king in the Aryan society of early India (a great raja); later used more generally to denote an important ruler.

**Mahayana** a school of Buddhism that promotes the idea of universal salvation through the intercession of bodhisattvas; predominant in north Asia.

***majlis*** a council of elders among the Bedouins of the Roman era.

**mandate of Heaven** the justification for the rule of the Zhou dynasty in China; the king was charged to maintain order as a representative of Heaven, which was viewed as an impersonal law of nature.

**mandates** a system established after World War I whereby a nation officially administered a territory (mandate) on behalf of the League of Nations. Thus, France administered Lebanon and Syria as mandates, and Britain administered Iraq and Palestine.

**Manichaeanism** an offshoot of the ancient Zorastrian religion, influenced by Christianity; became popular in central Asia in the eighth century C.E.

**manor** an agricultural estate operated by a lord and worked by peasants who performed labor services and paid various rents and fees to the lord in exchange for protection and sustenance.

**Marshall Plan** the European Recovery Program, under which the United States provided financial aid to European countries to help them rebuild after World War II.

**Marxism** the political, economic, and social theories of Karl Marx, which included the idea that history is the story of class struggle and that ultimately the proletariat will overthrow the bourgeoisie and establish a dictatorship en route to a classless society.

**mass education** a state-run educational system, usually free and compulsory, that aims to ensure that all children in society have at least a basic education.

**mass leisure** forms of leisure that appeal to large numbers of people in a society including the working classes; emerged at the end of the nineteenth century to provide workers with amusements after work and on weekends; used during the twentieth century by totalitarian states to control their populations.

**mass politics** a political order characterized by mass political parties and universal male and (eventually) female suffrage.

**mass society** a society in which the concerns of the majority—the lower classes—play a prominent role; characterized by extension of voting rights, an improved standard of living for the lower classes, and mass education.

**materialism** the belief that everything mental, spiritual, or ideal is an outgrowth of physical forces and that truth is found in concrete material existence, not through feeling or intuition.

**matrilinear** passing through the female line, for example from a father to his sister's son rather than his own, as practiced in some African societies; not necessarily, or even usually, combined with matriarchy, in which women rule.

**megaliths** large stones, widely used in Europe from around 4000 to 1500 B.C.E. to create monuments, including sophisticated astronomical observatories.

**Meiji Restoration** the period during the late 19th and early 20th century in which fundamental economic and cultural changes occured in Japan, tranforming it from a feudal and agrarian society to an industrial and technological society.

**mercantilism** an economic theory that held that a nation's prosperity depended on its supply of gold and silver and that the total volume of trade is unchangeable; therefore, advocated that the government play an active role in the economy by encouraging exports and discouraging imports, especially through the use of tariffs.

**Mesoamerica** the region stretching roughly from modern central Mexico to Honduras, in which the Olmec, Mayan, Aztec and other civilizations developed.

**Mesolithic Age** the period from 10,000 to 7000 C.E., characterized by a gradual transition from a food-gathering/hunting economy to a food-producing economy.

**mestizos** the offspring of intermarriage between Europeans, originally Spaniards, and native American Indians.

**metics** resident foreigners in ancient Athens; not permitted full rights of citizenship but did receive the protection of the laws.

**Middle Passage** the journey of slaves from Africa to the Americas as the middle leg of the triangular trade.

**Middle Path** a central concept of Buddhism, which advocates avoiding extremes of both materialism and asceticism; also known as the Eightfold Way.

***mihrab*** the niche in a mosque's wall that indicates the direction of Mecca, usually containing an ornately decorated panel representing Allah.

**militarism** a policy of aggressive military preparedness; in particular, the large armies based on mass conscription and complex, inflexible plans for mobilization that most European nations had before World War I.

***millet*** an administrative unit in the Ottoman empire used to organize religious groups.

**ministerial responsibility** a tenet of nineteenth-century liberalism that held that ministers of the monarch should be responsible to the legislative assembly rather than to the monarch.

**Modernism** the new artistic and literary styles that emerged in the decades before 1914 as artists rebelled against traditional efforts to portray reality as accurately as possible (leading to Impressionism and Cubism) and writers explored new forms.

**monotheistic/monotheism** having only one god; the doctrine or belief that there is only one god.

***muezzin*** the man who calls Muslims to prayer at the appointed times; nowadays often a tape-recorded message played over loudspeakers.

**mulattoes** the offspring of Africans and Europeans, particularly in Latin America.

**Munich syndrome** a term used to criticize efforts to appease an aggressor, as in the Munich agreement of 1938, on the grounds that they only encourage his appetite for conquest.

**mutual deterrence** the belief that nuclear war could best be prevented if both the United States and the Soviet Union had sufficient nuclear weapons so that even if one nation launched a preemptive first strike, the other could respond and devastate the attacker.

**mystery religions** religions that involve initiation into secret rites that promise intense emotional involvement with spiritual forces and a greater chance of individual immortality.

**nationalism** a sense of national consciousness based on awareness of being part of a community—a "nation"—that has common institutions, traditions, language, and customs and that becomes the focus of the individual's primary political loyalty.

**nationalities problem** the dilemma faced by the Austro-Hungarian Empire in trying to unite a wide variety of ethnic groups including, among others, Austrians, Hungarians, Poles, Croats, Czechs, Serbs, Slovaks, and Slovenes in an era when nationalism and calls for self-determination were coming to the fore.

**nationalization** the process of converting a business or industry from private ownership to government control and ownership.

**nation in arms** the people's army raised by universal mobilization to repel the foreign enemies of the French Revolution.

**nation-state** a form of political organization in which a relatively homogeneous people inhabits a sovereign state, as opposed to a state containing people of several nationalities.

**NATO** the North Atlantic Treaty Organization; a military alliance formed in 1949 in which the signatories (Belgium, Canada, Denmark, France, Great Britain, Iceland, Italy, Luxembourg, the Netherlands, Norway, Portugal, and the United States) agreed to provide mutual assistance if any one of them was attacked; later expanded to include other nations, including former members of the Warsaw Pact—Poland, the Czech Republic, and Hungary.

**natural laws** a body of laws or specific principles held to be derived from nature and binding upon all human society even in the absence of positive laws.

**natural rights** certain inalienable rights to which all people are entitled; include the right to life, liberty, and property, freedom of speech and religion, and equality before the law.

**natural selection** Darwin's idea that organisms that are most adaptable to their environment survive and pass on the variations that enabled them to survive, while other, less adaptable organisms become extinct; "survival of the fittest."

**Nazi New Order** the Nazis' plan for their conquered territories; included the extermination of Jews and others considered inferior, ruthless exploitation of resources, German colonization in the east, and the use of Poles, Russians, and Ukrainians as slave labor.

**negritude** a philosophy shared among African blacks that there exists a distinctive "African personality" that owes nothing to Western values and provides a common sense of purpose and destiny for black Africans.

**Neo-Confucianism** the dominant ideology of China during the second millennium C.E., it combined the metaphysical speculations of Buddhism and Daoism with the pragmatic Confucian approach to society, maintaining that the world is real, not illusory, and that fulfillment comes from participation, not withdrawal. It encouraged an intellectual environment that valued continuity over change and tradition over innovation.

**neocolonialism** the use of economic rather than political or military means to maintain Western domination of developing nations.

**Neolithic Revolution** the development of agriculture, including the planting of food crops and the domestication of farm animals, around 10,000 B.C.E.

**Neoplatonism** a revival of Platonic philosophy; in the third century C.E., a revival associated with Plotinus; in the Italian Renaissance, a revival associated with Marsilio Ficino who attempted to synthesize Christianity and Platonism.

**New Course** a short-lived, liberalizing change in Soviet policy to its Eastern European allies instituted after the death of Stalin in 1953.

**New Culture Movement** a protest launched at Peking University after the failure of the 1911 revolution, aimed at abolishing the remnants of the old system and introducing Western values and institutions into China.

**New Deal** the reform program implemented by President Franklin Roosevelt in the 1930s, which included large public works projects and the introduction of Social Security.

**New Democracy** the initial program of the Chinese Communist government, from 1949 to 1955, focusing on honest government, land reform, social justice, and peace rather than on the utopian goal of a classless society.

**New Economic Policy** a modified version of the old capitalist system introduced in the Soviet Union by Lenin in 1921 to revive the economy after the ravages of the civil war and war communism.

**new imperialism** the revival of imperialism after 1880 in which European nations established colonies throughout much of Asia and Africa.

**new monarchies** the governments of France, England, and Spain at the end of the fifteenth century, where the rulers were successful in reestablishing or extending centralized royal authority, suppressing the nobility, controlling the church, and insisting upon the loyalty of all peoples living in their territories.

**Nirvana** in Buddhist thought, enlightenment, the ultimate transcendence from the illusion of the material world; release from the wheel of life.

**nobiles** "nobles." The small group of families from both patrician and plebeian origins who produced most of the men who were elected to office in the late Roman Republic.

**Nok culture** in northern Nigeria, one of the most active early iron-working societies in Africa, artifacts from which date back as far as 500 B.C.E.

**nuclear family** a family group consisting only of father, mother, and children.

**nun** female religious monk.

**old regime/old order** the political and social system of France in the eighteenth century before the Revolution.

**oligarchy** rule by a few.

**Open Door notes** a series of letters sent in 1899 by U.S. Secretary of State John Hay to Great Britain, France, Germany, Italy, Japan and Russia, calling for equal economic access to the China market for all states and for the maintenance of the territorial and administrative integrity of the Chinese Empire.

**optimates** "best men." Aristocratic leaders in the late Roman Republic who generally came from senatorial families and wished to retain their oligarchical privileges.

**opium trade** the sale of the addictive product of the poppy, specifically by British traders to China in the 1830s. Chinese attempts to prevent it led to the Opium War of 1839–1842, which resulted in British access to Chinese ports and has traditionally been considered the beginning of modern Chinese history.

**orders/estates** the traditional tripartite division of European society based on heredity and quality rather than wealth or economic standing, first established in the Middle Ages and continuing into the eighteenth century; traditionally consisted of those who pray (the clergy), those who fight (the nobility), and those who work (all the rest).

**organic evolution** Darwin's principle that all plants and animals have evolved over a long period of time from earlier and simpler forms of life.

**Organization of African Unity** founded in Addis Ababa in 1963, it was intended to represent the interests of all the newly independent countries of Africa and provided a forum for the discussion of common problems until 2001, when it was replaced by the African Union.

**Paleolithic Age** the period of human history when humans used simple stone tools (c. 2,500,000–10,000 B.C.E.).

**pan-Africanism** the concept of African continental unity and solidarity in which the common interests of African countries transcend regional boundaries.

**pantheism** a doctrine that equates God with the universe and all that is in it.

**pariahs** members of the lowest level of traditional Indian society, technically outside the class system itself; also known as untouchables.

**pasha** an administrative official of the Ottoman empire, responsible for collecting taxes and maintaining order in the provinces; later, some became hereditary rulers.

**paterfamilias** the dominant male in a Roman family whose powers over his wife and children were theoretically unlimited, though they were sometimes circumvented in practice.

**patriarchal/patriarchy** a society in which the father is supreme in the clan or family; more generally, a society dominated by men.

**patriarchal family** a family in which the husband/father dominates his wife and children.

**patricians** great landowners who became the ruling class in the Roman Republic.

**patrilinear** passing through the male line, from father to son; often combined with patriarchy.

**patronage** the practice of awarding titles and making appointments to government and other positions to gain political support.

**Pax Romana** "Roman peace." A term used to refer to the stability and prosperity that Roman rule brought to the Mediterranean world and much of western Europe during the first and second centuries C.E.

**peaceful coexistence** the policy adopted by the Soviet Union under Khrushchev in 1955, and continued by his successors, that called for economic and ideological rivalry with the West rather than nuclear war.

**Pentateuch** the first five books of the Hebrew Bible (Genesis, Exodus, Leviticus, Numbers, and Deuteronomy).

**peoples' democracies** a term invented by the Soviet Union to define a society in the early stage of socialist transition, applied to Eastern European countries in the 1950s.

**perestroika** "restructuring." A term applied to Mikhail Gorbachev's economic, political, and social reforms in the Soviet Union.

**permissive society** a term applied to Western society after World War II to reflect the new sexual freedom and the emergence of a drug culture.

**Petrine supremacy** the doctrine that the bishop of Rome—the pope—as the successor of Saint Peter (traditionally considered the first bishop of Rome) should hold a preeminent position in the church.

**phalanx** a rectangular formation of tightly massed infantry soldiers.

**philosophes** intellectuals of the eighteenth-century Enlightenment who believed in applying a spirit of rational criticism to all things, including religion and politics, and who focused on improving and enjoying this world, rather than on the afterlife.

**plebeians** the class of Roman citizens who included nonpatrician landowners, craftspeople, merchants, and small farmers in the Roman Republic. Their struggle for equal rights with the patricians dominated much of the Republic's history.

**pluralism** the practice in which one person holds several church offices simultaneously; a problem of the late medieval church.

**pogroms** organized massacres of Jews.

**polis** an ancient Greek city-state encompassing both an urban area and its surrounding countryside; a small but autonomous political unit where all major political and social activities were carried out in a central location.

**political democracy** a form of government characterized by universal suffrage and mass political parties.

**politiques** a group who emerged during the French Wars of Religion in the sixteenth century; placed politics above religion and believed that no religious truth was worth the ravages of civil war.

**polygyny** the practice of having more than one wife at a time.

**polytheistic/polytheism** having many gods; belief in or the worship of more than one god.

**popular culture** as opposed to high culture, the unofficial, written and unwritten culture of the masses, much of which was passed down orally; centers on public and group activities such as festivals. In the twentieth century, refers to the entertainment, recreation, and pleasures that people purchase as part of mass consumer society.

**populares** "favoring the people." Aristocratic leaders in the late Roman Republic who tended to use the people's assemblies in an effort to break the stranglehold of the *nobiles* on political offices.

**popular sovereignty** the doctrine that government is created by and subject to the will of the people, who are the source of all political power.

***portolani*** charts of landmasses and coastlines made by navigators and mathematicians in the thirteenth and fourteenth centuries.

**Poststructuralism** a theory formulated by Jacques Derrida in the 1960s, holding that there is no fixed, universal truth since culture is created and can therefore be analyzed in various ways.

**praetorian guard** the military unit that served as the personal bodyguard of the Roman emperors.

**praetors** the two senior Roman judges, who had executive authority when the consuls were away from the city and could also lead armies.

**Prakrit** an ancient Indian language, a simplified form of Sanskrit.

**predestination** the belief, associated with Calvinism, that God, as a consequence of his foreknowledge of all events, has predetermined those who will be saved (the elect) and those who will be damned.

**price revolution** the dramatic rise in prices (inflation) that occurred throughout Europe in the sixteenth and early seventeenth centuries.

**primogeniture** an inheritance practice in which the eldest son receives all or the largest share of the parents' estate.

**principate** the form of government established by Augustus for the Roman Empire; continued the constitutional forms of the Republic and consisted of the *princeps* ("first citizen") and the senate, although the *princeps* was clearly the dominant partner.

**proletariat** the industrial working class. In Marxism, the class who will ultimately overthrow the bourgeoisie.

**Protestant Reformation** the western European religious reform movement in the sixteenth century C.E. that divided Christianity into Catholic and Protestant groups.

**purdah** the Indian term for the practice among Muslims and some Hindus of isolating women and preventing them from associating with men outside the home.

**Pure Land** a Buddhist sect, originally Chinese but later popular in Japan, which taught that devotion alone could lead to enlightenment and release.

**Puritans** English Protestants inspired by Calvinist theology who wished to remove all traces of Catholicism from the Church of England.

***querelles des femmes*** "arguments about women." A centuries-old debate about the nature of women that continued during the Scientific Revolution as those who argued for the inferiority of women found additional support in the new anatomy and medicine.

***quipu*** an Inka record-keeping system that used knotted strings rather than writing.

**raj** common name for the British colonial regime in India.

**raja** originally, a chieftain in the Aryan society of early India, a representative of the gods; later used more generally to denote a ruler.

**Ramadan** the holy month of Islam, during which believers fast from dawn to sunset; since the Islamic calendar is lunar, Ramadan migrates through the seasons.

**rationalism** a system of thought based on the belief that human reason and experience are the chief sources of knowledge.

**realism** in medieval Europe, the school of thought that, following Plato, held that the individual objects we perceive are not real but merely manifestations of universal ideas existing in the mind of God. In the nineteenth century, a school of painting that emphasized the everyday life of ordinary people, depicted with photographic realism.

**Realpolitik** "politics of reality." Politics based on practical concerns rather than theory or ethics.

**real wages/income/prices** wages/income/prices that have been adjusted for inflation.

**reason of state** the principle that a nation should act on the basis of its long-term interests and not merely to further the dynastic interests of its ruling family.

**reincarnation** the idea that the individual soul is reborn in a different form after death; in Hindu and Buddhist thought, release from this cycle is the objective of all living souls.

**relativity theory** Einstein's theory that holds, among other things, that (1) space and time are not absolute but are relative to the observer and interwoven into a four-dimensional space-time continuum and (2) matter is a form of energy ($E = mc^2$).

**Renaissance** the "rebirth" of classical culture that occurred in Italy between c. 1350 and c. 1550; also, the earlier revivals of classical culture that occurred under Charlemagne and in the twelfth century.

**rentier** a person who lives on income from property and is not personally involved in its operation.

**reparations** payments made by a defeated nation after a war to compensate another nation for damage sustained as a result of the war; required from Germany after World War I.

**revisionism** a socialist doctrine that rejected Marx's emphasis on class struggle and revolution and argued instead that workers should work through political parties to bring about gradual change.

**revolution** a fundamental change in the political and social organization of a state.

**revolutionary socialism** the socialist doctrine espoused by Georges Sorel who held that violent action was the only way to achieve the goals of socialism.

**rhetoric** the art of persuasive speaking; in the Middle Ages, one of the seven liberal arts.

**Rococo** a style, especially of decoration and architecture, that developed from the Baroque and spread throughout Europe by the 1730s. While still elaborate, it emphasized curves, lightness, and charm in the pursuit of pleasure, happiness, and love.

***ronin*** Japanese warriors made unemployed by developments in the early modern era, since samurai were forbidden by tradition to engage in commerce.

**rural responsibility system** post-Maoist land reform in China, under which collectives leased land to peasant families, who could consume or sell their surplus production and keep the profits.

**sacraments** rites considered imperative for a Christian's salvation. By the thirteenth century consisted of the eucharist or Lord's Supper, baptism, marriage, penance, extreme unction, holy orders, and confirmation of children; Protestant reformers of the sixteenth century generally recognized only two—baptism and communion (the Lord's Supper).

**samurai** literally "retainer"; similar to European knights. Usually in service to a particular shogun, these Japanese warriors lived by a strict code of ethics and duty.

**Sanskrit** an early Indo-European language, in which the Vedas were composed, beginning in the second millenium B.C.E. It survived as the language of literature and the bureaucracy for centuries after its decline as a spoken tongue.

***sans-culottes*** the common people who did not wear the fine clothes of the upper classes (sans-culottes means "without breeches") and played an important role in the radical phase of the French Revolution.

**sati** the Hindu ritual requiring a wife to throw herself upon her deceased husband's funeral pyre.

***satori*** enlightenment, in the Japanese, especially Zen, Buddhist tradition.

**satrap/satrapy** a governor with both civil and military duties in the ancient Persian Empire, which was divided into satrapies, or provinces, each administered by a satrap.

***satyagraha*** the Hindi term for the practice of nonviolent resistance, as advocated by Mohandas Gandhi; literally, "hold fast to the truth".

**scholar-gentry** in Song dynasty China, candidates who passed the civil service examinations and whose families were non-aristocratic landowners; eventually, a majority of the bureaucracy.

**scholasticism** the philosophical and theological system of the medieval schools, which emphasized rigorous analysis of contradictory authorities; often used to try to reconcile faith and reason.

**School of Mind** a philosophy espoused by Wang Yangming during the mid-Ming era of China, which argued that mind and the universe were a single unit and knowledge was therefore obtained through internal self-searching rather than through investigation of the outside world; for a while, a significant but unofficial rival to neo-Confucianism.

**scientific method** a method of seeking knowledge through inductive principles; uses experiments and observations to develop generalizations.

**Scientific Revolution** the transition from the medieval worldview to a largely secular, rational, and materialistic perspective; began in the seventeenth century and was popularized in the eighteenth.

**secularization** the process of becoming more concerned with material, worldly, temporal things and less with spiritual and religious things.

**self-determination** the doctrine that the people of a given territory or a particular nationality should have the right to determine their own government and political future.

**self-strengthening** a late-nineteenth-century Chinese policy, by which Western technology would be adopted while Confucian principles and institutions were maintained intact.

**senate/senators** the leading council of the Roman Republic; composed of about 300 men (senators) who served for life and dominated much of the political life of the Republic.

**sepoys** native troops hired by the East India Company to protect British interests in south Asia, who formed the basis of the British Indian Army.

**serf** a peasant who is bound to the land and obliged to provide labor services and pay various rents and fees to the lord; considered unfree but not a slave because serfs could not be bought and sold.

***Shari'a*** a law code, originally drawn up by Muslim scholars shortly after the death of Muhammad, that provides believers with a set of prescriptions to regulate their daily lives.

***sheikh*** originally, the ruler of a Bedouin tribe; later, also used as a more general honorific.

**Shi'ite** the second largest tradition of Islam, which split from the majority Sunni soon after the death of Muhammad, in a disagreement over the succession; especially significant in Iran and Iraq.

**Shinto** a kind of state religion in Japan, derived from beliefs in nature spirits and until recently linked with belief in the divinity of the emperor and the sacredness of the Japanese nation.

**shogun** a powerful Japanese leader, originally military, who ruled under the titular authority of the emperor.

**shogunate system** the system of government in Japan in which the emperor exercised only titular authority while the shogun (regional military dictators) exercised actual political power.

**Sikhism** a religion, founded in the early sixteenth century in the Punjab, which began as an attempt to reconcile the Hindu and Muslim traditions and developed into a significant alternative to both.

***sipahis*** in the Ottoman empire, local cavalry elites, who held fiefdoms and collected taxes.

**skepticism** a doubtful or questioning attitude, especially about religion.

**Social Darwinism** the application of Darwin's principle of organic evolution to the social order; led to the belief that progress comes from the struggle for survival as the fittest advance and the weak decline.

**socialism** an ideology that calls for collective or government ownership of the means of production and the distribution of goods.

**social security/social insurance** government programs that provide social welfare measures such as old age pensions and sickness, accident, and disability insurance.

**Socratic method** a form of teaching that uses a question-and-answer format to enable students to reach conclusions by using their own reasoning.

**Sophists** wandering scholars and professional teachers in ancient Greece who stressed the importance of rhetoric and tended toward skepticism and relativism.

**soviets** councils of workers' and soldiers' deputies formed throughout Russia in 1917; played an important role in the Bolshevik Revolution.

**sphere of influence** a territory or region over which an outside nation exercises political or economic influence.

**Star Wars** nickname of the Strategic Defense Initiative, proposed by President Reagan, which was intended to provide a shield that would destroy any incoming missiles; named after a popular science-fiction movie series.

**stateless societies** the pre-Columbian communities in much of the Americas who developed substantial cultures without formal nation states.

**State Confucianism** the integration of Confucian doctrine with Legalist practice under the Han dynasty in China, which became the basis of Chinese political thought until the modern era.

**Stoicism** a philosophy founded by Zeno in the fourth century C.E. that taught that happiness could be obtained by accepting one's lot and living in harmony with the will of God, thereby achieving inner peace.

**stupa** originally a stone tower holding relics of the Buddha, more generally a place for devotion, often architecturally impressive and surmounted with a spire.

**subinfeudation** the practice in which a lord's greatest vassals subdivided their fiefs and had vassals of their own, and those vassals, in turn, subdivided their fiefs and so on down to simple knights whose fiefs were too small to subdivide.

**Sublime Porte** the office of the grand vezir in the Ottoman empire.

***sudras*** the classes that represented the great bulk of the Indian population from ancient time, mostly peasants, artisans or manual laborers; ranked below brahmins, kshatriyas, and vaisyas, but above the pariahs.

**suffrage** the right to vote.

**suffragists** those who advocate the extension of the right to vote (suffrage), especially to women.

**Sufism** a mystical school of Islam, noted for its music, dance, and poetry, which became prominent in about the thirteenth century.

**sultan** "holder of power," a title commonly used by Muslim rulers in the Ottoman Empire, Egypt, and elsewhere; still in use in parts of Asia, sometimes for regional authorities.

**Sunni** the largest tradition of Islam, from which the Shi'ites split soon after the death of Muhammad, in a disagreement over the succession.

**Supreme Ultimate** according to Neo-Confucianists, a transcendent world, distinct from the material world in which humans live, but to which humans may aspire; a set of abstract principles, roughly equivalent to the Dao.

**surplus value** in Marxism, the difference between a product's real value and the wages of the worker who produced the product.

**Swahili** a mixed African-Arabian culture that developed by the twelfth century along the east coast of Africa; also, the national language of Kenya and Tanzania.

**syncretism** the combining of different forms of belief or practice, as, for example, when two gods are regarded as different forms of the same underlying divine force and are fused together.

**Taika reforms** the seventh-century "great change" reforms that established the centralized Japanese state.

**taille** a French tax on land or property, developed by King Louis XI in the fifteenth century as the financial basis of the monarchy. It was largely paid by the peasantry; the nobility and the clergy were exempt.

**Tantrism** a mystical Buddhist sect, which emphasized the importance of magical symbols and ritual in seeking a path to enlightenment.

**tariffs** duties (taxes) imposed on imported goods; usually imposed both to raise revenue and to discourage imports and protect domestic industries.

**tetrarchy** rule by four; the system of government established by Diocletian (284–305) in which the Roman Empire was divided into two parts, each ruled by an "Augustus" assisted by a "Caesar."

**theocracy** a government based on a divine authority.

**Theravada** a school of Buddhism that stresses personal behavior and the quest for understanding as a means of release from the wheel of life, rather than the intercession of bodhisattvas; predominant in Sri Lanka and Southeast Asia.

**three-field system** in medieval agriculture, the practice of dividing the arable land into three fields so that one could lie fallow while the others were planted in winter grains and spring crops.

**three kingdoms** Koguryo, Paekche, and Silla, rivals but all under varying degrees of Chinese influence, which together controlled virtually all of Korea from the fourth to the seventh centuries.

**three obediences** the traditional duties of Japanese women, in permanent subservience: child to father, wife to husband, and widow to son.

**tithe** a tenth of one's harvest or income; paid by medieval peasants to the village church.

**Tongmenghui** the political organization—"Revolutionary Alliance"—formed by Sun Yat-sen in 1905, which united various revolutionary factions and ultimately toppled the Manchu dynasty.

**Torah** the body of law in Hebrew Scripture, contained in the Pentateuch (the first five books of the Hebrew Bible).

**totalitarian state** a state characterized by government control over all aspects of economic, social, political, cultural, and intellectual life, the subordination of the individual to the state, and insistence that the masses be actively involved in the regime's goals.

**total war** warfare in which all of a nation's resources, including civilians at home as well as soldiers in the field, are mobilized for the war effort.

**trade union** an association of workers in the same trade, formed to help members secure better wages, benefits, and working conditions.

**transubstantiation** a doctrine of the Roman Catholic church that teaches that during the eucharist the substance of the bread and wine is miraculously transformed into the body and blood of Jesus.

**trench warfare** warfare in which the opposing forces attack and counterattack from a relatively permanent system of trenches protected by barbed wire; characteristic of World War I.

**tribunes of the plebs** beginning in 494 B.C.E., Roman officials who were given the power to protect plebeians against arrest by patrician magistrates.

**tribute system** an important element of Chinese foreign policy, by which neighboring states paid for the privilege of access to Chinese markets, received legitimation and agreed not to harbor enemies of the Chinese Empire.

**Truman Doctrine** the doctrine, enunciated by Harry Truman in 1947, that the United States would provide economic aid to countries that said they were threatened by Communist expansion.

**twice-born** the males of the higher castes in traditional Indian society, who underwent an initiation ceremony at puberty.

**tyrant/tyranny** in an ancient Greek *polis* (or an Italian city-state during the Renaissance), a ruler who came to power in an unconstitutional way and ruled without being subject to the law.

***uhuru*** "freedom" (Swahili), and so a key slogan in the African independence movements, especially in Kenya.

***uji*** a clan in early Japanese tribal society.

**ulama** a convocation of leading Muslim scholars, the earliest of which shortly after the death of Muhammad drew up a law code, called the Shari'a, based largely on the Koran and the sayings of the Prophet, to provide believers with a set of prescriptions to regulate their daily lives.

**umma** the Muslim community, as a whole.

**uncertainty principle** a principle in quantum mechanics, posited by Heisenberg, that holds that one cannot determine the path of an electron because the very act of observing the electron would affect its location.

**unconditional surrender** complete, unqualified surrender of a nation.

**uninterrupted revolution** the goal of the Great Proletarian Cultural Revolution launched by Mao Zedong in 1966.
**utopian socialists** intellectuals and theorists in the early nineteenth century who favored equality in social and economic conditions and wished to replace private property and competition with collective ownership and cooperation; deemed impractical and "utopian" by later socialists.

***vaisya*** the third-ranked class in traditional Indian society, usually merchants.
**varna** Indian classes, or castes. See caste system.
**vassal** a person granted a fief, or landed estate, in exchange for providing military services to the lord and fulfilling certain other obligations such as appearing at the lord's court when summoned and making a payment on the knighting of the lord's eldest son.
**veneration of ancestors** the extension of filial piety to include care for the deceased, for instance by burning replicas of useful objects to accompany them on their journey to the next world.
**vernacular** the everyday language of a region, as distinguished from a language used for special purposes. For example, in medieval Paris, French was the vernacular, but Latin was used for academic writing and for classes at the University of Paris.
**Vietnam syndrome** the presumption, from the 1970s on, that the U.S. public would object to a protracted military entanglement abroad, such as another Vietnam-type conflict.
***vizier*** (*also*, vezir) the prime minister in the Abbasid caliphate and elsewhere, a chief executive.
**volkish thought** the belief that German culture is superior and that the German people have a universal mission to save Western civilization from inferior races.

**war communism** Lenin's policy of nationalizing industrial and other facilities and requisitioning the peasants' produce during the civil war in Russia.
**War Guilt Clause** the clause in the Treaty of Versailles that declared that Germany (and Austria) were responsible for starting World War I and ordered Germany to pay reparations for the damage the Allies had suffered as a result of the war.
**Warsaw Pact** a military alliance, formed in 1955, in which Albania, Bulgaria, Czechoslovakia, East Germany, Hungary, Poland, Romania, and the Soviet Union agreed to provide mutual assistance. Dissolved in 1991, most former members eventually joined NATO.
**welfare state** a social/political system in which the government assumes the primary responsibility for the social welfare of its citizens by providing such things as social security, unemployment benefits, and health care.
**well field system** the theoretical pattern of land ownership in early China, named for the appearance of the Chinese character for "well," in which farmland was divided into nine segments and a peasant family would cultivate one for their own use and cooperate with seven others to cultivate the ninth for the landlord.
**wergeld** "money for a man." In early Germanic law, a person's value in monetary terms, which was paid by a wrongdoer to the family of the person who had been injured or killed.
**White Lotus** a Chinese Buddhist sect, founded in 1133 C.E., that sought political reform; in 1796–1804, a Chinese peasant revolt.
**women's liberation movement** the struggle for equal rights for women, which has deep roots in history but achieved new prominence under this name in the 1960s, building on the work of, among others, Simone de Beauvoir and Betty Friedan.
**world-machine** Newton's conception of the universe as one huge, regulated, and uniform machine that operated according to natural laws in absolute time, space, and motion.

**Yangshao** a Neolithic society from near the Yellow River in China, sometimes identified by its painted pottery.
**Young Turks** a successful Turkish reformist group in the late nineteenth and early twentieth centuries.

**zaibatsu** powerful business cartels formed in Japan during the Meiji era and outlawed following World War II.
**zamindars** Indian tax collectors, who were assigned land, from which they kept part of the revenue; the British revived the system in a misguided attempt to create a landed gentry.
**Zen Buddhism** (in Chinese, Chan or Ch'an) a school of Buddhism particularly important in Japan, some of whose adherents stress that enlightenment (satori) can be achieved suddenly, though others emphasize lengthy meditation.
**ziggurat** a massive stepped tower upon which a temple dedicated to the chief god or goddess of a Sumerian city was built.
**Zionism** an international movement that called for the establishment of a Jewish state or a refuge for Jews in Palestine.
**Zoroastrianism** a religion founded by the Persian Zoroaster in the seventh century C.E.; characterized by worship of a supreme god Ahuramazda who represents the good against the evil spirit, identified as Ahriman.

# Pronunciation Guide

**Abbasid** uh-BAH-sid *or* AB-uh-sid
**Abd al-Rahman** ub-duh-rahkh-MAHN
**Abu al-Abbas** uh-BOOL-uh-BUSS
**Abu Bakr** uh-boo-BAHK-ur
**Achebe, Chinua** ah-CHAY-bay, CHIN-wah
**Achilles** uh-KIL-eez
**Adenauer, Konrad** AD-uh-now-ur
**aediles** EE-dylz
**Aegospotami** ee-guh-SPOT-uh-mee
**Aeolians** ee-OH-lee-unz
**Aequi** EE-kwy
**Aeschylus** ESS-kuh-luss
**Aetius** ay-EE-shuss
**Afrikaners** ah-fri-KAH-nurz
**Agesilaus** uh-jess-uh-LAY-uss
**Agincourt** AH-zhen-koor
**Aguinaldo, Emilio** ah-gwee-NAHL-doh, ay-MEEL-yoh
**Ahlwardt, Hermann** AHL-vart, hayr-MAHN
**Ahuramazda** uh-hoor-uh-MAHZ-duh
**Aix-la-Chapelle** ex-lah-shah-PELL
**Ajanta** uh-JUHN-tuh
**Akhenaten** ah-khuh-NAH-tun
**Akhetaten** ah-khuh-TAH-tun
**Akkadians** uh-KAY-dee-unz
**Alaric** AL-uh-rik
**Alberti, Leon Battista** al-BAYR-tee, LAY-un buh-TEESS-tuh
**Albigensians** al-buh-JEN-see-unz
**Albuquerque, Afonso de** AL-buh-kur-kee, ah-FAHN-soh day
**Alcibiades** al-suh-BY-uh-deez
**Alcuin** AL-kwin
**Alemanni** al-uh-MAH-nee
**al-Fatah** al-FAH-tuh
**al-Hakim** al-hah-KEEM
**Alia, Ramiz** AH-lee-uh, rah-MEEZ
**al-Khwarizmi** al-KHWAR-iz-mee
**Allah** AH-lah
**al-Ma'mun** al-muh-MOON
**Almeida, Francesco da** ahl-MAY-duh, frahn-CHAYSS-koh
**al-Sadat, Anwar** ah-sah-DAHT, ahn-WAHR
**Aidoo, Ama Ata** ah-EE-doo, AH-mah AH-tah
**Amaterasu** ah-muh-teh-RAH-suh
**Amenhotep** ah-mun-HOH-tep
**Anasazi** ah-nuh-SAH-zee
**Andreotti, Giulio** ahn-dray-AH-tee, JOOL-yoh
**Andropov, Yuri** ahn-DRAHP-awf, YOOR-ee
**Anjou** AHN-zhoo
**Antigonid** an-TIG-uh-nid
**Antigonus Gonatus** an-TIG-oh-nuss guh-NAH-tuss
**Antiochus** an-TY-uh-kuss
**Antonescu, Ion** an-tuh-NESS-koo, YON
**Antoninus Pius** an-tuh-NY-nuss PY-uss
**Anyang** ahn-YAHNG
**apella** uh-PELL-uh
**Apollonius** ap-uh-LOH-nee-uss
**Aquinas, Thomas** uh-KWY-nuss
**Arafat, Yasir** ah-ruh-FAHT, yah-SEER
**aratrum** uh-RAH-trum
**Arawak** AR-uh-wahk
**Archimedes** ahr-kuh-MEE-deez
***Argonautica*** ahr-guh-NAWT-uh-kuh
**Aristarchus** ar-iss-TAR-kus
**Aristotle** AR-iss-tot-ul
**Arjuna** ahr-JOO-nuh
**Arsinoë** ahr-SIN-oh-ee
***artium baccalarius*** ar-TEE-um bak-uh-LAR-ee-uss
***artium magister*** ar-TEE-um muh-GISS-ter
**Aryan** AR-ee-un
**Ashikaga** ah-shee-KAH-guh
**Ashkenazic** ash-kuh-NAH-zik
**Ashoka** uh-SHOH-kuh
**Ashurbanipal** ah-shur-BAH-nuh-pahl
**Ashurnasirpal** ah-shur-NAH-zur-pahl
***asiento*** ah-SYEN-toh
***assignat*** ah-see-NYAH
**Assyrians** uh-SEER-ee-unz
**Astell, Mary** AST-ul
**Atahualpa** ah-tuh-WAHL-puh
**Attalid** AT-uh-lid
***audiencias*** ow-dee-en-SEE-uss
**Auerstadt** OW-urr-shtaht
**augur** AW-gurr
**Augustine** AW-guh-steen
**Aum Shinri Kyo** awm-shin-ree-KYO
**Aung San Huu Kyi** AWNG-sawn-soo-chee
**Aurelian** aw-REEL-yun
**Auschwitz-Birkenau** OW-shvitz-BEER-kuh-now
***Ausgleich*** OWSS-glykh
**auspices** AWSS-puh-sizz
**Austerlitz** AWSS-tur-litz
**Australopithecines** aw-stray-loh-PITH-uh-synz
**Austrasia** awss-TRAY-zhuh
**Autun** oh-TUNH
**Avalokitesvara** uh-VAH-loh-kee-TESH-vuh-ruh
**Avicenna** av-i-SENN-uh
**Avignon** ah-veen-YOHNH
**Ayacucho** ah-ya-KOO-choh
**Ayodhya** ah-YOHD-hyah
**Ayuthaya** ah-yoo-TY-yuh
**Azerbaijan** az-ur-by-JAN
**Ba'ath** BAHTH
**Baader-Meinhof** BAH-durr-MYN-huff
**Babeuf, Gracchus** bah-BUFF, GRAK-uss
**Babur** BAH-burr
**Bach, Johann Sebastian** BAKH, yoh-HAHN suh-BASS-chun
**Baden-Powell, Robert** BAD-un-POW-ul
**Bai Hua** by HWA
***bakufu*** buh-KOO-foo *or Japanese* bah-KOO-fuh
**Bakunin, Michael** buh-KOON-yun
**Balboa, Vasco Nuñez de** bal-BOH-uh, BAHS-koh NOON-yez day

**Ballin, Albert** BAH-leen
**Bandaranaike, Sirimavo** bahn-dur-uh-NY-uh-kuh, see-ree-MAH-voh
**Banque de Belgique** BAHNK duh bel-ZHEEK
**Ban Zhao** bahn ZHOW
***Bao-jia*** BOW-jah
**Barbarossa** bar-buh-ROH-suh
**Baroque** buh-ROHK
**Barth, Karl** BAHRT
**Basho** BAH-shoh
**Bastille** bass-STEEL
**Basutoland** buh-SOO-toh-land
**Batista, Fulgencio** bah-TEES-tuh, full-JEN-see-oh
**Bauhaus** BOW-howss
**Bayazid** by-uh-ZEED
**Bayle, Pierre** BELL, PYAYR
**Beauharnais, Josephine de** boh-ar-NAY, zhoh-seff-FEEN duh
**Beauvoir, Simone de** boh-VWAR, see-MUHN duh
**Bebel, August** BAY-bul, ow-GOOST
**Beccaria, Cesare** buh-KAH-ree-uh, CHAY-zuh-ray
**Bechuanaland** bech-WAH-nuh-land
**Bede** BEED
**Begin, Menachem** BAY-gin, muh-NAH-khum
**Beguines** bay-GEENZ
**Beiderbecke, Bix** BY-der-bek, BIKS
**Beijing** bay-ZHING
**Belarus** bell-uh-ROOSS
**Belgioioso, Cristina** bell-joh-YOH-soh
**Belisarius** bell-uh-SAH-ree-uss
**benefice** BEN-uh-fiss
**Benin** bay-NEEN
**Bergson, Henri** BAYRK-suhn, ahn-REE
**Berlioz, Hector** BAYR-lee-ohz, hek-TOR
**Berlusconi, Silvio** bayr-loo-SKOH-nee, SEEL-vee-oh
**Bernhardi, Friedrich von** bayrn-HAR-dee, FREED-reekh fun
**Bernini, Gian Lorenzo** bur-NEE-nee, JAHN loh-RENT-zoh
**Bernstein, Eduard** BAYRN-shtyn, AY-doo-art
**Bethman-Hollweg, Theobald von** BET-mun-HOHL-vek, TAY-oh-bahlt fun
**Bhagavad Gita** bah-guh-vahd-GEE-tuh
**Bharata Janata** BAR-ruh-tuh JAH-nuh-tuh
**Bhutto, Zulfikar Ali** BOO-toh, ZOOL-fee-kahr ah-LEE
**Bismarck, Otto von** BIZ-mark, OH-toh fun
**Blanc, Louis** BLAHNH, LWEE
***Blitzkrieg*** BLITZ-kreeg
**Blum, Léon** BLOOM, LAY-ohnh
**Boccaccio, Giovanni** boh-KAH-choh, joe-VAH-nee
**Bodichon, Barbara** boh-di-SHOHNH
**Boer** BOOR *or* BOR
**Boethius** boh-EE-thee-uss
**Boleyn, Anne** BUH-lin *or* buh-LIN
**Bolívar, Simón** boh-LEE-var, see-MOHN
**Bologna** boh-LOHN-yuh
**Bolsheviks** BOHL-shuh-viks
**Bora, Katherina von** BOH-rah, kat-uh-REE-nuh fun
**Borobudur** boh-roh-buh-DOOR
**Bosnia** BAHZ-nee-uh
**Bosporus** BAHSS-pruss
**Bossuet, Jacques** baw-SWAY, ZHAHK
**Botswana** baht-SWAH-nuh
**Botta, Giuseppe** BOH-tah, joo-ZEP-pay
**Botticelli, Sandro** bot-i-CHELL-ee, SAHN-droh
**Boulanger, Georges** boo-lahnh-ZHAY, ZHORZH
**boule** BOOL
**Bracciolini, Poggio** braht-choh-LEE-nee, POH-djoh
**Brahe, Tycho** BRAH, TY-koh
**Brahmo Samaj** BRAH-moh suh-MAHJ
**Bramante, Donato** brah-MAHN-tay, doh-NAH-toh
**Brandt, Willy** BRAHNT, VIL-ee
**Brasidas** BRASS-i-duss
**Brest-Litovsk** BREST-li-TUFFSK
**Brétigny** bray-tee-NYEE
**Brezhnev, Leonid** BREZH-neff, lyee-oh-NYEET
**Briand, Aristide** bree-AHNH, ah-ruh-STEED
**Broz, Josip** BRAWZ, yaw-SEEP
**Brunelleschi, Filippo** BROO-nuh-LESS-kee, fee-LEE-poh
**Brüning, Heinrich** BRUR-ning, HYN-rikh
**Bückeberg** BURK-uh-bayrk
**Bulganin, Nicolai** bool-GAN-yin, nyik-uh-LY
***Bund Deutscher Mädel*** BOONT DOIT-chur MAY-dul
**Bundesrat** BOON-duss-raht
**Burckhardt, Jacob** BOORK-hart, YAK-ub
***Burschenschaften*** BOOR-shun-shahf-tun
**Bushido** BOO-shee-doh
**Cabral, Pedro** kuh-BRAL, PAY-droh
***cahiers de doléances*** ka-YAY duh doh-lay-AHNSS
**Cai Yuanpei** TSY yoo-wan-PAY
**Calais** ka-LAY
**Calas, Jean** ka-LAH, ZHAHNH
**Caligula** kuh-LIG-yuh-luh
**caliph** KAY-liff
**caliphate** KAY-luh-fayt
**Callicrates** kuh-LIK-ruh-teez
**Calonne, Charles de** ka-LUNN, SHAHRL duh
**Cambyses** kam-BY-seez
**Camus, Albert** ka-MOO, ahl-BAYR
**Can Vuong** kahn VWAHNG
**Canaanites** KAY-nuh-nytss
**Cannae** KAH-nee
**Cao Cao** TSOW-tsow
**Capet, Hugh** ka-PAY, YOO
**Capetian** kuh-PEE-shun
**Caracalla** kuh-RAK-uh-luh
**Caraffa, Gian Pietro** kuh-RAH-fuh, JAHN PYAY-troh
***carbonari*** kar-buh-NAH-ree
**Cárdenas, Lázaro** KAHR-day-nahss, LAH-zah-roh
**Carolingian** kar-uh-LIN-jun
***carruca*** kuh-ROO-kuh
**Carthage** KAHR-thij
**Carthaginian** kahr-thuh-JIN-ee-un
**Cartier, Jacques** kahr-TYAY, ZHAK
**Casa de Contratación** KAH-sah day KOHN-trah-tahk-SYOHN
**Cassiodorus** kass-ee-uh-DOR-uss
**Castiglione, Baldassare** ka-steel-YOH-nay, bal-duh-SAH-ray
**Castro, Fidel** KASS-troh, fee-DELL
**Çatal Hüyük** chaht-ul-hoo-YOOK
**Catharism** KATH-uh-riz-um
**Catullus** kuh-TULL-uss
**Cavendish, Margaret** KAV-un-dish
**Cavour, Camillo di** kuh-VOOR, kuh-MEEL-oh dee
**Ceauşescu, Nicolae** chow-SHES-koo, nee-koh-LY
**celibacy** SELL-uh-buh-see
**cenobitic** sen-oh-BIT-ik
**Cereta, Laura** say-RAY-tuh, LOW-ruh
**Cerularius, Michael** sayr-yuh-LAR-ee-uss
**Cézanne, Paul** say-ZAHN, POHL
**Chacabuco** chahk-ah-BOO-koh
**Chaeronea** ker-uh-NEE-uh
**Chaldean** kal-DEE-un
**Chamorro, Violeta Barrios de** chah-MOH-roh, vee-oh-LET-uh bah-REE-ohss day

**Champlain, Samuel de** shonh-PLENH *or* sham-PLAYN, sahm-WEL duh
**Chandragupta Maurya** chun-druh-GOOP-tuh MOWR-yuh
**Chang'an** CHENG-AHN
***chanson de geste*** shahn-SONH duh ZHEST
**Chao Phraya** chow-PRY-uh
**Charlemagne** SHAR-luh-mayn
**Chateaubriand, François-René de** shah-TOH-bree-AHNH, frahnh-SWAH-ruh-NAY duh
**Châtelet, marquise du** shat-LAY, mahr-KEEZ duh
**Chauvet** shoh-VAY
**Chavín de Huántar** chah-VEEN day HWAHN-tahr
**Chechnya** CHECH-nyuh
**Cheka** CHEK-uh
**Chennai** CHEN-ny
**Chen Shuibian** CHEN-shwee-BYAHN
**Chiang Kai-shek** CHANG ky-SHEK
**Chichén Itzá** chee-CHEN-eet-SAH
**Chimor** chee-MAWR
**Chirac, Jacques** shee-RAK, ZHAHK
**Chongqing** chung-CHING
**Chrétien de Troyes** kray-TYEN duh TRWAH
**Chrétien, Jean** kray-TYEN, ZHAHNH
**Chrysoloras, Manuel** kriss-uh-LAWR-uss, man-WEL
**Cicero** SIS-uh-roh
**Cincinnatus** sin-suh-NAT-uss
***ciompi*** CHAHM-pee
**Cistercians** sis-TUR-shunz
**Cixi** TSEE-chee
**Clairvaux** klayr-VOH
**Claudius** KLAW-dee-uss
**Cleisthenes** KLYSS-thuh-neez
**Clemenceau, Georges** kluh-mahn-SOH, ZHORZH
**Clovis** KLOH-viss
**Codreanu, Corneliu** kaw-dree-AH-noo, kor-NELL-yoo
**Colbert, Jean-Baptiste** kohl-BAYR, ZHAHN-bap-TEEST
**Colonia Agrippinensis** kuh-LOH-nee-uh uh-grip-uh-NEN-suss
***colonus*** kuh-LOH-nuss
**Columbanus** kah-lum-BAY-nuss
***comitia centuriata*** kuh-MISH-ee-uh sen-choo-ree-AH-tuh
**Commodus** KAHM-uh-duss
**Comnenus** kahm-NEE-nuss
**Comte, Auguste** KOHNT, ow-GOOST
***concilium plebis*** kahn-SILL-ee-um PLEE-biss
**Concordat of Worms** kun-KOR-dat uv WURMZ *or* VORMPS
**Condorcet, Marie-Jean de** konh-dor-SAY, muh-REE-ZHAHNH duh
***condottieri*** kahn-duh-TYAY-ree
**Confucius** kun-FYOO-shuss
**conquistador** kahn-KEESS-tuh-dor
**consul** KAHN-sull
**Contarini, Gasparo** kahn-tuh-REE-nee, GAHS-puh-roh
***conversos*** kohn-VAYR-sohz
**Copán** koh-PAHN
**Copernicus, Nicolaus** kuh-PURR-nuh-kuss, NEE-koh-lowss
**Córdoba** KOR-duh-buh
**Corinth** KOR-inth
***Corpus Hermeticum*** KOR-pus hur-MET-i-koom
***Corpus Iuris Civilis*** KOR-pus YOOR-iss SIV-i-liss
***corregidores*** kuhr-reg-uh-DOR-ayss
**Cortés, Hernán** kor-TAYSS *or* kor-TEZ, hayr-NAHN
**Corvinus, Matthias** kor-VY-nuss, muh-THY-uss
**Courbet, Gustave** koor-BAY, goo-STAHV
**Crassus** KRASS-uss
**Crécy** kray-SEE
**Credit Anstalt** KRAY-deet AHN-shtahlt
**Crédit Mobilier** kray-DEE moh-bee-LYAY
**Croatia** kroh-AY-shuh
**Croesus** KREE-suss
***cum manu*** koom MAH-noo
**Curie, Marie** kyoo-REE
**Cypselus** SIP-suh-luss
**Cyrenaica** seer-uh-NAY-uh-kuh
**Dadaism** DAH-duh-iz-um
**Daimler, Gottlieb** DYM-lur, GUHT-leeb
**daimyo** DYM-yoh
**Dai Viet** dy VYET
**d'Albret, Jeanne** dahl-BRAY, ZHAHN
**Dalí, Salvador** dah-LEE, sahl-vah-DOR
**Dandin** DUN-din
**Danton, Georges** dahn-TONH, ZHORZH
**Dao de Jing** DOW-deh-JING
**Darius** duh-RY-uss
**Darmstadt** DARM-shtaht
**dauphin** DAW-fin
**David, Jacques-Louis** dah-VEED, ZHAHK-LWEE
**de Gaulle, Charles** duh GOHL, SHAHRL
***De Rerum Novarum*** day RAY-rum noh-VAR-um
**Debelleyme, Louis-Maurice** duh-buh-LAYM, LWEE-moh-REESS
**Debussy, Claude** duh-byoo-SEE, KLOHD
***décades*** day-KAD
***Decameron*** dee-KAM-uh-run
**decarchies** DEK-ar-keez
***decemviri*** duh-SEM-vuh-ree
**Deffand, marquise du** duh-FAHNH, mar-KEEZ doo
**Dei-Anang** DAY-ah-NAHNG
**Deir el Bahri** dayr-ahl-BAH-ree
**Delacroix, Eugène** duh-lah-KRWAH, oo-ZHEN
**Démar, Claire** DAY-mar
**Demosthenes** duh-MAHSS-thuh-neez
**Deng Xiaoping** DENG-show-PING
**Denikin, Anton** dyin-YEE-kin, ahn-TOHN
**Desai, Anita** dess-SY
***descamisados*** dayss-kah-mee-SAH-dohss
**Descartes, René** day-KART, ruh-NAY
**Dessau** DESS-ow
**d'Este, Isabella** DESS-tay, ee-suh-BELL-uh
**détente** day-TAHNT
***devshirme*** dev-SHEER-may
***dharma*** DAR-muh
**d'Holbach, Paul** dohl-BAHK, POHL
***dhoti*** DOH-tee
**Diaghilev, Sergei** DYAHG-yuh-lif, syir-GAY
**Dias, Bartholomeu** DEE-ush, bar-toh-loh-MAY-oo
**Diaspora** dy-ASS-pur-uh
**Diderot, Denis** dee-DROH, duh-NEE
**Ding Ling** DING LING
**Diocletian** dy-uh-KLEE-shun
**Disraeli, Benjamin** diz-RAY-lee
**Djibouti** juh-BOO-tee
**Djoser** ZHOH-sur
**Dollfuss, Engelbert** DAWL-fooss, ENG-ul-bayrt
**Domesday Book** DOOMZ-day book
**Domitian** doh-MISH-un
**Donatello, Donato di** doh-nuh-TELL-oh, doh-NAH-toh dee
**Donatist** DOH-nuh-tist
**Donatus** duh-NAY-tus
**Dopolavoro** duh-puh-LAH-vuh-roh
**Dorians** DOR-ee-unz

**Doryphoros** doh-RIF-uh-rohss
**Dostoevsky, Fyodor** dus-tuh-YEF-skee, FYUD-ur
**Douhet, Giulio** doo-AY, JOOL-yoh
**Dreyfus, Alfred** DRY-fuss
**Du Bois, W. E. B.** doo-BOISS
**Dubček, Alexander** DOOB-chek
**Dufay, Guillaume** doo-FAY, gee-YOHM
**Duma** DOO-muh
**Duong Thu Huong** ZHWAHNG too HWAHNG
**Dupleix, Joseph-François** doo-PLEKS
**Dürer, Albrecht** DOO-rur, AHL-brekht
**Dzerzhinksy, Felix** djur-ZHIN-skee
**Ebert, Friedrich** AY-bayrt, FREE-drikh
***ecclesia*** ek-KLEE-zee-uh
**Eckhart, Meister** EK-hart, MY-stur
***Einsatzgruppen*** YN-zahtz-groop-un
**Einstein, Albert** YN-styn
**Ekaterinburg** i-kat-tuh-RIN-burk
**Emecheta, Buchi** ay-muh-CHAY-tuh, BOO-chee
***encomienda*** en-koh-MYEN-duh
**Engels, Friedrich** ENG-ulz, FREE-drikh
**Enki** EN-kee
**Enlil** EN-lil
**Entente Cordiale** ahn-TAHNT kor-DYAHL
**entrepôt** ahn-truh-POH
**Epaminondas** i-PAM-uh-NAHN-duss
**Ephesus** EFF-uh-suss
**ephor** EFF-ur
**Epicureanism** ep-i-kyoo-REE-uh-ni-zum
**Epicurus** ep-i-KYOOR-uss
**episcopos** i-PIS-kuh-puss
**equestrians** i-KWES-tree-unz
***equites*** EK-wuh-teez
**Erasistratus** er-uh-SIS-truh-tuss
**Erasmus, Desiderius** i-RAZZ-mus, dez-i-DEER-ee-uss
**Eratosthenes** er-uh-TAHSS-thuh-neez
**eremitical** er-uh-MIT-i-kul
**Erhard, Ludwig** AYR-hart, LOOD-vik
**Estonia** ess-TOH-nee-uh
**Etruscans** i-TRUSS-kunz
**Euclid** YOO-klid
**Euripides** yoo-RIP-uh-deez
**exchequer** EKS-chek-ur
**Execrabilis** ek-suh-KRAB-uh-liss
**Eylau** Y-low
**Falange** fuh-LANJ
**Fang Lizhu** FAHNG lee-ZHOO
***fasces*** FASS-eez
***Fascio di Combattimento*** FASH-ee-oh dee com-bat-ee-MEN-toh
**Fatimid** FAT-i-mid
**Fedele, Cassandra** FAY-duh-lee
**Feltre, Vittorino da** FELL-tray, vee-tor-EE-noh dah
**Ficino, Marsilio** fee-CHEE-noh, mar-SIL-yoh
**Fischer, Joschka** FISH-ur, YUSH-kah
**Flaubert, Gustave** floh-BAYR, goo-STAHV
**Fleury, Cardinal** floo-REE
***fluyt*** FLYT
**Foch, Ferdinand** FUSH, fayr-di-NAWNH
**Fontainebleau** FAWNH-ten-bloh
**Fontenelle, Bernard de** fawnt-NELL, bayr-NAHR duh
**Fouquet, Nicolas** foo-KAY, nee-koh-LAH
**Fourier, Charles** foo-RYAY, SHAHRL
**Francesca, Piero della** frahn-CHESS-kuh, PYAY-roh del-luh
**Freud, Sigmund** FROID, SIG-mund *or* ZIG-munt
**Friedan, Betty** free-DAN
**Friedland** FREET-lahnt
**Friedrich, Caspar David** FREED-rikh, kass-PAR dah-VEET
**Froissart, Jean** frwah-SAR, ZHAHNH
**Fronde** FROHND
**Fu Xi** foo SHEE
**Fu Xuan** foo SHWAHN
***fueros*** FWYA-rohss
***Führerprinzip*** FYOOR-ur-prin-TSEEP
**Fujiwara** foo-jee-WAH-rah
***gabelle*** gah-BELL
**Gaiseric** GY-zuh-rik
**Galba** GAHL-buh
**Galilei, Galileo** GAL-li-lay, gal-li-LAY-oh
**Gama, Vasco da** GAHM-uh, VAHSH-koh dah
**Gandhi, Mohandas (Mahatma)** GAHN-dee, moh-HAHN-dus (mah-HAHT-muh)
**Garibaldi, Giuseppe** gar-uh-BAHL-dee, joo-ZEP-pay
**Gasperi, Alcide de** GAHSS-puh-ree, ahl-SEE-day day
**Gatti de Gamond, Zoé** gah-TEE duh gah-MOHNH, zoh-AY
**Gaugamela** gaw-guh-MEE-luh
**Gelasius** juh-LAY-shuss
**Genghis Khan** JING-uss *or* GENG-uss KAHN
***genin*** gay-NIN
**Gentileschi, Artemisia** jen-tuh-LESS-kee, ar-tuh-MEE-zhuh
**Geoffrin, Marie-Thérèse de** zhoh-FRENH, ma-REE-tay-RAYZ duh
***gerousia*** juh-ROO-see-uh
***Gesamtkunstwerk*** guh-ZAHMT-koonst-vayrk
**Gierek, Edward** GYER-ek, ED-vahrt
**Gilgamesh** GILL-guh-mesh
**Giolitti, Giovanni** joh-LEE-tee, joe-VAHN-nee
**Giotto** JOH-toh
**Girondins** juh-RAHN-dinz
***glasnost*** GLAHZ-nohst
***Gleichschaltung*** glykh-SHAHL-toonk
**Goebbels, Joseph** GUR-bulz
**Goethe, Johann Wolfgang von** GUR-tuh, yoh-HAHN VULF-gahnk fun
**Gokhale, Gopal** GOH-ku-lay, goh-PAHL
**Gömbös, Julius** GUM-buhsh
**Gomulka, Wladyslaw** goh-MOOL-kuh, vlah-DIS-lahf
***gonfaloniere*** gun-fah-loh-NYAY-ray
**Gonzaga, Gian Francesco** gun-DZAH-gah, JAHN frahn-CHES-koh
**Gorbachev, Mikhail** GOR-buh-chof, meek-HAYL
**Göring, Hermann** GUR-ing, hayr-MAHN
**Gottwald, Clement** GAWT-valt, klay-MENT
**Gouges, Olympe** GOOZH, oh-LAMP
**Gracchus, Tiberius and Gaius** GRAK-us, ty-BEER-ee-uss *and* GY-uss
***grandi*** GRAHN-dee
**Grieg, Edvard** GREEG, ED-vart
**Groote, Gerard** GROH-tuh
**Gropius, Walter** GROH-pee-uss, VAHL-tuh
***Grossdeutsch*** GROHS-doich
**Groza, Petra** GRO-zhuh, PET-ruh
**Guan Yin** gwahn-YIN
**Guangdong** gwahng-DUNG
**Guangxu** gwahng-SHOO
**Guangzhou** gwahng-JOH
**Guaraní** gwahr-uh-NEE
**Guicciardini, Francesco** gwee-char-DEE-nee, frahn-CHESS-koh
**Guindorf, Reine** GWIN-dorf, RY-nuh
**Guise** GEEZ
**Guizot, François** gee-ZOH, frahnh-SWAH
**Gujarat** goo-juh-RAHT

**Guomindang** gwoh-min-DAHNG
**Gustavus Adolphus** goo-STAY-vus uh-DAHL-fuss
**Gutenberg, Johannes** GOO-ten-bayrk, yoh-HAH-nuss
**Guzman, Gaspar de** goos-MAHN, gahs-PAR day
**Habsburg** HAPS-burg
***Hadith*** huh-DEETH
**Hadrian** HAY-dree-un
**Hagia Sophia** HAG-ee-uh soh-FEE-uh
***hajj*** HAJ
**Hammurabi** hahm-uh-RAH-bee
**Han Gaozu** HAHN gow-DZOO
**Han Wudi** HAHN woo-DEE
**Handel, George Friedrich** HAN-dul
**Hankou** HAHN-kow
**Hannibal** HAN-uh-bul
**Hanukkah** HAH-nuh-kuh
**Harappa** huh-RAP-uh
**Hardenberg, Karl von** HAR-den-bayrk, KARL fun
**Harun al-Rashid** huh-ROON ah-rah-SHEED
**Hassan ben Sabbah** khah-SAHN ben shah-BAH
**Hatshepsut** hat-SHEP-soot
**Haushofer, Karl** HOWSS-hoh-fuh
**Haussmann, Baron** HOWSS-mun
**Havel, Vaclav** HAH-vul, VAHT-slahf
**Haydn, Franz Joseph** HY-dun, FRAHNTS YO-zef
**Hedayat, Sadeq** hay-DY-yaht, sah-DEK
***hegemon*** HEJ-uh-mun
**Hegira** hee-JY-ruh
**Heian** hay-AHN
**Heisenberg, Werner** HY-zun-bayrk, VAYR-nur
**heliaea** HEE-lee-ee
**Hellenistic** hel-uh-NIS-tik
**helots** HEL-uts
**Heraclius** he-ruh-KLY-uss *or* huh-RAK-lee-uss
**Herculaneum** hur-kyuh-LAY-nee-um
**Herodotus** huh-ROD-uh-tuss
**Herophilus** huh-ROF-uh-luss
**Herzegovina** HAYRT-suh-guh-VEE-nuh
**Herzen, Alexander** HAYRT-sun
**Herzl, Theodor** HAYRT-sul, TAY-oh-dor
**Heshen** HEH-shen
**Hesiod** HEE-see-ud
**Hesse, Hermann** HESS-uh, hayr-MAHN
***hetairai*** huh-TY-ry
**Heydrich, Reinhard** HY-drikh, RYN-hart
**Hideyoshi, Toyotomi** hee-day-YOH-shee, toh-yoh-TOH-mee
**hieroglyph** HY-uh-roh-glif
**Hildegard of Bingen** HIL-duh-gard uv BING-un
**Hindenburg, Paul von** HIN-den-boork, POWL fun
**Hiroshima** hee-roh-SHEE-muh
**Hisauchi, Michio** hee-sah-OO-chee, mee-CHEE-OH
***Hitler Jugend*** HIT-luh YOO-gunt
**Ho Chi Minh** HOH CHEE MIN
**Höch, Hannah** HURKH
**Hohenstaufen** hoh-en-SHTOW-fen
**Hohenzollern** hoh-en-TSULL-urn
**Hohenzollern-Sigmaringen** hoh-en-TSULL-urn-zig-mah-RING-un
**Hokkaido** hoh-KY-doh
**Hokusai** HOH-kuh-sy
**Holtzendorf** HOHLT-sen-dorf
***Homo sapiens*** HOH-moh SAY-pee-unz
**Honecker, Erich** HOH-nek-uh, AY-reekh
**Hong Xiuquan** HOONG shee-oo-CHWAHN
**Honorius** hoh-NOR-ee-uss
**hoplites** HAHP-lyts
**Horace** HOR-uss
**Horthy, Miklós** HOR-tee, MIK-lohsh
**Hosokawa, Mirohiro** hoh-soh-KAH-wah, mee-roh-HEE-roh
**Höss, Rudolf** HURSS
**Hoxha, Enver** HAW-jah, EN-vayr
**Huang Di** hwahng-DEE
**Huayna Inca** WY-nuh INK-uh
**Huê** HWAY
**Huguenots** HYOO-guh-nots
**Huitzilopochtli** WEET-see-loh-POHCHT-lee
**Humayun** hoo-MY-yoon
**Husák, Gustav** HOO-sahk, goo-STAHV
**Ibn Saud** ib-un-sah-OOD
**Ibn Sina** ib-un SEE-nuh
**iconoclasm** y-KAHN-uh-claz-um
**Ictinus** ik-TY-nuss
**Ife** EE-fay
**Ignatius of Loyola** ig-NAY-shuss uv loi-OH-luh
***Il Duce*** eel DOO-chay
**Île-de-France** EEL-duh-fronhss
***illustrés*** ee-loo-STRAY
***illustrissimi*** ee-loo-STREE-see-mee
***imperator*** im-puh-RAH-tur
***imperium*** im-PEER-ee-um
***intendant*** anh-tahnh-DAHNH *or* in-TEN-dunt
**Irigoyen, Hipólito** ee-ree-GOH-yen, ee-POH-lee-toh
**Isis** Y-sis
**Issus** ISS-uss
**Iturbide, Agustín de** ee-tur-BEE-day, ah-goo-STEEN dat
**Itzamna** eet-SAHM-nuh
***ius civile*** YOOSS see-VEE-lay
***ius gentium*** YOOSS GEN-tee-um
***ius naturale*** YOOSS nah-too-RAH-lay
**Izanagi** ee-zah-NAH-gee
**Izanami** ee-zah-NAH-mee
***Izvestia*** iz-VESS-tee-uh
**Jacobin** JAK-uh-bin
**Jacquerie** zhak-REE
**Jadwiga** yahd-VEE-guh
**Jagiello** yahg-YEL-oh
**Jahn, Friedrich Ludwig** YAHN, FREED-rikh LOOD-vik
***jati*** JAH-tee
**Jaufré Rudel** zhoh-FRAY roo-DEL
**Jaurès, Jean** zhaw-RESS, ZHAHNH
**Jena** YAY-nuh
**Jiang Qing** jahng-CHING
**Jiang Zemin** JAHNG zuh-MIN
**Jiangxi** JAHNG-shee
***jihad*** jee-HAHD
**Jinnah, Mohammed Ali** JIN-uh, moh-HAM-ed ah-LEE
**Joffre, Joseph** ZHUFF-ruh, zhoh-ZEFF
***Journal des Savants*** zhoor-NAHL day sah-VAHNH
**Juana Inés de la Cruz, Sor** HWAH-nuh ee-NAYSS day lah KROOZ, SAWR
**Judaea** joo-DEE-uh
**Judas Maccabaeus** JOO-dus mak-uh-BEE-uss
**Jung, Carl** YOONG
**Junkers** YOONG-kurz
**Jupiter Optimus Maximus** JOO-puh-tur AHP-tuh-muss MAK-suh-muss
**Jurchen** roor-ZHEN
**Justinian** juh-STIN-ee-un
**Juvenal** JOO-vuh-nul
**Ka'aba** KAH-buh
**Kádár, János** KAH-dahr, YAH-nush

**Kalidasa** kah-lee-DAH-suh
***kamikaze*** kah-mi-KAH-zee
**Kanagawa** kah-nah-GAH-wah
**Kanchipuram** kahn-CHEE-poo-rum
**Kandinsky, Wassily** kan-DIN-skee, vus-YEEL-yee
**Kang Youwei** KAHNG yow-WAY
**Kangxi** GANG-zhee
**Kanishka** kuh-NISH-kuh
**Kant, Immanuel** KAHNT, i-MAHN-yoo-el
**Karisma Kapoor** kuh-RIZ-muh kuh-POOR
**Karlowitz** KARL-oh-vits
**Karlsbad** KARLSS-baht
**Kaunitz, Wenzel von** KOW-nits, VENT-sul fun
**Kautilya** kow-TIL-yuh
**Kazakhstan** ka-zak-STAN *or* kuh-zahk-STAHN
**Kemal Atatürk, Mustafa** kuh-MAHL ah-tah-TIRK, moos-tah-FAH
**Kenyatta, Jomo** ken-YAHT-uh, JOH-moh
**Kerensky, Alexander** kuh-REN-skee
**Keynes, John Maynard** KAYNZ
**Khadija** kaha-DEE-jah
**Khajuraho** khah-joo-RAH-hoh
**Khanbaliq** khahn-bah-LEEK
**Khomeini, Ayatollah Ruholla** khoh-MAY-nee, ah-yah-TUL-uh roo-HUL-uh
**Khrushchev, Nikita** KHROOSH-chawf, nuh-KEE-tuh
**Khubilai Khan** KOO-bluh KAHN
**Kikuya** ki-KOO-yuh
**Kilwa** KIL-wuh
**Kim Dae Jung** kim day JOONG
**Kim Il Sung** kim il SOONG
**Kirghiz** keer-GEEZ
***Kleindeutsch*** KLYN-doich
**Knesset** kuh-NESS-it
**Koguryo** koh-GOOR-yoh
**Kohl, Helmut** KOHL, HEL-moot
***koiné*** koi-NAY
**Koizumi, Junichero** koh-ee-ZOO-mee, joo-nee-CHAY-roh
***kokutai*** koh-kuh-TY
**Kolchak, Alexander** kul-CHAHK
**Kollantai, Alexandra** kul-lun-TY
**Kongxi** koong-SHEE
**Königgrätz** kur-nig-GRETS
**Kornilov, Lavr** kor-NYEE-luff, LAH-vur
**Koryo** KAWR-yoh
**Kosciuszko, Thaddeus** kaw-SHOOS-koh, tah-DAY-oosh
**Kosovo** KAWSS-suh-voh
**Kossuth, Louis** KAWSS-uth *or* KAW-shoot
**Kostunica, Vojislav** kuh-STOO-nit-suh, VOH-yee-slav
**Kosygin, Alexei** kuh-SEE-gun, uh-LEK-say
***kouros*** KOO-rohss
**Koyaanisqatsi** koh-YAH-niss-kaht-see
***Kraft durch Freude*** KRAHFT doorkh FROI-duh
**Kreditanstalt** kray-deet-AHN-shtalt
**Krishna** KRISH-nuh
***Kristallnacht*** kri-STAHL-nahkht
**Krupp, Alfred** KROOP
**Kuchuk-Kainarji** koo-CHOOK-ky-NAR-jee
**Kukulcan** koo-kul-KAHN
**kulaks** KOO-lahks
***Kulturkampf*** kool-TOOR-kahmpf
**Kun, Béla** KOON, BAY-luh
**Kundera, Milan** koon-DAYR-uh, MEE-lahn
**Kursk** KOORSK
**Kushanas** koo-SHAH-nuz
**Kwasniewski, Aleksander** kwahsh-NYEF-skee
**Kyangyi** kyang-YEE
**Kyoto** KYOH-toh
**Kyushu** KYOO-shoo
**la belle époque** lah BEL ay-PUK
**Lafayette, marquis de** lah-fay-ET, mar-KEE duh
**laissez-faire** less-ay-FAYR
**Lamarck, Jean-Baptiste** lah-MARK, ZHAHNH-bah-TEEST
**Lancaster** LAN-kas-tur
**Lao Tzu** LOW-dzuh
**La Rochefoucauld-Liancourt, duc de** lah-RUSH-foo-koh-lee-ahnh-KOOR, dook duh
**Las Navas de Tolosa** lahss nah-vahss day toh-LOH-suh
***latifundia*** lat-i-FOON-dee-uh
**Latium** LAY-shum
**Latvia** LAT-vee-uh
**Launay, marquis de** loh-NAY, mar-KEE duh
**Laurier, Wilfred** LOR-ee-ay
**Lavoisier, Antoine** lah-vwah-ZYAY, an-TWAHN
**Lazar** lah-ZAR
**Le Tellier, François Michel** luh tel-YAY, frahnh-SWAH mee-SHEL
***Lebensraum*** LAY-benz-rowm
**Lee Kuan-yew** LEE-kwahn-YOO
***Les Demoiselles d'Avignon*** lay dem-wah-ZEL dah-vee-NYOHNH
**Lespinasse, Julie de** less-pee-NAHSS, zhoo-LEE duh
**Lévesque, René** lay-VEK, ruh-NAY
***Leviathan*** luh-VY-uh-thun
**Leyster, Judith** LESS-tur
**Liège** lee-EZH
**Li Su** lee SOO
**Li Yuan** lee YWAHN
**Li Zicheng** lee zee-CHENG
**Liaodong** LYOW-doong
**Licinius** ly-SIN-ee-uss
**Liebenfels, Lanz von** LEE-bun-felss, LAHNTS fun
**Liebknecht, Karl** LEEP-knekht
**Liebknecht, Wilhelm** LEEP-knekht, VIL-helm
**Liliuokalani** LIL-ee-uh-woh-kuh-LAH-nee
**Lin Zexu** LIN dzeh-SHOO
**Lindisfarne** LIN-dis-farn
**Lionne, Hugues de** LYUN, OOG duh
**List, Friedrich** LIST, FREED-rikh
**Liszt, Franz** LIST, FRAHNTS
**Lithuania** lith-WAY-nee-uh
**Liu Bang** lyoo BAHNG
**Liu Ling** lyoo LING
**Liu Shaoqi** lyoo show-CHEE
**Livy** LIV-ee
**Longshan** loong-SHAHN
**L'Ouverture, Toussaint** loo-vayr-TOOR, too-SANH
**Louvois** loo-VWAH
**Lu Xun** loo SHUN
**Lucretius** loo-KREE-shus
**Luddites** LUD-yts
**Ludendorff, Erich** LOO-dun-dorf
**Lueger, Karl** LOO-gur
***Luftwaffe*** LOOFT-vahf-uh
***l'uomo universale*** LWOH-moh OO-nee-vayr-SAH-lay
**Luoyang** LWOH-yahng
**Lützen** LURT-sun
**Luxemburg, Rosa** LOOK-sum-boork
**Lyons** LYOHNH
**Maastricht** MAHSS-trikht
***Ma'at*** MAH-ut
**Macao** muh-KOW

**Machiavelli, Niccolò** mahk-ee-uh-VEL-ee, nee-koh-LOH
**Maginot Line** MA-zhi-noh lyn
**Magna Graecia** MAG-nuh GREE-shuh
**Magyars** MAG-yarz
**Mahabharata** muh-hahb-huh-RAH-tuh
**maharaja** mah-huh-RAH-juh
**Mahavira** mah-hah-VEE-ruh
**Mahayana** mah-huh-YAH-nuh
**Mahfouz, Naguib** mahkh-FOOZ, nah-GEEB
**Mahmud of Ghazni** MAHKH-mood uv GAHZ-nee
**Maimonides** my-MAH-nuh-deez
**Maistre, Joseph de** MESS-truh, zhoh-ZEF duh
***maius imperium*** MY-yoos im-PEE-ree-um
**Malaysia** muh-LAY-zhuh
**Malaya** muh-LAY-uh
**Malenkov, Georgy** muh-LEN-kuf, gyee-OR-gyee
**Mallarmé, Stéphane** mah-lahr-MAY, stay-FAHN
***Malleus Maleficarum*** mal-EE-uss mal-uh-FIK-uh-rum
**Malthus, Thomas** MAWL-thuss
**Mamallapuram** muh-MAH-luh-poor-um
**Manchukuo** man-CHOO-kwoh
**Manetho** MAN-uh-thoh
**Mao Dun** mow DOON
**Mao Zedong** mow zee-DOONG
**Marconi, Guglielmo** mahr-KOH-nee, gool-YEL-moh
**Marcus Aurelius** MAR-kuss aw-REE-lee-uss
**Marcuse, Herbert** mar-KOO-zuh
**Marie Antoinette** muh-REE an-twuh-NET
**Marius** MAR-ee-uss
**Marquez, Gabriel Garcia** mar-KEZ
**Marseilles** mar-SAY
**Marsiglio of Padua** mar-SIL-yoh uv PAD-juh-wuh
**Masaccio** muh-ZAH-choh
**Masaryk, Thomas** MAS-uh-rik
**Mästlin, Michael** MEST-lin
**Matteotti, Giacomo** mat-tay-AHT-tee, JAHK-uh-moh
**Maxentius** mak-SEN-shuss
**Maximian** mak-SIM-ee-un
**Maya** MY-uh
**Mazarin** maz-uh-RANH
**Mazzini, Giuseppe** maht-SEE-nee, joo-ZEP-pay
**Megasthenes** muh-GAS-thuh-neez
**Mehmet** meh-MET
**Meiji** MAY-jee
***Mein Kampf*** myn KAHMPF
**Meir, Golda** may-EER
**Melanchthon, Philip** muh-LANK-tun
**Menander** muh-NAN-dur
**Mencius** MEN-shuss
**Mendeleyev, Dmitri** men-duh-LAY-ef, di-MEE-tree
**Mensheviks** MENS-shuh-viks
**Mercator, Gerardus** mur-KAY-tur, juh-RAHR-dus
**Merian, Maria Sibylla** MAY-ree-un
**Merovingian** meh-ruh-VIN-jee-un
**Mesopotamia** mess-uh-puh-TAY-mee-uh
**Messiaen, Olivier** meh-SYANH, oh-lee-VYAY
**mestizos** mess-TEE-zohz
**Metaxas, John** muh-tahk-SAHSS
**Metternich, Klemens von** MET-ayr-nikh, KLAY-menss fun
**Mexica** meh-SHEE-kuh
**Michel, Louise** mee-SHEL
**Michelangelo** my-kuh-LAN-juh-loh
**Mieszko** MYESH-koh
***millet*** mi-LET
**Millet, Jean-François** mi-YEH, ZHAHNH-frahnh-SWAH
**Milošević, Slobodan** mi-LOH-suh-vich, sluh-BOH-dahn
**Miltiades** mil-TY-uh-deez
**Minamoto Yoritomo** mee-nah-MOH-toh, yoh-ree-TOH-moh
**Minseito** MEEN-say-toh
**Mirandola, Pico della** mee-RAN-doh-lah, PEE-koh DELL-uh
**Mishima, Yukio** mi-SHEE-muh, yoo-KEE-oh
***missi dominici*** MISS-ee doh-MIN-i-chee
**Mitterrand, François** MEE-tayr-rahnh, frahnh-SWAH
**Moche** moh-CHAY
**Moctezuma** mahk-tuh-ZOO-muh
**Mogadishu** moh-guh-DEE-shoo
**Mohács** MOH-hach
**Mohenjo-Daro** mo-HEN-jo-DAH-roh
**Moldavia** mohl-DAY-vee-uh
**Moldova** mohl-DOH-vuh
**Molière, Jean-Baptiste** mohl-YAYR, ZHAHNH-bah-TEEST
**Molotov, Vyacheslav** MAHL-uh-tawf, vyich-chiss-SLAHF
**Mombasa** mahm-BAH-suh
**Monet, Claude** moh-NEH, KLOHD
**Mongkut** MAWNG-koot
**Montaigne, Michel de** mahn-TAYN, mee-SHEL duh
**Montefeltro, Federigo da** mahn-tuh-FELL-troh, fay-day-REE-goh dah
**Montesquieu** MOHN-tess-kyoo
**Montessori, Maria** mahn-tuh-SOR-ee
**Morisot, Berthe** mor-ee-ZOH, BAYRT
**Mozambique** moh-zam-BEEK
**Mozart, Wolfgang Amadeus** MOH-tsart, VULF-gahng ah-muh-DAY-uss
**Muawiya** moo-AH-wee-yah
**Mudejares** moo-theh-KHAH-rayss
**Mughal** MOO-gul
**Muhammad** moh-HAM-ud *or* moh-HAHM-ud
**Mühlberg** MURL-bayrk
**Mukden** MOOK-dun
**mulattoes** muh-LAH-tohz
**Mumbai** MUM-by
**Müntzer, Thomas** MURN-tsur
**Murad** moo-RAHD
**Musharraf, Pervaiz** moo-SHAHR-uf, pur-VEZ
**Muslim** MUZ-lum
**Mutsuhito** moo-tsoo-HEE-toh
**Myanmar** MYAN-mahr
**Mycenaean** my-suh-NEE-un
**Nabonidas** nab-uh-NY-duss
**Nabopolassar** nab-uh-puh-LASS-ur
**Nagasaki** nah-gah-SAH-kee
**Nagy, Imry** NAHJ, IM-ray
**Nanjing** nan-JING
**Nantes** NAHNT
**Nara** NAH-rah
**Nasrin, Taslima** naz-REEN, tah-SLEE-muh
**Nasser, Gamal Abdul** NAH-sur, juh-MAHL ahb-DOOL
**Navarre** nuh-VAHR
**Nebuchadnezzar** neb-uh-kud-NEZZ-ur
**Nehru, Jawaharlal** NAY-roo, juh-WAH-hur-lahl
**Nero** NEE-roh
**Nerva** NUR-vuh
**Netanyahu, Benjamin** net-ahn-YAH-hoo
**Neumann, Balthasar** NOI-mahn, BAHL-tuh-zahr
**Neumann, Solomon** NOI-mahn
**Neustria** NOO-stree-uh
**Nevsky, Alexander** NYEF-skee
**Newcomen, Thomas** NYOO-kuh-mun *or* nyoo-KUM-mun
**Ngo Dinh Diem** GOH din DYEM
**Nguyen** NGWEN
**Nicias** NISS-ee-uss

**Nietzsche, Friedrich** NEE-chuh, FREED-rikh
**Nimwegen** NIM-vay-gun
**Ninhursaga** nin-HUR-sah-guh
**Nkrumah, Kwame** en-KROO-muh, KWAH-may
***nobiles*** no-BEE-layz
**Nobunaga, Oda** noh-buh-NAH-guh, OH-dah
**Nogarola, Isotta** noh-guh-ROH-luh, ee-ZAHT-uh
**Novalis, Friedrich** noh-VAH-lis, FREED-rikh
**Novotny, Antonin** noh-VAHT-nee, AHN-toh-nyeen
***novus homo*** NOH-vuss HOH-moh
***nuoc mam*** NWAHK MAHM
**Nyame** NYAH-may
**Nystadt** NEE-shtaht
**Oaxaca** wah-HAH-kuh
**Octavian** ahk-TAY-vee-un
**Odoacer** oh-doh-AY-sur
**Odysseus** oh-DISS-ee-uss
**Oe, Kenzaburo** OH-ay, ken-zuh-BOO-roh
**Olivares** oh-lee-BAH-rayss
**Olmec** AHL-mek *or* OHL-mek
**Omar Khayyam** OH-mar ky-YAHM
**Ometeotl** oh-met-tee-AH-tul
***optimates*** ahp-tuh-MAH-tayz
***Oresteia*** uh-res-TY-uh
**Orkhan** or-KHAHN
**Osaka** oh-SAH-kuh
**Osama bin Laden** oh-SAH-muh bin LAH-dun
**Osiris** oh-SY-russ
**Ostara** oh-STAH-ruh
***Ostpolitik*** OHST-poh-lee-teek
***ostrakon*** AHSS-truh-kahn
**Ostrogoths** AHSS-truh-gahthss
**Ovid** OH-vid
**Oxenstierna, Axel** OOK-sen-shur-nah, AHK-sul
**Pacal** pa-KAL
**Pachakuti** pah-chah-KOO-tee
**Paekche** bayk-JEE
**Pagan** puh-GAHN
**Paleologus** pay-lee-AWL-uh-guss
**Panaetius** puh-NEE-shuss
**Pankhurst, Emmeline** PANK-hurst
**papal curia** PAY-pul KYOOR-ee-uh
**Papen, Franz von** PAH-pun, FRAHNTS fun
**Paracelsus** par-uh-SELL-suss
***Parlement*** par-luh-MAHNH
**Parti Québécois** par-TEE kay-bek-KWAH
**Pascal, Blaise** pass-KAHL, BLEZ
**Pasternak, Boris** PASS-tur-nak, buh-REESS
**Pasteur, Louis** pass-TOOR, LWEE
**Pataliputra** pah-tah-lee-POO-truh
***paterfamilias*** pay-tur-fuh-MEEL-yus
***Pensées*** pahnh-SAY
**Pentateuch** PEN-tuh-took
**Pepin** PEP-in *or* pay-PANH
***perestroika*** per-uh-STROI-kuh
**Pergamum** PUR-guh-mum
**Pericles** PER-i-kleez
***perioeci*** per-ee-EE-see
**Perpetua** pur-PET-choo-uh
**Pétain, Henri** pay-TANH, AHN-ree
**Petite Roquette** puh-TEET raw-KET
**Petrarch** PEE-trark *or* PET-trark
**Petronius** pi-TROH-nee-uss
**phalansteries** fuh-LAN-stuh-reez
**philosophe** fee-loh-ZAWF
**Phintys** FIN-tiss
**Phoenicians** fuh-NEE-shunz
**Photius** FOH-shuss
**Picasso, Pablo** pi-KAH-soh
**Pietism** PY-uh-tiz-um
**Pilsudski, Joseph** peel-SOOT-skee
**Piscator, Erwin** PIS-kuh-tor, AYR-vin
**Pisistratus** puh-SIS-truh-tuss
**Pissarro, Camille** pee-SAH-roh, kah-MEEL
**Pizan, Christine de** pee-ZAHN, kris-TEEN duh
**Pizarro, Francesco** puh-ZAHR-oh, frahn-CHESS-koh
**Planck, Max** PLAHNK
**Plantagenet** plan-TAJ-uh-net
**Plassey** PLASS-ee
**Plato** PLAY-toh
**Plautus** PLAW-tuss
***plebiscita*** pleb-i-SEE-tuh
**Poincaré, Raymond** pwanh-kah-RAY, ray-MOHNH
***polis*** POH-liss
**politiques** puh-lee-TEEKS
**Pollaiuolo, Antonio** pohl-ly-WOH-loh
**Poltava** pul-TAH-vuh
**Polybius** puh-LIB-ee-uss
**Pombal, marquis de** pum-BAHL, mar-KEE duh
**Pompadour, madame de** POM-puh-door, mah-DAHM duh
**Pompeii** pahm-PAY
**Pompey** PAHM-pee
***pontifex maximus*** PAHN-ti-feks MAK-si-muss
**Popul Vuh** puh-PUL VOO
***populares*** PAWP-oo-lahr-ayss
***populo grasso*** PAWP-oo-loh GRAH-soh
**Postumus** PAHS-choo-muss
**Potosí** poh-toh-SEE
**Potsdam** PAHTS-dam
**Poussin, Nicholas** poo-SANH, NEE-koh-lah
***Praecepter Germaniae*** PREE-sep-tur gayr-MAHN-ee-ee
**praetor** PREE-tur
**Prakrit** PRAH-krit
***Pravda*** PRAHV-duh
**Primo de Rivera** PREE-moh day ri-VAY-ruh
**primogeniture** pree-moh-JEN-i-chur
**princeps** PRIN-seps
***Principia*** prin-SIP-ee-uh
**Procopius** pruh-KOH-pee-uss
**procurator** PROK-yuh-ray-tur
**Ptolemaic** tahl-uh-MAY-ik
**Ptolemy** TAHL-uh-mee
**Pugachev, Emelyan** poo-guh-CHAWF, yim-yil-YAHN
**Punic** PYOO-nik
**Putin, Vladimir** POO-tin
**Pyongyang** pyawng-YANG
**Pyrrhic** PEER-ik
**Pyrrhus** PEER-uss
**Pythagoras** puh-THAG-uh-russ
**Qajar** kuh-JAHR
**Qianlong** CHAN-loong
**Qin** CHIN
**Qin Shi Huangdi** chin shee hwang-DEE
**Qing** CHING
**Qiu Jin** chee-oo-JIN
**Qu** CHOO
***quadrivium*** kwah-DRIV-ee-um
***quaestors*** KWES-turs
***querelle des femmes*** keh-REL day FAHM
**Quesnay, François** keh-NAY, frahnn-SWAH
**Quetzelcoatl** KWET-sul-koh-AHT-ul
**Quraishi** koo-RY-shee

**Qur'an** kuh-RAN *or* kuh-RAHN
**Rabe'a of Qozdar** rah-BAY-uh uv kuz-DAHR
**Racine, Jean-Baptiste** ra-SEEN, ZHAHNH-buh-TEEST
**Rahner, Karl** RAH-nur
**Rajput** RAHJ-poot
**Rama** RAH-mah
**Ramayana** rah-mah-YAH-nah
**Ramcaritmanas** RAM-kah-rit-MAH-nuz
**Rameses** RAM-uh-seez
**Raphael** RAFF-ee-ul
**Rasputin** rass-PYOO-tin
**Rathenau, Walter** RAH-tuh-now, VAHL-tuh
***Realpolitik*** ray-AHL-poh-lee-teek
***Realschule*** ray-AHL-shoo-luh
**Reichsrat** RYKHSS-raht
**Reichstag** RYKHSS-tahk
**Rembrandt van Rijn** REM-brant vahn RYN
**Rémy, Nicholas** ray-MEE, nee-koh-LAH
**Renan, Ernst** re-NAHNH
**Rhee, Syngman** REE, SING-mun
**Ricci, Matteo** REE-chee, ma-TAY-oh
**Richelieu** REESH-uh-lyuh
**Ricimer** RISS-uh-mur
**Rig Veda** RIK-vee-duh
**Rikstag** RIKS-tahk
**Rilke, Rainer Maria** RILL-kuh, RY-nuh mah-REE-uh
**Rimbaud, Arthur** ram-BOH, ar-TOOR
***risorgimento*** ree-SOR-jee-men-toh
**Riza-i-Abassi** ree-ZAH-yah-BAH-see
**Robespierre, Maximilien** ROHBZ-pyayr, mak-see-meel-YENH
**Rococo** ruh-KOH-koh
**Rocroi** roh-KRWAH
**Röhm, Ernst** RURM
**Rommel, Erwin** RAHM-ul
**Romulus Augustulus** RAHM-yuh-luss ow-GOOS-chuh-luss
**Rossbach** RAWSS-bahkh
**Rousseau, Jean-Jacques** roo-SOH, ZHAHNH-ZHAHK
**Rurik** ROO-rik
**Ryswick** RYZ-wik
**Sacrosancta** sak-roh-SANK-tuh
**Saikaku** sy-KAH-koo
**Saint-Just** sanh-ZHOOST
**Saint-Simon, Henri de** sanh-see-MOHNH, ahnh-REE duh
**Sakharov, Andrei** SAH-kuh-rawf, ahn-DRAY
**Saladin** SAL-uh-din
**Salazar, Antonio** SAL-uh-zahr
**Sallust** SAL-ust
**Samnite** SAM-nyt
**Samudragupta** suh-mood-ruh-GOOP-tuh
**samurai** SAM-uh-ry
**San Martín, José de** san mar-TEEN, hoh-SAY day
**Sandinista** san-duh-NEES-tuh
***sans-culottes*** sahnh-koo-LUT *or* sanz-koo-LAHTSS
**Sarraut, Albert** sah-ROH, ahl-BAYR
**Sartre, Jean-Paul** SAR-truh, ZHAHNH-POHL
**Sassanid** suh-SAN-id
***sati*** suh-TEE
**satrap** SAY-trap
**satrapy** SAY-truh-pee
***Satyricon*** sa-TEER-uh-kahn
**Schaumburg-Lippe** SHOWM-boorkh-LEE-puh
**Schleswig-Holstein** SHLESS-vik-HOHL-shtyn
**Schlieffen, Alfred von** SHLEE-fun, AHL-fret fun
**Schliemann, Heinrich** SHLEE-mahn, HYN-rikh
**Schmidt, Helmut** SHMIT, HEL-moot
**Schönberg, Arnold** SHURN-bayrk, AR-nawlt
**Schönborn** SHURN-bawn
**Schönerer, Georg von** SHURN-uh-ruh, GAY-ork fun
**Schröder, Gerhard** SHRUR-duh, GAYR-hahrt
**Schuschnigg, Karl von** SHOOSH-nik, KAHRL fun
**Schutzmannschaft** SHOOTS-mahn-shahft
**Scipio Aemilianus** SEE-pee-oh ee-mil-YAY-nuss
**Scipio Africanus** SEE-pee-oh af-ree-KAY-nuss
**scriptoria** skrip-TOR-ee-uh
**Ségur** say-GOO-uh
**Sejm** SAYM
**Seleucid** suh-LOO-sid
**Seleucus** suh-LOO-kuss
**Seljuk** SEL-jook
**Seneca** SEN-uh-kuh
**Sephardic** suh-FAHR-dik
**Septimius Severus** sep-TIM-ee-uss se-VEER-uss
***serjents*** sayr-ZHAHNH
**Sforza, Ludovico** SFORT-sah, loo-doh-VEE-koh
**Shakuntala** shah-koon-TAH-lah
**Shalmaneser** shal-muh-NEE-zur
**Shandong** SHAHN-doong
**Shang** SHAHNG
***Shari'a*** shah-REE-uh
**Shen Nong** shun-NOONG
**Shi'ite** SHEE-YT
**Shidehara** shee-de-HAH-rah
**Shiga Naoya** SHEE-gah NOW-yah
**Shikoku** shee-KOH-koo
**Shimonoseki** shee-moh-noh-SEK-ee
**Shiva** SHIV-uh
**Shotoku Taishi** shoh-TOH-koo ty-EE-shee
**Sichuan** SEECH-wahn
**Siddhartha Gautama** si-DAR-tuh GAW-tuh-muh
**Sieveking, Amalie** SEE-vuh-king, uh-MAHL-yuh
**Sieyès, Abbé** syay-YESS, ab-BAY
**Sigiriya** see-gee-REE-uh
***signoria*** seen-YOR-ee-uh
**Silla** SIL-uh
**Silva, Luis Inácio Lula de** LWEES ee-NAH-syoh LOO-luh duh-SEEL-vuh
**Sima Qian** SEE-mah chee-AHN
***sine manu*** sy-nee-MAY-noo
***sipahis*** suh-PAH-heez
**Sita** SEE-tuh
**Slovenia** sloh-VEE-nee-uh
**Société Générale** soh-see-ay-TAY zhay-nay-RAHL
**Socrates** SAHK-ruh-teez
**Solon** SOH-lun
**Solzhenitsyn, Alexander** sohl-zhuh-NEET-sin
**Somme** SUM
**Song Taizu** SOONG ty-DZOO
**Soong, Mei-ling** SOONG, may-LING
**Sophocles** SAHF-uh-kleez
**Sorel, Georges** soh-RELL, ZHORZH
**Spartacus** SPAR-tuh-kuss
***Spartiates*** spar-tee-AH-teez
**Speer, Albert** SHPAYR
**Speransky, Michael** spyuh-RAHN-skee
**Spinoza, Benedict de** spi-NOH-zuh
***squadristi*** skwah-DREES-tee
**Srebrenica** sreb-bruh-NEET-suh
**stadholder** STAD-hohl-dur
**Staël, Germaine de** STAHL, zhayr-MEN duh
**Stakhanov, Alexei** stuh-KHAH-nuf, uh-LEK-say
**Stasi** SHTAH-see

**Stauffenberg, Claus von** SHTOW-fen-berk, KLOWSS fun
**Stein, Heinrich von** SHTYN, HYN-rikh fun
**Stilicho** STIL-i-koh
**Stoicism** STOH-i-siz-um
**Stolypin, Peter** stuh-LIP-yin
***strategoi*** strah-tay-GOH-ee
**Stravinsky, Igor** struh-VIN-skee, EE-gor
**Stresemann, Gustav** SHTRAY-zuh-mahn, GOOS-tahf
**Strozzi, Alessandra** STRAWT-see
**Struensee, John Frederick** SHTROO-un-zay
**Sturmabteilung** SHTOORM-ap-ty-loonk
**Sudetenland** soo-DAY-tun-land
***sudra*** SOO-druh *or* SHOO-druh
**Suger** soo-ZHAYR
**Suharto** soo-HAHR-toh
**Sui Wendi** SWEE wen-DEE
**Sui Yangdi** SWEE yahng-DEE
**Sukarno** soo-KAHR-noh
**Sukarnoputri, Megawati** soo-kahr-noh-POO-tree, meg-uh-WAH-tee
**Suleiman** SOO-lay-mahn
**Suleymaniye** soo-lay-MAHN-ee-eh
**Sulla** SUL-uh
**Sumerians** soo-MER-ee-unz *or* soo-MEER-ee-unz
***Summa Theologica*** SOO-muh tay-oh-LAH-jee-kuh
**Sun Yat-sen** SOON yaht-SEN
**Suppiluliumas** suh-PIL-oo-LEE-uh-muss
**Suttner, Bertha von** ZOOT-nuh, BAYR-tuh fun
**Swaziland** SWAH-zee-land
***Symphonie Fantastique*** SANH-foh-nee fahn-tas-TEEK
**Taaffe, Edward von** TAH-fuh, ED-vahrt fun
**Taban lo Liyong** tuh-BAN loh-lee-YAWNG
**Tacitus** TASS-i-tuss
**Tahuantinsuyu** tuh-HWAHN-tin-SOO-yoo
**Taika** TY-kuh
***taille*** TY
**Taiping** ty-PING
**Talleyrand, Prince** tah-lay-RAHNH
**Tanganyika** tang-an-YEE-kuh
**Tanizaki, Junichiro** tan-i-ZAH-kee, jun-i-CHEE-roh
**Tanzania** tan-zuh-NEE-uh
**Temuchin** TEM-yuh-jin
**Tenochtitlán** tay-nawch-teet-LAHN
**Teotihuacán** tay-noh-tee-hwa-KAHN
**Tertullian** tur-TUL-yun
**Texcoco** tess-KOH-koh
**Thales** THAY-leez
**Theocritus** thee-AHK-ruh-tuss
**Theodora** thee-uh-DOR-uh
**Theodoric** thee-AHD-uh-rik
**Theodosius** thee-uh-DOH-shuss
**Theognis** thee-AHG-nuss
**Theravada** thay-ruh-VAH-duh
**Thermopylae** thur-MAHP-uh-lee
**Thiers, Adolphe** TYAYR, a-DAWLF
**Thucydides** thoo-SID-uh-deez
**Thutmosis** thoot-MOH-suss
**Tiananmen** TYAHN-ahn-men
**Tianjin** TYAHN-jin
**Tiberius** ty-BEER-ee-uss
**Tiglath-pileser** TIG-lath-py-LEE-zur
**Tikal** tee-KAHL
**Tirpitz, Admiral von** TEER-pits
**Tisza, István** TISS-ah, ISHT-vun
**Tito** TEE-toh
**Titus** TY-tuss
**Tlaloc** tuh-lah-LOHK
**Tlaltelolco** tuh-lahl-teh-LOH-koh
**Tlaxcala** tuh-lah-SKAH-lah
**Toer, Pramoedya** TOOR, pra-MOO-dyah
**Tojo, Hideki** TOH-joh, hee-DEK-ee
**Tokugawa Ieyasu** toh-koo-GAH-wah ee-yeh-YAH-soo
**Tolstoy, Leo** TOHL-stoy
**Tongmenghui** toong-meng-HWEE
**Topa Inca** TOH-puh INK-uh
**Topkapi** tawp-KAH-pee
**Torah** TOR-uh
**Tordesillas** tor-day-SEE-yass
**Touré, Sékou** too-RAY, say-KOO
**Trajan** TRAY-jun
**Trevithick, Richard** TREV-uh-thik
**Tristan, Flora** TRISS-tun
**trivium** TRIV-ee-um
**Trotsky, Leon** TRAHT-skee
**Troyes** TRWAH
**Trudeau, Pierre** troo-DOH, PYAYR
**Trufaut, François** troo-FOH, frahnh-SWAH
**Tsara, Tristan** TSAHR-rah, TRISS-tun
**Tübingen** TUR-bing-un
**Tughluq** tug-LUK
**Tulsidas** tool-see-DAHSS
**Tutankhamun** too-tang-KAH-mun
**Tyche** TY-kee
**Uccello, Paolo** oo-CHEL-oh, POW-loh
***uhuru*** oo-HOO-roo
***uji*** OO-jee
**Ulbricht, Walter** OOL-brikht, VAHL-tuh
**Ulianov, Vladimir** ool-YA-nuf
**Umayyads** oo-MY-adz
***Unam Sanctam*** OO-nahm **SAHNK-tahm**
***universitas*** yoo-nee-VAYR-see-tahss
**Utamaro** OO-tah-mah-roh
**Uzbekistan** ooz-BEK-i-stan
***vaisya*** VISH-yuh
**Vajpayee, Atal Behari** VAHJ-py-ee, AH-tahl bi-HAH-ree
**Valens** VAY-linz
**Valentinian** val-en-TIN-ee-un
**Valéry, Paul** vah-lay-REE, POHL
**Valois** val-WAH
**Van de Velde, Theodore** vahn duh VEL-duh, TAY-oh-dor
**van Eyck, Jan** vahn YK *or* van AYK, YAHN
**van Gogh, Vincent** van GOH
**Vasa, Gustavus** VAH-suh, GUSS-tuh-vuss
**Vega, Lope de** VAY-guh, LOH-pay day
**Velde, Theodor van de** VEL-duh, tay-oh-DOR vahn duh
**Vendée** vahnh-DAY
**Venetia** vuh-NEE-shuh
**Verdun** vur-DUN
**Vergerio, Pietro Paolo** vur-JEER-ee-oh, PYAY-troh POW-loh
**Versailles** vayr-SY
**Vesalius, Andreas** vuh-SAY-lee-uss, ahn-DRAY-uss
**Vespasian** vess-PAY-zhun
**Vespucci, Amerigo** vess-POO-chee, ahm-ay-REE-goh
**Vesuvius** vuh-SOO-vee-uss
**Vichy** VISH-ee
**Vierzehnheiligen** feer-tsayn-HY-li-gen
**Virchow, Rudolf** FEER-khoh, ROO-dulf
**Virgil** VUR-jul
**Visconti, Giangaleazzo** vees-KOHN-tee, jahn-gah-lay-AH-tsoh
**Vishnu** VISH-noo
**Visigoths** VIZ-uh-gathz

**Voilquin, Suzanne** vwahl-KANH, soo-ZAHN
***Volk*** FULK
***Volkschulen*** FULK-shoo-lun
**Voltaire** vohl-TAYR
**Wafd** WAHFT
**Wagner, Richard** VAG-nur, RIKH-art
**Walesa, Lech** vah-WENT-sah, LEK
**Wallachia** wah-LAY-kee-uh
**Wallenstein, Albrecht von** VAHL-en-shtyn, AWL-brekht
**Wang Anshi** WAHNG ahn-SHEE
**Wang Shuo** wahng-SHWOH
**Wang Tao** wahng-TOW
**Wannsee** VAHN-zay
**Watteau, Antoine** wah-TOH, AHN-twahn
**Weill, Kurt** VYL
**Weizsäcker, Richard von** VYTS-zek-ur, RIKH-art
***wergeld*** WUR-geld
**Windischgrätz, Alfred** VIN-dish-grets
**Winkelmann, Maria** VINK-ul-mahn
**Witte, Sergei** VIT-uh, syir-GYAY
**Wittenberg** VIT-ten-bayrk
**Wojtyla, Karol** voy-TEE-wah, KAH-rul
**Wollstonecraft, Mary** WULL-stun-kraft
**Wu Zhao** woo-ZHOW
**Würzburg** VURTS-boork
**Wyclif, John** WIK-lif
**Xavier, Francis** ZAY-vee-ur
**Xerxes** ZURK-seez
**Xhosa** KHOH-suh
**Xia** SHEE-ah
**Xian** SHEE-ahn
**Xiangyang** SHYAHNG-yahng
**Ximenes** khee-MAY-ness
**Xinjiang** SHIN-jyahng
**Xiongnu** SHYAHNG-noo
**Xui Tong** shwee-TOONG
**Yahweh** YAH-way
**Yan'an** yuh-NAHN
**Yang Guifei** yahng gwee-FAY
**Yangshao** yahng-SHOW
**Yangtze** YANG-tsee
**Yayoi** yah-YO-ee
**Yeats, William Butler** YAYTS
**Yeltsin, Boris** YELT-sun
**Yi Jing** yee-JING
**Yi Song-gye** YEE song-YEE
**yishuv** YISH-uv
**Yuan Shikai** yoo-AHN shee-KY
**Yudhoyono, Susilo** yood-hoh-YOH-noh, soo-SEE-loh
**Yue** yoo-EH
***zaibatsu*** zy-BAHT-soo *or Japanese* DZY-bahtss
**Zanj** ZANJ
**Zanzibar** ZAN-zi-bar
**Zasulich, Vera** tsah-SOO-likh
**Zemsky Sobor** ZEM-skee suh-BOR
**zemstvos** ZEMPST-vohz
**Zeno** ZEE-noh
**Zenobia** zuh-NOH-bee-uh
**zeppelin** ZEP-puh-lin
**Zeus** ZOOSS
**Zhang Zhidong** JANG jee-DOONG
**Zhao Ziyang** JOW dzee-YAHNG
**Zhenotdel** zhen-ut-DEL
**Zhivkov, Todor** ZHIV-kuff, toh-DOR
**Zia ul-Haq, Mohammad** ZEE-uh ool-HAHK
**ziggurat** ZIG-uh-rat
**Zimmermann, Dominikus** TSIM-ur-mahn, doh-MEE-nee-kooss
**Zinzendorf, Nikolaus von** TSIN-sin-dorf, NEE-koh-LOWSS fun
**Zola, Émile** ZOH-lah, ay-MEEL
***zollverein*** TSOHL-fuh-ryn
**Zoroaster** ZOR-oh-ass-tur
**Zuanzong** zwahn-ZOONG
**Zuni** ZOO-nee
**Zwingli, Ulrich** TSFING-lee, OOL-rikh

# Map Credits

The authors wish to acknowledge their use of the following books as reference in preparing the maps listed here:

**SPOT MAP, PAGE 39** Geoffrey Barraclough, ed., *Times Atlas of World History*, (Maplewood, N.J.: Hammond Inc., 1978), p. 65.

**MAP 3.1** Geoffrey Barraclough, ed., *Times Atlas of World History*, (Maplewood, N.J.: Hammond Inc., 1978), p. 63.

**MAP 3.2** Hammond Past Worlds: *The Times Atlas of Archeology*, (Maplewood, N.J.: Hammond Inc. 1988), pp. 190–191.

**MAP 3.3** Conrad Schirokauer, *A Brief History of Chinese and Japanese Civilizations*, 2d ed. (San Diego: Harcourt Brace Jovanovich, 1989), p. 52.

**MAP 6.2** Michael Coe, Dean Snow and Elizabeth Benson, *Atlas of Ancient America* (New York: Facts on File, 1988), p. 144.

**MAP 6.3** Geoffrey Barraclough, ed., *Times Atlas of World History*, (Maplewood, N.J.: Hammond Inc., 1978), p. 47.

**MAP 6.4** Phillipa Fernandez-Arnesto, *Atlas of World Exploration*, (New York: Harper Collins, 1991), p. 35.

**MAP 6.5** Geoffrey Barraclough, ed., *Times Atlas of World History*, (Maplewood, N.J.: Hammond Inc., 1978), p. 47.

**MAP 7.3** Geoffrey Barraclough, ed., *Times Atlas of World History*, (Maplewood, N.J.: Hammond Inc., 1978), pp. 134–135.

**MAP 7.4** Geoffrey Barraclough, ed., *Times Atlas of World History*, (Maplewood, N.J.: Hammond Inc., 1978), p. 135.

**MAP 8.1** Geoffrey Barraclough, ed., *Times Atlas of World History*, (Maplewood, N.J.: Hammond Inc., 1978), pp. 44–45.

**MAP 8.4** Geoffrey Barraclough, ed., *Times Atlas of World History*, (Maplewood, N.J.: Hammond Inc., 1978), pp. 136–137.

**MAP 9.2** Michael Edwardes, *A History of India* (London: Thames and Hudson, 1961), p. 79.

**MAP 10.1** John K. Fairbank, Edwin O. Reischauer, and Albert M. Craig, *East Asia: Tradition and Transformation* (Boston: Houghton Mifflin, 1973), p. 103.

**SPOT MAP, PAGE 272** Albert Hermann, *An Historical Atlas of China* (Chicago: Aidine, 1966), p. 13.

**MAP 11.1** John K. Fairbank, Edwin O. Reischauer, and Albert M. Craig, *East Asia: Tradition and Transformation* (Boston: Houghton Mifflin, 1973), p. 363.

**MAP 13.1** Geoffrey Barraclough, ed., *Times Atlas of World History*, (Maplewood, N. J.:Hammond, Inc. 1978), p. 160.

**MAP 15.3** Geoffrey Barraclough, ed., *Times Atlas of World History*, (Maplewood, N. J.: Hammond, Inc. 1978), p. 173.

**MAP 16.1** Jonathan Spence, *The Search for Modern China*, (New York: W. W. Norton, 1990), p. 19.

**MAP 16.2** Conrad Schirokauer, *A Brief History of Chinese and Japanese Civilizations*, 2d ed., (San Diego: Harcourt Brace Jovanovich, 1989), p. 330.

**MAP 16.3** John K. Fairbank, Edwin O. Reischauer, and Albert M. Craig, *East Asia: Tradition and Tranformation*, (Boston: Houghton Mifflin, 1973), pp. 402–403.

**MAP 17.1** *Atlas of World History*, (New York: Harper & Row Publishers, 1987), p. 187.

**MAP 20.4** Geoffrey Barraclough, ed., *Times Atlas of World History*, (Maplewood, N. J.: Hammond, Inc. 1978), p. 235.

**MAP 21.2** John K. Fairbank, Edwin O. Reischauer, and Albert M. Craig, *East Asia: Tradition and Transformation*, (Boston: Houghton Mifflin, 1973), p. 451.

**MAP 21.4** Geoffrey Barraclough, ed., *Times Atlas of World History*, (Maplewood, N. J.: Hammond, Inc. 1978), p. 243.

# Documents

*Continued from page xx*

## Chapter 6



## Chapter 7



## Chapter 8



## Chapter 9

## CHAPTER 10



## CHAPTER 11



## CHAPTER 12

THE SIEGE OF JERUSALEM: CHRISTIAN AND MUSLIM PERSPECTIVES 344

*Chronicle of the First Crusade* by Foucher de Chartres. AMS Press, 1978.

A MEDIEVAL HOLOCAUST: THE CREMATION OF THE STRASBOURG JEWS 348

Excerpt from *The Jew in the Medieval World*, by Jacob Marcus. Copyright © 1972 by Atheneum. Reprinted with permission of the Hebrew Union College Press.

BONIFACE VIII'S DEFENSE OF PAPAL SUPREMACY 350

Excerpt taken from *Select Historical Documents of the Middle Ages*, by Ernest F. Henderson. Copyright © 1892 by George Bell & Sons.

## CHAPTER 13

THE PORTUGUESE CONQUEST OF MALACCA 368

From *The World of Southeast Asia: Selected Historical Readings* by Harry J. Benda and John J. Larkin, eds. Copyright © 1967 by Harper & Row, Publishers.

LAS CASAS AND THE SPANISH TREATMENT OF THE AMERICAN NATIVES 371

From *The Tears of the Indians*, Bartolome de Las Casas. Copyright © 1970 by The John Lilburne Company Publishers.

AN AZTEC'S LAMENT 372

From *The Tears of the Indians*, Bartolome de Las Casas. Copyright © 1970 by The John Lilburne Company Publishers.

KING OF SONGHAI 379

From *The Epic of Askia Mohammed*, by Thomas Hale, Indiana University Press, 1996, pp. 22–26.

A SLAVE MARKET IN AFRICA 382

From *The Great Travelers, vol. I*, Milton Rugoff, ed. Copyright © 1960 by Simon & Schuster. Used with permission of Milton Rugoff.

AN EXCHANGE OF ROYAL CORRESPONDENCE 386

From *The World of Southeast Asia: Selected Historical Readings* by Harry J. Benda and John A. Larkin, eds. Copyright © 1967 by Harper & Row, Publishers.

THE TIMELY END OF SULTAN ZAINAL-'ABIDIN 387

From *The World of Southeast Asia: Selected Historical Readings*, Harry J. Benda and John A. Larkin, eds. Copyright © 1967 by Harper & Row, Publishers.

THE MARCH OF CIVILIZATION 388

From *The Age of Reconnaissance* by J.H. Parry (International Thomson Publishing, 1969), pp. 233–234. "Journal of Captain James Cook" from *The Fatal Impact: An Account of the Invasion of the South Pacific: 1767–1840*, ed. by Alan Moorhead (New York: Penguin, 1966), p. 70.

## CHAPTER 14

LUTHER AND THE NINETY-FIVE THESES 396

Copyright © 1970 by E. G. Rupp and Benjamin Drewery. From *Martin Luther*, by E. G. Rupp and Benjamin Drewery. Reprinted with permission of Palgrave Macmillan.

A PROTESTANT WOMAN 399

Excerpt from *Not In God's Image: Women in History From the Greeks to the Victorians* by Julia O'Faolain and Lauro Martines. Copyright © 1973 by Julia O'Faolain and Lauro Martines. Reprinted by permission of the authors.

A WITCHCRAFT TRIAL IN FRANCE 405

From *Witchcraft in Europe, 1100–1700: A Documentary History* by Alan Kors and Edward Peters (Philadelphia: University of Pennsylvania Press, 1972), pp. 266–275. Used with permission of the publisher.

THE FACE OF WAR IN THE 17TH CENTURY 408

Excerpt from *The Adventure of Simplicius Simplissimus* by Hans Jacob Chistoffel von Grimmelshausen, translated by George Schulz-Behren, © 1993 Camden House/Boydell & Brewer, Rochester, New York.

PETER THE GREAT DEALS WITH A REBELLION 411

From James Harvey Robinson, *Readings in European History* (Lexington, Mass.: Ginn & Co.), 1934. Reprinted with permission of Silver, Burdett & Ginn, Inc.

THE BILL OF RIGHTS 414

From *The Statutes: Revised Edition* (London: Eyre & Spotiswoode, 1871), Vol. 2, pp. 10–12.

WILLIAM SHAKESPEARE: IN PRAISE OF ENGLAND 416

Excerpt from "Richard II" in *Shakespeare: The Complete Works* by G. B. Harrison, copyright © 1968 by Harcourt Brace & Company and renewed 1980 by G. B. Harrison, reprinted by permission of the publisher.

## CHAPTER 15

THE FALL OF CONSTANTINOPLE 421

From William H. McNeill and M. R. Waldham, *The Islamic World*, copyright © 1973 by The University of Chicago Press. Used with permission.

A PORTRAIT OF SULEYMAN THE MAGNIFICENT 424

From William H. McNeill and M. R. Waldham, *The Islamic World*, copyright © 1973 by The University of Chicago Press. Used with permission.

A TURKISH DISCOURSE ON COFFEE 430

From *The Balance of Truth* by Katib Chelebi, translated by G. L. Lewis, copyright 1927.

THE RELIGIOUS ZEAL OF SHAH ABBAS THE GREAT 432

From Eskander Beg Monshi in *History of Shah Abbas The Great, Vol. II* by Roger M. Savory by Westview Press, 1978.

THE MUGHAL CONQUEST OF NORTHERN INDIA 434

From *The Memoirs of Zehir-ed-din Muhammed Baber*, translated by John Leyden and William Erskine (London: Longman and Cadell, 1826).

A RELIGION FIT FOR A KING 436

From Abu'l Fazl, A'in-i-Akbare, pp. ii–iv, as cited in *Sources of Indian Tradition*, ed. by Ainslee Embree (New York: Columbia UP, 1988), pp. 425–427.

THE POWER BEHIND THE THRONE 438

From *Nur Jahan: Empress of Mughal India* by Ellison Banks Findly. Oxford University Print on Demand, 1993.

THE CAPTURE OF PORT HOOGLY 439

From *King of the World: a Mughal manuscript from the Royal Library, Windsor Castle*, trans. by Wheeler Thackston, text by Milo Cleveland Beach and Ebba Koch (London: Thames and Hudson, 1997), p. 59.

**THE HOUSING VENTURE OF OCTAVIA HILL 548**
Extract taken from *Human Documents of the Victorian Age* by E. Royston Pike. Copyright © 1967 by Frederick A. Praeger.

**ADVICE TO WOMEN: BE INDEPENDENT 552**
From Henrik Ibsen, *A Doll's House*, Act III, 1879, as printed in *Roots of Western Civilization* by Wesley D. Camp, John Wiley & Sons, 1983.

**ZAPATA AND LAND REFORM 556**
Excerpt from *Latin American Civilization* by Benjamin Keen, ed. (Boston: Houghton Mifflin, 1974), vol. 2, pp. 188–189.

**FREUD AND THE CONCEPT OF REPRESSION 562**
Reprinted from *Five Lectures on Psychoanalysis* by Sigmund Freud. Translated and edited by James Strachey, W. W. Norton & Company, Inc. Copyright 1909, 1910 by Sigmund Freud. Copyright © 1961 by James Strachey, renewed 1989.

**THE VOICE OF ZIONISM: THEODOR HERZL AND THE JEWISH STATE 564**
From Theodor Herzl, *The Jewish State*, 3rd ed. Sylvia D. Anigdor, trans., copyright © 1936.

**SYMBOLIST POETRY: ART FOR ART'S SAKE 565**
"The Drunken Boat" by Arthur Rimbaud from *Realism, Naturalism, Symbolism: Mode of Thought and Expression in Europe* by Roland N. Stromberg. English translation copyright 1968 by Roland Stromberg. Reprinted by permission of HarperCollins Publishers, Inc.

## CHAPTER 20

**WHITE MAN'S BURDEN, BLACK MAN'S SORROW 579**
From Rudyard Kipling, "The White Man's Burden," McClure's Magazine 12 (Feb. 1899). Edmund Morel, *Black Man's Burden*, Metro Books, 1972.

**INDIAN IN BLOOD, ENGLISH IN TASTE AND INTELLECT 583**
From *Speeches by Lord Macaulay, With His Minute on Indian Education* by Thomas B. MacAuley. AMS Press, 1935.

**THE EFFECTS OF DUTCH COLONIALISM IN JAVA 586**
From *Max Havelaar or the Coffee Auctions of the Dutch Trading Company* by Multatali, translated with notes by Roy Edwards. Penguin USA, 1995.

**THERE'S A EUROPEAN, THERE'S A EUROPEAN! 590**
From Mary E. Smith, *Baba of Karo: A Woman of the Muslim Hausa* (New Haven, CT: Yale University Press, 1981), pp. 66–68.

**THE NDEBELE REBELLION 591**
From Margery Perham, *Ten Africans* (London: Faber & Faber, 1963), pp. 72–75.

**THE CIVILIZING MISSION IN EGYPT 592**
From Leila Ahmen, *Women and Gender in Islam* (New Haven, CT: Yale University Press, 1992), pp. 152–160.

**TO RESIST OR NOT TO RESIST 595**
From Truong Buu Lam, *Patterns of Vietnamese Response to Foreign Intervention*, Monograph Series No. 11. Southeast Asian Studies, Yale University, 1967. Dist. By Cellar Book Shop, Detroit, MI.

## CHAPTER 21

**A LETTER OF ADVICE TO THE QUEEN 602**
Reprinted by permission of the publisher from *China's Response to the West: A Documentary Survey, 1839–1923*, by Ssu-yu Teng and John K. Fairbank, pp. 19, 24–27, Cambridge, Mass.: Harvard University Press. Copyright © 1954, 1979 by the President and Fellows of Harvard College, copyright © renewed 1982 by Ssu-yu Teng and John King Fairbank.

**AN APPEAL FOR CHANGE IN CHINA 604**
Excerpt from *Sources of Chinese Tradition* by William Theodore De Bary. Copyright © 1960 by Columbia University Press, New York.

**PROGRAM FOR A NEW CHINA 608**
Excerpt from *Sources of Chinese Tradition* by William Theodore De Bary. Copyright © 1960 by Columbia University Press, New York. Reprinted with permission of the publisher.

**A LETTER TO THE SHOGUN 614**
Excerpt from *Commodore Perry in Japan*, Robert L. Reynolds (New York: Harper & Row, 1963), p. 68.

**A PROGRAM FOR REFORM IN JAPAN 615**
From *Sources of Japanese Tradition* by William Theodore de Bary. Copyright © 1958 by Columbia University Press. Reprinted with permission of the publisher.

**IN THE BEGINNING, WE WERE THE SUN 618**
From John David Lu, *Sources of Japanese Tradition* (New York: McGraw-Hill, 1974), vol II, pp. 118–119, from *Chuo Koren*, November 1965, pp. 354–357.

**THE RULES OF GOOD CITIZENSHIP IN MEIJI JAPAN 619**
From Ryusaku Tsunoda et al., *Sources of Japanese Tradition* (New York: Columbia University Press, 1958), Vol. 2, p. 139.

**TWO VIEWS OF THE WORLD 622**
From MacNair, *Modern Chinese History*, pp. 530–534, quoted in Franz Schurmann and Orville Schell, eds., *The China Reader: Imperial China* (New York: Vintage, 1967), pp. 251–259.

## CHAPTER 22

**"YOU HAVE TO BEAR THE RESPONSIBILITY FOR WAR OR PEACE" 629**
From *The Western World: From 1700, Vol. II*, by W. E. Adams, R. B. Barlow, G. R. Kleinfeld, and R. D. Smith (Dodd, Mead, and Co., 1968), pp. 421–442.

**THE EXCITEMENT OF WAR 631**
From *The World of Yesterday* by Stefan Zweig, translated by Helmut Ripperger. Translation copyright 1943 by the Viking Press, Inc.

**THE REALITY OF WAR: TRENCH WARFARE 633**
*All Quiet on the Western Front* by Erich Maria Remarque. *Im Westen Nichts Neues*, copyright 1928 by Ullstein A.G.; copyright renewed © 1956 by Erich Maria Remarque. *All Quiet on the Western Front*, copyright 1929, 1930 by Little, Brown and Company; Copyright renewed © 1957 1958 by Erich Maria Remarque. All Rights Reserved.

**WOMEN IN THE FACTORIES 637**
From "Munition Work" by Naomi Loughnan in Gilbert Stone, ed., *Women War Workers* (London: George Harrap and Company, 1971), pp. 25, 35–38.

**SOLDIER AND PEASANT VOICES 640**
From Mark D. Steinberg, *Voices of Revolution*, 1917 (New Haven: Conn.: Yale University Press, 2001), pp. 291 and 302–303.

**THE VOICE OF PEACEMAKING: WOODROW WILSON 644**
Excerpts from *The Public Papers of Woodrow Wilson: War and Peace*, edited by Ray Stannard Baker. Copyright 1925, 1953 by Edith Bolling Wilson.

**THE GREAT DEPRESSION: UNEMPLOYED AND HOMELESS IN GERMANY 648**
From *Living Age*, Vol. 344, no. 4398 (March 1933), pp. 27–31, 34–38.

**HESSE AND THE UNCONSCIOUS 652**
From *Demian*, by Hermann Hesse. (New York: Bantam Books, 1966), p. 30.

## CHAPTER 23

**THE DILEMMA OF THE INTELLECTUAL 658**
From *The World of Southeast Asia: Selected Historical Readings*, Harry J. Benda and John A. Larkin, eds. Copyright © 1967 by Harper & Row, Publishers.

**A CALL FOR A MUSLIM STATE 661**
Excerpt from *The Sources of Indian Tradition*, Stephen Hay, ed. Copyright © 1988 by Columbia University Press, New York. Reprinted with permission of the publisher.

**MUSTAFA KEMAL'S CASE AGAINST THE CALIPHATE 663**
From *Atatürk's Speech to the Assembly*, pp. 432–433. A speech delivered by Ghazi Mustafa Kemal, President of the Turkish Republic, October 1927.

**THE PATH OF LIBERATION 668**
From *Vietnam: History, Documents, and Opinions on a Major World Crisis*, Marvin Gentleman, ed. (New York: Fawcett Publications, 1965), pp. 30–32.

**A CALL FOR REVOLT 671**
From *Selected Works of Mao Tse-Tung* (London: Lawrence and Wishart, Ltd., 1954), Vol. 1, pp. 21–23.

**AN ARRANGED MARRIAGE 674**
Excerpt from *Family* by Ba Jin. Copyright © 1964 Foreign Languages Press, 24 Baiwanzhuang Rd., Beijing 10037, P.R. China. Used with permission.

**IN SEARCH OF OLD JAPAN 676**
Excerpt from *Some Prefer Nettles*, Junichiro Tanizaki (New York: Medallion Books, 1960), pp. 96–98.

**A PLEDGE OF COOPERATION 679**
From Ruhl J. Bartlett, ed., *The Record of American Diplomacy* (New York: Knopf, 1952), pp. 551–552.

## CHAPTER 24

**PROPAGANDA AND MASS MEETINGS IN NAZI GERMANY 689**
Excerpt from *Mein Kampf* by Adolf Hitler, translated by Ralph Manheim. Copyright 1943, © renewed 1971 by Houghton Mifflin Company. From Norman Baynes, ed., *The Speeches of Adolf Hitler* (New York: Oxford University Press, 1942), 1:206–207.

**THE FORMATION OF COLLECTIVE FARMS 690**
From Sidney Harcave, *Readings in Russian History* (New York: Thomas Crowell & Co., 1962), pp. 208–210.

**THE MUNICH CONFERENCE 693**
From *Parliamentary Debates, House of Commons* (London: His Majesty's Stationery Office, 1938), vol. 339, pp. 361–369. From *Neville Chamberlain, In Search of Peace* (New York: Putnam, 1939), pp. 215, 217.

**JAPAN'S JUSTIFICATION FOR EXPANSION 695**
From *Sources of Japanese Tradition* by William Theodore de Bary. Copyright © 1958 by Columbia University Press.

**A GERMAN SOLDIER AT STALINGRAD 700**
From Vasili Chuikov, *The Battle of Stalingrad* (Grafton Books).

**HITLER'S PLANS FOR A NEW ORDER IN THE EAST 702**
From Hitler's Conversations, Hugh Trevor Roper, copyright © 1953 by New American Library, published by Octagon Books, a Division of Hippocrene Books, Inc.

**THE HOLOCAUST: THE CAMP COMMANDANT AND THE CAMP VICTIMS 707**
From *Commandant of Auschwitz: The Autobiography of Rudolph Hoss*, Cleveland World Publishing Company. From *Nazism: A History in Documents and Eyewitness Accounts, Vol. II* by J. Noakes and G. Pridham. Copyright © 1988 by Department of History and Archaeology, University of Exeter.

**JAPAN'S PLAN FOR ASIA 708**
From *Sources of Japanese Tradition* by William Theodore de Bary. Copyright © 1958 by Columbia University Press.

## CHAPTER 25

**THE TRUMAN DOCTRINE 725**
U.S. Congress, *Congressional Record, 80th Congress, 1st Session* (Washington, D.C.: U.S. Government Printing Office, 1947), Vol. 93, p. 1981.

**WHO LOST CHINA? 731**
From *United States Relations with China* (Washington, D.C., Dept. of State, 1949), pp. iii–xvi.

**THE CUBAN MISSILE CRISIS: KHRUSHCHEV'S PERSPECTIVE 737**
From *Khrushchev Remembers* by Nikita Khrushchev, copyright © 1970 by Little, Brown, & Company.

**A PLEA FOR PEACEFUL COEXISTENCE 738**
From G. F. Hudson et al., eds. *The Sino-Soviet Dispute* (New York: Frederick Praeger, 1961), pp. 61–63, cited in *Peking Review*, No. 40, 1959.

**COMBATING THE AMERICANS 739**
"Statement of the National Liberation Front of South Vietnam," *New Times* (March 27, 1965), pp. 36–40.

**A MANUAL FOR REVOLUTIONARIES 740**
From *Nationalism and Communism*, Norman Grabner, ed. Copyright © 1977 by D. C. Heath and Company.

**A NEW BEGINNING IN SINO-AMERICAN RELATIONS 743**
U.S. statement from *Public Papers: Jimmy Carter*, 1978, p. 2266. China statement from *Xinhua*, Dec. 16, 1978 in Foreign Broadcast Information Service, *Daily Report: People's Republic of China*, Dec. 18, 1978, p. A2.

**THE BREZHNEV DOCTRINE 744**
From *Moscow News*, Supplement to No, 30 (917), 1968, pp. 3–6.

## CHAPTER 26

**KHRUSHCHEV DENOUNCES STALIN 754**
From *Congressional Record, 84th Congress, 2nd Session*, Vol. 102, Part 7, pp. 9389–9402 (June 4, 1956).

**ONE DAY IN THE LIFE OF IVAN DENISOVICH 758**
From *One Day in the Life of Ivan Denisovich* by Alexander Solzhenitsyn, translated by Ralph Parker, translation copyright © 1963 by E. P. Dutton and Victor Gollancz, Ltd. Copyright renewed © 1991 by Penguin USA and Victor Gollancz, Ltd.

**SOVIET WOMEN: "IT'S SO DIFFICULT TO BE A WOMAN HERE" 760**
From *Moscow Women: Thirteen Interviews* by Carola Hansson and Karin Liden, edited by Gerry Bothmer, George & Lone Blecher, Text copyright © 1983 by Random House, Inc. Reprinted by permission of Pantheon Books, a division of Random House, Inc.

**LAND REFORM IN ACTION 766**
From Richard Solomon, *Mao's Revolution and the Chinese Political Culture*, pages 198–199. Copyright © 1971 Center for Chinese Studies, University of Michigan.

**MAKE REVOLUTION! 796**
From *Life and Death in Shanghai* by Nien Cheng (New York: Penguin, 1986).

**STUDENTS APPEAL FOR DEMOCRACY 772**
From a flyer in the archives of William J. Duiker.

**GLASS CEILING, CHINESE STYLE 778**
From Susan Vacca's translation of Ting Ling's "In the Hospital," *Chinese-English Translation Magazine*, No. 8, Autumn 1977, published by the Comparative Literature and Translation Centre, The Chinese University of Hong Kong.

**LOVE AND MARRIAGE IN CHINA 779**
From *Chinese Lives: An Oral History of Contemporary China*, by Zhang Xinxin and Sang Ye, copyright © 1987 by W.J.F. Jenner and Delia Davin. Used by permission of Pantheon Books, a division of Random House, Inc.

## CHAPTER 27

**MARGARET THATCHER: ENTERING A MAN'S WORLD 787**
From *The Path to Power* by Margaret Thatcher. Copyright 1995 by Margaret Thatcher.

**"I HAVE A DREAM" 792**
From Martin Luther King, Jr., 1963. Copyright © 1963 by Martin Luther King, Jr. Copyright renewed 1991 by Coretta Scott King. Reprinted by arrangement with the Estate of Martin Luther King, Jr., c/o Writers House, Inc. as agent for the proprietor, New York, NY.

**CASTRO'S REVOLUTIONARY IDEALS 796**
Excerpt from *Latin American Civilization* by Benjamin Keen, ed. (Boston: Houghton Mifflin, 1974), pp. 369–373.

**STUDENT REVOLT IN MEXICO 799**
Excerpt from *Latin American Civilization* by Benjamin Keen, ed. (Boston: Houghton Mifflin, 1974), pp. 226–227.

**"THE TIMES THEY ARE A-CHANGIN'": THE MUSIC OF YOUTHFUL PROTEST 802**
From *Bob Dylan, Lyrics 1962–1985* (New York: Alfred A. Knopf, 1992), p. 91. Copyright © 1963 by Warner Bros Inc. Copyright renewed 1991 by Special Rider Music. All rights reserved. International copyright secured. Reprinted by permission.

**THE VOICE OF THE WOMEN'S LIBERATION MOVEMENT 804**
From *The Second Sex* by Simone De Beauvoir, trans. H. M. Parshley. Copyright 1952 and renewed 1980 by Alfred A. Knopf, Inc.

**SMALL IS BEAUTIFUL: THE LIMITS OF MODERN TECHNOLOGY 811**
Excerpts from *Small Is Beautiful: Economics As If People Mattered* by E. F. Schumacher. Copyright 1973 by E. F. Schumacher.

## CHAPTER 28

**TOWARD AFRICAN UNITY 819**
From *Organizing African Unity* by J. Woronoff, pp. 642–649. Copyright © 1980 by Scarecrow Press, Inc. Used with permission of the publisher.

**STEALING THE NATION'S RICHES 820**
From *The Beautiful Ones Are Not Yet Born* by Ayi Kwei Armah (Heinemann, 1989).

**SOCIALISM IS NOT RACIALISM 823**
From Julius Nyerere, "The Arusha Declaration" in *Freedomways* (magazine) (Dar es Salaam: Second Quarter, 1970), pp. 124–127.

**AFRICA: DARK OR RADIANT CONTINENT? 830**
From *Heart of Darkness* by Joseph Conrad. Penguin Books, 1991. From *The Radiance of the King* by Camara Laye, translated from the French by James Kirkup. New York: Vintage, 1989.

**THE ROOTS OF TERRORISM 832**
Excerpt from "Algeria: Rethinking the Variables" by A. Bahmane in *El Watan*, 9/19/01, Algiers, in *World Press Review*, November 2001. Reprinted with permission from *World Press Review*.

**THE SUEZ CANAL BELONGS TO EGYPT! 834**
From a speech nationalizing the Suez Canal, Gamal Abdul Nasser, in *The Egyptian Gazette* (July 27, 1956), p. 5.

**ISLAM AND DEMOCRACY 844**
From M.J. Akbar, "Linking Islam to Dictatorship," in *World Press Review*, May 2004. Reprinted by permission.

**KEEPING THE CAMEL OUT OF THE TENT 846**
From *Nine Parts Desire: The Hidden World of Islamic Women*, by Geraldine Brooks (Doubleday, 1996).

## CHAPTER 29

**TWO VISIONS FOR INDIA 854**
From *Sources of Indian Tradition* by William Theodore De Bary. Copyright © 1988 by Columbia University Press, New York. Excerpt from Gandhi "Letter to Jawaharlal Nehru" pp. 328–331 from *Gandhi In India: In His Own Words*, Martin Green, ed. Copyright © 1987 by Navajivan Trust. Lebanon, NH: University Press of New England.

# Photo Credits

## CHAPTER 1

**1** © The British Museum **2** © Nik Wheeler/CORBIS **5** © AP/Wide World **8** Courtesy of the Hashemite Kingdom of Jordan, Dept. of Antiquities **11** © The British Museum **12** © Réunion des Musées Nationaux/Art Resource, NY **15TL** © Réunion des Musées Nationaux/Art Resource, NY **15TR** © Tom Till Photography **15BL** © Archivo Iconografico, S.S./CORBIS **15BR** © Michael Holford **19** Harvard MFA Expedition, Courtesy, Museum of Fine Arts, Boston **23** © British Museum **34** © Adam Wolfitt/Robert Harding Picture Library **27** © British Museum **31** © British Museum **33** © The Art Archive/Dagli Orti

## CHAPTER 2

**37** © The Trustees of the Chester Beatty Library, Dublin/ Bridgeman Art Library **40TL** © Borromeo/Art Resource, NY **40TR** Courtesy of William J. Duiker **40B** © Royal Smeets Offset, Weert **41** © Scala/Art Resource, NY **49** Courtesy of William J. Duiker **52** © Alison Wright/CORBIS **53L** © Freer Gallery of Art, Smithsonian Institution, Washington, DC **53R** © Scala/Art Resource, NY **54** © Robert Harding Picture Library **56** Courtesy of the British Library, Oriental and India Office Collection **60TL** © ephotocorp.com **60TR** © Vanni/Art Resource, NY **60B** Courtesy of William J. Duiker.

## CHAPTER 3

**64** ©Topham/The Image Works **66TR** Courtesy of William J. Duiker **66TL** Courtesy of William J. Duiker **67** © Werner Forman Archive, British Library/Art Resource, NY **69TL** © ChinaStock **69TR** Egyptian National Museum, Cairo, Egypt/Bridgeman Art Library **71** © British Museum **76** © Topham/The Image Works **92** © Bradley D. Appleby **89** Courtesy of William J. Duiker **85** Courtesy of William J. Duiker **86TL** Courtesy of William J. Duiker **86TR** Courtesy of William J. Duiker **88** Courtesy of William J. Duiker **90L** Courtesy of William J. Duiker **90R** © China Photos/ Getty Images

## CHAPTER 4

**95** © akg images/John Hios **98** © Erich Lessing/Art Resource, NY **100** © Michael Holford, London **101** © Scala/Art Resource, NY **105TR** © The Art Archive/Acropolis Museum Athena/Dagli Orti **105TL** Courtesy of William M. Murray **110** © Art Resource, NY **110B** © Michael Holford, London **111** © Scala/ Art Resource, NY **113** © The Metropolitan Museum of Art , Flecher Fund, 1931 (31.11.10) **116** © Réunion des Musées Nationaux/Art Resource, NY **121TL** © The Art Archive/Kanellopoulos Museum Athens/ Dagli Orti **121B** © Borromeo/Art Resource, NY **121BR** © The Metropolitan Museum of Art, Rogers Fund, 1909 (09.39)

## CHAPTER 5

**126** © Dulwith Picture Gallery, London/Bridgeman Art Library **130T** © Archivo Iconografico, S.A./CORBIS **130R** © China Tourism Press/Getty Images **128** © Photo AKG, London **131** © Réunion des Musées Nationaux/Art Resource, NY **135** © Scala/Art Resource, NY **137** © Photo Vatican Museums **140** Photo © Eberhard Thiem, Lotos-Film, Kaufbeuren, Germany **143TR** © Fred Mayer/Magnum Photos **143TL** © Michael S. Yamashita/CORBIS **145** © The Metropolitan Museum of Art/Rogers Fund, 1903 (03.14.5) **146** © Scala/Art Resource, NY **151** Fitzwilliam Museum, University of Cambridge **153** © Scala/Art Resource, NY **155TL** © British Museum **155TR** © British Library

## CHAPTER 6

**161** The Metropolitan Museum of Art, Fletcher Fund, 1947; The A.W. Bahr Collection (47.18.1) **162** © The Granger Collection, New York **164** Courtesy of Claire L. Duiker **165T** © Will & Deni McIntyre/Photo Researchers, Inc **165B** © Richard A. Cooke III **166** Courtesy of William J. Duiker **167** © Justin Kerr, 1997 **169BR** Courtesy of William J. Duiker **170** © British Museum, London **175** © The Granger Collection, New York **178** Courtesy of William J. Duiker **180L** Courtesy of Carol C. Coffin **180R** Courtesy of William J. Duiker **183** Courtesy of William J. Duiker

## CHAPTER 7

**187** © British Library. London/Bridgeman Art Library **188** © Mehmet Biber/Photo Researchers Inc **191** © British Library. London/Bridgeman Art Library **198L** British Library **198R** © Michael Nicholson/CORBIS **201T** © Giraudon/Art Resource, NY **201B** © Bildarchiv Preussischer Kulturbesitz/Art Resource, NY **205L** Courtesy of William J. Duiker **205R** © Nik Wheeler/CORBIS **206T** Courtesy of William J. Duiker **206Ctr** Courtesy of William J. Duiker **206B** Courtesy of William J. Duiker **207** © Scala/Art Resource, NY **209** © Erich Lessing/Art Resource, NY

## CHAPTER 8

**218** © Ariadne Van Zandbergen/Lonely Planet Images **221** © Robert Harding Picture Library **222** © Erich Lessing/Art Resource **224** © Frans Lemmens/CORBIS **227** Courtesy of William J. Duiker **231** © Bibliotheque Nationale, Paris **232** © Ariadne Van Zandbergen/Lonely Planet Images **234** Courtesy of William J. Duiker **236L** © Yale University Art Gallery **236R** © Werner Forman Archive, British Museum/Art Resource NY **238L** © Werner Forman/Art Resource, NY **238Ctr** © Réunion des Musées Nationaux/ Art Resource, NY **238R** © Borromeo/Art Resource, NY **239** © Angela Fisher/Robert Estall Photographs

## CHAPTER 9

**241** © Thomas J. Abercrombie/National Geographic Image Collection **243L** © Thomas J. Abercrombie/National Geographic Image Collection **243R** © Kimbell Art Museum/CORBIS **255L** Courtesy of William J. Duiker **249R** Courtesy of William J. Duiker **249L** Courtesy of William J. Duiker **250** Courtesy of William J. Duiker **255R** © Werner Forman/ Art Resource, NY **256** © S. Fiore/Explorer **257** © Marcello Berntinetti/Photo Researchers, Inc. **259** Courtesy of William J. Duiker **262** Courtesy of William J. Duiker **263** Clayton Fogel **265L** Courtesy of William J. Duiker **265R** Courtesy of William J. Duiker **266** Courtesy of William J. Duiker

## CHAPTER 10

**269** The Metropolitan Museum of Art, Fletcher Fund, 1947; The A.W. Bahr Collection (47.18.1) **272L** Courtesy of William J. Duiker **272R** Courtesy of William J. Duiker **274L** Courtesy of William J. Duiker **274R** Courtesy of William J. Duiker **276** © The Art Archive/ Topkapi Museum Istanbul/Dagli Orti **278** The Metropolitan Museum of Art, Fletcher Fund, 1947; The A.W. Bahr Collection (47.18.1) **282** © Museum of Fine Arts, Boston, Special Chinese and Japanese Fund, 12.886 **287** Courtesy of William J. Duiker **289T** © The Art Archive/British Museum **289B** Courtesy of William J. Duiker **294** © The Art Archive/ National Palace Museum Taiwan **295** Courtesy of William J. Duiker

## CHAPTER 11

**298** Yale University Library, Maurice Durand Collection of Vietnamese Art; **301L** Courtesy of William J. Duiker **301Ctr** Courtesy of William J. Duiker **301R** Courtesy of William J. Duiker **304** © Kyoto National Museum, Kyoto, with permission from the Kozan-ji Temple **305** Photograph © 2006 Museum of Fine Arts, Boston **306T** Courtesy of the Tokyo National Museum **306B** © Scala/Art Resource, NY **307** © Michael Holford, London **313TR** © Charles Gupton, Tony Stone Images/ Getty Images **313TL** Courtesy of William J. Duiker **313B** Courtesy of William J. Duiker **314** Courtesy of the Korean Cultural Service Library **315** Courtesy of William J. Duiker **317TL** © Archivo Iconografico, S.A./CORBIS **317TR** Courtesy of William J. Duiker **318** Yale University Library: Maurice Durand Collection of Vietnamese Art **319** Courtesy of William J. Duiker

## CHAPTER 12

**323** © Scala/Art Resource, NY **327** The Granger Collection **329L** © The Pierpont Morgan Library/Art Resource, NY **329R** © University Museum of Cultural Heritage, University of Oslo, Norway. Photograph by Eirik Irgens Johnsen **332B** © The Art Archive, from the collections at the British Museum **332T** Freer Gallery of Art, Smithsonian Institution, Washington, D.C.: Purchase F1954.21 **335** © Bibliotheque Nationale, Paris **340** © Bibliotheque Royale Albert ler (Ms IV 119, fol.72 verso) **342** © The Art Archive/Dagli Orti **343** © Sylvain Grandadam/ Photo Researchers, Inc. **349** © Bibliotheque Nationale, Paris/ Bridgeman Art Library **352T** © Scala/Art Resource, NY **352B** © Scala/Art Resource, NY **353** © Scala/Art Resource, NY

## CHAPTER 13

**361** © The Art Archive, London **362** Beinecke Rare Book and Manuscript Library, Yale University **365** Jomard, Les Monuments de la Geographie, Paris, 1862. Photo courtesy of the New York Public Library, Map Division, Stor, Lennox and Tilden Foundations **366L** Courtesy of William J. Duiker **366R** © National Maritime Museum, London **367L** Courtesy of William J. Duiker **367TR** Courtesy of William J. Duiker **367BR** Courtesy of Claire L. Duiker **369** © North Wind Picture Archive **370** © Gianni Dagli Orti/CORBIS **373L** Courtesy of William J. Duiker **373R** Courtesy of William J. Duiker **374** from the Collections of the Library of Congress **375T** Courtesy of William J. Duiker **375B** Bibliotheque Nationale, Paris **377R** Courtesy of William J. Duiker **377L** Courtesy of William J. Duiker **381L** Courtesy of Claire L. Duiker **381R** Courtesy of Claire L. Duiker **384T** Beinecke Rare Book and Manuscript Library, Yale University **384B** © The Art Archive, London **385** Courtesy of William J. Duiker

## CHAPTER 14

**392** © Bibliotheque Nationale, Paris/Bridgeman Art Library **394** Staatliche Landesbildstelle Hamburg **397** Staatliche Museen Bildarchiv Preussischer Kulturbesitz, Kupferstichkabinett, Berlin, Photo: Jorg P. Anders/Art Resource, NY **398** © Bibliotheque Publique Universitaire, Geneva **401** © Scala/Art Resource, NY **403** Courtesy of J. K. Wingfield Digby, Sherborne Castle **409L** © Réunion des Musées Nationaux/Art Resource, NY **409R** © Metropolitan Museum of Art, Rogers Fund, 1942 (42.141.2) Photo © 1980 The Metropolitan Museum of Art **410** © Giraudon/Art Resource, NY **413** Robert Walker, Oliver Cromwell, 1649. By Courtesy of the National Portrait Gallery, London. **415L** © Réunion des Musées Nationaux/Art Resource, NY **415R** © Scala/Art Resource, NY **416** Leyster, Judith (Dutch, 1609-1660) *Self Portrait*, c. 1630, oil on canvas, (9 3/8" x 25 5/8"): National Gallery of Art, Washington, Gift of Mr. and Mrs. Robert Woods Bliss

## CHAPTER 15

**419** © Ancient Art & Architecture **420** © Sonia Halliday Photographs **425L** © Ancient Art & Architecture **425R** © Oronoz Archivo **426** © Topkapi Palace Museum/ Bridgeman Art Library **429L** © Robert Harding Picture Library. Photo by Robert Frerck **429R** Courtesy of William J. Duiker **433** © The British Library, London **432** © George Holton/Photo Researchers, Inc. **437** © Arthur M. Sackler Gallery, Smithsonian Institution, Washington, D.C.: Purchase, F1942.15a **444** The Royal Collection © 2005 Her Majesty Queen Elizabeth II. **442L** Photo; Courtesy of Ian Bell **442R** Photo: Courtesy of Carol C. Coffin. **443** © Orde Eliason/Link India

## CHAPTER 16

**448** © Metropolitan Museum of Art, Rogers Fund, 1942 (42.141.2) Photo © 1980 The Metropolitan Museum of Art **452** Courtesy of William J. Duiker **456** © Marine Museum Stockholm/Dagli Orti/The Art Archive **459** City of Suzhou, China. **458** © Werner Forman Archive/Art Resource, NY **461R** © Dean Conger/National Geographic Image Collection **461L** Courtesy of William J. Duiker **462** Courtesy of William J. Duiker **464T** Courtesy of William J. Duiker **464Ctr** Courtesy of William J. Duiker **464B** © Collection Musee Guimet, Paris/

Photo Michael Holford, London **472** Gift of James A. Michener, Honolulu Academy of Arts **470** Photo; McGill University School of Architecture **471L** © Clarence Buckingham Collection, 1939.2152, Photograph © 1993, The Art Institute of Chicago **471R** © Scala/Art Resource, NY **473** Courtesy of William J. Duiker

## CHAPTER 17

**476** © Réunion des Musées Nationaux/Art Resource, NY **478L** Courtesy of the Lilly Library, Indiana University, Bloomington, Indiana **478R** Courtesy of the Lilly Library, Indiana University, Bloomington, Indiana **483** © Michael Holford, London **484** © Réunion des Musées Nationaux/Art Resource, NY **485** © Scala/Art Resource, NY **488R** © Erich Lessing/Art Resource, NY **488L** Collection of the Earl of Pembroke, Wilton House, Wilts., UK/Bridgeman Art Library **491** © The Granger Collection, NY **494** By courtesy of the National Portrait Gallery, London **496T** © Musee de la Revolucion Francais,Vizelle, France/Visual Arts Library, London/Bridgeman Art Library **496B** © School of Oriental & African Studies/Eileen Tweedy/The Art Archive **497** © Giraudon/Art Resource, NY **502** © Réunion des Musées Nationaux/Art Resource, NY

## CHAPTER 18

**511** V and A Picture Library **512** © Scala/Art Resource, NY **514** © Mansell/Time Pix **515T** © CORBIS **515B** Laurie Platt Whitney, Inc. **519** © CORBIS **525** Historisches Museum der Stadt, Wien **526** © Museo Nacional de Historia, Dagli Orti/The Art Archive **529** akg-images **531** Anton von Werner , Photo © Bildarchiv Preussischer Kutruabeitz, Berlin /Art Resource, NY **536** Nationalgalerie SMPK Berlin. Photo © Jorg P. Anders, © Bildarchiv Preussischer Kulturbesitz, Berlin /Art Resource, NY **537** © Erich Lessing/Art Resource, NY **538** Gemaldegalerie Neue Meister, Staatliche Kunstsammlungen Dresden; Photo by Reinhold, Leipzig-Molkau

## CHAPTER 19

**541** © Museum of the City of New York/Byron Collection/Getty Images **542** The Fotomas Index **547** Verein fur Geschichte der Arbeiterbewegung, Vienna **549** © CORBIS **550** Harrowgate Museums and Art Gallery, North Yorkshire, UK/Bridgeman Art Library **554** Courtesy, Vassar College Library **555** © Brown Brothers **561** © AP/Wide World Photos **566TL** © Erich Lessing/Art Resource, NY **566TR** © National Research Institute for Cultural Properties, Tokyo **566B** © The Museum of Modern Art/Licensed by Scala/Art Resource, NY **597TL** © The Museum of Modern Art/Licensed by Scala/Art Resource, NY © 2006 Estate of Pablo Picasso/Artists Rights Society (ARS), NY **567TR** Musee Barbier-Mueller, Photo: Pierre-Alain Ferrazzini **567B** The Solomon R. Guggenheim Museum, NY, Photograph David Heald © The Solomon R. Guggenheim Foundation, New York (37.245)/© 2006 Artist's Rights Society (ARS) ADAGP, Paris

## CHAPTER 20

**571** © Photo by Hulton Archive/Getty Images **574** © Singapore History Museum, National Heritage Board **577T** Bildarchiv Preussische Kulturbesitz, Berlin /Art Resource, NY **577B** © Bojan Brecelj/CORBIS **582** Courtesy of William J. Duiker **585** V and A Picture Library **587L** Durand Collection of Vietnamese Art, Yale University Library **587R** Courtesy of the British library, Oriental and India Office Collections **588L** Courtesy of William J. Duiker **588R** Courtesy of William J. Duiker **589** © Photo by Hulton Archive/Getty Images **591** © Mary Evans Picture Library **594** Emile Duboc, 35 mois de campagne en Chine, au Tonkin (1882-1885).

## CHAPTER 21

**599** National Maritime Museum, London **603** National Maritime Museum, London **605** Courtesy of Claire L. Duiker **606L** Courtesy of the Freer Gallery of Art, Smithsonian Institution, Wshington, D.C. **606R** National Portrait Gallery, London **607** Leslie's Weekly, 10/14/1900 **609** © Camera Press/Globe Photos **611** © Archive Photos/Popperfoto **612** Photograph courtesy of Peabody Essex Museum, Neg #A9939 **613** Boehringer Collection, The Mariners' Museum, Newport News, VA **616** Meiji Jingu, Hosankai **620** © Réunion des Musées Nationaux/Art Resource, NY **621** Seitoku Kinen Kaigakan Hekigashu, 1932, Meiji Jingu, Hosankai. **623** © Scala/Art Resource

## CHAPTER 22

**626** © Private Collection/Archives Charmet/Bridgeman Art Library **630** Librairie Larousse, Paris **634** © Roger-Viollet/Getty Images **635T** © Bettmann/CORBIS **635B** © Hulton Archive/Getty Images **636** © The Art Archive, London **639** © Sovfoto **641L** © Brown Brothers **641R** © Underwood & Underwood/CORBIS **643** © Hulton Archive/Getty Images **647** © Roger Viollet/Getty Images **650** © Erich Lessing/Art Resource, NY. © 2006 Artist's Rights Society (ARS), New York/VG Bild-Kunst, Bonn **652** © The Museum of Modern Art/ Licensed by Scala/Art Resource, NY. © 2006 Salvador Dali, Gala-Salvadore Dali Foundation/Artist's Rights Society (ARS), New York

## CHAPTER 23

**656** © AP/Wide World Photos **660** © AP/Wide World Photos **662** © Culver Pictures, Inc. **664** © Hulton-Deutsch Collection/CORBIS **665** © Illustrated London News **666** Agence Vietnamienne d'Information, Hanoi. **669L** YMCA of the USA Archives, University of Minnesota Libraries **669R** Courtesy of William J. Duiker **672L** © Earl Leaf/Rapho **672R** © David King Collection, London **675** Fortune Magazine, 1933. **680** © Hulton Archive/Getty Images **681** © Schalkwijk/Art Resource, NY © Estate of David Alfaro Siqueiros/SOMAAP, Mexico City/VAGA, NY

## CHAPTER 24

**684** © Time Life Pictures/Getty Images **686** © AP/Wide World Photos **688** Hugo Jaeger, Life Magazine © TimePix **692** © Bildarchiv Preussischer Kulturbesitz, Berlin /Art Resource, NY **694** Paul Dorsey, Life Magazine © 1938 TimePix **698** © AKG London **702** © Mainichi Shimbun, Tokyo **704** Library of Congress (2391, folder 401) **708** Imperial War Museum Photographic Archive, London. Neg Ref #D6246 **711L** © J.R. Eyerman/Time Life Pictures/Getty Images **711R** The Herald and Evening Times Picture Library, © SMG Newspapers Ltd. **713** © The Art Archive, London

## CHAPTER 25

**721** Courtesy of William J. Duiker **722** © The Art Archive, London **724** © CORBIS **726** © Hulton Archive/Getty Images **729** Jack Wiles, Life Magazine © 1945 TimePix **730** © David King Collection **733** © Black Star **735** © AP/Wide World Photos **736T** © AP/Wide World Photos **736B** © Bettmann/ CORBIS **741 F** © AP/Wide World Photos **741L** © Hoang Mai **742** © AP/Wide World Photos **745** © Judyth Platt, Ecoscene/ CORBIS

## CHAPTER 26

**750** Courtesy of William J. Duiker **753** Courtesy of William J. Duiker **756** Courtesy of William J. Duiker **757** Courtesy of William J. Duiker **761** Courtesy of William J. Duiker **763** Courtesy of William J. Duiker **768** © Private Collection/ Bridgeman Art Library **770** © AP/Wide World Photos **771L** © C. Raimond-Dityvon/Viva/Woodfin Camp & Associates **771R** Courtesy of William J. Duiker **775T** Courtesy of William J. Duiker **775B** © Vittoriano Rastelli/CORBIS **777** Courtesy of William J. Duiker

## CHAPTER 27

**783** © Bettmann/CORBIS **784** © Pierre Boulat-Cosmos/Woodfin Camp & Associates **786** © Mark Stewart/Camera Press, London **788** © AP/Wide World Photos **791** © Bob Adelman/Magnum Photos **795** © CORBIS **798** © CORBIS **801** © Popperfoto/ Hulton Archive/Getty Images **803** © AP/Wide World Photos **806L** © AP/Wide World Photos **806R** © AP/Wide World Photos **808** © Hans Namuth/Photo Researchers, Inc. **809** © Norman McGrath

## CHAPTER 28

**815** © Herbert M. Cole **827** Courtesy William J. Duiker **827** Courtesy William J. Duiker **825L** Courtesy William J. Duiker **825R** Courtesy William J. Duiker **824** Herbert M. Cole **828** Courtesy William J. Duiker **821L** Ajasi Alama; *Problems of Transport at Weya Rural Area*; 2005. Painting on board. Zimbabwe Artists Project **821R** Courtesy of Claire L. Duiker **836** Courtesy William J. Duiker **838T** © CORBIS/Abbas Imax **838B** © AP/Wide World Photos **843** © Alexandra Winkler/ Reuters/CORBIS **842** © Patrick Robert/Sygma/CORBIS

## CHAPTER 29

**851** Courtesy William J. Duiker **853** Courtesy William J. Duiker **857** Courtesy William J. Duiker **860** Courtesy William J. Duiker **864** Courtesy William J. Duiker **865** Courtesy William J. Duiker **866L** Courtesy William J. Duiker **866R** Jim Whitmer Photography **867** Courtesy William J. Duiker **868** © CORBIS **873** © Barry Cronin Newsmakers/Getty Images **877** Courtesy William J. Duiker **878** Courtesy William J. Duiker

# INDEX

**Italicized page numbers show the locations of illustrations.**